20th International Conference on Circuits, Systems, Communications and Computers (CSCC 2016)

MATEC Web of Conferences Volume 76 (2016)

Corfu Island, Greece
14-17 July 2016

Editors:

N. Mastorakis
A. Bulucea
V. Mladenov

ISBN: 978-1-5108-3166-7

Printed from e-media with permission by:

Curran Associates, Inc.
57 Morehouse Lane
Red Hook, NY 12571

Some format issues inherent in the e-media version may also appear in this print version.

Printed by Curran Associates, Inc. (2016)

For additional information, please contact EDP Sciences – Web of Conferences
at the address below.

EDP Sciences – Web of Conferences
17, Avenue du Hoggar
Parc d'Activité de Courtabœuf
BP 112
F-91944 Les Ulis Cedex A
France

Phone: +33 (0) 1 69 18 75 75
Fax: +33 (0) 1 69 28 84 91

contact-edps@webofconferences.org

Additional copies of this publication are available from:

Curran Associates, Inc.
57 Morehouse Lane
Red Hook, NY 12571 USA
Phone: 845-758-0400
Fax: 845-758-2633
Email: curran@proceedings.com
Web: www.proceedings.com

TABLE OF CONTENTS

Bifurcations of Equilibrium Forms of NEMS/MEMS as a Sensor of Microphysical Alterations

Dmitrii Skubov[1,2a], Alexey Lukin[2] , Ivan Popov[2] and Lev Shtukin[1,2]

[1]*Institute of the Problems of mechanical engineers IPME RAS, 199178 St.-Petersburg Russia*
[2]*St.-Petersburg Polytechnic University SPbPU, 195251, St.-Petersburg, Russia*

Abstract. In our work the results of analytical and numerical investigation of equilibrium forms of round conductive and ferromagnetic micro-membrane situated in uniform electrostatic or magnetic static field and also the branching of equilibrium forms of the system of two and three nano-layers with direct currents are described. The structure of this type is practically realizable and exercisable as a sensor of alteration of external and inner mechanical and electrical characteristics. Exactly in a case of nano/micro schemes it is necessary to take in account the nonlinearity of its interaction, which leads to significantly nonlinear effects. On a base of nonlinearity we can determine the alteration of mechanical and electrical characteristics. This type of nonlinear effects mostly unattainable in macroscale but in case of nano- or microscale their realization gets off on the first plan and appears as a sensor of small physical alteration.

1 Introduction

In recent time the development and achievement of micro- and nanoelectromechanical systems (MEMS and NEMS) appeal the great interest of physics, biologists, electricians. The use of these devices is connected with their high sensitivity for nano- and micro-scale alterations of physical and biological parameters [1-6]. For example, it's used as a determination of molecular mass, quantum states, biochemical reactions, production of some new molecules and others nanoparticles, and also their sensitivity for alteration of different types of external microphysical magnitudes. With help of miniature nano- and micro-sensors the supersensitive for extremely small forces and masses have been found: - for forces of the order some zepto-newton (1zN=10^{-21}N), for masses – some zepto-gram. Reaching of this sensitivity is connected with attainment of Mega and even Giga-Hertz diapason of eigen frequency of their dynamical characteristics. Increasing of eigen frequency until 1GHz gives the opportunity to avoid the influence of some physical noise on micro-sensors, such as, for example, a temperature and humid fluctuations. So silicon material with length 1μm, width 0.12μm and thickness 0.075μm has eigen frequency 1.03GHz with quality of order $Q \sim 10^4$ [3,4,12].

The important significance of the nano- and micro-actuators has been revealed [1,2] as micro-switches with forward or rotary movement. These devices may be membranes or cantilevers and other types, also a high speed rotational actuator - contactless micro-gyroscope.
It is necessary to say that not less important the micro-sensors based on «pull-in» effect have been obtained. This effect gives the opportunity to determine the micro-alteration of external or inner excitation [1]. «Pull-in» instability is an inherently nonlinear effect connected with disappearance of equilibrium forms of elastic part of sensitive and actuating mechanism. This effect occurs at achievement of electro or magneto static actions the determined critical value.

The great interest also is presented by the determination of multitude of equilibrium forms of elastic bodies, which are possible in MEMS/NEMS, their bifurcation and stability. The same mathematical task arises at the modeling of electromechanical devices including the ferromagnetic parts: cores and armatures of electromagnets, magnetically controlled materials (ferrite elastics) [10] and others.

In our work the results of analytical and numerical investigation of equilibrium forms of round conductive and ferromagnetic micro-membrane situated in uniform electrostatic or magnetic static field and also the branching of equilibrium forms of the system of two and three nano-layers (wires) with direct currents are described. The structure of this type is practically realizable [10] and exercisable as a sensor of alteration of external and inner mechanical and electrical characteristics. For example, it's one of the types of nano-resonators, used for measuring a mass of adhesing nanoparticle [11,12]. In this case the measuring of a mass of nanoparticle is realized based on the alteration of an eigen frequency of flexural oscillations of nanolayer.

It's important to note that exactly in a case of nano/micro schemes it is necessary to take in account the nonlinearity of interaction in them, which leads to

[a] Corresponding author: skubov.dsk@yandex.ru

significantly nonlinear effects. Namely on a base of nonlinearity we can determine the alteration of mechanical and electrical characteristics. This type of nonlinear effects mostly unattainable in macro scale but in case of nano- or microscale their realization gets off on the first plan and appears as a sensor of small physical alteration.

The change of mechanical and electrical characteristics of one of micro-layers MEMS/NEMS can bring to asymmetry in a form of bending flexure that is completely revealed with modern measuring equipment. With gradual change of magnetic induction in a case of ferromagnetic membrane deformation and the rise of current value in a case of wire deflection we again can obtain their symmetric, thereby determinate happened alteration in nano- or micro scales.

2 Branching of equilibrium forms of ferromagnetic membrane

2.1 Case of one magnet

The combined system of equations of linear elastic and nonlinear magneto-elastic tasks consists in equations of task of stationary distribution of magnetic field and the equation of elasticity of deformed body [19]. The ponderomotive forces are included in equations of deformation, which in technical applications should be related for undeformed body. For nearly situated sufficiently smooth surfaces of ferromagnetic bodies the surface forces are acted. The surface density q of which can be founded from expression $\frac{1}{2}H^2 \times \nabla\mu$ passaged to the limit, then we have a discontinuity of magnetic penetrability μ. With accuracy relatively of highest degree terms of $\frac{\mu_0}{\mu}$ the obtained expression for surface force, acting on ferromagnetic, have a next form:

$$q = \frac{1}{2}\mu_0 H_0^2 \boldsymbol{n} = \frac{1}{2}\left[\frac{\varphi(M)-\varphi_*(M)}{h(M)-u(M)}\right]^2 \boldsymbol{n} \qquad (1)$$

Here φ и φ_* - the scalar magnetic potentials of the close-fitting surfaces of ferromagnetic, $h(M)$ and $u(M)$ – initial distance between surfaces and displacement in a normal arise from their elastic deformation. The largest simplification is achieved for ideal ferromagnetic bodies (when in ferromagnetic we can assume, that $\mu = \infty$). Therefore the value of magnetic potentials φ and φ_* will be the same in all points of surfaces S and S_*. For the systems with nearly situated smooth surfaces with small flexure, as in a considerable case, the difference of potentials is equal to total current I, which is covered by power line of magnetic field, taken with corresponding sign. It is necessary to say that in this statement we neglect the boundary-layer effect, believing that the ratio of gap size to radius of membrane is very small.

The analogy propositions can be supposed believing that ferromagnetic membrane is situated nearly the pole of electromagnet. In this case the membrane may be considered as another pole. The same mathematical problem arises at investigation of equilibrium forms of conductive membrane in electrostatic field.

Thus we obtain the nonlinear boundary problem for determination the forms of membrane flexure with surface normal force, which itself depends on its deformation. The equilibrium equation and boundary conditions have a form:

$$\Delta u + \frac{1}{2}\frac{\mu_0 I^2}{T}\frac{1}{(h-u)^2} = 0, \quad u|_\Gamma = 0 \qquad (2)$$

Here u – displacement, T – tension in unit of distance, h - gap between a pole of electromagnet and undeformed surface of a membrane, Γ – contour of membrane. The further investigation is realized for round membrane. Having entered the dimensionless displacement $v = \frac{u}{h}$ and dimensionless parameter $\kappa^2 = \frac{1}{2}\frac{\mu_0 I^2}{Th^3}$ we obtain the equation:

$$\frac{\partial^2 v}{\partial r^2} + \frac{1}{r}\frac{\partial v}{\partial r} + \frac{1}{r^2}\frac{\partial^2 v}{\partial \theta^2} + \frac{\kappa^2}{(1-v)^2} = 0 \qquad (3)$$

Transforming to new unknown variable $w = 1 - v$ yields the equation:

$$\frac{\partial^2 v}{\partial r^2} + \frac{1}{r}\frac{\partial v}{\partial r} + \frac{1}{r^2}\frac{\partial^2 v}{\partial \theta^2} - \frac{\kappa^2}{w^2} = 0. \qquad (4)$$

Let's consider the axisymmetric case of deformation, believing that displacement does not depend on ϑ. The equation (4) with dimensionless argument $\rho = r/R$ takes a form:

$$\frac{\partial^2 v}{\partial \rho^2} + \frac{1}{\rho}\frac{\partial v}{\partial \rho} - \frac{\alpha^2}{w^2} = 0. \qquad (5)$$

where R – radius of membrane $\alpha^2 = \kappa^2 R^2$ and boundary conditions:

$$w'(0) = 0, \quad w(1) = 1. \qquad (6)$$

The numerical solution of boundary task (5),(6) is obtained with MATLAB program bvp4 (solver of "Boundary Value Problem for ordinary differential equations") [20].

The numerically obtained equilibrium forms at different values of parameter α are shown in Fig.1. It is important to note, that for some fixed value α, which characterizes the induction of external magnetic field, more than one equilibrium states of membrane are corresponded.

The equilibrium forms by solid and dotted lines with the same color, obtained at different angle of inclination of the membrane surface on its edge are shown in Fig.1.

The method of direct numerical solution described above doesn't perfectly satisfy a task of finding the complete quantity and stability of the equilibrium forms, corresponding to given value of parameter α. For achievement the complete solution of the described boundary task we can use a method of building a phase portrait, proposed in [19].

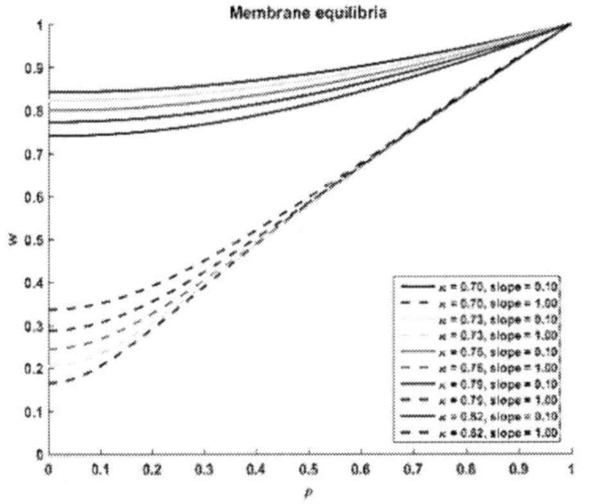

Figure 1. Equilibrium forms of ferromagnetic membrane

Using dimensionless radial coordinate $\tilde{\rho} = \alpha r$, we can transform the equilibrium equation in axisymmetric case (5) to the form:

$$\frac{d^2w}{d\tilde{\rho}} + \frac{1}{\tilde{\rho}}\frac{dw}{d\tilde{\rho}} - \frac{1}{w^2} = 0 \quad (8)$$

with boundary conditions:

$$w'(0) = 0, \quad w(\alpha) = 1. \quad (9)$$

The equation of the boundary problem (8) belongs to Emden-Fowler equations [16]

$$\frac{d}{d\tilde{\rho}}\left(\tilde{\rho}^k \frac{dw}{d\tilde{\rho}}\right) - \tilde{\rho}^m w^n = 0 \quad (10)$$

in our case $k = m = 1$, $n = -2$. This equation is integrated in quadrature only at some values of k, m other than zero. But it can be reduced to a system having excluded the argument $\tilde{\rho}$, that simplifies investigation. Let's input the new variables: argument τ and unknown function η with relations $\tilde{\rho} = ae^{-\beta\tau}$, $w = b\eta e^{-\tau}$. For equation (8) we have obtained $a = \kappa$, $\beta = \frac{3}{2}$, $b = \sqrt[3]{\frac{9}{4}\kappa^2}$. It's important to note, that in view of boundary conditions $\eta(0) = \frac{1}{b}$, consequently at $\alpha > \frac{2}{3}$ $b > 1$ and $\eta(0) < 1$, and on the contrary at $\alpha < \frac{2}{3}$ $b < 1$ and $\eta(0) > 1$. Transformed to function $\eta(\tau)$, we have obtained the next boundary problem:

$$\eta'' - 2\eta' + \eta - \frac{1}{\eta^2} = 0, \quad \eta(0) = \frac{1}{b} \quad (11)$$

For this boundary task it is necessary to add the condition of limitation of displacement in a center, that is corresponded to limitation of $\lim_{\tau\to\infty} \eta(\tau)e^{-\tau}$. The autonomous equation of a boundary problem (11) can be rearranged as a system:

$$\eta' = \vartheta, \qquad \vartheta' = 2\vartheta - \eta + \frac{1}{\eta^2} \quad (12)$$

On the phase plane for system (12) the critical point $\vartheta = 0$, $\eta = 1$ is an unstable focus. The derivative has a view:

$$\frac{d\vartheta}{d\eta} = 2 - \frac{\eta}{\vartheta} + \frac{1}{\vartheta\eta^2} \quad (13)$$

Thus the integral curve proceeding from focus, the part of which is corresponded to boundary task (11), at $\eta \to \infty$ asymptotically approaches to a straight $\vartheta = \eta$, remained below. The phase curve corresponding to boundary task is shown in Fig.2.

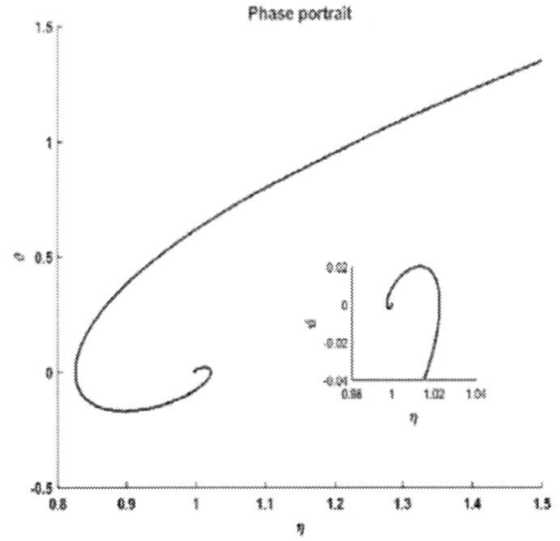

Figure 2. Phase curve corresponding to boundary task

On the appropriated integral curve

$$\frac{dw}{d\tilde{\rho}} = \frac{1}{\eta(0)}\frac{2}{3\alpha}(\eta - \vartheta)e^{\frac{1}{2}\tau}, \quad (14)$$

That corresponds to minimum of variable $w = 1 - v$, i.e. maximum of flexure in a center of membrane at it monotonically decreasing of flexure until zero on a boundary of membrane.

For found solution at prescribed value of parameter κ and, consequently $b = \sqrt[3]{\frac{9}{4}\kappa^2}$, it's necessary to take a vertical $\eta(0) = \frac{1}{b}$ on a phase plane of Fig.2. From the point of its crossing with integral curve, proceeding from the focus, and further along the corresponding phase trajectory segment, we have obtained the solution of axisymmetric boundary task. These crossings can be more than one, and consequently we have some solutions of our boundary problem.

At $\kappa < \frac{2}{3}$ this vertical is situated from the right of vertical $\eta = 1$ and from the left at $\kappa > \frac{2}{3}$. The exclusion is the equilibrium form corresponding $\kappa = \frac{2}{3}$ and, consequently $b = 1 = \eta(0)$. The solution of boundary task (11) in this case completely lies on the phase curve proceeding from the focus and asymptotically approaches to a bisecting line of the first quadrant of phase plane Fig.2. The equation of the flexure has a form $v(\tilde{\rho}) = 1 - (\frac{3\tilde{\rho}}{2})^{2/3}$. The membrane, accordingly bended, is similar to funnel with bevel in a center. This solution and close to it are considered as a formal not corresponding to initial assumption for smallness of curvature of deformed membrane.

The dependence of maximal flexure in a center of membrane v_m (or correspondingly zero of $w_m = 1 - v_m$) from the value of parameter κ is presented in Fig.3.

The building of bifurcation diagram gives the possibility to determine the number and a form of equilibrium axisymmetric forms of the membrane. The upper branch of diagram is responsible for stable equilibrium position.

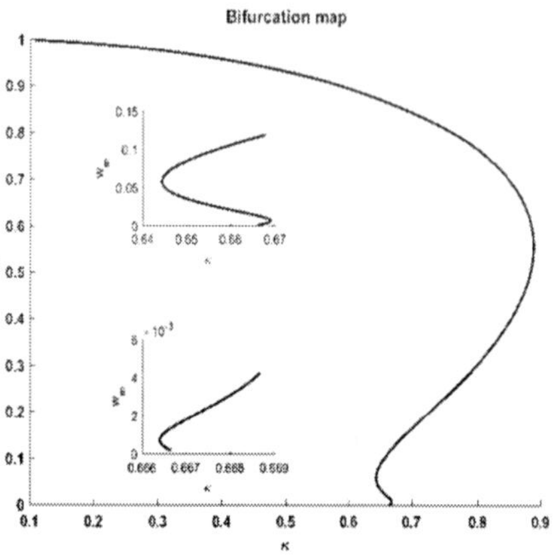

Figure 3. Diagram of branching of equilibrium positions

The found forms of equilibrium coincide with the results obtained by direct numerical solution of boundary problem (5),(6).

Owing to known theorem about non-existence of radial-asymmetrical solutions of nonlinear elliptic tasks in a ball of corresponding dimension (the round in our case) and at condition of nonnegative of external action $f(u)$ [7,8] the task of finding antisymmetric equilibrium forms doesn't have a solution. Our numerical and analytic results confirm the truth of this statement.

2.1 Case of two magnets

Let's consider a case of two magnets with identical poles facing to ferromagnetic membrane situated between them. Now the theorem [8] is unacceptable due to various signs of external ponderomotive action, which has a form

$$f(u) = \frac{1}{2}\frac{\mu_0 I^2}{T}\left[\frac{1}{(h-u)^2} - \frac{1}{(h+u)^2}\right] \quad (15)$$

Thereby in this case it is possible the existence of antisymmetric forms of equilibrium position.

Let's turn to study the diagram of bifurcation of this boundary problem

$$\Delta u + \frac{1}{2}\frac{\mu_0 I^2}{T}\left[\frac{1}{(h-u)^2} - \frac{1}{(h+u)^2}\right] = 0, \quad u|_\Gamma = 0 \quad (16)$$

Inputting to eq. (16) the dimensionless displacement $v = \frac{u}{h}$ and dimensionless parameter $\kappa^2 = \frac{1}{2}\frac{\mu_0 I^2}{Th^3}$ in analogy to previous case of one membrane we obtain the next equation for round membrane:

$$\frac{\partial^2 v}{\partial \rho^2} + \frac{1}{\rho}\frac{\partial v}{\partial \rho} + \frac{1}{\rho^2}\frac{\partial^2 v}{\partial \theta^2} + \alpha^2\left[\frac{1}{(1-v)^2} - \frac{1}{(1+v)^2}\right] = 0, \quad (17)$$

were $\alpha = \kappa R$. This task has a trivial solution $v \equiv 0$ at any value of parameter α. The points of bifurcation with appearance of nonzero solutions are determined at those parameters α at which the variation equation, built relatively to zero solution of (17), has nontrivial solution. This equation relatively a solution with k harmonics on the angle coordinate with boundary homogenous condition has a form:

$$\frac{d^2\xi_k}{d\rho^2} + \frac{1}{\rho}\frac{d\xi_k}{d\rho} + \left(4\alpha^2 - \frac{k^2}{\rho^2}\right)\xi_k = 0. \quad (18)$$

Boundary conditions $\xi_k(1) = 0$. This is a Bessel equation and its solution has a form $\xi_k = J_k(2\alpha\rho)$, which in a sense of boundary problem has an eigenvalue at $2\alpha = \lambda_{ki}, i = 1,2,...$, where λ_{ki} – the roots of Bessel function of k order $J_k(\lambda_{ki}) = 0$. The first point of bifurcation corresponds to $k = 0$ with axisymmetric form of deformation.

The task of direct finding of nontrivial forms of equilibrium states of the membrane (axisymmetric and antisymmetric) can be solved by numerical methods. For this aim the module of system MATLAB (Partial Differential Equations Toolbox), based on FEM [20] is applied. For definition of initial approximation for required solution at given value of parameter α we use a solution obtained at previous step of iteration procedure, obtained at less value α. This method gives an opportunity for finding all the branches of bifurcation diagram. Acquirement of the points of branching $\alpha = \frac{\lambda_{ki}}{2}$ obtained above analytically for different states of equilibrium essentially simplify this problem.

The symmetrical equilibrium forms of a membrane for $k = 0$ at some values of parameter α are shown in Fig.5(a,b). These branches of forms correspond to points of bifurcation $\alpha = \frac{\lambda_{01}}{2}, \frac{\lambda_{02}}{2}$. The antisymmetric forms with $k = 1$ corresponded to a branch issuant from $\alpha = \frac{\lambda_{11}}{2}, \frac{\lambda_{12}}{2}$ are shown in Fig.6(a,b). The corresponded diagram of branching is shown in Fig.7.

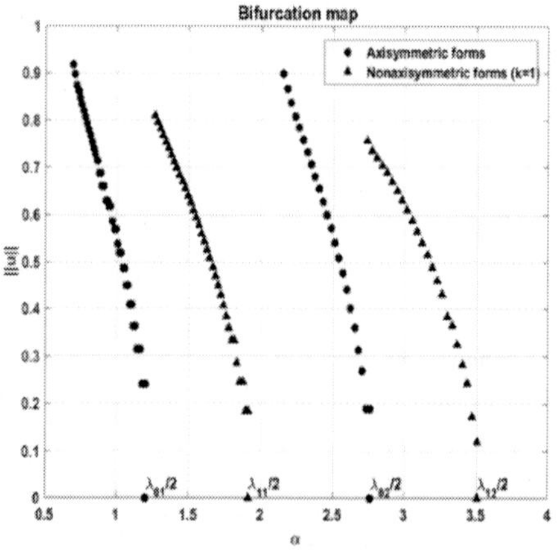

Figure 7. Bifurcation of the states of equilibrium

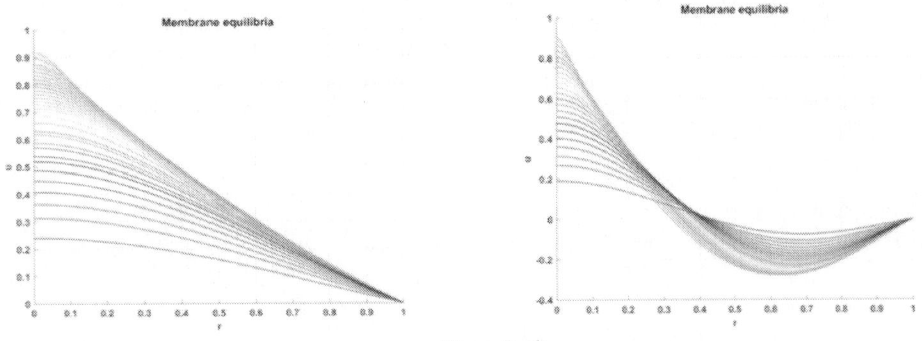

Figure 5. a,b

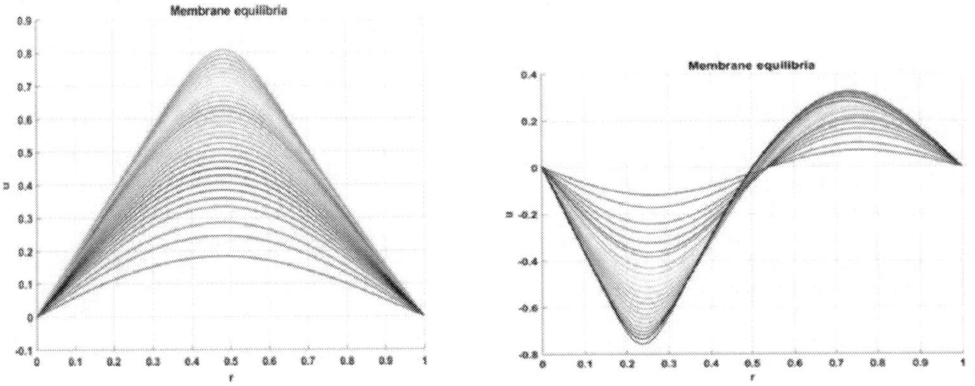

a) b)

Figure 6. a,b

It is interesting and is conform by the theory of branching that all nonzero forms are unstable. This result gives us the field of attraction of stable undeformed form of membrane. From this point of view it is important that the amplitude of nontrivial solution is increased at decreasing the value of parameter α, proportional to quadrate of induction of external magnetic field.

3 Branching of equilibriums of a system of nano-layers

In this paragraph we can investigate the branching of equilibrium forms of three parallel micro- nanolayers MEMS and NEMS with constant currents (Fig.9). The system of this type is workable even in the nanoscale [2]. This micro/nanostructure can be used as a sensor of external and internal mechanical and electrical characteristics at their small change or as one of types of nanoresonators, which are used for measuring the mass of adhering nanoparticles [11,12]. In last case the measuring of a mass of nanoparticle is possible due to change in the eigen frequency of mechanical oscillations.

It is important to note that in a case of micro- nano-circuits the nonlinear interaction between them must be considered, which leads to nonlinear effects. On the base of nonlinear effects it is possible to identify changing the mechanical and electrical characteristics. The nonlinear effects of this type are mostly unattainable in macroscales, but in a case of nano- microscales their implementation is coming to the first plan and taking place as a sensor of small physical changes.

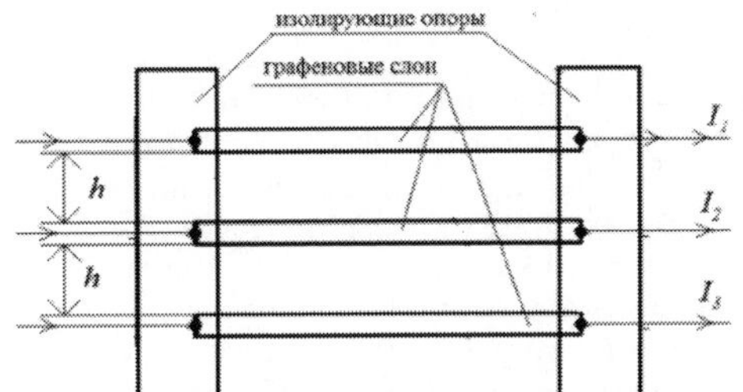

Figure 9. System of nanolayers

Changes in mechanical and electrical characteristics of one of the layers of MEMS/NEMS may cause asymmetry in the form of deflection, which is quite detectable by modern measuring equipment. With gradual change in a current in one of layers we can achieve their symmetry again, thereby identifying the changes in the micro/nanoscale.

Let's carry out the estimations of parameters of graphene nanostrings [5], at which their significant interaction is realized: the length of layer $l = 1000$ nm, width $\delta = 10$ nm, thickness $b = 0.3$ nm. Thus, the resonance frequency of string oscillations reaches 30 MHz with quality factor $Q \sim 100$. Using the expression for eigen frequency $\bar{\omega}$, we obtain the required tensile force

$$T = \rho_V S \frac{l^2 \bar{\omega}^2}{\pi^2} = 1{,}5 \cdot 10^{-12}\text{N}.$$

Using the expression for parameter $\lambda^2 = \frac{\mu_0 I^2}{2\pi T h^2}$, entered below and characterizing the strong interaction of layers, and setting, that its value corresponds to a gap of the order $h \sim 10$ nm, we get the current value

$$I_0 = \frac{h\lambda}{l}\sqrt{\frac{\pi T}{\mu_0}} = 40 \cdot 10^{-6}\text{A} = 40 \text{ мkA},$$

that is quite feasible in nanosystems.

In our work we study the static positions of the three parallel nano/microstrings with constant current and equal gaps between them, that in mathematical sense is close to consideration of equilibrium shapes of ferromagnetic membranes in a constant axisymmetric magnetic field [13].

Inputting the designation of currents in a case of their equality $I_1 = I_2 = I_3 = I = const$, we write the approximate expression for distributed attractive forces without regard to boundary effects

$$q = \frac{\mu_0 I^2}{2\pi}\frac{r}{r^2}, \tag{19}$$

here r – vector of distance between strings, which in a first approximation directs vertically to the strings [19]. The dynamical equation of a string with tension T, linear density ρ and force of attraction q in a vector form:

$$Tu'' - \rho\ddot{u} + q = 0 \tag{20}$$

The equations of equilibrium for three strings (without taking into account the interaction of extremes) are written in the form:

$$Tu_1'' + q_{12} = 0,$$
$$Tu_2'' + q_{21} + q_{23} = 0, \tag{21}$$
$$Tu_3'' + q_{32} = 0.$$

Here q_{ij} – the forces of attraction from j – th conductor with i –th, $u_i, i = 1,2,3$– displacements of the strings one by one due to their vertical deflection deformation, the derivative is taken along the length. The positive displacements of strings are directed vertically in the same direction as the positive direction of efforts. In the case of the attracting force difference currents are written in the form:

$$q_{12} = \frac{\mu_0 I_1 I_2}{2\pi}\frac{1}{(h + u_2 - u_1)}, \quad q_{21} = -q_{12},$$
$$q_{23} = \frac{\mu_0 I_2 I_3}{2\pi}\frac{1}{(h + u_3 - u_2)}, \quad q_{32} = -q_{23}, \tag{22}$$

here h – initial gap between conductors (strings). Inputting the dimensionless coordinates and displacements $s = x/l$, $v_i = u_i/h$ and the main dimensionless physical parameter $\lambda^2 = \frac{\mu_0 I^2 l^2}{2\pi T h^2}$, where I – a large scale of current value. Instead of the dimensional equations (21),(22) we will receive system of the equations in a dimensionless form:

$$v_1'' + \frac{\alpha_1\lambda^2}{1 + v_2 - v_1} = 0,$$
$$v_2'' - \frac{\alpha_1\lambda^2}{1+v_2-v_1} + \frac{\alpha_2\lambda^2}{1+v_3-v_2} = 0, \tag{23}$$
$$v_3'' - \frac{\alpha_2\lambda^2}{1 + v_3 - v_2} = 0,$$

The sum of derivations of deflections owing to symmetry of deformation of strings on length is equal to zero. And, therefore, the sum of deflections, owing to zero regional conditions, is also equal to zero:

$$v_1 + v_2 + v_3 = 0. \tag{24}$$

Let's enter the differences of deflections: $z_1 = v_1 - v_2$, $z_2 = v_2 - v_3$ and, subtracting the second equation from the first and third of the second, we will receive system of two nonlinear equations:

$$z_1'' + \frac{2\alpha_1\lambda^2}{1-z_1} - \frac{\alpha_2\lambda^2}{1-z_2} = 0,$$
$$z_2'' + \frac{2\alpha_2\lambda^2}{1-z_2} - \frac{\alpha_1\lambda^2}{1-z_1} = 0 \tag{25}$$

with zero boundary conditions. Deflections of each of strings, using the entered variables, are written in a form:

$$v_1 = \frac{2z_1+z_2}{3}, \quad v_2 = \frac{z_2-z_1}{3}, \; v_3 = -\frac{2z_2+z_1}{3}. \tag{26}$$

Obtained boundary problem (25) at equality of currents allows the symmetric solution with not deformed average string and the identical opposite directed deflections of extremes $v_2 = 0$, $v_1 = -v_3$ (extreme strings cave in towards), when $z_1 = z_2 = z_3$ and instead of two equations (25) we have one:

$$z'' + \frac{\lambda^2}{1-z} = 0 \tag{27}$$

with boundary conditions: $z(0) = 0$, $z(1) = 0$. The boundary problem (27) realized in a case $\alpha_1 = \alpha_2 = 1$ is completely equivalent to the problem of a deflection of two strings considered by us earlier with direct identical currents [19]. Its bifurcation diagram has two solution sat value of parameter $\lambda < \lambda_* \approx 1.54$ with a smaller steady and bigger unstable symmetric form of a deflection. Rewriting the equations (25) in a form:

$$z_1'' + 2z_2'' + \frac{3\lambda^2}{1-z_2} = 0, \; 2z_1'' + z_2'' + \frac{3\lambda^2}{1-z_1} = 0 \tag{28}$$

and multiplying the first equation on z_2' and second on z_1', we have obtained after summation the integral of energy:

$$(z_1')^2 + (z_2')^2 + z_1'z_2' - 3\lambda^2 \ln(1 - z_1) - 3\lambda^2 \ln(1 - z_2) = h = const, \tag{29}$$

having the symmetry relatively z_1, z_2. If to look for the private symmetric solution $z_1 = z_2 = z$, the integral is given to a form:

$$(z')^2 - 2\lambda^2 \ln(1 - z) = h = const, \tag{30}$$

what corresponds to a boundary task for two strings.

The solution of a boundary task (25) is passed numerically, using the subprogramme bvp4c MatLab, and Galerkin's method. The numerically obtained symmetric and asymmetric relatively average layer equilibrium states, corresponding to various value of λ are shown in Fig.12,13

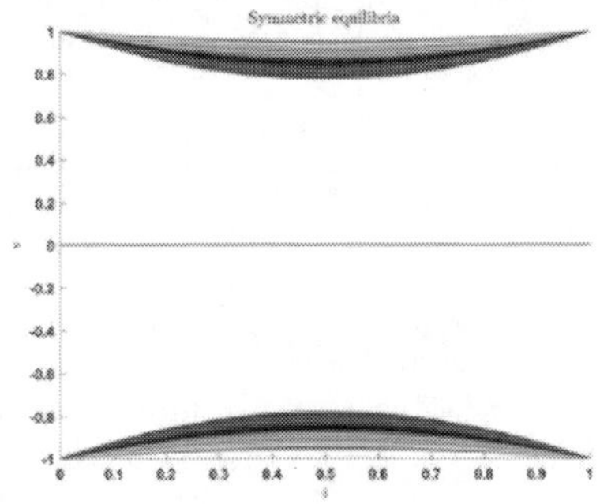

Figure 12. Symmetric equilibrium states

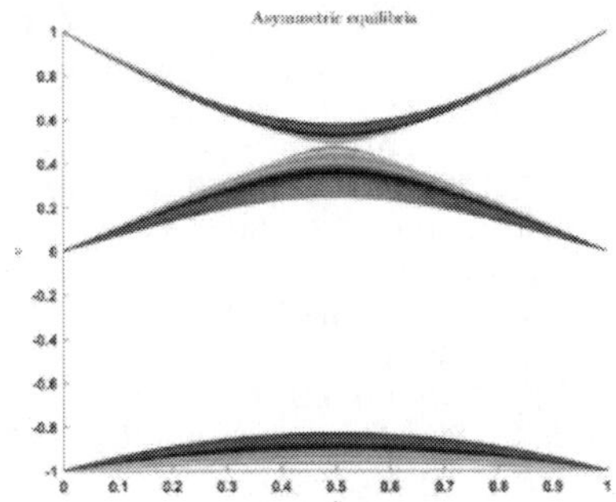

Figure 13. Asymmetric equilibrium states

Projective conditions on Galerkin in case of forms of a deflection, symmetric concerning the middle, are received at taking of the approximate solution at a form:

$$z_i = x_i sin\pi s, \quad i = 1,2. \tag{31}$$

Projective conditions of system (28) for the taken forms of deflections (31) have a form:

$$\begin{gathered} -\pi^2[2x_1 + x_2]\int_0^1 sin^2\pi s\, ds + 3\alpha_1\lambda^2\int_0^1 \frac{\sin\pi s}{1 - x_1 \sin\pi s} ds = 0 \\ -\pi^2[2x_2 + x_1]\int_0^1 sin^2\pi s\, ds + 3\alpha_2\lambda^2\int_0^1 \frac{\sin\pi s}{1 - x_2 \sin\pi s} ds = 0. \end{gathered} \tag{32}$$

In result the system (32) takes a form:

$$\begin{gathered} \frac{\pi^2}{2}[2x_1 + x_2] - \frac{3\alpha_1\lambda^2}{\pi x_1}\left[\pi\left(\frac{1}{\sqrt{1-x_1^2}} - 1\right) + \frac{2\arcsin x_1}{\sqrt{1-x_1^2}}\right] = 0, \\ \frac{\pi^2}{2}[2x_2 + x_1] - \frac{3\alpha_2\lambda^2}{\pi x_2}\left[\pi\left(\frac{1}{\sqrt{1-x_2^2}} - 1\right) + \frac{2\arcsin x_2}{\sqrt{1-x_2^2}}\right] = 0. \end{gathered} \tag{33}$$

The bifurcation diagram of solutions of a system (33) in a case of equal currents represents in Fig.14. By one color and one type of a marker in Fig.14 the equilibrium states of three layers which are realized in common are designated in one color.

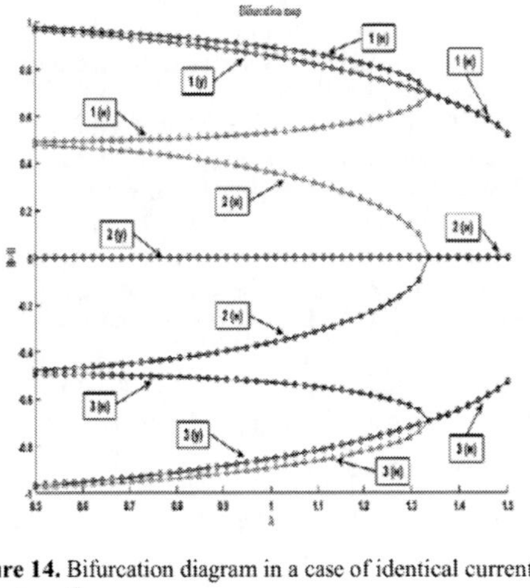

Figure 14. Bifurcation diagram in a case of identical currents: $\alpha_1 = \alpha_2 = 1$

The branching of forms of balance of three strings in a case of identical currents happens in the form of a threefold point with steady until value of parameter $\lambda_* \approx 1.34$ neutral zero position of the second (average) string. At the value of parameter λ, exceeding λ_*, the neutral position of a middle string became unstable and asymmetric forms, at which the average string is deformed, are vanished. At achievement of parameter λ the value 1.53 all equilibrium positions are disappeared, that physically corresponds to adhesion of strings (violation of the conditions of the studied model).

Transition through a symmetric case of identical currents is of special interest, at gradual (quasistationary) increasing of current in one of extreme strings. At the same time two boundary problems are solved. The first corresponds to smaller current in one of extreme strings, and identical in two others ($\alpha_1 < 1, \alpha_2 = 1$) the second - to bigger current in extreme, than in two others ($\alpha_1 > 1, \alpha_2 = 1$).

As entry conditions of the numerical solution of a boundary task the solution of the linearized system (25) was made. The linearized system at small deflections has the following appearance:

$$\xi_1'' + 2\lambda^2(1+\xi_1) - \lambda^2(1+\xi_2) = 0,$$
$$\xi_2'' + 2\lambda^2(1+\xi_2) - \lambda^2(1+\xi_1) = 0.$$

Or

$$\xi_1'' + \lambda^2(2 + 2\xi_1 - \xi_2) = -\lambda^2,$$
$$\xi_2'' + \lambda^2(2 + 2\xi_2 - \xi_1) = -\lambda^2. \quad (34)$$

The system (34) at zero boundary conditions, what, in fact, means equality $\xi_1 = \xi_2$, takes a form of one equation:

$$\xi'' + \lambda^2\xi = -\lambda^2. \quad (35)$$

Under zero boundary conditions the boundary task (35) has the solution:

$$\xi = -1 + \cos\lambda s + (1 - \cos\lambda)\frac{\sin\lambda s}{\sin\lambda}, \quad (36)$$

Linear approximation (36) suits for system (25) only at small currents - small λ and corresponds only to small deflections.

For search of points of branching it is necessary to investigate compliance of eigenvalues of the equations in variations concerning the found symmetric form with value of parameter λ [14,15]. Proceeding from the numerical solution of an uniform nonlinear boundary task (25), branching happens at values $\lambda = \lambda_* \approx 1.34$. This value coincides with value $\lambda = \lambda_{**}$ at which there is a bifurcation of symmetric forms of equilibrium - "contact" of static forms of middle string with one of extreme strings to further loss of the symmetric solution.

The variation equation for system (25) in case of the symmetric solution at $\lambda = \lambda_0$, $z = z_0(s)$ is written in a form:

$$\xi'' + \frac{\lambda^2}{(1 - z_0(s))^2}\xi = 0 \quad (37)$$

with uniform boundary conditions:

$$\xi(0) = \xi(1) = 0, \eta(0) = \eta(1) = 0.$$

The equation (37) with zero regional conditions is a linear boundary task with variable coefficient. Due to positivity of the variable coefficient in a differential equation (37) $(0 < z_0(s) < 1)$ the eigenvalue of variation task (25) decreases. The second item plays a role of the negative distributed modulus of foundation. The point of branching corresponds to coincidence of eigenvalue of a variation boundary task (37) with own value of parameter λ. Stability of asymmetrical forms is defined by calculation of eigen frequencies of the dynamic uniform tasks received by linearization of a system (25) concerning the asymmetrical nonlinear deflections [14].

$$\xi'' + \frac{2\alpha_1\lambda^2}{(1 - z_{10})^2}\xi + \frac{\alpha_2\lambda^2}{(1 - z_{20})^2}\eta - \varrho\ddot{\xi} = 0,$$
$$\eta'' + \frac{2\alpha_2\lambda^2}{(1 - z_{20})^2}\eta + \frac{\alpha_1\lambda^2}{(1 - z_{10})^2}\xi - \varrho\ddot{\eta} = 0. \quad (38)$$

Points of branching correspond to the equality to zero the eigen frequencies of linearized dynamic boundary task (38).

Important achievement of the real work is application of the theory of branching to new type nano - micro electromechanical schemes with possible using of the received structure of branching of the equilibrium forms for definition its nano- micro scale physical changes.

Acknowledgements

Work is performed with assistance of a grant of the RFBR 14-01-00845.

References

1. Wen-Ming Zhang, Han Yan, Zhi-Ke Peng, Guang Meng, *Electrostatic pull-in instability in MEMS/NEMS: A review* – Sensors and Actuators A **214** p.187–218 (2014)
2. Eom K., Harold S. Park (et al) *Nanomechanical resonators and their applications in biological/chemical detection: Nanomechanics principles.* Physics Reports, V. **503** p. 115 – 163 (2011)
3. Scott Bunch J. (et al) *Electromechanical Resonators from Graphene Sheets* V. **315** p. 490 – 493 (2007)
4. Chen C. (et al) *Performance of monolayer graphene,* Nature Nanotechnology, V. **4** p. 861-867 (2009)
5. He X.Q., Kitipornchai S., Liew K.M. *Resonance analysis of multi-layered graphene sheets used as nanoscale resonators*, Nanotechnology V.**16** p. 2086 – 2091 (2009)
6. John A. Pelesko, Tobin A. Driscoll *The effect of the small-aspect-ratio approximation on canonical electrostatic MEMS models* Journal of Engineering Mathematics, **53**, p. 239-25 (2005)
7. B. Gidas, Wei-Ming Ni, L. N. Nirenberg *Symmetry and Related Properties via the Maximum Principle* Commun. Math. Phys. **68** p.209-243 (1979)
8. Dong Ye., Feng Zhou *On a general family of nonautonomous elliptic and parabolic equations* Calc. Var. **37** p.259-274 (2010)
9. Griberg Ya.S. (et al) *Nanomechanical resonators,* Sucs.of Phys.Sience, 4 V.**182** p.407 – 436 (2012)
10. Raiher Yu.L., Stolbov O.V., Stepanov G.V. *Deformation of a round membrane (ferro-elastic) in uniform magnetic field*, Journ. Technic. Phys. V.**78**, issue 9, p.69-76 (2008)
11. Morozov N.F., Berinsrii I.E., Indeitsev D.A., Privalova O.V., Skubov D.Yu., Shtukin L.V. *Failure of oscillations of graphene resonator as a method of determination of its spectral characteristics*, DAS, V. **456**, № 5, p.537 - 540 (2014)
12. Shtukin L.V., Berinskii I.E., Indeitsev D.A., Morozov N.F., Skubov D.Yu. *Electromechanical models of nanoresonators*, Physic. Mezomechanics, V. **19**, № 1 (2016)
13. Skubov D.Yu., Lukin A.V., Popov I.A., Privalova O.V., Shtukin L.V. *Branching of equlibrium forms of nonlinear NEMS/MEMS* Proc. of III Intern. School-NDM, p. 274-281 (2016)

14. Vainberg M.M., Trenogin V.A. *The theory of bifurcation of nonlinear equations* – M.: Science, (1969)
15. Antman St., Keller J. B. *Bifurcation theory and nonlinear eigenvalue problems* – M.: World, (1974)
16. Sansone J. *Ordinary differential equations* – M.: In.Lit., (1953)
17. Bellman R. *Theory of stability solutions of differential equations* - M.: In.Lit. (1954)
18. Fridman V.M. Theory of elastic oscillations. Equations and methods – St.Petersb.: Sciece (2014)
19. Skubov D.Yu., Khodzhaev K.Sh. Nonlinear electromechanics –Springer-Verlag (2003)
20. Matlab Documentation, The MathWorks, Inc., 2015

MATEC Web of Conferences **76**, 01002 (2016) DOI: 10.1051/matecconf/20167601002
CSCC 2016

Polynomial Digital Control of a Series Equal Liquid Tanks

Vladimír Bobál[a], Stanislav Talaš, Petr Dostál and Marek Kubalčík

Tomas Bata Universty in Zlin, Faculty of Applied Informatics, Department of Process Control, Nad Stranemi 4511, 760 05 Zlin, Czech Republic

Abstract. Time-delays are mainly caused by the time required to transport mass, energy or information, but they can also be caused by processing time or accumulation. Typical examples of such processes are e.g. pumps, liquid storing tanks, distillation columns or some types of chemical reactors. In many cases time-delay is caused by the effect produced by the accumulation of a large number of low-order systems. Several industrial processes have the time-delay effect produced by the accumulation of a great number of low-order systems with the identical dynamic. The dynamic behavior of series these low-order systems is expressed by high-order system. One of possibilities of control of such processes is their approximation by low-order model with time-delay. The paper is focused on the design of the digital polynomial control of a set of equal liquid cylinder atmospheric tanks. The designed control algorithms are realized using the digital Smith Predictor (SP) based on polynomial approach – by minimization of the Linear Quadratic (LQ) criterion. The LQ criterion was combined with pole assignment.

1 Introduction

Time-delay may be defined as the time interval between the start of an event at one point in a system and its resulting action at another point in the system. Delays are also known as transport lags or dead times; they arise in physical, chemical, biological and economic systems, as well as in the process of measurement and computation.

Some technological processes in industrial practice are characterized by high-order dynamic behaviour or large time constants and time-delays. For control engineering, such processes can often be approximated by the FOTD (first-order-time-delay) model. Time-delay in a process increases the difficulty of controlling it. However, using the approximation of a high-order process by a low-order model with time-delay provides simplification of the control algorithms. In many cases the time delay is caused by the effect produced by the accumulation of a large number of low order systems.

Let us consider a continuous-time dynamical linear SISO system (single input $u(t)$ – single output $y(t)$) with time-delay L. The transfer function of a pure transportation lag is e^{-Ls} where s is a complex variable. Overall transfer function with time-delay is in the form

$$G_L(s) = G(s)e^{-Ls} \qquad (1)$$

where $G(s)$ is the transfer function without time-delay.

Historically first modifications of time-delay control algorithms were proposed for continuous-time (analog) controllers using various approaches. One of possible approaches to control of process with time-delay is Smith predictor [1]. In industrial practice, the implementation of the time-delay compensation algorithms on continuous-time technique is difficult. One of possible approaches to control of process with time-delay is digital Smith predictor based on polynomial theory.

This paper is oriented to design of a LQ control using polynomial theory [2, 3]. The minimization of LQ criterion is completed with pole assignment principle.

The digital pole assignment Smith predictor was designed using a polynomial approach in [4]. The design of this controller was extended by a method for a choice of a suitable pole assignment of the characteristic polynomial. Because the classical analog Smith predictor is not suitable for control of unstable and integrating time-delay processes, the polynomial digital LQ Smith predictor for control of unstable and integrating time-delay processes has been designed in [5].

It is obvious that the majority processes met in industrial practice are influenced by uncertainties. The uncertainties suppression can be solved either implementation adaptive control or robust control. Some adaptive (self-tuning) modifications of the digital Smith predictors are designed in [4, 6, 7]. Two versions of these controllers were implemented into MATLAB Toolbox [8, 9].

Main contribution of this paper is focused on the design of the digital polynomial control of a set of liquid cylinder atmospheric tanks. The paper is organized in the following way. The general problem of a control of the time-delay systems with regard to polynomial approach is described in Section 1. The high-order system (a set of n

[a] Corresponding author: bobal@fai.utb.cz

equal liquid cylinder atmospheric tanks) is analysed in Section 2. Section 3 contains description of identification procedures. The fundamental principle of digital Smith predictor is described in Section 4. The primary polynomial LQ controller, which is component of the digital Smith predictor, is proposed in Section 5. The simulation verifications of individual control-loops with their results are presented in Section 6. Section 7 concludes this paper.

2 Series of equal liquid tanks

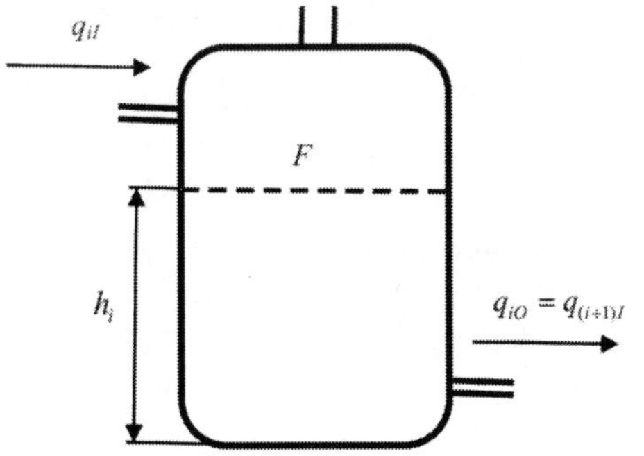

Fig. 1 Schema of liquid cylinder tank

In many cases in industrial practice the time-delay is caused by the effect produced by the accumulation of a large number of low-order systems. Consider a set of n equal cylinder atmospheric tanks, where a single tank is shown in Fig. 1 [10] and the whole set is shown in Fig. 2.

In this system, the output flow of tank i (q_{iO}) feeds tank $i + 1$; that is, the input flow tank $i + 1$ is $q_{(i+1)I} = q_{iO}$. If all the tanks have the same area (F) of crosscut and the individual tank levels are near to an operating point, then the dynamic behaviour of the level in each tank h_i can be modelled by a linear system

$$F\frac{dh_i}{dt} = q_{iI} - q_{io} \qquad q_{iO} = K_1 h_i \tag{2}$$

where K_1 is a constant that depends on the tank characteristics and $T = F / K_1$ is time constant.

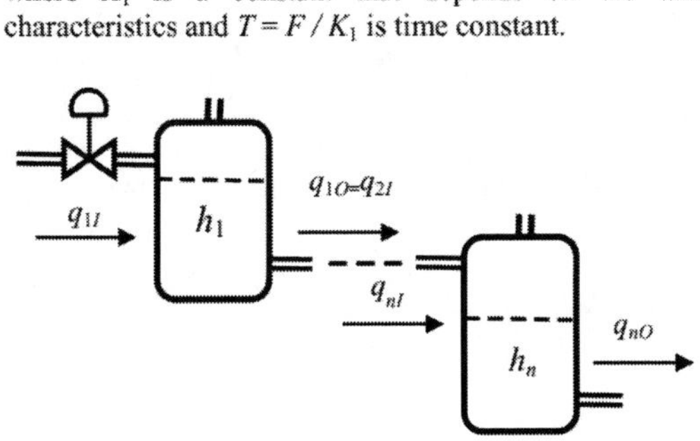

Fig. 2 Series of liquid cylinder tanks

Consider a set of n tanks as shown in Fig. 2. Thus, the transfer function relating the input follow in tank i and its level is given by

$$h_i(s) = \frac{1/K_1}{Ts+1} q_{iI}(s) \tag{3}$$

For tank 1 is

$$h_1(s) = \frac{1/K_1}{Ts+1} q_{1I}(s) \tag{4}$$

and for tank 2 using the second equation of (2)

$$h_2(s) = \frac{1/K_1}{Ts+1} q_{2I}(s) = \frac{1/K_1}{Ts+1} q_{1O}(s) = \frac{1/K_1}{Ts+1} K_1 h_1(s) \tag{5}$$

Then, using the expression (4) it follows

$$h_n(s) = G(s) q_{1I}(s) = \frac{K_g}{(Ts+1)^n} q_{1I}(s) \tag{6}$$

and the transfer function of the series of tanks system is

$$G(s) = \frac{h_n(s)}{q_{1I}(s)} = \frac{K_g}{(Ts+1)^n} \tag{7}$$

where $K_g = 1/K_1$ is static gain of the system (7).

Consider for simulation experiments of control model (7) the eight – order system, i. e. n = 8. Following parameters of the individual liquid tanks are considered (see Fig. 1):
high of tank h = 1.5 m;
diameter of tank d_T = 1 m;
tank area $F = \frac{\pi d_T}{4} = 0.785$ m^2;
time constant T = 2 min;
constant $K_1 = \frac{F}{T} = \frac{0.785}{2} = 0.3925$ m^{2}min^{-1};
static gain $K_g = \frac{1}{K_1} = \frac{1}{0.3925} = 3.08$ m^{-2} min.

The resulting transfer function is given by

$$G(s) = \frac{h_8(s)}{q_{1I}(s)} = \frac{3.08}{(2s+1)^8} \tag{8}$$

If (8) is the transfer function of a continuous-time dynamic system, then the following expression for the discrete transfer function with zero - order holder and sampling period T_0 is valid

$$G(z^{-1}) = \frac{b_1 z^{-1} + b_2 z^{-2} + \ldots + b_8 z^{-8}}{1 + a_1 z^{-1} + a_2 z^{-2} + \ldots + a_8 z^{-8}} \tag{9}$$

The transfer function (9) was approximated by the discrete second-order model with time-delay

$$G_L(z^{-1}) = \frac{B(z^{-1})}{A(z^{-1})} z^{-d} = \frac{b_1 z^{-1} + b_2 z^{-2}}{1 + a_1 z^{-1} + a_2 z^{-2}} z^{-d} \tag{10}$$

 DOI: 10.1051/matecconf/20167601002

3 Identification of series liquid tanks

3.1 Determination of number time-delay steps

The number of time-delay steps is obtained using an off-line identification by the least squares method (LSM). The measured process output (liquid level $h_8(k)[\mathrm{m}]$ near operating flow) is influenced by input – generator of white noise which excites changes of flow rate $q_{1I}(k)[\mathrm{m}^3\,\mathrm{min}^{-1}]$. The non-measurable system disturbances cause errors **e** in the determination of model parameters and therefore real output vector is in the form

$$\mathbf{y} = \mathbf{F}\boldsymbol{\Theta} + \mathbf{e} \tag{11}$$

The matrix **F** has dimension (*N-n-d*, 2*n*), the vector **y** (*N-n-d*) and the vector of parameter model estimates $\hat{\boldsymbol{\Theta}}$ (2*n*). *N* is the number of samples of measured input and output data, *n* is the model order. It is possible to obtain the LSM expression for calculation of the vector of the parameter estimates

$$\hat{\boldsymbol{\Theta}} = \left(\mathbf{F}^{\mathrm{T}}\mathbf{F}\right)^{-1}\mathbf{F}^{\mathrm{T}}\mathbf{y} \tag{12}$$

Equation (12), where $n = 8$, serves for calculation of the vector of the parameter estimates $\hat{\boldsymbol{\Theta}}$ using *N* samples of measured input-output data. The form of individual vectors and matrices in equations (11) and (12) are introduced in [11].

Consider that model (10) is the deterministic part of the stochastic process described by the ARX (regression) model

$$\begin{aligned} y(k) &= -a_1 y(k-1) - a_2 y(k-2) + \\ &+ b_1 y(k-1-d) + b_2 y(k-2-d) + e_s(k) \end{aligned} \tag{13}$$

where $e_s(k)$ is the random non-measurable component.

The vector of parameter model estimates is computed by solving equation (12)

$$\hat{\boldsymbol{\Theta}}^T(k) = \begin{bmatrix} \hat{a}_1 & \hat{a}_2 & \hat{b}_1 & \hat{b}_2 \end{bmatrix} \tag{14}$$

and is used for computation of the predicted output

$$\begin{aligned} \hat{y}(k) &= -\hat{a}_1 y(k-1) - \hat{a}_2 y(k-2) + \\ &\hat{b}_1 u(k-1-d) + \hat{b}_2 u(k-2-d) \end{aligned} \tag{15}$$

The quality of identification can be considered according to error, i.e. the deviation

$$\hat{e}(k) = y(k) - \hat{y}(k) \tag{16}$$

Continuous-time system (8) was identified by discrete model (10) using off-line LSM (12) for different time-delay dT_0; $T_0 = 1\,\mathrm{min}$. The White Noise Generator was used as excitation input signal. A criterion of the identification quality is based on sum of squares of error

$$J_{\hat{e}^2}(d) = \sum_{k=1}^{N} \hat{e}^2(k) \tag{17}$$

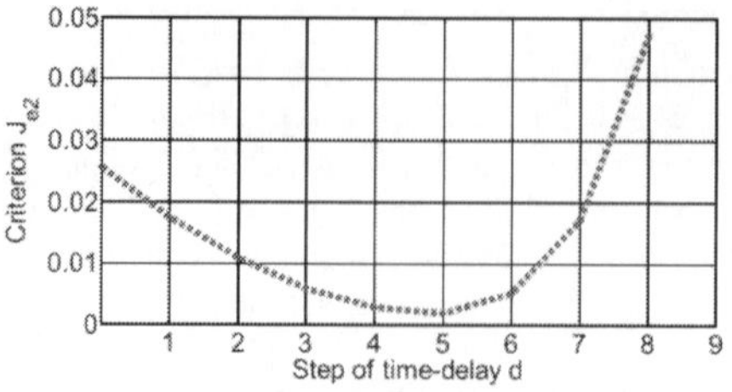

Fig. 3 Criterion of Quality Identification for $d \in [0,8]$

This criterion represents accuracy of process identification. It is obvious from Fig. 4 that minimum value of the criterion (21) is reached when the number of time-delay steps $d = 5$. Then it is possible to use model

$$\hat{G}_L\left(z^{-1}\right) = \frac{\hat{b}_1 z^{-1} + \hat{b}_2 z^{-2}}{1 + \hat{a}_1 z^{-1} + \hat{a}_2 z^{-2}} z^{-5} \tag{18}$$

for an approximation of model (8).

3.2 Identification procedure

The model (18) was used in off-line identification procedure for calculation of parameter estimates. This procedure was realized by the MATLAB function

$$x = \mathrm{fminsearch}('name\_fce', x_0) \tag{19}$$

from the MATLAB Optimization Toolbox. This function finds minimum of an unconstrained multivariable function using derivative-free method. Algorithm "fminsearch" uses the simplex search method of [12]. This is a direct search method that does not use numerical or analytic gradients.

The difference between static gain $K_g = 3.08$ of the continuous-time transfer function (8) and estimation of the static gain of discrete transfer function (18)

$$\hat{K}_g = \frac{\hat{b}_1 + \hat{b}_2}{1 + \hat{a}_1 + \hat{a}_2} \tag{20}$$

can serve as a good criterion for the quality of identification.

Results of experimental identification demonstrated that better the identification quality is obtained using "fminsearch" method. Discrete model for sampling period $T_0 = 1\,\mathrm{min}$

$$\hat{G}_L\left(z^{-1}\right) = \frac{0.0309 z^{-1} + 0.0286 z^{-2}}{1 - 1.777 z^{-1} + 0.7964 z^{-2}} z^{-5} \tag{21}$$

is obtained using this method with static gain (20) $K_g = 3.08$ is the same as in model (8). Comparison of step responses of continuous-time (8) and discrete model (21) is shown in Fig. 4. The input step signal $\Delta q_{1I} = 0.04\,\mathrm{m}^3\,\mathrm{min}^{-1}$ was chosen so that tank level is near to an operating point.

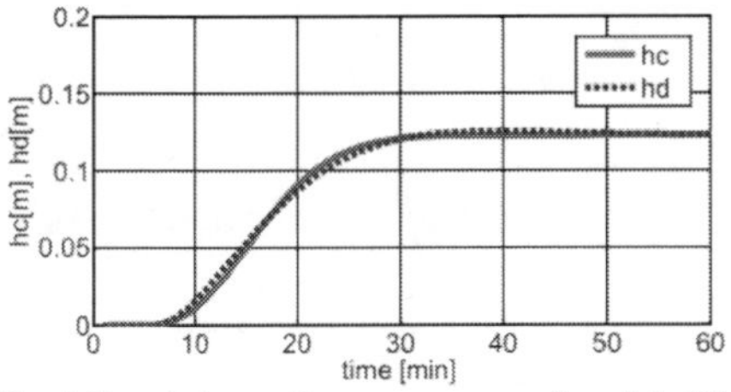

Fig. 4 Comparison of step responses of models (8) and (20)

It is obvious that linear model (20) was obtained without complying with valves contain hysteresis and other nonlinearities that the series liquid tanks system contains [13].

4 Fundamental principle of digital SP

The block diagram of a digital SP (see [4], [5]) is shown in Fig. 5. The function of the digital version is similar to the classical analogue version. In this paper, the second-order linear model (20) with the time-delay d = 5 is considered. The block $G_m(z^{-1})$ represents process dynamics without the time-delay and is used to compute an open-loop prediction. The numerator in transfer function $G_d\left(z^{-1}\right)$ is replaced by its static gain $B(1)$, i.e. for $z = 1$. This is to avoid problem of controlling a model with a $B(z^{-1})$, which has non-minimum phase zeros caused by a high sampling period or fractional delay. Since $B(z^{-1})$ is not controllable as in the case of a time-delay, it is moved out of the prediction model $G_m(z^{-1})$ and is treated together with the time-delay block, as shown in Fig. 5.

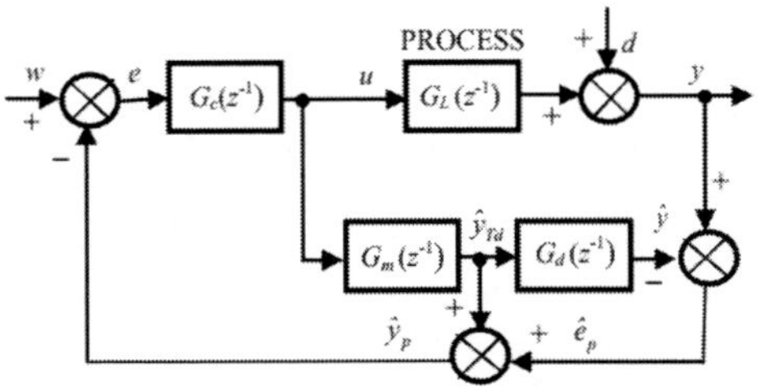

Fig. 5 Block diagram of a digital Smith predictor

The difference between the output of the process y and the model including time-delay $\hat{y}$ is the predicted error $\hat{e}_p$ as shown in Fig. 1, whereas e and d are the error and the measured disturbance, w is the reference signal. The primary (main) controller $G_c(z^{-1})$ can be designed by different approaches (for example digital PID control or methods based on polynomial approach). The detailed description of the block diagram (Fig. 5) is in [2].

5 Design of primary 2DOF controller

The design of the control algorithm is based on a general block scheme of a closed-loop with two degrees of freedom (2DOF) according to Fig. 6. The controller synthesis consists in the solving linear polynomial (Diophantine) equations [14]. From first polynomial equation

$$A(z^{-1})K(z^{-1})P(z^{-1})+B(z^{-1})Q(z^{-1})=D(z^{-1}) \qquad (22)$$

it is possible to compute 7 feedback controller parameters – coefficients of the polynomials Q, P. Polynomial $D\left(z^{-1}\right)$ is the characteristic polynomial and $K\left(z^{-1}\right)=1-z^{-1}$.

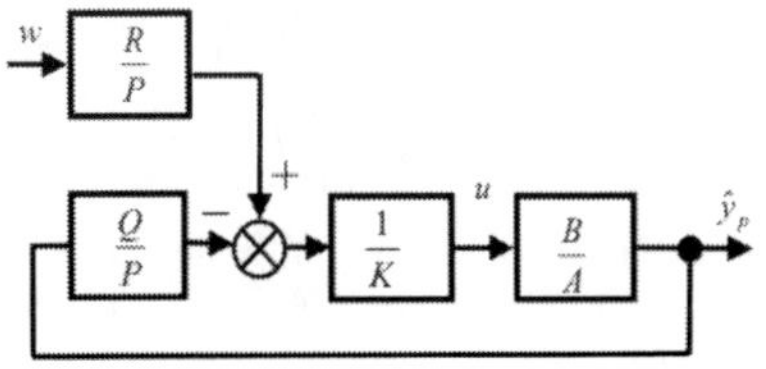

Fig. 6 Block diagram of a closed loop 2DOF control system

Asymptotic tracking of the reference signal w is provided by the feedforward part of the controller which is given by solution of the second following polynomial Diophantine equation

$$S(z^{-1})D_w\left(z^{-1}\right)+B(z^{-1})R(z^{-1})=D(z^{-1}) \qquad (23)$$

For a step-changing reference signal value, polynomial $D_w(z^{-1}) = 1 - z^{-1}$ and S is an auxiliary polynomial which does not enter into the controller design. Then it is possible to derive the polynomial R from equation (24) by substituting $z = 1$

$$R=r_0=\frac{D(1)}{B(1)} \qquad (24)$$

The 2DOF controller output is given by

$$u(k)=\frac{r_0}{K\left(z^{-1}\right)P\left(z^{-1}\right)}w(k)-\frac{Q\left(z^{-1}\right)}{K\left(z^{-1}\right)P\left(z^{-1}\right)}\hat{y}_p(k) \qquad (25)$$

The LQ control methods try to minimize the quadratic criterion which uses penalization of the value of the controller output

$$J=\sum_{k=0}^{\infty}\left\{\left[w(k)-\hat{y}_p(k)\right]^2+q_u\left[u(k)\right]^2\right\} \qquad (26)$$

where q_u is the so-called penalization constant, which gives the influence of the controller output to the value of the criterion. In this paper, criterion minimization (26) will be realized through the spectral factorization for an input-output description of the system

$$A(z)q_uA\left(z^{-1}\right)+B(z)B\left(z^{-1}\right)=D(z)\delta D\left(z^{-1}\right) \qquad (27)$$

where δ is a constant chosen so that $d_0 = 1$. $A(z)$, $B(z)$ are the second-order polynomials and $D(z)$ is also the second-order polynomial

$$D\left(z^{-1}\right)=1+d_1z^{-1}+d_2z^{-2} \qquad (28)$$

The design of the LQ controllers for control of the second-order system with time-delay (10) is in detail derived in [4, 15]. It is obvious from (28) that using spectral factorization of the second-order model, only two parameters d_1 and d_2 can be computed. Simulation experiments demonstrated that use of the second-order polynomial (28) leads to the oscillations of the controller output for control of the time-delay system (21). These oscillations it is impossible to eliminate not even by increasing of penalization factor q_u. This problem it is possible to solve by addition another pole into polynomial (28). It means to use the third order polynomial

$$D_3\left(z^{-1}\right)=1+d_1z^{-1}+d_2z^{-2}+d_3z^{-3} \qquad (29)$$

for controller design. The polynomial $D_3(z^{-1})$ is then to use in equations (22) and (23). The polynomial (29) may have three different real poles α, β, γ or one complex conjugated pole $z_{1,2}=\alpha\pm j\beta$ and one real pole γ. These poles must be included into polynomial $D_3(z^{-1})$ (29). A suitable pole assignment was designed for both types of the processes:

1st possibility:
Polynomial (29) has two different real poles α, β (computed from (27)) and user-defined real pole γ. Then it is possible to write polynomial (29) as a product root of factor

$$D_3(z)=(z-\alpha)(z-\beta)(z-\gamma) \qquad (30)$$

and its individual parameters can be expressed as

$$d_1=-(\alpha+\beta+\gamma);\quad d_2=\alpha\beta+\alpha\gamma+\beta\gamma;\quad d_3=\alpha\beta\gamma \qquad (31)$$

2nd possibility:
Polynomial (29) has the complex conjugate pole $z_{1,2}=\alpha\pm j\beta$ (computed from (27)) and user-defined real pole γ. Then polynomial (30) has the form

$$D_3(z)=(z-\alpha-j\beta)(z-\alpha+j\beta)(z-\gamma) \qquad (32)$$

and its individual parameters can be expressed as

$$d_1=-(2\alpha+\gamma);\quad d_2=2\alpha\gamma+\alpha^2+\beta^2;\quad d_3=-\left(\alpha^2+\beta^2\right)\gamma \qquad (33)$$

With increased penalization constant $q_u\geq 0$, the amplitude of the controller output decreases and thereby, the flow of the process output is smoothened and any possible oscillations or instability are damped.

6 Simulation verification and results

A simulation verification of the designed control algorithm was performed in MATLAB/SIMULINK environment. It is obvious from Section 5 that courses of the controlled variables are dependent not only on pole assignment obtained by spectral factorization (α, β), but also on the user-defined real γ and the penalization factor q_u.

6.1 Influence of pole γ on quality of control

The following individual simulation experiments were realized subsequently: the penalization factor was set as q_u = 10 and the user-defined real pole γ was increasing. The courses of the controlled process output and controller output for individual poles γ are shown in Fig. 7 – 9.

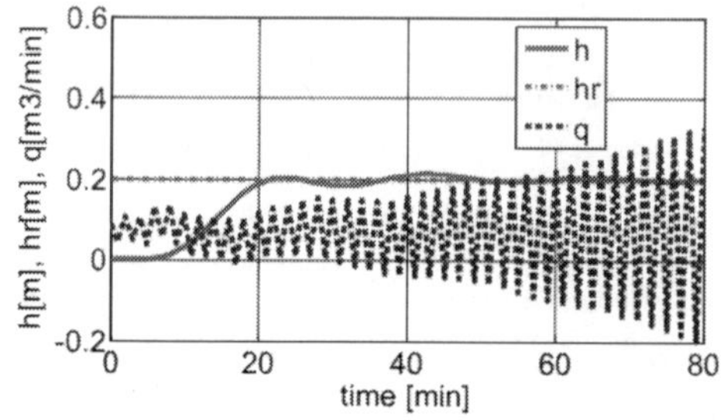

Fig. 7 Control courses for parameters $q_u=10;\ \gamma=0.01$

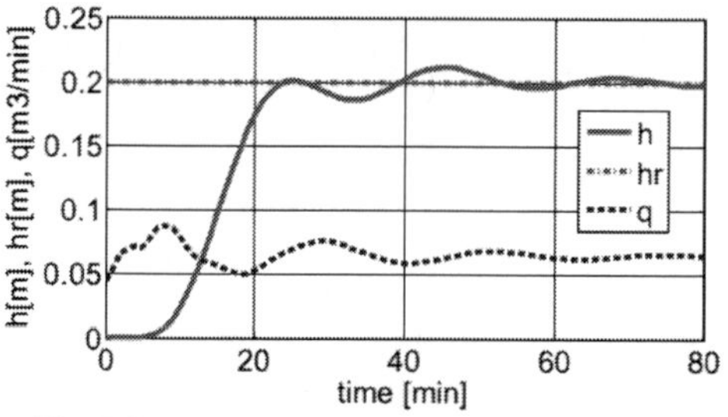

Fig. 8 Control courses for parameters $q_u=10;\ \gamma=0.5$

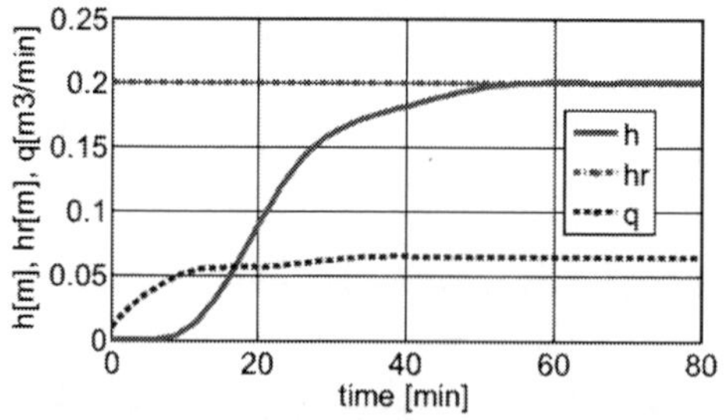

Fig. 9 Control courses for parameters $q_u=10;\ \gamma=0.9$

It is obvious from Fig. 7 - 9 that increasing the value of the pole γ caused a slowdown of the process output *y* and suppression of oscillations. Oscillations of the controller output were also suppressed.

6.2 Influence of penalization factor q_u on quality of control

The following simulation experiments were realized subsequently: the real pole was set as γ = 0.5 and the penalization factor q_u was increasing. The courses of the controlled process output and controller output for individual poles γ are shown in Fig. 10 – 12.

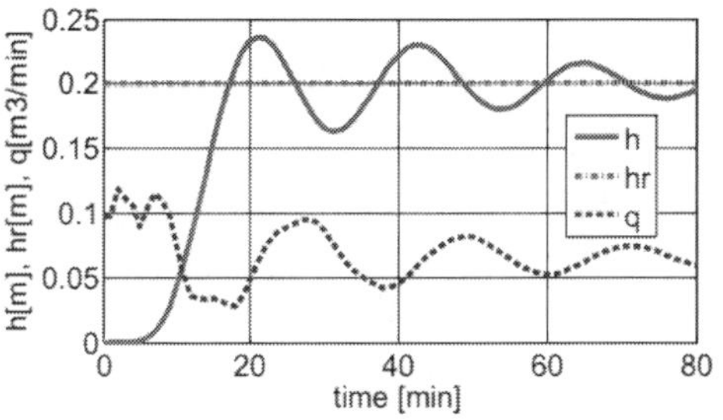

Fig. 10 Control courses for parameters $\gamma = 0.5; q_u = 1$

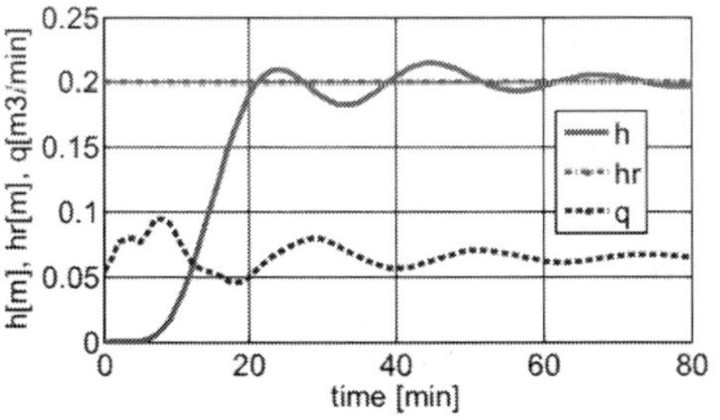

Fig. 11 Control courses for parameters $\gamma = 0.5; q_u = 5$

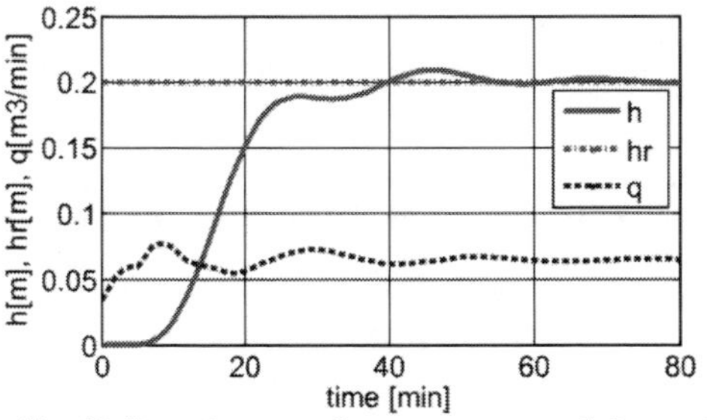

Fig. 12 Control courses for parameters $\gamma = 0.5; q_u = 100$

It is obvious from Fig. 10 - 12 that increasing the value of the penalization factor q_u caused a slowdown of both the process output y and the manipulated variable u and also suppression of oscillations.

7 Conclusion

The paper presents a simulation control of the high-order process (a set of equal liquid tanks). This process was identified by the second-order model with five time- delay steps. The designed control algorithm uses the digital LQ Smith predictor. A minimization of the LQ criterion was combined with the pole assignment principle. The designed controller was verified by simulation in the MATLAB/SIMULINK environment. The results of simulation verifications demonstrated very good control quality and robustness of the designed digital LQ algorithm. Another good property of the designed algorithm is the possibility of suitable penalization of the manipulated variable which prevents oscillations of the actuator (in this case the input valve). The main contribution of this paper is the finding that a high-order system, which is composed of a set of low-order systems, can be approximated by a low-order model with time-delay. For this approximated model it is possible to design relatively simple digital controllers. The polynomial controller was derived purposely by the analytical way (without utilization of numerical methods) in order to obtain an algorithm with easy feasibility in industrial practice.

References

1. J. Smith, Chem. Eng. Progress, **53**, 217-219, (1957)
2. M. Šebek, M. Hromčík, Int. J. of Robust and Nonlin. Contr., **17**, 679-681, (2007)
3. M. Šebek, V. Kučera, IEEE Trans. Automatic. Contr., **AC-27**, 1248-1250, (1982)
4. V. Bobál, P. Chalupa, P. Dostál, M. Kubalčík, Int. J. of Math. and Comp. in Simul., **5**, 342-351, (2011)
5. V. Bobál, P. Chalupa, P. Dostál, M. Kubalčík, Int. J. of Circ., Syst. and Sign. Proc., **8**, 424-432, (2014)
6. C.C. Hang, K.W. Lim, B. W. Chong, Automatica, **20**, 1-16, (1989)
7. C.C. Hang, H.L. Tong, K.H. Weng, *Adaptive Control*, Instrument Society of America, (1993)
8. V. Bobál, P. Chalupa, J. Novák, P. Dostál, *International Workshop on Applied Modelling and Simulation, Roma*, 44-49,(2012)
9. V. Bobál, P. Chalupa, J. Novák, Toolbox for CAD and Verification of Digital Adaptive Control Time-Delay Systems, Available from http://nod32.fai.utb.cz/promotion/Software_OBD/Time_Delay_Tool.zip
10. J.E. Normey Rico, E.F. Camacho, Control of Dead-time Processes, Springer-Verlag, (2007)
11. V. Bobál, M. Kubalčík, P. Dostál, J. Matějíček, Comp. and Math. with Applic., **66**, 165-176, (2013)
12. J.C. Lagaris, J.A. Reds, M.H. Wright, P.E. Wright, Siam J. of Optim., **9**, 112-147, (1998)
13. P. Chalupa, J. Novák, *Nostradamus: Modern Methods of Prediction, Modeling and Nonlinear Systems*, Springer-Verlag, 93-102 (2013)
14. V. Kučera, Automatica, **29**, 1391-1357, (1993)
15. V. Bobál, J. Böhm, J. Fessl, J. Macháček, *Digital Self-tuning Controllers: Algorithms, Implementation and Application*, Springer-Verlag, (2005)

Multivariable Predictive Control with Filtered Variables in Prediction Equations

Marek Kubalcik [1,a] and Vladimir Bobal[1]

[1] Tomas Bata University in Zlin, Faculty of Applied Informatics, Nam. T. G. Masaryka 5555, 760 05 Zlin, Czech Republic

Abstract. The paper is focused on an implementation of a multivariable predictive controller with a colouring filter *C* in a disturbance model. The filter is often essential for practical applications of predictive control based on input-output models. It is commonly considered as a design parameter because it has direct effects on closed loop performance. In this paper a computation of predictions for the case with the colouring filter is introduced. The computation is based on a particular model of the controlled system in the form of matrix fraction which is commonly used for description of a range of multivariable processes. Performance of closed loop system with and without the colouring filter in the disturbance model was compared.

1 Introduction

Typical technological processes require the simultaneous control of several variables related to one system. Each input may influence all system outputs. The design of a controller for such a system must be quite sophisticated if the system is to be controlled adequately. Simple decentralized PI or PID controllers largely do not yield satisfactory results. There are many different advanced methods of controlling multi-input–multi-output (MIMO) systems. The problem of selecting an appropriate control technique often arises. Perhaps the most popular way of controlling MIMO processes is by designing decoupling compensators to suppress the interactions [1] and the designing multiple SISO controllers [2] . This requires determining how to pair the controlled and manipulated variables. One of the most effective approaches to control of multivariable systems is model predictive control (MPC) [3], [4], [5]. An advantage of model predictive control is that multivariable systems can be handled in a straightforward manner. When using most of other approaches, the control actions are taken based on past errors. MPC uses also future values of the reference signals. It is essentially based on discrete or sampled models of processes. Computation of appropriate control algorithms is then realized especially in the discrete domain. The basic idea of the generalized predictive control [6], [7] is to use a model of a controlled process to predict a number of future outputs of the process. A trajectory of future manipulated variables is given by solving an optimization problem incorporating a suitable cost function and constraints. Only the first element of the obtained control sequence is applied. The whole procedure is repeated in following sampling period. This principle is known as the receding horizon strategy.

[a] Corresponding author: kubalcik@fai.utb.cz

An implementation of a multivariable predictive controller based on a matrix fraction model with a colouring filter *C* in a disturbance model is described in this paper. The filter is often essential for practical applications of predictive control based on input-output models. Surveys of practical applications of predictive control are presented in [8], [9], [10]. It is commonly considered as a design parameter because it has direct effects on closed loop performance. A computation of predictions for the case with the colouring filter is introduced. The computation is based on a particular model of the controlled system in the form of matrix fraction which is commonly used for description of a range of processes.The filtering of variables is the equivalent of the colouring filter in the noise model. It is practically very difficult to estimate the coefficients of the colouring filter. A model with the *C*-filter is then utilized as an example with filtering of input and output variables when the filter *C* is a tuning parameter. In the paper are derived prediction equations for an input-output model in the form of matrix fraction both for the case with the *C*-filter and without the *C*-filter. Performance of closed loop system with and without the colouring filter in the disturbance model was compared.

2 Model of the controlled system

Let us consider a two input – two output system. The two – input/two – output (TITO) processes are the most often encountered multivariable processes in practice and many processes with inputs/outputs beyond two can be treated as several TITO subsystems [11].

A general transfer matrix of a two-input–two-output system with significant cross-coupling between the control loops is expressed as:

$$G(z)=\begin{bmatrix} G_{11}(z) & G_{12}(z) \\ G_{21}(z) & G_{22}(z) \end{bmatrix} \quad (1)$$

$$Y(z)=G(z)U(z) \quad (2)$$

where $U(z)$ and $Y(z)$ are vectors of the manipulated variables and the controlled variables, respectively.

$$U(z)=[u_1(z),u_2(z)]^T \; Y(z)=[y_1(z),y_2(z)]^T \quad (3)$$

It may be assumed that the transfer matrix can be transcribed to the following form of the matrix fraction:

$$G(z)=A^{-1}(z^{-1})B(z^{-1})=B_1(z^{-1})A_1^{-1}(z^{-1}) \quad (4)$$

where the polynomial matrices $A\in R_{22}[z^{-1}], B\in R_{22}[z^{-1}]$ are the left coprime factorizations of matrix $G(z)$ and the matrices $A_1\in R_{22}[z^{-1}], B_1\in R_{22}[z^{-1}]$ are the right coprime factorizations of $G(z)$. The model can be also written in the form

$$A(z^{-1})Y(z)=B(z^{-1})U(z) \quad (5)$$

As an example a model with polynomials of second degree was chosen. This model proved to be effective for control of several TITO laboratory processes [12], where controllers based on a model with polynomials of the first degree failed. The model has sixteen parameters. The matrices A and B are defined as follows

$$A(z^{-1})=\begin{bmatrix} 1+a_1z^{-1}+a_2z^{-2} & a_3z^{-1}+a_4z^{-2} \\ a_5z^{-1}+a_6z^{-2} & 1+a_7z^{-1}+a_8z^{-2} \end{bmatrix} \quad (6)$$

$$B(z^{-1})=\begin{bmatrix} b_1z^{-1}+b_2z^{-2} & b_3z^{-1}+b_4z^{-2} \\ b_5z^{-1}+b_6z^{-2} & b_7z^{-1}+b_8z^{-2} \end{bmatrix} \quad (7)$$

A widely used model in general model predictive control is the CARIMA (controller autoregressive integrated moving average) model which we can obtain by adding a disturbance model as

$$A(z^{-1})y(k)=B(z^{-1})u(k)+C(z^{-1})\Delta^{-1}(z^{-1})n(k) \quad (8)$$

where n is a non-measurable random disturbance that is assumed to have zero mean value and constant covariance and

$$\Delta(z^{-1})=\begin{bmatrix} 1-z^{-1} & 0 \\ 0 & 1-z^{-1} \end{bmatrix} \quad (9)$$

in case of TITO system. C is the colouring polynomial matrix. For purpose of simplification it is often supposed to be equal to the identity matrix [3]. In a single input – single output case we have a colouring polynomial C instead of the matrix C.

$$\Delta A(z^{-1})y(k)=B(z^{-1})\Delta u(k)+C(z^{-1})n(k) \quad (10)$$

where A, B and C are polynomials and $\Delta=1-z^{-1}$. In Model Predictive Control it is also common to treat C as a design parameter [6], [7], [13]. Analogically the polynomial matrix C could be expected as the design parameters in a multivariable case. Nevertheless considering the polynomial matrix C as the design parameter is computationally unsolvable and practically inapplicable. A simplified model when the non-measurable random disturbance was a scalar was then considered

$$\Delta A(z^{-1})y(k)=B(z^{-1})\Delta u(k)+C(z^{-1})n(k) \quad (11)$$

Further will be compared cases when C is the identity matrix and when the input and output variables are filtered with a colouring polynomial C which is supposed as the design parameter.

3 Implementation of predictive controller

The basic idea of MPC is to use a model of a controlled process to predict N future outputs of the process. A trajectory of future manipulated variables is given by solving an optimization problem incorporating a suitable cost function and constraints. Only the first element of the obtained control sequence is applied. The whole procedure is repeated in following sampling period. This principle is known as the receding horizon strategy. The computation of a control law of MPC is based on minimization of the following criterion

$$J(k)=\sum_{j=N_1}^{N}e(k+j)^2+\lambda\sum_{j=1}^{N_u}\Delta u(k+j)^2 \quad (12)$$

where $e(k+j)$ is a vector of predicted control errors, $\Delta u(k+j)$ is a vector of future increments of the manipulated variable (for the system with two inputs and two outputs each vector has two elements), N is a length of the prediction horizon, N_u is a length of the control horizon and λ is a weighting factor of control increments. A predictor in a vector form is given by

$$\hat{y}=G\Delta u+y_0 \quad (13)$$

where $\hat{y}$ is a vector of system predictions along the horizon of the length N, Δu is a vector of control increments, y_0 is the free response vector. G is a matrix of the dynamics. It is given as

$$G=\begin{bmatrix} G_0 & 0 & \cdots & \cdots & 0 \\ G_1 & G_0 & 0 & \cdots & 0 \\ \vdots & & \ddots & \ddots & \vdots \\ \vdots & & & G_0 & 0 \\ G_{N-1} & \cdots & \cdots & \cdots & G_0 \end{bmatrix} \quad (14)$$

where sub-matrices G_i have dimension 2x2 and contain values of the step sequence.

The criterion (12) can be written in a general vector form

$$J=(\hat{y}-w)^T(\hat{y}-w)+\lambda\Delta u^T\Delta u \quad (15)$$

where w is a vector of the reference trajectory. The criterion can be modified using the expression (15) to

$$J=2g^T\Delta u+\Delta u^TH\Delta u \quad (16)$$

where the gradient g and the Hess matrix H are defined by following expressions

$$g^T=G^T(y_0-w) \quad (17)$$

$$H=G^TG+\lambda I \quad (18)$$

Handling of constraints is one of main advantages of predictive control. General formulation of predictive control with constraints is then as follows

$$\min_{\Delta u} 2g^T\Delta u+\Delta u^TH\Delta u \quad (19)$$

owing to

$$\boldsymbol{A}\Delta\boldsymbol{u} \le \boldsymbol{b} \tag{20}$$

The inequality (20) expresses the constraints in a compact form.

4 Computation of Predictions *C=I*

An important task in predictive control is computation of predictions for arbitrary prediction and control horizons.

The difference equation of the CARIMA model without the unknown term can be expressed as:

$$\begin{aligned} y_1(k+1) &= (1-a_1)y_1(k)+(a_1-a_2)y_1(k-1)+a_2y_1(k-2)- \\ &-a_3y_2(k)+(a_3-a_4)y_2(k-1)+a_4y_2(k-2)+ \\ &+b_1\Delta u_1(k)+b_2\Delta u_1(k-1)+b_3\Delta u_2(k)+b_4\Delta u_2(k-1) \\ y_2(k+1) &= (1-a_7)y_2(k)+(a_7-a_8)y_2(k-1)+a_8y_2(k-2)- \\ &-a_5y_1(k)+(a_5-a_6)y_1(k-1)+a_6y_1(k-2)+ \\ &+b_5\Delta u_1(k)+b_6\Delta u_1(k-1)+b_7\Delta u_2(k)+b_8\Delta u_2(k-1) \end{aligned} \tag{21}$$

These equations can be written into a matrix form

$$\begin{aligned} \boldsymbol{y}(k+1) &= \boldsymbol{A}_1\boldsymbol{y}(k)+\boldsymbol{A}_2\boldsymbol{y}(k-1)+\boldsymbol{A}_3\boldsymbol{y}(k-2)+ \\ &+\boldsymbol{B}_1\Delta\boldsymbol{u}(k)+\boldsymbol{B}_2\Delta\boldsymbol{u}(k-1) \end{aligned} \tag{22}$$

where

$$\boldsymbol{A}_1 = \begin{bmatrix} 1-a_1 & -a_3 \\ -a_5 & 1-a_7 \end{bmatrix} \quad \boldsymbol{A}_2 = \begin{bmatrix} a_1-a_2 & a_3-a_4 \\ a_5-a_6 & a_7-a_8 \end{bmatrix}$$

$$\boldsymbol{A}_3 = \begin{bmatrix} a_2 & a_4 \\ a_6 & a_8 \end{bmatrix} \tag{23}$$

$$\boldsymbol{B}_1 = \begin{bmatrix} b_1 & b_3 \\ b_5 & b_7 \end{bmatrix} \quad \boldsymbol{B}_2 = \begin{bmatrix} b_2 & b_4 \\ b_6 & b_8 \end{bmatrix}$$

It was necessary to directly compute three steps-ahead predictions in a straightforward way by establishing of previous predictions to later predictions. The model order defines that computation of one step-ahead prediction is based on the three past values of the system output.

$$\begin{aligned} \hat{\boldsymbol{y}}(k+1) &= \boldsymbol{A}_1\boldsymbol{y}(k)+\boldsymbol{A}_2\boldsymbol{y}(k-1)+\boldsymbol{A}_3\boldsymbol{y}(k-2)+ \\ &+\boldsymbol{B}_1\Delta\boldsymbol{u}(k)+\boldsymbol{B}_2\Delta\boldsymbol{u}(k-1) \\ \hat{\boldsymbol{y}}(k+2) &= \boldsymbol{A}_1\boldsymbol{y}(k+1)+\boldsymbol{A}_2\boldsymbol{y}(k)+\boldsymbol{A}_3\boldsymbol{y}(k-1)+ \\ &+\boldsymbol{B}_1\Delta\boldsymbol{u}(k+1)+\boldsymbol{B}_2\Delta\boldsymbol{u}(k) \\ \hat{\boldsymbol{y}}(k+3) &= \boldsymbol{A}_1\boldsymbol{y}(k+2)+\boldsymbol{A}_2\boldsymbol{y}(k+1)+\boldsymbol{A}_3\boldsymbol{y}(k)+ \\ &+\boldsymbol{B}_1\Delta\boldsymbol{u}(k+2)+\boldsymbol{B}_2\Delta\boldsymbol{u}(k+1) \end{aligned} \tag{24}$$

It is possible to divide computation of the predictions to recursion of the free response and recursion of the matrix of the dynamics. The free response vector can be expressed as:

$$\begin{aligned} \boldsymbol{y}_0 &= \begin{bmatrix} p_{11} & p_{12} \\ p_{21} & q_{22} \\ \hline p_{31} & p_{32} \\ p_{41} & p_{42} \\ \hline p_{51} & p_{52} \\ p_{61} & p_{62} \end{bmatrix} \begin{bmatrix} \Delta u_1(k-1) \\ \Delta u_2(k-1) \end{bmatrix} + \left[\begin{array}{cc|cc|cc} q_{11} & q_{12} & q_{13} & q_{14} & q_{15} & q_{16} \\ q_{21} & q_{22} & q_{23} & q_{24} & q_{25} & q_{26} \\ \hline q_{31} & q_{32} & q_{33} & q_{34} & q_{35} & q_{36} \\ q_{41} & q_{42} & q_{43} & q_{44} & q_{45} & q_{46} \\ \hline q_{51} & q_{52} & q_{53} & q_{54} & q_{55} & q_{56} \\ q_{61} & q_{62} & q_{63} & q_{64} & q_{65} & q_{66} \end{array}\right] \begin{bmatrix} y_1(k) \\ y_2(k) \\ \hline y_1(k-1) \\ y_2(k-1) \\ \hline y_1(k-2) \\ y_2(k-2) \end{bmatrix} = \\ &= \begin{bmatrix} \boldsymbol{P}_1 \\ \boldsymbol{P}_2 \\ \boldsymbol{P}_3 \end{bmatrix} \Delta\boldsymbol{u}(k-1) + \begin{bmatrix} \boldsymbol{Q}_{11} & \boldsymbol{Q}_{12} & \boldsymbol{Q}_{13} \\ \boldsymbol{Q}_{21} & \boldsymbol{Q}_{22} & \boldsymbol{Q}_{23} \\ \boldsymbol{Q}_{31} & \boldsymbol{Q}_{32} & \boldsymbol{Q}_{33} \end{bmatrix} \begin{bmatrix} \boldsymbol{y}(k) \\ \boldsymbol{y}(k-1) \\ \boldsymbol{y}(k-2) \end{bmatrix} = \boldsymbol{P}\Delta\boldsymbol{u}(k-1) + \boldsymbol{Q} \begin{bmatrix} \boldsymbol{y}(k) \\ \boldsymbol{y}(k-1) \\ \boldsymbol{y}(k-2) \end{bmatrix} \end{aligned} \tag{25}$$

The coefficients of the matrices $\boldsymbol{P}$ and $\boldsymbol{Q}$ for further predictions are computed recursively. Based on the three previous predictions it is repeatedly computed the next row of the matrices $\boldsymbol{P}$ and $\boldsymbol{Q}$ in the following way:

$$\boldsymbol{P}_4 = \begin{bmatrix} p_{71} & p_{72} \\ p_{81} & p_{82} \end{bmatrix} = \boldsymbol{A}_1\boldsymbol{P}_{31}+\boldsymbol{A}_2\boldsymbol{P}_{21}+\boldsymbol{A}_3\boldsymbol{P}_{11} \tag{26}$$

$$\boldsymbol{Q}_{41} = \begin{bmatrix} q_{71} & q_{72} \\ q_{81} & q_{82} \end{bmatrix} = \boldsymbol{A}_1\boldsymbol{Q}_{31}+\boldsymbol{A}_2\boldsymbol{Q}_{21}+\boldsymbol{A}_3\boldsymbol{Q}_{11} \tag{27}$$

$$\boldsymbol{Q}_{42} = \begin{bmatrix} q_{73} & q_{74} \\ q_{83} & q_{84} \end{bmatrix} = \boldsymbol{A}_1\boldsymbol{Q}_{32}+\boldsymbol{A}_2\boldsymbol{Q}_{22}+\boldsymbol{A}_3\boldsymbol{Q}_{12} \tag{28}$$

$$\boldsymbol{Q}_{43} = \begin{bmatrix} q_{75} & q_{76} \\ q_{85} & q_{86} \end{bmatrix} = \boldsymbol{A}_1\boldsymbol{Q}_{33}+\boldsymbol{A}_2\boldsymbol{Q}_{23}+\boldsymbol{A}_3\boldsymbol{Q}_{13} \tag{29}$$

The recursion of the matrix $\boldsymbol{G}$ is similar. The next element of the first column is repeatedly computed and the remaining columns are shifted. This procedure is performed repeatedly until the prediction horizon is achieved. If the control horizon is lower than the prediction horizon a number of columns in the matrix is reduced. The technique is apparent from the equations (30) and (31).

$$\begin{aligned} \boldsymbol{G}\Delta\boldsymbol{u} &= \left[\begin{array}{cc|cc} g(1,1) & g(1,2) & 0 & 0 \\ g(2,1) & g(2,2) & 0 & 0 \\ \hline g(3,1) & g(3,2) & g(1,1) & g(1,2) \\ g(4,1) & g(4,2) & g(2,1) & g(2,2) \\ \hline g(5,1) & g(5,2) & g(3,1) & g(3,2) \\ g(6,1) & g(6,2) & g(4,1) & g(4,2) \end{array}\right] \begin{bmatrix} \Delta u_1(k) \\ \Delta u_2(k) \\ \hline \Delta u_1(k+1) \\ \Delta u_2(k+1) \end{bmatrix} = \\ &= \begin{bmatrix} G(1,1) & 0 \\ G(2,1) & G(1,1) \\ G(3,1) & G(2,1) \end{bmatrix} \begin{bmatrix} \Delta\boldsymbol{u}(k) \\ \Delta\boldsymbol{u}(k+1) \end{bmatrix} \end{aligned} \tag{30}$$

$$\boldsymbol{G}_{41} = \begin{bmatrix} g_{71} & g_{72} \\ g_{81} & g_{82} \end{bmatrix} = \boldsymbol{A}_1\boldsymbol{G}_{31}+\boldsymbol{A}_2\boldsymbol{G}_{21}+\boldsymbol{A}_3\boldsymbol{G}_{11} \tag{31}$$

The predictions can be written in a compact matrix form

$$\begin{aligned} &\hat{\boldsymbol{y}}(k+j) = \boldsymbol{G}\Delta\boldsymbol{u}(k+j-1)+\boldsymbol{P}\Delta\boldsymbol{u}(k-1)+\boldsymbol{Q}\boldsymbol{y}(k-j+1) \\ &j \le N \end{aligned} \tag{32}$$

5 Computation of predictions with colouring filter *C*

Computation of predictions with colouring filter is solved for example in [14] for a single input–single output case. Including the *C*-filter the CARIMA model takes the form

$$\Delta\boldsymbol{A}(z^{-1})\boldsymbol{y}(k) = \boldsymbol{B}(z^{-1})\Delta\boldsymbol{u}(k) + C(z^{-1})\boldsymbol{n}(k) \tag{33}$$

As it was previously mentioned, a simplified model when the non-measurable random disturbance was a scalar was considered.

Equation (33) can be modified to

$$\Delta\boldsymbol{A}(z^{-1})\boldsymbol{y}(k)\frac{1}{C(z^{-1})} = \boldsymbol{B}(z^{-1})\Delta\boldsymbol{u}(k)\frac{1}{C(z^{-1})} + \boldsymbol{n}(k) \tag{34}$$

where the unknown term is supposed to be the white noise and the input and output variables are filtered. Using of (34) for prediction improves prediction accuracy.

The filtered variables are defined as

$$\begin{pmatrix} y_{1f}(k) \\ y_{2f}(k) \end{pmatrix} = \begin{pmatrix} y_1(k) \\ y_2(k) \end{pmatrix} \frac{1}{C(z^{-1})} \tag{35}$$

$$\begin{pmatrix} u_{1f}(k) \\ u_{2f}(k) \end{pmatrix} = \begin{pmatrix} u_1(k) \\ u_2(k) \end{pmatrix} \frac{1}{C(z^{-1})} \tag{36}$$

In this case the polynomial C is a design parameter. It is a stable polynomial. For the system with polynomials of the second degree (6), (7) it was chosen to be of the second degree as well

$$C(z^{-1}) = 1 + c_1 z^{-1} + c_2 z^{-2} \tag{37}$$

The input and output data are filtered before prediction. $1/C$ is a low-pass filter which reduces high frequency noise. It is easy to prove by simulation that the cases when the noise is coloured (33) and when the noise is white and the input and output variables are filtered (34) are equal.

The prediction equation for filtered variables takes the following form

$$\hat{\boldsymbol{y}}_f(k+j) = \boldsymbol{G}\Delta\boldsymbol{u}_f(k+j-1) + \boldsymbol{P}\Delta\boldsymbol{u}_f(k-1) + \boldsymbol{Q}\boldsymbol{y}_f(k-j+1) \quad j \le N \tag{38}$$

For practical application equation (28) is inapplicable. Prediction of the unfiltered output must be expressed by means of future control increments.

The relationship between filtered and unfiltered variables can be expressed as follows

$$\begin{pmatrix} y_{1f}(k) \\ y_{2f}(k) \end{pmatrix} = \begin{pmatrix} y_1(k) \\ y_2(k) \end{pmatrix} \frac{1}{1 + c_1 z^{-1} + c_2 z^{-2}} \tag{39}$$

$$\begin{pmatrix} y_1(k) \\ y_2(k) \end{pmatrix} = \begin{pmatrix} y_{1f}(k) + c_1 y_{1f}(k-1) + c_2 y_{1f}(k-2) \\ y_{2f}(k) + c_1 y_{2f}(k-1) + c_2 y_{2f}(k-2) \end{pmatrix} \tag{40}$$

For three step ahead predictions

$$\begin{aligned} \hat{\boldsymbol{y}}(k+1) &= \boldsymbol{y}_f(k+1) + c_1 \boldsymbol{y}_f(k) + c_2 \boldsymbol{y}_f(k-1) \\ \hat{\boldsymbol{y}}(k+2) &= \boldsymbol{y}_f(k+2) + c_1 \boldsymbol{y}_f(k+1) + c_2 \boldsymbol{y}_f(k) \\ \hat{\boldsymbol{y}}(k+3) &= \boldsymbol{y}_f(k+3) + c_1 \boldsymbol{y}_f(k+2) + c_2 \boldsymbol{y}_f(k+1) \end{aligned} \tag{41}$$

In a matrix form the equations (31) can be expressed as follows

$$\begin{pmatrix} \hat{y}_1(k+1) \\ \hat{y}_2(k+1) \\ \hat{y}_1(k+2) \\ \hat{y}_2(k+2) \\ \hat{y}_1(k+3) \\ \hat{y}_2(k+3) \end{pmatrix} = \overbrace{\begin{pmatrix} 1 & 0 & 0 & 0 & 0 & 0 \\ 0 & 1 & 0 & 0 & 0 & 0 \\ c_1 & 0 & 1 & 0 & 0 & 0 \\ 0 & c_1 & 0 & 1 & 0 & 0 \\ c_2 & 0 & c_1 & 0 & 1 & 0 \\ 0 & c_2 & 0 & c_1 & 0 & 1 \end{pmatrix}}^{C_c} \begin{pmatrix} \hat{y}_{1f}(k+1) \\ \hat{y}_{2f}(k+1) \\ \hat{y}_{1f}(k+2) \\ \hat{y}_{2f}(k+2) \\ \hat{y}_{1f}(k+3) \\ \hat{y}_{2f}(k+3) \end{pmatrix} + \overbrace{\begin{pmatrix} c_1 & 0 & c_2 & 0 & 0 & 0 \\ 0 & c_1 & 0 & c_2 & 0 & 0 \\ c_2 & 0 & 0 & 0 & 0 & 0 \\ 0 & c_2 & 0 & 0 & 0 & 0 \\ 0 & 0 & 0 & 0 & 0 & 0 \\ 0 & 0 & 0 & 0 & 0 & 0 \end{pmatrix}}^{H_c} \begin{pmatrix} \hat{y}_{1f}(k) \\ \hat{y}_{2f}(k) \\ \hat{y}_{1f}(k-1) \\ \hat{y}_{2f}(k-1) \\ \hat{y}_{1f}(k-2) \\ \hat{y}_{2f}(k-2) \end{pmatrix} \tag{42}$$

The relationship between filtered and unfiltered control increments can be expressed similarly. Using matrix notation we can define following equations

$$\hat{\boldsymbol{y}}(k+j) = \boldsymbol{C}_C \boldsymbol{y}_f(k+j) + \boldsymbol{H}_C \boldsymbol{y}_f(k-j+1) \tag{43}$$

$$\Delta\boldsymbol{u}(k+j) = \boldsymbol{C}_C \Delta\boldsymbol{u}_f(k+j) + \boldsymbol{H}_C \Delta\boldsymbol{u}_f(k-j+1) \tag{44}$$

where matrices $\boldsymbol{C}_c$ and $\boldsymbol{H}_c$ are defined as follows

$$\boldsymbol{C}_C = \begin{pmatrix} 1 & 0 & 0 & 0 & 0 & 0 \\ 0 & 1 & 0 & 0 & 0 & 0 \\ c_1 & 0 & 1 & 0 & 0 & 0 \\ 0 & c_1 & 0 & 1 & 0 & 0 \\ c_2 & 0 & c_1 & 0 & 1 & 0 \\ 0 & c_2 & 0 & c_1 & 0 & 1 \end{pmatrix} \tag{45}$$

$$\boldsymbol{H}_C = \begin{pmatrix} c_1 & 0 & c_2 & 0 & 0 & 0 \\ 0 & c_1 & 0 & c_2 & 0 & 0 \\ c_2 & 0 & 0 & 0 & 0 & 0 \\ 0 & c_2 & 0 & 0 & 0 & 0 \\ 0 & 0 & 0 & 0 & 0 & 0 \\ 0 & 0 & 0 & 0 & 0 & 0 \end{pmatrix} \tag{46}$$

From equations (43) and (44) we can express the filtered variables

$$\hat{\boldsymbol{y}}(k+j) = \boldsymbol{C}_C \boldsymbol{y}_f(k+j) + \boldsymbol{H}_C \boldsymbol{y}_f(k-j+1) \tag{47}$$

$$\Delta\boldsymbol{u}(k+j) = \boldsymbol{C}_C \Delta\boldsymbol{u}_f(k+j) + \boldsymbol{H}_C \Delta\boldsymbol{u}_f(k-j+1) \tag{48}$$

After substitution of equations (47) and (48) to equation (38) we obtain

$$\begin{aligned} &\boldsymbol{C}_C^{-1}\left(\hat{\boldsymbol{y}}(k+j) - \boldsymbol{H}_C \boldsymbol{y}_f(k-j+1)\right) = \\ &= \boldsymbol{G}\boldsymbol{C}_C^{-1}\left(\Delta\boldsymbol{u}(k+j-1) - \boldsymbol{H}_C \Delta\boldsymbol{u}_f(k-1)\right) + \\ &+ \boldsymbol{P}\Delta\boldsymbol{u}_f(k-1) + \boldsymbol{Q}\boldsymbol{y}_f(k-j+1) \end{aligned} \tag{49}$$

After modification we obtain resulting equation of the predictor

$$\begin{aligned} \hat{\boldsymbol{y}}(k+j) &= \boldsymbol{G}\Delta\boldsymbol{u}(k+j-1) + [\boldsymbol{C}_C \boldsymbol{P} - \boldsymbol{G}\boldsymbol{H}_C]\Delta\boldsymbol{u}_f(k-1) + \\ &+ [\boldsymbol{H}_C + \boldsymbol{C}_C \boldsymbol{Q}]\boldsymbol{y}_f(k-j+1) \end{aligned} \tag{50}$$

We can establish following substitutions

$$\tilde{\boldsymbol{P}} = [\boldsymbol{C}_C \boldsymbol{P} - \boldsymbol{G}\boldsymbol{H}_C] \tag{51}$$

$$\tilde{\boldsymbol{Q}} = [\boldsymbol{H}_C + \boldsymbol{C}_C \boldsymbol{Q}] \tag{52}$$

The prediction equation then can be written in the form

$$\hat{\boldsymbol{y}}(k+j) = \boldsymbol{G}\Delta\boldsymbol{u}(k+j-1) + \tilde{\boldsymbol{P}}\Delta\boldsymbol{u}_f(k-1) + \tilde{\boldsymbol{Q}}\boldsymbol{y}_f(k-j+1) \tag{53}$$

6 Simulation verification

Verification by simulation was carried out on a range of plants with various dynamics. The control of the model below is given here as an example.

$$\boldsymbol{G}(s) = \begin{bmatrix} \dfrac{3}{5s^2+6s+1} & \dfrac{2}{2s^2+4s+1} \\ \dfrac{7}{3s^2+10s+1} & \dfrac{5}{2s^2+8s+1} \end{bmatrix} \tag{54}$$

A corresponding discrete model in the form given by equations (6), (7) and (21) was obtained by recursive identification. Control in the initial adaptation phase then has worse quality. It does not exist a systematic way for

DOI: 10.1051/matecconf/20167601003

selection of the filter C. Its selection is mostly based on intuition. In our example the filter was chosen as

$$C\left(z^{-1}\right) = 1 + 0{,}8z^{-1} + 0{,}05z^{-2} \qquad (55)$$

The sampling period was tuned experimentally and the best value was $T_0 = 0{,}5\ s$. The controlled variable was affected by a noise with zero mean value and constant covariance. Simulation sampling of noise was 0,1 s.

In figures 1-6 are simulation results. Figures 1,3 and 5 show time responses of the control without the filtering of the variables introduced in section 4. Figures 2, 4 and 6 show time responses of the control with the filtering of variables described in section 5.

In figures 1 and 2 there is the response of the controlled variable taken by 0,1 s. It means with the same sampling period as the simulation noise. Simulation results in this figure are the closest to the reality. In figures 3 and 4 there is the controlled variable taken by 2 s. It means with the same sampling period which is used for the control. The data then simulates measured values. In figures 5 and 6 is the manipulated variable.

The tuning parameters that are lengths of the prediction and control horizons and the weighting coefficient λ were tuned experimentally. There is a lack of clear theory relating to the closed loop behavior to design parameters. The length of the prediction horizon, which should cover the important part of the step response, was set to N = 5. The length of the control horizon was also set to N_u = 5. The coefficient λ was taken as equal to 0,1.

It is necessary to emphasize that the displayed inputs and outputs in the graphs are not filtered. The filtered values are used only for computation of systems output predictions and consequently for computation of the control law. The displayed inputs and outputs are real unfiltered values.

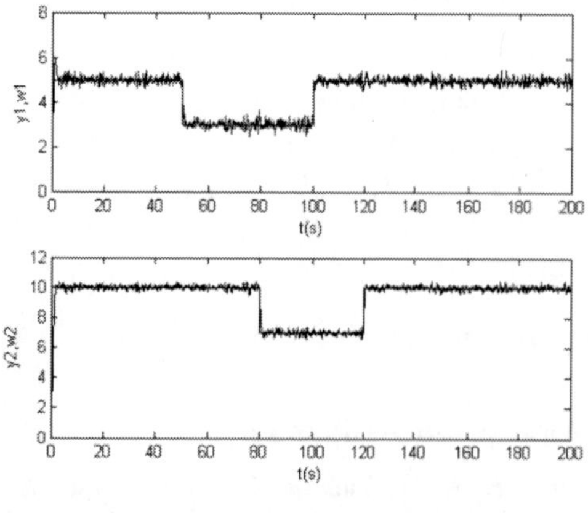

Figure 1. Controlled variables sampled by 0,1s – case without filtering of variables

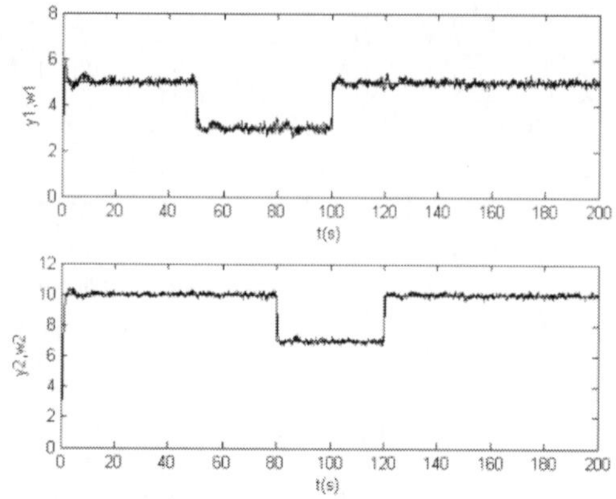

Figure 2. Controlled variables sampled by 0,1s – case with filtering of variables

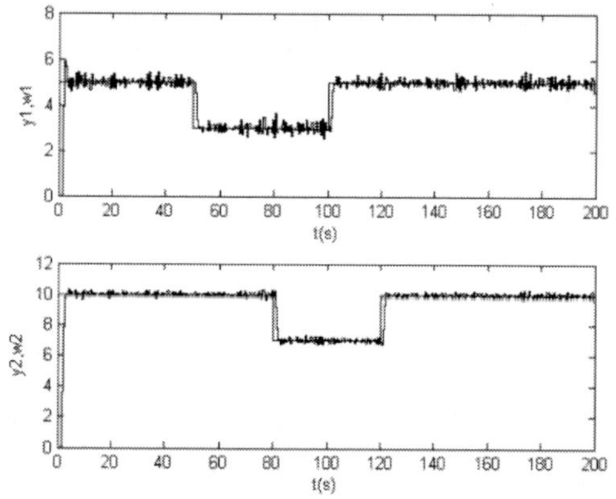

Figure 3. Controlled variables sampled by 0,5s – case without filtering of variables

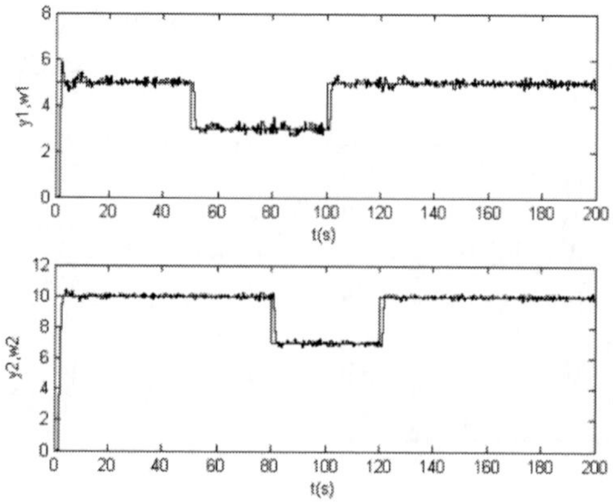

Figure 4. Controlled variables sampled by 0,5s – case with filtering of variables

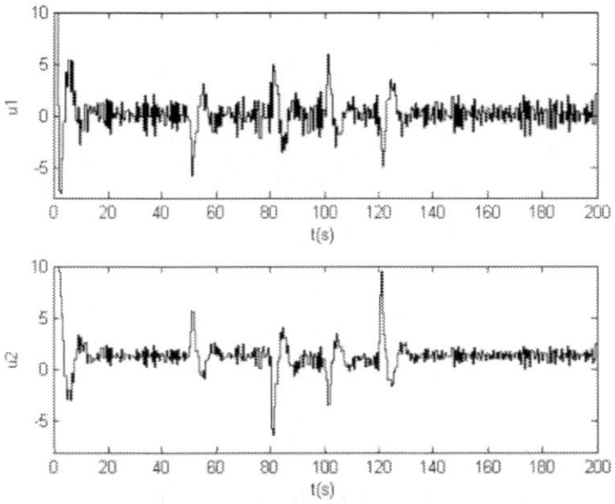

Figure 5. Manipulated variables – case without filtering of variables

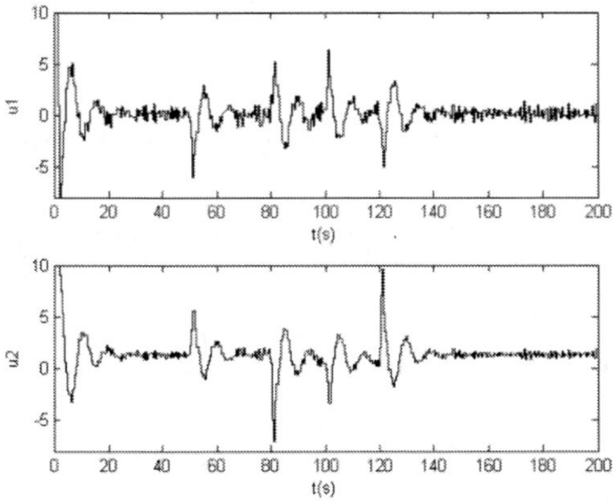

Figure 6. Manipulated variables – case with filtering of variables

7 Conclusion

Specific self-contained prediction equations for the input-output model in the form of matrix fraction were derived for the case with filtering of the input and output variables. Simulations, where the filtered variables are used for computation of the control law and the manipulated variable, were performed. In the simulation results are displayed real unfiltered variables. By simulation control of a range of systems were compared control results of cases with and without the C-filter. In the paper there is introduced one simulation example. The best achieved results are shown. The C-filter is a tuning parameter for which setting we do not have available any exact methodology. The filter was designed by try it and see approach as a low pass filter. Obviously better results were achieved in case with the C-filter particularly regarding rate of oscillations of the input and output variables. It is obvious that the variables are more settled in case with the C-filter. The filter reduces sensitivity of the closed loop system to high frequency noise. Cost for this improvement is a relatively difficult setting of the C-filter as a parameter.

Acknowledgement

This work was supported by the Ministry of Education, Youth and Sports of the Czech Republic within the National Sustainability Programme project No. LO1303 (MSMT-7778/2014) and also by the European Regional Development Fund under the project CEBIA-Tech No. CZ.1.05/2.1.00/03.0089 and also by the Programme EEA and Norway Grants for funding via grant on Institutional cooperation project nr. NF-CZ07-ICP-4-345-2016

References

1. P.R. Krishnawamy, et al., Ind. Eng. Chem. Res., **30**, 662 (1991)
2. W. L. Luyben, Ing. Eng. Chem. Process Des. Dev., **25**, 654 (1986)
3. E.F. Camacho, C. Bordons, *Model Predictive Control* (Springer-Verlag, London, 2004)
4. M. Morari, J.H. Lee, Computers and Chemical Engineering, **23**, 667 (1999)
5. J. Mikleš, M. Fikar, *Process Modelling, Optimisation and Control* (Berlin: Springer-Verlag, 2008)
6. D. W. Clarke, C. Mohtadi, P. S. Tuffs, Automatica, **23**,137 (1987)
7. D. W. Clarke, C. Mohtadi, P. S. Tuffs, Automatica, **23**,149 (1987)
8. S.J. Quin, T.A. Bandgwell, Proceedings of the Chemical Process Control – V., **93**, 232 (1996)
9. S.J. Quin, T.A. Bandgwell, Nonlinear Model Predictive Control (F. Allgöwer & A. Zheng, Ed.), 369 (2000)
10. S.J. Quin, T.A. Bandgwell, Control Engineering Practice, **11**, 733 (2003)
11. F. G. Shinskey, *Process Control System* (McGraw-Hill. New York, 1996)
12. M. Kubalčík, V. Bobál, IMechE Part I: J. Systems and Control Engineering, **220(17)**, 641 (2006)
13. T.W. Yoon, D.W. Clarke, International Journal of Control, **61**, 171 (1995)
14. J.A. Rossiter, *Model Based Predictive Control: a Practical Approach* (CRC Press, 2003)

Adaptive LQ Cascade Control of a Tubular Chemical Reactor

Dostal Petr, Vladimír Bobal and Jiri Vojtesek

Tomas Bata University in Zlin, Faculty of Applied Informatics, Nad Stranemi 4511, 760 05 Zlin, Czech Republic

Abstract. The paper deals with adaptive LQ cascade control design of a tubular chemical reactor with an exothermic consecutive reaction. The control is performed in primary and secondary control-loops where the primary controlled output of the reactor is the concentration of a main reaction product and the secondary output is the mean temperature of the reactant. A common control input is the coolant flow rate. The controller in the primary control-loop is a nonlinear P-controller with the gain calculated using simulated or measured steady-state characteristics of the reactor. The controller in the secondary control-loop is a LQ adaptive controller. The proposed method is verified by control simulations.

1 Introduction

Tubular chemical reactors (TCRs) are units frequently used in chemical industry, biotechnologies and some others. From the system theory point of view, TCRs belong to the class of nonlinear distributed parameter systems. Their mathematical models are described by sets of nonlinear partial differential equations (PDEs). The methods of modelling and simulation of such processes are described e.g. in [1] or [2]. Detailed analysis of the specific TCR is carried out for example in [3].

Tubular chemical reactors belong to hardly controllable processes. Difficulties associated with their control are given not only by their nonlinearity but also by the fact that concentrations of reactants cannot mostly be measured continuously. Here, the cascade control takes place as a suitable and effective control method.

The cascade control belongs to more complex control structures. It may be applied in such cases where more output variables can be measured and where only one input variable is available to the control. Principles of the cascade control are described e.g. in [4], [5] and [6].

In this paper, the TCR control strategy is based on the fact that concentrations of components of reactions taking place in the reactor depend on the reactant temperature. Moreover, the procedure assumes that the reactant temperature is measured at more points along the reactor from which is subsequently calculated mean reactant temperature. Then, in the cascade control-loop, the concentration of a main product of the reaction is considered as the primary controlled variable, and, the mean reactant temperature as the secondary controlled variable. The coolant flow rate represents a common control input. The primary controller determining the set point for the secondary (inner) control-loop is derived as a nonlinear proportional controller using the steady-state characteristics of the reactor. Since the controlled process is nonlinear, a continuous-time adaptive controller is used as the secondary controller. The procedure for the adaptive control design in the inner control-loop is based on approximation of a nonlinear model of the TCR by a continuous-time external linear model (CT ELM) with recursively estimated parameters. In the process of the parameter estimation, a corresponding delta model is used, see, e.g. [7], [8] and [9]. The resulting CT controller is derived on the basis of the LQ control theory, see, e.g. (10) and the polynomial method, see, e.g. [11] or [12]. The control is tested by simulations on the nonlinear model of the TCR with a consecutive exothermic reaction.

2 Model of the reactor

An ideal plug-flow tubular chemical reactor with a simple exothermic consecutive reaction $A \xrightarrow{k_1} B \xrightarrow{k_2} C$ in the liquid phase and with the countercurrent cooling is considered. Heat losses and heat conduction along the metal walls of tubes are assumed to be negligible, but dynamics of the metal walls of tubes are significant. All densities, heat capacities, and heat transfer coefficients are assumed to be constant. Under above assumptions, the reactor model can be described by five PDEs in the form

$$\frac{\partial c_A}{\partial t} + v_r \frac{\partial c_A}{\partial z} = -k_1 c_A \tag{1}$$

$$\frac{\partial c_B}{\partial t} + v_r \frac{\partial c_B}{\partial z} = k_1 c_A - k_2 c_B \tag{2}$$

$$\frac{\partial T_r}{\partial t} + v_r \frac{\partial T_r}{\partial z} = \frac{Q_r}{(\rho c_p)_r} - \frac{4U_1}{d_1 (\rho c_p)_r}(T_r - T_w) \tag{3}$$

Corresponding author: dostalp@fai.utb.cz

$$\frac{\partial T_w}{\partial t}=\frac{4}{(d_2^2-d_1^2)(\rho c_p)_w}\left[d_1U_1(T_r-T_w)+\right.$$
$$\left.+d_2U_2(T_c-T_w)\right] \qquad (4)$$

$$\frac{\partial T_c}{\partial t}-v_c\frac{\partial T_c}{\partial z}=\frac{4n_1d_2U_2}{(d_3^2-n_1d_2^2)(\rho c_p)_c}(T_w-T_c) \qquad (5)$$

with initial conditions

$c_A(z,0)=c_A^s(z)$, $c_B(z,0)=c_B^s(z)$, $T_r(z,0)=T_r^s(z)$,

$T_w(z,0)=T_w^s(z)$, $T_c(z,0)=T_c^s(z)$

and boundary conditions

$c_A(0,t)=c_{A0}(t)$ (kmol/m^3), $c_B(0,t)=c_{B0}(t)$ (kmol/m^3),

$T_r(0,t)=T_{r0}(t)$ (K), $T_c(L,t)=T_{cL}(t)$ (K).

Here, t is the time, z is the axial space variable, c stands for concentrations, T for temperatures, v for fluid velocities, d for diameters, ρ for densities, c_p for specific heat capacities, U for heat transfer coefficients, n_1 is the number of tubes and L is the length of tubes. The subscript $(\cdot)_r$ stands for the reactant mixture, $(\cdot)_w$ for the metal walls of tubes, $(\cdot)_c$ for the coolant, and the superscript $(\cdot)^s$ for steady-state values.

The reaction rates and heat of reactions are nonlinear functions expressed as

$$k_j=k_{j0}\exp\left(\frac{-E_j}{RT_r}\right), \mathrm{j}=1,2 \qquad (6)$$

$$Q_r=(-\Delta H_{r1})k_1c_A+(-\Delta H_{r2})k_2c_B \qquad (7)$$

where k_0 are pre-exponential factors, E are activation energies, $(-\Delta H_r)$ are reaction enthalpies in the negative consideration and R is the gas constant.

The fluid velocities are calculated via the reactant and coolant flow rates as

$$v_r=\frac{4q_r}{\pi n_1 d_1^2}, \quad v_c=\frac{4q_c}{\pi(d_3^2-n_1d_2^2)} \qquad (8)$$

The parameter values with correspondent units used for simulations are given in Table 1.

From the system engineering point of view, $c_A(L,t)=c_{A\text{out}}$, $c_B(L,t)=c_{B\text{out}}$, $T_r(L,t)=T_{r\text{out}}$ and $T_c(0,t)=T_{c\text{out}}$ are the output variables and $q_r(t)$, $q_c(t)$, $c_{A0}(t)$, $T_{r0}(t)$ and $T_{cL}(t)$ are the input variables. Among them, for the control purposes, mostly the coolant flow rate can be taken into account as the control variable, whereas other inputs entering into the process can be accepted as disturbances. In this paper, the mean reactant temperature

$$T_m(t)=\frac{1}{n_p}\sum_{p=1}^{n_p}T_r(z_p,t) \qquad (9)$$

is considered as the secondary (inner) controlled output. Here, z_p refers to measurement points and n_p is their number. The concentration c_B represents the primary controlled output.

Table 1. Parameters and input values.

$L = 8$ m	$n_1 = 1200$
$d_1 = 0.02$ m	$d_2 = 0.024$ m
$d_3 = 1$ m	
$\rho_r = 985$ kg/m^3	$c_{pr} = 4.05$ kJ/kg K
$\rho_w = 7800$ kg/m^3	$c_{pw} = 0.71$ kJ/kg K
$\rho_c = 998$ kg/m^3	$c_{pc} = 4.18$ kJ/kg K
$U_1 = 2.8$ kJ/m^{2}s K	$U_2 = 2.56$ kJ/m^{2}s K
$k_{10} = 5.61\cdot10^{16}$ 1/s	$k_{20} = 1.128\cdot10^{18}$ 1/s
$E_1/R = 13477$ K	$E_2/R = 15290$ K
$(-\Delta H_{r1}) = 5.8\cdot10^4$ kJ/kmol	$(-\Delta H_{r2}) = 1.8\cdot10^4$ kJ/kmol
$c_{A0}^s = 2.85$ kmol/m^3	$c_{B0}^s = 0$ kmol/m^3
$T_{r0}^s = 323$ K	$T_{cL}^s = 293$ K
$q_r^s = 0.15$ m^3/s	

For solution of PDEs, the finite differences method is employed. The procedure is based on substitution of the space interval $z \in <0, L>$ by a set of discrete node points $\{z_i\}$ for i = 1, , n, and, subsequently, by approximation of derivatives with respect to the space variable in each node point by finite differences. The procedure is in detail described in [3].

3 Control objective

Basic scheme of the cascade control is in Fig. 1. Here, NPC stands for the nonlinear proportional controller, AC for the adaptive LQ controller.

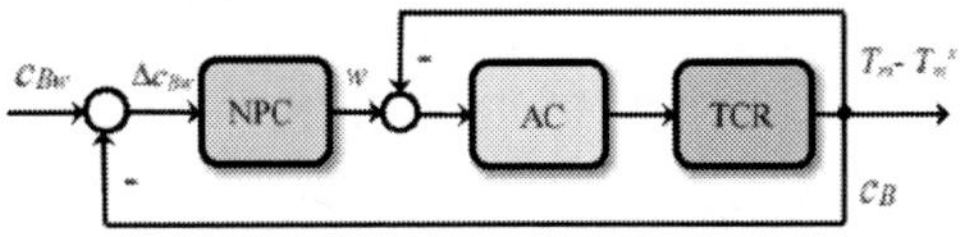

Figure 1. Cascade control scheme.

The control objective is to achieve a concentration of the component B as the primary controlled output near to its maximum. A dependence of the concentration of B on the mean reactant temperature is in Fig. 2.

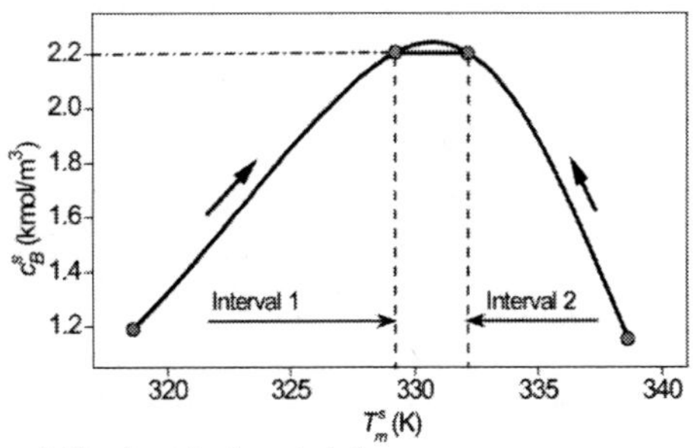

Figure 2. Steady-state characteristics.

There, the operating interval consists of two parts. In the first interval, the concentration B increases with increasing reactant temperature, in the second interval it again decreases. The endpoints defining both intervals are in Table 2.

It can be seen in Fig. 2 that the maximum value of c_B can be slightly higher than 2.2 kmol/m^3. However, the maximum desired value of c_B will be limited just by 2.2 kmol/m^3.

Table 2. Parameters and input values.

Interval	Temperature	Concentration
1	$318.7 \le T_m \le 329.3$	$1.193 \le c_B \le 2.2$
2	$332.4 \le T_m \le 338.7$	$2.2 \ge c_B \ge 1.142$

For purposes of later approximations, the mean temperature is transformed as

$$\xi = \frac{T_m - T_{m\min}}{T_{m\max} - T_{m\min}} \tag{10}$$

where $T_{m\min} = 318.7$ and $T_{m\max} = 338.7$.

The dependence of c_B on ζ is shown in Fig. 3.

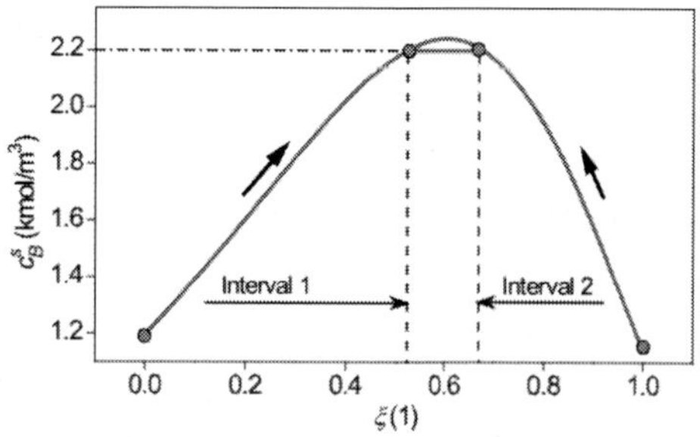

Figure 3. Transformed steady-state characteristics.

4 The NPC design

The procedure of the NPC design appears from polynomial approximation of transformed steady-state characteristics shown in Fig. 3. Approximate polynomials in both intervals are stated including their derivatives in Table 3.

Table 3. Approximate polynomials and their derivatives.

Interva l	Approximate polynomials
1	$c_B = 1.1954 + 1.7848\xi + 1.9554\xi^2 - 3.1818\xi^3$
	$c_B' = 1.7848 + 3.9108\xi - 9.5454\xi^2$
2	$c_B = -6.1051 + 31.0236\xi - 35.9335\xi^2 + 12.1564\xi^3$
	$c_B' = 31.023 - 71.867\xi + 36.4692\xi^2$

Now, a desired value of the mean reactant temperature in the output of the NPC can be computed for each c_B as

$$w = K_w (T_{m\max} - T_{m\min}) \left(\frac{dc_B}{d\xi} \right)^{-1} \Delta c_{Bw} \tag{11}$$

where $\Delta c_{Bw} = c_{Bw} - c_B$, $w = \Delta T_{mw}$, and K_w is a selectable gain coefficient.

5 CT and Delta external linear model

For the control purposes, the controlled output and the control input are defined as

$$u(t) = \Delta q_c(t) = q_c(t) - q_c^s \;, \quad y(t) = \Delta T_m(t) = T_m(t) - T_m^s$$

The CT ELM is proposed in the time domain on the basis of preliminary simulated step responses in the form of the second order differential equation

$$\ddot{y}(t) + a_1 \dot{y}(t) + a_0 y(t) = b_0 u(t) \tag{12}$$

and, in the complex domain, as the transfer function

$$G(s) = \frac{b_0}{s^2 + a_1 s + a_0} . \tag{13}$$

Establishing the δ operator

$$\delta = \frac{d-1}{T_0} \tag{14}$$

where δ is the forward shift operator and T_0 is the sampling period, the delta ELM corresponding to (12) takes the form

$$\delta^2 y(t') + a_1' \delta y(t') + a_0' y(t') = b_0' u(t') \tag{15}$$

where t' is the discrete time.

When the sampling period is shortened, the delta operator approaches the derivative operator, and the estimated parameters a', b' reach the parameters a, b.

6 Delta model parameter estimation

Substituting $t' = k - 2$, equation (15) can be rewriten to the form

$$\delta^2 y(k-2) + a_1' \delta y(k-2) + a_0' y(k-2) = b_0' u(k-2) \tag{16}$$

Establishing the regression vector

$$\mathbf{\Phi}_\delta^T(k-1) = \left(-\delta y(k-2) \quad -y(k-2) \quad u(k-2) \right) \tag{17}$$

where

$$\delta y(k-2) = \frac{y(k-1) - y(k-2)}{T_0} \tag{18}$$

the vector of delta model parameters

$$\mathbf{\Theta}_\delta^T(k) = \left(a_1' \; a_0' \; b_0' \right) \tag{19}$$

is recursively estimated by the least squares method with exponential and directional forgetting from the ARX model, e.g. [12].

$$\delta^2 y(k-2) = \mathbf{\Theta}_\delta^T(k) \mathbf{\Phi}_\delta(k-1) + \varepsilon(k) \tag{20}$$

where

$$\delta^2 y(k-2) = \frac{y(k) - 2y(k-1) + y(k-2)}{T_0^2}. \qquad (21)$$

7 Adaptive LQ controller

The secondary feedback control loop is depicted in Fig. 4. In the scheme, w is a sequence of step reference signals as outputs from the primary controller, e is the tracking error, u is output of the secondary controller, and y is the controlled output. The transfer function $G(s)$ of the CT ELM is given by (13).

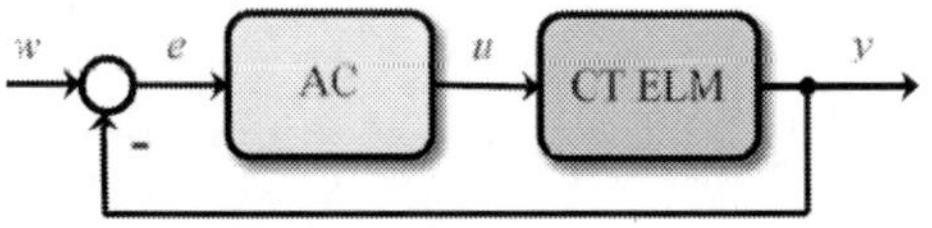

Figure 4. Feedback control loop.

The controller design is based on the polynomial approach and the LQ control theory. Procedure for designing can be briefly described as follows:

The transfer function of the AC is in the form

$$Q(s) = \frac{q(s)}{p(s)} \qquad (22)$$

where q and p are coprime polynomials satisfying the condition of properness $\deg q(s) \le \deg p(s)$. Such control law is sought that minimizes the quadratic cost function

$$S = \int_0^\infty \{e^2(t) + \varphi \dot{u}^2(t)\}\, dt \qquad (23)$$

where $\dot{u}(t)$ is the controller output derivative and φ is the weighting coefficient.

As known, the problem is solved by controller whose polynomials are given by a solution of the polynomial equation

$$a(s)p(s) + b(s)q(s) = d(s) \qquad (24)$$

with a stable polynomial $d(s)$ on the right side, and, where $p(s) = s\,\tilde{p}(s)$ for a step input signal.

Now, the polynomial $d(s)$ takes the form

$$d(s) = g(s)\,n(s) \qquad (25)$$

where $g(s)$ is a monic form of the polynomial $h(s)$ given by spectral factorization

$$[s\,a(s)]^* \varphi [s\,a(s)] + b^*(s)b(s) = h^*(s)h(s). \qquad (26)$$

The second polynomial $n(s)$ ensuring properness of the controller can be chosen as a result of spectral factorization

$$a^*(s)\,a(s) = n^*(s)\,n(s). \qquad (27)$$

For $G(s)$ with $a(s) = s^2 + a_1 s + a_0$, polynomials $h(s)$, $g(s)$ and $n(s)$ take forms

$$h(s) = h_3 s^3 + h_2 s^2 + h_1 s + h_0 \qquad (28)$$

$$g(s) = s^3 + g_2 s^2 + g_1 s + g_0,\ g_j = h_j / h_3 \qquad (29)$$

$$n(s) = s^2 + n_1 s + n_0 \qquad (30)$$

The polynomial $d(s)$ has the form

$$d(s) = s^5 + d_4 s^4 + d_3 s^3 + d_2 s^2 + d_1 s + d_0 \qquad (31)$$

where

$$\begin{aligned} d_0 &= g_0 n_0,\ d_1 = g_1 n_0 + g_0 n_1,\ d_2 = g_2 n_0 + g_1 n_1 + g_0 \\ d_3 &= g_3 n_0 + g_2 n_1 + g_1,\ d_4 = g_3 n_1 + g_2 \end{aligned} \qquad (32)$$

Then, the resulting strictly proper controller has the transfer function

$$Q(s) = \frac{q_2 s^2 + q_1 s + q_0}{s(s^2 + p_1 s + p_0)} \qquad (33)$$

with parameters computed as

$$\begin{pmatrix} 1 & 0 & 0 & 0 & 0 \\ a_1 & 1 & 0 & 0 & 0 \\ a_0 & a_1 & b_0 & 0 & 0 \\ 0 & a_0 & 0 & b_0 & 0 \\ 0 & 0 & 0 & 0 & b_0 \end{pmatrix} \times \begin{pmatrix} p_1 \\ p_0 \\ q_2 \\ q_1 \\ q_0 \end{pmatrix} = \begin{pmatrix} d_4 - a_1 \\ d_3 - a_0 \\ d_2 \\ d_1 \\ d_0 \end{pmatrix} \qquad (34)$$

The above procedure implies that the secondary controller parameters can be adjusted by single selectable parameter φ.

8 Simulations

All simulations were performed on nonlinear model of the TCR (1) – (5) with parameters in Table 1.. The concentration c_B is measured in the period τ_s (s). The aim of simulations is to show an effect of adjustable gain K_w, an effect of the period τ_s and an effect of adjustable weighting parameter φ on some control responses. At the start of simulations, the P controller with a small gain was used. For the δ-model parameter recursive identification, the sampling period $T_0 = 0.5$ s was chosen. In all cases, the reference signal w, the mean temperature T_m and the concentration c_B responses were simulated.

Starting value of the coolant flow rate was always chosen as $q_c^s = 0.48\,\text{m}^3/\text{s}$ and to it corresponding initial values $c_B^s = 1.194\,\text{kmol/m}^3$ and $T_m^s = 318.68\,\text{K}$. The desired value of c_B has been chosen as $c_{Bw} = 2.1$ kmol/m^3.

Effect of the parameter K_w on above responses is evident Figs. 5 – 7. It can be seen that an increasing K_w accelerates all signals in the control loop. However, its value is not unrestricted and its convenient value should be found experimentally.

An effect of the period τ_s can be seen in Figs. 8 – 10. Although shortening τ_s leads to faster control responses, its length is not freely selectable but it is determined by possibilities of a measurement.

The last group of simulations shows an effect of selectable weight coefficient φ on simulated responses. It can be seen that its influence is little significant. This fact is caused by small steps in the sequence of the reference.

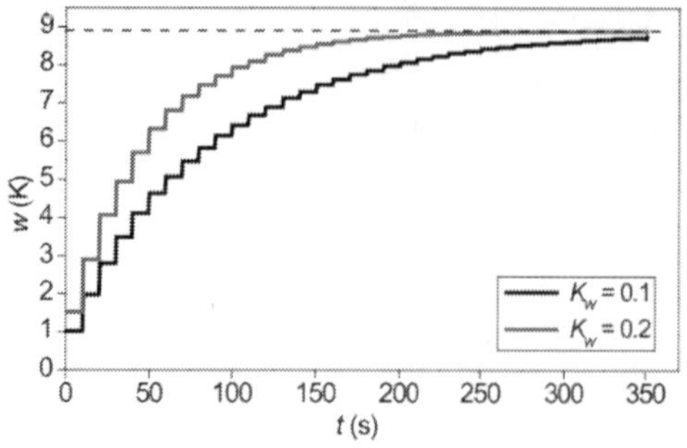

Figure 5. Sequence of step references ($\tau_s = 10$, $\varphi = 100$).

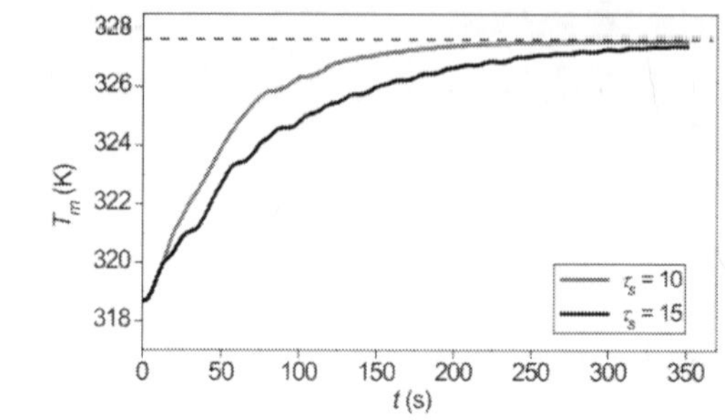

Figure 9. Mean reactant temperature responses ($K_w = 0.15$, $\varphi = 100$).

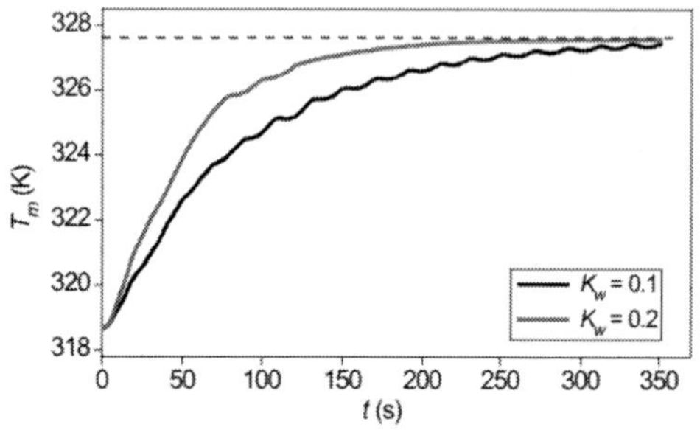

Figure 6. Mean reactant temperature responses ($\tau_s = 10$, $\varphi = 100$).

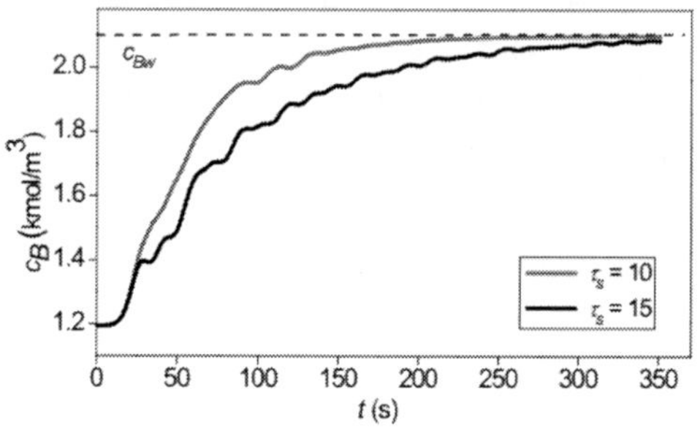

Figure 10. Concentration c_B responses ($\tau_s = 10$, $\varphi = 100$).

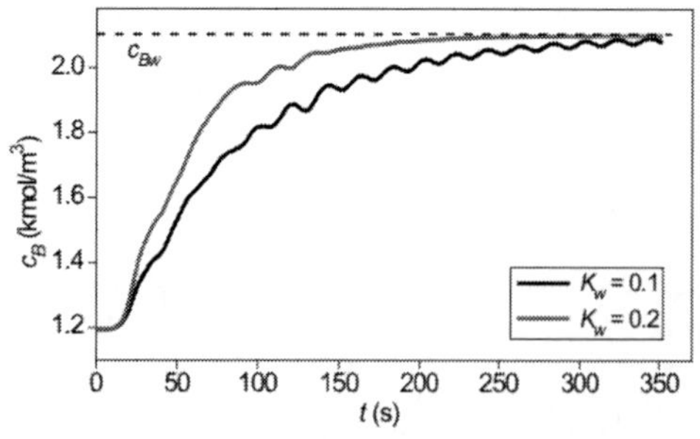

Figure 7. Concentration c_B responses ($\tau_s = 10$, $\varphi = 100$).

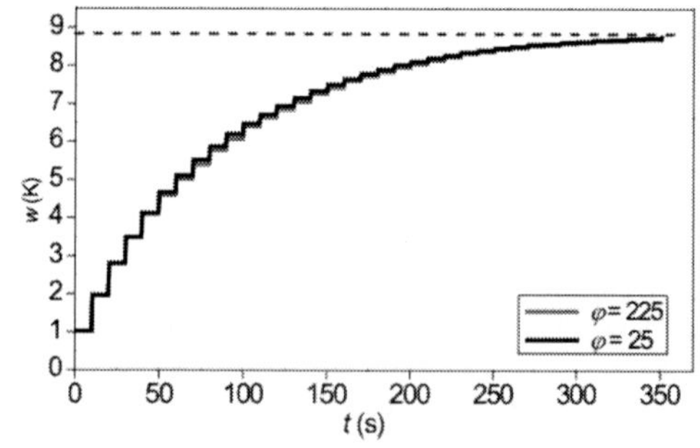

Figure 11. Sequence of step references ($K_w = 0.15$, $\tau_s = 10$).

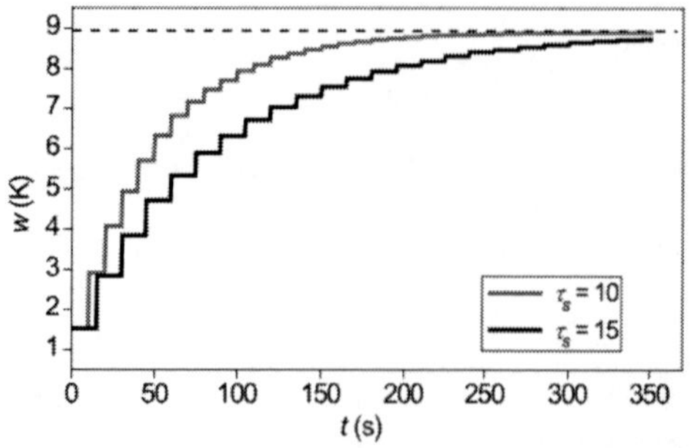

Figure 8. Sequence of step references ($K_w = 0.15$, $\varphi = 100$).

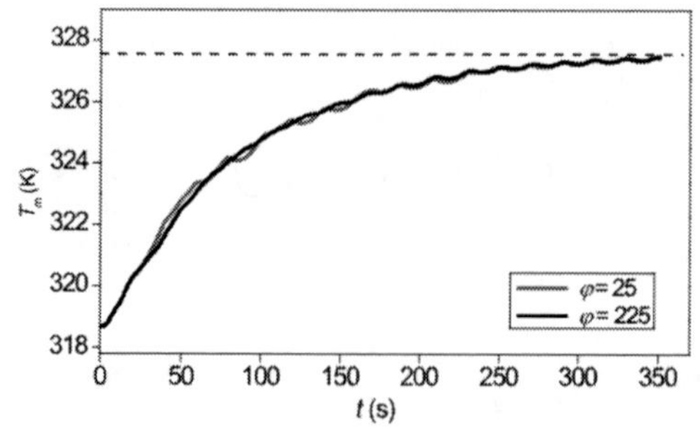

Figure 12. Mean reactant temperature responses ($K_w = 0.1$, $\tau_s = 10$).

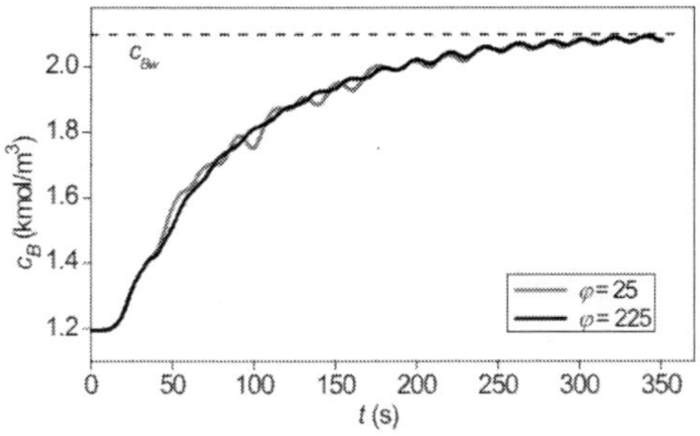

Figure 13. Concentration c_B responses ($K_w = 0.1$, $\tau_s = 10$).

9 Conclusions

The article presents the cascade control design of a tubular chemical reactor. The procedure is based on a possibility of measuring the concentration of a main product of a reaction taking place in the reactor and measuring the temperature of the reactant at multiple points along the reactor. The control is performed in the external (primary) and inner (secondary) closed-loops where the concentration of a main product on the output of the reactor is the primary and the mean reactant temperature the secondary controlled variable. A common control input is the coolant flow rate.

The controller in the external control-loop is a discrete nonlinear P-controller derived on the basis of simulated or measured steady-state characteristics of the reactor. The controller in the inner control-loop is an adaptive LQ continuous-time controller. In its derivation, the recursive parameter estimation of an external delta model of the reactor, the polynomial approach and the LQ control theory are applied.

The presented method has been tested by computer simulation on the nonlinear model of the tubular chemical reactor with a consecutive exothermic reaction.

References

1. W.L. Luyben, *Chemical reactor design and control* (John Wiley & Sons, Chichester, 2007)
2. D.E. Seborg, T.F. Edgar, D.A. Mellichamp, *Process Dynamics and Control* (John Wiley & Sons, Chichester, 1989)
3. P. Dostál, V. Bobál, J. Vojtěšek, *Proc. of 22nd European Conference on Modelling and Simulation*, 487-492, Cyprus (2008).
4. J. F. Smuts, *Process control for practitioners* (OptiControls Inc., New York, 2011)
5. M. King, *Process control: A practical approach* (John Wiley & Sons, Chichester, 2010)
6. R. Schmidt, *Chemical process design and integration* (John Wiley & Sons, Chichester, 2005)
7. H. Garnier, L. Wang (eds.), *Identification of continuous-time models from sampled data* (Springer-Verlag, London, 2008)
8. S. Mukhopadhyay, A.G. Patra, G.P. Rao, Int. J. Contr. **55**, (1992).
9. D.L. Stericker, N.K. Sinha, Control-theory and adv. Technol. **9**, (1993)
10. V. Kučera, D. Henrion, *Proc of IFAC Symposium Robust Control Design*, Prague (2000)
11. J. Mikleš, M. Fikar, *Process modellig, identification and control 2* (STU Press, Bratislava, 2004)
12. V. Bobál, J. Böhm, J. Fessl, J. Macháček, *Digital self-tuning controllers* (Springer Verlag, Berlin, 2005)

Comparison of Two Identification Models Used in Adaptive Control of Continuous-Stirred Tank Reactor

Jiri Vojtesek and Petr Dostal

Tomas Bata University in Zlin, Faculty of Applied Informatics, Nad Stranemi 4511, 760 05 Zlin, Czech Republic

Abstract. The goal of this paper is to compare two identification methods – continuous-time and discrete-time. The continuous-time identification model is more accurate but not very suitable for on-line identification. This disadvantage was overcome with the use of differential filters. On the other hand, discrete-time identification model has is more suitable for identification but less accurate. Compromise can be found in the delta model as a special type of the discrete-time model parameters of which are related to the sampling period. The adaptive approach is based on the choice of the External Linear Model, parameters of which are identified recursively which satisfies the adaptivity of this system. Proposed control strategy was applied on the mathematical model of the Continuous Stirred-Tank reactor as a typical nonlinear lumped-parameters system used in the industry.

1 Introduction

The continuous stirred-tank reactor (CSTR) is typical nonlinear equipment used in the chemical and biochemical industry for production of various chemicals, drugs etc. [1].

The modelling and simulation is great tool which helps with the observing of the system's behaviour and designing of the appropriate controller. The mathematical model of CSTR is usually described by the set of nonlinear ordinary differential equations (ODEs) which can be solved mathematically for example by the Runge-Kutta's method.

The adaptive control [2] used here for the control is one of the approaches used for the nonlinear systems because it produces good control results. Advantage of this method can be found in very good theoretical background and variety of modifications [3].

The approach used here is based on the choice of the External Linear Model (ELM) which describes controlled, originally nonlinear, process in the linear way for example by the discrete or the continuous transfer function (TF) [3]. Parameters of ELM are then identified recursively during the control and parameters of the controller are recomputed according to identified parameters of the system. The advantage of used polynomial synthesis is that it produces the structure and also relations for computing controller's parameters that reflect identified parameters of ELM.

Two identification models with the continuous-time (CT) model [4] and special type of the discrete-time (DT) model called delta/model [5] where discussed here. Parameters of input and output variables are related to the sampling period. It was proved that parameters of the delta model approach to parameters of the CT model for sufficiently small sampling period [6]. This combination of the continuous-time control synthesis with the discrete-time identification is called "Hybrid adaptive control" and some applications can be found for example in [7] and [8].

The recursive least-squares method is used for online identification. This method is widely used because it is easily programmable in standard programming languages at one hand but it produces sufficiently good identification results with various modifications.

All results in this paper are simulations made in the mathematical software Matlab, version 7.0.1.

2 Continuous Stirred-Tank Reactor

The system under the consideration is Continuous Stirred-Tank Reactor (CSTR) with so called Van der Vusse reaction inside [9]:

$$\begin{gathered} A \xrightarrow{k_1} B \xrightarrow{k_2} C \\ 2A \xrightarrow{k_3} D \end{gathered} \tag{1}$$

The mathematical model of this system comes from material and heat balances inside the reactor and results in the set of four nonlinear ordinary differential equations (ODE):

$$\frac{dc_A}{dt} = \frac{q_r}{V_r}\left(c_{A0} - c_A\right) - k_1 c_A - k_3 c_A^2 \tag{2}$$

$$\frac{dc_B}{dt} = -\frac{q_r}{V_r} c_B + k_1 c_A - k_2 c_B \tag{3}$$

$$\frac{dT_r}{dt} = \frac{q_r}{V_r}\left(T_{r0} - T_r\right) - \frac{h_r}{\rho_r c_{pr}} + \frac{A_r U}{V_r \rho_r c_{pr}}\left(T_c - T_r\right) \tag{4}$$

[a] Corresponding author: vojtesek@fai.utb.cz

$$\frac{dT_c}{dt} = \frac{1}{m_c c_{pc}} \left(Q_c + A_r U \left(T_r - T_c \right) \right) \qquad (5)$$

The mathematical model described by the set of ODE (2) - (5) have state variables concentrations c_A, c_B and temperatures of the reactant T_r and the cooling T_c. This system provides theoretically four input variables – a volumetric flow rate of the reactant, q_r, a heat removal of the cooling, Q_c, an input concentration c_{A0} and an input temperature of the reactant, T_{r0}. The last two are only theoretical and could not be used as an input variable from the practical point of view.

The scheme of this chemical reactor is in Figure 1.

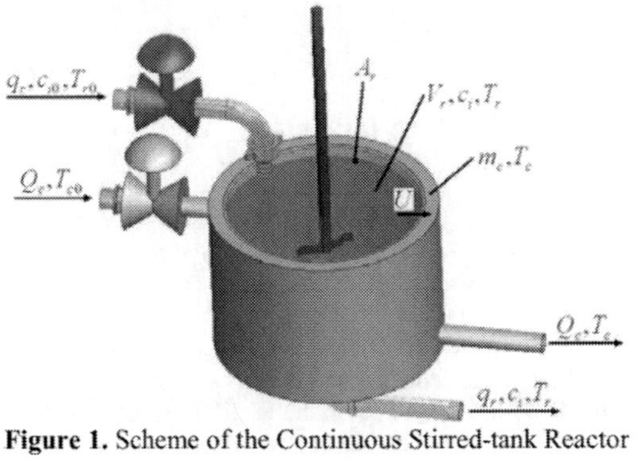

Figure 1. Scheme of the Continuous Stirred-tank Reactor

Due to the simplification of the mathematical model, other variables are supposed to be constant during the control. The volume of the reactor is denoted as V_r, A_r is the heat exchange surface, ρ_r is used for the density of the reactant, U is the heat transfer coefficient, c_{pc} and c_{pr} are specific heat capacities of the cooling and the reactant a mc is the weight of the cooling mass. Values of these fixed parameters are in Table 1 [9].

Table 1. Fixed parameters of the reactor

Variable	*Value*
Pre-exp. factor for react. 1	k_{01}=2.145•10^{10} min^{-1}
Pre-exp. factor for react. 2	k_{02}=2.145•10^{10} min^{-1}
Pre-exp. factor for react. 3	k_{03}=1.5072•10^{8} min^{-1}mol^{-1}
Activation ener. 1 to R	E_1/R = 9758.3 K
Activation ener. 2 to R	E_2/R = 9758.3 K
Activation ener. 3 to R	E_3/R = 8560 K
Enthalpy of reaction 1	h_1 =-4200 $kJ.kmol^{-1}$
Enthalpy of reaction 2	h_2 =11000 $kJ.kmol^{-1}$
Enthalpy of reaction 3	h_3 = 41850 $kJ.kmol^{-1}$
Volume of the reactor	V_r = 0.01 m^3
Heat capacity of reactant	c_{pr} = 3.01 $kJ.kg^{-1}.K^{-1}$
Heat transfer coefficient	U = 67.2 $kJ.min^{-1}m^{-2}K^{-1}$
Input concentration of A	c_{A0} = 5.1 $kmol.m^{-3}$
Input concentration of B	c_{B0} = 0 $kmol.m^{-3}$
Input temp. of reactant	T_{r0} = 387.05 K
Density of reactant	ρ_r = 934.2 $kg.m^{-3}$
Heat capacity of coolant	c_{pc} = 2.0 $kJ.kg^{-1}.K^{-1}$
Surface of cooling jacket	A_r = 0.215 m^2
Weight of coolant	m_c = 5 kg

The first step of the simulation is the steady-state analysis which observes behaviour of the system in the steady-state where state variable does not change. This analysis can help us with the choice of the optimal working point for control. Experiments in [8] have shown working point defined by the volumetric flow rate of the reactant q_r^s = 2.4•10^{-3} $m^3.min^{-1}$ and heat removal of the coolant Q_c^s = -18.56 $kJ.min^{-1}$.

The second, dynamic, analysis then observes the behaviour of the system after the step change of the input variable, in this case the heat removal of the coolant, ΔQ_c. The observed output is on the other hand the change of the reactant's temperature, T_r, i.e.

$$u(t) = \frac{Q_c(t) - Q_c^s}{Q_c^s} \cdot 100\,[\%], \quad y(t) = T(t) - T^s\,[K] \quad (6)$$

The results for various step changes of the input variable from the range $\Delta u(t)$ = <-100%; +100%> and results are in Figure 3.

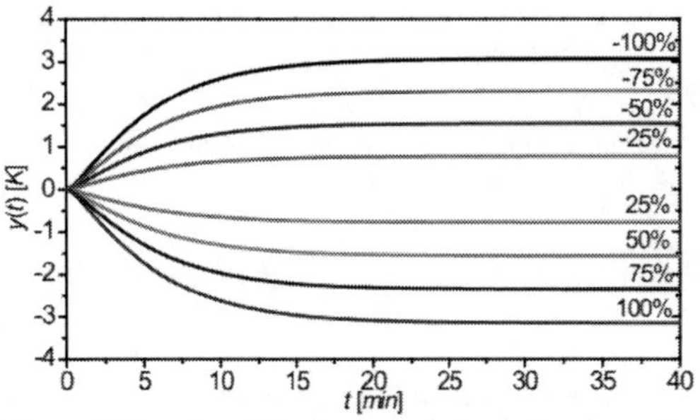

Figure 2. Results of the dynamic analysis for the various changes of the input variable $\Delta u(t)$

Results clearly shows, that all outputs could be described by the second order transfer function (TF) with relative order one in the polynomial form

$$G(s) = \frac{b(s)}{a(s)} = \frac{b_1 s + b_0}{s^2 + a_1 s + a_0} \qquad (7)$$

This will be later used for identification in the adaptive control.

3 Hybrid Adaptive Control

The control approach here is based on the term "Adaptivity" known from the nature, where plant, animals or even human beings "adapts" their behaviour to the actual environment.

At first we will start with the control synthesis which uses advantages of the polynomial synthesis [10] that satisfies basic control requirements such as stability, disturbance attenuation and reference signal tracking. Moreover, this method produces not only the structure of the controller, but also the relations for computing of controller's parameters.

The simplest, most common known control scheme with one degree of freedom (1DOF) [11] is shown in Figure 3. The controller is here represented by the TF $Q(s)$ and the controlled system is described by TF $G(s)$ from (7).

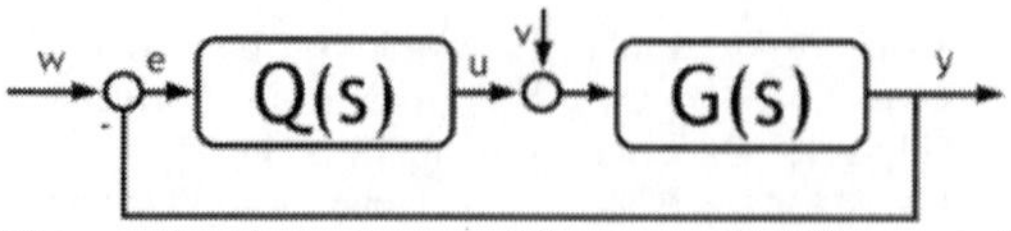

Figure 3. One degree-of-freedom (1DOF) control configuration

The signal w in Figure 3 is reference signal (i.e. wanted value), v denotes disturbance, u is an input and y an output variable. It can be seen, that controller is here only in the feedback part.

The TF of this controller Q(s) is generally:

$$Q(s)=\frac{q(s)}{p(s)} \tag{8}$$

where degrees of polynomials $p(s)$ and $q(s)$ must hold properness condition:

$$\deg q(s)\le \deg p(s) \tag{9}$$

The condition for the reference signal tracking is satisfied if the polynomial p(s) in the denominator of the controller's transfer functions (17) is divided into

$$p(s)=f(s)\cdot\tilde{p}(s) \tag{10}$$

where $f(s)$ is a least common divisor of the reference and the disturbance transfer functions. If we have these TF in the form of the step function, $f(s) = s$ and (17) could be rewritten into

$$Q(s)=\frac{q(s)}{s\cdot\tilde{p}(s)} \tag{11}$$

Parameters of controller's polynomials $\tilde{p}(s)$ and $q(s)$ are computed from Diophantine polynomial equation [10]

$$a(s)\cdot s\cdot\tilde{p}(s)+b(s)\cdot q(s)=d(s) \tag{12}$$

and they can be solved by the Method of uncertain coefficients. Polynomials $a(s)$ and $b(s)$ in (21) are known from the recursive identification which will be discussed in the next subchapter. The polynomial $d(s)$ on the right side of Diophantine equations (21) is stable optional polynomial which could affect the quality of the control.

Degrees of controller's polynomials $\tilde{p}(s)$ and $q(s)$ and the degree of the stable polynomial d(s) are

$$\deg\tilde{p}(s)=\deg a(s)-1 \quad \deg q(s)=\deg a(s)$$
$$\deg d(s)=2\cdot\deg a(s) \tag{13}$$

As it was already mentioned, polynomial $d(s)$ is optional polynomial which could be designed for example by the Pole-placement method, generally

$$d(s)=\prod_{i=1}^{\deg d(s)}(s+s_i) \tag{14}$$

where roots s_i are generally in the complex form $s_i = \alpha_i + \omega_i\ j$ and the stability is satisfied for $\alpha_i < 0$. If we want to obtain an aperiodic output response, ω_i must hold 0 and (14) is then

$$d(s)=(s+\alpha)^{\deg d} \tag{15}$$

The equation (15) is very general which could be disadvantage of this method – there is no recommendation for the choice of roots in polynomial $d(s)$. Our previous experiments [8] have shown that is good co connect the choice of this polynomial somehow with the controlled system. The Spectral factorization could be used for this task and it means that the polynomial $d(s)$ is divided into two parts

$$d(s)=n(s)\cdot(s+\alpha)^{\deg d-\deg n} \tag{16}$$

where one part is classic pole-placement method and $n(s)$ comes from the Spectral factorization of the polynomial $a(s)$ in the denominator of the controlled system's transfer function (7):

$$n^*(s)\cdot n(s)=a^*(s)\cdot a(s) \tag{17}$$

Advantage of the Spectral factorization can be also find in the feature, that the polynomial $n(s)$ is always stable even if the polynomial $a(s)$ is unstable. This could happen for example by inaccurate estimation at the beginning of the control when an estimator does not have enough information about the system.

4 Identification Models

It was already mentioned that the controller is based on the adaptivity. There are several adaptive approaches used in the control theory. The one used here is based on the online recursive identification of the External Linear Model (ELM) of the originally nonlinear system. Parameters of the controller are then recomputed according to identified parameters of the ELM. ELM could be for example TF in the form of (7).

There will be discussed two types of identification models – continuous-time (CT) and discrete-time (DT) in the next subchapters.

4.1. Continuous-Time Identification Model

The ELM of the controlled system is described by continuous-time TF $G(s)$ (7) and this relation is also described to the fraction of the the Laplace transform of the output variable, $Y(s)$, to the input variable, $U(s)$, the ELM in the (7) could be also rewritten to the form

$$a(\sigma)\cdot y(t)=b(\sigma)\cdot u(t) \tag{18}$$

where $u(t)$ denotes the input variable, $y(t)$ is the output variable and σ is the differentiation operator.

The identification of CT model in (18) is problem because the derivatives of the input and the output variables are immeasurable but they could be replaced by the filtered ones denoted by u_f and y_f and computed from

$$c(\sigma)\cdot u_f(t)=u(t)$$
$$c(\sigma)\cdot y_f(t)=y(t) \tag{19}$$

for a new stable polynomial $c(\sigma)$ that fulfils condition $\deg c(\sigma)\ge\deg a(\sigma)$, the Laplace transform of (19) is then

$$c(s)\cdot U_f(s)=U(s)+o_1(s)$$
$$c(s)\cdot Y_f(s)=Y(s)+o_2(s) \tag{20}$$

where polynomials $o_1(s)$ and $o_2(s)$ includes initial conditions of filtered variables. If we substitute (20) into the Laplace transform of the Equation (18), the relation for the Laplace transform of the filtered output variable, $Y_f(s)$ is

$$Y_f(s) = \frac{b(s)}{a(s)} U_f(s) + \Psi(s) \tag{21}$$

and $\Psi(s)$ is a rational function which contains initial conditions of both filtered and unfiltered variables.

The dynamics of the differential filters $c(s)$ in (20) must be faster than the dynamics of the controlled system [12] which is satisfied if parameters of this polynomial sufficiently small.

The values of filtered values are taken in the discrete time moment $t_k = k \cdot T_v$ for $k = 0, 1, 2, \dots N$. T_v is sampling period and the regression vector has $n+m$ parts where deg $a = n = 2$ and deg $b = m = 1$, i.e.

$$\varphi_{CT}(t_k) = \left[-y_f(t_k), -y_f^{(1)}(t_k), u_f(t_k), u_f^{(1)}(t_k)\right]^T \tag{22}$$

The vector of parameters

$$\theta_{CT}(t_k) = \left[a_0, a_1, b_0, b_1\right]^T \tag{23}$$

is computed from the differential equation

$$y_f^{(n)}(t_k) = \theta_{CT}^T(t_k) \cdot \varphi_{CT}(t_k) + \Psi(t_k) \tag{24}$$

where Ψ includes immeasurable errors.

4.2. Discrete-Time Identification Model

The discrete-time identification model is better for practical purposes – it is more simple to read input and output variables in the defined time intervals then continuously. We can find also compromise between practically better DT model and more accurate CT model in so called delta-models [8] that are special types of DT models where input and output variables are related to the sampling period.

A new complex variable γ is defined generally as [13]

$$\gamma = \frac{z-1}{\beta \cdot T_v \cdot z + (1-\beta) \cdot T_v} \tag{25}$$

for T_v as a sampling period and β an optional parameter which holds $0 \le \beta \le 1$. It is clear, that there could be an infinite number of delta-models as there is modifiability of β. One of the most used model is Forward delta-model for $\beta = 0$ was used here.

The complex variable γ is then

$$\gamma = \frac{z-1}{T_v} \tag{26}$$

It was proved for example in [6], that parameters of the delta-model approaches to the CT ones for sufficiently small sampling period T_v.

In delta-models, the CT model (18) can be rewritten to the form

$$a'(\delta) y(t') = b'(\delta) u(t') \tag{27}$$

where $a'(\delta)$ and $b'(\delta)$ are discrete polynomials and their coefficients are different from those in CT model but we suppose, that they are close to them because the sampling period is sufficiently small.

The regression vector is in this case for TF (7):

$$\varphi_\delta(k-1) = \left[-y_\delta(k-1), -y_\delta(k-2), u_\delta(k-1), u_\delta(k-2)\right]^T \tag{28}$$

and the vector of parameters is then

$$\theta_\delta(k) = \left[a_1', a_0', b_1', b_0'\right]^T \tag{29}$$

Parameters of this vector are computed again from the differential equation

$$y_\delta(k) = \theta_\delta^T(k) \cdot \varphi_\delta(k-1) + e(k) \tag{30}$$

for $e(k)$ as a general random immeasurable component.

4.3. Identification Method

The last what needs to be described is the online identification method which satisfies the adaptivity of the controller. The Recursive Least-Squares Method [14] could be used because it is simple, accurate with modifications and it is also easily programmable.

Presented method could be used for both CT and DT identification models described above. The RLS method used for estimation of vectors of parameters $\hat{\theta}_{CT}^T$ or $\hat{\theta}_\delta^T$ in (24) or (30) could be described generally by the set of equations:

$$\begin{aligned}
\varepsilon(k) &= y(k) - \varphi^T(k) \cdot \hat{\theta}(k-1) \\
\gamma(k) &= \left[1 + \varphi^T(k) \cdot \mathbf{P}(k-1) \cdot \varphi(k)\right]^{-1} \\
\mathbf{L}(k) &= \gamma(k) \cdot \mathbf{P}(k-1) \cdot \varphi(k) \\
\mathbf{P}(k) &= \frac{1}{\lambda_1(k-1)} \left[\mathbf{P}(k-1) - \frac{\mathbf{P}(k-1) \cdot \varphi(k) \cdot \varphi^T(k) \cdot \mathbf{P}(k-1)}{\frac{\lambda_1(k-1)}{\lambda_2(k-1)} + \varphi^T(k) \cdot \mathbf{P}(k-1) \cdot \varphi(k)}\right] \\
\hat{\theta}(k) &= \hat{\theta}(k-1) + \mathbf{L}(k)\varepsilon(k)
\end{aligned} \tag{31}$$

where ϕ is regression vector, ε denotes a prediction error, $\mathbf{P}$ is a covariance matrix and λ_1 and λ_2 are forgetting factors. For example constant exponential forgetting [14] uses $\lambda_2 = 1$ and

$$\lambda_1(k) = 1 - K \cdot \gamma(k) \cdot \varepsilon^2(k) \tag{32}$$

where K is a very small value (e.g. $K = 0.001$). This RLS modification was used in this work for the online estimation.

5 Simulation Experiment

Proposed adaptive controller with two identification models was tested by simulation on the mathematical model of CSTR presented in Chapter 2.

Due to comparability, both simulations were performed for the same simulation parameters. The sampling period was $T_v = 0.3$ *min*, the initial covariance matrix $\mathbf{P}(0)$ has on the diagonal $1 \cdot 10^6$ and starting vectors of parameters for the identification was chosen $\theta_{CT}(0) = \theta_{CT}(0) = [0.1; 0.1; 0.1; 0.1]^T$. The simulation was performed for 750 *min* and there were done 5 changes of the reference signal $w(t)$ during this time.

The controller needs some time for adaptation and our previous experiments have shown that it is good to insert the first change of the reference signal as an exponential function instead of the step function. The next changes were step functions The input signal $u(t)$ was limited to the values $u(t)$ = <-75%; +75%> due to physical limitations.

As it was mentioned, the tuning parameter for this adaptive controller is the position of the root α. There were observed courses of the output variable y for three values of α = 0.05; 0.08 and 0.4 for both identification models and results are shown in the following figures.

The first analysis was done for the CT identification model where the filtered polynomial $c(\sigma)$ was $c(\sigma) = s^2 + 1.4\,s + 0.49$.

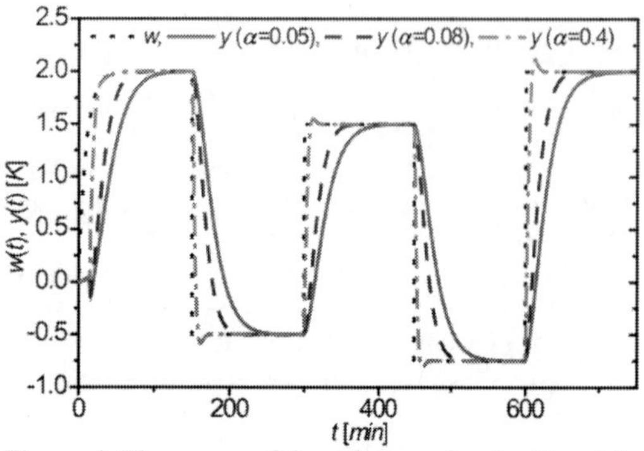

Figure 4. The course of the reference signal $w(t)$ and the output variable $y(t)$ for CT identification model and various parameter α

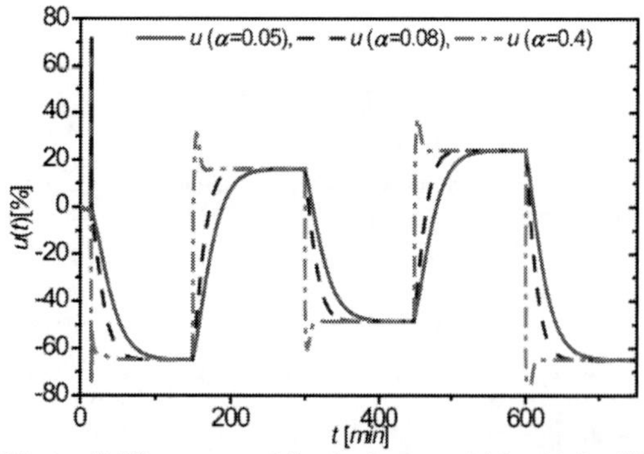

Figure 5. The course of the the input variable $u(t)$ for CT identification model and various parameter α

Results show that the tuning parameter α affect mainly the speed of the control. Increasing value of α produces quicker output response but could end with small overshoots which is evident for α = 0.4. On the other hand, a smaller value of α has smoother course of the input variable $u(t)$ in Figure 5 which is better from practical point of view.

The second analysis for DT delta model was performed for Forward delta model and the same tuning parameters α.

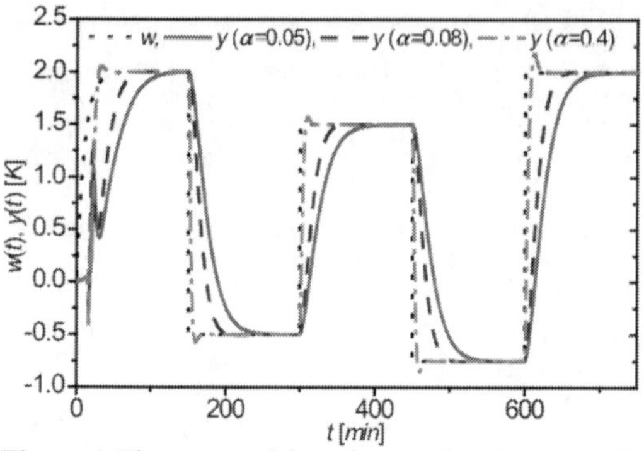

Figure 6. The course of the reference signal $w(t)$ and the output variable $y(t)$ for delta identification model and various parameter α

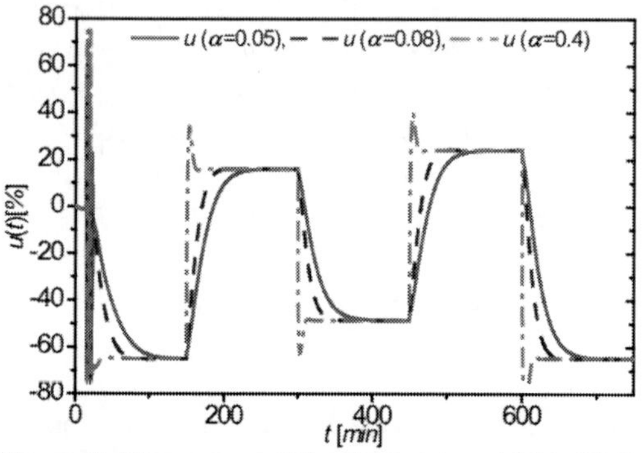

Figure 7. The course of the the input variable $u(t)$ for delta identification model and various parameter α

Obtained results are very similar to those in the previous analysis. The biggest value of α = 0.4 has again the quickest course but overshoots and their value depends on the height of the change. The course of the input variable is smoother for the lower values of tuning parameter.

Both studies have very good control results except the beginning of the control. This is caused by the inaccurate identification which starts from the general point and it needs some time for "adaptation". On the other hand, after initial 50 *min* the controller does not have problem with the online identification.

Courses of the identified parameters are in Figures 8 – 11. These figures show that recursive least squares method used for identification has no problem with the identification except the beginning of the control in the adaptation part.

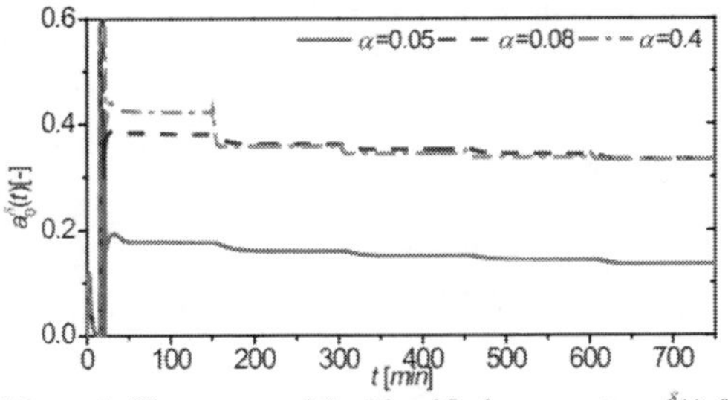

Figure 8. The course of the identified parameter $a_0^{\delta}(t)$ for various α in delta identification model

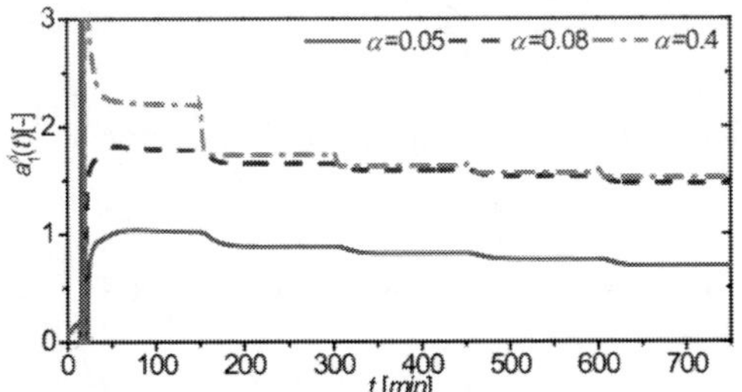

Figure 9. The course of the identified parameter $a_1^{\delta}(t)$ for various α in delta identification model

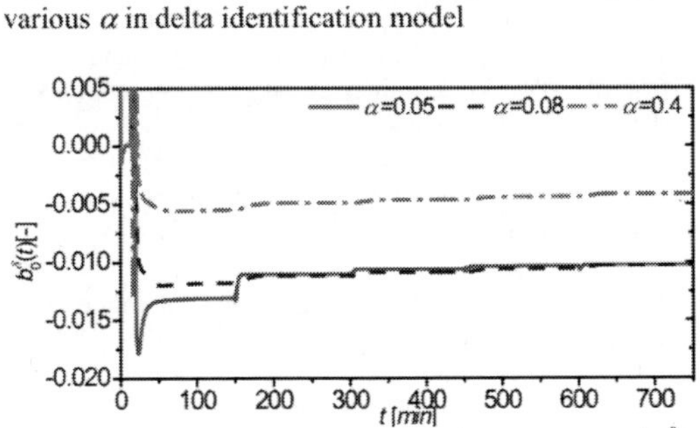

Figure 10. The course of the identified parameter $b_0^{\delta}(t)$ for various α in delta identification model

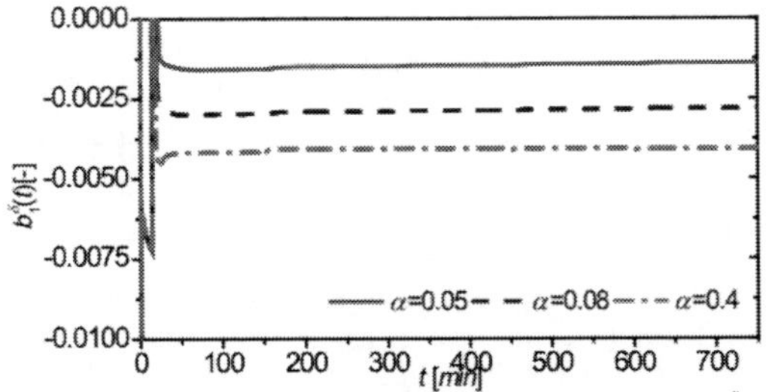

Figure 11. The course of the identified parameter $b_1^{\delta}(t)$ for various α in delta identification model

6 Conclusions

The paper shows one approach for controlling of the nonlinear process represented by the continuous stirred-tank reactor with the cooling in the jacket. The mathematical model of this reactor is described by the set of four nonlinear ODE that are easily solvable by the numerical methods. Proposed control strategy is based on the choice of the ELM parameters of which are identified recursively during the control and parameters of the controller are recomputed according to the identified ones. This controller could be tuned by the parameter α as a position of the root in the pole-placement method. The simulation experiments have shown that the increasing value of this parameter affect the speed of the control and overshoots – bigger value of α results in quicker output response but overshoots. Proposed controller produces good control results although this system has nonlinear behaviour and negative properties from the control point of view.

References

1. J. Ingham, I. J. Dunn, E. Heinzle, J. E. Prenosil. *Chemical Engineering Dynamics. An Introduction to Modeling and Computer Simulation.* Second. Completely Revised Edition. (VCH Verlagsgesellshaft. Weinheim, 2000).
2. K. J. Åström, B. Wittenmark 1989. *Adaptive Control.* (Addison Wesley. Reading. MA, 1989).
3. V. Bobal, J. Böhm, J. Fessl, J. Machacek. *Digital Self-tuning Controllers: Algorithms. Implementation and Applications.* Advanced Textbooks in Control and Signal Processing. (Springer-Verlag London Limited. 2005).
4. B. Wahlberg,., Automatica, vol. 26, 167-170 (1990).
5. R. H. Middleton, G. C. Goodwin. *Digital Control and Estimation - A Unified Approach.* (Prentice Hall. Englewood Cliffs, 2004).
6. D. L. Stericker, N. K. Sinha. *Control-Theory and Advanced Technology.* vol. 9. 113-125 (1993).
7. J. Vojtesek, P. Dostal. *Proceedings of 19th European Conference on Modelling and Simulation ECMS 2005.* Riga, Latvia, p. 591-598 (2005).
8. J. Vojtesek, P. Dostal. *Proceedings 25th European Conference on Modelling and Simulation ECMS 2011.* Nicosia: p. 501-507. ISBN 978-0-9564944-2-9 (2011).
9. H. Chen, A. Kremling; F. Allgöwer. *Proceedings of 3rd European Control Conference.* Rome, Italy (1995).
10. V. Kucera. *Automatica.* 29. 1361-1375 (1993).
11. M. J. Grimble *Robust industrial control. Optimal design approach for polynomial systems.* (Prentice Hall, London, 1994).
12. P. Dostal, V. Bobal; M. Blaha, M. *Proceedings of IFAC Workshop on Adaptation and Learning in Control and Signal Processing ALCOSP 2001*, 407-412, Cernobbio-Como, Italy, (2001).
13. S. Mukhopadhyay, A. G. Patra, G. P. Rao. *International Journal of Control*, vol.55, 1161-1187 (1992).
14. J. Mikleš, M. Fikar, *Process modellig, identification and control 2* (STU Press, Bratislava, 2004).

Area-efficient readout with 14-bit SAR-ADC for CMOS image sensors

Sassi Ben Aziza[1,a], and Daniel Dzahini[2]

[1] *STMicroelectronics, 12 rue Jules Horowitz, 38000 Grenoble, France*
LPSC, Université Grenoble-Alpes, CNRS/IN2P3, 53 rue des Martyrs 38026 Grenoble, France
[2] *LPSC, Université Grenoble-Alpes, CNRS/IN2P3, 53 rue des Martyrs 38026 Grenoble, France*

Abstract. This paper proposes a readout design for CMOS image sensors. It has been squeezed into a 7.5um pitch under a 0.28um 1P3M technology. The ADC performs one 14-bit conversion in only 1.5us and targets a theoretical DNL feature about +1.3/-1 at 14-bit accuracy. Correlated Double Sampling (CDS) is performed both in the analog and digital domains to preserve the image quality.
Keywords— CMOS Image Sensor, Successive-Approximation-Register ADC, Column-parallel architecture, CDS

1 Introduction

Recently introduced CMOS image sensors (CIS) have been following an evolutionary trend in the last years. One benchmark for this is the dramatic growth of patents mainly for process [1]. This technological breakthrough yields an added value along with new design solutions.

Applications like automotive, surveillance and broadcast cameras require high quality moving pictures in terms of speed, accuracy and compactness. This represents a good opportunity to exploit the process progress. Still mode for Digital Still Cameras (DSC) for instance is also an important development area were resolution can be justified until 14 or 16 bit.

Column-parallel readout is commonly used for a high frame rate and low power operation. Four main architectures can be distinguished for the Analog to Digital Converter (ADC) cells. : the Single Slope ADC (SS-ADC), the Successive-Approximation-Register ADC (SAR-ADC) [2-3], the Cyclic ADC (CY-ADC) and the Delta-Sigma ADC (ΔΣ-ADC). The SS-ADC is mainly bound by the clock high frequency required for high speed and high resolution applications. The CY-ADC suffers from high power consumption as the bit resolution increases due the open-loop gain requirements of the amplifier. ΔΣ-ADCs present intrinsic good noise performances coming with the noise shaping but they suffer from low speed operation and require also additional digital filters.

In this paper, a new architecture of column-parallel SAR-ADC adapted for CMOS image sensors is presented. Conversion time has been optimized to reach 1.5us over 14-bit resolution. In [3], a 14-bit SAR-ADC has been reported with a layout pitch of 11.2um as shown in Table1. In [2] ADC pitch reached 8.4um. In this work, the design has been squeezed into 7.5um pitch. The adopted solutions are also easily adaptable to a 12-bit 5.6um ADC pitch making it compatible with next generation automotive sensors.

In each column of the imager, a Programmable Gain Amplifier (PGA) is implemented just before the SAR-ADC to ensure different analog gains. Such an operation relaxes the constraints on the ADC input-referred noise. During our discussion, the PGA plus the SAR-ADC are called the readout.

The layout has been implemented both under Front Side Illumination (FSI) and Back Side Illumination (BSI) in a 1P3M 0.28um process. Another flexibility advantage of the design is the high voltage swing. It has been validated for 1V5 voltage swing and can be extended to 1V7 making it compatible with next generation pixels.

Table 1. State of art of 14-bit SAR-ADCs.

Ref.	ADC Type	Resolution	ADC Pitch (um)	Conversion Time (us)
[2]	SAR	14	8.4	1.7
[3]	SAR	14	11.2	-
This Work	SAR	14	7.5	1.5

In this paper, we will present in Section 2 the architecture of the image sensor with emphasis on the readout operation. Section 3 details a novel scheme 14-bit SAR-ADC architecture and design considerations. Section 4 gives an overview of layout solutions.

2 Image sensor architecture

2.1 Bloc diagram

The modular architecture of the image sensor is depicted in Figure 1(a). The present work consists on designing the pre-amplification and the SAR-ADC.

[a] Corresponding author: *sassi.benaziza@st.com*

DOI: 10.1051/matecconf/20167601006

(a) (b)
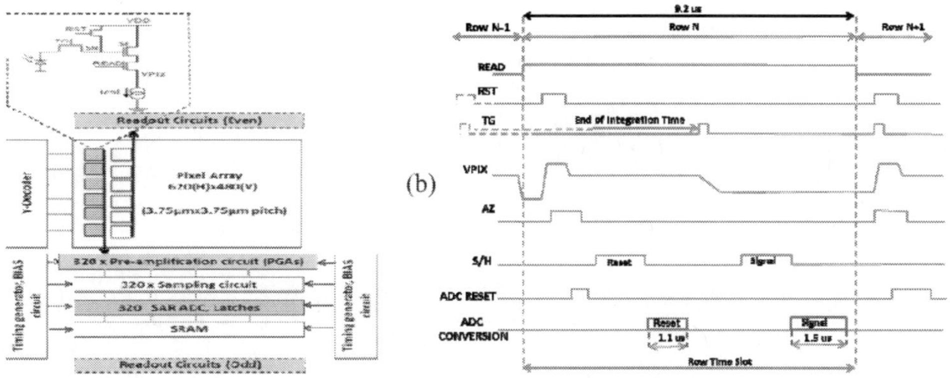

Figure 1. Image Sensor (a) Overall Architecture (b) Readout Operation

A Static Random Access Memory (SRAM) bloc is implemented to save data prior to the transfer out to a Field Programmable Gate Array (FPGA) for processing. The active pixel sensor array is based on a 4-transistor type pinned photo diode (PD) and is driven by a vertical driver (Y-Decoder). Signal RST for resetting, TG for charge transfer and READ for pixel reading can be set by the Y-Decoder. The pixel pitch is 3.75um. A top and bottom readout disposition is adopted so as to benefit from a double pitch layout.

2.2 Readout operation

The readout timing analysis is shown in Figure 1(b). A 9.2us line period has been reached. It includes the pixel, the PGA and the ADC operations.

A first TG pulse allows dumping out residual charges from the photodiode. The second one ensures charges transfer to the Sensing Node (SN) presented by the gate of the source follower (SF) shown in Figure 2. The PGA is first initialized by means of an auto-zero (AZ) signal. Various analog gains 2^0 .. 2^4 are ensured by the PGA by selecting binary weighed feed-back capacitors (CFB). The PGA output is sampled (S/H) prior to each ADC conversion. Two ADC conversions are performed: one for the reset and one for the signal so as to do a digital Correlated Double Sampling (CDS) operation. The reset conversion is performed over only 10-bit during 1.1us in order to save power.

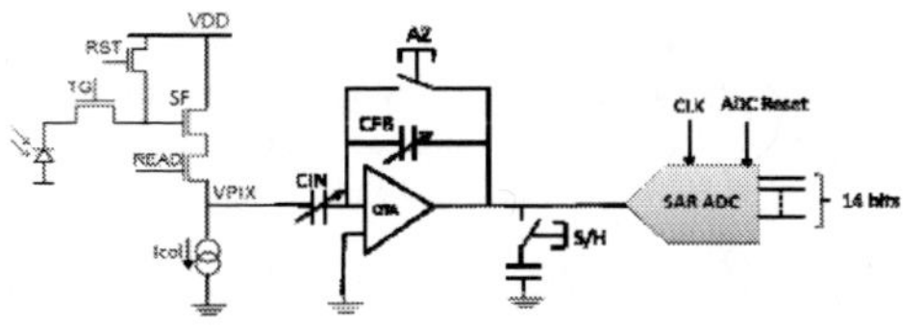

Figure 2. Simplified Schematic of the Pixel and the Readout

3 Compact 14-bit SAR-ADC

3.1 ADC architecture

The SAR-ADC consists of a Digital-to-Analog converter (DAC) and a multistage comparator (Preamp1, Preamp2 and a Latch) as shown in Figure 3(a). The preamplifiers preamp1 and preamp2 ensure the analog gain and mitigate the kick-back noise due to the Latch. The DAC consists of a charge distribution-based capacitor array.

This SAR architecture is developed to be suitable with imager's context where specific features should be taken into account namely:

- Compactness for 7.5um pitch design
- Low power operation to limit the dark current
- Common control of all ADCs
- Image quality considerations: Uniformity of ADCs across the imager, immunity to crosstalk, horizontal (X) and vertical (Y) droop effects, offsets and noise, dispersions, …

Compactness within 7.5um pitch has been ensured through a specific use of multiple reference voltages as depicted in Figure 3(a). This technique allowed reaching 14-bit resolution with only 7 binary weights $2^0 \ldots 2^6$. Two additional fractional references Vfractional1 and Vfractional2 are used in addition to the primary ones Vref0 and Vref1 that define the Dynamic Range (DR) of the ADC according to (1). Theses reference voltages are correlated as follows:

$$DR = Vref1 - Vref0 \qquad (1)$$

$$Vref0 = 0V \qquad Vref1 = 1.5V \qquad (2)$$

$$Vfractional0 = \frac{Vref1 - Vref0}{2^7} = \frac{DR}{2^7} \approx 11.71mV \qquad (3)$$

$$Vfractional1 = Vref1 + \frac{Vref1 - Vref0}{2^7} \approx 1.5V + 11.71mV \qquad (4)$$

ADC operation timing analysis is shown in Figure 3 (b) in the case of six bit conversion for simplicity. The 14-bit SAR conversion consists of two steps of classical SAR conversions of 7-bit resolution each. The first step extracts the seven Most Significant Bit (MSB). It is performed between the primary references Vref1 and Vref0. The second step is performed using Vfractional1 and Vfractional0 to extract the seven Least Significant Bit (LSB). An extra clock cycle is required between these two steps to ease the transition by means of Multi-Vrefs devices controlled by a common control signal. The final binary 14-bit word is obtained following a concatenation of both 7-bit words. Dynamic power consumption is optimized by a straight-forward SAR operation as depicted in Figure 3(c).

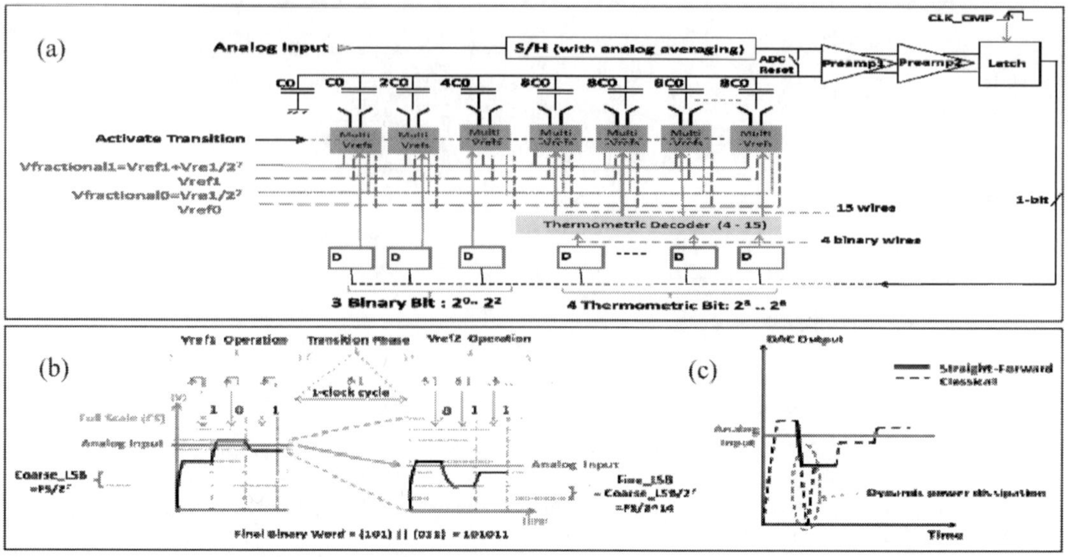

Figure 3. Novel scheme 14bit SAR-ADC(a) Architecture(b) ADC Operation for 6bit conversion(c) Straight-forwad switching scheme

3.2 Linearity analysis

Two main error contributors can be identified for the linearity issues: The DC accuracy of the reference voltages and the capacitors mismatching due to the fabrication process. In fact, the fractional reference voltages Vfractional1 and Vfractional0 have to be matched up to a 14-bit resolution with regard to the main references Vref1 and Vref0. According to (5) and (6), the module of δ1 and δ0 have to remain below one LSB given by (7). A calibration algorithm has been defined to correct for this issue and is beyond the scope of this paper.

$$Vfractional0 = Vfractional0\_Nom + \delta_0 \quad (5)$$

$$Vfractional1 = Vfractional1\_Nom + \delta_1 \quad (6)$$

$$LSB = \frac{Vref1 - Vref0}{2^N} = \frac{1.5V}{2^{14}} \approx 91uV \quad (7)$$

To illustrate this effect, a behavioral simulation of the ADC has been performed over the dynamic range with the parameters indicated in Figure 4(a). Comparatively, the fractional references induced Differential-Non-Linearity (DNL) error is given by (8).

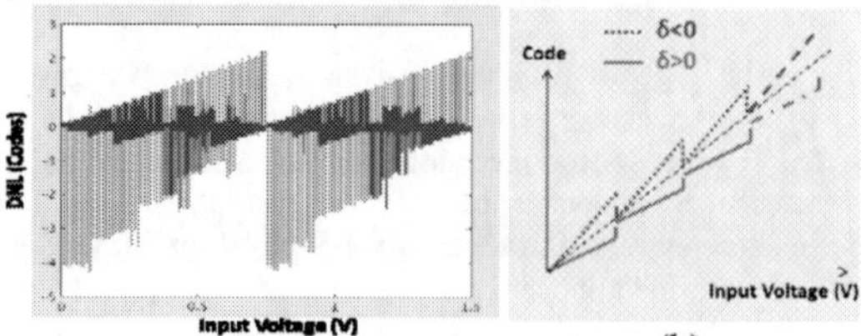

(a) (b)

Figure 4. DNL errors due to fractional reference voltages shift: (a) δ0= - 4LSB, δ1= +2LSB (b) Impact on transfer characteristic

To explain, any shift δ on either fractional references will result into a slope variation between the coarse and the fine operations as depicted in Figure 4(b).

At a unity gain ADC transfer characteristic if neglecting attenuations, one LSB error on the input voltage axis results into one code DNL error.

$$DNL\_error = \frac{\delta}{LSB} \quad (8)$$

Simultaneously, the capacitors dispersion affects the DNL where the process matching is generally limited to 10-bit. Based on matching figures from a similar technology, the proposed architecture has been simulated in a fully binary DAC configuration. The results are shown in Figure 5(a). Capacitors were assumed to have a mean value and an error term according to:

$$C = C_{Nominal} + \delta_{err} \quad (9)$$

With δerr assumed to be Independent Identically Distributed (i.i.d) binary weighed Gaussian Random Variables. Clearly, the simulations confirm the presence of missing codes and decision levels. For this purpose, thermometric decoding has been applied to the four MSB as shown in Figure 3(a). This choice is based on a trade-off between the layout feasibility and DNL performances. Final DNL simulation results are shown in Figure 5(b) where +1.3 /-1 features is obtained at a 14-bit accuracy.

Integral-Non Linearity (INL) is less critical in the imaging context since we are mainly bound by the linearity of the pixel ~1%. The proposed architecture with thermometric decoding reaches an INL feature about +5.3/-9 at a 14-bit accuracy. Such a result guarantees 1‰ of linearity which is ten times better than that of the pixel.

Constant gain dispersion between columns, however, could cause important image artefacts. In this work, the Photo Response Non-Uniformity (PRNU) has been considered as a reference. It characterizes the inherent gain mismatch between the pixels and is about 5‰. Consequently, we targeted 0.5‰ (11-bit) of gain dispersion across the imager for the readout including the PGA and the ADC.

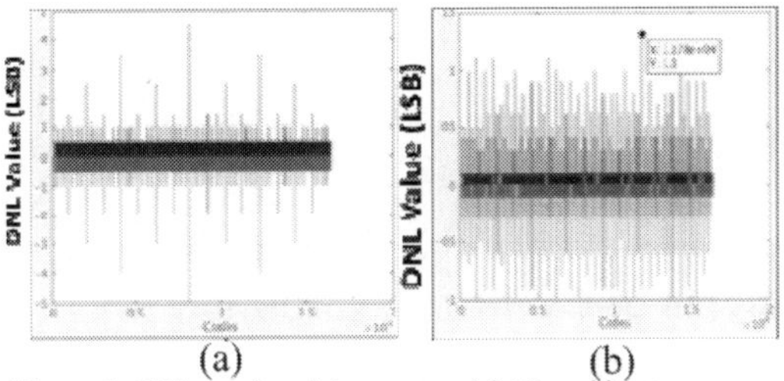

Figure 5. DNL results of the proposed SAR architecture: (a) Binary DAC (b) With thermometric decoding

4 Layout considerations

A prototype of 336 parallel readouts has been implemented respecting the 7.5um pitch. It is important to realize that the capacitor array is the most critical part especially in such a massive parallelism context. The array consists of 128 identical capacitive elements to ensure matching and thus DNL performances. This corresponds to 2^7xC0 of total DAC capacitance as already shown in Figure 3(a). Association between these elementary capacitors is made to form 2xC0, 4xC0 and 15 thermometric elements of value 8xC0. This association is made in a stamped way to further improve matching. The total length of the capacitor array is about 600um. To mitigate the gradient effect, thermometric 8xC0 elements are ordered one next to the other in the same order of the thermometric wires. In other words, it is only needed to ensure matching between two subsequent elements to preserve DNL.

With the Signal to Noise Ratio (SNR) and crosstalk in mind, plate capacitor technology has been adopted as shown in Figure 6(a). The idea consists on protecting the comparator input node from attenuation and noise. Metal2 has been chosen to route this node which benefits from low parasitic capacitance with respect to the ground. Post Layout Simulations (PLS) results show a DR of the ADC of 1.370V and a clipping at the end of the transfer characteristic due to attenuations as shown in Figure 6(b). Introducing the resulting DR in (7) gives (10). The SNR is then only decreased by 0.7dB compared to the initial LSB according to (11). ADC layout length reaches 1250um in a 7.5um pitch (Cf.Figure 6(c)).

$$LSB = \frac{1.370V}{2^{14}} \approx 84uV \quad (10)$$

$$SNR\_Loss = 20 * \log_{10}\frac{84}{91} \approx -0.7dB \quad (11)$$

Capacitors bottom plates, conveying reference voltages, are used as metal shielding as depicted in Figure7. The crosstalk worst case occurs when one column ADC converts zero signal whereas a maximum one is being converted by the two adjacent ADCs. PLS shown in Table2 indicate one code error on the middle column due to leakage problems during the 9.2us line timing which proves immunity to crosstalk.

Table 2. Output codes of PLS of three adjacent ADCs

ADC	Left ADC (Vin=1V5)	Middle ADC (Vin=0V)	Right ADC (Vin=1V5)
Output Code	11..111	00..001	11..111

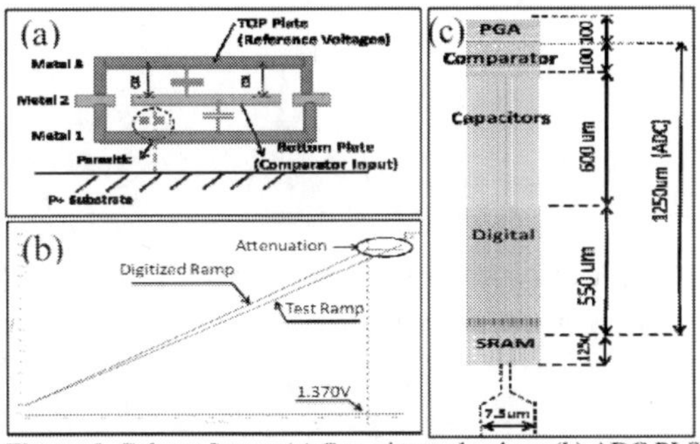

Figure 6. Column Layout(a) Capacitor technology (b) ADC PLS simulation of the transfer characteristic (c) 16 Columns layout

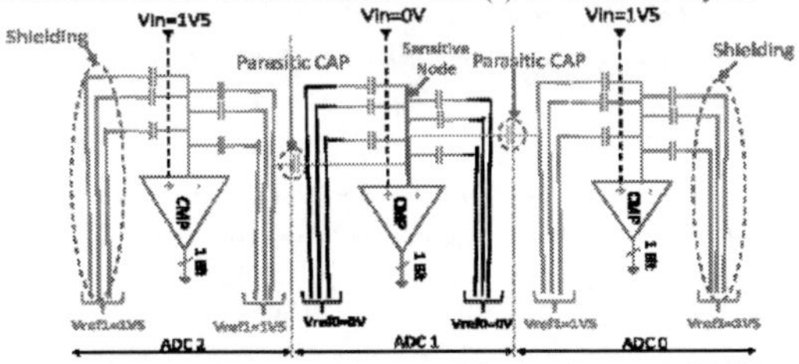

Figure 7. Worst case crosstalk and mitigation by metal shielding

5 Conclusion

In this work, a novel scheme SAR-ADC design for CMOS image sensors is proposed. It targets a DNL feature of +1.3/-1 over 14-bit. Our previous work [4] reported a DNL of +0.9/-0.7. This is due to trade-offs made in the layout phase. Final results will depend on the measurements of the prototype.

Future researches will be focused towards reference voltages. In addition to DC accuracy requirements mentioned above, drive capability remains a challenge to overcome mainly for a large columns number where steep current flows are needed. For the implemented 336 columns prototype, large reservoir capacitors have been used in addition to external reference voltages.

References

1. R. Fontaine, et al., ChipSelect for Image Sensors (ChipSelectIS) Subscription Service, Chipworks
2. S.Matsuo, T. Bales, M. Shoda, S. Osawa,K.Kawamura, A. Andersson, M. Haque, H. Honda, B. Almond, Y. Mo, J. Gleason, T. Chow, and I. Takayanagi, "8.9-megapixel video image sensor with 14-b column parallel SA-ADC," IEEE Trans. Electron Devices, vol. **56**, no. 11, pp. 2380–2389, Nov. (2009)
3. J. Kim, S. Hong and O. Kwon,"A Low-Power CMOS Image Sensor with Area-Efficient 14-bit Two-Step SA ADCs Using Pseudo-Multiple Sampling Method," IEEE Trans. on Circuits and Systems II, Jan.(2015)
4. S.Ben Aziza, D.Dzahini, L.Gallin-Martel, "A High Speed High Resolution Readout with 14-bits Area Efficient SAR-ADC Adapted for New Generations of CMOS Image Sensors", *Ph.D. Research in Microelectronics and Electronics (PRIME)*, (2015)

An Efficient Procedure for Transient Analysis of Electronic Circuits with Increased Precision

David Cerny[1,a] and *Josef* Dobes[1,b]

[1] *Czech Technical University in Prague*
Department of Radio Engineering
Technicka 2, 166 27 Prague 6, Czech Republic

Abstract. This article presents an efficient procedure allowing to increase the final accuracy of the electronic circuits simulation. To obtain Transient Analysis of a nonlinear circuit the simulator needs to perform various algorithms, from an evaluation of initial DC state through a nonlinear iterative algorithm, to a numerical integration. These complex computations have to be implemented effectively with regards to memory and processor usage. Direct implementation of arbitrary precision types can directly lead to increased simulation accuracy but also significantly decrease simulation performance. As a compromise, we suggest using an additional algorithm based on Newton Iteration method for the solution of matrix inversion. The method was modified to be comparable to direct LUF solver.

1 Introduction

Every year significant number of articles focus on simulation core of Spice and its device models is published . As interesting works on similar problematic to this article we can point out [1–4]. It is without a doubt that the accuracy of a simulation of the electronic circuits is essential. The primary importance can be seen in several aspects. The first one points to the band of the unknown variables that are simulated. They usually represent the real physical behavior of circuit devices, and their values can differ in magnitude by several orders. The difference can be in the extreme cases higher than a range of used floating point data type. To be able to simulate those extreme cases requires increasing precision of given datatype. The second aspect of the accuracy problems is related to the solution of linear systems. Although standard circuit state (i.e. OP) can be well established during transient analysis may occur situations when a circuit matrix is changed a lot. It makes a computation of specific time-points very problematic, especially in the case when matrix setup rapidly increases condition number. In that situation, some time-points may be affected by precision inaccuracies more than others.

2 Simulation Overview

In the Spice program, there are four basic analysis for simulation of electronic circuits: Transient Analysis, Operation Point (DC), Small Signal Analysis and Noise Analysis. All of them shares a common family of computation algorithms. As the most critical Transient analysis can be considered which uses the most time demanding operations. Spice simulation core to compute Transient analysis needs to evaluate a system of nonlinear differential equations defined by device models. It is done by Newton-Raphson iteration algorithm together with LU factorization (LUF) method capable of handling sparse matrices and pivoting.

Algorithm 1 Transient Simulation Procedure

```
Simulation definition
Modified Nodal Analysis
for Time do
  Initial value estimation
  DC Analysis (optional)
  if Non-linear System then
    repeat
      Generate Jacobian matrix
      Reordering and LU factorisation
      Evaluation of next value estimation
      Compute residual
    until Stopping criteria or convergence
  end if
end for
```

In particular cases, when time dependent devices enter a simulation, it also needs to enumerate numerical integration using Trapezoidal, Gear or another method. Algorithm 1 characterize simulation of the circuit with nonlinear devices performed by Transient analysis. It should be pointed out that computation of each time-step requires solution of the linear system produced by Jacobian ma-

[a] e-mail: cernyd1@fel.cvut.cz
[b] e-mail: dobes@fel.cvut.cz

Table 1. Comparison of Performance of NIM and LUF to Matrix Dimension

Dim.	LUF [s]	NIM [s]	LUF -O1 [s]	NIM -O1 [s]	LUF -Ofast [s]	NIM -Ofast [s]	ratio [%]
50	0.001643	0.00121	0.000539	0.000271	0.000405	0.000215	53.08641975
100	0.00785	0.008951	0.001903	0.001944	0.00192	0.000819	42.65625
150	0.023481	0.029905	0.00893	0.006858	0.005238	0.003025	57.75105002
200	0.030418	0.070165	0.018022	0.016332	0.009884	0.007513	76.01173614
250	0.053492	0.136668	0.016572	0.031944	0.010891	0.01431	131.3928932
300	0.07998	0.234934	0.035751	0.055234	0.021445	0.023843	111.1820937
350	0.174865	0.371465	0.046123	0.086999	0.031859	0.036893	115.8008726
400	0.206388	0.566372	0.075759	0.130182	0.042249	0.052848	125.0869843
450	0.291311	0.787467	0.109412	0.184372	0.0471	0.077378	164.2845011
500	0.482965	1.077401	0.137663	0.25123	0.064424	0.101362	157.3357755

trix. It is done by direct LU factorization method based on modified Crout algorithm.

3 Precision Problems

Floating point numbers are designed to be an efficient representation of the real numbers but with a limited accuracy that is directly related to their magnitude. It si perfect idea that works for most cases. For double precision numbers (64 bit machine) IEEE 1987 defines 52 significant bits plus 1 sign and 11 exponent bits. It gives us range from 10^{-323} to 10^{308}. It seems to be an enormous scale of numbers, but there is always a catch. Nevertheless, of scalability floating point numbers are precise only within some region of magnitude. It implies that the situation when precision goes wrong can occur, and, unfortunately, it have a higher probability to happen during simulation of electronic circuits. Floating point numbers can not be as precise as their real counterparts defined by mathematical apparatus. For example number, 0.1 will become

$$0.1000000000000000055511151231257827021181$$

and the even more different result can be obtained by definition of 1.1×10^{-8} that will become

$$1.0999999999999999237531434067779989582\,90 \times 10^{-8}$$

Although those numbers have a finite decimal representation, in computer memory they are an infinitely repeating numeric sequence. It is caused by the fact that they lie exactly between two representable floating point numbers and therefore in computer memory they have to be rounded to one of them. Floating point numbers also include several non-numeric definition as infinity for larger (or smaller) numbers than highest (or lowest) representative number, positive and negative zero and "not a number" (NaN) definition for undefined states (division by zero). There is another implication of problems caused by a limitting precision of the floating point numbers. In a case ill-conditioned linear systems the accuracy of the solution can be rapidly decreased. Although that matrix condition number is not directly related to the accuracy, it can be taken as an indicator that the solution may be affected by an error. For example, if we have a system:

$$\begin{cases} 4.012x_1 + 4.013x_2 = 4011 \\ 4.013x_1 + 4.013x_2 = 4012 \end{cases} \quad (1)$$

its computation using double precision will result in residual error r computed by L2 norm $r = 4.547474 * 10^{-13}$ it is significantly higher contrary to expected value $r < 10^{-15}$.

4 Precision of the Algorithm

The original mathematical definition of Newton Iteration Method (NIM) [5, 6] can be rewritten to the form applicable for implementation as an iterative algorithm for precision enhancement. Denoting Jacobian matrix as $\mathbf{J}$ and Identity matrix as $\mathbf{I}$, for inverted Jacobian matrix $\mathbf{J^{-1}}$ we can write

$$\mathbf{J}^{-1} = \mathbf{J}^{-1}(2\mathbf{I} - \mathbf{I}) = \mathbf{J}^{-1}(2\mathbf{I} - \mathbf{J}\mathbf{J}^{-1}). \quad (2)$$

For an arbitrary real matrix, $\mathbf{J}$, the above statement allows for each iteration step n to define a generalized inverse (pseudo inverse) denoted as $\mathbf{X_n}$

$$\mathbf{X_n} = \mathbf{J}^{-1} + \varepsilon_\mathbf{n} \Rightarrow \mathbf{X_{n+1}} = \mathbf{J}^{-1} + \varepsilon_{n+1}, \quad (3)$$

where ε_n is an error matrix. From that, we get to

$$\mathbf{J}^{-1} + \varepsilon_{n+1} = (\mathbf{J}^{-1} + \varepsilon_n)(2\mathbf{I} - \mathbf{J}(\mathbf{J}^{-1} + \varepsilon_n)). \quad (4)$$

The above form can be rewritten using $\mathbf{X_n}$ and $\mathbf{X}_{n+1}$ to a more readable form

$$\mathbf{X}_{n+1} = \mathbf{X}_n(2\mathbf{I} - \mathbf{J}\mathbf{X}_n). \quad (5)$$

It is obvious that previous equation will iterate to the solution if

$$0 < \|2\mathbf{I} - \mathbf{J}\mathbf{X}_n\| < 1. \quad (6)$$

There are two important remarks for this solution. First is connected to nature of Spice simulator. It does not compute matrix inversion of Jacobian matrix. Instead, it computes next iteration steps of NR algorithm directly evaluating equation

$$J(x_n)(x_{n+1} - x_n) = -F(x_n). \quad (7)$$

Table 2. Overview of Compiler Optimization Settings

option	optimization level
-O0	opt. for compilation time (default)
-O1 or -O	opt. for code size and execution time
-O2/O3	opt. more for code size and exec. time
-Os	opt. for code size
-Ofast	O3 with fast none accurate math calc.

The second remark is that the circuit matrix is going to be very sparse and more of that its density decrease with increasing matrix size. It concludes that computation of matrix inversion proves to be very inefficient for huge matrices from a point of view of memory handling. On the other hand stability of algorithm and simplicity of implementation together with possible optimization makes algorithm very efficient for computation with matrix dimension up to 200 (circuits with up to 200 independent voltage nodes). Putting it all together we finally receive final algorithm:

$$\begin{cases} \mathbf{X}_D = \mathbf{J}_D^{-1} \\ \mathbf{X}_{D+} = \mathbf{X}_D(2\mathbf{I} - \mathbf{J}_D\mathbf{X}_D), \end{cases}$$

where A^{-1} stands for inversion of the current computation of the Jacobian matrix in current precision that can be easily obtained from last LU factorization. This will be used as a starting point for linear solver. $\mathbf{X}_{D+}$ represents matrix inversion with increased precision. Both matrix multiplications in second line must be computed with increased arbitrary precision to achieve increased accuracy in $\mathbf{X}_{D+}$. Then more accurate solution of the time step is given by simple vector matrix multiplication

$$\mathbf{X}_{D+}\mathbf{y}_{RHS} = \mathbf{x}_{D+}$$

The simplicity of implementation of NIM allows to compiler optimize the code in such a way that performance can be rapidly increased, but with increasing of matrix dimension memory requirements of this method rapidly decrease performance. This can be visible from Table 3. The number of required iteration to obtain a result with particular precision, unfortunately, depends on initial estimation and matrix dimension. Therefore, this algorithm will offer best results only in a case of one iteration.

5 Performance

Adapt NIM algorithm as an efficient competitor to LUF is not an easy task. First of all, it's hard to optimize two matrix multiplications that must be performed during NIM computation. Secondly, with increasing size of sparse Jacobian matrix with also, increase unfortunately dense matrix J^{-1}. It is caused by the nature of matrix inversion, and there is no way to suppress it. Therefore, the best usage of the algorithm is for matrices with dimension up to 200 when it can be taken as dense. Although, optimization of efficiency can be done. Current compilers (e.g., GCC) offers various optimizations settings that can rapidly improve calculation performance and memory handling without a need of parallelisation or other techniques (Table 2). It should be noted that it does not directly concludes that higher optimization attribute equals more efficient result. It is nature and simplicity of NIM that it is so well optimizable. It is hard for iterative methods or even impossible to overcome direct one. Mainly it is because that direct methods evaluate directly to the solution contrary to the iterative algorithms that need several iteration loops before they obtain a result with sufficient precision. It is the reason why LUF is a better option than NIM for standard computation.

Algorithm 2 Modified Transient Procedure

```
Simulation definition
Modified Nodal Analysis
for Time do
  Initial value estimation
  DC Analysis (optional)
  NIM - Arbitrary (optional)
  if Non-linear System then
    repeat
      Generate Jacobian matrix
      LU of Jacobian matrix
      Evaluation of next value estimation
      Compute residual
    until Stopping criteria or convergence
  end if
  NIM - Arbitrary
end for
```

Another optimization can be done reducing the number of iterations. It is obvious that fewer iterations mean less computation time. Therefore, the algorithm was limited to only one iteration. There is computation of initial inversion matrix from already precomputed LUF followed by two matrix-matrix products. This algorithm is pretty simple and straightforward (no factorisation or precision comparison is needed). It gives to NIM for small matrice an advantage among over any other algorithms. Together with very straight convergence a simplicity of the algorithm allows very fast implementation of arbitrary precision numeric types. It will be shown that usage of arbitrary precision numbers in computation even for one iteration of NIM can directly improve resulting accuracy by factor two. For instance, if the final precision of LUF was around 10^{-16} next iteration with NIM could increase it up to 10^{-32}.

6 Results

In the Table 1 there is a comparison of computation times of LUF and one iteration of NIM for different optimization levels of GCC compiler. It is clearly visible how optimization attributes to improve performance. It can be seen that up to matrix dimension 200, implementation with NIM proves as a faster solution. It is also showed in the Figure 1. Table 3 gives a slight look on efficiency of different stages of NIM iterations for various matrix dimensions. It is visible that the most critical is a fact that several iteration loops are required. It is evident that the iteration loops

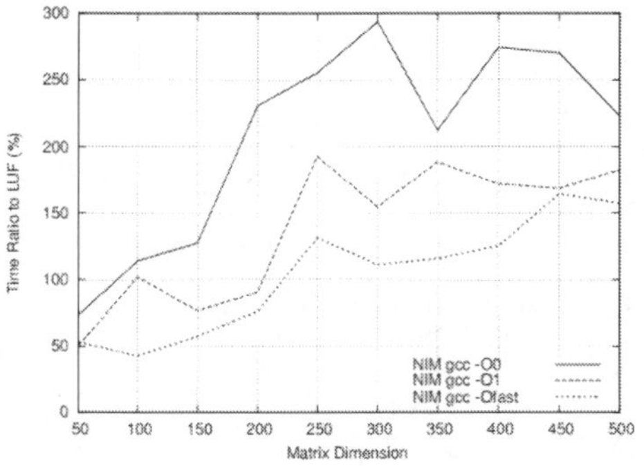

Figure 1. Time Ration of NIM to LUF vs Matrix Dimension

Table 3. Computation Times in Sec. of Individual Steps of NIM

Dim.	Initial Estim.	Residual	30 Iterations
50	0.000072	0.000072	0.004254
100	0.000414	0.000414	0.023759
150	0.001334	0.001334	0.086467
200	0.003287	0.003287	0.216549
250	0.006375	0.006375	0.412877
300	0.011092	0.011092	0.693523
350	0.017103	0.017103	1.07149
400	0.02443	0.02443	1.536133
450	0.034815	0.034815	2.190221
500	0.045693	0.045693	2.821963

Table 4. Accuracy Boost Given by One Iteration Loop of NIM with Arbitrary Precision

Dim.	Double	→ Arbit.	Long	→ Arbit.
50	1.47E-14	2.72E-28	1.56E-17	3.92E-30
100	1.14E-15	5.21E-29	2.86E-17	6.21E-30
150	6.32E-15	1.89E-29	2.54E-17	2.18E-31
200	2.03E-13	2.69E-27	1.58E-16	3.85E-29
250	2.16E-11	3.27E-24	8.96E-16	5.47E-28

can be taken as the most time demanding operation during entire evaluation. Not only from this reason NIM is not used for computation or as replacement of LUF method but only as a so-called precision booster that improves the accuracy of the result during a single iteration. In Table 4 is the comparison of the accuracy of LUF (column: Double and Long Double) and LUF with additional NIM cycle computed with arbitrary numbers (columns with → Arbitrary) to matrix dimension. It is clearly visible that accuracy was significantly increased for both data types (Double and Long Double). The adapted Transient analysis completed by single loop NIM with arbitrary precision is in Algorithm 2. It got an additional precision boost computed by NIM after each successful iteration time-step.

7 Conclusion

In this article, we presented an iterative method that increases the precision of analysis of electrical circuit by suppressing errors produced by floating point variables. It can be applied to the end of OP simulation or as a final procedure after each time-step of Transient analysis. It is clear that iterative NIM will always be outperformed by direct LUF method, especially in a case of sparse matrices. However, the achievable precision during computation with floating-point precision numbers is strictly limited by a size of the variable type. It has been demonstrated that because of precision problems caused by the nature of floating point numbers, we can achieve total accuracy only in very trivial cases. Mostly computation finish regardless on used numeric type with precision around 10^{-16} or less. The only way that can provide results with greater precision is to switch to arbitrary precision numbers. Arbitrary precision numbers allow to setup any precision but they are also very demanding from a point of view of performance. Standard LUF followed with a single iteration of NIM with arbitrary precision can definetely improve the accuracy with preserved performance for dense matrices. In a case of sparse matrices efficiency of NIM is discussable and will be decreasing with growing sparsity of the matrix. Therefore method is aplicable for small circuits only (up to 200 nodes).

Acknowledgment

This work was supported by the Grant Agency of the Czech Technical University in Prague, grant No. SGS15/161/OHK3/2T/13

References

[1] A. Subbiah, O. Wasynczuk, IEEE Transactions on Power Electronics **31**, 6351 (2016)

[2] I. Mejia, G. Gutierrez-Heredia, A.L. Salas-Villasenor, C.G. Alvarado-Beltran, C. Avila-Avendano, M.A. Quevedo-Lopez, IEEE Transactions on Electron Devices **63**, 1437 (2016)

[3] D. Bulakh, *Fast SPICE based circuit simulation using source code generation approach*, in *Internet Technologies and Applications (ITA), 2015* (2015), pp. 53–55

[4] X. Chen, L. Ren, Y. Wang, H. Yang, IEEE Transactions on Parallel and Distributed Systems **26**, 786 (2015)

[5] A. Ben-Israel, Mathematics of Computation pp. 452–455 (1965)

[6] A. Ben-Israel, D. Cohen, SIAM Journal on Numerical Analysis **3**, 410 (1966)

Optimisation of the Low-Frequency Response of a Multi-stage Bioelectric Amplifier for Electrocardiogram (ECG) Recording

Martin J. Burke[1,a] and Kerstin Kofler[2]

[1]Dept. of Electronic and Electrical Engineering, Trinity College, University of Dublin, College Green, Dublin 2, Ireland.
[2]Dept. of Engineering and IT, Medical Engineering, Carinthia University of Applied Sciences, 9020 Klagenfurt, Austria.

Abstract. This paper reports the optimisation of the low-frequency response of a multi-stage bioelectric amplifier intended for use in the measurement of the human electrocardiogram (ECG) using high-impedance un-gelled electrodes. The frequency response was optimised to meet international performance requirements for electrocardiographic recorders, in particular the International Electrotechnical Commission 60601 standards [1,2]. The pole and zero locations of a multi-stage amplifier configuration were optimised to meet both time and frequency domain specifications. The optimum assignment for a three stage amplifier, having two differential stages and a differential-to-single-ended conversion stage was established by evaluating the performance of a number of circuit configurations. The optimum configuration was found to be two differential stages with a gain of 20dB each and a differential-to single-ended output stage with unity gain. The -3dB pole is placed at 0.028Hz and a zero at 0.0028Hz in the first and second stages to give an overall -3dB bandwidth of 0.043Hz. In addition, the pole of the input ac coupling network was placed at 0.0028Hz in order to meet the undershoot and recovery slope requirements in the narrow pulse response.

1 Introduction

The low-frequency response of the bioelectric amplifier used in recording the human electrocardiogram (ECG) is of the utmost importance due to the clinical significance of such recordings. Appropriate magnitude and phase responses are needed in order to prevent distortion of the ECG signal profile and adverse changes in the waveform morphology. The nature of the distortion which can arise in the ECG signal due to poor low frequency response in the recording amplifier has been well documented for several decades and has serious diagnostic implications [3,4]. The type of distortion which results from poor low frequency response has a detrimental effect primarily on the T-wave, the S-T segment and the Q-T interval.

In addition to hospital oriented ECG recorders, there has been a substantial increase in recent years in the number of portable ECG recorders. Many of these are used in non-clinical scenarios such as general practice, sports medicine, physiology and even on the factory floor. This has led to an increase in battery-operated and low-power equipment with the associated changes in instrumentation design. Consequently trends have changed in the design of the electronic amplifiers for ECG recording. Lower power supply voltages have tended to make amplifier front-end stages ac coupled rather than dc coupled as in the past. This allows electrode polarisation voltages to be eliminated at the input so that they do not saturate the front-end stage of the amplifier. Recent advances in electrode technology have increased the magnitude of these polarisation voltages. Ac coupling also facilitates maintaining a high gain in the early stages of the amplifier to preserve the signal-to-noise ratio. Low-power technology has meant that the gain-bandwidth product of operational amplifiers has fallen so that the gain required in ECG amplifiers is often spread over several stages. This has led to an increase in multi-stage amplifier configurations and a consequent increase in the complexity of the associated frequency response at both the high and low ends of the spectrum. The authors have concentrated the effort in this paper on investigating the optimisation of the low-frequency response of multi-stage bioelectric amplifiers intended for use in ECG signal recording.

2 Background

Standards for the performance requirements of ECG recorders have been developed in the US by the American National Standards Institute (ANSI) with recommendations made by the American Heart Association (AHA) and in Europe by the International Electrotechnical Commission (IEC). These have changed much over the decades since they were first introduced and have taken account of technological developments. Most recent standards have made an effort to merge the US and EU requirements to make them almost identical. This has, in fact, added strength to both sets of standards

[a] Corresponding author: mburke@tcd.ie

and increased the usage of the IEC 60601 standard, which is now accepted worldwide [1,2].

2.1 Frequency domain requirements

Early standards for ECG recorder performance were based on recommendations issued by the AHA and the IEEE in 1967 [5,6]. These standards required that the magnitude of the frequency response be within ± 0.5 dB of the mid-band gain within the frequency range 0.67Hz–150Hz. The low-frequency value was based on a practical lowest-heart rate value of 40 beats-per-minute (bpm). The phase response was required to be no greater than that caused by a single-pole high-pass filter having a -3dB cut-off frequency of 0.05Hz [5,6]. These magnitude and phase response requirements are shown in Figure 1.

More recent standards issued by both the EU and the US [1,2] require that the amplitude response of an ambulatory ECG recorder shall be within ±3 dB of the response at 5Hz, within a frequency band of 0.05Hz to at least 55Hz. A phase response requirement is not specified but the merits of a single-pole high-pass filter having a cut-off frequency of 0.05Hz are still cited as example. Instead of the phase response requirement a time-domain specification has been introduced.

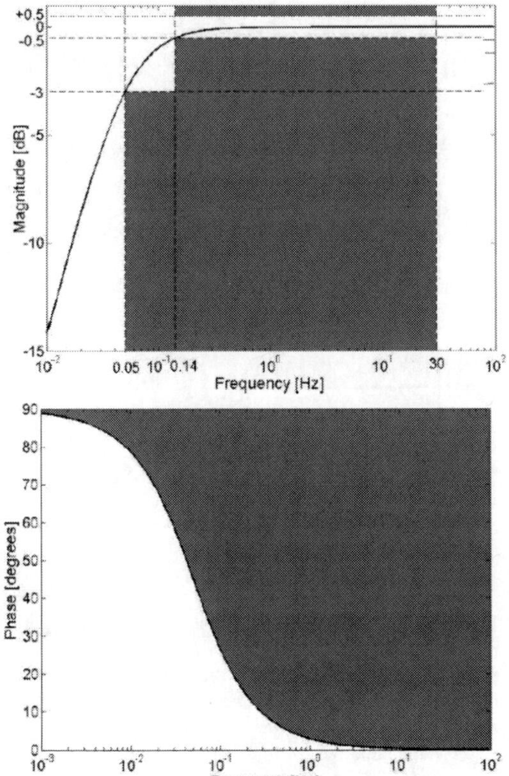

Figure 1. Magnitude and phase response requirements.

2.2 Time domain requirements

The IEC 60601 most recent standards, which are now closely aligned and merged with those of ANSI, have introduced two time-domain methods of testing ECG recorder performance. These are both shown in Figure 2. Method A was introduced in a previous IEC standard and allows a maximum baseline undershoot of 0.1mV in the transient response to a narrow rectangular pulse of 3mV amplitude and 100ms duration with a maximum recovery slope of 0.3mV/s between pulses, as can be seen in Figure 2. Method B, on the other hand, uses a triangular wave to model the QRS complex of the ECG. An isosceles triangular wave of peak amplitude of 1.5mV and a duration varying between 20ms and 200ms with a repetition rate of less than 1Hz is applied as input to the recorder. The amplitude of the peak of the triangle must maintain a variation within +0dB and -1dB (-10%) as the pulse duration is varied between 20ms and 200ms. This can be seen in Figure 2. In the studies carried out by the authors, the rectangular pulse of Method A was preferred.

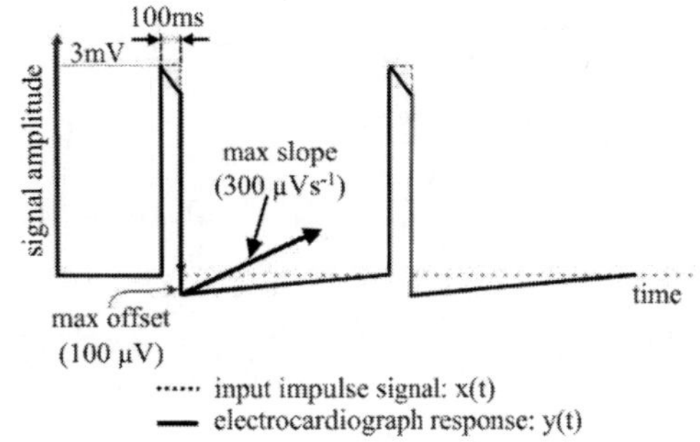

Method A: Rectangular Pulse

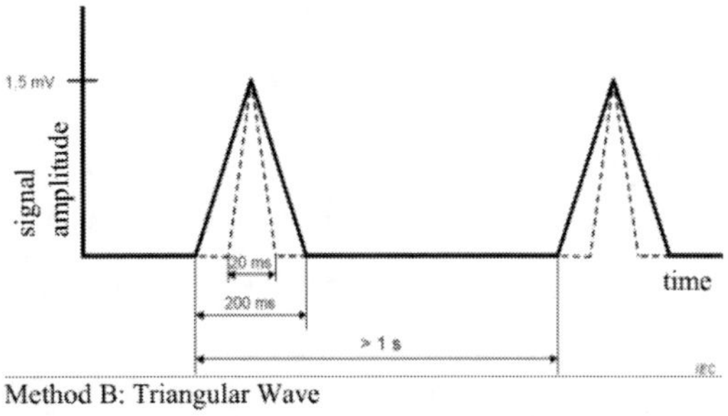

Method B: Triangular Wave

Figure 2. Transient response requirements [adapted from 1,2]

3 Single-stage amplifiers

3.1 Non-inverting high-pass filter

The first amplifier stage of interest is the simple 1st-order high-pass filter shown in Figure 3. This configuration was used as the reference standard in the early performance specifications [5,6] where the -3dB cut-off frequency was 0.05Hz. It is still cited as a comparative reference in more recent specifications [1,2]. The steady-state transfer function of this stage is of the form:

$$\frac{V_o}{V_i} = \frac{j\omega C_1 R_1}{1 + j\omega C_1 R_1} \qquad (1)$$

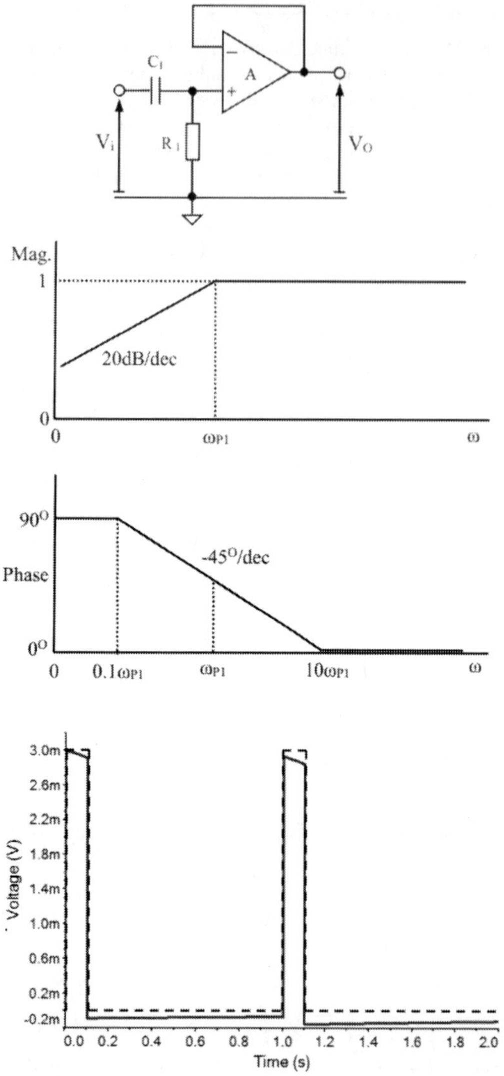

Figure 3. Magnitude, phase and pulse response of 0.05Hz HPF.

Idealised Bode plots of the magnitude and phase of the frequency response are also shown in Figure 3. The high-frequency pass-band gain is unity. It can be seen that there is a pole at a radian frequency of $\omega_{P1} = 1/(C_1R_1)$ which corresponds to the -3dB cut-off frequency of the high-pass response. The response of this filter in the time domain to the narrow input pulse which is defined in Figure 2 can also be seen in Figure 3. The undershoot in the response is 0.093mV and the recovery slope is 29μV/s. This indicates that this filter meets all of the performance criteria for ECG amplifiers.

3.2 Non-inverting high-pass amplifying stage

The next stage of interest is the 1st-order high-pass amplifier stage shown in Figure 4. This stage is ac coupled but has a gain in the pass band. It has a steady-state transfer function of the form:

$$\frac{V_o}{V_i} = \frac{[1 + j\omega C_1(R_1 + R_2)]j\omega C_3R_3}{(1 + j\omega C_1R_1)(1 + j\omega C_3R_3)} \quad (2)$$

It can be seen that this stage has an in-band high-frequency gain of $A_V = (R_1 + R_2)/R_1$. The -3dB pole in the high-pass response is again located at a radian frequency of $\omega_{P1} = 1/(C_1R_1)$. A Bode plot of the magnitude and phase of this stage is also shown in Figure 4. It can be seen that a network has been included at the input in the form of resistor R_3 and capacitor C_3 to ensure that the stage is ac coupled and that dc potentials do not appear at the input to the amplifier. If this network were omitted, the gain of this stage would level out at unity, at the zero in the frequency response which is located at a radian frequency of $\omega_{Z1} = 1/[C_1(R_1 + R_2)] = \omega_{P1}/A_V$. The zero also has the effect of restoring the phase back to zero as $\omega \rightarrow 0$, as shown by the dashed lines in Figure 4. In this case the amplifier stage could be saturated by electrode polarisation voltages at the input.

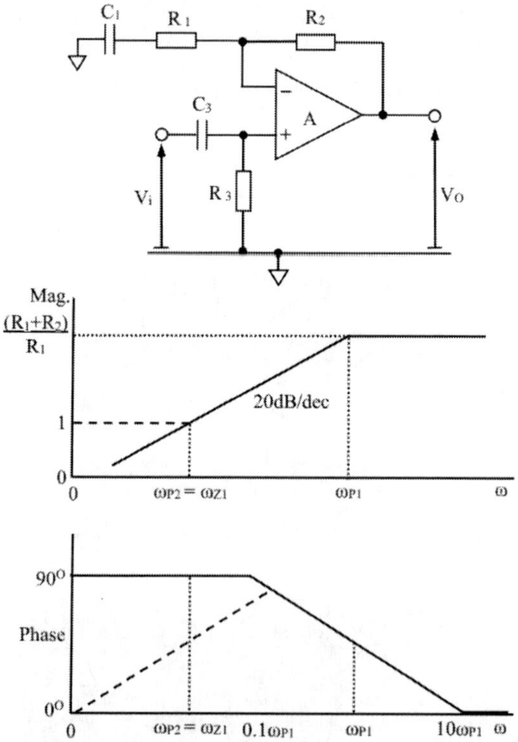

Figure 4. Magnitude and phase Bode plots of 1-stage amplifier

In order to get an overall response of the form of a high-pass filter, the lower frequency pole, ω_{P2}, of the input network is arranged to cancel the zero in the response of the feedback network by a choice of time constants such that $C_3R_3 = C_1(R_1 + R_2)$. In this case the transfer function of the stage becomes:

$$\frac{V_o}{V_i} = \frac{j\omega C_3R_3}{(1 + j\omega C_1R_1)} = \frac{j\omega C_1(R_1 + R_2)}{(1 + j\omega C_1R_1)} \quad (3)$$

This is depicted by the solid line responses in Figure 4.

It was decided to explore whether or not the frequency response of the single high-pass stage could be improved by not implementing an exact cancelation of the pole and zero, but to allow a degree of mismatch in their locations. In particular the effect on the phase of varying the location of the pole on either side of the zero was of interest. Figure 5 shows plots of the magnitude and phase of a single-stage amplifier having a non-inverting gain of 20dB.

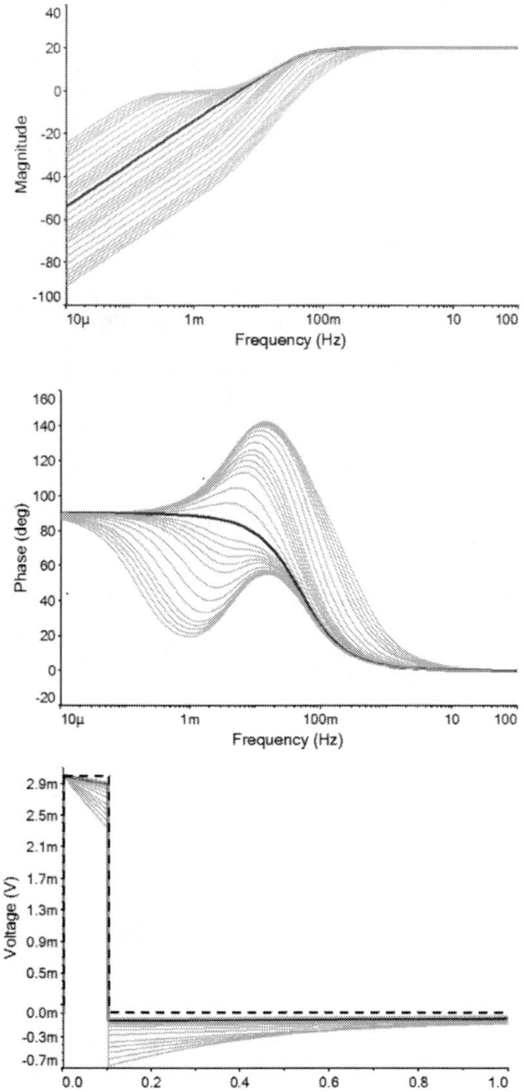

Figure 5. Magnitude, phase and pulse responses of 1-stage amp

An ideal op-amp model was used in MultiSim for circuit simulations so that its properties would not influence the results. The heavy curves in Figure 5 represent the case where $C_3R_3 = C_1(R_1 + R_2)$ with precise pole-zero cancellation. Moving the location of the pole above that of the zero increases the phase above the phase of the perfect cancellation curve, and also raises the -3dB cut-off frequency, which does not improve the response. Moving the location of the pole below that of the zero, on the other hand, lowers the phase compared with the perfect cancellation curve by a small amount at in-band frequencies and lowers the frequency at which the gain falls from 0dB. However, even when the frequency of the pole is lowered significantly, there is only a small reduction of the phase at in-band frequencies. The very small benefits gained in phase may be outweighed by the increased initialisation time of the amplifier. Figure 5 also shows the effect of varying the pole location on the response to the narrow 100ms pulse. It can be seen that lowering the frequency of the pole location gives a slight reduction in undershoot and recovery slope of the pulse response, which are again only marginal and barely noticeable.

4 Multi-stage amplifiers

4.1 Two-stage differential amplifier

The schematic diagram of a simple differential amplifier is shown in Figure 6. This has a single cross-coupled input stage with differential input voltages V_1 and V_2. This is followed by a differential-to-single-ended conversion stage providing the output voltage, V_O. The A and B designation of components will nominally have the same values.

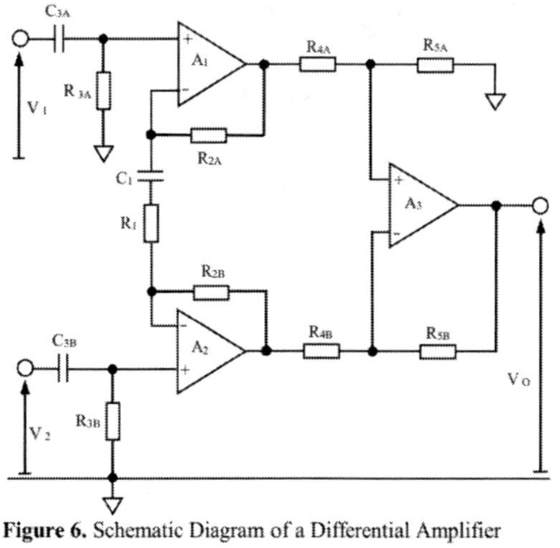

Figure 6. Schematic Diagram of a Differential Amplifier

The steady-state transfer function of this amplifier structure is given for a differential input $V_1 - V_2$ as:

$$\frac{V_o}{V_1 - V_2} = \frac{R_5}{R_4} \frac{[1 + j\omega C_1(R_1 + 2R_2)]j\omega C_3 R_3}{(1 + j\omega C_1 R_1)(1 + j\omega C_3 R_3)} \tag{4}$$

Very often $R_5 = R_4$ so that the output stage has unity gain, to maximize the CMRR. In this case the in-band differential gain of this stage is given as $A_V = (R_1 + 2R_2)/R_1$. The -3dB cut-off frequency is again located at $\omega_{P1} = 1/(C_1R_1)$ while the zero is located at $\omega_{Z1} = 1/[C_1(R_1 + 2R_2)] = \omega_{P1}/A_V$. The pole due to the input network, which is identical at each input terminal, is again located at a frequency $\omega_{P2} = 1/(C_3R_3)$. The same pole-zero cancellation as was implemented in the single stage amplifier can be obtained in the differential amplifier by choosing $C_3R_3 = C_1(R_1 + 2R_2)$. Plots of the magnitude and phase of the two stage differential amplifier are shown in Figure 7. Varying the location of the pole ω_{p2} has the same effect as in the equivalent single stage amplifier. The curves therefore show only two unmatched locations for this pole, one at the geometric mean of the pole ω_{P1} and the zero ω_{Z1} that is at a frequency $\omega = \sqrt{\omega_{P1}\omega_{Z1}}$ and the other below the zero by the same factor as the geometric mean is above it. The pulse response of Figure 8, shows the detail at the lower end of the trailing edge of the pulse. There is little benefit to be gained from lowering the location of the pole and it has negligible effect on the undershoot and recovery slopes. Increasing the frequency of the pole location causes the undershoot to exceed 100μV and the recovery slope to exceed $300\mu Vs^{-1}$. It therefore makes most sense to apply the pole-zero cancellation principle as in the case of the single-stage amplifier and choose $C_3R_3 = C_1(R_1 + 2R_2)$.

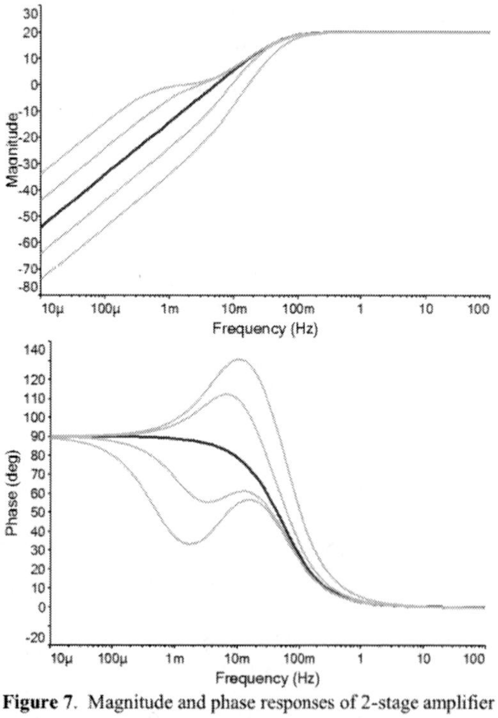

Figure 7. Magnitude and phase responses of 2-stage amplifier

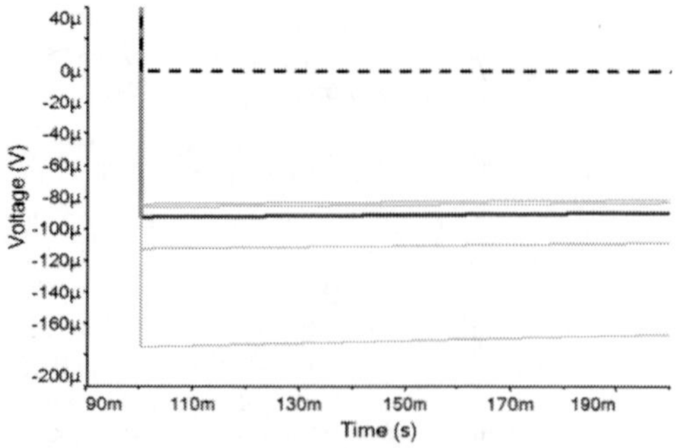

Figure 8. Trailing edge pulse response of 2-stage amplifier

4.2 Three-stage differential amplifier

The final configuration of interest is the 3-stage differential amplifier shown in Figure 9. This has a high-pass input stage and a differential-to-single-ended output stage identical to the two stage amplifier. There is a second differential stage which is dc coupled to the first so that the output dc bias potentials of the first stage will carry through to the second stage. The ac coupling of the first stage is sufficient to block any dc polarisation potentials at the input. The steady state transfer function of this three stage amplifier is given as:

$$\frac{V_o}{V_1 - V_2} = \frac{R_5}{R_4} \times \frac{[1 + j\omega C_1(R_1 + 2R_2)][1 + j\omega C_7(R_7 + 2R_6)]j\omega C_3R_3}{(1 + j\omega C_1R_1)(1 + j\omega C_7R_7)(1 + j\omega C_3R_3)} \quad (5)$$

where, R_6, R_7 and C_7 are the components in the second differential stage. It can be seen that the dc coupling in the second differential stage adds an additional pole and zero to the transfer function. If the output stage has unity gain and the overall gain is shared equally between the two differential stages then the poles and zeros of both of these stages are identical so that $\omega_{P1} = 1/(C_1R_1) = \omega_{P3} = 1/(C_7R_7)$ and $\omega_{Z1} = 1/[C_1(R_1 + 2R_2)] = \omega_{P1}/A_{V1} = \omega_{Z2} = 1/[C_7(R_7 + 2R_6)] = \omega_{P3}/A_{V2}$. The gains of the individual differential stages were kept at 20dB as for the two-stage amplifier so that the overall gain of the three-stage amplifier is 40dB. On the basis of the results of Figures 7 and 8 for the two-stage amplifier the pole-zero cancellation was maintained in the first differential stage by maintaining the choice $C_3R_3 = C_1(R_1 + 2R_2)$. If the intention, in the first instance, is to maintain the -3dB frequency of the three-stage amplifier at the same location as for the two-stage amplifier then it can be shown that:

$$\omega_{-3dB2} = \sqrt{\sqrt{2} - 1}\ \omega_{-3dB1} = 0.645\,\omega_{-3dB1} \quad (6)$$

where ω_{-3dB2} is the -3dB frequency of a single stage in a two-stage amplifier having identical stages and ω_{-3dB1} is the -3dB frequency of a single-stage amplifier which is equal to the overall -3dB frequency of the two-stage amplifier. If f_{-3dB1} = 0.05Hz then f_{-3dB2} = 0.032Hz to maintain an overall -3dB frequency of 0.05Hz for the three-stage amplifier. However, this choice does not allow the three-stage amplifier to meet the pulse response requirements. In order to accomplish this, it is necessary to lower the -3dB frequency of the three-stage amplifier to 0.043Hz which corresponds to a -3dB frequency for the individual differential stages of 0.028Hz. This gives an undershoot of 98μV and a recovery slope of $15\mu Vs^{-1}$. This can be seen in Figures 10 and 11 where the optimised response is represented by the bold curves. The magnitude and phase responses are shown in Figure 10, while the pulse response expanded in the region of the undershoot is shown in Figure 11. This heavy grey curves represents the corresponding responses of a single-stage amplifier with a -3dB frequency of 0.05Hz.

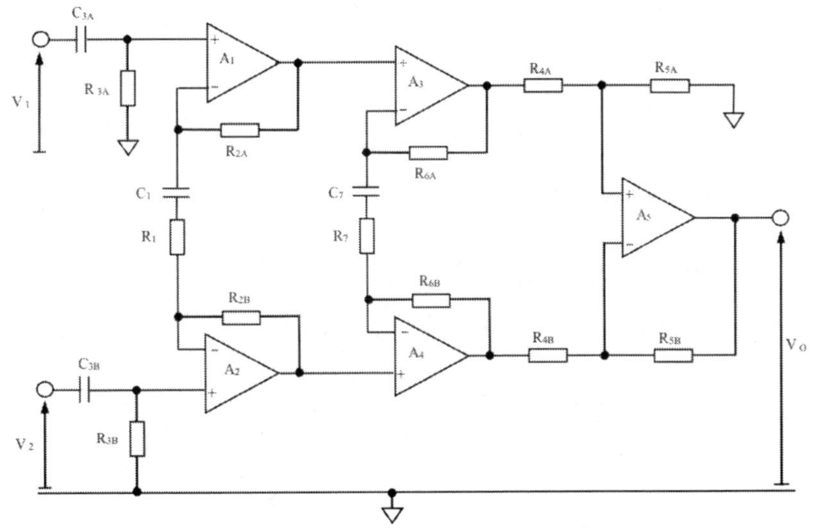

Figure 9 Schematic diagram of a 3-stage ECG amplifier

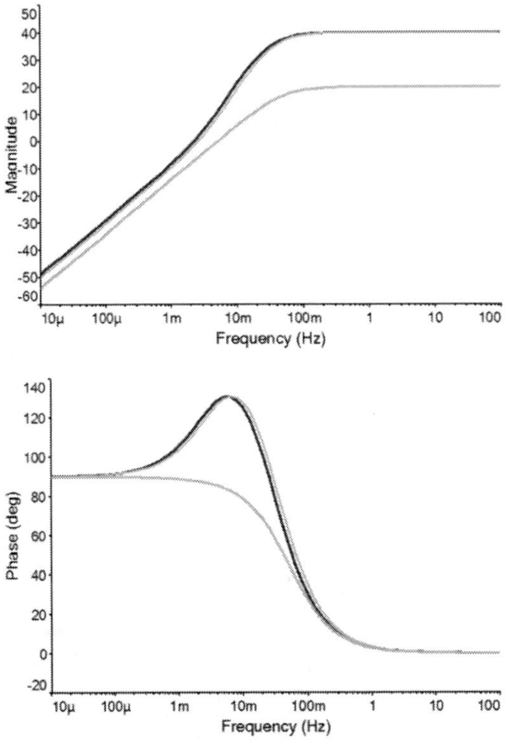

Figure 10 Magnitude and phase responses of 3-stage amplifier

5 Conclusion

A 3-stage ECG amplifier for use with unjelled electrodes has been designed which satisfies the IEC 60601 specification. The undershoot in the pulse response is less than 100μV and the recovery slope less than 300μVs^{-1}. The -3dB low cut-off frequency of two identical cascaded differential stages must be set at 0.028Hz in order to accomplish this.

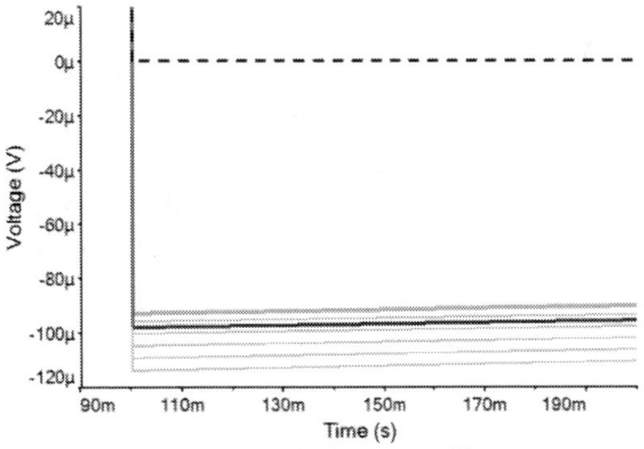

Figure 11 Pulse response of the 3-stage amplifier

References

1. International Electrotechnical Commission, Medical Electrical Equipment Std. 2-25. IEC 60601, 2011.
2. International Electrotechnical Commission, Medical Electrical Equipment Std. 2-47. IEC 60601, 2012.
3. A. S. Berson and H. V. Pipberger, 'The Low-Frequency Response of Electrocardiographs, A Frequent Source of Recording Errors'; Amer. Heart J.; **71**, 779-789, 1966.
4. D. Tayler and R. Vincent, 'Signal distortion in the electrocardiogram due to inadequate phase response', IEEE Trans. Biomed. Eng.; **30**, 352-356, 1983.
5. C. E. Kossmann et al., 'Recommendations for standardization of leads and of specifications for instruments in electrocardiograpy and vectorcardiography.; Circulation, **35**, 583–602, 1967.
6. H. V. Pipberger et al., 'Recommendations for standardization of instruments in electrocardiography and vectorcardiograhy, IEEE Trans Biomed. Eng.; **14**, 60-68, 1967.

An Improved Very Low-Power Electrode Contact Impedance Monitor

Martin J Burke[1,a], Cormac Molloy[1] and Helge Fossan[2]

[1]*Dept. of Electronic and Electrical Engineering, Trinity College, University of Dublin, College Green, Dublin 2, Ireland.*
[2]*Laerdal Medical AS, P.O. Box 337, Tanke Svilandsgate 30, N-4002 Stavanger, Norway.*

Abstract. This paper reports the design improvement of a circuit for monitoring the quality of contact of un-gelled stainless steel electrodes with a patient's skin in the measurement of the ECG. The circuit is intended to be incorporated into a heart rate monitor used prior to and during childbirth to measure the mother's heart rate. The revised design uses commercially available low-power technology to implement the circuit with a reduction in the power consumption by a factor of 20 over a previous design [1]. The circuit measures the quality of contact of electrode impedances up to 100kΩ and gives a visual indication when the contact impedance of either electrode is above this level. The impedance is measured using a signal injected through the electrodes via the input impedance of the amplifier at a frequency of 5kHz. The resulting signal present at the amplifier input at this frequency is then extracted and processed before threshold detection of the signal level which is used to indicate whether or not the quality of contact of the patient's fingers with the electrodes is acceptable for the purposes of heart rate measurement.

1 Introduction

The Safer Births Programme [2], sponsored by the Norwegian Research Council as part of a larger World Health Organization initiative [3], is an action plan aimed at eliminating preventable deaths of infants at birth, in developing countries. Many maternity hospitals in these locations are understaffed and are often forced to rely on midwives and nurses alone to contend with the clinical complications that arise around childbirth, without access to the assistance or equipment needed to deal with them. Few places have sufficient equipment for fetal monitoring such that fetuses in distress can be left unattended, adding to the burden of birth asphyxia and stillbirth. Many of the infants born may not be breathing correctly and have pulses which are difficult or impossible to detect manually. On occasions these infants can be misclassified as stillborn, when their hearts are still functioning and they could be resuscitated with suitable equipment. Laerdal Medical AS, based in Norway, designs and markets resuscitation equipment for use in the scenarios described above. One such product is the Moyo unit shown in Figure 1. This unit is a heart rate monitor which uses an ultrasonic transducer placed on the mother's abdomen to detect the infant's heart beat and indicates the fetal heart rate on a LCD. One common problem with ultrasonic heart rate monitors is that when the infant's heart beat is difficult to detect the transducer often picks up the mother's heart rate in error [4]. In order to overcome this problem the Moyo unit incorporates an ECG amplifier which is used to measure the mother's heart rate by way of an ECG signal picked up from her hands. This heart rate value is then indicated separately on the LCD. The Moyo unit is held by the mother giving birth who presses her fingers onto the stainless steel electrodes of the unit, which then detects her ECG and measures and displays her heart rate. The values of the two heart rates can then be compared by the midwife and used to discern whether or not the ultrasonic transducer is measuring the infant's heart rate reliably or the mother's heart rate in error. As the mother may be in distress during childbirth, the problem arises of ensuring that she maintains an adequate grip on the monitor to allow her ECG to be detected reliably.

It is intended to implement a mechanism in the Moyo unit which will verify that the electrical contact of the mother's fingers with the stainless steel un-gelled electrodes is acceptable. This is done by measuring the contact impedance of the skin-electrode interface at each electrode to assess whether or not the mother has pressed her fingers properly onto the electrodes. Surface contact

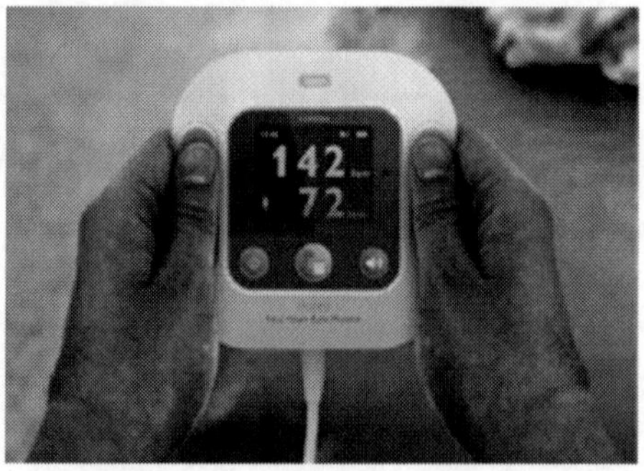

Figure 1. The MOYO Unit in Use

[a] Corresponding author: mburke@tcd.ie

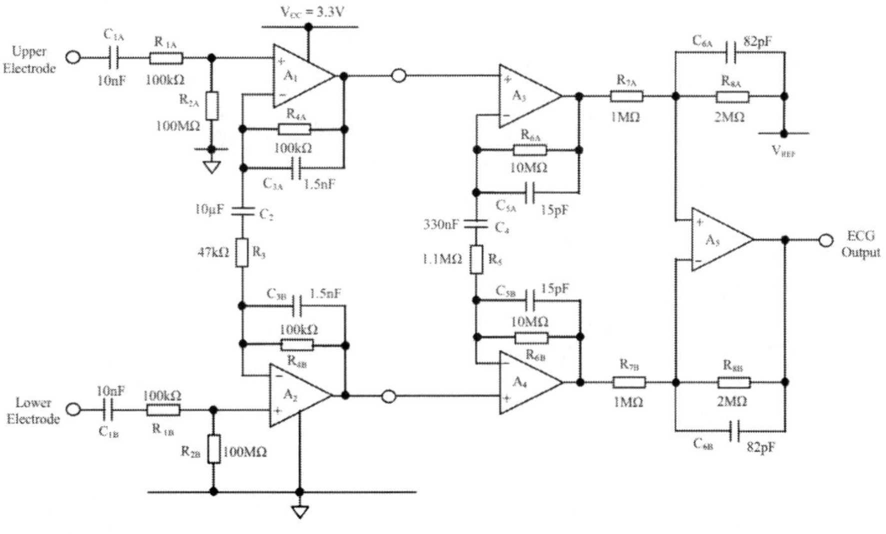

Figure 2. Schematic Diagram of the Original ECG Amplifier

impedance of each electrode is measured independently and a visual alarm is activated when the state of contact of either electrode is unsatisfactory for the purposes of reliable ECG measurement.

2 Background

2.1 Existing ECG Amplifier

The schematic diagram of the ECG amplifier originally used in the Moyo unit is shown in Figure. 2. This is a three-stage instrumentation ECG amplifier adapted from an earlier design by Burke & Gleeson [5] and later improved by Assambo & Burke [6]. The 46dB of differential gain is split primarily between the first stage with 14.4dB and the second stage with 25.6dB while the third stage provides 6dB of the gain with differential-to-single-ended conversion. The input stage provides a high differential-mode and common-mode impedance of 100MΩ in order to preserve adequate common-mode-rejection-ratio (CMRR) when interfacing with high-impedance dry electrodes. The amplifier operates from a single 3.3V supply rail and the input stages are biased to a mid-rail voltage of 1.65V using a separate dc-to-dc convertor chip not shown in the schematic. ESD protection and r.f. suppression elements are also omitted for clarity. The operational amplifier used in this design is the AD8648 (Analogue Devices Inc.) which is a quad amplifier package with each op-amp having a gain-bandwidth product of 24Mz and a quiescent current of 2mA. It also offers low offsets and noise and a CMRR of 84dB. The input impedance of each amplifier is unspecified, however.

2.2 Electrodes

The electrodes used in the Moyo unit shown in Figure 1 are made of stainless steel with a matt-finish surface, and are easily disinfected before use with an alcohol wipe. Electrical contact is made with the electrodes by the user gripping the unit in both hands with their fingers placed on the electrode surfaces. Only the firmness of the user's grip determines the contact pressure. In order to obtain an indication of the contact impedance of these electrodes a method formerly reported by Baba & Burke [7] was used to characterize the electrodes. An equivalent electrical model of the electrode is shown in Figure 3. This can be seen to contain two parallel C-R networks as well as two series resistors. The frequency response of the model is therefore characterized by two time constants. The values of these time constants are very large, which makes their evaluation in the frequency domain very difficult and consequently this was done in the time domain instead.

The current source shown in Figure 4 was used to inject a minute current of 2μA through the electrodes while being held by the user. The current was activated and then deactivated via the relay for a stable period in the region of 30s. A 10kHz sinewave signal was also used to allow the high frequency purely resistive elements to be evaluated. A program in MATLAB (MathWorks Inc.) was then used to fit a two time constant C-R model shown in Figure 3 to the recorded voltage waveforms and to determine the values of the individual components of the model.

This was done for measurements made on 20 subjects of varying age, sex, nationality and skin colour, in order to establish the extent of the variation of electrode impedance to be expected. Only the passive components of the model were of interest in this instance and the dc polarization potentials were not measured. The ranges of values measured for each component of the model are listed in Table.1 below. Plots of the magnitude and phase as functions of frequency of a single stainless steel electrode are shown in Figure 5. Plots are shown for a light grip on the electrode and for a falling current. The impedance varies considerably within the frequency range of the ECG signal. The magnitude falls off abruptly

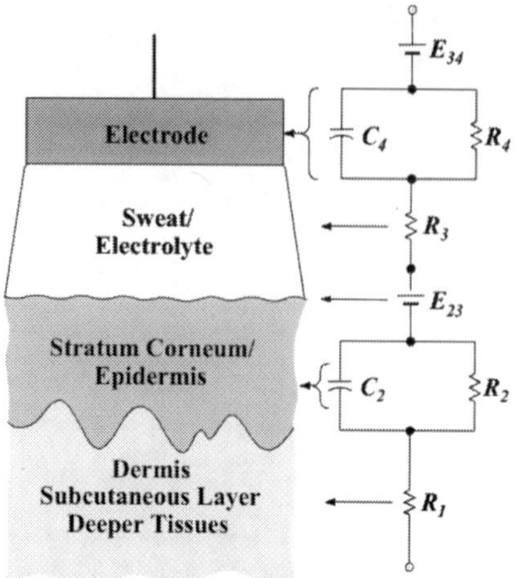

Figure 3. Equivalent Electrical Model of the Electrodes

above 1Hz and the phase falls off above 10Hz. It can be seen that the magnitude of the impedance is less than 30kΩ at frequencies above approximately 10Hz. This is considerably lower than the input common-mode resistance of the amplifier or of the protection resistor, R_1, shown in the schematic diagram of the amplifier in Figure 2. This indicates that the signal levels involved in measuring the contact impedance of such electrodes are by nature quite low.

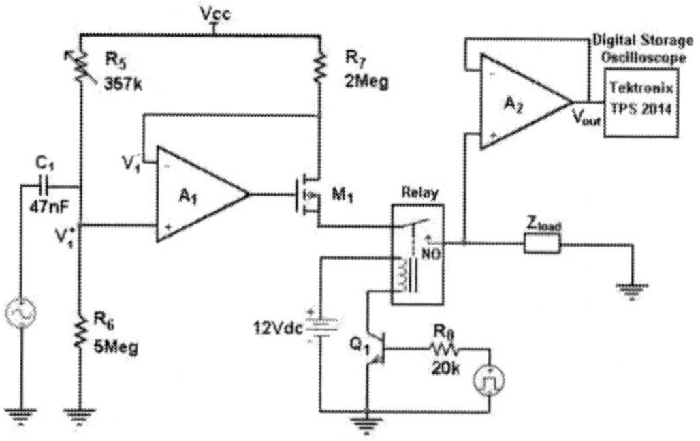

Figure 4. Electrode Impedance Measurement Circuit

Table 1. Range of Values for Electrode Model Elements

Element	Minimum	Maximum	Unit
$R_1 + R_3$	20	45	kΩ
R_2	2.03	331	kΩ
C_2	0.000619	891	μF
R_4	1.96	911	kΩ
C_4	0.00134	976	μF
τ_2	0.0000227	25.4	s
τ_4	0.00039	889	s

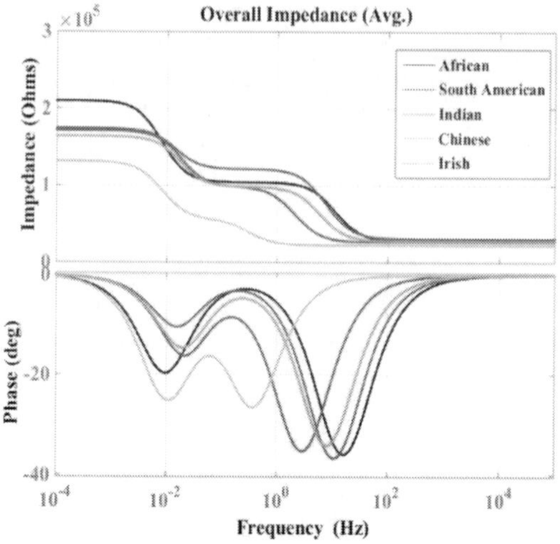

Figure 5. Impedance of Blasted Stainless Steel Electrodes

3 Methodology

A block diagram of the electrode contact monitoring system is shown in Figure 6. An oscillator and bandpass filter are used to provide a sinusoidal source signal for measurement purposes that is outside of the range of the ECG signal spectrum. This signal is then buffered in unity-gain inverting and non-inverting amplifiers to provide antiphase measurement sources. These antiphase signals are then fed through the common-mode input resistors of the ECG amplifier to the electrodes. The first stage of the ECG amplifier is also used to provide initial gain for the contact monitoring signal. Following this, bandpass filters are used to extract the sinusoidal signal from the ECG signal at the outputs of the first stage of the amplifier. The output signal of the upper and lower bandpass filters are then fed into separate half-wave rectifiers in order to provide a steady-state indication of the contact impedance at each electrode. The output voltages of the rectifiers are then compared with reference levels in separate threshold detectors in each channel. When the contact impedance of an electrode exceeds the reference value, the output of the corresponding threshold detector goes high. This output is then used to drive a LED via a suitable buffer circuit. LEDs were used to provide visual alarms in the prototype unit but this will implemented on the LCD display in the final unit to maintain very low power consumption.

4 Measurement Circuit

4.1. ECG amplifier modification

A full schematic diagram of the electrode contact monitoring system and its incorporation into the ECG amplifier is shown in Figure 7. ESD protection diodes, D_3 and D_4 and r.f. suppression capacitors, C_{15}, are also

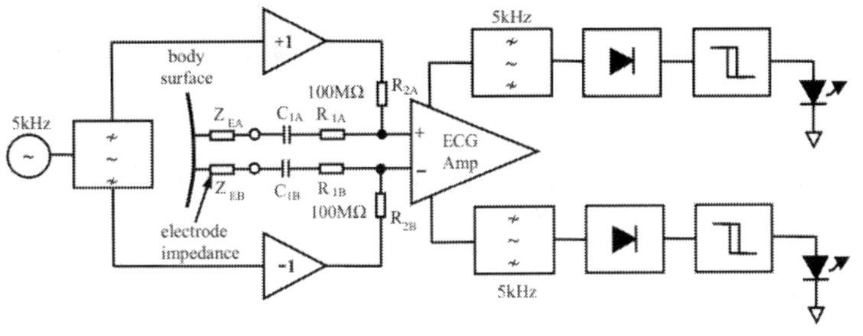

Figure 6. Block Diagram of the Electrode Impedance Measuremnt System

shown in each channel. It was decided to use the front-end stage of the ECG amplifier to provide the first phase of amplification for the electrode contact monitoring signal. The gains of the three stages of this amplifier were revised accordingly. The first stage gain was changed to 22dB, the second stage to 25dB and the third stage was revised to give unity gain. The revised component values set the 3dB lower cut-off frequency at 0.67Hz as required by the international standards for clinical heart-rate monitoring [8]. It also increased the CMRR by 6dB in the ECG signal bandwidth. The AD8619 (Analog Devices Inc.) op-amp was used in the first stage of the ECG amplifier as it has a gain-bandwidth product of 400kHz with a quiescent current of 38μA per channel. Its upper cut-off frequency was self-limited by the op-amp at greater than 10kHz, thus allowing full amplification of the 5kHz contact monitoring signal. The OPA4379 (Texas Instruments Inc.) op-amp was used in the second and third amplifier stages as it provides a gain-bandwidth product of 90kHz with a quiescent current of only 3μA per channel. The upper cut-off frequencies of the second and third stages of the amplifier were set at 350Hz and 480Hz respectively. This reduced the power consumption of the redesigned ECG amplifier by a factor of 120.

4.2. Measurement signal generation

An astable multivibrator built around the comparator A_6 is used to generate a square-wave at a frequency of 5kHz. The TLV3201 (Texas Instruments Inc.) is used as the comparator because of its high slew rate and rail-to-rail voltage swing with a low quiescent current of 40μA. The bandpass filter centred around op-amps A_7 and A_8 is a multiple feedback configuration having a centre frequency of 5kHz and a Q-factor of 12. This provides a sinusoidal source signal with an amplitude of 1.35V peak. The choice of contact monitoring frequency was a design compromise. A high frequency well above the ECG bandwidth is desirable as it is easy to extract and separate from the wanted ECG signal. However, the parasitic input capacitance of operational amplifiers and r.f. suppression capacitors have a significant shunting effect on the electrode contact impedance at higher frequencies so that the signal developed across this impedance is very small. The design value of 5kHz was chosen to allow a reasonable signal level for measurement, while at the same time maintaining the measurement frequency at least a decade above the ECG band.

4.3. Signal injection

The sinewave is then passed through two buffer amplifiers, a non-inverting unity-gain stage built around op-amp A_{10} and a unity-gain inverting stage built around op-amp A_{11}, which also have mid-rail bias voltages. The in-phase component is fed to the upper electrode point via the upper-channel common-mode input resistor R_{2A}. The inverted component is fed to the lower electrode contact point via the lower-channel common-mode resistor R_{2B}. Both resistors R_{2A} and R_{2B} of 100MΩ are bypassed by parallel capacitors of 1pF in order to lower the series impedance seen at the signal injection frequency of 5kHz to around 24MΩ. This method of feeding the contact monitoring signal to the electrodes preserves the high common-mode impedance at the ECG amplifier input and consequently the CMRR. The use of antiphase signals also allows the signal developed on the mother's body to be kept close to zero.

The levels of 5kHz signal present at the input terminals of the ECG amplifier are those developed across the contact impedances of each electrode namely, Z_{EA} and Z_{EB}. With good contact and low skin-electrode impedance the signal levels are extremely small as the impedance of resistor R_2 in parallel with capacitor C_{14} forms a potential divider with the electrode contact impedance, Z_E, at each terminal of the amplifier. In fact, most of the 5kHz signal present is actually developed across the protection resistor R_1 in each case. This has a value of 100kΩ, which is much greater than the typical contact impedance of the electrode itself.

4.4. Signal extraction

Under normal conditions with good electrode contact the signal at 5kHz present at the amplifier input terminals is of the order of 12mV. On the other hand, when electrode contact is lost altogether, a signal level of just less than 125mV is obtained at the inputs terminals of the amplifier.

If a maximum electrode contact impedance is set at 100kΩ, which is the same value as the resistor, R_1, then the maximum expected signal with good electrode contact appearing at the input of the ECG amplifier is of the order of 22mV. The gain of 22dB in the first stage of the ECG amplifier provides the initial gain for the contact monitoring signal, raising the signal level at the output of this stage to 268mV.

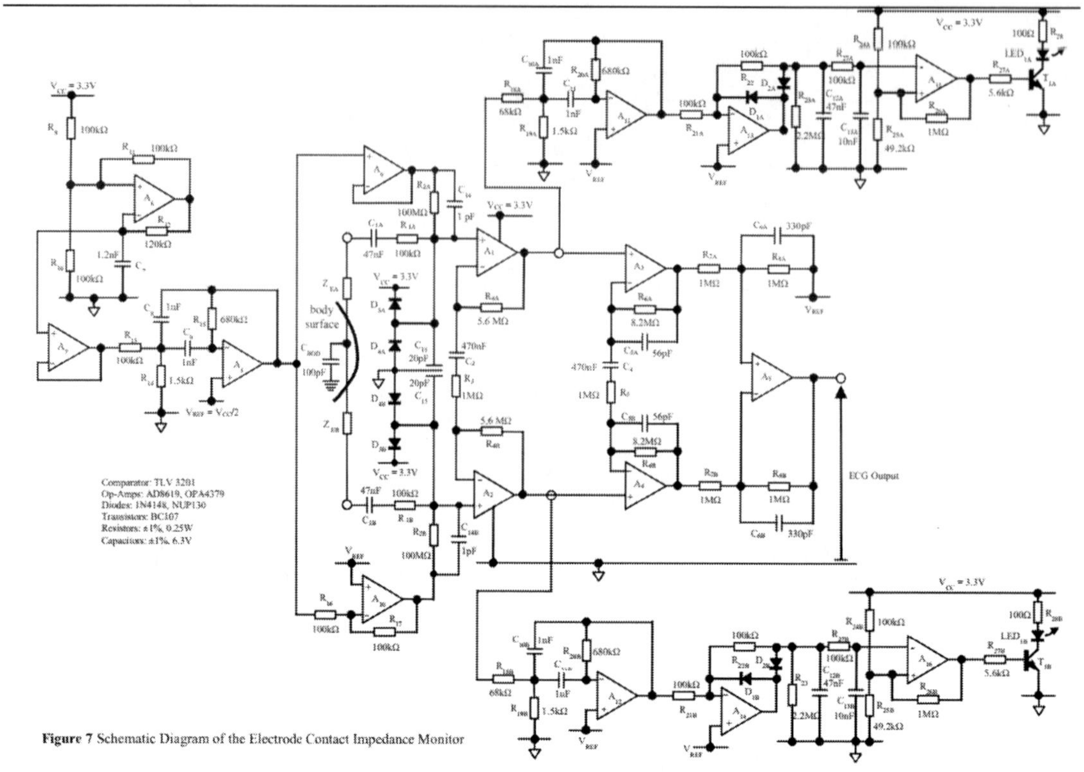

Figure 7 Schematic Diagram of the Electrode Contact Impedance Monitor

The electrode contact monitoring signals are extracted from the outputs of each side of the first stage of the ECG amplifier using band-pass filters built around op-amps A_{11} and A_{12}. These filters are multiple feedback structures having a centre frequency of 5kHz, a gain of 14dB at this frequency and a Q-factor of 12. All of the bandpass filters were implemented using the AD8619 op-amp. This provides an overall gain of 36dB or a factor of 60 to the signal developed across the resistor R_1 and the electrode impedance Z_E in series. The output signal level from the filters with good electrode contact is then of the order of 350mV. At the limit of poor electrode contact impedance of 100kΩ, this rises to approximately 660mV peak.

4.5. Signal level detection

The output sinewaves from the band-pass filters in each channel are then fed into precision half-wave rectifiers built around op-amps A_{13} and A_{14}. The rectification process has unity gain but is inverting and includes envelope detection of the sinewave by means of a C-R smoothing circuit having a time-constant of 1s. This provides a steady-state signal level representing the amplitude of the recovered sinewave at 5kHz. The rectified level is negative-going with respect to the reference voltage of half the supply, V_{REF} = 1.65V. Therefore, at the limit of poor electrode contact, the output voltage of op-amp A_{13} or A_{14} falls to 1V.

Finally, the rectified voltages in each channel are fed into threshold detectors built around op-amps A_{15} and A_{16}. The reference voltage of each threshold detector is set at 1.09V relative to ground by resistors R_{24} and R_{25} with approximately 40mV of hysteresis added by the positive feedback provided by resistor R_{26}. The action of the threshold detectors is also inverting. Consequently, when the rectified 5kHz signal level reaches a threshold of 700mV below V_{REF} or 1.09Vdc, the op-amp acting as a comparator changes state and its output goes from 0V representing good electrode contact, to the supply voltage of 3.3V representing poor electrode contact.

All of the op-amps used in the signal level assessment circuitry are AD8657s in order to minimise power consumption. This HI output voltage of the op-amp is then used to feed a bipolar transistor based light-emitting-diode (LED) driver that provides a current of 10mA to the activated LED. The LED will be replaced in the final design by a segment on the LCD in the Moyo unit.

5 Performance Verification

For test purposes, the electrodes were implemented as matched resistors in each channel, in the first instance. The value of these resistors were varied between 10kΩ and 10MΩ and the signal level at the output of the filters, V_{A11}, V_{A12}, the half-wave rectifiers, V_{R23A}, V_{R23B} and the threshold detectors, V_{A15}, V_{A16}, recorded as shown in Table 2. The threshold detector logic outputs, change state at a value of electrode resistance between 100kΩ and 200kΩ as required. Imbalance in the electrode resistance in each channel was also investigated and the output logic states of the threshold detectors are shown in Table 3. An electrode impedance above the threshold level in either channel caused the threshold detectors in both channels to register this. This is due to cross-coupling in the differential input stage of the amplifier.

Table 3. Threshold Detector State vs. Electrode Resistance

Upper → Lower ↓	10kΩ	100kΩ	200kΩ	10MΩ
10kΩ	LO/LO	LO/LO	HI/HI	HI/HI
100kΩ	LO/LO	LO/LO	HI/HI	HI/HI
200kΩ	HI/HI	HI/HI	HI/HI	HI/HI
10MΩ	HI/HI	HI/HI	HI/HI	HI/HI

References

[1] M. J Burke, C. Molloy and H. Fossan "High-Impedance Electrode Contact Monitoring" *Proc. 19th WSEAS Int. Conf. Circuits, Sys., Comm. & Comput.*, Zakynthos, Paper No. 581-6000, July 2015.

[2] http://www.saferbirths.com

[3] http://www.who.int/en

[4] M. M. Murray, "Maternal or Fetal Heart Rate? Avoiding Intrapartum Misidentification" *J. Obstet. Gynecol. & Neonatal Nurs.*, vol. **33**, pp33-104, 2004.

[5] M. J. Burke and D. T. Gleeson "A Micropower Dry-electrode ECG Pre-amplifier" *IEEE Trans. Biomed. Eng.*, vol. **47**, pp155-162, 2000.

[6] C. Assambo and M. J. Burke, "An Improved Very-Low Power Preamplifier for Use with Ungelled Electrodes in ECG Recording" *NAUN Int. J. Biol. & Biomed. Eng.*, vol. **1**, pp. 25-35, 2007.

[7] A. Baba and M. J. Burke, "Electrical Characterization of Dry Electrodes for ECG Recording" *Proc. 12th WSEAS Int. Conf. Circuits, Sys., Comms. & Comput.*, Crete, Paper No. 591-226, July 2008.

[8] International Electrotechnical Commission, Medical electrical equipment Part 2-27: Particular requirements for the safety, including essential performance, of electrocardiographic monitoring equipment, *IEC Std. IEC60 601-2-27*: 3rd ed., 2011.

Acknowledgement: This work was supported by the Norwegian Research Council Grant No. ES506110 under the Safer Births Program.

Table 2. Voltage at Key Circuit Nodes vs. Electrode Resistance

R_E (Ω)	V_{iA} (mV)	V_{iB} (mV)	V_{A1} (mV)	V_{A2} (mV)	V_{A11} (V)	V_{A12} (V)	V_{R27A} (V)	V_{R27B} (V)	V_{A15} (logic)	V_{A16} (logic)
10k	26	22	166	112	0.63	0.58	1.40	1.38	LO	LO
100k	40	25	285	226	0.88	0.81	1.24	1.27	LO	LO
200k	50	38	380	290	1.21	1.04	1.07	1.16	HI	HI
10M	64	54	608	588	2.68	2.12	0.51	0.73	HI	HI

MATEC Web of Conferences 76, 01010 (2016) DOI: 10.1051/matecconf/20167601010
CSCC 2016

Construction of compact step down voltage converter in terms of EMC

Peter Janku[1,a], Martin Pospisilik[1] and Tomas Dulik[1]

[1] *Toma Bata University in Zlin, Faculty of applied informatics, Nad Stranemi 4511, Zlin , Czech Republic*

Abstract. At the present there is a wide variety of step down converters on market. Due to differences in converter's prices, parameters and principles of function, it is not that easy to choose a proper one suitable for a concrete application. Moreover, really strict standards are applied in order to achieve high EMC compatibility between different devices. This article tries to show the possibilities of a really low-end DC/DC converter controller AOZ 1284. The set of measurements according to the set specifications and standard EN 61000-6-3 are presented together. Moreover, measures needed to comply to limits of the standard are shown along with it's results.

1 Introduction

In modern electronic designs, the low price and compact size are two basic requirements defined by customers. At the other side, modern electronic devices have to meet really strict limitations defined in local or global EMC standards. These two opposite requirements, in common with wide variety of custom integrated drivers available on market, makes the correct step-down converters design really tricky.

This paper follows the previously based study [1] in which two different step down voltage converters were described. In following sections the step down converter based on AOZ1284 is discussed. The main advantage of this controller is its wide range of working frequency. Thanks to this, one of the most voluminous parts - inductor, can be chosen with relatively low value. The second, but not least advantage is its price - selected controller due to its parameter is one of the cheapest available on the market. [6]

The measurements of real parameters of step down controller are presented in this paper. Moreover, the main disadvantage of this converter – EMC interference level is discussed common with design of measures. All measurements and measures were performed to meet the requirements placed by working conditions and the standard EN 61000-6-3.[2.3.4]

2 Description of the tested converter

The converter, which parameters and performance are discussed in this paper, was constructed according the specifications defined in section 2.1. These specifications were defined on a real embedded project requirements. In this project, new special secured access system will be developed in cooperation with specific company.

2.1 Operating requirements

As was told before, operating requirements were defined on real project base. Whole required electric characteristics are listed in Table 1. In addition, there were special requirement on size of whole DC/DC converter and finally the price had to be as low as possible.

Table 1. Electrical operating requirements.

Parameter	Value	
	Min.	**Max.**
Input voltage	12 V	24 V
Output voltage	5 V	5 V
Output current - continuous	150 mA	300 mA
Output current- peak	500 mA	800 mA
Power efficiency	80 %	-

2.2 Converter circuit description

The converter, which parameters and performance are discussed, is based on AOZ1284 controller. The whole design was performed with respect to the manufacturer's notes provided within the datasheet of the circuit [5]. The circuit diagram of this converter is depicted in Figure 1.

[a] Corresponding author: janku@fai.utb.cz

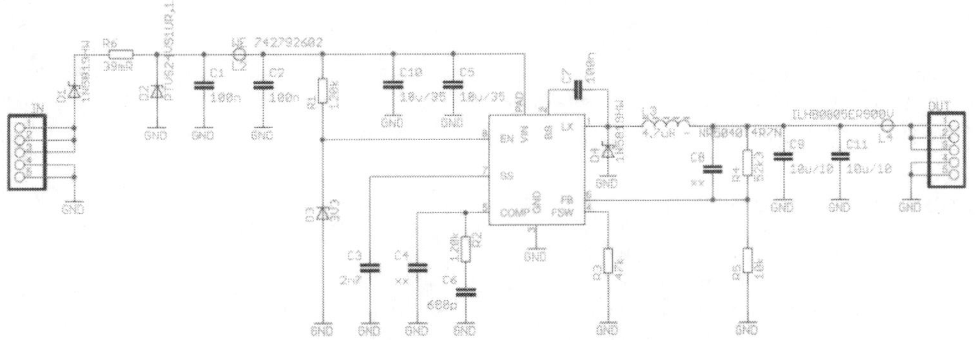

Figure 1. Circuit diagram of a voltage converter based on AOZ 1284.

As could be recognized from provided schematic, the switching transistor is integrated on the chip. The circuit operation is based on Continuous-Conduction Mode (CCM) in fixed frequency.

The inbuilt transistor is N-MOSFET switch. The inductor current is sensed by amplifying the voltage drop across the drain to source of this MOSFET. Output voltage is divided down by external voltage divider (defined by R5 and R4), it's internally compared with internal reference voltage source and amplified by the internal transconductance error amplifier. The error voltage is compared against the current signal, which is sum of inductor current signal and ramp compensation signal, at PWM input. If the current signal is less than the error voltage, the internal high-side switch is on. The inductor current flows from the input through the inductor to the output. When the current signal exceeds the error voltage, the high-side switch is off. The inductor current is freewheeling through the Schottky diode to output.[5,6]

As it is described above, the whole converter works on a fixed frequency defined by the internal oscillator. It can be programmed by external resistor connected to the FSW pin. In this specific circuit the operating frequency is set by R3 to value 961 kHz.

The circuit is equipped with filters (C1, L2 and C2) and with set of two protective diodes. The D1 take care about right input voltage polarization and the D2 works as overvoltage protection. Moreover, there is a Zener diode connected to the enable pin of converter, which is able to disable converter, when the input voltage is under the limit defined by manufacturer. [4,6,10,11]

3 Measurements and results

The described circuit was constructed as a functional sample and tested for achieving of the required parameters. Consequently a set of test was performed in order to gain data set needed for implementation of the DC converter into the final product. As in the previous research and in context of the requirements, the standard EN 61000-6-3 had been chosen, since the target use of the circuits was not specified.

The tests were as follows:

1. output voltage stability versus output load,
2. power efficiency at different output load and input voltages,
3. maximum output power according to the cooling capability of the components,
4. electromagnetic interference without a cover according to EN 61000-6-3,
5. interference currents on the input cables measured by a current clamp according to EN 61 000-6-3.

3.1 Measurement configurations

Three basic measurement network configurations were used in order to obtain the above described data:

1. Measurement of DC static parameters,
2. Measurement of radiated electromagnetic field,
3. Measurement of interferences on input cables.

3.1.1 DC parameters measurement network

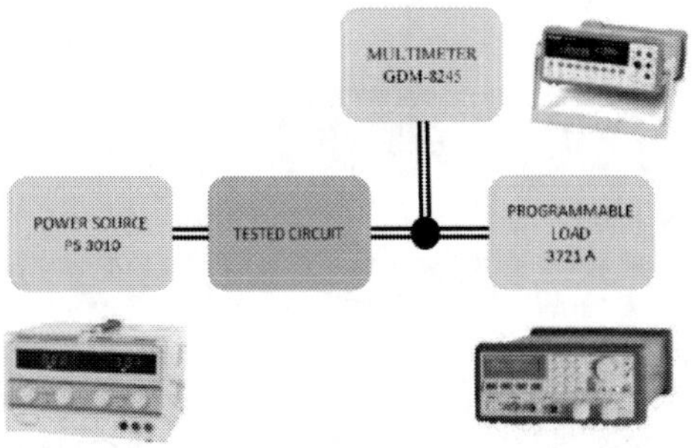

Figure 2. Configuration of measurement network for validating of converters static DC parameters. [1]

DOI: 10.1051/matecconf/20167601010

The DC parameters were measured by using stabilized laboratory power source Velleman PS3010 as converters voltage input. The converter output was stretched by programmable electronic load Array 3721A operating in constant current mode. The input voltage and current were measured by set of two RMS multimeters. The output parameters – voltage and current were measured directly by the electronic load. Its accuracy was randomly checked with another RMS multimeter.

3.1.2 Radiated electromagnetic field

The intensity of electromagnetic interference was measured in a semi anechoic chamber in order to avoid other signals ordinary presented in environment. The measurement network is visualised in Figure 3. As can be seen, it is composed of a bilogarthmical antenna Teseq Bilog CBL 6112 connected to the Rohde&Schwartz ESU 8 test receiver and spectral analyser. The measured controller was loaded by the electronic load Array 371A, that sunk a current of 0.2A and as power supply the lead battery was used. The potential interferences caused by the electronic load were excluded by additional measurement during which the converter was bypassed. All obtained data were collected and processed by means of EMC 32 software.[7,8,9]

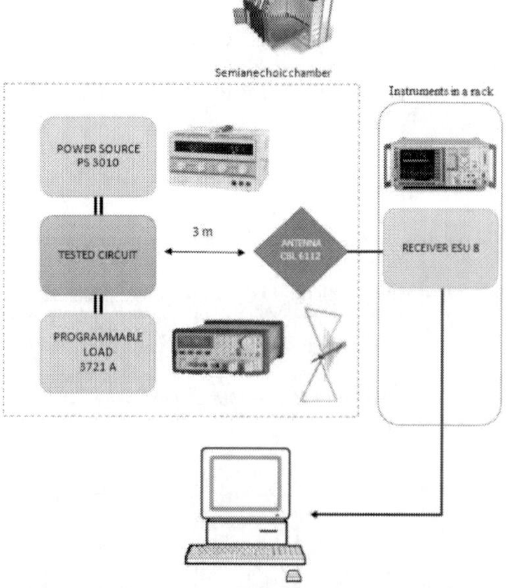

Figure 3. Configuration of the experiment consisting in measurement of electromagnetic field radiated by the tested voltage converters.[1]

3.1.3 Interferences on input cables

The third measurement configuration was built in two stages. In the first one the current probe F-52 was used as the sensor connected to the ESU 8 receiver. This configuration was used in previous research [1]. In the second stage, the current probe was replaced by a LISN Rohde&Schwarz ENV216 which can meet the requirements of CISPR 16-1-2, EN 55016-1-2. Both stages were compared with positive results – the same values were gained by both sensors. Therefore the second stage measurement network was selected as the one used for whole measuring of interferences on input cables.

The obtained data were collected in EMC 32 software and post processed in MS Excel. Tested circuit was powered by laboratory power source PS3010 and the output current was consumed by programmable load Array 3721A. Final experiment configuration is described in picture Figure 4.

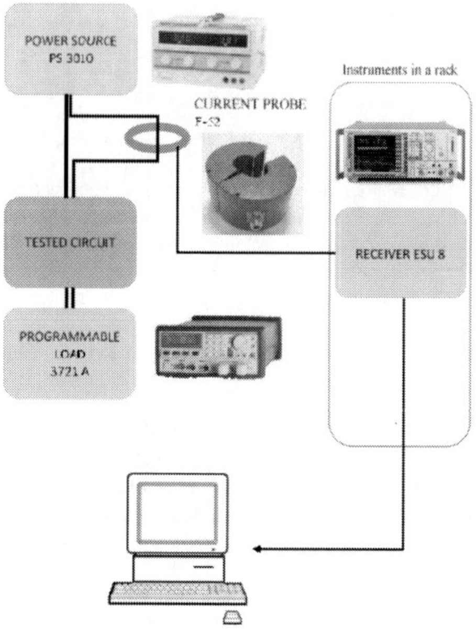

Figure 4. Configuration of measurement network used for measure on input wires by using current probe.[1]

3.2 Obtained results

By using measurement networks and devices described in previous parts of this paper, a large set of results was obtained. The most interesting and important results are presented in this section.

3.2.1 DC parameters

The first measurement was performed in order to verify required parameters of constructed converter. After static verification of output voltage, the load characteristic was measured. As can be seen in Figure 5, the output voltage naturally goes down together with rising output current load. Moreover, significant output voltage drop down was measured on 24 V input and 400 mA output current. Despite this fact, maximal voltage drop down achieved 44 mV (in case of 15 V input), which is absolutely acceptable level.

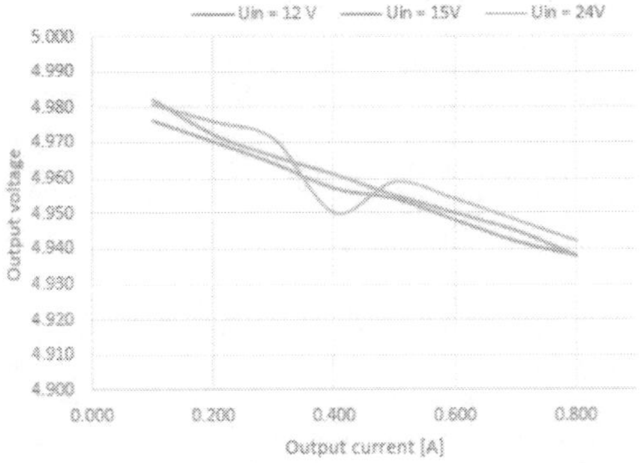

Figure 5. Output voltage dependence on the output current and input voltage.

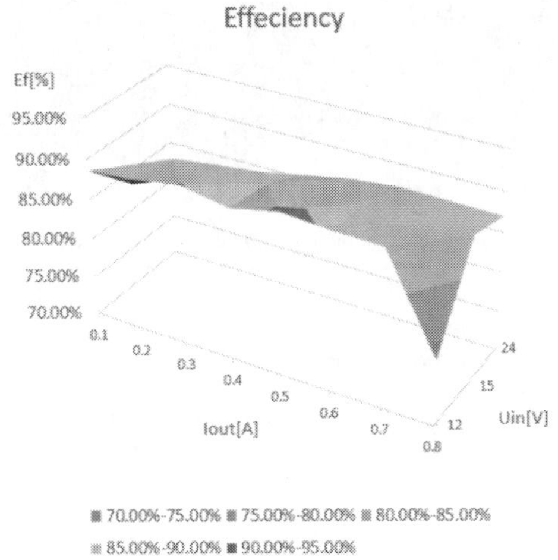

Figure 6. The converter efficiency in different working conditions.

The converter's power effeciency was calculated from the measured input and output power. It is despicted by Figure 6. As can be noticed, the average value of power effeciency is about 87%. The highest value was measured at the input level of 12 voltage and the output current of 500 mA (90.33%). At the other side, the lowest efficiency was observed at the input level of 12 voltage and the output current of 800 mA and at the input leve of 24 voltage and the output voltage of 100 mA.

During the measurements of the static DC characteristics, the temperature of the whole voltage converter was checked by thermocamera. The limited thermal picture is shown in Figure 7. As the most problematic part of voltage controller device, two schotky diodes were found. The first one worked as an input voltage polarity protection, the second one was used in main converters circuite described in section 2.2.

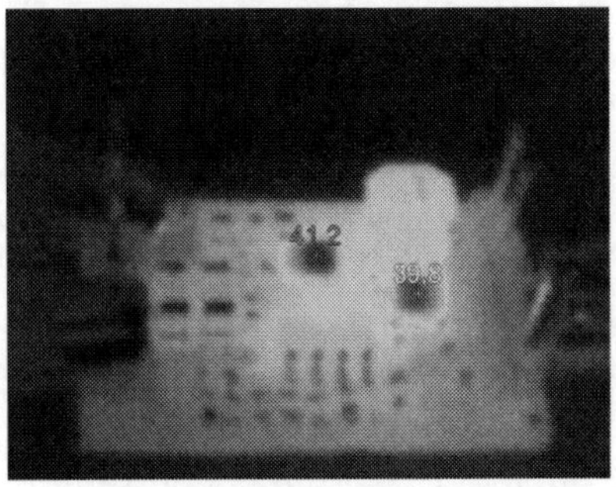

Figure 7. Thermal image of constructed converter.

3.2.2 Electromagnetic interferences

As it was described in previous sections, the electromagnetic interferences were measured according to the requirements of the standard EN 61000-6-3. The base band defined by this standard was from 30 MHz to 1 GHz and the measurement was performed on working prototype without any box or another shielding.

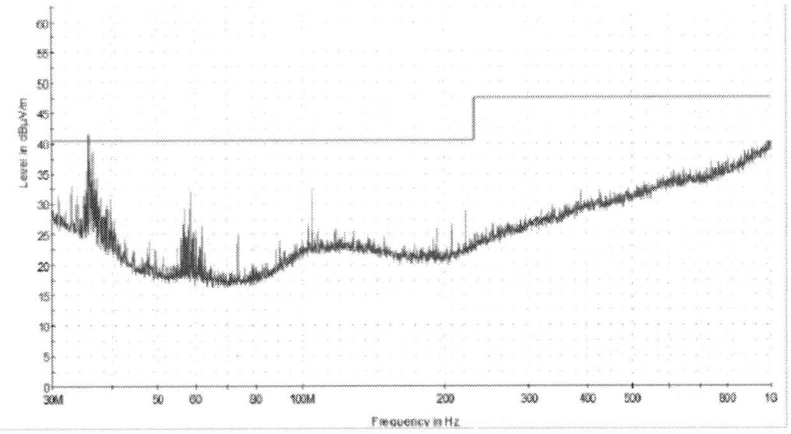

Figure 8. The electromagnetic interference spectrum.

The converter mostly passed the test with small exceptions. In the Figure 8 the worst test case result is shown. As can be seen, the only one problem is at the frequency of about 40 MHz, where the measured level exceed the limit over 1 dBuV/m. Nonetheless, the converter is expected to pass the test in real device with proper case.

It has to be mentioned, that together with measured sample, there were other devices in chamber (power source and programmable load. Theoretically, these two devices could produce some level of electromagnetic interferences. For this reason, the power source was replaced by a leaded battery. Moreover, the initial measurement was performed with bypassed converter in order to gain electromagnetic background in chamber. Because of significantly low level of electromagnetic interferences in chamber with bypassed converter, it could be claimed, that the measurement is correct and results are suitable.

3.2.3 Interferences on the input wires

According to the principle of operation of the converters the current ripples and/or voltage peaks are expected to occur at its input and output cables. Within the framework of the standard EN 61000-6-3, a large set of measurements is expected to be processed. Due to limited size of this paper, only data gained on positive power supply wire are discussed here. The measurement configuration was described in previous section. In additional, as was described, the measurement was performed with ENV 2016 LSN network and verified by using a current probe. Both results were the same; therefore, only data measured by ENV 216 LSN are presented.

In the Figures 10 and 11, the dependency of the measured voltage peaks spectrums on the output current (at a constant input voltage) is shown. It could be noticed from these pictures, that there are peaks starting from working frequency (about 961 kHz) and continuing on its harmonic frequencies up to 30 MHz. Moreover, most of these peaks break the limits defined by the standard. The most visible exceeded is noticeable at 24 voltage input and low output current. In this stage, the converter is working in a discontinuous mode and it is producing highest level of interferences.

Based on previous findings, it can be expected, that this converter will not pass the standard requiremetns of interferences on the input wires anymore. Therefore, a new input LC (inductor – capacitor) filter has been designed, built and, in the form of a functional sample, connected to the voltage convertor. The simulation of filter characteristic is depicted in Figure 9. After that all previous measurements on input wires were repeated.

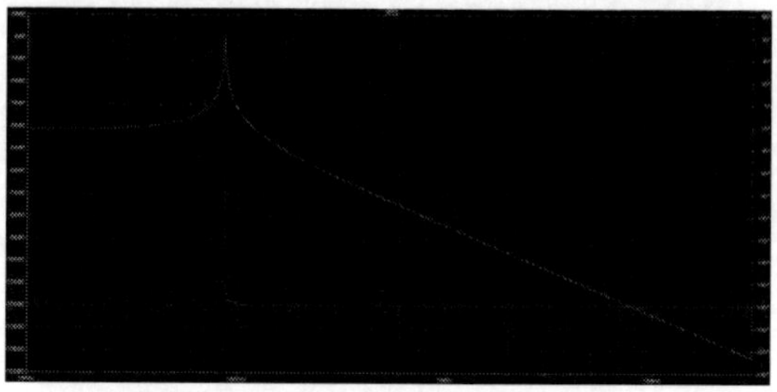

Figure 9. The simulation of input filter characteristics.

The second set of input ripple voltage spectrum measurements (after the filter was applied) is shown in pictures Figure 12 and Figure 13. It is clear, that the measured results are significantly better after the filter application then before. The whole spectrum is lowered down; especially the peaks on working frequency and another harmonics frequencies. In this consequence, it could be expected that the designed voltage converter with appropriate input filter will be able to pass the tests defined standard EN 61000-6-3.

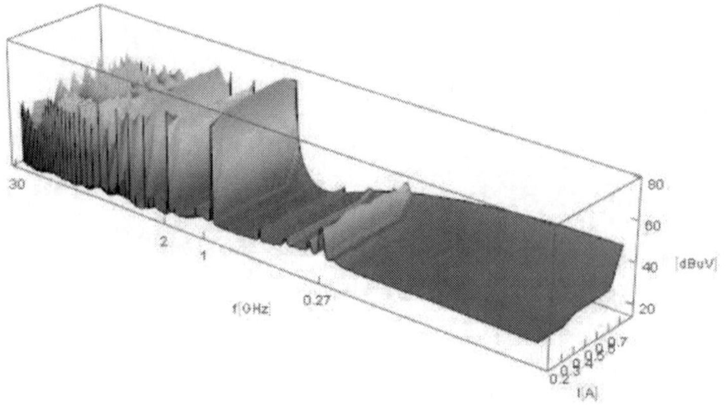

Figure 10. Ripple current spectrum on the input wire (constant input voltage 12V), no filter applied.

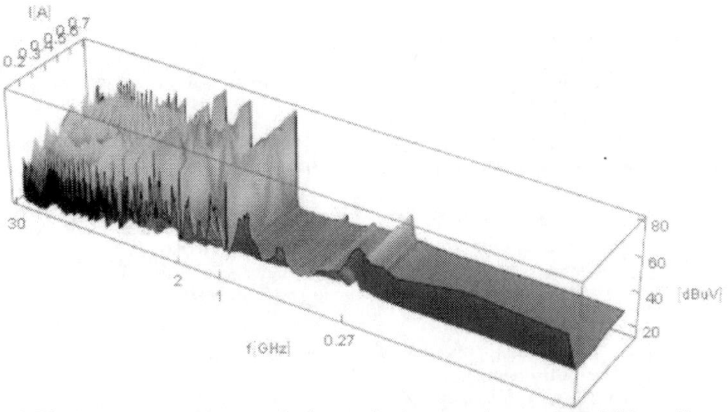

Figure 11. **Ripple current spectrum on the input wire (constant input voltage 24V), no filter applied.**

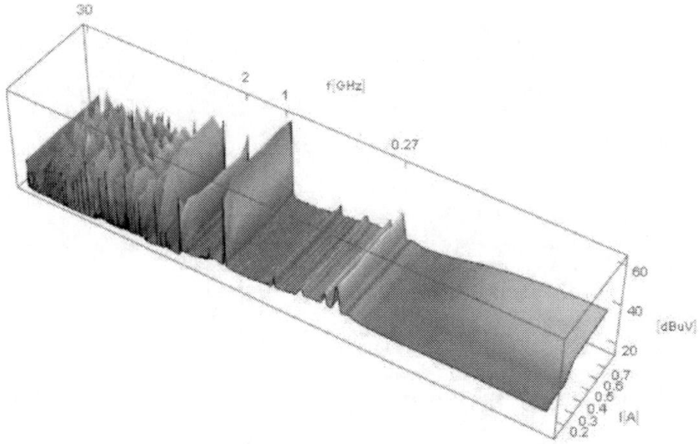

Figure 12. **Ripple current spectrum on the input wire (constant input voltage 12V), designed filter connected.**

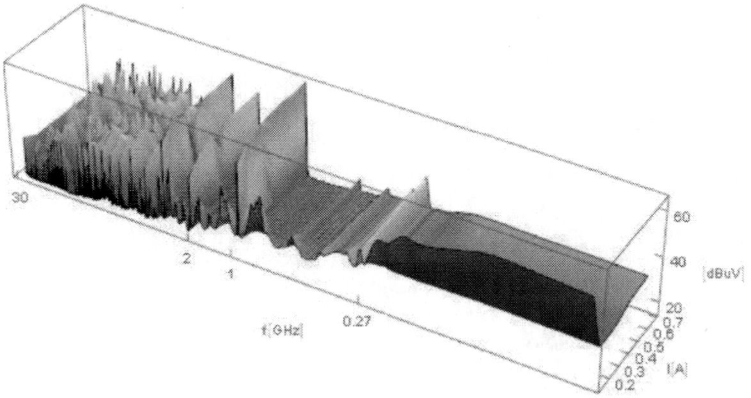

Figure 13. **Ripple current spectrum on the input wire (constant input voltage 24V), designed filter connected.**

4 Conclusion

This paper provides an overview about designing of a small cheap voltage converter, which can be useful for implementation into small embedded devices. As the basic driver, the small and simple controller the AOZ 1284 has been chosen. Based on the datasheets and manufacturers' recommendations, the DC/DC converter circuit was designed and the applicable sample was constructed. After that the static DC characteristics were verified, the set of control measurement of interferences was performed according to the requirements of the standard EN 61000-6-3.

The static DC measurements agree that all requirements defined in the start of this paper were fulfilled. The radiated electromagnetic field measurements shown, that the designed circuit is likely to meet the requirements defined by the standard. At the other hand, the measurement of interferences on input cables revealed a significant problem with the level of these interferences.

According to this information, the simple LC filter was designed and all necessary measurements were repeated. After the application of the filter, the level of interferences has been lowered.

Because of the level of the interferences produced by this converter also depends on the connected load and the PCB design, we did not continued in tuning of the input filter and converter into details.

According to the data we obtained it can be claimed, that the designed converter will be suitable for its designation; moreover, it can be expected, that it will be able to pass all requirements defined in standard EN61000-6-3 after small tuning of its parts. Together with the price of this converter (about 0.4 USD) and final size of whole design (2 cm x 3 cm), this converter can be used as a replacement for frequently used MC34063 drivers and it could be sufficient competition for products of other manufacturers.

As mentioned in the introduction, a comparison with other two converters that were subjects to research in the past is provided in this paper. Due to different requirements (output voltage, output current, etc.) on these converters, the results cannot be directly compared which ones obtained during this paper measurement. Despite this, previous paper has been used as a guide for all tests performed on designed converter.

Acknowledgement

This paper is supported by the Ministry of Education, Youth and Sports of the Czech Republic within the National Sustainability Programme project No. LO1303 (MSMT-7778/2014) and also by the European Regional Development Fund under the project CEBIA-Tech No. CZ.1.05/2.1.00/03.0089 and the Internal Grant Agency at TBU in Zlin, Project No. IGA/FAI/2016/036 .

References

[1] M. Pospisilik, M. Adamek, R. M. S. Silva, Different constructions of step down voltage converters in termsof EMC, *International Journal of Circuits, Systems and Signal Processing*, Volume **10**, (2016), p. 190-199, ISSN: 1998-4464

[2] J. Svacina, Electromagnetic Compatibility *[Elektromagneticka kompatibilita]*, Brno: VUT Brno, (2002).

[3] C. R. Paul, *Introduction to Electromagnetic Compatibility*, New York: John Wiley, (1992).

[4] P. A. Chatterton, M. A. Houlden, *EMC – Electromagnetic Theory to Practical Design*, New York: John Wiley, (1991).

[5] ALPHA & OMEGA Semicondutor (2012, March), AOZ1284 Datasheet[online]. Available: http://aosmd.com/res/data_sheets/AOZ1284PI.pdf

[6] M. Pospisilik., T. Dulik, *International Journal of Circuits, Systems and Signal Processing*, Volume **8**, (2014), pp 518 – 528

[7] M. Mann, B. Gutheil, J. Zastrau, P. Weiss, "Electromagnetic field measurements – Means of verification", In *Proc. of the 5th WSEAS/IASME Int. Conf. on Electric Power Systems, High Voltages, Electric Machines*, Tenerife, Spain, December 16-18, (2005), pp 591-595

[8] M. Pospisilik, J. Soldan, M. Adamek, Influence of the Properties of a Real Semi Anechoic Chamber on an Internal Electromagnetic Field Distribution, *WSEAS Transactions on Systems*, Volume **14**, (2015), pp 174 – 186, E-ISSN: 2224-2678

[9] J. A. Cartrysse, "Measuring method for the characterization of shielding gaskets", in *8th International Conference on Electromagnetic Compatibility*, pp 251 – 253, Heriot-Watt University, Edinburgh, UK, September (1992).

[10] Z. Trnka, *Theory of Electrical Engineering [Teoretická elektrotechnika]*. Bratislava: SNTL Alfa, (1972)

[11] V. Kus, Effects of Converters with Semiconductors to the Power System [Vliv polovodičových měničů na napájecí soustavu], Prague: BEN-Technicka literature, (2002), ISBN: 80-730-0062-8

Friction coefficient measurements of silencers on specialized duct tract

Stanislav Sehnalek[1,a], Pavel Drabek[1] and Martin Zalesak[1]

[1] *Tomas Bata University in Zlin, Faculty of Applied Informatics, Department of Automation and Control Engineering, Nad Stranemi 4511, Zlin, Czech Republic*

Abstract. This article describes test methods on air duct track in Laboratory of Environmental Engineering. It focuses on measurement of silencer parameter like is pressure loss coefficient. Firstly, the paper describe the measurement apparatus with description of calculation method by standard ISO 7235 and energy equation. Then the paper presents three ways how to accomplish measurement because such way is not covered by procedure in standard. Then follows the evaluation of results of measurements on three types of silencer designed for HVAC applications. The article is concluded with discussion over measured data with outline for further research.

1 Introduction

Aerodynamic properties of air is in the scope of interest of researchers for more than century. The air flow parameters was investigated by Hagen, Reyleigh, Reynolds [1], followed up by Prandtl, Moody [2], Colebrook [3], Von Karman [4] and many others. [5] The knowledge of concept properties concerning HVAC components is a prerequisite for successful design technique. In the draft of ventilation ducts the pressure loss is an important parameter to know based on different velocities of transported air. Determination of parameters for specific HVAC devices are in scope of specialized laboratories. Laboratory of such capabilities is maintained by authors of this article at Tomas Bata University in Zlin, Faculty of Applied Informatics and is involved in this paper. Special interest in actual development is focused in acoustic silencers for mounting in the ducts which are important element within HVAC systems. With the silencers there are two main parameters which should be taken care off, first one is a sound attenuation and second one are pressure losses. It is regrettable that those parameters are in opposition to each other. In facility of the authors the Laboratory of Environmental Engineering it is possible to test the silencers for both parameters and thus combine both parameters for better performances. In presented paper, the focus is on measurement methods described by standard ISO 7235 [6] and comparison of results obtained by this standard with analytical calculations with different approach. Mainly, this standard lacks any details how to accomplish such measurement of friction losses. Investigation of such procedure is the subject of presented paper, where three possible ways hot to executed measurement of silencers are compared.

In the presented article is firstly described the methods of measurement with the test track, with the description of calculation for losses by standard and alternative method. Above mentioned is linked with the description of measurement method with characterization of used samples. Then the measured results are described, followed by discussion. Article is wrapped up by conclusion of used methods and samples.

2 Methods

There is a possibility to measure minor loss coefficient of any equipment determined for installation inside a duct. For this measurements is used multiple-nozzle chamber to resolve flow rate through the duct configuration. There is taping mount on ducts for measurement of static pressure before and after surveilled object. Such measurements and consequential calculations are in scope of this article. Firstly, duct track will be covered followed by description of two options for determination of minor loss coefficient. At first by ISO 7235 [6] and subsequently by hydraulic

Figure 1. Controlling board for duct tract

[a]Corresponding author sehnalek@fai.utb.cz

 DOI: 10.1051/matecconf/20167601011

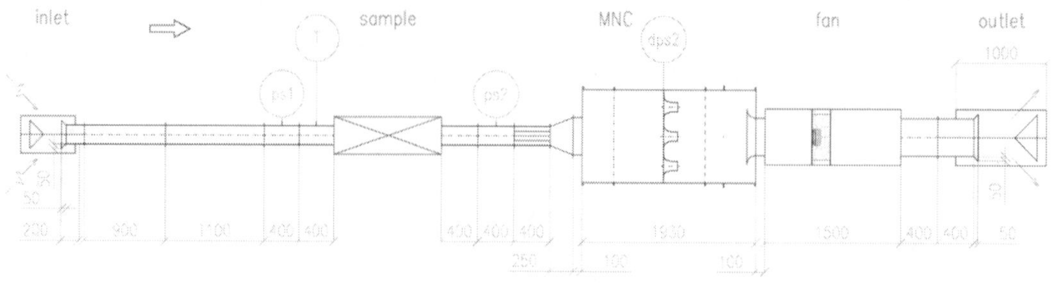

Figure 2. Track for measurement of friction loss coefficient

equation. At the end of this section will be a brief description of silencers which was used as samples.

2.1 Fan track

There are two available dimensions for the track. The diameters are 200*mm* and 400*mm*. For each dimension there are available several type of duct which could be connected with each other. This function lead to many variations for measurements. At the track could be done measurements of fan performance curve, loss coefficient, acoustic parameters, leakage and other measurements. All components of track are made in accordance with International standard ISO 5801. Controlling system of track is handled by PLC with touch panel including visualization. All measured data are periodically saved to local FTP server in form of CSV file. Whole controlling board is depicted on Figure 1. On the left could be seen frequency converters for fans, next to it is buttons for switching circuit breaker, then is touch panel with visualization for setting experiment and on the right is computer unit. For purpose of measurement was used an automated excel sheet, where the manually loaded data and all calculations are ensued by graphical output. The data collection is started after two minutes phase within is stabilized conditions and are collected for one minute every half second. This means that for each point were collected 120 values which are averaged afterwards.

Measurement track is depicted in Figure 2. The whole length without the sample is more than 9*m* long. It consist of inlet, ducts, sample, ducts, straightener, size extension, multiple-nozzle chamber (MNC), fan, duct and outlet. Ducts before MNC are of diameter 200*mm*, tract after MNC are of dimension 400*mm*.

2.2 Minor loss coefficient by CSN EN ISO 7235

In the following text will be described method to measure minor loss coefficient by international standard ISO 7235. [6] This norm is mainly used for duct silencers and describes the measuring of sound attenuation as well as the measurement of minor loss coefficient. Evaluation of friction coefficient is done by subtracting the pressure difference at substituted duct from static pressure difference of silencer. All computational steps are described by following equations.

$$\Delta p_{tot} = p_{s1(I)} - p_{s1(II)} \tag{1}$$

Where is			
	Δp_{tot}	total pressure	[Pa]
	$p_{s1(I)}$	pressure drop at measured device	[Pa]
	$p_{s1(II)}$	pressure drop of substituted duct	[Pa]

The value $p_{s1(I)}$ is the difference of static pressure between the measured sample. The value $p_{s1(II)}$ is same as before only performed on substituted duct. There is also included measurement between static pressure before sample and atmospheric pressure $p_{s1(a)}$ only for graphical representation of results. In the following equations 2, 3 can be seen how to calculate dynamic pressure and determine density of inlet air.

$$p_d = \frac{\varrho_{in}}{2} v^2 = \frac{\varrho_{in}}{2}\left(\frac{q_v}{A}\right)^2 \tag{2}$$

Where is			
	p_d	inlet dynamic pressure	[Pa]
	v	flow velocity	$[\frac{m}{s}]$
	A	area at the point of measurement of static pressure	[m]
	ϱ_{in}	density of inlet air	$[\frac{kg}{m^3}]$
	q_v	volumetric flow rate	$[\frac{m^3}{s}]$

$$\varrho_{in} = \frac{p_{s1} + p_a}{R(\theta_{in} + 273)} \tag{3}$$

Where is			
	R	gas constant	$287[\frac{N \cdot m}{kg \cdot K}]$
	θ_{in}	temperature of air before sample	$[°C]$

The coefficient of the total pressure loss ξ averaging over a range of flow rate is calculated from the equation (4).

$$\xi_{iso} = \frac{\Delta p_{tot}}{p_d} = \frac{\Delta p_{tot}}{\frac{\varrho}{2}\left(\frac{qv}{A}\right)^2} \tag{4}$$

Where is			
	ξ_{iso}	minor loss coefficient by ISO 7235	[-]
	A	area of duct	$[m^2]$

Mean loss coefficient is then calculated from equation (5).

$$\xi_{iso,m} = \frac{1}{N}\sum_{j=1}^{N}\frac{p_{s1(I)j}}{p_{dj}} - \frac{1}{M}\sum_{k=1}^{M}\frac{p_{s1(II)k}}{p_{dk}} \quad (5)$$

Where is	N	number of measured points of silencer	[-]
	M	number of measured points of substitution	[-]

2.3 Minor loss coefficient from Bernoulli equation

Other option could be the determination of ξ from energy equation which is summarized in (6), which is known also as Bernoulli Equation.

$$p_1 + \frac{\rho v_1^2}{2} + h_1\rho g = p_2 + \frac{\rho v_2^2}{2} + h_2\rho g + \Delta p_{loss} \quad (6)$$

Where is	p	static pressure	[Pa]
	h	elevation height	[m]
	g	acceleration of gravity	[$\frac{m}{s^2}$]
	Δp_{loss}	pressure loss	[Pa]

The focus is now on Δp_{loss} which is specified by equation (7).

$$\Delta p_{loss} = \Delta p_\lambda + \Delta p_\xi \quad (7)$$

Where is	Δp_λ	major loss	[Pa]
	Δp_ξ	minor loss	[Pa]

The equation (8) summarizes the Darcy-Weisbach Equation for calculation of major loss and in equation (9) is noted the calculation of minor loss .

$$\Delta p_\lambda = \lambda\frac{l}{d}p_d = \lambda\frac{l}{d}\frac{\rho}{2}v^2 = \lambda\frac{l}{d}\frac{\rho}{2}\left(\frac{q_V}{A}\right)^2 \quad (8)$$

Where is	λ	friction coefficient	[-]
	l	length of the duct	[m]
	d	hydraulic diameter of duct	[m]
	p_d	dynamic pressure	[Pa]

Minor loss coefficient also, known as friction coefficient, is dependent only on Reynolds number for laminar flow. For turbulent flow matters the friction coefficient function of Reynold number as well as of roughness of the duct. In 1937 Colebrook and White presented experiment of friction coefficient in roughness duct and established Colebrook-White formula [7]. There are at least three implicit formulas known by today literature. This article will present only best known of them; thus authors of this article compared results with all of implicit equations and there have been negligible aberration in results. Used equation is formulated in (10) which presented Collebrook in 1939.[3][8] There have been many attempts to provide explicit form in the past. Mainly because iterative process of implicit equation was complicated in time where there haven't been calculators. It would be possible to use so called Moody chart, which was laid out by prof Moody in 1944 as estimation from Colebrook-White formula. This chart made it easy to estimate friction coefficient and was extensively used by engineers for more than half century. [2][8] This changed with arrival of electronic chips and computers where was no problem to use iterative process. [8]

$$\Delta p_\xi = \xi_{be}p_d = \xi_{be}\frac{\rho}{2}v^2 = \xi_{be}\frac{\rho}{2}\left(\frac{q_V}{A}\right)^2 \quad (9)$$

Where is	ξ_{be}	minor loss coefficient by Bernoulli equation	[-]

$$\frac{1}{\sqrt{\lambda}} = -2\log\left(\frac{2,51}{Re\sqrt{\lambda}} + \frac{\varepsilon}{3,7}\right) \quad (10)$$

Where is	Re	Reynolds number	[-]
	ε	Roughness coefficient of duct	[m]

So called Reynold number was introduced in 1883 by Osborne Reynolds and it is transcribed in (11). As Reynolds number came to known by usage of Sommerfeld and Prandtl at the beginning of the last century. [1][5]

$$Re = \frac{vd}{\nu} = \frac{\rho vd}{\mu} \quad (11)$$

Where is	ν	kinematic viscosity of the fluid	[$\frac{m^2}{s}$]
	μ	dynamic viscosity of the fluid	[$\frac{Ns}{m^2}$]

From above equation (7) could be determined minor loss coefficient ξ_{be} by simple mathematical extraction and it is equal to (12). Also (13) could be used, particularly because there is unknown roughness coefficient for the silencers so λ should be neglected.

$$\xi_{be,\lambda} = \frac{2\Delta p_{loss}}{\rho v^2} - \lambda\frac{l}{d} \quad (12)$$

$$\xi_{be} = \frac{2\Delta p_{loss}}{\rho v^2} \quad (13)$$

2.4 Measurement practice

Measurement was performed in accordance with ISO 7235 and flow determination ISO 5801. [6][9] In the standards there is specified tapping to obtain average static pressure. Before tapping should be straight duct in length at least $5d$ or two meters long, depends which value is higher. It is also stated, that position of tapping should be $1,5d$ from entrance to tested object as well as at exit from it. Measurement of temperature inside the duct is specified as $2d$ in front of the tested specimen. [6]

In standard ISO 7235 is not specified method of reduction of flow, nor is stated if measurement should be done in-front or behind the fan. So in this articlethe measurement was performed at inlet side of fan, outlet side will be subject of further interest. Due to the nature of measurement tract it was possible to perceived three types of flow reduction. Description of those three category and naming is as follows:

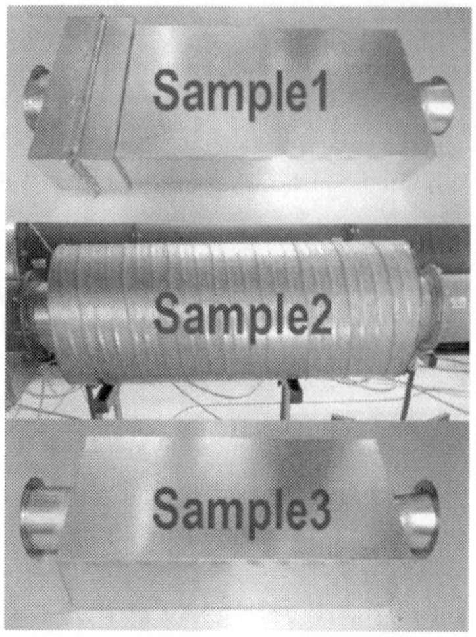

Figure 3. Silencers used as samples

- **InRedu** - Reduction of flow and static pressure is done by throttling at inlet duct.
- **OutRedu** - Reduction of flow and static pressure is done by throttling at outlet duct. Decreasing of flow was done based on FanRedu values of flow for comparison of results.
- **FanRedu** - Reduction of flow and static pressure is done by decreasing power of ventilator (this method could be persecuted from 100% to 20% of ventilator power, where selected steps for fan was by 10%).

2.5 Silencer specimens

Measurement was done on three types of silencers and they can be seen in Figure 3. Description of those samples is as follows:

- **Sample1** - This silencer is most complicated one, it has square outside shape with round inside silencing part. Its outlet is made from 9 small connections of diameter $80mm$. For purpose of measurement was created reduction chamber with $0,2m$ diameter outlet to fit to the measurement tract. The whole length is $1,45m$ and outer dimensions are $250x500mm$.
- **Sample2** - This silencer is round with centre body. Its length is $1,2m$ and outer diameter is $0,4m$.
- **Sample3** - The last silencer is same as first one, but outlet part with 9 connections is removed and it is directly connected to $0,2m$ fitting. The length is in this case $1,3m$.

3 Results

The following section contains results and findings during the performed measurements. Firstly will be mentioned method InRedu and its results. This will be forwarded with results of OutRedu and FanRedu methods for all samples.

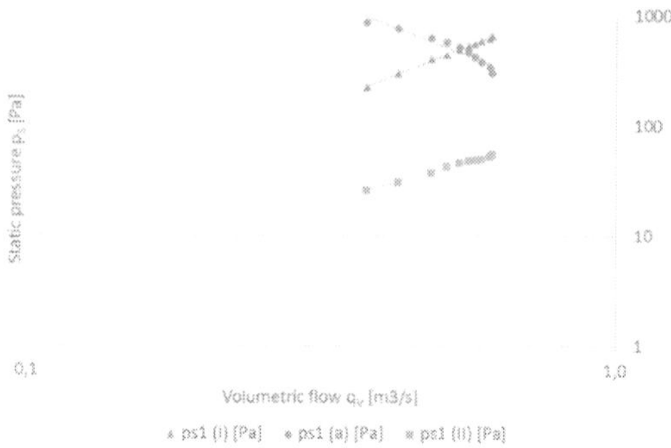

Figure 4. Log-log plot of inlet reduction for Sample1

All the presented graphs are in log-log scale. This section will conclude with comparison of two types of calculation which was described in Methods section and introduction to option for backward finding of roughness coefficient.

3.1 Results for InRedu method

This method was tested only on Sample1 and is depicted in Figure 4. The method could be hardly used for appropriate presentation of results, nevertheless the friction coefficient was in the end similar as in other methods which will be presented.

3.2 Results forOutRedu and FanRedu methods

Pressure drop and flow through the duct with method OutRedu and FanRedu are depicted in Figures 5, 6 and 7. Difficulty during measurement happened when there was a necessity to measure substituted duct with the FanRedu method. When was executed measurement of substituted duct it should proceed with same flow as sample which was at the beginning always around 60% with inequivalent steps. Reason of this is due to steep losses of supplementary duct. This is reflected by the substituted curve, which has less points because fan can not go less than 20% of power. From the figures could be seen that both methods are similar and could be commuted. This fact is also digested in Table 1, where could be seen differences in methods by friction coefficient. Most significant difference in methods was $\xi = 0,054$ and occurred with Sample2, which is careless amount.

Table 1. Comparison of methods with calculation by CSN

Sample	Method	$\xi_{csn}[-]$	diff [−]
Sample1	OutRedu	2,851	0,044
	FanRedu	2,808	
Sample2	OutRedu	2,598	0,054
	FanRedu	2,544	
Sample3	OutRedu	0,924	0,014
	FanRedu	0,911	

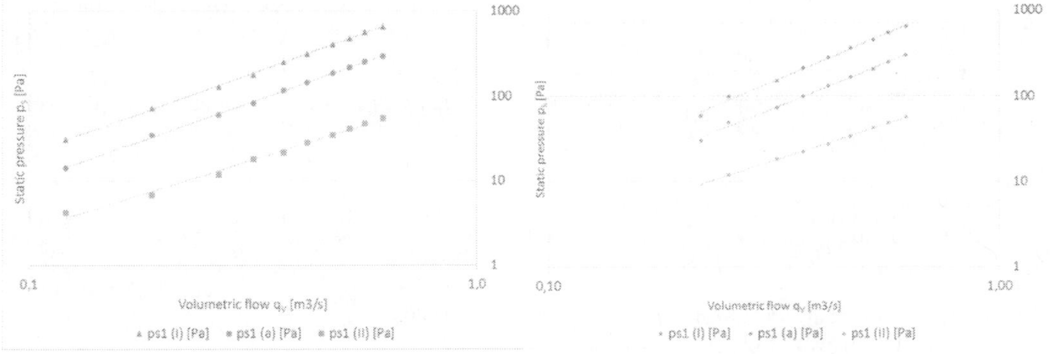

(a) OutRedu **(b)** FanRedu

Figure 5. Log–log plots for Sample1

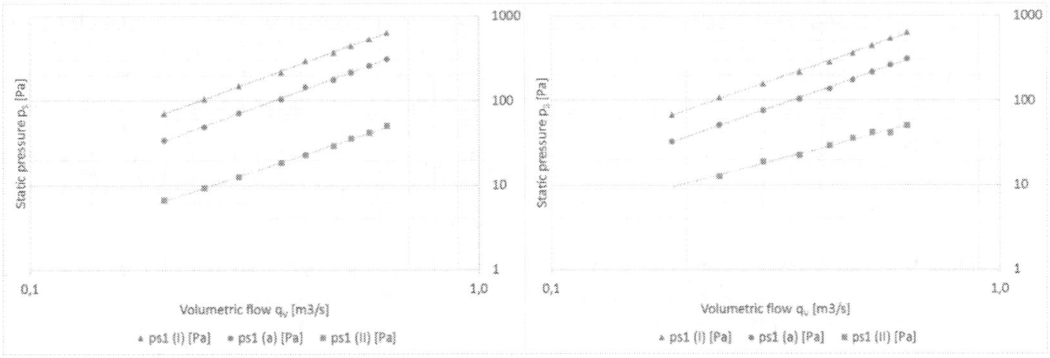

(a) OutRedu **(b)** FanRedu

Figure 6. Log–log plots for Sample2

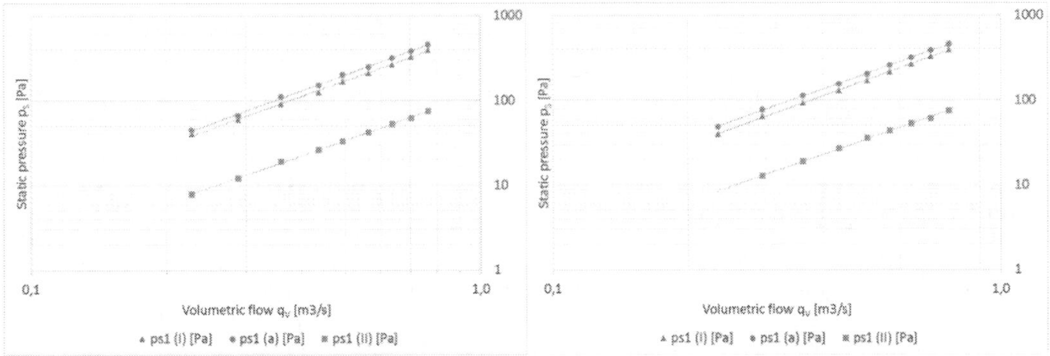

(a) OutRedu **(b)** FanRedu

Figure 7. Log–log plots for Sample3

From the Table 2 could be seen that all flows were in turbulent region based on Reynolds numbers.

Results concerning calculation of ξ_{be} are written in Table 3, where the most significant difference with Sample1

Table 2. Minimal and maximal Reynolds number for each sample and method

Sample	Method	Re min [−]	Re max [−]
Sample1	OutRedu	49 730	254 576
	FanRedu	89 678	257 955
Sample2	OutRedu	81 719	258 050
	FanRedu	76 512	258 035
Sample3	OutRedu	93 414	316 163
	FanRedu	95 922	317 042

is evident. The inequality with standard method is due to fact that method measured by subtracting pressure with substituted duct could include inaccuracy.

Table 3. Comparison of methods with calculation by BE

Sample	Method	$\xi_{be}[-]$	diff [−]
Sample1	OutRedu	3,099	0,117
	FanRedu	3,216	
Sample2	OutRedu	2,834	0,042
	FanRedu	2,876	
Sample3	OutRedu	1,154	0,007
	FanRedu	1,147	

In the Table 5 are compared two ways of calculation of ξ, namely equation (5) with (13). The difference is fluctuating around 0, 3. This diversity is mainly because in ξ_{csn} was taken total pressure subtracted by pressure of substituted duct as for opposition is taken only total pressure of sample for ξ_{be}.

There are significant differences of coefficients within the used method and samples. This is caused basically because there is difference in ξ calculated by both methods.

Table 4 summarize all friction loss coefficients. First line is used sample and method, thus S1-OR for Sample1 OutRedu method and so on. In some cases missing coefficients, this is due to nature of method where was low limit reached in different points. It is obvious that minor loss coefficient is independent on velocity inside the duct, this fact is valid only for velocity from 3 to $24\frac{m}{s}$. Thus in this range was execute the measurements. It would be interesting to accomplish measurement with velocity under the range achieved in this article.

Table 4. Match of loss coefficient for samples by method

S1-OR	S1-FR	S2-OR	S2-FR	S2-OR	S3-FR
2,6570	2,5516	2,5070	2,5112	0,8982	0,8987
2,7585	2,5658	2,5255	2,5225	0,9055	0,9030
2,7043	2,4402	2,5405	2,4592	0,8845	0,8917
2,7276	2,5009	2,5066	2,4307	0,8919	0,8848
2,7509	2,4317	2,7151	2,4446	0,9330	0,8731
2,8609	2,3580	2,5236	2,5303	0,8695	0,8971
2,7070	2,1497	2,7128	2,6119	0,9272	0,9442
2,7780	2,3227	2,6556	2,8450	0,9530	0,9925
3,1028	-	2,6998	-	1,0556	-
3,0284	-	-	-	-	-

Table 5. Comparison between option CSN and BE

Sample	Method	$\xi_{csn}[-]$	$\xi_{be}[-]$	diff [−]
Sample1	OutRedu	2,851	3,099	0,248
	FanRedu	2,808	3,216	0,409
Sample2	OutRedu	2,598	2,834	0,236
	FanRedu	2,544	2,876	0,332
Sample3	OutRedu	0,924	1,154	0,230
	FanRedu	0,911	1,147	0,236

4 Conclusion

In the article were mentioned three ways of measurement of silencers at the suction part. Comparison of friction coefficient calculation by standard ISO 7235. There were compared three types of measurement with three types of different silencers. Each silencer had diverse construction thus results have broad meaning. In the future should be done measurement on outlet side of the duct and make adequate practice for the effective outcome of measurement.

Acknowledgements

This work was supported by the Ministry of Education, Youth and Sports of the Czech Republic within the National Sustainability Programme project No. LO1303 (MSMT-7778/2014) and also by the Internal Grant Agency of Tomas Bata University in Zlin under the project No. IGA/CebiaTech/2016/001.

References

[1] O. Reynolds, Proceedings of the Royal Society of London **35**, 24 (1883)
[2] L.F. Moody, Transaction of the A.S.M.E. **66**, 14 (1944)
[3] C.F. Colebrook, Journal of the Insitution of Civil Engineers **11**, 29 (1939)
[4] T. Von Kármán, L. Edson, *The Wind and Beyond: Theodore Von Kármán, Pioneer in Aviation and Pathfinder in Space* (Little, Brown, 1967)
[5] P.A. Davidson, Y. Kaneda, K. Moffatt, K.R. Sreenivasan, *A voyage through turbulence* (Cambridge University Press, 2011)
[6] CSN EN ISO 7235, Standard, Czech office for standards metrology and testing, Prague, CZ (2010)
[7] C.F. Colebrook, C.M. White, Proceedings of the Royal Society of London A: Mathematical, Physical and Engineering Sciences **161**, 15 (1937)
[8] S. Genić, I. Arandjelović, P. Kolendić, M. Jarić, N. Budimir, V. Genić, FME Transactions **39**, 4 (2011)
[9] CSN EN ISO 5801, Standard, Czech office for standards metrology and testing, Prague, CZ (2009)

MATEC Web of Conferences **76**, 01012 (2016) DOI: 10.1051/matecconf/20167601012
CSCC 2016

Operations on Multiple Transition Faults without Enumeration

Theodoros Toulas[1,a] and Spyros Tragoudas[2]

[1]*Synopsys Inc, Mountain View, USA*
[2]*Southern Illinois University, Carbondale, USA*

Abstract. The multiple transition fault model has been used to represent alternative defective gate combinations in the circuit. However, the number of faults is very large even of modest size circuits and therefore the defective configuration may not be considered. It is shown that multiple transition faults can be stored compactly in Binary Decision Diagrams. Furthermore, important operations for identifying the location of failures are implemented without fault enumeration. Experimental results on some of the largest ISCAS'85, ISCAS'89, and ITC'99 benchmarks demonstrate the scalability of the proposed method.

1 Introduction

With the technology moving to nanometer regime, the task of testing and diagnosing failures in integrated circuits (ICs) has become very demanding. Reductions on the area of the chip combined with increase in the number of transistors can cause delay defects.

The process of identifying the location of failures in an IC is guided by a set of possible fault sites [1]. This process is guided by a set of possible fault sites in the IC called suspects. Methods like [2]-[3] are restricted to a single defect location. This is very unlikely to be the case in deep submicron.

The path delay fault model is used to delay defects in deep submicron since it allows for many small delay defects to be distributed along a failing path [4]-[5]. Although effective in testing, its use in identifying the defective locations is limited [6]-[8]. The transition fault model [9] is used, but the authors assume that only one fault is being generated at each node. This is rarely the case in deep submicron. This may turn out to be a restriction that may misguide the identification of the location of failures.

This paper uses the multiple transition fault model (MTF) along sensitized paths to represent alternative defective gate combinations in the circuit. The number of MTFs is much higher than the number of PDFs. Transition fault based approaches in [10]-[11] do not scale well to the complexity of this model.

Fault implicit algorithms on appropriate data structure are used in this paper, to cope with the such scalability challenges. In this paper, we use the term test vector to denote a pair of input test patterns. The main contributions of this paper are:

1. Algorithms to compute and store in a non-fault enumeratively manner the number of MTFs that are excited by a bad vector (the initial suspect set) as well as by a set of good vectors (the good set).
2. Algorithms to prune the suspect set using the good set and guide the identification of defective locations.
3. A thorough experimental evaluation to demonstrate the impact of the proposed method.

This paper is organized as follows. Section 2 gives an overview of the proposed method. Section 3 describes the proposed method. Section 4 gives experimental results and finally Section 5 concludes.

2 Overview of the proposed method

We define the hit rate as the frequency of a gate in the MTFs that are sensitized by a bad vector (also called the bad set). The proposed tool will produce the hit rate of all gates. Gates with higher hit rates are most likely to have a defect and the silicon debugger should first examine those gates.

Consider the circuit in Figure 1. For simplicity in the exposition, we assume that all nodes have unit delay. Furthermore, we assume that the total delay defect observed (along any path) is at most one unit. Therefore, we assume that defective nodes reside along paths with the longest number of nodes.

In this example there are no inverting nodes, and therefore, all transition faults are rising. For brevity, in the following we do not explicitly indicate that the faults are rising. In Figure 1, the bad vector T1 = {10100,11101} sensitizes rising transitions along paths P1 = {1-5-7-10-12} and P2 = {4-6-9-11-12}. MTFs occur along these paths and a delay of unit 1 is observed at gate 12. A possible MTF is {1,5}, where each number indicates the gate id. This MTF may occur because both gates belong to the same path and the sum of potential

[a] theodoros.toulas@synopsys.com

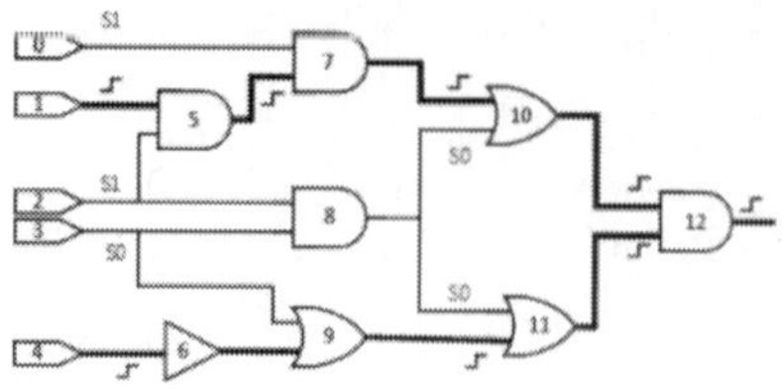

Figure 1. A long sensitized pdf along which MTFs are generated.

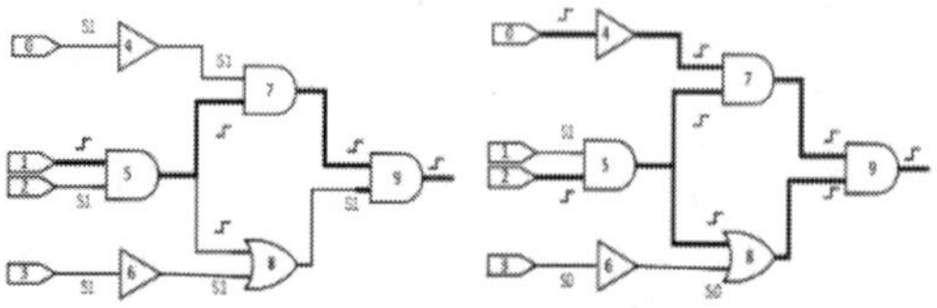

(a) Bad Vector (b) Good Vector

Figure 2. Pruning MTFs using good vectors.

defects associated to these gates may sum up to 1 unit. Another MTF is {1,4,5,7,9,10}. In this MTF possible delays on nodes 4 and 9 (which are on the same path) may sum up to 1 unit and possible delays on nodes {1,5,7,10} (which are on another path) may also sum up to 1 unit of defect.

In this example, MTF {1,4} may occur if one unit of defect is lumped on gate 1 and also one unit of defect is on gate 4. (Two gates are in different paths). The total number of MTF in this example is 511. In general, the total number of MTFs grows super-exponentially to the number of gates on the sensitized PDFs. It is a huge number even for a small number of paths. This paper presents algorithms that utilize the data structure in [12]. It is shown that is capable of storing very compactly a huge number of MTFs.

In Figure 1, the rising transitions faults at gates 1,4,5,6,7,9,10,11 and 12 have 256 hit rate in the total MTF initial suspect set $MTF_{initial}$. Therefore, there is no indication on which gate should be examined first for defects. The process may be assisted by good vectors. We will show a methodology on how to remove MTF from a suspect set and change the hit rate of fault sites in $MTF_{initial}$.

The example in Figure 2 illustrates the pruning process. The bad vector T_{bad} = {1011, 1111} sensitizes failing path Pf (1-5-7-9). Figure 2(b) shows a good vector T_{good} = {0100, 1110} that sensitizes paths P1 = {0-4-7-9}, P2 = {2-5-7-9} and P3 = {2-5-8-9}.

We define set $MTF_{initial}$ to be the union of all possible suspect MTFs. In the example of Fig 2 $MTF_{initial}$ = {{7}, {5}, {5,7}, {4}, {4,7}, {4,5}, {4,5,7}, {1}, {1,7}, {1,5}, {1,5,7}, {1,4}, {1,4,7}, {1,4,5}, {1,4,5,7}}. Each gate has same number of appearances in the $MTF_{initial}$.

The good vector sensitizes two long PDFs. Therefore, we include all possible MTF combinations along these PDFs. The union of all MTFs generated from the good vector in Figure 2(b) is the set MTF_{good}. Set MTF_{good} = {{0}, {4}, {0,4}, {2}, {5}, {2,5}, {0,2}, {0,5}, {0,2,5}, {2,4}, {4,5}, {2,4,5}, {0,2,4}, {0,4}, {0,2,4,5}, {2,8}, {5,8}, {2,5,8}, {0,7}, {4,7}, {0,4,7}, {2,7}, {5,7}, {2,5,7}, {0,2,7}, {0,5,7}, {0,2,5,7}, {2,4,7}, {4,5,7}, {2,4,5,7}, {0,2,4,7}, {0,4,7}), {0,2,4,5,7}, {7}, {0,8}, {4,8},{0,4,8}, {0,2,8}, {0,5,8}, {0,2,5,8}, {2,4,8}, {4,5,8}, {2,4,5,8}, {0,2,4,8}, {0,4,8}, {0,2,4,5,8}, {0,7,8}, {4,7,8}, {0,4,7,8}, {2,7,8}, {5,7,8}, {2,5,7,8}, {0,2,7,8}, {0,5,7,8}, {0,2,5,7,8}, {2,4,7,8}, {4,5,7,8}, {2,4,5,7,8}, {0,2,4,7,8}, {0,4,7,8}, {0,2,4,5,7,8}, {7,8}, {8}, {0,8,9}, {4,8,9}, {0,4,8,9}, {2,9}, {5,9}, {2,5,9}, {0,2,8,9}, {0,5,8,9}, {0,2,5,8,9}, {2,4,8,9}, {4,5,8,9}, {2,4,5,8,9}, {0,2,4,8,9}, {0,4,8,9}, {0,2,4,5,8,9}, {0,7,8,9}, {4,7,8,9}, {0,4,7,8,9}, {2,7,8,9}, {5,7,8,9}, {2,5,7,8,9}, {0,2,7,8,9}, {0,5,7,8,9}, {0,2,5,7,8,9}, {2,4,7,8,9}, {4,5,7,8,9}, {2,4,5,7,8,9}, {0,2,4,7,8,9}, {0,4,7,8,9}, {0,2,4,5,7,8,9}, {7,8,9}, {8,9}, {9}}.

We prune from the $MTF_{initial}$ all the MTFs that are also present in the MTF_{good}. In that way we also modify the number of gate hit rate in the set $MTF_{initial}$. The initial suspect set $MTF_{initial}$ had 15 MTFs. After pruning the suspect set deduced to MTF_{final} = {{1}, {1,7}, {1,5}, {1,5,7}, {1,4}, {1,4,7}, {1,4,5}, {1,4,5,7}} and the total number of MTFs reduced from 15 to 8. The hit rate of gate 1 is four, which is the highest frequency. The proposed tool guides silicon debug by considering this fault site first.

3 Generation, storage and manipulation of faults without enumeration

The advantage of the deductive method [16] is that all sensitized MTF by a single test vector, can be generated with a single topological traversal of the circuit netlist. Figure 3 shows an example of MTF generation using the deductive method. Let a test vector be T = {01, 11}. At each gate, all possible MTF that may occur until that gate are stored in ZBDD data structure [12]-[14].

Our method constructs two main MTF sets. One set is generated for the good set and one for the bad set. For the bad set we generate MTF along robust and non-robust PDFs. For the good set only long robust and validatable non-robust PDFs are considered [5]. The generation rules at each gate are the same for bad and good sets. A gate it is marked if it belongs to an appropriate PDF. The MTF generation takes into consideration only marked gates.

MTFs are generated non-enumeratively using basic operations in ZBDDs. Table 1 shows some basic ZBDDs operations being used in our approach. (More details about ZBDDs operators can be found in [12] and [13].) We represent the MTFs as combinational sets in the ZBDD. In Figure 4 we give an example of the representation of the MTFs on the sensitized circuit path of Figure 4(a) to its ZBDD shown in Figure 4(b). The ZBDD is a directed acyclic graph. Node 0 in Figure 4(b) is called its root. Nodes with the same label correspond to the same gate. There exist two terminal nodes, terminal 1 and terminal 0. In this example, there is only one sensitized PDF by test vector T = {01101, 11101}. The rising MTFs are stored in a ZBDD. Each MTF is a ZBDD path from root node 0 to terminal node 1. The doted lines indicate the absence of that particular gate in the MTF. For example, ZBDD path (solid line) 0-5-7-8 represent the MTF {0,5,7,8} and ZBDD path ¯0-5-7-¯8 (where ¯ is the doted line) represents MTF {5,7}.

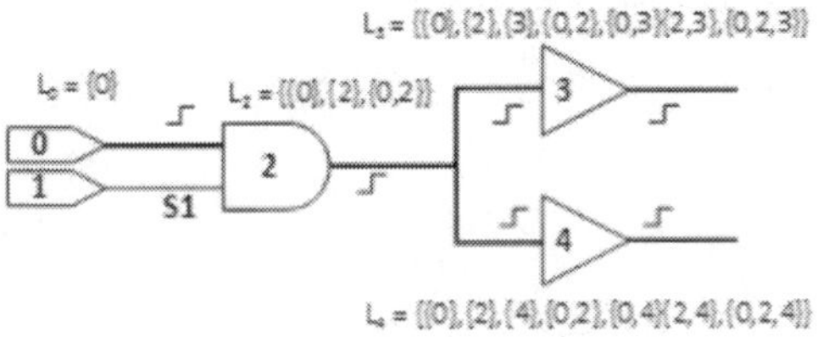

Figure 3. List of multiple transition faults in deductive method

Table 1. Basic ZBDD Operations

Operation	Symbol	Description
Union (A, B)	A U B	The union operation
Prod (A, B)	A ∩ B	The unate product operation
Subset (A, B)	A C B	The subset operation
Diff (A, B)	A - B	The set difference operation

The generation of the MTF obeys the rules showed in Table 2 for the case of an AND gate. (We generate tables for all gates in the same manner.) At each simulation test vector T, we traverse the circuit in a topological manner. For each gate, rules from Table 2 are used to generate an MTF. Let us assume a 2-input AND gate whose inputs are labeled a, b and its outputs labeled c. When addressing the gate MTF that have propagated until inputs a and b are stored explicitly in a ZBDD. The table shows how to generate the MTFs at output c. They are generated in a non-fault enumerative manner using the operators in Table 1, and are kept as list MTF_C in the ZBDD.

We illustrate the method circuit shown in Figure 5. Let test set T consists of three test vectors T = {T1, T2, T3}. Assume that vector T1 = {1010, 1000} is a bad vector and PDF P1 = {2-6-8-9-10} is sensitized as shown in Figure 5(a). For brevity, we do not list the type of the transition at each MTF but we list the gate id. For the bad vector T1 the marked gates are 2, 6, 8, 9, 10. Therefore the initial suspect set $MTF_{initial}$ = {{2}, {8}, {2,8}, {9}, {2,9}, {8,9}, {2,8,9}, {10}, {2,10}, {8,10}, {2,8,10}, {9,10}, {2,9,10}, {8,9,10}, {2,8,9,10}, {6}, {{2,6}, {6,8}, {2,6,8}, {6,9}, {2,6,9}, {6,8,9}, {2,6,8,9}, {6,10}, {2,6,10}, {6,8,10}, {2,6,8,10}, {6,9,10}, {2,6,9,10}, {6,8,9,10}, {2,6,8,9,10}}.

Let test T2 and T3 be the good sets. Test vectors T2 = {1011, 0010} and T3 = {1011, 1110} sensitize PDFs P2 = {3-8-9-10} and P3 = {1-5-9-10}, respectively.

PDF P1 is sensitized robustly [15]-[16], and therefore has no defect. Gates 3, 8, 9, 10 are marked. The MTF set RMTF10 contains all the generated MTFs which guaranteed to be good (no defect). Set RMTF10 = {{3}, {8}, {3,8}, {9}, {3,9}, {8,9}, {3,8,9}, {10}, {3,10}, {8,10}, {3,8,10}, {9,10}, {3,9,10}, {8,9,10}, {3,8,9,10}}.

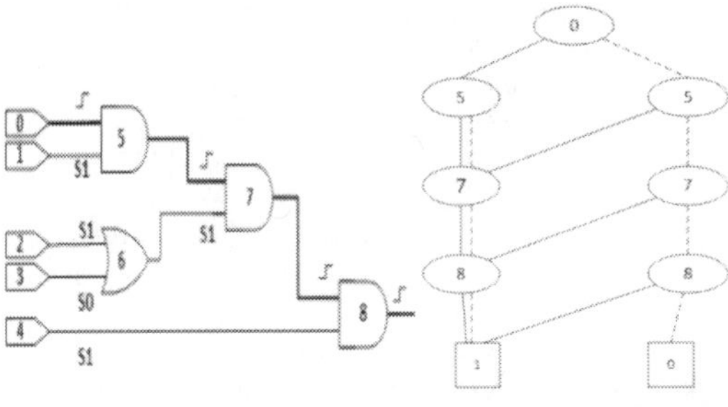

(a) A sensitized path delay fault (b) The MTF in ZBDD

Figure 4. MTF along a sensitized path stored in a ZBDD.

Table 2. Generating a list of MTF at the output of an AND gate using lists of MTF at its inputs

INPUTS		**OUTPUT**	**FAULT LIST**
a	b	c	MTF_C
0/1 or 1/0	S1	0/1 or 1/0	MTFa U c U (MTFa * c)
S1	0/1 or 1/0	0/1 or 1/0	MTFb U c U (MTFb * c)
0/1 or 1/0	1/0 or 0/1	1/0	MTFa U MTFLb U c U (MTFa * c U MTFb * U MTFa * MTFb)
0/1	0/1	0/1	MTFa U MTFb U c U (MTFa * c U MTFb * c U MTFa * MTFb)
1/0	1/0	1/0	MTFa * MTFb U c U ((MTFa * MTFb) * c)

Test vector T3 sensitizes a non-robust PDF P3 [15], [16]. We cannot guarantee that this PDF has no defect. However, P2 and P3 together they form a VNR test [5] and therefore, it is guaranteed that P3 has no defect. Gates 1, 3, 5, 8, 9, 10 are marked. MTF set RMTF10 contains all MTFs generated until that gate. RMTF10 = { {3}, {8}, {3,8}, {9}, {3,9}, {8,9}, {3,8,9}, {1}, {5}, {1,5}, {9}, {1,9}, {1,9}, {1,5,9}, {1,3}, {1,8}, {1,3,8}, {1,9}, {1,3,9}, {1,8,9}, {1,3,8,9}, {3,5}, {8,5}, {3,5,8}, {5,9}, {3,5,9}, {5,8,9}, {3,5,8,9}, {1,3,5}, {1,5,8}, {1,3,5,8}, {1,5,9}, {1,3,5,9}, {1,5,8,9}, {1,3,5,8,9}, {1,3}, {1,8}, {1,3,8}, {1,9}, {1,3,9}, {1,8,9}, {1,3,8,9},{1,3,5,8,9}, {10}, {3,10}, {8,10}, {3,8,10}, {9,10}, {3,9,10}, {8,9,10}, {3,8,9,10}, {1,10}, {5,10}, {1,5,10}, {9,10}, {1,9,10}, {1,9,10}, {1,5,9,10}, {1,3,10}, {1,8,10}, {1,3,8,10}, {1,9,10}, {1,3,9,10}, {1,8,9,10}, {1,3,8,9,10}, {3,5,10}, {5,8,10}, {3,5,8,10}, {5,9,10}, {3,5,9,10}, {5,8,9,10}, {3,5,8,9,10}, {1,3,5,10}, {1,5,8,10}, {1,3,5,8,10}, {1,5,9,10}, {1,3,5,9,10}, {1,5,8,9,10}, {1,3,5,8,9,10}, {1,3,10}, {1,8,10}, {1,3,8,10}, {1,9,10}, {1,3,9,10}, {1,8,9,10},{1,3,8,9,10}, {1,3,5,8,9,10}}. The good set MTF_{good} is the union of all MTFs generated by robust and VNR tests. Therefore, MTF_{good} = {VMTF10 U RMTF10}.

Once both MTFs for bad and good tests are generated, a simple set difference ZBDD operation takes place. Namely, $MTF_{final} = MTF_{initial} - MTF_{good}$. With this operation the initial suspect set $MTF_{initial}$ reduces to MTF set MTF_{final} = {{2}, {2,8}, {9}, {2,9}, {2,8,9}, {2,10}, {2,8,10}, {2,9,10}, {2,8,9,10}, {6}, {{2,6}, {6,8}, {2,6,8}, {6,9}, {2,6,9}, {6,8,9}, {2,6,8,9}, {6,10}, {2,6,10}, {6,8,10}, {2,6,8,10}, {6,9,10}, {2,6,9,10}, {6,8,9,10}, {2,6,8,9,10} }. It contains all the possible defect sites for silicon debug.

For a single vector our method runs one traversal to generate all the possible MTFs. Moreover, simple ZBDD operations and algorithms, that are not described in this paper, can produce the transition fault sites with the highest ranking rate. The frequency of appearance of a gate inside the set MTF_{final} determines the order of inspecting during silicon debug.

The frequency of all gates can be identified by traversals on MTF_{final} [17]. The gate with the highest hit rate that is used for silicon debug.

4 Experimental results

We experimented on a Unix machine with 8 GB memory and 2.40 GHz. The algorithms were implemented in C++. The ISCAS '85, ISCAS '89 and ITC '99 benchmarks were used as the circuits under test. In our experimentation, we had 3 bad vectors and 40,000 good vectors, for each benchmark. All gates were assumed to have unit delay. It was asserted that the total delay defect did not exceed two units of delay, and, therefore, MTFs generated only along the longest and second longest paths in each benchmark.

Table 3 reports our experimental results. Column 2 shows the size of $MTF_{initial}$, i.e., the number of MTF sensitized by bad vectors. Column 3 reports the total number of good MTF, i.e., the size of MTF_{good} consisting of MTFs from robustly and validatable non-robustly sensitized PDFs by the 40.000 good test vectors.

Column 4 shows the reduction in the suspect set using set MTF_{good}. In benchmarks such as s38584 and s9234 the number of total MTFs was huge and we could not enumerate them. Therefore, data structures such as arrays could not be used to store them efficiently. However, our method uses the ZBDD data structure and stored all the MTFs. The results for benchmarks s38584 and s9234 show the effectiveness of ZBDD data structure. Column 5 shows the percentage reduction in the suspect set $MTF_{initial}$. Observe that the average reduction of the suspect set is 83.41%. In circuit c6288, the reduction is only 0,5% but the number of eliminated suspect MTFs is 1.030e+16, which is a huge number.

Columns 6 and 7 show the impact of the proposed approach in silicon debug. The numbers in the cells are the gate labels and the characters in parenthesis are the type of the transition ({r} for rising and {f} for failing). Column 6 reports for each benchmark the top two transition fault sites in order that appear more often in the set $MTF_{initial}$. Column 7 shows the same information for MTF_{final}. In bold fonts we list all gates that do not appear in column 6. The results show the impact of pruning for silicon debug.

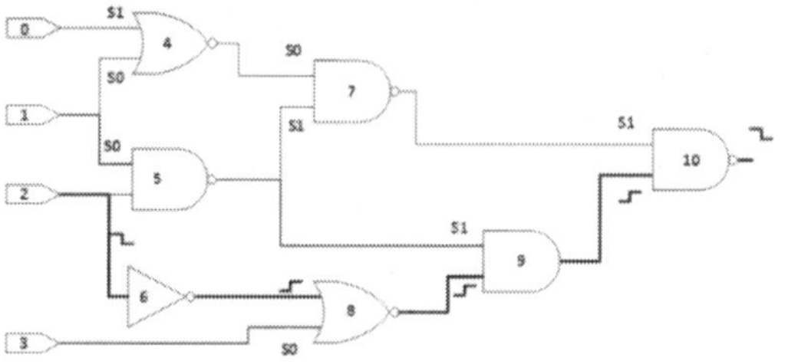

(a) The bad vector

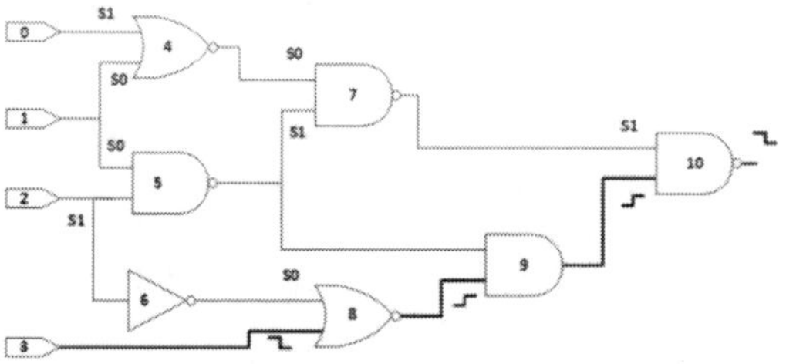

(b) The first good vector

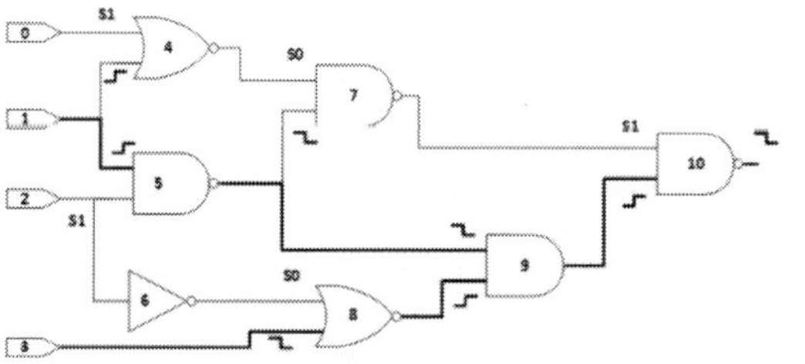

(c)The second good vector

Figure 5. Illustration of the proposed method with a bad vector and two good vectors

the transition ({r} for rising and {f} for failing). Column 6 reports for each benchmark the top two transition fault sites in order that appear more often in the set $MTF_{initial}$. Column 7 shows the same information for MTF_{final}. In bold fonts we list all gates that do not appear in column 6. The results show the impact of pruning for silicon debug.

Column 8 lists the total CPU time (in seconds) by the proposed method. Columns 2, 3 and 4 show the total number of MTFs generated. It is clearly shown that the approach is fault implicit.

5 Conclusion

A method to guide silicon debug for delay defects has been proposed in order to guide silicon debug for delay defects. The collection of suspect MTFs has been generated implicitly by considering appropriately sensitized path delay faults for the bad and the good vectors. A method to effectively prune the initial suspect collection of MTF faults has been proposed and its impact has been evaluated experimentally.

Table 3. Suspect Set Reduction and recommended defective

Ben/s	Number of MTF in $MTF_{initial}$	Number of MTF in MTF_{good}	Number of reduced Suspect MTF_{good}	(%) Reduction in suspect MTF	Top two hit rate gates before pruning	Top two hit rate gates after pruning	Time(sec)
c880	1.00664e+08	4.60744e+13	144	99.99	41(r),43(r)	20(r),**88(f)**	103.89
c3540	364190	4.58564e+25	987	99.72	13,62(r)	62(r),**152(f)**	1092.42
c5315	571305	2.02657e+21	7013	98.77	112(r),114(r)	**682(f),10(r)**	1420.58
c6288	1.89e+18	2.77873e+16	1.88e+18	0.54	16(r),11(r)	16(r),11(r)	7369.65
c7550	882760	1.24182e+26	25804	97.07	5(r),233(f)	**2728(f),640(f)**	2205.43
s1196	34138	2.689e+11	4600	86.52	5(r),4(r)	**18(r)**,4(r)	108.45
s1296	132649	3.34936e+13	203	99.84	26(f),27(f)	**553(f),579(f)**	84.26
s1493	640407	6.84848e+10	112	99.98	293(r),294(r)	**25(f),30(f)**	145.33
s1494	309201	1.85235e+11	785	99.74	10(r),17(r)	**9(r)**,10(r)	52.11
s3330	131427	1.64227e+16	8250	93.72	166(r),151(f)	166(r),**147(r)**	2952.35
s9234	6.2068e+15	3.29304e+40	5.16581e+15	16.77	25(r),1578(f)	**1638(r),1639(r)**	2788.71
s13207	3.868561e+17	7.82535e+36	3.2021e+20	17.22	1236(r),1273(r)	**8409(r),8410(r)**	9496.72
s38984	1.29549e+10	1.07208e+29	2.13368e+06	99.98	1759(f)1760(f)	**785(r),1599(r)**	18854.98
b09	420046	1.2011e+16	48283	88.50	4(f),3(f)	3(f),4(f)	338.57
b10	180520	1.97929e+06	32231	82.14	15(r),21(r)	21(r),15(r)	83.96
b11	1.05872e+06	1.54903e+13	886441	82.18	8(r),9(r)	**768(r),769(f)**	122.22
b13	207592	2.14798e+07	38929	81.24	80(r),81(r)	**95(f),84(r)**	120.30
b15	688366	3.45974e+08	389457	43.42	39(f),40(f)	**73(f),42(r)**	5571.10
b17	557434	1.70268e+11	262342	52.93	14088(r),14089(r)	**14199(f),14200(f)**	19612.10
b20	479130	5.04538e+14	54747	88.57	48(f),49(f)	**50(f),51(r)**	12897.27
b21	140898	2.26338e+16	16156	88.53	8343(r),20781(r)	**21020(r),20783(r)**	12928.26
Average				**83.41%**			

References

1. S. Venkataraman and S. B. Drummonds, POIROT: A logic fault diagnosis tool and its applications, in Proc. Int. Test Conf., (Oct. 2000), pp. (253 –262).
2. K. Yang and K.-T. Cheng, Timing-reasoning-based delay fault diagnosis, in Proc. Des. Autom. Test Eur., (Mar. 2006), **vol. 1**, pp. 418 –423.
3. Z. Wang, M. Marek-Sadowska, K. H. Tsai, and J. Rajski, "Delay-fault diagnosis using timing information,"IEEE Trans. Comput.-Aided Design Integr. Circuits Syst., **vol. 24**, no. 9, pp. 1315–1325), Sep. (2005)
4. P. Pant, Y. C. Hsu, S. K. Gupta, and A. Chatterjee, Path delay fault diagnosis in combinational circuits with implicit fault enumeration, IEEE Trans. Computer-Aided Design, **vol. 20**, pp. (1226–1235, Oct. 2001).
5. S. Padmanaban and S. Tragoudas, "An Implicit Path-Delay Fault Diagnosis Methodology," IEEE Trans. Computer-Aided Design Of Integrated Circuits, **Vol. 22,** No. 10, (Oct 2003)
6. A.M. Somashekar, S. Tragoudas, "Diagnosis of small delay defects arising due to manufacturing imperfections using path delay measurements," 14th International Symposium on Quality Electronic Design. pp.481–486, **4–6** (March 2013).
7. E.J Jang, J. Chung, and J.A. Abraham. Delay defect Diagnosis methodology using path delay measurements, In Proceedings of the 13th International Symposium on Integrated Circuits (ISIC), (2011)
8. V. J. Mehta,M. Marek-Sadowska, K. Tsai, J.Rajski, Timing-Aware Multiple-Delay-Fault Diagnosis, IEEE Trans. Computer-Aided Design,**vol. 28**, no. 2, Feb (2009)
9. J. A. Waicukauski, E. Lindbloom, B. Rosen, and V. Iyengar, Transition fault simulation, IEEE Des. Test. Comput., **vol. 4**, no. 2, pp. 32–38, (Apr. 1987).
10. J. B. Liu, A. Veneris, and S. Safarpour, "Diagnosing multiple transition faults in the absence of timing information," in Proc. 15th ACM Great Lakes Symp. VLSI, (2005), pp. 193–196.
11. Y. C. Lin, F. Lu, and K.-T. Cheng, "Multiple-fault diagnosis based on single-fault activation and single output observation," in Proc. Des. Autom. Test Eur., (Mar. 2006), pp. 1–6.
12. S. Padmanaban, M. Michael, and S. Tragoudas, "Exact path delay fault coverage with fundamental zero suppressed BDD operations," IEEE Trans. Computer- Aided Design, pp. 305 –316, (Mar. 2003)
13. S.-I. Minato, "Zero-suppressed BDD's for set manipulation in combinatorial problems," in Proc. Design Automation Conf., (1993), pp. 272 –277
14. S.-I. Minato, "Calculation of Unate Cube Set Algebra Using Zero-Suppressed BDDs," in Proc. Design Automation Conf., (1993), pp. 272–277
15. K. T. Cheng and H. C. Chen, "Classification and identification of nonrobust untestable path delay faults," IEEE Trans. Computer-Aided Design, **vol. 15**, pp. 845–853, (Aug. 1996)
16. Bushnell, M., Agrawal, Vishwani, "*Essentials of Electronic Testing for Digital, Memory and Mixed-Signal VLSI Circuits*"
17. D.Jaramayan, "Optimization Techniques for Performance and Power Dissipation in Test and Validation," Ph.D Dissertation , ECE , Southern Illinois University, (May 2012)

MATEC Web of Conferences **76**, 01013 (2016) DOI: 10.1051/matecconf/20167601013
CSCC 2016

Software for CCTV systems design

Milan Adamek [1,a] Michaela Barinova and Tomas Havir[1]

[1] *Tomas Bata University in Zlin, Faculty of Applied Informatics, Nam. T. G. Masaryka 5555, 760 05 Zlin, Czech Republic*

Abstract. The article is focused on the software, which is used in the design of the CCTV systems. It shows tools available online, tools for PC and mobile applications. It describes the basic components of the camera systems, their characteristics and current trends in CCTV systems. Moreover, it compares two selected software tools, their features and supported functions. In the practical part, these tools are used for the design of a CCTV system and the whole process is described in detail.

1 Introduction

CCTV systems help to protect the property, can provide evidence, inform about traffic situations, indicate suspicious behavior of people, etc. It is obvious that the application of CCTV systems will gradually expand in the future hand in hand with the development of new technologies and a gradual decrease in production costs.

Designing a CCTV system involves a number of calculations and specifications that are subsequently used for the selection of suitable components with desired properties. These basic parameters include the CCTV lens focal length, depth of field, CCTV viewing angle, parameters for identification of persons, data bandwidth capacity, voltage drop, the backup HDD storage space for various formats and also the minimum required upload of the internet connection to stream all the cameras in the designed CCTV system. The calculations do not have to be done manually, since there is a wide range of software tools that perform these calculations. Today's software applications, in addition to the calculation of the CCTV system component parameters, also allow modeling of selected objects.

There are online tools currently available that are usually open to the public at the websites of CCTV component manufacturers. And of course there are also sophisticated software tools that must be installed prior to their use on the computer.

The paper focuses on the analysis of online tools that can be used for the determination of parameters of individual CCTV components. Detailed comparison is provided of sophisticated software tools that can be used to create 3D models of an object, including their internal equipment. The CCTVs of required parameters are then placed to the models.

2 Online tools for CCTV systems design

2.1 Calculator of focal length

Through the calculator it is possible to calculate the appropriate focal length; to maintain the required image quality, the following input parameters must be specified: resolution (in pixels per meter), the height and width of the scene and its distance from the lens. The function of this tool is not only one-way to calculate the focal length, but quite the contrary; after entering the focal length it is possible to calculate any of the above parameters, Fig. 1.

Figure 1. AXIS Lens calculator [1]

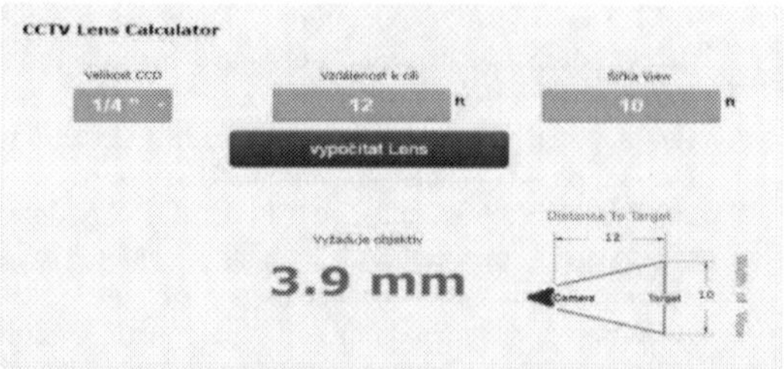

Figure 2. CCTV Lens calculator [2]

[a] Corresponding author: adamek@fai.utb.cz

2.2 CCTV Designer

Through this tool, you can design a CCTV system. It allows adding cameras, recording equipment, accessories or network elements to your own design; these elements can be selected from a list of components. A useful feature is specification of parameters of a new item. Designer lets you see a preview of the camera view; by a movement you can set the viewing angle, the height and distance of the monitored person. Depending on the CCTV and its parameters, a real shot of the person is displayed in the right side of the screen, which shows the image quality. You can also switch to a 3D mode, where the shot is displayed in 3D space. It is possible to move the graphical representation of the person's silhouette and check whether the image is of sufficient quality.

It is also possible to select the type of the scene; from the default scenes you can choose a busy street, parking place, office space, etc. Based on the choice made, the approximate size of one image is calculated. Depending on the CCTV number, type and time required for archiving, the needed storage capacity is calculated and a suitable recording device is selected accordingly.

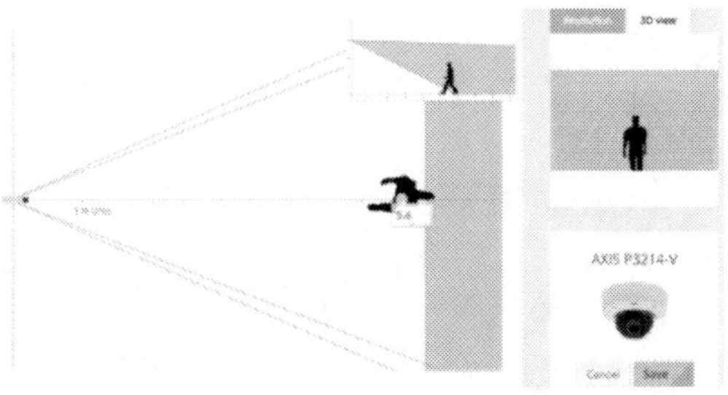

Figure 3. Design system [3]

2.3 HDDs Calculator

After entering the parameters of the selected CCTV system, the Calculator calculates the storage capacity of a hard drive in order to enter and save the time required for recording. This requires the following parameters: CCTV resolution, image frequency, number of CCTVs and required recording time. After entering of all said parameters, the Calculator calculates the required storage capacity.

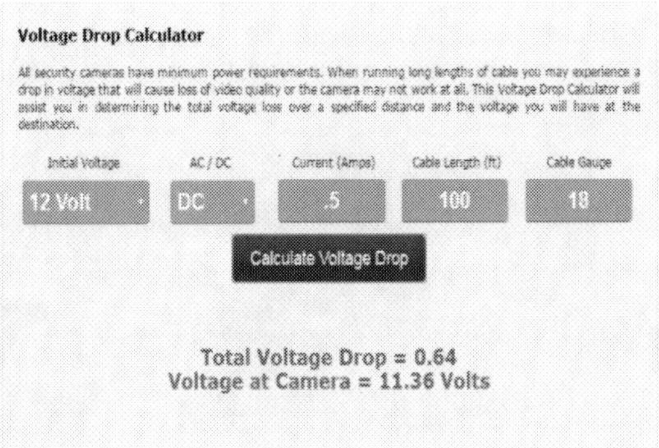

Figure 4. Voltage drop calculator

2.4 Voltage Drop Calculator

Calculator that can calculate the voltage drop across the transmission route. It is required to specify the values of voltage, current, cable length and cable gauge [4].

2.5 Calculator with a support for Google Maps

A tool that can display a security camera view on a map and its approximate image quality. It utilizes information from Google Maps and calculations which are performed on the basis of the specified parameters.

The camera can be placed anywhere in the world; if images captured for the Street View are available, a rough view of the scene will be showed on the right side of the screen. The tool also includes the function of automatic calculation of the pixel density and in the right side it shows a snapshot figure, which implies the quality of the image. The tool also allows changing the area that is monitored by the camera, and it accordingly recalculates the lens parameters and changes the image quality.

The CCTV properties can be defined manually and the parameters can be modified for various purposes. In the event that the software tool user decides on a particular CCTV model with predefined parameter settings, there is a choice of more than 2500 camera models from well-known manufacturers.

Figure 5 shows a camera capturing a scene between two streets Masarykova and Nádražní in Brno. The upper part of the figure shows the parameters that can be changed as needed. In the left you can see the camera image and in the right an approximation of the real picture. In the lower right corner you can see the image quality of a person captured on camera; the person is showed as a drawn human silhouette in the left within the green triangle. [5]

Figure 5. IPVM Calculator

3 Software for the PC

3.1 Microsoft Visio

A simple 2D tool, which can create CCTV designs. The program includes a number of predefined blocks, which are standardized. Of course, the user can generate their own blocks with defined parameters via a library. The blocks are connected by lines using the connecting points.

Data from individual blocks can be interconnected with other Microsoft programs, such as Microsoft Excel or Microsoft SQL.

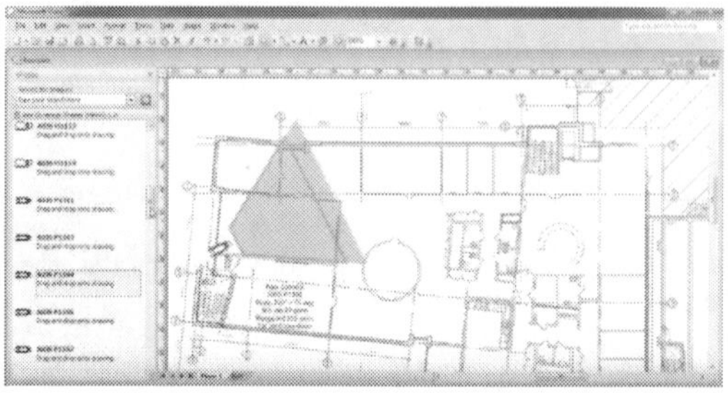

Figure 6. Example of CCTVs installation in Microsoft Visio [6]

3.2 SketchUP

Program for modeling in 3D space, which is not branch-specific, and therefore allows modeling of absolutely anything from individual interior elements for an entire house, or for example technical equipment or things that we use on daily basis.

Drawing is easier than in other professional design softwares such as CAD. Most models are created by drawing with classic tools such as pencil, ellipse or rectangle, and subsequently using the drag function allows creation of a 3D object. The sketchup contains a large library, in which you can find a lot of pre-defined objects created by users themselves. For example furniture, trees, equipment or individual instruments.

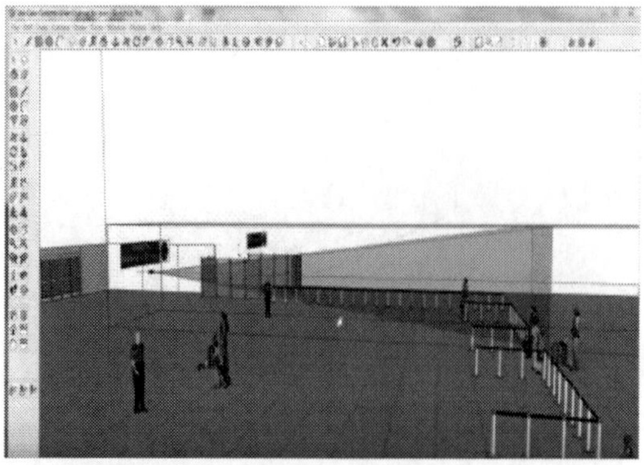

Figure 7. Example of SketchUP environment [7]

The feature that allows cooperation of the program with Google Earth enables the users to upload individual objects also from this application. For example, you can use the terrain, bumps or individual buildings. It is also possible to draw by means of importing photos. The resulting models can be exported into many file types. The dwg file types are also possible to use in CAD systems.

In CCTV systems, it is possible to insert individual cameras into 3D designs and monitor their properties. The camera can be modeled as a new object or you can download pre-defined cameras from Axis if needed. The creators of the program CCTVCAD developed an add-on for SketchUp that allows inserting cameras into objects objects and arbitrarily modify their properties. The result can be seen as a camera footage in 3D mode [7].

3.3 AutoCAD

Professional software which supports 2D drawing and 3D modeling.

The 3D modeling in this software has not become widely popular in the field of CCTV systems, mainly due to its complexity. However, drawing in 2D is quite the opposite and is used very frequently. It is mainly used for plotting of cable locations and placing of CCTV system components to a house layout. In AutoCAD you can also use the function for distance measurement for qualified estimation of the required amount of cabling.

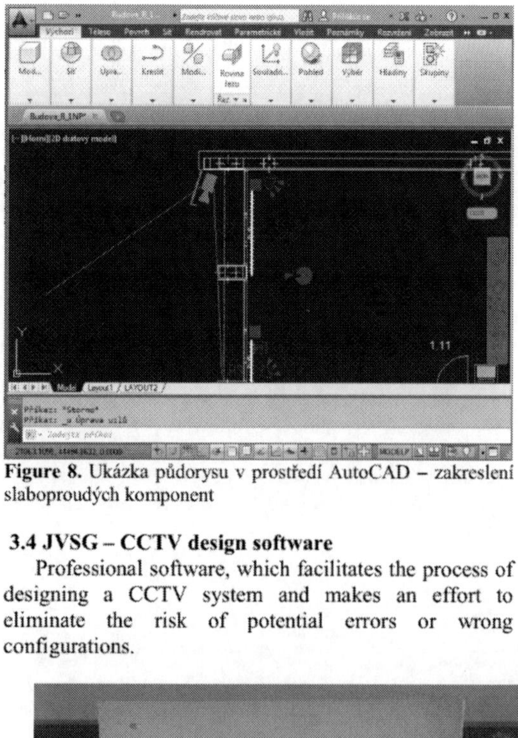

Figure 8. Ukázka půdorysu v prostředí AutoCAD – zakreslení slaboproudých komponent

3.4 JVSG – CCTV design software

Professional software, which facilitates the process of designing a CCTV system and makes an effort to eliminate the risk of potential errors or wrong configurations.

Figure 9. 3D objects in JVSG environment [7]

Although the original title contains IP CCTV systems, the tool serves also for the design of analog systems.

A 3D model is created based on the plans of the object into which we place cameras with defined configurations and parameters. During the modeling it is possible to import external 3D objects in Collada formats.

When working in this environment after loading the object layout in JPEG, PNG, BMP, PDF, MS Visio or Google Earth formats you can be model walls, rooms, windows, doors and more. Subsequently, equipment and other objects are added into the object. This is followed by adding cameras, the number of which in one project can reach up to 150; this number allows proposal of extensive CCTV systems. The tool can calculate fields of vision, viewing angles and focal lengths. In the visual field it can calculate the image quality in relation to the distance of captured object. The vision fields can be divided into zones, the colors of which represents the video quality for detection.

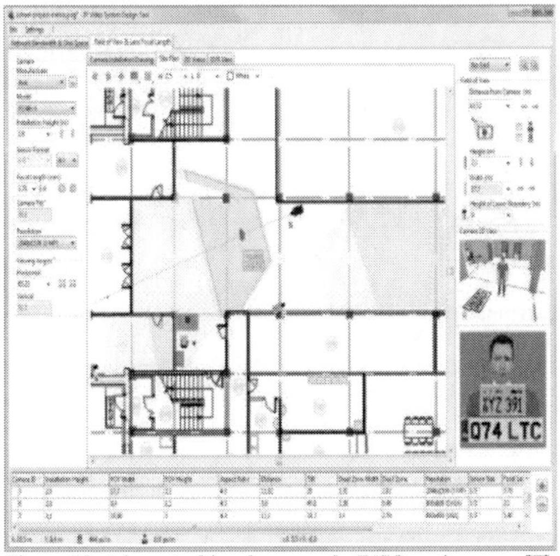

Figure 10. A layout with color zones in JVSG environment [7]

The software can display real views from all cameras in 3D mode and can also display the quality of a sample image in relation to the distance from the camera, all this in both day and night regimes. Another feature is displaying of the image quality when identifying the license plates of vehicles; this feature can be used, for example, when installing CCTVs at gates or entrances to buildings.

3.5 CCTVCAD

Comprehensive software for CCTV system designs which facilitates the calculations necessary for the selection of suitable system components. It can also calculate focal lengths, viewing angles and ranges of the cameras. Further it helps determine the parameters for the detection of persons, their identification or reading the license plates of vehicles.

Other features include calculating the depth of field, voltage drops and determination of the required light output for sufficient lighting of the scene.

Figure 11. Simulation of a camera view in CCTVCAD environment [8]

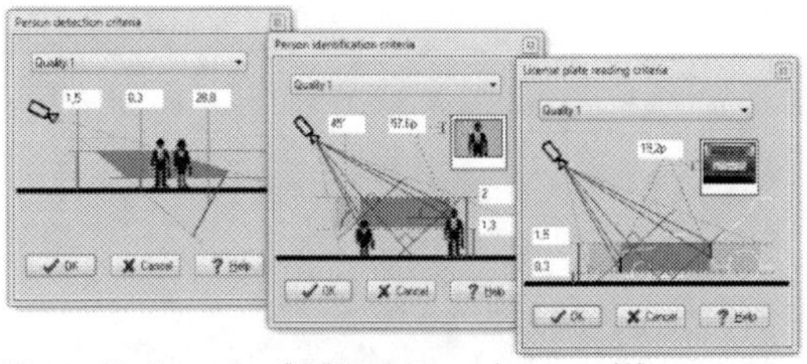

Figure 12. Example of CCTVCAD environment [8]

The entire facility can be drawn in 2D or 3D formats and the cameras can be placed in the designed model. They can be subsequently configured in order to see precise viewing angles, and realistic images in 3D. The images are displayed in a color corresponding to the image quality in relation to the distance from the camera. It is possible to set up our own color zones or choose from default options. The camera can be rotated in order to seek optimum angles to achieve the desired images. The software is also able of displaying zones of cameras that have lenses with high distortion.

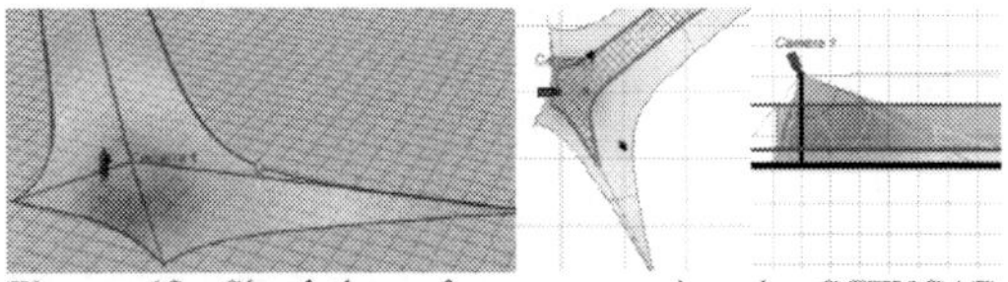

Figure 13. Simulation of a camera view in CCTVCAD environment [8]

Formats supported for the layout upload are BMP, JPG, EMF, WMF, PNG, GIF, TIF, PDF, DWG, DXF. Like the JVSG design tool, the CCTVCAD also contains its own 3D objects. Upload of external models into the layout is allowed from programs such as Autodesk 3Ds Max and SketchUp.

The software can simulate camera images based on camera settings and the parameters of the scene. For example, there are predefined scenes with artificial lighting, fog, reduced visibility, and others. Properties of light sources and camera sensitivities are also taken into consideration. You can also simulate infrared illumination of the cameras. According to the parameters, you can calculate the camera depth of field. Other displayed properties are image contrast, compression and rendering [8].

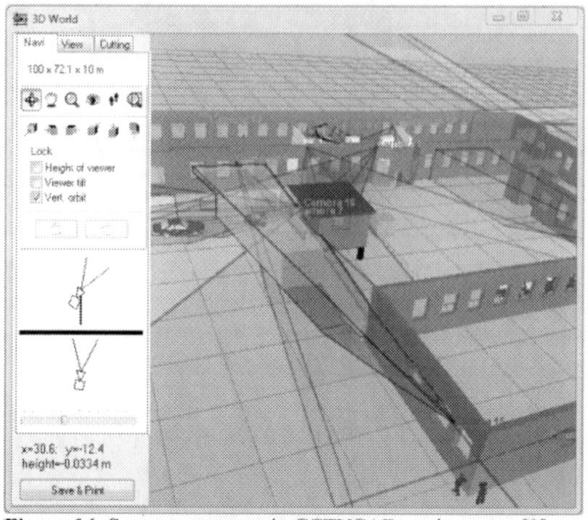

Figure 14. Scene parameters in CCTVCAD environment [8]

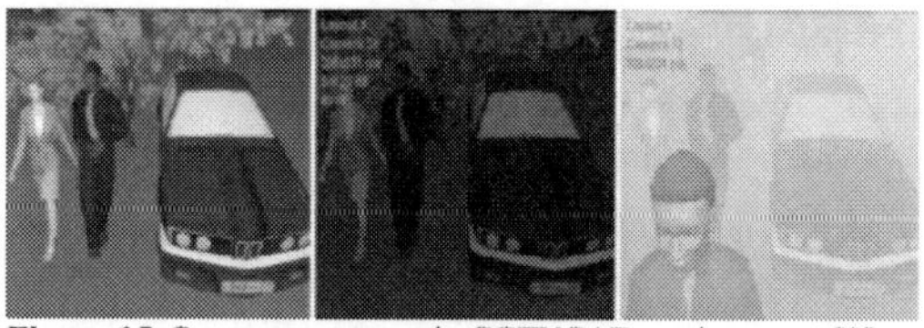

Figure 15. Scene parameters in CCTVCAD environment [8]

4 CCTV design using JVSG

An object layout created in AutoCAD was inserted as a background on which the object was modeled.

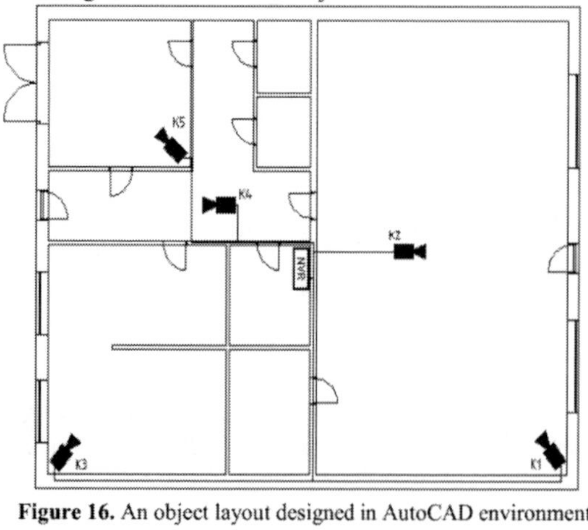

Figure 16. An object layout designed in AutoCAD environment

Individual offices in the building were equipped with office furniture using the sources from libraries in a Collada format. The building also includes storage rooms equipped with storage shelves and goods. Also the shelves were imported in the Collada format.

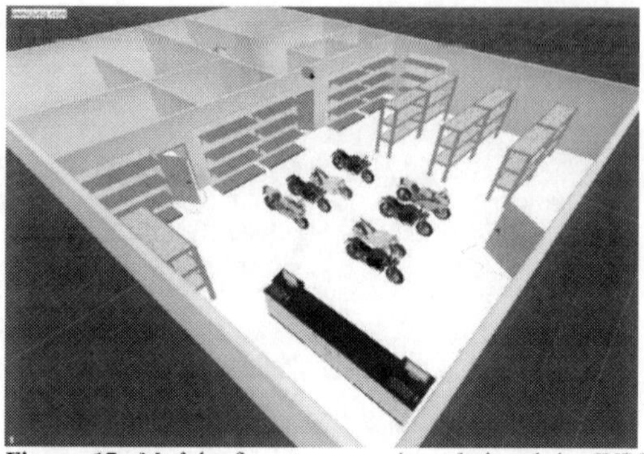

Figure 17. Model of a store premises designed in JVSG environment

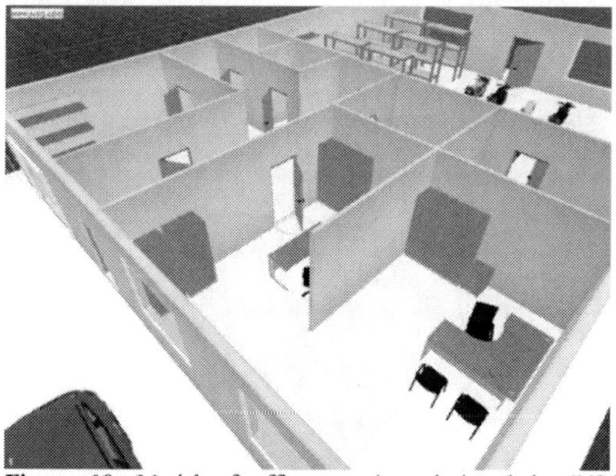

Figure 18. Model of office premises designed in JVSG environment

4.1 Choosing the cameras and their location in JVSG studio

The facility has been used Five IP cameras in a dome design were used in the building connected by twisted pair cabling to an NVR recording device in the utility room. Cameras 1 and 2 were located in the sale space. Camera 3 is located in an office with a safe with money placed in a closet. Camera 4 captures the corridor and camera 5 is placed in the service department.

Figure 19. Location of camera K1 in a storage room of modeled object, created in JVSG environment

The cameras of required properties (focal length) were chosen based on the simulation steps in JVSG environment and their locations within the model object were selected.

Figure 19 shows the location of camera K1 in the modeled object warehouse, Figure 20 represents the view of K1, which was created in JVSG Studio.

Figure 20 View of camera K1 in the modeled object warehouse designed in JVSG environment

The CCTV system includes five IP cameras that are connected via twisted-pair cabling to a NVR recording device. The NVR is located in the utility room and is equipped with a backup in case of power failure. A security and emergency alarm system (PZTS) centre is also present in the utility room, therefore this space is monitored by a PIR motion detector.

Cameras K1 to K5 represent IP cameras with varifocal lens of a 2.8 – 12 mm and image sensor of 1 / 2.8 "Sony. The cameras have a built-in IR illuminator, which reaches up to 30 meters, which is sufficient for the object distance. 12V / 1A is via PoE. The maximum camera resolution is 1080p and a compression of H.264 is set at a frequency of 15 images per second. The focal length settings of each camera is described in Table 1.

Table 1 Focal lengths of cameras K1 to K5

Camera	Focal length (mm)
K1	2,9
K2	6,3
K3	2,9
K4	2,9
K5	3

4.2 NVR recording device

For the CCTV system a network device was selected that can record simultaneously eight 2-megapixel cameras at a frequency of 15 images per second. All camera ports have PoE power connections, so it is not necessary to provide power for individual cameras. The NVR can be connected to Internet Network via a WAN port. The recording can be made on up to two 4TB drives. Supported are the Three types of compression are supported, namely the H.264, MPEG4 and MJPEG; the H.264 was chosen for the object [9].

4.3 Hard drive

The requirement for video record archiving is set up to the last four days. For installation, a hard drive with a capacity of 500 gigabytes was chosen, which is sufficient for that purpose. When a motion is detected within the camera field of vision, the cameras record at full quality; without motion detection they record at a lower resolution.

Rozlišení	Komprese	Velikost snímku*, KB	FPS	Dnů	Kamer	Šířka pásm...	Velikost na disku, GB	Datový tok, kbit/s
1280x720 (HD)	[illegible]	10,5	15	4	5	6,45	278,7	1290
1920x1080 (Full HD)	H.264-15 (High Quality)	24	15	4	1	2,95	127,4	2949

Celkem FPS	Místo na disku, GB	Šířka pásma, Mbit/s
90	406,1	9,4

Figure 21 Calculation of a hard drive capacity for record within the last four days

5 Conclusion

Online software tools for designing CCTV systems are tools that are easier to use and in most cases solved by means of calculators. The tools can usually calculate the basic parameters of a CCTV system, which are often not sufficient for modeling of objects in which the CCTV system is to be located. Second type is represented by software tools which, once installed on a PC, are much more sophisticated environment with support of a wide range of libraries. They allow creating of 3D models of buildings and their interior equipment. Cameras with defined parameters are subsequently placed into the models. The tools can then simulate the images captured by the cameras and show previews of real footage. The last type of software are mobile applications. They predominantly operate on the same principle as the online tools.

Acknowledgement

This work was supported by the Ministry of Education, Youth and Sports of the Czech Republic within the National Sustainability Programme project No. LO1303 (MSMT-7778/2014) and also by the European Regional Development Fund under the project CEBIA-Tech No. CZ.1.05/2.1.00/03.0089.

References

1. Axis - Portál nástrojů [online]. 2016 [cit. 2016-05-02]. In: http://www.axis.com/cz/cs/tools
2. Security Camera King - CCTV Calculators [online]. Boca Raton, 2016 [cit. 2016-05-02]. In: http://www.securitycameraking.com/calc.html
3. NAS Servery [online]. 2016 [cit. 2016-05-02]. In: http://www.nasservery.cz/

4. Security Camera King - CCTV Calculators [online]. Boca Raton, 2016 [cit. 2016-05-02]. In: http://www.securitycameraking.com/calc.html
5. Camera Calculator / Design Software [online]. Sanborn, 2016 [cit. 2016-05-02]. In: http://ipvm.com/calculator
6. SketchUP [online]. 2014 [cit. 2016-05-02]. In: http://www.cadtutorial.cz/sketchup/sketchup_uvod_do_3d_modelovani.php
7. JVSG: CCTV Design Software [online]. 2016 [cit. 2016-05-02]. In: http://www.jvsg.com/
8. CCTVCAD Software [online]. Perm, Russia, 2016 [cit. 2016-05-02]. In: http://www.cctvcad.com/
9. STASANET - Bezpečnostní technologie [online]. Praha, 2016 [cit. 2016-05-02]. In: https://www.stasanet.cz/

Optimization of the Document Placement in the RFID Cabinet

Maciej Kiedrowicz[1] Tadeusz Nowicki[1,a], Robert Waszkowski[1], Zbigniew Wesołowski[1], Kazimierz Worwa[1]

[1]*The Faculty of Cybernetics, Military University of Technology, 00-908 Warsaw, Kaliskiego 2, Poland*

Abstract. The study is devoted to the issue of optimization of the document placement in a single RFID cabinet. It has been assumed that the optimization problem means the reduction of archivization time with respect to the information on all documents with RFID tags. Since the explicit form of the criterion function remains unknown, for the purpose of its approximation, the regression analysis method has been used. The method uses data from a computer simulation of the process of archiving data about documents. To solve the optimization problem, the modified gradient projection method has been used.

1 Introduction

One of the important problems related to the use of the document archivization system with the RFID (Radio-frequency identification) technology [1,2], is the issue of such placement of the set of documents on particular shelves of the RFID cabinet that minimize the length of the time interval of registering the data about these documents in a database of an information system. To solve this problem, the standard optimization approach may be applied [3, 4]. One of the issues, which need to be solved by using such approach, is the problem of collecting data necessary for approximation of the criterion function. Since the process of data collection is time-consuming and laborious, to improve it, the stochastic simulation method has been applied [5-7]. It is based on generating pseudorandom real numbers, whose values are interpreted as the length of time intervals of archiving the information about the RFID-tagged documents. Thanks to such features as the ability to quickly generate a wide variety of data and flexibility in planning and performing various experiments, computer simulation has become in recent years a kind of modus operandi of many scientific specialties [8]. On the basis of the simulation data, local approximations of the criterion function are performed using the regression analysis method [9-11]. Thanks to applying the complete two-level plan of experiments [12, 13], the computational complexity of the estimation process of the local linear parameters of the regression functions was reduced.
Section 2 formulates the optimization problem. Section 3 describes the method for solving the problem. In particular, section 3.1 presents the method for estimation the parameters of the local linear regression functions, whereas section 3.2 describes an algorithm for solving the optimization problem reflecting the modified gradient projection method [14, 15].

Let $(\Omega, \mathcal{F}, P)$ be the probabilistic space, where all random variables are defined. Let us use the following notation: $\mathbb{N}$ - the set of natural numbers, $\mathbb{R}$ - the set of real numbers, $WN(0,\sigma^2)$ - the white noise with zero expected value and variation σ^2.

2 Formulation of the optimization problem

Let us assume that the RFID cabinet is composed of S, $S>0$, shelves for documents with the RFID tags. Let $\mathcal{S}=\{1,\ldots,S\}$ be a set of shelf numbers. Let m_s, $m_s \geq 0$ be the number of free spaces for the documents on shelf number s, $s \in \mathcal{S}$. Let x_s, $0 \leq x_s \leq m_s$ be the number of documents stored on shelf number s. We will assume that D, $D>0$, documents must be stored in the cabinet. Let $\mathcal{D}=\{1,\ldots,D\}$ be a set of numbers of such documents. The point is to placement the documents from set $\mathcal{D}$ in such a manner so that minimize the length of time interval of archiving the information about the RFID-tagged documents. Let $y \in \mathbb{R}$ means the length of the time interval.
The optimization issue can be formulated as follows

$$\mathrm{f}(\hat{\mathbf{x}}) = \min_{\mathbf{x}\in\mathcal{X}_0} \mathrm{f}(\mathbf{x}), \tag{1}$$

where:

- $\mathrm{f}:\mathbb{R}^S \to \mathbb{R}$ is the criterion function of unknown explicit form, whose the values are interpreted as the length of time intervals of archiving the information about the RFID-tagged documents from set $\mathcal{D}$;
- $\mathcal{X}_0$ is the set of feasible solutions in the form of

[a] Corresponding author: tadeusz.nowicki@wat.edu.pl

$$\mathcal{X}_0 = \{\mathbf{x} \in \mathbb{R}^S : \mathbf{x} \geq \mathbf{0}, \mathbf{g}(\mathbf{x}) \leq \mathbf{0}, g_{S+1}(\mathbf{x}) = 0\}, \quad (2)$$

and $\mathbf{g}(\mathbf{x}) = [g_1(\mathbf{x}), g_2(\mathbf{x}), \ldots, g_S(\mathbf{x})]^T$ is a vector constraint function, $g_s : \mathbb{R}^S \to \mathbb{R}$ is a constraint function in the form of $g_s(\mathbf{x}) = \mathbf{x}^T \mathbf{a}_s - m_s$, $\mathbf{a}_s = [0, \ldots, 0, \underset{s}{1}, 0, \ldots, 0]^T$, for $s \in \mathcal{S}$; $g_{S+1} : \mathbb{R}^S \to \mathbb{R}$ is a constraint function in the form of $g_{S+1}(\mathbf{x}) = D - \mathbf{x}^T \mathbf{1}$, $\mathbf{1}$ is a unit vector.

Subject 1. If $\sum_{s \in \mathcal{S}} m_s \geq D$, $m_s \geq 0$, $s \in \mathcal{S}$, $D > 0$, then the set of permissible solutions $\mathcal{X}_0$ (2) is not empty, closed and convex.

Proof. The set of $\mathcal{X}_0$ is closed, since the functions $\mathbf{x}^T \mathbf{a}_s \leq m_s$, $m_s \geq 0$, $s \in \mathcal{S}$, limit it from the top, and the limitations $\mathbf{x} \geq \mathbf{0}$ and $\mathbf{x}^T \mathbf{1} \geq D$ limit this set from the bottom. The set of $\mathcal{X}_0$ is not empty, since if $\sum_{s \in \mathcal{S}} m_s \geq D$ and $m_s \geq 0$, $s \in \mathcal{S}$, $D > 0$, then the set $\mathcal{X}_0$ includes points $\mathbf{x} \geq \mathbf{0}$ meeting the constraint criteria $\mathbf{x}^T \mathbf{a}_s \leq m_s$, $s \in \mathcal{S}$. The convexity of the set $\mathcal{X}_0$ is due to the fact that all limitations are linear.

3 Method for solving the optimization problem

Problem (1) is a nonlinear problem of the mathematical programming with linear constraints. If the mapping $f : \mathbb{R}^S \to \mathbb{R}$ is differentiable and set $\mathcal{X}_0$ is closed and convex, the problem may be solved by the modified gradient projection method. This method consists of generating a sequence of approximations:

$$\mathbf{x}^{k+1} = \mathbf{x}^k + \tau_k \mathbf{d}^k, \qquad k=0,1,\ldots, \quad (3)$$

where: $\mathbf{x}^0 \in \mathcal{X}_0$ is a predefined initial point, $\tau_k > 0$ is the kth step size, the value of which can be determined by the Armijo rule, $\mathbf{d}^k \in \mathbb{R}^S$ is the direction, in which the minimum of the criterion function f is searched. Since the form of this function is unknown, it is necessary to conduct a simulation experiment aimed at collecting statistical data, based on which it will be possible to perform approximation of the function f in the neighborhood $\mathbf{Q}(\mathbf{x}^k, \delta) = \{\mathbf{x} \in \mathbb{R}^S : \|\mathbf{x} - \mathbf{x}^k\| < \delta\}$ of the point $\mathbf{x}^k$ (3), where $\delta = S$. The approximation may be performed on the basis of the regression analysis method.

3.1 Local linear approximation of the criterion function

Let us assume that the probabilistic model for the process of changing the number of documents on the shelf s is a random variable $\xi_s : \Omega \to \mathbb{R}$, for $s \in \mathcal{S}$. The value of x_s is interpreted as a realization of the random variable ξ_s, i.e. $\xi_s = x_s$. Therefore, the value of vector $\mathbf{x} = [x_1, x_2, \ldots, x_S]^T$ is interpreted as a realization of the multi-dimensional random variable $\boldsymbol{\xi} = [\xi_1, \xi_2, \ldots, \xi_S]^T$, i.e. $\boldsymbol{\xi} = \mathbf{x}$. Let us further assume that the probabilistic model of the process of changing the length of time intervals of archiving the information about the RFID-tagged documents from set $\mathcal{D}$ is the random variable $\psi : \Omega \to \mathbb{R}$. The value of y is interpreted as a realization of this random variable, i.e. $\psi = y$.

Let us assume that the stochastic model of influence of independent random variables $\xi_1, \xi_2, \ldots, \xi_S$ on the dependent random variable ψ is the following equation

$$\psi = \eta(\xi_1, \xi_2, \ldots, \xi_S) + \varepsilon,$$

where: $\eta : \mathbb{R}^S \to \mathbb{R}$ is the response surface, $\varepsilon \sim WN(0, \sigma^2)$. The regression analysis method is often used to approximate the function η.

Theorem 1 (regression). If $\boldsymbol{\xi}$ and ψ are random variables defined in the probabilistic space $(\Omega, \mathcal{F}, P)$, whereas $\mathrm{E}(\psi) < \infty$, and if $f : \mathbb{R}^S \to \mathbb{R}$ is the measurable function, a mean-square error of the model, i.e.

$$Q(f) = \mathrm{E}\{[\psi - f(\boldsymbol{\xi})]^2\},$$

assumes the smallest value for the function f by the formula:

$$\hat{f}(\mathbf{x}) = \mathrm{E}(\psi | \{\boldsymbol{\xi} = \mathbf{x}\}).$$

The function $\hat{f}$ is called the regression model of the random variable ψ with respect to the random variable $\boldsymbol{\xi}$.

Let us assume that the unknown function η belongs to the class of functions H including all linear regression functions with the vector parameters $\boldsymbol{\beta} \in \mathbb{R}^{P \times 1}$. It means that the response surface meets the equation $\mathrm{E}(\psi) = \eta(\mathbf{x}, \boldsymbol{\beta})$. The main idea of the response surface methodology [16] consists in the planning of experiments in such a manner that the mean-square error of the model with the vector parameter $\boldsymbol{\beta}$ is minimized.

Let us assume that in the neighborhood $\mathbf{Q}(\mathbf{x}^k, \delta)$ of the point $\mathbf{x}^k$ (3), the local model of the response surface is the linear regression function in the form of

$$f^k(\mathbf{x}) = \mathbf{z}^T \boldsymbol{\beta}_k, \qquad \mathbf{x} \in \mathbf{Q}(\mathbf{x}^k, \delta), \quad (4)$$

where: $\mathbf{z} = [1, \mathbf{x}^T]^T$, $\boldsymbol{\beta}_k = [\beta_{k0}, \beta_{k1}, \ldots, \beta_{kS}]^T$ is vector of unknown parameters of the function f^k. The estimation of the model f^k is based on the estimation of the vector

$\boldsymbol{\beta}_k$. For that purpose, it is essential to come up with a plan of the simulation experiments allowing to collect the statistical data, based on which the estimation of this vector will be possible.
Let

$$P_k = \begin{pmatrix} \mathbf{z}_1 & \mathbf{z}_2 & \cdots & \mathbf{z}_N \\ p_{k1} & p_{k2} & \cdots & p_{kN} \end{pmatrix}, \quad \mathbf{x} \in \mathbf{Q}(\mathbf{x}^k, \delta) \quad (5)$$

be a normalized discrete plan of an experiment, where: $\mathbf{z}_1, \ldots, \mathbf{z}_N$ are focal points of the plan, in which the realizations of the random variable ψ are observed for the fixed realizations of the multi-dimensional random variable ξ, i.e. $\xi_{\omega_n} = \mathbf{x}_n$, for $n=1,\ldots,N$; $p_{k1}, \ldots, p_{kN}$ are weights selected in such a manner that $\sum_{n=1}^{N} p_{kn} = 1$. Let $\mathcal{N} = \{1, \ldots, N\}$ be a set of numbers of the focal points of the plan P_k. Let us assume that in the focal points, influence of the realizations of the random variable ξ on the realizations of the random variable ψ is described by the equations in the form of

$$y_n = \mathrm{f}^k(\mathbf{x}_n) + \varepsilon_n = \mathbf{z}_n^T \boldsymbol{\beta}_k + \varepsilon_n, \quad n \in \mathcal{N}, \quad (6)$$

where: y_n is the observed length of time intervals of archiving the information about the RFID-tagged documents from set $\mathcal{D}$ located on the shelves of the RFID cabinet in a manner determined by the value of vector $\mathbf{x}_n$, $\mathbf{x}_n \in \mathbf{Q}(\mathbf{x}^k, \delta)$; $\mathbf{z}_n = [1, \mathbf{x}_n^T]^T$; $\varepsilon_n \sim WN(0, \sigma^2)$.
We are looking for the linear regression model of mapping $\hat{\mathrm{f}}^k$ (6) in the form of

$$\hat{y}_n = \hat{\mathrm{f}}^k(\mathbf{x}_n) = \mathbf{z}_n^T \mathbf{b}_k, \quad n \in \mathcal{N}, \quad (7)$$

where $\mathbf{b}_k = [b_{k0}, b_{k1}, \ldots, b_{kS}]^T$.
Let us rewrite equations (6) in the following matrix form:

$$\mathbf{y} = \mathbf{Z}\boldsymbol{\beta}_k + \boldsymbol{\varepsilon},$$

where: $\mathbf{y} = [y_1, \ldots, y_N]^T \in \mathbb{R}^{N \times 1}$, $\mathbf{Z} = [\mathbf{z}_1^T, \mathbf{z}_2^T, \ldots, \mathbf{z}_N^T]^T$, $\boldsymbol{\varepsilon} = [\varepsilon_1, \ldots, \varepsilon_N]^T \in \mathbb{R}^{N \times 1}$.
On the other hand, the equations (7) will have the following matrix form:

$$\hat{\mathbf{y}} = \mathbf{Z}\mathbf{b}_k,$$

where: $\hat{\mathbf{y}} = [\hat{y}_1, \ldots, \hat{y}_N]^T \in \mathbb{R}^{N \times 1}$. Matrix $\mathbf{Z}$ is called the plan of an experiment.
The problem of estimating the model $\hat{\mathrm{f}}^k$ reduces to the issue of estimation of vector $\hat{\mathbf{b}}_k$ that minimizes the sum of squared errors of the model $\mathbf{e} = \mathbf{y} - \mathbf{Z}\mathbf{b}_k$.
This issue can be formulated as the optimization problem in the form of

$$\mathrm{q}(\hat{\mathbf{b}}_k) = \min_{\mathbf{b}_k \in \mathbb{R}^{(S+1)}} \left[\mathrm{q}(\mathbf{b}_k) = \mathbf{e}^T \mathbf{e} \right]. \quad (8)$$

Problem (8) is a linear squares issue [9-11]. Let us write the minimized sum of squared errors in the form of

$$\begin{aligned} \mathrm{q}(\mathbf{b}_k) &= (\mathbf{y} - \mathbf{Z}\mathbf{b}_k)^T (\mathbf{y} - \mathbf{Z}\mathbf{b}_k) \\ &= \mathbf{y}^T\mathbf{y} - \mathbf{y}^T\mathbf{Z}\mathbf{b}_k - \mathbf{b}_k^T\mathbf{Z}^T\mathbf{y} + \mathbf{b}_k^T\mathbf{Z}^T\mathbf{Z}\mathbf{b}_k \\ &= \mathbf{y}^T\mathbf{y} - 2\mathbf{b}_k^T\mathbf{Z}^T\mathbf{y} + \mathbf{b}_k^T\mathbf{Z}^T\mathbf{Z}\mathbf{b}_k. \end{aligned}$$

When we differentiate function q with respect to the vector $\mathbf{b}_k$, we obtain:

$$\frac{\partial \mathrm{q}(\mathbf{b}_k)}{\partial \mathbf{b}_k} = -2\mathbf{Z}^T\mathbf{y} + 2\mathbf{Z}^T\mathbf{Z}\mathbf{b}_k.$$

According to the above formula, we obtain the system of the normal equation:

$$\mathbf{Z}^T\mathbf{Z}\mathbf{b}_k = \mathbf{Z}^T\mathbf{y}.$$

If the matrix $\mathbf{Z}^T\mathbf{Z}$ is not singular, then the solution of problem (8) is the estimator in the form of

$$\hat{\mathbf{b}}_k = (\mathbf{Z}^T\mathbf{Z})^{-1}\mathbf{Z}^T\mathbf{y}. \quad (9)$$

To facilitate the estimation of parameter vector $\hat{\mathbf{b}}_k$ (9), the complete two-level plan of experiments are often used [13]. According to this method, it is assumed that the number of focal points N of plan P_k (5) is $N = 2^S$, and the components of the plan of experiment assume the values from the set {-1,1}. Let $\mathbf{U} = [u_{ij}]_{N \times (S+1)}$ be the plan of experiment, whose components u_{ij}, $i=1,\ldots,N$, $j=1,\ldots,S+1$, assume the values from this set. Figure 1 presents matrix$\mathbf{U}$ for $S=3$.

$$\mathrm{U} = \begin{pmatrix} 1 & -1 & -1 & -1 \\ 1 & 1 & -1 & -1 \\ 1 & -1 & 1 & -1 \\ 1 & 1 & 1 & -1 \\ 1 & -1 & -1 & 1 \\ 1 & 1 & -1 & 1 \\ 1 & -1 & 1 & 1 \\ 1 & 1 & 1 & 1 \end{pmatrix}$$

Figure 1. Model plan of experiment

For plan $\mathbf{U}$, the equivalent of the estimator $\hat{\mathbf{b}}_k$ (9) is the vector $\hat{\mathbf{a}}_k$ in the form of

$$\hat{\mathbf{a}}_k = (\mathbf{U}^T\mathbf{U})^{-1}\mathbf{U}^T\mathbf{y}, \quad (10)$$

where: $\hat{\mathbf{a}}_k = [\hat{a}_{k0}, \hat{a}_{k1}, \ldots, \hat{a}_{kS}]^T$, and the components $\hat{a}_{k1}, \hat{a}_{k2}, \ldots, \hat{a}_{kS}$ of this vector are equal to appropriate components of vector $\hat{\mathbf{b}}_k$, i.e. $\hat{a}_{ks} = \hat{b}_{ks}$, for $s=1,\ldots,S$. Since the covariance matrix $(\mathbf{U}^T\mathbf{U})^{-1}$ is:

$$(\mathbf{U}^T\mathbf{U})^{-1} = \frac{1}{N}\mathbf{I}_S,$$

the estimator (8) has the following final form

$$\hat{\mathbf{a}}_k = \frac{1}{N}\mathbf{U}^T\mathbf{y}, \quad (11)$$

where $\mathbf{I}_S$ is an $S\times S$ identity matrix.

3.2 Solution of the optimization problem

Let us write vector $\hat{\mathbf{a}}_k = [\hat{a}_{k0}, \hat{a}_{k1}, \ldots, \hat{a}_{kS}]^T$ (11) in the form of $\hat{\mathbf{a}}_k = [\hat{a}_{k0}, \hat{\mathbf{c}}_k^T]^T$, where $\hat{\mathbf{c}}_k = [\hat{a}_{k1}, \ldots, \hat{a}_{kS}]^T$. As can be seen, the gradient of function $\hat{f}^k$ (6) has, in the point $\mathbf{x}^k$, the following form

$$\nabla \hat{f}^k(\mathbf{x}^k) = \hat{\mathbf{c}}_k.$$

Applying algorithm (3) for solving problem (1) needs to determine a set of constraints active at the point $\mathbf{x}^k$ which is defined by a set of their indices

$$\mathcal{A}(\mathbf{x}^k) = \{i \in \{1, 2, \ldots, S+1\} : \mathbf{e}_i^T\mathbf{x}^k = n_i\},$$

where: $\mathbf{e}_i = \begin{cases} \mathbf{a}_i, & for\ 1 \le i \le S, \\ \mathbf{1}, & for\ i = S+1, \end{cases}$, $n_i = \begin{cases} m_i, & for\ 1 \le i \le S, \\ D, & for\ i = S+1. \end{cases}$

On the basis of set $\mathcal{A}(\mathbf{x}^k)$ defines a matrix $\tilde{\mathbf{A}}_k$, whose rows are vectors $\mathbf{e}_i$, for $i \in \mathcal{A}(\mathbf{x}^k)$. Next is created a matrix of constraints $\mathbf{A}_k$ significantly active in the point $\mathbf{x}^k$. This matrix is formed in such a way that linearly dependent rows are removed from matrix $\tilde{\mathbf{A}}_k$.

Direction $\mathbf{d}^k$ (3) is calculated according to the following formula:

$$\mathbf{d}^k = \begin{cases} -\mathbf{w}^k + \beta_k \mathbf{d}^{k-1}, & for\ k > 0, \\ -\mathbf{w}^k, & for\ k = 0, \end{cases}$$

where:

- β_k is a coefficient determined by the formula,

$$\beta_k = \begin{cases} 0, & for\ k = 0, \\ \dfrac{(\mathbf{w}^k)^T(\mathbf{w}^k - \mathbf{w}^{k-1})}{\|\mathbf{w}^{k-1}\|^2}, & for\ k > 0, \end{cases}$$

- $\mathbf{w}^k$ is a vector of the form,

$$\mathbf{w}^k = \begin{cases} \nabla \hat{f}^k(\mathbf{x}^k), & for\ k = 0, \\ \mathbf{P}_k \nabla \hat{f}^k(\mathbf{x}^k), & for\ k > 0, \end{cases}$$

- $\mathbf{P}_k$ is an orthogonal projection matrix in the form of

$$\mathbf{P}_k = \mathbf{I}_S - \mathbf{A}_k^T(\mathbf{A}_k\mathbf{A}_k^T)^{-1}\mathbf{A}_k.$$

Reapplication of the above procedure, consisting in applying the substitution $\mathbf{d}^k = \mathbf{w}^k$, is performed in the following cases:

- $\mathbf{d}^k$ is not a descending direction,
- when matrix $\mathbf{A}_k$ is changed, i.e. when $\mathbf{A}_k \ne \mathbf{A}_{k-1}$,
- when from the last round it was made of $S - \operatorname{rank}(\mathbf{A}_k)$ iterations.

The basic criterion for terminating the above procedure is when the norm of vector $\mathbf{w}^k$ reaches a zero value with accuracy ε>0, i.e. $\|\mathbf{w}^k\| \le \varepsilon$.

Example 1. Let us consider the issue of optimization the placement of the RFID-tagged documents in the cabinet equipped with S=4 document shelves. The numbers of free spaces on particular shelves are: $m_1 = 100$, $m_2 = 10$, $m_3 = 5$, $m_4 = 40$. Let us assume that we need to place D=100 RFID-tagged documents in the cabinet. On the basis of the simulation experiments and by applying the optimization algorithm described in section 3, the following solution is reached:

$$\hat{\mathbf{x}} = [45, 10, 5, 40]^T.$$

4 Summary and direction of further work

The optimization approach to the issue of placing the RFID-tagged documents ha been discussed in the work. Since the form of the criterion function is not explicitly known, to solve the optimization problem, the computer simulation method has been applied. On the basis of such data, the local linear approximation of the criterion function has been made by using the regression analysis method. The method required, among other things, to prepare the plans of the simulation experiments. For this, the complete two-level designs have been used.

Further work should focus on important from a practical point of view, the issues of grouping documents and their movement between different RFID cabinets. To solve these problems, the method of the facility location problem may be applied [17-19].

References

1. D. Hunt, A. Puglia, M. Puglia, RFID: *A Guide to Radio Frequency Identification* (Wiley-Blackwell, 2007)
2. C. Heinrich, *RFID and Beyond* (Wiley Publishing, Indianapolis, 2005)
3. W. I. Zangwill, *Nonlinear Programming: A Unified Approach* (Englewood Cliffs: Prentice-Hall, 1969)
4. E. Polak, *Computational Methods in Optimization: A Unified Approach* (Academic Press, 1971).
5. G. S. Fishman, *Discrete-Event Simulation: Modeling, Programming, and Analysis* (Springer, 2001)
6. G. A. Wainer, P. J. Mosterman (Eds.), *Discrete-Event Modeling and Simulation: Theory and Applications*, (CRC Press, 2010)
7. P. C. Kleijnen, *Design and Analysis of Simulation Experiments* (Springer, 2010)

8. B. Zeigler, H.S. Sarjoughian, *Guide to Modeling and Simulation of Systems of Systems* (Springer, 2012)
9. G.E.P. Box, G.M. Jenkins, G.C. Reinsel, *Time Series Analysis. Forecasting and Control* (John Willey and Sons, 2008)
10. J. Fan, Q. Yao, *Nonlinear Time Series. Nonparametric and Parametric Methods* (Springer-Verlag Inc., 2003)
11. L. Ljung, *System Identification. Theory for the User*, (PTR Prentice Hall, 1999)
12. F. Pukelsheim, *Optimal Design of Experiments* (Society for Industrial & Applied Mathematics, 2006)
13. M. Morris , *Design of Experiments: An Introduction Based on Linear Models* (Chapman & Hall/CRC Texts in Statistical Science, 2010)
14. M. A. Bhatti, *Practical Optimization Methods with Mathematica Applications* (Springer-Verlag Inc., 2000)
15. P. H. Calamai, J. J.Moré, *Projected Gradient Methods for Linearly Constrained Problems*, (Mathematical Programming, 39, 1987, pp. 93- 116)
16. G. E. P. Box, R. D. Norman, *Response Surfaces, Mixtures, and Ridge Analyses* (Wiley Series in Probability and Statistics. Wiley-Blackwell, 2007)
17. J. A. Eiman, *Models and Algorithms for the Capacitated Facility Location Problem: Basics, Concepts, Methods* (LAP LAMBERT Academic Publishing, 2014)
18. Ch. N. Vijeyamurthy, *Genetic Algorithm for Facility Location Problem* (LAP LAMBERT Academic Publishing , 2013)
19. R. Martin , *Facility Location and Related Problems* (Südwestdeutscher Verlag für Hochschulschriften, (2009)

MATEC Web of Conferences 76, 02002 (2016) DOI: 10.1051/matecconf/20167602002
CSCC 2016

Network model of security system

Piotr Adamczyk[1], Grzegorz Kiryk[1], Jarosław Napiórkowski[1], Andrzej Walczak[1 a]

[1]*Faculty of Cybernetics, Military University of Technology (WAT), Gen. Sylwestra Kaliskiego 2 Str., 00-908 Warsaw, Poland*

Abstract. The article presents the concept of building a network security model and its application in the process of risk analysis. It indicates the possibility of a new definition of the role of the network models in the safety analysis. Special attention was paid to the development of the use of an algorithm describing the process of identifying the assets, vulnerability and threats in a given context. The aim of the article is to present how this algorithm reduced the complexity of the problem by eliminating from the base model these components that have no links with others component and as a result and it was possible to build a real network model corresponding to reality.

1 Are the network models suitable for risk assessment? The information based on the standards.

One of the regulations describing the risk assessment techniques is the international standard PN-EN 31010: 2010 [1] "Risk management - Risk assessment techniques." It describes the concept and process of risk assessment and provides guidelines for the selection and application of the systematic and methodical risk assessment techniques [2, 3]. The examples include "brainstorming", Delphi technique, preliminary analysis of threats, Failure Mode and Effects Analysis, FMEA, Fault Tree Analysis, FTA, methods based on Bayesian statistics and Bayesian networks. Risk assessment carried out in accordance with this standard supports other measures of risk management. It shows the use of certain techniques, referring to other international standards, which describe in more detail the concept and application of these techniques. This standard, Table A.1 (Applicability of tools used for risk assessment) contains special classification, proposal of the techniques that can be applied at each stage of risk assessment and their usefulness. The techniques are classified according to their use at different stages:

- risk identification;
- analysis of the consequences at the stage of risk analysis;
- qualitative, quantitative or semi-quantitative estimation of the probability at the stage of risk analysis;
- analysis of control effectiveness at the stage of risk analysis;
- evaluation of risk level at the stage of risk analysis;
- risk assessment;

At each stage of risk assessment, it is possible to use various tools and methods.

The standard indicates 31 tools that can be used at each of these stages. Apart from the tools of the groups of supporting methods (Delphi technique), Business Impact Analysis, BIA, or functional analysis, the standard also provide for some statistical methods, including:

- Markov analysis,
- Monte-Carlo simulation,
- Bayesian statistics and Bayes Nets.

Only one of these tools is based on the network approach.

Methods based on Bayesian statistics and Bayesian networks are classified as non-applicable to risk identification of qualitative, quantitative or semi-quantitative estimation of the probability at the stage of risk analysis or risk assessment at the stage of risk analysis. At the same time, the standard shows them as having application to the analysis of the consequences at the stage of risk analysis and risk assessment.

According to the standard, one of the strong points of this approach is the fact that only the Bayes rule and knowledge of a priori probabilities are required.

What is more, the language is easy to understand and the method provides a mechanism for using subjective beliefs.

At the same time, it has some limitations, such as:

- defining dependency on the Bayesian network may not be feasible due to the complexity and costs related thereto;
- the Bayesian approach requires knowledge of a number of conditional probabilities, which are generally determined on the basis of expert knowledge. The software based on the Bayesian network can provide answers only on the basis of such assumptions.

The first limitation indicates a problem that all links need to be defined with the use of complex systems. Furthermore, even a relatively simple system allows

[a] Corresponding author: andrzej.walczak@wat.edu.pl

direct application of the Bayesian networks. The second limitation is the necessity of knowledge of many conditional probabilities, which are usually delivered by experts.

Taking an inventory of resources and identifying the processes of vulnerability and risks, the scale effect should be taken into account [4]. The size of the network representing expertise knowledge can also be a problem. Obviously, it would translate into the complexity of the algorithms, in particular the Bayesian network algorithms.

2 Networks - basic definitions and advantages of the network models

Network is the collection of all ordered triples:

$$S = \langle G, \{\Phi i\}, \{\Psi\} \quad (1)$$

where:

$$G = (X, E, P) \quad (2)$$

is an arbitrary graph

$$\{\Phi_i\} = \{\Phi_1, \dots, \Phi_I\} \quad (3)$$

is a set of functions defined on set X of vertices of graph G

$$\Phi_i : X \rightarrow R,\ i = 1 \dots \text{I and } \{\Psi_j\} = \{\Psi_1, \dots, \Psi_J\} \quad (4)$$

is a set of functions defined on set E on the edges of graph G

$$\{\Psi_j\} : \mathrm{E} \rightarrow R,\ i = 1 \dots \mathrm{I} \quad (5)$$

The function Φ can describe the type of vertex of the graph, e.g. resource, resource vulnerability, threat. While the function Ψ is usually, in practice, a function that builds a network graph on the basis of the links between the nodes of the graph and is used to express the characteristics of the links between the described graph arcs.

The degree of vertex

$$k(x_i) = k + (x_i) + \mathrm{k} - (x_i) + \mathrm{k}^{\sim}(x_i) + \mathrm{k}^{\circ}(x_i) \quad (6)$$

where:

$k + (x_i)$– the number of arcs "going out" of vertex x_i
$k - (x_i)$ – the number of arcs "going in" to vertex x_i
$\mathrm{k}^{\sim}(x_i)$ – the number of edges incident to vertex x_i
$\mathrm{k}^{\circ}(x_i)$ – the number of loops incident to vertex x_i

The graf is a network in which:

$$\{\Phi i\} = \{\Psi_j\} = \emptyset \quad (7)$$

(we omit such trivial functions as functions numbering vertex and branches)

In the surrounding reality, networks are understood as a set of vertices and branches representing the interaction between these vertices together with the ubiquitous functions assigned to the graph.

In the safety analysis of the system, we are looking for nodes with specific characteristics of connections between nodes, threats and vulnerability nodes.

Apart from the obvious advantage of the network model, which is the ability to visualize the links between the effects of hazards, the network models are also built to determine which probability distributions should be applied in a given network. Furthermore, if the links described by the edges are clearly defined - which is relatively easy in the network - the introduction of priors for performing the Bayesian analysis on such network is feasible and bears the characteristics of objectivity, not of a subjective expertise. However, the most important thing is that the network models are typical tools for analysing the situation, in which there is no valid characterization of probability based on tests with a given repetition. The security systems do not provide such models of probability. Therefore, the network feature, which gives a possibility of statistical analysis, not based on the prevalence of an event, predestines the networks to examine the safety issues.

Developing methods for building the network security models may prove to be a truly cost-effective method of analysis of potential security despite the above-mentioned limitations.

3 Model office - example of analysis

The inspiration for the development of the network risk analysis model was to establish the security analysis information for the model of an office, which would be used in case of the documents containing classified information:

- safe storage of existing documents,
- secure document flow with the prerogative of full accountability for both the document and the user,
- safe environment for work with documents,
- safe environment for drawing up new documents,

A model office was developed for storing and viewing classified documents using the RFID technology to mark media information stored in the office. Due to the sensitivity of the information produced and processed in the office, the primary goal was to make it an area isolated from the rest of the office building. The separated area, which the office has become, has a single protected input/output zone, equipped with electronic access control systems and monitoring of items that are brought in. Upon entering the office, there is an area inaccessible to people unauthorized to use it, i.e. the zone for storing the documents. Only the employees of the office may have access to this zone. The last zone, available to persons authorized to use the office, is the zone of the reading room, where one can work on documents taken from the storage or to produce new documents. All office areas are equipped with the systems for monitoring the movement of objects or documents protected by RFID tags [5].

In developing the concept of the model office, the basic criteria of its organization, which had to be taken into account, resulted from the Polish applicable law.

4 Reference model of the security system

The security model used in the Office applies the general reference model shown below.

Figure 1. Network reference model. Source: own elaboration.

This model reflects the general approach to inventory, including its vulnerability and identification of threats that may, based on such vulnerability, have negative impact on the resources.

5 Overview of the methodology

The vast majority of the presently used methodologies for risk analysis are based solely on the expertise of the person conducting this analysis. Assuming only such guarantee of safety, the in-built system can lead to serious deficiencies resulting from intentional or unintentional omission or failure to notice a threat. Equally dangerous could be failure to see vulnerability of the resources to certain threats. Risk assessment of threat implementation by the resource completely depends on the expert knowledge of the issues.

All these defects of the risk analysis method may lead to impairment of the protection system, which in turn can lead to loss of confidentiality, integrity or availability of the protected information.

The process of risk analysis requires, at every stage, the verification of the results by other experts. Interactivity and complexity of this process means that it takes a long time to be implemented (so it is costly) and there is no guarantee of its accuracy and completeness.

Expert analysis of any problem, including identification of the resources, their vulnerability and existing threats lead to extensive and complex semantic description of the problem.

Typically, all components listed in the diagram in Figure 1 are introduced by way of a description, with no strict rules of its creation. In addition, all components must be independent and the resulting links between them must be generated in accordance with the definition of the links in the form of all possible subsets of the Cartesian product of sets of threats, vulnerabilities and assets.

The complexity of this description makes the analysis of the impact of a particular threat on the whole system time-consuming and feasible only by an expert, who developed this description. This is due to the lack of consistent methodology formalizing the rules of impact of the threat description on the resources. As a result, any security consequences and risk analysis constitute a document of considerable volume, which is prepared only because such are the normative and legal requirements. On the other hand, the technique for creating this documentation may contain and usually contains infringement arising from subjective expert knowledge.

The work carried out for the constructed model of the secret office relied on the expert's:

- identification of assets,
- identification of risks,
- identification of vulnerability,

These works resulted in the identification of:

- 213 assets,
- 61 risks,
- 211 susceptibility threats.

Attempts have been made to automate the construction of risk analysis, which showed the complexity of the problem and indicated the key role of an expert. Additionally, a broader view of the obtained results allowed to note the following rule:

- assets described as nouns,
- threats described as nouns,
- vulnerability is described as adjectives or (in Polish) adjective participle or adjective phrase.

With regard to the reference model of the network we obtain the following context (in the sense of grammar) of the network model:

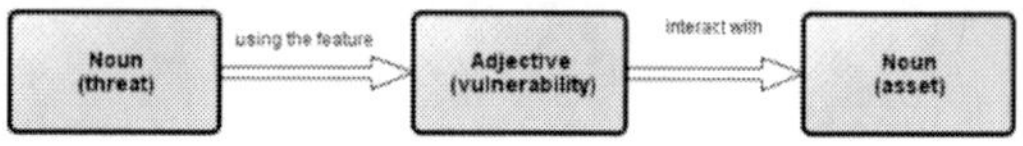

Figure 2. Context model of the network. Source: own elaboration.

The diagram shown in Figure 2 is an indication of the element of the methodology of the network security model.

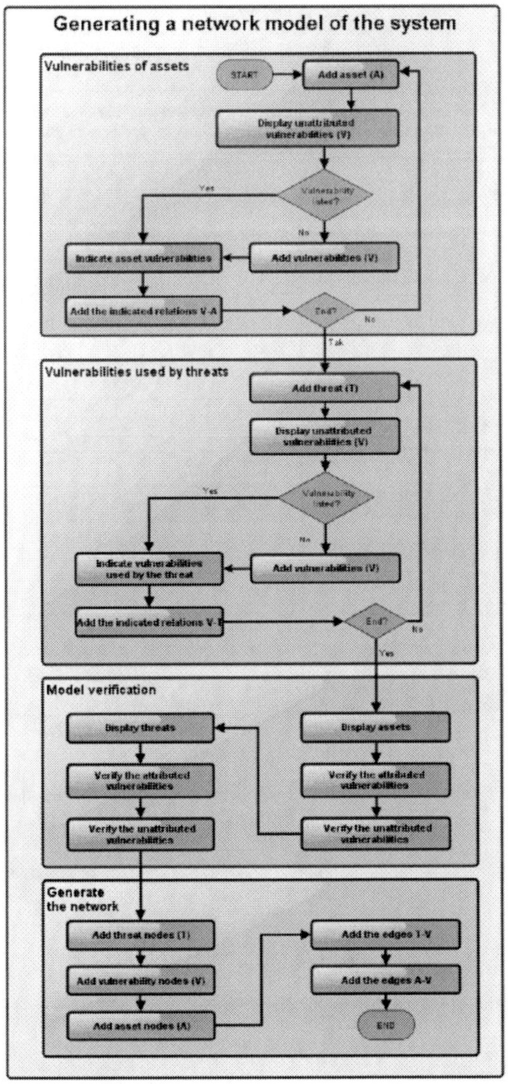

Figure 3. Generation diagram of the network model. Source: own elaboration.

The use of this model has led to the development of an algorithm that describes the process of identifying resources, vulnerability and threats in the context. This algorithm reduced the complexity of the problem by eliminating from the full Cartesian product these components that have no links. Therefore, it made it possible to build a real network model corresponding to reality.

Approval of the expert model is the foundation for building the network model, in which the nodes are the resources, risks and vulnerability. The key for the construction of the network model is the result of creating three pairs: resource - vulnerability and threat-vulnerability through links and connections leaving the nodes, showing the vulnerability, as in the diagram in Figure 2.

6 The use of the network model in the context under consideration

The adopted context model makes it finally possible to maintain an acceptable level of complexity and establish links in a controlled manner subject to the rule shown in Figure 2.

Only a fragment of the expert study was used for the purpose of clear imaging of the results. For this purpose, the following elements have been selected from different areas:

Threats:

- water supply system failure,
- AC system failure,
- heating system failure,
- back-up power system failure,
- emergency power supply system failure,
- external power supply system failure,
- device failure,
- IT system administrator failure.

Vulnerability:

- uncontrolled access of third party users,
- unauthorized access to telecommunications cabinets,
- insufficient physical protection of objects or their elements.

It seems that in the context of a full risk analysis, threats, the occurrence of which is possible rather incidentally, and vulnerability, which may also have to be marginalized, were identified. Therefore, an expert would define them. It turned out that by using the proposed model (risk - susceptibility - resource), the implementation of any of the eight selected threats, using any of the three identified vulnerability risks, may have impact on at least one resource of the 187 items identified in the model of the office.

During the construction of the network model, the fact that every threat affects the resource only based on the vulnerability that exists in this resource was considered. This means that a threat may affect an asset only in the context of specific vulnerability.

The data in Table 1 summarizes some threats and some vulnerability risks, which in the context of these threats will be able to interact with specific resources.

Table 1. Summary of threats and possibly contextually related vulnerability present in the constructed model office.

Threat (T)	Vulnerability (V)
T 0. Water supply system failure	V 70. Uncontrolled remote access of third party users
	V 74. Unauthorized access to telecommunications cabinets
	V 78. Insufficient physical protection of objects or their elements

T 1. AC system failure	V 70. Uncontrolled remote access of third party users
	V 74. Unauthorized access to telecommunications cabinets
	V 78. Insufficient physical protection of objects or their elements
T 2. Heating system failure	V 74. Unauthorized access to telecommunications cabinets
	V 78. Insufficient physical protection of objects or their elements
T 3. Back-up power system failure	V 70. Uncontrolled remote access of third party users
	V 78. Insufficient physical protection of objects or their elements
T 4. Emergency power supply system failure,	V 70. Uncontrolled remote access of third party users
	V 78. Insufficient physical protection of objects or their elements
T 5. External power supply system failure,	V 70. Uncontrolled remote access of third party users
	V 78. Insufficient physical protection of objects or their elements
T 6. Failure of equipment	V 70. Uncontrolled remote access of third party users
T 8. IT system administrator failure	V 70. Uncontrolled remote access of third party users

Table 2 shows a small portion of the statement concerning the vulnerability that can expose certain resources to threats. In such an uncomplicated model, the selected susceptibility exposes to risk almost all of the identified resources, which results in a considerable size of the table.

Table 2. Summary of the selected vulnerability and resources, in which such vulnerability exists, in the constructed model office.

Vulnerability (V)	Asset (A)
V 78. Insufficient physical protection of objects or their elements	A 181. Laptop
	A 182. Telephone line
	A 190. CCTV wiring
	A 192. LAN wiring (copper cable)
	A 193. LAN wiring (optical fibre cable)
	A 194. Intruder Alarm System (IAS) wiring
	A 195. Access control system wiring
V 70. Uncontrolled remote access of third party users	A 134. Firewall
	A 163. AC
	A 179. Back-up copies
	A 181. Laptop
	A 202. Cabinet software
	A 227. Router
	A 239. Alarm system
	A 242. Metal and electronic devices detection system (gate)
V 74. Unauthorized access to telecommunications cabinets	A 227. Router
	A 229. Surrounding
	A 245. Back-up power supply surveillance system
	A 295. Power supply

Comprehensive visualization of the network model is shown in the figure below (Fig. 4):

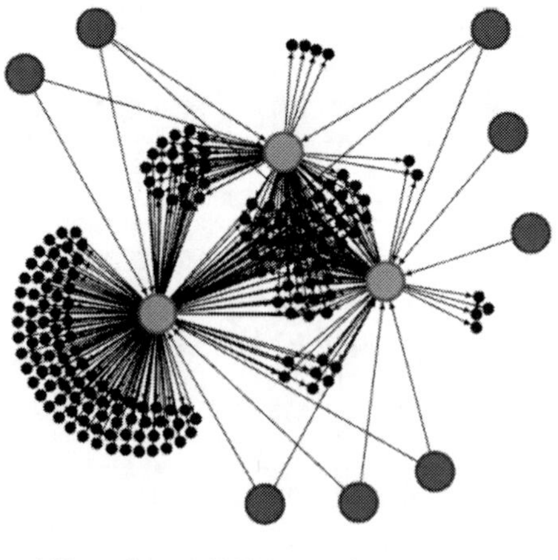

Figure 4. Network graph [6,7] for security model described in the office - selected portion of the assets. (black - asset node, green - vulnerability node, red - threat node). Source: own elaboration, Gephi ver. 0.9.1

A specially developed algorithm based on lexical system was used to create relevant data for the purpose of building a network graph out of the three contextual network models.

The research network algorithms frequently use the method for generating random graphs proposed by Barabasi and Albert [8]. Their model shows two causes - depending on the power series in the distribution of the number of edges coming out of the node. These causes constitute a gradual growth of the network and preferential attachment of the nodes.

Let us denote the network graph node as one vulnerability (V) of the object called asset (A). Let - in the selected V - the number of such recognized threats (T) be equal to m. If they are diagnostically equal (have equally significant impact on the likelihood of a threat), then m of such nodes modelling the risks will be attached to a node of vulnerability.

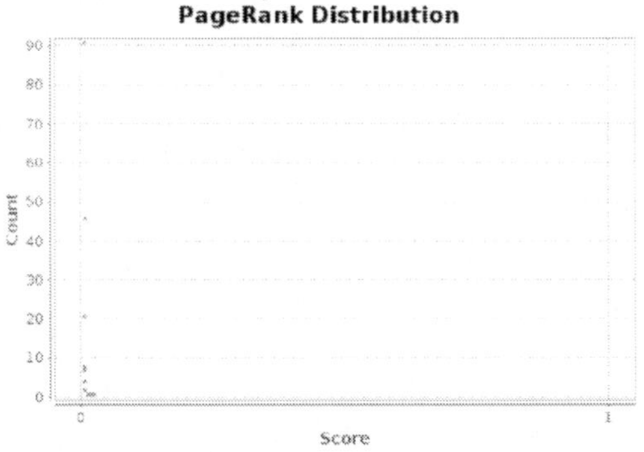

Figure 5. Result of PageRank algorithm. Algorithm: Sergey Brin, Lawrence Page, The Anatomy of a Large-Scale Hypertextual Web Search Engine, in Proceedings of the seventh International Conference on the World Wide Web (WWW1998):107-117, Source: own elaboration, Gephi ver. 0.9.1

Special training is prepared for the purpose of the work (Table 1). On the basis of the information contained in the database, a subnet considering the link with context three is built. In the study A.-L. Barabasi [9], the power distribution of Web was confirmed and the data analysis algorithm was used for indexing web pages developed by the founders of the company Google, Larry Page and Sergey Brin. The research shows that the network security model system shares some common properties with B-A networks.

During the work carried out in the Gephi environment, it turned out that the graph of the network was characterized by the power distribution of the degrees of vertices. As it can be observed, even the subnet shown in Figure 4 is characterized by the power distribution of the degrees of vertices shown in Figure 5. Apparently, this feature also describes the technical systems [10].

The power distribution, in contrast to, for example, the Gaussian, Poisson or exponential distribution, is a natural off-the-scale range. This means that talking about the average values of the degrees of vertices in such networks is ineffective, and, in many cases, the use of the concept of the medium degree leads to serious errors. In the network with the power distribution of the degrees of vertices, many nodes have only one edge, but it is possible to also find the nodes with a huge number of edges, the so-called hubs. This disproportion in an unusual way translates into properties of the off-the-scale networks and makes them very interesting objects of research (Figure 4). We can also observe the small-world phenomenon.

The network analysis can visualize the nodes that pose threats to the resources. It also allows to relatively easily identify a priori probabilities on finite and small set of nodes, which describe the threat.

7 Examples of security incidents - on the network (tripping hazard)

The data presented in Table 3 show the selected vulnerability (V 70. Uncontrolled remote third party user access) and seven threats that - in the context of this vulnerability - may affect the specific, identified assets.

Table 3. Threats and the associated contextual vulnerability present in the constructed model office.

Vulnerability (V)	Threat name (T)
V 70. Uncontrolled remote access of third party users	T 0. Water supply system failure
	T 1. AC system failure
	T 3. Back-up power system failure
	T 4. Emergency power supply system failure,
	T 5. External power supply system failure,
	T 6. Failure of equipment
	T 8. IT system administrator failure

The model of the network of the three, threat - vulnerability - asset was displayed in a way that radically changed its assessment and made it clear that the impact of the threat on the entire system was possible.

The graphic illustration in the system threat (T) - vulnerability (V) - asset (A) is much clearer than the presentation of the same problem in a tabular format. This forms additional grounds for usability of the network model.

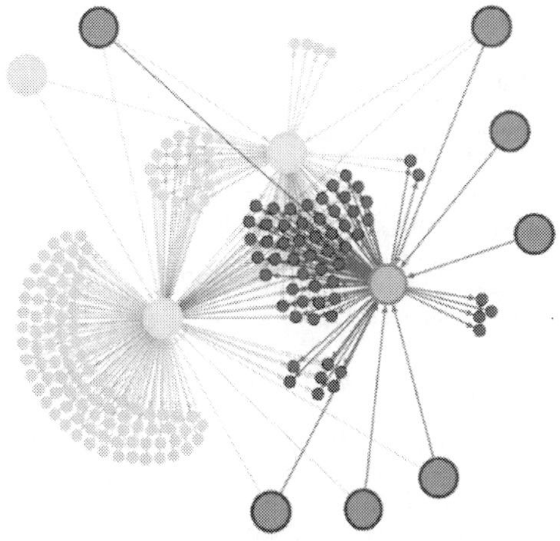

Figure 6. Assets that may be affected by the occurrence of one of the six above-mentioned threats in the context of vulnerability "Uncontrolled remote access of third party users." Source: own elaboration, Gephi ver. 0.9.1

In the above figure (Figure 6), it is easy to notice a group of resources that have one, two or three analysed vulnerability risks. There are also visible threats that can use only one, indicated susceptibility. In further stages of the safety analysis, it is possible to use this information to establish protection systems. They will be aimed at precisely selected vulnerability risks. The stage of establishing security must precede the full risk analysis.

8 Summary

On the example of the model office, including the documents of different classification levels [11], the construction of the network security model has been shown. For this purpose, the methodology procedure was developed, bearing the features of the new solution.

An analysis of the occurrence of a security incident and its impact on certain resources using the network model [12] is much more readable than the traditional tabular description. Additionally, it becomes apparent that the use of the Bayesian networks can be limited not to the full network configuration, but to its subgraph so as to include the selected hazards in the analysis. Basically, it will change the possibility of using the Bayesian networks in the safety analysis and determining priors.

While the grounds for restrictions in the normative documents concerning the use of the network could justify considerable complexity of the calculations (when we consider the full shape of the network with a number of elements that is determined by the Cartesian product $A \times V \times T$) and difficulty of assignment of probabilities by the Bayesian models, in drawings 5 and 7, the reduction of these restrictions to an acceptable level is clearly visible. Therefore, it was possible to develop a systematic methodology for the construction of networks. This indicates the possibility of a new definition of the role of the network models in the safety analysis.

References

1. *PN-EN 31010:2010 Risk management - Risk assessment techniques*
2. *PN ISO/IEC 27005 Information technology. Security techniques. Information security risk management*
3. *PKN–ISO GUIDE 73 Risk management - Terminology*
4. K. Liderman, *Risk Analysis and protection of information in computer systems* (2008)
5. M. Kiedrowicz (Editor), *Managing sensitive information* (2015)
6. A. Fronczak, P. Fronczak, *Świat sieci złożonych. Od fizyki do Internetu*, (Wydawnictwo Naukowe PWN, 2009)
7. R. Sinatra, P. Deville, M. Szell, D. Wang, A-L Barabási, *A century of physics*, Nature Physics, **11**, 791–796 (2015)
8. A.-L. Barabási, R. Albert, *Emergence of scaling in random networks*, Science, **286**, 509−512 (1999)
9. A.-L. Barabási, R. Albert, H. Jeong, G. Bianconi,, Science, **287**, 2115 (2000)
10. I. Eusgeld, C. Nan, S. Dietz , *"System-of-systems" approach for interdependent critical infrastructures*, Reliability Engineering and System Safety, **96**, 679-686 (2011)
11. J. Stanik J., M. Kiedrowicz, *Selected aspects of risk management in respect of security of the document lifecycle management system with multiple levels of sensitivity*, Information Management in Practice, 231-251, (2015)
12. Probabilistic Risk Assessment Procedures Guide for NASA Managers and Practitioners, NASA/SP-2011-3421, Sec.Ed (2011)

Efficient parameter estimation for anatomy deformation models used in 4D-CT

Elizabeth S. Zachariah[1], Ding-Yu Fei[2] and Alen Docef[1,a]

[1]Virginia Commonwealth University, Electrical and Computer Engineering, Richmond, Virginia 23284-3072, USA
[2]Virginia Commonwealth University, Biomedical Engineering, Richmond, Virginia 23284-3067, USA

Abstract. A critical feature of radiation therapy for cancerous tumors located in the thorax and abdomen is addressing tumor motion due to breathing. To achieve this goal, a CT study (ordinarily denoted as 4D-CT) showing tumor location, size, and shape against time is essential. Several 4D-CT reconstruction methods have been proposed that employ anatomy deformation models. The proposed method estimates temporal parameters for these models using an approach that does not require markers or manual designation of landmark anatomical features. A neural network is trained to estimate the parameters based on simple statistical features of the CT projections. The proposed method achieves an average estimation error of less than 0.02 seconds, corresponding to a spatial error of less than 1.3 mm. The accuracy of the proposed method is evaluated in the presence of several limiting constraints such as computational complexity and noise.

1 Introduction

Radiation therapy is the preferred method of eradicating cancerous tumors located in the thorax and abdomen. To accurately target radiation to the tumor, its size, shape and location have to be known for both planning and delivery [1, 2, 3, 4, 5]. Image-guided radiation therapy (IGRT) techniques, such as conformal radiation therapy and intensity modulated radiation therapy, use CT imaging to optimize coverage of the target volume without affecting surrounding healthy tissue [1, 6]. A critical feature of IGRT is addressing tumor motion. The most prevalent cause for motion in the thorax and abdomen is breathing [1, 7, 8]. Tumors can move up to 4 cm during the breathing cycle [1, 2] causing the target volume to move in and out of the dose targeting window [9, 10, 11]. Techniques like controlled breath hold or respiratory gating can be uncomfortable or require long treatment sessions [8, 12, 13, 14, 15]. By contrast, in tumor tracking, the delivery field follows the tumor during the entire breathing cycle, allowing the patient to breathe freely [16].

A critical requirement for tumor tracking is a time-dependent CT study, ordinarily denoted as 4D-CT. Numerous methods have been implemented to construct a 4D-CT model of the moving anatomy. Some methods include modeling respiratory motion with cosine models, or averaging multiple breathing periods to create one model period [9]. In actuality, respiratory motion is more complex, and breathing periods change during treatment [1]. The more common approach is to combine CT data with a respiratory trace and assume that anatomical motion occurs in synchrony with the trace [7, 14, 17]. The trace can be obtained by monitoring a physical marker (such as a reflecting block attached to the patient's abdomen) or by measuring the tidal volume using a spirometer [5].

In the conventional 4D-CT method, the breathing trace is collected as CT projections are acquired [2, 17, 18, 19]. Based on their temporal locations within a breathing cycle, the projections are partitioned into several bins [5]. Commonly, 10 time bins are used. A 3D CT image is reconstructed for each time bin using filtered back-projection, resulting in ten CTs covering a typical breathing period.

Model-based 4D-CT methods do not limit the 4D-CT to one typical period, thus addressing inter-period variations. They also provide much better temporal resolution, potentially providing images of the anatomy at arbitrary time instants. These methods use a reference 3D image S which is deformed by a time-dependent Displacement Vector Field (DVF) $d($ such that the anatomy at any time is

$$S'(\boldsymbol{r},t) = S(\boldsymbol{r} + \boldsymbol{d}(\boldsymbol{r},t)) \quad (1)$$

Here, $\boldsymbol{r}$ is the 3D spatial variable. In our notation all bold-faced variables are vectors in space.

The spatio-temporal DVF model employed in this research is the one introduced in [20, 21, 22]. This model employs DVF basis vectors $\boldsymbol{u}_i$ to model spatial variation in the DVF and the breathing trace ℓ to model temporal variation:

[a] Corresponding author: adocef@vcu.edu

$$d(r,t) = \sum_i a_i u_i(r) b(t - \theta_i) \quad (2)$$

Each spatial basis vector $u_i(r)$ is scaled by the amplitude a_i and modulated by the term $b(t-\theta_i)$, resulting in a DVF component that varies proportionally with breathing, with a delay θ_i. It has been shown that three basis vectors are sufficient for accurate representation of DVFs [22]. The basis vectors are obtained as follows: First, conventional 4D-CT is performed on the CT projection set. Pairs of consecutive projections are then registered, resulting in a set of 3D DVFs. Lastly, three basis vectors are computed from this set by means of Principal Component Analysis (PCA).

The model parameters and could be computed using a curve-fitting approach for anatomical landmarks (either fiducials or manually identified features); however, these are not available in realistic scenarios. Instead, projection-matching methods have been proposed in [21, 22]. These methods deform the reference image using a DVF model, compute simulated projections, and iteratively adjust the DVF model parameters to minimize the difference between simulated and actual projections. Each iteration involves a large number of computations, and the algorithm may converge to a local minimum.

A method is proposed for computationally efficient marker-less estimation of the temporal parameters. A neural network is trained to estimate the parameters based on simple statistical features of the CT projections. For projection-based parameter estimation, this method reduces the number of computations and the likelihood of convergence to local minima. For binning-based DVF interpolation, the method becomes a two-step non-iterative algorithm.

Details on the proposed method are presented in Section 2. The experimental results are discussed in Section 3 and the findings are summarized in Section 4.

2 Proposed Estimation Method

In a typical clinical scenario, a 4D-CT image set must be reconstructed from the following available data: a complete set of CT projections collected as the patient breathes freely, a digitized breathing trace, and an a priori 3D reference CT scan acquired for treatment planning. From these inputs, a complete 4D volumetric image must be computed. Usually, the reference is a fan-beam scan while the free-breathing scan is a cone-beam CT.

The temporal parameters for the model are estimated in this work using neural networks. Neural networks have been used successfully for prediction of breathing amplitudes and irregular breathing patterns [23, 24]. Given their proven ability to model temporal behavior, they are a good candidate for temporal parameter estimation. We next describe the method as used in two different scenarios.

Case 1: Use in projection matching 4D-CT. In this scenario, the spatial basis vectors in Eq. 2 are known; and are sought. A feature vector is first computed from the projection set $\{P_i, i = 1, \ldots,$ The features are then fed to a neural network trained to estimate the delay parameters . Once are known, the amplitudes are found using the projection matching approach. An initial guess of is assumed and a DVF is computed using Eq. 2. The DVF is used to deform the reference image at time instants $t_1, \ldots$ Simulated CT projections { are computed through the moving anatomy and compared to the actual projections . The parameters are iteratively adjusted to minimize the difference between the simulated and actual projections.

The features used to estimate are simple statistical features of the CT projections. In this paper, the mean, standard deviation, and centroid of each projection are computed and grouped in a vector of size . The neural network is trained using a large number of simulated projection sets corresponding to known values.

In contrast with existing projection matching methods [21, 20], the proposed method estimates and separately. Since the number of free parameters is reduced by half, projection matching is less likely to converge to a local minimum, requires fewer iterations, and fewer computations in each iteration. The single-step estimation of requires a comparatively insignificant amount of computation.

Case 2: Use in basis DVF computation. The proposed method can be used to simplify the process by which the DVF basis functions are obtained. The PCA method of [22] assumes no knowledge of the delays . The computations can be significantly simplified if are first estimated using the method described in Case 1. We next describe the method for computing and , when are known.

The method assumes that 3D DVFs are known at time instants $t_1, \ldots$ These have been computed from a conventional 4D-CT. Eq. 2 is applied times, resulting in a set of equations that can be written in matrix form as:

$$\boldsymbol{D} = \mathbf{BAU}, \quad (3)$$

where each row of matrix $\boldsymbol{D}$ is a DVF, each row of matrix $\boldsymbol{U}$ is a row basis vector, $\boldsymbol{A} = \mathrm{diag}(a_1, a_2, a_3)$ is a diagonal matrix of amplitude parameters, the matrix

$$\mathbf{B} = \begin{bmatrix} b(t_1-\theta_1) & b(t_1-\theta_2) & b(t_1-\theta_3) \\ b(t_2-\theta_1) & b(t_2-\theta_2) & b(t_2-\theta_3) \\ \vdots & \vdots & \vdots \\ b(t_N-\theta_1) & b(t_N-\theta_2) & b(t_N-\theta_3) \end{bmatrix} \quad (4)$$

contains values of the breathing trace, and θ_1, θ_2, θ_3 are the temporal parameters. In Eq. 3, the unknowns are the matrices $\boldsymbol{A}$ and $\boldsymbol{U}$. This is an over-determined system, and the least-square solution for the product $\boldsymbol{AU}$ is given by

$$\mathrm{AU} = \boldsymbol{B}^{+}\boldsymbol{D}, \quad (5)$$

where $\boldsymbol{B}^{+}$ is the Moore-Penrose pseudo-inverse of $\boldsymbol{B}$ [25]. Since u_i are unit vectors, they, together with a_i, can be computed by normalization of $a_i u_i$, the rows of $\boldsymbol{AU}$:

$$u_i = \frac{a_i u_i}{\|a_i u_i\|}, \quad a_i = \frac{a_i u_i}{\|u_i\|} \quad (6)$$

The method is non-iterative and involves computation of the pseudo-inverse of a small matrix (typically 10). By comparison, the PCA method of [22] processes vectors of size equal to the number of voxels in the image. More details about the pseudo-inverse method and its performance can be found in [26]. Note that in this context the proposed method can also be seen as a model-based DVF interpolation method.

3 Experimental Results

3.1 Experimental Setup

The proposed method is evaluated in the context of Case 1 described above. The CT images in real clinical settings are 3D, and cone-beam CT projections are 2D. In this paper, the feasibility of the proposed method is assessed in a simplified setting using 2D CT images. The projections are therefore 1D and the DVF in Eq. 2 is 3D (2D + time).

Since ground truth values are not available for real clinical data, a combination of real anatomy, real breathing, synthetic motion, and simulated projections was used, as follows:

- The reference static CT image S used in all experiments is an axial fan-beam CT slice of size 256×256. A cropped version of the image is shown in Figure 1.
- The real trace $b(t)$ previously used in [23] was chosen to model breathing and is shown in Figure 2. The trace was normalized to have zero mean and a maximum absolute value of 1.0. The scan time instants $t_1, \dots, t_N$ were chosen to uniformly cover two full breathing periods. The period was estimated to be $T = 3.1$ s based on the average interval between peaks.
- The synthetic motion corresponds to a DVF computed using Eq. 2 with two basis vectors: u_1 being an antero-posterior expansion and u_2 a lateral contraction of the anatomy. In both directions the maximum displacement was chosen to be 3.5 cm. For clarity, we hereafter denote the two vectors by u_x and u_y and the corresponding delays by θ_x and θ_y.
- For a given (θ_x, θ_y) pair, the DVF is computed and used to animate the reference image. A set of N simulated parallel projections is then computed at time instants $t_1, \dots, t_N$. The N projection angles uniformly cover a full gantry rotation. The algorithm is evaluated for N ranging from 8 to 64.
- For each projection, the features (mean, standard deviation, and centroid) are computed. The N triplets are merged into a single feature vector, then fed to the neural network, which estimates the two delays.

This approach made possible the comparison between the estimated and actual temporal parameters.

A feed-forward neural network with one hidden layer of 20 neurons was used. The network takes a vector of projection features as input and outputs the estimated delay parameters. The network is trained to minimize the estimation error in the Mean Square Error (MSE) sense. The testing data sets, consisting of representative input feature vectors and target delay parameters, were created as follows: A set of random $(\theta_x,$ delays is first generated with values ranging from $-T$ to $+T$ where is the period of the breathing trace. For each of these, a DVF is computed and used to animate the reference image, simulated projections are computed, and a feature vector is calculated. A total of 2200 samples were used to train and test the network, with 10-fold cross-validation. In all the experiments described below, the neural network is trained for 50 Levenberg-Marquardt iterations.

To evaluate the accuracy and robustness of the proposed method, multiple scenarios have been considered, with varying numbers of projections, projection resolutions, and levels of projection noise. The method's accuracy was quantified by means of the root MSE (rMSE) error.

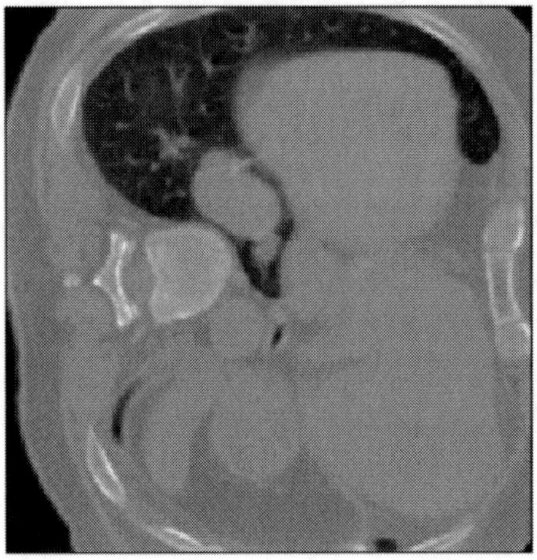

Figure 1. Reference CT image

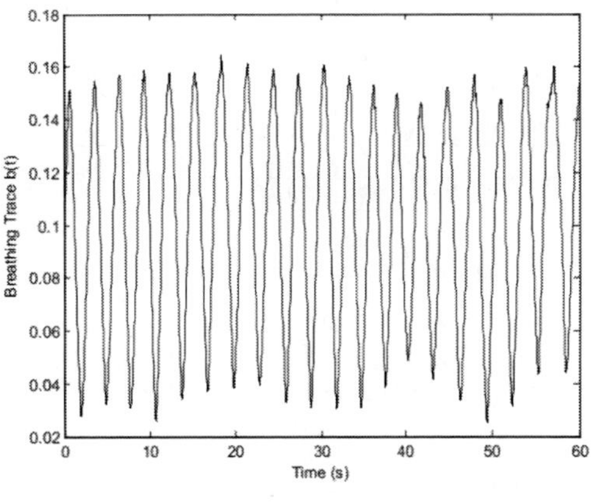

Figure 2. Breathing trace, in arbitrary dimensionless units.

3.2 Results

The *reference* scenario, against which all scenarios are evaluated, assumes that 32 full-resolution noise-free projections are available. The input to the neural network is the feature vector described previously. The rMSE values for θ_x and θ_y are 0.0188 and 0.0178 seconds, respectively.

The effect of the *number of projections* on accuracy is evaluated by changing the reference setting of $N =$ up to 64 and down to 16 and 8. The results are shown in Figure 3(a). As expected, as the number of projections decrease, the accuracy worsens. While the algorithm does not completely fail when fewer than 16 projections are used, such settings are probably of little practical use.

Next, to assess the necessary *projection resolution*, the CT projections are downsampled by a factor of 2, then 4. The resolution of the parallel projections in the reference setting is equal to the spatial resolution of the reference CT image. The results shown in Figure 3(b) indicate that downsampling by 2 is acceptable but the accuracy decreases significantly for higher ratios. The plot also suggests that higher resolution projections would have little benefit.

The method's robustness in the presence of *projection noise* is also evaluated. Zero-mean white Gaussian noise is added to the projections in increasing amounts (5%, 10%, 20%, and 40%). These noise levels represent the ratio between the standard deviations of noise and projection. The results in Figure 3(c) show, unsurprisingly, higher estimation errors for increased noise. Noise levels higher than 10% are unacceptable.

In an attempt to assess the *suitability of the features* chosen for temporal parameter estimation, a final experiment was carried out, comparing feature-based estimation to estimation based on the entire projection sequence. The dimension of a full projection set is prohibitive (for both statistical and computational reasons), therefore we chose to downsample the reference image to $32 \times$ and to use at most 8 noise-free projections. This is clearly not a practical setting, however, the results in Table 1 indicate that a larger feature set may achieve improved accuracy or allow the use of fewer projections.

Table 1. Suitability of the feature set

	Full Projections		Features	
Number of Projections	rMSE (θ_x)	rMSE (θ_y)	rMSE (θ_x)	rMSE (θ_y)
8	0.0042	0.0050	0.0849	0.0603
4	0.0109	0.0108	0.1178	0.1136

3.3 Discussion

To put these rMSE numbers in context, recall that the delays take values from $-T/2$ to $+T/2$, where $T = 3.1$. Thus the rMSE values for the reference setting are 0.6% of the breathing period, or 6% of the interval between the time bins of a typical conventional 4D-CT. An even more illuminating interpretation of these results is to consider the effect of the estimation error on the DVF accuracy.

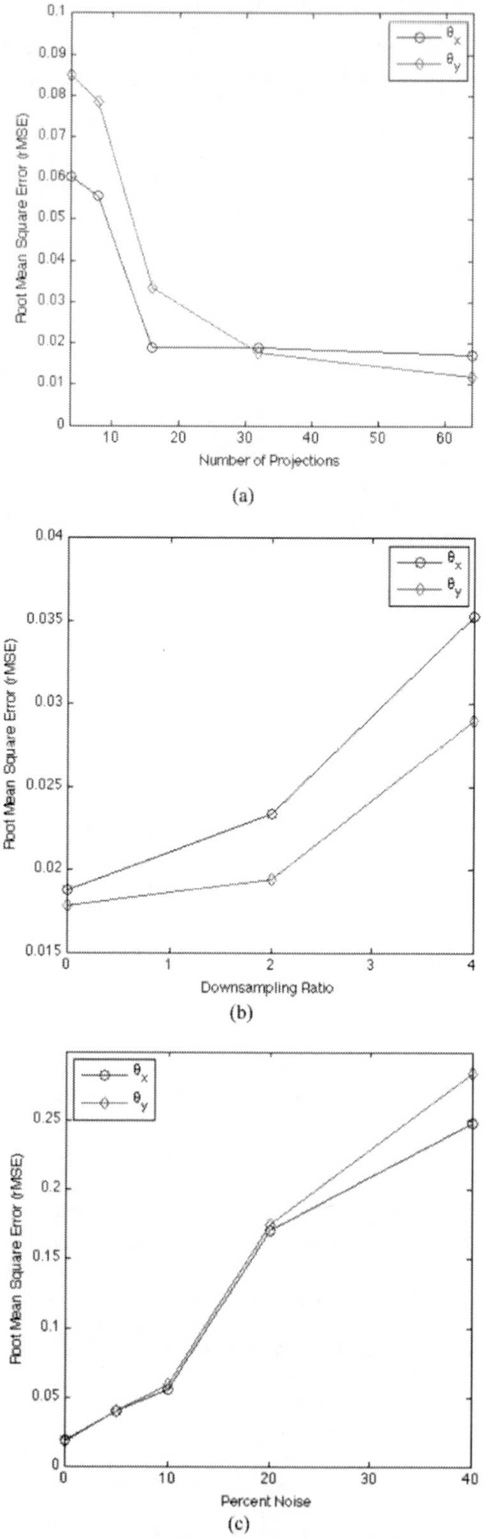

Figure 3. Estimation error as a function of (a) the number of projections, (b) the projection resolution and (c) noise level.

In a worst-case scenario, considering the maximum slope of the trace in Eq. 2 and a maximum deformation of cm, the maximum DVF error is found to be mm. This value is well within the accuracy of DVF estimation methods.

One limitation of the experimental setup is that the neural network is trained for a particular reference image and set of DVF basis vectors. When these change, it may therefore fail to accurately estimate values. Addressing this issue is beyond the scope of this feasibility study. However, the rather generic nature of the features and the substantial amount of a priori information that can be exploited (reference image, lengthy breathing trace, conventional 4D-CT) are grounds for optimism that the issue could be successfully addressed in future work.

Another minor limitation is that the test DVF is perfectly modeled by Eq. 2. However, it has been shown previously that the equation accurately models realistic breathing motion [22]. Real anatomical motion will be used in future work.

4 Conclusions

A neural network-based method for estimating temporal parameters of a DVF model has been proposed. The method's average estimation error is less than 0.02 seconds, and its worst-case DVF error is 1.3 mm. The accuracy of the proposed method has been evaluated in the presence of computational complexity constraints and CT projection noise.

References

[1] L. Xing, B. Thorndyke, E. Schreibmann, Y. Yang, T.-F. Li, G.-Y. Kim, G. Luxton and A. Koong, "Overview of Image-Guided Radiation Therapy," *Medical Dosimetry,* vol. 31, no. 2, pp. 91-112, 2006.

[2] L. A. Dawson and M. B. Sharpe, "Image-guided radiotherapy: rationale, benefits, and limitations.," *Lancet Oncology,* no. 7, pp. 848-858, 2006.

[3] L. A. Dawson and D. A. Jaffray, "Advances in image-guided radiation therapy," *J Cin Oncol,* vol. 25, pp. 938-946, 2007.

[4] M. Baumann, T. Holscher and D. Zips, "The future of IGRT - cost benefit analysis," *Acta Oncologica,* vol. 47, no. 7, pp. 1188-1192, 2008.

[5] M. Lecchi, P. Fossati, F. Elisei, R. Orecchia and G. Lucignani, "Current concepts on imaging in radiotherapy," *European Journal of Nuclear Medicine and Molecular Imaging,* vol. 35, pp. 821-837, 2008.

[6] D. Verellen, M. De Ridder and G. Storme, "A (short) history of image-guided radiotherapy," *Radiotherapy and Oncology,* vol. 86, pp. 4-13, 2008.

[7] G. S. Mageras, A. Pevsner and E. D. Yorke, "Measurement of lung tumor motion using respiration-correlated CT," *Int J Radiat Oncol Biol Phys,* no. 60, pp. 933-941, 2004.

[8] P. Keall, "4-dimensional computed tomography imaging and treatment planning," *Seminars in Radiation Oncology,* vol. 14, pp. 81-90, 2004.

[9] V. Boldea, G. C. Sharp, S. B. Jiang and D. Sarrut, "4D-CT lung motion estimation with deformable registration: Quantification of motion nonlinearity and hysteresis," *Medical Physics,* vol. 35, pp. 1008-1018, 2008.

[10] Y. Sun, S. Dieterich, B. Cho and P. J. Keall, "An analysis of thoracic and abdominal tumour motion for stereotactic body radiotherapy patients," *Physics in Medicine and Biology,* vol. 53, pp. 3623-3640, 2008.

[11] S. Mori, M. Endo, S. Komatsu, T. Yashiro, S. Kandatsu and M. Baba, "Four-dimensional measurement of lung tumor displacement using 256-multi-slice CT-scanner," *Lung Cancer,* vol. 56, pp. 59-67, 2007.

[12] A. Trofimov, E. Rietzel and H. Lu, "Temporo-spatial IMRT optimization: Concepts, implementation and initial results," *Phys Med Biol,* no. 50, pp. 2779-2798, 2005.

[13] E. M. Leter, F. Cademartiri, P. C. Levendag, H. Stam and P. J. Nowak, "Four-dimensional multislice computed tomography for determination of respiratory lung tumor motion in conformal radiotherapy," *International Journal of Radiation Oncology, Biology, Physics,* vol. 62, no. 3, pp. 888-892, 1 July 2005.

[14] J. Wong, M. B. Sharpe and D. A. Jaffray, "The use of active breathing control (ABC) to reduce margin for breathing motion," *Int J Radiat Oncol Biol Phys,* no. 44, pp. 911-919, 1999.

[15] R. Zeng, J. A. Fessler and J. M. Balter, "Respiratory motion estimation from slowly rotating x-ray projections: theory and simulation," *Medical Physics,* vol. 32, no. 4, pp. 984-991, April 2005.

[16] F. Khan, G. Bell, J. Antony, M. Palmer, P. Balter, K. Bucci and M. J. Chapman, "The use of 4DCT to reduce lung dose: a dosimetric analysis," *Medical Dosimetry,* vol. 34, no. 4, pp. 273-278, 2009.

[17] G. Chen, J. Tang and S. Leng, "Prior image constrained compressed sensing (PICCS): A method to accurately reconstruct dynamic CT images from highly undersampled projection data sets," *Medical Physics,* vol. 35, pp. 660-663, 2008.

[18] P. J. Keall, G. Starkschall and H. Shukla, "Acquiring 4D thoracic CT scans using a multislice helical method," *Phys Med Biol,* no. 49, pp. 2053-2067, 2004.

[19] E. Yorke, K. E. Rosenzweig, R. Wagman and G. S. Mageras, "Interfractional anatomic variation in patients treated with respiration-gated radiotherapy," *Journal of Applied Clinical Medical Physics,* vol. 6, pp. 19-32, 2005.

[20] A. Docef and M. J. Murphy, "Reconstruction of 4D

DOI: 10.1051/matecconf/20167602003

deformed CT for moving anatomy," *International Journal of Computer Assisted Radiology and Surgery,* no. 3, pp. 591-598, 2008.

[21] R. S. Brock, A. Docef and M. J. Murphy, "Reconstruction of a cone-beam CT via forward iterative projection matching," *Medical Physics,* vol. 37, 2010.

[22] D. Staub, A. Docef, R. S. Brock and C. Vaman, "4D Cone-beam CT reconstruction using a motion model based on principal component analysis," *Medical Physics,* vol. 38, no. 12, pp. 6212-6220, December 2011.

[23] M. J. Murphy and S. Dieterich, "Comparative performance of linear and nonlinear neural networks to predict irregular breathing," *Physics in Medicine and Biology,* vol. 51, no. 22, p. 5903, 21 Nov 2006.

[24] M. J. Murphy and D. Pokhrel, "Optimization of an adaptive neural network to predict breathing," *Medical Physics,* vol. 36, no. 1, pp. 40-47, January 2009.

[25] A. G. T. Ben-Israel, Generalized Inverses: Theory And Applications, Springer, 2003.

[26] E. Zachariah, "4-D Modeling of Displacement Vector Fields for Improved Radiation Therapy," 2010. [Online]. Available: http://scholarscompass.vcu.edu/etd/2323.

Seismic response of waste storage tanks

Kamila Kotrasova[1,a] and Eva Kormanikova[1]

[1]Department of Structural Mechanics, Institute of Structural Engineering, The Technical University of Kosice, Faculty of Civil Engineering, Vysokoskolska 4, 042 00 Kosice, Slovak Republic

Abstract. Ground- supported cylindrical tanks are used to store a variety of liquids. This paper provides the theoretical background for takes into account impulsive and convective (sloshing) actions of the fluid in concrete containers fixed to rigid foundations; it has been adopted in Eurocode 8. Seismic responses – base shears, the bending and overturning moments – are calculated by using the response spectra of the earthquake in Loma Prieta, California. As the examples is analyzed the ground supported cylindrical concrete tanks, where for constant fluid filling *H*, *R* are depended from parameters tank slenderness ratio $\gamma = H/R$.

1 Introduction

Ground-supported cylindrical tanks are strategically very important structures, since they have vital uses in industries, nuclear power plants and are connected to public life. Liquid storage tanks are used to store a variety of liquids, e.g. water for drinking and fire fighting, petroleum, oil, liquefied natural gas, chemical fluids, chemical and radioactive wastes. Seismic safely of liquid tanks is of considerable importance [1–8]. Water storage tanks should remain functional in the post earthquake period to ensure potable water supply to earthquake-affected regions and to cater the need for fighting demand. Industrial liquid tanks containing highly toxic and inflammable liquids and these tanks should not lose their contents during the earthquake. Satisfactory performance of tanks during strong ground shaking is crucial for there modern facilities. The seismic behavior of liquid storage tanks is highly complex problem due to liquid-structure interaction. Tanks that were inadequately designed or detailed have suffered extensive damage during past earthquakes [9–12].

2 Cylindrical tank and behaviour

Among the different structural forms of liquid containers, the ground supported upright cylindrical tank is the most commonly used type because it is very efficient in withstanding the hydrostatic load caused by the liquid content.

A typical cylindrical tank is shown in Figure 1. It essentially consists of a base plate rested on the ground and a vertically erected shell wall. Optionally, there may be a floating or fixed roof to protect the liquid content from the outside air, column(s) inside the tank to support the roof, ring girders to enhance the stiffness of the wall and to improve its stability, and anchorage along the border of the base plate to prevent uplift. For a broad tank with its diameter, and therefore the tank is generally left unanchored.

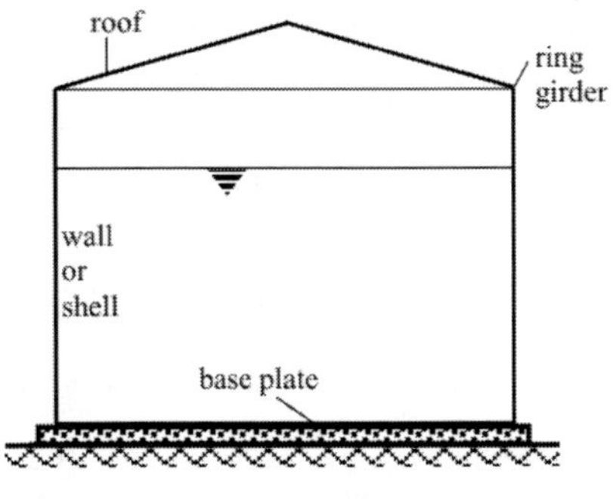

Figure 1. Typical cylindrical tank

Under the static condition, a cylindrical liquid storage tank is subjected to axisymmetric hydrostatic pressure caused by the liquid content acting radially outwards on the vertical tank shell wall. Hoop tensile force is developed in tank shell wall to withstand this pressure. In static design of a cylindrical tank, the required shell thickness of the shell wall is determined by the magnitude of this hoop tensile force. Under the static condition the base plate and the other parts of the tank structure bear no significant load and thus can be designed just to comply with the minimum structural requirements.

When a liquid storage tank is subjected to seismic load, vibration motion of the liquid content is developed due to the ground excitation acting on it via the tank

[a] Corresponding author: kamila.kotrasova@tuke.sk

structure. The first one, defined as the "impulsive mode", consists of the liquid particles moving in unison with the motion of the tank structure. The second one, defined as the "convective mode" or usually called "sloshing", consists of the liquid particles near the free surface oscillating vertically. The resultant load effect of the liquid motion is generally represented by a total base shear and an overturning moment. In response to the hydrodynamic load, axial compressive and tensile stresses as well as additional hoop stress are developed in the tank shell wall. These stresses are asymmetric and much greater than that due to the hydrostatic pressure under the static condition. For an unanchored tank subjected to a sufficiently large resultant overturning moment, a portion of the base plate will separate from the support foundation. Accompanying with the base plate uplift, extensive deformations with significant out-of round distortion occur in the tank shell wall. The phenomenon is called the "uplift mechanism". The "uplift mechanism" is highly nonlinear to the applied load. The significant deformation and violet motion of the tank structure in turn greatly affect the liquid motion, and thud the hydrodynamic load.

Based on field observations, the typical failure modes of liquid storage tanks can be summarized as follows [2]:

- failure of the base plate,
- buckling of the tank shell wall,
- rupture of the tank shell wall at anchorage,
- failure of anchorage,
- failure of roof,
- total collapse,
- failure off partial settlement of foundation,
- sliding walk-off of foundation due to rocking,
- damages to piping connections or other equipments.

For unanchored liquid storage tanks, buckling of the tank shell wall is the most common type of structure damage due to the narrow concentration and high magnitude of the compressive force developed in the tank shell wall when the tank base plate is partially uplifted from the ground support during an earthquake. Failure of the tank roof, due to the impact from the intense liquid sloshing and damage to piping connection, due to the large displacement of the tank structure during dynamic response, are also frequently reported for unanchored liquid storage tanks.

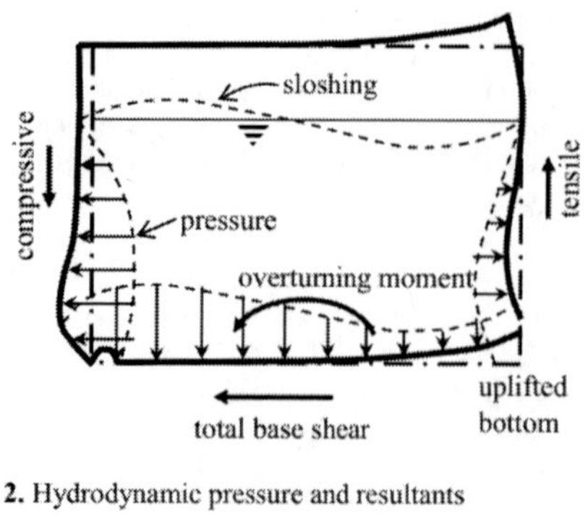

Figure 2. Hydrodynamic pressure and resultants

Figure 2 illustrates the typical hydrodynamic effect and resultants.

3 Mechanical model

The dynamic analysis of a liquid - filled tank may be carried out using the concept of generalized single - degree - of freedom (SDOF) systems representing the impulsive and convective modes of vibration of the tank - liquid system as shown in Figure 3. For practical applications, only the first convective modes of vibration need to be considered in the analysis, mechanical model. The impulsive mass of liquid m_i is rigidly attached to tank wall at height h_i. Similarly convective mass m_{cn} is attached to the tank wall at height h_{cn} by a spring of stiffness k_{cn}. The mass, height and natural period of each SDOF system are obtained by the methods described in [13].

4 Seismic analysis of liquid filled tanks

The seismic analysis of a liquid-filled tank may by carried out using the concept of generalized single-degree-of-freedom systems representing the impulsive and convective modes of vibration of tank-liquid system. The problem of fluid-structure interaction is very important in case of high tanks. The motion of fluid in the tank is possible to define using the simple quasistatic model, in which the inertial forces are defined by hydrostatic and hydrodynamic pressure on the tank wall.

4.1 Formatting the text

The seismic loads acting on wall and bottom of cylindrical tanks (Figure 2) can be divided into the following components:

- The rigid impulsive component, caused by the inertia of the liquid, if the rigid tank moves together with the foundation,
- the convective load component; the fluid vibration in the rigid tank (sloshing),
- the impulsive flexible tank shell (e.g. steel tanks) with the liquid.

The motion of the fluid contained in a rigid cylinder may by expressed as the sum of two separate contributions, called "rigid impulsive" and "convective", respectively. The "rigid impulsive" component satisfies exactly the boundary conditions at the walls and the bottom of the tank, but gives (incorrectly, due to the presence of the waves in the dynamic response) zero pressure at the original position of the free surface of the fluid in the static situation. The "convective" term does not alter those boundary conditions that are already satisfied, while fulfilling the correct equilibrium condition at the free surface. Use is made of a cylindrical coordinate system: r, z, θ, with origin at the centre of the tank bottom and the radius are denoted by H and R, respectively, ρ is the mass density of the fluid, while $\xi = r/R$ is dimensionless radius and $\zeta = z/H$ is nondimensional coordinate.

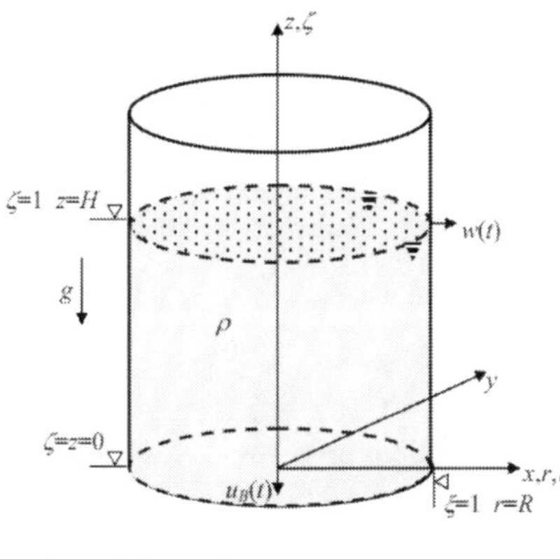

Figure 3. Cylindrical tank

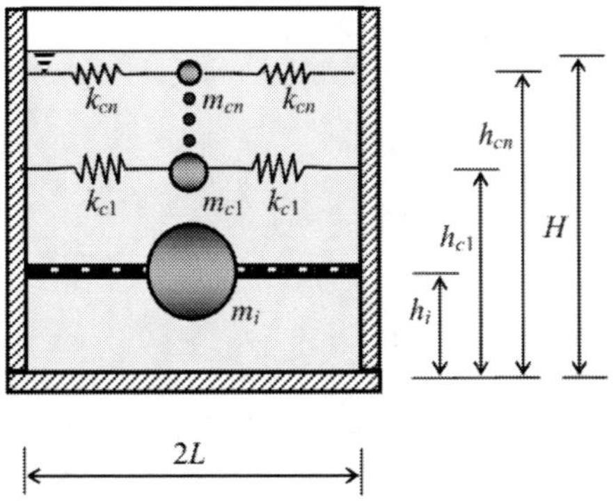

Figure 4. Liquid-filled tank modeled by generalized single degree of freedom systems

4.2 Rigid impulsive component

The seismic loads acting on wall and bottom of cylindrical tanks (Figure 2) can be divided into the following components:

The spatial-temporal variation of the "rigid impulsive" pressure is given by the expression

$$p_i(\xi,\zeta,\theta,t)=C_i(\xi,\zeta)\rho H\cos\theta A_g(t), \tag{1}$$

where

$$C_i(\xi,\zeta)=2\sum_{n=0}^{\infty}\frac{(-1)^n}{I_1'(\nu_n/\gamma)\nu_n^2}\cos(\nu_n\zeta)I_1\left(\frac{\nu_n}{\gamma}\xi\right), \tag{2}$$

$\nu_n=\pi\frac{2n+1}{2}$ and $\gamma=H/R$, $I_1(\cdot)$ is the modified Bessel function of order 1 and $I_1'(\cdot)$ is derivate can be expressed in terms of modified Bessel function of order 0 and 1 $I_1'(x)=\frac{dI_1(x)}{dx}=I_0(x)-\frac{I_1(x)}{x}$. The function C_i gives the distribution along the height of p_i. θ is angle of circumference, $\gamma=H/R$ is slenderness, $A_g(t)$ is the ground horizontal acceleration time-history in free-field with peak value denoted by a_g as a result of an equivalent single-degree-of-freedom system with a impulsive period T_i.

Impulsive base shear is at the base of the wall is given

$$Q_i(t)=m_iA_g(t), \tag{3}$$

m_i is termed impulsive mass, denoted the mass of the contained fluid which moves together with the walls and is given by the expression:

$$m_i=m2\gamma\sum_{n=0}^{\infty}\frac{I_1(\nu_n/\gamma)}{\nu_n^3 I_1'(\nu_n/\gamma)}, \tag{4}$$

where $m=\rho\pi R^2H$ is total contained mass of the fluid.

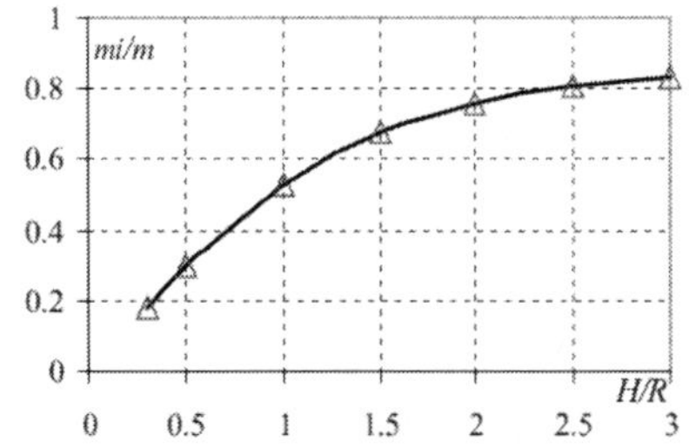

Figure 5. Ratios m_i/m as function of the parameter tank slenderness

The total moment with respect to an axis orthogonal to the direction of the seismic action motion, M_i^*, immediately bellow the tank bottom includes the contributions of the pressures on the walls from expression (1) and of those on the tank bottom. The total moment M_i immediately above the tank bottom includes only the contributions of the pressures on the walls.

Impulsive base moment immediately below the tank bottom:

$$M_i^*=m_ih_i^*A_g(t), \tag{5}$$

where

$$h_i^*=H\frac{\frac{1}{2}+2\gamma\sum_{n=0}^{\infty}\frac{\nu_n+2(-1)^{n+1}I_1(\nu_n/\gamma)}{\nu_n^4 I_1'(\nu_n/\gamma)}}{2\gamma\sum_{n=0}^{\infty}\frac{I_1(\nu_n/\gamma)}{\nu_n^3 I_1'(\nu_n/\gamma)}}. \tag{6}$$

Impulsive base moment immediately above the tank bottom:

$$M_i=m_ih_iA_g(t), \tag{7}$$

where

$$h_i=H\frac{\sum_{n=0}^{\infty}\frac{(-1)^nI_1(\nu_n/\gamma)}{\nu_n^4 I_1'(\nu_n/\gamma)}\left(\nu_n(-1)^n-1\right)}{\sum_{n=0}^{\infty}\frac{I_1(\nu_n/\gamma)}{\nu_n^3 I_1'(\nu_n/\gamma)}}. \tag{8}$$

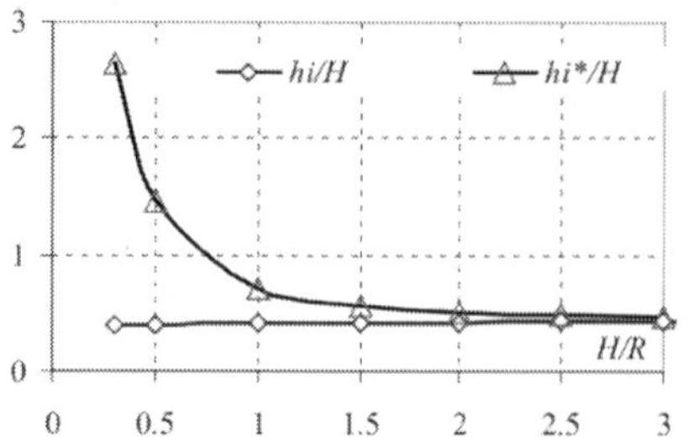

Figure 6. Ratios h_i/H and h_i^*/H as functions of the parameter tank slenderness

4.3 Convective component

The spatial-temporal variation of the "convective" pressure component is given by the expression

$$p_c(\xi,\zeta,\theta,t)=\rho\sum_{n=1}^{\infty}\psi_n\cos(\nu_n\gamma\zeta)J_1(\nu_n\xi)\cos\theta A_{cn}(t), \quad (9)$$

where

$$\psi_n=\frac{2R}{(\lambda_n^2-1)J_1(\lambda_n)\cosh(\lambda_n\gamma)}, \quad (10)$$

J_1 is Bessel function of the first order, λ_n are the roots of the first-order Bessel function of the first kind (λ_1=1.8412; λ_2=5.3314; λ_3=8.5363, λ_4=11.71, λ_5=14.66 and $\lambda_{5+i}=\lambda_5+5\ i$ (i=1,2,...)). $A_{cn}(t)$ is acceleration time-history of the response of a single degree of freedom oscillator having a circular frequency ω_{cn} was given by

$$\omega_{cn}=\sqrt{\frac{g\lambda_n\tanh(\lambda_n\gamma)}{R}}, \quad (11)$$

so

$$T_{cn}=\frac{2\pi}{\sqrt{\frac{g\lambda_n\tanh(\lambda_n\gamma)}{R}}} \quad (12)$$

and a damping ratio appropriate for the sloshing of the fluid.

Only the first oscillating, or sloshing, mode and frequency of the oscillating liquid (n=1) needs to be considered in expression for design purposes.

$$\omega_{c1}=4{,}2/\sqrt{R} \quad (13)$$

which, for the usual values of R yields periods of oscillation of the order of few seconds.

Convective base shear is given

$$Q_c(t)=\sum_{n=1}^{\infty}m_{cn}A_{cn}(t) \quad (14)$$

where

$$m_{cn}=m\frac{2\tanh(\lambda_n\gamma)}{\lambda_n\gamma(\lambda_n^2-1)} \quad (15)$$

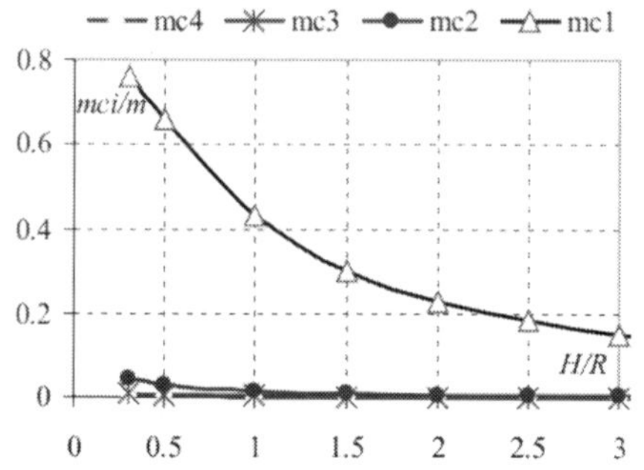

Figure 7. Ratios m_{ci}/m as function of the parameter tank slenderness for i = 1, 2, 3 and 4

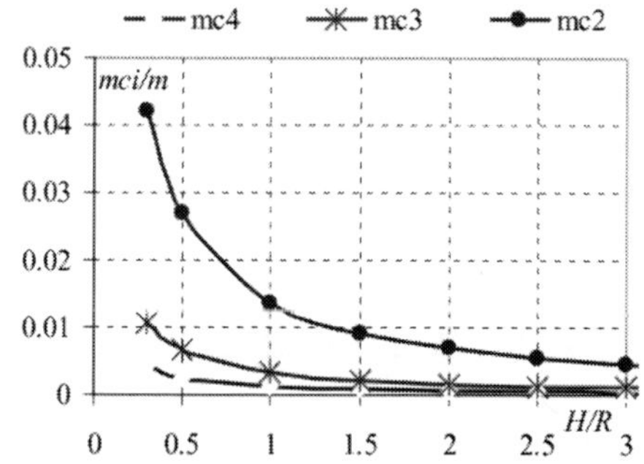

Figure 8. Ratios m_{ci}/m as function of the parameter tank slenderness for i = 2, 3 and 4

Only the first oscillating, or sloshing, mode and frequency of the oscillating liquid (n=1) needs to be considered in expression for design purposes.

$$\omega_{c1}=4{,}2/\sqrt{R} \quad (13)$$

which, for the usual values of R yields periods of oscillation of the order of few seconds.

Convective base shear is given

$$Q_c(t)=\sum_{n=1}^{\infty}m_{cn}A_{cn}(t) \quad (14)$$

where

$$m_{cn}=m\frac{2\tanh(\lambda_n\gamma)}{\lambda_n\gamma(\lambda_n^2-1)} \quad (15)$$

Moment immediately below the bottom plate of the tank:

$$M_c'(t)=\sum_{n=1}^{\infty}(m_{cn}A_{cn}(t))h_{cn}^{*}=\sum_{n=1}^{\infty}Q_{cn}(t)h_{cn}^{*} \quad (16)$$

where

$$h_{cn}^{*} = H\left(1 + \frac{2 - \cosh(\lambda_n \gamma)}{\lambda_n \gamma \sin(\lambda_n \gamma)}\right) \quad (17)$$

Moment in tank wall immediately above the bottom plate

$$M_c(t) = \sum_{n=1}^{\infty} (m_{cn} A_{cn}(t)) h_{cn} = \sum_{n=1}^{\infty} Q_{cn}(t) h_{cn} \quad (18)$$

where

$$h_{cn} = H\left(1 + \frac{1 - \cosh(\lambda_n \gamma)}{\lambda_n \gamma \sin(\lambda_n \gamma)}\right) \quad (19)$$

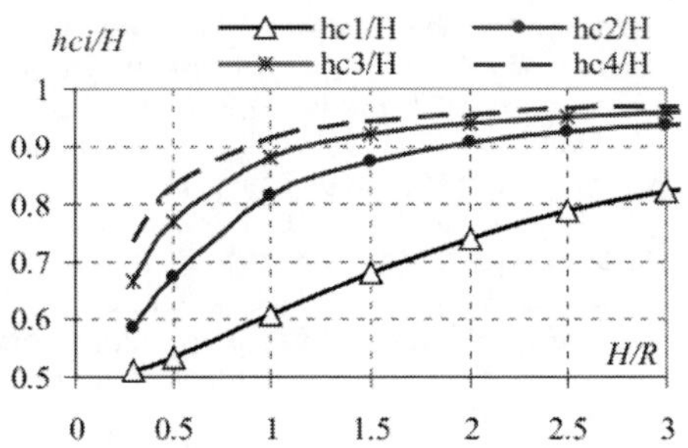

Figure 9. Ratios h_{ci}/H as functions of the parameter tank slenderness

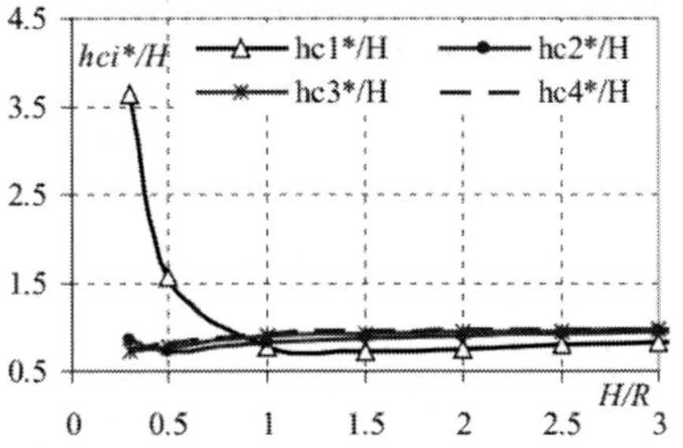

Figure 10. Ratios h_{ci}^{*}/H as functions of the parameter tank slenderness

The convective component of the response may be obtained from that of oscillators having masses m_{cn}, attached to the rigid tank through springs having stiffness $k_n = \omega_n^2 m_{cn}$. The tank is subjected to the ground acceleration time-history $A_g(t)$ and the masses respond with accelerations $A_{cn}(t)$. h_{cn}^{*} or h_{cn} is the level where the oscillator needs to be applied in order to give the correct value of M_{cn}^{*} or M_{cn}, respectively.

4.4 Flexible component

It is normally unconservative to consider the tank as rigid (especially for steel tanks). In flexible tanks the fluid pressure is usually expressed as the sum of tree contributions, referred to as: "rigid impulsive", "sloshing" and "flexible". The third satisfied the condition that the radial velocity of the fluid along the wall equals the deformation velocity of the tank wall, as well as the conditions of zero vertical velocity at the tank bottom and zero pressure at the free surface of the fluid. The dynamic coupling between the sloshing and the flexible components is very weak, due to the large differences between the frequencies of the sloshing motion and of the deformation of the wall, which allows determining the third component independently of the others.

The radial distribution of the flexible impulsive pressure on the tank bottom is qualitatively the same as for the rigid impulsive pressure. Assuming the modes as known, the flexible pressure distribution on the walls has the form

$$p_f(\zeta, \theta, t) = \rho H \psi \cos\theta \sum_{n=1}^{\infty} \cos(\nu_n \zeta) A_{fn}(t) \quad (20)$$

For a horizontal earthquake ground motion, the response of various SDOF systems may be calculated independently and then combined to give the base shear and overturning moment. The most tanks have the parameter tank slendernes γ, whereby $0,3 < \gamma < 3$. The parameter tank slendernes is given by relation $\gamma = H/L$, where H is the filling height of fluid in the tank and $2L$ is inside width of tank.

Values mi, h_i, h_i^{*}, m_{cn}, h_{cn}, and h_{cn}^{*} for rigid vertical circular tanks on ground, fixed to the foundation in Eurocode 8 - 4 [13] are shown in Figure 7 - 10.

5 Numerical example and results

In this study is analyzed fluids filling of ground supported cylindrical rigid tank. The characteristics of fluid filling for $H = 2$ m, where R - inner radiuses of cylindrical tanks are depended from tank slenderness ratios $\gamma = H/R$.

For tank slenderness ratio $\gamma = 0.3$, the inner radius of tank R is given 6.667 m,

- for $\gamma = 0.5$ ⇨ R is 4 m,
- for $\gamma = 0.7$ ⇨ $R = 2.857$ m,
- for $\gamma = 1$ ⇨ $R = 2$ m,
- for $\gamma = 2$ ⇨ $R = 1$ m,
- and for $\gamma = 3$, R is given 0.667 m.

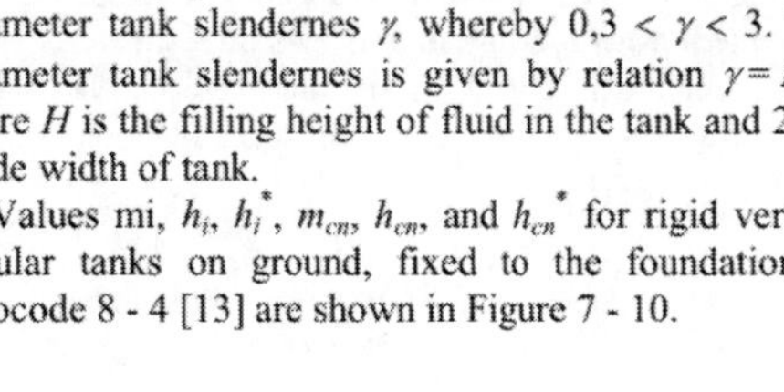

Figure 11. Accelerogram Loma Prieta, California

The material characteristics of fluid filling (H_2O) is density $\rho_w = 1\ 000$ kg/m^3. As the excitation input we consider horizontal earthquake load given by the accelerogram of the earthquake in Loma Prieta, California (18.10.1989), Figure 11. Seismic responses of tanks are calculated by using the response spectrums for the Loma Prieta accelerogram, California, Figure 12.

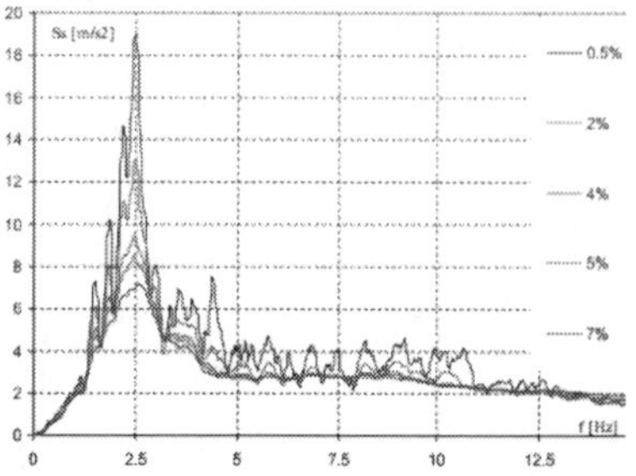

Figure 12. Response spectrums for the Loma Prieta accelerogram from Figure 11

The elastic response spectrums of the Loma Prieta accelerogram (Figure 11) were used for simulation of earthquake. The impulsive spectral accelerations are obtained from a 5% damped elastic response spectrum (for concrete tanks) and the convective spectral accelerations are obtained from a 0.5% damped elastic response spectrum.

Table1. comparison of the total base shears, the bending and overturning moments of fluid as functions of the tank slenderness

	D [m]	***V*** [kN]	***M*** [kNm]	M^* [kNm]
$\gamma = 0.3$	13.333	7643.55	7780.72	51013.9
$\gamma = 0.5$	8	7751.87	8284.86	23463.3
$\gamma = 0.7$	5.714	2153.03	2349.75	4352.12
$\gamma = 1$	4	1744.58	2065.91	2711.89
$\gamma = 2$	2	179.51	224.97	235.39
$\gamma = 3$	1.333	46.86	50.42	51.79

Comparison of the total base shears V, the bending moments M and overturning moments M^* of fluid as functions of the tank slenderness ratios for diameters $D = 2R$ are shown in Table 1.

6 Conclusions

The ground supported cylindrical tank was excited by ground motion of Loma Prieta in California. Basic responses of the interest were: the total base shears, the bending and overturning moments of fluid as functions of the tank parameter slenderness ratio.

Acknowledgment

This work was supported by the Scientific Grant Agency of the Ministry of Education of Slovak Republic and the Slovak Academy of Sciences under Project VEGA 1/0477/15.

References

[1] A. Di Carluccio, G. Manfredi, I. Iervolino, G. Fabbrocino, Fragility analysis of liquid storage steel tanks in seismic areas. *Proceedings of ISEC-4 - Innovations in Structural Engineering and Construction* (2008) **2**, p. 1049-1055.

[2] S. Dorafshan, F. Behnamfar, A. Khamesipour. M. Motosaka, *Condensed hyperelements method of non-vertical consistent boundaries for wave propagation analysis in irregular media. Earthquake engineering and engineering vibration* (2013) **12**, p. 547-559.

[3] G. Fabbrocino, I. Iervolino, I. Orlando, E. Salzano, Quantitative risk analysis of oil storage facilities in seismic areas (2005) **123 (1-3)**, Journal of Hazardous Materials, pp. 61-69.

[4] N. Jendzelovsky, N., L. Balaz, Numerical Modeling of Cylindrical Tank and Compare with Experiment. In: Applied Mechanics and Materials (2013) **617**, ISSN 1660-9336. p. 148-151.

[5] K. Kralik, J. Kralik jr., Probability assessment of analysis of high-rise buildings seismic resistance, Advanced Materials Research (2013) **712-715,** p. 929-936.

[6] M. Krejsa, P. Janas, V. Krejsa, Software application of the DOProC method In: International Journal of Mathematics and Computers in Simulation (2014) **8**, ISSN 1998-0159, p. 121-126.

[7] P. K. Malhotra, T. Wenk, M., Wieland, Simple procedure for seismic analysis of liquid-Storage tanks. Structural Engineering International, (2000) **3**, s. 197-201.

[8] J. Melcer, Experimental testing of a bridge. Applied Mechanics and Materials (2014) **486**, pp. 333-340.

[9] J., Michel, M. Mihalikova, Degradation of pipes properties in creep conditions. In: Acta Metallurgica Slovaca (2000) **2**, p. 108-115. ISSN 1335-1532.

[10] O. Sucharda, J. Brozovsky, Bearing capacity analysis of reinforced concrete beams, International Journal of Mechanics (2013) **7**, Issue 3, p. 192-200.

[11] B. Taraba, Z Michalec, V. Michalcova, T. Blejchar, M Bojko, M Kozubkova. CFD simulations of the effect of wind on the spontaneous heating of coal stockpiles. Fuel (2014) **118**, ISSN 0016-2361, p. 107-112.

[12] M. Zmindak, I. Grajciar, Simulation of the aquaplane problem. Computers and Structures (1977) **64**, Issue 5-6, p. 1155-1164.

[13] Eurocode 8 - Design of structure for earthquake resistance - Part. 4: Silos, tanks and pipelines. Januar 2006.

Operation analysis of AC traction motors in terms of electromagnetic torque capability on sustainable railway vehicles

Cornelia A. Bulucea[1,a], Doru A. Nicola[1], Marc A. Rosen[2], Nikos E. Mastorakis[3] and Carmen A. Bulucea[4]

[1] *University of Craiova, Faculty of Electrical Engineering, Craiova 200440, Romania*
[2] *University of Ontario Institute of Technology, Faculty of Engineering and Applied Science, Oshawa, ON, L1H 7K4, Canada*
[3] *Military Institutions of University Education (ASEI), Hellenic Naval Academy, Piraeus 18539, Greece*
[4] *University of Medicine and Pharmacy of Craiova, Faculty of Medicine, Craiova 200349, Romania*

Abstract. Sustainable operation of electric railway systems represents a significant purpose nowadays in the development of high power and high speed locomotives and trains. At present, high speed electric vehicles mostly work with three-phase induction motors or three-phase synchronous motors as traction motors. The two electric machine types have different efficiencies at different operation points, and experience differences with respect to safety, speed and power, energy use and exergy efficiency. An important issue that correlates these aspects is the electromagnetic torque developed by an electric traction motor. In order to provide an overview of the technical performance of the operation of sustainable railway systems, a detailed analysis is carried out of the electromagnetic torque capability of AC electric motors utilized as traction motors in modern locomotives of high power and/or high speed. The results of this work may help in enhancing the main criteria for optimising the safe and sustainable operation of electric railway traction systems.

1 Introduction

The final decades of the 20th century and the first decade of the 21st century were marked by a significant rise in the speed of electric railway vehicles due to progress in power electronics for electric locomotive technology [1-7]. Consequently, nowadays we are encountering a rethinking and redrawing of the architecture of electric railway vehicles, regardless of the type of the electric contact line (in DC or in AC). Under the vision of sustainable development and industrial ecology, the key points of operation of electric railway vehicles nowadays are related to the high electromagnetic torque developed by traction motors, energy savings and environmental impact mitigation, particularly through high exergy efficiency [1-2,4-6]. Moreover, the variable voltage/current variable frequency (VV/CVF) power conversion technology facilitates the use of on-board AC drives which ensure regenerative braking and thus make possible efficient management of energy supply of high speed trains [1-8]. But note that these advantages are met under the condition of using in traction drives the AC electric motors, namely of induction type or synchronous type, regardless of the contact line type.

The rivalry between the two three-phase AC traction electric motors, namely the induction motor and synchronous motor persists, each competing to be the safest, fastest and cheapest [4-7]. The two electric machine types have different efficiencies at different operation points in terms of electromagnetic torque [1-8]. An accurate insight into these two types of electric traction motors (three-phase induction motors and three-phase synchronous motors) is presented subsequently.

The three-phase induction motor with squirrel-cage rotor meets the criteria for an ideal traction motor, since it is robust and reliable, having fewer components than the DC traction motor. Moreover, for this type of electric motor the energy transfer between the stator and the rotor is performed without an electric contact, but instead just through the electromagnetic field, so that there are no limitations with respect to power, speed or voltage. Note that switching to the braking regime, or sense reversal, are achieved through the control logic of the power converters, without electromechanical contactors [1,4-7].

Further, a comparison of the traction motor with collector shows that the three-phase induction motor with a cage rotor presents an advantage in that, for the same useful power, the size and weight are lower.

The traction induction motors used on the locomotives and high speed/power trains are robust, with rated powers up to 1.5 MW. As a traction motor the induction motor must satisfy several criteria [1-2,4-7]:

- high torque developed at low speeds, even during start-up, and
- operation over a large range of the supply frequency, from roughly 0.4–1 Hz to 140–180 Hz, both as a motor and as a brake (generator).

[a] Corresponding author: abulucea@em.ucv.ro

The technology becomes significantly complicated in the range of low frequencies (under the rated frequency) because the motor is submitted to magnetic saturation at relatively small variations of supply voltage. For this reason, in the under-rated frequency range, the voltage will vary simultaneously with the supply frequency, in order to enable through the control system both the appropriate level of magnetic stresses and the required magnitude of the electromagnetic torque [1, 4-7].

But developments should be made in the range of over-rated frequencies for which, due to reasons of motor windings insulation and voltage stresses of power electronics, the supply voltage must be maintained constant at the level of rated voltage U_N. Consequently, when powered at the rated voltage U_N and over-rated frequencies, the induction motor operates with weakened flux, which leads to the torque overloading capability λ_M becoming increasingly lower and the rotor pulsation ω_r becoming increasingly higher. Besides, for the operation in the range of over-rated frequencies, the reaching of critical rotor pulsation ω_{rk} limits the higher value of the stator frequency to below the maximum f_{smax} [1-2,4-7].

The synchronous motor utilized as traction motor must develop significant high electromagnetic torques at variable speeds, namely from the starting to the maximum speed. Consequently it is compulsory the traction synchronous motor to be powered from a static converter with variable frequency so that the rotor, which controls the static converter to maintain the synchronization with the rotating magnetic field at any value of stator frequency [1, 8-9].

Following this idea means that the current converters with natural commutation which power the self-controlled three-phase traction synchronous motors are simple, being composed by six thyristorised branches connected as a three-phase bridge. Note that some problems concerning the natural commutation realisation appear at very low speeds, when the magnitude of the counter electromotive force (c.e.m.f) is small (insufficient to ensure the commutation). In such situations, from the starting regime up to roughly 5-10% of the maximum speed v_{max}, assisted commutation is necessary [1, 6, 8-9].

The self-controlled synchronous motor becomes competitive as a traction motor solely at high powers, which is exactly in the application field of electric railway locomotives/trains. Specifically, three-phase traction synchronous motors with unit powers up to 1300 kW (in continuous operation regime) with forced ventilation are manufactured, of axial type (being provided with axial channels in the stator ferromagnetic core).

In this study, we perform a detailed analysis of the electromagnetic torque developed by the three-phase induction motor and the three-phase synchronous motor, the most generally used traction AC electric motors in present-day railway systems. We focus here on these two types of AC motors, which are widely used as traction motors on electric railway transportation systems, with particular reference to electromagnetic torque analysis, since certain traits of the developed electromagnetic torque are strongly related to the safety, speed, exergy efficiency and energy savings of high power and speed locomotives and trains. The aim of this study is to enhance understanding of these motors and their use in railway systems. Consequently, we present in the paper some less known theoretical aspects of the operation at variable frequency of AC traction motors.

2 Analysis of electromagnetic torque developed by traction induction motor

To address meaningfully many of the problems facing railway vehicles, conditions for the performance of sustainable transportation systems must be formulated [2-3, 10]. Costs should reflect value, which is doubtless associated with sustainability aspects [10-12]. The sustainability of traction operation of the electric induction motor is related its exergy efficiency.

In physics and engineering, work is a specific form of action, and exergy is defined based on work, i.e. ordered motion, or ability to perform work [2,10-13]. While energy is a measure of quantity only, exergy is a measure of quantity and quality or usefulness. Since exergy is a measure of the potential of a system to do work, the electromagnetic torque M developed by an induction motor can be interpreted as the driving force of useful work, i.e. the electric motor output exergy [2-3,10,13].

In line with this idea, through the modeling of the electromagnetic torque developed by induction motor, this study supports the findings that electric traction drive systems using induction motors fed by VVVF inverters enhance the sustainable operation of railway trains.

In order to assess the electromagnetic torque developed by the traction induction motor, the vehicle regulation speed is determined by examining the VVVF inverter and electric machine as an assembly [1-3]. We have pointed out in previous studies [1-3,10,13] that a traction electric vehicle might be analyzed as an ecosystem, and the dynamic regimes in electric train operation, e.g. starting or braking processes, can be viewed as representing the industrial ecosystem movement among points of equilibrium. Since the traction motor speed regulation is based on stator voltage and frequency variation, in order to achieve high energy and exergy efficiencies, the first requirement of the train control system concerns passing of the motor operation equilibrium point from one mechanical characteristic to another [1-3,13].

If we note by $s = \frac{n_s - n}{n_s} = \frac{\omega_r}{\omega_s} = \frac{f_r}{f_s}$ the slip of rotor (having the speed n) in the rotating magnetic field (which has the synchronism speed $n_s = 60 \cdot f_s/p$), then the electromagnetic torque M developed by the traction induction motor at any current value of the stator frequency f_s and rotor slip s (respectively, rotor pulsation $\omega_r = s \cdot \omega_s$) is specified by $M = \frac{3p}{\omega_s} \cdot \frac{R_r'}{s} \cdot I_r'^2 = 3p \cdot \frac{R_r'}{\omega_r} \cdot I_r'^2$.

Neglecting the stator resistance ($R_s \approx 0$), the evaluation relation of the electromagnetic torque M becomes:

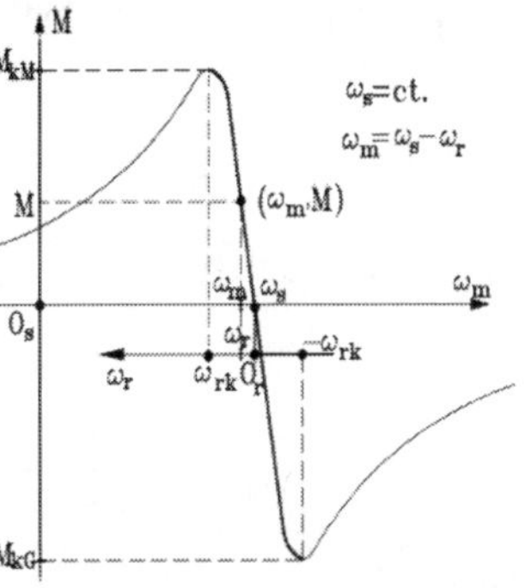

Figure 1. Mechanical characteristic $M = f(\omega_m)$ at ω_s=ct.

$$M = M(\omega_s,\omega_r) = 3p\cdot\frac{1-\sigma}{\sigma\cdot L_s}\cdot\frac{\left(\frac{U_s}{\omega_s}\right)^2}{\frac{R'_r}{\omega_r\cdot\sigma\cdot L'_r}+\frac{\omega_r\cdot\sigma\cdot L'_r}{R'_r}} \qquad (1)$$

With the notation $\omega_m = p\cdot\Omega_m = p\dfrac{2\pi\cdot n}{60}$, the torque characteristic of the induction motor, meaning the curve $M = f(\omega_m)$ for any constant pulsation/frequency $\omega_s = 2\pi f_s$ = ct. and $\omega_m = \omega_s - \omega_r$ is graphically illustrated in Figure 1. The specific points of the mechanical characteristic in Figure 1 have coordinates (for any constant value of the stator frequency f_s) given by:

- mechanical pulsation ω_m corresponding to the synchronism point (when $\omega_r = 0$) :

$$\omega_m = \omega_s = 2\pi\cdot f_s = 2\pi\frac{p\cdot n_s}{60} \qquad (2)$$

- critical rotor pulsations ω_{rk} (extreme points' abscissa of the graph in Figure 1):

$$\omega_{rk} = \omega_{rk\psi s} = \pm\frac{R'_r}{\sigma\cdot L'_r} \qquad (3)$$

- extreme values (as motor M_{kM} and respectively as generator M_{kG}, of the torque curve), given by:

$$M_k = M_{k\psi_s} = \pm\frac{3p}{2}\cdot\frac{1-\sigma}{\sigma\cdot L_s}\cdot\left(\frac{U_s}{\omega_s}\right)^2 \qquad (4)$$

Note in the above relation that the sign "+" refers to the motor regime (with index M in Figure 1) while the sign "-" refers to the generator regime (with index G in Figure 1).

2.1 Limits of variation of stator frequency

For the supply with variable frequency voltages it is important to assess the limit values of stator minimum frequency f_{smin} and maximum frequency f_{smax} (as in Figure 2, in the bottom part) among which the stable operation of the traction induction machine is possible.

2.1.1 Minimum frequency

The minimum frequency (for operation with constant stator flux, see Figure 2) is assessed taking into consideration that in a steady-state regime, at any value of stator frequency f_s, among rotor pulsation ω_r, stator pulsation $\omega_s = 2\pi\cdot f_s$ and mechanical pulsation $\omega_m = p\cdot\Omega_m = p\cdot 2\pi\cdot n/60$, the "Frequency Theorem" relation is valid:

$$\omega_s = \omega_m + \omega_r \qquad (5)$$

or

$$2\pi\cdot f_s = p\cdot\frac{2\pi\cdot n}{60} + \omega_r \quad\Rightarrow\quad n = \frac{60}{p}\cdot\left(f_s - \frac{1}{2\pi}\cdot\omega_r\right) \qquad (6)$$

For any stator frequency $f_s < f_N$, the rotor speed n_k corresponding to maximum electromagnetic M (meaning the abscissa of point K_M in Figure 2) is established with the relation:

$$n_k = \frac{60}{p}\cdot\left(f_s - \frac{1}{2\pi}\cdot\omega_{rk\psi_s}\right); \qquad n_k \geq 0 \qquad (7)$$

The minimum stator frequency f_{smin} (that still will ensure the above operation conditions) corresponds to the limit situation when $n_k = 0$. That means that the minimum stator frequency will be given by the relation:

$$f_{smin} = \frac{1}{2\pi}\cdot\omega_{rk\psi_s} = \frac{1}{2\pi}\cdot\frac{R'_r}{\sigma\cdot L'_r} \qquad (8)$$

Note that f_{smin} must be ensured by the supply source (VVVF) and depends solely on the parameters R'_r, L'_r and σ of the traction induction machine.

In Figure 2, the smooth starting manner (without shocks) is highlighted, through a progressive increase of the stator flux ψ_s (from 0 up to ψ_{sN}) at the minimum value f_{smin} = ct. (of the supply stator frequency), followed by an increase of the stator frequency f_s (at the constant stator flux a $\psi_s = \psi_{sN}$ = ct.) simultaneously with the increase of rotor speed.

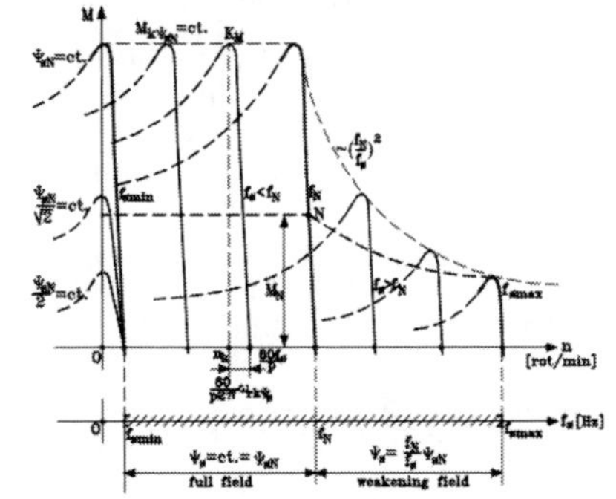

Figure 2. Overview of traction induction motor characteristics for operation at variable stator frequency f_s

2.1.2 Maximum frequency

The maximum stator frequency $f_{s\max}$ (higher than f_N) will be established by the condition of development (still) of an electromagnetic power P_M of magnitude equal to that of the motor rated operation.

Note that because of the voltage restriction on both supply inverter and induction machine winding insulation considerations, the stator voltage is limited and maintained at a constant magnitude $U_s = U_N$ when $f_s > f_N$ and the induction machine operates in weakened flux conditions [1-7]. Since the stator flux and stator pulsation exhibit an inverse proportionality relation, the machine torque capability is strongly affected (see Figure 2). This is the reason for the limited increase of stator frequency.

Simultaneously, due to the decrease of flux ψ_s on the basis of the law "$1/\omega_s$":

$$\psi_s = \psi_{sN} \cdot \frac{\omega_N}{\omega_s} \approx \frac{U_N}{\omega_s} \tag{9}$$

a reduction of the maximum electromagnetic torque occurs, and its equation (4) at over-rated frequencies $f_s > f_N$ becomes:

$$M_{k\psi_s} = \frac{3p}{2} \cdot \frac{1-\sigma}{\sigma \cdot L_s} \cdot [\psi_{sN} \cdot \frac{\omega_N}{\omega_s}]^2 = M_{k\psi_{sN}} \cdot (\frac{\omega_N}{\omega_s})^2 \tag{10}$$

In this context, the maximum value of the stator frequency f_{smax} is established from the electromagnetic power invariance condition $P_M = M \cdot \Omega_s = M \cdot \omega_s/p$ (transferred by air-gap) at different over-rated values of stator frequency f_s.

In order to maintain a constant electromagnetic power $P_M = M \cdot \Omega_s = M \cdot \omega_s/p$ (at nominal level P_{MN} = ct.) even for the maximum stator frequency f_{smax}, the following relation can be written:

$$M_N \cdot \frac{\omega_N}{p} = M_{f_{smax}} \cdot \frac{\omega_{smax}}{p} \tag{11}$$

If at the maximum frequency f_{smax} the condition $M_{f_{smax}} = M_{k\psi_s}$ is imposed, the following results:

$$M_N \cdot \frac{\omega_N}{p} = M_{k\psi_{sN}} \cdot (\frac{\omega_N}{\omega_{smax}})^2 \cdot \frac{\omega_{smax}}{p} \Rightarrow \omega_{smax} = \frac{M_{k\psi_{sN}}}{M_N} \cdot \omega_N \tag{12}$$

or taking into account the definition of the torque overload capacity λ_M we obtain:

$$\lambda_M = \frac{M_{k\psi_{sN}}}{M_N} \Rightarrow f_{smax} = \lambda_M \cdot f_N \tag{13}$$

Consequently, the increase of the maximum frequency f_{smax} can be achieved through the design and further construction of induction machines with increased torque overload capacity λ_M. For traction induction machines, λ_M can take on values of 2.5 to 3.0.

2.2 Torque capability and comparison at constant flux operation

Note that, at any frequencies, in the permanent harmonic regime, among the fluxes $\underline{\Psi}_s$, $\underline{\Psi}_u$, $\underline{\Psi}'_r$ and the currents $\underline{I}_s$, $\underline{I}'_r$ of any unsaturated induction machine with electric and magnetic symmetry, the following relations apply [1, 13]:

$$\begin{aligned} \underline{\psi}_s &= L_{s\sigma} \cdot \underline{I}_s + \underline{\psi}_u \\ \underline{\psi}_s &= \sigma \cdot L_s \cdot \underline{I}_s + \frac{L_u}{L_{r'}} \cdot \underline{\psi}'_r \\ \underline{\psi}'_r &= \underline{\psi}_u + L'_{r\sigma} \cdot \underline{I}'_r \\ 0 &= R'_r + j\,\omega_r \cdot \underline{\psi}'_r \end{aligned} \tag{14}$$

Accordingly, a phasor diagram is shown in Fig. 3 of the fluxes and currents for the induction machine operating in the motor regime. In the complex reference system, with real axis (+1) along the direction of phasor $\underline{\Psi}'_r$ (with $\underline{\Psi}'_r = \Psi'_r + j \cdot 0$; $\underline{I}_s = I_{sx} + j \cdot I_{sy}$ and $\underline{I}'_r = 0 - j \cdot I'_r$), from the geometry of the rectangular triangles OAA' and OBB' (see Fig. 3) one can write:

$$\begin{aligned} \psi_s^2 &= [\frac{L_u}{L_{r'}} \cdot \psi'_r + \sigma \cdot L_s \cdot I_{sx}]^2 + (\sigma \cdot L_s \cdot I_{sy})^2 \\ \psi_u^2 &= \psi'^2_r + (L'_{r\sigma} \cdot I'_r)^2 \end{aligned} \tag{15}$$

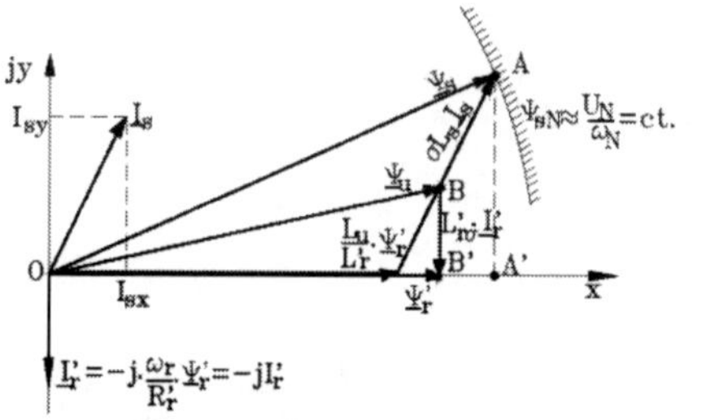

Figure 3. Phasor representation of induction motor fluxes and currents at $\omega_r > 0$

Furthermore, taking into consideration the components I_{sx} and I_{sy}, as well as the rotor current I'_r in accordance with the following relations:

$$I_{sx} = \frac{\psi'_r}{L_u};\; I_{sy} = \frac{\psi'_r}{L_u} \cdot \frac{L'_r}{R'_r} \cdot \omega_r;\; I'_r = \frac{\omega_r}{R'_r} \cdot \psi'_r \tag{16}$$

and, after mathematical calculations, the expressions for the fluxes Ψ_u and Ψ'_r can be determined:

$$\begin{aligned} \psi_u(\omega_r) &= \psi_s \cdot \frac{L_u}{L_s} \cdot \sqrt{\frac{1 + (\frac{L'_{r\sigma}}{R'_r} \cdot \omega_r)^2}{1 + (\frac{\sigma \cdot L'_r}{R'_r} \cdot \omega_r)^2}} \\ \psi'_r(\omega_r) &= \psi_s \cdot \frac{L_u}{L_s} \cdot \frac{1}{\sqrt{1 + (\frac{\sigma \cdot L'_r}{R'_r} \cdot \omega_r)^2}} \end{aligned} \tag{17}$$

Note that the fluxes Ψ_u and Ψ'_r depend on Ψ_s, as well on machine parameters and on ω_r. But any induction machine designed to be supplied with phase voltage U_N at stator frequency f_N ($\omega_N = 2\pi \cdot f_N$) will have the stator flux Ψ_s approximately constant, with magnitude Ψ_{sN}, where:

$$\psi_{sN} \approx \frac{U_N}{\omega_N} = ct. \tag{18}$$

Hence, for operation with constant stator flux ($\Psi_s = \Psi_{sN}$ = ct.), the reference levels of the fluxes Ψ_u=ct. and Ψ'_r = ct., respectively should set to values such that, over the entire variation range of rotor pulsation ω_r, the stator flux Ψ_s does not exceed the established limit value. Therefore, in Fig. 4 there are shown the dependence $\Psi_s = \Psi_{sN}$=ct. in accordance with (18), and $\Psi_u = f_1(\omega_r)$ and $\Psi'_r = f_2(\omega_r)$ according to (17) for the maximum variation range of ω_r ($|\omega_r| \le R'_r/L'_{r\sigma}$ when the induction machine has stable operation at Ψ_u=ct.).

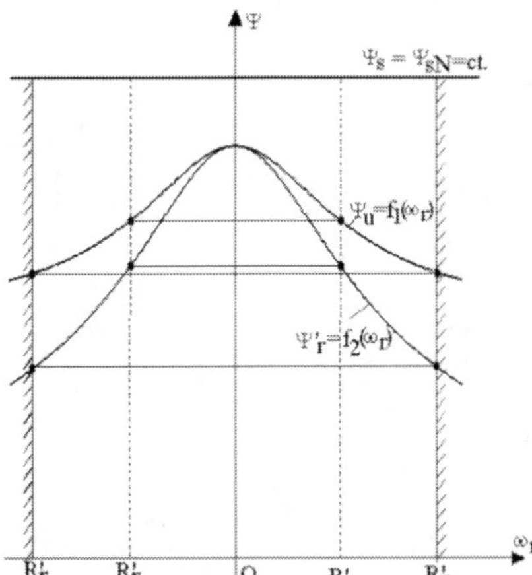

$-\frac{R'_r}{L'_{r\sigma}}$ $-\frac{R'_r}{\sigma L'_r}$ O $+\frac{R'_r}{\sigma L'_r}$ $+\frac{R'_r}{L'_{r\sigma}}$

Figure 4. Dependence of induction machine fluxes Ψ_s, Ψ_u and Ψ'_r on ω_r

Based on the curves of Fig. 4 and the above relations, the constant flux levels are determined:

$$\psi_s = \psi_{sN} = ct. \tag{19}$$

$$\psi_u = f_1(\pm\frac{R'_r}{L'_{r\sigma}}) = \psi_s \cdot \frac{L_u}{L_s} \cdot \frac{\sqrt{2}}{\sqrt{1+(\frac{\sigma L'_r}{L'_{r\sigma}})^2}} = ct.$$

$$\psi'_r = f_2(\pm\frac{R'_r}{L'_{r\sigma}}) = \psi_s \cdot \frac{L_u}{L_s} \cdot \frac{1}{\sqrt{1+(\frac{\sigma L'_r}{L'_{r\sigma}})^2}} = ct. \; (\psi'_r = \frac{\psi_u}{\sqrt{2}})$$

For these constant values of fluxes Ψ_s, Ψ_u and Ψ'_r, an exergetic analysis imposes the electromagnetic torque characteristics $M = f(\omega_r)$, and stator current characteristics $I_s = f(\omega_r)$ are compared for the stable operation intervals.

2.2.1 Electromagnetic torques comparison at Ψ_s = ct., Ψ_u=ct. and Ψ'_r = ct.

For the three subsequent cases, the electromagnetic torque M has the following expressions:

a) When stator flux is constant Ψ_s = ct.:

$$M = \frac{2 \cdot M_{k\psi_s}}{\frac{\sigma \cdot L'_r \cdot \omega_r}{R_{r'}} + \frac{R_{r'}}{\sigma \cdot L'_r \cdot \omega_r}} \tag{20}$$

$$M_{k\psi_s} = \frac{3p}{2} \cdot \frac{1-\sigma}{\sigma \cdot L_s} \cdot \psi_s^2$$

b) When useful flux is constant Ψ_u = ct.:

$$M = \frac{2 \cdot M_{k\psi_u}}{\frac{L'_{r\sigma} \cdot \omega_r}{R'_r} + \frac{R'_r}{L'_{r\sigma} \cdot \omega_r}} \tag{21}$$

$$M_{k\psi_u} = \frac{3p}{2} \cdot \frac{1}{L'_{r\sigma}} \cdot \psi_u^2$$

c) When rotor flux is constant Ψ'_r = ct.:

$$M = 3p \cdot \frac{\omega_r}{R'_r} \cdot \psi'^2_r \tag{22}$$

Moreover, according to the constant flux levels (19), between the maximum torques $M_{k\Psi s}$ and $M_{k\Psi u}$ the following recurrence relationship can be demonstrated:

$$\frac{M_{k\psi_s}}{M_{k\psi_u}} = \frac{1}{2} \cdot (\frac{\sigma \cdot L'_r}{L'_{r\sigma}} + \frac{L'_{r\sigma}}{\sigma \cdot L'_r}) \tag{23}$$

Also, since the electromagnetic torque is interpreted as output exergy, based on the observation $\Psi'_r = \Psi_u/\sqrt{2}$ = ct., at Ψ'_r = ct. a relationship for the electromagnetic torque M can be useful within the exergetic analysis:

$$M = M_{k\psi_u} \cdot \frac{L'_{r\sigma}}{R'_r} \cdot \omega_r \tag{24}$$

Graphically, curves of the induction machine electromagnetic torque $M/M_{k\Psi s} = f(\omega_r)$ at Ψ_s = ct., Ψ_u = ct., and Ψ'_r = ct., respectively, are presented in Fig. 5.

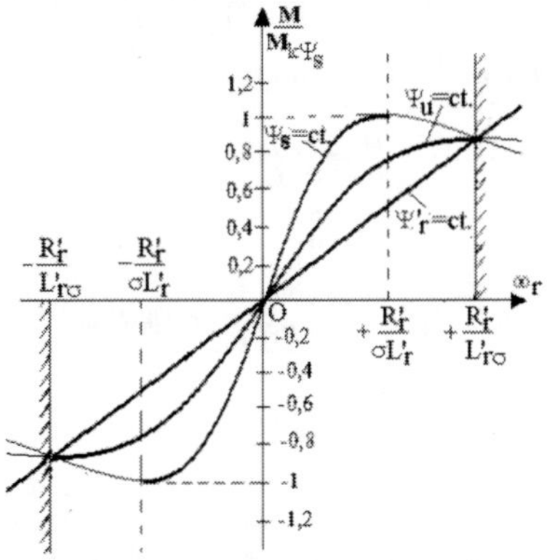

Figure 5. Curves of $M/M_{k\Psi s}=f(\omega_r)$ at constant flux

2.2.2 Stator currents comparison at Ψ_s = ct., Ψ_u=ct. and Ψ'_r = ct.

According to relationship (19) for constant flux levels, the stator current I_s expressions become as follows:

a) When stator flux is constant Ψ_s = ct.:

$$I_s = \frac{\psi_s}{L_s} \cdot \sqrt{\frac{1+(\frac{L'_r}{R'_r} \cdot \omega_r)^2}{1+(\frac{\sigma \cdot L'_r}{R'_r} \cdot \omega_r)^2}} \tag{25}$$

b) When useful flux is constant Ψ_u = ct.:

$$I_s = \frac{\psi_s}{L_s} \cdot \frac{\sqrt{2}}{\sqrt{1+(\frac{\sigma \cdot L'_r}{L_{r\sigma}})^2}} \cdot \sqrt{\frac{1+(\frac{L'_r}{R'_r} \cdot \omega_r)^2}{1+(\frac{L_{r\sigma}}{R'_r} \cdot \omega_r)^2}} \tag{26}$$

c) When rotor flux is constant Ψ'_r = ct.:

$$I_s = \frac{\psi_s}{L_s} \cdot \frac{1}{\sqrt{1+(\frac{\sigma \cdot L'_r}{L_{r\sigma}})^2}} \cdot \sqrt{1+(\frac{L'_r}{R'_r} \cdot \omega_r)^2} \tag{27}$$

Graphically, in Fig. 6 there are depicted the characteristics of stator current I_s at Ψ_s = ct., Ψ_u = ct., and

Ψ'_r = ct., respectively.

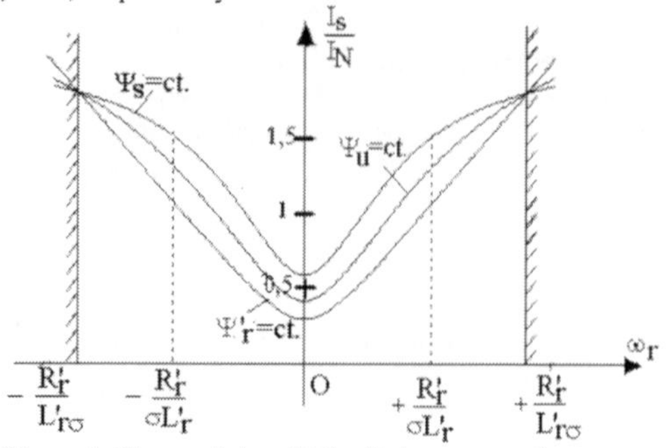

Figure 6. Characteristics of $I_s/I_N=f(\omega_r)$ at constant flux

2.2.3 Discussion of torques

The greatest magnitudes of electromagnetic torque are obtained when operating at Ψ_s=ct. Moreover, with the usual approximations $\sigma \cdot L'_r = L_{s\sigma} + L'_{r\sigma}$ and $L'_{r\sigma}$_$L_{s\sigma}$, the maximum torque relationship is obtained in the form:

$$M_{k\psi_u} \approx \frac{4}{5} \cdot M_{k\psi_s} \tag{28}$$

This emphasizes that the maximum electromagnetic torque in operating at Ψ_u = ct. is approximately with 20% smaller than the maximum torque in operating at Ψ_s = ct. The ratio of the critical rotor pulsations $\omega_{rk\Psi s}$ and $\omega_{rk\Psi u}$ is:

$$\frac{\omega_{rk\psi_s}}{\omega_{rk\psi_u}} = \frac{L'_{r\sigma}}{\sigma \cdot L'_r} \approx \frac{1}{2} \tag{29}$$

This means that an "inferior" maximum torque $M_{k\Psi u}$ is developed at the rotor pulsation with a double value that of the rotor pulsation corresponding to $M_{k\Psi s}$ ($\omega_{rk\Psi u} = 2 \cdot \omega_{rk\Psi s}$).

Moreover, at the imposed electromagnetic torque, the smallest value of rotor pulsation is obtained in operation with Ψ_s = ct.

From Fig. 6 similar observations are drawn with regard to the stator currents. Actually, the smallest values of stator currents I_s are obtained for operation with Ψ'_r = ct.

The analysis of induction machine operation with constant flux highlights that only at Ψ'_r = ct. do the mechanical characteristics not have extremum points; they are straight lines. These linear characteristics are preferable for applications which demand high sustainability dynamics in induction machine operation.

3 Analysis of electromagnetic torque developed by traction synchronous motor

Like a traction motor, the three-phase synchronous motor with salient poles is powered from a three-phase source, ideally with sinusoidal currents. In this case the current phasor I (through the reference stator winding) is specified by its magnitude |I|=I and the initial phase ψ to the axis q of the rotor, as in Figure 7. This means that implicitly the components I_d and I_q are specified of the stator current I [1, 9, 14-15].

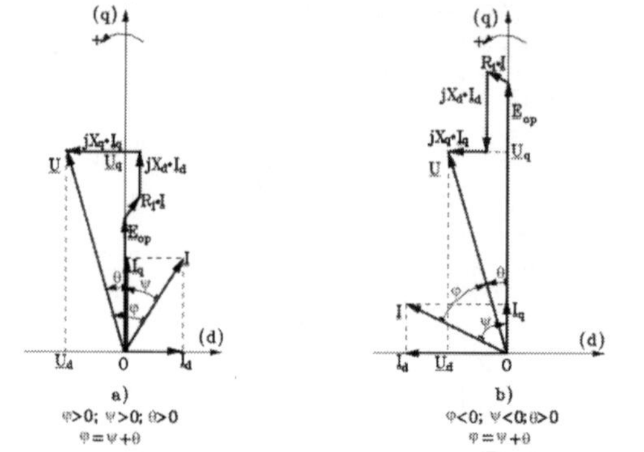

Figure 7. Blondel phasor diagram of synchronous motor with salient poles; a) under-excited operation (inductive current I); b) over-excited operation (capacitive current I)

In these conditions, the electromagnetic torque of the synchronous motor with salient poles M_I (at the current supplying) is determined as follows [1,9] :

$$M_I = \frac{3\cdot p}{\omega}[E_{0p}\cdot I \cdot \cos\Psi + (X_d - X_q)I^2 \cdot \sin\Psi \cdot \cos\Psi] \tag{30}$$

which can be put in the final form [1]:

$$M_I = \frac{3\cdot p}{\omega}\cdot[E_{0p}\cdot I \cdot \cos\Psi + \frac{1}{2}I^2(X_d - X_q)\cdot \sin 2\Psi] \tag{31}$$

On the whole, the presence of two components $M_I = M_I' + M_I''$ is noticed.

The main component:

$$M_I' = \frac{3\cdot p}{\omega}E_{0p}\cdot I \cdot \cos\Psi$$

depends on the excitation degree (namely, the magnitude of excitation current I_e), while the secondary component:

$$M_I'' = \frac{3\cdot p}{\omega}\cdot\frac{I^2}{2}\cdot(X_d - X_q)\cdot\sin 2\Psi$$

is determined by the magnetic asymmetry of the rotor, being present (non-zero) even in the absence of the synchronous motor excitation. At I=ct., f=ct. and excitation current I_e=ct. (when E_{0p}=ct.), the electromagnetic torque M_I depends solely on the load angle ψ.

For the salient pole synchronous motor, the characteristic $M_I = f(\psi)$ is represented in Figure 8 by a thick line.

In the case of non-salient pole motors, in which $X_d=X_q=X_s$ the secondary component will not appear and the load characteristic $M_I = f(\psi)$ is represented just by the main component with a cosine variation.

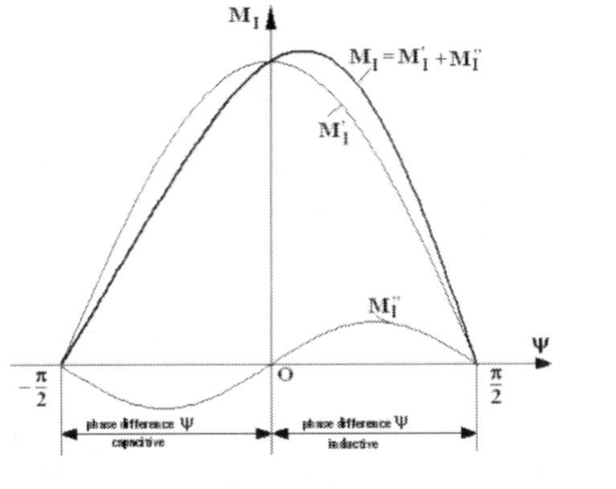

Figure 8. Characteristic representation $M_I = f(\psi)$ of synchronous motor with salient poles at powering from a three-phase source of sinusoidal currents

Note that if in formula (31) of the torque M_I we make the following substitutions:

$$E_{0p} = \omega \cdot (w_1 \cdot k_{w1} \frac{\Phi_{om}}{\sqrt{2}}); \quad X_d = \omega \cdot L_d \text{ and } X_q = \omega \cdot L_q \quad (32)$$

then the electromagnetic torque expression M_I (at the supply current) becomes:

$$M_I = 3p \cdot (w_1 \cdot k_{w1} \frac{\Phi_{om}}{\sqrt{2}}) \cdot I \cos \Psi + \frac{3p}{2} \cdot I^2 (L_d - L_q) \cdot \sin 2\Psi \quad (33)$$

In relations (32) and (33) the physical significance of the new quantities follows:

w_1 = the number of turns, in series, on a stator phase of synchronous motor;

k_{w1} = the winding factor of a stator phase;

Φ_{om} = the maximum value of the main magnetic flux, depending on the magnitude of excitation current I_e, namely $\Phi_{om}=f(I_e)$;

L_d = the longitudinal inductance of stator winding;

L_q = the transverse inductance of stator winding of synchronous motor.

Particularly, for $\psi=0$ (when $I_d=0$ and $I_q=I$), the expression (33) of the electromagnetic torque M_I becomes:

$$M_I = M_I' = 3p(w_1 \cdot k_{w1} \frac{\Phi_{om}}{\sqrt{2}}) \cdot I = K \cdot \Phi_{om} \cdot I \quad (34)$$

so that M_I takes on a form that is mathematically identical to the electromagnetic torque $M=C_m \cdot \Phi \cdot I$ developed by a DC motor (with collector) with separated excitation. In relation (34), with K has been denoted the constructive constant $K = 3p \cdot w_1 \cdot k_{w1} \frac{1}{\sqrt{2}}$ of the synchronous motor.

Expression (33) highlights that at I_e=ct., I=ct. and ψ=ct. the electromagnetic torque M_I is constant (and nonzero) and has the same magnitude regardless of the numerical value of the frequency f of the stator currents.

The existence of nonzero electromagnetic torque at the powering in current (by magnitude I phase shift ψ=ct. related to the counter-electromotive forces E_{op}) leads to the development of synchronous motor applications in electric traction.

On electric locomotives, the traction synchronous motor is powered from a current inverter (thyristorised), with natural commutation, determined exactly by the counter-electromotive forces E_{op} (induced in the stator windings of the synchronous motor).

In order to ensure the phase shift ψ (of the current fundamental I leading the counter-electromotive forces E_{op}), the control of the thyristors' conduction is based on the signals from a position transducer solidary with the rotor.

3.1 Diagram of currents for the traction synchronous motor

The synchronous motor will be over-excited and the three-phase induced counter-electromotive forces ($-e_{0A}$, $-e_{0B}$, $-e_{0C}$) of frequency $f=\omega/2\pi$ are able to drive the commutation of the current inverter thyristors at any speed $\Omega>\Omega_{min}$ without risk of losing synchronism between rotor and rotating magnetic field [1,4-6,9].

Specifically, at any speed "n" of the rotor of self-piloted synchronous motor (corresponding to the frequency $f=p \cdot n/60$ of stator currents) through the induced counter-electromotive forces the synchronous motor is piloting the converter which, from the DC current I_0, is distributing (on each of the three phases of the stator) current pulses of amplitude $\pm I_0$, duration T/3 and a repetition frequency $f=1/T=\omega/2\pi$ which is proportional to the angular mechanical speed of rotor rotation $\Omega=\omega/p$ (see Fig. 9).

The angular mechanical speed Ω of rotor results from the fundamental equation of motion:

$$J \cdot \frac{d\Omega}{dt} = M - M_{ex} \quad (35)$$

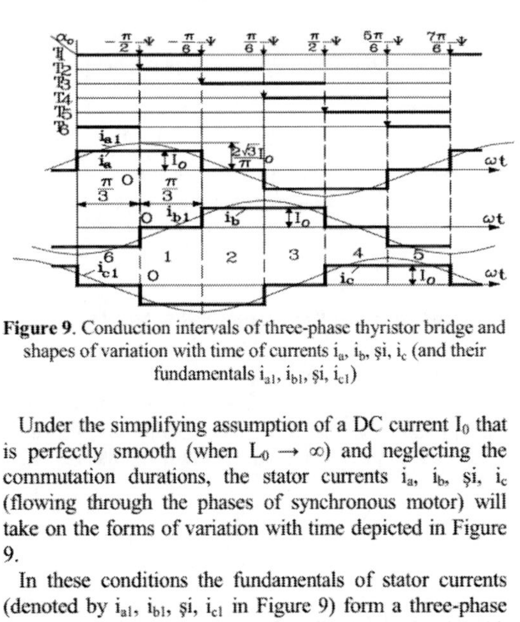

Figure 9. Conduction intervals of three-phase thyristor bridge and shapes of variation with time of currents i_a, i_b, şi, i_c (and their fundamentals i_{a1}, i_{b1}, şi, i_{c1})

Under the simplifying assumption of a DC current I_0 that is perfectly smooth (when $L_0 \rightarrow \infty$) and neglecting the commutation durations, the stator currents i_a, i_b, şi, i_c (flowing through the phases of synchronous motor) will take on the forms of variation with time depicted in Figure 9.

In these conditions the fundamentals of stator currents (denoted by i_{a1}, i_{b1}, şi, i_{c1} in Figure 9) form a three-phase symmetrical current system (by direct sequence) with frequency $f=\omega/2\pi$ and the effective I_1 value given by:

$$I_1 = \frac{\sqrt{6}}{\pi} \cdot I_0 \quad (36)$$

3.2 Synchronization of commands

Operation of the self-piloted synchronous motor is based on ensuring the capacitive shift phase ψ=ct. between the space phasor of stator currents and the axis q. This condition is verified six times during each time period T (by controlling the moments of thyristor ignition relative to the position $\alpha=\omega t+\alpha_0$ of the axis d of the rotor). For this purpose, a position transducer TP provides the rotor positions (with respect to a reference direction of the stator) at which the bridge thyristors of the current inverter IC are on [1,4-6,9].

Ideally, for harmonic variation of stator currents, their space phasor $\underline{i}_{1dq}$ (in the rotor referential (d,q)) is a fixed phasor, mathematically expressed by:

$$\underline{i}_{1dq}=\sqrt{2}I_1\cdot e^{j(\frac{\pi}{2}+\psi)} \quad \text{with} \quad I_1=\frac{\sqrt{6}}{\pi}\cdot I_0 \tag{37}$$

In the fixed stator referential the space phasor $\underline{i}_{1dq}$ matches the expression $\underline{i}_{1s}$:

$$\underline{i}_{1s}=\frac{2}{3}(i_{a1}+a\,i_{b1}+a^2 i_{c1})=\underline{i}_{1dq}e^{j\alpha}=\frac{2\sqrt{3}}{\pi}I_0\cdot e^{j(\frac{\pi}{2}+\psi+\alpha)} \tag{38}$$

with $\alpha=\omega t+\alpha_0$.

If the reference stator axis overlaps the magnetic axis of phase A, and the temporal origin (ωt=0) is chosen when the current i_{a1} (phase A) passes through a maximum (a moment that is coinciding with thyristor ignition timing), the space phasor $\underline{i}_{1s}$ will be of the form:

$$\underline{i}_{1s}=\sqrt{2}\cdot I_1\cdot e^{j\omega t}=\sqrt{2}\cdot(\frac{\sqrt{6}}{\pi}I_0)\cdot e^{j\omega t} \tag{39}$$

From the expressions (38) and (39), it follows that:

$$\frac{\pi}{2}+\psi+\alpha_0=0 \Rightarrow \alpha_0=-(\frac{\pi}{2}+\psi) \tag{40}$$

This angle represents the rotor position at the moment of ignition of thyristor T_2. The other thyristors will be switched on their natural succession (at successive positions of the rotor evenly shifted by $\pi/3$ electric radians) as in Figure 9.

3.3 Considering the sinusoidal currents

When considering only the fundamentals of stator current, the space phasor $\underline{i}_{1dq}$ (in the rotating referential d,q) is fixed and is subject to the expression (in polar form) given by (37). From this relationship, identifying the equivalent algebraic form:

$$\underline{i}_{1dq}=\sqrt{2}\cdot I_1\cdot e^{j(\frac{\pi}{2}+\psi)}=\sqrt{2}\cdot(I_{1d}+j\cdot I_{1q}) \tag{41}$$

where the effective values I_{1d} and I_{1q} of the orthogonal components are:

$$I_{1d}=-I_1\cdot\sin\psi=-(\frac{\sqrt{6}}{\pi}I_0)\sin\psi$$

$$I_{1q}=I_1\cdot\cos\psi=(\frac{\sqrt{6}}{\pi}I_0)\cos\psi$$

If further in the expression of the electromagnetic torque M the following substitutions are performed: $I_d=I_{1d}$ and $I_q=I_{1q}$, the following result holds for $M=M_1$:

$$M_1=3p\{\frac{\sqrt{6}}{\pi}\cdot I_0\cdot(K\Phi_{0m})\cdot\cos\psi-\frac{3}{\pi^2}\cdot I_0^2\cdot(L_d-L_q)\cdot\sin 2\psi\} \tag{42}$$

where the average value of current I_0 (which is established in the DC intermediary circuit) is calculated from the relationship:

$$I_0=\frac{U_{1d}-V_{d\alpha}}{R_0} \tag{43}$$

The sole problem of self-piloted synchronous motor is the starting regime [1,4-6,9]. At low rotational speeds, under 5% of Ω_{max}, the counter-electromotive force ($-e_{0p}$) becomes unable to ensure the commutation of the thyristors of the current inverter (CI). In this speed range, assisted commutation is applied, usually realized by the device AC through creative options.

3.4 Considering the non-sinusoidal currents

In very deed, the phase currents i_a, i_b, i_c are strongly distorted as against the ideal sinusoidal shape [1,9]. Actually, under the simplifying assumptions adopted, each phase current (i_a, i_b or i_c from Fig. 9) consists of "rectangular blocks" of amplitude $\pm I_0$ (and duration equal to $2\pi/3$) separated by intervals (by duration $\pi/3$) in which the currents are null.

Moreover, the fundamentals of phase currents (denoted by i_{a1}, i_{b1} and i_{c1} in Figure 9) have equal amplitudes (of magnitude $\frac{2\sqrt{3}}{\pi}I_0$) and they are shifted, one lagging another, with the same angle of $2\pi/3$, forming a symmetrical three-phase system of sinusoidal currents, by direct succession. One could notice that by I_0 is denoted the DC intensity from the DC intermediary circuit.

In the fixed stator referential $\alpha\beta$, with the real axis Oα overlapped to reference stator winding axis A and with the temporal origin (ωt=0) chosen at the moment when its current is passing through a maximum (when $i_{a1}=\frac{2\sqrt{3}}{\pi}I_0$), the space phasor $\underline{i}_{1s}$ of stator current fundamentals, calculated with the formula:

$$\underline{i}_{1s}(\omega t)=\frac{2}{3}\cdot(i_{a1}+a\cdot i_{b1}+a^2\cdot i_{c1})=\sqrt{2}(\frac{\sqrt{6}}{\pi})I_0\cdot e^{j\omega t} \tag{44}$$

is a rotating phasor (with the angular speed ω=ct) with the top-point describing the circle of radius equal to $\sqrt{2}(\frac{\sqrt{6}}{\pi})\cdot I_0=\frac{2\cdot\sqrt{3}}{\pi}\cdot I_0$ (represented by dashed line in Figure 10).

In the same time interval, still in the fixed stator referential $\alpha\beta$, the space phasor $\underline{i}_s$ (of non-sinusoidal currents) is completely different. For this reason, analytically it will proceed to an evaluation of this space phasor on each angular interval (by width $\pi/3$), in which the stator currents i_a, i_b and i_c remain constant. Thereby:

1. In the first interval $0 \leq \omega t \leq \pi/3$ when $i_a = +I_0$, $i_b = 0$ and $i_c = -I_0$ the space phasor $\underline{i}_s$ is fixed (position "0" in Figure 10) and has the expression:

$$\underline{i}_s(\omega t) = \frac{2}{3}(i_a + a \cdot i_b + a^2 \cdot i_c) = \frac{2}{3} \cdot (I_0 - a^2 \cdot I_0) = \frac{2}{\sqrt{3}} \cdot I_0 \cdot e^{j\frac{\pi}{6}}; \quad 0 \leq \omega t < \frac{\pi}{3}$$

(45)

2. In the interval (k+1) by width $\pi/3$, when ωt may be written as:

$$\omega t = k \cdot \frac{\pi}{3} + \omega t'; \quad 0 \leq \omega t' < \frac{\pi}{3}; \quad k = 1, 2, 3 \ldots \tag{46}$$

the space phasor $\underline{i}_s$ remains fixed (in position "k", k=1,2,3… in Figure 10) on whole duration $0 \leq \omega t' < \pi/3$.

Broadly speaking, for any ωt by type (46), the expression of space phasor $\underline{i}_s$ can be written as:

$$\underline{i}_s(\omega t) = \frac{2}{\sqrt{3}} \cdot I_0 \cdot e^{j(\frac{\pi}{6} + k \cdot \frac{\pi}{3})} \tag{47}$$

with $k = 0, 1, 2, 3 \ldots$

During each period $\omega T = 2\pi$, the space phasor $\underline{i}_s(\omega t)$ of non-sinusoidal currents will successively scan all 6 fixed positions (denoted by "0", "1", "2", "3", "4", "5" in Figure 10). At each position it will remain motionless for

$$t' = \frac{\pi}{3\omega} = \frac{\pi}{3}\left[\frac{T}{2\pi}\right] = \frac{T}{6},$$

that time being numerically equal to the duration between two successive commutations of the bridge, then instantly "jumps" to the next position.

Geometrically, over the duration of each period $\omega T = 2\pi$, the "jumping" space phasor $\underline{i}_s(\omega t)$ performs a complete rotation, like the rotating phasor $\underline{i}_{1s}(\omega t)$ of current fundamentals [1,9]. Accordingly, the virtual angular speed ω_{vir} (fictitious average) of rotation of "jumping" phasor of non-sinusoidal currents $\omega_{vir} = \frac{2\pi}{T} = 2\pi f = \omega$ is numerically equal to the rotation angular speed ω of the rotating phasor of stator current fundamentals. Consequently, this common value ω of angular speeds will be used at changing the referential of space phasors.

In the coordinates (d,q) rotating with angular speed ω, the space phasor $\underline{i}_{1s}$ will become $\underline{i}_{1dq}$, while the space phasor $\underline{i}_s$ will become $\underline{i}_{dq}$. At changing the referential, the relations among these phasors are as the form:

$$\underline{i}_{1dq} = \underline{i}_{1s} \cdot e^{-j\alpha}; \quad \alpha = \alpha_0 + \omega t \tag{48}$$

$$\underline{i}_{dq} = \underline{i}_s \cdot e^{-j\alpha}; \quad \alpha = \alpha_0 + \omega t \tag{49}$$

With expression (44) for $\underline{i}_{1s}$, the relation of phasor $\underline{i}_{1dq}$ given by (48) takes on the form:

$$\underline{i}_{1dq} = \sqrt{2} \cdot (\frac{\sqrt{6}}{\pi}) \cdot I_0 \cdot e^{j\omega t} \cdot e^{-j(\alpha_0 + \omega t)} = \frac{2\sqrt{3}}{\pi} I_0 \cdot e^{-j\alpha_0} \tag{50}$$

Similarly, for any ωt of the form: $\omega t = k \cdot \frac{\pi}{3} + \omega t'$

with $0 \leq \omega t' < \frac{\pi}{3}$.

and k = 0, 1, 2, 3, … when, in fixed coordinates, the space phasor $\underline{i}_s$ has the expression (47), it will result that, in synchronous rotating coordinates, the space phasor $\underline{i}_{dq}$ will be established by:

$$\underline{i}_{dq} = \frac{2}{\sqrt{3}} \cdot I_0 \cdot e^{j(\frac{\pi}{6} + k\frac{\pi}{3})} \cdot e^{-j(\alpha_0 + k \cdot \frac{\pi}{3} + \omega t')} = \frac{2}{\sqrt{3}} \cdot I_0 \cdot e^{j(\frac{\pi}{6} - \alpha_0 - \omega t')} \tag{51}$$

If the initial position α_0 it is chosen accordingly to relation (40), meaning $\alpha_0 = -(\frac{\pi}{2} + \psi)$, then in rotating coordinates (d,q), the space phasors $\underline{i}_{1dq}$ and $\underline{i}_{dq}$ become respectively:

$$\underline{i}_{1dq} = \frac{2\sqrt{3}}{\pi} \cdot I_0 \cdot e^{j(\frac{\pi}{2} + \psi)} = j \cdot \frac{2\sqrt{3}}{\pi} \cdot I_0 \cdot e^{j\psi} \tag{52}$$

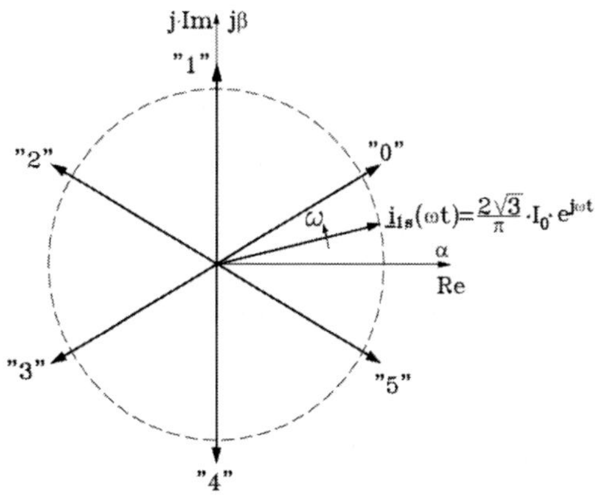

Figure 10. Rotating space phasor $\underline{i}_{1s}(\omega t)$ and the 6 fixed positions of non-sinusoidal current phasor $\underline{i}_s(\omega t)$ in the fixed stator referential

$$\underline{i}_{dq} = \frac{2}{\sqrt{3}} \cdot I_0 \cdot e^{j(\frac{\pi}{2} + \psi + \frac{\pi}{6} - \omega t')} = j \cdot \frac{2}{\sqrt{3}} \cdot I_0 \cdot e^{j(\psi + \frac{\pi}{6} - \omega t')} \tag{53}$$

Space phasors $\underline{i}_{1dq}$ and $\underline{i}_{dq}$ are geometrically represented in Figure 11, in the interval $0 \leq \omega t' < \frac{\pi}{3}$ (on the time duration $0 \leq t < \frac{\pi}{3\omega} = \frac{\pi \cdot T}{3 \cdot 2\pi} = \frac{T}{6}$), meaning that exactly the duration T/6 between two successive commutations of the bridge.

Figure 11 emphasizes that during the time between two successive commutations T/6 the space phasor $\underline{i}_{dq}$ rotates in opposite sense, with the angular speed ω=ct., its extremity describing the arc between the points 1 and 2 corresponding to an angle at the centre of $\pi/3$ electrical radians [1,9].

At the moment t'=0, the phasor $\underline{i}_{dq}$ starts from initial position **1** (corresponding to angle $\psi+30^0$) towards the final position **2** (corresponding to angle $\psi-30^0$), reached after t'=T/6. At each commutation of the bridge, the space phasor $\underline{i}_{dq}$ instantly returns from position 2 to position 1, then the oscillation around the fixed phasor $\underline{i}_{1dq}$ is repeated in an identical manner.

Accordingly, the electromagnetic torque M_I developed by the self-piloted synchronous motor will oscillate.

In order to evaluate the electromagnetic torque M_I, we first establish the effective values $I_d(t')$ and $I_q(t')$ of the orthogonal components of phasor $\underline{i}_{dq}$:

$$\underline{i}_{dq} = \sqrt{2}\cdot[I_d(t') + j\cdot I_q(t')] = j\cdot\frac{2}{\sqrt{3}}\cdot I_0\cdot e^{j(\psi+\frac{\pi}{6}-\omega t')} \qquad (54)$$

Then, by identifying terms, the following immediately is observed:

$$I_d(t') = -\sqrt{\frac{2}{3}}I_0\sin(\psi+\frac{\pi}{6}-\omega t') \qquad (55)$$

$$I_q(t') = \sqrt{\frac{2}{3}}I_0\cos(\psi+\frac{\pi}{6}-\omega t')$$

If in expression (30) of the electromagnetic torque M there are performed the substitutions $I_d = I_d(t')$ and $I_q = I_q(t')$ specified by (45), then the torque M_I takes on the form:

$$M_I(t') = 3p\left[(K\Phi_{0m})\cdot\sqrt{\frac{2}{3}}I_0\cos(\psi+\frac{\pi}{6}-\omega t') - \frac{I_0^2}{3}(L_d - L_q)\sin 2(\psi+\frac{\pi}{6}-\omega t')\right]$$

(56)

This expression of the torque is valid in each interval $0 < \omega t' < \pi/3$ between two successive commutations of the bridge. Overall, the torque M_I is irregular.

The non-uniformity of electromagnetic torque M_I is caused by the variation of the orthogonal components $I_d(t')$ and $I_q(t')$, according to (31), this variation being determined by the oscillation of space phasor $\underline{i}_{dq}$ around the fixed phasor $\underline{i}_{1dq}$. On each period T (of non-sinusoidal variation of currents) the electromagnetic torque M_I performs six pulsations of the type described by relationship (56).

In order to attenuate pulsations of electromagnetic torque one is searching for ways to limit the oscillation amplitude of phasor $\underline{i}_{dq}$ (for instance between $\psi+15^o$ and $\psi-15^o$). For this goal, the stator winding of synchronous motor is divided in two distinct three-phase windings (spatially shifted with $\pi/6$ electrical radians), each being separately supplied from a current inverter. If the two inverters provide current pulses shifted from each other by $\pi/6$ electric radians, then it could be achieved a system with the pulsation index q=2·6=12, consequently with a pulsation period of the electromagnetic torque equal to T/12. It follows implicitly that the amplitude of torque pulsation will be less.

4 Conclusions

Addressing the sustainability of operation of the AC traction electric motors constitutes a challenge in electric railway transportation research.

An electromagnetic torque capability analysis of the traction AC electric motors has been carried out in this study.

The analysis of the torque capability of the traction inductor motor emphasizes that the greatest magnitudes of electromagnetic torque are obtained for operation at a constant stator flux Ψ_s=ct. The study highlights that the

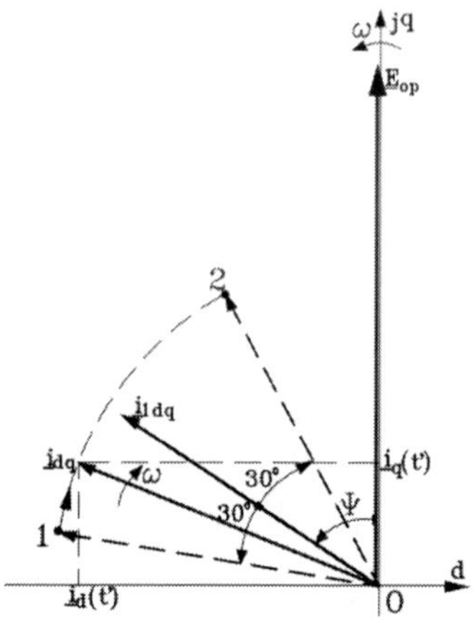

Figure 11. Oscillations of phasor $\underline{i}_{dq}$ around $\underline{i}_{1dq}$ in case of rectangular currents

maximum electromagnetic torque when the induction motor is operating at constant useful flux Ψ_u = ct. is approximately 20% smaller than the maximum torque when operating at Ψ_s = ct. Moreover, at the imposed electromagnetic torque, the smallest value of rotor pulsation is obtained for operation with Ψ_s = ct. The analysis of induction machine operation with constant flux highlights also that only at constant rotor flux Ψ'_r = ct. do the induction machine mechanical characteristics not have extremum points; rather they are straight lines. These linear characteristics are preferable for the applications which demand high sustainability dynamics in induction machine operation.

The study of traction synchronous motor emphasizes that electric traction drive systems using synchronous motors fed by current inverters provide high performance for high speed electric trains, in terms of both train dynamics and sustainability. With respect to the electromagnetic torque capability of the traction synchronous motor, the paper highlights that in order to synchronize the machine rotating field with the rotor (and avoiding the risk of losing the synchronism at any frequency value of stator currents) the synchronous motor will control the current inverter which is powering it, becoming in this way a self-piloted synchronous motor. Actually, the position of direct axis of synchronous motor rotor will be checked in an evolutionary sense in time (through position transducers) 6·p times during each complete rotation (at any value of rotor speed), by the ignition control of the thyristor of the current inverter bridge that is supplying the motor. Hence, the paper emphasizes that at electrically driven railway systems with traction synchronous motors the functions of amplitude adjustment are completely separate from those of the frequency control. As a consequence, the result is a simpler construction for both the power part and the control electronics of static converters.

The paper supports the findings that electric traction drive systems using three-phase induction and synchronous motors fed by variable voltage or current variable frequency inverters enhance the sustainable operation of electric railway trains. The results of this work may lead to enhancements of the main criteria for optimising the safe and efficient operation of railway electric traction systems.

References

1. D.A. Nicola, *Tractiune electrica (Electric Traction)*, Universitaria Publishing House, Craiova, Romania (2012).
2. M.A. Rosen, D.A. Nicola, C.A. Bulucea, D.C. Cismaru, *Sustainability*, *7*, 3441-3459 (2015).
3. C.A. Bulucea, D.A. Nicola, N.E. Mastorakis, M.A. Rosen, *Recent Researches in Energy and Environment: Proc. 6th IASME/WSEAS Int. Conf. on Energy and Environment*, Cambridge, UK, February 20-25, pp. 182-191 (2011).
4. R. Kaller, J.M. Allenbach, *Traction Electrique (Electrical Traction)*, Vol. 1-2, PPUR, Lausanne, (1995).
5. F. Perticaroli, *Sistemi elettrici per i transporti: Trazione elettrica (Electrical Systems for Transportation: Electric Traction)*. Ed. Masson, Milano-Parigi-Barcellona (1994).
6. J.A. Lozano, J.Félez, J.de Dios Sanz, J. M. Mera, *Railway Traction, Reliability and Safety in Railway*, Dr. Xavier Perpinya (Ed.), (2012), Available at: http://www.intechopen.com/books/reliability-and-safety-in-railway/railway-traction , Accessed on 15 February 2016.
7. T. Koseki, *The 2010 International Power Electronics Conference*, pp. 2836-2741 (2010), Available at: http://koseki.t.u-tokyo.ac.jp/report2010/141-146.pdf , Accessed on 10 February 2016
8. M. Georgescu, *Tracţiunea electrică de mare viteză cu motoare sincrone (High Speed Electric Traction with Synchronous Motors)*, Dacia Publishing House, Cluj-Napoca (2001).
9. C.A. Bulucea D.A. Nicola, D.C. Cismaru, N.E. Mastorakis, C.A. Bulucea, C. Brindusa, *Advances in Environmental Sciences, Development and Chemistry, Proc. 2014 Int. Conf. on Energy, Environment, Development and Economics (EEDS 2014)*, Santorini Island, Greece, July 17-21, pp. 21-28 (2014).
10. D.A. Nicola, M.A. Rosen, C.A. Bulucea, C. Brandusa, *Proc. 6th WSEAS Int. Conf. on Engineering Education (EE'09)*, Rhodes, Greece, July 22-24, pp. 124-132 (2009).
11. M.A. Rosen, *Proc. 3rd IASME/WSEAS Int. Conf. on Energy & Environment*, Cambridge, UK, Feb. 23-25, 136-142 (2008).
12. I. Dincer, M.A. Rosen, *Exergy: Energy, Environment and Sustainable Development*, 2d ed., Elsevier: Oxford, UK (2013).
13. C.A. Bulucea, D.A. Nicola, M.A. Rosen, N.E. Mastorakis, C.A. Bulucea, *Recent Advances in Environmental and Earth Sciences and Economics, Proc. 2015 Int. Conf. on Energy, Environment, Development and Economics (EEDE 2015)*, Zakynthos Island, Greece, July 16-20, pp. 108-115 (2015).
14. J. Chatelain, *Machines électriques (Electrical Machines)*, PPUR, Lausanne (1989).
15. D.A. Nicola, C.A. Bulucea, *Electrotechnics, Electrical Equipment and Machines*, Vol. II "Electrical Equipment", SITECH Publishing House, Craiova (2005).

MATEC Web of Conferences **76**, 02006 (2016) DOI: 10.1051/matecconf/20167602006
CSCC 2016

Environmental Management Systems and Sustainability in SMEs

Satya Shah[1,a], Elmira Ganji[1] and Syed Hasan[2]

[1]*Faculty of Engineering and Science, University of Greenwich, UK*
[2]*Industrial and Manufacturing Engineering, NED University of Technology, Pakistan*

Abstract. Environmental sustainability in manufacturing sector has been allocated a major consideration in the international literature. Due to growing concerns over the high effect of SMEs on world manufacturing industries and their contribution to pollution; this research attempts to focus on the key parameters that interact in the application of environmental management system, taking into account the main features of SMEs and also the integral role of industrial entrepreneurs in inspiring their firms' approaches. The paper explores the potential opportunities which enable these enterprises to move towards organizations with high level of responsibility regarding environmental protection in order to provide a healthier life for future generations. Case investigation is carried out on an adhesive manufacturing company, which covers a notable market share within the sector. The research identifies that the company requires developing both internal and external entities within an explicit plan to revolutionize the recruitment patterns. Given the lack of adequate studies in adhesive technology, more researches are recommended in the future to consider the sustainable innovations on a broader sample of adhesive manufacturing companies to perform the life-cycle analysis due to the harmful organic compounds and toxic vapours of the adhesive products.

1 Introduction

In the last two decades, the concept of sustainability and accountability has become an emerging characteristic of the enterprises worldwide. Improving significant aspects of a company success such as economic, social and environmental performance; sustainability defines a strategy to transform businesses towards long-term prosperity. The Brundtland Commission (WCED) defined sustainable development in 1987, as "seeking to meet the needs and aspirations of the present, without compromising the ability to meet those of the future" which became a classic and common definition [1]. Nowadays widespread idea of the triple P of business (Profit, People and Planet) which is delivered by [2], describes the term sustainability appropriately. Therefore, environmental sustainability would be a significant factor of every decision-making, from purchasing raw materials to products and services that firms provide. Going green is at the heart of the sustainability and involves some guiding principles to provide the deepest view of how the business can have impacts on our planet and build a better life for future generations [3]. In other words, green strategies focus on propelling just one of the sustainability goals which is environmental stewardship [4].

ISO is originally a Greek word meaning "Equal" and it was initially an organization for product development and safety standards which altered its traditional way by evolving a series of quality management standards [5]. Implementation of the EMS and adopting a certification such as ISO 14001 or EMAS act as sustainable evaluation tools to provide visual assessment, monitor the production waste and environmental performance. A comprehensive definition for EMS is given by ISO.org, as "organizational structure, responsibilities, practices, procedures, processes and resources for determining and implementing environmental policy". Thus, EMS would be the effective and positive bedrock for companies' continual improvements that also assist them on their path towards sustainability [6].

2 Literature Review

The review of literature seeks to outline the conceptual framework of the research by presenting a review of advantages, disadvantages, motivations, drivers and hurdles towards Environmental Management Systems (EMS) in order to prove the necessity of the environmental sustainability practices within the SMEs. In particular, adhesive technology characteristics considering major problems correlated with optimizing sustainability and its environmental impacts will be examined.

2.1 Importance of SME on Business Factors

Since the priority of any firm is its survivability and better performance, SMEs are not only an exception, but also have a significant impact in most of the market economies. Research studies indicated that SMEs make

[a] Corresponding author: s.shah@gre.ac.uk

up about 90% of all global enterprises and many of them are suppliers over the supply chain [7]. SMEs share of global environmental pollution is 70%, with the majority of manufacturing sector [8]. Moreover, 0.4% of all the SMEs belong to the enterprises with more than 100 employees. Climate change is seen as the greatest environmental challenge facing the world today and is considered as the key focus of international, European and UK policy. With climate change considered as an important factor within any environmental and governmental policies, the study aims towards focusing on the importance of Environmental and Climate change aspects through sustainable development and Environmental Management systems within SMEs.

The existing literature on the business response to climate change seems to be largely normative rather than empirical in nature and tends to focus towards larger firms rather than small and medium enterprises (SMEs). Similarly, government policies on climate change often focus predominantly on larger firms, with less emphasis on the roles that SMEs can play. Yet, as SMEs constitute 99% of UK businesses, provide 43% of private-sector employment and may account for 20% of total UK carbon emissions understanding their environmental impact and engagement, both generally and with respect to climate change, seems highly important [9].

Identifying a firm internal and external changes and profitability benefits through adoption of sustainable strategies are fundamental factors in healthy dynamic businesses. Hence, there is a growing concern to promote SMEs to make investments in sustainable business practices, particularly in developing countries as it has been noted that the industrial activities carried out within the SMEs contributes towards environmental pollution. This would be also as a result of poor financial resources, lack of regulations and inadequate expertise to deal with complex technologies. Utilising economical and simple solutions facilitate a foundation for developing countries to implement effective systems for environmental protection without the need to spend long time periods or having high scientific backgrounds, high costs and high level technologies. Scrutinizing SMEs characteristics to face green or environmental management issues and sustainability criteria, helps researchers recommend applicable mechanisms for such. On the other side, SMEs may confront many pressures on their management strategies to the way of being environmentally friendly. Inadequate financial resources, lack of technical expertise, low level of research and development, management weaknesses and their visions that SMEs have little environmental impact are the major barriers for SMEs social responsibility and competitive advantage [10]. Therefore, the strategic choices of entrepreneurs and managers play a vital role in organizational growth and sustainable development of the firm in the long-term perspective. This research seeks to address the gaps in literature regarding the actual effectiveness of considering environmental sustainability practices with a particular attention to the traditional management methods, lack of understanding of environmental risks and lack of proper information availability within SMEs, specifically in manufacturing sector. The author also tends to look at the recruitment practices in SMEs as a part of the research.

2.2 EMS Objectives for SMEs Performance

Numerous benefits of adopting EMS by SMEs have been categorized by [8] into two main groups: Internal Benefits and External Benefits. Internal benefits include many organizational improvements, financial savings and payback periods of investments within the company. Moreover, EMS implementation provides new interactions between personnel and management and results in intangible advantages such as employee morale and social responsibility (MSR) enhancement, communication and skills improvements, increasing knowledge and altering staff's attitude which are very important for SMEs performance. In terms of External benefits, companies find more competitive and business rewards. Therefore, they attract new business partners and increase satisfaction of customer requirements. In addition to the commercial benefits, companies find positive outcomes such as environmental achievements, assured legal compliance, energy consumption minimization and waste reduction. As a result, relationships with stakeholders, company image and reputation will be improved.

The main objectives of EMS which move companies towards systematic approaches development has been defined by [6]. Applying the concept of EMS not only assists SMEs to reduce energy consumption, pollution and hazardous wastes in the chemical industry; but also lead them into conservation of resources, increasing productivity and reducing costs. It develops awareness of environmental issues and responsibilities among entrepreneurs. Furthermore, SMEs will be encouraged to apply an environmental management system in their production processes. Research studies introduced EIS which help SMEs to review comprehensive environmental information relevant to the company operations and facilities. EIS can be used as an effective tool to measure, benchmark and monitor the environmental performance in a time sequence analysis. The environmental indicators enable company managers to detect the market prospect, cost reduction potentials, compare their firm with industrial standards and importantly, to better decision-making [6]. However, ISO 14001 does not require indicators development but they could be obtained through ISO 14001 standard. The studies pointed out that eco-mapping is a visual assessment tool particularly designed for SMEs to reduce their environmental documentation quantities. Using this tool includes maps for various entities of the company, such as water map, energy map, and material and resource flow map [6]. Furthermore, flowcharts such as process maps provide a general and instant overview of company operations, starting with material inputs ending up with waste disposal and distribution [11]. Both these evaluation tools assist and prepare SMEs on their journey to environmental management system and sustainability.

Quantitative evaluation of environmental management system is required to help us determine the effectiveness and value of such a system. Assisting particular sector if SMEs, helps to focus on homogenous tools and approaches without necessity of high cost modification or application. Moreover, using visual assessment and evaluation tools already exist and necessitate the contribution and commitment of all personnel which is a key success towards EMS implementation. These tools help manufacturing sector appropriately but they still remain heterogeneous and need to be integrated. In general, three main factors answer the "Why" it is necessary to adopt EMS by SMEs. Firstly, implementing EMS brings high efficiency and cost savings. Moreover, many bank insurance companies give predominance to organizations with low environmental risk. Secondly, market demand for products and services with better environmental preferences such as "green consumerism" would be another driver. Thirdly, effective EMS brings firms fewer risks of breaking the laws and also fewer environmental incidents [6].

2.3 SMEs Motivations towards Environmental Approaches

Different Scenarios exist for SMEs to optimize sustainability and create competitive advantages and were discussed by [7]. These motivations enable SMEs to develop into valuable sustainable investment target points for larger firms; therefore, they become sustainable suppliers in both global and local supply chain. If SMEs work collaboratively and create networked entities in sustainable marketplace, which is nowadays facilitated by globalization of communication technology, it can offer them the opportunities for better economic performance where the MNEs (Multinational Enterprises) are less successful.

Considering SMEs from an upstream view as buyers from suppliers, more pressures can be exert by them in order to take into account the three dimensions of sustainability in order to provide a sustainable supply chain [12]. Furthermore, other research studies also claim that motivations inspiring the sustainability concept for the SMEs are in a wide range, including internal organization improvements, legal requirements, competitive advantage, reputation concerns and increasing profitability [13]. Three fundamental phases and motivations have been identified for corporate sustainability by [14]. In this regard, sanitizing as compliance driven health or safety efforts, controlling as eco-efficiency driven environmental management and integration of all the components of the company into business decisions as a value creator have been mentioned.

Exploring the strong drivers such as customers, legislation and social responsibility of SMEs environmental processes like disposal, recycling and EMS, it is necessary to address their impact on company performance. Achieving this goal, a sample of 500 Turkish SMEs was investigated by [15] using a cross-sectional design. They considered regulation as a low-level motivator towards environmental pollution in Turkish SMEs. They pointed out that governments can also act with other beneficial techniques such as building waste treatment facilities in industrial areas and encourage the SMEs to develop their environmental projects. The important point is that besides environmental issues, government policy should also result in SMEs growth. Moreover, OEM as an element in supply chain could offer some help to their suppliers in order to provide green design, processes or certifications. In the factor analysis, the researchers have eliminated some of the drivers triggering environmental processes due to the poor loadings on their intended factor. Removing short-term profits allows long-term benefits to be more investigated along with market share, firm image and competitive advantage [15]. One significant problem which has not been solved yet is that SMEs are in an ambiguous situation and that the confusion among different entities controlling the environmental programs always exists, and some SMEs operate without accurate inspection. Moreover, a huge investment is needed to implement recycling processes or EMS.

Assessing the motivation of five German SMEs to implement and certify EMS was part of another research studies [16]. Among the small and medium-sized energy and gas companies in Germany, organizing companies to deal with environmental regulations and domestic competition, finding cost cutting opportunities and increasing efficiency for competitiveness enhancement are frequently mentioned as strong motivators to adopt EMS. These companies reported air and waste emissions reductions, energy and water conservation, safety and incidence reduction as positive consequences of ISO 14001. However, it is essential to perform more researches to explore whether the benefits and positive impacts of certifying environmental management system can accomplish the strong motivations of doing so. Furthermore, among all the benefits of SMEs, cost savings documentation, increased competitive advantages and operational improvements are more difficult to bring into focus.

2.4 Environmental and Sustainability Practices and Strategies

Key parameters and strategies which interact with implementation of environmental management tools have been described and analysed by taking into account the specific characteristics of the SMEs [10]. According to Figure1, in the First stage of the strategy it is noted that environmental tools adoption does not require extra financial support or access to capital [8] [10]; as SMEs may have higher risks, information limitations and higher costs for implementing EMS. Since the small firms usually consist of an operative unit which is being run by a single individual owner-manager having the absolute authority, the Second stage is to identify that the mind-set of the manager in risking, embracing change, innovation, growth and social responsibility exert a high influence on the development of firms and choice of strategies and policies.

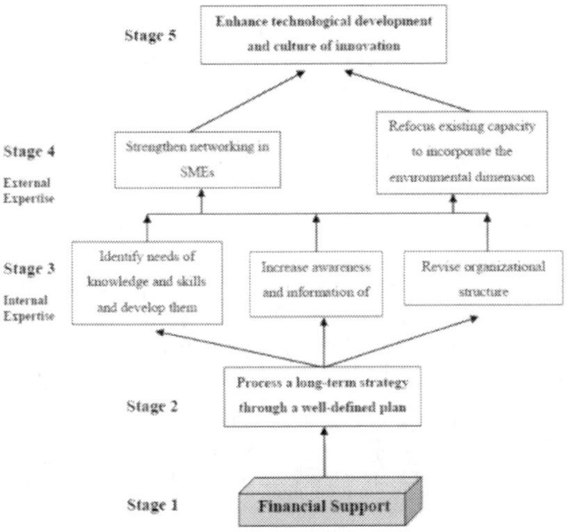

Figure 1. Proposed Strategy for Environmental Activities in SMEs [10].

The Third stage indicates the necessity of internal expertise, higher qualifications of managers, attracting high skill labour and increasing awareness on waste minimization in SMEs. Moreover, SMEs organizational structure need to be revised as a small team who is generally responsible for all the important aspects of the business including key decision makings, dealing with regulations and identifying markets. In doing so, SMEs have to shift responsibilities to qualified workers in order to facilitate collaboration and a democratic workplace which relies on high knowledge and expertise. In the Fourth stage, using the external expertise has been mentioned. Eventually on the Fifth stage, the need for technological development and a culture of innovation is illustrated. In general, in the case of packaging they mentioned that legislation, producer responsibility obligation and increasing pressure on companies related to environmental issues will result in attracting more expertise and advice in order to implement environmental management tools with the new regulations.

Strategy elements that address several important issues for adopting environmental management tools need more research, since they might develop or become invalid in the future. In SMEs, the transit packaging is used to supply materials and finished products that is the treat for the packaging waste. This information could also be utilised for developing an export system. Research investigated development practice and innovation theory within the SMEs which will lead sustainable innovations into practice. In that research it is shown that sustainable innovations mostly rely on technological processes improvements and reduction in production costs [17]. The case of PRIMA project (rubber and plastics industry) was selected, in order to interview with their 26 companies and gather the appropriate data to study the triple P in business through them. In the specified case the dominant role of the managers is considered as one of the SMEs behavioural advantages to undertake the sustainable innovation activities. Moreover, flexibility of the organization is another benefit for SMEs especially the smaller companies, as a little bureaucracy and personnel motivation will result in more efficiency in innovation projects.

In contrast, managers could have disadvantages regarding to their short-term focus and also weaknesses in managerial skills such as decision making. Plenty of sustainable innovation activities indicate that attaining a determined concept for sustainable innovation seems not to be easy in the short-term. Therefore, further researches should be done to compare the influence of internal and external factors in SMEs to the way of their sustainability corporations. Furthermore, better understanding of the sustainable innovation techniques, companies' stakeholders and staffs could perform tasks more effective to make developments in company performance.

2.5 Environmental Impacts of Adhesive Industry

Studies had sought to find out the concept of environmental sustainability within the adhesive industry. Adhesives are mostly consisting of polymers and derived from petroleum feedstock which is non-renewable resources [18]. Moreover, in their manufacturing process, a large-scale energy with pollutions including greenhouse gases used as input and emissions of organic pollutants will be generated in output. In terms of resources, studies also declare that adhesives produced from renewable vegetable and animal resources were being used for a long time. In addition, the pressures towards sustainable practices caused investigations to develop new polymers from renewable biomass, using fermentation techniques or controlled pyrolysis [18]. Adhesive products are a main source of volatile organic compounds which are harmful to the atmosphere as they cause photochemical smog and also lung diseases such as asthma. Furthermore, organic vapours have the same influence as greenhouse gases due to absorption of infra-red radiation [18].

However, several adhesives such as rubber to metal bonding which were produced as organic solvents are based on aqueous emulsions at present. Residues of some of the compounds used in additives and adhesives might be released into the environment and reported for disruption of endocrine system as well. According to European Union "REACH" regulations (Registration, Evaluation, Authorization and Restriction of Chemical); more obligations should be applied to the industries to substitute safer materials by endocrine disruptors.

Taking into account the two important factors including raw material inputs and discharging wastes outputs from and back to the ecosystem, the laws of the Thermodynamics can be considered. In accord with the second law of Thermodynamics, in this case, system begins with highly ordered raw materials with low entropy and moves towards increasing entropy and finally ends up with disordered wastes with maximum entropy which is called the state of "Thermodynamic Equilibrium". Therefore, the petroleum with low entropy is burnt to produce carbon dioxide with high entropy. On the other hand, constant rate of growth (size of the economy or resource) relies on the growth rate in mathematical terms. Therefore, it is clear that as long as the economic system pursues endless growth, sustainability could not be achieved by adhesive technology and this fact is well ensured by Thermodynamics laws. However, many researchers have tried to find a solution for environmental impact of particular adhesive products; still it is necessary to consider the total environmental aspects of the engineering framework in which the adhesive technology is being developed. Improving the engineering efficiency towards products sustainability and reducing the environmental impacts of adhesive industry, a complete "life-cycle analysis" would be found.

2.6 EMS Disadvantages for SMEs

The disadvantages of EMS have been grouped [8] into three categories. Some studies indicate that cost of certification/validation, cost and quality of advising consultant resulted in SMEs dissatisfaction with implementing the EMS. In this regard, lack of rewards, restriction of linking the EMS to quality systems and complexity of this approach are other factors which need to be taken into account. According to the research, legislation and regulators are more significant for environmental improvements in SMEs than customers and this fact shows the key role of regulations in SMEs environmental strategies [8]. Investigating the adoption of formal EMSs across the European Union, studies identified regarding EMAS and ISO 14001. According to reliable commercial sources, comparing ISO 14001 standard popularity to EMAS, it can be estimated that the percentage of SMEs registered to international guideline ISO 14001 would be higher than for European EMAS. This is also widely reported in the analysed studies. Due to the variety of enterprises in the SME sector, it is not evaluated as a homogenous group of companies.

Therefore, SMEs have a diverse and heterogeneous nature and the studies which probe this sector are too general. The paper conducted also identified the limitation and it is recommended that in the further research, specific sub-groups of SMEs in terms of size and sector diversity be considered [8]. In summary, the literature demonstrated that environmental management system and sustainability strategies have been mostly employed in developed countries such as European countries. Implementing EMS in SMEs, different techniques and strategies were studied in order to gain a perception about the criteria of the environmental sustainable practices. However, there is lack of literature regarding adhesive technology environmental impacts. Objective 1 and 3 was fulfilled through wide-ranging literature studies. In the next chapter, a detailed description of all features of the design and research settings will be presented through main principles for the research approach.

3 Research Methodology

This research is based on both qualitative and quantitative data which is facilitated through detailed company survey using site visits, themed interviews and questionnaire administration. Furthermore, reviewing the history and background of the company, all the publicity available materials such as company website and brochures were used within the research. The proposed research seeks to describe the characteristics of a sustainable manufacturing business by pursuing environmental management strategies based on the collected data from document research, industry association data from the interviews and also any government environmental regulations, therefore it would be a descriptive research.

The population of the study is the personnel of Company X consisting of the shareholders, senior managers, engineers and high-level personnel due to their primary knowledge; current, accurate and factual data they can present for the research purpose. As a result, the researcher will be able to draw assumptions and derive findings based on the existing information and perform the analysis in the higher steps. In Company X, five main parties were involved in meetings and helped the author to write up the observations and findings of the production line and surroundings during two days company visit; comprising HSE department (Health and Safety protection experts), quality control management, planning management, foreign purchasing management, and technical management. Moreover, the five owners (shareholders) and the board of director of the company offered an opportunity to ask some key questions and take their feedback regarding the most significant challenges they face in the company.

4 Results and Discussions

Different levels of managers and personnel were engaged in completing the survey questionnaires. The respondent to the survey questionnaire consisted of owners (17.5%), board of directors (3.5%), top managers (24%), engineers (27.5%) and other high-level personnel (27.5%). In total 29 responds were received for the Question 1, 2, and 3 for the further analysis. Question 4 was only administrated to the company owners, since it was only related to their job responsibilities. The key questions identified within the research study are as shown below:

1. In which department do you work? What is your task within that department?
2. How important are these stakeholders' pressures listed below in influencing your company attitudes towards environmental performance and are known as main drivers for adoption of formal EMS?
3. How important are the factors listed below in motivating your facility to seek for ISO 14001 and sustainability practices?
4. From your perspective, what are the top 5 challenges your firm faces generally?

DOI: 10.1051/matecconf/20167602006

4.1 Influence of Stakeholder's Pressures to adopt EMS

In accordance with the second question, all the 29 respondents were replied to all parts of the questions, and the respondents indicated that a variety of stakeholders exert strong influences on their environmental performance improvement.

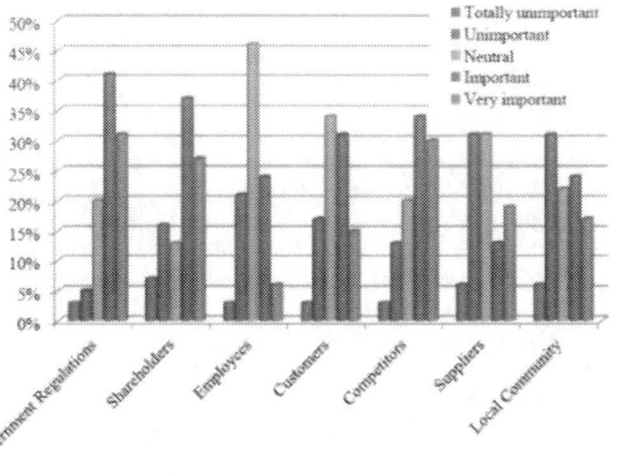

Figure 2. Influence of Stakeholders pressures towards adopting EMS.

As it is evident from figure 2, the three stakeholders commonly mentioned as applying pressure to undertake EMS were competitors, government regulations and shareholders with 31%, 30% and 27% respectively. The power of inspiration and significant role of these three entities in changing the whole SME approaches towards thinking about environmental concerns and working in a sustainable organization can be realized from the following chart. On the contrary, the local community and suppliers were mainly mentioned as unimportant components with no pressure and little influence on firm environmental attitude by 31% of each. With respect to the employees, the respondents recorded 46% neutral answers which can be interpreted that the environmental approach and awareness of the employees is not sufficient and they seem to have no orientation about these issues. This can be as a result of cultural and existing gaps in a developing country, meaning that it is not a long time that the public society got familiar with environmental importance of today's world.

4.2 Motivation towards adopting EMS

Figure 3 illustrates the significant business elements and their level of encouragement for the owners, top managers and the rest of the staff of Company which can revolutionize their way of thinking about the wide range of environmental program advantages and build a foundation for them to uptake a sustainable agenda and achieve its great results. Competitive advantage was most frequently rated as a very important motivator, by 31% of the respondents and only 10% of them judged it as unimportant. 24% noted that they can be highly motivated by profitability and cost savings.

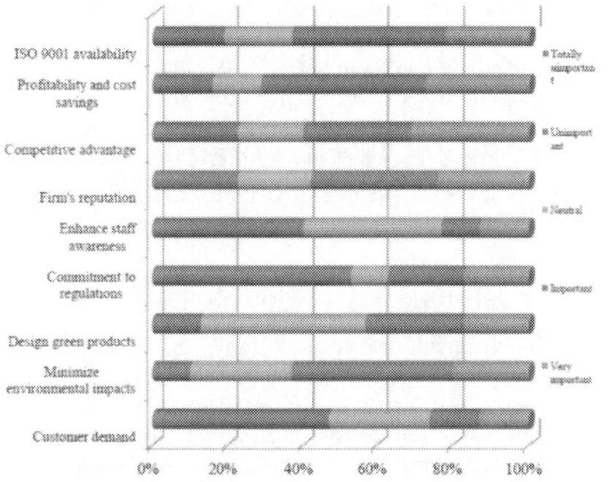

Figure 3. Motivation Factors towards adoption of EMS

By contrast, commitment to the government regulations was judged as totally unimportant by a massive 34% of the respondents. Considering the respond to customer demand, a large percentage of 37% mentioned it as an as an unimportant factor which is a surprising statistic showing that the house customers or even industrial customers do not consider the negative impacts on the environment or the green certificates the company might have. This is also mentioned by the planning manager of the Company X during site visits.

4.3 Business Owners Challenges

With regard to the fourth question, the total number of 5 participants including owners (shareholders) of the Company X participated to the questionnaire. The question has sought to discover the top 5 most challenging aspects that they currently have to tackle in their business.

Figure 4. Business Owners Challenges within their Environment

Figure 4 indicates that the top five challenges the managers encounter were strengthen the Razi brand (20%), increasing financial performance (20%), energy and water consumption (16%), providing equipment's (12%) and recycling development (12%). 8% of the respondents were also largely regarded to be so important by 24%. Hence, it is evident that employing expert staff, generating new products, increasing productivity and reducing raw material consumption have a minor priority and currently their key focus is towards competing with the growing market of SMEs to save their costs. This can be achieved by consultations with professional advisors and also employing high-skilled staff instead of those who are old and have old-fashioned insights into environmental sustainability issues.

5 Conclusions

The research was set out to scrutinize the concept of environmental sustainability and has determined the practicality of EMS within an SME in a developing country; explored the incentives and supply chain impressions for the standard system adoption, and the role and impact of management strategies on an organization sustainability and environmental developments. The study also has sought to argue the success of sustainable practices in SMEs which confront with internal and external hurdles of doing so. Main consideration was given to shifting managers' long-established attitudes, tackling the employees' indifference to environmental issues and also making coordination with the upstream and downstream stakeholders of supply chain. It would not be surprisingly that the findings of the research proved the significant role of owner-managers of SMEs as absolute authorities and decision makers in SMEs who have the power to embrace changes and address environmental risks by developing EMS. Hence, they need to be aware that their company exists not only to generate profit, but also to create a positive revolution in the world by actions to deal with the global issue of sustainability. They need to perceive that a sustainable business is more efficient, more robust and has closer ties with the stakeholders. In essence, based on the findings of the research; it seems that implementing EMS within the investigated SME absolutely has too many advantages that outweigh the disadvantages; such as improving firm images, enhancing environmental responsibility, achieving cost savings, profitability in the long-term and business prosperity.

The authors have attempted to discover appropriate answers concerning initial questions of the study which helps to delineate the scope of the research. The key question was to identify the factors which can motivate SMEs to adopt EMS. Moreover, advantages and disadvantages of environmental practices were compared together in order to find out the highest possible benefits that company can achieve through this journey. However, in the developing countries due to the economic, finance and cultural gaps still there is a long journey to the adaptation with the green management and sustainability practices to the businesses. The barriers of sustainable practices adoption in a developing country were explored, considering the major challenges of business entrepreneurs and the vulnerability of SMEs.

References

[1] Brundtland Commission, World Commission on Environment and Development (1987). Our Common Future. Oxford: Oxford University Press (1987)
[2] J. Elkington. Cannibals with Forks: The triple bottom line. Oxford Press Publishers: Capstone (1999)
[3] J. Kaplan, J. Greening Your Small Business: How to Improve Your Bottom Line, Grow Your Brand, Satisfy Your Customers-and Save the Planet. New York: Penguin Group, pp. 13 (2009)
[4] F. Roettgers, Going Green Together: How to Align Employees with Green Strategies. Environmental Pioneers (2011)
[5] G. Woodside, P. Aurrichio, P, J. Yturri. ISO 14001 Implementation Manual, McGraw-Hill, pp. 3 (1998)
[6] A. Zorpas. Environmental management systems as sustainable tools in the way of life for the SMEs and VSME, Bioresource Technology, 101(6), pp. 1544-1557 (2010)
[7] S.B. Moore, S.L. Manring. Strategy development in small and medium sized enterprises for sustainability and increased value creation. Journal of Cleaner Production, 17(2), pp. 276-282 (2009)
[8] R. Hillary. Environmental management systems and the smaller enterprise. Journal of cleaner production, 12(6), pp. 561-569 (2004)
[9] H. Williams, A. Schaefer, A. Small and Medium Sized Enterprises and Sustainability: Manager's Values and Engagement with Environmental and Climate Change Issues., Business Strategy and the Environment, Vol 22: pp 173-186 (2013)
[10] D. Perez-Sanchez, J.R. Barton, D. Bower. Implementing environmental management in SMEs. Corporate Social Responsibility and Environmental Management, 10(2), pp. 67-77 (2003)
[11] US EPA. Integrated environmental management systems: implementation guide. Washington DC: U.S. Environmental Protection Agency (2000)
[12] F. Ciliberti, P. Pontrandolfo, B. Scozzi. Investigating corporate social responsibility in supply chains: a SME perspective. Journal of cleaner production, 16(15), pp. 1579-1588 (2008)
[13] D. Dunphy. Organizational change for corporate sustainability. pp. 695-698. London: Routledge (2003)
[14] G. Keijzers. Business, Government and Sustainable Development. Oxford: Routledge (2005)
[15] Y. Agan, M.F Acar, A. Borodin. Drivers of environmental processes and their impact on performance: a study of Turkish SMEs. Journal of Cleaner Production, 51, pp 23-33 (2013)
[16] D. Morrow, D. Rondinelli. Adopting Corporate Environmental Management Systems: Motivations and Results of ISO 14001 and EMAS Certification. European Management Journal, 20(2), pp. 159-171 (2002)
[17] H.E.J. Bos-Brouwers. Corporate sustainability and innovation in SMEs: evidence of themes and activities in practice. Business Strategy and the Environment, 19(7), pp. 417-435 (2010)
[18] D.E Packham. Adhesive technology and sustainability. International Journal of Adhesion and Adhesives, 29(3), pp. 248-252 (2009)

MATEC Web of Conferences **76**, 02007 (2016) DOI: 10.1051/matecconf/20167602007
CSCC 2016

Procurement Practices in Project Based Manufacturing Environments

Satya Shah[1,a] and Syed Hasan[2]

[1]*Faculty of Engineering and Science, University of Greenwich, UK*
[2]*Industrial and Manufacturing Engineering, NED University of Technology, Pakistan*

Abstract. Procurement is one of the processes that cannot be separated in a business. To be able to run a business, it certainly needs to go through procurement stage that involves purchasing raw materials and services. There are many procurement practices in different kinds of business environment such as manufacturing business and construction business. Competitive strategies application within procurement in this manufacturing is very important in order to win a tender for material procurement required in projects. The paper examines how competitive strategies are applied within procurement practice in project-based manufacturing environment. This research studies in the literature of management in engineering, competitive strategy, procurement integration, and case study that takes a sample from the examples of procurement practice application in large organisation such as that of McDermott. The research aims to conduct a qualitative research method based on the discussion and analysis of literature reviews and case study to build conclusions. The findings suggest business players should have core competencies and develop factors such as superior quality, price advantage, on-time delivery, flexibility, and innovation through technology in order to win the competition.

1 Introduction

In the current unpredictable competition of project-based manufacturing environment, it is very important for business players (both suppliers and manufacturers) to start recognizing the importance of procurement practice because it is one of the most important stages in a business that always requires attention and continuous evaluation. Procurement facilitates acquisition or purchasing of goods and services. That is why, procurement is closely related to a purchase management. In the area of project-based manufacturing, procurement is the connection process of purchasing and arranging in bound movement of all items, supplies, materials, parts, finished inventory and general support services from the suppliers into manufacturing process or assembly plants or warehouses [1]. The final product created in project-based manufacturing is in the form of final result of a project. It is one of particular manufacturing styles that requires engineering design become unique and sometimes complex in specification. This requires a special attention to business players in implementing this stage. In addition, the actual procurement function is complex processes in which it manages the much wider supply between suppliers and manufacturers and not only buy raw materials and services as mentioned before. The activities in procurement involve the following stages from planning, estimating and identifying the needs; finding, request and evaluation of offers; review and award of contracts; contracting process and administration; until goods are delivered, and the agreement of contract has been reached [2]. Therefore, in recent years, many academics and business practitioners have shown a sense of interest to find out how organisations and suppliers have a control on the manufacturing environment, society, and the economy [3]. Many literatures have been discussed to the subject. From the current literature reviews, we can recognise the procurement practices and strategic principals that will contribute a company to develop the knowledge of linking procurement practices with competitive strategy.

There are a lot of studies about procurement practices in construction business. But it is very difficult to find the in-depth comprehension of procurement practices with the implementation of appropriate competitive strategies within every phase in a project-based manufacturing environment. Whereas the understanding of the competitive procurement strategy is very important to study more in detailed that contribute to competitive advantage of a business. It will help manufacturer to determine how competitive strategy in procurement practices implemented. Moreover, many companies that prefer to do a long-term relationship in the supplier selection process to supply materials required in the project because it is always conducting tendering process, is less effective and efficient. It is not only the partnership strategy can be used to obtain a competitive advantage, but also many factors need to consider by manufacturers in choosing suppliers, even to gain

[a] Corresponding author: s.shah@gre.ac.uk

competitive advantages. The main contribution of this research is to provide an in-depth knowledge about procurement practices within manufacturing environment between suppliers and manufacturers as a buyer and to establish the suitable competitive procurement strategy especially in required materials procurement during a project. The understanding on how to recognise the process between the manufacturers that conduct the procurement until supplier selection, in which it identifies the procurement steps and recognises factors that should be owned and developed by companies to gain competitive advantages. It also recognises different kinds of procurement strategies from long-term partnership strategy between suppliers and manufacturers to ensure continuous supply of materials and components until competitive strategies to have a success in procurement practices, business outcomes and how to develop it so that a company can find a favourable competitive position in businesses. The scope of this research is in areas of competitive strategy application in procurement practices that are used in project-based manufacturing environment. In order to achieve this, the authors make a limitation on the competitive-related strategy application in manufacturing environment between suppliers and manufacturers only, which conducts the procurement. Therefore, it considers to the given time and the limited availability of data. The strategies except competitive strategy will not be taken into consideration within this research study.

2 Literature Review

Effective and efficient procurement require good integrations in each procedure, from making tight cost control to emphasis innovation process by applying a variety of appropriate strategies. The main purpose of procurement practices is to coordinate and integrate every step to fulfil a need for goods and services in a right time with a minimum processing expense, so efficient procurement can be achieved. Hence, it is necessary to understand procurement procedures so that firms can determine suitable strategies to apply. Moreover, partner selection, contract formalization, payment, subcontractor selection, collaborative tools, and performance evaluation have been initiated in a previous research as a control of the project [4].

2.1 Procurement Procedures

Procurement procedures can be described as a system of sequential step or the life-cycle stages that begin with defining requirement of procurement, followed by activities involved in the real acquisition of goods or services, until the contract is reached. Because since there are serious implications when procurement procedures are not fulfilled, then it is important for the stakeholders, purchasing departments and others to contribute and interact with the procurement cycle. These are three different phases that can be separated later into different parts of the procurement each of which represent an important step of the procurement phase: Programme planning, procurement stage, and performance monitoring [5].

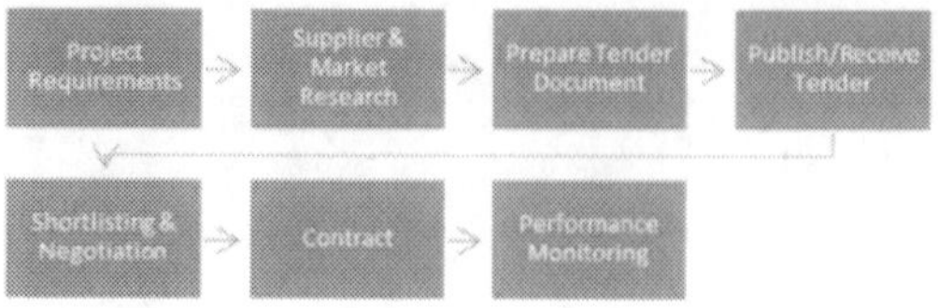

Figure 1. Procurement Process Lifecycle [5]

2.1.1 Programme Planning

The beginning phase in the procurement is a planning process which identifies the outcomes and objectives of the procurement. Firms define buying requirements based on the firm's final customer demand. In this step of collecting information, it is very important to define requirement and analyse the supply market because the complexity of this process will vary from case to case. To fulfil the requirement, firms need to define and explain what is needed and will be produced, gather information, identify the proper solution and determine the specification of goods and equipment.

2.1.2 Procurement Stage

Sourcing is emphasized in procurement stage. It is defined as a technical activity with the aim of identifying suitable products and services on the market also providing information of supplier qualification criteria to deliver goods and service. Processes such as short-listing, selection of a procurement strategy, supplier selection, negotiation and contract are contained included in this stage. In a contract phase, firms can achieve their efficiencies, flexibility, and sustainable competitive advantage with building supplier and supply chain relationships [6].

2.1.3 Performance Monitoring

The main purpose of performance monitoring is to promote economical and efficient procurement. To achieve efficient procurement, the performance of existing suppliers should be monitored continuously. Some firms have developed specific criteria in terms of monitoring supplier performance, for example: the quality of goods and services, delivery times or deadlines, after-sales service, documentation accuracy, responsive action and general collaboration. Firms use the criteria for making a fed back of future sourcing processes. Performance monitoring is also commonly used as firms' indicator for improving performances to achieve best value outcomes by making the service delivery more efficient and coordinated in the future.

2.2 Project-Based Manufacturing

Project-based manufacturing, which is also referred to engineer-to-order (ETO) is a manufacturing operation process designed to create similar artificial products with a low inventory level that can be managed as a project. It is one style of particular manufacturing in the industry. In

 DOI: 10.1051/matecconf/20167602007

ETO's manufacturing, every product which is created is the final result of a project [7]. The final product is created in a manufacturing environment that may require engineering design and the specifications prescribed by the customer and the engineers [8]. Therefore, in the ETO's environment, customer needs are unique and sometimes complex. It is a part of a combination of engineering and manufacturing process. Producing of products is only one part of the project manufacturing, many processes that should be done that need to be integrated to create a better planning and controls of the manufacturing project business [9].

In project-based manufacturing, the methods that are used for mass production planning and control are not suitable to apply in making of the project because the final product is a product that requires unique engineering design or significant customisation. Previous studies considered that an innovative approach to integrate manufacture and logistic with project management is important [10]. ETO sector includes various types of companies, designing, and manufacturing various kinds of products. This enables manufacturers to plan, organise and control the project to produce the final product. ETO companies typically have processes related with the tender, product design, manufacture, installation and contracting. The characteristics of ETO companies can be seen from their markets, products and internal processes of the company. Through the integration, design and product development to respond market demands, product performance improvisation, and a more affordable price to the customers so that the company can improve the efficiency of a product [11].

2.3 Competitive Strategy

Business competition determines the success or failure of the firms. Firm's activities such as innovation, a consistent culture, or good implementation take a contribution on its performance. In order to win competition and gain competitive advantages, firms must have proper and good strategy which creates such advantages. But in a business there are many tight and continuous challenges that are very difficult to predict forecast how competition will evolve, so it will be a rare possibility to know for sure whether that firms choose the right strategy or not. The decision of firms' strategy is very important to determine why a customer buys and experiences goods or services continuously over time, and firms must differentiate an organization's value from its competitors [12]. It is why firms must define its business objectives and gather as much information as possible to meet the value of competitive advantages in business. A firm's mission and objectives are a long-term purpose. Figure 2 shows how firms define its mission to get its competitive advantage.

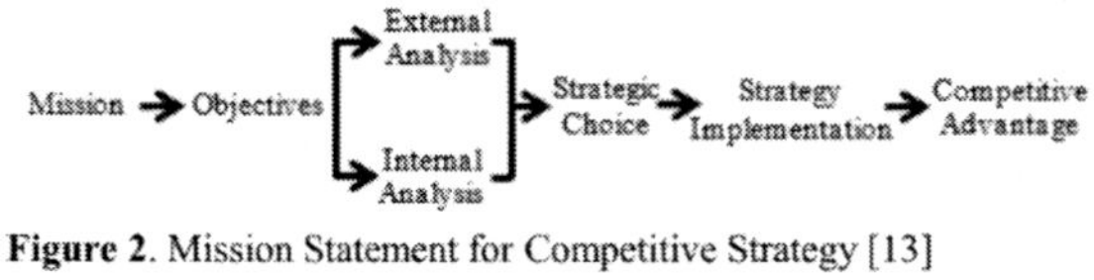

Figure 2. Mission Statement for Competitive Strategy [13]

Competitive advantage in general is when the firm can make more economic value than other competitors. Value is the satisfaction and benefits gained by customers (and other stakeholders) that buy and use firm's products and services [12]. This is important for firms to create unique value for its customer. With a purpose of achieving competitive advantage there is a phase in which firms must choose the strategy. In a large and diversified business, strategy is formulated, evaluated and implemented at three level of organisational strategy:

1. Corporate strategy (highest level)
2. Business strategy (mid – level)
3. Functional/operational strategy (lowest level)

How to succeed competence and achieve competitive advantage are emphasised in business-level strategy. Generally, the business strategy is how the firms develop its distinctive competences and competitive advantages of each unit and compete in the particular business area [14]. It is why firms must have its competitive strategy in the business in which environmental dynamism and manufacturing strategy form a mediating relationship cast in competitive strategy [15]. Competitive strategy is one of the company's efforts in finding a favourable competitive position in business, with the aims to create a profitable and sustainable position in the business competition against many variable forces [16, 17]. Many authors agree that environment determines the choice of competitive strategy which has a relationship with firm's performance. In their discussion, authors had shown that the dynamics of the environment has a positive relationship with the flexibility and capability of high manufacturers [18, 19].

2.4 Connection of Procurement Procedures with Competitive Strategies

The procurement procedures generally has the function as defining the characteristic of purchased materials, goods and services; selecting a supplier that can provide goods and service at favourable price and high quality goods; and managing all of aspects in procurement steps so that the goods or services are delivered in a right time. Furthermore, generally manufacturing firm spends around 60% of its sales on purchasing materials or services, so the importance of procurement significantly affects the successful of the firm's final product [20]. Procurement is now considered as a core of competency of many enterprises and be a main strategic importance [21]. A firm's competitive strategy allows firms determining operations decision that result the preferred performance. In order to gain competitive advantages, manufacturing strategy must be aligned with the company's competitive strategy. It is the same with a strategy in procurement practice, in which all the basic elements of the supply chain must be integrated in order to achieve competitive advantages. Companies can accomplish customer, supplier, and information integration to a higher or lesser level through the design process, purchasing practices like early supplier contribution.

DOI: 10.1051/matecconf/20167602007

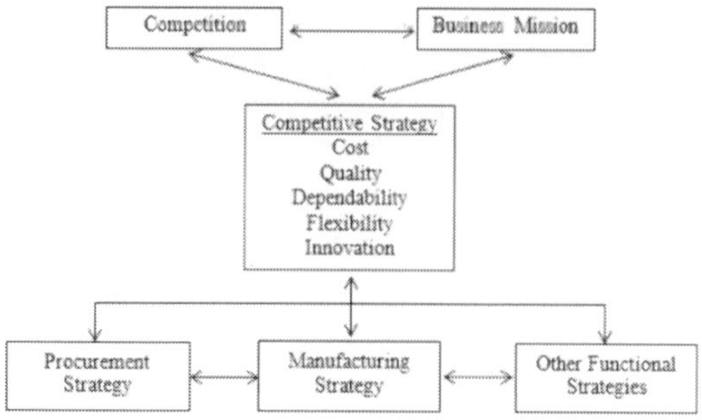

Figure 3. The Relationship of Competitive Strategy and Functional Strategy [22]

Procurement integration may require more than just the application of major purchasing practices such as supplier involvement, supplier development, supplier certification or supply base reduction. Integration in procurement focuses on internal orientation, which aims to align procurement practices with competitive priorities of the company. The procurement integration in the manufacturing and corporate strategy has been discussed into several conceptual frameworks, one of which is framework from existing research [22]. They emphasize the importance of procurement in the business strategy formulation and implementation.

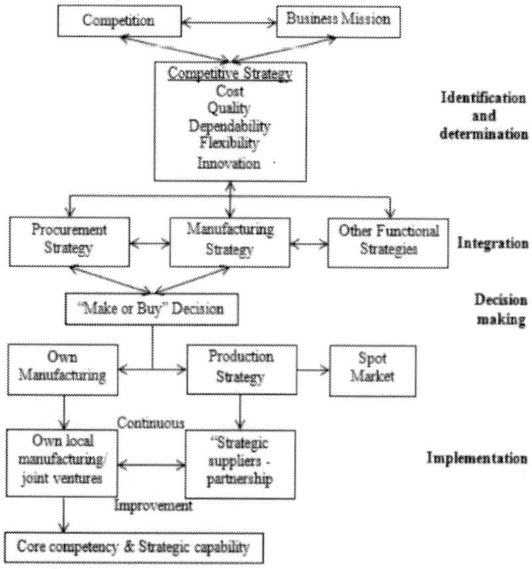

Figure 4. Development of Integrated Procurement Strategy Framework [23]

Since the main purpose of procurement is to support production and operation activities with continuous supply of material and service, so it is necessary to have the consistency between procurement and manufacturing strategy and they must be able to support the company's competitive strategy. The procurement strategy can be seen as a pattern of corporate decisions related to obtaining necessary goods or services for company's operational activities by using overall company's competitive strategies. The relationship of the competitive strategy and functional strategy diagram has shown significant changes in its development. There are four phases that the company must be executed so the competitive advantages are able to be achieved.

2.5 Supplier Selection

The project-based manufacturing business characterization makes procurement activities to have an important role in determining the competitiveness of enterprises. The efficient purchasing process in ETO supply chain plays a significant role because more than 60% of the total price of the product in this business environment is spent for components purchasing. Therefore, the company's performance in this business depends on the performance of its suppliers [24]. In the ETO procurement process, a selection of partners/suppliers is often based on the offers and negotiations, so that, sometimes there are many factors to be considered. Since the main purpose of procurement activities is to get materials/components with a minimum price and available when they are required.

Supplier selection is one of the most important decisions in the procurement of goods. Other studies conducted a broad analysis of the criteria and methods for supplier selection in general. Criteria often used include price, on time delivery and quality. Procurement process begins with the realization of the need for new suppliers, the formulation of decision criteria, manufacturers invite suppliers to make a bid [25]. Followed by a final selection process in monitoring suppliers and next, manufacturers decide to accept or make a counter offer to the selected supplier that will be continued on negotiation step until manufacturers and suppliers reach an agreement [26].

Manufacturers often conduct a study to make sure that they have chosen the right suppliers and applied supplier performance, because it is important for manufacturers to choose suppliers for strategic need and transactional interests and ensures a good corporation. By identifying all of stakeholders' needs of company and improving collaborative relationships between producers and a major supplier for the strategic partnership, it increases the efficiency and benefits of both partners. There are many ways and innovations that can be developed in this collaboration, for example:

1. Communications strategy is needed in the development of corporate strategy;
2. Managed competition is applied to reduce the number of suppliers and consolidate existing suppliers, also supply base segmentation into a more strategic and transactional role;
3. Continuous improvement is carried out through processes such as supplier performance management, in which the supplier's performance is monitored on a regular basis to achieve a certain performance quality level;
4. Value-based compensation is used to convince suppliers and manufacturers in achieving a mutual beneficial objective.

3 Research Methodology

This study focuses towards the use of qualitative research methods towards understanding the application of competitive strategies within procurement practices in project based manufacturing environment to succeed in a competitive sector. This study uses case study based approach with gathering information on procurement practices and competitive strategy application in project-based manufacturing environment. The research took samples of leading company engaged in the business of EPCI (engineering, procurement, construction and installation).

The case focuses on McDermott International, Inc. ("MII") which is one of the largest states of US-based engineering and construction ("E&C") companies which concentrates on the offshore upstream oil and gas sector, providing a fully integrated EPCI services. The study analyses different phenomenon and characteristics within the company to provide sufficient knowledge about the development of competitive strategies application in project-based manufacturing environment. The key focus of this study is to provide more detailed explanations of the competitive procurement strategies in project-based manufacturing which has not been fully explored in past studies. Many research studies only examine procurement in the industrial business environment that is usually referred as purchasing, but there is lack of focus towards project-based manufacturing environment.

4 Case Study Analysis

The research focuses on the case of McDermott International, Inc.; a leading engineering, procurement, construction and installation ("EPCI") company engaged in designing and implementing complex offshore oil and gas projects in the world. Most of their customers include national, major integrated and other oil and gas companies. Operating in the Atlantic, Caspian, Middle East and Asia Pacific countries (90% of projects are outside the United States) which are segmented based on regions' proximity, similarities in the environment of services provided, economic characteristics and supervisory responsibility. Providing fully integrated EPCI services, they also make fixed and floating production facilities, pipeline installations and subsea systems from concept to ordering.

Company's resources integration includes employees, various fleets of marine vessels, fabrication facilities and engineering offices. The company's activities are supported by comprehensive project management and procurement service. With abundant capital and company's special abilities in EPCI projects throughout the world create a significant barrier for competitors to enter the global market. However, the company also faces challenges such as tight competition from regional competitors and offshore construction services providers that are less integrated, for example, engineering companies, manufacturing facilities, pipe laying companies and shipbuilders as well as a number of companies that compete with McDermott in each separate phase in EPCI around the world. To encounter competition, the company build the joint venture with a third party through the partnership program becoming strength for the company [27]. The next is the fabrication stage, where on this stage the construction phase begins. For example, on an offshore facilities project, construction work includes packaging, warehousing, weld management, topside and onshore modules, jackets, piles and compliant towers, subsea production systems, also fabrication processes and procedures standardisation. After it is completed, the final process is the installation process, where there are many services offered by McDermott like single and dual heavy lift, float over and various diameter pipeline installation, dynamic positioning systems, subsea installation support. Once the project is completed, the company will conduct commissioning activity. All of data and information used for the project will be added into the historical database, so it is as sources which sometimes can improve the company's performance, scope of work and profitability in the future.

4.1 Project Operation

All of the company's operations require raw materials such as carbon and alloy steel in various shapes and components for assembly. The company purchases raw materials and components needed through individual contract. They do not rely on one source of supply for any important raw material. Industry environment where McDermott operates is a very competitive environment and has been contracted to a large number of fixed price projects. In many cases, the company is faced with projects involving complex design and engineering, significant procurement of equipment and supplies, broad construction management and other activities performed in a long period and sometimes in distant locations. So the costs incurred by the company for their projects sometimes exceed of the company's projection. It makes the company covering changes and cost increases with the cost of long-term contracts for labour, materials and services, as well as the estimated increase in costs that reflect to the price of the original contract or price increase clauses [27].

However, despite these efforts, there are still many variations and risks inherent in the industry result in declining profitability and the loss on the project. It is usually caused by a variation in the fixed price contract because of the performance of suppliers, contractors and subcontractors, the company's performance itself, changes in working conditions, unpredictable weather conditions, variations in labour and equipment productivity, and rising in the raw material price, particularly steel price, during the term of the contract.

4.2 Purchases and Contracts

Suppliers have a very important role for McDermott and the core business of a company, and contribute to deliver high quality, efficient and competitive solutions for customers. The company acquired all the equipment, supplies and services on the value basis, considering suppliers, vendors and sub-contractors fairly and without discrimination, except in some cases where the procurement process is given specifically to certain groups with the purpose of Socioeconomic. The Company applies the highest ethical standards in selecting source, negotiation, determining the award, also managing all purchasing activities so conflict of interest among the company or person can be minimized [27].

4.3 Procurement Strategies

Procurement is a very important phase in any McDermott's project, with spare parts and supplies purchased from all over the world and shipped to several international job sites, all parties have a role to play, as each stage of the procurement determines the success of the project. One wrong step happens, then all of which can lead to failure. One effective way arranged by the company to ensure that all steps of the project come together efficiently is EPCI, using one contractor to manage all engineering, procurement, construction and installation process. The company's approach aims to provide more quality control and scrutiny from materials, schedules, and personnel. McDermott's success cannot be separated from the outward expansion conducted by the company and getting competitive bids early. According to the company, it is the correct approach and provides the best opportunity to be competitive due to changing market conditions.

Due to the company's projects are located in different countries, the company continues to develop and use new local supply chain to accommodate the location of the installation as a whole. According to them, choosing the right supplier is a key component to get procurement succeeded. Sometimes they spend a lot of time in the pre-qualification because of their attention to things, like supplier's financial stability, quality of work, compliance with schedules and response to change. Procurement plan made by the company is also implementing a range of strategies on how they purchase equipment and supplies, how to speed up the requirements examination that will be needed, and how to modify it if there is a change in the project. EPCI approach applied by the company to be very valuable because of the projects, the economic environment and regulatory increasingly become complex, plus involved contractors and vendors, especially iron raw material price continues to fluctuate rapidly.

5 Analysis and Discussions

From the case study analysis, it shows that the company is an EPCI company that works in the same environment. McDermott International, Inc. engages in energy sector and complex processing industry. They manage and execute complex engineering and construction project. Most of their customers are large oil and energy companies. The supports of companies are a large capital, special abilities, comprehensive project management and procurement services. In providing good procurement service, the companies must have their own strategy in order to win the competition and create a significant barrier for competitors. The companies are no longer competing at the local level but at the global level so that they face many challenges. The companies run their business based on long-term relationships guidelines with customers and joint venture. The companies build partnerships for the company's force. Procurement becomes an important phase in EPCI project. It is necessary for the companies to make the appropriate competitive strategy in order to win the competition. The companies should be able to improve the integration of design, manufacturing and procurement. Through the integration, the companies can improve their product performances and respond to the market demands that the company can increase their project efficiency.

The products that are produced in a project-based manufacturing is engineered products, which require engineering design, the specifications defined by customers and engineers, and is managed as a project. Most of the tools needed in the projects are industrial tools. They require detailed technical specifications. Although the offered product types are same, but suppliers that offer varied innovations and variations will be able to create a unique advantage and gain a competitive advantage. Product innovation is sometimes required to meet customer's specific requirements that with technology development can do. Innovation used for customisation and products performance development to respond to the demands. Competition in the project-based manufacturing demands the companies to develop their products continuously, so it can compete with other globally. Sourcing innovation is needed to facilitate companies in analysing sourcing process complexities. Information in the portal facilitates the company in sourcing process. So when it is at tendering stage, competent suppliers will be directly able to submit bids for any offered projects. In the bidding stage, big companies will normally use E-procurement that has been commonly used in the tender submission stage.

6 Conclusions

The research focused towards the use of competitive strategy within procurement practices in project-based manufacturing environment, with a study of the relationship between competitive strategy and procurement procedures so that both suppliers and manufacturers can find their competitive advantages in business. One of the most effective way is for the company is to recognise their core competencies in order to provide satisfactory advantages to its customers. The authors recognise that the long-term partnership is the effort to make effective tendering process, but both suppliers and manufacturers must limit their dependence with each other so that they are able to reduce the risk of bargaining power threats of both suppliers and manufacturer. Moreover, manufacturers must accurately choose a supplier from the beginning, because a supplier selection can determine the smoothness and success of the procurement until a project is completed. Even though the relationship runs very well during a project, then it usually will form a partnership commitment based on trust. So the research identifies that supplier must have competitive strategies that are adapted with company's internal conditions and a competitive environment in order to sustain them continuously in competitions and achieving new businesses.

This study also highlights the need to conduct qualitative research in the future by using other types of strategy approach in order to enrich the content of strategy application literatures to win the tender in a procurement process. The research can be implemented only for the supplier's or manufacturer's point of view. A supplier can be used as a subject in obtaining competitive advantages because a supplier must compete with each other in getting the contract made by the manufacturer. While in a project-based manufacturing, a manufacturer also can turn as a supplier because a manufacturer works as a contractor that focus on a project from a project's owner, so a manufacturer must compete with other manufacturers to obtain project contracts held by the owner. The study also plans towards focusing on a global procurement, as procurement on a global level will be different compared to that of national/regional levels of application.

References

[1] D.J. Bowersox, D. Closs, M.B. Cooper. Procurement. In: Supply Chain Logistics Management, Second Edition. Singapore: McGraw-Hill, p. 32 (2007)

[2] UN Office for Project Services. Procurement Manual. Revision 4 ed. Copenhagen Denmark: P. P. Group (2010)

[3] H. Walker, W. Phillips. Sustainable Procurement: Emerging Issues. International Public Procurement Conference Proceedings (2006)

[4] P. Eriksson. Achieving suitable coopetition in buyer-supplier relationships: The case of AstraZeneca. Journal of Business to Business Marketing, 15(4), 425-454 (2008)

[5] S. Lenny Koh, A. Genovese, A. Acquaye. BIG Energy Upgrade: Procurement and Supply Chain report – Green Deal and Energy Efficiency Retrofitting Supply Chains Delivery, Sheffield Centre for Energy Environment & Sustainability (2012)

[6] G.N. Nyaga, J.M. Whipple, D.F. Lynch. Examining supply chain relationships: Do buyer and supplier perspectives on collaborative relationships differ. Journal of Operations Management, 28 (2), p. 101–114 (2010)

[7] C.S. Chen. Concurrent engineering-to-order operation in the manufacturing engineering contracting industries. Int. J. Industrial and Systems Engineering, pp. 37-58 (2006)

[8] N. Cameron, P. Braiden. Using business process re-engineering for the development of production efficiency in companies making engineered to order products. Int. J. of Production Economics, pp. 261-273 (2004)

[9] P. Blevins. Project-oriented manufacturing: how to resolve the critical business issues that impact organizational competitiveness. Virginia, APICS International Conference, US (1999)

[10] F. Caron, A. Fiore. Engineer to order companies: how to integrate manufacturing and innovative processes. Int. J. of Project Management, Issue 13 (5) (1995)

[11] N. Cameron, P. Braiden. Using business process re-engineering for the development of production efficiency in companies making engineered to order products. Int. J. of Production Economics, pp. 261-273 (2004)

[12] B.J Witcher, V.S Chau. Overview of strategic management. In: F. Rowe, ed. Strategic Management: Principles and Practice, 2nd edition. Hampshire: Andrew Ashwin, p. 5 (2014)

[13] J.B. Barney, W. Hesterly. Strategy and the Strategic Management Process. In: S. Yagan, ed. Strategic Management and Competitive Advantage. New Jersey: Pearson Education (2012)

[14] K. Lysons, B. Farrington. Business-level strategy. In: Purchasing and Supply Chain Management. Essex: Pearson Education Limited, pp. 41-48 (2012)

[15] N. Venkatraman. The concept of fit in strategy research: towards verbal and statistical correspondence. Int. J. of Academy of Management, 24 (4), p. 423–444 (1989)

[16] M.E. Porter. Competitive Strategy: The core Concepts. In: Competitive Advantage: Creating and Sustaining Superior Performance. New York: Free Press (2004)

[17] M.E. Porter. The Value Chain and Competitive Advantage: Creating and Sustaining Superior Performance. New York, 33-59 (2004)

[18] P. Swamidass, W. Newell. Manufacturing Strategy, Environmental Uncertainty and Performance: a path analytic model. Management Science, 33 (4) (1987)

[19] P. Ward, R. Duray, G. Leong, C. Sum, C. Business environment, operations strategy, and performance: an empirical study of Singapore manufacturers. J. of Operations Management, 13 (2), p. 99–115 (1995)

[20] D. Burt. Managing product quality through strategic purchasing Sloan Management Review. Sloan Management Review, Issue 30 (1), pp. 39-47 (1989)

[21] R. Tassabehji, A. Moorhouse. The changing role of procurement: Developing professional effectiveness. J. of Purchasing & Supply Management, 14, pp. 55-68 (2008)

[22] C. Watts, K. Kim, C. Hahn. Linking purchasing to corporate competitive strategy. Int. J. Purchasing and Materials Management, 28 (4), pp. 2-8 (1992)

[23] V.M. Virolainen. A survey of procurement strategy development in industrial companies. Int. J. of Production Economics, 56, pp. 677-688 (1998)

[24] J. Jahnukainen, M. Lahti. Efficient purchasing in make-to-order supply chains. Int. J. of Production Economics, 59, pp. 103-111 (1999)

[25] C.A. Weber, J.R. Current, W.C. Benton. Vendor selection criteria and method. European J. of Operations Research, 50, pp. 2-18 (1991)

[26] K.L. Choy, W.B. Lee. On the development of a case based supplier management tool for multinational manufacturers. Measuring Business Excellence, 6 (1), pp. 15-22 (2002)

[27] McDermott International Inc. McDermott International Inc., 2012 Annual Report on Building for Growth, Texas: McDermott International, Inc. c/o Investor Relations (2013)

 DOI: 10.1051/matecconf/20167602008

Evaluation of Agile Suppliers Using Fuzzy MCDM Approach

Mehtap Dursun[1,a]

[1]*Galatasaray University,Industrial Engineering Department, 34349, Ortakoy, Istanbul, Turkey*

Abstract. In today's competitive environment, supply chain need to be of high speed and flexibility, i.e., agile. Agility has been proposed as a response to the high levels of complexity and uncertainty in modern markets. It is a business-wide capability that embraces organizational structures, information systems and logistics processes. This study employs the hierarchical fuzzy MCDM algorithm proposed by Karsak and Ahiska for the evaluation of agile suppliers. This algorithm is based on the proximity to the ideal solution concept and it can address the problems containing both crisp and fuzzy data. The application of the decision making method is illustrated through a case study conducted in a privet hospital and the results are analysed.

1 Introduction

Supply chain is composed of a complex sequence of processing stages, ranging from raw materials supplies, parts manufacturing, components and end-products assembling, to the delivery of end products. In the context of supply chain management, supplier selection decision is considered as one of the key issues faced by operations and purchasing managers to remain competitive.

Supplier selection and management can be applied to a variety of suppliers throughout a product's life cycle from initial raw material acquisition to end-of-life service providers. Thus, the breadth and diversity of suppliers make the process even more cumbersome. Supplier selection process has different phases such as problem definition, decision criteria formulation, pre-qualification of potential suppliers, and making a final choice. The quality of the final choice largely depends on the quality of all the steps involved in the selection process.

Recently, industries face significant changes especially in marketing competition, technological innovation, and customer demands. Situations and possibilities are varied and organizations are responsible for adapting themselves to this various cases. Moreover, the scarce sources are considered as an important restriction faced by the companies. Agility is essential to deal with these problems. The term agility can be defined as an ability to give quick responses to changes and unpredictable situations. It is considered as the bearer competitive advantage in today's business environment. Companies have to be aligned with suppliers, customers, and competitors within the supply chain. Also, they should work together to achieve a level of agility.

Supply chain agility is implemented in which the ordered innovative goods with small volumes of high margin in addition to short product life cycle through a complex global supply chain network. It is applied an equilibrium solution which copes with the complexity in a limited coordination and cooperation through the links in the network. The agility of supply chain might be measured as how well supply chain elements, suppliers, customers and competitors are coordinated and collaborated in the network enhance four pivotal objectives of agile manufacturing which are customer enrichment ahead of competitors, achieving mass customization at the cost of mass production, mastering change and uncertainty through routinely adaptable structures, and leveraging the impact of people across enterprises through information technology [1].

This study aims to develop multi-criteria decision making approach for evaluating agile suppliers. Supplier evaluation process requires the consideration of multiple conflicting criteria, yielding in a multi-level hierarchical structure, incorporating vagueness and imprecision with the involvement of a group of experts. Fuzzy set theory is one of the effective tools to deal with uncertainty and vagueness in criteria values. The objective of this study is to propose a hierarchical fuzzy multi-criteria group decision making methodology for agile supplier evaluation.

In the literature, there are a few papers that evaluate agile suppliers. Wu et al. [2] proposed a two-stage approach, based on the application of analytic network process (ANP) and mixed integer multi-objective programming model, to solve the problem of partner selection in agile supply chains. Wu and Barnes [3] presented a four phase dynamic feedback model for supply partner selection in agile supply chains. Alminardi et al. [4] combined SWARA and VIKOR for supplier selection in an agile environment. Abdollahi et al. [5] integrated analytic network process (ANP) and data

[a] Corresponding author: mdursun@gsu.edu.tr

envelopment analysis (DEA), and DEMATEL method for evaluating suppliers considering lean and agile criteria. Lee et al. [6] employed fuzzy AHP and fuzzy TOPSIS to select suppliers. Beikkhakhian et al. [7] identified the criteria to evaluate agile suppliers and then they used fuzzy TOPSIS to rank alternative suppliers.

The rest of the paper is organized as follows. Section 2 analyzed the fuzzy decision making methodology employed in this study for the evaluation of agile suppliers. Section 3 presents the application of the proposed model. Finally, conclusions are provided in Section 4.

2 Hierarchical fuzzy MCDM approach

Real-world decision problems such as the supplier selection often involve the consideration of numerous performance attributes. When a large number of performance attributes are to be considered in the evaluation process, it may be preferred to structure them in a multi-level hierarchy in order to conduct a more effective analysis. In this study, the hierarchical distance-based fuzzy MCDM algorithm introduced by Karsak and Ahiska [8] is employed for evaluating agile suppliers. This MCDM algorithm is based on the proximity to the ideal solution concept and which can address the problems containing both crisp and fuzzy data. The origins of the proposed decision making procedure are found in the multi-criteria decision tool named TOPSIS [9].

The proposed fuzzy MCDM approach can be described as follows:

***Step* 1.** Construct the decision matrix that denotes the fuzzy assessments corresponding to qualitative sub-criteria and the crisp values corresponding to quantitative sub-criteria for the considered alternatives.

***Step* 2.** Normalize the crisp data to obtain unit-free and comparable sub-criteria values. The normalized values for crisp data regarding benefit-related as well as cost-related quantitative sub-criteria are calculated via a linear scale transformation as

$$y'_{ijk} = \begin{cases} \dfrac{y_{ijk} - y^-_{jk}}{y^*_{jk} - y^-_{jk}}, & k \in CB_j; i = 1,2,\ldots,m;\ j = 1,2,\ldots,n \\ \dfrac{y^*_{jk} - y_{ijk}}{y^*_{jk} - y^-_{jk}}, & k \in CC_j; i = 1,2,\ldots,m;\ j = 1,2,\ldots,n \end{cases} \qquad (1)$$

where y'_{ijk} denotes the normalized value of y_{ijk}, which is the crisp value assigned to alternative i with respect to the sub-criterion k of criterion j, m is the number of alternatives, n is the number of criteria, CB_j is the set of benefit-related crisp sub-criteria of criterion j and CC_j is the set of cost-related crisp sub-criteria of criterion j, $y^*_{jk} = \max_i y_{ijk}$ and $y^-_{jk} = \min_i y_{ijk}$. The normalized values for crisp data can be represented as $\tilde{y}_{ijk} = (y'_{aijk}, y'_{bijk}, y'_{cijk})$ in triangular fuzzy number format, where $y'_{aijk} = y'_{bijk} = y'_{cijk} = y'_{ijk}$.

***Step* 3.** Aggregate the performance ratings of alternatives at the sub-criteria level to criteria level as follows:

$$\tilde{x}_{ij} = (x_{aij}, x_{bij}, x_{cij}) = \frac{\sum_k \tilde{w}^1_{jk} \otimes \tilde{y}_{ijk}}{\sum_k \tilde{w}^1_{jk}}, \forall i, j \qquad (2)$$

where $\tilde{x}_{ij}$ represents the aggregate performance rating of alternative i with respect to criterion j, $\tilde{w}^1_{jk}$ indicates the average importance weight assigned to sub-criterion k of criterion j, and $\otimes$ is the fuzzy multiplication operator.

***Step* 4.** Normalize the aggregate performance ratings at criteria level using a linear normalization procedure, which results in the best value to be equal to 1 and the worst one to be equal to 0, as follows:

$$\tilde{r}_{ij} = (r_{aij}, r_{bij}, r_{cij}) = \left(\frac{x_{aij} - x^-_{aj}}{x^*_{cj} - x^-_{aj}}, \frac{x_{bij} - x^-_{aj}}{x^*_{cj} - x^-_{aj}}, \frac{x_{cij} - x^-_{aj}}{x^*_{cj} - x^-_{aj}} \right), \forall i, j \qquad (3)$$

where $x^*_{cj} = \max_i x_{cij}$, $x^-_{aj} = \min_i x_{aij}$, and $\tilde{r}_{ij}$ denotes the normalized aggregate performance rating of alternative i with respect to criterion j.

***Step* 5.** Define the ideal solution $A^* = (r^*_1, r^*_2, \ldots, r^*_n)$ and the anti-ideal solution $A^- = (r^-_1, r^-_2, \ldots, r^-_n)$, where $r^*_j = (1,1,1)$ and $r^-_j = (0,0,0)$ for $j = 1,2,\ldots,n$.

***Step* 6.** Calculate the weighted distances from ideal solution and anti-ideal solution (D^*_i and D^-_i, respectively) for each alternative as

$$D^*_i = \sum_j 1/2 \left\{ \max(w^1_{aj}\left|r_{aij} - 1\right|, w^1_{cj}\left|r_{cij} - 1\right|) + w^1_{bj}\left|r_{bij} - 1\right| \right\}, i = 1,2,\ldots,m \qquad (4)$$

$$D^-_i = \sum_j 1/2 \left\{ \max(w^1_{aj}\left|r_{aij} - 0\right|, w^1_{cj}\left|r_{cij} - 0\right|) + w^1_{bj}\left|r_{bij} - 0\right| \right\}, i = 1,2,\ldots,m \qquad (5)$$

***Step* 7.** Calculate the proximity of the alternatives to the ideal solution, P^*_i, by considering the distances from ideal and anti-ideal solutions as

$$P^*_i = D^-_i \Big/ \left(D^*_i + D^-_i\right), i = 1,2,\ldots,m. \qquad (6)$$

***Step* 8.** Rank the alternatives according to P^*_i values in descending order. Identify the alternative with the highest P^*_i as the best alternative.

3 Case study

In order to illustrate the application of the proposed decision making method, a case study conducted in a private hospital on the Asian side of Istanbul is presented. Benefiting from the literature, management capability, manufacturing capability, collaboration capability, and agility, and their related sub-criteria are identified as the selection attributes as in Table 1.

Table 1. Criteria and related sub-criteria.

Main criteria	Sub-criteria
Management capability (C_1)	Management and Organization (C_{11}) Financial position (C_{12}) Customer relation (C_{13}) Training aids (C_{14}) Reputation (C_{15})
Manufacturing capability (C_2)	Production capacity (C_{21}) Product diversity (C_{22}) R&D (C_{23}) Quality (C_{24})
Collaboration capability (C_3)	Delivery reliability (C_{31}) Warranties and claim policies (C_{32})
Agility (C_4)	Delivery speed (C_{41}) Delivery flexibility (C_{42}) Agile customer responsiveness (C_{43}) Collaboration with partners (C_{44}) Make flexibility (C_{45}) Source flexibility (C_{46})

The expert used the linguistic variables given in Figure 1 to evaluate the importance of the criteria and sub-criteria, and also the ratings of alternatives with respect to various subjective criteria and sub-criteria. There are 4 suppliers who are in contact with the hospital.

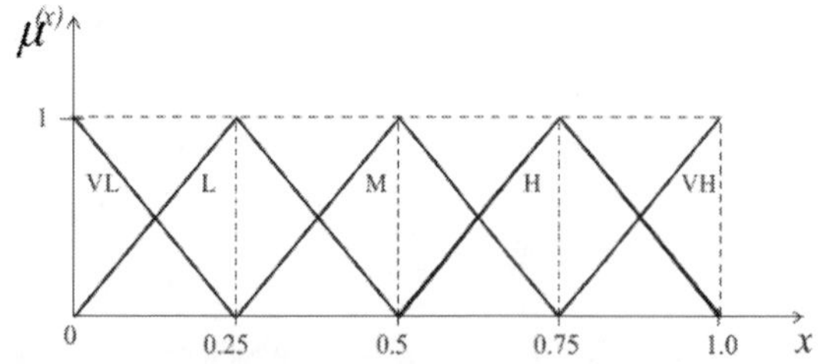

Figure 1. A linguistic term set where VL = (0, 0, 0.25), L = (0, 0.25, 0.5), M = (0.25, 0.5, 0.75), H = (0.5, 0.75, 1), VH = (0.75, 1, 1)

The evaluations are represented in Tables 2, 3, and 4.

Table 2. Importance weights of criteria.

Criteria	Importance weight
C_1	H
C_2	H
C_3	M
C_4	VH

Table 3. Importance weights of sub-criteria.

Sub-Criteria	Importance weight
C_{11}	VH
C_{12}	H
C_{13}	VH
C_{14}	M
C_{15}	H
C_{21}	H
C_{22}	VH
C_{23}	H
C_{24}	VH
C_{31}	H
C_{32}	H
C_{41}	H
C_{42}	H
C_{43}	VH
C_{44}	H
C_{45}	VH
C_{46}	VH

Table 4. Data related to agile supplier evaluation problem.

Sub-Criteria	S_1	S_2	S_3	S_4
C_{11}	M	M	M	H
C_{12}	VL	L	L	VH
C_{13}	VH	VH	VH	VH
C_{14}	M	H	H	H
C_{15}	VL	VL	VL	VL
C_{21}	VH	H	H	L
C_{22}	VH	H	H	M
C_{23}	M	M	L	H
C_{24}	L	L	M	M
C_{31}	VH	H	H	M
C_{32}	VH	H	H	M
C_{41}	VH	H	H	L
C_{42}	H	H	H	VH
C_{43}	H	H	H	H
C_{44}	M	M	H	H
C_{45}	H	VH	H	VH
C_{46}	H	M	M	H

Sub-criteria values are aggregated to criteria level using equation (2), and are represented in Table 5.

Table 5. Data related to agile supplier evaluation problem.

Criteria	S_1	S_2	S_3	S_4
C_1	(0.30,0.44,0.59)	(0.32,0.52,0.68)	(0.32,0.52,0.68)	(0.52,0.72,0.84)
C_2	(0.45,0.72,0.84)	(0.32,0.58,0.84)	(0.34,0.59,0.84)	(0.25,0.50,0.75)
C_3	(0.75,1,1)	(0.50,0.75,1)	(0.50,0.75,1)	(0.25,0.50,0.75)
C_4	(0.50,0.75,0.96)	(0.47,0.71,0.92)	(0.45,0.70,0.96)	(0.52,0.77,0.92)

The normalized values of these aggregate performance ratings are computed using equation (3). The ideal and the anti-ideal solutions are defined as A^*=((1,1,1), (1,1,1), (1,1,1), (1,1,1)) and A^-=((0,0,0), (0,0,0), (0,0,0), (0,0,0)), respectively. The weighted distances from ideal and anti-ideal solutions and the proximity of the alternatives to the ideal solution are calculated employing Eqs. (4)-(6). The results are shown in Table 6.

Table 6. Data related to agile supplier evaluation problem.

S_i	D_i^*	D_i^*	P_i^*	Ranking
S_1	1.354	2.586	0.656	1
S_2	1.624	2.119	0.567	3
S_3	1.626	2.014	0.553	4
S_4	1.508	2.470	0.621	2

The rank order of the suppliers is $S_1 \succ S_4 \succ S_2 \succ S_3$. According to the results of the analysis, supplier 1 is determined as the most suitable supplier, which is followed by supplier 4. Supplier 3 is ranked at the bottom due to inadequate financial position, reputation, and R&D.

4 Conclusions

In this study, the hierarchical fuzzy MCDM algorithm proposed by Karsak and Ahiska [8] has been employed for the evaluation of agile suppliers. In classical MCDM methods, the ratings and the weights of the criteria are assumed to be known precisely. In general, crisp data are inadequate to model real-life situations. Besides having the capability of considering numerous attributes that are structured in a multi-level hierarchy, the proposed decision framework enables the decision-makers to use linguistic terms.

Considering the fact that an alternative with the shortest distance from the ideal alternative may not have the farthest distance from the anti-ideal, Karsak and Ahiska's decision algorithm takes into account the weighted distances from both the ideal and anti-ideal simultaneously. Furthermore, Karsak and Ahıska's approach does not require the use of fuzzy number ranking methods, which may yield different results according to the ranking method selected for application purposes.

Further researches might focus on the extensions of the proposed methodology by employing both subjective and objective weight assessments of the criteria and related sub-criteria.

Acknowledgement

This work has been financially supported by Galatasaray University Research Fund 16.402.010.

References

1. Z. Nagy, T. Hartványi, Agility in supply chains, Acta Technica Jaurinensis Series Logistica, 1(2), 315-323, (2008).
2. C. Wu, D. Barnes, D. Rosenberg et al., An analytic network process-mixed integer multi-objective programming model for partner selection in agile supply chains, Production Planning & Control, 20(3), 254-275, (2009).
3. C. Wu, D. Barnes, A dynamic feedback model for partner selection in agile supply chains, International Journal of Operations & Production Management, 32(1-2), 79-103, (2012).
4. M. Alimardani, H.Z. Sarfaraz, M.H. Aghdaie, et al., A novel hybrid SWARA and VIKOR methodology for supplier selection in an agile environment, Technological and Economic Development of Economy, 19(3), 553-548, (2013).
5. M. Abdollahi, M. Arvan, J. Razmi, An integrated approach for supplier portfolio selection: Lean or agile?, Expert Systems with Applications, 42(1), 679-690, (2015).
6. J. Lee, H. Cho, Y.S. Kim, Assessing business impacts of agility criterion and order allocation strategy in multi-criteria supplier selection, Expert Systems with Applications, 1136-1148, (2015).
7. Y. Beikkhakhian, M. Javanmardi, M. Karbasian, et al., The application of ISM model in evaluating agile suppliers selection criteria and ranking suppliers using fuzzy TOPSIS-AHP methods, Expert Systems with Applications, 42(15-16), (2015).
8. E.E. Karsak, S.S. Ahiska, Fuzzy multi-criteria decision making approach for transport projects evaluation in Istanbul, Lecture Notes in Computer Science, 3483, 301 - 311, (2005).
9. C.L. Hwang, K. Yoon, Multiple attribute decision making: methods and applications, Heidelberg, (1981).

Using improved analytical programming algorithm for effort estimation in software engineering

Tomas Urbanek[1,a], Zdenka Prokopova[1], Radek Silhavy[1], and Ales Kuncar[1]

[1] *Tomas Bata University in Zlin, Faculty of Applied Informatics, Namesti T.G.Masaryka 5555, 760 01 Zlin, Czech Republic*

Abstract. This paper evaluates the usage of improved analytical programming algorithm for software effort estimation. The new model was generated by improved analytical programming and it was tested and compared with Karner's model to assess its properties. Least Absolute Deviation and random sub-sampling cross validation were used to assess the reliability to this experiment. The experimental results shows that the new model generated by analytical programming outperforms the Karner's equation about 40 %. Moreover, this work shows that improved analytical programming algorithm is feasible method for calibrating Use Case Points method. All results were evaluated by standard approach: visual inspection and statistical significance testing.

1 Introduction

Effort estimation is the activity of predicting the amount of effort required to complete a software development project [1].The reason for this research is to find effective method, which helps to project managers estimate effort more accurate. Accurate and consistent predictions are crucial point in project management for effective planning, monitoring and controlling the software development cycle. Project managers also used these predictions for better management decisions.

There are a great deal of factors which influencing the final prediction; for instance, the size of development team, used programming language, the complexity of requirements and other factors. One of the most substantial factor is human factor. In this point of view, the use of artificial intelligence could be a promising way for effort estimation in software engineering. Nowadays, using of artificial intelligence is very common in this research field. Hence, in this article the method of improved analytical programming for effort estimation is investigated.

In recent time we published study that examined a selection of fitness function for analytical programming and it was found that the best fitness functions are LAD, MSE and very common MMRE [2]. Therefore, in this work we use a LAD as accuracy measurement. This article is evolution of the published study [3]. In this article we investigated the one specific model from generated population. However, there were no statistical evidence of the better accuracy. This paper provides the comparison of Karner's model with models generated by the improved analytical programming algorithm [4]. In our best knowledge no previous study has investigated this improved analytical programming algorithm on real world dataset. Therefore, this study makes a major contribution to research of Use Case Points method, while the improved analytical programming algorithm is used.

[a] Corresponding author: turbanek@fai.utb.cz

2 Related work

Despite of a great deal of effort of scientists and software engineers, there is still no optimal and effective method for every software project. Some work has been done to enhance the effort estimation based on the Use Case Points method. These enhancements cover the review and calibrating the productivity factor such as the work of Subriadi et al. [5]. Another enhancement could be the construction investigation and simplification of the Use Case Points method presented by Ochodek et al. [6]. The recent work of Silhavy et al. [7] suggest a new approach " automatic complexity estimation based on requirements ", which is partly based on Use Case Points method. Very promising way is a research of Kocaguneli et al. [8], this paper shows, that ensemble of effort estimation methods could provide better results than a single estimator.

2.1 The Use Case Points method

This effort estimation method was presented in 1993 by Gustav Karner[9]. It is based on a similar principle to the function point method. Project managers have to estimate the project parameters to four tables. These tables are as follows:

- Unadjusted Use Case Weight (UUCW)
- Unadjusted Actor Weight (UAW)
- Technical Complexity Factor (TCF)
- Environmental Complexity Factor (ECF)

Due to the aims of this paper, the detailed description of well known Use Case Point method basic principles is insignificant and hence omitted. Please refer to [9], [2] for more detailed description of the Use Case Point method.

2.2 Differential evolution

Differential evolution is an optimization algorithm introduced by Storn and Price in 1995, [10]. This optimization method is an evolutionary algorithm based on population, mutation and recombination. Differential evolution is easy to implement and has only four parameters which need to be set. The parameters are: Generations, NP, F and Cr. The Generations Parameter determines the number of generations; the NP Parameter is the population size; the F Parameter is the weighting factor; and the Cr Parameter is the crossover probability [11]. In this research, the differential evolution is used as an individual generator for analytical programming.

2.3 Analytical programming

Analytical programming (AP), is a symbolic regression method. The core of analytical programming is a set of functions and operands. These mathematical objects are used for the synthesis of a new function. Every function in the analytical programming set core has its own varying number of parameters. The functions are sorted according to these parameters into General Function Sets (GFS). For example, GFS_{1par} contains functions that have only 1 parameter – e.g. *sin*(), *cos*(), or other functions. AP must be used with any evolutionary algorithm that consists of a population of individuals for its run [12], [13]. In this paper, we use improved analytical programming algorithm which is described in [4].

3 Problem statement

In this section the design of the research question is provided and can be outlined as follows:

- RQ-1: Analysing the effectiveness of models synthesised by improved analytical programming algorithm with Karner's model.

The research question (RQ-1) aims to obtain an insight on the estimation accuracy of improved analytical programming algorithm and understand the actual effectiveness of this technique with respect to the estimates by standard Use Case Points method. For this reason, the productivity factor will be set to the standard value of 20. Then the estimates will be calculated by improved analytical programming algorithm and then compared with standard Use Case Points method. One sample t-test and descriptive statistics is utilised to asses the statistical evidence of the effectiveness of this technique.

4 Experiment planning

The proposed experiment can be seen in the Figure 1. In this experiment we used repeated random sub-sampling cross validation. In one loop was generated one equation which was then verified on the rest of the dataset. The process begins with a cycle that loops through the 100 random sub-samples. In the data preparation loop, the random subsampling cross validation was used to split the dataset into two distinct sets (training set 60 % and testing set 40 %). In the second loop, the differential evolution process starts to generate an initial population. Analytical programming then uses this initial population to synthesize a new function with constants resolved. After that, the new function is evaluated by the least absolute deviation measure. If the termination condition, which can be the number of population, is met, one can assume that one has an optimal predictive model, and this model is then evaluated by the calculation of the least absolute deviation on the testing set. Then, the results are saved to file for further analysis.

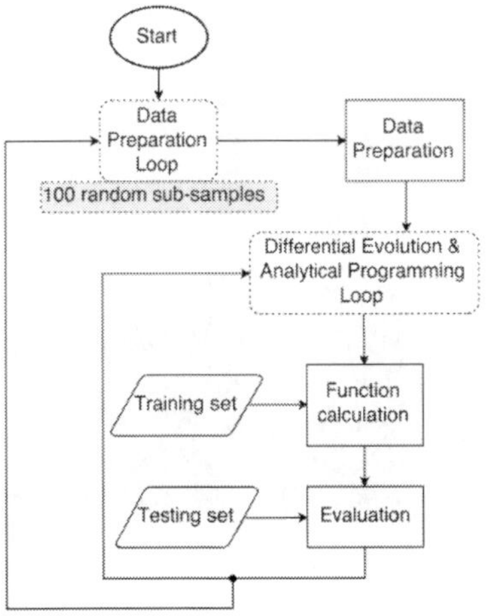

Figure 1. Diagram of proposed experiment.

4.1 Dataset

The data for this study was collected using document review. There are Use Case Points data from 86 software projects and five values for each project: UUCW, UAW, TCF, ECF and actual effort. The distribution of this dataset can be seen on Figure 2. On this figure can be seen bimodal distribution with two distinct peeks. First peek about roughly 700 man/hour and the second peek in roughly 1800 man/hour.

Table 1 shows the analytical programming set-up. The number of leafs (functions built by analytical programming can be seen as trees) was set to 20, which can be recognized as a relatively high value. However, one needs to find the model that will be more accurate than the Karner's model. There is no need to generate short and easily memorable model, but rather, model that will be more accurate.

Table 2 shows the set-up of differential evolution. The best set-up of differential evolution is the subject of further research.

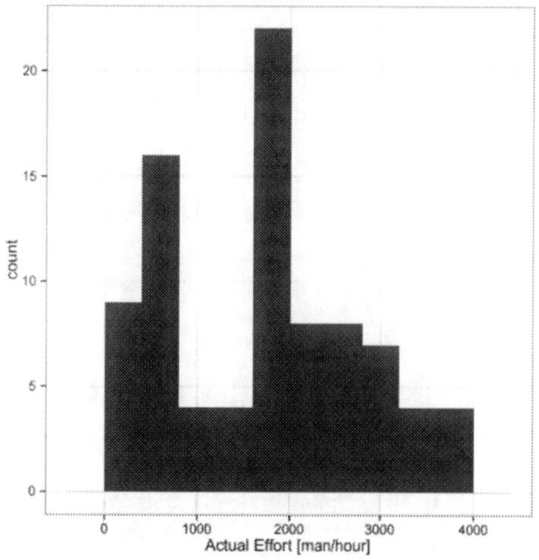

Figure 2. The distribution of actual efforts in dataset.

Table 1. Set-up of analytical programming.

Parameter	Value
Number of leafs	30
GFS - functions	Plus, Subtract, Divide, Multiply, Power, Sqrt, Abs, Sin, Cos
GFS - constants	UUCW, UAW, TCF, ECF, K
Constant K range	0-10

Table 2. Set-up of differential evolution.

Parameter	Value
NP	45
Generations	670
F	0.2
Cr	0.9

4.2 Fitness function

The new model built by the analytical programming method contains the following parameters: UUCW, UAW, TCF and ECF. There is no force applied to the analytical programming that the models have to contain all of these parameters.

$$LAD = \sum_{i=1}^{n} |y_i - \hat{y}_i| \tag{1}$$

,where n is equal to the number of projects in training set, $\hat{y}_i$ is prediction,y_i is actual effort

The Equation 1 is used for optimization task. When the Least Absolute Deviation result is closer to zero then the accuracy of the proposed model is higher.

5 Results

In this section, we present the result of our study. Descriptive statistical analysis and one sample t-test was utilized to describe research results. All the calculations was performed with repeated random sub-sampling cross validation on 86 software projects.

The LAD value for the Karner's equation on the whole dataset is 75744 man/hour. Hence the average error on one software project is 880 man/hour.

Table 3 provides the calculation of 5 point summary of least absolute deviation on training set, testing set and on the sum of training and testing set. The most interesting value is 41209 man/hour as a maximum of the sum of testing and training dataset with the comparison of Karner's equation LAD error. Also can be noted that medians and means of the calculation are very similar. This is also true for inter quartile ranges.

5.1 Statistical test

One sample t-test was conducted to provide the evidence that the new new created models had statistically lower LAD error than Karner's equation.

One Sample t-test
data: data$Complete
t = -184.5056, df = 99, p-value < 2.2e-16
Alternative hypothesis: true mean is less than 75744
95 percent confidence interval:
-Inf, 34681.93
Sample estimates:
mean of x
34309.05

As can be seen the p-value of the t-test has been $2.2 * 10^{-16}$. The null hypothesis that the Karner's equation had less true mean is not accepted. Hence, there is a statistical evidence that the new method produce more accurate models.

6 Discussion

This section begun with answering the question of whether improved analytical programming outperformed the standard UCP equation. This question is answered in the result section. If the productivity factor and the whole UCP method is set to default values, there is a possibility, that model built by analytical programming outperform the standard UCP equation.

There is question (RQ-1), which must be answered. For answering this question we need to study table 3 and statistical t-test from result section. From table 3 could be seen that, the value of maximum (statistically worst model) of the sum of testing and training dataset is 41209 man/hour. This is much lower LAD error than for the Karner's equation. The mean and median model have had values roughly 34000 man/hour. For this models is average LAD error for one software project 395 man/hour.

Table 3. The statistical summary of synthesized models.

	LAD Training set [52 projects]	LAD Testing set [36 projects]	LAD Training+Testing set
Min.	15297	9424	26990
1st Qu.	18675	12994	33358
Median	20027	14040	33849
Mean	20008	14301	34309
3rd Qu.	21331	15515	35316
Max.	24236	20366	41209

Hence, there is a 50% probability that, the improved analytical programming algorithm generate a 2.5 times more accurate equation than the standard UCP equation. The interesting result is the maximum values in table 3. There is no equation, which reaches the penalization. This can be seen as a property of the usage of the improved analytical programming algorithm. The t-test in result section also provides evidence of the accuracy improvement of generated equations.

Evidences provided by these statements could be probably false, when the productivity factor will be set to the optimal value. However the optimal value for productivity factor is not known and therefore in this paper we used standard productivity factor. When the productivity factor is set to standard value the new equations outperform the Karner's equation.

7 Conclusion

The current study discover that the prediction of effort estimation by improved analytical programming can be seen as a feasible method. However, this statement is true if and only if the UCP method is not optimized. The equations, which outperforms the Karner's equation in average 44 %, could be produced by this technique. The findings of this study have a number of important implications for future research of the using of the improved analytical programming as an effort estimation technique. More research is required to determine the efficiency of analytical programming for this task.

Acknowledgement

This work was supported by Internal Grant Agency of Tomas Bata University in Zlin under the project No. IGA/FAI/2016/035.

References

[1] J.W. Keung, Software Engineering Conference, 2008. APSEC '08. 15th Asia-Pacific pp. 495–502 (2008)
[2] T. Urbanek, Z. Prokopova, R. Silhavy, V. Vesela, SpringerPlus (2015)
[3] T. Urbanek, Z. Prokopova, R. Silhavy, A. Kuncar (2016), Vol. 465, pp. 261–272, ISBN 978-3-319-33620-6
[4] T. Urbanek, Z. Prokopova, R. Silhavy, A. Kuncar, 30th European Conference on Modeling and Simulation pp. 231–236 (2016)
[5] A.P. Subriadi, P.A. Ningrum, Journal of Theroretical and Applied Information Technology **59**, 735 (2014)
[6] M. Ochodek, J. Nawrocki, K. Kwarciak, Information and Software Technology **53**, 200 (2011)
[7] R. Silhavy, P. Silhavy, Z. Prokopova, PLOS ONE **10** (2015)
[8] E. Kocaguneli, T. Menzies, J.W. Keung, IEEE Transactions on Software Engineering **38**, 1403 (2012)
[9] G. Karner, Objective Systems SF AB pp. 1–9 (1993)
[10] R. Storn, K. Price, Vol. 11 (Technical Report TR-95-012, 1995), ISBN TR-95-012
[11] R. Storn, Proceedings of North American Fuzzy Information Processing pp. 519–523 (1996)
[12] I. Zelinka, D. Davendra, R. Senkerik, R. Jasek, Z. Oplatkova, (InTech, Rijeka, 2011), ISBN 978-953-307-171-8
[13] Z.K. Oplatkova, R. Senkerik, I. Zelinka, M. Pluhacek, Computers & Mathematics with Applications **66**, 177 (2013)

Effect of cloudiness on the production of electricity by photovoltaic panels

Pavel Chrobak[1,a], Jan Skovajsa[1] and Martin Zalesak[1]

[1]*Tomas Bata University in Zlin, Faculty of Applied Informatics, Namesti T.G.Masaryka 5555, 760 01 Zlin, Czech Republic*

Abstract. The paper deals with the influence of different types of cloud on the production of electricity by photovoltaic panels. In the introductory part of the paper, processes in the atmosphere are described, giving rise to various types of clouds and, consequently, to the formation of cloud. In the next section of the paper, the system is described on which the research and the methodology of acquisition and data evaluation were carried out. The last part of the paper summarizes the overall results of the research.

1 Introduction

Nowadays, there is an increasing development of photovoltaic power plants which serve as a source of clean energy for power, whether the large industrial enterprises or small houses. These photovoltaic plants convert sunlight to electricity by the various types of photovoltaic cells which differ both in used construction materials, efficiency and cost. Moreover, the increase of temperature is causing decrease of effectiveness of the photovoltaic panel. This phenomenon is a common property of photovoltaic panel. This declination of the efficiency and thus the production of electrical energy may vary according to the type of photovoltaic cell due to the increased surface temperature. The production of electric energy also affects the orientation, position, inclination, and the ambient climate conditions in which the photovoltaic panels are located.

In this post, we will focus mainly on the issue of the impact of changing climatic conditions for the production of electricity. These issues are often ignored while changing climatic conditions, in which the photovoltaic panels are located, may have significant impact on the total production of electricity in long time horizon. In particular, the incidence of various types of cloudiness which are formed during the day and at certain time intervals prevents impact of the direct solar radiation on the photovoltaic panels.

2 Processes leading to formation of cloudiness

From the surface of the water, soil and living organism, particles of water or ice evaporates into the atmosphere, and at a certain height above the ground surface gradually condensing into droplets or ice crystals that form clouds. Height, at which this process takes place, is variable and the boundary at which the water in the vapour phase transformed into liquid is called the dew point. This depends on the stability of the air and the percentage of moisture. The average particle size of water or ice crystals in a cloud is 0.01 mm [1, 2]. Clouds vary not only on the height in which is formed, but also on the appearance, properties and may consist of particles of different size and origin. Formation and development of the cloud is connected with the thermodynamic conditions occurring in the ambient atmosphere, and inside the cloud. Maximum water vapour concentration in the atmosphere is 4 percent, and if it is reached then we talk about a hundred percentage of humidity. The size of the droplets, that form clouds, is different depending on the types of individual clouds. Rain clouds (Nimbostratus) contain the largest droplets of size up to one hundred micrometre. The smallest droplets are about nine micrometres. These droplets are contained in the clouds of Cumulus type, and Stratus.

Basic international classification divides clouds into 10 cloud types. Given the observed differences in appearance and internal structure of the clouds, the clouds were further separated into 14 basic shapes. For this reason, the cloud observed in the sky may be labelled with the name of only one shape, which means that shapes of clouds are mutually exclusive. Certain shapes can also be found in several types of clouds. The clouds may also have particular characteristics, which are called varieties and distinction nine of them [3, 4]. These distinctive features are related to the different arrangement of cloud elements (for example the arrangement in the form of waves, etc.) and more or less translucency. The variety may again be common to several kinds of clouds. For some clouds, the withholding stripes, shreds of low clouds, etc. can occur directly in the cloud or outside the cloud. This certain characteristic

[a] Corresponding author: chrobak@fai.utb.cz

traits are referred to as peculiarities clouds. The following Figure 1 shows ten basic types of cloud [5].

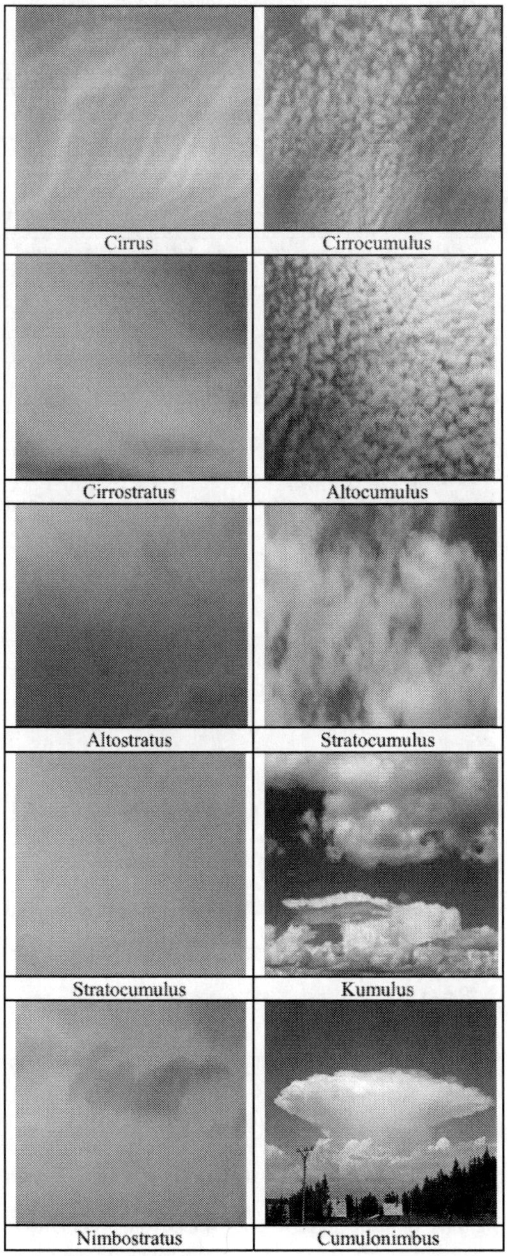

Figure 1. Types of clouds. [5]

According to the altitude of its occurrence, the clouds are classified into three levels. The first level is low, which is up to 2 km from the earth's surface. Second level is medium (2-7 km) and last is high (5-13 km). Part of the sky covered with clouds is called cloudiness [5]. Cloudiness can be given in the eights (meteorologists) or in the tenths (climatologists) and expresses the fraction of the sky covered with clouds. Completely clear sky has zero cloudiness. If the sky is completely covered with clouds, the cloudiness is on code eight according to the scale used by meteorologists. Individual degrees of cloudiness used in meteorology are shown in Table 1.

Table 1. The degree of cloudiness and their brands. [6]

Coverage x code	Meaning	Symbol
0/8 x 0	Sky completely clear	
1/8 x 1	Sky completely clear	
2/8 x 2	Almost sky completely clear	
3/8 x 3	Small cloudy	
4/8 x 4	Sky half cloudy	
5/8 x 5	Cloudy	
6/8 x 6	Cloudy	
7/8 x 7	Almost cloudy	
8/8 x 8	Sky completely cloudy	
x 9	Sky obstructed from view	

3 Description of the system

On the roof of the building FAI TBU is a small photovoltaic plant. The system consists of 9 photovoltaic panels with a total area of 11.25 square meters. The panels used, are of the type of polycrystalline photovoltaic cells. The producer of these panels has declared an energy efficiency of 15 % (for angle of the panels surface inclined from the horizontal one of 45 ° with the southeast azimuth of the normal direction to the panel surface).Installed panels are shown in figure 2.

Figure 2. Photovoltaic panels.

Surface reaches 750 W/m^2, the electric power produced by the panels should be P = 1265 W, based on the declared efficiency by the producer. The output DC voltage of the panels is converted by the AC voltage inverter in one phase AC current with the 230 V AC. This inverter is housed in the building faculty and in the laboratory of environmental engineering and energy efficiency is η_{euro} = 91.8 %. This value is measured under varying climatic conditions. Maximum efficiency were reached η_{max} = 93.5 % with the optimal measuring conditions (stable temperature conditions, nominal DC voltage and medium values of AC power). The rest of the converted energy is lost by the electrical conversion in the form of heat [7], [8].

4 Measurement

Collecting meteorological conditions occurred at the placement of photovoltaic panels in October, November, December, and January in year 2015 and 2016, respectively. For this purpose, the weather station on the building of FAI was used, which provided data on the average outdoor temperature and global solar radiation. Furthermore, the cloud amount occurring in Zlin was observed. Data were obtained from the Czech Hydrometeorological Institute (CHMI) that publishes this information on their website in the form of graphs. This includes a summary of the percentage coverage of the different types of cloudiness for high, medium, low and the total cloud cover for each hour occurring at the placement of photovoltaic panels. These data from graphs were regularly read out and written to the database. The last part of the record is complemented by information on the amount of electricity produced by photovoltaic panels. The following Table 2 shows the average amount of each type of cloudiness occurring in selected months of the year along with production of electricity with photovoltaic panels and the amount of solar radiation incident on a horizontal plane.

Table 2. Coverage cloudiness in selected months.

Months	Coverage cloudiness [%]				Global solar radiation [W/m²]	Production PV [kWh]
	low	medium	high	overall		
October	40.23	44.49	42.19	68.61	80.73	3.106
November	34.01	46.63	42.88	68.81	52.14	2.652
December	45.40	35.14	30.65	62.25	23.27	1.006
January	52.45	48.74	29.98	74.46	30.12	1.370

In the months of December and January, resulting values of production of electrical energy, global solar radiation and the degree of the sky clouded were adjusted for days in which power were not produced due to unfavourable weather conditions. Especially in days when the solar panels were covered with a thick layer of frost or snow, which made it impossible to produce electricity for a significant part of the day. Table 3 details the values of electrical energy production for selected day in the month of November.

Table 3. Production of electricity in different parts of the day.

Time [h:min]	Coverage cloudiness [%]				Global solar radiation [W/m²]	Production PV [kWh]
	low	medium	high	overall		
6:00	85	20	78	97	3.29	0.002
7:00	93	35	70	98	66.12	0.038
8:00	96	60	63	99	185.68	0.153
9:00	98	86	65	100	302.35	0.267
10:00	96	83	60	99	264.07	0.202
11:00	98	95	62	100	291.49	0.246
12:00	95	92	0	99	352.93	0.336
13:00	95	96	0	100	156.84	0.114
14:00	90	97	0	100	155.75	0.117
15:00	95	85	0	99	237.43	0.199
16:00	75	85	5	96	414.25	0.378
17:00	75	70	30	95	325.83	0.075
18:00	40	65	40	84	119.87	0.025
19:00	9	25	30	60	0.58	0.002
Average	81.43	71.00	35.93	94.71	205.46	0.150

Figure 3 shows the dependence of the total cloudiness on the intensity of solar radiation and power production in the month of November. Degree sky coverage cloud is here expressed in the eights.

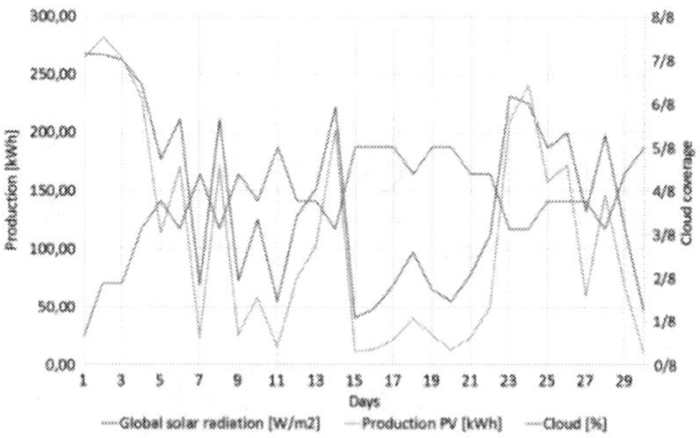

Figure 3. The dependence of the total cloudiness on production electrical energy.

5 Results

From the measured values, which are listed in table 2, the occurrence of cloudiness in the different parts of the year, showing that the overall power production in individual months affects irradiance photovoltaic modules. On the other hand, the individual cloudy days do not affect the overall production of electricity. Decisive in this case, that the average value of the solar radiation and the lighting time of photovoltaic panels which are different each part of the year. Table 3 lists grade cloud cover, solar radiation and the amount of electricity produced by photovoltaic panels for each hour. These values were measured for each day in months. From these data, the values of the percentage coverage of the sky by different types of cloudiness, solar radiation intensity and the amount of electricity produced had been selected only 12 hour for each day of the month. All these values had been summarized in the database and linear regression was used to determine the effects of the percentage coverage of the sky clouds on the production of electricity photovoltaic panels. The results showed that the production of electricity by photovoltaic panels at the same percentage sky coverage of clouds is random. These measured data cannot determine the dependence between cloudiness and the production of the electricity. The same procedure was applied to determine the dependence of the cloudiness on the intensity of the global solar radiation incident on a horizontal plane. Even in this case, it showed that the intensity of the solar radiation is random and these measured data cannot define the dependence between the cloudiness and the light intensity on the horizontal plane.

6 Conclusion

In our case, the determination of the percentage of the dependence between cloudiness and the production of the electricity of photovoltaic panels cannot be determined from the collected data in number of reasons. The measurement of the percentage of coverage cloudiness can determine what cloud cover it is whether it is high, medium or low, but we cannot determine the strength of cloud cover, type and density of clouds, which are in various heights. This information is clearly essential for determining the influence of individual kinds of cloudiness on the production of electricity by photovoltaic panels, because the strength and type of cloud very substantially affects the transmittance of sunshine through the cloud. Based on the results, it is impossible to determine the effect of different types of clouds on electricity production of photovoltaic panels. The measured data shows that the most negative effect on the daily production of electricity is low cloud cover, because it prevents the passage of most of sunlight. Other climatic conditions that affect the production of electricity are ambient temperature, humidity (mist) the degree of air pollution and the wind, which increases heat dissipation from the surface of photovoltaic panels in clear days, and thus increases efficiency.

Further research will focus on determining the passage of the solar radiation different types of clouds. On the basis of these results, model that will determine exactly how clouds influence production of photovoltaic power plants will be created.

Acknowledgement

This work was supported by the Ministry of Education, Youth and Sports of the Czech Republic within the National Sustainability Programme project No. LO1303 (MSMT-7778/2014) and also by the European Regional Development Fund under the project CEBIA-Tech No. CZ.1.05/2.1.00/03.0089 and also by internal grant agency of Tomas Bata University in Zlin no. IGA/CEBIA-Tech/2016/001.

References

1. Meteocentrum [Online]. Prague: 2014, [cit.2016-04-13]. Available: http://www.meteocentrum.cz/zajimavosti/encyklipedie/oblacnost.
2. Cloud atlas [Online]. Brno: 2005, [cit. 2016-04-10]. Available: http://mraky.astronomi e.cz/zvlastni.php
3. Weather station Maruska [Online]. Hostýnské vrchy: 2007 [cit. 2016-04-13]. Available: http://maruska.ordoz.com/meteorologie/oblacnost
4. Sunny [Online]. Ostrava: 2014, [cit. 2016-04-13]. Available: http://www.slunecno.cz/clanky/oblacnost-a-jeji-urcovani-83
5. My NASA Data [online]. [cit. 2016-04-22]. Available: http://mynasadata.larc.nasa.gov/science_projects/make-a-sky-mirror-to-observe-clouds-and contrails/
6. Weather news - Meteoblog [Online]. 2012 [cit. 2016-04-27]. Available: http://meteo-aktuality.blog. cz/1512/meteorologicke-znacky
7. P. Chrobak, M. Zalesak, M. Oplustil, S. Sehnalek, J. Vincenec. In: Proceedings of the International Conferences: Latest Trends on Systems - Volume **II**. 1. rel. Santorini Island, Greece, (2014), s. 581-587. ISBN 978-1-61804-244-6ISSN 1790-5117.
8. T. Habrovansky. *Control and monitoring of heating and cooling units in laboratory of building control systems*. Zlin (2014). Available: http://dspace.k.utb.cz/handle/10 563/ 6910

Model of Coupled Drives Apparatus – Static and Dynamic Characteristics

Petr Chalupa[a], Jakub Novák and Michal Jarmar

Faculty of Applied Informatics, Tomas Bata University in Zlín, 76001 Zlín, Czech Republic

Abstract. The paper presents an initial part of a modelling the Coupled Drives Apparatus CE108 developed by TecQuipment Ltd. The final model should be used in the process of control design for the apparatus. The model derived by the developers of the apparatus using first-principle modelling is used as a starting point for comparison of its properties with measured characteristics. The static and dynamic characteristics of the real-time apparatus are presented and discussed. Special attention is paid to principal differences between the model and the real-time apparatus. Real-time measurements are obtained using MATLAB / Simulink environment in connection with a Real-time Toolbox. Evaluation of the experiments is also performed in the MATLAB environment.

1 Introduction

Most current control algorithms use a model of a controlled plant [1]. It is obvious that some information about controlled plant is required to allow for design of a controller with satisfactory performance. A plant model can be also used to investigate properties and behaviour of the modelled plant without a risk of damage or violating technological constraints of the real plant. There are two basic approaches of obtaining plant model: the black box approach and the first principles modelling (mathematical-physical analysis of the plant).

The black box modelling [2], [3] is based on analysis of input and output signals of the plant. The main advantage of the black box approach consists in the possibility of usage the same identification algorithm for wide set of various controlled plants [4], [5].

On the other hand, the first principle modelling provides general models valid for whole range of plant inputs and states. A first principle model is created by analysing the modelled plant and combining physical laws [6]. Regrettably there are usually many unknown constants and relations when performing analysis of a plant. Therefore, first principle models are suitable for simple controlled plants with small number of parameters. First principle modelling can be also used for obtaining basic information about controlled plant (rage of gain, rank of suitable sample time, etc.). Some simplifications must be used to obtain reasonable results in more complicated cases. These simplifications must relate with the purpose of the model. The first principle modelling is also referred to as white box modelling.

The CE108 apparatus, which was developed by TecQuipment Ltd., is modelled by combination of both methods. Basic relations between plant inputs and outputs are taken over from the first-principle model derived by developers of the apparatus. The obtained model is confronted with the data obtained by real-time measurements. The model will be further improved to represent the real-time apparatus well. This approach is known as grey box modelling [7].

The goal of the whole work is to obtain a mathematical model of the CE108 Couple Drives Apparatus and design the model in MATLAB-Simulink environment. The resulting model should be used in the process of design of the controllers for the real-time control of the CE108 apparatus A model, which represents the plant well, can considerably reduce testing time of different control approaches because only promising control strategies are applied to the real plant and verified.

Controlling the tension and speed of interacting drive systems is a common task in industrial applications. The manufacture of continuous lengths of material can serve as an example. Textiles, paper, wire, metal sheet, plastic films are all processed in continuous lengths. The material is transported and processed through work stations by drive systems and the material speed and tension to be controlled to within defined limits at all times. In applications such as steel rolling mills the material becomes thinner and stretched as it passes through each roller. Each roller therefore has to be set at different speeds. [8]

The paper is organized as follows. Section 2 presents the modelled system – CE108 Coupled Drives Apparatus. The initial first-principle model is presented Section 3. Section 4 on focused on measurement of static and dynamic characteristics of the real-time apparatus. Finally, differences between the model and measured data are discussed in Section 5.

[a] Corresponding author: chalupa@fai.utb.cz

2 Coupled drives apparatus

A photo of the CE108 Coupled Drives Apparatus is presented in Figure 1.

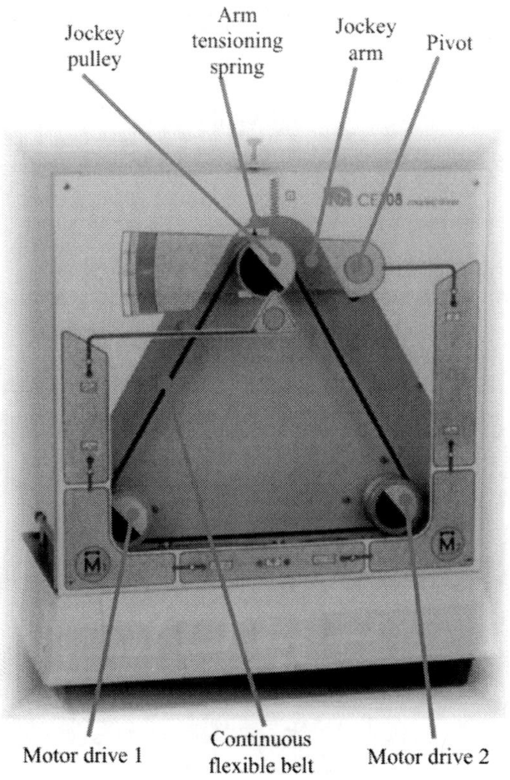

Figure 1. CE108 Coupled Drives Apparatus.

The apparatus consists of two drive motors (Motor 1 and Motor 2). These drives ae used to control the speed and the tension of a continuous flexible belt. The belt goes round three pulleys. Two of them are attached on the drive motor shafts and a jockey pulley. The jockey pulley is mounted on a swinging arm that is supported by a spring. The position of the arm corresponds to the tension in the drive belt [8].

The CE108 Coupled Drives Apparatus has two input signals:

- control voltage of motor M1,
- control voltage of motor M2.

The apparatus provides 4 output signals:

- speed of the belt, i.e. rotations of the jockey pulley,
- tension of the belt measured as an angle of the arm,
- rotations of the motor M1,
- rotations of the motor M2.

The rotations of the motors can also be considered states of the apparatus.

In the most often used setup, the apparatus is considered a Two Inputs Two Outputs (TITO) system with control voltages as the inputs and belt speed and tension as the outputs.

3 Initial first principle model

A scheme of the CE108 Coupled Drives Apparatus is shown in Figure 2 [8].

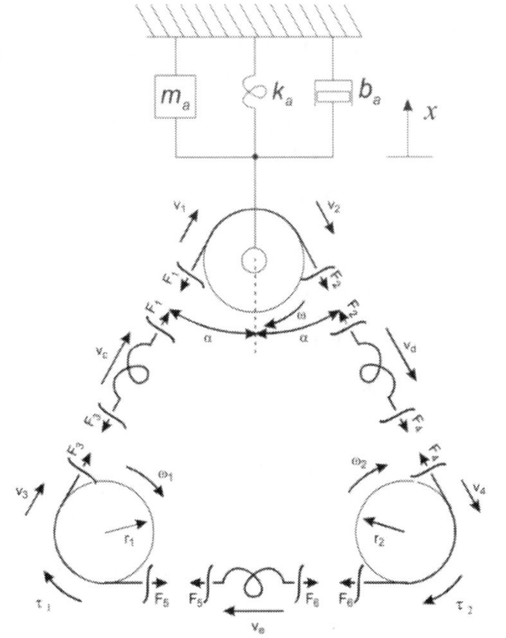

Figure 2. Scheme of the CE108 Coupled Drives Apparatus.

3.1 Notation

The following notation is used for derivation of the model of the apparatus:

m_a – the jockey arm and pulley mass,
k_a – the jockey arm spring stiffness,
b_a – the jockey arm bearing coefficient of friction,
x – the vertical position of the jockey pulley,
α – the angle of the belt sections with the vertical,
F_a – vertical force affecting the spring,
k – the stiffness of the belt,
I – the moment of inertia of a motor drive,
b – the friction coefficient of inertial of a motor drive,
ω_i – the rotational speed (angular velocity) of Drive i; $i \in \{1, 2\}$,
ω – the rotational speed (angular velocity) of the jockey pulley,
τ_i – the input torque of Drive i; $i \in \{1, 2\}$,
F_i – the tensions in the individual belt sections; $i \in \{1, 2, 3, 4, 5, 6\}$,
x_c – the extension of the belt section C,
x_d – the extension of the belt section D,
x_e – the extension of the belt section E,
v_i – velocity of the belt at a corresponding position; $i \in \{1, 2, 3, 4\}$,

p – the momentum of mass m_a,
h_i – the drive pulley/motor angular momenta; $i \in \{1, 2\}$.

3.2 Derivation of the model

This section presents short form of derivation of a first principle model of the CE108 apparatus. Details can be found in [8] and [9].

It is assumed that the pulley is light and rotates without friction:

$$F_1 = F_2 = F \tag{1}$$

Then vertical force affecting the spring can be written as follows:

$$F_a = 2F\cos(\alpha) \tag{2}$$

And from the conservation of power:

$$F_a \dot{x} = F(v_1 - v_2) \tag{3}$$

Combining (2) and (3) leads to

$$2\dot{x}\cos(\alpha) = v_1 - v_2 \tag{4}$$

The vertical force balance on jockey arm assembly leads to:

$$F_a = \dot{p} + k_a x + b_a \dot{x} \tag{5}$$

The force balance on belt sections C and D gives

$$F = kx_c = kx_d \tag{6}$$

where

$$F = F_1 = F_2 = F_3 = F_4 \tag{7}$$

The force balance of the belt in section E is described by (8):

$$F' = kx_e \tag{8}$$

where

$$F' = F_5 = F_6 \tag{9}$$

A torque balance on the drive pulleys gives

$$\tau_1 + F_3 r - F_5 r = \dot{h}_1 + b\omega_1 \tag{10}$$

$$\tau_2 + F_6 r - F_4 r = \dot{h}_2 + b\omega_2 \tag{11}$$

where

$$h_1 = I\omega_1 \tag{12}$$

$$h_2 = I\omega_2 \tag{13}$$

Angular velocities of motors and belt velocities are connected according to the following equations:

$$v_3 = \omega_1 r \tag{14}$$

$$v_4 = \omega_2 r \tag{15}$$

Combining equations (4) – (15) leads to state space description of the CE108 Coupled Drives Apparatus.

$$\begin{aligned}
\dot{h}_1 &= -\frac{b}{I}h_1 + rkx_c - rkx_e + \tau_1 \\
\dot{h}_2 &= -\frac{b}{I}h_2 - rkx_c + rkx_e + \tau_2 \\
\dot{x}_c &= \frac{1}{2}\left(-h_1\frac{r}{I} + h_2\frac{r}{I} + p\frac{2\cos(\alpha)}{m_a}\right) \\
\dot{x}_e &= \frac{r}{I}h_1 - \frac{r}{I}h_2 \\
\dot{x} &= \frac{p}{m_a} \\
\dot{p} &= 2\cos(\alpha)\,kx_c - k_a x - \frac{b_a}{m_a}p
\end{aligned} \tag{16}$$

It is possible to derive two transfer functions from the state equations:

$$\omega(s) = \frac{\tau_1(s) + \tau_2(s)}{2(sI + b)} \tag{17}$$

$$x(s) = \frac{kr\cos(\alpha)(\tau_2(s) - \tau_1(s))}{(Is^2 + b + 3kr^2)(m_a s^2 + b_a s + k_a + 2k\cos^2(\alpha)) - 2k^2 r^2 \cos^2(\alpha)} \tag{18}$$

The motor torques τ_1 and τ_2 are derived by the input signals u_1 and u_2. In the simplest case the motor actuator characteristic is linear:

$$\tau_1 = g_1 u_1 \tag{19}$$

$$\tau_2 = g_2 u_2 \tag{20}$$

The jockey arm deflection and belt speed are measured by a sensor with outputs y_x and y_ω respectively. The characteristics of the sensors is assumed to be linear:

$$y_x = g_x x \tag{21}$$

$$y_\omega = g_\omega \omega \tag{22}$$

It should be noted that it is assumed that the friction coefficients between the belt and motor pulleys is the same for both motor pulleys.

Combining equations (17) – (22) leads to the following statements concerning static characteristics of the system:

- The speed of the belt in the steady states is proportional to the sum of control inputs ($u_1 + u_2$).
- The tension of the belt in the steady states is proportional to the difference between control inputs (u_2 - u_1)
- The system is linear with respect to its control inputs

4 Static and dynamic characteristics

This sections presents several measurements of static and dynamic characteristics of the CE108 Coupled Drives Apparatus.

The measurements were performed using MATLAB / Simulink environment. The real-time behaviour of Simulink was guaranteed by using Real-Time Toolbox by Humusoft Ltd. A data acquisition PCI card MF624 was used as an interface between personal computer and the apparatus.

The measurements of static characteristics were performed for both increasing and decreasing sequence of control signal. Fast sampling time of T_0=0.01s was used for all measurements. Static characteristics was measured more than 30 times to obtain representative results for different setups. Typically, each setup was measured 3 times and the results were compared to state if averaging can be used.

An example of input signals courses is presented in Figure 3.

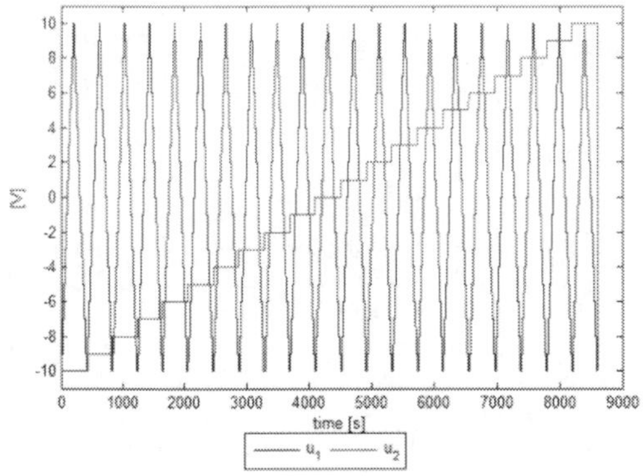

Figure 3. Course of input signals for measurement of static characteristics.

It can be seen that both signals are piece-wise constant. The signal u_2 is constant for the whole increase-decrease cycle of the signal u_1. Hence, the input u_1 is stated as the one with faster changes of its value. This single measurement lasted for 8610 s (i.e. almost 2,5 hours).

A typical static characteristics of belt speed is presented in Figure 4. In this case control inputs were coursed according to Figure 3. Steady states for increasing sequence of u_1 is presented.

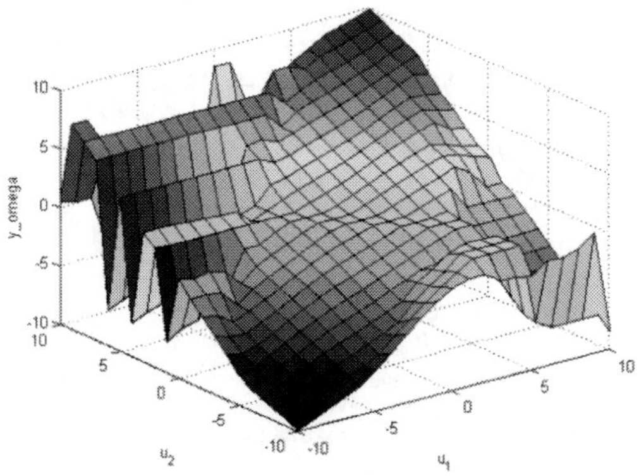

Figure 4. Static characteristics of belt speed (increasing u_1)

It can be observed that the system is not linear especially in the area where signs of input signals is different (i.e. u_1<0 and simultaneously u_2>0 or u_1>0 and simultaneously u_2<0). A linear area is observed in the neighbourhood of line u_1=u_2 with a small dead-zone close to origin (u_1=0, u_2=0).

The static characteristics for decreasing u_1 is presented in Figure 5.

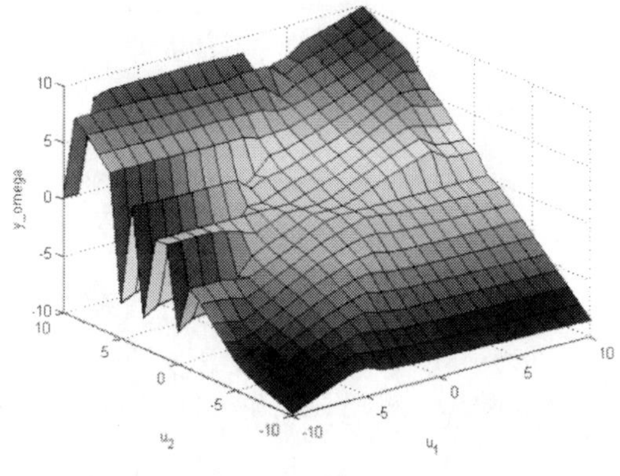

Figure 5. Static characteristics of belt speed (decreasing u_1)

It can be observed from comparison of Figure 4 and Figure 5 that the output value of the steady CE108 apparatus is dependant not only on the current steady inputs but also on their history. This statement is supported by measurement of static characteristics where input u_2 was changing faster – the courses of inputs were opposite to Figure 3. Resulting static characteristics of belt speed is presented in Figure 6.

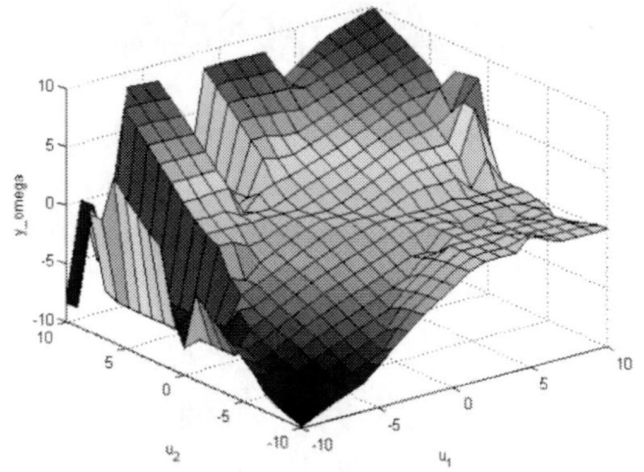

Figure 6. Static characteristics of belt speed (increasing u_2)

As the system behaviour was studied deeper it was found out that that for particular combinations of steady inputs the belt speed tends to be close to the speed of one of motors regardless of the speed of the other motor.
This situation can be observed in Figure 7. It can be seen that the bet speed is:

- close to speed of motor M1, or
- close to speed of motor M2, or
- close to zero.

Belt speed proportional to sum of input signal did not occur in this part of the measurement of static characteristics.

The same course with smaller time frame is presented in Figure 8. This figure can be used to study dynamic behaviour of the apparatus as the course contains several step responses of both belt speed and belt tension.

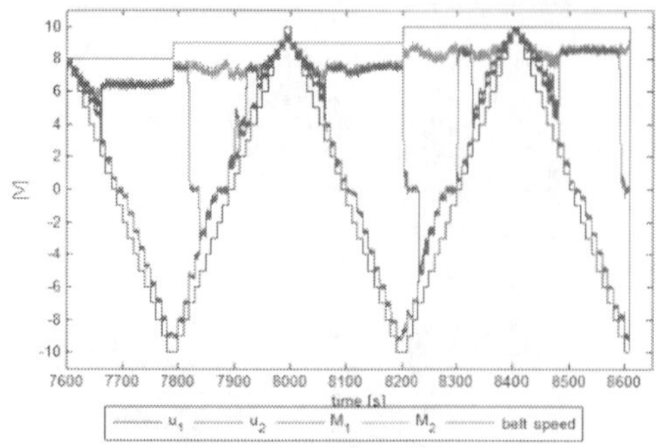

Figure 7. Measurement of static characteristic – course of input and output signals

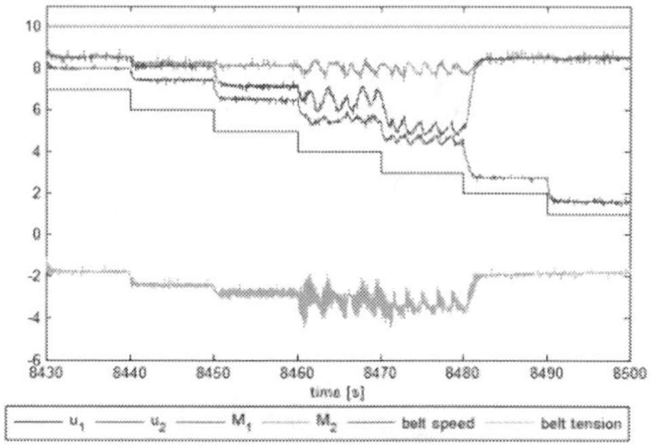

Figure 8. Dynamic behaviour of the CE108 apparatus

A typical static characteristic of belt tension is presented in Figure 9.

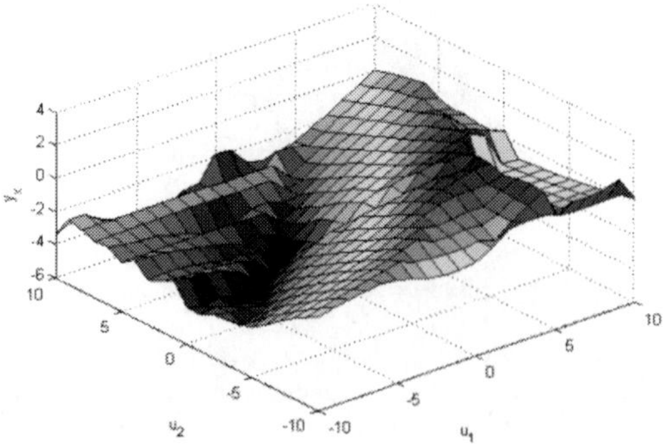

Figure 9. Typical static characteristics of belt tension

As for the linearity of the belt tension, the statement might be the same as for belt speed: A linear area is observed in the neighbourhood of line $u_1=u_2$.

5 Comparison of model and real-time apparatus

Several principal differences were observed when comparing behaviour of the first principle model with real-time measurements:

- The CE108 apparatus is not linear in whole range of its inputs
- The steady outputs of the CE108 apparatus do not depend only on the steady inputs but also on the previous course of the inputs
- The behaviour of the CE108 apparatus in the area where inputs have opposite sign is very far from deterministic. This area can be modelled only by stochastic approach
- Steady outputs are not reached for the steady inputs in some cases. This behaviour represents nonlinearity of the system (see Figure 8).

Conclusion

The CE108 Coupled Drives Apparatus was presented as well as its first principle model. Many static characteristics of the real-tome apparatus were measured and the behaviour of the real-time system was compared with the model. The comparison was focused on principal differences which cannot be omitted or suppressed by tuning parameters of the model. Significant differences occur especially in cases where the signs of the input were opposite.

Further work will be focused on improvement of the model to represent nonlinearities of the CE108 Coupled Drives Apparatus.

Acknowledgment

This work was supported by the Ministry of Education, Youth and Sports of the Czech Republic within the National Sustainability Programme project No. LO1303 (MSMT-7778/2014).

References

1. V. Bobál, J. Böhm, J. Fessl, J. Macháček, *Digital Self-tuning Controllers: Algorithms, Implementation and Applications* (2005)
2. G. P. Liu, *Nonlinear identification and control – A neural network Approach* (2001)
3. L. Ljung, *System identification: theory for the user. Upper Saddle River* (1999)
4. J. Mikleš, M. Fikar, *Process modelling, identification, and control* (2007)
5. B. Codrons, *Process modelling for control: a unified framework using standard black-box techniques* (2005)
6. D. M. Himmelblau. J. B. Riggs, *Basic principles and calculations in chemical engineering* (2004).
7. K.C. Tan, Y. Li, Control Engineering Practice **10,** 673–684 (2002).
8. H. Hagadoorn, M. Readman, *Coupled Drives 1: Basics* (2004), http://www.control-systems-principles.co.uk/whitepapers/coupled-drives1.pdf
9. H. Hagadoorn, M. Readman, *Coupled Drives 2: Control and analysis* (2004), http://www.control-systems-principles.co.uk/whitepapers/coupled-drives2.pdf

A comparison of possible exponential polynomial approximations to get commensurate delays

Libor Pekař[a] and Petr Chalupa

[1]Tomas Bata University in Zlín, Faculty of Applied Informatics, Nad Stráněmi 4511, 76005 Zlín 5, Czech Republic

Abstract. The paper is aimed at a comparative simulation study on three prospective ideas how to approximate a general exponential polynomial by another one having all its exponents in the exp-function as integer multiples of some real number. This work is motivated by spectral properties of neutral time-delay systems (NTDS) and the contemporary state of the knowledge about the spectrum of NTDS with commensurate delays which are characterized by the latter family of exponential polynomials. The three ideas are, namely, those: Taylor series expansion, the interpolation in points given by dominant roots estimates and the special extrapolation technique presented by the authors recently. The goal is to match dominant parts of both the spectra as close as possible. However, some properties from the so called strong stability point of view can not be, in principle, preserved. The presented simulation example demonstrates the accuracy and efficiency of all the methods.

1 Introduction

The characteristic quasipolynomial of a linear-time invariant time delay system (TDS) gives the fundamental information about the system's dynamics; for instance, its zeros coincide (under some conditions) with system poles (i.e. eigenvalues) [1, 2]. Much effort has been made to analyse the infinite spectrum of TDS of retarded as well as neutral type (NTDS), mainly when the endeavour to decide about system stability and its dependence on particular delays' values [3-8]. Compared to retarded ones, NTDS are much more advanced, tricky and intricate regarding spectral properties [1, 4, 9]. Namely, positions of vertical strips of poles are sensitive to infinitesimal delay changes, which give rise to the notion of strong stability [10, 11] that is affected i.a. by the rational dependence of delays [9].

These infinite vertical strips constitute the so called essential spectrum of a NTDS and they are unambiguously given by roots of the associated exponential polynomial [1]. While there are many analytical results on the (essential and whole) spectrum of systems with commensurate delays in the literature, see e.g. [6, 7], it is extremely difficult to find any exact laws for roots loci in the case of non-commensurate delays.

The goal of this work should be to establish a bridge between these two spaces by design of some possible ways how to approximate an exponential polynomial with non-commensurate delays by that with commensurate ones – which can be then analyzed easier. The accuracy of the approximation is measured by the matching of a subset of both the essential spectra with the most dominant poles. Roots loci are computed and displayed by means of the (advanced) Quasi-polynomial mapping Rootfinder (QPmR) [12] which is available as the *aqpmr* function in MATLAB.

We compare three methods in this contribution. As first, Taylor's series expansions of approximating and approximated exponential polynomial in the dominant root estimation point can be made, which is equivalent to the derivatives' equalities up to an appropriate order. As second, linear and quadratic extrapolation procedures based on the Taylor's series expansion again can be used. As third, the interpolation idea is another natural way how to cope with the problem. We present and compare two possibilities of the selection of points for the interpolation.

All these techniques require a sufficiently accurate estimation of dominant roots of the approximated exponential polynomial, which can be done e.g. by using our gridding algorithm [13]. Another problem is the selection of the value of the base delay for the commensuracy; hence, we provide the reader with a possible solution and give the comparison with some other options. Last but not least, obtained approximated roots do not constitute complex pairs due to complex-valued coefficients.

A simulation example preformed in the MATLAB/Simulink environment provides the reader with the comparison case study and it clearly indicates that some of the above introduced ideas are good enough for the approximation in question.

Throughout the paper, $\mathbb{C}$, $\mathbb{R}$, $\mathbb{N}$ and $\mathbb{N}_0$ denote the sets of complex, real, integer and natural numbers, respectively. For $s \in \mathbb{C}$, $\operatorname{Re} s$ denotes the real part of s.

[a] Corresponding author: pekar@fai.utb.cz

2 Preliminaries

2.1 NTDS spectrum

Let the transfer function $G(s) = \cdot / D(s)$ of a NTDS have no common zeros and poles. Consider the corresponding monic characteristic quasipolynomial of a NTDS as

$$D(s) = s^n + \sum_{i=0}^{n} \sum_{j=0}^{h_i} d_{ij} s^i \exp(-\tau_{ij} s) \tag{1}$$

where $d_{ij} \in \mathbb{R}$, $\tau_{i0} = 0$, $\boldsymbol{\tau} = (\tau_{01}, \tau_{02}, ..., \tau_{nh_n}) \in \mathbb{R}_+^L$ are general delays and $L = \sum_{i=0}^{n} h_i$. The associated exponential polynomial reads $D_a(s) = 1 + \sum_{j=1}^{h_n} d_{nj} \exp(-\tau_{nj} s) \notin \mathbb{R}$ for some $d_{nj} \neq 0$.

Define the spectrum of the NTDS and its essential spectrum as

$$\Sigma := \{s : D(s) = 0\}, \Sigma_e := \{s : D_a(s) = 0\} \tag{2}$$

respectively. Then it holds that [4, 9]:

- If there exists a nonzero pair d_{ij} for some *i*, *j*, then $|\Sigma| = \infty$.
- There exists a vertical chain of poles, $s_k \in \Sigma$, at $\gamma := \sup \operatorname{Re} \Sigma_e$ such that $\lim_{k \to \infty} \operatorname{Re} s_k = \gamma$, $\lim_{k \to \infty} \operatorname{Im} s_k = \infty$ for $|s_{k-1}| < |s_k|$.
- Let $s_k \in \Sigma$, $s_{e,k} \in \Sigma_e$, with $|s_{k-1}| < |s_k|$, $|s_{e,k-1}| < |s_{e,k}|$ then $\lim_{k \to \infty} |s_k - s_{e,k}| = 0$.
- The value of γ is not continuous with respect to $\boldsymbol{\tau}$.

Moreover, let us define some other useful notions. The spectral abscissa equals $\alpha := \sup \operatorname{Re} \Sigma$. If every delay in (1) can be written as $\tau_k = \lambda_k \tau_0$, $\lambda_k \in \mathbb{N}$, for some (fixed) base delay τ_0, delays are called commensurate. This notion is often confused with the so called rational dependency. Nonzero delays $\tau_1, \tau_2, ..., \tau_L$ are rationally dependent if there exist nonzero $\lambda_1, \lambda_2, ..., \lambda_L \in \mathbb{N}$ such that $\sum_{k=1}^{L} \lambda_k \tau_k = 0$ [14].

For commensurate delays, it is easy to see that if $s_{e,0} \in \Sigma_e$ then

$$s_{e,k} = s_{e,0} \pm \mathrm{i} \frac{2k\pi}{\tau_0} \in \Sigma_e \tag{3}$$

for any $k \in \mathbb{N}$.

2.2 NTDS stability

Regarding exponential stability, this notion coincides with the finite-dimensional case, i.e. a NTDS is exponentially stable if $\alpha < 1$ (including the limit of infinite vertical chains); however, other habitual types of stability (asymptotic, H_∞, etc.) are much more complicated, see e.g. [6, 14]. Moreover, there exists a specific stability notion for NTDS – strong exponential stability – expressing that it remains $\gamma < 0$ under small delay perturbations; note that isolated roots with $\operatorname{Re} s_k \in \Sigma > \gamma$ are not considered in this definition. The system is strongly (exponentially) stable if and only if

$$\xi := \sum_{j=1}^{h_n} |d_{nj}| < 1 \tag{4}$$

Moreover it holds for NTDS with rationally independent delays that $\xi > 0$ implies strong instability [15]. Hence, from this point of view, the rational independency is a rather stronger notion compared to the rational dependency. Notice that condition (4) does not include delay values.

Whereas the value of γ is not continuous with respect to delay values, this relation holds for the safe upper bound estimation on γ introduced e.g. in [12] as

$$c \in \mathbb{R} \to \sum_{j=1}^{h_n} |d_{nj}| \exp(-c\tau_{nj}) = 1 \tag{5}$$

In fact, the value of *c* calculated from (5) gives the relevant information about the exponential stability of $D_a(s)$.

3 Problem formulation and possible solutions

As introduced above, there exist many results on the (essential) spectrum of NTDS with commensurate delays but only a few on non-commensurate ones. Therefore, our intention is to approximate $D_a(s)$ with a general vector $\boldsymbol{\tau}$ by

$$D_A(s) = 1 + \sum_{k=1}^{k_{\max}} d_{A,k} \exp(-k\tau_0 s) \tag{6}$$

where $k_{\max}$ means the degree of commensuracy. Let us denote the spectrum of (6) as $s_{A,i} \in \Sigma_A$ and, analogously, the corresponding values $\hat{\gamma}$, $\hat{\xi}$, $\hat{c}$.

Three possible ways how to cope with this task follow.

3.1 Extrapolation method

This idea stems from the discrete formulation of $D_A(s)$. Assume the substitution $\exp(-\tau s) \to q^{\vartheta}$ where $\vartheta = \tau / \tau_0$ and the shifting operator *q* corresponds to the variable z^{-1} from the z-transform. Hence, one can write

$$z^{-\vartheta} = z^{-(\lfloor \vartheta \rfloor + l)} z^{(l - \overline{\vartheta})} \tag{7}$$

for some $l \in \mathbb{N}$ where $\overline{\vartheta}$ means the non-integer fractional part.

Then the Taylor's series expansion of the factor $z^{(l-\overline{\vartheta})}$ of the order *l* in a suitable point $z_0 \in \mathbb{C}$ can be made. In [16] we have presented analytic result for the linear

($l=1$) and quadratic case ($l=2$); both of them are used in this study yet not displayed herein the paper.

The dominant roots have the decisive impact to the dynamics. From one point of view, the rightmost poles coincide with the dominant ones. However, this is not the best conception for our case since there are infinitely many rightmost roots, see (3). Another idea is to measure the dominancy by the distance from the zero (i.e. the absolute value) which, however, is applicable to stable systems only. Thus, if $s_0 \in \mathbb{C}$ expresses the dominant root, then

$$z_0 = \exp(\tau_0 s_0), s_0 = \frac{1}{\tau_0}\log z_0 \quad (8)$$

3.2 Taylor's series expansion

Consider Taylor's series expansions $T_{D_a}(s)$ and $T_{D_A}(s)$ of $D_a(s)$ and $D_A(s)$, respectively, of the order l. The identity $T_{D_a}(s) = T_{D_A}(s)$ can also be expressed as

$$\frac{\mathrm{d}^i}{\mathrm{d}s^i}T_{D_a}(s) = \frac{\mathrm{d}^i}{\mathrm{d}s^i}T_{D_A}(s), i = 0,1...l \quad (9)$$

where derivatives are calculated in a suitable point s_0, for instance, again in the dominant root.

Whenever there exists a number $k_{\max}$ of unknown coefficients $d_{A,k}$ in (6), one can set $l = k_{\max} - 1$ (if linear algebraic equations (9) are independent) to get the unambiguous solution.

3.3 Interpolation method

Unknown coefficients of a prescribed $D_A(s)$ can be determined by the interpolation with $D_a(s)$ in the number of $l = k_{\max} - 1$ points $s_{0,i}$ as

$$D_A(s_{0,i}) = D_a(s_{0,i}),\ i = 1,2...,l \quad (10)$$

Let us choose two options. As first, consider the infinite chain of the rightmost roots (3). As second, try to take roots estimates with the minimum modulus (except for those in the chain with a high imaginary part), see the last paragraph of 3.1.

Due to (3), the exact imaginary parts can not be taken; otherwise, the set (10) would have no solution. Therefore, small deviations r_i in the imaginary parts are made.

3.4 Discussion on methods

The crucial task is the option of the base delay τ_0. From the z-transform point of view, it has the meaning of the sampling period, the recommended value interval of which for a second order finite-dimensional system reads

$$\tau_0 = \left[0.2|s_0|^{-1}, 0.5|s_0|^{-1}\right] \quad (11)$$

since $|s_0|$ agrees with the value of undumped oscillations frequency.

Option (11) is faced with other values of τ_0 in the example below; hence, let us denote

$$\tau_0 = \frac{1}{\lambda_0|s_0|}, \lambda_0 \in \mathbb{R} \quad (12)$$

On the other hand, it is a natural requirement that at least one delay in $D_a(s)$ has the same value as in $D_A(s)$, e.g. the smallest one, $\tau_{\min}$, is an integer multiple of τ_0. Then we can set $\tau_0 = \tau_{\min}/n_m \in \mathbb{N}$, which gives rise to the optimization problem

$$\min_{n_m} \arg\left|\frac{\tau_{\min}}{n_m} - \frac{1}{\lambda_0|s_0|}\right| \quad (13)$$

for some suitable selected real λ_0.

Another issue to be touched is that all the above methods result in complex-valued coefficients of the eventual exponential polynomial. This i.a. implies that roots are not symmetrical to the real axis. Thus, in the example, we benchmark the option to take $\operatorname{Re} s_0$ rather than s_0 in (7)-(10).

Assume an exponential term in (6), $\exp(-\tau s)$, and its linear approximation as

$$\exp(-\tau s) \approx a_k \exp(-k\tau_0 s) + a_{k+1}\exp(-(k+1)\tau_0 s) \quad (14)$$

where $k\tau_0 \le \tau < (k+1)\tau_0$ for some integer k.

Since the linear extrapolation method is based on the Taylor's series expansion, it can easily be deduced that this method coincides with (9) whenever the approximating exponential polynomial is constructed as in (14), see details in [16].

Apparently, strong stability condition (4) is not affected only if $|a_k| + |a_{k+1}| = 1$; however, it can be verified that it is satisfied only for $s_0 = 0$, i.e. $z_0 = 1$ [16]. Another problem is that there is the transition from non-commensuracy to commensuracy that yields rational dependency. Therefore, condition (4) becomes less strict than in the case of rational independency.

Last but not least, the approximation might be improved by the iterative use of the particular method via the re-calculation of the leading root estimation $s_0 \approx s_{A,0}$. Simply, the discretization described in the subsection 3.1 is used to get a polynomial and it is followed by the use of the function to (8) to get the eventual $s_{0,A}$.

4 Example

Consider the following exponential polynomial to be approximated

$$D_a(s) = 1 + 0.5\exp(-0.9s) - 0.4\exp\left(-\frac{2\pi}{3}s\right) \quad (15)$$

We are going to present several numerical test below. Let the initial dominant root estimation simply be $s_0 = 0$. Since the imaginary part is "unknown" in this case, set the default value $\tau_0 = 0.9$. In the interpolation method, let us set $s_{0,1} = 0$, $s_{0,2} = -1$. Corresponding results without and with iterations are displayed in Figure 1 and Figure 2, respectively, in the form of the dominant subset of Σ_A.

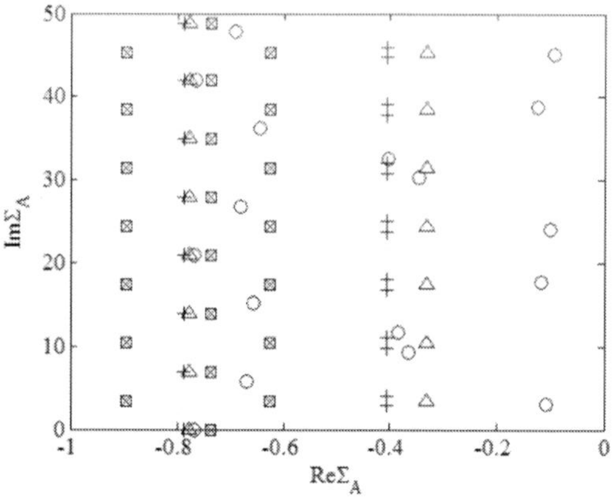

Figure 1. Σ_e, Σ_A for $\tau_0 = 0.9$, $s_0 = 0$ ($s_{0,1} = 0$, $s_{0,2} = -1$), non-iterative procedure.

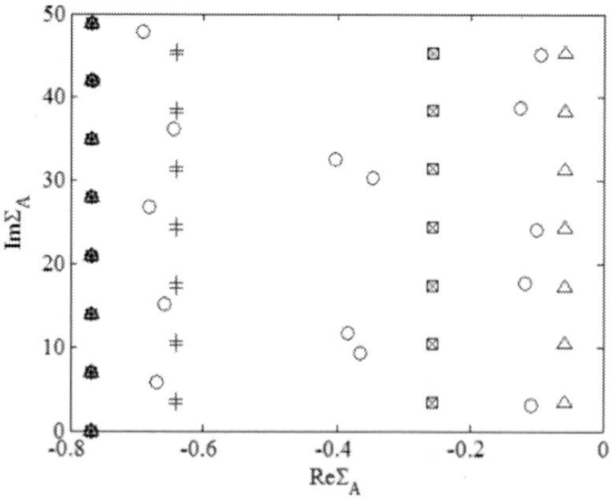

Figure 2. Σ_e, Σ_A for $\tau_0 = 0.9$, $s_0 = 0$ ($s_{0,1} = 0$, $s_{0,2} = -1$), iterative procedure.

In all figures of the paper, the legend is as follows: Roots of (15) are denoted by circles (○); those of the $D_A(s)$ obtained by using the linear and the quadratic extrapolation method are denoted by crosses (x) and plusses (+), respectively, Σ_A from the Taylor's series expansion is denoted by squares (□), and the interpolation method with the vertical chain of dominant roots $s_{0,i}$ and the roots $s_{0,i}$ with the minimum modulus give Σ_A denoted by triangles (∇, Δ), respectively.

Figures 1 and 2 clearly display very poor results where the non-iterative procedure has yielded the acceptable estimation of roots about $\operatorname{Re} s_e \approx -0.77$. The iterative procedure has resulted in almost exact estimation of these roots (but also some more not included in the original spectrum); however, the dominant rightmost roots of Σ_a have not been approached at all (except for the last submethod). Note that results for the interpolation method with roots $s_{0,i}$ in a vertical chain are not displayed since a part of the spectrum is quite far in the right half-plane.

As the second experiment, we attempt to get better initial estimation by the simple linear extrapolation (14) where a_k, a_{k+1} express the closeness of τ to $k\tau_0$ and $(k+1)\tau_0$, respectively. The dominant roots for $\tau_0 = 0.9$ then read

$$\begin{aligned} s_0 &= s_{0,1} = -0.6269847 + 3.490659i \\ s_{0,2} &= -0.6269847 + 10.471976i, s_{0,2} = -0.736792 \end{aligned} \tag{16}$$

Recall that last two values are the root estimate in the vertical chain and that with the second minimum modulus, respectively. The corresponding z-values via (8) are $z_0 = z_{0,1} = z_{0,2} = 0.568766, z_{0,2} = 0.515245$. Set the deviation in the imaginary part as $r_1 = 0.1$; hence,

$$\begin{aligned} s_{0,2} &= -0.626985 + 10.571976i \\ z_{0,2} &= -0.566464 - 0.05112i \end{aligned}$$

Results for $\lambda_0 = 5/3$ ($\tau_0 = 0.18$), $\lambda_0 = 1$ ($\tau_0 = 0.3$), $\lambda_0 = 1/3$ ($\tau_0 = 0.9$) and both non-iterative and iterative procedures are displayed in Figures 3 to 8. Clearly, the best one has been obtained for $\tau_0 = 0.3$ where almost all the (sub)methods have given a very close spectrum estimation; however, it has not been proved that the iterative procedure should have given better results in terms of our example. Notice that the linear extrapolation method and Taylor series expansion for (14) yield the same spectra, as mentioned above.

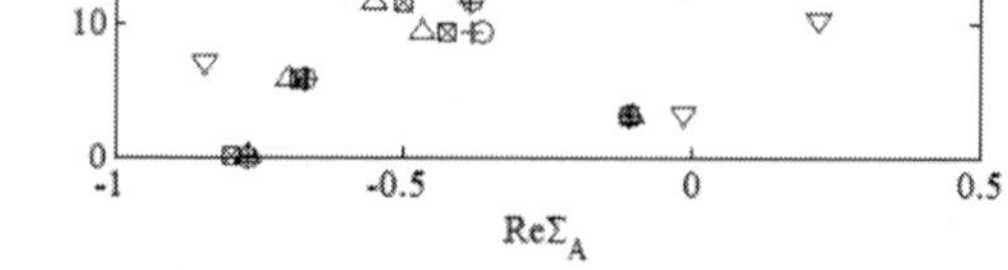

Figure 3. Σ_e, Σ_A for $\tau_0 = 0.18$, $s_{0,i}$ given by (16), non-iterative procedure.

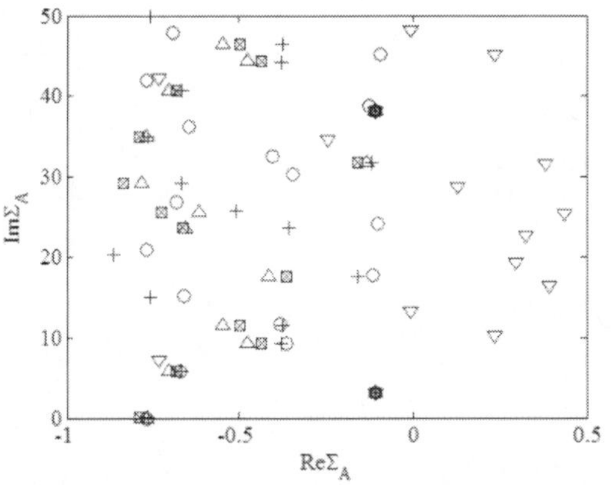

Figure 4. Σ_e, Σ_A for $\tau_0 = 0.18$, $s_{0,i}$ given by (16), iterative procedure.

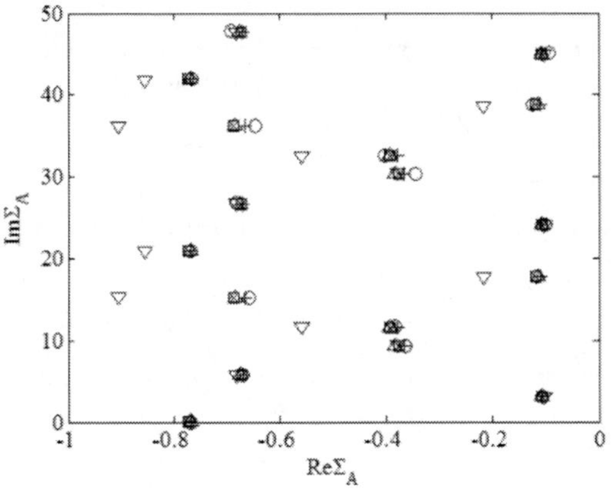

Figure 5. Σ_e, Σ_A for $\tau_0 = 0.3$, $s_{0,i}$ given by (16), non-iterative procedure.

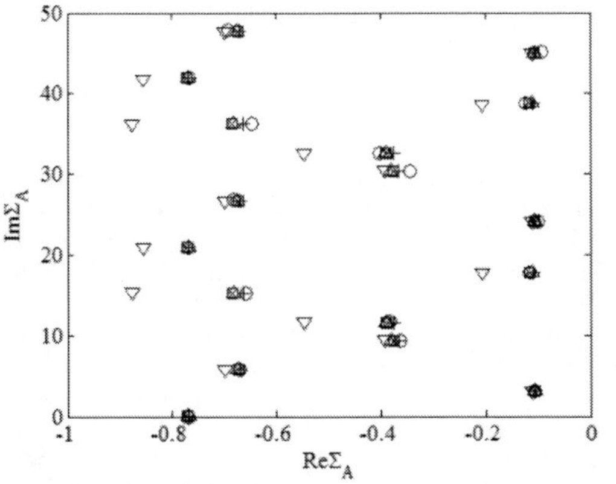

Figure 6. Σ_e, Σ_A for $\tau_0 = 0.3$, $s_{0,i}$ given by (16), iterative procedure.

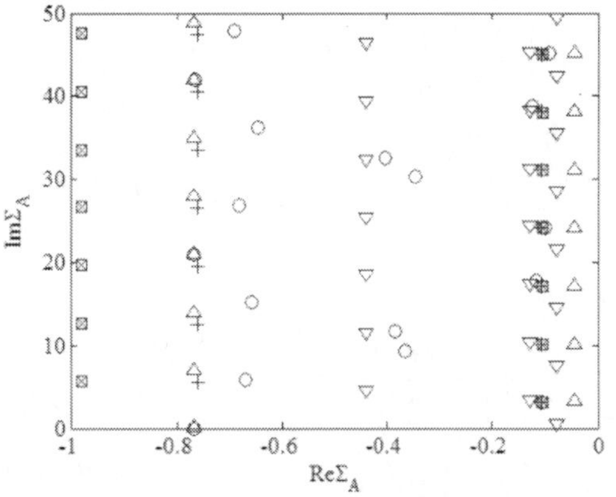

Figure 7. Σ_e, Σ_A for $\tau_0 = 0.9$, $s_{0,i}$ given by (16), non-iterative procedure.

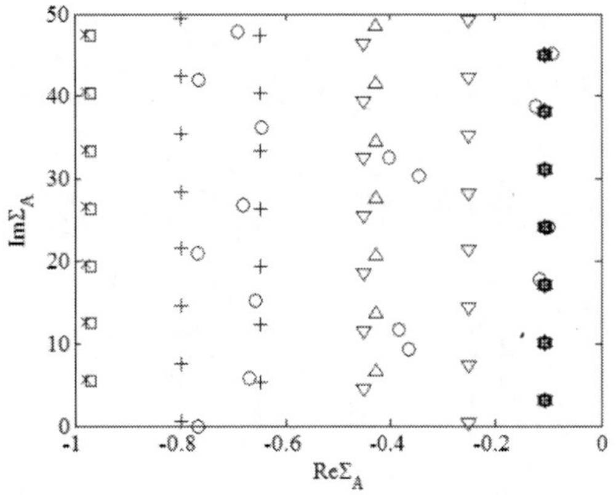

Figure 8. Σ_e, Σ_A for $\tau_0 = 0.9$, $s_{0,i}$ given by (16), iterative procedure.

Due to complex-values coefficients in $D_A(s)$, spectra are asymmetrical with respect to the real axis. More precisely, non-displayed roots are distributed according to (3). To get real-values coefficients, let us perform the last experiment in which all interpolations and extrapolations are made in $\operatorname{Re} s_0$ instead of s_0. However, $\operatorname{Im} s_0$ still plays a role in (12) and (13). With respect to the results from the experiment above, set $\tau_0 = 0.3$ and select two methods: The linear extrapolation one and the interpolation method with $s_{0,i}$ with the minimum modulus. The corresponding results are displayed in Figure 9 and Figure 10. Although the distribution of Σ_A in the complex plane is not as multifarious as in the previous experiment, positions of the roots give a very good estimation of Σ_e.

Eventual forms of $D_A(s)$ and some spectral and stability measures (see section 2) from the last two experiments for $\tau_0 = 0.3$ are given to the reader in Table 1.

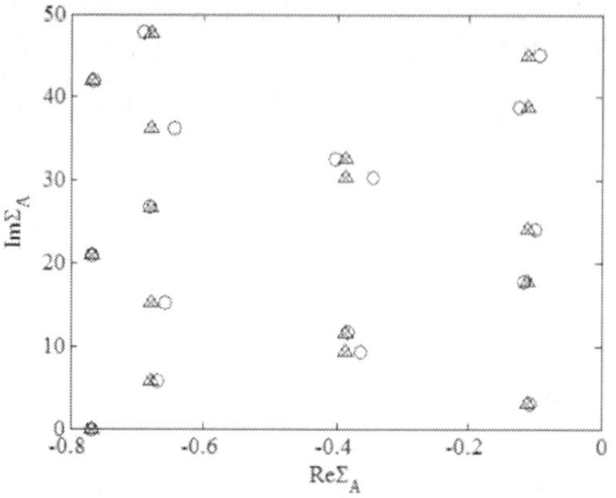

Figure 9. Σ_e, Σ_A for $\tau_0 = 0.3$, $s_{0,i}$ given by (16), real-valued coefficients in $D_A(s)$, non-iterative procedure.

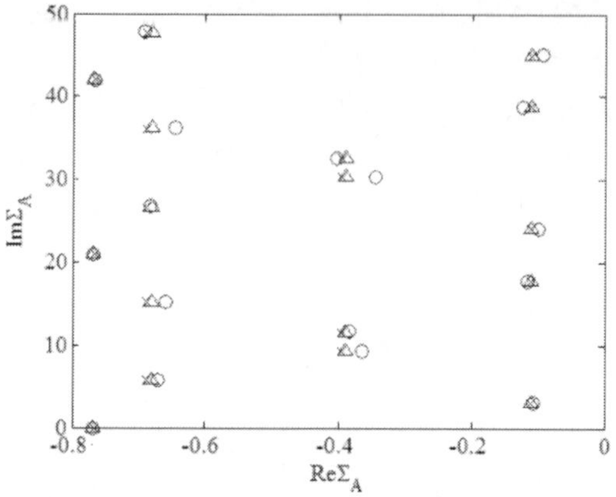

Figure 10. Σ_e, Σ_A for $\tau_0 = 0.3$, $s_{0,i}$ given by (16), real-valued coefficients in $D_A(s)$, iterative procedure.

Table 1. Resulting exponential polynomials and their measures.

Method	$D_A(s)$	α	ξ	c
I	$1+0.5\exp(-0.9s)+(-0.004613+0.006181i)\exp(-1.8s)$ $+(-0.392229-0.006943i)\exp(-2.1s)$	-0.107396	0.900007	-0.072978
I-R	$1+0.5\exp(-0.9s)-0.013108\exp(-1.8s)-0.38835\exp(-2.1s)$	-0.110071	0.901457	-0.071907
II	$1+0.5\exp(-0.9s)+(-0.00235+0.003148i)\exp(-1.8s)$ $+(-0.399557-0.007073i)\exp(-2.1s)+(0.00202+0.002917i)\exp(-2.4s)$	-0.107396	0.907096	-0.070089
III	$1+0.5\exp(-0.9s)+(-0.004613+0.006181i)\exp(-1.8s)$ $+(-0.392229-0.006943i)\exp(-2.1s)$	-0.107396	0.900007	-0.072978
IV	$1+0.5\exp(-0.9s)+(-0.025823+0.071838i)\exp(-1.8s)$ $+(-0.328624-0.027388i)\exp(-2.1s)$	-0.107396	0.906101	-0.069245
V	$1+0.5\exp(-0.9s)+(-0.007814+0.004075i)\exp(-1.8s)$ $+(-0.392076-0.003236i)\exp(-2.1s)$	-0.107395	0.900902	-0.072278
V-R	$1+0.5\exp(-0.9s)-0.008744\exp(-1.8s)-0.391348\exp(-2.1s)$	-0.107395	0.900092	-0.072925

In Table 1, method "I" and "I-R" means the linear extrapolation with complex- and real-valued coefficients, respectively; quadratic extrapolation method is denoted as "II"; the Taylor's series expansion is denoted as method "III"; and the interpolation methods with $s_{0,i}$ in a vertical chain and $s_{0,i}$ with the minimum modulus are denoted as "IV" and "V", respectively. Finally, the last one submethod giving real-valued coefficients is denoted as "V-R". The original $D_a(s)$ as in (15) has $\alpha = -0.107396$, $\xi = 0.9$, $c = -0.072978$.

All the methods give almost identical spectral abscissa that is, surprisingly, better than the original one. This is, however, due to the identified dominant root in the selected subset of the complex plane located left from the exact spectral abscissa. Another interesting result is given by method "II": A relatively high value of ξ and a low value of c. This is becase of a higher value of $k_{\max}$.

In general, strong stability becomes worse under the approximation.

5 Conclusions

Several possible methods of the characteristic exponential polynomial approximation for systems with neutral delays have been proposed and compared by an example. The goal has been to get commensurate delays for a simpler spectral properties determination.

We have i.a. found that the simple linear extrapolation procedure gives satisfactory results and almost keeps basic spectral and (strong exponential) stability measures compared to the original; moreover, it coincides with Taylor series expansion with the linear delay expansion. Both the approximated and approximating spectra are matched best via the quadratic extrapolation method and the interpolation method that uses the dominant roots with the minimum modulus. On the contrary, the interpolation in points given by the vertical strip of roots has given poor results. An idea how to obtain real-valued coefficients has also been given to the reader.

In the future research, the natural extension of this work may lie in a complex commensurate or a finite-dimensional approximation of the whole characteristic quasipolynomial.

Acknowledgements

This work was supported by the Ministry of Education, Youth and Sports of the Czech Republic within the National Sustainability Programme project No. LO1303 (MSMT-7778/2014) and also by the European Regional Development Fund under the project CEBIA-Tech No. CZ.1.05/2.1.00/03.0089.

References

1. J.K. Hale, S.M. Verduyn Lunel, *Introduction to functional differential equations* (Springer, New York, 1993)
2. K. Gu, V.L. Kharitonov, J. Chen, *Stability of time-delay systems* (Birkhäuser, Boston, 2003)
3. K.E. Walton, J.E. Marshall, IEE P-Contr. Theor. Ap. **134**, 2 (1987)
4. T. Vyhlídal, *Analysis and synthesis of time delay system spectrum* (Ph.D. thesis, Faculty of Mechanical Engineering, Czech Technical University in Prague, Prague, 2003)
5. D. Breda, S. Maset, R. Vermiglio, SIAM J. Sci. Comput. **27**, 2 (2005)
6. C. Bonnet, A.R. Fioravanti, J.R. Partington, SIAM J. Control. Optim. **49** (2011)
7. T. Vyhlídal, J.F. Lafay, R. Sipahi, *Delay systems: From theory to numerics and applications* (Springer-Verlag, New York, 2014)
8. S. Sönmez, S. Ayasun, C.O. Nwankpa, IEEE Trans. Power Syst. **31**, 1 (2015)
9. W. Michiels, S.-I. Niculescu, SIAM J. Control Optim. **45**, 6 (2007)
10. W. Michiels, K. Engelborghs, D. Roose, D. Dochain, SIAM J. Control Optim. **40**, 4 (2001)
11. W. Michiels, T. Vyhlídal, H. Nijmeijer, D. Henrion, SIAM J. Control Optim. **48**, 2 (2009)
12. T. Vyhlídal, P. Zítek, in *Delay systems: From theory to numerics and applications*, T. Vyhlídal, J.F. Lafay, R. Sipahi (eds.) (Springer, New York, 2014)
13. L. Pekař, in *Recent Advances in Systems* (*Proc. 19th Int. Conf. Systems*, Zakynthos, Greece) (IEEE, New Jersey, Piscataway, 2015)
14. W. Michiels, S.-I. Niculescu, *Stability and stabilization of time-delay systems* (SIAM, Philadelphia, 2007)
15. J.K. Hale, S.M. Verduyn Lunel, IMA J. Math. Control Inform. **19**, 1-2 (2002)
16. L. Pekař, P. Navrátil, in *Automation Control Theory Perspectives in Intelligent Systems* (*Proceedings of the 5th Computer Science On-line Conference 2016 (CSOC2016)* **3**), R. Šilhavý et al. (eds.) (Springer, 2016)

Mixed-integer MPC for the temperature control of the batch reactor

Jakub Novák[a] and Petr Chalupa

Faculty of Applied Informatics, Tomas Bata University in Zlin, 76001 Zlin, Czech Republic

Abstract. Discrete Model Predictive Control (MPC) became one of the most widespread modern control principles. Process controls with a finite number of admissible values are common in a large number of relevant applications. For this type of optimization problems, the computational complexity is exponential in the number of binary optimization variables. The solver is based on a standard branch-and-bound method and interior point method is used for solution of the relaxed problem. The simulation experiment involved controlling the temperature of a batch reactor by using two on/off input valves and a discrete-position mixing valve.

1 Introduction

Model Predictive Control (MPC) has become of the most widespread modern control strategies which have been successfully applied in many industrial applications. The idea of MPC is to determine an optimal control at the current time instant by solving an optimal control problem on a prediction horizon. The main reason for the wide-scale adoption of MPC is its ability to handle constraints on inputs and states that arise in most applications. MPC requires process model that allows it to react to future changes of the reference signal. MPC also naturally handles the multidimensional systems. Process controls with a finite number of admissible values are common in a large number of relevant applications. For example, chemical plants are equipped with valves that can be either open or closed. Hybrid systems represent a unified framework for modelling such processes that combine continuous and discrete dynamic with logical rules and appear in various applications like robotic systems and automotives. Bemporad and Morari [1] introduced a special class of hybrid systems called Mixed Logical Dynamical (MLD) systems. They can effectively model a variety of systems: hybrid automata, nonlinear systems with the nonlinearity represented by the piece-wise affine functions, linear systems with constraints, etc. The interest in hybrid systems has grown considerably during the last decade because of its potential impact on the industrial applications of control. Hybrid systems arise naturally in areas such as automotive systems [2], chemical systems [3] or power systems [4]. In all of these applications, there are several operation modes in the plant that justify the implementation of a hybrid MPC controller.

MPC is a general approach for control of hybrid systems. However, the optimization problem is no longer quadratic programming (QP) problem but a Mixed-Integer Quadratic Programming (MIQP) problem. The inclusion of integer variables turns the easily solved QP problem, into an NP-hard problem [2]. It has been demonstrated in the recent research that convex QP problem can be solved at high sampling rates on embedded computing platforms [5]. The main methods are tailored optimization methods for particular embedded platform. Several application of embedded MIQP solvers have been proposed in [6], [7]. Many methods have been developed for solution of the MIQP problem, however branch-and-bound method have proved superior to other methods such as decomposition method or logic-based method [8]. Authors in Ref [9] provide a review of computational methods of solving MIQP problems. CPLEX and GUROBI represent a commercial optimization software that is able to solve the MIQP problems and also several toolboxes for MATLAB exists (OPTI Toolbox which uses SCIP solver [10], Hybrid toolbox [11]).

In this paper, MLD approach is used for modelling and predictive control of a batch reactor as a switched linear system.

2 Mixed logical dynamical systems

The MLD modelling framework is based on the idea of translating logic relations, discrete/logic dynamics, A/D (analogue to digital (logic)), D/A conversion and logic constraints into mixed integer linear inequalities. These inequalities are combined with the continuous dynamical part, which is described by linear difference equations. The resulting MLD system is described by the following relations:

[a] Corresponding author: jnovak@fai.utb.cz

$$\begin{aligned} x(k+1) &= A\,x(k) + B_1\,u(k) + B_2\,\delta(k) \\ &\quad + B_3\,z(k) + B_0 \\ y(k) &= Cx(k) + D_1u(k) + D_2\delta(k) \\ &\quad + D_3z(k) + D_0 \\ E_2\delta(k) + E_3\,z(k) &\le A\,x(k) + E_1u(k) \\ &\quad + E_4x(k) + E_5 \end{aligned} \tag{1}$$

where

$x = \begin{bmatrix} x_c \\ x_b \end{bmatrix}, x_c \in R^{n_c}, x_b = \{0,1\}^{n_b}, n_x = n_c + n_b$ x are the system states,

$y = \begin{bmatrix} y_c \\ y_b \end{bmatrix}, y_c \in R^{p_c}, y_b = \{0,1\}^{p_b}, n_y = p_c + p_b$ are the system outputs combining contionuous and binary outptus and

$u = \begin{bmatrix} u_c \\ u_b \end{bmatrix}, u_c \in R^{m_c}, u_b = \{0,1\}^{m_b}, n_u = m_c + m_b$ are the command inputs and may also contain continuous and binary commands, δ and z are respectively auxiliary logical and continuous variables. The auxiliary variables are introduced when translating propositional logic into linear inequalities. In order to be well posed, the MLD system (1) must be such that for any given x(k) and u(k) the values of δ(k) and z(k) are defined uniquely.

3 Predictive control of MLD systems

In [12], Bemporad and Morari introduced a model predictive control of hybrid systems using mixed logical dynamical (MLD) system description and a mixed integer linear program solver. Assuming a quadratic cost function from the MLD model the optimization has the following form:

$$\min J(u,z,\delta) = \sum_{k=0}^{N-1} \begin{matrix} \|u(k) - u_e\|_{Q_1}^2 + \|z(k) - z_e\|_{Q_2}^2 + \\ + \|\delta(k) - \delta_e\|_{Q_3}^2 \end{matrix} \tag{2}$$

Subjected to equations which define the MLD system for N steps ahead predictions. The matrices Q_1, Q_2, Q_3, Q_4 are given weight matrices. This problem can be rewritten to a standard MIQP programing form:

$$\begin{aligned} &\min 0.5\left[\boldsymbol{x}_c^T, \boldsymbol{x}_i^T\right] \boldsymbol{H} \begin{bmatrix} \boldsymbol{x}_c^T \\ \boldsymbol{x}_i^T \end{bmatrix} + f^T \begin{bmatrix} \boldsymbol{x}_c^T \\ \boldsymbol{x}_i^T \end{bmatrix} \\ &x_c \in R^{n_c}, x_i \in N^{n_i} : \boldsymbol{a}_j^T \begin{bmatrix} \boldsymbol{x}_c^T \\ \boldsymbol{x}_i^T \end{bmatrix} + b_j = 0, \quad j = 1,\dots,m_{ec} \\ &\boldsymbol{c}_j^T \begin{bmatrix} \boldsymbol{x}_c^T \\ \boldsymbol{x}_i^T \end{bmatrix} + d_j \ge 0, \quad j = 1,\dots,m_{ic} \end{aligned} \tag{3}$$

where n_c and n_i define the numbers of continuous and integer variables, $\boldsymbol{H}$ is a positive definite matrix, $\boldsymbol{f}$ is the n-dimensional vector. The n-dimensional vectors a_j and c_j and vectors $\boldsymbol{b}$ and $\boldsymbol{d}$ are used to set up the constraints. The numbers of equality and inequality constraints are specified with m_{ec} and m_{ic}, respectively. The equality and inequality constraints define a feasible region in which the solution to the problem must be located in order for the constraints to be satisfied. The optimization procedure of (3) leads to problems with the following optimization vector :

$$\begin{aligned} x = [&u(k),\dots,u(k+N-1), \delta(k),\dots,\delta(k+N-1),\dots \\ &z(k),\dots,z(k+N-1)] \end{aligned} \tag{4}$$

Mixed Integer Quadratic Program (MIQP) represents a non-convex optimization problem with quadratic objective function and linear constraints. The non-convexity is caused by the fact that the optimized variables xi belong to the binary set. The only difference between the convex QP and MIQP is the presence of binary variables x_i which makes system non-convex. Fortunately, for relaxed or fixed binary variables the problem becomes convex and can be solved using methods for convex optimization. In practice a constrained QP is usually solved either using an interior point method or an active set method.

Active set method searches for optimum solution by scanning the boundary of the problem's feasible region. It moves from a point on the boundary to another point that has better value of the objective function. This process is repeated until the optimal solution is found. With the interior point method the solution that is obtained at each iteration never lies on the boundary of the feasible region. Interior point methods solve the general inequality constrained problem by converting it to an equality constrained problem. Solution is reached by solving KKT (Karush-Kuhn-Tucker) conditions of this problem. There are two famous types of interior point methods; Barrier method and Primal-Dual interior point method. Due to higher efficiency, the primal-dual interior method is used in the paper for the solution of the following problem:

$$\begin{aligned} &\min 0.5\boldsymbol{x}^T \boldsymbol{H} \boldsymbol{x} + \boldsymbol{f}^T \boldsymbol{x} \\ &x \in R^n : \boldsymbol{A}_c \boldsymbol{x} + \boldsymbol{b}_c = 0 \\ &\boldsymbol{C}_c \boldsymbol{x} + \boldsymbol{d}_c \ge 0 \end{aligned} \tag{5}$$

where A_c is a m_{ec} x n matrix describing the equality constraints and C_c is a m_{ic} x n matrix describing the inequality constraints. b_c and d_c are m_{ec} x n and m_{ic} x n vectors respectively.

The primal-dual method uses some variations to Newton methods. Newton's method is used to solve the KKT conditions of the constrained QP problem. The concept of Newton's method is to calculate a direction that points toward improving the value of the objective function. The strategy is improved with methods like central path and path-following. These modifications improve the speed of convergence by allowing the algorithm to take large steps in the calculated search direction.

Using a brute force approach to find the optimal solution all of the QPs (LPs) that are associated to all the feasible combinations of the discrete decision variables would have to be solved. The solution of MIQP would be the minimum of the solutions of all these problems. For n_i Boolean decision (input) variables, the number of possible QP (LP) problems is 2^{ni}.

Fortunately, efficient methods can be used for solution of this type of problem. Branch-and-bound has been the most used tool for solving large scale NP-hard combinatorial optimization problems since the branch-and-bound method is an order of magnitude faster than any of the other methods such as Generalized Benders Decomposition or Outer Approximation. The method is so fast due to the fact that that the QP subproblems are easy to solve. For MATLAB, free software like YALMIP [13] can be used. At any time in the solution process, the status of the solution is given by a pool of yet unexplored subset of the solution space and by the best solution that has been found so far. The algorithm dynamically generates a search tree, which initially contains only one node called the root. At each iteration of a classical branch-and-bound algorithm only one node that represents unexplored subspaces is processed. The iteration consists of two main components: selection of the next node to process and strategy for branching. The nodes that created via branching strategy are stored together with the bound of the currently processed node. The search stops when the pool of unexplored subset is empty and then the optimal solution is the one recorded as "current best".

There are two basic node selection strategies for next node to proceed. The first one is best-first-search, where the next node is always the one with the lowest dual bound. However, this method has high storage requirements. The second type of node selection strategies is the depth-first-search where warm-starting can be successfully applied since the subproblems are similar and also number of unexplored nodes is low, so this method does not require a lot memory for nodes storage. Branching on a variable involves choosing the branching variable of the current optimal solution of the relaxed problem and then adding a constraint to it. The maximum fractional branching strategy is used in the solver and this method uses the variable with the highest fractional part for branching. The scheme of branch-and-bound method is depicted in Figure 1.

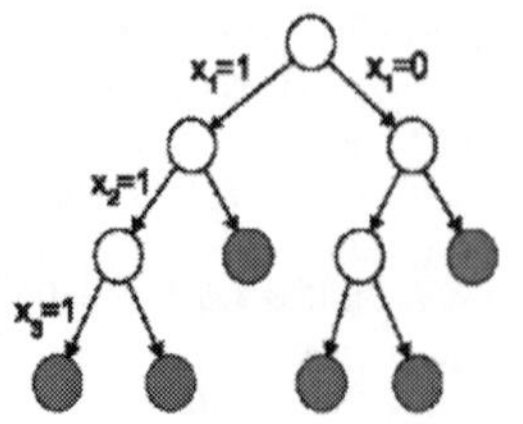

Figure 1. Branch-and-bound algorithm.

4 Relaxation of MIQP

In order to reduce the complexity of MIQP the constraints of binary variables can be relaxed, i.e. binary variables are allowed to span over the continuous interval [0,1] and the problem can be solved as a QP problem. In the receding horizon scheme only the first control action is applied so the later stages can be relaxed as result of trade-off of computation time for performance. For given prediction horizon H_p, after H_r ($H_r<H_p$) steps the binary variables are relaxed to the continuous interval [0,1].

5 Simulation results

The developed predictive controller was tested on a simulation example of a real batch reactor with the parameters from the paper [14]. The goal is to control the temperature of the ingredients stirred in the reactor core so that they synthesize into the final product. The main task is to control the temperature in the reactor as accurately as possible. A scheme of the batch reactor is shown in Figure 2. The reactor's core (temperature T) is heated or cooled through the reactor's water jacket (temperature Tw) in which there is a mixture of fresh input water, which enters the reactor through an on/off valve and reflux water. The dynamics of the system depend on the physical properties of the ingredients in the batch reactor's core. The temperature of the fresh input water T_{in} depends on two inputs: the positions of the on/off valves k_H and k_C. Only one of them can be open at a time. The ratio of fresh input water to reflux water is controlled by the mixing valve k_M. There are six possible ratios that can be set by the mixing valve. The share of fresh input water can be either 0, 0.01, 0.02, 0.05, 0.1 or 1. Therefore the system has two binary inputs, one input with six admissible values and two measurable outputs (T and T_w). Due to the dynamics of the process the sampling period was set to 10s.

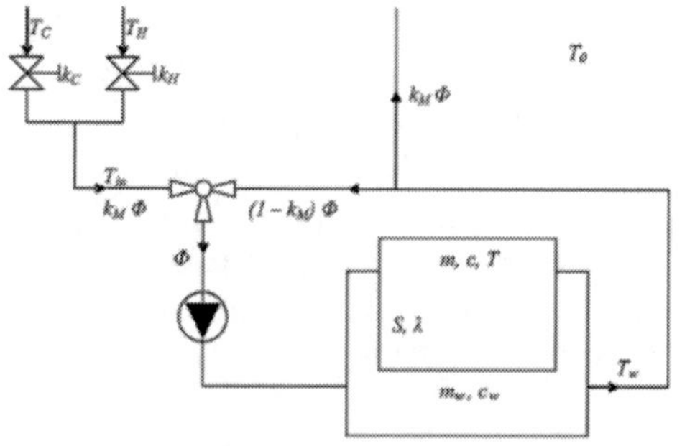

Figure 2. Scheme of batch reactor.

Hybrid linear model of the second order was developed in [15] by identification from the input –output data using the least-squares identification method. The model has the following form:

$$T_w(\mathrm{k}+1)=\begin{Bmatrix}\Theta_1[T_w(\mathrm{k})\ \mathrm{T(k)}\ \ k_M(\mathrm{k})\ 1]^T\ if\ k_C=0\\ \Theta_2[T_w(\mathrm{k})\ \mathrm{T(k)}\ \ k_M(\mathrm{k})\ 1]^T\ if\ k_C=1\end{Bmatrix}$$
$$T(\mathrm{k}+1)=0.9967T(\mathrm{k})+0.0033T_W(\mathrm{k}) \tag{6}$$
$$\Theta_1=\begin{bmatrix}0.9429 & 0.0395 & 10.5969 & 0.5273\end{bmatrix}$$
$$\Theta_2=\begin{bmatrix}0.9322 & 0.0466 & -7.8013 & 0.5650\end{bmatrix}$$

The set of possible input variables $[k_M\ k_H\ k_C]^T$ is defined in

$$M=\left\{\begin{matrix}\begin{bmatrix}0\\0\\1\end{bmatrix},\begin{bmatrix}0.01\\0\\1\end{bmatrix},\begin{bmatrix}0.02\\0\\1\end{bmatrix},\begin{bmatrix}0.05\\0\\1\end{bmatrix},\dots\\ \begin{bmatrix}0.1\\0\\1\end{bmatrix},\begin{bmatrix}1\\0\\1\end{bmatrix},\begin{bmatrix}1\\1\\0\end{bmatrix}\end{matrix}\right\} \tag{7}$$

Using the HYSDEL Toolbox [16], problem (3) for the piece-wise affine system (6) is translated into a mixed integer quadratic program (MIQP), i.e., into the minimization of a quadratic cost function subject to linear constraints, where some of the variables are constrained to be binary or integer. The optimization problem is solved in the extended ($x;\ u;\ z;\ \delta$) space subjected to constraints, which increase the size of the problem dramatically.

The weighting matrices were defined as follows:

$$Q_1=\begin{bmatrix}10&0&0&0\\0&10&0&0\\0&0&10&0\\0&0&0&10\end{bmatrix}$$
$$\mathrm{Q}_2=\begin{bmatrix}100&0&0&0\\0&100&0&0\\0&0&100&0\\0&0&0&100\end{bmatrix}, \tag{8}$$
$$Q_3=diag([0\ \ 100\ \ 0\ \ 100\ \ 0\ \ 100\ \ 0\ \ 100])$$

The weighting matrix Q_2 weights the event of changing fresh input water from hot to cool. The value was set higher than Q_1 to prevent changes of valves k_H and k_C but low enough to allow the on/off valves to change when a reference step occurs. Q_3 weights the error between the predicted temperatures and reference signals. The highest values of weights are set on the reactors core temperature *T*.

The prediction of N = 4 was chosen as control and prediction horizon for batch reactor. The resulting optimization problem has 4 discrete variables (positions of the valve k_M), 4 binary variables (position of the valve k_H) and 8 continuous variables (auxiliary variables *z*) and 76 constraints. Either k_C or k_H can be open so the value of the k_C is computed as the negation of k_H. If all possible combinations of input signal were computed the solver would have to solve 20736 problems.

$$M=6^4 2^4=20736 \tag{9}$$

from which only

$$M=7^4=2401 \tag{10}$$

are valid because only k_M = 1 is allowed for cold water k_C=1 as given in the value set (7). Increasing the horizons may increase the performance of the controller, but it increases the complexity of the mixed-integer programming procedure. The choice of prediction horizon offers reasonable values in terms of performance and speed. The optimization was performed in MATLAB using the solver we developed in [17]] and extended from binary variables to integer variables. The optimization is computed in 200 ms to700 ms using a computer with 3 GHz PENTIUM-4 processor and 8GB of RAM. In order to reduce the complexity of the problem only inputs related to the prediction horizon 2 steps are considered integer and binary and inputs related to the horizon steps 3 and 4 are considered continuous and in the range <0,1>. Thus the problem is reduced to an optimization problem with 2 discrete variables, 2 binary variables and 12 continuous variables is computed in less than 200 ms. The computation time are shown in Figure 3. For clarity only the first 2000s of the experiment are presented.

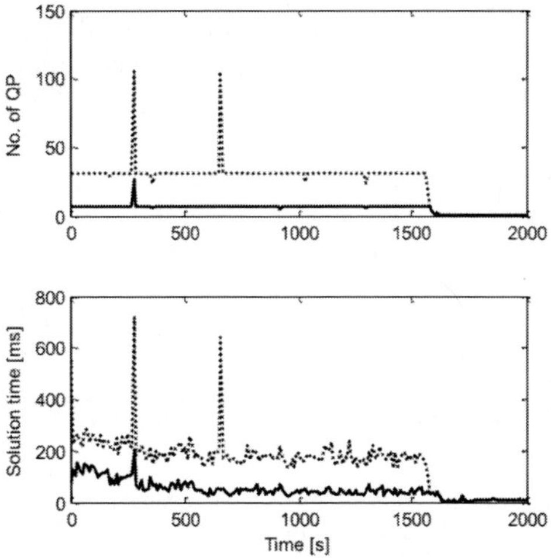

Figure 3. Optimization time and number of solved QP problems (original problem – solid line, reduced problem with relaxed variables – dotted line).

The initial value of the reference trajectory is set to 95 ∘C, so that the ingredients react at the optimal temperature. The control courses are presented on Figure 4. The similar control performance is obtained for control problem with horizon Hp=4 and for control problem with horizon H_p=4 but relaxed input variables from horizon H_r=3.

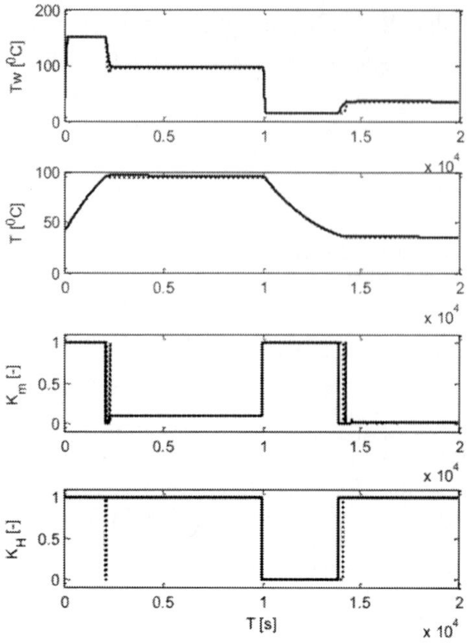

Figure 4. Control courses and input signals (relaxed problem – dotted line).

Conclusion

The predictive control of a batch-reactor system using MLD approach was evaluated. The temperature can be optimally controlled using MLD approach within the sampling period; however the complexity of mixed-integer optimization that appears in optimal control of MLD systems limits the application to short prediction horizon. With the relaxed constraints the suboptimal solution in general can be found, but as can be seen in the case of the batch reactor, the performance degradation may be minimal while the necessary computation times are reduced significantly.

Acknowledgment

This work was supported by the Ministry of Education, Youth and Sports of the Czech Republic within the National Sustainability Programme project No. LO1303 (MSMT-7778/2014).

References

1. A. Bemporad, M. Morari, Automatica **35,** 407-427 (1999)
2. F. Borrelli, A. Bemporad, M. Fodor, D. Hrovat, IEEE Transactions on Control Systems Technology **14**, 541-552 (2006)
3. J. Causaa, G. Karer, A. Núñez, D. Sáez, I. Škrjanc, B. Zupančič, Computers & Chemical Engineering **32**, 3254-3263 (2008)
4. J. Hlava, R. Horalek, Annals of DAAAM for 2009 & Proceedings of 20th DAAAM International Symposium Intelligent Manufacturing & Automation: Theory, Practice & Education (2009)
5. M. Kögel, R. Findeisen, Proceeding of the 50th IEEE Conference on Decision and Control and European Control Conference, 501–506 (2011)
6. D. Frick, A. Domahidi, M. Morari, Computers & Chemical Engineering **72**, 21-33 (2015)
7. J. Novak, P. Chalupa, Procedia Engineering **100**, 1649-1656 (2015)
8. O. V. Volkovich, V. A. Roshchin, and I. V. Sergienko. Cybernetics **23**, 289 – 305 (1987)
9. R.T. Meyer, M. Žefran and R. A. DeCarlo, IEEE Transactions on Control Systems Technology **22**, 1784-1800 (2014)
10. T. Achterberg, Mathematical Programming Computation **1**, 1-41 (2009)
11. A. Bemporad, Hybrid Toolbox - User's Guide,2004. http://cse.lab.imtlucca.it/~bemporad/hybrid/toolbox.
12. A. Bemporad, M. Morari, Automatica **35**, 407-427 (1999)
13. J. Lofberg, Proceedings of the IEEE International Symposium on Computer Aided Control Systems Design, 284-289 (2004)
14. G. Karer, I. Skrjanc, B. Zupancic, Chemical Engineering and Processing **47**, 2379–2385 (2008)
15. G. Karer, G. Music, I. Skrjanc, B. Zupancic, Journal of Intelligent Robotic System **20**, 297-319 (2007)
16. F.D. Torrisi, A. Bemporad, IEEE Transactions on Control Systems Technology **12**, 235-249 (2004)
17. J. Novak, P. Chalupa, International Journal of Cicrcuits, Systems and Signal Processing **10**, 200-207 (2016)

MATEC Web of Conferences **76**, 02014 (2016) DOI: 10.1051/matecconf/20167602014
CSCC 2016

Thermal energy storage in the form of heat or cold with using of the PCM-based accumulation panels

Jan Skovajsa[1,a], Martin Koláček[1] and Martin Zálešák[1]

[1]*Tomas Bata University in Zlin, Faculty of Applied Informatics, Department of Automation and Control Engineering, Nad Stranemi 4511, Zlin, Czech Republic*

Abstract. This article describes the usage of thermal energy storage in the form of heat and cold with an adaptation of the special device which is composed of the thermal panels. These panels are based on the phase change materials (PCM) for normal inner environment temperature in buildings. The energy for the thermal energy storage is possible to get from built-in electric heating foil or from the tube heat exchanger, which is build in the thermal panels. This technology is able to use renewable energy sources, for example, solar thermal collectors and air-to-water heat pump as a source of heat for heating of the hot water tank. In the cooling mode, there is able to use the heat pump or photovoltaics panels in combination with thermoelectric coolers for cooling.

1 Introduction

One of the biggest disadvantages of modern lightweight structures is the lack of thermal mass. It may cause overheating in the summer or problems with keeping the heat in the winter. This problem can be solved by using f the thermal energy storage, which can be defined as the temporary storage of thermal energy. It is the accumulation of heat in the materials, specifically in the building structures. [1] These structures transferring their heat to the surrounding when the ambient air temperature drops. During the planning of a building can be minimized the use of cooling devices or even avoid them, mainly due to good thermal accumulation parameters of construction materials.

Thermal energy can be accumulated as sensible or latent heat. Both are not special forms of energy. They describe exchanges of heat in terms of their effect on a material or a thermodynamic system. Sensible heat is heat exchanged by a thermodynamic system that changes the temperature of the system without changing some variables such as volume or pressure. The sensible heat possessed by an object is evidenced by its temperature. Latent heat is associated with changes of state, measured at almost constant temperature. PCMs use a combination of sensible and latent heat.

The main parameter of the accumulation of sensible heat is the specific heat capacity. This parameter determines an amount of energy needed to change the temperature of 1 kg of the substance by 1 K. The amount of sensible heat energy is calculated from the equation (1).

$$Q = m \cdot \int_{T_f}^{T_i} c_p \, \mathrm{d}T \qquad (1)$$

[a] Corresponding author: jskovajsa@fai.utb.cz

Where m is mass [kg]
T_i initial temperature [K]
T_f final temperature [K]
c_p specific heat capacity [$J \cdot kg^{-1}K^{-1}$]

In the case of accumulation of latent heat, latent heat is consumed or released during the phase change of the material. During this phase transition temperature remains almost constant and there is the possibility to store large amounts of energy into the material. However, there may be a slight change in volume. The total amount of stored energy is determined by changes in enthalpy. The amount of energy is determined from the enthalpy value during the phase change, in the solid state and in the liquid state, according to the following equation (2).

$$\Delta Q = m \cdot \Delta h \qquad (2)$$

Where m is mass [kg]
Δh enthalpy change [$J \cdot kg^{-1}$]

Figure 1 shows the principle of thermal energy storage in the form of latent and sensible heat in the PCMs.

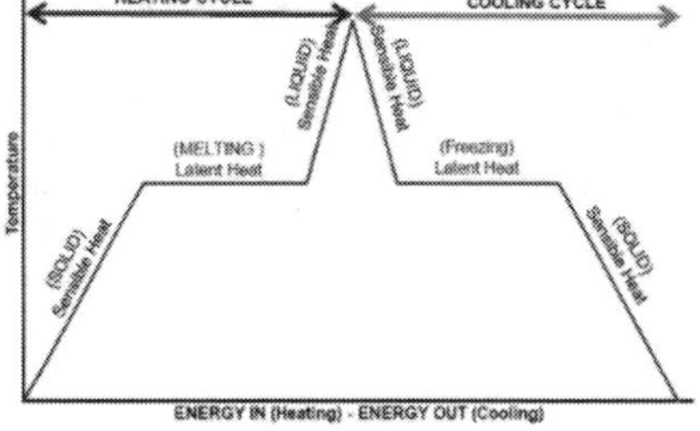

Figure 1. Heating and cooling of PCM. [2]

Essentially all materials can be considered for PCM. However, the characteristics required for effective and predictable thermal energy storage excludes a large number of materials. Suitable PCMs for households are paraffin, eventually salt hydrates.

Paraffin-based PCMs with a mixture of a polyethylene uses molecular-encapsulation, which is caused by high concentrations of the polymer compound of material. Molecules are designed to that the connection of the individual molecules of the wax creates a homogeneous mixture. Thus formed structure is a highly durable material with a wide operating temperature range from 0 °C to 40 °C. Molecular-encapsulation also allows drilling and cutting through the material without any PCM leakage. [3]

Today's classic cooling systems are used for room cooling, and these ensure that the rooms are cooled to a comfortable temperature in all environment climates. These systems are effective, but they would have a higher energy efficiency if they used the natural temperature differences between day and night for the purpose of cooling. In these cases, can be applied PCMs that reduce overheating of the room by storing the redundant heat during the day and releasing it during the night. [1]

The PCMs can be used to utilize by natural heat and cold sources, for example, solar energy for heating during the evening and night or the use of night cold for cooling during the day. Furthermore, PCM can use manmade heat or cold sources. In addition, there are different possible uses of the PCMs. In buildings can be placed building structures such as are walls or ceilings, or can be arranged into separate storages of heat or cold. In buildings, the PCMs are often used as passive systems. Using PCMs in separate heat or cold storages are usually based on active systems. Heat or cold is stored in separate storages outside the building and heat or cold transfer is on demand. An interesting option is a technology based on the active system with combination of renewable energy sources. [4]

Nowadays, accumulation of energy in the form of heat or cold is done with large heat storage tanks, or passive accumulation elements, e.g. PCM panels. These commercial PCMs can also be used in active systems, e.g. in ventilation systems, cooling ceilings, cooling beams etc. These active systems are affecting the temperature of the air flow around the element from PCM. It follows that the use of PCM for energy storage is possible and it has already used in some systems, or the new ways of utilization are developed and tested.

The technology, which is proposed in this article is based on commercial PCM panels. The used PCM panels are grouped to one active element including some other technical devices, allowing active management of deliveries of heat or cold, which is obtained from standard external energy sources. The fundamental difference between the standard solutions and proposed technology are the ability to use energy that is gained from any available energy sources including renewable energy sources, e.g. photovoltaics, heat pumps, solar thermal collectors or electrical thermocouples. Another difference is the ability of the active electric cooling, which is not quite common in the PCM devices.

2 Methods

2.1 Technology

Measurement of parameters was done on the active technology for heating and cooling with the accumulation of heat or cold, which is located in a laboratory at the Faculty of Applied Informatics of Tomas Bata University in Zlín in the Czech Republic. This system is composed of two thermal accumulation panels. Dimensions of one panel are 1.25 x 0.083 x 2.07 m and each of them is composed of 6 layers of PCM panels DuPont Energain. The rear part of panels is insulated and between layers of the PCM panels is imposed copper tube heat exchanger for heating and cooling. The heat exchanger is connected to the water tanks with cold or hot water. There are also imposed three electric heating foils inside the panels.

The mass of thermal panels is composed from mixture of polyethylene and paraffin wax. Paraffin wax is in the solid state at temperatures below 18 °C. When the temperature of panels rises above 18 °C, the wax begin to melt and absorb up to 515 kJ·m^{-2} of heat between 18 °C to 24 °C. Its melting point is about 22 °C, which corresponds to a standard indoor temperature conditions. [4]

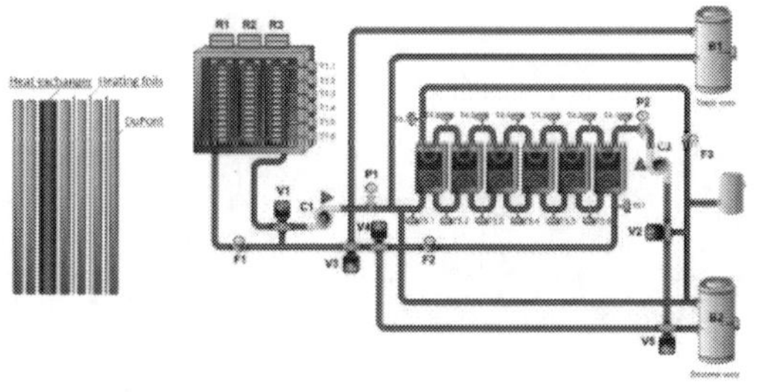

Figure 2. Storage panel and technology scheme. [6]

Figure 2 shows hydraulic connection technology that can use different heat sources, including renewable energy sources. The technology is powered from 230V AC power grid and it can also be powered from the photovoltaic system. The photovoltaic system consists of 9 polycrystalline photovoltaic panels with a total area of 11.25 m^2. Energy efficiency of a photovoltaic system was set at 11 to 13% in the earlier measurements.

Technology is further equipped with a thermoelectric coolers which may be powered by photovoltaic panels or from the power grid. Heating of the hot water tank is done by solar thermal collectors or air-to-water heat pump. The heat pump could be also used for cooling of the cold water tank.

2.2 Operation of technology

Technology for the accumulation of heat or cold can be operated in different modes which depend on requirements. The technology can be used as a standard passive system. In this mode, technology accumulates heat or cold and for reduction of the temperature peaks and keeps temperature stable in the monitored room during the day and night. The technology can also be operated in active mode. In this mode, the technology is able to influence the room temperature by accumulating of the heat or cold which is obtained from external sources. Individual operating modes are described in the following paragraphs of the text.

- **Heating of thermal panels by electric heating foils**
Electric heating foils are installed inside the panel and divided into three sections. Each section has an output of 600 W. Switching of individual sections depends on the temperature of the panel or on the performance of photovoltaics. [6]

- **Heating of thermal panels from the hot water tank**
Inside the thermal panels is tube heat exchanger to transfer heat from the hydraulic part of technology. The hot water tank can be heated by any other installed technology which is available. It is possible to use a heat pump, solar thermal collectors or an electric boiler in this case.

- **Cooling of thermal panels from the cold water tank**
The principle of this mode is similar to the previous mode. This mode also uses a heat exchanger and cold water tank can be cooled by the cooling mode of the heat pump.

- **Cooling of thermal panels by thermoelectric coolers**
Thermocouples are used for the cooling mode. They are able to reach a low temperature but it is necessary to ensure the cooling of their hot sides, because these sides produce large amounts of waste heat. The installed system uses a hydraulic circuit for removing of cold from the thermoelectric elements into thermal panels and a second circuit for waste heat dissipation. The number of switched on elements depends on the amount of supplied energy from photovoltaics. [6]

- **Removing of heat or cold from the thermal panels**
The technology can also be used without active cooling or heating for stored energy in the panels to be transferred into the hot or cold water tank.

2.3 Measurement

The aim of the measurement was to determine the changing of the ambient temperature during the heating mode and cooling. There were measured different parameters, but the most important were measurements of temperatures inside the panels, the temperatures of their surfaces, the flow of heat transfer fluid and its temperatures at the inlet and outlet of the exchanger. Furthermore, there was measured the temperature in the room and outdoor temperature by own weather station.

The surface of one panel is painted with black matt paint, see figure 3, which increases the emissivity of the surface and thus also the heat transfer coefficient. Previous research has established the average heat transfer coefficient to a value of 4.1 $Wm^{-2}K^{-1}$ for the unmodified surface and 8.3 $Wm^{-2}K^{-1}$ for the panel with a modified surface. Another important parameter is the time constant which is around 6.8 hours for the unmodified surface and around 5.5 hours for the modified surface. The time constant of one PCM panel is approximately 75 min. [8]

Figure 3. Thermal panels with the original and modified surfaces.

From the measured parameters it was possible to determine the amount of heat or power that was supplied into or removed from the thermal panels by the heat exchanger. The amount of heat and power can be calculated from the equation (1) and the following equation (3).

$$P = \dot{m} \cdot c_p \cdot \Delta\theta \qquad (3)$$

Where $\dot{m}$ is mass flow [$kg \cdot s^{-1}$]
c_p specific heat capacity [$J \cdot kg^{-1}K^{-1}$]
$\Delta\theta$ temperature difference [°C, K]

3 Results

Measurement of heating of PCMs has already been examined many times. Another specific utilization is the use of the PCMs in the form of cooling elements. Important parameter of heat accumulation of material is its specific heat capacity. The used PCM has this value around 6800 $Jkg^{-1}K^{-1}$ in the temperature range from 10 °C to 21 °C. The main limiting factor of cooling devices is the risk of condensation of water vapor. So it must be ensured that the surface temperature was at least 1 K above the dew point temperature.

Figure 4 shows the measurement results of piece of PCM plate which had been cooled to a temperature of 9 °C in a cooling chamber and then it was placed in a room with an air temperature of 23.5 °C. The test sample had dimensions of 0.5 x 0.5 meters and a thickness of 5 mm. The chart shows the behavior of the material, especially in terms of time which is required for reaching room temperature. This material represents nonstandard possibility of using in cooling systems, mainly due to its good parameters.

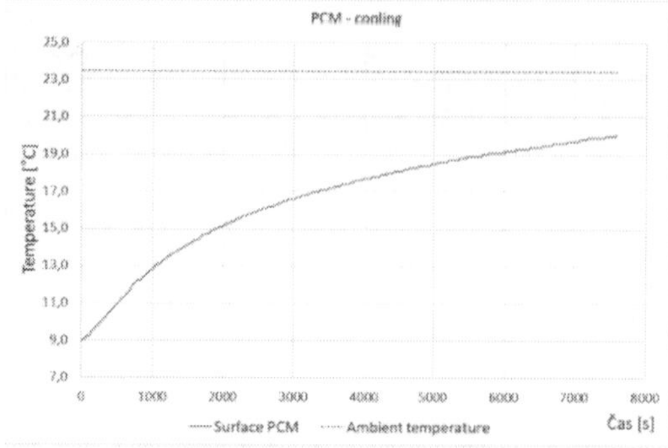

Figure 4. PCM with an initial temperature of 9 °C placed in a room with a constant temperature of 23.5 °C.

There were been done three different measurements on the technology. The first measurement represents the using of active heating mode, see figure 5. The second measurement represents standard passive mode, see figure 6. The last measurement represents active cooling mode, see figure 7. Heating and cooling of water in water tanks was made by the solar thermal collectors and heat pump.

Active heating mode in figure 5 shows the progress of heating of the thermal panels. At the beginning, it is possible to see that the surface temperature increased slightly, but then the temperature began to rise dramatically. This effect occurred when material has ceased to accumulate latent heat and has started to accumulate only sensible heat. Thermal panels were able to increase the temperature of the air in the room during the day and keep it during the following night. Energy supplied to the panels was 1.9 kWh. In passive mode, the thermal panels were able to keep an air temperature steadily, see figure 6.

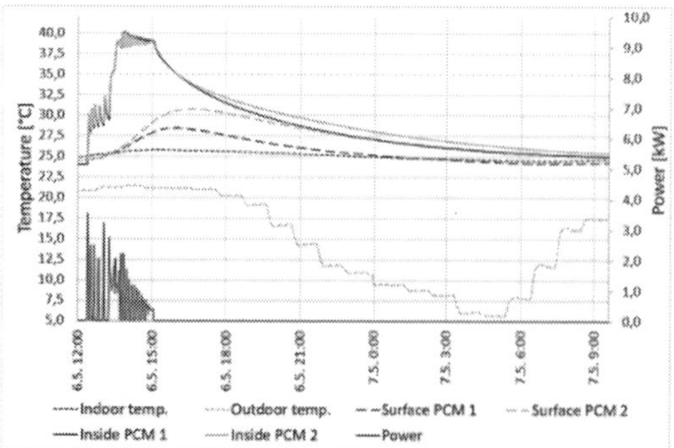

Figure 5. Active mode – heating.

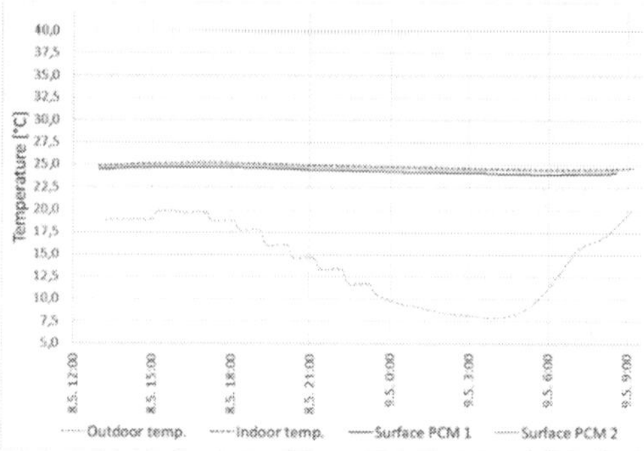

Figure 6. Passive mode.

Active cooling mode in figure 7 shows the progress of cooling of the thermal panels. It is possible to see the effect of surface modification. A time of change of the surface temperatures from 21.2 °C to 17.7 °C (unmodified surface) and from 22.4 °C to 19.8 °C (modified surface) was around 9 hours. During this cooling, the total amount of energy drained from thermal panels was 3.7 kWh. Heating time was approximately 24 hours.

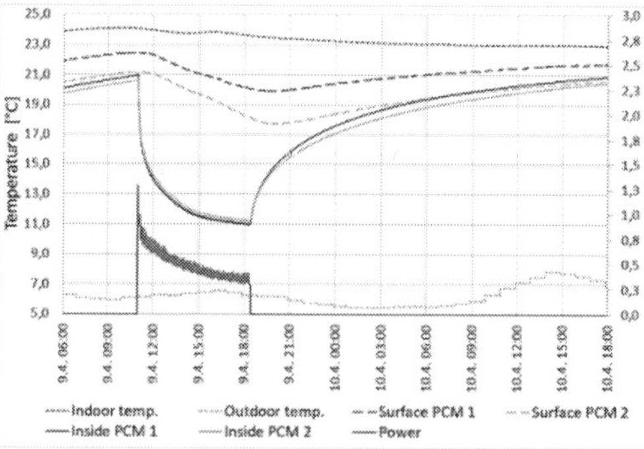

Figure 7. Active mode – cooling.

4 Conclusion

The main activity of this research was to measure parameters of the thermal panels based on PCMs.

The advantage of the proposed technology is optimizing parameters of thermal energy storage in buildings and the related achieving better thermal comfort inside the room. Furthermore, there is another advantage, which is the combination of passive and active systems with the use of renewable energy sources. Next advantage is the possibility to control the temperature in the monitored room, but unfortunately, it is possible only in a limited range. This problem is caused by low efficiency at a given size. The problematic factor is a low heat transfer coefficient. Deficiencies can be solved by forced convection and better position of accumulation panels.

The research will continue making changes to convective parameters and using the renewable energy sources.

Acknowledgement

This work was supported by the Ministry of Education, Youth and Sports of the Czech Republic within the National Sustainability Programme project No. LO1303 (MSMT-7778/2014) and also by the European Regional Development Fund under the project CEBIA-Tech No. CZ.1.05/2.1.00/03.0089 and also by internal grant agency of Tomas Bata University in Zlin no. IGA/CEBIA-Tech/2016/001

References

1. Joint Implementation Network, *Energy Storage: Phase Change Materials for Thermal Energy Storage* (ClimateTechWiki, 2010)
2. W. Sutterlin, *A brief comparison of ice packs, salts, paraffins and vegetable-derived phase change materials* (Plymount: PureTemp, 2014).
3. L. Sánchez, P. Sánchez, A.D. Lucas, M. Carmona, J.F, Colloid Polym Sci, **12**, 1377 – 1385 (2007)
4. A. Pasupathy, R. Velraj, R.V. Seeniraj. Renew. Sustainable Energy Rev., **12**, 39-64 (2008)
5. Energain® PCM *DuPontTM Energain® - A thermal mass solution that's ready to make its mark.* (2007)
6. T. Habrovanský, *Control and monitoring of heating and cooling units in laboratory of building control systems.* (Zlín, 2008)
7. P. Chrobák, S. Sehnálek, M. Zálešák, (Electrorevue, 2014)
8. M. Kolacek, M. Zalesak, IJMR. **3,** 7-12 (2016)

MATEC Web of Conferences **76**, 02015 (2016)
DOI: 10.1051/matecconf/20167602015
CSCC 2016

Modelling of pneumatic muscle actuator using Hill's model with different approximations of static characteristics of artificial muscle

Ján Piteľ[1,a] and Mária Tóthová[1]

[1]*Department of Mathematics, Informatics and Cybernetics, Faculty of Manufacturing Technologies, Technical University of Košice, Bayerova 1, 080 01 Prešov, Slovakia*

Abstract. For modelling and simulation of pneumatic muscle actuators the mathematical dependence of the muscle force on the muscle contraction at different pressures in the muscles is necessary to know. For this purpose the static characteristics of the pneumatic artificial muscle type FESTO MAS-20-250N used in the experiments were approximated. In the paper there are shown some simulation results of the pneumatic muscle actuator dynamics using modified Hill's muscle model, in which four different approximations of static characteristics of artificial muscle were used.

1 Introduction

Pneumatic muscle actuators for robotics and biomedical engineering applications [1,2] are usually designed as a kinematic structure, which corresponds to a one degree-of-freedom (DOF) system with one rotary axis [3]. These actuators are characterized by several appealing properties such as advantageous power/weight ratio, natural compliance, cleanness and structural simplicity. They consist of a pair of pneumatic artificial muscles (PAMs) arranged in antagonistic configuration (acting against themselves) in order to generate a retraction force or rotary movement (Figure 1) [4].

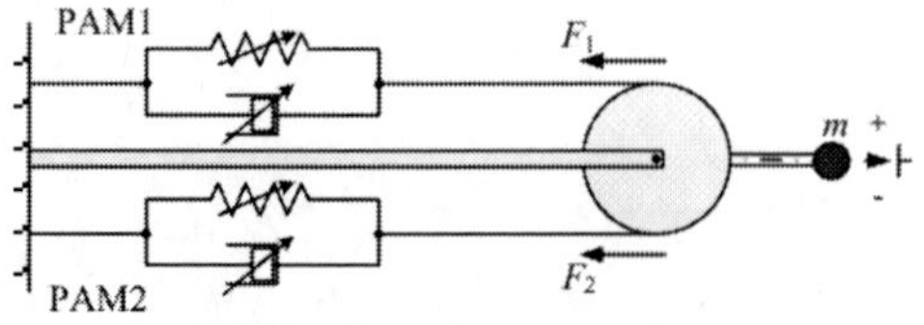

Figure 1. Model of antagonistic pneumatic muscle actuator using modified Hill's model

PAMs are made of rubber elastic tube with nonextensible braiding made of various materials (e.g. nylon), which defines an expansion in the context of increasing pressure. Depending on the actual construction of PAMs as well as operating condition, the highly nonlinear and also hysteretic properties may be more or less pronounced. Therefore it is necessary to use modeling for the better understanding the design parameters of PAMs in order to find dynamic muscle characteristics. These models are also important for simulation of the movement dynamics of the pneumatic muscle actuators and also for their control.

[a] Corresponding author: jan.pitel@tuke.sk

2 Modified Hill's muscle model

The modeling of PAMs as a main part of pneumatic muscle actuators was the subject of study from the very beginning of renewed interest about PAMs [5-9]. One of the simplest models of PAM is the simple geometric [10] and the advanced geometric [11] muscle model which dominate muscle modeling for simplicity and low demands on computing power. They depend on the geometrical properties of the muscle and physical processes running inside the muscle. The modified Hill's muscle model uses an engineering approach to muscle modeling, it is one of the oldest models and belongs to phenomenological models, that consists of a variable damper and a variable spring connected in parallel (Figure 1) [4]. Dynamic simulation model of antagonistic pneumatic muscle actuator using modified Hill's model was realized in Matlab/Simulink environment (Figure 2).

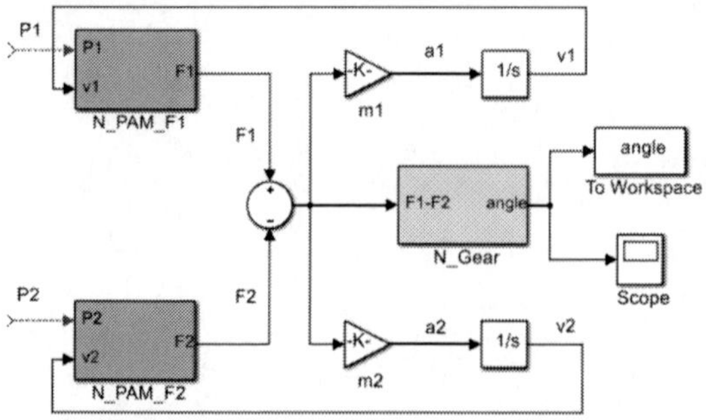

Figure 2. Simulation model of antagonistic pneumatic muscle actuator using modified Hill's model

The dynamics of the PAM system consists of the series-parallel combination of standard mechanical components [12]. It can be described by the following nonlinear differential equation based on the Newton's second law:

$$\ddot{y} = \frac{1}{m}\left[F_E - F_s(\kappa, P) - F_d(\dot{\kappa}, P)\right], \qquad (1)$$

where m is the moving mass, y is the muscle displacement [m], $F_s(\kappa, P)$ is the nonlinear term representing a variable spring force, $F_d(\dot{\kappa}, P)$ is the nonlinear term representing a damper force, F_E is the external force [N], P is the absolute muscle pressure [Pa] and κ is the muscle contraction (defined as $\kappa = \kappa_0 + {}^{y}\!/_{l_0}$, where κ_0 is the initial contraction [-] and l_0 is the initial muscle length [m].

The member F_E (external force) represents all forces to which a muscle is subjected. It can be for example the gravitational force of a load or the frictional force. In case of use muscles antagonistic connection, it is the force of the other muscle.

The force of variable spring $F_s(\kappa, P)$ represents an active member in the modified Hill's muscle model and it is described in section 3.

The force of damper $F_d(\dot{\kappa}, P)$ represents a passive member in the modified Hill's muscle model and it is a nonlinear (due to the multiplication) function of the velocity of muscle movement and the muscle pressure [12]:

$$F_d(\dot{\kappa}, P) = R \cdot P \cdot \dot{\kappa}, \qquad (2)$$

where R is the damping coefficient [$m^2 \cdot s$], P is the absolute muscle pressure [Pa] and $\dot{\kappa}$ is the muscle velocity [s^{-1}].

Modified Hill's muscle model does not include internal structure and function of the muscle. PAM in this model generates two types of forces, active F_s and passive F_d, which together form a resultant force of the muscle (Figure 3). The contractile member in Hill's muscle model is an active source of power which is controlled by the muscle pressure. Then the force of contractile element is a nonlinear function (f(u) in Figure 3) of two variables, contraction and pressure in the muscle [13].

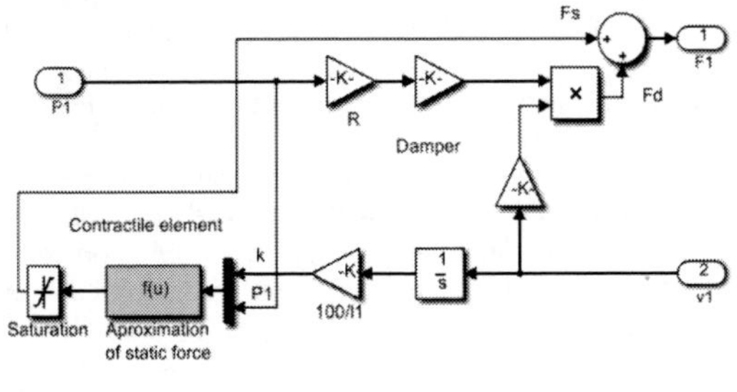

Figure 3. Subsystem N_PAM_F of the muscle force nonlinearity

3 Approximations of the PAM static characteristics

The muscle force dependence on the muscle contraction and pressure in the muscle (Figure 4) [14] was approximated using available software tools as Matlab Curve Fitting Toolbox and four obtained functions are expressed and used for modeling of pneumatic muscle actuator using modified Hill's muscle model.

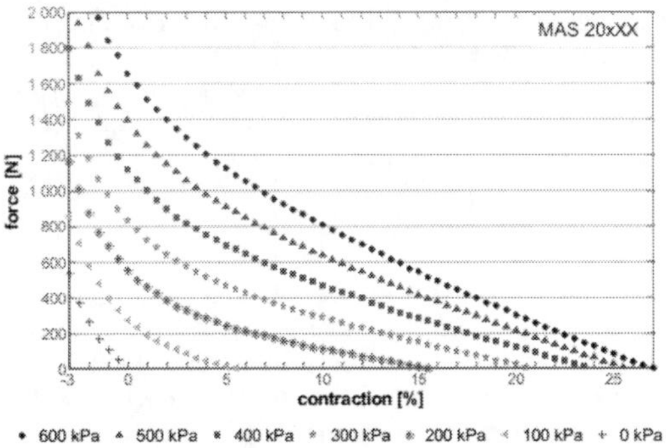

Figure 4. Static characteristics of PAM type FESTO MAS 20-200N 12

For practical use, the range of the muscle contraction is limited from 0% to 25%. At lower muscle contractions, the value of muscle force is already very high and it cause excessive stress materials of the muscle. At higher muscle contractions, there is decrease in the generated force very large. Figure 4 shows that PAM type FESTO MAS 20-20xXX can at the pressure of 600 kPa to exert the muscle force up to 2 000 N.

On the basis of physical laws and the geometric parameters of PAM, relation of the static characteristics was derived [7]:

$$F_s(\kappa, p) = \mu(\kappa) \cdot \pi \cdot r_0^2 \cdot p \cdot \left(a \cdot (1 - \varepsilon(p) \cdot \kappa)^2 - b\right) \qquad (3)$$

with member $\mu(\kappa)$ to obtain better approximation for small values of the pressure:

$$\mu(\kappa) = a_\kappa \cdot e^{-\kappa \cdot c_\kappa} - b_\kappa \qquad (4)$$

and the member $\varepsilon(p)$ to obtain better approximation for higher values of the pressure:

$$\varepsilon(p) = a_\varepsilon \cdot e^{-p} - b_\varepsilon, \qquad (5)$$

where p is the pressure in the muscle [Pa], κ is the muscle contraction [-], coefficients a_ε, b_ε, a_κ, b_κ, c_κ were determined using Matlab Curve Fitting Toolbox and values a, b have the form [7]:

$$a = \frac{3}{\tan^2 \alpha_0}, \qquad (6)$$

$$b = \frac{1}{\sin^2 \alpha_0}, \qquad (7)$$

where α_0 is the initial angle between the muscle axis and its fibers.

The muscle force as a function $F_s(\kappa, P)$ of the muscle contraction for different pressures in the muscles can be deducted also from the maximum muscle force F_{max} [6]:

$$F_s(\kappa, p) = F_{\max}(\kappa) - (p_{\max} - p) \cdot \left(\frac{a_0 - a_1\kappa}{a_2} \right), \qquad (8)$$

where p_{max} is the maximum and p is the actual pressure in the muscle [Pa], κ is the muscle contraction [-] and coeficients a_i, $i = 0,1,2$, were found using Matlab Curve Fitting Toolbox [15].

A fourth-order polynomial function for the response at the maximum pressure $p_{max} = 600$ kPa was derived for the maximum muscle force F_{max} and apply [6]:

$$F_{\max}(\kappa) = b_0 + b_1\kappa + b_2\kappa^2 + b_3\kappa^3 + b_4\kappa^4, \qquad (9)$$

where coeficients b_i, $i = 1,2,3,4$, were also found using Matlab Curve Fitting Toolbox [15].

The muscle force can be also approximated with a good precision using an exponential function with six different unknown parameters [16]:

$$F_s(\kappa, p) = (a_1 \cdot p + a_2) \cdot e^{a_3 \cdot \kappa} + \\ + a_4 \cdot \kappa \cdot p + a_5 \cdot p + a_6, \qquad (10)$$

where κ is the muscle contraction [-], p is the pressure in the muscle [Pa] and a_i, $i = 1,..,6$ are unknown coefficients which values were also found using Matlab Curve Fitting Toolbox [15].

The fourth method applied for approximation was a polynomial approximation. In order to approximate these static characteristics with good accuracy, a fifth-order polynomial function of two variables was used. This polynomial function contains twenty-one coefficients and its form is as follows [17]:

$$\begin{aligned} F_s(\kappa, p) &= a_{00} + a_{10} \cdot \kappa + a_{01} \cdot p + a_{20} \cdot \kappa^2 + \\ &+ a_{11} \cdot \kappa \cdot p + a_{02} \cdot p^2 + a_{30} \cdot \kappa^3 + a_{21} \cdot \kappa^2 \cdot p + \\ &+ a_{12} \cdot \kappa \cdot p^2 + a_{03} \cdot p^3 + a_{40} \cdot \kappa^4 + a_{31} \cdot \kappa^3 \cdot p + \\ &+ a_{22} \cdot \kappa^2 \cdot p^2 + a_{13} \cdot \kappa \cdot p^3 + a_{04} \cdot p^4 + a_{50} \cdot \kappa^5 + \\ &a_{41} \cdot \kappa^4 \cdot p + a_{32} \cdot \kappa^3 \cdot p^2 + a_{23} \cdot \kappa^2 \cdot p^3 + \\ &+ a_{14} \cdot \kappa \cdot p^4 + a_{05} \cdot p^5, \end{aligned} \qquad (11)$$

where κ is the muscle contraction [-], p is the pressure in the muscle [Pa] and the values of other coefficients in (11) were determined also using Matlab Curve Fitting Toolbox [15].

4 Simulation results

The designed simulation model of pneumatic muscle actuator based on modified Hill's muscle model was simulated in Matlab/Simulink environment [18] for four different approximations of static force $F_s(\kappa, P)$. The simulation results of the actuator arm position for different approximations of static characteristics are shown in Figure 5 and Figure 6. Responses obtained for approximation using an analytical modeling were created using (3), responses obtained for approximation deducted from the maximum force were created using (8) and (9), responses obtained for approximation using an exponential function were created using (10) and responses obtained for approximation using a polynomial function were created using (11).

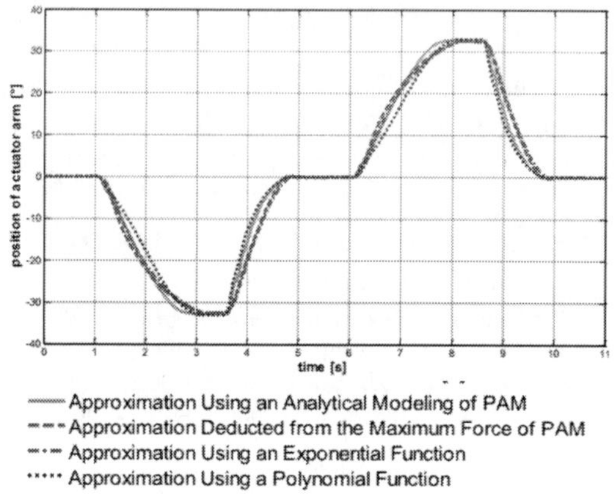

Figure 5. Dynamic responses of the actuator arm position for different approximations (maximum angle of actuator arm)

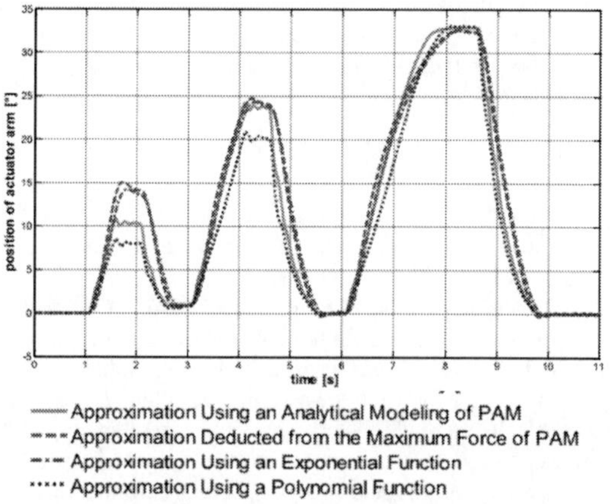

Figure 6. Dynamic responses of the actuator arm position for different approximations (different time periods of filling/discharging air pressure into/from the muscle)

It can be stated, that dynamic responses of the actuator arm position obtained by simulation of pneumatic muscle actuator for approximation deducted from the maximum force and using an exponential function are the similar. On the other hand there are some differences in the simulated responses for used analytical approximation and approximation using polynomial function especially in simulation for different time periods of filling/discharging air pressure into/from the muscle (Figure 6).

5 Conclusion

The muscle force dependence on the muscle contraction and pressure in the muscles was approximated for PAM produced by FESTO Company. Four different approximation functions were tested for possible approximation of the given static characteristics of muscle type MAS-20-200N (Figure 4). Analyses were carried out in Matlab Curve Fitting Toolbox. It can be stated from the obtained simulation results of the pneumatic muscle actuator dynamics using modified Hill's muscle model that the process of approximation of PAM static characteristics has been chosen correctly. The best results were achieved for approximations deducted from the maximum force and using an exponential function and that's why these two approximations are recommended for using in modeling of pneumatic actuators based on artificial muscles. Presented responses are highly non-linear which results high demands on the control algorithms of such actuators.

Acknowledgment

The research work is supported by grant VEGA 1/0822/16 „Research of intelligent manipulator based on pneumatic artificial muscles with three degrees of freedom“.

References

1. J.M. Hopen and A. Hošovský, "The servo robustification of the industrial robot", *in Annals of DAAAM for 2005 & Proceeding 16th International DAAAM Symposium "Intelligent Manufacturing & Automation: Focus on Young Scientists and Researchers"*, Vienna, 2005. pp. 161-162 (2005)
2. O. Líška, M. More, D. Janáčová, and H. Charvátová, "Design of rehabilitation robot based on pneumatic artificial muscles", *in Proceedings of Mathematical Methods and Optimization Techniques in Engineering*, Antalya, 2013. pp. 151-154 (2013)
3. A. Hošovský and M. Havran, "Dynamic modeling of one degree of freedom pneumatic muscle-based actuator for industrial applications", Tehnički Vjesnik - Technical Gazette, Vol. **19**, No. 3, 2012. pp. 73-681 (2012)
4. A. Hošovský and M. Havran, "Hill's muscle model-based modeling of pneumatic artificial muscle", *in Annals of DAAAM for 2011 & Proceedings of the 22nd International DAAAM Symposium*, Vienna, 2011. pp. 1005-1006 (2011)
5. J. Boržíková, "The determination of analytic dependence of static characteristic of PAM-based antagonistic actuator", *Acta Mechanica Slovaca*, Vol. **12**, No. 1-A, 2008. pp. 227-230. (2008)
6. V.T. Jouppila, S.A. Gadsden, and A. Ellman, "Modeling and identification of a pneumatic muscle actuator system controlled by an ON/OFF solenoid valve", *in Proceeding 7th International Fluid Power Conference*, Aachen, 2010, pp. 1-11 (2010)
7. T. Kerscher, J. Albiez, J.M. Zollner, and R. Dillmann, "Evaluation of the dynamic model of fluidic muscles using quick-release", *in Proceeding of International Conference on Biomedical Robotics and Biomechatronics (BioRob 2006)*, Pisa, 2006. pp. 637-642 (2006)
8. M. Tóthová, and J. Piteľ, "Dynamic simulation of pneumatic muscle actuator in Matlab/Simulink environment", *in Proceedings of the IEEE 12th International Symposium on Intelligent Systems and Informatics (SISY 2014)*, Subotica, 2014. pp. 209-213. (2014)
9. J. Sárosi, I. Biro, L. Nemeth, and I. Cveticanin, "Dynamic modeling of a pneumatic muscle actuator with two-direction motion", Mechanism and Machine Theory, Vol. **85**, 2015. pp. 25-34. (2015)
10. M. Tóthová and J. Piteľ, "Simulation of actuator dynamics based on geometric model of pneumatic artificial muscle", *in Proceedings of the IEEE 11th International Symposium on Intelligent Systems and Informatics (SISY 2013)*, Subotica, 2013. pp. 233-237 (2013)
11. M. Tóthová and J. Piteľ, Dynamic model of pneumatic actuator based on advanced geometric muscle model", *in Proceedings of the IEEE 9th International Conference on Computational Cybernetics (ICCC 2013)*, Budapest, 2013. pp. 83-87 (2013)
12. J. Piteľ, M. Balara, A. Hošovský, and M. Tothova, *Pneumatic muscle actuators: modelling, simulation and control* (Košice: TU, 275 p. 2015)
13. J. Boržíková, "Non-linear approximation of the static characteristic F = f (p,κ) of antagonistic system", *in Proceeding ARTEP 2008*, Stará Lesná, 2008. pp. 4-1–5 (2008)
14. Fluidic muscles DMSP-.../MAS-... [online] Available at: https://www.festo.com/cat/en-us_us/data/doc_enus/PDF/US/DMSP-MAS_ENUS.PDF (2016)
15. M. Tóthová, J. Piteľ, A. Hošovský, and J. Sárosi, "Numerical approximation of static characteristics of McKibben pneumatic artificial muscle", International Journal of Mathematics and Computers in Simulation, Vol. **9**, 2015. pp. 228-233 (2015)
16. J. Sárosi, "New approximation algorithm for the force of fluidic muscles", *in Proceeding 7th International Symposium on Applied Computational Intelligence and Informatics (SACI 2012)*, Timisoara, 2012, pp. 229-233 (2012)
17. A. Hošovský, *Methods of computational intelligence in the control and modeling of manipulators driven by artificial muscles* (Habilitation work, Prešov: TU, 135 p. 2014)
18. M. Tóthová and A. Hošovský, "Dynamic simulation model of pneumatic actuator with artificial muscle", *in Proceedings of the 11th IEEE International Symposium on Applied Machine Intelligence and Informatics (SAMI 2013)*, Budapest, 2013. pp. 47-51 (2013)

MATEC Web of Conferences **76**, 02016 (2016) DOI: 10.1051/matecconf/20167602016
CSCC 2016

The simulation of a non-linear unstable system of motion, utilising the Solid-Works and Matlab/Simulink extended libraries/toolboxes

Jiří Zátopek[1,a]

[1] *Tomas Bata University in Zlín, Faculty of Applied Informatics, Nad Stráněmi 4511, 760 05 Zlín, Czech Republic*

Abstract. This text discusses the use and integration of various support software tools for the purpose of designing the motion control law governing mechanical structures with strongly non-linear behaviour. The detailed mathematical model is derived using Lagrange Equations of the Second Type. The physical model was designed by using SolidWorks 3D CAD software and a SimMechanics library. It extends Simulink with modelling tools for the simulation of mechanical "multi-domain" physical systems. The visualization of Simulink outputs is performed using the 3D Animation toolbox. Control law - designed on the basis of the mathematical model, is tested for both models (i.e. mathematical and physical) and the regulatory processes' results are compared.

1 Introduction

Nowadays, a large amount of support software tools is available. These tools facilitate our work in analysing, modelling, simulating and designing a control law for complex mechanical structures. By connecting these resources a considerable simplification of the synthesis can be achieved as well as clarity by using visualisation in 3D space directly in the regulation process, or creating a physical model in Simulink directly from CAD software (SolidWorks), without the need to derive the equations of motion.

The system which is the object of our interest is called "Ball and beam", and the description of the dynamic behaviour is derived in the most general way as possible for use in the control of a real model. The ball and beam are mass objects and are thus situated in the 3D space - only the movement is limited to planar. The system is located in the Earth's gravitational field and has two degrees of freedom. The mass of the ball is chosen to have a significant impact on the movement changes of the beam; the beam may be unbalanced. The ball position is measured from the axis of rotation of the beam (i.e. the axis of the shaft of the driving motor). The Denavit-Hartenberg (DH) notation/method of placement for coordinate systems is used to determine the ball's position in a selected global coordinate system.

First, the whole system is sketched-out for the purpose of compiling a transformation matrix to determine the position of the ball in the global coordinate system. Using this transformation, the equations of motion of the system are derived - which include the moments of inertia, and the centrifugal/centripetal and Coriolis generalized forces or linear friction. Than, a 3D model was constructed in the CAD design software SolidWorks suite, including all kinematic constraints and the mass distribution of the whole assembly. This model is also useful for detecting the masses or matrices/moments of inertia of complex objects, which cannot be determined analytically. The subsequent CAD model is then export into the SimMechanics format in Matlab/Simulink, which leads to a physical model - including its kinematic link and the distribution of the mass of the whole assembly. This model subsequently tests the proposed control algorithm and compares the outputs with a mathematical model.

[a]e-mail: zatopek@fai.utb.cz

2 "Ball and beam" – the mathematical description

2.1 Transformation of coordinate systems

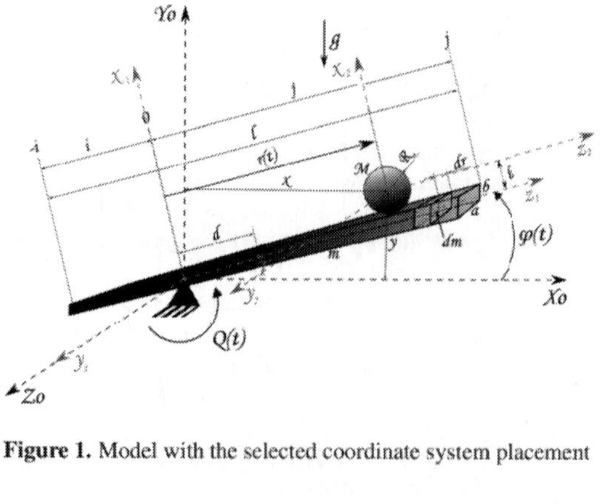

Figure 1. Model with the selected coordinate system placement

Figure 1 shows the system drawn for the purpose of determining the transformation matrix from the local coordinate system (x_2, y_2, z_2) to the global system (X_0, Y_0, Z_0). Rotation of the beam is only possible around the global axis Z_0; rolling the ball only in direction of local axis z_1 is ideal. The connection of the beam with the frame in the place where the torque actions provide controlled tilting of the beam (i.e. the first degree of freedom) is shown schematically. The second degree of freedom is the movement of the ball on the beam.

The resulting homogeneous transformation matrix between the coordinate systems is:

$$ {}^{0}\mathbf{T}_2 = \begin{bmatrix} -\sin\varphi(t) & 0 & \cos\varphi(t) & -h\sin\varphi(t) + r(t)\cos\varphi(t) \\ \cos\varphi(t) & 0 & \sin\varphi(t) & h\cos\varphi(t) + r(t)\sin\varphi(t) \\ 0 & 1 & 0 & 0 \\ 0 & 0 & 0 & 1 \end{bmatrix} \quad (1) $$

For determining the homogeneous coordinates of the ball position relative to the origin of the global coordinate system, the equation is:

$$ {}^{0}\mathbf{r} = {}^{0}\mathbf{T}_2 \cdot {}^{2}\mathbf{r} \Rightarrow \begin{bmatrix} X \\ Y \\ Z \\ 1 \end{bmatrix} = \begin{bmatrix} -\left(R + \frac{b}{2}\right)\sin\varphi(t) + r(t)\cos\varphi(t) \\ \left(R + \frac{b}{2}\right)\cos\varphi(t) + r(t)\sin\varphi(t) \\ 0 \\ 1 \end{bmatrix} \quad (2) $$

In order to determine the square-size of the absolute speed vector (in the global coordinate system), it is:

$$ |\mathbf{v}|^2 = \left(\dot{x}^2 + \dot{y}^2\right) = \left(\frac{2R+b}{2}\right)^2 \dot{\varphi}^2 + r^2\dot{\varphi}^2 + \dot{r}^2 - (2R+b)\dot{r}\dot{\varphi} \quad (3) $$

Note, the Ball and beam is only planar in this model (processes take place in 2D).

2.2 Motion equations

To be able to use Lagrange equations of the second kind, it is therefore necessary to determine the kinetic and potential energy of the whole system.

The kinetic energy of the balls is comprised of its translational and rotational motion:

$$ \mathbf{E}_{\mathbf{k}_{\mathbf{ball}}} = \frac{1}{2}Mv^2 + \underbrace{\frac{1}{2}\overbrace{J_{kul}}^{\frac{2}{5}MR^2}\ \overbrace{\omega_{kul}^2}^{\frac{\dot{r}^2}{R^2}}}_{\frac{1}{5}M\dot{r}^2} = \frac{1}{2}M\left[\left(\frac{2R+b}{2}\right)^2\dot{\varphi}^2 + r^2\dot{\varphi}^2 + \frac{7}{5}\dot{r}^2 - (2R+b)\dot{r}\dot{\varphi}\right] \quad (4) $$

The potential energy of the ball is:

$$ \mathbf{E}_{\mathbf{P}_{\mathbf{ball}}} = Mgy = Mg\left[\left(\frac{2R+b}{2}\right)\cos\varphi + r\sin\varphi\right] \quad (5) $$

The Beam is cuboid in shape, with an optionally-stored rotation axis as shown in Figure 1. Its inertia matrix has 3x3 moments of inertia, and is defined as:

$$ \mathbf{J} = \begin{bmatrix} J_{xx} & J_{xy} & J_{xz} \\ J_{yx} & J_{yy} & J_{yz} \\ J_{zx} & J_{zy} & J_{zz} \end{bmatrix} = \iiint_B \rho(x,y,z) \begin{bmatrix} J_{xx} & J_{xy} & J_{xz} \\ J_{yx} & J_{yy} & J_{yz} \\ J_{zx} & J_{zy} & J_{zz} \end{bmatrix} \quad (6) $$

in which $\rho(x, y, z)$ is the density of the material body. If a new coordinate system is selected such that all the deviance moments will be zero; the torques to the individual axes of the system will be equal to the polar moments of the inertia matrix with respect to these axes. A well established system already meets this assumption, it is not necessary to introduce a new coordinate system and the moment of inertia relative to the axis of rotation (axis Z_0) will be equal to the polar moment J_{zz}.

$$ \mathbf{J}_{\mathbf{beam}} = J_{zz} = \frac{1}{12}m\left[b^2 + 4\left(i^2 - ij + j^2\right)\right] \quad (7) $$

The kinetic energy of the beam is:

$$ \mathbf{E}_{\mathbf{k}_{\mathbf{beam}}} = \frac{1}{2}\dot{\varphi}^2 J_{beam} = \frac{1}{24}m\dot{\varphi}^2\left[b^2 + 4\left(i^2 - ij + j^2\right)\right] \quad (8) $$

The relationship between the mass element and the length element can be expressed as:

$$ \mathbf{dm} = \rho\, a\, b\, dr = \frac{m}{a\,b\,l}a\,b\,dr = \frac{m}{l}dr \quad (9) $$

The potential energy of the beam element is:

$$ \mathbf{dE}_{\mathbf{P}_{\mathbf{beam}}} = dm\, g\, \sin\varphi\, r = \frac{m\, g\, \sin\varphi}{i+j} r\, dr \quad (10) $$

The potential energy of the whole beam is:

$$ \mathbf{E}_{\mathbf{P}_{\mathbf{beam}}} = \int_{-i}^{j} dE_{P_{beam}} = \frac{1}{2}m\, g\, \sin\varphi(j-i) \quad (11) $$

The total kinetic and potential energy of the system is the sum of their partial energies:

$$ \mathbf{E}_{\mathbf{k}} = \frac{1}{24}m\dot{\varphi}^2\left[b^2 + 4\left(i^2 - ij + j^2\right)\right] + \frac{1}{2}M\left[\left(\frac{2R+b}{2}\right)^2\dot{\varphi}^2 + r^2\dot{\varphi}^2 + \frac{7}{5}\dot{r}^2 - (2R+b)\dot{r}\dot{\varphi}\right] \quad (12) $$

$$ \mathbf{E}_{\mathbf{p}} = Mg\left[\left(\frac{2R+b}{2}\right)\cos\varphi + r\sin\varphi\right] + \frac{1}{2}mg\sin\varphi(j-i) \quad (13) $$

The Lagrangian calculation is:

$$ \mathbf{L} = E_k - E_p = \frac{1}{24}m\dot{\varphi}^2\left[b^2 + 4\left(i^2 - ij + j^2\right)\right] + \frac{1}{2}M\left[\left(\frac{2R+b}{2}\right)^2\dot{\varphi}^2 + r^2\dot{\varphi}^2 + \frac{7}{5}\dot{r}^2 - (2R+b)\dot{r}\dot{\varphi}\right] - Mg\left[\left(\frac{2R+b}{2}\right)\cos\varphi + r\sin\varphi\right] - \frac{1}{2}mg\sin\varphi(j-i) \quad (14) $$

The linear friction - dependent upon the generalised speed (i.e. sliding friction with a friction factor k_1 and rolling resistance with a friction factor k_2) will be added to the system. The equations of motion are therefore:

$$ \frac{d}{dt}\left(\frac{\partial L}{\dot{q}_i}\right) - \frac{\partial L}{q_i} = Q_i \quad \Rightarrow \quad \frac{d}{dt}\left(\frac{\partial L}{\dot{r}}\right) - \frac{\partial L}{r} = 0 $$
$$ \frac{d}{dt}\left\{\frac{1}{2}M\left[\frac{14}{5}\dot{r} - (2R+b)\dot{\varphi}\right]\right\} - Mr\dot{\varphi}^2 + Mg\sin\varphi = 0 \quad (15) $$

$$ \frac{\mathbf{7}}{\mathbf{5}}\mathbf{M\ddot{r}} - \frac{\mathbf{2R+b}}{\mathbf{2}}\mathbf{M\ddot{\varphi}} - \mathbf{Mr\dot{\varphi}^2} + \mathbf{k_1\dot{r}} + \mathbf{Mg}\sin\varphi = \mathbf{0} \quad (16) $$

$$\frac{d}{dt}\left(\frac{\partial L}{\dot{q}_i}\right)-\frac{\partial L}{q_i}=Q_i \quad \Rightarrow \quad \frac{d}{dt}\left(\frac{\partial L}{\dot{\varphi}}\right)-\frac{\partial L}{\varphi}=0$$

$$\begin{aligned}&\frac{d}{dt}\left\{\frac{1}{2}M\left[\frac{(2R+b)^2}{2}\dot{\varphi}+2r^2\dot{\varphi}-(2R+b)\dot{r}\right]+\frac{1}{12}m\dot{\varphi}\left[b^2+\right.\right.\\&\left.\left.+4\left(i^2-ij+j^2\right)\right]\right\}+Mg\left[r\cos\varphi-\left(\frac{2R+b}{2}\right)\sin\varphi\right]+\\&+\frac{1}{2}mg\cos\varphi\,(j-i)=Q\end{aligned} \tag{17}$$

$$\begin{aligned}&\mathbf{M}\left(\frac{\mathbf{2R+b}}{\mathbf{2}}\right)^2\ddot{\varphi}+\mathbf{Mr^2}\ddot{\varphi}+\frac{\mathbf{1}}{\mathbf{12}}\mathbf{m}\left[\mathbf{b^2+4\left(i^2-ij+j^2\right)}\right]\ddot{\varphi}-\\&-\mathbf{M}\frac{\mathbf{2R+b}}{\mathbf{2}}\ddot{\mathbf{r}}+\mathbf{2Mr\dot{r}}\dot{\varphi}+\mathbf{k_2}\dot{\varphi}+\mathbf{Mgr}\cos\varphi-\\&-\mathbf{Mg}\left(\frac{\mathbf{2R+b}}{\mathbf{2}}\right)\sin\varphi+\frac{\mathbf{1}}{\mathbf{2}}\mathbf{mg(j-i)}\cos\varphi+\mathbf{2Mr\dot{r}}\dot{\varphi}=\mathbf{Q}\end{aligned} \tag{18}$$

After modification, we can write:

$$\begin{aligned}\ddot{\mathbf{r}}=&\frac{60A\begin{bmatrix}Q-k_2\dot{\varphi}+AMg\sin\varphi-Mgr\cos\varphi+\\+\frac{1}{2}mg(i-j)\cos\varphi-2Mr\dot{r}\dot{\varphi}\end{bmatrix}}{24MA^2+84Mr^2+7Bm}-\\&-\frac{5\begin{bmatrix}\left(12MA^2+12Mr^2+Bm\right)\cdot\\\cdot\left(k_1\dot{r}-Mr\dot{\varphi}^2+Mg\sin\varphi\right)\end{bmatrix}}{24M^2A^2+84M^2r^2+7BMm}\end{aligned} \tag{19}$$

$$\ddot{\varphi}=\frac{6\begin{bmatrix}14Q-14k_2\dot{\varphi}-10Ak_1\dot{r}+10AMr\dot{\varphi}^2+\\+4AMg\sin\varphi-14Mgr\cos\varphi+\\+7mg(i-j)\cos\varphi-28Mr\dot{r}\dot{\varphi}\end{bmatrix}}{24MA^2+84Mr^2+7Bm}$$

in which:

$$\mathbf{A}=\left(\frac{2R+b}{2}\right) \qquad \mathbf{B}=\left[b^2+4\left(i^2-ij+j^2\right)\right] \tag{20}$$

The block diagram in Simulink that corresponds to the derived non-linear mathematical model was created from the Equation (19). The modified equations of motion are part of the *r''* and *fi''* functional blocks, and it is also possible to choose non-zero initial conditions of the mathematical model.

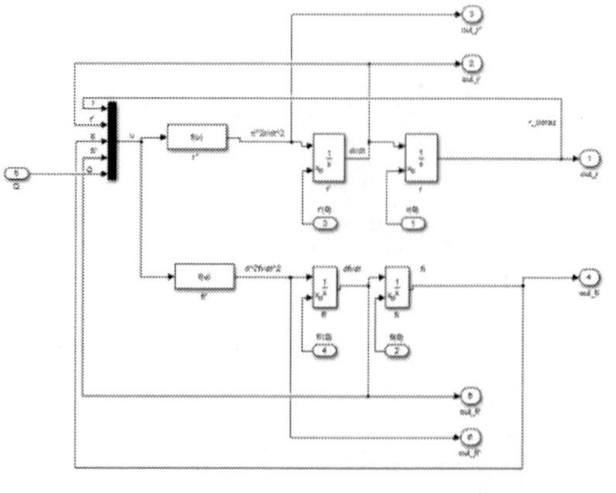

Figure 2. The non-linear mathematical model in Simulink

For the state vector: $[r\ v\ \varphi\ \omega]^T=[x_1\ x_2\ x_3\ x_4]^T$ and input signal: $Q=u$ the state-space representation will correspond to the shape of:

$$\begin{bmatrix}\dot{x}_1\\\dot{x}_2\\\dot{x}_3\\\dot{x}_4\end{bmatrix}=\begin{bmatrix}x_2\\ \dfrac{60A\begin{bmatrix}Q-k_2x_4+AMg\sin x_3-\\-Mgx_1\cos x_3+\frac{1}{2}mg(i-j)\cos x_3-\\-2Mx_1x_2x_4\end{bmatrix}}{24MA^2+84Mx_1^2+7Bm}-\dfrac{5\begin{bmatrix}\left(12MA^2+12Mx_1^2+Bm\right)\cdot\\\cdot\left(k_1x_2-Mx_1x_4^2+Mg\sin x_3\right)\end{bmatrix}}{24M^2A^2+84M^2x_1^2+7BMm}\\ x_4\\ \dfrac{6\begin{bmatrix}14Q-14k_2x_4-10Ak_1x_2+10AMx_1x_4^2+\\+4AMg\sin x_3-14Mgx_1\cos x_3+\\+7mg(i-j)\cos x_3-28Mx_1x_2x_4\end{bmatrix}}{24MA^2+84Mx_1^2+7Bm}\end{bmatrix} \tag{21}$$

From these equations, it can be determined that the system has only one unstable singular point and its steady-state is only given by the ball position on the lever/beam x_1.

All remaining state variables are zero in singular point. The singular (stationary) point is:

$$\begin{bmatrix}x_1^0 & x_2^0 & x_3^0 & x_4^0\end{bmatrix}^T=\begin{bmatrix}\dfrac{m(i-j)}{2M} & 0 & 0 & 0\end{bmatrix}^T \tag{22}$$

The Steady state is:

$$\begin{aligned}\mathbf{x_1^s}&=\frac{u^s}{Mg}+\frac{m(i-j)}{2M}\\\mathbf{u^s}&=Mgx_1^s-\frac{1}{2}mg(i-j)\end{aligned} \tag{23}$$

Linearisation in the working point x_1^s (i.e. steady state) can be obtained from the transmission of the linear model:

$$\mathbf{G(s)}=\frac{\mathbf{X_1(s)}}{\mathbf{U(s)}}=\frac{\mathbf{b_2s^2+b_0}}{\mathbf{s^4+a_3s^3+a_2s^2+a_1s+a_0}} \tag{24}$$

in which:

$$\mathbf{b_2}=\frac{60A}{24MA^2+336Mx_1^{s2}+7Bm}$$

$$\mathbf{b_0}=\frac{-60g}{24MA^2+336Mx_1^{s2}+7Bm}$$

$$\mathbf{a_3}=\frac{60MA^2k_1+240Mk_1x_1^{s2}+84Mk_2+5Bk_1m}{M\left(24MA^2+336Mx_1^{s2}+7Bm\right)^2}$$

$$\mathbf{a_2}=\frac{\begin{matrix}\left(12096AgM^3+20160Mk_1k_2\right)x_1^{s2}-\\-10080AgmM^2(i-j)x_1^s+864A^3M^3g+\\+1440A^2Mk_1k_2+420Bk_1k_2m+252ABgmM^2\end{matrix}}{M\left(24MA^2+336Mx_1^{s2}+7Bm\right)^2} \tag{25}$$

$$\mathbf{a_1}=\frac{-60Agk_1}{24MA^2+336Mx_1^{s2}+7Bm}$$

$$\mathbf{a_0}=\frac{-60Mg^2\begin{bmatrix}24MA^2+336Mx_1^{s2}+\\+7Bm-168m(i-j)x_1^s\end{bmatrix}}{\left(24MA^2+336Mx_1^{s2}+7Bm\right)^2}$$

Linearization is derived in the general position of the working point, so it is possible to continuously recalculate it.

3 "Ball and beam" – support software tools

3.1 SolidWorks

Figure 3. The complete assembly in SolidWorks

The considered system consists of three basic parts: the base, the beam and the ball. All of these parts are material. Ideally, a rigid base is connected to the frame so its physical properties are not relevant to the dynamic behaviour of the system.

3.2 The SimMechanics – physical model

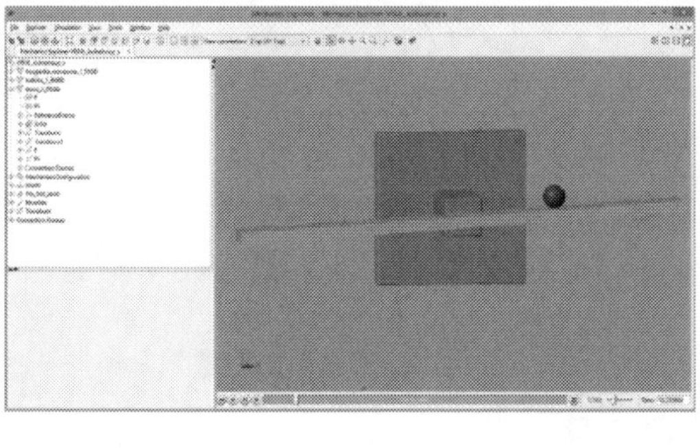

Figure 4. A Real-time visualisation using the SimMechanics Second Generation suite

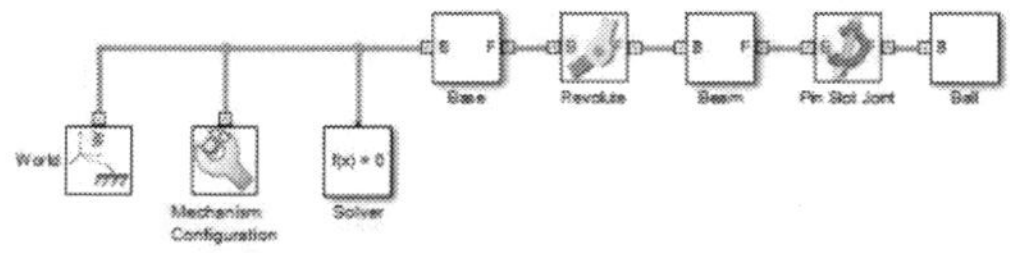

Figure 5. A separate model in the SimMechanics environment

The SolidWorks 3D CAD model (Figure 3) was exported in SimMechanics second generation *xml* format and then imported into the MATLAB/Simulink environment as a Simulink scheme (Figure 5). The link were revised because - between SolidWorks and SimMechanics; some are unknown or illicit.

3.3 3D Animation

Figure 6. Visualisation using a 3D Animation Toolbox in a web-browser

This model is also exported from the SolidWorks suite - but in the *wrl* format , which is loaded into a special block through the 3D Simulation toolbox. As inputs to this block are used, outputs from the mathematical model are converted through the transformation matrix (HD notation) into the translational and rotational motions of the individual parts of the assembly. Visualisation has more visualising options, e.g. a Web browser can also be used (Figure 6).

4 The "Ball and beam" – control

The large numbers of trigonometric functions and multiples of rounded state variables it contains leads to the generation of cumulative numerical error. Thus, despite placing the ball in equilibrium, the system will set itself into motion - as is apparent from Figure 7.

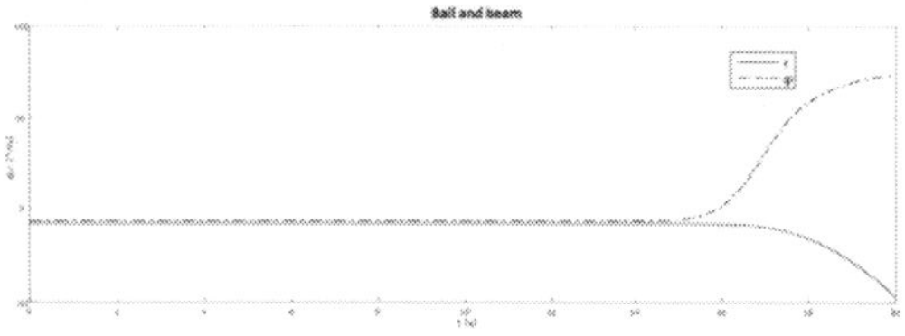

Figure 7. Cumulative Numerical Error

The system is controlled by a linear regulator with 1DOF designed by the pole placement with a continuous linearisation. The controller parameters - resulting from the transfer function, are derived generally so that they can be updating continuously. The final regulator then, has the form:

$$Q(s) = \frac{U(s)}{E(s)} = \frac{q(s)}{p(s)} = \frac{q_4 s^4 + q_3 s^3 + q_2 s^2 + q_1 s + q_0}{s\left(p_3 s^3 + p_2 s^2 + p_1 s + p_0\right)} \quad (26)$$

The step-changes in the reference value will be followed by step-changes in the control deviation; then there will be a problem with the physical realisation of a step

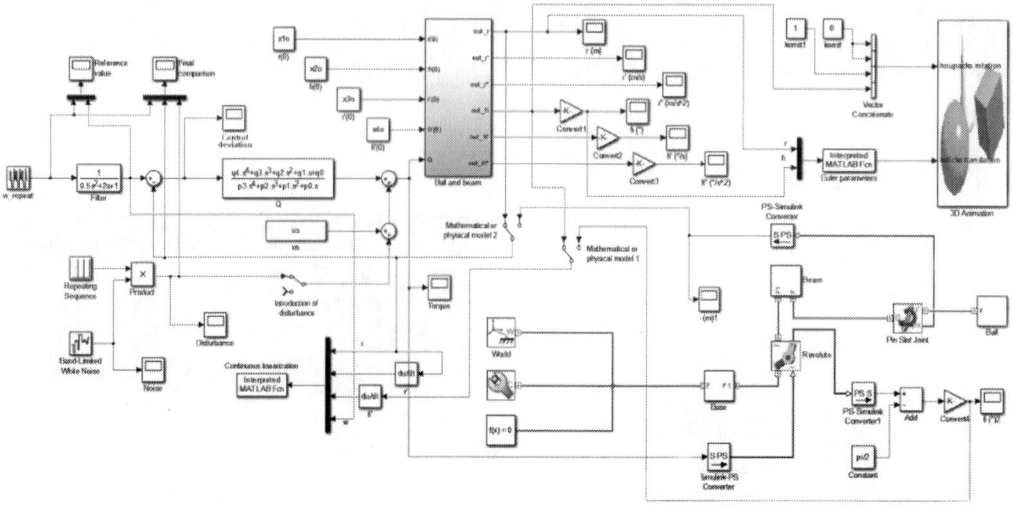

Figure 8. Complete Simulink scheme with SimMechanics and 3D Animation

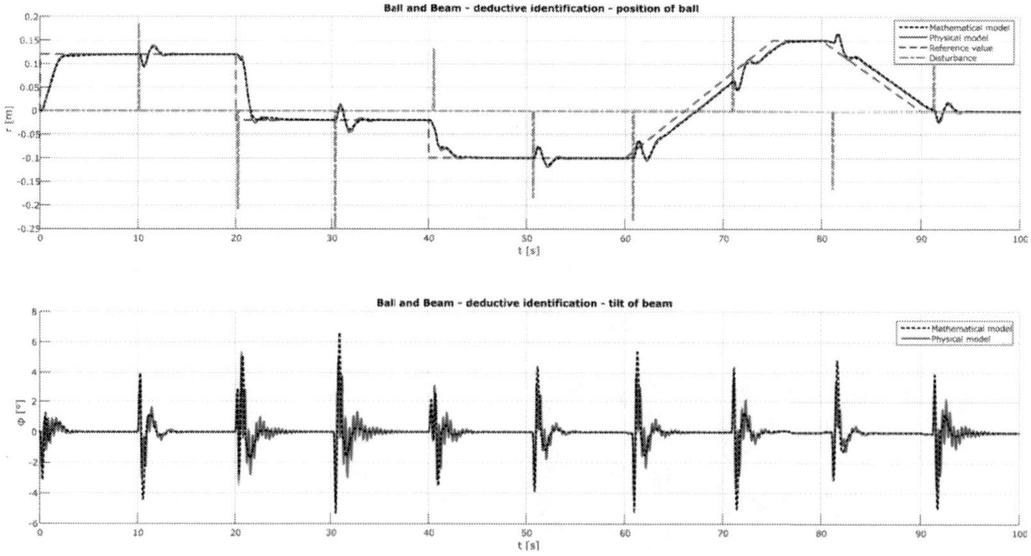

Figure 9. Control process for the mathematical and physical models

changes in the torque - and thus to the rapidly-changing tilt of the beam. In combination with the centrifugal forces and inertia of the system, the process will oscillate; and often will be an unmanageable state. Therefore, a filter that prevents such step-changes was introduced into the system.

As shown in Figure 9, the control processes (i.e mathematical and physical) of both models are nearly identical. The controller is designed to compensate for disturbance and the reference value is in the shape of a step-change, so a lag fault will appear in the transition part of the process at the ramp-shaped reference value. The trend of the reference value however, replicates very well.

5 Conclusion

This article contains a complete control design solution of a system known as a "Ball and beam" system, substantial part of the article relate to the derivation of systems motion equations from their energy balance. The model was - through to the definition of transmission, derived in a quite general manner and corresponds to motion equations linearised at the operating point. Therefore, it is possible to carry out a continuous linearisation efficiently - and with low computational effort. This description however, applies only in the area surrounding the working point. When this point changes, linearisation is needed again.

Linking with 3D CAD software and Matlab/Simulink, while using toolboxes for physical modelling (SimMechanics) and 3D visualisation outputs (3D Animation) is a very visual and effective control tool for the presentation of the results. In real time, it is possible to observe dynamic processes occurring in the system and for instance - for to slow then down or to pause them for the purpose of detailed motion analysis or the exploration of the energy interactions between system components.

The control methods designed a described herein are tested on a unbalanced system with variable reference course and disorders. To achieve the desired quality of regulation, it is necessary to eliminate a step-change in the control deviation and to stabilize the course of the regulatory process.

References

[1] S. Crandall, D. C, .Karnopp, E.F. Kurz, *Dynamics of mechanical and electromechanical systems* (McGraw-Hill, NewYork, 1968) 466

[2] H. K. Khali, *Nonlinear Systems* (Upper Saddle River, N.J: Pearson, 2001) 750

[3] Y. Shaoqiang, L. Zhong, L. Xingshan, Chinese Control Conference **27**, 161–165 (2008)

[4] Z. Úředníček, *Robotika* (Zlín, T. Bata university in Zlin, 2012) 284

[5] Z. Úředníček, *Elektromechanické akční členy* (Zlín, T. Bata university in Zlin, 2009) 127

[6] R. C. ROSENBERG, Journal of Dynamic Systems, Measurement, and Control **94**, 6 (1972)

[7] D. C. Karnopp, R. C. Rosenberg, *System dynamics* (A Unifies Approach. Wiley & Sons, New York, 1975) 372

[8] M. H. Loi Tran, International Mechanical Engineering Congress & Exposition **7**, 10 (2011)

The coordinate system transformation of a serial kinematic structures and use in the derivation of systems motion equations

Jiří Zátopek[1,a]

[1] *Tomas Bata University in Zlín, Faculty of Applied Informatics, Nad Stráněmi 4511, 760 05 Zlín, Czech Republic*

Abstract. This text discusses the use of transformation matrices to determine the motion equations of the complex mechanical structure. Use of the transformation matrix does not apply only to motion equations but has the general use in relative positions determine of objects in the 3D space. Analysed model is divided into seven physical objects, the transformation matrix and the corresponding inertia/pseudo-inertia matrix is included in each of them. This matrices are strictly necessary to the system dynamic description using the matrix form of Lagrange Equations of the Second Type. Another possibility to use the transformation matrix is shown in the camera system measurement. Model was designed in 3D CAD system SolidWorks, MATLAB was used for the mathematical calculations.

1 Introduction

Derivation of systems motion equations (deductive identification) is a crucial part of designing the motion control law of any mechanical structure. These structures are composed of mass objects and acts by not inconsiderable effect on other components of the system.

Each mass object has inertia in the motion. These inertias are reflected in the form of centrifugal/centripetal and Coriolis generalized forces with the combination of rotational movements - non-linearity into the system is introduced. The whole system has, therefore, highly non-linear behaviour during fast movements - non-linearities are bounded to the rate of change of state variables largely.

The system which is the object of our interest is called "Ball and plate", shown in Figure 1. To derive the equations of motion of the system the transformation matrices individual parts are advantageous to know. These transformation matrices can be further used for derivation of the inertia matrix, the position determining of the individual parts of the assembly in a 3D space, and non-measurable state variables obtaining - during the whole process procedure. The matrix form of Lagrange equations of the second type there will be used, which involves the use of the transformation matrices directly.

The Denavit-Hartenberg (DH) notation/method of placement for coordinate systems is used to determine the transformation matrices. The position measurement of the ball on the plate is realized using the camera system. As shown in Figure 10, with respect to the fixed location of the camera is necessary to transform the camera measured position of the ball to the actual position of the ball on the plate. Even in this case, the transformation matrix method is advantageously uses.

[a]e-mail: zatopek@fai.utb.cz

2 Ball and plate

2.1 3D model

Figure 1 shows a complete 3D assembly model. This model is created in SolidWorks and has 4 generalized degrees of freedom. Tilts of the plate are two of them. They are realized by two rotary kinematic pairs in perpendicular relation to their common normal. The ball position on the plate are other two generalized degree of freedom.

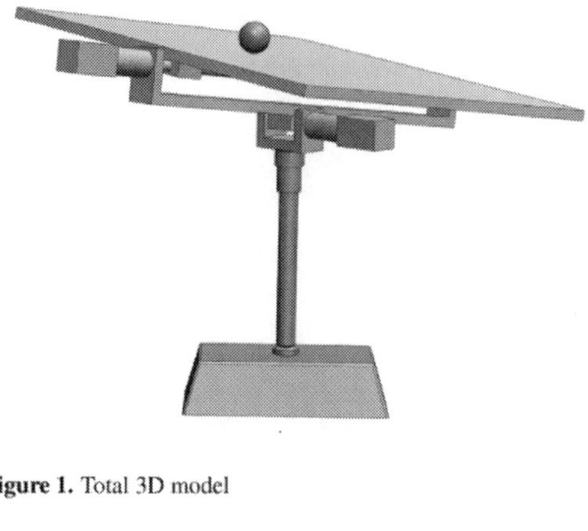

Figure 1. Total 3D model

For purposes of determining the system dynamic characteristics is preferably to simplify the system to the extent not too complicated equations of motion and at the same time the dynamic characteristics of the simplified model not be much different from the behaviour of the original system.

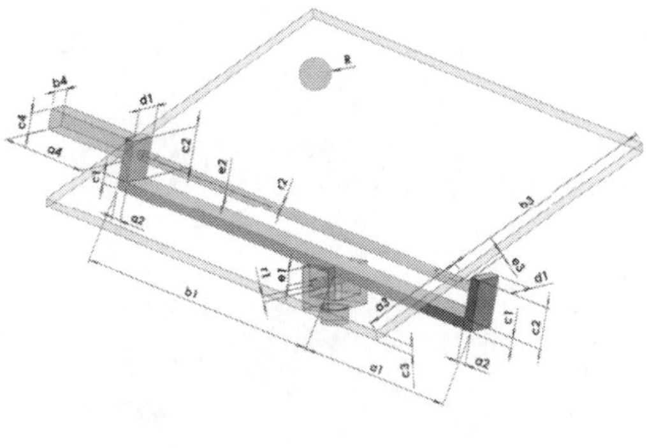

Figure 2. Simplified 3D model

The simplified model shown in Figure 2 contains only parts that have a major influence on its dynamics or serves as a global coordinate system base.

There are generally shown the basic dimensions that will be used in the coordinate system transformation - will be possible to change them in the resulting equation.

The stand as a base and the first motor need not be taken into account because they do not perform any movement (they are fixed) - as well as the connecting parts with negligible mass. The motor that moves the plate is replaced by cuboid.

2.2 Transformation of coordinate systems

The model is divided into seven parts for determining the homogeneous coordinates of the system. The part which is the transformation relates is always shown in the accompanying figures.

Used Denavit-Hartenberg (DH) notation/method of placement for coordinate systems is probably the most popular method used in robotics kinematics.

Table 1. DH parameters general table

Link	a_i	α_i	θ_i	d_i
1	a_1	α_1	θ_1	d_1
2	a_2	α_2	θ_2	d_2
...	...	...	...	...
n	a_n	α_n	θ_n	d_n

The calculation of the required transformations from the Table 1 is performed using the following relationships:

$$\mathbf{{}^{i-1}T_i} = \begin{bmatrix} \cos\theta_i & -\cos\alpha_i\sin\theta_i & \sin\alpha_i\sin\theta_i & a_i\cos\theta_i \\ \sin\theta_i & \cos\alpha_i\cos\theta_i & -\sin\alpha_i\cos\theta_i & a_i\sin\theta_i \\ 0 & \sin\alpha_i & \cos\alpha_i & d_i \\ 0 & 0 & 0 & 1 \end{bmatrix} \quad (1)$$

$$\mathbf{{}^0T_n} = {}^0T_1 \ldots {}^{n-2}T_{n-1}{}^{n-1}T_n \quad (2)$$

$$\mathbf{{}^Gr} = {}^GT_B \cdot {}^Br \quad (3)$$

The ball transformation in a global coordinate system is listed here as a pattern, other transformations have similar characteristics. The global coordinate system (X_0, Y_0, Z_0) is positioned at the rotation center axis of the first motor, as shown in Figure 3.

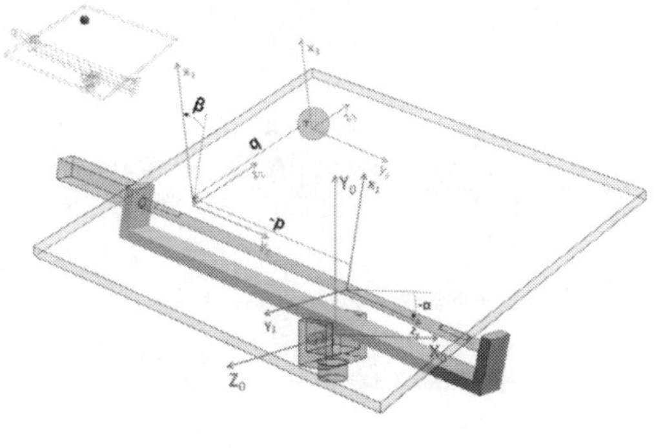

Figure 3. Coordinate system placement for the ball transformation - part 7

The gradual transformations from the Figure 3 can be written in Table 2. Utilising the relationship in the Equation 1 is found the transformation matrix between systems. Equation2 is used for finding the final transformation matrix from the local body coordinate system - chosen at the center of gravity, into the global coordinate system. It is possible to determine the position vector ball in the global coordinate system (ball position in 3D space) by using the Equation 3.

Table 2. DH parameters for ball transformation - part 7

Link	a_i	α_i	θ_i	d_i
1	$e_1 + r_1 + c_1 + e_2 + r_2$	$\frac{\pi}{2}$	$\frac{\pi}{2}$	$\frac{\pi}{2} + \alpha$
2	$r_2+e_3+c_3+R$	$\frac{\pi}{2}$	p	β
3	0	0	q	0

The matrix ${}^0T_3$ is listed in Equation 4. It is labelled as T_7 according to the selected assembly parts numbering.

$$\mathbf{T_7} = \begin{bmatrix} -\cos\beta\sin\alpha & \cos\alpha & -\sin\alpha\sin\beta & T_7^1 \\ \cos\alpha\cos\beta & \sin\alpha & \cos\alpha\sin\beta & T_7^2 \\ \sin\beta & 0 & -\cos\beta & T_7^3 \\ 0 & 0 & 0 & 1 \end{bmatrix} \quad (4)$$

in which:

$$\begin{aligned} T_7^1 &= p\cos\alpha - \sin\alpha(c_1 + e_1 + e_2 + r_1 + r_2) - \\ &\quad - q\sin\alpha\sin\beta - \cos\beta\sin\alpha(R + c_3 + e_3 + r_2) \\ T_7^2 &= \cos\alpha(c_1 + e_1 + e_2 + r_1 + r_2) + p\sin\alpha + \\ &\quad + q\cos\alpha\sin\beta + \cos\alpha\cos\beta(R + c_3 + e_3 + r_2) \\ T_7^3 &= \sin\beta(R + c_3 + e_3 + r_2) - q\cos\beta \end{aligned}$$

Transformation of the remaining parts of the assembly are given in Equations 5 - 10, Tables 3 - 8 and comes from Figure 4 - 9.

$$\mathbf{T_1} = \begin{bmatrix} -\sin\alpha & 0 & \cos\alpha & T_1^1 \\ \cos\alpha & 0 & \sin\alpha & T_1^2 \\ 0 & 1 & 0 & 0 \\ 0 & 0 & 0 & 1 \end{bmatrix} \quad (5)$$

DOI: 10.1051/matecconf/20167602017

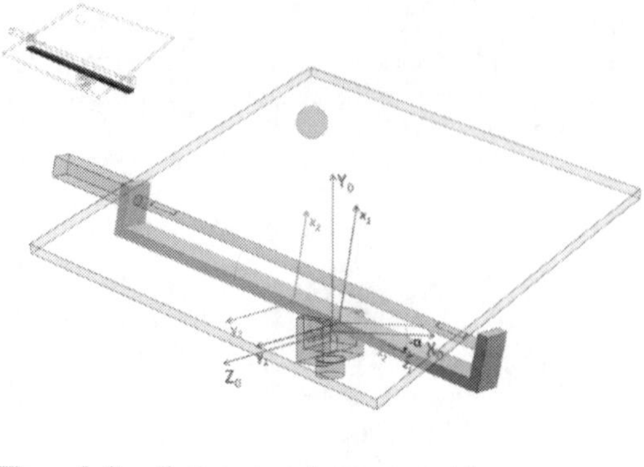

Figure 4. Coordinate system placement - part 1

Table 3. DH parameters - part 1

Link	a_i	α_i	θ_i	d_i
1	$e_1 + r_1 + \frac{c_1}{2}$	$\frac{\pi}{2}$	0	$\frac{\pi}{2} + \alpha$
2	0	0	$\frac{a_1 - b_1}{2}$	0

in which:

$$T_1^1 = \cos\alpha \frac{a_1 - b_1}{2} - \sin\alpha\left(\frac{c_1}{2} + e_1 + r_1\right)$$
$$T_1^2 = \sin\alpha \frac{a_1 - b_1}{2} + \cos\alpha\left(\frac{c_1}{2} + e_1 + r_1\right)$$

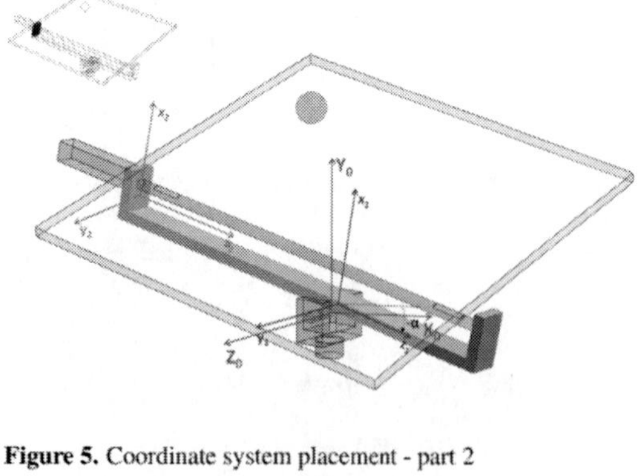

Figure 5. Coordinate system placement - part 2

Table 4. DH parameters - part 2

Link	a_i	α_i	θ_i	d_i
1	$e_1 + r_1 + \frac{c_1}{2}$	$\frac{\pi}{2}$	0	$\frac{\pi}{2} + \alpha$
2	$\frac{c_1+c_2}{2}$	0	$\frac{a_2}{2} - b_1$	0

$$\mathbf{T_2} = \begin{bmatrix} -\sin\alpha & 0 & \cos\alpha & T_2^1 \\ \cos\alpha & 0 & \sin\alpha & T_2^2 \\ 0 & 1 & 0 & 0 \\ 0 & 0 & 0 & 1 \end{bmatrix} \quad (6)$$

in which:

$$T_2^1 = \cos\alpha\left(\frac{a_1}{2} - b_1\right) - \sin\alpha\left(c_1 + \frac{c_2}{2} + e_1 + r_1\right)$$
$$T_2^2 = \sin\alpha\left(\frac{a_1}{2} - b_1\right) + \cos\alpha\left(c_1 + \frac{c_2}{2} + e_1 + r_1\right)$$

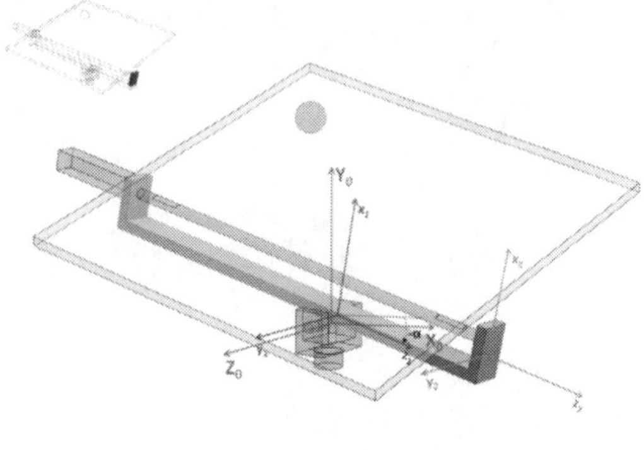

Figure 6. Coordinate system placement - part 3

Table 5. DH parameters - part 3

Link	a_i	α_i	θ_i	d_i
1	$e_1 + r_1 + \frac{c_1}{2}$	$\frac{\pi}{2}$	0	$\frac{\pi}{2} + \alpha$
2	$\frac{c_1+c_2}{2}$	0	$a_1 - \frac{a_2}{2}$	0

$$\mathbf{T_3} = \begin{bmatrix} -\sin\alpha & 0 & \cos\alpha & T_3^1 \\ \cos\alpha & 0 & \sin\alpha & T_3^2 \\ 0 & 1 & 0 & 0 \\ 0 & 0 & 0 & 1 \end{bmatrix} \quad (7)$$

in which:

$$T_3^1 = \cos\alpha\left(a_1 - \frac{a_2}{2}\right) - \sin\alpha\left(c_1 + \frac{c_2}{2} + e_1 + r_1\right)$$
$$T_3^2 = \sin\alpha\left(a_1 - \frac{a_2}{2}\right) + \cos\alpha\left(c_1 + \frac{c_2}{2} + e_1 + r_1\right)$$

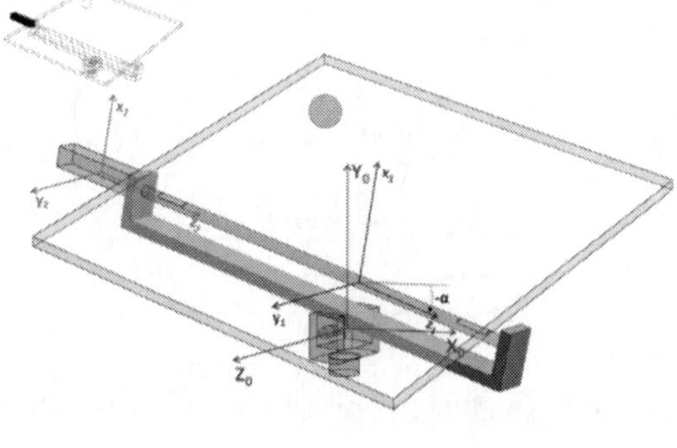

Figure 7. Coordinate system placement - part 4

Table 6. DH parameters - part 4

Link	a_i	α_i	θ_i	d_i
1	$e_1 + r_1 + c_1 + e_2 + r_2$	$\frac{\pi}{2}$	0	$\frac{\pi}{2} + \alpha$
2	0	0	$-b_1 - \frac{a_4}{2}$	0

$$\mathbf{T_4} = \begin{bmatrix} -\sin\alpha & 0 & \cos\alpha & T_4^1 \\ \cos\alpha & 0 & \sin\alpha & T_4^2 \\ 0 & 1 & 0 & 0 \\ 0 & 0 & 0 & 1 \end{bmatrix} \quad (8)$$

in which:

$$T_4^1 = -\sin\alpha\,(c_1 + e_1 + r_1 + e_2 + r_2) - \cos\alpha\left(b_1 + \frac{a_4}{2}\right)$$

$$T_4^2 = \cos\alpha\,(c_1 + e_1 + r_1 + e_2 + r_2) - \sin\alpha\left(b_1 + \frac{a_4}{2}\right)$$

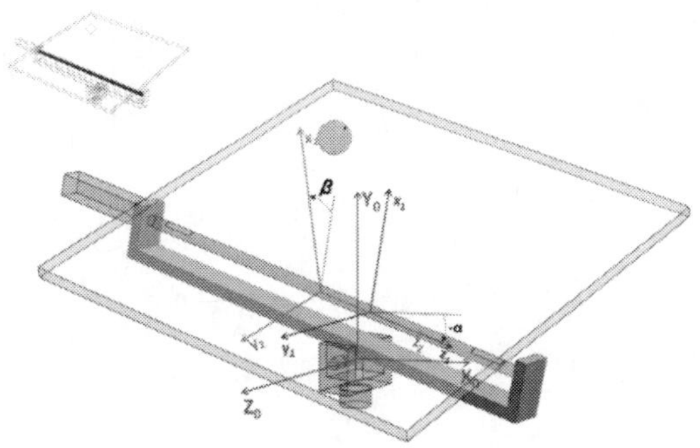

Figure 8. Coordinate system placement - part 5

Table 7. DH parameters - part 5

Link	a_i	α_i	θ_i	d_i
1	$e_1 + r_1 + c_1 + e_2 + r_2$	$\frac{\pi}{2}$	0	$\frac{\pi}{2} + \alpha$
2	0	0	$\frac{a_1 - b_1}{2}$	β

$$\mathbf{T_5} = \begin{bmatrix} -\cos\beta\sin\alpha & \sin\alpha\sin\beta & \cos\alpha & T_5^1 \\ \cos\alpha\cos\beta & -\cos\alpha\sin\beta & \sin\alpha & T_5^2 \\ \sin\beta & \cos\beta & 0 & 0 \\ 0 & 0 & 0 & 1 \end{bmatrix} \quad (9)$$

in which:

$$T_5^1 = \cos\alpha\frac{a_1 - b_1}{2} - \sin\alpha\,(c_1 + e_1 + r_1 + e_2 + r_2)$$

$$T_5^2 = \sin\alpha\frac{a_1 - b_1}{2} + \cos\alpha\,(c_1 + e_1 + r_1 + e_2 + r_2)$$

Table 8. DH parameters - part 6

Link	a_i	α_i	θ_i	d_i
1	$e_1 + r_1 + \frac{c_1}{2}$	$\frac{\pi}{2}$	0	$\frac{\pi}{2} + \alpha$
2	0	0	$\frac{a_1 - b_1}{2}$	β
3	0	$\frac{\pi}{2}$	0	0
4	$r_2 + e_3 + \frac{c_3}{2}$	0	$\frac{b_3 - a_3}{2}$	0

$$\mathbf{T_6} = \begin{bmatrix} -\cos\beta\sin\alpha & \cos\alpha & -\sin\alpha\sin\beta & T_6^1 \\ \cos\alpha\cos\beta & \sin\alpha & \cos\alpha\sin\beta & T_6^2 \\ \sin\beta & 0 & -\cos\beta & T_6^3 \\ 0 & 0 & 0 & 1 \end{bmatrix} \quad (10)$$

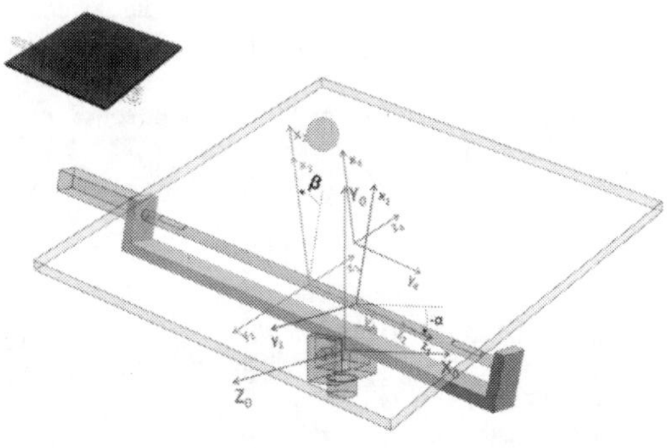

Figure 9. Coordinate system placement - part 6

in which:

$$T_6^1 = \cos\alpha\frac{a_1 - b_1}{2} - \sin\alpha\,(c_1 + e_1 + r_1 + e_2 + r_2) + \\ + \sin\alpha\sin\beta\frac{a_3 - b_3}{2} - \cos\beta\sin\alpha\left(r_2 + e_3 + \frac{c_3}{2}\right)$$

$$T_6^2 = \sin\alpha\frac{a_1 - b_1}{2} + \cos\alpha\,(c_1 + e_1 + r_1 + e_2 + r_2) - \\ - \cos\alpha\sin\beta\frac{a_3 - b_3}{2} + \cos\alpha\cos\beta\left(r_2 + e_3 + \frac{c_3}{2}\right)$$

$$T_6^3 = \cos\beta\frac{a_3 - b_3}{2} + \sin\beta\left(r_2 + e_3 + \frac{c_3}{2}\right)$$

2.3 Motion Equations

Motion equations matrix form of serial manipulator has the general form:

$$\mathrm{D}(\bar{\mathbf{q}}) \cdot \ddot{\bar{\mathbf{q}}} + \bar{\mathbf{H}}\left(\bar{\mathbf{q}}, \dot{\bar{\mathbf{q}}}\right) + \bar{\mathbf{G}}(\bar{\mathbf{q}}) = \bar{\mathbf{Q}} \quad (11)$$

in which:

$\mathrm{D}(\bar{\mathbf{q}})$ ... symmetric inertia matrix
$\bar{\mathbf{H}}\left(\bar{\mathbf{q}}, \dot{\bar{\mathbf{q}}}\right)$ ... bounded velocity vector
$\bar{\mathbf{G}}(\bar{\mathbf{q}})$ ... gravitational force vector
$\bar{\mathbf{Q}}$ ... non-potential (non-conservative) generalized forces causing change of $\bar{\mathbf{q}}$

Individual parts of the Equation 11 can be decomposed to the form:

$$\mathbf{D_{i,j}} = \sum_{r=max\{i,j\}}^{n} tr\left[\frac{\partial\,{}^0T_r}{\partial q_j} \cdot {}^r\bar{I}_r \left(\frac{\partial\,{}^0T_r}{\partial q_i}\right)^T\right] \quad (12)$$

$$\mathbf{H_i} = \sum_{k=1}^{n}\sum_{m=1}^{n} H_{ikm}\,\dot{q}_k\,\dot{q}_m \quad (13)$$

$$\mathbf{H_{ikm}} = \sum_{r=max\{i,k,m\}}^{n} tr\left[\frac{\partial^2\,{}^0T_r}{\partial q_k\,\partial q_m} \cdot {}^r\bar{I}_r \left(\frac{\partial\,{}^0T_r}{\partial q_i}\right)^T\right] \quad (14)$$

$$\mathbf{G_i} = -\sum_{r=i}^{n} m_r\left({}^0\bar{g}\right)^T \cdot \frac{\partial\,{}^0T_r}{\partial q_i} \cdot {}^r\bar{r}_r \quad (15)$$

in which:

n ... number of links
i, j ... state variables

$\bar{I}$ ... pseudo-inertia matrix
${}^0\bar{g}$ ... gravitational vector in global coordinate system
${}^r\bar{r}_r$ ... the center of mass position vector of link in the local coordinate system

The gravitational vector ${}^0\bar{g}$ is in the direction of the global axis Y, therefore:

$$ {}^0\bar{\mathbf{g}} = \begin{bmatrix} 0 \\ -g \\ 0 \\ 1 \end{bmatrix} \tag{16} $$

The center of mass position vector of link is zero in his local coordinate system - all the local coordinate systems are placed in the body center of mass:

$$ {}^r\bar{\mathbf{r}}_r = \begin{bmatrix} r_x \\ r_y \\ r_z \\ 1 \end{bmatrix} = \begin{bmatrix} 0 \\ 0 \\ 0 \\ 1 \end{bmatrix} \tag{17} $$

Only the last unknown parameter is missing in Equation 11 - the pseudo-inertia matrix $\bar{I}$.

2.3.1 *Inertia matrix*

The inertia matrix of individual assembly parts is also need to know to derive the pseudo-inertia matrices in their local coordinate system. Because the local coordinate system are always placed in the object center of mass the deviance moments (i.e. off-diagonal elements) of inertia matrices will be zero.

The numbering is similar as for the transformation matrices.

$$ \mathbf{I_1} = \frac{m_1}{12}\begin{bmatrix} (a_1+b_1)^2+d_1^2 & 0 & 0 \\ 0 & (a_1+b_1)^2+c_1^2 & 0 \\ 0 & 0 & c_1^2+d_1^2 \end{bmatrix} \tag{18} $$

$$ \mathbf{I_2} = \mathbf{I_3} = \frac{m_2}{12}\begin{bmatrix} a_2^2+d_1^2 & 0 & 0 \\ 0 & a_2^2+c_2^2 & 0 \\ 0 & 0 & c_2^2+d_1^2 \end{bmatrix} \tag{19} $$

$$ \mathbf{I_4} = \frac{m_4}{12}\begin{bmatrix} a_4^2+b_4^2 & 0 & 0 \\ 0 & a_4^2+c_4^2 & 0 \\ 0 & 0 & b_4^2+c_4^2 \end{bmatrix} \tag{20} $$

$$ \mathbf{I_5} = \frac{m_5}{12}\begin{bmatrix} 3r_2^2+(a_1+b_1-2a_2)^2 & 0 & 0 \\ 0 & 3r_2^2+(a_1+b_1-2a_2)^2 & 0 \\ 0 & 0 & r_2^2 \end{bmatrix} \tag{21} $$

$$ \mathbf{I_6} = \frac{m_6}{12}\begin{bmatrix} (a_3+b_3)^2+d_3^2 & 0 & 0 \\ 0 & (a_3+b_3)^2+c_3^2 & 0 \\ 0 & 0 & c_3^2+d_3^2 \end{bmatrix} \tag{22} $$

$$ \mathbf{I_7} = \frac{2}{5}m_7R^2\begin{bmatrix} 1 & 0 & 0 \\ 0 & 1 & 0 \\ 0 & 0 & 1 \end{bmatrix} \tag{23} $$

2.3.2 *Pseudo-inertia matrix*

$$ \bar{\mathbf{I}} = \begin{bmatrix} \frac{-I_{xx}+I_{yy}+I_{zz}}{2} & I_{xy} & I_{xz} & mr_x \\ I_{yx} & \frac{I_{xx}-I_{yy}+I_{zz}}{2} & I_{yz} & mr_y \\ I_{zx} & I_{zy} & \frac{I_{xx}+I_{yy}-I_{zz}}{2} & mr_z \\ mr_x & mr_y & mr_z & m \end{bmatrix} \tag{24} $$

The general definition of pseudo-inertia matrix is listed in Equation 24. Now there is all you need to derive the resulting motion equations - Equation 11.

$$ \mathbf{I_{1P}} = \begin{bmatrix} \frac{m_1c_1^2}{12} & 0 & 0 & 0 \\ 0 & \frac{m_1d_1^2}{12} & 0 & 0 \\ 0 & 0 & \frac{m_1(a_1+b_1)^2}{12} & 0 \\ 0 & 0 & 0 & m_1 \end{bmatrix} \tag{25} $$

$$ \mathbf{I_{2P}} = \mathbf{I_{3P}} = \begin{bmatrix} \frac{m_2c_2^2}{12} & 0 & 0 & 0 \\ 0 & \frac{m_2d_1^2}{12} & 0 & 0 \\ 0 & 0 & \frac{m_2a_2^2}{12} & 0 \\ 0 & 0 & 0 & m_2 \end{bmatrix} \tag{26} $$

$$ \mathbf{I_{4P}} = \begin{bmatrix} \frac{m_4c_4^2}{12} & 0 & 0 & 0 \\ 0 & \frac{m_4b_4^2}{12} & 0 & 0 \\ 0 & 0 & \frac{m_4a_4^2}{12} & 0 \\ 0 & 0 & 0 & m_4 \end{bmatrix} \tag{27} $$

$$ \mathbf{I_{5P}} = \begin{bmatrix} \frac{m_5r_2^2}{4} & 0 & 0 & 0 \\ 0 & \frac{m_5r_2^2}{4} & 0 & 0 \\ 0 & 0 & \frac{m_5(a_1-2a_2+b_1)^2}{12} & 0 \\ 0 & 0 & 0 & m_5 \end{bmatrix} \tag{28} $$

$$ \mathbf{I_{6P}} = \begin{bmatrix} \frac{m_6c_3^2}{12} & 0 & 0 & 0 \\ 0 & \frac{m_6d_3^2}{12} & 0 & 0 \\ 0 & 0 & \frac{m_6(a_3+b_3)^2}{12} & 0 \\ 0 & 0 & 0 & m_6 \end{bmatrix} \tag{29} $$

$$ \mathbf{I_{7P}} = \begin{bmatrix} \frac{m_7R^2}{5} & 0 & 0 & 0 \\ 0 & \frac{m_7R^2}{5} & 0 & 0 \\ 0 & 0 & \frac{m_7R^2}{5} & 0 \\ 0 & 0 & 0 & m_7 \end{bmatrix} \tag{30} $$

2.4 The ball position on the plate

Obviously, the transformation matrix using is not only refer to the motion equations. The system has four generalized degree of freedom as Section 2.1 shows. This state variable is need to know during all the regulation process.

Tilts of the plate are given by encoders on the motors which controls them. However, the ball position on the plate is unknown - it rolls independently in the direction of the fastest decrease in potential energy - a negative gradient. It is given by the tilt of the plane.

The ball position on the plate is measured by using a camera, which is placed as shown in Figure 10 - the optical axis of the camera is identical to the global axis Y_0 and the plate edges are parallel to the camera pixel array edges.

The ball coordinates on axes X_0 and Z_0 are measured by this placement, not the size of the p and q as shown in Figure 3.

The best way would be moving the camera and the plate together, but it is ineffective from the construction and control viewpoint. However, the p and q parameters is possible to calculate with the transformation matrices help.

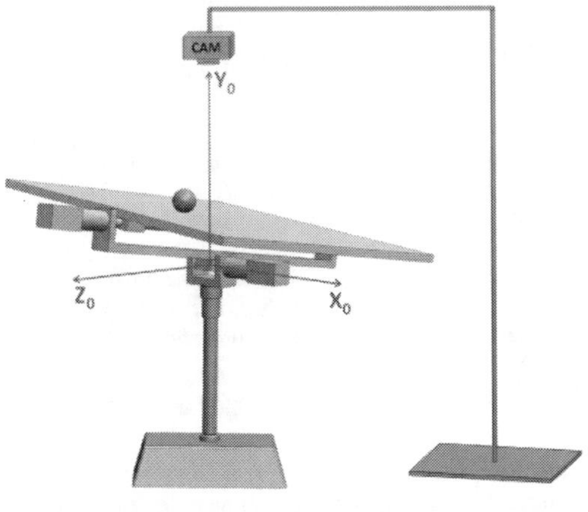

Figure 10. 3D Model with camera evaluation

The ball position in the global coordinate system is expressed from Equation 3.

$$\begin{aligned}\mathbf{X} &= p\cos\alpha - \sin\alpha\,(c_1 + e_1 + e_2 + r_1 + r_2) - \\ &\quad - q\sin\alpha\sin\beta - \cos\beta\sin\alpha\,(R + c_3 + e_3 + r_2) \\ \mathbf{Y} &= \cos\alpha\,(c_1 + e_1 + e_2 + r_1 + r_2) + p\sin\alpha + \\ &\quad + q\cos\alpha\sin\beta + \cos\alpha\cos\beta\,(R + c_3 + e_3 + r_2) \\ \mathbf{Z} &= \sin\beta\,(R + c_3 + e_3 + r_2) - q\cos\beta\end{aligned} \tag{31}$$

Parameters p and q are expressed from Equation 31, X and Z are measured by the camera system.

$$\mathbf{p} = \frac{X - \dfrac{\sin\alpha\sin\beta\,[Z - \sin\beta\,(R + c_3 + e_3 + r_2)]}{\cos\beta} + \sin\alpha\,(c_1 + e_1 + e_2 + r_1 + r_2) + \cos\beta\sin\alpha\,(R + c_3 + e_3 + r_2)}{\cos\alpha} \tag{32}$$

$$\mathbf{q} = \frac{\sin\beta\,(R + c_3 + e_3 + r_2) - Z}{\cos\beta}$$

All the state variables are already fully defined. If the vertical ball position is necessary to know in the global coordinate system, state variables p and q just put into Y in Equation 31.

3 Conclusion

The article contains derivations of the transformation, inertia matrices and all other required formalities necessary for the determine motion equations using the matrix form shown in Equation11. The substitution into the Equation11 and the resultant form is not listed here due to the high dimensionality of the resulting expression. This substitutions and mathematics adjustments are implemented in MATLAB.

The model is divided into 7 parts for ease identifying and acceptable inertia matrices form - each part is one of the basic shapes. These parts connection occurs during substituting into the Equation 11.Transformation matrices are designed to transform the local coordinate system position, associated with the object center of mass, to the global coordinate system. This transformation ensures zero inertia matrix deviance moments and therefore zero pseudo-inertia matrices off-diagonal elements.

Transformation matrices are also used in the regulated value determining, which is different from the actual values, with respect to the fixed camera location to the moving plate. It is used for conversion between the measured and the actual output/regulated value.

Suitable coordinate system placement and then the transformation matrix form is a key consideration as follows from the foregoing. It is important from the viewpoint of complexity of other calculations, from the perspective of finding potential errors or their further use - correctness of the transformation matrix can be easily geometrically verified, which can not be said about the system dynamics describing structures.

References

[1] S. Crandall, D. C, .Karnopp, E.F. Kurz, *Dynamics of mechanical and electromechanical systems* (McGraw-Hill, NewYork, 1968) 466

[2] H. K. Khali, *Nonlinear Systems* (Upper Saddle River, N.J: Pearson, 2001) 750

[3] M.-T. Ho, Y. Rizal, L.-M. Chu, International Journal of Advanced Robotic Systems & Exposition **10**, 16 (2013)

[4] M. Nokhbeh, D. Khashabi, H. A. Talebi, Final Project Report from Amirkabir University of Technology **1**, 22 (2011)

[5] Z. Úředníček, *Robotika* (Zlín, T. Bata university in Zlin, 2012) 284

[6] Z. Úředníček, *Elektromechanické akční členy* (Zlín, T. Bata university in Zlin, 2009) 127

[7] D. C. Karnopp, R. C. Rosenberg, *System dynamics* (A Unifies Approach. Wiley & Sons, New York, 1975) 372

[8] X. Dong, Y. Zhao, Y. Xu, Z. Zhang, P. Shi, Internacional Journal of Innovative Computing, Information and Control **7**, 13 (2011)

Micro-hardness of surface layer of irradiated Polybutene Terephthalate (PBT)

David Manas[1,a], Miroslav Manas[1], Martin Ovsik[1], Michal Stanek[1], Lenka Chvatalova[1], Pavel Stoklasek[1] and Lenka Hylova[1]

[1]Tomas Bata University in Zlin, Nam. T.G.Masaryka 5555, Zlin, 760 01, Czech Republic

Abstract. Using high doses of beta radiation for polybutylene terephthalate (PBT) and its influence on the changes of micromechanical properties of surface layer has not been studied in detail so far. The specimens of PBT were made by injection moulding technology and irradiated by high doses of beta radiation (0, 132, 165 and 198 kGy). The changes in the microstructure and micromechanical properties of surface layer were evaluated using WAXS and instrumented microhardness test. The results of the measurements showed considerable increase in micromechanical properties (indentation hardness, indentation elastic modulus) when high doses of beta radiation are used.

1 Introduction

Poly (butylene terephthalate), PBT, is a commercially important engineering polymer with a wide range of applications such as injection molding and extrusion. As a member of the polyester family, it is also often used as the matrix material in glass fiber reinforced composites, having attractive mechanical properties, good moldability and fast crystallization rate. PBT has some processing advantages over its chemical relative, poly (ethylene terephthalate), PET. The melting temperature of PBT is about 230°C, which is lower than PET, (ca. 270°C), allowing PBT to be processed at lower temperatures. In addition, PBT has a lower glass transition temperature, a faster crystallization rate [1-8].

And it is widely used as fiber, textile, bottle, video tape, food trays and automobile components, such as connectors. However, the disadvantages such as relatively low notched impact strength, poor photo-stability and low deformation temperature obstruct the application of PBT. Therefore, modification of PBT becomes an important consideration.

The most effective and feasible method to solve the high notch sensitivity of PBT problem is to blend it with appropriate elastomeric materials, which is often called polymer-polymer alloying technique. In order to improve compatibility of the blends, reactive modifiers were selectively applied because they can react with the carboxylic or hydroxyl end groups of PBT molecular chains. Among these reactive modifiers, core-shell structured particles functionalized with epoxy groups were usually chosen for PBT blend systems. Therefore, many research efforts have been put into improving the impact strength of PBT [3-10]. The principle of the radiation process is the ability of the high energy radiation to produce reactive cationts, anoints and free radicals in the material. The industrial application of the radiation process (Figure 1) on polymer and composites includes polymerization, crosslink-linking and degradation. The radiation process involves mainly the use of either electron beam from electron accelerators or gamma radiation from Cobalt – 60 sources.

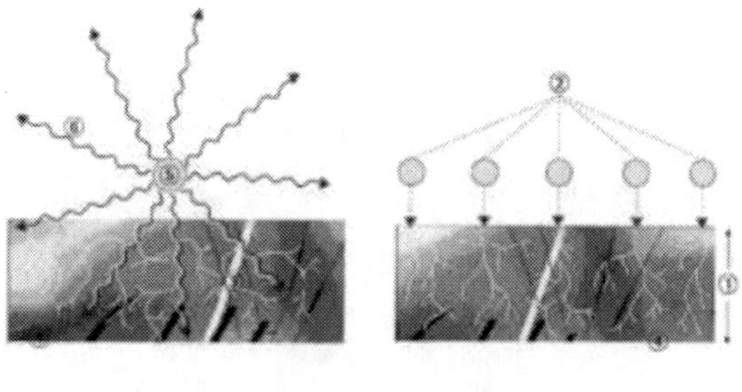

a) b)

Figure 1. Design of Gamma rays (a) and Electron rays (b).

a) 3 – secondary electrons, 4 – irradiated material, 5 – encapsulated Co – 60 radiation source, 6 – Gamma rays

b) 1 – penetration depth of electron, 2 – primary electron, 3 – secondary electron, 4 – irradiated materiál

The aim of this paper is to study the effect of ionizing radiation with different doses, on microhardness of surface layer of PBT and compare these results with those of non-irradiated samples. The study is carried out due to the ever-growing employment of this type of polymer PBT [3-10].

[a] Corresponding author: dmanas@ft.utb.cz

DOI: 10.1051/matecconf/20167602018

2 Experimental

2.1 Micro-indentation test

For this experiment polybutylene terephthalate (PBT) V-PTS-CREATEC-B3HZC * M800/25 nature; PTS Plastics Technologie Service, Germany was used. The material already contained a special cross-linking agent TAIC—triallylisocyanurate (6 volume %), which should enable subsequent cross-linking by ionizing β-radiation. Irradiation was carried out in the company BGS Beta Gamma Service GmbH & Co, KG, Germany with the electron rays, electron energy 10 MeV, doses minimum of 0, 132, 165 and 198 kGy on air the ambient temperature.

The samples (Figure 2) were made using the injection molding technology on the injection moulding machine Arburg Allrounder 420C. Processing temperature 245–295 °C, mold temperature 85 °C, injection pressure 80 MPa, injection rate 45 mm/s. [7-17]

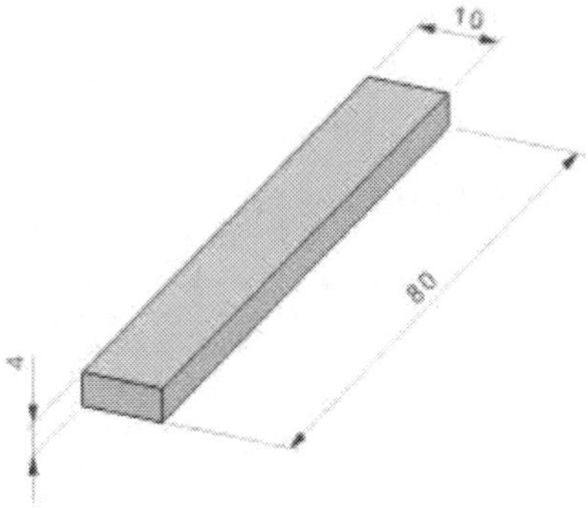

Figure 2. Dimension of sample.

2.2 Micro-indentation test

Micro-indentation test was done using a Micro Combi Tester (Figure 3), CSM Instruments (Switzerland) according to the CSN EN ISO 14577. Load and unload speed was 2 N/min. After a holding time of 90 s at maximum load 1 N the specimens were unloaded. The specimens were glued on metallic sample holders. Poisson's ratio (ν) of the polymer was 0.3. The indentation hardness (H_{IT}) was calculated as maximum load (F_{max}) to the projected area of the hardness impression (A_p) according to: [7-17]

$$H_{IT} = F_{max}/A_p \qquad (1)$$

2.3 Wide-angle X-ray scattering

Wide-angle X-ray diffraction patterns were obtained using a PANalytical X'Pert PRO X-ray diffraction system (Netherlands). The CuKα radiation was Ni-filtered. The scans (4.5 ° 2 Θ/min) in the reflection mode were taken in the range 5–30 ° 2 Θ. The sample crystallinity (X) was calculated from the ratio of the crystal diffraction peaks and the total scattering areas. Crystall size L100 of α most intensive peak at 100 was calculated using Scherrer equation. As a standard "perfect" crystal terephthalic acid with the peak at 2 Θ = 17.4 ° and the half maximum breadth 0.3 ° 2 Θ was chosen [7-17].

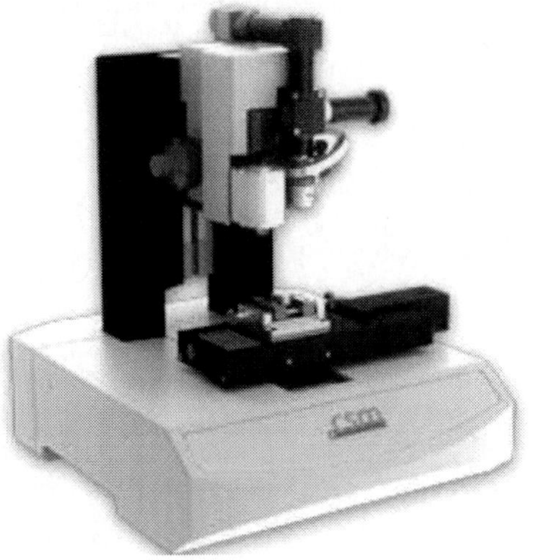

Figure 3. Nano-indentation tester.

3 Results and discussion

The development of micromechanical properties of irradiated polybutylene terephthalate was characterized by the instrumented test of microhardness (H_{IT}), as can be seen in Figure 4. The lowest values (84 MPa) of microhardness were found on polybutylene terephthalate irradiated with radiation dose of 198 kGy radiation dose, while the highest value of microhardness (110 MPa) was measured at 165 kGy radiation dose. The values (93 MPa) of microhardness were found on non-irradiated polybutylene terephthalate. The increase of microhardness at 165 kGy radiation dose was by 18 % compared to the non-irradiated polybutylene terephthalate.

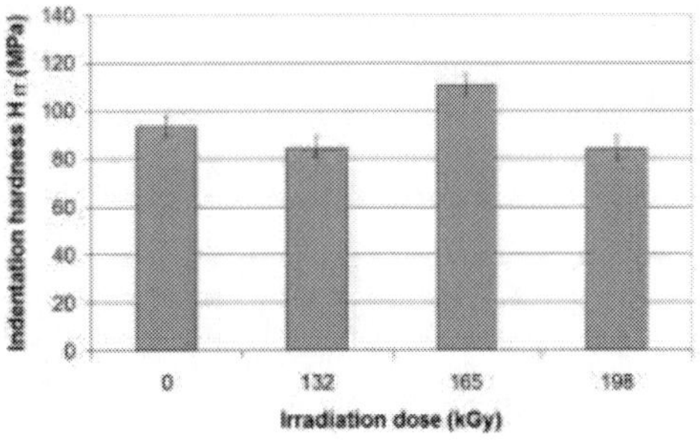

Figure 4. Indentation hardness H_{IT} vs. irradiation doses.

Similar development was recorded for microstiffness of specimens represented by the elastic modulus of indentation (E_{IT}) illustrated in Figure 5. The results of measurements show clearly that the lowest values of microstiffness were measured on the polybutylene terephthalate (1.23 GPa) irradiated with radiation dose of 198 kGy, while the highest values were reached in polybutylene terephthalate irradiated by 165 kGy dose (1.72 GPa). The value (1.54 MPa) of microstiffness were found on non-irradiated polybutylene terephthalate. A significant decrease of microstiffness (11 %) was recorded at the radiation dose of 33 kGy compared to the non-irradiated polybutylene terephthalate.

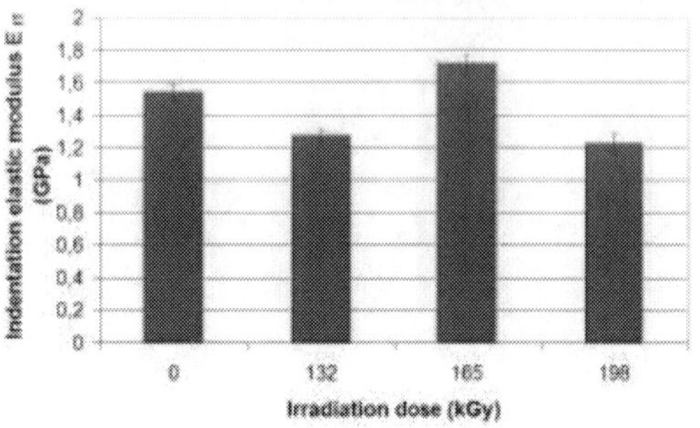

Figure 5. Indentation elastic modulus E_{IT} vs. irradiation doses.

Other important material parameters obtained during the micro-hardness test were elastic and plastic deformation work. The mechanical work W_{total} induced by the indentation is only partly consumed as plastic deformation work W_{plas}t. During the removal of the test force the remaining part is set free as work of the elastic reverse deformation W_{elast}.

Very important values were found for indentation creep (C_{IT}). For materials which creeps as polymers, a basic calculation of that creep can be measure during a pause at the maximum force. The creep is the relative change of the indentation depth when the test force is kept constant measured by instrumented test of microhardness showed (Figure 6) that the highest creep values were measured on non-irradiated polybutylene terephthalate (7.8 %), while the lowest creep value was found in polybutylene terephthalate irradiated by 198 kGy dose (5.7 %). The creep dropped by 27 % as a result of radiation, which represents a considerable increase of surface layer resistance.

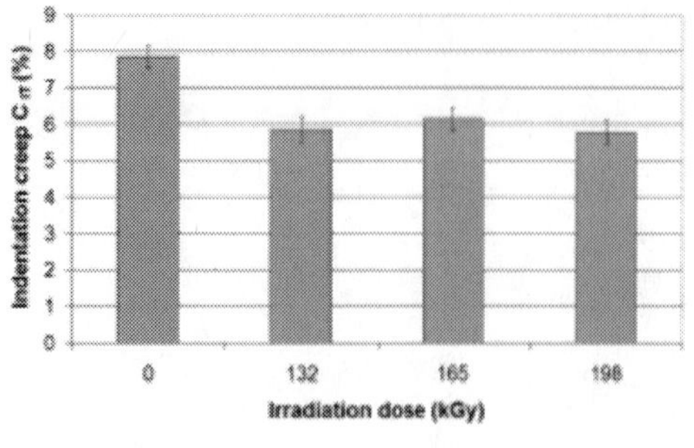

Figure 6. Indentation creep C_{IT} vs. irradiation doses.

The highest values of plastic deformation work were obtained for non-irradiated polybutylene terephthalate. The highest values of elastic deformation work were obtained for polybutylene terephthalate irradiated with radiation dose of 198 kGy. The lowest values of W_{el}, W_{pl} were obtained for polybutylene terephthalate irradiated with dose of 165 kGy. Radiation of specimens caused lower values of plastic deformation work which is in Figure 7.

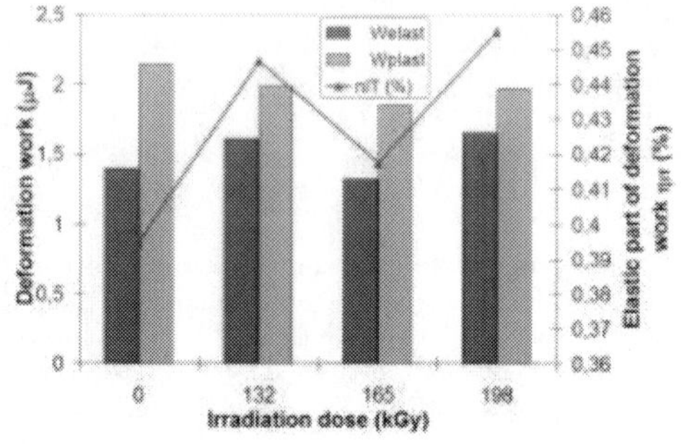

Figure 7. Deformation work vs. irradiation dose.

Higher radiation dose does not influence significantly the micro-hardness value. An indentation hardness increase of the surface layer is caused by irradiation cross-linking of the tested specimen. A closer look at the micro-hardness results reveals that when the highest radiation doses are used, micro-hardness decreases which can be caused by radiation induced degradation of the material.

When applying β-radiation the structure of polypropylene undergoes loss and then a grow of the crystalline phase. It can be assumed that the size of individual crystals will correspond with the loss of crystalline phase (crystalline value X calculated lay in the range 29-33 %). Cross-linking occurs in the remaining noncrystalline part which has a significant influence on the mechanical properties of the surface layer. The greatest size (Figure 9) of crystalline phase was found in the case at the radiation dose of 165 kGy (33 %). The lowest size of crystalline phase was found in the case at the radiation dose of 132 kGy (29 %). On the contrary the smaller size of crystalline phase was measured at non-irradiated (31 %). Its influence on the mechanical behavior is insignificant.

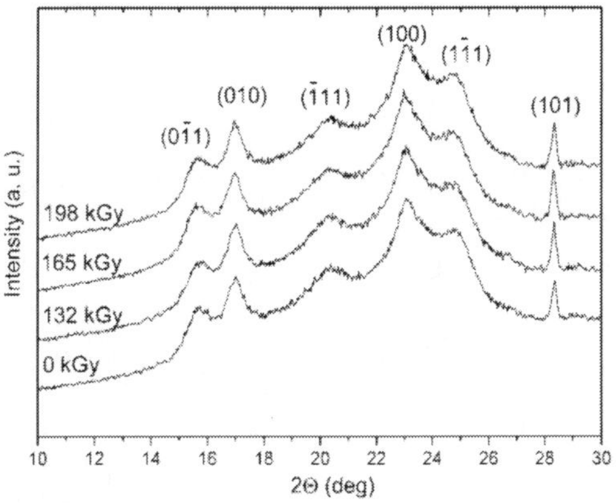

Figure 8. X- ray diffraction non-irradiated and irradiated PBT.

The figure 8 shows typical X-ray diffraction spectrum of the non-irradiated and irradiated polybutylene terephthalate. There is an apparent presence of α-phase in the non-irradiated specimen. The greatest grow of α-phase is seen at the radiation dose of 198 kGy (Figure 8).

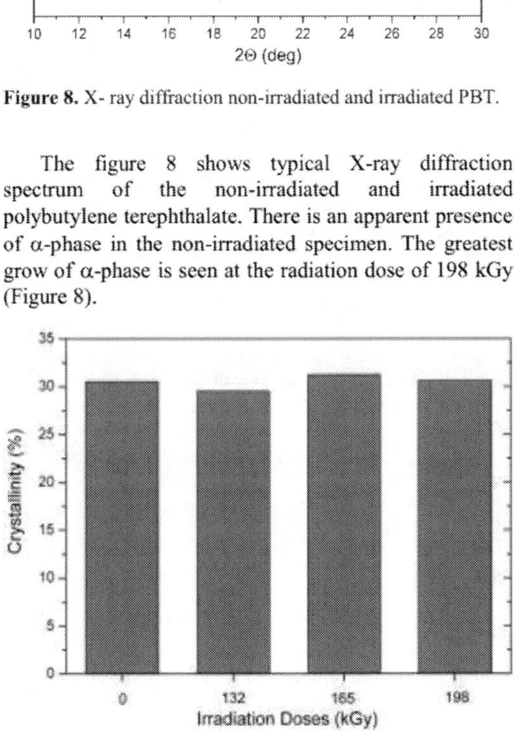

Figure 9. The crystallinity of non-radiated and irradiated PBT.

4 Conclusion

The experimental study deals with the effect of modification of the surface layer by irradiation cross-linking on the properties of the surface layer of polybutylene terephthalate. Polybutylene terephthalate was modified by beta irradiation at doses of 0, 132, 165, 198 kGy. The changes of micromechanical properties were found at the radiation dose of 198 kGy for indentation creep (which decreased by 27%) compared to the non-irradiated polybutylene terephthalate.

Improvement of mechanical properties in micro and macro scale of radiated polybutylene terephthalate has a great significance also for industry. The modified polybutylene terephthalate shifts to the group of materials which have considerably better properties. Its micromechanical properties make polybutylene terephthalate ideal for a wide application in the areas where higher resistance to wear, scratch are required.

Acknowledgment

This work was supported by the Ministry of Education, Youth and Sports of the Czech Republic within the National Sustainability Programme project No. LO1303 (MSMT-7778/2014) and also by the European Regional Development Fund under the project CEBIA-Tech No. CZ.1.05/2.1.00/03.0089 and the internal grant of TBU in Zlin No. IGA/FT/2016/010 funded from the resources of specific university research and by the Ministry of Education, Youth and Sports of the Czech Republic

References

1. Dj. Gheysari, Eur. Polym. J. **37** (2001) 295-302, (2001)
2. K. Makuuchi, S. Cheng. Wiley, Hoboken, 2011.
3. J.G. Drobny, Elsevier, Oxford, 2013.
4. D. Dobrotə, Energy Procedia, **100**, 1160-1166, (2015)
5. G. Zamfirova, V. Gaydarov, T. Zaharescu, L. G. Silva. Chemicke Listy, **104**, 283-286, (2010)
6. D. Manas, M. Hribova, M. Manas, M. Ovsik,M. Stanek, Thin Solid Films, **530**, 49-52,(2013)
7. O. Uzuna, U. Kölemena, S. Çelebi, N. Güçlü, Journal of the European Ceramic Society. **25**, 969–977, (2005).
8. W. C. Oliver, G. M. Pharr. J Mater Res, **7**. (6) 1564–1583, (1992)
9. E. Ragan, P. Baron, J. Dobránsky. Advanced Materials Research 383-390, 2813-2818, (2012).
10. H. Wang, L. Xu, R. Li, J. Hu, M. Wang, G. Wu, Radiation Physics and Chemistry, **125**, 41-49, (2016)
11. J. Dobránsky, L. Běhálek, P. Baron, Key Engineering Materials, **669,** 36-43, (2016)
12. Dobransky, J., Běhalek, L., Baron, P., Kočiško, M., Simkulet, V., Vojnova, E., Briančin, J. Metalurgija, **55** (3), pp. 449-452, (2016)
13. Dobránsky, J., Kočiško, M., Baron, P., Simkulet, V., Běhálek, L., Vojnová, E., Nováková Marcinčinová, Ľ. Metalurgija, **55** (3), pp. 477-480, (2016)
14. J. Čop, L. Fojtl, O. Bílek, V. Pata, Manufacturing Technology, **16** (2), pp. 334-338, (2016)
15. Singh, P. Kishore, M. Singh, A. Srivastava, Radiation Effects and Defects in Solids, **170** (10), 845-853, (2015)
16. S. Kashyap, D. Datta, International Journal of Plastics Technology, **19** (1), 1-18, (2015)
17. S. Zhang, R. Dubay, M. Charest, Expert Systems with Applications, **42** (6), 2919-2927, (2015)

Effect of Ionizing Beta Radiation on the Mechanical Properties of Poly(ethylene) under Thermal Stress

Martin Bednarik[1,a], David Manas[1], Miroslav Manas[1], Ales Mizera[1] and Martin Reznicek[1]

[1]*Tomas Bata University in Zlín, TGM 5555, 760 01, Zlín, Czech Republic*

Abstract. It was found in this study, that ionizing beta radiation has a positive effect on the mechanical properties of poly(ethylene). In recent years, there have been increasing requirements for quality and cost effectiveness of manufactured products in all areas of industrial production. These requirements are best met with the polymeric materials, which have many advantages in comparison to traditional materials. The main advantages of polymer materials are especially in their ease of processability, availability, and price of the raw materials. Radiation crosslinking is one of the ways to give the conventional plastics mechanical, thermal, and chemical properties of expensive and highly resistant construction polymers. Several types of ionizing radiation are used for crosslinking of polymers. Each of them has special characteristics. Electron beta and photon gamma radiation are used the most frequently. The great advantage is that the crosslinking occurs after the manufacturing process at normal temperature and pressure. The main purpose of this paper has been to determine the effect of ionizing beta radiation on the tensile modulus, strength and elongation of low and high density polyethylene (LDPE and HDPE). These properties were examined in dependence on the dosage of the ionizing beta radiation (non-irradiated samples and those irradiated by dosage 99 kGy were compared) and on the test temperature. Radiation cross-linking of LDPE and HDPE results in increased tensile strength and modulus, and decreased of elongation. The measured results indicate that ionizing beta radiation treatment is effective tool for improvement of mechanical properties of LDPE and HDPE under thermal stress.

1 Introduction

Ionizing radiation is radiation at which quanta have a high energy and can knock out electrons from atomic shell and ionize the substance. Electrically neutral atoms become positive and negative ions.

The crosslinking level can be adjusted by irradiation dosage and often by means of a crosslinking booster. The main difference between electron beta and photon gamma is in their different abilities of penetrating the irradiated material. Gamma rays have a high penetration capacity. The penetration capacity of electron rays depends on the energy of the accelerated electrons. Due to accelerated electron the required dose may be applied for seconds, whereas several hours are required on the gamma radiation plant. The electron accelerators operate on the principle of the Braun tube, whereby a hot cathode is heated in vacuum to such a degree that electrons are released [1-6].

As a result of ionizing radiation, linking macromolecular chains emerge and formate the spatial grid. From the results of previous studies it is apparent, that the radiation crosslinking is very efficient method for modifying the final properties of the polymers. However, some knowledge remains unexplained so far, and therefore each new finding about the effect of radiation crosslinking on the properties of polymer materials may contribute to a better understanding of the issue and thus can extend the field of new applications [7-14].

This paper evaluates the effect of ionizing beta radiation on the mechanical properties of LDPE and HDPE under thermal stress.

2 Experimental

2.1. Materials

For this experiment LDPE (DOW LDPE 780E) and HDPE (DOW HDPE 25055E) were used. The basic properties of used materials are shown in Table 1.

The samples were made using the injection molding technology on the injection molding machine Arburg Allrounder 470H 1000-400. The samples had the shape and dimensions according to the CSN EN ISO 527-2 (referring to: Fig. 1 and Tab. 3). Processing conditions during the injection moulding were according to the recommendation of the procedures (referring to: Tab. 2).

All samples were irradiated with electron (beta) rays (electron energy 10 MeV, radiation dose: 99 kGy) in the firm BGS Beta Gamma Service GmbH & Co, Saal am Danau – Germany [6, 8, 9].

[a] Corresponding author: mbednarik@ft.utb.cz

 DOI: 10.1051/matecconf/20167602019

Table 1. Properties of LDPE and HDPE.

LDPE	
Density [g/cm^3]	0.923
Molding shrinkage [%]	1.9
Tensile strength [MPa]	10.5
Shore hardness [Shore D]	49
Tensile impact strength [kJ/m^2]	286
HDPE	
Density [g/cm^3]	0.955
Molding shrinkage [%]	2.1
Tensile strength [MPa]	27
Shore hardness [Shore D]	65
Tensile impact strength [kJ/m^2]	55

Table 2. Injection conditions.

LDPE	
Injection pressure [MPa]	60
Injection rate [mm/s]	50
Injection time [s]	0.4
Cooling time [s]	30
Mold temperature [°C]	40
HDPE	
Injection pressure [MPa]	80
Injection rate [mm/s]	60
Injection time [s]	0.4
Cooling time [s]	20
Mold temperature [°C]	40

2.2. Tensile test

For testing the mechanical properties there was used a tensile test on the test machine Zwick 1456. Test conditions were according to the CSN EN ISO 527 – 1 and CSN EN ISO 527 – 2. Speed was 50 mm/min and test data was processed by Test Xpert Standard software and tensile strength (σt [MPa]), tensile modulus (E [MPa]) and elongation (εσt [%]) were determined [6, 8, 9].

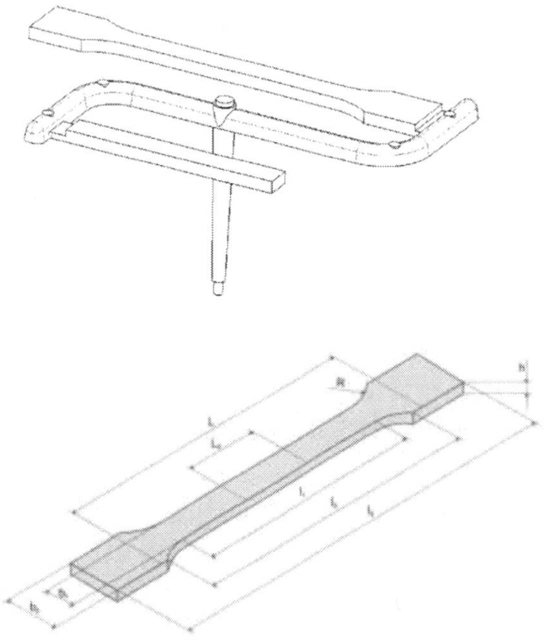

Figure 1. Testing specimens.

Table 3. Specimen dimensions.

Test specimen parameters	
b_1 - Width of Gage Length	10 ± 0.2 [mm]
b_2 - Width of Gripping End	20 ± 0.2 [mm]
l_1 - Length of gage Length	80 ± 2 [mm]
l_2 - Distance Between Gripping Ends	104-113 [mm]
l_3 - Specimen Length	≥ 150 [mm]
L_0 - Distance of Extensometers	30 ± 0.5 [mm]
L - Distance of Grips	115 ± 1 [mm]
h - Specimen Thickness	4 ± 0.2 [mm]
R - Radius	20 - 25 [mm]

3 Result and discussion

3.1. Mechanical properties – LDPE

Comparison of tensile strength, tensile modulus and elongation (at 23, 30, 40, 50, 60, 70, and 80 °C) of LDPE before and after irradiation is given in the Fig. 1, Fig. 2 and Fig. 3. The measured results clearly show, that irradiation increases tensile strength and tensile modulus of LDPE for all tested temperatures.

The highest increase in tensile strength was achieved at temperature 50 °C and the lowest change of tensile strength was measured at temperature 80 °C. In the case of temperature 50 °C the tensile strength increased from 6.8 MPa (non-irradiated samples) to 7.9 MPa (dose of 99 kGy), which is a hike of approximately 16 % (referring to: Fig. 2).

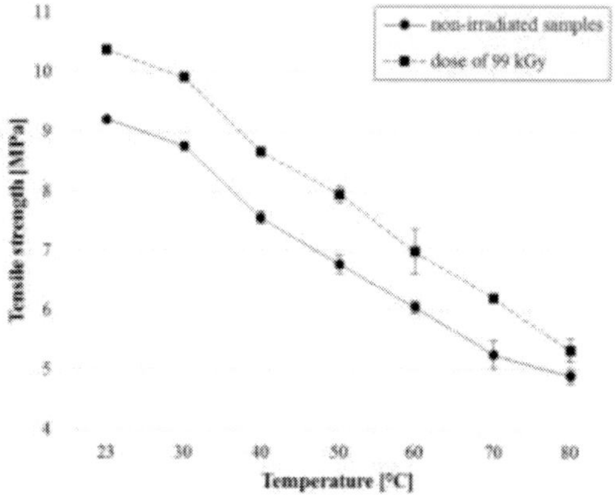

Figure 2. LDPE – variation of tensile strength (σ_t).

The highest increase in tensile modulus was achieved at temperature 30 °C and the lowest change of tensile modulus was measured at temperature 80 °C.

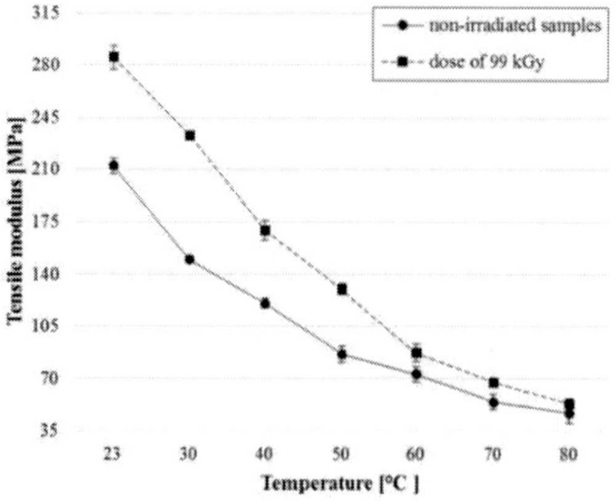

Figure 3. LDPE – variation of tensile modulus (E).

In the case of temperature 30 °C the tensile modulus increased from 149.9 MPa (non-irradiated samples) to 233.3 MPa (dose of 99 kGy), which is a hike of approximately 56 % (referring to: Fig. 3).

The highest decrease in elongation was achieved at temperature 40 °C and the lowest change of elongation was measured at temperature 60 °C. In the case of temperature 40 °C the elongation decreased from 78.3 % (non-irradiated samples) to 61.6 % (dose of 99 kGy), which is a drop of approximately 17 % (referring to: Fig. 4).

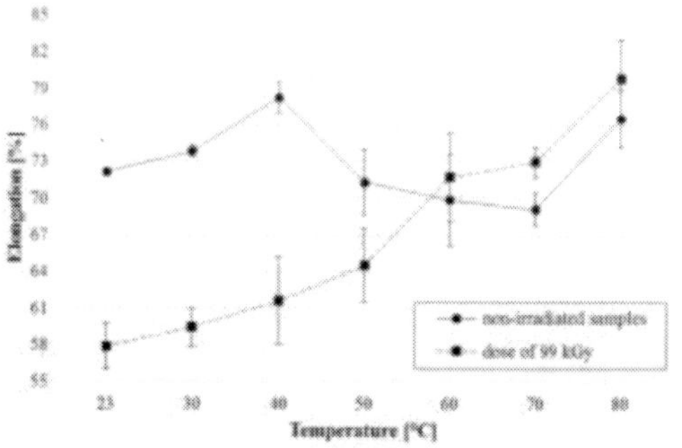

Figure 4. LDPE – variation of elongation (ε_{σ_t}).

3.2 Mechanical properties – HDPE

Comparison of tensile strength, tensile modulus and elongation (at 23, 30, 40, 50, 60, 70, and 80 °C) of HDPE before and after irradiation is given in the Fig. 5, Fig. 6 and Fig. 7. The measured results clearly show, that irradiation increases tensile strength and tensile modulus of HDPE for all tested temperatures.

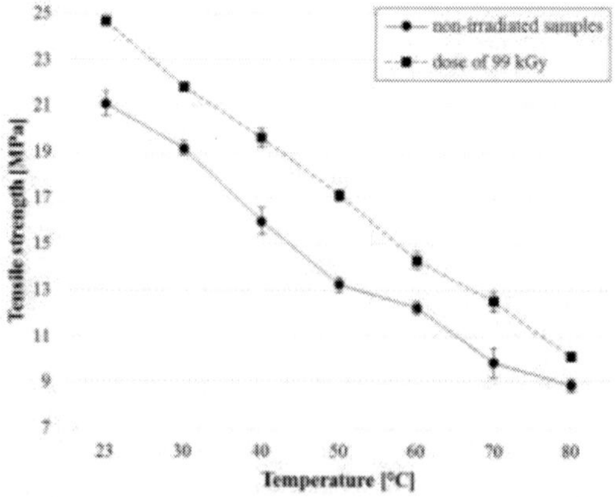

Figure 5. HDPE – variation of tensile strength (σ_t).

The highest increase in tensile strength was achieved at temperature 50 °C and the lowest change of tensile strength was measured at temperature 80 °C. In the case of temperature 50 °C the tensile strength increased from 13.3 MPa (non-irradiated samples) to 17.1 MPa (dose of 99 kGy), which is a hike of approximately 29 % (referring to: Fig. 5).

The highest increase in tensile modulus was achieved at room temperature (23 °C) and the lowest change of tensile modulus was measured at temperature 80 °C. In the case of temperature 23 °C the tensile modulus increased from 1065.4 MPa (non-irradiated samples) to 1299.9 MPa (dose of 99 kGy), which is a hike of approximately 22 % (referring to: Fig. 6).

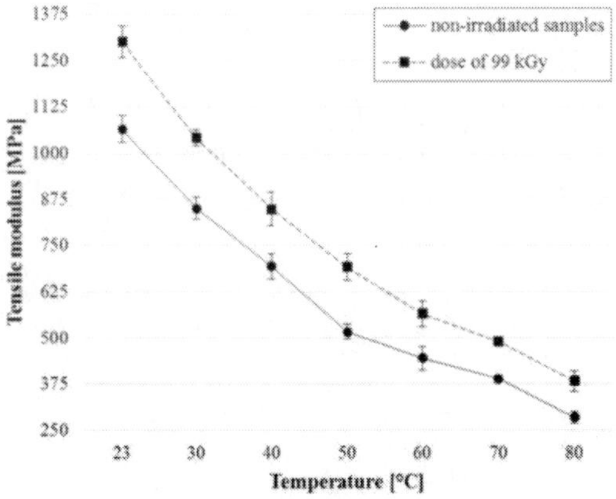

Figure 6. HDPE – variation of tensile modulus (E).

The highest decrease in elongation was achieved at temperature 80 °C and the lowest change of elongation was measured at temperature 30 °C. In the case of temperature 80 °C the elongation decreased from 22.4 % (non-irradiated samples) to 16.1 % (dose of 99 kGy), which is a drop of approximately 6 % (referring to: Fig. 7).

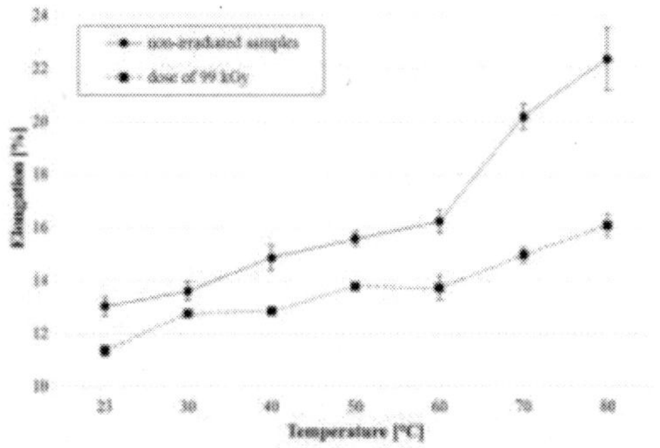

Figure 7. HDPE – variation of elongation ($\varepsilon_{\sigma t}$).

4 Conclusion

This article describes the effect of radiation crosslinking on the mechanical properties (tensile strength, tensile modulus and elongation) of LDPE and HDPE under thermal stress. From the measurement results follows, that the radiation crosslinking appears to be a very effective way to increase the tensile strength and tensile modulus, and decrease elongation. In the case of tensile strength was achieved of the highest increase (for LDPE and HDPE) at temperature 50 °C (a hike of approximately 16 % - LDPE and 29 % - HDPE) (referring to: Fig. 2 and Fig. 5). In the case of tensile modulus was achieved of the highest increase at temperature 30 °C (LDPE) and 23 °C (HDPE) (a hike of approximately 56 % - LDPE and 22 % - HDPE) (referring to: Fig. 3 and Fig. 6).

In the case of elongation was achieved of the highest decrease at 40 °C (LDPE) and 80 °C (HDPE) (a drop of approximately 17 % - LDPE and 6 % - HDPE) (referring to: Fig. 4 and Fig. 7).

The consequence of irradiation is the creation of the covalent bonds among the macromolecular strings which are more flexible during thermal load than intermolecular forces [6, 8].

Acknowledgments

This paper is supported by the internal grant of TBU in Zlin No.IGA/FT/2016/010 funded from the resources of specific university research and by the Ministry of Education, Youth and Sports of the Czech Republic within the National Sustainability Programme project No. LO1303 (MSMT-7778/2014) and also by the European Regional Development Fund under the project CEBIA-Tech No. CZ.1.05/2.1.00/03.0089.

References

1. J.G. Drobny, Radiation Technology for Polymers, CRC Press, Boca Raton (2003)
2. D. Manas, M. Manas, M. Stanek, T. Drga, Chem. Listy **101**, 2 (2007)
3. D. Manas, M. Ovsik, M. Manas, M. Stanek, J. Javorik, P. Kratky, Key Eng. Materials **586**, 4 (2014)
4. M. Manas, M. Stanek, D. Manas, M. Danek, Z. Holik, Chem. Listy **103**, 5 (2009)
5. M. Ovsik, P. Kratky, D. Manas, M. Manas, M. Stanek, M. Bednarik, Key Eng. Materials **606**, 4 (2014)
6. Z. Holik, M. Manas, M. Danek, J. Macourek, Chem. Listy **103**, 4 (2009)
7. Makuuchi, S. Cheng, Radiation Processing of Polymer Materials and its Industrial Applications, Wiley, Hoboken (2011)
8. Z. Holik, M. Danek, M. Manas, R. Lamborova, J. Cerny, K. Kyas, M. Krumal, M. Malachova, Chem. Listy **105**, 3 (2011)
9. M. Bednarik, D. Manas, M. Ovsik, M. Manas, M. Stanek, S. Sanda, P. Kratky, Key Eng. Materials **586**, 4 (2014)
10. D.W. Clegg, A.A. Collyer, Elsevier Science Publications (1991)
11. R.L. Clough, S.W. Shalaby, American Chem. Soc. (1996)
12. S.M. Tamboli, S.T. Mhaske, D.D. Kale, Indian J. Chem. Tech. **11**, 12 (2004)
13. H.A. Khonakdar, S.H. Jafari, U. Wagenknecht, D. Jehnichen, Radiat. Phys. Chem. **75**, 9 (2006)
14. S.P. Hlangothi, I. Krupa, V. Djoković, A.S. Luyt, Polym. Degrad. Stabil. **79**, 7 (2003)

Polymer fluidity influenced by type and amount of filler

Michal Stanek[1a], David Manas[1], Miroslav Manas[1], Adam Skrobak[1], Vaclav Janostik[1] and Vojtech Senkerik[1]

[1] *Tomas Bata University in Zlin, TGM 5555, 760 01 Zlin, Czech Republic*

Abstract. Delivery of polymer melts into the mold cavity is the most important stage of the injection molding process. This paper shows the influence of cavity surface roughness and technological parameters on the flow length of polymers into mold cavity. Application of the measurement results may have significant influence on the production of shaping parts of the injection molds especially in changing the so far used processes and substituting them by less costly production processes which might increase the competitiveness of the tool producers and shorten the time between product plan and its implementation. This research focused into the influence of technological parameters on filling of the injection mold cavity and the flow length respectively.

1 Introduction

Injection molding is one of the most extended polymer processing technologies. It enables the manufacture of final products, which do not require any further operations. The tools used for their production – the injection molds – are very complicated assemblies that are made using several technologies and materials. Working of shaping cavities is the major problem involving not only the cavity of the mold itself, giving the shape and dimensions of the future product, but also the flow pathway (runners) leading the polymer melt to the separate cavities. The runner may be very complex and in most cases takes up to 40% volume of the product itself (cavity). In practice, high quality of runner surface is still very often required. Hence surface polishing for perfect conditions for melt flow is demanded. The stated finishing operations are very time and money consuming leading to high costs of the tool production.

The fluidity of polymers is affected by many parameters (mold design, melt temperature, injection rate and pressures) and by the flow properties of polymers. Results of the experiments carried out with polypropylene contained different amount of filler proved a minimal influence of surface roughness of the runners on the polymer melt flow. This considers excluding (if the conditions allow it) the very complex and expensive finishing operations from the technological process as the influence of the surface roughness on the flow characteristics does not seem to play as important role as was previously thought.

A plastic nucleus is formed by this way of laminar flow, which enables the compression of the melt in the mold and consecutive creeping. A constant flowing rate given by the axial movement of the screw is chosen for most of the flows. During filling the mold cavity the plastic material does not slide along the mold surface but it is rolled over. This type of laminar flow is usually described as a "fountain flow" (Figure 1).

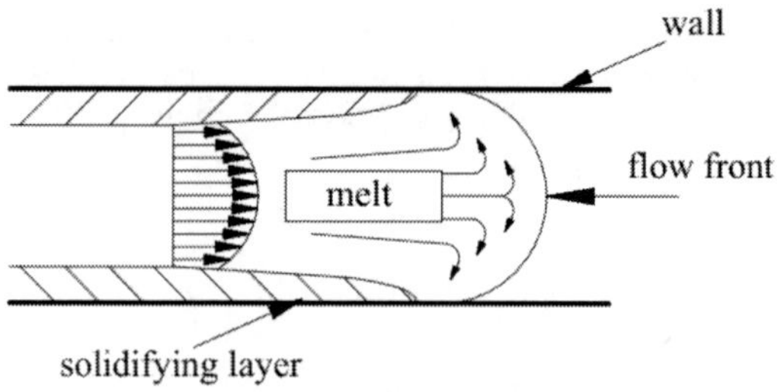

Figure 1. Fountain flow.

2 Injection molding technology

The injection mold for was designed for the easiest possible manipulation both with the mold itself and during injection molding while changing the testing plates, size of the mold gate, pressure and temperature sensors etc. The injection mold is inserted into a universal frame (Figure 2) which was designed for use with many different injection molds that fit the size of the frame. This makes the change of the separate injection molds easier, because the frame remains clamped to the injection molding machine and only the shaping and ejection parts of the molds are changed. Attaching right and left sides of the frame to fixed and moving plates of the injection molding machine is done using four adjustable clamps on each side.

[a] Corresponding author: stanek@ft.utb.cz

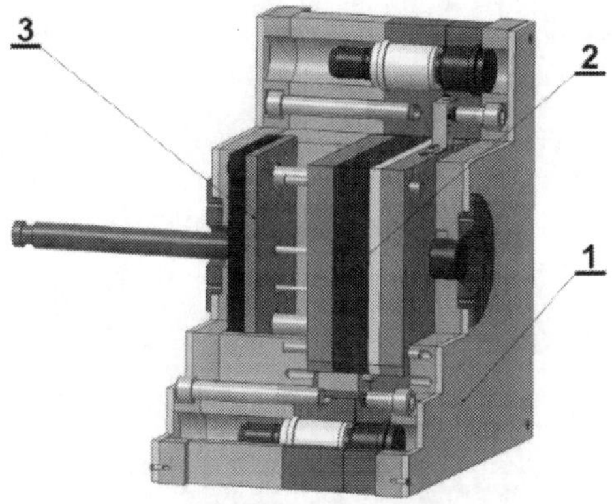

Figure 2. Assembly of injection mold.

1 – frame, 2 – injection mold, 3 – ejection system.

The shaping part of the injection mold is composed of right and left side. The most important parts of the injection mold concerning the measurements are: testing plate, cavity plate and a special sprue puller insert.

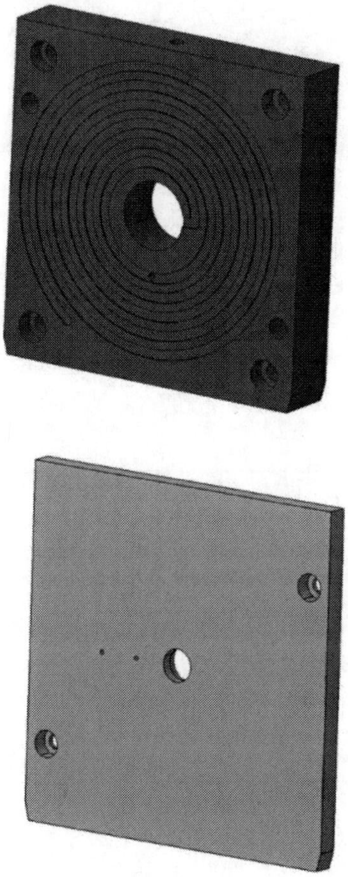

Figure 3. Cavity plate – spiral shaping plate (top), testing plate (bottom).

The cavity (Figure 3) of injection mold for is in a shape of a spiral with the maximum length of 2000 mm and dimensions of channel cross-section: 6x1 mm. The cavity is created when the injection mold is closed, i.e. when shaping plate seals the testing plate.

The surface of the plates was machined by four different technologies, which are most commonly used to work down the cavities of molds and runners in industrial production. These technologies are polishing, grinding, milling and two types of electro-spark erosion – fine and rough design (Table 1). The testing plates are made from tool steel whose are used for simple and fast changing the surface of the mold cavity.

Table 1. Surface of testing plates.

Surface	Ra [μm]	Surface photo
Polished plate	0,102	
Ground plate	0,172	
Electro – spark machined plate with a fine design	4,055	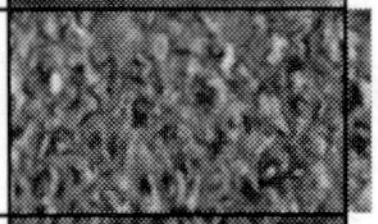
Milled plate	4,499	
Electro – spark machined plate with a rough design	9,566	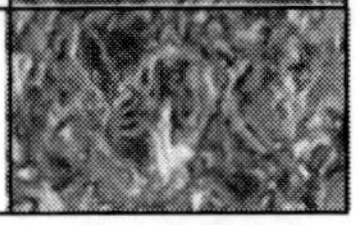

2.1 Injection molding machine

Injection molding machine Arburg Allrounder 420C – 1000 has been used for testing sample preparation. Melt temperature of all materials has been set on 240°C and temperature of mold was 30°C.

2.2 Tested polymers

Natural polypropylene (Moplen) and polypropylene (Hostacom) with different amount and type of filler – glass fibers and talc (5%, 10%, 15%, 20%, 25%, 30%, 35%, 40% of short glass fibers and talc) has been used for the experiment.

3 Results

The aim of the measurements was to find out the influence of separate parameters, especially the quality of the injection mold cavity surface, filler type and filler amount, on the flow length. The main results of the measurement and testing are given on the following pictures.

3.1 Influence of material fluidity on surface roughness.

Influence of the flow length on surface quality is shown on the next figures. The surface quality was changed by the testing plates with different surface roughness.

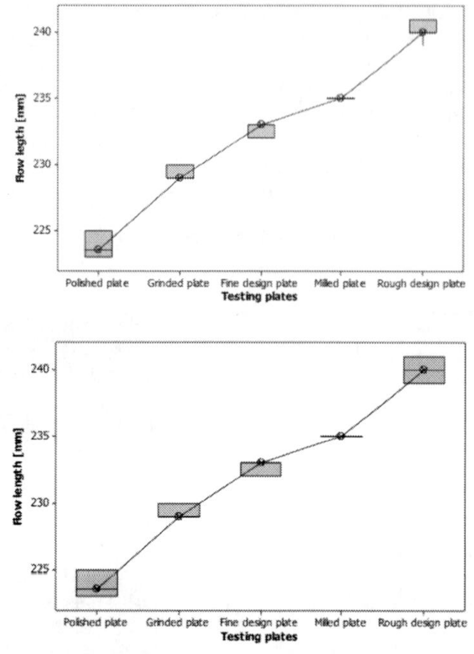

Figure 4. Influence of the flow length on surface quality (0% - GF top, talc bottom).

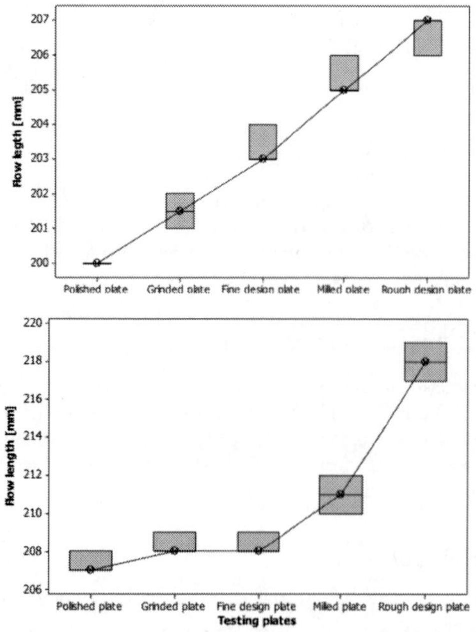

Figure 5. Influence of the flow length on surface quality (20% - GF top, talc bottom).

The amount of glass fibers filler and talc was for the demonstration selected only with 0%, 20% and 40%. The other results were similar – the best fluidity had rough design plate and the worse fluidity had polished plate.

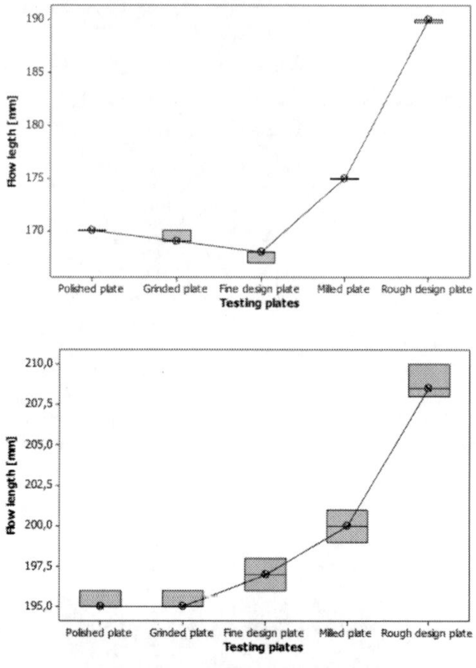

Figure 6. Influence of the flow length on surface quality (40% - GF top, talc bottom).

3. 2 Influence of material fluidity on filler amount

Influence of the testing samples length on glass fibers filler and talc amount (0, 5, 10, 15, 20, 25, 30, 40%) is shown on the next pictures. The results are displayed separately for each testing plate because of better comparison.

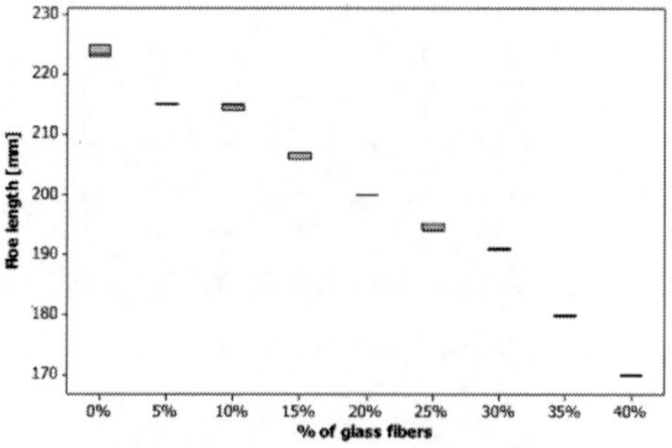

DOI: 10.1051/matecconf/20167602020

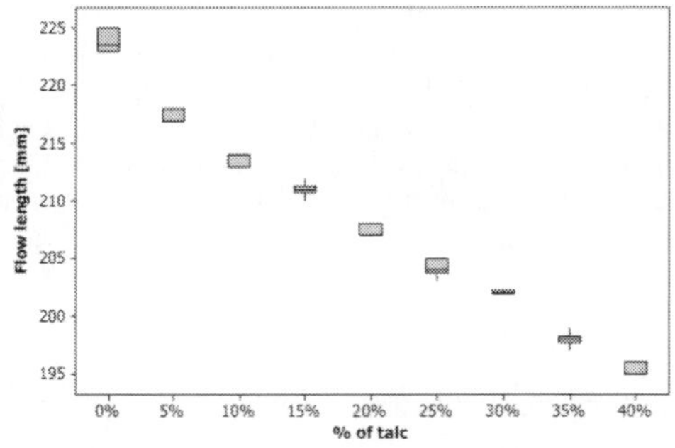

Figure 7. Influence of the flow length on filler amount (Polished plate)

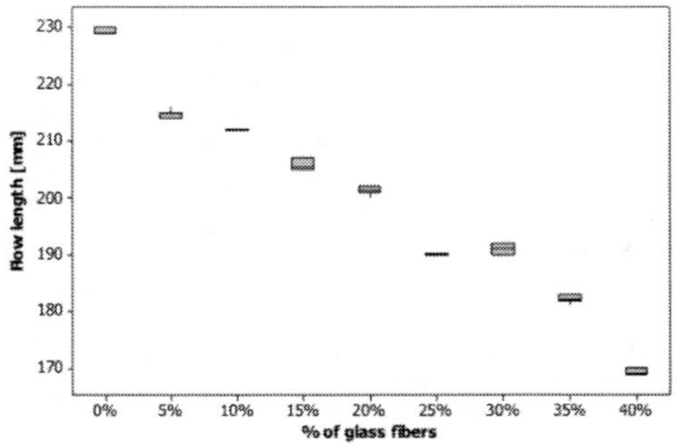

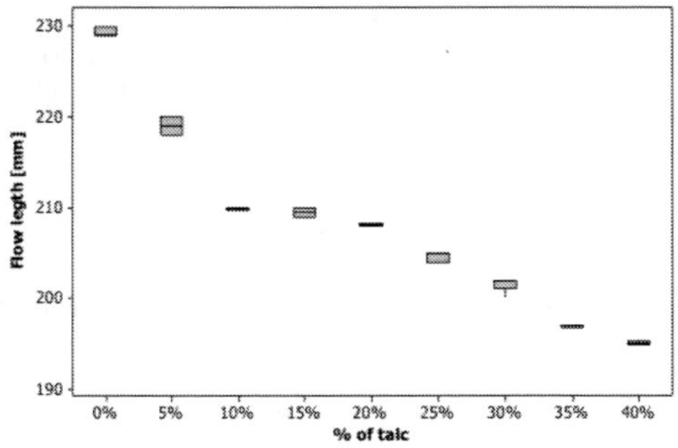

Figure 8. Influence of the flow length on filler amount (Grinded plate).

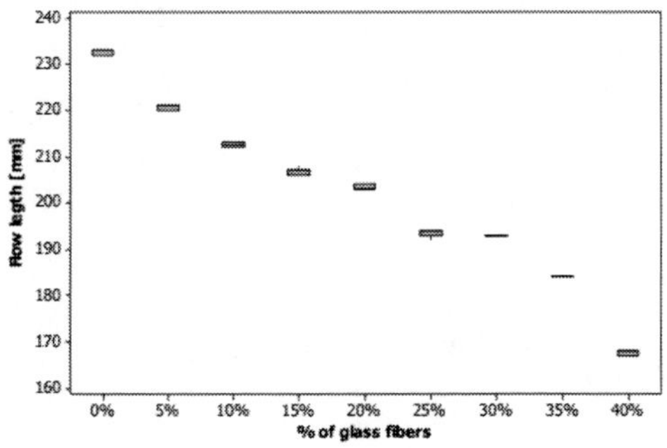

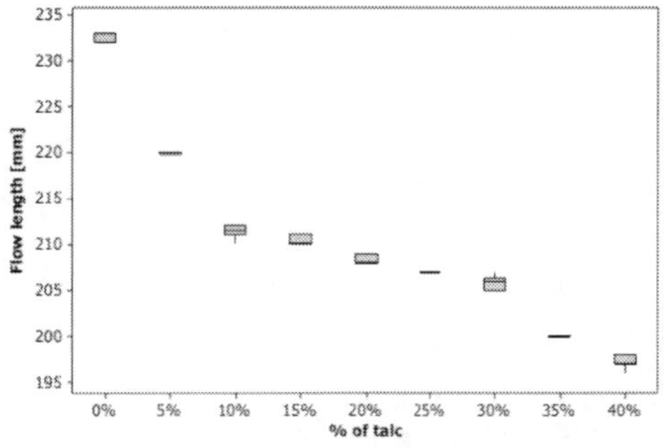

Figure 9. Influence of the flow length on filler amount (Fine design plate)

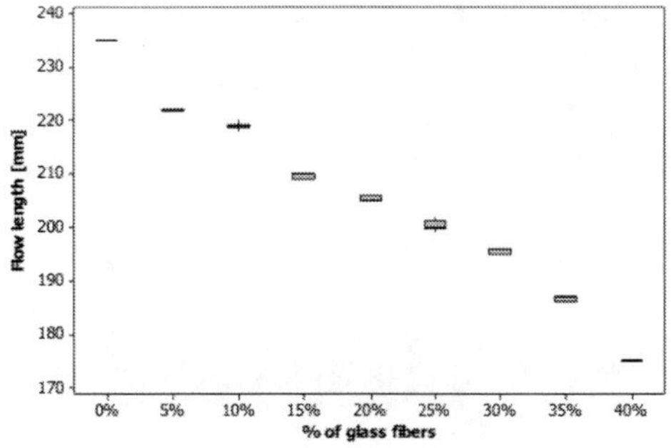

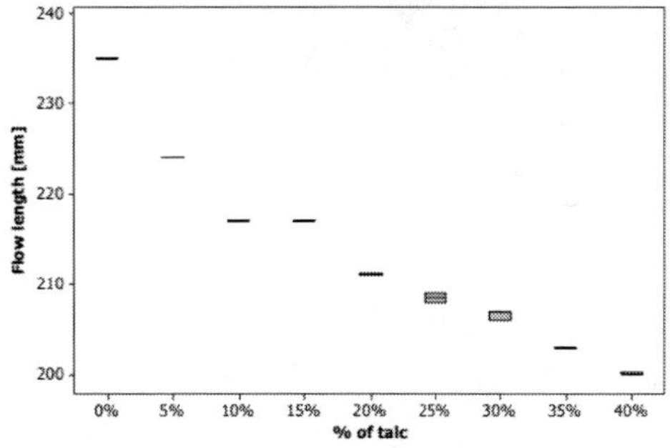

Figure 10. Influence of the flow length on filler amount (Milled plate).

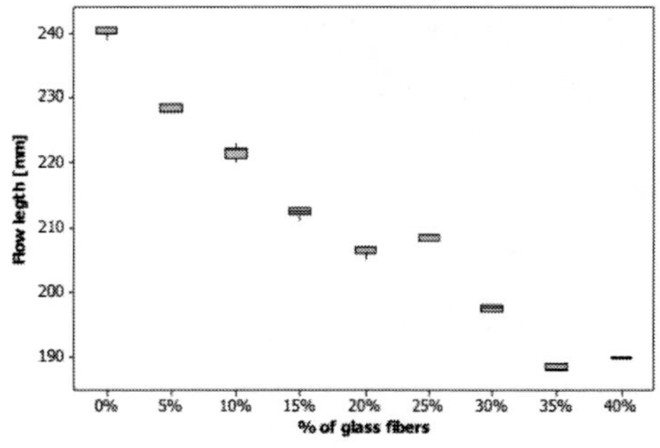

DOI: 10.1051/matecconf/20167602020

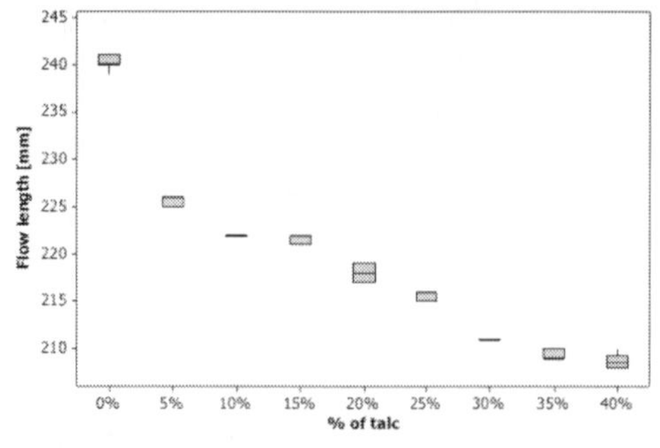

Figure 11. Influence of the flow length on filler amount (Rough design plate).

The fluidity was better in all ways with smaller amount of glass fibers and talc as well. In case of glass fibers and talc used as filler in polymer materials there is significant influence on worse flow material properties. On the other hand the final product form the filled material has better mechanical properties and of course lower percentage of shrinkage.

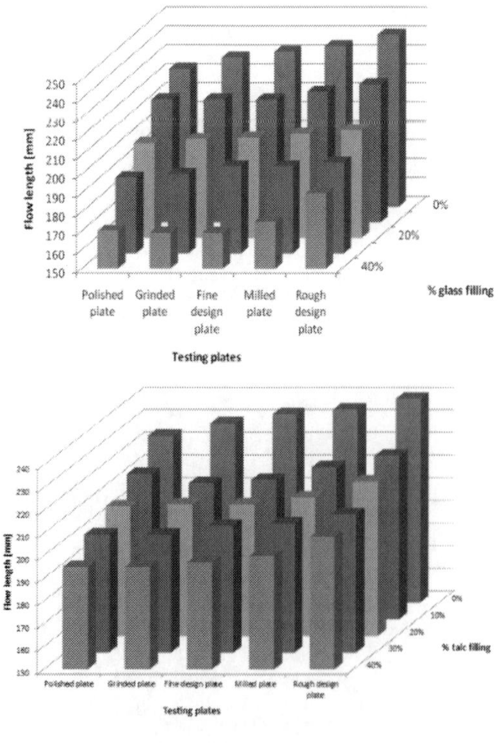

Figure 12. Dependence of the flow length on surface quality and filler amount.

4 Conclusion

This research looked into the influence of technological parameters on filling of the injection mold cavity and the flow length respectively. The differences in flow lengths at the testing cavity plates with different surface roughness were very small, rather higher in case of rougher surfaces. But there is demonstrable difference of worse flow properties on each testing plate with increasing percentage of filler (GF – glass fibers or talc). The measurement shows that surface roughness of the injection mold cavity or runners have no substantial influence on the length of flow. This can be directly put into practice. It also suggests that final working and machining (e.g. grinding and polishing) of some parts of the mold, especially the flowing pathways, are not necessary.

Acknowledgement

This work was supported by the Ministry of Education, Youth and Sports of the Czech Republic within the National Sustainability Programme project No. LO1303 (MSMT-7778/2014) and by the European Regional Development Fund under the project CEBIA-Tech No. CZ.1.05/2.1.00/03.0089 and also by the internal grant of TBU in Zlin No. IGA/FT/2016/010 funded from the resources of specific university research.

References

1. D. Manas, M. Stanek, M. Manas, V. Pata, J. Javorik, KGK – KautschukGummiKunststoffe, 62. Jahrgang, (2009)
2. M. Ovsik, D. Manas, M. Manas, M. Stanek, M. Hribova, K. Kocman, D. Samek, Chemicke listy 106, (2012)
3. M. Stanek, M. Manas, D. Manas, V. Pata, S. Sanda, V. Senkerik, A. Skrobak, Chemicke listy, (2011)
4. V. Pata, M. Manas, D. Manas, M. Stanek, Chemicke listy 105, (2011)
5. M. Stanek, D. Manas, M. Manas, O. Suba, Intl. J. of Math. and Computers in Simul., (2011)
6. J. Javorik, M. Stanek, Intl. J. of Math. and Computers in Simul., (2011)
7. M. Stanek, D. Manas, M. Manas, J. Javorik, Intl. J. of Math. and Computers in Simul., (2011)
8. K. Kyas et al., Simulation of rubber injection molding process, Chem. Listy S J. 105, (2011)
9. M. Ovsik, D. Manas, M. Manas, M. Stanek, M. Bednarik, P. Kratky, Key Engineering Materials 586, (2014)
10. M. Manas, D. Manas, M. Stanek, A. Mizera, M. Ovsik, Asian Journal of Chemistry, (2013)
11. Dj. Gheysari, Eur. Polym. J. **37** (2001) 295-302, (2001)
12. G. Zamfirova, V. Gaydarov, T. Zaharescu, L. G. Silva. Chemicke Listy, **104**, 283-286, (2010)
13. D. Manas, M. Hribova, M. Manas, M. Ovsik,M. Stanek, Thin Solid Films, **530**, 49-52,(2013)
14. Dobransky, J., Běhalek, L., Baron, P., Kočiško, M., Simkulet, V., Vojnova, E., Briančin, J. Metalurgija, **55** (3), pp. 449-452, (2016)
15. J. Čop, L. Fojtl, O. Bílek, V. Pata, Manufacturing Technology, **16** (2), pp. 334-338, (2016)
16. S. Kashyap, D. Datta, International Journal of Plastics Technology, **19** (1), 1-18, (2015)

Influence of length of glass fibers in recycled polypropylene on tensile properties

Vojtech Senkerik[1,a], Michal Stanek[1], David Manas[1], Miroslav Manas[1], Vaclav Janostik[1] and Martin Ovsik[1]

[1]*Tomas Bata University in Zlin, nam. T. G. Masaryka 5555, 76001 Zlin, Czech Republic*

Abstract. The purpose of this article is to show the influence of grinded glass fibers in polymer material. Tested samples were processed by injection molding. Waste from this production was subsequently ground and a mixture was obtained with different size of crushed material. These particles contains glass fibers of similar length as the specific size of particle. Thus very small particles contain very short fibers. Investigation was carried out by testing tensile properties on material polypropylene with 30% glass fibers. Testing was conducted at ambient temperatures. The effect of reprocessing of material is mainly represented by fiber shortening. As a result, considerable reduction of tensile properties can be observed. The reduction is most evident in the modules of elasticity and ultimate tensile strength.

1 Introduction

Products made by injection molding have either character of final product or are semi products for consequent assembly into next complex product. Products made by injection molding are distinguished by very precise dimensions and shape, and also by great reproducibility of mechanic and physical properties. Injection molding technology is most wide-spread technology in plastic manufacturing; it is discontinuous and cyclic process. Almost all kinds of thermoplastics can be injected. Some thermosetting polymer and rubbers can be injected as well.

Defective injects, waste and runner system originating during injection molding can be processed several times. This way of processing is frequently used because of high portion of the waste, especially while manufacturing small injects. For this reason is unpolluted waste cut and crushed. Material modified by this process is once again granulated and mixed with pure granulate and consequently utilized. Using this mixed material has usually no significant influence on physical-mechanical properties or surface appearance. Level of properties degradation depends on levels of crushed material in original material. Transparent and highly stressed materials cannot be mixed, because of high demands.

Injected product can be made even with fifteen to thirty percent amount of waste in origin material without significant influence on its properties. Material properties gradually decrease with higher percents of waste in mix. In some cases (low-end simple injects) parts can be made even from hundred percent of waste.

Mechanical recycling consists in recovering waste material by means of thermos-physical processes. This recycling of plastics presents several technical, economical and marketing challenges.

Mechanical recycling is the most common method of recycling. Here plastics are physically ground back to a suitable size (regrind) and reprocessed. The end use can be the original one or something different.

In the plastics industry it has long been common practice to reprocess waste material arising from normal production. This in-house recycling, known as primary recycling, makes economic sense as it reduces both production waste and utilisation of raw materials. For example, with injection moulding, regrind from start-up waste and production waste such as reject parts, can be fed directly back into the production machine.

In general, variability of product composition and color leads to difficulties in obtaining a product with a consistent set of properties, and sourcing an adequate supply of a reasonably clean feedstock is often the crucial step in determining the economics of the recycling process and the quality of the recycled products. Processability and physical properties of recycled products can be considerably deteriorated with respect to virgin polymers. This is mainly due to the following effect polymer degradation.

Degradation of polymers are subject to negative changes in their macroscopic properties due to subtle modification of molecular structure that can result from the following environmental factors: thermal-oxidative processes that can occur during molding or even at room temperature, attack by pollutant gasses, chemical interaction with liquid contents, and others.

[a] Corresponding author: vsenkerik@ft.utb.cz

Degradative processes are often accelerated by the presence of certain impurities.

Glass fibers are one of the most cost-effective reinforcements for plastics. Chopped glass fibers can be compounded with thermoplastics to obtain products with improved property sets. They are easily obtainable from a range of manufactures and their production process is quite energy efficient, so that their use into products does not significantly affect the environmental performance.

Mechanical recycling of thermoplastics materials with glass fibers consists of granulating and re-molding, without separating reinforcing fibers from matrix. Then the material is reused still as composite. The fiber length distribution and the bonding between the glass fibers and the polymer are affected by the injection molding process. Bonding can be improved by using coupling agents or by incorporating recycled material into virgin material, but fiber shortening constitutes an important issue for safely using recycled fiber reinforced materials. [1-11]

2 Experiment

The aim of this work is to study the effect of particle size of recycled polymeric material to mechanical properties. The goal is to perform an experiment in which the products of the studied polymer will be crushed to crushed material (recycled material) and then reprocessed into new products. These are then subjected to tensile mechanical testing.

Polymer used for this work is an injection molding grade Syntegum 2030 AFV. It is compound on homopolymer polypropylene, reinforced with 30 percentage chemical couple glass fibers. And this PP is suitable for the production of high-technological products, which in normal working conditions are submitted to high temperatures and considerable mechanical stress.

The in-plant recycling of the virgin polypropylene consisted of grinding of tensile test specimens in a knife mill type GK 2218 from producer Maskain AB Rapid. The output of the knife mill was mixed crushed material containing many particles of various sizes up to a fine powder.

Sieving of material immediately follows grinding. The purpose of the sifting was to group the particles of certain sizes of non-sieved crushed recycled material. Sieving was carried out on laboratory sieve shakers AS 200 Basic. The specimens were prepared by the injection molding technology on the injection molding machine. Process conditions were set according to the recommended values according to the material manufacturer.

3 SPECIMENS

Different compositions were prepared for the measurements of tested mixtures with differing sizes of sieved particles.

Virgin PP - material directly from the manufacturer which has not yet been processed in any way, it is taken as a referential material, length of cylindrical granules is 3.5mm.

PP 5 – 4 mm – sieved recycled material with a particle size bigger than 4 mm – this particles stay on sieve with holes 4 mm and chopped fibers are at least due to the length size of the polymer particles (in Figure 1).

PP 4 – 3 mm – sieved recycled material with a particle size from 4 mm to 3 mm, these particles are similar in size as the original virgin granule.

PP 3 – 2 mm – sieved recycled material with a particle size from 3 mm to 2 mm.

PP 2 – 1 mm – sieved recycled material with a particle size from 2 mm to 1 mm.

PP 1 – 0 mm – sieved recycled material with a particle size from 1 mm to 0 mm, containing very small to dust particles and therefore the shortening of the fibers is the greatest (in Figure 2).

Non-sieved crushed PP – this recycled material is collected directly from the knife mill, contains particles of all sizes, from large particles to dust particles and therefore is heterogeneous.

Figure 1. PP 5 – 4 mm mixture.

Figure 2. PP 1 – 0 mm mixture.

Figure 3 shows the weight ratio of particle size of the total grinded mixture. It shows that the largest proportion of the recycled particles between 4-3 mm, of the total volume of them present in almost half.

Particles 3-2 mm representing a further 41% by weight. Other particles represent only a small percentage. Finally, the dust particles occupy only 1% of the total weight.

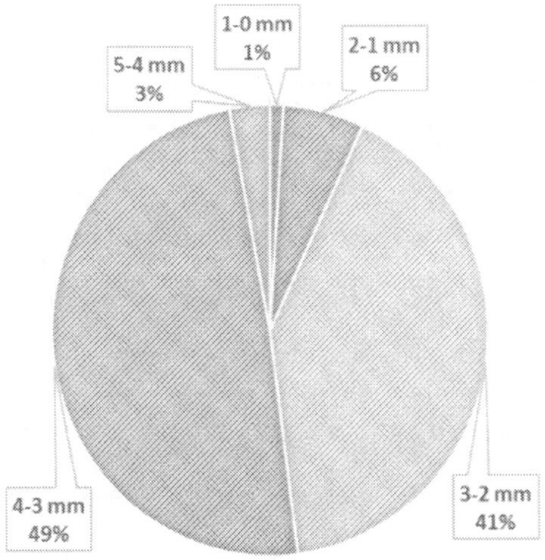

Figure 3. Weight ratio of particle size of the total grinded mixture.

4 Testing

Mechanical testing consisted of tensile test. Tensile properties were measured in accordance with the procedure in EN ISO 527 standard on a universal tensile testing machine 1456 from Zwick / Roel. Testing was conducted at ambient temperature 23°C.

5 Results

All graphs are normalized that the virgin material is 100%. Other values are scaled to this value.

5.1 Elastic tensile modulus

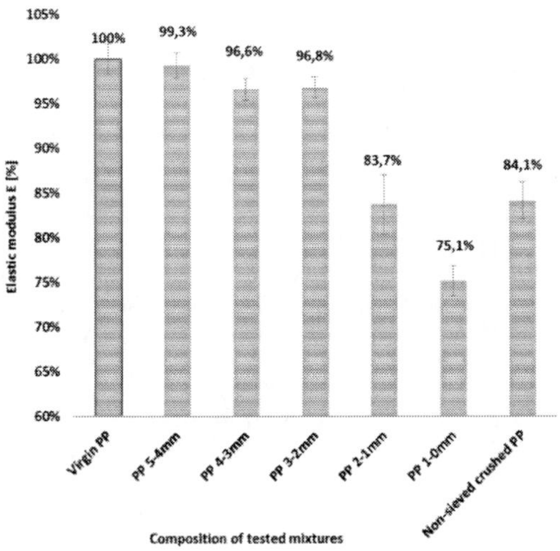

Figure 4. Elastic modulus.

From Figure 4 is can be seen that elastic modulus is reduced by only about 3% for mixtures with crushed size greater than 2 mm, from the original value 6530 MPa to 6300 MPa. This reduction leads to further reducing the particle size to a value of 4900 MPa for the smallest size of particles, which when compared with the virgin PP represents a reduction of 25%.

Negative effect of particle size when decreasing the particle size can be seen on rapid deterioration of elastic modulus at room temperature of the tested material. In non-sieved crushed material containing both small and large particles the modulus is decreased by 16%.

5.2 Ultimate tensile strength

In Figure 5 shows the effect of fillers on tensile strength at room temperature. From results it can be observed even greater influence on the composite with small particle size, which is changed to 28% from the virgin PP.

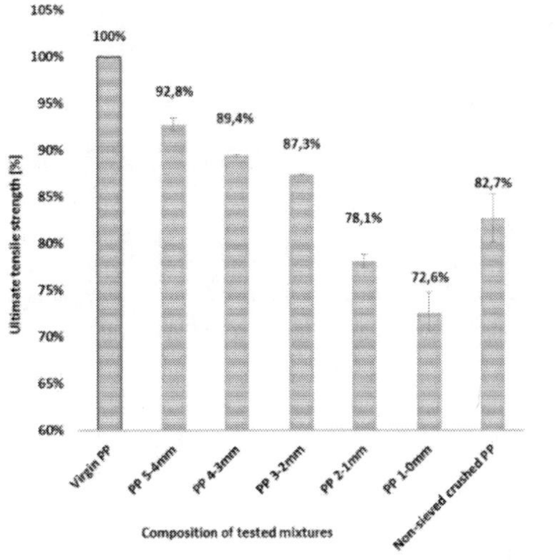

Figure 5. Ultimate tensile strength.

For the composite with the greatest length recycled material and therefore the least shortening of glass fibers was reduced strength only 7%. Overall, there was a significant drop in tensile strength at room temperature of 89 MPa for virgin PP to the 65 MPa. Non-sieved crushed material shows similar reduction in tension as in the previous case of tensile modulus.

5.3 Strain

The decreasing strength and tensile modulus also entails disadvantages in the form of increasing strain (Figure 6). Mixture with particle size 5-4 mm has been reduced by only 1% compared to the virgin PP. Non-sieved crushed mixture shows a similar elongation.

Further reducing particle size and therefore the filler size decreased elongation in tension up to 5% of its initial value. From the obtained results can be concluded that the lower the value of modulus respectively tensile strength leads to a greater resulting strain.

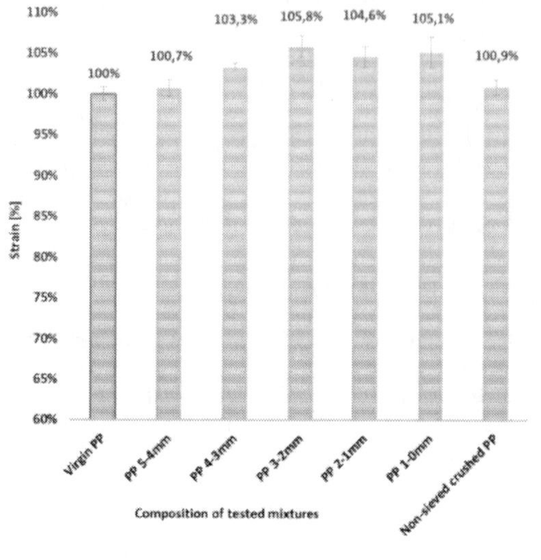

Figure 6. Strain.

6 Summary

The main objective of this study was to define the influence of particle size of recycled material with a filler. This filler is glass fiber. The polymeric matrix used was polypropylene PP. Polymer waste from industrial products was crushed, followed by sieving. Thus combination of mixtures were obtained, which differed from each other in particular size of the individual mixtures. These mixtures contain glass filler and for example very small particles contain very short fibers. This way prepared and processed mixtures were subjected to tensile tests.

From the viewpoint of tensile behavior for all prepared mixtures was observed decrease of stiffness and strength. For the elastic modulus there was quite a large drop in values for mixtures with small particles, this is decrease 25 %. The presence of small particles of recycled material had same impact to ultimate strength.

Adverse change in tensile behavior was further confirmed by a larger elongation of test specimens. The values of elongation increased gradually with decreasing particle size.

Results showed applicability recycled material with larger particles. For mixtures of dust and small particles of 2-1 mm is too large decrease in tensile properties. These particles contains only a very small part of the total weight of the whole non-sieved crushed mixture and causing a large drop of tensile properties.

This decrease is mainly due to the shortening of fiberglass grinding. Because of the pure polymer without glass fibers occurs after the first recycling only to reduce the tensile properties only on a smaller scale. [8, 9] Therefore, if they were removed from the crushed mixture, there would be no great reduction in tensile properties.

Acknowledgment

This paper is supported by the internal grant of TBU in Zlin No. IGA/FT/2016/010 funded from the resources of specific university research and by the Ministry of Education, Youth and Sports of the Czech Republic within the National Sustainability Programme project No. LO1303 (MSMT-7778/2014) and also by the European Regional Development Fund under the project CEBIA-Tech No. CZ.1.05/2.1.00/03.0089.

References

1. L. Scelsi, A. Hodzic, C. Soutis, S.A. Hayes, S. Rajendran, M.A. Alma'adeed, R. Kahraman. *A Review on Composite Materials Based on Recycled Thermoplastics and Glass Fibres*. Plastics, Rubber and Composites. (2011), vol. **40**, ISSN:1465-8011.
2. V. Goodship, Introduction to plastics recycling. 2nd ed. Shawbury, U.K.: Smithers Rapra, (2007), 174 p. ISBN 978-1-84735-078-7.
3. J. Brandrup (ed.): *Recycling and recovery of plastics*, Munich, Hanser Verlag, (1996).
4. M. K. Loultcheva, M. Proietto, N. Jilov and F. P. La Mantia: Polym. Degrad. Stab., (1997).
5. F. P. La Mantia. Recycling of plastic materials. Toronto: ChemTec Pub., (1993), **vi**, 189 p. ISBN 18-951-9803-8.
6. A. Bernasconi, P. Davoli, D. Rossin, C. Armanni. *Effect of Reprocessing on the Fatigue Strength of a Fibreglass Reinforced Polyamide*. Composites Part. (2007), vol. 38, no. **3** s. 710-718. ISSN:1359-835X
7. JC Arnold. Reprocessing. In: Ballie C, editor. Green composites. Polymer composites and the environment. Cambridge: CRC Press, Woodhead Publishing Ltd; (2004).
8. V. Senkerik, M. Stanek, D. Manas, M. Manas, A. Skrobak, J. Navratil. *Size effect of recycled material to tensile properties of PC* (2014) Advanced Materials Research, 1025-1026.
9. V. Senkerik, M. Stanek, D. Manas, M. Manas, A. Skrobak, J. Navratil. *Comparison of mechanical properties of different particle sizes of recycled polycarbonate at higher temperature* (2014) International Journal of Mechanics, **8** (1), pp. 268-275.
10. D. Bryce. Plastic injection molding: manufacturing process fundamentals. Dearborn, Mich.: Society of Manufacturing Engineers, (1996), **xvi**, ISBN 08-726-3472-8.
11. M. Ovsik, D. Manas, M. Manas, M. Stanek, K. Kyas, K., M. Bednarik, A. Mizera. *Microhardness of HDPE influenced by Beta Irradiation*, International Journal of Mathematics and Computers in Simulation, Volume **6**, Issue **6**, (2012), p. 566-574, ISSN 1998-0159.

The Influence of runner system on production of injection molds

Vaclav Janostik[1,a], Michal Stanek [1], David Manas[1], Miroslav Manas[1] and Vojtech Senkerik[1]

[1] *Tomas Bata University in Zlin, TGM 5555, 760 01 Zlin, Czech Republic*

Abstract. This experimental study describes the influence of runner system on rheological properties during the injection molding process. Economic effects on the amount of production are discussed as well. Autodesk Moldflow Synergy 2016 (Moldflow) was used for the study of the injection process. Three suggestions of the runner system, cold runner system, hot runner system and the combination of cold–hot runner system have been promoted. These three variants underwent the rheological and economic analysis. As a result, recommendations for the application of the runner system for the required amount of production have been suggested

1 Introduction

Injection molding is a thermodynamic cyclic process forming of polymer materials wherein material from a solid phase in a granular form is transferred into plastic state (a state of melt) under the action of thermal and mechanic (dissipative) energy. Afterwards the material in a plastic state is injected at a high speed in a closed cavity of a mould which is tempered for injecting of thermoplastic at a significantly lower temperature than the temperature of the melt.

The price of an injected part plays an important role. The price depends on the amount of the production, difficulty of injection mold, multiplicity of injection mold and the quantity of the used material. The aim of this experiment to determine the suitability of a runner system based on the amount of the production for the specific part.

The technology of injection is used for the production from hundreds to millions products. Any particular saving on the time or quantity of the used material causes an important financial saving.

2 Process setting

Experiments were processed in a moldflow program. Very similar injecting conditions were set for all the types of experiments. Product was projected in 3D mesh. The vertices were 1,5 mm distant. Trajectory tempering circuits were the same as well. Diameter of a tempering channel was 6 mm. Tempering medium was the solution of ethylene glycol and water in the ratio of 1:4. Material of the product was selected from MID - Range polymers PA66 filled with 30% of glass fiber by Ultramid A3EG6. The weight of one piece of the product is 21g. Total weight is 84g because the conception is quadrupled. The rest is waste.

Table 1. Process parameters.

Process parameter	CRS	HRS	HRSCG
Filling time [s]	2	1,3	1,4
Pressure controlled [%]	90	90	90
Melt temperature [°C]	300	300	300
Ejection temperature [°C]	195	195	195
Max pressure [MPa]	15	18,87	34,2
Cooling [s]	30	30	30

3 Experiment

3.1. Cold runner system (CRS)

The first variant was a cold runner system which is one of the most simple from the construction point of view. No necessary special construction parts or components forming the runner system are needed. This advantage is very important for the price of the injection mold.

Inlet system is formed by runner insert which guarantees leakage of injection mold with a plasticizing unit of the injection molding machine. Furthermore, the anchoring plates milled inlet channels. The aim of this channel is to distribute polymer melt into shaped mold cavities. The last section of the runner system is a gate locatio, which can influent the shear rate for filling the cavity. Determination of suitable place can minimize pressures required for the transport of the polymer melt.

The final price consists of the price of injecting mold, quantity of material consumption for the production and consumption of energy. In this case, the option with the cold runner system means a consumption of material of 120 g for one cycle. Total weight of a product is 84 g.

[a] Corresponding author: vjanostik@ft.utb.cz

DOI: 10.1051/matecconf/20167602022

The big part of this number is waste. It is 36 g which is 30% of total weight of material used.

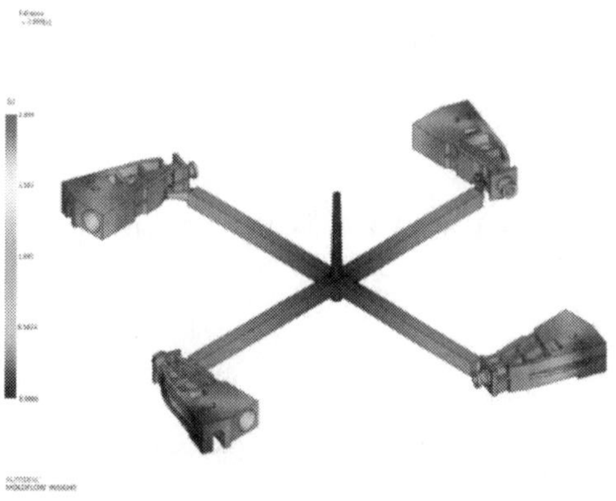

Figure 1. Cold runner system.

3.2. Hot runner system (HRS)

The second option for the analysis is the injection mold with a hot runner system. This conception is much more complex if compared with a cold distribution system. There is a need of additional plates of the injecting mold, such as spacers. Furthermore, special constructions parts of inlet system, which are usually heat resistant, are used. These constructions parts are very expensive and therefore it increases the final price of machine. Design of part placement in mold is similar to the first variant. The cold runner system is substituted by hot distribution system consisting of a hot distribution block and four hot nozzles. The significant advantage of this option is no waste.

The weight of material needed for fulfilling one cycle is 84 g. Due to using the special construction parts, this injection form is 4 800 € more expensive than within the cold runner system.

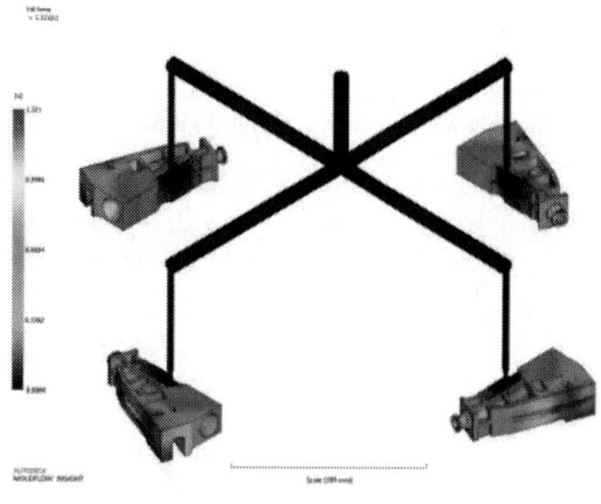

Figure 2. Hot runner system.

3.3. Combination of a hot runner system and a cold gate location (HRSCG)

The third variant is the combination of a hot runner system and a cold gate zone. This variant combines the advantages of a hot runner system and cold gate zone. There is also a benefit of using a cold gate zone as it is a low price part of a relatively simple construction. Inlet system is formed by hot distribution system, two nozzles and a gate zone which is milled on the anchor plate. Compared to Experiment 1, this is also an expensive design but still cheaper than Experiment 2 with a hot distribution system. A runner block of type 1 and only two nozzles perform in this option.

Total weight of a product is 84 g and the number of waste is minimized to 6%, only. From the economic point of view, the amount of waste is acceptable. The final price is about 2 500 € higher than in Experiment 1.

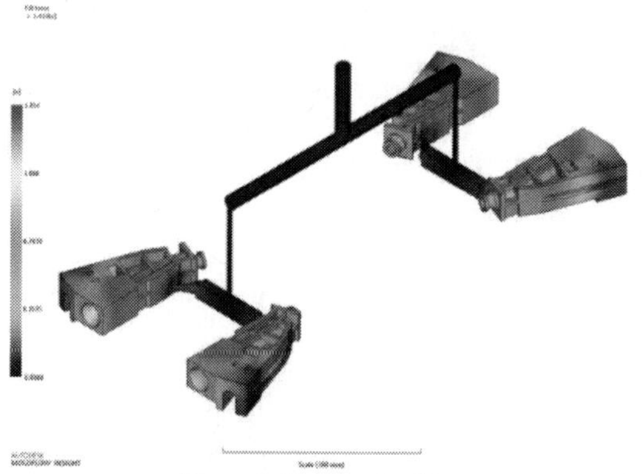

Figure 3. Combination Hot.

4 Results

4.1. Economic results

The options described above have been compared from the economic point of view. The most important factor is the amount of production. The price and consumption of the material and energy required for the heating of elements are included as well.

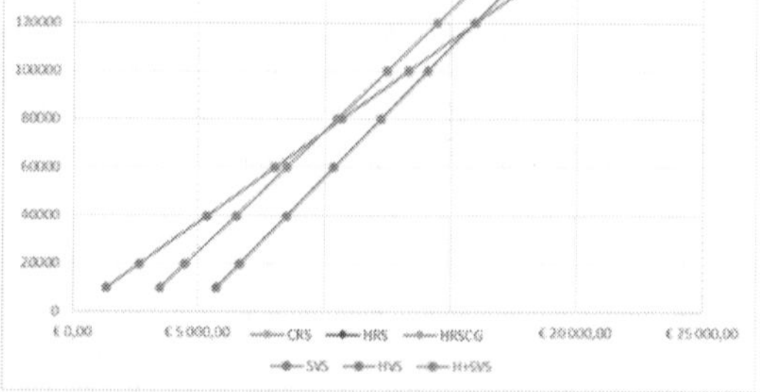

Figure 4. Economic index.

For the number of products up to 80 000, the option described in Experiment 1 should be performed, although the amount of waste represents 36%. It could be decreased by using the variant with a combined system where the waste is only 6%. But the financial savings due to the lower consumption of the material are not so significant.

Within the production over 80 000 pieces it is profitable to use the option with a combined runner system. There is a smaller amount of waste and special construction parts of a runner system and materials would be saved as well. There are lower costs associated with recycling the waste.

Regarding the production over 350 000 pieces savings precautions could be performed by using an injecting mold with a hot runner system.

4.2 Technical results

4.2.1 Pressure at injection

The following figure shows the progress of the pressure during the injection cycle. The injection cycle was optimized to provide an optimal progress of the pressure in the mold cavity. At the beginning there is a steep increase of pressure during the filling phase. The value of the highest pressure is called an injection pressure. Followed by a slight decrease during a replenishment of the melt, it leads to the compression of the melt inside the mold cavity. Then the sharp decrease of pressure occurs due to freezing inlet orifice. It is followed by a cooling phase and by fixing the product in the final shape. After that, the mold is opened and the moldings are ejected.

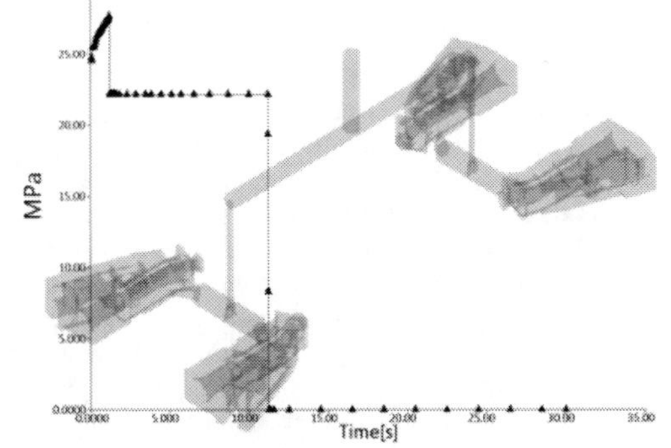

Figure 5. Pressure at an injection location.

4.2.2 Clamp force

The following graph describes the process of clamping force in injection cycle. When the mold is in the injection phase and the injection pressure counteract to the closing force, the closing force have to be the biggest. The melt tends to open the form and against the acting closing force. The value of the maximum closing force of the machine is 2 000 kN. The closing force required at the time of injection is only 190 kN. There is a lot of space for clamping force.

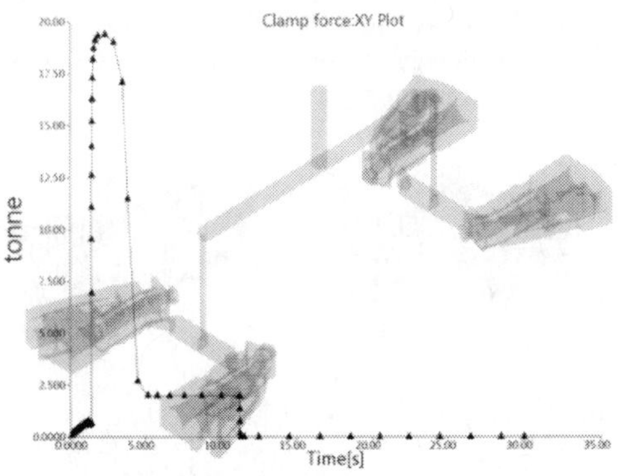

Figure 6. Clamp Force.

4.2.3 Deformation

The level of deformation is characterized by the difference in dimensions of forms and dimensions of the resulting moldings. The shrinkage value is influenced by both the type of polymer, the shape of the ejection and by the injection mold (gating, holding pressure and choice of tempering channels). The total deformation of operating pressures, material shrinkage and the influence of annealing is 0.5 mm. This value is relative to the central axis of a system model. To achieve preservation of dimensions of the products the mold cavity should be increased by a shrinkage value.

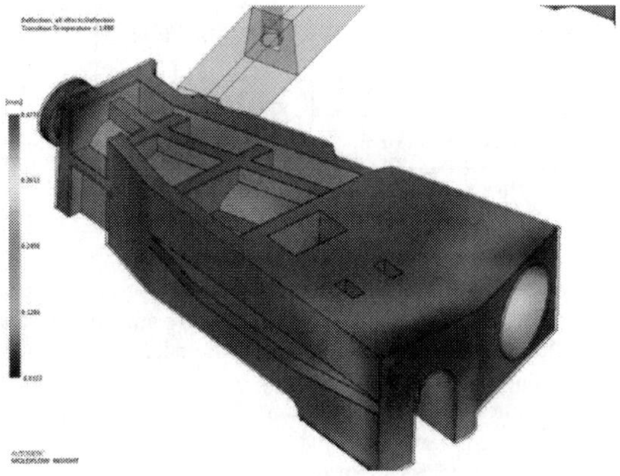

Figure 7. Absolute deformation.

4.2.4 Welld lines

The cold seal is formed by a collision of the front of the melt, such as wrapping cores. It is caused by local lower strength product. The following figure shows the placement of the collision of two faces melt and the formation of the cold joints. The most serious are the furthest cold joints. Due to long flow paths the fronts of the cooled polymer melt is cooled at this point and metallic additional coating is located there as well. The temperature of the polymer melt front at this point is 298°C. Due to such a high temperature of the polymer melt a cold seal with a significantly lower strength is not created.

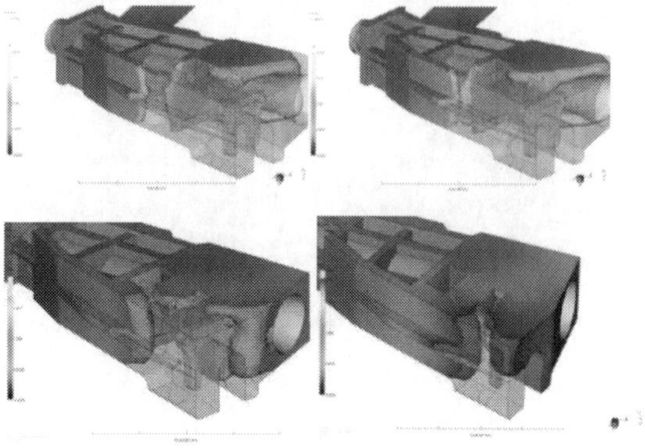

Figure 8. Welld lines.

Table 2. Results.

Result	CRS	HRS	H+SVS
Fill time [s]	2	1,3	1,4
Max Pressure [MPa]	14,88	18,87	34,52
Clamp force [tonne]	13,70	12,26	24,30
Max share rate [1/s]	18 916	11 369	21 349
Shear stress at wall [MPa]	0,22	0,19	0,24
Circuit flow rate[lit/min]	1,4	1,4	1,4
Warp deflection [mm]	0,51	0,39	0,47

5 Conclusion

Because of the similar design aspects, such as the location of the inlet orifice, choice of the temperature and technological conditions, technological results are similar.

Time of filling is the same for all analysed options and ranged between 2 and 1.3 s. The highest pressure inside the intake system is the variant with a combination of a hot distribution channel with the cold-air intake opening. This phenomenon has occurred because of the great complexity of the flow paths. With the size of the pressure inside the cavity the size of the closing force is related. It is the opposite of the force of the pressure and prevents the injection mold from opening. The largest speed shear deformation is also the variant of HRSCG. This value is not approaching the limit value of the rate of shear deformation which is satisfactory. From the economic point of view it is best to use the option of HRSCG. It suits all the technological parameters and economic requirements. The amount of the production is a significant value. With the knowledge of this information, the injection mold could be designed to perform significant financial and time savings.

Acknowledgement

This work was supported by the Ministry of Education, Youth and Sports of the Czech Republic within the National Sustainability Programme project No. LO1303 (MSMT-7778/2014) and by the European Regional Development Fund under the project CEBIA-Tech No. CZ.1.05/2.1.00/03.0089 and also by the internal grant of TBU in Zlín No. IGA/FT/2016/010 funded from the resources of specific university research.

References

1. M. Ovsik, D. Manas, M. Manas, M. Stanek, M. Hribova, K. Kocman, D. Samek, Irradiated Polypropylene Studied by Microhardness and WAXS, Chemicke listy 106, (2012)
2. M. Stanek, M. Manas, D. Manas, V. Pata, S. Sanda, V. Senkerik, A. Skrobak, How the Filler Influence the Fluidity of Polymer, Chemicke listy, (2011)
3. M. Stanek, D. Manas, M. Manas, O. Suba, Optimization of injection molding process, Intl. J. of Math. and Computers in Simul., Vol.5, No.5, (2011)
4. J. Javorik, M. Stanek, The shape optimization of the pneumatic valve diaphragms, Intl. J. of Math. and Computers in Simul., Vol.5, No.4, (2011)
5. M. Stanek, D. Manas, M. Manas, J. Javorik, Simulation of injection molding process by cadmould rubber, Intl. J. of Math. and Computers in Simul., Vol.5, No.5, (2011)
6. M. Ovsik, D. Manas, M. Manas, M. Stanek, M. Bednarik, P. Kratky, Effect of beta irradiation on microhardness of polyamide 6, Key Engineering Materials, vol. 586, (2014)
7. M. Manas, D. Manas, M. Stanek, A. Mizera, M. Ovsik, Modification of polymer properties by irradiation properties of thermoplastic elastomer after radiation cross-linking, Asian Journal of Chemistry, vol. 25, Issue 9, (2013)
8. Tim A. Osswald, International Plastics Handbook: the Resource for Plastics Engineers (fourth ed.) Hanser Publishers, Munich (2006)
9. Dobransky, J., et al. Comparison of Cooling Variants by Simulation Software. Advanced Materials Research. Vol. 801 (2013). pp. 75-80. ISSN 1022-6680.
10. Behalek, L. and Dobránsky, J. Conformal cooling of the injection moulds. Applied Mechanics and Materials. Vol. 308 (2013). pp. 127-132. ISSN 1660-9336.

Mechanical Properties of Injection Molded and Compression Molded Samples from Nature-Butadiene Rubber

Adam Skrobak[1,a], Václav Janoštík[1], Michal Stanek[1], David Manas[1], Martin Ovsik[1], Vojtech Senkerik[1] and Martin Reznicek[1]

[1]*Tomas Bata University in Zlin, TGM 5555, 760 01 Zlin, Czech Republic*

Abstract. The aim of this paper is to show what extent there is an impact on the mechanical properties (tensile strength and tear strength) of a standardized testing sample made of rubber compound based on nature rubber and butadiene rubber produced by injection molding in comparison with a sample produced by classic preparation (cutting out a compression molded plate) according to the standard ISO 23529. For realization of this study it was necessary to design and produce an injection mold for all types testing samples. Subsequently, mechanical properties such as the tensile stress-strain and tear strenght of compression molded samples and injection molded samples were studied, compared and discussed.

1 Introduction

When producing rubber products it is necessary to watch and check the mechanical properties whether it be the properties of the processed material, i.e. the rubber compound, or properties of the product itself. This control aims primarily on how the mechanical properties are influenced by the preparation of the rubber-processing compounds itself, or the change of technological conditions, e.g. the curing time, the curing temperature etc. However, it does not deal with the impact of changing the whole production technology. One of the very productive technologies, which is coming forth, is the production by injection molding. Control of the mechanical properties of rubber products produced by injection molding is mostly performed on testing samples produced in another way, i.e. cutting off a compression molded plate. [1-13] This distinct way of producing testing samples and final products can result in different mechanical properties. Injection molding of rubber compounds is used mainly in the automotive industry to produce a large assortment of products which are more demanding as for the shape and dimensional precision. Injection molding is most effective in continuous production operations. Injection molding differs from compression molding mainly in different remolding of the material. During the injection molding the rubber compound comes in the mold cavity, having been preheated to a higher temperature, i.e. with lower viscosity, and owing to the injection speed and pressure it is subject to higher shear stress. [14-23] This distinct way of remolding can result in a different disposition of macromolecules in the material structure and different internal strain, which has an impact on the resulting properties of the final product. [24-33]

2 Experiment

For this research, a rubber compound on based nature rubber and butadiene rubber (curing agent - sulphur) appointed for production of automotive parts was chosen. Approximate composition of the compound shown in Table 1. This compound shows sufficient scorch time and fluidity, which were verified by a measurement on RPA (Rubber Process Analyzer). The curing temperature 160 °C was chosen for both technologies (compression molding and injection molding).

Table 1. Composition of the compound.

Nature rubber (NR)	35 %
Butadiene rubber (BR)	20 %
Plasticizer	6,5 %
Filler (carbon black)	27 %
Sulphur curing agent	11,5 %

[a] Corresponding author: skrobak@ft.utb.cz

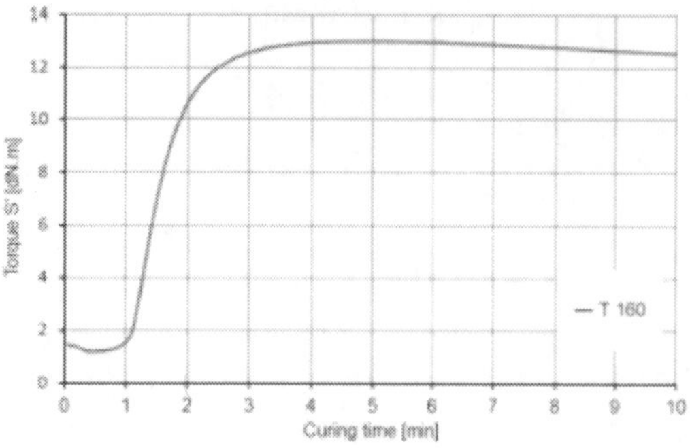

Figure 1. Curing curve for 160 °C

Optimum of cure at this temperature is approximately 2.4 minutes. Curing parameters of the compound are listed in Table 2.

Table 2. Curing specification for 160 °C.

Max. torque S'	13.01 dN.m
Scorch time (t_S)	1.04 min
10% cure (t_{10})	1.14 min
50% cure (t_{50})	1.50 min
90% cure (t_{90})	2.40 min

2.1 Production of testing samples

For this research, the mechanical tension test according to the standard ISO 37 was chosen. The standard also prescribes the shapes and dimensions of testing samples. To perform this test, the testing sample dumbbell – type 1 (Fig. 2a) has been selected. Another test confirming the mechanical properties is the test determining tear strength according to the standard ISO 34-1. To perform this test, the samples crescent, graves and trousers were chosen (Fig. 2b, c, d).

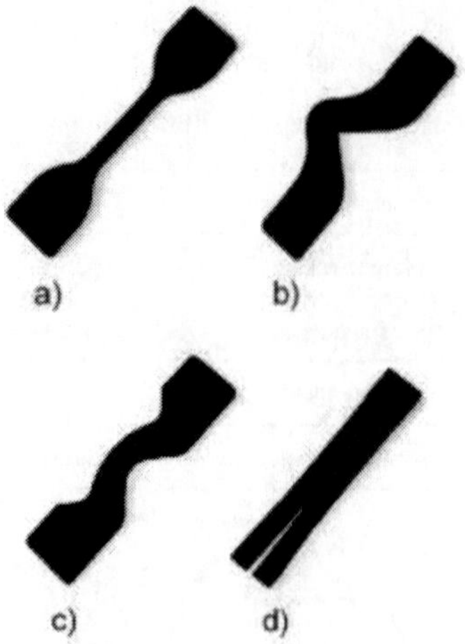

Figure 2. Test samples: a) dumbbell (type 1); b) crescent; b) graves; d) trouser

To carry out the experiment, it was necessary to design and produce an injection mold for all types testing samples. The designed mold includes a universal frame, into which mold plates for given shapes of samples are inserted as necessary. The production of samples was carried out as follows. In case of compression molding, it was first necessary to remold the rubber compound with the assistance of a roll mill and to prepare the required thickness. Next the raw products were cut out in shape of the sheet. Then the raw products were inserted into the pre-heated molding machine and the sheets with dimensions 120 x 120 mm, 2 mm thick, were compression molding. Finally the testing rubber samples were cut out with the assistance of a shape knife, in the line of the material orientation to prevent mistaking the anisotropy direction.

In case of injection molding the pre-plasticated compound, 4 mm thick, was cut into belts 3 cm wide to fill in the injection molding machine REP V27/Y125. Then the injection molding itself was performed. The injection molded samples after opening the mold are demonstrated in Fig. 3. After injection molding the runner system was removed. The samples were produced from one charge of rubber compound.

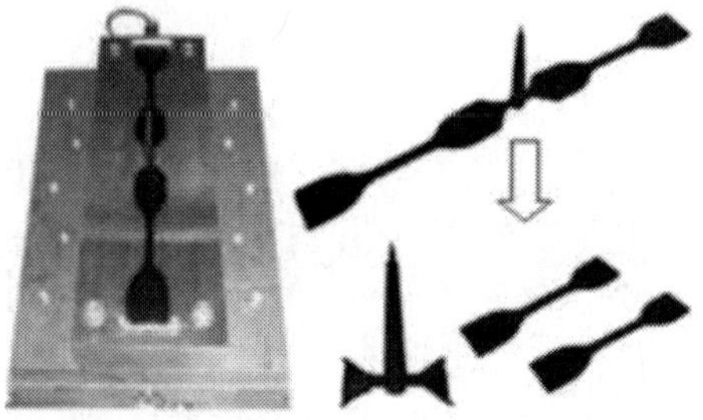

Figure 3. Production of testing samples by injection molding

Table 3. Process conditions of production

		Compression molding	Injection molding
Temperature	Mold	160 °C	
	Rubber compound	23 °C	100 °C[1])
Pressure	Closing	20 MPa	-
	Injection	-	20 MPa
Curing time		2; 3; 4; 5; 6; 7; 8; 9; 10 min[2])	

[1]) Time of preheating the rubber compound in plastication unit was 30 seconds.
[2]) Individual curing times were chosen in the same range (1 min).

DOI: 10.1051/matecconf/20167602023

Figure 4. Injection molding machine REP V27/Y125 with injection mold

2.2 Mechanical tests

After producing of the testing samples a test was carried out to determine the tensile stress-strain properties and also the test to determine the tear strength. In both cases the testing samples were clamped into jaws at both ends in the tensile stress machine Tensometer 2000 by Alpha Technologies. (Fig. 5). Test sample dumbbell was stretched by the prescribed constant speed 500 mm/min until they were torn.

In case of test sample crescent, graves and trouser, stretching speed was 100 mm/min. As for both groups of compression molded and injection molded testing samples, 9 series of measurement with different curing time (2 up to 10 minutes) were carried out, with the repeatability of ten samples to one series of measurement.

Figure 5. Tensile stress machine Tensometer 2000

3 Results and discussion

The evaluated data of the tensile test (Fig. 6) indicate that with the growing curing time the tension necessary to tear the testing sample grows. When the curing time of 3 minutes is exceeded the ultimate tensile strength decreases gradually in case of both preparation methods. The decreasing tendency of the tensile strength is caused by over-curing of the compound. This supports the fact that the vulcanizate based on India rubber obtains better mechanical properties with a longer curing time, but only until the reversal occurs, i. e. until the gradual decay of cross links and degradation of most of the mechanical properties.

The results also show that samples produced by injection molding have higher strength (by 12.4 % in approximately optimal curing time of 3 minutes) than compression molded samples.

Other obtained results show the tear strength of the graves sample (Fig. 7), the crescent sample (Fig. 8) and the trouser sample (Fig. 9) in dependence on the curing time.

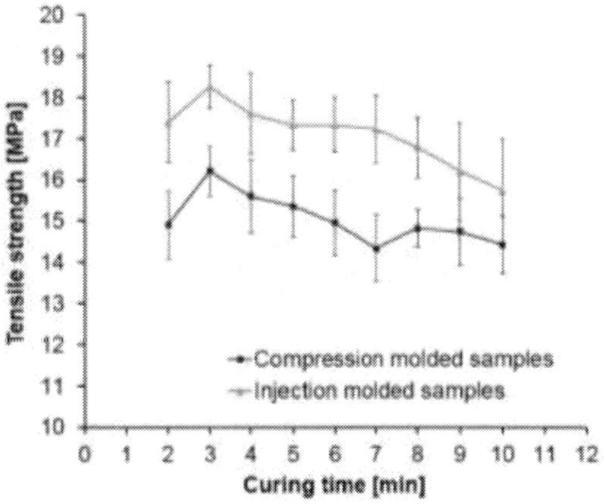

Figure 6. Tensile strength vs. curing time

With the growing curing time the tear strength of the graves, crescent and trouser samples does not significantly change. This means that the degree of crosslinking of the vulcanizate does not have a substantial impact on the tear strength, which supports the information quoted in literature. However, there are evident differences between individual preparation methods. The tear strength of the injection molded graves samples decreased during the optimum cure by 14.4 % compared to the compression molded samples.

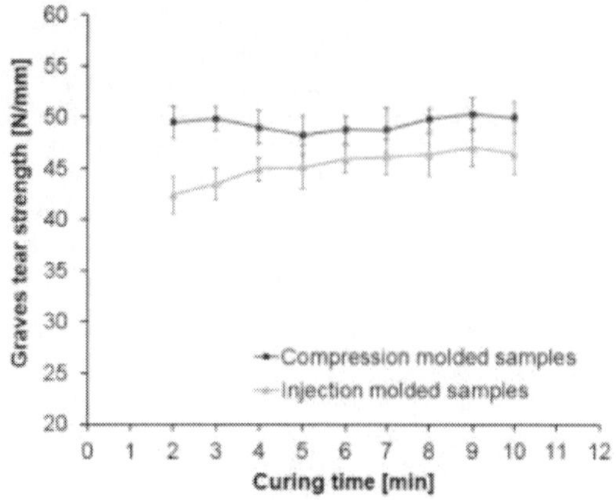

Figure 7. Graves tear strength vs. curing time

To the contrary the tear strength of the injection molded crescent samples during the same curing time increased by 24.4 % and in case of the trouser tear strength the difference is 17.3 % in favor of injected samples. The crescent samples do not have significant notches that would contribute to concentration of the tension. During stretching the deformation energy is mainly used for stretching of the sample rather than for broadening the cracking. This is why the tear strength of this type of sample reaches generally higher values.

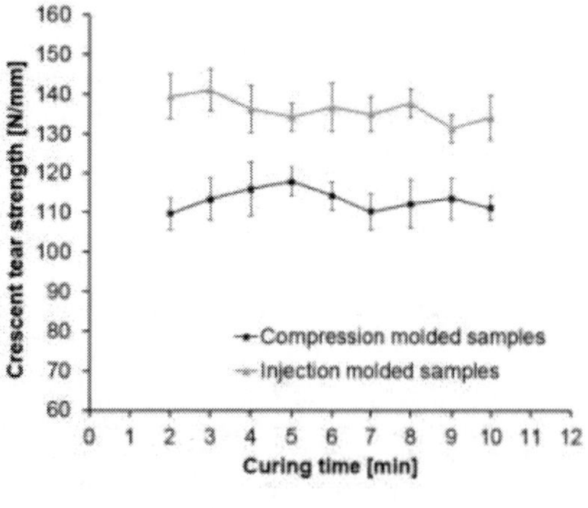

Figure 8. Crescent tear strength vs. curing time

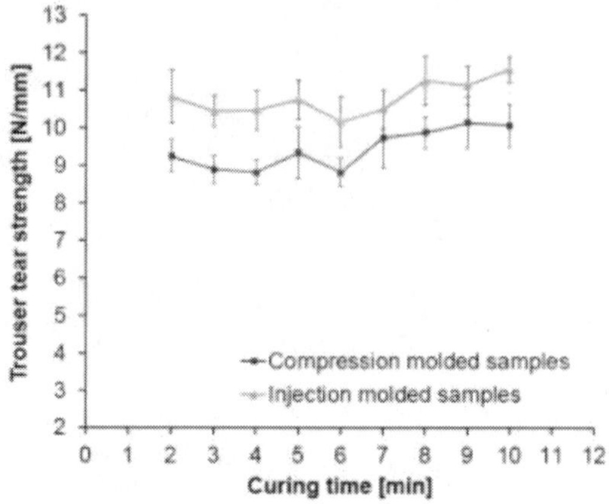

Figure 9. Trouser tear strength vs. curing time

The obtained results of tests performed on the produced testing samples showed certain differences in mechanical properties. To provide clearer evaluation there is a table (Tab. 4) which shows the increase (+) or decrease (-) in percentage of the measured properties of injected samples with respect to the samples produced by the standard method. The table evaluates the quantities measured in the time close to the optimum cure (3 minutes).

Table 4. The relative increase (decrease) in the measured properties of injection molded samples.

Measurement property	Injection molding
Tensile strength	+13 %
Graves tear strength	-14,4 %
Crescent tear strength	+24,4 %
Trouser tear strength	+17,3 %

4 Conclusion

The results of the performed tests showed that the standard preparation method used in case of testing samples (cutting out of the compression molded plate) can be applied also on compounds appointed to the production of injected products. However, the properties of samples produced by this method are not wholly objective, mainly in case of tear strength. The results of the tensile test prove that in the optimum of cure the injected samples have higher tensile strength than samples produced by a standard method. This is probably caused by a higher degree of cross-linking. This also supports the hypothesis that owing to pre-heating of the compound in the plasticizing unit of the injection molding machine the degree of cross-linking is in case of injected samples within the same curing time higher than in case of samples produced by the standard procedure, like compression molding.

The stated results of this research open new possibilities of the testing samples preparation in rubber-making industry, mainly in companies where the injection molding technology is used. It was determined that the preparation method of injection molded samples is viable and for testing of rubber compounds, or products made of such compounds, is more evident than in case of samples prepared by the standard method used up to the present time. In view of the results of this research, when producing injection molded rubber products, it is also recommended to use injection molded testing samples to test their tear properties.

Acknowledgment

This paper is supported by the internal grant of TBU in Zlin No. IGA/FT/2016/010 funded from the resources of specific university research and by the Ministry of Education, Youth and Sports of the Czech Republic within the National Sustainability Programme project No. LO1303 (MSMT-7778/2014) and also by the European Regional Development Fund under the project CEBIA-Tech No. CZ.1.05/2.1.00/03.0089.

References

1. Sezna J. A. Rubber testing for injection molding. Rubber World, **207(4)**, 12-19 (1993)
2. A. Arrillaga, A. M. Zaldua, A. S. Farid, A. S. Evaluation of injection molding simulation tools to model the cure kinetics of rubbers. J. Appl. Pol. Sci., **123(3)**, 1437-1454. (2012)
3. K. Kyas, M. Stanek, M. Manas, M. Stanek, M. Krumal, Z. Holik. Simulation of rubber injection molding process. Chemicke listy, **105(15)**, 354-356 (2011)
4. A. Skrobak, M. Stanek, D. Manas, O. Ovsik, V. Senkerik, M. Reznicek. Mechanical Properties of Rubber Samples. Key Eng. Mater., **606**, 249-252 (2014)
5. E. Ragan, P. Baron, J. Dobránsky. Advanced Materials Research 383-390, 2813-2818, (2012).
6. H. Wang, L. Xu, R. Li, J. Hu, M. Wang, G. Wu, Radiation Physics and Chemistry, **125**, 41-49, (2016)
7. J. Dobránsky, L. Běhálek, P. Baron, Key Engineering Materials, **669**, 36-43, (2016)
8. Dobransky, J., Běhalek, L., Baron, P., Kočiško, M., Simkulet, V., Vojnova, E., Briančin, J. Metalurgija, **55** (3), pp. 449-452, (2016)
9. Dobránsky, J., Kočiško, M., Baron, P., Simkulet, V., Běhálek, L., Vojnová, E., Nováková Marcinčinová, Ľ. Metalurgija, **55** (3), pp. 477-480, (2016)
10. J. Čop, L. Fojtl, O. Bílek, V. Pata, Manufacturing Technology, **16** (2), pp. 334-338, (2016)
11. Singh, P. Kishore, M. Singh, A. Srivastava, Radiation Effects and Defects in Solids, **170** (10), 845-853, (2015)
12. S. Kashyap, D. Datta, International Journal of Plastics Technology, **19** (1), 1-18, (2015)
13. S. Zhang, R. Dubay, M. Charest, Expert Systems with Applications, **42** (6), 2919-2927, (2015)
14. J.G. Drobny, Radiation Technology for Polymers, CRC Press, New York, (2003).
15. M. Ovsik, D. Manas, M. Manas, M. Stanek, M. Hribova, K. Kocman, D. Samek, Irradiated Polypropylene Studied by Microhardness and WAXS, Chemicke listy 106 (2012), 507-510.
16. O. N. Tretinikov, S. Ogata, Y. Ikada, Surface Crosslinking of Polyethylene by Electron Beam Irradiation in Air, Polymer 39 24 (1998.
17. G. Zamfirova, V. Gaydarov, T. Zaharescu, L. G. Silva, Microindentation study of Electron Beam Irradiated Polyamide Samples, Chemicke Listy 104 (2010).
18. W.C. Oliver, G.M. Pharr, Measurement of Hardness and Elastic Modulus by Instrumented Indentation, Journal of Materials Research 19 (1) (2004).
19. D. Manas, M. Hribova, M. Manas, M. Ovsik, Stanek, Thin Solid Films 530 (2013).
20. Sefidmazgi NR, Bahia HU. Mechanisms of failure in uniaxial repeated creep test and the relationship to aggregate packing. RILEM Bookseries ,11:757-71, (2016).
21. Ren, W., Zhang, D., Wang, G. and CHeng, H. Mechanical and thermal properties of bamboo pulp fiber reinforced polyethylene composites. BioResources, 11, pp. 4117-4127, (2014).
22. Ge H, Le J-, Mantell SC. Numerical modeling of stress corrosion cracking of polymers. Eng Fract Mech , 160:199-212, (2016).
23. E. Morales, J.R. White, J. Mater. Sci., 44 (17) (2009), pp. 4734–4742
24. Ge, H., Li, H., Mantell, S.C.,Annual technical conference - ANTEC, conference proceedings, 2, 1281 - 1286p., (2014).
25. Apollonio C, Covas DIC, de Marinis G, Leopardi A, Ramos HM. Creep functions for transients in HDPE pipes. Urban Water J, 11,:160-6,(2014).
26. M. Ovsik, D. Manas, M. Manas, M. Stanek, M. Hribova, K. Kocman, D. Samek, Chem. listy, 106 (2012)
27. A. Lalande, D. Gardette Nucl. Instrum. Methods Phys. Res. B, 222 (2004)
28. D. Manas, M. Manas, M. Stanek, M. Danek, Arch. Mater. Sci. Eng., 32 (2) (2008)
29. D. Manas, M. Stanek, M. Manas, V. Pata, J. Javorik, KGK – KautschukGummiKunststoffe, 62. Jahrgang, (2009)
30. M. Ovsik, D. Manas, M. Manas, M. Stanek, M. Hribova, K. Kocman, D. Samek, Chemicke listy 106, (2012)
31. M. Stanek, M. Manas, D. Manas, V. Pata, S. Sanda, V. Senkerik, A. Skrobak, Chemicke listy, (2011)
32. V. Pata, M. Manas, D. Manas, M. Stanek, Chemicke listy 105, (2011)
33. M. Stanek, D. Manas, M. Manas, O. Suba, Intl. J. of Math. and Computers in Simul., (2011)

MATEC Web of Conferences **76**, 02024 (2016) DOI: 10.1051/matecconf/20167602024
CSCC 2016

Micro-Hardness of PBT Influenced by Beta Radiation

Martin Ovsik[1,a], Lenka Hylova[1], David Manas[1], Miroslav Manas[1] and Michal Stanek[1]

[1] *Tomas Bata University in Zlin, TGM 5555, 760 01 Zlin, Czech Republic*

Abstract. Cross-linking is a process in which polymer chains are associated through chemical bonds. Radiation, which penetrated through specimens and reacted with the cross-linking agent, gradually formed cross-linking (3D net), first in the surface layer and then in the total volume, which resulted in considerable changes in specimen behaviour. This research paper deals with the utilization of electron beam irradiated PBT on the micro-indentation test. Radiation doses of 66, 132 and 198 kGy were used for unfilled PBT with the 5% crosslinking agent (triallyl isocyanurate). Individual radiation doses caused structural and micro-mechanical changes which have a significant effect on the final properties of the PBT tested. The highest values of micro-mechanical properties were reached radiation dose of 132 kGy, when the micro-mechanical values increased by about 30%.

1 Introduction

Polybutylene terephthalate (PBT) is a semi-crystalline thermoplastic of the polyester family, which crystallizes very slowly and is therefore available in an amorphous-transparent or crystalline-opaque condition, depending on the processing method [1-2].

PBT are characterized by their high strength and rigidity, dimensionally stable, low tendency to creep, very good frictional and wear resistance, good impact strength, very low coefficient of thermal expansion, good chemical resistance to acids, very good electrical characteristics, very low moisture absorption, good adhesion and welding ability. Furthermore, PBT, like all polyesters, has very good frictional and wearing properties. Compared to PET, PA6 has a better impact strength - particularly at low temperatures [2-4].

Cross-linking is a process in which polymer chains are associated through chemical bonds. Cross-linking is carried out by chemical reactions or radiation and in most cases the process is irreversible. Ionizing radiation includes high-energy electrons (electron beam - β-rays) (Fig. 1) and gamma rays (γ-rays) (Fig. 2). These not only are capable of converting monomeric and oligomeric liquids into solids, but also can produce major changes in properties of solid polymers. [3]

Common PBT, when exposed to the effect of the radiation cross-linking, degrades and its mechanical properties deteriorate. Using cross-linking agent TAIC (triallyl isocyanurate) produces a cross-linking reaction inside the PBT structure. The utility properties of PBT improve when the non-crystalline part of PBT is cross-linked.

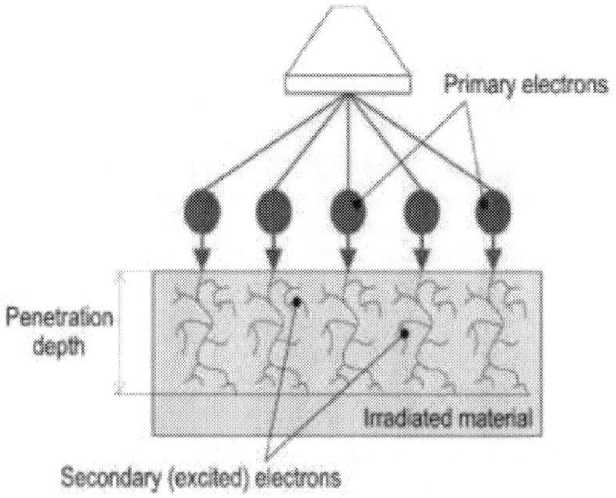

Figure 1. Radiation crosslinking by electrons rays

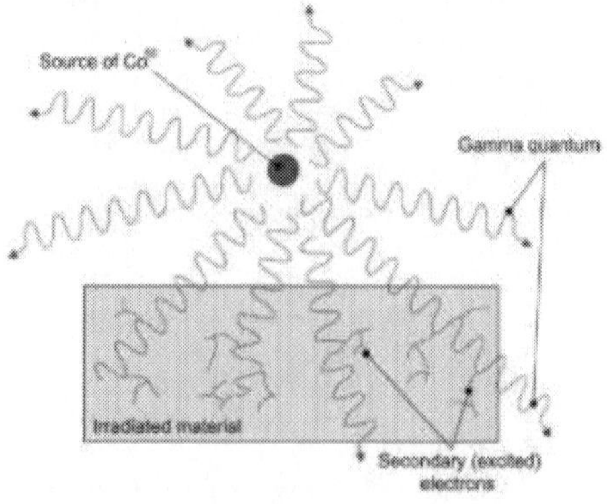

Figure 2. Radiation crosslinking by Gamma rays

[a] Corresponding author: ovsik@ft.utb.cz

The thermoplastics which are used for production of various types of products have very different properties. Standard polymers which are easy obtainable with favorable price conditions belong to the main class. The disadvantage of standard polymers is limited both by mechanical and thermal properties. The group of standard polymers is the most considerable one and its share in the production of all polymers is as high as 90% [1] [5].

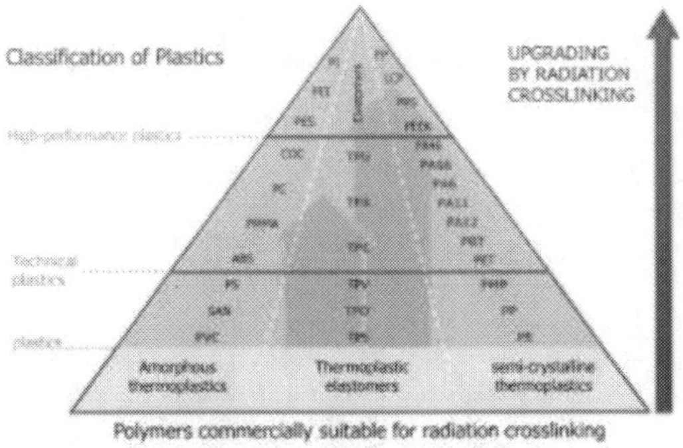

Figure 3. Upgrading properties by radiation cross-linking

The aim of this paper is to study the effect of ionizing radiation with different doses, on micro-mechanical properties of PBT and compare these results with those of non-irradiated samples. These tested polymers find a broad application in many branches of industry and in daily life as well.

2 Experimental

2.1 Material

For this experiment Polybutylene terephthalate PBT V-PTS-CREATEC-B3HZC * M800/25, PTS Plastics Technology Service, Germany, was used. The material already contained a special cross-linking agent TAIC (5 volume %), which should enable subsequent cross-linking by ionizing β – radiation.

2.2 Sample preparation

The samples were made using the injection molding technology on the injection molding machine Arburg Allrounder 470H. Processing temperature 225–255 °C, mold temperature 70 °C, injection pressure 90 MPa, injection rate 50 mm/s. It was used normalized specimen measuring 80x10x4 mm.

2.3 Irradiation

The prepared specimens were irradiated with doses of 0, 66, 132 and 198 kGy at BGS Beta-Gamma Service GmbH & Co. KG, Germany.

2.4 Micro-indentation

Micro-indentation test were performed using a Micro-indentation tester (Micro Combi Tester), CSM Instruments (Switzerland) according to the CSN EN ISO 14577. The tip is made of diamond having the shape of a cube corner (Vickers). In the present study, the maximum load used was 0.5 N and loading rate (and unloading rate) was 1 N/min. A holding time was 90 s at the indentation and 21600 s at the creep.

Figure 4. Micro-indentation tester

The indentation hardness (H_{IT}) was calculated as maximum load (F_{max}) to the projected area of the hardness impression (A_p) and the indentation modulus (E_{IT}) is calculated from the Plane Strain modulus (E^*) using an estimated sample Poisson's ratio (ν) according to [5-7]:

$$H_{IT} = \frac{F_{max}}{A_p} \quad (1)$$

$$E_{IT} = E^* \cdot (1 - \nu_s^2) \quad (2)$$

Measurement of all above mentioned properties was performed 10 times to ensure statistical correctness.

3 Results and discussion

Radiation, which penetrated through specimens and reacted with the cross-linking agent, gradually formed cross-linking (3D net), first in the surface layer and then in the total volume, which resulted in considerable changes in specimen behaviour.

Micro-indentation characteristics determined by DSI method are depicted in Fig. 1 and 2. They characterize course of loading force in dependence on indentor penetration depth, which gives an idea about course of instantaneous values of observed micro-mechanical properties.

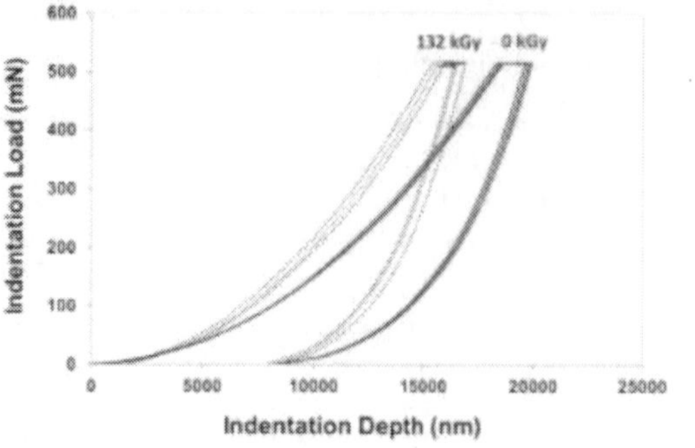

Figure 5. Indentation characteristic of irradiated PBT

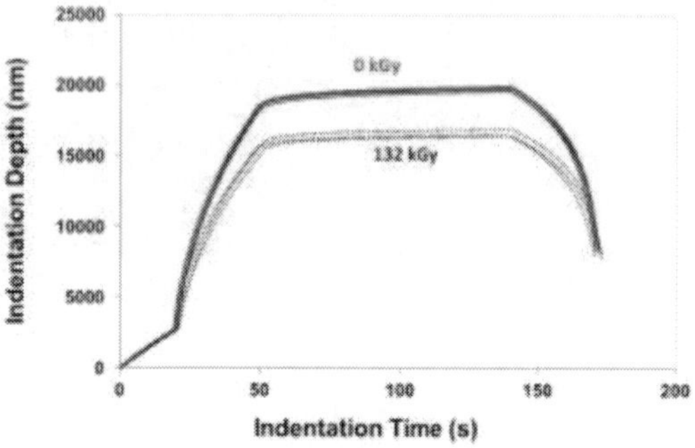

Figure 6. Indentation characteristic of irradiated PBT

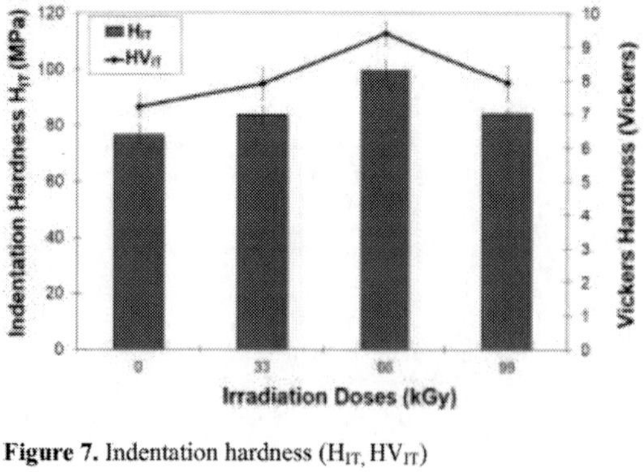

Figure 7. Indentation hardness (H_{IT}, HV_{IT})

It demonstrated the influence of radiation on the change of micro-mechanical properties in the surface layer of specimens. The non-irradiated material showed low hardness as well as increasing impression of the indenter in the surface layer. On the contrary, the irradiated PBT showed considerably smaller depth of the impression of the indenter which can signify greater resistance of this layer to wear (Fig. 5 and Fig. 6).

The values measured during the micro-indentation test showed that the lowest values of indentation hardness and Vickers hardness (H_{IT} = 76 MPa, HV_{IT} = 7 Vickers) were found for the non-irradiated PBT. On the contrary, the highest values of indentation hardness and Vickers hardness (H_{IT} = 100 MPa, HV_{IT} = 9 Vickers) were obtained for PBT irradiated by a dose of 132 kGy (by 30% higher in comparison with the non-irradiated PBT), as can be seen at Fig. 7.

In the case of indentation modulus the highest value was found for PBT irradiated by the radiation dose of 132 kGy (E_{IT} = 1.8 GPa). The smallest value of indentation modulus was found for non-irradiated PBT (E_{IT} = 1.4 GPa). The increase of the value of PBT irradiated by the radiation dose of 132 kGy was by 31% in comparison to the non-irradiated PBT (Fig. 8).

Very important values were found for indentation creep (C_{IT}). The lowest value of indentation creep was measured at radiation dose of 132 kGy (C_{IT} = 14.7%). The highest indentation creep value measured at non-irradiated PBT (C_{IT} = 28.2%). Decrease in creep values was 92% for irradiated PBT compared to the non-irradiated one as is seen at Fig. 11.

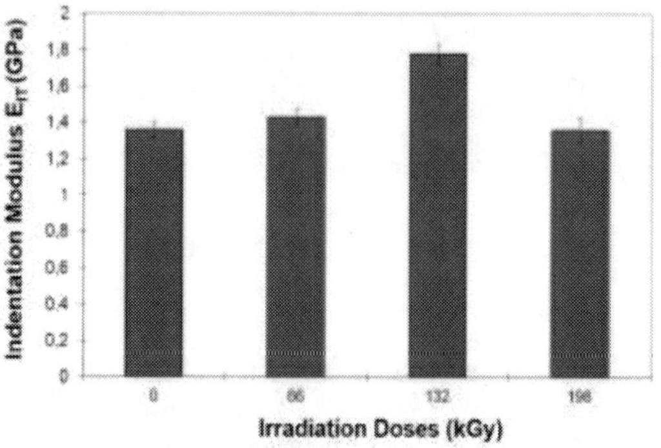

Figure 8. Indentation Modulus (E_{IT})

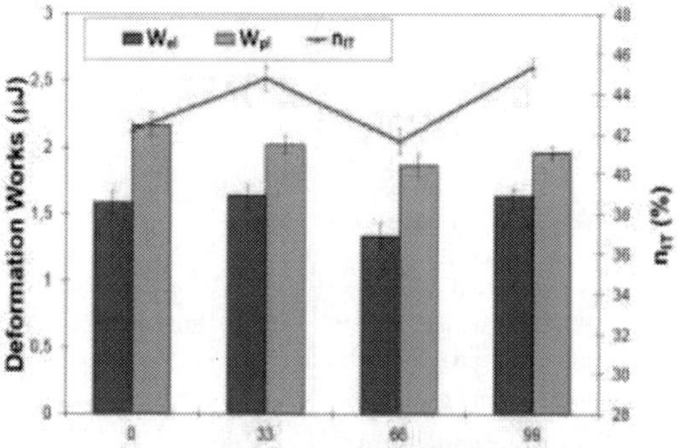

Figure 9. Elastic and plastic part of deformation work

Other important material parameters obtained during the micro-indentation test were elastic and plastic deformation work. The greatest values of plastic and elastic deformation work and coefficient of back deformation η_{IT} were obtained for non-irradiated PBT (W_{el} = 1.6 µJ, W_{pl} = 2.2 µJ, n_{IT} = 42.2 %,). The lowest values of W_{el}, W_{pl} and η_{IT} were obtained for PBT irradiated with dose of 132 kGy (Wel = 1.3 µJ, Wpl = 1.9 µJ, nIT = 41.6 %,). Radiation of specimens caused lower values of elastic as well as plastic deformation work which is apparent in Fig. 9.

Radiation cross-linking creates changes in the PBT structure by creating 3D net. Beta radiation gradually penetrates more deeply into the PBT structure through the surface layer. The surface layer undergoes changes which have a considerable influence on the micro-mechanical properties of PBT.

Higher radiation dose does not influence significantly the micro-mechanical properties. An indentation hardness increase of the surface layer is caused by irradiation cross-linking of the tested specimen. A closer look at the micro-hardness results that when the highest radiation doses are used, micro-mechanical properties decreases which can be caused by radiation induced degradation of the material.

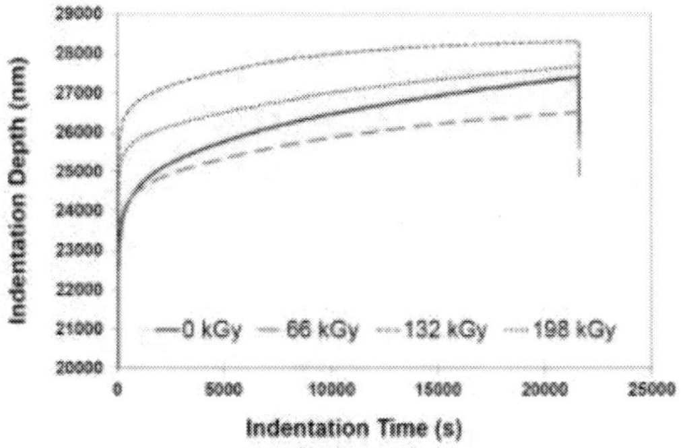

Figure 10. Indentation creep (C_{IT})

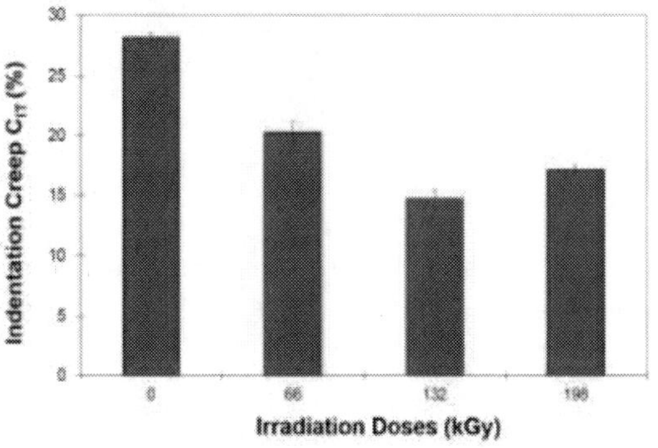

Figure 11. Indentation creep (C_{IT})

4 Conclusion

This research paper investigates influence of modified polymer material (beta radiation) on the micro-indentation test. The surface layer of PBT is modified by β – radiation with doses of 66, 132 and 198 kGy.

Radiation, which penetrated through specimens and reacted with the cross-linking agent, gradually formed cross-linking (3D net), first in the surface layer and then in the total volume, which resulted in considerable changes in specimen behaviour.

Irradiation of PBT with a β - radiation influences the micro-mechanical properties in the following way:

- Radiation of specimens caused improvement values of indentation hardness and indentation modulus.
- The highest values of indentation hardness and indentation modulus were achieved at the PBT irradiated with dose of 132 kGy (The micro-hardness values were increased by 30% and indentation modulus increased significantly by 31% as a result of radiation).
- Higher radiation dose does not influence the indentation hardness and indentation modulus significantly, on the contrary due to degradation processes the properties deteriorate.
- Values of indentation hardness and indentation modulus correspond to the deformation works.

The results of micro-mechanical properties of surface layer of modified PBT show that it can be used in more difficult applications in some industrial fields, in particular where there are high requirements for strength, stiffness and hardness of surface layer which appears to be the most suitable area of application

Acknowledgment

This paper is supported by the internal grant of TBU in Zlin No. IGA/FT/2016/010 funded from the resources of specific university research and by the Ministry of Education, Youth and Sports of the Czech Republic within the National Sustainability Programme project No. LO1303 (MSMT-7778/2014) and also by the European Regional Development Fund under the project CEBIA-Tech No. CZ.1.05/2.1.00/03.0089.

References

1. J.G. Drobny, Radiation Technology for Polymers, CRC Press, New York, (2003).
2. M. Ovsik, D. Manas, M. Manas, M. Stanek, M. Hribova, K. Kocman, D. Samek, Irradiated Polypropylene Studied by Microhardness and WAXS, Chemicke listy 106 (2012).
3. O. N. Tretinikov, S. Ogata, Y. Ikada, Surface Crosslinking of Polyethylene by Electron Beam Irradiation in Air, Polymer 39 24 (1998).
4. G. Zamfirova, V. Gaydarov, T. Zaharescu, L. G. Silva, Microindentation study of Electron Beam Irradiated Polyamide Samples, Chemicke Listy 104 (2010).
5. W.C. Oliver, G.M. Pharr, Measurement of Hardness and Elastic Modulus by Instrumented Indentation, Journal of Materials Research 19 (1) (2004).
6. D. Manas, M. Hribova, M. Manas, M. Ovsik, Stanek, Effect of Beta Irradiation on Morphology and Microhardness of Polypropylene Thin Layers, Thin Solid Films 530 (2013).
7. G. M. Pharr, Measurement of mechanical properties by ultra-low load indentation, Materials Science and Engineering (1998).

MATEC Web of Conferences **76**, 02025 (2016) DOI: 10.1051/matecconf/20167602025
CSCC 2016

Influence of measurement conditions and used devices on consequential creep modulus

Martin Reznicek[1, a], Martin Bednarik[1], Lenka Hylova[1] and David Manas[1]

[1] *Tomas Bata University in Zlin, Nam. T.G. Masaryka 5555, Zlin, 760 01 Czech Republic*

Abstract. This research deals with study of the possibilities of the creep properties measurement on dedicated devices for the creep measurement and on devices, which enable the creep properties measurement. A comparison of these two different measurement methods show the influence of boundary conditions on the measurement result. Simultaneously, the effort to shorten the long-term tests, because of time saving during research and development of new materials, is confronted here. Radiation crosslinking samples of high-density polyethylene (HDPE), which enable the change of the internal structure to the spatial network by the influence of beta radiation, were chosen as an example for comparison.

1 Introduction

The present trend of research and development of new materials is among one of the most developing area of science and technology. The ever greater requirements of product properties make challenging demands on the material, which are produced from. Recent years progress in the area of material engineering enabled development of new devices. Testing devices, which were used in the past, are connected in the one unit with several basic methods or procedures for evaluation of material properties. Testing devices, which are used for present research and development, dispose of whole range of progressive methods, primarily with a big amount for evaluation of suitability of using material in many applications. These testing methods are mostly know-how of the company, which is protected by the patents. Commercial devices, which are sold as a one unit, represent a significant initial investment in a comparison with devices, which is possible to make them yourself and the data to evaluate relatively cheaply from these measurement. [1-5]

Commercial programs for evaluation of data have great requirements for knowledges in the area of the structure of the work in program, more specifically, knowledge of the program in the background. This phenomenon is often called as Black Box, where the measured data is evaluated without more operator intervention. This fact may seem appropriate from the viewpoint of simplicity of evaluation, but it is undesirable from the viewpoint of effort better understanding of the material.

For this reason, some research institutes produce their own testing devices, which are more interesting from the viewpoint of the financial sector.

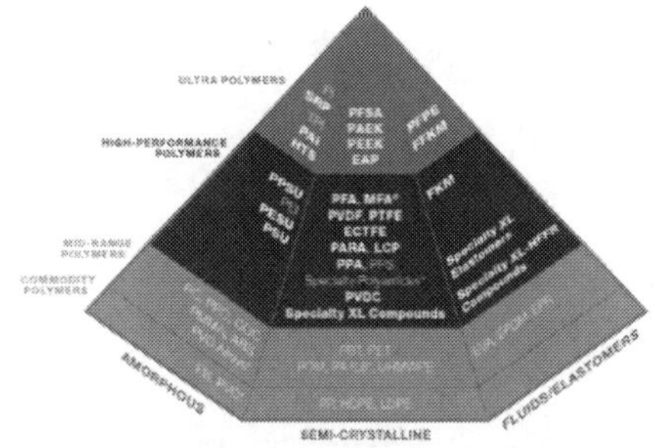

Figure 1. Separation of polymer.

It is possible to save substantial funds using correct interpretation of the results. By comparing the results of various procedures, it is possible to interpret better the conclusion obtained from own device because of detailed knowledge of the device. [6-9]

Design and realization of the proposed devices comply with specific requirements, which are required by the company or the measuring institution. By this targeted construction and mainly during evaluation of the background lead to effective use of funds, which are invested to the devices. It is very common situation that the company is very closely specialized and it is forced by customize to buy the device which is not subsequently fully utilized at 100 %. The measuring device has the advantage of the disposition of the possibilities which are required. The advantage of these solutions is closely profiled software which is very simple for the use and thus make lower demands on personnel qualification requirements.

[a] Corresponding author: mreznicek@ft.utb.cz

2 Methods

The crosslinked material was chosen for the measurement of creep properties for comparison of various options. High-density polyethylene from the company DOW was chosen as a material. Testing samples were made from this material according to a standard ISO 527-2 1BA for the tensile test. The processes of injection molding and radiation cross-linking were performed with the minimum time gap to avoid the influence on the measurement surroundings.

Process conditions were set according to the manufacturer. During subsequent quality control of specimens was detected an excessive trough in the stress part of the specimen. This undesirable effect, which could then affect the results of the measurements had to be removed. This removal is performed by changing the molding process conditions namely by increasing the holding pressure. This pressure was increased by a total of 5 MPa which is reflected in the subsequent quality control of specimens as sufficient.

These samples were molded by the injection molding machine ARBURG Allrouder 170U according to the same process conditions.
Process conditions:

Table 1. Process conditions.

Parameter	Value
Injection temperature	200 °C
Barrel temperatures	195 °C, 190 °C, 180 °C
Mold temperature	40 °C
Injection velocity	40 mm/s
Injection pressure	60 MPa
Cooling time	45 s

Apart from using a standardized sample, it was necessary to use the second part of sample too, because of the reason of restrictions loading forces on one testing device (DMA). As can be seen in Figure 2, this part had the dimensions 5 × 3 × 60 mm.

This dimension during clamping proved very useful, mainly because of the need to use special screws for clamping the specimens in the fixed and movable jaws. The length of the test specimen must then be more shortened, so as to allow the use of a closing part of the test chamber.

All these samples were sent to the company B. G. S. to Germany, where the samples were irradiated by doses 33 kGy, 66 kGy, 99 kGy, 132 kGy, 165 kGy, 198 kGy. The concurrent measurement followed after irradiation on the device DMA1 from the Company Mettler Toledo and on the device for measurement of creep properties of own produce.
The most common method of loading sample is cycling loading. The construction of this device enables to test the samples at various temperatures or in various environments.

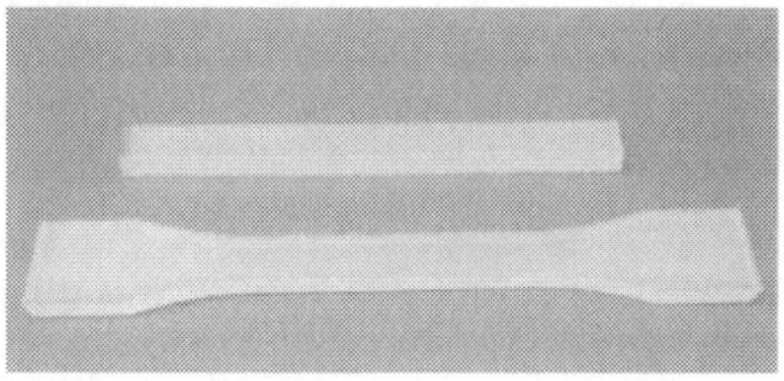

Figure 2. Samples of measurement.

Dynamic mechanical analysis (DMA) is one of the possible methods for measurement of dynamic properties. The samples for this kind of test can be exposed to tension, compression, bending and shear.

Figure 3. Mettler Toledo DMA1.

The device disposes with the mode TMA, which enables to measure the expansion, creep and relaxation time. The device DMA1 in Figure. 3 was used for measurement.

The device DMA1 enables the measurement of brittle and though materials, which are suitable for these type of loading, and it enables evaluation in the program STAR.

The load modul enables loading from 0.001 to 10 N. The frequency generator enables the variable adjustment of oscillation from 0.001 to 300 Hz.

Figure 4. Clamping of sample.

DOI: 10.1051/matecconf/20167602025

The total measuring range of deformation (displacement jaws) is ± 1 mm from the middle neutral position sensor. Whole unit can be equipped with an external device for adjusting the test temperature from -190 to 600 °C. For the chosen radiation cross-linked material was selected initial voltage value 7 N. Before the measurement, the sample was loaded only by clamping force, which was used for demarcation of clamping and determine the initial position of the sensor extension. Test duration was set for 6 hours at 22 ° C. In Figure 5, the results can be seen.

Table 2. Parameters of Allrouder 170U.

Parameter	Value
Clamping force	150 kN
Maximal size of mold	170 x 170 x 200 mm
Screw diameter	22 mm
Maximal injection volume	34 cm^3

3 Data of results

Figure 5 shows the values of the minimum and the maximum progress, which have the same trend. The value of the arithmetic average is calculated from all measurements and was used for calculating of creep modulus during the test. This progress is calculated from the equation:

$$E_t = \frac{FL_0}{A(\Delta L)_t} \tag{1}$$

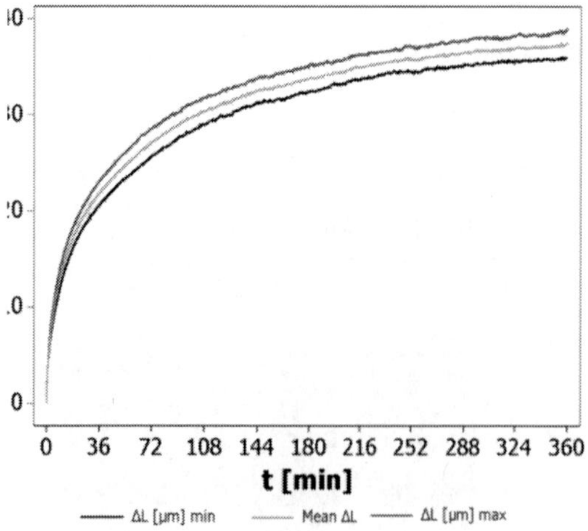

Figure 5. Results of measurement DMA for HDPE 132 kGy.

Where E_t is creep modulus in time t, L_0 is initial value 10 mm, A is initial cross-section of testing sample 15 mm^2.

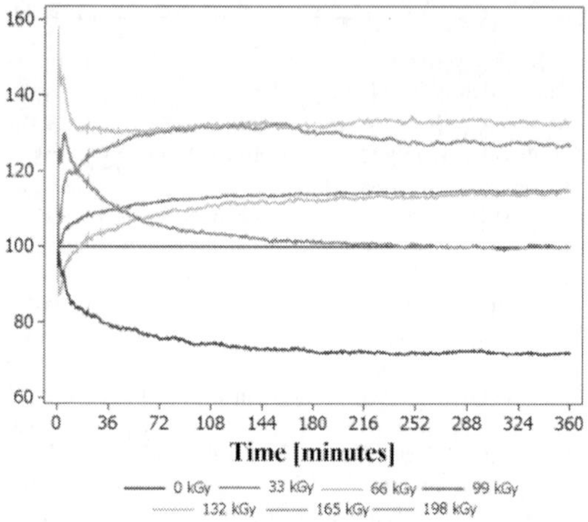

Figure 6 DMA tensile creep modulus.

4 Measurement of creep properties in the longer term

As a second option of the research of creep properties is its measurement on device, which is used for long-term measurement of deformation of the sample.

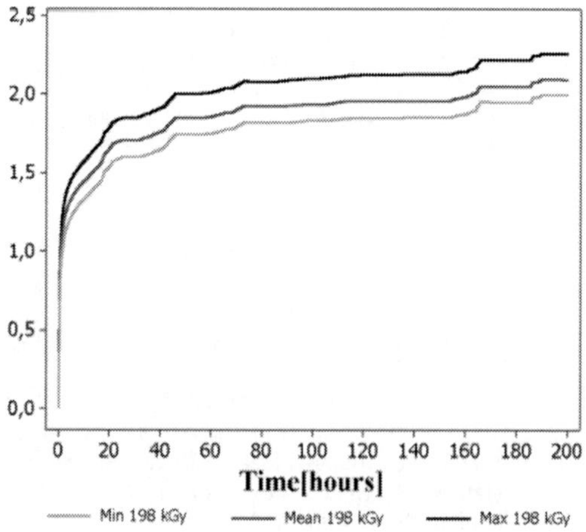

Figure 7. Illustration of results of measurement on simple device.

These devices are generally intended for one type of the test and therefore their construction is simple. The basic parameters of these measuring units are often closely linked with the intended purpose of use. The parameters of each device may vary mainly in the values of loading, reading accuracy and the complexity of the operation. The example of this type of the test is shown in Figure 7.

In Figure 8 can be seen the curve extension for HDPE irradiated by different doses. Each curve represents the mean value of the measured data in terms of the median.

Sample size was eight measurements. As can be seen in comparison with Figure 9, these results closely correspond.

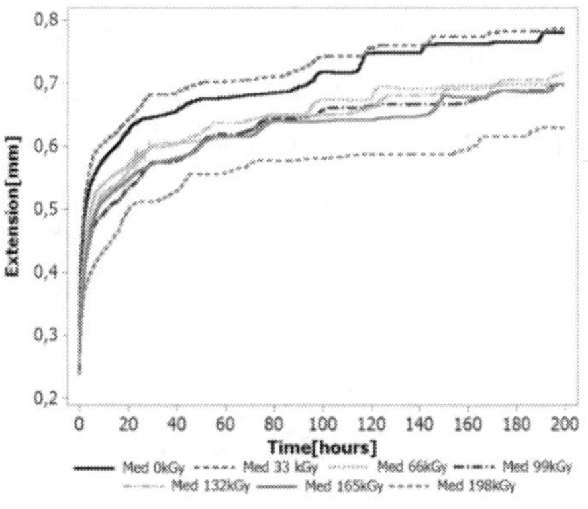

Figure 8 Extension for normal creep test.

Unirradiated material (indicated as 0 kGy) is compared to the dose of 66 kGy and more throughout the measurement worse. Only at doses 33 kGy since the beginning of the measurement worsening, which may explain the low degree of crosslinking and a high degree of decay of the original chains.

5 Conclusion

Figure 6 and 9 shows the results of various improvement of creep modulus in time. The results, which were measured on devide DMA1, show the differences in the primary test phase. Stabilization of creep modulus, which do not change rapidly, appears in the secondary test phase.

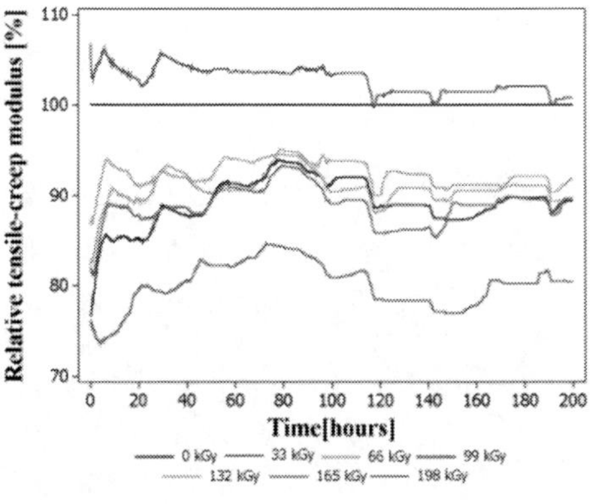

Figure 9 Tensile-creep modulus.

From the progress, the proportion of cross-linked layer is evident and the stabilization rate, which increases with the dose of irradiation.

Relative progress of the creep modulus on dedicated device does not show so rapid primary and secondary phase of test as results from the device DMA1, but it enables to imagine better progress in longer term with rapidly lower equipment costs and the progress of the test.

The choice of the device and the measurement procedure depends on the manner of use the material. Figure 6 and 9 shows the various influence of the irradiation dose on the creep properties, which is primarily caused by duration of test and posibility of stabilization of the whole process. The amount of the irradiation dose has the influence on creep modulus in time too, which is more suitable with lowest doses. These results are decisive for establishing the threshold and degradation of the spatial network.

Using a suitable measuring device can significantly shorten measurement time and also the development time of each material intended for applications where the material is subjected to creep. Based on this short measurement can already predict the next course with a certain probability. To verify the final properties is always advisable to use long-term tests.

Acknowledgments

This paper is supported by the internal grant of TBU in Zlin No. IGA/FT/2016/010 funded from the resources of specific university research and by the Ministry of Education, Youth and Sports of the Czech Republic within the National Sustainability Programme project No. LO1303 (MSMT-7778/2014) and also by the European Regional Development Fund under the project CEBIA-Tech No. CZ.1.05/2.1.00/03.0089.

References

1. Sefidmazgi NR, Bahia HU. Mechanisms of failure in uniaxial repeated creep test and the relationship to aggregate packing. RILEM Bookseries ,**11**:757-71, (2016).
2. Ren, W., Zhang, D., Wang, G. and CHeng, H. Mechanical and thermal properties of bamboo pulp fiber reinforced polyethylene composites. *BioResources*, **11**, pp. 4117-4127, (2014).
3. Ge H, Le J-, Mantell SC. Numerical modeling of stress corrosion cracking of polymers. *Eng Fract Mech* , **160**:199-212, (2016).
4. E. Morales, J.R. White, J. Mater. Sci., **44** (17) (2009), pp. 4734–4742
5. Ge, H., Li, H., Mantell, S.C.,Annual technical conference - ANTEC, conference proceedings, **2**, 1281 - 1286p., (2014).
6. Apollonio C, Covas DIC, de Marinis G, Leopardi A, Ramos HM. *Creep functions for transients in HDPE pipes*. Urban Water J, **11**,:160-6,(2014).
7. M. Ovsik, D. Manas, M. Manas, M. Stanek, M. Hribova, K. Kocman, D. Samek, Chem. listy, **106** (2012)
8. A. Lalande, D. Gardette Nucl. Instrum. Methods Phys. Res. B, **222** (2004)
9. D. Manas, M. Manas, M. Stanek, M. Danek, Arch. Mater. Sci. Eng., **32** (2) (2008)

Regulation and temperature dependency of the light sources

Jiri Vincenec[1,a] and Martin Zalesak[1]

[1] *Tomas Bata University in Zlin, Faculty of Applied Informatics, Department of Automation and Control Engineering, Nad Stranemi 4511, Zlin, Czech Republic*

Abstract. The paper focuses on the regulation effect on the photometric properties of the artificial light sources generally used in administrative and residential buildings. If energy consumption is one of leading areas of usage, there is an area for improvement and energy savings. There are several approaches how to achieve this aim. This attempt for energy saving is limited by standards which regulate the quality of the luminous environment; for example, illuminance level, uniformity illuminance, the colour rendering respectively colour temperature or glare requirements.

1 Introduction

Nowadays, when electric energy is used almost in all areas, higher efficient is required from electric devices. One of the leading areas of usage is Illumination. According to Şahin, 19 % of total amount of energy consumed is for illumination [1]. This quantity of energy encourages for improvement of the lighting solutions installed in buildings.

For example, Şahin described the usage of artificial neural networks for calculating the efficiency of the used lighting solution and the uniformity of its illuminance and as a result of these calculations optimal period of maintenance can be decided [1]. Another approach is optimisation of interior lighting as described Madia, in this solution, genetic algorithms were used for optimising illuminance and uniformity with no interventions to a building [2].

On the other hand, several studies compare different control approaches. Pandharipande described two architectures for lighting control centralised and distributed [3]. Roisin deal with individual daylight dimming system, movement detection switching, movement detection dimming and its combinations [4].

During daytime is appropriate using daylight. Han describing new developments in illuminations; for example, solar tubes or Mini-dish optical-fiber solar system for indoor illumination [5]. The shading control of daylighting through windows is described in several studies; for example, the subdivided window design with light shelves, which divide window to two parts, one with static light shelves and the second part with light shelves controlled by the occupant is presented by Sanati [6].

Due to this approach, our intention is to discover the effect of regulation on the photometric properties of the light sources. Because, no matter what approach is chosen, the light environment must fit the standards; for example, CSN EN 12464-1 [7].

2 Methods

This study was performed for common light sources used in residential buildings. Every light source was measured in a climatic chamber for several temperatures, specifically 0, 5, 10, 15 and 20 °C. Temperatures below 0 °C were not chosen due to impossibility measured photometric properties with provided measure head.

The measurement began with a time period when the light source was switch on with 100 % regulation level and the climatic chamber was set on one of the temperatures. This period lasts minimally 25 minutes.

Figure 1 shows inside of the climatic chamber. Due to stainless steel walls inside the climatic chamber, these walls were covered with paper.

Figure 1. Climatic chamber with modification

During the measurement were recorded illuminance levels, colour temperature, spectral luminous efficiency,

[a] Corresponding author: vincenec@fai.utb.cz

voltage, current and for verification temperature inside the climatic chamber. Those parameters were measured for the possibility to describe temperature effect on the photometric properties.

The attributes of the measured light sources are given in Table 1, those attributes were read out from the wrapper.

Table 1. Attributes of the light sources

Light source	Power [W]	Colour temperature [K]	luminous flux [lm]
Bulb	75	2700	940
Classic ECO halogen	53	2700	840
LED Premium	14	2500	995

Figure 2 illustrate a diagram of the regulation circuit used for measurement. As could be seen only light source and measurement heads were inside the climatic chamber, regulation elements were stated out of the chamber.

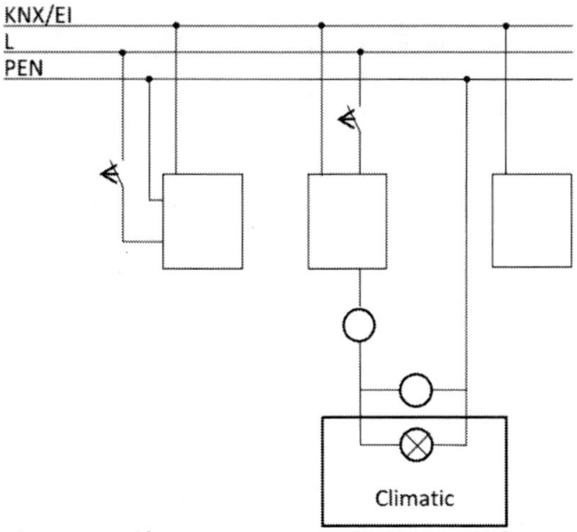

L	-	Phase	V_1,V_2	-	Voltmeter
PEN	-	Protective earth, neutral	A	-	Ammeter
REG	-	Regulation element			

Figure 2. Diagram of the regulation circuit used for measurement

3 Results

This article provides relative illumination in selected regulation levels, colour temperature and spectral composition of artificial lighting at different temperatures.

3.1 Bulb

The first artificial light source was the bulb. Figure 3 summarises relative illumination in selected regulation levels and temperatures. From this figure conclude no obvious dependency on temperature. In several regulation levels, there is a small difference between relative illuminance but this difference is probably caused by measurement error.

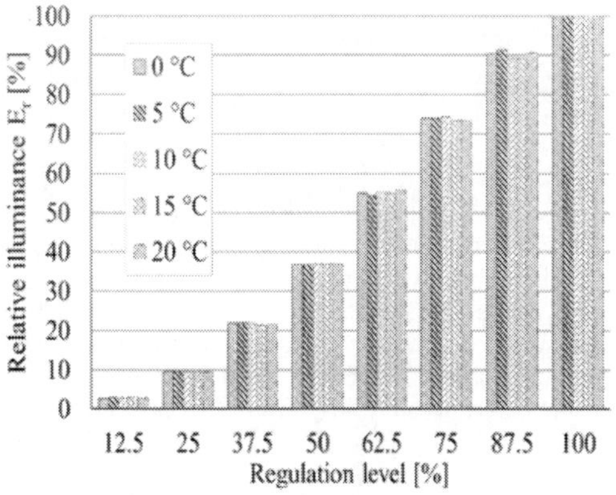

Figure 3. Relative illumination in selected regulation levels and temperatures (Bulb)

Following Figure 4 colour temperature dependency on regulation levels and temperature shows difference at the lowest regulation levels, when the light source provides the lesser colour temperature at the lower temperature. Higher regulation levels, above 37.5 %, provide the equal colour temperature at all measured temperatures.

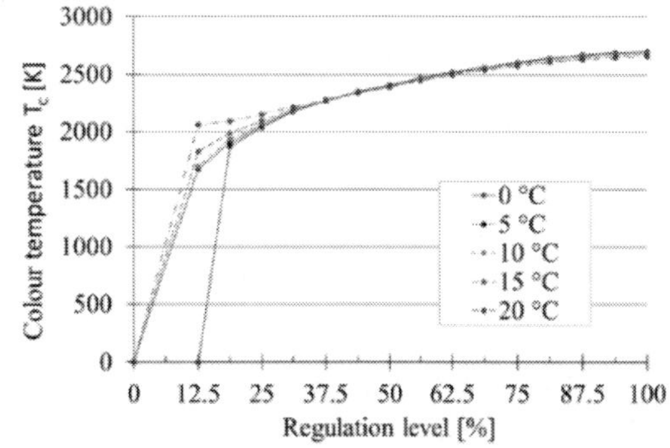

Figure 4. Colour temperature dependency on regulation levels and temperature (Bulb)

Figure 5 shows the spectral composition of artificial light (Bulb) at different temperatures and V(λ). This figure provides us only with the spectral composition at 50 % and 100 % regulation level. As can be seen there in no difference in spectral composition, the difference is only when the regulation level is changed.

DOI: 10.1051/matecconf/20167602026

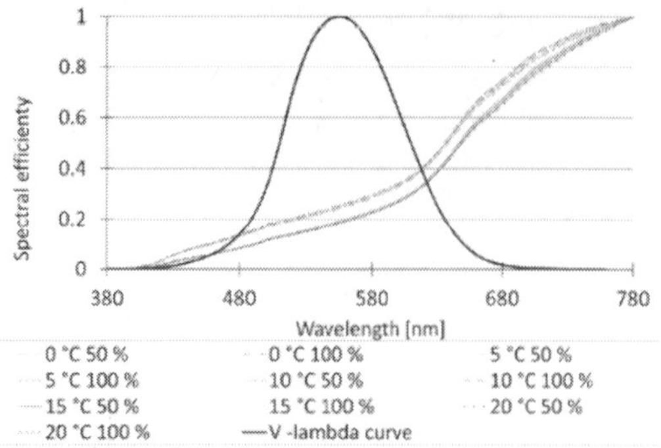

Figure 5. Spectral composition of artificial light source at different temperatures and V(λ) curve

3.2. Classic ECO halogen

The second light source was classic ECO halogen. Figure 6 presents relative illumination in selected regulation levels and temperatures. As can be seen, there is also no obvious dependence on temperature as was not which bulb artificial light source. A small difference in several regulation levels is probably caused also by measurement error.

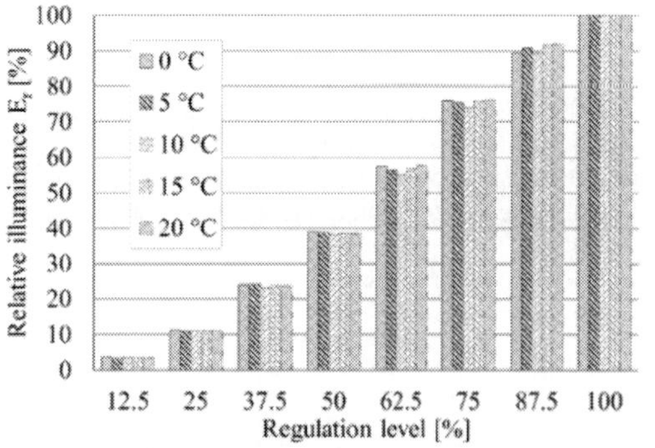

Figure 6. Relative illumination in selected regulation levels and temperatures (Classic ECO halogen)

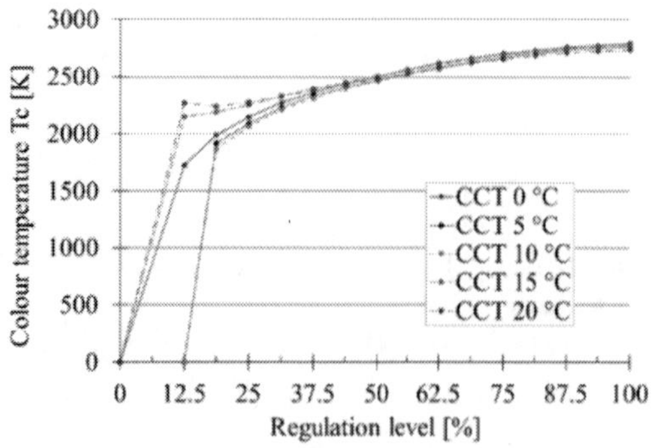

Figure 7. Colour temperature dependency on regulation level and temperatures (Classic ECO halogen)

Figure 7 illustrates colour temperature dependency on regulation level and temperature. According to the figure, the difference is only at lower regulation levels, but in this case, it is not the truth that the lower temperature provides lower colour temperature. Also higher regulation levels, above 43.75, provide the equal colour temperature at all measured temperatures.

Figure 8 shows the spectral composition of artificial light at different temperatures and V(λ) curve. This figure provides us only with the spectral composition at 50 % and 100 % regulation level. As can be seen there in no difference in spectral composition, the difference is only when the regulation level is changed.

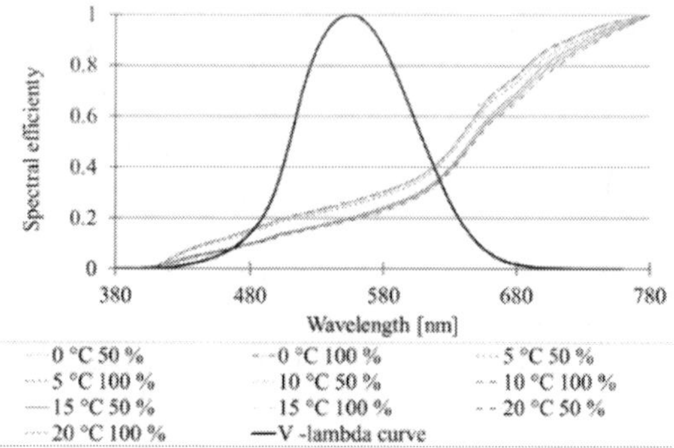

Figure 8. Spectral composition of artificial light source (Classic ECO halogen) at different temperatures and V(λ) curve

3.3 LED Premium

The third artificial light was LED premium. Figure 9 shows relative illumination in selected regulation levels and temperatures. The figure illustrates no obvious dependence on temperature as were not in previous measurements. Same as in previous measurements there is a small difference in several regulation levels which is probably caused also by measurement error.

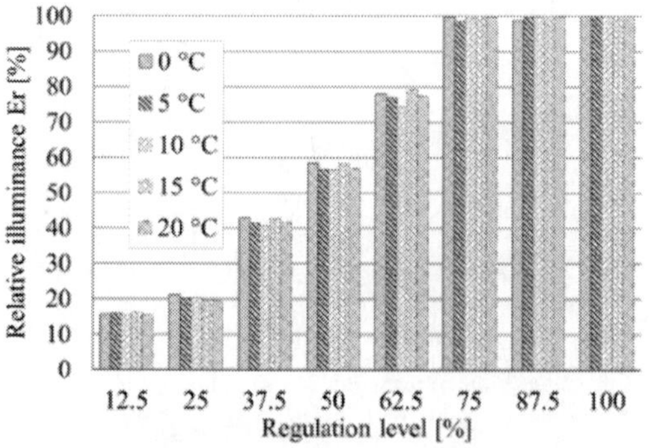

Figure 9. Relative illumination in selected regulation levels and temperatures (LED Premium)

Figure 10 illustrates colour temperature dependency on regulation level and temperature. According to the figure, there is no difference in colour temperature in chosen regulation levels and temperatures.

DOI: 10.1051/matecconf/20167602026

Figure 11 show us spectral composition of artificial lighting at different temperatures and V(λ) curve. In this case, there is no difference in spectral composition of LED Premium artificial light source. Even different regulation levels do not have an effect on the spectral composition of LED Premium artificial light source.

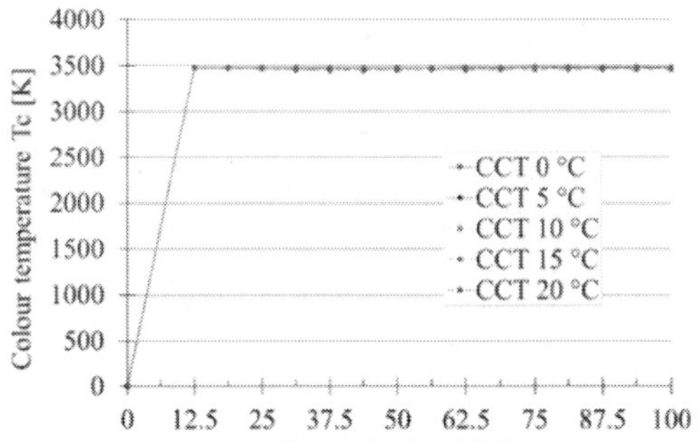

Figure 10. colour temperature dependency on regulation level and temperatures (LED Premium)

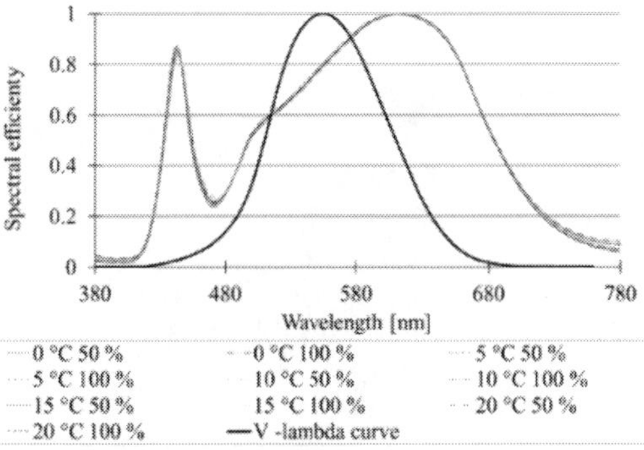

Figure 11. spectral composition of artificial light source (LED Premium) at different temperatures and V(λ) curve

4 Conclusion

This article describing. temperature effect on the photometric properties. As can be seen from Figures 3, 6 and 9 shows that the temperature in the range between 0 °C to 20 °C do not have an effect on the illumination, the small difference in regulation levels is probably caused by measurement error, due to this difference is under 2 %. Figures 4, 7 and 10 summarises colour temperature dependency on regulation level and temperature. For bulb and classic ECO halogen, there is the difference in lower regulation levels; however, due to low levels of illumination in this regulation levels, use of those regulation levels are limited. For LED premium, there is no difference in measured points and colour temperature is constant; however, the difference can be seen between value what was measured and what producer provide. The rest Figures 5, 8 and 11 present spectral compositions of the artificial light source at different temperatures. As can be seen from those figures temperature does not have an effect on spectral compositions. An effect on spectral composition have only regulation levels, but only for the bulb and the classic Eco halogen, for the LED premium the spectral composition is almost comparable to each regulation level and temperature.

As introduce above the measurement was performed for the temperatures in the range between 0°C to 20 °C, the temperatures in which those light sources will be commonly used. The measurement should be done for compact fluorescent light, but due to undefined regulation problems the measurement will be repeated shortly. In future research, the temperature below 0 °C will be measured for clarification effect on the photometric properties.

Acknowledgements

This work was supported by the Ministry of Education, Youth and Sports of the Czech Republic within the National Sustainability Programme project No. LO1303 (MSMT-7778/2014) and also by the Internal Grant Agency of Tomas Bata University in Zlin under the project No. IGA/CebiaTech/2016/001.

References

1. M. Şahin,Y. Oğuz, Energy and Buildings **116**, 13 (2016)
2. E. D. Madias, P. A. Kontaxis, F. V. Topalis, Energy and Buildings **125**, 9 (2016)
3. A. Pandharipande, D. Caicedo, Energy and Buildings **104**, 9 (2015)
4. B. Roisin, M. Bodart, A. Deneyer, P. D'Herdt, Energy and Buildings **40**, 10 (2008)
5. H.J. Han, Y.I. Jeon, S.H. Lim, W.W. Kim, K. Chen, Energy **35**, 7 (2010)
6. L. Sanati, M. Utzinger, Building and Environment **64**, 10 (2013)
7. CSN EN 12464-1, Standard, Czech office for standards, metrology and testing, Prague, CZ (2012)

Measuring robot kinematics description and its workspace

Zdeněk Úředníček[1] and, Rudolf Drga[2]

[1]UTB FAI ve Zlíně, Department of Automation and Control Engineering, Nad Stráněmi 4511760 05 Zlín, Czech Republic,
[2]UTB FAI ve Zlíně, Department of Security Engineering ,Nad Stráněmi 4511760 05 Zlín, Czech Republic,

Abstract. Text deals with 6 degree of freedom measuring robot kinematics description enabling manipulation with measuring effector in 3D space. Mentioned description flowing from Denavit- Hartenberg notation for serial ordering of ideally stiff bodies connected by kinematic pairs, makes possible to create complete set of transformation matrices for coordinates transformation from distal to the adjoining proximal Cartesian coordinate system, which enables to calculate the coordinates of arbitrary structure point by means of joints' coordinates. Thenceforth it makes possible to determine standby and available robot workplace and mainly to perform the analysis of one fundamental control system problem of such robots- i. e. solving inverse kinematic problem.

1 Introduction

On solving of problem deal with parameters collection in defined 3D space points, or with theirs influence, there're not only in laboratory conditions, but also in real practice exploited robotic systems enabling to smartly adjust required measuring or active effector position.

Knowledge in kinematic relationships among required effector position and robotic system joints' coordinates enables to determine both basic robot workspaces, which is important in light of measuring robotic system proposal. A primarily, it makes possible to define, to analyse and eventually to solve so - called inverse kinematic problem. I.e. determination robot joint coordinates for effector required position in 3D space.

2 Kinematic structure make-up

Figure 1 shows described measuring robot real kinematic structure make-up. This make-up is created that way, that it isn't possible to divide formulated problem solving to manipulator problem ensuring so-called wrist point position in 3D space and standard wrist created by three rotary kinematic pairs with orthogonal axis decussate in one point – wrist point.

Two rotary joints are orthogonal and intersect always in one point, third rotary joint axis generally intersects only one axis from previous and not orthogonally yet.

As a consequence is further mentioned direct kinematic problem description (algebraic relation among joint coordinates and point effector Cartesian coordinates), which is solvable (if ever) only numerically. It complicates for example control system operation in case of need on-line generation of requested values of joint coordinates at autonomous robot behaviour.

Figure 1 Real measuring robot mechanical structure.

2.1 Co-ordinate systems according to Denavit-Hartenberg

Figure 2 shows select ordering of Cartesian co- ordinate systems on described kinematic structure and basic dimensions and Table 1. shows then associated Denavit - Hartenberg parameters (DH).

Corresponding author: urednicek@fai.utb.cz

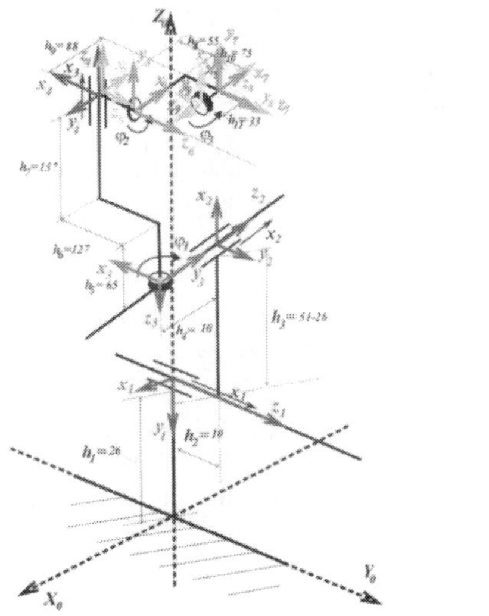

Figure 2 Measuring robot DH co-ordinate systems introduction.

Table 1 DH parameters of axis systems.

N° \ parametr	a_i	α_i	d_i	Θ_i
1	$z_0 \to z_1$ along x_1=0	$z_0 \to z_1$ around x_1 =-90°	$x_0 \to x_1$ along z_0=h_1	$x_0 \to x_1$ around z_0=0°
2	$z_1 \to z_2$ along x_2= h_3	$z_1 \to z_2$ around x_2 =90°	$x_1 \to x_2$ along z_1⇒ h_2+x_1	$x_1 \to x_2$ around z_1=-90°
3	$z_2 \to z_3$ along x_3=0	$z_2 \to z_3$ around o x_3 =90°	$x_2 \to x_3$ along z_2= -h_4-x_2	$x_2 \to x_3$ around z_2=-90°
4	$z_3 \to z_4$ along x_4= h_6	$z_3 \to z_4$ around x_4 =180°	$x_3 \to x_4$ along z_3⇒ -(h_7+ h_5+ x_3)	$x_3 \to x_4$ around z_3=φ_1
5	$z_4 \to z_5$ along x_5=0	$z_4 \to z_5$ around x_5 =90°	$x_4 \to x_5$ along z_4=0	$x_4 \to x_5$ around z_4=-90°
6	$z_5 \to z_6$ along x_6=0	$z_5 \to z_6$ around x_6 =0°	$x_5 \to x_6$ along z_5⇒ h_8	$x_5 \to x_6$ around z_5=0°
7	$z_6 \to z_7$ along x_7= h_9	$z_6 \to z_7$ around x_7 =0°	$x_6 \to x_7$ along z_6⇒ h_{10}	$x_6 \to x_7$ around z_6=φ_2
8	$z_7 \to z_8$ along l x_8=0	$z_7 \to z_8$ around x_8 =90°	$x_7 \to x_8$ along z_7⇒ 0	$x_7 \to x_8$ around z_7=90°
9	$z_8 \to z_9$ along x_9=0	$z_8 \to z_9$ around x_9 =180°	$x_8 \to x_9$ along z_8⇒ -h_{11}	$x_8 \to x_9$ around z_8=-φ_3

2.2 Homogenous transformation matrices

Because for transformation homogenous matrix for coordinates of proximal and distal neighbouring systems reads

$$ {}^{i-1}T_i = \begin{bmatrix} \cos\theta_i & -\cos\alpha_i \sin\theta_i & \sin\alpha_i \sin\theta_i & a_i \cos\theta_i \\ \sin\theta_i & \cos\alpha_i \cos\theta_i & -\sin\alpha_i \cos\theta_i & a_i \sin\theta_i \\ 0 & \sin\alpha_i & \cos\alpha_i & d_i \\ 0 & 0 & 0 & 1 \end{bmatrix} \quad (1) $$

it is possible to write for homogenous transformation matrices among particular coordinate systems from Figure 2

$$ {}^0T_1 = \begin{bmatrix} 1 & 0 & 0 & 0 \\ 0 & 0 & 1 & 0 \\ 0 & -1 & 0 & h_1 \\ 0 & 0 & 0 & 1 \end{bmatrix}; \quad {}^1T_2 = \begin{bmatrix} 0 & 0 & -1 & 0 \\ -1 & 0 & 0 & -h_3 \\ 0 & 1 & 0 & h_2 + x_1 \\ 0 & 0 & 0 & 1 \end{bmatrix}; \quad (2a) $$

$$ {}^2T_3 = \begin{bmatrix} 0 & 0 & -1 & 0 \\ -1 & 0 & 0 & 0 \\ 0 & 1 & 0 & -h_4 - x_2 \\ 0 & 0 & 0 & 1 \end{bmatrix} \quad (2b) $$

$$ {}^6T_7 = \begin{bmatrix} \cos\varphi_2 & -\sin\varphi_2 & 0 & h_9 \cos\varphi_2 \\ \sin\varphi_2 & \cos\varphi_2 & 0 & h_9 \sin\varphi_2 \\ 0 & 0 & 1 & h_{10} \\ 0 & 0 & 0 & 1 \end{bmatrix}; \quad {}^7T_8 = \begin{bmatrix} 0 & 0 & 1 & 0 \\ 1 & 0 & 0 & 0 \\ 0 & 1 & 0 & 0 \\ 0 & 0 & 0 & 1 \end{bmatrix} \quad (2c) $$

$$ {}^8T_9 = \begin{bmatrix} \cos\varphi_3 & -\sin\varphi_3 & 0 & 0 \\ -\sin\varphi_3 & -\cos\varphi_3 & 0 & 0 \\ 0 & 0 & -1 & -h_{11} \\ 0 & 0 & 0 & 1 \end{bmatrix} \quad (2d) $$

Resulting homogenous transformation matrix ${}^0T_9$ from effector co-ordinate system to the global co-ordinate system is

$$ {}^0T_9 = \begin{bmatrix} \cos(\varphi_1)\cdot\sin(\varphi_2)\cdot\cos(\varphi_3) - \sin(\varphi_1)\cdot\sin(\varphi_3) & -\cos(\varphi_1)\cdot\sin(\varphi_2)\cdot\sin(\varphi_3) - \sin(\varphi_1)\cdot\cos(\varphi_3) & \cos(\varphi_1)\cdot\cos(\varphi_2) & t_{14} \\ -\sin(\varphi_1)\cdot\sin(\varphi_2)\cdot\cos(\varphi_3) - \cos(\varphi_1)\cdot\sin(\varphi_3) & \sin(\varphi_1)\cdot\sin(\varphi_2)\cdot\sin(\varphi_3) - \cos(\varphi_1)\cdot\cos(\varphi_3) & -\sin(\varphi_1)\cdot\cos(\varphi_2) & t_{24} \\ \cos(\varphi_2)\cdot\cos(\varphi_3) & -\cos(\varphi_2)\cdot\sin(\varphi_3) & -\sin(\varphi_2) & t_{34} \\ 0 & 0 & 0 & 1 \end{bmatrix} $$

where

$$ \begin{aligned} t_{14} &= x_2(t) + h_4 + \cos[\varphi_1(t)]\cdot\{h_{11}\cdot\cos[\varphi_2(t)] - h_9\cdot\cos[\varphi_2(t)]\} + (h_8 + h_{10} - h_6)\cdot\sin[\varphi_1(t)] = \\ &= x_2(t) + h_4 - (h_9 - h_{11})\cdot\cos[\varphi_1(t)]\cdot\cos[\varphi_2(t)] + (h_8 + h_{10} - h_6)\cdot\sin[\varphi_1(t)] \\ t_{24} &= x_1(t) + h_2 - \sin[\varphi_1(t)]\cdot\{h_{11}\cdot\cos[\varphi_2(t)] - h_9\cdot\cos[\varphi_2(t)]\} + (h_8 + h_{10} - h_6)\cdot\cos[\varphi_1(t)] = \\ &= x_1(t) + h_2 + (h_9 - h_{11})\cdot\sin[\varphi_1(t)]\cdot\cos[\varphi_2(t)] + (h_8 + h_{10} - h_6)\cdot\cos[\varphi_1(t)] \\ t_{34} &= x_3(t) + h_1 + h_3 + h_5 + h_7 + h_9\cdot\sin[\varphi_2(t)] - h_{11}\cdot\sin[\varphi_2(t)] = \\ &= x_3(t) + h_1 + h_3 + h_5 + h_7 + (h_9 - h_{11})\cdot\sin[\varphi_2(t)] \end{aligned} $$

2.3 Robot kinematic behaviour description

For any point **X**, whose coordinates in co-ordinate system $\mathbf{O_{x_9y_9z_9}}$ are

$$ {}^9X = \begin{bmatrix} x \\ y \\ z \end{bmatrix} $$

its global coordinates (coordinates in system $\mathbf{O_{X_0Y_0Z_0}}$) are

$$ {}^0X = \begin{bmatrix} x_0 \\ y_0 \\ z_0 \end{bmatrix} $$

where

$$ \begin{aligned} x_0 &= x_2(t) + h_4 - (h_9 - h_{11})\cdot\cos[\varphi_1(t)]\cos[\varphi_2(t)] + (h_8 + h_{10} - h_6)\cdot\sin[\varphi_1(t)] + \\ &+ x\cdot\{\cos[\varphi_1(t)]\cdot\sin[\varphi_2(t)]\cdot\cos[\varphi_3(t)] - \sin[\varphi_1(t)]\cdot\sin[\varphi_3(t)]\} + \\ &+ y\cdot\{-\cos[\varphi_1(t)]\cdot\sin[\varphi_2(t)]\cdot\sin[\varphi_3(t)] - \sin[\varphi_1(t)]\cdot\cos[\varphi_3(t)]\} + \\ &+ z\cdot\{\cos[\varphi_1(t)]\cdot\cos[\varphi_2(t)]\} \end{aligned} \quad (3a) $$

$$ \begin{aligned} y_0 &= x_1(t) + h_2 + (h_9 - h_{11})\cdot\sin[\varphi_1(t)]\cdot\cos[\varphi_2(t)] + (h_8 + h_{10} - h_6)\cdot\cos[\varphi_1(t)] + \\ &+ x\cdot\{-\sin[\varphi_1(t)]\cdot\sin[\varphi_2(t)]\cdot\cos[\varphi_3(t)] - \cos[\varphi_1(t)]\cdot\sin[\varphi_3(t)]\} + \\ &+ y\cdot\{\sin[\varphi_1(t)]\cdot\sin[\varphi_2(t)]\cdot\sin[\varphi_3(t)] - \cos[\varphi_1(t)]\cdot\cos[\varphi_3(t)]\} + \\ &+ z\cdot\{-\sin[\varphi_1(t)]\cdot\cos[\varphi_2(t)]\} \end{aligned} \quad (3b) $$

$$ \begin{aligned} z_0 &= x_3(t) + h_1 + h_3 + h_5 + h_7 + (h_9 - h_{11})\cdot\sin[\varphi_2(t)] + \\ &+ x\cdot\{\cos[\varphi_2(t)]\cdot\cos[\varphi_3(t)]\} + \\ &+ y\cdot\{-\cos[\varphi_2(t)]\cdot\sin[\varphi_3(t)]\} + \\ &+ z\cdot\{-\sin[\varphi_2(t)]\} \end{aligned} \quad (3c) $$

If this point will be on axis $\mathbf{z_9}$, then

$$ \begin{aligned} x_0 &= x_2(t) + h_4 - (h_9 - h_{11})\cdot\cos[\varphi_1(t)]\cos[\varphi_2(t)] + (h_8 + h_{10} - h_6)\cdot\sin[\varphi_1(t)] + \\ &+ z\cdot\{\cos[\varphi_1(t)]\cdot\cos[\varphi_2(t)]\} \\ y_0 &= x_1(t) + h_2 + (h_9 - h_{11})\cdot\sin[\varphi_1(t)]\cdot\cos[\varphi_2(t)] + (h_8 + h_{10} - h_6)\cdot\cos[\varphi_1(t)] + \\ &+ z\cdot\{-\sin[\varphi_1(t)]\cdot\cos[\varphi_2(t)]\} \\ z_0 &= x_3(t) + h_1 + h_3 + h_5 + h_7 + (h_9 - h_{11})\cdot\sin[\varphi_2(t)] + \\ &+ z\cdot\{-\sin[\varphi_2(t)]\} \end{aligned} \quad (4) $$

So, if we will require any position on effector rotation axis achievement in global coordinate system, it is possible, by means of these equations, to specify joints' coordinates, by which is possible to reach hereof point?

This nonlinear algebraic equations system and its solvability investigation in general case exceeds framework of presented paper [11], [12], [13].

We state only, that in general is possible to regard this structure as solvable only numerically (see below).

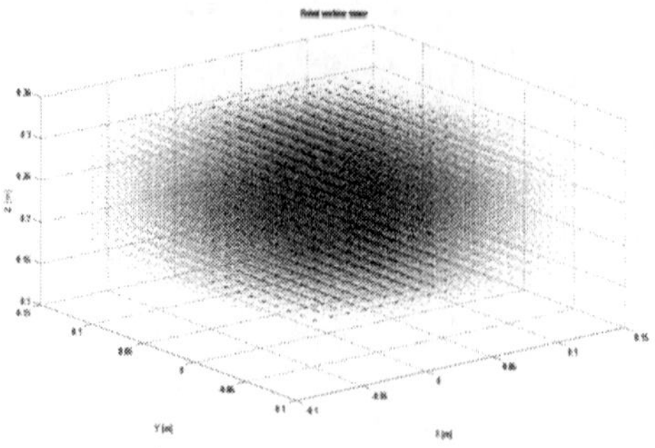

Figure 3 Calculated robot standby working place.

For any joints' coordinates possible configuration

$$[x_1 \; x_2 \; x_3 \; \varphi_1 \; \varphi_2 \; \varphi_3]^T$$

is possible by means of (3) or (4) to evaluate any effector point in global coordinates (and then determine its global velocity size and then kinetic and potential energy).

The set of all effector co-ordinate system $\mathbf{O_{x9y9z9}}$ origin points for whole joints' coordinates range is substantial part of robot's standby working space and it's displayed on Figure 3.

2.4 Inverse kinematic problem and its solution

On the contrary, the system of equations (3) or (4), do it enables, for any required cartesian coordinates configuration of any effector point

$$[x_0 \quad y_0 \quad z_0]^T$$

to establish such joints' coordinates

$$[x_1 \; x_2 \; x_3 \; \varphi_1 \; \varphi_2 \; \varphi_3]^T,$$

which will provide its required position in 3D space ?

Answer to this question is answer on the question about existence and unicity of solving so-called inverse kinematic problem and its result determines required position values' dependence on time for individual joints. Real translational or angular joint position is then job of inverse dynamic problem solving, which isn't aim hereof paper.

From equations (3) is evident, that generally any required effector point absolute position

$$[\mathrm{x}_0 \quad \mathrm{y}_0 \quad \mathrm{z}_0]^T$$

faces to the 3 nonlinear algebraic equations' system for 6 unknowns and analysis its general solution and its unicity generally exceeds scope hereof paper.

We will accent only basic fact, that kinematic structure created this way presents effector body orientation inseparability from manipulator position. Thenceforth on examples we will show, that chosen trajectories of chosen effector point is possible to achieve by diverse joints control.

2.4.1 Movement control demonstration only by means of translational joints

We'll discover equations (4) solution for required coordinates' trajectory

$$[x_0(t) y_0(t) z_0(t)]^T$$

effector point, which lies on axis $\mathbf{z_9}$ in the distance 5.10^{-2} m from the origin of $\mathbf{O_{x9y9z9}}$. Effector body orientation is given by constant angles

$$\varphi_1 = -15^o \, ; \, \varphi_2 = 20^o \, ; \, \varphi_3 = -20^o$$

We will perform the solution only by means of translational articulated coordinates' time changes

$$[x_1(t) \; x_2(t) \; x_3(t)]^T,$$

whereas the point with the coordinates $[x_0(t) y_0(t) z_0(t)]^T$ describes circle with radius $3{,}5.10^{-2}$m around axis passing through origin $\mathbf{O_{x9y9z9}}$ parallel with axis $\mathbf{X_0}$, in the plane parallel with global plane $\mathbf{Y_0}$,$\mathbf{Z_0}$ in the distance 5.10^{-2} m from the origin, with constant peripheral speed of $4{,}3982.10^{-1}$ m/s. See Figure 4.

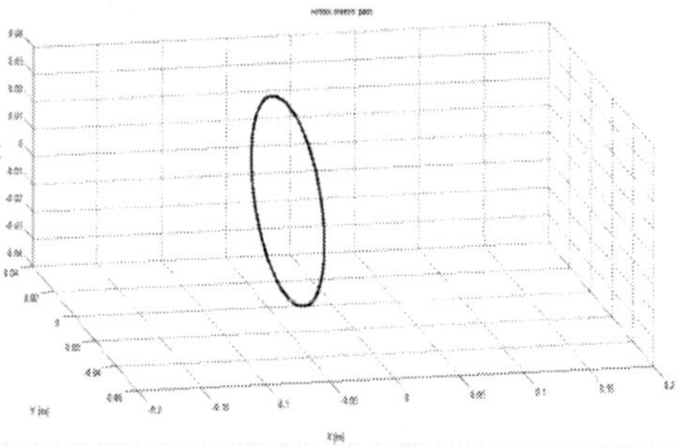

Figure 4 Required robot effector point path.

Is evident that happens an trivial situation corresponding cartesian robot type. Figure 5. shows time dependence, just as make the system (4) solution.

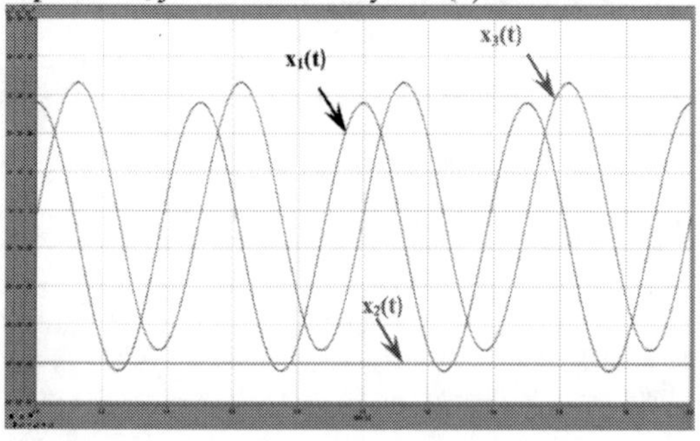

Figure 5 $[x_1(t) \; x_2(t) \; x_3(t)]^T$ as time functions for given parameters.

On effector orientation modification, the joints' coordinates trajectories will change, but it will conserve its form (harmonics courses), because joints' coordinates

$$[x_1(t) \; x_2(t) \; x_3(t)]^T$$

copy point effector trajectory.

2.4.2 Demonstration of movement control only by means of rotational joints

Try to find equations (4) solution for required trajectory with coordinates

$$[x_0(t)y_0(t)z_0(t)]^T$$

of effector point on z_9 axis with fixed joins' coordinates

$$x_1 = 0\,m;\ x_2 = -2.10^{-2}\,m;\ x_3 = 0\,m$$

We require to extended effector axis in 1m distance arcs the curve from Figure 5.

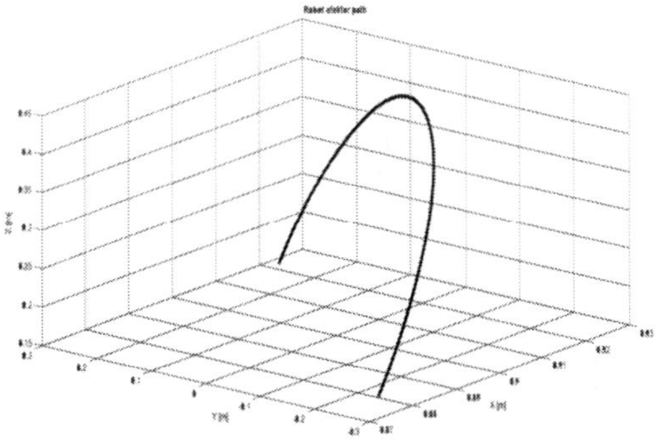

Figure 6 Required robot effector point path.

We perform the solution only by means of rotary joints, i.e. we search

$$\varphi_1(t);\ \varphi_2(t);\ \varphi_3(t)$$

satisfying our requirement. First of all we see that we can achieve this trajectory only by means of first two rotary joints. Trajectory logically not depends on third rotary joint rotation.

From third equations (4) we can solve angle $\varphi_2(t)$. Then second from equations (4) can be modified to form

$$y_0 - (x_1(t) + h_2) =$$
$$= \{(h_9 - h_{11} - z)\cdot cos[\varphi_2(t)]\}\cdot sin[\varphi_1(t)] + (h_8 + h_{10} - h_6)\cdot cos[\varphi_1(t)]$$

This equation is

$$a\,cos\varphi_1 + b\,sin\varphi_1 = c$$

type and it can be solve easily (multivalued). So we can obtain angle φ_1.

On the Figure 7 we can see the time dependence of the first two angles φ_1, φ_2.

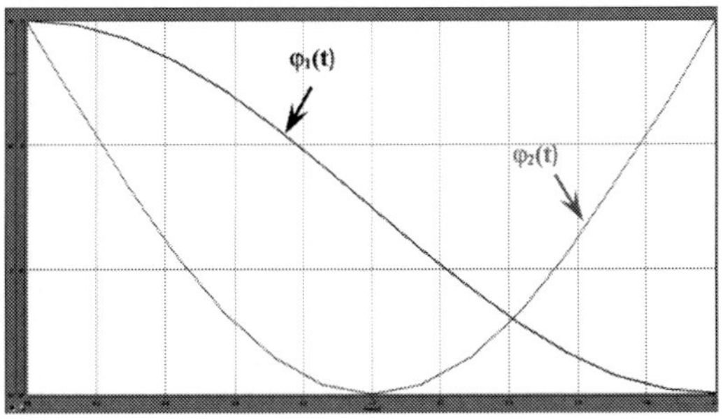

Figure 7 Rotational angles required for trajectories on Figure 6.

3 Conclusions

Mentioned paper is focused on measuring robot kinematic description. Robot serves to software-controlled measuring effector movement in 3D space. Except basic exercise standby and available working space determination, also they are in paper described basic aspects of so-called inverse kinematic problem by means of appropriate DH notation and transformation matrices. I.e. required joints' coordinates finding.

Paper doesn't deal with direct and inverse dynamic problem, which concurs on kinematic problem. Motional equations derivation and control laws proposal will be subject of next parts work.

References

1. S. Crandall, D. C, .Karnopp, E.F. Kurz,. *Dynamics of Mechanical and Electromechanical Systems*, McGraw-Hill, NewYork (1968).
2. D. C Karnopp, R. C. Rosenberg. *System dynamics*. A Unifies Approach. Wiley & Sons, (1975).
3. R. C. Rosenberg,, Multiport Models in mechanics. Trans. ASME, (sept 1972)
4. Z. Úředníček, *Modelling and simulation. Simulation experiment utilization at mechatronics systems' proposal*, (In Czech) Inaugural dissertation. Transport and communications university ZILINA, (1997)
5. J.U. Liceaga-Castro, I. I Siller-Alcalá., J. Jaimes-Ponce, R., Alcántara-Ramírez, and A. Ferreyra-Ramírez, Proceedings of the 11th WSEAS International Conference on Circuits, Systems, Electronics, Control & Signal Processing (CSECS '12). Montreux, Switzerland. December 29-31, (2012)
6. H.A. Darweesh, M. Roushdy , H.M. Ebied, and B.M. Elbagoury, Proceedings of the WSEAS International Conference Mathematical Applications in Science and Mechanics. Dubrovnik, Croatia, June 25-27, (2013)
7. S. Hubalovsky, P.Kadlec, L. Mitrovic, and P. Hanzalova, Proceedings of the 3rd International Conference on Mathematical Models for Engineering Science (MMES '12). Paris, France, December 2-4, (2012)
8. Z. Úředníček, *Robotics* (in Czech), T. Bata university in Zlin, Zlin (2012), ISBN 978–80–7454–223–7
9. Kohli D. and Osvatic M., ASME J. Mech. Design, (1993), 115: 922–931
10. Raghavan M. and Roth B., *Kinematic analysis of the 6R manipulator of general geometry*, Proc. 5th International Symposium on Robotics Research, edited by H. Miura and S. Arimoto, MIT Press, (1990), Cambridge
11. Lee H. Y. and Reinholtz C. F., ASME J. Mech. Design, (1996), 118: 396– 404

12. Yan Wang, Lu bin Hang, and Ting-li Yang. Frontiers of Mechanical Engineering in China, 1:115–124, (2006). 10.1007/s11465-005-0022-7.
13. L. Bláha. *Groebnerova báze a teorie řízení*. PhD dissertation, Cybernetics' department, FAV, ZCU Plzen, (2011).

MATEC Web of Conferences 76, 02028 (2016) DOI: 10.1051/matecconf/20167602028
CSCC 2016

Mechanical properties change of thermoplastic elastomer after using of different dosage of irradiation by beta rays

Ales Mizera[1,a], Miroslav Manas[1], David Manas[1], Pavel Stoklasek[1], Martin Bednarik[1] and Lenka Hylova[1]

[1]*Tomas Bata University in Zlin, nam. T. G. Masaryka 5555, 76001 Zlin, Czech Republic*

Abstract. Radiation processing of polymers is a well-established and economical commercial method of precisely modifying the properties of polymers. The industrial applications of the radiation processing of plastics and composites include polymerization, cross-linking, degradation and grafting. Radiation processing mainly involves the use of electron beams from electron accelerators. The Thermoplastic Elastomer (TPE) was used in this research and the mechanical properties were investigated at the ambient temperature. Results demonstrate that TPE has higher values of tensile strength with the increased irradiation dose and it has decreased elongation at break. This behaviour leads to the expansion of these materials in the automotive and electrical industry.

1 Introduction

Polymers rank among a construction materials which find use in industry branches. The advantage of polymers is a low weight together with the excellent mechanical properties, very good chemical resistance and other properties, which assign them for various applications. Disadvantage is mainly low temperature stability which significantly reduces usage of these polymers.

Every property improvement especially temperature stability helps to increase application possibilities. In addition, property modifications of standard polymers, which are relatively cheap products, give them advantage for another usage.

The cross-linking of rubbers and thermoplastic polymers is a well-proven process of the improvement of the thermal properties. The chemical cross-linking or rubber vulcanization is normally induced by the effect of heating after processing with the presence of a curing agent. The cross-linking process for thermosets is very similar. In thermosets the polymer molecules are also chemically linked due to heat after processing. Cross-linked rubbers have a wide-meshed molecular network that keeps them soft and their properties change only slightly on a wide temperature scale. On the other hand, thermosets are characterized by a very narrow-meshed network. Due to this fact they hardly change their high level of stiffness on a wide temperature scale [1].

Radiation cross-linking with accelerating electrons offers several advantages when compared to other radiation sources, particularly gamma rays and X-rays. The process is very fast, clean and can be controlled with a great deal of precision. In contrast to gamma rays and X-rays the electron beam can be steered relatively easy, thus allowing irradiation of variety of physical shapes. The large advantage includes flexibility and controllability in operation, beneficial economics, high throughput capability and the ability to switch off the source of radiation [1, 2].

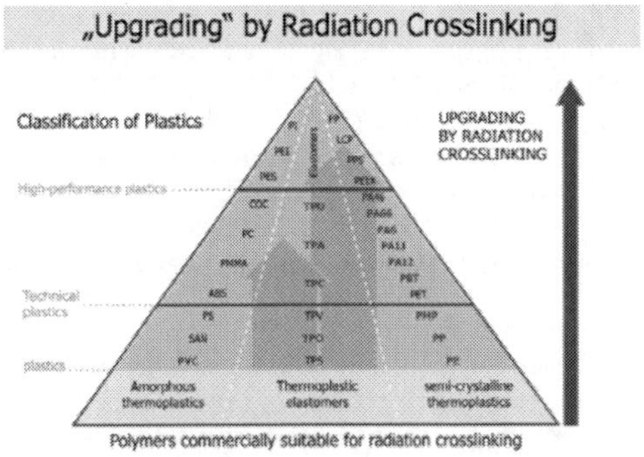

Figure 1. Pyramid of polymers [1].

The thermoplastics which are used for production of various types of products have very different properties. The special group of polymers which exhibit elastic behaviour to similar that of vulcanized conventional elastomer and can be processed as thermoplastics (i.e. by melt processing) are called thermoplastic elastomers (TPEs). The most thermoplastic elastomers are essentially phase-separated systems. Usually one phase is hard and solid at ambient temperature whereas the other is an elastomer. Often, the phases are bonded chemically by block or graft polymerization. In other case a fine dispersion of the phases is apparently sufficient. The hard phase gives these TPEs their strength and represents physical crosslinking. Without it the elastomer phase would be free to flow under stress and the polymer would be practically unusable. TPE has good physical properties

[a] Corresponding author: mizera@fai.utb.cz

of elastomers along processing characteristics of thermoplastic [3, 4].

A team of Indian scientists examined the influence of electron beam technology on blends of polyethylene and ethylene-vinyl acetate copolymer. These scientists discovered that tensile strength and E-modulus increased while elongation at the break initially increased followed by decrease with increase in the radiation dose at the constant monomer level and blend ratio [4]. López-Quintana from Spain and his colleagues investigated the effect of beta radiation on mechanical properties of metallocene elastomers/PA 6 blends and they found out that TPE with excellent mechanical properties and thermal stability can be obtained by beta irradiation technology [5]. In Indian institute of technology was examined the effect of electron beam irradiation on silica-filled LDPE-EVA based thermoplastic elastomer. They discovered that all filled TPE system represented rise of E-modulus with increase in radiation dose and that rise of E-modulus with the increase in radiation dose is attributed to radiation cross-linking of the silica-filled TPE system [6].

This research paper deals with a possibility of using radiation cross-linked TPE as a suitable material for pipes in automotive industry, especially from point of view mechanical testing and temperature stability.

2 Experimental

As the basic polymer material was used thermoplastic elastomer (TPE, V-PTS-UNIFLEX-E25D/M*M800/20 natur). An ARBURG Allrounder 420C Advance Injection molding machine was used for sample preparation, with the processing conditional to comply with the TPE producer's recommendations.

Irradiation of tested TPE was performed with the kind help of BGS Germany, in the BGS Wiehl plant using accelerated electrons with a dosage range of 0 to 198kGy. Samples with the dosage of irradiation higher than 99 kGy were exposed temperature 200°C during one hour and then these samples were cooled spontaneously to ambient temperature.

Mechanical properties before and after temperature load and temperature stability of irradiated thermoplastic elastomer after irradiation has been tested. The thermo-mechanical properties were measured. Perkin – Elmer Thermal Analyser TMA7 was used for the thermo-mechanical analysis, heated from 50°C to 400°C at 20°C/min, hold for 1 min at 50°C. The tensile behaviour of temperature non-loaded and loaded samples of TPE were measured at the ambient temperature. Tensile test was carried out on tensile test machine ZWICK 1456 for TPE according to standard CSN EN ISO 527-1, 527-2 with used rate 50 mm/min. Test data was processed by Test Expert Standard software and tensile strength [MPa] and elongation at break [%] were determined. The test of hardness was measured using a HPE – A Berreiss hardness tester type, Shore A method. The shape and dimensions of the testing samples were according to the CSN 621431 standards.

3 Results and discussion

3.1. Temperature stability

Temperature stability of polymers is very low in comparison with other construction materials. Experiments done in this project show that irradiation cross-linking markedly affects the temperature stability of studied TPE. The higher is the dose of irradiation the best is temperature stability of this polymers.

Irradiation affects the thermomechanical properties of the studied TPE (Figure 2). Already small dose of radiation (up to 33 kGy) move the softening point up to 210 °C. TPE irradiated by the dose of 198 kGy evinces the significant improvement of the temperature stability. Irradiation TPE with the dose 198 kGy holds temperature stability up to 360 °C for short time. The temperature stability of TPE was measured. The temperature stability was evaluated by visual observation in the temperature chamber. The visual observation of sample behaviour after two hours exposition at 200 °C is given on Figure 3.

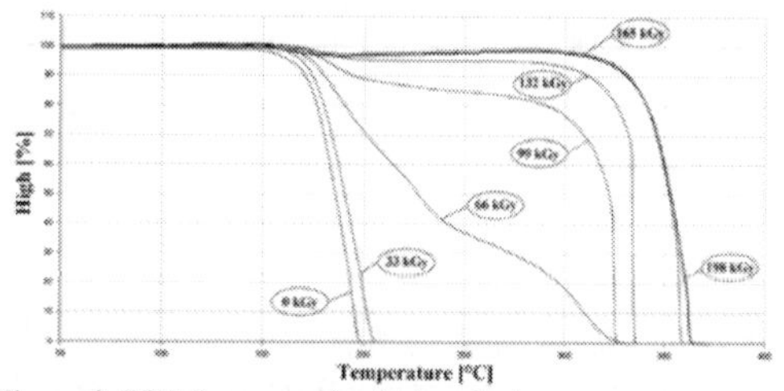

Figure 2. TPE thermomechanical analysis.

Specimens are fitted horizontally in the temperature chamber and loaded by the bending moment both form its own weight and the weight on the end of specimen. Specimen deformation is decreasing with increasing dose of radiation at elevated temperature (Figure 3). At 200 °C the specimen from not irradiated TPE is totally melted while the polymer irradiated by the dose of 198 kGy keeps its cross-section without changes, there is only deformation by its own weight. The surface quality worsens.

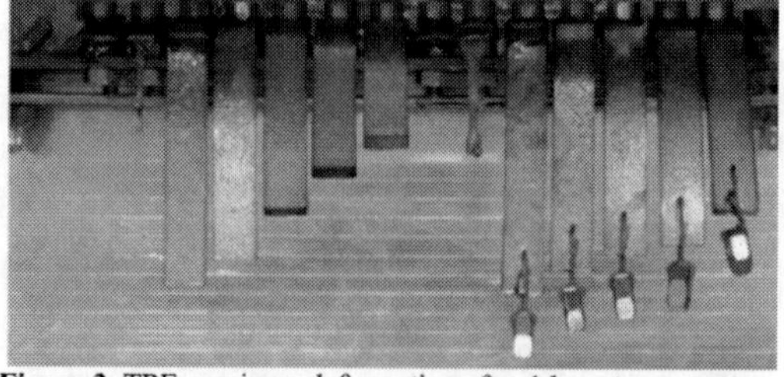

Figure 3. TPE specimen deformation after 1 hour temperature exposure 200 °C.

On Figure 4 is displayed surface of irradiated TPE by 99 kGy after 15 minutes at 200 °C. There is not any change of colour and surface quality. However, after 1 hour at the same temperature the surface changes colour to yellow-brown (Figure 5) and also surface quality is worse.

Figure 4. 100 times magnified surface of TPE irradiated by 99 kGy after 15 minutes at 200 °C.

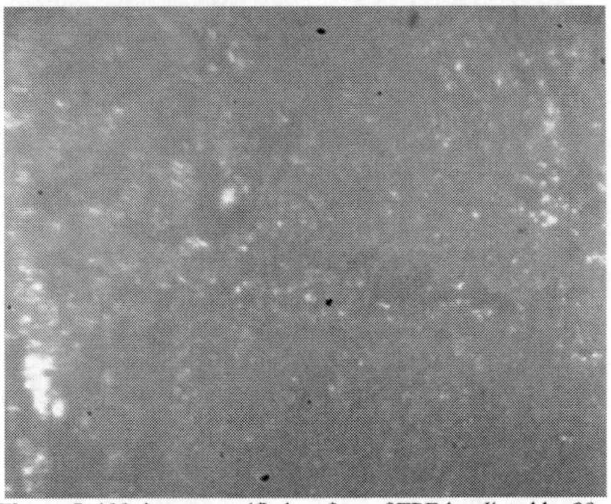

Figure 5. 100 times magnified surface of TPE irradiated by 99 kGy after 1 hour at 200 °C.

On another pictures (Figure 6 and Figure 7) there are depicted similar changes of surface quality after 15 and 60 minutes. However, irradiated TPE with the dose 198 kGy after 1 hour at 200 °C has smoother surface than irradiated TPE by 99 kGy. It can be caused higher degree of cross-linking bonds.

3.2. Tensile behaviour

The tensile behaviour of TPE, before and after irradiation, was studied. For easier of evaluation of the measured data, and the comparison of the irradiated polymer with a non-irradiated one, the changes of measured were used on some graphs. The property of the non-irradiated polymer had the value of 100 %, while others were expressed in % as the ratio of measured property of irradiated polymers to the same property of non-irradiated polymer.

The tensile strength rises more than 40 % after irradiation with the dose of 66 kGy (Figure 9). Although the gel content (Figure 8) rises with the dose of irradiation the tensile strength goes down with the dose higher than 66 kGy. Then with the dose of 132 kGy and higher the value of tensile strength oscillates around the value of not irradiated polymer. From the point of view of tensile strength the dose of irradiation of 66 kGy looks to be optimal.

Figure 6. 100 times magnified surface of TPE irradiated by 198 kGy after 15 minutes at 200 °C.

Figure 7. 100 times magnified surface of TPE irradiated by 198 kGy after 1 hour at 200 °C.

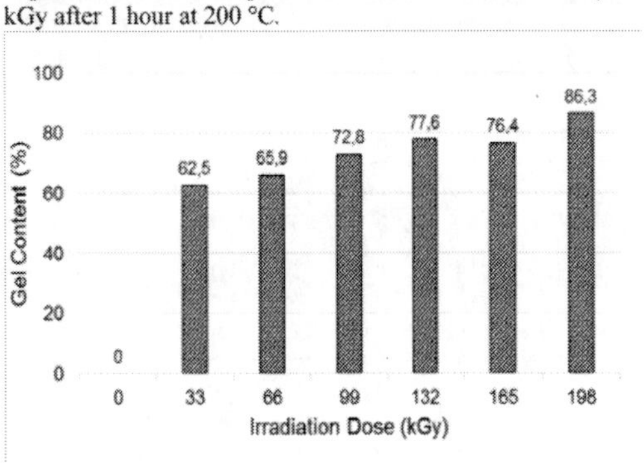

Figure 8. Gel content of irradiated TPE by beta rays.

Tensile strength of TPE after temperature load with increasing dose of irradiation decreases. However, the value of tensile strength is about 2 MPa lover in comparison with temperature non-loaded TPE which was irradiated by 99 kGy.

Elongation at break of TPE goes down continually with the dose of irradiation. By the highest applied dose of irradiation (198 kGy) the elongation is only 22 % of former (non-irradiated) polymer before temperature load. Due to irradiation of the studied TPE loses significantly its flexibility (Figure 10). After temperature load there is the same tendency as before temperature load.

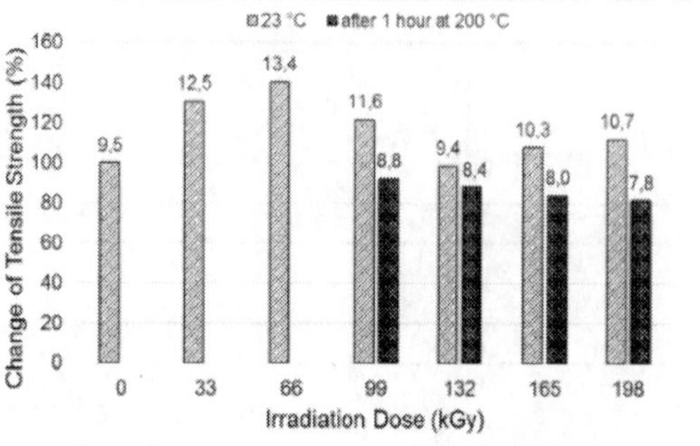

Figure 9. Change of tensile strength before and after temperature load.

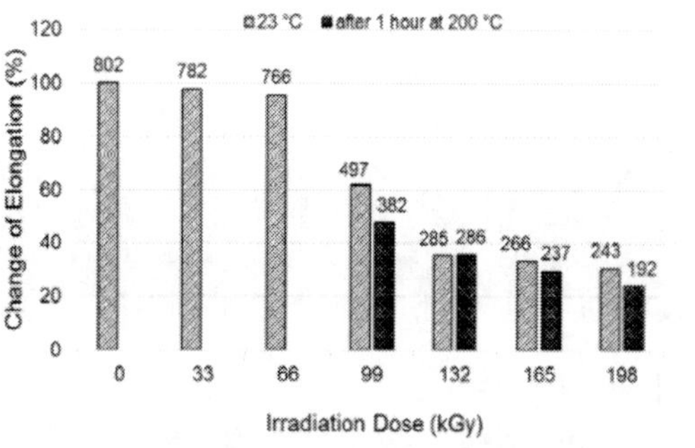

Figure 10. Change of elongation at break before and after temperature load.

3.3. Hardness

Change of Shore A hardness is showed on the Figure 11. Shore A hardness rises with increasing dose of irradiation up to 66 kGy then decreases slowly along irradiation.

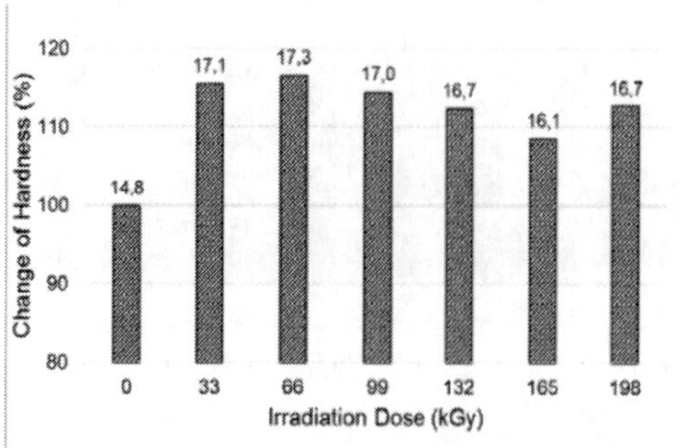

Figure 11. Change of Shore A hardness before and after temperature load.

4 Summary

Plastics are by far the largest group of polymeric materials being processed by electron beam irradiation. Cross-linking of polyolefins, PVC, polyesters, polyurethanes, polyamides, fluoropolymers and fiber-reinforced composites are a common practice. Radiation cross-linking of polyamides requires considerably less overall energy and space, and is faster, more efficient and more environmentally acceptable. The disadvantage of electron beam cross-linking is a more or less nonuniform dose distribution. This can happen, particularly in thicker objects, due to intrinsic dose-depth profiles of electron beams. Another problem can be a nonuniformity of rotation of cylindrical objects as they traverse a scanned electron beam. However, the mechanical properties often depend on the mean cross-link density.

Results of the measurements of TPE after irradiation show significant changes of mechanical and thermomechanical properties. Tensile strength rises of 40 % after irradiation by the dose of 66 kGy. Elongation at break is going down gradually with the dose of irradiation. The lowest value of elongation at break was registered after irradiation by the dose of 198 kGy and reaches only 25 % of elongation of non-irradiated polymer. Very important is improvement of temperature stability of TPE after irradiation. Tested polymer irradiated by the dose of 198 kGy shows no dimensional changes even by the temperature of 200 °C. This significantly moves application possibilities of TPE to area with service temperature much higher than former melting point of tested polymers.

Acknowledgment

This paper is supported by the internal grant of TBU in Zlin No. IGA/FT/2016/010 funded from the resources of specific university research and by the Ministry of Education, Youth and Sports of the Czech Republic within the National Sustainability Programme project No. LO1303 (MSMT-7778/2014) and also by the European Regional Development Fund under the project CEBIA-Tech No. CZ.1.05/2.1.00/03.0089.

References

1. J.G. Drobny, *Radiation Technology for Polymers* (CRC Press, Boca Raton, 2003)
2. D.W. Clegg, A.A. Collyer, *Irradiation effects on polymers* (Elsevier Applied Science, London, 1991)
3. J.G. Drobny, *Handbook of Thermoplastic Elastomers* (William Andrew Publishing, Norwich NY, 2007)
4. S. Chattopadhyay, T.K. Chaki, Anil K. Bhowmick, J. Appl. Polym. Sci. **79**, 1877 (2001)
5. S. López-Quintana, C. Rosales, I. Gobernado-Mitre, J.C. Merino, J.M. Pastor, Polymer **45**, 8041 (2004)
6. S. Hui, S. Mushtaq, T.K. Chaki, S. Chattopadhyay, J. Appl. Polym. Sci. **119**, 8041 (2004)

MATEC Web of Conferences 76, 02029 (2016) DOI: 10.1051/matecconf/20167602029
CSCC 2016

Improvement of handle grip using reverse engineering, CAE and Rapid Prototyping

Pavel Stoklasek[1,a], Ales Mizera[1], Miroslav Manas[1] and David Manas[1]

[1]Tomas Bata University in Zlin, nam. T.G. Masaryka 5555, 76001 Zlin, Czech Republic

Abstract. The overwhelming majority of manual operations is even nowadays performed by using manual hand tools. These tools can be divided into 2 groups – hand tools designed for general use or a single-purpose hand tools for special operations. Tool described in this paper is used in assembling operation in the completion of electric motor. During the design of the existing tools the requirements for a functional part of the tool (lifespan, inability to damage the engine installation) were fully considered, demands for ergonomic grip area, however, were not taken into account. Long-term use of incorrectly designed tool causes carpal tunnel syndrome, hand-arm vibration syndrome, diminished sensitivity or tingling in the fingers of workers. These difficulties can be reduced or entirely eliminated due to proper design of the grip of hand tool. Most authors focus on adjusting the grip for optimum ergonomics at individual types of grips (cylindrical, palmar, lateral, etc.). However, as already mentioned, there are tools for specific operations when the working area is limited by space or a specific type of load on the grip is needed. In some cases, it is often necessary to change the type of grip or combine different types of grips. This paper describes the design of an optimal grip of hand tool used for specific operation when assembling motors. Design of prototype mold and production of functional prototypes for ergonomics assessment directly in the workplace were realized. New design of handle should reduce the risk primarily of developing carpal tunnel in long-term use.

1 Introduction

Tool handles have been improving for thousands of years. People have tried to modify the tool handles for improving effectiveness of the work with them. Proper design of the handle is important for comfortable work. Companies producing tools often disregard the ergonomic requirements of individual consumers. Handles of these tools are often too small, stiff, sharp or misplaced. There are many different sizes of hands and every person is holding a tool according to habit.

Tools are often used differently than were designed, the contact between the hand and the tool handle is wrong or inaccurate. At first feeling improperly designed thickness, length and position of the handle can be detected. The functional and ergonomic requirements must be effectively interconnected when developing new hand tools. Grip should be designed with consideration to ergonomic which has a significant effect on muscle problems in the wrist. [1, 2]

Handle length should be at least 10 to 15 cm to cover the entire width of the palm. The diameter of the tool handle for maximum performance is for an adult male 30 – 45 mm. The shape of the handle should have a cylindrical or spherical cross-section due to good contact with the hand. Most tools has a designed area for the thumb and the combined area for other fingers, which prevents unintentional twisting of the hand. The general rule is to eliminate sharp edges and elevated places in contact with the hand. Properly designed handle should transfer the best possible strength of hand into tool and also ensure the best possible safety while working. Elevations may be used on the edge of the handle to prevent slipping of the hand and accidental injuries. The smooth surface is used on the handles, along which the hand moves and rotates. Rough surface is used on some products purposely to fix the arm in correct place. These are only general recommendations – every new handle tool design must be individually adapted to the needs of the specific operation and comfort of the worker. [3-9]

2 Experimental

2.1. Original tool

The existing tool consists of two main parts - the handle and the working part. The handle is made of pertinax - composite material made of paper impregnated with a plasticized phenol formaldehyde resin. The handle is made by combining machining, cutting and grinding. The working part is made of tool steel. Both parts are connected with two screws.

[a] Corresponding author: pstoklasek@fai.utb.cz

 DOI: 10.1051/matecconf/20167602029

Figure 1. Original tool.

2.2. Design of improved tool

First, a handle shape of modeling clay was created on the working part of the tool. Two combined grip types (cylindrical and palmar) were chosen based on videoanalysis of work and workers comments. The handle was enlarged and anatomically shaped for a new type of grip. The handle enlarging had increased contact area in the palm. In comparison with the original tool, new design fully respects the general requirements for ergonomics.

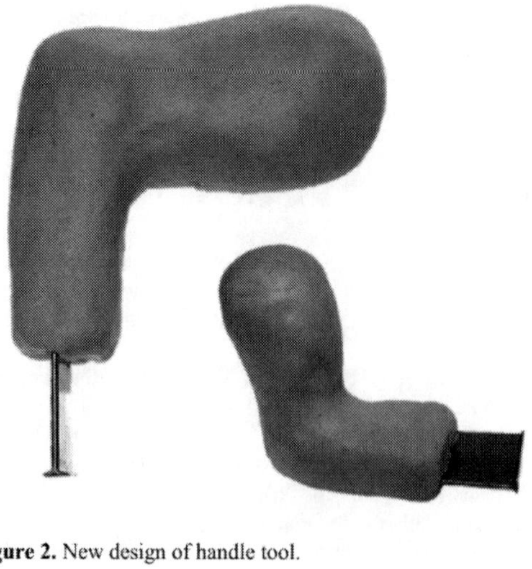

Figure 2. New design of handle tool.

Clay model was scanned by using a contactless 3D scanner ATOS II TripleScan 5M (GOM, Germany). The final model consisted of 16 scans (8 shots on each half of the model). The entire surface of the model was modified in the program GOM Professional (GOM, Germany) to eliminate minor irregularities and patch small holes. The data was then exported in STL format. The total scanning time was 7 minutes, the time of postprocessing operations was 10 minutes.

The surface of the model was smoothed in the program Geomagic Design X (3D Systems, USA). Based on surface analysis a plane of symmetry was created. This plane is also used as the parting plane of future mold. Due to left-handed and right-handed use of new tool it is necessary to have a symmetrical shape at this stage of design. One of halves of the model was removed and replaced by a mirror copy of the original half. The created model was again smoothed (especially in the area of parting plane) and using a standard reverse engineering steps converted to a volumetric 3D model. Total time of handle reverse engineering operations was 35 minutes.

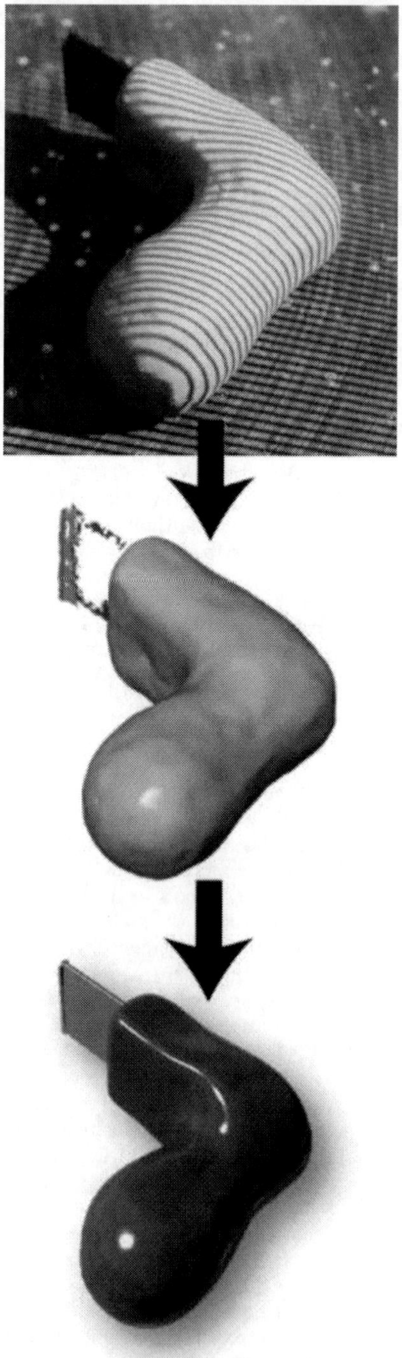

Figure 3. Workflow: 3D scanning – STL export – CAD model.

2.3. Mold design

Mold was designed in Autodesk Inventor Professional 2016 (Autodesk, USA). The cavity was created by using Boolean difference model of the handle and block of mold. When designing mold it is necessary to specify both the position the gate and the position of the handle during the injection of polyurethane foam. The vents 4 must be in the highest position of the mold cavity. Figure 4 shows CAD design of injection mold of new handle tool where metal functional part 3 is molded into polyurethane grip element. Mold parts, particularly gate 1 and the leader pins 2 are for increasing resistance to abrasion and deformation made of metal. Mold fully complies with the demands on the technology of polyurethane injection. [10]

Total time of mold design was 3 hours.

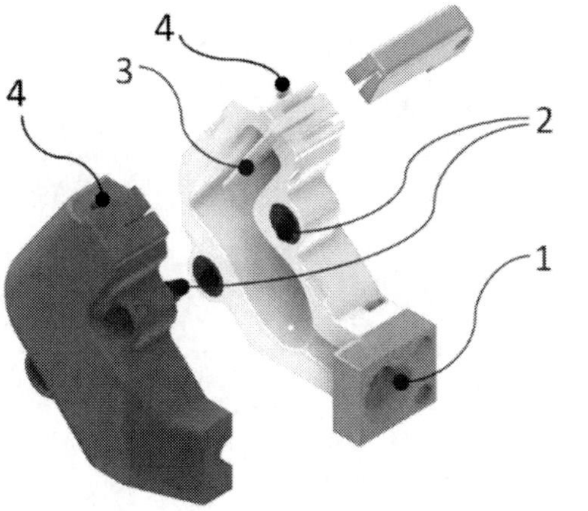

Figure 4. Prototype mold design.

Fortus 900mc (Stratasys, USA) was used for mold building. Due to sufficient temperature resistance ABS was used as a building material. Maximum temperature of injected PUR foam is not higher than 90° C. The height of the print layer was 0.17 mm. After printing the support material was chemically removed in ultrasonic cleaner. Total time of mold 3D printing and support removing was 20.5 hours (18 hours printing, 2.5 hours postprocessing operations).

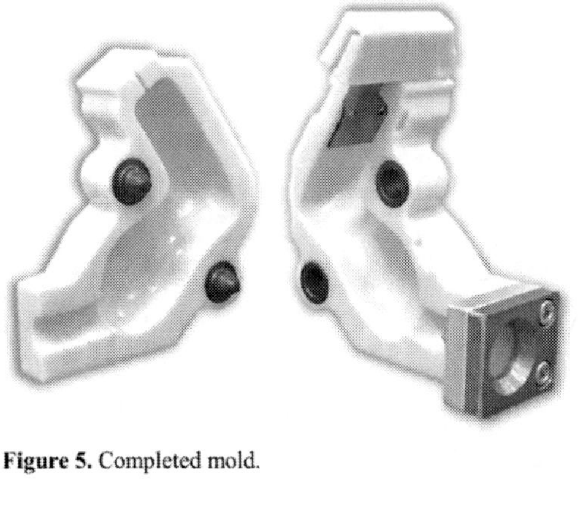

Figure 5. Completed mold.

Figure 5 shows the completed mold. All parts of mold were sandblasted and chemically smoothed in acetone vaporizer. After surface finishing the mold cavity was coated with thick layer of PUR foam separator which was soaked into material and filled micro-cavities and surface roughness. The separator was removed after 10 minutes and mold was dried. Before injecting of the polyurethane normal layer of separator was applied. Separation is used to removing injected part without difficulty. Total time of mold cavity postprocessing and mold completing took about 2.5 hours.

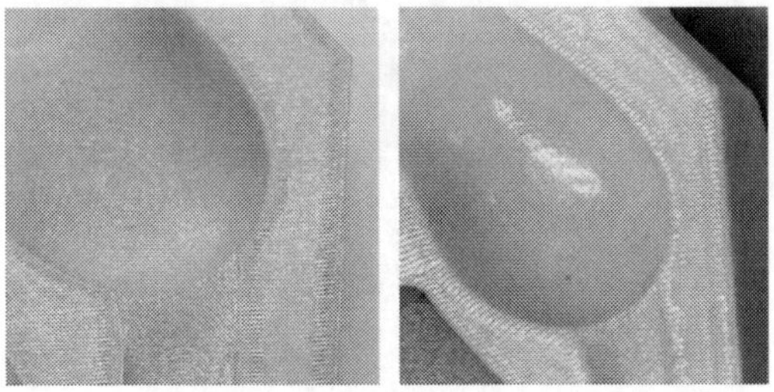

Figure 6. Surface comparison (before/after aceton smoothing).

Before the injection molding process it is necessary to heat the mold to 50° C. The prepared mold was placed in an oven for 15 minutes. In case of repeated injection is not necessary to repeat this operation. Production cycle of one part is 7 minutes. After each removal of the part the separation the process must be repeated.

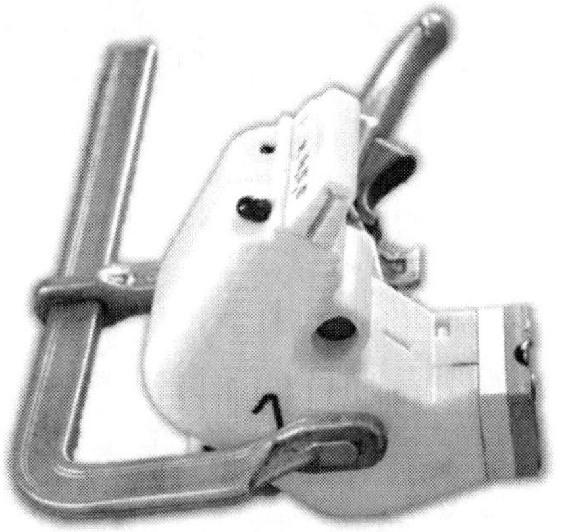

Figure 7. Mold after injection of PUR foam.

3 Results and conclusion

Combination of optical digitalization and rapid prototyping methods were used to minimize the manufacturing time of mold. These methods are applicable to the most of currently used manufacturing processes and can save significant amount of resources mainly in field of pre-production and early design processes. In this article, the methods were applied to specific problem of ergonomic and functional design of hand tool. New tool design is shown on the Figure 5. It was manufactured about 20 prototypes for ergonomics assessment directly in the workplace.

Main advantages of the new solution were observed on comfort of workers. According to the survey 74 % of workers stated improvement of muscle load in hand area. Also manufacturing process of new tool is shorter and does not need any conventional milling operations which are not so productive as injection PUR molding.

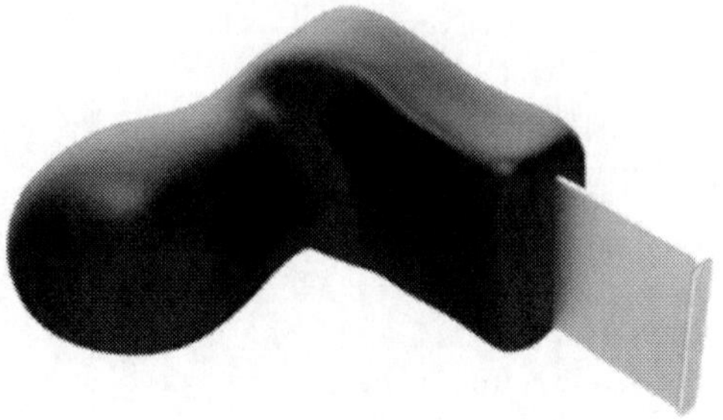

Figure 8. New tool.

Figure 9. Mold cavity after injection of 20 parts.

Table 1. Time summary of all operations.

Operation	Time (h)
3D digitizing, postprocessing	0,6
polygonal data processing, reverse engineering	0,8
mold design	3,0
3D printing time, postprocessing	20,5
mold completing	2,5
production cycle	0,1
TOTAL	**27,5**

Acknowledgments

This paper is supported by the internal grant of TBU in Zlin No. IGA/FT/2016/010 funded from the resources of specific university research and by the Ministry of Education, Youth and Sports of the Czech Republic within the National Sustainability Programme project No. LO1303 (MSMT-7778/2014) and also by the European Regional Development Fund under the project CEBIA-Tech No. CZ.1.05/2.1.00/03.0089.

References

1. G. Harih, B. Dolšak, Int J Ind Ergonom, **43**, 288 (2013)
2. A.G. González, J. G. Sanz-Calcedo, O. López, D.R. Salgado, I. Cambero, J. M. Herrera, Procedia Eng. **132**, 1014 (2015)
3. M. Patkin, HFESA, **15** (2001)
4. K. A. Grant, D. J. Habes, L. L. Steward, , Int J Iind Ergonom, **10**, 199 (1992)
5. Y. Kong, B. D. Lowe, Int J Iin Ergonom, **35**, 495, (2005)
6. R. G. Dong, J. Z. Wu, D. E. Welcome, T. W. McDowell, Med Eng Pphys, **30**, (2008)
7. B. Wimer, R. G. Dong, D. E. Welcome, Ch. Warren, T.W. McDowell, Med Eng Phys, **31**, 695 (2009)
8. M. Motamedzade, A. Choobineh, M. A. Mououdi, S. Arghami, Int J Int Ergonom, **37**, 581 (2007)
9. I. Dianat, M. Nedaei, M. A. M. Nezami, Int J Int Ergonom, **45**, 13 (2015)
10. J. Dobránsky, L. Běhálek, Key Eng Mat, 669, **95** (2016)

MATEC Web of Conferences 76, 02030 (2016) DOI: 10.1051/matecconf/20167602030
CSCC 2016

Nano-hardness of Electron Beam Irradiated Polyamide 11

Martin Ovsik[1,a], Lenka Hylova[1], David Manas[1], Miroslav Manas[1] and Michal Stanek[1]

[1] Tomas Bata University in Zlin, TGM 5555, 760 01 Zlin, Czech Republic

Abstract. Cross-linking is a process in which polymer chains are associated through chemical bonds. Radiation, which penetrated through specimens and reacted with the cross-linking agent, gradually formed cross-linking (3D net), first in the surface layer and then in the total volume, which resulted in considerable changes in specimen behaviour. In this study there was found that ionizing beta radiation increased the nano-mechanical properties of polyamide 11 (PA11). The measurement results indicated that ionizing beta radiation (66kGy, 132kGy and 198kGy) was a very effective tool for improvement of indentation hardness, indentation modulus, indentation creep and deformation works of studied polymers. The best results were achieved by irradiation at doses of 132 kGy (increase about 40%) by which the highest nano-mechanical properties of PA11 were achieved.

1 Introduction

Polyamides are one of the most commonly used polymers. Due to their very high strength and durability polyamides are commonly used in textiles, carpets and floor coverings or automotive. Probably more familiar name designation is nylon. Polyamide 11 (PA11) is a semi-crystalline thermoplastic material with very high toughness, good chemical stability and impact resistance. PA11 is also a good electrical insulator and as other polyamide insulating properties will not be affected due to moisture. It is also resistant to corrosion. PA11 has many features and enhancements in terms of plasticization of improved varieties. Polyamide 11 is thanks to its very good mechanical properties, which can be even improved as shown in the results, suitable for applications with great demand on the stiffness and resistance of surface layers for instance friction parts used in automotive industry [1-3].

Polyamides are polymers whose repeating units are characterized by the amide group. Through radiation cross-linking, thermoplastic polyamides are turned into plastics which behave like elastomers over a wide temperature range. Cross-linking makes the originally thermoplastic product able to withstand considerably higher temperatures of up to 350 °C. The dimensional stability under thermal stress is also improved. Radiation cross-linked polyamide can often replace thermosetting plastics or high-performance plastics such as PPS, PEI, LCP, etc. One application that has proved most useful over the years is radiation cross-linked components for the electrical industry, e.g. switch components, and the automotive industry, for instance components for the engine compartment [1-3].

Electron beams (β-rays) generated by accelerators are monoenergetic and the absorbed dose is greatest just below the surface of the irradiated material and falls rapidly at greater depths in the material (Fig. 1). The energy range of electron beams used in radiation processing is from 0.15 to 10 MeV. Compared with gamma irradiation, electron accelerators have advantages of higher power and directional beams. The time of irradiation by β-rays is in seconds. The limited penetrating power of electron beams means that they are mainly used for irradiating relatively thin objects like wires and cable insulation [1-4].

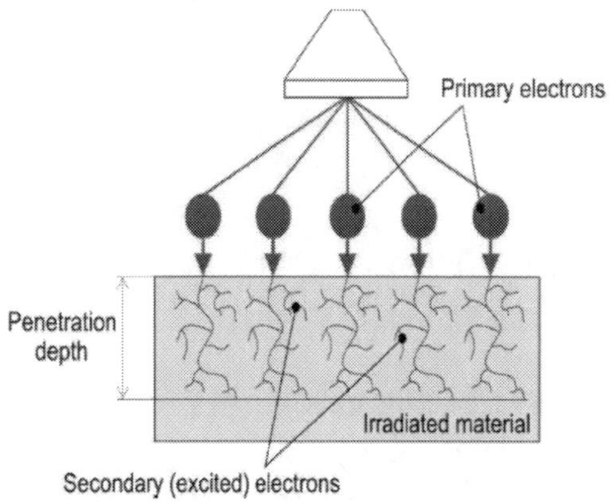

Figure 1. Radiation crosslinking by electrons rays

In general, copolymers cross-link more readily than polyamide. Common PA11, when exposed to the effect of the radiation cross-linking, degrades and its mechanical properties deteriorate. Mechanical properties

[a] Corresponding author: ovsik@ft.utb.cz

of polyamides are modified by irradiation, as seen by reduced tensile strength (50% loss when irradiated in air, 16% under vacuum). Aromatic polyamides retain strength better than aliphatic polyamides. Using cross-linking agent TAIC (triallyl isocyanurate) produces a cross-linking reaction inside the PA11 structure. The utility properties of PA11 improve when the non-crystalline part of PA11 is cross-linked [1-4].

The aim of this paper is to study the effect of ionizing radiation with different doses, on nano-mechanical properties of polyamide 11 and compare these results with those of non-irradiated samples. The study is carried out due to the ever-growing employment of this type of polymer (polyamide 11).

2 Experimental

2.1 Material

For this experiment Polyamide 11 PA11 V-PTS-Creamid-11-AMN 0 TLD, that were supplied by PTS Plastics Technology Service, Germany was used. The material already contained the special cross-linking agent TAIC - triallyl isocyanurate (6 volume %), which should enable subsequent cross-linking by ionizing β – radiation.

2.2 Sample preparation

The samples were made using the injection molding technology on the injection molding machine Arburg Allrounder 470H. Processing temperature 240–260 °C, mold temperature 60 °C, injection pressure 90 MPa, injection rate 50 mm/s. It was used normalized specimen measuring 80x10x4 mm.

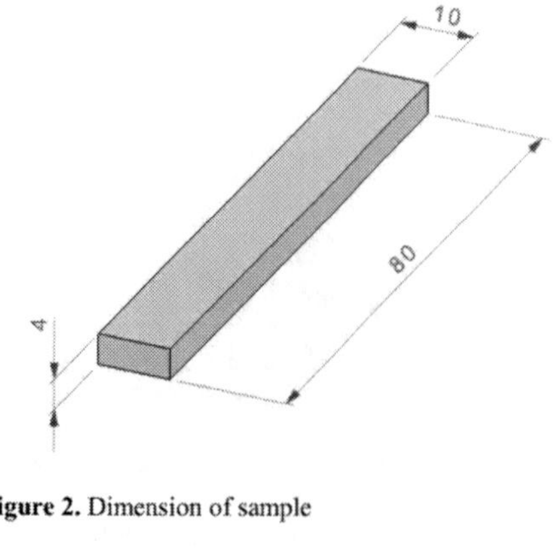

Figure 2. Dimension of sample

2.3 Irradiation

The prepared specimens were irradiated with doses of 0, 66, 132 and 198 kGy at BGS Beta-Gamma Service GmbH & Co. KG, Germany.

2.4 Nano-indentation

Nano-indentation test were performed using a Nano-indentation tester (NHT), CSM Instruments (Switzerland) according to the CSN EN ISO 14577. The tip is made of diamond having the shape of a cube corner (Vickers). In the present study, the maximum load used was 50 mN and loading rate (and unloading rate) was 100 mN/min. A holding time was 90 s at the indentation and 21600 s at the creep.

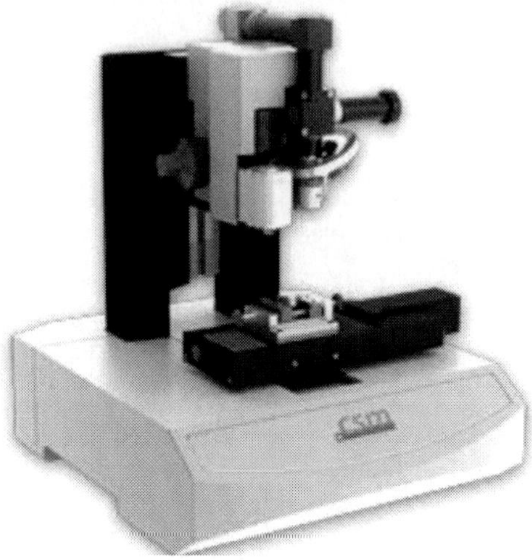

Figure 3. Nano-indentation tester

The indentation hardness (H_{IT}) was calculated as maximum load (F_{max}) to the projected area of the hardness impression (A_p) and the indentation modulus (E_{IT}) is calculated from the Plane Strain modulus (E^*) using an estimated sample Poisson's ratio (ν) according to [4-6]:

$$H_{IT} = \frac{F_{max}}{A_p} \tag{1}$$

$$E_{IT} = E^* \cdot (1 - \nu_s^2) \tag{2}$$

Measurement of all above mentioned properties was performed 10 times to ensure statistical correctness.

3 Results and discussion

Radiation cross-linking creates changes in the polyamide 11 structure by creating 3D net. Beta radiation gradually penetrates more deeply into the PA11 structure through the surface layer. The surface layer undergoes changes which have a considerable influence on the nano-mechanical properties of PA11.

The Fig. 4 and Fig. 5 shows a very important correlation between the force and the depth of the indentation. The correlations provide very valuable information on the behavior of tested material and the modified surface layer. The correlation between the force and the depth of the indentation in PA11 also proved very interesting. It demonstrated the influence of radiation on the change of nano-mechanical properties in the surface layer of specimens. The non-irradiated material showed low hardness as well as increasing impression of the indenter in the surface layer. On the contrary, the irradiated PA11 showed considerably smaller depth of the impression of the indenter which can signify greater resistance of this layer to wear.

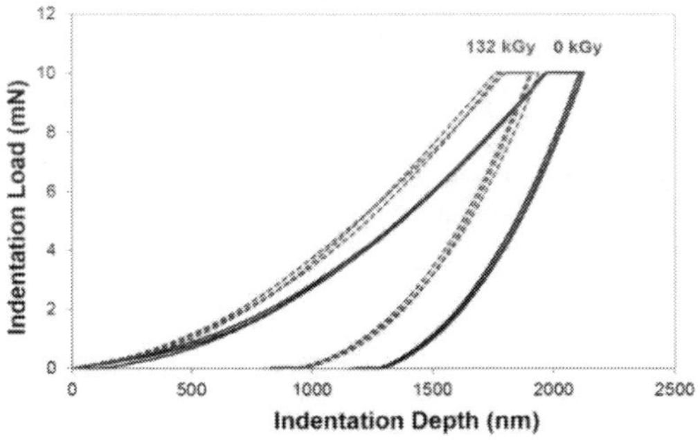

Figure 4. Indentation characteristic of irradiated PA11

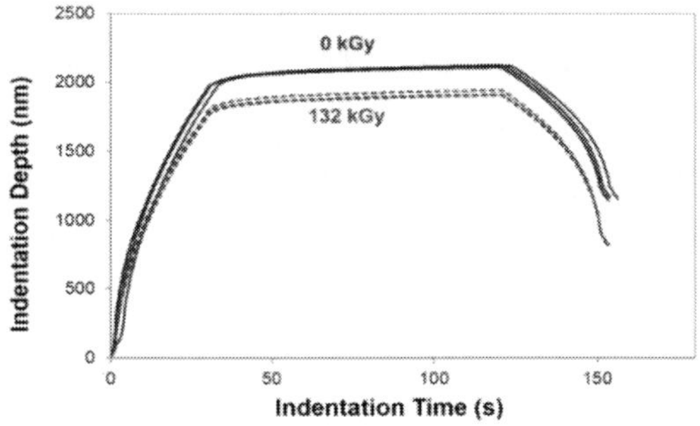

Figure 5. Indentation characteristic of irradiated PA11

The greatest values of nano-hardness test were obtained for PA11 irradiated with dose of 132 kGy as is apparent in Table 1.

Table 1. Summary of measured values

Irradiation doses	0kGy	66kGy	132kGy	198kGy
H_{IT} [MPa]	110,0	132,4	153,5	134,1
HV_{IT} [Vickers]	10,4	12,1	14,6	12,9
E_{IT} [GPa]	1,8	2,0	2,1	2,0
C_{IT} [%]	7,4	7,8	7,5	7,2
W_{el} [pJ]	2984,8	2887,7	3266,7	3039,6
W_{pl} [pJ]	5350,2	5224,2	4490,4	4974,4

Nano-indentation test of PA11 modified by beta radiation showed that the highest values of indentation hardness and Vickers hardness were found for PA11 modified by the radiation dose of 132 kGy (H_{IT} = 153.5 MPa, HV_{IT} = 14.6 Vickers). The smallest value of indentation hardness a Vickers hardness was found for non-irradiated PA11 (H_{IT} = 110.0 MPa, HV_{IT} = 10.4 Vickers). The increase of indentation hardness value for PA11 irradiated by the dose of 132 kGy was by 40% (Fig. 6, Fig. 7) in comparison with the non-irradiated PA11.

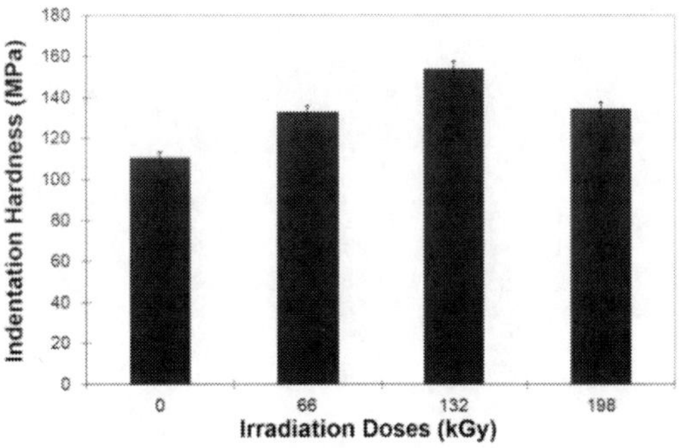

Figure 6. Indentation hardness (H_{IT})

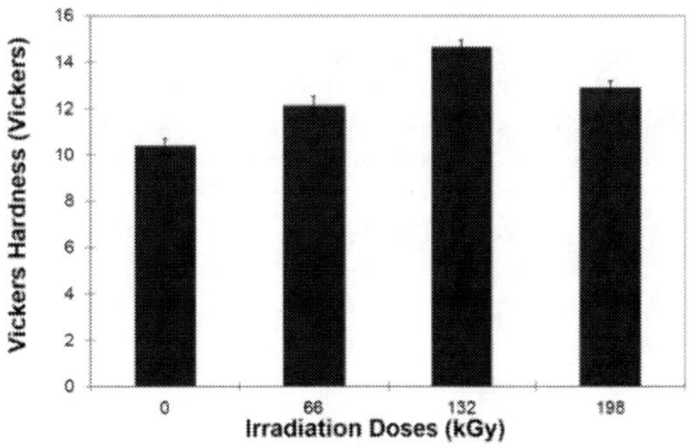

Figure 7. Vickers hardness (HV_{IT})

Similar behaviour was found for indentation modulus E_{IT} according to Oliver and Pharr method (see Fig. 8), which also increases with increasing irradiated doses. Values of stiffness showed the highest value 2.1 GPa at 132 kGy radiation dose, while the lowest stiffness value 1.8 GPa was found in non-irradiated PA11. This represents increase in indentation modulus by 17%.

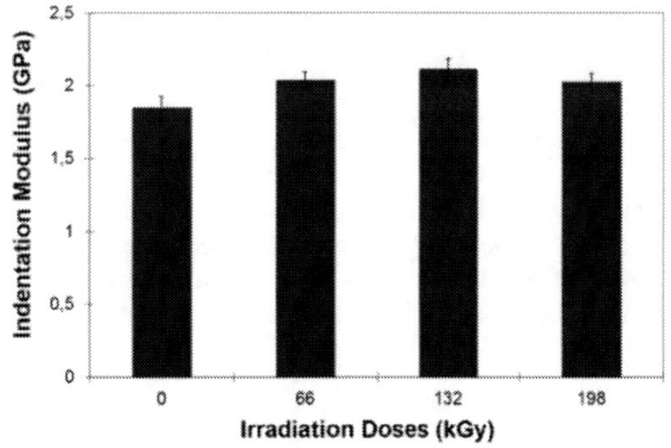

Figure 8. Indentation modulus (E_{IT})

Very important values were found for indentation creep (C_{IT}). The lowest value of indentation creep was measured at radiation dose of 198 kGy (C_{IT} = 7.2%). The highest indentation creep value measured at non-irradiated PA11 (C_{IT} = 7.8%). Decrease in creep values was 9% for irradiated PA11 compared to the non-irradiated one as is seen at Fig. 9.

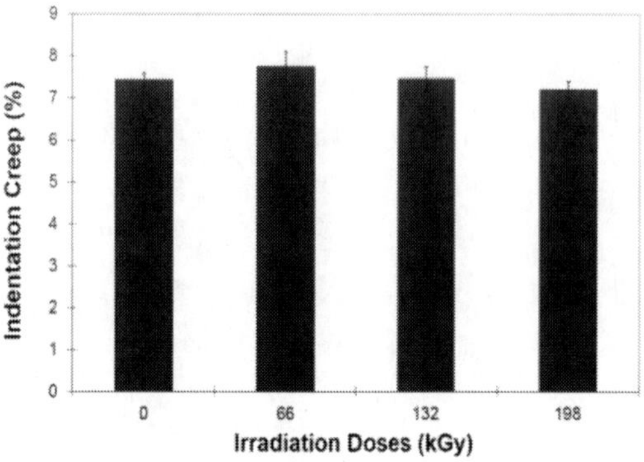

Figure 9. Indentation creep (C_{IT})

Interesting results were found for elastic and plastic part of deformation work. The highest value of elastic and plastic deformation work was measured for non-irradiated PA11. The lowest value at both deformation work was found when the highest value of radiation dose of 132 kGy was applied (Fig. 10).

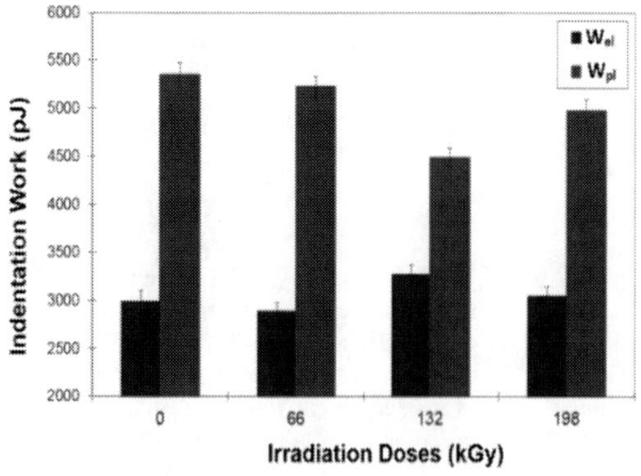

Figure 10. Elastic and plastic part of deformation work

Higher radiation dose does not influence significantly the nano-mechanical properties. An indentation hardness increase of the surface layer is caused by irradiation cross-linking of the tested specimen. A closer look at the nano-hardness results reveals that when the highest radiation doses are used, nano-mechanical properties decreases which can be caused by radiation induced degradation of the material.

4 Conclusion

This research paper investigates influence of modified polymer material (beta radiation) on the nano-indentation test. The surface layer of PA11 is modified by β – radiation with doses of 66, 132 and 198 kGy.

Radiation, which penetrated through specimens and reacted with the cross-linking agent, gradually formed cross-linking (3D net), first in the surface layer and then in the total volume, which resulted in considerable changes in specimen behavior.

The nano-mechanical properties of surface layer of PA11 modified by beta radiation improved significantly. The nano-hardness values increased by about 40% (132 kGy). Stiffness of surface layer increased significantly by 17% (132kGy) as a result of radiation. Also different depths of indentation in the surface layer of tested specimen were significantly different. The highest values of nano-mechanical properties were reached at radiation dose of 132 kGy. It also proved the fact that higher doses of radiation do not have very positive effects on the nano-mechanical properties, on the contrary due to degradation processes the properties deteriorate.

Acknowledgment

This paper is supported by the internal grant of TBU in Zlin No. IGA/FT/2016/010 funded from the resources of specific university research and by the Ministry of Education, Youth and Sports of the Czech Republic within the National Sustainability Programme project No. LO1303 (MSMT-7778/2014) and also by the European Regional Development Fund under the project CEBIA-Tech No. CZ.1.05/2.1.00/03.0089.

References

1. J.G. Drobny, Radiation Technology for Polymers, CRC Press, New York, (2003).
2. M. Ovsik, D. Manas, M. Manas, M. Stanek, M. Hribova, K. Kocman, D. Samek, Irradiated Polypropylene Studied by Microhardness and WAXS, Chemicke listy 106 (2012), 507-510.
3. O. N. Tretinikov, S. Ogata, Y. Ikada, Surface Crosslinking of Polyethylene by Electron Beam Irradiation in Air, Polymer 39 24 (1998.
4. G. Zamfirova, V. Gaydarov, T. Zaharescu, L. G. Silva, Microindentation study of Electron Beam Irradiated Polyamide Samples, Chemicke Listy 104 (2010).
5. W.C. Oliver, G.M. Pharr, Measurement of Hardness and Elastic Modulus by Instrumented Indentation, Journal of Materials Research 19 (1) (2004).
6. D. Manas, M. Hribova, M. Manas, M. Ovsik, Stanek, Effect of Beta Irradiation on Morphology and Microhardness of Polypropylene Thin Layers, Thin Solid Films 530 (2013).

MATEC Web of Conferences **76**, 02031 (2016) DOI: 10.1051/matecconf/20167602031
CSCC 2016

Mechanical properties and temperature stability of modified polybutylene terephthalate by beta rays

Ales Mizera[1,a], Miroslav Manas[1], David Manas[1], Pavel Stoklasek[1], Martin Bednarik[1] and Lenka Hylova[1]

[1]*Tomas Bata University in Zlin, nam. T. G. Masaryka 5555, 76001 Zlin, Czech Republic*

Abstract. The presented article deals with the research of mechanical properties before and after temperature load and temperature stability of modified polybutylene terephthalate by radiation cross-linking. The mechanical properties were measured, at the ambient temperature, by the tensile test on samples which were non-irradiated and irradiated by different doses of the beta radiation and then were temperature loaded. Results demonstrate that PBT has higher values of tensile strength with the increased irradiation dose and it has decreased elongation at break sharply. The purpose of the article is to consider to what extent the irradiation process influences the resulting mechanical properties and temperature stability. The PBT tested showed significant improvement of temperature stability after irradiation. This behaviour leads to the expansion of these materials in the automotive and electrical industry.

1 Introduction

Radiation processing of polymers is a well-established and economical commercial method of precisely modifying the polymer properties. The industrial applications of the radiation processing of plastics and composites include polymerization, cross-linking, degradation and grafting. Radiation processing mainly involves the use of either electron beams from electron accelerators or gamma radiation from Cobalt-60 sources [1, 2].

During the last few decades the industrial use of radiation crosslinking for polymers have rapidly increased. Radiation cross-linking cause a noticeable improvement in the properties of polymers, e.g. their mechanical, chemical and thermal properties [3]. The electron beam radiation process is practically free of waste products and therefore is no serious environmental hazard. The main difference between beta and gamma rays is in their different abilities to penetrate the irradiated material. Gamma rays have a high penetration capacity. The penetration capacity of electron rays depends on the energy of the accelerated electrons. Due to electron accelerators, the required dosage can be applied within seconds, whereas several hours are required in the gamma radiation plant [1, 2].

As a result, we can optimise properties of commodity and engineering polymers and impart them the properties of high performance polymers. Irradiation of polymers turned out to be interesting because of economic reasons, production costs and a life time of products. However, these benefits depend on the type of irradiated polymer and the radiation dosage. Behaviour of each material is different after irradiation. We cannot expect the improvement in all areas (mechanical, thermal and chemical). Most of polymers are not suitable for irradiation because of degradation and deterioration of their properties [4].

Radiation processing of polymers involves treatment of polymer materials with ionizing radiation to modify their physical and chemical properties to make property improvement. Therefore, using of ionizing radiation has found a very wide range of applications in medicine, agriculture and industry. Many scientists have examined the issues of polymer radiation cross-linking. They discovered that some of polymer materials exposed to the ionizing radiation tend to either improve or worsen their mechanical properties. It depends on chemical structure if polymers cross-link or degrade predominantly. Degradation is an undesirable process which may cause significant deterioration of crucial properties for some applications. Effect of radiation cross-linking significantly improves temperature stability. Because of that, materials which belong to group of commodity polymers can be used in applications, which would be in term of temperature stability intended only to engineering thermoplastic polymers [5, 6, 7, 8].

Beta radiation is used for irradiation of PBT in this research. Although many research papers are written about radiation cross-linking of numerous of polymers [9, 10, 11], not so many research papers are written about irradiation of polybutylene terephthalate. A small amount of research which is written about radiation cross-linking of polybutylene terephthalate is written [12, 13] but it does not examine mechanical properties and thermal resistance. These research papers study dielectric constant, thermal degradation and flames retardant additives [12], the effect of gamma irradiation on

[a] Corresponding author: mizera@fai.utb.cz

DOI: 10.1051/matecconf/20167602031

dielectric surface breakdown of PBT under reduced pressure [13].

This research paper deals with a possibility of using radiation cross-linked PBT as a suitable material for automotive industry, especially from point of temperature stability.

2 Experimental

As the basic polymer material was used polybutylene terephthalate (PBT, V-PTS-CREATEC-B3HZC*M800/ /25 natur). An ARBURG Allrounder 420C Advance Injection molding machine was used for sample preparation, with the processing conditional to comply with the PBT producer's recommendations.

Irradiation of tested PBT was performed with the kind help of BGS Germany, in the BGS Wiehl plant using accelerated electrons with a dosage range of 0 to 198 kGy. Then samples were exposed temperature 200 °C during one hour and after that these samples were cooled spontaneously to ambient temperature.

Mechanical properties before and after temperature load and temperature stability of irradiated polybutylene terephthalate after irradiation has been tested. The thermo-mechanical properties were measured. Perkin – Elmer Thermal Analyser TMA7 was used for the thermo-mechanical analysis, heated from 50 °C to 400 °C at 20 °C/min, hold for 1 min at 50 °C. The tensile behaviour of temperature non-loaded and loaded samples of PBT were measured at the ambient temperature. Tensile test was carried out on tensile test machine ZWICK 1456 for PBT according to standard CSN EN ISO 527-1, 527-2 with used rate 50 mm/min. Test data was processed by Test Expert Standard software and E-modulus [MPa], tensile strength [MPa] and elongation [%] were determined.

3 Results and discussion

3.1. Temperature stability

Temperature stability of polymers is very low in comparison with other construction materials. Experiments done in this project show that irradiation cross-linking markedly affects the temperature stability of studied PBT. The higher is the dose of irradiation the best is temperature stability of this polymers.

The temperature stability of PBT was measured. The temperature stability was evaluated by TMA measurement and by visual observation. The graphical depiction of TMA results and description of a test record of the temperature stability inside a temperature chamber are described the dose of radiation from 0 to 198 kGy. Irradiation affects the thermo-mechanical properties of the studied PBT (Figure 1). Non-irradiated and irradiated PBT sample with the dose of irradiation 33 kGy are melted at the temperature 230 °C. PBT with the increased dose above 132 kGy is not lost the temperature stability up to 300 °C. Irradiated PBT specimens above the dose of irradiation 132 kGy evince the significant improvement of temperature stability.

The visual observation of sample behaviour after one hour exposition at 250 °C is given on Figure 2. Specimens are fitted horizontally in the temperature chamber and loaded by the bending moment both form its own weight and the weight on the end of specimen. Specimen deformation is decreasing with increasing dose of radiation at elevated temperature. At 250 °C the specimen from not irradiated PBT is totally melted while the polymer irradiated by the dose of 198 kGy keeps its cross-section without changes, there is only deformation by its own weight. The surface quality worsens and the colour of polymer specimen change due to thermo-oxidation.

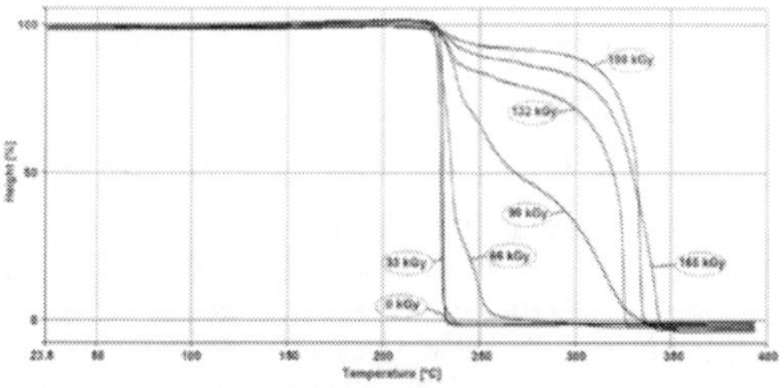

Figure 1. PBT thermomechanical analysis.

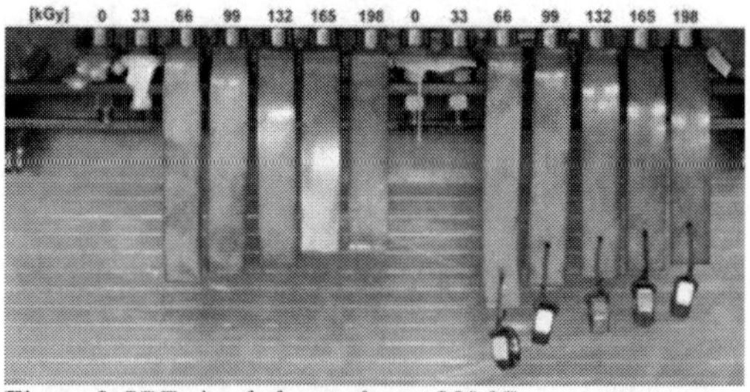

Figure 2. PBT visual observation at 250 °C.

On Figure 3 hot penetration test is displayed at temperature 250 °C. Change of colours is not visible, however, on Figure 4, in the centre of penetration there is beginning of termo-oxidative degradation at 300 °C.

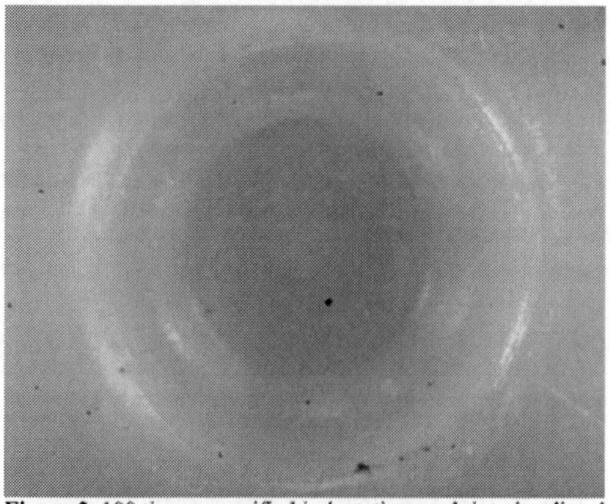
Figure 3. 100 times magnified indentation mark into irradiated PBT by 132 kGy after 5 seconds of penetration at 250 °C.

The surface quality worsens and the colour of polymer specimen change due to thermo-oxidation more and more with increasing temperature as it can be seen on

Figure 5 and 6. It was observed that another irradiated PBT samples changed colours with increasing temperature almost the same as at 132 kGy.

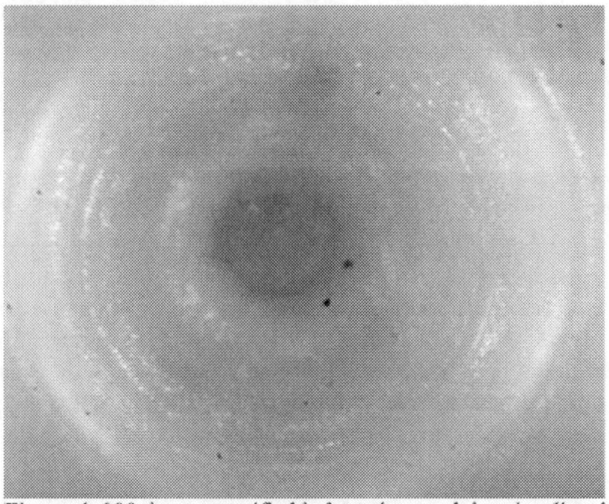

Figure 4. 100 times magnified indentation mark into irradiated PBT by 132 kGy after 5 seconds of penetration at 300 °C.

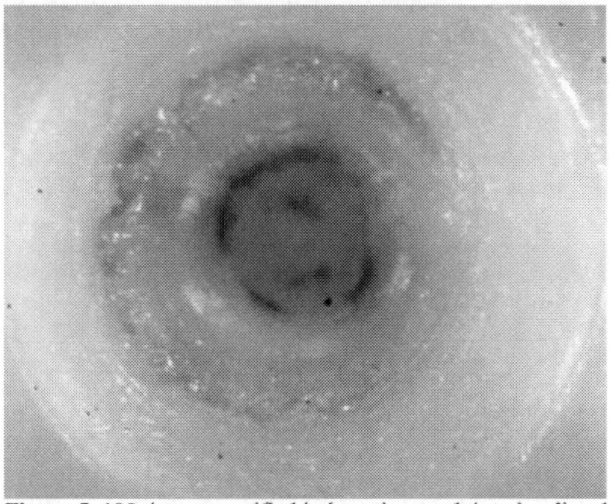

Figure 5. 100 times magnified indentation mark into irradiated PBT by 132 kGy after 5 seconds of penetration at 350 °C.

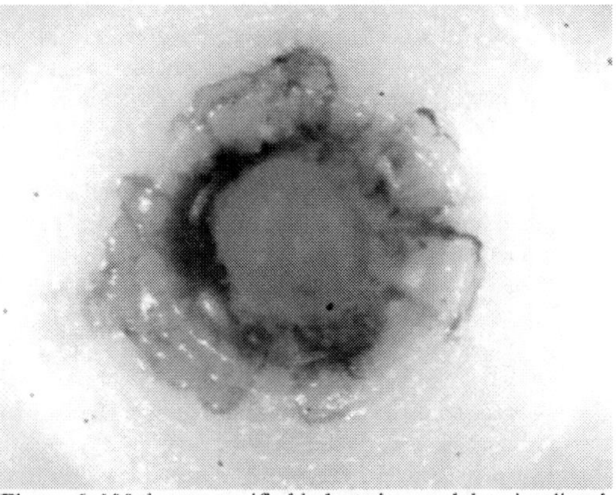

Figure 6. 100 times magnified indentation mark into irradiated PBT by 132 kGy after 5 seconds of penetration at 400 °C.

3.2. Tensile behaviour

The tensile behaviour of PBT, before and after irradiation, was studied. For easier of evaluation of the measured data, and the comparison of the irradiated polymer with a non-irradiated one, the changes of measured were used on some graphs. The property of the non-irradiated polymer had the value of 100 %, while others were expressed in % as the ratio of measured property of irradiated polymers to the same property of non-irradiated polymer.

After performing the tensile test at ambient (23°C) temperature the observed parameter (E-modulus) was compared. As can be seen from Figure 7, there was a significant growth of the E-modulus with increasing doses of irradiation. It was a progressive increase from 1703 MPa to 2022 MPa and from 1989 MPa to 2149 MPa for temperature loaded PBT at the dose of irradiation 198 kGy. The E-modulus rises by 19 and 27 % after irradiation with a dosage of 198 kGy in comparison with non-irradiated PBT.

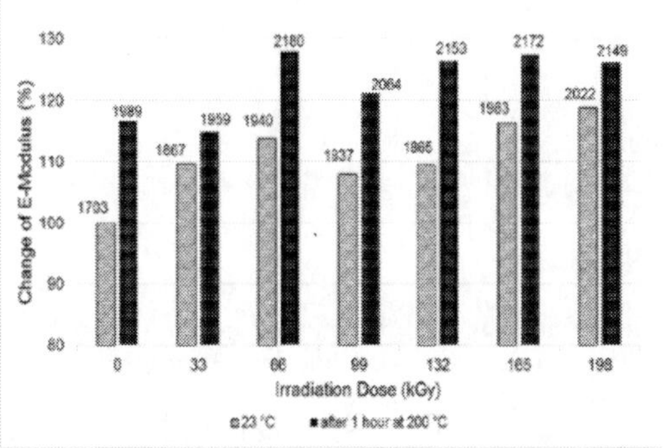

Figure 7. Change of E-modulus before and after temperature load.

After performing the tensile test at ambient (23°C) temperature the observed parameter (tensile strength) was compared. As can be seen from Figure 8, there was a significant growth of the tensile strength with increasing doses of irradiation up to 132 kGy then tensile strength is almost constant with increasing dose of irradiation for both types of measurement. The tensile strength rises by 7.1 and 3.2 MPa for temperature non-loaded and loaded PBT, respectively, after irradiation with a dosage of 198 kGy in comparison with non-modified PBT.

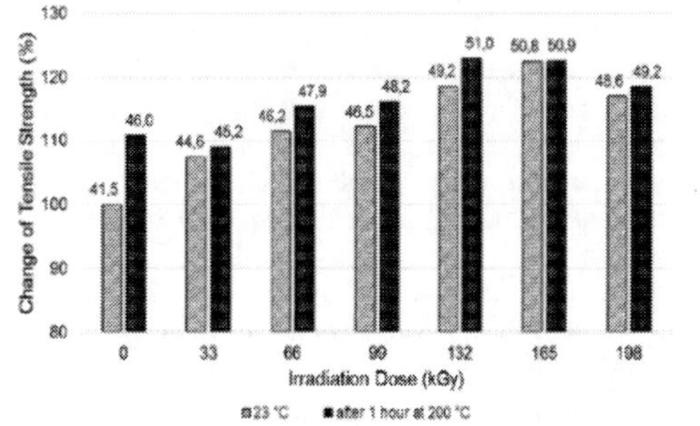

Figure 8. Change of tensile strength before and after temperature load.

After performing the tensile test at ambient (23°C) temperature the observed parameter (elongation at break) was compared. As can be seen from Figure 9, there was a significant decline of the elongation at break with increasing doses of irradiation and also with temperature load. It was a sharp decrease from 119 % to 17 % at the dose of irradiation 66 kGy then the elongation at break was almost constant. The elongation at break decreases by 80 % after temperature load at 200 °C in comparison with non-modified PBT.

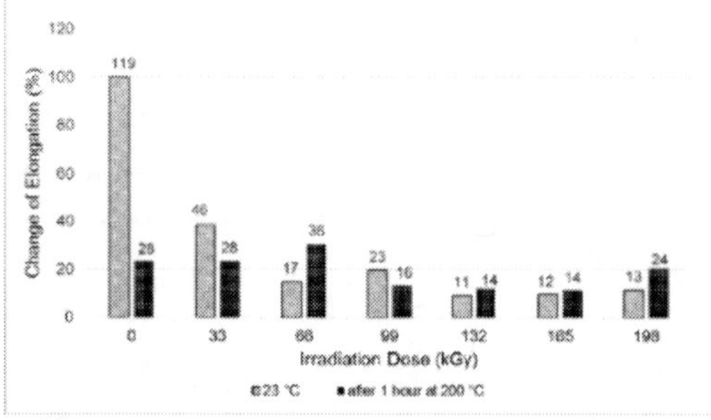

Figure 9. Change of elongation at break before and after temperature load.

4 Summary

Plastics are by far the largest group of polymeric materials being processed by electron beam irradiation. Cross-linking of polyolefins, PVC, polyesters, polyurethanes, polyamides, fluoropolymers and fiber-reinforced composites are a common practice. Radiation cross-linking of polyamides requires considerably less overall energy and space, and is faster, more efficient and more environmentally acceptable. The disadvantage of electron beam cross-linking is a more or less nonuniform dose distribution. This can happen, particularly in thicker objects, due to intrinsic dose-depth profiles of electron beams. Another problem can be a nonuniformity of rotation of cylindrical objects as they traverse a scanned electron beam. However, the mechanical properties often depend on the mean cross-link density [1].

The temperature stability of polymers is very low in comparison with other construction materials. Experiments done in this project showed that irradiation cross-linking markedly affected the temperature stability of the PBT studied. The higher the irradiation dosage, the better the temperature stability of studied polymers is. As can be seen from the tests results, the irradiation cross-linking improves the PBT tensile behaviour. The improvement is more considerable in case of higher temperature (200 °C), as a consequence of creation of cross-link (during irradiation cross-linking) resulting in protraction of macromolecular chain, which is thus more flexible during thermal load than individual shorter macromolecular chains.

As can be seen from the tests results, the irradiation cross-linking improves the PBT tensile behaviour. The results of the measurements of PBT after irradiation showed significant changes of tensile strength, E-modulus and elongation at break. The tensile strength rises by 23 %, after irradiation with a dosage of 165 kGy at the both temperatures (23 and 200 °C). The E-modulus rises by 19 and 27 %, after irradiation with a dosage of 198 kGy at the ambient and elevated temperature, respectively. The elongation at break decreases by 80 % after temperature load at 200 °C in comparison with non-modified PBT.

A very important point is the improvement of the PBT specimens' temperature stability, after irradiation. The tested polymer, when irradiated by a dosage of 198 kGy showed no dimensional changes - even at a temperature of 250°C. This significantly moves the application possibilities of the PBT specimens we tested to an area with service temperatures much higher than their former melting-point. However, this study dealt with PBT material only, hence more polymer materials and a wider range of temperature will be investigated to confirm or deny these findings.

Acknowledgment

This paper is supported by the internal grant of TBU in Zlin No. IGA/FT/2016/010 funded from the resources of specific university research and by the Ministry of Education, Youth and Sports of the Czech Republic within the National Sustainability Programme project No. LO1303 (MSMT-7778/2014) and also by the European Regional Development Fund under the project CEBIA-Tech No. CZ.1.05/2.1.00/03.0089.

References

1. K. Makuuchi, S. Cheng, Radiation Processing of Polymer Materials and Its Industrial Applications (Wiley, Hoboken, 2011)
2. J.G. Drobny, Ionizing Radiation and Polymers: Principles, Technology and Applications (Elsevier, Oxford, 2013)
3. Joachim Gehring, Radiat. Phys. Chem. 57, 361 (2000)
4. Z. Holik at al., Chem. Listy 105(S), 269-271 (2011)
5. D.W. Clegg, A.A. Collyer, Irradiation effects on polymers (Elsevier Applied Science, London, 1991)
6. J.G. Drobny, Radiation Technology for Polymers (CRC Press, Boca Raton, 2003)
7. R.L. Clough, S.W. Shalaby, Irradiation of Polymers: Fundamentals and Technological Applications (American Chemical Society, 1996)
8. H.A. Khonakdar et al., Indian J. Chem. Tech. 75, 78 (2006)
9. D. Manas, M. Hribova, M. Manas, M. Ovsik, M. Stanek, D. Samek, Thin Solid Films 530, 49 (2013)
10. S. Nakamura, K. Tokumitsu, T. Yamaguchi, J. Appl. Polym. Sci. 130, 4318 (2013)
11. J. Chen, M. Czayka, R.M. Uribe, Radiat. Phys. Chem. 74, 31 (2005)
12. Z. Hooshangi, S.A.H. Feghhi, N. Sheikh, Radiat. Phys. Chem. 108, 54 (2015)
13. B.X. Du, H.J. Liu, Y. Liu, IEEE Transactions on Dielectrics and Electrical Insulation 14, 696 (2006)

MATEC Web of Conferences 76, 02032 (2016)
CSCC 2016
DOI: 10.1051/matecconf/20167602032

Prosumers strategy for DHC energy flow optimization

Lubomir Vasek[1] and Viliam Dolinay[1,a]

[1] *Tomas Bata University in Zlín, Faculty of Applied Informatics, Nad Stranemi 4511, 760 05 Zlin, Czech Republic*

Abstract. This article introduces the proposal of discrete model of district heating and cooling system (DHC) for energy flow optimization. The aim is to achieve the best solution of the objective function, usually determined by minimizing the production and distribution costs and providing meets the needs of energy consumers. The model also introduces the idea of general prosumers strategy, where all active elements within the modern DHC system are representing by prosumers object. The prosumers are perceived as objects able to actively participate in the planning of production and consumption of energy. It is assumed that the general behaviour of the object in DHC is the same, no matter how they differ in sizes and designs. Thus, all the objects are defined by two characteristics - the ability to produce and consume. The model based on this basic principle, of course, with the most accurate information about the particular values at a time, object properties and other, should provide tools for simulation and control of modern DHC, possibly superior units as Smart Energy Grids - understood as a system integrating Smart Grids (electricity) and Smart Thermal Grids (heat a cool).

1 Introduction

At present, the primary goal of sustainability and efficiency in the field of energetics is to lower consumption of primary energy. The main obstacles to these goals are mainly technical capabilities and the economic performances of individual countries [2]. However, if the countries want to behave ecologically and foresight into the future, they must seek these goals.

An effort to saving also means the introduction of new technologies and principles. In the area of district heating and cooling variety of producers grows, smaller and usually more ecological sources are involved, for example geothermal, solar, wind sources, industrial waste heat recovery, etc. [10-12]. Also role of consumers is more important, because only mutual cooperation of all DHC elements can bring the expected benefits [4, 8]. These upgraded and improved technologies require support from new and intelligent approaches in control. However, the modern concept of control cannot be understood only as an algorithm implemented in a specific object, but the entire hierarchy in which objects collaborate to achieve common goals. On the other hand, such a large and often disparate systems as DHC is not appropriate to centralize. It seems better to distribute the competence and ensure cooperation.

2 The requirements of the energy sector

The interest in all modern countries in the field of energetics is to behave ecologically and use its resources as effectively as possible.

2.1 European Union's energy policies

The European Union's energy policies are driven by three main objectives:

- secure energy supplies to ensure the reliable provision of energy whenever and wherever needed,
- ensure that energy providers operate in a competitive environment that ensures affordable prices for homes, businesses, and industries,
- energy consumption to be sustainable, through the lowering of greenhouse gas emissions, pollution, and fossil fuel dependence

EU has formulated targets for 2020, 2030, and 2050.Each target quantify the environmental benefits and the expectations are not small, for example, the EU aims to achieve an 80% to 95% reduction in greenhouse gasses compared to 1990 levels by 2050 [2].

2.2 Energy efficiency

By using energy more efficiently, Europeans can lower their energy bills, reduce their reliance on external suppliers of oil and gas and help protect the environment. Energy efficiency has to be increased at all stages of the energy chain from generation to final consumption. At the same time, the benefits of energy efficiency must outweigh the costs, for instance those involved in renovations [2].

Energy efficiency has a fundamental role to play in the transition towards a more competitive, secure and sustainable energy system with an internal energy market

[a] Corresponding author: vdolinay@fai.utb.cz

at its core. While energy powers our societies and economies, future growth must be driven with less energy and lower costs.

3 District heating and cooling

Fill stated targets means to promote and implement many changes at all levels of management of energy, however this article primarily focuses on the area of heat and cold supply, therefore it is necessary to mention a DHC area - District heating and cooling systems need to be more efficient, intelligent and cheaper. It is necessary to develop and deploy intelligent systems using smart metering and control solutions for optimization and consumer empowerment and exploiting multiple energy resources, including waste heat recovery, heat pumps, thermal storage, cogeneration and renewable energy integration, and to roll-out solutions for the integration of intelligent thermal network with smart electricity grids [2, 6, 7]. Achieving these goals requires a fresh new look at the way the production, distribution and consumption. This involves expand and improve existing concepts. It is necessary to move into the next generation of understanding of district heating. This generally means to shift into the 4th generation of District Heating.

3.1The 4th Generation District Heating

The 4th Generation District Heating (4GDH) system is defined as a coherent technological and institutional concept, which by means of smart thermal grids assists the appropriate development of sustainable energy systems [4]. 4GDH systems provide the heat supply of low-energy buildings with low grid losses in a way in which the use of low-temperature heat sources is integrated with the operation of smart energy systems. See figure1. The concept involves the development of an institutional and organizational framework to facilitate suitable cost and motivation structures [1].

In the context of the 4th generations, we can also talk about Smart Thermal Grids or in combination with electric power is also used term Smart Energy Grid.

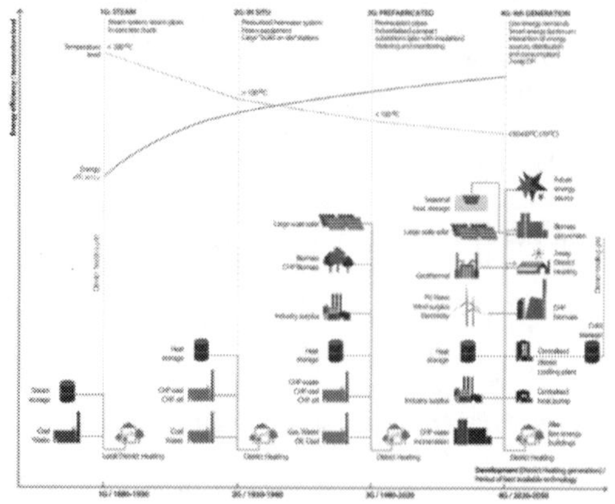

Figure 1. A timeline of district heating evolution [1].

3.2 Prosumer definition

Generally the term prosumer encapsulates the meaning of words proactive producer and consumer. The originator of the phrase "prosumers" is considered futurist Alvin Toffler who coined this phrase in his 1980 book, The Third Wave. The original meaning was "people who blurred the line between consuming and producing by actively collaborating to improve or design the goods and services of the marketplace, transforming it and their roles as consumers" [9].

A deeper look of this definition shows that it describes well the role of the prosumer in Smart Energy (Thermal) Grids and DHC, where the prosumer can be generally characterized as unit able to produce thermal energy, but also consume (hence the term **pro**ducer-con**sumer**). An example might be modern buildings (active or zero), which in bad weather conditions consume energy from external sources (behave as consumers), but most of the time the energy they produce, are themselves unable to consume and may offer it to other network elements. Their active collaboration improves functioning and increases efficiency of the entire energy network.

4 Analysis of the DHC

Consider DHC in which distribution network interconnect N elements – prosumers.

To analysis processes in the production, distribution and consumption of thermal energy in such DHC, which can be characterized as dynamic, rather complex and complicated system, are preferably used modelling techniques. This article is devoted to the formulation of one of the possible models, in the form of a mathematical model applicable for the description and examining behaviour of such DHC system. This model is designed and built in order to optimize production and distribution of heat in accordance with the desired demand (consumption). The model is designed in accordance with the modelled system as a distributed and discretized. Distributed approach will be implemented in holonic structure.

4.1. Distributed - holonic system

As already mentioned, the model as well as real DHC system is understood as distributed. For controlling of such systems is useful to use also distributed manner, for example holonic approach. In general comprehension, it can be understood as a form of multi-agent control, but it is necessary to respect some of its specifics [3, 5].

Holon, in this context, could be defined as an autonomous and co-operative building block of the system for transforming, transporting, storing and/or validating information and physical objects. The holon consists of an information processing part and often a physical processing part. A holon can be part of another holon. It is also possible to see it as a model of a particular element, i.e. part of the model of the entire system. In this sense is holon used in this article.

The internal structure of holons can be made up of a group of other holons, which can be described as "subholons". Any such subholon is, of course, full holon. This allows a very flexible way to define entire holonic system.

The most important features of holon are autonomy and co-operation. Autonomy is characterized by its ability of self-regulation, i.e. the capability to apply the flexible strategy which allows holon to respond differently to changes in its relevant environment [5].

4.2 Prosumers concept

For the purpose of modelling processes in DHC in the production, distribution and consumption of heat presented in this article can be as prosumer identified also element that can be used either just as a source of thermal energy or only as an consumer (without production). Such kind of elements are usually termed by other names – on the one hand local sources or even heating plant, formerly acting as a central source of heat, on the other hand classic heated buildings - residential, office buildings and others.

When a certain (higher) level of abstraction is applied prosumer tag may be given also to other DHC element - to thermal energy storage (accumulator). This is because at a certain time it acts as a consumer - receives and stores heat, at another time it acts as a source - stored heat can deliver to the grid. From the above follows that the characteristics of the processes of production and the heat consumption in various types of prosumer may vary considerably or their proactive role may not be obvious. However, this is not a significant problem in the proposed holonic model, where the individual prosumers will be modelled by different types of holons.

5 Formulation of the distributed model of DHC

This chapter describes the two fundamental components of the proposed model of DHC – set of prosumer and distribution network. For all the elements are described their characteristic attributes which further specify their properties relevant for the modelling and analysis of DHC behaviour.

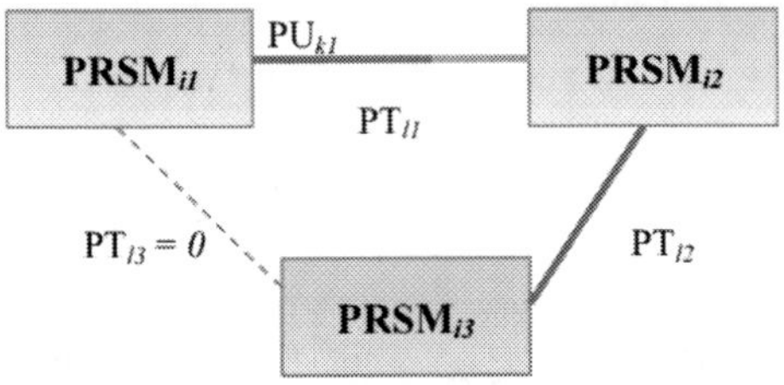

Figure 2. An example of the description of the DHC network topology.

Proposed description of the modelled system was shown in figure2 and will be explained in detail in the following paragraphs.

5.1 Prosumers role

Mark as PRSMi each prosumer in the system, where i = 1, 2, ... N. Each PRSMi is characterized in relation to the analysed processes of production, distribution and consumption of heat with a number of attributes that can be divided into two groups - producer attributes and consumer attributes.

Most of these attributes are function of time. First should be declared one general remark regarding this fact. Discretization of the model over time is achieved by providing the necessary data for example in the form of a table of values for a suitably selected time interval TI. These values then in TI remain constant or can be interpolated using linear function (complex interpolation function is also applicable, but due to the accuracy of the entire model inadequate)

1. Producer attributes - for $PRSM_i$ it is necessary to know the following:

a. Performance data for each source as a function of time *t* and any other parameters, referred to as a vector *PP* (production parameters). They are specific for the process of heat production in a given source and affect produced quantities – for example the intensity of sunlight at the solar source, the intensity of the wind for wind turbines, etc.

- P_{min} (*t, PP*) – minimal supplied power
- P_{opt1} (*t, PP*) – lower limit of the optimal power supplied range
- P_{opt2} (*t, PP*) – upper limit of the optimal power supplied range
- P_{max} (*t, PP*) – maximal supplied power

b. Price data of the supplied energy for each source, again as a function of time *t* and any other parameters referred to as a vector *PP*

- c_{min} (*t, PP*) – price in the range of supplied power $<P_{min}, P_{opt1}>$ per unit of energy supplied
- c_{opt} (*t, PP*) – price in the range of supplied power $<P_{opt1}, P_{opt2}>$ per unit of energy supplied
- c_{max} (*t, PP*) – price in the range of supplied power $<P_{opt2}, P_{max}>$ per unit of energy supplied

2. Consumer attributes

Data on the required consumption of each consumer as a function of time *t* and any other parameters *CP* (consumption parameters)

- D_{min} (*t, CP*) – minimal required energy
- D_{opt} (*t, CP*) – optimal required energy
- D_{max} (*t, CP*) – maximal consumed energy

5.2 Distribution network

Another important part of DHC and therefore its model is distribution network. It connects individual prosumers and allows the transfer of thermal energy between them in a desired direction and time varying quantities. The distribution network is characterized by a topology which is generally very stable and varies, if at all, only in very specific points in time - the physical reconstruction of the network, connecting or disconnecting certain prosumer etc.

The data required to model the distribution network are stored in the following structures:

- Sections of the distribution network. The entire distribution network is divided into individual sections - the set of the K sections U_k, k = 1, 2, ..., K. For each section is determined its "distribution capacity", i.e. the amount of the thermal power PU_k, which is the given section able to transmit. In general it is contemplated that the size of the transmitted power PU_k is dependent on the time *t* and any other parameters specified in vector *DP* (*distribution parameters*), so PU_k (*t, DP*). In practical conditions the value PU_k will be constant in most cases.
- For each section are defined distribution costs CU_k which must be considered when distributing the thermal power through a given section
- Connection lines (routes) between prosumers are captured in the square matrix R = $\{r_{ij}\}$, where the rows and columns are the individual prosumers. The value of r_{ij} element then indicates the appropriate connection ID (route number *l*) for transfer thermal energy. If the connection does not physically exist, the value of this element is zero (or blank ID).
- The link between sections and routes are defined in matrix S = $\{s_{ij}\}$, where the rows are individual routes, columns sections and value s_{ij} indicate whether the particular route *i* passes through a section *j* (s_{ij} = 1) or not (s_{ij} = 0).
- Distribution costs CT_l for individual routes can be calculated from values CU_k and matrix S.

6 Optimization of energy flow in DHC

Model specified in the previous section is used to find the optimal distribution of energy flows between the individual prosumers to satisfy their consumption demands and apply the most efficient use of production capacity of each prosumer (as produced). There should be highlighted that the solutions are being sought for dynamic system, i.e. these energy flows are changing over time. Result (solution) is captured in the matrix X(t) = $\{x_{ij}(t)\}$, which has a similar structure as the matrix R. The value of $x_{ij}(t)$ is the amount of energy transmitted from the supplier to the consumer *j* (at time t) ($x_{ij}(t) >= 0$).

The solution will satisfy the condition of minimum objective function. That is, in this case the value of the total cost CF which is calculated as sum of cost CP to produce and the cost CT to transfer whole needed amount of heat energy between prosumers for the entire time period of heating, thus

$$CF = min(CP + CT) \quad (1)$$

If the time interval TI is divided into M particular time intervals identified as $\Delta t_k = t_{k+1} - t_k$, $k = 1, 2, \dots, M$, the equation for the production costs is

$$CP = \sum_{k=1}^{M} \left(\sum_{i=1}^{N} \sum_{j=1}^{N} x_{ij}(t) * c_i(t) \right) \Delta t_k \quad (2)$$

here $c_i(t)$ are costs (the cost of one unit of heat energy producing in source (prosumer) *i* in the corresponding time interval Δt_k.

Similarly, for transportation (distribution) is obtained equation

$$CT = \sum_{k=1}^{M} \left(\sum_{i=1}^{m} \sum_{j=1}^{n} x_{ij}(t) * ct_l(t) \right) \Delta t_k \quad (3)$$

where $cd_l(t)$ are the cost of the transport of energy unit through route *l* - their tag (index) is stored in matrix R.

Obtained solutions X must fulfil the following conditions:

- Producers must not exceed its maximal performance, i.e.

$$\sum_{j=1}^{N} x_{ij}(t) \leq P_{max,i}(t) \quad (4)$$

for each *i* and *t* in whole *TI*

- The produced power should vary inside of the optimal area, i.e.

$$P_{opt1,i} \leq \sum_{j=1}^{N} x_{ij}(t) \leq P_{opt2,i}(t) \quad (5)$$

for each *i* and *t* in *TI*

- Customer requirements must be met, i.e.

$$\sum_{i=1}^{N} x_{ij}(t) \geq D_{min,j}(t) \quad (6)$$

for each j and *t* in *TI*

- Consumable energy of consuming prosumer must not be exceeded, i.e.

$$\sum_{i=1}^{N} x_{ij}(t) \leq D_{max,j}(t) \quad (7)$$

for each *j* and *t* in *TI*

- Power consumption should be close to optimal, i.e.

$$\sum_{i=1}^{N} x_{ij}(t) \cong D_{opt,j}(t) \quad (8)$$

for each *j* and *t* in *TI*

- The energy flow through each section of distribution net must be lower as its "distribution capacity". If the energy flow for route *l* is

$$P_l = \sum_{i=1}^{N} \sum_{j=1}^{N} x_{ij}(t) \times \delta_{ij} \quad (9)$$

where $\delta_{ij} = 1 \;\; for r_{ij} = l and \delta_{ij} = 0 \; for r_{ij} \neq l$

then

$$\sum_{l=1}^{L} P_l \times s_{lk} \leq PU_k \quad \text{for } k = 1, 2, \ldots K \quad (10)$$

An example of the solution matrix for the sample topology presented in Figure 3 is shown below.

Note: Diagonal matrix elements indicate prosumer part of production to cover its own needs. If there is higher production, the surpluses are offered to others. Non-existent connections are indicated by zero.

.	.	$PRSM_{i1}$	.	$PRSM_{i2}$	.	$PRSM_{i3}$	.
	.	.	.	.	.	.	.
$PRSM_{i1}$	.	x_{i11}	.	x_{i12}	.	0	.
.	.	.	.	.	.	.	.
$PRSM_{i2}$	.	x_{i21}	.	x_{i22}	.	x_{i23}	.
.	.	.	.	.	.	.	.
$PRSM_{i3}$	.	0	.	x_{i32}	.	x_{i33}	.
.	.	.	.	.	.	.	.

Figure 3. Solution matrix.

7 Proposal for the solution of the scheduling of energy flow

The purpose of the proposed model is its use for solving the optimal allocation of energy flows in modern conceived DHC systems. As shown in chap. 5 and 6 of this paper, proposed model represents the relatively complicated mathematical structure whose solution using analytical techniques would be very difficult, if not impossible. Moreover, it should be noted that, as already mentioned, it is a dynamic system in which the processes are running in real time. Also the relevant environment of DHC and its influence is constantly changing. It is therefore expected that the used computational algorithms must be simple enough to allow repeat the calculations in a sufficiently short time period.

The issues defined in previous equations belongs into the category of tasks that are generally involved in the planning of production or services with a limited set of constrained resources (employees, assets, time and money). Usually the aim is to optimize such planning to do more business with less resources. This is known as Constraint Satisfaction Programming (which is part of the Operations Research discipline).

An example might be a job shop scheduling in manufacturing system, where can be used as optimize goals minimum manufacturing costs, minimal work in process (WIP) or maximum machine utilization. In the production can be used only limited manufacturing resources (employees, machines, manipulators etc.) and a number of constraints must be respected (length of work shifts, succession of scheduled operations, etc.)

This type of task falls into the class of so-called NP-complete or Harder problems. NP-complete problem means:

• It's easy to verify a given solution to a problem in reasonable time.

• There is no silver bullet to find the optimal solution of a problem in reasonable time.

To solve such tasks usually means to define a function (target or purpose function). Very often this function is defined in economic terms as a cost function that calculates the necessary cost for given solution. A solution is determined by set of, mostly integer, parameters which characterize the process. If the values of parameters are such, that the restrictive conditions come true, the solution is defined as feasible solution. It is usually possible to find it by a heuristic method. However, very difficult is to find the optimal solution. Such solution is characterized in that the selected target function for it acquires its most extreme, usually minimum value.

Theoretically, it is easy to find the optimal solution by calculating all the possible variants and determine if it is a feasible solution. For feasible solution calculate the value of the target function and choose the one in which reaches the target function extreme value – it is so called the Brute Force algorithm. It is clear, however for the larger scheduling task the amount of possible variants is huge and this method is not due time requirements practically applicable.

In our case, when the parameters (transferred thermal power or amount of heat energy) are not integer values, the situation is more complicated becausethe number of possible variants can grow beyond all bounds. Thereafter the only possible way is to find a suitable procedure based on the heuristic methods and tries to find in reasonable time the solution, which is good enough, because there is in general unfortunately not guarantee finding the optimal one.

7.1 Methods

Searching the best variant of scheduling energy flows will be designed as a suitable procedure based on the set of heuristic methods. Methods will be developed to explore feasible solution. Such methods may vary either by using different algorithms, or, in case that the used algorithms are parametrized, only vary the values of those parameters. The search process then proceed in a way that successively, by a suitable mechanism, will individual heuristics methods propose their solutions and the best result will be sought - evaluation will be performed using the chosen target function. The mechanism to prepare sequence of used methods can be established on the basis of the results obtained previously and of course, it can interfere with human - the dispatcher. The search progress will be stopped after a predetermined time and selected the best of the calculated variants.

The first heuristic method is designed as parameterized method "to satisfy the demands according to the volume (quantity)" - **Highest Demand First (HDF)**

HDF has two parameters:

- *red*, percentage reduction of demand D_j of heat supply for consumer j . For this reduced demand is looking for suppliers in one step of algorithm.
- D_{min}, minimum demand, which will be not more reduced

The algorithm of the scheduling method involves the following steps:

- Step 1: Find the customer with the largest heat supply volume demand D_j. If the requested size $D_j > D_{min}$, a reduced amount of this request is determined $D_{jact} = D_j * red$, which will be satisfied in this step, otherwise $D_{jact} = D_j$
- Step 2: Find the suppliers who are able to meet this demand by their production P_i. This means that the requirement D_{jact} splits into increment corresponding values of the solution x_{ij}. The order of selection of suppliers is carried out by their costs of production and distribution of heat c_{ij}. However, of course conditions (4), (5), (9) and (10) must be met.
- Step 3: The demand D_j is decreased by the size of the satisfied amount D_{jact}. If there is any unsatisfied D_j, means $D_j > 0$, finding process continues by returning to the step 1. If all $D_j = 0$, scheduling process is completed.

It is likely that the choice of different values of the above parameters can find a variety of feasible solutions. Search for the solution, which is good enough and which may replace the optimal solutions using this method so makes sense. Similarly, it is possible to define further heuristics – Lower Demand First (LDF), Highest Production First (HPF) or Lowest Production First (LPF).

8 Conclusions

This paper presents a method for modelling and optimizing the flow of energy in DHC system. New trends in the field of heating and cooling systems were analysed, built the mathematical description of the problem and on that basis prepared the first version of the model. Also was shown the process for flow optimization based on heuristic methodsHowever, the ideas presented in this paper is still under development and will be further improved and tested with real data to verify the proposed methods and principles.

Acknowledgment

This work was supported by the Ministry of Education, Youth and Sports of the Czech Republic within the National Sustainability Programme project No. LO1303 (MSMT-7778/2014).

References

1. 4DH, 4GDH Definition, Available from: *<http://www.4dh.dk/about-4dh/4gdh-definition>*
2. European Commission, Energy Strategy, Available from: *<http://ec.europa.eu/energy/en/topics/energy-strategy>*
3. A. Giret, V. Botti, In *Journal of Intelligent Manufacturing*, p. 645-659 (2004)
4. H. Lund, S. Werner, R. Wiltshire, S. Svendsen, J. E. Thorsen, F. Hvelplund, B. V. Mathiesen, 4th Generation District Heating (4GDH): Integrating smart thermal grids into future sustainable energy systems, *Energy*, **68**, (2014),
5. L. Vasek, V. Dolinay, In *Recent Advances in Systems*. New Jersey, Piscataway, p. 559-563, (2015)
6. P. Navratil, J. Klapka, J. Balate, P. Konecny, In: *Proceedings of the 18th International Conference on Soft Computing MENDEL*, p. 356-362, (2012)
7. M. T. Tsaya, W. M. Linb, *Elect. Power Energy Syst.*, **22**, p. 367–373, (2000)
8. C. Johansson, F. Wernstedt, P. Davidsson, Deployment of Agent Based Load Control in District Heating Systems. *First International Workshop on Agent Technologies for Energy Systems*, (2010)
9. S. Fawkes, The Rise of the Energy Prosumer, Available from: *<http://www.heatconference.co.uk/index.php/blog/entry/the-rise-of-the-energy-prosumer>* (2015)
10. D. Janacova, H. Charvatova, K. Kolomazník, V Vasek, P. Mokrejs, R. Drga, In *International Journal of Mathematical Models and Methods in Applied Sciences*, **5**, p. 1094-1101, (2011)
11. M. F. Ezzat, I. Dincer, In *Solar Energy*, **134**, p. 95-106, 2016
12. J. Novak, P. Chalupa, V. Bobal, In *IEEE Transactions on Power Systems*, **4**, p. 2450-2459, 2011

MATEC Web of Conferences 76, 02033 (2016) DOI: 10.1051/matecconf/20167602033
CSCC 2016

Modular control system for embedded applications

Petr Dostálek[1,a], Jan Dolinay[1] and Vladimír Vašek[1]

[1]Tomas Bata University in Zlín, Faculty of Applied Informatics, Nad Stráněmi 4511, 760 05 Zlín, Czech Republic

Abstract. This paper deals with hardware design of a modular control system intended for embedded applications demanding high computational power while maintaining low cost. The control system central unit is based on 32bit microcontroller MK60DN512 with ARM Cortex-M4 core manufactured by NXP Semiconductor. Module provides all the necessary signals on the two 2-row 40 pin headers and Ethernet communication interface in the form of a small daughter board. It is connected to the mainboard which must always contain 5 V stabilized power supply; other circuits are application specific. In our application the mainboard is equipped with SD card slot, RS232 and RS485 interface which is used for high speed interconnection with up to 15 expansion peripheral modules. This concept enables high flexibility to specific application demands without necessity of redesigning the control system. Controller is freely programmable in C language using any compatible integrated development environment – NXP Kinetis Design Studio, for example. Software development and debugging is simplified by our support program libraries including necessary routines for control and monitoring tasks.

1 Introduction

Present-day very rapid progress in electronics and computer science influences all areas of human activities. Production technology improvements of new microcontrollers lead to their miniaturization, increased central processor unit performance, decreased power consumption and price. Thus modern 8bit one-chip microcontrollers have enough computing power not only for simple control loops consisting of fixed parameters controllers like PS or PSD. They are able to handle tasks from the origin of modern control methods such as adaptive control [1]. However the second mentioned area is on the memory and computational power limit of most 8bit microcontrollers for more complex algorithms. New possibilities in this area are brought by modern 32bit ARM core based microcontrollers which can provide Ethernet, USB and other interfaces for communication and data storage enabling data presentation using simple web server, data logging to SD card and many other useful functionality.

Due to some limitations, mainly in main memory capacity and computational power in double precision floating point format, microcontrollers cannot fully substitute powerful industrial PCs or special programmable logic controllers, which can work with number of control loops simultaneously and realize highly sophisticated control algorithms. However, area of microcontroller usage is a bit different – in embedded systems, that is in systems where the emphasis is on low price, compact dimensions, low power consumption, high reliability and immunity against environmental influences and other specific requirements.

[a] Corresponding author: dostalek@fai.utb.cz

This work presents hardware design of a modular control system intended for embedded applications. The main idea is to combine advantageous properties of modular programmable logic controllers (configuration variability perfectly meets application requirements) and embedded systems (freely programmable in C language, very low cost). To fulfil main requirements of high computational power, Ethernet communication capabilities and low cost of the whole control system 32bit Kinetis microcontroller MK60DN512 with ARM Cortex-M4 core by NXP Semiconductor was chosen as a main part of the central unit.

First section of the paper describes hardware design of all the components of the control system – central unit, digital input / output and analog input / output extension modules representing basic configuration of the system. Last chapter deals with software support of the device which is necessary for effective programming of control and monitoring applications.

2 Control system hardware design

Design of the control system is adapted to easy functionality modification on the basis of the specific application requirements. This is achieved by splitting the whole control system to two main components:

- Central unit consisting of mainboard and microcontroller daughter board.
- Expansion modules which are connected with central unit using high speed RS485 communication bus.

Control system structure is depicted in Figure 1.

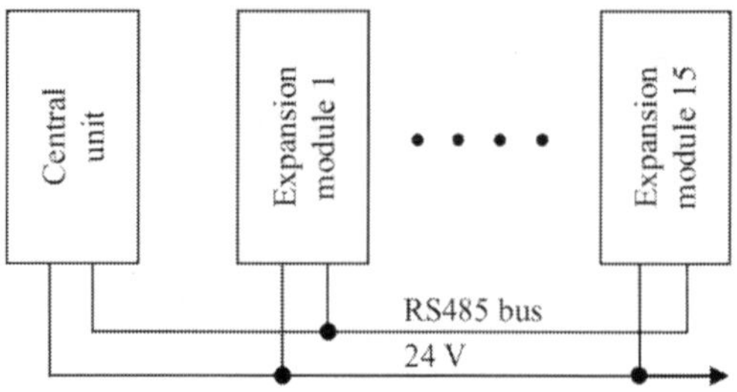

Figure 1. Modular control system structure.

2.1 Central unit

Central unit of the modular control system is based on low power 32bit microcontroller NXP Semiconductors MK60DN512 with ARM Cortex-M4 core with DSP instructions providing computational power of 1.25 Dhrystone MIPS per MHz. These microcontrollers have integrated on the chip 512 KB program FLASH memory, 128 KB RAM memory and many peripherals such as:

- Two 16bit A/D converters
- 12bit D/A converter
- Three analog comparators
- 16bit timer subsystem with PWM, quadrature encoder, periodic interrupt generation
- Real-time clock
- Ethernet controller with MII and RMII interface to external PHY
- USB interface full/low speed
- Two CAN modules
- Three serial peripheral interfaces (SPI)
- Two I2C modules
- Five asynchronous serial communication interfaces (UART)
- Secure Digital Host controller (SDHC)
- 66 general purpose I/O pins [2]

Central unit consists of two separable printed circuit boards: microcontroller daughter board and mainboard connected together using two 2-row 40 pin headers. Complete block schematic of the unit is depicted in the Figure 2.

Daughter board contain main microcontroller MK60DN512 connected via RMII interface with Ethernet PHY DP83848 by Texas Instruments supporting auto-MDIX feature for communication speed of 10/100 Mb/s. Status of the interface is indicated by three LEDs with the following meaning:

- D1 – Link good
- D2 – Speed, ON = 100 Mb/s
- D3 – Interface activity

Clock source for the PHY in RMII mode must provide 50 MHz reference clock signal with frequency tolerance and stability of ±50 ppm to the X1 pin. This requirement fulfils for example crystal clock oscillator ACHL-50.000MHz-EK which is currently used in the circuit. Clock output pin named 25MHz_OUT (in RMII mode provides 50 MHz) is connected to clock input pin EXTAL0 of the main microcontroller. TD+, TD- and RD+, RD- signals of the PHY PMD interface are connected to LAN magnetics module (transformer) B78476A8065A003 with 1:1 turn ratio and inductance of min. 350 µH followed by standard RJ-45 connector. Reference voltage of 2.5 V for A/D converter is provided by precision voltage reference REF03 by Analog Devices and connected to pin VREFH. Internal real-time clock is backed up when system power is down by lithium cell CR2032 with nominal voltage of 3 V. Microcontroller programming and application debugging can be done through 10 pin Kinetis debug port using compatible debug communication interface. Last part of the microcontroller daughter board is power supply circuit based on low drop linear voltage regulator AP1117D with output voltage of 3.3 V and 1 A current capability. Board power state is indicated by two LEDs for 3.3 V and 5 V rails separately.

The purpose of the mainboard is to provide to microcontroller daughter board stabilized 5 V supply voltage and necessary communication interfaces for the whole system functionality. Power supply was designed with respect to minimization of power losses as a step-down converter based on controller MC34063. On its output is generated stabilized DC voltage of 5 V which is in the next stage regulated to 3.3 V using linear voltage regulator AP1117D. Input supply voltage of the central module can be due to utilization of step-down converter in the wide range from 12 V to 40 V DC. Nominal supply voltage of control system is 24 V DC. Physical layer of the RS485 communication interface is implemented by RS485 transceiver SN65HVD10 operating at 3.3 V supply voltage which supports communication speed up to 32 Mb/s. Bus connection pins A and B are on the chip internally protected against ESD and short circuit from -7 V to 12 V. Serial asynchronous interface RS232 utilizes standard voltage level converter MAX3232 which can operate with supply voltage in range from 3.0 V to 5.5 V. It supports communication speed up to 120 kb/s while maintaining RS232 output levels. Integrated dual charge pump requires four external 100 nF capacitors.

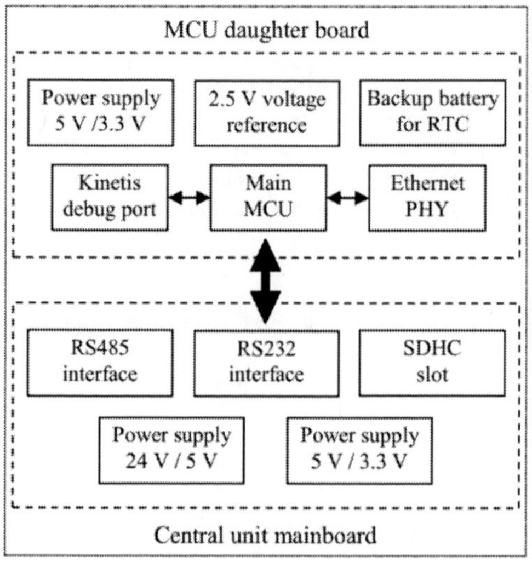

Figure 2. Central unit block schematics.

Mainboard is also equipped with slot for SD or SDHC card which can be used for data storage purposes. Maximum number of expansion modules connected to central unit is 15. Photograph of the completed central unit with removed top cover is in the Figure 3.

Figure 3. Photograph of the central unit.

2.2 Analog input / output module

Analog input / output expansion module is based on 8bit microcontroller NXP MC9S08QE16 which was chosen due to integrated 12bit A/D converter [3]. Input unified voltage signal with range from 0 V to 10 V first enters to resistor divider which adapts it to 0 V to 3.1 V range suitable for A/D converter of the microcontroller. After voltage divider follows non-inverting amplifier with gain set to 1 and simple first order low-pass filter for high frequency ripple rejection. Then the signal enters to the corresponding input channel of the A/D converter. Analog outputs are implemented using two 2 channel 12bit D/A converters MCP4822 [4] which are connected with microcontroller via serial peripheral interface (SPI). Analog signal from the converter is amplified using non-inverted amplifier with gain of 4.9 to achieve unified output voltage signal in range from 0 V to 10 V. RS485 communication interface utilizes same bus transceiver type SN65HVD10 as central unit. Firmware of the microcontroller can be updated via 6pin BDM interface. Input supply voltage with nominal value of 24 V is converted to 5 V by DC-DC converter Mean Well SMU01N-05 with power of 1 W. Because the digital circuits work with 3.3 V it is necessary to lower 5 V output from converter with low-drop linear voltage regulator AP1117D. Module address is selected in binary form by DIP switch with four positions. Valid address range is from 1 to 15 (address 0 is reserved for central unit only).

Photograph of the completed analog input / output module with removed top cover is in the Figure 4.
Module properties:

- 8 analog inputs with voltage range 0 V to 10 V
- 4 analog outputs with voltage range 0 V to 10 V
- 12bit resolution of A/D converter
- 12bit resolution of D/A converter
- RS485 communication interface for connection with central unit at speed of 625 kb/s
- 24 V DC supply voltage

Figure 4. Photograph of the analog I/O module.

2.3 Digital input / output module

Digital input / output expansion module is based on microcontroller MC9S08SH32 by NXP Semiconductor. It is 8bit microcontroller with 32 KB of program FLASH memory and 1 KB of RAM memory. On the chip the following peripherals are integrated: 10bit A/D converter, analog comparator, serial communication interface (SCI), serial peripheral interface (SPI), I2C, timer subsystem, real-time counter and others [5]. Digital inputs of the module are galvanically isolated by two 4 channel optocouplers TLP283-4 with output electrooptical transistor. Input voltage for logical 1 should be in wide range from 3.3 V to 24 V providing compatibility with both TTL and relay logic. Digital outputs of the microcontroller are connected with Darlington transistor array ULN2803A which makes possible directly switch loads with total current up to 500 mA – for example 24 V relays. Maximum voltage which can be connected to the outputs is 50 V DC. Communication interface and power supply is designed identically as in analog I/O module.

Photograph of the completed digital input / output module with removed top cover is in the Figure 5.
Module properties:

- 8 galvanically separated digital inputs
- 8 digital outputs with open collector (NPN)
- PWM signal generation support on digital outputs
- Pulse counting support on digital inputs
- RS485 communication interface for connection with central unit at speed of 625 kb/s
- 24 V DC supply voltage

Figure 5. Photograph of the digital I/O module.

3 Control system software

The software for the control system is based on the library created at our institute, named UCP [6]. This library was designed with three main requirements in mind:

- Provide discrete controllers usable in many common MCU applications
- Easy to use programming interface
- Easily portable to different MCUs

The library can be divided into three main parts:

- controller modules (functions)
- template code for user application
- software-PWM generator
- supporting code (drivers)

There are three main software layers in the control application above the microcontroller hardware: user code, library template files and device drivers [7]. Considering just the library code, there are two main parts: application (ucp_app) and hardware abstraction layer (ucp_hal).

3.1 Controller modules

Controller modules are the fundamental part of the software. By module we mean a set of functions and the data used by those functions enclosed into a source and header file. From the logical point of view a module is one type of a controller, e.g. a discrete PID controller. Typically it contains two C functions: one function which takes care of the initialization of the controller and one function which calculates the output of the controller in each step.

3.2 User application templates

The library also recommends a preferred way of using the controllers. This is accomplished by template files, which contain skeleton code of a control application. The user is advised to include these template files in his/her program and implement the application-specific and hardware-specific code as outlined in the templates. Example applications are also provided which show how to implement this code.

However, the user is not required to use this application template or any other particular style of programming. He is free to use any part of the library separately, e.g. just the controller module(s), which are C functions and therefore can be simply called from any C program.

3.3 Utility code

There is also utility code, which was developed during the development of the library for testing its functions. An example of such a code is a driver for serial communication interface (UART).

The utility code can be used directly in user applications, or it may provide starting point and working examples of the code which will be very likely needed when using the library.

4 Conclusions

This paper presented design of a universal modular control system intended for embedded applications demanding high computing power, wide communication possibilities and configuration flexibility while preserving low cost. These requirements are best fulfilled by a system consisting of a central unit and individual functional modules which number and type depends on target application. Developed prototype control system central unit is based on 32bit microcontroller MK60DN512 with ARM Cortex-M4 core with DSP instructions providing computational power of 1.25 Dhrystone MIPS per MHz. It is a part of a small daughter board including Ethernet communication interface and two 2-row 40 pin headers for connection with mainboard. The purpose of the mainboard is to provide to daughter board stabilized 5 V supply voltage and the required communication interfaces (RS232, RS485, SD card slot) for the whole system functionality. The RS485 interface is used for high speed interconnection with up to 15 expansion peripheral modules. Two types of expansion modules are now available: analog input / output module and digital input / output module which can cover most process control applications.

The controller is freely programmable in C language using any compatible integrated development environment, for example, NXP Kinetis Design Studio. Software development and debugging is simplified by our support program libraries named UCP which include various modules for control and monitoring tasks.

Acknowledgment

This work was supported by the Ministry of Education, Youth and Sports of the Czech Republic within the National Sustainability Programme project No. LO1303 (MSMT-7778/2014) and also by the European Regional Development Fund under the project CEBIA-Tech No. CZ.1.05/2.1.00/03.0089.

References

1. P. Dostálek, J. Dolinay, V. Vašek, L. Pekař, Int. J. of Math. Models and Methods in A. S., **4**, 274 (2010)
2. NXP Semiconductors, *K60 Sub-Family Reference Manual* (Freescale Semiconductor, Tempe, 2012), http://www.nxp.com
3. NXP Semiconductors, *MC9S08QE16 Reference Manual* (Freescale Semiconductor, Tempe, 2011), http://www.nxp.com
4. Microchip Technology, *12-Bit Dual Voltage Output Digital-to-Analog Converter* (Microchip Technology, Chandler, 2010), http://www.microchip.com
5. NXP Semiconductors, *MC9S08SH32 MC9S08SH16 Data Sheet* (Freescale Semiconductor, Tempe, 2014), http://www.nxp.com
6. J. Dolinay, P. Dostálek, V. Vašek, Latest Trends on Systems, **2**, 488 (2014)
7. T. D. Morton, *Embedded Microcontrollers* (Prentice-Hall, New Jersey, 2001)

MATEC Web of Conferences 76, 02034 (2016) DOI: 10.1051/matecconf/20167602034
CSCC 2016

Fuzzy logic as support for security and safety solution in soft targets

Lucia Ďuricová[1] and Martin Hromada[2]

Tomas Bata University in Zlin, Faculty of applied informatics, Nad Stranemi 4511, Zlin, 76005, Czech Republic

Abstract. Security and safety situations in objects, which are categorized as soft targets, is difficult. The current solving is based on several different type of solving. Soft targets are specific objects, and it requires special software solution. The proposal is based on fuzzy logic. Fuzzy logic could apply more expert's knowledges and it could help owners and managers with adequate responses in critical situation, and also definition of adequate preventive actions. System solving could help effectivity of proposed measures. The decision making is based on this fuzzy logic support and aim is explained in paper.

1 Fuzzy logic

Fuzzy logic is based on fuzzy set theory which is generalization of the classical set theory [8]. The classical sets are also called clear sets, as opposed to fuzzy, and by the same token classical logic id also known as Boolean logic or binary logic. In fuzzy logic are used to examining whole range of values. In classical theory are identified only two states. The first is when element belongs to group, or the second element doesn't belong to group.

2 Support for decision making

In security and safety sectors special links are identified which could have impact to developing security situation in object. This special links and relations have special conditions which could be some different in different kinds of objects. Soft targets are specified objects which don't have to implemented special security solution in process. This objects have specific properties which could make reaction more difficult. This properties are identified in next table 1.

Table 1. The properties of soft targets object.

The property	The specification
Public	Object has in same time and at the same bordered area or place a lot of uncontrolled moving visitors.
Distinction	Objects has different aim and it relate with interest groups of visitors.
Integration	Object don't have to integrate special technics which could help experts with solving security crises. Experts don't have to know situation in object. The training of intervention is vulnerable.
Localization	Objects cannot be linking with other object in group and efficiency of measures is nod adequate.

[a] Corresponding author: duricova@fai.utb.cz

In fuzzy logic are known fuzzy reasoning which is known as approximate reasoning. Reasoning is based on fuzzy rules that are expressed in natural language using linguistic variables which definition have been given above. A fuzzy rule has the form:
If x ϵ A and y ϵ B then z ϵ C, with A, B, and C fuzzy sets.

For example for one specified object:
If (safety measures are high) and (security option are medium) then (solving in object is secure).

The variable "solving" belongs to the fuzzy set "secure". The degree depends on the degree of validity of the premise, i.e. the membership degree of the variable "safety" to the fuzzy set "high" and membership degree of the variable "security" to fuzzy set "medium". The underlying idea is that more prepositions in premise are checked, the more the suggest output actions must be applied. To determine the degree of truth of the proposition fuzzy "solving will be secure", the fuzzy implication must be defined.

The fuzzy system designer must choose among the wide choice of fuzzy implications already defined, or set it by hand. In the security and safety proposal fuzzy implications are proposed which will be setting by hand.

The result of the application of a fuzzy rule depends on three factors:

1. The definition of fuzzy implication which were chosen.
2. The definition of membership function, of the fuzzy set, of the proposition located, at the conclusion of the fuzzy rule.
3. The degree of validity of propositions located premise.

When fuzzy operators (and, or, not) are defined, the premise of fuzzy rule may be formed from a combination of fuzzy propositions. All the rules of a fuzzy system is called the decision matrix. On the table 2 are defined examples for security and safety proposal.

Table 2. Examples for decision matrix.

Fuzzy statement	**Result**
If (*safety requirements* are high) and (*safety measures* are low)	Then (*situation in object* is hazardous).
If (*safety requirements* are medium) and (*safety measures* are medium)	Then (*situation in object* is optimising).
If (*safety requirements* are medium) and (*security requirements* are medium)	Then (*implemented measures* must be medium).
If (*implemented measures* must be high) and (*risk of incident* is high)	Then (*reaction* must be implementation immediately measures).

Fuzzy statement defines specific area of values and operators between this statements. Result consider of evaluation fuzzy statements and definition fuzzy implications. The result can help experts with making decision in crises and difficult situations.

2.1 The defuzzification in the proposal

For defuzzification is possible chosen among several possible definitions of defuzzification. In this paper will be presented some primary methods of defuzzification.

Defuzzification is based on converting fuzzy grade to crisp output. It is last part of this process.

The first method is often called Center of area or Center of gravity. We can see it on Figure 1.

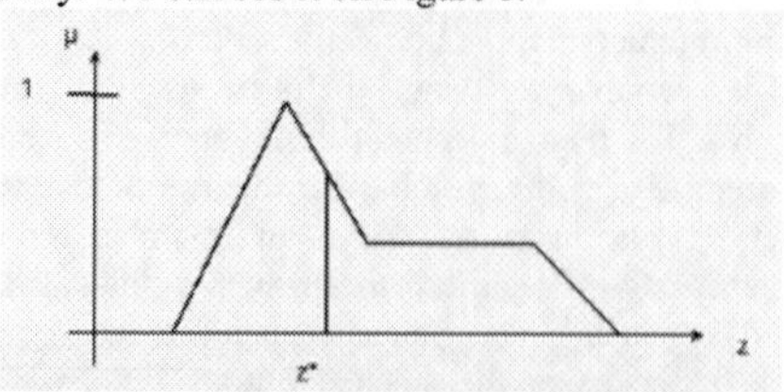

Figure 1. Defuzzification with centre of gravity.

This method for defuzzification is possible formulates with next equation.

$$z^* = \frac{\int \mu_c(z) \times z dz}{\int \mu_c(z) dz} \quad (1)$$

The next method is known as height method and based on max-membership principal which we can see on Figure 2.

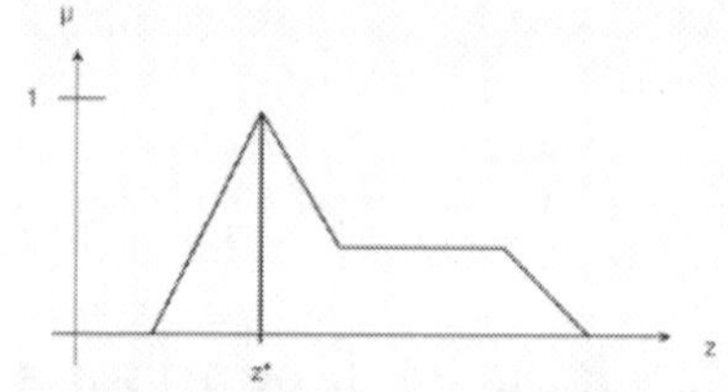

Figure 2. Defuzzification with heigh method.

The heigh method is possible formulates with next equation.

$$\mu_c(z^*) \geq \mu_c(z) for allz \in Z \quad (2)$$

The next defuzzification method is based on weighted average method which is valided for symmetrical output membership functions. On the figure 3 we can see graph, which formed maximum membership value in each functions.

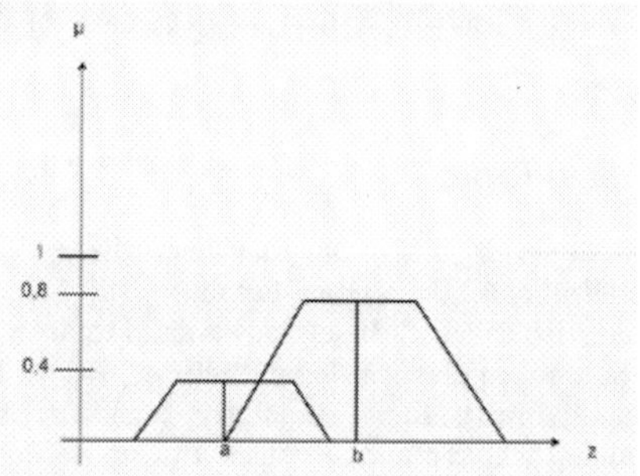

Figure 3. Defuzzification with weighted avarage method.

The next equipment formulates principle of this defuzzification method.

$$z^* = \frac{\sum \mu_c(\bar{z}) \times \bar{z}}{\sum \mu_c(\bar{z})} \quad (3)$$

In the next equipment is written model of example which is on grpah.

$$z^* = \frac{a(0,4) + b(0,8)}{0,4 + 0,8} \quad (4)$$

In this process is possible used to more methods, which aren't described in paper. For example:

- Middle of maxima.
- Center of sums.
- Center of largest area.
- First or last of maxima.

3 The proposal of software solving

The software solving is supported program for decision making in objects in category soft targets. Soft targets are objects which has specifics with common characteristic point:

- A lot of people in the same time at the same place.

 DOI: 10.1051/matecconf/20167602034

- Object without specific safety and security requirements for object (specific requirements are defined in fire protection category, and it is requiring from law requirements).
- The people moving isn't manage and monitoring depends upon manager or owner of object.
- The intervention of integrated emergency system is not regularly rehearsed.

The aim of this system is supporting experts and visualization possible scenarios in next incidents. This system may define level of measures and requirements of object must be implemented into measures. It means that integration safety and security measures could be in other category of object different and in the same category can be solving different too. This is reason for developing this proposal of system. Studies of dependencies are not possible, because this solving and decision making depends on expert's experiences and on specific conditions in object too. On the figure 4 is presented the proposal of system integration.

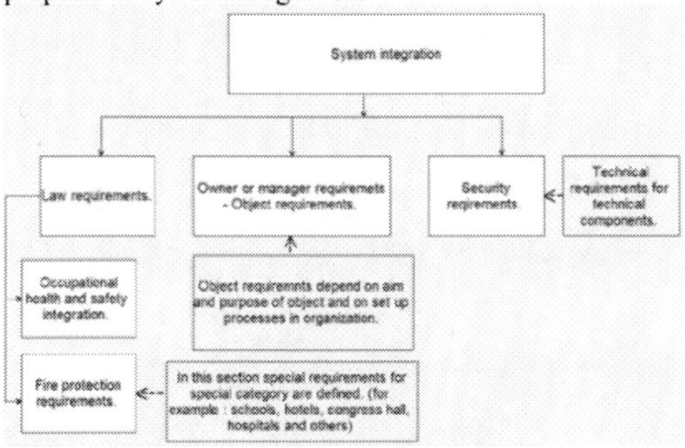

Figure 4. The proposal of system integration.

For proposal of solving incidents or security and safety situation we need to know about object next definition and characteristics:

- How is aim of object and how were processes set up?
- How is access managing? How is object divided?
- How are technical security components in object?
- Information about city and localization – it is called as External inputs parameters.
- Information about last incidents and problems.
- Information about human resources and job descriptions.
- And others.

After input parameters system can define requirements for object. The first and primary are law requirements. The next are security requirements, which are defined from level of security requirements. Level of security requirements experts can define after categorization object. Every category could have special parameters which are talked about situation and requirements and every object has one specific security number which is talked about situation in object only. The real situation is presented on figure 5.

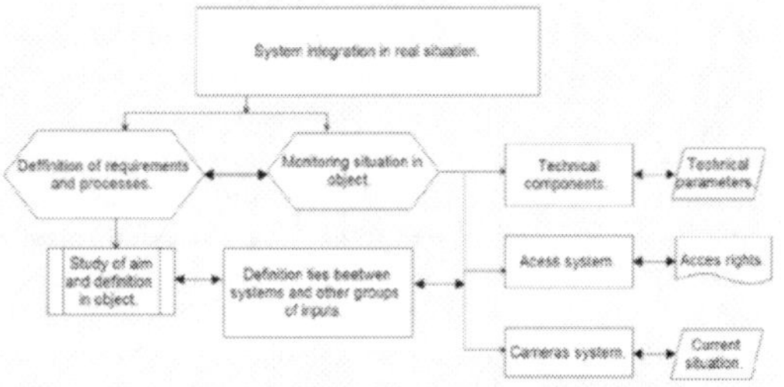

Figure 5. System integration process in real situation.

System integration in real situation is based on system solving and integration technical components to one system. This could achieved more effectivity of security and safety measurements.

If in the system will be implemented experiences from experts, system could be more intelligent and security manager needn't know more knowing in this system, but could be aimed to object requirements.

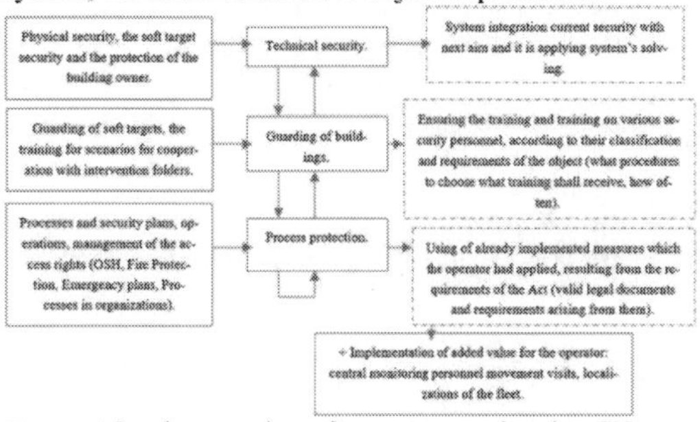

Figure 6. Implementation of experts experiencies. [2]

It is necessary to examine every object, but the aim is the examining and determining the security parameter. On the figure 6 is presented integration of technical security, guarding of building and process protection. The fuzzy logic can be used, because it necessary to know and work with a lot of plans and a lot of experts in one systems. It is a wide range of numerical values too, and a lot of technical components. It is important to define parameters and it is not about two values, but is about a lot of values, and it is reason for fuzzy logic use. This system will be adaptable with other methods, therefore every inputs can be set up and mechanism can be set up to. Then is the implementation of results from other group of security, for support solutions. [2]

4 The other approach to solving

Current situation is based on legislative requirements, which owners and managers must fulfilment. In the other hand next requirements are from owners and managers. It means requirements for achieving safety situation in object and to achieve avoiding to critical situations. Risk we could transport to other organization, accept or minimize to acceptable level. This system want to achieve maximize effect of measurements and achieve more effectivity of processes and no only security and safety processes.

Developing special methods for system solution is one of next and supported action in process of developing this system. Special and next methods and approach have not effect if this methods are not supported by system integration. In this proposal will be implemented more methods and approaches which are specific for specific objects. The reason is simple. Every object has special conditions and special own requirements which result of aim of object. System should not define requirements which could negatively impact operation in object. [2]

In object are used software tools, which is specified for one group of safety and security requirement. For example for Fire protection it is software for authorized persons, which could help them with definition fire safety solving of building. Other systems are for security analysis and other for choosing correct technical components, for example. This proposed system is different, because it could help owners and managers more effectively choosing security and safety solution. System transformed expert's experiences to every object which have this software in management. System support making decision in every installed object. Eventual effect is effective solution and less financially depending. Requirements for operators are lower and it could eliminate problems which was identified in incidents. It was low level of security education and persons weren't trained for specified incidents. For owners and managers it could be tool for setting correct system in every law requirements and also in other requirements.

5 Conclusion

The paper describes proposed system for solving security and safety incidents in objects, which are categorized as soft targets. The system is based on software support and on expert's experiences. It is reason why was chosen fuzzy logic as operate language. Incidents in soft targets are different and solving this incidents require more groups of knowledges and experiences. This system could use more expert's experiences, and system doesn't have to solve mathematical dependencies of this statements. At the end paper is described current situation in soft targets and benefits which this solving could supply managers and owners by system.

Acknowledgments

This work was supported by the European Regional Development Fund under the project CEBIA-Tech Instrumentation No. CZ.1.05/2.1.00/19.0376 and also by the Internal Grant Agency of Tomas Bata University under the project No. IGA/FAI (CEBIA)/2016/12.
This work was supported by the research project VI20152019049 "RESILIENCE 2015: Dynamic Resilience Evaluation of Interrelated Critical Infrastructure Subsystems", supported by the Ministry of the Interior of the Czech Republic in the years 2015-2019 too.

References

1. F. Dernoncourt, *Introduction to Fuzzy Logic* (2013)
2. L. Duricova, M. Hromada, *The Proposal of the Soft Targets Security.Advences in Intelligent Systems and Computing, Automation Control Theory Perspectives in Intelligent Systems*, **3**, 337-345 (2016)
3. G. J. Klir, B. Yuan, *Theory and Application*, 574 (1995)
4. L. Duricova, M. Hromada, *Proceeding of 3rd CER Comparative*, **2**, 30–33 (2015)
5. F. Rosenberg, Nice Solutions for Critical Facilities (2014)
6. T. Takagi, M. Sugeno, *Syst. Man. Cybern.* **1**, 116–132 (1985)
7. J. Valouch, *Int. J. Circ. Syst. Signal Process.*, **9**, 205–2010 (2015)
8. L. A. Zadeh, *Inf. Control*, **8**, 338–353 (1965)

Detection of emergent situations in complex systems represented by algebras of transformations

Jiri Bila[1], Martin Novak[1] and Jan Vrba[1]

[1]Department of Instrumentation and Control Engineering, FME, CTU in Prague, Technicka 4, 166 07 Prague 6, Czech Republic

Abstract. In this paper we will investigate emergent situations in complex systems represented by algebras of transformations. Though algebras of transformations seem to be rather distanced from a modeled complex system we show that it is representation very effective and for our application very appropriate. The paper continues in recent published works where the detection of an emergent situation was done by indication of violence of so called structural invariants. In this paper is used only one type of structural invariant Matroid and Matroid Bases (M, BM). A simple calculus for the emergent situation appearance computation is introduced. The application of the presented approach and computation method is demonstrated for the case of a possible collapse of the selected ecosystem.

1 Introduction

The paper continues in topics and technologies introduced in papers [1], [2], [3] and [4]. Especially papers [2] and [4] are needed for the effective reading and the understanding this paper. Similarly as in paper [1] we start here with 5 working hypotheses:

Hypothesis 1(H1): The emergent phenomenon is induced by a sharp change of complex system structure ("jump on the structure"). ♦

Hypothesis 2(H2): In case that we accept *H1*, the eventuality of an emergent phenomenon appearance may be detected as a sharp violence of complex system structure (or the violence of Structural Invariants respectively). ♦

Hypothesis 3(H3): The appearance of emergent situation is detected as the possibility of extension (reduction) of the basis of the matroid (matroid formed on the complex system) by at least one element. ♦

Hypothesis 4(H4): One of possibilities how to represent detection of appearance of emergent situation by extension of a matroid basis is to anticipate the increase of number of interacting elements in so called basic group (compartment). ♦

Hypothesis 5(H5): In order to attain an emergent phenomenon (by an extension (reduction) of a matroid basis) the complex system increases the number of elements (transformations, properties, processes) in *basic group* (compartment) by a minimum number of elements (transformations, properties, processes). ♦

Notes to organization of the paper. In section 2 there are introduced some works that are relevant to the topic of our paper. The description of the theory and computation method is introduced in section 3. In section 4, is a case study for application of the method for a possible collapse of the selected ecosystem.

2 Related works

The proposed paper is associated especially with results published in works [1, 2, 3] and [4]. In these papers is presented as well theoretical material for computing with emergent situations as application of the developed method in phenomena of macro-world (10^{-2}m÷10^{2}m) and also in phenomena of supermicro-world (10^{-10}m÷10^{-15}m).

General background for conceptual constructions in the field of Complex Systems are published in [5, 6, 7].

Work [10] forms the background for application of our method in the field of ecosystems. It is fair to introduce attempts for the description of irregularities in the ecosystem quantifying them by means of some special variables, e.g., fractal dimension, [11, 12]. The application of the proposed detection method for the considered ecosystem (Trebon basin in South Bohemia, Czech Republic) is easy to deploy for the super ecosystem of the planet and compare the results with existing results acquired from quantitative models (e.g., [13]).

A (small) common negative point of all cited works (including this proposed paper) is an absence of a chaotic phase and self-organizing phenomenon from expression (1).

3 Background for the detection of emergent situations

The simple scheme for the detection of emergent situations by means of algebras of transformations [2] is

[1]Corresponding author: jiri.bila@fs.cvut.cz

the following one:

G1→(G1⊕g)→Chaotic phase→EP→SOP→ G2, (1)

where G1, G2 are algebras of transformations characterizing complex system in situations of balances and g is a set of transformations that extends (reduces) kernel part of G1. (In case that is used matroid approach the kernel part will be the basis of the matroid.) Symbol ⊕ has no specific significance and depends on a real case of method application. EP symbolizes "emergent phenomenon" and SOP is "self organizing process".

In paper [1] were discussed problems of "chaotic phases" and "self-organizing processes" that need more detailed investigation however not necessarily introduced here.

For the description of the discussed complex system will be applied state model. Transformations transfer the system from one state to another state and the only problem is to detect a possible appearance of an emergent situation. For it is used a common decision rule:

IF (#g ≥ min Δ f(RN)) ⇒ THEN (PAES), (2)

where "min Δ f(RN)" is a minimal difference between further and actual Ramsey number and PAES is "a possible appearance of an emergent situation".

According to *H1* (from Introduction) – the emergent phenomenon is induced by a sharp change of complex system structure, i.e., by "a jump on the structure" and the eventuality of an emergent phenomenon appearance may be detected as a sharp violence of complex system structure (or the violence of so called Structural Invariants respectively – *H2*).

There have been tested the following violences of SIs that induce the appearance of Emergent Situation (EMS).

- (Matrix, Rank of Matrix) – the addition of linearly independent row or column.
- (Matroid, Bases of Matroid) – the addition of at least one element to basis.
- (Dulmage-Mendelsohn Decomposition, Tree Ordering) – violence of tree ordering.
- (Hasse Diagram, Set of Associated Rules) – violence of set of rules,
- (Set of Situations, Algebra of Transformations) - the deformation of group operation and as a consequence - construction a false element into the group carrier.

In the following sub-section we will deal only with one SI - (Matroid, Bases of Matroid) – (M, BM).

3.1. Structural Invariant (B, BM) and its violence

At first a few general facts:

Matroid has the following pleasant properties:

- It is possible to construct it for each set of elements (carrier of the system) when we have the relation of independence or when they are given independent sets.
- If we have relation of independence, there are investigated all elements (of the system) with regard to relation of independence.
- If the relation of independence exists it is easy (in most cases) to associate it with a semantic content (according to real conditions).
- Matroid is usually introduced as the following structure

$$M = \langle X, IND, \{N_1, N_2, \dots, N_n\}\rangle = \langle X, B\rangle, \quad (3)$$

where X is the ground set of elements (components), IND is a relation of independence, $N_1, N_2, \dots, N_n$ are independent sets and B is a set of matroid bases. Matroid bases are maximum (according to cardinality) independent sets.

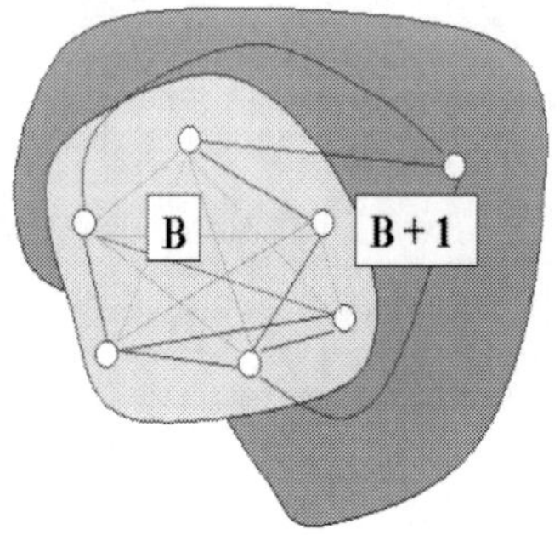

Figure 1. Extension of a matroid basis by one element.

The violence of this SI is considered (in this paper) *as an extension of a matroid basis* at least by one element (and it will be considered as an indicator of emergent situation appearance).

In case that relation IND is considered as a *binary relation* it is possible to use the following consequences:

The bases (**B**) will be constructed as perfect sub-graphs (in a perfect graph on X).

The independent and dependent elements in the perfect graph are easy constructed by coloring the edges by *two* colors and the formalism of Ramsey numbers – R(#*B*, #Y)), $B \in \boldsymbol{B}$ is offered to be used.

The extension of one of bases $B \in \boldsymbol{B}$ by one element is illustrated in Fig.1. The perfect graph in Fig.1 has six nodes and 15 (brown) edges. Coloring the edges by green and blue colors, there appears at least one perfect sub-graph with 3 nodes and 3 edges (basis ***B***) – for example the green one. For extension of ***B*** by one element (into ***B+1*** with 4 nodes) we need to add at least 3 elements (that are invisible here).

Historical note: Till now there are known only some Ramsey numbers (RNs), e.g.: R(3, 3) = 6, R(3, 4) = 9, R(3, 5) = 14, R(3, 6) = 18, .., R(3, 15) = [73, 78], …, R(4, 4) = 18, R(4, 11) = [96, 191], …, R(6, 10) = [177, 1171], …, R(10, 10) = [798, 23 556], …, R(19, 19) ≥ 17 885. The brackets [., .] denote intervals of integer numbers. (In computations in section 4 will be used known table quantities from [9].)

Note 3.1: According to hypothesis H4 (from the Introduction) the system selects as optimal those Ramsey numbers for which is needed to add the minimum elements for the extension of basis by one element.

 DOI: 10.1051/matecconf/20167602035

Example 3.1.: #X = 1600. (#**B** = 11 for #X ≥ 1597) and for one element extension of Basis (#**B** = 12 for #X ≥ 1637) is needed to add at least 40 elements.

4 Detection of a possible collapse of an ecosystem

In paper [10] has been modeled the situation of the violence of so called Short Water Cycle in a selected ecosystem (Trebon basin in South Bohemia, Czech Republic). The Short Water Cycle (SWC) refers to the behavior of the local ecosystem (e.g., the Trebon region), in which the volume of water that comes into the ecosystem is evaporated and falls back into this system. In the Trebon ecosystem, the evaporated water rises quickly inside the transport zone and does not have time to recondense before it is transported outside the ecosystem to the distant mountains, where it condenses spontaneously in the rising air streams. (Due to the enormous volumes of vapor that are transported, the condensation is very dynamic and sometimes leads to torrential downpours).

The ecosystem was described (for the conditions of the violence of SWC) by 19 states – Table. 1.

Table 1. States of the modeled ecosystem.

Field of observation	***Content of the state***
Name of the state	
Air humidity and water	
S1	*Low local humidity*
S2	*Medium local humidity*
S3	*High local humidity*
S4	*Local fog*
S5	*Regional fog (covering an area greater than 20 km2)*
S6	*High volume of water absorbed in the soil*
S7	*Local floods*
S8	*Violation of the small water cycle (SWC)*
Weather	
S9	*Rain*
S10	*Snow*
S11	*Longtime local dry atmosphere, (arid soil)*
S12	*Semi-clear weather*
S13	*Very cloudy weather and overcast*
S14	*Strong wind*
S15	*Storm*
Evaporation	
S16	*High evaporation (nearly no water goes back into the ecosystem)*
S17	*Medium evaporation – (some of the evaporated water returns back)*
S18	*Low evaporation*
S19	*Diminished evapotranspiration*

Note 4.1: The number of states could be substantially larger however after a few experiments we recognized that substantially larger number of states do not bring substantially greater amount of information.

In the introduced set of states has been discovered (with help of a qualified expert) the set of transformations – Table. 2 ("1" transformation possible, "0" transformation impossible, "*" irrelevant question).

Table 2. Matrix of transformations in considered ecosystem.

	S1	**S2**	**S3**	**S4**	**S5**	**S6**	**S7**	**S8**	**S9**	**S10**	**S11**	**S12**	**S13**	**S14**	**S15**	**S16**	**S17**	**S18**	**S19**
S1	1	1	0	0	0	0	*	*	*	*	1	*	*	*	*	1	1	1	1
S2	0	1	1	1	0	0	*	0	1	0	0	0	1	*	0	0	1	1	0
S3	0	1	1	1	1	1	1	0	*	*	0	*	*	*	*	1	1	0	0
S4	0	0	1	1	1	*	*	*	1	1	0	1	1	*	0	0	1	1	0
S5	0	1	1	1	1	*	*	0	1	1	0	1	1	*	1	0	0	1	0
S6	0	1	1	1	0	1	1	0	*	*	0	1	1	*	*	0	1	1	0
S7	0	1	1	1	0	1	1	0	1	0	0	1	1	1	1	0	0	1	0
S8	1	0	0	0	0	0	1	1	0	0	1	0	0	1	0	1	0	0	1
S9	0	1	1	1	1	1	1	0	1	1	0	1	0	1	1	1	0	1	0
S10	0	0	0	0	0	1	1	0	1	1	0	1	1	0	0	0	0	1	0
S11	1	0	0	0	0	0	0	1	0	0	1	0	1	0	0	0	0	0	1
S12	*	*	*	0	0	1	*	*	1	1	0	1	1	0	0	0	1	1	0
S13	*	*	*	0	0	*	*	0	0	0	0	1	1	1	*	0	1	1	0
S14	*	*	*	0	0	*	*	*	*	*	0	1	1	1	1	1	0	0	0
S15	0	0	1	1	0	0	1	0	1	0	0	0	0	0	1	0	0	1	0
S16	1	1	0	0	0	0	0	1	0	0	1	1	0	*	1	1	1	0	1
S17	1	1	0	1	1	1	0	0	1	1	0	1	0	*	1	0	1	1	0
S18	1	0	0	0	0	0	*	1	0	0	1	1	0	*	1	0	0	1	0
S19	1	0	0	0	0	0	0	1	0	0	1	*	*	*	*	1	0	0	1

Now we apply the theory from section 3.
The number of transformations in Table.2 is **141**. Using Ramsey numbers from [9] we find a few possible results for basis of matroid with 141 elements: #B ∈ {4, 5, 7, 10, 14}. (R(4, 10) ∈ [80, 149], R(4, 14) ∈ [141, 349], R(5, 7) ∈ [80, 143], R(5, 10) ∈ [141, 442].)
The minimal number of transformations that is necessary to add to X (in order to attain an emergence phenomenon by extension of the matroid basis by one element) is **12** (R(4, 14) ∈ [141, 349], R(4, 15) ∈ [153, 417].
We may find in Table.2 additional transformations (τ_{ai}), not discovered still, that could be really *dangerous* for the ecosystem:

$$\tau_{a1} = S1 \rightarrow S14, \quad (4)$$
$$\tau_{a2} = S1 \rightarrow S15, \quad (5)$$
$$\tau_{a3} = S2 \rightarrow S14, \quad (6)$$
$$\tau_{a4} = S2 \rightarrow S15, \quad (7)$$
$$\tau_{a5} = S1 \rightarrow S16, \quad (8)$$
$$\tau_{a6} = S14 \rightarrow S18, \quad (9)$$
$$\tau_{a7} = S12 \rightarrow S19, \quad (10)$$
$$\tau_{a8} = S5 \rightarrow S11, \quad (11)$$
$$\tau_{a9} = S11 \rightarrow S6, \quad (12)$$
$$\tau_{a10} = S3 \rightarrow S11, \quad (13)$$
$$\tau_{a11} = S3 \rightarrow S14, \quad (14)$$
$$\tau_{a12} = S12 \rightarrow S7. \quad (15)$$

The description of the introduced ecosystem by 19 states represents rather an approximation of a state model. The needed number of states could be for about 100 (and as a consequence it induces large number of transformations). Nevertheless even in our case has already been seen that the higher number of elements in the carrier of transformation algebra brings

- higher variability of emergent phenomenon (here registered only by a change of elements and by number of elements in the matroid basis),
- higher number of elements that are necessary to add to matroid carrier for the extension of matroid basis.

The second item could be understood as a reason why the standard ecosystems are relatively stable and *sufficiently distanced from collapse situations*.
State description that has been used is a qualitative knowledge based description. (Expert used a knowledge based concepts as "Local floods", "Semi-clear weather", etc. that are on the used ontology understandable however they have rather complicated internal structure. This is a great advantage of such qualitative description not to be obliged to consider interaction of an enormous number of elements of ecosystem.)
Another direction for the discussion could be done by question "why was not used technology of Markov chains or fuzzy logic?". Well-they could be used. But we are not interested in state trajectories of the system. We are interested in sharp structural changes of the system that we consider as emergent phenomena or appearance of emergent situations. From this point of view Markov chains technology and also fuzzy logic would not bring any new information.
Detection of emergent situations in ecosystems is a very actual field of research especially in relation to climate changes. However it requires clear and simple methods.

The presented approach is a small contribution to this trend.

5 Conclusions

In continuation of paper [2] there was applied in this paper the detection method for emergent situations appearances in complex systems. The method introduced in [1] was reduced here only for computation with numbers of matroid bases (without relations to the power of emergent phenomena). The proposed method provides only a necessary condition for an emergent situation appearance. The sufficient condition depends on self-organizing process that forms an external view of emergent situation (and it is not discussed here).

The proposed method has been applied for a selected ecological system. The model of this system was developed as an expert knowledge based state model. This state model decreased complexity of the original ecosystem (without necessity to consider all relevant elements and bonds). For such a model was easy to apply proposed detection method. (The same approach has been used for ant colonies and bee communities though the elements of these systems seemed to be more attainable.)

Acknowledgement: The development of this paper has been supported by Research Grant SGS12/177/OHK2/3T/12. This support is very gratefully acknowledged.

References

1. J. Bila, Int. J. of Enhanced Research in Science, Technology and Engng. **3**, 7, pp.1-17 (2014).
2. J. Bila, M. Mironovova, R. Rodriguez, J. Jura, Int. J. of Enhanced Research in Science, Technology and Engng., **4**, 9, pp. 38-46 (2015).
3. J. Bila, P.Krist, *17th Int. Conf. on Soft Computing – Mendel 2011,* Brno, Czech Republic, pp. 528-533 (2011).
4. J.Bila, 20th Int. Conf. on Soft Computing – Mendel 2014, Brno, Czech Republic, 395-401 (2014).
5. M. Svitek, Neural Network World, **26**., pp.5–33, (2015).
6. G. Ellis, http://www.mth.utc.ac.za/~ellis/cos0.html.
7. H. Ultsch, *6th Int. Workshop on Self-Organizing Maps – WSOM 2007*, http://bielcoll.ub.uni-bielefeld.de. (2007).
8. J.G. Oxley, *Matroid Theory*, (Oxford Science Publications, Oxford 2001).
9. W. Weinstein, *Ramsey Number*. A Wolfram Web, http:/mathword.wolfram.com/RamseyNumber.html.
10. J. Bila, J. Pokorny, J. Jura, I. Bukovsky, Ecol. Model., **222**, pp.3640–3650 (2011).
11. J. Jura, A. A. Kubena, M. Novak, *Mendel 2016: 22nd International Conference on Soft Computing*, Brno, Czech Republic, **2016** (2016).
12. J. Jura, J. Bila, Mendel 2010: 16th International Conference on Soft Computing, Brno, pp. 225-230, **2010**, (2010).
13. F.M. Viola, S.L.D. Paiva, M.A. Savi, Ecol. Model., **221**, pp. 1964-1978 (2010).

Remote controlled gate controller using a GSM network and Arduino platform

Martin Pospisilik[1,a], Tomas Smekal[1], Milan Adamek[1], Petr Neumann[1] and Tomas Dulik[1]

[1]*Faculty of Applied Informatics, Tomas Bata University in Zlin, Nad Stranemi 4511, 76005 Zlin, Czech Republic*

Abstract. Most remote controllers for entrance gates operate on free frequencies 433 or 868 MHz. However, this technology limits the user comfort, as it is usually not common that bi-directional communication is established. A higher comfort of controlling the entrance gates can be achieved by employing the GSM network for transmission of commands and messages between the gate controller and the user. In this case, only a conventional GSM cellular phone is needed to control the gate. A description of such a controller based on the GSM module and Arduino controller is provided in this paper.

1 Introduction

Not only in Europe, the GSM (Global System for Mobile Communication) is widely spread, allowing to transfer speech signals but supporting data transfers as well. The most common devices to be connected to this network are cellular phones. On the other hand, there exist other devices that embody the interface needed to establish the connection. The broadest possibilities are then given by standalone GSM modules that are designed to be embedded into arbitrary devices. In this work, GSM shield based on SIM900 chip has been used.

1.1 GSM network

The block diagram of the GSM network is depicted in figure 1. The description of the abbreviations is provided in table 1.

The brief description of the operation of the GSM network is as follows: The mobile station is always identified by its IMEI (International Mobile Equipment Number) and its user is identified by his SIM (Subscriber Identification Module). By means of a radio connection it is connected to the system of base stations (BSS). The BSS is connected to the Network Switching Subsystem (NSS). The BTS stations of the BSS are spread around the covered area, creating a cellular system of transceivers. While the BSS is responsible for maintaining the connection between the mobile stations and the network, the NSS is responsible for authorization of the devices connected to the network (using HLR, AUC and VLR) and for switching the data in the communication network. The service of the whole system is then provided by the Operational and Support Subsystem (OSS).

1.1.1 Data transfers in GSM network

The development of the GSM network has been launched in 1982. Although it was intended to be used for speech transfers, the packetizing of the digital speech signal allowed to extend its functionality for transferring of general data. In 2000 the standard GPRS (General Packet Radio Service) has been implemented, mainly to allow more comfortable connection of the mobile stations to the Internet.

Table 1. Description on abbreviations depicted in figure 1.

Abbreviation	Desctiption
MS	Mobile station
BTS	Base transceiver station
BSC	Base station controller
TC	Transcoder
BSS	Base station subsystem
NSS	Mobile switching centre
MSC	Mobile switching centre
GMSC	Gateway mobile switching centre
VLR	Visitor location register
SS7	Signalling system 7
IWF	Interworking functionality
EIR	Equipment identity register
HLR	Home location register
AUC	Authentication centre
SMSC	SMS centre
PSTN	Public switched telephone network
ISDN	Integrated services digital network
OSS	Operation subsystem
OMC	Operation and maintenance centre
NMC	Networking management centre
ADC	Administrative centre

[a] Corresponding author: pospisilik@fai.utb.cz

DOI: 10.1051/matecconf/20167602036

The GPRS system is designed to use the already set system of radio channels, but it treats the physical layer of the system in a different way. The implementation of the GPRS system in GSM networks is depicted in figure 2. As depicted, the implementation of the GPRS system to the GSM network consisted in adding several functionalities most of which are based on software. The Base Station Controllers must have been equipped with

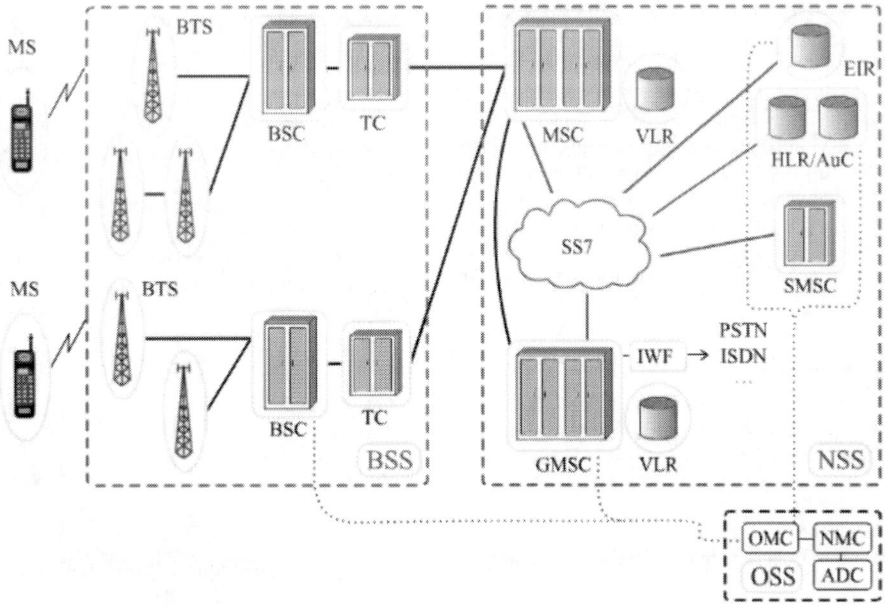

Figure 1. GSM network structure [4].

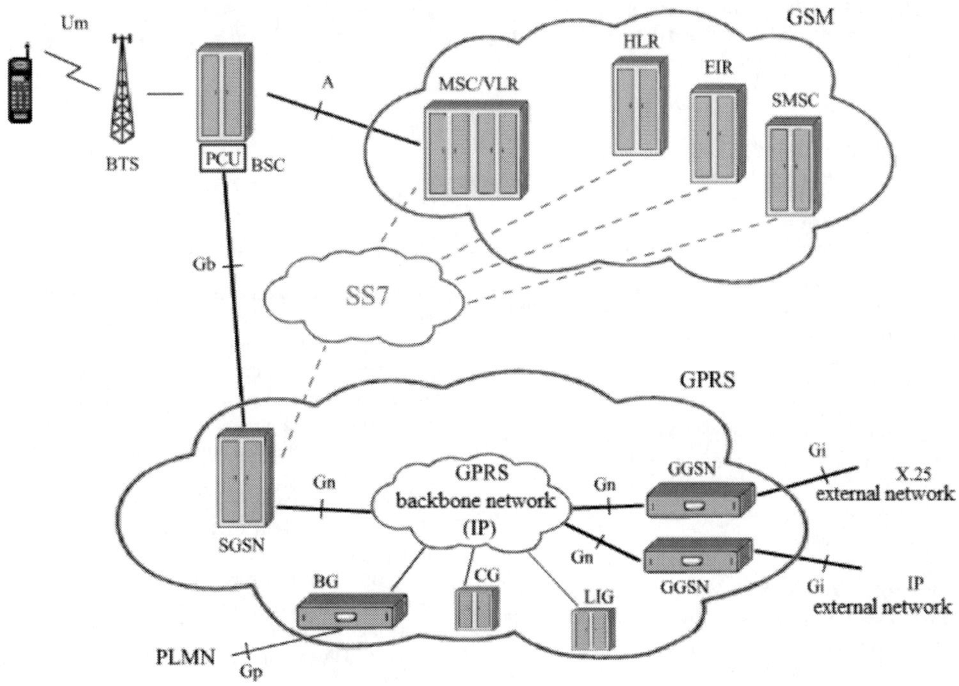

Figure 2. Implementation of GPRS system to the GSM network [4].

the hardware modules called PCU (Packet Controller Unit) that provided interface to the GPRS system. On the side of the GPRS, the interface is provided by SGSN (Servicing GPRS Support Node) that acts similar to MSC (Mobile Switching Centre). The signalization and controlling is provided also by the SS7 signalization protocol and from the GSM network, the following parts are used to identify the user and establish a communication with his mobile station: HLR, EIR, SMSC. The interface between the GPRS network and the networks based on different protocols (IP, X.25, etc.) is then provided by GGSN (Gateway GPRS Support Node). The system also incorporates the following units: BG (Border Gateway) that enables connection to other networks (roaming), CG (Charging Gateway) that stores and processes information on the amount of transferred data and the LIG (Legal Interception Gateway) that enables interception of the data transfers by the authorities (applied in several countries).

1.1.2 Security in GSM network

The level of security of the services provided by the GSM network is limited by several aspects. Generally, the authentication of the device is processed by means of a pre-shared key and response to the request. The communication between the base station and the user's mobile station may be encrypted. The authentication of the user is performed by means of his SIM card, PIN (Personal Identification Number) and PUK (PIN Unlocking Key). All devices are also given their unique IMEI number (International Mobile Equipment Identity) that is stored in both the mobile device and the EIR (see Table 1). Several encryption methods are applied to the data transferred by the GPRS. The details can be found in [3]

1.2 Remotely controlled gates

The remotely constructed gates are usually based on one of the following constructions:

- Rail based,
- Self-supporting.

Both of these types are usually equipped with unified actuators that enable opening and closing of the gates together with supplementary functions as giving the information on the position and/or movement of the gate, self-diagnostics, etc. The area of the gate's range is monitored by sensors detecting obstacles that could collide with the gate when opening or closing. Usually the sensors based on infrared rays.

The example of the construction of the remotely controlled gate is depicted in Fig. 3.

The conventional remote controllers operate at the frequency of 433 or 868 MHz respectively. The transceivers are distinguished by the unique code. Three types of authentication can be applied:

- Fixed code; the receiver and the transmitter use always the same code,
- Floating code; every time the transmitter is required to send a command, it uses different code. The receiver never accepts the same code again,
- Floating code with Antiscan; if the aggressor tries to guess the code, the receiver is blocked.

Application of controllers employing the GSM network can widen the functionality in the following aspects:

- A list of numbers being accepted can be set at the receiver.
- There is a possibility of bidirectional data transfers and sending messages to the user, for example when the gate is violently opened.
- The communication with the gate's controller can be processed easily by means of the user's cellular phone. The example of this solution can be found in [11].

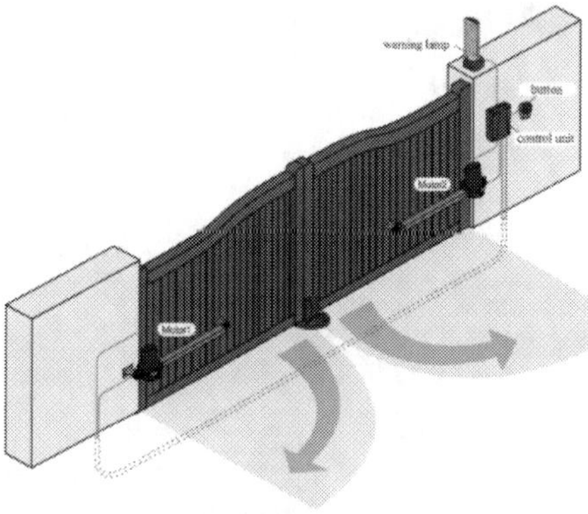

Figure 3. Example of construction of a remotely controlled gate with two drivers [5].

1.3 Arduino

Arduino is an open-source project that started in 2005 in Interaction Design Institute as a low cost development kit for applications with microcontrollers by Atmel. It is a physical platform with a microcontroller and several peripherals that is programmed by means of a simple development environment. Modular construction allows to connect expansion boards, called also as "shields". When programming, also the language C++ can be applied. More information on Arduino project can be found in [6].

For the purposes of this project, the Arduino model UNO has been selected. It is based on the microcontroller Atmel ATmega328p. It is equipped with 14 I/O pins. Some of these pins support PWM, analog inputs and/or connecting of a 16 MHz crystal. Using the shields, the following peripherals can be embedded in the unit: Ethernet, Bluetooth, LCD display, and, not least, the GSM module.

The parameters of Arduino Uno are provided in the table 2.

Table 2. Parameters of Arduino Uno.

Parameter	Value
Input voltage (operational)	7 - 12 V
Input voltage (limit)	6 – 20 V
Digital I/O pins	14
Analog inputs	6
Maximum current per a pin	40 mA
Flash memory	32 kB
SRAM	2 kB
EEPROM	1 kB
Clock	16 MHz
Dimensions (flat plane)	68.6 x 53.4 mm
Height	25 g

1.4 GSM shield

The GSM shield applicable for Arduino Uno that was used in this project, is based on the controller SIM900 by SIMCOM. It supports GSM/GPRS standards and operates at the frequencies of 850, 900, 1,800 and 1,900 MHz. The shield can be connected directly to the board of Adruino Uno by set of pins mounted at the bottom of the printed circuit board.

More information can be found in [7].

2 Project description

The hereby described project consists in development of a low-cost remote controlled driver for opening and closing of the gates. For the development, the above mentioned development kit Arduino Uno equipped with a GSM shield has been used. However, it was necessary to create another shield to provide interface between the controlling unit and the motors of the gate's driver unit.

The block diagram of the project solution is depicted in figure 4. The main development work consisted in making the Power section shield hardware, creating the software for the Arduino Uno board and making a model of the gate being controlled by the developed unit.

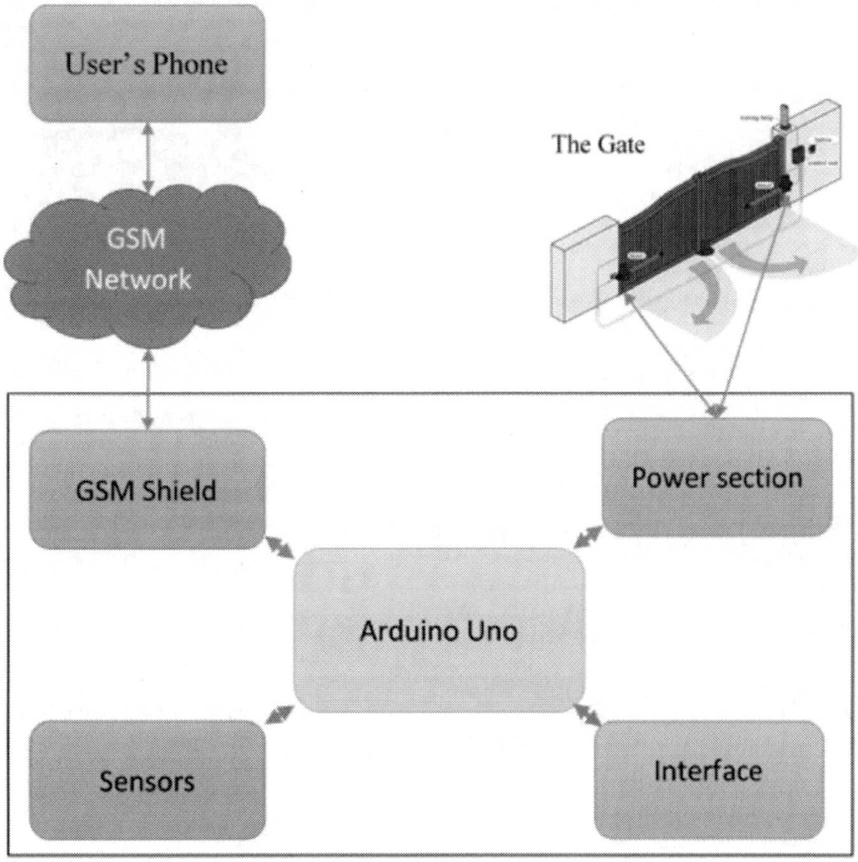

Figure 4. Concept of the remote controller using GSM network.

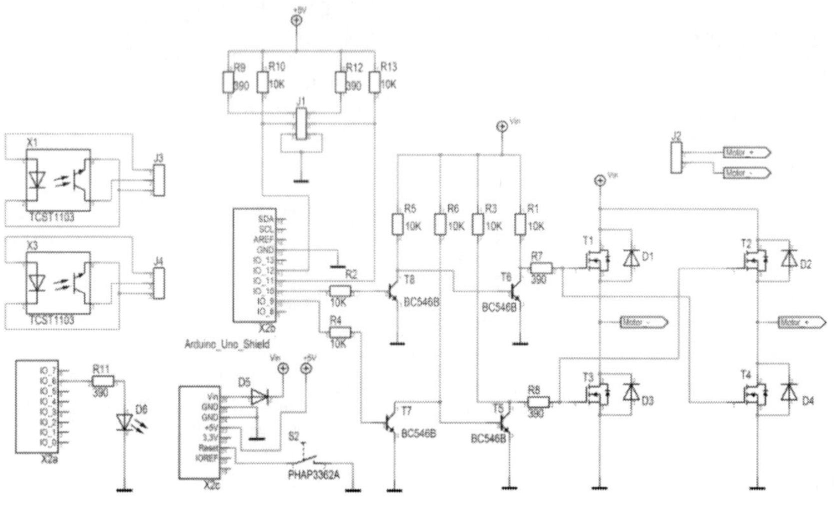

Figure 5. Connection diagram of the Power section shield [5].

3 Implementation

Within this chapter, hardware and software implementation is described.

3.1 Hardware

As noted above, as the Arduino Unit and its GSM shield were bought as the submodules, the another shield with the Power section had to be made in that way so it fit the Arduino Unit PCB directly by means of the connectors. Moreover, separated optical sensors were also created to check the obstacles in the area of the gate.

The connection diagram of the Power section shield is depicted in figure 5. The shield can be stacked to the units by means of the connectors X2a, X2b and X2c. The power section itself consists of a H-bridge, that is created by means of transistors T1 to T4 and the drivers of these transistors, that are made with transistors T5 to T8. The bridge is driven directly from the Arduino unit, using a PWM modulation that enables the possibility of controlling the speed of the gate's propulsion. The position of the gate is monitored by a pair of photocells that are connected to the connector J1. In the figure 5 the connection of these photocells is also depicted in the form of standalone circuits. The photocells employ TCST1103 modules that are marked as X1 or X3 in the diagram. Because the power consumption of the model of the gate is not high, the power supply to the Power unit is taken directly from the power supply network of the Arduino unit. The protection diode D5 was added to suppress the voltage ripples generated by the driven motor that could get back to the Arduino unit. If the output current of the driver is insufficient, more powerful H-bridge can be connected to the power output of the shield. The power output is conducted through the connector J2.

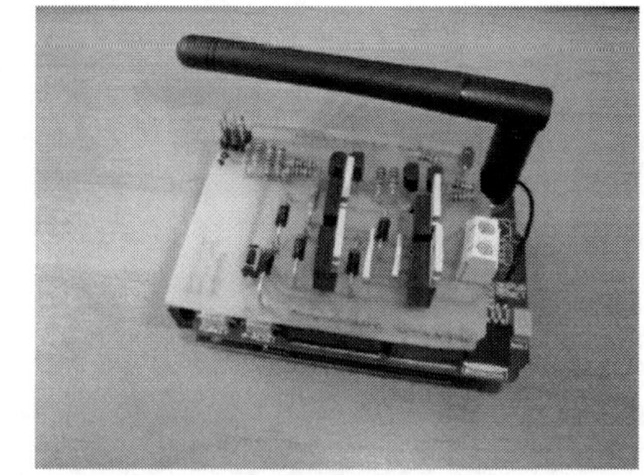

Figure 6. Completed gated controller [5].

The stack of three printed circuit boards can be seen in the figure 6. The PCBs are (from the top):

1. Power section shield,
2. GSM/GPRS shield,
3. Adruino Uno.

3.2 Software

The software implemented in the Arduino unit must distinguish between the following states:

- Opened – the gate is opened, the motor is off, the stop sensor of this position gives logical 1 at its output,
- Closed – the gate is closed, the motor is off, the stop sensor of this position gives logical 1 at its output,

- Opening – both stop sensors give logical 0 at their outputs and the motor is turning in the direction to open the gate,
- Closing – the stop sensors give logical 0 at their outputs and the motor is turning in the direction to close the gate,
- Error – occurs when both stop sensors give the logical 1 at their outputs or both sensors give the logical 0 at their outputs and the motor is off.

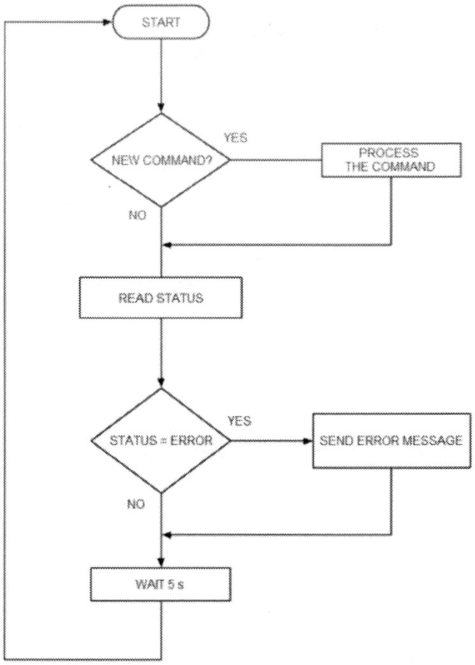

Figure 7. Flowchart of the software loop [5].

In this project, communication by means of SMS has been chosen. Therefore, the software must support the following commands that are sent via SMS:

- Open – calls the method gate.Open() that process opening of the gate,
- Close – calls the method gate.Close() that process closing of the gate,
- Slower – this command is determined by the set of characters "-" entered consecutively. By this command the speed of the gate's movement is decreased according to the number of the characters sent. The information on required speed of the gate is stored in the memory.
- Faster - this command is determined by the set of characters "+" entered consecutively. By this command the speed of the gate's movement is increased according to the number of the characters sent. The information on required speed of the gate is stored in the memory.
- Status – this command calls the method gate.Status() the result of which is to send the information on the status of the gate to the user by means of the SMS.

The application is repeated in a loop the diagram of which is depicted in the figure 7.

The Arduino's producer provides an open-source library GSM_GPRS_GPS_Shield that includes a set of classes for treating the GSM modules based on the controllers SIM900 and/or SIM908.

4 Conclusions

This paper provides a description on construction of the controller of the remotely controlled entrance gates that can be commanded via the user's cellular phone, employing data transfers in GSM network. In the framework of this project the functional sample was created on the basis of the development kit Arduino Uno and two embedded shields. The picture of the completed unit can be found in the figure 6.

The created sample is fully operational, providing large possibilities to implement expansion functionalities. For example, as the hardware supports connection of additional units, a logging unit can be added to monitor all attempts to control the driver. Another option is adding of the LAN unit that would allow to connect the driver to the LAN network.

Acknowledgements

This work was supported by the Ministry of Education, Youth and Sports of the Czech Republic within The National Sustainability Programme Project No. LO1303 (MSMT-7778/2014) and also by The European Regional Development Fund under the project CEBIA-Tech No. CZ.1.05/2.1.00/03.0089.

References

1. S. F. Barrett, *Arduino microcontroller: processing for everyone!* (Morgan, 2012, ISBN 978-160-8458-592)
2. B. Evans, *Beginning Arduino programming: writing code for the most popular microcontroller board in the world* (Apress, 2011, ISBN 978-1-4302-3777-8)
3. T. Halonen, J. Melero, J. Romero, GSM, GPRS and EDGE Performance: Evolution Towards 3G/UMTS, 2nd Edition (John Wiley, 2003, ISBN 04-708-6694-2)
4. Richtr, T., *Basic structure of GSM network* (Online: URL http://tomas.richtr.cz/mobil/gsm-strukt.htm)
5. Smékal, T., *The Remote control of gates using a GSM unit* (Diploma Thesis, 2015, Supervizor: M. Pospisilik)
6. Arduino - ArduinoBoardUno. (Online: URL http://www.arduino.cc/en/Main/ArduinoBoardUno)
7. SIM900 Quad-Band GPRS shield with Micro SD card slot - Epalsite Wiki (Online: URL http://wiki.epalsite.com/index.php?title=SIM900_Quad-Band_GPRS_shield_with_Micro_SD_card_slot)

 DOI: 10.1051/matecconf/20167602037

RFID reader immunity test against electrostatic discharge

Martin Pospisilik[1,a], Zdenek Korytak[1], Peter Janku[1] and Rui Miguel Soares Silva[2]

[1]Faculty of Applied Informatics, Tomas Bata University in Zlin, Nad Stranemi 4511, 76005 Zlin, Czech Republic
[2]Laboratório Ubi-NET, Campus do Instituto Polytécnico de Beja, Apartado 6155, 7800-295, Beja, Portugal

Abstract. This paper provides a description of an immunity test against the electrostatic discharge according to the standard EN 61000-4-2 that was applied to an RFID reader. The RFID reader was primarily developed for access systems, employing the on-board recognition of the RFID tags. The results obtained by the test are described hereby as well as the discussion on the security of this solution. The results of this experiment are beneficial for the developers of RFID devices, as these devices are endangered by the electrostatic discharge brought by their users. The hereby described results also shown a security hole in a simple access system based on the RFID technology. Details can be found in the paper.

1 Introduction

The issues on electrostatic discharges have been solved since the beginning of the 19th century when several paper mills had faced the accidents caused by ignition of the paper dust by spark discharges. Even earlier, the effects on spark discharges on gunpowder have also been known [3]. However, the problems of the electrostatic discharges have been comprehensively tackled since the first field-effect semiconductors begun to be employed. Nowadays the electrostatic discharge (ESD) protection is one of the most important issues at the electronic devices' development as the current semiconductors exhibit high sensitivity to the energy released during the discharge.

At present, testing of devices on the immunity to electrostatic discharges falls within the tests performed within the framework of electromagnetic compatibility (EMC) testing. In European Union the conditions and criteria of testing on the ESD immunity are described by the standard EN 61000-4-2. This standard prescribes the criteria that must be fulfilled when the tested device is in operation as well.

2 Local electrostatic discharge

The local electrostatic discharge occurs between two surfaces provided there is a significant difference between their charges that are determined by the number of accumulated electrons. Lightning is probably the most dramatic effect of ESD, but in practice, even in much smaller discharges high powers are dissipated, which can result in unpleasant consequences. Although the typical energy released at one ESD reaches the order of mJ, due to very short discharge times (nanoseconds) the levels of voltage and current are destructive to most of the semiconductor devices. According to [2] the charge on the surface of a human body can reach up to 15 kV when walking or rubbing on clothing. A typical current waveform when ESD occurs is depicted in figure 1.

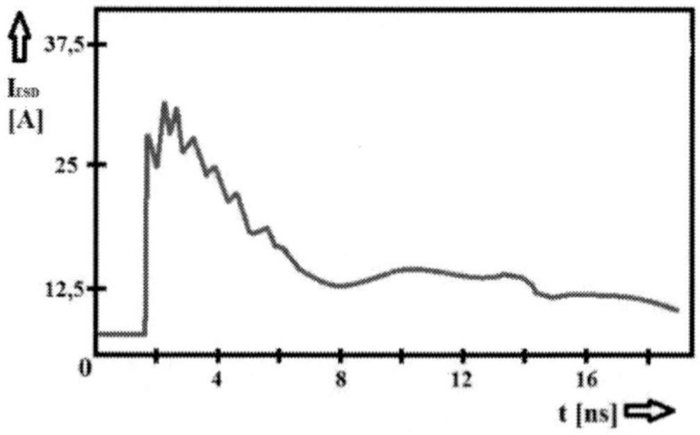

Figure 1. Typical current waveform during the electrostatic discharge [2].

The electrostatic discharge may occur both naturally and artificially as a result of operation of the device. With the participation of the human element, the following cases can occur:

- Electrostatic discharge between two entities provided one of them is charged and the other one is grounded, typically when a technician touches a part of the circuit with some instruments.
- Electrostatic discharge between the charged human body and the grounded electrical circuit, typically when an operator touches the control elements.

[a] Corresponding author: pospisilik@fai.utb.cz

In order to prevent the above mentioned situations, a set of test that must be underwent by the tested devices, is prescribed by the standard EN 61000-4-2.

3 Standardization

As mentioned above, testing of any electronic device's immunity against ESD falls among the issues on electromagnetic susceptibility. The generic standard EN 61000-6-1 defines functional criteria according to which the performance of the tested device can be objectified. The description of these criteria is provided in the table below.

Table 1. Functional criteria according to EN 61000-6-1.

Criterion	Description
A	No influence of the external energy to the operation of the device has been observed.
B	The device operates according to the specification, but some of its characteristics are partially affected by the interferences. The interferences do not change data in the memory of the device nor its operating state. Once the interference disappeared, the proper operation of the whole device is restored without the operator's intervention.
C	The interference interrupted the proper operation of the device or its part and the operator's intervention is needed to recover the device to its normal operation.
(D)	The interference caused damage to the device or its part.

The ESD immunity test is defined by the standard EN 61000-4-2. By means of this standard, the voltage levels, pulse waveforms and the configuration of the experiment are prescribed as well as the steps of the experiment. As the source of energy ESD simulators are used. Generally, three types of ESD tests can be applied, as described in the subchapters below.

3.1. Direct discharge through air gap

The principle of the direct discharge through an air gap is depicted in Fig. 2. The tested device (EuT) is placed on a wooden table the surface of which is covered by a grounded metal plate. On the floor of the testing area the grounded reference metal plate must be placed as well.

The discharge is generated by means of the ESD simulator, which is in the figure denoted by the letter "S". The block diagram of the simulator is depicted in Fig. 3. The main part of the simulator is the accumulating capacitor C_0 the capacity of which must be 150 pF. The capacitor is charged from the high voltage source. The output voltage of this source must be adjustable at least from 2 to 15 kV. The charging resistor R_0 limits the charging current as well as the output current of the simulator once the capacitor is discharged. Its resistance must be as high as 50 to 100 MΩ. According to the Czech version of EN 61000-4-2 the discharge resistor R must embody the resistance of 330 Ω.

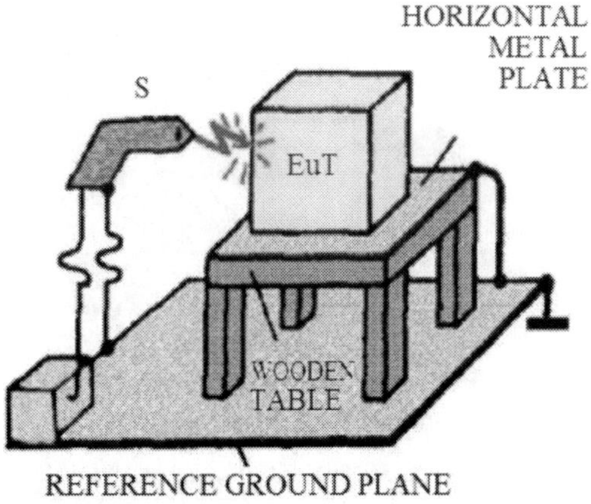

Figure 2. Direct discharge through the air gap – experiment configuration [1].

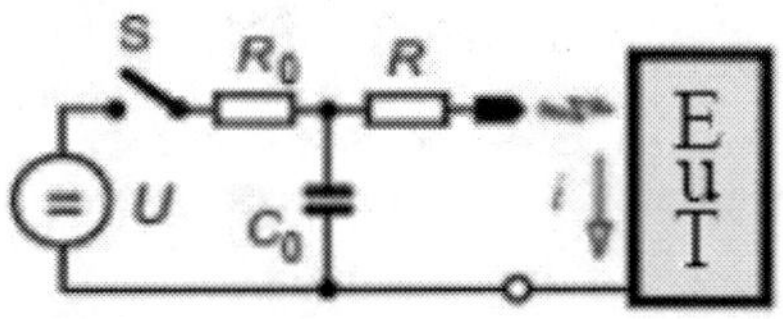

Figure 3. Block diagram of the ESD simulator generating the discharge through the air gap [1].

When processing the experiment, the operator moves the tip of the simulator toward to the tested device. Once the dielectric strength of the air gap is overcome, the energy stored in the capacitor C_0 is dissipated to the tested device by means of the discharge.

However, this type of experiments is not preferred due to its poor repeatability. When repeated, the waveform of the dissipation current can differ according to the air humidity, speed of the simulator tip's movement, air pressure and other variables.

3.2 Discharge through the contact

This experiment eliminates the disadvantages of the test by means of the discharge through the air gap. The ESD simulator touches the tested device by means of a conductive contact. This configuration allows better control over the amount of the dissipated energy and the time course of its handover.

The configuration of the experiment is depicted in Fig. 4. The placement of the tested device is the same as in the previous case as well as the configuration of the whole experiment, but the operator touches the device (EuT) by the conductive tip of the simulator and triggers the discharge by the "trigger" contact.

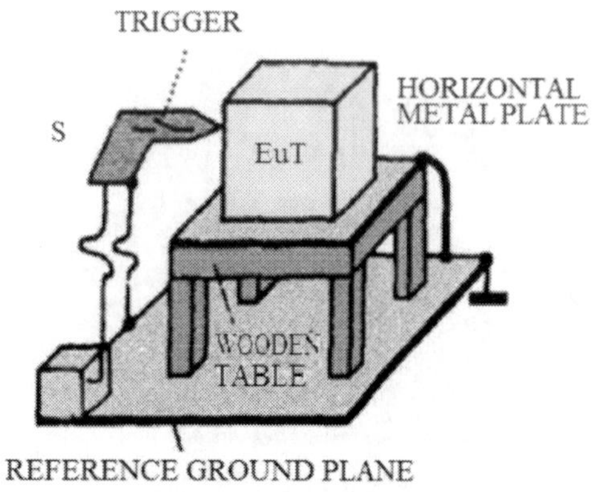

Figure 4. Discharge through the contact – experiment configuration [1].

The block diagram of the simulator is depicted in Fig. 5. The principle of its operation is the same as described in the subchapter above. Also the values of the devices R_0, C_0 and R are the same, but there is a switch denoted as "K" that triggers the discharge to the tested device (EuT).

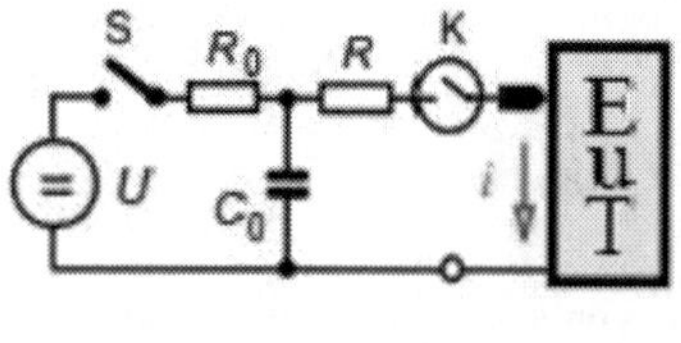

Figure 5. Block diagram of the ESD simulator generating the discharge through the direct contact [1].

The typical discharge current time course at this kind of experiment is depicted in Fig. 6. The levels of the currents I_{30} and I_{60}, referring to the time period of 30 and 60 ns after the discharge was triggered, are dependent on the voltage on the capacitor C_0. The theoretical levels are enlisted in Table 2.

Table 2. Theoretical current pulse parameters.

Charge voltage [V]	I_{max} [A]	I_{30} [A]	I_{60} [A]
2	7.5	4	2
4	15	8	4
6	22.5	12	6
8	30	16	8

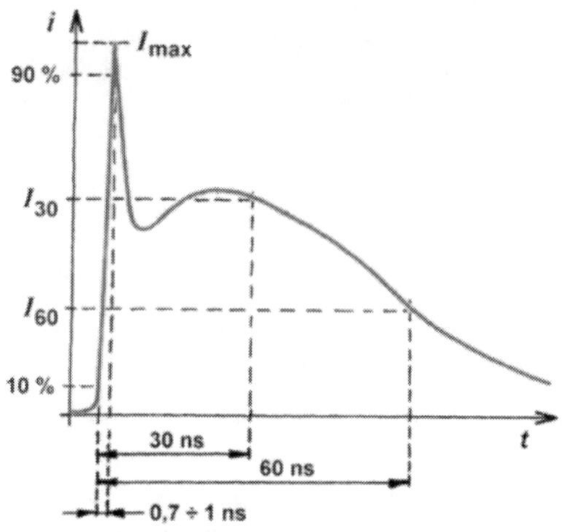

Figure 6. Typical time course of the discharge current at the direct discharge experiment [1].

3.3 Indirect discharge

This experiment simulates the situation in which the device is not directly hit by the electrostatic discharge, but some other objects in its neighbourhood are. The configuration of this experiment is depicted in Fig. 7.

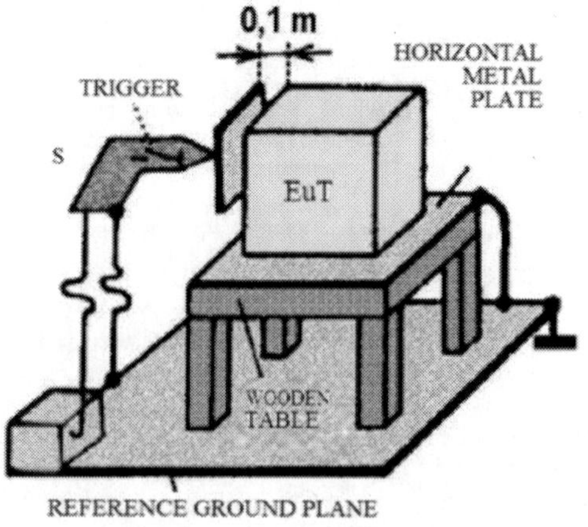

Figure 7. Indirect discharge – experiment configuration [1].

In this experiment, the horizontal coupling plane is placed 0.1 m far from the tested device. This plane is driven by the direct contact discharge. The experiment is repeated ten times for each side of the device. The construction of the simulator is as depicted in Fig. 5.

 DOI: 10.1051/matecconf/20167602037

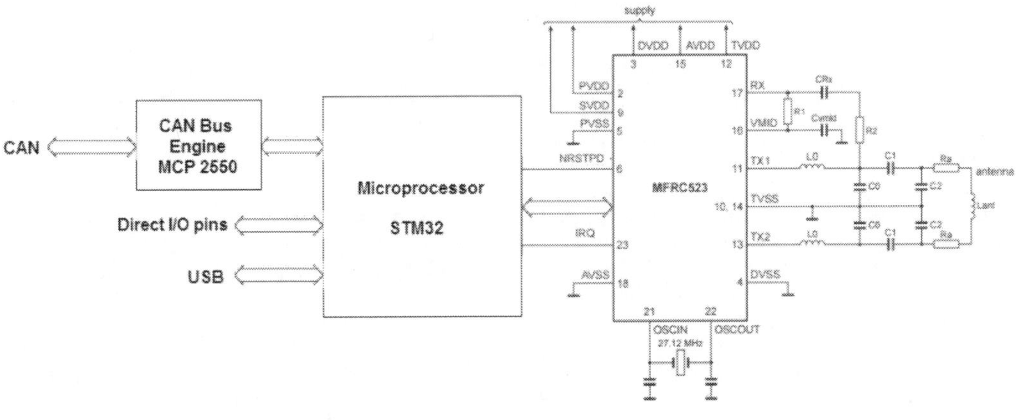

Figure 8. Simplified schematic diagram of the RFID reader.

3.4 Selection of testing points

The type of the experiment as well as the points of the tested device that are exposed to the ESD are selected according to the expected method of the device's use. Usually, the following critical parts of the device are tested:

- AC/DC mains terminals,
- Signal terminals,
- Control elements,
- Cover of the device.

4 Tested RFID reader

This chapter describes the RFID reader that was a subject to the ESD testing. The block diagram of the reader is depicted in Fig. 8.

The heart of the reader is the microprocessor from the family STM32F that has a direct connection to the RFID reader chip MFRC523. This chip provides a complete RFID interface for reading of tags implemented in access cards. The detailed description of this chip can be found in [4]. The data interface of the reader is assured by several ports:

- CAN Bus based on the engine MCP 2550,
- USB implemented directly in the microprocessor,
- Direct parallel port connected to the microprocessor's I/O pins.

To simplify the test, the following algorithm has been implemented to the reader. The microcontroller periodically requests the RFID chip to check whether there is a readable tag. Once the tag is enclosed to the reader's antenna, its unique number is read and when it is recognized, a set of logical bits is sent to the direct parallel port of the reader. This implementation cam be for example used in simple authentication systems where the actuator (door opening etc.) is driven directly by the RFIR reader. Moreover, there is a LED connected to one of the output pins to indicate the logical level at the appropriate output.

5 Experiment description

The experiment was held according to the requirements specified by the standards EN 61000-6-1 and EN 61000-4-2. The configuration of the experiment was held according to the figures 2, 4 and 7. To process the experiment, the test generator Haeffely ONYX 16 was employed. It embodies the following features:

- Replaceable tip for both type of discharges – with and without the air gap,
- Adjustable voltage from 1 to 16 kV,
- Plus or minus polarity.

The tested RFID reader was supplied from a laboratory power source. The configuration of the experiment is depicted in Fig. 9.

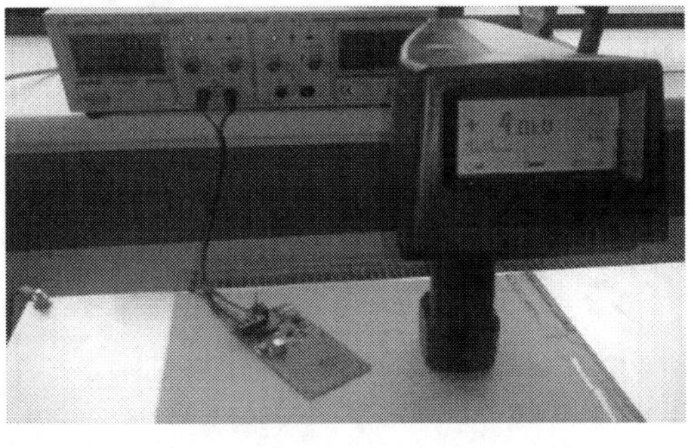

Figure 9. The RFID reader and the ESD generator ONYX 16 [5].

The test voltages were increased from the basic level of 1 kV up to the levels prescribed by the above mentioned standards:

- ± 4 kV for a contact discharge,
- ± 8 kV for a discharge through the air gap.

The ESD was applied to the following parts of the RFID reader:

- Input and output pins,
- Status LED,

- RFID antenna.

6 The results

The results achieved at the test are enlisted in the Table 3. The functional criteria have been evaluated according to Table 1.

To fulfil all the requirements of the standard EN 61000-4-2, the worst achieved result should not be worse than B. As obvious from the Table 3, in one case this requirement has not been met. However, it must be considered, that the tested device was operated without the proper cover and the contact discharge was targeted directly to the receiver's antenna. This problem can be solved by enclosing the reader into a suitable cover.

After processing of the test the device has been checked for its proper operation and it has been found that no permanent damage occurred.

Unfortunately, the test shown another problem that is not covered by the requirements of the standard. When the device was influenced by the ESD, several logical 1 states occurred at the direct parallel bus. That means that there exists a real risk if the RFID reader is used directly to drive the actuators (for example the door lock), consisting in the fact that the attacker would bypass the authentication by giving the ESD shock to the RFID reader. On the other hand, this risk can be eliminated by using the modulated and/or encoded output peripherals as the CAN bus or USB. In this case, the RFID reader only gives the information on reading of the tag to another device that manages the actuators driving and the existence of accidental pulses on the communication bus cause no harm to the safety of the authentication system.

7 Conclusions

In this paper a description of the ESD immunity test on a typical construction of the RFID reader is provided. The results of the test indicate, that if the RFID reader is intended to be used in a safety critical application, for example as a controller of the door lock, the phenomenon of the electrostatic discharge cannot be omitted, as the ESD can be generated deliberately as a kind of attack to the system. In this test a possibility of generating a false positive signals at the output of the reader was confirmed. Therefore we recommend not to use the RFID reader directly to recognize the tags, but to process the information on the tags in the neighbourhood of the reader's antenna by the remote device.

Acknowledgements

This work was supported by the Ministry of Education, Youth and Sports of the Czech Republic within The National Sustainability Programme Project No. LO1303 (MSMT-7778/2014) and also by The European Regional Development Fund under the project CEBIA-Tech No. CZ.1.05/2.1.00/03.0089.

References

1. J. Svacina, *Electromagnetic compatibility [Elektromagneticka kompatibilita]* (VUT Brno, 2001, ISBN 80-21418737)
2. P. Horsky, *Electrostatic discharge and testing of its influence on integrated circuits [Elektrostatický výboj a testování jeho vlivu na elektromagnetické pole]* (Online, 2014, URL: http://design.georgius.cz/sites/infocube/eem/horsky_eem081.pdf)
3. I. Poole, *ESD Protection* (Online, 2014, URL: https://radio-electronics.com)
4. MFRC523 (datasheet, 2016)
5. Z. Korytak, *Testing the Electromagnetic Susceptibility of Electrical Appliances* (Diploma thesis, Supervisor: M. Pospisilik)

Table 3. Results of the test.

Point of ESD application	Charge voltage	Discharge type	Polarity	Result
I/O pins	4 kV	Contact	(+)	B
			(-)	B
LED (output state indicator)	4 kV	Contact	(+)	B
			(-)	B
RFID antenna	4 kV	Contact	(+)	C
			(-)	B
The whole reader through a vertical coupling plane	4 kV	Vertical coupling plane	(+)	A
			(-)	B
I/O pins	8 kV	Air gap	(+)	B
			(-)	B
LED (output state indicator)	8 kV	Air gap	(+)	B
			(-)	B
RFID antenna	8 kV	Air gap	(+)	B
			(-)	B

MATEC Web of Conferences **76**, 02038 (2016)
CSCC 2016 DOI: 10.1051/matecconf/20167602038

Design of active feedback for rehabilitation device

Ondrej Liska[1a] Marcel More[1] Dagmar Janacova[2,] and Vladimir Vasek[2]

[1] *Technical University of Kosice, Faculty of Mechanical Engineering, Department of Automation, Control and Human Machine Interaction, Letná 9, 04200 Košice, Slovakia*
[2] *Tomas Bata University in Zlín, Faculty of Applied Informatics, nám. T.G.Masaryka 5555, 760 01 Zlín. Czech republic*

Abstract. Sensor systems are an essential part of automated equipment. They are even more important in machines that come in contact with people, because they have a significant impact on safety. This paper describes the design of active feedback for rehabilitation device driven by pneumatic artificial muscles. Here are presented three methods for measuring the load of the robot. The first is a system composed of Force Sensitive Resistors (FSR) placed in the handle of the device. Two other methods are intended to measure the load of the actuator composed of artificial muscles. The principle of one method is to measure the difference in filling pressures of the muscles, second is based on strain measurement in the drive cables. The paper describes advantages and disadvantages of using each of these methods in a rehabilitation device

1 Introduction

Musculoskeletal rehabilitation is an essential part of the healing process of patients who have experienced a traumatic injury or stroke limiting their range of motion. But rehabilitation exercises carried out by a physiotherapist are time-consuming and expensive. For these reasons, there is an endeavor to at least partially automate this task with usage of robotic rehabilitation devices. Their advantage is that the patient himself can choose the time and intensity of the exercise and especially in the case of simpler devices it is also possible to use them at the patient's home.

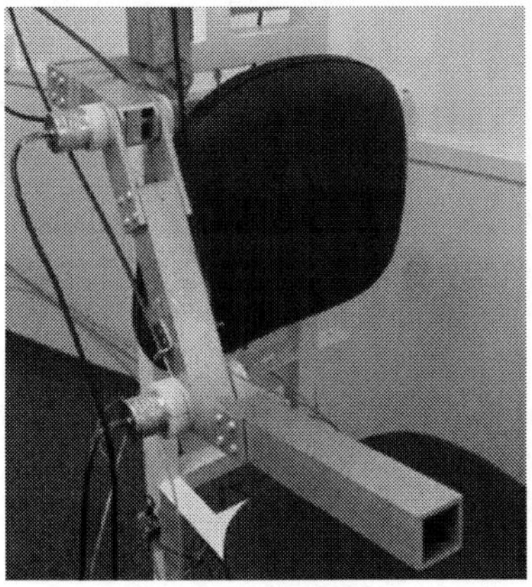

Figure 1. Rehabilitation device driven by pneumatic artificial muscles

In our department we are developing device for rehabilitation of the upper limb joints. It is designed for exercising shoulder and elbow joint at the same time. It's in the form of exoskeleton, so its kinematics reproduces kinematics of the human arm. The main specific of this device is actuator used to drive him - pneumatic artificial muscles.

Figure 2. Rehabilitation device driven by pneumatic artificial muscles - rear view

[a] Corresponding author: ondrej.liska@tuke.sk

 DOI: 10.1051/matecconf/20167602038

Device as is shown in Figure 1and 2 can perform passive rehabilitation exercises. For these exercises, it is sufficient that the device have a control loops for position and speed control of the device joints. But at some stage of recovery, it is necessary to start with active exercises in which the patient has to use his own strength. For the automated rehabilitation system, this means that this force should be measured and regulated. However, force measurement is problematic part in the design of sensor system. Since this device is specific by its purpose (rehabilitation) and also because of its drive (pneumatic muscles), there are no ready-made solutions that can be directly applicable. Because measured values should be used for direct control, this method must provide them in real time, without significant delay and without so called time errors.

2 Analysis of force measurement

Principled model of robotic arm with one joint driven by a pair of antagonistically connected artificial muscles is shown in Figure 3. On this model there are shows possible placements of force measuring system. In this case, the load is considered to be solely on the end of the robots arm.

The load can be measured on these three places:

1. at the point of contact,
2. at the robots arm - measurement of deformation,
3. in the actuator - measurement of load.

2.1 Measuring deformation of the robots arm

In this method, the force is measured indirectly as a deformation of the robots arm. For small deformation measurement in experimental mechanics but also in practical applications there are used strain gauges and load cells. For measuring the load of rehabilitation robot we considered two methods. The first is application of strain gauges directly to the robots arm. But this includes one difficult task. It is necessary to create the point, in which the deformation will be sufficient for measurement with satisfying resolution, while maintaining the strength of this element. This disadvantage can be eliminated by usage of bending load cell. These sensors mostly consist of a steel body on which the strain gauges connected to Wheatstone bridge are mounted. They are designed to measure strain in their nominal range but they can withstand some overload (typically 150-200%) [1]. Sensor like this can be embedded in the robots arm. The disadvantage of this solution is its dimensions and weight. Because of the material of load cell (mostly steel), the sensor placed on the end of kinematic chain can create significant torque.

2.2 Measurement of actuator's load

Rehabilitation device is designed so that each member of the kinematic chain has one degree of freedom. This is where the actuator operates and also where we need to measure load. In conventional robots that use electric actuators, the load is mostly determined indirectly by measuring the current that passes through the motor. When using a pneumatic actuator this solution can't be used. But in the devices driven by artificial muscles other variables specific to this type of drive can be measured. Application of external forces to such an actuator leads both to change of pressure in both pneumatic muscles and also to change of stress in other components such as cables, chain, pulleys, etc.

3 Methods selected for further evaluation

For further consideration, we have selected three measurement methods. We choose these methods based on their advantages but also for their affordability and suitability for incorporation into existing rehabilitation device.

3.1 Force Sensitive Resistors (FSR)

FSR are passive electronic components that change their resistance according to applied force. These sensors consist of several thin layers of polymer so that application of force to the active area results in reduction of electrical resistance. Mechanically and also by range of measurement are these sensors designed to measure force of human touch. FSRs are not intended to accurate measurements like strain gauges.

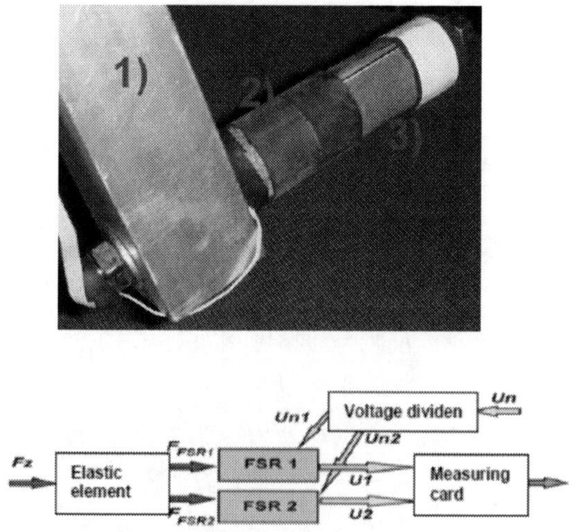

Figure 3. FSR sensors mounted on handle – 1) robots arm, 2) handle, 3) FSR

The force between rehabilitation device and patient is transferred mainly through the handle. This is place where direct contact occurs on relatively small area, which can be covered by conventional sizes of these sensors (0.25 to 25 cm^2). Output characteristic of the sensor (resistance dependence on the strength) is roughly linear, so simple algorithms are sufficient for the signal

processing. Because this is a simple passive element, this characteristic can be modified by various electrical connections. If necessary, it is also possible to create different types of output - voltage, current, frequency and so [2]. To determine the force in the direction of one axis, it is necessary to know the values measured in opposing sensors (F_{x1}, F_{x2}).
The force on this axis is then the difference of their values ΔF_x.

$$\Delta F_x = F_{x1} - F_{x2} \tag{1}$$

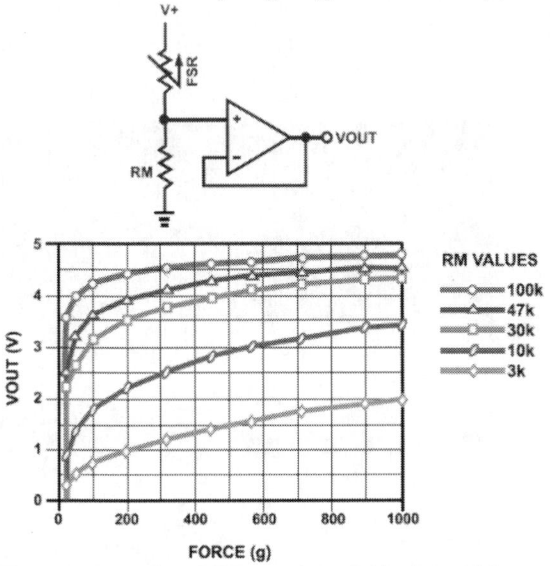

Figure 4. Connection of FSR to voltage divider (up) and its output characteristics (down) [2]

Key parameters, which determine if these sensors will be used in rehabilitation device, are accuracy and repeatability they can achieve. Accuracy, as stated by one of the manufacturers of these sensors [2], is generally between ±5 to ± 25%. This value depends on the particular measuring system, on the way as the force is applied and also on the quality of the sensor. Significant increase in accuracy can be achieved by calibrating the sensors mounted directly in the system, in which it will be used. The second important parameter is the repeatability. This largely depends on variations in location and distribution of the load. The more consistent the load is the better results can be obtained with repeated measurements. But in rehabilitation we are not able to provide the same grip of the handle even when exercising same patient. This problem gets even worse if the same machine has to serve multiple users. We can reduce these impacts by constructing appropriate handle with proper placement of sensors. The use of thin layers of flexible material, which overlays the active area of the sensors, can more or less (depending on the thickness of the layer) distribute the load. Another option is to use auto calibration system before each exercise, which would eliminate differences between patients.

3.2 Measuring actuator's load based on pneumatic pressure

When the force is applied to the muscle, it changes its length. With the change of length it also changes its volume, which in a closed system leads to a change in pressure. This means that we can determine load of the robot by measuring values of pneumatic pressure in muscles. The process of calculating force from pressure is described bellow. First, we must determine value of the nominal difference between the pressures in the muscles ΔP_n at given position (measured by encoder). For this purpose it is necessary to assemble the model or mathematical dependence of pressure on the angle of the joint φ.

$$\Delta P_n = f(\varphi) \tag{2}$$

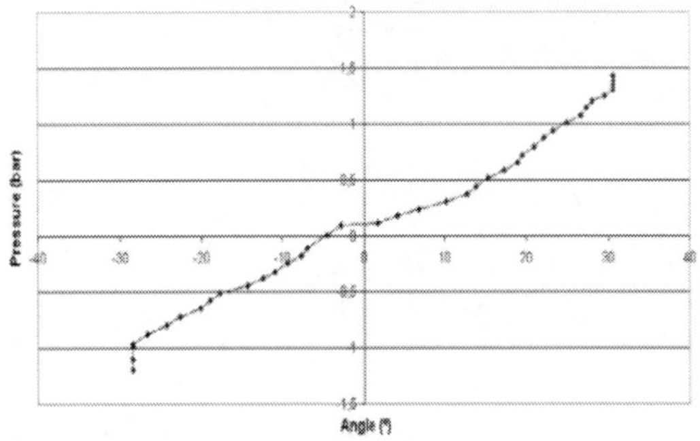

Figure 5. Dependence of pressure difference on angle of the joint

A complication in this step can be a various non-linear properties, which are characteristic for these actuators. However, it has significant impact on accuracy of this method of measurement. The next step is to calculate the actual pressure difference betwee values ΔP_s of pressure in these muscles (P_1, P_2).

$$\Delta P_s = P_1 - P_2 \tag{3}$$

Finally we can calculate the torque *(M)* as the function of difference between real and nominal pressure differences. Because the ratio of transmission is known and constant, we can then calculate the force.

$$M = f(\Delta P_s - \Delta P_n) \tag{4}$$

Different types of sensors can be used for pressure measurement. It is possible to use differential sensor, which provide directly the difference between two pneumatic pressures. But here, the more useful solution is to use single ended sensor for each muscle so it can be used also for different tasks (like in algorithm, which prevents complete exhaust of muscle). The disadvantage of this measuring method is that the measured values can be affected by pressure fluctuations caused by pneumatic valves during operation. This phenomenon is less significant when we use control methods that change the pressure in muscles smoothly (proportional valves, etc.). Another optimization can be done by mounting sensor in proper location. Since the pressure fluctuations are largest near the valve, pressure sensor should be connected as close to the muscle as possible (Fig. 6 left). However, best location is on the other side of the muscle, opposite to the opening where the valve is connected (Fig. 6 right). But for this, it is necessary to use muscle that is opened on booth sides.

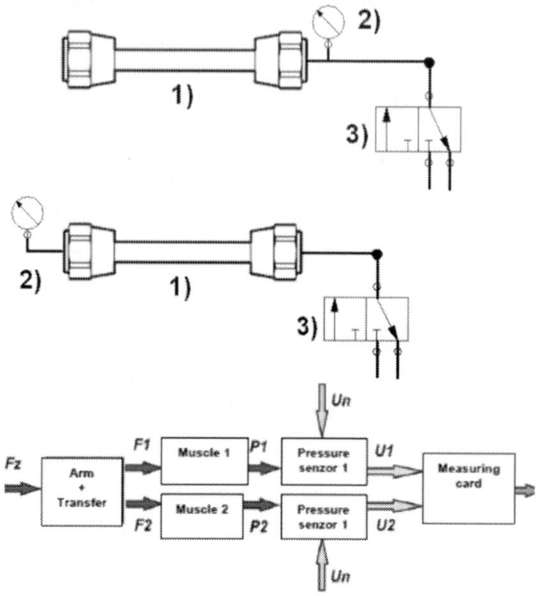

Figure 6. Options for placement of pressure sensor on muscle opened on one (up) and booth ends (down)

3.3 Measuring actuator's load based on strain in cables

Strain in the cables can be measured by load cells. Sensors for measuring tensile forces are small in size and relatively light and thus can be easily incorporated into the system. On Fig. 7 it is possible to see an example of their placement between pneumatic muscle and cable. Dimensions of this sensor are Ø34x18mm, so it does not increase the outline of a muscle in diameter and only slightly increases its length. Since booth muscle and cable transfer force only in one axis, sensor can be loaded only by tensile stress. Although the sensor is placed on the moving component, the movement of the muscle is in the order of centimeter, so the supply and signal conductors don't limit its use. Also measurement apparatus can be placed relatively close to the sensors.
Processing of measured values is similar to the previous case. For the determination of the force it is necessary to calculate the difference ΔF between forces in each cable (F_1, F_2).

$$\Delta F = F_1 - F_2 \tag{5}$$

Even if the forces measured on unloaded arm should be theoretically balanced, in the practical implementation it is necessary to consider the effect of gravity. This affects the robots arm differently depending on its position and also on the position of other members of the kinematic chain.

Therefore, as in the previous case, it is necessary to determine a dependence of the force (F_G) on the position of the arm (φ).

$$F_G = f(\varphi) \tag{6}$$

Then the effect of this force is subtracted from the measured values to get the real value of force exerted by the patient (F_P).

$$F_P = \Delta F - F_G \tag{7}$$

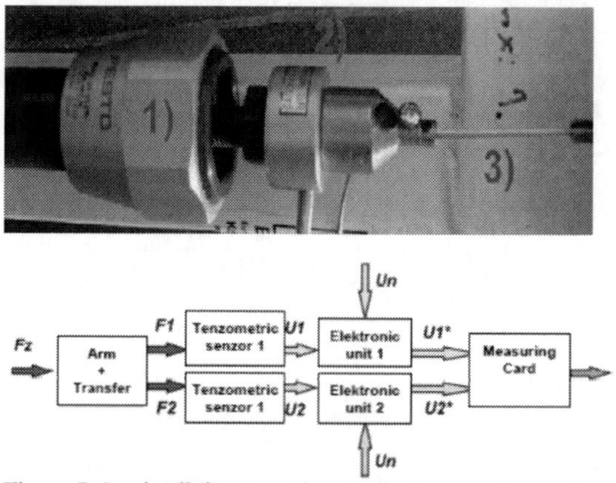

Figure 7. Load cell for measuring tensile forces – 1) muscle, 2) load cell, 3) cable

4 Conclusion

Force feedback is essential for the automated device that is intended for active rehabilitation. But in the device driven by pneumatic artificial muscles, we can not use the force measuring system used in conventional robots. It is therefore necessary to assemble a measuring system which takes into account his specific characteristics and requirements. Analysis of the available options shows that load can be measured in three locations: at the point of contact, at the robot's arm or in the drive. For closer comparison we selected three methods. The first is measurement in the handle of the device using FSR sensors. Other two methods use the fact that the force applied to the robot arm creates appropriate response in the drive. In case of actuator composed of pneumatic muscles, this load can be determined from the change in filling pressure in each muscle. Because the pressure sensors are a standard part of systems containing pneumatic circuits, such measurement requires no additional hardware components. Application of the load also results in the strain in mechanical parts of the drive and can be measured by load cells. Although this method is relatively complex, it gives results least influenced by other processes and random errors. These three methods will be evaluated in our department to determine the most suitable method for measuring force in unconventional rehabilitation device.

Acknowledgement

The research work is supported by the Project of the Structural Funds of the EU, Operational Programme Research and Development, Measure 2.2 Transfer of knowledge and technology from research and development into practice. Title of the project: „Research and development of intelligent nonconventional actuators based on artificial muscles", ITMS code: 26220220103, by the Slovak Grant Agency VEGA contract Nb. 1/0911/14 "Implementation of wireless technologies into the design of new products and services to protect human health" and by the Ministry of Education, Youth and Sports of the Czech Republic within the National Sustainability Programme project No. LO1303 (MSMT-7778/2014) and also by the European Regional Development Fund under the project CEBIA-Tech No. CZ.1.05/2.1.00/03.0089

References

1. Emsyst Shear-web Load Cell EMS30. Avalibe:http://emsyst.sk/images/snimace_sily/standartne/EMS30a.pdf
2. Interlink Electronics: *FSR Force Sensing Resistor Integration Guide and Evalution* Parts Catalog. Available: http://www.imagesco.com/sensors/fsr/
3. A. Erwin et al.: Interaction Control For Rehabilitation Robotics via a Low-Cost Force Sensing Handle, in: *DSCC2013 Proceedings of the ASME 2013 Dynamic Systems and Control Conference* Available: http://mahilab.rice.edu/sites. (2013)
4. F. Trebuna, P. Sivak, Experimentálne metódy mechaniky: *Tenzometria, Košice* : TU, ISBN 978-80-553-1378-8. (2012)
5. A. Hosovsky et al.: Model-based Evolution of a Fast Hybrid Fuzzy Adaptive Controller for a Pneumatic Muscle Actuator, in: International Journal of Advanced Robotic Systems. Vol. **9** (56). pp. 1-11. – ISSN 1729-8806. (2012)
6. I. Mack et al.: Interactive Force Sensing Feedback System for Remote Robotic Laparoscopic Surgery, in: Haptic Audio visual Environments and Games. (2009) Available: http://ieeexplore.ieee.org/stamp
7. T. Kelemenova et al.: Model based design and HIL simulations, in: American Journal of Mechanical Engineering. Vol. 1 pp. 276-28. ISSN 2328-4102. (2013)
8. K. Zidek, A. Hosovsky: Wireless Device Based on MEMS Sensors and Bluetooth Low Energy (LESmart) *Technology for Diagnostics of Mechatronic Systems*, In: *Applied Mechanics and Materials*. Vol. 460, pp. 13-21. ISSN 1660-9336. (2014)
9. L. Vasek, V. Dolinay Simulation model of heat distribution and consumption in municipal heating network, *International Journal of Mathematical Models and Methods in Applied Sciences*, Volume 4, 4, pages 240-248 (2010)
10. P. Berkelman et al.: A Miniature Microsurgical Instrument Tip Force Sensor for Enhanced Force Feedback During Robot-Assisted Manipulation, In: *IEEE Transactions On Robotics And Automation*. (2003)
11. M. Tothova, J. Pitel: Dynamic model of pneumatic actuator based on advanced geometric muscle model, in ICCC 2013: *IEEE 9th International Conference on Computational Cybernetics, IEEE* pp. 83-87. ISBN 978-1-4799-0060-2. (2013)
12. M. Dalvand et al.: Force Measurement Capability for Robotic Assisted Minimally Invasive Surgery Systems, in: Proceedings of the World Congress on Engineering and Computer Science. (2013)

Credit Risk Assessment Model Based Using Principal component Analysis And Artificial Neural Network

Abeer Hamdy [1,2], Walid B. Hussein[1]

[1]*Faculty of Informatics and Computer science, The British University in Egypt, Cairo, Egypt*

[2] *Department of Computers and Systems, Electronics Research Institute, Cairo, Egypt*

Abstract. Credit risk assessment for bank customers has gained increasing attention in recent years. Several models for credit scoring have been proposed in the literature for this purpose. The accuracy of the model is crucial for any financial institution's profitability. This paper provided a high accuracy credit scoring model that could be utilized with small and large datasets utilizing a principal component analysis (PCA) based breakdown to the significance of the attributes commonly used in the credit scoring models. The proposed credit scoring model applied PCA to acquire the main attributes of the credit scoring data then an ANN classifier to determine the credit worthiness of an individual applicant. The performance of the proposed model was compared to other models in terms of accuracy and training time. Results, based on German dataset showed that the proposed model is superior to others and computationally cheaper. Thus it can be a potential candidate for future credit scoring systems.

Keywords. Credit scoring, ANN, PCA, credit risk, German data.

1 Introduction

Credit risk assessment has gained increasing attention in recent years. Banks and financial institutions have extensively started to consider the credit risk of their customers in order to make decisions to grant credit to new applicants, extend credit or increase credit limit for existing customers and under what terms. If the customer starts to fall behind in his repayments what actions should the financial institution take? Techniques that help with such decisions are called credit and behavioral scoring models [1]. The information that is available in making a credit scoring decision includes both of the applicant's application form details and the information held by a credit reference agency on the applicant. Credit scoring models analyze the applicant's information and classify him into either applicant with good credit or applicant with bad credit. Applicant with good credit has great possibility to repay financial obligation, while, applicant with bad credit has high possibility of failing. The accuracy of credit scoring model is critical for financial institution's profitability. A one percent improvement on the accuracy of credit scoring of applicants may protect the financial institution from a great loss. Parametric statistical methods particularly Linear Discriminate Analysis (LDA) and Logistic Regression (LR) have been utilized in developing credit scoring models [2-6]. The weakness of the LDA and LR is due to the assumption of linear relationship between response and predictor variables, which is usually nonlinear and the sensitivity to the deviation from the multivariate normality assumption. Recently, artificial intelligence (AI) and data mining approaches have been utilized in developing credit scoring models, and numerous studies revealed that AI based models outperform the classical statistical models. Neutral networks is one of the AI techniques that have been applied to credit scoring due to their ability to model both of linear and non-linear functions [8-16]. However, ANNs are often criticized as being a ''black box'', computationally expensive and may suffer over fitting problem. Support vector machines SVMs, firstly developed by Cortes and Vapnik (1995) ,is another modern classification

Corresponding author: abeer.hamdy@bue.edu.eg

technique applied to credit scoring [17- 23]. SVMs do not suffer from over fitting problem like ANN and consequently can generalize well. However they are still computationally expensive. Genetic algorithms was also tried in the field of credit scoring [24].
According to the literature review, it is easy to find that almost all classification methods can be used for credit risk assessment and they demonstrate comparable performance. However, some hybrid AI techniques, which integrate two or more single classification methods or cluster and classification methods have shown higher predictability than individual methods. Recent examples are neural discriminate technique [25], Neurofuzzy [26,27], neural network ensemble [28,29], evolving neural network [30], fuzzy SVM , that integrates the theory of fuzzy sets with SVM [31] and with LSSVM [32] classifiers to increase their sensitivity to outliers and generalization capabilities. Harris [33] utilized clustered SVM (CSVM) in order to reduce the computational complexity required to train the non linear SVM using large datasets.

As AI techniques are computationally expensive relative to traditional statistical methods like LDA and LR, especially when it comes to classifying massive data sets like the ones used in developing credit scoring systems, it is known that many financial institutions and banks have millions of customers and they hold the information of their credit history and application forms.. The contribution of the paper is proposing a hybrid model to discriminate good from bad customers in customer credit evaluation. The model consists of an ANN classifier fed by attributes determined by a feature extraction technique called principal component analysis PCA. The hybrid technique accomplishes the following:

1. A credit scoring system that outperforms previous systems in terms of accuracy.
2. Reduction in the computational complexity of the ANN by reducing the dimension of the feature space using PCA.
3. Parametric study to the impact of the number of Principal components (PCs) on the model accuracy and training time
4. An analysis to the significance of each of the credit scoring attributes commonly used in building credit scoring models.

We compared our achievements to Harris [33] for the following reasons: 1. He utilized the open source data set we utilized in this paper, 2. His motivation is same as ours (improve predictive accuracy and reduce training time) and 3. He trained several other classifiers and outlined their performance.

The remainder of the paper is organized as follows: Section 2 presents the model, dataset and the performance criteria. Section 3 discusses our findings. Section 4 concludes the paper and outlines possible directions for future research.

2 Background

2.1 Artificial neural networks

Artificial neural network (ANN) is an information processing paradigm that is inspired by human brain nerve cells, their communication and techniques in processing information. ANN is composed of a large number of highly interconnected processing elements (neurons) working together to solve specific problem. ANN, like people, learn by examples; they generalize from previous experiences to new ones, and can make decisions [34]. The most common type of ANN consists of three layers of units: input layer, hidden layer, and output layer. It is called multilayer perceptron (MLP). A layer of ''input'' units is connected to a layer of ''hidden'' units, which is connected to a layer of ''output'' units. The input nodes represent the raw information that is fed into the network. The input of each hidden node is determined by the outputs of the input units and the weights on the connections between the input and the hidden units. The output layer consists of nodes that represent the system's classification decisions. The outputs of the output nodes are determined based on the outputs of the hidden layer and the weights between the hidden and output layers. Figure 1 shows an example of three-layer neural network including input, output, and one hidden layer. The weight adjustments process of the ANN is known as training the ANN. The training process consists of running input values over the network with predefined classification output nodes. The predicted outputs for each training sample are calculated, and compared to the corresponding target outputs. The weights are then adjusted so that the error rate will be reduced next time when the training samples are presented to the network. Thus, the training algorithm finds out the properties of the ANN that are most relevant to learning the classification model. Testing samples are used to verify the performance of the trained network.

2.2 Principal component analysis (PCA)

Due to the multivariate nature of the samples, the computational time of designing and operating a classifier is challenging. Therefore, a PCA is applied to the dataset to find the best low dimension space that conveys maximum useful information, and to define the underlying attributes that influence the samples.

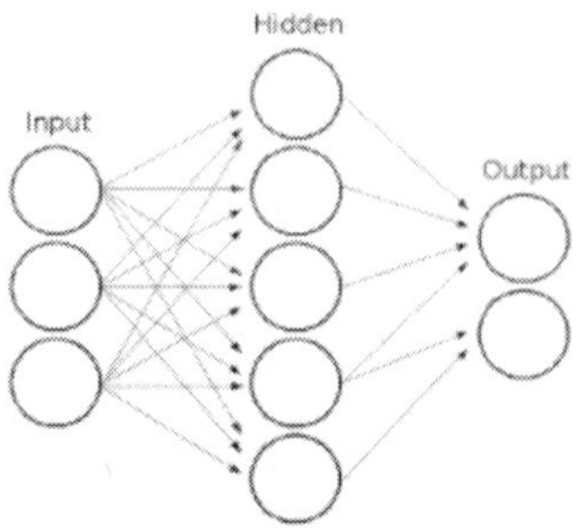

Figure 1. Three layers, two outputs an ANN architecture.

PCA is a mathematical procedure uses orthogonal decomposition and transformation to project a set of observations of possibly correlated attributes (i.e., high dimensional data) into a set of values of linearly uncorrelated attributes (i.e., low dimensional data) called principal components PCs. PCs are linear combinations of original attributes in which the weights allocated to the linear combinations of those original attributes are termed eigenvector. The number of PCs is less than the number of original attributes. The projection is performed in a least square sense, where the large (i.e. principal) variability in the data is captured, while the small variability is ignored. As a result, the first principal component (PC1) will be in the direction of maximum variance in the input space. The second principal component (PC2) is orthogonal to (PC1) and coincides the direction of the second maximum variance. Subsequent principal components are found according to the remaining maximum variance down to the last PC (i.e., PC24) which is the one represents the lowest variance of the data. PCA proved its effectiveness in various applications, for example [35-37] more and elaborated details about PCA algorithm are found in [38,39].

3 Methodology

3.1 Dataset

A German credit scoring dataset was taken from the UCI Machine Learning Repository. This dataset consists of 700 examples of creditworthy applicants and 300 examples of customers who should not have been granted credit. In addition, it presents twenty (20) categorical attributes for each credit applicant, which are:

- The status of the client's existing checking account,
- The duration of the credit period in months,
- The client's credit history,
- The purpose for the credit,
- The credit amount requested,
- The client's savings account/bonds balance,
- The client's present employment status,
- The client's personal (marital) status and sex,
- Whether the client is a debtor or guarantor of credit granted by another institution,
- The number of years spent at present residence,
- The type of property possessed by client,
- The client's age in years,
- Whether the client has other installment plans,
- The client's housing arrangements (i.e. own their home, rent, or live for free)
- The number of existing credits the client has at the bank,
- The client's job,
- The number of people for whom the client is liable to provide maintenance for,
- Whether the client has a telephone,
- Whether the client is a foreign worker.

3.2 Experimental Approach

Two types of models were trained for credit scoring. The first one of them is an ANN fed with the 24 attributes German data. The second type is a hybrid model consists of a PCA and ANN classifier. PCA is fed with the 24 attributes German dataset while ANN is fed with a set of PCs as shown in figure 2.

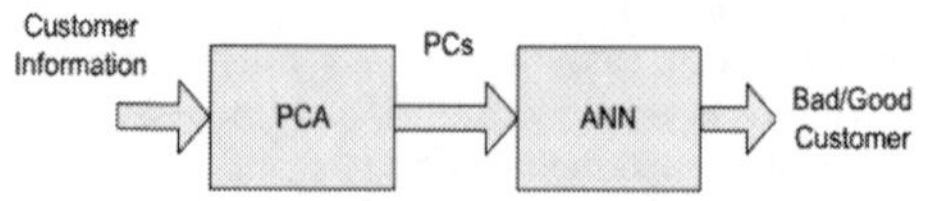

Figure 2. PCA-ANN model for credit scoring

For each attribute in the German dataset, the enclosed values were normalized in the range [-1,1] to prevent the ANN from being dominated by the input attributes with large values (in case of using ANN only). If the attributes will be fed to PCA, normalization guarantees that PCs will be independent as PCA is sensitive to the relative scaling of the original attributes. Normalization is carried out by removing the feature's average and then dividing by its standard deviation using equation 1.

$$x' = \frac{x - \text{mean}}{\text{standard deviation}} \quad (1)$$

Where x and x′ are the old and new value of each feature in the data set respectively.

Afterwards, the data were divided into 65% for training the model, 15% for validation, and 20% for testing the performance of the trained model.

3.3 Performance Metrics

A number of performance metrics could be used to report the performance of the credit scoring classifiers including predictive accuracy, confusion matrix and AUC metrics.

3.3.1 Predictive accuracy

Predictive accuracy metric measures how accurately the model classifies credit applicants on the dataset and is defined by equation 2.

$$\text{Predective accuracy} = \frac{TP + TN}{P + N} \quad (2)$$

Where,

TP: true positive (the number of correct predictions that a customer is good);

TN: true negative (the number of correct predictions that a customer is bad);

P, N : are the number of positive and negative samples respectively.

Predictive accuracy is not a reliable metric for the real performance of the classifiers specially, in case of imbalanced data sets (this is the case of credit scoring data).

3.3.2 Confusion matrix

Confusion matrix is one of the methods that provides more detailed analysis than the accuracy metric to the results of the classifiers. Confusion matrix is explained in figure 3. Where, FP: false positive (the number of bad customers who are predicted as good customers); and FN: false negative (the number of good customers who are predicted as bad customers)

3.3.3 AUC

AUC, the Area under the Receiver Operating Characteristic (ROC) curve, metric has emerged as one of the most promising and widely accepted evaluation metric for binary classifiers in general and in the field of credit scoring [21]. AUC was first used by the American army after the attack on Pearl Harbour, to detect Japanese aircraft from radar signals. Its main advantages over other metrics is it's insensitivity to unbalanced datasets. ROC curve is a two dimensional measure of classification performance where the sensitivity (the fraction of actual positives predicted as positive), as in equation 3 and the specificity (the fraction of actual negatives predicted as negative), as in equation 4 are plotted on the Y and X axis, respectively. The AUC measure is calculated as in equation 5, where, S1, represents the sum of the ranks of the creditworthy clients. Here, a score of 100% indicates that the classifier is able to perfectly discriminate between the classes, and a score of 50% indicates a classifier of insignificant discriminatory quality.

$$\text{Sensitivity} = \frac{TP}{TP + FP} \quad (3)$$

$$\text{Specifity} = \frac{TN}{FP + TN} \quad (4)$$

$$AUC = \frac{S1 - \text{Sensitivity} * (\text{Sensetivity} + 1) * .5}{\text{Sensitivity} * \text{Specificity}} \quad (5)$$

Predicted Classification		Actual classification: Positive (Good Customers)	Actual classification: Negative (Bad Customers)
	Positive (Good Customers)	True Positive (TP)	False Positive (FP)
	Negative (Bad Customers)	False Negative (FN)	True Negative (TN)

Figure 3. Confusion matrix.

4 Results and Discussions

4.1 ANN model

The neural network was designed of three layers, input, hidden, and output layers with 24 neurons in the input layer for the 24 input credit scoring attributes. Fifteen neurons in the hidden layer with

 DOI: 10.1051/matecconf/20167602039

Tansig activation function (equation 6) and one neuron in the output layer with linear transfer function to linearly scale the output values to the interval [0,1].

$$a = \frac{2}{1+e^{-2n}} - 1 \qquad (6)$$

Where, n and a are the input and output of each neuron in the hidden layer; respectively.

The training algorithm is the back propagation algorithm [41]. Iterations were performed on the weights and bias of each neuron in the network until the mean squared error for the validation samples dropped to the possible minimum value. Figure 4 shows that the minimum mean square error was 0.14 at epoch number 2. At other epochs either the mean square error is high (epochs number1 and 2). At epochs 4 and more, the mean square error of the model on the training data is decreased while it increases on the validation data which means that the generated models suffer over fitting problem. The performance of the best model (at epoch 2) was evaluated against the testing dataset. Figures 5 and table 6 show the ROC curve of the resulting classifier and its confusion matrix. It could be observed that the ROC curve of the trained classifier is above the diagonal line (line of no discrimination or random classifier) which implies that the ANN classifier can produce a good classification results.

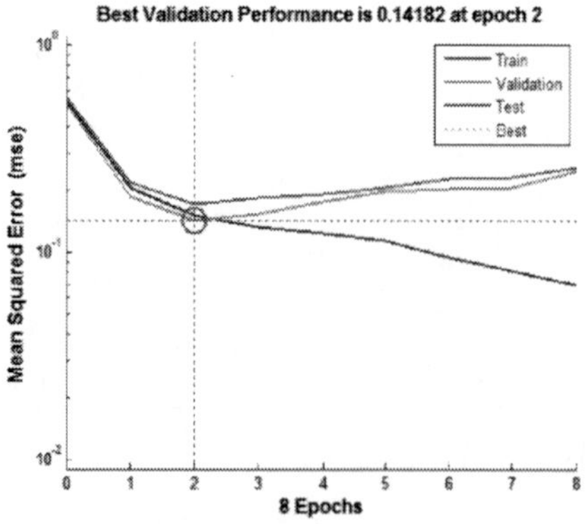

Figure 4. MSE of the trained ANN models at different epochs on each of the training, validation and testing datasets.

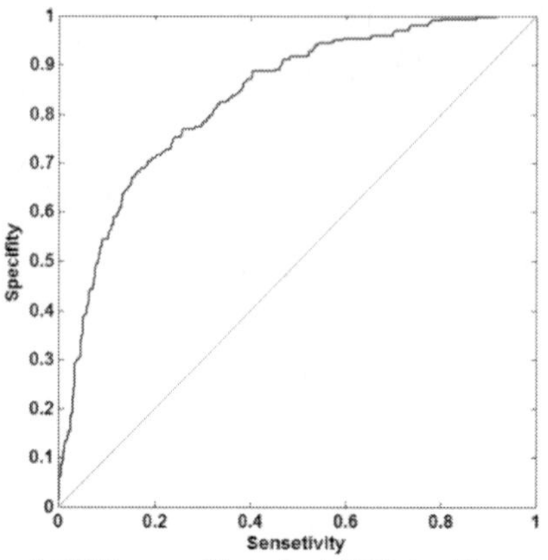

Figure 5. ROC curve of the trained ANN classifier

Table 1. Confusion matrix of the trained ANN classifier

		Actual classification	
		Positive (Good Customers)	**Negative (Bad Customers)**
Predicted Classification	**Positive (Good Customers)**	622 62.2%	104 10.4%
	Negative (Bad Customers)	78 7.8%	196 19.6%

4.2 PCA-ANN models

PCA was applied on the normalized data set. Figure 6 shows the significance of the resulting PCs with respect to data variation. The Y axis represents the normalized weight of each PC. It was found that the highest weight is equal to 861.75 and the lowest weight is equal to 0.015. It could be observed that the first three PCS account for as much of the variability in the data; their cumulative weights is equal to 1073.512.

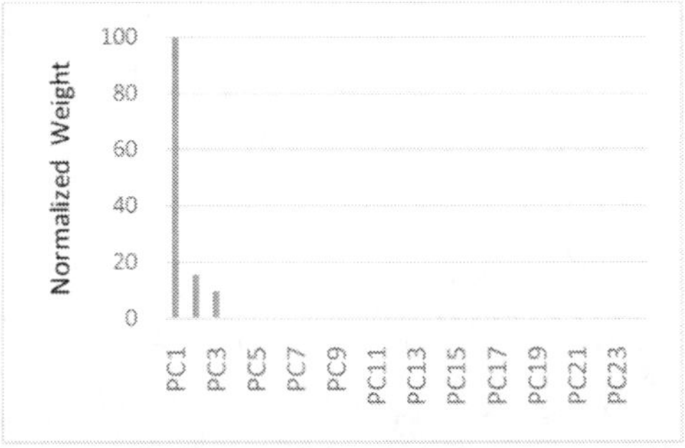

Figure 6. Significance of the principal components with respect to the data variation

Five PCA-ANN models were trained. The models differ from each other in the number of PCs that were fed to a three layer ANN. The structures of the five trained PCA-ANN models are listed in table 2. Figure 7 shows the AUC metric values for each of the ANN model and the five PCA-ANN models. It is clearly observed that the best model based on the AUC metric is the ANN model (AUC = .856). While the worst performance model is PCA-ANN#5 which uses 3 PCs only and results in AUC value equal to .625. PCA-ANN#4 which uses 6 PCS improves the performance dramatically (AUC = 0 .779), the more PCs included the closer the performance to the ANN model. Figure 8 shows the ROC curves of the models PCA-ANN#4 and PCA-ANN#5 and it is obvious the less the number of PCs included the closer the ROC curve to the diagonal which indicated less capability on diffrentitaing between good and bad clients.

Table 2. Description of PCA-ANN models.

Model	PCs number (Input neurons)	Hidden neurons
PCA-ANN #1	20	15
PCA-ANN# 2	10	5
PCA-ANN# 3	8	5
PCA-ANN# 4	6	2
PCA-ANN #5	3	2

Figure 9. Shows the training time (in seconds) of each model, as observed PCA-ANN#5 model is the most expensive model computationally as ANN was not able to generalize quickly with the few number of input features. However, all PCA-ANN models generalize faster than ANN only and the more PCs included the more training time required.

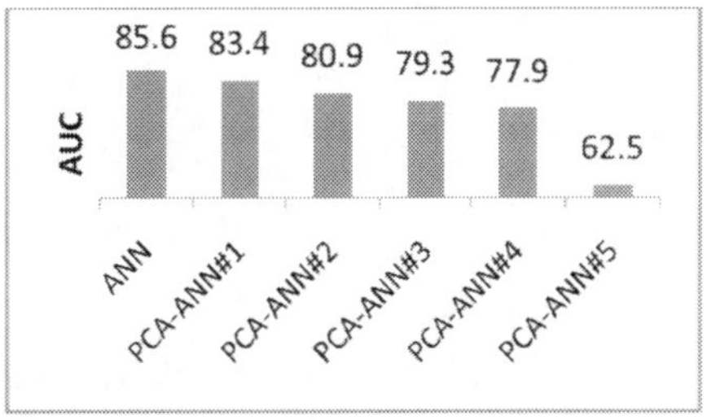

Figure 7. AUC metric values of the 6 trained models

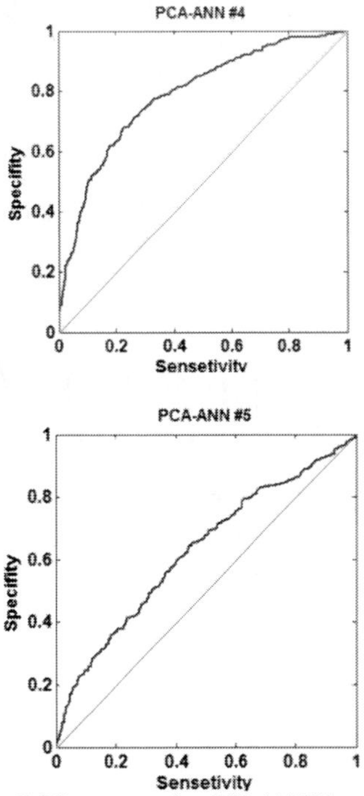

Figure 8. ROC curves for PCA-ANN#4 and PCA-ANN#5.

Figure 10 shows a comparison ,based on AUC, among the performance of our 6 trained models and 8 models of Harris [33]. The models of Harris are: logistic regression (LR), K-means plus logistic regression (K-means + LR), clustered support vector machine with a RBF kernel (CSVM-RBF), K-means plus support vector machine with a RBF kernel (K-means + SVM-RBF), support vector machine with a RBF kernel (SVM-RBF), linear clustered support vector machine (CSVM-linear), K-means plus support vector machine with a linear kernel (K-means + SVM-linear), and a linear support vector machine (SVMlinear). As observed all our models, except the model PCA-AN #5, outperform Harris models. We could not compare the training time of our models to models in Harris [33] due to the difference between our platform and his.

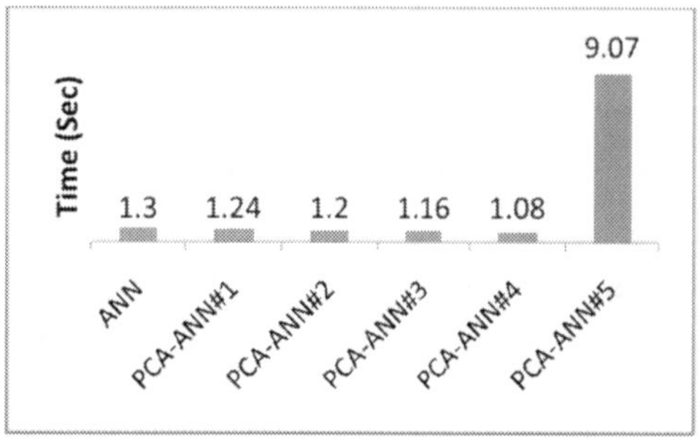

Figure 9. Training time (seconds) of the proposed models

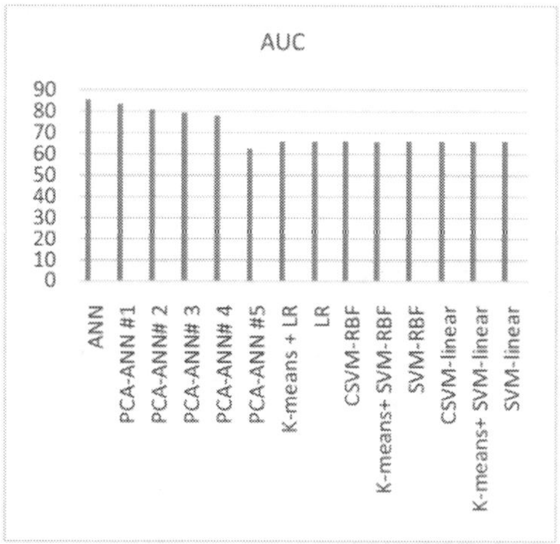

Figure 10. Performance of our trained credit scoring models compared to performance (in terms of AUC) of models provided in Haris [33].

4.3. Credit scoring attributes analysis

Although data mining techniques are useful in analyzing the credit worthiness, the selection of the best set of independent attributes to be included in the model building is essential to improve the performance of the model, speed up the learning process and save the storage space especially with the large amount of data. Same as PCA is a technique that can find a smaller size attribute space that represents a set of observations; it can also be helpful in analyzing an existing attribute space and determine the significance of each of these attributes. This significance is determined based on the dominant attributes in the dominant PCs, which are responsible for the most variability in the dataset. Figure 11 shows the significance, weights, of the different attributes in each of PC1, PC2 and PC3. It is obvious that some attributes contribute minimally to PC1, PC2 and PC3; consequently, their contribution to the credit-scoring model is minimal too and could be ignored.

It is noteworthy that when a NNET was trained using the attribute space of the German dataset (without pre-PCA), it gave a weight to each input attribute without any consideration to the actual impact of each attribute (as shown in figure 12), and this is in general a drawback of any ANN based model, where it develops a models that maps any nature of inputs to any nature of outputs. But with PCA analysis, significance of each input attribute is taken into consideration to develop a realistic model.

5 Conclusion

Credit scoring model is a mean to measure the risk related to a potential customer, by analyzing his data to determine the probability of him paying his debits back to the financial institution. The paper discussed the development of a credit-scoring model based on PCA and ANN to achieve better performance than existing models and reduce the computational complexity of the ANN through using PCA analysis. . Numerous studies have proven that ANN perform remarkably better than any other statistical approach, such as logistic regression or discriminant analysis however they are computationally expensive. So a PCA The proposed model showed its ability to generalize well to the credit-scoring problem and its performance, in terms of AUC, outweighed many other previous models. Preceding ANN with PCA reduces the number of inputs to the ANN and reduces its training time. Moreover, PCA provides a mean for analyzing the importance of each attribute to the model which helps in reducing the input space size and save storage.

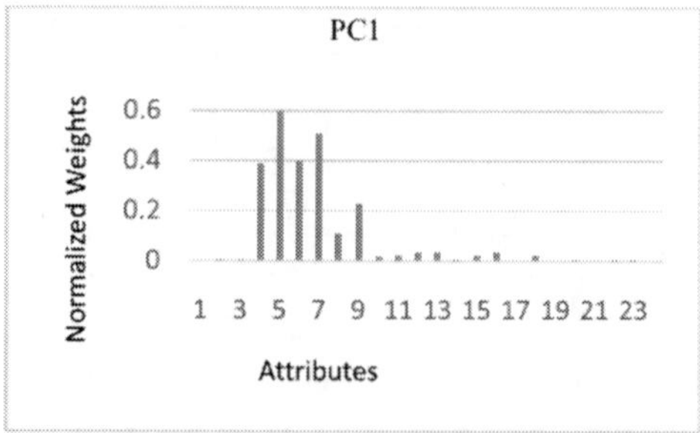

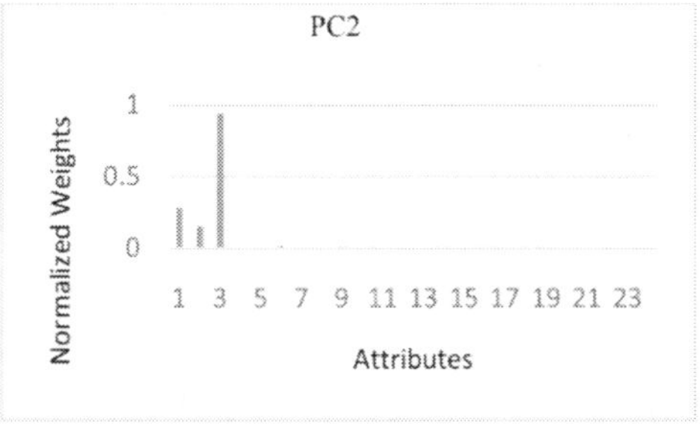

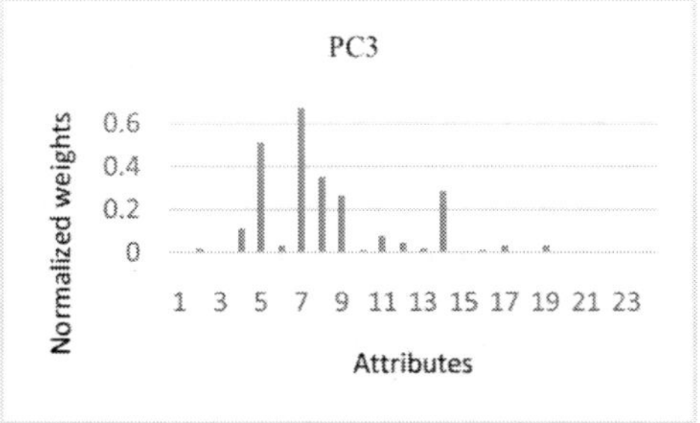

Figure 11. Relative significance of each German dataset attribute in the calculation of PC1 , PC2 and PC3.

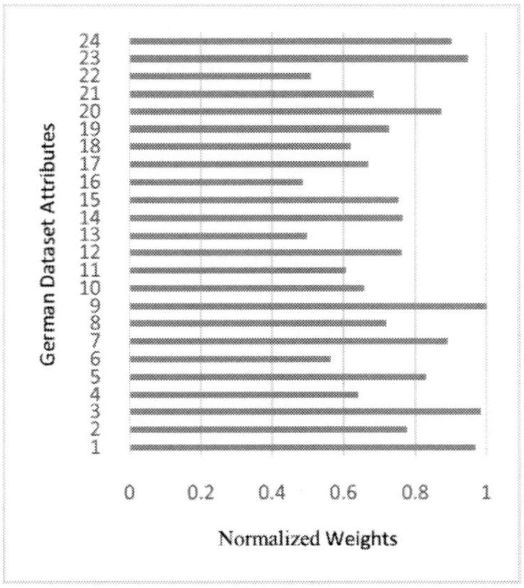

Figure 12. Normalized input weights of the trained ANN.

References

1. Lyn C. Thomas, A survey of credit and behavioral scoring: forecasting financial risk of lending to consumers,International Journal of Forcasting, vol. 16, issue2,pp.149-172,April-June 2000.
2. E. I. Altman, "Financial ratios, discriminant analysis and the prediction of corporate bankruptcy,"Journal of Finance, vol. 23, pp. 89–609, 1968
3. Kleimeier, S., & Dinh, T. A. (2007). Credit scoring model for Vietnam's retail banking market. International Review of Financial Analysis, 16(5), 471–495.
4. Rayo, S., Lara, J., & Camino, D. (2010). A credit scoring model for institutions of microfinance under the Basel II normative. Journal of Economics, Finance & Administrative Science, 15(28), 89–124.
5. Viganò, L. A. (1993). Credit scoring model for development banks: An African case study. Savings and Development, 17(4), 441–482.
6. Vogelgesang, U. (2003). Microfinance in times of crisis: The effects of competition, rising indebtness, and economic crisis on repayment behaviour. World Development, 31(12), 2085–2114.
7. Lee, T. S., & Chen, I. F. (2005). A two-stage hybrid credit scoring model using artificial neural networks and multivariate adaptive regression splines. Expert Systems with Applications, 28(4), 743–752.
8. Yu, L., Wang, S. A. and Lai, K. K. 2008. Credit risk assessment with a multistage neural network ensemble learning approach. Expert systems with applications. vol. 34. pp. 1434-1444.
9. Tsai, C.-f. and Wu, J.-w. 2008. Using neural network ensembles for bankruptcy prediction and credit scoring. Expert systems with applications. vol. 34. pp. 2639-2649.
10. Angelini, E., Tollo, G. D. and Roil, A. 2008. A neural network approach for credit risk evaluation. The quarterly review of economics and finance. vol. 48. pp. 733-755.
11. Antonio Blanco, Rafael Pino-Mejías, Juan Lara, Salvador Rayo, Credit scoring models for the microfinance industry using neural networks:Evidence from Peru, Expert Systems with Applications 40 (2013) 356–364
12. Zongyuan Zhao a, Shuxiang Xu a, Byeong Ho Kang b, Mir Md Jahangir Kabir a, Yunling Liu, Rainer Wasinger a Investigation and improvement of multi-layer perceptron neural networks for credit scoring, Expert Systems with Applications 42 (2015) 3508–3516
13. Z. Huang, H. Chen, C.-J. Hsu, W.-H. Chen, and S. Wu, "Credit rating analysis with support vector machines and neural networks: A Market Comparative Study," Decision Support Systems, vol. 37, no. 4, pp. 543–558, 2004.
14. K. K. Lai, L. Yu, S. Y. Wang, and L. G. Zhou, "Neural network meta-learning for credit scoring," inIntelligent Computing, vol. 4113 of Lecture Notes in Computer Science, pp. 403–408, 2006. View at Google Scholar
15. R. Malhotra and D. K. Malhotra, "Evaluating consumer loans using neural networks," Omega, vol. 31, no. 2, pp. 83–96, 2003. View at Publisher · View at Google Scholar · View at Scopus
16. Z. Huang, H. Chen, C.-J. Hsu, W.-H. Chen, and S. Wu, "Credit rating analysis with support vector machines

and neural networks: A Market Comparative Study," Decision Support Systems, vol. 37, no. 4, pp. 543–558, 2004.
17. K. K. Lai, L. Yu, L. G. Zhou, and S. Y. Wang, "Credit risk evaluation with least square support vector machine," in Rough Sets and Knowledge Technology, vol. 4062 of Lecture Notes in Artificial Intelligence, pp. 490–495, 2006.
18. K. K. Lai, L. Yu, W. Huang, and S. Y. Wang, "A novel support vector machine metamodel for business risk identification," in PRICAI 2006: Trends in Artificial Intelligence, vol. 4099 of Lecture Notes in Artificial Intelligence, pp. 480–484, 2006.
19. R. Malhotra and D. K. Malhotra, "Differentiating between good credits and bad credits using neuro-fuzzy systems," European Journal of Operational Research, vol. 136, no. 1, pp. 190–211, 2002.
20. L. Zhou, K. K. Lai, and L. Yu, "Least squares support vector machines ensemble models for credit scoring," Expert Systems with Applications, vol. 37, no. 1, pp. 127–133, 2010.
21. L. Zhou, K. K. Lai, and L. Yu, "Credit scoring using support vector machines with direct search for parameters selection," Soft Computing, vol. 13, no. 2, pp. 149–155, 2009.
22. L. Yu and X. Yao, "A total least squares proximal support vector classifier for credit risk evaluation," Soft Computing, vol. 17, no. 4, pp. 643–650, 2013.
23. L. Yu, X. Yao, S. Wang, and K. K. Lai, "Credit risk evaluation using a weighted least squares SVM classifier with design of experiment for parameter selection," Expert Systems with Applications, vol. 38, no. 12, pp. 15392–15399, 2011.
24. Vaclav Kozeny, Genetic algorithms for credit scoring: Alternative fitness function performance comparison" Expert Systems with Applications, vol. 42, pp. 2998-3004, 2015.
25. T.-S. Lee, C.-C. Chiu, C.-J. Lu, and I.-F. Chen, "Credit scoring using the hybrid neural discriminant technique," Expert Systems with Applications, vol. 23, no. 3, pp. 245–254, 2002.
26. Malhotra, R., & Malhotra, D. K. (2002). Differentiating between good credits and bad credits using neuro-fuzzy systems. European Journal of Operational Research, 136(1), 190–211
27. S. Piramuthu, "Financial credit-risk evaluation with neural and neurofuzzy systems," European Journal of Operational Research, vol. 112(2), pp. 310–321, 1999
28. K. K. Lai, L. Yu, S. Y. Wang, and L. G. Zhou, "Credit risk analysis using a reliability-based neural network ensemble model," in Proceedings of the International Conference on Artificial Neural Networks (ICANN '06), vol. 4132 of Lecture Notes in Computer Science, pp. 682–690, 2006.
29. L. Yu, S. Wang, and K. K. Lai, "Credit risk assessment with a multistage neural network ensemble learning approach," Expert Systems with Applications, vol. 34, no. 2, pp. 1434–1444, 2008.
30. R. Smalz and M. Conrad, "Combining evolution with credit apportionment: a new learning algorithm for neural nets," Neural Networks, vol. 7, no. 2, pp. 341–351, 1994.
31. Y. Wang, S. Wang, and K. K. Lai, "A new fuzzy support vector machine to evaluate credit risk," IEEE Transactions on Fuzzy Systems, vol. 13, no. 6, pp. 820–831, 2005.
32. Lean Yu, 2014, Credit Risk Evaluation with a Least Squares Fuzzy Support Vector Machines Classifier
33. Terry Harris , Credit scoring using the clustered support vector machine, Expert Systems with Applications, 2015.
34. S.Haykin, Neural Networks: A comprehensive foundation, Prentice Hall , 1998.
35. L. Yu, J.-h. Zhu, L.-j. Chen Parametric study on PCA-based algorithm for structural health Prognostics & System Health Management Conference, Macao (2010), pp. 1–6.
36. M.A. Rassam, A. Zainal, M.A. Maarof An adaptive and efficient dimension reduction model for multivariate wireless sensor networks applications Applied Soft Computing, 13 (2012), pp. 1978–1996
37. Jie Wang, Jun Wang, Forecasting stock market indexes using principal component analysis and stochastic time effective neural networks, *Neurocomputing, Volume 156, 25 May 2015, Pages 68-78*
38. Abdi. H., & Williams, L.J. (2010). "Principal component analysis.". *Wiley Interdisciplinary Reviews: Computational Statistics*, 2: 433–459.
39. T. Jolliffee, Principal Component Analysis , Springer Secaucus, NJ,USA,2002.
40. Hussein A. Abdou1,* and John Pointon , credit scoring, statistical techniques and evaluation criteria: a review of the literature
41. Rumelhart,D.E. G.E. Hinton, R.J. Williams Learning internal representation by error propagation Parallel Distrib. Process., 1 (1986), pp. 318–362

E-Government Applications for Integrated Access to Complex Data Resources Using Multi-Agent Systems

Roumen Trifonov [1] and Radoslav Yoshinov [2]

[1] *Department Computer Systems at Technical University – Sofia, 1000 Sofia, Bulgaria*
[2] *Telematics Laboratory at Bulgarian Academy of Sciences, 1000 Sofia, Bulgaria*

Abstract. Currently the main focus of e-Government in Bulgaria is aimed at the provision of electronic administrative services to citizens and businesses. The development aimed at streamlining and optimizing the work of administration and information support of processes of decision-making is still unregulated. They are not conducted any serious research. The paper points out one of the activities which according to the authors may fruitfully contribute to the development in this direction. It is about an integral approach to access to complex information resources (databases), supported by different systems, including in different countries. For realization of this approach the authors propose the application of multi-agent systems in an environment of semantic Web services.

1 Introduction

According to the latest strategy of the Bulgarian government: "E-governance is the transformation of state structures through the use of information and communication technologies, entirely geared towards consumers. It is done in parallel with organizational changes and the acquisition of new knowledge to improve public services and democratic processes and the creation and implementation of state policy."

Actually, the main aspect of e-Government in Bulgaria is focused to the provision of electronic administrative services to citizens and businesses. The development aimed at streamlining and optimizing the work of administration and information support of processes of decision-making is still unregulated. They are not conducted any serious research.

At the same time, the experience of some advanced countries [1] [2] shows that automation of the processes of decision-making in administrative structures has potential not less than the services in order to enhance the public effectiveness. By the way, while in executive agencies and municipal administration the services for citizens and businesses occupy a significant place, in the activities of the ministries these functions almost absent.

The observations of the authors in the process of collaboration with the administrative authorities (particularly at the central level) allow the conclusion that perhaps the most fruitful direction in the automation of the process of decisions making by administrative authorities would be the organization of effective integration of data from heterogeneous information sources, organized by various technologies and various target functions [3].

Proceeding from these circumstances, the present article attempts to indicate one of the possible directions for informational support of decision making in administration. On the base of international experience, the authors suppose that this may be a combination of two technologies. On the one hand, the application of so called Semantic Web technologies. On the other hand, as management tool for the environment of Semantic Web services the present article proposes to use system of autonomous intelligent agents.

2 The basis of the proposed approach

Intelligent agents and semantic web services are two technologies with great potential. Striking new applications can be developed by using the tools and techniques they provide. However, Semantic Web Services need for an upper software entity able to deal with them and, on the other hand agent technology has historically suffered from a number of drawbacks that must be addressed. Integrating these two technologies in a joint environment can overcome their problems while strengthening their advantages [4].

The Semantic Web aims at adding semantics to the data published on the Web, so that machines are able to process these data in a similar way a human can do. For this, ontologies are the backbone technology.

Traditionally, the Web has been conceived as a distributed source of information. The emergence of Web Service Technology has permitted to extend it to a distributed source of functionality. Web Services make applications available on the Web in a standard way so that they can be accessed regardless of the operating

[a] Corresponding author: r_trifonov@tu-sofia.bg

system they are deployed on and the programming language they are implemented in.

The joint application of Semantic Web and Web Services in order to create intelligent Web Services is referred to as Semantic Web Services. Semantic Web Services consist of describing Web Services with semantic content so that service discovery, composition and invocation can be done automatically by, for example, the use of intelligent agents able to process the semantic information provided. The W3Consortium is currently examining various approaches with the purpose of reaching a standard for the Semantic Web Services technology. The recently proposed W3C recommendation SAWSDL (Semantic Annotations for WSDL and XML Schema [5] identifies some WSDL and XML Schema extension attributes that support the semantic description of WSDL components.

The Intelligent Agent (IA) and Multi-Agent System (MAS) area has received ever-increasing attention by researchers over the last few years. This field emerged due to the promising benefits of having applications with a technology that allows systems to decide for themselves what they need to do in order to satisfy their design objectives. A common accepted definition of the term 'Agent' determines that an agent is a computer system situated in some environment and capable of autonomous action in this environment in order to meet its design objectives [6]. It is necessary to highlight that an agent has to fulfil some properties in order to become intelligent: reactivity (i.e. the ability to perceive its environment and respond to changes in it in a timely fashion), pro-activeness (i.e. the ability to exhibit goal-directed behaviour by taking the initiative), and social ability (i.e. the ability to interact with other agents).

During the process of transforming web services into agents or boxing them into agents, the web service description may be retrieved automatically by examining its description in WSDL (web service description language). Converted agent description can be extended with specific ontologies. Agents can be connected to web services by using a gateway agent which keeps two directories – one that serves the agent world and another that serves the web service world.

3 The functioning of the proposed approach

There is currently a great quantity of independent and heterogeneous data resources, accessible through the Internet, covering information, which can be useful for administration in order to decision making. Most of this information is stored in databases, although in the last years some ontologies have been developed to harmonise the terminology used in the different databases and to promote integrated access and interoperability among different information resources and applications.

The increasing number of independent and heterogeneous databases produced high inefficiency when the developers wanted to search for information across different databases. So, finding relevant information was rather difficult due to the terminological diversity. Given this situation, different entities that had developed their own databases often work together to define a common vocabulary for modelling how terms might be annotated.

Despite their ability to provide a high degree of interoperability across platforms and operating systems, Semantic Web Services infrastructures possess neither enough degree of autonomy nor ability to automatically adapt to changing situations. In these settings, agents can contribute to make systems more autonomous and dynamic, thus maximising their perceived utility. In line with this, the approach presented here comprises both Intelligent Agents and Semantic Web Services working cooperatively in the same environment. Ontologies act as the facilitating technology thus making it possible to exploit the advantages these technologies offer separately. This solution stems from a basic underlying hypothesis: Intelligent Agents and Semantic Web Services were conceived for quite different purposes, and so, they must lie on different abstraction layers. The main idea behind Agent Technology was not for Intelligent Agents to be able to provide services, but to act as autonomous entities that incorporate intelligence and cognitive capacities, which allow them to show a goal-oriented pro-active behaviour and to establish, either competitive or cooperative, interaction processes with other software entities in order to satisfy their design objectives. On the other hand, Web Services involved a further evolution in the distributed computing field and their only purpose is to provide accessible functionality.

These conceptual differences between Agent Technology and Semantic Web Services Technologies lead to the need to have both technologies working in an integrated environment and glimpse the advantages of their combination in the development of complex systems. Ontologies [7] are the paramount technology in the presented approach as they operate as the 'glue' that binds the remaining components of the architecture.

The ontologies function as universal vocabularies so that Web Services and agents share the same interpretation of the terms contained in the messages that they exchange. From the Web Services point of view, ontologies are useful to semantically describe Web Services' capabilities and processes.

This semantic description can then be automatically processed by software entities, so that Web Service discovery, composition, selection, execution and monitoring can be done without human intervention. On the other hand, from the perspective of the agents, the local domain-related knowledge of each agent may be extracted from, or built upon, the application domain ontology. Moreover, inter-agent communication may be carried out by means of a common vocabulary based on an agreed ontology.

The negotiation processes between agents may take place in accordance with protocols represented in an ontology and by using the related strategies also stored in an ontology.

The practical implementation of the proposed approach has as main objective to develop an agent-based knowledge manipulation framework. One of possible architectures of this framework can consist of following modules (Fig. 1):

- ontology design component with user friendly interface;
- agent-based Web Service search module;
- knowledge Database (KDB);
- Semantic Web Service composition module;
- user interface for displaying the results.

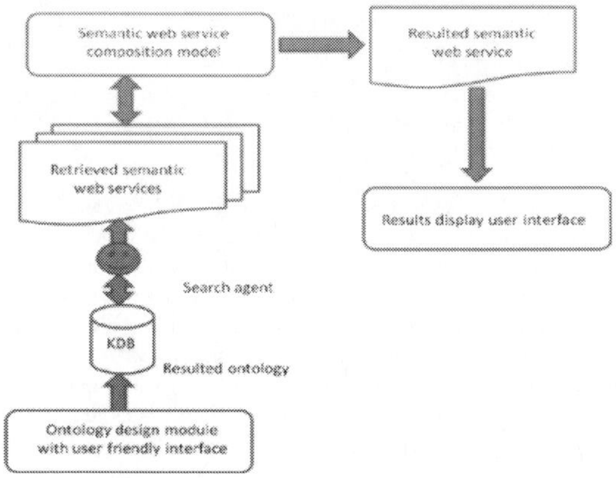

Figure 1. Architecture of agent-based knowledge manipulation framework

In order for intelligent agents to successfully carry out their assigned tasks, those ones must have access to various data repositories containing the knowledge that is necessary to fulfil the assignment. These repositories can be either local or external to the system. As data repositories, four kinds of ontologies have been included within the platform:

1. Application and domain ontology - the application ontology contains the knowledge entities (i.e. concepts, attributes, relationships, and axioms) that model the application in which the framework is to be employed. On the other hand, the domain ontology, represents a conceptualisation of the specific domain the framework is going to be applied in. This ontology supports the communication among the components in the framework without misinterpretations.

2. Agent local knowledge ontology - it contains, for each agent, the knowledge about the environment it possesses. This ontology generally includes knowledge about the assigned tasks, as well as the mechanisms and resources available to achieve those tasks.

3. Negotiation ontology - it comprises both negotiation protocols and negotiation strategies that constitute the negotiation mechanisms agents must use to coordinate their interactions. With this ontology, agents can choose the best mechanism to use for coordinating their actions, which highly depends on the problem under question and the application domain.

4. Semantic Web Services ontologies - in this repository (that can be comprised of various ontologies distributed all over the Internet) the ontologies that contain the semantic description of Web Services are stored. The framework does not impose any restriction in terms of the kind of Semantic Web Services specification to be used.

4 Conclusions

The objective of the present paper is to contribute for overcoming the unilaterally understanding of e-Government, limited to electronic administrative services for citizens and business.

It should be borne in mind that there is a fundamental difference in the computing processes that underlie these activities. While the provision of services can be attributed to a category "Real Time Information Processing" and there are a pre-domination of formalized procedures, structured information and mode kindred to real-time; the decision-making process belongs to the category "Knowledge Management". There are a pre-domination of analytical and synthetic procedures, unstructured information, non-formalized data and non-regulated time periods for solutions generation.

As about the semantic interoperability of processes, the service delivery uses deterministic processes based on registers, performing the role of "data clearinghouse" and semantic filters, the role of which is performed by UEEDE. In the case of decisions making the semantic interoperability is based on a stochastic approach.

This determines differences in the instruments for implementation of these two types of activities.

References

1. The Role of Business Intelligence in Government: A Case Study of Swedish Municipality Contact Centers, Trollhattan (March 2010)
2. e-Government Intelligence "Ca' Foscari" University of Venice (2010)
3. United Nations E-Government Survey 2014 E-Government for the Future We Want, New York, (2014), 264 p., ISBN: 978-92-1-123198-4
4. Shalini.L, Femila Goldy.R Efficient Discovery of Semantic Web Services, International Journal of Innovative Research in Science, Engineering and Technology Volume 3, Special Issue 3, (March 2014) ; ISSN: 2319 - 8753
5. Semantic Annotations for WSDL and XML Schema W3C Recommendation (28 August 2007)
6. Agent Technology: Enabling Next Generation Computing A Roadmap for Agent Based Computing AgentLink (2003)
7. Web Service Modeling Ontology (WSMO) W3C Member Submission (3 June 2005)

Exploring the Consistent behavior of Information Services

Sarantos Kapidakis[1a]

[1]*Laboratory on Digital Libraries and Electronic Publishing, Department of Archive, Library and Museum Sciences, Faculty of Information Science and Informatics, Ionian University, 72 Ioannou Theotoki Str., Corfu 49100, Greece*

Abstract. Computer services are normally assumed to work well all the time. This usually happens for crucial services like bank electronic services, but not necessarily so for others, that there is no commercial interest in their operation. In this work we examined the operation and the errors of information services and tried to find clues that will help predicting the consistency of the behavior and the quality of the harvesting, which is harder because of the transient conditions and the many services and the huge amount of harvested information. We found many unexpected situations. The services that always successfully satisfy a request may in fact return part of it. A significant part of the OAI services have ceased working while many other serves occasionally fail to respond. Some services fail in the same way each time, and we pronounce them dead, as we do not see a way to overcome that. Others also always, or sometimes fail, but not in the same way, and we hope that their behavior is affected by temporary factors, that may improve later on. We categorized the services into classes, to study their behavior in more detail.

1 Introduction and Related work

The computer services do not always have the right behavior. The users may notice delays or unavailability – but they have no idea how often these happen, and assume that each problem is rare and temporary.

The users usually have higher operation expectations from the commercial services than from the free services. Therefore, the non commercial service providers do not have the same motivation, and even no resources, to ensure reliable and fast operation.

The big diversity of computer services, their different requirements, designs and interfaces and also network problems and user-side malfunctions, make it hard to know when a service behavior is normal or not and what to measure in each case.

To overcome some of these restrictions, we examined the behavior of a large number of similar services of a specific type: data providers using the Open Archives Initiative Protocol for Metadata Harvesting (OAI-PMH).

Metadata harvesting is used very often, to incorporate the resources of small or big providers to large collections. The metadata harvesters, like Science Digital Library and Europeana, accumulate metadata from many collections (or sources) through the appropriate services, belonging to metadata providers mostly memory institutions, by automatically contacting their services and storing the retrieved metadata locally. Their goal is to enable searching on the huge quantity of heterogeneous content, using only their locally store content. Metadata harvesting is very common nowadays and is based on the Open Archives Initiative Protocol for Metadata Harvesting. As examples, we mention the Directory of Open Access Repositories (OpenDOAR) that provides an authoritative directory of academic open access repositories[a], and the OAIster[b] database of OCLC with millions of digital resources from thousands of providers.

The reliability of the services is important for ensuring current information. If the metadata harvesting service is not responding, the corresponding metadata records will not be updated at that time. If the reason is temporary, this may not be a very serious deficiency, as the updates will eventually be performed on the next successful metadata exchange, and will be normally used afterwards. Nevertheless, the unreliability - downtime of the metadata harvesting services usually indicate a proportional unreliability or downtime of the resource providing service, which always resides on the local sites, where both the local and the harvested metadata link to. When the resources are not available, the corresponding user requests are not satisfied, affecting the quality of the service.

In [7] Lagoze et al. discuss the NSDL development and explains why OAI-PMH based systems are not relatively easy to automate and administer with low people cost, as one would expect from the simplicity of

[a] Corresponding Author : sarantos@ionio.gr

[a] http://www.opendoar.org
[b] http://www.oclc.org/oaister.en.html

the technology. It is interesting to investigate the deciciencies of the procedure.

National or large established institutions consistently try to offer their metadata and data reliably and current and to keep the quality of their services as high as possible, but local and smaller institutions often do not have the necessary resources for consistent quality services – sometimes not even for creating metadata, or for digitizing their objects. In small institutions, the reliability and quality issues are more prominent, and decisions often should also take the quality of the services under consideration.

The behavior and the reliability of a service, as well as the quality of its content, is important to the outcome and the satisfaction from the service. The evaluation and quality of metadata is examined as one dimension of the digital library evaluation frameworks and systems in the related literature, like [2], [8] and [11]. Fuhr et al. in [2] propose a quality framework for digital libraries that deal with quality parameters. The service reliability falls under their System quality component, and the metadata update under their Content quality component.

In [9] Ward describes how the Dublin Core is used by 100 Data Providers registered with the Open Archives Initiative and shows that is not used to its fullest extent. In [4] Kapidakis presents quality metrics and quality measurement tool, and applied them to compare the quality in Europeana and other collections, that are using the OAI-PMH protocol to aggregate metadata. In [5] Kapidakis further studies the responsiveness of the same OAI services, and the evolution of the metadata quality over 3 harvesting rounds between 2011 and 2013.

From the different aspects of the quality of digital library services, the quality of the metadata has been mostly studied. Some approaches are applied on OAI-PMH aggregated metadata: Bui and Park in [1] provide quality assessments for the National Science Digital Library metadata repository, studying the uneven distribution of the one million records and the number of occurrences of each Dublin Core element in these. Another approach to metadata quality evaluation is applied to the open language archives community (OLAC) in [3] by Hughes that is using many OLAC controlled vocabularies. Ochoa and Duval in [9] perform automatic evaluation of metadata quality in digital repositories for the ARIADNE project, using humans to review the quality metric for the metadata that was based on textual information content metric values.

In [6] Kapidakis examines how solid is the metadata harvesting procedure, making 17 harvesting rounds, over three years, from 2014 to 2016, and exploiting the results to conclude on the quality of their metadata as well as on their availability, and how it evolves over these harvesting rounds. The list of working services was decreasing every month almost constantly, and less than half of the initial services continued working.

Nevertheless, the services did not have a solid behavior, which make any assumption and conclusion harder to reach. In this work we explore the behavior of the information services over a small period of time, so that no permanent changes to their behavior are expected and we are able to study their consistency without considering their evolution.

The rest of the paper is organized as follows: In section 2 we describe our methodology and the data we collected for that purpose. In section 3 we analyze the data to find patterns of behavior. In section 5 we classify the services into classes according to their behavior over consecutive observations, in many harvesting rounds, and study each class for further behavior details. We conclude on section 5.

2 Methodology and Collected Data

It is difficult to understand, analyze or predict the behavior of network services, because it depends on many factors, many of which may be external to the service and unknown. Nevertheless, there may be some significant factors of the service configuration or maintenance, or their environment (including the accessing network) that can be considered.

To reveal common behavior patterns, we used several harvesting rounds, where on each one we asked each of the 2121 OAI-PMH sources listed in the official OAI Registered Data Providers[c] on January of 2014 for a similar task: to provide 1000 (valid) metadata records. Such tasks are common for the OAI-PMH services, which periodically satisfy harvesting requests for the new or updated records, and involve the exchange of many requests and responses, starting from the a negotiation phase for the supported features of the two sides.

Our sequential execution of all these record harvesting tasks from the corresponding services, usually takes more then 24 hours to complete, and sometimes some tasks time out (we set a timeout deadline to 1 hour for each task, and interrupted any incomplete task just afterwards, so that it will not last forever) resulting to abnormal termination of the task.

Ideally, a task will complete normally, returning all requested metadata records – 1000, or all records if fewer (even zero) are only available on that service. Other behaviors are also possible - and of interest when studying the behavior of each service. A task may return an error, declaring that the final task goal cannot be satisfied. We also consider as error the situation of the abnormal termination of a timed out task, as it is not clear if any useful part of the requested goal was completed, and if the communication sides have the same view about it. If, because of an erroneous situation, both communication sides do not agree on the harvested records, the have to be re harvested in the future, and are not useful in the meanwhile.

Finally, it is also possible to have a situation that the service actually returns less records than the ones available and requested, but reports that the task completes normally. Nevertheless, we classify this behavior with the successful ones, because both sides acknowledge the harvesting of these records, and on periodic normal harvesting – while the remaining of the records will eventually also be harvested, even on a later effort. This situation looks also similar to the expected

[c] https://www.openarchives.org/Register/BrowseSites

behavior of returning all available records, when they are fewer than the requested ones, and the two can only be distinguished when examining other responses of the same service.

We repeat a new harvesting round with all the task to the services in constant intervals, asking the exact same services every three days for a period of two months. We selected this interval so that we do not overload the services and also leave enough time for the services to correct temporary problems – especially if they need human attention.

Below, the behavior of the participating services is examined collectively, to better understand the possible outcomes, and their likelihood.

3 Collective Behavior of the Services

On our 44541 tasks on all 21 harvesting rounds, 21478 tasks (48%) completed declaring a success, with average response time 60.5 seconds, although only 20409 (95%) of them returned records. For tasks that returned records, the minimum response time was less than a second and the maximum was 3175 seconds, in a case that the information service returned only 200 of the 1000 records, while there were more records (as they were returned on all other requests). Because of the short interval between our harvesting records, in most cases neither the service software nor the records in each service were modified between rounds. We still consider responses with fewer than the requested records as successful, because the remaining of the requested records can be returned on a successive request, in the common OAI-PMH configuration.

We study the successful responses for each harvesting round, to detect if some of the rounds had much higher or lower success rates: the successful responses on each of the 21 rounds range from 977 to 1040, with an average of 1022.8 and standard deviation 15.8. The similar results from all rounds indicate that there was no special conditions (possibly on our network) that will affect the outcome of our tasks and contaminate our analysis. Otherwise, we should have excluded them.

We study the distribution of the number of records returned by each service for common values, other than the requested records, 1000. Figure 1 presents the distribution of the number of records returned by each of the 1079 services that responded successfully on any of the 21 rounds. 324 of the services were successful only on some rounds, and 125 of them were successful on all rounds, but did not provide the same number of records on each round. In these cases, the maximum number of records returned was considered. The remaining 630 services always returned the same number records. The more rounds a service responded successfully – especially when their maximum is repeated in many rounds, the safer it is to assume that we have found the number of records that should be returned on each task.

Only 633 of the 1079 services returned 1000 records, and may actually have more records. On the other hand, 61 services always returned 0 records, and considered it as a successful task. It is not clear if all their records are deleted, or there is an incompatibility on accessing the service that is not detected properly. The remaining 385 services returned from 2 to 994 records (217 of them consistently in all 21 rounds – the others occasionally returned less) and with no obvious pattern: as can be seen in Figure 1, 203 services had a unique number of records, 55 pairs of services shared the number of returned records, etc, and, on the maximum, 6 services returned the same number of records (34). The number of returned records seems to vary unpredictably.

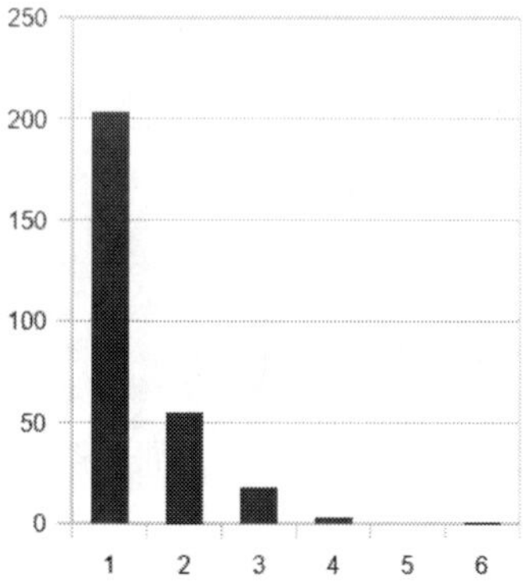

Figure 1. The distribution of the number of records returned by a service and its frequency for the 385 services.

The other 23063 times the service ended with an error: in 22073 (96%) of these tasks, no records were retrieved at all, while the remaining 990 times some records (57 distinct numbers ranging from 20 to 1000, with an average around 400 – in most cases it was a round number though) were indeed returned. Among these cases, in 62 the service did not terminate but timed out after an hour of trying, and out of them in 45 cases, no records were retrieved at all, while the remaining 17 times some records (ranging 20 to 1000) were indeed returned. The records that were returned when the service ended with an error were ignored in our study.

As each task consists of many actions, its outcome may not be trivially classified as full success or failure, but may be something in between, with contradicting indicators, like when retrieving records and getting an error status, or when retrieving no records and getting a success status, resulting to partial success or failure. Therefore, the success and the failure of a task has to be clearly defined, so that it can be used later on. In this work, we decided to adopt the status returned from the task in order to characterize it as success or failure, not considering the number of records actually returned. This has the advantage that on the failures we can interpret the returned error status to further explore the reason for the failure. The outcome of a task is further classified into more cases later on.

When a task reports a failure, there is a variety of errors that appear, as returned by each service, that are briefly listed in Table 1 with their frequencies. The error messages are service specific and the exact semantics of each error message is not globally defined, although we can assume the semantics of most errors by their complete message.

Apart from the normal responses and the timed-out responses, we present the remaining errors by splitting them into two categories, the ones related to the network communication, that may apply to more services, and the ones that are specific to the OAI-PMH operation, and its data interpretation and exchange. There are errors that their short name is too generic to explain. In order to decide in which category each error belong, we examined the complete error message, although on the table we only show its short form, as returned by the software of the service.

Table 1. The error messages by category.

Error short name	*Frequency*
Normal Completion	
	21478
Timed-out Execution	
Timeout	62
Communication Errors	
Error	170
error	332
IncompleteRead	10
HTTPError	6985
SSLError	48
URLError	7401
OAI-PMH Protocol Errors	
UnicodeEncodeError	125
BadArgumentError	356
BadStatusLine	54
BadVerbError	3507
CannotDisseminateFormatError	42
NoRecordsMatchError	682
XMLSyntaxError	2771
DatestampError	438
BadResumptionTokenError	80

We observe that the communication errors are about twice more often than the OAI-PMH protocol errors.

Some of the errors may be permanent, requiring human intervention (in the data or the software) to correct them, while other errors are temporary, and may not occur on another request. The temporary errors may affect not only the successful tasks, but also those with permanent errors, temporarily hiding them, making the analysis of each behavior more complex.

4 Consistency in the Behavior

We want to consider the behavior of each service over time, our harvesting rounds, to see how consistent it is. The temporary errors may hide the permanent behavior , but there are many services with a consistent behavior: in fact, we found that 1668 of the services had the "same" behavior each time: either they always succeeded or they always failed with the same way - by timeout or by reporting the same error. We did not expect the behavior of these services to change much.

To get a more accurate picture, we split our services into groups, according with their response behavior, that we called classes, and made a separate analysis for each one of these classes, which are shown in Table 2 with the number of services in each class.

Table 2. Services by behavior type.

#	class	services
1	full	630
2	some	125
3	both	324
4	fail	129
5	dead	913
	total	**2121**

The classes are defined as follows:

1. full: the services that always succeeded and always returned the same number of records, been as consistent as one could wish for.
2. some: the services that always succeeded but did not always return the same number of records each time. Their behavior is good, but could be improved to be more consistent.
3. both: the services that sometimes succeeded and sometimes failed and reported an error. Their errors should be temporary, as they do not prevent the successful behavior on other times.
4. fail: the services that always fail, but report different reason / errors – some of the errors should be temporary, but also some permanent errors may be hidden below them.
5. dead: the services that always fail, but always report the same error – which must be (in most cases) permanent.

The class with the most services (913) is the dead class, the services that seem to have stopped responding for one specific reason. The second class in size is the full class (with 630 services), with the services that work as expected. The classes with more transient / less consistent behavior follow in size. The behavior characteristic of each class can be further examined.

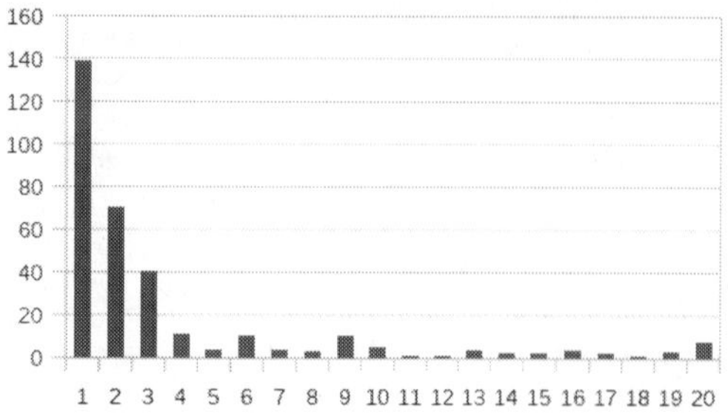

Figure 2. The number of failed tasks per service (class both).

We initially examine the return status of the tasks: only in class both, the successful and failed tasks coexist for each service, as the other classes contain the services that always failed or always succeeded. The number of failed tasks per service for class both is shown in Figure 2. We observe that, although most services failed just one time, and a significant number of them two or three times, there are services that failed even all but one time. Although most services fail occasionally, some of them only succeed occasionally.

The number of failed tasks per round for class both is shown in Figure 3. The average number of failed tasks per round is 56.2, with minimum 39 and maximum 102. Rounds 4 and 6 had a higher number of failures, but not too high to indicate a problem on the client side.

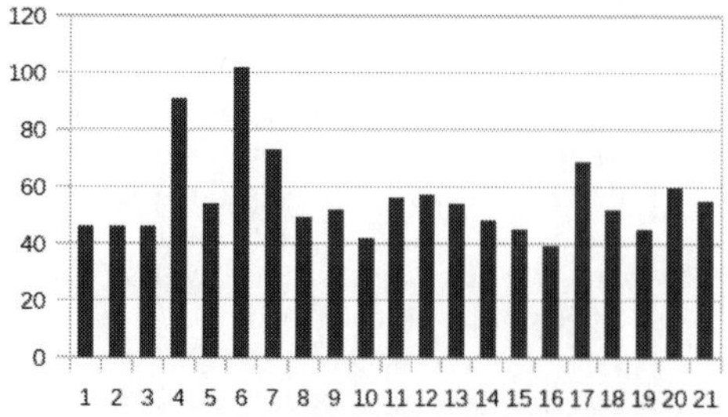

Figure 3. The number of failed tasks per round (class both).

We also examine the outcome of the harvesting: the average records retrieved from each successful task for the services of each class are presented in Table 3. Their number always ranges from 0 to 1000, and the average and standard deviation shows that the services in the class full usually provide more records, than the other, less consistent, services. It looks like the consistency problems affects the number of returned records.

Table 3. Records per successful task.

class	min	max	average	sdev	#tasks
full	0	1000	752.175	394.709	13230
some	0	1000	381.698	317.244	2625
both	0	1000	681.923	420.788	5623

In Table 4 we examine for each service the number of times that the number of returned records is different from that of the previous harvesting round (that was only 3 days earlier , and in most cases denote a problem in the harvesting and not a change in the records).

Table 4. Record changes per service.

class	min	max	average	sdev	#services
full	0	0	0.0	0	630
some	1	15	2.712	2.764	125
both	0	17	0.481	1.728	324

For the 630 services in the class full, this is, by definition, 0: only these services are included in the class. In the class some, this is from 1 up to 15, but with a much lower average and standard deviation. Similarly for class both, although it may be as high as 17, its average is less than 0.5.

In class some all tasks are successful, but some of them only partially, returning less records than those available and requested. The number of partially successful tasks per service is shown in Figure 4. We observe that the services may partially succeed quite often, from 1 to the maximum of 20 times, and on average 11.7 times (standard deviation is 6.7), often having more often partially than complete success. The partial success of the tasks seems quite unpredictable.

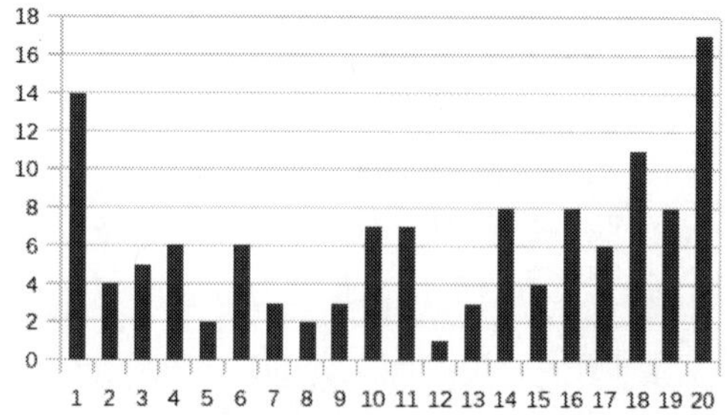

Figure 4. The number of partially successful tasks per service (class some).

The number of failed tasks per round is shown in Figure 5. It looks like that the services get improved on each round, and decrease the number of partial success, and increase the number of complete success on each round. The strict decrease of the number of partial success was not predicted. We assume that the class contains mostly services that do not work perfectly, but are improved somehow, while the services that get worse will eventually fail and will be classified under the class both.

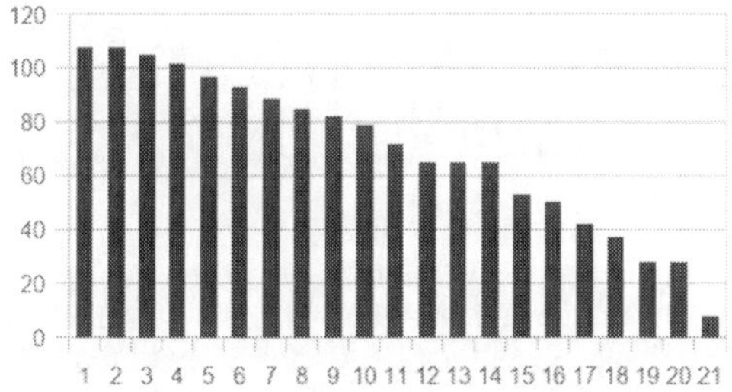

Figure 5. The number of partially successful tasks per round (class some).

The response time of the 21478 successful tasks, per service class, is shown in Table 5 . We observe that the average response time is smaller on the classes that are not consistently returning all the asked records, probably because they perform less work in this case, and return less records on the average. We conclude that some services are consistently more stable than others, although they so a similar job and often use similar software.

Table 5. Response time per successful task.

class	min	max	average	sdev	#tasks
full	0.43	2669.9	65.53	149.5	13230
some	0.34	234.5	27.82	32.7	2625
both	0.07	3175.4	63.95	122.1	5623

The remaining 23063 tasks return an error. These errors are shown in Table 6 and their frequency per service class. From the class dead, we see that only the errors IncompleteRead and Timeout are not always persistent in the same service, and all others may be persistent, which usually happen in the permanent errors. We cannot claim that a specific error occurs more often in the services of any class, even considering the total number of errors in each class.

Table 6. Frequency of service errors in each class.

error / class	both	fail	dead
BadArgumentError		20	336
BadResumptionTokenError	17		63
BadStatusLine	11	1	42
BadVerbError	99	384	3024
CannotDisseminateFormatError			42
DatestampError	7	158	273
Error	25	19	126
HTTPError	297	934	5754
IncompleteRead	10		
NoRecordsMatchError	140	143	399
SSLError		6	42
Timeout	37	25	
URLError	400	449	6552
UnicodeEncodeError		20	105
XMLSyntaxError	101	486	2184
error	37	64	231

Finally, we examine how often the errors do change to a different error (or to a success), between successive tasks of a service. This, by definition of the classes, only happens in services of the classes both and fail, and does not change in the other 3 classes.

Table 7. Service error changes per service

class	min	max	average	sdev	#services
both	1	13	3.056	1.931	324
fail	1	12	2.612	1.724	129

In Table 7 we examine for each service the number of times that the returned error is different from that of the previous harvesting round. Although it can change as high as 13 times, on average it changes from 2.5 to 3 times, with higher average and standard deviation on the class both: this class seems to have more unpredictable behavior.

5 Conclusions and Future Work

Communication of user and services through networking is complex, and we often do not have a picture of all the involved factors and situations. Understanding how the services behave, either qualitatively or quantitatively, help us understand the current situation and better design future services.

We studied the behavior of the services in many rounds of record harvesting, which is a complex procedure, with many requests through the network. We examined the number of returned records, and realized that in some cases less records are returned. Also, the service may report an error, and still some of the requested records may have been transferred. Therefore, the successful task is not obvious, and we had to define it, considering what is "successful enough".

The tasks are executed in multiple rounds, which are close enough to each other to avoid significant changes on the services. Analyzing the success of the tasks in a round demonstrates if unexpected circumstances occurred during this round. The behavior of a service over multiple rounds of tasks is not always consistent, and it is not rare that it changes from round to round, because of temporary problems. We categorized the services into classes according to the consistency of their behavior, and how the inconsistent behavior varies, and studied aspects of the behavior that appear in each class.

No obvious patterns of behavior were detected. Nevertheless, that some services are consistently more stable than others, although they do a similar job and often use similar software.

In the future, we plan to further analyze the errors as permanent or temporary, exclude the tasks with the temporary errors and analyze the others for more permanent characteristics, as well as to examine the error distribution per service.

References

1. Y. Bui & J. Park, *An assessment of metadata quality: a case study of the National Science Digital Library Metadata Repository*, In Haidar Moukdad (Ed.) CAIS/ACSI 2006 Information Science Revisited: Approaches to Innovation. Proceedings of the 2005 annual conference of the Canadian Association for Information Science held with the Congress of the Social Sciences and Humanities of Canada at York University, Toronto, Ontario (2005)
2. N. Fuhr, G. Tsakonas, T. Aalberg, M. Agosti, P. Hansen, S. Kapidakis, P. Klas, L. Kovács, M. Landoni, A. Micsik, C. Papatheodorou, C. Peters and I. Sølvberg, *Evaluation of Digital Libraries*, International Journal of Digital Library, Springer-Verlag, vol. **8**, no 1, November 2007, pp. 21-38 (2007)
3. B. Hughes, *Metadata quality evaluation: experience from the open language archives community*, Berlin: Springer. *Lecture Notes in Computer Science* vol. **3334**. ISBN 978-3-540-24030-3. doi: 10.1007/b104284 (2005)
4. S. Kapidakis, *Comparing Metadata Quality in the Europeana Context*, Proceedings of the 5th ACM international conference on PErvasive Technologies Related to Assistive Environments (PETRA 2012), Heraklion, Greece, June 6-8 2012, ACM International Conference Proceeding Series; vol. **661** (2012)
5. S. Kapidakis, *Rating Quality in Metadata Harvesting*, Proceedings of the 8th ACM international conference on PErvasive Technologies Related to Assistive Environments (PETRA 2015), Corfu, Greece, July 1-3 2015, ACM International Conference Proceeding Series; ISBN 978-1-4503-3452-5 (2015)
6. S. Kapidakis, *Exploring Metadata Providers Reliability and Update Behavior*, Proceedings of the International Conference on Theory and Practice of Digital Libraries (TPDL 2016), September 5-9, to appear (2016)
7. C. Lagoze, D. Krafft, T. Cornwell, N. Dushay, D. Eckstrom & J. Saylor, *Metadata aggregation and "automated digital libraries": a retrospective on the NSDL experience"* Proceedings of the 6th ACM/IEEE-CS joint conference on Digital libraries (JCDL 06), pp. 230-239 (2006)
8. B. L. Moreira, M. A. Goncalves, A. H. F. , Laender & E. A. Fox, *Automatic evaluation of digital libraries with 5SQual*, Journal of Informetrics, vol. 3, 2, pp. 102-123 (2009)
9. X. Ochoa & E. Duval, *Automatic evaluation of metadata quality in digital repositories*, International Journal on Digital Libraries, vol. **10**(2/3), pp. 67–91 (2009)
10. J. Ward, *A quantitative analysis of unqualified dublin core metadata element set usage within data providers registered with the open archives initiative*, Proceedings of the 3rd ACM/IEEE-CS joint conference on Digital libraries (JCDL 03), ISBN:0-7695-1939-3, pp. 315-317 (2003)
11. Y. Zhang, *Developing a holistic model for digital library evaluation*, Journal of the American Society for Information Science *and Technology*, vol. **61**, 1, pp. 88-110 (2010)

A qualitative survey for the academic libraries in the throes of a great recession

Petros Kostagiolas[1], Christina Banou[2], Stella Vazaiou[3], Nikolaos Kapellas[4]

[1]Assistant Prof. Dep. Archives, Library Science and Museology, Faculty of Information Science and Informatics, Ionian University. Greece
[2]Assistant Prof. Dep. Archives, Library Science and Museology, Faculty of Information Science and Informatics, Ionian University. Greece
[3]MSc. PhD candidate Dep. Archives, Library Science and Museology, Faculty of Information Science and Informatics, Ionian University. Greece
[4]MSc. Dep. Archives, Library Science and Museology, Faculty of Information Science and Informatics, Ionian University. Greece

Abstract. Over the last years the economic crisis affected the wide range of activities and services that Academic Libraries provide. On the other hand the demand for such services is increasing due to the reduced individual income of the librarie's users. The management of libraries is sometimes forced to make agonizing decisions regarding further shrinkage or/and mergers. An alternative to this scenario involves a strategy for advocating the value and developing alliances and collaborations among the Academic Libraries. The paper focuses on academic libraries in Greece during the economic crisis of the last five years with the aim to investigate problems and difficulties as well as challenges; changes brought about are discussed proposing at the same time a framework not only for overcoming the difficulties but also for exploiting the new opportunities. Initially, an overview of the role and function of academic libraries is presented with emphasis on their social character. Key leadership issues are explored in the context of on going restructuring attempts in order to establish viable operational models for academic institutions.

1 Introduction

The global economic crisis of 2008 has variously affected the Greek economy over the last few years. Economic phenomena have complicated socioeconomic roots that raise a wide array of issues and questions. These questions are related to values, comprehending existing problems, social conditions and cultural as well as political issues. As it has been shown from the global economic recessions of the past, hard times apart from problems create opportunities and form challenges while roles are constantly redefined [1].Undeniably, the hard economic pressures in Greece and elsewhere call for solutions through innovation and creativity. Academic libraries are expected not only to survive but mainly to take a leading role in higher education, scholarly dissemination and communication, information literacy and reading policy etc. [2].For this purpose, the exploitation of new information technologies as well as synergies has undeniably been among the opportunities presented up to this point. But pressing questions that call for answers set the scene in a world where economies sometimes in certain historical junctures collapse, as expectations and needs of the readers may grow slower than technologies.

The so-called "public debt crisis" mainly affected Greece, Ireland, Spain, Portugal and Italy. Regarding Greece, the economic crisis appeared in 2009, and has been actually related to innate structural deficiencies of the Greek public sector and its potential inability to control its ballooning debt [3].In a broader sense, however, this is a Euro zone economic crisis related to the European Monetary Union (EMU) structure as well as in the strategy for safeguarding a "good euro" as a world currency. Greece was forced to resort to the Financial Support Mechanism in March 2010, with the participation of other Eurozone countries, the European Central Bank (ECB) and the International Monetary Fund (IMF). After five years of recession in Greece, the current economic crisis has influenced every aspect of the public and private life, leading to a decrease in the living standards of most citizens and to new consumer patterns, reinforcing feelings of uncertainty, and most significantly creating a different social and cultural framework [3].

It must, though, be pointed out that it is not possible to fully evaluate the impact and the extent of this economic crisis since the recession phenomenon is still ongoing and its consequences in many sectors are uncontrollable [4].As data collection remains an important challenge, it is widely acknowledged that the recession has already influenced, and will further

[a] Corresponding author: pkostagiolas@ionio.gr

influence the operation and services of Academic Libraries leading to re-evaluation of their strategies and re-construction of their policies [5].Taking into consideration the continuous emergence of new information and communication technologies, the long-awaited recovery may come in a time when libraries will be probably different to what they were before 2008 [6]; this is not surprising and in hardly constitutes a unique occurrence. This paper initially provides an overview of the economic crisis impact on academic libraries and finally proceeds by presenting the results of an empirical survey. This survey is based on a similar research conducted by University College of London (UCL) and attempting to include all academic libraries in Greece. The survey is conducted through semi-structured interviews in a sample of Academic Libraries' directors that finally participated. The aim of this research is to record the perceptions on the top library management executives in light of the economic crisis presenting their efforts to advance innovation, implement alternative leadership practices within the present financial and social vortex by relying on their creativity and viable cooperation schemes.

2 Libraries as treasuries of knowledge in a globalised environment

Academic libraries over their long history played a dynamic role by serving the research and educational needs of the academic community being simultaneously at the peak of innovation and by exploring new technologies and opportunities.For a better understanding of their leading role, we must bear in mind that their policies and profile, being often relatively exempt from political or economic restrictions, led to the production of innovative, even revolutionary ideas and methods [7]. In Renaissance North Italy, for example, academic libraries, apart from being enriched with printed copies of the current the scientific output, evolved due to complex scientific and social reasons so as to better serve the scientist's needs. During the 19th century in Great Britain among the members of the famous Bibliographical Society were librarians that, apart from their knowledge and experience, offered a systemized approach to book and library studies playing thus a dynamic role in the study of the book and the function of libraries. *"Free to all, open to all"* libraries have been a common value of the Western World concerning libraries and a privilege gained for all people from the Enlightenment and the Industrial Revolution till now. It is noteworthy that libraries existed and exist in the centre the cities, library buildings being among of the most recognizable urban structures declaring in this way the strength of knowledge and the value of information [8].

The mission and values of academic libraries are certainly interrelated with the role of universities and more specifically, apart from the research and the teaching, with their policies that have in turn economic and social impact. The so-called decline nowadays of humanistic sciences may be one of the faces of Janus, while some point out the significance of what on first glance appears not to be useful or practical or financially valuable. Moreover, libraries ought to utilize other types of intangible resources for innovation and development. In a world in which the information is the main product and access to information is of significant value, new information technologies and services offer innovative opportunities for value creation [9]. Nowadays, above and beyond the economic crisis, the ever-changing information environment creates probably the most important challenge for libraries. Digitization may be one of them [10]; additionally, the social media that build communities of readers create a new framework for the libraries which in their turn have to exploit the opportunity for attracting library users and empower their presence in the local community. Recession actually forces people to visit *"free to all, open to all"* libraries. Furthermore, the knowledge economy may indeed increase the social value of information institutions providing opportunities for growth [11].Problems and challenges seem though to go hand in hand; it must also be clarified that highlighting the opportunities related to the recession does not mean rejecting its inevitable negative effects to information institutions [12].

Libraries have always been treasuries of knowledge and librarians and information scientists have been considered gatekeepers to the treasures of knowledge, of information presented mainly in the traditional form of the printed word. Thus, libraries are dynamic institutions of memory that strive to provide access to information and knowledge to all that care to use their resources. As libraries are still treasuries of the memory of the community and of knowledge, being historically at the centre of the cities, towns and universities, they hold another important role: that of exhibiting and making use of the tradition and history of the local community [13]. This provides an opportunity to the library to explore alternative funding strategies. Indeed, active participation of the library in the educational and research university processes may go hand in hand with the development of reading policies especially in times when the demand of library services is increasing. Apart from these ways of reaching the reading audience, creating readers and then allowing them to develop, social media nowadays offer the opportunity of building communities of readers who take an active dynamic role by expressing their attitudes and exchanging opinions. Libraries have always been striving for a more active participation of readers; nowadays engagement of the reader is further encouraged by information technologies, multimedia, augmented multimedia and social media. Library services have to be constantly updated, collections ought to be developed and technologies to be implemented as soon as they are made available.

Libraries through the centuries have developed collaborations and co-operations so as to share, exchange, solve, develop and re-develop policies, discuss, plan and act. They are sharing tangible and intangible resources and develop economies of scale and scope. For example, library alliances negotiate better with publishers and other stakeholders so as to get more favorable agreements [14]; moreover, they can commonly use information resources and infrastructure [15] and develop innovative services [16]; cataloguing and documentation are shared for decades. Actually, among the advantages that alliances have for Academic Libraries we may recognize the following [17]: sharing information and other resources, companionship programs promoting teamwork within the library, associations with other libraries whether of the same kind and interest or/and located in the same area, collaboration programs based on relations that the library establishes with other units and staff members within the university, links with libraries and organizations of the same type and nature in other countries. More specifically, library consortiums may take different forms and have different dynamics [17]: they may be internal, among staff members, between the library and other libraries [18] [19] [20] between the library and other units or departments of the academic institution [21], between the users and the library [15] and finally between the library and the wider community [17]. Developing viable cooperative operational models and reinforcing already existing ones may prove to be profitable during the recession through the creation of economies of scale [22].

3 A brief overview of the economic crisis impact on Academic Libraries

The economic crisis has not affected only the Academic libraries in Greece, but has impacted the libraries all over the world and certainly in Europe [23] [24] [25]. The most profound impact is related to budget reductions and results from the corresponding fiscal crisis. Just to mention only a few, academic libraries with budget reductions include the academic Library of East Tennessee [26] as well as the reductions in the academic libraries of Emory University and the University of Washington [27]. Moreover, it is generally accepted that the number of staff allocated in the academic libraries will never be the same again [28]. In Great Brittan the library services have been affected by the economic crisis [29]. In Ireland, after a period of prosperity, the academic libraries have also been hit by the economic crisis [24].

The reduction in research funding, as well as, in higher education institutional budgets increases the competition for the allocation of funding within the institutions. In most cases, the aforementioned background of competition reinforces budget reductions in academic libraries [30]. However, the true extend of the economic crisis impact is difficult to estimate [5].

On the other hand the economic crisis may also be seen as an opportunity for innovation and adjustments based on the new information technologies such as digitization [10]. The sustainability of an Academic Library may also depend on its ability to develop cooperation's and alliances with other institutions and organizations [17]. The academic libraries need synergies of many types in order to "communicate" and prove their value in the wider socioeconomic environment. According to Nicholas et al. [31] during the economic crisis, academic libraries should share openly ideas and experiences and promote cooperations [20] [18] [19] [27]. These can be among the academic library and other university units [21] [32]; among the academic library and other private or public organizations [17]; and also among the library and its' users [15]. The economic crisis can further urge innovation capabilities and promote an outreach culture for library management [34]. The professional communities need to advocate the role of academic libraries in promoting teaching and research; while the central role of the library in any university should be made clear [33]. On the other hand, the more the economic crisis deepens the demand for the services provided by the academic libraries increases due to the reduced income of the individuals, e.g. students of all levels etc. [2]. This phenomenon of increased demand in library services can actually provide an excellent argument for the important socioeconomic role of the libraries in periods of economic recession [12] [35] [36]. Therefore, the basic goals of the academic libraries still include the management of scholarly information and communication, the improvement of research and educational tools as well as the development of new ones.

4 The impact of the economic crisis on academic libraries in Greece: Empirical evidence

The largest part of Academic Library financing in Greece comes from the budget of higher and technical education institutions and thus they are fully dependent upon state funding. Budget cutbacks are the most obvious consequence of reducing state expenses. In Greece, higher education budgets receive further cuts every year of the recession. Additionally, European Development programs which significantly helped Academic Libraries have concluded by May 2009. According to the available information, in the year 2010 there was an overall total reduction of 31.3% in state funding, as compared to 2006. A comparative analysis of total annual expenses demonstrates the existence of an upward trend for University Libraries until 2009; however, this trend was suddenly discontinued in the following years (2010-2012) marking a sharp fall of around 50%. For academic libraries in Technical Education Institutes this unfavorable situation had started one year before, in 2008, with a significant drop which reached about 50% in the year 2009 and remained at the same levels afterwards. In the past two years, operational expenses were also significantly reduced around 50.0%; while staff members dropped of around 20% in 2010, mainly due to the dismissal of many contract agents employed through European Programs, which closed approximately in May 2009.

4.1. Profile and methodology

In Greece there are Academic Libraries in 22 Higher Education Institutions and 15 higher Technical Education Institutes.The survey was conducted during the summer of 2013, more specifically from the middle of July till the end of August and was partly based on a similar research conducted by University College London [23]. The aim of the research was to record and study the opinions and experience of directors of academic libraries in Greece in a moment when the economic crisis was more than ever present, influencing deeply library services. The research was conducted through interviews with the directors either through the telephone or, if requested by the directors, via email. More specifically, twenty directors participated and answered to the following seven questions:

I. Which are your estimations for the growth/evolution of the Greek economy in the next couple of years?
II. Which influences do you consider more significant and unfavourable / negative on the operation of the academic libraries?
III. According to your estimations, will more cutbacks at the academic libraries take place?
IV. According to your estimations, is it possible mergers or even shutdown of academic libraries to take place?
V. Do you consider the economic crisis as a challenge too for (the) academic libraries?
VI. Do you base your decisions primarily on economic criteria or according to other factors?
VII. Do you believe that collaborations between (the) academic and / or another kind of libraries could encourage the development of libraries during the economic crisis?

4.2. Results

Results are representative of the present situation experienced by Greek academic libraries. In that framework of the economic recession and its influence on the management of these libraries through mergers and cutbacks, directors were called to express their opinions and estimations. Actually, the reality for all libraries, including the academic ones, is budget cutbacks that have inevitably influenced the policy and the strategies of libraries. From this point on, there are various representative examples.

Regarding the first question, the perspective of the growth of the Greek economy in the next couple of years responses were characterized as negative or in the context of the cutbacks that are planned from the Government giving sometimes an optimistic point of view because of the stability at the existing levels of development.

Regarding the influence that the economic crisis had on the operation of academic libraries, answers given were focused on the cutbacks of budget but also on the reduction of personnel/staff. This is, however, not only a feature in Greece. According to statistical data provided by LAMPOST [37] and published by the Loughborough University, at the beginning of the crisis in the United Kingdom there was a reduction of employees amounting to 2.6% in 2009 and 1.8% for information scientists. In Ireland, a decade of Academic Library progress was followed by the crisis [24] and libraries were obliged to cut back their staff by 9% by the end of 2011, as compared to the number of their staff members in 2008.In Greece, the reduction of staff is in cases dramatic due to the fact that significant part of the personnel had not a permanent position at the libraries. Furthermore, cutbacks in the acquisitions either of printed or of electronic material are changing the function and the operation of libraries; in economically hard times libraries are supposed to widen their audience by encouraging new readers to join as members; but if the libraries cannot satisfy their needs and meet their expectations, then part of the challenge is lost.

In that framework, library directors have identified among the problems difficulties in the creation of academic repositories. Moreover, many of them have expressed the fear that the conditions will get worst and cutbacks will continue reducing the active participation of academic libraries in the educational and research process in universities. Regarding the possibility of mergers and close-ups of libraries, the majority of the directors participating in the survey estimate they will take place in the near future. Mergers were also considered in the possibility of larger institutional mergers.

It is noteworthy that the economic crisis was perceived as a challenge for libraries too, giving thus another point of view. More specifically, it was identified that the crisis forces people and institutions to be more competitive and creative, to demonstrate the value of libraries and to imagine operating in a more rational manner having developed strategies and implemented internal restructuring. Furthermore, the knowledge economy may indeed increase the social value of information institutions providing opportunities for growth [11]. From this point of view, collaborations and synergies between academic libraries or between academic and other types of libraries could be positive as vehicles of development in hard economic times. Successfully utilizing the opportunities presented by technology, institutions values and their intellectual capital could lead to collaborations that could benefit all stakeholders. For example, the HEAL-Link federation is the largest academic library consortium in Greece and is constituted from the total sum of 37 Academic Institutions (22 Universities and 15 Technological Institutions), 14 Research Institutions, the Academy of Athens, the National Library of Greece, the Hellenic Parliament Library, the Pedagogical Institute, the National Agricultural Research Foundation, and the University of Cyprus. Another example is the Hellenic Economic Library Network H.E.LI.N. The mission of the Network is to promote cooperation among the member libraries, with the consent and support of their respective administrations, in order to exchange services and resources related to their collections and various sources of economic content. The ultimate goal of the member libraries is to provide higher quality and more effective services to their user communities.

4.3. Discussion

The majority of the directors estimate that in ensuing years the problems will increase, mainly due to expected budget cutbacks. Among the difficulties they stress recognize is staff reduction, cutbacks in acquisitions, and problems in the function of libraries; mergers are also mentioned as a negative perspective. On the other hand, the crisis creates challenges; among these are the augmented needs and expectations of readers who turn to libraries. The demand for library services is really increasing but at the same time opening hours are in many cases reduced due to the reduction of staff, while cutbacks in acquisition policies practically mean that the library cannot always satisfy the needs of the readers. Meanwhile virtual and on site visits per person increase; that is the challenge for libraries which in their turn have to continue, empower and enrich their role as treasuries of knowledge. New information and communication technologies undeniably help them while collaborations and synergies form part of the challenges.

Undoubtedly, the economic crisis has influenced the daily operation of libraries, bringing about several changes, for example, in acquisitions, open hours, staff etc. What the crisis could not change is the role of libraries which is further empowered creating thus a historical continuity between the "open to all, free to all" libraries of the Enlightenment - Industrial Revolution and the Digital Revolution of our era. Furthermore, reading policy should be high in the priorities of the management of libraries giving emphasis not always in attracting and nurturing new readers, which is the first step, but also encouraging reader development. In that framework, new information technologies, especially social media, may help towards this aim by building communities of readers. Libraries already use them for strengthening the relationship between them and their users, for example via book blogs and book clubs. What we may ask our selves is whether the crisis is only economic and not as well a crisis of values. In this framework, what does the library mean and what is the distance between info-poor and info-rich? As in the publishing industry, problems that seem to be new are rather old, options that seem to be innovative are already used for centuries; in this context, old strategies are rediscovered in a time when digital libraries, thus services without physical appearance, seem to take a leading role. On the other hand, the library as a meeting place, as a place of various activities, in the centre of tows/cities, as a symbol not only of knowledge but mainly of the "free to all, open to all" access to information services continues to have a strong impact.

5 Conclusions

Economic perspectives need to be combined with the needs, priorities and values of library users. In this framework, in periods of recession and crisis, promoting the value of libraries and non-profit organizations seems to be of high importance [38]. At the same time, and most distressingly, libraries run the risk of failing to meet users' expectations being thus marginalized within their community if they do not manage to take advantage of the challenges and satisfy the readers' needs. Successful application of new information technologies and social media, creativity, synergies, collaborations are among the challenges. Undeniably, the non-profit character of academic libraries makes them part of an operational model that utilizes public funding so as to serve the University to which they belong [13]. Taking always into consideration the different traditions, policies and approaches of each institution, academic libraries in Greece ought to have a common policy regarding important issues in the heart of which there is the need for demonstrating library value. The creation of novel highly valued services can be based on the intellectual capital of the library [39] also highlights the need of library management to focus on human capital in times of crisis. Furthermore, active participation of the academic libraries in the educational and research university processes will promote achievements in research and further encourage cooperation with other institutional units [9]. Due to the recession, some of the main goals of academic libraries, such as providing access to high quality academic information, developing research tools, providing educational infrastructures, may be served and supplemented in alternative ways, through cooperation.

References

1. W. Grant, G. Wilson, *The global financial crisis: The Rhetoric of reform and regulation.* Oxford University Press. (2012)
2. P. Kostagiolas., E. Papadaki, G. Kanlis, S. Papavlasopoulos, Advances in Librarianship, *Responding to Crises with Alliances: Evidence from an Academic Library Survey in Greece.*, **36**, pp. 247-279 (2012)
3. M.G Arghyrou, J.D. Tsoukalas, CESifo Working Papers, *The Greek debt crisis: Likely causes, mechanics and outcomes*, **3266** (2010)
4. R, Harper, S. Corrall, New Review of Academic Librarianship, *Effects of the economic downturn on academic libraries in the UK: Positions and projections in mid-2009.* **17, 1**, pp. 96-128 (2011)
5. D.M. Davis, Chicago, IL: American Library Association, *The condition of U.S. libraries: Academic library trends, 1999-2009.* (2009). http://www.ala.org/ala/research/librarystats/academic/Condition_of_Libraries_1999.20.pdf
6. J. J. Regazzi, The Journal of Academic Librarianship U.S. *Academic Library Spending, Staffing and Utilization during the Great Recession 2008–2010,* **39,** pp. 217–222. (2013)
7. M Kumaran. Chandos Publishing, Oxford, Information Professional Series, *Leadership in Libraries.* (2012)
8. J. R. Matthews portal: Libraries and the Academy, *Valuing information, information services, and the Library: Possibilities and realities*, **13, 1**, pp. 91–112. (2013)
9. Y. Noh Aslib Proceedings,*The impact of university library resources on university research achievement outputs.* **64, 2,** pp. 109 – 133 (2012)
10. A. Powell, Journal of Library Administration *Times of crisis accelerate inevitable change.* **51, 1,** pp. 105-129 (2011)

11. P.A. Kostagiolas, Oxford, UK: Chandos *Managing intellectual capital in libraries: Beyond the balance sheet.* (2012)
12. Goulding, Journal of Librarianship and Information Science, *Credit crunch: The impact on A libraries*, **41, 3,** pp. 3-6. (2009)
13. Arts Council England *Evidence review of the economic contribution of libraries*. (2014)
14. C. Banou, P. Kostagiolas, Proceedings ELPUB2007 Conference on Electronic Publishing, *Managing Expectations for Open Access in Greece: Perceptions from the Publishers and Academic Libraries*, (2007)
15. N.J Meyer, I.R. Miller, College & Undergraduate Libraries *The Library as service learning partner: A win-win collaboration with students and faculty*, **15, 4**, pp. 399-413 (2008)
16. J. W. Marcum, The Bottom Line: Managing Library Finances, *Partnering for innovation and sustainability*, **21, 3,** pp.82-84. (2008)
17. , L.M. Anglada Library Management, *Collaborations and alliances: Social intelligence applied to academic libraries*, **28**, pp. 406-415. (2007)
18. R.M. Dougherty, American Libraries, *Prescription of financial recovery: The current economic crisis holds opportunities*. **40, 6,** pp. 50-53. (2009)
19. T. Kidd, The Serials Librarian,*The view from the UK: The economic crisis and serials acquisitions on an offshore island*, **59, 3/4,** pp. 384-393. (2010)
20. E. Cryer, K.S. Grigg, Journal of Electronic Resources in Medical Libraries *Consortia and journal package renewal: Evolving trends in the "big package deal?"*. **8, 1,** pp. 22-34. (2011)
21. S.E. Montgomery, J. Miller, College & Undergraduate Libraries, *The third place: The library as a collaborative and community space in a time of fiscal restraint*, **18, 2/3,** pp. 228-238. (2011)
22. W. Günter, R. Erway Museum Management and Curatorship, *Think Global, Act Local-Library, Archive and Museum Collaboration*. **24,4**. (2009)
23. Charleston Observatory *The economic downturn and Libraries: Survey findings*. University College London. (2009). http://dx.doi.org/10.1108/PMM-05-2015-0016
24. J. Cox, An Leabharlann, The Irish Library *Academic libraries in challenging times*. **19, 2,** pp. 7-13. (2010)
25. American Library Association. *Academic libraries in the United States: Statistical trends*. Chicago, IL(2011). http://www.ala.org/ala/research/librarystats/academic/academiclibraries.cfm
26. L. Adebonojo, M. Ellis, K. Campbell, M. Hawkins, Reference Services Review, *Redirecting library instruction based on socioeconomic data*. **38, 3,** pp. 398 416. (2010)
27. M. K Throumoulos, The Bottom Line: Managing Library Finances, *Exceptional service during and after deep serial cuts*, **23, 1,** pp. 24–28. (2010)
28. Medeiros, N., OCLC Systems and Services: International digital library perspectives *Transformation: Next generation technical services at the University of California Libraries.*, **27, 1** , pp. 6–9 (2011)
29. I. Mori, *The impact of the economic recession on university library and IT services: Final report for JISC, SCONUL and UCISA*. (2009). http://www.jisc.ac.uk/media/documents/publications/libsitimpacts.pdf
30. M. Reid, The Bottom Line: Managing Library Finances *Building an academic library fundraising program "from scratch"*, **23, 2,** pp. 53–56 (2010)
31. D. Nicholas, I. Rowlands, M. Jubb, H. R. Jamali, The Journal of Academic Librarianship, *The impact of the economic downturn on libraries: with special reference to university libraries*, **36, 5**, pp. 376-382 (2010)
32. S.M. Pritchard, Library and the Academy *Crises and opportunities*, **9, 4,** pp. 437-440 (2009)
33. R. Volentine, C. Tenopir, Aslib Proceedings, *Value of academic reading and value of the library in academics' own words*, **65, 4,** pp. 425–440(2013)
34. P.A. Kostagiolas, A. Margiola, A. Avramidou, Library Review, *A library management response model against the economic crisis: The case of public libraries in Greece*, **60 6,** pp. 486-500(2011)
35. C. Rooney-Browne, Library Review, *Rising to the challenge: A look at the role of public libraries in times of recession*, **58, 5,** pp. 341–352 (2009).
36. P. Kostagiolas, Library Management, *Managing knowledge capital in public libraries for a knowledge-driven socioeconomic environment*, **34 8/9**, pp. 677–689(2013)
37. LAMPOST (2012), Loughborough University, *Libraries, Archives, Museums and Publishing Online Statistics Tables*, http://www.lboro.ac.uk/microsites/infosci/lisu/lampost10/exp10.html
38. P. Calvert, A. Goulding, Performance Measurement and Metrics, *Narratives and stories that capture the library's worth*, **16, 3,** pp. 276–288 (2015)
39. P.A. Kostagiolas, S. Asonitis, A. Woodsworth, Advances in Librarianship *Managing intellectual capital in libraries and information services*, **33**, vol. 31-50 (2011)

Multivariable decoupling set-point approach applied to a wastewater treatment plant

Ramon Vilanova[1,a] and *Orlando* Arrieta[2]

[1] *Departament de Telecomunicació i d'Enginyeria de Sistemes, Escola d'Enginyeria, Universitat Autònoma de Barcelona, 08193 Bellaterra, Barcelona, Spain.*
[2] *Instituto de Investigaciones en Ingeniería, Facultad de Ingeniería, Universidad de Costa Rica, 11501-2060 San José, Costa Rica*

Abstract. This paper presents a formulation for the inclusion of the second degree of freedom for MIMO system for decoupling purposes. The proposal is specially effective when combined with decentralized feedback controllers. Loop interaction is of the major problems in the control of MIMO systems, as interaction can be considered as a disturbance coming from all other loops, the design of the decentralized feedback controller is better understood as a disturbance rejection design. In this approach the set-point tracking capabilities may be not as good as expected. The proposed Two-Degree-of-Freedom (2-DoF) formulation provides a complement to the existing controller that can be automatically determined in terms of the available process and feedback controller information.

1 Introduction

Despite the great developments of advanced process control techniques, [1], [2], it is widely recognized that PI/PID control is still the most commonly adopted control approach in the process industry. The main reason is the fact that this controller is easily understandable and its few parameters have easy interpretation for *hand*-tuning. This popularity has been inherited in the control of Multi-Input Multi-Output (MIMO) processes, specially for Two-Input-Two-Output (TITO) processes, being decentralized PI/PID controllers the most popular. Within this MIMO context, the decentralized option obviously requires fewer parameters than the full multivariable case. Another side advantage of decentralized PI/PID controllers is that of loop failure tolerance of the resulting closed-loop system [3].

Even the extensive advances on single-loop PI/PID control tuning methods [4–7] all these methods cannot be directly applied to the design of decentralized control systems because of the existence of interaction among loops. Effectively, the presence of interactions among the loops introduce an inherent difficulty to the design of these local controllers. In the presence of strong interactions the effectiveness of the decentralized controllers can be seriously deteriorated or even cause instability. This fact has motivated the extension of single-loop tuning rules to decentralized control systems an active area of research.

A common approach is to tune an individual controller for each loop and then detune each loop by a detuning factor in order to account for interactions. This is the well known Biggest Log modulus (BLT) method of Luyben [8]. Other similar methods [9] design the controllers on the basis of the diagonal elements and do a further detuning on the basis of the RGA elements. Another different approach is to account for loop interactions when designing the individual control loops. In the sequential design method [10], for example, each designed individual loop is closed an subsequent controllers are designed by looking at the generated disturbance. The main drawback of the approach is that the designer has to proceed on a very ad-hoc manner and decisions are taken on the basis of loops already closed. Therefore the order the loops are being designed may have influence on the system performance. Other researches formulate the design problem as an optimization problem by using Linear Matrix Inequalities [11, 12], genetic algorithms [13], Neural Networks [14], Fuzzy approaches [15]. All these methods suffer from the problem of being too much dependent on the objective control function formulated or the order the loops are being closed. These controllers may result in an unstable system under the case of loop-failure or even when the loops are closed in a different order.

A common concern in all these approaches is, in addition to the inherent difficulties of MIMO control, to achieve a suitable trade-off between the disturbance rejection (also needed to minimize process interaction) and the tracking performance. This trade-off is better tackled within a 2-DoF framework. Despite several advanced procedures do exists in literature; see for example the works on [16–18] for 2-DoF controller design on a general set-

[a] Corresponding author: Ramon.Vilanova@uab.cat

ting, however it is sometimes desirable to keep the design of both degrees of freedom separated and with as much independence as possible. It is in this sense that we propose to add a second degree of freedom for designing a 2-DoF controller. From this alternative perspective, some approaches can be found in the literature aiming at the design of a suitable prefiltering or feedforward control action aimed to improve the set-point following performance of an existing feedback controller. These approaches ranges form the introduction of a reference prefiltering action [19, 20] to the design of complementary feedforward control actions: [21].

Even the idea of improving tracking performance by adding complementary parts to an existing controller structure is appealing (it preserves the performance and design principles of the original design) results and can only be found for the Single-Input Single-Output (SISO) case. The only exception is the recent result provided in [22] where an extension of the SISO results of [21] are worked out. The method however requires the solution of a multiobjective optimization problem in order to determine a feasible feedforward control actions. In this paper, a 2-DoF MIMO controller is proposed where the feedback part is assumed to be implemented as a decentralized feedback controller and the part that operates on the prefilter/feedforward paths is conceived with a special structure that allows a possible automatic tuning from the existing feedback control. As it will be seen the resulting overall MIMO controller consists of the same number of elements as that of MIMO controller but distributed along the feedback, prefilter and feedforward terms. Assuming the feedback part is already in place, the determination of the complementary prefilter/feedforward terms will be done by borrowing some recent results on Internal Model Control (IMC) based feedforward control ([23].

The rest of the paper is organized as follows. First of all the problem formulation set up is presented in section 2, whereas section 3 presents the determination of the decoupling strategy for set-point following on the basis of feedforward control principles. The derivation is first presented for the TITO case and further generalized to a square MIMO system. Section 4 presents some examples of application and section 5 exemplifies the method on a non-linear Activated Sludge Process (ASP). Section 6 closes the paper by presenting main conclusions and outlines possible further developments.

2 Feedforward based Set-point decoupling 2-DoF controller

In this section, the feedforward control design ideas presented in [23] will be applied within the context of a multivariable system. In fact, one can see the control signal generated in one of the loops as a disturbance generator for the rest of the loops. Therefore, one possible way of tackling this interaction is by the inclusion of a feedforward control action from one of the loops to the rest in order to attenuate the effect of the existing interaction. In that sense, the application of the ideas proposed in [23] result to a compensation scheme as it is shown in figure (1) for a TITO system. In this figure $Q_{12}^{ff}(s)$ and $T_{12}^{ff}(s)$ are suitable transfer functions (to be defined below) that constitute the feedforward compensation. The same scheme will apply for the compensation that goes from the second to the first loop. In this later case the feedforward blocks will read $Q_{21}^{ff}(s)$ and $T_{21}^{ff}(s)$, but are not shown for clarity.

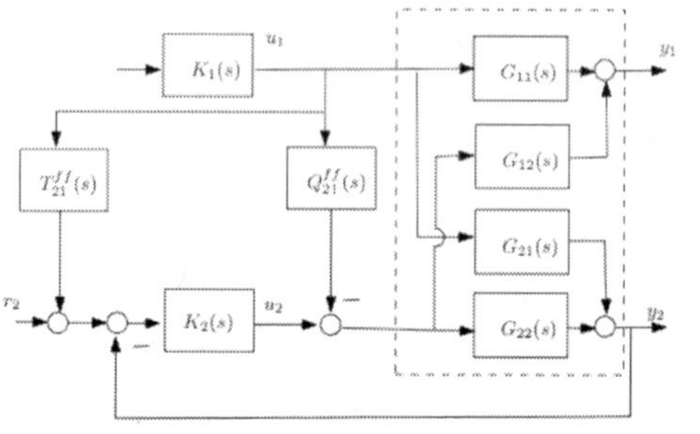

Figure 1. Incorporation of Feedforward corrective actions on a decentralized TITO control scheme.

It is important to note that the application of feedforward control on a single-loop setting has no implications on the stability of the resulting control system (as long as the added blocks are themselves stable). However, within a multivariable approach, like the one concerned here, the addition of these two blocks will introduce new feedback loops that may have repercussions on the final stability. It is therefore needed to workout concrete expressions for these new loops and derive conditions for maintaining stability. The final design of the feedforward terms will therefore need to deal with the unavoidable constraint of maintaining stability and, at the same time, try to improve the attenuation of the interaction effects. Obviously the added stability constraint will make the whole design more complex. In order to avoid this extra complexity and try to have a feedforward approach that is as direct as possible, the following observation is made.

Assume the feedback controllers, $K_1(s)$ and $K_2(s)$, have been designed on the basis of $G_1(s)$ and $G_2(s)$ (they can be the direct through transfer functions $G_{11}(s)$, $G_{22}(s)$ or the effective transfer functions if other previously closed loops are taken into account). An estimation of the generated control action on the face of a reference change can be generated by using their associated Internal Model Control (IMC) parameters $Q_1(s)$ and $Q_2(s)$. It is well known within the IMC framework that the feedback controller and IMC parameter are elated by means of:

$$K_i(s) = \frac{Q_i(s)}{1 - G_i(s)Q_i(s)} \tag{1}$$

$$Q_i(s) = \frac{K_i(s)}{1 + G_i(s)K_i(s)} \tag{2}$$

being the reference to control relation given by $u_i = Q_i(s)r_i$. Therefore, in order to recover a full feedforward action, instead of applying the feedforward compensation directly from the control signal, it is proposed to be generated from the corresponding reference signal. On that basis figure (1) is redrawn as figure (2).

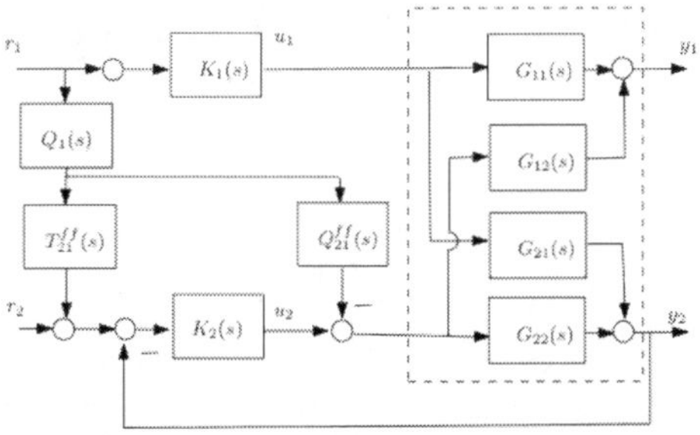

Figure 2. Reference signal based feedforward corrective actions on a decentralized TITO control scheme.

The importance of this change of scenario comes from the generation of the compensating feedforward signal completely *from the outside*. In this case from the reference signal.

2.1 Design of the Feedforward Decoupling terms

Previous section has presented the different terms involved on the feedforward correction that is generated from the first loop into the second loop. Although the same idea applies on the other direction (second loop to the first one), the design equations that follow will only concentrate, for simplicity, on the situation depicted in the figures. Afterwards, a generalization will be presented that will also show how the approach do generalize to a square system of arbitrary dimension.

According to [23], the $Q_{21}^{ff}(s)$ transfer function is, in fact, the feedforward controller to be designed. The design is carried out in two steps

1. Design a feedforward controller, $\overline{Q_{21}^{ff}}(s)$ on the basis of the models, $G_{22}(s)$ and $G_{21}(s)$. This design can be done by trying to approximate the ideal feedforward controller $\overline{Q_{21}^{ff}}(s) = G_{21}(s)/G_{22}(s)$ by existing model matching procedures such as the $\mathcal{H}_2$ optimal design of [2] or a min-max approach along the lines of [6]. Here we will use the approach based on [6], where the $\overline{Q_{21}^{ff}}(s)$ is defined as:

$$\overline{Q_{21}^{ff}}(s) = \arg\min_{Q(s)} \|W(s)(G_{21}(s) - Q(s)G_{22}(s))\|_\infty \tag{3}$$

   Ideal feedforward controllers are usually defined in terms of the inverse of the plant. However this usually introduces excessive control actions and high frequency behavior. In turn, this approximate inversion is proposed here where the weighting function $W(s)$ defines the frequency range where the desired inversion error carried out by the feedforward controller is to be penalized.

2. Augment the obtained feedforward controller by a low pass filter $F_{21}^{ff}(s) = 1/(\lambda_{21}^{ff}s + 1)^n$ in order to obtain the final feedforward controller as $Q_{21}^{ff}(s) = \overline{Q_{21}^{ff}}(s)F_{21}^{ff}(s)$. The filter order is chosen in order to make the controller transfer function strictly proper. On the other hand, the filter time constant λ_{21}^{ff} is chosen in order to tradeoff the reduction of the feedforward control action bandwidth against the loos of achieved nominal performance.

On the other hand, the $T_{21}^{ff}(s)$ term is automatically determined once the feedforward controller $Q_{21}^{ff}(s)$ is calculated. The definition of $T_{21}^{ff}(s)$ is simply as the error incurred by $Q_{21}^{ff}(s)$ on trying to approximate the ideal controller:

$$T_{21}^{ff} = (G_{21}(s) - Q_{21}^{ff}(s)G_{22}(s)) \tag{4}$$

Therefore, problem (3) can alternatively be written as

$$\overline{Q_{21}^{ff}}(s) = \arg\min_{Q(s)} \|W(s)T_{21}^{ff}(s))\|_\infty \tag{5}$$

2.2 Generic Feedforward-Decoupling configuration

The ideas presented in the previous section can be given a more compact form by introducing the following matrices:

$$K(s) = \begin{pmatrix} K_{11}(s) & 0 \\ 0 & K_{22}(s) \end{pmatrix} \quad Q(s) = \begin{pmatrix} Q_{11}(s) & 0 \\ 0 & Q_{22}(s) \end{pmatrix} \tag{6}$$

$$Q^{ff}(s) = \begin{pmatrix} 0 & Q_{12}^{ff}(s) \\ Q_{21}^{ff}(s) & 0 \end{pmatrix} \quad T^{ff}(s) = \begin{pmatrix} 0 & T_{12}^{ff}(s) \\ T_{21}^{ff}(s) & 0 \end{pmatrix} \tag{7}$$

If we now denote the vector signals as $\mathbf{r} = (r_1\ r_2)^T$, $\mathbf{u} = (u_1\ u_2)^T$ and $\mathbf{y} = (y_1\ y_2)^T$, we can write:

$$\mathbf{u} = K(s)(\mathbf{r} + T^{ff}(s)Q(s)\mathbf{r} - \mathbf{y}) + Q^{ff}(s)Q(s)\mathbf{r} \tag{8}$$
$$= K(s)((I + T^{ff}(s)Q(s))\mathbf{r} - \mathbf{y}) + Q^{ff}(s)Q(s)\mathbf{r} \tag{9}$$

with

$$K(s) = diag\{K_{11}(s), K_{22}(s)\} \tag{10}$$
$$Q(s) = diag\{Q_{11}(s), Q_{22}(s)\} \tag{11}$$

and the $Q^{ff}(s)$ and $T^{ff}(s)$ matrices will be completely *off-diagonal* matrices defined as:

$$Q^{ff}(s) = \begin{pmatrix} 0 & Q_{12}^{ff}(s) \\ Q_{21}^{ff}(s) & 0 \end{pmatrix} \tag{12}$$

$$T^{ff}(s) = \begin{pmatrix} 0 & T_{12}^{ff}(s) \\ T_{21}^{ff}(s) & 0 \end{pmatrix} \tag{13}$$

being each one of the feedforward controllers $Q_{ij}^{ff}(s)$ designed on the basis of:

$$\overline{Q_{ij}^{ff}}(s) = \arg\min_{Q(s)} \|W_j(s)(G_{ij}(s) - Q(s)G_{ii}(s))\|_\infty \qquad (14)$$

therefore

$$T_{ij}^{ff}(s) = (G_{ij}(s) - Q_{ij}^{ff}(s)G_{ii}(s)) \qquad (15)$$

Some remarks have to be made with respect to the resulting final controller structure. The design starts from the diagonal matrix $K(s)$, designing an independent controller, $K_{ii}(s)$, for each one of the diagonal process terms $G_{ii}(s)$. Once we have this controller, its corresponding IMC parameter, $Q_i(s)$, is computed:

$$Q_{ii}(s) = \frac{K_{ii}(s)}{1 + K_{ii}(s)G_{ii}(s)} \qquad (16)$$

and their associated diagonal matrix, $Q(s)$, can also be generated. On the other hand, the $Q^{ff}(s)$ matrix is fully *off*-diagonal, having each one of its elements got as the solution to (14). Again, once the $Q_{ij}^{ff}(s)$ are calculated, the $T^{ff}(s)$ matrix can be automatically generated from (15).

3 Application to an Activated Sludge Process

The Activated Sludge Process (ASP) is arguably the most popular bioprocess utilized in the treatment of polluted water, using microorganisms present within the treatment plant in the biological oxidation of the wastewater. With the provision of adequate oxygen supply, this process can be maintained to degrade the organic matter in the pollutant. Most modern wastewater treatment plants is of this type and consists of a series of bioreactors and settlers. In this report the configuration of a single bioreactor connected to a single secondary clarifier is considered. See fig. (3). The simplified but still realistic and highly non-linear four-state multivariable model considered here is the Activated Sludge Process (ASP) [24].

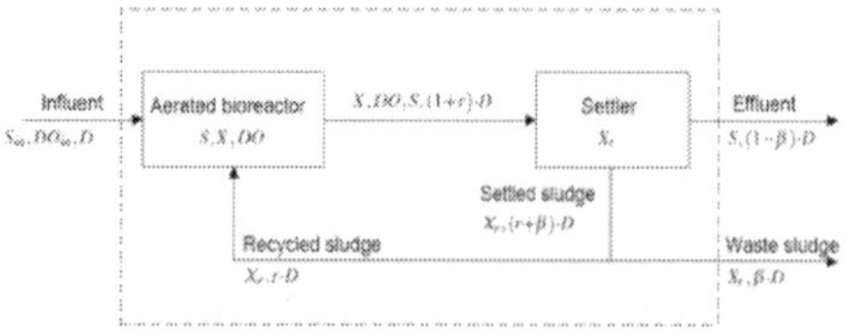

Figure 3. Activated Sludge Process layout

3.1 Activated Sludge Process (ASP) Description

The mathematical model considered in this paper is given in [24]. The ASP process comprises an aerator tank where microorganisms act on organic matter by biodegradation, and a settler where the solids are separated from the wastewater and recycled to the aerator. The layout is shown in figure (3). The component balance for the substrate, biomass, recycled biomass and dissolved oxygen provide the following set of non-linear differential equations:

$$\frac{dX(t)}{dt} = \mu(t)X(t) - D(t)(1 + r)X(t) - rD(t)X_r(t) \qquad (17)$$

$$\frac{dS(t)}{dt} = -\frac{\mu(t)}{Y}X(t) - D(t)(1 + r)S(t) + D(t)S_{in} \qquad (18)$$

$$\frac{dDO(t)}{dt} = -\frac{K_o\mu(t)}{Y}X(t) - D(t)(1 + r)DO(t) + K_{La}(DO_s - DO(t)) + D(t)DO_{in} \qquad (19)$$

$$\frac{dX_r(t)}{dt} = D(t)(1 + r)X(t) - D(t)(\beta + r)X_r(t) \qquad (20)$$

$$\mu(t) = \mu_{max}\frac{S(t)}{k_S + S(t)}\frac{DO(t)}{k_{DO} + DO(t)} \qquad (21)$$

where $X(t)$ - biomass, $S(t)$ - substrate, $DO(t)$ - dissolved oxygen, DO_s - maximum dissolved oxygen, $X_r(t)$ - recycled biomass, $D(t)$ - dilution rate, S_in and DO_in - substrate and dissolved oxygen concentrations in the influent, Y - biomass yield factor, μ - biomass growth rate, μ_{max} - maximum specific growth rate, k_S and k_{DO} - saturation constants, $K_{La} = \alpha W$ - oxygen mass transfer coefficient, α - oxygen transfer rate, W - aeration rate, K_o - model constant, r and β - ratio of recycled and waste flow to the influent. The model parameterization is according to tables (1) and (2). On the other hand,the influent concentrations are set to S_{in} = 200 mg/l and DO_{in} = 0.5 mg/l.

Biomass	$X(0)$=215 mg/l
Substrate	$S(0)$=55 mg/l
Dissolved Oxygen	$DO(0)$=6 mg/l
Recycled Biomass	$X_r(0)$ = 400 mg/l

Table 1. Initial Contitions

$\beta = 0.2$	K_c=2 mg/l
$r = 0.6$	K_s=100 mg/l
$\alpha = 0.018$	K_{DO}=0.5
$Y = 0.65$	DO_s = 0.5 mg/l
$\mu_{max} = 0.15\ h^{-1}$	

Table 2. Kinetic parameters

With respect to the control problem definition, the waste water treatment process is considered under the assumption that the dissolved oxygen, $DO(t)$, and substrate, $X(t)$, are the controlled outputs of the plant, whereas the dilution rate, $D(t)$, and aeration rate $W(t)$ are the two manipulated variables.

3.2 Linearized model

For controller design purposes, the previous model is linearized around the operating point defined by the steady-state inputs of D_{ss} = 0.0825 and W_{ss} = 90 . The resulting linear model will have a transfer function matrix of the form:
such that

$$\begin{pmatrix} S(t) \\ DO(t) \end{pmatrix} = \begin{pmatrix} G_{11}(s) & G_{12}(s) \\ G_{21}(s) & G_{22}(s) \end{pmatrix} \begin{pmatrix} D(t) \\ W(t) \end{pmatrix} \qquad (22)$$

The $G_{ij}(s) = n_{ij}(s)/d(s)$ transfer function components are given as:

$$G_{11}(s) = \frac{134.0243s^3 + 295.3529s^2 + 53.5176s + .5855}{s^4 + 2.4617s^3 + 0.9859s^2 + 0.1107s + 0.0008} \quad (23)$$

$$G_{12}(s) = \frac{-0.0312s^2 - 0.0062s - 0.0001}{s^4 + 2.4617s^3 + 0.9859s^2 + 0.1107s + 0.0008} \quad (24)$$

$$G_{21}(s) = \frac{-9.2834s^3 - 15.0312s^2 - 2.6325s - 0.0123}{s^4 + 2.4617s^3 + 0.9859s^2 + 0.1107s + 0.0008} \quad (25)$$

$$G_{22}(s) = \frac{0.0699s^3 + 0.0340s^2 + 0.0042s + 2.910^{-5}}{s^4 + 2.4617s^3 + 0.9859s^2 + 0.1107s + 0.0008} \quad (26)$$

3.3 Decentralized PI control

As a first step, two PI feedback controllers are designed. The design is based on the 2DoF PI tuning approach presented in [25] and within the ASP process in [26]. Due to space constraints, just the tuning for both controllers is provided as well as the time responses achieved for such tuning in comparison with a well known multivariable PID technique such as that of [27]. The resulting PI tuning parameters are: $K_{p1} = 0.006$, $T_{i1} = 3.0$ and $\beta_1 = 0.67$ for substrate loop, whereas $K_{p2} = 3.13$, $T_{i2} = 0.8$ and $\beta_2 = 1$ ar got for the dissolved oxygen loop.

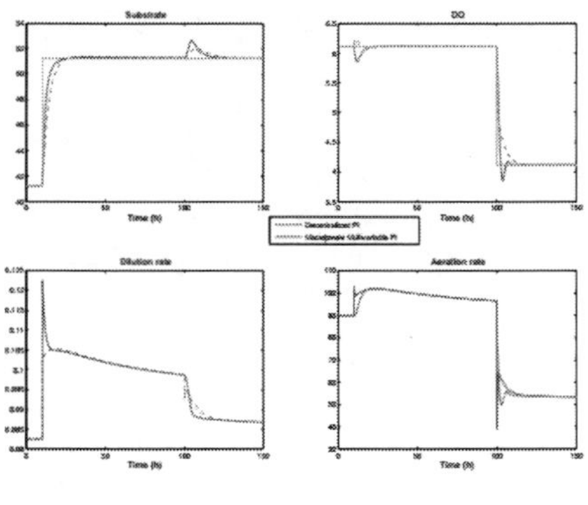

Figure 4. Comparison of the decentralized PI tuning and the Multivariable PI method of Maciejowski

Now, in order to improve the performance where set-point changes are applied, the proposed feedforward decoupling controllers are applied. In this case, as $G_{22}(s)$ and $G_{21}(s)$ share the same denominator a straightforward choice for Q_{21}^{ff} results as:

$$Q_{21}^{ff} = \frac{n_{22}(s)}{n_{21}(s)} \frac{1}{(\lambda_{21}^{ff} s + 1)} \quad (27)$$

where λ_{21}^{ff} is the tuning parameter associated with the feedforward compensator. The tuning of this parameter can be done by observing it has to be in accordance with the expected control signal bandwidth. This way, the poles of $Q_{11}(s)$ (the IMC parameter of $K_{11}(s)$) are computed and λ_{21}^{ff} is chosen, for example, five times smaller than the corresponding fastest time constant of $Q_{11}(s)$. By applying such simple rule the following values are obtained for the feedforward filter time constants: λ_{21}^{ff}=0.4 and λ_{12}^{ff}=0.2. The resulting improvement in interaction compensation is shown in figure (5). The figure axis have been magnified in order to have a better look at the difference with respect to the purely decentralized control case. It is important to notice that the change incurred in the corresponding control actions it is not really large and basically introduced anticipatory control action (as expected).

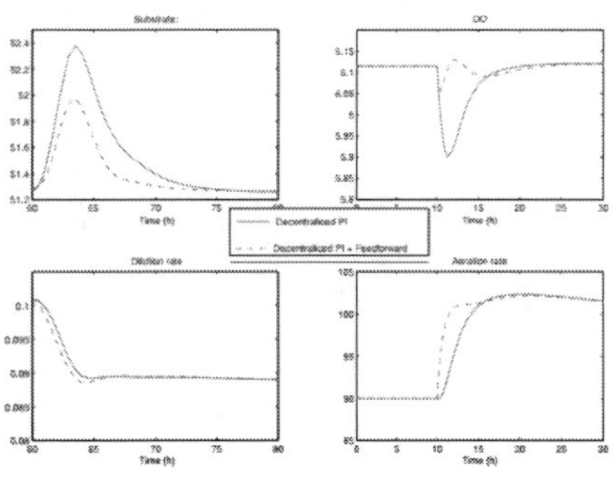

Figure 5. Interaction reduction by using the reference-driven feedforward actions.

It is important to remark that the generated feedforward signals are based on:

- The linear models of the process, therefore only retaining local information.
- The generation of the expected control signal from the applied reference input. This generation is also performed on the basis of linear models.

However, as it is shown in figure (6) if we compare the performance of the feedforward corrections by directly using the control signal or by using the proposed generation from the reference signal, it is seen that both performances are comparable and, in some cases, even better for the reference-driven case.

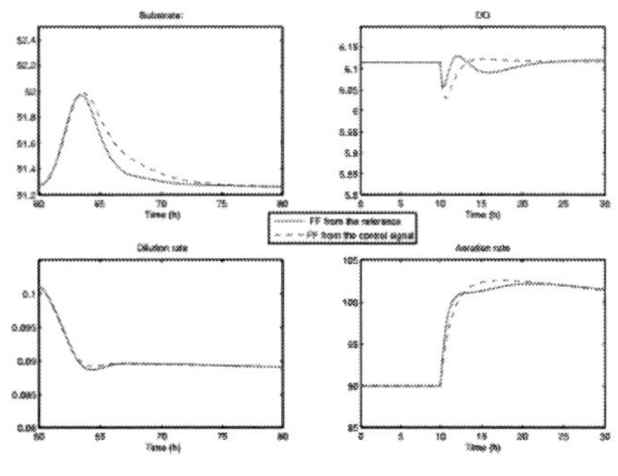

Figure 6. Comparison of the reference-driven and control signal-driven feedforward actions.

4 Conclusions

This paper has presented a formulation for the incorporation of feedforward control action from the reference signal in multivariable control in order to alleviate the effects of process interaction and improve the performance for set-point following.

The approach has special appealing for decentralized PI/PID control based on IMC-*like* tuning methods. In such cases, the tuning is directed by the desired closed-loop bandwidth. It is this parameter that is used for the tuning of the feedforward filters. The overall resulting control configuration has the same components as a full multivariable controller. However just the diagonal part of the controller remains within the loop, whereas the rest is located outside. Therefore there is no need to incorporate additional stability considerations.

Future efforts are directed towards a simultaneous design of the feedback and feedforward parts, as well as the exploration of possibilities regarding the inclusion of such feedforward actions within the loop and its use for interaction effects attenuation also when dealing with external disturbances.

Acknowledgments

The financial support from the University of Costa Rica, under the grants 322-B4-218 and 731-B4-213, is greatly appreciated. Also, this work has received financial support from the Ministerio de Economia e Innovacion of Spain under project DPI2013-47825-C3-1-R.

References

[1] E. Camacho, C. Bordons, *Model Predictive Control in the Process Industry* (Springer-Verlag, 1995)

[2] M. Morari, E. Zafirou, *Robust Process Control.* (Prentice-Hall International, 1989)

[3] S. Skogestad, M. Morari, Automatica **25**, 119 (1989)

[4] S. Skogestad, Modeling, Identification and Control **25(2)**, 85 (2004)

[5] K. Astrom, T. Hagglund, Journal of Process Control **14**, 635 (2004)

[6] R. Vilanova, Journal of Process Control **18**, 61 (2008)

[7] K. Åström, T. Hägglund, *Advanced PID Control* (ISA - The Instrumentation, Systems, and Automation Society, 2006)

[8] W. Luyben, Ind Eng. Chem Des. Dev. **25**, 654 (1986)

[9] I. Chien, H. Huang, J. Yang, Ind. Eng. Chem. res. **37** (1999)

[10] M. Hovd, S. Skogestad, Automatica **30**, 1601 (1994)

[11] J. Bao, J. Forbes, P.J., Ind. Eng. Chem. res. **38** (1999)

[12] S. Tong, Q. Zhang, Int. J. Innovative Computing, Information and Control **4**, 3385 (2008)

[13] C. Vlachos, D. Williams, J. Gomm, IEE- Proc on Control Theory and Applications **146** (1999)

[14] Y. Abe, J.I. M. Konishi, R. Hasagawa, M. Watanabe, H. Kamijo, Int. J. Innovative Computing, Information and Control **4**, 2649 (2008)

[15] S. Tong, W. Wang, L. Qu, Int. J. Innovative Computing, Information and Control **3**, 657 (2007)

[16] M.J. Grimble, *Robust Industrial Control. Optimal design Approach for Polynomial Systems* (Prentice-Hall International, 1994)

[17] D. Limebeer, E. Kasenalli, J. Perkins, Automatica **29**, 157 (1993)

[18] R. Vilanova, I. Serra, C. Pedret, R. Moreno, IET-Control Theory and Applications **1**, 1322 (2007)

[19] A. Leva, L. Bascetta, Automatica **11**, 1984 (2007)

[20] L. Bascetta, A. Leva, Journal of Process Control **18**, 465 (2008)

[21] A. Visioli, Journal of Process Control **14**, 457 (2004)

[22] S. Piccagli, A. Visioli, Journal of Process Control **19**, 978 (2009)

[23] R. Vilanova, O. Arrieta, P. Ponsa, ISA- Transactions **48**, 439 (2009)

[24] F. Nejjari, A. Benhammou, B. Dahhou, G. Roux, Int. J. Adapt. Control Signal Process. pp. 347–365 (1999)

[25] V. Alfaro, R. Vilanova, O. Arrieta, *Analytical Robust Tuning of PI Controllers for First-Order-Plus-Dead-Time Processes*, in *13th IEEE International Conference on Emerging Technologies and Factory Automation* (2008), Hamburg-Germany

[26] R. Vilanova, R. Katebi, V. Alfaro, *Multi-loop PI-based control strategies for the Activated Sludge Process*, in *14th IEEE International Conference on Emerging Technologies and Factory Automation* (2009), Mallorca, Spain

[27] J.M. Maciejowski, 1st edition, Addison Weslew, Wokingham (1989)

Emerging opportunities: the internet, marketing and museums

Evdoxia Richani[1], Georgios Papaioannou[2], Christina Banou[3]

[1]*BSc, MSc LIS-Museology, Dep. Archives, Library Science and Museology, Faculty of Information Science and Informatics, Ionian University. Greece*
[2]*Assistant Prof. Dep. Archives, Library Science and Museology, Faculty of Information Science and Informatics, Ionian University, Greece*
[3]*Assistant Professor, Dep. Archives, Library Science and Museology, Faculty of Information Science and Informatics, Ionian University, Greece*

Abstract. The tremendous impact of applying new technologies is obvious when it comes to museums. Internet forms an integral part of museums everyday life and decision making. Websites, online communities, social media, and mobile applications comprise elements of the modern museum's digital self, which complements the real museum of permanent and temporary exhibitions, storage rooms, visitors' facilities, laboratories and, most important, museum objects. This environment inevitably affects museum marketing strategies and creates relevant opportunities.

1 Introduction

This paper attempts to discuss a triparted cultural relationship: museums, marketing and the Internet. Museums have served as guardians of objects and people's identities. In the last few decades museums attempt to transform into multidimensional cultural centers by listening to current cultural identities. This is achieved by thematic temporary exhibitions, educational programs and regular collaborations with different ethnic groups. Towards this end, museums have recently adopted digital technologies and the Internet. Documentation, multimedia-based exhibitions, websites, special needs applications contributed towards to the modern museum's "socially relevant objectives and basic principles...toward making a population aware of its identity, strengthening that identity, and instilling confidence in a population's potential for development."[1]. New technologies have also been used for museum educational programs.

New information technologies in the last few years have changed the way people communicate, think, read, write and act. Online communities have emerged. Social networking has provided tools for information sharing. Recommendation technologies have further encouraged user participation. Museums have used technologies that provide instant access to information in various ways. "From providing visitors with handheld devices to instantly access more information about a work of art to using cards tagged with RFID chips to automatically create a personal website based on the visitors' interests, museums are experimenting with ways these new technologies can enhance the visitor experience on site and at home." [2]. Visitors' profiles, skills and needs have therefore been affected and altered. [3] "Web 2.0 technologies enable audiences to access and interpret museum information in their own time and on their own terms and to add their personal stories and memories to this body of knowledge, liberating collections from their academic and institutional context in the traditional museum space." [4]. The evolution of digital technologies and the Internet have provided museum access across the world. "...in the past decade the role of the online/web environment has grown exponentially, offering a space free of opportunities, which represents today a benefit for the exhibition's audience and offers museums a venue for fresh improvement" [5].

In this paper we discuss museums, marketing and the internet as a triparted base for museum-related opportunities.

2 Museum marketing and the Internet

Museum types have been categorized in four large domains: private museums, government museums, museums of nonprofit organizations and university museums [6]. According to ICOM's estimations, there are roughly more than 55.000 museums in 202 countries around the globe [7]. Most of them were created and run

[a] Corresponding author: evarichani@ionio.com

thanks to government funding and support, but new needs and realities led to government funding shortage and the need for extra funding, and this factor boosted marketing concepts in the museum world. Marketing was not initially received well in the museum society [8], but government underfunding led to museum marketing firstly in the USA and shortly afterwards in Europe [9].

Successful management in museums nowadays requires the use of marketing. It seems this is not an option; it is a necessity. From its early appearance in the 20th century [10], different museum marketing strategies have been planned and applied depending on general and individual museum needs. A common parameter seems to be the need to attract visitors and gradually increase visitors' flow [11], as well as visitors' engagement and participation.

Towards attracting visitors, internet marketing seems to be a valuable tool. Museum websites used to have a prominent role in attracting museum audiences. Museum website have added a digital self in museum realities by presenting the museum online and receiving virtual visitors that may (or may not) become real visitors. Marty and Jones state: "Virtual museum visitors are different from those that actually visit museums onsite; there are different motivations, different reasons and different expectations from the interaction with the museum." [12].

Digitized museum objects available online can support the museum's educational character. Museum marketing and the use of Internet can serve the primary museum aim as commonly accepted: "a museum is a non-profit, permanent institution in the service of society and its development, open to the public, which acquires, conserves, researches, communicates and exhibits the tangible and intangible heritage of humanity and its environment for the purposes of education, study and enjoyment." [13]. Museums are bound to objects, but their purpose is to disseminate knowledge and educate. "Virtual exhibits are not substitutes for exhibits in museums. They are opportunities for people who have seen the real exhibits to revisit them electronically and learn more." [14]. Students can gain much from this. "The development and maintenance of a virtual museum is an ideal way to provide a student-centered constructivist learning environments. It allows students to make choices about what they want to study and provides meaningful topics that incorporate academics and culture while providing a way to get families and the community involved in their education." [15]

Mass media presence and content industries comprise fields of museum marketing and the Internet. Modern museums, in their attempts to be an integral part of the societies they are in, have become active, have undertaken new activities and they communicate them to the public. Museums affiliate themselves with mass media by forming museum content industries. These industries create and disseminate material that can be conveyed by media. "[...] museums and other collectors of art, graphics, etc., become content producers when they produce images of their art for use by consumers." [16].

Connectedness and interaction are also enhanced. "Connectedness does not merely mean to link objects together but to give visitors the opportunity to focus on their special interests by pursuing them in an interactive dialog with the museum." [17]. Museums use the internet not only to provide access to information but also to interact with visitors by getting feedback, comments, ideas and contributions. Social media play a key role in building communities of visitors who share information and develop taste. Whether having visited the museum or not, visitors can express their attitudes and share comments and information. "People do not participate merely for the fun of it. They care about having their voice heard. Museums need to respond to visitors' participation. [...] Visitor participation, whether in the gallery or online through social media, is an important part of the museum's quest to remain relevant in society. Tools, such as the participatory aspect of social media, are strategies that allow museums to be as relevant to their audiences as possible."[18]. Visitors' view may affect museums' policies, aims, objectives, strategies and futures.

Let us not underestimate the marketing's key role: funding. Nowadays most museums are partly or completely self-financed. "In the 1990s, moreover, the policy focus increasingly shifted from merely encouraging private support to a more full-blown privatization or de-governmentalization of public cultural institutions – a trend that was particularly evident in Central and Eastern Europe [...]. [19]. Internet can be (and may already have been) a necessary factor in the museum's financial life, since it offers ways to increase museum finances. "Museums through the internet can reach global markets, which allow consumers to purchase products and services from museums throughout the world. Global marketing breaks down national boundaries, encouraging museums to interact with another across the world". [20]

3 Internet and museums

At the beginning, museum websites were mostly used as brochures to invite the public to visit, to promote new exhibitions and inform about collections and activities. Later on, photographs of museum artifacts started to be included in museum websites along with some information. Global communication via the World Wide Web provided museums the opportunity to contact each other fastly and in an economic way, using new means of contact, such as computer mediated conferencing (CMC), e-mail lists, discussion boards, bulletin boards and chat rooms, which were used to support many types of discursive or collaborative activities. Nowadays, social networking is used for offering and sharing information as well as for creating online communities [21].

Every museum curator, even with the smallest budget, must nowadays pursue an online representation of the museum. [22] As stated before one of the simplest presence of museums online was the "brochure museum". This type of museums usually informs people about visiting hours, tickets' prices and says a few words about their collection. Later on, a new museum form was introduced on the web, "the content museum". Many museums have at their collections millions of artifacts. This type of museums presents a part of the collection and invites virtual visitors to explore. "Content museums" usually display online the most special artifacts in order to intrigue people to go and see these artifacts in person. One step further is the "learning museum". At this type, "the site is didactically enhanced and linked to additional information that motivates the virtual visitor to learn more about a subject they are interested in and to revisit the site." [23].

The latest development comes in the form of virtual museums, also noted as hyper museums, digital museums, cyber museums or web museums. A virtual museum can be the World Wide Web self of traditional museums (e.g., displaying digital representations of existing collections or exhibits), or it can be created from digital content such as net art, virtual reality and digital art. "A virtual museum is a construction, a code in itself, which is encoded technically by the website developer and socially by the curator. [...] Just like in a traditional museum, curators are responsible for what is included, and what is excluded from a body of knowledge." [24]. Virtual museums offer virtual visits and virtual activities, such as virtual games for students based on CVE (collaborative virtual environments).[25].

At the communication end, museums in the last decade have moved towards incorporating the benefits of social media. "Social media indeed gives museums additional opportunities to build online communities, both on their own websites and on popular international networks like Facebook or Twitter, which potentially can extend their cultural outreach beyond national borders." [26]. Social media has revolutionized communications by providing a stable and affordable platform for ongoing dialogue that goes beyond national boundaries among countries around the world. This communication could be established by museum professionals and at the same time by simple visitors without cultural, social, political and geographical boundaries.

In the last few years museums entered the world of mobile (smart)phones, tablets, applications and services. Mobile applications for museums are rapidly increasing. "The use of mobile apps opens up new channels of communication between the cultural institution and the user, which extent to his or her personal space and go beyond the boundaries of the museum's walls." [27].

4 Strategic marketing and museums

During the last quarter of the 20th century a new term was introduced to museum societies: new museology, a concept that shifted museums' centre from objects to society. These thoughts were the outcome of the post World War II shift in museum identity within the broader European society and the world [28], and introduced new ways of expressions and new roles in the relationship of museums and society [29], including an advanced educational role of museums [30]. Today museums actively contribute to social, cultural and economic life of a society [31]. Within this new role and given the funding shortages, museums seek new funds and sustainability [32]. Towards this end, museums apply marketing techniques and strategies [33].

The strategic marketing process is a very hard and worth-working process, having long term results and benefits. Marketing helps museum people to set aims and objectives, forces them to face the difficulties and exploit opportunities, helps to develop a more distinctive structure and makes good use of all different professions in a museum. Marketing is used not only to increase finance, but also to attract visitors, to penetrate into new audiences, to gain feedback from visitors so as to understand and measure needs and expectations, enriching the visitor's experience and widening the borders of the museum [34, 35, 36].

5 Some concluding thoughts

"The ways in which historical, art historical, and scientific studies are changing through the use of technology are legion. The difficulty of recalling past research on a given topic is problematic and mounts with each passing year" [37].

The advantages of applying new technologies in museums are certainly many. Going online means for a museum to exploit all the given possibilities. First of all, by using the web a museum offers free access to the artifacts for everyone. This is especially important for people who are physically and/or economically disabled or live far away from the actual museum. For them it might not be possible to gain access in a specific museum and its artifacts otherwise. Secondly, by exposing virtually its artifacts, museums provide a safe way for everyone to explore these artifacts, and augment symbolic capital. Thirdly, the internet provides access to artifacts which are kept in storage rooms or are not safe to be displayed. Fourth, by using all the potentials that multimedia provide, artifacts can be virtually re-composed and re-exposed in innumerable ways. Fifth, people can work with the artifacts displayed in front of them on a computer screen in various ways, e.g. put them nest to each other and play with them. Finally, new information technologies and multimedia encourage visitors to participate and be further engaged; thus the role of the visitors is upgraded, especially if we consider the social media and the potential of creating and organizing online communities, especially with the contribution of young people [38].

On the other end, museums tend to design their digital representations in a "much prettier" way than the actual thing. As years go by, real artifacts are becoming increasingly remote for safekeeping, forcing them to appear less real and secluded. Visiting a real museum is often more exciting, because of the actual presence of other people and of activities and services there.

Marketing in the world of museums can help

towards making the most of and for visitors. Services marketing [39] of tangible and intangible museum assets [40, 41], real and digital, will offer museums a chance to overcome funding difficulties, set new aims and objectives, and make real and virtual visitors more satisfied.

References

1. A. Hauenchild, *Claims and reality of new museology: Case studies in Canada, the United States and Mexico* http://museumstudies.si.edu/claims2000.htm#2.Elements
2. W. Witschey, Museums in transition: Emerging technologies as tools for free – choice learning, *Science Museum of Virginia*,p.3 (2006)
3. Giannoutsou, N. Avouris, *7th Greek Convention with International participation « The ICTs in Education »*, p.3 (2010)
4. J. Verboom, P. Arora, *Museum 2.0: A study into the culture of expertise within the museum blogosphere*, , s.e., s.l., p.8 (2015)
5. Cap Sciences and TEC-Lab, *Technology and the public. Evaluation of ICT in museums* no. 5, ,p.8 (2013) http://online.ibc.regione.emilia-romagna.it/I/libri/pdf/LEM5th-report-technology-and-the-public.pdf
6. G. Edson, 'Museum Management', *Running a museum: a practical handbook*, ICOM, France, pp. 133-146 (2004) http://icom.museum/uploads/tx_hpoindexbdd/practical_handbook.pdf
7. *Frequently asked questions,* ICOM (2010-2015) http://icom.museum/resources/frequently-asked-questions/
8. R. Rentschler, *Museum marketing: no longer a dirty word* (2013) http://www.researchgate.net/publication/237721763_Museum_marketing_no_longer_a_dirty_word
9. V. D. Alexander, A delicate balance: Museums and the marketplace, *Museum management and marketing,* 400-405 (2007) http://upir.ir/934/Museum-Management.pdf
10. E. Hooper – Greenhill, Museum and communication: an introductory essay, *Museum, media, message*, Routledge, p. 1-12 (1995) http://samples.sainsburysebooks.co.uk/9781134640751_sample_517927.pdf
11. A. Gilmore, R. Rentschler, Changes in museum management: a custodial or marketing emphasis, *Journal of management development,* vol. 21, no. 10, pp. 745-760 (2002) http://dro.deakin.edu.au/eserv/DU:30008525/rentschler-changesinmuseum-post-2002.pdf
12. P. F. Marty, K. Burton Jones, *Museum Informatics : people, information, and technology in museums*, Taylor & Francis Group LCC, s.l., p. 192 (2009)
13. ICOM, *Museum definition*, http://icom.museum/the-vision/museum-definition/
14. B. Finn, Digitising museum collections *Artefacts Consortium*, p.167 http://www.artefactsconsortium.org/Publications/PDFfiles/Vol4Pics/4.10.Pictures-Finn,Digitizing75ppiWEBF.pdf
15. Dr. G. Jones, M. Christal, *The future of Virtual Museums: On-Line, Immersive, 3D Environments*, Created Realities Group, p. 9 (2002) http://ww.w.created-realities.com/pdf/Virtual_Museums.pdf
16. L. Kueng, R. Picard & R. Towse, *The internet and the mass media*, Sage Publications LTD, London, p.7, (2008)
17. W. Schweibenz, The "Virtual Museum": New Perspectives For Museums to Present Objects and Information Using the Internet as a Knowledge Base and Communication System, *Proceedings des 6. Internationalen Symposiums für Informationswissenschaft,* p.189 (1998), http://www.intelyway.com/administrator/arhivi/Vid_Gajsek-MUZEJI/14_isi-98-dv-schweibenz-saarbruecken.pdf
18. Rebecca Whelan, *The Use of Social Media in Museums,* (2011) http://trentcentre.ca/documents/public/4157FinalReport.pdf
19. S. Toepler, V. Kirchberg, *Museum marketing: competing in the global marketplace,* pp. 160-166 (2007)
20. N. G. Kotler, P. Kotler, W. I. Kotler, *Museum and marketing strategy: designing missions, building audiences, generating revenue and resources*, Jossey-Bass, p.34 (2008)[2]
21. K. Walker, Structuring Visitor Participation, *Digital Technologies and the Museum Experience: Handheld Guides and Other Media,* Altamira Press, pp. 109-124 (2008) http://www.lkl.ac.uk/people/kevin/book_chapter7.pdf
22. *Making the Most of the Web – a Guide for Small Museums* http://www.chr.org.uk/pdfs/webforsmallmuseums07part1.pdf
23. W. Schweibenz, The development of Virtual museums, *ICOM NEWS,* ICOM, no. 3, p. 3 (2004) http://icom.museum/fileadmin/user_upload/pdf/ICOM_News/2004-3/ENG/p3_2004-3.pdf
24. D. Langlais, *Cybermuseology and intangible heritage*, p.75 http://www.yorku.ca/etopia/docs/conference/Langlais.pdf
25. D. Economou, Understanding social interaction and informing the design of virtual actors in collaborative virtual environments (CVEs) for learning",*Technology in service of cultural heritage, Kaleidoskopio*, pp. 241-249(2008)
26. N. Grincheva, *The "Starfish" of cultural diplomacy: social media in the toolbox of museums* http://www.culturaldiplomacy.org/acd/content/articles/2011loam/participant-papers/the_starfish_of_cultural_diplomacy_-_social_media_in_the_toolbox_of_museums.pdf

27. M. Economou, E. Meintani, *Promising beginnings? Evaluating museum mobile phone apps* http://www.idc.ul.ie/techmuseums11/paper/paper8.pdf
28. A. Desvallées, F. Mairesse (eds), *Key Concepts of Museology*, Armand Colin (2010) http://icom.museum/fileadmin/user_upload/pdf/Key_Concepts_of_Museology/Museologie_Anglais_BD.pdf
29. V. MacCall, C. Gray, Museums and the 'new museology': theory, practice and organisational change, *Museum Management and Curatorship*, vol. 29, no. 1, pp. 1–17 (2013) http://www2.warwick.ac.uk/fac/arts/theatre_s/cp/staff/gray/research/new_museology_article.pdf
30. P. Vergo, *The new museology*, Reaktion Books Ltd, London (1989)
31. A. Timothy, P. Crispin, *Museum basics,* Routledge, London (2012) https://books.google.gr/books?id=POtDB4VkZK0C&printsec=frontcover&redir_esc=y#v=onepage&q&f=false
32. R. Rentschler, Museum and Performing Arts Marketing: A Climate of Change *Journal of Arts Management, Law and Society*, vol. 28, no 1, pp. 83–96 (1998) http://search.proquest.com/openview/d2e2061ea4b28f0279d987ac78e992b0/1?pq-origsite=gscholar
33. N. G. Kotler., P. Kotler, W. I. Kotler, *Museum Marketing and strategy: Designing Missions Building Audiences Generating Revenue and Resources,* Jossey-Bass (2008)
34. K. M. Ekström., Marketing of Museums', *Proceedings of the 37th Macromarketing Conference, Marketing of Museums,* The Macromarketing Society, Inc., Germany, pp. 207-210 (2012) http://s3.amazonaws.com/academia.edu.documents/30231388/macromarketing2012proceedings.pdf?AWSAccessKeyId=AKIAJ56TQJRTWSMTNPEA&Expires=1454092124&Signature=DNeSpPwJARW4tU0Q3NftDd1sBAI%3D&response-content-disposition=inline%3B%20filename%3DConstructivism_in_Advertising_Exposing_I.pdf#page=208
35. R. C. Blattberg, C. J. Broderick. Marketing of Art Museums, *The Economics of Art Museums,* University of Chicago Press, pp. 327–346 (1991) http://www.nber.org/books/feld91-1
36. F. McLean, *Marketing the museum* Routledge, London. (1997)
37. M. L. Anderson, Museums of the future: The impact of technology on Museum practices, *Journal of the American Academy of Arts and Sciences,* pp.129-162 (1999) http://www.columbia.edu/itc/anthropology/schildkrout/6353/client_edit/week14/anderson.pdf
38. D. Tsichritzis, S. Gibbs, Virtual museums and virtual realities, *International Conference on Hypermedia & Interactivity in Museums,* Archives & Museum Informatics, pp. 17-25 (1991) http://www.archimuse.com/publishing/hypermedia/hypermedia.Ch3.pdf
39. A. M. Rushton, D. J. Carson, The Marketing of Services: Managing the Intangibles, *European Journal of Marketing,* vol. 19, Iss: 3, pp. 19 – 40 (1985). http://www.emeraldinsight.com/doi/abs/10.1108/EUM0000000004748
40. J. A. Cohen., *Intangible assets: Valuation and Economic Benefit* , John Wiley & Sons Inc., New Jersey (2005)
41. O. A. Aghan. Marketing intangible heritage to museum publics: the case of folklore. *ICOM MPR conference,* ICOM (2006) http://network.icom.museum/fileadmin/user_upload/minisites/mpr/papers/2006-Papers.pdf

SOME characteristic properties of analytical method of magnetic control of ferroimpurities in various primary and technological media

Anna A. Sandulyak[1a] , Alexander V. Sandulyak[1], Hasan Bulut[2], Haci Mehmet Baskonus[3], Maria N. Polismakova[1], Darya A. Sandulyak[1]

[1] *Moscow Technological University, 107996 Moscow, Stromynka, 20, RF*
[2] *Department of Mathematics, Firat University, 23119, Elazig, Turkey*
[3] *Faculty of Engineering, Tunceli University, 62100, Tunceli, Turkey*

Abstract - The paper demonstrates that when defining the content of ferroimpurities in the analyzed media by magnetic control based on measuring the ferroimpurities masses *m*, which are extracted from the media sample step-by-step, it is crucial to define a functional view of the obtained dependence m on the operation order number *n*. It allows receiving additional forecast data m by extrapolating this dependence. With corresponding calculations being done, it enables determining the sought total mass of ferroimpurities (including their residual mass). We consider alternate solutions of practical tasks which yield magnetic control results in case of linear and piecewise-linear views (in semi-logarithmic coordinates) of the control mass-operational characteristics.

1 Introduction

Many industries face a challenge of inevitable presence of ferroimpurities in primary and technological media. Deteriorating the quality of these media and thus impoverishing the quality of the final product, such impurities can also seriously destabilize the technological process and the performance of manufacturing equipment. Therefore, it is important to ensure valid control of ferroimpurities content. The classification of a medium by normative quality targets greatly depends on solution of this problem which also influences the timely decisions and efficient removal of ferroimpurities (e.g. with the help of magnetic separators [1-6]). Besides, it is important for modeling of the process of magnetic impact on ferroimpurities [7-13].

It is common practice for control methods to use a test-method control based on magnetic extraction of ferroimpurities from the sample of the medium analysed (magnetophoresis), measuring their masses and further evaluation of their mass share (concentration). For a more complete removal of ferroimpurities, the magnetophoretic operations are as a rule performed several times, recurrently, cyclically with determining the accumulated mass of the ferroimpurities removed from the sample. In such a case, there is assigned some recommended 'sufficient' number n of such operations.

However, we believe that such recommendations are not to be taken for granted, but they are to be discussed. The matter is, after performing even an increased *n* number of magnetophoretic operations, a sample of a medium still contains a residual (not-removed) mass of ferroimpurities. As far as the *n* number increases, the value of this mass (from general physical concepts it is always present) surely reduces (and the quality of control improves), but we have to admit it reduces asymptotically nearing zero only when the number of operations is infinitely unlimited.

Yet such an approach stipulating multiple (reasonably limited by practically substantiated number of operations) magnetic removal of ferroimpurities from the sample of the medium analyzed is justified. Herewith, it becomes effective to the extent required if it is followed by obtaining an experimental dependence (decreasing) of the measured operational masses m of removed ferroparticles on the sequence order number n of the operation. It is similar to the process when we study the nature of reducing ferroparticles concentration progressively as wefurther

[a] Corresponding author: anna.sandulyak@mail.ru

execute multiple magnetophoretic operations for removing ferroparticles from liquids [14]. This particular dependence can serve as a basis for substantiating and execution of the experimental and calculating method of ferroimpurities magnetic control.

2 Main results and their discussion

Obtaining experimental dependence of operational masses *m* of extracted ferroimpurities on the operation sequence number *n* is one of the first steps in the experimental and calculating method of ferroimpurities magnetic control considered here. The second step required for the method is identifying the functional view of dependence *m* on *n*. Thus, its functional legalization allows for objective extrapolation up to any value *n*, no matter how big it is, and consequently, it affords obtaining values m lying beyond actual experiment by calculating [15].

Many experimental dependences of *m* on *n*, in particular, the ones depicted in Fig. 1*a* – 4*a* (obtained during multiple operations of magnetic separation of ferroimpurities from flour, quartz sand, petrol, engine oil), linearize quite well in semilogarithmic coordinates (Fig. 1*b* – 4*b*). This proves the regularity of operational masses exponential reduction:

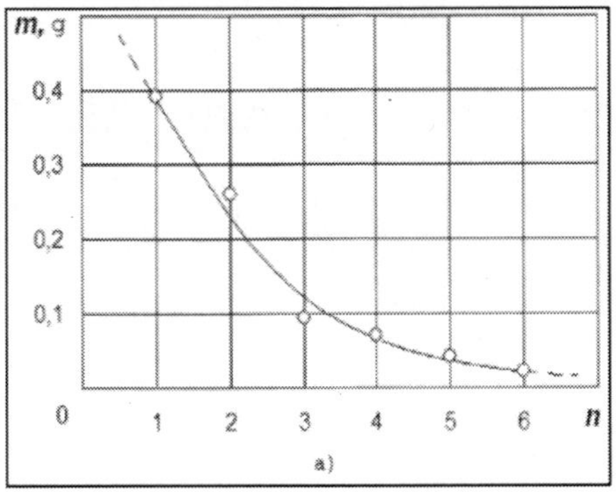

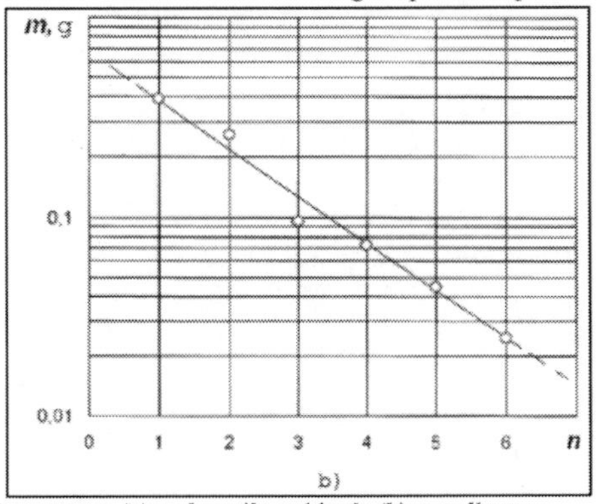

Figure 1. Experimental data of ferroimpurities masses removed from flour after each magnetophoretic operation – in common (a) and semilogarithmic (b) coordinates.

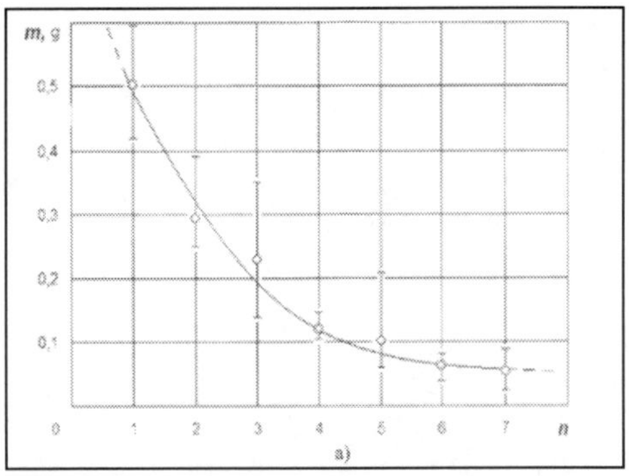

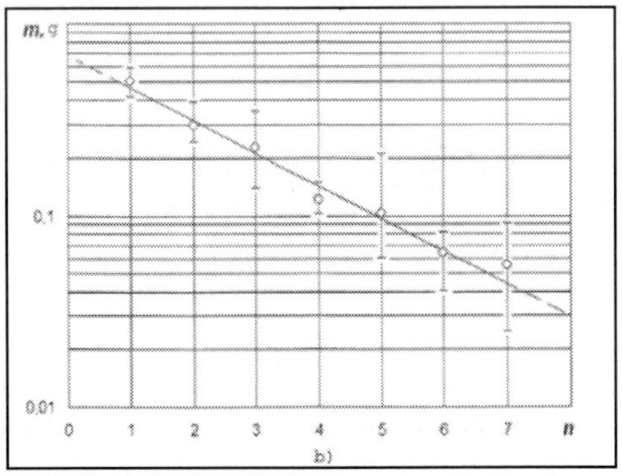

Figure 2. The same data as in Fig. 1 but for quartz sand.

$$m=A\cdot\exp(-k\cdot n), \qquad (1)$$

Summing up the experimental data (Fig. 1 – 4), expression (1) actually provides an extrapolational forecast of values of further operational masses. At that for specific cases of ferroimpurities magnetic control, parameter A in (1) is determined graphically as a fictitious starting (n=0) ordinate which is 'linearized' in logarithmic coordinates of dependence m on n (Fig. 1*b* – 4*b*). Another parameter in (1) is k, which is defined by inverse recalculation with an arbitrary pair (Fig. 1 – 4) of corresponding values of n and $m=mn$, i.e. $k=[-\ln(mn/A)]/n$. Besides, it is also possible to employ Excel spreadsheet to develop expression (1) with its inherent particular values of parameters A and k during ferroimpurities magnetic control in some medium.

After determining expression (1) we can have at our disposal the data on total aggregate value of ferroimpurities masses, including residual (not extracted) masses as well.

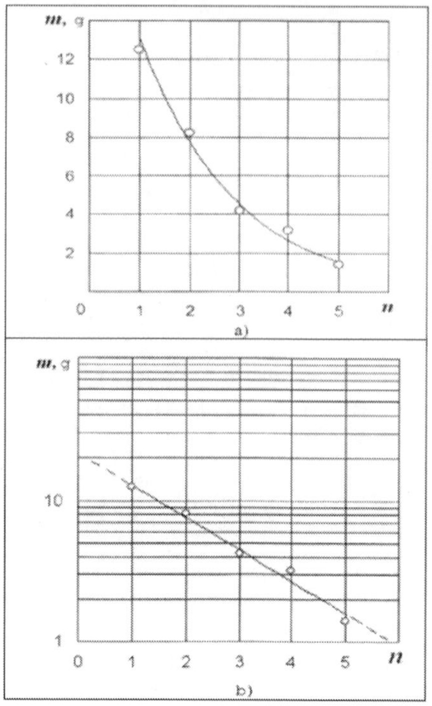

Figure 3. The same data as in Fig. 1 but for engine oil.

At the first glance, it may seem that we would need to sum up as many as possible members of discrete dependence (1), up to n→∞.

Having said that, we still claim this summing up is easily done if we take into consideration that discrete dependence (1) is a quantitative series represented as a decreasing geometric progression. Consequently, with the known first member of this progression m1=A·exp(-k·1) and its ratio q=exp(-k) the mass of ferroimpurities in the medium analyzed is determined as a total potential mass of residue m1…∞, which could be obtained with virtually unlimited number of operations (n→∞), i.e.

$$m_{1...\infty} = \sum_{n=1}^{\infty} m_n = \frac{m_1}{1-q} = \frac{A}{\exp k - 1}. \quad (2)$$

Further, with known values of volume V and mass M of the analysed medium sample, we can find true values of volume and/or mass-concentrations C_V and C_M respectively: cV =m1…∞/V, cM=m1…∞/M.

In case when a limited number of operations n is performed, employing the same discrete dependence (1) we can find the mass of the ferroimpurities removed from the sample analysed m1…nas a sum of the limited number of geometric progression members:

$$m_{1...n} = \sum_{n=1}^{n} m_n = \frac{m_1 - m_n \cdot q}{1-q} = A\frac{1-\exp(-k \cdot n)}{\exp k - 1}. \quad (3)$$

In which case, with the account for (1) and (3) we can assess the corresponding error ε1…n=(m1…∞-m1…n)/m1…∞ =exp(-k·n) (x100%) for the case when we take into consideration only the data for some number n of actually performed magnetophoretic operations.

It is noteworthy, that the afore-described methodology of magnetic control (its calculating part) is true not for all media. Thus, similar experiments on poly-operational extraction of ferroimpurities from a sample of other media, e.g. feldspar, demonstrated the following. The obtained mass-operational dependence (Fig. 5*a*) was at first sight a decreasing and asymptomatically nearing zero one, but as a whole, it was functionally different from the basic dependence (1). We also proved it true that in test semi logarithmic coordinates (Fig. 5*b*) this dependence could not be fully linearized. However, it can be partially linearized as two sections with clearly expressed 'kink', which actually suggests that the described experimental and calculating method of magnetic control can be possibly adapted to working with such specific media.

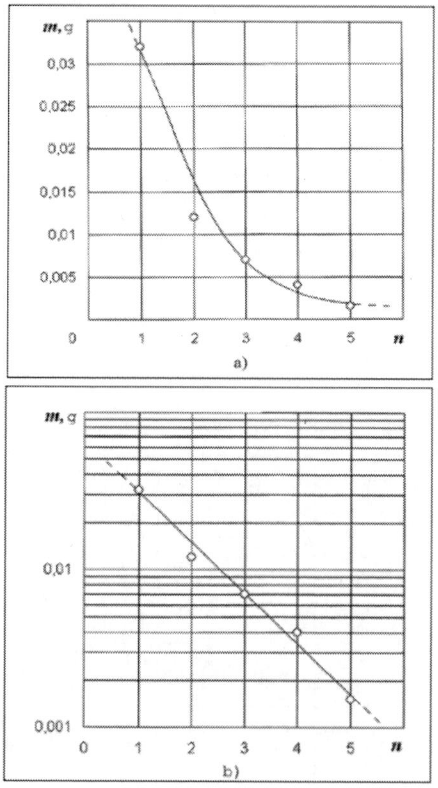

Figure 4. The same data as in Fig. 1 but for petrol.

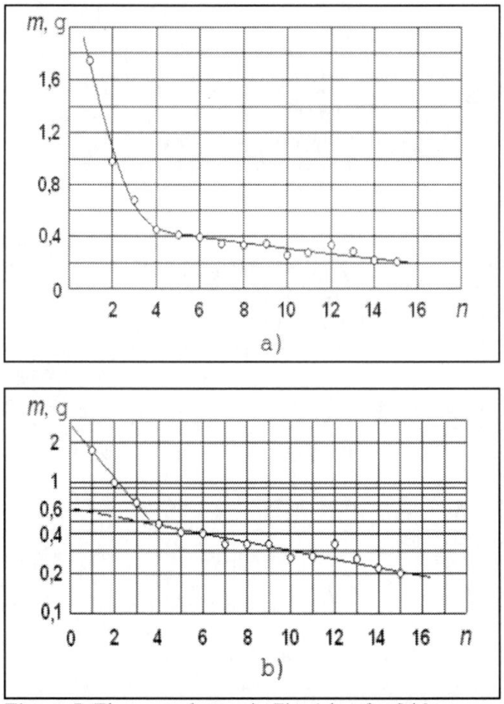

Figure 5. The same data as in Fig. 1 but for feldspar.

Essentially, such adaptation comes down to the following. Total mass $m_{1...\infty}$ of ferroimpurities in the sample analysed is obviously (Fig. 5*b*):

$$m_{1...\infty} = m_{1...n} + m_{(n+1)...\infty} . \quad (4)$$

Providing the 'kink' of *m*, *n* – dependence (Fig. 6*b*) falls on some value *n*, as a rule, a small one (Fig.5*b*, n =4), then value $m_{1...n}$ (for the first steeply descending initial section) can be easily determined immediately by a simple summation of factual data of operational masses, i.e. $m_{1...n} = m_1 + m_2 + ... + m_n$. Whereas when calculating mass $m_{(n+1)...\infty}$ (for the next, second section, including the data of extrapolated operations) we should subtract a some what insignificant initial part of the second downward flat section (in Fig. 2 it is shown by a dash-line preceding this second, plateau section), using formulae (2) and (3) for this task:

$$m_{(n+1)...\infty} = m_{1...\infty} - m_{1...n} = A\frac{\exp(-kn)}{\exp k - 1} , \quad (5)$$

i.e.$m_{1...n}$ here (in contrast with the aforementioned analogous symbol) is the formal isolated mass which should have belonged to the second (flat) section if that section had been the only one and let us repeat again, had begun with $n = 1$, but not e.g. with $n = 5$ (Fig. 5*b*). Herewith, empirical parameters A and k are the parameters of this flat section.

Then, for the given case of magnetic control of ferroimpurities in feldspar, the calculating formula (5) takes the following view:

$$m_{1...\infty} = m_{1...n} + A\frac{\exp(-kn)}{\exp k - 1} . \quad (6)$$

This formula allows determining actual content of ferroimpurities (both extracted and residual ones) in the feldspar sample, and naturally, in the samples of likewise media (as is seen in Fig. 6, a dependence similar in view is observed

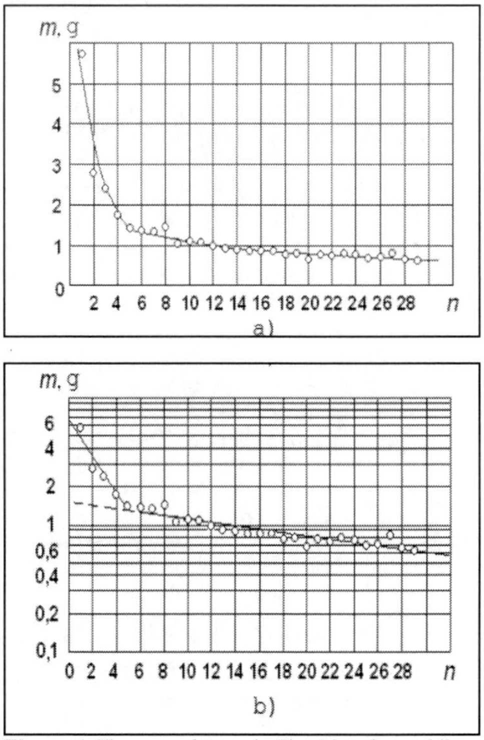

Figure 6. The same data as in Fig. 1 but for molding sand mixture in foundry production.

at magnetic control of ferroimpurities in sand and clay moulding mixtures for foundry production). As the research manifests, these quite peculiar media (feldspar, moulding mixes etc.) feature ferroparticles with a wide array of granularity, i.e. relatively 'easily-removed' and 'hard-to-remove' particles which eventually determine the 'piecewise-linear' view of *m*, *n* – dependences.

3 Conclusion

In this paper, it has been submitted to the literature that magnetic control of ferroimpurities of various granular and liquid media presupposes such as performing multiple operations of magnetic separating ferroimpurities from the sample of the medium analysed, obtaining a discrete dependence of ferroimpurities masses removed from the medium analysed on the sequence number of the magnetophoretic operation, functional legalisation of this dependence, employing this functional dependence for developing calculating formulae which allow defining total aggregate mass (including residual one) of ferroimpurities in a sample of given volume and/or mass have been observed. The method considered in the manuscript has been tested in such media as flour, grounded tealeaf, quartz sand, petrol, engine oil, feldspar, moulding sand mix for foundry production.

Acknowledgement

The research is conducted with financial support from RFFI within the frameworks of research project № 16-38-60034 mol_a_dk, the RF Ministry of Education and Science by the State Assignment in scientific activities №9.1189.2014/K.

References

1. D. Norrgran, T. Shuttleworth, G. Rasmussen. Updated magnetic separation techniques to improve grinding circuit efficiency, Minerals Engineering, **17** (2004).
2. P. Todd , R.P.Cooper, J.F. Dooyle, S. Dunn, J. Vellinger, M.S. Deuser, Multistage magnetic particle separator, Journal of Magnetism and Magnetic Materials, **225** (2001).
3. V. Zezulka, P. Straka, P. Mucha. A magnetic filter with permanent magnets on the basis of rare earth, Journal of Magnetism and Magnetic Materials, **268** (2004).
4. D. Norrgran. Magnetic filtration: producing fine high-purity feedstocks, Filtration and Separation, **45** (6), (2008).
5. J.M.D. Coey. Permanent magnet applications, Journal of Magnetism and Magnetic Materials, **248** (2002).
6. S. Nedelcu, J.H. Watson. Magnetic separator with transversally magnetized disk permanent magnets, Mineral Engineering, **15** (2002).
7. S. Sharma, A. Gaur, U. Singh, V. K. Katiyar. Modeling and Simulation of Magnetic Nanoparticles Transport in a Channel for Magnetic Drug Targeting, *Proceedings of the 12th International Conference on Heat Transfer*, Thermal Engineering and Environment (HTE '14).
8. O. Hidehiko, M. Kazunari, O. Takeshi, R. **Evan, W. Hiroshi. Computational Fluid** Dynamics Simulation of High Gradient Magnetic Separation, Separation Science and Technology, **40** (2005).
9. J.G. Rayner, T.J. Napier-Munn. A mathematical model of concentrate solids content for the wet drum magnetic separator, International Journal of Mineral Processing, **70** (2003).
10. J. Svoboda. A realistic description of the process of high-gradient magnetic separation, Minerals Engineering, **14** (2001).
11. V.Murariu, J.Svoboda, P.Sergeant. The modeling of the separation process in a ferrohydrostatic separator, Minerals Engineering, **18** (2005).
12. K.Nandy, S.Chaudhuri, R.Ganguly, I.K.Puri. Analytical model for the magnetophoretic capture of magnetic microspheres in microfluidic devices, Journal of Magnetism and Magnetic Materials, **320** (2008).
13. R. Goleman. Macroscopic model of particles' capture by the elliptic cross-section collector in magnetic separator, Journal of Magnetism and Magnetic Materials, **272-276**, (2004).
14. Patent 4492921 US. Method of Determining the Quantity of Solid Fraction of Ferromagnetic Matter in a Fluid. Sandulyak A.V., Garaschenko V.I., Korkhov O.J. Published 1985.
15. A.A. Sandulyak, D.A. Sandulyak, A.E. Ablaeva, A.V. Sandulyak. A Phenomenological Model of Experimental and Computational Magnetic Control of Ferrous Impurities in Foodstuffs, *Proceedings of the 4th International Conference on Agricultural Science, Biotechnology, Food and Animal Science* (Dubai, ABIFA15).

MATEC Web of Conferences 76, 02046 (2016) DOI: 10.1051/matecconf/20167602046
CSCC 2016

Stability results for sets of uniqueness in binary tomography

Paolo Dulio[1,a] and *Silvia M.C.* Pagani[1,b]

[1] *Dipartimento di Matematica "F. Brioschi", Politecnico di Milano, Piazza Leonardo da Vinci 32, I-20133 Milano*

Abstract. The recovery of an unknown density function from the knowledge of its projections is the aim of tomography. In many cases, considering the problem from a discrete perspective is more convenient than employing a continuous approach: discrete tomography, and in particular binary tomography, is therefore exploited. One of the main goals of tomography is guaranteeing that the produced output coincides with the scanned object, namely, one wants to achieve uniqueness of reconstruction, even when only a few directions, from which projections are taken, are employed. Relying on a theoretical result stating that special sets of just four lattice directions are enough to uniquely reconstruct a binary grid, we prove that such sets are stable, in the sense that a small discrete perturbation of the components of the directions returns sets which again ensure uniqueness of reconstruction. Examples are provided.

1 Introduction

Tomography takes its practical foundation from the following request: reconstruct the interior of an object which is not directly accessible (for instance, a human brain) without opening and/or damaging it. Tomography is therefore a branch of the inverse problems, and was born thanks to the theoretical work done by Johann Radon [1], who gave a formula to reconstruct a function from its line integrals. This continuous approach is known as *computed tomography*. In order to achieve the reconstruction, X-rays are sent from a source to a detector, and what we measure is their attenuation coefficient, meaning that the ray encountered some kind of obstacle in its trajectory.

The continuous framework in which Radon inversion formula takes place, however, reveals not to be the best way of modeling reality. The most important drawback in the continuous approach is the necessity of considering projections from all angles in $[0, 2\pi)$, which is of course not achievable in the real world. This reflects into performing some kind of discretization, leading to *discrete tomography*, where integrals are replaced by finite sums, and different models can be employed according to the different ways of representing pixels and X-rays. As a special case of discrete tomography we have *binary tomography*, where one is interested in detecting the presence or the absence of the object itself. This paper deals with binary objects.

A fundamental issue of tomography is uniqueness of reconstruction, namely, one wants to ensure that the reconstructed object is exactly the original one. Generally speaking, the reconstruction problem is ill-posed. Ambiguities descend from the fact that the Radon transform is injective only if projections are available for all angles in $[0, 2\pi)$. If some angles are missing, then the kernel of the Radon transform is not trivial. In the discrete case, this reflects in the presence of non-zero images, having null projections along the considered directions. Such images are known as *ghosts*. The presence of ghosts was the input to investigate which parts of the object could be anyway reconstructed; this problem has been developed in [2–4].

In binary tomography, however, one can exploit the upper bound on the number of allowed grey levels in order to get some extra conditions. This has been done by Brunetti, Dulio and Peri in [5] (and later generalized to higher dimensions in [6]), who prove that just four suitably chosen valid directions guarantee uniqueness of reconstruction. Their main theorem is reported and explained in Section 3.

Starting from that result, we want to address another common issue which arises when facing the real world: that of stability, namely, what happens when a small perturbation affects four directions which ensure uniqueness. This problem is closely related to that of the presence of noise. In this paper, we prove that sets ensuring uniqueness are stable under the action of a small lattice perturbation.

The paper is organized as follows. In Section 2 we recall the main definitions concerning discrete tomography and lattice directions. In Section 3 the main uniqueness theorem of [5] is reported, while Section 4 shows the new results concerning stability. In Section 5 examples are depicted and commented; Section 6 focuses on possible further work and concludes the paper.

[a] e-mail: paolo.dulio@polimi.it
[b] e-mail: silviamaria.pagani@polimi.it

2 Definitions

2.1 Main models for discrete tomography

We restrict our investigation to the two-dimensional case, so the object we aim to reconstruct is an *image*, occupying a subset of the lattice $\mathbb{Z}^2$, say a rectangular grid $\mathcal{A}$. We can therefore say that an image is a map $f : \mathcal{A} \to \mathbb{Z}$. By an abuse of notation, we will sometimes say that we reconstruct $\mathcal{A}$ instead of f.

The image is represented as a column vector $\mathbf{x} \in \mathbb{R}^N$, where N is the number of the pixels composing the image. The projection data are collected in a vector $\mathbf{p} \in \mathbb{R}^M$, where M corresponds to the sum of the lengths of the arrays gathering the measurements along each direction. So, the tomographic reconstruction problem is modeled as an equivalent linear system

$$A\mathbf{x} = \mathbf{p}, \tag{1}$$

where A is the $M \times N$ matrix such that its entry a_{ij} is related to the contribution that the j-th pixel gives to the i-th equation. In general, such an approach is severely underdetermined, and many solutions are allowed for a given set of projections. Usually this leads to rely on iterative methods, such as ART, DART and SIRT (see for instance [7]).

Different ways of computing a_{ij}s give different models for discrete tomography. We recall the two we will employ throughout the paper; in both of them, a pixel is considered to be a-dimensional, namely, collapsed into a point of the lattice, say its bottom-left corner.

In the *discrete strip model* (see Figure 1(a)), X-rays are strips of given width w. Here $a_{ij} = 1$ if the pixel x_j belongs to the i-th strip, and $a_{ij} = 0$ otherwise. Therefore, p_i sums the values of the lattice points falling in the corresponding strip.

For $w \to 0$, we get the *grid model* (see Figure 1(b)), where therefore X-rays are lattice lines. Consequently, $a_{ij} = 1$ if the pixel x_j belongs to the i-th line, and $a_{ij} = 0$ otherwise. This model is the basic discrete theoretical model.

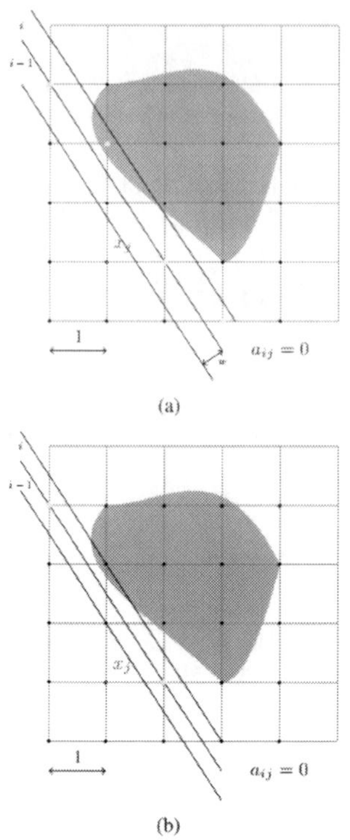

Figure 1. Different models for discrete tomography. (a) The discrete strip model. (b) The discrete line model, or grid model.

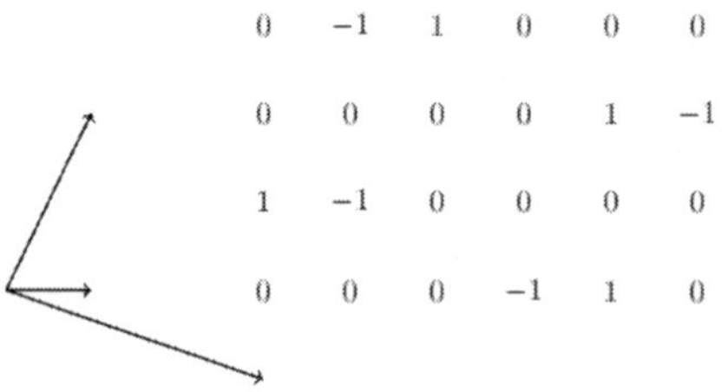

Figure 2. A ghost associated to the three depicted directions. The non-null pixels are the ones of the associated bad configuration.

2.2 Valid directions

As previously said, the presence of ghosts causes ambiguities in the reconstruction. Ghosts' non-null pixels form the so-called *(weakly) bad configurations*, namely, pairs of sets of pixels having the same projections along the considered directions (see Figure 2 for an example). The presence of weakly bad configurations prevents an image from being uniquely reconstructed. We call S-bad configuration a bad configuration associated to a set S of directions. If pixels can be counted with multiplicity greater than one, we deal with S-weakly bad configurations.

It is known from [8] that a grid $\mathcal{A}$ is uniquely determined by a set S of directions if and only if no S-bad configuration can be constructed inside $\mathcal{A}$.

However, uniqueness can be trivially achieved, even with just one direction: for instance, if one takes a direction u whose slope is such that each line parallel to u has at most one intersection with the grid $\mathcal{A}$, then the resulting linear system (1) has only one solution (see Figure 3). In real tomographic applications, however, non-valid directions are undesirable, since each detector should collect information point by point. We therefore consider a different approach.

In 2001, Hajdu and Tijdeman [9] introduced an algebraic approach to discrete tomography, which shows how ghosts can be treated in terms of polynomials.

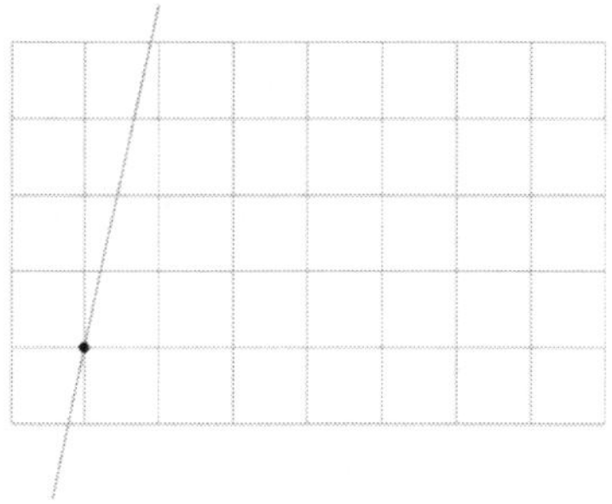

Figure 3. A single direction can ensure uniqueness of reconstruction.

Fix a lattice grid $\mathcal{A} = \{(z_1, z_2) \in \mathbb{Z}^2 \mid 0 \leq z_1 < m, 0 \leq z_2 < n\}$. A direction is modeled as a pair (a, b) of coprime integers; coordinate directions are represented by the pairs $(1, 0)$ (the horizontal one) and $(0, 1)$ (the vertical one). We can assume without loss of generality that $a \geq 0$.

Definition 1 *A set $S = \{(a_r, b_r) \mid r = 1, \ldots, d\}$ of d lattice directions is said to be* valid *for the grid $\mathcal{A}$ if*

$$\sum_{r=1}^{d} a_r < m \quad \text{and} \quad \sum_{r=1}^{d} |b_r| < n. \tag{2}$$

Therefore, valid sets are the ones that allow us to construct a ghost inside the grid.

3 A uniqueness result for binary tomography

Since valid sets of directions imply the presence of bad configurations inside the image, they cannot lead to uniqueness of reconstruction. To do so, we need to add other constraints. A commonly employed one is the prior knowledge of the number of grey levels of the image; in particular, one is often interested in detecting the presence or the absence of a body, reflecting in the presence of just two shades, say black and white. This is the framework of binary tomography.

This kind of prior knowledge reveals to be fundamental in order to get uniqueness results with valid directions. The result we are going to recall, due to Brunetti, Dulio and Peri ([5]), characterizes the smallest sets of binary uniqueness, namely, sets of valid directions which ensure uniqueness of reconstruction for binary images. Such sets are composed of just four directions, built in a peculiar way; we now define the tools which will be employed in the characterization theorem.

First of all, sets S of directions have to satisfy a necessary condition: one of the directions has to be the sum of the other three, or the sum of two of them must equal the sum of the other two. This means that $S = \{u_1, u_2, u_3, u_4 = u_1 + u_2 \pm u_3\}$. Note that u_4 has to be a direction, namely, a pair of coprime integers, so not all triples u_1, u_2, u_3 are allowed. This condition on the directions reflects in the fact that a minimal bad configuration associated to the set S has a pixel which is counted twice, so its value is 2 or -2. This is not allowed in a binary fashion, so such a bad configuration cannot be constructed inside a binary grid.

Set $u_r = (a_r, b_r)$, $r = 1, 2, 3, 4$, and

$$\sum_{r=1}^{4} a_r =: h, \qquad \sum_{r=1}^{4} |b_r| =: k.$$

Consider the set $D = \pm S \cup \hat{S}$, where

$$\pm S = \{\pm u_1, \pm u_2, \pm u_3, \pm u_4\}$$

and

$$\hat{S} = \{\pm(u_1 - u_4), \pm(u_2 - u_4), \pm(u_1 + u_2)\}.$$

Note that the set D is a set of pairs, so its elements are not necessarily directions.

Define the subsets A, B of D as follows:

$$\begin{aligned} A &:= \{(a, b) \in D \mid |a| > |b|\}, \\ B &:= \{(a, b) \in D \mid |b| > |a|\}. \end{aligned}$$

Moreover, if $|a| = |b|$, for some $(a, b) \in D$, we then include (a, b) in A if $\min\{m - h, n - k\} = m - h$, while $(a, b) \in B$ otherwise. Thus D is the disjoint union of A and B, where one of the two sets may be empty.

We can now state the uniqueness theorem.

Theorem 2 ([5], Theorem 6) *Let $S = \{u_1, u_2, u_3, u_4 = u_1 + u_2 \pm u_3\}$ be a valid set for the lattice grid $\mathcal{A} = \{(z_1, z_2) \in \mathbb{Z}^2 \mid 0 \leq z_1 < m, 0 \leq z_2 < n\}$. Then every binary image defined on $\mathcal{A}$ is uniquely determined if and only if*

$$\min_{(a,b) \in A} |a| \geq \min\{m - h, n - k\}, \tag{3}$$

$$\min_{(a,b) \in B} |b| \geq \min\{m - h, n - k\}, \tag{4}$$

and

$$\begin{aligned} m - h < n - k \; &\Rightarrow \; \forall (a, b) \in B : \\ &|a| \geq m - h \text{ or } |b| \geq n - k, \end{aligned} \tag{5}$$

$$\begin{aligned} n - k < m - h \; &\Rightarrow \; \forall (a, b) \in A : \\ &|a| \geq m - h \text{ or } |b| \geq n - k, \end{aligned} \tag{6}$$

where, if one of the sets A, B is empty, the corresponding condition (3) *or* (4) *drops.*

Denote by $\mathcal{S}(\mathcal{A})$ the collection of sets of binary uniqueness for a grid $\mathcal{A}$. We wish to exploit Theorem 2 to solve the linear system (1), which will have a unique binary solution.

4 Stability results

In view of applications, given a lattice grid $\mathcal{A}$, it would be desirable to have different sets from $\mathcal{S}(\mathcal{A})$, in order to select the set S which better fits with the faced constraints. Therefore, we wish to investigate how S could be changed without affecting uniqueness.

A first simple but useful result is the following.

Theorem 3 *Let $\mathcal{A} = \{(z_1, z_2) \in \mathbb{Z}^2 \mid 0 \le z_1 < m, 0 \le z_2 < n\}$ be a lattice grid, and let $S = \{u_1, u_2, u_3, u_4\} \in \mathbb{S}(\mathcal{A})$. Denote by $\mathbf{p}_S$ the projection vector obtained by employing the directions of S. Then there exist continuous intervals J_i, $i = 1, 2, 3, 4$, such that $u_i \in J_i$, and, for all $S' = \{u'_i \mid u'_i \in J_i\}$, the linear system $A\mathbf{x} = \mathbf{p}_{S'}$ has only one solution, which equals the unique binary solution of $A\mathbf{x} = \mathbf{p}_S$.*

Proof. Slightly changing the directions in S, we can always obtain a set S' formed by directions which are not valid for the $m \times n$ lattice grid $\mathcal{A}$. This can be easily achieved by replacing some (possibly all) $u_i = (a_i, b_i) \in S$, $i = 1, 2, 3, 4$, with $u'_i = (a'_i, b'_i)$ (see Figure 4), such that

$$\frac{b'_i}{a'_i} = \tan\gamma = \frac{w}{L} = \begin{cases} \dfrac{b_i}{n(a_i^2 + b_i^2)} & \text{if } b_i > a_i \\ \dfrac{a_i}{m(a_i^2 + b_i^2)} & \text{if } b_i < a_i. \end{cases}$$

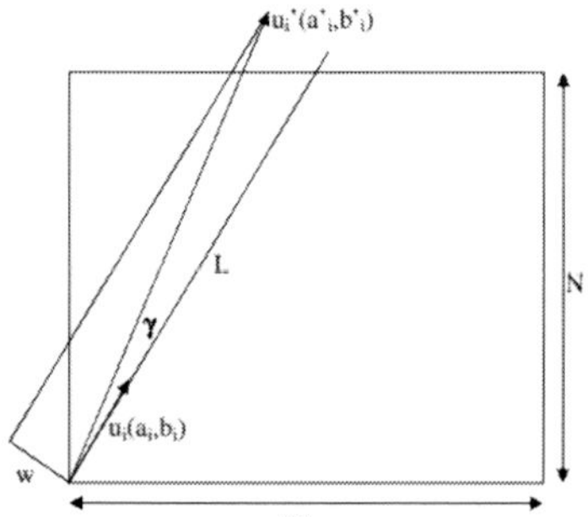

Figure 4. Angle γ between a non valid direction $u' = (a'_i, b'_i)$ obtained by a slight change of $u_i = (a_i, b_i) \in S$.

In fact, in this case, each line in direction u'_i intersects the grid in a segment completely included in the strip bounded by two adjacent lattice lines parallel to the direction u_i. Since S' contains non-valid directions, then S' does not satisfy condition (2). Therefore, S' is a set of general (not necessarily binary) uniqueness, meaning that the linear system $A\mathbf{x} = \mathbf{p}_{S'}$ has just one solution. □

Remark 4 *We have already said that non-valid directions are not desirable. However, instead of regarding Theorem 3 as a stable noise-free reconstruction result, we could interpret it as an exact reconstruction result for X-ray affected by some noise.*

As previously observed, in the grid model X-rays count the number of lattice points belonging to lines having rational slopes. In view of real applications we should also remark that, moving from source to detector, X-rays can be affected by deviations from the straight line paths, due to mechanical and physical phenomena. This means that a single X-ray, in fact, counts more points than in the usual grid model, since its trajectory meets different lattice lines. Trajectories could be highly different from ray to ray, so, in order to model the various behaviors, we assume that each X-ray path is confined in a strip of prescribed width w, and that each point in the strip cannot be visited twice. This means that the number of lattice points included in a given strip represents an upper bound on the corresponding detected projection.

This can be interpreted as a discrete strip model of the continuous approach, where a ray issuing from a given source P could be detected by any point of the line segment L_P of length w, and axis of symmetry passing through P. In term of back-projection, the strip orthogonal to L_P is spanned, and consequently a noise, depending on the width of the strip, is introduced with respect to the corresponding grid-model reconstruction process. This suggests to interpret the discrete strip model as a kind of noisy grid model, where the width w of the strips corresponds to the amount of noise that affects the grid model projections.

Now we want to show that a small *discrete* perturbation of a valid set of uniqueness, that preserves the validity of the employed directions, also preserves uniqueness. To this, we need to introduce a notion of *lattice perturbation* of a lattice direction.

Definition 5 *Let $d = (d_1, d_2)$ be a given lattice direction. For each $\epsilon = \frac{a}{b} \in \mathbb{Q} \cap [0, 1]$, and $\delta_x, \delta_y \in \{0, 1\}$, the ϵ-*lattice perturbation *of d is the vector $d(\epsilon, \delta_x, \delta_y)$, parallel to $d + \delta_x(\epsilon, 0) + \delta_y(0, \epsilon)$, given by*

$$d(\epsilon, \delta_x, \delta_y) = (d_1 b + a\delta_x, d_2 b + a\delta_y).$$

Note that

$$\frac{d_2}{d_1 + \epsilon} \le \frac{d_2}{d_1} \le \frac{d_2 + \epsilon}{d_1},$$

and also

$$\begin{aligned} \frac{d_2}{d_1 + \epsilon} &\le \frac{d_2}{d_1 + \epsilon\delta_x} \le \frac{d_2 b}{d_1 b + a\delta_x} \\ &\le \frac{d_2 b + a\delta_y}{d_1 b + a\delta_x} \le \frac{d_2 b + a\delta_y}{d_1 b} \le \frac{d_2 + \epsilon}{d_1}, \end{aligned}$$

so that the slope of $d(\epsilon, \delta_x, \delta_y)$ is sufficiently close to the slope of d. Therefore, $d(\epsilon, \delta_x, \delta_y)$ is a lattice vector (not necessarily a lattice direction), bounded in a small angular neighbor of d.

Theorem 6 *Let $\mathcal{A}$ be a lattice grid, and let $S = \{u_1, u_2, u_3, u_4\} \in \mathbb{S}(\mathcal{A})$. Let $S' = \{u'_1, u'_2, u'_3, u'_4\}$ such that $u'_1 = u_1(\epsilon, \delta_x, \delta_y)$, $u'_2 = u_2(\epsilon, \delta_x, \delta_y)$, $u'_3 = u_3$ and $u'_4 = u'_1 + u'_2 + u'_3$ if $u_4 = u_1 + u'_2 + u_3$, or $u'_4 = u'_1 + u'_2 - u'_3$ if $u_4 = u_1 + u_2 - u_3$. If S' is a set of valid directions for $\mathcal{A}$, then $S' \in \mathbb{S}(\mathcal{A})$.*

Proof. Assume $u_r = (a_r, b_r)$, $u'_r = (a'_r, b'_r)$, and consider the case when $u_4 = u_1 + u_2 + u_3$. We have

$$\begin{aligned} h' &= 2(a'_1 + a'_2 + a'_3) \ge 2(a_1 + a_2 + a_3) = h \\ k' &= 2(|b'_1| + |b'_2| + |b'_3|) \ge 2(|b_1| + |b_2| + |b_3|) = k, \end{aligned}$$

and consequently

$$\begin{aligned} \min\{m - h', n - k'\} &\le \min\{m - h, n - k\}, \\ \max\{m - h', n - k'\} &\le \max\{m - h, n - k\}. \end{aligned}$$

Now, consider the set $D' = \pm S' \pm \widehat{S'} = A' \cup B'$. For each $d' = (d'_1, d'_2) \in D'$ let $d = (d_1, d_2) \in D$ be the corresponding vector. Note that $d'_1 \geq d_1$ and $d'_2 \geq d_2$.

Now, let $d' \in D' = A' \cup B'$. There are several cases to be considered.

Case 1: $d' \in A'$. Since $S \in \mathcal{S}(\mathcal{A})$, we have two subcases.

Case 1a: If $d \in A$, then $|d_1| \geq \min\{m-h, n-k\}$, so that

$$|d'_1| \geq |d_1| \geq \min\{m-h, n-k\} \geq \min\{m-h', n-k'\}.$$

Case 1b: If $d \in B$, then $|d_2| \geq \min\{m-h, n-k\}$, so that

$$|d'_2| \geq |d_2| \geq \min\{m-h, n-k\} \geq \min\{m-h', n-k'\}$$

and, since $d' \in A'$, $|d'_1| \geq |d'_2|$, so that $|d'_1| \geq \min\{m-h', n-k'\}$ as in subcase 1a.

Therefore, for all $d' \in A'$, it is

$$|d'_1| \geq \min\{m-h', n-k'\},$$

and consequently

$$\min_{(a',b') \in A'} |a'| \geq \min\{m-h', n-k'\},$$

so that condition (3) in Theorem 2 holds.

Case 2: $d' \in B'$. Since $S \in \mathcal{S}(\mathcal{A})$, there are two subcases again.

Case 2a: If $d \in A$, then $|d_1| \geq \min\{m-h, n-k\}$, so that

$$|d'_1| \geq |d_1| \geq \min\{m-h, n-k\} \geq \min\{m-h', n-k'\}$$

and, since $d' \in B'$, $|d'_2| \geq |d'_1|$, so that $|d'_2| \geq \min\{m-h', n-k'\}$.

Case 2b: If $d \in B$, then $|d_2| \geq \min\{m-h, n-k\}$, so that

$$|d'_2| \geq |d_2| \geq \min\{m-h, n-k\} \geq \min\{m-h', n-k'\},$$

as in subcase 2a.

Therefore, for all $d' \in B'$, it is

$$|d'_2| \geq \min\{m-h', n-k'\}$$

and consequently

$$\min_{(a',b') \in B'} |b'| \geq \min\{m-h', n-k'\},$$

so that condition (4) in Theorem 2 holds.

Now, suppose that $\min\{m-h', n-k'\} = m-h'$, and consider any $d' \in B'$. If $d \in A$, then, by condition (3) in Theorem 2, we have $|d_1| \geq \min\{m-h, n-k\}$, so that

$$\begin{aligned} |d'_1| \geq |d_1| &\geq \min\{m-h, n-k\} \\ &\geq \min\{m-h', n-k'\} = m-h'. \end{aligned}$$

If $d \in B$, and $\min\{m-h, n-k\} = m-h$, then, by condition (5) in Theorem 2, it may be $|d_1| \geq m-h$, so that

$$|d'_1| \geq |d_1| \geq m-h \geq m-h',$$

or $|d_2| \geq n-k$, so that

$$|d'_2| \geq |d_2| \geq n-k \geq n-k'.$$

If $d \in B$, and $\min\{m-h, n-k\} = n-k$, then, by condition (4) in Theorem 2, we have $|d_2| \geq n-k$, so that

$$|d'_2| \geq |d_2| \geq n-k \geq n-k'.$$

Therefore, we have

$$\forall d' \in B' : |d'_1| \geq m-h' \text{ or } |d'_2| \geq n-k'$$

and condition (5) in Theorem 2 holds.

Similarly, if $\min\{m-h', n-k'\} = n-k'$, consider any $d' \in A'$. If $d \in A$ and $\min\{m-h, n-k\} = m-h$, then, by condition (3) in Theorem 2, we have $|d_1| \geq m-h$, so that

$$|d'_1| \geq |d_1| \geq m-h \geq m-h'.$$

If $d \in A$ and $\min\{m-h, n-k\} = n-k$, then, by condition (6) in Theorem 2, it could be $|d_1| \geq m-h$, so that

$$|d'_1| \geq |d_1| \geq m-h \geq m-h',$$

or $|d_2| \geq n-k$, so that

$$|d'_2| \geq |d_2| \geq n-k \geq n-k'.$$

If $d \in B$, then, by condition (4) in Theorem 2, we have $|d_2| \geq \min\{m-h, n-k\}$, so that

$$\begin{aligned} |d'_2| \geq |d_2| &\geq \min\{m-h, n-k\} \\ &\geq \min\{m-h', n-k'\} = n-k'. \end{aligned}$$

Therefore, we have

$$\forall d' \in A' : |d'_1| \geq m-h' \text{ or } |d'_2| \geq n-k',$$

and condition (6) in Theorem2 holds.

A similar proof works for $u_4 = u_1 + u'_2 - u_3$. □

Theorem 7 *Let $S = \{u_i = (a_i, b_i) \mid i = 1,2,3,4\}$ be a set of lattice directions, and r_1, r_2 be such that*

$$\begin{array}{ll} a_1 = \min_i a_i & b_1 = \min_i b_i \\ a_2 = a_1 + r_1, & b_2 = b_1 + s_1, \\ a_3 = a_1 + r_2, & b_3 = b_1 + s_2, \\ a_4 = a_1 + a_2 + a_3 & b_4 = b_1 + b_2 + b_3 \\ r_1 + r_2 \geq \frac{m-7a_1}{2} & s_1 + s_2 \geq \frac{n-7b_1}{2}. \end{array}$$

Then $S \in \mathcal{S}(\mathcal{A})$.

Proof. The set S is of the form $S = \{u_1, u_2, u_3, u_4 = u_1 + u_2 \pm u_3\}$, therefore we must prove that the assumptions of Theorem 2 hold.

Consider the set $\widehat{S} = \{\pm(u_1 - u_4), \pm(u_2 - u_4), \pm(u_1 + u_2)\}$. Since $a_1 = \min_i a_i$, and $b_1 = \min_i b_i$, then, for each $\widehat{s} = (\widehat{s_1}, \widehat{s_2}) \in \widehat{S}$, we have $\widehat{s_1} \geq a_1$ and $\widehat{s_2} \geq b_1$. Therefore, for any vector $d = (d_1, d_2) \in D = \pm S \cup \widehat{S} = A \cup B$, it results $d_1 \geq a_1$ and $d_2 \geq b_1$.

Now, note that

$$h = a_1 + a_2 + a_3 + a_4 = 6a_1 + r_1 + r_2$$

and

$$k = b_1 + b_2 + b_3 + b_4 = 6b_1 + s_1 + s_2.$$

Therefore, it results

$$\begin{array}{rcccl} m-h &=& m-6a_1-r_1-r_2 &\leq& a_1 \\ n-k &=& n-6b_1-s_1-s_2 &\leq& b_1. \end{array}$$

Assume that $\min\{m-h, n-k\} = m-h$. If $u_1 \in A$, then

$$a_1 \geq b_1 \geq n-k \geq m-h.$$

Consequently, if $(d_1, d_2) \in A$, then $d_1 \geq a_1 \geq m-h$, and Condition (3) in Theorem 2 holds. If $(d_1, d_2) \in B$, then $d_2 \geq b_1 \geq m-h$, and Condition (4) in Theorem 2 holds. Moreover, $d_1 \geq a_1 \geq m-h$, so that the first inequality of Condition (6) in Theorem 2 holds.

Suppose now that $\min\{m-h, n-k\} = n-k$. If $u_1 \in A$, then

$$a_1 \geq b_1 \geq n-k \geq m-h.$$

Consequently, if $(d_1, d_2) \in A$, then $d_1 \geq a_1 \geq n-k$, and Condition (3) in Theorem 2 holds. Moreover, $d_2 \geq b_1 \geq n-k$, so that the second inequality of Condition (5) in Theorem 2 holds. If $(d_1, d_2) \in B$, then $d_2 \geq b_1 \geq n-k$, and Condition (4) in Theorem 2 holds. Moreover, $d_1 \geq a_1 \geq m-h$, so that the first inequality of Condition (6) in Theorem 2 holds.

Therefore, all conditions in Theorem 2 hold, and consequently $S \in \mathcal{S}(\mathcal{A})$. □

In the experimental section we will provide a few examples of lattice perturbations.

5 Experimental results

In the following experiments, performed in a noise-free context, we employed ϵ equal to 1. This choice is due to the fact we reconstruct small images (11×11 and 15×15, respectively), so that greater values for a, b (recall that $\epsilon = \frac{a}{b}$) make the set S' non-valid for the grid $\mathcal{A}$.

In the first experiment, we consider the set

$$\begin{array}{rcl} S &=& \{u_1, u_2, u_3, u_1+u_2-u_3\} \\ &=& \{(1,5), (2,-3), (0,1), (3,1)\}, \end{array}$$

which is a set of binary uniqueness for an 11×11 grid. For $\epsilon = 1$ and a suitable choice of the values of δ_xs and δ_ys, the first two directions are modified as follows:

$$\begin{array}{rcl} u_1 = (1,5) \mapsto u_1' &=& (1\cdot 1 + 1\cdot 1, 5\cdot 1 + 1\cdot 0) \\ &=& (2,5), \\ u_2 = (2,-3) \mapsto u_2' &=& (2\cdot 1 + 1\cdot 1, -3\cdot 1 + 1\cdot 1) \\ &=& (3,-2). \end{array}$$

The third direction of the new set S' is the same as the third one of set S, and so we get

$$u_4' = u_1' + u_2' - u_3' = (5,2).$$

The set $S' = \{(2,5), (3,-2), (0,1), (5,2)\}$ is again a set of binary uniqueness for $\mathcal{A}$. An example of reconstruction is shown in Figure 5.

In the second experiment, we deal with an 15×15 grid $\mathcal{A}$, and initial set of uniqueness is

$$\begin{array}{rcl} S &=& \{u_1, u_2, u_3, u_1+u_2-u_3\} \\ &=& \{(1,-1), (3,-5), (0,1), (4,-7)\}. \end{array}$$

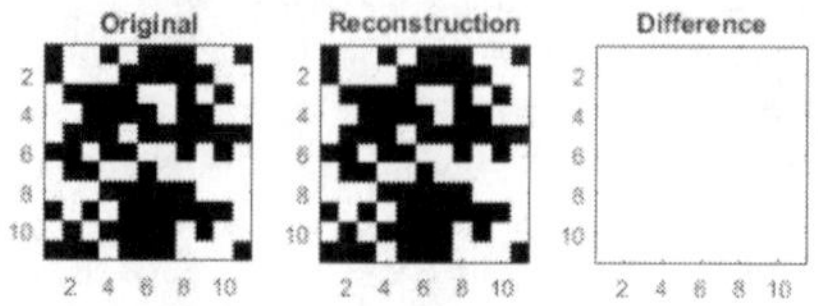

(a)

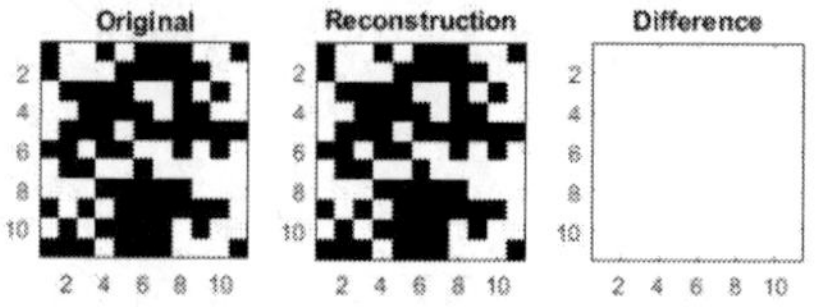

(b)

Figure 5. Reconstruction performed with different sets of directions on an 11×11 grid. In each line, the leftmost image is the original phantom, the central image is the reconstructed one, and the rightmost image shows the difference between the previous two (white pixel means exactly reconstructed pixel). (a) $S = \{(1,5), (2,-3), (0,1), (3,1)\}$. (b) $S' = \{(2,5), (3,-2), (0,1), (5,2)\}$.

Also in this case, we consider $\epsilon = 1$; the second direction is not modified (namely, we choose $\delta_x = \delta_y = 0$ in that case), while the first one becomes

$$u_1 = (1,-1) \mapsto u_1' = (2,-1).$$

The new set is therefore

$$S' = \{(2,-1), (3,-5), (0,1), (5,-7)\}.$$

Again, it satisfies all conditions of Theorem 2, so that S' is a set of binary uniqueness for $\mathcal{A}$. Figure 6 shows an example.

6 Conclusions and new directions of research

In this paper we have proven some results concerning the stability of sets of uniqueness in binary tomography, together with some experimental results. Sets of four directions, ensuring uniqueness for binary images defined on a

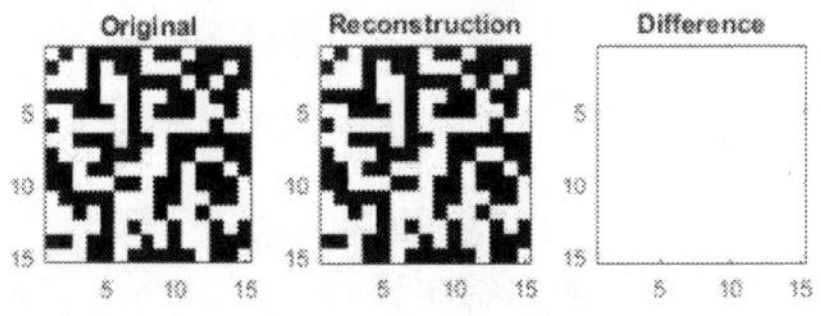

(a)

(b)

Figure 6. Reconstruction performed with different sets of directions on a 15×15 grid. (a) $S = \{(1,-1),(3,-5),(0,1),(4,-7)\}$. (b) $S' = \{(2,-1),(3,-5),(0,1),(5,-7)\}$.

given lattice grid $\mathcal{A}$, are shown to be robust with respect to lattice perturbations. This could represent an interesting way of recovering sets of binary uniqueness, whose complete enumeration is still missing (see for instance [10]).

Further work can be done. First of all, noise could be introduced in the reconstruction process, so one has to face modifications not only of the lattice directions, but also in the entries of the projection vector **p**.

Also, it would be interesting to combine the obtained stability results with another kind of investigation, relying on some preliminary results provided in [11, Theorem 2.5 and Corollary 2.1], which in turn rely on [12]. Here, the binary rounding of the solution obtained by pseudo-inversion (via iterative methods) is taken into account, and different sets of binary uniqueness may play a role in the speed of convergence of the iterations.

References

[1] J. Radon, Ber. Verh. Sächs. Akad. Wiss. Leipzig Math.-Phys. Kl. pp. 262–277 (1917)
[2] P. Dulio, A. Frosini, S.M. Pagani, in *Discrete geometry for computer imagery* (Springer, Cham, 2014), Vol. 8668 of *Lecture Notes in Comput. Sci.*, pp. 285–296
[3] P. Dulio, A. Frosini, S.M. Pagani, Inverse Problems **31**, 125011 (2015)
[4] P. Dulio, A. Frosini, S.M. Pagani, LNCS pp. 105–116 (2016)
[5] S. Brunetti, P. Dulio, C. Peri, Discrete Appl. Math. **161**, 2281 (2013)
[6] S. Brunetti, P. Dulio, C. Peri, Discrete Appl. Math. **183**, 20 (2015)
[7] K.J. Batenburg, J. Sijbers, IEEE Trans. Image Process. **20**, 2542 (2011)
[8] P.C. Fishburn, J.C. Lagarias, J.A. Reeds, L.A. Shepp, Discrete Math. **91**, 149 (1991)
[9] L. Hajdu, R. Tijdeman, J. Reine Angew. Math. **534**, 119 (2001)
[10] S. Brocchi, P. Dulio, S.M. Pagani, Recent Advances in Systems, in: Recent Advances in Electrical Engineering Series **52**, 393 (2015)
[11] S.M. Pagani, *From uniqueness results to reconstruction and characterization algorithms in discrete tomography* (PhD thesis, Politecnico di Milano, 2016)
[12] K.J. Batenburg, W. Fortes, L. Hajdu, R. Tijdeman, Discrete Appl. Math. **161**, 2236 (2013)

MATEC Web of Conferences **76**, 02047 (2016) DOI: 10.1051/matecconf/20167602047
CSCC 2016

A 4-D Hyperchaotic Memristive Dynamical System

Dimitrios Prousalis[1,a], Christos Volos[1,b], Ioannis Stouboulos[1,c], and Ioannis Kyprianidis[1,d]

[1] *Department of Physics, Aristotle University of Thessaloniki, Thessaloniki, GR-54124, Greece*

Abstract. A new 4-D memristive system is presented in this paper. The peculiarity of the model is that it displays a line of equilibrium points and it has hyperchaotic dynamics in a particular range of the parameters space. The behavior of the proposed system is investigated through numerical simulations, by using phase portraits, Lyapunov exponents and Poincaré sections. Furthermore, we have designed and implemented an electronic circuit to verify the feasibility of the proposed system.

1 Introduction

Chua introduced the missing fourth circuit element, the memristor, in 1971 according to the theory of electrical circuits combining the charge q and the flux ϕ [1]. A general concept of memristive systems was developed by Chua and Kang [2]. However until 2008 when Strukov *et al* at Hewlett-Packard Laboratories [3] reported a solid-state implementation of the memristor, the research on memristors was not broad enough. In 2009, Ventra *et al* [4] proposed other "mem-elements", such as memcapacitor memcapacitor and meminductor. Since then, many potential applications about memristors have been found based on their properties. Non-volatile memory applications, crossbar latches as transistor replacements or augmentors, analog computation and circuit applications, as well as memristor-based neural networks are some of them. Also, the design of memristor-based chaotic oscillators, by replacing the nonlinear part of chaotic dynamical systems with memristors has been introduced [5]-[7]. So, research on memristor-based chaotic systems becomes a focal research topic in both the technological and the application domain [8]-[16].

Furthermore, in recent years a new classification of chaotic dynamics has been introduced. According to this, there are two types of attractors: self-excited attractors and hidden attractors. A self-excited attractor has a basin of attraction that is excited from unstable equilibria. In contrast, hidden attractor cannot be found by using a numerical method in which a trajectory starts from a point on the unstable manifold in the neighbourhood of an unstable equilibrium [17]. Studying hyperchaotic systems with hidden attractors is still an open research topic. Motivated by complex dynamical behaviors of hyperchaotic systems, noticeable characteristics of memristor and unknown features of hidden attractors, a memristive hyperchaotic system with a line of equilibrium points is proposed in this paper.

This research work is organized as follows. In Section 2 a 3-D four-wing chaotic system, the model of the memristive system, as well as the new hyperchaotic system are presented. In Section 3 presents the simulation results of the memristive system. In Section 4 the circuit realization of the system is described in detail and Section 5 concludes this work with a symmary of the main results.

[a] e-mail: dprou@physics.auth.gr
[b] e-mail: volos@physics.auth.gr
[c] e-mail: stouboulos@physics.auth.gr
[d] e-mail: imkypr@auth.gr

2 The New 4-D Hyperchaotic Memristive System

2.1 The 3-D Four-Wing Chaotic System

In 2015 Li *et al* [18] announced a 3-D four-wing system which is described by the equations:

$$\begin{aligned} \dot{x} &= ax + y + yz \\ \dot{y} &= -xz + yz \\ \dot{z} &= -z - mxy + b \end{aligned} \tag{1}$$

The system of differential equations (1) is a chaotic nonlinear system with four quadratic nonlinearities, three linear terms and especially with none in the second equation.

It has been shown by Li *et al* [18] that the 3-D system (1) displays the following features.

- It generates a four-wing chaotic attractor with fractal structure for some choices of the parameters.
- In a selected parameter region, it displays robust chaos with periodic Arnold tongues, and the strange attractor varies among a symmetric pair of single-wing attractors, a double-wing butterfly attractor, and a four-wing attractor.
- There is a hidden parameter in the coefficient of a quadratic nonlinearity in the system, whereby an obvious constant term controls the amplitude of all variables.

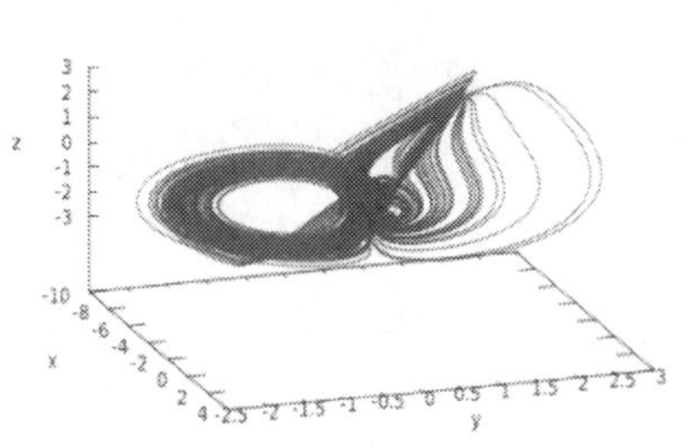

Figure 1. Phase space in $x - y - z$, for $a = 0.4$, $b = 3$, $c = 0.1$, $d = 6$, $e = 1$.

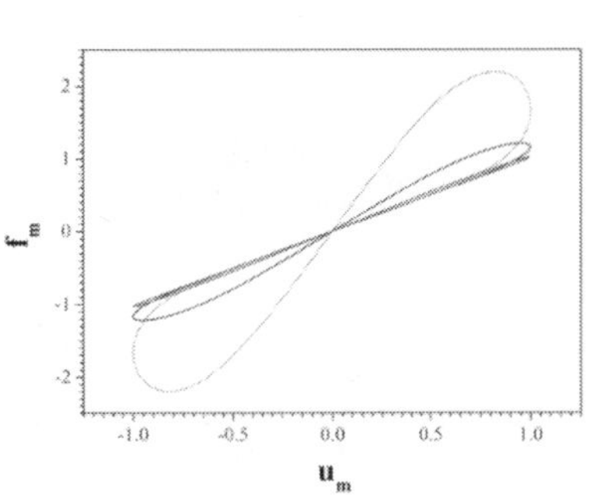

Figure 2. Hysteresis loops of the proposed memristive system driven by a sinusoidal stimulus with $A = 1$ and $w_0 = 0$, for $f = 0.1$ (green line), $f = 0.2$ (blue line), $f = 0.5$ (red line).

The attractor resembles two groups of butterfly shapes, which is different from other reported four-wing systems. The Figure 1 shows that system's (1) four wings are built in different way.

2.2 Model of the Memristive System

As it is mentioned, Chua and Kang introduced the memristive system by generalizing the original definition of a memristor [2]. A memristive system can be described as:

$$\begin{aligned} \dot{w}_m &= F(w_m, u_m, t), \\ f_m &= G(w_m, u_m, t)u_m \end{aligned} \tag{2}$$

where w_m, f_m and u_m denote the state of memristive system, output and input, respectively. The function G is a continuous and n-dimensional scalar function and F is a vector function. So in this work the following form of a memristive system has been used:

$$\begin{aligned} \dot{w}_m &= u_m, \\ f_m &= (1 + 0.25w_m^2 - 0.002w_m^4)u_m. \end{aligned} \tag{3}$$

In order to investigate the behavior of the memristive system an external bipolar period signal u_m is applied. The form of u_m is:

$$u_m = Asin(2\pi ft) \tag{4}$$

where A is the amplitude and f is the frequency. From the first equation of the system (3) we can find w_m:

$$w_m = w_m(0) + \tfrac{A}{2\pi ft}(1 - cos(2\pi ft)) \tag{5}$$

where $w_m(0) = \int_{-\infty}^{0} u_m(\tau)d\tau$ is the initial condition of the internal state w_m.

Substituting (4) and (5) into (3), it is easy to derive the output of the memristive system. Therefore, the output y_m depends on the frequency and amplitude of the applied input stimulus. Figure 2 shows the hysteresis loops of the memristive system (3) when it is driven by a periodic signal (4) with different frequencies. Obviously, the proposed memristive system exhibits a pinched hysteresis loop in the input-output plane.

2.3 The New Hyperchaotic Memristive System

Finally, according to the aforementioned 3-D chaotic system and memristive system, the following 4-D memristive system is presented.

$$\begin{aligned} \dot{x} &= ax + by + yz \\ \dot{y} &= -xz + yz - cf \\ \dot{z} &= -z - dxy + e \\ \dot{w} &= y \end{aligned} \tag{6}$$

where $y = u_m$, $w = w_m$ and $f = f_m$.

The 4-D memristive system (6) for every a, b, c, d, e has a line of equilibrium points $E(0, 0, e, w_m)$. As a result, this memristive hyperchaotic system can be considered as a dynamical system with hidden attractors because it is impossible to verify the chaotic attractor by choosing an arbitrary initial condition in the vicinity of the unstable equilibria [18].

The Four-Wing hyperchaotic attractor in the (x, y, z) phase space, for $a = 0.5$, $b = 3$, $c = 0.1$, $d = 6$, $e = 1$ is depicted in Fig. 3.

By using the Wolf *et al* [19] algorithm the Lyapunov exponents have been calculated as: $L_1 = 0.35891$, $L_2 = 0.00239$, $L_3 = 0$ and $L_4 = -4.1826$. So, there are two positive Lyapunov exponents as a result the system is hyperchaotic. In addition the Kaplan-Yorke dimension of the system is found as:

$$D_{KY} = 3 + \frac{L_1 + L_2 + L_3}{|L_4|} = 3.0864 \tag{7}$$

As it is shown in Fig. 3 the new 4-D memristive system has the same "butterfly" shape.

3 Simulation Results

In order to study the behavior of the new system, usual assets of the theory of dynamical systems such as phase portaits, Poincaré maps, bifurcation diagrams and and diagram of Lyapunov exponents.

The bifurcation diagram of y versus α, for $b = 3$, $c = 0.1$, $d = 6$, $e = 1$, is presented in Fig. 4. Also

DOI: 10.1051/matecconf/20167602047

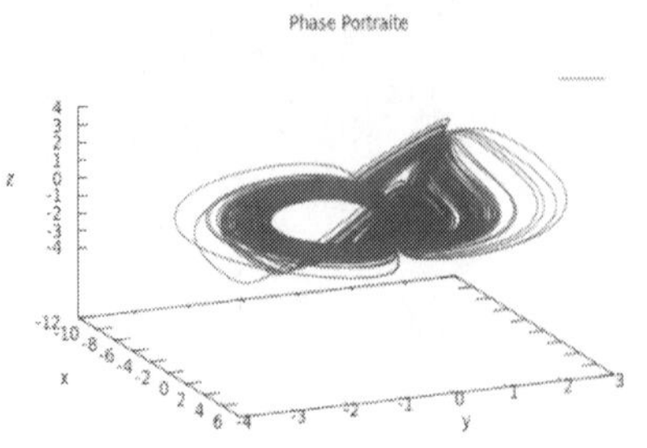

Figure 3. Hyperchaotic attractor in (x, y, z) phase space, for $a = 0.5$, $b = 3$, $c = 0.1$, $d = 6$, $e = 1$.

the diagram of system's (6) Lyapunov exponents versus α is depicted in Fig. 4. This diagram confirms system's dynamical behavior as it is presented in the respective bifurcation diagram. At the Lyapunov diagram (Fig. 5) the fourth Lyapunov exponent is ignored because it takes negative values far from the zero value.

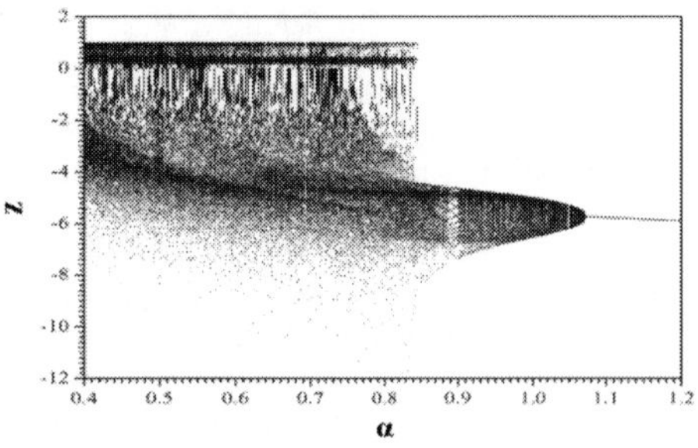

Figure 4. The bifurcation diagram of y versus α for $b = 3$, $c = 0.1$, $d = 6$, $e = 1$.

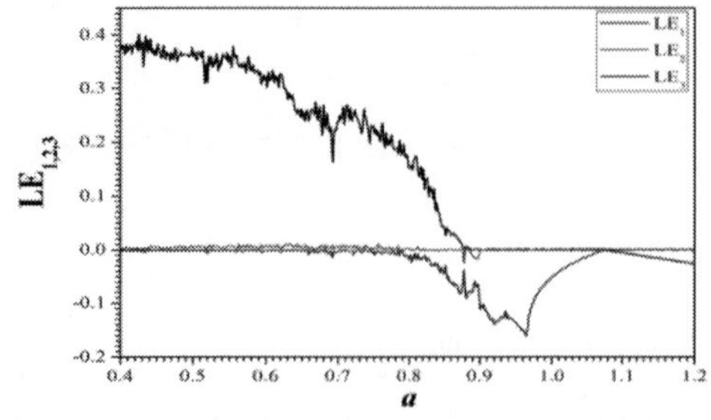

Figure 5. The Lyapunov Diagram of y versus α for $b = 3$, $c = 0.1$, $d = 6$, $e = 1$.

In more details, system (6) presents the following dynamical behavior:

- a region of periodic behavior for $a > 1.07$ (Fig. 6). .
- a region of quasi-periodic behavior for $0.91 < a < 1.07$ (Fig. 7).
- a region of periodic behavior for $0.89 < a < 0.91$.
- a region of chaotic behavior for $0.85 < a < 0.89$ (Fig. 8).
- a region of hyperchaotic behavior for $0.4 < a < 0.85$ (Fig. 9).

Especially, the hyperchaotic behavior is shown in the Lyapunov diagram of Fig. 5 in the region where two Lyapunov Exponents become positive and one zero.

4 Circuit Realization of the Memristive Hyperchaotic System

The electronic circuit, which emulates the mathematical model of the proposed memristive hyperchaotic system (6), is presented in this section, in order to show its feasibility. The designed circuit, which is built by using off-the-shelf electronic components, is an effective way for discovering dynamics of the theoretical model practically. Circuital design, especially of hyperchaotic systems plays an important role on the field of nonlinear science due to its applications in many fields, such as in secure communication, signal processing, random bit generator, or path planning for autonomous mobile robot etc [20]-[24]. In addition, circuital implementation of chaotic/hyperchaotic systems is also provide an effective approach for investigating dynamics of such theoretical models [25], [26]. For example, hyperchaotic attractors can be observed on the oscilloscope easily or experimental bifurcation diagrams can be obtained by varying the values of variable resistors [27], [28].

Figure 10 depicts the schematic of the circuit. The main circuit that realizes the system (6), has four integrators (U1 - U4) and two inverting amplifiers (U5, U6), which are implemented with the operational amplifier TL084, as well as three signals multipliers (U8 - U10) by using the analog multiplier AD633. Also, the circuital realization of the memristor's function f of Eq. (2), is also depicted in Fig. 10. Indeed the sub-circuit of the proposed memristive system only emulates the memristive function because there is not any commercial off-the-shelf memristive device in the market yet. So, the memristor's function is realized by using an inverting adder amplifier (U7) and three signals multipliers (U11 - U13). By applying Kirchhoff's circuit laws, the corresponding circuital equations of the designed circuit can be written as:

$$\begin{aligned}
\dot{x} &= \tfrac{1}{R\cdot C}[\tfrac{R}{R_a}x + \tfrac{R}{R_b}y + \tfrac{R}{10V\cdot R_1}y\cdot z] \\
\dot{y} &= \tfrac{1}{R\cdot C}[-\tfrac{R}{10V\cdot R_1}x\cdot z + \tfrac{R}{10V\cdot R_1}y\cdot z - \tfrac{R}{R_c}f] \\
\dot{z} &= \tfrac{1}{R\cdot C}[-z - \tfrac{R}{10V\cdot R_d}x\cdot y + V_e] \\
\dot{w} &= \tfrac{1}{R\cdot C}y
\end{aligned} \tag{8}$$

where

$$f = [\tfrac{R}{10V\cdot R_1}V_f + \tfrac{R}{(10V)^2\cdot R_2}w^2 - \tfrac{R}{(10V)^4\cdot R_3}w^4]y \tag{9}$$

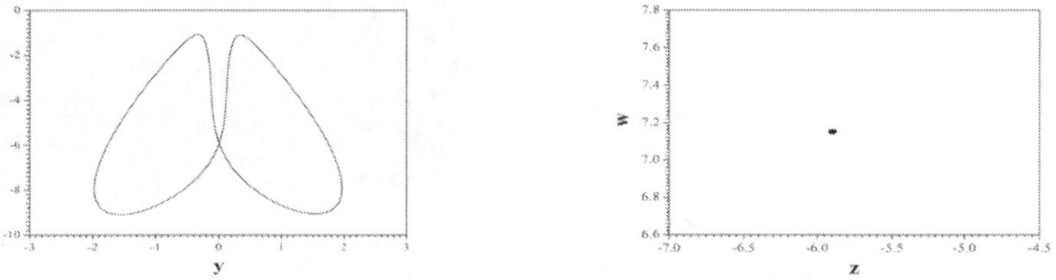

(a) (b)

Figure 6. (a) Phase portrait and (b) Poincaré map, for a = 1.2, b = 3, c = 0.1, d = 6, e = 1.

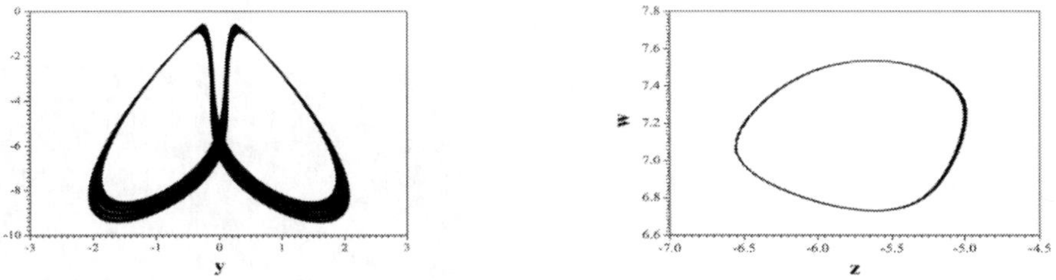

(a) (b)

Figure 7. (a) Phase portrait and (b) Poincaré map, for a = 1, b = 3, c = 0.1, d = 6, e = 1.

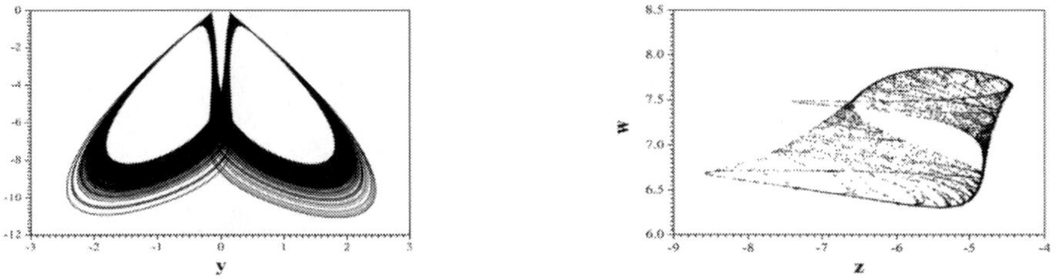

(a) (b)

Figure 8. (a) Phase portrait and (b) Poincaré map, for a = 0.85, b = 3, c = 0.1, d = 6, e = 1.

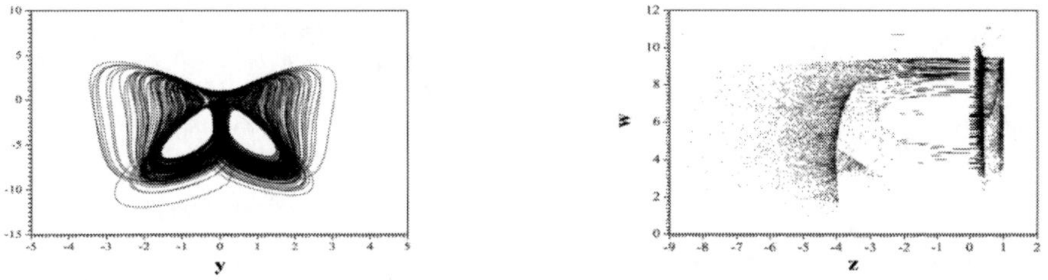

(a) (b)

Figure 9. (a) Phase portrait and (b) Poincaré map for a = 0.5, b = 3, c = 0.1, d = 6, e = 1.

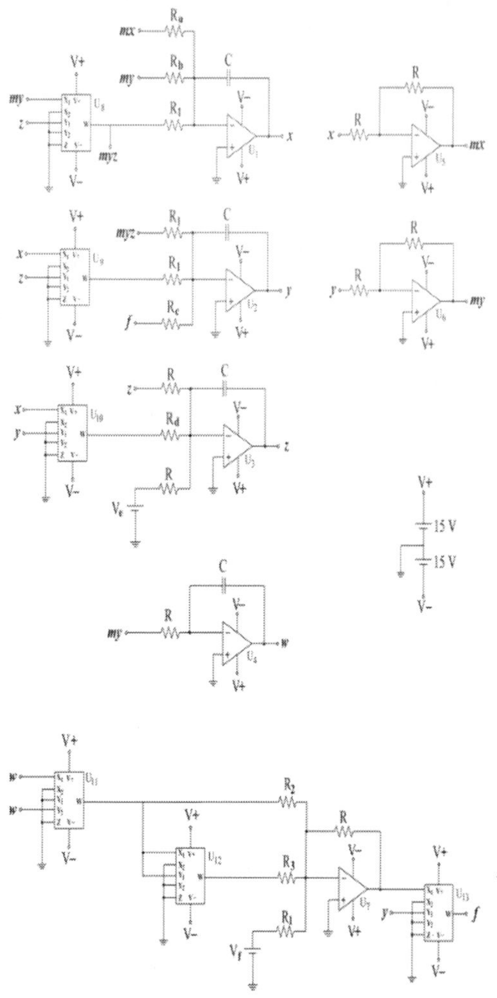

Figure 10. Schematic of the circuit which emulating the memristive hyperchaotic system.

In system (8), the variables x, y, z and ω correspond to the voltages in the outputs of the integrators $U1 - U4$. Normalizing the differential equations of system (8), by using $\tau = t/RC$, we can see that this system is equivalent to the system (6), with $a = R/R_a, b = R/R_b, c = R/R_c$ and $d = R/(10V \cdot R_d)$. The circuit components have been selected as: $R = 10k\Omega$, $R_1 = 1k\Omega$, $R_2 = 0.4k\Omega$, $R_3 = 0.5k\Omega$, $R_a = 20k\Omega$, $R_b = 3.333k\Omega$, $R_c = 100k\Omega$, $R_d = 0.166k\Omega$, $C = 10nF$, $V_e = V_f = -1V_{DC}$, while the power supplies of all active devices are $15V_{DC}$. For the chosen set of components the system's (6) parameter is $a = 0.5$, $b = 3$, $c = 0.1$, $d = 6$, $e = 1$. The designed circuit is implemented in the electronic simulation package MULTISIM and the obtained results are displayed in Figs. 11-12. Theoretical attractors (see Fig.9a) are similar with the circuital ones (see Fig. 12).

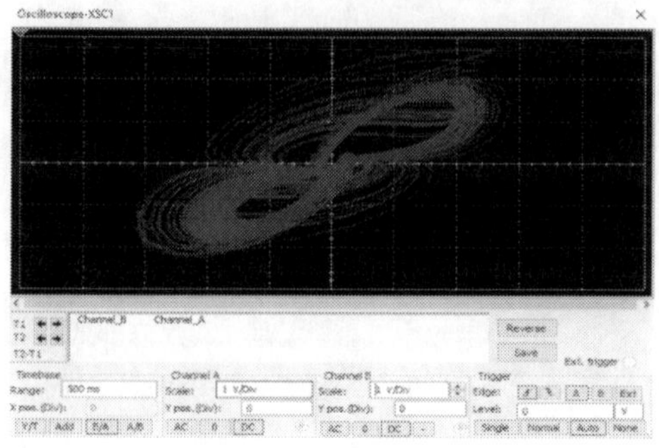

Figure 11. Hyperchaotic attractor of the designed circuit obtained from MULTISIM in the (x, y)-phase plane, for $a = 0.5$, $b = 3$, $c = 0.1$, $d = 6$, $e = 1$.

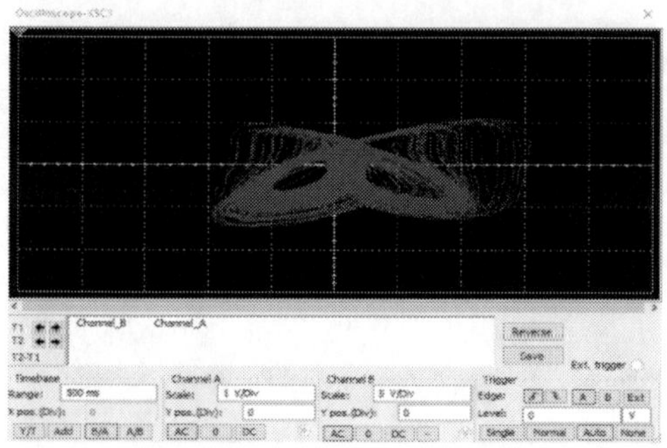

Figure 12. Hyperchaotic attractor of the designed circuit obtained from MULTISIM in the (x, z)-phase plane, for $a = 0.5$, $b = 3$, $c = 0.1$, $d = 6$, $e = 1$.

5 Conclusion

The existence of a memristor-based hyperchaotic system with line of equibria has been studied in this paper. Although 4-D memristive systems often only generate chaos, the presence of a memristive device leads the proposed system to a hyperchaotic system with hidden attractors. The system has rich dynamical behavior as confirmed by the example of attractor reported and by the numerical Poincaré map presented. Also, the designed circuit emulates very well the proposed hyperchaotic memristive system. Because there is little knowledge about the special features of such system, future works will continue focusing on dynamical behaviors, as well as the possibility of control and synchronization of such system.

References

[1] L.O. Chua, "Memristors-the missing circuit element," IEEE Trans. Circuit Theory, **vol. CT-18**, pp. 507–519, (1971).

[2] L.O. Chua and S.M. Kang, "Memristive devices and systems," Proceeding of the IEEE, **vol. 375**, no 23, pp. 209–223, (1976).

[3] D.B. Strukov, G.S. Snider, G.R. Stewart, and R.S. Williams, "The missing memristor found," Nature,**no 453**, pp. 80–83, (2008).

[4] M.D. Ventra, Y.V. Pershin, and L.O. Chua, "Circuit elements with memory: memristors, memcapacitors, and meminductors," Proceedings of the IEEE, **no. 97(10)**, pp. 1717–1724, (2009).

[5] M. Itoh and L.O. Chua, "Memristor oscillators," Int J Bifurc Chaos, **vol. 18**, pp. 3183–3206, (2008).

[6] Y.B. Zhao, C.K. Tse, J.C. Feng, and Y.C. Guo, "Application of memristor-based controller for loop filter design in charge-pump phase-locked loop," Circuits Syst Signal Process, **vol. 32**, pp. 1013–1023, (2013).

[7] A.L. Wu, J.N. Zhang, and Z.G. Zeng, "Dynamical behaviors of a class of memristor-based Hopfield networks," Physics Letters A, **vol. 375**, pp. 1661–1665, (2011).

[8] C.K. Volos, I.M. Kyprianidis, and I.N. Stouboulos, "The Memristor as an Electric Synapse Synchronization Phenomena," *In Proc. Int. Conf. DSP'2011 (Confu, Greece)*, pp. 1–6, (2011).

[9] J.J. Yang, D.B. Strukov, and D.R. Stewart, "Memristive Devices for Computing," Nature Nanotechnology, **vol. 8**, pp. 13–24, (2013).

[10] T. Driscoll, J. Quinn, S. Klein, H.T. Kim, B.J. Kim, Y. V. Pershin, M. Di Ventra, and D. N. Basov, "Memristive Adaptive Filters," Applied Physics Letters, **vol. 97**, pp. 093502-1–3, 2010.

[11] L. Wang, C. Zhang, L. Chen, J. Lai, and J. Tong, "A Novel Memristor-Based rSRAM Structure for Multiple-Bit Upsets Immunity," IEICE Electronics Express, **vol. 9**, pp. 861–867, (2012).

[12] Y. Shang, W. Fei, and H. Yu, "Analysis and Modeling of Internal State Variables for Dynamic Effects of Nonvolatile Memory Devices," IEEE Transactions on Circuits and Systems I: Regular Papers, **vol. 59**, pp. 1906–1918, (2012).

[13] S. Shin, K. Kim, and S.M. Kang, "Memristor Applications for Programmable Analog ICs," IEEE Transactions on Nanotechnology, **vol. 10**, pp. 266–274, (2011).

[14] C. Cepisca, N.G. Bardis., *Measurement and control in street lighting* (ELECTRA publication, 2011).

[15] Bogdan MARIA, Mariana BUGA, Rares MEDIANU, Costin CEPISCA, Nikolaos BARDIS, "Obtaining a Model of Photovoltaic Cell with Optimized Quantum Efficiency,"Scientific Bulletin of the Electrical Engineering Faculty, **No. 2 (16)**, ISSN 1843-6188, (2011).

[16] Costin CEPIŞCĂ, Sorin Dan GRIGORESCU, Stergios GANATSIOS, Nikolaos G. BARDIS,"Passive and Active Compensations for Current Transformers," METROLOGIE, pp. 5-10, (4/2008)

[17] S. Jafari and J.C. Sprott, "Simple chaotic flows with a line equilibrium," Chaos, Solitons and Fractals, **vol. 57**, pp. 79–84, (2013).

[18] C. Li, I. Pehlivan, J.C. Sprott, and A. Agkul, "A novel four-wing strange attractor born in bistability," IEICE Electronics Express, **vol.12**, no 4, pp. 2011116-20141116, (2015).

[19] A. Wolf, J.B. Swift, H.L. Swinney, and J. Vastano, "Determining Lyapunov exponents froma timeseries," Physica D, **vol. 16**, no. 3, pp. 285–317, (1985).

[20] M. Barakat, A. Mansingka, Radwan, A.G., and Salama, K.N. "Generalized hardware post processing technique for chaos–based pseudorandom number generators", ETRI Journal, **vol. 35**, pp. 448-458, (2013).

[21] L. Gamez-Guzman, C. Cruz-Hernandez, R. Lopez-Gutierrez, and E. E. Garcia-Guerrero, "Synchronization of Chua's circuits with multiscroll attractors: application to communication". Commun. Nonlinear Sci. Numer. Simul. , **vol. 14**, pp. 2765-2775, (2009).

[22] S. Sadoudi, C. Tanougast, M. S. Azzaz and A. Dandache, "Design and FPGA implementation of a wireless hyperchaotic communication system for secure realtime image transmission". EURASIP J. Image and Video Processing, **vol. 943**, pp. 1-18, (2013).

[23] C.K. Volos, I.M. Kyprianidis, and I.N. Stouboulos, "A chaotic path planning generator for autonomous mobile robots," Robot. Auto. Systems, **vol. 60**, pp. 651-656, (2012).

[24] M. E. Yalcin, J.A.K. Suykens, and J. Vandewalle, "True random bit generation from a double-scroll attractor," IEEE Trans. Circuits Syst. I, Regular Papers, **vol. 51**, pp. 1395-1404, (2004).

[25] A. Buscarino, L. Fortuna, and M. Frasca, "Experimental robust synchronization of hyperchaotic circuits," Physica D, **vol. 238**, pp. 1917-1922, (2009).

[26] V. Sundarapandian and I.Pehlivan, "Analysis, control, synchronization, and circuit design of a novel chaotic system", Math. Comp. Modelling, **vol. 55**, pp. 1904-1915, (2012).

[27] S. Bouali, A. Buscarino, L. Fortuna, M. Frasca, and L.V. Gambuzza, "Emulating complex business cycles by using an electronic analogue". Nonl. Anal.: Real World Applications, **vol. 13**, pp. 2459-2465, (2012).

[28] L. Fortuna, M. Frasca, and M.G. Xibilia, "Chua's circuit implementation: Yesterday, today and tomorrow", *World Scientific*, Singapore, (2009).

Implementation of a Hyperchaotic System with Hidden Attractors into a Microcontroller

Angelos E. Giakoumis, Christos K. Volos[a], Ioannis N. Stouboulos, Ioannis K. Kyprianidis

Department of Physics, Aristotle University of Thessaloniki, GR-54124, Greece

Abstract. In this work, the implementation of a hyperchaotic oscillator by using a microcontroller is proposed. The dynamical system, which is used, belongs to the recently new proposed category of dynamical systems with hidden attractors. By programming the microcontroller, the three most useful tools of nonlinear theory, the phase portrait, the Poincaré map and the bifurcation diagram can be produced. The comparison of these with the respective simulation results, which are produced by solving the continuous dynamical system with Runge-Kutta, verified the feasibility of the proposed method. The algorithms could be easily modified to add or substitute the hyperchaotic system.

1 Introduction

In the last decades, nonlinear systems and especially chaotic systems have aroused tremendous interest because of their applications in many scientific fields, such as in social sciences, ecology, electronic circuits, lasers, chemical reactions, fluid dynamics, mechanical systems, etc. [1, 2], but also of many other interesting applications such as in secure communication schemes, cryptography and robotics [3-5].

At the same period, there has been an exponential use of embedded systems due to the advances in technology, new communication networks and cost-effective solutions. In general, an embedded system is a computer system used for a specific application such as a washing machine, robotics, automotive, television, cameras, etc. [6-8]. It is basically a compound of a microprocessor, memory and peripherals. In recent years, there are several embedded applications based on microcontroller such as in military, industry, banking transference, e-commerce, biometric systems, cryptography, robotics, telemedicine, and computing [6], [9-18].

Literature presents in the last few years some advances of implementing chaotic systems and their applications with a microcontroller. In 2012, two works based on a microcontroller have been presented, in which the authors presented a simple implementation of the logistic map [19, 20]. Each one of the above papers presents the implementation of a chaotic cryptosystem. The same year, Stanciu and Datcu presented an Atmel AVR microcontroller implementation of a new encryption algorithm based on chaos [21]. In 2013, Volos *et al.* investigated experimentally the coverage performance of a chaotic autonomous mobile robot for fast scanning of the robots workspace with unpredictable way, in which each one of the two robot's independent active wheels is driven by two chaotic logistic maps implemented with Arduino Uno microcontroller [22]. In the same year, Chiu *et al.* proposed an experimental implementation in a microcontroller of the chaotic Lorenz system in order to demonstrate that this kind of chaotic oscillator can be achieved in a digital system like this [23]. Also, in 2013, Volos presented a microcontroller implementation of a chaotic random bit generator with very good statistical results [24].

In 2014, Ketthong and San-Um presented a new random-bit generator based on a new signum-based piecewise-linear chaotic map [25]. Also, in 2014, the same authors proposed a generalization of four chaotic maps with absolute value nonlinearity [26], which is experimentally implemented by using an Arduino microcontroller. Furthermore, Andreatos and Volos in 2014 presented a microcontroller implementation of a text encryption algorithm based on a chaotic Chua system [27]. In 2015, Zapateiro *et al.* [28] presented an experimental realization of a chaos-based secure communication by using Arduino microcontroller.

In this paper, the implementation of a hyperchaotic oscillator with hidden attractors, by using a microcontroller, is proposed. Hidden attractors cannot be localized by using the standard computational procedure; therefore it is difficult to predict the existence of them in a considered system [29, 30]. Furthermore, there has been a significant interest in studying hidden attractors because they play an important role both in theoretical problems and practical engineering applications [31, 32]. Hidden attractors appear in numerous dynamical systems such as Chua's circuit [33], van der Pol–Duffing oscillators [34], model of drilling system actuated by induction motor [35], Lorenz–like system describing convective fluid motion [36], or multilevel DC/DC converter [37].

[a] Corresponding author: volos@physics.auth.gr

This paper is organized as follows. In Section 2 the proposed hyperchaotic system with hidden attractors is analyzed. Section 3 presents the realization of the system with the microcontroller as well as the phase portraits, the Poincaré maps and the bifurcation diagram, which are obtained from the microcontroller. Finally, the conclusions are drawn in Section 4.

2 The Proposed System

In this work, the simplest four-dimensional hyperchaotic Lorenz-type system, which has been proposed by Gao and Zhang [38], is used. This system is an extension of a modified Lorenz system, which was studied by Schrier and Maas as well as by Munmuangsaen and Srisuchinwong [39, 40]. The proposed system is described by the following set of differential equations.

$$\begin{cases} \dot{x} = y - x \\ \dot{y} = -xz + u \\ \dot{z} = xy - a \\ \dot{u} = -by \end{cases} \quad (1)$$

It is structurally a very simple four-dimensional dynamical system having only two independent parameters (a, b). Also, it has many interesting properties not found in other proposed systems, such as:

- It has very few terms, only seven with two quadratic nonlinearities, and two parameters.
- All its attractors are hidden.
- It exhibits hyperchaos over a large region of parameter space.
- Its Jacobian matrix has rank less than four everywhere in the space of the parameters.
- It exhibits a quasiperiodic route to chaos with an attracting torus for some choice of parameters.
- It has regions in which the torus coexists with either a symmetric pair of strange attractors or a symmetric pair of limit cycles and other regions where three limit cycles coexist.
- The basins of attraction have an intricate fractal structure.
- There is a series of Arnold tongues [41] within the quasi-periodic region where the two fundamental oscillations mode-lock and form limit cycles of various periodicities.

In this Section the system's dynamic behavior is investigated numerically by employing a fourth order Runge-Kutta algorithm. For this reason, the bifurcation diagram, which is a very useful tool from nonlinear theory, is used. In Figure 1(a) the bifurcation diagram of the variable y versus the parameter b, for $a = 2.5$, reveals the richness of system's dynamical behavior. Besides limit cycles, the system (1) has quasiperiodicity, chaos, and hyperchaos.

Figure 1(b) shows the Lyapunov exponents' spectra, which is produced by using the Wolf's algorithm [42] for the chosen value of the parameter a ($a = 2.5$). As we can see, when the system has a periodic behavior all the Lyapunov exponents are $L_i \leq 0$ (i = 1, 2, 3, 4), while when it has chaotic or hyperchaotic behavior the system appears one or two positive Lyapunov exponents. So, from Fig. 1(b) the system's hyperchaotic behavior is found for example in the range of $b \in [0.313, 0.462]$, where the system has two positive Lyapunov exponents, as it is shown in the embedded diagram in Fig. 1(b).

In more details, as a value of a decreased from $a = 0.9$ the system goes from a period-1 steady state, through a quasi-periodic route, to the chaotic state. The limit cycle of period-1 and the quasiperiodic attractor in (y, z)-plane are shown in Fig. 6(a) and Fig. 7(a) for $b = 0.9$ and $b = 0.8$, respectively. Also, the chaotic behavior of the proposed system is confirmed by the attractor in (y, z)-plane, for b = 0.55, which is shown in Fig. 8(a). However, a very interesting feature of the specific system is the existence of hyperchaotic attractor for the range of parameter b, which is mentioned before, as it is shown in the phase portraits of Fig. 9(a).

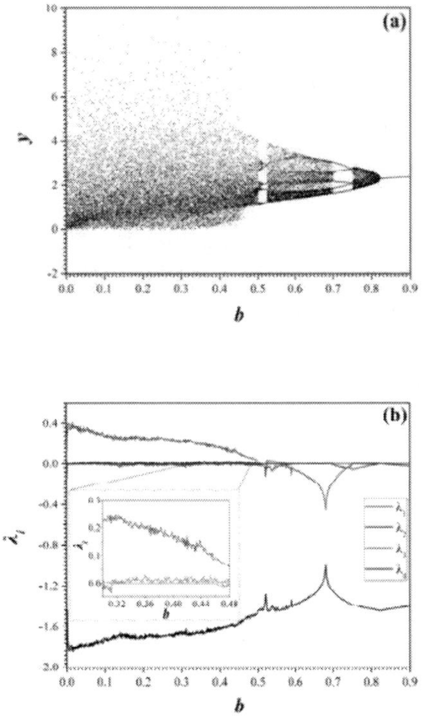

Figure 1. (a) Bifurcation diagram of y versus b, and (b) the diagram of Lyapunov exponents (λ_i) versus the parameter b, for $a = 2.5$.

3 Experimental Results

In this work, we use the PIC32MX795F512H 32-bits microcontroller from Microchip with up to 80 MHz of bus frequency on the Maximite board, which is a small and versatile computer board running MM Basic, a powerful Basic interpreter with floating point arithmetic and 128K working memory (Fig. 2). The data are stored in a .dat file in a 1MB SD card.

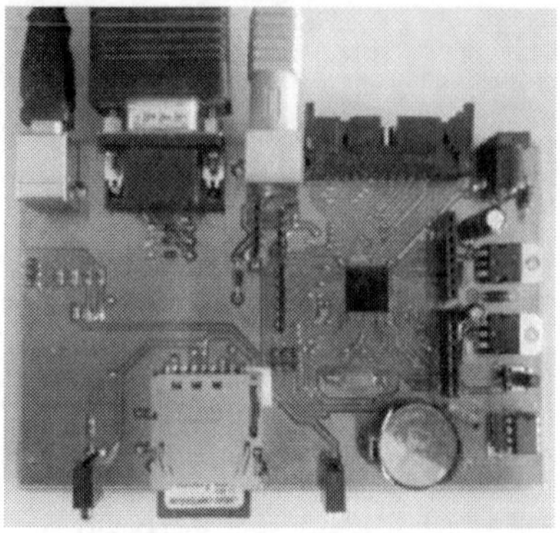

Figure 2. The PIC32MX795F512H 32-bits microcontroller from Microchip on the Maximite board.

In order to implement the oscillator with hidden attractors into the microprocessor, we use the four-dimensional hyperchaotic Lorenz-type system in discrete mode, using the Euler method [43]. So, the system takes the form

$$\begin{cases} X(k+1) = X(k) + h\left[Y(k) - X(k)\right] \\ Y(k+1) = Y(k) + h\left[-X(k)Z(k) + U(k)\right] \\ Z(k+1) = Z(k) + h\left[X(k)Y(k) - a\right] \\ U(k+1) = U(k) + h\left[-bY(k)\right] \end{cases} \tag{2}$$

Here $X(k)$, $Y(k)$, $Z(k)$ and $U(k)$ make up the system state, with the same parameters values, a, b, while h = 0.002 is the sampling time.

Next, the procedure with which the phase portrait, the Poincaré map and the bifurcation diagram produced, are described in details.

3.1 Phase Portrait

To test the implementation, the code shown in Fig. 3 was implemented using the MM Basic interpreter. Therefore, a file containing the $X(k)$, $Y(k)$, $Z(k)$ and $U(k)$ of system (2), which result to the variables $x(t)$, $y(t)$, $z(t)$ and $u(t)$ of the continuous dynamical system (1), is taken.

Figures 6(b), 7(b), 8(b) and 9(b) display the phase portraits in (Y, Z)-plane for a = 2.5 and for the same values of parameter b, as for the respective phase portraits in (y, z)-plane, which were produced by solving the system (1). From the comparison of the two series of phase portraits a very good agreement between them has been observed.

3.2 Poincaré Map

Next, the well-known Poincaré map, which is also a very useful tool in nonlinear theory, is used. This diagram is generated when system's trajectory intersects a selected plane in the phase space (X = 0) with $X(k + 1) > 0$. In this way, the program code shown in Fig. 4 was implemented using the MM Basic interpreter. So, from the microcontroller, a series of files containing the variables $Y(k)$, $Z(k)$ and $U(k)$, produced with the aforementioned procedure, for a = 2.5 and for various values of parameter b, are taken. From these files the Poincaré maps of Fig. 10, which confirm the expected dynamical behavior, are produced.

```
Rem  PROGRAM  BIFURCATION
xn1 = 0.2
yn1 = -0.1
zn1 = 0.3
wn = 0.1
c = 2.5
d = 0.9
h = 0.002
NTR = 200000
OPEN "php.DAT"  FOR OUTPUT  AS #1
FOR I = 1 TO 1200000
xn = xn1
yn = yn1
zn = zn1
wn = wn1
xn1 = xn + h*(yn - xn)
yn1 = yn + h*(- xn*zn + wn)
zn1 = zn + h*(xn*yn - c)
wn1 = wn + h*(-d*yn)
IF 1 > NTR  THEN  PRINT #1, xn1, yn1, zn1, wn1
NEXT I
CLOSE #1
END
```

Figure 3. Program code used to extract the variables X, Y, Z, U for system's phase portrait with the microcontroller.

```
Rem  PROGRAM  POINCARE
xn1 = 0.2
yn1 = -0.1
zn1 = 0.3
wn = 0.1
c = 2.5
d = 0.8
h = 0.002
OPEN "poin.DAT"  FOR OUTPUT  As #1
NTR = 200000
FOR I = 1  TO  20000000
xn = xn1
yn = yn1
zn = zn1
wn = wn1
xn1 = xn + h*(yn - xn)
yn1 = yn + h*(- xn*zn + wn)
zn1 = zn + h*(xn*yn - c)
wn1 = wn + h*(-d*yn)
dy = 0.001
IF I > NTR THEN
IF xn > -dy And xn < dy  THEN
IF (yn - xn) > 0 THEN
PRINT  #1,  yn1, zn1, wn1
EndIf
EndIf
EndIf
NEXT I
CLOSE #1
END
```

Figure 4. Program code used to extract the variables Y, Z, U, for system's Poincaré map with the microcontroller.

3.3 Bifurcation Diagram

Finally, a third code shown in Fig. 5 was implemented using the MM Basic interpreter. With this code the microcontroller was programmed to generate a bifurcation diagram by extracting in a file the variables Y, Z and U versus the parameter b. The bifurcation diagram produced by obtained sequential Poincaré maps as the bifurcation parameter (b) decreased with step 0.001. In Fig. 11 the bifurcation diagram, which is produced by the capturing from the microcontroller data, is depicted. From the comparison of this diagram with the bifurcation diagram (Fig. 1(a)), which is produced by solving with Runge-Kutta the continuous system (1), a good agreement between them can be observed. However, a slightly different dynamical behavior can be

DOI: 10.1051/matecconf/20167602048

observed in some small regions of parameter b, which occurred due to the different integrating methods.

```
Rem  PROGRAM  BIFURCATION
xn1 = 0.2
yn1 = -0.1
zn1 = 0.3
wn = 0.1
c = 2.5
d = 0.8
h = 0.002
OPEN "bif.DAT"  FOR  OUTPUT  As #1
DO
NTR = 200000
FOR  I = 1  TO  2000000
xn = xn1
yn = yn1
zn = zn1
wn = wn1
xn1 = xn + h*(yn - xn)
yn1 = yn + h*(- xn*zn + wn)
zn1 = zn + h*(xn*yn - c)
wn1 = wn + h*(-d*yn)
dy = 0.001
IF I > NTR THEN
IF xn > -dy And xn < dy  THEN
IF (yn - xn) > 0 THEN
PRINT  #1,  yn1, zn1, wn1
EndIf
EndIf
EndIf
NEXT I
IF d >= 0 THEN  d = d - 0.001
LOOP UNTIL d < 0
CLOSE #1
END
```

Figure 5. Program code used to extract the variables *Y*, *Z*, *U*, for system's bifurcation diagram with the microcontroller.

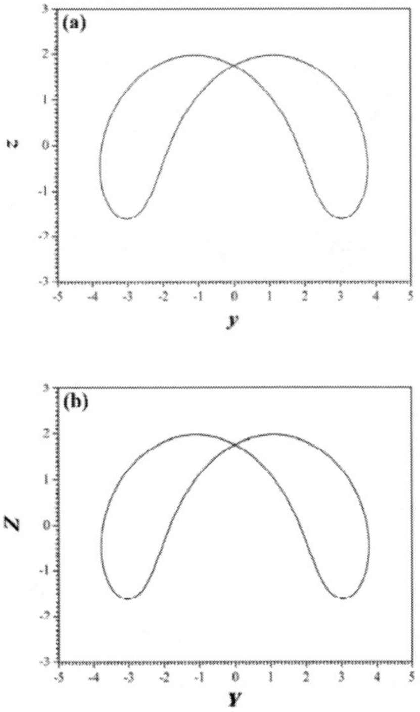

Figure 6. (a) Phase portrait of *z* versus *y* and (b) phase portrait of *Z* versus *Y*, for $a = 2.5$ and $b = 0.9$ (period-1 state).

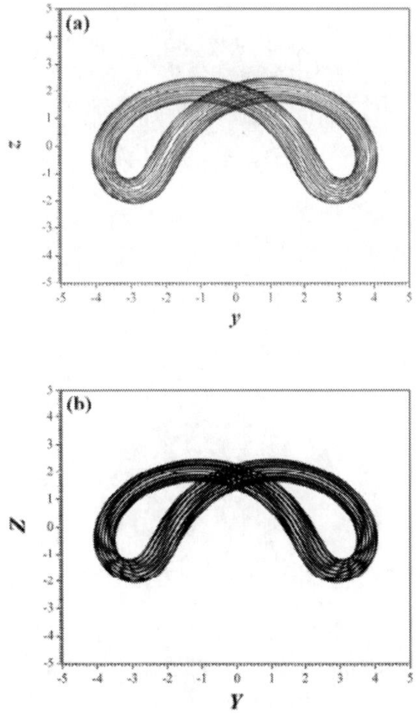

Figure 7. (a) Phase portrait of *z* versus *y* and (b) phase portrait of *Z* versus *Y*, for $a = 2.5$ and $b = 0.83$ (quasiperiodic state).

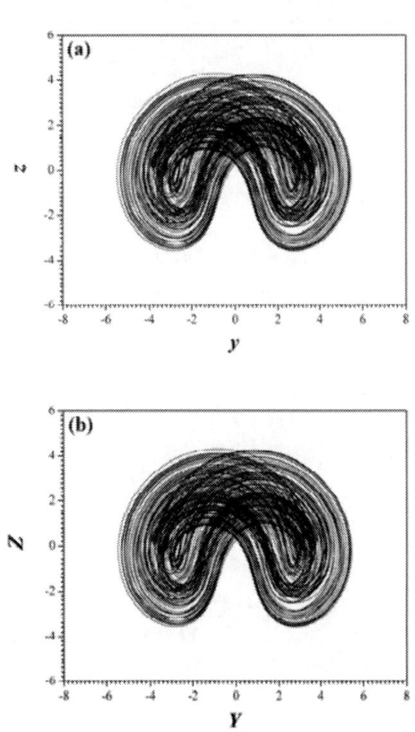

Figure 8. (a) Phase portrait of *z* versus *y* and (b) phase portrait of *Z* versus *Y*, for $a = 2.5$ and $b = 0.55$ (chaotic state).

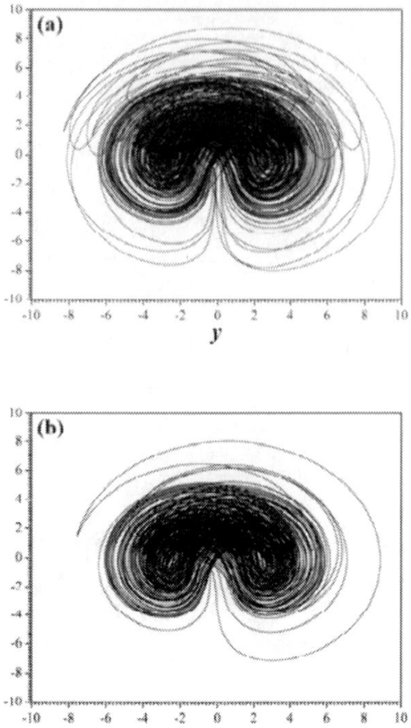

Figure 9. (a) Phase portrait of z versus y and (b) phase portrait of Z versus Y, for $a = 2.5$ and $b = 0.45$ (hyperchaotic state).

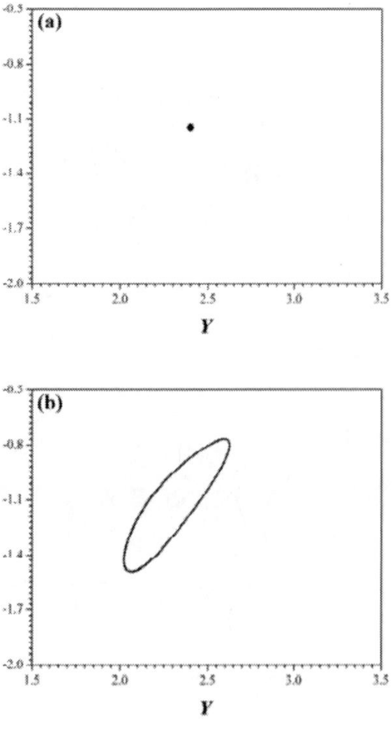

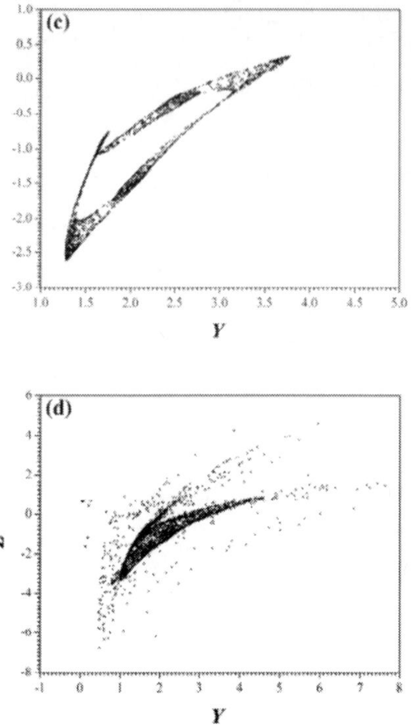

Figure 10. Poincaré maps of Z versus Y, for (a) $b = 0.9$, (b) $b = 0.8$, (c) $b = 0.55$ and (d) $b = 0.45$, produced using the microcontroller.

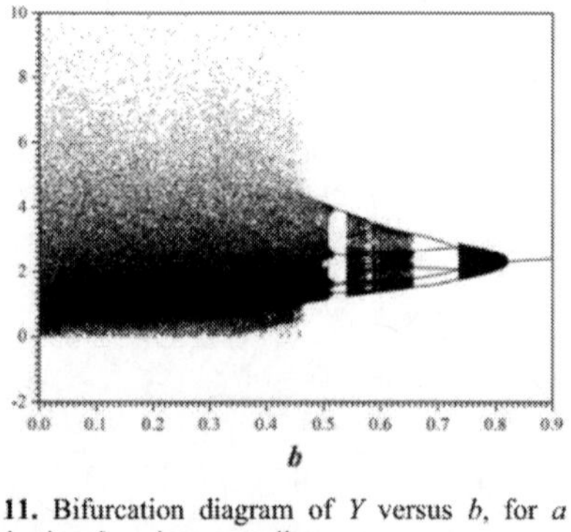

Figure 11. Bifurcation diagram of Y versus b, for $a = 2.5$, produced using the microcontroller.

4 Conclusion

In this work, a microcontroller was used in order to realize a hyperchaotic oscillator, which belongs to the recently new proposed category of dynamical systems with hidden attractors. By programming the microcontroller, the three most useful tools of nonlinear theory, the phase portrait, the Poincaré map and the bifurcation diagram was produced. The comparison of these with the respective simulation results, which were produced by solving the continuous dynamical system with Runge-Kutta, verified the feasibility of the proposed method. As a future work, the modifications of the algorithms so as to add or substitute the hyperchaotic system will be examined.

References

1. L.D. Kiel and E.W. Elliott, *Chaos theory in the social sciences: Foundations and applications* (Michigan University Press, 1997)
2. S. Banerjee, *Applications of chaos and nonlinear dynamics in engineering* **1**, (Springer, 2011)
3. C. Grebogi, J. Yorke, *The impact of chaos on science and society* (United Nations University Press, 1997)
4. T. Yang, Int. J. Comput. Cogn. **2**, 81-130 (2004)
5. L. Kocarev, IEEE Circ. Syst. Mag. **1**, 6-21 (2001)
6. T. Bräunl, *Embedded robotics: mobile robot design and applications with embedded systems* (Springer Science & Business Media, 2008)
7. W. Wolf, B. Ozer, T. Lv, Computer **35**, 48-53 (2002)
8. R. Alur, K.E. Arzen, J. Baillieul, T.A. Henzinger, *Handbook of networked and embedded control systems* (Springer Science & Business Media, 2007)
9. P. Marwedel, *Embedded system design: Embedded systems foundations of cyber-physical systems* (Springer Science & Business Media, 2010)
10. T. Choudhury, G. Borriello, S. Consolvo, D. Haehnel, B. Harrison, B. Hemingway, L. LeGrand, IEEE Pervasive Computing, **7**, 32-41 (2008)
11. D. Estrin, R. Govindan, J. Heidemann, S. Kumar, *Next century challenges: Scalable coordination in sensor networks*, In: Proceedings of the 5th Annual ACM/IEEE International Conference on Mobile Computing and Networking, 263-270 (1999)
12. R. Bastide, D. Navarre, P. Palanque, A. Schyn, P. Dragicevic, *A model-based approach for real-time embedded multimodal systems in military aircrafts*, In: Proceedings of the 6th International Conference on Multimodal Interfaces, 243-250 (2004)
13. D. Stepner, N. Rajan, D. Hui, *Embedded application design using a real-time OS*, In: 36th IEEE Design Automation Conference, 151-156 (1999)
14. M. Wolf, Newnes (2014)
15. A. Mifdaoui, F. Frances, C. Fraboul, IEEE Trans. Ind. Inform. **6**, 534-547 (2010)
16. C. Cepisca, N.G. Bardis, *Measurement and control in street lighting* (ELECTRA publication 2011)
17. M. Bogdan, M. Buga, R. Medianu, C. Cepisca, N. Bardis, Scientific Bulletin of the Electrical Engineering Faculty, **2**, (2011)
18. C. Cepisca, S.D. Grigorescu, S. Ganatsios, N.G. Bardis, Metrologie **4**, 5-10 (2008)
19. A.K. Aboul-Seoud, E.A. El-Badawy, A. Mokhtar, W. El-Marsy, M. El-Barbry, A.E.D.S. Hafez, *A simple 8 bit digital microcontroller implementation for chaotic sequence generation*, In: Proceedings of the 28th National Radio Science Conference, National Telecomunication Institute, 1-9 (2011)
20. J.D. Serna, A. Joshi, Phys. Educ. **47**, 1-6 (2012)
21. M. Stanciu, O. Datcu, *Atmel AVR microcontroller implementation of a new enciphering algorithm based on a chaotic Generalized Hénon Map*, In: 9th International Conference on Communications, 319-322 (2012)
22. C.K. Volos, I.M. Kyprianidis, I.N. Stouboulos, Robot. Auton. Syst. **61**, 1314-1322 (2013)
23. R. Chiu, M. Mora-Gonzalez, D. Lopez-Mancilla, IERI Procedia **4**, 247-252 (2013)
24. C.K. Volos, J. Comput. Model. **3**, 115-136 (2013)
25. P. Ketthong, W. San-Um, *A robust signum-based piecewise-linaer chaotic map and its application to microcontroller-based cost effective random-bit generator*, In: Proceedings of the International Electrical Engineering Congress 2014, 1-4 (2014)
26. W. San-Um, P. Ketthong, *The generalization of mathematically simple and robust chaotic maps with absolute value nonlinearity*, In IEEE Region Conference TENCON 2014, 1-4 (2014)
27. A.S. Andreatos, C.K. Volos, *Secure text encryption based on hardware chaotic noise generator*, In: 2nd International Conference on Cryptography and Its Applications in the Armed Forces (2014)
28. M. Zapateiro De la Hoz, L. Acho, Y. Vidal, Scientif. World J. **2015** (2015)
29. V.O. Bragin, V.I. Vagaitsev, N.V. Kuznetsov, G.A. Leonov, J. Comput. Syst. Sci. Int. **50**, 511-543 (2011)
30. G.A. Leonov, N.V. Kuznetsov, Int. J. Bifurcat. Chaos **23** 1330002 (2013)
31. T. Kapitaniak, G.A. Leonov, Eur. Phys. J. Special Topics **224**, 1405-1408 (2005)
32. D. Dudkowski, S. Jafari, T. Kapitaniak, N. Kuznetsov, G. Leonov, A. Prasad, Phys. Rep. doi: 10.1016/j.physrep.2016.05.002 (2016)
33. G.A. Leonov, N.V. Kuznetsov, V.I. Vagaitsev, Phys. D **241**, 1482-1486 (2012)
34. S. Brezetskyi, D. Dudkowski, T. Kapitaniak, Eur. Phys. J. Special Topics **224**, 1459-1467 (2015)
35. G.A. Leonov, N.V. Kuznetsov, M.A. Kiseleva, E.P. Solovyeva, A.M. Zaretskiy, Nonlinear Dyn. **77**, 277-288 (2014)
36. G.A. Leonov, N.V. Kuznetsov, T.N. Mokaev, Eur. Phys. J. Special Topics **224**, 142101458 (2015)
37. Z.T. Zhusubaliyev, E. Mosekilde, Comput. Simulat. **109**, 32045 (2015)
38. Z. Gao, C. Zhang, J. Jishou Univ. (Natural Science Edition) **32**, 65-68 (2011)
39. G. Van der Schrier, L.R.M. Maas, Phys. Nonlin. Phenom. **141**, 19-36 (2000)
40. B. Munmuangsaen, B. Srisuchinwong, Phys. Lett. A **373**, 4038-4043 (2009)
41. V. Paar, N. Pavin, Phys. Rev. E **57**, 1544-1549 (1998)
42. A. Wolf, J.B. Swift, J.A. Vastano, Physica D **16**, 285-317 (1985)
43. J.C. Butcher, *Numerical Methods for Ordinary Differential Equations* (John Wiley & Sons 2003)

Ecological Design of Cooperative Human-Machine Interfaces for Safety of IntelligentTransportSystems

Aleksandr Orekhov[1, a], *Anastasiia* Orekhova[1], and *Vyacheslav* Kharchenko[1,2]
[1]Department of computer systems and networks, National Aerospace University " KhAI", Kharkiv, 61070, Ukraine
[2]Centre for Safety Infrastructure Oriented Research and Analysis, Kharkiv, 61085, Ukraine

Abstract. The paper describes research results in the domain of cooperative intelligent transport systems. The requirements for human-machine interface considering safety issue of for intelligent transport systems (ITS)are analyzed. Profiling of the requirements to cooperative human-machine interface (CHMI) for such systems including requirements to usability and safety is based on a set of standards for ITSs. An approach and design technique of cooperative human-machine interface for ITSs are suggested. The architecture of cloud-based CHMI for intelligent transport systems has been developed. The prototype of software system CHMI4ITSis described.

1 Introduction

1.1 Motivation and work related analysis

Different vendors on IT market offer the advanced driver assistance systems [1, 2]. Such systems as a collision warning system, parking assistant, aredesigned for improvement of safety during the driving and reducing the driver's strain. [3].

One of the development lines of such systems is the improvement of the interaction between the driver and the vehicle control system "human-machine" (Human-Machine Interaction) and the provision information about the current situation on the road in real time for driver (Real-Time Traffic and Travel Information (RTTI).

The provision this sort of information leads to an increase of situational awareness of vehicle driver. Awareness implies existence of operational information about the vehicle state and road conditions. Sufficient level of situational awareness is required for risk assessment and hazard analysis, planning, goal-setting, etc.

Situational awareness includes levels:

– the level of perception of the situation, which is provided by monitoring the status of various objects around the vehicle;

– the level of conclusions, which determines the ability of vehicles to integrate various sources of information and to make assessments of situations on this basis (this level is provided by the decision-making about the current dangers and risks for the vehicle);

– the level of prediction, on which the forecast of dangerous situation risks is carried out.

Increasing of situational awareness leads to overall risk lowering (collisions, overturning, etc.), since it is possible to detect and predict hazardous situations, determine precautions for their reducing in real time.

Great importance for enhancing of situational awareness has issues for construction of secure dynamic human-machine interfaces (HMI) [4, 5].

At the same time, the point is that are two sides of the safe HMI:

– firstly, the development and evaluation of interfaces according to the requirements of the normative documents and safety standards;

– secondly, reporting succinct information about objects in the area of the vehicle movement to the driver, which can threat him (area of potential hazard (APH)).

It is also necessary to take into account the ability of an HMI to adapt to the situation on the road, to take into account the state of the driver, its features, driving experience, behavior peculiarities in critical situations, habits, etc., i.e. increasing of its adaptability.

The high amount of data used in the intelligent transportation system, leads to the necessity of improvement of information access for all traffic participants.

Improvement of situational awareness, risk assessment in the real-life improvement requires the use of large computing facilities for the storage, processing and analysis of data [6, 7].

It is very importantly that these facilities are not always available, even for modern on-board computing equipment of vehicle.

One of the nowadays challenges in the HMI creation domain is a development of green (or ecological) human-machine interfaces (GHMI). In contrast to the

[a] Corresponding author: a_orehov@rambler.ru

traditional HMIs they have such properties as environmental friendliness, adaptability, safety, reliability, etc. Scalable and flexible interfaces of the operator's panels allow integrating into the GHMI different systems monitoring and control functions.

GHMI for the automobile informational systems improves the traffic safety by decreasing the driver's informational overload, and thus minimizing the distractions.

Reliability of on-board software is also an additional safety factor in the ITS. It is necessary to consider additional precautions to enhance safety, including the possibility of using modern cloud computing for information processing in the framework of the ITS.

1.2 Goal of the paper

The goal of the paper is to raise the awareness of the vehicle driver about the road situation through the development and implementation of the cooperative human-machine interfaces for the intelligent transport systems based on the cloud computing. The paper is structuring by the following way. Second section describes requirements to the HMI for ITS and forms requirement profile. Third section is dedicated to development of cooperative HMI and cloud-based architecture. Fourth section presents some safety assessment results for CHMI. The last section concludes and discusses the future steps.

2 Requirements to the HMI for the ITSs

The international standardization process is an essential mean of ensuring the compatibility of the separate transport telematics systems.

The standards for ITSs are as follows:

– ISO/TR 10992:2011 Intelligent transport systems - Use of nomadic and portable devices to support ITS service and multimedia provision in vehicles;

– ISO/TR 12859:2009 Intelligent transport systems - System architecture - Privacy aspects in ITS standards and systems;

– ISO 15662:2006 Intelligent transport systems - Wide area communication - Protocol management information;

– ISO/TS 17419:2014 Intelligent transport systems - Cooperative systems - Classification and management of ITS applications in a global context;

– ISO/TS 17423:2014 Intelligent transport systems - Cooperative systems - ITS application requirements and objectives for selection of communication profiles;

– ISO/TS 17427:2014 Intelligent transport systems - Cooperative systems - Roles and responsibilities in the context of cooperative ITS based on architecture(s) for cooperative systems;

– ISO/TS 19321:2015 Intelligent transport systems - Cooperative ITS - Dictionary of in-vehicle information (IVI) data structures;

– ISO 21213:2008 Intelligent transport systems - Communications access for land mobiles (CALM) - 3G Cellular systems;

– ISO 24978:2009 Intelligent transport systems - ITS Safety and emergency messages using any available wireless media - Data registry procedures.

The main design manuals regarding the HMI for vehicles are European Statement of Principles on Human Machine Interface [8], JAMA – Japan Automobile Manufacturers Association Guidelines for InVehicle Display Systems [9] and Alliance of Automobile Manufacturers (AAM) [10]. These manuals summarize the key aspects of safety applicable for the human-machine interfaces of the automobile and communication systems.

The parameters and requirements for the CHMI for the ITSs identified as a result of the analysis into the standards, recommendations and the context of the use are given in the table 1.

Table 1. Requirements for the HMI for the ITSs.

Parameter	Requirement description
Usability	The feedback between the system and the driver should be timely and recognizable. The driver should be given the information about the current state of the system and any system malfunction. Visual information should be displayed in a way that the driver can assess special details within few sights. The driver should anytime have the possibility to keep at least one hand on the steering wheel when interacting with the system.
Safety	The system should help the driver and should prevent the possible dangerous behavior of the driver or other road users. The system should not distract the driver and draw his attention that should be focused on monitoring the road situation. The system should not provide the driver with the information that can cause the dangerous behavior of the driver or other road users. The system should provide the driver with high-priority information rather than the information related mostly to the safety.
Simplicity	The system instructions should be simple, correct and easy to understand. The visual information should be given piece by piece to ensure the step-by-step control of the system.
Cognitive compati-bility	The interface should not cause the driver's mixed reaction. The result of the drivers' actions should not be different from what he expects.

3 Development of cooperative HMI

3.1 Cooperative HMI

As noted above, the cooperative systems are such systems that wirelessly communicate with other cars.Therefore, under the term of a cooperative HMI we will
consider an interface system, distributed among several vehicles [11]. An additional monitor is installed on each vehicle or a compact unit is embedded into the existing HMI to provide information about safety in APH, which gives the information about the safety level.

This informationis formed and dynamically adjusted basing on the overall situation for each car (the state of the vehicle, driver and road conditions), which is in the danger zone.

It is clear that these must be adaptive HMI, which reflect not only information about the condition of the car, but of the driver as well. If a driver starts to doze off or falls asleep, it is necessary to wake him up and inform the drivers of motor vehicles that are nearby.

The property of adaptability in the HMI becomes apparent in several forms: changes in the content of the information provided, dialogue, sharing of tasks between man and machine, the speed of adaptation [12].One of the variants of cooperative HMI architecture is based on use of cloud computing (CC).

Cooperative HMI provides the measure values of the parameters of vehicle and driver state in real time via the Internet into the "cloud." Here, the data from all the cars is dynamically processed and transmitted to motoring public.

Information from the HMI of one vehicle passes through the "cloud" and is displayed on the HMI of another vehicle. In turn, the information from the HMI of another vehicle, is also transferred to the HMI of the first vehicle. This information is taken into account when the risk analysis of each vehicle is performed.

There are important issues in developing of HMI: optimization of the information necessary for driver for the safe driving mode; determination of the information views, which stimulate the driver; control and prevention of the driver's detraction.

3.2 Architecture of the system

The system consists of three projects combined in a single solution:

– server end – the decision support system (DSS);

– client end – the user HMI;

– Core-project that includes data models for the communication protocol and the common utility functions.

The server end is the web-application, the core of which is the DSS. The web-application is managed by the Apache Tomcat server that supports the HTTP protocol. The protocol allows the interaction between the client and the server. The client end is implemented for the Android platform and it stands for the user interface. The ground map is the key element. The data exchange is performed wirelessly using the data types specified in the general Core-project. Java serves as the platform for creating the system in question. The figure 1 shows the architecture of the system.

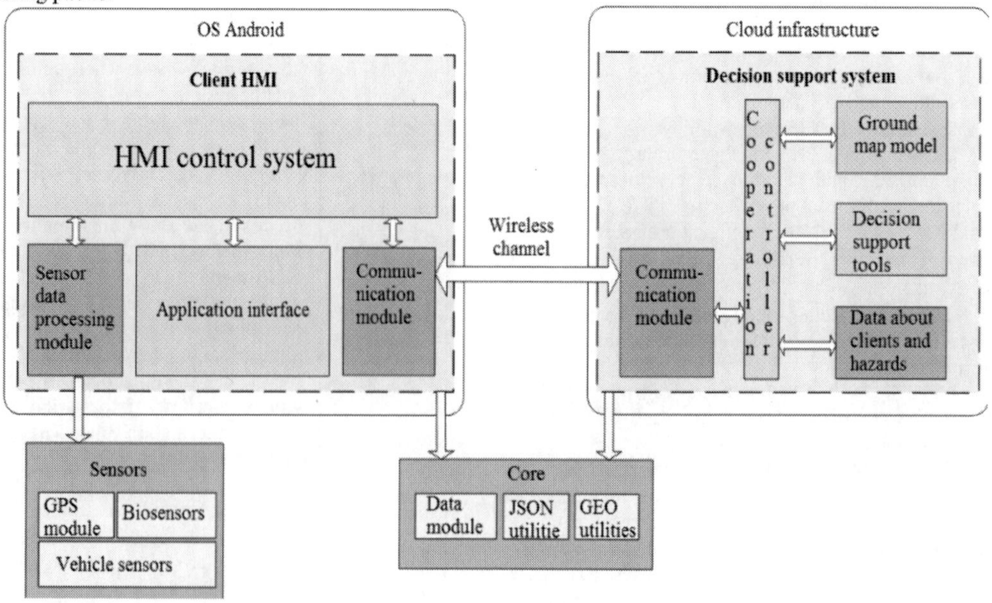

Fig 1. Architecture of the cooperative HMI based on cloud computing.

The client and the server cooperate wirelessly through the module for communication. The general convenience functions and data models for packetizing can be found in the Core-project that is used by the both sides.

Since the communication protocol should provide equal rights for the client and the server, it has been agreed to implement the communication protocol based on TCP from the specification Java EE – WebSocket.

The protocol ensures the free data exchange: two equal participants exchange data, each one working independently and sending data to the other one when necessary.

3.3 Interface design

The human-machine interface provides the driver with the information about the road situation, the driver's state and the vehicle's state. At the first start of the client application the registration form is displayed where the driver needs to enter his personal data (nickname, age, sex).

The working area on the display is covered with the ground map (fig. 2).

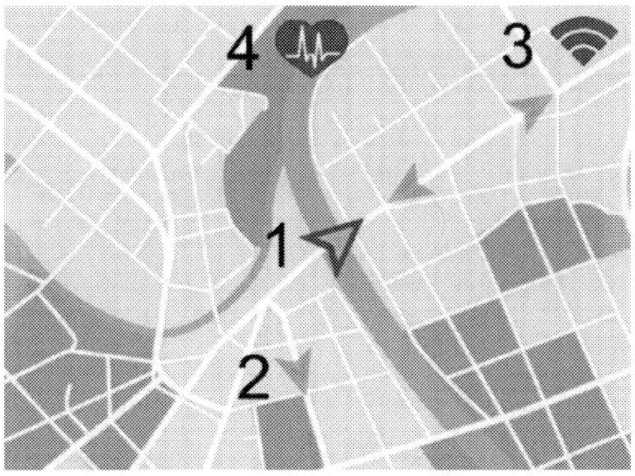

Fig 2. Visual interface. 1 – current position; 2 – other vehicle; 3 – server connection indicator; 4 – driver's state indicator.

The current state and the direction of the vehicle is marked on the map with the help of the special arrow indicator. The map is to be centered according to the current position. The position of other vehicles is displayed by means of arrows having different colours.

The driver's state is displayed by a special indicator. The HMI provides for the feature of manual signals to other drivers about the dangerous road stretch by pressing a button with the schematic representation of hazards types on a special board.

The speech recognition has been adopted in the HMI for the voice hazard signal transfer. The command for signal transfer consists of two fields: key phrase and hazard type. The key phrase should be brief and easy to pronounce. The possible key phrases are: "OK, motor", "Go, machine" or simply "Danger", "Danger ahead". According to the survey results, the majority of the drivers prefer to set their own key phrases for the control commands.

Hazards are indicated on the map with markers displaying the hazard type (table 2). The marker is coloured according to the hazard level.

Table 2. Hazard level.

Poor road	**Ice condition**	**Fog**	**Caving**	**Aggressive driver**
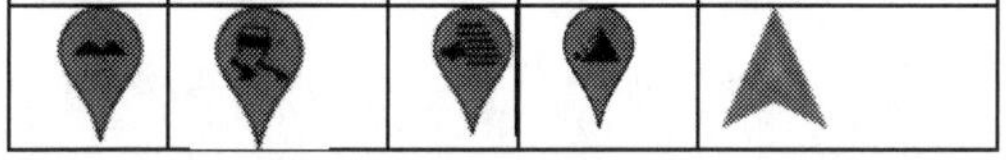				

Map scale should be set according to the range of the lowest hazard level. When the hazard description is queried, an informative message with the enlarged hazard marker and the distance to the hazard object is displayed.

A new hazard occurred is accompanied by the short voice signals. If the hazard level is high, the driver is informed by the voice messages communicating the hazard, for example: «Aggressive driver ahead, distance one hundred fifty meters, speed 90 kmph», «Fog in a hundred meters». Voice messages should repeat at a 10 second interval.

The driver is provided with the possibility to query the hazard description using voice commands like "Voice the hazard", "Describe the hazard".

The map scale can be configured, the voice and sound messages and volume level can be set or disabled.

Display brightness and contrast should be adjusted to the daytime. The voice messages volume level is to be adjusted to the noise level in the car.

The overall picture of the road is at the driver's disposal. He can see the ground map, monitor other vehicles moving on a real-time basis. The driver's awareness is improved as the position of the cars undetected through the glass or by the mirror can be obtained. The blind spot issue is resolved. Due to the voice description of the hazards the cognitive load is reduced, the probability of the driver's distraction of the display is lowered.

3.4 Development of the client end for the human-machine interfaces prototype

The client HMI subsystem is implemented on OS Android. It consists of several modules that interact via the HMI control system.

The vehicle's sensors data is obtained from the board computer through the wired interfaces. The requests to the biosensors can be done through wireless interfaces. The current coordinates are obtained from the GPS receiver through the wire communication channel.

The module for communication is responsible for receiving and transmitting the messages to the server. The packets are formed by the client subsystem using the data models from the Core-project.

The interface of the application includes the following modules:

1. Visual interface responsible for displaying the following elements on the monitor:

– registration page (personal data filling);

– ground map, current position and position of other participants, hazard objects on the ground map;

– indicators of the driver's state and server connection;

– hazards panel;

– signals setup control panel.

2. Speech synthesizer responsible for voice warnings generation.

3. Speech recognition responsible for voice commands recognition.

4. Sounds management responsible for sound warnings.

The HMI control system is responsible for the interaction with other modules in the system. It obtains the data from the sensor interfaces and transmits it to the communication module where packetizing takes place and the packets are sent to the server.

The user setup control module is responsible for the configuring and storing the personal data and parameters of the signals. The hazard control module is responsible for the refreshing of the hazards list provided by the server.

The emulation module is responsible for the emulation of the vehicle movement and the data obtained from the biosensors.

Figure 3 stands for the connection between the client, the server and the core modules.

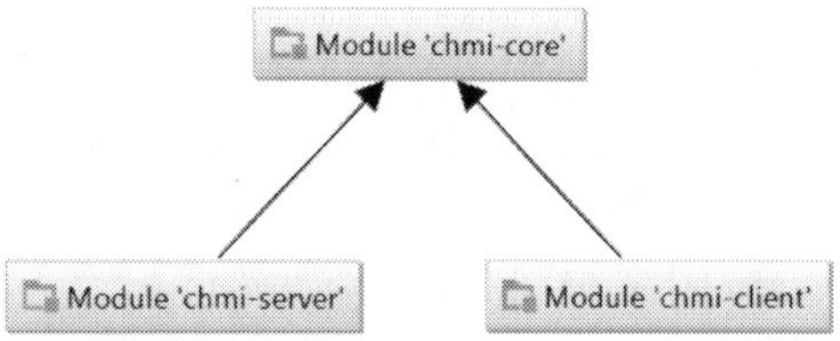

Fig 3. Module structure of the system.

The common classes for the client and the server applications are specified in the Core-project.

4 Research and assessment of safety

4.1 Automobile safety survey

At the interface design stage, the questionnaire has been conducted involving 93 vehicle drivers, in which the respondents have been offered to assess the types of signals about the hazards and the ways of interaction with the system.

The survey involved 93 people, of which 70% were male and 30% female. 69% of respondents were of the age from 20 to 30, 23% – from 30 to 40 and 8% had more than 40 years. 50% of respondents experienced a road accident at least once, 28% - several times, 5% - a lot of times and only 16% never had an accident on the road.

The results of hazards ranking show that the ice condition and the poor state of the road pavement are considered as the most dangerous situations, and the reconditioning work are ranked as the least dangerous.

The results of ranking the ways of interaction show that the sound and voice signals are more preferable along with the combinations of different types.

The results of the assessment of the ways of interaction with the interface show that the mechanical and voice interaction as well as the combinations are more preferable, while interaction by gestures is the least appropriate.

The most preferable key phrase for the voice commands is the combination of the welcoming word and the name of the vehicle which can be set by the driver.

4.2 GOMS method adaptation and human-machine interface efficiency assessment

The client HMI time indicators assessment model is given in the table 3.

Table 3.GOMS method adaptation for the HMI.

№	Operator	Code, time young / elderly
1	Mental psych-up	Mental M = 1.50 /2.55 s
	Compare the hazard description with the position on the map	
	Assess the most dangerous objects on the map	
2	Reach the monitor with the hand	Reach D = 0.45 / 0.77 s
3	Mark the position on the monitor with the finger	Mark Y = 0.80 / 1.36 s
4	Find the marker on the map	Search P = 2.30 / 3.91 s
5	Find the control element on the monitor	
6	Press the object on the map	Press H = 1.2 / 2.04 s
7	Press the button	
8	Wait for a response from the interface	Interface response O = 0.1 s
9	Say the key voice command aloud	Voice command G = 1.5 s
10	Say the signal voice command aloud	
11	Listen to the message about the hazard	Listen s = 3.5 s
12	React to the situation	Rection PE (experimental)

The quantitative evaluation of the HMI shows that the hazard signal is passed more effectively using the voice commands. The execution of the signalsetting task should be optimized through the voice commands, and thus less time will be spent by the driver. Additionally, we can conclude that the voice description requires more time compared to the situation of the driver executing the task of the ground map assessment. However, in this case the driver pays his attention to the map far more quickly which allows him to react to the situation faster.

5 Conclusion

In this work, the analysis into the available solutions regarding the cooperative intelligent transport systems and their human-machine interfaces has been conducted. The standards and recommendations in the area of transport systems interfaces design have been analysed. The requirements to the HMI for the cooperative ITSs have been formulated. The features of the such interfaces have been identified.

The prototype of the system "Cooperative human-machine interface for intelligent transport systems" based on the cloud computing has been developed.

The HMI prototype in question has been examined in the laboratory conditions. The assessment using the GOMS method has allowed to calculate the time to execute the task of user interaction with the system. The resulting data showed that the interface needs to be improved further.

The system "Cooperative HMI for ITSs" allows enhancing the vehicle safety and reducing the number of the road accidents.

Safety is improved by increasing the driver's awareness about the road situation and the possible hazards on a real-time basis through the human-machine interface.

Future steps will be related to experimental research of the software system and more infrastructure-oriented assessment by development and modeling different scenarios for ITSs considering vehicle failures, driver problems and so on.

References

1. *Opel and project UR:BAN: improvement of safety andcost-effectiveness on moving in cities*,(2014), www.opel.ru/experience/ob-opel/novosti opel.
2. *What technical innovations has Volvo implemented forlast 10 years*, (2011), www.autoconsulting.com.ua/news.
3. *Toyota Motor Corporation presents new systems of vehicle safety*, (2013), www.major-toyota.ru/news.html.
4. A. Orekhova, Information processing systems, **1**, 267 (2013).
5. A. Orekhova, V. Kharchenko, V. Tilinskiy, *Reliability: Theory & Applications*, **3**, 27 (2012).
6. Oleksandr P. Markovskyi, Nikolaos Bardis, Nikolaos Doukas, Sergej Kirilenko, *Congress on Information Technology, Computational and Experimental Physics CITCEP 2015*, 266, (2015).
7. Nikolaos G. Bardis, Oleksandr P. Markovskyi, Nikolaos Doukas, Athanasios Drigas, *IEEE IX International Symposium on Telecommunications*, (2012).
8. Off. J. Eur. Union,**32**, 200 (2007).
9. *JAMA - Japan Automobile Manufacturers Association Guidelines for In-Vehicle Display Systems*, (2004).
10. *Alliance of Automobile Manufacturers (AAM) Statement of Principles, Criteria and Verification Procedures on Driver Interactions with Advanced In-Vehicle Information and Communication Systems*, (2006),
11. V. Kharchenko, A. Orekhov, E. Brezhnev, A. Orekhova, V. Manulik, *EWDTS'2014*, 82 (2014).
12. A. Anokhin, E. Marshall, *EMCSR*, 185 (2012).

Risk Matrix-Based Method for Critical Infrastructure Safety Assessment Taking into Account Interdependencies

Eugene Brezhnev[1,2,a], Bogdan Chernetskiy[1]

[1]Department of computer systems and networks, National Aerospace University " KhAI", Kharkiv, 61070, Ukraine
[2]RPC Radiy, Kirovograd, 25006, Ukraine

Abstract. This paper is devoted to development of method for critical infrastructure (CI) safety assessment taking into account the different types of interdependencies: logical, physical, geographical, etc. There are many existing approaches for CI safety assessment. But the limited number of them consider the interdependencies focused on safety. Only few of them focus on interdependencies formalization. The suggested approach is based on application of risk matrixes built for each CI systems. Criticality of state is considered as safety value. The risk matrixes are developed for each CI life stage. The initial risk matrix is developed during CI design stage. All operational risk matrixes are built based on fuzzy logic and system field data.

1 INTRODUCTION

1.1 Motivation

Modern society has become widely dependent on the reliability and safety of critical infrastructure (CI). Critical infrastructure refers to processes, systems, facilities, technologies, networks, assets and services essential to the health, safety, security or economic well-being of people and the effective functioning of government. Critical infrastructure can be stand-alone or interconnected and interdependent within and across provinces, territories and national borders. There are many types of CI. These CIs are: telecommunications, electrical power systems, gas and oil storage and transportation, banking and finance, transportation, water supply systems, etc.

Disruptions of critical infrastructure, decrease of its safety could result in catastrophic loss of life, adverse economic effects and significant harm to public confidence. These CIs are supported by an array of physical assets, functions, information, people, and systems, forming what has been called the nation's critical infrastructures. These infrastructures have grown complex and interconnected, meaning that a disruption in one may lead to disruptions in others.

The significant increase in disasters of a natural and/or technological origin seen today has serious consequences for CI, the population, the environment, and the economy. These consequences have been exacerbated by the development of sociotechnical systems such as transport networks and industrial plants, their interdependencies, and their sensitivity to major hazardous events.

Many CI accidents are aggravated by systems interdependencies, when risk (safety) of one system is determined by risk (safety) of other system. Interdependence is a major challenge for risk management in CI. This gives rise a phenomenon known as “cascading events” – that is, once one disruption occurs, others are likely to follow within systems and processes that are connected to the infrastructure affected by the initial disruption. There is a strong need to consider the interdependencies in CI for safety and risk assessment.

1.2 Work Related Analysis

There is a significant number of risk assessment methodologies for CIs. In general the approaches that are used rather common and linear, consisting of some main elements: Identification and classification of threats, identification of vulnerabilities and evaluation of impact. These are well known and established

[a] Corresponding author: e.brezhnev@csis.org.ua

approaches for evaluating risks it is the backbone of almost all risk assessment methodologies.

Better Infrastructure Risk and Resilience [1]. The methodology covers the facilities in many critical infrastructure sectors (Energy, critical manufacturing etc.). This methodology has a sectoral approach that goes down to the assets level and gives priority on the protection measures that are applied mainly against terrorist threats. Concluding, this methodology is excellent for being applied to assets of critical infrastructures, it does not consider the interdependencies between safety states of systems.

Protection of Critical Infrastructures - Baseline Protection Concept [2] sets as basis the cooperation between infrastructures operators and state for reassuring the smooth operation of infrastructures with importance to the whole society. It is mentioned that infrastructure operators are the ones that should implement security measures as they have in-depth knowledge of their infrastructure and the way it operates. To this end, it provides recommendations on the identification of threats, vulnerable points and risk management elements, but safety is not considered and interdependencies that can undermine CI safety values aren't considered as well.

Counteract [3] is focused on assets and operators of any size, thus excluding an approach at the systems level. The security risk assessment is divided in two parts, the risk analysis and the vulnerability assessment.

The risk analysis focuses on the probability of an event and the impact it may have, while the vulnerability assessment evaluates the safeguards in place for the corresponding risks for the various assets. It is a rather different approach as to what is risk assessment with respect to what is widely acceptable.

This approach is not focused on interdependencies analysis between CI safety states.

1.3 Goal of the Paper

The aim of this paper is development of method for CI safety assessment considering the interdependencies among systems.

2 METHOD FOR CI SAFETY ASSESSMENT CONSIDERING THE INTERDEPENDENCIES

2.1 Interdependencies type description

There are four primary classes of interdependencies [4, 5, 6]:

– Physical Interdependency – two infrastructures are physically interdependent if the state of each depends upon the material output(s) of the other;

– Cyber Interdependency – an infrastructure has a cyber interdependency if its state depends on information transmitted through the information infrastructure. The computerization and automation of modern infrastructures and widespread use of supervisory control and data acquisition systems have led to pervasive cyber interdependencies [7, 8];

– Geographic Interdependency – infrastructures are geographically interdependent if a local environmental event can create state changes in all of them. This implies close spatial proximity of elements of different infrastructures, such as collocated elements of different infrastructures in a common right-of-way;

– Logical Interdependency – two infrastructures are logically interdependent if the state of each depends upon the state of the other via some mechanism that is not a physical, cyber, or geographic connection.

All of these types of interdependencies shall be considered for possible influence on system safety state. System safety state is considered as state when all risks are controlled or eliminated. These interdependencies influence the system safety in different way during different system life stage. Criticality of system state is considered as a safety value for systems in CI. The more system criticality is the less its safety. The typical risk (criticality) matrixes (FMECA like) usually allow to allocate system in particular boxes giving a clear understanding of the current safety state.

2.2 Description of the method stages

At each stage of CI life cycle the criticality assessment and adjustment of risk matrixes, taking into consideration probable changes, are carried out. A set of CI criticality matrixes failures is divided into two subsets:

- the subset of subsystem failures that criticality is located above the diagonal of the criticality matrix M^S_{crt} (the set of critical failures), and

- the subset, where criticality – under the diagonal of M^S_{crt} (the set of noncritical failures).

The hierarchy of risk matrixes is based on system hierarchy considering the real risks of each system (subsystems, components).

The sequence of carrying out CI safety assessment taking into account interdependencies between systems is shown in Fig. 1. The approach is bottom – up. The safety assessment is carried out from bottom up to the system top level. It allows considering the negative effects of components' failures on system as a whole.

Existing approaches for CI safety assessment do not consider any relation between subsystem failures of one hierarchy level. In this regard, the interdependencies when subsystem failures of i-level (on subsystem failure criticality of the same level) and its influence on subsystems of (i-1)-level (higher) is important.

The uncertainty takes into consideration information incompleteness and uncertainty related to the conditions that cause CI accidents, insufficient knowledge about CI, nature of new risks, etc.

The results of CI safety assessment are represented as risk matrixes' hierarchy.

CI initial safety assessment is done during CI development (or design) stage. Existing methods of criticality analysis for systems use standard algorithms of reliability analysis, one of which is FMECA.

Constructing the hierarchy of design criticality matrixes, CI project safety assessment, obtaining the safety value are tasks done during CI development stage.

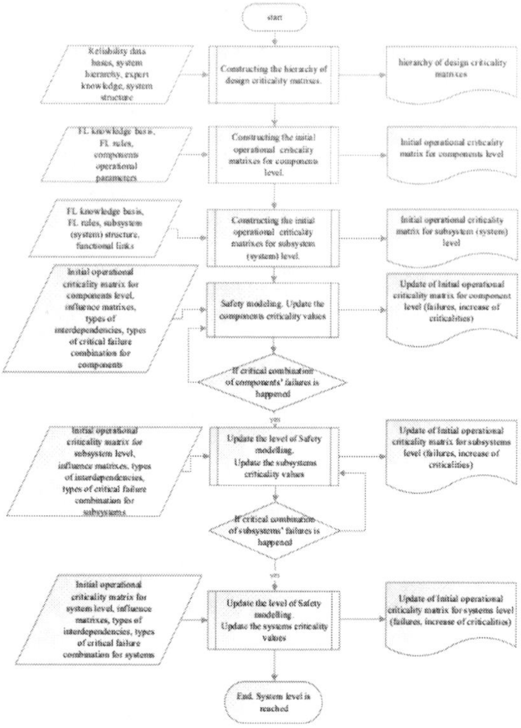

Fig 1. Algorithm of method.

As far as the stage of design analysis is characterized by high level of uncertainty, criticality design assessment can differ from CI safety operating values. This fact can be explained by inefficiency of reliability design measures at design stage when conditions of system operation are not expected or different (change of environment parameters).

In CI systems, there is a possibility for diagnostics of technical state of subsystem and components in accordance with results of physical measurement defining object operation. So, decrease of uncertainty of system safety state leads to changes of values of initial subsystem criticality assessment presented within the criticality matrix hierarchy.

It should be noted that CI failure effects severity can be both external and internal. The external severity is a result of dependent infrastructure damage made by the power system. Failure effect severity will be called internal if the power system compensates it using resources. Internal damage that cannot be compensated by CI is considered internal.

Initial data for revising of CI safety values are its operation parameters and conditions. It is done by application of fuzzy logic approach.

2.3 Description of the Fuzzy logic approach for components (subsystems) criticality assessment

It is proposed to use fuzzy logic definitions to evaluate failure criticality on different CI levels. They will allow to evaluate criticality indexes and arrange a failure set by a potential risk value. The safety assessment is done from the lowest possible level when all (or important operational parameters) are known for operator.

By means of operations $\bigcup$ and $\bigcap$ the FL rule set can be written as follows:

$$\bigcup_{p=1}^{k_j}\left[\bigcap_{i=1}^{n}(x_i = a_i^{jp})\right] \rightarrow y = d_j,\ j = \overline{1,m}. \qquad (1)$$

where $d_j(j=\overline{1,m})$ - linguistic evaluation of Y output (safety) variable determined out of D term-set;

a_i^{jp} - linguistic evaluation of xi input (operational parameters) in p-th line of the disjunction selected out of corresponding Ai term-set,

$$a_i^{jp} \in A_i, i=\overline{1,n}, j=\overline{1,m}, p=\overline{1,k_j}; \qquad (2)$$

kj – quantity of rules that define a value of y=di output variable.

This fuzzy approach is used in the two ways.

At first, as the suggested method is bottom up, the fuzzy logic is used to assess a criticality value of each component (lowest CI level). Fuzzy logic approach takes the real parameters of each components and returns its criticality values. It allows to locate each component into risk matrix on the lowest level of criticality matrix hierarchy. It is done for each systems' components. The lowest level criticality matrix is built.

At the second, this fuzzy approach is used to locate the all higher-level systems into criticality matrixes. This idea is straightforward. When we know the risks associated with each system components we can elaborate the risks associated with all system as a whole. FL approach takes the criticalities of each components and returns the criticality of whole system.

2.4 Approach to revising of systems criticality values due to interdependencies

The linguistic approach based on fuzzy sets has given very good results for qualitative risk-analysis of critical information control system based on FMECA. It is an approximate technique in its essence, which represents qualitative aspects as linguistic values by means of linguistic variables, that is variables whose values are not numbers but words or sentences in a natural or artificial language.

A linguistic aggregation operator based on the extension principle acts according to

$$S^n \xrightarrow{\tilde{F}} F(R) \xrightarrow{app_1(\cdot)} S \quad (3)$$

where S^n symbolizes the n Cartesian product of S, $\tilde{F}$ is an aggregation operator based on extension principle, F(R) the set of fuzzy sets over the set of real number R, $app_1: F(R) \rightarrow S$ is a linguistic approximation function that returns a label from the linguistic term S whose meaning is the closest to the obtained unlabeled fuzzy number and S is the initial term set. Fuzzy sets C_j (the new values of criticality) are obtained by the means of fuzzy arithmetic for triangular fuzzy numbers. The fuzzy numbers characterize the semantic of linguistic values. Multiplication of two fuzzy numbers P (fuzzy probability) and L (fuzzy severity) may be obtained as $L \odot P \overset{def}{=} C$, where membership function equals

$$\mu_C = \sup_{\substack{x_1, x_2 \\ y = x_1 \cdot x_2}} \min\{\mu_L(x_1), \mu_P(x_2)\} \quad (4)$$

This fuzzy approach allows to update all systems criticalities values when any systems fail. This approach uses linguistic values to formalize the interdependencies and initial criticality values. All interdependencies are formalized as linguistic values (high, medium, low) located in the matrix of influence.

2.5 Assessment of the occurrence of system failures critical combination

It is important to check if there is a critical failure combination after each update of systems criticality. Any systems might have a certain level of resilience, capacity to withstand the occurrence of its systems (components) failures. But each system has its own set of critical failures combination when a whole system fails. In term of the suggested in this thesis approach it asks for updating of level of CI safety analysis. The set of critical failures combination is determined by expert knowledge.

Thus, for instance if all critical components of subsystem fail then it is considered that subsystem fails. In this case we update the level of safety modelling. After this all of stages mentioned above are repeated for next level of CI.

2.6 Description of the case study

As a result of these researches a desktop software has been developed that allows to perform a safety assessment of CI considering new risk parameter – interdependencies. The program was developed in C # in Visual Studio design environment in 2012.

The program has the following features:

- set the number of objects;
- set object parameters (probability of failure and the severity of the consequences);
- drawing objects on the panel;
- the ability to create relations between objects (material and information);
- change parameters of objects;
- simulated failure of the object;
- step-change comparison objects;
- system reset.

To prove the approach to the CI safety assessment considering the interdependencies, Russian Sayano–Shushenskaya HPP accident was reviewed. The software was used as a tool to perform a case study taking into account the interdependencies between its hydro units (HUs).

As the approach is bottom up then we use a Fuzzy logic for distributing all HU components inside the risk matrix. The physical interdependencies are considered. It allows to revise the criticality states of all HUs. The system failures occurrence is modeled after obtaining the criticality matrixes for HUs. During this modelling the focus was made on HU 2 (which cause the real accident).

When any failures are happened then this failures are analyzed by software.

Simulation stator stanchion (S_{121}) failure leads to the fact that the criticalities of states of bearing (S_{124}) and other components (S_{128}) are increased.

Simulation upper and lower stator belt (S_{122}) and bearing (S_{124}) failure leads to the fact that the criticality of states of cover fastener systems (S_{127}) and the turbine cover (S_{125}) increases.

The results of HU-2 components' safety modelling is shown on Figure 2.

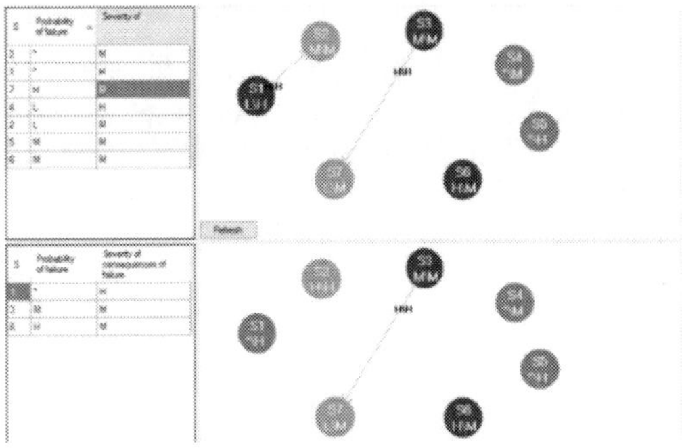

Fig.2. Modeling HU-2. Simulation upper and lower stator belt (S_{122}) and bearing (S_{124}) failure.

After checking for occurrence the critical combination failures the safety modelling level was updated (upper level, station level, HU as systems), from the level of hydro unit component to the next level, the level of hydraulic units. The critical failures combination is occurred and HU-2 fails (see Fig.3 below).

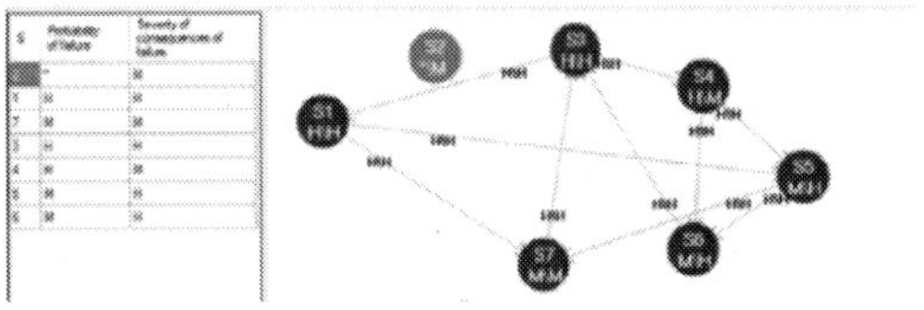

Fig 3. Modeling Sayano-Shushenskaya HPP. Out of order HU- 2 failure.

When HU-2 failure occurred the level of safety modelling was updated. Next, the safety modelling was done considering functional interdependency between HU-2 and other HUs.

HU-2 (S_2) failure leads to the fact that the criticalities of states of all HUs are increased.

The change of systems criticality values:

$S_2^* \rightarrow S_1\uparrow\ S_3\uparrow\ S_4\uparrow\ S_5\uparrow\ S_6\uparrow\ S_7\uparrow$.

The results obtained from this modelling tell us that even if HU was not thrown away and technical room was not flooded then its failure would have led to all HPP unavailability (but without such losses).

3 Conclusion and Future Work

As a result of method application – uncertainties of CI risk assessment is decreased by consideration on new parameter – type of interdependencies. All types of interdependencies are considered in method.

As this method allows for risk visualization then it becomes a good safety assessment tool for CI operators. The results of case study performed have shown that if these HUs were equipped with devices for measuring all (or most important) operational parameters then the application of this software would allow to on-line risk assessment and taking the preventive measure to decrese the high consequences of this accident.

Next step of method enhancement will be related to consideration of system multiple failures for criticality analysis and development of decision making tool-based system.

Further development of the software is to add it with the feature that suggest a set of preventive measures to decrease risks and its propagation on other CI levels.

References

[1] J. Sagoff, *Better infrastructure risk and resilience*, http://www.anl.gov/articles/better-infrastructure-risk-and-resilience, (2010)

[2] Federal Ministry of the Interior, *Protection of Critical Infrastructures – Baseline Protection Concept*, http://www.preventionweb.net/files/9266_2967ProtectionofCriticalInfrastruct.pdf, (2013)

[3] ForeScout, *ForeScout CounterAct*, https://www.forescout.com/products/counteract/, (2012)

[4] D. Dudenhoeffer, M. Permann, M. Manic, *CISMS: A Framework for Infrastructure Interdependency Modeling and Analysis*, (2006)

[5] R. Bloomfield, N. Chozos, P. Nobles, *Infrastructure interdependency analysis: introductory research review*, (2009)

[6] R. Zimmerman, *Decision-Making and The Vulnerability Of Interdependent Critical Infrastructure*, (2004)

[7] Nikolaos G. Bardis, Nikolaos Doukas and Olexander. P. Markovskyi, *"Effective method to restore data in distributed data storage systems", IEEE / MILCOM (2015)*

[8] Nikolaos G. Bardis, Nikolaos Doukas and Olexander. P. Markovskyi, *"Efficient burst error correction method for application in low frequency channels and data storage units", 17th International Conference on Digital Signal Processing (DSP) IEEE, DOI: 10.1109/ICDSP.2011.6004970, Corfu 2011*

MATEC Web of Conferences **76**, 02051 (2016) DOI: 10.1051/matecconf/20167602051
CSCC 2016

Diversity for security: case assessment for FPGA-based safety-critical systems

Vyacheslav Kharchenko[1,2], Oleg Illiashenko[1,a]

[1]*National Aerospace University "KhAI", 61070 Kharkiv, Ukraine*
[2]*Centre for Safety Infrastructure Oriented Research and Analysis, 61085 Kharkiv, Ukraine*

Abstract. Industrial safety critical instrumentation and control systems (I&Cs) are facing more with information (in general and cyber, in particular) security threats and attacks. The application of programmable logic, first of all, field programmable gate arrays (FPGA) in critical systems causes specific safety deficits. Security assessment techniques for such systems are based on heuristic knowledges and the expert judgment. Main challenge is how to take into account features of FPGA technology for safety critical I&Cs including systems in which are applied diversity approach to minimize risks of common cause failure. Such systems are called multi-version (MV) systems. The goal of the paper is in description of the technique and tool for case-based security assessment of MV FPGA-based I&Cs.

1 Introduction

1.1 Four challenges for I&C safety assessment and assurance

Industrial safety critical instrumentation and control systems (I&Cs) such as reactor trip systems, on-board aviation systems, railway blocking and signaling systems, etc. are facing more with information (in general and cyber, in particular) security threats and attacks. It concerns most sensitive in point of view safety nuclear domain [1]. Nowadays there is a gap in understanding how to assess safety of industrial I&Cs considering the following:

- firstly, the security issues; security related threats are more and more challengeable for safety critical application. As a result security informed safety conception is intensively developed the last years, in particular for NPP I&Cs [2];
- secondly, the features of FPGA technology and FPGA-based systems as a specific target for intruders. Security aspects for FPGA design and implementation are analyzed in [3-5]. These works allow to systemize different vulnerabilities and threats, and better to understand which of them should be taken into account to assure security;
- thirdly, an application of diversity approach as a mean of minimizing common cause failure risks. In this case two (or more) channels are used in different combinations for obtaining the needed functionality and ensuring of required level of safety. Techniques of development and safety assessment of FPGA-based multi-version industrial systems (MVI&Cs) are researched in [6-8]. However, it is required to analyze influence and features of diversity application in point of view security;
- fourthly, using of case-based proved paradigm. Really, to assure trustworthiness of security assessment for such extremely complex systems, more formalized (and independent in sense of expert errors and uncertainties) techniques are required.

1.2 Researched domains. Goal of the paper

The paper represents research results in the domains of safety, security, diversity and FPGA with representation of methodology of cybersecurity assessment based on cases. The figure 1 shows research fields and the targeted area encircled by red line. Additionally, dashed line describes area of case-based approach application to assessment of safety and security.

Figure 1. Targeted area of research

[a] Corresponding author: o.illiashenko@csn.khai.edu

Another research aspect is providing effective risk mitigation strategy by use of countermeasures (see Figure 2 where area of countermeasures for FPGA-based MV I&C systems is encircled by red as well, and dashed line describes area of case-based approach application to choice and prove effectiveness of countermeasures).

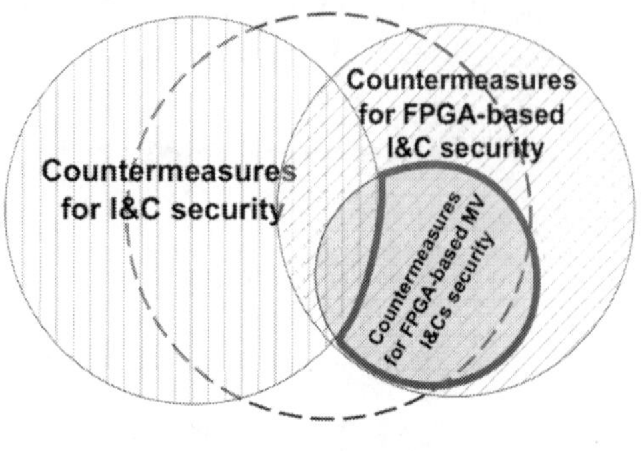

Figure 2. Targeted area for countermeasures.

Thus, goal of the paper is to suggest technique and tool for case-based security assessment of FPGA-based MVI&Cs. Structure of the paper is following.

Second section describes normative base (ISO, IEC and IAEA standards), classification and analysis of application of diffrent diversity kinds for safety and security assessment and assurance for FPGA-based I&Cs.

Third section is dedicated to case development and descridiscusses an example of ASAC application for security analysis and assessment.

The last section concludes the paper and presents directions of future researches.

2 Diversity for safety and security of FPGA-based I&Cs

Diversity is a part of more general principle D3 (Defense-in-Depth&Diversity) [8] applied to provide trusted, fault- and intrusion-tolerant design and operation of I&Cs. Defense-in-Depth is a horizontal/sequential echelon of defense, diversity is a vertical/parallel part of once [11].

2.1 Diversity related standards for safety and security

There are a lot of international standards and national guides containing requirements for implementation and assessment of diversity. Among them are:

a) IEC standards:

- IEC 61513:2001. NPPs - I&Cs important to safety – general requirements for systems;

- IEC 60880 2006. NPPs - I&Cs important to safety - SW aspects for computer-based systems performing category A functions;

- IEC 61508 :2011. Functional Safety of Electrical/Electronic/Programmable Electronic Safety-related Systems;

b) IAEA standards :

- IAEA NS-G-1.1:2001. Software for Computer Based Systems Important to Safety in NPPs;

- IAEA NS-G-1.3:2002. I&Cs important to safety in NPPs;

- IAEA NP-T-1.5:2009. Protecting against CCFs in Digital I&C Systems of NPPs ;

c) IEEE and NUREG (USA) standards :

- IEEE std.7-4.3.2:2003. IEEE standard criteria for digital computers in safety systems of NPPs;

- NUREG/CR-7007:2009. Diversity Strategies for NPP I&C Systems, NUREG/CR-7007 ORNL/TM-2009/302.

d) National guides and norms :

- DI&C-ISG-02, Diversity and Defense-in-Depth Issues, Interim Staff Guidance (USA);

BTP 7-19, Guidance for Evaluation of D&DiD In Digital I&C Systems (USA);

- NP 306.5.02/3.035. Requirement on nuclear and radiation safety for I&Cs important to safety in NPPs (Ukraine), etc.

There are standards for other critical domains where diversity as an approach is postulated or requirements to its application are described. For example, requirements to diversity for automotive systems are determined by standard IEC 26262. This standard contains requirements regarding application of software and hardware diversity for on-board vehicle systems.

Generally, the standards are not enough detailed to make all necessary decisions concerning diversity: type of diversity selection and combining, process and product diversity volume assessing and grounding, etc. It is very importanty that they do not take into account two issues :

- features of FPGA technology what complicates their application and

- security issues for safety assessment.

2.2 Assessment of safety and security of FPGA-based I&Cs

2.2.1 Comparison of diversity for SW- and FPGA-based I&Cs

FPGA-based technology provides new possibilities for implementation of diversity principle and additional options [7, 8]. The features of FPGA technology increase a number of diversity kinds and enlarge a set of possible diversity-oriented decisions.

General diversity classification scheme was presented by "cube of diversity" with three coordinates: "stage of the life cycle" – "level of project decisions" and "type of version redundancy" [8]. Using this classification we can analyse safety and security issues for FPGA-based systems and traditional SW-based I&Cs, first of all, for NPPs.

Table 1 summarizes variety of diversity attributes from NUREG-CR/7007:2009 for NPP I&Cs and their accordance with kinds of version redundancy of FPGA-based systems.

Table 1. Diversity attributes and correspondent FNI&Cs version redundancy kinds.

DIVERSITY ATTRIBUTES (NUREG-CR/ 7007:2009)	KINDS OF VERSION REDUNDANCY (FPGA-BASED I&Ss)
Design	**Diversity of electronic elements (EE)**
Different technologies	Different manufacturers of EEs; Different technologies of EEs production
Different approaches within a technology	Different technologies of EEs production
Different architectures within a technology	Different families of EEs
Equipment Manufacturer	**Diversity of electronic elements (EE)**
Different manufacturers of fundamentally different equipment designs	Different manufacturers of EEs
Same manufacturer of fundamentally different equipment designs	Different families of EEs
Different manufacturers of same equipment design	Different manufacturers of EEs
Same manufacturer of different versions of the same equipment design	Different EEs of the same family
Logic Processing Equipment	**Diversity of project development languages**
Different logic processing architectures	
Different logic processing versions in same architecture	
Different component integration architectures	Joint use of graphical scheme language and hardware description language (HDL)
Different data flow architectures	Joint use of graphical scheme language and HDL
Function	**Diversity of CASE-tools**
Different underlying mechanisms to accomplish safety function	Combination of couples of diverse CASE tools and SSs
Different purpose, function, control logic, or actuation means of same underlying mechanism	Different SSs
Different response time scale	
Life-Cycle	**Diversity of CASE-tools**
Different design companies	Combination of couples of diverse CASE-tools and HDLs
Different management teams within the same company	Combination of diverse CASE-tools and HDLs
Different designers, engineers, and/ or programmers	Different HDLs
Different implementation/ validation teams	
Signal	**Diversity of CASE-tools, Diversity of scheme specification (SS)**
Different reactor or process parameters sensed by different physical effect	Combination of couples of diverse CASE tools and SSs
Different reactor or process parameters sensed by the same physical effect	
The same process parameter sensed by a different redundant set of similar sensors	
Logic	**Diversity of CASE-tools, Diversity of scheme specification (SS)**
Different algorithms, logic, and program architecture	Combination of couples of diverse CASE-tools and HDLs
Different timing or order of execution	Different CASE tools configurations
Different runtime environments	Different CASE tools
Different functional representations	Different HDLs

2.2.2 Diversity and security

Table 2 shows results of research on diversity attributes from NUREG-CR/7007 which could be applied to mitigate CCF in diverse SW- and HW/FPGA-based systems with the same vulnerabilities in both versions. Different vulnerabilities in both versions have four grades: VH – very high, H –high, M – medium, L – low.

Gradation is based on risk reduction after appliance of a certain diversity attribute. In this case diversity is considered as a countermeasure for elimination of harmful consequences after successful attacks.

2.3 Diversity as a countermeasure

Table 3 summarizes some attacks on FPGA-based I&Cs and results of security assessment using IMECA-analysis [2,8]. Countermeasures are employed to thwart such tampering attacks. The table contains countermeasures strategies which could be applied as a requirements from Regulatory Guide 5.71:2010 (Cyber Security Programs For Nuclear Facilities, U.S. NRC) to eliminate the attack causes and, moreover, FPGA-based MV I&Cs diversity kind and its attributes as a countermeasures.

Thus diversity of FPGA-based MV I&Cs is reviewed as a countermeasure and mitigation strategy for ensuring of security and safety of systems. Criticality matrix (see Fig.3) shows how application of different FPGA-based I&Cs diversity kinds and its attributes will decrease the level of overall risk.

3 Security case development

3.1 Advanced security assurance case

The idea of cybersecurity case for evaluation of security of MV I&Cs lays in appliying of Advanced Security Assurance Case ASAC proposed by [9] which is built taking into account requirements to version kinds of systems.

Table 2. Diversity attributes as a countermeasure.

DIVERSITY ATTRIBUTES (NUREG-CR/ 7007:2009)	VULNERABILITIES			
	Software		Hardware	
	common vulnerability	different vulnerabilities	common vulnerability	different vulnerabilities
Design				
Different technologies	H	H	H	H
Different approaches within a technology	M	M	M	M
Different architectures within a technology	L	L	L	L
Equipment Manufacturer				
Different manufacturers of fundamentally different equipment designs	H	H	H	H
Same manufacturer of fundamentally different equipment designs	HM	HM	HM	HM
Different manufacturers of same equipment design	M	M	M	M
Same manufacturer of different versions of the same equipment design	L	L	L	L
Logic Processing Equipment				
Different logic processing architectures	H	H	H	H
Different logic processing versions in same architecture	HM	HM	HM	HM
Different component integration architectures	M	M	M	M
Different data flow architectures	L	L	L	L
Function				
Different underlying mechanisms to accomplish safety function	H	H	H	H
Different purpose, function, control logic, or actuation means of same underlying mechanism	M	M	M	M
Different response time scale	L	L	L	L
Life-Cycle				
Different design companies	H	H	H	H
Different management teams within the same company	HM	HM	HM	HM
Different designers, engineers, and/ or programmers	M	M	M	M
Different implementation/ validation teams	L	L	L	L
Signal				
Different reactor or process parameters sensed by different physical effect	H	H	H	H
Different reactor or process parameters sensed by the same physical effect	M	M	M	M
The same process parameter sensed by a different redundant set of similar sensors	L	L	L	L
Logic				
Different algorithms, logic, and program architecture	H	H	H	H
Different timing or order of execution	HM	HM	HM	HM
Different runtime environments	M	M	M	M
Different functional representations	L	L	L	L

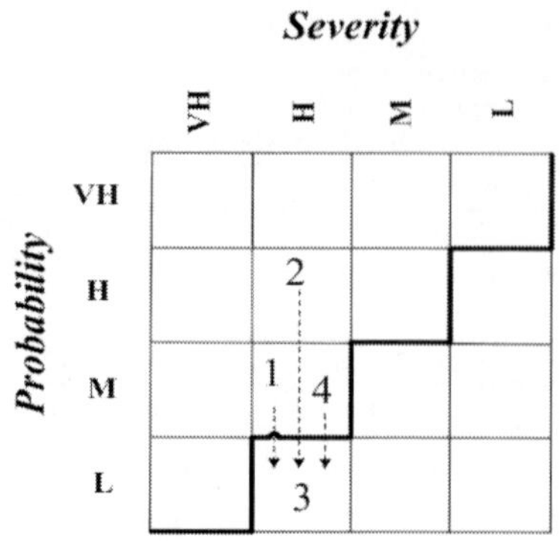

Figure 3. Criticality matrix.

DRAKON was used as a graphical modeling language for representation of cybersecurity case based on ASAC. It was developed from former USSR space program Buran (analogue of Space Shuttle). DRAKON, stands for "friendly algorithmic language that provides clarity." Initially DRAKON was developed for capturing requirements and building software that controls spacecraft [10]. As a language of requirements modeling was chosen IDEF0 notation. Notation IDEF0 allows to show the steps of the evaluation unambiguously (in the form of a directed graph), for each step to determine the evaluated property and evidences necessary for the evaluation, the subjects of assessment, and standards.

If the assessment is subject to a complex (composite) requirement, so each step (or block of IDEF0-diagram) can be decomposed for a detailed description of sub-properties evaluation procedure.

Table 3. IMECA-analysis of attacks on FPGA-based I&Cs.

No	Attack mode	Attack nature	Attack cause	Occurrence probability	Effect severity	Type of effects	Countermeasures (including RG 5.71)	FPGA-based I&C diversity kinds and its attributes
1	Readback	Active	Absence of chip security bit and/ or availability of physical access to chip interface (e.g., JTAG)	M	H	Obtaining of secret information by adversary	• The use of security bit; • Application of physical security controls; (B.1.18 Insecure and Rogue Connections, Appendix B to RG 5.71, Page B-6)	Diversity of (EE): •Different technologies of EEs production
2	Cloning	Active	Storing of decoded configuration	H	H	Obtaining of configuration data by adversary	• Checking of chip's internal ID before powering up an electronic design; • Encoding of configuration file; • Storing of configuration file within FPGA chip (requires internal power source)	Diversity of EE: •Different technologies of EEs production; •Different element kinds of EE families
3	Brute force	Active	• Search for a valid output attempting all possible key values; • Exhaustion of all possible logic inputs to a device in order; • Gradual variation of the voltage input and other environmental conditions	L	M	Leak of undesirable information	Detecting and documenting unauthorized changes to software and information, (C.3.7, Appendix C to RG 5.71, Page C-7)	Diversity of project development languages •Combination of couples of diverse CASE-tools and HDLs
4	Fault injection (glitch)	Active	•Altering the input clock; •Creating momentary over- or under-shoots to the supplied voltage	M	H	•Device to execute an incorrect operation •Device left in a compromising state •Leak of secret information	•Making sure all states are defined and at the implementation level, verifying that glitches cannot affect the order of operations; •Detection of voltage tampering from within the device; •Clock supervisory circuits to detect glitches	Diversity of EE: •Different manufacturers of EEs; •Different technologies of EEs production; Diversity of SS •Different SSs; •Combination of diverse CASE tools and SSs

3.2 Building of ASAC

The result of the analysis of requirements of assurance class "Vulnerability analysis" AVA_VAN.3 from International Standard ISO/IEC 15408 is presented in the form of ontological graph (see Fig. 4). The graph accurately and unambiguously (in the accepted notation) describes the subject area (i.e. basic notions/concepts and relations between them). It contains diversity requirements for ensuring of cybersecurity of I&Cs (as countermeasures, Table 3) marked in light-blue fillings.

Completeness of scope of assessment is ensured by using ontological graphs of two kinds of object-oriented and process-oriented ontology. Requirements of assurance class "Vulnerability analysis" AVA_VAN.3 from IEC 15408 are depicted in form of properties (Fig. 5), evidences (Fig. 6) and corresponding actions of an expert (Fig. 7) as results of ontological analysis of diversity requirements for secure I&Cs (marked with blue and dark-blue) and represented in established ASAC form on figure.

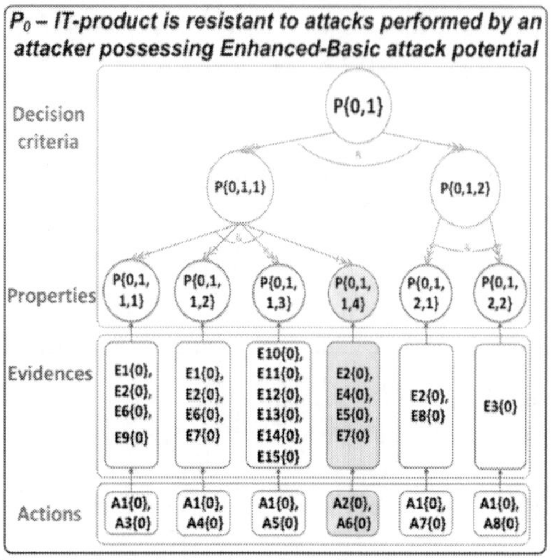

Figure 4. Ontological model in form of graph.

P{J}	PROPERTIES
P{0}	Resistant of the TOE to attacks performed by an attacker possessing Basic attack potential
P{0,1}	Readiness of the TOE for testing
P{0,1,1}	Consistent of the TOE with ST
P{0,1,1,1}	Conformity of the TOE reference with the CM capabilities (ALC_CMC) sub-activities and ST introduction
P{0,1,1,2}	Consistent of the all TOE configurations with ST
P{0,1,1,3}	Conformity of the testing environment to the security objectives for the operational environment described in the ST
P{0,1,1,4}	Conformity of the TOE to diversity requirements
P{0,1,2}	Accuracy of the TOE installing
P{0,1,2,1}	Successfulness completion of the AGD_PRE.1
P{0,1,2,2}	Successfulness of the TOE install and start up, using the supplied guidance only

Figure 5. Properties of ASAC represented in tabular form.

Ei{J}	EVIDENCES
E1{0}	TOE is suitable for testing
E2{0}	Security Target
E3{0}	Guidance documentation
E4{0}	Information is publicly available to support the identification of potential vulnerabilities
E5{0}	Current information regarding potential vulnerabilities (e.g. from an evaluation authority)
E6{0}	Basic functional specification
E7{0}	Security architecture description
E8{0}	Implementation representation of the TSF
E9{0}	Basic modular design
E10{0}	Applicability of different technologies of EEs production
E11{0}	Applicability of different element kinds of EE families
E12{0}	Applicability of different manufacturers of EEs
E13{0}	Applicability of different SSs
E14{0}	Applicability of combination of diverse CASE tools and SSs
E15{0}	Applicability of combination of couples of diverse CASE-tools and HDLs

Figure 6. Evidences of ASAC represented in tabular form.

Ai{J}	ACTIONS
A1{0}	Obtain the evidences
A2{0}	Obtain the diversity applicability evidences
A3{0}	Check the conformity of the TOE reference with the CM capabilities (ALC_CMC) sub-activities and ST introduction
A4{0}	Check the consistent of the all TOE configurations with ST
A5{0}	Check the conformity of the testing environment to the security objectives for the operational environment described in the ST
A6{0}	Check the conformity of the TOE to diversity requirements
A7{0}	Check the successfulness completion of the AGD_PRE.1
A8{0}	Check the successfulness of the TOE install and start up, using the supplied guidance only

Figure 7. Actions of ASAC represented in tabular form.

4 Conclusions

The paper describes cybersecurity assurance technique of multi-version FPGA-based I&Cs. Requirements profile is formulated using the best practices from the following international regulations. The paper summarizes research results on using of security informed safety assessment of FPGA-based MV I&Cs by development of security case based on ASAC. This case considers requirements from Common Criteria and added requirements for diversity as a countermeasure and CCF risk reduction strategy.

Security assurance case tends to reducing of uncertainty of safety assessment taking into account influence of security (cybersecurity) to safety.

It is characterized by introduction of technique of decision making, which is easy to scale, modify, it's in compliance with standards requirements to the

Future steps of research and development will be connected with creation integrative intsrumentation tool to assess secuirty and safety at the all life cycle stages considering features of FPGA-based industrial I&Cs where application of diversity is defined by standard requirements. Other direction of future work is concerned to improve and completely assure computer-based implementation of ASAC-based technique.

References

1. V. Sklyar, Cyber Security of Safety-Critical Infrastructures: A Case Study for Nuclear Facilities, Information & Security An international Journal, **28**, 1 (2012)
2. V. Kharchenko, O. Illiashenko, A. Kovalenko, et. al. Security Informed Safety Assessment of NPP I&C Systems: GAP-IMECA Technique, ICONE 22, Prague, Czech Republic (2014)
3. B. Badrignans, J. Danger, V. Fischer, G. Gogniat, L. Torres, *Security Trends for FPGAs* (Springer, 2011)
4. T. Huffmire, C. Irvine, T. Nguyen, T. Levin, R. Kastner, T. Sherwood, *Handbook of FPGA Design Security* (Springer, 2010)
5. M. Tehranipoor, C. Wang (edits), *Introduction to Hardware Security and Trust* (Springer, 2012)
6. NUREG/CR-7007 ORNL/TM-2009/302 (2009)
7. V. Kharchenko, V. Sklyar (edits). *FPGA-based NPP Instrumentation and Control Systems: Development and Safety Assessment*, (KhAI , 2008)

8. M. Yastrebenetsky, V. Kharchenko (edits). *NPP I&S for Safety and Security*, (IGI-Global, USA, 2014)
9. O. Illiashenko, O. Potii, D. Komin. Advanced security assurance case based on ISO/IEC 15408, DepCoS-RELCOMEX, Brunów, Poland (2015)
10. V. Parondzhanov, *How to improve the work of your mind* (Delo, Russia, 2001)
11. N. G. Bardis, N. Doukas, O. P. Markovski. Burst Error Correction Using Binary Multiplication without Carry, MILCOM 2011 Military Communications Conference, Baltimore, MD (2011)

Investigation of Torsional Oscillations in Railway Vehicles

Tomáš Fridrichovský[1,a], and Bohumil Šulc[1]

[1]*Czech Technical University in Prague Faculty of Mechanical Engineering, Technická 4, 166 07 Prague 6, Czech Republic*

Abstract. The development of semiconductor electro-technics during last decades allowed us to produce railway vehicles with very high tractive power. High performances reveal new problems that were unknown until these days. One of these problems are torsional oscillations of running wheelsets, which may appear and compromise the safety of railway vehicles. This article analyzes dynamical events that may occur in drives of the vehicles and that are bound with transmission of the torque to the wheels during the operation of the vehicle, which is exposed to the variable external influences (adhesion conditions, track irregularities, variation of wheel forces, etc.). This is based on the idea of a model of simplified drive of the real railway vehicle, which is used for simulation purposes. The model serves for the parametric analysis of individual components, to make an effective design or control remedy.

1 Introduction

High travel velocities bring a requirement on high tractive power, which is demanded to be produced and transmitted from the traction motor to the wheels. In 2009 a slightly relative rotation between the wheel and the axle has been discovered on one of the DB (German Railways) locomotives during the maintenance. This issue has been then discovered on some other locomotives of the same type. Discovered rotation was relatively small, but it meant a big security risk due to its seriousness, especially when this problem has appeared on more vehicles. The main risk is a fact that the relative rotation between the wheel and the axle means losing friction and the failure of the whole press-fitted joint.

Figure 1. The detail of a relative rotation of the wheel disc on a modern electric locomotive (see yellow indication mark in the red ellipse on the right part of the picture) (source [1]).

It means that a wheel can move almost freely along the axle in transversal direction in that moment, during interaction of a guiding force. In such situation the distance between both wheels (wheelset gauge) can decrease and make vehicle derailed.

Investigation has been made when the problem has been discovered, but there weren't found any manufacture problems or failures [1]. Attention was turned to the phenomenon called "torsional oscillations of wheelsets". Torsional oscillation is a situation when both of the wheels start to oscillate one against the other (in an opposite phase). This event leads to slightly twisting of the axle.

Torsional oscillations requires an impulse to appear. This can happen when the adhesion on one of the wheels is lost. In case of a locomotive this may happen, when the vehicle runs with a high tractive effort and the adhesion force between a wheel and a rail is exceeded. Another reason is a situation when the vehicle passes through a small radius curvature. Oscillations with opposite phase may also merge during different slip velocities when the vehicle runs without tractive effort or breaking force [2]. Long lasting or periodically repeating oscillations may also lead to the creation and developing of fatigue failures in the press-fitted joint.

2 Analysis of torsional oscillations and finding a way of their reduction

There has been made an intensive research of sources and ways to reduction because of the seriousness of this problem. Simulation methods are a major type of the research because of experimental measurements on a real vehicle are very expensive and require a lot of time as well. Another advantage of simulation methods is a possibility to consider the wheelset as a part of the whole drive, which is represented as a controlled dynamic system. This allows to apply design processes that are based on the theory of system control. This approach has been used by Böcker, Amann and Schulz

[a] Corresponding author: tomas.fridrichovsky@fs.cvut.cz

 DOI: 10.1051/matecconf/20167602052

[3] for presentation of a design of an active reduction of torsional oscillations in a drivetrain of a car. This uses an estimation regulator with help of the Kalman filter. The research was based on a simplified and idealized interpretation of flexible and inertial properties of the used components.

Situation in railway vehicles is much more difficult. Railway vehicles work with proportionally higher values of the torque, which is influenced by much higher values of inertia momentum. External influences are specific for operation of railway vehicles (effect of wind, uncompensated centrifugal forces…), especially during creation of the model of torque transmission on the tractive effort.

One of the first publications focused on torsional oscillations was the article written by authors Kaderavek and Pernicka [1]. In this article the phenomenon was described on a general level. There was mentioned history of this phenomenon and its general specification, namely verbal description and some of the necessary conditions. More detailed description, objected on physical principle of this phenomenon, was written by authors Benker and Weber [4] who paid attention to this phenomenon in some of their articles. These articles were mainly aimed on a wheelset that was presented as a force excited mechanical oscillator.

Possibility of detection of the oscillations has been described by authors Markovic, Kostic and Bojovic [5]. Authors made a simplified model of the class 444 locomotive, propelled via DC motors. The model was created as a scheme of transmission of the torque, using the set of parts connected via torsional elastic elements, representing the wheelset, the gearbox and the traction motor. Results of the simulations showed that in the moment when the adhesion is decreased enough and the wheelset starts to slip, the voltage of the motor increases above its nominal value. Closer look at the voltage course shows that the voltage oscillates with a small amplitude and a specific frequency. This frequency corresponds to the natural frequency of the wheelset and appears only in the moment of losing the wheelset adhesion.

Possibility of reduction of the oscillations has been described by authors Bieker, Dede, Dörner, Klein and Pusnik [6]. Authors have dealt with an idea of using of brake discs elastically connected to the wheels that may serve as additional oscillators. These oscillators, suitably configured, should start to oscillate instead of the wheelset when the adhesion is lost. This means the axle shouldn't twist at all. Then brake discs can serve as absorbers of the wheelset torsional oscillations. This may work only on condition when all the parameters are well set. This may be problematic because of diameter of the wheel that may differ during the vehicles lifetime, which causes changes of the wheelset natural frequency. Another problem is a fact that the natural frequency depends on the value of tangential forces between the wheel and the rail, the concept of the drive, and velocity of the vehicle [2, 7, 8].

3 Idealization used in presented approach to the modelling of torsional oscillations

The problem seems to be related only to the wheelset, but there are more factors that may have influence on it. These factors are necessary to be considered because of complexity of the models, in simplified form with certain degree of idealization or, because of difficulty of mathematical description, fully neglected. For example a vehicle body may interact with an elastically connected two-axle bogie. The wheel force, interacting between the wheel and the rail, and the pulling force may then differ during the operation. These influences are not considered in the presented model, which is used for further analysis. The major attention has been aimed on the model of the whole drive chain and the adhesion between the wheel and the rail.

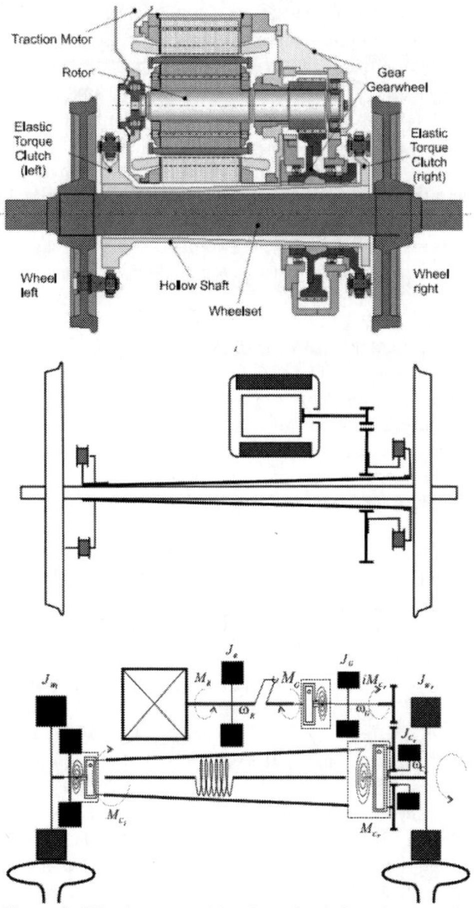

Figure 2. Wheelset – transition from the design sketch to the substitute idealized concept.

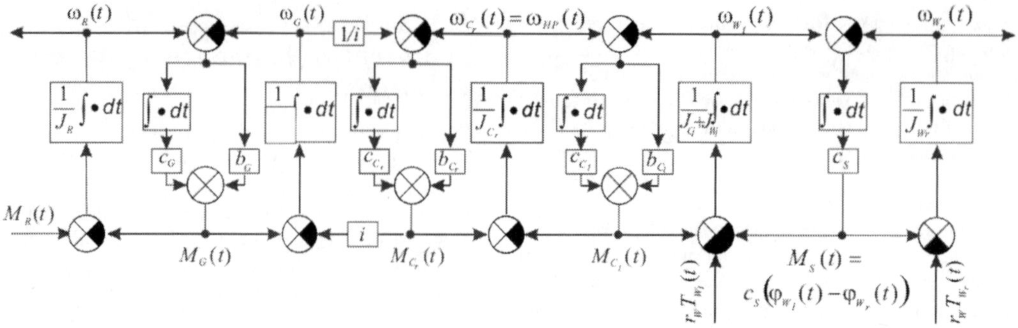

Figure 3. Block scheme of the model of the torque transmission from the traction motor to the wheels.

Design scheme of the drive chain containing cross section view is shown on Figure 2. As a support of the models creation, the decomposition on the base elements has been made as it can be seen in the mid part of Figure 2. The drive chain is here divided into fundamental parts, namely a traction motor, a gearbox, clutches, a hollow shaft, an axle and wheels.

Schematically shown substitute concept of the torque transmission, in the lower part of the image is the fundamental part of the creation of the mathematical model. The components, which are passing a rotary motion, are idealized and their mechanical properties are centralized into fundamental elements. These elements represent moments of inertia, torsional stiffness and torsional damping. The two rails on the bottom of the picture represent a requirement to include the adhesion model.

The model of drive chains dynamics is composed of three connected subunits:

- model of transmission of the torque on the wheelset including the model of the gearbox
- model of transmission of the toque on the adhesion force between the wheel and the rail
- model of the traction motor

The creation of the model was based on the idea that the schematically shown mechanical components are massless and rigid and are unable to resist to the rotary motion. All of these resists are made via connected elements that represent these concentrated properties.

These elements are resolved with different line thickness or bordered with the dashed line on the Figure 2. Continuously distributed properties (moment of inertia, torsional stiffness, torsional damping) are replaced with three idealized elements: massless spiral spring with a constant torsional stiffness c, rotary hydraulic dumper with an incompressible fluid with the dumping coefficient b, rotating disc with the moment of inertia J. These three elements create a fictional component that is connected into the modelled component of the drive, so it is not disrupting the functionality of the transmission of the rotary motion. The respective component is then considered as ideally rigid and massless.

The equation description, which is based on the mentioned substitute concept, is a shortened description of the increment interpretation of all variables in the symbolic labelling of all the values that are characterizing the rotary motion (the angle of rotation $\varphi(t)$, the rate of its change $\omega(t) = \dot{\varphi}(t)$). It means all the values are the increments – deviations from the nominal values. The usually used symbol Δ has been suppressed because of shortening of the description.

The increment model of the drive is described with following equations. Symbols in brackets show where is the value belonging to – rotor (R), gearbox (G) right torsional clutch (C_r) hollow shaft (HP), left wheel (W_l), the axle (S) and right wheel (W_r).

$$J_R\dot{\omega}_R(t) = M_R(t) - M_G(t) \tag{1}$$

$$M_G(t) = c_G(\varphi_R(t) - \varphi_G(t)) + b_G(\omega_R(t) - \omega_G(t)) \tag{2}$$

$$J_G\dot{\omega}_G(t) = M_G(t) - iM_{C_r}(t) \tag{3}$$

$$M_{C_r}(t) = c_{C_r}\left(\frac{1}{i}\varphi_G(t) - \varphi_{C_r}(t)\right) + b_{C_r}\left(\frac{1}{i}\omega_G(t) - \omega_{C_r}(t)\right) \tag{4}$$

$$J_{C_r}\dot{\omega}_{C_r}(t) = M_{C_r}(t) - M_{HP}(t) \tag{5}$$

$$\varphi_{HP_r}(t) = \varphi_{HP_l}(t) = \varphi_{HP}(t) \quad \omega_{HP_r}(t) = \omega_{HP_l}(t) = \omega_{HP}(t)$$
(1)

$$\varphi_{HP_r}(t) = \varphi_{HP_l}(t) = \varphi_{HP}(t) \quad \omega_{HP_r}(t) = \omega_{HP_l}(t) = \omega_{HP}(t) \tag{6}$$

$$M_{C_l}(t) = c_{C_l}(\varphi_{HP}(t) - \varphi_{W_l}(t)) + b_{C_l}(\omega_{HP}(t) - \omega_{W_l}(t)) \tag{7}$$

$$(J_{W_l} + J_{C_l} + \frac{1}{2}J_S)\dot{\omega}_{W_l}(t) = M_{C_l}(t) - M_{W_l}(t) \tag{8}$$

$$M_S(t) = c_S(\varphi_{W_l}(t) - \varphi_{W_r}(t)) \tag{9}$$

$$(J_{W_r} + \frac{1}{2}J_S\dot{\omega}_{W_r}(t) = M_{C_l}(t) - r_W T_{W_r}(t) - M_S(t) \tag{10}$$

Dynamic changes of the angular velocities of the wheels make changes of the tangential forces which depend on them.

The model of the transmission of the tangential forces between the wheel and the rail is based on Polach theory [9]. Tangential forces are transmitted via friction which is bounded with a slight slip of the wheels on the rails. The amount of friction and the tangential forces as well is based on a friction coefficient μ.

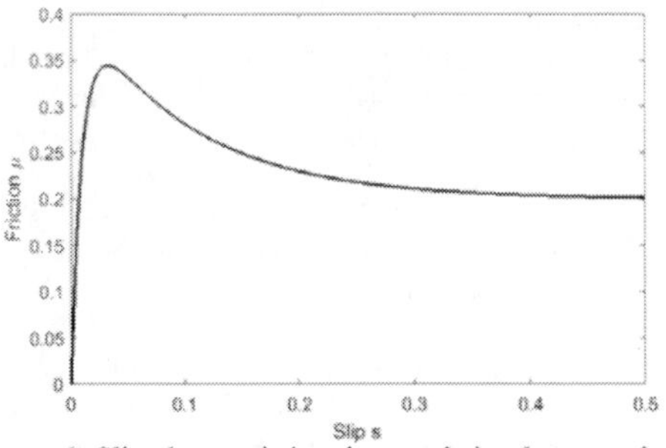

Figure 4. Slip characteristics shows relation between the slip and the friction. The characteristics is described via eq. (11).

The relation between the slip and the friction is expressed via slip characteristics, which has been analytically described for the simulation purposes with a sum of two exponential functions.

$$\mu(s) = \mu_{MAX}\left(1 - e^{\frac{-s}{\tau_1}}\right) - \mu_{RED} h(s - 0{,}01)\left(1 - e^{-\frac{(s-0{,}01)}{\tau_2}}\right) \quad (11)$$

The variability of the slip conditions for a dry or wet rail may be well expressed with appropriate chosen parameters μ_{MAX}, μ_{RED}, τ_1, τ_1. The slip s is defined as a dimensionless ratio of a perimeter speed of the wheel and the vehicle velocity *v(t)* and is described with the following equation

$$\Delta s(t) = \frac{r_w \Delta\omega_w(t) - \Delta v(t)}{r_w \omega_{w0}} \quad (12)$$

This adhesion model is based on an assumption that the vehicle is in a steady state. This means the vehicle moves with a constant velocity v_0, the pulling force of the vehicle, divided on single wheels is constant as well as the tangential forces T_{w0}, which correspond with the engine torque M_{w0}. Then the slip must have a steady value s_0 so the friction coefficient $\mu_0 = g^{-1}T_{w0}/m_w$ corresponds with the requested value of the tangential force T_{w0} coinciding with the vehicle mass divided onto single wheels m_w.

The angular velocity of the wheel differs by an increment in the non-steady state. This velocity is bounded with an angular acceleration and a moment of inertia J_w during imbalance of the dynamic change of the torque on the wheel $\Delta M_w(t)$, transmitted through the drive, and change of the torque that occurs during changes of the slip $m_w g \Delta s(t)$.

The calculation of the slip differences is then necessary to be completed with a dynamics of the velocity changes that depends on drive resists. The drive resist (the roll and the aero dynamical resist) can be expressed with a parabolic relation for a single vehicle or the whole train with an equation $m_s(a+bv(t)+cv^2(t))$. This drive resist is necessary to be linearized according to an increment form of the model and then divided into single drives or wheels.

The model of the asynchronous motor is based on a real traction motor type ML 4550 K/6 whose parameters are following

Power output	1 600	kW
Nominal speed	1 825	min-1
Maximum torque	10 000	Nm
Nominal torque	8 400	Nm

The complex model of the traction motor has been replaced with a linear approximation of the relation between the torque and speed due to the fast dynamics of the initial simulations.

4 Results

The experiments were focused on the situation when the torque is rapidly changed from its steady state. This corresponds to the situation when the adhesion is decreased and the stick slip protection makes an intervention (the torque of the motor is decreased or increased in this moment).

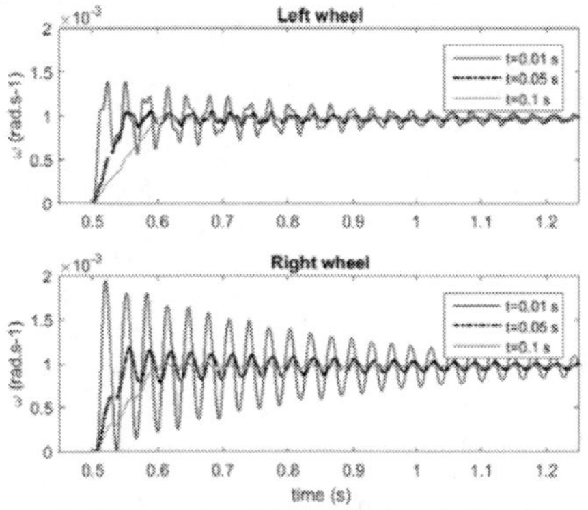

Figure 5. Time courses of the oscillations during change of the motor torque. Torque increment is 500 N.m.

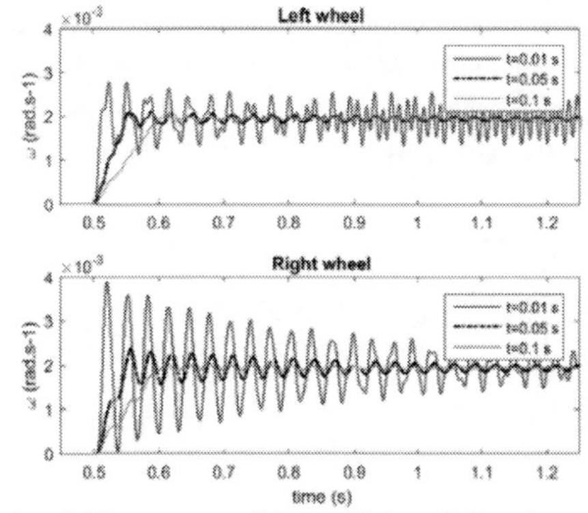

Figure 6. Time courses of the oscillations during change of the motor torque. Torque increment is 1000 N.m

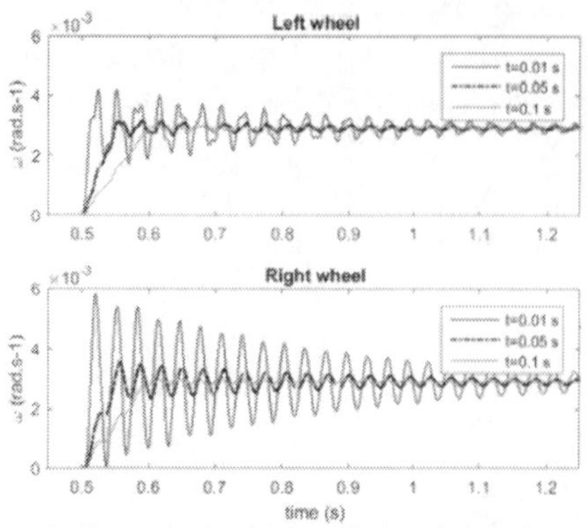

Figure 7. Time courses of the oscillations during change of the motor torque. Torque increment is 1500 N.m

The simulations took into account different size of the actual torque changes and different speed of these changes. Enclosed figures show following

- Faster the speed of the change is, the greater the amplitudes of the oscillations are.
- Higher the change of the torque is, the greater the amplitudes of the oscillations are.

These oscillations have relatively small amplitudes but they may be dangerous when the torque control changes the value of the torque repeatedly in quick during the operation of the vehicle. As a result, this may lead to very high oscillations created in the drive of the vehicle.

5 Conclusions

From a series of experiments that have been carried out are presented those focused on the angular velocities of the wheels. These velocities can be expected as a possible consequences of a rapid change of the motor torque. The motor torque is the most important and easiest exploitable way how to supress possible occurrence of oscillations by means of control circuit using the motor torque as a manipulated variable.

Created simulation model includes a model of running behaviour that is respecting change of the adhesion conditions and detailed model of the asynchronous motor. This allows to study the influence of the level of knowledge of the known parameters. This is then used to assess an impact of different design settings or control actions required for reduction of the torsional oscillations.

Acknowledgement

The paper was created with the financial support SGS grant No. SGS14/184/OHK2/3T/12 and of the Technology Agency of the Czech Republic, project No TE01020038 "Competence Centre of Railway Vehicles".

References

1. P. Kaderavek, J. Pernicka, Torsion oscillations of powered wheelsets, *Railvolution*, 34-37 (2013)
2. J. Kolář, Design of a Wheelset Drive, Transaction on Electrical Engineering, **4**, 11-19 (2015)
3. J. Böcker, N. Amann, B. Schulz, Active Suppression of Torsional Oscillations, *EEE/ASME Transactions on Mechatronics*, **9**, 6 (2004)
4. T. Benker, T. Weber, Torsionsschwingungen von Raddsätzen - eine Herausforderung?, *Eisenbahn-ingenieur*, 47-52 (2015)
5. P. Markovic, D. Kostic, N. Bojovic, One Method for Detection of Torsional Oscillations of Driving Axles of Electrical Locomotives, *Proceedings of the 22nd international conference on Current problems in Rail vehicles – PRORAIL 2015*, **1**, 27-35 (2015)
6. G. Bieker, J. Dede, D. Dörner, H. Klein, A. Pusnik, Bremsscheibe als Tilger für Radsatz-torsionsschwingungen, *ZEV Rail*, 381-387 (2014)
7. J. Kolář, Problems with modellling of the influence of the vertical track irregularities on the dynamics of the vehicle drive, *Proceedings of the 22nd international conference on Current problems in Rail vehicles – PRORAIL 2015*, **1**, 275-286 (2015)
8. J. Kolář, Dynamics of Wheelset with Axle Gearbox, *Proceedings of the 22nd international conference on Current problems in Rail vehicles PRORAIL 2015*, vol. **2**, 139-148 (2011)
9. O. Polach, Creep forces in simulations of traction vehicles running on adhesion limit, *Proceedings of the 6th International Conference on Contact Mechanics and Wear of Rail/Wheel Systems (CM2003)*, 279-285 (2003)

The subsystems design of methods for solving a problem of non-stationary waves propagation in solid bodies

Zhanar Akhmetova[1,a], Gulmira Baenova[2], Assel Omarbekova [3]

[1] *L.N.Gumilyov Eurasian National University, Department of Information Systems, 010000 Satpaev 2, Astana, Kazakhstan*
[2] *L.N.Gumilyov Eurasian National University, Computer Science Department, 010000 Satpaev 2, Astana, Kazakhstan*
[3] *L.N.Gumilyov Eurasian National University, Department of Informatics and Information security, 010000 Satpaev 2, Astana, Kazakhstan*

Abstract. In this paper is considered the design of information subsystem of method bicharacteristics, and also their numerical solution and computer visualization. The bicharacteristics method is one of the most convenient methods for software creating. This information subsystem combines the results of the solutions of practical tasks in the dynamics of a homogeneous elastic media, with the aim of creating digital collections for use in calculations of building constructions in engineering practice and also in problems of mechanical engineering and in general for researches in respective industries.

1 Introduction

Today world progress in information technologies, widespread introduction of computer facilities and new level of developments of applied and scientific researchers have made significant changes in the organization of scientific process. There was opportunity to solve many physical experiments and complex challenges in the field of economy, ecology, physics, biology, etc. with the help of appropriate software, computer simulation and visualization.

Examples of such implementations can serve a variety of electronic library with online access that contains unique text-based information, and non-specific, for example, a microfilm. [1,2].

In this paper is considered the association of private methods for solving problems of solid mechanics in one information subsystem.

The need for qualitative and quantitative analysis of the dynamic effects of the stress- strained state is increasing because of the connection with the various fields of engineering, structural elements, working in the dynamic load duty. As a result of the dynamic loads an elastic wave takes place in the testing body. And a reliable calculation of it helps in evaluating the strength and reliability of the entire design and technology.

Nowadays the numerical methods of spatial characteristics, finite element, the boundary integral equation and etc. are used for solving dynamic problems in elastic media [3-6].

In this paper is considered the design of information subsystem which integrates implemented methods and numerical and graphical results.

In this paper, we offer the bicharacteristicsmethod with the usage of ideas of splitting method for solution of the homogeneous isotropic elastic body. The advantage of this method is that it allows approaching the maximum dependence domain of the final and differential equation to the dependence area of the initial differential equation [3,4].

Novelty of development of a subsystem consists in use of a numerical method of bicharacteristics which is one of the most convenient for an application creation.

2 Statement of problem

In this paper we consider the solution of problems relating to the propagation of non-stationary waves in solid bodies, and combining the results in one subsystem to development a digital library in the future.

This subsystem is intended for physicists, engineers who engages in calculations of building constructions and solves different problems of mechanical engineering and others.

The functionality of this subsystem allows the use of the proposed methods, and manage through changing parameters such as density, temperature, and other, for their own research.

[a] Zhanar Akhmetova: zaigura@mail.ru

3 The method of calculating the spatial characteristics

Currently, for solving dynamic problems in elastic medium there widely used the numerical methods of spatial characteristics [10], finite element [1], the boundary integral equation [2] and etc.One of the most convenient methods in applications is bicharacteristics method with the use of splitting method ideas [5,6,7]. This method allows approaching dependence domain of the final and differential equation to the dependence area of the initial differential equation as much as possible.

In this paper we reviewed the non-stationary problem solution of the homogeneous isotropic elastic body dynamics in the Cartesian coordinate system using the bicharacteristics method. Let us introduce the following notations:

x_i – Cartesian coordinates, t - time, σ_{ij} – tension tensor, ϑ_i– velocity vector, u_i – displacement vector. Let us consider an elastic semi-strip of final width which in the Cartesian system of coordinates x_1Ox_2 occupies the area of $0 < x_2 < \infty$, $|x_1 < l|$. In the initial time point the body is at state of rest.

$$\vartheta_i = 0, \sigma_{ij} = 0, (i,j=1,2) \quad (1)$$

At any other time on the site $N_1 \le x_2 \le N_2$, $x_1 = l$ of border BN the uniformly distributed transient normal load $f(t)$ has its influence, which varies according to sine law

$$\sigma_{22}(t) = \begin{cases} -A\sin(\omega t) 0 \le t \le S_1 \\ 0, \; t \ge S_1 \end{cases} \quad (2)$$
$$\sigma_{21}(t) = 0.$$

Where S_1– loadings action time and $\omega = \pi/S_1$. The other part of the semi-strip border is free from any influence:

$$\sigma_{11}(t) = 0, \quad \sigma_{12}(t) = 0, \quad x_1 = 0, \quad |x_1| \ge l,$$
$$\sigma_{22}(t) = 0, \quad \sigma_{21}(t) = 0, \quad 0 \le x_1 \notin (N_1, N_2) |x_2| = l \quad (3)$$

Under existing conditions it is necessary to investigate an elastic body tension at $t>0$.

A. The defining equations. In order to solve the problem along with entry and boundary conditions, we used the system of the equations consisting of the movement and ratios equations of the generalized Hooke's law:

$$\sigma_{i\beta,\beta} = \rho \frac{\partial^2 u_i}{\partial t^2}, \quad (4)$$

$$\sigma_{ij} = \lambda u_{\beta,\beta}\delta_{ij} + \mu(u_{i,j} + u_{j,i}) \quad (5)$$

Where ρ – density, λ, μ – Lama's constants, δ_{ij}– Kronecker delta.

After the non-dimensional variables integration, the motion equations (4) and correlations of the generalized Hooke's law differentiated by time (5) take the following form:

$$\{\dot{\vartheta}_1 = \sigma_{11,1} + \sigma_{12,2}, \dot{\vartheta}_1 = \sigma_{21,1} + \sigma_{22,2}, \dot{\sigma}_{11} = \vartheta_{1,1} + \gamma_{11}\sigma_{2,2}, \dot{\sigma}_{22} = \gamma_{11}\vartheta_{1,1} + \sigma_{2,2}, \dot{\sigma}_{12} = \gamma_{12}^2(\vartheta_{1,2} + \vartheta_{2,1}) \} \quad (6)$$

Indexes after the comma denote the partial derivatives on Cartesian coordinates and the point from the top shows the partial derivatives on time.

B. The equations of bicharacteristics. In order to obtain bicharacteristics equation and conditions on them, let us split the two-dimensional system (6) on the single-dimensional one. Applying ideas of K.A.Bagrinovski and S.K.Godunov on splitting multidimensional t-hyperbolic systems on single-dimensional systems where $x_k = const$ [9], we will have:

$$\begin{Bmatrix} \dot{v}_i - \sigma_{ij,j} = a_{ij} \\ \dot{\sigma_{ij}} - \lambda_{ij}^2 v_{i,j} = b_{ij} \end{Bmatrix} \quad (7)$$

From here, using notorious methods to obtain differential bicharacteristics equations and conditions on them, we obtain:

$$dx_j = \pm\lambda_{ij}dt,$$
$$d\sigma_{ij} \mp \lambda_{ij}dv_i = (b_{ij} \mp \lambda_{ij}a_{ij})dt \quad (8)$$

C. Selection of a point scheme and a pattern. This body is divided into square cells, sides of which are $\Delta x_1 = \Delta x_2 = h$. In the double points, the function values ϑ_i, σ_{ij} are searched at various time points with step of τ. The dot grid (on the basis of which the difference scheme is built, other than those mentioned double points) contains points formed by the intersection of bicharacteristics with hyperplanes $t = const$.

D. Resolving differential equations. The integration of equations (6) from the point O to the point A and the relations (8) from the point $E_{ij}^{\pm}$ to the point A by trapezoid method allows us to obtain the expression of the following form.

$$\vartheta_i = \vartheta_i^0 + \frac{\tau}{2}(\sigma_{ij,j} + a_{ij} + \vartheta_i^{\dot{0}}),$$
$$\sigma_{ij} = \sigma_{ij}^0 + \frac{\tau}{2}(\lambda_{ij}^2 v_{i,j} + b_{ij} + \sigma_{ij}^{\dot{0}}), \quad (9)$$

$$\sigma_{ij} - \sigma_{ij}^{\pm} \mp \lambda_{ij}(v_i + v_i^{\pm}) = \frac{\tau}{2}(b_{ij} + b_{ij}^{\pm} \mp \lambda_{ij}[a_{ij} + a_{ij}^{\pm}]) \quad (10)$$

Excluding from (9) ϑ_i, σ_{ij} by means of (10), we will receive:

$$\lambda_{ij}^2 v_{i,j} \mp \lambda_{ij}\sigma_{ij,j} = b_{ij}^{\pm} - \sigma_{ij}^0 \pm \lambda_{ij}(v_i^0 - a_{ij}^{\pm} + \frac{2}{\tau}(\sigma_{ij}^{\pm} - \sigma_{ij}^0 \pm \lambda_{ij}[v_i^0 - v_i^{\pm}]) \quad (11)$$

Values of unknown quantities in non-nodal points of expression (12) are calculated on Taylor's formula near a double point of 0 with accuracy to the second order concerning a step τ, therefore, we will have:

$$\lambda_{ij}^2 v_{i,j} \mp \lambda_{ij}\sigma_{ij,j} = \lambda_{ij}^2(v_{i,j}^0 + \tau \dot{v}_{i,j}^0) \mp \lambda_{ij}(\sigma_{ij,j}^0 + \tau \dot{\sigma}_{ij,j}^0 \quad (12)$$

Summing up and subtracting each system equation (13) with identical indexes pair, we will receive

$$v_{i,j} = v_{i,j}^0 + \tau(\sigma_{ij,jj}^0 + a_{ij,j}^0)$$
$$\sigma_{ij,j} = \sigma_{ij,j}^0 + \tau(\lambda_{ij}^2 v_{i,jj}^0 + b_{ij,j}^0) \quad (13)$$

Procedure of receiving the equations allowing systems in double points of the studied body in time moment $t = t_n + \tau$ is various for internal, boundary and angular points of the studied area. We should recognize that the given problem in general case should be investigated as part of an axially symmetric deformation. However, the numerous experimental results confirm that during the process of well compaction, any geometric shape of the well base (rectangle, triangle, circle, etc.) affects only the numerical results. Qualitatively, the deformation process is practically repeated almost in all cases. With this in mind, and having developed an algorithm for solving the location of planar linear dynamic problems of deformable bodies, the process of soil compaction was investigated in this paper [7-9].

4 The computer visualization bicharacteristics method for the special case

As an example of solving one of the problems with using the method bicharacteristics implemented in Fortran and obtained graphical visualization of normal and tangent tensions isolines in several moment of time. On figures 1 and 2 you can see the isolines of normal σ_{11} and tangent σ_{12} tension corresponding to a time point $t = 20\tau$.

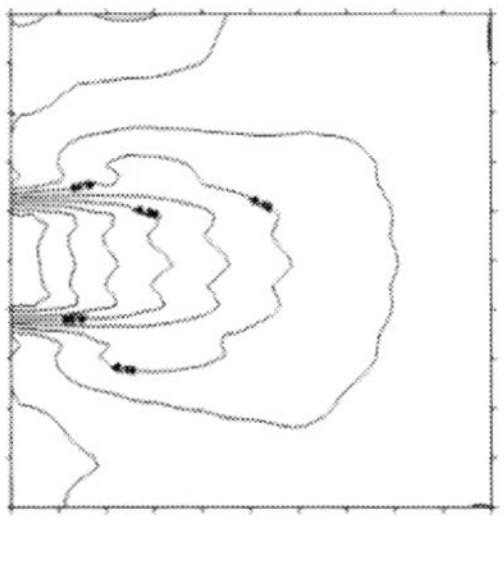

Figure 1. Isolines of normal tension

During this time, the boundary perturbance extending from influence local site travel a distance *10h* and reach opposite border.

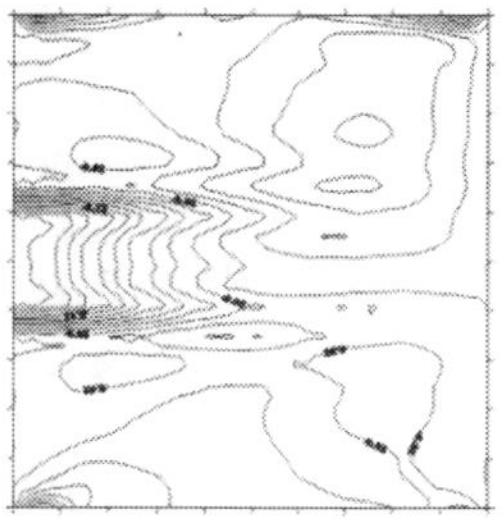

Figure 2. Isolines of tangent tension

In a timepoint of $t=40\tau$ tension fields symmetry, characteristic for $t=20\tau$, to an axis of $x_1 = 12h$ are still looked through near a symmetry axis. With removal from this axis symmetry of isolines are broken. This result is explained by influence on nature of distribution of tension from a free end AB in the field of $x_1 \leq N_1$ and absence of similar effects in the field of $x_1 \leq N_2$[10].

5 The design of Information Subsystem

In order to classify the obtained solutions and their graphic images, it was decided to combine them into one information system, the core of which is a digital library containing a collection of software and analytical methods of wave propagation for different environmental settings and their corresponding graphic image.

This system allows physicists, engineers and related professionals to use the methods and manage through changing parameters such as density, temperature and others, for their own studies.

During architecture selection and database creation, solved such tasks as the creation of infrastructure and technological solutions and access as to the actual methods and graphical solutions. Therefore, interface design is another direction in building an information system. In our case the interface of the program needs to solve both user and functional tasks [11].

In [12] considered a system development of user interfaces. This work belongs to the early studies. It was supposed to develop an integrated environment for the creation and management of various user interfaces. This system is called the system user interface design (UIDS - User Interface Development Systems). For the first time interactive communication between human and machine was proposed by W. Newman in 1968.

Simple interfaces designed standard components, which occurs by the user directly. Modern software products have complex interfaces containing various styles of user interaction. For example, the management object that represents application data, support for graphical data representation, management dialog boxes, etc. Than bigger the app, the more tools and interface features integrated into it, the harder it is amenable to the study of the interface.

One of the common methods of developing user interfaces is the model-based design, consisting of several stages (Fig.3) [13]. In the first stage, organizational and collaborative tasks are modeled using high-level specifications. In the second stage, tasks are specified and the level of detail increases. And finally, the last stage is modeled by the interaction between individual user and the application using the system tree of parallel tasks [14].

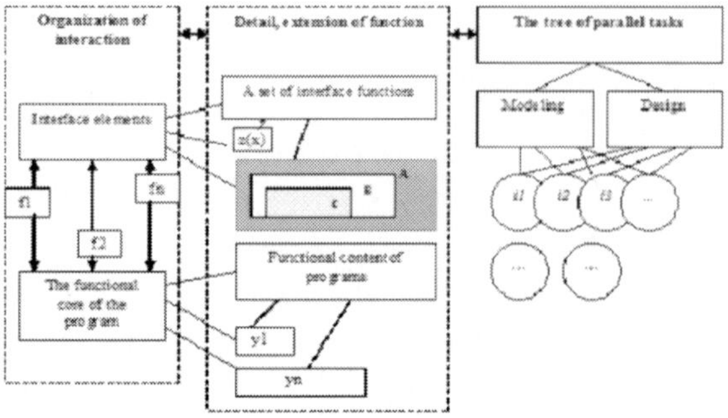

Figure 3. The abstract model of interface design

6 Final remarks

The main purpose of this subsystem is designed to bring together the spatial characteristics of methods and their graphic solutions.

The software subsystem technology is implemented in Java in the database development environment - Microsoft SQL Server.

The digital collection of this subsystem includes numerical methods for transient wave propagation in solids and their visualization.

During further research it is planned to expand a set of methods by calculation of waves in solid media.

This subsystem will be of interest to various researchers not only as a finished instrument, but also from the point of view of further optimization of the algorithms.

7 Conclusions

In the design and construction of engineering structures for more economical use of materials it is necessary to consider not only the statistical burden on facilities , but also dynamic, which may occur , for example , at the location of facilities in areas with high seismic activity. Power dynamic load cannot be determined without a full study of the space- time picture of the state of stress of the object appearing in the propagation of elastic waves in solids.

In this paper, information subsystem was proposed, which is a digital collection of numerical methods bicharacteristics for solving problems of dynamic wave propagation in an elastic medium.

References

1. O. Syuntyurenko. Electron. Lib. Electronic information resources: new technologies and applications, **1**, (2011)
2. W. Y. Arms. Digital Libraries. MA: The MIT Press, Cambridge (2000).
3. G. T. Tarabrin. Construction mechanics and calculation of constructions, **6**, pp. 53-58 (1980)
4. G. T Tarabrin. Stroit. Mechanics and calculation of constructions. **4**, pp. 38-43 (1981)
5. G. T Tarabrin. Metallurgical science. **3**, pp. 193-199 (1979)
6. Sh. Aytaliyev, L. Alekseeva, Sh. Dildabayev, N. Zhanbyrbayev. Metod of the boundary integrated equations in problems of dynamics elastic many connected ph. Alma-Ata, pp.238 (1992)
7. Z. Akhmetova, S. Boranbayev., S. Zhuzbayev, Advances in Intelligent Systems and Computing. The visual representation of numerical solution for a non-stationary deformation in a solid body. **448**, pp 473-482 (2016)
8. S.Boranbayev, S. Altayev, A. Boranbayev. Applying the method of diverse redundancy in cloud based systems for increasing reliability, Proceedings of the 12th International Conference on Information Technology: New Generations, pp.796-799 (2015)
9. S.Boranbayev, A.Boranbayev, S.Altayev, A.Nurbekov. Mathematical model for optimal designing of reliable information systems, Proceedings of the 8th IEEE International Conference on Application of Information and Communication Technologies, pp.123-127 (2014)
10. Z. Akhmetova, S. Zhuzbayev, S. Boranbayev., Acta Physica Polonica A , The method and software for the solution of dynamic waves propagation problem in elastic medium (To be published)
11. D. Raskin. Interface: New directions in designing of computer systems: Transl. from English.pp. 272 (2007)
12. Q. Mao. Micro-UIDT: A user interface development tool. Eurographics Association, pp. 3-14 (1989)
13. I.Molina Ana, M.Redondo, M. Ortega. A methodological approach for user interface development of collaborative applications: A case study. Science of Computer Programming, **74**, pp. 754-776 (2009)
14. G.Tidwell. Development of user interfaces: TRANS. from English. Pp. 416 (2008)

Effects on phased arrays radiation pattern due to phase error distribution in the phase shifter operation

Giuseppe Coviello[1,a], Gianfranco Avitabile[1], Giovanni Piccinni[1], Giulio D'Amato[1], Claudio Talarico[2]

[1]*Politechnic of Bari, Department of Electrical and Information Engineering, 70125 Bari, Italy*
[2]*Gonzaga University, Spokane, USA*

Abstract. A comprehensive study on the role of the phase errors distribution on the performances of the phased array systems has been produced. The analysis is brought out using a complete and behavioural model for radiation-pattern characteristics. The study has shown how the phase errors distribution actually affects the performances demonstrating that the rms phase error is a valuable figure of merit of phased array systems but it is not sufficient to completely describe the behaviour of a real system. The paper demonstrates that the antennas array beam shape is depending by the actual error phase distribution and that a good phase shifter has to have the phase errors as constant as possible and with a low rms value.

1 Introduction

Phased array antennas play an important role in many applications. Their success is mainly due to high agility in reconfiguring pattern and quick steering capability. Many phased-array antennas are designed to use digital or digitalized phase shifters in which the phase shift varies in discrete steps rather than continuously. As a consequence of using digital phase shifter, the beam can be steered only in discrete steps and the granularity [1], defined as the finest realizable increment between adjacent beam positions, depends on the number of bits and the number of antennas. Furthermore, the phase shifts produced by the phase shifter are not ideal, because a phase shifter itself is affected by errors and non-idealities and this implies that the radiation pattern characteristics are further altered.

Usually [2]-[3], the phase accuracy is synthetically presented in terms of rms phase error defined as in (1). Let's denote $\theta\Delta i$ the i-th error phase shift, so the rms phase error can be defined as

$$\theta_{\Delta rms} = \sqrt{\frac{1}{N-1}\sum_{i=2}^{N}|\theta_{\Delta i}|^2} \qquad (1)$$

where the phase of an arbitrary channel is chosen as the reference for the calculations of the errors in the other channels.

This figure of merit, even being a significant feature of the phase shifters, it is not satisfactory to describe consistently the behavior of real phased array systems. Indeed, an important role on determining the radiation-pattern characteristics is played by the phase errors distribution which can be defined as a vector with the length equal to the number of possible phase shifts and with the i-th element equal to the phase error corresponding to the i-th ideal phase shift.

The phase shifter with a low rms phase error is a challenging building block, expressly at high frequencies [4]. It is easy to understand as the achievement presented in this study is an important key aspect to be taken into account designing a high performances phased array systems such as those used to achieve high directivity and high suppression of sidelobes for satellite, RADAR and wireless communications systems.

An advanced model, thus, must account for the non-idealities and the afore mentioned aspects related to phase errors distribution in the introduced phase shifts, besides of the classical parameters affecting the radiation-pattern characteristics, such as number of antennas, number of bits, and so on. In this chapter this complete and advanced behavioral model, developed in MATLAB® is presented and discussed. This tool is able to predict antenna array performance in terms of beam shape, directivity, side lobe levels, main lobe deviation etc. considering also the phase errors distribution.

Another important feature of the tool is the possibility to get the project specification of a phased array, starting from the radiation–pattern characteristics. In particular, the user can specify the minimum value of the side-lobe level, the maximum value of the lobe deviation and the maximum value of the half power beam width and the tool gives all those ideal values that satisfy the conditions imposed. For this type of simulation it was decided to limit the output to combinations of number of bit and

[a] Corresponding author: giuseppe.coviello@poliba.it

DOI: 10.1051/matecconf/20167603002

number of antennas, fixing to 0.5 λ the distance between the antennas. The reasons are:

- to reduce the simulation time
- as will be described below the modification of the distance between the elements in the array can be advantageous for some parameters but inconvenient for other parameters; for this reason, a good compromise is setting the inter-element spacing equal to 0.5 λ.

The paper is organized as follows: the model is described in Section 2; the analysis and results of the proposed study are presented in Section 3, while in the Section 4 the conclusions are given.

2 Model description

Matlab® furnishes a high-level technical computing language and an interactive environment for algorithm development, data visualization, data analysis, and numeric computation. For sake of clarity, every detail of the complete model is discussed in the following paragraphs.

2.1 Array configuration

The tool takes into account the array factors of linear arrays and it is based on basic antenna array theory. The array configuration is shown in Figure 1 where the elements, considered as point sources, are positioned on the horizontal axis.

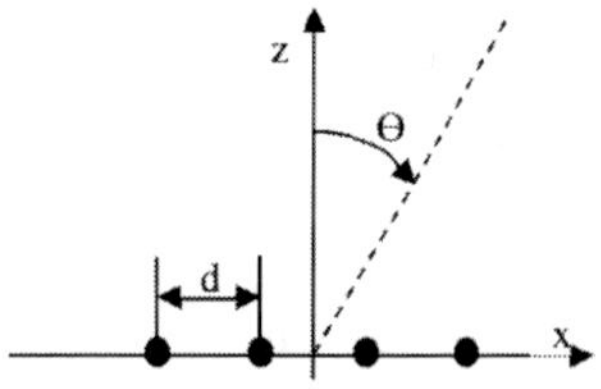

Figure 1. Array configuration.

The angle Θ represents the elevation angle which is the angle of the beam with respect to the z axis. The scan angle is the elevation angle imposed.

2.2 Results plot types

At the end of the simulations, the user can plot the obtained radiation-patterns in various formats: classical rectangular plot, classical polar plot or unconventional two-dimensional color graph representation in Cartesian coordinate system. Conventionally, radiation patterns are represented in two dimensions (2D), in Cartesian or polar coordinate systems. In the Cartesian coordinate system, the magnitude of the radiated field, usually in decibels (dB), is indicated on the Y axis, whereas the angular parameter, the elevation angle θ or the quantity u=sin(θ), governs the X axis. In the polar coordinate system, the radius usually represents the magnitude of the radiated field while the angle represents the elevation angle. When a comparison is required or a parametric simulation is carried out, several curves are plotted on the same graph or, alternatively, another dimension is added. If we use another axis as a third dimension, the extrapolation of the data is not easily done, considering that the three dimensional representation is actually two dimensional on a planar surface [5]. An attractive representation adds the colors used for the graphs as the third dimension, which represents the variable or the parameter of user's interest. As a clarifying example, consider the case of a not parametric simulation in which the user aims to study the array factor of a sixteen element array with the inter-element spacing equal to half a wavelength and exact phase at each element, over a range of scan angles. Assume, in our example, that the elevation start angle is -90°, the elevation stop angle 90°, the elevation increment angle 0.2°, the start scan angle 0°, the stop scan angle 70° and the increment scan angle 0.5°. Two different representations of the same results are shown in Figure 2, where Figure 2a is the classical representation with the overlap of all simulation in different color in rectangular and polar representation and Figure 2b is the proposed unconventional plot with the color scale in dB.

In this latter representation, the wanted elevation scan angle is the parameter on the Y axis, while on the X axis there is the elevation angle and finally the color indicates the magnitude in dB. Thus, each horizontal line corresponds to the array factor calculated for the relative wanted elevation scan angle. In such a representation it is easy to visualize the main lobe, sidelobes, nulls, and half-power-beamwidth (HPBW) variation when the scan angle changes and if there are some grating lobes . Particularly, with the help of the black contour line at the -3dB level, the user can notice the widening of the HPBW with the increase in the scan angle. Referring to Fig. 2 for comparison, it is almost impossible to extrapolate the results related to a single simulation.

It is clear the advantage in using the two dimensional color plot which gives more legibility to the graphical representation when, in general, a parametric or comparative simulation is required. This is only an example of the tool capabilities which depend on the characteristics the user wants to focus on.

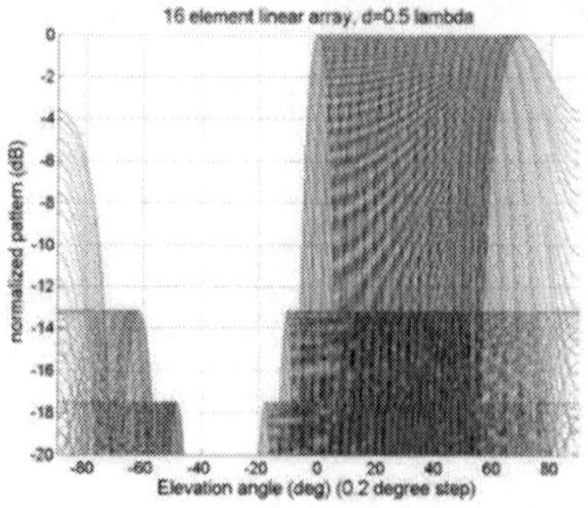

a)

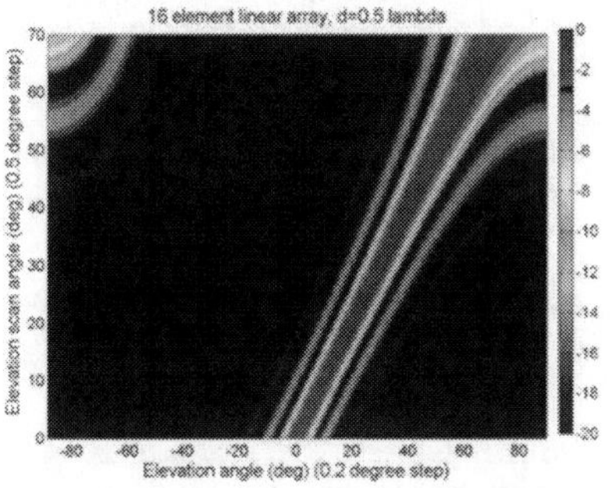

b)

Figure 2. a) Overlapped simulations in a rectangular classical plot. b) Unconventional color polar plot.

It is clear the advantage in using the two dimensional color plot which gives more legibility to the graphical representation when, in general, a parametric or comparative simulation is required. This is only an example of the tool capabilities which depend on the characteristics the user wants to focus on.

2.3 Round-off technique

The user can choose the preferred round-off technique among the following for each of the simulations described in the next section:

1. *Exact phase at each element:* this is the ideal situation represented by an ideal analog phase shifter. With this type of simulation the user can study the geometry of the array without worrying about the non-idealities of the phase shifter;

2. *Ideal quantization:* most phase shifters are digital devices or, at least, are digitally controlled. Therefore only discrete values of phase shift are allowed, and they may not be the precise values required. This simulation takes into account the errors due to an ideal quantization;

3. *Real simulated quantization:* the real digital phase shifts fed to each element are not ideal and they depend on the phase shifter adopted. A figure of merit is the rms error of the phase generation of the phase shifter. Starting from the ideal quantization, a casual and random error distribution, with the imposed rms, is added to the phase shifts in order to obtain the simulated allowable phase states;

4. *Measured values:* it is possible to insert the measurements taken by a prototype phase shifter in order to test the behavior of the real phase shifter and the resulting array pattern.

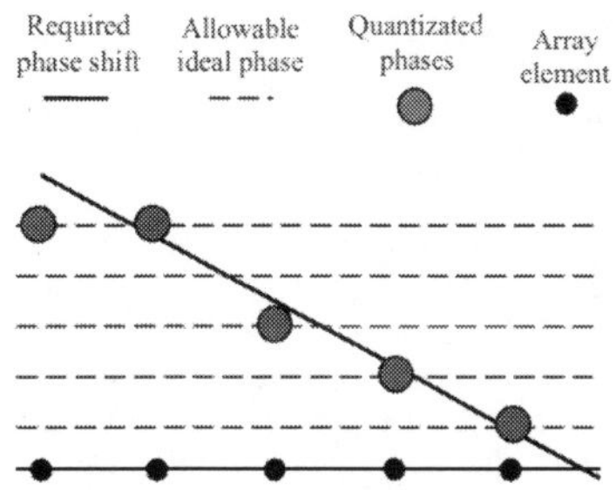

Figure 3. Allowable phase states due to ideal quantization

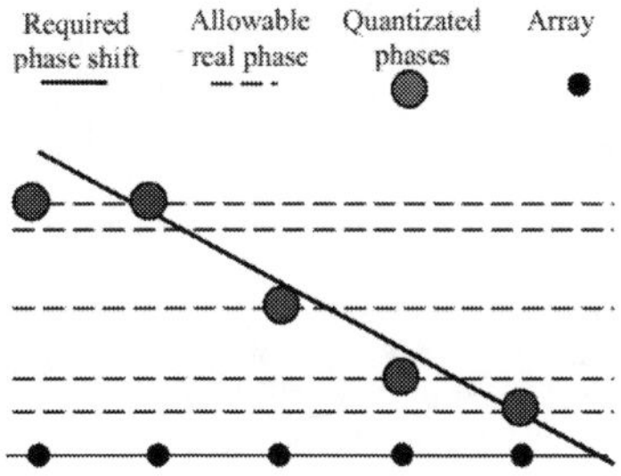

Figure 4. Allowable phase states due to simulated real quantization

2.4 Type of simulation

The model presented is very complete [6], in fact it accepts as input, according to the simulation type chosen, the range of elevation angles for pattern calculation, the number of antennas and the inter-element spacing between the antennas, the type of phase shifts fed at the antennas (ideal phase shift which simulates an ideal analog phase shifter, ideal quantization which simulates an ideal digital phase shifter, calculated real quantization which implements a simulated real digital phase shifter and finally real quantization obtained by inserting a vector of real digital phase shifter measurements and which implements a real measured phase shifter), the wanted elevation angle (scan angle) or range of scan angles.

The program is organized in menu; first of all the user can choose the type of simulation a subset of those is composed by:

1. *Variable number of antennas:* it is a parametric simulation which has as parameter the number of the antennas. The particular parameters required are the antenna start number, the antenna stop number and the antenna increment number. The other parameters that have to be inserted are the elevation start angle, the elevation stop angle, the elevation increment angle, the elevation start scan or start steering angle, the stop scan angle, the increment scan angle, the antenna spacing.

2. *Variable value of rms error:* it is a parametric simulation which varies the rms error added to the ideal phase shifter in order to simulate a real phase shifter and to analyse the impact of the rms phase error introduced by a non-ideal phase shifter, on the radiation-pattern characteristic. This type of simulation, respecting the common practice, uses the rms phase error value as the only figure of merit of a phase shifter goodness while a more exhaustive study about this concept is achieved using the simulation option number 7 below described. In this case the parameters required are the number of simulation and the rms value to be used in those simulations. This is one of the most interesting feature of the program because it gives the opportunity to investigate if there is a particular relation between the rms phase error of the phase shifter and some parameter of the radiation-pattern [5]. The other parameters required are the elevation start angle, the elevation stop angle, the elevation increment angle, the elevation start scan, the stop scan angle, the increment scan angle, the number of the antennas, the inter-element antenna spacing.

3. *Variable number of bit:* also in this case there is a parametric simulation which has as input the start number of bits, the stop number of bits and the increment. Such a simulation is the key point in those application where a great precision is required during the scan. In fact the more are the bits, the more is the scan precision till the ideal situation of analog phase shifter which could be assimilated to a phase shifter with infinite number of bits. So this type of simulation could be used as a dimension tool or as an instrument to study how effective is the increment of the number of bits and what is the impact on the radiation-pattern. The parameters required are the elevation start angle, the elevation stop angle, the elevation increment angle, the elevation start, the stop scan angle, the increment scan angle, the number of antennas and the inter-element antenna spacing.

4. *Rms behaviour study:* this type of simulation is very important in studying the impact of the effective phase error distribution on the beam shape. In fact for a generic phase shifter, it is often given the rms phase error as the only figure of merit, but this parameter does not represent the phase error distribution in an unambiguous way because there are infinite distribution with the same value of rms error, and different distributions can lead at significant different beam shapes. This simulation has as peculiar inputs the phase error vector or distribution defined as the difference between the measured or simulated phase distribution and the ideal one; the simulation consists in combining the values of ideal phase shifts with the values of the phase errors in a different way for every simulation. The user can choose the type of this combination and in particular he can choose if the all permutations have to be used or a circular shift has to be used; the first option is only practical for situation where the number of phase is less than about 5 due to time and memory required by the simulation. As an example, let's consider a 6-bit phase shifter; the total phase shift are 2^6=64 that corresponds to 1,2e89 permutations (64!=1,2e89) and 64 circular shifts; in this case it has to be chosen the circular shift mode. The other parameter that have to be inserted are the number of antennas, the inter-spacing antenna, the elevation start angle, the elevation stop angle, the elevation increment angle, the elevation start scan, the stop scan angle, the increment scan angle.

5. *case study:* this type of simulation examines all possible parameters of a phase shifter that meet certain requirements of the beam. The input parameters are the side lobe level, the lobe deviation and the half power beam width and the outputs are the combination of the number of antennas and the number of bits. Other inputs are the range of the number of antennas, the increment for the antenna variation, the range of number of bit, the increment for the bit variation, the bit-equivalent rms error to add iteratively at the simulations. The graphical representation shows immediately the combinations of number of antennas and number of bits that satisfies the beam requirements. As example in Figure 4 it is shown the output results as a function of bit-equivalent rms error for Lobe deviation<0.005; HPBW<=3°; sll>=-13dB.

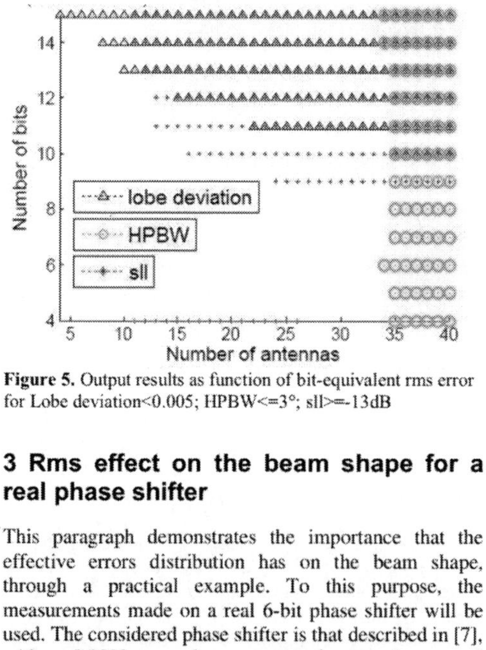

Figure 5. Output results as function of bit-equivalent rms error for Lobe deviation<0.005; HPBW<=3°; sll>=-13dB

3 Rms effect on the beam shape for a real phase shifter

This paragraph demonstrates the importance that the effective errors distribution has on the beam shape, through a practical example. To this purpose, the measurements made on a real 6-bit phase shifter will be used. The considered phase shifter is that described in [7], with a 0.223° rms phase error and a maximum and minimum phase error equal to about ±0.5° as shown in Figure 6. Different prototypes of the same architecture showed the same rms phase error, approximately, but certainly they don't have the same errors distribution that is, in this context, the vector containing the phase errors associated to vector of the possible phase shifts.

With the simulation number 4, called "Rms behavior study" explained in the previous paragraph (with the option of circular shift due to the great number of possible phase shifts), we are able to study the beam shape variations determined by a 64 different phase errors distribution with the same rms phase error. In this way, the i-th simulation uses the vector of the phase errors inserted with a circular shift of exactly i places.

As it is obvious, the rms phase error of the various distributions is the same for each simulation because the values of the phase errors are the same and only the positions in the vector are changed. The hypothesis is that we have 16 identical phase shifters for the 16 antennas. The simulation setup is shown in Table I, while Figure 7 report the results of the simulations.

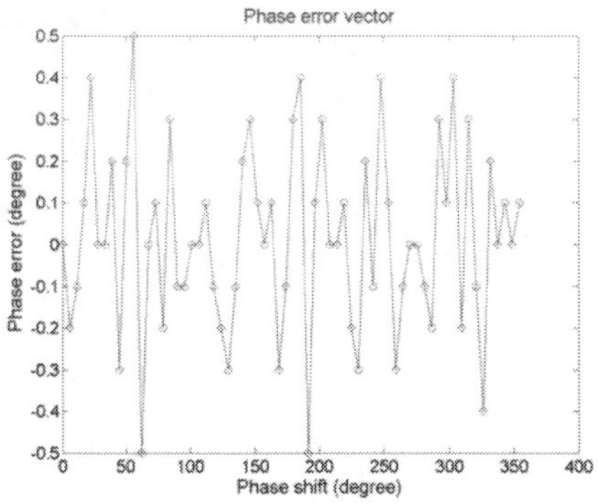

Figure 6. Phase shifter error vector.

An exhaustive and complete representation of the simulation results are reported in Figure 7a, Figure 7b and Figure 7c, where it has been used the unconventional color plot described in the previous section. In those type of plots all simulation results have been used without any significant loss of information.

Table 1. Summary of the simulation setup

Parameter	Variable error vector
Elevation start angle (degree)	-90
Elevation stop angle (degree)	90
Elevation increment angle (degree)	0.001
Scan start angle (degree)	0
Scan stop angle (degree)	70
Scan increment angle (degree)	0.1
Number of antennas	16
Inter-element distance	0.5
Simulation type	circular
Number of simulation	64

In Figure 7a it is reported the lobe deviation as a function of the number of simulations; the elevation scan angles in degrees are on the X axes, while on the Y axes there is the number of the simulations and the color bar represents the value of the main lobe deviation in degrees.

Thus, on each horizontal line are the lobe deviations related to the single simulation over the entire span of scan angles. On each vertical line the lobe deviations related to the single elevation scan angle over all the simulations are reported.

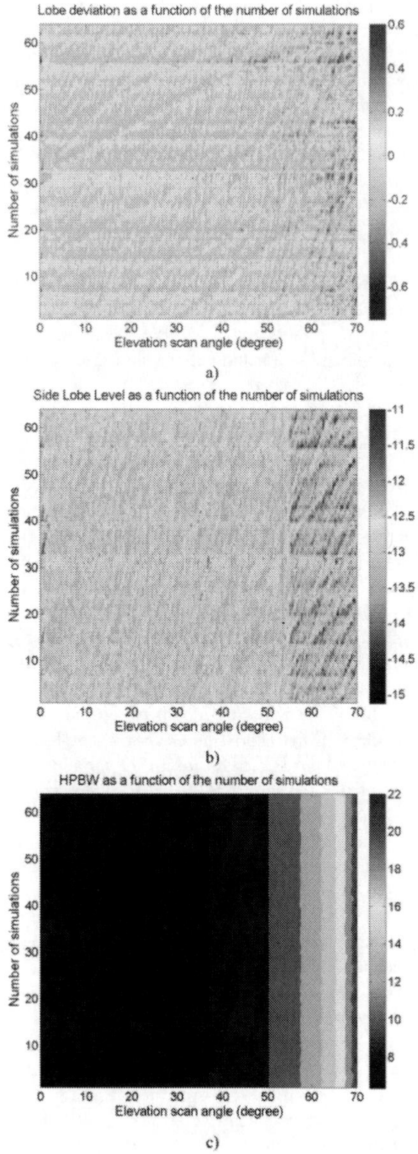

Figure 7. Simulation results obtained changing the error phase vector. a) Lobe deviation. b) Side Lobe Level. c) Half Power Bandwidth.

In Figure 7b it is represented the side lobe level as a function of the number of simulation; on the X axes there are the elevation scan angles in degrees, on the Y axes there is the number of the simulations, the color bar represents the value of the side lobe level in dB. Thus, on each horizontal line the side lobe level relates to each of the simulations over the entire span of scan angles and on each vertical line there are the side lobe level related to the single elevation scan angle over all the simulations.

In Figure 7c it is represented the lobe deviation as a function of the number of simulations: on the X axes there are the elevation scan angles in degrees, on the Y axes there is the number of the simulations, the color bar represents the value of the HPBW in degrees. So on each horizontal line there are the HPBW levels related to the single simulation over the entire scan angles span and on each vertical line there are the HPBW values related to the single elevation scan angle over all the simulations.

It is evident that the comparison among different simulations is very simple giving the opportunity to evaluate what are the critical angles.

The reported simulations demonstrate that the phase error rms value itself, even being an important figure of merit, it is not enough to evaluate antenna performances because the beam shape characteristics are strictly dependent on the actual phase errors vector.

Ideally, in absence of differences between the simulations, in Figure 7a, Figure 7b and Figure 7c would have shown perfectly matched vertical lines with the same colors; but the variations between the simulations are evident in the cited figures. For example, the lobe deviation and the SLL have significant variations for high values of the elevation angles, where there are red and blue zones for the same scan angle. The HPBW represented in Figure 7c seems to be not changed varying the simulations since the graph is composed by vertical line of almost the same color. Actually, this is not true and it is determined by the great span of the HPBW represented, which doesn't give the opportunity to appreciate little changes.

As a consequence of these results we can say that for a phase shifter a little rms phase error value is not the only key issue but a good phase shifter should have the phase error vector as flat as possible, that means that each phase error should be very similar to another. The ideal condition is a constant phase error over all the possible phase shifts [7].

4 Conclusion

In this paper it has been demonstrated that the beam shape of an array of antennas depends on the actual phase errors distribution and that a good phase shifter must exhibit phase errors with low rms values and as constant as possible. The model presented is an optimum tool to be used in order to investigate how sensible an application is to the phase errors distribution and which parameters of the beam shape are mainly affected.

Moreover the tool can be used for a yield analysis of sensitivity, simulating different implementation of the same architecture assuming that each phase shifter sample has a fixed rms phase error value but different phase errors vector.

References

1. Burrel R. Hatcher, Granularity of beam positions in digital phased array, *proceedings of the IEEE*, **56** (1968)
2. Kwang-Jin Koh and Gabriel M. Rebeiz, 0.13-μm CMOS Phase Sfhiters for X-,K*u*-, and K-Band Phased Array, *IEEE Journal of Solid-state Circuits*, **42**, 2535-2542 (2007)
3. J. K. Ryoo and S. H. Oh, Broadband 4-bit Digital Phase Shifter Based on Vector Combining Method, *Proceeding SBMO/IEEE MTT-S International*, **1**, 17-19 (2003)
4. G. Avitabile, F. Cannone, G. Coviello, Low-power Tx module for high-resolution continuous programmable phase shift, *Electronics Letters*, **44**, 1052-1054 (2008)
5. M. Clénet, G. A. Morin, Visualization of radiation-pattern characteristics of phase arrays using digital phase shifters, *IEEE antennas and propagation magazine*, **45** (2003)
6. G. Coviello, F. Cannone, G. Avitabile, A study on the Phase Errors Distribution in Phased Array Systems Based on a Behavioral Model of Radiation-Pattern Characteristics, *15th IEEE Mediterranean Electrotechnical Conference* (2010)
7. G. Avitabile, F. Cannone, G. Coviello, A novel 2.4 GHz high-resolution and low-power phase array transmitter, *39th European Microwave Conference*, (2009)

MATEC Web of Conferences **76**, 03003 (2016) DOI: 10.1051/matecconf/20167603003
CSCC 2016

Antenna Spatial Structure Influence on Communication System Capacity in Consideration of Transmitting Antenna Rotation

Yuri Parshin[1], Sergey Gusev [1] and Sergey Kolesnikov [1 a]

[1] *Ryazan State Radio Engineering University, Department of Radio Engineering Devices, 390095 Ryazan, Russia*

Abstract. Questions of technical implementation of communication system with different antenna spatial structures are discussed. The paper reviews the design of a system for data transmission from a rotating object to the ground receiving station with various spatial MIMO antenna structures. Different variants of the onboard antenna array with a different number of antennas are investigated. Values of the channel matrix for the communication system for the object rotating around the longitudinal axis are calculated. Transmission rate averaged over the period of rotation according to the position of the object on the trajectory and spatial structure of the ground receiving station is calculated.

1 Introduction

Design of high-speed data transmission system to a ground receiving station from rotating object requires solution of various research problems [1,2]. A feature of functioning conditions for information transmission system for some types of research equipment cargo is the rapid rotation of the object around the longitudinal axis specially implemented in order to stabilize the object when moving all over the path or just unwanted and uncontrolled rotation due to piloting malfunction. Also, when moving object changes orientation relative to ground reception point. All of this complicates the work of the information transmission system, requires matching directivities of onboard and ground-based antenna systems with the character of object motion, accounting of influence of changes in their relative orientation on the information transmission channel capacity.

The paper [2] outlines the problems associated with varying orientation of the object relative to ground reception point, which leads to lower data transmission efficiency. During object rotation the antenna blockage effect with object body may cause the interruption of information transmission. To improve the reliability of operation multiple ground reception points are used, and it leads to significant costs.

In this paper, in order to improve the quality of information transmission data MIMO technology [3], which has received widespread in mobile communication systems, is used. A special feature of the problem is the presence of multiple antennas on the rotating object to transmit information to a ground receiving station. Therefore, an actual problem is to optimize the transmitting part of the system that can be realized by space-time coding [3,4].

The objective is to obtain capacity limit value in information transmission system from a rotating object with various spatial structures of antenna systems and recommendations on the technical implementation of the researched system.

2 Problem Statement

Let the object rotation axis be perpendicular to the plane of the receiving points. The rotation of the object is made with a certain angular velocity Ω. Transmitting antennas are located on the object surface having form of a cylinder with radius r uniformly along the circumference. Angular coordinates of antennas $\gamma_{Tm} = 2\pi(m-1)/N_T$, $m = 1,...,N_T$ (Fig.1). The receiving antennas are located in the plane of object rotation by arc of radius R uniformly in angular sector $\Delta\gamma_R$, angular coordinates of antennas $\gamma_{Rn} = \Delta\gamma_R(n-1)/N_R$, $n = 1,...,N_R$.

Directivity of transmission antennas is determined by the type of radiators, location on the cylinder surface, influence of currents spreading on the cylinder surface, as well as the mutual influence of the radiators [2,5]. In the simple case, it can be assumed that the object body completely obscures the antenna and radiation pattern of transmitting antenna radiators in the plane of rotation is given by the expression

$$D(\gamma) = \begin{cases} \cos\gamma, \ \cos\gamma > 0 \\ 0, \quad \cos\gamma < 0 \ . \end{cases} \qquad (1)$$

[a] Corresponding author: sergey_v.k@mail.ru

During object rotating the orientation of m-th transmit antenna relative to n-th receiving antenna is defined by an antenna on the object and the receiving antenna on terrain

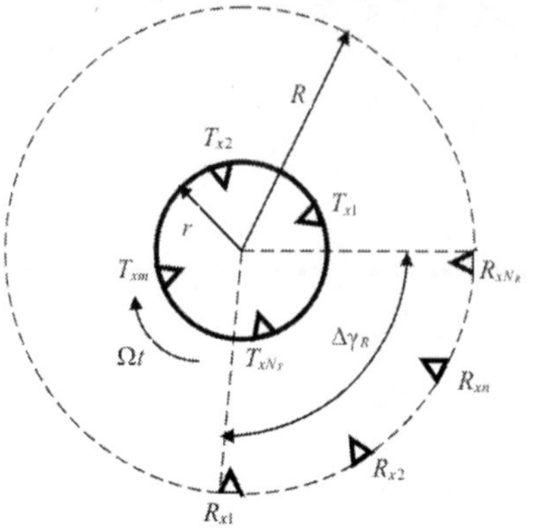

Figure 1. Spatial location of transmitting and receiving antennas

object slewing angle and angular positions of the transmitting respectively: $\gamma_{nm} = \Omega t + \gamma_{Tm} - \gamma_{Rn}$. Channel matrix coefficients are determined assuming direct line of sight between receiving and transmitting antennas and depend on the orientation of transmitting antennas in the direction of receiving antennas, and depend on the distance between the phase centers R_{nm} of each pair of m-th transmitting and n-th receiving antennas [6]. Assuming that $R_{nm} >> r$ and variance of distance between antennas while rotating the object has almost no effect on the amplitude of received signal, we can write channel coefficient as:

$$\underline{H}_{nm} = D(\gamma_{nm}) e^{-j\frac{2\pi}{\lambda}R_{nm}} \tag{2}$$

where

$$R_{nm} = [(R\cos\gamma_{Rn} - r\cos(\Omega t + \gamma_{Tm}))^2 + \\ + (R\sin\gamma_{Rn} - r\sin(\Omega t + \gamma_{Tm}))^2]^{1/2} \tag{3}$$

The capacity of communication channel is given by [3]:

$$C = \log_2 \det\left(\mathbf{I}_{N_R} + \frac{q}{N_T}\underline{\mathbf{H}}\underline{\mathbf{H}}^H\right) \text{ bit/symbol,} \tag{4}$$

where $\mathbf{I}_{N_R}$ – the unit diagonal matrix of dimension N_R, $q = D_X / D_N$ – system power budget, which is the ratio of signal power radiated from all transmitting antennas D_X to the noise power at each receiving antenna D_N, $\underline{\mathbf{H}} = \{\underline{H}_{nm},\ n = 1,\dots,N_R,\ m = 1,\dots,N_T\}$ – matrix of channel coefficients.

3 Simulation Results

Figures 2a, 2b, 2c and 2d show the dependence of channel capacity on the object rotation angle on the axis of rotation in a time equal to the period of object rotation at various number of receiving N_R and transmitting antennas N_T. Receiving antennas are located in sector $\Delta\gamma_R = \pi/4$, $R = 10^6\lambda$, $r = 5\lambda$.

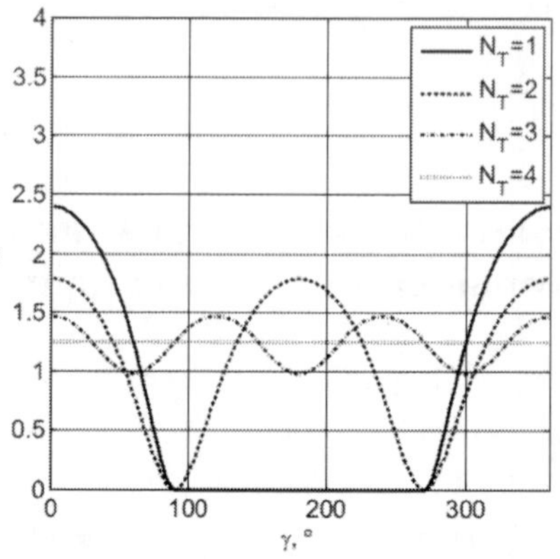

Figure 2a. Channel capacity vs object angular position for $N_R = 1$

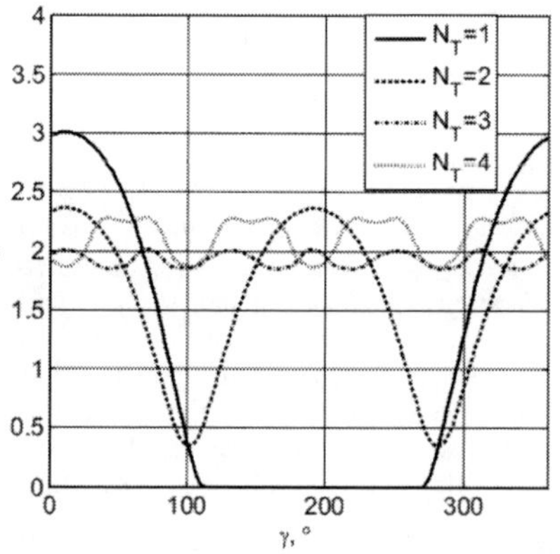

Figure 2b. Channel capacity vs object angular position for $N_R = 2$

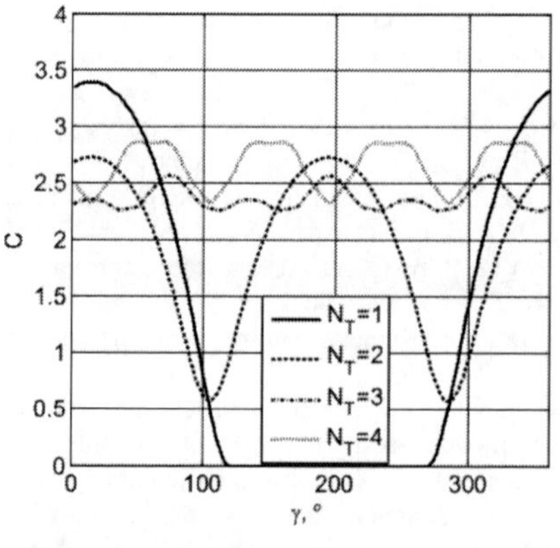

Figure 2c. Channel capacity vs object angular position $N_R = 3$

DOI: 10.1051/matecconf/20167603003

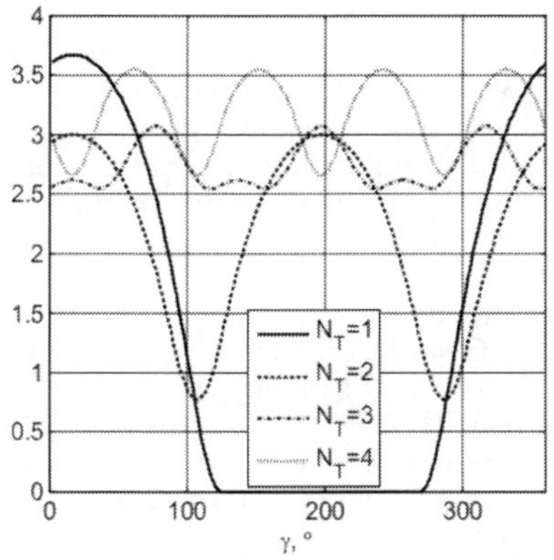

Figure 2d. Channel capacity vs object angular position for $N_R = 4$

At high speed rotation of the object practical interest represents the average for the period of rotation information transmission channel capacity. In this case, the potential capacity may be obtained by using interleaving in a combination with efficient error correcting coding. Figures 3a, 3b, 3c, 3d, 3e, and 3f show the dependence of average capacity on the angular position of the receiving antennas sector at different numbers of receiving N_R and transmitting antennas N_T.

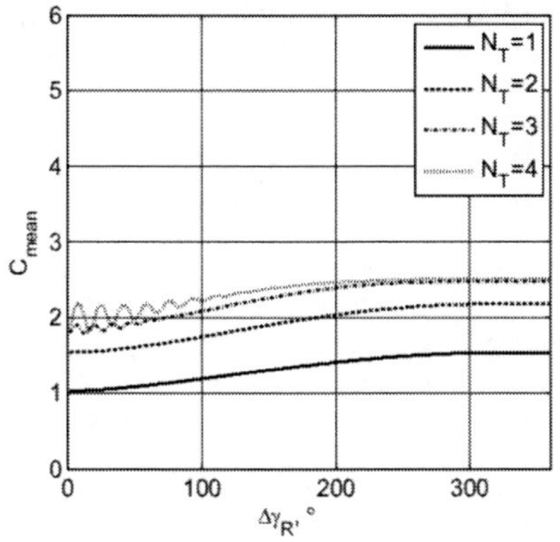

Figure 3a. Average channel capacity vs angular position of the receiving antennas for $N_R = 2$

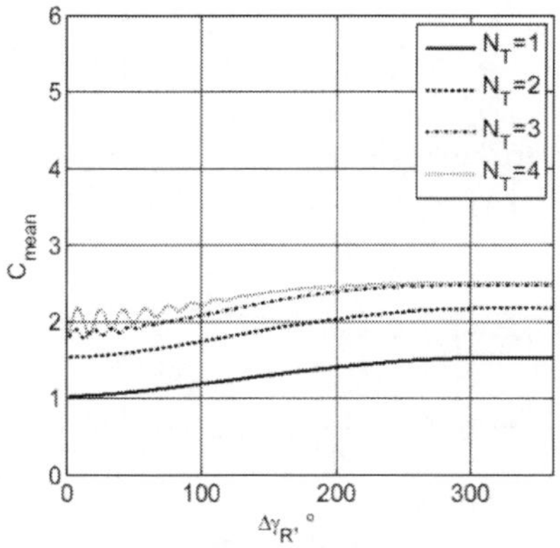

Figure 3b. Average channel capacity vs angular position of the receiving antennas for $N_R = 3$

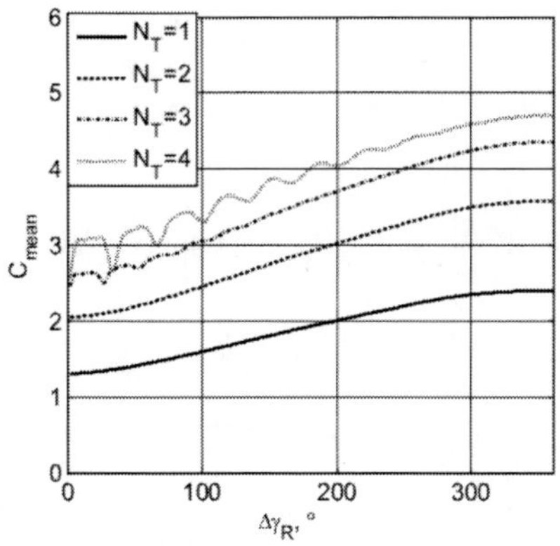

Figure 3c. Average channel capacity vs angular position of the receiving antennas for $N_R = 4$

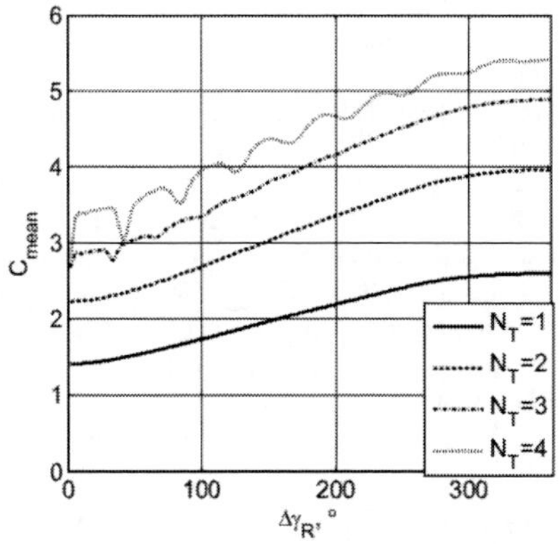

Figure 3d. Average channel capacity vs angular position of the receiving antennas for $N_R = 5$

DOI: 10.1051/matecconf/20167603003

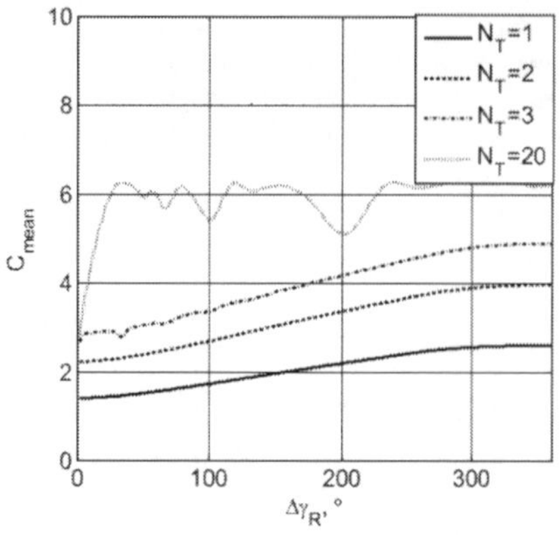

Figure 3e. Average channel capacity vs angular position of the receiving antennas for $N_R = 5$

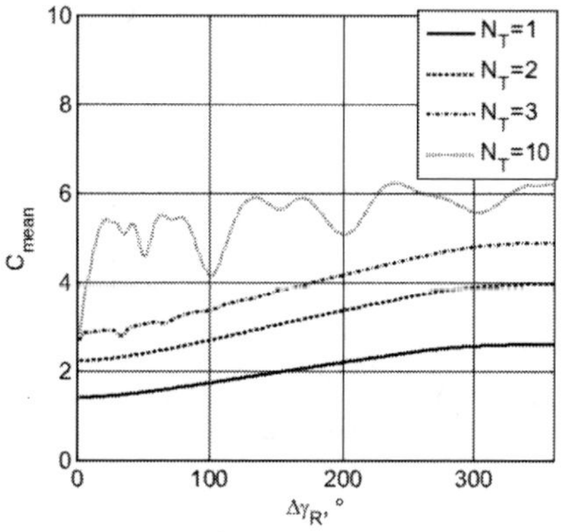

Figure 3f. Average channel capacity vs angular position of the receiving antennas for $N_R = 5$

4 Conclusion

Based on the research of instantaneous and mean capacity depending on antenna spatial structure two modifications for technical implementation of high-speed data transmission system for a rotating object are advised.

In the first case it is assumed placement on board filled circular antenna array with antenna pattern, free from dips and diffraction lobes. In this case, minimum variation of instantaneous capacity depending on the object orientation and the maximum capacity is provided. At the same time limitations on mechanical strength of the object body and the complexity of implementing the transmission path, containing N_T power amplifiers or microwave path for power distribution and phasing of antenna array elements from a single-channel transmitter does not allow to implement this variant with a large number of antennas. Besides, the implementation of multi-channel transmitter and microwave channel of phasing and power distribution with necessary efficiency is difficult because of limitations on the weight and size parameters of equipment.

The second variant of high-speed data transmission system assumes placing on object few-element circular antenna array and multiposition ground receiving system. The high mean capacity achieved using effective error-correcting coding. The realization of the encoding and decoding, which provides necessary data transmission rate may require significant computational resources. The main disadvantages of this method are extremely high requirements to memory volume of encoder, which is a part of transmitting equipment. The volume of required memory grows proportional to the square of object rotation period. The considered method is sensitive to width and number of deep dips of more than 10 dB in radiation pattern of onboard transmitting antenna array. In the presence of deep nulling the accuracy of transmitted information sharply reduced. An additional limitation of the second method is the necessity to measure coefficients of channel matrix with frequency depending on object speed and the requirement for the corresponding reverse link.

The research is carried out in the project of the Ministry of Education and Science of the Russian Federation №8.1697.2014/K

References

1. N. N. Bulgakov, V. G. Alybin ; A. A Krivoshein, Design features of the spacecraft vehicle onboard equipment of the command-measuring system to control it in the zone of its coverage from a ground station and outside it Microwave and Telecommunication Technology (CriMiCo), 2014 24th International Crimean Conference. Sevastopol, Crimea. – pp. 6-9.
2. E.P. Kolesnikov, Features of energy budget calculation of telemetry systems for missile launch, *Radiotekhnika*, 2004, **№6**, pp. 70-80.
3. Kuhn V. Wireless Communications over MIMO channels. Applications to CDMA and multiple antenna systems - John Wiley & Sons, Ltd. 2006.
4. A.M. Shloma, M.G. Bakulin, V.B. Krejndelin, A.P. Shumov, Novye algoritmy formirovaniya i obrabotki signalov v sistemah podvizhnoj svyazi. Pod. red. prof. A.M. Shloma. Moscow: Goryachaya liniya-Telekom, 2008
5. G.T. Markov, D.M. Sazonov, Antenny: Uchebnik dlya studentov radiotekhnicheskih special'nostej VUZov. Moscow: Energiya, 1975.
6. Yu.N. Parshin, A.V. Ksendzov, "Effect of spatial correlation on the optimization efficiency of the spatial structure of multiple antenna system with receive diversity", *Bulletin of Ryazan State Radio Engineering Academy*, 2006, **№19**, pp. 54-62.

MATEC Web of Conferences 76, 03004 (2016) DOI: 10.1051/matecconf/20167603004
CSCC 2016

An evaluation of the proposed ITS system for the city of São Paulo based on the 2015 tender

Mauricio Consulo[1], Maria L. R. P. D. Scoton[1], Jilmar A. Tatto[1], Eduardo M. Dias[1]

[1] *GAESI –Grupo de Automação Elétrica em Sistemas Industriais, Escola Politécnica da Universidade de São Paulo, Av. Prof. Luciano Gualberto, trav. 3, nº 158, CEP 05508-970, São Paulo/SP, Brazil, http://www.gaesi.eng.br*

Abstract. The Secretary of Transportation of the city of São Paulo recently released a public consultation for the city's Urban Mobility plan. This consultation is quite broad in scope, addressing many different areas of the bus public transportation modal in the city, including the operation itself, control and bus terminal administration. The proposal contains guidelines to reorganize the actual services using the infrastructure already deployed. This article will bring to light the development stages of the ITS in the United States, Europe, and Japan while focusing on the technology portion of the São Paulo tender such as: (i) planning and scheduling systems, (ii) operational control center and its technologies to monitor and control the operation, (iii) the on-board technologies, and (iv) the integration to the existing track and location (T&L), control and reporting system called SIM – Sistema Integrado de Monitoramento (Integrated Monitoring System). The main goal of this article is to map the proposed ITS system for the city of São Paulo and compare it to the world class systems operating in the major cities in the world highlighting the areas of excellence and the ones with room for improvement.

1 Introduction

Nowadays, it is extremely difficult to decouple Intelligent Transportation Systems (ITS) from the concept of smart cities. The major cities around the world are addressing the Urban Mobility as a key component of their planning and governance. Most cities worldwide were not built with the vision for expansion, such as new streets and avenues, bus lanes, or Bus Rapid Transit (BRT). As a result, even the construction of monorails and subways lines can be onerous and inefficient due to the need to renovate overall infrastructures around these cities in order to accommodate new public transportation options. For example, streets in the downtown area of many cities in Latin America are narrow and contain landmark buildings, which restricts construction area wise as well as in capital.

A balance of construction and technology needs to be achieved. However, in the Latin American scenario the technology and the intelligent transportation systems play a more important role in this equation and both necessary to improve road network capacity. The correct use of technology can boost the correlation of the road network, bus lanes, BRT and its clients. As a result, the ITS systems can become more data driven, making the traffic management system more efficient, convenient, safe and reliable.

ITS provides the ability to gather, organize, analyze, use, and share information about transportation systems and it can be used by decision makers and planners in order to increase their awareness of the benefits as well as the prerequisites of ITS. Its ability is decisive and effectual for the economical construction and operation of transportation systems and to their efficient use.

2 Outlook of ITS in the U.S.A, Europe and Japan

The fundamental reasons for introducing ITS are similar in many countries across the world. Numerous governments are seeking to increase efficiency, safety and to reduce the environmental impact.

The ITS deployment was led by United States of America, Europe and Japan. The incentive for these regions has many similarities, including the economical interest supported by technology, the need to expand the transportation systems, and a coordinated effort between the industry, government, and academia.

2.1 United States of America

In the United States of America (U.S.A.), the ITS systems began with the electronic route guidance system (ERGS) in 1967 [2] from a study performed by the Bureau of Public Roads of the US Department of Transportation (USDOT). ITS started to become an important part of major highway transportation laws. Later, in 1991, the USDOT included the Intermodal Surface Transportation Efficiency Act (ISTEA, 1991)

[a] Corresponding author: mconsulo@gmail.com

and the Transportation Equity Act for the 21st Century (TEA-21, 1998).

In 1997, the Intelligent Vehicle Initiative (IVI) had its debut by the USDOT, "this initiative aims to accelerate the development, availability, and use of integrated in-vehicle systems that help drivers of cars, trucks, and buses operate more safely and effectively" [3]. Afterward, the Vehicle Infrastructure Integration (VII) project [4] was proposed. The main goal of this project was to provide a standardized communication channel between the physical surroundings and the vehicles on the road in order to improve safety. Another US program, called Cooperative Vehicle-Highway Automation Systems (CVHAS) [5], is also supported by the US federal pooled fund program and has focus on improving the safety, mobility, and other essential concerns, followed the VII.

The "ITS Joint Program Office (ITS JPO), within the Office of the Assistance Secretary for Research and Technology (OST-R), is in charge of executing the Subtitle C- Intelligent Transportation System Research of Public Law 109-59 - Safe Accountable, Flexible, Efficient Transportation Equity Act: A Legacy for Users, enacted August 10, 2005, which requires the Department to: Conduct an ongoing intelligent transportation system program to research, develop, and operationally test intelligent transportation systems and to provide technical assistance in the nationwide application of those systems as a component of the surface transportation systems of the United States"[6].

The USDOT has a complete and comprehensive Intelligent Transportation Systems (ITS) strategy plan for 2015 to 2019. This "plan is built on the success of the 2010 to 2014 plan and presents a wide array of technical, policy, institutional, and organizational concepts. It provides a comprehensive perspective that is based on an inclusive, collaborative, interactive, and iterative process, with a wide mix of stakeholder engagement opportunities that ensured that the Strategic Plan reflects the aspirations of the multi-faceted ITS community across the nation." [7]. For the next four years, this proposal has a clear vision to "transform the way society moves". This is a very bold foresight, which reflects the American pragmatism, and the way they organize their future. This vision is supported by two primary strategies: (i) Realizing Connected Vehicle (CV) Implementation and (ii) Advancing Automation.

These two primary strategies are supported by the following themes adopted by the USDOT as priorities:

- enable Safer Vehicles and Roadaways;
- enhance mobility;
- limit Environmental Impacts;
- promote Innovation; and
- Support Transportation Systems Information Sharing.

A more comprehensive and complete study about the USDOT Intelligent Transportation Systems (ITS) strategy plan for 2015 to 2019 is the subject for a future article. The objective of this session is to illustrate the state of development and planning of the ITS systems in the United States of America.

2.2 Europe

The ITS systems had its genesis back in the early 1970s, and one of the first projects was the Road Transport Informatics (RTI) [8]. Other projects such as the Dedicated Road Infrastructure for Vehicle Safety in Europe (DRIVE) [9] also took place in the 80s. In 1991, the EU launched its European Road Transport Telematics Implementation Coordination Organization (ERTICO) to promote ITS development. eSafety [10] is a representative program under ERTICO that aims to provide vehicle-based intelligent safety systems to improve road safety.

Europe plays a very active role in the regional and international ITS activities to advance its ITS, specially with the standards. "The European Committee for Standardization (Comité Européen de Normalisation – CEN) has a technical committee (TC278 – Road Traffic and Transport Telematics) focused on ITS standards issues. TC278 works in close cooperation with the ITS Technical Committee (TC204) of ISO. Many ITS standards items are developed in parallel by ISO/TC204 and CEN/TC278" [11].

[11] also states that "Europe has been very successful in establishing partnerships" to conduct tests and demonstrations among European national and city governments, vehicle manufacturers and suppliers, and universities. Europe has also succeeded in establishing a robust industry for ITS infrastructure systems and end-user products, with customers worldwide".

2.3 Japan

Like Europe, Japan started its ITS efforts in the 1970s. At the time, the ITS research was to build a safe, eco-friendly, transport system. In 1998, an ITS application named Vehicle Information and Communication System (VICS) [12] was deployed to collect traffic information and deliver it to drivers. Japan's complex and congested road system has made this program particularly attractive to the driving public.

In the early 21st century, Japan started a national program called Smartway [13] to promote Japan's ITS development. The promotion of ITS in Japan today is led by four Ministries and Agencies. The National position on ITS promotion was laid down in 1995 in the "Basic Guidelines on the Promotion of an Advanced Information and Telecommunications Society." [11]

Also, "Japan recognizes ITS as an opportunity to advance its industrial and trade interests, as well as a means to improve domestic transportation. Japan pursues international ITS standardization with a view to encourage international competition and safeguarding Japan's competitive position." [11]

It is interesting to see that each region has its goals and approach in the use and deployment of ITS. This analysis will be helpful to build a parallel with the project has been developed and implemented in Europe, U.S.A and Japan versus in Latin America, more specifically São Paulo, Brazil.

3 Urban mobility in Brazil

Brazil, as many other countries in Latin America, does not have a national plan or strategy for ITS. Many different cities in Brazil, particularly the capitals, are building their own ITS tenders without a clear direction from the government. The Agência Nacional de Transportes Terrestres (ANTT – National Land Transportation Agency) has started initiatives, however, they are geared towards infrastructure and not technology. The Agência Nacional de Transportes Urbanos ANTU – National Urban Transport Agency) has a more technological focus and has released a publication entitled: "The best practices for the new Urban Mobility". Both agencies are working towards creating best practices and guidelines for the development Urban Mobility in Brazil.

In 2012, Brazil issued a federal law addressing Urban Mobility, Federal Law 12.587/2012. According to this law, the municipalities have until the end of 2015 to prepare and submit their Urban Mobility plan.

This Urban Mobility law has some key points as follow [14]:

- the prioritization of public transportation over private transportation projects and the drivers for integrated urban development;
- fare policy must have a contribution of direct and indirect beneficiaries to fund service operations;
- the pay rate is determined by the price (public rate) charged to the user plus revenue from other sources of funding
- the fare adjustments and revisions of the parameters used in the calculation will have the frequency established by the government in the announcement and in the concession for granting the service
- it is permitted to subsidize bus fares, which should be covered by non-ticket revenue, alternative revenues, budgetary or cross subsidies, intra sectorial and inter-sectorial subsidies.;
- the government is required to disclose in a systematic and regular basis the impact in the allowance in the fare paid by the user;
- the Federal, State and Local governments, and the Federal District have an obligation to contest the illegal transport of passengers and may sign agreements for this purpose;
- the government may establish restrictions, access control, temporary or permanent entry of motorized vehicles in certain locations;
- exclusive spaces on public roads for public transportation of passengers;
- companies may provide discounted fares, including seasonal promotions;
- surveillance of public transport services should be held preferably in conjunction with the federal and state governments.

Brazil has a government program called PAC that stands for Programa de Aceleração de Crescimento (Growth Acceleration Program) in which the Urban Mobility plans must be submitted. The PAC was created in 2007, during President Lula's second term (2007-2010). PAC promoted the resumption of the planning and execution of social projects, as well as projects related to urban infrastructure, logistics and energy, contributing to its growth and sustainable development [15]. In addition, PAC has allocated R$ 22.4 Billion Reals for Urban Mobility in the large cities of Brazil and R$ 7 billion Reals for the mid size cities. Brazil has 75 municipalities that are eligible to receive the funds of PAC, in which 71 have already requested the funds for their projects. These 71 municipalities serve nearly 27 million inhabitants and are concentrated mainly on the southeast region Brazil along the coast [16].

Also, according to [14], Brazil has 107.000 buses with an average age of 4.2 years and 1.800 private bus operators. These private bus operators are responsible for 537.000 direct jobs, and their buses transport close to 40 million passengers daily in 3.311 cities that have an established bus transportation system. In Brazil, the buses are responsible for 86.8% of the passengers transported via mass transportation systems and 85.2% of the municipalities with more than 100 thousand inhabitants have electronic fair collection systems.

It is safe to say that Brazil is a highly dependable country on the modal bus as a mass transportation system, even though the number of users has declined drastically from the 1990s [17] due to some incentives and an increase in line of credit allowing more people to purchase cars. The Fig. 1 shows the decline of the passengers transported per month.

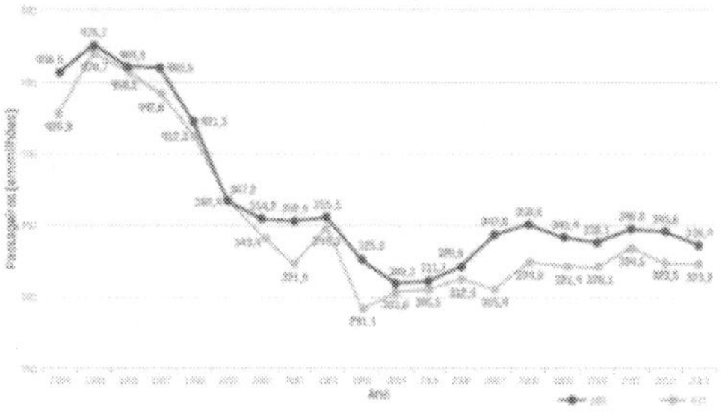

Figure 1. Passengers transported per month 1.

The above numbers are concerning when compared to Figure 2, which demonstrates that the distance covered per month is about the same as it was back in the 1990s, while the number of passengers was much higher than in the 2010s [17].

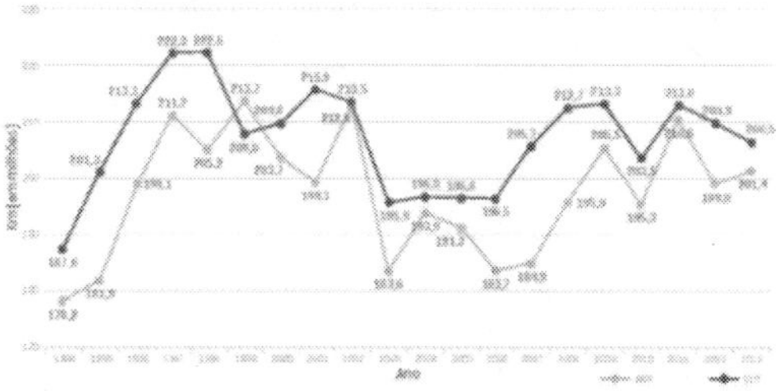

Figure 2. Km covered per month.

Fig. 3 demonstrates that the cost of fuel has also increased when compared to the 1990s [17].

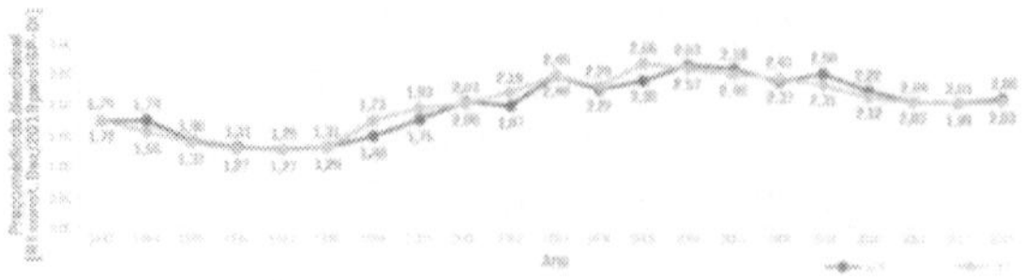

Figure 3. Cost of fuel.

Using these three elements: (i) passengers transported per month, (ii) Km covered per month, and (iii) the cost of fuel, one can infer that in order to be competitive and profitable, the private bus operators must find new ways to cut costs and operational inefficiencies. Intelligent Transportation Systems, including infrastructure and technology, have been presented as a possibility to the bus operators to optimize their operations and to become more efficient. The next session of this article briefly describes benefits that are brought by infrastructure innovations.

4 The mass transportation system in São Paulo

The city of São Paulo and its metropolitan area (39 municipalities) are home for 21 million people within an area of 8.000 km2. The Empresa Metropolitana de Transporte Urbano (EMTU), by Companhia Paulista de Trens Metropolitanos (CPTM), feeds the mass transportation system of São Paulo city and Companhia do Metropolitano de São Paulo (METRÔ). The city of São Paulo itself has São Paulo Transportes S.A. (SPTRANS) as its Transit Authority. The buses in São Paulo city cover more than 17 km of routes and in 10 rapid bus lanes with 110km of extension, in which Expresso Tiradentes is the only one with the BRT characteristics. São Paulo has 28 bus terminals, 1500 routes, and 19 thousand bus stops serving 9 million passengers per day. Customers can use the SPTRANS, CPTM and METRÔ systems with just one fare card know as Bilhete Único (BU). Figure 4 shows the rapid bus lanes in São Paulo and Figure 5 demonstrates the subway system [18].

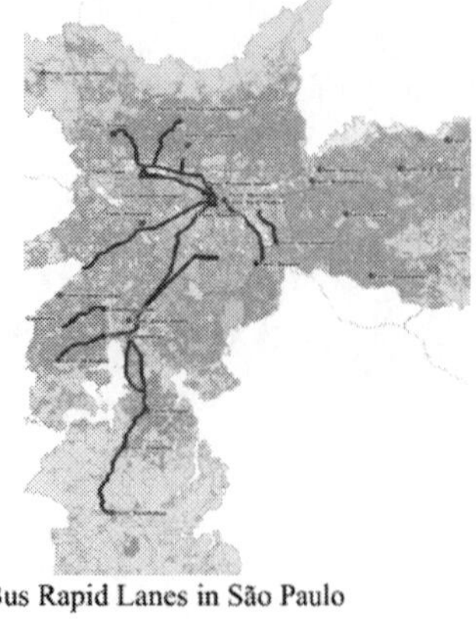

Figure 4. Bus Rapid Lanes in São Paulo

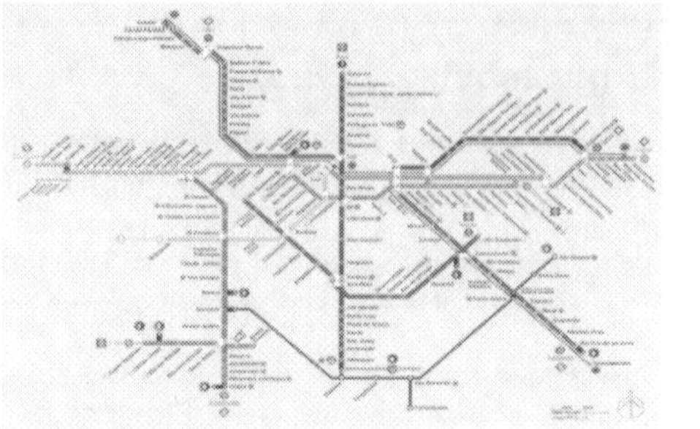

Figure 5. Subway system in São Paulo

4.1. A bus lane implementation and results in São Paulo

An ITS project consists of many different components, including civil construction, vehicles, sensors, on-board technology, command centers and personnel, just to list a few. In São Paulo, Companhia de Engenharia de Tráfego – CET [19] developed a project to create Bus Lanes (BL) in the city, and since the beginning more than 479 km of Bus Lanes were deployed in the city of São Paulo. The creation of Bus Lanes on the right side of the streets generated positive results to the modal bus, and consequently to the population. In 2013, CET reported a decrease in the total time travelled by bus in São Paulo decreased 38 minutes per day. Conversely, in 2014 this number increased to 40.7 minutes per day while the fuel consumption decreased by 8.8%.

Before the Bus Lanes deployed in 2014, the average speed on the route was 12.1 km/h. After the implementation of the Bus Lanes, the average speed jumped to 20.3 km/h, an improvement of 67.5%. The following routes have shown the most significant improvements:

- Best performance – Av. Jaguaré
  - average speed jumped from 10.8km/h to 44.9km/h; an improvement of 317.3%;
  - this Bus Lane has 12 routes transports 50.508 passengers per day, and serves 52 buses per hour during peak hours.
- Highlight – av. Belmira Marim
  - average speed increased from 9.5km/h to 25.2 km/h, an improvement of 165.7%;
  - this Bus Lane has 23 routes, transports 202.000 passengers per day, and serves 159 buses per hour during the peak hours.
- Largest extension – Av. Vila EMA/ Rua do Orfanato
  - 2.5km of Bus Lane
  - average speed leaped from 12.2 km/h to 21.4 km/h;
  - this Bus Lane has 6 routes, transports 77.031 passengers per day, and serves 56 buses per hour during the peak hours.

The overall average speed of the city of São Paulo went from 14.3km/h before the Bus Lanes, to an astounding 20.3km/h after Bus Lanes were adopted. This represents a 42% improvement in speed. The Bus Lanes also helped decrease the sluggishness of the city of São Paulo as shown in table 1.

Table 1. Decrease in sluggishness.

Year	Km/h	%
2011	115	-
2012	132	14,8
2013	142	7,8
2014	146	2,8

As previously mentioned, civil construction in the cities is limited, and therefore, major improvements are difficult. In order to achieve a quantum leap in the transportation system, more advanced technology is necessary to better support the ITS initiatives, such as the Bus Lanes in São Paulo.

5 Actual ITS system for the city of São Paulo

According to [18], São Paulo's focus on ITS started in 1976 with the creation of Companhia de Engenharia de Tráfego (CET). In 1995, SPTRANS was created. In 2001, Municipal Law 13.241 organized the mass transportation system in the city. In 2004, Electronica fare collection was deployed in the city with Bilhete Único, initially using a magnetic strip followed thereafter by modern touch-less technologies. By 2005, the BU was also accepted by the CPTM and the METRÔ. The next big leap happened in 2008, with the implementation of the Sistema Integrado de Monitoramento (SIM), an integrated monitoring system using Automatic Vehicle Location (AVL) technology to track and locate the buses throughout the city. With the AVL technology, it was also possible to deploy LED signs in bus terminals and bus stops for Real Time Passenger Information (RTPI).

The creation of a Portal to provide RTPI and work as a channel of communication with SPTRANS and its customers. The SIM is outdated, therefore, a modernization request has been made in the new tender released for São Paulo's ITS system.

5.1 Sistema Integrado de Monitoramento (SIM)

Per [18], SIM is an integrated management system designed to monitor, control and supervise the quality of the service offered to the population. It collects and provides real time information about the buses, bus terminals to passengers and other systems. SIM has six subsystems, as follow:

- Integrated Control Center (ICC);
- Bus Terminal Operation Center (BTOC);
- Intelligent Bus Lanes (IBL);
- Concessionaires Operational Centers (COC);
- Fleet Management (FM); and
- On-board equipment a.k.a AVL (AVL).

The figure 6 shows the integration among the INFOTRANS (databases) and the SIM.

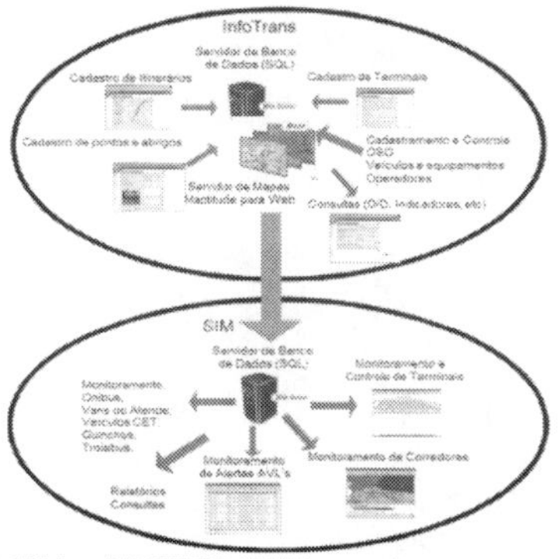

Figure 6. SIM and INFOTRANS Integration

As previously stated, the SIM system is outdated and the same is true for the on-board system that supports it. One out of the two hardware suppliers for the city of São Paulo is no longer providing any support to the on-board devices. This alone substantiates a great challenge for the bus operators to keep the system running and avoid the substantial penalties placed by SPTRANS when their buses are not communicating with the main bus system. Figure 7 shows the on-board equipment that is currently running in São Paulo's buses.

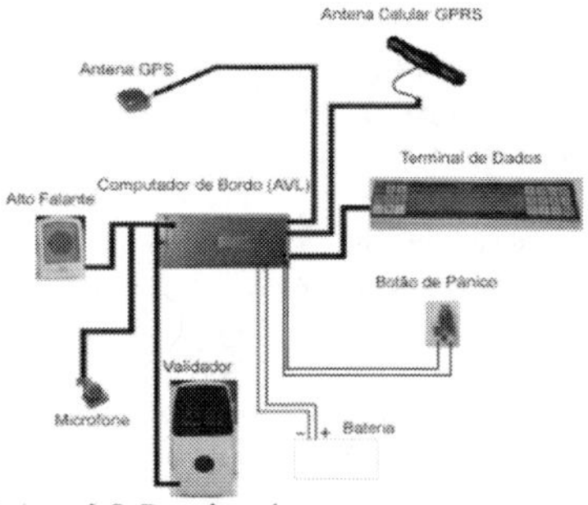

Figure 7. Actual O-Board equipment

The bus terminals have a Closed Circuit Television (CCTV) as shown on the figure 8.

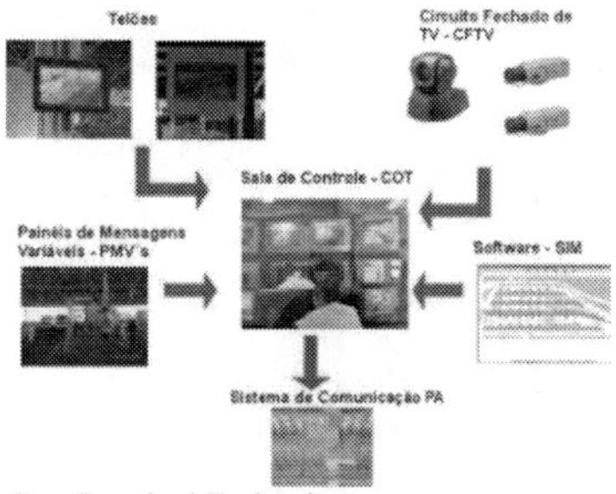

Figure 8. Bus Terminal Technology

The bus terminals are equipped with a CCTV, LED signs and LCD monitors for RTPI, a PA system and a

SIM client. Even though the RTPI prediction is set for two minutes, there are many discrepancies in the accuracy due to the outdated on-board technology, which can be seen at the terminals and bus stops with the system. Another point of consideration is the fact that the analysis of the cameras is entirely done by people and lack intelligent systems, such as face recognition and pattern analyses.

SIM is not a system designed to take action, but rather to supervise and report. For example, there is no feature or functionality to self-regulate the operation. SPTRANS plays a passive role in the system and most of the bus garages have their own Operational Command Center (OCC) to monitor operation; SPTRANS only receives and consolidates the data.

Communication is another obstacle with the actual system. There is no VOIP implemented, preventing effective communication with the bus drivers. When the OCC attempts to contact a bus driver, the system stops providing real time bus location, prioritizing voice communication. Additionally, the command to restore the location of the bus does not work, asking for human intervention. As observed, communication with the bus drivers is done via Nextel radio or cellular phone.

Not all the reports are real time in SIM and most of the information is D+1. The other concern is system reliability, which as been a recurrent complaint.

6 Proposed new ITS sytems to the city of São Paulo

Annex 7-A of the tender for São Paulo [18] brings on item 7.1.6, which include the following goals for the new ITS system for the city of São Paulo: (i) to renew the entire on-board system of the bus fleet in São Paulo, (ii) the adoption of a planning and scheduling system, a dispatching system, the construction of an Operational Control Center, and (iii) the deployment of all the hardware, software, data center and communication infrastructure.

The Operational Command Center (OCC) will have an area greater than 8.000m2 where it will host the servers, links and the entire infrastructure necessary for the operation. It is also important to mention that the OCC will interface with other entities related directly or indirectly with the transportation system in São Paulo, such as: CET, Sistema de Atendimento Móvel de Urgência (SAMU), First Responders, Police, Fire Department among others.

Item 7.2.1.1 [18] describes the on-board architecture for the new ITS system of São Paulo as seen on the Fig. 9.

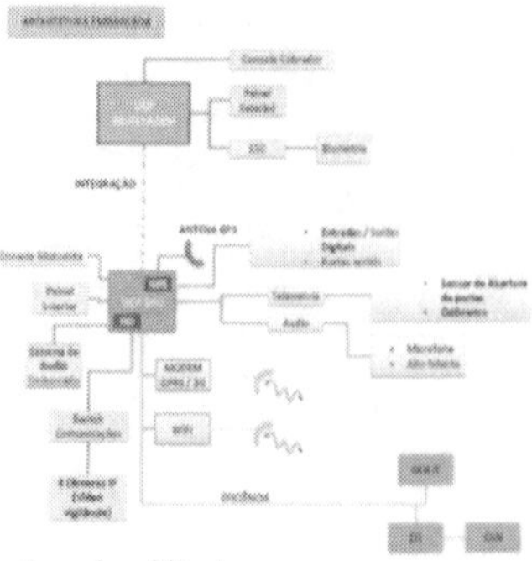

Figure 9. On-board architecture

The proposed on-board architecture is considerably more advanced and brings substantial enhancements when compared to the current deployed system (Fig. 7). The first and the most important difference is that the new system uses an on-board computer rather than a tracking device. This on-board computer brings the possibility to embed systems and bring intelligence to the bus, which will control other sub-systems, such as the internal passenger's information, public WiFi, VOIP, CCTV, emergency alarm, ticketing, Automatic Passenger Counting systems (APC) and telematics.

The specification is a high level solution, and escalates the ITS requirements for São Paulo to a world class system. From the big picture perspective, this tender follows the organization of the model proposed on [20], in which Stage 1 describes the benefits and motivations, and Stage 2 portrays the ITS applications and requirements. However, its limitation lies on the evaluation and implementation of the ITS system, shown below in Fig. 10.

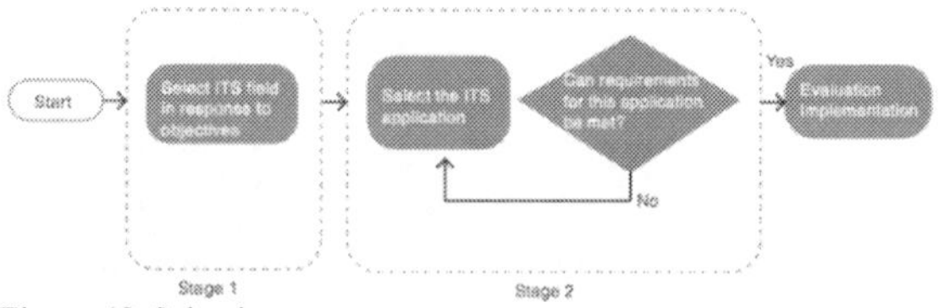

Figure 10. Selection process

For example, decoupling the on-board computer from the software seems to be a great solution when you consider that the current fleet of São Paulo has close to 15.000 buses [18]. The possibility of choosing the on-board hardware empowers the bus operators to choose the technology that best fits their operation needs. In order to guarantee the integration among the different hardware platforms, SPTRANS created a certification process to guarantee that the hardware will meet the minimum requirements. This certification process is divided into three phases: (i) Documentation analysis, (ii) bench tests for hardware and software and (iii) the SIM integration. This is brings some complexity to the solution, regarding interoperability, but offers rubusticity when it comes to the on board certification process and all the international standards that must be followed.

It is yet necessary to define the rules and standards when it comes to ITS functionalities and processes. That will be of great use in terms of interoperability.

Another proposition worth of highlighting in this tender includes the creation of a gateway to guarantee the communication of all CPUs, the current SIM system, and the future OCC software as see in Fig.11.

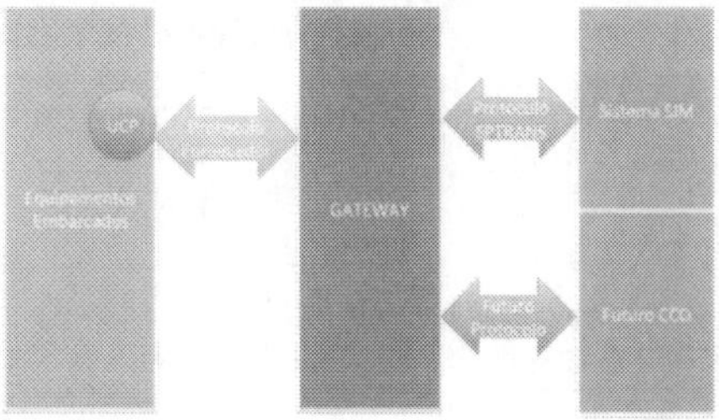

Figure 11. Selection process

This proposition is totally in line with open standards and will created mechanisms to foster a better interaction among the different on-board hardware. This gateway still does not solve the hardware/software compatibility issue described before but it is a step forward in terms of integration and open standards.

7 Conclusion

The tender released in São Paulo is an initiative to improve the chaotic traffic of the city and the metropolitan area. The changes in the civil infrastructure of the roads have already brought benefits to the city. These changes alone cannot produce additional benefits, so the need for the technology becomes apparent. São Paulo's tender demonstrated a regional action to update its on-board system and mimic the state-of-the-art ITS system in the world. This tender was a first step towards São Paulo ITS modernization. A great benefit was the development of a gateway to guarantee the communication of the SIM and the future OCC, favouring open standards. However, modernization is an on going process, so the work needs to evolve and approach other defying questions, like interoperability and description of features and functionalities.

Thinking country wise, Brazil would benefit from having a national plan or strategy for ITS, as do developed countries.

References

1. D. A. Rosen, F. J. Mammano, R. Favout, An electronic route-guidance system for highway vehicles. *IEEE Trans Veh Technol*, **19**, 143–152 (1970)
2. C. Little, The intelligent vehicle initiative: advancing "human-centered" smart vehicles. Public Roads, **61** (1997). http://www.fhwa.dot.gov/publications/publicroads/97septoct/p97sept18.cfm
3. Intelligent Vehicle Initiative: Strategic Planning Overview, Draft, (1997).
4. R. Kandarpa, M. Chenzaie, J. Anderson, Final Report: Vehicle Infrastructure Integration Proof-of-Concept Results and Findings. C Infrastructure. Technical Report FHWA-JPO-09-057 (2009).
5. Y. F. Yin, M. A. Miller, S. E. Shladover, Assessment of the applicability of cooperative vehicle-highway automation systems to freight movement in Chicago. In: The 83rd TRB Annual Meeting, Washington, DC (2004).
6. US Department of Transportations: http://www.its.dot.gov/its_program/about_its.htm
7. US Department of Transportation: http://www.its.dot.gov/strategicplan.pdf
8. I. Catling, B. McQueen. Road transport informatics in Europe-major programs and demonstrations. *IEEE Trans Veh Technol*, **40**, 132–140 (1991).
9. Oxley P R, Mitchell C G B. Final report on elderly and disabled drivers information telematics. R & D Programme Telematics System in the Area of Transport (DRIVE II), Commission of the European Communities CEC, Brussels (1995).
10. A. Carrotta (ERTICO). Report on the Progress of the 28 eSafety Recommendations. Brussels (2008).
11. T. Yokota, ITS Technical Note for Developing Countries – Technical Note 1, NRI.
12. T. Tanaka, T. Yamamoto, S. Fukuda. Onboard system devices for a vehicle information and communication system. *FUJITSU TEN Tech J*, **7**, 26–34 (1995).
13. T. Bar, D. Nienhuser, R. Kohlhaas, Probabilistic driving style determination by means of a situation based analysis of the vehicle data. In: The 14th International IEEE Conference on Intelligent Transportation Systems, Washington, DC, 1698–1703 (2011).
14. NTU – Dados do transporte público: http://www.ntu.org.br/novo/AreasInternas.aspx?idArea=7&idSegundoNivel=18
15. Ministério do Planejamento: http://www.pac.gov.br/sobre-o-pac
16. Critérios técnicos na seleção de projetos. Apresentado pela SEMOB / Ministério das cidades: http://thecityfixbrasil.com/files/2012/11/8CRITÉRIOS-DE-SELEÇÃO-DE-PROJETOS_SEMOB.pdf
17. NTU – Indicadores de desenpenho: http://www.ntu.org.br/novo/ListaDadosPorRegiao.aspx?idArea=7&idSegundoNivel=17
18. SPTRANS: http://www.sptrans.com.br
19. Companhia de Engenharia de Tráfego: http://www.cetsp.com.br/consultas/da-licenca-para-o-onibus/o-programa.aspx#
20. T. Yokota, Two stage Selection Model for ITS Applications– Technical Note 2, NRI.
21. 2015-2019 DoT Strategic Plan www.its.dot.gov

MATEC Web of Conferences **76**, 03005 (2016) DOI: 10.1051/matecconf/20167603005
CSCC 2016

One electronic document accepted by importer and exporter authorities: Blue Path as an element of integration and traceability

Maria L. R. P. D. Scoton[1, a], Anderson O. de Souza[1], Flávia R. P. de Lima[1], Vidal A. Z. C. Melo[1], Luiz N. Rossi[1], Eduardo M. Dias[1]

[1] *GAESI - Grupo de Automação Elétrica em Sistemas Industriais, Escola Politécnica da Universidade de São Paulo, Av. Prof. Luciano Gualberto, trav 3, n°. 158, CEP 05508-970, São Paulo/SP, Brazil, http://www.gaesi.eng.br.*

Abstract. The Blue Path (CA-e) is an document created and transmitted electronically that contains all necessary data to allow the sanitary authority to analyze the requirement of exportation that will result on the sanitary clearance of the animal protein for exportation. Actually it is in use in Brazil. However, even though the data exists electronically, when it is send to the importer country some must be sent on paper, because the bilateral agreements do not allow the exchange of electronic documents. The present work proposals the extension of the CA-e, as an element of integration and traceability, that will allow the automation of the communication between private and public systems not only at Brazil, the country of the origin of the animal protein exported, but also between and at the country of destiny. Based on the number presented by the adoption of the CA-e at Brazil, it is fair to conclude that this communication machine/machine would bring great economy and optimization for the supply chain.

1 Introduction

Electronic documents (e-Docs) are not novelties; however, their level of adoption is still low if compared with its potential. [1] An example of that are the international trades that demand the use of paper documents instead of electronic ones. Observe Brazilian animal protein supply chain that, on 2012, had about 200 million heads of cattle and 22 million cattle slaughtered, and, on 2010, generated a turnover of US$167.5 billion. [2] Brazilian animal protein exportation process demands documents on electronic format, such as the electronic invoice, known in Brazil by the acronymic NF-e, but, also demands paper documents, like the International Health Certificate, CSI, acronymic from its name in Portuguese. [2]

As verified by a pilot project, the dependency of documents on paper resulted on an extra 57 hour on the exportation through Port of Santos (at city of Santos, state of São Paulo), and on an extra 109 hour on the exportation through Port of Navegantes (city of Florianopolis, state of Santa Catarina). [3] Brazil has to improve its process to be more competitive, considering he was the 124 country, between 189 analyzed, on the business regulations aspect, which "measures the time and cost (excluding tariffs) associated with exporting and importing a standardized cargo of goods by sea transport. The time and cost necessary to complete every official procedure for exporting and importing the goods are recorded; however, the time and cost for sea transport are not included. All documents needed by the trader to export or import the goods across the border are also recorded". [4]

The cause of this extra time was the necessity to make the inspection request, called "request for exportation" (RE), and all the papers that accompany it, get to the International Agricultural Surveillance, known in Brazil as Vigiagro. Vigiagro is the institution responsible for analysing the RE. This document results on the cargo being granted or not a heath certificate to exportation. This analysis, as timed during the pilot took around 4 minutes. No analysis took more than 30 min. [3]

In a nutshell: the bureaucratic process can occur independently of the physical one. This is what is shown of Fig. 1 [3]:

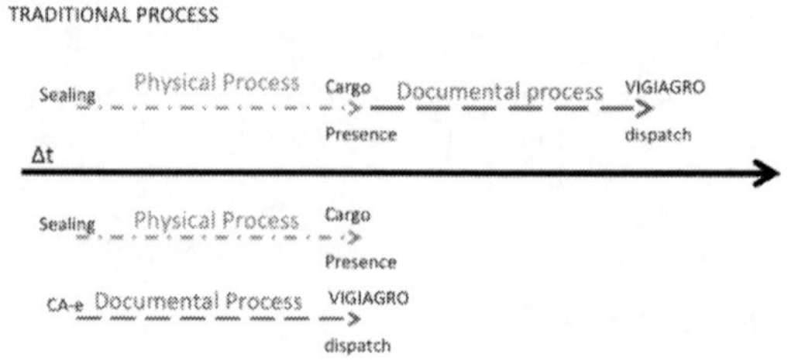

Figure 1. Graphic comparison between the traditional process and the proposed process (CA-e) [3]

Therefore, if Brazilian animal protein supply chain adopt an e-Doc that (a) will be available as soon as transmitted to the back office; and (b) contains all

[a] Corresponding author: lidiadias@pea.usp.br

information necessary for Vigiagro's analysis, it will be possible to Vigiagro to analyze the RE just after this cargo is sealed. Therefore, the following process will no longer happen:

1. Collection of the documents that accompanied the cargo by a employee of the customs broker;
2. Delivery of the collected documents to the customs broker;
3. Issue RE, by the customs broker;
4. Delivery of the RE to the Vigiagro at a Vigiagro's unit; and
5. Withdraw dispatch at Vigiagro

The only thing that will remain from the conventional process is the analysis and dispatch of the RE by a Vigiagro agent, which will be available on line.

This, as verified on some practical cases represents a significant gain of time because, by having the documents available electronically, the RE analysis can occur independently of the cargo physically arriving on the terminal, which will optimize the clearance of the cargo. Fig. 2 presents the days that took to complete the conventional process (based on paper, red line) and the electronic process (with CA-e, green line). Based on that, it also shows the time economy in days for the protein exportation to the listed countries (purple line). The blue columns represent the total of containers measured per country.

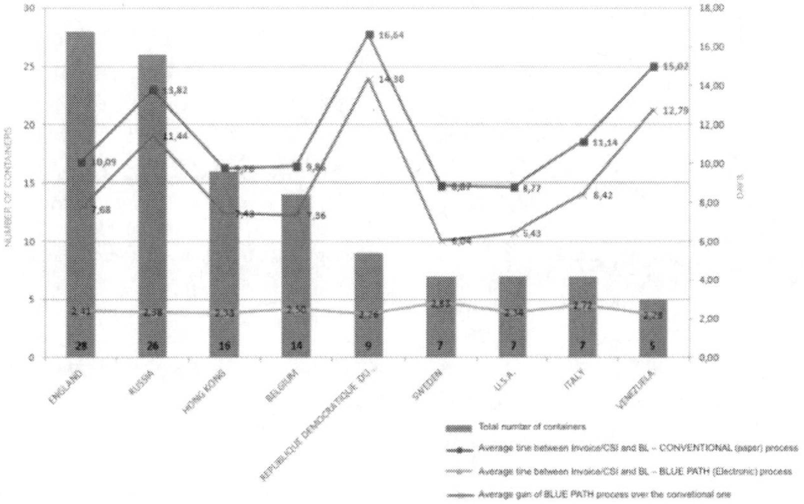

Figure 2. Time economy of electronic process based on data collection of days necessaries to complete conventional process and process with Blue Path

Those are the time economy measured only at the Brazilian part of the process. However, this process will continue on the importer country. The need for a paper document can occur because of requirements inside of a country, but also requirements inside of the importer country. This depends of bilateral agreements between those countries. If the importer country does not accept the electronic document, a paper document will have to be issued anyway to be sent to the importer (or its representative). Thus, the level of bureaucracy probably will be higher than it could, impacting on the competitiveness of that supply chain.

Having in mind the animal protein international commerce, the present work proposes to extend the adoption of the CA-e, extending its function as an element of integration and traceability since the industry until the port of destiny. This will allow the information to get faster to the importer and authorities of the importer country, in a more secure and efficient manner. Given the CA-e is based on machine/machine communication, it will diminish errors, inefficiency and reworks.

2 CA-e

It is possible to diminish the amount of bureaucracy through Brazilian beef supply chain by adopting an e-Doc that allows the analysis of the required information before the arrival of the cargo at the border; the CA-e is an example of that [2 e 3].

Actually, the CA-e acts over animal protein exportation supply chain, more exactly over the health clearance of the cargo. Besides the parties of the contract of purchase and sale, this process involves industry, Ministry of Agriculture, and Provisioning of the Land (MAPA) broker, transportation companies and ports. So far, it does not involve the Internal Revenue Service of Brazil (RFB) or the port of destiny.

At the industry, as shown on Fig. 3, the following steps are taken: 1. fabrication of the product; 2. load unitization; and, 3. generation of traditional operational documents.

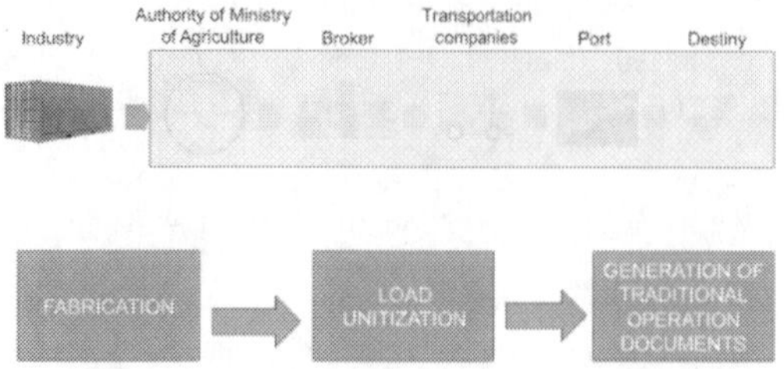

Figure 3. Brazilian animal protein exportation supply chain: processes realized at the industry.

At the exit of the industry acts the fiscal of the MAPA, who, as shown on Fig. 4, must: 1. verify cargo and documents; 2. seal the container; 3. generate the CA-e; and, 4. transmit the CA-e to the system BackOffice. By doing so, the information will automatically be available for those previously registered on CA-e system.

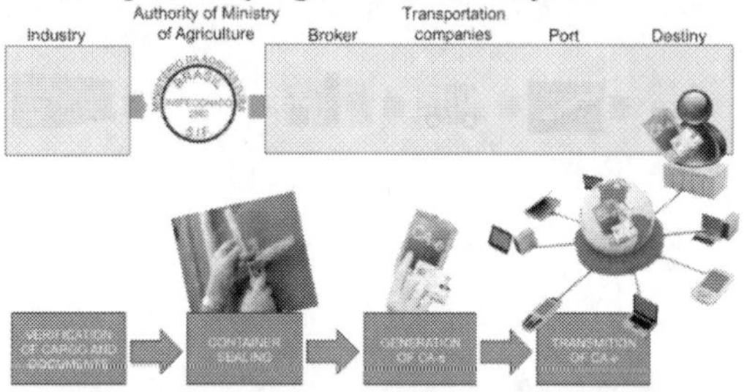

Figure 4. Brazilian animal protein exportation supply chain: processes realized at the exit of the industry by an authority of MAPA.

The CA-e operational model is explained on Fig. 5 and Fig. 6.

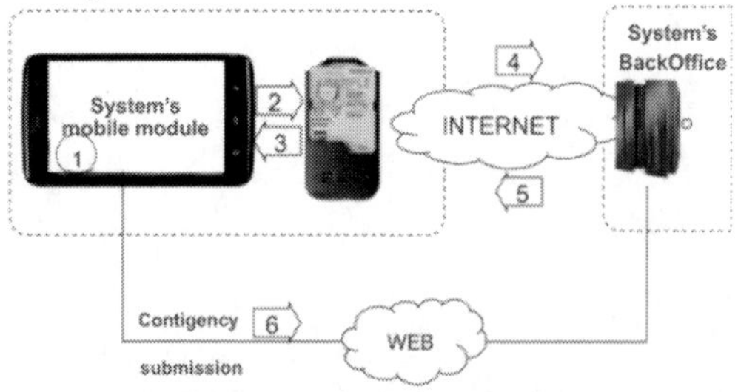

Figure 5. CA-e operational model: creation of a CA-e

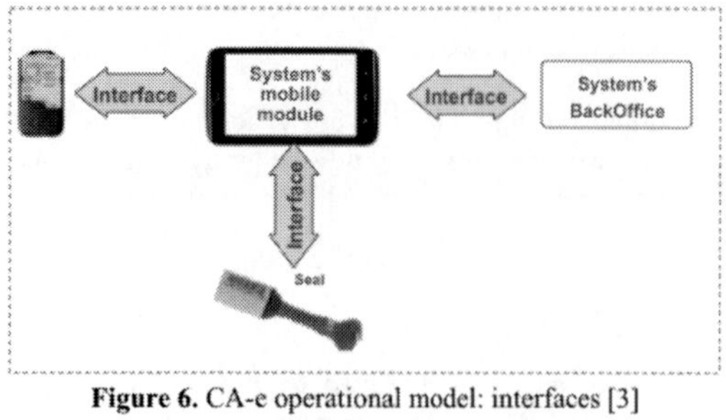

Figure 6. CA-e operational model: interfaces [3]

Note that the applied technologies are [2 and 3]:

1. RF-ID: Radio Frequency Identification
2. NFC: Near Field Identification
3. Cloud Computing
4. ICP-BRASIL: Public Keys Infrastructure
5. Mobility: mobile devices for field
6. Tamper proof: electronic detection of violations
7. XML: eXtensible Markup Language

After that, as shown in Fig. 7, the exporter (or his representative, usually a broker) will: 1. electronically receive the information contained at the CA-e; 2. realize the traditional operational dispatch; and, 3. electronically receive a status return of the system.

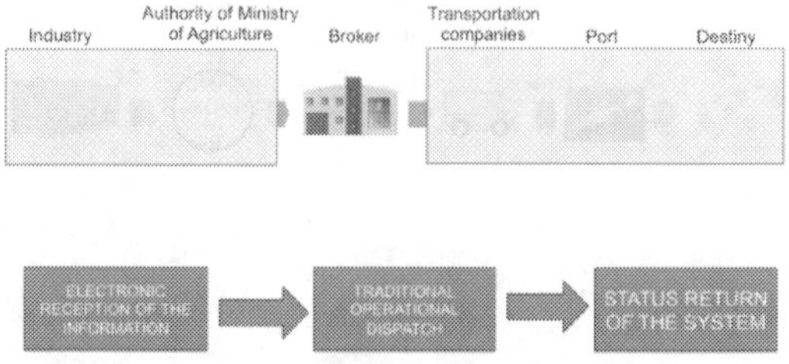

Figure 7. Brazilian animal protein exportation supply chain: processes realized by the broker

The transportation companies, as presented by Fig. 8, will take the cargo to the Port. During that way they can be subjected to non-intrusive inspection, by passing through a Radiofrequency Identification (RFID) portal.

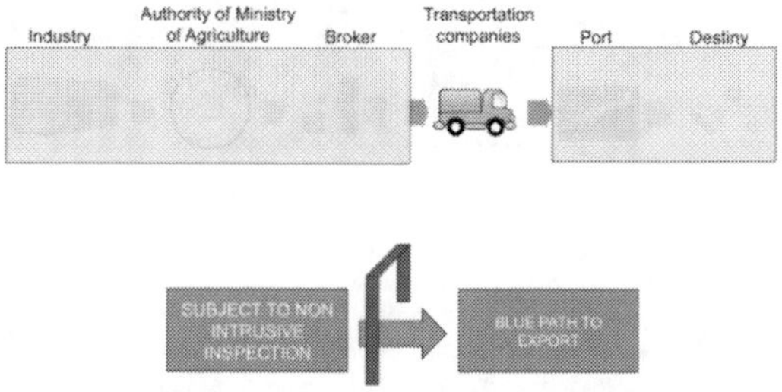

Figure 8. Brazilian animal protein exportation supply chain: processes realized by transportation companies

At last, as shown in Fig. 9, the sealed container arrives at the Port of Origen, where will be read the RFID on its seal. When the seal is read, the terminal operator can verify if the truck is clear to board or not, or if it has to be physically inspected by an agent of Vigiagro.

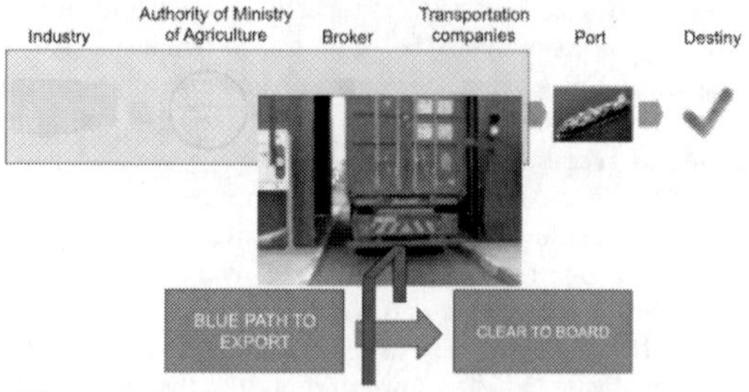

Figure 9. Brazilian animal protein exportation supply chain: processes realized at the Port

3 CA-e as an element of integration and traceability

As said before, it is possible to diminish the amount of bureaucracy through Brazilian beef supply chain by adopting the CA-e on Brazilian territory. But, its adoption abroad can also diminish the bureaucracy of the process on the importer territory.

CA-e is a document "that exists exclusively in the digital format, is stored and delivered through electronically means, in order to document an operation of container sealing by SIF, with legal validity guaranteed by the digital signature based on digital certificates issued by ICP-BRAZIL.

ICP-BRAZIL is the official public key infrastructure in Brazil, since 2001, allowing electronic documents to be signed and recognized all over the national territory." [3] [5] [6]

It makes an interface between public and private systems, applying a communication machine-machine. Private systems are those of operational and supervision layers, such as SAP, Oracle, J. D. Edwards and others proprietary systems. Public systems are those of control layer, those that support compliance and procedures, such as governmental systems that users must input information to fulfill requirements. Brazilian examples are: Vigiagro's system (SIGVIG) and RFB's system (SISCOMEX). Fig. 10 presents reference architecture and technology: private and public layers. Fig. 11 presents CA-e function in those terms.

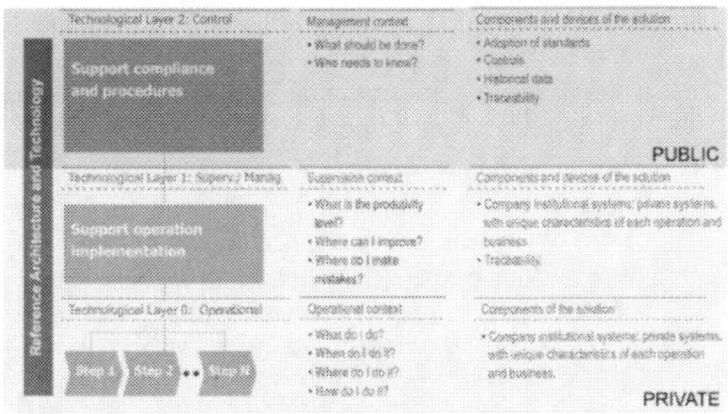

Figure 10. Reference architecture and technology: private and public layers

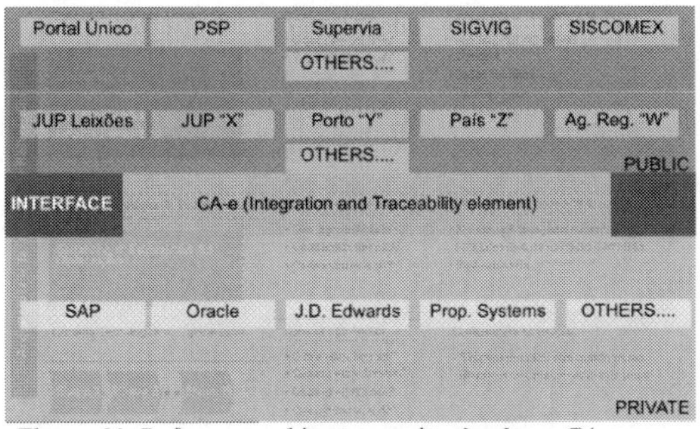

Figure 11. Reference architecture and technology: CA-e as an element of integration and traceability

In other words, it substitutes communications that nowadays still happens man-man or man-machine. Just by doing so, it avoids inefficiency, errors and rework.

4 Proposed Solution

Acting as an element of integration and traceability, the CA-e can optimize the supply chain. It can transfer all necessary information electronically, as presents Fig. 12.

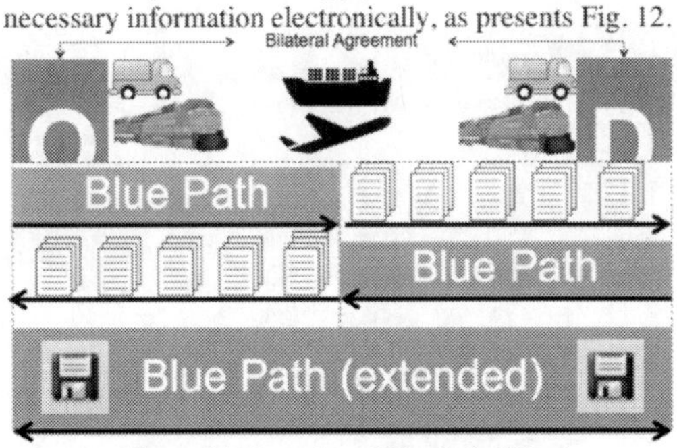

Figure 12. Extension of Blue Path (CA-e)

Presently the CA-e is in use in Brazil, so the information regarding the health supervision can be presented electronically as soon as an agent of SIF (an institution of MAPA) generates the CA-e. However, that e-Doc is not accepted at the destiny port, because of the absence of a bilateral agreement that allows so.

The extended CA-e would work on the following manner, as shown on Figs.:

1. The data present on a private system at the Origen is used to create the CA-e.
2. The data is automatically transferred to CA-e system.
3. The data is automatically transferred to the public system.
4. The public institution analyzes the data and, if everything is OK, that cargo receives health clearance.

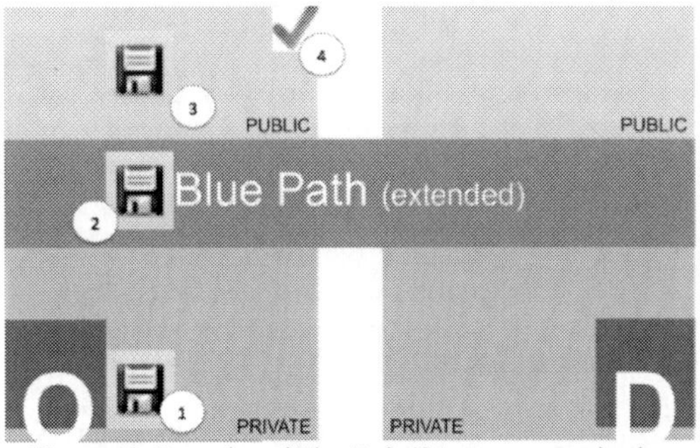

Figure 13. Extension of Blue Path (CA-e) - communication process at Origen

5. The data is automatically sent to the system at the destiny.
6. The data is automatically sent to the private system at the destiny.

7. The private system recognizes the cargo as theirs and automatically informs the public system that he is going to receive such cargo.
8. Thus, the public system is ready to analyze and decide for the inspection, clearance or denial of the cargo.

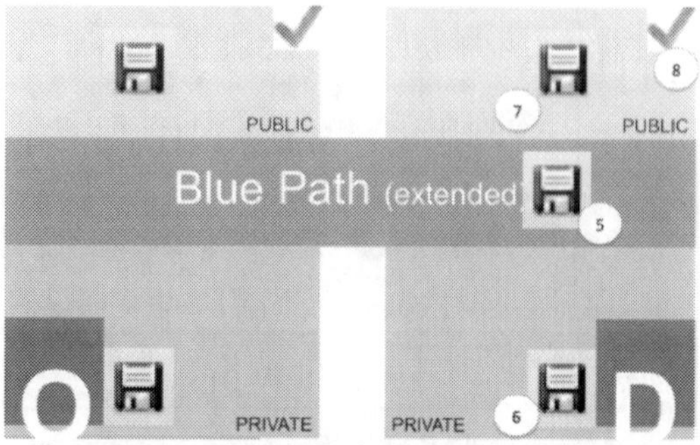

Figure 14. Extension of Blue Path (CA-e) - communication process at Destiny

9. Being cleared by the public authorities at the destiny, it will mean that the cargo was released prior to its arrival at the port of origin, because all the process will begin when the cargo leaves the industry. (Fig. 15)

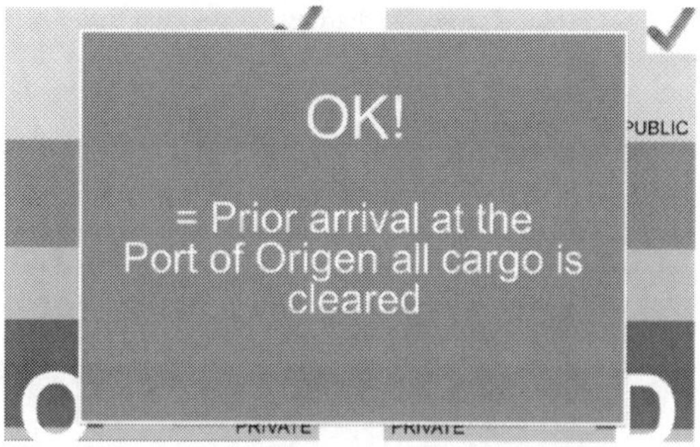

Figure 15. Extension of Blue Path (CA-e) - communication process, result expected

As previously said, the importer country can be impacted by the requirement of paper documents for the nationalization of the product, which would justify reviewing bilateral agreements to contemplate the acceptance by the authorities of an electronic document instead.

5 Conclusions

The CA-e is a tool that allows the automation of the communication between systems. It allows the communication machine/machine between systems. By substituting communications man/man and man/machine, it reduces errors, inefficiency and rework.

By extending the CA-e for the importer country all the exportation process will be followed, from beginning to end. In the case of the animal protein supply chain that means from the industry, passing through transportation companies, port of origin and destiny, until it gets to the importer.

That means that the CA-e guarantees traceability and visibility along the entire logistic chain, which makes powerful tool to improve its management efficiency, including the capacity to anticipate problems or errors and to reduce operational costs.

However, bilateral agreements must be changed in order to allow the adoption of e-Docs through the whole exportation and subsequently nationalization process.

References

1. A. Perego and A. Salgaro, *Assessing the benefits of B2B trade cycle integration: a model in the home appliances industry*. Benchmarking: An International Journal, **Vol. 17** Iss 4 pp. 616 - 631 (2010). Available at <http://dx.doi.org/10.1108/14635771011060611>. Accessed on 22/08/2014.
2. M. L. R. P. DIAS et al. *Blue Path for exports of animal protein*, Proceedings of the 12th WSEAS International Conference on Information Security and Privacy (ISP '13), Recent Advances in Computer Science (ISBN 978-960-474-354-4), pp. 134 - 140 (2013). Available at <http://www.wseas.us/e-library/conferences/2013/Nanjing/ACCIS/ACCIS-21.pdf>. Accessed on 30/04/2016.
3. M. L. R. P. DIAS et al. *Customized e-Doc to expedite the Brazilian animal protein export process by sea*, International Journal of Systems Applications, Engineering & Development (ISSN: 2074-1308), **v. 8**, pp. 221 - 229 (2014). Available at <http://www.naun.org/main/UPress/saed/2014/a062014-150.pdf>. Accessed on 30/04/2016.
4. *The World Bank. "Trading Across Borders"*. Available at <http://www.doingbusiness.org/data/exploretopics/trading-across-borders>. Accessed on 30/04/2016.
5. BRAZIL. Presidency of the Republic. Provisional Measure (MP) n. 2200-2 of 08/24/2001. Published on August, 24 of 2001. Available at <http://www.planalto.gov.br/ccivil_03/mpv/Antigas_2001/2200-2.htm>. Accessed on 30/04/2016.
6. ITI (National Institute of Information Technology). *Official public key infrastructure in Brazil* (ICP-BRASIL). Available at <http://www.iti.gov.br/icp-brasil/o-que-e>. Accessed on 30/04/2016.

A Simple Dual Decomposition Method for Resource Allocation in Telecommunication Networks

Igor Konnov[1,a], Aleksey Kashuba[2] and Erkki Laitinen[3]

[1]*Department of System Analysis and Information Technologies, Kazan Federal University, Kazan 420008, Russia*
[2]*LLC "AST Povolzhye", Kazan 420029, Russia*
[3]*Department of Mathematical Sciences, University of Oulu, 90014 Oulu, Finland*

Abstract. We consider a problem of optimal resource allocation in a wireless communication network divided into zones (clusters). The network manager aims to distribute some homogeneous resource (bandwidth) among users of several zones in order to maximize the total network profit, which takes into account payments from users and implementation costs. As a result, we obtain a convex optimization problem involving capacity and balance constraints. By using the dual Lagrangian method with respect to the capacity constraint, we reduce the initial problem to a suitable one-dimensional problem, so that calculation of its cost function value leads to independent solution of zonal problems, treated as two-side auction models with one trader. We show that solution of each zonal problem can be found exactly by a simple arrangement type algorithm even in the case where the trader price is not fixed. Besides, we suggest ways to adjust the basic problem to the case of moving nodes. Some results of computational experiments confirm the applicability of the new method.

1 Introduction

The current development of telecommunication systems creates a number of new challenges of efficient management mechanisms for efficient allocation of limited communication networks resources. In fact, despite the existence of powerful processing and transmission devices, increasing demand of different communication services and its variability lead to serious congestion effects and inefficient utilization of network resources (e.g., bandwidth and batteries capacity), especially in wireless telecommunication networks. This situation forces one to replace the fixed allocation rules with more flexible mechanisms, which are based on proper mathematical models; see e.g. [1-3]. The problem is to suggest such models and to develop suitable solution methods. Usually, the decision making processes are based on solutions of the corresponding optimization problems. At the same time, experience of dealing with these very complicated and spatially distributed systems usually shows that these problems have to utilize a proper decomposition/clustering approach, which can be based on zonal, time, frequency and other attributes of nodes/units; see e.g. [4, 5].

In this paper, we consider one of such problems, i.e. optimal allocation of a homogeneous resource in a zonal telecommunication network such that the income received from users payments is maximized and the implementation costs of the network operator are minimized; see [6, 7]. The network manager problem consists in optimal distribution of the resource shares among zones in order to maximize the total network profit. As a result, we obtain a convex optimization problem involving capacity and balance constraints. By using the dual Lagrangian method with respect to the capacity constraint, we reduce the initial problem to a suitable one-dimensional problem, so that calculation of its cost function value leads to independent solution of zonal problems, treated as two-side auction models with one trader. We show that solution of each zonal problem can be found exactly by a simple arrangement type algorithm even in the case where the trader price is not fixed. In such a way we develop a new dual decomposition approach for solution finding, whose implementation is simpler essentially in comparison with the methods from [6, 7]. We present results of computational experiments which confirm the applicability of the new method.

[a] Corresponding author: konn-igor@yandex.ru

2 Notation and the problem statement

Let us consider a telecommunication network with nodes attributed to users (consumers) which is divided into zones (clusters). The problem of a manager of the network is to find the optimal allocation of a limited homogeneous network resource among the zones. That is, the optimal shares should maximize the value of the total profit containing the total income received from consumers' fees and negative resource implementation costs.

Let us use the following notation:

- n is the number of zones;
- I_k is the index set of users (currently) located in zone k ($k = 1,\dots,n$);
- B is the total resource supply (the total bandwidth) for the system (network);
- x_k is an unknown quantity of the resource allotted to zone k with the upper bound b_k and $f_k(x_k)$ is the cost of implementation of this quantity of the resource for zone k ($k = 1,\dots,n$);
- y_i is the resource amount received by user j with the upper bound a_i and $\varphi_i(y_i)$ is the charge value paid by user j for the resource value y_i.

The problem of the network manager can be written as follows:

$$\max \to \mu(x,y) = \sum_{k=1}^{n}\left[\sum_{i\in I_k}\varphi_i(y_i) - f_k(x_k)\right], \qquad (1)$$

subject to

$$\sum_{i\in I_k} y_i = x_k, k = 1,\dots,n; \qquad (2)$$

$$0 \le y_i \le a_i, i \in I_k, k = 1,\dots,n; \qquad (3)$$

$$\sum_{k=1}^{n} x_k \le B; \qquad (4)$$

$$0 \le x_k \le b_k, k = 1,\dots,n. \qquad (5)$$

That is, (2) provides the balance for demand and supply in each zone, (3) and (5) are capacity constraints for users and network supply values in each zone, respectively, and (4) gives the upper bound for the total resource supply. The goal of the network manager is to maximize the total network profit subject to all these constraints.

In what follows we assume that there exists at least one feasible point satisfying conditions (2)–(5), each function $f_k(x_k)$ is convex and differentiable, and all the functions $\varphi_i(y_i)$ are affine, i.e.

$$\varphi_i(y_i) = \alpha_i y_i + \beta_i, \alpha_i > 0, i \in I_k, k = 1,\dots,n. \qquad (6)$$

This means that the prices (marginal utilities) α_i of the users are fixed, but the manager can vary the prices depending on volumes, so that each zonal price is a non-increasing function.

3 Dual solution method

Under the basic assumptions of the previous section, (1)–(5) is a differentiable convex optimization problem, which has a solution since its feasible set is bounded. Hence it can be found by a great number of iterative methods; see e.g. [8, 9]. However, the problem of selection of an efficient decomposition method here is not trivial task since problem (1)–(5) has $n+1$ functional constraints (2) and (4) and many box type ones. For instance, utilization of the standard duality approach which is based on defining the Lagrangian function with respect to all the functional constraints leads to a non-smooth dual convex optimization problem in $n+1$ dual variables, whose solution may cause certain difficulties. For this reason, we intend to apply a special dual method, which takes into account peculiarities of this problem and does not require hard implementation procedures.

Let us first define the Lagrange function of problem (1)–(4) as follows:

$$L(x,y,\lambda) = \mu(x,y) - \lambda\left(\sum_{k=1}^{n} x_k - B\right),$$

i.e. we insert only the term corresponding to the the upper bound constraint for the total resource supply (4) with the Lagrangian multiplier λ. At the same time, we keep the zonal balance constraints (2) as well as the capacity constraints (3) and (5).

Hence, we can write the one-dimensional dual problem:

$$\min_{\lambda\ge 0} \to \psi(\lambda), \qquad (7)$$

where

$$\psi(\lambda) = \sup_{(x,y)\in W} L(x,y,\lambda)$$

$$= \sup_{(x,y)\in W} \sum_{k=1}^{n}\left[\sum_{i\in I_k}\varphi_i(y_i) - f_k(x_k) - \lambda x_k\right]$$

$$+\lambda B;$$

where

$$W = \left\{ (x,y) \;\middle|\; \begin{array}{l} \sum_{i\in I_k} y_i = x_k, \\ 0 \le y_i \le a_i, i \in I_k, \\ 0 \le x_k \le b_k, k = 1,\dots,n \end{array} \right\}.$$

By duality (see e.g. [8, 9]), problems (1)–(5) and (7) have the same optimal value. However, solution of (7) can be found by one of well-known one-dimensional optimization algorithms based on calculation of values of $\psi(\lambda)$. We now discuss this problem in more detail. The main element in calculation of $\psi(\lambda)$ is a solution of the problem:

$$\max \to \sum_{k=1}^{n}\left[\sum_{i\in I_k}\varphi_i(y_i) - f_k(x_k) - \lambda x_k\right] \qquad (8)$$

subject to

$$\sum_{i\in I_k} y_i = x_k, 0 \le y_i \le a_i, i \in I_k,$$

$$0 \le x_k \le b_k, k = 1,\dots,n.$$

However, this problem decomposes into n independent zonal convex programming problems

$$\max \rightarrow \left[\sum_{i \in I_k} \varphi_i(y_i) - f_k(x_k) - \lambda x_k \right] \tag{9}$$

subject to

$$\sum_{i \in I_k} y_i = x_k, 0 \le y_i \le a_i, i \in I_k,$$

$$0 \le x_k \le b_k,$$

for $k = 1,\dots,n$. Hence, we have to suggest a simple and efficient algorithm for the basic problem (9).

Set $y(k) = (y_i)_{i \in I_k}$,

$$W_k = \left\{ (x_k, y(k)) \left| \begin{array}{l} \sum_{i \in I_k} y_i = x_k, \\ 0 \le y_i \le a_i, i \in I_k, \\ 0 \le x_k \le b_k \end{array} \right. \right\},$$

then

$$W = \prod_{k=1}^{n} W_k.$$

The necessary and sufficient optimality condition for problem (9) in view of (6) is written in the form of the variational inequality: find $(\bar{x}_k, \bar{y}(k)) \in W_k$ such that

$$\begin{array}{l} (f_k'(\bar{x}_k) + \lambda)(x_k - \bar{x}_k) - \sum_{i \in I_k} \alpha_i (y_i - \bar{y}_i) \ge 0 \\ \forall (x_k, y(k)) \in W_k. \end{array} \tag{10}$$

This is a two-sided auction type equilibrium problem with one seller and several buyers; see e.g. [10, 11]. It is equivalent to the problem of finding a feasible vector $(\bar{x}_k, \bar{y}(k)) \in W_k$ and a cutting price $\bar{p}_k$ such that

$$f_k'(\bar{x}_k) + \lambda \begin{cases} \ge \bar{p}_k & if \quad \bar{x}_k = 0, \\ = \bar{p}_k & if \quad \bar{x}_k \in (0, b_k), \\ \le \bar{p}_k & if \quad \bar{x}_k = b_k, \end{cases} \tag{11}$$

and

$$\alpha_i \begin{cases} \le \bar{p}_k & if \quad \bar{y}_i = 0, \\ = \bar{p}_k & if \quad \bar{y}_j \in (0, a_i), \quad i \in I_k. \\ \ge \bar{p}_k & if \quad \bar{y}_j = a_i, \end{cases} \tag{12}$$

Since buyers' prices are fixed, we can re-arrange them to be non-increasing and then find easily an intersection point of the staircase-wise inverse common demand and offer price $f_k'(x_k) + \lambda$ lines; see also [11]. Therefore, an exact solution of problem (10) or (9) (hence (8)) can be found explicitly by simple ordering type algorithms, although (9) contain a non-linear function in general. In other words, calculation of values of $\psi(\lambda)$ can be accomplished by several independent simple ordering type algorithms. Notice that the re-arrangement of bid prices α_i in each zone should be made only one time that reduces the computational expenses essentially in comparison with the general duality approach. So, having the optimal value λ^* of problem (7), we can find a solution of problem (1)–(5) by solving problem (8) with $\lambda = \lambda^*$, i.e. it is accomplished within the main calculation process for (7).

4 Adjustment for the case of moving nodes

In the above model it was assumed that users locations are fixed. We now intend to suggest some adjustments of the above model to networks with more complex and non-stationary behavior of users (nodes), which is typical for various modern wireless telecommunication systems; see e.g. [2, 12].

We consider the above problem of the network manager for some time slot. In this case we need some additional information about the behavior of users (nodes). It was suggested by I. Konnov (see e.g. [13]) to treat each moving node in a wireless network as a separate Markovian chain.

In order to create such a model, we determine a suitable grid G covering the domain of the network so that G_k denotes the index set of all the cells belonging to zone k. Next, we consider the discrete time model and suppose that, given a user (node) j, we can determine the starting probability vector $\pi^{j,(0)}$, whose components $\pi_\sigma^{j,(0)}$ give its probabilities to be in cell $\sigma \in \mathsf{G}$ by time slot (stage) 1, and the probability $\tilde{\pi}_{\sigma\tau}^j$ (for the simplicity of exposition, it is supposed to be independent of time) of the one stage transition $\sigma \rightarrow \tau$ for each pair $\sigma, \tau \in \mathsf{G}$. Knowing the starting and transition probability vectors for each node j, we can calculate its probability $\pi_\sigma^{j,(t-1)}$ to be in cell $\sigma \in \mathsf{G}$ by a selected slot t via the standard Markovian chain technique (see e.g. [14]). Afterwards we calculate the value

$$\tilde{p}_k^{j,(t-1)} = \sum_{\sigma \in \mathsf{G}_k} \pi_\sigma^{j,(t-1)}$$

for each zone k and assign user j to zone l where the probability $\tilde{p}_l^{j,(t-1)}$ is maximal, i.e. then $j \in I_l$.

Therefore, we can solve the same problem (7)–(9) with this assignment and obtain the desired resource allocation for time slot t in the case of moving nodes.

Similarly, if

$$\lim_{m \to \infty} (\Pi^j)^m = \overline{\Pi}^j \tag{13}$$

for each probability matrix $\tilde{\Pi}^j = (\tilde{\pi}_{\sigma\tau}^j)_{\{\sigma,\tau \in \mathsf{G}\}}$, behavior of each user is stable and we can evaluate the optimal resource allocation for a long-time stationary period by calculation of the limit probabilities

$$\overline{\pi}_{\tau}^{j} = \sum_{\sigma \in G} \pi_{\sigma}^{j,(0)} \overline{\pi}_{\sigma\tau}^{j} \ for \ \tau \in G$$

and set

$$\overline{p}_{k}^{j} = \sum_{\sigma \in G_k} \overline{\pi}_{\sigma}^{j}$$

for each j. Then we can assign user j to zone l where the probability $\overline{p}_{l}^{j}$ is maximal, i.e. then $j \in I_l$ and solve problem (7)–(9) with this assignment and obtain the long-time resource allocation strategy.

However, this approach can not be used if the limit in (13) does not exist. Then we can apply the statistical approach and calculate the probabilities on-line as it was suggested in [15]. After t time slots we can determine the value

$$p_{k}^{j,t} = s_{j,k}(t)/t,$$

for each user j and for each zone k, where $s_{j,k}(t)$ denotes the number of time slots when user j was in zone k. It is treated as some approximation of the probability of user j to be in zone k. We set

$$\overline{p}_{k}^{j} = p_{k}^{j,t}$$

if

$$\left\{ \sum_{j \in I} \sum_{k=1}^{n} (p_{k}^{j,t} - p_{k}^{j,t-1})^2 \right\}^{1/2} \le \delta$$

for $\delta > 0$ small enough, where I denotes the index set of all the users. Then we utilize the values $\overline{p}_{k}^{j}$ as above in order to assign each user j to some zone l. Solution of problem (7)–(9) with this assignment gives the long-time resource allocation strategy.

5 Numerical experiments

In order to evaluate efficiency of the new method we made several series of computational experiments. Since the case of moving nodes yields the same mathematical model (1)–(5) we restricted ourselves with the fixed case.

We utilized the golden section method for solving the single-dimensional optimization problem (7). The programs were coded in C++ with a PC with the following facilities: Intel(R) Core(TM) i7-4500, CPU 1.80 GHz, RAM 6 Gb.

The initial intervals for choosing the dual variable λ were taken as $[0,1000]$. Values of b_k were chosen by trigonometric functions in $[1,11]$, values of a_i were chosen by trigonometric functions in $[1,2]$. The functions $f_k(x_k)$ were chosen to be convex quadratic, all the coefficients of $f_k(x_k)$ and $\varphi_i(y_i)$ were chosen with the help of trigonometric functions. The number of zones was varied from 5 to 105, the number of users was varied from 210 to 1010. Users were distributed in zones either uniformly or according to the normal distribution. The processor time and number of iterations, which gave an approximate solution of problem (7) within the same accuracy, were not significantly different for these two cases of distributions. We made calculations with 1000 test examples for each set of parameters, their average values are indicated in each row of the tables.

Further we report the results of tests, which include the time and number of iterations needed to find a solution of problem (7) within some accuracies. Let ε denote the desired accuracy of finding an approximate solution of problem (7). Let J denote the total number of users, N_ε the number of upper iterations in λ, T_ε the total processor time in seconds. The results of computations are given in Tables 1–3. In Table 1, we vary the accuracy ε, in Tables 2 and 3 we vary the total number of users and the number of zones, respectively.

Table 1. Results of testing with $J = 510$, $n = 70$.

ε	N_ε	T_ε
10^{-1}	20	0.0003
10^{-2}	24	0.0004
10^{-3}	29	0.0008
10^{-4}	34	0.0007

Table 2. Results of testing with $n = 70$, $\varepsilon = 10^{-2}$.

J	N_ε	T_ε
210	24	0.0001
310	24	0.0003
410	24	0.0004
510	24	0.0004
610	24	0.0008
710	24	0.0012
810	24	0.0011
910	24	0.0014
1010	24	0.0018

Table 3. Results of testing with $J = 510$, $\varepsilon = 10^{-2}$.

n	N_ε	T_ε
5	24	0.0001
15	24	0.0002
25	24	0.0001
35	24	0.0001
45	24	0.0002
55	24	0.0002
65	24	0.0002
75	24	0.0002
85	24	0.0003
95	24	0.0004
105	24	0.0002

From the results we can conclude that the performance of the new method is satisfactory for applications.

6 Conclusions

Equations should be centred and should be numbered with the number on the right-hand side. In this work, we considered a problem of managing limited resources in a zonal wireless telecommunication network and gave its constrained convex optimization problem formulation. We proposed a new dual decomposition method, which reduces the initial problem to a sequence of simple zonal convex optimization problems, they can be solved by efficient ordering type algorithms despite the nonlinear cost network functions. The results of the numerical experiments confirmed the rapid convergence of these methods. We also suggested ways to adjust the problem to the case of moving nodes.

References

1. Courcoubetis, C., Weber, R.: *Pricing Communication Networks: Economics, Technology and Modelling.* John Wiley & Sons, Chichester (2003)
2. Stańczak, S., Wiczanowski, M., Boche, H.: *Resource Allocation in Wireless Networks. Theory and Algorithms.* Springer, Berlin (2006)
3. Wyglinski, A.M., Nekovee, M., Hou, Y.T.: (eds.) *Cognitive Radio Communications and Networks: Principles and Practice.* Elsevier, Amsterdam (2010)
4. Chen, Y., Liestman, A.L.: A zonal algorithm for clustering ad hoc networks, Int. J. Found. of Computer Sci. **14**, pp.305–322 (2003)
5. Rohloff, K., Ye, J., Loyall, J., Schantz, R.: A hierarchical control system for dynamic resource management, Proceedings of the 12th IEEE Real-Time and Embedded Technology and Applications Symposium (RTAS 2006) Work in Progress Symposium, San Jose, CA (2006)
6. Konnov, I.V., Kashina, O.A., Laitinen, E.: Optimisation problems for control of distributed resources. Int. J. Model., Ident. and Contr., vol.**14**, pp.65–72 (2011)
7. Konnov, I.V., Kashina, O.A., Laitinen, E.: Two-level decomposition method for resource allocation in telecommunication network. Int. J. Dig. Inf. Wirel. Comm., vol.**2**, pp.150–155 (2012)
8. Polyak, B.T.: *Introduction to Optimization.* Nauka, Moscow, 1983 (Engl. transl. in Optimization Software, New York, 1987)
9. Minoux, M.: *Programmation Mathématique. Théorie et Algorithmes.* Bordas, Paris (1989)
10. Konnov, I.V.: On variational inequalities for auction market problems. Optim. Lett., vol.**1**, pp.155–162 (2007)
11. Konnov, I.V.: Optimisation of network resources with zonal auctions. Int. J. Knowl. Engin. Soft Data Parad., vol.**4**, pp.297–305 (2014)
12. X. Cheng, X. Huang, D.-Z. Du, Eds., *Ad Hoc Wireless Networking*, Kluwer, Dordrecht (2004)
13. I.V. Konnov, O. A. Kashina, Optimization based flow control in communication networks with moving nodes, Proc. of The Fourth Moscow Conference on Operations Research, MaxPress, Moscow, 2004, pp.116–118 (2004)
14. J.G. Kemeny, J.L. Snell, *Finite Markov Chains*, Van Nostrand, Princeton (1960)
15. I.V. Konnov, E. Laitinen, O. Pinyagina, Equilibrium based flow control in wireless networks with moving users, Proc. of the Finnish Operations Research Society 40th Anniversary Workshop (FORS40), Ed. by M.Collan, J.Hamalainen, P.Luukka. Lappeenranta, 2013, pp.30–33 (2013)

MATEC Web of Conferences **76**, 03007 (2016) DOI: 10.1051/matecconf/20167603007
CSCC 2016

Efficiency Estimation of MIMO Communication System Channel Coefficients Based on Markov Model

Yuri Parshin, Vladislav Kudryashov

Ryazan State Radio Engineering University, Department of Electronic devices, 390005 Ryazan, Russian Federation

Abstract. Based on Markov model of MIMO data transmission system channel coefficients from moving object held synthesis and analysis of channel coefficients error estimation. The model takes into account distribution configuration of reflectors in area, reception center and moving object location at a given time, kind of trajectory and speed of the moving object. A theory discrete Markov processes linear filtration is used by the development of estimation algorithm. Posteriori dispersions matrix is calculated. The simulation of filtering algorithm for different signal-interference situations is carried out.

1 Introduction

Due to the expansion of applications of mobile objects to accumulate various types of information arises the problem of transmitting information from mobile object to receiving station. Transmission of optical images and radar high-resolution images in real-time shows increased requirements to channel capacity. Implementation of required bandwidth causes difficulties due to multipath propagation of radio waves from mobile object to receiving station. In these conditions data transmission systems based on MIMO technology [1] are widely used. To realize MIMO channel potential performance it is necessary to measure channel coefficients from each transmit antenna to each receive antenna with high accuracy. The channel estimation errors has a significant impact on channel capacity [2–4]. The reduction of channel coefficients estimation errors can be realize by the most complete account of their statistical properties, as well as development of optimal estimation algorithm. The statistical description of channel coefficients most frequently uses Gaussian probability density distribution. However, the usage of correlation properties of channel coefficients and their dependence on speed of object movement in the estimation algorithm design is not enough to allow potential accuracy. Determination of the optimal mode of channel coefficients matrix estimation is considered in [5], but the possibility of accounting channel coefficients correlation in their estimation also not implemented.

The purpose of the article is to increase the MIMO data transmission system capacity by reduction of channel coefficients estimation error, which is achieved by using the optimal algorithm for filtering channel coefficients based on the Markov model.

2 Statement of the Problem

To describe the signal propagation in MIMO channel a geometric one-ring scattering model (Figure 1) [6] is used. Complex channel coefficients between antennas form a channel matrix

$$\underline{\mathbf{H}} = \{h_{nm} = a_{nm} e^{j\psi_{nm}}, n = 1,\ldots,N_R,\ m = 1,\ldots,N_T\},$$

where a_{nm} – signal amplitude transmission coefficient, ψ_{nm} – phase shift of signal, N_R, N_T – numbers of receive and transmit antennas respectively. Terrestrial antenna system operates in receive mode, and contains N_R elements of the coordinates x_n, y_n in the coordinate system O_1, associated with terrestrial antenna system. The antenna system of moving object operates in transmit mode, and contains N_T elements of the coordinates x_m, y_m, $m = 1,\ldots,N_T$, in the coordinate system O_2, associated with the moving object. The coordinate system O_2 is located at point (S,H), which characterizes the position of the moving object, and its dependence on time sets its trajectory. Each of the N scatterers located on a circle of radius R centered at the point O_2; coordinates of scatterers are: $x_n = R\cos\phi_n$, $y_n = R\sin\phi_n$. Angular scatterers coordinate $\phi_n = n\frac{2\pi}{N}$, $n = 1,\ldots,N$, specify to the uniform distribution of the scatterers along the circumference.

[a] Corresponding author: parshin51@mail.ru, yachmen@mail.ru

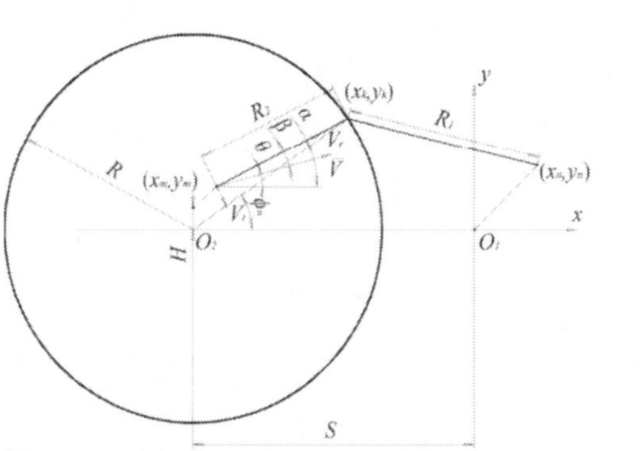

Figure 1. A geometric one-ring scattering model

In accordance with the model, channel matrix coefficient is determined by the following expression:

$$\underline{h}_{nm}(t)=\frac{1}{\sqrt{N}}\sum_{k=1}^{N}a_{nm}e^{i2\pi\frac{R_{nk}(t)}{\lambda}}e^{i2\pi\frac{R_{mk}(t)}{\lambda}}e^{i[2\pi f_{d,k}(t)t+\theta_k]}=\frac{1}{\sqrt{N}}\sum_{k=1}^{N}\underline{A}_k(t)e^{i\theta_k}$$

where $e^{i2\pi\frac{R_{mk}(t)}{\lambda}}$ – the coefficient describes the phase shift of the signal from the transmitting antenna to one of scatterers; $e^{i2\pi\frac{R_{nk}(t)}{\lambda}}$ – coefficient describes the phase shift of the signal from one of the scatterers to the receiving antenna, $R_{nk}(t)=\sqrt{(x_k(t)-x_n(t))^2+(y_k(t)-y_n(t))^2}$ – distance from the receiving antenna to one of scatterers, $R_{mk}(t)=\sqrt{(x_k(t)-x_m(t))^2+(y_k(t)-y_m(t))^2}$ – distance from the transmitting antenna to one of scatterers, $\lambda=c/f_0$ – wavelength. Similarly, we write channel transmission rate at time $t+\tau$: $\underline{h}_{nm}(t+\tau)=\frac{1}{\sqrt{N}}\sum_{k=1}^{N}\underline{B}_k(t+\tau)e^{i\theta_k}$. The Doppler frequency shift is determined by radial component of the moving object speed in the direction of the terrestrial antenna system, $f_{dk}=f_{\max}\cos\beta_k$ – the value of the Doppler shift for the k-th scatterer, $\cos\beta_k=\frac{(x_k-x_m)\cos\theta-(y_k-y_m)\sin\theta}{\sqrt{(x_k-x_m)^2+(y_k-y_m)^2}}$, $f_{\max}=Vf_0/c$ – the maximum Doppler frequency, V – the speed of moving object, $c=3\times10^8$ m/s – the speed of wave propagation. Phase shift θ_k, introduced by each scatterer, are independent and identically distributed random variables with uniform distribution law in the interval $[0,2\pi)$, and it is assumed to be constant when the calculation of channel coefficients. Attenuation of the signal amplitude when passing from the transmitter to the scatterer, from the scatterer to the receiver, and the reflection coefficient is not take into account when the calculation of the normalized correlation function.

The behavior of channel coefficients in time is important when estimating channel coefficients and capacity of MIMO data transmission system. In general, changes are specified correlation function of each of coefficients, which reflects the rate of change over time and especially changes of module and argument of complex channel coefficients:

$$\underline{K}_{nm}(t,\tau)=\mathbf{M}\{\underline{h}_{nm}(t)\underline{h}_{nm}^{*}(t+\tau)\}=$$
$$=\frac{1}{N}\sum_{k_1=1}^{N}\sum_{k_2=1}^{N}\underline{A}_{k_1}(t)\underline{B}_{k_2}^{*}(t+\tau)\mathbf{M}\{e^{j(\theta_{k_1}-\theta_{k_2})}\}.$$

Because phase shift introduced by each scatterer, are independent and identically distributed random variables with uniform distribution law in the interval $[0,2\pi)$, have the equality:

$$\underline{K}_{nm}(t,\tau)=\frac{1}{N}\sum_{k=1}^{N}\underline{A}_k(t)\underline{B}_k^{*}(t+\tau). \quad (1)$$

3 Development of Channel Coefficients Model And Filtering

Values of the MIMO communication system channel coefficients matrix correlation $\underline{K}_{nm}(t,\tau)$, $n=1,...,N_R$, $m=1,...,N_T$, obtained in accordance with (1). Figure 2 shows the dependence of channel coefficient correlation function at $m=n=1$, the radius of scatterer ring $R=50$ m, the sampling time interval $\Delta t=1$ µs, the number of scatterers $N=5000$, center frequency of transmitter $f_0=2{,}4$ GHz, the initial distance from the transmitting antenna to reception of the axes $S=1000$ m, $H=100$ m, the velocity of moving object $V=10...40$ m/s. This parameters are typical characteristics of moving objects for urban environment and indoor as well. Represent channel coefficients model in the form of a Markov sequence

$$\underline{\mathbf{H}}_k=\{\underline{H}_{ki}=\underline{h}_{nm}(k), i=(n-1)N_R+m\}\rightarrow\underline{\mathbf{x}}_k, k=1,2,... .$$

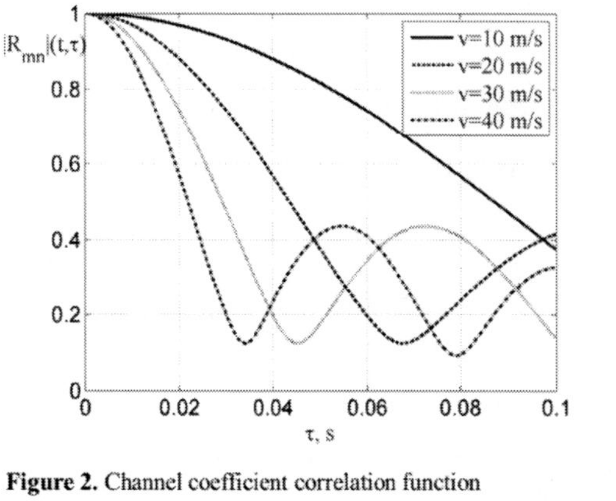

Figure 2. Channel coefficient correlation function

Given M correlation matrix values $\underline{\mathbf{K}}_j$, $j=0,...,M$, state vector of the dynamic system $\underline{\mathbf{x}}_k$, $k=1,2,..$, forming all channel coefficients. Dimension of channel coefficients vector is equal $L=N_TN_R$. We also believe that relocation of mobile object is insignificantly during the filtration interval, which suggests that channel coefficients are stationary. The state vector is formed by means of transformation of input sequence in the form of discrete uncorrelated noise $\underline{\mathbf{w}}_k$ with a diagonal intensities matrix $\mathbf{M}\{\underline{\mathbf{w}}_k \underline{\mathbf{w}}_k^{\mathrm{H}}\} = \mathbf{I}$:

$$\underline{\mathbf{x}}_{k+1} = \underline{\mathbf{A}}\underline{\mathbf{x}}_k + \underline{\mathbf{G}}\underline{\mathbf{w}}_k, \quad k = 1,2,..... \tag{2}$$

To ensure the independence of channel coefficients the size of discrete noise column vector $\underline{\mathbf{w}}_k$ is equal to the number of different channel coefficients $N_{TX}N_{RX}$. Submission process being evaluated in the form of (2) is widely used in optimal filtration theory [7-9].

Matrix of forming filter of size $L \times L$ can be calculated from measurements of correlation matrices with different delays into time [10,11]: $\underline{\mathbf{A}} = \left(\sum_{j=0}^{M-1} \underline{\mathbf{K}}_{j+1}\underline{\mathbf{K}}_j^{\mathrm{H}}\right) \times \left(\sum_{j=0}^{M-1} \underline{\mathbf{K}}_j \underline{\mathbf{K}}_j^{\mathrm{H}}\right)^{-1}$. Assuming a stationary random process matrix $\underline{\mathbf{G}}$ is solution of the following equation $\underline{\mathbf{K}}_0 = \underline{\mathbf{A}}\underline{\mathbf{K}}_0\underline{\mathbf{A}}^{\mathrm{H}} + \underline{\mathbf{G}}\underline{\mathbf{G}}^{\mathrm{H}}$ by Cholesky decomposition: $\underline{\mathbf{G}} = \mathrm{Chol}(\underline{\mathbf{K}}_0 - \underline{\mathbf{A}}\underline{\mathbf{K}}_0\underline{\mathbf{A}}^{\mathrm{H}})$. Thus completely determined stochastic differential equation (2), specifies time variation of channel coefficients.

Priory correlation matrix of stationary channel coefficients is equal [10] $\underline{\mathbf{K}}_j = \underline{\mathbf{A}}^j \underline{\mathbf{P}}$, where priory variances matrix determined from the linear algebraic equation:

$$\underline{\mathbf{P}} = \underline{\mathbf{A}}\underline{\mathbf{P}}\underline{\mathbf{A}}^{\mathrm{H}} + \underline{\mathbf{G}}\underline{\mathbf{Q}}\underline{\mathbf{G}}^{\mathrm{H}} = \underline{\mathbf{A}}\underline{\mathbf{P}}\underline{\mathbf{A}}^{\mathrm{H}} + \underline{\mathbf{G}}\underline{\mathbf{G}}^{\mathrm{H}}.$$

Single out the terms containing the matrix posteriori variances:

$$\underline{\mathbf{P}} - \underline{\mathbf{A}}\underline{\mathbf{P}}\underline{\mathbf{A}}^{\mathrm{H}} = \underline{\mathbf{M}}\underline{\mathbf{P}} = \left\{\underline{P}_{ij} - \sum_{k_1=1}^{L}\sum_{k_2=1}^{L} \underline{A}_{ik_2}\underline{P}_{k_2k_1}\underline{A}_{jk_1}, \; i,j = 1,...,L\right\}. \tag{3}$$

To solve this equation, it is advisable to introduce a matrices $\underline{\mathbf{P}}$, $\underline{\mathbf{A}}$ in vector form in rows:

$$\underline{\mathbf{P}}^{\mathrm{V}} = \{\underline{P}_k^{\mathrm{V}} = \underline{P}_{ij}, \; i,j = 1,...,L, \; k = j + (i-1)L\},$$

$$\underline{\mathbf{A}}^{\mathrm{V}} = \{\underline{A}_k^{\mathrm{V}} = \underline{P}_{ij}, \; i,j = 1,...,L, \; k = j + (i-1)L\}.$$

Represent equation (3) in a vectorized form: $\underline{\mathbf{M}}^{\mathrm{V}}\underline{\mathbf{P}}^{\mathrm{V}} = (\underline{\mathbf{G}}\underline{\mathbf{G}}^{\mathrm{H}})^{\mathrm{V}}$, where vectorized matrix is the Kronecker product $\underline{\mathbf{M}}^{\mathrm{V}} = \underline{\mathbf{A}} \otimes \underline{\mathbf{A}}^{\mathrm{H}}$. Solution vectorized equation is: $\underline{\mathbf{P}}^{\mathrm{V}} = (\mathbf{M}^{\mathrm{V}})^{-1}(\underline{\mathbf{G}}\underline{\mathbf{G}}^{\mathrm{T}})^{\mathrm{V}}$.

For optimal criterion of minimum mean squared error channel coefficients estimates used the method of Markov filtering of discrete random sequences [7-9], using developed dynamic model of channel coefficients in the form of a stochastic difference equation (2). The measured values $\underline{\mathbf{Y}}_k = \underline{\mathbf{H}}_k + \underline{\mathbf{E}}_k$ of channel coefficients at each discrete point in time contain measurement error $\underline{\mathbf{E}}_k$, which is assumed to be uncorrelated Gaussian random variable with correlation matrix $\mathbf{M}\{\underline{\mathbf{E}}_k\underline{\mathbf{E}}_k^{\mathrm{H}}\} = \underline{\mathbf{R}} = D_R\mathbf{I}$. Recursive filtering algorithm is given by [8]:

$$\hat{\underline{\mathbf{x}}}_k = \underline{\mathbf{A}}\hat{\underline{\mathbf{x}}}_{k-1} + \underline{\mathbf{K}}_k(\underline{\mathbf{Y}}_k - \underline{\mathbf{A}}\hat{\underline{\mathbf{x}}}_{k-1}), \tag{4}$$

where a posteriori variance of channel coefficients estimation determined by the difference equation:

$$\underline{\mathbf{V}}_k = (\mathbf{I} - \underline{\mathbf{K}})\tilde{\underline{\mathbf{V}}}_{k-1}, \; \tilde{\underline{\mathbf{V}}}_k = \underline{\mathbf{A}}\underline{\mathbf{V}}_{k-1}\underline{\mathbf{A}}^{\mathrm{H}} + \underline{\mathbf{G}}\underline{\mathbf{Q}}\underline{\mathbf{G}}^{\mathrm{H}}. \tag{5}$$

Expressions (4) and (5) compose optimal filtering algorithm, and matrix $\underline{\mathbf{V}}_k$ sets the channel coefficients posteriori dispersion, and its diagonal coefficients are estimation error variance.

4 Analysis of Channel Coefficients Estimating Errors

If channel coefficients are formed by difference equation (2), the channel coefficient estimation error variance determined by diagonal matrix elements $\underline{\mathbf{V}}_k$. Variances matrix of channel coefficient estimation errors can also be obtained by means of statistical modeling filtration equation (4) and averaging over N_S realizations:

$$\underline{\mathbf{D}}_{ps\_x} = \frac{1}{N_S}\sum_{k=1}^{N_S}(\underline{\mathbf{x}}_k - \hat{\underline{\mathbf{x}}}_k)(\underline{\mathbf{x}}_k - \hat{\underline{\mathbf{x}}}_k)^{\mathrm{H}}.$$

For more comprehensive taking into account the properties of channel coefficients can, it is necessary to use values $\underline{\mathbf{H}}$ for recording the measured values at discrete time $\underline{\mathbf{Y}}_k = \underline{\mathbf{H}}_k + \underline{\mathbf{E}}_k$, and equation (4) when the simulation. Matrix of posteriori variances

$$\underline{\mathbf{D}}_{ps\_H} = \frac{1}{N_S}\sum_{k=1}^{N_S}(\underline{\mathbf{H}}_k - \hat{\underline{\mathbf{H}}}_k)(\underline{\mathbf{H}}_k - \hat{\underline{\mathbf{H}}}_k)^{\mathrm{H}}.$$

is obtained by the simulation and it is more accurate than $\underline{\mathbf{D}}_{ps\_x}$, since more fully take into account the form of the correlation function (1).

When technical implementation of channel coefficients estimation algorithms (4) and (5) must perform a certain number of arithmetic operations in real time. This requires computing power of embedded processor: computing speed and amount of memory. Equations (5) can be solved in advance and results stored in memory, the volume of which is equal $L(L-1)/2$ complex words. To compute channel coefficients vector estimates (4) is necessary to make $L(2L+1)$ additions and $2L^2$ multiplications of complex words. Bit depth representation of result would provide a digital representation error is not more of optimal estimation error. Processor performance is determined by time of formation of a valid channel coefficients estimation, which for modern communication systems is 0.1...100 μs.

Considering the example of MIMO system with $N_{TX} = N_{RX} = 2$ and 8-core TMS320C6678 signal processor with 1 GHz clock speed, it can be shown that necessary computing time can be 68 ns. Comparing this time with time interval necessary to update channel coefficients (Figure 1), which is about 50 μs, we conclude that technical implementation of proposed algorithm is possible.

5 Conclusion

Investigated Markov model of MIMO data transmission system channel coefficients from mobile object, taking into account different conditions of radio waves propagation and reflections. Application of channel coefficients filtering algorithm provides potential estimation accuracy. However, for implementation of optimal estimation algorithm need to know correlation properties of channel coefficients that as shown in this work depend on specific practical situations. Computational costs for technical implementation of proposed channel coefficients estimating algorithm are realized with modern signal processors.

Research performed in part of grant of the Russian Scientific Foundation, project № 14-19-01263.

References

1. I. Emre Telatar. *Capacity of multi-antenna Gaussian channels*, European Transactions on Telecommunications, **vol. 10**, No 6, (1999), pp.585–595.
2. V.T. Ermolayev, A.G. Flaksman, I.P. Kovalyov, I.M. Averin. *Weight error loss in MIMO systems using eigenchannel technique*. Proceedings of the 1st International Conference on Antenna Theory and Techniques (ICATT'03), Sevastopol, Ukraine, (2003), pp. 333–336.
3. D.D.N Bevan., V.T. Ermolayev, A.G. Flaksman. *Analysis of weight error loss with a multichannel beamformer processor*. IEE Proceedings - Radar, Sonar and Navigation, (1998), **vol. 145**, No 1, pp. 63–72.
4. D.D.N Bevan., V.T.Ermolayev, A.G. Flaksman. *Coherent multichannel reception of binary modulated signals with dependent Rician fading*. IEE Proceedings Communications, (2001), **vol. 148**, No 2, pp. 105–111.
5. Yu.N.Parshin, V.I. Kudryashov. *Analysis of information transmission channel capacity from unmanned aerial vehicle with incorrect channel matrix*. Journal of Ryazan State Radio Engineering University, (2015), No 52, pp. 19–24.
6. M. Patzold, B. O. Hogstad. *A space-time channel simulator for MIMO channels based on the geometrical one-ring scattering model*. Wireless Communications and Mobile Computing. Special Issue on Multiple–Input Multiple–Output (MIMO) Communications, (2004), **vol. 4**, No 7, pp. 727–737.
7. M.S. Yarlykov. *Application of Markov nonlinear filtering theory in radio*. – M .: Sov. radio, (1980). – 360 p.
8. A.P.Sage, J.L. Melse. *Estimation Theory with Application to Communication and Control*. – N.–Y.: McGraw-Hill, (1972). – 496 p.
9. Yu.G. Sosulin. *Detection and Estimation Theory of Stochastic Signals*. – M.: Sov. radio, (1978). – 320 p.
10. R.I. Ivanovsky. *Theory of Probability and Mathematical Statistics. Basics, Practical Aspects with Examples and Problems in MathCad Environment*. – SPb: BHV–Petersburg, (2008) – 528 p.
11. Kuznetcov D.F. Numerical Simulation of Stochastic Differential Equations and Stochastic Integrals. – SPb .: Science, 1999. – 458 p.

MATEC Web of Conferences **76**, 03008 (2016) DOI: 10.1051/matecconf/20167603008
CSCC 2016

High throughput satellites in 5G and MIMO interference limited communications

Ana Pérez-Neria[1,2,a], Miguel A. Lagunas[1,2] and Miguel A. Vázquez[1]

[1]*CTTC, Centre Tecnològic de Telecomunicacions de Catalunya, 08860 Castelldefels, Spain*
[2]*UPC, Universitat Politècnica de Catalunya, 08034 Barcelona, Spain*

Abstract. Classically, thermal noise has been the workhorse of satellite communications due to the long distances to be covered between the satellite and the user terminal (UT). Lately, LDPC (Low-Density Parity-Check) codes allow the noise threshold to be set very close to the Shannon limit for the memory-less satellite channel; thus, solving the noise problem that turbo codes were not able to solve. However, recently, the high target rates in next generation 5G wireless terrestrial system are pushing the required spectral efficiency in Satellite Communications; therefore, shifting the SatCom paradigm towards an interference limited one. This paper revisits the 5G scene and the role of next generation satellite communications, with a special focus on high throughput satellites (HTS) together with the future accompanying MIMO interference mitigation techniques.

1 Introduction

5G is conceived as a composition of: i) enhanced mobile broadband; ii) ultra-reliable and low latency communications; iii) massive machine type communications [1]. However and more importantly it is seen as a new infrastructure that will bring a new unique network and service capability to provide an order of magnitude improvement in different key performance indicators. While too much focus has been set so far in urban scenarios, the 5G ecosystem should continue to adapt their mobile use cases and deployments. Emerging use cases that have been identified are: rural infrastructure, high bandwidth because of many users, but low bandwidth to each one, broadband mobile connectivity. The satellite component can have many things to say in the use cases aiming at helping to bridge the digital divide in parts unreachable by terrestrial, whilst optimizing the value for money to the end-users [2-3]. Ubiquitous coverage, together with resilient overlay communications and disaster relief are the three main assets that satellite can complement terrestrial communications.

Satellite orbits can be classified mainly into three main types: Geostationary (GEO) orbits (36.000 km above the equator), Medium earth orbits (from 6000 to 25000 km altitude) and Low earth orbits (<1500 km altitude). Whenever these orbits are combined, hybrid orbits arise. Concerning the services they provide, Fixed Satellite Services (FSS) operate at C band (3-6 GHz), whenever extreme wide coverage and/or resilience to bad weather conditions are needed. This band was the first to be used and currently FSS are moving to Ku band (12-18 GHz) and Ka band (26.5-40 GHz), mainly to provide backhauling services to terrestrial operators. Mobile Satellite Service (MSS) operate primarily in L band (1-2 GHz) and S band (2-4 GHz). They offer services to both handheld and vehicle mounted terminals as well as some fixed terminals. In the past the air interfaces and networks have been mainly proprietary (e.g. BEGAN for MSS) and recently satellite systems have adopted standards within the DVB-S, ETSI and ITU. Either in FSS or in MSS, the supported services by SatCom are not limited to basic data speeds (with a 5G target of up to 1Gbps in average per user for mobile broadband) and voice services, but also for machine type communications, broadcast and narrow band services (up to 100 Kbps per user in machine type communications).

So far, the major business and focus are: FSS-DTH (Direct To Home) for new High Definition (HD), Ultra HD, 3D TV. Another important market is IP trunking to connect parts of the backbone, either for internet or for VoIP, at 310 Mbps. Residential broadband is another important data communication application with 2.20 Mbps for the end user that are evolving towards higher rates. Cellular backhauling for connecting cellular radio towers to the core network are currently working at 2 Mbps and, finally, corporate and public VSAT for connecting a site to the IT network of a private or public organization. These applications are carried out through GEO satellites and, while C-band use keeps flat in forthcoming years, Ku and Ka band use increases.

When talking about non-GEO constellations, there are existing LEO constellations that target lower capacity global services. Also, new Mega-constellations are being developed (e.g. OneWeb (640), LeoSat (80-100), SpacEx (4000), Samsung (4600), SSI (80), etc.) and foresee to

[a] Corresponding author: ana.perez@cttc.es

reach by 2020 a Global market with high capacity and low latency services.

Figure 1 sketches a satellite communication system. The Forward Link supports communications from a Gateway (GW) to the Users. The Return Link supports the communications from the Users to the GW. The main features with respect to a terrestrial system are: i) long propagation delay (i.e. 500 ms from ground station to the satellite and back, known as Round Trip Delay); ii) Doppler effects are relevant for LEO and MEO constellations (i.e. 200KHz for high speed UEs). Whenever a hybrid terrestrial/satellite system is the target, new interfaces should accommodate these features to the baseline terrestrial system. In fact, more than a mere relay, the satellite should be an integral part of the network [4].

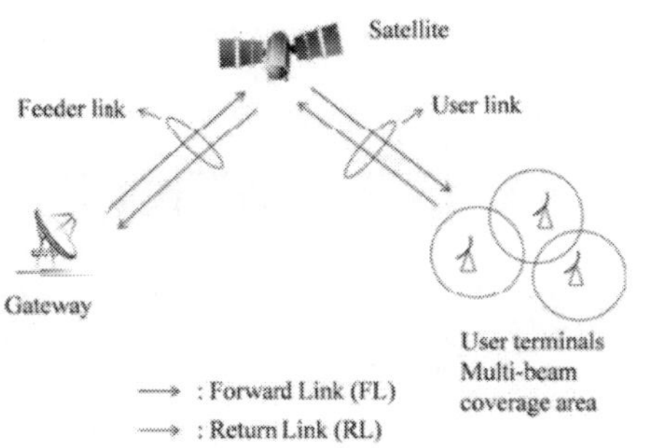

Figure 1. Satellite system.

A possible classification of the satellites focuses on their beam topology, namely: number of beams, radius of each beam and flexibility when configuring the beams. High Throughput Satellites (HTS) are considered the next generation of GEO satellites [5-6], which split the service area into a multi-spot service area to exploit a high order of frequency reuse and use the ensuing satellite antenna gain to deliver more capacity for given satellite resource. HTS systems can be classified by the capacity they provide. The 1st generation offered an aggregate capacity of up to a few 10's of Gbit/s. The 2nd generation, led by Ka-Satellites, offers approx. 100Gbit/s. To satisfy the technology agnostic consumer, the system must deliver services comparable to fiber-to-the-home and 3rd generation HTS systems will go a step further and offer a few hundred Gbit/s. Because of its broadband nature and potential to lower the cost per bit, HTS is a potential wild card to help in attaining many of the 5G network requirements.

2 High Throughput Satellites

The most valuable asset in any given orbital location is spectrum. High throughput satellites employ multiple spot beams to enable "frequency re-use". This is achieved typically with 4 color re-use (two frequency slots and two polarizations) and high gain spot beams. Whilst GEO-HTS multi-spot/beam satellite configurations can be applied to Ku and C frequency bands, such systems are particularly applicable to the Ka frequency band, which allows: better use of the reflector aperture size, very small beam sizes of increased gain with high roll-off to neighboring beams and benefit from smaller and lighter feed technologies that enable accommodation of tightly packed beams. Currently they have around 100 beams and provide an aggregate rate of 100 Gbps at Ka band. Higher gains allow for improvements to spectrum efficiency via higher order coding and modulation (16APSK vs 8SPK for example). Future GEO-HTS systems will use exclusive and shared Ka-bands [4], flexible power distribution, dynamic beamforming, beam hopping, etc…

In HTS, user service areas are typically located over a large region and therefore a large number of cells are required. Frequency Reuse (FR) is applied such that the same frequency on a given polarization is reused several times. This is achieved through separation of the cells to control the intra-system interference. This is achieved typically with 4 color re-use (two frequency slots and two polarizations) and high gain spot beams. Figure 2 shows an example of HTS Europe coverage. For HTS systems, in order to provide good performance, the antenna should have high gains with steep roll-offs and low side lobes that result in good C/I. The figure plots only the footprints of each beam. Active antennae's could help in the efficient use of spacecraft power.

The feeder link (see Figure 1) is considered ideal in terms of Signal to Noise Ratio (SNR) and it is only bandwidth limited. The user link is limited by the additive noise, in terms of SNR, and by the generated interference, in terms of Signal to Interference Ratio (SIR). Therefore its link budget determines the performance. In each beam/color, the downlink user signal is typically a time multiplex signal e.g. DVB-S2 such that at the satellite level, this can be considered as a single continuous signal from fixed angular offsets. Assuming infinite lattice of 4 color reuse, Figure 3 shows that each cell has 6 first order neighbors of the same color. With the signal structure this implies that interference for a given location in the wanted center cell is static. The performance is a function of the location of the terminal in the cell and is further degraded by the repeater C/I effects and the inter-spot interference.

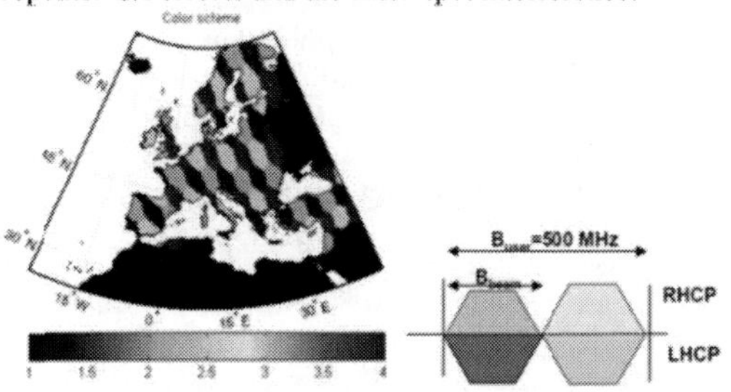

Figure 2. HTS applied to a European coverage with 500 MHz user bandwidth divided in 4 colours. Each color is up to 250MHz on one polarization.

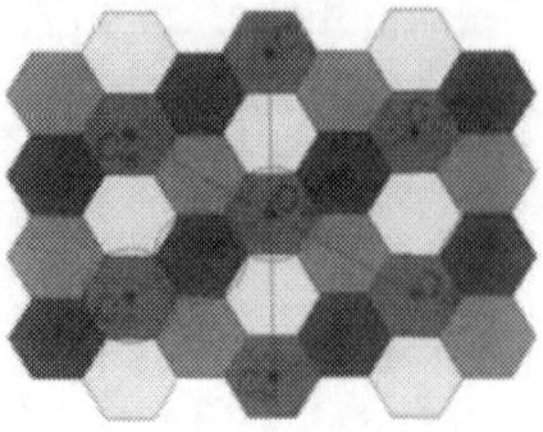

Figure 3. First order cluster of interfering cells with FR=4.

In order to increase capacity, next HTS systems are considering more aggressive frequency reuse (i.e. the target is reuse 1 or 2); thus, increasing interference. In other words, in order to make full use of diversity schemes, orthogonality is not imposed anymore. This fact urges the need for advanced interference management techniques that enable the satellite system to work in an interference limited scenario, rather than in a noise limited one. New LDPC codes allow to approach the theoretical Shannon limit (DVB-S2, S2X, RCS2, …), but are not able to properly handle interference on its own. Before getting into the study of PHY layer alternatives to manage interference, we devote the rest of this section to revisit one of the major features of HTS, which is its ability to have flexible payloads. This aspect is considered key in order to have higher throughput per satellite. Tremendous evolution in HTS payload capabilities is foreseen: in 2003 typical systems offered 2-4 Gbps, while in 2016, 1000 Gbps are proposed.

In order to lower the cost per bps, the key aspect in multi beam HTS is its flexibility to control the peak rate per spot beam while guaranteeing an average rate within the service area and minimum rate at the edges. In order words, HTS takes advantage of hot and cold spots. The capacity depends on many system choices: antenna size, technology, network dimensioning … The traffic profile is highly time and region dependent; thus, traffic peaks are not geographically synchronous. For instance, while with one wide footprint a peak rate of 54 Mbps and a maximum of 5475 users can be reached. With 8 beams covering the same area, the attained sum peak rate can be 123 Mbps. Traffic peaks also present a daily repetition. Namely, the flexibility introduced by HTS helps counteract the regional peak demands per beam. Concerning the cost, a possible approach here is to leverage on the traffic statistics for reducing the DC Power consumption and to reflect this on the price to be paid by the user. We note that broadcast bent-pipe payload architectures do not have this need or problem.

Payload flexibility techniques are relatively well-used in the current generation of HTS systems in order to: i) reconfigure the bandwidth allocation per beam (i.e. thanks to digital or analogue on-board switching and filtering); ii) reconfigure the power allocation with the user of Flex amplifiers. In future systems, beam hopping will be possible in order to jointly allocate time, power and bandwidth to each beam. Also, flexible beam coverage is foreseen.

Additional payload flexibility requires On Board Processing (OBP) in order to regenerate the signal and to carry out beamforming at the satellite. The goal is to have further SNR and SIR gains. However, OBP has a cost and a trade-off with other system and business case aspects needs to be done to justify that cost factor.

Beam hopping is one of the most popular actual alternatives in order to confer flexibility to the system. It means: time sharing according to a beam hopping pattern. In other words, at any given time, only a subset of beams is illuminated. The illumination time of any beam can be changed according to the traffic request of that beam. In addition, power and bandwidth can be flexibly allocated. The constraint is that the total illumination time of the set of beams served by a High Power Amplifier (HPA) has to stay constant. Therefore, the flexibility of throughput is within the set of beams illuminated by the same HPA. There is a total number of time slots that that can be assigned to the beams connected by the same switch. The minimum slot duration depends on the minimum switching time and defines the minimum capacity granularity of the network. By assigning different time slots to different beams the capacity per beam is adjusted. Figure 4 depicts an example of time and beam assignment for beam hopping within 6 time slots.

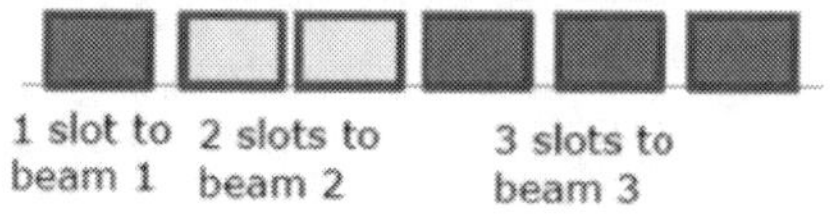

Figure 4. Time and beam assignment for beam hopping within 6 time slots.

The capacity values of a beam hopping and a frequency division multiplex are the same if the number of beams, HPAs and user bandwidth, are identical. However, such two systems would correspond to a different overall payload mass, resulting heavier the frequency division multiplex.

When selecting appropriate technologies and architectures for flexible HTS payloads the network architecture and its resulting impacts to geographical connectivity need to be considered. Currently, new Mesh or Open Architectures are being researched by payload manufacturers in order to get advantages over the classical Star or Closed Architectures. In mesh or Open Architectures:

- Satellite Capacity (MHz) and Uplink access are provided.
- The User is responsible for network definition and operations.
- Payload / Repeater need to provide geographical connectivity implying a mesh connectivity matrix
- Digital payload or beam hopping adds value to manage complex connectivity.

In contrast, when using the satellite within a star architecture conception:

- The operator defines the network and sells end to end service based on Mbps
- The access to the network is through operator gateways

- Payload / Repeater is typically a star network with well-defined gateway to user beam paths

Therefore, connectivity matrices between any uplink channel and any downlink beam, as shown in Figure 5, can become major payload design drives as the number of beams in an HTS system increases.

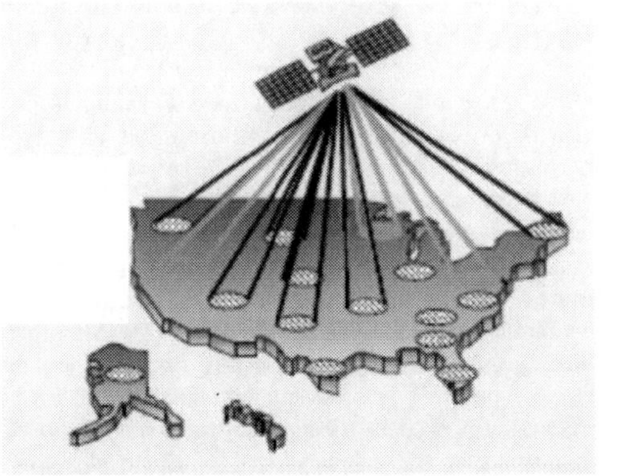

Figure 5. The satellite in a Mesh architecture

Digital processing capabilities at the satellite are desirable to have full flexibility. Topics of current research are: channelization and connectivity, digital on board beamforming, low consumption DAC and ADC, optimization of input gain and dynamic range (i.e. trade-off between noise figure and dynamic range), currently there is a total signal power limit of -8dBm/500MHz and gain must be sufficient to map small carriers above port quantization noise floor. Finally, the radio frequency payload performance to manage has to be analyzed as there are multiple additional potential degradations to payload Es/No to manage, such as: Phase Noise, Frequency Stability impacts for narrow band channelization, Gain frequency response & Group Delay, Clock Jitter, Alias Band Folding. It is important to understand the relative impact of these in order to optimize the balance between payload performance and equipment cost.

In short, HTS and flexible payloads open a variety of topics to explore. Section 4 summarizes those that are related to signal processing. Before that, next Section 3 focuses on those signal processing techniques that are being researched in order to manage interference. HTS stresses the spectrum usage in order to reduce costs; thus, changing the noise limited paradigm of satellite communications into interference limited.

3 Interference Mitigation Techniques: MIMO processing

HTS and multi-beam satellites in general will change the TV distribution business in coming years, among others. One aspect of HTS that has been mentioned in the previous section is the introduction of greater amounts of radio frequency interference, primarily through frequency reuse with multiple spot beams on the same frequency [7]. As a result, beam to beam interference becomes the limiting factor. This fact translates the paradigm of satellite communications as noise limited ones into interference-limited communications; thus, attracting more research efforts towards these systems.

There are various means by which interference can be managed. In this section we focus on those situations where the satellite communication can be modelled as a Multiple Input Multiple Output (MIMO) system [8-12]. Thus, multiple signals coexist geographically in time and in frequency. The goal is first to set up the capacity bounds that are benchmarking the system. Next, an overview of the signal processing techniques that solve the interference problem come. The radio resource management that should be considered to optimize the usage of code, power, bandwidth and beams in a dynamic way is out of the scope of this paper and interesting techniques can be found in [13]. This section compiles these different aspects with the aim to help in future research.

3.1 System model

Let us assume that at a given time instant and frequency bean, K signals, $s_i, i = 1 \dots K$, are to be simultaneously transmitted through different physical channels. The K received signals are $x_i, i = 1 \dots K$. The base-band transmission can be modelled as

$$\boldsymbol{x} = \boldsymbol{H}\boldsymbol{B}\boldsymbol{s} + \boldsymbol{w} \qquad (1)$$

where $\boldsymbol{x}$ and $\boldsymbol{s}$ are complex vectors that contain the received and transmitted signals respectively. Vector $\boldsymbol{w}$ contains thermal noise samples of Gaussian distribution with zero mean and variance equal to N_o Watts. The elements of matrix $\boldsymbol{H}$ are $h_{ij}, i, j = 1 \dots K$, and model de equivalent channel gains that affect the transmission of symbol s_j when it is received by therminal i. These gains are random variables, whose statistics depend on the specific situation that they are modelling. If matrix $\boldsymbol{H}$ is not diagonal, each terminal i will not only receive its intended signal s_i, but also interference from the others. The role of matrix $\boldsymbol{B}$ is to counteract this interference and its design is the focus of study of MIMO precoding techniques.

Depending on the system architecture and constraints that (1) is modelling, additional MIMO processing has to be carried out at reception on signal $\boldsymbol{x}$. Finally, if (1) faces a multiuser system, scheduling techniques should be designed in order to select the most suitable set of K users out of a bigger set of N possible users. Model (1) is a time and frequency snapshot, therefore it only contains a spatial model as bandwidth or time allocations are out of the scope of the present review.

First, it is of interest to analyze when model (1) is suitable for a satellite transmission. In this respect, there were initial studies promoted by the European Space Agency with this purpose [8-9]. The conclusion is that direct application of MIMO to satellite in a single-user scenario is rather limited due to: i) strong LOS component and ii) absence of rich scattering environment. Therefore, the resulting MIMO channel $\boldsymbol{H}$ is rank deficient and the optimal design is to transmit a single stream and use beamforming in order to point to the desired user. In other words, there is not MIMO processing as such. MIMO processing is needed only in situations where there is significant movement and multipath appears. One example is GEO maritime transmission [14].

Still, if either the Multi Beam dimension, or the Multi Satellite dimension, or the Multiple Gateway dimension, or even the Hybrid satellite-Terrestrial networks are considered, MIMO processing is needed. All these situations use to be multiuser communications instead of single user ones.

Before getting into the MIMO processing techniques, next some capacity bounds from (1) are considered [15].

3.2 MIMO Capacity

Whenever model (1) can be applied, if the spatial degrees of freedom are properly used, there is additional capacity per Hz and second. In a scenario with N total users and K possible simultaneous transmissions (i.e. K transmitters and K receivers), if the transmitter has all the channel state information (CSIT) and so the receiver does (CSIR), the maximum attained spectral efficiency is

$$C_{SNR\to\infty} = min(N,K)\log(SNR) \quad (2)$$

$$C_{N\to\infty} = K\log\log(NK) \quad (3)$$

Whereas, if only CSIR is availble, the maximum spectral efficiency is

$$C_{SNR\to\infty} = N\log(SNR) \quad (4)$$

$$C_{N\to\infty} = 0 \quad (5)$$

In expressions (3) and (5) the total number of users tends to infinite in order to highlight the so-called multiuser diversity gain: whenever the set of users that require transmission is high, there is an inherent system gain, even though the system can only set transmission with one user at a time. Note that there is no multiuser capacity gain if only CSIR is available (i.e. (5) is zero).

Next section gets into the signal processing techniques that are required to approach the mentioned bounds. As the goal is to study the multiple beam scenarios, which is a multiuser scenario, next section focuses on this multiple user case.

3.3 MIMO multiuser in multi-beam satellite

As it has been previously commented, in order to increase capacity, next HTS systems are considering more aggressive frequency reuse (i.e. the target is reuse 1 or 2); thus, increasing interference.

3.3.1 On ground processing for MIMO precoding

Let us consider frequency reuse 1 with the simplest satellite system configuration when only one gateway is serving K users (as Figure 1 depicts). With frequency reuse 1, the GW aims to serve simultaneously K users, all of them sharing the same 500 MHz band, and different information is to be conveyed to each user (so-called unicast transmission). The specific model for $\boldsymbol{H}$ can be found in [9]. In this situation MIMO processing can be done in the forward link at the transmitter in order to diminish the interference with a suitable design of matrix $\boldsymbol{B}$ in (1). If full CSIT is available, linear processing techniques such as Zero-Forcing or its regularized version: the MMSE (Minimum Mean Square Error) precoding can be implemented [16]

$$\boldsymbol{B}_{ZF} = G_{ZF}\boldsymbol{H}^H(\boldsymbol{H}\boldsymbol{H}^H)^{-1} \quad (6)$$

$$\boldsymbol{B}_{MMSE} = G_{MMSE}\boldsymbol{H}^H(\alpha\boldsymbol{I} + \boldsymbol{H}\boldsymbol{H}^H)^{-1} \quad (7)$$

If more complex processing is allowed, non-linear precoding alternatives can be applied in order to attain a performance close to the bounds in (2) and (3). If only partial channel state information is available at the transmitter, opportunistic beamforming is another very interesting alternative [17]. Figure 6 depicts the total average throughput that is obtained with these precoding techniques and compares them with the frequency reuse 4 scenario that serves as a reference. Note that precoding improves performance both in terms of throughput and availability, especially with the linear MMSE precoder. An important aspect is that in this scenario the satellite behaves just as a transparent payload; thus no on board processing is needed. All the pre-processing is carried out on ground, at the gateway. In [16] the reader can find further studies on how to cope with: imperfect CSIT, fairness, availability and bigger number of feeds at the satellite than K users to simultaneously transmit. Current challenges are to match these designs with the DVB S2x frame, where all simultaneous users should use the same spatial precoder instead of the K different ones that are encompassed in equations (6) and (7). In other words, the design should be multicast instead of unicast and the same precoder must fulfill different Quality of Service at the same time [18-19].

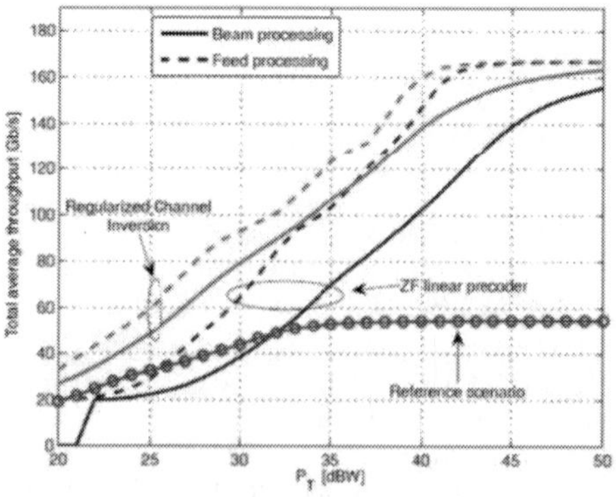

Figure 6. GEO satellite for FSS. Total average throughput in a 500 MHz system with frequency reuse 1 and MIMO precoding on ground. Results are compared with a frequency reuse 4 reference system.

The more users can be served in the user link, the higher the capacity should be in the feeder link. This fact is currently motivating research in two directions: go up to Q/V and optical bands in the feeder link or, use multiple gateways to give service to the same number of beams. This later topic triggers further research on MIMO processing because a proper cooperation and channel information exchange has to be designed to make the system practicable [20].

3.3.2 Multiuser decoding at the user terminal

In the previous section, the transmitter was in charge of pre-cancelling the interference; therefore, all the processing complexity remained at the gateway. Another alternative is to increase the complexity of the user terminal, which will carry out multiuser decoding in order to eliminate interference. In other words, whenever the user terminal receives its desired signal contaminated by interferences that operate in the same frequency band one alternative is to demodulate them so that they can be properly subtracted from the incoming signal (i.e. the so-called Sequential Interference Canceller or SIC). In this way, the desired stream can be recovered finally clean from interference. The stronger the interference, the better it can be cancelled with this strategy. Next we consider single antenna user terminals (UTs), techniques with array processing at the UT are also possible at the cost of increasing complexity [21].

Let us consider, for instance, a frequency reuse 2, such as in Figure 7, which shows the footprints of a multi-beam satellite over European coverage in this case.

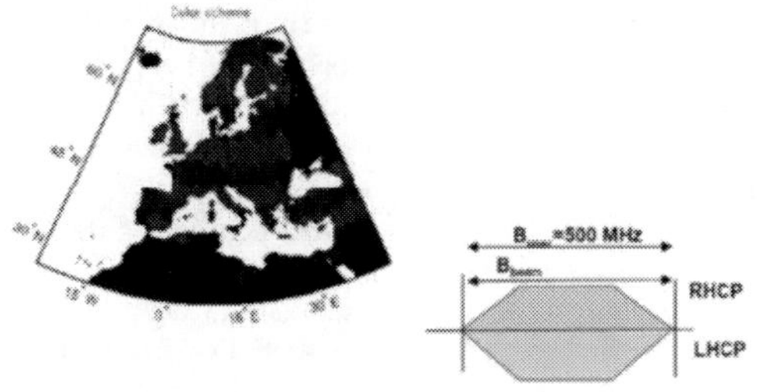

Figure 7. HTS applied to a European coverage with 500 MHz user bandwidth divided in 2 colours. Each color is up to 500MHz on one polarization.

In this situation multiple beams serve simultaneously overlapped areas. Depending on the position of the user within each beam coverage area, the level of interference will vary. Figure 8 plots the distribution of possible $\frac{C}{I_1}$.

Table 1. Interference levels up to the 6th tear for FR=2,4.

	Reference	Int. 1	Int. 2	Int. 3	Int. 4	Int. 5
FR=2	P	$\frac{C}{I_1}$ = 6dB	$\frac{C}{I_2}$ = 27dB	$\frac{C}{I_3}$ = 26dB	$\frac{C}{I_4}$ = 27dB	$\frac{C}{I_5}$ = 30dB
FR=4	P	$\frac{C}{I_1}$ = 22dB	$\frac{C}{I_2}$ = 22dB	$\frac{C}{I_3}$ = 22dB	$\frac{C}{I_4}$ = 22dB	$\frac{C}{I_5}$ = 22dB

Users located in the intersection of beams can benefit from multi-user detection together with scheduling techniques to boost capacity.

In the implementation of the multiuser decoding the modulation and coding of the desired signal and that of the interference matters in practice. Figure 9 and 10 show the different performance that can be obtained [22-24]. Therefore, multiuser detection has to be carried out together with joint adaptive modulation. In order to allow a practical user scheduler, one possible strategy is to to use both signals (transmitted from two co-channel beams) to carry useful information for the considered user. Then, both transponders (beam 1 and beam 2) are used to serve one user at a time. Figure 11 shows that with this joint detection and scheduling strategy capacity increases with respect to the frequency reuse 4 baseline scenario.

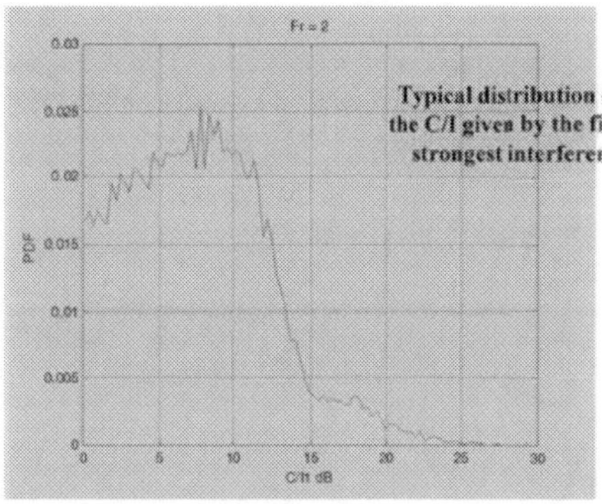

Figure 8. Probability Density Function of the Carrier to main Interference Ratio ($\frac{C}{I_1}$) with frequency reuse 2.

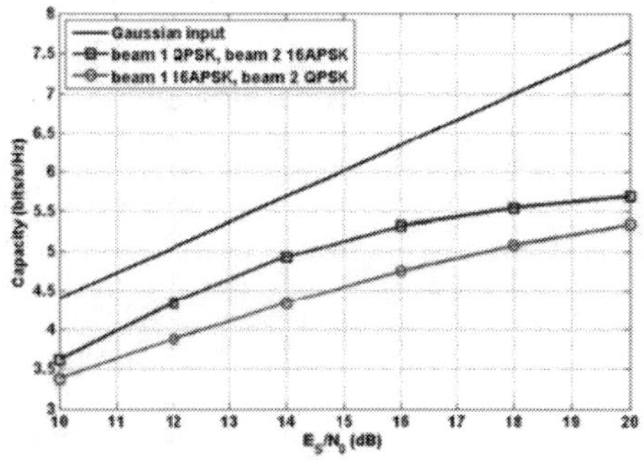

Figure 9. Capacity for user in beam 1 when beam 2 reuses the frequency and acts as an interference with ($\frac{C}{I_1}$)=0 dB.

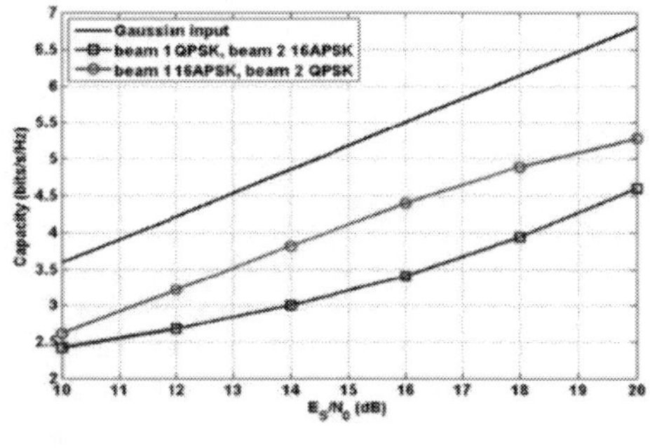

Figure 10. Capacity for user in beam 1 when beam 2 reuses the frequency and acts as an interference with ($\frac{C}{I_1}$)=10 dB.

3.3.3 Joint transmit and receive MIMO processing

In the forward link of a multi-beam satellite networks we have differentiated so far between techniques employed at the transmitter (gateway, GW) and techniques employed at the receiver (UT). If the goal is to attain rate performance close to the capacity bounds, the system should take advantage of both and carry out a joint precoding/detection design: i) the scheduler considers the possibility of superposition coding or joint ACM among the different beams; ii) the precoder uses power control and the interference rejection capabilities of the receivers. This is a matter of future research.

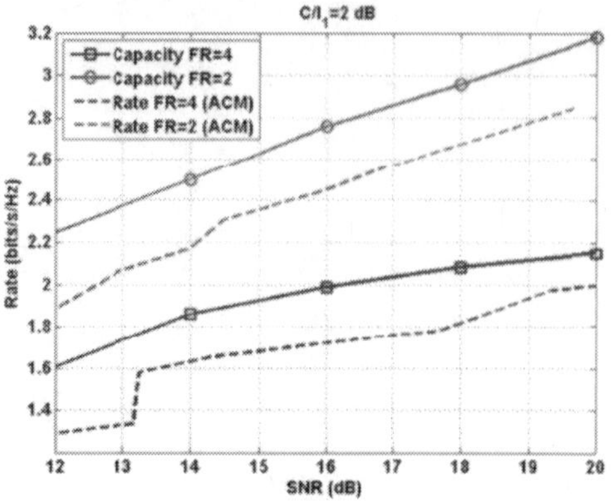

Figure 11. Aggregate capacity and rate for FR=2 with joint multiuser decoding and scheduling. In the FR=4 scenario the detection is single user.

4 Signal Processing Challenges

Next Generation wireless terrestrial networks will not provide ubiquitous communications. In contrast, satellite networks provide coverage, disaster relief and resilience and therefore, both networks are complementary. The novelty and challenges are [25] : 1) New network architectures and constellations, LEO, MEO; 2) Aeronautical and Professional Link Designs for Satellite Systems at Extremely High Frequency Bands; 3) Seamless services over hybrid terrestrial-satellite networks; 4) Optical free-space communications, 5) On-board signal processing and 6) Multiple Gateway architectures.

In each of the challenges that have been identified novel tailored solutions for the satellite segment have to be studied. If we focus now on the physical layer aspects and the associated signal processing problems,

- concerning the integration of terrestrial and satellite systems in future 5G networks, there are different aspects to be considered from a waveform perspective because frequency assignments range from 300 MHz up to 100 GHz and both, Single- and multi-carrier solutions have to be studied, together with
- Licensed/shared/unlicensed spectrum access.
- As in the wireless arena, not only orthogonal but also non-orthogonal multiple access can be useful to increase the spectral efficiency; thus, creating the need for interference management techniques.
- There are also several impairments in a satellite channel to be dealt with: phase noise, non-linearities, on-board filtering.

We talk about tailored solutions because it has to be studied: i) how do the proposed air interface(s) performs in the presence of typical satellite channel impairments and ii) how do the proposed countermeasures devised for terrestrial channel impairment fit satellite architectures. In this latter issue, note that satellite communications present, not only a different channel, when compared to the wireless terrestrial one, but also, as it has been commented along the text, there are some specificities such as:

- long round trip delay (that can be overcome by addressing the proper service and cache management);
- satellite high power amplifiers (HPAs) effects on the signal;
- Limited on-board power, mass and accommodation yields to limitation in terms of HPAs, when dealing with high-frequency re-use and precoding;
- frame structure that encompasses many users under the same channel code in order to properly combat noise (that forces many times a multicast configuration rather than a unicast one);
- GW scheduler strategies modification to be in line with precoding techniques;
- geographical and time traffic variations that are different from the terrestrial only communications (e.g. a satellite can serve geographical areas that are in different time-slots and with complementary traffic needs);
- trade-offs between capacity, availability and fairness requirements that become more relevant than in the terrestrial arena;
- channel variations that depend not only on the user terminal, but also on the satellite orbit and can range from very slow ones for GEO satellites and FSS to high Doppler with LEO satellites;
- synchronization and time recovery issues different from the wireless terrestrial segment for channel estimation and interference cancellation;
- on-ground and on-board complexity considerations.

Finally, and in addition to the mentioned aspect, if TeraHertz communications are targeted, Very HTS are around the corner and will bring new situations to be solved in order to properly work in Q/V band (40/50 GHz), W band (70/80 GHz) and optical bands, with photonics optimized payload mass [26].

Acknowledgements

This work has been developed within the network of Experts SATNEX IV (http://www.satnex4.org/) that is supported by the European Space Agency. This work has also received funding by the Spanish Ministry of Economy and Competitiveness (Ministerio de Economia y Competitividad) under project TEC2014-59255-C3-1-R (ELISA); and from the Catalan Government (2014SGR1567).

References

1. 5GPPP Association, *5G Vision Brochure*, www.5g-ppp.eu, (2015)
2. NetWorld2020's-SatCom WG, *The role of satellites in 5G*, http://www.networld2020.eu (2014)

3. NGMN Alliance, NGMN White Paper, www.ngmn.org/ (2015)
4. www.sansa-h2020.eu/
5. Y. Vasavada, R. Gopal, C. Ravishankar, G. Zakaria and N. BenAmmar, *Architectures for next generation high throughput satellite systems*, International Journal of Satellite Communications and Networking (2016)
6. P. M. French, *High Throughput Satellites (HTS) are pushing open the satellite market door*, guest column Near Earth LLC. (2012).
7. T. Glynn et al, *Multi-beam satellite communications system*, US patent 20040166801 A1 (2004)
8. G. Gallinaro, G. Caire, M. Debbah, L. Cottatellucci, R. Muller, R. Rinaldo, *Perspectives of adopting interference mitigation techniques in the context of broadband multimedia satellite systems*, in *Proc. 23rd AIAA Int. Commun. Satell. Syst. Conf.*, ICSSC (2005).
9. N. Zorba, M. Realp, A. Perez-Neira, *An improved partial CSIT random beamforming for multibeam satellite systems, in* Proc. 2008 10th International Workshop on Signal Processing for Space Communications (2008).
10. A. Perez-Neira, C. Ibars, A, del Coso, M. Caus, *MIMO channel modeling and transmission techniques for multi-satellite and hybrid satellite-terrestrial mobile networks*, Physical Communication **4** (2011) 127–139, Elsevier (www.elsevier.com/locate/phycom)
11. K. P. Liolis, J. Gómez-Vilardebó, E. Casini, A. Pérez-Neira, *Statistical Modeling of MIMO Land Mobile Satellite Channels*, IEEE Trans. on Comm., vol. **58**, issue 11 (2010)
12. D. Pantelis et al., *MIMO over Satellite: A Review*, IEEE Communications Surveys & Tutorials, Volume:**13** , Issue: 1, (2011)
13. *Digital Satellite Communications*, ed. By G. Corazza, Springer (2007)
14. P. Henarejos, A. I. Pérez Neira, *Dual Polarized Modulation and Reception for Next Generation Mobile Satellite Communications*, IEEE Transactions on Communications (Volume:**63** , Issue: 10) (2015)
15. M.A. Lagunas, A. Pérez-Neira, *MIMO processing*, class notes at http://www.cttc.es/research-development/training/graduate-and-undergraduate-lectures/
16. J. Arnau, B. Devillers, C. Mosquera, A. Pérez-Neira, *Performance study of multiuser interference mitigation schemes for hybrid broadband multibeam satellite architectures*, EURASIP Journal on Wireless Communications and Networking (2012)
17. N. Zorba Barah, M. Realp Campalans, A. Perez-Neira, *Beamforming technique for broadband satellite communications*, US8310980 B2 patent (2012)
18. N. Zorba, A. Pérez-Neira, *Performance Evaluation of MIMO Multiuser Opportunistic Schemes under QoS requirements*, in 4G Mobile & Wireless Communications Technologies, River Publishers, Aalborg, Denmark (2008) ISBN 978-8792329028.
19. D. Christopoulos, S. Chatzinotas, G. Taricco, M. Á. Vázquez, A. I. Pérez-Neira, P. Arapoglou, A. Ginesi, *Multibeam joint precoding: Frame-based design*, Chapter in Cooperative and Cognitive Satellite Systems", edited by Symeon Chatzinotas, Bjorn Ottersten, Riccardo De Gaudenzi, published by Elsevier. **11** (2015). ISBN: 978-0-12-799948-7.
20. V.Joroughi, M. Á. Vázquez, A. I. Pérez-Neira, *Multiple Gateway Precoding with Per Feed Power Constraints for Multibeam Satellite Systems* , in *Proceedings of European Wireless 2014* (EW'14), 14-16 May 2014, Barcelona (Spain).
21. J. Grotz, *Interference Mitigation and Synchronization for Satellite Communications*, PhD Thesis (2008)
22. M. Caus, A. I. Pérez-Neira, M. Angelone, A. Ginesi, *An innovative interference mitigation approach for high throughput satellite systems, Proc. IEEE International Workshop on Signal Processing Advances in Wireless Communications*, SPAWC (2015).
23. G. Cocco, M. Angelone, A. I. Perez-Neira, *Co-channel interference cancellation at the user terminal in multibeam satellite systems*, in *Proc. 7th Advanced Satellite Multimedia Systems Conference and the 13th Signal Processing for Space Communications Workshop (ASMS/SPSC)*, (2014), pp. 43–50.
24. M. Angelone, A. Ginesi, M. Caus, A. I. Perez-Neira, J. Ebert, *System Performance of an advanced multi-user detection technique for high throughput satellite systems, Proc. 21st Ka band and broadband communication conference* (2015).
25. EURASIP, *Position Paper on Signal Processing Challenges for Communications beyond 5G*, Joint Expert Group and 5G Vision Working Group Workshop, Bologna 16 April (2016)
26. O. Vidal et al., *Next Generation High Throughput Satellite System based on Optical Feeder Links, Proceedings of the Ka and Broadband Communications, Navigation and Earth Observation Conference* (2015)

MATEC Web of Conferences **76**, 03009 (2016) DOI: 10.1051/matecconf/20167603009
CSCC 2016

Automated design of IoT Wi-Fi FSS filter

Pavel Tomasek[1,a]

[1] *Tomas Bata University in Zlin, Faculty of Applied Informatics, Nad Stranemi 4511, 76005 Zlín 5, Czech Republic*

Abstract. This work is presenting a technique of automated design of a Frequency Selective Surface aimed at shielding wireless communication under a very new standard of IEEE 802.11ah. This standard is primarily focused on rapidly growing network of communicating electrical devices called Internet of Things. Shielding of such a communication can be, in certain situations, very important for elimination of the possibility of eavesdropping.

1 Introduction

The standard from the Institute of Electrical and Electronics Engineers (IEEE) with the label of 802.11ah is a quite hot topic in the field of the Internet of Things (IoT). For the purpose of communication between even very small electrical appliances a very special energy saving way of communication has been developed.

The world of IoT is full of electrical devices, sensors, accessories, wearables, security elements, various appliances utilizable in Smart Home (for instance lighting, cooking, heating) and also agriculture monitoring, industrial automation and smart metering. The number of mentioned devices is supposed to raise rapidly in the near future what is related with potentially significant security risks.

Therefore the main goal of this study is aimed at possible ways of shielding communication under this standard against eavesdropping outside a room or a building.

This study is partially based on the previous work [1] where the goal was to reflect wireless communication under older standard IEEE 802.11b,g.

This article includes the following content: section 2 contains brief description of IEEE 802.11ah. In section 3, there are very simply described some possible ways of shielding of this type of wireless communication. Section 4 informs about a chosen way of optimization of a filter based on a Frequency Selective Surface. And finally Section 5 presents synthetic results and section 6 concludes the whole idea presented in this study.

2 IEEE 802.11ah

The IEEE standard of 802.11ah, also called "Wi-Fi HaLow", has a great potential of usability in the area of IoT because of two main reasons [2]:

- Low power consumption thanks to a native power saving mechanism with sleep modes (should consume much less energy than Bluetooth or Wireless-Fidelity (Wi-Fi) of earlier standards b, g, a or n)
- Long range (can penetrate walls much more easily), the penetration and range of various Wi-Fi standards is depicted in Figure 1.

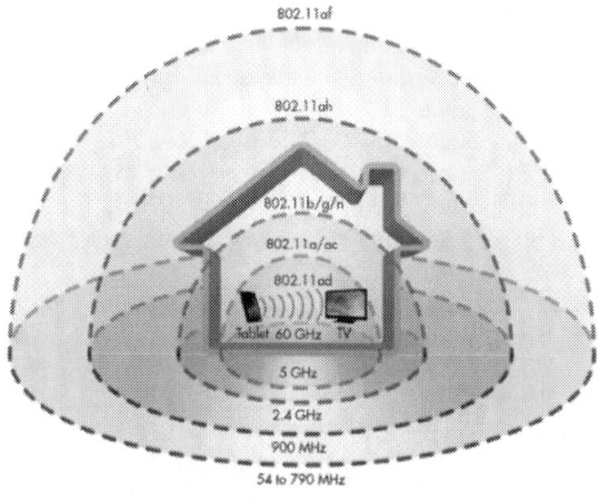

Figure 1. Comparison of different Wi-Fi ranges [3].

Both items mentioned above are based on the key technological features of IEEE 802.11ah [4]:

- Sub 1 GHz frequency
- Design of new Physical Layer (PHY layer) and Media Access Control Layer (MAC layer). These new layers include several modifications with respect to consolidated IEEE standards. The IEEE 802.11ah MAC layer incorporates most of the main IEEE 802.11 characteristics, adding some novel power management mechanisms.
- Typical range of IEEE 802.11ah is 100 – 1000 m

[a] Corresponding author: tomasek@fai.utb.cz

- Transmission power is from <10 mW to <1 W (depending on the country's regulations)
- Battery operation should be from months to years (also thanks to long sleeping periods)

The mentioned standard is very new. It was standardized and introduced in January 4 2016 [5] (the first IEEE 802.11 standard was released in June 1997). The first certified devices should come soon (probably in 2017 or 2018). Due to these data, the topic of this study is unique and potentially very important and interesting from the point of view of secure communication.

3 Shielding

Considering wireless communication between electrical sensors or generally devices using IEEE 802.11ah, the first idea of how to shield a communication in a room, in a small building or area is to use

A) a very simple Faraday cage or

B) a very specific and hard to develop wallpaper reflecting only a desired frequency range.

3.1 Faraday cage

Faraday cages are named after the English scientist Michael Faraday. Faraday shield (cage) is an enclosure made from a conductive material or by a mesh of such material to block electric fields.

These shields – cages can be used to protect different kinds of electronic equipment from electrostatic discharges. They cannot block magnetic fields like Earth's magnetic field, but they can protect the interior from electromagnetic radiation coming from the outside. An external electrical field leads to rearrangement of the charges, and this cancels the field inside. Electric fields (applied externally) create forces on electrons in the conductor, creating a current, which will further result in charge rearrangement. The current will cease when the charges rearrange and the applied field inside is cancelled [6].

This approach is cheap but has several very negative side effects. First of all, whole frequencies coming to or from a cage are reflected, generally:

- Global System for Mobile (GSM)
- Universal Mobile Telecommunications System (UMTS)
- Long-Term Evolution (LTE)
- all frequencies of Wi-Fi (sub 1 GHz, 2.4 and 5 GHz)
- Bluetooth
- and possibly also the visible light if not using a dense mesh

This approach may go against the original aim to use IEEE 802.11ah in longer distances.

3.2 FSS

Frequency Selective Surfaces (FSSs) are important spatial filters, which can efficiently filter desired band of frequencies. Therefore these can play a significant role in electromagnetic related problems.

Frequency selective surfaces can be used and adjusted to prepare a structure reflecting just a desired narrow range of a spectrum.

To briefly sketch the history, the beginning of FSS relates to Ben A. Munk who was the guru of this approach [7]. In the last decade, the idea of FSS has spread out into many applications. Example of a band-pass FSS is in [8] where the goal was to transmit GSM signals through energy efficient windows. One of the first FSS absorbers was presented by Salisbury and Jaumann [9]. Great research has been already done in the field of FSS including also the analysis of frequency characteristics of dielectric period structures [10] and another analysis of characteristics of dielectric grating of left-handed and right-handed materials [11]. FSS are also used in the antenna theory and experiments like analysis of ultra wide band planar monopole antenna and its design [12].

Back to shielding: this second idea of how to shield the communication (using FSS) is to use a special pattern/wallpaper selectively attenuating just the frequency range used in IEEE 802.11ah.

With respect to the design, rules and law of various countries the frequency range for Europe is 863 – 868 MHz (for example in USA it is 902 – 928 MHz and in China it is 755 – 787 MHz) [13]. Figure 2 presents the ranges in more detail.

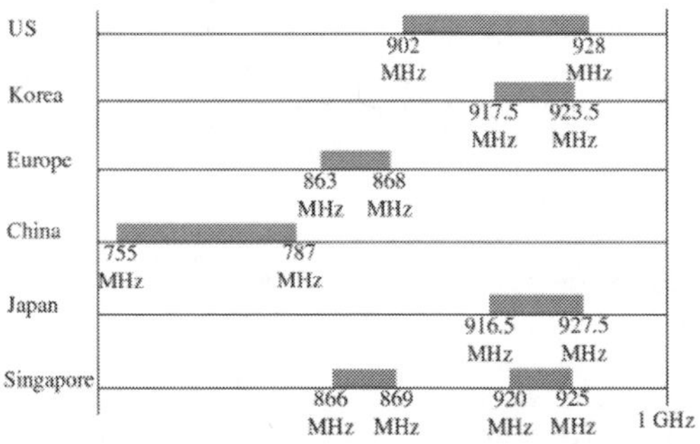

Figure 2. Sub 1 GHz spectrum specified in the IEEE 802.11ah channelization [13].

The standard of IEEE 802.11ah is operating in sub-gigahertz frequencies in comparison with traditional IEEE 802.11b or IEEE 802.11g working at 2.4 GHz and IEEE 802.11a working at 5 GHz.

The schema of a typical FSS structure: simple cross and a Jerusalem-cross is presented in Figure 3. Both models consist of simple rectangular elements. Theoretically, the second geometry may have better reflection. Moreover double-layer should provide a more narrow band-stop filter. Several comparisons have been presented in [14].

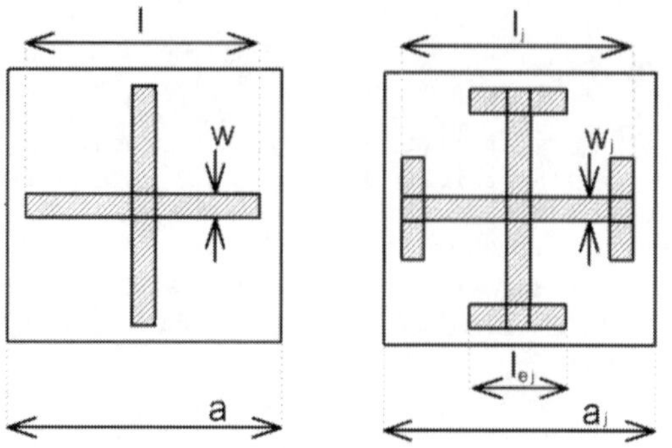

Figure 3. Schema of a cell containing the simple cross (on the left) and the Jerusalem-cross (on the right).

In Figure 3, a and a_j represent the width and height of a cell (a cell is just one square element of the whole structure of FSS; index j relates to the structure depicted on the right: the Jerusalem-cross), l and l_j is the total width and height of the cross, w and w_j is the width of an arm and l_{ej} represents the length of the bar connected to the end of an arm of the Jerusalem-cross.

There is a special software suitable for optimization of FSS elements. It is FSSMR software [15], which was developed at Tomas Bata University in Zlin and which analyses the planar periodic structures and tries to optimize them with respect to defined optimization goals. Therefore this software is suitable for estimation of proper values of design variables (a_j, l_j, w_j, and l_{ej}) to meet the optimization goals (and thus to reflect the desired frequency band in this case of IEEE 802.11ah).

There are also some shortages in this approach. One of the most questionable aspects of the FSS approach is the influence of the angle of incidence which must be also examined. Another problem is with windows when attempting to secure a room against transmitting sub 1 GHz frequencies outside the room.

4 Optimization

A frequency range, an initial geometry with design variables (e.g. width and height of the arms of the cross) and optimization goals must be set before performing the optimization of an FSS filter.

The transmission coefficient depends on frequency and other parameters forming the parameter vector of the filter which specifies the geometry (defined by design variables). An optimization method searches for the set of parameters which satisfies the given objectives, at least approximately, being thus in a certain sense optimal.

An optimization goal is defined by a frequency range where the transmission coefficient must be lower or greater than a defined threshold value.

In our experiment three optimization goals were modelled (also graphically presented by green color in Figure 4 together with results of the initial configuration):

Table 1. Description of design parameters related to the geometry of the Jesrusalem-cross FSS filter (see Figure 3).

Var.	Description	Initial Value	Lower Bound	Upper Bound
a_j	The width and height of a cell [m]	0.15	0.1	0.2
w_j	The width of an arm [m]	0.0055	0.001	0.010
k_{1j}	The width parameter ($k_{1j} = l_j/a_j$)	0.85	0.7	1.0
k_{2j}	The length parameter ($k_{2j} = l_{ej}/l_j$)	0.35	0.2	0.5

1. To transmit frequencies from 0.1000 to 0.8222 GHz (threshold: -2.5 dB)
2. To reflect frequencies from 0.8223 to 0.9088 GHz (this range relates to the Q factor equal to 10, $f_{stop\ range} = f_c/10 = 86.55MHz$; threshold: -20.0 dB)
3. To transmit frequencies from 0.9089 to 3.0000 GHz (threshold: -2.5 dB)

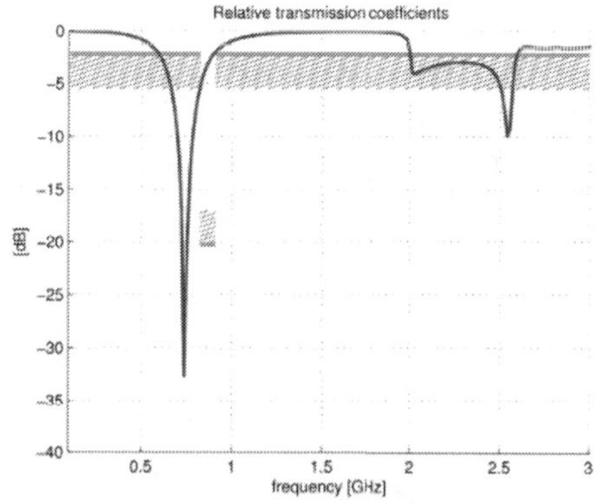

Figure 4. Transmission coefficients of the initial geometry of the FSS IEEE 802.11ah filter.

The initial values of design parameters with lower and upper bounds were guessed (by the earlier professional experiences with FSS filters) and they are mentioned in Table 1 where $l = ka$, $l_j = k_{1j}a_j$ and $l_{ej} = k_{2j}l_j$.

In this work, optimization was performed numerically using an implementation of local optimizer of Levenberg-Marquardt (a possible alternative is *fmincon* [16] or *fminsearchbnd* [17] which can be directly used in Matlab, evolutionary algorithms are another possible way).

The settings of the optimization process:

- Optimization technique: Levenberg-Marquardt
- FunTol = 10^{-3}, this represents the threshold tolerance
- MaxIter = 100, this constant defines the maximal number of iterations

- NormStep = 0.06, this is the constraint on maximal norm of a step
- Constraints on design variables a_j, w_j, k_{1j} and k_{2j} respect the lower and upper bounds mentioned in Table 1
- Cost function uses the method of moments [7, 18] to analyse and estimate the FSS transmission coefficients

All computations by optimization were based on perpendicular angle of incidence only.

In this study, FSSMR software [15] was used. It was developed at Tomas Bata University in Zlin and it analyses the planar periodic structures and tries to optimize them with respect to the optimization goals.

5 Results

The optimization procedure results in a filter which suppresses well the central channels. The attenuation is below -20 dB what can be considered as a very good filter. The final transmission coefficients are presented in Figure 5. The process of optimization in Matlab took at about 5 hours using an average computer (mainly depends on the amount of computed frequency points and the density of mesh cells in computation).

There is also some kind of an unwanted low subsidiary attenuation between 2.5 and 3.0 GHz.

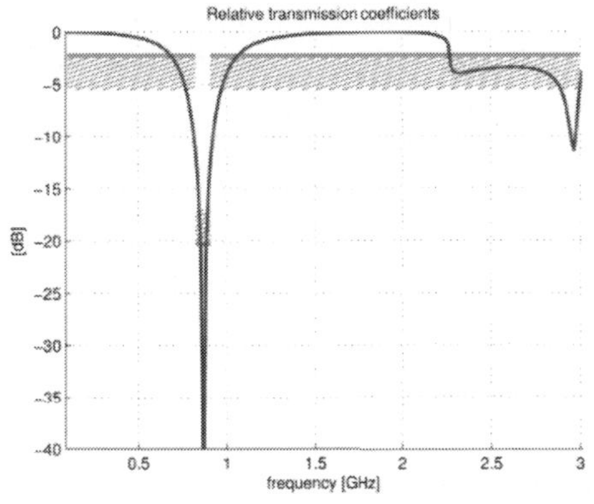

Figure 5. Transmission coefficients of the optimized geometry of the FSS IEEE 802.11ah filter.

The optimized values of design parameters of Jerusalem-cross FSS filter are presented in the list below:

- $a_j = 0.132m$
- $w_j = 0.007m$
- $k_{1j} = 0.85$
- $k_{2j} = 0.35$

Furthermore, from the design parameters the lengths l, l_j and l_{ej} can be computed in the following way:

- $l_j = k_{1j}a_j$; $l_j = 0.1122m$ (the total width and height of the Jerusalem-cross)
- $l_{ej} = k_{2j}l_j$; $l_{ej} = 0,03927m$ (the total length of the outer arms)

6 Conclusion

A very new standard for wireless communication suitable for the Internet of Things, IEEE 802.11ah, has been introduced in this preliminary study together with possible ways of how to shield communication under mentioned standard. A theoretical concept of a wallpaper with a deep practical impact has been revealed. A technique of how to generate an optimized geometry of an FSS filter with adaptation to the narrow specific range of frequencies used in IEEE 802.11ah has been presented. Also, some shortages of this approach have been described.

The boom of the Internet of Things is coming. It can make life simpler (like other technologies in the history), but it also contains a great portion of a threat of abuse. This article points this out.

Further analysis with practical experiments and measurements are proposed as a possible further work in this domain.

Acknowledgment

This work was partially supported by Internal Grant Agency of Tomas Bata University under the project No. IGA/CebiaTech/2016/004. This work was supported by the Ministry of Education, Youth and Sports of the Czech Republic within the National Sustainability Programme project No. LO1303 (MSMT-7778/2014).

References

[1] P. Tomasek, S. Gona, in *PIERS* (Electromagnetics Academy, Cambridge, 2013), pp. 221–224, ISBN: 9781934142264

[2] E. Khorov, A. Lyakhov, A. Krotov, A. Guschin, Computer Communications **58**, 53 (2014), ISSN: 0140-3664

[3] J.J. DeLisle, Microwaves and RF **54**, 69 (2015), ISSN: 0745-2993

[4] T. Adame, A. Bel, B. Bellalta, J. Barcelo, M. Oliver, IEEE Wireless Communications **21**, 144 (2014), ISSN: 1536-1284

[5] *Wi-Fi Alliance(R) introduces low power, long range Wi-Fi HaLow(TM)* (2016), URL: http://www.wi-fi.org/news-events/newsroom/wi-fi-alliance-introduces-low-power-long-range-wi-fi-halow [accessed: 2016-03-30]

[6] *Faraday Cage* (2016), URL: http://www.faradaycage.org/ [accessed: 2016-03-30]

[7] B. Munk, ed., *Frequency selective surfaces – theory and design* (New York, USA: Willey & Sons, 2000), ISBN: 978-0-471-37047-5

[8] G. Kiani, L. Olsson, A. Karlsson, K. Esselle, M. Nilsson, IEEE Transactions on Antennas and Propagation **59**, 520 (2011), ISSN: 0018-926X

[9] R. Haupt, IEEE Transactions on Antennas and Propagation **54**, 1807 (2006), ISSN: 0018-926X

[10] R. Mehrnejad, R. Razmjoueian, in *ACMIN'12 Proceedings of the 14th international conference on Automatic Control, Modelling & Simulation, and Proceedings of the 11th international conference on Microelectronics, Nanoelectronics, Optoelectronics* (WSEAS, Stevens Point, Wisconsin, USA, 2012), pp. 187–190, ISBN: 978-1-61804-080-0

[11] R. Mehrnejad, R.Razmjoueian, in *ACMIN'12 Proceedings of the 14th international conference on Automatic Control, Modelling & Simulation, and Proceedings of the 11th international conference on Microelectronics, Nanoelectronics, Optoelectronics* (WSEAS, Stevens Point, Wisconsin, USA, 2012), pp. 205–208, ISBN: 978-1-61804-080-0

[12] M. Rahim, T. Masri, H. Majid, O. Ayop, F. Zubir, WSEAS Transactions on Communications, WSEAS **10**, 212 (2011), ISSN: 1109-2742

[13] W. Sun, M. Choi, S. Choi, Journal of ICT Standardization **1**, 83 (2013), ISSN: 2246-0853

[14] P. Tomasek, International Journal of Circuits, Systems and Signal Processing **8**, 594 (2014), ISSN: 1998-4464

[15] S. Gona, V. Kresalek, COMITE **14** (2008)

[16] MathWorks, *Find minimum of constrained nonlinear multivariable function - matlab* (2016), URL: http://www.mathworks.com/help/optim/ug/fmincon.html [accessed: 2016-03-30]

[17] J. D'Errico, *fminsearchbnd, fminsearchcon - File Exchange - MATLAB Central* (2012), URL: http://www.mathworks.com/matlabcentral/fileexchange/8277-fminsearchbnd--fminsearchcon [accessed: 2016-03-30]

[18] T.K. Wu, ed., *Frequency selective surfaces and grid arrays* (New York, USA: Willey & Sons, 1995), ISBN: 0-471-31189-8

A Parallelized Phase-Frequency Detector based Modified LSPF-DPLL for Wireless Communication – Comparative Study with Modified LSPF-DPLL

Sabyasachi Bhattacharyya[1,a], Aradhana Misra[1], Kandarpa Kumar Sarma[2] and Nikos Mastorakis[3]

[1]*Gauhati University Institute of Science and Technology, Department of Electronics and Communication Engineering, Guwahati, India*
[2]*Gauhati University, Department of Electronics and Communication Technology, Guwahati, India*
[3]*Technical University of Sofia, Bulgaria*

Abstract. In recent times, communication technologies have evolved at a brisk rate. 3G and 4G networks have already been widely deployed. However, with increase in user number and applications, alternative strategies in the form of 5G systems have been devised. Thus, it is desirable to have communication systems which can provide low error levels with minimum delay. DPLL based systems play a versatile role in modern day communication receivers. Popular DPLL receiver packages based on Zero Crossing (ZC) and Least Square Polynomial Fitting (LSPF) techniques have been recently proposed to serve standalone reception in communcation setups. Such systems involve intensive computations and thus show excellant error performance ; but are bottlenecked by poor time performance. The LSPF-DPLL system was aided by a Modified Phase Resolving Numerically Controlled Oscilator (MPR-NCO) to achieve both improved error and time performance in another subsequent DPLL design that was proposed of late. This design is modified in the DPLL system proposed here by incorporating a Parallelized LSPF based Phase-Frequency Detector to achieve furhter improvements in time performance while maintaining the system's error performance.

1 Introduction

Digital Phase Locked Loops (DPLLs) are the sampled domain extraction of the Phase Locked Loops (PLLs) realized by means of a digital Phase-Frequency Detector (PFD) [1,2]. Popularly referred to as an FM demodulator, DPLL plays diverse roles in communication systems which include recovering carrier information in non-coherent systems where the channel state is not known to the receiver [2], symbol retrieval in coherent links for known channel [3], multi-clock synchronization and clock distribution into different sub-systems using divider unit in PLLs besides time synchronizing such systems [2]. DPLL based packages have therefore been emphasized as standalone means of reception in recent wireless communication setups [3].

A ZC-DPLL has been proposed in [4] for high Doppler environments which incorporates a hyperbolic non-linearity block and a sigma-delta modulator unit which helps the loop filter to adapt better. The proposed system exhibits improved time jitter performance and widened lock-in range. The ZC-DPLL proposed for Rayleigh faded channels in [3] utilizes the conclusions of ZC Algorithm in its PFD and retrieves the original phase of transmitted QPSK symbols. The system exhibits excellent error rates but the intensive Left/Right (L/R) Shift algorithm leads to poor time performance. Similarly, a highly intense L/R Shift algorithm based Numerical Controlled Oscillator (NCO) and LSPF based PFD aided DPLL based signal recovery system is presented in [2]. This system also shows excellent error performance but lacks time efficiency. An MPR-NCO based LSPF-DPLL system is proposed in [1] for wireless fading environments and emerges as an improved design over the existing LSPF-DPLL [2] with better error and time performance.

The recent trend in wireless communications as can be seen in [1,4] is time efficient symbol recovery. Certain DPLL designs however emphasize on significant reduction in BER levels and therefore involve intensive computations which lead to poor time performance [2, 3]. The LSPF-DPLL in [2] additionally also involves another hugely time-intensive LSPF based PFD unit. An MPR-NCO based LSPF-DPLL has been recently proposed in [1] and exhibits improved error and time performance over the existing design in [2]. The time efficiency improvement in [1] is solely due to the incorporation of the MPR-NCO. The design presented here tries to further improve system time performance by parallelizing the operations of intensive LSPF based PFD in [1] using the different cores of a Quad Core processor while maintaining the system's error performance.

The following sections constitute the remaining portion of this paper. Section 2 discusses the proposed system model for the Parallelized Phase Frequency Detector based Modified LSPF-DPLL system in terms of

[a] Sabyasachi Bhattacharyya: sabya005@gmail

its crucial components and their functioning, different mathematical relationships involved, parameters settings for simulation and the modifications made to parallelize the DPLL in [1] are also discussed in details. Section 3 analyzes the performance of the proposed system and a comparative study of the system with the MPR-NCO based LSPF-DPLL system in [1] is also presented here. Section 4 deals with the advantages and limitations of the system proposed and finally Section 5 concludes the discussion.

2 System Model

The proposed DPLL system with parallelized PFD is subjected to degraded QPSK modulated symbols under the combined effects of Rayleigh and Rician faded wireless environments and Additive White Gaussian Noise (AWGN).

2.1 System Architecture

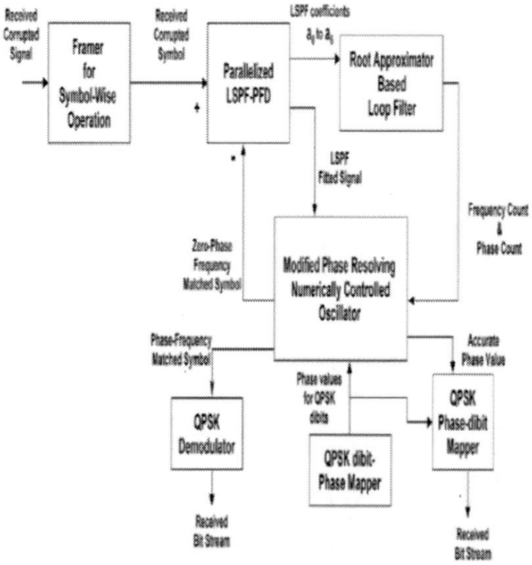

Figure 1. Parallelized PFD based Modified LSPF-DPLL

The architecture overview for the proposed DPLL system is depicted in Figure 1. It consists of a framer for symbol-wise operation, a Parallelized version of the LSPF based Phase-Frequency Detector (LSPF-PFD) in [1], a Root Approximator (RA) based Loop Filter (RA-LF) and an MPR-NCO which are integrated for proper system functioning. QPSK dibit-phase and phase-dibit mapper units aid the proposed DPLL topology. The Framer unit splits the received signal into frames of length same as QPSK symbol period. The time-intensive LSPF-PFD proposed in [1,2] is modified here by parallelizing the PFD action in [1] using the different cores of a Quad core processor as shown in Figure 2. The time efficient parallelized PFD provides the best fit coefficients a_0 to a_6 containing ZC information of the incoming signal. The RA-LF utilizes these coeeficients to measure the frequency and phase counts associated with the incoming degraded symbols. It does so by extracting the roots and Eigen values of the best-fit estimate. The MPR-NCO uses the frequency and phase counts from RA-LF and fitted signal from the LSPF-PFD and provides three crucial outputs.

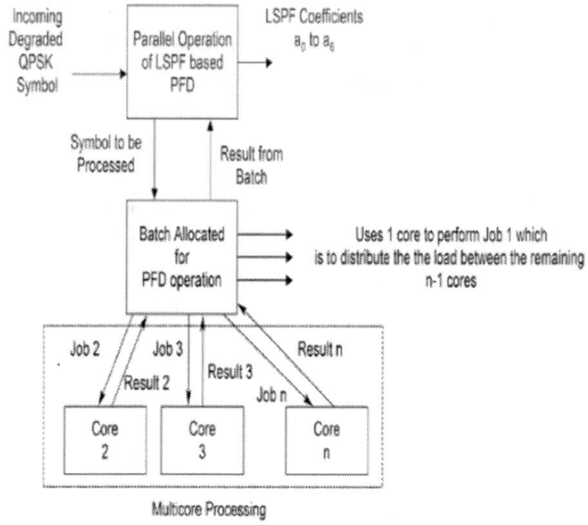

Figure 2. Proposed model for Parallelized PFD in LSPF-DPLL

They are the zero-phase frequency matched signal which is fed back to the LSPF-PFD, the phase-frequency matched signal with original modulation information and also the accurate phase value associated with the received symbol computed from the phase count of RA-LF. The NCO determines the accurate phase value using the look-up information of dibit-phase mapper. The accurate phase is further mapped to the correct dibits using the phase-dibit mapper to reduce the need for complicated branched QPSK demodulation as suggested in [2, 3, 5].

2.2 Parallel PFD based LSPF-DPLL Analysis

The modified LSPF-DPLL with Parallelized PFD proposed for QPSK modulated symbols recovers digital intelligence under degraded effects of Rayleigh and Rician fading channels and AWGN noise.

2.2.1 QPSK signal model

Quadri-phase signals significantly conserve bandwidth by transmitting dibits and also maintain low error rates using distinct decision boundaries as elaborated in [2,6,7]. The proposed system is thus inspected for QPSK modulated symbols. A QPSK modulated signal is mathematically represented as in eq. (1)

$$q(t) = A\cos(2\pi f_c t + \theta_i) \quad (1)$$

$$0 \le t \le T, i = 1,2,3,4$$

$$\theta_i = \frac{(2i-1)\pi}{4}$$

where, A is the signal amplitude, f_c is the transmission carrier frequency and θ_i is the QPSK phase. The four possible phases are : $\frac{\pi}{4}, \frac{3\pi}{4}, \frac{5\pi}{4}, \frac{7\pi}{4}$.

2.2.2 Rayleigh and Rician Fading Model

Rayleigh and Rician fading models provide accurate estimates of the wireless fading environment prevelant in urban, sub-urban and rural areas [5,7]. The proposed Parallel PFD based modified DPLL system is tested under degraded effects of Rayleigh and Rician fading.

The received signal $s(t)$ under Rayleigh faded NLOS transmission scenario between transmitter and receiver is depicted in eq. (2):

$$s(t) = \sum_{k=1}^{N} a_k \cos(\omega_c t + \omega_{dk} t + \phi_k) \quad (2)$$

where a_k is the gain in the kth path, ω_c is the angular carrier frequency for transmission, ω_{dk} is the Doppler Frequency due to relative motion in between the transmitter and receiver for k^{th} path and ϕ_k is the random phase for the kth path [2,5].

Similarly, the received signal under Rician faded wireless environment composite of NLOS and LOS paths is depicted as shown in eq. (3) :

$$r(t) = s(t) + k_d \cos(\omega_c t + \omega_d t) \quad (3)$$

where $s(t)$ represents the contribution due to the NLOS components, k_d indicates the strength of the LOS component, and ω_d is the Doppler frequency component in the direct path[1, 2, 5].

2.2.3 Component wise analysis of Proposed Model

The proposed Parallel PFD based Modified LSPF-DPLL depicted in Figure 1 incorporates *five* functional blocks as already mentioned in Section 2.1. The Framer Unit provides symbol-wise DPLL operation. The detailed functioning of the four major units are elaborated below.

Parallelized LSPF based PFD

The LSPF based PFD performs phase-frequency detection at moderate sampling rates over ZC based designs as suggested in [1, 2]. The presented 6th order polynomial fitting PFD [2] however involves intensive computations and thus leads to poor time performance of the PFD. The design presented in [1] incorporates an MPR-NCO which leads to improvements in processing time. The phase-frequency detection process in [1] was realized using the intensive LSPF unit and so in addition to the time efficiency achieved due to the MPR-NCO, there remained scope for further improvement in time performance with necessary modifications made in the PFD unit in [1]. To achieve this improvement in system performance, the intensive computations involved in the serial LSPF-PFD unit of [1] are parallelized using the different cores of a Quad Core Processor. The parallelized version of the LSPF-PFD provides the best-fit coefficients a_0 to a_6 which are indicative measures of phase and frequency content associated with the incoming symbol.

If (t_1,y_1), (t_2,y_2)........(t_n,y_n) represent the corrupted signal samples of received QPSK sybmols along with time index, the received symbol can therefore be fitted to a 6th order polynomial, such that the sum of squared residuals S is minimized as discussed in [2]. The fitted signal is mathematically expressed as in eq. (4):

$$\hat{y} = a_0 + a_1 t + a_2 t^2 + ... + a_6 t^6 \quad (4)$$

$$S = \sum_{i=1}^{N} [y_i - \hat{y}]^2 \quad (5)$$

On partially differentiating S in eq. (5) with respect to best-fit coefficients a_0 to a_6, and equating each of them to zero, an important matrix equality is obtained in eq. (6) from which the coefficients a_0 to a_6 can be obtained.

$$\begin{bmatrix} ns & \sum t_i & \sum t_i^2 & \sum t_i^3 & \sum t_i^4 & \sum t_i^5 & \sum t_i^6 \\ \sum t_i & \sum t_i^2 & \sum t_i^3 & \sum t_i^4 & \sum t_i^5 & \sum t_i^6 & \sum t_i^7 \\ \sum t_i^2 & \sum t_i^3 & \sum t_i^4 & \sum t_i^5 & \sum t_i^6 & \sum t_i^7 & \sum t_i^8 \\ \sum t_i^3 & \sum t_i^4 & \sum t_i^5 & \sum t_i^6 & \sum t_i^7 & \sum t_i^8 & \sum t_i^9 \\ \sum t_i^4 & \sum t_i^5 & \sum t_i^6 & \sum t_i^7 & \sum t_i^8 & \sum t_i^9 & \sum t_i^{10} \\ \sum t_i^5 & \sum t_i^6 & \sum t_i^7 & \sum t_i^8 & \sum t_i^9 & \sum t_i^{10} & \sum t_i^{11} \\ \sum t_i^6 & \sum t_i^7 & \sum t_i^8 & \sum t_i^9 & \sum t_i^{10} & \sum t_i^{11} & \sum t_i^{12} \end{bmatrix} \times \begin{bmatrix} a_0 \\ a_1 \\ a_2 \\ a_3 \\ a_4 \\ a_5 \\ a_6 \end{bmatrix} = \begin{bmatrix} \sum y_i \\ \sum t_i y_i \\ \sum t_i y_i^2 \\ \sum t_i y_i^3 \\ \sum t_i y_i^4 \\ \sum t_i y_i^5 \\ \sum t_i y_i^6 \end{bmatrix} (6)$$

Eq. (6) provides the optimum LSPF coefficients a_0 to a_6, which contains phase and frequency contents of the received QPSK symbol. Moreover, it computes the LSPF best fit curve which was additionally incorporated in [1] to obtain information about whether the signal phase being tracked is below or beyond π radians. As can be seen, a number of intensive computations are involved in eq. (6) to compute the best fit LSPF coefficients. Sequential execution of such intense computations using a single core of the processor leads to hugely degraded time performance. So, these intense computations of the PFD are distributed for parallel execution on multiple processor cores as depicted in Figure 2. A Quad core processor is used to achieve speed up in the PFD and thus overall time performance improvement over [1]. The proposed system incorporates *batch mode of processing* to initiate a batch consisting of n cores. Each PFD computation is termed as a *job*. The batch uses *one* core to execute its own workload distribution and result accumulation process whereas the remaining n-1 cores are used to parallely execute n-1 jobs at a time as shown in Figure 2. Upon completion of all the necessary jobs (computations), the results of all the jobs are combined together to provide the PFD output, i.e., the LSPF coefficients a_0 to a_6 (fed to RA-LF) and the fitted signal $\hat{y}$ (fed to MPR-NCO). It is important to note that the computations in eq. (6) are to be performed per symbol of the received QPSK signal. The parallelization and subsequent speed up are therefore achieved for each received symbol. This speed up achieved per symbol of received data, will definitely lead to an overall time performance improvement for a standard transmission with multiple QPSK symbols [2]. The computation time is directly related to the number of signal samples *ns* used to represent each incoming symbol and thus the variation of processing time with *ns* has been analyzed.

RA based LF

The Loop Filter Unit for the proposed DPLL is realized using a Root Approximation unit as proposed in [1, 2]. It utilizes a matrix M_{RA} formed by the coefficients a_0 to a_6 from the PFD unit to compute the roots signifying signal zero crossing index as shown in eq. (7) below.

$$M_{RA} = \begin{bmatrix} \frac{-a_1}{a_0} & \frac{-a_2}{a_0} & \frac{-a_3}{a_0} & \frac{-a_4}{a_0} & \frac{-a_5}{a_0} & \frac{-a_6}{a_0} \\ 1 & 0 & 0 & 0 & 0 & 0 \\ 0 & 1 & 0 & 0 & 0 & 0 \\ 0 & 0 & 1 & 0 & 0 & 0 \\ 0 & 0 & 0 & 1 & 0 & 0 \\ 0 & 0 & 0 & 0 & 1 & 0 \\ 0 & 0 & 0 & 0 & 0 & 1 \end{bmatrix} \quad (7)$$

From the matrix in eq. (7), six eigen values e_1 to e_6 are computed and further using eq. (8) six roots r_1 to r_6 are evaluated as below.

$$r_i = \frac{1}{e_i} \quad (8)$$

As elaborated in [1,2], the frequency and phase counts, f_{cnt} and p_{cnt} , are computed from the significant roots r_2 to r_5 using eq. (9) and (10).

$$f_{cnt} = \frac{1}{r_3 - r_1} \quad (9)$$

$$p_{cnt} = \frac{\pi}{r_3 - r_2} \times r_2 \quad (10)$$

The MPR-NCO uses the computed values of f_{cnt} and p_{cnt} for further processing as shown in Figure 1.

MPR-NCO

The Parallelized DPLL system incorporates the Modified NCO proposed in [1] to compute accurate phase values associated with incoming QPSK symbols by avoiding sample-wise reorientation [8, 9, 10] resulting in improved time as well as error performance [1]. The MPR-NCO uses f_{cnt} and p_{cnt} from RA-LF, $\hat{y}$ from Parallelized PFD unit and possible phase values from look up table of QPSK dibit-phase mapper unit. It performs the following steps for proper phase and frequency matching as suggested in [1].

- It uses f_{cnt} to regenerate the carrier zero-phase carrier which acts as free running NCO signal.
- It studies the first zero crossing of $\hat{y}$ to set a flag f as either '0' or '1' as elaborated in [1].
- The estimated phase est_p is thus computed using eq. (11) in a similar manner to [1].

$$est_p = p_{cnt} + (f \times \pi) \quad (11)$$

- The accurate phase acc_p is finally computed as the phase value from the look-up table having minimum difference with est_p. Using acc_p and f_{cnt}, the modified NCO generates the phase frequency matched signal. acc_p is fed to dibit-phase mapper unit for simpler bit recovery [1].

QPSK dibit-phase and phase-dibit mapper

A similar dibit-phase and phase-dibit mapper unit as proposed in [1] is incorporated here for simpler bit recovery by avoiding branched demodulation structure suggested in [2,11,12]. The dibit-phase mapper aids NCO action by providing different possible phases whereas the phase-dibit mapper uses the look-up table of dibits and phases shown in Table 1 to map acc_p to the correct dibits facilitating simpler recovery of digital data.

Table 1. QPSK dibit-phase look-up table

Dibit	Phase Associated
00	$\frac{\pi}{4}$
01	$\frac{3\pi}{4}$
10	$\frac{5\pi}{4}$
11	$\frac{7\pi}{4}$

2.2.3 Simulation Parameter Settings

The Modified LSPF-DPLL system proposed with Parallelized PFD is tested under *non-coherent transmission scenario*. Table 2 shows the different parameters and corresponding specifications under which the proposed system has been simulated.

Table 2. Simulation Parameters

Parameters	Values or specification
Modulation Scheme	QPSK
Carrier Frequency	900 *MHz*
Fading	Rayleigh and Rician (5 and 10 path)
AWGN Noise	-10 to 10 dB (SNR)
Number of bits in simulation	20000
LOS factor	0.5
LSPF order	6
Processor Used	Intel Core i5, Quad Core, 4 GB (RAM), 64-bit, 2.4 *GHz*
Number of cores used to parallelize	three and four
Sample size variation (per QPSK symbol)	20,00000 to 2,60,00000 (in steps of 20,00000)
Parallelization Method Used	Batch Processing

As depicted in Table 2, the number of cores used for parallel execution of the load is varied between *three and four*. The mode of processing is batch type, so *one* core is always used to execute the batch process. Therefore, when *three* cores are used, effectively the PFD load is distributed between *two* cores. Similarly, the load is divided between *three* cores when the total number of cores used is *four*.

3 Results and Discussion

The analysis presented in this section can be broadly classified into *two* parts. Firstly, the system performance improvement due to parallelization of PFD unit is studied in terms of CPU utilization, processing time requirement and percentage speed up achieved with respect to the serial DPLL [1]. Secondly, the error performance of the system is analyzed in terms of a comparative BER analysis under different fading conditions to ensure that BER levels of Serial DPLL [1] are preserved.

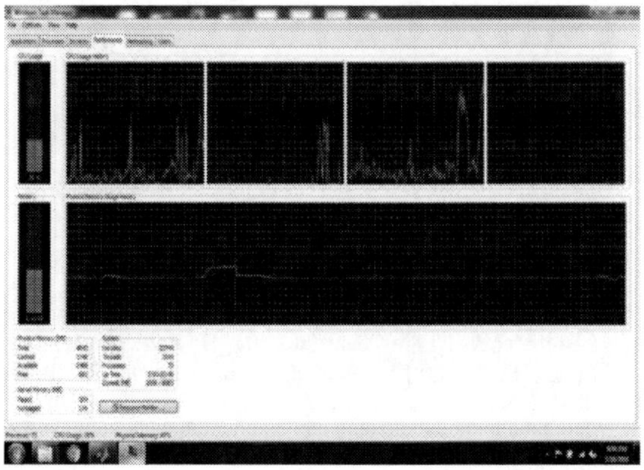

Figure 3. CPU processing for Serial DPLL (40,00000 samples)

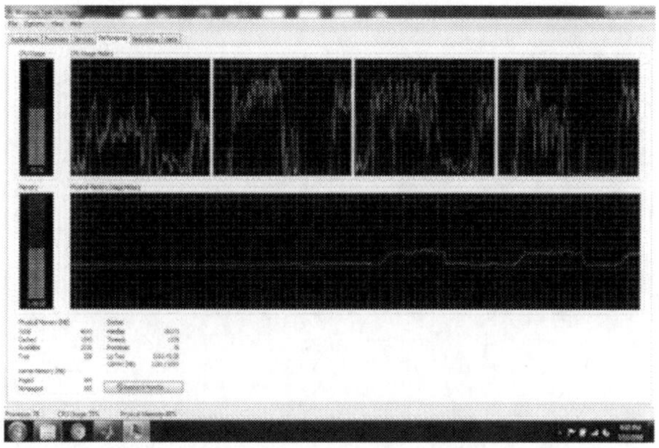

Figure 4. CPU processing in Parallel DPLL (40,00000 samples)

Figures 3 and 4 depict the CPU processing carried out for Serial and Parallel DPLL respectively. The sample size in each case is 40,00000. It can be very clearly seen that for Serial DPLL in Figure 3, only one processor is being used and the CPU cores are not utilized properly. On the other hand, for Parallel DPLL in Figure 4, all the processor cores are utilized properly resulting in better CPU utilization.

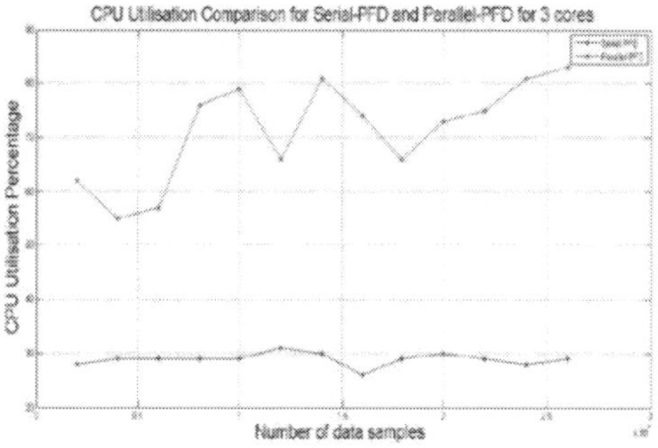

Figure 5. CPU utilization for Serial and Parallel DPLL (3 core)

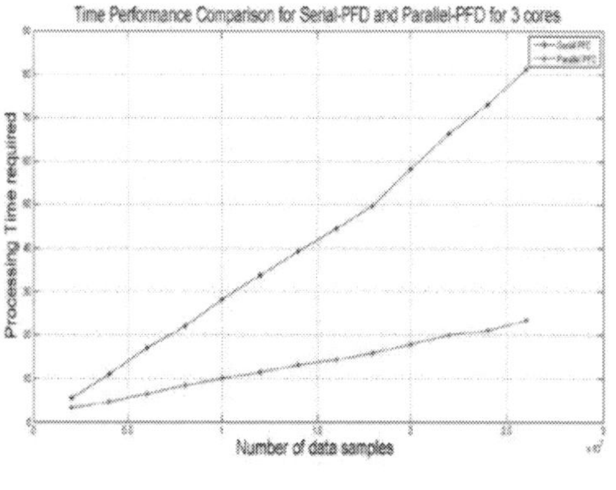

Figure 6. Processing time for Serial and Parallel DPLL (3 core)

Figures 5 and 6 exhibit average improvement in CPU utilization by *43 %* and speed-up as high as *71 %* for Parallel DPLL over Serial DPLL under 3-core parallelization.

DOI: 10.1051/matecconf/20167603010

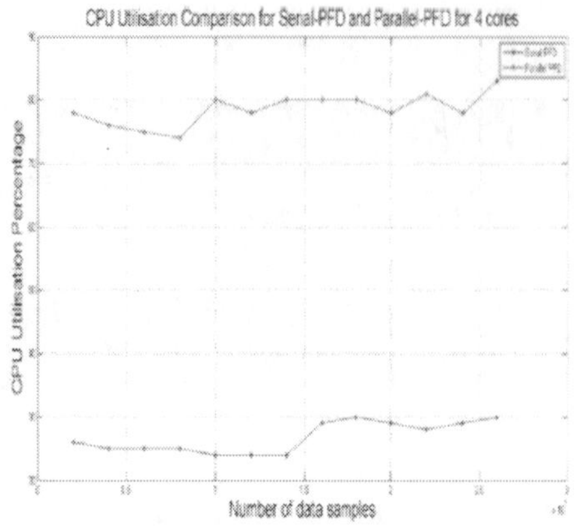

Figure 7. CPU utilization for Serial and Parallel DPLL (4 core)

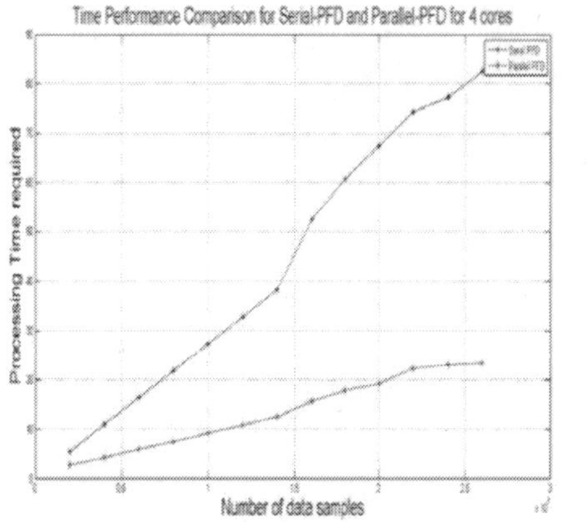

Figure 8. Processing time for Serial and Parallel DPLL (4 core)

Figures 7, 8 and Table 3 show average improvement in CPU utilization for Parallel DPLL over Serial DPLL by *53 %* and speed up as high as *72 %* with 4 cores.

Table 3. CPU utilization and Time Performance Comparison

Sample Size	CPU Utilization (%)		4-core Processing Time (seconds)	
	Serial DPLL	**Parallel DPLL (4 cores)**	**Serial DPLL**	**Parallel DPLL** (4 cores)
2000000	26	78	5.449	2.729
6000000	25	75	16.353	5.882
8000000	25	74	21.846	7.501
12000000	24	78	32.834	10.787
26000000	30	83	82.499	23.328

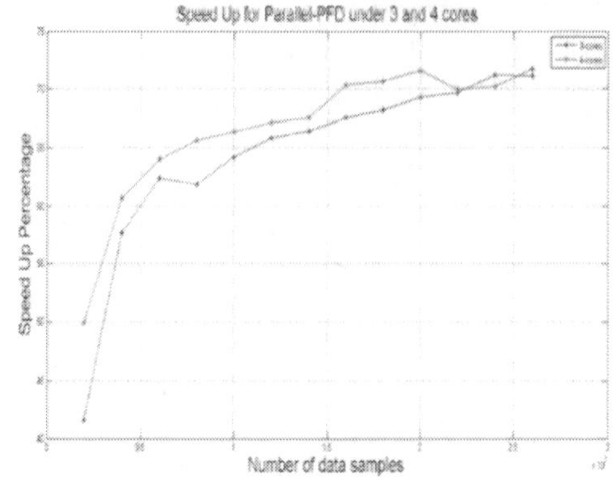

Figure 9. Speed up for Parallel DPLL under 3 and 4 cores

Figure 9 depicts a comparative analysis of the speed up achieved for the proposed DPLL with Parallel PFD under 3 and 4 cores. It is quite clear that speed up achieved is more with 4 cores than that with 3 cores because with increase in number of cores, the speed up increases.

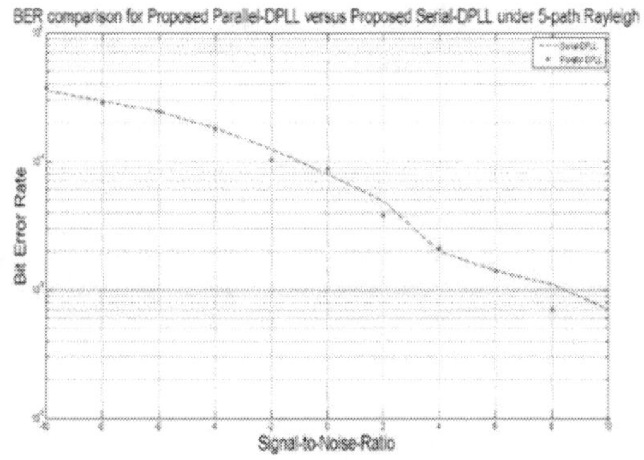

Figure 10. BER comparison under 5-path Rayleigh (3 core)

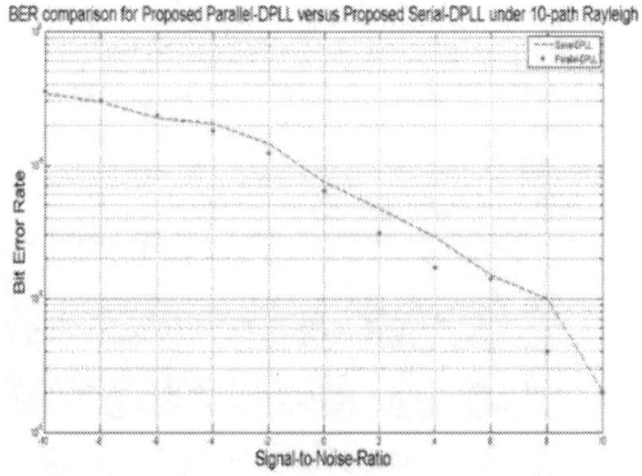

Figure 11. BER comparison under 10-path Rayleigh (3 core)

Figures 10, 11 and 12 clearly indicate that the proposed system with 3 cores maintains the BER levels exhibited by the Serial DPLL [1] under 5-path Rayleigh, 10-path Rayleigh and 10-path Rician respectively in addition to providing improvements in time performance and CPU utilization.

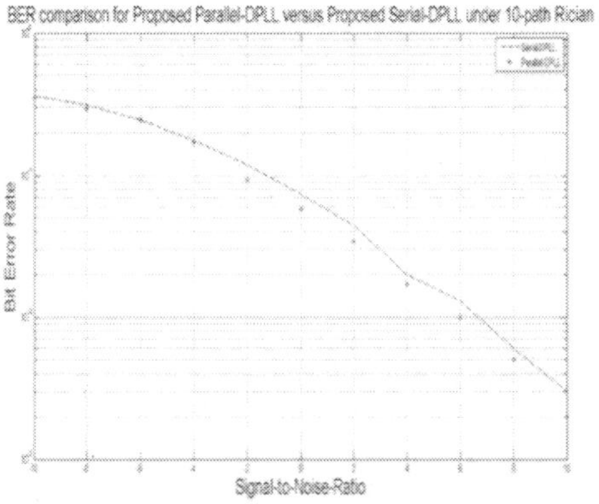

Figure 12. BER comparison under 10-path Rician (3 core)

Table 4 depicts the comparative BER analysis of the proposed Parallel DPLL with Serial DPLL [1] under 4-core parallelization. As in case of 3 core, the proposed system maintains BER levels similar to those of Serial DPLL proposed in [1] for 4 core case also.

Table 4. BER Comparison under 10-path Rayleigh and Rician

SNR (in dB)	BER under 10-path Rayleigh		BER under 10-path Rician	
	Serial DPLL	Parallel DPLL (4 cores)	Serial DPLL	Parallel DPLL (4 cores)
-10	0.3430	0.3350	0.3600	0.3480
-4	0.2070	0.1790	0.1780	0.1790
0	0.0750	0.0650	0.0740	0.0570
2	0.0470	0.0430	0.0440	0.0330
4	0.0290	0.0220	0.0200	0.0120
6	0.0150	0.0100	0.0130	0.0070
10	0.0020	0.0020	0.0030	0.0010

Thus, the different results and illustrations presented in this section are substantial evidences for us to claim the Modified LSPF-DPLL proposed with Parallelized PFD as an improved design over the Serial LSPF-DPLL with MPR-NCO[1].The proposed system exhibits performance improvement in terms of processing time, percentage speed up and CPU utilization while maintaining BER levels similar to the Serial DPLL [1].

4 Advantages and Limitation

The proposed system has certain advantages and also some limitations which are outlined below.

4.1 Advantages

In addition to possessing the advantages suggested in [1], the system also exhibits the following features:

- Reduced computational load per core due to distribution of PFD operations into different cores of the Quad core processor.
- Further improvement in processing speed as compared to the Serial DPLLs presented in [1] [2].
- Improved CPU resource utilization over systems proposed in [1,2]; serves as a dedicated receiver package for DPLL based communications.

4.2 Limitation

In some specific cases where either the sample size per QPSK symbol or the total number of such symbols transmitted are comparatively smaller than the data sizes for a standard transmission, the parallelization overheads may consume more time leading to ineffective parallelization and thus degraded time performance.

5 Conclusion and Future Direction

This paper proposes a Parallelized PFD based LSPF-DPLL system. The previously proposed Serial DPLL with MPR-NCO [1] is modified here by incorporating a new parallel processing aided LSPF-PFD unit to time efficiently track accurate phase values for retrieving digital intelligence. The system is tested under varying conditions of Rayleigh and Rician fading. Specifically, the performance of PFD unit is rigorously tested under different number of cores and with varying sample sizes. The proposed DPLL system is found to exhibit improvements in time performance, percentage speed up and CPU utilization over the Serial DPLL in [1] making it a suitable for today's technology focussed on minimizing delays. In addition to this, the system also maintains similar BER levels to those suggested in [1]. The proposed work could be extended further by analyzing the system under realistic estimates of Nakagami-*m* fading channels composite of Rayleigh and Rician behaviour.

Acknowledgement

The authors are thankful to Mr. Basab Bijoy Purkayastha, Dept. of Physics, Indian Institute of Technology Guwahati, Mr. Kaustubh Bhattacharyya, Dept. of ECE, School of Technology, Assam Don Bosco University for their valuable suggestions and also to the Ministry of Communication and Information Technology, Govt. of India, for facilitating the research.

References

1. S.Bhattacharyya, A. Misra, K. K. Sarma, "A Modified NCO based LSPF-DPLL Phase Resolver for Wireless Communication", *3rd IEEE International Conference on Recent Advances in Information Technology*, 1-7, Dhanbad (2016)
2. B.B. Purkayastha, K.K. Sarma, *A Digital Phase Locked Loop based Signal and Symbol Recovery System for Wireless Communication* (Springer India, 2015)
3. S.Bhattacharyya, R.N. Ahmed, B.B. Purkayastha, K. Bhattacharyya, " Zero Crossing Algoritm based Phase Recovery for DPLL based Wireless Communication", *IEEE International Conference on Computation, Communication and Automation,* 1220-1226, Greater Noida (2015)
4. E. Salahat, M.A. Qutayri, S.R. Al-Araji, H. Saleh, "A Zero Crossing Digital Phase Locked Loop Architecture with Hyberbolic Non-Linearity for High Doppler Environments", *21st IEEE International Conference on Electronics, Circuits and Systems*, 56-59, Marseille (2014).
5. B. B. Purkayastha, K. K. Sarma, "A Digital Phase Locked Loop based System for Nakagami-m Fading Channel Model", Int. J Comp. App., **42(9)**: 1-8 (2012).
6. E. Salahat, S. R. Al-Araji, M. Al-Qutayri, " A Frequency Synthesizer based on Zero Crossing Digital Phase Locked Loop", *20th IEEE International Conference on Electronics, Circuits and Systems*, 835-838, Abu Dhabi (2013).
7. S. Kandeepan, " Steady State Distribution of a Hyperbolic Digital Tanlock Loop for Wireless Communications", IEEE Trans. Wir. Comm., **8(2)** : 890-897 (2009).
8. Q. Nasir, S. Al-Araji, " Linearized Phase Detector Zero Crossing DPLL Performance Evaluation in Faded Mobile Channels", Circ. and Sys., **2(3)** : 139-144 (2011).
9. S. R. Al-Araji, E. Salahat, D. Kilani, S. A. Yasin, H. Alkhoja, J. Aweya, " Adaptive Zero Crossing Digital Phase Locked Loop for Packet Synchronization", *11th IEEE International New Circuits and Systems Conference*, 215-221, Paris (2013).
10. S. Levantino, C. Samori, " Non-Linearity Cancellation in Digital PLLs", *IEEE Custom Integrated Circuits Conference*, 1-8, San Jose (2013).
11. E. Salahat, M. A. Qutyari, S. R. Al-Araji, " Robust Hyperbolic Σ-Δ Based No Delay Tan Lock Loop for Wireless Communication", *80th IEEE Vehicular Technology Conference*, 512-517, Vancouver (2014).
12. C. C. Hung, S.I. Liu, " A 40 *GHz* Fast Locked All Digital Phase Locked Loop using Modified Bang-Bang Algorithm", IEEE Trans. Circ. And Sys., **58(6)** : 321-325 (2011).

Using microcomputers for lighting appliance control using a DALI bus

Tomas Sysala[1,a], Jan Pribyslavsky[1] and Petr Neumann[2]

[1] *Tomas Bata University in Zlin, Faculty of Applied Informatics, Department of Automation and Control Engineering, nam. T.G.Masaryka 5555, 760 01 Zlin, Czech Republic*
[2] *Tomas Bata University in Zlin, Faculty of Applied Informatics, Department of Electronics and Measurements, nam. T.G.Masaryka 5555, 760 01 Zlin, Czech Republic*

Abstract. Article concerns the DALI bus theoretical and practical aspects. The DALI bus is a modern technology developed especially for illumination systems control. Authors are outlining communication basic principles related to the physical layer and going up to more complex data transactions among particular devices. The article main topic is aimed at two device models development based on microcontroller and exploiting that technology. The first of those two devices is a DALI slave unit enabling the light source or multi switch with light indication components control via DALI bus. The second device measures the ambient illumination intensity and it also detects errors in the load.

1 Introduction

The electric illumination is a common furnishing of every habitable building nowadays. Nevertheless, it is necessary to bear in mind that the classic concept of light with corresponding switch has been implemented practically in the same arrangement and design since the end of 19th century when it starts spreading in residential buildings. It is quite a peculiar phenomenon because other electro-technology or informatics based designs have gone through a tremendous development. In spite of that, we can witness a wide range of technologies development aimed at the area of illumination control in course of last two decades.

We are more and more often encountering the notion "smart building" recently. These buildings providing occupiers with optimal indoor environment are economy and energy effective, and the frequently offer a multipurpose use of. All of that is possible due to modern technologies related to informatics, automation and control, not excepting sophisticated illumination ways realisation.

We deal with devices and smart building control algorithms development in our research project. One of many possibilities is the whole smart building parameters to be controlled with a programmable automaton (PLC) [1-2]. Such solution is comprehensive, but it suffers from high costs. Providing we want to control only one segment from the wide range of controllable parameters, we can use a cheaper solution.

This article does not deal with smart building issues as such, but it only strives to describe one alternative related to illumination systems control.

2 DALI bus

The illumination control design is based on a device incorporating microcontroller and controlled components which mutually communicating via DALI bus.

The DALI bus (Digital Addressable Lighting Interface) corresponding with the international standard IEC 62386 is a digital bus designated for illumination framework control. It is an open protocol system what means that various manufacturers can use it for their products. The DALI bus offers a unified interface for all bus participants. The coordination scheme respects the master slave hierarchy.

The master usually acts as a controlling unit starting communication, and approaching individual slave devices. There must be at least one master unit in any DALI bus system. The slave device is a remote unite acting according to master unit commands. The slave can send data back, but only as a response for preceding inquiry [3-6].

2.1 Physical layer

The DALI bus data and commands transfer runs via two wires, and devices are parallel connected to that two wire link. One link segment can bear up to 64 unit connections in an arbitrary combination of masters and slaves. The communication rate is fixed to 1200 Bd. The DALI protocol has been developed with an idea that the data link is realized with same wires as for 230 VAC power supply distribution in one cable.

[a] Corresponding author: sysala@fai.utb.cz

2.2 Manchester coding

The bus data transfer uses Manchester coding scheme which codes with transitions between levels. The leading edge codes the bit logic symbol 0, and the trailing edge codes the bit logic symbol 1. The signal voltage levels are typically 0-16 Volts [5].

2.3 Frames

There are composed frames from individual bits in DALI bus during transfer. The frame can be either the controlling one which serves for the master unit to approach slave devices, or the backward frame for the slave response.

The first bit in every frame is the start bit, and the frame ends with two stop bits. The time slot for one bit is constant what means 833.33 µs at the data rate of 1200 Bd. The acceptable tolerance of bit duration is +/- 10%.

2.4 Addresses, groups and commands

Any DALI bus slave device has its own address. If master device sends the control frame containing the particular slave device address in the frame address segment, the corresponding slave device responses. As a general rule, the slave device response procedure includes the frame data segment reading to check for a command to be performed. The frame data segment has 8 bits so that there could be in general one of 256 various commands to be performed [6].

Besides its own address, every device can be assigned to one or more groups. The total group number is 16. In case the master unit sends a frame with group identification code in address segment, the response comes from every member of that particular group. This is how there is possible to approach more than one device with only one inquiry unlike individual approach with corresponding number of message frames.

2.5 Topology

The DALI bus topology usually comprises a parallel interconnection of all devices in one network. The term network represents in our case the formation of no more than 64 units, the DALI bus power supply, DALI controller, and at least one device acting as a light source. That controller can be connected to another extensive system via a different bus. Providing we need to control more than 64 devices in our DALI bus, we have to extend it by means of other separate DALI bus interconnected via a gateway, or as the case may be, there can be more DALI bus systems unified using their master units that communicate mutually in another way.

3 The slave design concept

There is necessary to solve several problems in course of a new device for the DALI bus. Those problems are related both to the physical layer realisation aspect, and to the processing of packets in Manchester encoding.

In view of the fact that all devices are electrically isolated in the DALI bus system, it should be taken into account for circuit design. It is also necessary to ensure that the DALI bus signal conductors are independent on the polarity. The design of that can be inspired by some ready to use solutions. The DALI slave board OM13026 by NXP in Fig. 1can serve as an illustrative example.

The goal within our project was to utilize any DALI Master control unit that was able to communicate with DALI slave devices using standard commands, and that was meeting all above mentioned attributes. The project focus was to bring for being new DALI slave units.

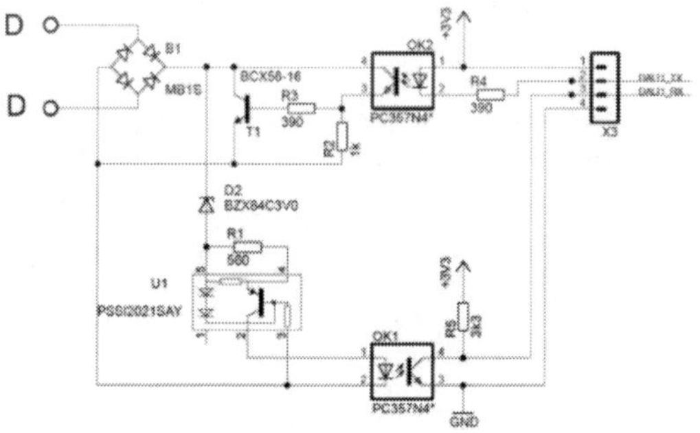

Figure 1. The DALI bus physical layer realization using OM13026 module circuit diagram [8].

As there is evident in the Fig. 1, the galvanic isolation is realized with optocouplers (OK1 a OK2) where each data transfer direction uses one of them. It is a cheap and efficient solution which enables voltage levels conversion to a required range at the same time like in this case to 0 – 3.3 Volts.

For the sake of both master and slave unit realisation is requisite to use one of up-to-date microcontrollers. DALI_RX and DALI_TX signals in Fig. 1 can be connected to such controller. Nevertheless, the Manchester encoding could be a problem for realization because not any microcontroller is able to process it directly. The LPC1343 circuit which OM13026 module incorporates can communicate only in the standard UART mode. That is why there was necessary to employ our own solution. The data transmission with DALI1_TX signal has software solution without any sophisticated hardware peripheral. The data reception DALI1_RX signal is fetched to the LPC1343 timer input set to the periodical level sampling of that signal. The samples are software-evaluated afterwards.

The communication exclusively software solution has advantage for the case that microcontroller does not provide any hardware support for given serial protocol in. It is thus possible to apply that method for every microcontroller with regards to its memory size and to its computing power.

The remarkable disadvantage of such solution is the fact that each bit processing consumes an appreciable part of computing power. The communication protocol supporting software also reduces the memory space what can matter in some applications. Much better solution represents the selection of microcontroller with inbuilt hardware Manchester encoded data processing support.

The microcontroller market offers an acceptable assortment of microcontrollers with Manchester encoded data processing support. The model from AT90PWM family [9] by Atmel [10] can be one of them. That family has been particularly designed for illumination applications, and every member of that family provides the extended function of the UART module for 16/17 bit communication in the DALI bus. Even though it is an 8-bit microcontroller which unlike the 32-bit LPC1343 does not provide such a computing power, the hardware level DALI communication handling compensates that disadvantage. The price of AT90PWM family circuits is comparable with LPC13 family members.

3.1 The DALI Slave I/O unit concept

The DALI Slave I/O unit has been designed in two variants with the same concept. One of those two variants has to provide the light source control via DALI bus, the other one has to provide the multi switch function with indicating elements. That is a user choice whether he decides to use that module either as a light source or as a multi switch.

The DALI Slave unit physical layer has been adopted from the OM13026 module. The other part of circuitry originates from the reference design by Atmel.

The DALI interface has been realized with regard to galvanic isolation with an optocoupler just as all I/O modules.

The I/O unit block diagram is illustrated in the following Fig. 2.

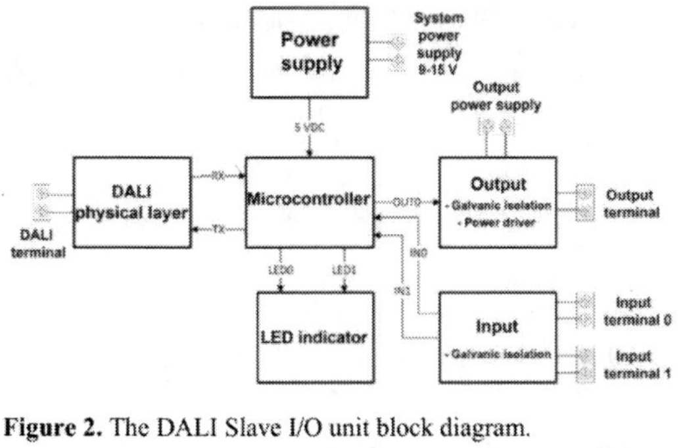

Figure 2. The DALI Slave I/O unit block diagram.

3.2 The DALI Slave sensor unit concept

The sensor unit originates both in hardware and software concept mostly from the I/O unit. However, it has brought the following modifications in comparison to it:

- It does not incorporate the user entries (push-buttons).
- It has no output galvanic isolation.
- There is an output load current measurement resistor added.
- There is a voltage divider with photoresistor for ambient illumination intensity measurement added.

Besides the ambient illumination intensity measurement and load error detection indicated with load current out of expected value, the third DALI slave unit adding in the system offers one possibility more – the DALI group utilization. In case we decide to operate only two Slave units separately in two different groups, from the practical point of view, there is no difference between the access via a direct address or via the group address.

The sensor unit concept has been generated in a block diagram form similarly to the I/O unit concept one.

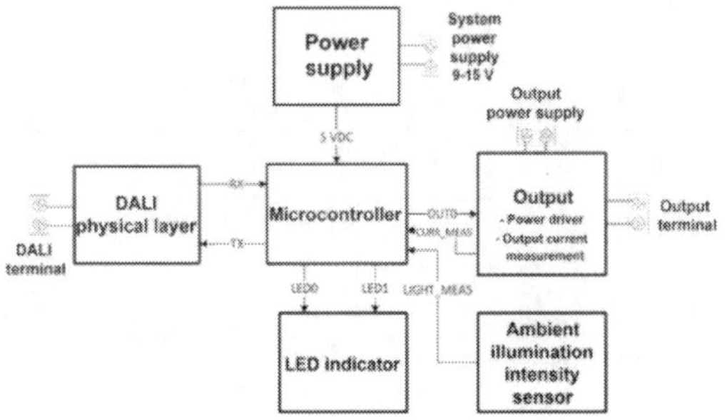

Figure 3. The DALI Slave sensor unit block diagram.

3.2.1 The ambient illumination value measurement

The DALI Slave sensor unit is equipped with a voltage divider composed from a photoresistor and a common resistor in series for ambient illumination intensity measurement.

The divider input was connected directly between the microcontroller supply voltage rail and the ground rail.

That arrangement is surely not a best one. However, it serves sufficiently when the simplicity and the only indicative ambient illumination measurement have main priority. The accuracy improvement would require either a voltage reference for voltage divider input or the specialized integrated circuit designed for such purpose with the digital output of measured values.

The VT93N2 photoresistor has been selected. Its nominal dark value is 500 kilo ohms [11].

The divider output voltage is the voltage of the two components in series common node. The output of that voltage divider was directly connected to the microcontroller AD converter input without any supplementary components for voltage level modification. There was necessary to take into account not only the AD input nominal voltage range, but also the working range of ambient illumination values for the second resistor value calculation.

4 Microcontroller

The DALI Slave units have as a core part ATMega88 (IC5) microcontroller with other components supporting its function. There are decoupling capacitors (C1, C6, C7 a C8) connected to microcontroller supply voltage pins. LED indication diodes (LED1 and LED2) are also directly connected to microcontroller. The 6-pin SPI connector has been added to the circuitry for firmware loading possibility. It provides not only SPI bus communication possibility, but also ensures a special DebugWire serial interface.

The microcontroller individual pin function overview brings the following table (Tab 1).

Table 1. Microcontroller pins function.

Pin	Data direction	Signal	Description	Note
PC2	DI	DALI RX	DALI data reception	
PC6	DI	Reset	Microcontroller Reset	
PB0	DI	IN1	Digital input push-buttons	I/O unit exclusively
PB1	DO	DALI TX	DALI data transmission	
PB2	DO	OUT0	PWM output for load control	
PB3	DO	MOSI	SPI data input (FW update)	
PB4	DI	MISO	SPI data output (FW update)	
PB5	DI	SCK	SPI clock signal (FW update)	
PB6	DO	LED1	Indication LED 1 output	
PB7	DO	LED2	Indication LED 2 output	
PD5	DI	IN0	Digital input push-buttons	I/O unit exclusively
PC0	AI	CURR _MEAS	Current measurement input	Sensor unit exclusively
PC1	AI	LIGHT _MEAS	Illumination intensity measurement input	Sensor unit exclusively

5 Final DALI Slave board

The following picture displays the final DALI Slave I/O assembled module after PCB manufacturing and component insertion and soldering.

Figure 4. The ready to use DALI Slave I/O unit photo [3].

6 DALI Slave unit firmware

From the architectural point of view, firmware is divided into three main segments:

- Drivers –physical layer signals processing
- DALI services –DALI frames processing
- DALI application – DALI Slave unit functions realization

The basic architecture as it was adopted from the reference design is illustrated in the following picture:

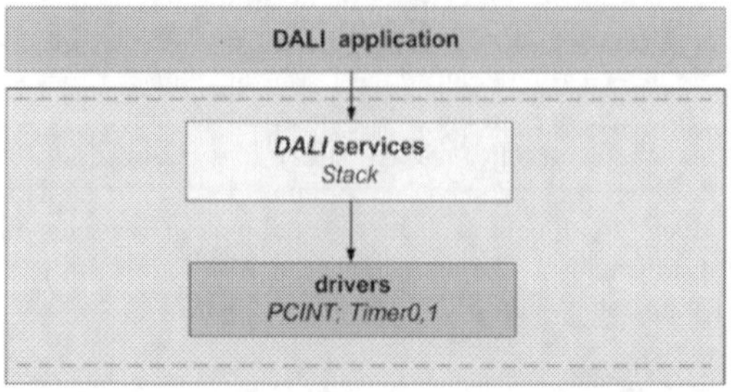

Figure. 5. DALI Slave unit firmware architecture [12].

6.1 Physical layer signals processing (drivers)

As the employed ATMEGA88 microcontroller is not endowed with any hardware interface for a direct Manchester encoded serial communication processing, it was necessary to ensure it in a purely software way. Microcontroller uses the PCINT hardware peripheral and the timer 0.

PCINT is an interrupt that is activated at any value change on microcontroller input pin. In our case, it is PC2 pin which is DALI_RX signal brought to. That signal is a direct output from the DALI physical layer. The physical layer has been adopted from the OM13026 module.

6.2 Frames processing (DALI services)

The DALI frames processing is implemented as a finite state machine which functions realizing states evaluation and the transition between them has to be periodically activated from higher software layers.

The finite state machine for frames processing is in non active state most of time (Idle state) waiting for frame arrival. If a frame comes, it is processed, and the state machine transits in other possible states depending on coming data – reception repeat, answer sending, or back to idle state as the case may be.

IEC62386-100 standard requires the obligatory pause between individual states transition. Our design respects that requirement. Standard also sets down that arriving frame is only valid providing it is obtained two times in course of a 100 milliseconds period. The reason for that is the erroneous data reception exclusion. Provided that condition is fulfilled, the frame related command is executed, and state machine transits in idle state. If there is not possible to receive same frame within 100 milliseconds, the state machine transits in idle state directly.

6.3 Application layer (DALI application)

The term "application layer" in our project is to be understood as all what is on the highest level from the software architecture point of view, and what implements the functionality as such. The application layer term in our project is to be understood from the software point of view as a highest level implementing the Slave unit functionality as such from the user position. There has been created several smaller software modules which task is to mediate for application layer the microcontroller hardware components access.

The list of those software modules is as follows: LEDs.c, inputs.c, sensing.c.

6.4 Supported DALI commands

Any command captured during arriving DALI frames processing is transferred to the application layer for further processing.

Every command has its value within enumeration type (enum), and its particular implementation is located within a switch block where is to be jumped according to the "enum" value to.

Because of simplicity, there are only a few remarkable commands presented in the following table (Table 2).

Table 2. Selected DALI Slave unit commands list.

Comm. code	Command name (enum)	Command description
0	OFF	Immediate output setting to 0 value, device switching over to "OFF" mode
1	UP	Gradual lightening for 200ms period providing device is in "ON" mode
2	DOWN	Gradual dimming for 200ms period providing device is in "ON" mode
3	STEP_UP	Lightening of one step in the range of 1-254 providing device is in "ON" mode
4	STEP_DOWN	Dimming of one step in the range of 1-254 providing device is in "ON" mode
32	RESET	Device Reset to initial state
144	QUERY _STATUS	Device state inquiry
231	SET _INDICATION _LED_1	Indication LED 1 switch on
232	CLEAR _INDICATION _LED_1	Indication LED 1 switch off

7 The entire system test

The test fixture for assembled modules has been created. As was mentioned above, the commercial unit OM13046 by NXP was selected as the DALI Master device. It is practically a converter between the DALI bus and the USB interface. It is based on the LPC134x microcontroller. That device is supplied directly via USB port, and it uses the HID (Human Interface Device) class for communication with a PC. That concept makes PC software development much easier because there is possible to make use of Windows and NET platform native drivers.

From the hardware point of view, that OM13046 module includes the DALI bus physical layer with optocouplers galvanic isolation.

The test fixture comprises of following components:

- 2pcs DALI Slave I/O unit
- 1pc DALI Slave sensor unit
- 1pc DALI-Master unit
- 24VDC adaptor for DALI bus power supply
- 9VDC adaptor for DALI units power supply
- 3pcs light source
- 4pcs push-button

Test fixture enables particularly following functions:

- User entry via 4 individual push-buttons.
- 3 light sources power control (9V LED „bulbs").
- User adjustable events indication with 6 LED indicators.
- One failure detection (load disconnect) at one light source.
- Ambient illumination intensity sensing.
- DALI bus power supply.

There were tested all commands individually and communication possibilities by means of this set.

Acknowledgements

This work was supported by the Ministry of Education, Youth and Sports of the Czech Republic within the National Sustainability Programme project No. LO1303 (MSMT-7778/2014) and also by the European Regional Development Fund under the project CEBIA-Tech No. CZ.1.05/2.1.00/03.0089.

Conclusion

Article describes some aspects of DALI bus application for illumination systems control.

According to the most convenient concept, there were created two unit types for communication via DALI bus. The functionality of those units was demonstrated on the test fixture comprising both those units and other accessories forming together with units a complete DALI system.

There has been also designed and implemented PC application for that DALI system configuration and control within the bounds of our project. All parts of our project were successfully implemented so that the system functionality can be extended in the future.

References

1. T. Sysala, M. Pospichal P. Neumann, *Proceedings of the 17th International Carpathian Control Conference - ICCC'2016*, **1**, 706-710, (2016)
2. P. Navratil, L. Pekar, *Proc. of the 16th WSEAS International Conference on Circuits*, **1**, (2012)

3. J. Pribyslavsky, *diploma work at Tomas Bata University in Zlin*, (2016)
4. Semiconductors, NXP, Application note - DALI slave using the LPC111x, *NXP Semiconductors*, (2012).
5. S. Husain, Application note - Digitally Addressable Lighting Interface (DALI) Communication. [PDF] *Microchip Technology Inc.*, (2012)
6. Philips, Introduction to DALI. [PDF], *Philips*, (2008)
7. T. Sysala, P. Neumann, J. Pribyslavsky, M. Adamek, *International Journal of Circuits, Systems and Signal Processing*, **7**, (2013)
8. NXP Semiconductors N.V., [Online]. Available: http://www.mouser.com/pdfdocs/AN11174.pdf, (2012)
9. Atmel Corporation, 8-bit Atmel Microcontroller with 8K Bytes In-SystemProgrammable Flash, [PDF], (2013)
10. Atmel Corporation. [Online] Available: http://www.atmel.com/, (2016)
11. Optoelectronics, PerkinElmer. [Online] http://www.farnell.com//datasheets/919043.pdf, (2012)
12. Corporation, Atmel, [Online] Available: http://www.atmel.com/images/atmel-42071-dali-slave-reference_design_application-note_at01244.pdf, (2012)

MATEC Web of Conferences **76**, 03012 (2016) DOI: 10.1051/matecconf/20167603012
CSCC 2016

Knowledge Base for an Intelligent System in order to Identify Security Requirements for Government Agencies Software Projects

Beltrán G. Adán[1,a], Lombana C. Cristhian[1], Calvo L. Mario[1], Ordoñez S. Sonia[1], Caviativa C. Yaneth[1] and Garcés Jairo[1]

[1] *Grupo de Investigación en Ingenieria de Software. Vicerrectoría de Investigaciones. Universidad Manuela Beltrán. Av. Circunvalar No. 60-00, Bogotá, Colombia*

Abstract. *It has been evidenced that one of the most common causes in the failure of software security is the lack of identification and specification of requirements for information security, it is an activity with an insufficient importance in the software development or software acquisition We propose the knowledge base of CIBERREQ. CIBERREQ is an intelligent knowledge-based system used for the identification and specification of security requirements in the software development cycle or in the software acquisition. CIBERREQ receives functional software requirements written in natural language and produces non-functional security requirements through a semi-automatic process of risk management. The knowledge base built is formed by an ontology developed collaboratively by experts in information security. In this process has been identified six types of assets: electronic data, physical data, hardware, software, person and service; as well as six types of risk: competitive disadvantage, loss of credibility, economic risks, strategic risks, operational risks and legal sanctions. In addition there are defined 95 vulnerabilities, 24 threats, 230 controls, and 515 associations between concepts. Additionally, automatic expansion was used with Wikipedia for the asset types Software and Hardware, obtaining 7125 and 5894 software and hardware subtypes respectively, achieving thereby an improvement of 10% in the identification of the information assets candidates, one of the most important phases of the proposed system.*

1 Introduction

It has been shown that the most common causes of application security vulnerabilities are the incomplete identification of requirements and bad specification of requirements. In Colombia, the government entities have been subject of several information security incidents. The root cause of those incidents has been identified as a bad requirements engineering practice. A simple study of the Request For Proposals (RFP) used to contract software development and software acquisition written by government entities, shows that security requirements are underspecified. Most of the documents ask for a "secure implementation" or a "secure configuration", but they do not describe in detail the concrete aspects of such request.

In this article we describe the knowledge base of an intelligent system for the identification and specification of security requirements in software applications. The knowledge base was designed using elements of semantic web, natural language processing, knowledge management and cross sourcing. The purpose of the intelligent system is to allow government entities to identify and define, together with the software provider, the security requirements that application and systems must meet.

The article is organized as follows, section II presents the state of the art regarding knowledge bases developed for cybersecurity. Section III discusses the methodology used to build the knowledge base. In section IV we describe the ontology used to build the knowledge base for the proposed system and shows how the system interacts with the knowledge base.

[a] Corresponding author: adan.beltran@docentes.umb.edu.co

2 State of the Art: Knowledge Bases for Cybersecurity

In [1] an ontology of information security is proposed. The ontology includes the most relevant concepts of the domain as Asset, Vulnerability, Threat and Control. It also discriminates between tangible and intangible assets; and allows modeling of the physical infrastructure of the organization with information such as the place where the asset is located. The ontology has 500 concepts and 600 formal restrictions, and was derived from best practice guidelines and standards for information security, including Internet Security Glossary (RFC 2828); German IT Grundschutz Manual; The United Nations Standard Products and Services Code; National Institute of Standards and Technology Special Publication 800-12; ISO / IEC 27000; among others.

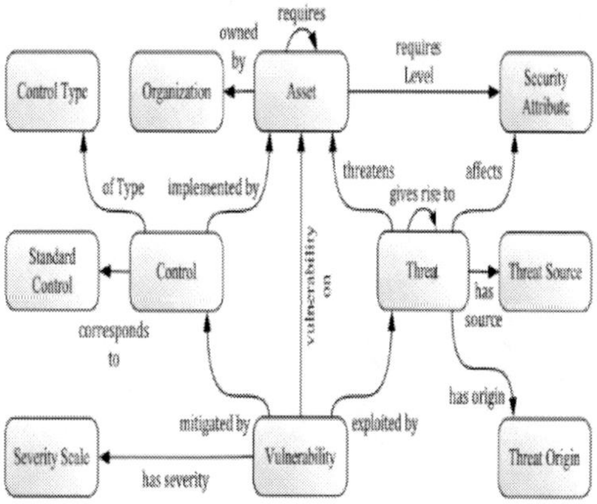

Figure 1. Security relationships [1].

In [2] the authors present a framework composed of several ontologies. These ontologies are used to represent, store and reuse safety requirements. The first ontology presents knowledge for risk analysis following the ISO 27002 standard (see Fig. 2) As a result the ontology identifies five main elements: assets, threats associated with the asset, protection measures to address threats, valuation dimensions (attributes that make an asset valuable) and valuation criteria (measure of the importance of an asset to the organization).

The second ontology has classified requirements according to IEEE standards. In the combination of these two ontologies, each security requirement has an associated asset together with threats and protection measures. Additionally, each requirement has the information of valuation dimensions, and valuation criteria for each asset associated with the requirement

In [3] an ontology of security incidents is proposed. The ontology describes a conceptual framework with the following elements: Agent, Attack, Security Incident, Tools Vulnerability and Access. These elements are related as follows: an agent performs an Attack that can cause a Security Incident. In order to perform an Attack,the agent uses a Tool, which exploits a Vulnerability, in order to get Access. The Incident has a Consequence, on an Asset, and happens at a specific Time.

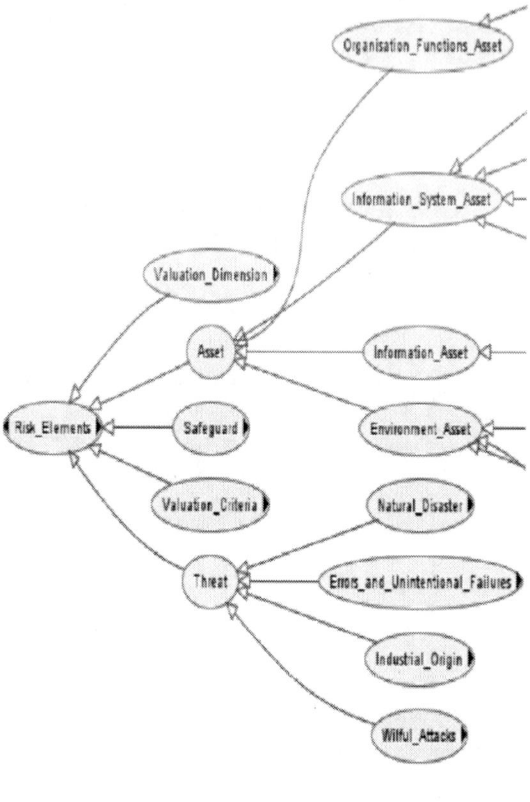

Figure 2. Taxonomy of the elements of the risk analysis ontology [2].

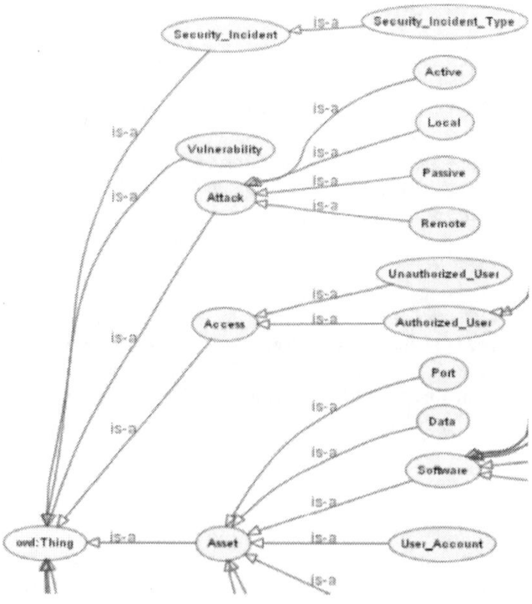

Figure 3. The security incident ontology conceptual model [3].

In [4] an initial work is presented for a unified security ontology. First, the study identifies the basic requirements that the ontology should have.

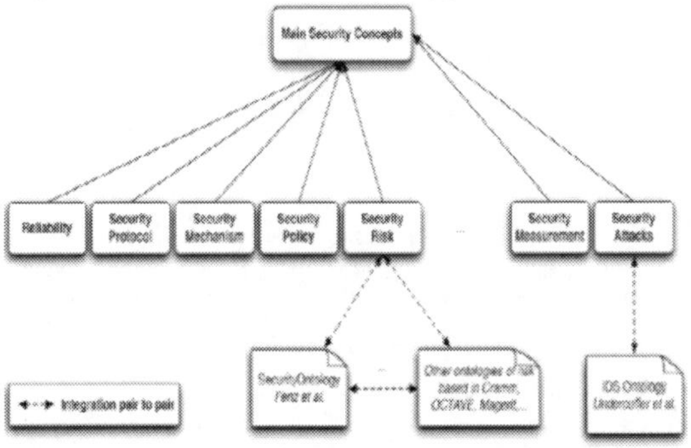

Figure 4. Overlapping between security domains for integrated security ontology [4].

To identify such requirements the study uses OntoMetric to create a comparative analysis of existing proposals. These requirements are: static knowledge, dynamic knowledge and reusability. Second, a process for ontology integration was applied. Following such process overlapping areas between ontologies were identified (see Fig. 4), related concepts and consistency of the result were verified.

3 Design Methodology for the Ontology

For the design of ontology the methodology described in [5] was used. The following steps are carried out.

A. What is the domain the ontology will cover?

Definitions of functional requirements to acquire or develop an application.

B. For what we use the ontology?

To identify information security requirements.

C. What types of questions the information in the ontology should answer?

- What are the vulnerabilities for an asset?
- What are the threats that can exploit a vulnerability?
- What are the controls that can minimize a vulnerability?
- What are the types of risk that may materialize?

a. Enumerate the important concepts in the domain

Information asset, environment, threat, vulnerability, inherent risk, impact, control, residual risk, accepted risk, encryption algorithm, encryption software, cryptographic hash algorithm, cryptographic-summary software, log audit, log traceability, application, application code, database, table, communications link, issuer, receiver, owner of information asset, switch, router, firewall, antimalware, malware.

b. Define the classes and the class hierarchy

Information asset: information; hardware; software; person, service.

Threats: human intentional (STRIDE), human unintentional, hardware, nature, among others.

Vulnerability: unencrypted data, unsigned data, absence of audit, lack of traceability, lack of access control, data without cryptographic summary, absence of capture fields validation, absence of output data validation, among others.

Risk: damage or loss of assets, excessive costs, loss of income, loss of business, image loss, legal sanctions, wrong decisions, impact, level of involvement for the company can be measured in money, percentage levels, among others.

Controls: rules, procedures, policies, implementation guidelines, standards, cryptography, logs, monitoring, access control, disciplinary sanctions, backups, alternate center, redundancy, among others.

4 Results

A. CyberSecurity Ontology

This section describes the ontology that was designed following the methodology described above (see Fig. 5).

We now define in detail the classes (concepts) and properties (relations) of the ontology.

1) Classes

Asset type: Electronic Data, Physical data, Hardware, Software, Service, Person.

Vulnerability: Unrestricted access, Absence of antivirus, Absence of backup, Absence of logging and auditing, Weak passwords, Disgruntled employee, Typos, Lack of secure deletion policy, Installing unauthorized software, Unprotected network point, Vulnerabilities in the operating system and/or PC applications, among others.

Threat: Intrusive access to the PC, Alteration or removal, Accidental damage, Natural disasters, Terrorism or public disorder, Information leakage, Infection or malware, among others.

Control: Enable audit logs, Apply Active Directory policies, User training, Defining roles and user roles, Record file deletion, Implementing encryption in storage, Implement UPS or power plant, Implement firewall, Backups policy, Secure wiring policy, Procedure for defining strong passwords, Record of failed attempts to access network resources, among others.

Risk type: Competitive disadvantage, Loss of image or credibility, Economic risks, Strategic risks, Operational risks, Legal sanctions.

2) Properties

Can have: the relation *can have* is defined as follows: an Asset Type can have a Vulnerability.

Exploits. The relation *exploits* has Threat as domain and a conjunction between Asset Type and Vulnerability as range.

Minimize. In the relation *minimize* the domain is Control and Vulnerability is the range. A control minimizes a vulnerability.

Can be materialized. The relation *can be materialized* has Risk Type as domain and Asset Type as range.

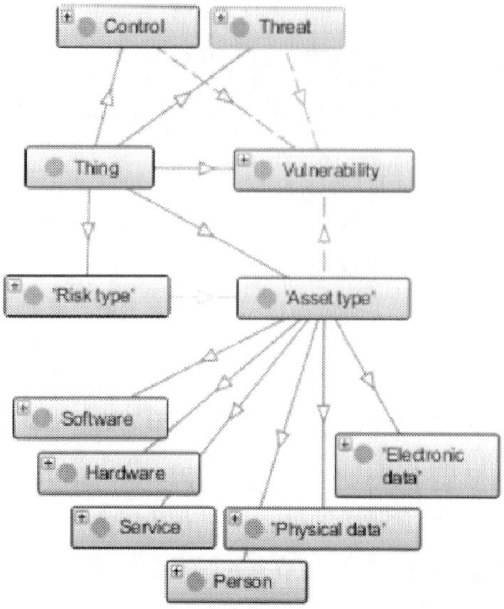

Figure 5. Top level concepts and relationships in the ontology.

A concrete example of the type of information that can be extracted from the ontology is:

The asset type 'Electronic data' can have a vulnerability of 'Absence of backup', which is exploited by the threat 'Alteration or deletion' and is minimized by the control 'Backups Policy'. The risk that can be materialized in this case is 'Operational risk'.

The ontology has 361 concepts, which are broken down into six types of assets, six types of risks, 95 vulnerabilities, 24 threats and 230 controls. In addition, there are 515 relationships between concepts.

The following link shows the complete ontology description that was developed using Protégé [6]: http://webprotege.stanford.edu/#Edit:projectId=1530e338-671c-474f-a01e-4f77808ce63b

B. Knowledge-based Intelligent System

The intelligent system based on the ontology is called "CIBERREQ". CIBERREQ is a tool for the identification and specification of security requirements for projects of software development or software acquisition in government entities.

The system receives as input functional requirements written in natural language and, using the knowledge represented in the knowledge base, supports domain experts or users in the definition and specification of security requirements.

CIBERREQ uses the knowledge base for (Fig. 6):

- *Identify the information assets candidates*, found in the functional requirements.
- *Identify vulnerabilities* related to specific assets.
- *Identify threats* that exploit vulnerabilities.
- *Identify the controls* that minimize vulnerabilities.
- *Identify the types of risks* that may materialize.

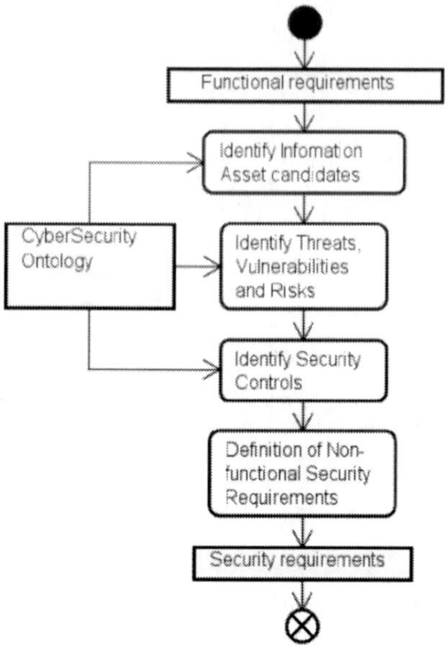

Figure 6. Process for identification of security requirements to CIBERREQ.

Following there is a description of an example of the application of the CIBERREQ tool in a real project:

Given the following functional requirement: "it is required a functionality that allows for the initial loading of parametric tables that make up the databases Base1 and BD2; the system identifies semi-automatically, using natural language processing techniques and validation from security experts, the following information assets: BD1 (unique client base), BD2 (membership database), parametric tables. These three correspond to the asset type 'Electronic Data'.

For these assets the tool identified the vulnerability: "password administration inadequate"; and the threat: "non-authorized access", and the control: "to implement strong passwords in the access control established for the equipment".

For the preceding information the following risks were identified: "damage or loss of assets due to non-authorized access in Base2 due to inadequate password administration"; "legal sanctions for non-authorized access in Base2 due to inadequate password administration".

Considering the previous information, the security expert, using the mentioned tool, defined the following non-functional security requirements: "confidential information that is processed and transmitted must be encoded with strong cryptographic algorithms"; "authorized users must enter the system using authentication based on the specific role"; "a profile, historical and tracing register must be generated".

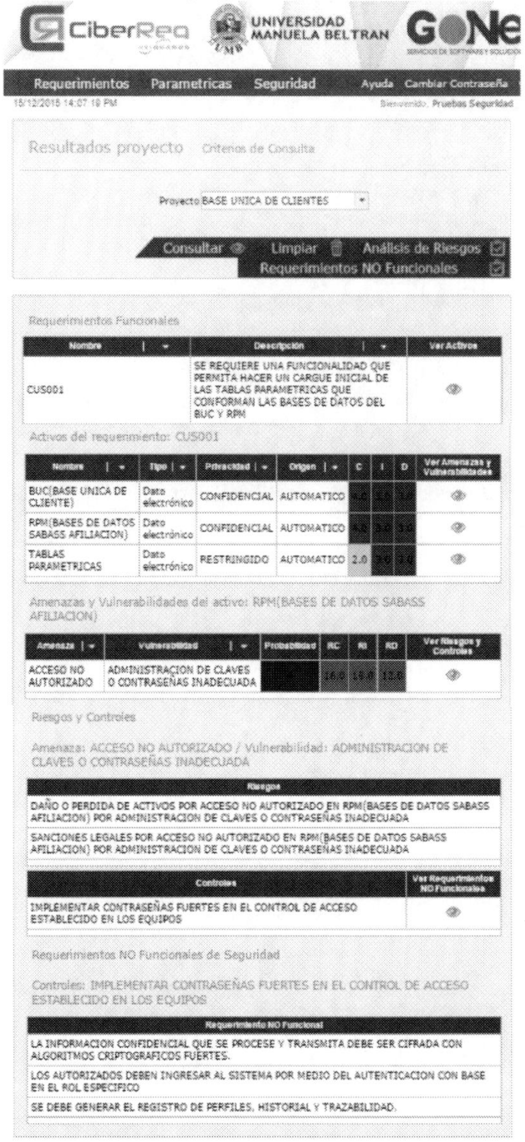

Figure 7. CIBERREQ tool.

Figure 7 shows the process developed with the CIBERREQ tool for the case previously described.

C. Ontology expansion with Wikipedia

Additionally, with the object of enriching the ontology, some terms were automatically expanded using Wikipedia's API.

In Wikipedia, every page has one or more associated categories, and each category can have subcategories or supercategories [7]. For this expansion, category trees were extracted of up to 7 depth levels for the asset types Software and Hardware, obtaining 7125 subtypes of Software and 5894 subtypes of Hardware. This allowed an improvement in identifying the information assets candidates of 10%, one of the most important phases in the system.

5 Discussion

The use of ontologies in building the knowledge base facilitates maintenance, expansion and extension of the system to other more specific contexts of information security to improve accuracy throughout the process of identifying security requirements.

Therefore, this knowledge base can be used for other projects that are not government.

6 Conclusion

We have presented the design of an ontology for information security, and a tool that uses the ontology in order to aid in the identification and specification of security requirements. The ontology was developed collaboratively by domain experts and users, and was later expanded automatically with Wikipedia, producing a 10% improvement in the precision of the phase of information asset identification of the CIBERREQ tool. The resulting ontology is a general model that is not specific for a platform or technology. Thus it can be used to develop other intelligent knowledge-based systems.

The knowledge base was validated with different experts and officials from state agencies, in addition, the system was used in a real project of a state entity, but as previously said the knowledge base can be specified and adjusted for other not necessarily governmental contexts, and the fact that part of this ontology is based and expanded with terms in Wikipedia allows validation by the expert community in the subject.

Acknowledgment

This research is financed jointly by Colciencias (Fondo Francisco Jose de Caldas), Ministry of Information and Communication Technologies of Colombia (MinTic), Universidad Manuela Beltrán and Ubiquando – Project No. 1263-668-44906

References

[1] S. Fenz and A. Ekelhart. "Formalizing Information Security Knowledge." In *Proceedings of the 4th International Symposium on Information, Computer, and Communications Security*, 2009, 183-194.

[2] J. Lasheras, R. Valencia-García, J. T. Fernández-Breis, and A. Toval. "Modelling reusable security requirements based on an ontology framework."

Journal of Research and Practice in Information Technology, vol. 41, no. 2, pp. 119–133, 2009.

[3] A. Martimiano and E. Moreira. "An owl-based security incident ontology." in *Proceedings of the Eighth International Protege Conference*, 2005, pp. 43–44.

[4] C. Blanco, J. Lasheras, E. Fernández-Medina, R. Valencia-García, and A. Toval, "Basis for an integrated security ontology according to a systematic review of existing proposals," *Computer Standards & Interfaces*, vol. 33, no. 4, pp. 372–388, 2011.

[5] N.F. Noy and D.L. McGuinness. "Ontology Development 101: A Guide to Creating Your First Ontology". Stanford Knowledge Systems Laboratory Technical Report KSL-01-05 and Stanford Medical Informatics Technical Report SMI-2001-0880, March 2001.

[6] Protégé. http://protege.stanford.edu/. [Oct. 01, 2015]

[7] T. Zesch, I. Gurevych and M. Mühlhäuser. "Analyzing and Accessing Wikipedia as a Lexical Semantic Resource." *Data Structures for Linguistic Resources and Applications*, pp. 197-205, 2007.

Standardized headings as a foundation for semantic interoperability in EHR

Amra Halilovic[1,a] and Annika Terner[2]

[1]*Dalarna County Council, Falun, Sweden, amra.halilovic@ltdalarna.se*
[2]*Uppsala County Council and Department of Public Health and Caring Sciences, Uppsala University, Uppsala, Sweden*

Abstract. The new Swedish Patient Act, which allows patients to choose health care in county councils other than their own, creates the need to be able to share health-related information contained in electronic health records [EHRs) across county councils. This demands interoperability in terms of structured and standardized data. Headings in EHR could also be a part of structured and standardized data. The aim was to study to what extent terminology is shared and standardized across county councils in Sweden. Headings from three county councils were analyzed to see to what extent they were shared and to what extent they corresponded to concepts in SNOMED CT and the National Board of Health and Welfare's term dictionary [NBHW's TD). In total 41% of the headings were shared across two or three county councils. A third of the shared headings corresponded to concepts in SNOMED CT. Further, an eighth of the shared headings corresponded to concepts in NBHW's TD. The results showed that the extent of shared and standardized terminology in terms of headings across the studied three county councils were negligible.

Keywords. Terminology, Snomed CT, Electronic Health Records, Healthcare Information and Management Systems, Health Informatics, Data Engineering.

1 Introduction

The 21 county councils in Sweden are responsible for ensuring that everyone living in Sweden has access to good health care. The principle of local self-government gives each county council the right to design health care services with reference to local conditions [1]. Most county councils have one joint electronic health record [EHR) system for all health-related documentation in hospitals, psychiatry and primary care.

The Patient Act 2104 [2] is a new law in Sweden, the aim of which is to empower patients and to promote patients' rights to privacy, self-determination, and participation. According to the law a patient has the right to choose health care in county councils other than their own which creates the need to be able to share health-related information in EHRs across county councils.

EHR is defined as an electronic record of health-related information on an individual which conforms to nationally recognized interoperability standards and which can be created, managed, and consulted by health care professionals across health care organizations. Health-related information means among others: treatment and discharge summaries, investigation results and reports, prescriptions and health care professional notes [3].

The main keys to interoperability are structured and standardized data. The Patient Act has been the driving force towards interoperability in health care. Interoperability allows the right information to be available to the tight people at the right time across products and organisations [4].

1.1 Interoperability and headings

Interoperability for EHRs is defined here as the ability of EHRs to send, receive, share and interpret structured and standardized health-related information [5]. There are several categories of interoperability, e.g. technical, semantic, organizational and legal interoperability [6]. Semantic interoperability means that the information is unambiguously understood in content, meaning, and purpose by the receiver. This demands standardized terminology as a path to structured, encoded and on a semantic level interoperable health data [7].

To structure the data EHRs should have templates [8-11] which consist of headings in a tree-structure [12, 13]. The templates and headings support the user to enter collected data in a structured way [14] into larger or smaller parts [15]. They also provide collected data with context [16] because a heading briefly defines the data in

[a]Amra Halilovic: amra.halilovic@ltdalarna.se

the part as a label on a box [15]. An EHR without structure obstructs the possibility to find collected data about the patient when and where it is needed.

Headings constitute a crucial part of the terminology employed in EHRs. The headings are predefined according to medical specialists' [16-20] and professional groups' [16], [21-26] perceived needs of necessary information to provide high-quality health care [17]. When professional groups and medical specialties independently define headings there are risks for synonyms i.e. different terms for the same concept [22], [27-30] or for homonyms i.e. different concepts for the same term [22, 27]. This has resulted in headings not being standardized.

The Swedish National Board of Health and Welfare (NBHW), mandated by the Government, has the objective to develop and provide health care with a standard in terms of Common Information Structure (CIS) including National Information Structure (NIS) and National Language for Specific Purposes (NLSP). NIS includes descriptions at an overall level of the health care process and the information to be dealt with during the process. NLSP consists of nationally agreed concepts and terms published in the NBHW's term dictionary (TD). It also consists of SNOMED CT's (translated into Swedish) established statistical classifications and code systems. Methods for the development, management, and rules for use are also included in the CIS [31].

1.2 Problem

The need to be able to share health-related information across county councils in Sweden has become more important since the new Patient Act came into force. A prerequisite for sharing health-related information across county councils is interoperability which demands structured and standardized data. Headings structure the data in the EHRs and are therefore a crucial part of the terminology employed in the EHRs. However, to fulfill the request for standardized data the same terminology must be employed by all the county councils sharing health-related information. The question is: Do county councils employ the same terminology?

2 Aim

The aim of this paper is to study to what extent terminology is shared and standardized across county councils in Sweden. The specific research questions were: To what extent are headings shared across county councils? To what extent do the identified shared headings correspond to concepts in SNOMED CT and NBHW's TD?

3 Methods

A descriptive design was chosen for the study. At the time of data collection all county councils in Sweden had implemented EHRs for hospitals, psychiatry, and primary care. Three of these county councils (County A, County B, and County C) were chosen for the study.

3.1 Data collection and analyses

In January 2016 administrators in the chosen counties with access to EHR databases were asked for the headings stored in the databases. The obtained headings were compiled into a spreadsheet data file. The data consisted of a total of 32,228 headings consisting of single terms, multiple terms, expressions, or phrases. The spreadsheet data file was used for calculations and descriptive statistics.

The headings studied were obtained from databases. No patient information or health care professional information were obtained for the study.

3.1.1 Shared headings across the county councils

The number of headings which county B and C shared with County A as well as the proportions of shared headings were calculated and described. The criterion for sharing a heading with County A was that the studied headings in County B and/or C were spelled exactly the same as in County A. Headings sharing the same meaning but not spelled exactly the same were in this study not considered as shared with County A.

3.1.2 Shared headings corresponding to concepts in SNOMED CT and NBHW's TD

To examine how the shared headings corresponded to concepts in SNOMED CT and NBHW's TD each heading as a concept was searched for in SNOMED CT and NBHW's TD. A heading found in SNOMED CT or NBHW's TD as a concept with the same spelling, in an adequate category in SNOMED CT and with a similar description as the heading was deemed to have a corresponding concept in SNOMED CT and/or NBHW's TD.

4 Results

The collected data from County A included 588 headings, County B had 15,778 headings and County C had 15,862. When duplications were eliminated County B had 14,906 headings and County C had 5,809. These numbers of heading for each county are used in the presentation of the results.

4.1 Shared headings across the county councils

In total 41% (n=241) of County A's 588 headings were shared with County B and/or County C. All three counties shared 130 headings (22%). County A shared 174 headings with County B and 197 headings with County C, see Table 1.

Table 1: The distribution of shared headings in proportion to each county's number of headings

	County A n=588	County B n=14906	County C n=5809
County A n=588		30% (174)	34% (197)
County B n=14906	1% (174)		
County C n=5809	3% (197)		

4.2 Shared headings corresponding to concepts in SNOMED CT and NBHW's TD

In total 35% (n=86) of the 241 headings in County A, shared with County B and/or County C, corresponded to concepts in SNOMED CT and 13% (n=31) corresponded to concepts in NBHW's TD. Thirteen headings (5%) were found both in SNOMED CT and NBHW's TD, see Table 2. Further, in total 45% (n=59) of the 130 headings shared across the three counties corresponded to concepts in SNOMED CT and 15% (n=20) corresponded to concepts in NBHW's TD. Ten headings (7%) were found both in SNOMED CT and NBHW's TD, see Table 2.

Table 2: The distribution of shared headings corresponding to SNOMED CT and NBHW's TD in proportion to headings shared with County B and/or County C and headings shared with County B and C

	SNOMED CT	NBHW's TD	SNOMED CT & NBHW's TD
Headings shared with County B and/ or County C n=241	36% (86)	13% (31)	5% (13)
Headings shared with County B and C n=130	45% (59)	15% (20)	7% (10)

5 Discussion

The results show that the headings in County B and C to a negligible extent were shared with County A. Only a third of the shared headings correspond to concepts in SNOMED CT. Further, only an eighth of the shared headings correspond to concepts in NBHW's TD. Thirteen headings (5%) of 241 shared headings were found both in SNOMED CT and NBHW's TD.

The study was based on a large set of data comprising 32,228 headings from three county councils. The headings in County B and C were compared to the headings in County A. County A had the smallest number of headings (n=588) and the authors considered that this was sufficient to fulfil the aim in the study. Therefore the authors decided not to compare the headings between County B and County C. Further, there is the question of whether all these headings correspond to the needs of health and health care.

Semantic interoperability is crucial in EHRs. This was the basis for the decision to only accept concepts in SNOMED CT and terms in NBHW's TD with exactly the spelling as the shared headings; only under this criterion were the headings regarded as shared. However, the amount of standardized headings in the studied EHRs is negligible.

5.1 Conclusion and Future Work

The results show that the extent of shared and standardized terminology in terms of headings across the studied three county councils is negligible. Consequently, the studied county councils do not employ the same terminology. These headings are a crucial part of a standardized terminology and medical specialists and professional groups have lengthy experience of employing headings. However, common and standardized headings should be employed and shared between different EHRs. Therefore our recommendation is to use headings as a tool for implementing a National Language for Specific Purposes as NBHW's standard.

The plan for the next study is to involve all 21 county councils and analyze the extent headings with the same meaning (including headings not spelled exactly the same) are common across the counties.

References

[1] Socialstyrelsen. *God vård – om ledningssystem för kvalitet och patientsäkerhet i hälso- och sjukvården* In: Socialstyrelsen, Stockholm (2006)

[2] European Commission. *Semantic Interoperability for Better Health and Safer Healthcare*. Research and deployment roadmap for Europe. In: Commission E, (2009)

[3] The National Alliance for Health Information Technology. Report to the Office of the National Coordinator for Health Information Technology on *Defining Key Health Information Technology Terms*, Available at: http://cdm16064.contentdm.oclc.org/cdm/ref/collection/p266901coll4/id/2086 (2008)

[4] M. Stroupe, *What is EHR Interoperability and Why Should I Care?* A reference document for Urgent Care and Occupational Health Providers (2011)

[5] Healthcare Information and Management Systems Society. *Interoperability Definition and Background*. Available at http://www.himss.org/ResourceLibrary/ResourceDetail.aspx?ItemNumber=9265 (2005)

[6] European Commission. *Interoperability Solutions for European Public Administrations*. Available at: http://ec.europa.eu/isa (2016)

[7] European Commission. eHealth Governance Initiative, *Making Use of SNOMED CT: Key Questions And Status As Of September 2013*. Available at: ec.europa.eu/health/ehealth/events/ev_20131119_en.htm.

[8] D. Andreen, L. Dobie, J. Jasperson, T. Lucas, C. Wubbenhorst. *The conversion to electronic hospital notes at Mayo Clinic. Overcoming barriers and challenges.* JHIM, **24(3)**, pp. 57-64 (2010)

[9] K. Bernstein, M. Bruun-Rasmussen, S. Vingtoft, S. K. Andersen, C. Nøhr. *Modelling and implementing electronic health records in Denmark.* IJMI, **74(2)**, pp 213-20 (2005)

[10] D.R. Boulware, A.S. Dekarske, G.A. Filice, *Physician Preferences for Elements of Effective Consultations.* JGIM, **25(1)**, pp:25-30 (2010)

[11] V.K. Goradia. *Electronic Medical Records for the Arthroscopic Surgeon.* Arthroscopy: The Journal of Arthroscopic and Related Surgery, **22(2)**, pp 219-24 2006

[12] J.C. Denny, Iii A. Spickard, K.B. Johnson, N.B. Peterson, J.F. Peterson, R.A. Miller. *Evaluation of a Method to Identify and Categorize Section Headers in Clinical Documents.* JAMIA, 16(6), pp 806-15 (2009)

[13] E. Törnvall, S. Wilhelmsson, *Nursing documentation for communicating and evaluating care.* JCN, **17(16)**, pp 2116-24. (2008)

[14] C. Cusack, *Electronic Health Records and Electronic Prescribing: Promise and Pitfalls.* OBSTET GYN CLIN N AM, **35(1)**, pp 63-79 (2008)

[15] M. Nordman, *Överskrift, titel, namn eller rubrik? Några beteckningar i teori och praktik.* In: Nuopponen A TB, Myking J, editor. I terminologins tjänst Festskrift för Heribert Picht på 60-årsdagen Vaasa: Vasa universitet, pp. 110-7 (2000).

[16] K. Häyrinen, K. Harno, P. Nykänen, *Use of headings and classifications by physicians in medical narratives of EHRs: An evaluation study in a Finnish hospital.* ACI, **2(2)**, pp 143-57 (2011)

[17] H. Ahlfeldt, M. Ehnfors, L. Ridderstolpe, *Towards a Multi-professional Patient Record – A Study of the Headings Used in Clinical Practice.* (1999). Available at: http://citeseerx.ist.psu.edu

[18] A.B. De Luna, G. Wagner, Y. Birnbaum, K. Nikus, M. Fiol, A. Gorgels, et al. *A new terminology for left ventricular walls and location of myocardial infarcts that present Q wave based on the standard of cardiac magnetic resonance imaging: A statement for healthcare professionals from a committee appointed by the International Society for Holter and Noninvasive Electrocardiography.* Circulation, **114(16)**, pp. 1755-60 (2006)

[19] A.J. Maxwell, N.T. Ridley, G. Rubin, M.G. Wallis, F.J. Gilbert, M.J. Michell, *The Royal College of Radiologists Breast Group breast imaging classification.* CLIN RADIOL, **64(6)**, pp. 624-7. (2009)

[20] M. Schargus, F. Grehn, *The European Glaucoma Society Glaucocard project: Improved digital documentation of medical data for glaucoma patients based on standardized structured international datasets.* Albrecht Von Graefes Arch Klin Exp Ophthalmol, **246(12)**, pp. 1757-68 (2008)

[21] A. Ehrenberg, M. Ehnfors, I. Thorell-Ekstrand, *Developing a national integrated classification of health care interventions in Sweden.* IJMI, **74(11-12)**, pp. 973-9 (2005)

[22] J. Ozbolt, M.L. Wilson, D O'Brien, *Much Ado About Terminology Standards.* J. Perianesth. Nurs., **22(4)**, pp. 280-4 (2007)

[23] A. Thoroddsen, M. Ehnfors, A. Ehrenberg, *Content and Completeness of Care Plans After Implementation of Standardized Nursing Terminologies and Computerized Records.* CIN, **29(10)**, pp. 599-607 (2011)

[24] American Occupational Therapy Association. *Uniform terminology for occupational therapy.* Third edition. Am J Occup Ther., 48(11), pp. 1047-54 (1994)

[25] R. Buyl, M. Nyssen, *Structured electronic physiotherapy records.* IJMI, **78(7)**, pp. 473-81. (2009)

[26] K.R. Goeg, R. Chen, A.R. Hojen, P.Elberg, *Content analysis of physical examination templates in electronic health records using SNOMED CT.* IJMI, **83(10)**, pp. 736-49 (2014)

[27] T. Watkins, R. Haskell, C. Lundberg, J. Brokel, M. Wilson, N.Hardiker, *Terminology use in electronic health records: basic principles,* Urol Nurs, **29(5)**, pp. 321-6; quiz 7. (Sep-Oct 2009)

[28] A. Tapuria, D. Kalra, S.Kobayashi, *Contribution of Clinical Archetypes, and the Challenges, towards Achieving Semantic Interoperability for EHRs.* HIR, **19(4)**, pp. 286-92 (2013)

[29] J. Zeleznik, B. Agard-Henriques, B. Schnebel, D.L. Smith, *Terminology Used by Different Health Care Providers to Document Skin Ulcers: the Blind Men and the Elephant.* Journal of WOCN, **30(6)**, pp. 324-33. (2003)

[30] A-B. Jensdóttir, P. Jónsson, A. Noro, E. Jonsén, G. Ljunggren, H. Finne-Soveri, et al. *Comparison of nurses' and physicians' documentation of functional abilities of older patients in acute care - Patient records compared with standardized assessment.* SJCS, **22(3)**, pp. 341-7 (2008)

[31] Socialstyrelsen. *Nationell informationsstruktur* (2016) Available at: http://www.socialstyrelsen.se/nationellehalsa/nationellinformationsstruktur.

Composite laminate under influence of temperature and moisture

Eva Kormaníková[1,a] and Kamila Kotrasová[1]

[1]*TUKE, Faculty of Civil Engineering, Department of Structural Mechanics, Vysokoškolská 4, 04200Košice, Slovakia*

Abstract. The static response of simply supported carbon/epoxy composite plates in a hygrothermal environment is carried out using the general purpose finite element program COSMOS. The static load model and the hygrothermal incorporation are solved separately. The hygrothermal effect is introduced by using empirical relations for degrading the material stiffness properties of the matrix. The corresponding ply properties are calculated using Mori-Tanaka method. A parametric study is conducted by varying the fiber volume fraction and the fiber orientation of the angle plies in the laminate.

1 Introduction

The use of composite materials in the modern engineering applications has been increasing rapidly. Bridges, aerospace structures are few examples of their application. Steel bridges are replaced by composite materials due to their superior qualities like higher strength-to-weight ratio.

A laminate is a stack of lamina, with different fiber orientations, bonded together to attain desired properties. Laminates can be classified as symmetric, unsymmetric, balanced and unbalanced composites. In a symmetric laminate, the material and orientation of layers above the mid plane are identical to those below. In a symmetric laminate the bending-stretching coupling is absent. This is not true for unsymmetric laminates.

The analysis of composite structures is more complex and several theories have been proposed for the analysis of laminated composites. Composite laminates have larger planar dimensions, so they can be treated as plate elements. Therefore, plate theories can be applied in the analysis of laminated composites and it is very important to study the response of these materials to environmental conditions like temperature and moisture.

As alternative to the experimental determination of material properties of fiber matrix composite material is usage of various homogenization techniques. Many analytical homogenization techniques are based on the equivalent eingenstrain method, which considers the problem of a single inclusion embedded in an infinite elastic medium. Homogenization has been accomplished by using various techniques including the Fourier series technique, variational principles etc. Most fiber matrix composites have random arrangement of the fibers [2] (Fig. 1).

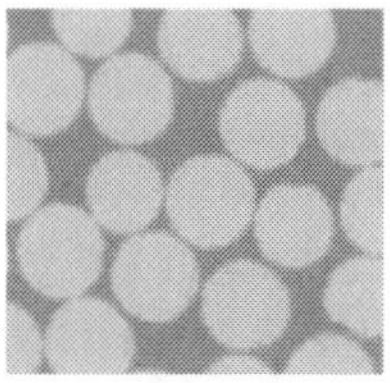

Figure 1. Randomly distributed fibers.

2 Mori-Tanaka Method

In the last decade, effective media theories, widely used in classical continuum micro mechanics, have been recognized as an attractive alternative to FE based methods. Since its introduction the Mori-Tanaka (MT) method has enjoyed a considerable interest in a variety of engineering applications. These include classical fiber matrix composites too [2].

General description of the Mori-Tanaka method in the framework of elasticity is treated in this section. The Mori-Tanaka method takes into account the effect of phase interactions on the local stresses by assuming an approximation in which the stress in each phase is equal to that of a single inclusion r embedded into an unbounded matrix subjected to as yet unknown average matrix strain or stress.

The constitutive equation $\sigma = \mathbf{C}\varepsilon$ we can write in the following form:

$$\begin{Bmatrix} \sigma_1 \\ \sigma_2 \\ \sigma_3 \\ \sigma_4 \\ \sigma_5 \\ \sigma_6 \end{Bmatrix} = \begin{bmatrix} n & l & l & 0 & 0 & 0 \\ l & (k+m) & (k-m) & 0 & 0 & 0 \\ l & (k-m) & (k+m) & 0 & 0 & 0 \\ 0 & 0 & 0 & m & 0 & 0 \\ 0 & 0 & 0 & 0 & p & 0 \\ 0 & 0 & 0 & 0 & 0 & p \end{bmatrix} \begin{Bmatrix} \varepsilon_1 \\ \varepsilon_2 \\ \varepsilon_3 \\ \varepsilon_4 \\ \varepsilon_5 \\ \varepsilon_6 \end{Bmatrix} \tag{1}$$

[a] Corresponding author: eva.kormanikova@tuke.sk

Material characteristics we can solve from the following equations:

$$k = -\left(1/G_{23} - 4/E_{22} + 4\nu_{12}^2/E_{11}\right)^{-1}, \quad l = 2k\nu_{12},$$

$$m = G_{23}, \quad n = E_{11} + 4k\nu_{12}^2 = E_{11} + l^2/k, \quad p = G_{12}. \quad (2)$$

3 Hygrothermal analysis

Prolonged exposure to a hygrothermal environment has two major effects on a polymer matrix composite (PMC) structure. The first one is of a residual nature. The second significant effect of an increased hygrothermal condition is the degradation of the mechanical properties of a PMC ply. Again it is the matrix that bears the brunt of this degradation while the fiber properties remain nearly unchanged. The degradation occurs in both the stiffness and strength values of the matrix and consequently in the corresponding values of the lamina. In the present paper only this degradation effect is considered while ignoring the residual stresses. It is observed from various studies that the exposure to high moisture and temperature do not significantly affect the fiber related properties, but, the matrix properties get affected considerably. Therefore, the loss in performance can be related to temperature and moisture content of the matrix material.

In this paper, the relations given by Chamis [1, 3] are used to calculate the degraded properties of composite due to hygrothermal conditions. The hygrothermal strains in the longitudinal direction and transverse the fibre direction of a lamina are not equal since the effective elastic moduli E_L and E_T and also the thermal and moisture expansion coefficients $\boldsymbol{\alpha}$, $\boldsymbol{\beta}$ respectively, are different.

The stress-strain relations of a unidirectional (UD) lamina, including temperature differences are given [3]

$$\begin{bmatrix} \sigma_{xx}^T \\ \sigma_{yy}^T \\ \sigma_{xy}^T \end{bmatrix} = \begin{bmatrix} Q_{11} & Q_{12} & Q_{16} \\ Q_{21} & Q_{22} & Q_{26} \\ Q_{61} & Q_{62} & Q_{66} \end{bmatrix} \begin{bmatrix} \varepsilon_{xx}^0 + z\kappa_x - \alpha_x \Delta T \\ \varepsilon_{yy}^0 + z\kappa_y - \alpha_y \Delta T \\ \gamma_{xy}^0 + z\kappa_{xy} - \alpha_{xy} \Delta T \end{bmatrix} \quad (3)$$

where ΔT is the temperature change, where $\bar{\varepsilon}$ and $\boldsymbol{\kappa}$ are vector of strain and curvature of mid-plane, respectively.

The internal forces in the laminate with the influence of temperature are following form

$$\begin{bmatrix} N_x \\ N_y \\ N_{xy} \end{bmatrix} = \begin{bmatrix} A_{11} & A_{12} & A_{16} \\ A_{21} & A_{22} & A_{26} \\ A_{61} & A_{62} & A_{66} \end{bmatrix} \begin{bmatrix} \varepsilon_{xx}^0 \\ \varepsilon_{yy}^0 \\ \gamma_{xy}^0 \end{bmatrix} + \begin{bmatrix} B_{11} & B_{12} & B_{16} \\ B_{21} & B_{22} & B_{26} \\ B_{61} & B_{62} & B_{66} \end{bmatrix} \begin{bmatrix} \kappa_x \\ \kappa_y \\ \kappa_{xy} \end{bmatrix} -$$

$$- \begin{bmatrix} A_{11} & A_{12} & A_{16} \\ A_{21} & A_{22} & A_{26} \\ A_{61} & A_{62} & A_{66} \end{bmatrix} \begin{bmatrix} \alpha_x \\ \alpha_y \\ \alpha_{xy} \end{bmatrix} \Delta T = 0$$

$$\begin{bmatrix} M_x \\ M_y \\ M_{xy} \end{bmatrix} = \begin{bmatrix} B_{11} & B_{12} & B_{16} \\ B_{21} & B_{22} & B_{26} \\ B_{61} & B_{62} & B_{66} \end{bmatrix} \begin{bmatrix} \varepsilon_{xx}^0 \\ \varepsilon_{yy}^0 \\ \gamma_{xy}^0 \end{bmatrix} + \begin{bmatrix} D_{11} & D_{12} & D_{61} \\ D_{21} & D_{22} & D_{26} \\ D_{61} & D_{62} & D_{66} \end{bmatrix} \begin{bmatrix} \kappa_x \\ \kappa_y \\ \kappa_{xy} \end{bmatrix} -$$

$$- \begin{bmatrix} B_{11} & B_{12} & B_{16} \\ B_{21} & B_{22} & B_{26} \\ B_{61} & B_{62} & B_{66} \end{bmatrix} \begin{bmatrix} \alpha_x \\ \alpha_y \\ \alpha_{xy} \end{bmatrix} \Delta T = 0 \quad (4)$$

The stress-strain relations of a unidirectional (UD) lamina, including moisture differences are given

$$\begin{bmatrix} \sigma_{xx}^H \\ \sigma_{yy}^H \\ \sigma_{xy}^H \end{bmatrix} = \begin{bmatrix} Q_{11} & Q_{12} & Q_{16} \\ Q_{21} & Q_{22} & Q_{26} \\ Q_{61} & Q_{62} & Q_{66} \end{bmatrix} \begin{bmatrix} \varepsilon_{xx}^0 + z\kappa_x - \beta_x \Delta c \\ \varepsilon_{yy}^0 + z\kappa_y - \beta_y \Delta c \\ \gamma_{xy}^0 + z\kappa_{xy} - \beta_{xy} \Delta c \end{bmatrix} \quad (5)$$

where Δc is weight of moisture absorption per unit weight of the lamina.

The internal forces in the laminate with the influence of moisture are following form

$$\begin{bmatrix} N_x \\ N_y \\ N_{xy} \end{bmatrix} = \begin{bmatrix} A_{11} & A_{12} & A_{16} \\ A_{21} & A_{22} & A_{26} \\ A_{61} & A_{62} & A_{66} \end{bmatrix} \begin{bmatrix} \varepsilon_{xx}^0 \\ \varepsilon_{yy}^0 \\ \gamma_{xy}^0 \end{bmatrix} + \begin{bmatrix} B_{11} & B_{12} & B_{16} \\ B_{21} & B_{22} & B_{26} \\ B_{61} & B_{62} & B_{66} \end{bmatrix} \begin{bmatrix} \kappa_x \\ \kappa_y \\ \kappa_{xy} \end{bmatrix} -$$

$$- \begin{bmatrix} A_{11} & A_{12} & A_{16} \\ A_{21} & A_{22} & A_{26} \\ A_{61} & A_{62} & A_{66} \end{bmatrix} \begin{bmatrix} \beta_x \\ \beta_y \\ \beta_{xy} \end{bmatrix} \Delta c = 0$$

$$\begin{bmatrix} M_x \\ M_y \\ M_{xy} \end{bmatrix} = \begin{bmatrix} B_{11} & B_{12} & B_{16} \\ B_{21} & B_{22} & B_{26} \\ B_{61} & B_{62} & B_{66} \end{bmatrix} \begin{bmatrix} \varepsilon_{xx}^0 \\ \varepsilon_{yy}^0 \\ \gamma_{xy}^0 \end{bmatrix} + \begin{bmatrix} D_{11} & D_{12} & D_{61} \\ D_{21} & D_{22} & D_{26} \\ D_{61} & D_{62} & D_{66} \end{bmatrix} \begin{bmatrix} \kappa_x \\ \kappa_y \\ \kappa_{xy} \end{bmatrix} -$$

$$- \begin{bmatrix} B_{11} & B_{12} & B_{16} \\ B_{21} & B_{22} & B_{26} \\ B_{61} & B_{62} & B_{66} \end{bmatrix} \begin{bmatrix} \beta_x \\ \beta_y \\ \beta_{xy} \end{bmatrix} \Delta c = 0 \quad (6)$$

4 Tsai-Wu Failure Criterion

A more general form of the failure criterion for orthotropic materials under plane stress is expressed as

$$F_{01}\sigma_1 + F_{11}\sigma_1^2 + 2F_{12}\sigma_1\sigma_2 + F_{02}\sigma_2 + F_{22}\sigma_2^2 + F_{44}\tau_{12}^2 < 1 \quad (7)$$

where

$$F_{01} = \frac{1}{X_t} - \frac{1}{X_c}, \quad F_{11} = \frac{1}{X_t X_c}, \quad F_{02} = \frac{1}{Y_t} - \frac{1}{Y_c},$$

$$F_{22} = \frac{1}{Y_t Y_c}, \quad F_{12} = -\frac{1}{2}\frac{1}{\sqrt{X_t X_c Y_t Y_c}}, \quad F_{44} = \frac{1}{S^2}$$

The failure criterion for an orthotropic material under a strain is expressed as

$$G_{01}\varepsilon_1 + G_{11}\varepsilon_1^2 + G_{12}\varepsilon_1\varepsilon_2 + G_{02}\varepsilon_2 + G_{22}\varepsilon_2^2 + G_{44}\gamma_{12}^2 < 1 \quad (8)$$

where

$$G_{01} = F_{01}E_{11} + F_{02}E_{12}$$

$$G_{02} = F_{02}E_{22} + F_{01}E_{12}$$

$$G_{11} = F_{11}E_{11}^2 + F_{22}E_{12}^2 + F_{12}E_{11}E_{12}$$

$$G_{22} = F_{22}E_{22}^2 + F_{11}E_{12}^2 + F_{12}E_{22}E_{12}$$

$$G_{12} = 2E_{12}(F_{11}E_{11} + F_{22}E_{22}) + 2F_1(E_{12}^2 + E_{11}E_{22})$$

$$G_{44} = F_{44}E_{44}^2$$

When $F_{12} = \frac{-1}{2X_t^2}$, the Tsai-Wu criterion is reduced to the Tsai-Hill criterion, and when $F_{12} = \frac{-1}{2X_tX_c}$ the Tsai-Wu criterion is reduced to the Hoffman criterion [4, 7].

These failure criteria are used to calculate a failure index (FI) from the computed stresses and user-supplied material strengths. The failure index as a response of quantity is used for several FEA packages and it is defined as

$$I_F = \frac{\text{stress}}{\text{strength}} \tag{9}$$

Failure criteria predict the first occurrence of failure in one of the laminate layers. A value less than 1 denotes no failure and failure is predicted when IF$\geq$ 1. The strength ratio is the inverse of the failure index.

It is important to distinguish between the fibre failure (FF) and the inter-fibre failure (IFF). In the case of shear plane stress, the IFF criteria discriminates three different modes [4]. The IFF Mode A is when perpendicular transversal cracks appear in the lamina under transverse tensile stress with or without in-plane shear stress. The IFF Mode B denotes perpendicular transversal cracks, but in this case they appear under in-plane shear stress with small transverse compression stress. The IFF Mode C indicates the start of oblique cracks when the material is under significant transversal compression.

The FF and the three IFF modes yield separate failure indices. The failure index for FF is defined as

$$I_{FF} = \begin{cases} \sigma_1 / X_t & if \quad \sigma_1 > 0 \\ -\sigma_1 / X_c & if \quad \sigma_1 < 0 \end{cases} \tag{10}$$

For IFF with positive transverse stress, Mode A is active. The failure index in this case is defined as

$$I_{IFF,A} = \sqrt{\left(\frac{\tau_{12}}{S}\right)^2 + \left(1 - p_{6t}\frac{Y_t}{S}\right)^2\left(\frac{\sigma_2}{Y_t}\right)^2} + p_{6t}\frac{\sigma_2}{S} \quad if \quad \sigma_2 \geq 0 \tag{11}$$

where $p_{6t} = 0.3$.

Under negative transverse stress, either Mode B or Mode C is active, depending on the relationship between in-plane shear stress and transversal shear stress. The failure indices are defined as

$$I_{IFF,B} = \frac{1}{S}\left[\sqrt{\tau_{12}^2 + (p_{6c}\sigma_2)^2} + p_{6c}\sigma_2\right] \quad \text{if} \quad \begin{cases} \sigma_2 < 0 \\ \left|\frac{\sigma_2}{\tau_{12}}\right| \leq \frac{F_{2A}}{F_{6A}} \end{cases} \tag{12}$$

$$I_{IFF,C} = -\frac{Y_c}{\sigma_2}\left[\sqrt{\left(\frac{\tau_{12}}{2(1+p_{2c})S}\right)^2 + \left(\frac{\sigma_2}{Y_c}\right)^2}\right] \quad \text{if} \quad \begin{cases} \sigma_2 < 0 \\ \left|\frac{\sigma_2}{\tau_{12}}\right| \geq \frac{F_{2A}}{F_{6A}} \end{cases} \tag{13}$$

where $p_{6c} = 0.2$.

The limit between Mode B and Mode C is defined by the relation F_{2A} / F_{6A},

where

$$F_{2A} = \frac{S}{2p_{6c}}\left[\sqrt{1 + 2p_{6c}\frac{Y_c}{S}} - 1\right] \tag{14}$$

$$F_{6A} = S\sqrt{1 + 2p_{2c}} \qquad p_{2c} = p_{6c}\frac{F_{2A}}{S}. \tag{15}$$

5 Numerical example and results

It was considered the laminate made of 8 layers $[0/\theta/-\theta/90]_s$ and $[0/\theta/-\theta/90/0/\theta/-\theta/90/]$. Constituent properties of Carbon fiber and Epoxy matrix are listed in the Table 1. Each Carbon/epoxy composite layer has the same material characteristics, that were obtained from Mori Tanaka method and listed in the Tables 2 and 3. The temperature change ΔT = 20°C and moisture change Δc = 1.5%. The reinforcement angle θ is changed from 0° to 90°. The results of hygrothermal conditions are solved for simply supported square laminate plate with L = 0.8 m and thickness h = 0.008 m.

Table 1. Constituent mechanical properties of Carbon fiber and Epoxy matrix.

Property	Carbon fiber	Epoxy matrix (Dry)
Modulus of elasticity, E [GPa]	228	3 GPa
Poisson's ratio, ν [–]	0.3	0.36

Table 2. Mechanical properties of Carbon/epoxy composite layer.

E_1 [MPa]	E_2 [MPa]	G_{12} [MPa]	ν_{12}[–]	ν_{21}[–]
1.38e+5	1.032e+4	4.389e+3	0.343	0.0257

Tables 3. Hygrothermal properties of Carbon/epoxy composite layer.

α_1 [(m/m)°C]	α_2 [(m/m)°C]	β_1 [m/m]	β_2 [m/m]
-3.00e-7	2.80e-5	0.01	0.3

σ_{Lu}^t [MPa]	σ_{Lu}^c [MPa]	σ_{Tu}^t [MPa]	σ_{Tu}^c [MPa]	σ_{LTM} [MPa]
2000	1200	50	170	70

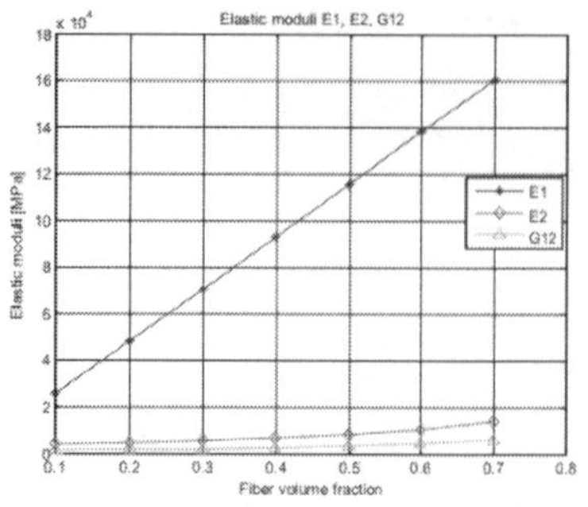

Figure 2. Elastic moduli versus fiber reinforced angle.

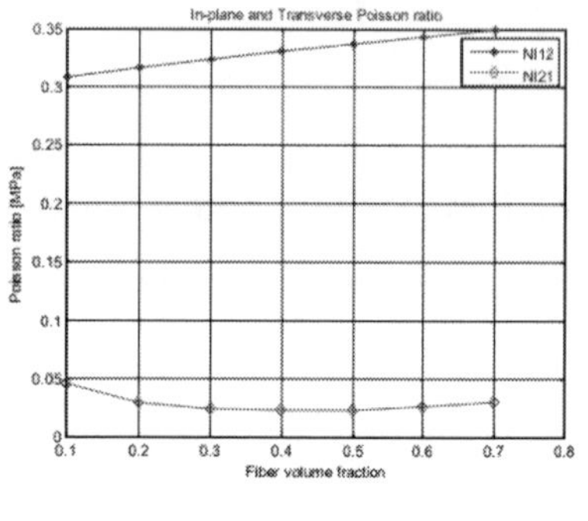

Figure 3. Poisson ratio versus fiber reinforced angle.

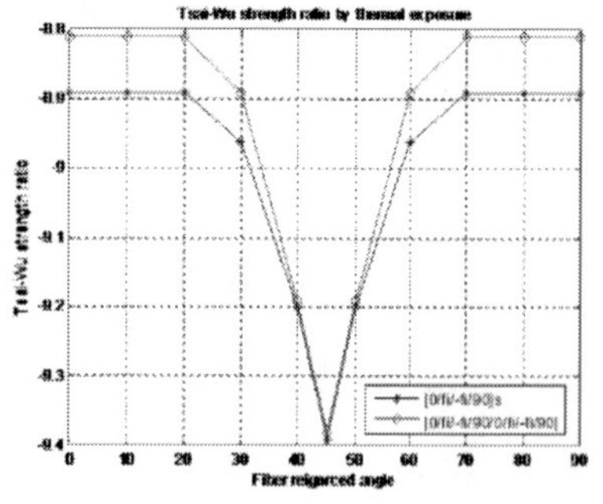

Figure 4. Moisture strength of ratio versus fiber reinforced angle.

Table 4. Bending moments of mechanical and hygrothermal exposure for $[0/45/\text{-}45/90]_S$.

Property	M_x [MNm/m]	M_y [MNm/m]	M_x [MNm/m]
q	$6.15 \cdot 10^{-5}$	$2.33 \cdot 10^{-5}$	$5.41 \cdot 10^{-5}$
Δc	0	0	0
ΔT	0	0	0

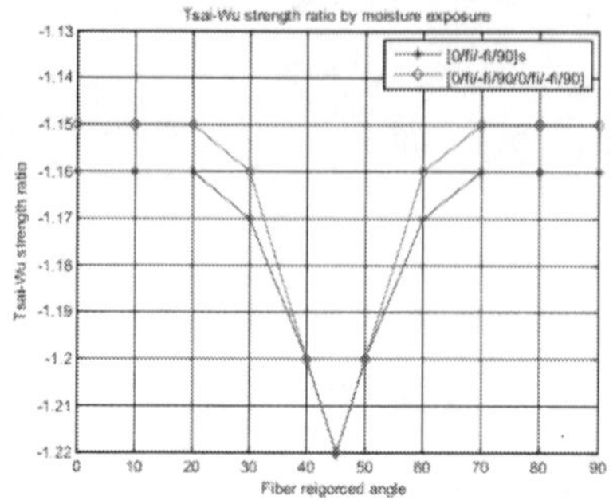

Figure 5. Thermal strength of ratio versus fiber reinforced angle.

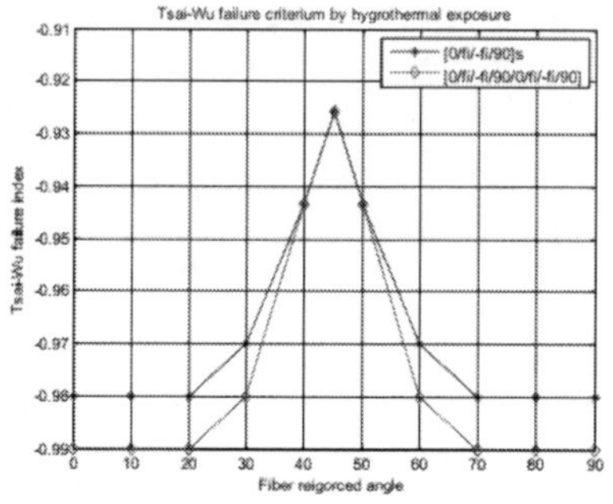

Figure 6. Mechanical and hygrothermal failure index versus fiber reinforced angle.

Table 5. Normal forces of mechanical and hygrothermal exposure for $[0/45/\text{-}45/90]_S$.

Property	$N_x = N_y$ [MN/m^2]	N_{xy} [MN/m^2]
q	0	0
Δc	$3.37 \cdot 10^{-1}$	0
ΔT	$2.79 \cdot 10^{-2}$	0

Table 6. Bending moments of mechanical and hygrothermal exposure for [0/45/-45/90/0/45/-45/90/].

Property	M_x [MNm/m]	M_y [MNm/m]	M_{xy} [MNm/m]
q	$1.2 \cdot 10^{-5}$	$2.54 \cdot 10^{-5}$	$-6.29 \cdot 10^{-6}$
Δc	$3.1 \cdot 10^{-5}$	$-3.1 \cdot 10^{-5}$	$1.1 \cdot 10^{-5}$
ΔT	$1.39 \cdot 10^{-5}$	$-1.39 \cdot 10^{-5}$	$0.461 \cdot 10^{-5}$

Table 7. Normal forces of mechanical and hygrothermal exposure for [0/45/-45/90/0/45/-45/90/].

Property	N_x [MN/m^2]	N_y [MN/m^2]	N_{xy} [MN/m^2]
q	$2.84 \cdot 10^{-2}$	$3.22 \cdot 10^{-2}$	$1.26 \cdot 10^{-3}$
Δc	$3.37.10^{-1}$	$3.37.10^{-1}$	0
ΔT	$2.79.10^{-2}$	$2.79.10^{-2}$	0

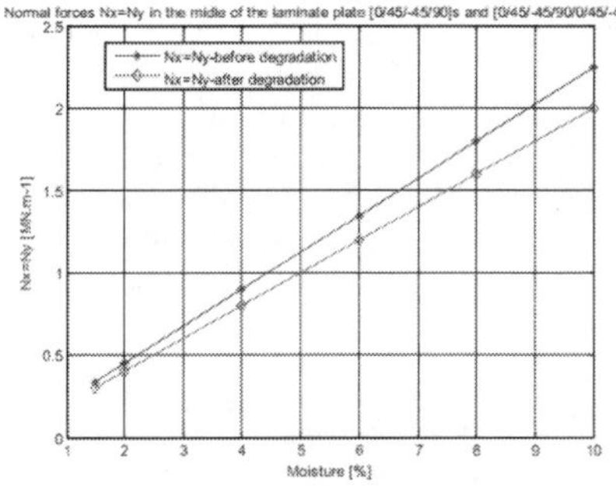

Figure 7. Normal forces $N_x = N_y$ of symmetric and asymmetric laminates versus change of moisture.

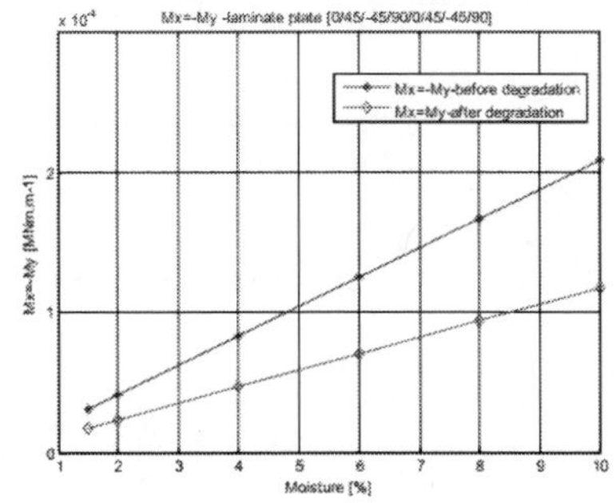

Figure 8. Bending moments $M_x = -M_y$ of unsymmetric laminates versus change of moisture.

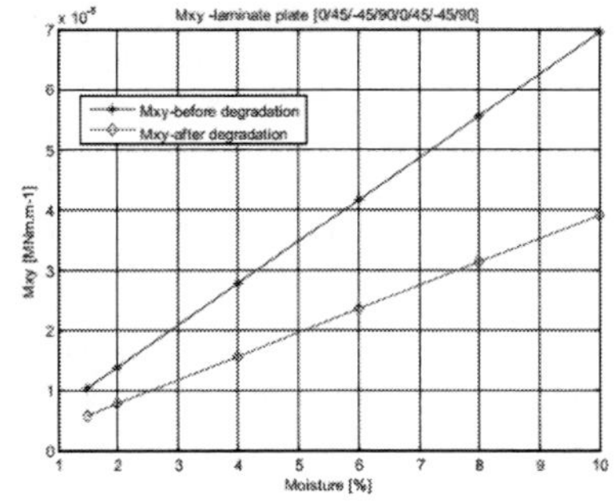

Figure 9. Bending moments M_{xy} of unsymmetric laminates versus change of moisture.

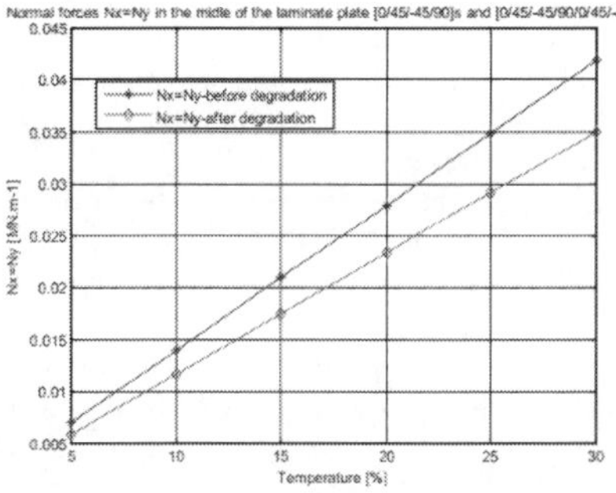

Figure 10. Normal forces $N_x = N_y$ of symmetric and asymmetric laminates versus change of temperature.

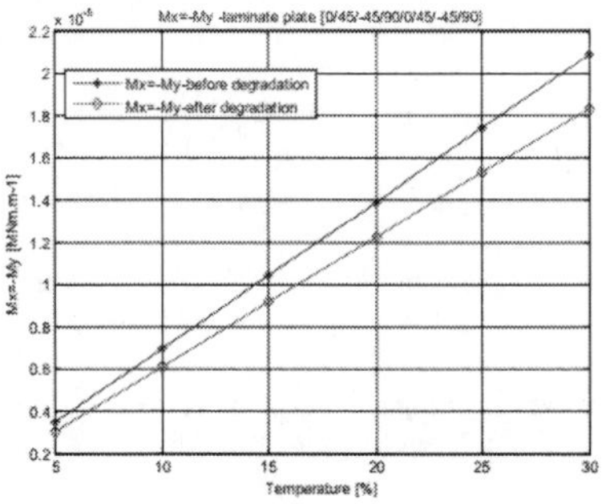

Figure 11. Bending moments $M_x = -M_y$ of unsymmetric laminates versus change of temperature.

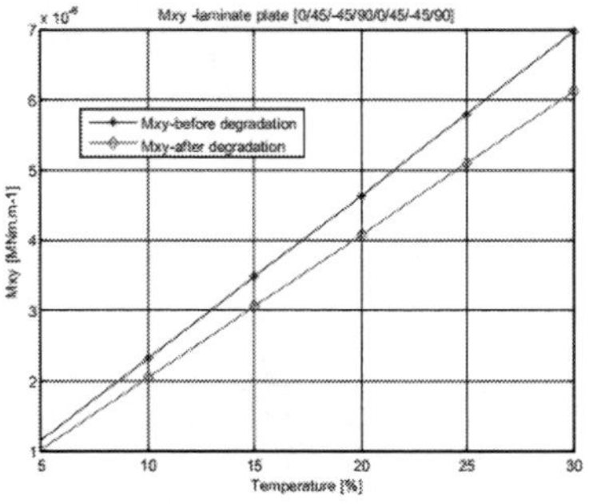

Figure 12. Bending moments M_{xy} of asymmetric laminates versus change of temperature.

6 Conclusion and discussion

There was investigated the laminates made of 8 layers $[0/\theta/-\theta/90]_s$ and $[0/\theta/-\theta/90/0/\theta/-\theta/90/]$ in the paper. Each layer consists of Carbon fibers and Epoxy matrix. Effective material characteristics [11 - 13] for dry and wet laminate were establish using the program, that works under Mori-Tanaka method [2]. The material characteristics of undegraded laminate layer versus fiber volume fraction can be seen in Figs. 2, 3. The longitudinal modulus and longitudinal Poisson ratio have minor difference between undegraded and degraded values. The transverse modulus and in-plane shear modulus have considerable differences between undegraded and degraded values. For the optimization process [5, 6], the symmetric and unsymmetric laminates with fiber volume fraction 0.6 was taken into account. In the example there was calculated the influence of fiber reinforced angle change on strength ratio or failure index (Figs. 4-6). It is seen the best laminates are $[0/45/-45/90]_S$ and [0/45/-45/90/0/45/-45/90/].

The mechanical and hygrothermal analysis was performed using the program MATLAB. The response of laminated composite to hygrothermal conditions was investigated to validate the hygrothermal aspect of the model. The internal forces without degradation of material characteristics are written in the Tables 4 - 7. The symmetric laminate has any coupling effect between normal forces and bending moments (Tabs. 4, 5), opposite the unsymmetric laminate with coupling effect (Tabs. 6, 7) [7 - 9]. Then the degradation process caused by temperature and moisture was investigated (Figs. 7-12). In the case of simply supported square laminate plates $[0/45/-45/90]_S$ and [0/45/-45/90/0/45/-45/90] subjected to hygrothermal environment we can observe the difference between normal forces to 12.6% and between bending moment to 77.6%. Based on these results a designer can choose the right ply orientations to control behavior of laminated plates [14 - 18]. It is possible to minimize the environmental effect by judiciously selecting the laminate configuration. Consequently, it is preferable to use the symmetric laminate panels for exterior utilization.

Acknowledgment

This work was supported by the Scientific Grant Agency of the Ministry of Education of Slovak Republic and the Slovak Academy of Sciences under Projects VEGA 1/0477/15 and 1/0078/16.

References

1. C. C. Chamis, Simplified Composite Micromechanics Equations for Hygral, Thermal and Mechanical Properties, Houston, TX, 1-10, (1983)
2. J. Sykora, M. Sejnoha, J. Sejnoha, Homogenization of coupled heat and moisture transport in masonry structures including interfaces, Appl. Math. and Comp. **219** (13), p. 7275-7285, (2013)
3. P. K. Kavipurapu, *Forced Vibration and Hygrothermal Analysis of Composite Laminated Beams under the Action of Moving Loads*, Morgantown, West Virginia, (2005)
4. V. Las, *Mechanics of Composite Materials*, West Bohemia University, (2008)
5. J. Kralik, Optimal design of npp containment protection against fuel container drop, Adv. Mat. Res. **688**, p. 213-221, (2013)
6. M. Krejsa, P. Janas, I. Yilmaz, M. Marschalko, T. Bouchal, The use of the direct optimized probabilistic calculation method in design of bolt reinforcement for underground and mining workings, *The Scientific World Journal*, Article number 267593, (2013)
7. M. Zmindak, Z. Pelagic, M. Bvoc, Analysis of high velocity impact on composite structures, Appl. Mech. and Mat. **617**, p. 104-109, (2014)
8. K. Tvrda, Probability and sensitivity analysis of plate, Appl. Mech. and Mat. **617**, p. 193-196, (2014)
9. J. Melcer, G. Lajcakova, Comparison of finite element and classical computing models of reinforcement pavement, Adv. Mat. Res. **969**, p. 85-88, (2014)
10. M. Sejnoha, J. Zeman, Micromechanical modeling of imperfect textile composites, Int. Jour. of Eng. Scien. **46** (6), p. 513-526, (2008)
11. J. Ma, S. Sahraee, P. Wriggers, , L. De Lorenzis, Stochastic multiscale homogenization analysis of heterogeneous materials under finite deformations with full uncertainty in the microstructure, Comp. Mech. **55**, Issue 5, p. 819-835, (2015)
12. C. Maruccio, L. De Lorenzis, L. Persano, D. Pisignano, Computational homogenization of fibrous piezoelectric materials, Comp. Mech. **55**, Issue 5, p. 983-998, (2015)
13. S. Tang, Y. Yang, X. H. Peng, X. X. Huang, K. Elkhodary, A semi-numerical algorithm for instability of compressible multilayered structures, Comp. Mech. **56**, Issue 1, p. 63-75, (2015)
14. E. Kormanikova, I. Mamuzic, Optimization of laminates subjected to failure criterion, Metal. **50** (1), p. 41-44, (2011)
15. R. Dhabale, V. S. Jatti, Optimization of material removal rate of AlMg1SiCu in turning operation using genetic algorithm, WSEAS Transactions on Appl. and Theor. Mech. **10**, p. 95-101, (2015)
16. A. M. Valuev, Models and methods of multiobjective optimization in problems of quarry design and planning, WSEAS Trans. on Math., **13**, p. 557-566, (2014)
17. E.A. Vorontsova, A projective separating plane method with additional clipping for non-smooth optimization, WSEAS Trans. on Math., **13**, p. 115-121, (2014)
18. Lovíšek, J. Králik, J., Optimal Control for Elasto-Orthotropic Plate. Contr. and Cyber. **2**, p. 219-278, (2006)

MATEC Web of Conferences **76**, 04003 (2016) DOI: 10.1051/matecconf/20167604003
CSCC 2016

Business processes in the RFID-equipped restricted access administrative office

Waszkowski Robert[1,a], Kiedrowicz Maciej[1], Nowicki Tadeusz[1], Wesołowski Zbigniew[1] and Worwa Kazimierz[1]

[1]*Military Academy of Technology, Faculty of Cybernetics, Kaliskiego 2, 00-908 Warsaw, Poland*

Abstract. The paper presents business processes in the RFID-equipped restricted access administrative office. The presented diagrams are the result of the analytical work performed by the multidisciplinary team of experts. The team was composed of IT specialist, security systems specialists and employees of the secret office. The presented models include the fact that the facilities in the secret office (cabinet, sluice, photocopier, desks) are equipped with the RFID reader, which allows to immediately read the documents that are within their reach.

1 Introduction

The second decade of the twenty-first century is a time of increasingly widespread use of electronic documents. Electronic applications, certificates and invoices have become a natural part of reality for Polish enterprises.

However, paper documents still remain of great importance. Agreements, certificates, securities, deeds, records of employees are some of the examples of the documents stored in paper form.

Both storage and archiving of such documents as well as access management constitute a challenge and very often require the use of certain IT-supported procedures.

The offices of modern enterprises are equipped with hardware and software to effectively manage open and classified documents. Complementing the currently used solutions with the opportunity to identify each document using the RFID tags makes it possible to obtain an automated document management system. It offers great opportunities in the field of document security, accountability and traceability.

This paper presents business processes in the restricted access administrative office equipped with the RFID readers placed in cabinets, desks and entrance sluices. By using these readers, it is possible to automatically and immediately read the content of the cabinets, identify documents on the desk and register facts of entry/exit of the document. Taking into account such innovative technological advances, the new business processes of the administrative office were proposed.

The basic functionalities of the system include:

- remote identification of unclassified and classified data storage devices labelled for real-time radio-reading at the storage and work location;
- automatic inventory of unclassified and classified documents arranged in piles and filed, including automatic detection of relocation;
- control of the movement of data storage devices as well as unclassified and classified documents across security zones, including access control of unclassified and classified documents;
- protection of data storage devices and documents against unauthorized relocation;
- automatic identification of data storage devices and documents not only at the storage location, but also at workstations;
- protection against repeated copying of unclassified and classified documents;
- control of printing of unclassified and classified documents with a copy limit;
- identification of the location of individual unclassified and classified documents with a pre-set accuracy of a file or volume location.

The document lifecycle management, built on the basis of the Business Process Management System, is used by the personnel of the restricted access to an administrative office, where the system is to be implemented. The system co-operates with the following external systems: CrossTalkAppCenter and Cosmos. It is integrated via adequate programming interfaces (Web service). The document flow management system also has a graphic user interface (GUI) accessible from the Internet browser level. CrossTalkAppCenter and Cosmos also have user interfaces enabling their control and configuration (Figure 1.).

[a] Corresponding author: robert.waszkowski@wat.edu.pl

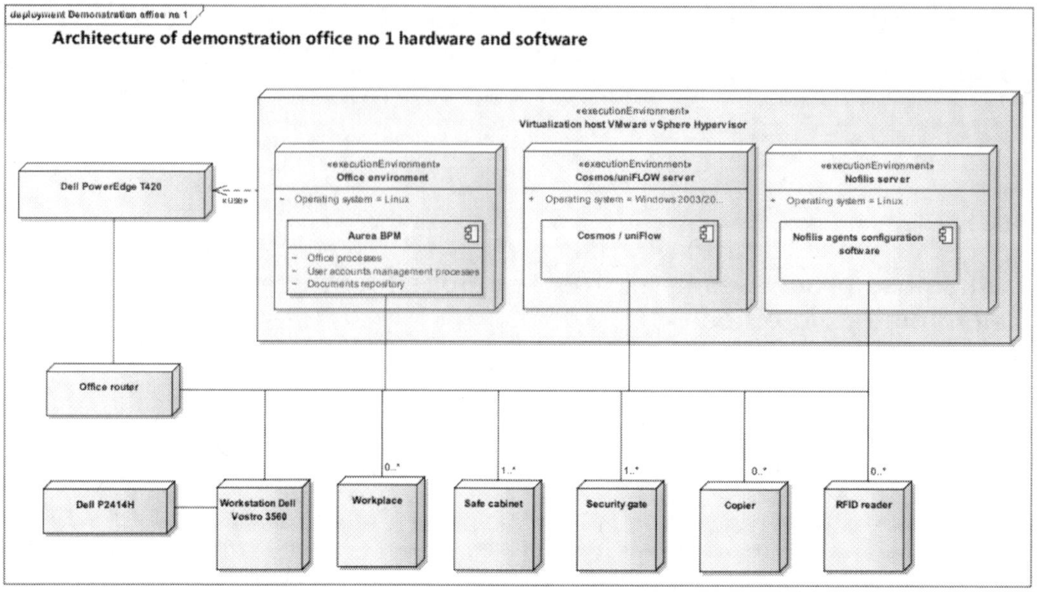

Figure 1. Architecture of the classified document lifecycle management system

2 Business processes of the RFID-equipped restricted access administrative office

As a result of the analytical work, the following business processes of the secret office equipped with the RFID devices have been defined:
- acceptance of the document or documents with the RFID tags from a natural person,
- acceptance of a parcel with documents including the RFID tags, with traces of opening,
- performance of standard procedures when receiving the RFID tagged documents,
- registration of correspondence in the form of the RFID tagged documents,
- classification of the RFID tagged documents,
- registration of the created RFID tagged documents,
- processes related to the storage of the RFID tagged documents,
- preparation for dispatch of the RFID tagged documents,
- sending of the RFID tagged documents via a carrier,
- making the RFID tagged documents available,
- destruction of the RFID tagged documents.

The subsequent chapters outline the most important of these processes.

3 Parcel receipt business process

The parcel receipt business process (Figure 1) is implemented according to the following scenario:

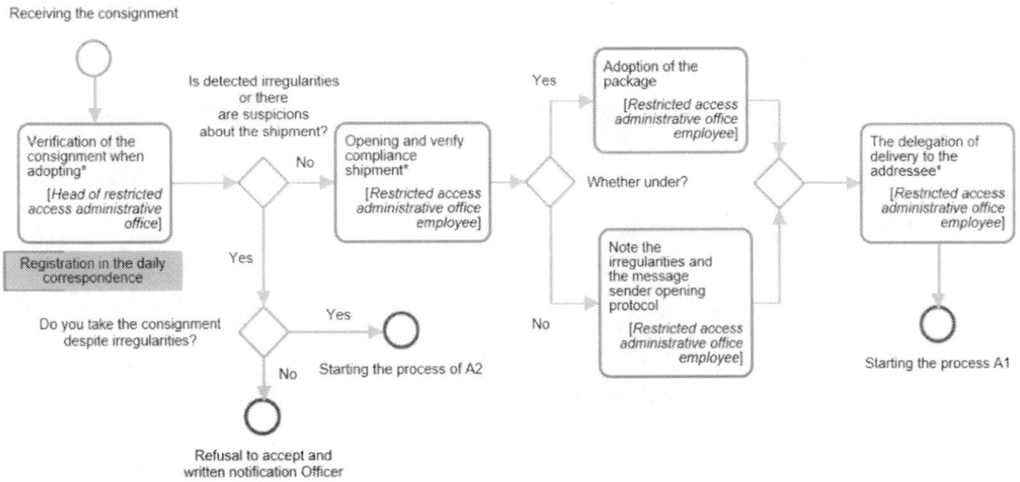

Figure 2. Parcel receipt (source: own elaboration).

1. The process is initiated at the time of shipment acceptance by an employee of the restricted access administrative office (K), who prepares a start-up form on the date of acceptance of the consignment, enters the data into the records of delivery / schedule of shipments and approves the task.
2. Then the Director receives the consignments and checks them on entry. (S)he introduces the data upon receipt, whereas the sender acknowledges safe receipt of the shipment and enters the data to verify the compliance of the consignment.
3. The head of the secret office notes if the irregularities were detected during the check or if there are suspicions about the shipment.
   a. If Yes (go to step 4).
   b. If Not (go to step 5).
4. The head of the secret office decides whether to accept the consignment or not, despite certain irregularities:
   a. If not, (s)he refuses to accept the shipment and does not notify the authority in writing. This ends the process.
   b. If yes, (s)he starts the process of "acceptance of the damaged or opened parcel".
5. The secret office manager hands over the parcel to an employee of the secret office.
6. The employee opens the parcel.
7. The secret office employee checks the compatibility between the contents of the consignment and the locator numbers inside the envelope.
8. The secret office employee verifies the number of pages, attachments and pages of appendices according to the numbers indicated on the individual cryptographic media.
   a. If the employee finds any irregularities, (s)he makes an entry into the parcel opening register, describing the existing irregularities and includes this information in the official correspondence. Subsequently, (s)he attaches the opening confirmation letter to the cryptographic materials. Then (s)he sends the opening confirmation letter to the original parcel sender (go to step 10).
9. The secret office employee accepts the parcel.
10. The secret office employee forwards the parcel in the following manner:
    a. If it is an urgent parcel, go to step 11.
    b. If it is an ordinary parcel, an office worker may be in no hurry with the transfer of the consignment. The employee stars the process of the "registration of the document in the restricted access administrative office".
11. The secret office employee passes the parcel immediately. (S)he includes this fact in the notes of the muster apparatus specifying the date and time of the delivery. The employee starts the process of the "registration of the document in the restricted access administrative office".

4 Business process registration of the document in the restricted access administrative office

The business process - "Registration of the document in the restricted access administrative office" (Figure 2) is implemented according to the following scenario:

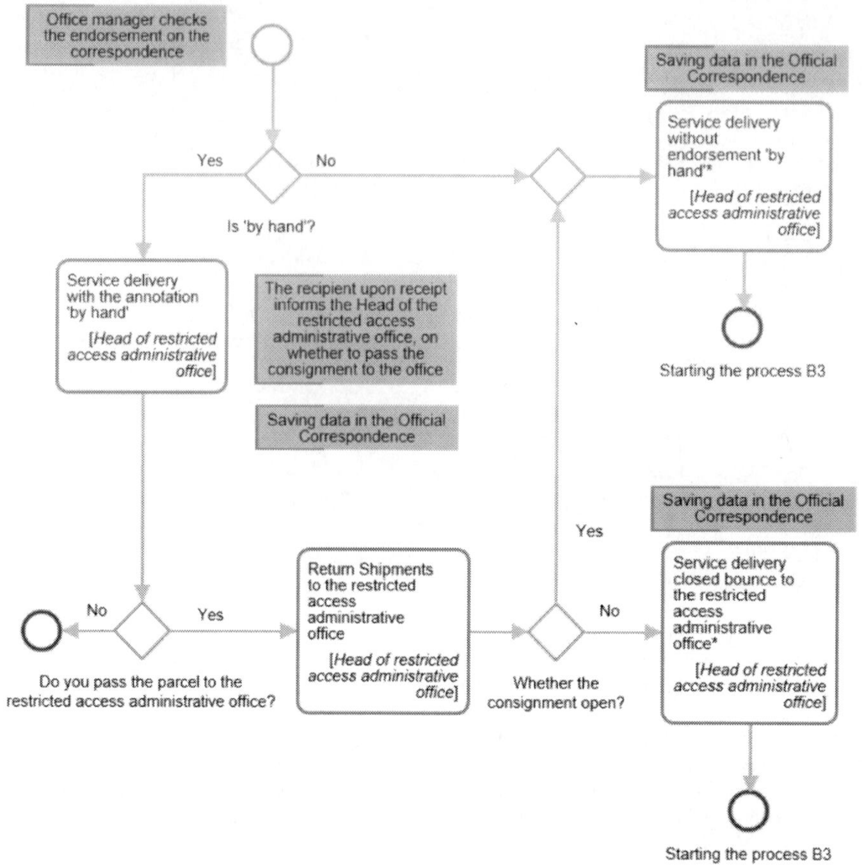

Figure 3. Registration of the document in the restricted access administrative office (source: own elaboration).

1. The head of the secret office or other authorized employee verifies whether the correspondence contains the notation 'by hand':
   a. If not, go to 2.
   b. If yes, go to 7.
2. The head of the secret office or other authorized employee applies a stamp effect on the first page of the cryptographic material.
3. The head of the secret office or other authorized employee makes seal imprints on the annexes.
4. The head of the secret office or other authorized employee completes more items in the official correspondence.
5. The head of the secret office or other authorized employee enters the date of registration in the document.
6. The head of the secret office or other authorized employee enters the item the "document storage" is initiated.
7. The head of the secret office or other authorized employee leaves the shipment in a closed inner wrapping.
8. The head of the secret office or other authorized employee includes in the official correspondence the information contained in the inner packaging.
9. The head of the secret office or other authorized employee includes in the official correspondence date of receipt.
10. The head of the secret office or other authorized employee puts the notation 'by hand' in the Comments section.
11. The head of the secret office or other authorized employee puts the stamp imprints on the consignment.
12. The head of the secret office or other authorized employee includes a registration number in the official correspondence.
13. The head of the secret office or other authorized employee puts the date information on the consignment.
14. The head secret office or other authorized employee transfers the load directly to the addressee or authorized person.
15. The recipient or authorized person decides whether the consignment will be sent back to the office:
    a. If yes, go to 16.
    b. If not, end the process.

16. The recipient or person authorized returns the parcel to the office:
    a. Parcel opened (go to 2).
    b. Parcel closed (go to 17).
17. If the service delivery is closed the shipment is returned to the office. The head of the secret office or other authorized employee puts the stamp imprints in the form of round numbers or their names.
18. The head of the secret office or other authorized employee notes that the consignment is stored in the form of a sealed package in the "Remarks" section in the official correspondence. The process of the "document storage" is initiated.

5 Business process "Security classification granting"

The business process - "Security classification granting" (Figure 3) is implemented according to the following scenario:

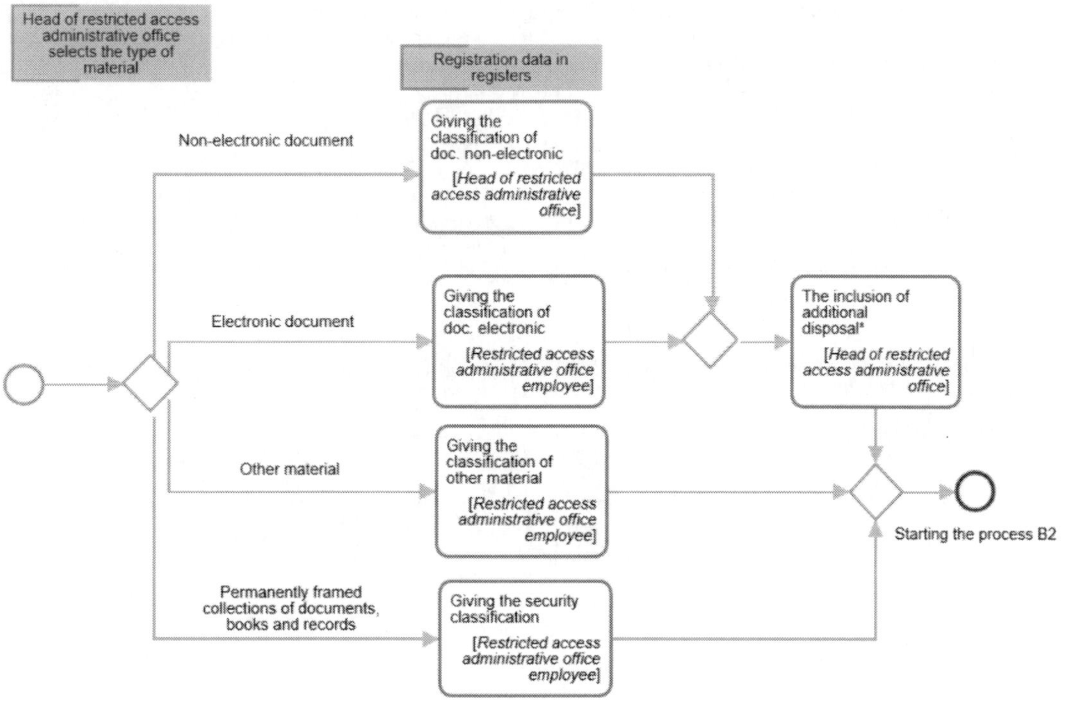

Figure 4. Security classification granting (source: own elaboration).

1. The person responsible for assigning clauses on the start-up form selects the type of material and approves the task:
    a. If a non-electronic document is selected, the task "Classifying the doc. as non-electronic" is started. The head of the restricted access administration office enters the following data:
        i. On each page - go to 2.
        ii. On the first page - go to 7.
        iii. On the last page of the content - go to 10
    b. If an electronic document is selected, the task "Classifying the doc. as electronic" is started (go to 15).
    c. If other materials are selected, the task "Classifying other material" is started (go to 24).
    d. If a tightly sealed set of documents, books and records are selected, the task "Security classification" is started (go to 25).
2. The responsible person puts the security classification at the centre, as the first element in the header and footer.
3. The responsible person types the copy number, or, in case of a single copy, enters "Single".
4. The responsible person affixes a digital signature.
5. The responsible person enters page numbers and the number of pages in the entire document.
6. The responsible person adds additional instructions.
7. The responsible person enters the name of the entity or organizational unit.
8. The responsible person enters the name of the place and date of signing the document.
9. In the case of a document that has been provided in the course of the correspondence, the responsible person enters his/her name or the name of the recipient.
10. The responsible person enters the number of attachments and number of pages.

11. The responsible person enters the security classification attachments with the numbers under which they were registered.
12. The responsible person enters the position and name of the person authorized to sign the documents.
13. The responsible person enters the number of copies made and recipients of individual copies.
14. The responsible person enters the name of the contractor. Then, (s)he adds the supplementary information and starts the process of the "registration of the produced materials".
15. The responsible person enters the security classifications in the metrics form.
16. The responsible person affixes a digital signature.
17. The responsible person enters the name of the entity or organizational unit.
18. The responsible person enters the document's registration date.
19. In the case of a document that has been provided in the course of the correspondence, the responsible person enters his/her name or the name of the recipient.
20. The responsible person enters the security classification attachments with the numbers under which they were registered.
21. The responsible person enters the position and name of the person authorized to sign the documents.
22. The responsible person enters his/her name and the name given to the document or the signature of the author.
23. The responsible person enters the name given to the document or determines which document is discussed. The responsible person enters the supplementary information and then starts the process of the "registration of the on-site prepared materials".
24. The responsible person enters the classification and affixes the digital alphanumeric signature by way of stamping/printing/permanent marking on the casing or packaging. The process of the "registration of the on-site prepared materials" starts.
25. The responsible person enters the classification clause on the outer walls of the cover and the title page. The process of the "registration of the on-site prepared materials".

6 Business process "Shredding of cryptographic documents"

The business process – "Shredding of cryptographic documents" (Figure 4) is implemented according to the following scenario:

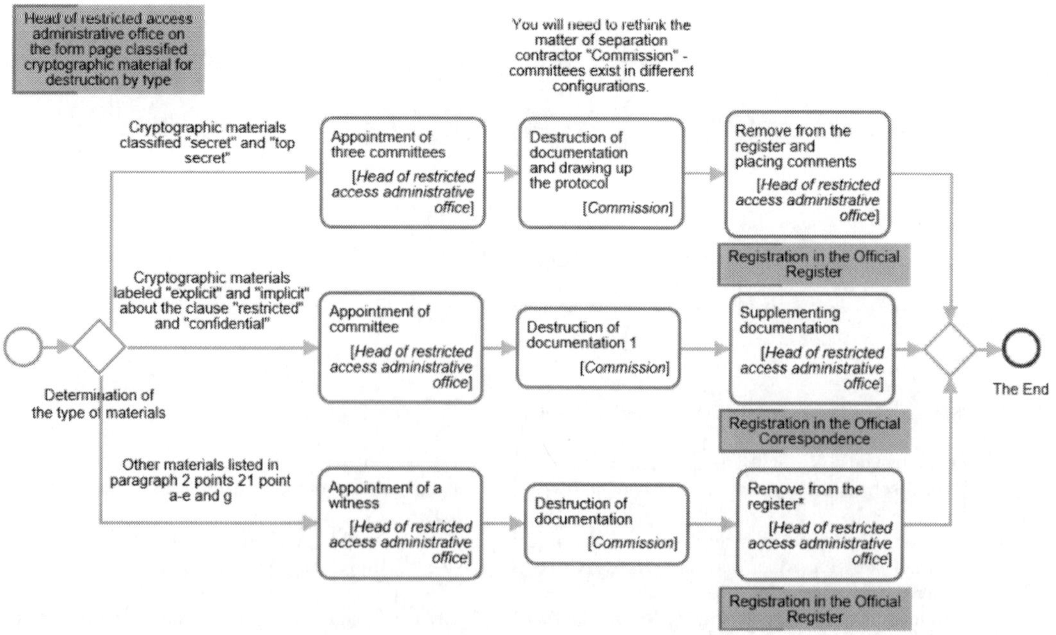

Figure 5. Shredding of cryptographic documents (source: own elaboration)

1. On the start-up form, the head of the secret office classifies the materials to be destroyed by their type (the documents stored in the computer databases are not to be destroyed):
   a. If the cryptographic material is classified as SECRET and TOP SECRET, the task Appointment of three commission members (go to step 2) is initiated.
   b. If the cryptographic materials designated as EXPLICIT and CLASSIFIED, the task to set up the commission (go to step 6) is initiated.

c. Other materials: cryptographic system components (block module, component and auxiliary cryptographic devices), cryptographic products, publications and cryptographic technical documentation, cryptographic systems and products, forms and other registration devices to start the task aimed at calling a witness (go to 10).

2. The head of the organizational unit is appointed and at least 3 persons from the commission.
3. The commission shreds the documentation.
4. The commission draws up the minutes.
5. The manager of the organization removes documentation from the register and the information about this event is included therein. The process ends.
6. The manager of the organization appoints a committee composed of the office staff or contractor.
7. The commission shreds the documentation.
8. The manager of the organization enters in the "Remarks" muster apparatus annotation that reads: "destroyed by ...".
9. The manager of the organization completes the date and ensures that the legible signatures of the persons involved in the destruction of the cryptographic materials are affixed. The process ends.
10. The manager of the organization appoints a witness: Deputy Chief Registry Officer or any other person holding a security clearance.
11. The commission destroys the documentation.
12. The manager of the organization confirms the destruction on the form AF 21 PL.
13. The manager of the organization removes documentation from the register and the information about this event is included therein. The process ends.

7 Conclusion

The management of the classified and non-classified document flow, the document access control, supervision of their copying as well as the document access management constitute basic functions of the solution proposed in the research project,

The results of the project will be used in the document management systems, local organizations, banks, government organizations. These systems store personal data or corporate data as well as support document flow between different organizations.

The measurable social benefits are also important. The increased confidence of the third party institutions, such as public, government and non-government organizations, cooperating associations, companies and corporations, state authorities, is also worth mentioning.

Both the increasing of the security level of the documents as well as the authorized persons will improve the quality of the entire process associated with the document flow. The most tangible result of these actions will be the reduction (eventually - total liquidation) of incidents related to the uncontrolled disclosure of the classified documents and data. It is of great importance from the point of view of state safety, which nowadays may be even related to terrorist threats. Poland, as a member of the European Union and NATO, is obliged to exert certain efforts to protect the processing of sensitive information.

An additional advantage of the proposed solutions, apart from providing better control over the storage and document sharing, will be a possibility of tracing the document flow between safety zones, with knowledge of the authorized persons that have been using the documentation. Mapping of the flow of the classified documents, in case of an incident, will allow effective investigation of the causes of their occurrence and making a list of the persons potentially responsible thereof.

The main users of the system will be units of state administration, including institutions subordinate to the Ministry of National Defence and the Ministry of the Interior and Administration. An important field of application of the results of the project will also include the area of justice and health care institutions.

Potential customers interested in deploying the results are the following institutions: Ministry of National Defence, Ministry of Internal Affairs, Internal Security Agency, Foreign Intelligence Agency, National Police and Polish Border Guard.

In addition, the following institutions would be interested in the project results: hospitals, libraries, national archives, colleges, and universities.

Despite the increasingly popular use of electronic documents, there are still areas where it is necessary to store paper documents. For example, the whole area of justice - the police, prosecutors, ordinary and administrative, regional, district and appellate courts use documents in paper form. In accordance with the Polish and European legislation, most of the paper documents constitute evidence in the police investigation, prosecution and court proceedings, and, consequently, it is impossible to convert them into an electronic form – they have to remain in their traditional paper form.

Another example are various medical records produced by different institutions participating in the healing process. Taking into account the size of the produced medical records, their current storage and backup, clinics and hospitals are faced with a serious challenge. Therefore, the use of the results of the project would provide huge benefits for this industry thanks to automation of document processing operations.

The national archives, which are part of the public administration, manage documents that are a perpetual source of providing information on the historical society, history of the Polish nation and our statehood. The purpose of the state archives today is also to secure archival materials created in the public sector. The application of the project to check archival resources already at its creation in the institutions that have archival materials, will allow to secure historical resources through supervision and control of the movements of the labelled media. Miles and miles of archives collected in different archives (for example, churches, political parties, etc.) secured and recorded by the system are part of the strategic objectives specified by the Executive Director of the State Archives in the document issued on December 29, 2010 entitled "National Archives Strategy for the period 2010-2020". The use of the project will allow the documents to be more effectively protected against any damage or theft both during their storage and access.

The system, based on the RFID technology, may also be applied to other institutions, which store archival materials, such as libraries, museums and documentation centres, etc. The library may also use the system for securing individual cards of valuable antique books.

The implementation of the system will contribute to the growth and competitiveness of the sector of workflow systems in Poland. This is due to the fact that the advanced solutions based on the radio and automatic document identification does not exist in Europe. With such technology, Polish institutions and companies become a leading supplier of the solutions for the European market, and later also worldwide.

Acknowledgements

This work was created as part of the project: DOBR-BI04/006/13143/2013 supported by NCR&D.

References

1. Finkenzeller K., RFID Handbook: Fundamentals and Applications in Contactless Smart Cards and Identification, Second Edition, John Wiley & Sons (2003)
2. Cole P.H., Ranasinghe D.C., Networked RFID Systems and Lightweight Cryptography, Springer (2008)
3. Zhang Y., Yang L.T., Chen J., RFID and Sensor Networks Architectures, Protocols, Security and Integrations, CRC Press (2009)
4. Paret D., RFID at Ultra and Super High Frequencies. Theory and application, John Wiley & Sons (2009)
5. Bolic M., Simplot-Ryl D., Stojmenovic I., RFID Systems Research Trends And Challenges, John Wiley & Sons (2010)
6. Miles S.B., Sarma S.E., Williams J.R., RFID Technology and Applications, Cambridge University Press (2008)
7. noFilis "CrossTalk AppCenter 3.0 Installation and Administration Guide"
8. Canon UniFLOW documentation - www.canon.com
9. Aurea BPM system documentation - aurea-bpm.com
10. Braude E.J., Bernstein, M.E., Software engineering: modern approaches, J. Wiley & Sons (2011)
11. Larman, C., Applying UML and Patterns: An Introduction to Object-Oriented Analysis and Design and Iterative Development, 3/e, Pearson Education India (2012)
12. http://aurea-bpm.com

MATEC Web of Conferences 76, 04004 (2016) DOI: 10.1051/matecconf/20167604004
CSCC 2016

Data flow between RFID devices in a modern restricted access administrative office

Waszkowski Robert[1,a], Chodowska Agata[2], Kiedrowicz Maciej[1], Nowicki Tadeusz[1], Wesołowski Zbigniew[1], Worwa Kazimierz[1]

[1]*Military Academy of Technology, Faculty of Cybernetics, Kaliskiego 2, 00-908 Warsaw, Poland*
[2]*Tecna Sp. z o.o., Kasprowicza 103a/9, 01-823 Warsaw, Poland*

Abstract. The paper presents models of data flow between RFID devices in a modern restricted access administrative office. The presented diagrams are the result of the analytical work performed by the multidisciplinary team of experts. The team was composed of IT specialist, security systems specialists and employees of the secret office. The presented models include the fact that the facilities in the secret office (cabinet, sluice, photocopier, desks) are equipped with the RFID reader, which allows to immediately read the documents that are within their reach.

1 Introduction

This paper presents models of data flow between RFID devices in a modern restricted access administrative office.

The research results are part of an R&D project, partially supported by the National Centre for Research and Development under grant No. DOBR-BIO4/006/13143/2013.

The science project – entitled "Electronic system for life-cycle management of documents of various level of confidentiality" – focuses on the use of the latest information and communication technologies related to Radio-Frequency Identification (RFID) and biometrics. The aim of completing this research project is to build and implement a prototype of a modern secret office designed to manage documents of various levels of confidentiality. The project covers all processes that take place in a secret office and the use of devices equipped with the RFID transmitter / receiver modules. The focus of the research is not only on documents and data carriers, but also on all secret office equipment (cabinets, desk, copying machines and entry/exit control devices) and appropriate software (the RFIDoc system).

The integration of all software and hardware components in a single system using the dedicated software involves the need to establish strict rules for data exchange between them. In the following chapters, the data flow between these components is described for different cases of application in the office.

2 Types of interfaces between RFIDoc systems and office devices

2.1 Monitoring

The monitoring interface receives every event sent by special devices in the secret office. The device sends signals thanks to CrossTalk system agents. The information on events is received from the following devices:

- Cabinet
  - Switching on the cabinet
  - Opening the door
  - Closing the door
- Sluice (entry/exit zones)
  - Closing the entrance door
  - Closing the exit door
- Trays
  - Switching on the device
  - Placing the document on tray
  - Taking the document from the tray
- Tunnel
  - Switching on the device
  - Placing the document in tunnel
  - Taking the document from the tunnel
- Photocopier
  - Which documents are copied and by whom

The monitoring interface communicates through http protocol. If any event occurs, the device sends an XML message to the rfiDoc system.

2.2 Authentication

The authentication interface authenticates access to various devices in the secret office, in particular to :

1. Passage through sluices:

When a person enters a sluice, the system sends the following types of signals:

[a] Corresponding author: robert.waszkowski@wat.edu.pl

- The OK signal means consent for passage and opens the exit door, and then allows a person to enter the next zone.
- The NOK signal means lack of consent and re-opens the entrance door and allows the person to leave the sluice.

2. Opening cabinets
When placing an ID card on a special spot in the cabinet, the cabinet sends a request for authentication. The cabinet opens the door once it receives permission from the rfiDoc system.

3. Copying documents
The interface communicates with the device and informs which materials may be copied, in which number and by whom.
Once the copy button is pressed, the photocopier saves in a special output folder (Archive-OUT) the documents that are to be copied as pdf files, with the following formal name:
[sequential_number(pages)]_[JobId]_[user's_identification_number]_[id_tagu_rfid].pdf
Where:
- sequential_number(pages) – paper sheet number
- JobId – internal identification number of the task
- user's_identification_number – ID number of the ID card
- id_tagu_rfid – ID of the RFID tag of the document

The verification process may commence once the following file appears: [jobId].ok
After the rfiDoc system recognizes the file [jobId].ok, it starts the verification process and checks which documents may be copied. After verification, the system copies the verified files from the output folder (keeping the file names) into the input folder (Archive-IN). The rfiDoc system signalizes the end of the verification process by placing the [jobId].ok file in the input folder w (Archive-IN). Once the photocopier recognizes the file, it starts copying

3 Data flows between the system and RFID devices

The rfiDoc system communicates with the devices via CrossTalk AppCenter and Cosmos. The Cosmos system ensures communication between the photocopier and rfiDoc, whereas CrossTalk AppCenter supports communication between rfiDoc and such devices as sluice, cabinet, tray and tunnel.

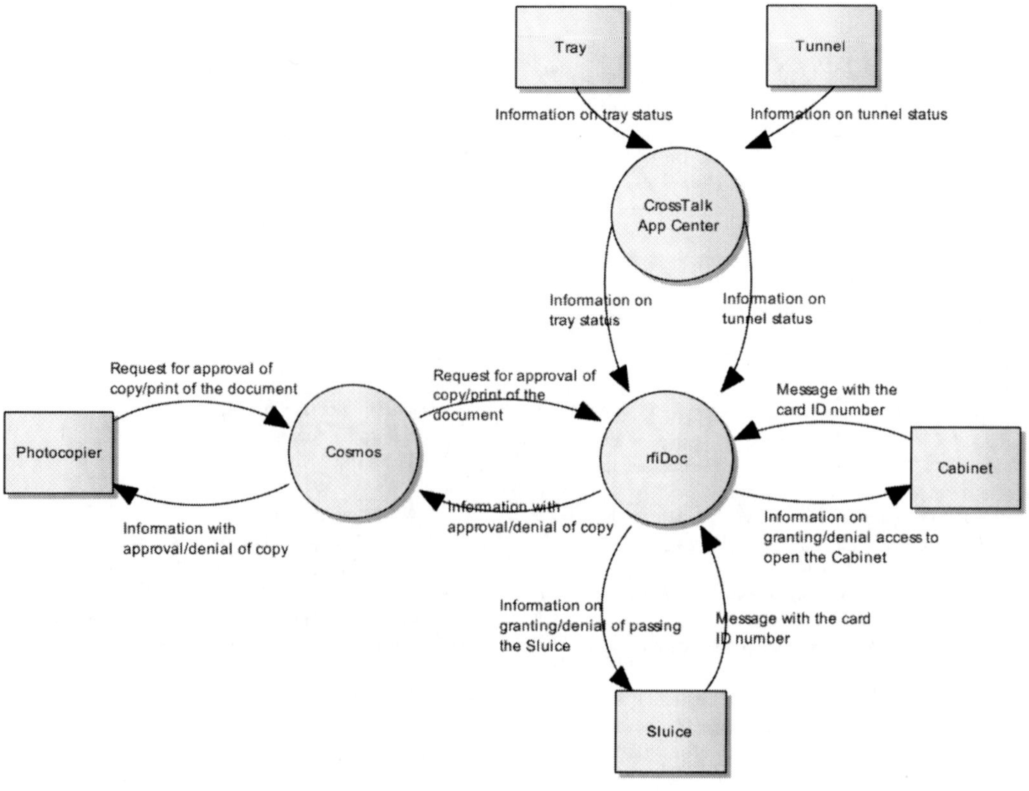

Figure 1. Diagram of flows between the rfiDoc system and Cosmos and CrossTalk systems as well as devices used in the secret office. Source: own elaboration.

The following subchapters describe communication and data flow between the rfiDoc system and other devices in the secret office.

3.1 Switching on the sluice

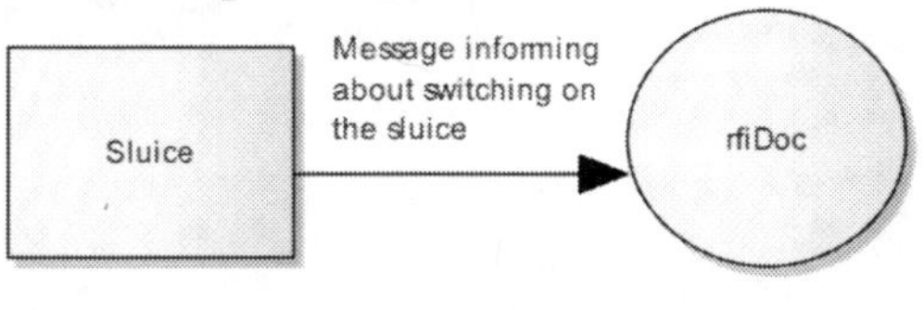

Figure 2 Diagram of data flow between the sluice and rfiDoc system – switching on the sluice

The following table presents the types and informational scope of the messages used when switching on the sluice.

Type of event	Type of message	Description
Switching on the sluice	Event	When switching on the sluice, the signal informing about the event, together with the list of all RFID tags currently on the device, is sent.

Example of the text of the HTTP POST request in the form of XML:


```
<events>
  <event type='com:nofilis:crosstalk:event:tag-observation'
    timestamp='1425475430717' uuid='B6887BED-1518-E3A6-C3ED-1461BB2D3A61'
    locationId='SAFETY_LOCK_1.I'
objectId='4000E005C701B004'>
    <property id='first-read'
value='1425475414927' />
    <property id='last-read'
value='1425475414927' />
    <property id='observationUUID'
value='2D9CCFB4-496E-AB2E-99E9-FF5526B1843D' />
    <property id='reads' value='1' />
    <property id='user' value='4000E005C701B004'
/>
  </event>
  <event type='com:nofilis:crosstalk:event:read-report' timestamp='1425475430718'
    locationId='SAFETY_LOCK_1.I' uuid='96F7DF8F-2A3E-FC35-245C-3E4316FFAC7E'
    objectId='2D9CCFB4-496E-AB2E-99E9-FF5526B1843D'>
    <property id='start-time'
value='1425475407372' />
    <property id='stop-time'
value='1425475430716' />
    <property id='start-event'
value='PROCESS_START' />
    <property id='stop-event' value='null' />
    <property id='condition' value='1' />
    <property id='tag-count' value='1' />
  </event>
</events>
```


3.2 Access to the secret office

Only duly authorized persons will have access to the secret office. Every person visiting the secret office must produce an ID card with the RFID chip. To enter the secret office, it is necessary to go through a sluice. The sluice is composed of the entrance door (outside), which allow to enter the secret office from its environment, and exit door (inside), which allow to exit the secret office to its environment.

When entering the secret office through the sluice, a given person is verified by the rfiDoc system in terms of his/her authorization. At this time, the sluice sends a message about closing the entrance door. The system verifies the authorization of the person entering the secret office and then sends a message about consent or lack of consent to enter the secret office. If the person is authorized to enter the secret office, the exit door opens. Otherwise, when the person may not enter the secret office – the entrance door allowing to leave the sluice opens.

The following diagrams show data flows between the sluice and the rfiDoc system. The first diagram shows the data flow in the event when the person entering the secret office is not duly authorized.

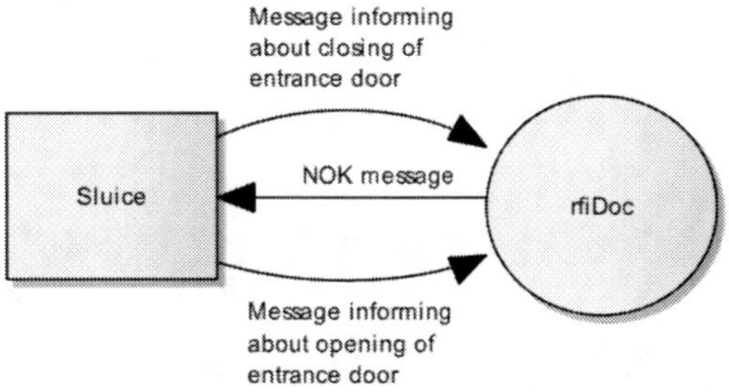

Figure 3 Diagram of data flow between the sluice and the rfiDoc system – no authorization to enter the secret office

In case of no authorization to enter the secret office, the sluice sends messages in the following form:

Type of event	Type of message	Description
Opening of the entrance door	Event	When opening the entrance door of the sluice, the device sends the information about this event, together with the information that did it and the list of all RFID tags currently on the device.

Example of the text of the HTTP POST request in the form of XML:


```
<events>
    <event
type='com:nofilis:crosstalk:event:door-in-open'
timestamp='1425475430717'
        locationId='SAFETY_LOCK_1'>
        <property                    id='user'
value='4000E005C701B004' />
    </event>
</events>
```


Closing of the entrance door	Event	When closing the entrance door of the sluice, the device sends the information about this event, together with the information that

		did it and the list of l RFID tags currently on the device.

Example of the text of the HTTP POST request in the form of XML:

```
<events>
  <event  type='com:nofilis:crosstalk:event:tag-
observation'
    timestamp='1425475430717'      uuid='B6887BED-
1518-E3A6-C3ED-1461BB2D3A61'
    locationId='SAFETY_LOCK_1'
objectId='4000E005C701B004'>
    <property                     id='first-read'
value='1425475414927' />
    <property                      id='last-read'
value='1425475414927' />
    <property                id='observationUUID'
value='2D9CCFB4-496E-AB2E-99E9-FF5526B1843D' />
    <property id='reads' value='1' />
    <property id='user' value='4000E005C701B004'
/>
  </event>
  <event type='com:nofilis:crosstalk:event:read-
report' timestamp='1425475430718'
    locationId='SAFETY_LOCK_1'    uuid='96F7DF8F-
2A3E-FC35-245C-3E4316FFAC7E'
    objectId='2D9CCFB4-496E-AB2E-99E9-
FF5526B1843D'>
    <property                     id='start-time'
value='1425475407372' />
    <property                      id='stop-time'
value='1425475430716' />
    <property                   id='start-event'
value='DOOR_IN_CLOSED' />
    <property id='stop-event' value='null' />
    <property id='condition' value='1' />
    <property id='tag-count' value='1' />
  </event>
</events>
```

The second diagram presents the data flow in the event when the person entering the secret office is duly authorized.

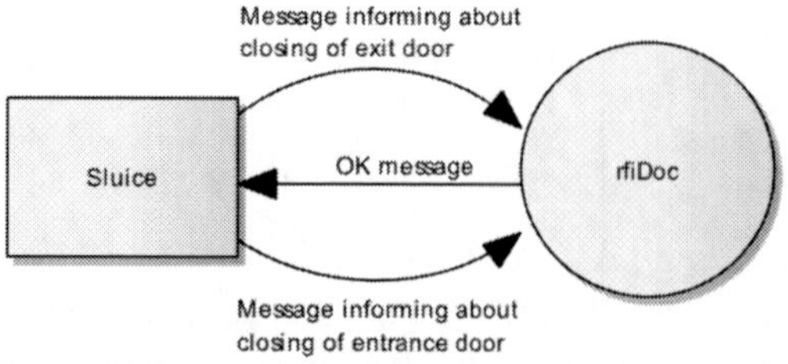

Figure 4 Diagram of data flow between the sluice and the rfiDoc system – positive authorization to enter the secret office

In case of positive authorization to enter the secret office, the sluice sends messages in the following form:

Type of event	Type of message	Description
Closing of the entrance door	Event	When closing the entrance door of the sluice, the device sends the information about this event, together with the information who did it and the list of all RFID tags currently

		on the device

Example of the text of the HTTP POST request in the form of XML:

```
<events>
  <event  type='com:nofilis:crosstalk:event:tag-
observation'
    timestamp='1425475430717'      uuid='B6887BED-
1518-E3A6-C3ED-1461BB2D3A61'
    locationId='SAFETY_LOCK_1'
objectId='4000E005C701B004'>
    <property                     id='first-read'
value='1425475414927' />
    <property                      id='last-read'
value='1425475414927' />
    <property                id='observationUUID'
value='2D9CCFB4-496E-AB2E-99E9-FF5526B1843D' />
    <property id='reads' value='1' />
    <property id='user' value='4000E005C701B004'
/>
  </event>
  <event type='com:nofilis:crosstalk:event:read-
report' timestamp='1425475430718'
    locationId='SAFETY_LOCK_1'    uuid='96F7DF8F-
2A3E-FC35-245C-3E4316FFAC7E'
    objectId='2D9CCFB4-496E-AB2E-99E9-
FF5526B1843D'>
    <property                     id='start-time'
value='1425475407372' />
    <property                      id='stop-time'
value='1425475430716' />
    <property                   id='start-event'
value='DOOR_IN_CLOSED' />
    <property id='stop-event' value='null' />
    <property id='condition' value='1' />
    <property id='tag-count' value='1' />
  </event>
</events>
```

Opening of the entrance door	Event	When opening the exit door of the sluice, the device sends the information about this event, together with the information who did it and the list of all RFID tags currently on the device

Example of the text of the HTTP POST request in the form of XML:

```
<events>
    <event
type='com:nofilis:crosstalk:event:door-out-open'
timestamp='1425475430717'
        locationId='SAFETY_LOCK_1'>
        <property                         id='user'
value='4000E005C701B004' />
    </event>
</events>
```

3.3 Exit from the secret office

The person leaves the secret office through the sluice. The inside door of the sluice opens each time, whereas the outside door opens depending on whether the person leaving the secret office takes with him/her any documents or not, to do which such person is authorized. Any attempt to take the documents without proper

authorization is signalized by the rfiDoc system, and, additionally affects the decision to open the outside door of the sluice.
The person leaving the secret office with or without documents, with respect to which (s)he is authorized, may freely go through the sluice and leave the area of the secret office. The system verifies the authorization of such person and then „allows" the sluice to open the outside door. After closing the entrance door of the sluice, a message informing about the rfiDoc system about this event is sent. The rfiDoc system sends the information about allowing or forbidding to exit the secret office. The information is passed in the form of the NOK and OK messages.
The following diagrams present the data flow between the sluice and the rfiDoc system. The first diagram shows the data flow when the person leaving the secret office does not take any documents.

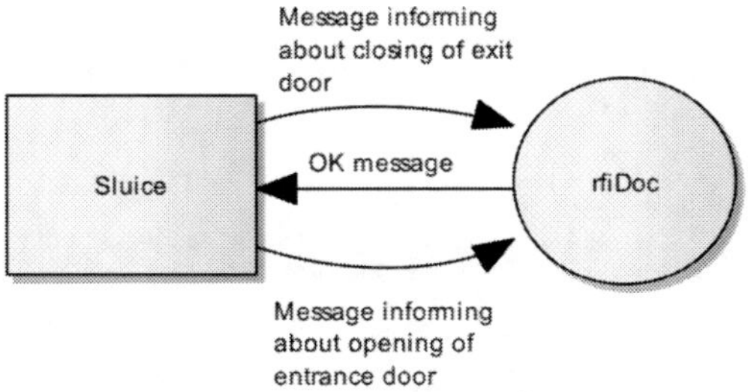

Figure 5 Diagram of data flow between the sluice and the rfiDoc system – leaving the secret office without any documents

In the event when the person leaving the secret office does not take any documents, the sluice sends messages with the following content:

Type of event	Type of message	Description
Closing of the entrance door	Event	When closing the entrance door of the sluice, the device sends the information about the event, together with the information who did it and the list of all RFID tags currently on the device

Example of the text of the HTTP POST request in the form of XML:


```
<events>
  <event  type='com:nofilis:crosstalk:event:tag-observation'
    timestamp='1425475430717'    uuid='B6887BED-1518-E3A6-C3ED-1461BB2D3A61'
    locationId='SAFETY_LOCK_1'
objectId='4000E005C701B004'>
    <property                    id='first-read'
value='1425475414927' />
    <property                     id='last-read'
value='1425475414927' />
    <property               id='observationUUID'
value='2D9CCFB4-496E-AB2E-99E9-FF5526B1843D' />
    <property id='reads' value='1' />
    <property id='user' value='4000E005C701B004'
/>
  </event>
  <event type='com:nofilis:crosstalk:event:read-report' timestamp='1425475430718'
    locationId='SAFETY_LOCK_1'    uuid='96F7DF8F-2A3E-FC35-245C-3E4316FFAC7E'
    objectId='2D9CCFB4-496E-AB2E-99E9-FF5526B1843D'>
    <property                    id='start-time'
value='1425475407372' />
    <property                     id='stop-time'
value='1425475430716' />
    <property                   id='start-event'
value='DOOR_IN_CLOSED' />
    <property id='stop-event' value='null' />
    <property id='condition' value='1' />
    <property id='tag-count' value='1' />
  </event>
</events>
```


Closing the exit door	Event	When closing the exit door of the sluice, the device sends the information about this event, together with the information who did it and the list of all RFID tags currently on the device

Example of the text of the HTTP POST request in the form of XML:


```
<events>
  <event  type='com:nofilis:crosstalk:event:tag-observation'
    timestamp='1425475430717'    uuid='B6887BED-1518-E3A6-C3ED-1461BB2D3A61'
    locationId='SAFETY_LOCK_1'
objectId='4000E005C701B004'>
    <property                    id='first-read'
value='1425475414927' />
    <property                     id='last-read'
value='1425475414927' />
    <property               id='observationUUID'
value='2D9CCFB4-496E-AB2E-99E9-FF5526B1843D' />
    <property id='reads' value='1' />
    <property id='user' value='4000E005C701B004'
/>
  </event>
  <event type='com:nofilis:crosstalk:event:read-report' timestamp='1425475430718'
    locationId='SAFETY_LOCK_1'    uuid='96F7DF8F-2A3E-FC35-245C-3E4316FFAC7E'
    objectId='2D9CCFB4-496E-AB2E-99E9-FF5526B1843D'>
    <property                    id='start-time'
value='1425475407372' />
    <property                     id='stop-time'
value='1425475430716' />
    <property                   id='start-event'
value='DOOR_OUT_CLOSED' />
    <property id='stop-event' value='null' />
    <property id='condition' value='1' />
```

```
    <property id='tag-count' value='1' />
  </event>
</events>
```


The second diagram presents the data flow in the event when the person leaving the secret office is authorized to take documents outside the area of the secret office.

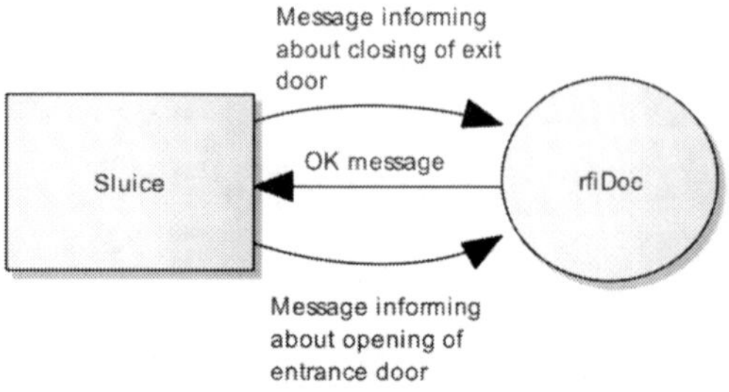

Figure 6 Diagram of the data flow between the sluice and the rfiDoc system – authorized exit from the secret office with the documents

In the event when the person leaving the secret office takes the documents, to do which (s)he is authorized, the sluice sends messages with the following content:

Type of event	Type of message	Description
Closing of the entrance door	Event	When closing the entrance door of the sluice, the device sends the information about this event, together with the information who did it and the list of all RFID tags currently in the

Example of the text of the HTTP POST request in the form of XML:


```
<events>
  <event  type='com:nofilis:crosstalk:event:tag-
observation'
    timestamp='1425475430717'     uuid='B6887BED-
1518-E3A6-C3ED-1461BB2D3A61'
    locationId='SAFETY_LOCK_1'
objectId='4000E005C701B004'>
    <property                    id='first-read'
value='1425475414927' />
    <property                     id='last-read'
value='1425475414927' />
    <property               id='observationUUID'
value='2D9CCFB4-496E-AB2E-99E9-FF5526B1843D' />
    <property id='reads' value='1' />
    <property id='user' value='4000E005C701B004'
/>
  </event>
  <event  type='com:nofilis:crosstalk:event:read-
report' timestamp='1425475430718'
    locationId='SAFETY_LOCK_1'    uuid='96F7DF8F-
2A3E-FC35-245C-3E4316FFAC7E'
    objectId='2D9CCFB4-496E-AB2E-99E9-
FF5526B1843D'>
    <property                    id='start-time'
value='1425475407372' />
    <property                     id='stop-time'
value='1425475430716' />
    <property                   id='start-event'
value='DOOR_IN_CLOSED' />
    <property id='stop-event' value='null' />
    <property id='condition' value='1' />
    <property id='tag-count' value='1' />
  </event>
</events>
```


Closing of the exit door	Event	When closing the exit door of the sluice, the device sends the information about this event, together with the information who did it and the list of all RFID tags currently on the device

Example of the text of the HTTP POST request in the form of XML:


```
<events>
  <event  type='com:nofilis:crosstalk:event:tag-
observation'
    timestamp='1425475430717'     uuid='B6887BED-
1518-E3A6-C3ED-1461BB2D3A61'
    locationId='SAFETY_LOCK_1'
objectId='4000E005C701B004'>
    <property                    id='first-read'
value='1425475414927' />
    <property                     id='last-read'
value='1425475414927' />
    <property               id='observationUUID'
value='2D9CCFB4-496E-AB2E-99E9-FF5526B1843D' />
    <property id='reads' value='1' />
    <property id='user' value='4000E005C701B004'
/>
  </event>
  <event  type='com:nofilis:crosstalk:event:read-
report' timestamp='1425475430718'
    locationId='SAFETY_LOCK_1'    uuid='96F7DF8F-
2A3E-FC35-245C-3E4316FFAC7E'
    objectId='2D9CCFB4-496E-AB2E-99E9-
FF5526B1843D'>
    <property                    id='start-time'
value='1425475407372' />
    <property                     id='stop-time'
value='1425475430716' />
    <property                   id='start-event'
value='DOOR_OUT_CLOSED' />
    <property id='stop-event' value='null' />
    <property id='condition' value='1' />
    <property id='tag-count' value='1' />
  </event>
</events>
```


The third diagram presents the data flow in the event when the person leaving the secret office is not authorized to take the documents outside the area of the secret office.

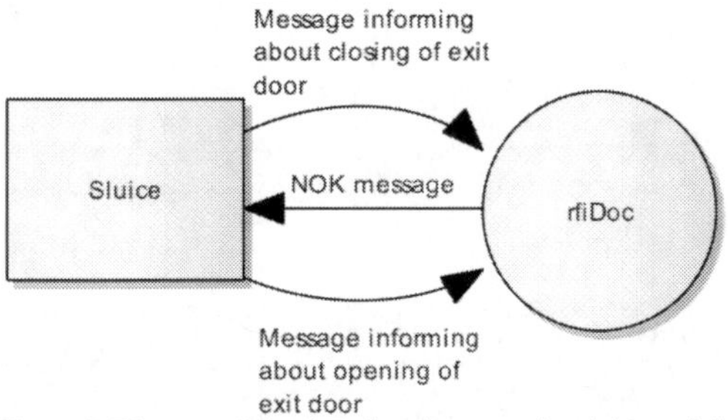

Figure 7 Diagram of the data flow between the sluice and the rfiDoc system - unauthorized exit from the secret office with the documents

Type of event	Type of message	Description
Opening of the exit door	Event	When opening the exit door of the sluice, the device sends the information about this event, together with the information who did it and the list of all RFID tags currently on the device

Example of the text of the HTTP POST request in the form of XML:

```
<events>
    <event
type='com:nofilis:crosstalk:event:door-out-open'
timestamp='1425475430717'
        locationId='SAFETY_LOCK_1'>
        <property                          id='user'
value='4000E005C701B004' />
    </event>
</events>
```

Closing of the exit doors	Event	When closing the exit door of the sluice,

Example of the text of the HTTP POST request in the form of XML:

```
<events>
  <event  type='com:nofilis:crosstalk:event:tag-
observation'
    timestamp='1425475430717'     uuid='B6887BED-
1518-E3A6-C3ED-1461BB2D3A61'
    locationId='SAFETY_LOCK_1'
objectId='4000E005C701B004'>
    <property                    id='first-read'
value='1425475414927' />
    <property                     id='last-read'
value='1425475414927' />
    <property               id='observationUUID'
value='2D9CCFB4-496E-AB2E-99E9-FF5526B1843D' />
    <property id='reads' value='1' />
    <property id='user' value='4000E005C701B004'
/>
  </event>
  <event type='com:nofilis:crosstalk:event:read-
report' timestamp='1425475430718'
    locationId='SAFETY_LOCK_1'    uuid='96F7DF8F-
2A3E-FC35-245C-3E4316FFAC7E'
    objectId='2D9CCFB4-496E-AB2E-99E9-
FF5526B1843D'>
    <property                    id='start-time'
value='1425475407372' />
    <property                     id='stop-time'
value='1425475430716' />
    <property                   id='start-event'
value='DOOR_OUT_CLOSED' />
    <property id='stop-event' value='null' />
    <property id='condition' value='1' />
    <property id='tag-count' value='1' />
  </event>
</events>
```

3.4 Handling the cabinet

The rfiDoc system provides control over authorization of the persons working with documents stored in the cabinets in the secret office. Every person staying within the area of the secret office must produce the ID card with the RFID chip. The devices in the secret office are equipped with the RFID reader, which allows full control of the operations performed in the secret office.

Only authorized persons may take the document out of the cabinet or put it back. Both operations are preceded by identification by the ID card with the RFID chip. Depending on the rights vested with the person working The cabinet sends to the rfiDoc system a message about an identifier of the card of the person trying to get access to the documents and information about closing and opening of the cabinet. The system sends the following messages to the cabinet:

- OK- if the person is authorized to open the cabinet,
- NOK- if the person is not authorized to open the cabinet,
- The message about the exceeded time for opening the cabinet.

Each of the above-mentioned cases was presented on the following diagrams. The first diagram shows the data transfer between the cabinet and the rfiDoc system in the event when the access to the cabinet is authorized.

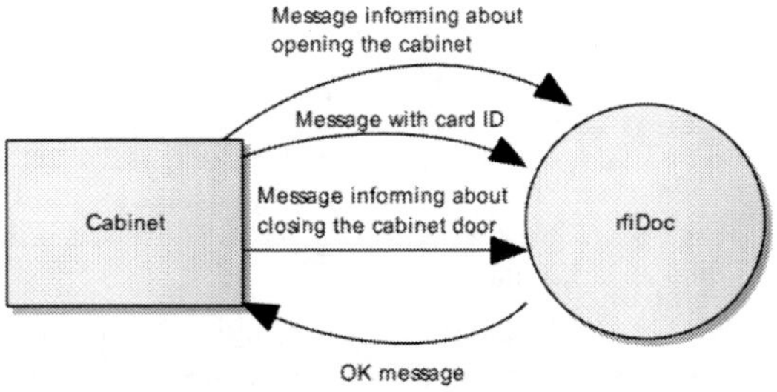

Figure 8 Diagram of the data flow between the cabinet and the rfiDoc system – authorized opening of the cabinet

Type of event	Type of message	Description
Opening of the door	Event	When opening the door of the cabinet, the device sends the information about this event, together with the information who did it and the list of the RFID tags currently in the cabinet

Example of the text of the HTTP POST request in the form of XML:

```
<event    type='com:nofilis:crosstalk:event:door-
open' timestamp='1417780472942'
      locationId='CABINET_3'>
      <property                          id='user'
value='4001E00543CBC01B' />
</event>
```

Closing the door	Event	When closing the door, the device sends the information about this event, together with the information who did it and the list of the RFID tags currently in the cabinet

Example of the text of the HTTP POST request in the form of XML(addition of RFID tag):

```
<events>
  <event   type='com:nofilis:crosstalk:event:tag-
observation'
    timestamp='1417780472942'    uuid='83B3B520-
59A1-5DA0-56FF-F149CF891032'
    locationId='CABINET_3.A'
objectId='001DEEC0'>
    <property                     id='first-read'
value='1417780464499' />
    <property                      id='last-read'
value='1417780464499' />
    <property               id='observationUUID'
value='4467A9DA-03BF-DB1D-F6A0-CDB1B55E8EE9' />
    <property id='reads' value='5' />
    <property id='user' value='4001E00543CBC01B'
/>
  </event>
  <event  type='com:nofilis:crosstalk:event:read-
report' timestamp='1417780472975'
    locationId='CABINET_3.A'     uuid='98487206-
19B6-4E0F-D462-D4F8B75F3A81'
    objectId='4467A9DA-03BF-DB1D-F6A0-
CDB1B55E8EE9'>
    <property                     id='start-time'
value='1417780463949' />
    <property                      id='stop-time'
value='1417780472938' />
    <property                    id='start-event'
value='DOOR_CLOSED' />
    <property id='stop-event' value='null' />
    <property id='condition' value='1' />
    <property id='tag-count' value='1' />
  </event>
</events>
```

Example of the text of the HTTP POST request in the form of XML(removal of RFID tag):

```
<events>
  <event   type='com:nofilis:crosstalk:event:tag-
observation'
    timestamp='1417780472942'    uuid='83B3B520-
59A1-5DA0-56FF-F149CF891032'
    locationId='CABINET_3.R'
objectId='001DEEC0'>
    <property                     id='first-read'
value='1417780464499' />
    <property                      id='last-read'
value='1417780464499' />
    <property               id='observationUUID'
value='4467A9DA-03BF-DB1D-F6A0-CDB1B55E8EE9' />
    <property id='reads' value='5' />
    <property id='user' value='4001E00543CBC01B'
/>
  </event>
  <event  type='com:nofilis:crosstalk:event:read-
report' timestamp='1417780472975'
    locationId='CABINET_3.R'     uuid='98487206-
19B6-4E0F-D462-D4F8B75F3A81'
    objectId='4467A9DA-03BF-DB1D-F6A0-
CDB1B55E8EE9'>
    <property                     id='start-time'
value='1417780463949' />
    <property                      id='stop-time'
value='1417780472938' />
    <property                    id='start-event'
value='DOOR_CLOSED' />
    <property id='stop-event' value='null' />
    <property id='condition' value='1' />
    <property id='tag-count' value='1' />
  </event>
</events>
```

Pressing ID card	Question - answer	When pressing the ID card, the device sends the information about this event together with the card identifier, which cause the event. The device waits for approval to open the door of the cabinet.

Example of the text of the HTTP POST request in the form of XML:

```
<event type='com:nofilis:crosstalk:event:access'
timestamp='1417780472942'
     locationId='CABINET_3'>
     <property                          id='user'
value='4001E00543CBC01B' />
</event>
```

The second diagram refers to the case when the ID card holder is not authorized to open the cabinet.

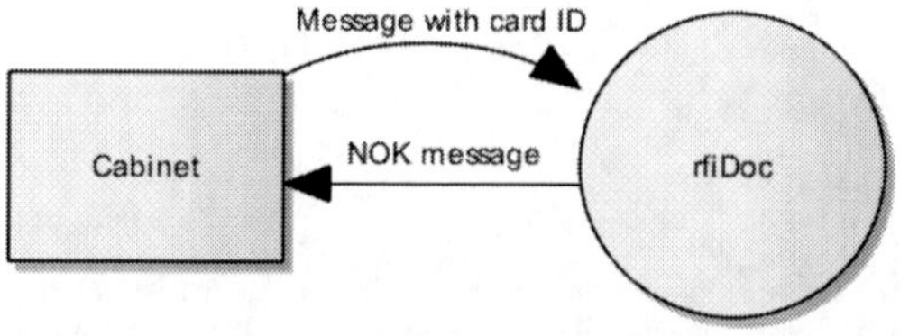

Figure 9 Diagram of data flow between Cabinet and rfiDoc system – not authorized access to the cabinet

Type of event	Type of message	Description
Pressing ID card	Answer - question	When pressing the ID card, the device sends the information about this event, together with the card identifier, which caused the event. The device waits for

		approval to open the door of the cabinet

Example of the text of the HTTP POST request in the form of XML:


```
<event type='com:nofilis:crosstalk:event:access'
timestamp='1417780472942'
     locationId='CABINET_3'>
     <property                                    id='user'
value='4001E00543CBC01B' />
</event>
```


3.5 Copying of documents

The rfiDoc system stores authorization to the documents that are in the secret office. The following operations may be performer on the document: copying, printing or scanning. The copying and scanning is performed with the use of a special photocopier including the RFID reader.
To copy the document, authentication by means of the RFID chip card is essential. The photocopier sends to the rfiDoc system the information containing the data identifying the person who wants to copy the document. The copying process commences, during which the rfiDoc system verifies rights to certain documents. The documents, to which the copying party is authorized, are transferred to the Archive-IN folder and only such documents will be copied. Other documents are not copied.
The following diagrams show the data flow between the photocopier and the rfiDoc system. The first diagram shows the data flow for the event when the copying party is authorized to copy the document.

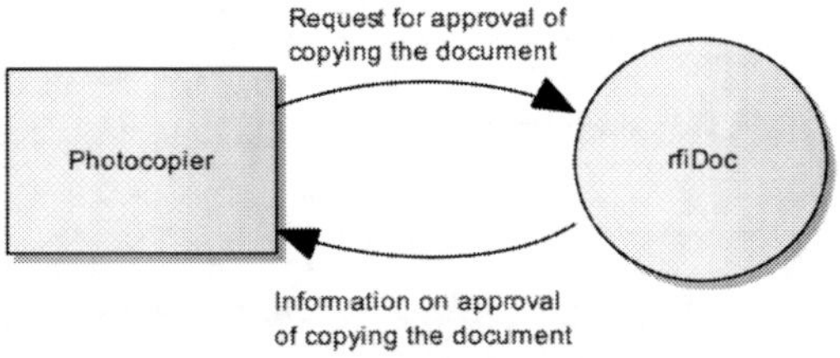

Figure 10 Diagram of the data flow between the photocopier and the rfiDoc system – authorized copying

The second diagram shows the data flow for the event when the copying party is not authorized to copy the document.

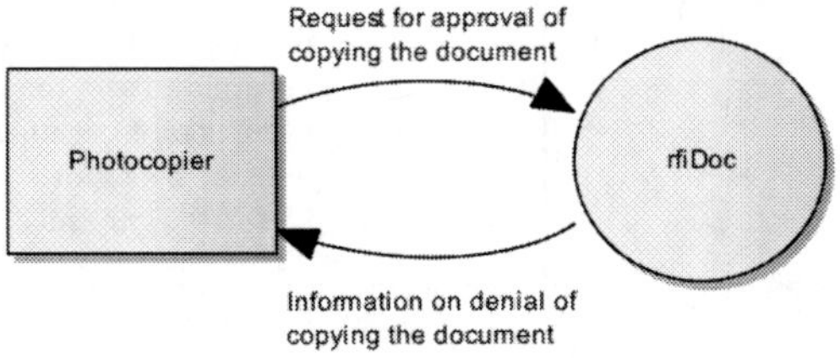

Figure 11 Diagram of the data flow between the photocopier and the rfiDoc system – unauthorized copying

3.6 Switching on the tray

After switching on the tray, the device sends the signal informing about this event. The message contains a list of the RFID tags on the device.

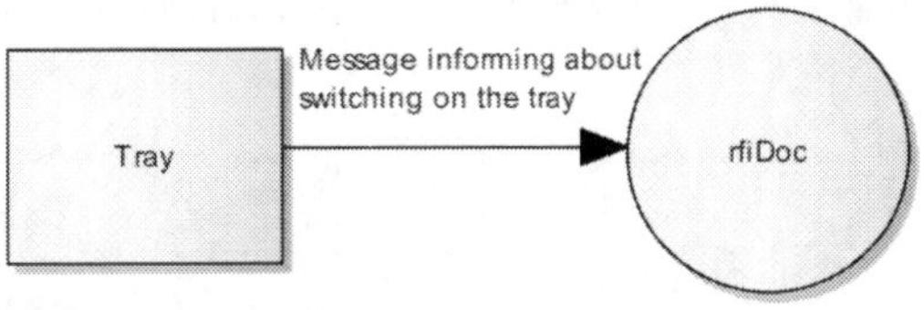

Figure 12 Diagram of the data flow between the tray and the rfiDoc- switching on the tray

Type of event	Type of message	Description
Switching on the device	Event	When switching on the device, the signal informing about this event, together with the list of all RFID tags currently on the device

Example of the text of the HTTP POST request in the form of XML:


```
<events>
     <event
type='com:nofilis:crosstalk:event:tag-
observation'
          timestamp='1417780472975'
uuid='4AF6AB5B-604B-75DD-E929-CD0C27FBB632'
          locationId='TRAY_1.I'
objectId='4001E00543CBC01B'>
          <property                id='first-read'
value='1417780464603' />
          <property                 id='last-read'
value='1417780464603' />
          <property            id='observationUUID'
value='4467A9DA-03BF-DB1D-F6A0' />
          <property id='reads' value='1' />
     </event>
     <event
type='com:nofilis:crosstalk:event:read-report'
timestamp='1417780472975'
          locationId='TRAY_1.I'    uuid='98487206-
19B6-4E0F-D462-D4F8B75F3A81'
          objectId='4467A9DA-03BF-DB1D-F6A0-
CDB1B55E8EE9'>
          <property                id='start-time'
value='1417780463949' />
          <property                 id='stop-time'
value='1417780472938' />
          <property               id='start-event'
value='PROCESS_START' />
          <property  id='stop-event'  value='null'
/>
          <property id='condition' value='1' />
          <property id='tag-count' value='1' />
     </event>
</events>
```


3.7 Placement of the document on tray

Each document stored in the secret office has an appropriate RFID tag. All metadata of the documents are stored in the rfiDoc system. The rfiDoc system has data

concerning the location of the documents in the secret office. The secret office clerk identifies the documents in the secret office by using the tray.
The placement of the documents on the tray causes automatic sending of the data with the RFID tag placed on the document to the CrossTalk system. The CrossTalk system sends the received data to the rfiDoc system. The data flow between the tray and the systems is shown on the diagram below.

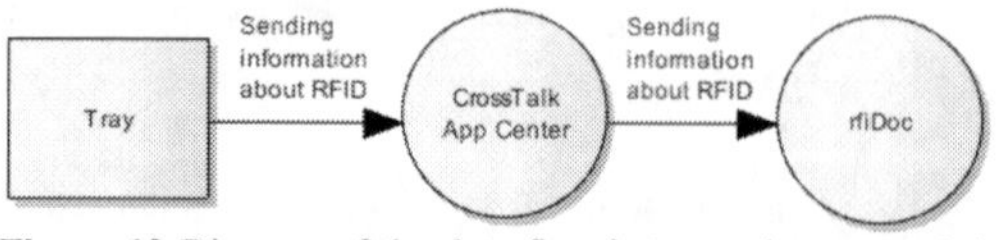

Figure 13 Diagram of the data flow between the tray and the CrossTalk and the rfiDoc

Type of event	Type of message	Description
Placement of the document	Event	When placing the document, the device sends the information about this event, together with the list of all RFID tags currently on the device

Example of the text of the HTTP POST request in the form of XML:


```
<events>
    <event
type='com:nofilis:crosstalk:event:tag-
observation'
        timestamp='1452698270796'
uuid='DA5E8CA7-24AC-912B-2ECA-3E4B75E1E1C4'
        locationId='TRAY_1.A'
objectId='4001E00528F8C01B'>
        <property                    id='first-read'
value='1452698270780' />
        <property                     id='last-read'
value='1452698270780' />
        <property              id='observationUUID'
value='7F701933-FF3F-8B9B-8E8A' />
        <property id='reads' value='1' />
    </event>
    <event
type='com:nofilis:crosstalk:event:read-report'
timestamp='1452698270796'
        locationId='TRAY_1.A'   uuid='ECAB62A6-
8388-3696-27CC-1CE54D5A5A2D'
        objectId='7F701933-FF3F-8B9B-8E8A'>
        <property                    id='start-time'
value='1452698270780' />
        <property                     id='stop-time'
value='1452698270796' />
        <property                   id='start-event'
value='null' />
        <property  id='stop-event'  value='null'
/>
        <property id='condition' value='0' />
        <property id='tag-count' value='1' />
    </event>
</events>
```


Removal of the document	Event	When removing the document, the device sends the information about this event, together with the list of all RFID tags currently on the device

Example of the text of the HTTP POST request in the form of XML:


```
<events>
    <event
type='com:nofilis:crosstalk:event:tag-
observation'
        timestamp='1452698270796'
uuid='DA5E8CA7-24AC-912B-2ECA-3E4B75E1E1C4'
        locationId='TRAY_1.R'
objectId='4001E00528F8C01B'>
        <property                    id='first-read'
value='1452698270780' />
        <property                     id='last-read'
value='1452698270780' />
        <property              id='observationUUID'
value='7F701933-FF3F-8B9B-8E8A' />
        <property id='reads' value='1' />
    </event>
    <event
type='com:nofilis:crosstalk:event:read-report'
timestamp='1452698270796'
        locationId='TRAY_1.R'   uuid='ECAB62A6-
8388-3696-27CC-1CE54D5A5A2D'
        objectId='7F701933-FF3F-8B9B-8E8A'>
        <property                    id='start-time'
value='1452698270780' />
        <property                     id='stop-time'
value='1452698270796' />
        <property                   id='start-event'
value='null' />
        <property  id='stop-event'  value='null'
/>
        <property id='condition' value='0' />
        <property id='tag-count' value='1' />
    </event>
</events>
```


3.8 Switching on the tunnel

After switching on the tunnel, the device sends the signal informing about this event. The message also contains the status of tags on the device.

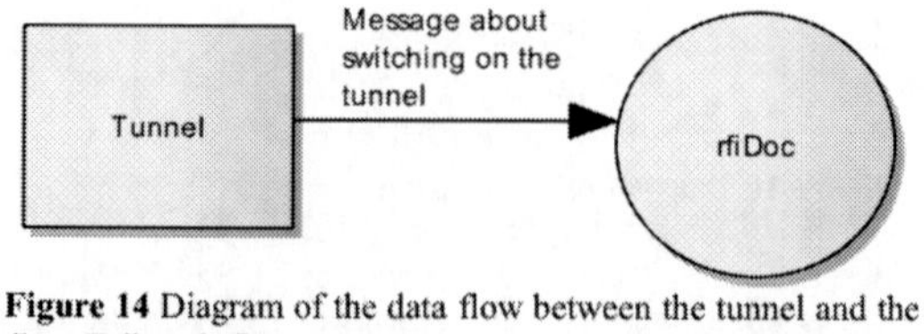

Figure 14 Diagram of the data flow between the tunnel and the CrossTalk and rfiDoc systems

Type of event	Type of message	Description
Switching on the device	Event	When switching on the device, the signal informing about this event is sent, together with the list of all RFID tags currently on the device

 DOI: 10.1051/matecconf/20167604004

Example of the text of the HTTP POST request in the form of XML:

```
<?xml version="1.0" encoding="UTF-8"?>
<events>
     <event
type="com:nofilis:crosstalk:event:tag-
observation"
          timestamp="1418306935411"
uuid="131D54A5-8C40-192B-F714-A8A8ACE4816C"
          locationId="TUNNEL_1.I"
objectId="4001E00541AAC01C">
          <property                  id="first-read"
value="1418306935406" />
          <property                   id="last-read"
value="1418306935406" />
          <property             id="observationUUID"
value="E89BF652-6F7A-3227-6FEF-E5A4DE4D8B17" />
          <property id="reads" value="1" />
     </event>
     <event
type="com:nofilis:crosstalk:event:read-report"
timestamp="1418306935411"
          locationId="TUNNEL_1.I"
uuid="F23966A6-21D7-F408-0E17-2E4AC93FA44C"
          objectId="E89BF652-6F7A-3227-6FEF-
E5A4DE4D8B17">
          <property                  id="start-time"
value="1418306935406" />
          <property                   id="stop-time"
value="1418306935411" />
          <property                 id="start-event"
value="PROCESS_START" />
          <property  id="stop-event"  value="null"
/>
          <property id="condition" value="0" />
          <property id="tag-count" value="1" />
     </event>
</events>
```

3.9 Moving the document through the tunnel

All documents stored in the secret office have appropriate tunnelRFID tags allowing their identification and placement. Taking the document out of the secret office is possible only upon prior grant of authorization. The document may be taken out of the secret office if the person carries it through the sluice or tunnel. The tunnel identifies the documents, which are stored therein. When the documents are moved through the tunnel, it affects the transfer of data with the RFID tags on the documents through the tunnel. Therefore, the control of the movement of the documents inside different zones of the secret office or outside the office is maintained.
The following diagram present the data flow between the tunnel and the CrossTalk and rfiDoc systems.

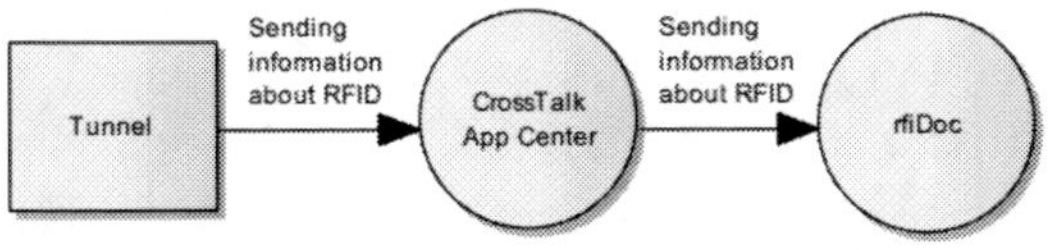

Figure15 Diagram of the data flow between the tunnel and the CrossTalk and rfiDoc systems

Type of event	Type of message	Description
Detection of the document	Event	After detecting the document, the device sends the information about this event, together with the list of all RFID tags currently on the device

Example of the text of the HTTP POST request in the form of XML:

```
<events>
  <event  type="com:nofilis:crosstalk:event:tag-
observation"
    timestamp="1418306935411"    uuid="258E9DFF-
7365-3812-BAB3-2D90D23CA8B8"
    locationId="TUNNEL_1.A"
objectId="4001E0052A1BC01C">
    <property                        id="first-read"
value="1418306935406" />
    <property                         id="last-read"
value="1418306935406" />
    <property                  id="observationUUID"
value="E89BF652-6F7A-3227-6FEF-E5A4DE4D8B17" />
    <property id="reads" value="1" />
  </event>
  <event type="com:nofilis:crosstalk:event:read-
report" timestamp="1418306935411"
    locationId="TUNNEL_1.A" uuid="F23966A6-21D7-
F408-0E17-2E4AC93FA44C"
    objectId="E89BF652-6F7A-3227-6FEF-
E5A4DE4D8B17">
    <property                        id="start-time"
value="1418306935406" />
    <property                         id="stop-time"
value="1418306935411" />
    <property id="start-event" value="null" />
    <property id="stop-event" value="null" />
    <property id="condition" value="0" />
    <property id="tag-count" value="1" />
  </event>
</events>
```

Deletion of the document	Event	After deleting the document, the device sends the information about this event, together with the list of all RFID tags currently on the device

Example of the text of the HTTP POST request in the form of XML:

```
<events>
  <event  type="com:nofilis:crosstalk:event:tag-
observation"
    timestamp="1418306935411"    uuid="258E9DFF-
7365-3812-BAB3-2D90D23CA8B8"
    locationId="TUNNEL_1.A"
objectId="4001E0052A1BC01C">
    <property                        id="first-read"
value="1418306935406" />
    <property                         id="last-read"
value="1418306935406" />
    <property                  id="observationUUID"
value="E89BF652-6F7A-3227-6FEF-E5A4DE4D8B17" />
    <property id="reads" value="1" />
  </event>
  <event type="com:nofilis:crosstalk:event:read-
report" timestamp="1418306935411"
    locationId="TUNNEL_1.A" uuid="F23966A6-21D7-
F408-0E17-2E4AC93FA44C"
    objectId="E89BF652-6F7A-3227-6FEF-
E5A4DE4D8B17">
```

```
    <property                    id="start-time"
value="1418306935406" />
    <property                    id="stop-time"
value="1418306935411" />
    &lt;property id="start-event" value="null" /&gt;
    &lt;property id="stop-event" value="null" /&gt;
    &lt;property id="condition" value="0" /&gt;
    &lt;property id="tag-count" value="1" /&gt;
  &lt;/event&gt;
&lt;/events&gt;
```

Conclusions

The dedicated monitoring and authenticating interfaces ensure complete data flow between the devices, which support the work of the secret office and the rfiDoc system. The operations of the secret office are supported by the rfiDoc system and the following equipment: sluice, cabinet, tray, tunnel and photocopier.
The rfiDoc system exchanges with the devices the information on the authorization rights and messages concerning their operation in the secret office. The lack of authorization to operate the device or handle the document stored in the secret office is signalized by way of certain messages sent by the system, which affect the behavior of the equipment. Unauthorized actions are blocked by the rfiDoc system.

References

1. Orłowski A. Analiza tendencji rozwoju technik RFID oraz laboratorium badawcze technik RFID, Warszawa 2008
2. Patrick J. Sweeney II „RFID for Dummies" Wiley Publishing 2005
3. Szczurkowski M. Roz. Zdalna identyfikacja radiowa obiektów w oparciu o RFID. W: Wytwarzanie i sterowanie polami magnetycznymi dla radiowej identyfikacji obiektów RFID. Rozprawa doktorska, Kraków 2010
4. Techniki inwigilacji, Paweł Kałużny, ISBN/ISSN: 978-83-01-15317-5 , Wydawnictwo Naukowe PWN, Rok wydania 2008
5. Wolf-Ruediger Hansen, Frank Gillert, „RFID for the Optimization of Business Processes,,, str. 95 – 120 (roz. V), Wiley
6. noFilis "CrossTalk AppCenter 3.0 Installation and Administration Guide"
7. Canon UniFLOW documentation - www.canon.com
8. Aurea BPM system documentation - aurea-bpm.com
9. Finkenzeller K., RFID Handbook: Fundamentals and Applications in Contactless Smart Cards and Identification, Second Edition, John Wiley & Sons (2003)
10. Cole P.H., Ranasinghe D.C., Networked RFID Systems and Lightweight Cryptography, Springer (2008)
11. Zhang Y., Yang L.T., Chen J., RFID and Sensor Networks Architectures, Protocols, Security and Integrations, CRC Press (2009)
12. Paret D., RFID at Ultra and Super High Frequencies. Theory and application, John Wiley & Sons (2009)
13. Bolic M., Simplot-Ryl D., Stojmenovic I., RFID Systems Research Trends And Challenges, John Wiley & Sons (2010)
14. Miles S.B., Sarma S.E., Williams J.R., RFID Technology and Applications, Cambridge University Press (2008)

Business process modeling for processing classified documents using RFID technology

Jarosław Koszela[1,a]

[1]*Military University of Technology, Faculty of Cybernetics, Institute of Computer and Information Systems, Warsaw, Poland*

Abstract. The article outlines the application of the processing approach to the functional description of the designed IT system supporting the operations of the secret office, which processes classified documents. The article describes the application of the method of incremental modeling of business processes according to the BPMN model to the description of the processes currently implemented ("as is") in a manual manner and target processes ("to be"), using the RFID technology for the purpose of their automation. Additionally, the examples of applying the method of structural and dynamic analysis of the processes (process simulation) to verify their correctness and efficiency were presented. The extension of the process analysis method is a possibility of applying the warehouse of processes and process mining methods.

Keywords: business process modeling, BPMN, RFID, Classified Registry/secret office, workflow system, business process simulation, warehouse of processes, process mining

1 Introduction

At the time of building IT systems supporting the operations of an organization, it is essential to apply the methods and tools which allow to determine the needs and functions of the system for the purpose of mitigating the risk of its failure and more precise assessment of the system's complexity and cost. The article outlines the application of the processing approach to the description of the functionality of the secret office in organization. The example describes the business process modeling method from the current state (manual processes) to the target state (automated processes using the RFID technology [1], [2]) and the use of the tool for structural and dynamic process analysis (business process simulation, warehouse of process, process mining).

The application of the RFID (Radio-Frequency Identification) technology for processing the documents with different sensitivity levels was caused by insufficient level of protection of sensitive documents and the process of handling such documents, which are currently implemented. The application of RFID increases the level of security of the documents as well as the efficiency of their processing and flows in the secret office and other organizations, where the document archiving and workflow are crucial for their functioning. Since such solutions are rather complex and consist of many different components, which differ in terms of technology and the scope of their functioning and impact [3] (i.e. IT, ICT, electronic, mechanical, organizational, formal and legal systems), it is required to apply the method for describing the system's functionalities and their analysis.

Therefore, the objective is to verify a possibility of modeling main activities performed in the secret office in the traditional form (without automation) and when using process automation systems, including ICT systems (workflow system [4], [5], [6], registers and date resources [7], [8]), RFID technology and a possibility of checking their compliance with the BPMN [9] model, also by applying the process simulation method.

[a] Corresponding author: jkoszela@wat.edu.pl

2 Business processes modeling – phases of life cycle

The PDCA model [10] may be used to manage business processes in organization. The model describes the life cycle of the process and consists of the four main steps (Figure 1): Plan, Do, Check, Act. The model presents a closed cycle of the process management, where the processes should be constantly modified and improved.

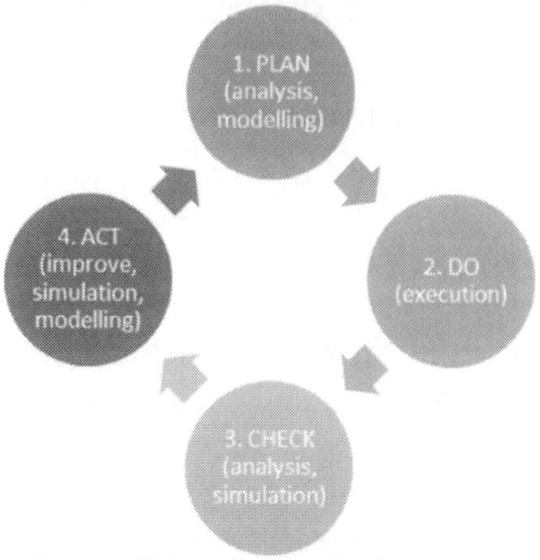

Figure 1. PDCA - life cycle of business process

The modeling of the business processes according to BPMN for the secret office in the operating organization may be divided into two main phases (Figure 2) [11], [12]: modeling of the processes that are currently implemented in the organization ("as is") and modeling of the processes for the target model of the organization's functioning model ("to be"). It means that the change of the current processes to target processes must be defined by determining which mainly business goals are to be achieved (e.g. increasing efficiency of the organization's operations, decreasing the costs, reducing the execution time, increasing safety, etc.).

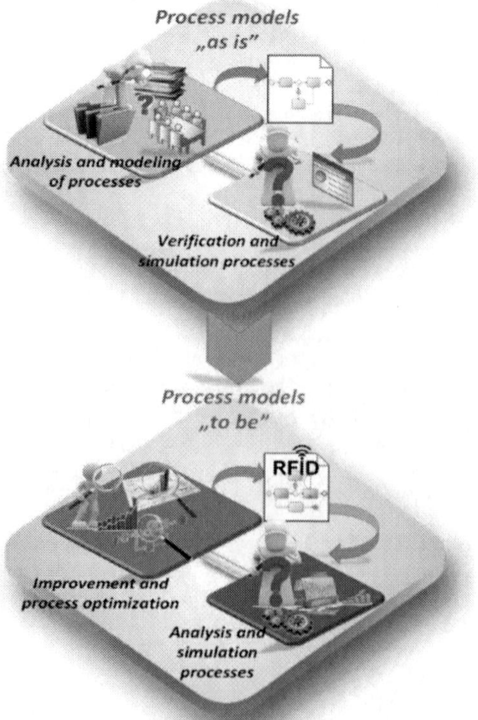

Figure 2. Modeling processes from « as is » to « to be » phase

The developed processes may be used for their automation by applying the process automation system (i.e. workflow process) as well as for the analysis and exploration of the processes (Figure 3) [5], [6], [13].

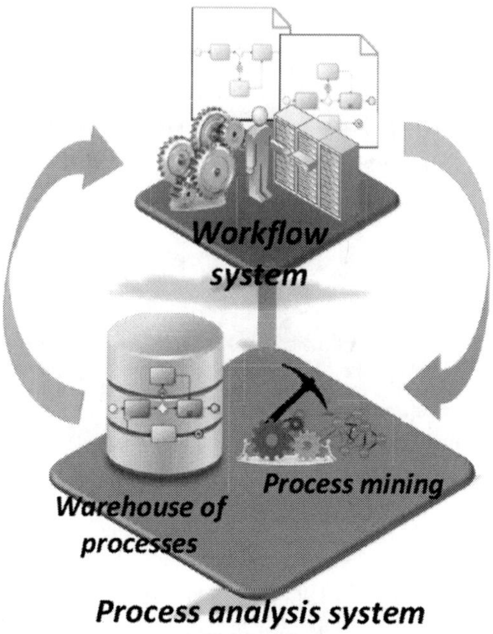

Figure 3. Execution (workflow system) and analysis (process system architecture

The main function of the warehouse of processes and process mining, being one of the tools supporting the decision-making process, is a possibility of conducting analyses of the collected resources, such as [13]:

- in the area of the process definition analysis:

1) suggesting model definitions of the processes during the modeling based on the already used elements of the process and set of models,
2) semantic similarity measures of the process definition or fragments thereof,
3) structural similarity measures of process definition or fragments thereof,
4) validation of the correctness of the process definition by analyzing the graph created on the basis of this definition,
5) analysis of the construction of the process definition by analyzing the graph created on the basis of this definition,
6) the level of detail of the definition defined as: readability - the number of vertices of a single graph and component subgraphs, complexity - the number of resources assigned to the graph or component graph,
7) determination whether a gridlock may occur when two activities are mutually waiting for their completion,
8) including all cases in the definition,

- in the area of the process implementation analysis (instances):

a) process mining: discovering new process definitions based on the instance of the process execution, execution deviations from the process definition, searching for models and their rare and common sequence of events;

b) quantitative analyses: execution time, delays, use of resources, how many instances can be appointed within an hour, what is the average flow time, how many additional resources may be needed, how many particular types of resources are consumed during working days, similarity measures of the sequence of events, analysis of the adequacy of the process in a ratio (whether the given process in effect gives the expected results), identification of problems (e.g. congestion) and their causes.

3 Business processes of the secret office

The operations of the secret office (SO), which is by nature responsible for processing classified documentation, include many processes related to the document flow. The developed processes are in compliance with applicable Polish law. The basic processes in the form of the process hierarchy were presented below:

- A Acceptance of the parcel
  - A1 Registration of the correspondence received in the secret office,
  - A2 Acceptance of the parcel which was damaged/bears traces of opening,

- B Creation of the material,
  - B1 Confidentiality clause,
  - B2 Registration of the created material,
  - B3 Storage,
    - o B3.1 Destruction of the cryptographic material,
      - B3.2 Sending of the material via carrier with sub-process B3.2.1 Explanation of failure in delivery of the parcel,
      - B3.3 Receipt of the request to share the document and sub-process: B3.3.1 Sharing of the material, B3.3.1.1 Return of the material,
- B3.4 Inventory (stocktaking),

- C Issuance of Cryptographic Access Certificate
  - C1 Storage of the Certificate,
    - o C1.1 Issuance of the Certificate for the working purposes,
    - o C1.2 Cancellation of the Certificate,

3.1. Business process model – phase "as is"

Figure 4 shows the business process model for making the documents available in the secret office in the "as is" phase. The process describes legitimate activities that are performed manually, without any IT systems or RFID, for the purpose of their automation.

The structural and dynamic analyses of the developed processes were also conducted in this phase. The dynamic analysis of the processes was based on the process simulation, including the parameters estimated during the sample analysis of the secret office. According to the general analysis, it is evident that the "as is" phase covers 41 business processes, which include over: 240 processes/sub-processes, 75 gateways and 160 events.

The Bizagi Modeler v2.9 [14] software was used to model business processes according to BPMN v2.0 and simulate the processes according to BPSim v1.0.

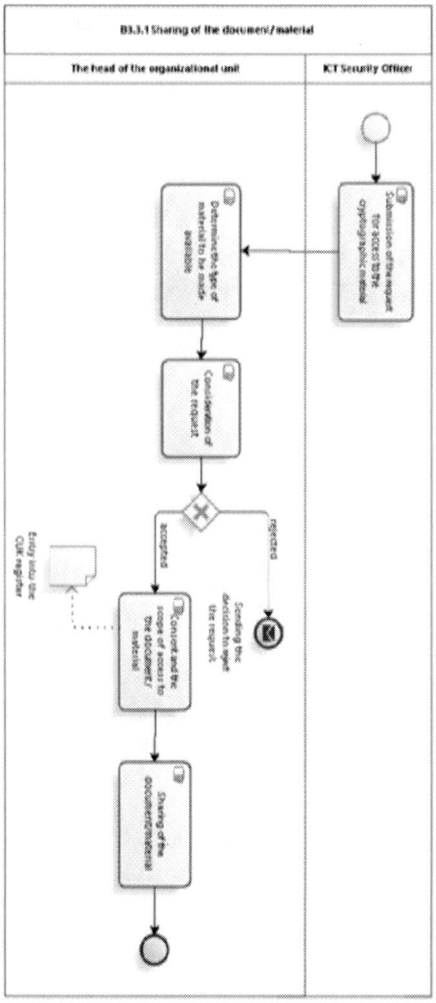

Figure 4. **BPMN process: Sharing** of the **document - phase "as is"**

3.2. Business process model – phase "to be"

Figure 5 shows the business process model for making the documents available in the secret office, using RFID and IT systems - phase "to be". The developed models in the "to be" phase extend the functionality of the "as is" phase by incorporating actions with the use of the RFID technology and include a possibility of work in case of failure of the IT and RFID systems.

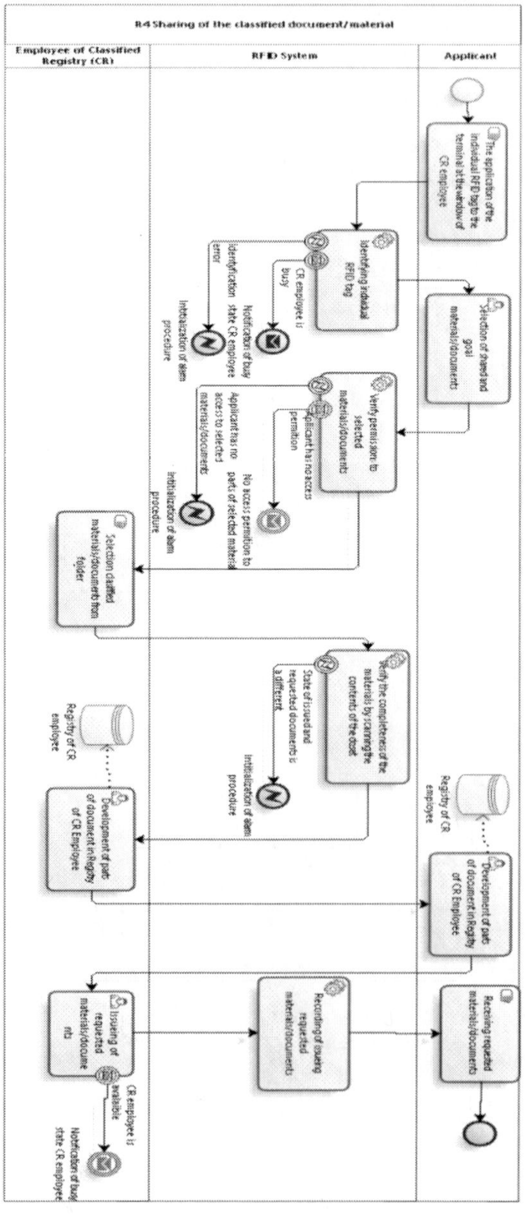

Figure 5. BPMN process: Sharing document with RFID- phase "to be"

Similarly to the business process models of the "as is", the structural and dynamic analysis of the business process models of the "to be" phase was performed. In this phase, 66 business processes were performed, in which over: 390 processes/sub-processes, 169 gateways, 288 events were applied.

The process simulation was used to verify changes resulting from the application of the RFID technology in the secret office in the modeled processes. The test included estimation of the execution time necessary for one case in the discussed processes. The results of the simulation showed that the estimated average time of execution of the availability process performed using the traditional method was 31 min., whereas in case of the RFID-supported process - the time was shorter by half, i.e. 15 min. When bearing in mind the 8-hour working time in the secret office, it is apparent that the technology should increase the efficiency and quality of handling the matters in the SO, including high reliability of the whole supporting system, using the RFID technology.

4 Conclusion

The availability of the new technologies contributes to their wide spreading in many different institutions. The application of the RFID technology in the processes of the secret office not only improved the functioning of the entire office, but also ensured better protection of the materials stored therein. Furthermore, the work capacity improved, which was demonstrated in the simulation. Nonetheless, it should be remembered that such systems are not 100% reliable. To avoid a situation, when the secret office is obliged to discontinue its operations due to failed technology, an alternative way of implementing the processes should be always available. In such case, it is worth using the process implemented in a traditional manner, which is in accordance with the effective legal standards.

The RFID technology offers cost-effective means of electronically tagging documents while maintaining remote identification capabilities. Moreover the utilization of such technology provides more convenient ways to organize and tag documents in comparison with QR codes. The simplicity of RFID scanning process and the possibility of faster and more accurate, close range object identification, makes the technology more convenient for large document storages.

The RFID system, as every other technology, ceases to meet the expectations with time, therefore, it is worth continuing further research to find other types of systems for the management and handling of the office processes so that the information contained in the sensitive documents is not disclosed to any unauthorized parties.

The analysis of the processes as the definition and implemented instances constitute the further direction of the research. Their analysis by developing different methods and tools will allow, for example [13]: to define trends, similarities and anomalies, and by applying the feedback method in the process of building the systems using the process approach, it is possible to improve the quality and efficiency of the implemented processes in the automated ICT environment.

References

1. V. D. Hunt, A. Puglia i M. Puglia, *RFID-A guide to radio frequency identification*, Hoboken, New Jersey: John Wiley & Sons, Inc. (2007)
2. S. Edwards i M. Fortune, *A Guide to RFID in Libraries*, London: Book Industry Communication (2008)
3. M. Kiedrowicz, *Zarządzanie informacjami wrażliwymi - wybrane aspekty organizacyjne, prawne i techniczne ochrony informacji niejawnych*, Warszawa, WAT, (2015)
4. M. Weske, *Business Process Management. Concepts, Languages, Architectures*, Berlin, Springer-Verlag (2007)
5. B. Gawin, *Systemy informatyczne w zarządzaniu procesami Workflow*, Warszawa, PWN (2015)
6. W. van der Aalst i K. van Hee, *Workflow Management. Models, Methods, and Systems*, Massachusetts London, The MIT Press Cambridge (2002)
7. M. Kiedrowicz, Organizacja i dostęp do heterogenicznych, publicznych zasobów danych, *Projektowanie systemów informatycznych: modele i metody*, Warszawa, WAT (2014)
8. M. Kiedrowicz, Rejestry i zasoby informacyjne wykorzystywane przez organy odpowiedziane za wykrywanie i przeciwdziałanie przestępczości, *Jawność i jej ograniczenia: Zadania i kompetencje*, Warszawa, C.H.Beck Sp. z o.o. (2015)
9. OMG, BPMN - standard documents. [Online] http://www.omg.org/spec/BPMN/2.0/ (2011)
10. R. Moen i C. Norman, *Evolution of the PDCA Cycle* (2009)
11. A. Arsanjani, N. Bharade, M. Borgenstrand, P. Schume, J. K. Wood i V. Zheltonogov, *Business Process Management Design Guide. Using IBM Business Process Manager*, USA, IBM Corporation (2015)
12. A. Sidnev, J. Tuominen i B. Krassi, *Business Process Modeling and Simulation*, Espoo, Otamedia Oy (2005)
13. G. Bliźniuk, M. Chmielewski, T. Gzik i J. Koszela, Warehouse of processes, *Studia Informatica*, **33-2A**, 111-127 (2012)
14. Bizagi, [Online] http://www.bizagi.com (2016)

MATEC Web of Conferences **76**, 04006 (2016) DOI: 10.1051/matecconf/20167604006
CSCC 2016

Patient Safety versus Computer Diagnosis

Andrzej Wałczak[1,a] and Karol Antczak[1]

[1] *Institute of Computer and Information Systems, Military University of Technology, Warsaw, Poland*

Abstract. The development of the Internet technology has caused telemedicine diagnosis systems to be commonly available. The most crucial aspect of the patient's safety in such systems is a problem of safe diagnosis. There are two factors at the stake here. The first one is a human factor in the form of user; it is especially severe when the user is not a physician. The second one is the accuracy of the diagnosis process. The best way to handle possible diagnosis errors is to apply measures of sensitivity, specificity and ROC (Receiver Operating Characteristic) curve. We examine these measures on a sample diagnosis system against a real-life data. It turns out that values of these measures are strictly associated with another measure: an indication threshold. Therefore, the accuracy of diagnosis may be to a large extent determined by the chosen threshold. We propose several methods for minimizing the impact of this factor.

1 Introduction and Motivation

We are all witnesses to the software boom in telemedicine technology. A significant part of this technology is used for diagnostic data transmission. Such transmission allows proliferation of the measured data and creates wide audience for proper final diagnosis. However, there is also another aspect of telemedicine. Plenty of diseases are widely described on the Internet, which is quite often used for self-diagnosis. What is worse, there are multiple telemedicine services used for the same purpose. A study by Pew Research Center says that 35 % of American adults have used the Internet to figure out their or someone else's medical condition - they are the so-called "online diagnosers" [1]. About half of the online diagnosers talked with a clinician to confirm or deny their findings. Only 41% of them had their diagnosis confirmed.

Abuse of the self-diagnosis seems to be the source of potential danger for patients who are trying to diagnose themselves. This danger comes from two sources. The first one are the patients themselves. The activity of such online diagnosers can cause unfounded escalation of concerns about common symptomatology. The media coined a special term known as "cyberchondria" to name such condition; it is suggested that it can affect medical decisions and anxiety level of online diagnosers or their loved ones [2].

The second source of potential danger comes from the very process of self-diagnosis. One of the problems is its accuracy, or - more precisely – the issue of how to measure its reliability. A standard approach to medical diagnosis normally involves a combination of the research evidence with a physician's personal opinions and experience. Though nonetheless empirical to some degree, this process is highly dependent on subjective factors. As a result, the final decision may vary from clinician to clinician. Moreover, there is no objective measure of impact of the evidence.

With the advent of the Evidence Based Medicine (EBM), the emphasis was put on further objectivization of the decision-making process by applying a scientific method. The EBP uses tools such as statistical measures for objective evidence evaluation. It allows to rate diagnostic tests using sensitivity and specificity metrics as well as the Receiver Operating Characteristic curves.

A very important feature of medical diagnosis (both traditional and evidence-based) is that, in fact, each diagnosis is a kind of measurement - in quite clear, scientific sense. Yet, sorry to say, medicine does not apply proper measurement descriptions. What is measured are the diagnostic tests, but not the diagnosis itself. The history of medicine did not teach the tradition to describe a diagnosis with proper accuracy. A common use of the "diagnosis" is not in the form of measurement of symptoms, but rather a physician's decision. Such decision is made as a result of a single or multiple measurements of the disease symptoms using different tools or methods. The basic grounds for this decision are always similarities between the observed symptoms of the registered and gathered disease descriptions.

2 Background

Determination of diagnose accuracy is not easy. The exact definitions of sensitivity and specificity of a

[a] Corresponding author: andrzej.walczak@wat.edu.pl

diagnosis are sometimes determined for diagnostic methods, e.g. diagnostic tests. To obtain these values, the test is evaluated by comparison with the so-called "gold standard" test, which is the best test available under reasonable conditions.

The test sensitivity (also known as the "true positive ratio") is defined as a proportion of patients correctly diagnosed with a disease (TP) to all patients having the disease (TP + FP). The above may be noted down in using the following formula:

$$sensitivity = \frac{|TP|}{|TP|+|FN|} \tag{1}$$

Specificity is defined as ratio of patients correctly ruled out by test (TN) to all patients not having disease (TN + FP). This can be expressed as:

$$specificity = \frac{|TN|}{|TN|+|FP|} \tag{2}$$

Sensitivity is used to express the test's ability to confirm a disease, while specificity relates to its ability to rule out certain cases. Both of these measures can be combined to create the Receiver-Operating Characteristic (ROC) curves. Such curves are an excellent way to compare diagnostic tests. The British initially developed such tests for radar receiver testing during World War II. The sensitivity describes the "true positive rate" while (1-specificity) describes the "false positive rate" obtained during patients' population examination.

The above metrics are the result of the clinical examination. We suggest applying the sensitivity and specificity to describe accuracy of the diagnosis. In case of computer diagnostic systems, "nameplates" are generated, with the parameters providing descriptions analogous to those of diagnostic tests. As a consequence, the systems will be more "evidence-based" and hence, more secure for the patients.

Note, though, that the sensitivity and specificity depend on where we make the cut-point (a threshold for the assumed level of the rejected results). Let us explain the complicated links between the sensitivity, specificity and cut-point. In table 1, we have placed the values of similarities measured by means of the Jaccard coefficient:

$$d^{J}_{AB} = \frac{|A \cap B|}{|A \cup B|} = \frac{|A \cup B| - |A \cap B|}{|A \cup B|} \tag{3}$$

Table 1. Jaccard coefficient between sample illnesses chosen from a medical database.

Illness code	B36	B85	C84.0	H26.8	L13.0	L20.0
B36	1,00	0,91	0,78	0,72	0,12	0,13
B85	0,91	1,00	0,85	0,77	0,14	0,14
C84.0	0,78	0,85	1,00	0,90	0,12	0,13
H26.8	0,72	0,77	0,90	1,00	0,12	0,12
L13.0	0,12	0,14	0,12	0,12	1,00	0,61
L20.0	0,13	0,14	0,13	0,12	0,61	1,00

Similarities exposed in table 1 illustrate that each patient's diagnosis should result in a set of indications containing different diseases. Obviously, the level of similarity between the disease and the patient's examination will be different for each indication. The example of such similarity may be as in fig.1, with the help of two different classifiers.

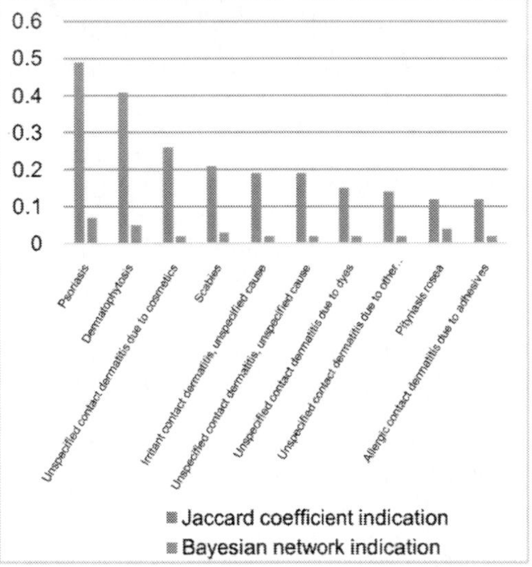

Figure 1. Similarities between the disease and the patient's examination.

A cut-point set in the classifiers' indications in figure 1 results in different choices for each classifier, whereas the threshold displacement causes different sensitivity and specificity. For the purpose of a safer diagnosis, proper values of the threshold must be used to obtain the expected sensitivity and specificity. In such sense, safer diagnosis seems to be a part of the Evidence Based Medicine. Speaking of the EBM, one of its important traits is that it involves the search for the most specific evidence - that is, the most unambiguous proof of a given disease. However, one should note that only in some cases we are able to perform the screening tests to evaluate the evidence in a form as shown in table 1. In many situations, it is necessary to depend only on a collection of clinical cases, which are not usually identical in terms of clinical research. This leads to the reduction of quality of the acquired data. Moreover, what can be considered a rule is the patient's state described by a set of several distinct proofs. It is generally impossible to assess sensitivity and specificity for each of them.

Another important factor is the approach presented in fig. 1, which contains some hidden information resulting from the inter-individual response to the cause of the disease. It means that even the diagnostic test, which confirms the existence of the evidence does not necessarily mean that a given patient is sick and vice versa: the test excluding the evidence does not entail certainty that the patient will not have a disease. Even such factor as the time difference between performing the tests, symptom incubation period and the patient's reaction strongly influences the result of the observation.

3 Tasks, methods and models

Let us examine how different cut-point values result in different quality of the classification. We have used a neural network to classify a set of 81 clinical cases from medical database of respiratory diseases. We evaluated neural network classifier by measuring its sensitivity and specificity for different cut-point values. The results are shown on fig 2. As one can see, there is a link between the sensitivity, specificity and cut-point. The higher is the cut-point value, the more increases the sensitivity, but at the expense of lower specificity. The more indications does the classifier propose, the more chance that a correct disease will be found among them.

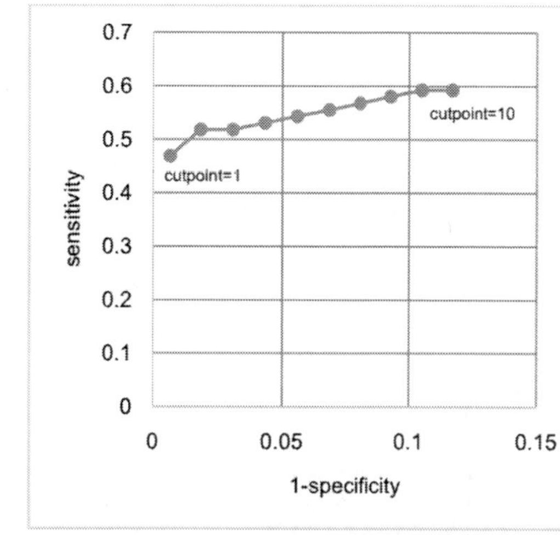

Figure 2. ROC curve for neural network classifier with various cut-point values.

How to make the classification more resistant to different cut-point values? We are unable to completely eliminate this dependency, but we may weaken it. The basic method is to increase the selectivity of indications. The selectivity can be measured as a standard deviation between the indication values. We can modify it so that one of the two indications has considerably higher values than the other. Thus, the changing of the cut-point to some extent will not change the set cut-point and the final classification will remain the same.

The selectivity varies between various classification methods. As we can observe on fig 1, the indications of the Bayesian Network have higher selectivity than the ones of the Jaccard coefficient. This is due to the fact that the Jaccard coefficient takes in consideration only amount of the symptoms, ignoring their significance. The Bayesian Network is able to extract the hidden information concerning the symptoms. In a way, this classifier works similarly to the EBM. We can improve the selectivity of the classifier by explicitly using the symptom weights during the classification process. The extraction of the hidden information to improve the selectivity may also be achieved by way of data pre-processing, as demonstrated by Walczak and Paczkowski [3]. They make the weights of the symptoms by introducing the concept of "medical diamonds". Using such terminology, a "diamond of the first kind" is the symptom that identifies only one disease. On the other hand, the "diamond of the second kind" uniquely identifies one disease, but is also present in a few other ones. The "diamond of the third kind" defines a group of symptoms, which is always associated with a specific illness. This categorization allows weighing the symptoms and hence extracting some of their hidden properties.

Creating an ensemble of classifiers can also increase the selectivity. The ensemble of classifiers (also known as a "conference of classifiers") is a set of classifiers connected in such a manner so as to produce single output resulting from the combined outputs from the base classifiers. Typically, this combination involves some kind of voting. As a result, the ensemble of classifiers may have better sensitivity and specificity than any of its base classifiers. The exact explanation of this feature was given by Dietterich [4]. It turns out, that ensemble can also improve the selectivity of indications. This phenomenon is based on the Pareto principle: the majority of good indications occur in the first few places. Fig. 3 shows the occurrence of this principle for the Jaccard coefficient and neural network. As shown by Antczak, in the ensembles of classifiers based on voting methods (namely Borda Count and Highest Rank), common indications of base classifiers are promoted, while the differences between them are leveled [5].

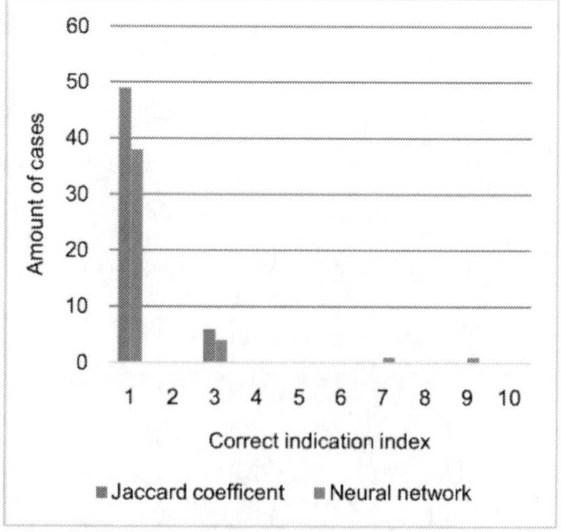

Figure 3. Amounts of correct indication indices for the Jaccard coefficient and neural network

Other methods developed in the recent years and extensively researched, are the Deep Learning techniques. It is a group of biologically inspired methods for pattern recognition and classification of complicated, high-level models. They work by "feature extraction" - in the medical diagnosis, these features can constitute the hidden information about symptoms. DL algorithms are able to extract it in a hierarchical fashion. The algorithms are useful for modeling the aforementioned medical diamonds and other "hidden" data features.

The problem of the cut-point influence can also be approached in a completely different way: instead of dealing with the selectivity, one can create a "solver" which will adjust the cut-point to ensure the sensitivity and specificity as required by a physician. This way the classifier would work as a diagnostic test, with strictly measured accuracy. The explicit formula binding the sensitivity, specificity and cut-point can be hard to obtain. It is, however, possible to use the probabilistic optimization methods (e.g. simulated annealing) to find a cut-point for the desired sensitivity and specificity.

4 Conclusions

The term "patient safety" means not only the proper protection of the patient's data, but also, what seems to be even more important, safe diagnosis. It is a vital aspect of the diagnosis as such and even more important in case of the Computer Diagnosis Support Systems. Since the diagnosis may not always be precise, the best way to control the risk is a clear determination of the properly described diagnosis errors. A part of such approach has been described above as the necessity to determine the "sensitivity-specificity-threshold" triplet. However, these measures may not be considered independently, as they are interrelated. Furthermore, a level of this association, interpreted as the selectivity of indications, may affect overall quality of the diagnosis. To minimize the impact of this factor, we proposed several methods, which mainly rely on the extraction of the hidden information about the symptoms. This approach would allow controlling the values of the sensitivity, specificity and threshold, thus, improving safety of the diagnosis.

It seems reasonable to further investigate the issue of maximizing the diagnosis selectivity. A more detailed comparative analysis of the various classification methods in terms of their selectivity can produce a lot of interesting findings. Additionally, the Deep Learning methods seem to be a promising direction of research. They already have some impressive applications, achieving human-level control [6]. It would be an interesting task to build a DL-based classifier for medical diagnosis and to test its ability as regards extracting the hidden features.

References

1. S. Fox and M. Duggan, *Health Online 2013*, (Pew Research Center 2013).
2. R. W. White and E. Horvitz, *AMIA Annu. Symp. Proc*, **2009**, pp. 696-700 (2009).
3. A. Walczak and M. Paczkowski, *BioAlgorithms and MedSystems*, **16**, 1, (2016)
4. T. G. Dietterich, "Ensemble Methods in Machine Learning," (Oregon State University 2000)
5. K. Antczak, "Rank Threshold in Classifier Ensmbles in Medical Diagnosis," *Computer Science & Mathematical Modelling*, **III**, no. 1 (2016, to be published)
6. V. Mnih et al., "Human-level control through deep reinforcement learning," *Nature*, 518, p. 529–533, (2015)

MATEC Web of Conferences **76**, 04007 (2016) DOI: 10.1051/matecconf/20167604007
CSCC 2016

Developing an expert system integrated into the information portal to evaluate reactivity of organic molecules in radical reactions

Vladimir E. Tumanov[1], Elena S. Amosova[1] and Andrei I. Prokhorov[1,a]

[1]*Department of Computing and Information Resources, Institute of Problems of Chemical Physics RAS, 142432, Chernogolovka, Semenov ave, 1, RUSSIAN FEDERATION*

Abstract. This paper presents an approach to develop a production expert system integrated into the information portal using the fuzzy inference machine to predict reactivity of organic molecules in the radical reactions of abstraction in the liquid phase based on theoretical and experimental data. The intelligent agent technology is used to develop the expert system. The intelligent agents have their own fuzzy knowledge bases. General description of the knowledge base structure and its relations to the information portal databases are presented. Fuzzy inference models used by the intelligent agents of the expert system are listed.

1 Introduction

Knowing reactivity of organic compounds in radical reactions is an important theoretical and practical problem for basic research in physical chemistry as well as for application in chemical engineering.

Making experiments to quantify reactivity of molecules in radical reactions is expensive and hard. Quantum chemical calculations take much times and their resulting data is not sufficiently reliable. Methods of radical process simulation based on kinetic schemes require knowledge of the rate constants of elementary radical reactions. Experimental values of the rate constants of radical reactions are known only for a limited number of organic compounds in the gaseous phase [1] and liquid phase [2].

Therefore developing new approaches and tools for evaluation of reactivity of organic molecules in radical reactions based on the experimental and theoretical data is one of the most important topics of research in physical chemistry. Authors use the expert systems and fuzzy logic [3] to solve the given problem.

Papers [4,5] discuss using the expert systems and fuzzy logic in chemistry.

2 Problem formulation

Authors developed a concept of expert systems integrated into the information portal to evaluate reactivity of organic molecules in radical reactions using multiagent technology, empiric models of radical reactions and artificial neural networks [3].

In experiments reactivity of an organic molecule in a radical reaction is defined by the activation energy (E_i) or classical potential barrier (E_{ei}), which are related as follows:

$$E_{ei} = E_i + 0.5(hL\nu_i - RT) \quad (1)$$

Rate constant (k) of the chemical reaction is calculated by the Arrhenius formula:

$$k = nA_0 \exp(-E_i/RT), \quad (2)$$

where A_0 is the frequency of collisions per one reaction bond and n is the number of equireactive bonds.

Empiric models proposed in [6] evaluate classical potential barrier of radical reactions by the formulas

$$\text{if } \alpha \neq 1: \quad \sqrt{E_{ei}} = \frac{br_e}{1-\alpha^2}\left[1-\alpha\sqrt{1-\frac{\Delta H_e(1-\alpha^2)}{(br_e)^2}}\right] \quad (3)$$

$$\text{if } \alpha = 1: \quad \sqrt{E_{ei}} = \frac{1}{2}br_e + \frac{\Delta H_e}{2br_e} \quad (4)$$

Within the proposed empiric models of radical reactions the variables have the meaning [6].

According to the review within the model of intersecting parabolas the radical reaction of abstraction

$$H^{\circ} + R_1H \rightarrow RH + R^{\circ}_1 \quad (5)$$

is characterized by the following parameters:

1) **Enthalpy of reaction**:

$$\Delta H_e = D_i - D_f + 0.5(hL\nu_i - hL\nu_f), \quad (6)$$

where ν_i is the frequency of the stretching vibration of the breaking bond, ν_f is the frequency of the stretching vibration of the forming bond, h is Planck's constant, L is the Avogadro constant, D_i is dissociation energy of the

---

[a] Corresponding author: aipro@icp.ac.ru

breaking bond, $D_{ei} = D_i + 0,5hLv_i$, D_f is dissociation energy of the forming bond, $D_{ef} = D_f + 0,5hLv_f$.

2) **Classical potential barrier** E_{ei}:

$$E_{ei} = E_i + 0.5(hLv_i - RT), \qquad (7)$$

is measured from the minimum of the potential curve of the breaking bond to the minimum point of the transition state. R is the gas constant, T is the thermodynamic temperature in K, E_i is the experimental value of activation energy of the radical reaction.

3) **Distance** r_e between the vertices of the potential curves in the coordinate system: the range of stretching vibrations of atoms is potential energy.

4) **Coefficients**:

$$b = \pi(2\mu_i)^{1/2} v_i \text{ and } b_f = \pi(2\mu_f)^{1/2} v_f, \qquad (8)$$

describe the dependance of the potential energy from the range of stretching vibrations of atoms along the breaking (i) and forming (f) valence bond, $2b^2$ is force constant of the bond, μ_i is the reduced atom mass of the breaking bond, μ_f is the reduced atom mass of the forming bond.

5) **Coefficient**

$$\alpha = b/b_f \qquad (9)$$

The main correlation ratio of the model of intersecting parabolas for the elementary act is:

$$br_e = \alpha(E_e - \Delta H_e)^{1/2} + E_e^{1/2} \qquad (10)$$

The br_e value is called **kinetic parameter of the structurally similar radical reactions.**

Formula to evaluate measurement error of the potential barrier of the reaction is:

$$\Delta q = \Delta br_e \sqrt{\left(\frac{1}{1+\alpha}\right)^2 + \frac{\alpha^2}{4}\left(\frac{q}{br_e}\right)^2}, \qquad (11)$$

where $q = E_{ei}^{1/2}$.

Disadvantage of such approach is that for a wide range of compounds the kinetic parameter br_e is assumed constant, which leads to considerable error in determining the classical potential barrier.

In research using the artificial neural network technology authors have attempted to escape generalized class characteristics of radical reactions. But using artificial neural networks complicates the interpretation of the derived results.

Authors' research shows that using fuzzy logic and knowledge base on its basis solves this problem.

The purpose of this paper is to propose an approach to develop expert systems integrated into the information portal to evaluate reactivity of organic molecule in radical reactions of abstraction.

The proposed approach of using multiagent technologies is the defining point of the research. This approach complies with chemistry and physics of radical reactions. Thus R+RH reactions in the liquid phase depend on the environment of the reaction. Mamdani's model of fuzzy inference functions well for hydrocarbon solvents. However in water (acid environment) a strong dependence from pH is observed, which suggests using the TSK (Takagi, Sugeno, Kang) model with polynomial dependence. Thus each intelligent agent should have its own knowledge base and make inference on the input data.

3 Problem solution

The proposed by authors approach to develop expert systems integrated into the information portal is based on using multiagent technology [3]. The expert system built in to the information portal is its active intelligent component.

During the first stage of operation the expert system should identify reagents of the radical reaction. This problem is solved using the production rules and metadata stored in the information portal thesaurus. After reagent identification their thermochemical characteristics in the knowledge base tuples are determined. Then the reaction center indexes of reactions are defined and acquired set of parameters is sent to one of the intelligent agents. The agent returns the result.

3.1 Using the knowledge base

The knowledge base of the expert system is distributed and consists of several parts: shared by all agents and linked directly to intelligent agents.

The first part of the knowledge base includes two thesauri that can be considered as domain ontologies. Thesauri contain tuples related to identification of organic molecules and radicals (atoms). They contain indexes to physical and chemical properties stored in the information portal database: bond dissociation energies and rate constants of radical reactions of abstraction. Process of reaction identification includes determination of a radical (atom), forming bond type, indexes to values of thermochemical characteristics of reagents.

Then it is checked whether database contains rate constants that satisfy the request. If such data is found in the database, it is extracted and provided to the user.

If such data is not found in the database, the shared part of the knowledge base is used to determine the reaction center index of the reaction and its characteristics. This part of the knowledge base consists of the classical production rules of the following structure:

Rule Type 1:

IF reaction class is R_1+ RH **AND** organic molecule is "alkane" **AND** molecule reaction center is «-CH_2CH_3» AND radical reaction center is «-$CH_2C^{\bullet}H_2$» **THEN** kinetic parameter of reaction (br_e) = 14.93 **AND** preexponent per one equireactive bond = 10^9 **AND** α=1.0.

Then the expert system attempts to obtain thermochemical data (bond dissociation energies) from the information portal database. If such data is not found, it is proposed to the users to enter their own evaluations and the flag of high risk for the obtained results is set.

Then depending on the reaction class proper intelligent agent is chosen to calculate.

Each agent has its own knowledge base of fuzzy production rules. Depending on the reaction class, fuzzy production rules may be created using:

Mamdani's fuzzy inference machine:

RULE:

IF bond dissociation energy about "432" **AND** bond formation energy about "412" **AND** kinetic parameter of reaction about "17.3" **THEN** classical potential barrier about "40".

TSK Type 1 inference machine:

IF bond dissociation energy about "432" **AND** bond formation energy about "412" **AND** kinetic parameter of reaction about "17.3" **THEN** classical potential barrier is calculated by formulas in [7].

In case if there is no suitable intelligent agent, control is given to the agent that calculates classical potential barrier by formula (1) by the production rule:

IF bond dissociation energy about "432" **AND** bond formation energy about "412" **AND** kinetic parameter about "17.3" **THEN** classical potential barrier is calculated by formulas (3,4).

3.2 Software and technology architecture of the expert system

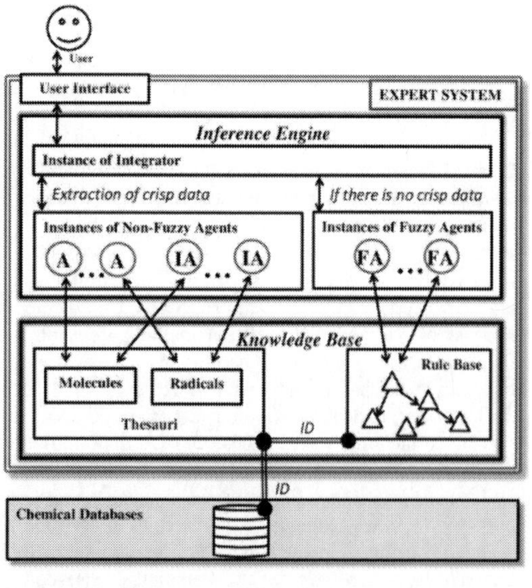

Figure 1. The architecture of the expert system

Designed originally for the portal, databases of physical and chemical properties of molecules and radicals are the factual part of thesauri for the knowledge base. Thesauri, the rule base, the chemical databases are linked identifiers that uniquely identifies the molecule, radical, or fragments thereof in the portal. If the system can respond to the user at his request with crisp data on the basis of existing knowledge, the system displays the data. If needed to predict the data, then fuzzy logic agents are invoked with attempt to predict the parameters of a radical reaction. In this case, the integrator displays the predicted parameters and their accuracy.

4 Conclusions

The proposed approach of developing the expert system integrated into the information portal to evaluate reactivity of organic molecules in radical reactions of abstractions is based on building and using the multilevel knowledge base.

The knowledge base combines shared by intelligent agents components built on the classical production rules and agents' separate knowledge bases build on various methods of fuzzy inference.

Our approach of developing the expert system integrated into the information portal combines fuzzy logic and classical production expert systems, which definitely is a new move in developing distributed applications for the use in the Internet.

Acknowledgment

The study was supported by RFBR, research project No. 15-07-08645.

References

1. J.A. Manion, R.E. Huie, R.D. Levin, D.R. Burgess, Jr., V.L. Orkin, W. Tsang, W.S. McGivern, J.W. Hudgens, V.D. Knyazev, D.B. Atkinson,. E. Chai, A.M Tereza, C.-Y. Lin, T.C. Allison, W.G. Mallard, F. Westley, J.T. Herron, R.F. Hampson, D.H. Frizzell, National Institute of Standards and Technology, Gaithersburg, Maryland, 20899-8320.: http://kinetics.nist.gov/
2. V.E. Tumanov, A.I. Prokhorov, D.Yu. Lazarev, M.E. Solov'eva, Institute of Problems of Chemical Physics RAS, 142432, Chernogolovka, Russian Federation.: http://lion.icp.ac.ru/
3. V.E. Tumanov, WSEAS Transactions on Computers. **15**, 9 (2016)
4. M.C. Hemmer, *Expert system in chemistry research*, (CRC Press, Taylor & Francis Group, 2008)
5. D.H. Rouvray, *Fuzzy Logic in Chemistry*, (Academic Press, 1997)
6. E.T. Denisov, Uspekhi Khimii, **66**, 957 (1997)
7. V.E. Tumanov, E.S. Amosova, B.N. Gaifullin, A.I. Prokhorov, International Journal of Mathematical and Computational Methods, (to be published in 2016)

MATEC Web of Conferences **76**, 04008 (2016) DOI: 10.1051/matecconf/20167604008
CSCC 2016

Derivation of Event-B Models from OWL Ontologies

Eman H. Alkhammash[1,a]

[1] *Department of Computers and Information Technology, University of Taif, Taif, Saudi Arabia*

Abstract. The derivation of formal specifications from large and complex requirements is a key challenge in systems engineering. In this paper we present an approach that aims to address this challenge by building formal models from OWL ontologies. An ontology is used in the field of knowledge representation to capture a clear view of the domain and to produce a concise and unambiguous set of domain requirements. We harness the power of ontologies to handle inconsistency of domain requirements and produce clear, concise and unambiguous set of domain requirements for Event-B modelling. The proposed approach works by generating Attempto Controlled English (ACE) from the OWL ontology and then maps the ACE requirements to develop Event-B models. ACE is a subset of English that can be unambiguously translated into first-order logic. There is an injective mapping between OWL ontology and a subset of ACE. ACE is a suitable interlingua for producing the mapping between OWL and Event-B models for many reasons. Firstly, ACE is easy to learn and understand, it hides the math of OWL and would be natural to use by everybody. Secondly ACE has a parser that converts ACE texts into Discourse Representation Structures (DRS). Finally, ACE can be extended to target a richer syntactic subset of Event-B which ultimately would facilitate the translation of ACE requirements to Event-B.

1 Introduction

The derivation of formal specifications from informal requirements is difficult. Informal requirements are often vague, incomplete, and ambiguous. To bridge the gap between informal requirements and formal specification, we propose an approach that makes use of OWL ontologies to describe requirements in a more precise way and to map OWL ontologies into Event-B models using ACE. An ontology is a formal specification of the concepts in a given domain and the relationships between them [1]. ACE is a subset of natural language that can be transformed to discourse representation structures [2]. Event-B is a formal method for modeling and verifying consistency of systems [3].

Ontologies have been used in different activities in requirements engineering and found to be beneficial in reducing ambiguities, inconsistency, and incompetence of requirements. Many studies have explored the use of ontologies in requirement engineering [4, 5]. Some studies adopted ontologies during the elicitation process to reduce ambiguous and incomplete requirements [4, 5]. Other studies build ontologies for describing the structure of requirements specification documents in order to reduce the insufficient requirements specification [4, 5]. Furthermore, application domain ontologies have been used to represent the application domain knowledge and enable the reuse of the requirements for the applications of the same domain [4, 5].

[a]e-mail: eman.kms@tu.edu.sa

In this paper, we propose an approach that use ontologies to derive clear, concise, consistent and unambiguous requirements to develop Event-B formal models. There are three stages of this approach. Firstly, we convert OWL ontology to OWL/XML using OWL syntax parser [6]. Secondly, we convert OWL/XML into Attempto Controlled English (ACE) text using OWL verbalizer Converter [7]. Thirdly, we produce the Event-B modelling concepts that correspond to the ACE representation.

This paper is structured as follows: Sect. 2 gives an overview of OWL, OWL verbalization, and Event-B formal method. Sect. 3 introduces the methodology employed in this paper. Sect. 4 illustrates the application of the presented approach to a case study. Conclusions ad future work are drawn in Sect. 5.

2 Preliminaries

2.1 OWL

The worldwide web consortium (W3C) created OWL that became a W3C recommendation in 2004. OWL is an important language in semantic web, which facilitates creating, modifying, linking and importing ontologies in different environments [8]. OWL is derived from descriptive logic that uses formal semantics and vocabulary to allow machines to perform automatic reasoning [8]. OWL extends the Resource Description Framework (RDF) and RDF Schema and can be processed by the wide range of XML and RDF tools already available [8]. OWL ontologies consist of concepts (classes), roles (properties), and set of individuals (instances). Every individual in the

OWL world is a member of the class called *Thing*, thus each user-defined class is implicitly a subclass of *Thing*. There are various OWL language constructs such as class disjointness, functional constraint, class union and intersection, property restrictions, and the like. Figure 1 shows a small example that demonstrates the syntax of OWL:

```
< owl : Class rdf : ID = "OrangeJuice" >
    < rdfs : subClassOf rdf : resource = "&food; PotableLiquid" / >
    < rdfs : subClassOf >
        < owl : Restriction >
          < owl : onProperty rdf : resource = "#madeFromOrange" / >
          < owl : minCardinality rdf : datatype =
                  "&xsd; nonNegativeInteger" > 1
          < /owl : minCardinality >
        < /owl : Restriction >
    < /rdfs : subClassOf >
...
< /owl : Class >
```

Figure 1. Defintion of the class "OrangeJuice"

This example gives definition for the class *OrangeJuice*. *OrangeJuice* is a *PotableLiquid* (i.e *OrangeJuice* is a subclass of *PotableLiquid* class). The cardinality constraint provided in *owl : minCardinality* says that *OrangeJuice* is made from at least one Orange.

2.2 OWL Verbalization

OWL verbalization is the process of transforming OWL into Atempto Controlled English (ACE) [9]. ACE is a controlled natural language designed to serve as expressive knowledge representation language [2]. The mapping of OWL constructs into ACE constructs is injective (i.e. ACE can be parsed and converted back to OWL) [9]. ACE can be converted into Discourse Representation Structures (DRS) and automatically reasoned about. ACE includes some construction rules that define its syntax and some of interpretation rules that disambiguate constructs. The verbalization assumes that all names used in the ontology are English words [9]. The *individuals* are denoted by singular proper names (preferably capitalized). The *classes* are denoted by singular countable nouns, and (object) *properties* are map to active and passive verbs. Statement *ACE-S1* and statement *ACE-S2* are examples of ACE that describe the domain and range of properties.

ACE-S1	Everybody who writes something is a human.
ACE-S2	Everything that somebody writes is a book.

ACE statements perceive the reasoning results obtained on the OWL ontology [10, 11]. Statement *ACE-S1* and statement *ACE-S2* are valid but inconsistency is caused when we add the following ACE statements *ACE-S3-ACE-S5*:

ACE-S3	John who is a man writes a paper.
ACE-S4	Every man is a human.
ACE-S5	No paper is a book.

Inconsistency is caused because statement *ACE-S5* says that the input argument *paper* is outside the range*book*.

Statement *ACE-S6* describes inverse functional property. Inverse functional property means that every instance in the range is associated with at most one instance of the domain.

ACE-S6	Everything is ordered by at most one thing.

Inconsistency can be seen if we add the following statements *ACE-S7-ACE-S10*:

ACE-S7	Mary orders a book X.
ACE-S8	Bill orders the book X.
ACE-S10	Mary is not Bill.

2.3 Event-B

Event-B [3] is a formal method developed by Jean-Raymond Abrial, which uses set theory and predicate logic to provide a formal notation for the creation of models of discrete systems and the undertaking of refinement steps. Event-B is supported by the Rodin toolset [12], which includes various plugins for features such as theorem-proving, model-checking, model composition and decomposition and translation of diagrammatic representations to textual representation. An abstract Event-B specification can be refined by adding more detail and bringing it closer to an implementation. A refined model in Event-B is verified through a set of proof obligations expressing that it is a correct refinement of its abstraction. Event-B may be used for parallel, reactive or distributed system development. Event-B models contain two constructs: a context and a machine. The context is the static part of a model in which fixed properties of the model (sets, constants, axioms) are defined. The dynamic functional behaviour of a model is represented in the machine part, which includes variables to describe the states of the system, invariants to constrain variables, and events to specify ways in which the variables can change. The outline of an event used in this paper is shown in Figure 2. The event takes parameters *t*, that satisfies the guard and then executes the body. The guard is predicate on the machine variables and event parameters and an action updates machine variables atomically.

any *t* where *guard* then *action* end

Figure 2. The outline of an event

3 Methodology

This paper proposes an approach that uses clear, concise, consistent and unambiguous requirements extracted from OWL ontologies to build Event-B formal models. We transform OWL ontologies into Event-B formal models where it can be verified, developed and consecutively transformed into executable code. The steps used in the proposed approach are:

Figure 3. The architecture of the proposed approach

1. Convert OWL ontology to OWL/XML format using OWL Syntax Converter [6]
2. Convert OWL/XML into Attempto Controlled English (ACE) text using OWL verbalizer Converter [7]
3. Produce the Event-B modelling concepts that correspond to the ACE representation (requirements)

Table 1 shows some ACE statements (requirements) that parsed using OWL verbalizer and the corresponding Event-B modelling concepts for these sentences. The given ACE statements are borrowed from several tutorials that describe the process of writing OWL ontologies in ACE [9]. They are extracted from various OWL constructs. We use them to give an overview about the proposed approach. ACE can express a domain and a range of a property. Requirement *R3* expresses domain of *order* property and requirement *R4* expresses the range of the same property. A property can be functional and inverse functional, functionality in ACE means that for a given subject, the object of the property (verb) is always the same whereas inverse functionality means that for a given object the subject must always be the same. Requirement *R5* expresses functionality property whereas requirement *R6* expresses inverse functional property. A symmetric property is a property for which holds that if the pair (x, y) is an instance of P, then the pair (y, x) is also an instance of P. Requirement *R14* is example of a symmetric property. Equivalent properties state that two properties have the same property extension. They are expressed by declaring the two properties to be superproperties of each other. Requirements *R25(a, b)* are examples of equivalent properties. The transitivity property means that if a pair (x,y) is an instance of P, and the pair (y, z) is also instance of P, then we can infer the the pair (x, z) is also an instance of P. Requirement *R26* is an example of transitivity property. A property can be disjoint from another property as shown in *R24*. Disjointness of classes can be expressed via ACE as shown in requirement *R22*. Cardinality expressed in ACE as shown in requirements *R8-12*. Individuals of a class are expressed in ACE as in *R23*.

ACE	**Event-B modelling concepts**
R1 everything, something; thing.	*Thing* is a carrier set
R2 nothing.	no individuals $Thing = \{\}$
R3 If X orders Y then X is an orderer.	$dom(orders) = Orderer$
R4 If X orders Y then Y is an ordered-item.	$ran(orders) = Items$
R5 Everybody orders at most one thing.	$orders \in Orderer \rightarrow Items$
R6 Everything is something that at most one thing orders.	$order \in Orderer \rightarrowtail Items$
R7 Every millionaire owns at least 2 cars.	$owns \in millionaire \leftrightarrow car \wedge \forall i. i \in dom(owns) \implies card(owns[\{i\}]) \geq 2$
R8 something that owns at least v.	$card(Thing) \geq v$
R9 something that owns at most v.	$card(Thing) \leq v$
R10 something that owns more than v.	$card(Thing) > v$
R11 something that owns less than v.	$card(Thing) < v$
R12 something that owns exactly v.	card(Thing)=v
R13 Common noun e.g. cat.	*cat* set
R14 If somebody X loves somebody Y then Y loves X.	$love = love^{-1}$
R15 Every narcissist likes himself.	$id(narcissist) \subseteq likes$
R16 Something that is not a cat.	$Thing \setminus cat$
R17 Something that is not a cat and something that is a camel.	individuals in $camel \setminus cat$
R18 something that is a cat or that is a camel or that ...	individuals in $cat \cup camel$...
R19 Everything that a carnivore eats is a meat.	$eats[\{carnivore\}] \subseteq meat$
R20 Every man is human.	$man \subseteq human$
R21 Every human is a male or is a female.	$human \subseteq (male \cup female)$
R22 No dog is a cat.	$dog \cap cat = \{\}$
R23 John is a student and Mary is a student.	$\{John, Mary\} \subseteq student$
R24 Nothing that is child-of something is spouse-of it. . . .	$\forall x. spouseOf[\{x\}] \cap childOf[\{x\}] = \{\}$
R25 *(a)* Everybody who hates somebody despises him/her. *(b)* Everybody who despises somebody hates him/her.	$\forall x, y. (x \mapsto y) \in hate \implies (x \mapsto y) \in despite$ $\forall x, y. (x \mapsto y) \in despite \implies (x \mapsto y) \in hate$

ACE	Event-B modelling concepts
R26 If something X is taller than something Y and Y is taller than something Z then X is taller than Z.	$taller; taller \subseteq taller$

Table 1. Table 1: ACE requirements and the corresponding Event-B modelling concepts

The Event-B modelling concepts described in Table 1 represent data types. In Event-B, events are used to specify ways in which the variables can change. Suppose that we have intersecting sets which are *superclass* which is the parent of class *subclass* and *subsubclass* is a subclass of *subclass*. Then we introduce the following event to add an individual *c* to *subsubclass*.

event *add_Member*
then
$superclass := superclass \cup \{c\}$
$subclass := subclass \cup \{c\}$...
$subsubclass := subsubclass \cup \{c\}$...
$property_i := property_i \cup \{c \mapsto a\}$...
$property_n := property_n \cup \{b \mapsto c\}$
end

Any properties that represent a relation of members (individuals) of a class of which the individual *c* is going to be added, should be updated as well. Properties ($property_i$...$property_n$) are binary relations on individuals of *subsubclass*. *a* is an individual that belongs to the range of the property $property_i$ and *b* is an individual belongs to the domain of $property_n$.

To add an individual to a class that is disjoint from other classes, then we only need to add the individual to that class and its superclass and not to the disjoint classes.

To delete an individual from a class we introduce *Delete_Member* event.

event *Delete_Member*
then
$superclass := superclass \setminus \{c\}$
$subclass := subclass \setminus \{c\}$...
$subsubclass := subsubclass \setminus \{c\}$...
$property_i := property_i \setminus \{c \mapsto a\}$...
$property_n := property_n \setminus \{b \mapsto c\}$
end

4 The application of the proposed approach to an OWL ontology

In this section we apply the proposed approach to Pizza ontology. Pizza ontology is well-known ontology developed in the Protégé-OWL tutorial [13]. Pizza classifies several types of pizzas. In this case study we focus on two classes: *Food* and *PizzaTopping*. *Food* class has subclasses *VegetarianPizza* and *NonVegetarianPizza*. The *PizzaTopping* has subclasses: *MushroomTopping*, *MozzarellaTopping* and *TomatoTopping*. The properties are: *hasIngredient* which is a transitive property and *hasTopping* which is an inverse property that maps *Pizza* class to *PizzaTopping* class. In order to apply our approach to transform the Pizza ontology to Event-B formal models, we convert Pizza ontology to controlled English using the ACE converter using step 1 and 2 mentioned in Section 3 and then we select the following requirements to formalize them in Event-B models (step 3 in Section 3).

Requirements *REQ1, REQ2* and *REQ3* are described as follows:

REQ1	Every Pizza is a Food.
REQ2	Every PizzaBase is a Food.
REQ3	Every PizzaTopping is a Food.

Requirements *REQ1, REQ2* and *REQ3* can be mapped to the following Event-B set variables:

$Food \subseteq Thing$ where *Thing* is a set defined in the context *c*
$Pizza \subseteq Food$
$PizzaBase \subseteq Food$
$PizzaTopping \subseteq Food$

Requirements *REQ4, REQ5* and *REQ6* are described as follows:

REQ4	Everything that hasIngredient something is a Food.
REQ5	Everything that is isIngredientOf by something is a Food.
REQ6	If X isIngredientOf something that isIngredientOf Y then X isIngredientOf Y.

Requirements *REQ4* and *REQ5* define *hasIngredient* and its inverse *isIngredientOf* and identify the domain and the range. In Event-B we can use relation/function to define the domain and the range of a property and to infer the inverse property. There is no requirement says that *hasIngredient* is functional. Therefore, we introduce relation called *hasIngredient* and define it as follows:

$$hasIngredient \in Food \leftrightarrow Food$$

The domain of relation *hasIngredient* is the set of *Food* parts of all the pairs in *hasIngredient* (i.e. *dom(hasIngredient)*). Whereas, the range of relation *hasIngredient* is the set of second parts of all the pairs in *hasIngredient* (i.e. *ran(hasIngredient)*). We can use relational inverse of *hasIngredient* to obtain *hasIngredient* inverse as follows: $hasIngredient^{-1}$

Requirement *REQ6* shows that *hasIngredient* is transitive. Therefore we add the following predicate:

$$hasIngredient; hasIngredient \subseteq hasIngredient$$

Requirements *REQ7-REQ10* are described as follows:

REQ7	If X hasTopping Y then Y isToppingOf X.
REQ8	If X isToppingOf Y then Y hasTopping X.
REQ9	Everything that hasTopping something is a Pizza.
REQ10	Everything that is hasTopping by something is a PizzaTopping.

Requirements *REQ7*, and *REQ8* identify two properties: *hasTopping* and its inverse *isTopping*. *REQ9* identifies the domain of *hasTopping*. Requirement *REQ10* identifies that *PizzaTopping* is the range of *hasTopping*. Therefore we define *hasTopping* as relation property as follows:

$$hasTopping \in Pizza \leftrightarrow PizzaTopping$$

The domain of relation *hasTopping* is the set of *Pizza* parts of all the pairs in *hasTopping* (i.e. *dom(hasTopping)*). The range of relation *hasTopping* is the set of second parts of all the pairs in *hasTopping* (i.e. *ran(hasTopping)*). The relational image of set *Pizza* under relation *hasTopping* ($hasTopping^{-1}[Pizza]$) gives the image of a set *Pizza* under the relation *hasTopping* (i.e. determine all the toppings associated with set *Pizza*).

Requirement *REQ11* identifies that *hasIngredient* is a subproperty of *hasTopping*.

REQ11	If X hasTopping Y then X hasIngredient Y.

The corresponding Event-B predicate is as follows:

$$hasTopping \subseteq hasIngredient$$

Requirements *REQ12-REQ16* introduce different types of pizza toppings.

REQ12	Every FishTopping is a PizzaTopping.
REQ13	Every MeatTopping is a PizzaTopping.
REQ14	Every TomatoTopping is a PizzaTopping.
REQ15	Every MozzarellaTopping is a PizzaTopping.
REQ16	Every MushroomTopping is a PizzaTopping.

The Event-B modelling concepts correspond to requirements *REQ12-REQ16* are as follows:

$$\begin{array}{l} FishTopping \subseteq PizzaTopping \\ MeatTopping \subseteq PizzaTopping \\ TomatoTopping \subseteq PizzaTopping \\ MozzarellaTopping \subseteq PizzaTopping \\ MushroomTopping \subseteq PizzaTopping \end{array}$$

Requirements *REQ17* and *REQ18* introduce the definition of *NonVegetarianPizza*.

REQ17	Every NonVegetarianPizza is a Pizza that is not a VegetarianPizza.
REQ18	Every Pizza that is not a VegetarianPizza is a NonVegetarianPizza.

The Event-B modelling concepts correspond to requirement *REQ17* and requirement *REQ18* is as follows:

$$partition(Pizza, VegetarianPizza, NonVegetarianPizza)$$

Requirement *REQ19* and requirement *REQ20* introduce the definition of *VegetarianPizza*.

REQ19	Every VegetarianPizza is a Pizza that does not hasTopping a FishTopping and that does not hasTopping a MeatTopping.
REQ20	Every Pizza that does not hasTopping a FishTopping and that does not hasTopping a MeatTopping is a VegetarianPizza.

The Event-B modelling concepts correspond to requirement *REQ19* and requirement *REQ20* is as follows:

$$VegetarianPizza = Pizza \setminus (hasTopping^{-1}[FishTopping] \cup hasTopping^{-1}[MeatTopping])$$

Requirement *REQ21* defines *Mushroom*.

REQ21	Every Mushroom is a NamedPizza.
REQ22	Every NamedPizza is a Pizza.

The Event-B modelling concepts correspond to requirement *REQ21* and requirement *REQ22* is:

$$\begin{array}{l} Mushroom \subseteq NamedPizza \\ NamedPizza \subseteq Pizza \end{array}$$

Requirements *REQ23-REQ26* are:

REQ23	Every Mushroom hasTopping an MozzarellaTopping.
REQ24	Every Mushroom hasTopping a MushroomTopping.
REQ25	Every Mushroom hasTopping a TomatoTopping.
REQ26	Everything that is hasTopping by a Mushroom is something that is an MozzarellaTopping and that is a MushroomTopping and that is a TomatoTopping.

The Event-B modelling concepts correspond to requirements *REQ23-REQ26* are:

$$hasTopping[Mushroom] = (MozzarellaTopping \cup MushroomTopping \cup TomatoTopping)$$

In Event-B the partition predicate is introduced to identify enumerated sets. Therefore, we can use partition predicate in the machine level to identify the enumerated sets as follows:

```
partition(Food, partition(Pizza, VegetarianPizza, NonVegetarianPizza, ...)
partition(NamedPizza, Mushroom, ...),
partition(PizzaTopping, MushroomTopping, MozzarellaTopping,
        TomatoTopping)...
```

The first argument in the *partition* predicate is the superclass. Other classes are subsets of the superclass class. Partition predicate can be nested to show that subclasses can be parent of other classes as shown in *Pizza* partition that has *Food* as parent class.

Now, we need to define the events. We can introduce *portobello_mushrooms* as a new member in *Mushroom* class. This can be achieved using the following event:

```
event add_portobello_mushrooms
then
   Mushroom := Mushroom ∪ {portobello_mushrooms}
   NamedPizza := NamedPizza ∪ {portobello_mushrooms}
   Food := Food ∪ {portobello_mushrooms}
   MozzarellaTopping := MozzarellaTopping ∪ {portobello}
   hasTopping := hasTopping ∪ {portobello_mushrooms ↦ portobello}
end
```

5 Conclusions and future work

In this paper we proposed an approach that extract clear, concise, consistent and unambiguous requirements from OWL ontologies and transform them to Event-B formal models. The approach consists of three steps: the first step is based on converting the ontology into OWL format. The second step is based on converting the OWL ontology into ACE texts. The third step links ACE requirements to Event-B modelling concepts. We applied this approach to convert Pizza ontology to Event-B models. In the future we are going to develop a tool to automatically transform ACE texts generated from OWL ontologies to Event-B models. Another direction for future work is to work on ACE texts and convert large subset of ACE's texts into Event-B modelling concepts. Moreover, we plan to explore an approach of deciding the construction of refinements steps from ACE requirements extracted from OWL ontologies.

References

[1] W.N. Borst, *Construction of Engineering Ontologies for Knowledge Sharing and Reuse* (Enschede, The Netherlands, 1997)

[2] N. Fuchs, K. Kaljur, G. Schneider, *Attempto Controlled English Meets the Challenges of Knowledge Representation, Reasoning, Interoperability and User Interfaces*, in *In Proceedings of 19th International Florida Artificial Intelligence Research Society Conference* (2006)

[3] J. Abrial, *Modeling in Event-B - System and Software Engineering* (Cambridge University Press, 2010), ISBN 978-0-521-89556-9

[4] V. Castaneda, L. Ballejos, L. Caliusco, M.R. Galli, Global Journal of Researches in Engineering specification **10, no 6**, 2 (2010)

[5] D. Dermeval, J. Vilela, I. Bittencourt, J. Castro, S. Isotani, P. Brito, A. Silva, Requirements Engineering pp. 1–33 (2015)

[6] U. of Manchester, *Wl syntax converter*, http://owl.cs.manchester.ac.uk/converter/

[7] K. Kaljurand, *Verbalizing OWL in (controlled) english*, http://attempto.ifi.uzh.ch/site/docs/verbalizing_owl_in_controlled_english.html (2007)

[8] J. Heflin, K. Words, *An introduction to the owl web ontology language* (2007)

[9] K. Kaljur, N. Fuchs, *Verbalizing OWL in Attempto Controlled English*, in *In Proceedings of OWLED07* (2007)

[10] *Writing OWL ontologies in ACE*, http://attempto.ifi.uzh.ch/site/docs/writing_owl_in_ace.html, accessed: 2016-07-17

[11] N.E. Fuchs, U. Schwertel, *Reasoning in Attempto Controlled English*, in *Principles and Practice of Semantic Web Reasoning, International Workshop PPSWR 2003* (2003), pp. 174–188, ISBN 978-3-540-20582-1

[12] J. Abrial, M. Butler, S. Hallerstede, T. Hoang, F. Mehta, L. Voisin, STTT **12**, 447 (2010)

[13] M. Horridge, *A practical guide to building OWL ontologies using Protege 4 and CO-ODE tools edition 1.3* (2011)

MATEC Web of Conferences 76, 04009 (2016) DOI: 10.1051/matecconf/20167604009
CSCC 2016

Method for assessing software reliability of the document management system using the RFID technology

Maciej Kiedrowicz[1], Tadeusz Nowicki[1], Robert Waszkowski[1], Zbigniew Wesołowski[1], Kazimierz Worwa[1,a]

[1] *The Faculty of Cybernetics, Military University of Technology, 00-908 Warsaw, Kaliskiego 2, Poland*

Abstract. The deliberations presented in this study refer to the method for assessing software reliability of the document management system, using the RFID technology. A method for determining the reliability structure of the discussed software, understood as the index vector for assessing reliability of its components, was proposed. The model of the analyzed software is the control transfer graph, in which the probability of activating individual components during the system's operation results from the so-called operational profile, which characterizes the actual working environment. The reliability structure is established as a result of the solution of a specific mathematical software task. The knowledge of the reliability structure of the software makes it possible to properly plan the time and financial expenses necessary to build the software, which would meet the reliability requirements. The application of the presented method is illustrated by the number example, corresponding to the software reality of the RFID document management system.

1 Introduction

The software reliability is one of the most important indicators of the software quality. One of the methods for modeling software reliability is to treat the software as monolithic entirety, while considering its interactions with the external environment, without trying to model the internal structure of the software. Such approach is inappropriate for modeling larger IT systems, with complex internal architecture. There is a demand for the modeling techniques of the software reliability, using the knowledge of its internal structure, e.g. module structure. The basic unit for determining the software structure is its component - often a module - understood as a logically independent software element, which performs well a specific function. It means that the modules may be designed, implemented and examined independently.

The behavior of the software, depending on the manner, in which different software modules affect each other, is defined by the software architecture. The interactions between different modules in the form of mutual control transfer are present only during the execution of the computer program. The software architecture may also contain some information on frequency of activation of the individual modules. When the software is working, some emergency situations related to software errors may occur. The software error may be connected with the implementation of any module or transfer of control between the two modules. A possibility of occurrence of some emergency situations during the use of the software is described by various software reliability indicators. The knowledge of the component (module) structure of the examined software allows using the indicators, whose values depend on such structure and the reliability indicators of its particular elements. Depending on the method applied in that respect, it is possible to distinguish two approaches to the reliability modeling process, on the basis of: the structure set by the source code instructions, structure based on logical paths [6].

The models based on the architecture set by the source code for modeling the software architecture use the so-called control transfer graph, illustrating a possibility of transferring control between the blocks of the source code. The nodes on the structure are indicated by the so-called program control guidelines. It is often assumed in the models of the discussed class that the control transfer between them may be described by the Markov chains. This assumption means that the control transfer after implementation of a specific module to other modules does not depend on previous activation of the program blocks. The software architecture is modeled by the Markov chain, e.g. discrete in states and in time. The representative examples of such models may be found in studies [1, 5, 9, 11, 13].

In the models based on the logical path concept, the software architecture is also created by separate blocks of the source code, e.g. by the modules, which are not - however - analyzed as independent components, but as sequences of components executed one by one in case of activation of a given path by an appropriate set of input data. Knowing the values of the reliability indicators of the components that create a given logical path, it is possible to determine the value of the reliability indicator

[a] Corresponding author: kazimierz.worwa@wat.edu.pl

of the whole software, using the knowledge of the architecture of the software. The representative examples of the models based on logical paths may be found in studies [8, 17, 23].

It is worth mentioning that apart from the above-mentioned methods for modeling the software reliability, models alternative to the models based on the software architecture and results of the software errors observed, e.g. during the software tests, are applied in practice. On such basis, the hypotheses concerning working time distribution between the moments of the occurrence of the two subsequent errors are formulated. The representative examples of such models may be found in studies [4, 10, 12, 14, 20, 22, 24].

On the basis of the software engineering practice, it is evident that the software quality is the function of the time and expenses incurred during the production process, regardless of the applied methodology and production technology. Due to the fact that the process is usually executed with limited budget, the available funds should be used in a manner that maximally improves the quality of the produced software. A method often used in practice to achieve this objective is identification of the key components - for the purpose of proper functioning of the entire software - and paying special attention to the process of their production. It is worth mentioning that the solution of the issue of reducing the time and expenses required in the software production process may be significantly facilitated by applying formal methods of mathematical modeling and operational research. The examples of such approach may be found, for example, in [3-4,6-7,15, 21].

The subject of the deliberations in this study is the allocation of funds for the production of the document management software, using the RFID technology, with a known component structure, assuming that the software production process covers independent production of its components. In further deliberations, the components of the discussed software will be called software modules or just modules. In accordance with the previous idea, the allocation of the aforesaid funds includes the impact of the particular modules on the correct functioning of the whole software. The model of the discussed software is the control transfer graph, in which the probability of activating particular component modules during the operation of the system results from the so-called operation profile of the software, characterizing its actual working environment. Identification of the modules, whose execution has the largest impact on the proper functioning of the entire software system, will be made on the basis of an analysis of the so-called software reliability structure, understood as the components. The optimum structure will be established as a result of the solution of a specific mathematical software task. The knowledge of the software reliability structure of the document management system, with the RFID technology, allows proper planning of time and expenses required for its production. It should be emphasized that the approaches found in the literature [1], for example to determine the meaning of particular component modules of the software, are based on the results of the so-called sensitivity analysis, i.e. the analysis of the impact of changing the values of the reliability indicators of particular modules on the value of the adopted indicator of the software quality.

2 Characteristics of the examined software

It is assumed that the examined software has a module structure, where the term "module" has the meaning generally given in the software engineering, i.e. a logically independent software component, which usually executes one function. The logical independence means, among other things, technological independence, i.e. the module may be designed, implemented and tested independently. The typical production process of the software with the above-described module structure consists in identification and separation of the component modules, independent performance of the individual modules and their subsequent integration (usually during the integration testing) into one.

For the purpose of this study, the analyzed software will be represented by the graph, with a set of vertices corresponding to the numbers of the selected component modules and a set of arcs, characterizing a possibility of transferring control between the modules during the execution of the software. Without compromising the deliberations herein, it is possible to assume that the discussed software has one input and one output module. In the literature, the graph with the provided values is called the control transfer graph of the software [1, 16].

Let $\boldsymbol{M} = \{ 1,2,3,...,m,...,M \}$ mean a set of the module numbers of the examined software, where - for the purposes of simplification - the input module has number 1, and the output module – number M.

The reliability structure of the examined software will be understood as vector $\boldsymbol{R} = (R_1, R_2, R_3,..., R_m,..., R_M)$, whose particular components are the reliability indicators of the component modules, where the reliability indicator of the module constitutes probability of its correct, single execution during the execution of the software. The execution of the software for the specific set of its input data consists in activating a certain, corresponding sequence of modules, which created the so-called logical path of the software. It is assumed that the measure of reliability of the examined software is probability of its proper execution for a single set of input data. The probability is equal to a product of probabilities of the proper execution of the modules, which are part of the path from the initial to the final module, activated by a given set of input data. The reliability of the software module is a function of many factors, such as qualifications and experience of its designers, applied production technology, amount of time and expenses incurred, etc. It is assumed in the study that the process of transferring control between the modules during the software execution is the Markov chain. In particular, it means that the probability of the p_{ij} event consisting in the fact that after the execution of the$i$-th module, the j-th module will be next, does not depend on what happened before the control transfer to the$i$th module. The probability of transfers p_{ij},

$i, j \in \boldsymbol{M}$ between the software component modules in the process of its execution results from the so-called operational profile of the software, characterizing its actual working environment. When adding to the software control graph two additional statuses corresponding to the proper and improper completion of the software execution, respectively, the Markov chain is obtained with two absorbing statuses, whereas - in accordance with the previous assumptions - the reliability indicator of the software, defined as the probability of its proper execution for a single set of input data, may be calculated as the probability of achieving by the discussed Marvov process the absorbing status corresponding to the proper and improper completion of the software execution. The examined Markov chain explicitly characterizes the transfer matrix, which - in accordance with the adopted assumptions - is of the form

$$\overline{\boldsymbol{P}}(\boldsymbol{R}) = \begin{bmatrix} & C & F & 1 & 2 & \ldots & m & \ldots & M \\ C & 1 & 0 & 0 & 0 & \ldots & 0 & \ldots & 0 \\ F & 0 & 1 & 0 & 0 & \ldots & 0 & \ldots & 0 \\ 1 & 0 & 1-R_1 & 0 & R_1 p_{12} & \ldots & R_1 p_{1m} & \ldots & R_1 p_{1M} \\ \ldots & \ldots & \ldots & \ldots & \ldots & \ldots & & \ldots & \ldots \\ m & 0 & 1-R_m & 0 & R_m p_{m2} & \ldots & R_m p_{mm} & \ldots & R_m p_{mM} \\ \ldots & \ldots & \ldots & \ldots & \ldots & \ldots & \ldots & \ldots & \ldots \\ M-1 & 0 & 1-R_{M-1} & 0 & R_{M-1} p_{M-1,2} & \ldots & R_{M-1} p_{M-1,m} & \ldots & R_{M-1} p_{M-1,M} \\ M & R_M & 1-R_{M-1} & 0 & 0 & \ldots & 0 & \ldots & 0 \end{bmatrix}$$

in which the first two lines and the first columns correspond to the proper and improper completion of the software execution, respectively, for a single set of input data.

Let ***P(R)*** mean the matrix obtained by rejecting from matrix $\overline{\boldsymbol{P}}(\boldsymbol{R})$ the first two lines and the first two columns. It may be shown that the reliability indicator of the software *R(**R**)* with reliability structure ***R***, understood as the probability of its proper execution for a single set of input data, is defined by formula [6]

$$R(\boldsymbol{R}) = S_{1M}(\boldsymbol{R})R_M\,, \qquad (1)$$

where S_{1M} is an element located at the intersection of the first line and the *M*-th column of matrix *S(R)*, defined in the following manner:

$$\boldsymbol{S}(\boldsymbol{R}) = \boldsymbol{I} + \boldsymbol{P}(\boldsymbol{R}) + \boldsymbol{P}^2(\boldsymbol{R}) + \ldots = \sum_{k=o}^{\infty} \boldsymbol{P}^k(\boldsymbol{R}), \qquad (2)$$

where ***I*** is a unit matrix of the same category as matrix ***P(R)***.

3 Optimization of the software reliability structure

Let K_m mean the cost of production of the *m*-th software component module, with the reliability indicator of R_m, $m \in \boldsymbol{M}$.

When assuming that the production costs of the particular modules are the known functions of their reliability indicators $K_m = f_m(R_m)$, $m \in \boldsymbol{M}$, it is possible to determine - by way of an appropriately formulated mathematical programming - the software reliability structure, which may be understood as a kind of the production plan, and form the practical point of view, especially two tasks might be useful:

- one-criterion optimization task consisting in maximizing the value of the software reliability indicator as the function of objective, with the maximum, allowed cost of the software production being the limitation;
- two-criteria optimization task, with the software reliability indicator and the cost of its production as the vector function of objective, ensuring determination of the allowed software reliability structure, i.e. ensuring achievement of the required, minimum reliability level and not exceeding of the maximum, allowed cost of the software production.

The knowledge of the optimum software reliability structure, at the stage of planning its production, allows to identify the modules of the greatest importance for the reliability of the whole software and hence allows to allocate the available funds in such a manner that the produced software fully meets the assumed reliability requirements.

When considering the introduced designations and assumptions made, the first of the aforementioned optimization tasks may be formulated in the following manner:

$$\text{maximize} \quad R(\boldsymbol{R}) = S_{1M}(\boldsymbol{R})R_M \qquad (3)$$

considering limitation

$$K(\boldsymbol{R}) = \sum_{m=1}^{M} K_m(R_m) \le K_{max}\,, \qquad (4)$$

where

$$\boldsymbol{R} = (R_1, R_2, R_3, \ldots, R_m, \ldots, R_M),\; 0 \le R_m \le 1,\; m \in \boldsymbol{M}\,.$$

The formulation of the second of the aforementioned optimization tasks may be in the following form:

$$(\mathbf{R}, F, \Psi), \qquad (5)$$

where:

R - set of allowed solutions, defined in the following manner:

$$\mathbf{R} = \{\boldsymbol{R} = (R_1, R_2, R_3, \ldots, R_m, \ldots, R_M),\; 0 \le R_m \le 1,\; m \in \boldsymbol{M}\},$$

F - solution quality indicator:

$$F(\boldsymbol{R}) = (K(\boldsymbol{R}), R(\boldsymbol{R})), \qquad (6)$$

where values*R(**R**)*, *K(**R**)* are defined in the following manner:

$$R(\boldsymbol{R}) = S_{1M}(\boldsymbol{R})R_M\,, \quad K(\boldsymbol{R}) = \sum_{m=1}^{M} K_m(R_m) \qquad (7)$$

Ψ - the dominance relationship is as follows:

$$\Psi = \{y_1, y_2) \in \boldsymbol{Y} \times \boldsymbol{Y} : y_1^1 \le y_2^1,\; y_1^2 \ge y_2^2\}, \qquad (8)$$

where $y_1 = (y_1^1, y_1^2)$, $y_2 = (y_2^1, y_2^2)$,

where***Y*** is the so-called criterial space defined in the following manner:

$$\boldsymbol{Y} = \{y = (K(\boldsymbol{R}), R(\boldsymbol{R})) : \boldsymbol{R} \in \mathbf{R}\}. \qquad (9)$$

The first of the formulated tasks is the one-criterion optimization. Its nature, and hence - the manner of solution - strongly depend on the class (analytical form) of the software reliability indicator $R(\mathbf{R})$ and the cost of its production $K(\mathbf{R})$. The second of the formulated tasks is the non-linear two-criteria optimization task. Its solution may be determined in accordance with the generally adopted methodology for solving the optimization tasks [18]. In accordance with this methodology, the solution of task (5)-(9) may, in particular, require the determination of the following data:

- set of dominating strategies,
- set of non-dominated strategies,
- set of compromise strategies.

Due to the nature of correlations (7), which define the component critertial functions $R(\mathbf{R})$ and $K(\mathbf{R})$ the subject task, it should be expected that the set of the dominant solutions would be empty. Therefore, in the discussed situation, the issue of determining the set of non-dominated solutions and its potential narrowing, e.g. by setting the set of compromise solution, becomes of practical importance [18]. The reliability structure $\mathbf{R}^*$, being the solution to task (3) - (7), additionally maximizes the value of the software reliability indicator $R(\mathbf{R})$ and minimizes the value of the function of the cost of $K(\mathbf{R})$ its production.

4 Case study - software reliability of the document management system, using the RFID technology

The presented method for determining the software reliability structure will be illustrated by a number example, which is in accordance with the reality of the document management system software, using the RFID technology. The control transfer graph of the discussed software will be defined as in *Fig. 1*.

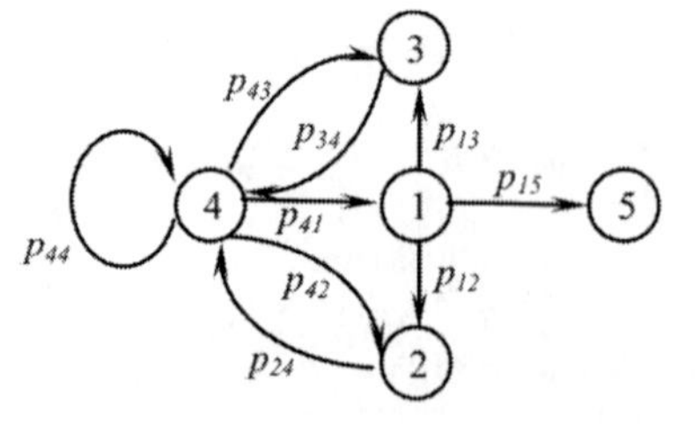

Figure 1. Control transfer graph of the discussed software

According to Fig. 1, it is evident that the set of numbers of the modules of the discussed software is in the form of $\mathbf{M} = \{1,2,3,4,5\}$, where module 1 is the initial module, and module 5 - the final module. The module structure of the software is defined by vector $\mathbf{R} = (R_1, R_2, R_3, R_4, R_5)$. Let probabilities p_{ij} of the control transfer between the modules, during the execution of the software be in the form of:

$p_{11}=0,\ p_{12}=0.6,\ p_{13}=0.3,\ p_{14}=0,\ p_{15}=0.1,$

$p_{21}=0,\ p_{22}=0,\ p_{23}=0,\ p_{24}=1,\ p_{25}=0,$

$p_{31}=0,\ p_{32}=0,\ p_{33}=0,\ p_{34}=1,\ p_{35}=0,$

$p_{41}=0.3,\ p_{42}=0.2,\ p_{43}=0.4,\ p_{44}=0.1,\ p_{45}=0.$

Using correlation (1), the software reliability indicator with the reliability structure$\mathbf{R}$ may be defined based on formula $R(\mathbf{R}) = S_{15}(\mathbf{R})R_5$, where value S_{15} may be set on the basis of correlation (2) or programming package *Mathematica* [19], which allows performing symbolic calculations.

The use of the above-mentioned package for the module structure from *Fig. 1* and the above-mentioned probabilities of transfers p_{ij} provides the following dependency on probability S_{15}

$$S_{15} = \\ = \frac{0{,}1R_1 - 0{,}01R_1R_4 - 0{,}02R_1R_2R_4 - 0{,}04R_1R_3R_4}{1 - 0{,}1R_4 - 0{,}2R_2R_4 - 0{,}18R_1R_2R_4 - 0{,}4R_3R_4 - 0{,}09R_1R_3R_4} \quad (10)$$

For the purpose of formulating the previously discussed optimization tasks, it is assumed that cost $K_i(R_i)$ of the production of the i-th module with the reliability indicator R_i is in the form of

$$K_i(R_i) = KS_i + \alpha_i e^{\beta_i R_i}, \quad i \in \mathbf{M} = \{1,2,3,4,5\} \quad (11)$$

where:

KS_i – fixed component of the production cost of the i-th module, independent of the level of its quality R_i,

α_i, β_i – co-efficient of the curve shape of the production cost of the i-th module, depending i.a. on its complexity, used technology, qualifications of the design and programming team, etc.

Let figures of value KS_i, α_i i β_i and K_{max} be defined as in *Table 1*.

For the module structure of the software in *Fig. 1* and numerical data in *Table 1*, the solutions of the optimization tasks, formulated in the previous sub-chapter, i.e. the one-criterion optimization tasks (3) - (4) and polyoptimization tasks (5) - (9), will be determined.

Table 1. Figures of value KS_i, α_i, β_i, K_{max} used for calculations

i	1	2	3	4	5
KS_i	1000.0	400.0	1500.0	2500.0	900.0
α_i	50.0	35.0	25.0	30.0	40.0
β_i	5.0	2.0	8.0	10.0	4.0
K_{max}	160 000.0				

When using the possibilities created by modern computer technology, both tasks may be solved by the full review method. For that purpose, a set of all possible reliability structures will be created $\mathbf{R} = (R_1, R_2, R_3, R_4, R_5)$, for $R_i \in [0.95, 1.00]$, $i \in \{1,2,3,4,5\}$, to two decimal places. The number of vectors in this set is $6^5 = 7776$, out of which *7770* meet the restriction (4).

Table 2. Solution of the one-criterion optimization task

R_1	R_2	R_3	R_4	R_5	***R(R)***	K_1	K_2	K_3	K_4	K_5	***K(R)***
0.98	1.00	1.00	1.00	1.00	0.8305	7,714.49	658.62	76023.95	76023.95	3,083.93	163,504.93 €
1.00	1.00	0.99	1.00	0.96	0.8362	8,420.66	658.62	70,294.28	76,023.95	2,761.02	158,158.52 €
1.00	1.00	0.99	1.00	0.97	0.8449	8,420.66	658.62	70,294.28	76,023.95	2,836.97	158,234.47 €
1.00	0.99	1.00	1.00	0.95	0.8488	8,420.66	653.50	76,023.95	76,023.95	2,688.05	163,810.10 €
1.00	1.00	0.99	1.00	0.98	0.8536	8,420.66	658.62	70,294.28	76,023.95	2,916.02	158,313.52 €
1.00	0.99	1.00	1.00	0.96	0.8578	8,420.66	653.50	76,023.95	76,023.95	2,761.02	163,883.07 €
1.00	1.00	0.99	1.00	0.99	0.8623	8,420.66	658.62	70,294.28	76,023.95	2,998.29	158,395.79 €
0.99	1.00	1.00	1.00	0.95	0.8628	8,058.75	658.62	76,023.95	76,023.95	2,688.05	163,453.31 €
1.00	0.99	1.00	1.00	0.97	0.8667	8,420.66	653.50	76,023.95	76,023.95	2,836.97	163,959.02 €
1.00	**1.00**	**0.99**	**1.00**	**1.00**	**0.8711**	**8,420.66**	**658.62**	**70,294.28**	**76,023.95**	**3,083.93**	**158,481.43 €**
0.99	1.00	1.00	1.00	0.96	0.8719	8,058.75	658.62	76,023.95	76,023.95	2,761.02	163,526.28 €
1.00	0.99	1.00	1.00	0.98	0.8756	8,420.66	653.50	76,023.95	76,023.95	2,916.02	164,038.07 €
0.99	1.00	1.00	1.00	0.97	0.8810	8,058.75	658.62	76,023.95	76,023.95	2,836.97	163,602.23 €
1.00	0.99	1.00	1.00	0.99	0.8846	8,420.66	653.50	76,023.95	76,023.95	2,998.29	164,120.35 €
0.99	1.00	1.00	1.00	0.98	0.8901	8,058.75	658.62	76,023.95	76,023.95	2,916.02	163,681.28 €
1.00	0.99	1.00	1.00	1.00	0.8935	8,420.66	653.50	76,023.95	76,023.95	3,083.93	164,205.98 €
0.99	1.00	1.00	1.00	0.99	0.8992	8,058.75	658.62	76,023.95	76,023.95	2,998.29	163,763.56 €
0.99	1.00	1.00	1.00	1.00	0.9083	8,058.75	658.62	76,023.95	76,023.95	3,083.93	163,849.19 €
1.00	1.00	1.00	1.00	0.95	0.9500	8,420.66	658.62	76,023.95	76,023.95	2,688.05	163,815.22 €
1.00	1.00	1.00	1.00	0.96	0.9600	8,420.66	658.62	76,023.95	76,023.95	2,761.02	163,888.19 €
1.00	1.00	1.00	1.00	0.97	0.9700	8,420.66	658.62	76,023.95	76,023.95	2,836.97	163,964.14 €
1.00	1.00	1.00	1.00	0.98	0.9800	8,420.66	658.62	76,023.95	76,023.95	2,916.02	164,043.19 €
1.00	1.00	1.00	1.00	0.99	0.9900	8,420.66	658.62	76,023.95	76,023.95	2,998.29	164,125.47 €
1.00	1.00	1.00	1.00	1.00	1.0000	8,420.66	658.62	76,023.95	76,023.95	3,083.93	164,211.10 €

Table 2 shows the values of the software reliability indicator (1) and the production cost of the model software, indicated in accordance with dependency $K(\boldsymbol{R}) = \sum_{i=1}^{5} K_i(R_i)$, where the cost of $K_i(R_i)$ is defined in formula (11), for the most important (from the point of view of the solution sought) fragment of the above set of the reliability structures of the analyzed software. The lines corresponding to the forbidden solutions, i.e. vectors $\boldsymbol{R} = (R_1, R_2, R_3, R_4, R_5)$, in case of which restriction (4) is not met, are marked in lighter color. Vector $\boldsymbol{R}^* = (1.00, 1.00, 0.99, 1.00, 1.00)$ is the optimum solution of the one-criterion optimization task (3) - (4). The corresponding line in *table 1* was shaded. The value of the software reliability indicator corresponding to the optimum solution is $R(\boldsymbol{R}^*)=0.87$, with the production cost of the software $K(\boldsymbol{R}^*)=158\ 481.43$ €.

For the purpose of the analysis to obtain optimum solution $\boldsymbol{R}^*$, the sensitivity evaluation of the software reliability indicator was performed: $R(\boldsymbol{R})$ with respect to a single change of the value of the reliability indicator of particular modules for the two levels of values of indicator $R(\boldsymbol{R})$. The results are presented in *Table 3*. It is noticeable that the ratio of the growth value of indicator $R(\boldsymbol{R})$ to the cost of its achievement is the least beneficial for module number *3*. It means that increasing the value of indicator R_3 is the most costly. It is worth mentioning that this fact is reflected in the value structure of optimum solution $\boldsymbol{R}^*$.

Due to the fact that the component criterial functions present in the two-criteria optimization task (5)-(9) are of opposite nature (the cost of the software production is reduced, while the value of the software reliability indicator is maximized), the set of dominating solutions to this task is empty. Therefore, the solutions must be sought among the non-dominated solutions.

Table 3. The unitary increase in the value of the software reliability indicator and the cost of its production for ΔR_i=0,01 and: a) R_i=0,95; b) R_i=0,99

	i	*1*	*2*	*3*	*4*	*5*
a)	$\Delta R(\Delta R_i)$	0.0073	0.0055	0.0063	0.0136	0.0026
	$\Delta K(\Delta R_i)$	296.31 €	4.73 €	4.160,60 €	4.160,60 €	72.97 €
b)	$\Delta R(\Delta R_i)$	0.0394	0.0436	0.0548	0.1230	0.0061
	$\Delta K(\Delta R_i)$	361.91 €	5.12 €	5.729.67 €	5.729.67 €	85.63 €

The set of the non-dominated solutions to the polyoptimization task (5)-(9) is presented in *Fig. 2*. Every point in bold fragment of the contour of *Fig. 2* is a non-dominated solution.

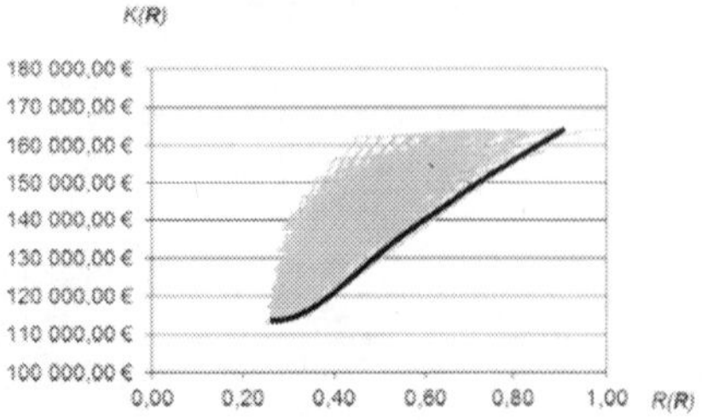

Figure 2. The non-dominated solution set of the optimization task (5)-(9)

To narrow the set to one solution only, the compromise solution, which is the closest (in terms of the Euclidean space) to the so-called ideal point [18] will be indicated. For that purpose, both components of the vector criterial function $(K(\boldsymbol{R}), R(\boldsymbol{R}))$ will be standardized, in result of which both indicators will have values in the range of $[0, 1]$:

$$\overline{K(\boldsymbol{R})} = \frac{K(\boldsymbol{R}) - K_{min}(\boldsymbol{R})}{K_{max}(\boldsymbol{R}) - K_{min}(\boldsymbol{R})},$$

$$\overline{R(\boldsymbol{R})} = \frac{R(\boldsymbol{R}) - R_{min}(\boldsymbol{R})}{R_{max}(\boldsymbol{R}) - R_{min}(\boldsymbol{R})}, \qquad (12)$$

where

$$K_{min}(\boldsymbol{R}) = \min_{\boldsymbol{R}\in\mathfrak{R}} K(\boldsymbol{R}), \quad R_{min}(\boldsymbol{R}) = \min_{\boldsymbol{R}\in\mathfrak{R}} R(\boldsymbol{R}) \quad (13)$$

$$K_{max}(\boldsymbol{R}) = \max_{\boldsymbol{R}\in\mathfrak{R}} K(\boldsymbol{R}), \quad R_{max}(\boldsymbol{R}) = \max_{\boldsymbol{R}\in\mathfrak{R}} R(\boldsymbol{R}). \quad (14)$$

In terms of the discussed task, the ideal point $(\overline{K^*(\boldsymbol{R})}, \overline{R^*(\boldsymbol{R})})$, being an element of the so-called extended standardized criterial space, is in the form of $(\overline{K^*(\boldsymbol{R})}, \overline{R^*(\boldsymbol{R})}) = (0, 1)$.

The solution of the polyoptimization problem (5)–(9), with cost limitation $K(\boldsymbol{R}) \leq 160\,000$ € is presented in *Table 3*. The shaded line corresponds to vector $\boldsymbol{R}^* = (1.00, 1.00, 0.95, 1.00, 1.00)$, being the compromise solution, i.e. the closest to the ideal point *(0, 1)*, where distance $d[(\overline{K(\boldsymbol{R})}, \overline{R(\boldsymbol{R})}, (0,1)]$ is defined by the following formula

$$d[(\overline{K(\boldsymbol{R})}, \overline{R(\boldsymbol{R})}, (0,1)] = \sqrt{[\overline{K(\boldsymbol{R})}]^2 + [\overline{R(\boldsymbol{R})} - 1]^2}. \quad (15)$$

The following

$$\boldsymbol{R}^* = (1.00, 1.00, 0.95, 1.00, 1.00)$$

values of the component criterial functions correspond to the compromise solution: $K(\boldsymbol{R}^*) = 139\,42.05$ € and $R(\boldsymbol{R}^*) = 0.5872$.

Table 4 shows the solution of the analyzed polyoptimization problem, with additional limitation to the minimum, allowed level of the software reliability in the form of $R(\boldsymbol{R}) \geq 0{,}8$. In this case, the compromise solution is vector $\boldsymbol{R}^* = (1.00, 1.00, 0.99, 1.00, 1.00)$, with the values of the component criterial functions: $K(\boldsymbol{R}^*) = 158\,481.43$ € and $R(\boldsymbol{R}^*) = 0.8711$. It is apparent that the solution coincides with the solution of the one-criterion optimization problem (3) - (4).

Table 4. Solution of the two-criteria optimization task K(**R**) ≤ 160 000 €

R_1	R_2	R_3	R_4	R_5	$\overline{R(\boldsymbol{R})}$	$\overline{K(\boldsymbol{R})}$	$d[(\overline{K(\boldsymbol{R})}, \overline{R(\boldsymbol{R})}, (0,1)]$
1.00	1.00	0.95	0.99	0.99	0.3425	0.41	0.773068
1.00	1.00	0.95	0.99	1.00	0.3493	0.41	0.768180
1.00	1.00	0.95	1.00	0.95	0.4116	0.51	0.780266
1.00	1.00	0.95	1.00	0.96	0.4194	0.51	0.775334
1.00	1.00	0.95	1.00	0.97	0.4272	0.52	0.770492
1.00	1.00	0.95	1.00	0.98	0.4350	0.52	0.765742
1.00	1.00	0.95	1.00	0.99	0.4428	0.52	0.761089
1.00	**1.00**	**0.95**	**1.00**	**1.00**	0.4506	0.52	0.756537
1.00	1.00	0.96	0.95	0.95	0.1251	0.11	0.882228
1.00	1.00	0.96	0.95	0.96	0.1299	0.12	0.877656
1.00	1.00	0.96	0.95	0.97	0.1347	0.12	0.873097
1.00	1.00	0.96	0.95	0.98	0.1395	0.12	0.868551
1.00	1.00	0.96	0.95	0.99	0.1443	0.12	0.864019
1.00	1.00	0.96	0.95	1.00	0.1491	0.12	0.859502
1.00	1.00	0.96	0.96	0.95	0.1647	0.20	0.857755

Table 5. Solution of the two-criteria optimization task K(**R**) ≤ 160 000 €, R(**R**) ≥ 0,8

R_1	R_2	R_3	R_4	R_5	$\overline{R(\mathbf{R})}$	$\overline{K(\mathbf{R})}$	$d[(\overline{K(\mathbf{R})}, \overline{R(\mathbf{R})}, (0,1)]$
1.00	1.00	0.99	0.99	0.99	0.5888	0.77	0.876889
1.00	1.00	0.99	0.99	1.00	0.5981	0.78	0.874058
1.00	1.00	0.99	1.00	0.95	0.7705	0.88	0.909792
1.00	1.00	0.99	1.00	0.96	0.7821	0.88	0.908320
1.00	1.00	0.99	1.00	0.97	0.7936	0.88	0.907053
1.00	1.00	0.99	1.00	0.98	0.8052	0.88	0.905995
1.00	1.00	0.99	1.00	0.99	0.8168	0.89	0.905147
1.00	1.00	0.99	1.00	1.00	0.8284	0.89	0.904515
1.00	1.00	1.00	0.95	0.95	0.2088	0.51	0.942643
1.00	1.00	1.00	0.95	0.96	0.2145	0.51	0.938661
1.00	1.00	1.00	0.95	0.97	0.2201	0.52	0.934730
1.00	1.00	1.00	0.95	0.98	0.2258	0.52	0.930854
1.00	1.00	1.00	0.95	0.99	0.2315	0.52	0.927034
1.00	1.00	1.00	0.95	1.00	0.2372	0.52	0.923273
1.00	1.00	1.00	0.96	0.95	0.2720	0.59	0.939384

5 Summary

The references include a description of the method for determining the optimum software reliability structure of a known module structure, assuming that the software production process covers independent creation of its component modules, where the software reliability structure is understood as the vector of the reliability indicators of the software component modules. The knowledge of the optimum reliability software structure allows proper planning of time and expenses required for the purpose of the software production, if the assumed reliability and cost requirements are met. The optimum reliability software structure is determined based on the solution to a specific one- or multi-criteria optimization problem. To establish the criterial functions or limitations of such mathematical programming problem, the program analyzed by the control transfer graph is modeled, where the probability of activation of the particular component modules in the software execution process result from the so-called operational profile of the software, which characterized the actual working environment of the software. Such graph model of the software allows, in particular, obtaining analytical dependency, defining the probability of the correct, single execution of the software on the basis of the Marvon chain theory.

The numerical example, which illustrates the above-described deliberations, confirmed a possibility of obtaining the optimum reliability software structure by way of solving the mathematical programming problem, whereas - in accordance with the expectations - the structure, indicated as the solution to the on-criterion optimization problem, turned out to be the same as in case of the solution to the polyoptimization problem.

References

1. R.C. Cheung, *A user-oriented software reliability model*. IEEE Transactions on Software Engineering, **SE-6**, 2, 118-125 (1980)
2. D.W. Coit, *Economic allocation of test times for subsystem level reliability growth testing*. IEEE Transactions on Software Engineering, **30**, 12, 1143-1151 (1998)
3. Y. S. Dai, M. Xie, K.L. Poth, B. Tang, *Optimal testing-resource allocation with genetic algorithm for modular software systems*. The Journal of Systems and Software, 66, 47-55 (2003)
4. W. Everett, *Software component reliability analysis*, in: Proceedings of the Symposium on Application-specific Systems and Software Engineering Technology (ASSET'99), 204–211 (1999)
5. S. Gokhale, W.E. Wong, K. Trivedi, J.R. Horgan, *An analytical approach to architecture based software reliability prediction*, in: Proceedings of the Third International Computer Performance and Dependability Symposium (IPDS'98), 13–22 (1998)
6. K. Goseva-Popstojanova, K.S.Trivedi, *Architecture-based approach to reliability assessment of software systems*. Performance Evaluation, 45, 179-204 (2001)
7. C.Y. Huang, J.H. Lo, *Optimal resource allocation for cost and reliability of modular software systems in the testing phase*. The Journal of Systems and Software, 79, 653-664 (2006)
8. S. Krishnamurthy, A.P. Mathur, *On the estimation of reliability of a software system using reliabilities of its components*, in: Proceedings of the Eighth International Symposium on Software Reliability Engineering (ISSRE'97), 146–155 (1997)

9. P. Kubat, *Assessing reliability of modular software*, Operations Research Letter, 8, 35–41 (1989)
10. W. Kuo, V.R. Prasad, *An annotated overview of system reliability optimisation*. IEEE Transactions on Software Engineering, **49**, 2, 176-187 (2000)
11. J.C. Laprie, *Dependability evaluation of software systems in operation*, IEEE Transactions on Software Engineering, **10**, 6, 701–714 (1984)
12. Y.W. Leung, *Dynamic resource-allocation for software-module testing*. The Journal of Systems and Software, **37**, 2, 129-139 (1997)
13. B. Littlewood, *Software reliability model for modular program structure*, IEEE Transactions on. Reliability, **28**, 3, 241–246 (1979)
14. J.D. Musa, *Software–Reliability-Engineered Testing Practice*. McGraw-Hill, New York (1998)
15. H. Ohtera, S. Yamada, *Optimal allocation & control problems for software-testing resources*. IEEE Transactions on Software Engineering, **39**, 2, 171-176 (1990)
16. J. Rajgopal, M. Mazumdar, *Modular operational test plans for inferences on software reliability based on a Markov model*. IEEE Transactions on Software Engineering, **28**, 4, 358-363 (2002)
17. M. Shooman, *Structural models for software reliability prediction*, in: Proceedings of the Second International Conference on Software Engineering, 268–280 (1976)
18. J. Stadnicki, *Teoria i praktyka rozwiązywania zadań polioptymalizacji*, WNT (2006).
19. S. Wolfram, *The Mathematica book*. Cambridge University Press and Wolfram Media (1996)
20. K. Worwa, *Application of mathematical modelling to the solution of software testing problems*, in: Proceedings of the XII International Conference System-Modelling-Control (2009)
21. K. Worwa, *Estimation of the program testing strategy*. Postępy Cybernetyki, 3-4, 155-188 (1995)
22. M. Xie, C. Wohlin, *An additive reliability model for the analysis of modular software failure data*, in: Proceedings of the Sixth International Symposium on Software Reliability Engineering, 188–194 (1995)
23. S. Yacoub, B. Cukic, Ammar H., *Scenario-based reliability analysis of component-based software*, in: Proceedings of the 10th International Symposium on Software Reliability Engineering, 22–31 (1999)
24. S. Yamada, T. Ichimori, M. Nishiwaki, *Optimal allocation policies for testing-resource based on a software reliability growth model*. International Journal of Mathematical and Computer Modelling, **22**, 10, 295-301 (1995)

MATEC Web of Conferences 76, 04010 (2016) DOI: 10.1051/matecconf/20167604010
CSCC 2016

Risk management system as the basic paradigm of the information security management system in an organization

Romuald Hoffmann[1,a], Maciej Kiedrowicz[1], Jerzy Stanik[1]

[1] *The Faculty of Cybernetics, Military University of Technology, 00-908 Warsaw, Kaliskiego 2, Poland*

Abstract. Risk is an inherent part of the functioning of every organization therefore the risk management should be a natural activity at each level of management. A common mistake in the management process of an organization is separating the security system, including the risk management system, and treating it as an isolated element. The article presents the place and role of the risk management system in the context of safety of the IT resource of an organization. A model of the risk management system was developed as the basic element of the organization management system and function supporting the continued operation in terms of IT safety of modern organizations.

Introduction

With the increase of changes in the surrounding environment, the management boards of various enterprises and organizations start to notice more risks of different type connected with business activities and start to pay more attention to the issue of security, including the information security. The issues related to the risk management system become an important element of the strategic management of enterprises and, in many cases, they are crucial for rationalizing the business activities and continued operations.

A common mistake in the management process of an organization is separating the security system, including the risk management system, and treating it as an isolated element. Our organizations already have different systems for process management, quality management, project management, objective management as well as control and internal audit, which on one hand are the perfect source of data for risk analysis, and on the other - provide knowledge of risks, vulnerability and potential of the said areas.

Many misunderstandings in the evaluation of the organization's safety often result from the lack of awareness and improper line of reasoning.

In the course of many disputes and proving one's reasons, the interlocutors often forget that the safety is not a state, but a constantly changing process, whose internal and external conditions to a different extent depend on an organization, to which they directly refer. Therefore, an important element in the process of ensuring internal and external security is the information security management system, which plays a key role in solving critical or crisis situations.

The knowledge of the level of the information security of particular business processes in the organization, including IT systems, allows to efficiently manage security by using dedicated risk management systems. To effectively manage the risk in the organization, it is crucial to be aware of the place and role of the risk management in the security management system.

The approach to the place and role of the risk management in the security system outlined in this study was presented in consideration of the fact that with the improvement of the functioning of the risk management system in the information security and the process undergoing therein, this place and role will be subject to change.

This document defined the essence of the risk, system components, model of the risk management process, role of the risk analysis team and approach to assessing the information security.

1 Organization as the system

The organization is a system aimed at achieving certain goals, whose subordinated parts/sub-systems co-contribute to the success of the entirety, and the success of the entirety is an important condition for success of every single part. The organization constitutes an internally integrated whole (system) composed of five basic parts (Fig. 1):

1. objectives and tasks – strategy system,
2. people (their efforts and patterns of behavior) - intellectual resources system,
3. material and technical equipment – technology system,
4. formal structure – structure system,
5. management element ensuring achievement of goals, survival and development of an organization in the conditions of the changing

[a] Corresponding author: maciej.kiedrowicz@wat.edu.pl

DOI: 10.1051/matecconf/20167604010

environment and requirements for the organization – management system.

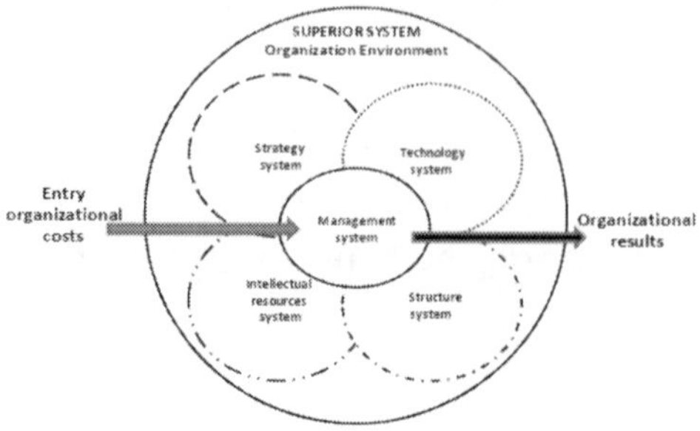

Figure 1 Model of organization in process terms

Environment of the organization - superior system composed of all external elements, directly or indirectly interacting therewith. The type of links between the organizations and the external elements allow differentiating the *closer environment* and *further environment.*

The management system is a set of operations:

1) performed within the area of the management function (planning, organizing, motivating, controlling) aimed at the resources of the organization (human, financial, material and informational), performed with the intention to achieve the objectives of the organization in an efficient and quick manner,
2) aimed at shaping fruitful cooperation inside the organization and matching these efforts with the requirements of its environment, in compliance with which the organization needs to function if it wants to survive.

The point of the management is to re-configure the functioning of the organization - using digital technology - in such a way that it is possible to use the full potential of the employees, business partners and clients to create and manufacture products and services with parameters satisfactory for the potential recipients in the second and next decades of the 21st century. The management changes the functioning of the organization in all its dimensions: from the organizational structures, communication, relationships with the personnel, through *information systems*, team work, arrangements with contractors, to relationships with the clients and public administration units.

For the purposes hereof, the organization is considered the system including the following sub-systems (Fig. 2):

1. The decision sub-system (control, regulation, management) - aimed at analyzing the conditions and inside of the organization, and making decisions with respect to the goals and missions as well as methods and programs of their implementation. It regulates the functioning of the organization by modifying appropriate stimuli compensating certain deviations (determined goals), which occurred during the operations of the system. It covers managerial position, hierarchical arrangements (organizational structure), and division of powers. The decision-making process requires from the decision-maker to define, analyze, assess and *take risk* as well as implement efficient measures. Due to its specificity, the system is closely related to the informational system. It is impossible to manage any organization (enterprise) with the information flow.
2. The information sub-system - an essential component of the efficient functioning of the organization, since - as mentioned above - the exchangeof information is a prerequisite for proper cooperation. The role of the informational system is to satisfy the informational needs of the decision-makers, since to make the right decision, they need to be provided with the necessary data. The informational system integrates technology with human actions in the organization. It covers all elements related to the exchange of information, i.e.: sources of origin of the information, its flow and manner of transfer, points of its collection and transformation processes. The informational management system is a set of operations and measures for collecting, finding, storing, sending and processing the information in such a manner so that it is possible to make decisions and manage an enterprise on the basis thereof.

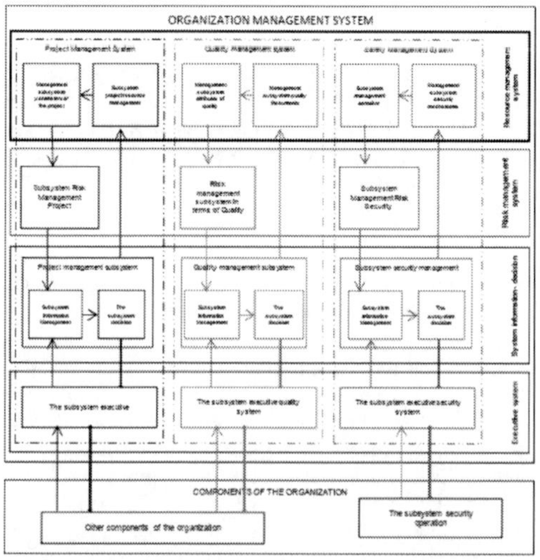

Figure 2 Sub-systems of the organization management system

3. Executive sub-system, which implements the tasks determined by the management arrangements. Its aim is to process the materials, raw materials and other resources during the technological processing. It includes direct production units, executive units, support services and other entities having direct impact on the transformation (processing) of resources and performance of services.
4. Risk management sub-system/system.

The levels of area-oriented security of the components of the organization determine the security level of the functioning of the organization. The functioning of every component (area-oriented) of the organization may be disrupted by the following:

- natural threats: floods, weather conditions, windstorms, etc.;
- technical failures of the devices and systems, e.g. interruption of power supply, IT breakdown, etc.;
- hazards of civilization: chemical, radiation, communication, etc.;
- threats results from the location and regional specificity, among other things, e.g. smuggling, ethnic and/or religious conditions, etc.;
- destructive human activity.

The particular types of risks may occur at the same time and negatively impact the components of the organization. Furthermore, they might interact synergistically, which should not be omitted in the analysis of comprehensive safety of the organization. The security of the functioning of the organization is ensured by:

- continuous prevention of occurrence of particular types of threats to the functioning of the components of the organization (facilities);
- proper preparation of the facilities and services responsible for the area-oriented protection of the organization against any potential types of risks;
- undertaking of efficient remedial actions in case of their occurrence;
- restoration of the functionality of the facilities affected by some risks after their elimination.

The security level of the organization, within the comprehensive meaning, depends on the area-oriented levels of security. A specific, area-oriented level of security of the organization may be obtained in a number of ways - not only by ensuring certain efficiency of the security system directly preventing some of the occurring events. Its value may be affected by the following:

- prevention of the occurrence of a given type of risks;
- preparation of an entity for the potential activation of a given risk;
- security in the form of an event (education, location and availability of prevention measures);
- increase in efficiency of the security measures and mechanisms, while combating the effects of a given event;
- efficiency of actions aimed at removing the effects of a given event.

Therefore, we have a possibility of shaping the area-oriented and comprehensive level of security. In this case, the controllable values are the parameters characterizing the factors affecting the security level of the organization, i.e. connected with the following:

- prevention of any potential threats to safety of the organization;
- preparation of the organization in case these threats activate;
- security mechanism combating such threats;
- removal of the effects of a given event.

2 Model of the security management system of the organization

Many misunderstandings in the evaluation of the organization's safety often result from the lack of awareness and improper line of reasoning.

In the course of many disputes and proving one's reasons, the interlocutors often forget that the safety is not a state, but a constantly changing process, whose internal and external conditions to a different (sometimes large) extent depend on an organization, to which they directly refer. Therefore, an important element in the process of ensuring internal and external security is the information security management system, which plays a key role in solving critical or crisis situations.

The security management system of the organization is a part of the entire management system, based on an approach as resulting from the business risk, referring to the establishment, implementation, use, monitoring, maintenance and improvement of the security of the organization (Fig. 3).

It is assumed that the objective of the security management sub-system of the organization is to maintain the required security level of the organization as the functional entirety and to ensure security of the sensitive materials. This objective may be achieved by current control of the executive sub-system of security measures. The security management sub-system of the organization is composed of the following sub-systems (Fig. 3):

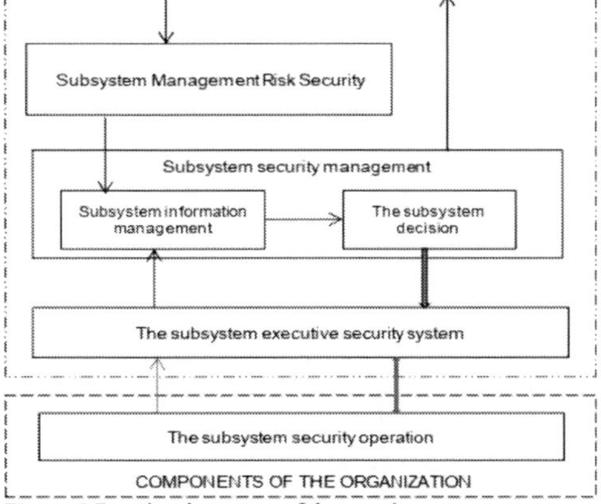

Figure 3 Functional structure of the security system

[*Organization Security Management System*]

- the security management sub-system, which implements the information and decision process, determining the manner of ensuring safety of the individual facilities in the organization by means of the executive sub-system,
- the executive sub-system, which consists of various measures for implementing executive processes,
- the security management sub-system,
- the management sub-system of sensitive materials,
- the risk management sub-system,
- the technical system supporting the management system and other components of the organization,

- the IT systems supporting the management system and other components of the organization.

The security management process in the organization should be performed in a continuous manner, constantly improved and implemented according to the plan, including the determination of the risk level, i.e. the tolerance threshold that - in case of exceeding - will make it necessary to manage this risk.

3 Model of risk management

A common mistake in the management process of an organization is separating the risk management system/process and treating it as an isolated element. Our organizations already have different systems for process management, quality management, project management, objective management as well as control and internal audit, which on hand are the perfect source of data for risk analysis, and on the other - provide knowledge of risks, vulnerability and potential of the said areas.

For the purposes hereof, the following definition of the risk management system of the organization was adopted:

"The risk management system of the organization is a set of rules, mechanisms and tools (including i.a. the policies and procedures concerning risk identification, measurement, monitoring and control) used for risk review processes in the organization".

The main task of the risk management system in the organization is risk identification, measurement or assessment and monitoring of the risk in a business activity of the organization, aimed at ensuring correctness of the process of rending office services.

3.1 Objectives, tasks, elements of the risk management system

The objective of the risk management system is permanent risk reduction, protection of sensitive resources, systems and processes, as well as protection against any potential effects of such risks. The risk management system should allow retrospective evaluation of the efficiency of actions undertaken with respect to:

- business process of the organization,
- employees and users in the organization,
- appropriate technologies.

The main tasks of the system include:

- provision of the information about risks and their profiles;
- performance of preventive actions reducing the risk and its consequences;
- monitoring of the acceptable risk level.

The elements of the operational risk management system of the organization are the following:

- strategy and policy rules of the organization with respect to risk management;
- by-laws and procedures defining the risk management process;
- the risk management structure defining the management levels as well as the scope of competency and responsibility of the persons involved in the risk management process;
- employees involved in the risk management process (their credentials);
- IT support of the process;
- management information;
- system control.

The strategy, including the policy contained therein, determines the objectives, basic rules and a set of guidelines concerning risk management. It provides grounds for developing detailed regulations and procedures.

3.2 Model of the risk management process concerning security of the organization

"Risk management" means the planned application of the management policy, procedures and practices as part of the activities concerning the risk analysis, valuation and control (Fig. 4). The risk management process supports and improves the operational efficiency of the management of the organization, as it helps to understand and assess serious risk factors. Therefore, the point of the risk management in the organization should be:

- obtaining the information about potential risks and their impact on the future form of the outside environment of the entity;
- defining the effects of the current events, which may have some impact on the functioning and the results of the organization;
- developing appropriate operational procedures (preparation for the consequences) for emergency situations, in particular for unpredictable risks.

The risk management process is a continuous process, which should be in the form of an ordered sequence of subsequent events, actions, decisions, resulting in a positive value, i.e. the security of the entity. Therefore, identification of a potential risk (crisis) is the key task aimed at avoiding surprise, such as, for example, a crisis situation. We should be aware of the fact that to efficiently deal with the risk analysis, it is crucial to define this risk as precisely as possible, by determining its causes, scope, limits and type of potential threats that may affect the achievement of the objectives stipulated by the entity.

We should realize that the risk analysis is a fundamental element of the risk management system in the organization, since during the risk analysis process, we obtain the information indispensable to make right decisions concerning the strategy of handling the risk, efficient choice of the risk reduction measures, assessment of the transfer validity, acceptance or avoidance of the rusk. From the perspective of the organization management, this important information, obtained in the course of the risk analysis, also indicates the priorities for the development of the security systems, security measures and control in the organization. Therefore, the statement that the risk analysis is used for the purpose of the mitigation (optimization) of the losses connected with the operational risk seems justified. At this point, we may ask the question why there is more and more emphasis on the risk management. The answer is pretty simple - the "real life" examples show that in case of uncertainty and a possibility of risk optimization by removing often unnecessary, inefficient, yet expensive protection measures - such approach seems to be reasonable. The traditional protection of all activity areas of the organization seems to be excessively costly and inefficient, as usually there are not enough resources (cost-effective variants). Therefore, it is necessary to not only avoid and reduce the risk, but also to efficiently manage the risk.

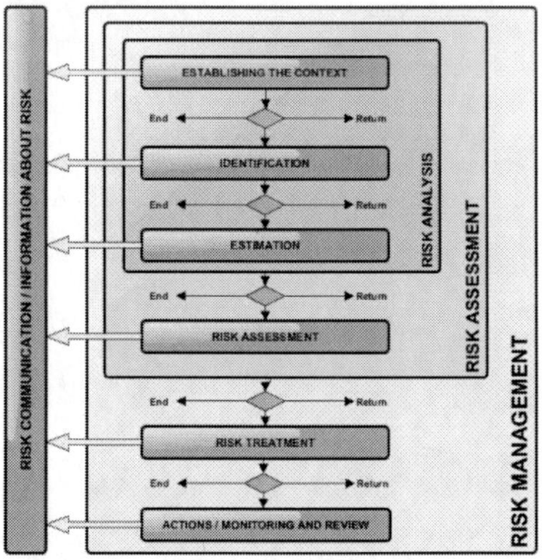

Figure 4 Model of the risk management process in the organization.

As shown in Fig. 4, the risk management process referring to the security of the organization may be iterative. The iterative approach to the risk assessment process may be in the form of increasing the level of detail of each iteration or stopping the process - after each phase/stage, there are decision points (continue, end, return).

The iterative approach ensures beneficial balance between the reduction of time and efforts spent on identifying some security measures and the certainty of the correct assessment of large risks. First, we need to set the context. Then, the risk assessment is performed. If as a result of the risk assessment, the sufficient information is obtained to determine the actions necessary for the purpose of modifying the risk to the acceptable level, then the task is considered completed and the risk handling process may commence. If the information is insufficient, the risk assessment iteration is performed once again in the changed context (e.g. risk assessment criteria, risk acceptance criteria or effect criteria), if possible, in the limited part of the entire scope. The risk acceptance should ensure that the residual risks are deliberately accepted by the management of the organization. It is especially important in the event when the security measures are not implemented or their implementation is postponed, e.g. due to costs. The efficiency of the risk handling process depends on the results of the risk assessment. It is possible that handling the risk will not lead directly to the acceptable level of the residual risk. In such case, if necessary, the next iteration of the risk assessment with the changed context parameters (e.g. risk assessment criteria, risk acceptance criteria or effect criteria) may be required, and only after this iteration, the risk is processed again.

Conclusions

Nowadays, the risk management processes with respect to the security of information should be an integral part of daily operations of every organization. To make these processes efficient, it is crucial to determine which management actions, method, techniques or tools will be the best for the organization. To efficiently implement the risk management policy in the organization, it is important to first define the objective and tasks of these units within the scope of risk management and make them compatible with the general strategy of the organization. Since the risk is an inherent part of the functioning of every organization, the risk management should be a natural activity at each level of management. It is a common opinion that the risk is always managed, but not always intentionally.

The process or processes of the risk management system constitute an element of the decision-making process, which make it easier for the managerial staff to make intentional and right decisions, determine the priority actions and recognize alternative ways of actions in case of present threats, events or critical situations.

Thanks to the risk management system, it is possible to improve the integrated security and quality management system, show the directions of the necessary changes that need to be introduced in the environment, indicate some priority actions and potential losses, if such event occurred. Such analysis enables to take preventive measures, which lead to the mitigation of the losses.

The risk analysis and assessment is the first element in the risk management process. The results of such process help to choose the appropriate systems or security methods as well as to minimize or eliminate the identified risk factors.

The risk management policy to a large extent depends on the nature of the business activity, its approach and tendency to take risks, also known as the "appetite" for risk, and business environment conditions. To support the process of introducing and maintaining the efficient risk management, it is indispensable to reach "common understanding" of the risk management system within the entire organizational unit and its environment. Without a common ground for discussion on the risk management system in the business operations of the organization, it is not possible to ensure powerful communication and introduce efficient risk management process within the entire organizational unit. It is impossible to manage something that is not explicitly defined and identified or understood in the same way by all employees of the organization. The risk management system is perceived in a different manner by the employees working on different levels of the organizational structure (higher management, medium management, average workers), responsible for particular business process (main, auxiliary processes) or located in different organization units (headquarter, branches) of the same organization. The practical solution to find the "common understanding" of the risk management system in the entire organization is to apply the standard valuation model and risk assessment model.

References

1. M. Bielski, *Podstawy teorii organizacji i zarządzania* (C.H. Beck, 2002)
2. A. Białas, *Bezpieczeństwo informacji i usług w nowoczesnej instytucji i firmie* (WNT, 2007)
3. K. Jajuga, *Zarządzanie ryzykiem* (PWN, 2009)
4. A. Korczowski, *Zarządzanie ryzykiem w projektach informatycznych. Teoria i praktyka* (Helion, 2013)
5. P. Matkowski, *Zarządzanie ryzykiem operacyjnym* (Wolters Kluwer Polska, 2006)
6. J. Monkiewicz, L. Gąsiorkiewicz, *Zarządzanie ryzykiem działalności organizacji* (Uczelnie Techniczne, 2010)
7. O. Patrick, *ISO 31000:2009 Risk management – Principles and guidelines*
8. J. Stanik, M. Kiedrowicz, *Selected aspects of risk management in respect of security of the document lifecycle management system with multiple levels of sensitivity*, Information Management in Practice, 231-251 (2015)
9. *PN ISO/IEC 27001 Information security management. Requirements*
10. *PN ISO/IEC 27005 Information technology. Security techniques. Information security risk management*
11. *PN-ISO 31000 Zarządzanie ryzykiem – Principles and guidelines*
12. *PKN–ISO GUIDE 73 Risk management – Vocabulary*

MATEC Web of Conferences **76**, 04011 (2016)
CSCC 2016 DOI: 10.1051/matecconf/20167604011

Evaluation of information safety as an element of improving the organization's safety management.

Romuald Hoffmann[1,a], Maciej Kiedrowicz[1], Jerzy Stanik[1]

[1] *The Faculty of Cybernetics, Military University of Technology, 00-908 Warsaw, Kaliskiego 2, Poland*

Abstract. The article discusses the problem of risk management in the context of safety of an organization's information assets. Assuming system of information risk management as a basic element of organization management in the aspect of information safety of modern organizations, this document focuses on methods and techniques of qualitative risk estimates. Basic standards and good practice from areas of risk management and ensuring information safety in the organization were recalled.

Introduction

Assuming that risk is an objective regularity that simple objects, processes and real world organizations are characterized by, in the age of rapid development of information technology and increasingly widespread use of IT systems, it becomes necessary to develop effective strategies, methods, evaluation systems or risk management related to operation of those facilities or systems, where the risk is defined as a threat, that the information technology used will not function the way it is expected to function.

Awareness of the risk level of organization's individual business processes or information systems within the organization allows for the effective management of such risk through the use of dedicated risk management systems for such purpose. In order to effectively manage security risk in the organization management it is necessary to determine, in a most objective manner, the level of such risk. Currently, there are many methods of the organization risk assessment, processes of information processing in the said organization or IT systems, but none of them, however, is a universal method, suitable for analysis of risks associated with an operation of both a small organization - a company, as well as complex organizations. In addition, none of the methods of analysis and risk assessment currently employed does not take into consideration, in a direct and comprehensive manner, factors such as quantitative, qualitative, economic or sociological - social factors, which on one hand is the strength of approaches currently employed through their focus on selected aspects of security, on the other hand, constitutes their weakness through far-reaching simplification of the adopted models or conditions for their development.

The proposed approach to risk assessment in security contained herein, also known as elements of "good practice" have been developed with the knowledge that along with the improvement in the system of risk management in information security and processes therein, they are subject to change.

This document defines the nature of risk, components of the system, model of risk management process, the role of risk analysis group and approaches to estimating safety of information.

1 The approach to risk assessment in information security

Risk assessment can be regarded as a process (see figure 1).

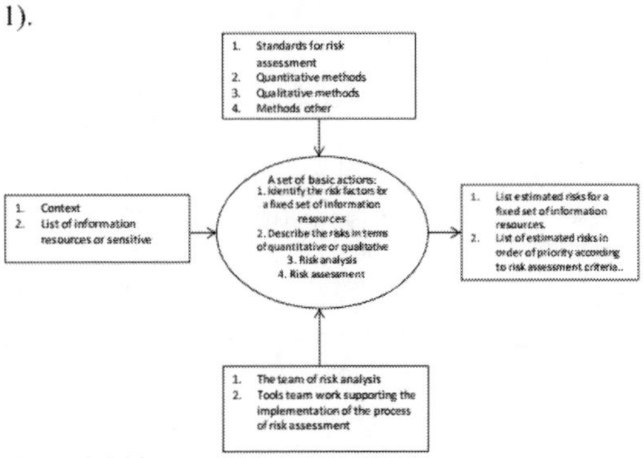

Figure 1. Risk assessment as a process.

Due to size limitations of this article only the basic elements of this process will be characterized in the remainder of this section, namely:

- Context,
- Identification of risk factors,
- Estimation of risk / Method of estimation.

[a] Corresponding author: maciej.kiedrowicz@wat.edu.pl

MATEC Web of Conferences **76**, 04011 (2016) DOI: 10.1051/matecconf/20167604011
CSCC 2016

2 Context

Establishing a context comes down to implementing the following tasks:

A. Determining the basic criteria needed for risk management in information security.
B. Defining the scope and limits of the risk management system.
C. Establish appropriate organizational structure dealing with risk management in information security.

As part of task A. (*Determination of basic criteria needed for risk management in information security*), the following operations need to be performed:

I. Choose or develop an appropriate approach to risk management, relating to the basic criteria, such as:
    1) criteria of risk management,
    2) results criteria,
    3) criteria of risk acceptance.

   While developing risk assessment criteria in information security in the organization, you should consider the following factors:
    1. The current map of business processes of the organization (figure 2.),
    2. Strategic business value of information processes,
    3. Importance of the information assets involved,
    4. Legal requirements resulting from the regulations and contractual obligations,
    5. A list of sensitive resources, as well as business and operational importance of their security attributes: availability, confidentiality, integrity, indisputability and accountability,
    6. Negative consequences for the image and reputation of the organization.

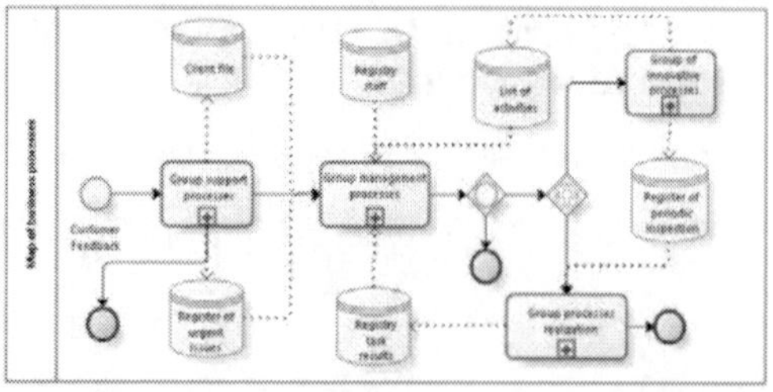

Figure 2. Sample map of business processes for a hypothetical organization.

II. Develop and determine the criteria for accepting risks taking into account the policies and objectives of the organization and the interest of the organization's employees.

III. Determine your own scale for levels of risk acceptance taking into account the following factors:
   - the criteria for accepting risks may include multiple threshold values having a desired target level of risk, but with the privilege of top company officers to accept risks exceeding the given level in certain circumstances,
   - criteria for accepting risk can be expressed as the ratio of estimated profit (or other business benefits) against the estimated risk;
   - different criteria for accepting risks may apply to different classes of risk, e.g. the risks which may result in non-compliance with regulations or provisions of law may not be accepted, whereas high risks may be accepted, if it is specified as a requirement under the contract;
   - criteria for accepting risks may include requirements relating to further additional proceedings, e.g. the risk may be accepted, if actions to reduce the risk to an acceptable level within a certain period of time are approved and carried out as an obligation.

IV. Determine a set of criteria for accepting risk, taking into account:
   - business criteria,
   - legal aspects and the resulting internal regulations,
   - usage,
   - technology,
   - finance,
   - social and human factors.

As part of task B. (*Defining a scope and limits of the risk management system)* the following steps need to be performed:

I. Determine the scope of the risk management process in information security, in order to ensure that the risk assessment takes into account all relevant assets.
    1. Basic assets:
       - Processes and business activities,
       - Information.
       - The supporting assets (which are based on the basic elements within the scope) of all kinds: Hardware, Software, Network, Personnel, Headquarter, and Organizational Structure.

II. In determining the scope and limits the organization should consider the following information:
    1. Strategic business objectives, strategies and policies,
    2. A list of key business processes,
    3. Information assets,
    4. Legal and contractual requirements resulting from the regulations and those applicable to the organization,
    5. The organization's information security policy,
    6. The organization's comprehensive approach to risk management,
    7. Locations of the organization and their geographical characteristics,
    8. Restrictions regarding the organization,
    9. Expectations of participants,
    10. Sociocultural environment,
    11. Interfaces (i.e. exchange of information with the environment).

As part of task C. (*Establishment of appropriate organizational structure dealing with risk management in information security*), it is necessary to perform the following:

I. The establishment and maintenance of the organization in addition to scope of responsibilities for the risk management process in information security. The main roles and responsibilities of such organizational structure are as follows:
   1. The development of the risk management process in the security information in a manner appropriate for the organization.
   2. Identification and analysis of the participants.
   3. Defining the roles and responsibilities of all parties, both internal and external in relation to the organization.
   4. Establishment of the required relationship between the organization and the participants, as well as interfaces to the highest management levels dealing with risk management (e.g. operational risk management) and interfaces to other relevant projects or activities.
   5. Defining decision escalation paths
   6. Defining accumulated records.

II. Establish / estimate whether the organization has the necessary Risk Analysis Team (RAT) - "*An agent of action*" - the necessary intellectual resources allowing for:
   1. Performing risk assessment and development of a strategy for dealing with risk.
   2. Define and implement policies and procedures, including the implementation of selected security.
   3. Monitoring of security measures.
   4. Monitoring the risk management process in information security.

3 Risk factors identification

The purpose of identifying risk factors is to determine what may happen causing potential loss, as well as gaining knowledge of how, where and why the loss might occur. The general scheme of the identification process is shown in Figure 3.

In order to carry out the identification of risk factors, it is recommended to conduct workshops often to discuss the list and definitions adopted for individual internal and external risks, to discuss the reasons for their occurrence and to determine the significance of individual risks for organizations and likelihood of their occurrence.

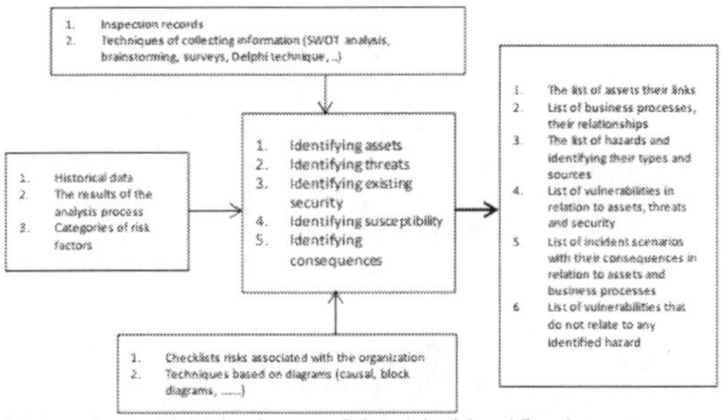

Figure 3. A general scheme of the risks identification process

These workshops allowed direct confrontation of opinions on internal and external risks inherent in the Organization formulated by the people having the most experience in working for the organization stemming from work in different areas of its operations. Collected results of the Workshops constitute a listing of risks associated with the activities of the Organization, according to importance of individual risks with detailed definitions assigned and causes for occurrence of particular risks. Manner of conducting individual risk identification is not a key element constituting its validity.

3.1 Identification of assets

Assets are anything of value to the organization and therefore require protection. When identifying assets it is recommended to take into account the fact that the information system also consists of elements other than hardware and software.

Identification of assets must be carrying out at the appropriate level of detail that will provide sufficient information for risk assessment. The level of detail used to identify the assets will have an impact on the total amount of information gathered during the risk assessment. This level of detail can be clarified in subsequent iterations of risk assessment. Each identified information resource should have its so-called "owner of the asset". The owner of the assets may not have the ownership of assets, however, (s)he is responsible for the development, maintenance and safety within the framework of assigned duties. The owner of assets is often the most appropriate person to assign a value to assets they have for the organization. After the identification of assets, the next step is a coordination of scale and criteria for the assignment of a specific point on the scale to all assets, based on the valuation of assets. Given the variety of assets operating in most organizations it is likely that part of the assets can be attributed to a specific value expressed in money, and for some you can only indicate a range of values, for example, from "very low" to "very high". The decision to use quantitative or qualitative scale depends on the preferences of the organization, but it is recommended to have a reference to the assets. Both types of assigning value can be used for the same assets. This work assumes, as the basis for valuation of assets, the costs incurred as a result of loss of confidentiality, integrity and availability as consequences of an incident. It is also recommended to consider adequate repudiation, authenticity and reliability. Such an approach takes into account essential elements during valuation of assets, as a complement to a replacement cost, based on the estimation of negative business consequences that could result from incidents related to information security, assuming a particular set of circumstances. It is emphasized that this approach takes into account the consequences that are factors introduced into the risk assessment. After determining the criteria to be taken into account, you need to align the scale uniformly throughout the organization. The first step is a decision on the number of levels to be used in the scale. There are no rules regarding the selection of the most appropriate number of levels. More levels means greater detail, but sometimes too detailed diversity makes it difficult to obtain consistent estimates for the entire organization. Usually, any number between 3 (e.g. low, medium, high) and 5 can be used as long as it remains consistent with the organization's approach to the whole process of risk assessment. Each organization can define their own limits for asset values, such as "0-low", "0,5-average" or "1-high". It is recommended that these limits are estimated according to selected criteria limits (e.g. for a potential financial loss it is recommended that the limits are expressed in pecuniary values, but to consider such risks as the risk of personnel safety, a financial valuation may be complex and not always appropriate for each organization). Finally, only the organization can decide what is considered "low" or "high" consequence. A result, which can be disastrous for a small organization, may be small or even negligible for a very large organization. Cost values assigned to each security attributes are placed in the matrix in an orderly manner. An example is shown below. For more information on identifying and evaluation of assets in relation to information security can be found in Annex B of ISO 27005 standard: 2013.

Table 1. An example of asset valuation for organization called XXX

Name of resource XXX	Financial expenses		Non-financial expenses			
Resource's safety attribute	Financial loss	Deterioration of business performance	Law violation	Personal data protection violation	Image losses	Other
Confidentiality	0	0	0.5	1	0.5	0
Availability	1	0.5	0	0	0.5	0.5
Integrity	0.5	0.5	0	0	0	0
Indisputability	0	0	0	0	1	0.5
Sum according to criteria:	1.5	1	0.5	1	2	1
Asset value:	7					

3.2 Threat identification

The threat may be a potential cause of damage to assets such as information, processes and systems, and in consequence to the organization. Threat sources may be natural or human, accidental or deliberate. It is necessary to identify both accidental and deliberate threat sources. The threat may occur inside or outside the organization. It is recommended to identify risks of general nature and by type (e.g. unauthorized actions, physical damage, technical failures) and, where appropriate, to identify individual threats within the general category identified earlier. This approach means that it will not omit any threat, including the unexpected, whereas the workload will be limited. The following table shows examples of typical threats.

Table 2. Examples of typical threats

Type	Threat	Source
Violation of information security	Law / statute violation	Accidental threat, deliberate threat
	Media or documents theft	Deliberate threat
	Data distortion	Deliberate threat
	Back-up from re-used or discarded storage carriers	Deliberate threat
	Data from unreliable sources	Accidental threat, deliberate threat
	Software forgery	Accidental threat, deliberate threat

Some risks may relate to more than one type of assets. In such cases they may cause varying results depending on the assets to which they relate. Input data used to identify threats and to estimate the likelihood of occurrence can be obtained from the asset owners or users, employees of personnel departments, administrators of facilities and information security specialist, experts on physical security, as well as from other organizations, including legal institutions, meteorological services, insurance companies and government administration bodies. While describing threats it is proper to consider environmental and social aspects. It might be useful to take into account the listing of threats (specific for the organization of the industry) during completion of general threats, if these are applicable. Catalogs and statistics of threats can be shared by industry organizations, state governments, legal institutions, insurance companies, etc..

After conducting threat identification we need to align the scale and criteria for the assignment of a specific point on the scale to each threat, based on evaluation of threats. Given the variety of threat factors occurring in the organization it is likely that some part of risks can be assigned a specific value expressed in money, and for some you can only indicate a range of values, for example, from "very low" to "very high". Normally, any number between 3 (e.g. Low, medium, high) and 5 (e.g. very low, low, medium, high, very high) can be used as long as it remains consistent with the organization's approach to the entire process of risk assessment . Each organization can define their own limits for the risk values, such as "L - low," "M - medium" or "H - high." It is recommended that these limits are estimated according to selected criteria limits (e.g. for a potential financial loss it is recommended that the limits are expressed in pecuniary values, but to consider such risks as the risk of personnel safety, a financial valuation may be complex and not always appropriate for each organization). Finally, only the organization can decide what is considered "low" or "high" consequence. A result, which can be disastrous for a small organization, may be small or even negligible for a very large organization. Threat values in the scope of individual security attributes assigned by experts are placed in the matrix in an orderly manner. An example is shown below. For more information about the types of threats and their evaluation can be found in Annex C of ISO 27005 standard: 2013.

Table 3. An example of risk valuation by experts in relation to XXX resource

Information asset: **XXX** Name of threat for the asset	Threat impact of security attribute	Expert's assessment 1	Expert's assessment 2	Expert's assessment 3	Expert's assessment 4	Expert's assessment 5	Average evaluation for a given threat
1. Law / statute violation	Confidentiality	H	H	M	H	H	H
2. Theft of media or documents	Confidentiality, Availability, Integrity	H	M	M	M	H	M
3. Data distortion	Integrity	L	M	M	M	M	M
4. Back-up from re-used or discarded storage carriers	Confidentiality, Indisputability	H	M	M	M	H	M
5. Data from unreliable sources	Confidentiality, Availability, Integrity, Indisputability	L	M	L	L	M	L
Assessment of risk to the information resource:							**M**

3.3 Identification of vulnerability

The very fact of existence of vulnerability does not cause any harm, as what is necessary is the risk using such vulnerability. The vulnerability, in case of which no relevant risk appears, may not require implementation of any security measures, yet, it is recommended to recognize it and monitor any changes with respect thereto. It is worth remembering that any security measure, which has been implemented incorrectly or functions incorrectly or is used incorrectly may cause vulnerability. The security measure may be efficient or inefficient depending on the environment, in which it operates. And vice verse, a threat without any matching vulnerability may not cause any risk. The vulnerability may be related to the properties of the assets, which may be used in an intentional manner or otherwise, at the time of purchase or creation of the assets. It becomes necessary to consider the vulnerability of the assets caused by different sources, for example, internal or external. The vulnerability may be identified within the following areas: ICT equipment, software or devices, personnel, organization, processes and procedures, management practices, physical environment, configuration of the information system, third party dependencies. The examples and assessment methods are presented in the tables below.

Table 4. Examples of vulnerability of the information resource XXX

Type of medium	Examples of vulnerability	Examples of threats
Electronic equipment	Unsecured devices for data storage	Theft of media or documents
	Lack of diligence when disposing of media	Theft of media or documents
	Uncontrolled copying	Theft of media or documents
Software	No logging out when leaving the workstation	Abuse of rights
	Use of application programs for outdated data	Data distortion
Personnel	Lack of monitoring mechanisms	Illegal data processing
	Work of third party personnel or cleaning staff without supervision	Theft of media or documents

The following table presents the examples of the vulnerability of the information resource, whose medium may be electrical equipment, software or a person.

Table 5. Example of assessment of vulnerability of the information resource XXX

Information asset: XXX Name of vulnerability of the resource	Expert's assessment 1	Expert's assessment 2	Expert's assessment 3	Expert's assessment 4	Expert's assessment 5	Average assessment of vulnerability
Unsecured devices for data storage	M	H	M	H	M	H
Lack of diligence when disposing of media	H	M	M	M	H	M
Uncontrolled copying	H	M	H	H	M	H
No logging out when leaving the workstation	H	M	M	M	H	M
Use of application programs for outdated data	H	M	H	H	M	H
Assessment of vulnerability of the information resource:						**H**

After the identification and vulnerability assessment process, the following is obtained:

1. List of vulnerability risks with respect to the assets, threats and security measures;
2. List of vulnerability risks, which do not refer to any identified threat, for the purpose of review; the vulnerability, with respect to which no relevant risk occurs, may not require implementation of the security measure, however, it is recommended to recognize it and monitor any changes with respect thereto.

The vulnerability may be related to the properties of the assets, which may be used in an intentional manner or otherwise, at the time of purchase or creation of the assets. It becomes necessary to consider the vulnerability of the assets caused by different sources, for example, internal or external.

The examples of vulnerability and methods of assessment of vulnerability are in Appendix D, ISO 27005: 2013.

4 Estimation of risk/methods of estimation

The risk analysis may be conducted at different levels of detail, depending on the criticality of the assets, level of vulnerability and incidents, which the organization experienced in the past. Depending on the circumstances, the methodology of estimation may be qualitative, quantitative or mixed. In practice, the qualitative estimation is often applied first to obtain the general indication of the risk level and to disclose serious risks. Later on, it may be necessary to perform a more specific or quantitative analysis of such serious risks, since the qualitative analysis is usually less complex and cheaper than the quantitative analysis. Below you may find a more detailed description of the methodology of estimation.

4.1 Quantitative estimation

The quantitative estimation applies a numerical scale (contrary to the description scale used in the qualitative estimation) for both the consequences and probabilities, using the data from various sources. The quality of analysis depends on the accuracy and completeness of the figures as well as correctness of the used models. In the majority of cases, the quantitative estimation uses some historical data about the incidents, thanks to which the estimation may directly address the objectives of the information security and problems of a given organization. However, the lack of such data for new risks or vulnerability related to the information security may be considered a disadvantage. The disadvantage of the quantitative estimation may appear in the event, when the actual and verifiable data are not available, hence the illusion of value and accuracy of the risk assessment is created. The quantitative methods use numerical measures, such as specific amounts of the values of the IT resources, frequency of incidents or probability of their occurrence. One of the first methods was Courtney's method published in 1975, also known as the ALE (Annual Loss Exposure).

The ALE parameter is calculated based on the following formula:

$$ALE = SLE \cdot ARO \quad (1)$$

where:

SLE (Single Loss Expectancy) – expressed in the currency, expected annual loss caused by a single incident,

ARO (Annualized Rate of Occurrence) – frequency of occurrence of an event causing loss.

SLE is expressed by the following formula:

$$ALE = AV \cdot RF \quad (2)$$

where:

AV (Asset Value) – value of an asset

RF (Exposure Factor) – percentage of the value of an asset, which will be lost due to a single event.

In the course of the risk analysis by Courtney's method, the following formula is applied to calculate ARO for the purpose of simplification:

$$ALE = \frac{10^{f+i-3}}{3} \quad (3)$$

where:

f – rate of occurrence

i - rate of loss value

The rate values are provided in table 6.

Table 6. Values of rates f and i

Rate i	Rate of occurrence	Rate f	Rate of loss
1	once per 300 years	1	$10
2	once per 30 years	2	$100
3	once per 3 years	3	$1000
4	once per 100 days	4	$10000
5	once per 10 days	5	$100000
6	once per day	6	$1000000
7	10 times per day	7	$10000000
8	100 times per day	8	$100000000

4.2 Qualitative estimation

The qualitative estimation uses qualitative attributes to describe the true scale of the potential consequences (e.g. low, medium and high) and the probability of their materialization. An advantage of this estimation is that it is easy to understand by practically all the competent employees, but it also depends on the subjective choice of the scale of attributes, which is a disadvantage. The scale may be adapted according to the circumstances, and, what is more, different descriptions may be applied to different types of risks. The qualitative estimation may be used as:

- initial review action (E.1) to identify the risks, which require a more detailed analysis (*General risk assessment concerning the information security*),
- basic action (E.2) to assess different variants of risk handling (*Detailed risk assessment concerning the information security)*.

It is recommended to use the available, actual data and information in the qualitative analysis.

E.1 General risk assessment concerning the information security

The general risk assessment allows to determine the priorities and sequence of actions. For various reasons, such as the budget, the implementation of all security measures at the same time may not be possible and only the most critical risks may be tackled during the risk handling procedure. Furthermore, it may be too early to start the detailed risk management if the management is anticipated in a year or two years time. The general risk assessment considers the business value of the information assets and the risks related to the business activity of the organization. A number of factors allow to determine whether the general risk assessment is appropriate for handling the risk:

1. business objectives, which are to be achieved by using different information assets;
2. extent to which the business activity of the organization depends on particular information assets, i.e. whether the functions considered critical for the existence of the organizations or their efficient business operations depend on the said assets or confidentiality, integrity, availability, non-repudiation, accountability and reliability of the information of the information stored and processed by such assets;
3. investment expenses incurred with respect to particular information assets, in the field of development, maintenance or replacement of assets.
4. The information assets are the assets with the directly ascribed value by the organization.

Another reason for starting the general risk assessment is its synchronization with other plans related to the change management (or continued operation). For example, full protection of the organization, system or application is not rational in the event when they are to be outsourced in the nearest future. However, it may still be worthwhile to assess the risk for the purpose of an outsourcing agreement. The iteration properties of the general risk assessment may be the following:

1. The general risk assessment may refer to the overall picture of the organization and its information systems, including the technological aspects, independent of the business issues. Therefore, the contextual analysis may concentrate better on the business and operational environment instead of the technological elements.
2. The general risk assessment may refer to a more restricted list of threats and vulnerability risks grouped into the defined categories or, to speed up the process, it may focus on the risk or attack scenarios instead of their elements.
3. The risks recognized in the general risk assessment are often more general risk areas than particular, specifically defined risks. The handling of risk is then mainly directed at selecting common security measures applicable in the entire system.
4. However, the general risk assessment, due to the fact that it refers to technological details, is more appropriate for indicating organizational and non-technical security measures as well as technical or key management aspects or common technical security measures, such as back-up copies and anti-virus software.

The advantages of the general risk management are the following:

1. an introduction of a original, simple approach increases the chances to obtain approval of the risk assessment program.
2. a possibility of creating a strategic picture of the information security in the organization, i.e. efficient planning support.
3. It is possible to allocate the resources and finances there, where they would bring the highest profits, whereas the systems, which probably need protection the most, will be addressed in the first place.

Since the initial risk analyses are conducted on a high level, which is potentially less accurate, the only possible defect of such approach may be the fact that a part of the business process or systems may not be identified as needing the second, more detailed assessment. It may be avoided if the relevant information on all aspects of the organization and its information systems, including the data obtained on the basis of the incident assessment related to the information security, is provided. If such factors are assessed, the decision becomes easier. In the event when the objectives of the asset data are especially important for further business operations of the organization or if the assets face significant risk, it is recommended to perform another iteration, detailed risk assessment of the indicated information assets (or part thereof). The general rule to apply: if the lack of security of the information causes negative consequences for the organization, its business processes or assets, the second risk assessment iteration, at a more detailed level, is required for the purpose of identifying potential risks.

E.2 Detailed risk assessment concerning the information security

The detailed risk assessment process concerning the information security covers in-depth identification and evaluation of assets, assessment of threats for such assets and assessment of vulnerability. The results of such activities are later used for the risk assessment and identification of variants of handling the risk. The detailed activities usually require a lot of time, efforts and skills, therefore, they are more suitable for the high-risk information systems. Many methods use tables and combine the subjective and empirical measures. It is important for the organization to apply the method, which is the most convenient and reliable for the organization and which produces repeatable results. One of the methods/techniques based on tables is presented below.

Assumptions

Z1. The risk may be described by the following relations:

$$R : \mathrm{Z} \times \mathrm{P} \times S \to \mathrm{N} \tag{4}$$

where:

R - function of relations, defined as follows:

$$r(z, p, s) = n; z \in \mathrm{Z}, p \in \mathrm{P}, s \in S \tag{5}$$

Z ={L, M, H}; - a set of values reflecting the level of risk to a resource (a possibility of materialization of the risk): L- low risk level, M – medium risk level, H – high risk level;

P={L, M, H};- a set of values reflecting the criterion for easiness of use of the information resource by the risk (a level of vulnerability of the resource, where: L- low use level, M – medium use level, H – high ruse level);

S={1, 2, 3, 4, 5, 6, 7, 8, 9,...};- a set of values reflecting a level of losses, in case of loss of the security attributes ascribed to the resource,

N - a set of numbers reflecting the risk measures on the adopted scale, e.g. from 1 to 13 for each combination.

Z2. Relations of R and the values of the risk measures are on the matrix - table 6, with the predefined values, in an organized way.

Table 7. Risk matrix - example

	Risk possibility	Low (L)			Medium (M)			High (H)		
	Easy use	L	M	H	L	M	H	L	M	H
Resource value (level of losses)	1	**1**	**2**	**3**	**2**	**3**	**4**	**3**	**4**	**5**
	2	**2**	**3**	**4**	**3**	**4**	**5**	**4**	**5**	**6**
	3	**3**	**4**	**5**	**4**	**5**	**6**	**5**	**6**	**7**
	4	**4**	**5**	**6**	**5**	**6**	**7**	**6**	**7**	**8**
	5	**5**	**6**	**7**	**6**	**7**	**8**	**7**	**8**	**9**
	6	**6**	**7**	**8**	**7**	**8**	**9**	**8**	**9**	**10**
	7	**7**	**8**	**9**	**8**	**9**	**10**	**9**	**10**	**11**
	8	**8**	**9**	**10**	**9**	**10**	**11**	**10**	**11**	**12**
	9	**9**	**10**	**11**	**10**	**11**	**12**	**11**	**12**	**13**

The colors in the above table have the meaning defined below:

- grey - area of acceptable risk,
- white - area of unacceptable risk,
- red - area of unacceptable risk of critical values.

Using these risk assessment methods, the current or suggested assets are evaluated in terms of replacement costs (i.e. quantitative measurements). The costs are then represented on the same qualitative scale as the scale used for the information resources of the information (see 3.1.). The applicable vulnerability and corresponding threats are considered for each type of assets. If there is vulnerability without a corresponding threat or a threat without corresponding vulnerability, currently, there is no risk (yet it is still recommended to monitor the changes of such situation). The correct line in the matrix is defined by the value of assets, and the correct column - by a possibility of materialization of a threat and easiness of use. For example, if the given assets have value 3, the risk is "high (H)" and vulnerability low "L", then the risk measure is 5. Let us assume that the given assets have value 2, e.g. for the purpose of modification, the level of risk is "low" and the easiness of use defined as high "H", then the risk measure is 4. The size of the matrix, from the point of view of the number of the risk probability category and the number of the asset evaluation category, may be adapted to the needs of the organization. Additional lines and columns may define, if necessary, additional risk measures. The advantage of such approach is the obtaining of the risk ranking, which should be addressed in the further steps.

5 Summary of the risk assessment process

In the risk assessment process, the following is defined:

1) value of the information assets,
2) identification of applicable risks,
3) existing (or potential) vulnerability,
4) identification of existing security measures and their impact on identified risk,
5) potential consequences,
6) indication of priorities of the obtained risks and their order in accordance with the criteria of risk assessment set during determined during the context setting.

The risk assessment is often performed in two (or more) iterations:

1) the first one consists in the general assessment performed to identify potentially high risks, which give a possibility of further assessment.
2) the second one covers subsequence, more detailed considerations regarding potentially high risks disclosed in the first iteration.

If it does not provide sufficient information for the risk assessment, a further, more detailed analysis is performed, presumably for the part of the entire scope and possibly using another method. The choice of the risk assessment approach, including the objectives of the risk assessment, depends on the organization.

Conclusions

The risk analysis and management (risk management system) constitute grounds for the management activities in the organization, aimed at minimizing the losses related to a critical situation or risk of the information security. It is a tool (element) supporting the indication of such area of activity of the organization, which should be verified and analyzed in the first place.

Regular and continuous risk analysis and management contribute to the improvement of efficiency and obtaining of consistent, comparable and reliable results. It should be remembered that the action-based approach to risk management may cause materialization of some serious undetected risks. Unfortunately, it is a difficult issue, which requires careful preparation and determination of a set of possible risk factors, building of awareness and proper merit-based approach of persons who analyze the risks in the security and quality management processes of the organization. It is necessary to apply the right approach, including comprehensive risk management in the organization, and not just risk assessment for some individual areas. At this point, it is important to analyze the basic rules of risk management in the context, whose application brings profits to the organization.

The risk analysis and management concerning the information security must be an integral part of the decision-making process, which contributes to the making of conscious and right choices, establishment of priorities of activities and recognition of alternative directions of actions in case of the existing threats, events and critical situation. The correct risk analysis is based on the best practices and available sources of information, such as historical data, experiences, feedback information from all the interested parties, observations, forecasts and opinion of experts, including their variety and limitations, hence, it at the same time, contributes to the collection of data from many sources, including and explicitly defining a level of their uncertainty.

The risk analysis and assessment constitute the first element in the risk management process. The results of this process help to choose the right systems of security methods and to minimize or eliminate the identified risk factors. The risk management policy to a large extent depends on the nature of business, its approach and tendency to take risk, also known as the risk "appetite", and business environment. To support the process of introducing and maintaining efficient risk management, it is indispensable to work out a "common understanding" concerning the risks within the entire organizational unit and its environment. Without a common ground for discussion on the risks accompanying business operations of the organization, it is not possible to ensure powerful communication and introduce efficient risk management process within the entire organizational unit. It is also impossible if the subject concept is not understood in the same way by all employees of the organization. The risk is perceived in a different manner by the employees working on different levels of the organizational structure, responsible for particular business process (or located in different organization units of the same organization. The practical solution to find the "common understanding" concerning the risks within the entire organization is to use the standard valuation and risk assessment model.

References

1. T. Aven, *Risk assessment and risk management: Review of recent advances on their foundation*, European Journal of Operational Research, **253**: 1-13 (2016)
2. J. Aagedal, D. Braber, T. Dimitrakos, B. Gran, D.Raptis, K. Stolen, *Model-based risk assessment to improve enterprise security. In: Proceedings of the sixth international enterprise distributed object computing conference.* EDOC'02. 51–62, (2002)
3. F. Baiardi, C. Telmon, D. Sgandurra, *Hierarchical, model-based risk management of critical infrastructures*, Reliability Engineering and System Safety, **94**, 1403-1415 (2009)
4. A. Białas, *Bezpieczeństwo informacji i usług w nowoczesnej instytucji i firmie*, (WNT, 2007)
5. I. Eusgeld, C. Nan, S. Dietz., *"System-of-systems" approach for interdependent critical infrastructures, Reliability Engineering and System Safety*, **96**, 679-686 (2011)
6. K. Jajuga, *Zarządzanie ryzykiem*, (PWN, 2009)
7. A. Korczowski., *Zarządzanie ryzykiem w projektach informatycznych. Teoria i praktyka*, (Helion, 2013)
8. P. Matkowski, *Zarządzanie ryzykiem operacyjnym*, (Wolters Kluwer Polska, 2006)
9. J. Monkiewicz, L. Gąsiorkiewicz, *Zarządzanie ryzykiem działalności organizacji*, (Uczelnie Techniczne, 2010)
10. O. Patrick, *ISO 31000:2009 Risk management – Principles and guidelines* (2009)
11. J. Stanik, M. Kiedrowicz, *Selected aspects of risk management in respect of security of the document lifecycle management system with multiple levels of sensitivity*, Information Management in Practice, **18**, 231-251 (2015)
12. *PN ISO/IEC 27001 Information security management systems. Requirements*
13. *PN ISO/IEC 27005 Information technology. Security techniques. Information security risk management*
14. *PN-ISO 31000 Zarządzanie ryzykiem – Zasady i wytyczne*
15. *PKN–ISO GUIDE 73 Risk management - Terminology*
16. *Probabilistic Risk Assessment Procedures Guide for NASA Managers and Practitioners*, NASA/SP-2011-3421, Sec.Ed. (2011)

MATEC Web of Conferences 76, 04012 (2016) DOI: 10.1051/matecconf/20167604012
CSCC 2016

Software simulator for property investigation of document management system with RFID tags

Maciej Kiedrowicz[1], Tadeusz Nowicki[1,a], Robert Waszkowski[1], Zbigniew Wesołowski[1], Kazimierz Worwa[1]

[1]The Faculty of Cybernetics, Military University of Technology, 00-908 Warsaw, Kaliskiego 2, Poland

Abstract. The study outlines the method for examining the properties of the RFID-tagged document management system. The system is composed of computers, where the software for supporting processes of the RFID-tagged documents was installed. Furthermore, the system cooperates with many other elements of the secret office (cabinets, sluices, photocopiers, desks). The examination of the properties of the RFID-tagged document management system is, in this case, complex due to the number of a possible examination scenarios. The simulation method for examining the system properties was proposed. It allows to conduct the examination of the properties in a short period of time for numerous testing scenarios.

1 Introduction

The flow of paper documents in public administration, commercial companies and other organizations is connected with the registration of many important legal deeds or personal documents, administrative decisions, bank decisions, etc. It is also worth mentioning that even though such documents are more and more often replaced by their electronic equivalents, the paper documentation is still required from the formal point of view. At different levels of public administration, the secret offices are established to collect the documents for the purpose of their efficient archivization and quick identification of their properties in that respect.

For some time now, the RFID (radio-frequency identification) (Heinrich [6]) tags have been used for the document flow processes. It is of great importance for both the public administration (Maniva et. al. [8]) and other organizations (Bose et. al. [4]), including health care (Wang et. al. [13]), logistic (Whang [14] and Stambaugh et. al. [12]), production (Araújo Filho et. al. [2]) and other institutions.

The technology allows to permanently attach the RFID markers (labels, tags) to documents, which - when subject to radiation from waves generated by appropriate antennas - send signals from such markers registering their presence in a certain distance from the antennas. Thus, the RFID-tagged documents are passive objects. If there is no radiation from the antennas, they do not send any signals across the ether. If the antennas work properly, the reading system allows identification of many tags present at the same time within the reading field.

It is also worth adding that, nowadays, the RFID tags are not something much different from traditional documents, without such markers. The RFID tags have recently undergone a substantial transformation in terms of their size. The RFID-tagged document shown in Fig. 1 does not differ much from a traditional document, and the size of the RFID tag is getting smaller and smaller, to approximately 10 square centimeters.

However, when bearing in mind the fact that the RFID antennas send signal with certain frequency, it is possible to establish a modern system for managing the RFID-tagged documents. Such system allows to register a number of events in a room, where the RFID-tagged document management system with the RFID antennas is located. The basic events include:

- occurrence of new documents with the RFID tags,
- taking away of a single RFID-tagged document or a package thereof outside the area of the antennas,
- relocation of the RFID-tagged document within the area of operation of the antennas,
- registration of new documents with the RFID tags,
- etc.

The implementation of the RFID-tagged document management system requires specialist environment, composed of a couple of elements, which creates a computer-assisted identification process of the document flow within a certain predefined area.

One of the most important examination of the properties of the RFID-tagged document management system consisted in developing a number of scenarios of events, which may appear during the operation of the system. There may be many of such scenarios. It must be remembered that in the course of the examination, the following should be taken into consideration:

- the number of the RFID-tagged documents may be changed,

[a] Corresponding author: tadeusz.nowicki@wat.edu.pl

- the location of the documents in particular cabinets may be each time different,
- the changes of location of the RFID-tagged documents may be subject to various activities of their users,
- different activities are registered in many locations in the databases of the system,
- every activity is the implementation of the adopted business processes,
- some new RFID-tagged documents appear in the system and some of them disappear from the system.

All of this creates an increase of the different variants of examining the properties of the system. The examination would entail a large number of the scenarios of activities of the system users. The examination of the properties would last too long. It also should be remembered that some of the characteristics of the use of the RFID-tagged documents are not homogeneous in time. They change quite often, which is caused by the fact that some RFID-tagged documents disappear from the system and the new ones appear. The frequency of use of particular documents also changes, since their relevance changes. It means that after some time, the examination of the system properties should be repeated.

Therefore, a concept of building a simulator (Fishman [5] and Perros [9]) of signals informing about different activities of the users of the RFID-tagged document management system emerged. The simulator may operate in the network environment (Sinclair [11]). It allows to prepare a number of program scenarios of physical implementation of activities of the users. The program scenarios of activities may be generated automatically. Their number is not limited, since what will be examined are the reactions of the RFID-tagged document management system, which takes place in a practically insignificant period of time. Such examination of the system properties is usually performed when we deal with the research into the IT systems with a large number of possible external and internal events.

The study outlines the simulation method for examining the properties of the RFID-tagged document management system, allowing to conduct complex research into its significant user features in a relatively short period of time.

2 Environment of the RFID-tagged document management system

We assume that the registration of the RFID-tagged documents is within the area of the widely understood secret office of the public administration. We may attempt to outline the structure of such secret office. Its elements, apart from the typical components, using the RFID technology, are the following:

- entrance sluice with the RFID antennas as the access terminal to the secret office,
- cabinets with the RFID antennas with the control unit,
- cabinets with the RFID antennas without the control unit,
- reading tunnel for the RFID-tagged documents,
- RFID tray reader,
- specialist photocopier with the RFID module,
- printer server,
- software server for registering RFID tags,
- software server of the RFID-tagged document management system.

The entrance sluice with the RFID antennas is for registering the documents brought into or taken away from the secret office. The person entering or leaving the secret office also has the RFID tag in the form of a special personal chip. The cabinets with the RFID antennas are natural storage for the documents in the secret office. The reading tunnel for the documents is used by the users of the secret office to file the documents brought and left in the office, including removal of the already held documents from the catalog. Similarily, the tray reader is used for registering single documents with the RFID tags. The specialist RFID printer registers the fact of copying a document. Thanks to its in-built verification system, it may check whether the document can or cannot be copied, by whom and in which number of copies.

Fig. 1 presents the architecture of the model execution environment for the computer RFID-tagged document management system. At the bottom of the figure, some symbolic external devices with the RFID-tagged documents are presented. They include:

- computer workstation for an employee of the secret office,
- cabinets with the RFID antennas with the control unit,
- cabinets with the RFID antennas without the control unit,
- reading tunnel for the RFID-tagged documents,
- RFID tray reader,
- specialist photocopier with the RFID module,
- entrance sluice to the secret office,
- manual RFID tag reader,
- and printer server.

All these devices connect with the RFID-tagged document management system via a computer network controlled by the network router.

The RFID-tagged document management system is composed of the following elements:

- Aurea BPM server describing potential activities of the system users,
- Cosmos server responsible mainly for the printer (photocopier) operations in the system,
- Nofilis server allows to configure the system (indication of the compatible devices in the secret office) and receive signals from the devices with the RFID-tagged documents.

The servers create a computer environment responsible for the RFID-tagged document flows in the system. The server software is the result of the work of the designers of the RFID-tagged document management system.

 DOI: 10.1051/matecconf/20167604012

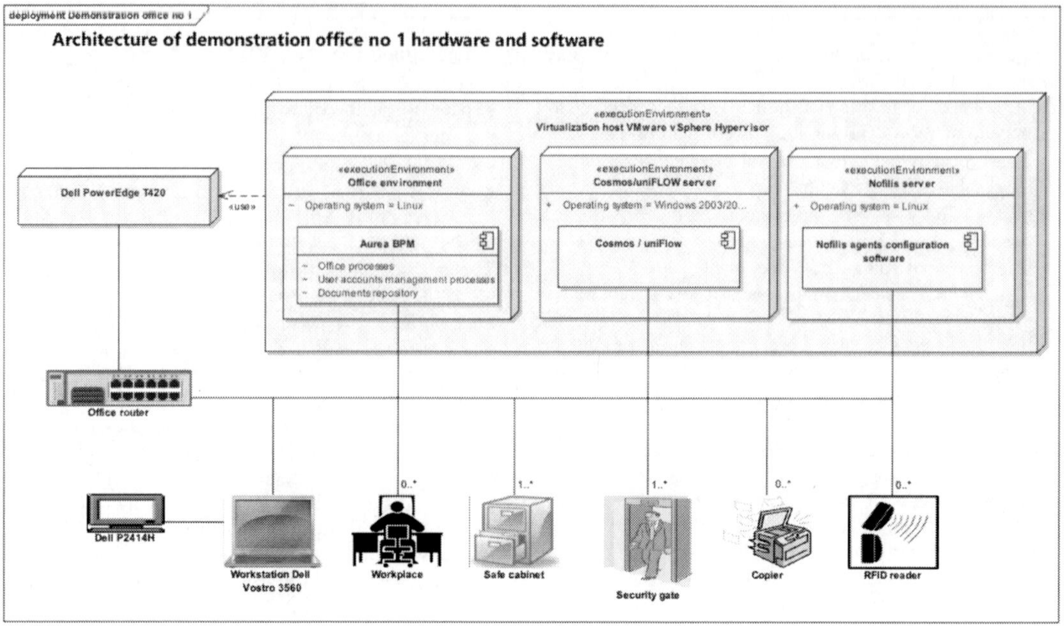

Fig. 1 Model execution environment of the computer RFID-tagged documents management system. Source: own elaboration.

The manner of communication between the devices of the servers of the system needs to be explained. CrossTalk is responsible for such communication. Every device in the secret office is accompanied by the CrossTalk agent, which sends the information to the system in case of any action involving the RFID-tagged documents or other action, such the opening or closing of the cabinet, entering of the user to the sluice, copying of the document, etc.

The messages are in the form of XML character strings. The XML documents in CrossTalk are used to describe the data and events in the system. They are sent over the network to the Aurea server. The server identifies and archives the documents in its database. Fig. 2 shows an example of the XML message.

```
<?xml version="1.0" encoding="UTF-8"?>
<events>
<event type="com:nofilis:crosstal
k:event:tag-observation"
timestamp="1417780363293" uuid="CCDEDBCA-
6D07-2076-5CAE-C1DBC42DEE5D" loca-
tionId="CABINET_3.R" objectId="C01B2916">
<id="first-read" value="1417780363291" />
<id="last-read" value="1417780363291" />
<id="observationUUID" value="73B00D24-C3B6-
25FB-CFD1-F59157FC3856" />
<id="reads" value="1" />
</event>
</events>
```

Fig. 2 Model XML documents defining the manner of handling an event

The XML message attributes, including their values, are contained in the following table.

Table 1. Descriptions of attributes of the XML documents defining the manner of handling an event

No.	Attribute	Description of the attribute value
1	timestamp	The value of this attribute is a timestamp of the RFID tag reader of the document. The value of the timestamps is expressed in the Unix time.
2	uuid	The value of this attribute is an event identifier - *tag-observation*.
3	objectId	The value of this attribute is the RFID tag of the document.
4	locationId	The values of this attribute are names of storage locations of the RFID-tagged documents and names of operations performed on these documents. The value of *[Cabinet name].A* means that from the cabinet called*name* the RFID tag of the document was read. The value of this tag is saved in the form of the value of attribute *objectId*. The value of*[Cabinet name].R* means that from the cabinet called *name*the RFID-tagged document was removed, whose value is equal to the value of attribute *objectId*.

5	id="first-read"	The value of this attribute is the timestamp of the read-out of the first RFID tag of the document from the set of documents located in a place defined by the value of attribute *locationId*. The value of the timestamps is expressed in the Unix time.
6	id="last-read"	The value of this attribute is the timestamp of the read-out of the RFID tag of the document from the set of documents located in a place defined by the value of attribute *locationId*. The value of the timestamps is expressed in the Unix time.
7	id="observationUUID"	The value of this attribute is the identifier of the read-out session of the RFID tags of the documents located in a place defined by the value of attribute *locationId*.
8	id="reads" value="1"	The value of this attribute is the number of read-outs of single RFID tags executed by technical devices included in the RFID cabinet. The default value of this attribute is 1.

The XML messages are the only results, from the point of view of the system, of the activities of the user in the secret office, involving the RFID-tagged documents. Therefore, the generation of the XML messages from the simulator and sending them to Aurea will make the system register the activities of the users in the secret office, even though they have not actually occurred.
It will allow to quickly examine the practical and functional properties of the RFID-tagged document management system, without the necessity of undertaking long-term activities by the users, hence developing complex and numerous scenarios of the functioning of the secret office. This is the approach applied by the simulation method for examining the properties of the RFID-tagged document management system.

3 Workflow processes in the secret office with the RFID-tagged documents

The fundamental concept of executing the computer system supporting the RFID-tagged document flow management is based on the definition of the business processes related to the document flow in the secret office. Development of the models of the document flow processes allows to automate the registration procedure in the secret office. Thanks to a user-friendly interface of the system, the employees of the secret office, do not need to fill out any detailed forms related to the receipt, issuance, creation, etc. of the documents, but only select and tick certain options available in the graphic user interface. Any entries made into the system with respect to the description of the operations made on the documents, their names, purpose, flow history, modifications, moments of incorrect identification, etc., are automatically implemented by the system.
The case models concerning document flows also allow to monitor the status of the RFID-tagged documents held in the secret office. It is possible to turn on the frequency option for monitoring the document status in the secret office, which will be automatically initiated from time to time. In case of any irregularities, the alarm signal will be sent. Obviously, at the beginning of the operations of the secret office, when the personnel is not sufficiently trained, such signals will occur on a daily basis. However, with time, they should be completely eliminated.
The process models related to the flow of the RFID-tagged documents may be also used for examining the characteristics of the document flow, which is the main issue discussed herein. It should be also stressed that at the stage of defining the document flow processes, no significant features are noticeable with respect to the capacity and reliability of the support system in the secret office.
The main business processes related to the functioning of the secret office in terms of the RFID-tagged documents, include the following:

- acceptance or the RFID-tagged document or documents from a natural person,
- acceptance of the parcel including the RFID-tagged documents, bearing some traces of opening,
- performance of standard activities when accepting the RFID-tagged documents,
- registration of correspondence in the form of the RFID-tagged documents,
- inclusion of a confidentiality clause in the RFID-tagged documents,
- registration of the created RFID-tagged documents,
- processes related to the storage of the RFID-tagged documents,
- preparation of the RFID-tagged documents for sending,
- sending of the RFID-tagged documents by a carrier,
- sharing of the RFID-tagged documents,
- destruction of the RFID-tagged documents.

The procedure of accepting the parcel containing the documents may be a good example of the business process related to the functioning of the secret office. The example was presented in Fig. 3

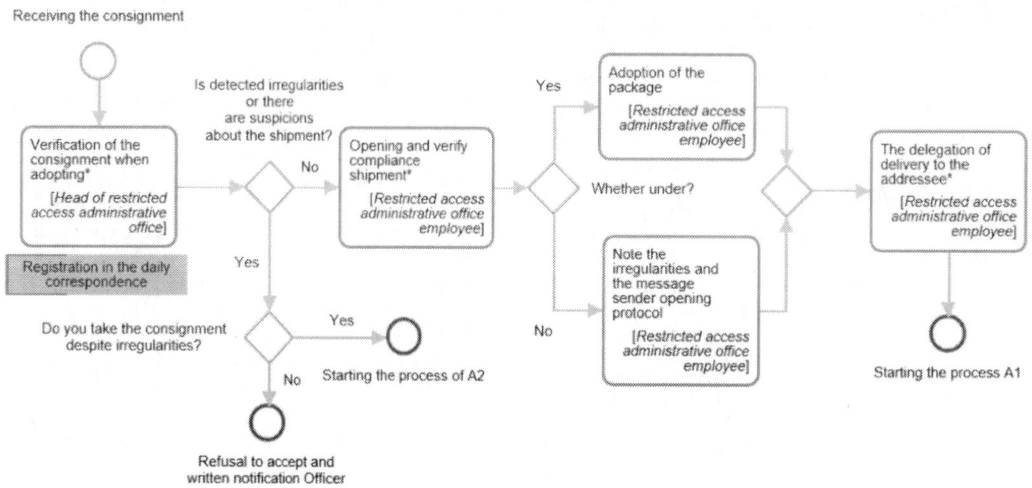

Fig. 3 Acceptance of the parcel containing the RFID-tagged document. Source: own elaboration.

The process is based on the following steps, which must be performed by an employee of the secret office. The process is initiated at the time of accepting the parcel by the employee of the secret office, who enters the date of receipt in the initial form and puts other information in the book of deliveries/list of delivered parcels, and approves the action. Subsequently, the Manager of the SO accepts the parcel and checks its contents. The Manager enters the information on the sender and recipient, confirms safe receipt of the parcel and includes the information about checking the compliance of the parcel. The Manager of the SO checks if any irregularities were found during the verification procedures or whether any suspicions exist with respect thereto. If so, the Manager decides on whether the parcel should be accepted, despite such irregularities, or not (If not, the Manager refuses to accept the parcel and informs thereof a responsible person in writing. The end of the process. If yes, the process of "acceptance of the parcel including the RFID-tagged documents, bearing some traces of opening" is initiated). If not, the Manager provides the employee of the secret office with the parcel. The employee of the secret office must open the parcel and check its contents in terms of the serial numbers listed in the inside envelope. The employee must verify which documents in the parcel already have the RFID tags. The employee must verify the number of pages, appendices and pages of appendices in accordance with the number indicated on particular materials. If the employee finds any irregularities, (s)he will make a relevant entry in the parcel opening report, defining the defects and making a comment about this fact in the correspondence logbook. Subsequently, the employee must attach the aforesaid reports and send them to the sender. The employee must accept the parcel. If necessary, the employee must put the RFID tags on the documents, which lack such markers, but should have them. The employee of the secret office must send the parcels to the addressees in different manners, depending on whether the matter is urgent or not. The process of the "registration of correspondence in the form of the RFID-tagged documents" is initiated. The employee must put a note about this fact in the "Comments" of the recording device. The process of the "registration of correspondence in the form of the RFID-tagged documents" is initiated.

To illustrate the complexity of the RFID-tagged document flow processes in the secret office, we may show the procedure related to the registration of the RFID-tagged documents in administrative office (Fig. 4).

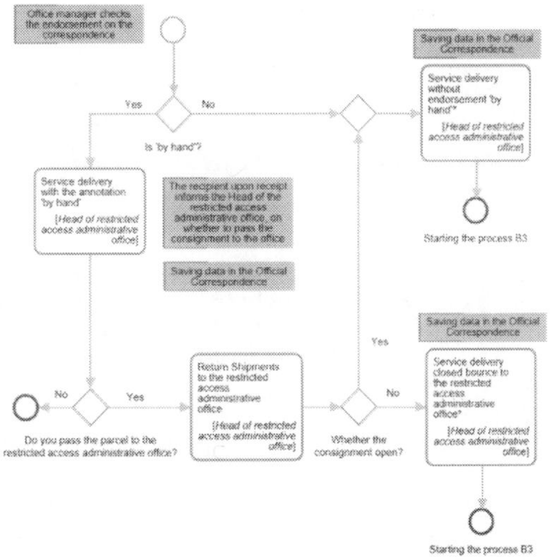

Fig. 4 Process related to registration of the RFID-tagged documents in administrative office.
Source: own elaboration.

4 Investigation of the workflow processes of the RFID-tagged document management system

The main issue concerning the examination of the characteristics of the document flow processes is to define the capacity and reliability properties on the support system implemented in the secret office. In natural conditions, the examination of the software properties would be very time-consuming. However, it is necessary before the accepting the system for use.

The basic features subject to the examinations and the capacity and reliability properties. As part of the examination of capacity and reliability,using previously developed methodologies and reliability characteristics, the following will be subject to examination:

- remote identification of documents and media, open and classified, in locations of storage and real-time work,
- automatic inventory of documents and media, open and classified, stacked up,
- automatic detection of relocation of marked documents and media,
- control system of the document and media flow,
- verification of the procedures and mechanisms for authentication of persons and documents,
- electronic system for protecting documents and media against unauthorized relocation and identification of documents and media at workplaces,
- method of protection against multiple copying of documents and printing with a limited number of copies,
- identification of location of a single document and medium with predefined accuracy,
- proper functioning of the sluice.

As part of the capacity examination, among other things, the following will be checked:

- efficient volume (number) of sets of marked documents in the selected procedures of their flow,
- duration of identification of the set of the marked documents and media in the selected procedures of their flow,
- analysis of significance of the impact of typical and random changes of the system working conditions (disruptions) on its correct functioning.

5 Simulation method for examining the workflow processes

To achieve this objective, the original working environment of the secret office was changed, according to Fig. 5. In such case, it would be necessary to implement a number of scenarios of events related to the messages sent between the RFID software agents from the third party device to the RFID system server. Furthermore, it would be indispensable to track the reactions of the server of the document flow system to the occurring events. The number of the examined scenarios, together with their internal diverse repeatability, would be so large that the study would take months.

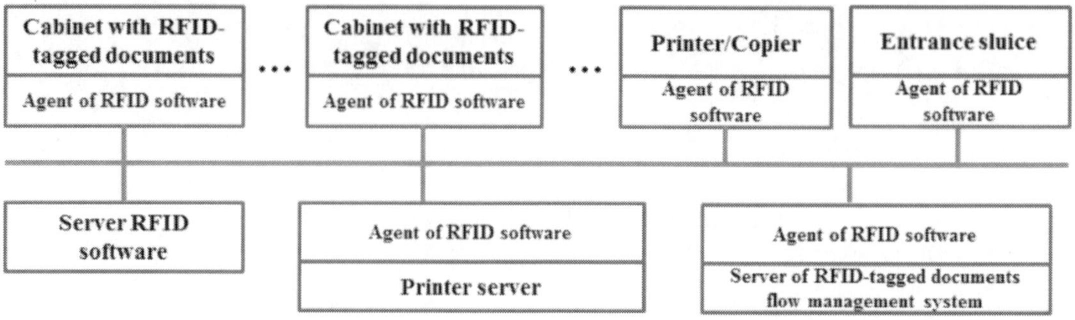

Fig. 5 System supporting the RFID-tagged document flow. Source: own elaboration.

It was decided to apply an innovative method of examination of the reliability and capacity properties of the system. We constructed a simulator imitating the events related to the document flow and - in this case - generating the signals about the change of the location of RFID-tagged documents in the system of the secret office. The event simulators imitating the functioning of the technical system were described, among other things, in terms of a model in the monograph (Fishman [5]) or (Ross [10]), and in terms of implementation - in (Abu-Taieh et. al. [1]) and (Sinclair [11]).
Normally, the RFID server is only used for the purpose of configuration of the environment, where the devices being the components of the secret office, are defined. On the other hand, the existence of the RFID-tagged documents are registered thanks to the fact that the RFID antennas send messages to the RFID software agents, which in turn send the signals to the document flow system. The messages are in the form of XML character strings. Therefore, the idea to build the simulator of the XML messages, imitating the existence or non-existence, or relocation of the documents in the system, was conceived.
The support system for the RFID-tagged document flow was thus transformed from Fig. 5 to artificial environment illustrated in Fig. 6.

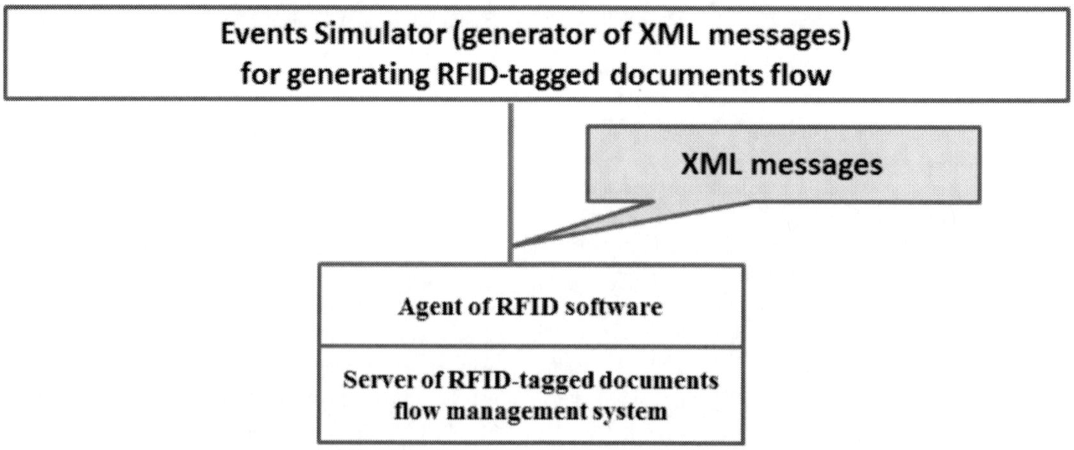

Fig. 6 Process related to the storage of the RFID-tagged documents Source: own elaboration.

It created a possibility of earlier creation of the scenarios related to the examination of the RFID-tagged documents held in the secret office, including their location. In such a way, it is possible to examine - in a definite and short period of time - the capacity and reliability properties of the system in the secret office, in terms of the application software of the document flow management server and correct functioning of the entries in the database. Without the aforesaid modification, the examination of such properties would be very time-consuming.
Obviously, the examination of the proper functioning of some peripheral devices, such as the cabinets, printer, sluices, etc. is performed in a standard manner, yet the number of experiments is relatively small and takes little time. The structure and basic functionality of the simulator was shown in Fig. 7.

 DOI: 10.1051/matecconf/20167604012

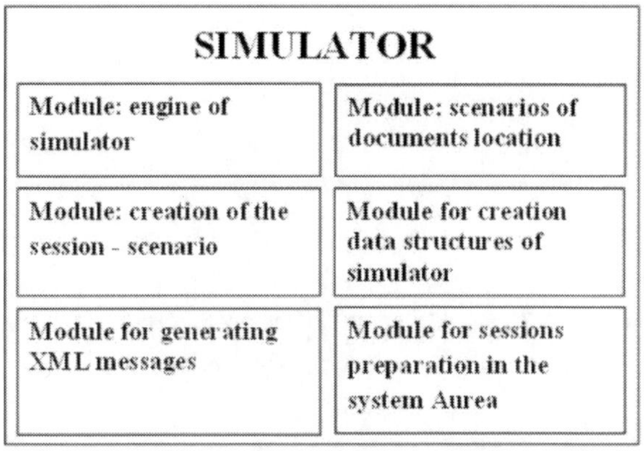

Fig. 7 Structure of the simulator for the information flow about the documents. Source: own elaboration.

6 Conclusions

The main functions of the suggested solution include the RFID-tagged document flow management , access control to the documents and supervision of their copying, as well as access management. The additional benefit of the designed solution, apart from the better control of the document storage and access, will be a possibility of tracking the flow paths of the open and classified media and documents between the safety zones, with the indication of persons authorized to use the documentation. Obviously, the main users of the system will be public administration units, including those subordinate to the Ministry of Defense and the Ministry of the Interior and Administration. An important field of interest as regards the results of the discussed project will be also the area of justice and health care institutions.

The implementation of the results will contribute to the development and increase of competitiveness of the sector of document flow in Poland, mainly because such advance solutions, based on radio and automatic identification of the documents, are not available in Europe. Thanks to the said technology, many Polish institutions and enterprises, not only state-owned, but also private, may become the leading suppliers of the subject solutions on the European market and later - also worldwide.

References

1. E.M. Abu-Taieh, A.A.R. El Sheikh, *Handbook of research on discrete event simulation environments: Technologies and applications*, IGI Global, Hershey, New York (2010)
2. F.W.C.Araújo Filho, X.L. Travassos, P.S. Figueiredo, *Use of the RFID technology to overcome inefficiencies in the production process: an analysis of a microcomputer company in Ilhéus – Bahia*, Journal of Information Systems and Technology Management. Vol. 11, No. 1, pp. 65-84 (Jan/Apr., 2014)
3. D. Barnard-Wills, D. Ashenden, *Public sector engagement with online identity management*, Identity in the Information Society, Volume 3, Issue 3, pp. 657-674 (December 2010)
4. I. Bose, E.W.T. Ngai, T.S.H. Teo, S. Spiekermann, *Managing RFID projects in organizations*, European Journal of Information Systems 18, pp. 534-540 (December 2009)
5. G.S. Fishman, *Discrete event simulation. Modeling, programming and analysis*, Springer, New York, (2001)
6. C. Heinrich, *RFID and Beyond*. Wiley Publishing, Indianapolis (2005)
7. J. Kannry, S. Emro, M. Blount, M. Ebling, *Small-scale Testing of RFID in a Hospital Setting: RFID as Bed Trigger*, AMIA Annual Symposium Proceedings Archive, pp. 384–388 (2007)
8. T. Maniva, H. Sugano, M. Kato, *Mass Data Read/Write Technology for UHF-Band RFID Tags*, Fujitsu Sci. Tech. J., 43,4,p.464-468 (October 2007)
9. H. Perros, *Computer simulation techniques – the definitive introduction*, North Carolina State University, Raleigh (2009)
10. S. M. Ross, *Simulation*, Elsevier Inc. (2006)
11. B. Sinclair, *Simulation of Computer Systems and Computer Networks: A Process-Oriented Approach*, University Press, Cambridge UK (2004)
12. C.T. Stambaugh, F.W. Carpenter, *Wireless innovation in inventory monitoring and accounting*, Strategic Finance, Vol. 91(6), pp. 35-40 (2009)
13. S. Wang, W. Chen, C. Ong, L. Liu, Y. Chuang, *RFID Application in Hospitals: A Case Study on a Demonstration RFID Project in a Taiwan Hospital*, In Proceedings of the 39th Annual Hawaii International Conference on System Sciences - Volume 08, (4-7 January 2006)
14. S. Whang, *Timing of RFID Adoption in a Supply Chain*, Management Science, vol. 56, No. 2, pp. 343-355 (2010)

Methods of Profile Cloning Detection in Online Social Networks

Michał Zabielski[1], Rafał Kasprzyk[1], Zbigniew Tarapata[1,a], Krzysztof Szkółka[1]

[1] *Institute of Computer and Information Systems, Military University of Technology, Warsaw, Poland*

Abstract. With the arrival of online social networks, the importance of privacy on the Internet has increased dramatically. Thus, it is important to develop mechanisms that will prevent our hidden personal data from unauthorized access and use. In this paper an attempt was made to present a concept of profile cloning detection in Online Social Networks (OSN) using Graph and Networks Theory. By analysing structural similarity of network and value of attributes of user personal profile, we will be able to search for attackers which steal our identity.

1 Introduction and Motivation

Problem of the privacy violation on the Internet exists from the time, when first mechanisms to store user personal data was developed [1]. This issue is an important part of discussion field on the Online Social Networks (OSN) domain, which are depending mostly on the Web.

The results of analyses indicate a wide range of techniques, that allows people to take an unauthorized access to user personal data. In general, we can classify them into two groups: local and global. Local mechanisms of privacy violation in OSNs are focused on analysing person and their direct neighbourhood i.e. friends in this network. This allows us, for example, to reveal hidden attribute values of user social profile. An example of this method is described in [2].

Using global techniques, by contrast, is a different approach to deal with that issue. They are based on the entire structure of the acquired social network. This allows for using additional groups of algorithms, starting from machine learning techniques to the ones based on the similarity of graphs and networks. As a result of such actions, we can gain data not only directly from the user's profile and other people within the network, but also from the similarities of network structures across multiple Online Social Networks. This method is capable of detecting phenomena, which are difficult to be examined with the use of local methods, such as cloning profiles. An example of using global techniques for finding evidence of identity theft was presented in [3].

A profile of the user in the Online Social Network can be represented as a set of features and links between other profiles that describe the person in that network. Depending on the type of OSN, a set of attributes and relationships that make up the profile may be different. This proves there is no profile of a unique social network for a person on the Internet today, which gives the possibility of impersonating that particular person in different OSNs.

The complexity of the considerations about violating privacy in Online Social Networks intensifies the phenomenon of social network aggregation. It is a situation in which a person can have totally different profiles in different social networks. This potentially increases the chance of cloning a profile or impersonating another user, hindering the possibility for reliable comparisons of users' profiles in Online Social Networks. These and other problems led to creation of mechanisms for detecting violations of privacy.

As there is no clear definition of privacy, it can be variously interpreted. For the purposes of this study, privacy can be understood as an opportunity for individuals or group of individuals to maintain their personal data as well as habits and behaviours which are undisclosed to the public [4].

But in order to design solutions mentioned before, it is necessary to understand the phenomena with which we are dealing. In addition, it is complicated by the fact that violating privacy is not guided by one of the predetermined procedure. This process consists of a number of factors: from the structural description of the individual with the use of a social network profile to the dynamics of building relationships with others, and thus formation of links between the nodes. This proves that there are at least a few methods of privacy violation. One of them is the cloning the user profile.

The method of cloning a user profile in a social network involves impersonating a victim by creating the best possible copies of their social profile. In the simplest scenario, it includes building relationships and sharing profile data in the same manner as in the victim profile from another social network. As a result, an attacker is able to steal the identity of the victim in another social network.

[a] Corresponding author: zbigniew.tarapata@wat.edu.pl

The paper is organized as follows. In section 2 we present short background for profile cloning detection problem being considered. Section 3 contains proposition for revealing hidden attributes of social profile. In section 4 we describe node similarity measure function. Section 5 contains description of graph structural similarity. In section 6 we present the concept of profile cloning detection using methods described in sections 3, 4 and 5.

2 Background

Nowadays there are some methods that allows us to detect a profile cloning event [3,5]. Most of them are based on Machine Learning algorithms [6,7]. This, in most cases, results in analysing persons in social network without taking into account aspects of relations between considered person and his friends.

Another way of thinking about aspect of profile cloning is designing a set of methods how to prepare this kind of cyberattack. It is explained by the fact that having a knowledge about how hackers works gives us an opportunity to detect susceptibilities of their method, which eventually implicates developing a solution to stop them. This approach is well described in [8].

Using the results from presented solutions, we developed method that take into account not only static social profile part, such attributes values, but also a dynamical part, which consists of relation between person and other people in OSN. Implemented methods of profile cloning attacks give us basics to analyse them and take into consideration in our methods of detecting them.

3 Revealing hidden attribute values of social profile

For detecting a profile cloning it is important to have a complete information about user personal profile in Online Social Network.

Most often the reason of hidden attribute value are mechanisms, provided by Online Social Networks, which give us an opportunity to show values of attributes only for user-defined group of people in network. In most cases this approach is implemented by Access Control Lists (ACL). Despite their usability in protecting privacy aspect, this situation complicates our analysis in sense of profile cloning detection.

To provide a situation, when we know all about attribute values for each personal profile in particular Online Social Network, we provide a method, based on network model and k-nearest neighbours' algorithm, which allows us to estimate a hidden values of attributes for appropriate personal profile. A general procedure for this show Figure 1.

First of all, we have to provide analysing network, where nodes represents persons and edges describe a relation between two people. Moreover, a set of functions on nodes, which represents an attributes of social profile and one function on edge, which defines force of relation has to be defined. In that network we choose a node, for which we want to reveal hidden attribute values – we denote it as w_s.

Next, we get the nearest neighbours of node w_s – that is an set of direct friends of considered person – and calculate for them an similarity measure between person w_s and his neighbors. The similarity function can be any function that gives a higher value for nodes that are similar in sense of attribute values. In our approach, we use function described by equation:

$$s(w_s, w) = d(w_s, w) * \sum_{a_i \in A} p_{a_i}(w_s, w) \qquad (1)$$

where:
$d(w_s, w) \in (0,1]$ – force of relation between person w_s and w . It can be measured, for example, as a number of messages sent to person w by w_s divided by numbers of whole messages sent in OSN by node w_s,

$$p_{a_i}(w_s, w) = \begin{cases} 1 \; if \;\; a_i(w) = a_i(w_s) \wedge a_i(w) \; known \\ 0 \; if \; a_i(w) \neq a_i(w_s) \vee a_i(w) \; unknown \end{cases} \qquad (2)$$

$a_i(w)$ – value of the i-th attribute of personal profile of person w;
A – set of personal profile attributes.

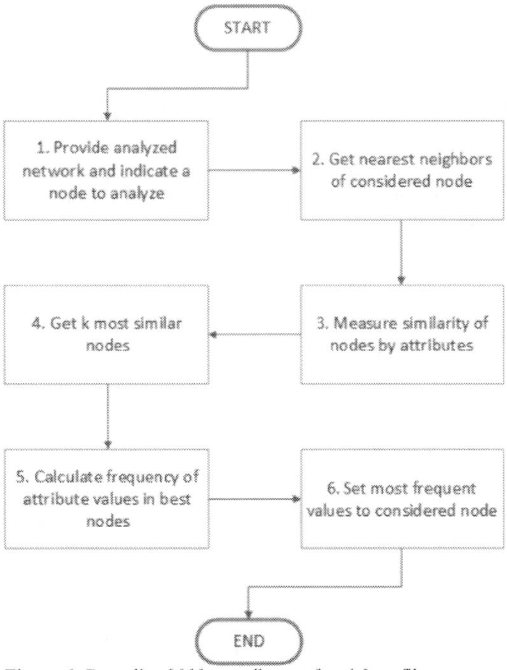

Figure 1. Revealing hidden attributes of social profile procedure.

When a similarity is calculated for every neighbour, we choose k nodes (the best nodes) with the highest similarity measure to consider their attributes values. Using a parameter k gives us confidence that calculated value of hidden attributes for node w_s will not be dominated by only one in Online Social Network. After choosing appropriate nodes, we calculate a frequency of appearing every value from the best nodes that are connected with hidden attributes. The most frequent value is taking as an answer. If we have more options to choose a value, we take a value with better similarity measure. We can repeat this procedure for every attribute that value is hidden.

The whole algorithm of revealing hidden values of attribute can be used for every node in a network, giving us an opportunity to estimate value for every attribute in every personal profile in OSN.

There are some important issues, that are worth discussing for best use of this model. Firstly, because this method is partially derived from *k*-neighbours' algorithm, it is good to choose a parameter *k* that is odd. This approach ensures that chance to get a value using only a frequency of appearing value in best nodes is high, which gives us better estimation of attribute hidden value. From our experiments, it is also good to choose parameter *k* from range [3,9], depend on nearest neighbour amount of considered node. The more neighbours' person has the higher value of parameter *k* should be. Secondly, it is good to know which kind of attribute values we can get. A similarity measure defined in (1) is good for discrete values, but it can give worst results for continuous values. If we have knowledge about a value range for attributes, we can use mix of similarity measures, which probably gives us a better estimation for continuous values of attributes.

4 Node similarity

After revealing all values of attributes in user social profile, we have to provide a measure, that helps us to detect an appropriate person from pattern network in our analysed network. To achieve this, we have to use a function which fulfil following conditions:

- it allows to simply compare attribute values between persons;
- it should be easy to interpret, which means that by using them we will be able to decide which personal profile, in sense of attribute values, is most similar to considered person's profile without any additional transformation of measuring function values;
- it should use a characteristic which are easy to obtain from network model.

According to the presented assumptions, for our purposes, we use a node similarity function, which is described by (3):

$$ID(w_s, w) = \sum_{i=1}^{m} I_i p_{a_i}(w_s, w) \in [0,1] \qquad (3)$$

where:

m – number of attributes in personal profile;

$I_i \in [0,1]$ – the importance of the *i*-th attribute $\sum_{j=1}^{m} I_j = 1$;

$p_{a_i}(w_s, w)$ – comparing function defined by (2).

Function $ID(w_s, w)$ meet all the conditions defined for node similarity measure function. By using only simple comparing of attribute values, it is reduced to compare vectors of attributes that creates user personal profile. Interpretation of (3) is easy, because $ID(w_s, w)$ can take values from range [0,1]. Finally, using only attribute value and significance, we provide a method, which base only on characteristics described directly on network.

Having a measure of similarity between nodes we can obtain a global measure of node similarity between two networks (pattern and analysed networks) *S* and *S'*, which gives us a better understanding of similarity of whole network. To do this we can formulate and solve (using for example Hungarian algorithm) optimal assignment problem to find the best allocation matrix $X = [x_{ij}]_{|W_G| \times |W_{G'}|}$ of nodes from network *S* to nodes from network S':

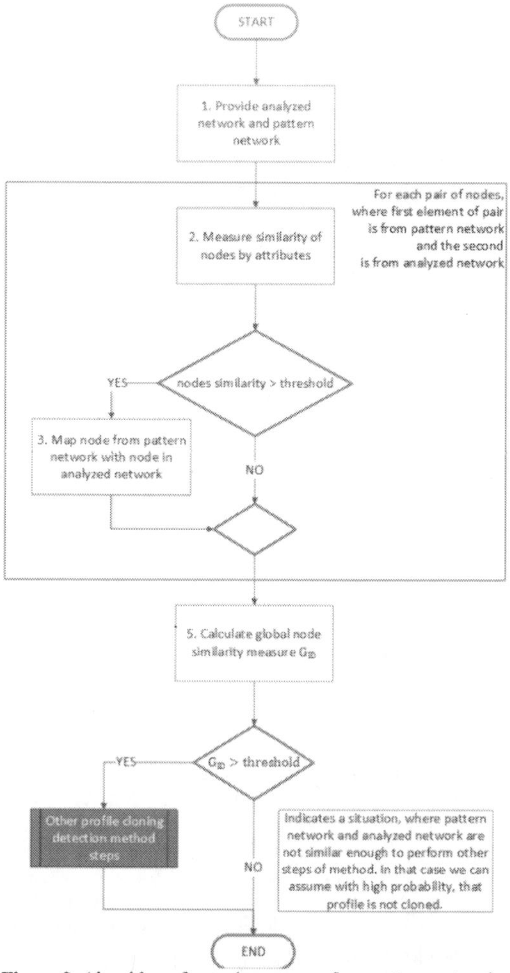

Figure 2. Algorithm of mapping persons from pattern network to analysed network in profile cloning detection method.

$$G_{ID} = \sum_{i=1}^{|W_G|} \sum_{j=1}^{|W_{G'}|} ID(i,j) \cdot x_{ij} \rightarrow max \qquad (4)$$

with constraints:

$$\sum_{i=1}^{|W_G|} x_{ij} \leq 1, j = \overline{1, |W_{G'}|} \qquad (5)$$

$$\sum_{j=1}^{|W_{G'}|} x_{ij} \leq 1, i = \overline{1, |W_G|} \qquad (6)$$

$$\bigwedge_{i \in \{1,\dots,|W_G|\}} \bigwedge_{j \in \{1,\dots,|W_{G'}|\}} x_{ij} \in \{0,1\}$$

where:
W_G – set of nodes in pattern network S;
$W_{G'}$ – set of nodes in analysed network S'.
Thanks that, we will be able to assess a "percentage" of similarity between considered networks and their persons.

It is important to remember that solutions provided in (3) and (4) are only some kind of proposals how to calculate a similarity at the vertices and network level, which we use in our specific implementation. For profile cloning detection method, which will be described in detail in chapter 6, we can define any other methods, which fulfils the conditions described earlier. Some of them are defined in details in [9]. In general, a procedure which is used in our profile cloning method is illustrated in Figure 2.

5 Graph structural similarity

There are a lot of measures that we can use to assess similarity of graphs nowadays. In this section, we present most popular of it. Other methods and models presented in this paper are independent of the algorithm that is used for measuring graph similarity.

We propose general classification of graph similarity measures as shown in Figure 3.

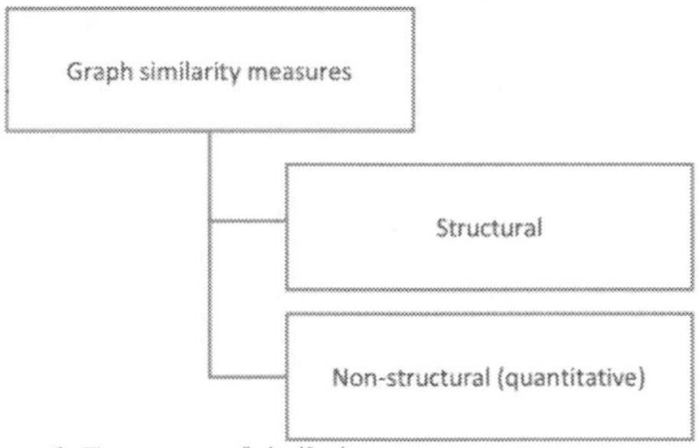

Figure 3. Taxonomy of similarity measures.

In short, structural similarity measures are used for graph and quantitative similarity measures for network (weighted graph) analysis. In the former only graph structure (topology) is examined. On the other hand, with quantitative similarity measures, we can consider node and edge weights (attributes). Graph isomorphism [12][13], maximum common subgraph [12], minimum common supergraph [12], edit distance [12][13], topological measures [12][13] and iterative methods [10][12][13] are examples of structural graph similarity measures. Non-structural graph similarity measures, in most cases, are based on iterative structural measures. Examples of these are presented in [5][11].

For the purpose of this research we propose graph structural similarity measure based on node neighbour matching. It is classified as one of iterative measures. The idea of it is as follows: two nodes are considered similar if they neighbours are similar [8][9][14].

Let structural similarity measure over the nodes of two networks S and S' be represented as [9][13]:

$$P_{node}(S,S') = [s_{ij}]_{|W_G|\times|W_{G'}|} = \lim_{k\to+\infty} Z_{2k} \quad (7)$$

where:

$$Z_{k+1} = \frac{BZ_kA^T + A^TZ_kB}{\|BZ_kA^T + A^TZ_kB\|}, k \geq 0,$$

A and B - transition matrices of S and S', Z_0=**1** (matrix with all elements equal 1); A^T – matrix A transposition; $\|y\| = \sqrt{\sum_{i=1}^{|W_G|}\sum_{j=1}^{|W_{G'}|} y_{ij}^2}$. Element z_{ij} of the matrix Z describes similarity score between the i-th node of the S' and the j-th node of the S. The greater value of z_{ij} the greater similarity between the i-th node of the S' and the j-th node of the S.

Having matrix $P_{node}(S,S')$, optimal assignment problem can be formulated and solved (using for example Hungarian algorithm) to find the best allocation matrix $X = [x_{ij}]_{|S|\times|S'|}$ of nodes from graphs S and S':

$$P(S,S') = \sum_{i=1}^{|W_G|}\sum_{j=1}^{|W_{G'}|} s_{ij}\cdot x_{ij} \to max \quad (8)$$

with constraints:

$$\sum_{i=1}^{|W_G|} x_{ij} \leq 1, j = \overline{1,|W_{G'}|} \quad (9)$$

$$\sum_{j=1}^{|W_{G'}|} x_{ij} \leq 1, i = \overline{1,|W_G|} \quad (10)$$

$$\bigwedge_{i\in\{1,\ldots,|W_G|\}}\bigwedge_{j\in\{1,\ldots,|W_{G'}|\}} x_{ij} \in \{0,1\}$$

The $P(S,S')$ is the value of structural similarity measure of graphs S and S'.

It is worth notice that analysed nodes could be part of the same or different graph. In the proposed method only shared nearest neighbours (first level neighbours) are taken into consideration. It can be easily extended to include neighbours of nearest neighbours (second level neighbours) and further. As an another extension we could propose to include node neighbours weights (attributes) when similarity of nodes is calculated.

6 The concept of profile cloning detection

For better understanding of provided approach, we introduce a following notation:
S – pattern network;
S' – analysed network;
$t_s \in [0,1]$ – threshold parameter for structural similarity of networks;
$t_{ID} \in [0,1]$ – threshold parameter for nodes global similarity;
w_s – person in analysed network that we are going to check if his identity was stole nor not;
$P(S,S')$ – structural similarity of network S and S';
i^{max} – maximum amount of iterations that algorithm should take;

DOI: 10.1051/matecconf/20167604013

ε- minimal allowed increase of structural similarity, that continues iteration of algorithm;
$t_S^{old} \in [0,1]$ – structural similarity value between network S and S' from previous iteration.

With this in mind, we provide an approach to detect profile cloning, by using an method illustrated on a diagram in Figure 4.

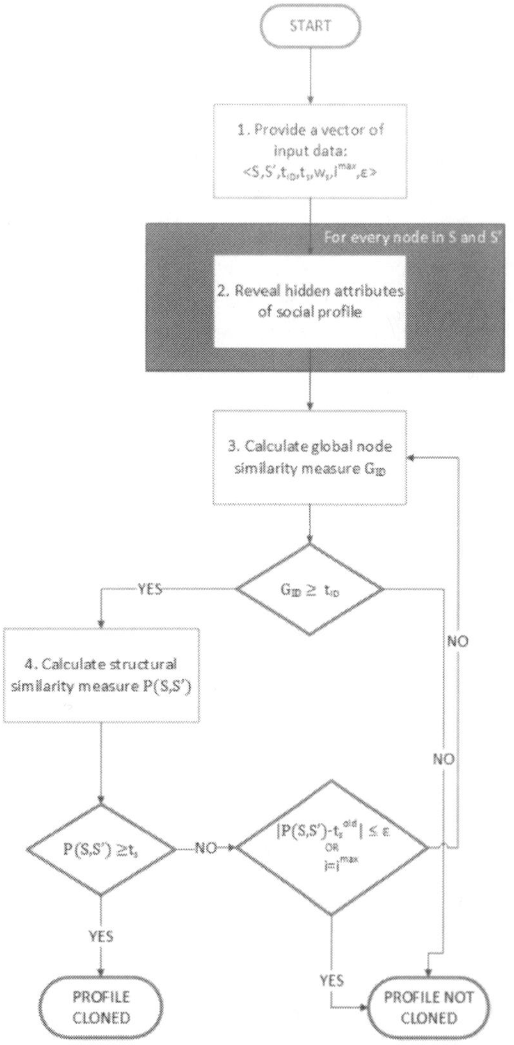

Figure 4. Profile cloning detection algorithm.

The general procedure is as follows. After providing an input data, we are using a method to reveal hidden values of attributes for every node in analysed network. A mechanism how to do it was described in chapter 3. Next, we calculate a global node similarity function to check whether analysing network is similar enough to pattern network. If this similarity is low, then we can assume that in analysed network there are not enough information to detect a profile cloning or the structure of this network, in sense of social profile, is too different so that the possibility of cloning a profile is low.

In situation when the G_{ID} value is greater than defined threshold, we can consider another steps of method. In that case, we calculate a structural similarity measure between pattern network and structural network. If this value is high enough, then we can assume, that the personal profile of person w_S is nearly the same in analysed network than in pattern network. This situation could happen in two scenarios. First is when the considered person create an account in analysed OSN and started to make a relations with his friends. Another case is when someone creates an account in analysed network and tries to recreate a social profile of person w_S. Second situation appears when a profile cloning has place, so we can say that we detect profile cloning.

Other part of algorithm consists of conditions to stop the method when a profile cloning didn't have a place. For this purpose we use two approaches. First is to set an maximum for amount of iteration. This gives us an opportunity to stop executing of method, but will also cause a risk, that algorithm will stop before detect a profile cloning. Another option used in our solution is to check whether an increasing of similarity measures are significant enough to continue searching. In that case, we assume that if we cannot obtain appropriate similarity of networks, then there is not any possibility that user's personal profile, in sense of attributes and relations between him and other people in OSN, was cloned. Because there is a risk that a second approach will not converge enough to stop executing an algorithm, a composition of first and second solution is used.

7 Conclusions

Presented approach shows that detecting a profile cloning using analytical methods is possible. This allows us to develop a solutions, which gives us opportunity to automate the process of discovering identity stealing in Online Social Networks. Moreover, a revealing hidden attributes values model, which is a part of detecting profile cloning procedure, can be also useful in analysing networks with lack of information about users and gives us also opportunity to analyse a procedure used by attackers to detect hidden attribute values. If we know how hackers are working to steal people identity, we can define a vulnerabilities of their action, which helps us to design methods to prevent from an unauthorized access to our attribute values.

Despite the effectiveness of considered approach, it is still place to extend presented method. For example, it will be good to design specialized structural similarity measures dedicated directly for Online Social Networks, which take into account a social profile characteristics and attributes. In our future work, we also plan to add ability to predict creation of relation between people in considered OSN. An example of predictor for making relations between people in Online Social Networks is described in details in [16]. This allows us to forecast an incident of profile cloning before this process will be completed by attacker. Thanks that, we will be able to prevent hacker from stealing user identity, which will definitely increase a value of implemented solution.

References

1. L. Faith Cranor, Internet privacy, Communications of the ACM, **42**, p. 28-38, (1999)
2. M. Mo, D. Wang, B. Li, D. Hong, I. King, Exploit of Online Social Networks with Semi-Supervised Learning, *The 2010 International Joint Conference on Neural Networks (IJCNN)*, 1-8, (2010)
3. M. Khayyambashi, F. Rizi, An approach for detecting profile cloning in online social networks, *e-Commerce in Developing Countries: With Focus on e-Security (ECDC)*, (2013)
4. H. Jeff Smith, *Managing Privacy: Information Technology and Corporate America*, UNC Press Books, (1994)
5. G. Kontaxis, I. Polakis, S. Ioannidis and E. P. Markatos, Detecting social network profile cloning, *IEEE International Conference on Pervasive Computing and Communications Workshops (PERCOM Workshops)*, Seattle, WA, 295-300, (2011)
6. X. Zhu, Z. Ghahramani, J. Lafferty, Semi-Supervised Learning Using Gaussian Fields and Harmonic Functions, *Proceedings of the Twentieth International Conference on Machine Learning*, 912-919, (2003)
7. A. Blum, Sh.Chawla, *Learning from Labeled and Unlabeled Data using Graph Mincuts*, Computer Science Department, paper 163, (2001)
8. L. Bilge, T. Strufe, D. Balzarotti, E. Kirda, All your contacts are belong to us: automated identity theft attacks on social networks, *Proceedings of the 18th international conference on World wide web (WWW '09)*, ACM, New York, NY, USA, 551-560, (2009)
9. Z. Tarapata, R. Kasprzyk, An application of multicriteria weighted graph similarity method to social networks analyzing, *Proceedings of the 2009 International Conference on Advances in Social Network Analysis and Mining*, Athens (Greece), IEEE Computer Society, 366-368, (2009)
10. V. Blondel, A. Gajardo, M. Heymans, P. Senellart, P. Van Dooren, A Measure Of Similarity Between Graph Vertices: Applications To Synonym Extraction And Web Searching, SIAM Review, **46** (4), 647–666, (2004)
11. M. Nikolić, Measuring similarity of graph nodes by neighbor matching, Intelligent Data Analysis, **16** (6), 865-878, (2012)
12. G. Jeh, J. Widom, SimRank: a measure of structural-context similarity, *Proceedings of the eighth ACM SIGKDD international conference on Knowledge discovery and data mining*, Edmonton, 538-543, (2002)
13. Z. Tarapata, Multicriteria weighted graphs similarity and its application for decision situation pattern matching problem, *Proceedings of the 13th IEEE/IFAC International Conference on Methods and Models in Automation and Robotics*, 1149-1155, (2007)
14. L. Zager, *Graph similarity and matching*, PhD thesis, MIT, (2005)
15. C. Bartosiak, R. Kasprzyk, Z. Tarapata, Application of Graphs and Networks Similarity Measures for Analyzing Complex Networks, Biuletyn Instytutu Systemów Informatycznych, **7**, 1-7, (2011)
16. D. Liben-Nowell, J. Kleinberg, The Link-Prediction Problem for Social Networks, Journal of the American Society for Information Science and Technology, **58** (7), 1019-1031, (2007)

Applications of RFID technology in dismounted soldier solution systems – study of mCOP system capabilities

Mariusz Chmielewski[1,a], Marcin Kukiełka[1]

[1]*Military University of Technology, Cybernetics Faculty, gen. S. Kaliski Street, Warsaw, Poland*

Abstract. This paper discusses application of RFID technology in Dismounted Soldier Solutions gathered from the development and demonstration of mCOP platform. The software has been developed to elaborate Network Enabled Capabilities in tactical environments. Presented research was a part of demonstration prepared for the European Defence Agency. The main aim of the tool is the delivery of command support capabilities utilizing data fusion and integration mechanisms implemented in heterogeneous military mobile networks. Application of military integration standards such as JC3IEDM, NFFI and TSO supports interoperability with BMS class systems. Utilisation of RFID technology in mCOP software has several purposes, mainly used for process automation of authorisation and personal identification. Indirectly such functionalities can be used for implementation of UAV supported - Blue Force Tracking and IFF services. This research elaborates a set of implemented ideas for such solutions. Developed system serves as a multi-level and multi-platform command and control system supporting military and crisis operations. A crucial part of the system - mCOP, the handheld application for tactical level commanders, serves as personal toolkit for location monitoring and combat situation distribution and management. The tool delivers a set of tailored functionalities supporting commander's situation awareness and decision making process. The mCOP hosting device equipped with RFID delivers also means of tactical, emergency, micro network communication.

1 Introduction and Main Concept

The main concept which has been driving the development of mCOP is to utilise commonly available mobile platforms and equip them with secure, fully functional application supporting main activities during combat missions. Military operations in 21st century require more and more information technology support in order to share information and decision superiority. Deployment of C4ISR systems in military has been conducted for almost three decades and the availability of smaller, smarter and more powerful handheld devices provides new opportunities for ICT tools. The deployment is constantly progressing moving downwards from operational unit command centres to tactical level command posts and further to task groups and even individual soldier. Such solutions (Dismounted Soldier Solutions) do not provide established, referenced functionalities as they represent research projects rather than deployed solutions. Also, the majority of them concentrate on integration of weapon systems rather than command and decision support or location and biomedical monitoring.

Described solution mCOP is a part of larger iCOP distributed C2 platform, delivered in form of a SOA environment available through stateful web portal. The technology used for implementation, was one of the crucial aspects tested in the research. The preferably more valuable part of research is connected with the design and composition of functionalities for mobile personal application, carried by task force members and utilised directly on the tactical level.

The availability of handheld devices and their usage during combat is often considered as a supplementary form of supporting soldiers and commanders. Especially in case of a crisis situations where any form of communication, monitoring, data sharing can be a valuable issue. Such observation was the base assumption for mCOP application, which should be treated as a tool for data fusion and integration but mainly the production of soldier's situation awareness during operation.

The security issues connected with processing of classified or potentially sensitive data, were one of the problems considered during architecture design and software development phase. Many of such problems could not be addressed due to many features of the devices such as utilisation of commercially available hardware platforms and operating systems. However, conducted research is aimed at utilising any available computing means, which can be used to help and support individuals during combat or crisis, at the same time maintaining acceptable security levels. Such compromise rises from the main assumption: deliver software, easily installable which can be used as a portable combat support tool. The ideal case assumes that any member of

[a] Corresponding author: mariusz.chmielewski@wat.edu.pl

a task group is able to acquire and configure the mCOP application on his personal or tactical handheld. To simplify configuration a RFID technology has been applied, which serves as remote identification mechanism. Using RFID soldier can log in to C2 system and preconfigure all GIS and mission data. RFID technology simplifies also integration with the logistics system/module where user obtains combat gear, ammunition and communication equipment. Depending on C2 system's The configuration and registration automation features are able to shorten TSU (Tactical Small Unit) combat preparation and departure time by almost 30%.

2 Concepts and features of Dismounted Soldier Solutions

A Dismounted Soldier Solution is a class of system going beyond only a software platform, as it multi-layer, wirelessly interconnected computer system integrated with weapons and specialised observation and reconnaissance gear. A valuable summary of such systems has been presented in [14]. The definition itself has not yet been unified and systems such as Land Warrior [15], ISW Tytan [14], IdZ-ES [14], FIST [17], FÉLIN [16] and many more, has been developed as technology demonstrators and testbeds for researching operational capabilities. Going into design details each and every system has been aimed at increasing higher combat effectiveness of the individual and by application of NEC concepts the unit itself. However, different systems emphasise various functional elements such as weapon system, camouflage capabilities, survivability, observation and sight equipment. For the purpose of this work we will discuss mainly ICT related capabilities of such solutions as the innovation and technology opportunity lies not in the tactical gear itself but extending the features of that gear with computer technology. In case of NEC concept implementation in DSS systems aim mainly at time constrained data distribution, sensor data utilisation and combat information sharing. The development of technology and processing power delivered new types of intelligent sensors and equipment, which in conjunction with wireless integration mechanisms and large data processing power give new opportunities for mobile platforms usage in combat.

The iCOP platform and mainly mCOP mobile application addresses rather different approach to software utilisation in combat, concentrating on functionalities mainly connected with soldier's situation awareness, decision support and mission guidance.

Available DSS systems maximise data sharing functions interconnecting soldiers within TSU and delivering:

- integration with command C4ISR systems,
- combat situation distribution,*
- voice communications,
- tactical picture or recon video sharing,
- reconnaissance and surveillance information delivery,
- mission report notifications,
- location monitoring
- GIS information delivery.

Such functions offer preliminary set of information required during combat especially in dynamic asymmetric conflict environment. However, soldiers may require additional set of services, which will assist them in three stages of operation:

- the briefing and departure,
- execution,
- post-reporting.

The requirements on each and every phase should support the soldier or commander and simplify activities indirectly connected with the mission itself. One of the crucial features of DSS system is to facilitate data sharing while delivering only useful and eligible information.

3 Situation awareness as a DSS –mCOP implemention [18]

Situation Awareness (SA) has been defined in [1] as "the perception of the elements in the environment within a volume on time and space, the comprehension of their meaning and projection of their status in near future" and is now being a subject of study in a number of domains [2,7,12]. This concept is a key feature around which presented work has been organised. mCOP system utilizes handhelds at the lowest levels of command for the development of near real-time tactical picture and soldier's situation awareness.

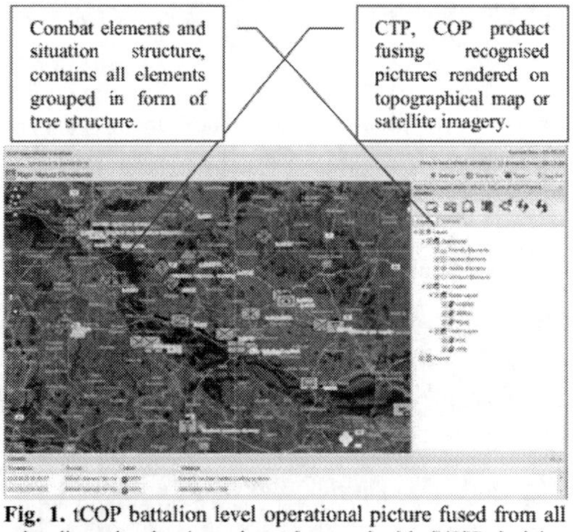

Fig. 1. tCOP battalion level operational picture fused from all subordinate level units and supplemented with C4ISR decision recommendation

The mCOP application automates many monitoring activities such as geo-location, intensity of activity, speed, bearing and even vital functions of a commander or a soldier. The process consists of two concurrent activities. The first one is aimed at the battlefield situation's data acquisition and delivery. The data provided by the sensors and obtained from the subordinates is derived and filtered on the handheld device itself and then sent to the tCOP server for further processing. The data describes the movement parameters of a given unit based on the fused data from the unit's staff. The second activity is oriented at acquisition of the battlefield situation's data from the server. The tCOP server obtains data from the automatized processes as well as from the template-based messages and other sources. The tCOP server filters collected data to match the situation in the vicinity of the user. Then the data is sent to the mCOP devices via sustained feedback connection.

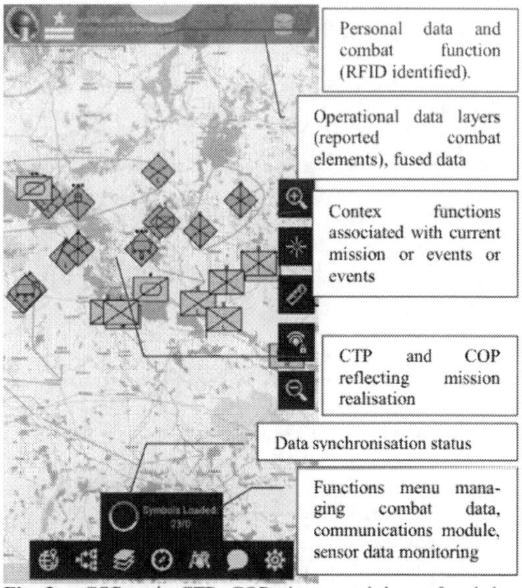

Fig. 2. mCOP main CTP, COP view containing – fused data and GIS information

The enrichment of users' SA is achieved by presenting inertial sensor data and using Augmented Reality perspectives containing the operational information. For SA development we combined common handheld sensors' data such as GPS, magnetometer, accelerometer, and gyroscope. Furthermore mCOP delivers efficient route planning capabilities and combat scenario simulation assessment.

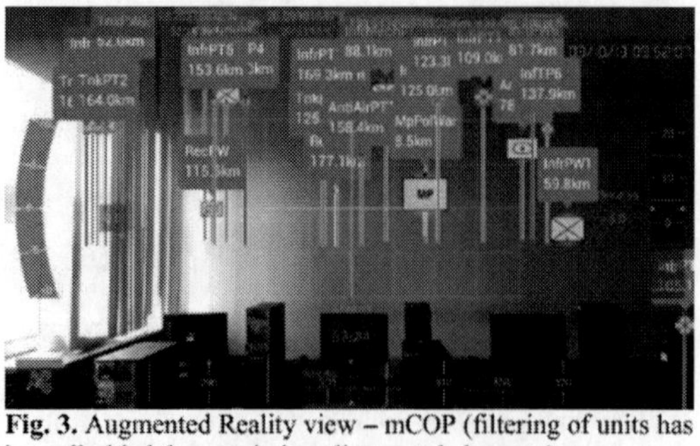

Fig. 3. Augmented Reality view – mCOP (filtering of units has been disabled thus rendering all reported elements)

To enrich the communication capabilities within the tactical network mCOP and tCOP provides secure and reliable template-based ADat-P3 military messaging.

Military operations are conducted mostly in difficult conditions in terms of the environment and the information. In such situation the lack of visibility and proper orientation locating and identifying enemy and friendly forces may be-come problematic; better situational awareness is required for effective operation. Believing that situational awareness in these circumstances cannot be met by using traditional approaches we decided to research Augmented Reality View.

The Augmented Reality view provides the data fusion products in form of one picture on which the application evaluates the positions of allied and enemy forces within the range of operation supplemented with the current observer location and device orientation. This information can be further semantically pro-cessed to recommend a commander the most efficient course of action or movement route. Augmented Reality is a construct built using data about battle-field, location, data derived from sensor fusion and above all the camera view. To create the AR View there is a need to describe the vertical and horizontal field of the camera's view. This is done by measuring the visible angle one meter away from the camera. Specifying the angles and maximum distance to the shown units allows further view creation.

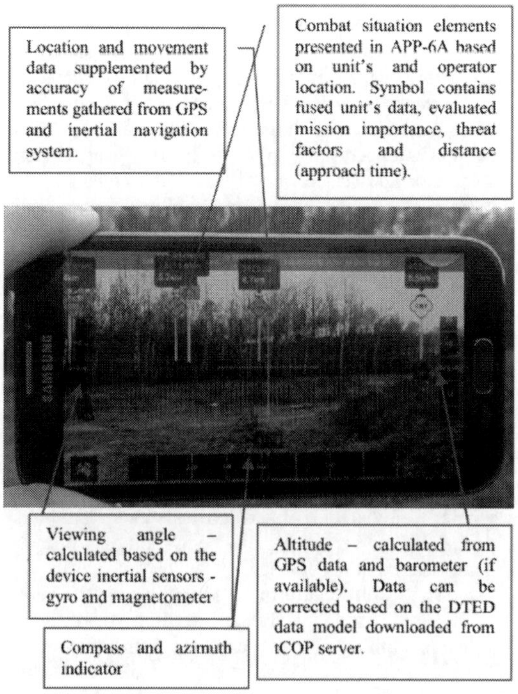

Fig. 4. Augmented Reality view rendering elements from CTP and COP products and viewing situation actors and evaluated SA characteristics

Implemented rendering mechanisms determines if the object should be shown on the screen and how to show the icons expressed in tactical symbology, evaluating their locations, azimuth, distance, and most of all mission importance and threat status (Fig. 3, 4).

4 RFID technology area of application

RFID [19,20] technology is well recognised standard for secure, wireless, remote identification and tagged objects tracking. In crisis operations such features can be utilised in many areas such as casualty identification, equipment or object tracking, combat gear configuration and assembly. Presented research discusses utilisation of this technology for handhelds supporting combat missions.

The mCOP application utilises RFID based features in three areas personal data identification, near field communications (serving as a backup emergency channel) and prototype IFF (Identification Friendly Foe) and BFT (Blue Force Tracking) services performed by assisting UAVs.

RFID in any DSS solution can be used to configure personal handheld which represents individual (using unique identifier and stored profile) which can be utilised for information access and crucial during medical assistance especially in the combat zone. The mCOP implementation solves time consuming authentication (perimeter control) and configuration issues during mission preparation and execution. The key advantage in such scenarios is connected with the simplification of tasks leading to mission preparation. The automation of such activities relief the operators and help them concentrate directly on the mission itself.

The mCOP toolkit utilising RFID mechanisms and functionality simplifies the departure and configuration phase by automation of soldier identity and credential verification. Using handheld with RFID or NFC technology user confirms the equipment and weapons acceptance for the mission, during which the logistics system checks if the equipment configuration is correct. Such functionality can be extended towards not only personal equipment but also vehicles. System supports also distribution of final forces and equipment TSU setup which normally is reported manually.

There are also application areas where RFID can be used dually as an emergency communication channel. Based on the near-field features of the RFID radio the mCOP can utilise such peer-to-peer channel for data transmission. Employing specialised algorithm and mechanisms for data aggregation and verification we can obtain means of communication on the lowest levels during radio-interference. For such case mCOP offers optimised tactical chat communications enabling dedicated means of communicating within TSU.

RFID can increase the efficiency of operation by providing each soldier in the squad with a tool for digital identity carrier and reader. Applying correctly configured RFID modules and utilising tactical UAV's, we can obtain which individuals are members of friendly forces which can be a form of simplified personal IFF service. To achieve such functionality a set of algorithms of location estimation must be developed and a specialised AR viewer functionality delivered.

Despite blue force tracking issue there are several areas in which RFID implementation can improve significant processes or even provide additional battlefield information.

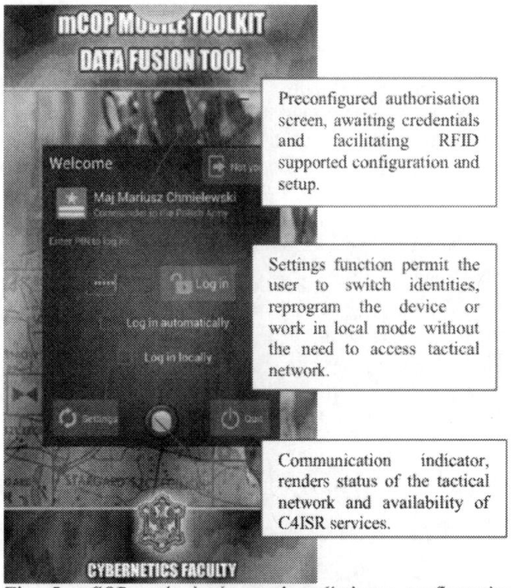

Fig. 5 mCOP authorisation and preliminary configuration screen rendered after device restart or mCOP activation.

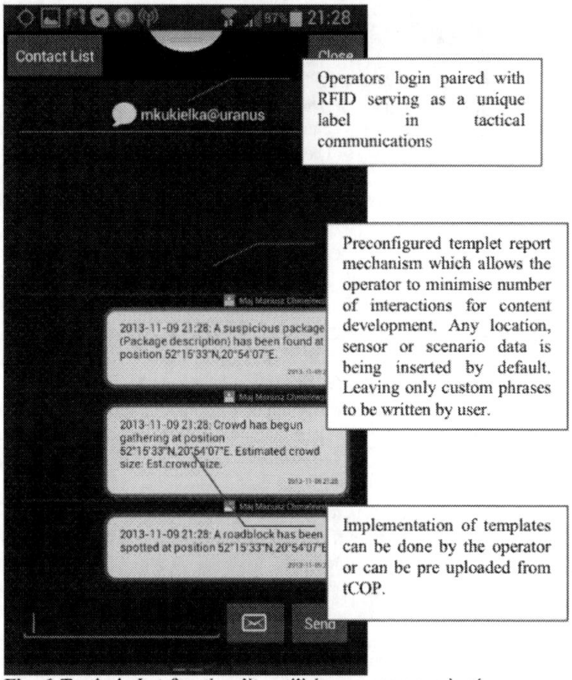

Fig. 6 Tactical chat functionality utilising any communication channel including tactical IP network, GSM, WiFi Direct and RFID based data sharing within TSU.

5 Battlespace data fusion and integration

Creating advanced sensor based views requires fusing the sensors output in order to obtain a reliable information. In created solution data from inertial sensors and magnetometer are utilized to obtain the position of the handheld in 3-dimensional space described by the Euler angles, pitch, roll and yaw, with yaw being nothing else than the azimuth. Moreover these angles have to be appropriate despite of the orientation of the phone, meaning that the coordinates system is changing along with orientation of the device. When the device is held flat the azimuth is based on the direction that the top of the device is pointing. To smoothen the sensor data a low-pass filter has been applied.

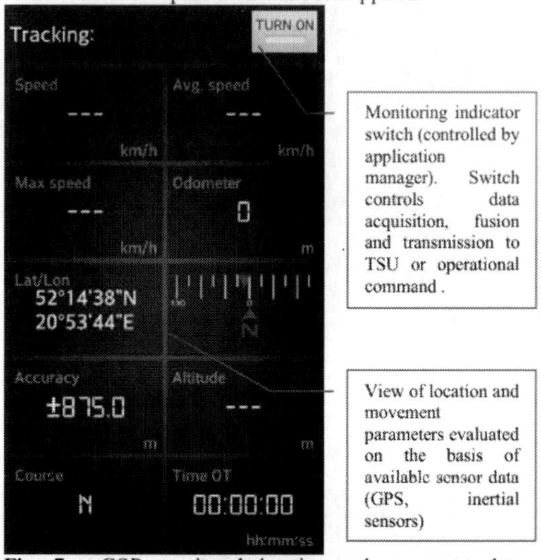

Fig. 7. mCOP monitored location and movement data, collected and retransmitted during mission execution. .

The fact that the operational data is often supplied from various, heterogeneous sources causes many integration problems on technical, syntax and semantics level. Implemented data fusion process provides data association and state estimation methods. Data processed in such way are more reliable and accurate which is significant in terms of developing multiresolution operational picture for crisis management support.

Data association is commonly used in cluttered environments (meaning that targets are close to one another). These situations hinder tracking targets and accurately determine their position. It is worth mentioning that data association is the key element due to higher levels of fusion process, like e.g. state estimation, which leads to incorrect behaviour if data association is incoherent. In order to improve the reliability of developed environment, we used three data association techniques and algorithms: nearest-neighbour algorithm, K-means algorithm and probabilistic data association including credibility factor. Obtained results are passed through majority voting mechanism. This approach reduces disadvantages of separately used methods providing reliable and accurate data association.

State estimation techniques have been used in order to determine, a state of the target especially while moving. The ultimate goal of these methods is to obtain a global state of the target basing on the given observations. During the revision of available sources for conducting an estimation process, one of most flexible methods has been applied – the particle filter. They cope successfully with both non-linear dependences and non-Gaussian density functions in dynamic systems and noise. Nevertheless, in order to obtain low variance, the filter needs huge quantities of data, which comes at the cost of computational power. To reduce the amount of particles a significant assumption has been made - tracking of the targets is processed individually with an assumption that they do not interfere with any particles. Estimated state of the target enriches the COP product and provides additional information to support a decision maker. In developed prototype this method is used mainly to estimate the route of the object and determine its combat potential.

Utilised heterogeneous data sources deliver data, which can be considered to be insignificant or invalid. We implemented methods which extract the important data by utilizing fusion techniques. Such algorithms support the reliability and accuracy of the Common Operational Picture and situation awareness [3] development thus improving decision support tools. An important aspect of the system is its data integration and acquisition capabilities. Such features in tCOP have been implemented as NFFI standard services and JC3IEDM compliant database.

NFFI (NATO Friendly Force Information) [4] is an interoperability standard initiated in 2005 by Allied Command Transformation (ACT) in response to an urgent need to exchange friendly force tracks between national Command and Control Information System (C2IS) within the ISAF coalition. TSO (Tactical Situation Object) [5] defines standard for data representation and a semantic model of a situation representation for crisis management and dispatching system perceived by a particular observer at a particular time. It is utilised to transfer data from such a view to console system or a dispatcher.

6 Architecture and implementation technology stack

The rendering of a COP utilizes data fusion algorithms and integration connectors. The major functionality of any military decision support system is GIS referenced data and functionalities for reflecting current or planned operational situation expressed in tactical symbology (APP-6A or country specific standard). It represents combat scenarios in form of pure relational data requires additional algorithms to present the situation picture, which can further be reused by the decision makers [7]. These tools enable allied (NATO) commanders to increase their Situation Awareness (SAW), which in case of our system can be understood as a perception of battlespace environment within a volume of time and space, and the projection of their status in the near future [8]. Such an approach enables collaboration between environment elements, improves synchronization and reduces delays of the communication. mCOP simplifies the delivery of CTP and COP to every soldier in that particular military unit. Usage of smartphones and wireless tactical networks improves the availability of toolkit. Services provided by the tCOP command system provides current situation including both military and civilian objects, information concerning both in Area of Responsibility – AOR and in Area of Interest – AOI. All requirements for COP and CTP products have been described in [9].

After review and analysis of set of available technologies on the market has been selected, fulfilling requirements for GIS tools with operational symbology editor capabilities and a stateful GUI, delivered through a browser. The tCOP a command centre application has been developed as a multilayer Java Enterprise system supplemented with GWT and Sencha GXT libraries facilitating GIS user interface. The choice of technology stack has been made based on the availability of open source libraries, flexibility of extensions and vendor-neutral characteristics. tCOP has been designed and developed according to multi layered architecture so as to allocate the different responsibilities of software to different layers. Client side has been developed according to the concept of RIA (Rich Internet Application). This model utilizes desktop application approach delivered as AJAX based client components executed in any web browser. GWT (Google Web Toolkit) is a set of tools and components supporting the development of RIA applications in Java language. The resulting GWT application consists of client side layer - HTML and JavaScript generated by GWT transformation engine from Java code and set of server side services (mostly asynchronous). The framework provides support for communication with server using GWT-RPC mechanism wrapped for AJAX calls from client to server side, providing stateful user interface and rapid application delivery.

Security characteristics in case of combat support application is one of crucial elements, especially when software is deployed on commercial equipment. Server side utilizes security layer consisting of authentication and authorization services for mobile application functionalities as well as for integration services responsible for data exchange and integration. The security layer utilizes also SSO (Single sign-on) infrastructure to simplify distributed and multiplatform authentication. Such approach in conjunction with RFID technology reduces time needed for logging and registering with-in the tactical network and simplifies user access within military C4ISR systems domain.

Business logic layer consists of SOA based services implemented using Enterprise Java Beans (EJB 3.1) components. tCOP web client layer backend software communicates with EJB's using Business Delegate object's implemented over HTTP standard: JAX-WS web services and GWT-RPC servlets.

Persistence layer have been implemented using Java Persistence API (JPA 2.1) standard approach for Object to Relational Mapping (ORM) as well as EclipseLink, which has been used for both management and auditing of data.

The solution provides extensive GIS mechanisms in form of SOA components dedicated at obtaining spatial data and maps. Moreover it is capable of rendering both raster and vector type terrain layers in the same time with possibility of setting order of them. User has ability both to use one of many predefined web mapping services' sources: OpenStreetMap, Bing, Landsat7 or any other custom web map service consistent with either WMS or WFS standards. To further expand the capabilities of the spatial data visualization, KML and GML standards have been used to describe spatial data sources.

tCOP solution allows visualization of operational situation in terms of military and civilian objects, their actions as well as equipment and supplies. It reflects the situation both by placing objects on the map and in the scenario objects widget representing formation's command chain, all objects and administrative structure. tCOP provides mechanism to visualize both military and civilian objects matching APP-6A or TSO standards. Described solution is not only a tool for visualization of current battlespace situation, but also a robust application mechanism for mission planning (adding units, infrastructures and tasks).

All data and messages are encrypted using RSA algorithm to ensure high level of security. Tactical voice or message communication in the system has been provided in form of tactical chat. To facilitate and speed up the messaging process tCOP provides messages' templates often used in both military and civilian communication.

0Presented solution iCOP provides scalable environment capable to develop and deliver COP and CTP products for the tactical and operational level commands. Crucial features of the environment deliver distributed SOA based and reliable set of integration and decision support be used as ort services, tuned for web and mobile access. The application of new technologies has been done intentionally in order to verify the Network Enabled Capabilities concepts in military tactical networks supporting civilian, commercially available technologies for dedicated security-oriented solutions.

Server-oriented tCOP is dedicated for a decision support of tactical level command. System has been developed using state of the art technologies and best practices. Supplied tools enable allied (NATO) commanders to increase their productivity of mission planning and operation execution. tCOP is one of few web-based applications used for heterogeneous data integration and Common Operational Picture development. mCOP mobile application is dedicated to the lowest levels of command, supporting efficient operational data flow and automatic monitoring of forces. The solution supports delivery of detailed battlespace information concerning objects, units, equipment and installations their combat potentials and tasks. Using the application the soldier is able to gather specific tactical information on equipment, warfare as well as unit resources and tasks. Furthermore, detailed combat information contains not only static data, but also description of unit's behavior in time (tasks).

7 Summary

Presented family of mission support tools (tCOP, mCOP) provides the information infrastructure for military and civilian crisis operation support. The tools utilise means of applying new technologies to increase the efficiency of combat operations on any stage of mission execution. The tool is able to consume and produce standardised data sources in form of NFFI and JC3IEDM data messages and TSO dispatch services which delivers standardised interfaces for COP and CTP acquisition. The demonstrator have been validated in several deployment configurations utilising ad-hoc tactical networks, server environments and variety of android devices (also ruggedized). The iCOP platform is able to process and refine operational scenario elements fusing the data from many heterogeneous data sources. Application of AR to support situation awareness of TSU member delivers new means of information rendering increase of the decision making efficiency during combat exercises. Application RFID standards simplified many activities connected with mission configuration and preparation phase. A handheld device can be used as a secure identification device storing crucial personal (including medical, ER) data. The tools have been demonstrated to EDA officials. Further research will be organised in three main areas extending the decision support capabilities, RFID applications for facilitating local communications as well as IFF and BFT service implementations. Furthermore the availability of RFID technology variants e.g. NFC, gives new opportunities for dual applications especially on the handheld market.

References

1. M. Endsley, „Design and Evaluation for Situation Awareness Enhancement," w Proceedings of the Human Factors and Ergonomics Society Annual Meeting, 1998.
2. M. R. Endsley, D. J. Garland, Situation Awareness Analysis and Measurement, CRC Press, 2000.
3. M. Chmielewski, „Ontology Applications for Achieving Situation Awareness in Military Decision Support Systems," Lecture Notes in Computer Science, nr DOI: 10.1007/978-3-642-04441-0_46, pp. 528-539, 2009.
4. NATO, NATO Fiendly Force Interoperability standard, STANAG 5527.
5. CEN WS/ISDEM, Definition of the OASIS Tactical Situation Object, 2006.
6. CEN, Disaster and emergency management - Shared situation awareness - Part1: Message structure., 2009.
7. M. G. D. Endsley, Situation Awareness Analysis and Measurement: Analysis and Measurement., Lawrence Erlbaum Associates, 2000.
8. M. Chmielewski, „Data fusion based on ontology model for common operational picture using OpenMap and Jena semantic framework," w Proceedings of the Military Communications and Information Systems Conference, Cracow, 2008.
9. NATO, NATO Common Operational Picture (NCOP) - NC3A, 2006.
10. M. Chmielewski, A. Gałka, „Semantic Battlespace Data Mapping Using Tactical Symbology," Advances in Intelligent Information and Database Systems, DOI: 10.1007/978-3-642-12090-9_14, pp. 157-168, 2010.
11. W3C, Web Service Glossary, 2011.
12. „Shared situation awareness – Part1: Message structure," CEN.
13. M. J. Zieniewicz ; D. C. Johnson ; C. Wong ; J. D. Flatt, "The Evolution of Army Wearable Computers", IEEE, Pervasive Computing, vol.1, no. 4, pp. 30-40, 2002, doi: 10.1109/ MPRV.2002. 1158276
14. K. Frącik, New technologies and means of combat shaping modern military operations, Journal of KONBiN 3(19), 2011, ISSN 1895-8281
15. N.L. Clifton Jr., D.W. Copeland, The Land Warrior Soldier System: A Case Study for the Acquisition of Soldier Systems, Monterey, California, MBA Professional Report, 2008
16. FELIN soldier system, Sagem Défense Sécurité brochure, available online, 2008.
17. FIST – Future Infantry Soldier Technology, http://www.army-technology.com/projects/fist/
18. M. Chmielewski, et.al. Development of Operational Picture in DSS Using Distributed SOA Based Environment, Tactical Networks and Handhelds; Information Systems Architecture and Technology: Selected Aspectss of Communication and Computational Systems, 2014, Wrocław, ISBN/ISSN: 978-83-7493-856-3
19. S.A.Weis, RFID (Radio Frequency Identification): Principles and Applications, 2007, MIT CSAIL
20. I. Angell, J. Kietzmann, RFID and the end of cash?. Communications of the ACM 49 (12): 90–96. 2006, doi:10.1145/1183236.1183237.

MATEC Web of Conferences 76, 04015 (2016) DOI: 10.1051/matecconf/20167604015
CSCC 2016

Applying Moving Objects Patterns towards Estimating Future Stocks Direction

Dahab Galal[1,a], Nada Hassan[1] and Doaa S. Elzanfaly[1]

[1]*Information Systems, Informatics and Computer Science, British University in Egypt*

Abstract. Stock is gaining vast popularity as a strategic investment tool not just by investor bankers, but also by the average worker. Large capitals are being traded within the stock market all around the world, making its impact not only macro economically focused, but also greatly valued taking into consideration its direct social impact. As a result, almost 66% of all American citizens are striving in their respective fields every day, trying to come up with better ways to predict and find patterns in stocks that could enhance their estimation and visualization so as to have the opportunity to take better investment decisions. Given the amount of effort that has been put into enhancing stock prediction techniques, there is still a factor that is almost completely neglected when handling stocks. The factor that has been obsolete for so long is in fact the effect of a correlation existing between stocks of the same index or parent company. This paper proposes a distinct approach for studying the correlation between stocks that belong to the same index by modelling stocks as moving objects to be able to track their movements while considering their relationships. Furthermore, it studies one of the movement techniques applied to moving objects to predict stock movement. The results yielded that both the movement technique and correlation coefficient technique are consistent in directions, with minor variations in values. The variations are attributed to the fact that the movement technique takes into consideration the sibling relationship

1 Introduction

Capitalizing in the stock market has always been a powerful investment tool that is gaining popularity fast. However, the one characteristic all stock markets have in common is uncertainty; an effect of the stock's short and long term states. Such a trait is undesirable yet unavoidable if people are to participate in the stock market; this is when prediction techniques for the stock market become a major point of interest.

There already exists a number of computational techniques which aim to enhance the stock prediction process including but not limited to; Linear Regression, Artificial Neural Networks (ANN) and Support Vector Machines (SVM). Another approach to stock prediction involves the use of Database Management Systems such as real time database characteristics. Databases in which the stock data is stored. Given the amount of techniques that are used to enhance stock prediction, the effect of a correlation that exists between stocks of the same index or mother company is a factor that is almost completely neglected in most of the aforementioned techniques.

This paper aims to study a new perspective of stock modelling that focuses on the correlation between stocks within the same index or parent company as a key factor to draw better predictions. The proposed approach considers stocks as objects that constantly move in accordance with their values, thus becoming moving objects. The idea is that by applying prediction patterns of moving objects such as "Following Pattern" and "Attraction & Avoidance Pattern", all the stocks involved in a relationship would be used to predict each stock's future direction relative to the rest of the 'sibling' stocks. If a stock is said to have an attraction/avoidance relationship with another stock, it means that when the first stock rises/falls in value, then the second stock would follow accordingly.

This paper is organized as follows; section two provides a brief literature review of the various techniques that were applied for stock prediction. Section three discusses the proposed model and how the movement technique is applied to the model. Section four evaluates the test results and experiments, lastly, section five provides a conclusion and sdiscussing the future work.

2 Literature Review

Current prediction techniques concerning stocks vary between psychological, financial and technical models. These techniques are applied to a stock's collected values over a period of time to predict its future value. Most of these techniques are in fact based on data mining techniques.

[a] Corresponding author: Dahab.Galal@bue.edu.eg

The most commonly used technique is that of linear regression. Linear regression allows analysts to predict the volume of a given stock taking into consideration the fluctuations in its values over a large period of time [12]. It is further used to detect patterns that occur with respect to actual and target stock values. The identified patterns allow for further prediction of stock values. One significant limitation of this technique is the fact that the dataset needs to be large to produce meaningful results. Furthermore, it projects the data onto a straight line, disregarding outliers and their impact on the determined patterns [7].

Artificial Neural Networks (ANN) is another technique that is employed in stock prediction. This technique has the added benefit of predicting the direction in which the stock value would move, meaning whether it would increase or decrease [11]. One issue with this technique is that it does not provide accurate results with respect to prediction of stock values. Another issue lies in its susceptibility to noisy data. An attempt to handle those limitations was to integrate ANN with Support Vector Machines (SVMs) that were introduced in stock prediction to tackle stock market movement as well as the variation in price indices [7]. The work done by [2] at al. shows that SVMs outperformed various other techniques including case based reasoning and ANNs with respect to prediction of stock direction.

In order to model the time aspect of stocks, real time databases were considered. Transactions stored within real time databases have strict time constraints [5]. Such transactions are referred to as tardy constraints and later overload the system. The issues with this representation include its improper handling of abortion and recovery of transactions. Furthermore, there is a constant trade-off between security and performance [1]

A common technique for measuring correlation between stocks the correlation coefficient. It is defined as follows:

$$Correlation = p = \frac{Cov(x,y)}{\sigma x \, \sigma y} \quad (1)$$

Where Cov (x, y) is the covariance between X and Y, σx is the standard deviation of X and σy is the standard deviation of Y [3]. As with previous techniques, the correlation coefficient technique only takes into consideration the stocks' closing price, which is a single dimension. It doesn't investigate how incorporating more than one dimension would affect the correlation between the two objects.

All of the above mentioned techniques have an important aspect in common, which is the fact of drawing assumptions about the future estimate of a stock, they use the history of the same individual stock as well as the possible fluctuations of the market. This discards any correlation between stocks of the same index or mother-company to be a significant factor. This leads to the main problem, which is the lack of techniques that take into consideration the correlation between stocks and how such a relation can aid the enhancement of stock prediction.

3 Modelling Stocks as Moving Objects

To overcome the limitations of the aforementioned stock prediction techniques, we propose a distinct approach for studying the correlation between stocks that belong to the same index by modelling them as a set of interrelated moving objects where the index is treated as a parent and stocks within it to be siblings to be able to track their movements while considering their relationship. Modelling stocks as moving objects has a threefold aim: first, getting benefits of the enriched capabilities of the object-oriented data model especially the inheritance property to model the parent-child and sibling relationships. Second, keeping track of the temporal and spatial aspects of the moving objects along with maintaining their hierarchy and relationships. Third, applying different movement patterns on moving stocks and determine its impact on stock value predictions.

A stock can be abstracted as <point, instance> where the point represents the stock and the instance represents its value in a certain time. The trajectory, that is the path a moving object follows through space as a function of time, represents the motion of a moving point in a discrete form [6]. Thus, trajectories of moving points are often defined as a sequence of (x, y, t) rows:

$$T = \{(x1, y1, t1), (x2, y2, t2), \ldots, (xn, yn, tn)\} \quad (2)$$

Where x, y ∈ R and t1 < t2 <... < tn, [13]. The trajectory of each object represents a sequence of locations each coupled with a certain timestamp. In our case, the object is a stock that is represented by its closing value coupled with the volume sold at that value.

As it has been briefly discussed above, if stocks are to be modelled and handled as points of moving objects, both the temporal and spatial factors would be taken into consideration where each stock would be managed as a moving entity over a period of time. As a result the proposed model could offer a significance advantage over Real-Time databases as stocks get to keep their relationships, their timestamp factor and adds to that their fluctuation of prices can be modelled as movement, this movement can be analysed by using different Moving Objects data model techniques.

3.1 Stock Movement Patterns

In the context of moving object, a number of movement patterns have recently been identified [9], most notable of which are the "Following" pattern and the "Attraction/Avoidance" pattern. The "Following" pattern shows the dynamic relationship between objects following the idea of how a predator follows its prey [10]. This pattern is limited by the fact that it defines a one-sided relationship. This implies that if one object follows the other, the reverse is not guaranteed. Furthermore, it does not specify a movement direction for the object in question.

On the other hand, the "Attraction/Avoidance" pattern is a technique that identifies whether two objects attract or avoid each other. This relationship would result from their dependence on each other in some way [8, 10]

The Attraction/Avoidance technique takes into consideration the two moving objects and the distance between them in order to determine when they [9]. A threshold is defined, dictating the maximum allowed distance between the two objects so as to consider that they have met. For this work, the designated threshold is in fact a particular time frame. The two stocks are considered to have met when the closing value and volume pair for each of the stocks occur within the specified time frame. The number of times that they occur within that time frame is considered the meeting frequency of those two stocks.

As an example, given the threshold of four days, stock A has closing price of 2.00$ with an associated volume of 5000 stocks; while stock B has closing price of 4.00$ with an associated volume of 3000 stocks. As such, stock A and stock B will meet if these same values occur again within the predetermined four days. The number of times that that condition evaluates to true would in turn represent the meeting frequency of those two stocks. It is however infeasible to directly measure the relationship between two trajectories using meeting frequency. This is because two objects may seem to be frequently meeting when in fact there are other issues that cause the excessive meetings (I.e. Outliers or noisy data).

To further achieve this notion, a permutation test is performed with the null hypothesis that the two movement sequences of the two stocks are independent. The null hypothesis is in fact the baseline for comparison. The permutation test involves randomly shuffling the movement sequences of the one of the two stocks and then checking whether the null hypothesis holds or not. If the hypothesis holds, then it is concluded that the two stocks are independent. Otherwise, it is proven that the stocks have a certain relationships which needs to be further classified as either attraction or avoidance.

In order to determine whether two stocks attract or avoid each other, the significance value is calculated as indicated by the algorithm. The calculated value is based on the actual meeting frequency as well as the permuted frequency. The resulting significance value lies in one of three ranges; either the resulting value is greater than 0.5 , is equal to 0.5, or is less than 0.5, thus emphasizing that only two ranges are of interest. If the significance value is greater than 0.5 then the two stocks are attract. Conversely, as the value decreases, the stocks avoid each other.

4 Model Evaluation

To evaluate the proposed model, an application has been built as an adaptation of the algorithms of a tool called MoveMine that was created by a team in Pennsylvania university to measure the movement of animals and their preys to then be displayed using Google Earth [8 - 10].

The application has been developed to track a certain pattern which is the "Attraction and Avoidance" pattern in the S&P 500 stock market index data set [4]. The S&P 500 Index is managed by S&P Dow Jones Indices. The S&P 500 stock market index represent 502 common stocks that are issued by 500 large-cap companies and are traded on the American Stock Exchange Market; some of which include IBM, Apple, and EMC. The S&P 500 companies takes up 75 percent of the American Equity market by Capitalization. Although the index is called S&P "500", it actually contains 502 stocks. This particular data set was chosen for the existence of siblings' relationship to validate the research hypothesis.

The dataset contained the Ticker, the opening stock value, the highest stock value, the lowest stock value, the closing stock value, and the volume (number of stocks sold). Each record of the above values was recorded for a single day. The dataset represents each of the 502 stocks over the period of 365 days.

Those values were chosen for two reasons; firstly because they are the most used values when it comes to stock prediction and secondly they are the most representative of a stocks state given a certain point in time. The values were further uniformly normalized (values lie between 0 and 1) so as to apply the attraction/avoidance technique. It was taken into consideration that the stocks were from the same industry, which is the information technology industry.

A number of pairs of stocks were selected to investigate the accuracy of modelling stocks as moving objects. In order to determine the quality of results, the resulting significance values were compared to correlation coefficient values [14]. Correlation coefficient values are between -1 and 1, where 0 indicates independence. Positive values indicate that the two stocks move in the same direction, while negative values indicate that they move in opposite directions. As such, this technique was used as a standard of comparison. The correlation coefficient values were normalized to values between 0 and 1.

In Figure 1, it is clear that both the Attract/Avoid technique and the correlation coefficient technique yield the same values with respect to their avoidance. The discrepancy between the values produced by each technique are attributed to the fact that the attract/avoid technique takes into consideration aspects that were otherwise ignored. This shows that the siblings' relationship does in fact add value to the prediction as it does not deviate drastically from the correlation coefficient values.

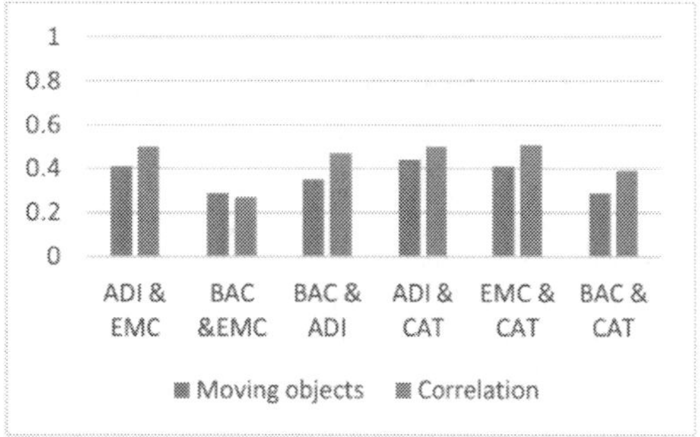

Figure 1. Stock Movement Prediction showing the proposed approach as comparison with the correlation equation

Among the set of stocks that were chosen, there was one particular stock that when compared with others, always yields different results than those produced by the correlation coefficient, as shown in Figure 2. This implies that there are certain characteristics provided by the "Attraction/Avoidance" technique that may cause skew for certain objects. This is consistent with the permutation step that is applied to ensure that two stock objects are truly attracted/avoid each other. This further proves that for this stock, the correlation coefficient does not take into consideration possible outliers that may affect the identified movement pattern.

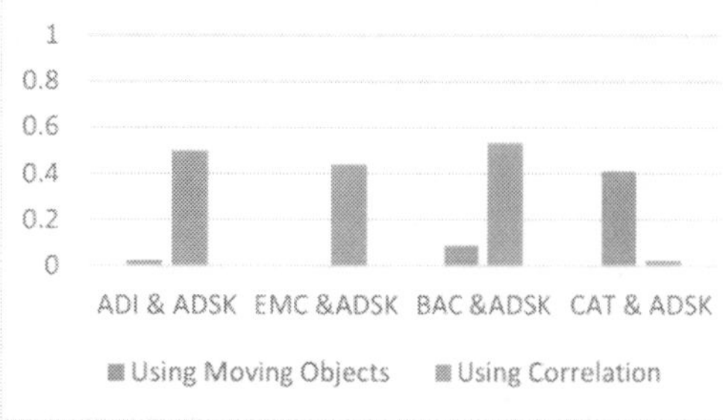

Figure 2. Stock movement prediction showing anomalist

By taking a closer look at the resulting values, stocks BAC and EMC have very close values with a lesser correlation value. This shows that the Attract/Avoid pattern identifies the avoidance for what it is and yet takes the value one step further to include the two stocks' history as siblings. This aspect was unaccounted for in the correlation coefficient technique

5 Conclusion and Future Work

In conclusion, it can be established that the use of the object oriented data concepts to model related stocks has positively affected stock prediction. The limitations of previous stock prediction techniques did not take into consideration the possible dependencies between different stocks. The dependencies are a result of the fact that a number of stocks may all belong to the same index, making those stocks siblings. Stocks were modelled as moving objects and were represented by their closing value and volume. One of the movement pattern techniques was selected to assess whether applying the moving object model holds for stock. The Attract/Avoid technique was selected due to its significance with respect to the model in question. The results shows that treating stocks as moving objects took into consideration aspects that were otherwise ignored by the correlation coefficient. Furthermore, the results prove that with respect to predicting movement direction, both techniques yield the same direction.

It is intended to study further the anomaly presented by some of the stocks, to determine the cause of such behaviour. Furthermore, more movement patterns can be applied and investigated to further enhance stock prediction.

References

1. Akdere, M., Cetintemel, u., & Upfal, E. (2009, August). Database-Support for Continuous Prediction Queries over Streaming Data. Providence, Rhode Island, USA.
2. Chen, A., Leung, M., & Daouk, H. (2003). Application of Neural Networks to an Emerging FInancial Market: Forecasting and Trading the Taiwan Stock Index. Computers & Operations Research, 901-923.
3. Cherewyk, P. (2015). Calculating Covariance For Stocks. Retrieved from Investopedia: http://www.investopedia.com/articles/financial-theory/11/calculating-covariance.asp
4. Economic Research Federal Reserve Bank of St. Louis. 2000. S&P 500© (SP500). [ONLINE] Available at: https://research.stlouisfed.org/fred2/series/SP500/downloaddata. [Accessed 15 July 15].
5. Hajari, H., & Hakimpour, F. (February 2014). A Spatial Data Model For Moving Objects Database. International Journal of Database Management Systems (IJDMS) Vol.6, No.1.
6. Imfeld, S., & P., L. (2002). Analyzing Relative Motion within Groups of rackable Moving Point Objects. Information Systems.
7. Kara, Y., Boyaciglu, M. A., & Baykan, O. K. (2011). Predicting Direction of Stock Price Index Movement Using Artificial Neural Networks and Support Vector Machines. Expert Systems with Applications, 5311-5320.
8. Kays, R., Li, Z., Ji, M., Lee, J.-G., Tang, L.-A., Yu, Y., & Han, J. (2011). MoveMine: Mining Moving Objects Database. Illinois.
9. Kin, T., Wu, F., Li, Z., & Han, J. (2013). MoveMine 2.0: Mining Object Relationships From Movement Data. Penssylvania & Illnois.
10. Li, Z., Ding, B., Wu, F., Lei, T. K., Kays, R., & Crofoot, M. C. (2014). Attraction and Avoidance Detection From Movements. Pennsylvania, USA.
11. Mahajan, K. S., & Kulkarni, R. (2013). A Review: Application of Datamining Tools For Stock Market. Kolhapur, India: Institude of Business Education & Research Center.
12. Olaniyi, A. S., Adewole, K. S., & Jimoh, R. G. (2011). Stock Trend Prediction Using Regression Analysis: A Data Mining Approach. ARPN Journal of Systems and Software, 4.
13. Pena, J. H., & Santos, M. Y. (2011). Representing, Storing and Mining Moving Objects Data. World Congress on Engineering . London: WCE.
14. Stock Charts. (2015). Technical Indicators and Overlays. Retrieved from Stock Charts: http://stockcharts.com/school/doku.php?id=chart_school:technical_indicators:correlation_coeffici

MATEC Web of Conferences 76, 04016 (2016) DOI: 10.1051/matecconf/20167604016
CSCC 2016

A Combined AHP and Source of Power Schemes for Prioritising Requirements Applied on a Human Resources

Osman Ibrahim and Ann Nosseir[1]

[1] *faculty of informatics and computer science (ICS), British University in Egypt, Cairo, Egypt*

Abstract. Abstract. There are a number of scenarios where prioritising is one of the critical activities. The requirements engineering process domain uses different approaches to prioritise requirements. Most of these approaches overlook the influence of the stockholders politics and power among dimensions of the process. This paper expands the scope of Analytic Hierarchy Process (AHP) and uses the source of power approach that accounts for the political and authoritative powers typically found among stakeholders. The suggested model weaves both approaches using a well-defined process model and applies this model on a case of prioritising the requirements of human resources software in a multinational company.

1 Introduction

Requirements Engineering (RE) is software engineering process, which covers all of the activities involved in discovering, documenting and maintaining a set of requirements for a computer-based system [1]. It is defined as the process of identifying stakeholders and their needs, and documenting these in a form that is amenable to analysis, communicate, and subsequent implement [2] & [3].

RE process is difficult because businesses operate rapidly in a changing environment. Accordingly, requirements change continuously and consequently that increases the vagueness of what is exactly required. Having multiple stakeholders with different goals is another reason to raise more arguments. More often, the requirements identifications and prioritisations are influenced by political and organizational factors that stakeholders will not admit publicly [1].

The RE process involves main four activities, which are requirements discovery, requirements classification, prioritisation and negotiation, and requirements documentation activities. In the requirements discovery, software engineers interact with stakeholders to discover their requirements. This is followed by requirements classification and organisation activity. In that respect, requirements are grouped and organised into coherent clusters. Afterward, in the prioritisation and negotiation, members of the project group subjectively do the process of requirements prioritisation, which is the process of finding an order relation on the set of requirements. The prioritisation involves negotiation among the stakeholders to resolve conflicts and to decide the ranking according to information available about budget, time and technical constraints, and stakeholder expectations [1].

Prioritising requirements means categorising raw potential requirements from the standpoint of importance into essential and desirable requirements. Essential requirements must be included because it would reduce system effectiveness if they were left out and desirable requirements will make the system more desirable to certain stakeholder[1]. "Negotiation and consensus are important to eliminate unnecessary potential "requirements" [2] (i.e., goals, desires, and "nice-to-haves" that do not merit the mandatory nature of true requirements) [1]. After finishing negotiating the set of requirements and their priories, requirements documentation ends this RE process.

Different technical approaches are used to automatism the AHP approach. More specifically, in prioritising requirements different techniques are used such as Analytic Hierarchy Process (AHP) [5], Bubble Sort [6], and Case Based Ranking [7].

These approaches represent an abstract and a mechanistic view of the prioritisation process and don't represent the real final decision of the ranked list. The final decision of ranking involves discussions and negations among different teams who are involved in projects. For instance, technical group like Information Technology (IT) group will have different ranking from the business groups such as marketing or finance groups. Each group prioritises according to its objectives that could introduce conflict and the power of politics among groups plays an important role to have the final set of prioritise requirements. Pairwise and other mechanistic approaches overlook this reality.

This paper proposes a novel approach that adds to the mechanistic pairwise technique i.e. AHP the weight power model. It is structured as follows. It starts with introducing the problem. The following section describes the related work and identifies the prioritising approaches. Then we present the details of our weighted political model followed by a case study to explain the implementation of the model and to perform an initial validation of the model. The final part discusses the implementation of model and finishes by concluding remarks.

2 Related work

Advancements in the software product management have pushed the industry to add updated releases of planning activity. One of the key steps in release planning is requirements prioritisation and several techniques are applied to do this step.

Pairwise comparison-based approaches are the pivotal pillar for a lot of models and frameworks to prioritise the requirements [1],[3],[4],[5],[6],&[7]. The most commonly used approach is Analytic Hierarchy Process (AHP). It

[a] Corresponding author: author@e-mail.org

compares all unique pairs of requirements to determine which of the two is of higher priority and to what extent [5]. Bubble Sort compares two requirements and swaps them if they are in the wrong order [6] & [8]. Case Based Ranking exploits a machine-learning algorithm to guide the elicitation of user preferences during the prioritisation process [7]. In the Cost-Value approach, each requirement is determined based on its value to the users and the cost of implementing. It also uses the AHP technique [6] & [9]. MoScoW (Museum of Soviet Calculators on the Web) MoScoW is a type of numerical assignment technique. It prioritises based on four priority groups, which are MUST have, SHOULD have, COULD have and WONT have [10] & [11]. Binary Search Tree Binary search tree method by Hopcroft, Aho and Ullman [11] is another technique used for sorting requirements. Berander and Andrews [12] suggested simple ranking requirement prioritisation technique. In simple ranking, requirements are ranged from 1 to n where n is any integer value. Adaptive Fuzzy Hierarchical Cumulative Voting technique uses fuzzy logic with adaptive mechanism.it analyses the different self-adaptive properties like self-heal, self-configure, self-optimize, self-protect [13].

AHP based approaches have the advantage of quantifying stakeholders' judgments and it works well as a computational process. In addition, it could be easily mixed with other models to introduce more robust model. The AHP is a subjective tool to analyse, based on a crisp 9-point scale, the qualitative criteria needed to generate alternative priorities and preferences [3]. The AHP enables decision makers to structure complex problems in a simple hierarchical form, and to evaluate a large number of quantitative and qualitative factors in a systematic manner despite the presence of multiple conflicting criteria. However, it lacks the representation of the rationale and justification for decisions and the negotiation among the stakeholders.

In reality, requirements identification and prioritisation involve politics because defining requirement represents different views and involves bargaining and negotiation to reach the final set of requirements. Models tend to simplify the process and overcome representing conflicts and differences of opinion. Team behaviour and decisions are usually presented as rational however, this is not the case. Individuals in organisations are not honest about their political motivations. Power relations are so embedded in our daily lives. In that respect, we find it is hard to talk about directly.

AL-Ta'ani and Razali [15], in their conceptual framework, have touched this point and they considered the stakeholders' characteristics, which are trust, knowledge, learning, experience and authority, as an environmental factor. It is one of the factors that affect the process and the final product of requirements prioritisation process in agile methods [16]. However, they didn't show the power relationship and didn't have a mathematical formula to calculate this framework.

Milne and Maiden work [16] shows a framework that defines the structure of power relationships networks. This can be used to describe the relationship between stakeholders in Requirements Engineering (RE) process. The framework shows structure of power relations and the process of decision-making by applying it to a case study [16].

Milne and Maiden [16] believe that politics played a role in forming decision-making process and present their framework about straightforward source of power. They use the French and Raven's[17] concept of sources of power that defines five powers: Legitimate, which is formal authority, Reward which is the ability to bestow rewards, Coercive which is the ability to punish, Expert which is possession of skill or knowledge, Referent from personal characteristics [17].

Figure 1 is an example that represents the actors and their power relationship. The most straightforward of the relationships shown in Figure. 1 is the legitimate links between actors. These links reflect the formal power structure of the organisation and it is usually documented in organisational charts and formal job descriptions. In Figure. 1, we see, B has legitimate authority over A and C, and A over F and E. The remaining power relationships within this simple network are based on informal ties. C has power over A by means of Expert power only — perhaps C might control the production of reports required by A. Actor F has power over E through Referent power—based upon interpersonal skills rather than any formal authority. E might rely on F's ability to manage relationships with other actors. The model of power described in Figure 1. implies a straightforward unidirectional exercise of power between actors. This framework can be used to add relative power importance of each stakeholder to the AHP based approach.

Figure 1. Social Network with sources of power [16].

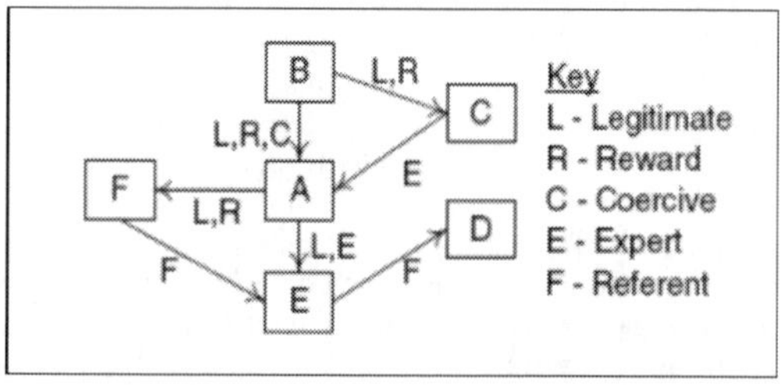

Our proposed model combines both AHP and the source of power mechanism in one scheme. We also tie both with a proposed clear supporting process model. Our approach AHP provides the stable and sound mathematical foundation for supporting individual's judgement on relative importance of pairs of requirements to come out, using simple mathematical manipulation, with a vector that reflects a specific stakeholder view of priorities of a list of requirements. The source of power clarifies the overlooked political merit inherent in the prioritisation process and adds the missing dimension from AHP. We call our scheme Power Analytic Hierarchy Process (PAHP).

Figure 2. The process of developing a hybrid matrix of the PAHP model

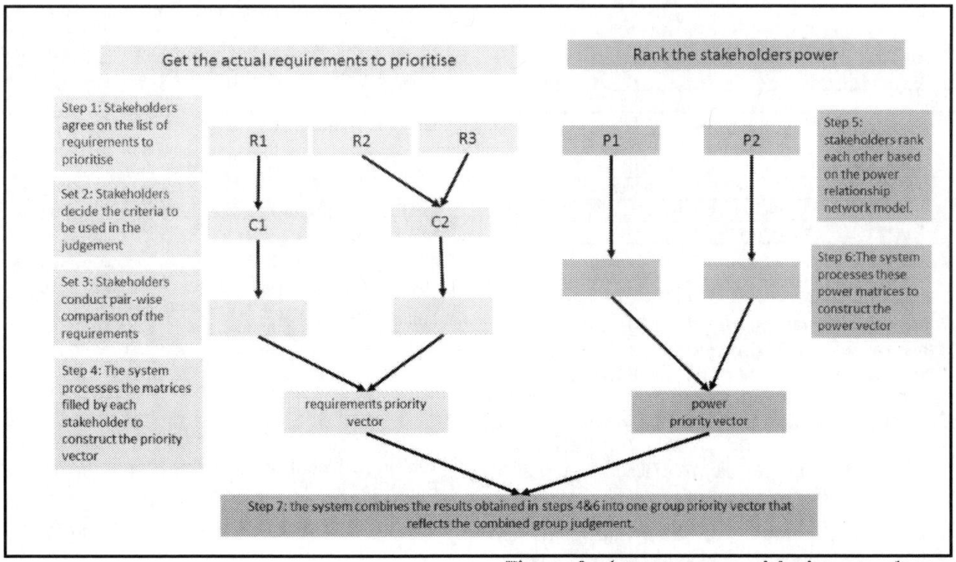

3. Power Analytic Hierarchy Process (PAHP)

3.1 Multi-level hierarchy decision problems &PAHP

Prioritising requirements by a group of stakeholders who may have different goals, is a kind of a decision problem. One efficient solution for such a problem is structuring. Hierarchical structuring techniques can play a pivotal role in solving this problem. The AHP method can perfectly fit because the AHP employs hierarchical structuring and the underlying problem needs such an abstraction technique.

Power Analytic Hierarchy Process (PAHP) models the process of group decision making and reflects the power structure in prioritise the requirements. In other words, it models the process of aggregating the opinions from all experts to get a consensus or compromise results through mutual interaction.

Power Analytic Hierarchy Process (PAHP) is multi-level hierarchy decision problems. The number of levels and what each level, it represents, depends on the nature of the problem and the sought solution. In our case, the problem is to choose and prioritise requirements based on some criteria and the prioritisation is done by a set of stakeholders who have power relationships. We can view this case as a structure that includes four main levels:

- Level 1: the root of the problem (prioritising requirements).
- Level 2: criteria on which judgment is based.
- Level 3: the requirements list to prioritise.
- Level 4: the power types that reflect the weights of the stakeholders

Figure 2 abstracts our model elements along with it process. Steps detailing such a process are presented below.

3.2 The PAHP Model Process

Our model process of combining individual stakeholder judgement into one group of prioritised requirements is viewed in two major activities. Each activity has a number of steps. The first major activity is the one where the actual requirements prioritisation process occurs. The second major activity is the process of ranking stakeholders themselves who will prioritise the requirements. Ranking of stakeholders is based on power relations among participating stakeholders. Both activities are employing AHP based theme as shown in Fig 2. These activities are broken down into six steps to produce the final priorities of the requirements set.

Step 1:Stakeholders agree on the list of requirements to prioritise

This is done in one or more sessions and may require the engagement in an elicitation effort. The outcome of this step is a set of requirements to priortise.

Step 2: Stakeholders decide the criteria to be used in the judgement

Stakeholders then agree on the criteria they will consider to prioritise the requirements. Similar to the previous step, stakeholders choose from criteria collected and agree on those criteria.

Step 3: Stakeholders conduct pair-wise comparison of the requirements

Based on the agreed criteria, each stakeholder is presented with an instance of the problem in the form of a matrix that each includes requirements to prioritise and the criterion against which the requirements pairs are to be compared. Comparison values are drawn from a 9-point scale (see TABLE I).

For example, for three criteria, each stakeholder is required to develop three matrices. In each of these three matrices, stakeholders assign relative importance to each requirement with respect to the other requirement

TABLE I. SCALE AND ITS DESCRIPTION

Scale	Compare factor i and j
1	Equal Importance
3	Weak Importance
5	Strong Importance
7	Very Strong Importance
9	Extreme Importance
Reciprocal	If the comparison value is $a_{ij}, a_{ji}=1/a_{ij}$

Step 4.The system processes the matrices filled by each stakeholder to construct the priority vector.

In this step, a priority vector for each stakeholder reflecting her/his individual judgment is produced following the AHP[5] steps described briefly below. Once all individual stakeholders are done, the system will use individual priority vectors to produce the final group priority vector showing the priority of each requirement with respect to all other requirements.

These (global) priorities of the requirements are obtained by manipulating the importance matrix resulting from the pairwise comparisons. The result of this manipulation is a vector of priorities that has an entry for each requirement.

While n requirements are assumed, n (n-1)/2 elements of the pairwise comparison must be derived. Let C_1, C_2, …, Cn denote the set of requirements to be prioritised against some criteria, while a_{ij} represents a quantified judgment on a pair of requirements C_i, C_j.. This yields an n-by-n matrix A see Equation (1).

$$A=\left[a_{ij}\right]=\begin{array}{c} \\ C_1 \\ C_2 \\ \vdots \\ C_n \end{array}\begin{array}{c} \begin{array}{cccc} C_1 & C_2 & & C_n \end{array} \\ \left[\begin{array}{cccc} 1 & a_{12} & \cdots & a_{1n} \\ 1/a_{12} & 1 & \cdots & a_{2n} \\ \vdots & \vdots & \ddots & \vdots \\ 1/a_{1n} & 1/a_{2n} & \cdots & 1 \end{array}\right] \end{array} \quad (1)$$

To calculate the priorities vector, given the importance matrix M, the priority vector is given by the normalised principal eigenvector of M. The principal eigenvector is the eigenvector corresponding to the largest eigenvalue λ max. The mathematical justification for this result is beyond the scope of this study. For details, please refer to [5]. The desired eigenvector is given by the normalised row sum of the limiting power of the importance matrix. This is obtained by raising the matrix into some arbitrary large power and dividing the sum of each row by the sum of the elements of the matrix.

Since the cost of this kind of computation is expensive in terms of time, some other methods are used that give crude estimates of the required vector. One of these methods called averaging over the normalised columns is summarised in the following stages:

1. Sum each column in the importance matrix M.
2. Divide each element in M by the sum of the column it belongs to obtaining MI.
3. Sum each row in MI, the result is a vector v.
4. Divide v by the sample size of n columns, the result is the required priority vector.

For example, let (gearboxes, horsepower, fuel consumption, air bags) be the list of alternative criteria to choose a car. We follow the earlier steps to prioritise the alternative criteria. After creating the pairwise comparisons, we get A matrix in Equation (2).

$$A=\begin{pmatrix} 1 & 4 & 2 & 5 \\ 1/4 & 1 & 1/4 & 3 \\ 1/2 & 4 & 1 & 4 \\ 1/5 & 1/3 & 1/4 & 1 \end{pmatrix} (2)$$

1: Sum each column in the importance matrix M in Equation (3).

$$M=(1.9 \quad 9.33 \quad 3.5 \quad 13)\ (3)$$

2: Divide each element in M by the sum of the column it belongs to obtaining MI in Equation (4).

$$MI=\begin{pmatrix} 0.51 & 0.42 & 0.5 & 1.89 \\ 0.12 & 0.10 & 0.07 & 0.53 \\ 0.25 & 0.42 & 0.28 & 1.27 \\ 0.1 & 0.35 & 0.7 & 0.28 \end{pmatrix} (4)$$

3 & 4: Sum each row in MI, the result is a vector v; Divide v by the sample size of n columns, the result is the required priority vector in Equation (5).

$$\text{Priority vector} = \begin{pmatrix} 0.47 \\ 0.13 \\ 0.31 \\ 0.07 \end{pmatrix} (5)$$

The priority goes for the gearboxes (0.47) then fuel consumption (0.31) and that is followed by the horsepower (0.13) and air bags (0.07).

Step 5. Stakeholders rank each other based on the power relationship network model.

Stakeholders rank each other's power. Each stakeholder produces five matrices for the five types of power defined by French and Raven i.e., Legitimate (L), Reward (R), Coercive(C), Expert (E)and, Referent(F).

To embed the source of power to PAHP model, TABLE 2 suggests numerical values for each sources of power based on their definition [18]. We use the same 9-point scale in TABLE I for the pairwise comparison. Legitimate or formal authority has the highest value because there is no Legitimate without Reward and/or Coercive [19] that takes the value 9. In some cultures, Expert has almost equal power as Legitimate but still does not have the full control. This is why we set it with the value 7. Referent effect depends upon the culture and the environment and interpersonal skills however, it is not as influential as Expert and knowledge, so we give it the value 5. The Reward power which is the ability to bestow rewards, has higher influence than Coercive power, which is the ability to punish [19].We scale reward with 3 and coercive with 1.

TABLE 2. THE SOURCE OF POWER EXPLANATION

Source of power	scale	Explanation
L C= Coercive	1	the ability to punish,
R= Reward	3	the ability to bestow rewards,
F= Referent—from personal characteristics	5	Referent affection is depending upon the culture and the environment
E= Expert—possession of skill or knowledge,	7	In some cultures, Expert has almost equal power as Legitimate,
L= Legitimate—formal authority	9	There is no Legitimate without Reward and/or Coercive,

In this step, power matrices are established for each stakeholder and each power type. Each stakeholder establishes one matrix for each type of power that reflects power weights of stakeholders as expressed by this stakeholder in matrix M in Equation (6).

$$M = (pij)\begin{pmatrix} 1 & p12 & & p1n \\ 1/p12 & 1 & \cdots & p2n \\ \vdots & & \ddots & \vdots \\ 1/p1n & 1/p2n & \cdots & 1 \end{pmatrix} (6)$$

Step 6.The system uses these power matrices to process the power vector.

If we have 10 stakeholders and 5 types of power, 50 matrices are produced. The previous Equations 1, 2, 3, 4, &5 are applied to produce an eigenvector for each power per one stakeholder. Then one priority vector that represents the group decision about power relationships.

Step 7. The system combines the results obtained in steps 4&6 into one group priority vector that reflects the combined group judgement.

This step combines both activities "actual prioritisation of requirements" and "ranking the stakeholders" and products one set of prioritised requirements that could map realistic one.

CASE STUDY

To explain the process model and clarify the steps in details, we describe the steps with an example of setting and prioritising a list of requirements to develop a human resources software in a multinational company.

Step 1:Stakeholders agree on the list of requirements to prioritise

In a multinational company, they want to develop a new human resources system. The panel, that has to decide on prioritising these requirements, consists of the following stakeholders: A (Marketing), B (Sales), C (Finance), and D (IT and Development) departments' representatives and each has different authority. Stakeholders have set seven main requirements that the system need to have. The requirements are R1 customer ease of use, R2 scalability, R3 performance, R4 cost, R5 security, R6 modifiability, and R7 ease of installation.

1) Step 2: Stakeholders decide the criteria to be used in the judgement

In that respect, in a session, stakeholders discussed the requirements and agreed to consider money is the criterion.

Step 3: Stakeholders conduct pair-wise comparison of the requirements

In this step, requirements' matrices are collected from each stakeholder.

Step 4.The system processes the matrices filled by each stakeholder to construct the priority vector.

Here, the eigenvector is calculated, and consistency test is checked as in [5].

$$\text{Stakeholder A} = \begin{bmatrix} 1 & 0.143 & 0.333 & 0.333 & 1 & 0.143 & 0.5 \\ 7 & 1 & 5 & 5 & 5 & 3 & 5 \\ 3 & 0.2 & 1 & 2 & 2 & 0.2 & 3 \\ 3 & 0.2 & 0.5 & 1 & 3 & 0.2 & 1 \\ 1 & 0.2 & 0.5 & 0.333 & 1 & 0.2 & 2 \\ 7 & 0.333 & 5 & 5 & 5 & 1 & 5 \\ 1 & 0.2 & 0.333 & 1 & 0.2 & 0.2 & 1 \end{bmatrix}$$

CI/RI = 0.088/1.32 = 0.067

$$\text{Stakeholder B} = \begin{bmatrix} 1 & 3 & 0.333 & 0.2 & 0.333 & 3 & 2 \\ 0.333 & 1 & 0.2 & 0.2 & 0.2 & 0.5 & 0.333 \\ 3 & 5 & 1 & 2 & 2 & 5 & 3 \\ 5 & 5 & 0.5 & 1 & 0.5 & 5 & 3 \\ 5 & 5 & 0.5 & 2 & 1 & 5 & 3 \\ 0.333 & 2 & 0.2 & 0.2 & 0.2 & 1 & 0.333 \\ 0.5 & 03 & 0.333 & 0.333 & 0.333 & 3 & 1 \end{bmatrix}$$

CI/RI = 0.089/1.32 = 0.068

$$\text{Stakeholder C} = \begin{bmatrix} 1 & 0.167 & 0.143 & 5 & 0.143 & 0.111 & 7 \\ 6 & 1 & 0.333 & 7 & 3 & 0.333 & 7 \\ 7 & 3 & 1 & 7 & 5 & 0.5 & 8 \\ 0.2 & 0.143 & 0.143 & 1 & 0.125 & 0.167 & 3 \\ 7 & 0.333 & 0.2 & 8 & 1 & 0.2 & 9 \\ 9 & 3 & 2 & 6 & 5 & 1 & 7 \\ 0.143 & 0.143 & 0.125 & 0.333 & 0.1111 & 0.143 & 1 \end{bmatrix}$$

CI/RI = 0.093/1.32 = 0.070

$$\text{Stakeholder D}=\begin{bmatrix} 1 & 0.5 & 2 & 2 & 0.333 & 5 & 0.2 \\ 2 & 1 & 3 & 2 & 0.333 & 5 & 4 \\ 0.5 & 0.333 & 1 & 2 & 0.2 & 5 & 0.143 \\ 0.5 & 0.5 & 0.5 & 1 & 0.333 & 5 & 5 \\ 3 & 3 & 5 & 3 & 1 & 5 & 0.333 \\ 0.2 & 0.2 & 0.2 & 0.2 & 0.167 & 1 & 0.1111 \\ 5 & 4 & 7 & 6 & 3 & 9 & 1 \end{bmatrix}$$

CI/RI = 0.075/1.32 = 0.057

All calculated eigenvector for the seven requirements of each stakeholder and put in one matrix (S)

$$S=\begin{bmatrix} 0.038706 & 0.099632 & 0.065454 & 0.08404 \\ 0.38039 & 0.036411 & 0.160784 & 0.161207 \\ 0.108828 & 0.280928 & 0.25934 & 0.063748 \\ 0.085427 & 0.205461 & 0.034073 & 0.121476 \\ 0.05806 & 0.245183 & 0.131788 & 0.196178 \\ 0.280723 & 0.045538 & 0.326521 & 0.01863 \\ 0.047866 & 0.086846 & 0.02204 & 0.354722 \end{bmatrix}$$

2) Step 5. Stakeholders rank each other based on the power relationship network model.

The 5 stakeholders, namely A (Marketing), B (Sales), C (Finance), and D (IT and Development) departments' representatives, have different authority. In the network of power, Fig.3 shows the different power each stakeholder has of legitimate, reward, coercive, expert, and referent.

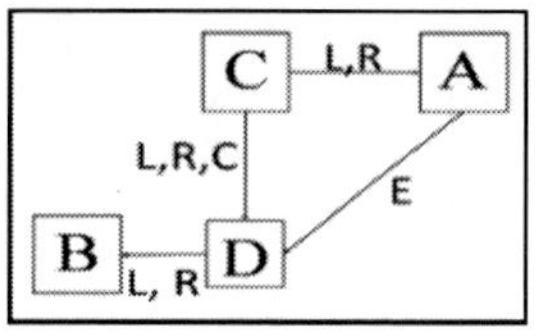

Fig. 3. Assumed model power

Step 6. The system uses these power matrices to process the power vector.

Because of the technical aspects of the system, the expert is the determine power. The expert matrix is calculated based on the figure 3 network of power. Accordingly, the eigenvector is calculated. Furthermore, the consistency test is checked.

$$\text{Power (E)}=\begin{bmatrix} 1 & 3 & 4 & 7 \\ 0.333 & 1 & 3 & 5 \\ 0.25 & 0.333 & 1 & 4 \\ 0.143 & 0.2 & 0.25 & 1 \end{bmatrix}$$

CR=0.0638

$$\text{The eigenvalue is}=\begin{bmatrix} 0.53445 \\ 0.267823 \\ 0.143703 \\ 0.054024 \end{bmatrix}$$

3) Step 7. The system combines the results obtained in steps 4&6 into one group priority vector that reflects the combined group judgement

In this step, the system multiples the produced matrix in step 4 that has the eigenvector for the seven requirements by the eigenvector of the expert power calculated in step 6.

Priorities =

$$\begin{bmatrix} 0.038706 & 0.099632 & 0.065454 & 0.08404 \\ 0.38039 & 0.036411 & 0.160784 & 0.161207 \\ 0.108828 & 0.280928 & 0.25934 & 0.063748 \\ 0.085427 & 0.205461 & 0.034073 & 0.121476 \\ 0.05806 & 0.245183 & 0.131788 & 0.196178 \\ 0.280723 & 0.045538 & 0.326521 & 0.01863 \\ 0.047866 & 0.086846 & 0.02204 & 0.354722 \end{bmatrix} * \begin{bmatrix} 0.53445 \\ 0.267823 \\ 0.143703 \\ 0.054024 \end{bmatrix} =$$

$$\begin{bmatrix} 0.061316 \\ \mathbf{0.244865} \\ 0.174114 \\ 0.112143 \\ 0.126232 \\ 0.210157 \\ 0.071172 \end{bmatrix}$$

The produced vector shows that R2 scalability is the first then R6 modifiability, R3 performance, R5 security, R4 cost, R7 ease of installation, and finally R1 customer ease of use.

4. Discussions

The theme of our proposed approach in tackling the requirements prioritisation activity deals with the problem in wider spectrum than currently practiced. First, it combines technical quantitative judgment method that is based on sound mathematical basis, with commonly overlooked realistic factors that affect the outcome of the whole prioritisation process which is the power relationships among stakeholders. To the best of our knowledge, this is the first work to combine both aspects in one scheme.

Second, we managed to express the power relationships using the same mathematical basis that the AHP adopts which led to our ability to rank stakeholders using priority vector derived from power relationships. This manipulation enabled us to get a homogenous combined priority vector for the whole process that encompasses the group judgment regarding the set of the requirements and also embedded power relations among stakeholders.

As for the process itself, all what is required from stakeholders is agreeing on the set of requirements to be prioritised and the criteria to be used in the judgment process. Once agreed, each stakeholder is presented with an instance of the problem structure and is actually engaged in the prioritisation that is mostly mechanised. For example, a stakeholder is required to fill only half of a comparison matrix and the system will automatically fill the other half. From this point on, the system performs the rest of the computations automatically until produces the final group combined priority vector.

One might question the cost of such a process especially with the commonly adopted agile approaches of software developments. However, requirements prioritisation is traditionally a required activity with large systems that have many stakeholders whose goals may be contradicting and this even goes with small agile system. For example in Scrum, the prioritisation activity could be part of the project planning or release planning activities to select features to be included in the project.

Currently, we are working on a prototype of a software tool that implements and supports this model and its process and evolves gradually into a complete system. We intend to use the system in sizable projects in cooperation with. This will enable us to get realistic result and measure the effectiveness and the viability of our approach. We will report on the obtained results.

5. Conclusions

Prioritising requirements is a critical activity in requirements engineering that mandates devising effective methods and techniques that take into account different dimensions of the endeavor and provide automated support for the process. In this paper, we presented a combined scheme for prioritising requirements that is based in part on the mathematical basis of the AHP method while weaving in the process an overlooked aspect which is the power authority and its effect on the outcome of the process.

Our proposed combined scheme does not only account for ranking requirements based on a mathematical model, but also ranking stakeholders engaged in the prioritisation process using the same mathematical model. The application of our scheme and its process will yield prioritisation of requirements, while embedding the overlooked power authorities with its different interpretations.

Currently we are engaged in developing a prototype that implements our scheme model and process that will be evolved into a complete system. The completed system will be used to run experimentations using realistic software development projects.

As a future work, we intend to formalise the scalability of our scheme as the set of the requirements gets larger. We also intend to study the refinement of the outcome result of our proposed scheme by the project's identified risks so that judgment criteria do not conflict with critical risks. We believe that more elaboration is needed to answer many questions in order to use our scheme in agile based development project.

References

1. Sommerville and P. Sawyer Requirements Engineering: A Good Practice Guide, John Wiley & Sons, Inc.: New York,1997.
2. Firesmith, Donald. "Prioritizing Requirements." Journal of Object Technology 3.8 (2004): 35-48.
3. Nuseibeh and S. Easterbrook. "Requirements engineering: a roadmap" ACM, the Conference on The Future of Software Engineering (ICSE '00). New York, NY, USA, 35-46. 2000.
4. S. M. Easterbrook, and B. A. Nuseibeh, "Managing Inconsistencies in an Evolving Specification." Second IEEE Symposium on Requirements Engineering, York, UK, March 27-29,pp. 48-55, 1995.
5. T.L., Saaty, "The Analytic Hierarchy Process", New York,NY: McGraw-Hill, 1980.
6. J. Karlsson, "Software requirements prioritizing" 2nd IEEE Int. Conf. on Requirements Eng. pp. 110–116, 1996.
7. P. Avesani, A. Perini and A. Susi, "Supporting the Requirements Prioritization Process: A Machine Learning Approach,". 16th International Conference on Software Engineering and Knowledge engineering, Banff, Alberta, June 2004.
8. J. Karlsson and K. Ryan, "Prioritizing requirements using a cost-value approach", IEEE Software vol 14:5, pp. 67–74, 1997.
9. J. Karlsson and K. Ryan.A "Cost-Value Approach for Prioritizing Requirements", IEEE Software, September/October 1997, pp. 67-74. 1997.
10. Dsdm Public version 4.2, from www.dsdm.org, Tech. Rep., Retrieved, 6 June, 2015.
11. A.V. Aho, J.D. Ullman and J.E.Hopcroft, data structure and algrithems, Reading, MA: Addison-Wesley, January 11, 1983.
12. P. Berander and A. Andrews. "Requirements prioritization".In Engineering and Managing Software Requirements, Aurum A. and Wohlin C. (eds). Springer,chap. 4, 2005.
13. G. Eason, B. Noble, and I.N. Sneddon, "On certain integrals of Lipschitz-Hankel type involving products of Bessel functions," Phil. Trans. Roy. Soc. London, vol. A247, pp. 529-551, April 1955. (*references*)
14. E. Bagheri, M. Asadi, D. Gasevic, and S. Soltani, (?). Stratified Analytic Hierarchy Process: Prioritization and Selection of Software Features
15. R. H. AL-Ta'ani and R.Razali "Prioritizing requirements in agile development:A conceptual framework" The 4th International Conference on Electrical Engineering and Informatics (ICEEI 2013) Procedia Technology, vol 11, pp. 733 – 739, 2013.
16. Milne and N. Maiden "Power and politics in requirements engineering: embracing the dark side?" Requirements Eng vol. 17 p.83–98, 2012.
17. J. R.P. French and B. Raven. Bases of Social Power." Studies in Social Power. Ed. Dorwin Cartwright. University of Michigan, Ann Arbor,1959.
18. J.L. Gibson, J.M. Ivancevich, JH. Donnelly, and R. Konopaske Organizations: Behavior, Structure, Processes. 14, NY : McGraw-Hill, 2012.
19. R. J Lewicki,., D. M., Saunders, and J. W. Minton, Negotiation. 3rd ed., Boston: Irwin-McGraw Hill 1999.

MATEC Web of Conferences **76**, 04017 (2016)
CSCC 2016
DOI: 10.1051/matecconf/20167604017

Employing finite-state machines in data integrity problems

Andrey Malikov[1,a], Vladimir Voronkin[1], and Nikolay Shiryaev[1]

[1]*Department of Applied Information Science, North-Caucasus Federal University. 1, Pushkin Street, Stavropol, Russian Federation.*

Abstract. This paper explores the issue of group integrity of tuple subsets regarding corporate integrity constraints in relational databases. A solution may be found by applying the finite-state machine theory to guarantee group integrity of data. We present a practical guide to coding such an automaton. After creating SQL queries to manipulate data and control its integrity for real data domains, we study the issue of query performance, determine the level of transaction isolation, and generate query plans.
Keywords: database, integrity, finite-state machine, finite-state automaton, directed graph, SQL query

1 Problem formulation

The most common definition of a data model includes a combination of three interrelated components [1]: the structural component that defines the structural contents of objects used in the model; the manipulation component, which describes the operators that manipulate the model's objects; the integrity component, which consists of rules that guarantee data integrity.

In context of a relational data model, the structural component defines a data object as an a-nary relation built on a set of domains. Relations contain unorganized sets of tuples, which are identified with a primary key.

The manipulation part of the model consists of relational calculus and relational algebra. The most popular declarative language aid for data access is the Structured Query Language – SQL.

The integrity component is vital for the functioning of informational systems. Despite our inability to fully match all qualities and properties of real-life objects in our model, this component will ensure that these properties are consistent and non-contradictory.

There are three types of integrity rules in relational databases: entity integrity – no primary key attribute of a basic relation should have a NULL value; referential integrity – any value of a foreign key in a relation must match the value of a primary or candidate key in the parent relation or be comprised solely of NULL values and corporate integrity constraints – additional rules for data consistency defined by the data domain.

The first two rules are already implemented in relational DBMS quite effectively and efficiently. Typically, these data integrity mechanisms focus on correctness of singular tuples and data values.

Corporate integrity constraints may demand the tuples be in some group consistency, while remaining individually correct and strictly correspond to the real-life object of the data domain, for example: the overall salary of employees in one department must not exceed some limit and the individual salaries of each employee must be in a certain range; hiring and firing heads of departments should only be performed in conjunction with hiring or firing the inferior staff; managing complex objects (described by more than one tuple) when you need to maintain a chain of tuples, linked by binary relations of order. For example, a table of traffic light colors should be ordered like this: "red" then "yellow" then "green".

There are some special cases when it comes to organizing relations, such as managing temporal data [2], hierarchical data [3], and the combination of the two [4]. The mentioned cases bring structural limitations to the model. That is why it is necessary to maintain group integrity of tuples. Let us examine each case closely.

Constraining temporal data, is when you need to maintain the right chronological order. In this case, every tuple corresponds to a state of an object at a point in time; the subset of these tuples describe the changes that the object undergoes during some period of time. It is necessary, therefore, to make sure that any pair of tuples is not in a temporal contradiction, and that the full subset of tuples creates a logically sound chain like: "state 1" before "state 2" before "state 3" etc. As an example, let us look at the stages a student goes through during their study at a university: "enrolling at the university" then "moving up a year" then "…" and finally "graduating".

Constraining hierarchical data is needed to guarantee correct subordination of all objects. A typical example is the chain of command in a company from "head" to "deputy" to "assistant".

Constraining temporal hierarchical data is simply maintaing the chain of subordination throughout the timeline.

Providing data integrity is relevant not only for relational data models. The currently popular NoSQL DBMS (such as MongoDB [5]) either does not support the ACID transaction management model or supports in only partially

[a]Corresponding author: AMalikov@ncfu.ru

[6]. A database designer interacts with simple-structure documents, identifiable by a unique id (key-value model). Interrelations between documents can be created based on their nesting-levels or by using key references, and that is why we are also considering the issue of group integrity of documents.

We can create a binary relation for each of the mentioned cases on the tuple-subset level, i.e. we can compare any pair of tuples from the subset, while the subset itself is ordered. This fact lets us apply automata theory [7] to achieve integrity of any subset of tuples. Introducing new mechanisms of constraining data integrity deviates us from the classical definition of a relation, because tuples stop being completely independent.

Typically, when solving such problems, corporate logic is implemented as a servicing application. This spreads the database interaction logic on both the application and the database. With time, such a system becomes more difficult to maintain.

A much simpler way is to implement corporate logic on one level.

The most reasonable way for large systems that operate numerous queries and procedures is to realize the update logic on the database level and put all the rest in the application.

A quite thorough description of finite automata, logics of several orders, and their uses is given in L.Libkin's book [8]. A model of finite automata theory elements in databases is described in V.Vianu's paper [9].

Using finite state machines doesn't just have uses in corporate integrity control. There are applications in the banking sector [10], uses for modelling trading systems [11], and creating recursive queries [12] for tasks like graph processing.

2 Implementing the finite-state machine in a relational database

Let us consider the realization of a finite state machine to constrain group data integrity using the Transact-SQL language in the MS SQL Server DBMS.

The finite state machine is set as $(Q, \sum, \delta, q_0, F)$ [7], [13], where: Q is the finite set of possible states of the machine;

$\sum$ is the alphabet of the automaton;

δ is a transition function, and $\delta : Q \times \sum \rightarrow Q$

q_0 is the start state.

F is the set of possible final states, $F \subseteq Q$

Let us examine the following example (without giving up the generic nature of our model) – a finite state machine of student statuses (fig. 1). The program module that tracks the chronology of students' movement is used in the information and education hub at the North-Caucus Federal University in Stavropol, Russia. Websites [14], [15] provide specialized educational content for students of over 500 schools and universities in the Stavropol region as well as providing consistent data processing of student movement for over 500 000 students.

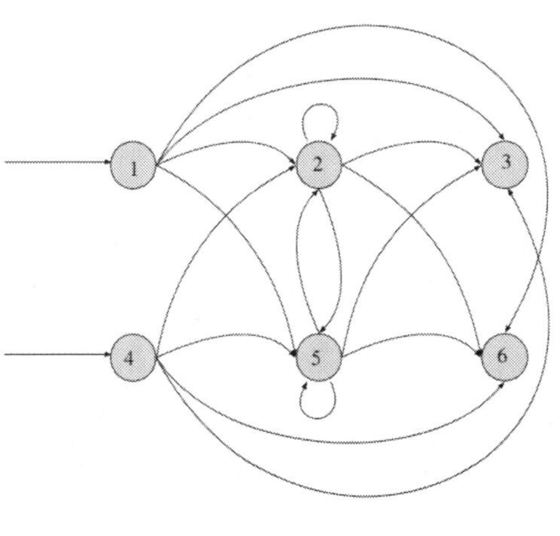

Figure 1. The finite-state machine of student statuses during their education

Table 1. The transition matrix for the machine

Alphabet	Machine state						
	start	1	2	3	4	5	6
1	1						
2		1	1		1		1
3		1	1		1		1
4	1						
5		1	1		1		1
6		1	1		1		1

The set of states consists of six elements $Q = \{1$ – (enrolling); 2 – (moving up a year); 3 – (expulsion due to graduation); 4 – (transfer from another university); 5 – (transfer to another university); 6 – (left to repeat the course)$\}$. (1) and (4) are start states and (3), (5) are final states. The alphabet $\sum$ in our case, is a set of characters that matches the set of possible stages Q. The automaton reads a word $w = (a_1, a_2, \ldots, a_n)$, $a_i \in \sum$ – a time-sorted sequence of states. The machine only accepts the word w, if by the end of starting word the machine ends up in an allowed state.

The transition matrix for the machine is presented in table 1.

To implement a finite-state machine in a relational database, one needs to create special tables, in which the machine's structure is coded by at least one of the following means [16], [3]:

First, the "parent-child" concept for coding the graph's adjacency matrix. The advantage of this method is its versatility in modelling complex graph structures. The weakness is lower query performance compared to the "materialized path" method. Another shortcoming is the difficulty of restoring valid words via a declarative language. However, this method is considered to be universal and can be used to model any arbitrary finite-state machine.

Table 2. An example of the "*movement*" table

idMov	idSchoolboy	idPr	dateMov
1	1	1	01.09.2014
2	1	2	01.07.2015

Second, the materialized graph path concept. The strengths of this method are data visualization, which makes it easier to comprehend, because each materialized path has a valid word attached to it, and high performance handling graph models when using index structures like B+tree. However, there are two disadvantages to this method. The first is rapid growth of relationship cardinality, which, in the worst case, will grow exponentially, depending on the properties of the machine. The second major disadvantage is the inability to code cycles and cyclical transitions – their presence would lead to a word with infinite length. Nevertheless, this method is the best alternative for modelling large machines with no cycles.

Third, the "ancestor-successor" concept for coding the graph's reachability matrix. This method has all of the pros and cons of previously mentioned methods.

3 Coding the machine in the parent-child model

Let us examine the specificity of using a finite-state machine that will check for data integrity and is coded in the parent-child model. We will require three tables:

First, the index-table of automaton states: *process (idPr int, name varchar(max))*.

Second, a table with the machine itself, two foreign keys of which refer to *process.idPr: automaton (idPar int, idCh int)*. The pair *(idPar int, idCh int)* is the primary key of the "*automaton*" table. According to fig. 1 the "*automaton*" table will have 20 entries; starting states are coded as (0,1) and (0,4), final states – as (3,0) and (5,0). Here are the contents of table "*automaton*" {(0,1), (1,5), (1,3), (1,2), (1,6), (2,2), (2,3), (2,5), (2,6), (0,4), (4,2), (4,6), (4,5), (4,3), (6,2), (6,6), (6,3), (6,5), (3,0), (5,0)}.

Third, a table of student movement. The foreign key will refer to *process.idPr: movement (idMov int, idSchoolboy int, idPr int, dateMov date)*. Here, *idSchoolboy* is the student's id; *dateMov* is the date of movement.

Table 2 contains an example of the "*movement*" table for student *idSchoolboy=1*. Group integrity of tuples is intact, because chronologically, the student was first admitted to the university, and then moved up a year.

According to Table 2, an attempt at adding the row (3, 1, 5, '01.09.2015') will result in success, but trying to add (3, 1, 5, '01.06.2015') will end in failure, because there would be a contradiction, where the final state is between the intervening ones.

Implementing a finite-state machine with this model does not allow us to effectively restore the list of acceptable words via a declarative language. In the worst case, cyclical transitions will make this list infinitely large (refer to fig.1).

We will use two lemmas to judge the acceptability of words, based on their fragments.

Lemma 1 - Word fragment lemma

If $P^n(V', E')$ is a path on graph $G = (V, E)$ of a finite-state machine $V' \subseteq V, E' \subseteq E, v_i' \in V', i = 0..n$; and $P^m(V'', E'')$ is a path on graph $G = (V, E)$ of a finite-state machine $V''' \subseteq V, E''' \subseteq E, v_i''' \in V''', i = 1..k$, so that,

1. $\exists(v_n', v_1'''), (v_n', v_1''') \in E$, or $|V'| = 0$;
2. $\exists(v_k''', v_1''), (v_k''', v_1'') \in E$, or $|V''| = 0$;

then $P = P^n \bigcup P^k \bigcup P^m$ is an acceptable path on graph G.

Consequence of lemma 1: a compound path exists on a graph, if all component paths exist and the condition of chronological order is met.

Lemma 2 – Lemma of the first fragment of an expectable word:

If in lemma 1 $q_0 \in P^n$, then P is the prefix of an expectable word.

According to the lemmas, it is necessary and sufficient to: check whether the new entry is allowed to change from the old state into the new state or if it is placed in the starting position; in order to allow parallel processing of transactions, including simultaneous access to the same word, it is necessary to introduce the following rule: transactions that manipulate data (adding, editing and deleting) should block the range of entry pairs, between which the manipulated entry lies, according to binary ordering relationship.

Let us create a query to add a single tuple. This will be a successful try (the initial state of the "*movement*" table is presented in Table 2)

Query 1:

```
declare @idSchoolboy int,
        @dateMov dateTime,
        @idPr int
set @idSchoolboy=1
set @dateMov='01.09.2015'
set @idPr=5
set transaction isolation level
    serializable

insert into movement (
        idSchoolboy,
        dateMov,
        idPr)
select @idSchoolboy, @dateMov, @idPr
from automaton previousConnection,
     automaton nextConnection
where previousConnection.idCh=@idPr
    and previousConnection.idPar=
        isnull((select top 1 idPr
    from movement b
    where b.idSchoolboy=@idSchoolboy
        and b.dateMov<=@dateMov
    order by dateMov desc),0) and
   nextConnection.idPar=@idPr and
   nextConnection.idCh=
      isnull((select top 1 idPr
```

```
        from movement b
    where b.idSchoolboy=@idSchoolboy
        and b.dateMov>=@dateMov
    order by dateMov asc),
    case isnull((select top 1 idPr
      from movement b
      where b.idSchoolboy=@idSchoolboy
          and b.dateMov<=@dateMov
      order by dateMov desc),0) when 0
    then (select top 1 idCh
      automaton anyConnection
      where idPar=@idPr)
    else 0 end)
```

And now, and attempt at adding an entry, which will fail the integrity check.

Query 2:

```
declare @idSchoolboy int,
        @dateMov dateTime,
        @idPr int
set @idSchoolboy=1
set @dateMov='01.06.2015'
set @idPr=5
set transaction isolation level
    serializable

insert into movement (
                idSchoolboy,
                dateMov,
                idPr)
select @idSchoolboy, @dateMov, @idPr
from automaton previousConnection,
        automaton nextConnection
where previousConnection.idCh=@idPr and
  previousConnection.idPar=
    isnull((select top 1 idPr
    from movement b
    where b.idSchoolboy=@idSchoolboy
      and b.dateMov<=@dateMov
    order by dateMov desc),0) and
  nextConnection.idPar=@idPr and
  nextConnection.idCh=
    isnull((select top 1 idPr
      from movement b
    where b.idSchoolboy=
      @idSchoolboy and
      b.dateMov>=@dateMov
    order by dateMov asc),
    case isnull((select top 1 idPr
      from movement b
      where b.idSchoolboy=
        @idSchoolboy and
        b.dateMov<=@dateMov
      order by dateMov desc),0) when 0
    then (select top 1 idCh
        from automaton anyConnection
        where idPar=@idPr)
    else 0 end)
```

The main purpose of this SQL-query is to find adjacent entries between which we are adding a new item. If the machine allows the transition from a previous state to the new one and from the new one to the next one, then the operation will be successful. The exceptions are trying to add a starting or a final state. In the first case, we only need to check if it is consistent with the following states, and in the second – we only need to verify consistency with states before it. If the algorithm finds inconsistency, the operation fails.

The query consists of four parts:

1. Preparation of data to be added into the target table:

```
insert into movement (idSchoolboy,
                      dateMov, idPr)
select @idSchoolboy, @dateMov, @idPr
```

2. The table with data about the structure of the automaton is opened under two pseudonyms to search for states before and after the one in question:

```
from automaton previousConnection,
        automaton nextConnection
```

3. Verifying that the previous sates are acceptable or that the entry is in a starting state:

```
where previousConnection.idCh=@idPr and
  previousConnection.idPar=
    isnull((select top 1 idPr
    from movement b
    where
      b.idSchoolboy=@idSchoolboy and
      b.dateMov<=@dateMov
    order by dateMov desc),0) and
```

4. Verifying that the following sates are acceptable or that the entry is in a final state. Also, performing the consistency check for a case when the entry we are adding is the very first one in the group:

```
  nextConnection.idPar=@idPr and
  nextConnection.idCh=
    isnull((select top 1 idPr
    from movement b
    where b.idSchoolboy=@idSchoolboy
    and b.dateMov>=@dateMov
    order by dateMov asc),
    case isnull((select top 1 idPr
      from movement b
      where b.idSchoolboy=
        @idSchoolboy and
        b.dateMov<=@dateMov
      order by dateMov desc),0) when 0
    then (select top 1 idCh
      from automaton anyConnection
      where idPar=@idPr)
    else 0 end)
```

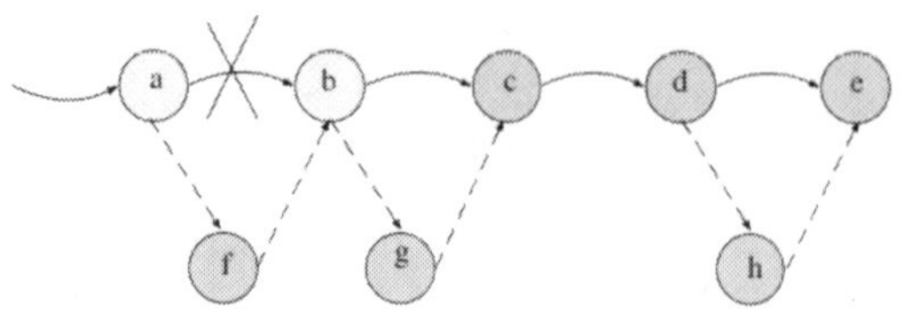

Figure 2. Parallel execution of transactions that alter the same word

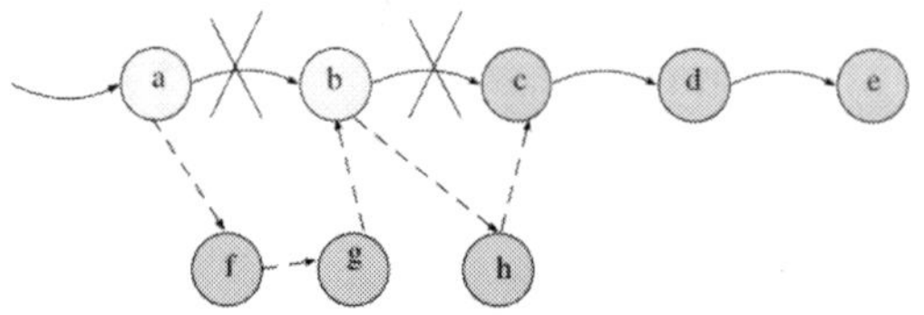

Figure 3. Batch loading of several symbols into a word

4 The issue of query performance and parallel transaction processing

Let us examine the issue of paralleling transactions that alter the same word simultaneously and the issue of implementing batch data loading transactions.

When dealing with parallel transaction processing, it is necessary to establish blocking rules, which would deny access to joint characters while the transaction of adding new characters is in processing. Fig. 2. presents a case of parallel processing of three transactions: tr1, tr2, and tr3, each one trying to add one symbol to alter the word 'abcde'. Transaction tr1 destroys the fragment 'ab' by creating a new one – 'afb'. This leads to a blocking of a range of entries with symbols 'a' and 'b'. That is why any transaction that alters the fragment 'ab' cannot be processed simultaneously with tr1. Transaction tr2 must run after tr1 because it will wait for the entry with 'b' to be unblocked. Transactions tr1 and tr3 can be processed at the same time, because they do not block shared entries.

In the case of batch loading of data, where one transaction attempts to add several symbols to a word, it is important to note that new word fragments are created with already existing symbols as well as new ones. Fig. 3. presents a situation, where tr1 blocks the range of entries with symbols 'a', 'b', and 'c' by destroying fragment 'abc' and creating a new one – 'afgbhc'.

To make sure that all transactions are executed correctly, we will need a SERIALIZABLE level of transaction isolation. It would block a range of keys that meet the following conditions [17]: instructions cannot read data that was just altered by another transaction but not yet formalized; other transactions cannot alter data that is being read by the current transaction until it finishes; other transactions cannot create new rows with key values that are in the range of keys being read by the instruction of the current transaction until it finishes.

Analysis of queries (1, 2) shows ways of improving performance of data processing operations. Taking into account query predicates and chosen fields, we will need to create the following B+tree type indexes:

– A clustered composite index with uniqueness support – *automaton.IX_idCh_idPar(idCh, idPar)*. It will be used to search for previous states when we know current ones and will ensure that the composite primary key {idCh, idPar} is unique.

– A non-clustered composite index *automaton.IX_idPar_idCh (idPar, idCh)*. It will be used to search for following states when we know the current ones.

– A non-clustered compound index *movement.IX_idSchoolBoy_dateMov_idPr(idSchoolBoy, dateMov)* with included column *ipPr*. It will be used to search data by students and their movement dates.

The relevant part of a query plan is shown in Fig. 4. It uses index searching to access data. Analysis operators that check whether a new tuple is consistent with previous sates are in box number one, the ones checking consistency with the next states are in box number two, and the ones checking the newly added starting and final states are in box three.

Now let us create a query to add a set of tuples containing symbols, which will alter the initial word (the initial state of the "*movement*" table is presented in Table 2)

Query 3:

```
declare @movement_new table (idMov int,
  idSchoolboy int, dateMov dateTime,
  idPr int)
insert into @movement_new (idMov,
  idSchoolboy, dateMov, idPr)
    values (-1, 1, '01.10.2014', 1)
insert into @movement_new (idMov,
  idSchoolboy, dateMov, idPr)
    values (-2, 1, '01.10.2015', 2)
insert into @movement_new (idMov,
  idSchoolboy, dateMov, idPr)
    values (-3, 1, '01.11.2015', 3)
set transaction isolation level
serializable;

begin transaction;
with movement_tmp (idMov,
  idSchoolboy, dateMov, idPr, isNew)
as
(select idMov, idSchoolboy,
        dateMov, idPr, 1
 from @movement_new
   union all
 select idMov, idSchoolboy,
        dateMov, idPr, 0
 from movement
   where idSchoolboy in
     (select distinct idSchoolboy
      from @movement_new))
insert into movement (idSchoolboy,
```

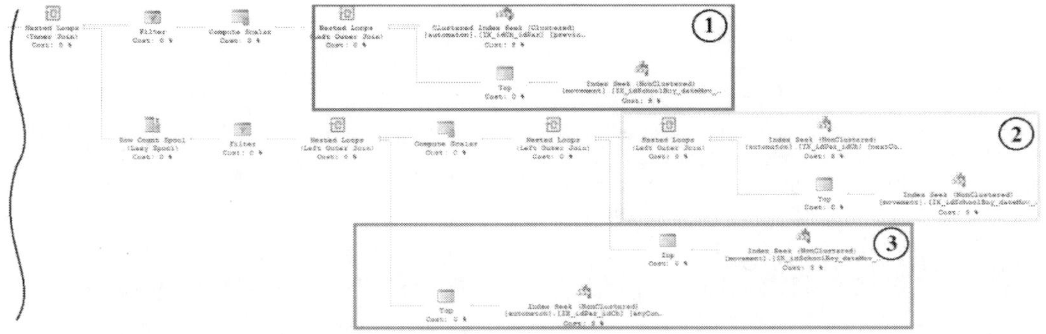

Figure 4. The relevant part of query plan to add a single tuple

```
                dateMov, idPr)

select movement_tmp.idSchoolboy,
  movement_tmp.dateMov,
  movement_tmp.idPr
from automaton previousConnection,
  automaton nextConnection,
  movement_tmp
where movement_tmp.isNew=1 and
  previousConnection.idCh=
    movement_tmp.idPr and
  previousConnection.idPar=
    isnull((select top 1 idPr
      from movement_tmp b
      where b.idSchoolboy=
        movement_tmp.idSchoolboy
        and b.dateMov<=
          movement_tmp.dateMov and
        b.idMov<>movement_tmp.idMov
      order by dateMov desc),0) and
  nextConnection.idPar=
    movement_tmp.idPr and
  nextConnection.idCh=
    isnull((select top 1 idPr
      from movement_tmp b
      where b.idSchoolboy=
        movement_tmp.idSchoolboy and
        b.dateMov>=
          movement_tmp.dateMov
        and b.idMov<>
          movement_tmp.idMov
      order by dateMov asc),
    case isnull((select top 1 idPr
      from movement_tmp b
      where b.idSchoolboy=
        movement_tmp.idSchoolboy and
          b.dateMov<=
            movement_tmp.dateMov
          and b.idMov<>
            movement_tmp.idMov
      order by dateMov desc),0) when 0
    then (select top 1 idCh
          from automaton anyConnection
```

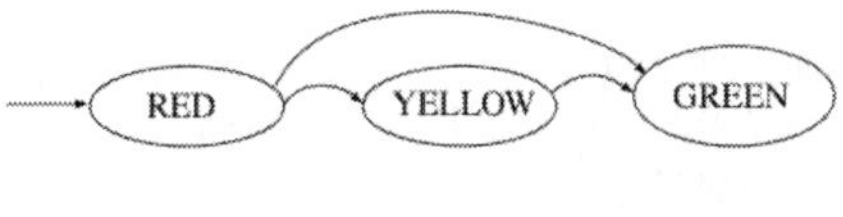

Figure 5. A finite-state machine of traffic light configurations

```
          where idPar=
            movement_tmp.idPr)
    else 0 end)
commit transaction;
```

This SQL-query is very similar to the one we examined previously. There are several differences between the query to add a single tuple and this one. Firstly, we declare a *table* type variable to which we add tuples with candidate-symbols to be added to a word. The generalized table expression *movement_tmp* contains a predicted result of the operation, which is further specified by the insert command. We use *movement_tmp.isNew* as an attribute for identifying candidate-symbols and already existing characters. The result of *insert* is a new word in the movement table – a word that was altered only with new characters from *@movement_new* which passed the automaton.

Operations of deletion and updating are implemented similarly.

5 Coding a finite-state machine using materialized paths

Let us look closely at using a finite-state machine, a model of which utilizes materialized paths of a graph in relational system. This case demands there be no cycles, like in Fig. 5 – a model of traffic light configurations (either with two or three lights)

We will need three tables in order to code this machine in a relational database:

1. An index table of colors named *color (idC int, name varchar(max))*. The table will contain { (1, red), (2, yellow), (3, green) }.

2. A table with the machine itself, done in the materialized path model. The key of the path *graphKey* is primary

Table 3. the *trafficLight* table

idTL	idC
1	1
1	3

for the relation. The clustered B+tree type index is built on this key. Every byte of it contains a value for each individual color of the traffic light, coded from left to right: *(idC int, graphKey varchar(max))*. According to Fig. 5. the automaion table will have four entries: {(1,'1'), (2,'12'), (3,'13'), (3,'123')}. Materialized path values in final states are valid words; and values in interim stages are word prefixes.

3. A traffic light table with a foreign key referring to *color.idC: trafficLight (idTL int, idC int)*. In our case, idTL is an id of a traffic light and (idTL, idC) is the primary key.

An example of the *trafficLight* is in table 3.

According to Table 3, attempting to add (1, 2) will be successful, because it will create an acceptable three-coloured traffic light *idTL = 1* out of an acceptable two-coloured light. Trying to add (1, 3) will fail, because the system will realize that we are trying to make a traffic light with two red lights.

In this case, we already know all valid words and prefixes. The integrity check will consist of just creating a word and checking if it exists in the *automaton* table. Adding new entries will be done through a table type variable *@light_new* that holds candidate-entries to be added to the *trafficLight* table. Note that the system will react differently to adding new entries than our previous example. The parent-child method assumes that we can add individual symbols that pass the machine, whereas materialized paths allow characters to be added and edited in groups – if all new symbols meet the machines restrictions, then they all get in the word, otherwise, if at least one character does not satisfy the machine's criteria, the entire operation is declined.

Let us create a query to add a set of tuples as a batch. These tuples contain characters that would modify the existing word. Initial state of the *trafficLight* table is given in Table 3.

Query 4:

```
declare @light_new table (idTL int,
                          idC int)
insert into @light_new (idTL, idC)
  values (1, 2)
insert into @light_new (idTL, idC)
  values (2, 1)
insert into @light_new (idTL, idC)
  values (2, 3)
set transaction isolation level
  serializable;

begin transaction;
with trafficLight_tmp (idTL, idC)
as
(select idTL, idC
  from @light_new
union all
select a.idTL, a.idC
  from trafficLight a
  where a.idTL in (select
                   distinct idTL
                   from @light_new))

insert trafficLight
select tl_new.idTL, tl_new.idC
from @light_new tl_new,
     (select distinct idTL
      from trafficLight_tmp) tl,
        automaton au
where au.graphKey=
  (select top 1
    (select convert(char(1),b.idC)
      from trafficLight_tmp b
        where b.idC<=a.idC and
          a.idTL=b.idTL
        order by 1 FOR xml path(''))
        from trafficLight_tmp a
        where a.idC=(select max(idC)
          from trafficLight_tmp b
          where a.idTL=b.idTL) and
            a.idTL=tl.idTL) and
        tl_new.idTL=tl.idTL
commit transaction;
```

In this case, an attempt at adding two traffic lights will be successful, because we are creating a valid tree-colored traffic light idTL = 1 out of a valid two-colored light and adding a new two-colored light idTL=2 with an acceptable set of colors.

The main purpose of this SQL-query is to form new words and prefixes out of candidate-symbols and already existing characters, then search for this word or prefix in the machine's table. If it finds a match, then it lets the symbols through; if not – ignores them. The query consists of four parts:

1. Preparing data to be added into the target table.

```
declare @light_new table (idTL int,
                          idC int)
insert into @light_new (idTL, idC)
  values (1, 2)
insert into @light_new (idTL, idC)
  values (2, 1)
insert into @light_new (idTL, idC)
  values (2, 3)
```

2. Forming a generalized table expression with an expected outcome of the operation.

```
with trafficLight_tmp (idTL, idC)
as (select idTL, idC
  from @light_new
union all select a.idTL, a.idC
  from trafficLight a where a.idTL in
    (select distinct idTL
     from @light_new))
```

3. Forming a word out of the expected result for each object

```
(select top 1
  (select convert(char(1),b.idC)
   from trafficLight_tmp b
     where b.idC<=a.idC and
       a.idTL=b.idTL
     order by 1 FOR xml path(''))
       from trafficLight_tmp a
       where a.idC=(select max(idC)
         from trafficLight_tmp b
         where a.idTL=b.idTL) and
           a.idTL=tl.idTL)
```

4. If this word is one of the values of *automaton.graphKey*, then all new symbols are added into the target table

```
insert trafficLight
select tl_new.idTL, tl_new.idC
from @light_new tl_new,
  (select distinct idTL
   from trafficLight_tmp) tl,
     automaton au
```

Operations of deletion and updating are implemented similarly.

6 Conclusion

This paper tackles the issue of providing data integrity. Corporate integrity constraints often demand tuples of certain relationships be consistent and non-contradictory as a group. This paper presents a new method of achieving integrity in logically connected subsets of data in relational databases using finite-state machines.

Implementation the automaton in flat tables can be achieved using several models: 'parent-child', 'ancestor-successor' or with materialized paths on a graph. The 'parent-child' model supports cycles in graphs but requires recursive restoration of valid words of the machine. This model works well when we need to check, whether a word fragment is valid for a given machine. In addition, it lets us add only those symbols that are acceptable to the machine. The 'materialized paths on a graph' model lets us store and process valid words and prefixes more clearly but does not support cycles. This model is preferred for cases where symbols are added as a group and when we need to verify that all new symbols are acceptable.

We provide examples of data management queries and integrity check queries using the Transact SQL language in the MS SQL Server DBMS. We looked at query performance, stated index requirements, and determined the necessary level of transaction isolation.

All models, data structures, and code presented in this paper are used successfully in a number of informational and educational outlets of the North-Caucasus Federal University and schools in the Stavropol Region, Russia (such as http://eCampus.ncfu.ru, http://olymp.ncfu.ru).

References

[1] J.D. Christopher, *Relational Theory for Computer Professionals (Theory in Practice)* (O'Reilly Media, 2013)

[2] C. Date, H. Darwen, *Time and Relational Theory: Temporal Databases in the Relational Model and SQL* (Morgan Kaufmann Publishers Inc., 2014)

[3] J. Celko, *Joe Celko's Trees and Hierarchies in SQL for Smarties* (Morgan Kaufmann Publishers Inc, 2004)

[4] A. Malikov, M. Sugakov, D. Parkhomenko, Y. Gulevskiy, *Temporal tree and its use in the conceptual modeling of databases* (2010), Vol. 2, pp. 99–104

[5] *Mongodb*, `https://www.mongodb.org/`

[6] B.G. Tudorica, C. Bucur, *A comparison between several NoSQL databases with comments and notes*, in *Roedunet International Conference (RoEduNet), 2011 10th* (2011), pp. 1–5

[7] T. Kam, T. Villa, R.K. Brayton, A. Sangiovanni-Vincentelli, *Synthesis of Finite State Machines: Functional Optimization* (Kluwer Academic Publishers, 2013)

[8] L. Libkin, *Elements of Finite Model Theory* (Springer-Verlag Berlin Heidelberg, 2004), ISBN 978-3-662-07003-1

[9] V. Vianu, *Databases and Finite-Model Theory*, in *In descriptive complixity and finite models* (American Mathematical Society, 1997), pp. 97–148

[10] I. Ion, C. Cristian, P. Sorin, *Collaborative Systems - Finite State Machines* (2011), Vol. 15

[11] M. Dippery, *Modeling states and transitions in relational databases* (2014)

[12] N. Deininger, *Finite-State Machines with recursive SQL* (2013), `https://ef.gy/fsm-recursive-sql`

[13] H. Straubing, *Finite Automata, Formal Logic, and Circuit Complexity* (Birkhauser Verlag, Basel, Switzerland, Switzerland, 1994)

[14] *Educational and informational hub of the north-caucasus federal university*, `http://eCampus.ncfu.ru`

[15] *Hub for university and school student competitions*, `http://olymp.ncfu.ru`

[16] V. Tropashko, *Nested Intervals with Farey Fractions* (2004), `http://arxiv.org/html/cs/0401014`

[17] J. Celko, *Joe Celko's SQL for Smarties: Advanced SQL Programming* (Morgan Kaufmann Publishers Inc., 2010)

E-commerce in Healthcare: A Case Study on Promoting the Therapeutic Hardware

Azza Abdel Monem[1,a]

[1]*Faculty of Computer & Information Sciences, Ain Shams University, Abbassia, 11566, Cairo, Egypt*

Abstract. The E-commerce and Internet permit enormous organizations to act like little ones and little organizations to act huge. The test to organizations is to make exchanges in the form of transactions less expensive and simpler for themselves as well as less demanding and more advantageous for clients and suppliers. This paper introduces a proposition for the foundation of a business that will encourage the offer of restorative hardware to social insurance organizations in the United Arab Emirates UAE. This case concentrates on the offer of different therapeutic hardware including wheelchairs, restorative programming, medicinal equipment's, in vitro calibrators as additional medicinal gadgets. The medicinal gadgets can be loaded by the business will consolidate items from various producers to provide food to serve the fluctuating purchaser taste and inclinations. The business who desires to require the backing of financial specialists in the business which is through Internet, so as to subsidize the foundation of a remarkable unique endeavour for the individuals working in for a business.

Key Words. E-commerce, E-Business, Management Information Systems, Healthcare, Medical Devices, Information System.

1 Introduction

The online world is another set of repeated exercise that consolidates the use of Web 2.0 to encourage deals in the form of sale. The fresh pattern is alluded to as Sales 2.0 that has expanded the ability to sell online. Besides, Web 2.0 dispense a rough and ready stage that is proper for putting sales into operation online. Web 2.0 offers a development that fuses the dynamic increment in the refinement of innovation because of the immense selection of the web, in this manner the influence is evident on the association of individuals in the present world. Essential mainstays of Web 2.0 is joint effort along these lines allowing individuals from everywhere throughout the world to cooperate and open out information in a way that was beforehand inconceivable [5]. This has permitted individuals to share their mental impressions, trusts, considerations and dreams subsequently rendering them open to different gatherings on the web.

The business will go for tackling the ability to do something given by Web 2.0 and to put these capabilities to build the promotion and sales strengths of the business. The online community proposition will help in the expansion of comprehension and association with various customers and subsequently expand the business sector for the offer of medicinal hardware online [8].

The web has brought about a considerable revamp in the costs of products, the information and presentation that is given to the clients and gave a fitting estimation of the reaction of various shoppers to the modifications in the business sector inclinations. It is imperative to note that there is an amendment in personalizing publicize information in the form of advertisements of products, the retail rehearse and the adaptability of sales to clear the learning path. The utilization of online stages is noteworthy to encourage the exploration of the business sector patterns via the investigation of the sales and purchaser inclinations from the hunt devices gave on the Internet stage [13]. This has brought about a variety in the costing schemes utilized as a part of online sales.

Information systems will undoubtedly enhance the execution of the business through helping with the advancement of new items and venture into upcoming markets for the business. The expansion in openness of the business sector will undoubtedly enhance the execution of the business [22]. It is fundamental to make a note that an Internet store does not exist in the United Arab Emirates that practices the sale of therapeutic (medicinal) hardware. In this way, the business will

[a] Corresponding author: azza_monem@hotmail.com

undoubtedly pick up prominence from the sale of restorative hardware on the web.

Information Systems have likewise demonstrated influential in the data capacity as well the data examination in detail that might be placed in the storage. Accordingly, the information systems will be utilize by the business and stockpiling of accounts in the repository as well business data examination will take place, keeping in mind the end goal is to encourage the fulfilment of precise results.

Online networking sites permit people to speak with each other keeping in mind the end goal to create individual connections. At the point when organizations interface these social sites, purchasers are capable partner with them specifically. That association can be near customers than standard methodologies connected in outbound promoting and showcasing. In this manner the business will apply online networking sites in showcasing the business to build the customers [13].

Online networking correlation destinations develop as verbal relationship with various people both universally and provincially. Individual to individual correspondence and web diaries allow the members to "tweet again and again" or "post again and again" on the comments made by people online, for this situation, the comments that are made in line to the business [6]. Through reiterating the message, the customer's affiliations can watch the message, then getting viral to many other peoples. More movement is passed on the entity or firm based on the information that is shown there about that entity. Through individual to individual correspondence ends points, association's connection with people can take place who are keen on the items sold by the organization. This joint effort which is individual based can build a divergence of trust of supporters and potential customers in the business exercises. In like manner, by picking whom to take after on these destinations, items can accomplish surprisingly expansive target gathering of people.

Long range casual correspondence, similarly, fuse an unfathomable data measure about what items and organizations arranged clients might be keen on. Through the usage of new Semantic Analysis progressions, promoters can perceive obtaining inclinations, for instance, substance ration out by people and request posted on the web. Cognizance of obtaining signs can offer the business some assistance with targeting correlated prospects and publicists run scaled down scale concentrated on promoting effort.

The business will likewise utilize comparative sites and healing (hospitality) facility sites to build the compass of the business to individuals having comparative intrigues accordingly might frame potential customers for the business. It is necessary that the promoting effort incorporate the business contact data to guarantee that individuals can call the business if there should be an occurrence of any request.

The strategy for success displayed goes for giving an online stage to encourage the selling of medical gadgets on the web. Therapeutic (Medical) gadgets fuse a scope of contraption and instruments that are utilized to encourage treatment for patients confronting distinctive infirmities. Along these lines, medical gadgets incorporate every one of the instruments mechanical assembly, in vitro gear and embeds that are connected in the treatment, conclusion and examination of various restorative conditions [9]. It is essential to note that medical gadgets don't bring about any concoction activity when connected in therapeutic (medical) applications; therefore, they can't be named drugs [15].

Keeping in mind the end goal to comprehend the business, the most indispensable thing is to acknowledge the meaning of a therapeutic (Medical) gadgets as exhibited by WHO (World Health Organization):

Medical gadget is any instrument, hardware, apparatus, machine, insert, programming, or other connected, proposed by the maker for the accompanying points:

- Conclusion, evasion, recognition, treatment or administration of ailment or harm
- Analysis, replacement, regulation, or bolster anatomical or physiological exercises.
- supporting or look after life
- Disinfection of hardware with respect to healthcare [16].

The paper is sorted out as takes after: the following segment introduces the writing audit concentrating on the qualities of e-commerce and the hypothetical establishments, trailed by the contextual investigation model depiction. The ensuing sections depict the targeted objective, model procedure, aftereffects of the contextual investigation model and conclusions, including the clients' study about applying this model.

2 Background

While examining, we receive a wide meanings of e-commerce to incorporate the exchanges and relevant intelligent business forms which might have happened previously, then after the fact those exchanges, using Internet, handheld cell phones and remote correspondence systems to lead the exchanges [18]. This segment will talk about the e-commerce methodologies, Business to Business (B2B) human services e-commerce and the advantages of e-wellbeing.

2.1 Strategies of E-commerce

The desires of customers when it comes to quality healthcare are high due to the quick headway in technology [14]. Doctor's facilities, clinical centres and other health care suppliers need to meet the customer desire whilst doing it in the most cost-productive way. In [6] clarified the huge effect e-commerce might impact cost, proficiency, as well distinction of the general type of administration and conveyance of health care administrations. Effectiveness picks up inside of the health care world which is credible to the use of IT (Information Technology) and, most particularly, the Internet. [6] The proper e-commerce plans of action redid and grew in like manner, it would achieve the objective of productive healthcare administration at lower expenses. In [6] discuss the advantages e-commerce (also called e-health) effect health care. E-commerce procedures usage will bolster healthcare suppliers work all the more productively particularly the ones utilizing back-dated systems which are paper-based [14]. The advantages are that clinics and specialists can see a patient's complete medicinal record of previous history and give the right finding. This spares the patient a lot of time. 'Briggs and Early3 talked about how Internet technology improvements had influenced the way healthcare is given.' In [3] characterizes the electronic health record (EHR) as "an electronic longitudinal accumulation pertaining to an individual wellbeing information generally taking into account the individual, entered or acknowledged by medicinal services suppliers, which can be circulated over various locales or collected at a specific source". EHR, a component that incorporates victim information into the up and coming era of health information advances with respect to the new technologies, containing Computerized Physician Order Entry (CPOE) and Clinical Decision Support Systems (CDSS), and by and large enhance the nature of purpose of-consideration choice making [14].

With the utilization of appropriate IT framework and information frameworks (systems), conventional paper-based frameworks will be minimized or dispensed with later on. [23] recorded the IT-drove framework change is fixated on different crossing advances(technologies) that might be gathered as tracking(following up), entry, choice backing and reporting:

- "Following or Tracking" or distinguishing advancements (technologies), for example, standardized tags and going with scanners emphatically recognize medications, measurements and patients(sufferers) [14]. (RFID) Radio Frequency Identification illustrated as "track and follow" advances might swap standardized tag technologies for recognizing assignments and permit further tracking of medications and, possibly, patients.

- "Passage" advancements are spoken to by automated doctor request section termed as (CPOE) systems, here CPOE stands for computerized physician order entry, that maintain a strategic distance from drug blunders brought on by crabbed and additional recording botches [17].

- "Choice bolster innovations or decision support technologies" (CDSS) are developed request section systems that have vanished their inactivity and related drug communication info, data from EHR, or treatment models, (for example, clinical practice rules), and which offer sensible favourable circumstances over basic CPOE systems [14]. Relevant are intelligent gadgets, for example, apparatuses utilized for tele-care that gather and keep track of information from remote patients and trigger future assessment and solve the health issue through appropriate treatment.

- "Reporting" systems accommodate unfavourable occasion and medicinal blunder divulgence and reporting and encourage results research. [23] Illustrated in writing about the development rate in Internet access and every one of the enhancements in execution coming about because of fresh technologies, specifically in the ranges of telemedicine and in correspondence in the middle of patient and healthcare experts. Advanced IT influences the conveyance of healthcare, as well as can essentially impact the specialist (doctor) – tolerant (patient) relationship [17].

2.2 Business 2 Business Healthcare & Supply Chain Management Systems

As e-commerce incomplete existence exploited/boosted to its maximum capacity because of individuals not having the capacity to completely let go of custom and grasp fresh technologies [14]. The way to the achievement lies generally in the full cooperation of purchasers and medicinal services suppliers. Medicinal services: B2B. B2B health care e-commerce incorporates exchanges and the trading of information among sellers, healing facilities, protection organizations, state and government controllers, and specialists' workplaces where patients—the end buyers—are not straightforwardly included. A decent approach to begin is for hospitals, clinical centres, drug stores and other medicinal services establishments to consolidate e-commerce and (SCM) Supply Chain Management. From the point of view of Operations Management, [10] expressed the centre in the medicinal services part focused on advancing individual procedures.

Examples are the utilization of operations exploration systems to improve stock levels of medications and strategies for upgrading the requesting procedure of safe keeping related items and pharmaceuticals. In [18] clarified that these days information and correspondence (communication) advances can assume a critical part in enhancing supply chains in health and it will be of nothing unexpected that numerous medicinal services associations have begun up ventures in the field of health supply chains. With the watchful usage of SCM, costs will decay. A SCM framework would deal with the medicinal services supplier's association with suppliers particularly since most choice making spin around the overseeing of therapeutic (medicinal) items and supplies. They can share data about requests, creation, stock levels, conveyance of items and administrations. The objective is to convey the perfect measure of item to the destination with minimal measure of time and most reduced expense. Therefore, a stock renewal framework could be actualized where the framework (system) keeps a day by day record of stock-levels and naturally arranges for new or future stock, sent and conveyed when required.

[14] The utilization of Skype and online video administrations is for the most part for social motives, correspondence in the middle of loved ones part or for business motive (video-conferencing). Specialists can use this technology for patients' standard registration, to give the patient their analysis and an electronic remedy for minor cases like flu, cough, nourishment harming and so forth. This technology could likewise be utilized for subsequent treatment and in addition sparing time and transportation costs. E-health can oversee intense and unending conditions, Electronic infection administration projects are an essential part of the e-health upset, and are intended to modify the conveyance of consideration using technology to screen patients day by day to decide their health status, remind them to take their drugs, and handle issues before they turn out to be more genuine.' [1]While the world's populace expands, assets are getting scarcer. E-commerce is an astounding answer for medicinal services, since it utilizes rare assets as a part of the most productive way that can manage the soundness of a country. In [19] investigated the use of e-commerce to the industry of healthcare from the shoppers' and suppliers' perspectives. They talked about the dangers of e-trade and survey people in general and private reactions to handle these worries. E-health guarantees to enhance effectiveness, encourage correspondence in the middle of specialist and patient, screen consistence with therapeutic regimens, and absolutely effect on the nature of the given health administrations and the general soundness of the patient [14].

2.3 The Advantages of E-health

Numerous advantages of e-health are noted. They are that organizations and healthcare suppliers have an edge over contenders. Through CRM and SCM daily operations are coordinating exceptionally with focused technologies [14]. The medical field is very competitive integrating technology in the daily operations. The capacity to oversee patient's consistence, drug-regimens, and full health status and alarms human experts of required involvement, a shopper's entrance to clinical guidance, authority's referrals, conclusion test results, drug models and antagonistic responses. Effective utilization of assets empowers specialists, doctor's facility staff and medicinal services experts to treatment conventions and correspondence difficulties and status of patient. More noteworthy patient reaction and advancement with respect to treatment involvement, endorsed over the-counter meds and reactions to instructive endeavors by specialists. Specialists can bolster enhance patients' adherence to plans of treatment, convey better care, decrease expenses, and upgrade general consumer loyalty. Creating nations and rising economies can advantage since technology separates hindrances and allows them to get profitable therapeutic (medical) information and administrations like wealthier created countries. In [20] talks about the (WHO) World Health Organization and (OSI) the Open Society Institute, a part of the Soros Foundation, have collaborated with driving data suppliers, ISI and Silver Platter, and other open and private accomplices to give access to excellent experimental data by means of the Internet, for exploration focuses in creating nations like Africa, Central Asia, and Eastern Europe. 'This is a section of the United Nations program named as Health-Inter-Network which plans to upgrade worldwide [14] Research, and distributing the knowledge increased through its endeavours, is basic to enhancing open health.'[20] E-health and M-Health are illustrations of associating health of human with technology which is online. These method for correspondence are both useful yet one is more practical than the other. With the end goal this should work, it'll take the support and eagerness of numerous medicinal services suppliers and customers [14]. While E-health utilizes systems like the web and video conferencing, M-health is portable health which utilizes specialized devices like phones and remote systems [12]. M-health could be connected for general purposes just, there are confined ways and numerous obstructions/limitations contrasted with E-health. In [11] article, Eric Rock remarked that he trusts marks/watchwords like "M-health", "portable" have a constrained time frame of realistic usability and as existing apart from everything else, he trusts E-health has a much higher rate of progress. In the article [12] it talks about how e-commerce has affected the medicinal segment, which is still in an exceptionally fundamental manner.

3 Case Study Description

The business will join the offer of therapeutic (medical) gadgets through an online stage. The medicinal gadgets that will be sold join diverse gadgets having changing applications and unpredictability. The business will stock an assortment of gadgets including wheelchairs, expendable gloves, tongue depressors and therapeutic thermometers. Likewise, the business will offer complex therapeutic gadgets incorporating PCs to help with the examination of inside and outside states of the body. Because of the affectability of restorative (medical) gadgets there is a development of the regulation of medical gadgets in UAE. It is necessary to ensure that the medicinal gear that are sold meet the security prerequisites to guarantee that they are alright for using them in various restorative organizations all inclusive. Mention that the security of medicinal gadgets is relative since all medicinal gear conveys a level of danger; subsequently, there might be a rise of issues in given circumstances. In this manner, it is basic to guarantee that the gadget sold by means of the organization site meets the details that are put aside by both neighborhood and global norms.

3.1 Objective

The business goes for encouraging the little scale and huge scale supply of medicinal hardware in UAE. The customers will be required to buy the organizations utilizing the online stage that will be made. What's more, the customers will require imparting on their area and location that will join their delivery data. The principle finding of this model plans to expand the openness of the merchandise that are brought in from various makers. Thus, the business will speak with the customers to clear up any subtle elements that the customer may wish to examine in reference to the request put. It is essential to make a note on the utilization of online stages will undoubtedly build the scope of the business to various customers from all over U.A.E since anybody that wishes to get to the items that are offered by the business just require to get to the organization site [1].

3.2 Local Market

The market which is proposed for the medical devices that will be sold by the business is the United Arab Emirates neighborhood market. The business sector for the items is assessed as Table 1. Along these lines, the business must overhaul the supply systems to guarantee that there is an adequate stream of products into the business sector. What's more, the business will go for ensuring so as to expand their compass that differing natures of customers are considered in the improvement of the business objectives. Case in point, the business merchandise ought to be reasonable to the run of the mill shopper and expansive scale purchasers shape the online stage.

Table 1: Financial projection for the business.

	Year 1	Year 2	Year 3
Estimated Sales	$500,000	$1,000,000	$1,500,000

3.3 Model Processes

Information organization is key to keeping up a productive business with respect to the 21st century. Every last business system can now be mapped and dismembered by data organization programming to propel business objectives and encourage the best possible administration of the business issues which are most complex. These data systems oblige information originators with a solid establishment in both business methods and Information Technology. Information systems (IS) and IT frameworks assume an indispensable part in advancing business forms including the administration of representatives and information on the business customers [24].

MIS/IT fortify the mix of various business procedures and exercises. As indicated by that, the organization arrangements to execute the requesting satisfies process keeping in mind the end goal to encourage and associate the execution and exercises of sales, bookkeeping and conveyance offices. Ordering satisfies process orchestrates business exercises in practical grouping. After create orders by sales division, sales submit it to bookkeeping that check and favor the instalments with a specific end goal to prepare and convey the items by conveyance office. As represented underneath in Fig. 1.

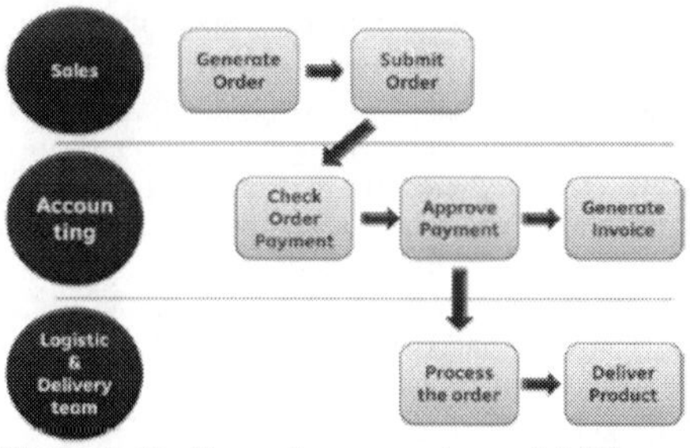

Figure 1: On-line order processing and fulfilment diagram

3.4 Findings

With an end goal to lead a business sector overview, 50 members were issued with a survey (see Table 2) which were went for analyzing the condition of the business sector and the buyer acknowledgment of the offer of therapeutic gear on the web. The consequences of this review will undoubtedly help in the change of the methodology towards the sale of medicinal gadgets online in the proposed business. The questionnaire results are summarized in Fig. 2.

Table 2: Questionnaire

1- Do you like to purchase your home use social insurance gear through the web or from Pharmacies/Healthcare Companies Showroom?
□ YES □ NO
2- What is the most advantageous installment payment path for you?
□ Cash □ Credit
3- Do you incline toward restorative gear's incorporate programming which is associated with your PC to exchange results and slants and for SW overhaul?
□YES □ NO
4- What is the worthy conveyance period?
□ 2 Days □ 1 Week □1 Month
5- Do you favor sites or portable applications?
□Web □Site □Mobile Application

From the review, 32 individuals favored purchasing form online stages. This pattern might be credited to the expanded assortment and simplicity of finding things in online stages. It is central to note that online stage give a perfect hunt streamlining in this manner furnishing the customer with a scope of things structure distinctive makers and diverse costs. Rather than logged off (offline) purchasing, customers can get to a scope of information that they can then utilize to look for options. Besides, there is an expansion in the availability of technological gadgets that are utilized to get to the web. Accordingly, the web has developed as a basic correspondence and exchanging stage for customers since it takes into consideration exchanging at the solace and comfort of the customer. The adaptability that is given by online sales will undoubtedly pull in customers in UAE.

28 individuals among those who responded wanted to pay for the endless supply of the products while 22 individuals wanted to pay before the conveyance of the merchandise. Online sales suffers from instabilities since the general population might question the quality of trusting and believing the online shop, especially toward the starting. In any case, the criticism that is gotten structure the customers has been ended up being a suitable strategy for gaging the validity of online shops. Subsequently, the business will go for supplying the merchandise to the customer in a solid way that will undoubtedly build the shopper trust in the item.

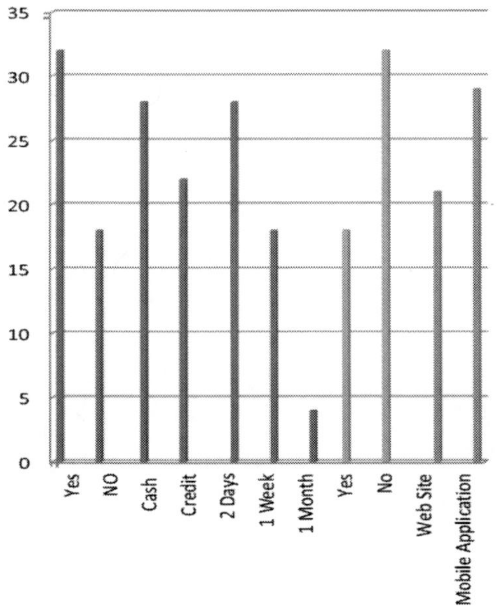

Figure 2: Questionnaire result diagram

Amid the review, the members were additionally requested that react to the time that they might want assign to conveyance of the item. The customers favored a shorter conveyance time to diminish the instability and improve the openness of the items after buy. It is clear that customers have a tendency to incline toward the enhancement of openness of the item. The trust of the buyers on the items sold online by the business will undoubtedly get expanded. Notwithstanding, it is indispensable to note that the lessening in the time taken for conveyance will undoubtedly expand the conveyance cost. Consequently, the business will see this as a venture to expand the shopper sales and trust in the organization [4].

The study additionally uncovered that 21 individuals favored utilizing sites while 29 individuals favored utilizing cell phone applications. This has uncovered the expansion in the gadgets that are accessible to get to the web therefore provoking the consolidation of cell phone applications. Hence, the business will add to a cell phone application that the clients can use in getting to the online store set up by the business. This will undoubtedly build the range of the business and expansion the prevalence and simplicity with which customers can buy products from the business on the web.

4 Conclusion and Future work

The strategies for success to venture into worldwide business sector. In any case, this requests more noteworthy interest with a specific end goal to encourage advertising and transportation of the items to various areas all inclusive. The UAE market shows an unexploited business sector that will undoubtedly encourage development of the business. Be that as it may, there is a need to expand the speculation on showcasing utilizing both online and logged off intends to build the quantity of customers. The economies of scale will be used by the business to guarantee that the items that are supplied by them is low in expense when compared to those created by the contenders.

Putting resources into MIS/IT expand association's productivity through minimizing the expense to maintain the business, give exact information to the leader and expansion consumer loyalty by coordinating their needs and convey a high values.

We have several ongoing activities, all concerned with extending our work to be more powerful and applicable. In what follows, we present some of these activities.

Linking this business with Telemedicine System will facilitate the consultation of doctors based on the kinds of the medical devices; online clinical interactive consultation and distance learning for special devices. A promising venue of research is to use Social Media for online buying decision. Social network such as Facebook, LinkedIn, Twitter, Google+, Pinterest, etc. have become an easy to login and purchase. Moreover, the customers can stay updated via the posts published on this media.

Further, the advertising & promotions on these social sites has increased the opportunities to success of generating transactions to many folds. One of the most important design goals of this research is to add Business Intelligence (BI) approach to this business. It will help the business to apply E-commerce, mobile apps and mobile payments and banking.

References

1. Amir, R. (n.d.), (2003) Market Structure, Scale Economies and Industry Performance. SSRN Journal.
2. Aggarwal AK1, Travers S., (2001) E-commerce in healthcare: changing the traditional landscape, J Healthc Inf Manag. Spring;15 (1):25-36.
3. Australian National Electronic Health Records Taskforce, A Health Information Network for Australia, Report to Health Ministers by the National Electronic Health Records Taskforce (Commonwealth Department of Health and Aged Care, Canberra, 2000) p 21 (hereinafter Taskforce).
4. Carrere, C. (2014). Regional Agreements and Welfare in the South: When Scale Economies in Transport Matter. Journal of African Economies, 23(3), pp.321-345.
5. Da Xu, L. (2014). Advances in e-business engineering management. Information Technology and Management.
6. Elmer, G. (2015). Going Public on Social Media. Social Media + Society, 1(1).
7. Ellen Hope Kearns, Suzanne C. Holmes, and Gerene Schmidt,(2002) The role of e-commerce in health care, Clinical report, SB & E, Inc. (Science Business & Education), Spokane, WA, U.S.A. CLMA/ ASCP, New Orleans, LA, June 26-29, 2002.
8. Fenton, N. (1991). Shaping the Future. Business Design through Information Technology. J Inf Technol, 6(3-4), pp.237-237.
9. Ivanov, I. (2007). Pharmaceutical and Medical Biotechnology. Biotechnology & Biotechnological Equipment, 21(1), pp.74-79.
10. Jan de Vries and Robbert Huijsman, (2011) Supply chain management in health services, Supply Chain Management: An International Journal Volume 16 • Number 3 • 159–165.
11. Jeff Kagan, (2011), Why Don't Doctors and Patients eConnect Yet ? E-Commerce Times.
12. Jeff Kagan, (2011) The Fuse Is Lit for the mHealth Industry Explosion, E-Commerce Time.
13. Kauffman, R., Liu, J. and Ma, D. (2015). Technology investment decision-making under uncertainty. Information Technology and Management, 16(2), pp.153-172.
14. Luzanna C. and Rashad Y., (2011) Ecommerce's Important Role in the Medical Sector, International Conference on Information Communication and Management, IPCSIT vol.16 IACSIT Press, Singapore.
15. Medical equipment & supplies. (1991). Journal of Air Medical Transport, 10 (3), pp.62-63.
16. Mdnr.sfda.gov.sa, (2015). MDNR [Online] Available at: https://mdnr.sfda.gov.sa/MDNR/Public/MedicalDevice.aspx [Accessed 20 May 2015].
17. Journal of Legal Medicine, Vol. 12, No. 1, 2004. Available at SSRN: http://ssrn.com/abstract=1265025.
18. Schneller, E.S., Schmeltzer, L.R. and Burns, L.R. (2006), Strategic Management of the Health Care Supply Chain, Jossey-Bass, San Francisco, CA.
19. Suzanne C. Holmes and Renee H. Miller, (2003), International Journal of Services Technology and Management, Volume **4**, Numbers 4-6 , pages507 – 517.
20. Suman Kapur, (2001) The Internet: Its Role in Medicine and Healthcare, Journal, Indian Academy of Clinical Medicine Vol. 2, No. 3 July-September , 10, p. 133-138.
21. Tarasewich P, Nickerson RC and Warkentin M (2002) Issues in mobile. Commerce Communications of the Association for Information Systems 8(2002), 41–64.
22. Tan, F. (1995). The responsiveness of information technology to business strategy formulation: an empirical study. J Inf Technol, 10(3), pp.171-178.
23. Terry, Nicolas P., (March 8, 2004), Electronic Health Records: International, Structural and Legal Perspectives.
24. Vidgen, R. and Wang, X. (2006). From business process management to business process ecosystem. J Inf Technol, 21(4), pp.262-271.

25. Luigi T.De Luca, *Propulsion physics* (EDP Sciences, Les Ulis, 2009)
26. F. De Lillo, F. Cecconi, G. Lacorata, A. Vulpiani, EPL, **84** (2008)

Unifier register to protect an efficient modular exponentiation algorithm

David Tinoco Varela[1,a]

[1] *Universidad Nacional Autónoma de México*
Campus Cuautitlán.
Cuautitlán Izcalli, Edo. Mex., México.

Abstract.
Simple power analysis (SPA) attacks are widely used against several cryptosystems, principally against those based on modular exponentiation. Many types of SPA have been reported in the literature in the recent years. There is a real necessity to eliminate the vulnerabilities of cryptosystems, such as CRT-RSA or the Elliptic Curve Cryptosystem, that make them susceptible to these attacks. There are many modular exponentiation algorithms that try to reinforce the security of these systems, of which one was proposed by Da-Zhi et al.

Da-zhi's algorithm was presented as a secure and efficient countermeasure against side channel attacks; however, recently it was shown that its security can be defeated. In this paper, a means of protecting the algorithm is presented. The proposed technique can be applied in any algorithm that computes dummy operations through its execution.

Keywords – Cryptography, modular exponentiation algorithms, side channel attacks, fault attacks, Jacobi symbol.

1 Introduction

A large amount of data are broadcasted daily through electronic communication channels. All of this information must be protected because of the importance and sensitivity of the transmitted data. The best way to protect such information is via high security cryptographic systems.

There are many strong cryptographic systems; two of the most important systems used currently are the RSA cryptosystem, proposed by *Rivest Shamir* and *Adleman* [1]; and the Elliptic Curve Cryptosystem.

A cryptographic system bases its security on many important aspects, such as the mathematical concepts on which it was founded, the computational difficulty needed to obtain the secret keys that ensure data protection, the transmission channel and, in many cases, the use chosen by the final user. Previously, a security system could be considered trustworthy if its mathematical argument was reliable, and the computational difficulty of finding the keys was high; however, this idea was proven false in 1996, when *Kocher* opened the door to a new type of attacks, called the *side channel attacks* (SCA) [2].

SCA are based on a new and different attack methodology that does not depend on formal mathematical concepts or computing power. This new attack scheme is based on observations of the execution time of an electronic device that is running up the modular exponentiation algorithm.

Kocher knew that the execution time of the device could be observed and measured and that from these measurements, it is possible to obtain information as valuable as the secret key of the system. Later, based on this first attack scheme, the extraction of important data from electronic devices by measuring the power consumption of the crypto devices was presented [3].

The measurement of electronic device power consumption at the moment that an algorithm is executed inside of the device created numerous opportunities for physical attacks based on measuring, analyzing, and interpreting any physical signals emanating from the device. Signals such as power consumption, heat emanation, electromagnetic signals, and any other possible signals issued by the device can be measured and used to breach the security of the information systems.

SCA were quickly used to break down the security of cryptosystems based on modular exponentiation (*Add and double* in the elliptic curve cryptosystem), such as RSA, and the method of secure exchange of cryptographic keys *Diffie-Hellman* [4].

[a] Corresponding author: dativa19@hotmail.com

After the SCA, *Bonhe, DeMillo* and *Lipton* presented *Fault attacks* (FA) [5]. FA are more aggressive than SCA because FA physically disturb the execution of the device that is running the cryptographic algorithm.

Many modular exponentiation algorithms have been proposed to avoid these types of physical attacks. The *Square-and-Multiply Always algorithm* developed by *Coron* [6] was the first algorithm specifically designed to avoid such attacks; however, this algorithm was attacked by *Safe error attack* (SEA) [7]. SEA uses dummy operations that the algorithm calculates to break the security of the system. A dummy operation is an operation that is calculated through execution but does not affect the final result of the algorithm's execution.

There are many physical attacks ([8], [9], [10], [11]) trying to break the different modular exponentiation algorithms ([12], [13], [14], [15], [16], [17]) but in 2006 *Boreale* [18] presented a new type of attack, his attack uses a combination between FA and SCA, and according to him, it is possible to get the binary string of the secret key d using the *Jacobi symbol* concept. He attacked the *Square and Multiply Right-to-Left* modular exponentiation and he proved that his attack is effective even in the presence of message blinding. *Schmidt* and *Medwed* [19] used the Jacobi symbol to create an attack which breaks the security of the Montgomery ladder in its blinded form. In the same way *Chong Hee Kim* designed an attack in 2010 [20], based on the Jacobi symbol too, to break the security of the *Add-Only* and *Add-Always* algorithms, both algorithms proposed by Joye in 2007 [21].

Sun Da-Zhi et al. developed an efficient algorithm against *simple power analysis* [22] that uses two binary strings instead of one to calculate modular exponentiation; however, in [23] was presented a way to defeat the security of Da-Zhi's algorithm. The threat was implemented in four steps. It is important to highlight that this assault was designed by observing the behavior of the basic characteristics of Da-zhi's algorithm.

2 Preliminaries

2.1 Quadratic residues and Jacobi symbol

For any prime number p, x is a quadratic residue if $gcd(x, p) = 1$ and $x = y^2 \ mod \ p$ for some y. If $gcd(x, p) = 1$ but x is not a quadratic residue mod p, then x is called a quadratic non-residue modulo p.

In order to illustrate this concept, we will use a modulo $n = 17$. The residues modulo 17 of $1^2, 2^2, ..., 16^2$ are 1, 4, 9, 16, 8, 2, 15, 13, 13, 15, 2, 8, 16, 9, 4, 1; therefore, the quadratic residues modulo 17 are 1, 2, 4, 8, 9, 13, 15, 16.

To determine if a value a is a quadratic residue modulo p, the *Legendre symbol* is used.

$\left(\frac{a}{p}\right)$ is called the *Legendre symbol* of a mod p and has the following properties:

$$\left(\frac{a}{p}\right) = \left\{ \begin{array}{ll} 1 & \text{If } a \text{ is a quadratic residue mod } p \\ -1 & \text{If } a \text{ is a quadratic non-residue mod } p \\ 0 & \text{If there is a common factor} \end{array} \right\}$$

Then, we have that $\left(\frac{a}{n}\right) = \left(\frac{a}{p_1}\right) \cdots \left(\frac{a}{p_k}\right)$ is the Jacobi symbol (JS), where $n = p_1 \cdots p_k$, and p's are prime factors. The Jacobi symbol is a generalization of the Legendre symbol.

2.2 Modular exponentiation

Modular exponentiation is the core of several cryptographic algorithms, and it is also the principal intrusion point of different physical attacks. The classical modular exponentiation algorithm is the *Square and Multiply Right-to-Left*, given as the algorithm 1. This kind of algorithm can be classified into two types: *left-to-right* and *righ-to-left*, depending on the position of the binary string at which the algorithm begins its execution.

Algorithm 1 Square and Multiply Right-to-Left.

```
1: Input m, d = (d_{n-1}, ..., d_0)_2
2: Output s = m^d
3: R_0 ← 1; R_1 ← m
4: for 0 to n − 1 do
5:    if d_i = 1 then
6:       R_0 ← R_0 · R_1 mod N
7:    end if
8:    R_1 ← R_1^2 mod N
9: end for
10: Return R_0
```

There are many variations of the modular exponentiation algorithm, all designed to make the security protocol safer.

Chevallier et al. proposed the atomicity technique for modular exponentiation in 2004 [24]. This technique, according to the authors, is a generic scheme and is virtually applicable to any algorithm. The idea says that a process can be seen as a sequence of instructions, and each is equivalent to all other instructions. Hence, they cannot be differentiated through an analysis such as side channel attack; this technique is shown in the algorithm 2.

2.3 Jacobi symbol attacks

As there are many modular exponentiation algorithms, there are also many physical attacks attempting to undermine the security of the exponentiation algorithms.

Algorithm 2 SaM protected by the atomicity technique.

```
Input m, d, N, with d = (d_{n-1} ··· d_0)_2
Output S = m^d mod N
R[0] ← 1
R[1] ← m
k = 0
i = n − 1
while i ≥ 0 do
    R[0] ← R[0] · R[k] mod N
    k ← k ⊕ d_i
    i ← i − k̄
end for
Return R[0]
```

After the apparition of SCA and FA, attacks that used one of these two techniques but were also based on a combination of mathematical and numerical concepts were developed, such as the attack proposed in [8].

Other types of attacks that combine physical attacks with numerical concepts use the Jacobi symbol to defeat cryptographic security.

Attacks using the Jacobi symbol began with *Boreale*, when he attacked the binary Square and Multiply Right-to-Left modular exponentiation (Algorithm 1) in 2006 [18]. He puts a fault z in R_1 when a squaring is executed in iteration $i-1$ of the Square-and-Multiply algorithm, and then, depending on the calculation of (S/N), where S is the output value of the algorithm and N is the modulus, it is possible to know what value of the bit d_i was attacked. This scheme works by assuming that $\left(\frac{m}{N}\right) = 1$, and its behavior is similar to the *Safe error*: if the bit in iteration i is equal to 0, the fault does not affect the calculation of the JS of (R_{0_i}/N), and z is squaring, so that $(z^2/N) = 1$, but if $d_i = 1$, z affects the register R_{0_i} and can have the JS value $(R_{0_i}/N) = -1$. Then, z can be or not be a quadratic residue. If z is a quadratic residue, then the final result will be $(S/N) = 1$, but if it is a quadratic non-residue, the final result will be $(S/N) = -1$. For this reason, his attack is a probabilistic model.

After Boreale, *Schmidt* [19] proposed an attack that entailed sending a message m with $(m/N) = -1$ to the *Fumaroli-Vigilant algorithm* [25] and skipping the operation $R_{d_i} = R_{d_i}{}^2$ in the algorithm. By observing the JS of the resulting value, it is possible to learn about the values of d_i and d_{i-1}. If (S/N) is equal to -1, then $d_i = d_{i-1}$.

The attacks mentioned above are easy to implement, and they are powerful because they require only the JS in the returned value by the attacked algorithm to breach the security of a cryptosystem. However, a way to avoid this kind of attack was shown in [26].

2.4 Attack on Da-zhi's algorithm

Sun Da-Zhi et al. published a modular exponentiation algorithm that separates the original binary string of the exponent d into two binary strings d_1 and d_2. The algorithm is given as algorithm 3, where $sq^{(y)}(A)$ means performing y modular squares on the integer A [22].

Algorithm 3 Sun Da-zhi's algorithm [22].

```
1: Input m, d, N with d_1 = d_{⌈k/2⌉,1} ··· d_{1,1} and d_2 = d_{⌈k/2⌉,2} ··· d_{1,2}
2: Output C = m^d mod N
3: s = m
4: C_0 = C_1 = C_2 = C_3 = 1;
5: C_{2·d_{1,2}+d_{1,1}} = s · C_{2·d_{1,2}+d_{1,1}}
6: for 2 to ⌈k/2⌉ do
7:     s = s · s
8:     C_{2·d_{i,2}+d_{i,1}} = s · C_{2·d_{i,2}+d_{i,1}}
9: end for
10: C_1 = C_1 · C_3
11: C_2 = C_2 · C_3
12: C = sq^{(⌈k/2⌉)}(m^{C_1}) · m^{C_2}
```

The key idea in algorithm 3 is to separate the k-bit binary string d into two $(\lceil k/2 \rceil)$-bit binary strings d_1 and d_2, and depending on the values of d_1 and d_2 in each iteration, four registers $C_0 \cdots C_3$ can be utilized to calculate the exponentiation. If $d_{i,1}$ and $d_{i,2}$ (Where $i,1$ is the i-bit of d_1 and $i,2$ is the i-bit of d_2) are equal to 0, the chosen register is C_0; if $d_{i,1} = 1$ and $d_{i,2} = 0$, the chosen register is C_1, and so on, for each register.

Algorithm 3 was presented as a secure algorithm against SCA. However in [23] was demonstrated that the security of the algorithm can be defeated using an attack consisting of four steps. The attack is described below:

1. When $d_{i,1} = d_{i,2} = 0$, register C_0 is used. Every time this register is picked, Da-zhi's algorithm executes a dummy operation. If an attacker performs a FA when C_0 is selected, then the final result will not be affected. Thus, an attacker can determine the bits combination relative to the point attacked; thus, he can find a quarter of the total binary string.

2. We can see at line 12 from algorithm 3, that the register C_1 is always squared. Therefore, if any FA is put over that register and alters its JS, Jacobi symbol value in the final calculation will always become 1 because all negative JS change to a positive JS due to the operation $C = sq^{(\lceil k/2 \rceil)}(m^{C_1})$. Thus, by performing several FA and studying the behavior of the returned value, an attacker can easily identify where the Register C_1 was used; therefore, he can know one of four bits combinations that the algorithm uses.

3. To use the register C_2, it is necessary that $d_{i,1} = 0$ and $d_{i,2} = 1$. To use the register C_3, it is necessary that $d_{i,1} = 1$ and $d_{i,2} = 1$. It can be noted that for both registers, the value of the bit $d_{i,2}$ in i will always be equal to 1; therefore, it is possible to determine that all of the unknown values of the bits in d_2 are equal to 1.

4. One quarter, on average, of the values of the binary string d are unknown, but these can be found via different algorithms in the literature[27].

3 Protecting Da-zhi's algorithm using a unifier register

As described previously, the first step in attacking the Da-zhi's algorithm is to determine the position of the exponent's binary string in which a dummy operation is executed. To avoid this situation, it is necessary to unify all of the algorithm's registers $C_0 ... C_3$ to prevent a dummy operation from being used.

We realized that using the register C_0 in an independent manner can permit the unification of the registers; this value can later be allocated in any other register used by algorithm 3. Due to the necessity of making the C_0 register independent, a first approach to solving this problem involved the use of the technique called *atomicity*, proposed in [24]. As mentioned previously, this technique requires that each iteration of an algorithm is equal in time and power consumption to the others. The implementation of this concept alone does not solve the problem, but it can allow us to work with the C_0 register separately.

In algorithm 4, we can see the implementation of the atomicity technique over the Da-zhi's algorithm.

Algorithm 4 Da-zhi's algorithm with atomicity.

Input m, d, N with $d_1 = d_{\lceil n/2 \rceil,1} \cdots d_{1,1}$ and $d_2 = d_{\lceil n/2 \rceil,2} \cdots d_{1,2}$
Output $C = m^d \ mod \ N$
$C_0 = m$
$C_1 = C_2 = C_3 = 1;$
$i = k = 1;$
while $i \leq \lceil i/2 \rceil$ **do**
  $k = k \oplus [d_{i,1} \ OR \ d_{i,2}];$
  $C_{2kd_{i,2}+kd_{i,1}} = C_0 \cdot C_{2kd_{i,2}+kd_{i,1}};$
  $i = i + k;$
end while
$C_1 = C_1 \cdot C_3$
$C_2 = C_2 \cdot C_3$
$C = sq^{(\lceil n/2 \rceil)}(C_1) \cdot C_2$

Algorithm 4 uses all of the registers to correctly calculate of the exponentiation result. Thus, it does not matter which is the altered register as the final result will always be inaccurate. This is an advantage over the original algorithm because in the original algorithm, if one fault was placed at C_0, the final result was unaltered. It should also be noted that the C_0 register is executed in each iteration of algorithm 4, which is an important feature of this algorithm. Despite its characteristics, this algorithm is insecure against Jacobi symbol attacks. This vulnerability will be explained in the next section.

After a way was found to manipulate C_0 in an independent form, algorithm 4 was modified to make it safe against FA and JS attack, thus obtaining the algorithm 5, where $\oplus$ represents the binary operation OR exclusive. This algorithm avoids the use of dummy operations through an interconnection of all the registers used in its execution, meaning that a dummy operation is converted into an operation that alters the final result of the calculation.

Algorithm 5 Da-zhi's algorithm with atomicity and the unifier register.

Input m, d, N with $d_1 = d_{\lceil n/2 \rceil,1} \cdots d_{1,1}$ and $d_2 = d_{\lceil n/2 \rceil,2} \cdots d_{1,2}$
Output $C = m^d \ mod \ N$
$C_0 = m$
$C_1 = C_2 = C_3 = C_4 = 1;$
$i = k = b = 0;$
while $i \leq \lceil i/2 \rceil$ **do**
  $k = \bar{k} \ AND \ (b \oplus [d_{i,1} \ OR \ d_{i,2}]);$
  $b = k \ OR \ \bar{b};$
  $C_{3k+b-2kd_{i,2}-kd_{i,1}} = C_0 \cdot C_{3k+b-2kd_{i,2}-kd_{i,1}};$
  $i = i + k;$
end while
$C_1 = C_1 \cdot C_4^{-1};$
$C_3 = C_3 \cdot C_1$
$C_2 = C_2 \cdot C_1$
$C = sq^{(\lceil n/2 \rceil)}(C_3) \cdot C_2$

Algorithm 5 has a higher number of registers than algorithm 3, including the C_4 register. However, the increase in registers is minimal because this modification will provide security for any information system in which this idea can be implemented. In other words, a minimum amount of memory is sacrificed, but a guarantee of security will be obtained.

Now, we will see how the algorithm 5 avoids the dummy operation. When a fault is allocated into C_0, the fault will modify the value of this register. Such erroneous values always disturb the final result. To obtain the general disturbance, C_0 will multiply to C_1 and C_4 when $d_{i,1} = d_{i,2} = 0$. Therefore, C_0 will not be multiplied by itself anymore (the importance of this fact will be described in the next section). This means that when an FA is allocated into C_0, this erroneous value will join another register through the algorithm's execution. As a result, it will be altering all of the necessary values involved in the calculation of the exponentiation. Thus, C_0 becomes a *unifier register*. Registers can be unified, and the erroneous value in C_0 will disturb the final result of the operation, thereby eliminating the dummy operations of the algorithm's execution.

C_4 register is used to contain a multiplicative inverse of C_0, which will eliminate the C_0 value from C_1 at line 12 of algorithm 5. We can also see that only one register is protected with the value of C_0 and so, it was not necessary to protect all of the remaining registers.

It is easy to see that the register selection is different than that of the algorithm 3. In this algorithm, when $d_{i,1} = d_{i,2} = 0$, the registers C_1 and C_4 are used; when $d_{i,1} = 1$ and $d_{i,2} = 0$, C_3 is used; when $d_{i,1} = 0$ and $d_{i,2} = 1$, C_2 is used; and finally, when $d_{i,1} = 1$ and $d_{i,2} = 1$, C_1 is used. C_0 is executed in all the bits combinations. First, C_0 is calculated. Then, the register corresponding to the combination is used.

This algorithm is only slightly more complex than the original one. The first step in its design was to determine the expressions to calculate b and k to make the algorithm performs three multiplications when $d_{i,1} = d_{i,2} = 0$ and two multiplications in any other case. Both formulas were obtained with the help of *Karnaugh maps*.

The unifier register is not limited to the Da-zhi's algorithm. It can be used in any algorithm that makes dummy operations through its execution to avoid FA.

4 Analysis of the displayed algorithm

The Jacobi symbol has been used to attack many exponentiation algorithms. The general form of the attack consists of putting an FA through the algorithm's execution, calculating the JS of the obtained result, verifying the JS values 1 and -1, repeating the same attack many times, and comparing the obtained JS from those attacks. Thus, an attacker can obtain the secret key's binary string.

To verify the security of Da-zhi's algorithm modified with the atomicity technique (algorithm 4) and to compare it with our algorithm implemented with the unifier register (algorithm 5), Jacobi symbol attacks were made over them. The attack is described below.

When we performed safety tests of the algorithm 4 with respect to the JS, we realized that it was effective against common FA; however, it allows attacks by the JS concept. If a fault is placed in C_0 when $d_{i,1} = d_{i,2} = 0$, the next operation in the iteration $i + 1$ of the algorithm is $C_0 = C_0 \cdot C_0$. Hence, if the erroneous value had a JS equal to -1 in i, in the iteration $i + 1$ the JS will be changed to 1. The other three combinations of $d_{i,1}$ and $d_{i,2}$ do not exhibit this behavior because the $JS = -1$ of C_0 always affects one of three registers in the next step such that $C_{2kd_{i,2}+kd_{i,1}} = C_0 \cdot C_{2kd_{i,2}+kd_{i,1}}$ (where $2kd_{i,2} + kd_{i,1} \neq 0$, for this case). Based on these data, we can determine that if a fault was placed when $d_{i,1} = d_{i,2} = 0$, the algorithm will always have a $JS = 1$ in the output value.

Although the implementation of the atomicity technique over Da-zhi's algorithm is very useful and witty, it has vulnerabilities against attacks that use the JS. The algorithm implemented with the unifier register (algorithm 5) does not present vulnerabilities against these types of attacks because it does not perform the operation $C_0 = C_0 \cdot C_0$. Thus, a negative JS in C_0 is unified with others registers. In the same manner that an FA can be propagated through the algorithm's execution, a JS value can be propagated through the calculations, and can disturb any final result (as explained previously). This avoids the identification of any specific bits combinations as all of them alter the JS of the final result. For this reason, an algorithm with unifier register has a better security level.

Because the algorithm has an atomized behavior, it is a regular algorithm and is secure against simple side channel attacks.

The version of Da-zhi's algorithm presented here has different characteristics than the original. Table 1 shows a summary of the characteristics of such algorithms.

In table 1 the multiplications and the squaring are considered a multiplication. In the column "number of variables" d_1, d_2, k, i, m, d and N are not counted because they are variables inherent in the modular exponentiation and are not related to their implementation.

Many modular exponentiation algorithms execute more calculations, whereas the binary form of the exponent has more 1's. For this reason, binary representations with less 1's are sought. *Non adjacent form* (NAF) [28] is a signed binary representation that can be used to reduce the quantity of 1's inside of a binary string. NAF has two main characteristics: First, the quantity of 1's in any binary string is $n/3$ on average, where n is the bit length. Second, this form has a bit length of $1 + n$ bits. We can see this behavior in the next example:

Decimal	Binary	NAF
98274	10111111111100010	10-1000000000-100010

The last characteristic can be a disadvantage when considering that many crypto devices that execute modular exponentiation algorithms are designed to work with a specific exponent's bit length (secret key). This means that they are designed to operate with 1024 bits, not 1025. In other words, an electronic device that executes a cryptographic algorithm would have to be redesigned to work properly with signed binary representations, a very expensive situation.

Table 1. Caracteristichs of the modified algorithms.

Algorithm	Number of multiplications	Inversions	Number of Variables
Algoritmo 3	$1.5n + 2$	0	5
Algoritmo 4	$1n + (3/8)n + 3 = 1.375n + 3$	0	4
Algoritmo 5	$1.5n + (1/8)n + 4 = 1.625n + 4$	1	6

Thus, it is important to note that the modified algorithm by the unifier register is not compatible with signed binary representations, such as NAF. As stated previously, the algorithm 5 makes three operations when the bit combination is $d_{i,1} = d_{i,2} = 0$. Therefore, while more bits equal to 0 exist, more operations are performed, and their execution times are longer. In this case, it is not necessary to search alternate binary representations that minimize the quantity of 1's. This can be considered an advantage over other algorithms because it can work more efficiently with unsigned binary representations. Hence, it can be in concordance with crypto devices that use standard bit lengths to function.

5 Conclusions

In this work we have presented a way to protect algorithms in right-to-left form that use dummy operations in their execution. When the unifier register is used, the algorithm's security is greater than that in the algorithms that are not protected. The protected algorithms can be incompatible with signed binary representations, such as NAF. This means that they are more efficient when the binary string has few bits equal to 0. However, this characteristic can be seen as an advantage if the implementation over crypto devices that use standard key bit lengths to execute an encryption algorithm is considered. Therefore, it is not necessary to change the hardware to use the unifier register, which may be a very important property.

In the specific case of the Da-zhi's algorithm, this simple modification avoids that the bits of the binary string which represents the secret key can be obtained as described by [23].

Additionally, this algorithm is secure against simple side channel attacks due to atomicity.

Acknowledgments

The authors thank PAPIIT IN 113316, PIAPI1634, and Program PCIC of the UNAM.

References

[1] RL Rivest, A. Shamir and L. Adleman. "A method for obtaining digital signatures and public-key cryptosystems". *Communications of the ACM*, **21**(2):120-126 (1978).

[2] P. Kocher. "Timing attacks on implementations of Diffie-Hellman, RSA, DSS, and other systems". *In Koblitz, N., ed.: Advances in Cryptology-CRYPTO 96*, **1109** of Lecture Notes in Computer Science:104-113, Springer (1996).

[3] P.C. Kocher, J. Jaffe and B. Jun. "Differential Power Analysis". *In Wiener, M., Ed.: Advances in Cryptology-CRYPTO '99.* **1666** *of Lecture Notes in Computer Science. Proceedings of the 19th Annual International Cryptology Conference on Advances in Cryptology*: 388-397, Springer (1999).

[4] Whitfield Diffie and Martin E. Hellman. "New directions in cryptography". *IEEE Transactions on Information Theory*, **22**(6):644-654, IEEE (1976).

[5] D. Boneh, R. DeMillo and R. Lipton. "On the importance of checking cryptographic protocols for faults". *In Fumy, W., Ed.: Advances in Cryptology-EUROCRYPT'97.* **1233** *of Lecture Notes in Computer Science*, pages 37-51, Springer (1997).

[6] J.S. Coron. "Resistance against differential power analysis for elliptic curve cryptosystems". *In Koç, Ç., Paar, C., Eds.: Cryptographic Hardware and Embedded Systems-CHES 2002.* **1717** *of Lecture Notes in Computer Science*, pages 292-302, Springer (1999).

[7] S.M. Yen, S. Kim, S. Lim and S. Moon. "A countermeasure against one physical cryptanalysis may benefit another attack". *Information Security and Cryptology-ICISC 2001*, **2288** of Lecture Notes in Computer Science:414-427, Springer (2001).

[8] S.M. Yen, W.C. Lien, S.J. Moon and J.C. Ha. "Power analysis by exploiting chosen message and internal collisions–vulnerability of checking mechanism for RSA-decryption". *Progress in Cryptology–Mycrypt 2005*, **3715** of Lecture Notes in Computer Science:183-195, Springer (2005).

[9] C.H. Kim and J.J. Quisquater. Fault attacks for CRT based RSA: New attacks, new results, and new countermeasures. *Information Security Theory and Practices. Smart Cards, Mobile and Ubiquitous Computing Systems*, 4462:215-228, Springer (2007).

[10] S. Chari, J. Rao and P. Rohatgi. "Template attacks". *Cryptographic Hardware and Embedded Systems-CHES 2002*, **2523** of Lecture Notes in Computer Science:12-28, Springer (2002).

[11] S.M. Yen and M. Joye. "Checking before output may not be enough against fault-based cryptanalysis". *IEEE Transactions on Computers*, **49**(9):967-970 (2000).

[12] H. Mamiya, A. Miyaji and H. Morimoto. "Efficient countermeasures against RPA, DPA, and SPA".

Cryptographic Hardware and Embedded Systems-CHES 2004, **3156** of Lecture Notes in Computer Science:343-356, Springer (2004).

[13] C.C. Lu, S.Y. Tseng and S.K. Huang. "A secure modular exponential algorithm resists to power, timing, C safe error and M safe error attacks". *In 19th International Conference on Advanced Information Networking and Applications, 2005. AINA 2005*, **2**, pages 151-154, IEEE (2005).

[14] C.H. Kim and J.J. "Quisquater. How can we overcome both side channel analysis and fault attacks on RSA-CRT?". *Workshop on Fault Diagnosis and Tolerance in Cryptography*, pages 21-29, IEEE (2007).

[15] A. Boscher, R. Naciri and E. Prouff."CRT RSA algorithm protected against fault attacks". *Information Security Theory and Practices. Smart Cards, Mobile and Ubiquitous Computing Systems*, **4462** of LNCS: 229-243, Springer (2007).

[16] J.C. Ha, C.H. Jun, J.H. Park, S.J. Moon and C.K. Kim. "A New CRT-RSA Scheme Resistant to Power Analysis and Fault Attacks". *Third 2008 International Conference on Convergence and Hybrid Information Technology*:351-356, IEEE (2008).

[17] A. Boscher, H. Handschuh and E. Trichina. "Blinded fault resistant exponentiation revisited". *In L. Breveglieri, S. Gueron, I. Koren, D. Naccache, and J.-P. Seifert, editors, Workshop on Fault Diagnosis and Tolerance in Crptography - FDTC'09*, pages 3-9, IEEE (2009).

[18] M. Boreale. "Attacking right-to-left modular exponentiation with timely random faults". *Fault Diagnosis and Tolerance in Cryptography*, **4236** of LNCS: 24-35, Springer (2006).

[19] Jörn-Marc Schmidt and Marcel Medwed. "Fault Attacks on the Montgomery Powering Ladder". *13th Annual International Conference on Information Security and Cryptology, Proceedings*, LNCS, Springer (2010).

[20] C.H. Kim. "New fault attacks using Jacobi symbol and application to regular right-to-left algorithms". *Information Processing Letters*, **110**(20):882-886, Elsevier (2010).

[21] M. Joye."Highly regular right-to-left algorithms for scalar multiplication". *Cryptographic Hardware and Embedded Systems-CHES 2007*, **4727** of Lecture in Notes in Computer Science:135-147, Springer (2007).

[22] D.Z. Sun, J.P. Huai, J.Z. Sun and Z.F. Cao. "An efficient modular exponentiation algorithm against simple power analysis attacks". *Consumer Electronics, IEEE Transactions on*, **53**(4):1718-1723 (2007).

[23] D. Tinoco Varela. "How to break down the security of an efficient modular exponentiation algorithm". *Recent advances in computer science*, Proceedings of the 19th International Conference on Computers: 81-85, INASE (2015).

[24] B. Chevallier-Mames, M. Ciet and M. Joye. "Low-cost solutions for preventing simple side-channel analysis: Side-channel atomicity. *IEEE Transactions on Computers*, **53**(6): 760-768, IEEE (2004).

[25] G. Fumaroli and D. Vigilant. "Blinded fault resistant exponentiation". *Fault Diagnosis and Tolerance in Cryptography*, **4236** of Lecture Notes in Computer Science:62-70, Springer-Verlag (2006).

[26] D. Tinoco Varela. "Blinded Montgomery Powering Ladder Protected Against the Jacobi Symbol Attack". *International Journal of Security (IJS)*, **6**(3), 15-27 (2012).

[27] Johannes Blömer and Alexander May. "New partial key exposure attacks on RSA". *Advances in Cryptology-CRYPTO 200*, **3**:27–43, Springer (2003).

[28] G.W. . Reitwiesner. "Binary arithmetic" . *Advances in computers*, **1**: 231-308, Elsevier (1960).

Simulation, analysis and service quality in carrier voice networks

Marius Popescu[1], Andrei Gabor[1] and Antoanela Naaji[1,a]

[1]"Vasile Goldis" Western University of Arad, Engineering and Computer Science Department, 86 Rebreanu Str., Romania

Abstract. Due to existing national regulations in the field of telecommunications, sometimes conflict situation arise between telecommunication operators. In these cases performing simulations and quality analysis are required. The paper describes the ways and means of changing caller ID in the relationship established between two telecommunication operators of different ranks, which have concluded a service agreement. Simulating the mode of interconnection between operators, based on an interface represented by Voice Gateway, and through various settings on a dial plan, one can establish a real operation. Finally, traffic trends are studied over a period of time, analyzing the conflicts started between the two telecommunications operators regarding traffic and quality of services.

1 Introduction

After 2000, Europe has seen the emergence of operators developing their own telecommunication networks, which have helped improve speed in accessing telecommunication services, quickly attaining the appropriate level of user requirements. During this time, in Romania the national regulatory authority in telecommunications (ANCOM) defined:
- carrier operators and/or service providers as those with "significant power ... of broadband electronic communication services and public telephone services at fixed points", who can directly provide users with Internet access services;
- dominant operators as those with "significant market power in terms of access to their mobile network in order to terminate calls", requiring interconnection with any other carrier operator and/or telecommunication service provider.

As a result, agreements have emerged between carrier operators and/or service providers and dominant operators, stipulating the installation of bi-directional communication streams (e.g. 30 channels, E1 [1]), without establishing details on how to identify and resolve deviations from prerequisites such as exceeding the value of daily traffic (e.g. traffic exceeding 30,000 minutes/month), forced route "maturing" (e.g., provided after 6 months), etc. Services required by service provider operators from the dominant operator were:
- termination of calls originated by customers of the carrier operator and /or service provider to the dominant operator's network;
- termination of calls originated by the dominant operator's network to the geographic numbers allocated to the carrier operator and/or service provider (for example, Romania: 021 569 xxxx where xxxx=0,1, ... 9);
- routing calls originated by the dominant operator's network to the carrier operator and/or service provider's exchange for calls with carrier selection;
- termination of calls originated by the dominant operator network to non-geographic numbers allocated to the carrier operator and/or service provider (e.g., green numbers 0800 120 xxx, prepaid cards 0808 810 xxx, or value added services 0903 030 xxx, where x = 0 1, ..., 9); allocation of short xxxx numbers, callable from the dominant operator's network, and which are routed to non-geographic numbers of the carrier operator and/or service provider, providing various services to customers depending on the set category.
- line services leased between customers and the company of the carrier operator and/or service provider through the dominant operator's network.

In our paper we present a real situation, in which traffic estimates for services established between the dominant operator and the service provider operator was 400,000 minutes/month in the first 3 months, of which 100% voice – to – voice calls, which in turn was distributed in a proportion of 70 % over the 08-18 time slot and 30% over the 18-08 time slot. Transmission hours were spread evenly from Monday to Sunday, with peak traffic from 10 am to 4 pm. The maximum number of simultaneous calls was 70, and the prospects for traffic increase were determined, depending on services, at 2 million minutes per month for the next eight months. We used numerical simulation for the quality analysis because in some cases there is no possibility to make this evaluation directly on equipment. For testing the method, we compared the results with those obtained through experimental evaluation. As conclusion, we demonstrated that the increasing trends of traffic over a short period of time (e.g. 20 days) resulted in the dominant operator taking additional measures to monitor traffic and

[a] Corresponding author: anaaji@uvvg.ro

DOI: 10.1051/matecconf/20167604020

moderate its growth. This fact caused discontent in the carrier operator and/or service provider, the latter mentioning that the traffic of their subscribers is a process that evolves in a probabilistic manner which cannot be controlled, and therefore requiring a new interconnection agreement for national and international call routing to the dominant operator's network.

2 Hardware and software used by telecommunications operators

2.1 Methods and equipment for the interconnection of telecommunication operators

The physical equipment (hardware) used by the carrier operator and/or service provider to connect with the dominant operator was an Ericsson ANS Translocal R420R2 exchange [2] with Diax A/S NMLCM v5 .43 support/OS/software, using SS7 CCS7v2.2 signalling, which allowed routing national and international calls to the dominant operator's network. Equipment used (in 2004, similar to Alcatel equipment) by the dominant operator had the following specifications: SW releases [3] SW of the platform (according to existing HW) are: Evolium SSP release R272.3.4.2/V9 (E10), Evolium RCP release R909 (EP8) and Evolium M HLR release GB910 (EP9). The gatekeeper, which provides call control for endpoints, more streamlined for incoming calls, is preceded by other equipment. Thus, VoIP calls incoming from interconnection lines of the input port, where transmission is performed by packets, were taken from an IP switch (DJAX-AS) layer 2 or 3 and, if the numbers were specific to the dominant operator, they were then routed to the receiving interface port. In the case of the service operator, the IP switch type (DJAX-AS) was layer 3 (in OSI - Open Systems Interconnection architecture) and therefore it could provide, in addition to the outgoing address, the input port address and not that of the caller. Figure 1 shows the configuration of interconnections in the case of incoming calls in the carrier operator and/or service provider network from other national and international networks.

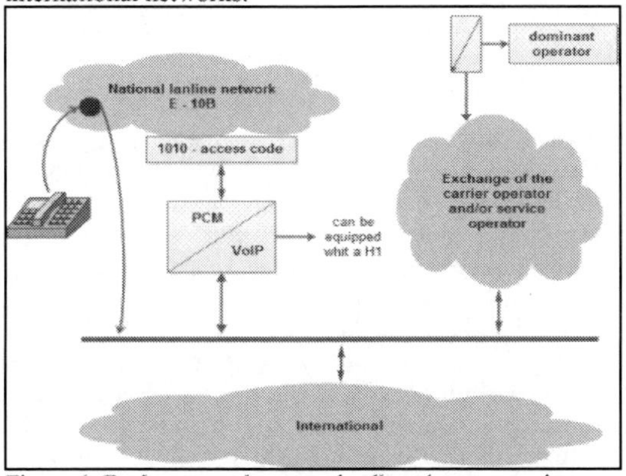

Figure 1. Explanatory scheme on the direct interconnection between the carrier operator and/or service provider network and the landline network (Alcatel) via an adapter (of the same type as for the interconnection with the dominant operator.

The access code in 2004, established under the interconnection agreement of the carrier operator and/or service provider with the national landline network, was changed in 2008 by ANCOM into access code 1010, according to the National Numbering Plan.

The equipment used proved that the carrier operator and/or service provider does not preserve caller ID (e.g., 021-BPQMCDU), introducing its own authorized numbering (021-569xxxx). Or, in order to change caller ID, the operation might be assigned (allocated) to either:
a) the layer 3 switch of the VoIP equipment (the carrier operator and/or service provider exchange);
b) or directly in the channel interface - 1 - MUX converter PCM/VoIP used for interconnecting the VoIP exchange with the mobile and landline network (gatekeeper).

In the first case, each incoming channel from platform 1010 is assigned from the outset a specific numbering on the VoIP network of the carrier operator and/or service provider, such as 021569111x (authorized numbering, the tranche of numbers used being highlighted in bi-annual reports of the carrier operator and/or service provider to ANCOM). In case of the carrier operator and/or service provider declares that the number of its subscribers is 11, 12 or 15, is sufficient to be used and allocated as ID to incoming channels on the landline or international network.

In the second case, if a simple converter is used, with no processing capacity, the ID change is performed within the layer 3 switch, the other numbering problems being the same as in the previous case. Connection with the dominant operator on the output of the VoIP - PCM converter is equipped with a 30-channel MUX, and not E1 stream. For calls originating in the dominant operator's network, calls will be connected directly via VoIP network – 4 – bypassing platform 1010 (Figure 2). H.323 (1996) is a suite of protocols that includes both signalling protocols (signalling and controlling point-to-point and multi-point conferences – calling, data bandwidth, etc.), as well as transport protocols. The H.323 standard describes a series of functional components, which can be implemented separately in different equipment, or can be grouped into one multi-purpose equipment.

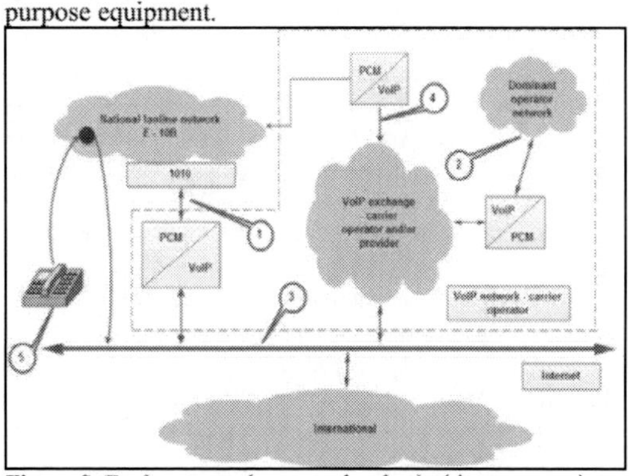

Figure 2. Explanatory scheme on the physical interconnection of the network operator and/or service provider network with the Internet data network.

For the first 10 months, the numbering plan used by the carrier operator and/or service provider analyzed in this case was limited to 10,000 call numbers (required by the equipment used [4]). Thus, as recommended by ITU-T (International Telecommunication Union), it could not be considered a public telecommunication service operator, but at most a VPN (Virtual Private Network) [5] implemented in the network of another dominant operator or a service provider between networks (ISP - Internetwork Service Provider). The carrier operator and/or service provider could allow routing, through its network, national and international calls from other national telecommunication operators to subscribers of the dominant operator with which they concluded an agreement, but only if this behavior was tolerated by the dominant operator.

2.2 Simulating an interconnection situation

Since it is not possible to carry out experimental simulations on a model that has its 2004 configuration, mainly for the analysis of an E1 stream as a link between a communication service distributor (Ericsson Diax Ans) and the dominant operator network as transit network (Alcatel 1000 E10 OCB 283 HC [1]), under certain circumstances, different software can be used to simulate the situation described earlier in this paper. Specifically to achieve such goals, a medium that simulates the infrastructure of some operators was used, in this case the connection between the dominant operator and the carrier operator.

Emulator GNS3 [6] and the application Cisco Unified Communication Manager (CUCM) [7] were used for simulation, the latter being an integrated communication system, based on voice, video and data IP, also allowing the exchange of information between operators. CUCM standardized components, by levels, are:

- infrastructure containing the routers, switches and Voice Gateway; the infrastructure level enables exchange of data, voice and video between network devices and applications.
- call control which is responsible for handling calls, controlling device and managing dialing plans.
- an application that is an independent level of the call control, which allows applications to run anywhere on the network, such as Voice Mail, Cisco Unified Meeting Place, Cisco Emergency Responder, as well as of the integration of SOAP, Q.SIG, H.323, MGCP and SIP protocols. The CUCM node in this simulation was located in the carrier operator's website. GNS3 emulator was used to configure the Cisco 3725 router and voice gateway, and Cisco IP Communications application to simulate calls [8].

In the proposed simulation scenario, both locations responsible for each operator simulate the connection to dial the number corresponding to operators, each location having a specific set numbering plan. CUCM was installed on a VMWare virtual machine, with a storage space of 160G and 8 GRAM. The idea was to simulate an environment as similar as possible to that described in paragraph 2.1., based on the H.323 protocol and SIP (Session Initiation Protocol) on the VoIP part. SIP, a signalling protocol, found in the application layer of the OSI stack, was used to create, modify, and terminate sessions between two or more participants in the conversation. The H.323 protocol was used between the routers and SIP. Topology was created in GNS3, and CUCM was the connection between the node and the Vmnet8 interface of the virtual machine. Routers were configured to provide connections based on H.323 protocol and SIP to CUCM. Ethernet port configuration and protocol H.323 activation for Voice Gateway are described below:

```
VoiceGateway(config-if)#ip      add      10.10.10.10
255.255.255.0
VoiceGateway(config-if)#no shut
%LINK-3-UPDOWN:
Interface Ethernet1/0, changed state to up
%LINEPROTO-5-UPDOWN:  Line  protocol  on  Interface
Ethernet1/0,
changed state to upno shtdo
VoiceGateway(config)#ip   route   0.0.0.0   0.0.0.0
10.10.10.1
...
VoiceGateway(config)#voice call send-alert
VoiceGateway(config)#voice rtp send-recv
VoiceGateway(config)#voice service voip
VoiceGateway(conf-voi-serv)#h323
VoiceGateway(conf-serv-h323)#end
VoiceGateway#
H.323 service is up
 This gateway  is not registered to any gatekeeper
Alias list (CLI configured) is empty
Alias list (last RCF) is empty
...
VoiceGateway(conf-voi-serv)#allow-connection h323 to
sip
VoiceGateway(conf-voi-serv)#allow-connections sip to
h323
VoiceGateway(conf-voi-serv)#voice translation-rule 1
VoiceGateway(cfg-translation-rule)#rule 1 /^9(.*$\)/
/\1/
VoiceGateway(cfg-translation-rule)#voice
translation-profile OUT
VoiceGateway(cfg-translation-profile)#translate
called 1
...
VoiceGateway(config)#dial-peer voice 4021555 voip
VoiceGateway(config-dial-peer)#destination-pattern
4021555
VoiceGateway(config-dial-peer)#session target
ipv4:10.10.10.10
VoiceGateway(config-dial-peer)#codec g711ulaw
VoiceGateway(config-dial-peer)#exit
VoiceGateway(config)#write
```

It can be considered that within the carrier network to Voice Gateway, the numbering of the caller and the call recipient may be stored according to SIP. It is possible that, by processing ID and numbering, the interconnection interface between operators can change the identity of the call source. SIP is widely used today as a signalling protocol for VoIP. Use of a PBX (Private Branch Exchange) by the dominant operator, which does not support SIP Trunking, will require a Voice Gateway to connect to the SIP provider. The gateway was placed between the PBX and the SIP provider, using an E1 ISDN (Integrated Services Digital Network) stream via the IP protocol [9]. These settings are not complete and are only the initial setup of voice characteristics. H323 calls are activated to SIP and SIP to H323 for Voice Gateway and R1, respectively. Subsequently, the connection for CUCM was configured. Cisco Unified Communications Manager supports several types of Cisco gateways. To configure Voice Gateway, they are used for communication terminals when IP telephony infrastructure communicates with PSTN (Public Switched Telephone Network) or other devices such as PBXs, analogue phones, fax machines, etc. The interfaces specify how the gateway communicates with the PSTN or other devices. The route plan is one of the most important components of a CUCM system. It is an integral part of all call processing operations. Generally, the route plan is the decision maker and instructs the call processing on how to route the calls (Figure 3).

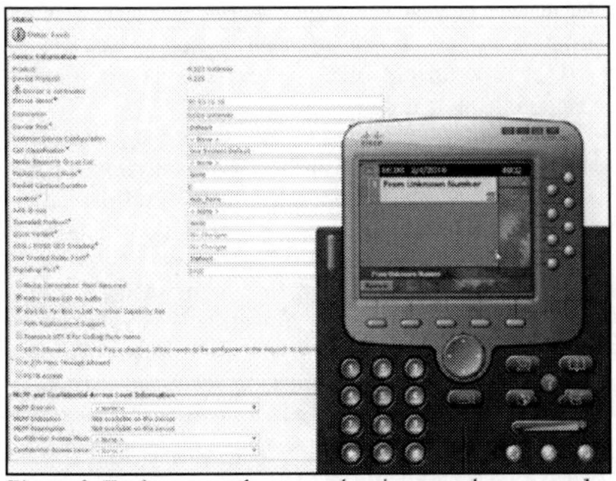

Figure 3. Explanatory scheme on showing an unknown number on the phone display in absence of a routing plan. Sources: Display Capture.

The dial plan describes how calls are processed and routed. This plan can be described based on certain main functions [10], of which the following are listed:
- Endpoint addressing;
- Calling;
- Path selection;
- Digit manipulation, the number of the source can be modified to remove the prefix (Figure 3);
- Call coverage;
- Patterns, the absence of a patterns route, can determine display an unknown number.

2.3 Testing an interconnection situation

Since it was not possible to run tests on a mockup with exactly the above-mentioned configuration, similar equipment was used to test those previously described in the paper. In order to attain our goals, we used an environment simulating the infrastructure of some operators, namely the connection between the dominant and the carrier operator. The tests were performed for 3 relevant situations:

Case 1: - one unaltered and one altered port. The call is initiated on a phone with the number 0132 130 002 – port 1 (unaltered port), and the recipient mobile phone shows the unaltered number 96 850 112, which is also registered in the logs (ABOIN).

The explanatory configuration on the recipient phone screen and the number registration in logs, is described below:

```
ABOIN: CEN=1/91-09-16/03 H 24 MN 52/INTERROG.
CARACTERISTIQUES D'ABONNES
@ND=96850112:
  TRAITEMENT TGLAIN ACC
      ND=96850112          NE =085-00-112
           CAT= NAT2+CLAB4
            MAR=ASD
             DS= 96 850212   <96850215
                      +96850991    <96850995
                TRAITEMENT TGLAIN EXC
              @URAIL:
 CEN=1/91-09-16/03 H 36 MN 25/LISTAGE EQUIPEMENTS U.R.A.
              @AFCN=85-0<20:
                NE= 085-00-096 < 085-00-111 NEQ
                NE= 085-00-112 ND=    96850112 ACP
                NE= 085-00-113 < 085-00-127 NQA
              ....
              *  ^R0809/054/'      '/LIBERATION DU TERMINAL
              ....
              @ABOIN:
           CEN=1/91-09-16/04 H 16 MN 57/INTERROG.
CARACTERISTIQUES D'ABONNES
              @ND=96850112:
                TRAITEMENT TGLAIN ACC
                  CAT= IAM+ CAM2+ NAT2+CLAB4
                      MAR=ASD
                    NDS= 96850212   <96850215
                      +96850991    <96850995
                TRAITEMENT TGLAIN EXC
```

The call is initiated on a phone with the number 0132 140 005 – port 2 (altered port), and the recipient mobile phone shows the altered number (the number set in the switch application), i.e. number 96 850 991.

Case 2: - both ports are altered. The call is initiated on a phone with the number 0132 130 002 – port 1 (altered port), and the recipient mobile phone shows the altered number 96 850 991 (the number set in the switch application) which is registered, and thus featured in the logs (ABOIN). The call is initiated on a phone with the number 0132 140 005 – on port 2 (altered port), and the recipient mobile phone shows the altered number (the number set in the switch application), i.e. the number 96 850 991, which was also noticed in the logs (ABOIN)

Case 3: - both ports altered. The call is initiated on a phone with the number 0132 130 002 – port 1 (altered), and the recipient mobile phone shows the altered number 96 850 991 (the number set in the switch application) which was also noticed in the logs (ABOIN) The call is initiated on a phone with the number 0132 140 005 – port 2 (altered), and the recipient mobile phone shows the altered number (the number set in the switch application), i.e. the number 96 850 995, which was also seen in the logs (ABOIN).

3 Traffic and voice transmission quality analysis

3.1 The carrier operator and/or service provider has routed into the dominant operator's network international traffic and/or national traffic originated in other networks than its own

Following the ANCOM decision on the standardization of national and international rates (2007), the carrier operator and/or service provider has reduced traffic (starting in the 36th month, Figure 4), but only for a short time period.

a) One argument for the major increase in traffic compared to the amount established in the agreement (30,000 minutes/month) is given by the small number of subscribers declared by the carrier operator and/or service provider in relation to the dominant operator.

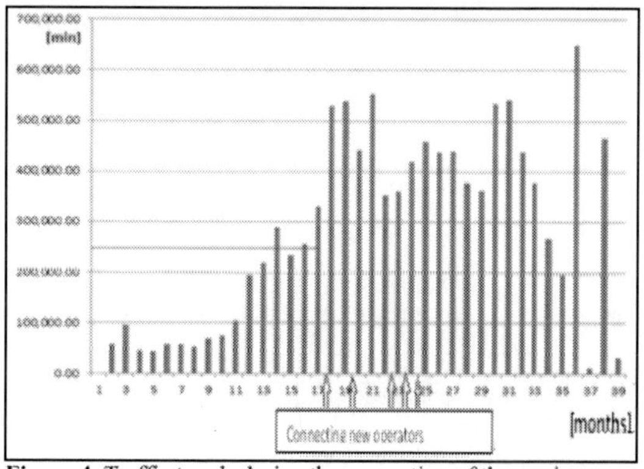

Figure 4. Traffic trends during the connection of the carrier operator and/or service provider with the dominant operator

Thus, during traffic monitoring by the dominant operator the given traffic values (Figure 5) are real, i.e. in accordance with the number of subscribers declared by the carrier operator and/or service provider.

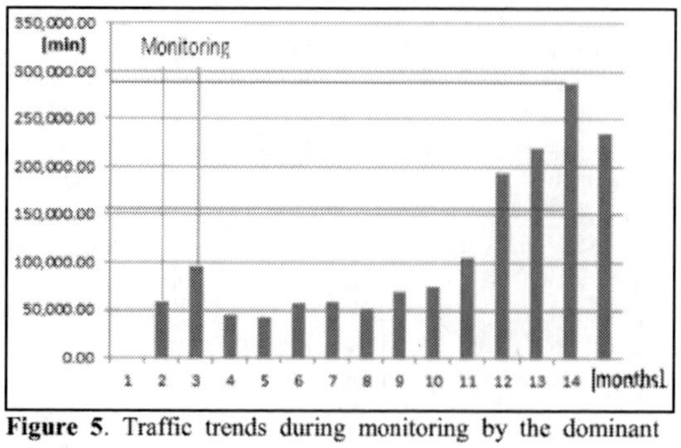

Figure 5. Traffic trends during monitoring by the dominant operator.

b) During the period under review, according to the existing agreement between the carrier operator and/or service provider and another dominant operator on the market, prepaid cards and smart calls are also used by subscribers of those networks. The service operator, offering conditions for routing traffic for subscribers of the other dominant operator and international traffic to subscribers of the dominant operator. The carrier operator and/or service provider would use card count-type cards by which the subscriber, dialing a phone number, after entering the account number, could access any other number in the telecommunication networks connected to the card issuer (card issuer identifier code), these short numbers being called carrier selection code. By using the smart call service, a subscriber can dial the desired number after previously entering a "short" phone number. The caller's ID may be replaced with another, pertaining to the carrier operator and/or service provider network, so that when reaching destination, the caller may be considered to be the carrier operator and/or service provider's own subscriber.

c) Use of traffic routing through VoIP protocol (allows changing caller identity upon entering another network), by the carrier operator and/or service provider, illustrates the fact that the carrier operator and/or service provider will be able to route national and international traffic to the dominant operator's network.

Thus, after converting voice signals and preparing the packets, upon entry into the operator's network operator and/or service provider, the true identity of the caller is replaced with an ID (caller number) pertaining to the transit network (of the carrier operator and/or service provider), and upon destination/reception the call appears as coming from the transit network and not the real one. Although ITU-T recommendations require just one signalling change for establishing communications in a national area, it can be noted that two changes are made in the signalling system, namely, into and out of the carrier operator and/or service provider network.

d) During the period under review, the carrier operator and/or service provider concluded a large number of interconnection agreements with various companies providing telecommunication services, concentrating and routing their traffic to subscribers of the dominant operator network. Routing other operators' traffic to the dominant operator network is also apparent from Figure 5, where traffic increases are highlighted every time a new network connects to the carrier operator and/or service provider network [4].

e) In addition to the amount of incoming traffic (Figure 6a), the dominant operator also monitored the average duration of incoming calls (Figure 6b) tolerating the behavior of the carrier operator and/or service provider.

Thus, there is a sudden increase in the average duration of calls from 1.5 minutes in the first 20 days to more than 4 minutes in the next 5 days, which indicates that the carrier operator and/or service provider began to route additional traffic (possibly international traffic) from the one originated in the home network to the dominant operator network.

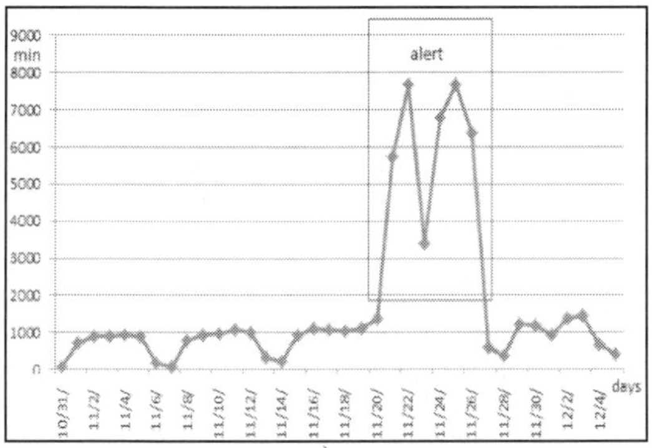

a)

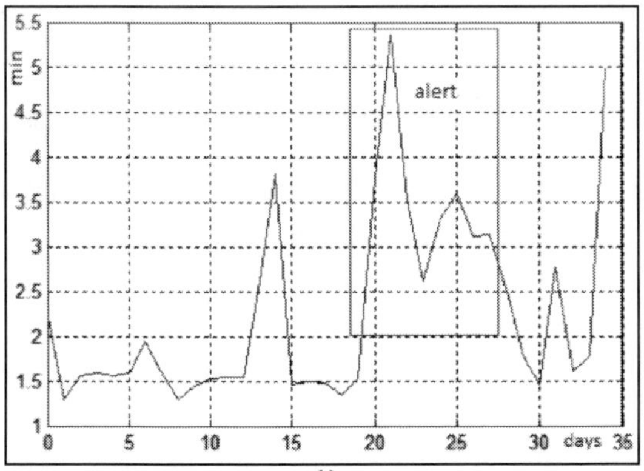

b)

Figure 6. Explanatory scheme on incoming traffic (a) and average duration of calls (b).

3.2 The quality of VoIP communications, the relationship between the carrier operator and/or service provider and the dominant operator

a) Quality parameters established for national and international communications, valid for both the carrier operator and/or service provider and the dominant operator, are [11]:

- the link upload domain, necessary to enable the carrier operator and/or service provider to use VoIP [12], with values ranging between 0.2 - 0.4 Erlang [13]; exceeding the upper threshold involves increasing waiting "queue" and thus loss of packets;
- the route loading indicator, ranging between 10-90% Erlang B, determines the probability for a call to be blocked; very high values will highlight the poor quality of equipment and software used by the carrier operator and/or service provider; reaching the upper limit cannot be accepted even in the case of route transport capacity falling below 20%;
- the percentage of erroneous seconds < 1.4% (14 missed calls in 1,000); reaching the upper limit is not acceptable for national/international traffic;
- Answer Seizure Ratio (ASR)> 50%, being dependent on the subscriber's presence in the network.

The above values, listed in the studied VoIP communications, do not meet the quality requirements desired by subscribers and do not fall into the general characteristics of voice communications, namely, ID change, interruptions and lengthy shutdowns.

b) The above-mentioned parameters as quality indicators are insufficient to ensure that the traffic routed through and originated on the carrier operator and/or service provider network maintains its quality levels upon arrival to the dominant network. VoIP-based service quality was contested by many international operators. Quality problems have only reached acceptable levels in 2008, by implementing Internet Protocol version 8 (IPv8), which allowed controlling packets carrying voice information and reducing the number of lost packets. Full implementation of this version, by all users, was due to be completed in 2013, which never happened.

c) As the transmission of voice packets can be affected by lack of synchronization occurring between the telecommunication network and telecommunication terminal adapters, resulting in loss of packets, VoIP communications are regarded as having a "best effort" quality level. However, if the bandwidth is much larger than that of an E1 stream (>2Mbps), then communications are not affected by packet loss, and transmission performance is "premium rate".

d) The existence of two changes in the signalling system drastically affects the quality of communications. In this respect, reference is made to the poor quality of communications before 1989, in Romania, when analogue communication systems were used, requesting two changes in the signalling system (Rotary [14] and Pentaconta technologies).

4 Conclusions

Performing simulations is required for the numerical analysis of the conflict situation arising between telecommunication operators. Thus, it has been observed that there is a possibility that numbers in a VoIP network be converted into another numbering plan based on pre-established settings. If the call source number does not correspond to a specific predefined pattern, the dominant operator may convert that number into one of its own network. Using a prefix to access the dominant operator network can result in conversion of the call source number to match the numbers in that network by removing the prefix and changing it. In the case presented in our paper, during the period under review, the carrier operator and/or service provider routed both traffic originated in other national networks than its own and international traffic to the dominant operator network, and the dominant operator allowed the routing of this traffic voluntarily and knowingly. The quality of VoIP communications, in the connection between the dominant operator and the carrier operator and/or service provider, did not meet the quality parameters required for national and international communications. The quality standard for this type of communication was achieved only after the implementation of Internet Protocol version 8, started in 2009 and expected to be completed in 2013, although currently in Romania there are communication networks using old versions of the Internet Protocol, namely IPv6.

References

1. M. Popescu, *Telecommunications (in Romanian)* Ed. Universitaria, Craiova (2008)
2. *ANS TransLocal for optimal flexibility*, Ericsson Diax A/S (2010) http://archive.ericsson.net/service/internet/picov/get?DocNo=1/28701-FGC101591&L.
3. M.M. Eissa, M. M. Elmesalawy, M.M.A. Hadhoud, Wide Area Monitoring System based on the third generation Universal Mobile Telecommunication System for event identification, *International Journal of Electrical Power & Energy Systems*, **69**, pp 34–47 (2015)
4. V. Croitoru, D. Geleriu, The report expertise in telecommunications specialty (not published), Bucharest (2013).
5. J. Snader, *VPNs Illustrated: Tunnels, VPNs and IPsec*, Ed. Addison Wesley Professional (2005)
6. GNS3 software, https://www.gns3.com/
7. Cisco Unified Communications Manager http://www.cisco.com/c/en/us/products/unified-communications/unified-communications-manager-callmanager/index.html
8. Cisco IP Communicator http://www.cisco.com/c/en/us/products/collaboration-endpoints/ip-communicator/index.html
9. S. Brent, *CCNA Voice Lab Manual*, Cisco Press, Indianapolis, Indiana (2013)
10. J. Cioara, V. Michael, *CCNA Voice 640-461 Official Cert Guide*, Cisco Press, Indianapolis, Indiana (2011)
11. T. Vaughan, *Multimedia: Making It Work*, 8th Edition, Ed. McGraw-Hill (2011)
12. P. Carden, *Building Voice over IP*, Network computing (2000) http://www.networkcomputing.com/netdesign/1109voipfull.html#two
13. M.C. Popescu, N. Mastorakis, *New Aspect on Wireless Communication Networks*, International Journal of Communications, Issue 1, **3**, pp.34-43, (2009) http://www.naun.org/journals/communications/
14. A. Calvo, *Compañia Telefónica Nacional de España: From subsidiary to leader*, in Telecommunications Conference (HISTELCON), Second IEEE Region 8 Conference on the History of, pp.1–7, Madrid (2010)

MATEC Web of Conferences 76, 04021 (2016) DOI: 10.1051/matecconf/20167604021
CSCC 2016

Diseases Diagnosis Using Medical Palmistry Fuzzy Model

Zainab Othman[1,a] and Sarmad Saleem[1]

1Department of Computer Science, Science College, University of Basra, Iraq.

Abstract. The design n, implementation, and use of biomedical information systems in the form of computer – aided decision support have become essential and widely used over the last two decades. Medical decision support systems play an increasingly important role in medical practice by assisting physicians who make clinical decisions. Medical scientists discovered that the hand can be used as an indicator for medical problems and the palm is the reflection of activities going on brain. The purpose of this research is to design and implement a decision support model for healthcare on the basis of medical palmistry to diagnose the diseases from palm colors. Database palm images for patients infected with specific disease is created from capturing live images from hospitals. Digital image processing techniques on input images are applied. Fuzzy Inference System is used to present medical knowledge as network diseases connected with each other by logical relations. The model is built to assist medical practitioners for taking diagnosis decision for four special diseases. The results obtained from this work are confidence.

1 Introduction

Computer – aided diagnosis is rapidly became a part of the routine clinical works for the detection of disease. The computer output is used as a "second opinion" in assisting for diagnosis a different diseases. Generally the proposed algorithm consists of many procedures that may include image feature analysis, and data classification via the use of tools such as fuzzy logic or artificial neural network (ANN) which are referred to as "artificial intelligence" [1]. One of the fields to identify disease is analysis of the color of human palm. Medical science studies the palm for various coloration of different region to get assistance in decision making. Different colors existing at different regions in palm are based on blood circulation at that region as well as presence of disease in human body. The computer will give more accurate results than human vision, because it overcomes the limitations of human eye like subjectivity and resolution power [2]. There are many previous attempts had been done to diagnose the disease from palm. But the researches in this field are still in the beginning.

B. Shanmugapriya *et al* [3]. Presented about the handling of valuable information from human hand image in various fields like biometrics, prophesy and medical diagnosis. A.Navpat *et al* [4]. Discussed the design of a system that helps in predicting the palmistry details by scanning an image of the palm. H. Pandit et *al* [5]. Explained a prototype for human

Palm based on digital image processing and analysis in field of healthcare. D. Desai et al [6].Applies digital image processing techniques on input palm images to identify certain features in the image and by using knowledge base of medical palmistry it analyzes certain features in image and predicts probable disease. In this paper new Fuzzy model is proposed to identify certain features in the palm images depending on knowledge base of medical palmistry. Database for live palm images had been created from Basra hospitals. This database contained palm images for patients had diseases in heart, kidney, lung, and obstruction in the circulation of the blood.

2 Palmistry Basics

Medical science has found that the palm contains more nerves cells than any other portion of the nervous system. So that, palm is the reflection of activities going on in brain. Thus, whatever is indicated in palm is result of biological and psychological changes in the human system [7]. A normal palm has color a light red color or a pinkish red with a shiny and smooth texture. While the following colors denote there are abnormal conditions [8].

[a] Corresponding author: zai_nab_alfahad@yahoo.com

a. **Pale White**: A palm appearing pale white in color indicates anemia or possibly occult bleeding.
b. If the palm looks white, this usually indicates lung disease or inflammation in the body.
c.**Blue:** A Blue palm usually indicates intestinal obstruction.
d. **Dark Green:** A Palm with a dark green color usually indicates obstruction in the circulation of the blood.
e. **Yellow:** A sallow yellow palm usually indicates chronic disease. This is because chronic disease typically affects the spleen and stomach. A palm that looks yellowish brown and has no sheen indicates the possibility of cancer.
e. **Black Red:** If the whole palm is covered with dark red or purple spots, this is usually seen in liver disease
f. **Purple:** When the subcutaneous tissue of the palm shows prune colored purple, it indicates serious infectious shock.
g. **Grey:** Thin Cigarette-ash like spots on the palm
h. **Black Brownish:** A palm that looks Brownish is often seen in kidney disease.

3 Database for Color Palm Images

Palmistry technique acts as one of the aid tools for diagnosing purposes. The Internet does not have like database for color palm images influenced with disease. Then to collect diseased palm images, it is practically to get them live from patients in hospitals. This caused a big problem, because most patients don't cooperate in this project. Also official approvals were difficult and take long time.

The specific Basra hospitals departments had been visited which are related with this work and a collection of color palm images are accumulated. The database includes images of normal persons and patients between the ages of 20 and 80 years. About 20% percentage of images are taken from female and the rest are for male. The images are captured for right and left palms. This operation built a Database for normal and diseased color palm images.

4 Limitation in Capturing Palm Images

Mainly there are two capturing devices. First, CCD based scanner and the second, is digital camera. The CCD based scanner device is not available in Basra hospitals, so the digital camera is the only solution to capture palm images. In this work, samples of palm images are digitally captured under standard and control environment. So many limitations are considered to capture a palm image using Digital Camera. These limitations are:

a. Image capturing is at the morning.
b. The light intensity must be controlled to suitable value.
c. The camera was placed at a distance of 40 to 50 cm directly above the hand palm of respondent.

Special Black Board is made to locate the palm on it before capturing the image. Figure (1) shows the black board using with capturing palm images. Some patients refused to put their hands on this black board. So black cushion was used for this purpose.

Figure 1. Black Board used in Capturing Color Palm Image.

5 The Proposed Model

The proposed model structure is designed to have the following architected as shown in Figure (2).

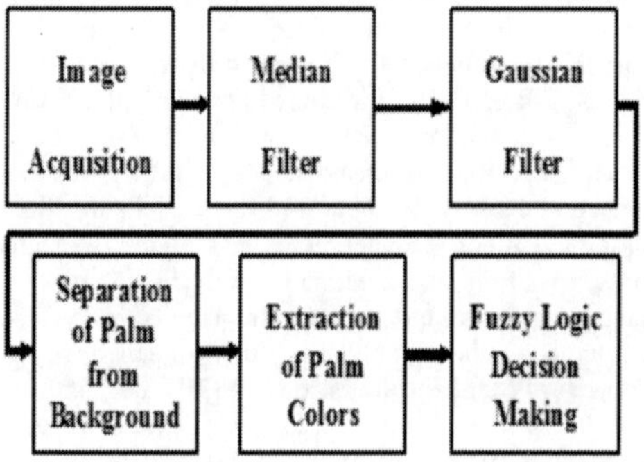

Figure 2. Block Diagram for Proposed Model

6 Image Acquisition

Digital camera of type Nikon d7100 with 24.1 megapixel is used to collect palm images from patients.

More than 500 images are captured from patients and only 436 obviously of them are used in this paper. Four diseases are concerned in this paper:

a. Lung disease.
b. Obstruction in the circulation of The blood.
c. Kidney disease.
d. Heart disease.

The RGB image for size 12 M Byte is formatted and saved as jpg format. The total capacity of the obvious palm images is more than 5G byte. Figure (3) shows sample of color palm images.

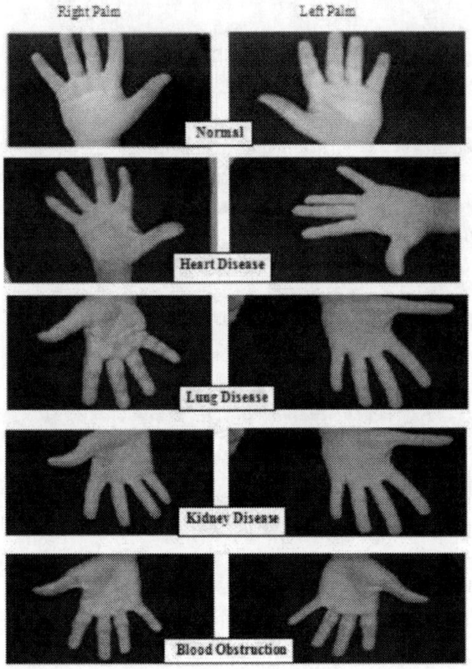

Figure 3. Samples of Palm Images

7 Filtering Results of Median

Median filter is a denoising filter used to remove salt and pepper noises from digital image [9]. The Median Filter is a two dimension filter, so it can't use for color image. To avoid this problem the color image is extracted to the individual red, green, and blue channels. In the RGB color model, each color appears in its primary spectral components of red, green, and blue. Each color is treated alone by Median Filter and then reconstruction is used to produce denoised free image.

Different window sizes are taken, but the best result is obtained when the window size is 3x3. The algorithm of Median Filter is shown as below:

Algorithm : processing median filter
Input: RGB Color Palm Image
Output: Denoising RGB Color Palm Image
Begin

1. ***read RGB Palm Image***
   image=imread(C:\palm1.jpg)
2. ***extract the individual red,green and blue color channels***
   redchannel = image(:,:,1)
   greenchannel=image(:,:,2)
   bluechannel=image(:,:,3)
3. ***median filter the channels***
   redmf=medfilt2(redchannel,[3 3])
   greenmf=medfilt2(greenchannel,[3 3])
   bluemf=medfilt2(bluechannel,[3 3])
4. ***reconstruct the denoise free RGB image***
   image =cat(3,redmf,greenmf,bluemf)

End.

Median Filtering have a good edge preserving ability, and does not introduce new pixel values to the processed image. As well as Median Filter reduces the blurring of edges. Median Filter reduces the blurring of edges. Figure (4) presents the operation of the Median Filter for a sample of palm images.

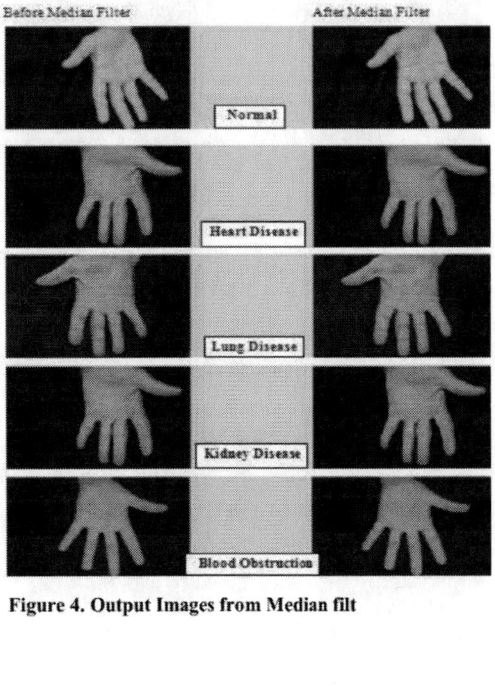

Figure 4. Output Images from Median filt

8 Filtering Results of Gaussian

One kind of noise which occurs in all recorded images to a certain extent is detector noise and visible as grains in the image. It may arise in the image as effects of basic physics-like photon nature of light or thermal energy of heat inside the image sensors [10]. The output images from Median Filter are used as input to Gaussian Filter. Figure 5 shows samples of images processing by Gaussian Filter. The Algorithm used to process Gaussian Filter is shown as below:

Algorithm : processing Gaussian filter
Input : RGB Color Palm Image after Processing by Median filter
Output : Denoising RGB color Palm Image
Begin
1. ***Get RGB Palm Image from Median filter***
   Image1=image
2. ***Processing image by Gaussian filter***
   h= fspecial('gaussian',[7,7],3)
   image=imfilter(image1,h)

End.

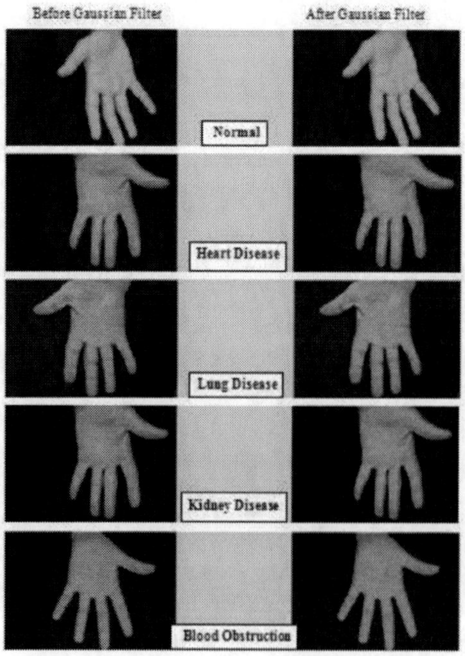

Figure 5. Output Images from Gaussian filter

9 Separation Palm from Background

The main difficulty with trying to separate an image from its background is that there are pixels which cover an area of the picture which is partly Foreground and partly background. With any of the methods, a pixel must be declared whether either foreground or background, even though it may be both. Threshold is actually a pretty good method to extract palm from background.

Actually all palm images are captured using black fixed background. But this operation is no sufficient to separate the palm image from background. So threshold method is used for this purpose. In the palm image of human, by eye's observation of RGB of palm. It is easy conclude that, red component having higher value than green and blue components. This observation is used as criteria to store all those pixels that satisfy the above condition. Figure 6 shows samples of images after separation processing .The following is Matlab code used in separation process.

Algorithm : separation Palm from Image
Input : Get denoising Image from Gaussian filter
Output : Palm Image separation from background
Begin
Image1=image
1. ***Get the image dimension number of color bands should be=3***
   [rows, columns ,number of Color bands]=size(image)
2. ***Extract the individual red , green , blue color Channels***
   Redchannel = image(:,:,1)
   Greenchannel = image(:,:,2)
   Bluechannel = i mage(:,:,3)
3. ***Separate background from palm image using threshold***
   k=0
   For I =1:rows
   For j = 1:columns
   If redchannel(i,j)>40||greenchannel(i,j) >40 ||bluechannel (i,j)>40
   k=k+1
   Else
   Redchannel (i,j)=0;greenchannel (i,j) = 0; bluechannel (i,j)=0
   end
   end
   end
4. ***Reconstruct the free RGB image after separation from background***
   Image=cat(3,redchannel,greenchannel, bluechannel)

End.

 DOI: 10.1051/matecconf/20167604021

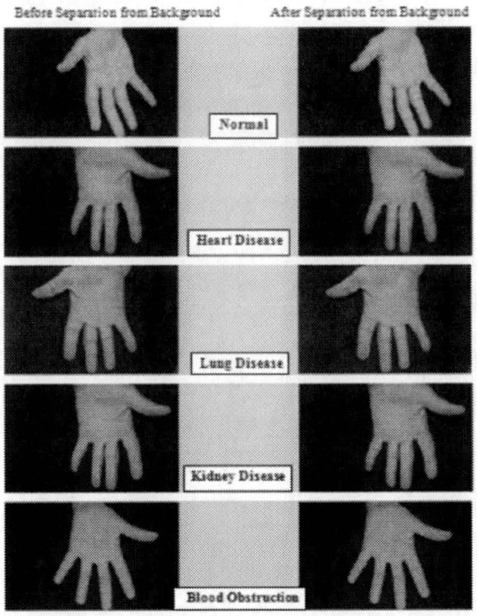

Figure 6. Images after Separation processing

10 Extraction of Palm Colors

Color images have multiple color intensity values stored per pixel. Different colors are generated by combination of red, green, and blue colors. In this model four diseases are chosen for detection. These diseases are chosen depending on available database .The chosen diseases are:

1. Lung disease: this disease causes the palm to get Pale White color with RGB value around [248,248,255]. I.e. High red, high green, and high blue.

2. Obstruction in the circulation of the Blood: this disease paints palm with dark green color and RGB value almost [0, 100, 0]. I.e. Low red, medium green, and Low blue.

3. Heart Disease: palm has grey color when the human is infected with this disease and the RGB value is about [128,128,128]. i.e. medium red, medium green, and medium blue.

4. Kidney Disease: this disease infects the human and produces a nearly brownish color with RGB value less than [160, 42, 42]. i.e. medium red, low green, and low blue.

11 Design of Fuzzy Inference System

There are two types of Fuzzy Inference Systems (FIS):

(a) Mamdani.

(b) Sugeno.

The color of the normal palm is light red or pinkish and RGB value is concerning [255, 80,150], i.e. high red, low green, and medium blue. Note that, these values of RGB are taken from RGB color codes chart presented in Internet web sites. These two types of inference systems vary somewhat in the way outputs are determined .Mamdani-type inference, as defined for the toolbox, expects the output membership functions to be fuzzy sets. After the aggregation process, there is a fuzzy set for each output variable that needs defuzzification. While Sugeno-type systems can be used to model any inference system in which the output membership functions are either linear or constant [11].

In this paper Mamdani-type inference system is used to diagnostic system with three inputs and single output. Also four rules are suggested each rule is noted to specific disease. Figure (7) shows the design of FIS in Matlab.

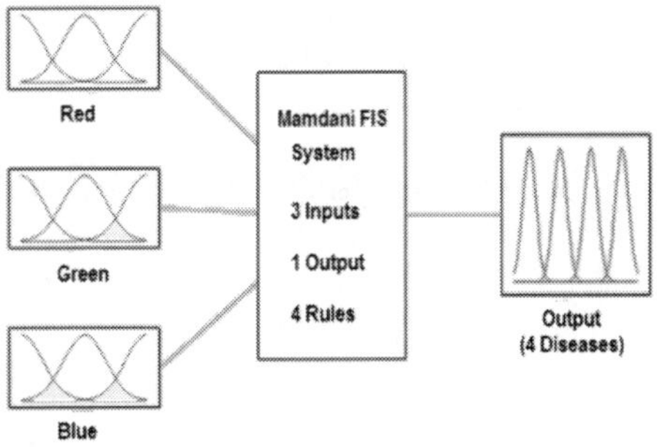

Figure 7. Matlab FIS for Diagnosis System.

Membership functions are used in the fuzzification and defuzzification steps of a FIS, to map the non-fuzzy input values and output value to fuzzy linguistic terms. An important characteristic of fuzzy logic is that a numerical value does not have to be fuzzified using only one membership function. In other words, a value can belong to multiple sets at the same time.

So color values can be considered as "High", "Medium", and "Low" at the same time with different degree of memberships. The most common types of membership functions are triangular, trapezoidal, and Gaussian shapes. These three shapes (a, b, c) are shown in Figure (8) and considered in this paper.

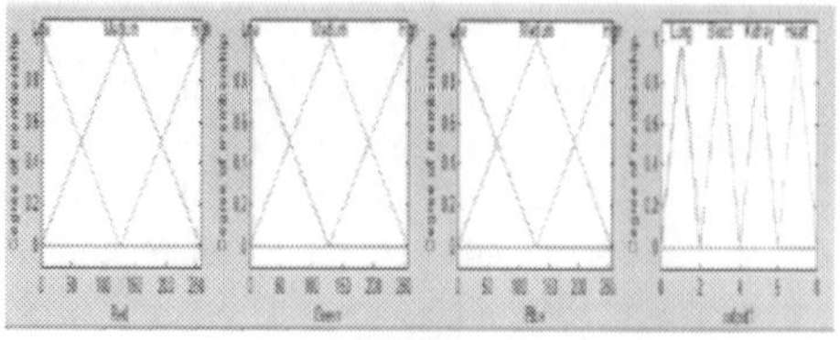

(a) Triangular Membership.

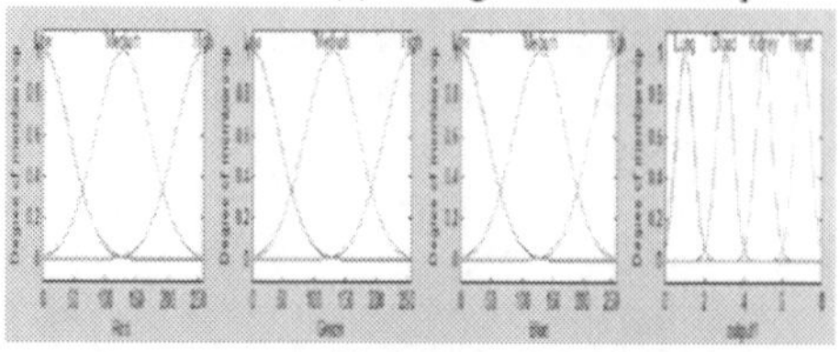

(b) Gaussian Membership.

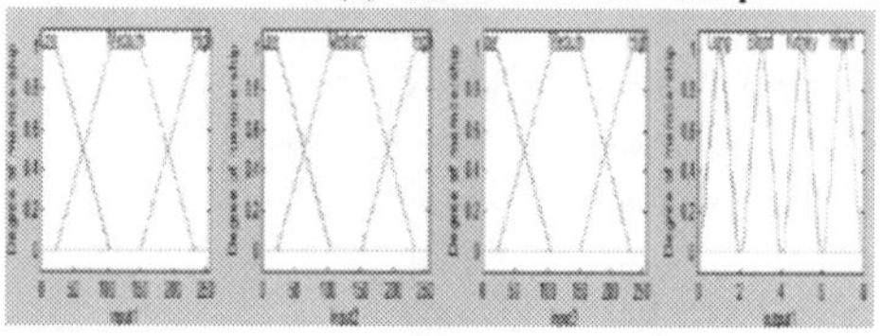

(c) Trapezoidal Membership.

Figure 8. Memberships Used in the Proposed Model.

In a FIS, a rule base is constructed to control the output variable. A fuzzy rule is a simple IF-THEN rule with a condition and a conclusion. In Table 1, fuzzy rules for FIS is presented.

Table 1. Fuzzy Rules for Diagnostic System.

Fuzzy Rules
1- IF (Red is High) and (Green is High) and (Blue is High) then (Output is Lung)
2- IF (Red is Low) and (Green is Medium) and (Blue is Low) then (Output is Blood)
3- IF (Red is Medium) and (Green is Low) and (Blue is Low) then (Output is Kidney)
4- IF (Red is Medium) and (Green is Medium) and (Blue is Medium) then (Output is Heart)

Table (2) shows the matrix representation of the fuzzy rules for the used FLS. This matrix is 3D matrix, but it is converted into 2D for simplicity.

Table 2. Fuzzy Matrix for Diagnostic System.

Green Blue \ Red	L.L	L.M	L.H	M.L	M.M	M.H	H.L	H.M	H.H
L	Normal	Normal	Normal	**Blood**	Normal	Normal	Normal	Normal	Normal
M	**Kidney**	Normal	Normal	Normal	**Heart**	Normal	Normal	Normal	Normal
H	Normal	Normal	Normal	Normal	Normal	Normal	Normal	Normal	**Lung**

The inference procedure is called as the "compositional rule of inference". The inference is determined by two factors; "implication operator" and "composition/aggregation operator". In Mamdani : Mamdani implication is **min** for each rule:

Rule1 $m1= \min\{\mu red(x),\mu green(x),\mu blue(x)\}$ (1)

Rule2 $m2= \min\{\mu red(x), \mu green(x),\mu blue(x)\}$ (2)

Rule3 $m3= \min\{\mu red(x), \mu green(x),\mu blue(x)\}$ (3)

Rule4 $m4= \min\{\mu red(x), \mu green(x),\mu blue(x)\}$ (4)

Mamdani aggregation is **max** for aggregation four outputs:

$\mu output (z) = Max \{m1, m2, m3, m4)$ (5)

Figure (9) shows the Rule viewer in FIS:

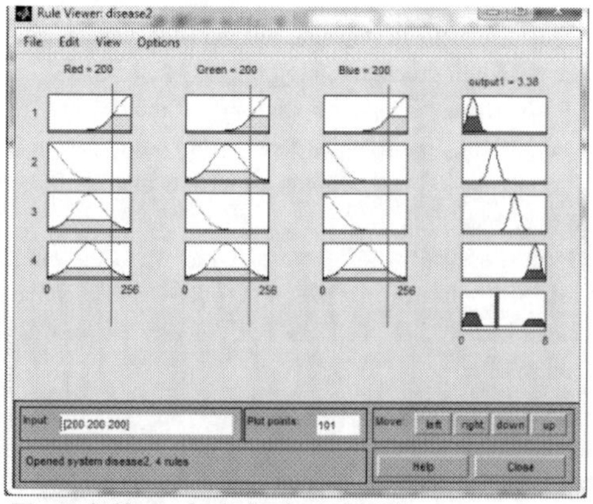

Figure 9. Shows the Rule viewer in FIS:

There are different algorithms for defuzzification. The purpose is to obtain a crisp value, represented with a dot in the figure, from this fuzzy result.

DOI: 10.1051/matecconf/20167604021

One of the most common is the center of gravity (or center of area).

$$COG(N) = \frac{\sum_{i=1}^{k} xi\,\mu(xi)}{\sum_{i=1}^{k} \mu(xi)} \quad \ldots (6)$$

Where

xi specifies element of output universal set,

μ(xi) represents the membership degree of element xi, and k specifies the number of elements in the universal set.

From FIS the results of disease diagnosed are obtained. The Gaussian Membership gives the best results. Table (3) presents the results obtaining from this membership.

Table (3). FIS Results using Gaussian Membership.

Actual values		Predicted Values from Model					Accuracy
Disease Type	No. of Live Images	As Heart	As Lung	As Blood Obstruction	As Kidney	As Normal	
Heart	140	135	0	0	0	5	96%
Lung	48	24	18	0	0	6	37.5%
Blood Obs.	56	20	0	23	0	3	50%
Kidney	92	43	8	2	31	8	33.6%
Normal	100	17	3	0	0	80	80%

12 Performance of Proposed System

In order to investigate the performance of the proposed model, the actual number of each disease is presented with these diagnosed by the proposed model. The comparisons between actual results and predicted results are presented in Figure (10), Figure (11), and Figure (12) using Triangular, Gaussian, and Trapezoidal Memberships respectively. The figures show the accuracy of different memberships.

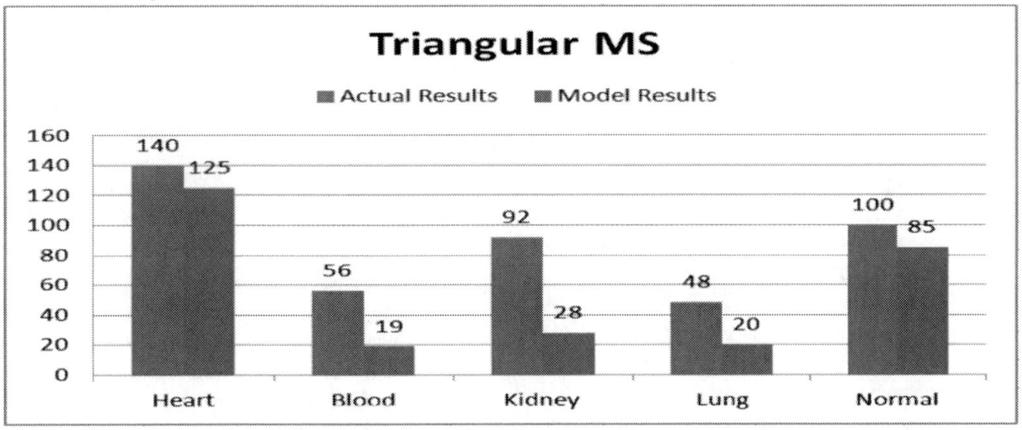

Figure 10. Results obtained using Triangular Membership

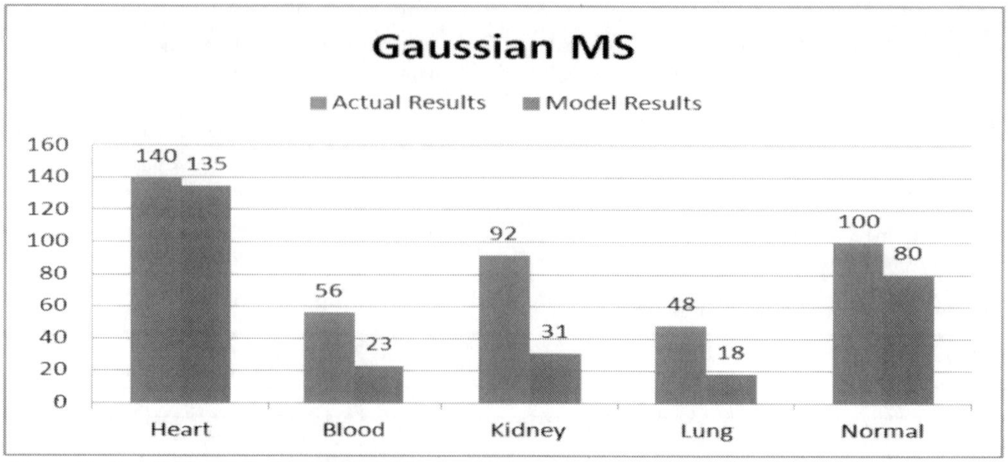

Figure 11. Results obtained using Gaussian Membership.

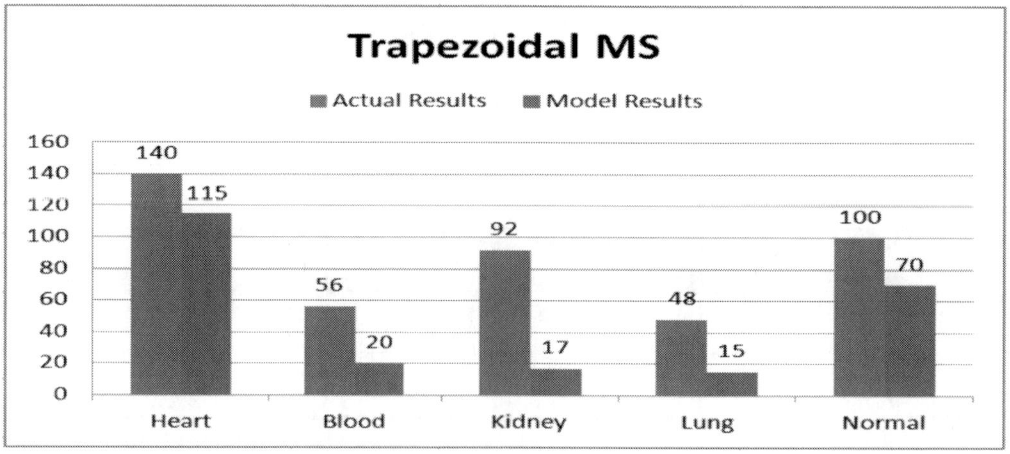

Figure 12. Results obtained using Trapezoidal Membership.

From these results, the following points are important to focus on:

1. Using Gaussian Membership in input and output of FIS gives more accurate results from Triangular and Trapezoidal Memberships.
2. Diagnosis of Heart disease in this Model have highest accuracy than the other diseases.
3. When Some Normal cases are diagnosed in this Model, it gives Heart disease. This happen because Normal cases are collected for persons they believe are Normal persons but perhaps there are such disease without they know that.
4. It is impossible to diagnosis more than one disease from single color palm image.
5. Most diseased palm images (about 80% of them) are captured for old ages patients. So most of them are infected with Heart disease and another disease. The proposed Model can specify only one disease from single palm image, so the Heart disease appears on the palm rather than other disease. i. e. Heart disease influence palm color instead on the any other disease.
6. The accuracy results for diagnosis of Lung, Kidney, and Obstruction in the Circulation of Blood diseases can be increase if the collection of their images from young patients have not Heart disease but are infected with one these diseases.
7. There are not study in this field obtaining final results, so comparison between this work and the other study is not existed.
8. The performance of proposed Model is confidence and the Model will give more accurate results if database of collection color palm images is increased with more and more images.

Conclusions and future works

The medical diagnosis model is built to assist medical practitioners for taking diagnosis decision. So, the final and important decision is related to doctor. Many conclusions are obtained from this work the chosen of excellent image acquiring device is necessary in capturing obvious palm image. The CCD scanner device is very important in capturing color palm image. So, Basra hospitals must advice them to buy this device. Also, denoising filters are important to get better extraction features from image. The filter must be chosen very careful in order to prevent the destroying the palm information.Using expert system like Fuzzy Logic System is significant in decision. These expert systems have ability to give less risk decision. In the end medical palmistry field needs more discuss and investigation.

In the future there are many interesting works that can be suggested in this field. As example, we mention the Palm image can be segmented corresponding to its mounts and then enlarged to get better observation .therefore, Implement a computer program to automatically search the palm image to indicate the symbols in the palm.we can Build large database for palm image infected with diseases and investigate the other diseases related to palm color and palm symbol. Finally The system can be developed by focusing on the palm lines which contain rich information and can be used to get more accurate diagnosing decisions.

References

1. J. Shiraishi, Q. Li, D. Appelbaum, and K. Doi , "*Computer-Aided Diagnosis and Artificial Intelligence in Clinical Imaging*", Seminars in Nuclear Medicine, Elsevier Inc, Vol. **41**, No. 6 (2011)
2. H. Pandit and D. Shah, " *The Model of nail color analysis – An application of Digital Image Processing*", International Journal of Advanced Research in Computer Science and Software Engineering, ISSN: 2277-128, Vol. **3**, Issue 5, May (2013)
3. B. Shanmugapriya and R. Rajesh, "*Survey: Applications of Bravura Information in Human Hand*", International Journal of Wisdom Based Computer, Vol. **1**(3) (2011)
4. A. Navpat, R. Mukherjee, V. Pandita and S. Gupta, "*Application of Prediction Software in Palmistry*", MPGI National Multi Conference, Proceeding Published by International Journal of Computer Applications ISSN: 0975-8887 (2012)
5. H. Pandit and D. Shah, "*A System for Palm Color Analysis Healthcare*", International Journal of Advanced Engineering Technology, E-ISSN: 0976-3945, Vol. **V**, Issue I (2014)
6. D. Desai, M. Parekh, D. Shah, V. Sawant, and A. Nagare, "*Automated Madical Palmistry System Based on Image Processing Techniques*", International Journal of Advanced Research in Computer Science and Software Engineering, Vol. **5**, Issue 1, ISSN: 2277-128X (2015)
7. F. Ahamad, K. Jhansi and S. Varali, "*Traditional Chinese Medicine and Its Significance*", Medicinal Chemistry, ISSN: 2161-0444, Vol. **5**, Issue 2 (2015)
8. X. Zong and G. Liscum – "*Chinese Medical Palmistry-Your Health in Your Hand*", Blue Poppy Press, ISBN: 0-938185-64-3 (1995)
9. R. Khanna, "*A Review of Image Restoration Techniques for Salt and Pepper Noise with Test Results*", IJARECE, ISSN: 2278 – 909X, Vol. **4**, Issue 2 (2015)
10. M. Huber, Nonlinear Gaussian Filter: Theory Algorithms and Application, Habilitation, Karlsruher Institut für Technologie, Publish by (KIT) Fakultt für Informatik, (2015)
11. N. Mishra, "*A Reviw on the Applications of Fuzzy Expert System for Disease Diagnosis*", International Journal of Advanced Research in Engineering and Applied Sciences, ISSN: 2278-6252, Vol. **3**, No. 12 (2014)

MATEC Web of Conferences **76**, 04022 (2016) DOI: 10.1051/matecconf/20167604022
CSCC 2016

Information and Communication Technology in Education - Current Trends

Eva Milkova[1], and Simona Pekarkova[2], Abdel-Badeeh M. Salem[3,a]

[1]*University of Hradec Kralove, Faculty of Science, Rokitanskeho 62, Hradec Kralove, Czech Republic*
[2]*University of Hradec Kralove, Faculty of Education, Rokitanskeho 62, Hradec Kralove, Czech Republic*
[3]*Ain Shams University, Faculty of Computer and Information sciences, Abbassia, Cairo, Egypt*

Abstract. The paper is aimed at current approaches toward using of information and communication technology in education. Firstly, nowadays usage of computers in education is introduced on the basis of an overview and survey of the researches presented on the recent conference Computers in Education organized by the Asia-Pacific Society for Computers in Education. Last research in the following areas is discussed here: computer-supported personalized and collaborative learning, seamless learning, level of attention and learning efficiency, learning analytics, application of innovative educational technologies in STEM education, and online game-based learning in school education. Despite the geographical orientation many issues may be inspirational for scholars from western countries. On the other hand, from research papers presented by researchers from Asia-Pacific region it is evident that they have been focusing on very similar topics in education as scientists in western countries do. Secondly, some observation concerning usage of information and communication technology in Egypt education as well as recent research works examined within the doctoral study program information and communication technology in Education provided by the University of Hradec Králové, Czech Republic, are presented in the paper in the light of the mentioned survey.

1 Introduction

The Department of Informatics of the Faculty of Science at the University of Hradec Králové (UHK) provides doctoral study program of ICT in Education (guaranteed by the first author of the paper) in cooperation with the Faculty of Education at the UHK and others three Czech Faculties of Education. This unique study program, recognized as the only one in the Czech Republic, is focused on preparation of experts in the major of information and communication technologies in education. Furthermore, it is also concentrated on their independent creative work in the field of science, research and their good prerequisite for further development of the area of information and communication technology (ICT) in Education.

Graduates of pre-gradual studies will expand their knowledge of detailed content and methods of main areas of informatics. They will particularly increase understanding of theoretical basis of aforementioned science field. They also acquire more in-depth knowledge of new trends in pedagogical and psychological subjects. ICT in Education is a very new and extremely fast developing area. In this field, it is necessary to explore and develop qualitatively different attitudes that have their roots in scientifically validated theories based on results of many foreign researches.

Thanks to the fact that one of our doctoral students, the second author of the paper, had chance to spent several months in China and during the stay took part at the 23nd International Conference on Computers in Education (ICCE 2015) held in Hangzhou last December, we had an opportunity to collect findings presented at the conference.

The aim of the paper is to introduce this conference search in the line with the latest Czech doctoral research works dealing with ICT usage in education as well as with observation concerning the mentioned area in Egypt education presented in works of the third author.

1.1 Conference on Computers in Education

The conference was organized by the Asia-Pacific Society for Computers in Education (APSCE). This society was established in 1989 and organizes conferences related to the aforementioned topic every year. Since the first year of establishing of APSCE the conferences have become a major event and great opportunity for researchers and scholars from all over the world to connect with each other and to develop and deploy ideas that span the field of Computers in education.

This time more than 163 papers from 24 countries related to use of information and technology for education were accepted. Most of them were presented by researchers from Asia-Pacific region, mostly from Japan, Taiwan, China and Thailand. The West part of the

[a] Corresponding author: abmsalem@yahoo.com

world was represented by 17 papers. Despite the geographical orientation many researchers from Asia-Pacific region have been focusing on very similar topics in education as scientists in western countries do.

In spite of the wide variety of papers some similar topics attracted researcher's attention. Those issues were mentioned in many papers; therefore we may introduce them briefly in section 2.

2 Current Trends within ICT in Education

2.1 Computer-supported personalized and collaborative learning

The importance of computer-supported personalized and collaborative learning was a highly discussed topic. Regarding this field some research papers were based on identifying the effects and impacts of flipped classrooms on pupils and student's achievements in different areas. Flipped classroom is described as an innovative and effective approach which engages students in a lesson and learning process actively and also changes the role of teacher. A teacher is considered to be more a guide or couch than that the one who is providing all-knowing to students and they only passively listen to.

Teachers often create videos and use websites, tutorials and new technologies to enhance problem-solving ability, discussion, cooperation and interaction among students. Students watch the video before the class and use the class time to solve complex concepts, answer question and students are encouraged to learn actively [1].

Using this new approach for teaching means that a teacher should handle new challenges of this creative and interactive way of education. Some research raised a question whether this method is equally efficient for students of different ages (younger people, middle age people and old age people). The results showed that the effectiveness of the method was influenced by will and personal preferences of participants. Nevertheless, all groups reached better results in learning.

The second research The Role of Social Presence in a Flipped Classroom to Facilitate Oral Skills of Language Learners [2] also confirmed positive effects of flipped learning. The results revealed that the combination of online learning community and flipped learning not only supported social and interpersonal communication and collaboration but also enhanced the participants' oral proficiency. This approach made the participants more competent and motivated in interactive learning activities (online or in-class interaction, collaboration and discussion).

Possibilities how to enhance collaboration and cooperation were mentioned many times. Some of other researches using computer-supported and collaborative learning (CSCL) have scrutinized impact of this method on promoting of interaction, collaboration, help each other, motivation and interests in learning. For example, Study of GS-Based "Factor" Collaborative Learning in a Primary School [3] proved positive effects of CSCL in aforementioned aspects.

2.2 Seamless learning

Many researches were driven with the idea to uncover opportunities of support of seamless learning. This is an approach in which learners can create relationships between their formal and informal learning. To support seamless learning, some seamless learning systems have been proposed, as for example aforementioned method flipped classrooms which tries also to incorporate and use this principle. Some researchers describe seamless learning system as a system based on the learners' textbooks (teaching materials) which can be prepared as e-Book. Learners can record their learning in class and the system allows them to link up what they have learned in class and what they have experienced outside of the class by providing quizzes or book information. One of such works devoted to this topic was e-Book Based on Seamless Learning System. [4]

2.3 Level of attention and learning efficiency

Other groups of research works were based on exploring the field of level of attention and learning efficiency. These works often used the comparison between traditional and digital learning materials. One of the goals of these works was to understand how different types of teaching materials affect learners' attention and how particular materials can unfold their potentials faster than others. The preliminary experiment described in the paper *A Study of Attention Difference between Traditional and Digital learning Materials Using Brainwave Measuring Devices*, showed that the attention level was higher when studying digital materials compared to traditional printed materials. [5] Electroencephalography (EEG) was used for collecting data that were analysed later and they showed significant differences in brainwaves while working with different types of materials.

Very similar results were shown in the other pilot experiment *The Effect of a Mobile Mathematical Game on the Mathematic Learning of the Student with Intellectual Disability* [6]. Intellectual deficit is often manifested by lowered ability of concentration, short-term memory and other cognitive skills. It means that many areas needed for efficient learning are impaired and acquiring of new information is very demanding for learning and also teaching. A digital game used as a tool for learning had positive impact on participant 's learning gains, he was able not only to learn a new concept in mathematics but this fact positively influenced his self-esteem and confidence for next learning. To sum up, it may change the personal attitude of someone with disabilities towards education.

Although many research and preliminary experiments have had positive results and often confirmed their positive hypothesis, it is worth mentioning researches those results were opposite and so provoking critical thinking and new questions for those who would be otherwise too optimistic or uncritical positive towards new technologies and computer-supported leaning. One of the research with different outcomes is following.

The Comparison of students' perceptions of small group discussion in online and face-to-face environments [7] was targeted on understanding of students' experience in online and face-to-face discussion. The researchers compared their perceptions towards these two environments in five aspects: learning, affection, reading and writing skills, critical thinking skills and efficacy. Although online tools have been often accepted by many as mainstream of collaborative learning during recent years, this research has showed that the students having the opportunity to choose between these types of discussion still prefer to participate in face-to face interaction.

2.4 Learning analytics

Digital data was an issue that has been discussed very often. On the one hand it is becoming very powerful and its good analysing can bring new opportunities in education. However, on the other hand, we must be aware of its dark side. Not only researchers but also teachers at all levels of schooling find the topic of learning analytics very important and potentially extremely beneficial for teachers and their students to unfold their potentials. Regarding to this issue let us mention the research and project about Lea's Box, *A Competency-oriented Approach to Facilitate Learning Analytics in School Settings* [8]. Lea's Box is a research and a development project funded by the European Commission. The project has focused on the fact that school-based teaching and learning are producing the digital data but tools for analytics of the data (which can lead to enhancing and individualizing of teaching process) are still missing. This new tool enables teachers not only to collect but also to analyse and visualise educational data of their pupils. Thanks using this technology, a teacher can tailor education for each student more specifically and make better and more suitable decisions about their pupils. The goal is to evaluate individual achievements and competencies and provide the learners with the best possible individual support and teaching. Besides the schools from Austria some schools from the Czech Republic and Turkey also participated in this project.

2.5 Application of innovative educational technologies in STEM education

Next area which was filled with wide numbers of research was application of innovative educational technologies in STEM (Science, Technology, Engineering, and Mathematics) education. STEM education is vital for nation´s competitiveness in the global economy. Therefore, STEM has been recognized as a part of education which should be changed in order to become more effective.

Both of the following research stressed the need of increasing mathematical critical-thinking. Moreover, the authors of the first research consider mathematical thinking as a skill necessary for the 21st century skills.

The first research related to STEM, *Non Numerical Aspects of School Mathematics* [9], claims that shifting the focus from numeracy (acquiring of basic mathematical ability) to consideration of mathematics as much wider cognitive ability is necessary.

Intended learning may fail to be achieved for many reasons and if the purpose of the mathematical tasks is confined or limited to 'solving', rather than 'learning from solving', it is likely that learners may neither learn nor enjoy engaging with the problem.

The authors underpin that the core of enhancing mathematical thinking is conscious questioning where the numbers do not have to be used. Students need to apprehend vocabulary, definitions and implement/shift aspects of a problem situation into understanding, solving and then connecting new knowledge into their mental concepts. Deeper questioning is the means for students can make sense of mathematics and digital tools should be effectively used to promote student questioning.

The second research, *Integration of Reciprocal Teaching-ICT Model To Improve Students' Mathematics Critical Thinking Ability* [10], is focused on integrating ICT with reciprocal teaching. Reciprocal teaching use four strategies to increase and maintain good engagement of students in learning process- These four strategies are:

1. summarizing what they read and identifying the main idea,
2. inquiring in order to ensure they understand the material,
3. clarifying parts of the text that may be confusing,
4. predicting what text they may or should read as a following step.

Students in the experimental class where reciprocal teaching- method and ICT were used reached better scores in all indicators (thinking, questioning, connecting, evaluating). The students had a lot of chance to ask questions, develop the problem that made them think more critical and were more active comparing with the control group.

Both two aforementioned researches concluded independently that for better acquiring mathematical skills and mathematical thinking a non-number concept – questioning is irreplaceable.

2.6 Online game-based learning in school education

In the last part of this article we would like to introduce the topic of constructivist online game-based learning in school education which gained attention of many participants at the conference.

The research Implementation of Mario-like Digital Game in Chemistry Education: Results on Students' Perception [11] presents the effectiveness of a digital game which was used for enhancing student knowledge in chemistry. Researchers observed influence and impact of digital game on six related areas: perceived learning, perceive ease of use, flow, playfulness, enjoyment and perceived satisfaction. The instruction is based on Bloom´s taxonomy that presents pedagogical and psychological background and could motivate students´

learning. „Mario like" is a digital game which has four levels of playing corresponding with four dimensions of Bloom taxonomy – Remember, Understand, Apply, Analyse.

The findings of the research showed successful improving in all observed areas and revealed positive impact of using digital game-based learning in education.

The next research which is worth mentioning, also using game-based learning as the previous research is *The Development of a Game-Based Formative Assessment Mathematical Algebra Tutorial App* [12]. In addition, the researchers included mobile learning and formative assessment. The principal goal of this study is to explore effects of formative assessment strategy on the learning effectiveness of a student. One of the conclusions for the game-based formative assessment mathematical algebra tutorial app is adoption and development of the mechanism of feedback and scoring. There is necessary to find balance and accurate ratio between teaching and game playing. It means to avoid more attention on game playing than on the teaching contents. The research concentrates not only to deepen the basic knowledge of mathematics, but also to promote learners´ ability of analysis and answering questions.

3 Current Trends within ICT in Egypt education

In this section let us present issues that have attracted attention of the second author and his colleagues from Egypt in recent years, see [13], [14].

3.1 Artificial intelligence in education (AI-ED)

The main goal of this multidisciplinary field of study AI–ED is to develop intelligent software which is capable to model human mind and thanks to it can be very beneficial in educational process. This development of knowledge-based software which can be used in real education (teaching, leaning and skill training) is the vital point of many research that have been carried out in one of the main seven areas which are namely: Intelligent Educational Systems (IES), Teaching Aspects, Learning Aspects, Cognitive Science, Knowledge Structure, Intelligent Tools, Shells and Interfaces.

Different intelligent learning applications have been already developed in order to improve students´ skills and to enable them faster enquiring of knowledge about complex problems. For instance, such learning applications are URI, CANCER or Heart. These tools are cased-based intelligent learning systems for diagnoses of particular diseases. The last mentioned intelligent learning application provides not only description of symptoms, but also treatments proven successful in similar cases and possible alternative causes of the pain are explained.

One of the main domain of artificial intelligence in education, to which gradually more research pay attention, is to create computer systems that can be used as collaboration tools and can enable to acquire new knowledge and skills in very effective way. The issue of motivation strengthening is also crucial topic for Artificial Intelligence. In addition, many researches in this area have been dealt with the issue of providing of assessment of learning outcomes. It is evident that artificial intelligence and its new paradigm and approaches such as case-based reasoning and intelligent data mining aiming to support individualized needs of learners and have been also recognized as an important aspect in e-learning technologies.

3.2 Intelligent Tutoring Systems (ITS)

Using Artificial Intelligence concepts and new forms of educational software can allow the computer to act as an intelligent tutor. Intelligent tutoring system (ITS) can adjust its tutorial to the student´s knowledge, experience, to minimize their weaknesses and boost their strengths.

ITS has been focusing on acquiring and building knowledge with a new approach called case-based reasoning (CBR). CBR means reasoning which has its origins in own experiences or in solving strategies of previous cases or problems. Research outcomes underpin the natural way of learning by fact that students learn best when they are presented with examples of problem-solving knowledge and are then required to apply the knowledge into real situations. This case-based reasoning is the opposite attitude to so called rule-based reasoning which represents a learning style when required knowledge has been already described by "knowledge experts" and learners´ own experience is not needed. In this type of reasoning learners are asked to use most of all their memory and recall the rules or facts that did learn previously. Whereas the case-based reasoning provides realistic problem-solving situations, presents them to the students as virtual simulations and so enhances students´ thinking.

Intelligent tutoring system also allows flexibility in teaching methods, achieving many of the same benefits as one-on-one instruction. Moreover, ITS and case-based reasoning approach enable to compose lessons with different levels of knowledge by following the school curriculum. The system can recognize learner´s knowledge level from previous results and can choose and adapt difficulty of lesson that fits to student´s actual knowledge. Additionally, ITS enhances productivity and allows to cope individually with bigger number of students than one teacher can cope.

3.3 Data mining Technology in Education

For most of Artificial Intelligence areas it is crucial to collect data, extract information from data set and transform it into an understandable structure for further use. Therefore the field of data mining technology and techniques seems to be indispensable because of its compounding of artificial intelligence, database system and statistics. There are many technics of collecting and analyzing data such as: clustering, regression models, classification, summarization, link analysis, sequence analysis, sequential pattern mining (SPM), text mining and association rules mining (ARM). This field of data mining is beneficial for e-learning educational methods. Moreover, a good adjusted e-learning system can contribute to effective solving of some acute problems in educational field. In countries when the number of learners is increasing and there is lack of educational institutions and lack of qualified teachers eLearning presents a chance for involving more students in higher education and prevent them from dropping out of the educational system early.

4 Doctoral study program ICT in Education

With regard to above-mentioned issues we can emphasize that the research topics realised within the doctoral study program ICT in Education closely correspond with them. Let us introduce some of actual research topics conducted within our doctoral study program:

There are the following main areas on which we have concentrated:

1. Mobile technology Applied in Education (e.g. [15])
2. Technology Enhanced Natural Science Teaching and Learning (e.g. [16])
3. Technology Enhanced Foreign Language Teaching and Learning (e.g. [17])
4. Programming techniques (e.g. [18])
5. Social and cultural impact of modern communications for education (e.g. [19])

To give better insight into works of our students, let us introduce abstracts of dissertation works defended in the last two academic years.

Interactive web applications as means towards increasing the efficiency of chemistry instruction [20]
The Internet and its web interface have brought new possibilities into chemistry instruction. Learning computer models (LCM) seem to be an efficient means towards increasing the clearness and stimulation of pupils′ cognitive activity but their applications within the process of instruction have not been researched to a large extent in the Czech Republic. That is why this dissertation project focuses on LCMs of acid-base titrations. In the dissertation thesis we dealt with types of questions what and under what conditions the pupil can learn being supported by LCM of acid-base titration. We supposed the LCM could make the process of acquiring the learning content easier on all knowledge levels which were operated in chemistry (symbolic – microscopic – macroscopic level) as well as they could be a relevant means for introducing learning situations where the activity and responsibility for learning were turned over the pupil.

E-learning in Foreign Language Teaching at Universities [21]
The dissertation describes research focused on the implementation of information and communication technologies (ICT) in learning and teaching English for Specific Purposes (ESP) at universities. Its theoretical part deals with an analysis of the current situation in education, concentrating on the elements of this complex system and on the influence of technologies on the educational system. Based on the conclusions of the theoretical part, a practical design for the implementation of technologies that support the active role of students of foreign languages was created with the aim of strengthening their motivation for learning by applying a cooperative form of work. The empirical research was conducted in the form of a case study that validates the proposed learning activities supported by Web tools in education and provides the information which helps us understand the processes occurring within this specific form of learning. The aim of this work is to enrich the e-learning of foreign languages with the use of currently available Web tools in tasks simulating activities students are apt to encounter after university and to contribute to the development of theoretical knowledge in the field of methodology and ICT in education.

Prevention of Software Piracy of Primary School Pupils and Secondary School Students [22]
The dissertation is focused on infringing copyright by primary school pupils and secondary school students. The dissertation brings the answer to the question whether sufficient knowledge of main legal aspects related to software, musical work and films affects behaviour and attitude of pupils and students to software, music and film piracy. The theoretical part of this work explains some basic terms related to the mentioned issue. It gives information about the current legislation concerning copyright infringement in the Czech Republic, EU, the USA and in the international law. It provides evaluation of the current state of the issue being solved in available information sources, curricular documents and in preventive activities of ministries and non-governmental organizations.

The practical part of this work includes a pilot study, definition of the research problem and specification of research questions and hypotheses. It presents the course of the pilot study and main study as well as their results and conclusions. The data are analysed in the following part of the work and the relation between knowledge of pupils and students and their attitude to the software piracy is studied. Based on the research results and the relation analysis that prove the urgency and seriousness of the research issue, preventive and corrective measures are presented. These measures are in the form of a suggestion concerning the scope of curriculum and expected outputs of school educational programmes with a view to get basic knowledge of the legal aspects connected with the software, music and film piracy. The proposed scope of curriculum was proved by experimental teaching.

Possibilities of Language Skills Development within the Framework of Communicative Competence Mastering in E-learning Language Courses [23]
The dissertation focuses on the difficult issues connected with implementing techniques for testing used by foreign language teaching methodology to practice and reinforce receptive language skills in reading and listening comprehension. Furthermore, the paper is also focused on

productive writing skills in e-learning language courses using a basic variety of technological exercises. The purpose of the research was to determine the effect on the practice of the aforementioned language skills when applying different pairs of testing techniques with various types of technological exercises within the process of the implementation. The analysis of pre-tests, progress tests, post-tests and feedback questionnaires proved that some pairs are more suitable for practicing and strengthening of language skills than other pairs. A description of the most suitable pairs provided at the end of the dissertation may be a significant contribution for authors of e-learning language courses as a convenient guide in the preparation of learning materials.

The influence of educational system applications for measurement using a computer on the popularity of physics at the elementary school [24]
The dissertation focuses on the impact of educational system applications for measurement using computers in a school science lab on popularity of physics at the elementary school. The theoretical part describes systems for measurement using a computer and an own system called SMPS as configurable alternatives to commercial products. It introduces the didactic and technological aspects of scientific experiments with the help of systems for measurement using a computer.

5 Conclusion

In the paper we presented an overview of today's research connecting to topic ICT in Education. To sum up, increasing number of professionals have recently become to be aware that the use of technology in education has had a significant impact on early childhood learning. However, the early childhood education including the use of ICT has not been largely explored research area so far. There is a growing expectation that preschool teachers and researchers will find the integration of theories and practices and will be able to recognize effective tools and implement them into the early childhood education. In the paper *The role of kindergarten teacher in using technology in mathematic teaching classroom* [25] was clearly revealed that the teacher represents a key role for integrating of technology.
Teacher provides appropriate tool at the right time for children to explore and extend their play to a meaningful learning. Technology did not interfere children's learning but accelerate and narrow the achievement gap between low-income children and other affluent peers.

Acknowledgements

This research has been supported by Specific research project of the University of Hradec Kralove, both Faculty of Science and Faculty of Education in 2016.

References

1. G-H. Hwang, B. Chen, Ch-W. Sung, T-H. Kuo, 'To Explore the Effect of Age on Cognitive Load When Using Social Websites to Conduct Flipped Classrooms on Musical Instrument Performance Teaching - Taking Amateur Erhu Learners as an Example', Proceedings of the 23rd International Conference on Computers in Education (ICCE 2015), Hangzhou, China, pp.1-8 (2015)
2. M-Y. S. Chen Hsieh, W-Ch. V. Wu, S-M. G. Chwo 'The Role of Social Presence in a Flipped Classroom to Facilitate Oral Skills of Language Learners', Proceedings of the 23rd International Conference on Computers in Education (ICCE 2015), Hangzhou, China, pp. 9-13 (2015)
3. Ch-P. Lin, W. Chen, Ch-Ch. Lin 'Study of GS-Based "Factor" Collaborative Learning in a Primary School', Proceedings of the 23rd International Conference on Computers in Education (ICCE 2015), Hangzhou, China, pp. 14-20 (2015)
4. M. Kiyotaa, K. Mourib, H. Ogatac 'A Proposal of e-Book Based Seamless Learning System', Proceedings of the 23rd International Conference on Computers in Education (ICCE 2015), Hangzhou, China, pp. 611-616 (2015)
5. S-Ch. Cheng, Ch-T. Liang, Y-P. Jheng 'A Study of Attention Difference between Traditional and Digital Learning Materials Using Brainwave Measuring Devices', Proceedings of the 23rd International Conference on Computers in Education (ICCE 2015), Hangzhou, China, pp. 85-94 (2015)
6. Ch-P. Wu, Y-Ch. Liu 'The Effect of a Mobile Mathematical Game on the Mathematic Learning of the Student with Intellectual Disability', Proceedings of the 23rd International Conference on Computers in Education (ICCE 2015), Hangzhou, China, pp. 105-109 (2015)
7. Y-Ch. Tseng, S. W-Y. Lee, A. Wang 'The Comparison of students' perceptions of small group discussion in online and face-to-face environments', Proceedings of the 23rd International Conference on Computers in Education (ICCE 2015), Hangzhou, China, pp. 307-310 (2015)
8. M.D. Kickmeier-Rust. M. Bedek, D. Albert 'A Competency-oriented Approach to Facilitate Learning Analytics in School Settings', Proceedings of the 23rd International Conference on Computers in Education (ICCE 2015), Hangzhou, China, pp. 372- 379 (2015)
9. Khan, K., Mason, J. 'Non Numerical Aspects of School Mathematics', Proceedings of the 23rd International Conference on Computers in Education (ICCE 2015), Hangzhou, China, pp. 477-482 (2015)
10. E.S. Alim, K. Umam, S. Rohim 'Integration of Reciprocal Teaching-ICT Model to Improve Students' Mathematics Critical Thinking Ability', Proceedings of the 23rd International Conference on Computers in Education (ICCE 2015), Hangzhou, China, pp. 483-487 (2015)
11. S. Kitchwalit, N. Srisawasdi 'The research Implementation of Mario-like Digital Game in Chemistry Education: Results on Students' Perception', Proceedings of the 23rd International

Conference on Computers in Education (ICCE 2015), Hangzhou, China, pp. 696-703 (2015)
12. G-H. Hwang, Ch-Y. Lee, T-H. Kuo 'The Development of a Game-Based Formative Assessment Mathematical Algebra Tutorial App', Proceedings of the 23rd International Conference on Computers in Education (ICCE 2015), Hangzhou, China, pp. 729-738 (2015)
13. A-B. M. Salem 'Intelligent Methodologies and Technologies for e-Learning, IEEE 10th International conference on Emerging eLearning Technologies and Applications', pp. 331-337 (2012)
14. A-B. M. Salem, H.S. Katoua 'Case-Based Reasoning Approach for Intelligent Tutoring Systems', Proceedings of Recent Techniques in Educational Science, WSEAS, Educational Technologies Series pp. 21-26 (2013)
15. M. Manenova, R. Spilka 'Tablet in preschool education for children with special needs', Proceedings of EDULEARN15 Conference, Barcelona, Spain: IATED, pp. 2205-2212 (2015)
16. E. Widenska 'Efficiency of practicing with materials using ICT and paper ones in mathematics', Journal on Efficiency and Responsibility in Education and Science, vol. 7, no. 2, pp. 37-43 (2014)
17. D. El-Hmoudova 'Assessment of Individual Learning Style Preferences with Respect to the Key Language Competences', Procedia - Social and Behavioural Sciences, vol. 171, pp. 40 – 48 (2015)
18. E. Milkova, O. Korinek 'Future ICT Teachers - Programming Aptitude', Proceedings of the 11th International Conference Efficiency and Responsibility in Education (ERIE 2014), Prague, pp. 456-462 (2014)
19. P. Kalibova, E. Milkova 'Internet Addictive Behaviour of Adolescents', International journal of education and information technologies, vol. 10, 2016, pp. 139–143 (2016)
20. M-Y. Shen, H-Y. Wei 'The Role of Kindergarten Teacher in Using Technology in Mathematic Teaching Classroom', Proceedings of the 23rd International Conference on Computers in Education (ICCE 2015), Hangzhou, China, pp. 787-789 (2015)
21. V. Machkova Interactive web applications as means towards increasing the efficiency of chemistry instruction, Hradec Kralove: Faculty of Education, University of Hradec Kralove, 135 p., thesis (2014)
22. S. Pavlikova E-learning in Foreign Language Teaching at Universities, Hradec Kralove: Faculty of Education, University of Hradec Kralove, 127 p., thesis (2014)
23. J. Skop Prevention of Software Piracy of Primary School Pupils and Secondary School Students, Hradec Kralove: Faculty of Education, University of Hradec Kralove, 111 p., thesis (2014)
24. P. Hercik, Possibilities of Language Skills Development within the Framework of Communicative Competence Mastering in E-learning Language Courses, Hradec Kralove: Faculty of Education, University of Hradec Kralove, 90 p., thesis (2015)
25. R. Nemec, The influence of educational system applications for measurement using a computer on the popularity of physics at the elementary school, Hradec Kralove: Faculty of Education, University of Hradec Kralove, 123 p., thesis (2015)

A Mobile-based Platform for Big Load Profiles Data Analytics in Non-Advanced Metering Infrastructures

Sherin Moussa [1,a]

[1] *Faculty of Computer and Information Sciences, Information Systems Department, Ain Shams University 11566 Cairo, Egypt*

Abstract. With the rapidly increase of electricity demand around the world due to industrialization and urbanization, this turns the availability of precise knowledge about the consumption patterns of consumers to a valuable asset for electricity providers, given the current competitive electricity market. This would allow them to provide satisfactory services in time of load peaks and to control fraud and abuse cases. Despite of this crucial necessity, this is currently very hard to achieve in many developing countries since smart meters or advanced metering infrastructures (AMIs) are not yet settled there to monitor and report energy usages. Whereas the communication and information technologies have widely emerged in such nations, allowing the enormous spread of smart devices among population. In this paper, we present mobile-based BLPDA, a novel platform for big data analytics of consumers' load profiles (LPs) in the absence of AMIs' establishment. The proposed platform utilizes mobile computing in order to collect the consumptions of consumers, build their LPs, and analyze the aggregated usages data. Thus, allowing electricity providers to have better vision for an enhanced decision making process. The experimental results emphasize the effectiveness of our platform as an adequate alternative for AMIs in developing countries with minimal cost.

1 Introduction

A keen attention has been directed in the last decades towards the utilization and optimization of electricity sources, especially with the tremendous increase of demand on the different levels of granularity. Thus, automatic meter reading (AMR) came about in the middle of 80s as an automated mechanism to gather basic electric meter-reading data, instead of depending on the individual collectors of the electricity providers to pass by one-by-one household to get its reading that represents the monthly energy consumption [1]. AMRs tended to be dedicated for collection only on either a monthly or daily basis, without any facilities of control messages or broadcast commands. In 2005, advanced metering infrastructure (AMI) technology has arisen in many countries, evolving from the foundations of AMR [2]. AMIs allow automated, real-time record and send of consumers' consumption data to a central computer in order to analyze and control user consumption.

The analysis of the high velocity, volume and variance of collected AMI data has allowed accurate aggregations for seasonal / long term usage trends, and provided a pattern of the total demands with many associated innovative analytical outcomes, including load profiling, peaks identification, abnormal usages, demand forecasting, electrical thefts, and intelligent pricing tariffs [3-4]. Thus, it allows operators to optimize the energy supply. Due to the lack of satisfactory nation-wide infrastructure and budget to establish their AMIs, many developing countries are still counting on individual collectors to record consumers' consumptions. Besides missing the vital bundle of advantages formerly discussed, this approach is always subject to the physical presence of the consumer at his premises at the time of the collector's visit and to human errors.

In this study, we present our novel mobile-based Big Load Profiles Data Analyzer (mBLPDA) platform, which is considered to be a cost-effective alternative for AMIs in developing countries. mBLPDA platform uses the widely-spread smart mobile devices to allow each consumer to securely submit his own reading within a predefined duration allowance, associated with some automatically-captured data for the reading to verify the submitted data. The submitted readings are verified then aggregated per consumer to build his load profile (LP) into a central cloud-based server, where further analysis is performed using R language packages. The rest of the paper is organized as follows; section 2 overviews the different studies related to the LPs.

Section 3 discusses our proposed platform, whereas section 4 presents the associated experiments and results to evaluate our proposed platform. Finally, section 5 concludes our study and highlights our future work.

2 Related Work

Many researches have been directed towards the analysis of smart meter readers' data for different purposes. Table

[a] Corresponding author: sherinmoussa@cis.asu.edu.eg

1 represents a comprehensive summary for the main studies related to electrical load profiles, clarifying the study area with the applied analytical approaches. Electricity production and consumption were investigated to forecast electricity load consumption in [5] using a genetic algorithm, in [6] using a data-based methodology, and in [7] using support vector machine for regression (SVR) and multilayer perceptron (MLP) for district or single household level. Whereas in [8], a semi-parametric approach based on generalized additive models theory was suggested. In [9], an incremental time series clustering technique using ARIMA time series forecasting model, along with a novel affinity score for determining cluster similarity of time series datasets was proposed. An Incremental Summarization and Pattern Characterization (ISPC) framework was introduced in [10] to incrementally characterize patterns in a data stream of electric meter reader and correlate these across time through incremental learning. Authors in [11-12] proposed a threat model and a predictive usage analytical toolkit for smart meter management applying time series analysis predictive modeling and regression analysis respectively, using data analytics on data collected by AMI in order to identify abnormal consumption trends and possible fraud to reduce electricity theft.

Another methodology for distribution feeder identification was presented in [13] to provide correctness improvement of distribution primary feeder connectivity by identifying the groups of customer meters connected to the same primary distribution feeder. K-means and self-organizing maps (SOMs) were applied in [14] to analyze load profiling in order to provide more customized tariff offers for customers pricing and supply availability. A profile identification, short-term load forecasting, and customer segmentation methodology was proposed in [15] to compute the daily profiles from estimated models. Another cloud-based Dynamic Demand Response (D^2R) platform was introduced in [3] to perform curtailment strategy selection, intelligent demand-side management and forecasting, visualize LP patterns, and to relieve peak load. In [16], Fourier transforms and Gaussian time series techniques were investigated to forecast domestic electricity system demand by analyzing LPs. Models were proposed in [17-19] to construct LPs for household electricity in order to determine energy use, forecast usage, predict charge in future energy use, design the power network, and to improve efficiency of energy build structure.

Table 1. Summary of main LPs analytical studies.

Rf No	Objective	Study Area	Techniques
5	Forecast energy consumption	Turkey	Genetic algorithm
8		France	Semi-parametric approach
9		LA, USA	ARIMA time series forecasting model
10		Australia	IPCL and SOMs
7		Ireland	SVR and MLP
6		Finland	SOMs, k-means and hierarchical clustering
14	Customized tariff offers	UK	K-means and SOMs
16	Demand forecasting and peak loads	Ireland	Fourier transforms and Gaussian time series
3		LA, USA	Cloud-based Dynamic Demand Response (D^2R) platform
15		Belgium	K-means, DB scan, and one-step-ahead prediction
18		Romania	K-means and agglomerative clustering
17		Sweden	Matlab Modelling
19		BC, Canada	Conditional demand analysis
32	Analyze energy consumption profiles	Slovenia	Hierarchical clustering, FCM, and PNNs
34		Monte Carlo-type Simulation	Beta Probability Distribution function
35		Southern Ontario, Canada	Auto-regressive time series modelling on Hadoop
36		Public data set	OpenTSDB, Hbase and Hadoop
33		UK	Clustering
13	Improve distribution of primary feeder	Thailand	K-means, hierarchal clustering, FCM, SOMs, and SVM
12	Identify abnormal consumption trends	NY, USA	Time series analysis, predictive modeling, and regression analysis
11		USA	Average Detector, ARMA-GLR, Nonparametric Statistics, and LOF
23	Classify customers' consumption patterns	Norway	PNNs and FCM
25		Ireland	K-means, K-medoid, SOM, SPSS, and Matlab
28		Spain	Frequency-based indices and SOMs
27			SOMs, Matlab, and frequency transform
30		Romania	Modified Follow-The-Leader algorithm, and SOMs
29			Frequency–domain technique
24		Slovenia	PNNs, Wavelet multi-resolution analysis, pattern recognition, and FCM
31			Hierarchal clustering
26		Ireland	Feature extraction and SOMs
20	Reduce energy consumption	Hong Kong	Non-linear algorithm
22		Salo, Finland	K-means and SOMs
21		Norway	Demand response analysis

A non-linear algorithm was used in [20] to characterize the growth pattern of household electricity consumption and calculate the power at a certain time to identify the reasons of consumption increase, in addition to the approaches developed in [21-22] to reduce the total energy consumption in periods of expected peak load.

On the other hand in [23-24], Probabilistic Neural Networks (PNNs) and Fuzzy C Means (FCM) clustering algorithm were used to determine and allocate the typical LPs to consumers. Unsupervised learning based on SOMs have been used in [25-27] to classify, filter and identify customers' consumption patterns in order to learn both their distribution and topology, and segment the demand patterns for electrical customers. Additionally frequency-based indices and hourly LP curve methods were proposed in [28]. In [29-30], authors have modified the Follow-The-Leader algorithm and proposed a frequency–domain approach with SOMs for consumption pattern-based classification of electricity consumers in order to know accurate knowledge of the customers' consumption patterns. Hierarchal clustering was also considered in [31] to determine customers' daily LP in order to cluster the similar units of measured LPs. A hierarchical cluster tree was constructed using the distances between profiles to divide or group each pair of near LPs until coherent clusters were formulated.

In [32], hierarchical clustering and FCM with PNNs were used in order to study the distribution of deviations between the estimated purchased electricity at the power market and the actual consumption. In [33-34], a probabilistic model using beta probability distribution function (beta pdf) and a formulating method for energy LP for domestic buildings were proposed respectively to analyze residential consumer loads. Clustering has been applied based on the proposed scenarios of occupancy patterns. Whereas Hadoop was used in [35] to introduce an auto-regressive time series modelling technique, and in [36] to build a smart meter data analytics approach using OpenTSDB, Hbase in order to store time series data and to compute electricity consumption profiles from residential smart meter data, combined with temperature data and the occupants' daily habits.

Although the previous researches investigated various analytical studies for the LPs and consumption patterns of electricity consumers, however all studies counted on the existence of an AMI to provide the data required for such analysis. Thus, this completely waives all territories having non-AMIs from getting benefits out of their LPs' analytical studies. One main reason for the uniqueness of the proposed research is that it provides an alternative platform for AMIs and individual collectors' visits that require consumers' physical existence to get their meter's readings, allowing developing regions to analyze and control their LPs for better decision making, optimized service in case of peaks, and energy theft detection.

3 Mobile-based BLPDA

In this section, we present our proposed mobile-based platform for big LPs data analytics (mBLPDA). This platform allows non-AMIs environments to track and analyze their energy consumptions for better decision making when AMIs are infeasible. A cloud-based server is utilized to manage and store the big LPs data, where all connections are made through JSON web services between the different sub-systems. A web-based interface is considered for the administrative services required for the system at the energy provider's side, providing the main analytical results with the appropriate graphical representations. As shown in figure 1, the system architecture of our proposed mBLPDA platform is composed of two main components explained as follows. This architecture can be considered for any energy domain having metering devices, i.e. electricity, gas, water… etc.

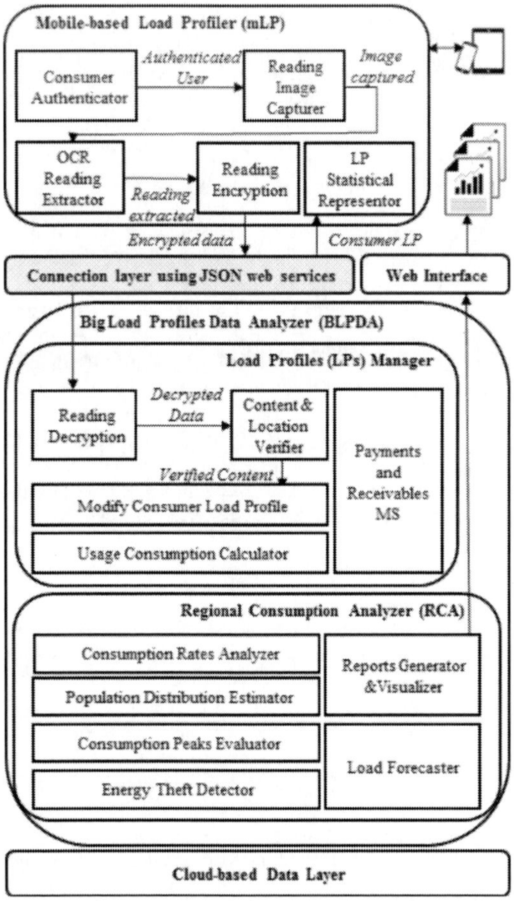

Figure 1. Mobile-based BLPDA Platform System Architecture.

3.1. Mobile-based Load Profiler (mLP)

A mobile-based application has been designed to allow building a secured LP for consumers having non-smart meter devices. This mobile load profiler app (mLP) allows the authenticated users to use their smart mobile devices to capture images with a pre-defined frame size according to the size of the meter device's reading window. An OCR module is integrated to mLP in order to extract the reading digits and the meter device ID out of the captured image. Once the reading digits and ID are extracted, mLP wraps them together with the date, timestamp, and exact longitude and latitude of capturing the reading image, in addition to the digital signature of the authenticated user. Advanced Encryption Standard (AES) algorithm is then applied to encrypt the wrapped content, which is directly sent to BLPDA server [37]. Thus, readings are secured and associated with the user's authenticated identity during transmission. mLP allows consumers as well to track their consumptions, invoices, and payments on a monthly basis, and to get main analytical insights about their usage patterns.

3.2 Big Load Profiles Data Analyzer (BLPDA)

This represents the core engine of our proposed platform, where big data analytic approaches are investigated to deal with the huge volume of LPs data. It is responsible for the LPs management and the associated analysis per region. BLPDA consists of the following sub-modules.

3.2.1 Load Profiles (LPs) Manager

LPs Manager receives the encrypted readings that are sent simultaneously from the authenticated users through their mLP. The content is first decrypted and verified to confirm that the extracted meter device ID and location match successfully with the registered profile of the authenticated user. The verified data is then accumulated to the consumer's LP according to the date of reading in order to compute his energy consumptions. Hence, LPs are constructed per consumer and distributed based on the geographical location of the meter devices. A payments and receivables management system can be integrated to generate invoices and handle the payment processes.

3.2.2 Regional Consumption Analyzer (RCA)

Considering the LPs accumulated for consumers, RCA uses R language packages to perform two main categories of analysis; per region and per household within a region analytics [38].

(i) Per region: RCA clusters the huge volume of consumption rates within a region using k-means approach, and forecasts the expected load demand for the next 12 months using time series analysis. Accordingly, usage peaks can be predicted in order to avoid service malfunctioning under load pressures.

(ii) Per household within a region: RCA estimates an overall approximation for the population distribution within a region using correlation, and detects possible energy theft cases using anomaly detection approach through the new R anomalous package [39-40]. This takes into consideration the LPs' patterns and the local average of consumption per individual.

Analytical reports and graphs are aggregated on a monthly and quarterly basis to visualize the outcomes at the energy provider side as well as the consumer side through mLP. Figure 2 clarifies the system flowchart of mBLPDA platform.

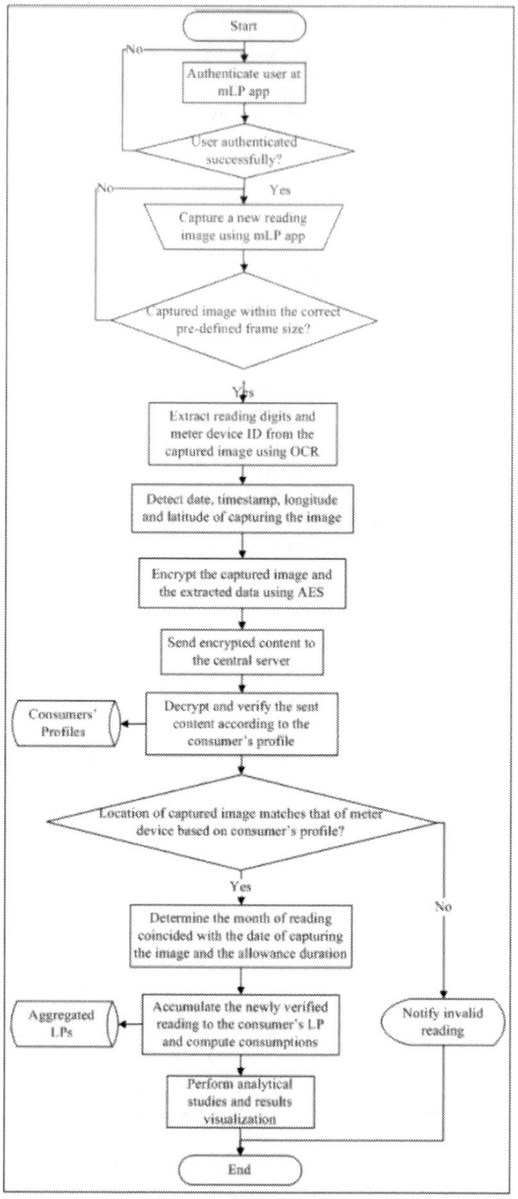

Figure 2. Mobile-based BLPDA Platform System Flowchart.

4 Experiments and Results

In order to evaluate our proposed platform, we operated mBLPDA for 6 months in 4 different regions. 1,648,576 electrical meter readings were collected through mLP Android app. Although mBLPDA architecture is generic for any energy domain having meter devices, we focus in our experiments on the electricity domain in order to pre-define the frame size of capturing to match the local electric meter devices. We have considered one of the most popular electrical meter device models as shown in figure 3, with the edge corners of the adjusted frame size of capturing. Moreover, a customized OCR module is integrated to mLP to extract the reading digits and meter device ID out of the captured image, having the specific font type and size of the local electric meter devices.

Figure 3. Sample electrical meter device with the pre-defined frame size of capturing.

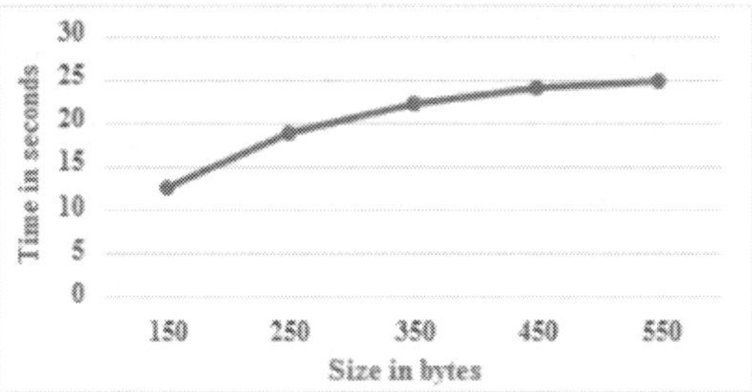

Figure 4. Time in seconds consumed by mLP to process and transmit readings versus the size of content to handle.

Experimental results indicate that mBLPDA platform can provide most of the essential analytical insights as in AMIs. Figure 4 shows the average time in seconds versus the size of content to handle in bytes in order to process a captured reading image by extracting and encrypting the associated content (i.e., reading digits, meter device ID, in addition to the date, timestamp, longitude, and latitude of image capturing), and then to transmit all of these processed data into the central cloud-based server. mLP app takes an average of 12.57 seconds to process and transmit 150 bytes on average, and increases till it reaches around 25.11 seconds for an average size of 550 bytes. Thus, mLP app consumes an overall average time equals to 20.63 seconds for the processing and transmission of one reading. Whereas Figure 5 presents the consumers' LPs collected through mLP app during the pilot duration for 4 the regions, having average consumptions ranged from 4,617,388 KW to 8,886,716.042 KW per month/ region.

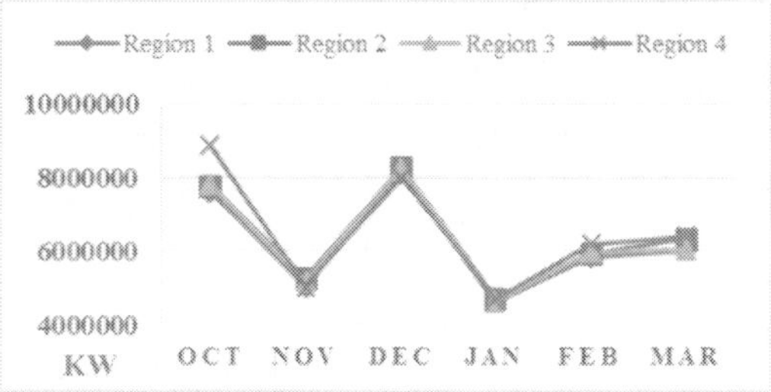

Figure 5. Accumulated LPs using mLP app.

We have used Rand Index (RI) as a measure to evaluate the quality of consumption rates clustering. RI is considered since it equally weighs false positives and false negatives, where both are false, as in the equation below [41]:

$$RI = TP + TN / TP + FP + FN + TN \quad (1)$$

Where *TP* represents the number of true positives, *TN* is the number of true negatives, *FP* is the number of false positives, and *FN* is the number of false negatives. Consumptions rates are clustered into 3 main clusters (i.e., minimal, normal, and high consumption, thus k=3). As shown in figure 6, mBLPDA platform has achieved RI values ranged from 0.88 till 0.93, which indicates coherent and high-quality clusters with an overall RI average equals to 0.9. Regarding the evaluation of peaks prediction in mBLPDA platform, we applied F-measure criteria, where it combines both recall and precision parameters to assess the prediction results according to the following equations respectively [42]:

$$F\text{-}measure = 2 x [(Precision\ x\ Recall) / (Precision + Recall)] \quad (2)$$

$$Precision = TP / (TP + FP) \quad (3)$$

$$Recall = TP / (TP + FN) \quad (4)$$

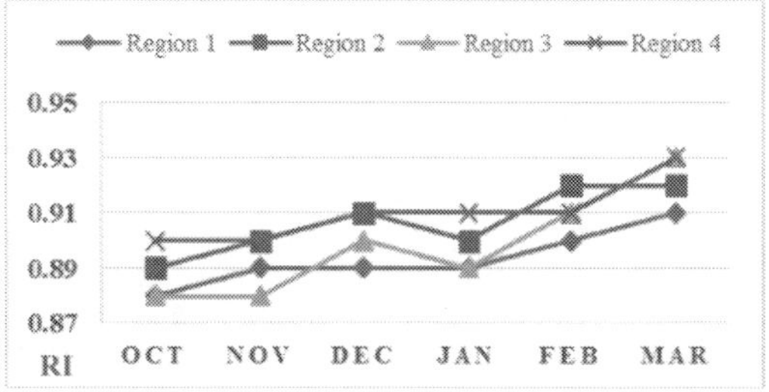

Figure 6. RI results for the quality of consumption rates clustering.

As shown in figure 7, mBLPDA platform successfully achieves F-measure results for consumptions' peaks prediction with a minimum value of 0.71 and a maximum value of 0.95. This indicates a high prediction capability of an overall F-measure value equals to 0.83. We have performed additional experiments as well to investigate anomaly detection at mBLPDA on the household's level, as a preparation for energy theft detection when accompanied with payments control. A sample anomaly detected on a household's level is presented in figure 8, where the average consumption rate for this consumer during 5 months is 120 KW. The reading recorded for December is 243 KW, which is a way beyond the normal average consumption rate.

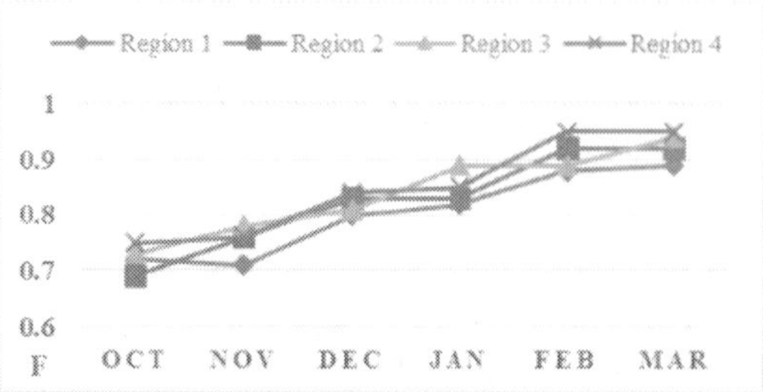

Figure 7. F-measure results for consumption peaks prediction.

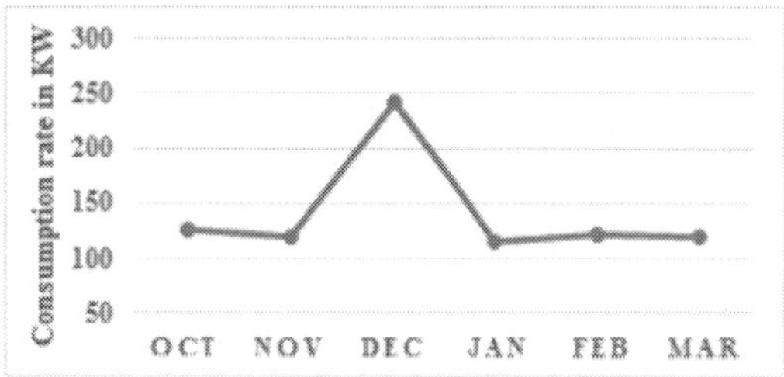

Figure 8. A sample anomaly detected at a household's level.

5 Conclusion and Future Work

Managing and analyzing the energy consumptions of energy providers among the world has become a dramatically increasing demand, where AMIs have supported during the last years to provide useful analytical insights. In this paper, we tackle the problem of building energy LPs in the non-AMIs environments. Many developing countries have not yet settled their AMIs, depending on individual collectors to record readings.

We propose our mobile-based big LPs data analyzer (mBLPDA) platform, where consumers can use mLP smart app to securely submit their own meter reading within an average of 20.63 seconds for the processing and transmission of one reading. Readings are all aggregated on cloud-based server that applies R language packages to analyze consumption rates, forecast load demands and peaks, and to detect energy theft, with an approximated population distribution estimation based on the built LPs. A popular design for local electric meter devices is used. Experiments show that our proposed mBLPDA platform successfully clusters LPs with an average RI equals to 0.9, whereas it predicts peak loads with an average of F-measure equals to 0.83.

As our future work, we investigate considering most of the designs of the local electric meter devices, including other energy meter devices for gas and water, and adding more analytical studies that increase the visibility of energy providers to support their decision making processes for a better service.

References

1. H. Sui, et al. An AMI system for the deregulated electricity markets, IEEE Transactions on Industry Applications **45.6**, 2104-2108 (2009)
2. M. Popa, Data collecting from smart meters in an Advanced Metering Infrastructure, *15th IEEE International Conference on Intelligent Engineering Systems (INES)*, (2011)
3. Y. Simmhan, et al. Cloud-based software platform for big data analytics in smart grids, Computing in Science & Engineering, **15.4**, 38-47 (2013)
4. D. Alahakoon, X. Yu, Advanced analytics for harnessing the power of smart meter big data, *IEEE International Workshop on Intelligent Energy Systems (IWIES)*, (2013)
5. M. Çunkaş, U. Taşkiran, Turkey's electricity consumption forecasting using genetic programming, Energy Sources, Part B: Economics, Planning, and Policy **6.4**, 406-416 (2011)
6. T. Räsänen, et al. Data-based method for creating electricity use load profiles using large amount of customer-specific hourly measured electricity use data, Applied Energy **87.11**, 3538-3545 (2010)
7. S. Humeau, et al. Electricity load forecasting for residential customers: Exploiting aggregation and correlation between households, *IEEE Sustainable Internet & ICT for Sustainability (SustainIT)*, (2013)
8. Y. Goude, R. Nedellec, N. Kong, Local short and middle term electricity load forecasting with semi-parametric additive models, IEEE Transactions on Smart Grid, **5.1**, 440-446 (2014)
9. Y. Simmhan, M. U. Noor, Scalable prediction of energy consumption using incremental time series clustering, *IEEE International Conference on Big Data*, (2013)
10. D. De Silva, et al. A data mining framework for electricity consumption analysis from meter data, IEEE Transactions on Industrial Informatics **7.3**, 399-407 (2011)
11. D. Mashima, A. A. Cárdenas, Evaluating electricity theft detectors in smart grid networks, *Research in Attacks, Intrusions, and Defenses*, Springer Berlin Heidelberg. 210-229 (2012)
12. H. Li, et al. Usage analysis for smart meter management, *8th IEEE International Conference & Expo on Emerging Technologies for a Smarter World (CEWIT)*, (2011)
13. K. Y. Khumchoo, W. Kongprawechnon, Cluster analysis for primary feeder identification using metering data, *6th IEEE International Conference of Information and Communication Technology for Embedded Systems (IC-ICTES)*, (2015)
14. I. Dent, U. Aickelin, T. Rodden, Application of a clustering framework to UK domestic electricity data, arXiv preprint arXiv, 1307.1079 (2013)

15. M. Espinoza, et al. Short-term load forecasting, profile identification, and customer segmentation: a methodology based on periodic time series, IEEE Transactions on Power Systems, **20.3**, 1622-1630 (2005)
16. F. McLoughlin, A. Duffy, M. Conlon, Evaluation of time series techniques to characterise domestic electricity demand, Energy **50**, 120-130 (2013)
17. J. Widén, et al. Constructing load profiles for household electricity and hot water from time-use data—Modelling approach and validation, Energy and Buildings **41.7**, 753-768 (2009)
18. E. C. Bobric, G. Cartina, G. Grigoras, Clustering techniques in load profile analysis for distribution stations, Advances in Electrical and Computer Engineering **9.1**, 63-66 (2009)
19. K. H. Tiedemann, Using conditional demand analysis to estimate residential energy use and energy savings, *Proceedings of the CDEEE* (2007)
20. T. M. Lai, et al. Electricity consumption in Hong Kong: trend analysis and greenhouse gases emission, HKIE Transactions, **21.2**, 81-88 (2014)
21. H. Sæle, O. S. Grande, Demand response from household customers: experiences from a pilot study in Norway, IEEE Transactions on Smart Grid **2.1**, 102-109 (2011)
22. T. Räsänen, J. Ruuskanen, M. Kolehmainen., Reducing energy consumption by using self-organizing maps to create more personalized electricity use information, Applied Energy **85.9**, 830-840 (2008)
23. D. Gerbec, S. Gašperič, F. Gubina, Allocation of the load profiles to consumers using probabilistic neural networks, IEEE Transactions on Power Systems, **20.2**, 548-555 (2005)
24. D. Gerbec, et al. Determining the load profiles of consumers based on fuzzy logic and probability neural networks, *IEEE Proceedings-Generation, Transmission & Distribution* **151.3**, 395-400 (2004)
25. F. McLoughlin, A. Duffy, M. Conlon, A clustering approach to domestic electricity load profile characterisation using smart metering data, Applied energy, **141**, 190-199 (2015)
26. C. Beckel, L. Sadamori, S. Santini, Towards automatic classification of private households using electricity consumption data, *Proceedings of the Fourth ACM Workshop on Embedded Sensing Systems for Energy-Efficiency in Buildings,* (2012)
27. S. V. Verdú, et al. Classification, filtering, and identification of electrical customer load patterns through the use of self-organizing maps, IEEE Transactions on Power Systems **21.4**, 1672-1682 (2006)
28. S. V. Verdű, et al. Characterization and identification of electrical customers through the use of self-organizing maps and daily load parameters, *Power Systems Conference and Exposition, IEEE PES*, (2004)
29. E. Carpaneto, et al. Electricity customer classification using frequency–domain load pattern data, Int. J. of Electrical Power & Energy Systems **28.1**, 13-20 (2006)
30. G. Chicco, et al. Load pattern-based classification of electricity customers, IEEE Transactions on Power Systems **19.2**, 1232-1239 (2004)
31. D. Gerbec, S. Gašperič, F. Gubina, An approach to customers daily load profile determination, IEEE Power Engineering Society Summer Meeting **Vol. 1**, (2002)
32. D. Gerbec, S. Gašperič, F. Gubina, Determination and allocation of typical load profiles to the eligible consumers, *IEEE Power Tech Conference Proceedings*, Bologna. **Vol. 1**, (2003)
33. R. Yao, K. Steemers, A method of formulating energy load profile for domestic buildings in the UK, Energy and Buildings **37.6**, 663-671 (2005)
34. S. W. Heunis, R. Herman, A probabilistic model for residential consumer loads, IEEE Transactions on Power Systems **17.3**, 621-625 (2002)
35. O. Ardakanian, et al. Computing Electricity Consumption Profiles from Household Smart Meter Data, *EDBT/ICDT Workshops,* (2014)
36. S. Prasad, S. B. Avinash, Smart meter data analytics using OpenTSDB and Hadoop, *IEEE Innovative Smart Grid Technologies-Asia (ISGT Asia),* (2013)
37. J. Daemen, and V. Rijmen, *The design of Rijndael: AES-the advanced encryption standard*, Springer Science & Business Media, (2013)
38. R Documentation, https://stat.ethz.ch/R-manual/R-devel/library/stats/html/00Index.html
39. R package for detecting unusual time series, http://robjhyndman.com/hyndsight/anomalous/
40. R. J. Hyndman, et al. Large-scale unusual time series detection, *Proceedings of International Conference on Data Mining series*, (2015)
41. W. M. Rand, Objective criteria for the evaluation of clustering methods, Journal of the American Statistical Association **66 (336)**, 846–850 (1971)
42. D. M. Powers, Evaluation: from precision, recall and F-measure to ROC, informedness, markedness and correlation, (2011)

MATEC Web of Conferences **76**, 04024 (2016) DOI: 10.1051/matecconf/20167604024
CSCC 2016

Design and Implementation of Distress Prevention System using a Beacon

Imsu Lee[1], Kyeonhoon Kwak[1], Jeonghyun Lee[1], Sangwoong Kim[1], Daehan Son[1] , Eunju Park[1] and Hankyu Lim[1,a]

[1]*Department of Multimedia Engineering, Andong National University, Republic of Korea*

Abstract. It was proven that human accidents due to mountain climbing occupy large proportion of recently occurred man-made disasters. This paper designed and implemented an application that tells users about a variety of accidents that frequently occur in mountain and shows dynamic information about mountain climbing. It designed 'distress prevention system using beacon'. When using beacon, it can dynamically express information without using GPS. It has advantage of supporting BLE and has little Smartphone battery consumption. The application was developed based on Android as a prototype. We expect that the application developed in this paper can contribute to the protection of precious lives by helping quick rescue in case of emergency such as distress. Manager of mountain can control data regarding the mountain climbing accident where the related functions are provided through view and user authority setup in DBMS.

1 Introduction

As perception about the importance of health gets stronger, the number of people interested in mountain climbing is increasing. Accordingly, mountain climbing accidents or distress in mountain is becoming more frequent. '2013 Disaster Yearbook' by the Ministry of Public Safety and Security regarding the situation of human disaster occurrence indicates very high frequency of human damage from mountain climbing, along with car accidents, falling and bicycle accidents [1]. However, national point number system that marks location information with signs is the best response to mountain climbing accidents as of now which has location limits as it has a form of sign [2]. In this situation, prompt response is almost impossible when accidents or critical situation happens. Hence, this paper attempts to provide dynamic and quick information regarding mountain climbing by using beacon to decrease accidents occurrence and help quick rescue in case of critical situation. Moreover, we believe that mountain climbing information can be made to data to be accumulated when using this application and that they can be used as other contents based on Big Data. Implementation in this paper a test application developed based on Android as a prototype.

2 Related Application

'Rambler' by Bientus and 'Sanddara Baramddara' by Baramgaebi are the representative domestic applications that are related to mountain climbing [3][4]. Figure 1 shows the implementation look of 'Rambler' and 'Sanddara Baramddara'.

'Rambler' is a service that marks users' record on mountain climbing activity on the map by using GPS[5]. Users can obtain information about mountain trail through map and can also see information about mountain trail that other users recorded alongside media. The recorded information can be used as diverse statistics data and they are linked to web service.

Figure 1. The Famous Application of Mt. Climbing

'Sanddara Baramddara' is an application that provides information about nationwide mountains, similar to most of the mountain-related applications. Without special function, it helps users search for desired mountains easily and supports communication such as comment.

[a] Corresponding author: hklim@anu.ac.kr

DOI: 10.1051/matecconf/20167604024

In this paper, basic information about domestic mountains is provided and records on mountain climbing activity are implemented. As a major function, mountain climbing information is shown to users in real time through beacon.

3 Major Function and Restriction Element

Major function of the system implemented in this paper contains the following. First is information notification service through beacon. Second is record on mountain climbing activity. Third is record on distress.

Figure 2 shows the principles of service function of beacon [6].

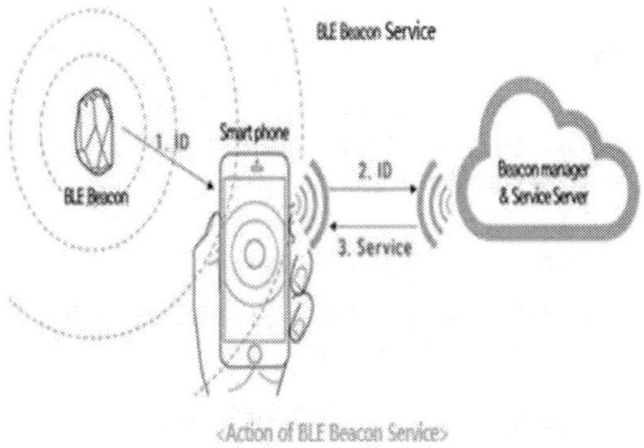

Figure 2. Beacon Service

Beacon is a location-based communication technology that attempts Bluetooth communication in one direction to user application SDK as shown in Figure 2 [7]. Beacon is a simple device that delivers only id values to users. Id value is identified in SDK and communication with server is made by using this value as a factor.

The role of beacon is to prepare a chance for communication with server when user enters into a relevant range. Here, the relevant range is the Bluetooth communication distance, which is up to 70m. In this paper, beacon signal captured by Bluetooth function while mountain climbing is analyzed to extract id values and the corresponding data are retrieved from DB to provide adequate application table and push message.

The second major function is record on the mountain climbing activity. The application implemented in this paper shows information about mountain, date and time of mountain climbing and passage.

Finally, the most important function, that is, the function in case of distress is as follows. Beacon is installed in locations that is not mountain trail or is a zone susceptible to distress and warning is given when user enters this point. Here, the previously stored GPS coordinate of beacon is expressed on map to indicate the user's current location and direction for the route back to mountain trail is provided along with a compass. As this function is map information that is provided with the stored data, no GPS sensor is necessary. In case of injury or when call is required, user can easily contact management office with the provided calling connection function. If communication is not possible, call can be made through server by using call button. Moreover, if there is no movement at the spot for a certain period of time or if one crosses the distress point more than twice, it is regarded as emergency situation and user information and location information are transferred to the server. It is expected that management office can easily recognize the information and promptly respond to the situation. To use this kind of function, users should always turn on Bluetooth while mountain climbing. The current BLE beacon has a feature of little battery consumption of Smart mobile devices compared to previous Bluetooth protocols [8]. Table 1 below presents the limiting factors in the process of system design in this paper.

Table 1. Restriction Element

Restriction Element		Reflection Contents
Theme	Social	Development for wide use
	Economy	Minimizing development cost with Android open source
External	Ethics	Information based on Ethics
	Beauty	Considering UI, UX based on beauty
SW	Security	Minimizing and securing private information
	Productivity	iOS 7.0, Android 4.3, Bluetooth
	Standard	Observing mobile app. standard

4 Design

4.1 Data Flow Diagram (DFD)

Figure 3 and Figure 4 below shows the schematization of system data flow.

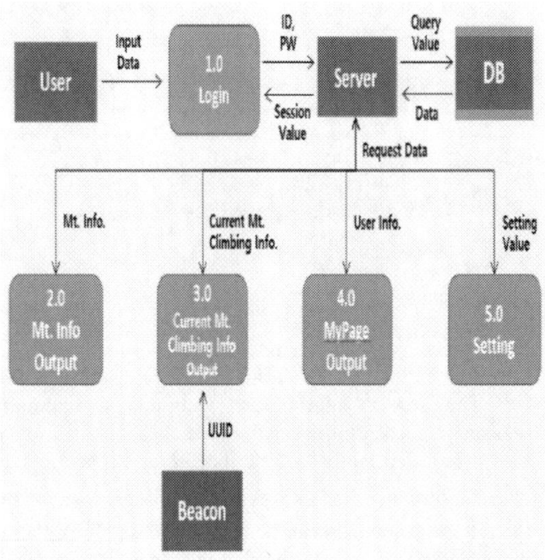

Figure 3. DFD scheme

DOI: 10.1051/matecconf/20167604024

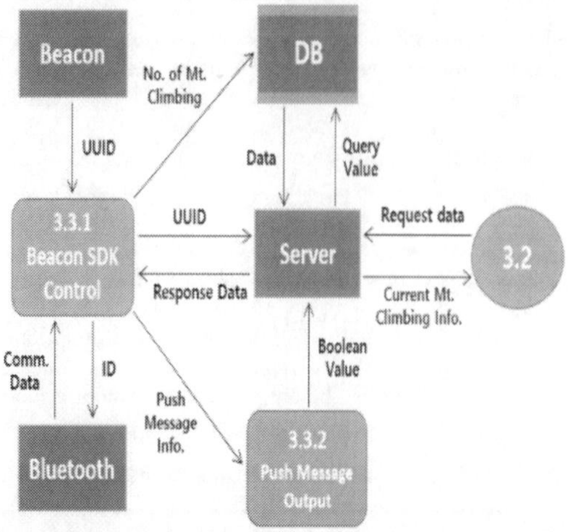

Figure 4. Beacon process DFD

4.2 Flow Chart and Scenario

Figure 5 below shows the overall flow chart of this system.

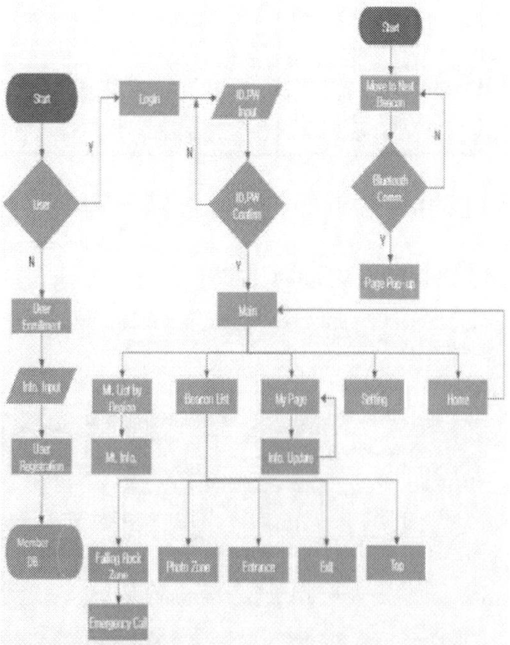

Figure 5. Flowchart

First, users apply for membership with simple personal information that can be helpful in case of distress and log on. The log-in information continuously maintains session in local domain. Afterward, beacon function is turned on at entrance and entrance beacon is recognized with an 'entrance finding' button. From here, beacons in the relevant mountain can be recognized and information is provided. It is designed such that Bluetooth is automatically turned on and turned off once mountain climbing finishes.

Next, there are six types of beacon that is recognized in case of mountain climbing, which include 'peak', 'photo zone', 'hazard zone', 'distress point', 'exit' and 'entrance'. 'Entrance' provides the relevant entrance information and begins counting the mountain climbing time. 'Peak' provides relevant peak information and notifies peak

arrival time. 'Photo zone' provides information about the surrounding landscape with image and recommends spots for taking pictures. 'Hazard zone' tells risk of relevant location such as frozen road, falling rock zone and steep slope to prevent accidents in advance. As was mentioned earlier, 'distress point' provides map information along with compass and has a calling function. Finally, when the user arrives at exit, 'exit' beacon is perceived to store the record on the mountain climbing activity so far and lists them to display. A push message is also serviced which connects to a relevant table once a beacon is perceived. Even when user climbs mountain while shutting the Smartphone screen off, he/she can dynamically receive mountain climbing information from the push message.

4.3 Entity Relationship Diagram (ERD)

The application in this paper consists of a total of nine tables whose relationship is depicted in Figure 6.

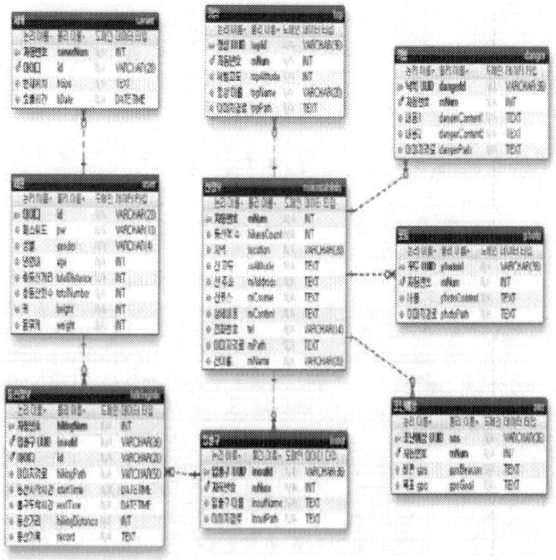

Figure 6. ERD

5 Implementation

'Distress prevention system using beacon' application was implemented by using java-based Android programming. Figure 7, Figure 8 and Figure 9 below show the actual screen implemented in Smartphone.

Figure 7. Mt. List and Mt. Information

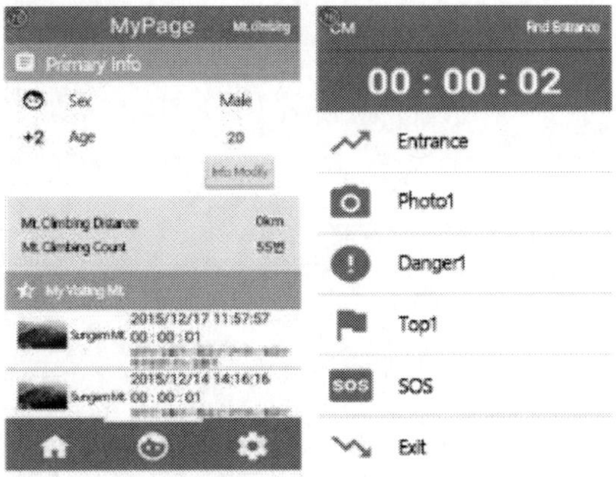

Figure 8. User Info. and Beacon Info. List

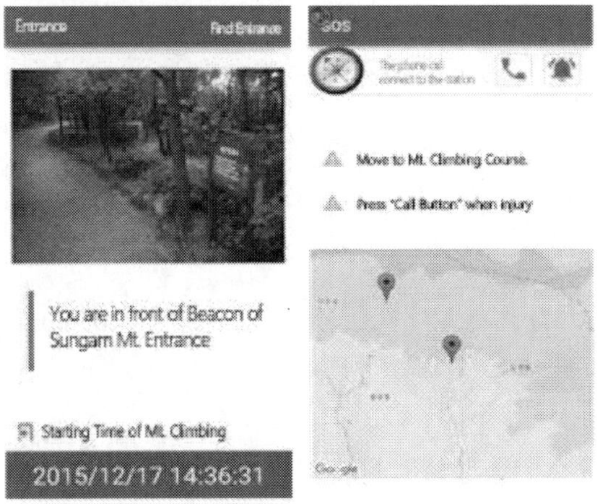

Figure 9. Activated Page with Beacon

Figure 10 shows the captured screen of implementation source of beacon scan function of the application. The function captures beacon signal by using Bluetooth library of Android and returns requested data.

```
private void sendRequestRecord(final String _minor) {
    String tag_string_req = "req_listview";
    StringRequest strReq = new StringRequest(Request.Method.POST, AppConfig.URL_RECORD,

        @Override
        public void onResponse(String response) {
            try {
                JSONObject jObj = new JSONObject(response);
                boolean error = jObj.getBoolean("error");
                if(!error) {
                    setRecord(response);
                }else{
                    String errorMsg = jObj.getString("error_msg");
                    Toast.makeText(getApplicationContext(),
                            errorMsg, Toast.LENGTH_LONG).show();
                }
            }catch (JSONException e){
                e.printStackTrace();
            }
        }
    }, new Response.ErrorListener(){
        @Override
        public void onErrorResponse(VolleyError error) {
            Toast.makeText(getApplicationContext(),
                    error.getMessage(), Toast.LENGTH_LONG).show();
        }
    }){
        protected Map<String, String> getParams(){
            Map<String, String> params = new HashMap<>();
            params.put("minor", _minor);
            return params;
        }
    };
    AppController.getInstance().addToRequestQueue(strReq, tag_string_req);
}
```

Figure 10. Beacon Scanning Source Code

This system provides data on mountain climbing accident through view and user authority setup in DBMS. Figure 11 shows the implementation of 'user view' and 'mountain climbing information view' of DBMS. View table is created to provide only the information that can be given to administrator.

```
mysql> Create view user_view(id, gender, age, totalDistance, totalNumber, height, weight)
    -> As select id, gender, age, totalDistance, totalNumber, height, weight
    -> From user;
Query OK, 0 rows affected (0.02 sec)

mysql> Create view hikingInfo_view(id, startTime, endTime, hikingDistance, record)
    -> As select id, startTime, endTime, hikingDistance, record
    -> From hikingInfo;
Query OK, 0 rows affected (0.04 sec)

mysql> select * from user_view;
+---------+--------+-----+---------------+-------------+--------+--------+
| id      | gender | age | totalDistance | totalNumber | height | weight |
+---------+--------+-----+---------------+-------------+--------+--------+
| abcd    | Male   |  20 |             0 |          80 |      0 |      0 |
| disa    | Male   |  10 |             0 |           0 |      0 |      0 |
| disms   | Male   |  20 |             0 |           0 |      0 |      0 |
| dismsl  | Male   |  20 |             0 |           0 |      0 |      0 |
| dismslee| Male   |  20 |             0 |          55 |      0 |      0 |
| kjfdre  | Male   |  10 |             0 |           0 |      0 |      0 |
| leesms  | Male   |  20 |             0 |           0 |      0 |      0 |
| qqq     | Male   |  20 |             0 |           0 |      0 |      0 |
| qqqq    | Male   |  20 |             0 |           0 |      0 |      0 |
| rusgns  | Male   |  20 |             0 |           0 |      0 |      0 |
+---------+--------+-----+---------------+-------------+--------+--------+
10 rows in set (0.00 sec)
```

Figure 11. 'User View' and 'Mt. Climbing View'

Figure 12 implements the authority given to administrator so that administrator can directly use the information coming to web server table in a limited manner.

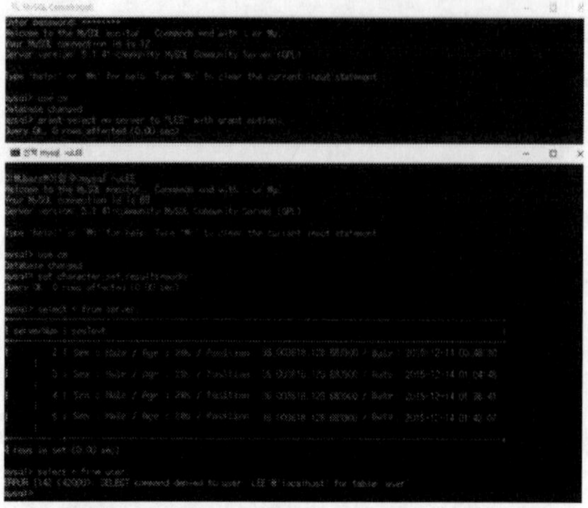

Figure 12. Managing Authority with 'LEE'

6 Conclusion

This paper designed 'distress prevention system using beacon' and implemented it in a form of application. When using beacon, it can dynamically express information without using GPS. Moreover, it has advantage of supporting BLE (Bluetooth Low Energy) and has little Smartphone battery consumption. Moreover, manager of mountain can control data regarding the mountain climbing accident where the related functions are provided through view and user authority setup in DBMS.

Using the system implemented in this paper, developing contents based on Big Data is also possible by accumulating information about when and how a certain age group went to mountain climbing. Moreover, it is expected to grow to be ICT convergence contents that can replace the national point number system.

Acknowledgments: This work was supported by a grant from 2016 Seoul Accord Project (R0613-16-1148) of MISP (Ministry of Science, ICT and Future Planning) and IITP (Institute for Information and Communication Technology Promotion).

References

1. Ministry of Public Safety and Security, "2013 Disaster Yearbook-Human Disaster", Ministry of Public Safety and Security (2013)
2. Ministry of the Interior Blog, http://mogahablog.net/11811027
3. Bientus' Rambler, http://www.rambler.com/web/main
4. Baramggabi's Sanddaramulddara, https://play.google.com/store/apps/details?id=windmill.windmill&hl=ko
5. K. Kwak, M. Yoon, Y. Lim, H. Lim, "A Design and Implementation of Vertical SNS for Student Backpackers", Proceedings of the International Conference on Communications and Computers, Oct. 2015, pp. 11 - 13
6. Beacon Principle, http://blog.lgcns.com/565
7. S. B. Han, J. H. Song, "Product Information Push Technique using Beacon MacAddress", Journal of The Society of Convergence Knowledge, Vol. 4, No. 1 (2016)
8. H. Namgung, "A System of Measurement Signal Analysis and Comparison using Bluetooth Low Energy Beacon", Graduate School of Hannam University (2015)

MATEC Web of Conferences **76**, 04025 (2016) DOI: 10.1051/matecconf/20167604025
CSCC 2016

CFD Problems Solving Parallel Approaches on Supercomputers

Tatiana Kudryashova[a], Sergey Polyakov and Viktoriia Podryga

Keldysh Institute of Applied Mathematics RAS, Miusskaya sq. 4, Moscow 125047, Russia

Abstract. The work is devoted to developing and testing parallel algorithms, suit of computer programs for numerical solution of CFD-problems on modern supercomputers. The paper summarizes our experience in solving various practical problems of gas dynamics. These problems include research of gas flow around bodies of complex shape by viscous gas flows with radiation processes near the surface of the bodies, calculations of jet streams in the open space and flows in micro channels of technical systems. We have developed approaches combining unstructured grids, domain decomposition technique, parallel implementation via MPI technology, OpenMP, CUDA. Calculations are performed on the heterogeneous computer systems with Graphical Processing Units, classical microprocessors (Central Processing Units) and use advanced parallel approaches.

1 Introduction

At present time there is a rapid increase in productivity of computer and supercomputer hardware. For example, some mobile or desktop systems utilizing the GPU have performance of the order of 1 teraflop and higher. Peak performance of the most powerful supercomputer system reaches about 50 PFLOPS (Guangzhou, China; 1 PFLOP means 10^{15} floating point operations per second, 1 TERAFLOPS = 0,001 PFLOPS, 1000 PFLOPS = 1 EXAFLOP) [1]. Supercomputer technologies provide a progress both in the defense and civilian sectors of science and technology. Ultra-high-performance systems allow us to simulate natural and technological processes with fine detailing, simultaneous consideration of different nature factors and fast analysis of numerous possible variants. Therefore, we can get information about studied process with a high degree of accuracy, and as close as possible to real-life situations. In the field of fundamental science, the supercomputer technologies give us possibility to explore previously inaccessible for detailed modeling the phenomenon, such as problems in astrophysics, direct modeling of turbulence, genome deciphering and others.

Recently, a new methodology of interaction of supercomputer modeling techniques and experiments are formed. According to it, a detailed comparison of the calculated data and experimental data is carried out. As a result of this comparison, reliable mathematical models and computer programs are developed and in the further, they replace experiment by calculations. The further investigations are performed using computational experiment. This is a problem of storing and analyzing the huge amount of data. In this case the computational complexity of the problem increases several times (non-linearly). The growth depends on the number of taken into account factors. These problems, for example, include an analysis of the situation in the near-Earth space (space debris), analysis of the transport situation in cities and etc.

Heterogeneous computing systems with performance about 5-10 PFLOPS widespread recently. In order to reduce the cost and power consumption, the main processing core of such systems together with conventional Central Processing Units (CPUs) constitute special calculators - Vector Processing Unit (VPU) or Graphical Processing Unit (GPU). However, combined use of CPU, GPU or VPU is complicated by a number of problems. For example, the VPU and GPU have its own memory and it differs from the CPU memory address space. Therefore, the applications must explicitly copy the data in memory VPU or GPU and back. This communication is slow and inefficient. The introduction of heterogeneous systems with coherent memory has not yet led to their mass extension and use. Thus, at present the developments of special parallel approaches to the implementation of the calculations on heterogeneous systems with different topologies and architectures are relevant [2, 3].

In this paper the Computational Fluid Dynamics (CFD) tasks on supercomputers with hybrid architecture of computing nodes, including CPU, VPU or GPU solving parallel technology is presented. Technology suggests that the discrete mathematical model of the CFD-process uses unstructured mesh and can be strongly spatially inhomogeneous. In this case, optimization techniques for balance of the computational load per a single node or a calculator inside node are implemented. To solve this problem, dynamic load balancing

[a] Corresponding author: kudryashova@imamod.ru

algorithms and block methods of exchange among the different devices of random access memory are proposed.

2 Problem definition

For investigating different CFD-problems we used system of Quasi Gas Dynamics (QGD) equations [4] and its approximations on hybrid meshes, which suppose adaptive, locally thickening meshes including both rectangular and triangular cells. The QGD system of equations is a generalization of Navier-Stokes model including additional dissipative terms with a small parameter τ acting as an artificial regularizer.

The QGD system has a form of the conservation laws and is presented in a common form as (1-6):

$$\frac{\partial \rho}{\partial t} + div\mathbf{j}_m = 0, \qquad (1)$$

$$\frac{\partial(\rho\mathbf{u})}{\partial t} + div(\mathbf{j}_m \otimes \mathbf{u}) + \nabla p = div\mathbf{\Pi} + \mathbf{F}, \qquad (2)$$

$$\frac{\partial}{\partial t}\left[\rho\left(\frac{\mathbf{u}^2}{2}+\varepsilon\right)\right] + div\left[\mathbf{j}_m\left(\frac{\mathbf{u}^2}{2}+\varepsilon\right)\right] = div(\mathbf{\Pi}\otimes\mathbf{u}) - div\mathbf{q} + Q \qquad (3)$$

Mass flux density vector is expressed as:

$$\mathbf{j}_m = \rho\mathbf{u} - \tau\left(div(\rho\mathbf{u}\otimes\mathbf{u}) + \nabla p\right), \qquad (4)$$

shear stress tensor has the following form

$$\begin{aligned}\mathbf{\Pi} &= -\tau div(\rho\mathbf{u}\otimes\mathbf{u})\otimes\mathbf{u} - \tau(\nabla p\otimes\mathbf{u}) + \\ &+\tau\left[div(\rho\mathbf{u}\otimes\mathbf{u}\otimes\mathbf{u}) + (\nabla\otimes p\mathbf{u}) + (\nabla p\mathbf{u})^T\right] + \\ &+\mathbf{I}\tau div(p\mathbf{u}),\end{aligned} \qquad (5)$$

heat flux vector:

$$\mathbf{q} = -\chi\nabla T - \tau p\nabla\left[\frac{p}{\rho}+\varepsilon\right] - \tau p\mathbf{u}\left[(\mathbf{u}\cdot\nabla)\varepsilon + p(\mathbf{u}\cdot\nabla)\left(\frac{1}{\rho}\right)\right] \qquad (6)$$

Here

$E = \rho|\mathbf{u}|^2/2 + p\varepsilon,\ \varepsilon = c_V T \quad p = Z\rho(R/M)T,\ \tau = \mu/p,$

μ is the viscosity coefficient, M is the molar mass, R is the universal gas constant, ⊗ – a sign of inner product and **I** – unity matrix. **F** – momentum vector of external forces, Q – power density of external energy sources, ρ – density, **u** – vector of velocity, Z – compressibility factor, c_V – coefficient of heat capacity at constant volume, χ – coefficient of thermal conductivity, T – temperature.

System (1)–(6) is completed by the equations of state for gas, suitable boundary conditions and the expressions for the coefficients of viscosity, heat conductivity and τ coefficient.

For special problems QGD system is supplemented by additional terms. In this paper we consider two applied tasks: radiation transfer and gas mixture flows.

2.1 Radiative Gas Dynamics

Many space programs are carried out today. They include launches of interplanetary stations (ExoMars 2016) and International Space Station flights (MKS, Soyuz Flight VS14) [5]. Therefore, scientific explorations of this area are quite relevant.

Returning to Earth after a flight into space is a fundamental problem, that demands to take into account gas-dynamic flow processes and the effects associated with radiation. Investigations of flows around a re-entry vehicle entering the atmosphere are traditional for high temperature gas dynamics because superheating proved a serious problem.

Development of space vehicles thermal insulation is important aspect of designing spacecraft. It requires accurate prediction of environmental gas parameters. An accurate description of the aero thermal environment is required to minimize the weight and price of the Thermal Protection System. The inability of test facilities to reproduce the high enthalpy flow coupled with the prohibitive expense of flight tests leads to the use of an analytical method, namely CFD, to describe the flow.

Radiative Gas Dynamics (RGD) approach is implemented for computing. The model includes QGD equations system and radiation transfer equations. The radiation transfer is realized with the diffusion approximation model [6-9]. The diffusion approximation model was coupled with the gas dynamic model by including the radiation energy $Q = div\vec{W}$ in the energy equation (3', 7, 8):

$$\frac{\partial}{\partial t}\left[\rho\left(\frac{\mathbf{u}^2}{2}+\varepsilon\right)\right] + div\left[\mathbf{j}_m\left(\frac{\mathbf{u}^2}{2}+\varepsilon\right)\right] = \\ = div(\mathbf{\Pi}\otimes\mathbf{u}) - div\mathbf{q} - div\mathbf{W}, \qquad (3')$$

where

$$\mathbf{W} = \int_0^\infty d\nu \int_{4\pi} I_\nu \mathbf{\Omega} d\mathbf{\Omega}, \qquad (7)$$

$$\mathbf{\Omega}\nabla I_\nu = \chi_\nu\left(I_{\nu p} - I_\nu\right), \qquad (8)$$

where ν is photon frequency, **Ω** – the direction of photon propagation, I_ν – radiation intensity, corresponding to a specific frequency, $I_{\nu p}$ – the intensity of the equilibrium radiation, χ_ν – absorption coefficient.

The diffusion equation (8) can correspond either individual spectral lines or a number of frequency intervals [6, 7]. We use the second approach and set 600 frequency groups for air. Tabulated data from [8] have been used for our early computations [9, 10]. Database supports approximately 10^5 meanings of the absorption coefficients. The four species accounted in these calculations are O_2, N_2, NO, N_2^+. Initial conditions of the free stream for calculations are presented in Table 1.

For realization of our mathematical approach the special parallel software was used [11-14].

Table 1. The initial conditions of the free stream.

Background gas temperature $T_0(K)$	266
Temperature of head shield $T_1(K)$	2000÷3300
Pressure $p_0(Pa)$	4.3*10
Density $\rho_0(kg/m^3)$	5.63*10^{-4}
Characteristic size of problem $L(m)$	5.035*10^{-1}
Mach number M_∞	12; 24

Gas flow is investigated inside free form closed volume. The boundaries are made of triangles or rectangles in 2D and 3D space. The unstructured locally-condensing meshes are applied. The number of nodes in the used meshes varies up to 10^6 in 2D case and more 10^6 in 3D case [9, 10]. Computational domains for 2D and 3D cases are shown in Figure 1, 2.

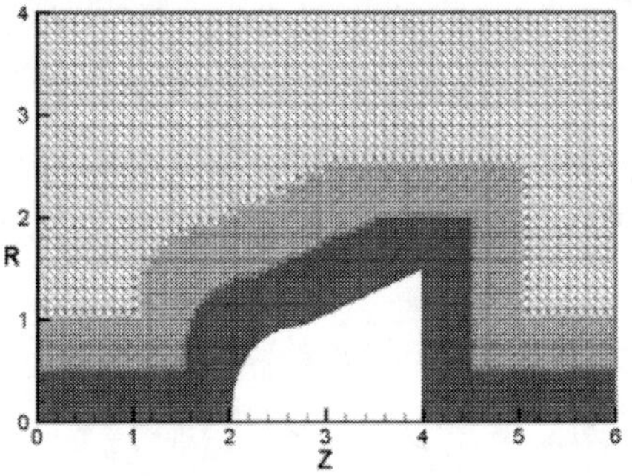

Figure 1. Computational domain with grid for 2D variant.

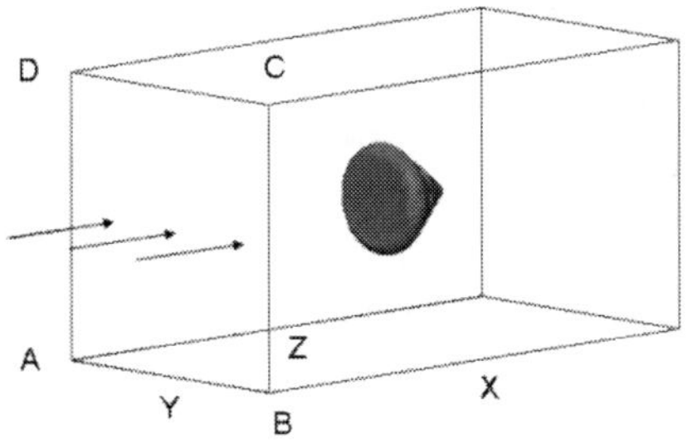

Figure 2. Computational domain.

For QGD equations a time explicit conservative numerical scheme was developed. Explicit schemes are very convenient for parallel computing. The main technique of parallelization is domain decomposition. Inter-communications among cluster nodes are performed with MPI library and OpenMP technology. For RGD calculations we realized parallelizing by groups: linear systems of each spectral group are computed by their own CPU cores. Then the sum of independent results is calculated. Advantages of this approach: simple realization, high computation speed, free selection of linear system solution method and pre-conditioner. Disadvantages are: inability to utilize more CPU cores than spectral group count (600), absence of load balancing. Other variant is the use of parallel algorithms for solving linear equations systems. This allows us to increase number of CPU cores but efficiency of these methods significantly decreases when the number of cores grows.

General parallel algorithm integrates the advantages of previous two methods. All available CPU cores are divided into groups and each group processes its own set of linear equations systems. Parallel algorithm for linear equations systems solving is used within each group and all the data are stored distributively.

2.2 Gas mixture flows

Another problem in which we used a developed parallel approach is related to modeling flows of gas mixtures in microchannels technical systems. Here we present the study of the evolution of a binary supersonic gas jet that is propagated in a vacuum. The computing complexity of such flows is associated with the violation in some parts of the computational domain of continuity hypothesis.

Using a multiscale approach is a way to overcome the problem of discontinuity [15-20]. We propose method that integrates a macroscopic approach and a method of molecular dynamics (MMD) [21-23]. Macroscopic approach is based on the QGD system [4]. The flow parameters are corrected with MMD. The system of molecular dynamic equations is used as a subgrid algorithm. At first step for MMD we assume that the molecules are distributed uniformly in space. Velocities of the molecules are distributed according to the Maxwell equilibrium function. Computational domain is shown in Figure 3.

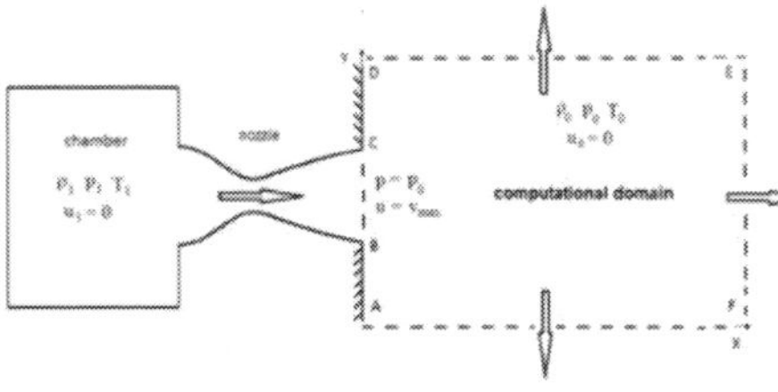

Figure 3. Computational domain.

The QGD equations of binary gas mixture dynamics are written as following (1)-(3), where F and Q are formulas (9, 10):

$$\mathbf{F}_a \equiv \mathbf{S}_a^u = \nu_{ab}\rho_a\left(\mathbf{u}_a^* - \mathbf{u}_a\right), \quad \mathbf{F}_b \equiv \mathbf{S}_b^u = \nu_{ba}\rho_b\left(\mathbf{u}_b^* - \mathbf{u}_b\right); \quad (9)$$

$$Q_a \equiv S_a^E = \nu_{ab}\left(E_a^* - E_a\right), \quad Q_b \equiv S_b^E = \nu_{ba}\left(E_b^* - E_b\right). \quad (10)$$

A mixture consists of two gases: a and b with numerical densities n_a and n_b and mass densities $\rho_a = m_a n_a$ and $\rho_b = m_b n_b$, respectively, here m_a and m_b are the masses of molecules of the gases a and b. Each of the gases is characterized by its temperature T_l and the macroscopic velocity – $\mathbf{u}_l$. The gas constant is equal to $\Re_l = k_B / m_l$, where k_B is the Boltzmann constant, γ_l is the specific heat ratio, Pr is the Prandtl number, τ is a relaxation parameter containing the dimension of time.

Here $\mathbf{S}_a^u$, $\mathbf{S}_b^u$, S_a^E, S_b^E are the exchange terms (5)-(6). $\mathbf{u}_l^*, E_l^*$ – vector of velocity and the total energy density, allowing us to take into account redistribution of momentum and energy between the components of the mixture. These parameters will be determined through MMD below. ν_a and ν_b – the frequency of mutual collisions between the molecules of one kind, ν_{ab} – the frequency of collisions between the molecules of *a* kind and the molecules of *b* kind, ν_{ba} – the frequency of collisions between the molecules of *b* kind and the molecules of *a* kind.

The calculation gas parameters are shown in the Table 2.

Table 2. The gas parameters.

Diameter (BC), μm	Pressure into chamber p_1, Pa	Temperature into chamber, T_1, K	Pressure into domain p_0, Pa	Temperature into domain T_0, K
6÷300	10^5	273	10^3	273

The parallel algorithm is based on "domain decomposition" technique and on splitting into physical processes. Splitting on physical processes means that QGD equations are processed by CPUs and MD is processed by CPUs, VPUs or GPUs. Gas dynamics is calculated on CPU units. For MMD parallelization an equal number of particles is sent to each computing unit. According to the algorithm the molecular dynamic calculations do not require exchanges.

Domain decomposition on computational domain is used for QGD equations. We take into account four levels on parallelization: nodes of system → CPUs → CPU cores → CPU threads. Node of system and GPU or VPU get the same subdomains. GPU or VPU computes the exchange terms. If GPU or VPU is unavailable these calculations are produced by CPU threads.

Parallelization of MD calculations is produced by splitting the set of molecules into groups with the same power. Each GPU or VPU produces a few molecular groups.

3 Results

For solution of described problems, we constructed the parallel software suite that is based on hybrid technology. The technology combines MPI, OpenMP and CUDA. The parallel testing techniques developed by us were performed using various computing systems. For demonstration of hybrid calculations, two systems were implemented: the K-100 hybrid cluster with CPU and GPU set at Keldysh Institute of Applied Mathematics RAS (Moscow), the MVS-10P supercomputer at Joint Super Computer Center of RAS based on CPUs and VPUs. The results of our studies for each of these tasks are presented below.

3.1. Radiative Gas Dynamic computing

Early for solution of RGD problem we used two parallel systems SKIF MSU and MVS-100k. Group parallelizing efficiency using 600 CPU cores was 84%. Hybrid parallelizing (groups consisting of 8 CPU cores) reached 79% efficiency using 600 CPU cores and 66% efficiency using 1200 cores.

Now we use the PETAFLOPS-system MVS-10P with CPU and VPU devices. The system has 207 nodes. Each node has two CPU Intel Xeon E5-2690 (8 cores and 16 threads per one CPU) and two VPU Intel Xeon Phi 7110X (41 cores and 244 threads per one VPU). Parallelization scheme was based on domain decomposition technique. Program realization was based on MPI and OpenMP technologies. For parallelization on spectral groups we used threads of CPU or VPU. The results of testing of our parallel software on space 3D grid with $48*10^6$ hybrid cells are shown in Figure 4. These results confirm that the CPU calculations are more effective. However the using of all devices on each node allows minimizing the computation time. And as summary, high possibilities of modern hybrid computer systems allows solving large RGD-problems.

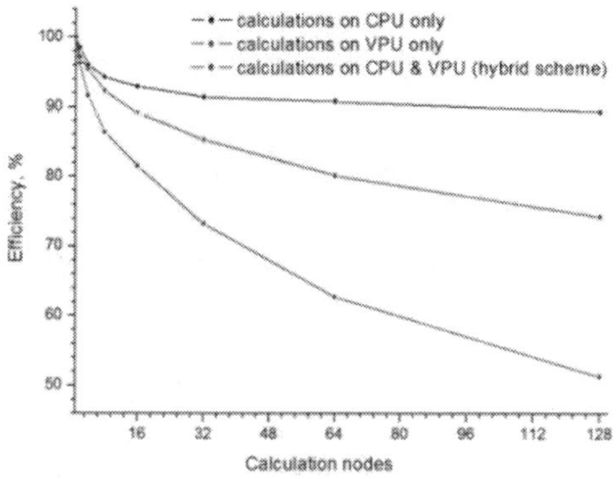

Figure 4: Efficiency of RGD algorithm parallelized with the help of hybrid approach (on group and on space).

3.2 Calculation of gas mixture flows

Calculations of gas mixture flows were provided on K100 hybrid cluster with CPU and GPU. Each node of the cluster has two CPU Intel Xeon X (6 cores and 12 threads per one CPU) and three GPU NVidia Tesla C2050 (448 CUDA cores per one GPU). We tested of our software on 3D Cartesian grid with sizes 240x240x720 cells. The calculations were connected with evolution of nitrogen and hydrogen jet in nickel microchannel with sizes 30x30x90 microns. Each grid cell in dependence on physical conditions can consist of 500 - 50000 gas particles. The results of testing are shown in Figure 5. These results confirm also that using of CPU systems is more effective. Perhaps the using of GPU allows reducing calculation time by 6 - 10 times. The using of more modern GPU devices (NVidia Tesla K40 or K80) allows decreasing calculation times by 20-40 times [24].

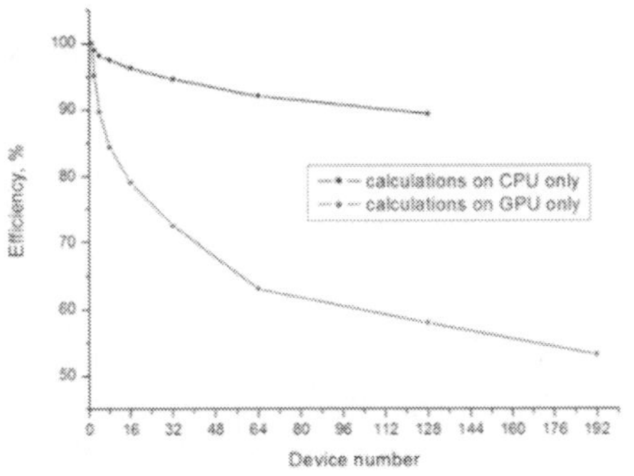

Figure 5: Efficiency of QGD-MD algorithm obtained by separate calculations on CPUs and GPUs.

4 Conclusions

Supercomputing can accelerate scientific research in important areas such as physics, material sciences, biology, and etc. Supercomputer simulations can augment or replace experimentation in cases where experiments are hazardous, expensive, or even impossible to perform. High performance systems allow us to solve large problems in the reasonable time.

They provide great computing power and possibility. To use them we need special tools and approaches. In our work we presented parallel algorithms and realization methods of the algorithms on high performance computer systems with different processors. Numerical results and data of efficiency reflect the correct direction of researches.

As computational power increases, fewer compromises are made, and more accurate results can be obtained. Therefore, in many application domains, there is essentially no limit to the amount of compute power and many contemporary challenges can be overcome.

Acknowledgements

This work was supported by Russian Foundation for Basic Research (grants № 15-29-07090-ofi_m and 16-07-00206-a).

References

1. http://www.top500.org/list/2015/06/
2. http://www.parallel.ru
3. https://www.ot.ru/en/solutions/hybrid-supercomputer/
4. T.G. Elizarova, *Quasi-Gas Dynamic Equations* (Springer-Verlag, Berlin Heidelberg New York, 2009)
5. http://www.arianespace.com/mission/ariane-flight-vs14
6. B.N. Chetverushkin, *Mathematical modeling of problems in the dynamics of a radiating gas* (Science, Moscow, 1985) [In Russian]
7. T.K. Bose, *High Temperature Gas Dynamics* (Springer, Cham, Heidelberg, New York, Dordrecht, London, 2014)
8. I.V. Avilova, L.M. Biberman, et al., *Optical Properties of Hot Air* (Science, Moscow, 1970) [In Russian]
9. T.A. Kudryashova, S.V. Polyakov, A.A. Sverdlin, Math. Models Comput. Simul., **1**(4), 445–452 (2009)
10. T.A. Kudryashova, S.V. Polyakov, E.M. Kononov, Math. Models and Comput. Simul., **1**(5), 551-560 (2009)
11. METIS-Family of Multilevel Partitioning Algorithms, http://glaros.dtc.umn.edu/gkhome/views/metis (2009)
12. S. Balay, K. Buschelman, W.D. Gropp, D. Kaushik, M.G. Knepley, L. Curfman McInnes, B.F. Smith, H. Zhang, http://www.mcs.anl.gov/petsc (2001)
13. H. Si, *TetGen: A Quality Tetrahedral Mesh Generator*, http://tetgen.berlios.de/ (2009)
14. K. Lipnikov, Yu. Vassilevski, Engineering with Computers, **20**(3), 193–201 (2004)
15. V.A. Titarev, Comput. Math. Math. Phys., **49**(7), 1197–1211 (2009)
16. M.K. Borg, D.A. Lockerby, J.M. Reese, J. Fluid Mech., **768**, 388–414 (2015)
17. K. Morinishi, Computers and Fluids, **35**(8-9), 978–985 (2006)
18. A. Patronis, D.A. Lockerby. J. Comput. Phys., **270**, 532–543 (2014)
19. S.Y. Docherty, M.K. Borg, D.A. Lockerby, J.M. Reese, Int. J. Heat and Fluid Flow, **50**, 114–125 (2014)
20. A. Alexiadis, D.A. Lockerby, M.K. Borg, J.M. Reese, Comput. Methods Appl. Mech. Eng., **264**, 81–94 (2013)
21. Yu.N. Karamzin, T.A. Kudryashova, V.O. Podryga, S.V. Polyakov, Math. Model., **27**(7), 65–74 (2015) [In Russian]
22. Yu. Karamzin, T. Kudryashova, V. Podryga, S. Polyakov, Int. Conf. Eng. Comput. Tech. (ECT 2014), **28**, (Civil-Comp Press, Stirlingshire, Scotland, 2014)
23. T. Kudryashova, Yu. Karamzin, V. Podryga, S. Polyakov, Adv. Eng. Software (to be published)
24. http://www.nvidia.co.uk/object/k80-gpu-test-drive-uk.html

 DOI: 10.1051/matecconf/20167604026

Computation of Equilibrium Paths in Nonlinear Finite Element Models

Zdeněk Kala[1,a]

[1]*Brno University of Technology, Department of Structural Mechanics, Veveří 95, 60200 Brno, Czech Republic*

Abstract. In the present paper, equilibrium paths are simulated applying the nonlinear finite element model. On the equilibrium paths, there are identified critical points which contribute to understanding and quantification of stability processes in a nonlinear system. By means of nonlinear solution, bifurcation points from which two equilibrium path branches emanate and so there is no unique tangent were identified and drawn. Mutual position of limit and bifurcation points was identified. The paper describes multidisciplinary problems of the analysis of limit states of nonlinear systems. The methods of stochastic and sensibility analyses which are frequently applied to assessment of the safety and reliability of supporting structural systems are discussed.

1 Introduction

The stability of slender bars is a phenomenon associated with buckling [1]. Even though the failure mechanism of a steel bar may appear to be a fundamental problem, its basis has often eluded researchers and practitioners. No matter how slender a steel bar, it does not reach its ultimate static resistance (load-carrying capacity) under elastic buckling, but rather after sufficient yielding of the critical cross-section under combined compression and bending [2].

In reality, steel bars are not perfectly straight, but are invariably subjected to some degree of initial crookedness. The shape of the steel bar is typically defined by the path denoted as "Imperfect bar" plotted in Fig. 1. Results of theoretical and experimental research present an important source of data for sensitivity analyses [3-6], assessment of structural reliability [7-10], and for multiple-criteria decision analyses, see, e.g., [11-16]. Results of experimental research of the load-deflection path have been published, e.g., in [17-19].

Specific scenarios of post-buckling behaviour are frequently attributed to certain structural types, like columns, shells or plates [1]. Structural post-buckling response has strong implications on the structural load carrying capacity, sensitivity to imperfection, structural safety, and is of great significance to current design procedures [1].

The nonlinear finite element solution performed using current software is, as a result of the instabilities of high von Mises truss, numerically demanding, and discrepancies could exist between the obtained result and experimental results [19]. In general, the phenomenon of loss of stability is present in the deforming structure regardless of whether the loading process is controlled by force [5, 7] or by displacement [20]. The geometrically nonlinear solution performed on the basis of increasing the deflection reliably investigates the full path of beam imperfection, see Fig. 1. Upon reaching the peak, the force decreases and the deformation increases. Reaching the peak of the load-deflection path can result in numerical problems for common software based on the geometrically nonlinear finite element solution, especially in cases, when the loading process is controlled by load increments.

The geometrically nonlinear finite element method, which has proven to be suitable for solving stability types of problems of the von Mises trusses [21], was applied in the presented article. The system load-deflection paths were evaluated using this method. The resulting outputs of the geometrically nonlinear solution are the static equilibrium states.

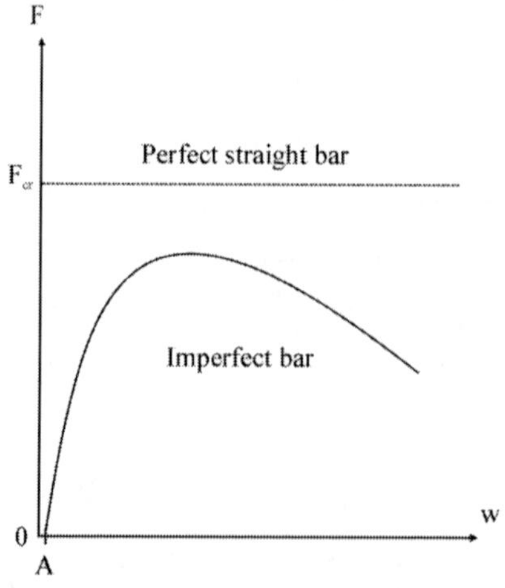

Figure 1. Load-deflection path of pin-ended model.

[a] Corresponding author: kala.z@fce.vutbr.cz

2 Bifurcation and limit points

Light weight steel structures often work in a nonlinear range; this is due to always increasing requirements for low price and high strength. The stability analysis of slender steel members is the key aspect of safety and reliability of constructional solution. The structure stability is often determined by singular points in its equilibrium path. These points can represent severe problems for common geometrically nonlinear finite elements methods based on increase of load actions which are routinely applied to engineering designs [22-24].

Each point of an equilibrium path represents an equilibrium state. Along a static equilibrium path of a conservative system, transition from stability to instability can occur at critical points only. Critical points are divided into limit and bifurcation points, see Fig. 2 and Fig. 3.

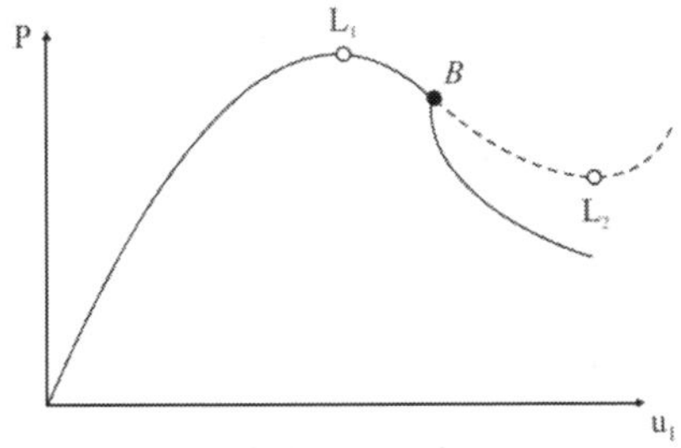

Figure 2. P vs u_1 plane: Limit point before bifurcation.

The parameter P which controls the structural behaviour in dependence on displacement u_1 is introduced to vertical axes. The identification of critical points is well known [24]. When applying the finite elements method, critical points can be identified using tangent stiffness matrix K. The matrix K is symmetric and real. The critical point takes place at the moment when matrix K is singular. The value of determinant of matrix K is the fundamental criterion for the identification of critical points. The isolated critical point has only one zero eigenvalue of matrix K. The multiple critical point has two or more zero eigenvalues of matrix K. The structure with multiple critical point is more sensitive to imperfections in the vicinity of that critical state [25]. The matrix of toughness K of the regular point of equilibrium path is nonsingular.

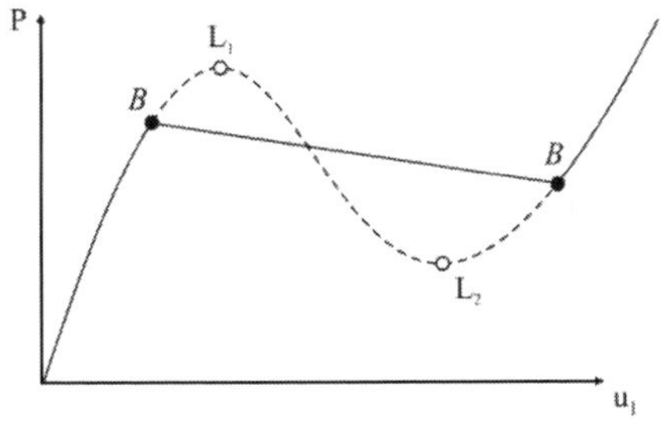

Figure 3. P vs u_1 plane: Bifurcation point before limit point.

Bifurcation point, also called branch point or branching point, is point from which two equilibrium path branches emanate and so there is no unique tangent. Bifurcation of equilibrium is characterized by the sudden transition from one deformation regime to another regime.

General understanding of the basic characteristics of the elastic buckling and postbuckling behaviour of members that become unstable as a result of bifurcation can be obtained by considering the simple model in Fig. 4. The object of the present paper is computing of equilibrium paths of pin-ended slender elastic von-Misses truss. The imperfect truss was considered as symmetrical, so only one half of the structure is plotted, see Fig. 4. The determination of failure load of the slender strut requires to take the influence of initial curvature of the bar axis into consideration and to consider the entire nonlinear load deflection curve of the structure, see Fig. 4.

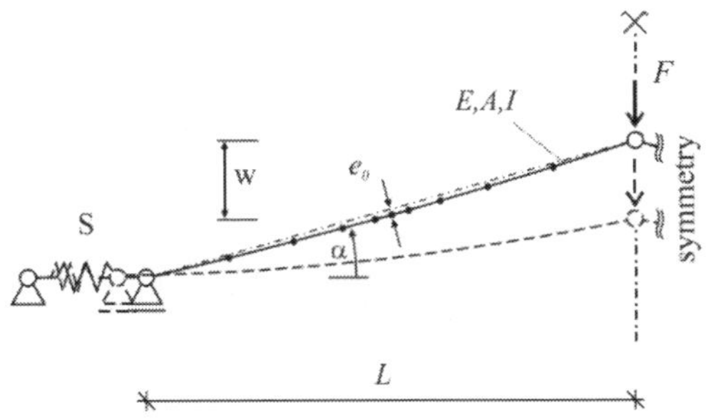

Figure 4. Bifurcation-buckling model of imperfect system.

3 Post buckling analysis

The planar truss with member HEA 200 and initial angel α=15° was analyzed, see Fig. 4. The HEA 200 is the cross-section with second moment of area I_z=13.36E6 mm^4 and section area A=5380 mm^2. Young's modulus is E=210 GPa. The bar has initial imperfection of bar axis. The one half sine function with aplitude e_0 was used for this imperfection. The computing of equilibrium paths of these geometrically nonlinear systems was solved using the software created by the author of the present paper, see Fig. 5.

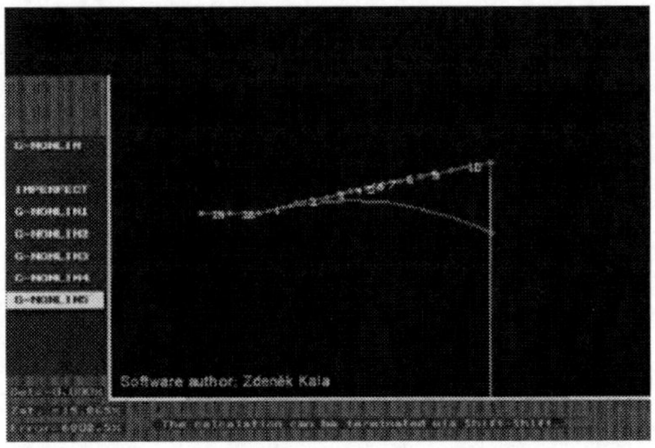

Figure 5. Computer program for bifurcation-buckling analysis.

The full-line black curve in Fig. 6 corresponds to the truss with e_0=0 (without initial imperfections). During increasing the load we reach the point "A" as the top of load-deflection curve. If we increase the load, the jump must occur and the displacement will be fixed in the point "D". Then, we can continue increasing the load. The jump is the so called snap-trough effect [26]. Buckling in the bar with e_0=0 will occur by bending about minor axis in the moment when the axial force in bar is equal to the Euler critical force N_{cr} = 1.54 MN. The bifurcation point at which buckling will occur, is marked by the black point "B", see Fig. 6.

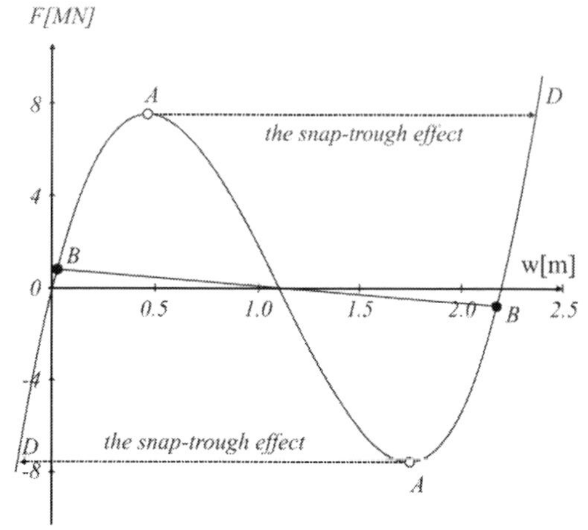

Figure 6. The snap-trough effect of von Misses truss.

After the bifurcation point, there follows the bifurcation of equilibrium, based on which buckled or unbuckled configuration of bar deformation is possible. Limit points of imperfect (e_0>0) bars are illustrated in hollow manner on dashed lines, see Fig. 7.

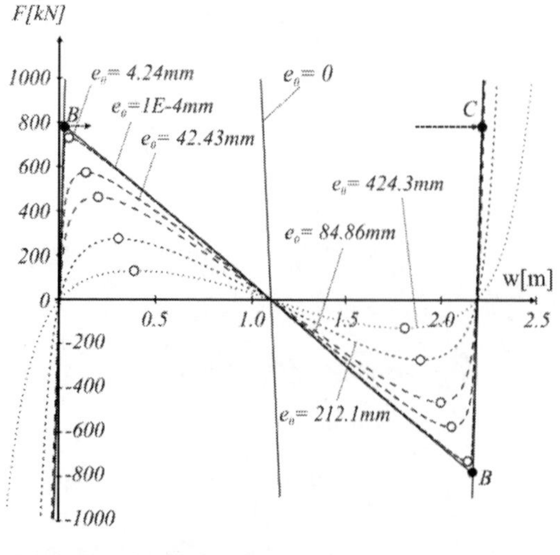

Figure 7. Load-deflection curves for $S = \infty$.

The bifurcation point and limit points lie on the straight line. After buckling, there will take place the snap from the point B → B due to the negligible increase of force F or there will be decreasing F due to increasing w, see Fig. 7. Snap-through instability mechanism of structure deformation is unstable under force F control of loading but it is stable under displacement w control of loading.

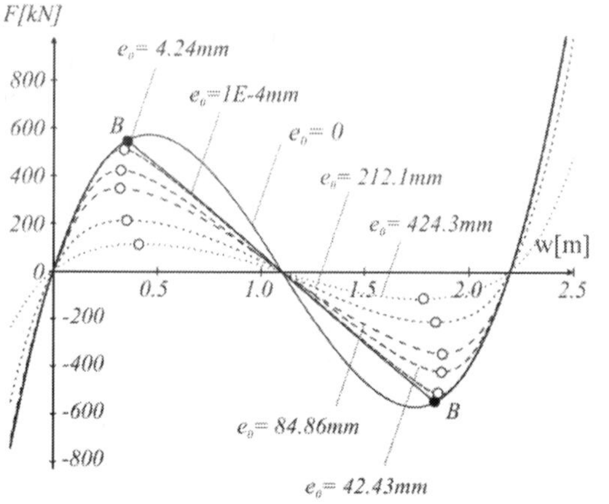

Figure 8. Load-deflection curves for $S = 21.21$ MNm^{-1}.

The full-line black curve in Fig. 8 corresponds to the truss with e_0=0 (without initial imperfections) for stiffness $S = 21.21$ MNm^{-1}. The bifurcation point and limit points are not presented on the straight line. The connection of configuration both of bifurcation point and limit points with initial imperfection and stiffness S can be analysed. When comparing Fig. 7 with Fig. 8, it is evident that the bifurcation point and limit points change their configuration from the position on the straight line to the situation on the curve. Finding dependences between e_0, S and limit points forms the basis for the analysis of equilibrium paths without application of nonlinear finite elements models.

4 System stability and randomness

A stable structure is the one which remains stable for any conceivable (imaginable) system of loads. The stability is mostly examined on a structure without imperfections. The result of common stability analysis is the value of critical loading at which the structure buckles. If the critical load is remarkably higher than the load action of structure, then the structure service is reliable and safe. Stability analysis should be carried out for all load action states, which can be counted up to thousands. Engineering computation and evaluation of results can be complicated, in particular if there occur multiple critical points. A large number of loading states in real structures represents a complication which is overcome by the engineers by means of approximate methods.

4.1. Buckling length

The static resistance of bars under compression stress can be computed by using the so-called buckling length.

Buckling length is represented by the structure parameters which take into consideration the influence of initial imperfections on the resistance decrease. Although there exist sophisticated approaches how to calculate the buckling length, it is always the engineer who estimates the structure as for ultimate limit states, who is responsible for their resulting choice. The occurrence of multiple critical points can cause the incorrect and dangerous assessment of buckling lengths. An alternate parameter to the buckling length is the slenderness of the bar, for the application of which the same cautiousness is valid as that for buckling lengths.

4.2 Failures and stability phenomenon

Many failures of building structures are caused by the stability loss. Many times repeated loading, which causes repeated buckling of slender elements and fatigue crack, is dangerous above all [27]. This phenomenon is met in bridge structures. Safety and reliability of slender bridge structures gets degraded in time, and enforces regular inspection checking up. The lifetime of bridge structures must be always specified, based on results of each inspection checking up which helps detect fatigue cracks and other failures occurring in bridges.

4.3 Imperfections and initial imperfections

In literature, the notions "imperfection" [28] and "initial imperfections" [3-5] are frequently met. In general, material and geometrical imperfections are distinguished [29]. Whereas an imperfection can be both small and large, an initial imperfection is assumed, as a rule, to be very small, in particular when geometrical imperfections are concerned. The size of initial imperfections always influences the safety and reliability of structures. Ultimate limit states are sensitive to the variability of initial imperfections less than serviceability limit states.

4.4 Stochastic computational models

The general development of theory and methods of design of structures is remarkable due to its multidisciplinary approach the tendency of which is the step by step transition from deterministic approach through semiprobabilistic conception to the direct probabilistic computation method. The development of computer technology enables to elaborate numerically demanding computer simulations of nonlinear systems based on computer modelling, non-linear systems, stochastic systems, neural networks, fuzzy systems, evolutionary computation, systems theory, soft computing, lightwave engineering and mathematical theory of stability. Stochastic calculation models consist of the deterministic nonlinear computation model (usually based on the nonlinear finite elements method), and on the numerical simulation method of Monte Carlo type. It is not possible to find the real value of structure failure probability; therefore it is being worked with its theoretical value. The calculation of probability of structure failure is always possible with a certain accuracy only. Therefore it is frequently spoken on the assessment of failure probability which testifies to the structure reliability, and provides information for decision makers. The lower fuzzy uncertainty of input data and of parameters of computation models, the more credible can be the assessment of structure reliability.

4.5 Sensitivity analysis

Sensitivity analysis is the crucial part of sophisticated computation models the influences of input quantities on the model output of which cannot be understood by simple intuition. Research [3-7] showed that the evaluation of the ultimate limit state by the sensibility analysis based on correlation between load carrying capacity and geometrical imperfection would lead to incorrect results. It is due to the fact that the imperfection decreasing or increasing from zero decreases the load carrying capacity.

The dependence and the correlations cannot be interchanged, nevertheless, a correlation can be chosen as the sensitivity indicator of the first choice in numerically demanding nonlinear computation models which other sophisticated approaches cannot be applied to.

5 Conclusion

In the paper, there were identified load-deflection curves of a geometrically nonlinear model with imperfections, and problems of multiple critical points were discussed. The probability of occurrence of multiple critical points can indicate high sensitivity of response of the system to initial imperfections [25]. The basic methods of stability analysis of nonlinear systems used in engineering practice were described in the present paper. The failures of slender structural system caused by stability loss frequently cause the decrease of safety and reliability. Modern methods of stability analysis are important instruments to ensure function reliability and general effectiveness of modern structural systems.

Acknowledgment

This result was achieved with the financial support of the projects No. LO1408 "AdMAs UP" and GA15-07730S and FAST-S-16-3779.

References

1. T.V. Galambos, Stability Design Criteria for Metal Structures, 911 (1998)
2. L.H. Teh, B.P. Gilbert, J. Constr. Steel. Res. 117, (2016)
3. Z. Kala, J. Kala, WSEAS Transactions on Applied and Theoretical Mechanics 4, 3 (2009)
4. Z. Kala, Arch. Civ. Mech. Eng. 15, 4 (2015)
5. Z. Kala, J. Civ. Eng. Manag. 22, 3 (2016)
6. R. Sousa, J. Guedes, H. Sousa, Arch. Civ. Mech. Eng. 15, 2 (2015)

7. Z. Kala, J. Kala, A. Omishore, International Journal of Mechanics 10, (2016)
8. Z. Kala, A. Omishore, International Journal of Mathematics and Computers in Simulation 10, (2016)
9. A. Omishore, Proc. of the 4th WSEAS Int. Conf. on EMESEG'11, pp.284-288 (2011)
10. M. Kvíčala, K. Frydrýšek, M., Štamborská, International Journal of Thermophysics 36, 2-3 (2015)
11. J. Antucheviciene, Z. Kala, M. Marzouk, E.R. Vaidogas, Math. Probl. Eng. 2015, 362579 (2015)
12. J. Antucheviciene, Z. Kala, M. Marzouk, E.R. Vaidogas, Math. Probl. Eng. 2015, 160569 (2015)
13. F. Baño, Á. Mena, F. Viscaino, J. Rubio, G. Rodríguez-Bárcenas, International Journal of Economics and Statistics 4, (2016)
14. E. Castillo, J.A. Lozano-Galant, M. Nogal, J. Turmo, J. Civ. Eng. Manag. 21, 6 (2015)
15. D.B. Hammad, N. Shafiq and M. F. Nuruddin, MATEC Web of Conferences 15, 01018 (2014)
16. M. Medineckiene, E.K. Zavadskas, F. Björk, Z. Turskis, Arch. Civ. Mech. Eng. 15, 1 (2015)
17. M. Štrba, M. Karmazínová, International Journal of Mechanics 9, (2015)
18. M. Karmazínová, J. Melcher, WSEAS Transactions on Applied and Theoretical Mechanics 9, (2014)
19. O. Sucharda, J. Vasek, J. Kubosek, International Journal of Mechanics 9, (2015)
20. Z. Kala, M. Kalina, International Journal of Mechanics 10, (2016)
21. Z. Kala, J. Civ. Eng. Manag. 18, 1 (2012)
22. V. Zakovorotny, WSEAS Transactions on Applied and Theoretical Mechanics 10, (2015)
23. J. Shi, Computers & Structures 58, 1 (1996)
24. Z.P. Bažant, L. Cedolin, Stability of structures: Elastic, inelastic, fracture and damage theories, (1991)
25. Z.P. Bazant, Y.Y. Xiang, Journal of Structural Engineering ASCE 123, 4 (1997)
26. J. Ravinger, Stability & Vibration, 135 (2012)
27. Z. Kala, J. Kala, M. Škaloud, B. Teplý, J. Civ. Eng. Manag. 11, 2 (2005)
28. A. Steinboeck, X. Jia, G. Hoefinger, H.A. Mang, Comput. Meth. Appl. Mech. Eng. 197, 45-48 (2008)
29. Z. Kala, Eng. Struct. 31, 6 (2009)

MATEC Web of Conferences 76, 04027 (2016) DOI: 10.1051/matecconf/20167604027
CSCC 2016

Development of optimization method for plate heat exchanger with undulation

Václav Dvořák[1,a]

[1] Technical university of Liberec, Faculty of mechanical engineering, Department of Power Engineering Equipment. Address: Studentska 2, 46117, Liberec, Czech Republic

Abstract. The article deals with optimization of undulated heat transfer surface of plate heat exchanger. The goal of optimization is not only to increase effectiveness of heat transfer but also to reduce the pressure drop. A combined pattern of undulation which combines herringbone pattern and wavy pattern was optimized and best values of four parameters were found; angle of herringbone pattern, number, phase and amplitude of longitudinal waves of wavy pattern. The optimization procedure looked for maximum of objective function which was a linear combination of effectiveness and pressure drop. We used simple Monte Carlo method and the optimum was searched for four values of reference pressure drop. Four different optimization were run and we investigated the effect of various definition of objective function and parameters of undulation. It was found that during optimization of combined pattern, the herringbone pattern is more favoured than wavy pattern. It is caused by the fact that herringbone pattern was described by the only one free parameter, which was the angle of undulation, and therefore it is more likely to be found by a stochastic method. This assumption was confirmed when simple wavy pattern was optimized and higher values of objective function and effectiveness were found.

1 Introduction

Energy recovery during air ventilation is one of the ways to reduce the energy consumption of buildings. Heat recovery can substantially reduce energy consumption needful for heating during cold seasons or air conditioning during hot seasons. The main component of any energy recovery devices are heat exchangers. Development of recuperative heat exchangers in recent years has focused on increasing their effectiveness. Another challenge is the development of so-called enthalpy exchangers for simultaneous heat and moisture transport, i.e. transport of both sensible and latent heat, as presented by Vít et al. in work [1]. To develop heat exchangers, methods of computational fluid dynamics are increasingly used, but there are still some problems to transfer the calculation results to the design and manufacturing processes.

To simulate a heat exchanger, it is necessary to create a model and a computational mesh and then use computational fluid dynamic (CFD) software. When assembling the heat exchanger, complicated and irregular narrow channels are created. These channels are split into small volumes (elements). The final meshes are structured or unstructured with different element sizes. Most of researchers use unstructured meshes for their calculations.

Gherasim et al., in work [2], presented a comparison of various grids for a plate heat exchanger modelled by a tetrahedral mesh. In order to assess the influence of the grid resolution on the solution, five grids were created and tested by meshing the volumes with different interval sizes. Laminar and turbulent regimes were simulated. It was discovered that the two grids with the smallest elements provided very similar results. In terms of temperature, the obtained results were close for grids with smaller elements. For pressure, quite a large difference between the grid with smallest elements and the grid with the largest ones was discovered.

Subsequent researchers have used numerical simulations to investigate plate heat exchangers with chevron (undulated) profiles, as it is presented in Figure 1. Tsai [3] and Liu [4], for example, dealt with these heat exchangers and their different geometries. Their conclusions regarding temperature and pressure loss were similar to Gherasim [2].

Similarly Giurgiu et al. in work [5] used CFD to study the influence of geometric characteristics of the two plates on the intensification process of heat transfer. They used SST k-ω turbulence model and non-structural high-density mesh and modelled only small part of the heat exchanger to analyse mini channels with the inclination angles of 30° respectively 60°. They carried out also a session of experimental measurements which confirms the results obtained through numerical simulation that the

[a] Corresponding author: vaclav.dvorak@tul.cz

plate heat exchanger model using mini channels with inclination angle of $\beta = 60^{\circ}$ provides best heat transfer. Kumar et al. [6] experimentally investigated the effect of symmetric and mixed chevron angles in a plate heat exchanger on heat transfer rate ratio, friction losses and many others quantities. Experimental observation confirmed previously known optimum for enhancement in heat transfer.

Rios Iribe et al. [7] investigated, using CFD and hexahedral meshes, momentum and heat transfer of a non-Newtonian fluid in steady laminar regime through a plate heat exchanger at constant wall temperature. They investigated the effect of number of plates and distance between plates on the heat transfer and the pressure drop and developed empirical correlations. Although the flow pattern was highly complex, under an adequate definition of the characteristics parameters, it was possible to establish simple correlations between the dimensionless numbers that characterize the thermal-hydraulic behavior of plate heat exchangers.

Al-Waked et al. [8] investigated numerically conjugate heat and mass transfer processes across membrane heat exchangers of variable mass transfer resistance. The authors studied effects of channel height, Reynolds number and flow direction on heat exchanger thermal effectiveness and energy recovered. A hybrid mesh was used.

Novosád and Dvořák [9], investigated the influence of oblique waves in herringbone pattern on the heat transfer surface. The main difficulty faced in this work was the creation of custom geometry. Each version had to be modelled, meshed, loaded into the solver, set the boundary conditions and subsequently perform the numerical simulation separately.

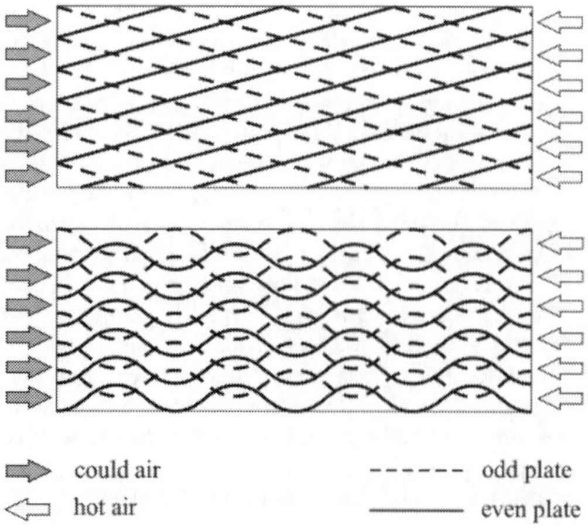

Figure 1 Two basic types of undulation; up – herringbone pattern, down – wavy pattern with sinusoidal waves.

Waves in herringbone pattern are widely used for steal plate heat exchanger. The reason is that forming the plates provides efficient and reliable way to increase the heat transfer area of the heat exchanger. Another pattern is the wavy pattern, visible down in Figure 1, which provides the same advantages. Although it is often used in plastic and aluminium plate heat exchangers in air ventilation systems, it is overlooked by researchers and it is not clear, which of both patterns is better, i.e. has higher heat transfer and lower pressure drop.

Therefore the aim of this work is to develop a method and optimize the combined pattern to answer these questions.

2 Methods

2.1 Methods of grid generation

To optimize a plate heat exchanger, we needed to model, mesh and compute a lot of computational variants. However, there are several disadvantages of repeated generation of computational meshes: Demanding and time consuming work and parameterization of the model is problematic. Further, even a small change of geometry requires to do again the whole process of model creation and mesh generation. Furthermore, meshes are not similar, i.e. the size, shape, and height of cells adjacent to walls are not the same for different topologies and numerical error which is added to the solution and influence evaluation of objective function.

Therefore, we used method, developed by Dvořák [10], for generating computational variants. This method is based on a dynamic mesh, which is provided by Ansys Fluent software. The meshes were created by pull procedure, which is similar to the own production process, i.e. the pulling direction is perpendicular to the plates. The main advantage is that this type of mesh generation is automatic and controlled by in-house software. All computational variants thus have the same mesh.

In this paper, we discuss the case of a counter flow heat exchanger, which does not have a symmetrical heat transfer area. It is because undulation cross each other, as it is obvious form Figure 1. To simulate flow and heat transfer in such heat exchanger, we need to create model containing two plates, as it is shown in Figure 2.

The heat transfer surface was divided into two parts. Input and output portions with length of $L_0 = 0.05$ m were fixed, remained flat and served for developing velocity profiles before and after central part.

The central part which was provided by undulation had length $L = 0.15$ m. Input boundary conditions were specified by velocities of 3 m/s, the output boundary conditions were specified as pressure outlets with static pressure 0 Pa. Bottom and upper boundary conditions were periodic, thus a heat exchanger with infinite number of plates was simulated. The width of the model was $B = 0.05$ m. We used mesh density, element size and count of cell layers according to recommendations from Dvořák and Novosád [11].

In this study, we used turbulence model SST k-ω, medium was air considered as incompressible gas. As a results, we obtained pressure, velocity, turbulence and temperature fields inside the computational domain for given inlet velocity.

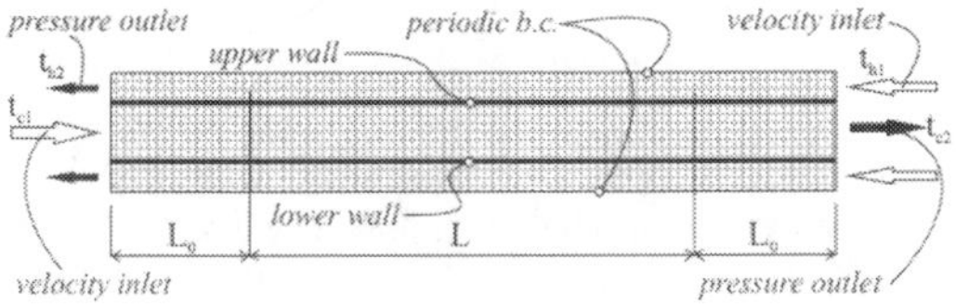

Figure 2 Model of heat exchange surface of counter flow recuperative heat exchanger.

In this work, the undulation was created as combination of two patterns, as it is indicated in Figure 3. Firstly, it was undulations in herringbone pattern, see top of Figure 1, defined by angle of undulation α (rad). Secondly, it was undulation in wavy patter, see bottom of Figure 1, defined by number of longitudinal waves n (1), their amplitude a (m) and phase f (1).

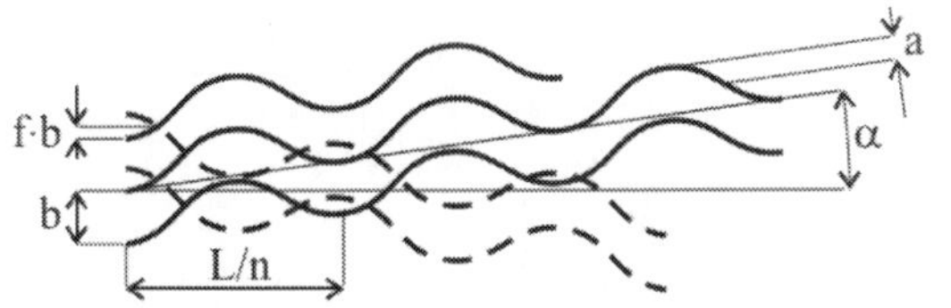

Figure 3 Parameters of plate undulation for optimization.

The shape of the middle part of plates was defined as vertical displacement z (m) of points on the wall according to equation

$$z = \frac{p}{2}\left[\cos(2\pi\, m) + s\right], \tag{1}$$

where $p = 0.003$ m is plate pitch, $s = 1$ for upper wall of the model and $s = -1$ for lower wall. m (1) represents wave number, which is calculated from horizontal coordinates (x, y) of points on the wall and set of parameters according to relation

$$m = \frac{f}{2} + \frac{1}{b}\left[s\,y + \frac{a}{2}\cos\left(2\pi\frac{n\,x}{L}\right) + y'\right], \tag{2}$$

where f (1) is phase, which is important especially for wavy corrugation, $b = 0.006$ m is pitch of corrugation, see Figure 3. a (m) is amplitude and n (1) count of longitudinal waves according to the same figure, while L (m) is the length of the middle part of the model heat exchanger. These parameters are needful for wavy corrugation.

For angled corrugation in herringbone patter, parameter y' is implied as

$$y' = -x\tan\alpha\,. \tag{3}$$

Amplitude of wavy corrugation was determined by two ways. First, it was defined as multiplication of pitch of corrugation according to relation

$$a = \zeta_1 b\,, \tag{4}$$

but this way can make it difficult to find optimal ζ_1 together with optimal count of longitudinal waves n. Therefore we also tried relation

$$a = \zeta_2 \frac{L}{n}\,, \tag{5}$$

in which the amplitude depends on parameter ζ_2 and the length of longitudinal waves. The method of grid transformation according to relations (1) to (5) are described in work [10].

2.2 Method for optimization of plate heat exchanger

Two optimize a heat exchanger, we need an objective function F. Producers of heat exchangers often require as high heat transfer as it is possible for given pressure drop. Therefore and according to previous works [12], we used linear combination of two main characteristic properties of a heat exchanger in the form of

$$F = \eta - C_F\left(\frac{\left|\Delta p - \Delta p_R\right|}{\Delta p_R}\right)^R, \tag{6}$$

where Δp (Pa) is calculated or measured pressure drop, Δp_R (Pa) is reference or required pressure loss, η (1) is calculated or measured coefficient of effectiveness, C_F (1) penalty coefficient and R (1) is parameter by which we can control peak of objective function. Thus, obtained effectiveness is penalized by the difference between obtained and required pressure drop.

The pressure drop was defined as pressure difference

$$\Delta p = \bar{p}_{01} - \bar{p}_2\,, \tag{7}$$

where $\bar{p}_{01}$ (Pa) is mass-averaged total pressure in the inlet and $\bar{p}_2$ (Pa) is area-averaged static pressure at the pressure outlet.

The coefficient of effectiveness (or effectiveness) is the efficiency of sensible heat transfer. Most recuperative heat exchangers in air conditioning systems work in isobaric mode, where mass flow rates of hot and cold air are equal, i.e. $\dot{m}_h = \dot{m}_c$. Assuming parity between specific heat capacities $c_{p\,h} = c_{p\,c}$, we can write the effectiveness as

$$\eta = \frac{t_{h\,1} - t_{h\,2}}{t_{h\,1} - t_{c\,1}}\,, \tag{8}$$

where t_{h1} (°C) and t_{h2} (°C) are inlet and outlet temperatures of hot air, t_{c1} (°C) is outlet temperature of cold air.

The task of optimization dealt with finding of optimal values of four parameters according to Figure 3; angle of undulation α, number of longitudinal waves n, their amplitude a and phase f, while plate pitch p, often defined by requirement on material consumption, and pitch of undulation b, which is usually defined by deformability of plate material and technology of pressing, remained constant during optimization.

As optimization method, we used a simple Monte Carlo algorithm. To emphasize searching for local optimum, we used modification that favoured variants closer to the last best variant found according to relations

$$\pi_i^n = \pi_i^{best} - ran^2(\pi_i^{best} - \pi_i^{low}), \quad (9)$$

$$\pi_i^n = \pi_i^{best} + ran^2(\pi_i^{up} - \pi_i^{best}), \quad (10)$$

where π_i^n is a new value of optimization parameter π_i, π_i^{best} is the value of the parameter for the last best variant, π_i^{low} and π_i^{up} are lower and upper limit of the same parameter respectively, and $ran = \langle 0;1 \rangle$ is random number. The use of equations (9) and (10) were alternated also randomly.

3 Results

The model of plate heat exchanger was optimized for four values of reference pressure, $\Delta p_R = 100, 150, 200$ and 250 Pa. The optimization was initialized by values of parameters: $\alpha = 5°$, $n = 4$, $\zeta_1 = 0.5$, which corresponds to $\zeta_2 = 0.08$, and $f = 0.25$.

There are a typical course of first 100 steps of optimization in Figure 4, where pressure drop, effectiveness and objective function are presented for reference pressure drop $\Delta p_R = 100$ Pa and parameters of equation (6) $R = 1$ and $C_F = 0.5$. We can see how the objective function is reduced while pressure drop varies significantly from reference pressure.

Figure 5 shows development of parameters of best variants for the same optimization. We can observe, how the phase f and angle α become negligible while the amplitude of longitudinal waves represented by ratio $a/b = \zeta_1$ increased. It means that the wavy undulation was found as optimal in this case.

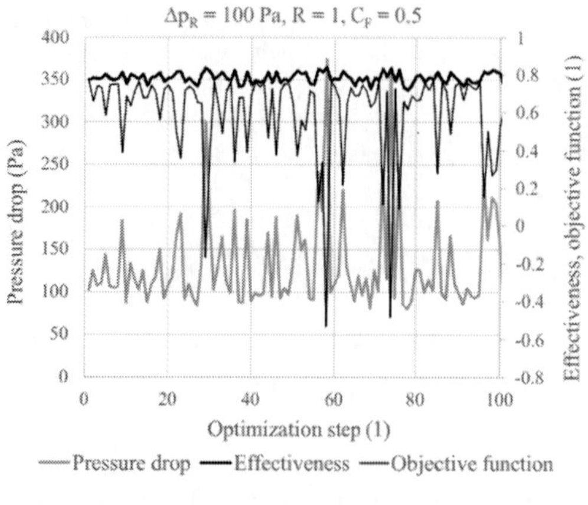

Figure 4 Course of optimization for reference pressure $\Delta p_R = 100$ Pa, $R = 1$ and $C_F = 0.5$.

Resulsts of optimization for different refference pressure are in Table 1. We can see that for refference pressure 150 and 200 (Pa), the angle is high, while parameter a/b is low. It means that herringbone pattern was found as optimal in these cases. The results for refference pressure 250 (Pa) show combination of both patterns.

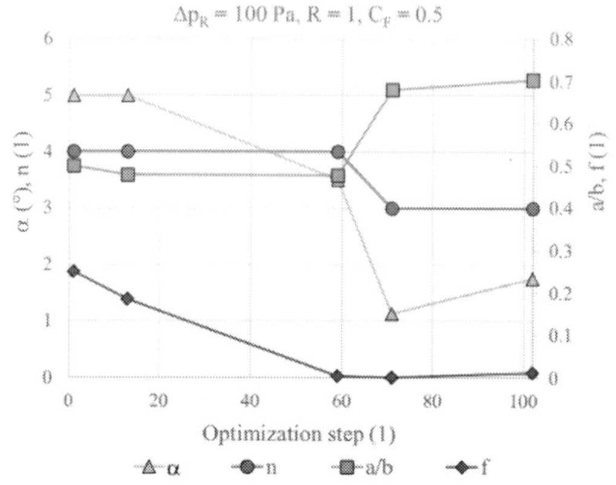

Figure 5 Development of parameters of best variants during optimization for reference pressure $\Delta p_R = 100$ Pa, $R = 1$ and $C_F = 0.5$.

Table 1. Results of optimization no. 1 for various values of reference pressure Δp_R, $R = 1$ and $C_F = 0.5$.

Δp_R (Pa)	100	150	200	250
No. of steps	102	93	109	17
η (1)	0.7719	0.8117	0.8263	0.8309
Δp (Pa)	100.2	150.0	200.0	251.1
F (1)	0.7709	0.8116	0.8263	0.8288
α (°)	1.8	22.7	28.8	29.9
n (1)	3	3	2	5
a/b (1)	0.70	0.12	0.10	0.49
f (1)	0.01	0.07	0.29	0.30

Because the peak of the objective function is quite steep and narrow, the parameters of equation (6) were changed in the second run of optimization. We used $R = 2$ and $C_F = 5$. Results of the second run of optimization are given in Table 2. Around five hundred variation were calculated, but the last best variants were found much earlier.

We can see from Table 2 that parameter a/b was reduced almost to zero for three lower values of required pressure. Thus undulation in herringbone pattern was found as optimal in these cases with angle α increasing with reference pressure. Waves were necessary only in case of the highest reference pressure 250 Pa. In that case, angle of undulation almost reached its maximum, 30°, and waves were necessary to increase obtained pressure drop. We can also see that obtained values of objective function were higher for the second run of optimization. It indicates that parameters $R=2$ and $C_F=5$ better suite the optimization procedure.

Table 2. Results of optimization no. 2 for various values of reference pressure Δp_R, $R=2$ and $C_F=5$.

Δp_R (Pa)	100	150	200	250
No. of steps	126	161	76	90
η(1)	0.7789	0.8123	0.8268	0.8317
Δp (Pa)	101.0	151.2	201.1	251.5
F (1)	0.7784	0.8120	0.8266	0.8315
α (°)	10.5	23.1	28.9	29.5
n (1)	7	3	6	7
a/b (1)	0.01	0.02	0.00	0.36
f (1)	0.34	0.18	0.26	0.37

If we compare results of Table 1 and Table 2, we find differences in values of obtained parameters. For the second run of optimization, herringbone pattern was found, while for the first run, it seems that combination of pattern was preferred. Therefore, the third run of optimization worked with different definition of amplitude a of longitudinal waves, and parameter ζ_2 defined by relation (5) was used instead of ζ_1.

Table 3. Results of optimization no. 3 for various values of reference pressure Δp_R, $R=2$, $C_F=5$ and $\zeta_2=0.08$ as initial value.

Δp_R (Pa)	100	150	200	250
No. of steps	176	117	76	74
η(1)	0.7794	0.8120	0.8268	0.8381
Δp (Pa)	101.1	150.9	201.1	256.4
F (1)	0.7787	0.8118	0.8266	0.8349
α (°)	10.8	23.0	28.9	1.6
n (1)	5	5	6	8
$n\cdot a/L$ (1)	0.00	0.00	0.00	0.27
f (1)	0.48	0.47	0.26	0.17

We can see from Table 3 that results of the third run of optimization were almost the same as for the second run. The only one difference are results for the highest reference pressure for which wave pattern with negligible angle $\alpha = 1.6°$ was found in the third run of optimization. Nevertheless, this exception lead to higher objective function and because it was still unclear which pattern is more advantage a fourth optimization was run with angle $\alpha = 0$ to optimize only the wave pattern.

Results of optimization of wavy pattern are collected in Table 4. Firstly, we can see that the best variants were changing even after more than 250 steps. Such slow optimization is probably connected with complexity of wavy pattern which is described by three parameters. So it seems that during optimization of combined pattern, undulation in herringbone patter is more favoured and more likely to be the result of optimization. Secondly, values of obtained effectiveness and objective function are higher than values obtained while undulation in herringbone patter was found.

Table 4. Results of optimization of wavy pattern for various values of reference pressure Δp_R, $R=2$, $C_F=5$, $\alpha=0$, $\zeta_2=0.08$ as initial value.

Δp_R (Pa)	100	150	200	250
No. of steps	236	273	269	279
η(1)	0.7796	0.8135	0.8282	0.8402
Δp (Pa)	100.0	153.3	202.5	248.8
F (1)	0.7796	0.8112	0.8274	0.8401
α (°)	0			
n (1)	5	4	5	5
$n\cdot a/L$ (1)	0.05	0.18	0.23	0.26
f (1)	0.24	0.20	0.18	0.25

Figure 6 Optimized shapes of heat transfer surfaces for reference pressures 100, 150, 200 and 250 Pa.

4 Conclusions

An undulated heat transfer surface of recuperative heat exchanger was optimized to obtain as high coefficient of effectiveness of heat transfer as possible. We optimized a combined pattern of undulation which combines herringbone pattern and wavy pattern. The task of optimization was to find optimal values of four parameters; angle of herringbone pattern, number, phase and amplitude of longitudinal waves of wavy pattern.

The optimization procedure looked for maximum of objective function which was a linear combination of effectiveness and pressure drop. We used simple Monte Carlo method and the optimum was searched for four values of reference pressure drop. Four different optimization were run and we investigated the effect of various definition of objective function and parameters of undulation.

It was found that during optimization of combined pattern, the herringbone pattern is more favoured than wavy pattern. It is probably caused by the fact that herringbone pattern was described by the only one free parameter, which was angle of undulation, and therefore it is more likely to be found by a stochastic method. This assumption was confirmed when simple wavy pattern was optimized and higher values of objective function and effectiveness were found. Nevertheless, optimization of wave pattern, which was defined by three free parameters, took longer time.

In further work, it would be beneficial to combine Monte Carlo method with a local optimization method to find optimums more precisely.

Acknowledgment

This publication was written at the Technical University of Liberec, Faculty of Mechanical Engineering with the support of the Institutional Endowment for the Long Term Conceptual Development of Research Institutes, as provided by the Ministry of Education, Youth and Sports of the Czech Republic in the year 2016.

References

1. T. Vít, P. Novotný, V.V. Nguyen, V. Dvořák, WSEAS, Recent Advances in Energy, Environment, Economics and Technological Innovation, 34-38 (2013)
2. I. Gherasim, N. Galanis, C.T. Nguyen, Int. Jour. of Thermal Science. **50**, 1499-1511 (2011)
3. Y.Ch. Tsai, F.B. Liu, P.T. Shen, Int. Commun. in Heat and Mass Transfer **36**, 574–578 (2009)
4. F.B. Liu, Y.Ch. Tsai, Heat Mass Transf. **46**, 585–593 (2010)
5. O. Giurgiu, A. Pleşa, L. Socaciu. Energy Procedia **85**, 244-251 (2016)
6. V. Kumar, A.K. Tiwari, S.K. Ghosh. Energy Conversion and Manag. **118**, 142–154 (2016)
7. E.Y. Rios-Iribe, M.E. Cervantes-Gaxiola, E. Rubio-Castro, O.M. Hernández-Calderón, Applied Thermal Eng. (in press)
8. R. AL-Waked, M.S. Nasif, G. Morrison, M. Behnia, Applied Thermal Eng. **84**, 301–309 (2015)
9. J. Novosád, V. Dvořák, EPJ Web of Conferences **67**, 020 85 (2014)
10. V. Dvořák, Recent Advances in Computer Science **1**, 193-198 (2014)
11. V. Dvořák, J. Novosád, Recent Advances in Computer Science, pp 115-120 (2015)
12. V. Dvořák, Applied Mechanics & Materials **752-753**, 820-827 (2015).

MATEC Web of Conferences 76, 04028 (2016) DOI: 10.1051/matecconf/20167604028
CSCC 2016

The Use of Multi-instrumental Approach to Teaching Physics

Radek Nemec[1], Filip Sramek[1] and Andrea Berkova[1]

[1]*University of Hradec Kralove, Faculty of Education, Czech Republic*

Abstract. This article describes the results of research focused on the impact of the use of multi-instrumental approach to teaching physics. This multi-instrumental approach to teaching physics is utilized by tools of CAA (Computer-aided assessment) and SMPSL (Systems for measurement using a computer). The effect of connecting the CAA and SMPSL as variable was examined through a pedagogical experiment to confirm the positive effect of using this multi-instrumental approach on the quality of elementary school pupils´ knowledge of physics.

1 Introduction

Multi-instrumental approach means connecting different instruments. In this case, system CAA (Computer-aided assessment) [1] and (SMPSL) systems for measurement using a computer [2] were interconnected. The aim of this research is to find out whether using the interconnected multi-instrumental approach influences the quality of elementary school pupils´ knowledge of physics.

Pre-test and post-test will be used for data collection. Before teaching with the help of multi-instrumental approach, a pre-test will be given to pupils. Post-test will be conducted after lessons where multi-instrumental approach was used. The test will be distributed among parallel groups. Multi-instrumental approach will not be applied to the control group (teaching will be in the traditional way without help of CAA and SMPSL systems). Multi-instrumental approach will be used in the experimental group. The results will be compared and conclusions will be drawn from them concerning the effect of multi-instrumental approach on pupils´ knowledge of physics.

2 Used Instruments

CAA (Computer-aided assessment) platforms are suitable for testing and practicing mathematical knowledge. An example of such system is the platform Maple T. A. (Testing and Assessment), which was established by integrating computational capabilities of computer algebra system Maple to CAA system. CAA platforms can help consolidate student understanding, support self-directed learning and make it easier for instructors to manage growing class sizes [3]. Mathematical platforms CAA also contain special features useful for testing mathematical knowledge such as working with graphs, series and mathematical symbols. In addition to practicing mathematical knowledge it is also available to use CAA platforms in physics.

SMPSL (Systems for measurement using a computer) is system that enables the collection, management and processing of data obtained by the measuring device that is connected to the computer. Such experiments are also called computer-aided experiments. The SMPSL (Measurement System Using a Computer in School Lab) enables using sensors connected to the hardware of the system to a PC evaluation program. The evaluation is created using a graphical representation of values from the computer.

2.1 Methodology of Research

As already mentioned, for examining differences in pupils' knowledge an objectively scored didactic tests were created, which were used as pre and post-tests. For the creation of didactic test the CAA system Maple TA was used. Maple T.A (Web-based Testing and Assessment for Math Courses) is an educational system distributed by Maplesoft to support training mathematics and science subjects [4]. Maple T.A provides students rich interactive environment using CAS (Computer Algebra System) Maple. Questions of various types were included in the tests.

To maintain objectivity, mainly closed questions (e.g. multiple choice) and exceptionally open questions with brief answers were selected.

3 Pre-test

Before the execution of research, a pre-test was conducted to determine comparable knowledge of control and experimental groups.

The results are summarized in the following tables.

[a] Corresponding author: radek.nemec@uhk.cz

DOI: 10.1051/matecconf/20167604028

Table 1 shows the test results of the control and experimental group. Point range was from 0 to 10 points.

Table 1. Points of Pre-test

Number of pupil	Control gr.	Exp. gr.
1	10	10
2	10	9
3	9	9
4	9	9
5	8	9
6	8	8
7	8	8
8	7	8
9	7	8
10	6	7
11	6	6
12	6	6
13	5	5
14	5	5
15	4	5
16	4	5
17	4	4
18	4	4
19	3	3
20	3	3
21	1	2
22	0	2
23		1
24		0

Table 2. F-test of Pre-test

	Contr. gr.	*Exp. gr.*
Expected value	5,773	5,667
Variance	7,613	8,232
Observation	22	24
Difference	21	23
F	0,925	
P(F<=f) (1)	0,431	
F krit (1)	0,485	

Hypothesis of identical variances was not rejected because the test criterion F was smaller than F crit. It was further applied to the two-sided T-test to determine whether pupils from both the control and experimental groups have comparable knowledge before the experiment. The reader can get acquainted with the results in Table 3.

Table 3. T-test of Pre-test

	Contr. gr.	*Exp. gr.*
Expected value	5,773	5,667
Variance	7,613	8,232
Observation	22	24
Common variance	7,936	
Hyp. Median difference value	0,000	
Difference	44,000	
t Stat	0,128	
P(T<=t) (1)	0,450	
t krit (1)	1,680	
P(T<=t) (2)	0,899	
t krit (2)	2,015	

The test criterion t is less than t crit and therefore the hypothesis of identical means is not rejected. It is assumed that pupils from both the control and experimental groups have comparable knowledge before teaching itself.

In the following table the basic statistics can be seen (Table 4).

Table 4. Descriptive statistics of Pre-test

Control group	
Expected value	5,773

Standard error of the mean	0,588
Median	6
Modus	4
Standard deviation	2,759
Variance	7,613
Kurtosis	-0,503
Skewness	-0,279
Minimum	0
Maximum	10
Suma	127
Total	22
Significance level (95,0%)	1,223
Experimental group	
Expected value	5,667
Standard error of the mean	0,586
Median	5,5
Modus	9
Standard deviation	2,869
Variance	8,232
Kurtosis	-0,975
Skewness	-0,297
Minimum	0
Maximum	10
Suma	136
Total	24
Significance level (95,0%)	1,212

For clarity, the reader can see the histogram. Table 5, 6, Figure 1, 2.

Table 5. Histogram of Pre-test

Control gr.		
Points	*Frequency*	*Cumul. %*
2	2	9,09%
4	6	36,36%
6	5	59,09%
8	5	81,82%
10	4	100,00%

Table 6. Histogram of Pretest

Exp. Gr.		
Points	*Frequency*	*Cumul. %*
2	4	16,67%
4	4	33,33%
6	6	58,33%
8	5	79,17%
10	5	100,00%

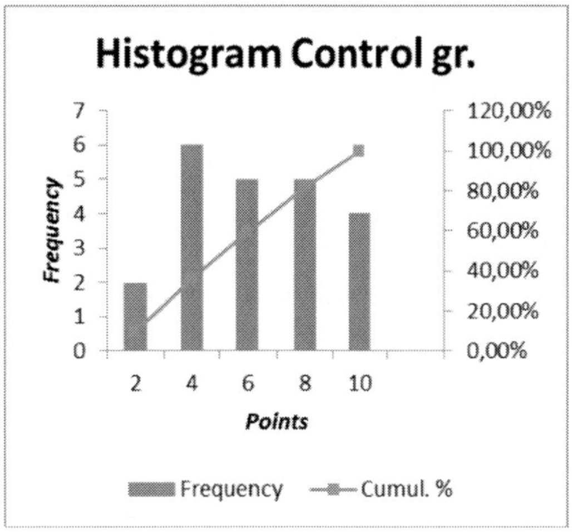

Fig. 1. Histogram of Pretest Control gr.

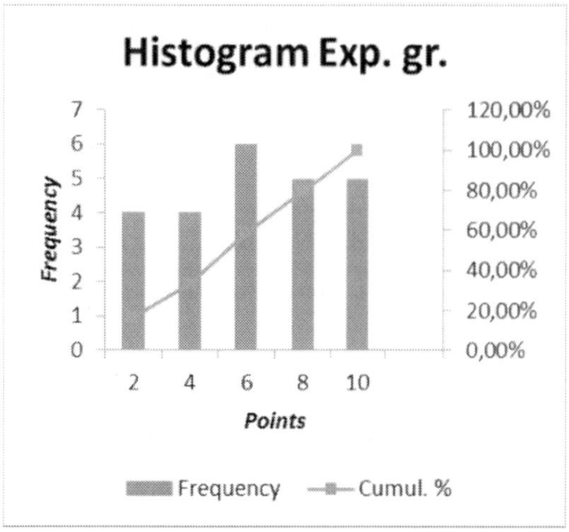

Fig. 2. Histogram of Pre-test Experimental gr.

4 Post-test

The experiments use of research focused on the impact of CAA and the use of measurement systems using computers in school science laboratories to acquire more knowledge than when teaching without CAA and measurement system using a computer are as follows.
The results are summarized in the following tables.

Therefore an experiment was subsequently conducted - teaching control and experimental groups ended with post-test (pre-test identical).

Table 7 shows the test results of the control and experimental group. Point range was from 0 to 10 points.

Table 7. Points of Post-test

Number of pupil	Control gr.	Exp. gr.
1	10	10
2	9	10
3	9	9
4	8	9
5	7	9
6	7	9
7	7	8
8	6	8
9	6	8
10	6	8
11	6	7
12	5	7
13	5	7
14	5	7
15	4	6
16	3	6
17	3	5
18	3	5
19	2	4
20	1	4
21		2

Table 8. F-test of Post-test

	Contr. gr.	*Exp. gr.*
Expected value	5,600	7,048
Variance	5,937	4,548
Observation	20,000	21,000
Difference	19,000	20,000
F	1,305	
P(F<=f) (1)	0,279	
F krit (1)	2,137	

The hypothesis of identical variance whereas the F test criterion is smaller than F crit is not rejected (Table 8). Therefore, T-test can be used again (Table 9).

Table 9. T-test of Post-test

	Control gr.	**Exp. gr.**
Expected value	5,600	7,048
Variance	5,937	4,548
Observation	20,000	21,000
Common variance	5,224	
Hyp. Median difference value	0,000	
Difference	39,000	
t Stat	-2,027	
P(T<=t) (1)	0,025	
t krit (1)	1,685	
P(T<=t) (2)	0,050	
t krit (2)	2,023	

Based on these results it is suggested that students in the experimental group showed acquisition of more knowledge than when teaching without measurement system using a computer. This can be seen in the box plot (Fig. 3).

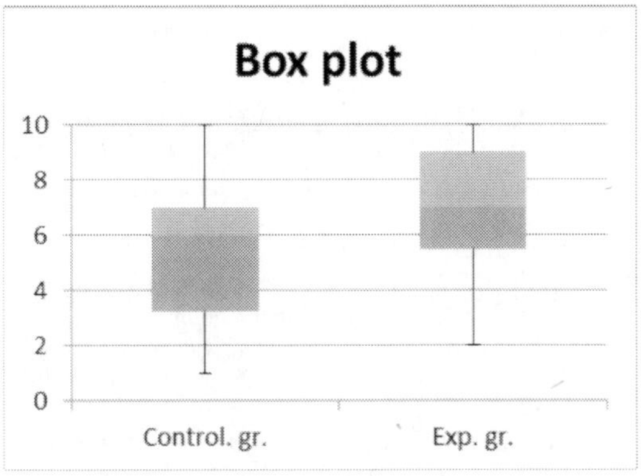

Fig. 3. Boxplot of Posttest.

In the following table the basic statistics can be seen (Table 10).

Table 10. Descriptive statistics of Post-test

Control group	
Expected value	5,600
Standard error of the mean	0,545
Median	6
Modus	6
Standard deviation	2,437
Variance	5,937
Kurtosis	-0,574
Skewness	-0,062
Minimum	1
Maximum	10
Suma	112
Total	20
Significance level (95,0%)	1,140
Experimental group	
	7,048
Expected value	0,465
Standard error of the mean	7
Median	9
Modus	2,133
Standard deviation	4,548
Variance	-0,006
Kurtosis	-0,684
Skewness	
	2
Minimum	10
Maximum	148
Suma	21
Total	0,971
Significance level (95,0%)	

For clarity, the reader can see the histogram. Table 11, 12, Figure 4, 5.

Table 11. Histogram of Post-test

Control gr.		
Points	*Frequency*	*Cumul. %*
2	2	10,00%
4	4	30,00%
6	7	65,00%
8	4	85,00%
10	3	100,00%

Table 12. Histogram of Post-test

Exp. Gr.		
Points	*Frequency*	*Cumul. %*
2	1	4,76%
4	2	14,29%
6	4	33,33%
8	8	71,43%
10	6	100,00%

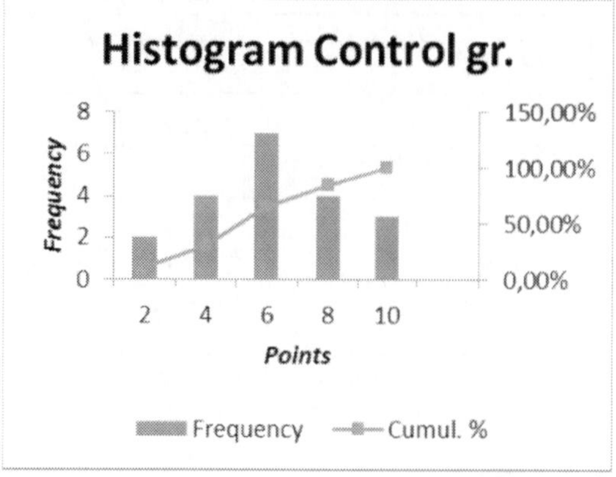

Fig. 4. Histogram of Post-test Control gr.

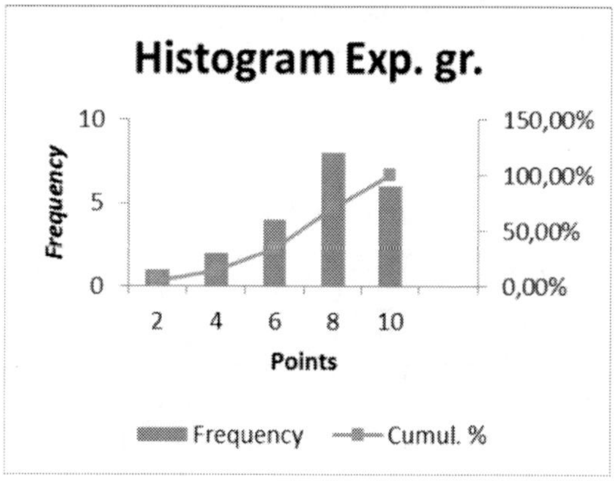

Fig. 5. Histogram of Post-test Experimental gr.

5 Conclusion

Use of CAA and system for measurement using a computer, as indicated by the research found a positive effect on the acquisition of knowledge in the Czech secondary schools. The test results of the experimental group, as shown by the Box plot, are considerably higher. The reader can find similar interesting approaches to teaching in papers [4-6]. It would certainly be interesting for future arrangement to evaluate this experiment with regard to students' approaches to learning and studying such as in [7].

ACKNOWLEDGMENT

This research work has been supported by specific research project of the University of Hradec Kralove, Faculty of Education in 2016 (No. 2142).

References

1. A. Berkova, (2014) 'Approaches To Learning And Studying In Mathematical Analysis Classes', *INTED 2014 Proceedings (8th International Technology, Education and Development Conference)*, IATED, Valencia, pp. 2978-2982.
2. R. Nemec, J. Triska, J. Sedivy. *System SMPSL*. In: The 4th NAUN International Conference on CIRCUITS, SYSTEMS, CONTROL, SIGNALS (CSCS '13). Valencia, 2013, ISBN: 978-960-474-318-6. P. 43-47.
3. Technical Whitepaper. (2015) 'Challenges and Solutions in Automated STEM Assessment', [Online], Maplesoft, a division of Waterloo Maple Inc. 2015, Available: http://www.maplesoft.com/contact/webforms/Whitepapers/STEMAssessment.aspx [15 February 2016].
4. *Maple T.A. - Web-based Testing and Assessment for Math Courses* - Maplesoft. [online]. [cit. 2016-02-26]. Available: http://www.maplesoft.com/products/mapleta.
5. R. Nemec, A Berkova, S. Hubalovsky, *The Use of Method of Multidisciplinary Approach, Modeling and Simulation in Learning of Gear Ratios*. International Journal of Mathematics and Computers in Simulation, volume 10, 2016 ISSN: 1998-0159
6. R. Nemec, A. Berkova, P. Hanzalova, (2016) '*The Connection of System SMPSL (System for measurement using a computer in the school laboratory) and CAA (Computer Aided Assessment) for Demonstration of Mathematical Modeling of Angle*'. *WSEAS Transactions on Information Science and Applications*. ISSN 1790-0832.
7. A. Berkova, J. Kulicka, (2015) '*Modelling and Simulation in Teaching of Future Teachers of Mathematics*', *ICERI 2015 Proceedings* (*8th International Conference of Education, Research and Innovation)*, IATED, Seville, pp. 7525-7533.

A time performance comparison of particle swarm optimization in mobile devices

Luis Antonio Beltrán Prieto[1,a], Zuzana Komínkova-Oplatková[1], Rubén Torres Frías[2] and Juan Luis Escoto Hernández[2]

[1]*Faculty of Applied Informatics, Department of Informatics and Artificial Intelligence, Tomas Bata University in Zlín, Nad Stráněmi 4511,76005 Zlín, Czech Republic*
[2]*Department of Systems and Computing, Technological Institute of Celaya, Av. Tecnológico y A. García Cubas S/N, 38010, Celaya, México*

Abstract. This paper deals with the comparison of three implementations of Particle Swarm Optimization (PSO), which is a powerful algorithm utilized for optimization purposes. Xamarin, a cross-platform development software, was used to build a single C# application capable of being executed on three different mobile operating systems (OS) devices, namely Android, iOS, and Windows Mobile 10, with native level performance. Seven thousand tests comprising PSO evaluations of seven benchmark functions were carried out per mobile OS. A statistical evaluation of time performance of the test set running on three similar devices –each running a different mobile OS– is presented and discussed. Our findings show that PSO running on Windows Mobile 10 and iOS devices have a better performance in computation time than in Android.

1 Introduction

The aim of this paper is to compare the performance of three implementations of a single C# mobile application which examines the Particle Swarm Optimization (PSO) algorithm running on three mobile devices, each with a different mobile operating system installed, specifically Android, iOS, and Windows Mobile 10. One thousand simulations of PSO evaluating seven benchmark functions were carried out per mobile OS, thus 21, 000 tests were performed in total. Xamarin platform made it possible to develop a single application in C# and deploy it to different mobile OS devices.

Smartphones are multitasking mobile devices in which installed applications should have an efficient use of resources, including CPU, memory, and sensors, in order to increase performance and maximize their battery life. Most of the time, if a mobile application is slow or consumes too many resources, e.g. mobile data, battery, or storage, it is either uninstalled from the mobile device or scored with a low review by the user in the mobile app store. Moreover, decision-making applications, such as travel destination recommenders and games, are may require intensive computing in order to get the best choice, or at least an optimal one. Even though most of the time a more powerful device, e.g., a server, deals with this task –giving the mobile device the assignment of only presenting the results to the user–, sometimes the mobile device requires to process information on its own, with no aid of external server. In other words, dealing with data and finding the best choice among different options are problems which mobile applications are not excluded to solve.

PSO is an optimization technique developed by Kennedy and Eberhart [1] inspired by the collective behaviour of animal groups, such as swarms of insects, in order to build a swarm of particles, i.e., a set of candidate solutions which flow through the parameter space generating trajectories driven by the best individuals. The initial population (swarm) consists of random solutions (particles) for the problem and is considered as a population of homogeneous agents which interact locally with other individuals without any central control. As a result, collective behaviour is generated, thus evolution relies on cooperation and competition among individuals through the different epochs (generations). Each particle defines trajectories in the parameter space according to a motion function which is affected by velocity, inertia, cognitive coefficient and social coefficient. The objective is to find the global best solutions by stochastic weighting of the aforementioned elements. The process is iterative until a stopping criterion is met.

Xamarin Platform is a mobile application development tool used to build native and cross-platform applications which can be deployed to Android, iOS, and Windows Mobile devices with native-level performance, native user interface, and a full access to the APIs of each platform. These applications are written once in C# language, sharing the same code across multiple mobile operating systems. Not only the business logic can be shared when building a mobile application with Xamarin, but also the user interface can be distributed by writing it either in C# or in eXtensible Application Markup

[a] Corresponding author: beltran_prieto@fai.utb.cz

Language (XAML). When deployed and tested into a specific platform, the application presents a native user interface, e.g., a Xamarin.Forms.Button is depicted as a UIButton on iOS, as an Android.Widget.Button on Android, and as a System.Windows.Controls.Button on Windows Mobile devices.

This paper is organized as follows. In the first section, a theoretical background on smartphones, particle swarm optimization, and Xamarin platform is presented. Afterwards, the methods and methodology that was used for this comparison are described. Then, evaluation results, statistical comparison and discussion are presented together. Finally, conclusions are shown at the end of the paper.

2 Background information

Smartphones are an important lifestyle device. There are almost 3.5 billion of smartphone subscriptions worldwide [2], and the trend is expected to double in size in the next lustrum. People use their smartphones on a daily basis in order to make their lives easier anytime and anywhere, for example, online purchases can be done while commuting thanks to a mobile application, thus it is not necessary to wait until a destination is reached and then use a PC. Another example of the advantages given by a smartphone is that it allows people to be communicated all the time.

Despite of the fact that smartphones are limited devices, they offer a PC user-experience, that is, they provide capabilities such as multitasking, video streaming, audio streaming, and web browsing, among others [3]. Therefore, they can be used intensively through the day while requiring a substantial usage of resources in order to work. When there are many applications working in the background, available memory can be significantly reduced. As a consequence, the smartphone's usability isn't user-friendly. In order to overcome this problem, the dispatcher, which is a privileged component of the operating system, terminates low-priority applications and frees resources until it determines that the available memory is enough to continue working. Moreover, battery life can be drained faster if there are too many programs running concurrently or if an application does not perform optimally. If a mobile app is killed by the dispatcher, it is not guaranteed that it would be properly closed as it didn't complete its lifecycle, so non-stored information will be lost and unrecoverable.

Artificial Intelligence (AI) algorithms, methods and techniques can be applied to build smart applications which delivers valid results to a user's request [4]. For instance, a geospatial analysis can be obtained by combining the use of geometric design with sensors and components from a smartphone, such as GPS, accelerometer, and camera [5]. Moreover, a deep learning neural network can perform effective human activity recognition with the aid of smartphone sensors [6]. Furthermore, Genetic Programming (GP) has been used to create a customized smartphone user-experience [7]. As can be seen, AI methods provide solutions for today's mobile world challenges.

2.1 Particle Swarm Optimization

Particle Swarm Optimization (PSO) is an example of stochastic optimization inspired by the social behaviour of animal groups [8]. Initially developed by Kennedy and Eberhart in 1995 [1], this technique has proven to be effective for neural networks weight calculation [9], business optimization [10], and parameter estimations [11]. Both behaviour and efficiency of the algorithm rely on the parameters shown in Table 1 [1]. Meta-optimization of the parameters has been used to tune them and find the best values which benefit PSO's performance in particular scenarios [12-15].

Table 1. Particle Swarm Optimization parameters.

Parameter	**Meaning**	**Typical Range** [8]
ω	Inertia weight	[0.8, 1.2]
c_1	Cognition learning rate	[0, 4]
c_2	Social learning rate	[0, 4]
N	Number of particles	[20-40]

The algorithm works as follows: First, a population of random N candidate solutions $\{x_1, x_2, ..., x_N\}$ is generated. Each individual is an N-dimensional vector (N > 1) with values within the problem bounds. Moreover, each particle contains a velocity vector v_i, which is also randomly initialized. By performing fitness evaluation, the best position at the moment, b_i, is obtained for each individual along with the best global position h_i. The iterative process starts by generating two random values, r_1, r_2, which are used to update each particle's velocity and position according to equations (1) and (2), respectively:

$$v_i = \omega v_i + c_1 r_1 (b_i - x_i) + c_2 r_2 (h_i - x_i) \quad (1)$$

$$x_i = x_i + v_i \quad (2)$$

Fitness evaluation is performed again in order to determine both the best position for each particle and the best global particle. The iterative process is repeated until a stopping criterion, such as a predetermined number of generations, is met. There are several variants of the PSO algorithm [16]. For instance, v_i in (1) is not affected by ω in the original version of the algorithm. Another variation consider the initialization of the particles as the most important element in order to improve the performance of the algorithm [17]. Opposition-based learning, a term that describes an individual's exact contrary, has also been considered as an enhanced variant of PSO which accelerates convergence [18-20] by replacing individuals which are far to the optimal solution by their opposite, which is closer in distance to the solution.

2.2 Xamarin Platform

Xamarin is a novel cross-platform mobile application development tool which can be used to build native Android, iOS and Windows applications that rely on a shared C# codebase. One of the main advantages of Xamarin is that allows developers to write an application once and deploy it to different mobile OS platforms without having to rewrite it in an completely different programming language, operating system or application programming interface (API) [21]. Even though all the platforms share similarities, such as graphical user interface (GUI) presentation, device sensors, and gestures interaction, each of them incorporates many differences, including navigation, user-experience, and fragmentation [22]. Xamarin's development of cross-platform solutions is possible mainly because of the Mono project, an open-source implementation of Microsoft's .NET Framework that can run on Linux, Windows, and Mac OS X [23] which is considered as the core of Xamarin, comprising three sets of .NET libraries: Xamarin.Mac, Xamarin.iOS, and Xamarin.Android. Xamarin.Forms (XF) allows developers to write code capable of being compiled and deployed to mobile devices, regardless of their OS. A basic XF application contains separate projects per desired target mobile platform -currently, Android, iOS, Windows Phone 8.1, Windows 8.1, and Universal Windows Platform platforms are supported [24]- plus another project which contains the common code that will be compiled and used at runtime by each specific platform together with the code contained in the project platform. Both the user-interface (UI) and the business logic (BL) can be developed in C# language, while eXtensible Application Markup Language (XAML) can also be used for the UI. On the one hand, the UI refers to the views or controls that will be shown on the device screen. On the other hand, the BL includes all the functionality of the application. It is also worth mentioning that platform-specific code can be added to the project to address key platform differences, such as screen sizes, navigation issues and push notifications, and device differences, for instance, sensors functionality, social networks interaction, and geo-location support.

3 Methods and methodology

The objective of this experiment is to evaluate the performance of an implementation of the Particle Swarm Optimization algorithm running on 3 smartphones with different mobile OS each (Android, iOS, and Windows Mobile) which evaluates 7 well-known benchmark functions for optimization (Ackley [25], Goldstein-Price [26], Rastrigin [27], Rosenbrock [28], Rotated Hyper-Ellipsoid [29], Sphere [30] and Sum Squares [31]). Table 2 provides a brief overview of the tested benchmark functions, while Table 3 outlines the relevant specifications of the 3 mobile devices [32] used for the analysis. Except for the Goldstein-Price function, which by definition operates only in a 2-dimensional space, all benchmarks were evaluated in a 10-dimensionall space

A C# version of the PSO algorithm was programmed and included in a mobile application developed with Xamarin platform using the Visual Studio Community 2015 IDE. Figure 1 shows the structure of the solution. Four projects were included in the solution. The first one, PSO, contains all the shared code. The other three, PSO.Droid, PSO.iOS, and PSOUWP represent the specific projects that were deployed to the particular mobile OS, namely Android, iOS, and Windows 10, respectively. It is worth mentioning that no code was added to the three projects due to Xamarin's code-sharing leveraging technique.

In all cases, $\omega = 0.729$, $N = 40$, $c_1 = 1.49445$, $c_2 = 1.49445$ values were used. For the benchmark functions, the search domain was set for the range indicated in Table 2. Finally, during the experiment, each mobile had neither processes working in the background nor background services and sensors active, except for the PSO mobile application developed in Xamarin and the Wi-Fi signal because the computation times were sent to an Azure SQL cloud database for further analysis.

One thousand simulations of the Particle Swarm Optimization full algorithm per benchmark function evaluation and per mobile OS were carried out, i.e., each time a new random initial population was generated and evolved in order to solve a benchmark function. Figure 2 depicts the process of a single run of the app in each device, while Figures 3 and 4 show the application being executed on Windows Mobile 10 and Android devices, respectively.

4 Results and discussion

The findings of the analysis are summarised in Table 4. A comparison of the average running time of 1000 simulations of PSO evaluating one benchmark function at a time on a mobile device is presented. The best (fastest) results in each case are marked in bold, while the worst ones are shown in italics. On the one hand, it is clearly seen that the Android device was far outperformed by both iOS and Windows Mobile 10 devices approximately two times, except for Rosenbrock and Rotated functions, in which average times are closer. On the other hand, the iOS and Windows Mobile 10 devices had similar performances in terms of time, with the latter being the fastest in 4 out of the 7 benchmark evaluations.

As iOS and Windows Mobile 10 computation times look similar, a statistical analysis can be performed to determine if there are significant differences between them. Firstly, an extended Shapiro-Wilk test [33] was conducted in order to assess the normal distribution of both samples. Table 5 and Table 6 show the findings of this test at the significance level of 0.05. The null hypothesis, H_0, in each case is set as "the computation times of a given benchmark-function evaluation on a mobile device are normally distributed".

Table 2. Tested benchmark functions.

Benchmark function	Equation	
Ackley	$$f(x) = -a\,exp\left(-b\sqrt{\frac{1}{d}\sum_{i=1}^{d} x_i^2}\right) - exp\left(\frac{1}{d}\sum_{i=1}^{d}\cos(cx_i)\right) + a + \exp(1) \quad (8)$$	
	Recommended values	a = 20, b = 0.2, c = 2π
	Global Minimum	f(x*) = 0, at x* = (0, …, 0)
	Search domain	$x_i \in [-32{,}768, 32768]$
Goldstein-Price	$$f(x) = [1 + (x_1 + x_2 + 1)^2(19 - 14x_1 + 3x_1^2 - 14x_2 + 6x_1x_2 + 3x_2^2)] \times [30 + (2x_1 - 3x_2)^2(18 - 32x_1 + 12x_1^2 + 48x_2 - 36x_1x_2 + 27x_2^2)] \quad (11)$$	
	Minimum	f(x*) = 3, at x* = (0, –1)
	Search domain	$x_i \in [-2, 2]$
Rastrigin	$$f(x) = 10d + \sum_{i=1}^{d}[x_i^2 - 10\cos(2\pi x_i)] \quad (10)$$	
	Minimum	f(x*) = 0, at x* = (0, …, 0)
	Search domain	$x_i \in [-5.12, 5.12]$
Rosenbrock	$$f(x) = \sum_{i=1}^{d-1}[100(x_{i+1} - x_i^2)^2 + (x_i - 1)^2] \quad (12)$$	
	Minimum	f(x*) = 0, at x* = (1, …, 1)
	Search domain	$x_i \in [-5, 10]$
Rotated Hyper-Ellipsoid	$$f(x) = \sum_{i=1}^{d}\sum_{j=1}^{i} x_j^2 \quad (13)$$	
	Minimum	f(x*) = 0, at x* = (0, …, 0)
	Search domain	$x_i \in [-65.536, 65.536]$
Sphere	$$f(x) = \sum_{i=1}^{d} x_i^2 \quad (13)$$	
	Minimum	f(x*) = 0, at x* = (0, …, 0)
	Search domain	$x_i \in [-5.12, 5.12]$
Sum Squares	$$f(x) = \sum_{i=1}^{d} i x_i^2 \quad (13)$$	
	Minimum	f(x*) = 0, at x* = (0, …, 0)
	Search domain	$x_i \in [-5.12, 5.12]$

*W** stands for the observed test statistic value. As can be seen, the statistical test clearly indicates that all benchmark-function evaluations on both mobile OS follow a normal distribution because our proposed null hypothesis is accepted, as $p(W^*) > 0.05$ in all cases.

Secondly, a Bartlett's test for variances homogeneity [34] can be performed. In this case, our null hypothesis, H_0, is set as "The variances of two samples of given benchmark-function evaluations running on different mobile OS devices are homogeneous".

Table 3. Relevant specifications of the smartphones used in the analysis.

Model	Brand	Mobile OS	Chipset	CPU	Memory
Lumia 930	Nokia	Windows Mobile 10	Qualcomm MSM8974 Snapdragon 800	Quad-core 2.2 GHz Krait 400	2 GB RAM
Nexus 5	LG	Android 6.0	Qualcomm MSM8974 Snapdragon 800	Quad-core 2.3 GHz Krait 400	2 GB RAM
iPhone 5s	Apple	iOS 8.4	Apple A7	Dual-core 1.3 GHz Cyclone (ARM v8)	1 GB RAM

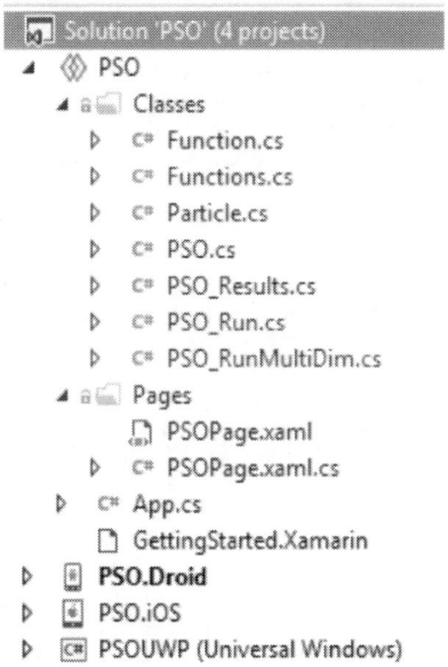

Figure 1. Solution structure of the PSO mobile application.

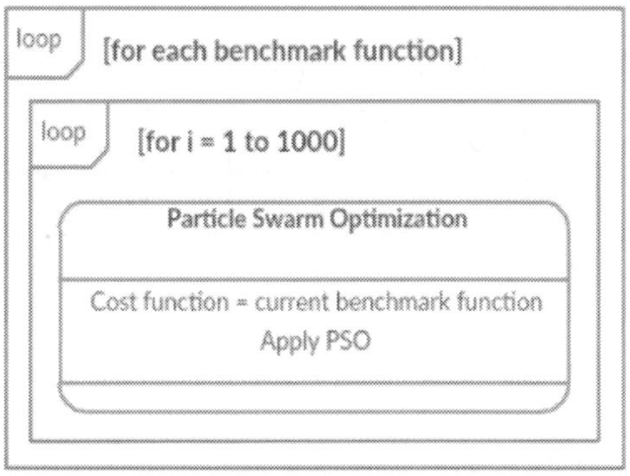

Figure 2. Solution structure of the PSO mobile application.

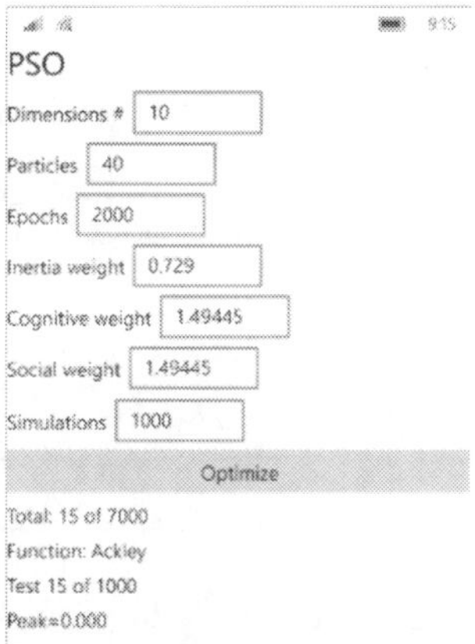

Figure 3. PSO app running on a Lumia 930.

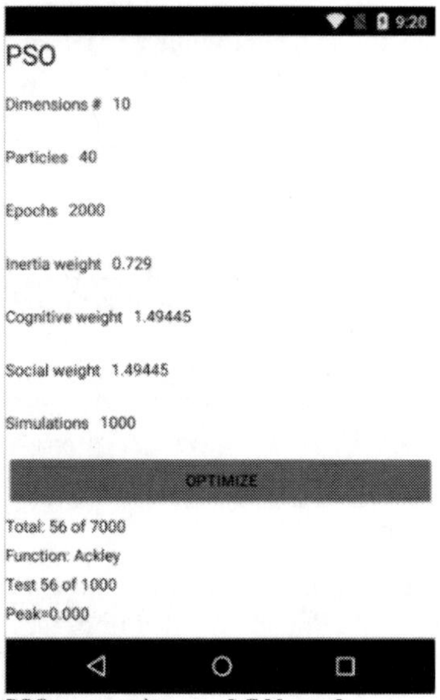

Figure 4. PSO app running on a LG Nexus 5.

Table 4. Average (mean) computation time (in miliseconds) taken by each mobile device to evaluate PSO using a benchmark function.

Benchmark Function	Android	W10	iOS
Ackley	*1496.77*	**711.696**	742.21
Goldstein-Price	*1205.98*	457.78	**432.64**
Rastrigin	*1482.86*	**685.69**	697.83
Rosenbrock	*1895.84*	**1433.79**	1452.47
Rotated	*3002.09*	2774.83	**2608.03**
Sphere	*1368.26*	**666.28**	682.59
Sum Squares	*1389.05*	617.17	**603.72**

Table 5. Shapiro-Wilk test for normal distribution of mean computation times (in miliseconds) in Windows 10 device.

Function	Mean	W*	p-value	H_0: p > 0.05?
Ackley	711.70	0.99825	0.4012	**Yes**
Goldstein-Price	457.78	0.99855	0.5887	**Yes**
Rastrigin	685.69	0.99734	0.09953	**Yes**
Rosenbrock	1433.8	0.99791	0.2471	**Yes**
Rotated	2774.8	0.99856	0.5924	**Yes**
Sphere	666.28	0.99759	0.1505	**Yes**
Sum Squares	617.17	0.997	0.05737	**Yes**

Table 6. Shapiro-Wilk test for normal distribution of mean computation times (in miliseconds) in iOS device.

Function	Mean	W*	p-value	H₀: p > 0.05?
Ackley	742.21	0.99787	0.2324	Yes
Goldstein-Price	432.64	0.99897	0.8563	Yes
Rastrigin	697.83	0.99788	0.2367	Yes
Rosenbrock	1452.47	0.99815	0.3528	Yes
Rotated	2608.03	0.99785	0.2255	Yes
Sphere	682.59	0.99769	0.1758	Yes
Sum Squares	603.72	0.99799	0.2787	Yes

For example, we want to test whether the evaluations of the Ackley function in Windows Mobile 10 have the same variance as the evaluations of the same benchmark function in iOS or not. Table 7 outlines the variances of each benchmark function per mobile device as well as the Bartlett's test at the 0.05 significance level, with one degree of freedom ($k - 1 = 1$, where k is the number of samples, in this case, 2), i.e., $\chi_{0.95,1} = 3.8414$. B^* stands for the observed test statistic value. As can be seen from the table, the test clearly indicates that all except one pair of benchmark-function evaluations on both mobile OS, namely the Rotated-function evaluation, don't have homogeneous variances because our proposed null hypothesis is rejected, as $\chi_{0.95,1} > B^*$ in 6 out of 7 cases. In other words, only the variances of the Rotated-function comparison between iOS and Windows Mobile 10 are homogeneous.

Table 7. Bartlett's test for variances homogeneity of computation times (in miliseconds).

Benchmark function	Variance W10	Variance iOS	B*	H_0: $\chi_{0.95,1} > B^*$?
Ackley	159.6535	289.12	100.99	No
Goldstein-Price	664.7554	1352.602	169.52	No
Rastrigin	311.917	218.3957	40.683	No
Rosenbrock	2477.584	5458.145	91.039	No
Rotated	1847.163	1578.721	0.48789	Yes
Sphere	348.5762	271.1668	30.404	No
Sum Squares	1310.597	1759.304	9.9097	No

In order to use the Analysis of Variance (ANOVA) statistical test between the running times in each mobile OS device, there are two assumptions for the populations: first, they have to follow a normal distribution; second, their variances have to be similar. On the one hand, the previous Shapiro-Wilk test proved that the first requirement is accomplished. On the other hand, the aforementioned Bartlett's test demonstrated that the second condition is not met, though. For that reason, a non-parametric Friedman statistical test [35] can be used to detect differences between our samples. Table 8 outlines the results of the Friedman test at the 0.05 significance level with one degree of freedom ($k - 1 = 1$, where k is the number of samples, in this case, 2). This test also relies on the chi-square critical value, i.e., $\chi_{0.95,1} = 3.8414$. Our null hypothesis, H_0, for each case is set as "there is no significant difference between Windows Mobile 10 and iOS evaluations of a given benchmark function". As shown in the previous table, the null hypothesis is certainly accepted in all evaluations, meaning that there is no significant difference between the computation times of the benchmark-function evaluations in both mobile OS.

Table 8. Friedman test for benchmark-functions running times in each mobile OS device.

Benchmark function	Q*	H_0: $\chi_{0.95,1} > Q^*$?
Ackley	0.784	Yes
Goldstein-Price	0.4	Yes
Rastrigin	0.256	Yes
Rosenbrock	0.576	Yes
Rotated	0.004	Yes
Sphere	0.016	Yes
Sum Squares	0.064	Yes

5 Conclusion

Smartphone applications require a careful management of resources in order to provide a proper user-experience. Despite of the fact that huge workloads are often assigned to servers, mobile devices are also capable of accepting time-consuming tasks which most of the time run in the background as the response time of a mobile app should be fast. In this study, we implemented Particle Swarm Optimization algorithm in order to test and compare their performance when being executed on three devices with different mobile OS, namely Android, iOS and Windows Mobile 10. Our findings show that Android got the worst performance, while a statistical analysis of iOS and Windows Mobile 10 computation times revealed that there was no significant difference between them. Future research will be focused on implementing PSO in Java and Swift, which are Android and iOS programming languages used for developing native apps respectively. Further, another statistical comparison of both the native and the C#-cross-platform current implementation in Xamarin that was shown in this paper can be done in terms of computation time and performance.

Acknowledgement

This work was supported by the Ministry of Education, Youth and Sports of the Czech Republic within the National Sustainability Programme project No. LO1303 (MSMT-7778/2014) and also by the European Regional Development Fund under the project CEBIA-Tech No. CZ.1.05/2.1.00/03.0089, further it was supported by Grant Agency of the Czech Republic—GACR 588 P103/15/06700S and by Internal Grant Agency of Tomas Bata University in Zlin under the project No. IGA/CebiaTech/2016/007.

References

1. J. Kennedy, R. C. Eberhart. *Proceedings of IEEE Int'l. Conf. on Neural Networks*, pp. 1942-1948 (1995)
2. Ericsson 2016 Mobility Report. http://www.ericsson.com/mobility-report [Online: accessed 16-Abr-2016]
3. S. Li, S. Mishra. J. of Par. and Dist. Comp., (2016)
4. R. Malaka. Workshop Notes of AIMS200, pp. 5-6 (2000)
5. S. Higuera de Frutos, M. Castro. Transp. Res. Part C Emerg. Technol. **38** (2014)
6. C. A. Ronao, S.-B. Cho. Expert Syst. Appl. **59**, pp. 235-244 (2016)
7. P. Valencia, A. Haak, A. Cotillon, R. Jurdak. Appl Soft Comput. **25** pp. 86-96 (2014)
8. X. Hu. Particle Swarm Optimization Home Page http://www.swarmintelligence.org [Online: accessed 16-May-2016]
9. M. Meissner, M. Schmuker, G. Schneider, BMC Bioinformatics **7**, 125 (2006)
10. X. S. Yang, S. Deb, S. Fong. *Proceedings of the 3rd Int'l. Conf. NDT2011*, pp. 53–66 (2011)
11. R. Susuki, F. Kawai, C. Nakazawa, T. Matsui, E. Aiyoshi. *Proceedings of SICE Annual Conf.*, pp. 1981-1988, (2008)
12. M. Schwaab, E. C. Biscaia Jr., J. L. Monteiro, J. C. Pinto. Chem. Eng. Sci. **63**, 1542–1552, (2008)
13. F. Marini, B. Walczak. J. Chemometr. **25**, 366–374, (2011)
14. A. N. Skvortsov. J. Chemometr. **28**, 727–739, (2014)
15. Q. Shen, J.-H. Jiang, C.-X. Jiao, G.-L. Shen, R.-Q. Yu. Eur. J. Pharm. Sci. **22**, 145–152, (2004)
16. M. Imran, R. Hashim, N. E. A. Khalid. Procedia Eng. **53**, 491-496, (2013)
17. N. Q. Uy, N. X. Hoai, R. McKay, P. M. Tuan. *Proceedings of IEEE C EVOL COMPUTAT*, pp. 1985-1992 (2007)
18. H. Jabeen, Z. Jalil, A.R Baig. *Proceedings of GECCO 2009*, pp. 2047- 2052 (2009)
19. M. G. H. Omran, S.al-Sharhan. *Proceedings of IEEE SIS 2008*, pp 16 (2008)
20. C. Zhang, Z. Ni, Z. Wu, L. Gu. *Proceedings of IFITA '09*. pp. 325-330 (2009)
21. C. Petzold. *Creating Mobile Apps with Xamarin.Forms. Cross-platform C# programming for iOs, Android, and Windows Phone*. (Microsoft Press, 2015)
22. S. Mansfield-Devine. Network Security, **2012**, 10, pp. 5-12 (2012)
23. Mono-Project. About Mono. http://www.mono-project.com/docs/about-mono [Online: accessed 22-Abr-2016]
24. Xamarin Inc. Xamarin + Universal Windows Platform. https://developer.xamarin.com [Online: accessed 24-Abr-2016]
25. D. H. Ackley. *A Connectionist Machine for Genetic Hillclimbing* (Kluwer Academic Publishers, 1987)
26. P. Serra, A. F. Stanton, S. Kaisb. J Chem Phys, **106** pp. 7170–7177, (1997)
27. L. A. Rastrigin. In Theoretical Foundations of Engineering Cybernetics Series (1974)
28. H. H. Rosenbrock. Comput. J., **3**, 3, pp. 175–184 (1960)
29. A. K. Qin, V. L. Huang, P. Suganthan. IEEE Trans. Evol. Computat. **13**, 2, pp. 398-417 (2009).
30. D. Simon. *Evolutionary Optimization Algorithms: Biologically Inspired and Population-Based Approaches to Computer Intelligence* (Wiley, 2013)
31. G. A. Jones, J. M. Jones. *Elementary Number Theory* (Springer SUMS, 1998)
32. GSMArena.com Finder. http://www.gsmarena.com [Online: accessed 22-Abr-2016]
33. A. C. Elliott, W. A. Woodward. *Statistical analysis quick reference guidebook with SPSS examples*. (Sage Publications, 2007)
34. M. S. Bartlett. J R Stat Soc Ser A Stat Soc. **160**, pp. 268–282 (1937)
35. M. Hollander, D. A. Wolfe. *Nonparametric Statistical Methods* (John Wiley & Sons, 1973)

Attribute Selection via a Novel Interval Based Evaluation Algorithm: Applied on Real life data sets

Mostafa A. Salama[1,a] and *Ghada* Hassan[1,b]

[1] *The British University in Egypt, Cairo, Egypt*

Abstract. Real life problems handled by machine learning deals with various forms of values in the data set attributes, like the continuous and discrete form. Discretization is an important step in the pre-processing stage as most of the attribute selection techniques assume the discreetness of the input values. This step could change the internal structure of the input attribute values with respect to the classification problem, and thus the quality of this step directly impact the quality of the selected features. This work discusses the problems existing in the current discretization techniques and proposes an attribute evaluation and selection technique to avoid these problems. Attributes are evaluated in its continuous form directly without biasing its internal structure and enhances the computational complexity by eliminating the discretization step. The basic insight of the proposed approach relies on the inverse relationship between class label distribution overlap and the relative information content of a given attribute. In order to estimate the validity of this assumption, a series of data sets were examined using several standard approaches including our own implementation, and the approaches ranked with respect to the overall classification accuracy. The results, at least with respect to the testing data sets deployed in this study, indicate that the proposed approach outperformed other methods selected for evaluation in this study. These results will be examined over a wider range of continuous attribute data sets from non-medical domains in order to investigate the robustness of these results.

1 Introduction

Attributes in real life data set have various forms that require a pre-processing stage before applying machine learning techniques. The quality of the classification techniques in machine learning and resulted accuracy is limited by the characteristics of the input attributes [1, 2]. The first characteristic is the type of the input attributes, discrete, ordinal, and continuous attributes[3]. Then the second aspect is the relevance of the input attributes to the targeted classification problem. Some attributes may contain irrelevant or redundant attributes that do not contribute to effective classification. Irrelevant attributes could have a negative effect on the resulted classification accuracy and its existence in the data set increases the effort and complexity in the machine learning technique applied [4, 5]. Attribute reduction technique is applied to select only the relevant attributes to the target class labels. Attribute selection algorithm is applied on two stages, First the attribute evaluation followed by the subset attribute subset selection. An attribute evaluation function ranks the attributes and removes the attributes that do not achieve an adequate score, while subset selection searches the set of possible attributes for an optimal subset. Most of the attribute evaluation techniques as statistical techniques have to be preceded by a discretization method. Few type of algorithms are in-dependent on the attribute selection and discretization process like for instance, genetic algorithm (GA), as it may be applied as a attribute selection wrapper to search for an optimal attribute subset for dimensionality reduction [7] [8]. But due to the high number combinations of attributes (subsets) these methods are computationally expensive in many real life cases. Some approaches integrate the attribute selection method directly into the classification pipeline. Techniques like ChiMerge attribute selection method utilize an internal discretization approach. Another method [9] tries to find the attribute ranks without discretization but this method is dependent on Information gain, which is only applicable for nominal data.

The main problem that lies in Discretization algorithms is its alteration of the internal structure of the attribute values. This can weakened the interdependency between the attribute values and the target class labels. And thus it can potentially influence subsequent classification results [6]. Discretization algorithms are either un-supervised or supervised algorithms. Un-supervised discretization is performed independently of the attribute selection and the classification tasks and performs an equal frequency or width discretization. Supervised discretization like information-gain, entropy-based, statistics based algorithms that are based on measuring the number class specific values for each attribute. Another technique like Class-Attribute Dependent Discretizer (CADD) measures

[a] e-mail: mostafa.salama@bue.edu.eg
[b] e-mail: ghada.hassan@bue.edu.eg

the dependency between each class and each interval of attribute values. Other than the descritization step is considered an extra step in the Data mining process that increases its time complexity, these techniques are considered of a high complexity cost.

This study proposes a supervised attribute evaluation technique that can be applied directly on all forms of attribute values. The purpose of this technique is to avoid the use of the discretization method in the pre-processing stage to decrease the computational complexity and to preserve the information quality. The algorithm of the attribute evaluation here is based on evaluating attributes according to number of class specific values or range of values. In other words, as the intervals of sorted attribute values related to a specific class increases as the importance of this attribute increases. The high lengths of the non-overlapped intervals for each attribute show the ability of this attribute on discriminating the classification of the instance. The discrimination power of this attribute is an evidence for the important of this attribute.

This algorithm operates on the premises that attributes are sorted, and then the number of adjacent values that have a single class label (not overlapped with other classes) is calculated. It quantizes the entire space of the class-dependent feature values into non-overlapping intervals. The resulted intervals generated by a different method from the Vector quantization method. The algorithm in this work search for the highest length regions that could exists in-between each adjacent group of points. While vector quantization divides a large set of points into groups of adjacent points; each group is represented by a centroid point as in k-means algorithm. It models the probability density function of the points? distribution. The length of the region in-between each two adjacent groups is not considered in vector quantization. This approach set the default number of intervals is three, but this number may not appropriate in some cases (data sets). Thus, the algorithm is repeated for up-to 10 intervals until the maximum classification accuracy is reached.

The approach adopted here (termed interval based attribute selection) will be compared with standard discretization based approaches such as IB, Relief Feature, ChiMerge and Information Gain. The comparison criteria will be applied by evaluating which attribute selection method yields maximal classification accuracy with the smallest number of attributes. More than ten bench mark data sets will be used in the comparison study, and the same classification techniques will be used after all the applied pre-processing techniques for fairness guarantee. The classification methods used here is Naive Bayesian Tree method, it is considered as an evaluation function for the forward attribute selection method. This method is implemented in the Weka suite of machine learning tools. The results from this study indicate that the approach adopted in this technique is superior to traditional based discretization methods in terms of the classification accuracy of standard classifiers.

The rest of this paper is organized as follows. Section 2 is a literature review on the problems existing in different attribute selection techniques and discretization techniques. Section 3 shows the proposed interval based attribute selection method. Classification results and comparisons with different attribute selection methods are illustrated in section 4. Lastly, Conclusion is discussed in section 5.

2 Literature review

Pre-processing stage include two independent steps which are the attribute discretization step and the attribute evaluation and selection step. Most of the attribute selection and machine learning techniques are performing on data in a discrete form. Several problems appears in the discretization techniques that have a direct negative effect on the classification accuracy results. First, two famous attribute evaluation techniques are demonstrated to show the dependence on the values to be in a discrete form. Then a brief discussion on the current discretization techniques and the existing problems in these techniques is provided.

2.1 Attribute evaluation techniques

The chi-Square χ^2 method measures the lack of independence between each attribute and the target class. ChiMerge or Chi2-Square is a χ^2-based discretization method [10] [11]. It uses the χ^2 statistic to discretize numeric attributes repeatedly until some inconsistencies are found in the data. Adjacent intervals with the least χ^2 values are merged together, because low χ^2 values for a pair indicates similar class distributions. This merging process proceeds recursively until all χ^2 values of all pairs exceeds a parameter *signlevel* (initially 0.5). Then repeat the previous steps with a decreasing *signlevel* until an inconsistency rate is exceeded, where two patterns are the same but classified into different categories.

The mutual information *MI* (also called cross entropy or information gain) is a widely used information theoretic measure of the stochastic dependency of discrete random variables [12] [13]. The mutual information $I(A;C)$ between values of attribute A and the set of classes C can be considered as a measure of the amount of knowledge of C provided by A (or conversely on the amount of knowledge of A provided by C). In other words $I(A;C)$ measures the interdependence between A and C as $H(C)$ - $H(C|A)$, where The entropy $H(C)$ measures the degree of uncertainty entailed by the set of classes C , and The conditional entropy $H(C|A)$ measures the degree of uncertainty entailed by the set of classes C given the set of attribute values A.

2.2 Discretization techniques

The discreteness of the input attributes is an important factor in many of the classification techniques. The nature of real life data usually has continuous spectrum of data values in the attribute vectors. Discretization method is applied by setting a set of cut points to partition the range of values into a small number of intervals. The term cut point is a real value inside a range of values that divides this range into two separate intervals. The algorithm of the discretization method has to preserve both, the information and statistical quality of the data. The information quality ensures that the internal structure of the continuous values according to the present classification problem is preserved. While the statistical quality guarantees that the number intervals is the minimum number and data values generalization is sufficient for the investigated problem. Discretization methods are either non-supervised or supervised by the target class label. The non-supervised methods divide the data values into equal range of values or into equal number of values. The number of intervals in these methods is a user defined threshold that is based on the domain problem. Example of the non-supervised methods is based on the k-mean clustering algorithm. This method randomly assigns k data values in the continuous range of values to be centers of the k intervals. The rest of the values in this range are assigned to the intervals of the nearest corresponding k-values. On the other hand, the supervised methods divide the data values based on the target class labels. The Entropy-based and chi-square based algorithms are examples of supervised partitioning. Entropy-based partitioning calculates the entropy for all the points in a range of values and selects the split point that has the lowest entropy value. The entropy value is based on the probability of the instances on both sides of the points are belonging to each class label. The ChiSquare partitioning merges two adjacent intervals of values into one interval if these intervals are independent on the target class label. Both of these two supervised discretization methods are binary splitting the continuous spectrum of data values until a splitting criterion is satisfied. The splitting criteria are dependent on user defined value based on the domain problem. A refinement stage in the discretization method is the test of the generated splits through an evaluation method. Classifiers test are applied as evaluation were the point of the minimum error rate is selected as the split point. Another way to make use of the evaluation tests is using of different discretization method and selecting the best fitting method for the domain data attributes [14, 15]. One general problem in non-supervised and supervised discretization method is the user interference during the process. The user interference could identify the number of intervals in non-supervised discretization or identify a threshold as a stopping criterion in supervised discretization. Although a default value can used for general cases, this shows inaccurate classification results in machine learning. The independence of the unsupervised techniques on the target class label leads to the loose of the internal structure of the attribute values and decreases the information quality of the data. The resulted intervals after applying the discretization method may contain values that are corresponding to different classes. This leads to ignoring several data values that could be helpful in classification accuracy results in machine learning. The interference of the target class labels in the discretization process is important to define the correct boundaries between the different data value. On the other hand, supervised methods suffers problems specific to each method. For example, the chimerge algorithm tests each adjacent interval only before deciding the interval merge and ignores the other surrounding intervals. This could leads to the formation of large intervals that do not correctly represent the correct class-based structure of the data distribution. Another example is the information entropy algorithm that tests each value in all the existing attributes, and iteratively does this test several times until the stopping condition is reached. On the other hand, Class-Attribute Dependent Discretizer (CADD) measures the estimated joint probability of the event that a value belongs to a particular class and a particular range of values. These algorithms are relatively expensive, as number of values of attributes in real life problems is very high. Another general problem is that the addition of extra step in the pre-processing stage, which is discretization, increases the effort in the machine learning process. It is required to decrease the number of steps in the machine learning techniques in order to easily identify the problem behind the classification accuracy error.

3 Interval based attribute selection technique

3.1 Discrimination concept

The interval based (I.B.) attribute selection technique developed in this work is an attribute evaluation techniques that does not require a preceding discretization technique. The technique evaluates each attribute separately and uses the target class labels for evaluating the discrimination power of this attribute. The algorithm of this technique works for discrete and continuous values equally, as it considers the range of the values in the attribute even if this range contains a single value. The proposed technique is based on a concept that is implemented by supervised attribute discretization and evaluation algorithms as shown here in sections 2. Theoretically, this concept states that if a specific attribute value appears for only a single target class label, then this value discriminates the class of the containing instance. And as the discriminating value increases in an attribute, then the value of this attribute increases. Discretization methods group the adjacent discriminating continuous values together in a single partition or interval. And also group the adjacent class independent values in a single interval. This concept is implemented in various techniques and proved practically in different areas. The proposed technique uses this concept in an evaluation technique that is applied directly on the continuous values, and avoids the drawbacks of the currently evaluation techniques. Accordingly, the applied algorithm in this technique sorts the values in each attribute and detects the intervals where the values appears in a single class and the intervals that contains and intersection between classes. As the intersection between attribute value ranges of different class labels decreases as the importance of this attribute increases.

The rationale for this approach is that if an attribute has a certain continuous range of values which appears only in the case of a specific class label, then this attribute is necessary as it provides required information for the given class label. Further, the length of the range of values increases in proportion to the information content, this content is in terms of the classification accuracy. In order to clarify the applied concept in this technique, figure 1 shows the range of sorted values of a single attribute. This example assumes the existence of three classes in the problem, and the range of values corresponding to each class label is as shown in the figure. In this figure, the dashed areas show the ranges of values that are not overlapped between multiple classes; only a single class label is assigned to this label. As the length of this dashed area increases as the importance of this attribute increases. These non-overlapped intervals are summed, and the rank of the attribute is the resulted sum relative to the total interval of values of this attribute.

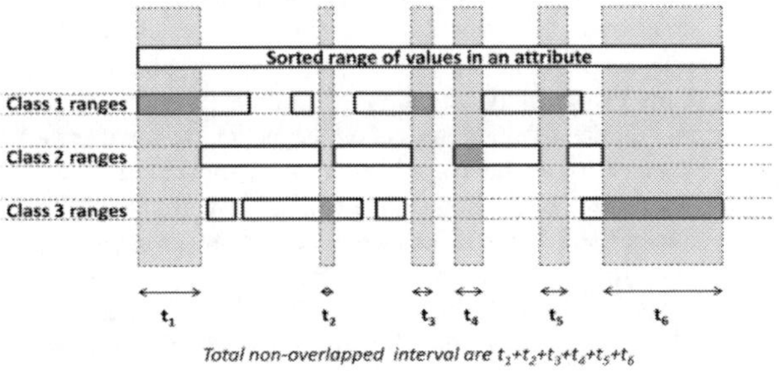

Figure 1. The non-overlapped intervals of an attribute categorized into three classes example

Equation 1 shows mathematically the evaluation of an attribute a based on calculated non-overlapped as shown in figure 1. In this equation, the μ value represents the evaluation of the attributes and it is measured for every attribute in the input data set.

$$\mu_a = \frac{1}{max_a - min_a} * \sum_{i \in I_n} t_i \quad (1)$$

μ_a represents the rank of attribute a;
max_a is the maximum value of the attribute a;
min_a is the minimum value of the attribute a;
I_n is set of non-overlapped intervals;
t_i is the length of non-overlapped interval i in I_n;
Theoretically, as the number of discriminating values in the attribute increases, as the attribute importance to the classification problem increases. It is clear in equation 1 that μ value is directly proportional to number of values lies in each class solely. The division by the total length of values of the attribute is for the normalization of the resulted value. This step standardizes the attribute rank to guarantee the fairness in the comparison to the other attributes ranks.

3.2 Algorithm implemented

Algorithm 1 formalizes the steps of evaluating a single attribute a by calculating μ_a in equation 1. This algorithm is applied on every attribute in the data set, and the attributes of the highest μ is selected based on the forward feature selection algorithm. The number of the intervals in an attribute is referred to as d. This number is directly proportional to the number of values in the attribute. The factor of proportionality is a user defined value. The number of attribute' intervals of the example in figure 1 is four. For simplicity, the value d is an input in algorithm 1.

Assume the number of intervals for each class is d
μ_a : Attribute a's rank, initial value is 0
l_a: length of range of values in attribute a, i.e. max_a-min_a
x_a and n_a : max and min values of attribute a
for Each Class label c **do**
  Sort values of attribute a corresponding to class c in an ascending order
  n_c :number of values in attribute a corresponding to class c, a_c
  Create array $D[n_c]$: array of difference between each value a_c and the previous value in the sorted list of values of attribute a
  Search and locate the maximum d values in array $D[n_c]$
  Create a two dimensional array $R_c[d, 2]$, each of d pairs of values $[s,e]$
  Where s and e are the located values containing the maximum value in array $D[n_c]$
end for
Sort values of attribute a in an ascending order
$t = 0$: non-overlapped interval
for Each Class label c **do**
  for Each interval $[s,e]$ in array $R_c[d,2]$ do **do**
    Find interval $[s_i,e_i]$ that has no intersection with other intervals in the rest of the class labels
    $t = t + (e_i - s_i)$
  end for
end for
$\mu_a = t/l$
return μ_a

Algorithm 1: Calculate Interval based rank μ_a of attribute a

The removal of misleading values in Algorithm 2 is an optional step as the accuracy depends on the collection methodologies. This step decreases the sensitivity to outliers by removing the values that are farthest away from the average value of the attribute values. This step should remove only a small percentage of the values in the attribute in order to ensure maximization of the overall classification accuracy.

Finally, the proposed technique sorts the attributes according to their μ value in a descending order, and select the best attributes using forward feature selection algorithm.

Input : *Inteval* values of an attribute a for objects lies in class c
Output : avg average of the values of an attribute a in a class c
for $x * IntervalLength$ values **do**
Remove the value of max difference from the average avg .
end for
Algorithm 2: Remove percentage x of misleading

3.3 Comparison to other attributes evaluation methods

It is well established that the classification accuracy increases as the number of selected attributes increases up to a point [2]. In many instances, including additional attributes may actually reduce the overall classification accuracy [17]. This behavior is depicted in figure 2.

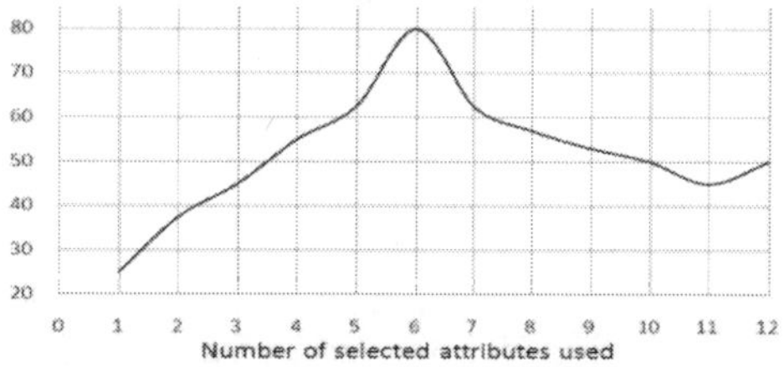

Figure 2. Classification accuracy versus the number of selected attributes

One explanation for the lack of a linear dependence of attribute number and classification accuracy is that certain attributes possess conflicting information with respect to the decision classes. Further, when the attributes of highest rank (relevance) are used the classification accuracy increases while the correlated or non-informative attributes can behave like noise in the data, thereby degrading classifier performance. In this work, the behavior of the attribute selection approach is examined in order to determine whether this non-linear relationship between attribute cardinality and classification accuracy exists across a set of three attribute selection methods. It should be noted that from an operational perspective, the best attribute selection method should adhere to the following criteria:

- The peak (maximum accuracy) is reached with the smallest number of attribute.
- The peak is of the highest value among other attribute evaluation methods.

The comparison will be validated by multiple training and testing runs. Further, initially, the data set will contain only the most relevant attribute (as determined empirically through the various comparative approaches), followed by the inclusion of the other lower ranked attributes until all have been included. This method could be considered as a semi-wrapper method as the evaluation will be applied only on a certain subset of attributes. The wrapper-based approaches employ an induction classifier as a black box using cross-validation or bootstrap techniques. Other related approaches include the deployment of genetic algorithm to evaluate the attribute subset candidates [8]. This approach has issues with respect to the high computational costs, and also has the added difficulty of not dealing with data sets containing continuous attributes. Therefore, in this work, three different classifiers will be applied: a Naive Bayesian Tree, a support vector machine and multi-layer perceptron (both via Weka implementations). Both have been extensively used as classification tools with a great deal of success from object recognition. The attribute selection methods used are Chi-merge, gain ration, and information gain attribute selection methods.

4 Experimental results and discussion

4.1 Practical Evaluation of the Interval Based Feature Evaluation

Two criteria will be used to evaluate the proposed interval based feature evaluation technique. The first criterion is the classification accuracy percentage of the selected attributes. The second criterion, in case the same classification accuracy is resulted from the usage two different feature evaluation technique, the number of selected features is considered as a discrimination factor. The feature evaluation technique that leads to the lowest number of features is considered better than the others.
Seven different benchmark data sets are used to compare the proposed technique to three other different techniques. The data sets are representing real life problems from different domains. Each contains a number of continuous valued attributes which are typically discretized when analyzed [16]. Further, these data sets are realistic in other ways, in that they typically do not possess specific distribution (at least one is not required typically for analysis) of values and may contain misleading and/or missing values, due to an error in calibrations or collection of data. The used data sets are obtained from the UCI machine learning repository [18] which are parkinsons, sonar, ringnorm, bupa, Hebatitis, NSLKDD, Thrombosis, wdbc, and ionosphere data sets. The number of features and the number of instances in each data set are as following respectively, parkinsons 96 22, sonar 208, 60, ringnorm 7400, 20, bupa 288, 6, Hebatitis 66, 19, wdbc 424, 30, NSLKDD 2000, 15, and Ionosphere 250, 34. The used feature evaluation techniques used in this experimental study are the ReliefF, the ChiMerge and the InfoGain techniques. Forward feature selection algorithm is used for the selection of the lowest number of feature that leads to the highest classification accuracy percentage. Finally, Naive Bayesian Tree classification method is used as the evaluation function. The classification accuracy was calculated by dividing the number of correctly classified objects divided by the total number of objects in the testing data set. 10-fold training and testing of the input data set method is used to generate a consistent classification accuracy percentage results. Also, in order to ensure the

Table 1. Classification accuracy and number of features comparison, d=3

Data set	IBFE	ReliefF	ChiMrg	InfoGain
parkinsons	94.79 19	94.79 20	93.75 2	92.70 3
sonar	81.73 25	81.25 6	80.28 14	79.80 17
ringnorm	97.70 20	97.62 19	97.51 19	97.22 19
bupa	67.36 4	62.5 4	56.25 5	56.25 5
Hebatitis	66.66 1	65.15 1	65.15 1	65.15 1
NSLKDD	90.2 13	89.55 14	89.60 13	89.35 15
Thrombosis	44.11 1	44.11 2	44.11 2	44.11 2
wdbc	95.04 12	96.46 4	94.81 16	94.81 16
ionosphere	90.4 21	91.2 7	89.2 2	89.6 3

fairness of the test, instances are divided equally into two class labels. An important note to be discussed later in this practical evaluation of the model is number of intervals. The number of intervals for all the data sets used in table 1 is three intervals only. This table shows for each data set the classification accuracy after feature selection, and the number of selected features below. For example, when using the IBFE feature selection technique on the parkinsons data set, the classification accuracy is 94.79% and the number of selected features are 19.

For some data sets like HS_AS_MR and HS_AR_MS in [19], the usage of three intervals only may be too small to lead to high classification accuracy percentages. In case of using six intervals $d = 6$ in algorithm 1 for the HS_AS_MR and HS_AR_MS data sets, the classification accuracy shows a higher percentages than in case of using three intervals only and than the other 'compared to' feature evaluation techniques. Figure 3 shows how the classification accuracy and number of selected features varies according to the used number of intervals. This figure shows that the lowest number of feature and the highest classification accuracy is reached when the number of intervals is 6 intervals.
Also in case of an increasing value d for the indian-diabetes data sets from [18], the classification accuracy shows a similar output like other feature evaluation techniques, but the number of features decreased from 8 to 7 features only. The number of features and the number of instances of data sets are HS_AS_MR 100, 74, HS_AR_MS 100, 74 and indian-diabetes 8, 536. Table 2 shows the results of the classification accuracy and the corresponding number of features # that leads to the highest classification accuracy.

Table 2. Classification accuracy and number of features comparison, d>3

Data set	IBFE	ReliefF	ChiMrg	InfoGain
HS_AS_MR	94.59 13	93.24 4	93.24 11	91.89 5
HS_AR_MS	86.48 69	86.48 8	83.78 15	86.48 7
Indian-diabetes	77.79 7	77.79 8	77.79 8	77.79 8

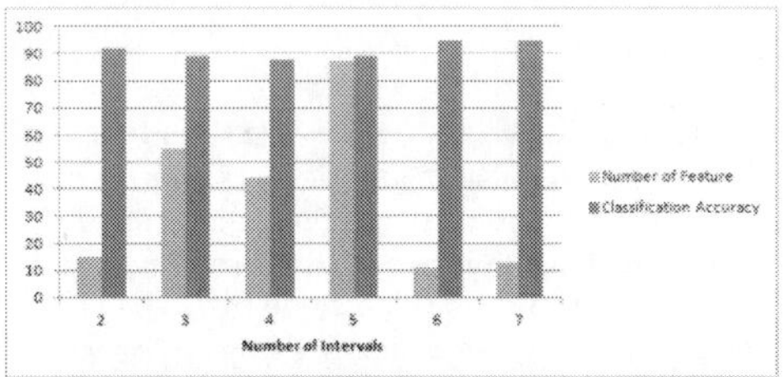

Figure 3. The variation of the classification accuracy and number of selected features according to the number of intervals

Finally, another test is applied for other classification techniques, like SVM for Support Vector Machine, mlp for Mult-Layer Perceptron and j48 for Decision Tree. The resulted classification accuracy for svm and mlp is the same as the other feature evaluation technique. But it is noticed that the classification accuracy of j48 after selecting features using the proposed evaluation technique is lower than the ReliefF, chimerge and InfoGain techniques. After increasing the number of intervals, the accuracy percentage after applying the proposed techniques is higher than the other techniques. The reason of such behavior can be justified based on the characteristics of the Decision Tree. The input attributes to the Decision Tree should be in a discretized form. As the discreteness of the values in the attribute increases, as the number of intervals should increases. And Dealing with the attribute values as continuous using the interval based evaluation method could decrease the quality of the Decision Tree classifier.

5 Conclusion

Most of the attribute evaluation techniques depend on the assumption the input data set is in a discrete form. The application of discretization method preceding the evaluation technique is crucial in these cases. If the discretization method is avoided, the alteration of the internal structure resulted from this method and the extra pre-processing are avoided.The results from this study support this general claim echoed loudly across the data mining community at large. The approach developed in this work relies on calculating the number of adjacent values that are class specific. The approach was compared with known attribute reduction methods and classifiers. The performance was evaluated with respect to the classification accuracy and as a function of the number of selected attributes. The approach was applied to a set of 12 publicly available data sets from different domains. The results demonstrate that the proposed attribute selection scheme was superior to the other approaches, regardless of the classifier deployed. After applying the proposed feature evaluation selection, the classification accuracy percentages are high and the numbers of feature are low in comparison the usage of the other feature evaluation techniques. These results were clearly present across all the twelve data sets. This provides a wide range of very diverse data sets that contain a variety of levels of sparseness and mixtures of ordinal, discrete, and continuous data sets.

References

[1] Michael K. Ismail, Vic Ciesielski, An Empirical Investigation of the Impact of Discretization on Common Data Distributions, Proceedings of the Third International Conference on Hybrid Intelligent Systems (HIS 03), pp. 692-701, 2003.

[2] Andreas G. K. Janecek and Wilfried N. Gansterer and Michael A. Demel and Gerhard F. Ecker, On the Relationship Between Feature Selection and Classification Accuracy, JMLR: Workshop and Conference Proceedings, vol.4, pp. 90–105, 2008.

[3] Manuel Mejia-Lavalle, Guillermo Rodriguez, Feature Selection with Interactions for Continuous Attributes and Discrete Class, Proceeding CERMA 07 Proceedings of the Electronics, Robotics and Automotive Mechanics Conference, pp. 318-323, 2007.

[4] Mostafa A. Salama and Aboul Ella Hassanien and Aly A. Fahmy, Pattern-based Subspace Classification Model, Proceedings of The Second World Congress on Nature and Biologically Inspired Computing, IEEE Xplore Digital Library, Kitakyushum, pp. 357-362, Dec. 2010.

[5] Mithun Nagendra Prasad and Arcot Sowmya and Inge Koch, Designing Relevant Features for Continuous Data Sets Using ICA, International Journal of Computational Intelligence and Applications, vol. 7, pp. 447-468, 2008.

[6] Huan Liu and Rudy Setiono, Feature Selection via Discretization, IEEE Transactions on Knowledge and Data Engineering, vol. 9, pp. 642-645, Aug. 1997.

[7] Khan, A., and Revett, K., Data mining the PIMA dataset using rough set theory with a special emphasis on rule reduction, bookIEEE International Multitopic Conference (INMIC 2004), Islamabad, Pakistan, pp. 334-338, 2004.

[8] Chi-ho Tsang and Sam Kwong and Hanli Wang, Genetic-fuzzy rule mining approach and evaluation of feature selection techniques for anomaly intrusion detection, Pattern Recognition, vol. 40, pp. 2373-2391, 2007.

[9] Manuel Mejda-lavalle and Eduardo F. Morales and Gustavo Arroyo, Two Simple and Effective Feature Selection Methods for Continuous Attributes with Discrete Multi-class, bookMexican International Conference on Artificial Intelligence, pp. 452-461, 2007.

[10] Huan Liu and Rudy Setiono, Chi2: Feature Selection and Discretization of Numeric Attributes, bookInternational Conference on Tools with Artificial Intelligence, Virginia, USA, pp. 388-392, 1995.

[11] Abdelwadood Moh'd, Chi Square attribute Extraction Based Svms Arabic Language Text Categorization System, Journal of Computer Science, vol.3, pp. 430-435, 2007

[12] Hanchuan Peng and Fuhui Long and Chris Ding, Feature selection based on mutual information: criteria of max-dependency, max-relevance, and min-redundancy, bookIEEE Transactions on Pattern Analysis and Machine Intelligence, vol. 27, pp. 1226-1238, 2005.

[13] Jin-Jie Huang and Yun-Ze Cai and Xiao-Ming Xu, A parameterless attribute ranking algorithm based on MI, bookNeurocomputing, vol.71, pp. 1656-1668, 2008.

[14] Sotiris Kotsiantis, Dimitris Kanellopoulos, Discretization Techniques: A recent survey, GESTS International Transactions on Computer Science and Engineering, Vol.32 (1), pp. 47-58, 2006.

[15] Rajashree Dash, Rajib Lochan Paramguru, Rasmita Dash, Comparative Analysis of Supervised and Unsupervised Discretization Techniques, International Journal of Advances in Science and Technology, Vol. 2, No. 3, 2011.

[16] K. Revett, M.S. Szczuka, P. Jahankhani, and V. Kodogiannis, Attribute Selection for EEG Signal Classification Using Rough Sets and Neural Networks, bookThe 5th International Conference Rough Sets and Current Trends in Computing (RSCTC 2006), Kobe, Japan, pp. 408-417, 2006.

[17] Mostafa A. Salama, Abol Ellah Hassanien, Aly E. Fahmy, Pattern-based Subspace Classification Model, Proceeding of the second World Congress on Nature and Biologically Inspired Computing (NaBIC), Kitakyushum, Japan, pp. 357-362, Dec. 2010.

[18] UCI, Machine Learning Repository, http://archive.ics.uci.edu/ml/datasets.html.

[19] Maglogiannis I, Loukis E, Zaropoulos E and Stasis A., Support vectors machine-based identication of heart valve diseases using heart sounds. Comput. Methods Programs Biomed, pp. 47-61, Mar 6. 2009 .

[20] Tamilarasan, A., S. Mukkamala, A.H. Sung and K. Yendrapalli, Feature Ranking and Selection for Intrusion Detection Using Artificial Neural Networks and Statistical Methods, Proceedings of the International Joint Conference on Neural Networks, pp. 4754-4761, 2006.

MATEC Web of Conferences 76, 04031 (2016) DOI: 10.1051/matecconf/20167604031
CSCC 2016

Comparison of tracking algorithms implemented in OpenCV

Peter Janku[1,a], Karel Koplik[2], Tomas Dulik[1], and Istvan Szabo[3]

[1] *Tomas Bata University in Zlin, Faculty of Applied Informatics, Nad Stranemi 4511, 760 05 Zlin*
[2] *Brno University of Technology, Faculty of Information Technology, Bozetechova 2, 612 66 Brno*
[3] *UNIS, a.s., Jundrovská 33, 624 00 Brno, Czech Republic*

Abstract. Computer vision is very progressive and modern part of computer science. From scientific point of view, theoretical aspects of computer vision algorithms prevail in many papers and publications. The underlying theory is really important, but on the other hand, the final implementation of an algorithm significantly affects its performance and robustness. For this reason, this paper tries to compare real implementation of tracking algorithms (one part of computer vision problem), which can be found in the very popular library OpenCV. Moreover, the possibilities of optimizations are discussed.

1 Introduction

The problem of object tracking is an important area of computer vision. Tracking algorithms can be used for various applications like traffic control and analysis, face and full-body person recognition, image matching etc. Although methods of object tracking has been studied for decades and many algorithms were developed, the current state of the art is far from having a perfect, universal solution for every use case. Because of enormous set of variables, parameters and environments (background, illumination, characteristics of the tracked objects, etc.), it is nearly impossible to develop universal tracking algorithm. [1, 12, 15]

Moreover, the selection of proper algorithm depends not only on the algorithm principle, but also on its implementation. Programming language, compiler and manual optimization can significantly affect the performance and robustness of the algorithm. For this reason, we decided to carry out an analysis of pre-implemented tracking algorithms available in OpenCV library.

The OpenCV is a well known library, which integrates necessary structures and tools for computer vision algorithms; in addition, it integrates large set of different pre-implemented algorithms solving different parts of object tracking problem. Moreover, different optimization methods including parallel programming, GPU computing etc. can be used for tuning the selected algorithm performance. [17]

This paper tries to bring a comparison of tracking algorithms implementations, which are included in the OpenCV library. Moreover, basic principles of presented algorithms and optimizations are discussed.

[a] Corresponding author: janku@fai.utb.cz

2 Algorithms description

While tracking is a very common computer-vision problem and OpenCV is a widely used C++ computer-vision library, sadly, only few algorithms are available in the library. For our testing, we have used three feature detectors, three pure trackers and one complex tracking framework.

2.1 Feature detectors

Feature detectors are not really trackers, they only try to detect a specified object in each frame individually. It works like this: we have two images, one is an image of the object we want to track and the other is the first frame of a video or frame obtained from live stream. We can obtain the first image from the second image by making rectangular selection.

Feature detectors then try to detect some features in the object image and try to find the best mapping of these features in the current frame. This works very well if the object image is large enough and the object itself has detectable features such as edges and texture. The object can be even freely rotated in the frame plane or slightly rotated in other planes while facing approximately the same direction. In OpenCV, we use functions *findHomography()* to find the transform between matched keypoints and function *perspectiveTransform()* to map the points. We have used a slightly improved code from OpenCV documentation example [6] to test feature detectors in the role of tracker.

The reason why we cannot say feature detectors are really trackers is their inconsistency between frames. Trackers follow trajectory, detectors only detect the best match for two images which leads to them being very unstable, especially when mistaking the tracked object for something at the moment more similar to the originally defined object.

The other problem with mere detectors could occur when tracked object is the same as one or more objects in the picture or is a part of repeating structure (e.g. windows, fences, etc.). This can become a problem with tracking in general but it can be helped by focusing on object's location. A this is were the trackers come in.

In OpenCV, there are currently three useful feature detectors: SURF [4], SIFT [2] and ORB [7]. The first two use floating point numbers but are patented. The third one uses integers and is therefore less precise but is faster and has more friendly licence. The basic concepts of SIFT and SURF algorithms and their usage with OpenCV implementation can be found in [5] and [3].

2.2 Pure trackers

For better distinction between this and the following subsection, we will use the term *pure trackers* for trackers which only do tracking and nothing else. Trackers are designed to track the object by following its trajectory and predicting its future locations. This includes correcting an error in the process.

The major problem with *pure trackers* is that they run into difficulties when the camera moves too fast or the object suddenly changes speed or direction. In that case, they may try to detect the object in more predictable location and find something similar instead.

In OpenCV, there are currently three useful pure trackers: MIL [8], Boosting [10] and MedianFlow [9].

2.3 Tracking frameworks

Tracking frameworks are algorithms which attempt to provide the most complex solution for the tracking task at hand. They can be considered as ready-to-use products. They are designed to overcome major tracking problems by constantly adapting to new conditions and correcting all crucial errors. Their disadvantage is bigger memory and processing power consumption, but this is the price to pay for all their advantages.

In OpenCV, there is currently one useful tracking framework: TLD. This algorithm is divided into three mostly independent parts - Tracking - Learning - Detecting. The tracker tries to track a blob of pixels from one frame to another. The detector tries to find similar observed object and correct tracker if necessary, and the learning estimates the detectors errors and updates it in order to avoid errors in future. Thanks to this, TLD can provide stable tracking in long term. Additionally, it is able to adapt to tracked blob changes. [11, 16]

Three basic parts of TLD can run simultaneously, each on separate processor and/or as a separate task. Moreover, each part can be optimized (parallelized) separately due to its character. [11, 16]

Table 1. List of Problems

Abbr.	Name	Description
IV	Illumination Variation	The illumination in the target region is significantly changed.
SV	Scale Variation	The ratio of the bounding boxes of the first frame and the current frame is out of the range.
OCC	Occlusion	The target is partially or fully occluded.
DEF	Deformation	Non-rigid object deformation.
MB	Motion Blur	The target region is blurred due to the motion of target or camera.
FM	Fast Motion	The motion of the ground truth is larger than limit.
IPR	In-Plane Rotation	The target rotates in the image plane.
OPR	Out-of-Plane Rotation	The target rotates out of the image plane.
OV	Out-of-View	Some portion of the target leaves the view.
BC	Background Clutters	The background near the target has the similar color or texture as the target.
LR	Low Resolution	The number of pixels inside the ground-truth bounding box is below limit.

3 Measurement methods

As it was already stated before in similar papers (e.g. [12], [13]), doing a complex comparison of tracking algorithms can be rather tricky. The main reason for that is that tracking itself can be used for many different purposes (tracking faces, people, vehicles etc.) in many different environments and situations (airport, inside a building, roads, nature, fog, day / night, etc.) while the cameras can be of low / high quality, near / far, colour / grey-scale, moving / stabilized and so on. What's more, tracking itself consists of overcoming different types of problems such as rotation or partial occlusion of tracked object, changing light conditions, blurred frame due to a fast camera movement, etc. The above stated means that a very large dataset is needed. Fortunately, Yi Wu et al. already managed to collect most commonly used testing videos and offer it freely with annotations [14]. In [12], they use this dataset to test tracking algorithms which are available with source code. Each video in the dataset has been described by listing major problems which has to be dealt with when implementing a good tracking algorithm. We include their problem definitions in Table 1 [12].

3.1 Success evaluation

In each video we had used the following formula for each frame: $C_{suc}(f) = \frac{|r_t \cap r_g|}{|r_t \cup r_g|}$ where $C_{suc}(f)$ is a success criterion function for frame f; r_t is bounding rectangle returned from tracker and r_g is the bounding rectangle provided by ground truth. We basically take the area of the interception and divide it by the area of the union of above defined rectangles. This will give as the overlapping ratio which is be considered a success when larger than 0.5. [12]

3.2 Precision evaluation

As a measure of algorithm precision, we decided to use the scale of rectangle obtained from the tracker considering the ground truth while the best precision is equal to 1 if we use this formula: $C_{prec}(f) = \frac{|r_t|}{|r_g|}$ where $C_{prec}(f)$ is the precision criterion function for the currently processed frame f.

3.3 Time demands evaluation

To objectively measure time demands of each algorithm, we propose to simply measure time for each frame: $C_{tim}(f) = t$ where $C_{tim}(f)$ is the algorithm time demands criterion function; t is the time it took to process the current frame f.

3.4 Performance evaluation

How did algorithms performed while facing each of the problems defined in Table 1 was evaluated in the same way as with the $C_{suc}(f)$ (see above) but only with relevant videos.

3.5 Difficulties

A few issues had to be resolved before collecting and processing data. The initial idea was to compare how much do the bounding rectangle provided by the tracker and the ground truth bounding rectangle overlap while also measuring the processing time. The first problem was that sometimes the tracker rejects the object from the ground truth when being initialized or completely looses the object during tracking. Since each frame produces data, even when tracking unsuccessfully, it can then imply the tracker was not able to deal with all tracking problems in the currently processed video. Typically, during benchmarking this is fixed by triggering reinitialization after a few failed frames. We decided to set retrigger threshold at 30 failed frames. This may mean that some trackers will appear more effective (the ground truth should not be available) but, as we supposed, 30 frames were enough to substantially penalize them. Other problems were discovered when trackers on very rare occasions behaved unpredictably and the output data were out of expected boundaries. Sometimes, it took several seconds to process a relatively small frame or the object turned out to supposedly cover almost whole frame while the ground truth bounding rectangle was much smaller. Such output was reclassified as failure and the data were constricted so they could both serve as score penalty and reasonable statistical record.

4 Results

In this section, we are going to discuss all of the benchmarking results. With great advantage, we used box-and-whisker type of charts to compare algorithms with each other, because this type of chart allows us to nicely compare the acquired data. The box represents the range of 50% of results. Inside each box, the horizontal line depicts the middle value, and the bottom-most and top-most lines are minimum and maximum values.

4.1 Success

In each video, we had counted number of frames which had results within the defined limits ($C_{suc}(f) \geq 0.5 \wedge C_{scale}(f) < 2.0 \wedge t(f) < 1$) and divided this number by the total number of frames. Surprisingly, TLD did not turn out to be the best algorithm (see Figure 1) despite being so complex.

There may be two reasons for this. The first one may be, that algorithms MIL and Boosting, categorized by us as *pure trackers*, were more successful due to reinitialization from the ground truth. The second reason could be, that TLD is so heavily correcting itself, that the bounding rectangle in each frame shifts a lot and therefore does not follow the ground truth bounding rectangle so nicely (the intersection is often less then 50%). It doesn't mean that TLD looses the object, the opposite is true, but it fails to center the object in its bounding rectangle.

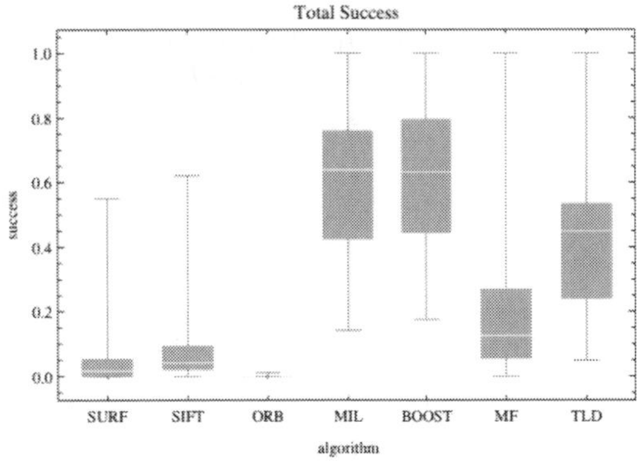

Figure 1. Total success chart

4.2 Precision

To measure precision of each algorithm, we decided to use the scale ratio. If the object is located precisely, the bounding rectangle dimensions should be more similar to the ground truth than if it is not. For this criterion, we had eliminated all the unsuccessful data, which means that the maximal acceptable scale ratio was 2. As you can see at Figure 2, all algorithms had their extreme values bellow this upper limit and above the lower limit, which was, off course, 0. To tell which algorithm did well according to this criterion, we need to look how close is their middle value to 1.0 and how small is the range between their minimal and maximal values.

 DOI: 10.1051/matecconf/20167604031

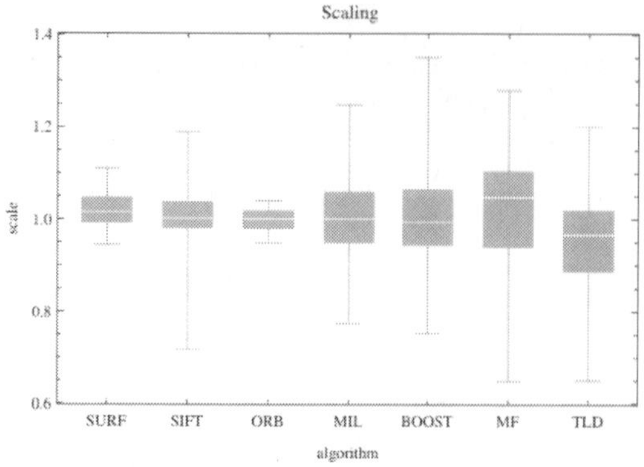

Figure 2. Scale chart

4.3 Time demands

For this criterion, we had measured the time each algorithm needs for processing a single frame. It was necessary to eliminate very short but also very long times because the box-and-whisker chart would be too stretched towards the extremes. You can see at Figure 3 that SIFT and SURF are very slow. That's because they work with floating point values and their inner calculations take more time. The rest of the algorithms are faster, while the slowest one is TLD. Slowness of the TLD algorithm is caused by its relative robustness and lack of optimizations of its OpenCV implementation.

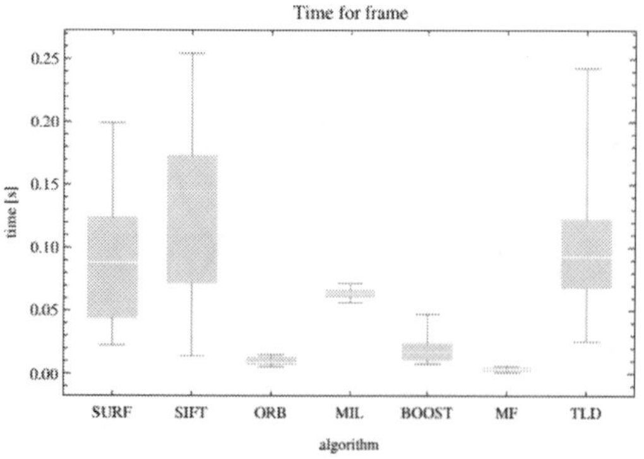

Figure 3. Time demands chart

4.4 Performance

In this section, we present results for each algorithm's performance when dealing with major tracking problems. As shown at Figure 4, the algorithms' success was not so different from their total success. To have a better overview, the Table 2 also shows the average success for each algorithm and problem.

Table 2. Problems' success table

	SURF	SIFT	ORB	MIL	BOOST	MF	TLD
IV	0.057	0.065	0.000	0.644	0.596	0.138	0.372
SV	0.076	0.089	0.001	0.549	0.559	0.218	0.409
OCC	0.051	0.068	0.000	0.572	0.586	0.185	0.400
DEF	0.023	0.044	0.000	0.616	0.596	0.146	0.388
MB	0.099	0.075	0.001	0.521	0.560	0.114	0.425
FM	0.083	0.086	0.001	0.506	0.521	0.165	0.394
IPR	0.064	0.079	0.001	0.500	0.567	0.206	0.366
OPR	0.053	0.060	0.001	0.562	0.585	0.231	0.372
OV	0.158	0.094	0.002	0.468	0.486	0.124	0.293
BC	0.066	0.076	0.001	0.692	0.661	0.153	0.374
LR	0.100	0.081	0.002	0.488	0.545	0.312	0.373

5 Algorithm optimizations

Because this paper deals with specific implementations of algorithms included in OpenCV, it has to be mentioned, that the final speed of algorithms depend not only on its principle, but also on the style of implementation and/or on used optimizations.

The OpenCV library contains one important method for parallelization of operations in computer vision algorithms. It is a set of virtual functions and classes, by which the performed operation, usually programmed using *for* loop, is defined as parallelisable operation. Thanks to this, when the OpenCV library is compiled with some parallelization framework, the marked section of algorithm is automatically distributed into parallel execution.

5.1 Available optimizations in OpenCV

The set of available optimization frameworks, which can be used as OpenCV background slightly depends on the platform. All optimizations can be divided into two basic categories. The first category of optimizations works with CPU. Inside this category are the multimedia instructions (SSE, NEON) together with multi-core parallelism methods (OpenMP, TTB). By using multimedia instruction, the one simple mathematical operation can be performed on multiple data concatenated into one processor word. For example if we have a processor with 64 bit wide registers, we can calculate a sum either in one instruction with eight numbers 1 byte wide or with numbers 2 byte wide or 2 numbers 4 byte wide. On the other hand, the multi-core parallelism methods are suitable when we have a CPU with multiple cores. In that way, the algorithm is divided into proper number of independent execution queues.

The second category of optimization uses GPUs as a computing devices. In OpenCV, the support for CUDA (NVidia graphics cards) and OpenCL(Intel and ATI graphic cards) is implemented. Moreover, the Vulcan (universal graphical card computing framework) will be available soon. The principle of this optimization lies in moving the graphical calculation on the GPU cores placed on the graphic card, where the amount of cores is significantly higher than in CPU.

6 Conclusion

The real aspects of implementation of tracking algorithms were discussed in this paper. Selected algorithms were

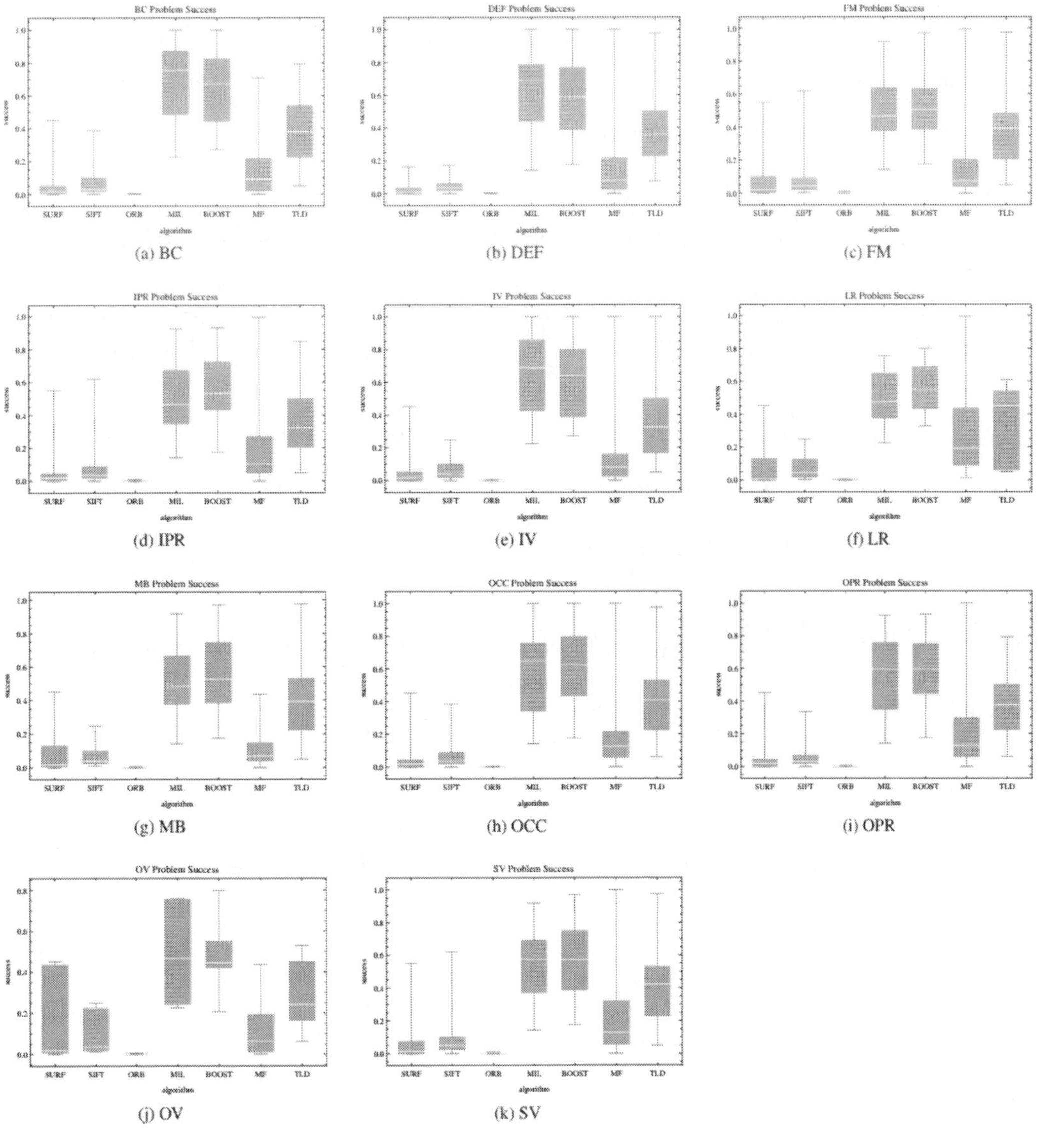

(a) BC (b) DEF (c) FM
(d) IPR (e) IV (f) LR
(g) MB (h) OCC (i) OPR
(j) OV (k) SV

Figure 4. Problems chart

tested and compared in different conditions and from different points of view.

Already the first criterion - *success* brings unexpected results. The TLD algorithm, which can be considered as the best one from the previous research base, was not as good as expected. It was partly caused by its complexity (it was not able to aim the target blob correctly because of adaptations), and partly by its insufficient implementation in OpenCV.

The second criterion - *precision*, brings constant results from the mean value point of view. At the other hand significant differences can be found on minimum and maximum levels of this measurement. These results can be marked as predictable on the previous research base.

As was described in previous sections, the time comparison of defined algorithms shows that the slowest algorithm was SIRF, directly followed by SURF algorithm. Surprisingly, the TLD algorithm was nearly as slow as the previous two. After deep analysis, it was recognized that the speed of TLD algorithm is limited by its complexity and/or its imperfect implementation, which does not use parallel loops available in OpenCV for speed optimization.

Because of the uncovered imperfections and limitations in algorithm implementation, the more detailed analysis will be created. The future work on this research will be focused of detailed analysis of implementation of these algorithms, including used programming techniques and memory and computing efficiency.

Acknowledgement

This paper is supported by Technology Agency of the Czech Republic (TA ČR) within the Visual Computing Competence Center - V3C project No. TE01020415, by Ministry of Education, Youth and Sports of the Czech Republic within the National Sustainability Programme project No. LO1303 (MSMT-7778/2014) and also by the European Regional Development Fund under the project CEBIA-Tech No. CZ.1.05/2.1.00/03.0089 and the Internal Grant Agency at TBU in Zlin, Project No. IGA/FAI/2016/036.

References

[1] D. Li, B. Liang, a W. Zhang, „Real-time moving vehicle detection, tracking, and counting system implemented with OpenCV", in 2014 4th IEEE International Conference on Information Science and Technology, 2014, s. 631–634.

[2] Lowe, D. G., "Distinctive Image Features from Scale-Invariant Keypoints", International Journal of Computer Vision, 60, 2, pp. 91-110, 2004.

[3] "OpenCV: Introduction to SIFT (Scale-Invariant Feature Transform)", Retrieved May 24, 2016, from http://docs.opencv.org/3.1.0/da/df5/tutorial_py_sift_intro.html

[4] Bay, H. and Tuytelaars, T. and Van Gool, L., "SURF: Speeded Up Robust Features", 9th European Conference on Computer Vision, 2006.

[5] "Introduction to SURF (Speeded-Up Robust Features)", Retrieved May 24, 2016, from http://docs.opencv.org/3.0-beta/doc/py_tutorials/py_feature2d/py_surf_intro/py_surf_intro.html

[6] "Features2D + Homography to find a known object", Retrieved May 24, 2016, from http://docs.opencv.org/2.4/doc/tutorials/features2d/feature_homography/feature_homography.html

[7] Ethan Rublee, Vincent Rabaud, Kurt Konolige, Gary R. Bradski: ORB: An efficient alternative to SIFT or SURF. ICCV 2011: 2564-2571.

[8] B. Babenko, M-H. Yang, and S. Belongie, "Visual Tracking with Online Multiple Instance Learning", In CVPR, 2009.

[9] Z. Kalal, K. Mikolajczyk, and J. Matas, "Forward-Backward Error: Automatic Detection of Tracking Failures", International Conference on Pattern Recognition, 2010, pp. 23-26.

[10] Friedman, J. H., Hastie, T. and Tibshirani, R., "Additive Logistic Regression: a Statistical View of Boosting.", Technical Report, Dept. of Statistics, Stanford University, 1998.

[11] Z. Kalal, K. Mikolajczyk, and J. Matas, "Tracking-Learning-Detection," Pattern Analysis and Machine Intelligence 2011.

[12] Wu, Yi et al., "Object Tracking Benchmark", IEEE Trans. Pattern Anal. Mach. Intell. 37 (2015): 1834-1848.

[13] Wu, Ye et al., "Online Object Tracking: A Benchmark", The IEEE Conference on Computer Vision and Pattern Recognition (CVPR), 2013, pp. 2411-2418.

[14] "Visual Tracker Benchmark. (n.d.)", Retrieved May 23, 2016, from http://cvlab.hanyang.ac.kr/tracker_benchmark/datasets.html.

[15] Z. Kalal, K. Mikolajczyk, a J. Matas, „Face-TLD: Tracking-Learning-Detection applied to faces", in 2010 IEEE International Conference on Image Processing, 2010, s. 3789–3792.

[16] Z. Kalal, K. Mikolajczyk, a J. Matas, „Tracking-Learning-Detection", IEEE Transactions on Pattern Analysis and Machine Intelligence, roč. 34, č. 7, s. 1409–1422, čvc. 2012.

[17] I. Culjak, D. Abram, T. Pribanic, H. Dzapo, a M. Cifrek, „A brief introduction to OpenCV", in 2012 Proceedings of the 35th International Convention MIPRO, 2012, s. 1725–1730.

Application of finite difference method in the study of diffusion with chemical kinetics of first order

Juan Carlos Beltrán-Prieto[1,a], Karel Kolomazník[1]

[1] *Department of Automation and Control Engineering, Faculty of Applied Informatics, Tomas Bata University in Zlín, nám. T. G. Masaryka 5555, 760 01 Zlín, Czech Republic*

Abstract. The mathematical modelling of diffusion of a bleaching agent into a porous material is studied in the present paper. Law of mass conservation was applied to analize the mass transfer of a reactant from the bulk into the external surface of a solid geometrically described as a flat plate. After diffusion of the reactant, surface reaction following kinetics of first order was considered to take place. The solution of the differential equation that described the process leaded to an equation that represents the concentration profile in function of distance, porosity and Thiele modulus. The case of interfacial mass resistance is also discused. In this case, finite difference method was used for the solution of the differential equation taking into account the respective boundary conditions. The profile of concentration can be obtained after numerical especification of Thiele modulus and Biot number.

1 Introduction

Bleaching is a chemical process performed to make a material whiter or lighter [1]. Some of the common bleaching agents used in the industry (i.e. paper coatings, oils, pulp, industrial wastewater, waxes) are sulfur dioxide, calcium hypochlorite, sodium hydrosulfite, hydrogen peroxide or sodium peroxide, ozone, among others) [2]. It is normally carried out by immersing the desired material in a recipient containing the bleaching agent which diffuses through the porous of the solid by random atomic motion.

The governing equation for the mass transfer of this process can be described by the Fick's second law which solution depends on the boundary conditions [3]. The mathematical description of this process is important for the proper quantification of the concentration of the bleaching agent and to understand its effect on the solid surface after the reaction takes place.

2 Description of the mathematical model

A microscopic mass balance for the concentration of bleaching agent is performed by considering the accumulation, convective mass transfer and diffusive transfer of bleaching solution through the pores of the solid and the reaction term as expressed in (1). The rate of reaction can be expressed as the disappearance of bleaching agent. Accordingly, it is possible to monitor the decrease in color of the material using a spectrophotometer.

The reaction rate term is considered in the equation because of the existence of an interaction between the solute and the surface of the solid. Assuming that a first order reaction takes place during the bleaching process, the reaction rate per unit of volume of the solid is described in (2)

$$\frac{\partial c}{\partial \tau} + V\nabla c = \nabla(D\nabla c) + R \quad (1)$$

$$-\frac{\partial c}{\partial \tau} = kc \quad (2)$$

where c represents the concentration of bleaching agent, τ the time, V the volume, D is the diffusivity, and k is the rate constant.

For the purpose of modeling this phenomena, we consider that the diffusion of the well stirred bleaching agent solution occurs in one dimension through a symmetrical flat plate with homogeneous and isotropic properties (the physical and mechanical properties are equal in all orientations of the solid), that the diffusivity is constant (independent of concentration), without interfacial resistance to the mass transport. Accordingly, we consider a steady state situation, in which the concentration will not change in time. Additionally, we suppose the absence of flow of mass due to convection, the equation (1) is transformed into (3) [4]

$$D\frac{\partial^2 c}{\partial x^2} - kc = 0 \quad (3)$$

The previous equation describes that the concentration (c) is a function of position(x). It is a linear partial differential equation (parabolic) that can be solved for a given settings (initial and boundary conditions)[5]. This is a two-point boundary value problem, therefore the

[a] Corresponding author: prieto@fai.utb.cz

concentration needs to be specified at both x=0 and x=L, as described in equations (4) and (5)

$$x = 0,\ \frac{dc}{dx} = 0 \quad (4)$$

$$x = L,\ c = \varepsilon \cdot c_L \quad (5)$$

The first condition expresses that at the center of the solid there is no diffusion flux and therefore express a condition of symmetry. The second condition describes the case of diffusion in a well-stirred media, in which the concentration on the surface of the solid(c) is equal to the concentration of the bulk c_L with the proper consideration of the porosity of the solid (ε).

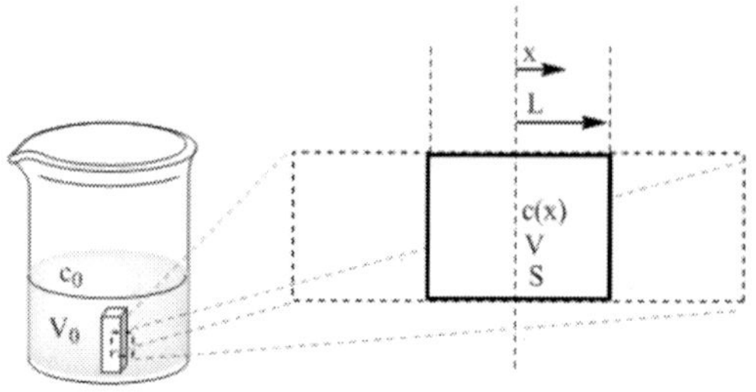

Figure 1. Geometric representation of the system under study.

For the solution of the problem, the mass balance equation and boundary conditions are expressed in dimensionless form using the parameters described in (6):

$$X = \frac{x}{L},\ C = \frac{c}{\varepsilon \cdot c_L} \quad (6)$$

As a result: $x = X \cdot L$, $c = C \cdot \varepsilon \cdot c_L$, $dx = L \cdot dX$, $dc = \varepsilon \cdot c_L \cdot dC$, and $\frac{d^2c}{dx^2} = \frac{d}{LdX}\left[\frac{\varepsilon \cdot c_L \cdot dC}{LdX}\right]$, therefore we obtain (7)

$$\frac{d^2c}{dx^2} = \frac{\varepsilon \cdot c_L \cdot d^2C}{L^2 dX^2} \quad (7)$$

Substitution of (7) and previous dependences into (3) leads to (8):

$$\frac{d^2C}{dX^2} - \frac{kL^2}{D}C = 0 \quad (8)$$

from where we can define the dimensionless parameter of Thiele module (φ), which represents the ratio of the rate of reaction to the rate of diffusion [6] as expressed in (9).

$$\varphi^2 = \frac{kL^2}{D} \quad (9)$$

The boundary conditions in dimensionless values adopt the form of the next equations:

$$X = 0,\ \frac{dC}{dX} = 0 \quad (10)$$

$$X = 1,\ C = 1 \quad (11)$$

Equation (8) has the form of the characteristic equation $m^2 - \varphi^2 = 0$ giving a set of conjugate roots $m_1 = \varphi$ and $m_2 = -\varphi$. As a result, the general solution of the differential equation is (12)

$$C = c_1 e^{\varphi X} + c_2 e^{-\varphi X} \quad (12)$$

For the purpose of applying boundary conditions, it is often convenient to represent equation (12) using hyperbolic functions. As a result, equation (12) is transformed into (13)

$$C = c_1 \cosh \varphi X + c_2 \sinh \varphi X \quad (13)$$

The value of the constants C_1 and C_2 can be determined taking into considerations the boundary equations (10) and (11). As a result $C_1 = (1 - C_2 sinh\varphi)/cosh\varphi$ and $C_2 = 0$. Substitution of the previous values in equation (12) leads to (14) (expressed in the original variables)

$$c = \frac{\varepsilon \cdot c_L \cdot \cosh \varphi \frac{x}{L}}{\cosh \varphi} \quad (14)$$

This equation allows us to obtain the concentration profile (*c*) as a function of distance (*x*) for a given values of porosity as represented in Figure 1 and for given values of Thiele modulus.

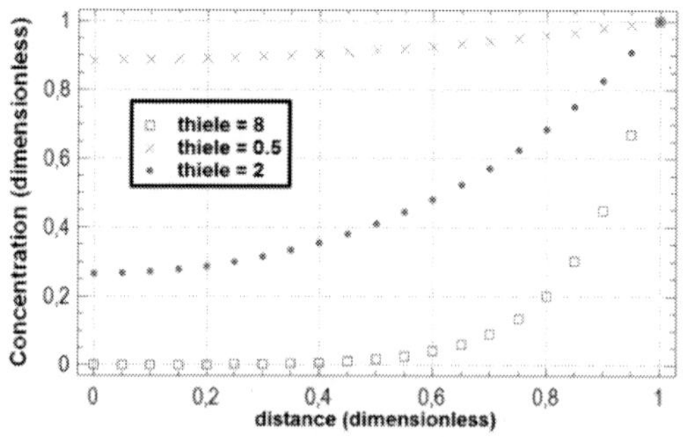

Figure 2. Plot of dimensionless concentration profile as a function of distance for different Thiele values (□ :0.8, x :0.5, and ● :2).

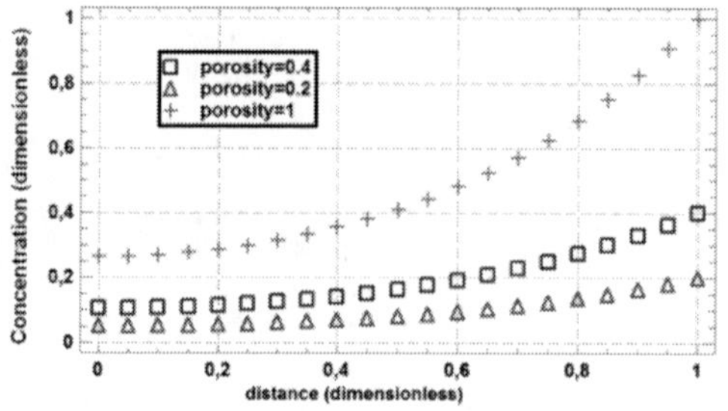

Figure 3. Plot of dimensionless concentration profile as a function of distance using different values of porosity (□ :0.4, Δ :0.2 and +:1).

Following we proceed to determine the effectiveness factor (η), which indicates the ratio between the reaction rate and the reaction rate without resistance to diffusion [7], [8] as described in (15)

$$\eta = \frac{-r}{-r_s} = \frac{actual\ reaction\ rate}{reaction\ rate\ without\ diffusion} = \frac{1}{\varphi^2}\frac{dC}{dX}\bigg|_{X=1} \quad (15)$$

Solving equation (14) leads to equation (16)

$$\eta = \frac{1}{\varphi^2}\left(\frac{1}{\cosh\varphi}(\varphi \cdot \sinh\varphi X)\right)\bigg|_{X=1} = \frac{1}{\varphi}\left(\frac{\sinh\varphi}{\cosh\varphi}\right) = \frac{\tanh\varphi}{\varphi} \quad (16)$$

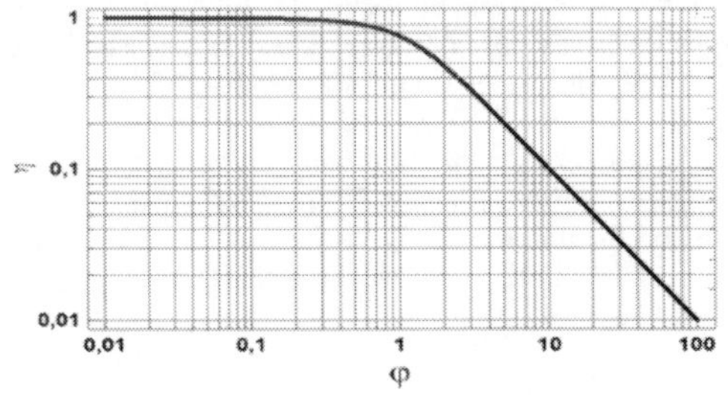

Figure 4. Plot of effectiveness factor as a function of Thiele modulus in logarithmic scale.

The reaction rate without diffusion is also the reaction rate at the surface of the solid, therefore the overall reaction rate is calculated by multiplying the intrinisic reaction rate per unit volume and the effectiveness factor as described in equation (17) and finally in (18)

$$r = \eta \cdot r_s = \eta \cdot k \cdot c \quad (17)$$

$$r = \frac{\tanh\varphi}{\varphi} \cdot k \cdot c = \frac{\tanh\sqrt{\frac{kL^2}{D}}}{\sqrt{\frac{kL^2}{D}}} k \cdot c \quad (18)$$

In the case that there is interfacial mass resistance, then the boundary condition is given by $x = 0,\ \frac{dc}{dx} = 0;$ and $x = L, -D\frac{dc}{dx} = k_s \cdot \varepsilon(c - c_L)$ where k_s represents the mass transfer coefficient. Accordingly, the same dimensionless parameters still apply and the boundary conditions are transformed in:

$$X = 0,\ \frac{dC}{dX} = 0\ ;\ X = 1,\ \frac{dC}{dX} = -\frac{L \cdot k_s}{D}(C \cdot \varepsilon - 1) \quad (19)$$

Where the quantity $-L \cdot k_s/D$ is also known as the mass transfer Biot number Bi_m which represents the ratio of internal diffusion resistance to external convection resistance [9]. In this case, equation (8) with boundary conditions expressed in (19) can be solved using finite difference method [10]. In this case, we used 4 interior nodes

$$Node\ 1 \rightarrow \frac{c_2 - c_1}{\Delta X} = 0 \quad (20)$$

$$Node\ 2 \rightarrow \frac{c_3 - 2c_2 + c_1}{\Delta X^2} - \varphi^2 c_2 = 0 \quad (21)$$

$$Node\ 3 \rightarrow \frac{c_4 - 2c_3 + c_2}{\Delta X^2} - \varphi^2 c_3 = 0 \quad (22)$$

$$Node\ 4 \rightarrow \frac{c_5 - 2c_4 + c_3}{\Delta X^2} - \varphi^2 c_4 = 0 \quad (23)$$

$$Node\ 5 \rightarrow \frac{c_6 - 2c_5 + c_4}{\Delta X^2} - \varphi^2 c_5 = 0 \quad (24)$$

$$Node\ 6 \rightarrow \frac{c_6 - c_5}{\Delta X} = Bi_m(C \cdot \varepsilon - 1) \quad (25)$$

ΔX is calculated from equation (26)

$$\Delta X = 1/(n+1) \quad (26)$$

Where n is the number of interior nodes, therefore ΔX is 0.2. Equations (20) to (26) results in a system of linear equations represented in equation (27)

$$\begin{pmatrix} -5 & 5 & 0 & 0 & 0 & 0 \\ 25 & -50-\varphi^2 & 25 & 0 & 0 & 0 \\ 0 & 25 & -50-\varphi^2 & 25 & 0 & 0 \\ 0 & 0 & 25 & -50-\varphi^2 & 25 & 0 \\ 0 & 0 & 0 & 25 & -50-\varphi^2 & 25 \\ 0 & 0 & 0 & 0 & 5 & -5-Bi_m \end{pmatrix} \begin{pmatrix} C_1 \\ C_2 \\ C_3 \\ C_4 \\ C_5 \\ C_6 \end{pmatrix} = \begin{pmatrix} 0 \\ 0 \\ 0 \\ 0 \\ 0 \\ -Bi_m \end{pmatrix} \quad (27)$$

The solutions of the previous system of equations leads to find the profile of concentration after numerical especification of Thiele modulus and Biot number. For numerical simulation we consider porosity equal to 1 and values of $\varphi^2 = 4$, and $Bi_m = 16$ and $\varphi^2 = 8$, and $Bi_m = 0.4$. This is represented in Figure 5.

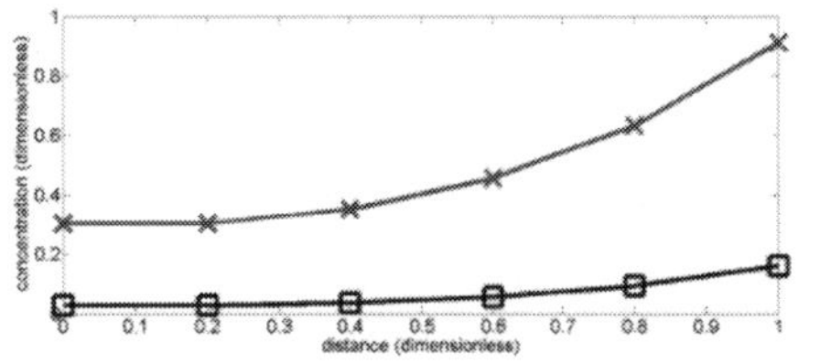

Figure 5. Plot of concentration profile for two cases. Case 1: $\varphi^2 = 4, Bi_m = 16$ (cross) and case 2: $\varphi^2 = 8$, $Bi_m = 0.4$ (square).

3 Conclusions

The study of diffusion of a liquid into a porous material with a first order reaction taking place has been studied. In order to determine the effect of mass transfer on the overall reaction rate, an effectiveness factor was determined. This factor is also important to describe how far the reactant diffuses into the solid before the reaction takes place.

When the values of η are near to 1, the reaction is surface reaction limited but if this value is small (η <<1) the reaction is diffusion limited. If Thiele modulus is large, internal diffusion limits the overall rate of reaction, but if it is small, surface reaction is rate limiting. The case of boundary condition with interfacial resistance was studied. This is present in the case that the bulk fluid moves slowly. Finite difference method was used for the solution of a problem describing the mass transport and reaction with this boundary condition.

Acknowledgements

This work was supported by the Ministry of Education, Youth and Sports of the Czech Republic within the National Sustainability Programme project No. LO1303 (MSMT-7778/2014).

References

1. International Food Information Service, *IFIS Dictionary of Food Science and Technology* (International Food Information Service, Wiley - Blackwell, Reading, 2009).
2. M. Ash, I. Ash, *Handbook of Paper and Pulp Chemicals* (Synapse Information Resources, Inc., New York, 2013).
3. R. B. Bird, W. E. Stewart, E. N. Lightfoot, *Transport Phenomena* (John Wiley and Sons, Inc, New York, 2002).
4. J. Welty, C. Wicks, R. Wilson, *Fundamentals of Momentum, heat, and Mass Transfer*, (John Wiley and Sons, Mexico, 2008).
5. Y. A. Cengel, *Heat And Mass Transfer: A Practical Approach* (McGraw-Hill, New York, 2006).
6. I. Tosun, *Modeling in Transport Phenomena* (Elsevier, The Netherlands, 2007).
7. B. Godongwana, PloS One, **11**, 1-13 (2016)
8. G. A. Adagiri, G. Babagana, A. A. Susu, Int. J. Res. Rev, Applied. Sci. **13**, 716-739 (2012).
9. R. G. Rice, D. D. Do, *Applied mathematics and modeling for chemical engineers*, (John Wiley & Sons, Inc, New Jersey, 2012).
10. R. L. Burden, J. D. Faires, *Numerical Analysis* (Brooks Cole, United Kingdom, 2002).

Modeling of the partial oxidation of glycerol by estimation of its transfer function

Juan Carlos Beltrán-Prieto[1,a], Karel Kolomazník[1], Roman Slavík[2]

[1] *Department of Automation and Control Engineering, Faculty of Applied Informatics, Tomas Bata University in Zlín, nám. T. G. Masaryka 5555, 760 01 Zlín, Czech Republic*
[2] *Department of Environmental Engineering Protection, Faculty of Technology, Tomas Bata University in Zlín, nám. T. G. Masaryka 275, 762 72 Zlín, Czech Republic*

Abstract. The reaction pathway for the conversion of glycerol into different products, namely glyceraldehyde, glyceric acid, glycolic acid, mesoxalic acid and tartronic acid was studied by means of electrochemistry. Multiple Pulse Amperometry technique was used to control the potential during the electrooxidation reaction. The estimation of the transfer function was realized on the basis of dynamic models for the oxidation reaction. The equations obtained in the s-domain were expressed in the time domain using Inverse Laplace transformation to describe the variation of glycerol and products concentration.

1 Introduction

The partial oxidation of glycerol via heterogeneous redox reaction is a process that is carried out under mild conditions. This allows the minimization of energy waste and by-products generation. This process has been intensively studied by several authors [1–7]. In mentioned works, glyceric acid, CO_2, hydroxypyruvate, tartronic acid, mesoxalic acid, glyceraldehyde, or formic acid are among the main products obtained. Although there are reports on glycerol oxidation, there is no record of glyceraldehyde production by electrochemical means on at least pilot plant level.

This makes the research into the production of pure glyceraldehyde a very complicated matter but at the same time more interesting. Most of the publications do not deal in detail with possible mechanism of partial glycerin oxidation and its subsequent quantitative description including experimental verification of the proposed mathematical models.

Determination of transient responses from the models can be performed by using Laplace transform technique; however the solutions obtained are particular to every set of initial conditions. [8] Therefore, the proposal of expressions that can describe the dynamic relation between the input and the output of a process model while being independent of the initial conditions is considered to be valuable. The transfer function is a mathematical representation of a process used in linear time-invariant systems to describe the dynamic properties of the system.

In this study, the electrochemical oxidation of glycerol was analyzed in a three electrode system using platinum as a working electrode.

[a] Corresponding author: prieto@fai.utb.cz

Analysis of reaction products formed during the sustained electrolysis was performed by High Performance Liquid Chromatography (HPLC). Multiple pulse amperometry technique was used to control the potential during the electrooxidation reaction. Proposal of a reaction pathway was performed in order to determine the rate constants, followed by the estimation of the transfer function calculated on the basis of dynamic models for the anodic oxidation.

2 Materials and methods

Reagents used for the experiment were purchased from Sigma-Aldrich (Czech Republic), deionized water was used in all procedures (Millipore). Electrochemical oxidation experiments were carried out using an EmStat Potentiostat (made by PalmSens) with computerized control by PSTrace Software to record the data from multiple pulse amperometry measurements.

Analysis of samples for quantification purposes was performed using a Shimadzu HPLC instrument with automatic injection. The system comprised a degassing unit DGU-20A 5R, a pump LC-20AD, an auto sampler SIL-30AC, a column oven CTO—20rA, a Refractive index detector RID-10A, an UV Detector SPD-20A and a communications bus module (control unit) CBM-20A. Data analysis and acquisition was performed with LabSolutions Software.

The HPLC column used was a reversed-phase Aminex HPX-87C (300mm x 7,8mm). Electrochemical experiments were performed as described in [9]. Samples were taken at specific intervals of time and the analysis of the glycerol oxidation products was performed using a recent published method [10].

According to the experimental results obtained from electrochemical experiments, a set of differential equations were proposed to test a first-order rate equation considering reversible reactions. A concentration-time curve for the reaction mechanism proposed was obtained by analytical solution of the equations and numerical simulation. The predicted values of the model were compared with the experimental data and the transfer function for the oxidation of glycerol was proposed.

3. Results

3.1 Oxidation at controlled potential by Multiple Pulse Amperometry

The products formed after the electrochemical reaction were identified and quantified by means of HPLC using two different detectors (Ultraviolet and Refractive index detectors) to ensure the validity of the results. Agreement between both detectors in the quantification of products was always presented.

Figure 1 presents the HPLC chromatogram using Ultraviolet detector of the reaction blend after the partial oxidation of glycerol. Glycerol peak is not present as it does not show absorption at the wavelength applied (210 nm) but it can be easily determined using Refractive index detector. The peak at 8.3 min is related to the solvent peak.

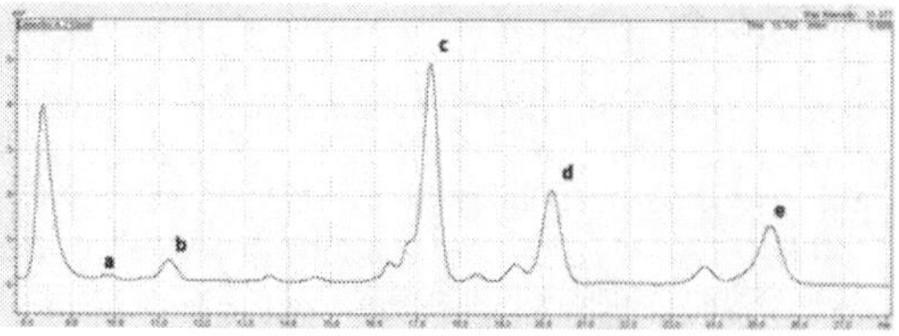

Figure 1. HPLC chromatogram after 5 hours of controlled potential; a) mesoxalic acid, b)tartronic acid, c)glyceraldehyde, d)glyceric acid, e)glycolic acid.

3.2 Mathematical model and mechanism

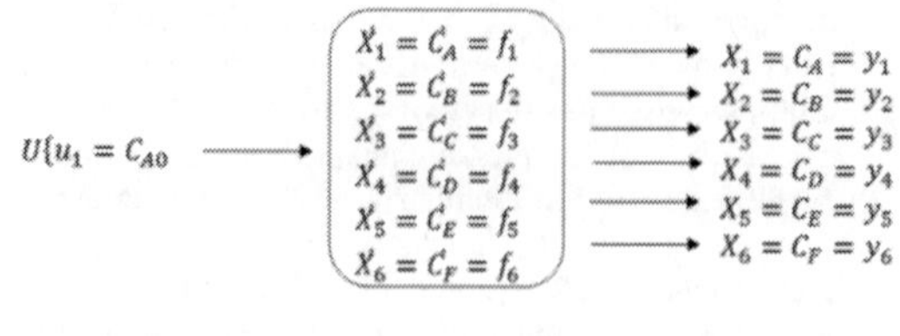

Figure 2. Description of the system including the input, state variable and output.

Figure 2 describes the input-output block diagram of the system. The input is the initial concentration of glycerol. The state and output variables are considered to be the concentration of glycerol (C_A), glyceraldehyde (C_B), glyceric acid(C_C), tartronic acid (C_D), glycolic acid (C_E), and mesoxalic acid (C_F). The reaction mechanism proposed is presented in Figure 3, considering the oxidation of glycerol into five different products.

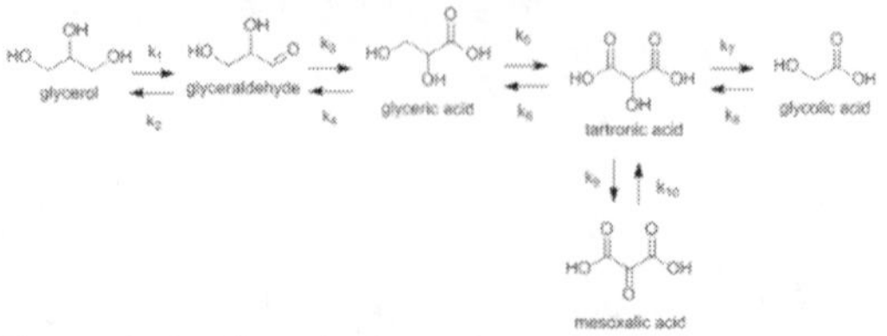

Figure 3. Anodic oxidation pathway proposed considering reversible reactions.

As a result, the mechanism can be described by the set of differential equations presented through (1) to (6)

$$dC_A/dt = -k_1 C_A + k_2 C_B \quad (1)$$

$$dC_B/dt = k_1 C_A - k_2 C_B - k_3 C_B + k_4 C_C \quad (2)$$

$$dC_C/dt = k_3 C_B - k_4 C_C - k_5 C_C + k_6 C_D \quad (3)$$

$$dC_D/dt = k_5 C_C - k_6 C_D - k_7 C_D + k_8 C_E - k_9 C_D + k_{10} C_F \quad (4)$$

$$dC_E/dt = k_7 C_D - k_8 C_E C_E \quad (5)$$

$$dC_F/dt = k_9 C_D - k_{10} C_F\, C_F \quad (6)$$

The previous equations can be solved numerically to approximate the solutions of the set of ordinary differential equations and to calculate the concentration of glycerol and products formed after evaluation of the respective reaction rate constant. The evaluation of the kinetic constant rates was performed using ERA 3.0 software, which uses the weighted sum of squares as objective function in order to minimize the weighted sum of squares of residual deviations.

Figure 4 present the model fitting to experimental data for concentrations of glycerol and products using the rate constants of k_1=0.04516 h^{-1}, k_2= 0.4263 h^{-1}, k_3=3.473 h^{-1}, k_4=4.3917 h^{-1}, k_5=6.269 h^{-1}, k_6=115.176 h^{-1}, k_7=38.413 h^{-1}, k_8=4.345 h^{-1}, k_9=3.674 h^{-1}, k_{10}=8.576 h^{-1}. Data is presented in dimensionless values considering the initial concentration of glycerol. Since the anodic oxidation is a heterogeneous process, the rate of the reaction is dependent of the surface concentration of the reactant.

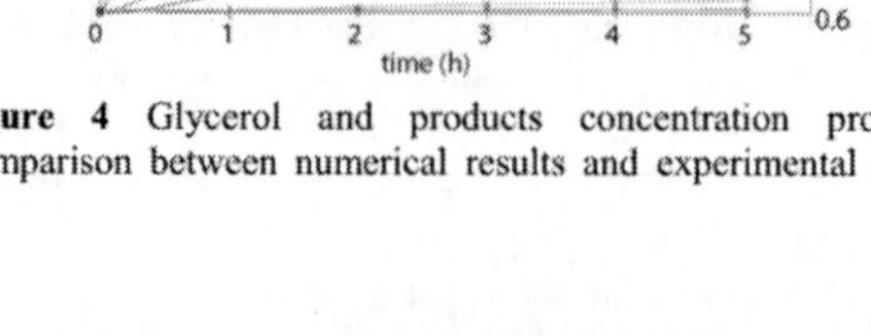

Figure 4 Glycerol and products concentration profile. Comparison between numerical results and experimental data

for the mechanism proposed Glycerol (●) and products (■C_B; ▲C_C; ▼C_D; ♦C_E; *C_F) concentration profile is displayed in the right y-axis and left y-axis respectively.

Equations (1) to (6) represent a vector differential equation as shown in (7) to (15). Considering that the input includes a defined initial concentration of glycerol we obtain the system represented in (10):

$$\frac{dC}{d\tau} = A \cdot C \qquad (7)$$

$$\tau = 0, \;\; C = C_0 \qquad (8)$$

$$\begin{pmatrix} \frac{dC_A}{d\tau} \\ \frac{dC_B}{d\tau} \\ \frac{dC_C}{d\tau} \\ \frac{dC_D}{d\tau} \\ \frac{dC_E}{d\tau} \\ \frac{dC_F}{d\tau} \end{pmatrix} = \begin{pmatrix} -k_1 & k_2 & 0 & 0 & 0 & 0 \\ k_1 & -(k_2+k_3) & k_4 & 0 & 0 & 0 \\ 0 & k_3 & -(k_4+k_5) & k_6 & 0 & 0 \\ 0 & 0 & k_5 & -(k_6+k_7+k_9) & k_8 & k_{10} \\ 0 & 0 & 0 & k_7 & -k_8 & 0 \\ 0 & 0 & 0 & k_9 & 0 & -k_{10} \end{pmatrix} \begin{pmatrix} C_A \\ C_B \\ C_C \\ C_D \\ C_E \\ C_F \end{pmatrix} \qquad (9)$$

$$\begin{pmatrix} C_A(0) \\ C_B(0) \\ C_C(0) \\ C_D(0) \\ C_E(0) \\ C_F(0) \end{pmatrix} = \begin{pmatrix} C_{A0} \\ 0 \\ 0 \\ 0 \\ 0 \\ 0 \end{pmatrix} \qquad (10)$$

Equations (9) and (10) are represented by the system of equations described in (11)

$$\begin{gathered} \Delta\dot{X}_{6x1} = A_{6x6}\Delta X_{6x1} + B_{6x1}\Delta U_{1x1} \\ \Delta Y = \Delta X \end{gathered} \qquad (11)$$

Where A is the state matrix of dimension 6×6 and B is the control matrix of dimension 6×1. The elements of both matrices A and B correspond to the system presented in (9) and (10) respectively:

By application of the Laplace transform to equation (7) we get:

$$C_L - C_0 = A \cdot C_L \qquad (12)$$

$$C_L = (sI - A)^{-1} C_0 \qquad (13)$$

Therefore, in order to determine the transfer function *G(s)* we need to calculate $(s) = (sI - A)^{-1}B$, as presented next:

$$(sI - A) = \begin{pmatrix} s & 0 & 0 & 0 & 0 & 0 \\ 0 & s & 0 & 0 & 0 & 0 \\ 0 & 0 & s & 0 & 0 & 0 \\ 0 & 0 & 0 & s & 0 & 0 \\ 0 & 0 & 0 & 0 & s & 0 \\ 0 & 0 & 0 & 0 & 0 & s \end{pmatrix} - \begin{pmatrix} -k_1 & k_2 & 0 & 0 & 0 & 0 \\ k_1 & -(k_2+k_3) & k_4 & 0 & 0 & 0 \\ 0 & k_3 & -(k_4+k_5) & k_6 & 0 & 0 \\ 0 & 0 & k_5 & -(k_6+k_7+k_9) & k_8 & k_{10} \\ 0 & 0 & 0 & k_7 & -k_8 & 0 \\ 0 & 0 & 0 & k_9 & 0 & -k_{10} \end{pmatrix} \qquad (14)$$

$$(sI - A) = \begin{pmatrix} s+k_1 & -k_2 & 0 & 0 & 0 & 0 \\ -k_1 & s+(k_2+k_3) & -k_4 & 0 & 0 & 0 \\ 0 & -k_3 & s+(k_4+k_5) & -k_6 & 0 & 0 \\ 0 & 0 & -k_5 & s+(k_6+k_7+k_9) & -k_8 & -k_{10} \\ 0 & 0 & 0 & -k_7 & s+k_8 & 0 \\ 0 & 0 & 0 & -k_9 & 0 & s+k_{10} \end{pmatrix} \qquad (15)$$

After obtaining the value of $(sI - A)^{-1}$ and multiplying by matrix B, the transfer function of the system can be determined. In this case, numerical values for the transfer function are estimated using the specific values of C_{A0} (dimensionless value of 1) and rate constants (k) calculated previously. As a result, the corresponding transfer functions are given by the following set of equations:

From input u=C_{A0} to output:

$$y_1 = C_A \rightarrow G(s) = \frac{s^5+184.744s^4+3653.0028s^3+23865.09s^2+48439.5s+8034.97}{s^6+184.79s^5+3661.33s^4+24026.6s^3+49460.26s^2+9935.52s-1.7785^{-10}} \qquad (16)$$

$$y_2 = C_B \rightarrow G(s) = \frac{0.04516s^4+8.1669s^3+133.813s^2+673.1926s+851.1834}{s^6+184.79s^5+3661.33s^4+24026.6s^3+49460.26s^2+9935.52s-1.7785^{-10}} \qquad (17)$$

$$y_3 = C_C \rightarrow G(s) = \frac{0.15684s^3+26.6918s^2+293.4246s+673.1243}{s^6+184.79s^5+3661.33s^4+24026.6s^3+49460.26s^2+9935.52s-1.7785^{-10}} \qquad (18)$$

$$y_4 = C_D \rightarrow G(s) = \frac{0.98323s^2+12.7044s+36.638}{s^6+184.79s^5+3661.33s^4+24026.6s^3+49460.26s^2+9935.52s-1.7785^{-10}} \qquad (19)$$

$$y_5 = C_E \rightarrow G(s) = \frac{37.769s+323.9067}{s^6+184.79s^5+3661.33s^4+24026.6s^3+49460.26s^2+9935.52s-1.7785^{-10}} \qquad (20)$$

$$y_6 = C_F \rightarrow G(s) = \frac{3.6124s+15.6959}{s^6+184.79s^5+3661.33s^4+24026.6s^3+49460.26s^2+9935.52s-1.7785^{-10}} \qquad (21)$$

Accordingly, the zero state response can be determined. For this, we firstly require to perform partial fraction expansion of equations (16) to (21) to get:

$$Y_1(s) = -\frac{0.0003}{s+163.4955} + \frac{0.0003}{s+9.5843} + \frac{0.0003}{s+8.2891} + \frac{0.0002}{s+3.4065} + \frac{0.1908}{s+0.2246} + \frac{0.8087}{s} \qquad (22)$$

$$Y_2(s) = \frac{0.0003}{s+163.4955} - \frac{0.003}{s+9.5843} + \frac{0.0012}{s+8.2891} - \frac{0.0039}{s+3.4065} - \frac{0.0802}{s+0.2246} + \frac{0.0856}{s} \qquad (23)$$

$$Y_3(s) = -\frac{0.0031}{s+9.5843} + \frac{0.0015}{s+8.2891} + \frac{0.0002}{s+3.4065} - \frac{0.0691}{s+0.2246} + \frac{0.0677}{s} \qquad (24)$$

$$Y_4(s) = \frac{0.0001}{s+3.4065} - \frac{0.0039}{s+0.2246} + \frac{0.0037}{s} \qquad (25)$$

$$Y_5(s) = -\frac{0.0004}{s+9.5843} - \frac{0.0001}{s+8.2891} + \frac{0.0037}{s+3.4065} - \frac{0.0358}{s+0.2246} + \frac{0.0326}{s} \quad (26)$$

$$Y_6(s) = -\frac{0.0002}{s+9.5843} + \frac{0.0003}{s+8.2891} - \frac{0.0017}{s+0.2246} + \frac{0.0016}{s} \quad (27)$$

Following, the previous equations in the s-domain are then expressed in the time domain using Inverse Laplace transform tables:

$$Y_1(t) = -0.0003e^{-163.4955t} + 0.0003e^{-9.5843t} + 0.0003e^{-8.2891t} - 0.0002e^{-3.4065t} + 0.1908e^{-0.2246t} + 0.8087 \quad (28)$$

$$Y_2(t) = 0.0003e^{-163.4955t} - 0.003e^{-9.5843t} + 0.0012e^{-8.2891t} - 0.0039e^{-3.4065t} - 0.0802e^{-0.2246t} + 0.0856 \quad (29)$$

$$Y_3(t) = -0.0031e^{-9.5843t} + 0.0015e^{-8.2891t} + 0.0002e^{-3.4065t} - 0.0691e^{-0.2246t} + 0.0677 \quad (30)$$

$$Y_4(t) = 0.0001e^{-3.4065t} - 0.0039e^{-0.2246t} + 0.0037 \quad (31)$$

$$Y_5(t) = -0.0004e^{-9.5843t} - 0.0001e^{-8.2891t} + 0.0037e^{-3.4065t} - 0.0358e^{-0.2246t} + 0.0326 \quad (32)$$

$$Y_6(t) = -0.0002e^{-9.5843t} + 0.0003e^{-8.2891t} - 0.0017e^{-0.2246t} + 0.0016 \quad (33)$$

When analyzing the engineering tasks of process operation and design of control systems, it is important to analyze if the transfer function obtained gives full information of the system. The response of the output/input relation for the variation of glycerol concentration and oxidation products is presented in Figure 5. It is clearly seen a correspondence with the behavior of the experimental and modeling data (Figure 4). As a result, the transfer function obtained describes properly the dynamic relation between the input and output of the oxidation process. Therefore, the partial oxidation of glycerol by electrochemistry demonstrated to be a process that can be modeled by transfer functions.

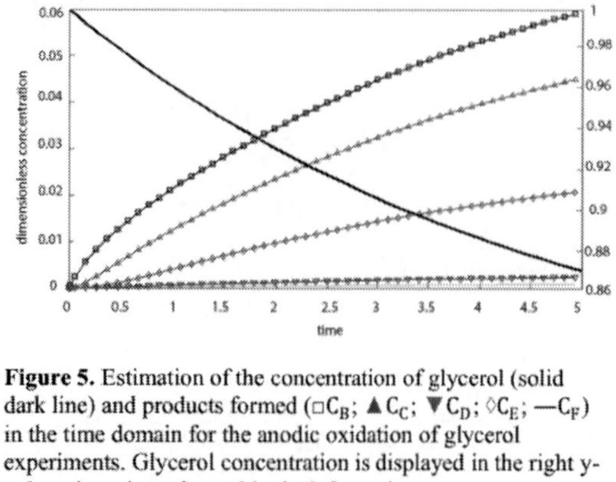

Figure 5. Estimation of the concentration of glycerol (solid dark line) and products formed (□C_B; ▲C_C; ▼C_D; ◇C_E; —C_F) in the time domain for the anodic oxidation of glycerol experiments. Glycerol concentration is displayed in the right y-axis and products formed in the left y-axis.

4. Conclusion

The estimation of the transfer function for the proposed kinetic model of partial oxidation of glycerol was useful in modeling the variation of glycerol derivatives concentration in time. The determination of the system transfer functions and representation of equations in the time domain avoids the analytical solution of the differential equations proposed in the kinetic modeling, which in the case of the full reversible mechanism in every step of the reaction would involve complicated mathematical treatment. Values of rate constants were estimated and agreement between numerical data (from mathematical modeling), experimental data and output using the respective transfer function was observed. As a result, the determined transfer function of the system demonstrated to fully describe the process.

Acknowledgements

This work was supported by the Ministry of Education, Youth and Sports of the Czech Republic within the National Sustainability Programme project No. LO1303 (MSMT-7778/2014) and also by the European Regional Development Fund under the project CEBIA-Tech No. CZ.1.05/2.1.00/03.0089

References

1. J. Schnaidt, M. Heinen, D. Denot, Z. Jusys, R. Jürgen Behm, J. Electroanal. Chem. **661,** 250–264 (2011).
2. Y. Kwon, S.C.S. Lai, P. Rodriguez, M.T.M. Koper, J. Am. Chem. Soc. **133,** 6914–6917 (2011).
3. M. Mougenot, a. Caillard, M. Simoes, S. Baranton, C. Coutanceau, P. Brault, Appl. Catal. B Environ. **107,** 372–379 (2011).
4. J. Song, S. Fan, J. Yu, K. Ye, C. Xu, Int. J. Electrochem. Sci. **7,** 10842–10850 (2012).
5. A. Serov, U. Martinez, P. Atanassov, Electrochem. Commun. **34,** 185–188 (2013).
6. Z. Zhang, L. Xin, W. Li, Appl. Catal. B Environ. **119-120,** 40–48 (2012).
7. Z. Zhang, L. Xin, J. Qi, D.J. Chadderdon, W. Li, Appl. Catal. B Environ. **136-137,** 29–39 (2013).
8. E.D. Seborg, T.F. Edgar, D. Mellichamp, *Process Dynamics and Control,* (John Wiley and Sons, Inc. New Jersey, 1989).
9. J.C. Beltran-Prieto, R. Slavik, K. Kolomaznik, Int. J. Electrochem. Sci. **9,** 6910–6923 (2014).
10. J.C. Beltrán-Prieto, J. Pecha, V. Kašpárková, K. Kolomazník, J. Liq. Chromatogr. Relat. Technol. **36,** 2758–2773 (2013).

Mathematical Model of Non-stationary Heat Conduction in the Wall: Asymmetric Problem with the Boundary Conditions of Imperfect Heat Transfer

Hana **Charvátová**[1,a] and Martin **Zálešák**[2]

[1] *Tomas Bata University in Zlín, Faculty of Applied Informatics, Regional Research Centre CEBIA-Tech, nám. T. G. Masaryka 5555, 760 01 Zlín, Czech Republic*
[2] *Tomas Bata University in Zlín, Faculty of Applied Informatics, Department of Automation and Control Engineering, nám. T. G. Masaryka 5555, 760 01 Zlín, Czech Republic*

Abstract. This paper deals with the study of a non-stationary heat conduction in the solid wall. It is focused on mathematical modelling of its asymmetric heating and cooling by imperfect heat transfer to both sides of the wall. It describes method used for deriving of the long time analytical solution describing temperature distribution in the heated (cooled) wall by use Laplace transform and verification of its validity by numerical calculation with COMSOL Multiphysics software. In the tested example, the maximum difference between analytical and numerical solution was about 3.5 % considering the possible maximum and minimum temperatures in the wall under the given conditions.

1 Introduction

Non-stationary heat conduction in a wall made of the solid material is a phenomenon that can occur all around us. It is part of many technological operations, but also also takes place within the walls of heated or cooled building structures, in components of many electronic devices, in heating and cooling equipment etc.

Knowledge of these processes course is necessary to ensure optimal heat supplying or heat dissipation and the associated avoidance of damage to materials or reduce energy intensity etc.[1].

But course of heating and cooling depends on many factors such as the dimensions and material properties of the walls but also the intensity of heat transfer between the wall surface and the surroundings [1–4].

To assess the course of non-stationary phenomena is often advantageous to use a combination of an experimental testing and computer simulation study done for the required initial and boundary conditions. In the paper [5] we dealt a mathematical model of non-stationary heat conduction under the condition of symmetric heating or cooling and also with asymmetric heating or cooling under the conditions of perfect heat transfer between surface of the wall and ambient liquid on the both sides of the wall.

In this paper we also deal with mathematical modelling of a heat conduction in the solid wall during its asymmetric heating and cooling but we will suppose conditions of the imperfect heat transfer to both sides of the wall, which significantly influences time course of the studied process.

2 Description of a Studied Model

In the following text we describe a mathematical model of the transient heat conduction in a solid wall which is made of isotropic material. Geometrical sketch of the studied model is depicts in Figure 1.

The length and width of the wall are order of magnitude larger than its thickness. The wall of the initial temperature t_p, being subjected to a sudden thermal effect of surrounding liquid, wherein the constant ambient temperature t_{o1} exerted on the left side of the wall is different than the constant ambient temperature t_{o2} on the right side of the wall. Moreover, the heat transfer coefficients α_1, α_2 on both sides of the wall are mutually different. Temperatures of both the surrounding environments are independent of time and they are different from the initial temperature considered wall.

We will suppose the following cases of heating or cooling of the wall:

$$t_p < t_{o1} < t_{o2} \wedge \alpha_1 \neq \alpha_2,$$
$$t_p < t_{o2} < t_{o1} \wedge \alpha_1 \neq \alpha_2,$$
$$t_p > t_{o1} > t_{o2} \wedge \alpha_1 \neq \alpha_2,$$
$$t_p > t_{o2} > t_{o1} \wedge \alpha_1 \neq \alpha_2.$$

Mathematical model of the studied problem is represented by a linear parabolic partial differential equation (1) [6], with initial condition (2) and boundary conditions (3) - (4) of imperfect heat transfer between surfaces of the wall and the surroundings:

[a] e-mail: charvatova@fai.utb.cz

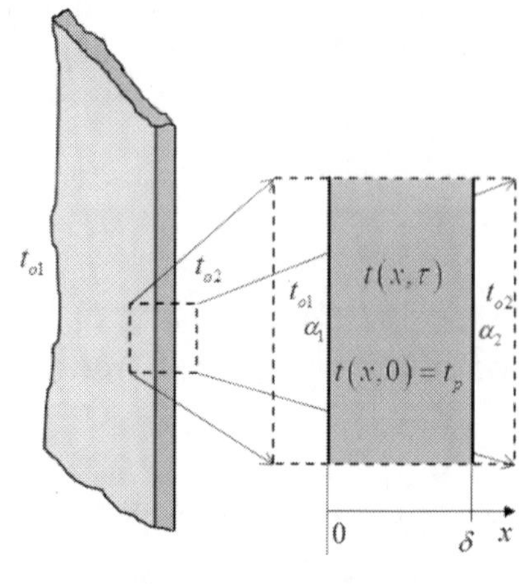

Figure 1. Geometrical sketch of the studied model of non-stationary heat conduction in the solid wall.

$$\frac{\partial t(x,\tau)}{\partial \tau} = a\frac{\partial^2 t(x,\tau)}{\partial x^2}, \quad 0 \le x \le \delta,\ \tau > 0 \tag{1}$$

$$t(x,0) = t_P \tag{2}$$

$$-\lambda \frac{\partial t(0,\tau)}{\partial x} = -\alpha_1 (t(0,\tau) - t_{oI}) \tag{3}$$

$$-\lambda \frac{\partial t(\delta,\tau)}{\partial x} = \alpha_2 (t(\delta,\tau) - t_{o2}) \tag{4}$$

The symbols used in equations (1) - (4) mean:
a - thermal diffusivity, $[\mathrm{m}^2.\mathrm{s}^{-1}]$;
t - time dependent temperature of the wall, [°C];
t_p - initial temperature of the wall, [°C];
t_{o1} - ambient temperature on the left side of the wall, [°C];
t_{o2} - ambient temperature on the right side of the wall, [°C];
x - space coordinate, [m];
α_1 - heat transfer coefficient on the left side of the wall, $[\mathrm{W.m}^{-2}.\mathrm{K}^{-1}]$;
α_2 - heat transfer coefficient on the right side of the wall, $[\mathrm{W.m}^{-2}.\mathrm{K}^{-1}]$;
δ - thickness of the wall, [m];
λ - thermal conductivity of the wall, $[\mathrm{W.m}^{-1}.\mathrm{K}^{-1}]$;
τ - time, [s].

3 Method Used for the Model Solving

For solving of the above described mathematical model we applied the Laplace transform technique for parabolic partial differential equation described in literature [7], [8].

The Laplace transform of a function $f(\tau)$, defined for all real numbers $\tau \ge 0$, is the function $F(s)$, which is a unilateral transform defined by equation (5):

$$F(s) = \int_0^\infty \exp^{-s\tau} d\tau. \tag{5}$$

According to [7], the long time solution can be obtained by expansion theorem in the Laplace domain as $F(s)$:

$$F(s) = \frac{p(s)}{q(s)}. \tag{6}$$

In our case, a polynomial $q(s)$ has an infinite number of roots. If $s = \mu_0$, $n = 1 \ldots \infty$ are the distinct roots of $q(s)$, $q(s)$ can be factorized as:

$$q(s) = (s-\mu_1)(s-\mu_2)\ldots(s-\mu_n)\ldots(s-\mu_\infty). \tag{7}$$

Assuming that order of polynomial $q(s)$ is greater than order of $p(s)$, the equation (6) can be converted to partial fractions as:

$$F(s) = \frac{B_1}{s-\mu_0} + \frac{B_2}{(s-\mu_0)^2} + \sum_{n=1}^{\infty} \frac{A_n}{s-\mu_n}. \tag{8}$$

Where

$$B_1 = \lim_{s\to\mu_0} \left(\frac{d}{ds}\left(\frac{p(s)(s-\mu_0)^2}{q(s)}\right)\right), \tag{9}$$

$$B_2 = \lim_{s\to\mu_0} \left(\frac{p(s)(s-\mu_0)^2}{q(s)}\right), \tag{10}$$

$$A_n = \frac{p(\mu_n)}{q'(\mu_n)}. \tag{11}$$

The analytical solution in time domain can be obtained by inverse Laplace transform as [7]:

$$f(s) = \mathcal{L}^{-1}(F(s)) = B_1 \exp(\mu_0\tau) + B_2\tau \exp(\mu_0\tau) + \sum_{n=1}^{\infty} A_n \exp(\mu_n\tau). \tag{12}$$

The procedure described by equations (6) - (12) we programmed in the user interface of MAPLE software. By calculation with the software Maple we derived analytical solution in a relatively complicated form. A simplified form of the analytical solution is described by the equation (13):

$$t(x,\tau) = Q_1 + \sum_{n=0}^{\infty} 2\,\frac{\mathrm{e}^{-Q_2\tau}(Q_3+Q_4+Q_5-Q_6)}{Q_7}. \tag{13}$$

Symbols $Q_1 - Q_7$ represent the following parts of the equation (13):

$$Q_1 = \frac{\alpha_2 t_{o2}\lambda + \alpha_1\lambda t_{oI} + \alpha_1\alpha_2(t_{o2}x - t_{oI}x + t_{oI}\delta)}{\alpha_2\lambda + \alpha_1\lambda + \alpha_1\alpha_2\delta}, \tag{14}$$

$$Q_2 = \frac{{q_n}^2 a}{\delta^2}, \tag{15}$$

$$Q_3 = (t_P - t_{o2}) \sin\left(\frac{q_n x}{\delta}\right) \alpha_2 \alpha_1 a^2 q_n + \\ (t_{o1} - t_P) \cos(q_n) \sin\left(\frac{q_n x}{\delta}\right) \alpha_2 \alpha_1 a^2 q_n, \tag{16}$$

$$Q_4 = \left(-t_P + \cos\left(\frac{q_n x}{\delta}\right)(-t_{o1} + t_P)\right) \sin(q_n)\, \alpha_2, \alpha_1 a^2 q_n \tag{17}$$

$$Q_5 = i\left(-\frac{{q_n}^2 a}{\delta^2}\right)^{3/2} \lambda \sqrt{a} \sin(q_n) - \\ \frac{a^2 {q_n}^2 (\alpha_2 + \alpha_1) \cos(q_n)\, t_P \lambda}{\delta}, \tag{18}$$

$$Q_6 = \left(t_{o1} - t_p\right) \alpha_1 \sin\left(\frac{q_n x}{\delta}\right) \sin(q_n)\, {q_n}^2 a^2 \lambda \delta^{-1} \\ + ((-t_P + t_{o2})\, \alpha_2)\, {q_n}^2 a^2 \lambda \delta^{-1} \\ + (t_{o1} - t_P)\, \alpha_1 \cos(q_n) \cos\left(\frac{q_n x}{\delta}\right) {q_n}^2 a^2 \lambda \delta^{-1}, \tag{19}$$

$$Q_7 = \frac{{q_n}^4 a^2 \lambda^2 \cos(q_n)}{\delta^2} + \\ i\sqrt{a}\left(-\frac{{q_n}^2 a}{\delta^2}\right)^{\frac{3}{2}} \delta \lambda \sin(q_n)(5\lambda + \alpha_1 \delta + \alpha_2 \delta) + \\ i a^{\frac{3}{2}} \sqrt{-\frac{{q_n}^2 a}{\delta^2}}\, (3\, \alpha_1 \alpha_2 \delta \sin(q_n)) + \\ i a^{\frac{3}{2}} \sqrt{-\frac{{q_n}^2 a}{\delta^2}}\, (q_n \cos(q_n)(4\lambda(\alpha_2 + \alpha_1) + \alpha_1 \alpha_2 \delta)). \tag{20}$$

The positive roots q can be calculated from a transcendental equation (21):

$$q = \frac{ia\left(\alpha_2 \cos(q)\, q \lambda \delta - \lambda^2 q^2\right)}{\left(\sqrt{-\frac{q^2 a}{\delta^2}}\right)\delta^2} + \\ \frac{ia\left(\sin(q)\,\delta^2 + \alpha_1 \lambda q \cos(q)\,\delta\right)}{\left(\sqrt{-\frac{q^2 a}{\delta^2}}\right)\delta^2}. \tag{21}$$

In the Figure 2 is shown computed temperature distribution in the wall during its heating. Figure 2a depicts 3D temperature distribution, Figure 2b depicts temperature curves in required times of cooling.

Temperature distribution in the wall in case of the cooling is shown in the Figure 3.

4 Verification of the Model Solution Validity

For the verification of the derived solution accuracy we compared data obtained by analytical solution (13) using MAPLE with results of computer simulation of the same model by COMSOL Multiphysics software, which performs calculations of physical processes numerically by finite element method.

Results based on analytical solution (13) and computer simulation are shown in Figure 4. The temperature fields during heating and cooling of the wall calculated by both procedures were similar. In the example shown in Figure 4, the maximum difference was about 0.7 °C, which makes the difference of 3.5 % relative to the possible maximum and minimum temperatures in the wall under the given conditions.

5 Discussion

The above-described method which was used for the derivation of analytical solution (13) is suitable for long time solution heating (cooling) of the wall [7]. In this case, solution appears to be sufficiently accurate. To derive an analytical solution in case of short time heating (cooling), the used mathematical method should be modified [7].

The derived analytical solution is valid for asymmetric heating, provided that both ambient temperatures are higher than the initial temperature of the wall or one of the ambient temperatures may be equal to the initial wall temperature. Similarly, when cooling is required, both to ambient temperatures were lower than the initial temperature of the wall. Alternatively, one of ambient temperatures may be equal to the initial temperature of the wall.

Special case of a transient heat conduction in the wall can occur if the wall is heated from one side and cooled simultaneously from the other side heated (i.e. for $t_{o1} < t_p < t_{o2}$ or $t_{o1} > t_p > t_{o2}$).

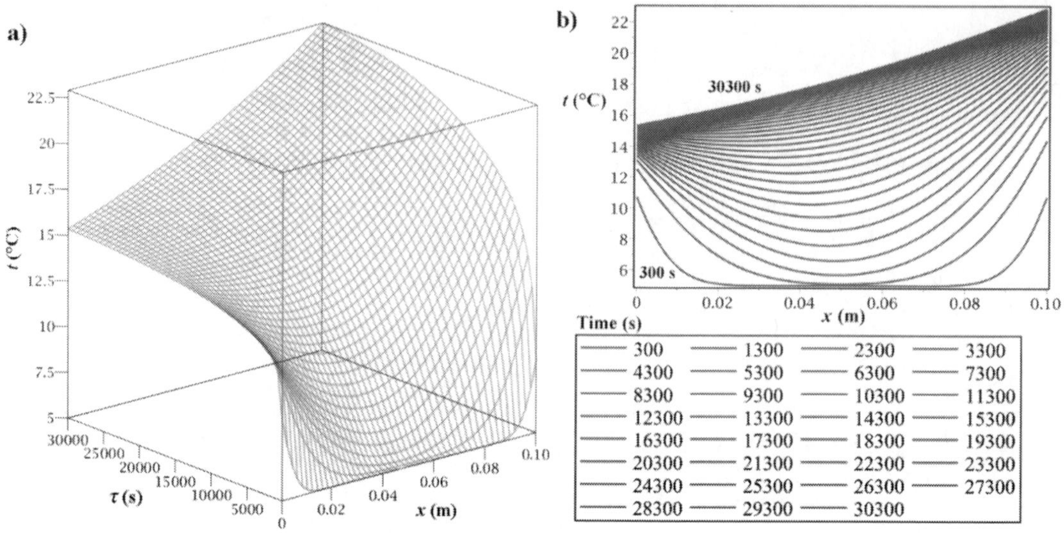

Figure 2. Heating of the wall; a) 3D temperature distribution, b) temperature curves in required times of heating. The used parameters: t_p = 5 °C, t_{o1} = 15 °C, t_{o2} = 25 °C, δ = 0.1 m, α_1 = 30 W.m^{-2}.K^{-1}, α_2 = 10 W.m^{-2}.K^{-1}, λ = 0.2 W.m^{-1}.K^{-1}, ϱ = 1140 kg.m^{-3}, c_p = 1200 J.kg^{-1}.K^{-1}.

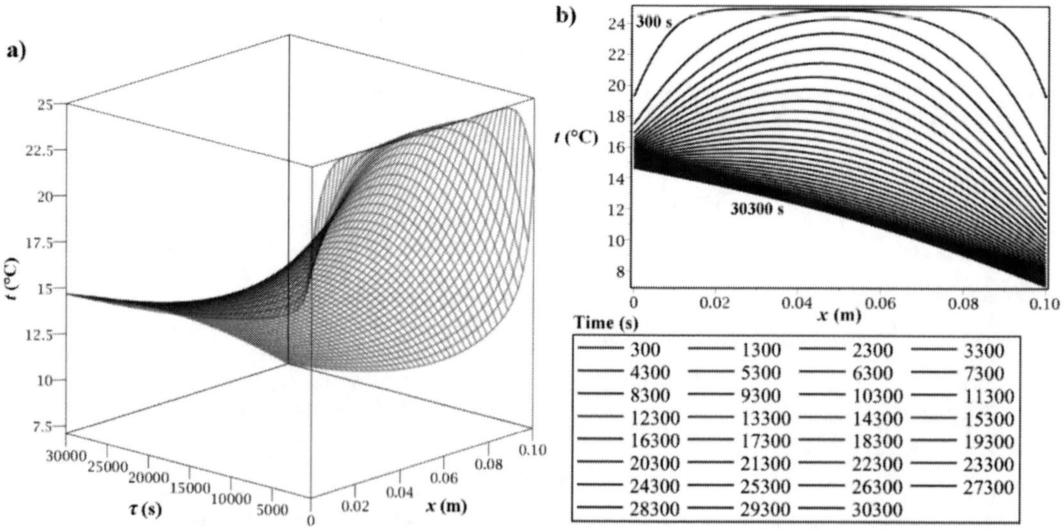

Figure 3. Cooling of the wall; a) 3D temperature distribution, b) temperature curves in required times of cooling. The used parameters: t_p = 25 °C, t_{o1} = 15 °C, t_{o2} = 5 °C, δ = 0.1 m, α_1 = 30 W.m^{-2}.K^{-1}, α_2 = 10 W.m^{-2}.K^{-1}, λ = 0.2 W.m^{-1}.K^{-1}, ϱ = 1140 kg.m^{-3}, c_p = 1200 J.kg^{-1}.K^{-1}.

6 Conclusion

This paper presented mathematical model of a heat conduction in the solid Wall during its asymmetric heating and cooling by imperfect heat transfer to both sides of the wall. The analytical solution of the studied model was derived by using Laplace transform and its validity was verified by numerical calculation with COMSOL Multiphysics software.

The derived analytical solution is suitable for the description of long time processes. Therefore, further studies will focus on the derivation of an analytical solution for the short time processes.

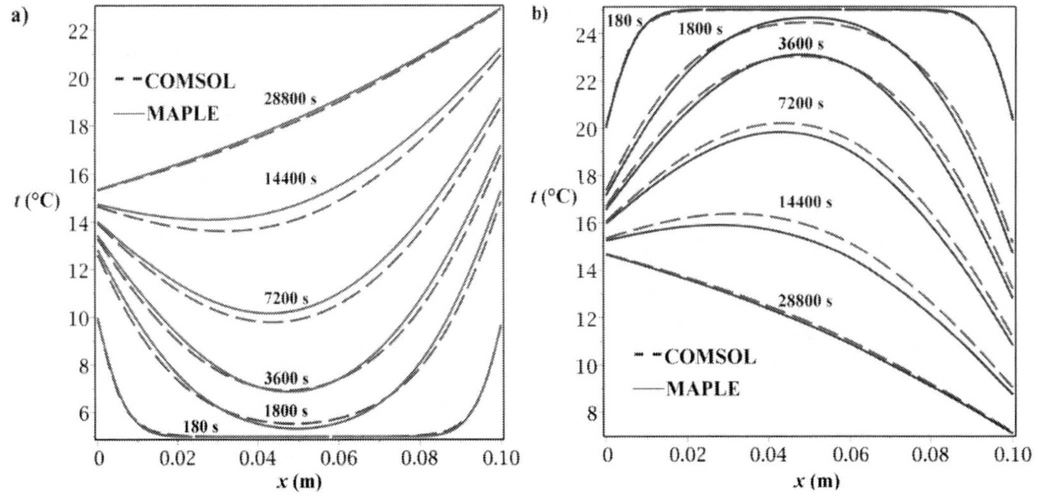

Figure 4. Comparing of analytical solution for model of transient heat conduction solved in Maple and numerical solution obtained by the simulation with software COMSOL Multiphysics; temperature field a) for heating, b) for cooling of the wall. The used parameters: a) t_p = 5 °C, t_{o1} = 15 °C, t_{o2} = 25 °C, δ = 0.1 m, α_1 = 30 W.m^{-2}.K^{-1}, α_2 = 10 W.m^{-2}.K^{-1}, λ = 0.2 W.m^{-1}.K^{-1}, ϱ = 1140 kg.m^{-3}, c_p = 1200 J.kg^{-1}.K^{-1}; b) t_p = 25 °C, t_{o1} = 15 °C, t_{o2} = 5 °C, δ = 0.1 m, α_1 = 30 W.m^{-2}.K^{-1}, α_2 = 10 W.m^{-2}.K^{-1}, λ = 0.2 W.m^{-1}.K^{-1}, ϱ = 1140 kg.m^{-3}, c_p = 1200 J.kg^{-1}.K^{-1}.

Acknowledgement
This work was supported by the Ministry of Education, Youth and Sports of the Czech Republic within the National Sustainability Programme project No. LO1303 (MSMT-7778/2014).

References

[1] K. Kolomazník, V. Vašek, D. Janáčová, *Proceedings of the 13th WSEAS International Conference on computers*, (Rhodes, Greece: WSEAS Press, 2009), p. 550

[2] O. Šuba, L. Sýkorová, Š. Šanda, M. Staněk, *Proceedings of the 13th WSEAS International Conference on Automatic control, modelling & simulation*, (Lanzarote, Canary Islands: WSEAS Press, 2011)

[3] L. Vašek, V. Dolinay, *Proceedings of the 14th WSEAS International Conference on Systems. Latest Trends on Systems.Volume II*, (Rhodes, Greece: WSEAS Press, 2010) pp. 439-442

[4] L. Xue, G.Dui, B. Liu, J. Zhang, Mechanics of Advanced Materials and Structures, **10**, 23 (2016)

[5] H. Charvátová, D. Janáčová, K. Kolomazník, *WSEAS Transactions on Heat and Mass Transfer* **6(1)**, pp. 11-20 (2011)

[6] H. S. Carslaw, J. C. Jaeger, *Conduction of Heat in Solids*. (Clarendon Press, Oxford, 1986) pp. 510

[7] R. E.White, V. R.Subramanian, *Computational Methods in Chemical Engineering with Maple*. (Springer-Verlag, Berlin Heidelberg, 2010) pp. 859

[8] R.G. Rice, D.D. Do, *Applied Mathematics and Modeling for Chemical Engineers*. (John Wiley & Sons, Inc., Chichester, 1995) pp. 719

[9] C.P. Naveira, M. Lachi, R.M. Cotta, J. Padet, International Journal of Heat and Mass Transfer, **1-2**, 52 (2009)

[10] E.C. Mladin, D. Stanciu, J.Padet, *Proceedings of the Romanian Academy Series A - Mathematics Physics Technical Sciences Information Science*, **2**, 11 (2010)

 DOI: 10.1051/matecconf/20167604035

Adaptive individual handling for neural network synthesis

Pavel Vařacha[1,a]

[1]Tomas Bata University in Zlín, Faculty of Applied Informatic, nám. T. G. Masaryka 5555

760 01 Zlín, Czech Republic

Abstract. Neural Network Synthesis is an algorithm capable of creating and learning and artificial neural networks as well as optimizing their structures and connections. The method is based on Analytic Programming and asynchronous implementation of Self-Organising Migration Algorithm. Such approach already recorded several successful application considering practical casers of modelling and simulation. This results vindicate efforts for its further development. This paper explores a possibility to make it more effective by adaptive individual handling. The main idea is an intelligent control the process based on complexity of processed neural network structure.

Keywords: neural; network; synthesys; SOMA; adaptive; strategy; structural; optimization

1. Introduction

Neural Network Synthesis (ANN synthesis) is an algorithm capable of creating and learning and artificial neural networks as well as optimizing their structures and connections. To describe this method in all details would significantly exceed a possible extend of this paper. Nevertheless ANN synthesis mechanisms are very well elaborated in papers [1] and [2]. An interested reader is respectfully asked to study this previous publications as are referred at the end of the paper.

ANN synthesis is based on Analytic Programming (AP) and asynchronous implementation of Self-Organizing Migration Algorithm (SOMA). Important facts about AP which are necessary for basic understanding of an idea proposed in the paper as an adaptive individual handling are described in chapters 2. And 3. For better understanding of SOMA, please, refer paper [3] or [4].

This paper explores a possibility to make it more effective by adaptive individual handling. The main idea is an intelligent control of the ANN synthesis based on complexity of processed neural network structure.

2. Analytic programming

The main principle (core) of AP is based on a discrete set handling (DSH) (Fig. 1). DSH shows itself as a universal interface between the EA and the symbolically solved problem. This is why AP can be used almost by any evolutionary algorithm. In the case of ANN synthesis the algorithm is SOMA.

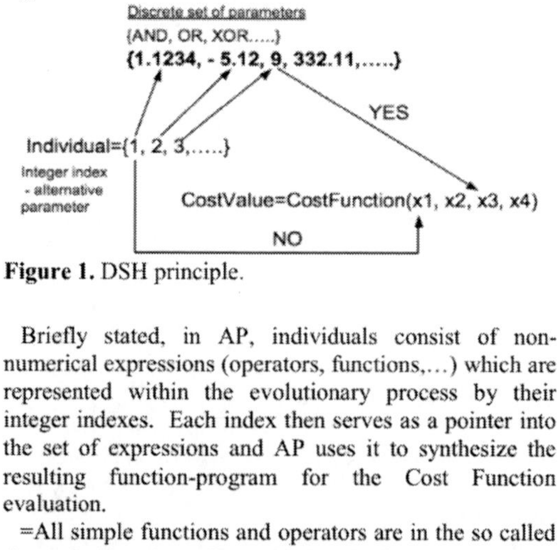

Figure 1. DSH principle.

Briefly stated, in AP, individuals consist of non-numerical expressions (operators, functions,...) which are represented within the evolutionary process by their integer indexes. Each index then serves as a pointer into the set of expressions and AP uses it to synthesize the resulting function-program for the Cost Function evaluation.

=All simple functions and operators are in the so called General Function Set (GFS) divided into groups according to the number of arguments which can be inserted during the evolutionary process to create subsets GFS3, GFS2...GFS0.

[a] Corresponding author: varacha@fai.utb.cz

Table 1. Example of GFS and its subsets.

GFS Degree	Contains
GFSall	f(x1, x2, x3), +, -, *, /, Power, Abs, Round, Sin, Cos, t, K, τ, 1, 2
GFS3	f(x1, x2, x3)
GFS2	+, -, *, /, Power
GFS1	Abs, Round, Sin, Cos
GFS0	t, K, τ, 1, 2

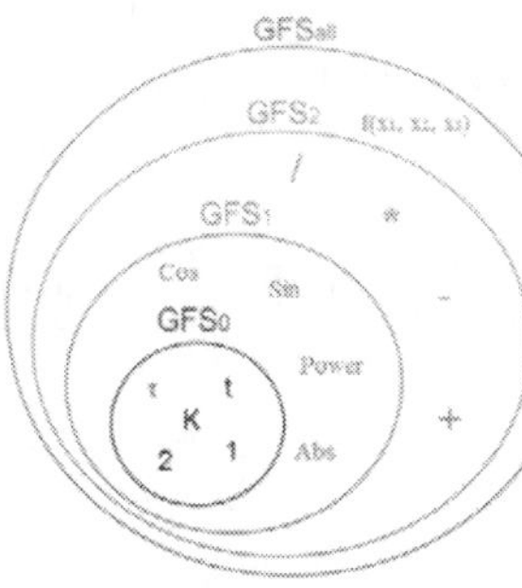

Figure 2. GFS subsets hierarchy.

The functionality of AP can be seen in the specific example in Figure 3:

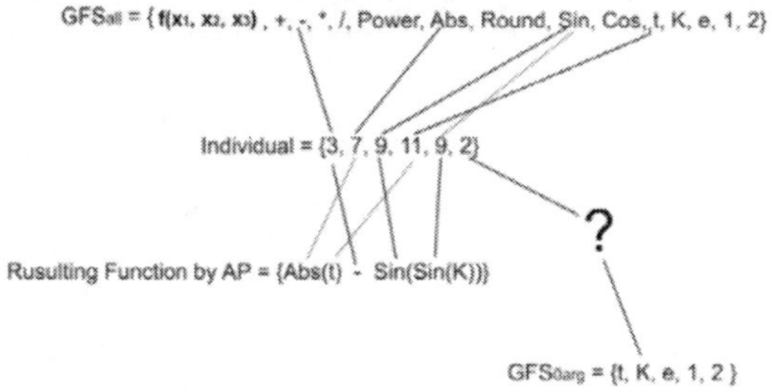

Figure.3. Main principles of AP.

The individual consists of 6 arguments (indices, pointers to GFS). The first index is 3, meaning that it is taken from the set of functions GFS_{all}. The function *minus* has two arguments; therefore indexes 7 and 9 are arguments of *minus*.

$$6 + 7 \quad (1)$$

Index 7 is then replaced by *Abs* and index 9 by *Sin*.

$$Abs + Sin \quad (2)$$

Abs and *Sin* are one-argument functions. Then, index 9 follows index 11, which is replaced by *t*.

$$Abs(t) + Sin \quad (3)$$

Sin is also a one-argument function. Then, after index 11, the individual takes index 9, which is replaced by *Sin* and this *Sin* becomes an argument of the previous *Sin*.

$$Sin(Tan) + Sin(Sin(\quad (4)$$

The last index is 2, but in this case there is the function *Plus*. *Plus* needs two arguments to work properly. AP will not allow this, as there is not any other free pointer to be used as the argument. Instead of *Plus*, AP will jump into the subspace, in this case directly to the GFS_{0arg}. In the GFS_{0arg} it finds the second element, which is *K*. And by doing so, we get (5).

$$Abs(t) + Sin(Sin(K)) \quad (5)$$

The number of pointers actually used from an individual before the synthesized expression is closed is called *depth*. This example is based on the relevant and previously published work in.

3. Neural network synthesis

The previous chapter described basic concepts of AP. Such concepts can be easily employed to synthetize different ANN structures as can be seen from Figure 4. This process of structural synthesis as well as ANN learning is well described for example in [3] and [4].

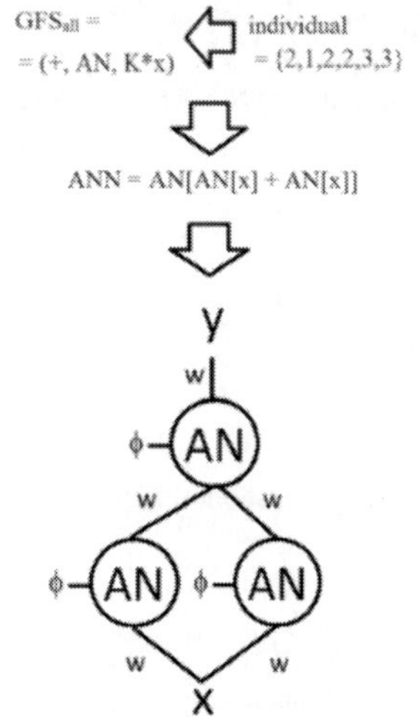

Figure 4. An Example of ANN synthesis.

4. Experiment designed for adaptive individual handling

Processes described in chapters 2. and 3. have to be optimized by a specific evolutionary algorithms. In case of ANN synthesis it basically means to try variously complex ANN structures (individuals in AP) to improve them in evolutionary way. In place of such evolutionary algorithm ANN synthesis commonly employ SOMA. An algorithm which is well described in [3] and [4]. However SOMA is not anyhow adaptive to coop with various lengths of individuals in AP. SOMA simply treat all such individuals as an individual of constant length (typically 100). For this paper one control parameter of SOMA was chosen to improve this behavior.

An adaptive individual handling proposed in this paper aim to influence control parameter of SOMA named PRT to improve its ability to deal with different lengths of individuals. For each individual SOMA will used different setting of PRT bases on length of a solved individual itself.

Commonly, SOMA is set on PRT = 0.1. In contradiction this paper proposes adaptive strategy so PRT will differ from individual to individual PRT = 1 / depth.

In order to statistically evaluate this new adaptive handling approach the function approximation problem was chosen as an aim of the experiment. The function (6) proposed by [5] as an appropriate approximation benchmark was chosen to be approximated by the ANN.

$$y = x_i^5 - 2x_i^3 + x_i \quad (6)$$
$$\text{where } x_i \text{ is in } <-1, \text{by the step } 0.04, 1>$$

Figure 5 (automatically generated by ANN synthesis software) shows an example of synthetized ANN approximating (6). The difference between the ANN and (7) is depicted as a red area which could be minimized by the process of synthesis. An goal of ANN synthesis in this case can be simply described as founding smallest possible ANN able to approximate given function. Simplicity of such function is purely purposeful here as the main goal is not test ability of ANN synthesis to solve complicated tasks but to test how the method improve while applying proposed adaptive strategy.

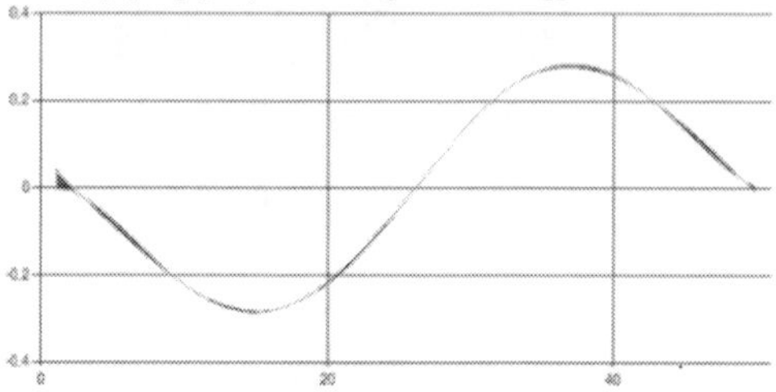

Figure 5. Approximation of (7) by synthetized ANN.

AP was executed 100 times (physically on 8 cores of the Super Micro Server) to produce an ANN with the RMSD < 0.005. The main intention was to find such an ANN which met this condition and which simultaneously used as few AN as possible. All SOMA's control parameters required for repetition of this experiment are described in following tables. The setting of Asynchronous SOMA used as the EA for AP can be seen in Table 2. and SOMA setting used for ANN learning in Table 3.

Table 2. Setting of SOMA used as EA for AP.

Number of Individuals	48
Individual Parameters	100
Low	0
High	3
PathLength	3
Step	0,11
PRT	Based on **experiment**
Divergence	0.01
Period	1

Table 3. Setting of SOMA used to optimize Kn.

Number of Individuals	number ofKn* 0.5 (at least 10)
Individual Parameters	100
Low	-10
High	10
PathLength	3
Step	0,11
PRT	$1/K_n$
Divergence	0.01
Period	6

Based on experiment setting PRT which SOMA used to optimize Kn is set either conservatively to PRT = 0.1 or adaptively PRT = 1 / depth

5. Results

The adaptive strategy for individual handling consists in replacement of the static PRT value by the value which inversely depends on depth of a currently operated individual.

Table 4. PRT strategy for individual handling.

	PRT = 1/ depth	PRT = 0.1
Average time needed for synthesis	194 s	373s
Average number of used AN	9	13

A total of 1,189,870 evaluations of AP individual fitness were completed during 100 AP executions while the PRT was set to 0.1 and the separate SOMA run was performed for all of them to set their Kn value. Without the adaptive PRT, AP was able to find an optimal ANN in only 1 case in comparison with 4 successful cases in the original experiment.

Conclusion

ANN synthesis already recorded several successful application considering practical casers of modelling and simulation [6] – [9]. It was also applied on large set of widely recognized benchmark functions [10], [11] with respect to the function approximation, prediction and problems. This results vindicate efforts for its further development.

Obtained results of experiment considered in this paper proves an ability of proposed adaptive individual handling to further improve ANN synthesis. It can significantly improve ANN synthesis ability to overshadow concurrent method of ANN optimization as are [12] – [17].

The method of adaptive individual handling proved in this paper are going to be applied on a practical industrial example and comparison of the improved ANN synthesis is to be subjected by a future study.

Acknowledgements

This work was supported by the Ministry of Education, Youth and Sports of the Czech Republic within the National Sustainability Programme project No. LO1303 (MSMT-7778/2014).

References

1. Zelinka I., Vařacha P., Oplatková Z., Volná, E. *12th International Conference on Soft Computing*. Czech Republic, VUT Brno, 25-30 (2006)
2. Vařacha P. *Recent Researches in Automatic Control*. Montreux : WSEAS Press, 377-382 (2011)
3. Šenkerik R., Zelinka I., Davendra D., Oplatkova Z. *Computers & Mathematics with Applications*, **60**, Issue 4, 1026-1037, ISSN 0898-1221, doi 10.1016/j.camwa.2010.03.059. (2010)
4. Šenkeřík R. Oplatkova Z., Zelinka I, Davendra D., Mathematical and Computer Modelling, ISSN 0895-7177, 10.1016/j.mcm.2011.05.030 (Available online 27 May 2011)
5. Vařacha P., Zelinka I. *IEEE Proceedings 7th International Conference Computer Information Systems and Industrial Management Applications*. Ostrava : IEEE Computer Society, 99-100 (2008)
6. Prechelt L., *Proben1—A Set of Neural Network Benchmark Problems and Benchmarking Rules*, Universität Karlsruhe, Germany (1994)
7. Mangarianm O.L., Wolberg W.H., *Cancer diagnosis via linear programming*, SIAM News, **23**, Number 5, , p. 1-18 (1990)
8. Král E., Dolinay V., Vašek L., Vařacha P. *14th WSEAS International Conference on Systems. Latest Trands on Systems*. **2**, Rhodes, WSEAS Press (GR) . 657-659 (2010)
9. CHRAMCOV, Bronislav. *Recent Researches in Automatic Control*. Montreux: WSEAS Press, 346-351 (2011)
10. Zelinka I., *Studies in Fuzziness and Soft Computing*, New York : Springer-Verlag, (2004)
11. Koza J. R., *Genetic Programming*, MIT Press, ISBN 0-262-11189-6 (1998)
12. Jui-Yu W., *MIMO CMAC neural network classifier for solving classification problems*, Applied Soft Computing, **11**, Issue 2, The Impact of Soft Computing for the Progress of Artificial Intelligence, p. 2326-2333 (2011)
13. Falco D.I., Cioppa E., Tarantino, *Discovering interesting classification rules with genetic programming*, Applied Soft Computing 1, p. 257–269 (2002)
14. Brameier M., Banzhaf W., *A comparison of linear genetic programming and neural networks in medical data mining*, IEEE Transactions on Evolutionary
15. Turner et al., *Grammatical Evolution of Neural Networks for Discovering Epistasis among Quantitative Trait Loci Evolutionary Computation, Machine Learning and Data Mining in Bioinformatics Book Series Title*: Lecture Notes in Computer Science Publisher: Springer Berlin / Heidelberg, 86 – 97 (2010)
16. Vonk E., Jain L.C., Johnson R.P *Advances in Fuzzy Systems – Applications and Theory*, **14**, World Science, ISBN: 981-02-3106-7 (1997)
17. Koza J. R. et al. *Genetic Programming III*; *Darwinian Invention and problem Solving*, Morgan Kaufmann Publisher, (1999)

Simulation of the PIR detector active function

Rudolf Drga[1,a], Dagmar Janacova[2] and Hana Charvatova[3]

[1]*Tomas Bata University in Zlín, Faculty of Applied Informatics, Department of Security Engineering, nám. T. G. Masaryka 5555, 760 01 Zlín, Czech Republic*
[2]*Tomas Bata University in Zlín, Faculty of Applied Informatics, Department of Automation and Control Engineering, nám. T. G. Masaryka 5555, 760 01 Zlín, Czech Republic*
[3]*Tomas Bata University in Zlín, Faculty of Applied Informatics, Regional Research Centre CEBIA-Tech, nám. T. G. Masaryka 5555, 760 01 Zlín, Czech Republic*

Abstract. The work deals with the behaviour of the PIR detector in an environment with great influence of a thermal background. It was necessary to perform simulations of the thermal behaviour of the sensor by COMSOL Multiphysics in different modes of heating the room to be able to prove that the PIR detector can function as an active detector with improved detection possibilities of intruders who would be invisible to a detector under normal circumstances. This confirms the detector's ability to work on the principle of active detector, i.e. as transmitter and receiver of thermal radiation and evaluation of heat flux changes depending on the type of the heater and the shrouding.

1 Introduction

This paper deals with the function of the passive PIR detector that can function as an active detector under certain conditions, which enhance its possibilities in terms for detecting intruders, who could successfully mask under normal circumstances and they would become invisible for the detector.

2 Principle of the PIR detector

The principle of the PIR detector is shown in Fig. 1. The detector consists of pyroelement 1 which is receiving radiation from an intruder. This radiation passes through the filter 2, which suppresses radiation of wavelength less than 8 micron and greater than 12 micron and is therefore permeable for the 8 to 12 microns with a maximum of 10 microns wavelength, which corresponds to the temperature of the intruder, i.e. about 37 ° C. Infrared optics detector 3 performs the concentration of thermal radiation on pyroelement while creating segments 4, wherein the detector "see" and "not see". If intruder moves tangentially 5 over these areas, this leads to intermittent radiation after passing through the filter to generate pyroelement charge whose magnitude is measured after signal processing 6 and then the signal is sent as an alarm message on I&HAS security system.

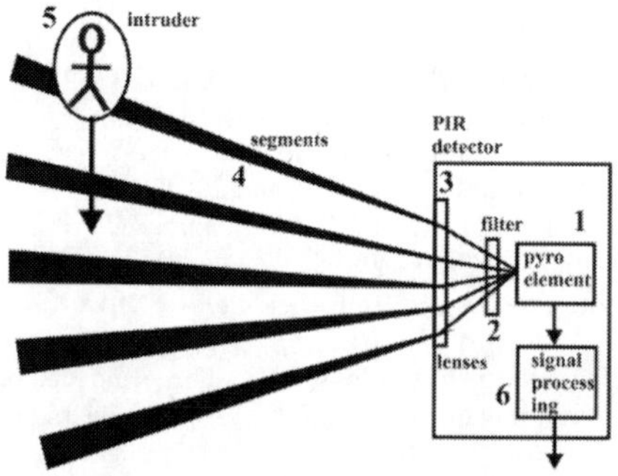

Figure 1. Principle of PIR detector.

3 Principle of active function of the PIR detector

The main function of the PIR detector is relatively easy to disrupt such a way that object (intruder) does not transmit thermal radiation. This can be relatively easily realized as an intruder uses curtain that hides the intruder in the direction of the PIR detector. In Fig. 2 are shown infrared images of various materials for the intruder masking. On left side is a man dressed in neoprene, in middle in winter clothes and on the right man disguised in an insulated liner.

[a] Corresponding author: rdrga@fai.utb.cz

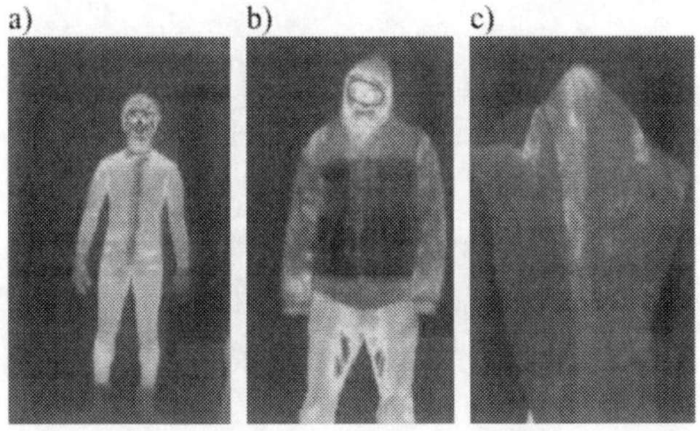

Figure 2. Masked intruder dressed in a) neoprene, b) winter clothing, c) isothermal foil.

Fig. 3 shows the principle of active PIR detector. A source of thermal radiation is in the background. It transmits radiation in the range of 10 μm wavelength. If the masked intruder moves in front of this background, there is a change of the heat flux from the background so that it obscures the individual segments, which quality PIR detector measures as a change of the incident radiation and activates the alarm condition.

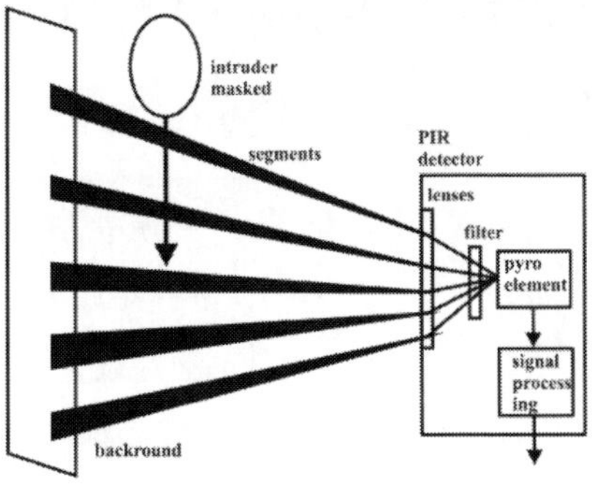

Figure 3. Principle of active PIR detector

4 Mathematical model of heating sensor by radiation

Thermal radiation incident on the sensor is partially reflected and partially absorbed by the sensor, thereby to ensure that the temperature measured at the beginning of the measurement does not fully effective temperature.

We used the Stefan-Boltzmann law for the quantitative description of the temperature distribution in the pyroelement inside the detector, which is heated by radiation. According to Stefan-Boltzmann law, the density of heat flux between the source and the heated surface is expressed as (1) [3]:

$$q(\tau)=\sigma.C(T_2^4-T_1^4) \tag{1}$$

where:

σ - Stefan-Boltzmann constant, $\sigma = 5.67.10^{-8}$ W m^{-2} K^{-4}

C – constant which characterizes emission surface and geometric properties, [1]

T_2 – source temperature, [K]

T_1 – temperature of heated surface, in this case the surface temperature, [K] .

Mathematical model of the sensor (pyroelement) heating can be described by equations (2) – (5):

$$\frac{\partial T}{\partial \tau}=a.\frac{\partial^2 T}{\partial x^2},\ (0\leq x\leq b, 0<\tau) \tag{2}$$

$$\left(\frac{\partial T}{\partial x}\right)_{x=0}=0 \tag{3}$$

$$\lambda\left(\frac{\partial T}{\partial x}\right)_{x=b}=q \tag{4}$$

$$T=T_p \text{ for } \tau=0 \tag{5}$$

where:

b - half thickness of the sensor, [m]

x - direction coordinate, [m].

Analytical solution of non-stationary temperature field for sensor plate shape symmetrically heated by radiation has been obtained by Laplace transform as:

$$\frac{T-T_p}{T_c-T_p}=K_i\left[Fo+\frac{1}{2}\left(\frac{x}{b}\right)^2-\frac{1}{6}-2\sum_{n=1}^{\infty}\frac{\cos\left(\frac{x}{b}p_n\right)}{p_n^2\cos(p_n)}e^{(-Fop_n^2)}\right] \tag{6}$$

where K_i is Kirpičev criterion (7)

$$K_i=\frac{qb}{\lambda(T_c-T_p)} \tag{7}$$

T_c is medium temperature of radiators.

Fourier criterion Fo represents the dimensionless heating time which can be calculated according to equation:

$$Fo=\frac{a\tau}{b^2} \tag{8}$$

where:

τ - time of heating, [s]

a - thermal diffusivity of sensor, [m^2.s^{-1}]

The thermal diffusivity is given by equation:

$$a = \frac{\lambda}{\rho c_p} \tag{9}$$

where:
λ - the thermal conductivity of sensor, [W.m^{-1}.K^{-1}]
ρ - the density of the sensor material, [kg.m^{-3}]
c_p - the specific heat capacity of the sensor material, [J.kg^{-1}.K^{-1}].

Members p of the analytical solution of (6) are determined from equation (10):

$$p_n = n \cdot \pi \ . \tag{10}$$

According to the solution (6) it is evident that with increasing time of heating, the influence of endless series elements decreases, i.e., we can also expect Fourier criterion Fo for which influence endless series may be neglected and for $Fo > Fo_k$ the temperature at any point in the wall is almost linear function of time and temperature profile across the pyroelement (in x-axis direction).

5 Simulations in Comsol Multiphysics

The aim of simulations was to compare the incident heat radiation to the surface of pyroelement, if the intruder was in the room, or not. It was considered both heated and unheated room with vertical or floor heater.

Fig. 4 shows room with an unheated vertical heating. Fig. 4a depicts the layout position of the heater, pyroelement and intruder. Fig. 4b shows the distribution of incident heat flux to the surface pyroelement and in Fig. 4c is seen course of the heat flux in vertical section of the pyroelement.

Fig. 5 shows the same situation as in Fig. 4 for the heated room.

Fig. 6 shows the results of simulations for an unheated room with underfloor heating. which in Fig. 6a is drawing position of underfloor heating, pyroelement and intruder inside the room. Fig. 6b depicts the distribution of incident heat flux to the surface of pyroelement and in Fig. 6c is shown course of the heat flux in a vertical section of the pyroelement.

Fig. 7 shows the same situation as Fig. 6 for room heated by underfloor heating.

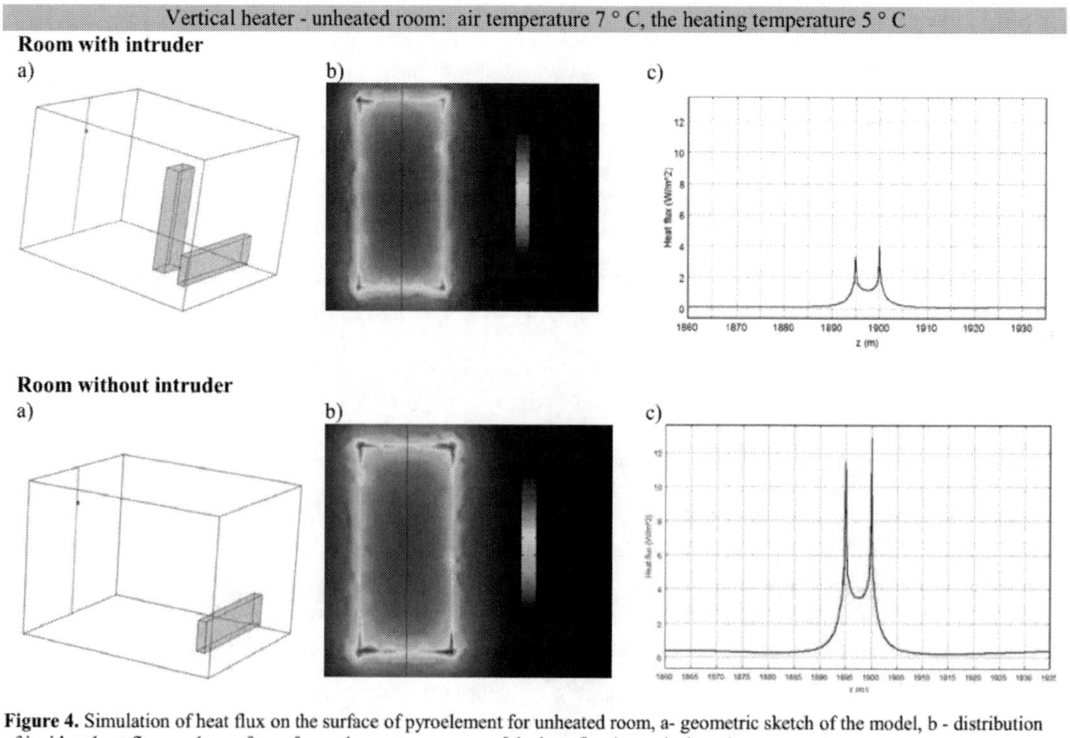

Figure 4. Simulation of heat flux on the surface of pyroelement for unheated room, a- geometric sketch of the model, b - distribution of incident heat flux on the surface of pyroelement, c - course of the heat flux in vertical section.

 DOI: 10.1051/matecconf/20167604036

Vertical heater - heated room: air temperature 24 ° C, heating temperature 37 ° C

Room with intruder

a) b) c)

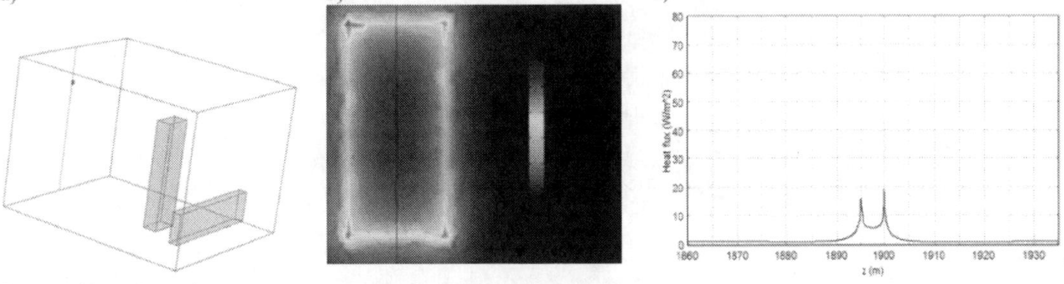

Room without intruder

a) b) c)

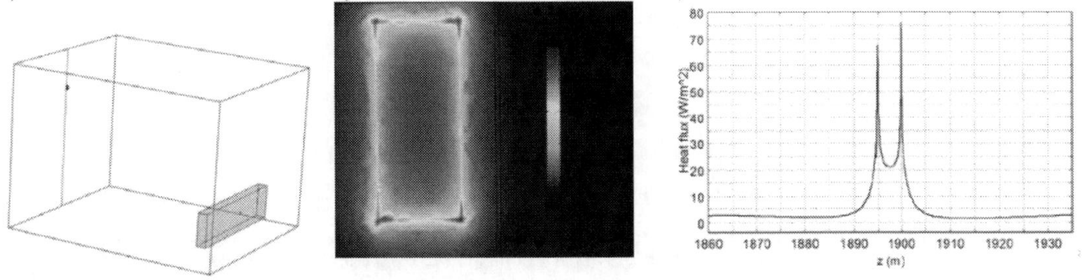

Figure 5. Simulation of heat flux on the surface of pyroelement for heated room, a- geometric sketch of the model, b - distribution of incident heat flux on the surface of pyroelement, c - course of the heat flux in vertical section.

Floor heating - unheated room: air temperature 7 ° C, the heating temperature 5 ° C

Room with intruder

a) b) c)

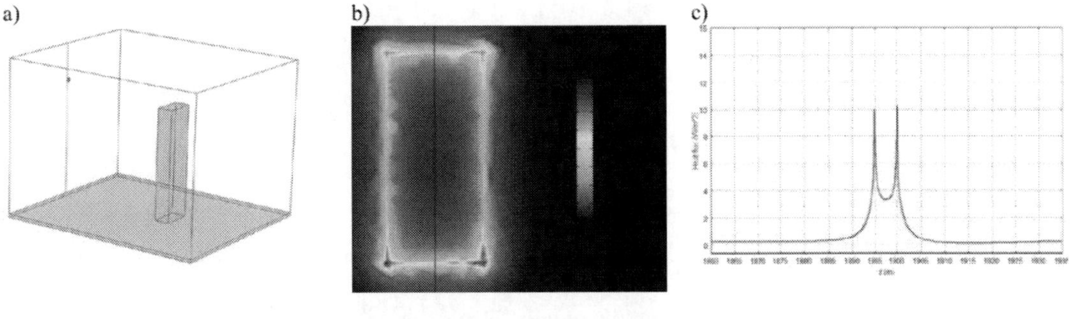

Room without intruder

a) b) c)

Figure 6. Simulation of heat flux on the surface of pyroelement for unheated room, a- geometric sketch of the model, b - distribution of incident heat flux on the surface of pyroelement, c - course of the heat flux in vertical section.

DOI: 10.1051/matecconf/20167604036

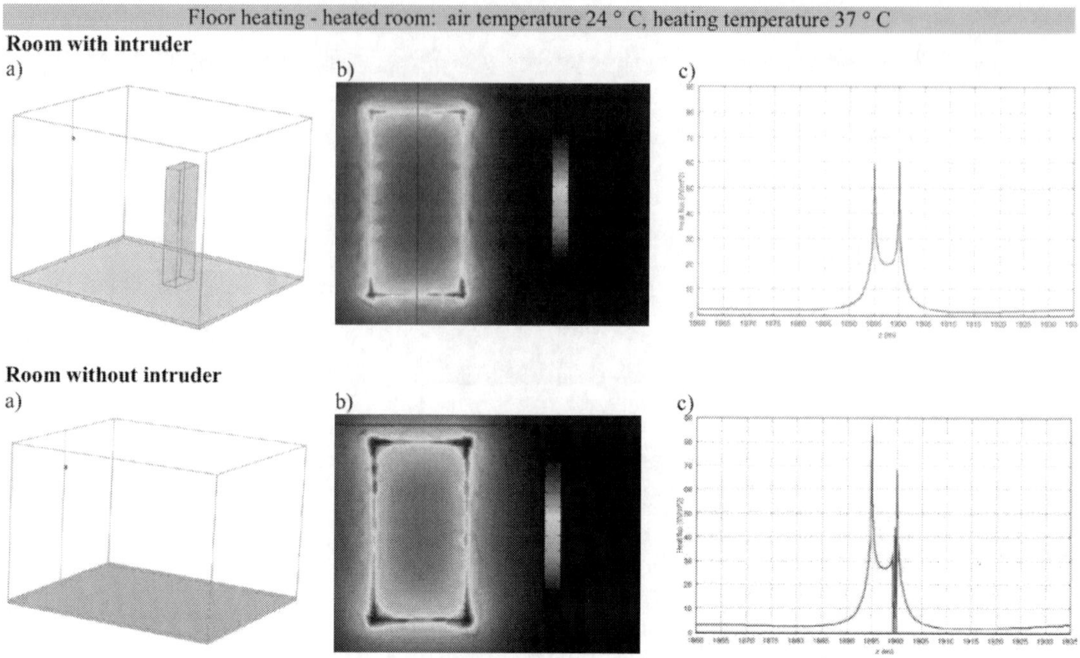

Figure 7. Simulation of heat flux on the surface of pyroelement for heated room, a- geometric sketch of the model, b - distribution of incident heat flux on the surface of pyroelement, c - course of the heat flux in vertical section.

The table 1 shows a summary of the simulation results which are shown in Figs. 4 – 7. The column 2 of the Table1 gives the values of the heat flux in the middle of pyroelement that corresponds to a minimum simulated value.

In the presence of intruder before heater, the heat flux incident on a surface of pyroelement decreased about a significant value which the PIR detector is able to measure.

Table 1. Minimum values of the heat flux on the surface of pyroelement determined by computer simulations.

Vertical heating	
Unheated room without intruder	3.7 W/m^2
Unheated room with intruder	1.3 W/m^2
Heated room without intruder	21 W/m^2
Heated room with intruder	6 W/m^2
Floor heating	
Unheated room without intruder	4.2 W/m^2
Unheated room with intruder	3.75 W/m^2
Heated room without intruder	27 W/m^2
Heated room with intruder	20 W/m^2

6 Conclusion

Based on results of simulations and measurements can be stated that the difference in heat flux incident on a surface of the pyroelement in the room both with the intruder, and also without the intruder will activate the PIR detector. In this way, the intruder can be detected and masked. This confirms the detector's ability to work on the principle of active detector, i.e. as transmitter and receiver of thermal radiation and evaluation of heat flux changes depending on the type of the heater and the shrouding.

Acknowledgments

This work was supported by the Ministry of Education, Youth and Sports of the Czech Republic within the National Sustainability Programme project No. LO1303 (MSMT-7778/2014) and also by the European Regional Development Fund under the project CEBIA-Tech No. CZ.1.05/2.1.00/03.0089.

References

1. J. D. Vincent, *Fundamentals of infrared detector operation and testing*. (WILEY, USA, Texas, 1990)
2. G. F. Knoll, *Radiation detection and measurement*. (WILEY, USA, Texas, 2000)
3. B. Saleh, *Fundamentals of photonics*. (WILEY, USA, Texas, 2007)
4. K. Kolomazník, *Teorie technologických procesů III. (in Czech)*. (University of Technology in Brno, Brno, 1978)
5. A, R. Jha, *Infrared technology*. (WILEY, USA, Texas, 2006)
6. C. Hotz, *Přenos tepla zářením (in Czech)*, (SNTL, Prague, 1979)
7. M. Fodor, O. Líška, *Proceedings of 8th International Symposium on Applied Machine Intelligence and Informatics*, (Herľany, Slovakia, 2010)

MATEC Web of Conferences 76, 04037 (2016) DOI: 10.1051/matecconf/20167604037
CSCC 2016

Modelling of the simple pendulum Experiment

L.Palka [1] ,F. Schauer [2] and P. Dostal[1]

[1]*Tomas Bata University in Zlin, Zlin, Czech Republic*
[2]*Trnava University in Trnava, Slovak Republic*

Abstract. Abstract - work focuses on the design of the simulation embedded in remote experiment "Simple pendulum " built on the Internet School Experimental System (ISES). This platform is intended for wide educational purposes at schools and universities in order to provide the suitable measuring environment for students using conventional computing resources Informatics.

1 Introduction

The modern trend in scientific and teaching experimentation are the remote e-laboratories and e-stores for their HW and SW components[2,4]. For the purpose of management of remote laboratories the interconnected datacentres, creating the seed of the integrated net of remote laboratories for EU programme is being built [5]. Why do we deal with the matter?

Traditional teaching methods for students at schools and universities are outdated and not effective enough. Students often expect faster and more understandable teaching methods in the field of physics, biology, chemistry and electro-engineering, which can help them to better perceive real world phenomena. The problem is also an accessibility of the educational materials, especially for distant students who nowadays prefer studying scientific topics using their computers via the Internet. These problematic points are effectively solved by the remote laboratories (RLs) so called e-laboratories. The RLs built on the ISES platform are developed longer time by the RL Consortium consisted of three universities (Charles University in Prague, Tomas Bata University in Zlín and Trnava University in Trnava) for educational purposes. The ISES is an advanced tool deployed for real-time operation, data acquisition, data processing, hardware (HW) controlling and visualizing.

The platform is an open system consisting of the ISES hardware and software components intended for hands-on experiments called ISES WIN. However, there is also an alternative for using remote experiments (REs), the ISES WEB Control Kit. Both types of the experiments are built as the burst (fast) and normal (slow) to offer students a wider spectrum of knowledge. The initial version of ISES RLs has been developed by Charles University in Prague. When the ISES RL became the time-proven educational tool, it was significantly improved to a higher level tool by Tomas Bata University in Zlín in cooperation with Charles University in Prague. They implemented features for the new user environment, EASY REMOTE-ISES, in order to simply building REs by laymen [4][16].

Let us describe the ISES RL concept. It consists of six units as the HW components (convertor, control board, physical modules categorized as meters, sensors and devices), Measureserver, Imageserver, Webserver, Datawarehouse and Webclient. More technical details and deployed applications are available in [1][2][3][4][6] and [7]. All the ISES RLs were recently integrated into a new platform so called Remote Laboratory Management System (REMLABNET). It provides autonomous units as services to the ISES RL administrators and clients. The schematic arrangement of all the involved units and corresponding communication is presented in Figure B.

The layout of the paper is following. In Chapter 1, the typical scheme of the communication of a typical remote experiment (RE) , built as the finite-state machine (FSM) [2], using the Datawarehouse and Internet School Experimental System (ISES) physical hardware, is described[10] (for the ease of reading we will next denote the set of the individual remote experiment by the word rig). Also, the control program compiling and the type of the data generated and transferred is shortly described. More details may be found in corresponding literature [2][3]

The Chapter 2 is devoted to describing the architecture Remote Experiments and the corresponding integrating management system, called for our purposes Remote Laboratory Management System (RLMS) [10]. The Chapter 3 is devoted to the actual communication design and database scheme of remote laboratories. The Chapter 4 is then focused on the simulation of a simple pendulum in remote experiments linked to RemLabNet environment. The chapter 5 is oriented on acquainting the reader with the results of a simulation of a simple pendulum in remote experiments linked to RemLabNet environment. The final chapter 6 is focused on the use of

[a] Corresponding author: lukas.palka@email.cz

data mining from simple pendulum, use in RemLabNet projection system and the results on the portal.

2 State of the art

Only recently has emerged a serious problem stemming from analysis of research data. ISES is a powerful tool for process and experiments control, acquisition, collecting and data processing in real time. Let us mention the basic features of the ISES system, more detailed description may be found elsewhere [2][10]. The basis of the system is ISES board, which is available in several versions, differing depending on the number of inputs/outputs and also on type of communication with the control PC (by PCI card, USB connector, Wi-Fi). To this board are, by a unique connector, plugged in sensors like: ammeter, voltmeter, thermometer, position sensor, ohmmeter, load cell, anemometer, microphones, sonar, light gate, pH meter, conductivity meter, heart rate monitor, etc. [8]. The layout arrangement of the RE is in Figure A.

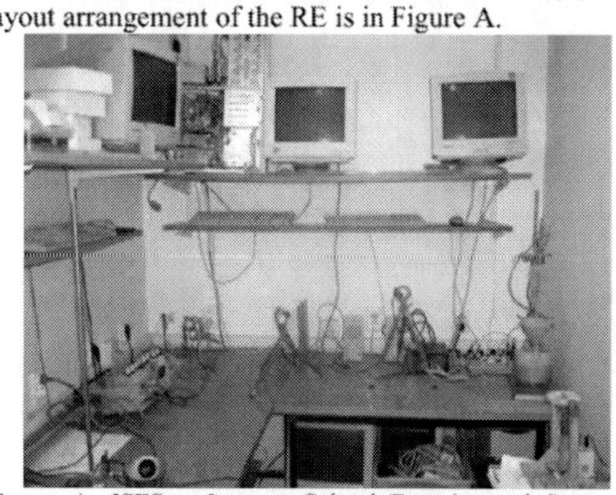

Figure A. ISES – Internet School Experimental System e-laboratory in MFF UK in Prague.

The most important component is the Measureserver module, functioning as finite-state machine (FSM) controlled by the controlling program of the PSC script file. The main feature of the Measureserver, is to communicate with the physical hardware and to check the setup of the ISES panel and its sensors/meters and to take care about their data collection and processing. Other parts of the system are ImageServer for life view of the remote experiment, Web server for the communication between RE and the client. Also, aprt of the RE is the communication web page as the interface communicating with the RE over the Internet by the client.

The inevitable part of the RE system is the data warehouse for the storage of data for all above systems. It is a centralized repository service to Measureserver, web server, image server and other components of the solution.

In this article we will discuss this last part of the system with respect of data security, but not only from the perspective a single RE, but of the whole RLMS. The layout arrangement of the RE is in Figure B.

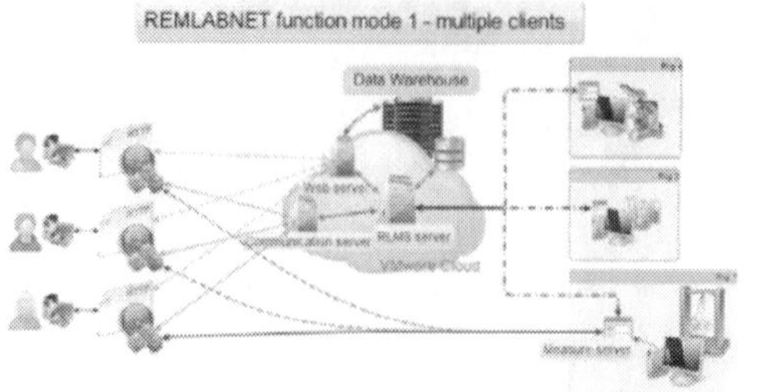

Figure B. REMLABNET function mode 1 – multiple clients.

A serious problem stemming from security aspects of e-laboratories has emerged only recently [19]. Let us describe first the data generated and that are processed in every ISES rig working on the communication principle server-client and the functioning of the superordinate Remote Laboratory management system (RLMS). The controlling of every rig by client is enabled via Web interface, by means of which the user can perform the appropriate settings, options, and starting or stopping of the remote experiment (RE).

The measured data from the experiment delivered from the MeasureServer are stored in the data storage . RLMS is a system for a database-driven Web application. This is seen from the figure 2, where LMS is divided terms of safety in three parts. Database-driven Web applications are very common in today's Web-enabled society. LMS consist of a back-end database with Web pages that contain server-side script written in a programming language that is capable of extracting specific information from a database depending on various dynamic interactions with the user.

Remote experiments problematic is the topic of scientific activities of the group since 2005, when the first remote experiment started to be built. We relied on the enormous know-how of Assoc. Prof. F. Lustig from Department of Physics Education of Faculty of Mathematics and Physics, Charles University in Prague, where the universal and very useful modular computer oriented set Internet School Experimental System (ISES) was designed at the beginning of 90th [21].

3 Phenomen simulation concept

The project deals with classical simple pendulum with adjustable amplitude and low damping, enabling experiments with duration of app. till 1 hour. The output is in form of the instantaneous angle of deflection (red curve in Figure A 1.2) on time and the counter of number of swings (blue marks). All data are available for downloading.

In the description of the use of the system a RemLabNet is the remote experiment simple pendulum with multipurpose use, starting from the measurement of acceleration of gravity, kinematics (instantaneous velocity and acceleration with its tangential and normal components), dynamics (acting forces, equation of motion), and energy (potential and kinetic energy, energy conservation law, work of dissipative forces) of curvilinear motion. Experiment is suitable as a demonstration experiment in the lectures, in the seminars as the data source for calculations and in the laboratory exercises.

Figure C. RemLabNet simple pendulum experiment.

The following figure shows a simple pendulum, where you can see a workable solution in practice in the lab.

The following illustration shows the description and amplitudes during the course of a simple pendulum. They are seen here with runs pendulum course of its amplitude and data that were generated by the pendulum. Public version of the data is in Chapter VII.

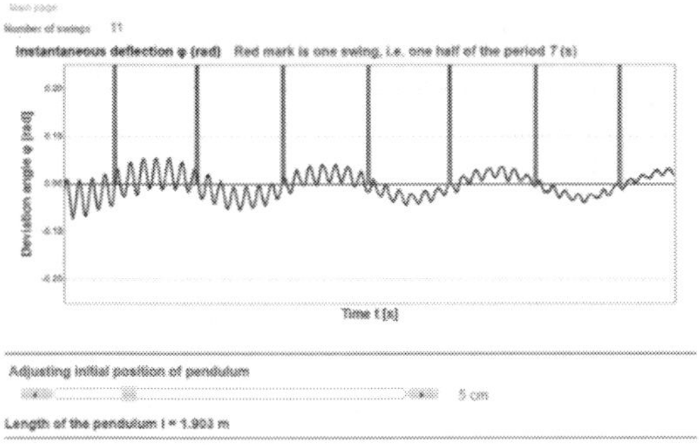

Figure D. amplitude easy course pendulum.

4 Simple pendulum model in easy java simulations - Theory

Classical simple pendulum with adjustable amplitude and low damping, enabling experiments with duration of app. till 1 hour. The output is in form of the instantaneous angle of deflection (red curve in Figure A 1.2) on time and the counter of number of swings (blue marks). All data are available for downloading.

Description of the use:

The remote experiment simple pendulum with multipurpose use, starting from the measurement of acceleration of gravity, kinematics (instantaneous velocity and acceleration with its tangential and normal components), dynamics (acting forces, equation of motion), and energy (potential and kinetic energy, energy

conservation law, work of dissipative forces) of curvilinear motion. Experiment is suitable as a demonstration experiment in the lectures, in the seminars as the data source for calculations and in the laboratory exercises.

We simulate the motion of a pendulum which has a fixed obstacle in the trajectory of its arm. For simplicity, we assume the obstacle is aligned vertically with the turning point of the pendulum. See the figure above.

The resulting motion can be considered as the superposition, to each side of the obstacle, of the motion of tow pendula, each with a different arm length. Hence, the differential equation of the interrupted pendulum is just:

$$\frac{d \cdot \theta}{dt} = \omega$$

$$\frac{d \cdot \omega}{dt} = -\frac{g}{l}\sin(\theta)$$

if only the value of l is different when the pendulum is at each side of the obstacle. Moreover, the collision of the pendulum's arm with the obstacle produces a sudden change of the angular velocity of the pendulum (while the linear velocity of the pendulum bob remains does not change as result of the collision). We will treat this collision by means of an event.

5 Theoretical background kinematics the curvilinear motion

Equations should be centred and should be numbered with the number on the right-hand side.

The velocity of a curvilinear motion is defined

$$\mathbf{v} = \frac{\mathbf{d}\mathbf{r}}{\mathbf{d}t}, \qquad (1)$$

where $\boldsymbol{r}$ is the position vector. The direction of the velocity $\boldsymbol{v}$ is given by the tangent to the trajectory (Figure 1).

The basic property of any curvilinear motion (even those with constant velocity) is its non zero normal acceleration $\boldsymbol{a}_n$. It is due to the fact that the direction of the unit vector of the velocity is not constant and changes with time.

$$\mathbf{a}_n = \frac{\mathbf{d}\left(\frac{\mathbf{v}}{v}\right)}{\mathbf{d}t} \qquad (2)$$

Its value is

$$\mathbf{a}_n = \frac{v^2}{R}, \qquad (3)$$

Where v is the value of the instantaneous velocity and R is the radius of the curvature of the trajectory in and its direction is the normal to the trajectory.
If the motion has variable velocity, then we introduce, similarly as with linear motion, the tangential acceleration

$$\mathbf{a}_t = \frac{dv}{dt}. \qquad (4)$$

With the direction given by the tangent to the trajectory.

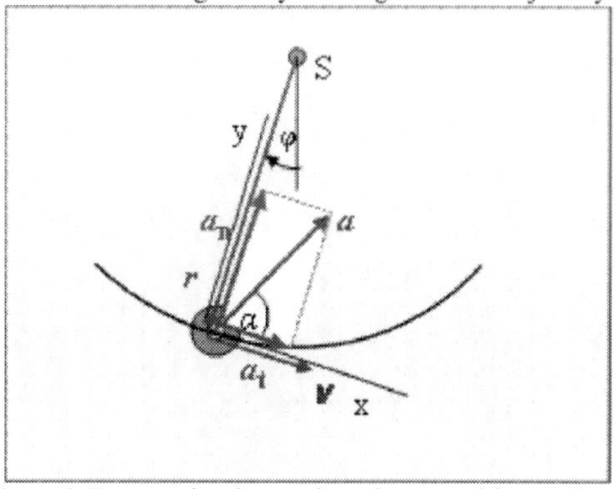

Figure 1*. Tangential and normal acceleration of the curvilinear motion (the angle of deflection in the figure is ?<0)*

To study the curvilinear motion we will use the simple pendulum (Figure 1). It is a weight of the mass m, hanging on the suspension of the length r. The pendulum is moving under the influence of the force of weight $\boldsymbol{G}$ by the harmonic motion, described by the angular displacement ? (> < 0!)

$$\varphi = \varphi_o \sin(\Omega t), \qquad (5)$$

where $?_o$ is its amplitude and ? is the angular frequency

$$\Omega = 2\pi f = \frac{2\pi}{T} = \sqrt{\frac{r}{g}},$$ where g is the acceleration due to the weight.
For the normal acceleration we can then write, using eq.(5), (Figure 2)

$$a_n = \mathbf{r}\omega^2 = r\left(\frac{\mathbf{d}\varphi}{\mathbf{d}t}\right)^2 = r(\varphi_o\Omega\cos\Omega t)^2, \quad (6)$$

where r is the radius vector value and $\omega = \frac{d\varphi}{dt}$ is the angular velocity of the pendulum motion.
For the tangential acceleration, using the angular acceleration $\varepsilon = \frac{d^2\varphi}{dt^2}$, we have

$$a_t = \mathbf{r}\varepsilon = r\left(\frac{\mathbf{d}^2\varphi}{\mathbf{d}t^2}\right) = -r(\varphi_o\Omega^2\sin\Omega t) \qquad (7)$$

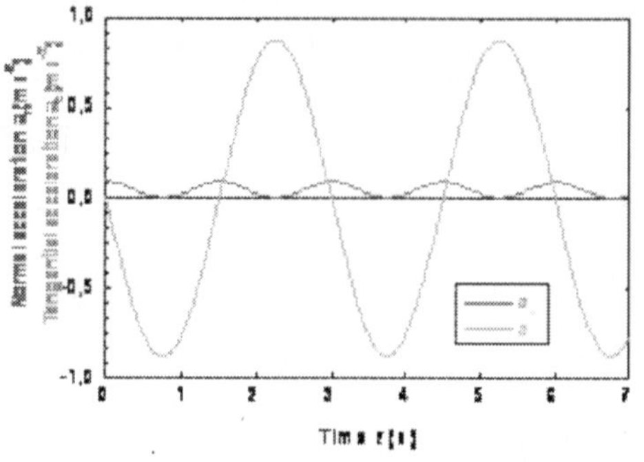

Figure 2. Tangential and normal acceleration of the simple pendulum, eq.(6) and (7);

r = 2m, $?_o$= 0,1rad T = 3s, m = 0,1 kg

Dynamics of the curvilinear motion
Why is the simple pendulum moving according to eq.(5)? The equation of motion (2. Newton' law of motion), expressing the action of forces from other bodies on the motion of a body is

$$\sum_i \mathbf{F}_i = m\mathbf{a}\ , \qquad (8)$$

where $\boldsymbol{a}$ is the acceleration of the body. For a simple pendulum from Figure3 the eq.(8) reads for the x axis (?

$$G\sin(\varphi) = -ma_t \qquad (9)$$

whereas for the y axis

$$T - G\cos(\varphi) = ma_n. \qquad (10)$$

Equation (9) is the differential equation for the angular displacement ? (where we used eq.(6))

$$\left(\frac{\mathbf{d}^2\varphi}{\mathbf{d}t^2}\right) = -\frac{g}{r}\sin(\varphi). \qquad (11)$$

The eq.(11) is analytically not soluble, but for small angular displacements (??) = ? and the solution is (see eq.(5))

$$\varphi = \varphi_o \sin(\Omega t).$$

Then we can write, using eqs. (5) and (6) for the pull T in the suspension of the pendulum the important for the measurement expression (see Figure 3 and its dependence in Figure 4)

$$T = mg\cos[\varphi_o\sin(\Omega t)] + mr(\varphi_o\Omega\cos\Omega t)^2. \ (12)$$

 DOI: 10.1051/matecconf/20167604037

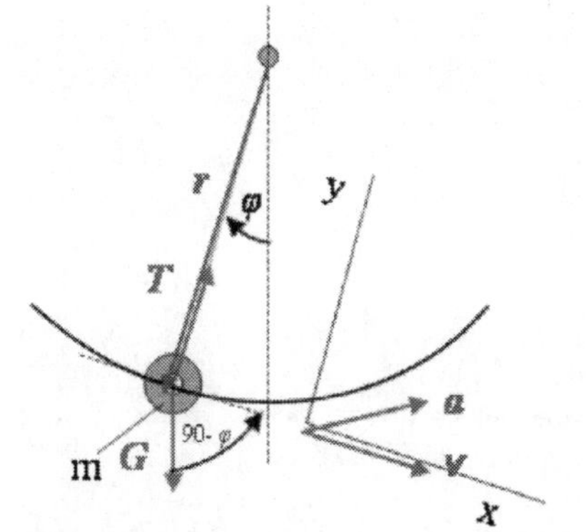

Figure 3. *Dynamics of the simple pendulum motion*

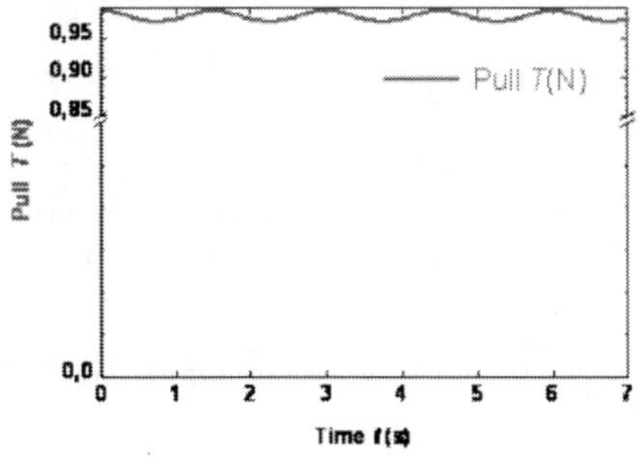

Figure 4. *Time dependence of the pull T in the suspension of the pendulum, eq.12;*
r = 2m, ?₀= 0,1rad T = 3s, m = 0,1 kg

Energy of the curvilinear motion

The kinetic energy of the pendulum is, using eq. (5) and the definition of the angular velocity

$$E_k = \frac{1}{2}mv^2 = \frac{1}{2}m(r\omega)^2 = \frac{1}{2}m[r\varphi_0\Omega\cos(\Omega t)]^2. \quad (13)$$

The potential gravitation energy of the weight of the pendulum is, using the expression for the pendulum position *h* above the reference level (taken as the lowest point of the pendulum swing) *h* = *l*(1-cos *?(t)*) (Figure 5)

$$E_p = mgh = mgr[1-\cos(\varphi(t))] = mgr\{1-\cos[\varphi_0\sin(\Omega t)]\}. \quad (14)$$

For the pendulum motion the law of the conservation of the mechanical energy is fulfilled (Figure 6)

$$E_{k1} + E_{p\ weight1} = E_{k2} + E_{p\ weight2}, \quad (15)$$

6 Simple pendulum model in easy java simulations - results

Motion of a Pendulum

This simulation models the motion of a simple pendulum. You can change the mass of the pendulum bob, the length of the string, the acceleration due to gravity, and the initial deflection of the pendulum. You then can observe the resulting oscillations of the pendulum, as well as see bar graphs of the kinetic, potential and total mechanical energy and plots of the pendulum's angular position, angular speed, and angular acceleration as a function of time.

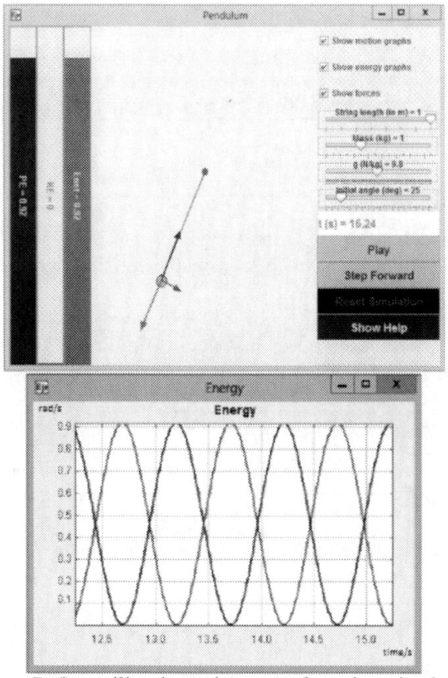

Figure D. Controlling the environment of easy java simulation and output to EJ.

Let us describe individual phases of the knowledge mining process in more detail.

Model:

Variables

We formulate the following basic set of variables:

- *t* - the time, *h* - the increment for the time at each evolution step, and *g* the acceleration due to gravity.
- *m*- the mass of the pendulum bob, *lTotal* -the full length of the pendulum, and *d*- the distance from the turning point to the obstacle. *?*
- *leftSide* is a boolean flag that indicates whether the pendulum is to the left side of the obstacle.
- *l* is the current value of the pendulum length to be used in the differential equation.
- *theta* and *omega* are the angular magnitudes.
- Finally, *x1* and *y1* are the Cartesian coordinates of the folding point of the (broken) pendulum, and *x2* and *y2* are the coordinates of the position of the pendulum bob.

The table of variables is then:

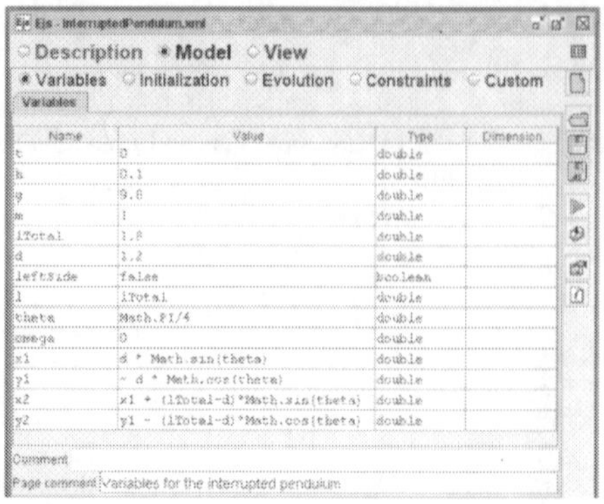

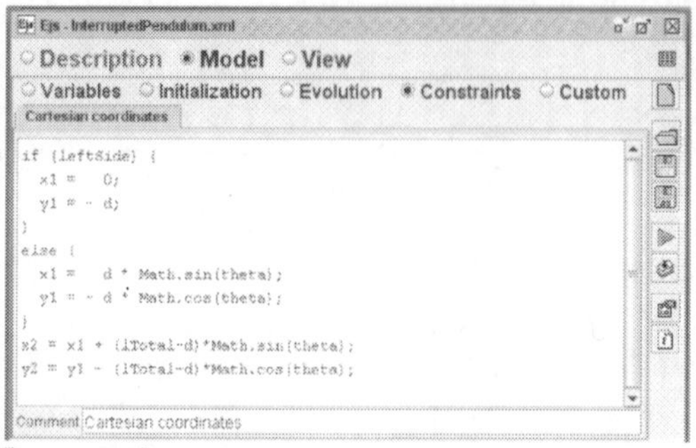

Custom code
No custom code required.

Initialization
The variables have been correctly initialized in the table of variables.

Evolution
The evolution needs a page of ordinary differential equations (ODE) with an event. The ODE editor looks as in the figure:

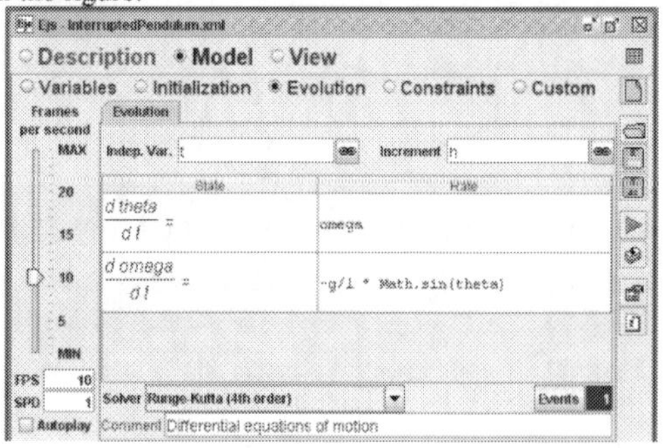

The event is defined by the event page:

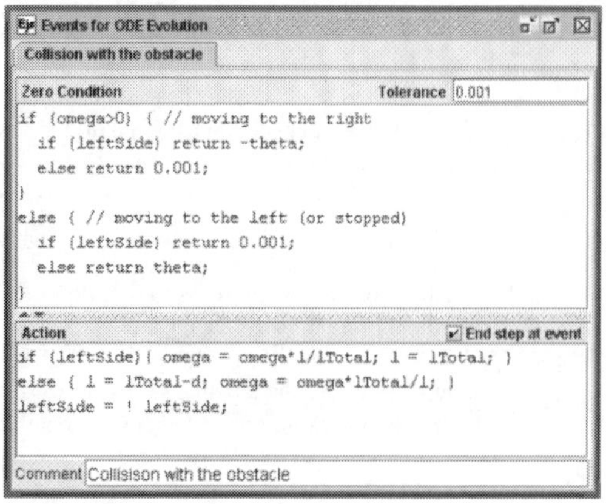

Notice how the collision computes the new angular velocity after the collision and adjust the value of *l* to use.

Constraints
A page of constraints is required to compute the Cartesian coordinates from the angular ones.

View
The view starts with the compound element based on a drawing panel with a default particle. We have added to the drawing panel a second particle to display the obstacle, and two strings (arrows with the *Style* property set to *SEGMENT*) to complete the scene.

A plotting panel displayed in a separate Dialog window will plot the time evolution of the angle of the pendulum. (This is rather standard and we give no further details here.)

The complete *Tree of Elements* is displayed in the figure below:

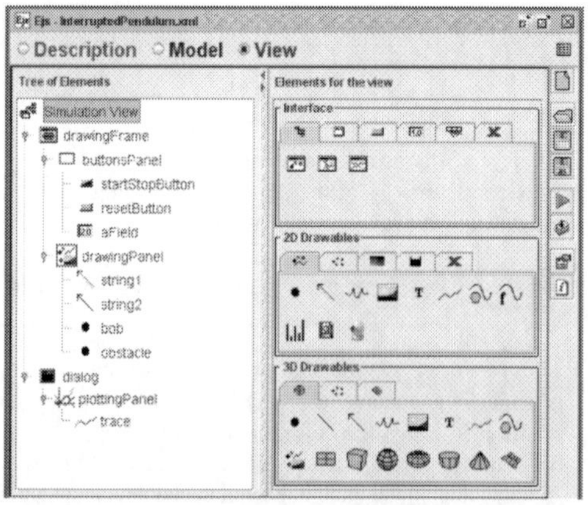

For simplicity we have suppressed interaction with our view elements. The main properties that need to be modified are shown in the colo fields of the property panels below:

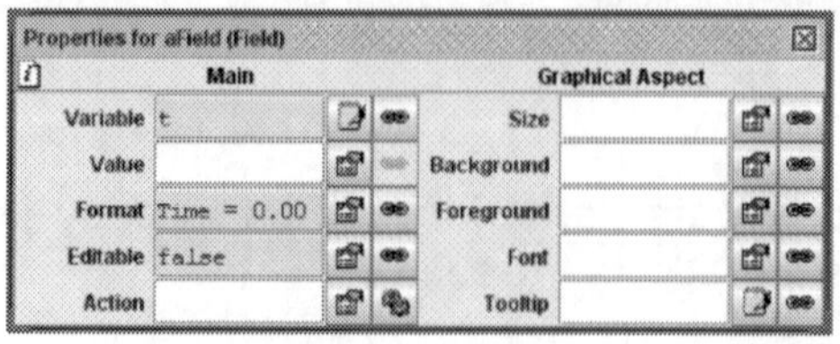

7 Simple pendulum model in data warehouse for remlabnet

Here we show the simple pendulum environment in RemLabNet day with output to data warehouse. Data are stored in OLAP cubes in the transaction concept store in the database. OLAP cubes are chosen due to the speed of analysis, which require immense computing power and access data stored on the measureserver. Data dimensional cubes to store our proposed method, where rows and columns are paired in three space and thus compare the cube to cube. Of course, the dice may be only 3 dimensional, but the number of dimensions is X. For our work but sufficient dimension 3. Structure of tables and data is protected compartment of our system, that is not public. Outcomes data are of course fully public and the needs of users.

Figure E. RemLabnNet simple pendulum experiment.

public version of the data is as follows:

Time t [s]	Deviation	[rad]	Time t [s]	Swing No.
1.351	-0.042	1.351	0	
1.371	-0.075	1.371	0	
1.391	-0.095	1.391	0	
1.411	-0.087	1.411	0	
1.431	-0.058	1.431	1	
1.451	-0.053	1.451	1	
1.471	-0.066	1.471	1	
1.491	-0.088	1.491	1	
1.511	-0.077	1.511	2	
1.531	-0.061	1.531	2	
1.551	-0.056	1.551	2	
1.570	-0.068	1.570	2	
1.591	-0.071	1.591	3	
1.611	-0.058	1.611	3	
1.631	-0.053	1.631	3	
1.650	-0.060	1.650	3	
1.671	-0.069	1.671	4	
1.691	-0.060	1.691	4	
1.711	-0.051	1.711	4	
1.730	-0.054	1.730	4	
1.751	-0.058	1.751	4	
1.771	-0.059	1.771	5	
1.791	-0.059	1.791	5	
1.811	-0.057	1.811	5	
1.831	-0.052	1.831	6	
1.851	-0.053	1.851	6	
1.871	-0.060	1.871	6	
1.891	-0.064	1.891	6	
1.911	-0.053	1.911	7	
1.931	-0.045	1.931	7	
1.951	-0.055	1.951	7	
1.971	-0.060	1.971	7	
1.991	-0.054	1.991	8	
2.011	-0.046	2.011	8	
2.031	-0.049	2.031	8	
2.051	-0.054	2.051	9	
2.071	-0.056	2.071	9	
2.091	-0.050	2.091	9	
2.111	-0.049	2.111	9	
2.131	-0.049	2.131	10	

Real running a simple pendulum experiment understandable model for the comparison of the simulations. Behavior, respectively, compared simulations and calculations from the actual operation is fascinating. So compare the article that focuses on the simulation of realistic simulation run. The picture is output in real measured data, which we can compare the result of the simulations. Measurement data in thousands of reported values is because of similar simulations, but in certain parts of the chart we see other shifts in behavior and real experiment.

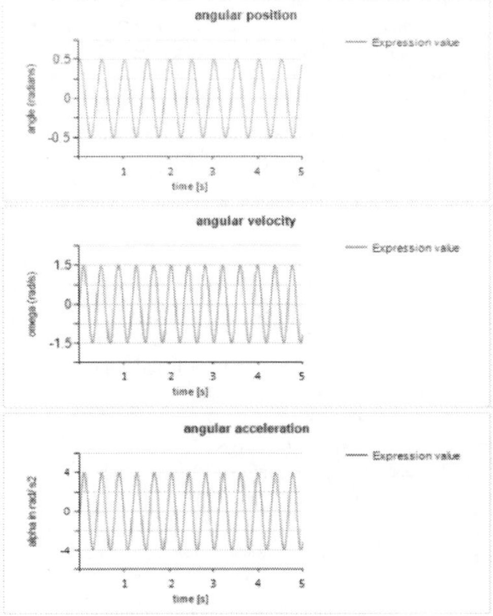

Figure F. graph of DW RemLabNet.

8 Conclusions

A simple pendulum mathematical model described above. It is a model of environmental RemLabNet, where the lessons we describe the theory and practice in simulation environments with remote experiments and analyzing the output data into the data warehouse RemLabNetu. From the article, it is obvious how the system works, all described by the theory, through calculation, via simulation to the real operation. Outputs are data from simulated and real environments from the measured data. Comparison of the results are fascinating. Great importance is being experinetů distant relative of both simulation and real factor systems running. In this article, however, we focus primarily on the simulation, which is described mathematically calculate all the characteristics and conditions and as such simulations in an environment easyjava simulation.

Acknowledgments

The paper was published thanks to the Grant of the Internal Agency of UTB No IGA/2016/. One of us acknowledges the partial support of the Slovak Research and Development Agency, project no. APVV-0096-11, the Scientific Grant Agency VEGA, project no.

2/0157/12, and the KEGA Agency projects No 011TTU-4/2012 and 020TTU-4/2013..

References

1. The whole system is detail described in the project proposal Submitted Project Grant Agency of the Czech Republic: INFORMATICS MEANS FOR GRID OF e-LABORATORIES – PROJECT REMLABNET, 2013.
2. KRBEČEK, Michal. Possible utilization of the artificial intelligence elements in the creation of remote experiments. [online]. 2012, č. 1 [cit. 2013-06-26]
3. Grid Remote Laboratory Management System. Sahara Reaches Europe. 2013, č. 1
4. Database-Level Roles [online]. 2012 [cit. 2013-06-26], http://msdn.microsoft.com/en-us/library/ms189121.aspx
5. ALEXANDER, David, Amanda FINCH, David SUTTON a Andy TAYLOR. Information Security Management Principles. 2. vyd. bcs, 2013. ISBN 9781780171753
6. SCHULZ. Cloud and Virtual Data Storage Networking. teChapterChapterbooks, 2011. ISBN 978-1439851739
7. Data Warehouse [online]. 2013 [cit. 2013-06-26], http://en.wikipedia.org/wiki/Data_warehouse
8. SCHAUER, František, František LUSTIG a Miroslava OŽVOLDOVÁ. Innovations 2011: World Innovations in Engineering Education and Research: Internet Natural Science Remote e-Laboratory (INTRE-L) for Remote Experiments. USA: iNEER, 2011, s. 51-68. 1. ISBN 978-0-9818868-2-4.
9. SCHAUER, František a Miroslava OŽVOLDOVÁ. Plug and play system for hands on and remote laboratories. In: Proceedings of 8th International Conference on Hands-on Science. Ljubljana: University of Ljubljana, 2011, s. 17-21. ISBN 978-989-95095-7-3
10. KRBEČEK Michal, František SCHAUER, Roman JAŠEK. Security aspects of remote e-laboratories. Zlín: UTB ve Zlíně, Fakulta aplikované informatiky, 2012
11. PÁLKA Lukáš,Data Warehouse services [online]. 2013 [cit. 2013-06-26], http://datawarehouse.cz/Data_warehouse
12. Data Warehouse [online]. 2013 [cit. 2013-06-25], http://www.1keydata.com/datawarehousing/datawarehouse.html
13. PÁLKA Lukáš, Methods and Tools Related to Data Security and the Protection of Microsoft SQL Servers. Zlín UTB, 2012
14. LABERGE, Robert. The Data Warehouse Mentor: Practical Data Warehouse and Business Intelligence Insights. -: 2011. ISBN-10: 0071745327
15. CLARKE, Justin. SQL Injection Attacks and Defense. USA: Elsevier, 2012. ISBN 978-1-59749-963-7.
16. GERŽA Michal, František SCHAUER, Roman JAŠEK. Security of ISES MeasureServer© module for remote experiments against malign attacks, Zlín: UTB ve Zlíně, Fakulta aplikované informatiky, 2013.
17. BRUCHEZ, Rudi. Microsoft SQL Server 2012 Security Cookbook. UK: Packt Publishing, 2012. ISBN ISBN 978-1-84968-588-7
18. HARKINS, Malcolm. Managing Risk and Information Security: Protect to Enable. LLC: Apress Media, 2013. ISBN 978-1430251132
19. Paper REV 2014 - 31102013 – F. Schauer 2014
20. T. Dulík, M. Bližňák, "Security measures in virtual laboratory of microprocessor technology," DAAAM International Vienna, Proceedings of the 21st International DAAAM Symposium "Intelligent Manufacturing & Automation: Focus on Interdisciplinary Solutions", Vienna, 2010, pp. 1203-1204, ISBNISSN 978-3-901509-73-5
21. D. Lowe, P, Newcombe and B. Stumpers, "Evaluation of the Use of Remote Laboratories for Secondary," Res. Sci. Educ/Science Education, Springer Science and Business Media B.V. 2012, DOI 10.1007/s11165-012-9304-3.
22. Lustig, F.: "Počítačem podporované školní experimenty s měřícím systémem ISES pod Windows", In: sborník MEDACTA 97 - vzdělávanie v meniacom sa svete, 404-408, Ústav didaktickej technológie, PF UKF v Nitre, Nitra, ISBN 80-967339-9-0, 1997 and Lustig, F. and Schauer, F.: "Creative laboratory experiments for basic physics using computer data collection and evaluation exemplified on the ISES", Proceedings first european conference on Physics Teaching in Engineering Education, 125-131, Copenhagen, Denmark, ed. Oehlenschlaeger, 1997

MATEC Web of Conferences **76**, 04038 (2016) DOI: 10.1051/matecconf/20167604038
CSCC 2016

Optimization of suspensions filtration with compressible cake

Dagmar Janacova[1,a], Pavel Mokrejs[2], Karel Kolomaznik[1], Vladimir Vasek[1], Rudolf Drga[1], Ondrej Líska[3] and Jiri Krenek[1]

[1] *Tomas Bata University in Zlín, Faculty of Applied Informatics, nám. T.G.Masaryka 5555, 760 01 Zlín. Czech Republic*
[2] *Tomas Bata University in Zlín, Faculty of Technology, nám. T.G.Masaryka 5555, 760 01 Zlín. Czech Republic*
[3] *University of Košice, Faculty of Mechanical Engineering, Letná 9, 04200 Košice, Slovak Republic*

Abstract. In this paper there is described filtering process for separating reaction mixture after enzymatic hydrolysis to process the chromium tanning waste. Filtration of this mixture is very complicated because it is case of mixture filtration with compressible cake. Successful process strongly depends on mathematical describing of filtration, calculating optimal values of pressure difference, specific resistant of filtration cake and temperature maintenance which is connected with viscosity change. The mathematic model of filtration with compressible cake we verified in laboratory conditions on special filtration device developed on our department.

1 Introduction

Filtration belongs to the most common cases practically making use of phenomena taking place during the flow of liquid through a layer of granular material. Its industrial application is similar to laboratory filtration performed on filter paper in a filter funnel. The objective is to separate solid particles from the liquid in which they are dispersed. This separation is achieved during filtration by forcing the liquid containing solid particles through a porous barrier. Solid particles get caught in pores of the barrier and gradually build up a layer on it. Liquid passes through the particle layer and porous barrier and leaves, gradually freed of its solid phase.

2 Filtration

A suspension of solid particles in liquid is brought to the filter, and filtrate and filter cake are drawn off [5]. Let us designate: m_F - mass of filtrate, m_S - mass of suspension, m_K - mass of filter cake, w_F - mass fraction of solid phase concentration in filtrate, w_S - mass fraction of solid phase in suspension, w_K - mass fraction of solid phase in cake. Balance relationships are balances of whole flows as well as balances of both phases. If the filter operates efficiently, value w_F is very small and negligible in relation to the others and the quantity of filtrate can then be determined from the quantity of suspension and concentrations of solid particles in suspension and filter cake:

$$m_F = m_S\left(1-\frac{w_S}{w_K}\right) \quad (1)$$

$$p_1 - p_2 = \rho\left(\frac{\lambda h A v_F^2}{8\varepsilon^3} + gh\right) \quad (2)$$

where: p_1 - pressure before cake, p_2 - pressure behind cake, ρ - density, v_F - velocity, λ - friction coefficient, ε -porosity of layer, g - gravitational constant, h - thickness of cake, A - surface density of articles.

Term gh usually has no significance in filtration as the hydrostatic pressure produced by height of suspension level is generally negligible when compared with a pressure difference produced by industrial means [1], [4]. Provided the particles are sufficiently firm and do not undergo deformation, porosity remains constant throughout filtration and the filter cake is regarded as incompressible. Constant C and cake properties, i.e. porosity and surface density, then combine into a single constant:

$$\alpha = CA^2 / \varepsilon^3 \quad (3)$$

after simplification:

$$p_1 - p_2 = \alpha h \mu\, v_F \quad (4)$$

Practical account is taken of the difference between p_1 and p_3. When passing through this screen, filtrate changes its pressure from p_2 to p_3 because the screen offers resistance to its flow

$$p_2 - p_3 = R v_F \quad (5)$$

Combining equations for filter cake and screen, we obtain the filtration equation:

[a] Corresponding author: janacova@fai.utb.cz

$$p_1 - p_3 = (\alpha h \mu + R) v_F \quad (6)$$

The flow of filtrate through cake is described as a flow of liquid through a layer of granular material [7]. This equation is used more practically in the form containing volume of
filtrate:

$$\frac{dV_F}{d\tau} = \frac{(p_1 - p_3) S^2}{\beta \mu (V + V_{EKV})} \quad (7)$$

where

$$\beta = \alpha \tau \frac{V_K}{V_F} \quad (8)$$

and V_{EKV} is the resistance of filter screen expressed by means of equivalent thickness of filter cake. Integration of (7) gives:

$$V^2 + V_{EKV} V = 2K\tau \quad (9)$$

where $$K = \frac{(p_1 - p_2) S^2}{\beta \mu} \quad (10)$$

With a constant rate of filtrate flow, the solution of (7) is:

$$V^2 + V_{EKV} V = K\tau \quad (11)$$

Accordingly, the deformation of particles has to be taken into account as this affects particle porosity. In that case specific resistance of the filter cake is not constant. On passage through the cake, filtrate pressure drops from value p_1 to p_2. Deformation of the cake is caused by a resistive force when the stream flows past particles in a layer placed on a firm screen. The intensity of resistance F'_R equals the difference in pressures (p_1-p_2) multiplied by flow cross-section, S - area of filter:

$$F'_{R=}(p_1 - p_2) S \quad (12)$$

As pressure p decreases when going from the interface with suspension to interface with screen, resistive force in the same direction increases and this is the force causing deformation of particles. This deformation then affects value of α and/or β. A certain value is found only across a differential section of the cake between h' and $h' + dh'$ described by equation:

$$-dp = \alpha \eta v_F dh \quad (13)$$

Integration across the whole thickness of cake and substitutions $dp' = -dp$ and $dh = -dh'$ give:

$$\int_0^{p-p_2} \frac{dp}{\alpha} = -\int_0^{-h} -\mu v_F dh \Rightarrow p_1 - p_2 = \rangle \alpha \langle \eta v_F h \quad (14)$$

where $<\alpha>$ is the mean value of α.

The mean value of $\alpha(\beta)$ is determined from the dependence on p'. It is found by filtration tests in an apparatus where value of p' can be altered. This dependence is usually expressed in the form as follows:

$$\alpha = \alpha_0 \left[1 + \beta (p)^\gamma\right] \quad (15)$$

Equation for rate of filtration:

$$v_F = \frac{p_1 - p_2}{\langle\alpha\rangle \mu h + R} = \frac{\Delta p . S^2}{\langle\beta\rangle \mu (V + V_{EKV})} \quad (16)$$

$$p_s = \frac{1}{\tau_1 - \tau_2} \int_{\tau_2}^{\tau_2} f(\tau) d\tau \quad (17)$$

Calculated mean values are presented in the following table [2]. Parameter β characterizes filter cake resistance. If this does not change when pressure differences during filtration change, the cake in question is incompressible; on the contrary, it is compressible if resistance changes. We adapted the filtration equation for a constant pressure difference [1, 6]:

$$\frac{dV_i}{dt} = \frac{\Delta p . S_f^2}{\mu \beta . V_i} \quad (18)$$

Assuming that $\Delta p = p_{si}$, and that β_i, μ, Δp and S_f^2 are constant within individual intervals and can be substituted by K_i, Constant K enabled us to determine:

$$\beta_i = \frac{\Delta p . S_f^2}{\mu . K_i} \quad (19)$$

The dependence was approximated by a dx potential

$$\beta = 1{,}76.10^{14} . e^{7{,}7275.10^5 . p_s} \quad (20)$$

For industrial application, the best advantage is gained at greatest rate (maximum filtrate in time). Therefore, the given equation was differentiated with respect to pressure difference:

$$\Delta p: \quad \frac{dv}{d\Delta p} = \frac{S_f^2}{\mu . V_F} . \frac{B.e^{C.\Delta p} - \Delta p . B . C . e^{C.\Delta p}}{\left(B.e^{C.\Delta p}\right)^2} \quad (21)$$

3 Experimental part

In laboratory conditions we verified recycling technology of leather shavings treatment. On the figure 1 is shown easier technology scheme of enzymatic hydrolysis [1].

The laboratory filtration model was designed to meet following requirements [3]:
- constant temperature of 30-80 °C in filtering space,
- filter underpressure recording (approx. 0,6 kPa),
- filtrate volume 5 l.

DOI: 10.1051/matecconf/20167604038

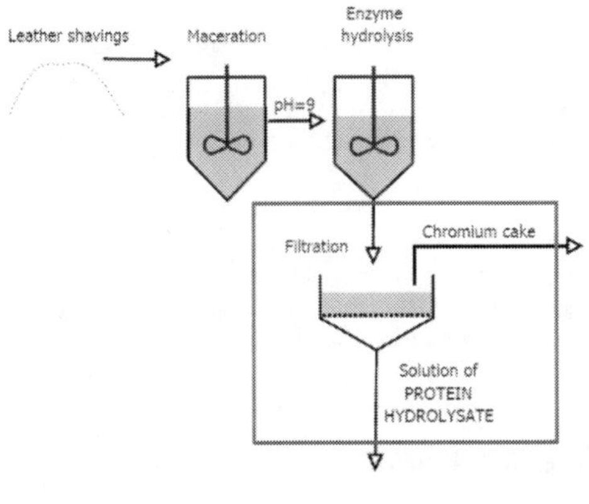

Figure 1. Process of enzymatic hydrolysis - scheme.

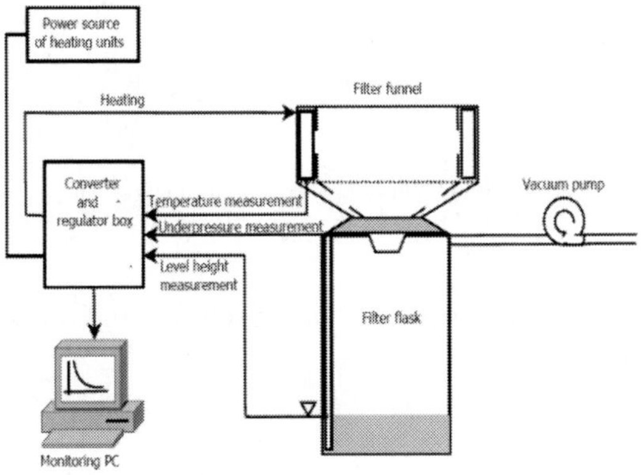

Figure 2. Laboratory arrangement of filtration.

The model consists of parts as follows:

- temperature-controlled heated filter funnel,
- filtration flask,
- underpressure measurement,
- level height measurement,
- unified signal conversion,
- data storage.

The filter funnel of circular shape consists of two main parts, the funnel proper and filter screen. Both parts were made of dural, which is light and conducts heat well [3], [4].

The basic dimensions of the funnel are inside diameter of 16,5 cm and funnel edge of 8cm height. It can be filled at a time with 1.7 litres of the filtered suspension. The funnel wall is provided with 4 holes drilled symmetrically from the bottom side for holding heating elements. Another two holes are asymmetrically drilled there for resistance thermometers. One of these is located in the close vicinity of a heating element, the second is precisely between these elements. The resistance thermometers are connected in series, which in the chosen spacing permits better determination of the funnel average temperature.

Complete sealing during filtration induced by underpressure under the funnel is provided by two rubber packing. The first of annulus shape is between the funnel proper and filter screen. The second, suitably shaped packing is mounted between the filter funnel and mouth of filtration flask [3].

Heating was provided by 4 heating elements fed by 24V a.c., each of 60 W power. The heating bodies were divided into two parallel sections, each containing two bodies connected in series. The heating bodies were powered through an external transformer.

Filtration was performed while the funnel was heated to 50°C. Properties of the suspension were as follows:

density $\rho = 2500$ kgm^{-3}, dynamic viscosity $\mu = 0{,}001$ Pas.

Primary filtration proceeded for the first 100 seconds without external underpressure, merely under own hydrostatic pressure. After 100 seconds, underpressure was produced by the vacuum pump. At the time when an underpressure decrease characterizing stoppage of filtration appeared, the value of underpressure was increased. This was repeated until the cake cracked and filtration stopped. An analogous procedure was employed in secondary filtration.

Primary filtration is the term applied to filtration in progress during the first stage of enzymatic dechromation, secondary filtration applied to that during the second stage. The pressure difference means value of produced underpressure or value at the beginning of hydrostatic pressure and both terms are interchangeable.

The course of pressure differences during primary filtration of first-stage suspension is depicted in Figure 3.

Four stages are obvious in primary filtration. The first (0-100 s) without underpressure, second (100-460 s) with underpressure exerted for the first time. Further underpressure increases occurred in the third (460-920 s) and fourth (920-2490 s) stages. A drop in underpressure follows stage four - the already mentioned filter cake rupture.

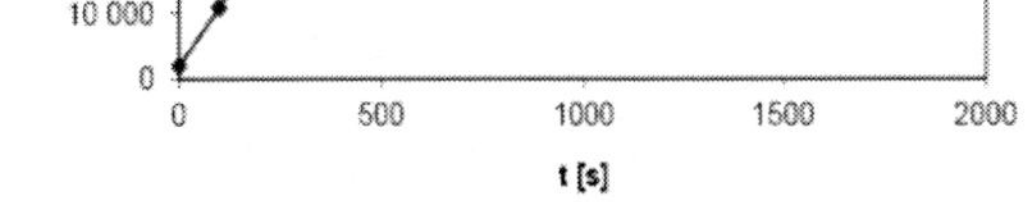

Figure 3. Course of underpressure during primary filtration

This signifies that the specific resistance of filter is independent of pressure difference $\Delta p = 12940 Pa$ (equation 21).

DOI: 10.1051/matecconf/20167604038

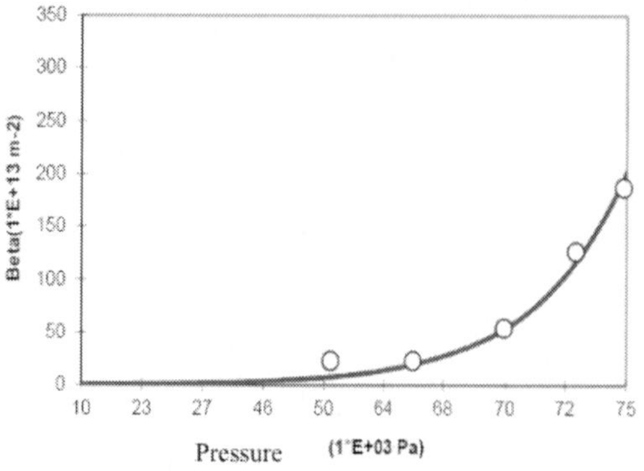

Figure 4. Dependence of parameter β on difference approximation by exponential curve (equation 20)

The procedure in secondary filtration of hydrolysate was the same as in primary filtration. Calculated values are presented in the table as follows.

Table 1. Calculated values for primary filtration.

Interval No.	τ_1 [s]	τ_2 [s]	P_s [Pa]	β [m^{-2}]
I	0	50	1 962	4,3E+12
II	50	80	10 802	2,4E+12
III	80	300	26 813	5,6E+12

Filtration of a similar volume of suspension proceeded much faster (about 22 times). Values of the cake specific resistance varied merely within the same order; the cake, therefore, was further considered to be incompressible. The general expression for calculating optimal values of pressure difference we used for control of primary filtration of suspension. The process having started, filtration runs without external cause only due to its own hydrostatic pressure. When the defined sampling period has elapsed, constant K is and the value of inductive force is increased by a difference defined in advance. With this first incrementation, the source of force changes from pressure to underpressure. Constant K is again calculated after this period, namely by recording changes in height of level. The preceding value of K is compared with the present. If it fails to comply with the specified condition, underpressure is increased again, and K is newly calculated after the time difference has elapsed. The cycle is terminated upon condition being met. A further condition follows, comparing actual underpressure with the value of optimal underpressure found in identifying filtration. Control is finished upon reaching accordance within a certain tolerance. If values of underpressures differ, the value found during process modelling is set up and control is finished. Parameter x of the first condition is chosen a priori and has an influence on underpressure being possibly exceeded. If x were chosen with a value approaching 1 from below, filtration would last too long.

4 Conclusion

In this contribution we have successfully solved the problem of separation of heterogeneous mixtures after enzymatic hydrolysis in the case of production of gelatine protein. By using controlled filtration during her constant speed, we have increased production of gelatine protein. We determined optimal underpressure and parameter β for filtration process with compressible cake. The filtration process we verified on our developed filtration equipment in laboratory conditions. For another suspensions with compressible cake we can determine optimal parameters: underpressure, specific resistanceβ and time of filtration also.

Acknowledgement

This work was supported by the Ministry of Education, Youth and Sports of the Czech Republic within the National Sustainability Programme project No. LO1303 (MSMT-7778/2014) and also by the European Regional Development Fund under the project CEBIA-Tech No. CZ.1.05/2.1.00/03.0089

References

1. K. Kolomazník, Recovery and recycling of chromium and protein from liquid and solid wastes from leather industry, *ERB 3512 PL 940974 (COP 974)*, (1996)
2. D. Janacova, K. Kolomaznik, V. Vasek, Optimization of liquids consumption at washing. *6th International Carpathian Control Conference*. Miskolc-Lilafuered, Hungary, ISBN 963-661-644-2. (2005)
3. V. Vasek, K. Kolomaznik, D. Janacova, Optimization and Automatic Control of Chromium Recycling Technology, *WSEAS Transactions on Systems*, **5** (11), ISSN 2651-2654. (2006)
4. J. Dolinay, P. Dostalek, V. Vasek, New Embedded Control System for Enzymatic Hydrolysis, *Proceedings of the 8th WSEAS International Conference on Applied Informatics and Communications*, Rhodes, Greece, p. 174, ISBN: 978-960-6766-94-7. (2008)
5. L. Vasek, V. Dolinay Simulation model of heat distribution and consumption in municipal heating network, *International Journal of Mathematical Models and Methods in Applied Sciences*, Vol. **4** (4), p. 240-248. (2010)
6. J. Pitel, J. Borzikova, Mizak, J. Biomass combustion process control using artificial intelligence techniques, *Proceedings of XXXV. Seminar ASR'2010 Instruments and Control*. (2010)
7. K. Kyas, J. Cerný, M. Stanek, M. Manas, D. Manas, V. Senkerik, A. Skrobak, Measuring of temperature and pressure in injection mold, *International Journal of Mathematics and Computers in Simulation.*, Vol. **6** (6), p. 600-607. (2012)

Priority Derivation from Pairwise Comparison Matrices by Multi-Objective Evolutionary Computing

Ludmil Mikhailov[a]

Manchester Business School, University of Manchester, Manchester, United Kingdom

Abstract. The paper investigates the application of evolutionary algorithms (EA) for solving prioritisation problems, in the framework of the Analytical Hierarchy Process. A new two-objective prioritization (TOP) method was proposed recently by the author, where the prioritisation problem is formulated as an optimization task for minimization of the Euclidean norm and the number of rank violations. The TOP method derives Pareto optimal solutions, which requires the application of efficient computational algorithms. We propose two evolutionary computing approaches, based on single-objective and multi-objective evolutionary algorithms. Our preliminary results from a Monte-Carlo simulation show that the multi-objective EA outperforms the single-objective solution approach with respect to accuracy and computational efficiency.

1 Introduction

The assessment of weights of criteria and scores of alternatives is one of the most important tasks in the multicriteria decision-making. In the Analytical Hierarchy Process (AHP), proposed by Saaty [1], the values of weights and scores are assessed indirectly from comparison judgments. The elicitation process for both weights and scores is the same, so they are often called *priorities*.

The pairwise comparison process in the AHP assumes that the decision-maker can compare any two elements at a given hierarchical level and to provide a numerical value of the ratio of their importance. Comparing any two elements E_i and E_j, the decision-maker assigns a ratio a_{ij}, which represents a judgment concerning the relative importance of preference of the decision element E_i over E_j. If E_i is preferred to E_j then $a_{ij} > 1$, otherwise $0 < a_{ij} \leq 1$.

A full set of ratio-scale judgments for a level with n elements requires $n(n-1)/2$ comparisons. In order to derive a priority vector $w = (w_1, w_2, ..., w_n)^T$ from a given set of judgments, Saaty constructs a positive reciprocal matrix $A = \{a_{ij}\}$.

With the exception of the traditional Eigenvector prioritization method, all other methods for deriving priorities in the AHP are based on some optimization approach. The optimal prioritization methods, as the Goal programming, the Direct Least Squares, the Logarithmic Least Squares and the Fuzzy Preference Programming introduce an objective function, which measures the degree of approximation or the distance between the initial judgments and the solution ratios [2]. Thus the problem of priority derivation is formulated as an optimization task of minimizing the objective function, subject to normalization and some additional constraints.

Despite the multicriteria nature of the requirements, regarding the properties of their solutions, all optimal prioritization methods optimize a *single* objective function. However, a single objective function cannot encompass and satisfy all requirements about the quality of solutions.

A new two-objective prioritization (TOP) method was proposed recently by the author [3], where the prioritisation problem is formulated as an optimization task for minimization of the Euclidean norm and the number of rank violations. The TOP method derives Pareto optimal solutions, which requires the application of efficient computational algorithms.

The paper investigates the application of evolutionary computing for solving the TOP problem. In order to eliminate the drawbacks of the numerical methods, we propose two evolutionary computing approaches. In the first one, the TOP problem is transformed into a single-objective one, which is then solved by a standard single-objective EA. The second approach applies a multi-objective EA for solving the TOP problem without such transformation.

[a] Email address: ludmil.mikhailov@manchester.ac.uk

In order to compare the solution approaches, we perform Monte-Carlo simulation experiments, by randomly generating a large number of pairwise comparison matrices. The paper presents some initial results from this simulation. Both computational approaches are also illustrated also by a numerical example.

2 The two objective prioritisation problem

Let $S = \{a_{ij} | j > i\}$ be a set of pairwise comparison judgments. The feasible set Q is defined as the set of all priority vectors $w = (w_1,...,w_n)^T$, which satisfy the normalization and non-negativity constraints:

$$Q = \left\{ (w_1,...,w_n) \middle| w_i > 0, \sum_{i=1}^{n} w_i = 1 \right\} \quad (1)$$

The accuracy of the each priority vector $w \in Q$, approximately satisfying the comparison judgments can be measured by the Total deviation criterion:

$$T(w) = \sum_{i=1}^{n-1} \sum_{j=i+1}^{n} (a_{ij} - \frac{w_i}{w_j})^2 \quad (2)$$

This criterion is equivalent to the squared Euclidean distance for the upper triangular part of a Saaty's reciprocal comparison matrix.

The rank preservation properties of the solutions can be measured by the Number of Violations criterion [2]:

$$NV = \sum_{i=1}^{n-1} \sum_{j=i+1}^{n} v_{ij} \quad (3)$$

where

$$v_{ij} = \begin{cases} 1, & \text{if } w_i > w_j \text{ and } a_{ij} < 1, \text{ or } w_i < w_j \text{ and } a_{ij} > 1, \\ 1/2, & \text{if } w_i = w_j \text{ and } a_{ij} \neq 1, \text{ or } w_i \neq w_j \text{ and } a_{ij} = 1, \\ 0, & \text{otherwise.} \end{cases}$$

The Number of Violations criterion (3) can be represented in the following compact form:

$$V(w) = \frac{1}{2} \sum_{i=1}^{n-1} \sum_{j=i+1}^{n} \left| signum(a_{ij} - 1) - signum(\frac{w_j}{w_j} - 1) \right|$$

where the *signum* function is defined as:

$$signum(b) = \begin{cases} 1, & \text{if } b > 1 \\ 0, & \text{if } b = 0 \\ -1, & \text{if } b < 1. \end{cases}$$

The two-objective prioritization (TOP) problem [3] is to find a feasible priority vector that 'simultaneously' minimizes the Total deviation and the Number of violations:

$$\begin{aligned} &\textit{minimize } T(w) \text{ and } V(w) \\ &\textit{subject to } w \in Q, \end{aligned} \quad (4)$$

where $T: R^n \to R^1$ and $V: R^n \to R^1$ are real-valued objective functions.

Each feasible vector $w \in Q$ determines a unique value of the objective function vector $y = (T(w), V(w))$. Therefore, the feasible set Q in the space of decision variables can be transformed into a *payoff set* Y in the two-dimensional objective space. The payoff set represents a feasible region of the admissible values of $T(w)$ and $V(w)$, and can be considered as the image of the feasible set Q in the objective space.

The payoff set Y of the TOP problem consists in parallel line segments, as the function $V(w)$ takes non-negative discrete values in some range, and the function $T(w)$ is bounded.

3 Computational approaches for solving the TOP problem

Some classical multi-objective optimization (MOO) methods, which can be applied for finding Pareto optimal solutions to the TOP problem are the Weighting Method, the ε-Constraint Method, the Goal Programming Method or the Proper Equality Constraints method [4]. Generally, the main strength of classical MOO methods is their efficiency and ability to generate strong Pareto optimal solutions. However, these methods have some weaknesses in generating the Pareto optimal solutions, when specific problem knowledge is not available. Additionally, they cannot generate all Pareto optimal solutions with non-convex surfaces. From computational point of view, many optimization runs are required to obtain an approximation set of the Pareto optimal solutions [5].

Recently, the evolutionary algorithms have become an alternative to the classical methods for generating Pareto optimal solutions; since they can eliminate some of the drawbacks of the classical MOO methods.

Taking into account the specific properties of the TOP problem, we can transform it into a single-objective optimisation problem, which is easily solved by standard single-objective EA.

The TOP problem can be transformed into a single-objective problem by associating weights *k* and *(1-k)* to both objective functions, where $k \in (0,1)$. The modified objective function

$$J(w) = kT(w) + (1-k)V(w) \quad (5)$$

is used as a fitness function of a single-objective EA, where the value of the weight coefficient is given by the user. This value represents his preferences with respect to the relative importance of those two objectives.

Some multi-objective EA, as the Vector Evaluated Genetic Algorithm (VEGA), the Non-dominated Sorting Genetic Algorithm (NSGA), the Niched Pareto GA (NPGA), the Multi-objective Genetic Algorithm (MOGA) [5] and the Pareto Envelope-based Selection Algorithm (PESA II) [6].

However, it is well known that the presence of constraints scientifically affects the performance of multi-objective EA. Additionally, as opposed to the single objective case, the ranking of a population in the multi-objective case is not unique [7].

In order to assess the applicability of EA for solving the TOP problem, we perform a series of computational experiments by Monte-Carlo simulation. In our study we use the PESA-II, which has some advantages compared to other EA. PESA-II follows the standard procedures of an EA, but with the difference that two populations of solutions are maintained: an internal population (IP) of fixed size, and an external population (EP) of non-fixed but limited size. The internal population's job is to explore new solutions, and it achieves this by the standard EA processes of reproduction and variation (i.e., recombination and mutation). The purpose of the external population is to store and exploit good solutions; it does this by maintaining a large and diverse set of the non-dominated solutions discovered during search [8].

4 Monte-Carlo simulation

Monte-Carlo simulation experiments have been carried out, consisting in generation of comparison matrices with different dimensions and applying the single-objective and multi-objective evolutionary approaches. Initially random consistent pairwise matrices are generated; then they are perturbed by a user-driven parameter, denoted as p, which determines the degree of inconsistency.

The matrices for this comparison study are of dimensions n=3, 4, 5, 6, 7, 8 and 9. For every value of n the parameter p takes 9 values, p=10, 20,…, 90 and each combination of $\{n, p\}$ is replicated 30 times, which gives a total number of 810 n-dimensional matrices with different degrees of inconsistency. The overall number of generated random matrices is 5670.

The single-objective EA (a standard Genetic Algorithm) and PESA-II have been applied for solving the TOP problem for each pairwise comparison matrix, using the jMetal toolkit [9]. In the single-objective EA each chromosome is represented by a string of n components, associated with the n-dimensional priority vector w. The EA performs the basic genetic operators, which are roulette wheel selection, crossover with random mating and simple mutation.

Elitism has also been applied as an additional selection strategy, to make sure that the best performing chromosome always survives. The elitism has been realized by comparing the fitness of chromosomes from the current population and the fitness of the corresponding offspring. The fittest chromosome from the initial population survives for the next generation.

At the beginning of each cycle, all chromosomes are normalised, so that the values of their genes sum up to one. The stopping condition is the number of generations, which is selected to be equal to 100. The experimental results show that the single-objective EA converges to the optimal solution for less than 50 generation cycles.

The high-level pseudocode, showing the main steps in the PESA-II algorithm, is given below [8]:

PESA-II pseudocode

- initially set IP and EP to be empty
- randomly generate ipsize solutions and evaluate them
- store the nondominated solutions in EP
- do (until stopping criterion is met) {
- for 1 to ipsize do{
- select a niche uniformly at random in EP and select a solution
- uniformly at random from within it; place the solution in IP}
- for each pair of solutions in IP do{
- with probability pc, crossover the pair and replace them with the two children created
- mutate both solutions}
- for each solution s in IP do{
- evaluate s
- update EP with s{
- if s dominates one or more solutions in EP; add s to EP and remove the dominated ones
- else if s is dominated by one or more solutions in EP; do nothing
- else {
- if EP has less than epsize solutions; add s to EP
- else if s is in a less crowded niche than a solution in EP; add s to EP and discard a randomly chosen solution from a most crowded niche}

}
}
- return EP, a set of nondominated solutions

END

5 Numerical results

Consider a problem with 5 comparison elements [8], where the DM provides the following pairwise comparison matrix:

$$A=\begin{array}{c} \\ \end{array}\begin{matrix} E_1 & E_2 & E_3 & E_4 & E_5 \\ \end{matrix}$$

$$A=\begin{bmatrix} 1 & 5 & 1/3 & 7 & 2/3 \\ 1/5 & 1 & 2 & 1/2 & 4 \\ 3 & 1/2 & 1 & 1/2 & 1/4 \\ 1/7 & 2 & 2 & 1 & 1/3 \\ 3/2 & 1/4 & 4 & 3 & 1 \end{bmatrix}\begin{matrix} E_1 \\ E_2 \\ E_3 \\ E_4 \\ E_5 \end{matrix}$$

The TOP problem is formulated as a single-objective one (5) by the Weighting method and solved by the single-objective EA. The parameters of the EA are selected as follows:

- Population size = 100;- Crossover probability=0.9;
- Mutation probability=0.01.

The results obtained are given in Table 1.

Table 1. Pareto optimal solutions obtained by a single-objective evolutionary algorithm

w_1	w_2	w_3	w_4	w_5	T	V
0.309	0.113	0.096	0.135	0.347	50.048	2
0.344	0.075	0.109	0.111	0.361	39.806	3
0.345	0.058	0.140	0.071	0.386	29.717	4
0.363	0.067	0.146	0.058	0.367	26.962	5
0.381	0.076	0.139	0.062	0.342	26.720	6

PESA-II was applied for solving the same problem. A 30-bit Gray code was used to represent each of the five weights, giving a 150-bit binary chromosome. Uniform crossover was applied with probability 0.2 and a bit-flip per-gene mutation rate of 0.01 was used. It was found that PESA-II is not sensitive to these parameters, and other values give similar performance.

The values of the PESA-II parameter settings are:

IPsize=10; EPsize=100; Generations=50; pm=0.01; Pc=0.2; #grid-cells (niches)=100; representation=30-bits per weight.

The best values of the priority vectors obtained from 20 runs of PESA-II are shown in Table 2.

Table 2. Pareto optimal solutions obtained by PESA II

w_1	w_2	w_3	w_4	w_5	T	V
0.356	0.096	0.096	0.096	0.356	39.469	2
0.362	0.078	0.099	0.100	0.362	38.631	3
0.358	0.065	0.149	0.065	0.363	27.438	4
0.361	0.074	0.144	0.060	0.361	26.622	5
0.398	0.083	0.158	0.065	0.296	26.479	6

By comparing the values of T for each value of V, it is seen that PESA-II solutions outperform those obtained by the single-objective EA, with respect to the accuracy.

Regarding the computational efficiency, the average processing time of the single-objective EA for this example is 1325 milliseconds, while the PESA II algorithm requires 622 milliseconds to find the optimal solution.

The performance comparison was obtained using an Intel-based PC with a Core2Duo T5500 CPU running at 1.66GHz and 2GB of physical memory. The tests were executed on Windows 7 with Java NetBeans IDE running in parallel.

The preliminary results from the Monte-Carlo simulation show that the multi-objective EA gives better accuracy than the single-objective EA, especially for high-dimensional and rather inconsistent pairwise comparison matrices.

Regarding the computation time, both approaches have rather similar performance for pairwise comparison matrices of lower dimension, n=3 and n=4. When the size of the matrices increases, PESA–II strongly outperforms the single-objective EA. The single-objective EA is particularly slower in inconsistent and non-transitive problems with many Pareto optimal solutions.

Conclusions

The paper investigates the application of evolutionary algorithms for solving the TOP problem and sows that they are very good alternatives to the numerical multi-objective optimization methods. The numerical example and the preliminary results from a Monte-Carlo simulation experiment show that the multi-objective EA outperforms the single-objective EA with respect to the computational efficiency and accuracy of solutions.

References

1. T. Saaty, A caling method for priorities in hierarchical structures, Journal of Mathematical Psychology, **15**, 234-281 (1977)
2. B. Golany, M. Kress, A multicriteria evaluation of methods for obtaining weights from ratio-scale matrices, European Journal of Operational Research, **69**, 210-220 (1993)
3. L. Mikhailov, Deriving priorities from ratio-scale comparison judgements: A multiple objective approach, *Proceedings of the 17th International Conference on Multiple Criteria Decision Making MCDM'2004*, August 2004, Whistler, Canada
4. Y. Sawaragi, H. Nakyama, T. Tanino, *Theory of multiobjective optimization*. Academic Press, Orlando (1985)
5. K. Deb, *Evolutionary algorithms for multi-criterion optimization in engineering design*. John Wiley & Sons, Chichester, UK (1999)
6. D. Corne, N. Jerram, J. Knowles, M. Oates, PESA-II: Region-based Selection in Evolutionary Multiobjective Optimization, *Proceedings of the Genetic and Evolutionary Computation Conference*, 283-290 (2001)
7. C. Fonseca, P. Fleming, Multiobjective optimization and multiple constraints handling with evolutionary algorithms, part 1: A unified formulation, IEEE Transactions on SMC, **28**, 26-37 (1998)
8. L. Mikhailov, J. Knowles, Priority Elicitation in the AHP by a Pareto Envelope-based Selection Algorithm. *Multiple Criteria Decision Making for Sustainable Energy and Transportation Systems* (M Ehrgott, B Naujoks, T Stewart, and J Wallenius eds.), Springer's Lecture Notes in Economics and Mathematical Systems, **634**, 249-258, Springer-Verlag, London (2010)
9. J. Durillo, A. Nebro, F. Luna, B. Dorronsoro, E. Alba, jMetal: *A Java Framework for Developing Multi-Objective Optimization Metaheuristics*, Departamento de Lenguajes y Ciencias de la Computación, University of Málaga (2006)

MATEC Web of Conferences 76, 04040 (2016) DOI: 10.1051/matecconf/20167604040
CSCC 2016

Rack-Scale Storage Fabric: A Practical Way to Build Best-Fit Infrastructure for High-Performance Data Processing

Ruiquan Ding[1], Xiao Hu[2,a], Guofeng Chen[1], Zhiwen Xiao[1], Jiajun Zhang[1], Chao Liu[1], Jian Wang[2], Huan Zhou[2] and Jun Zhang[2]

[1]Baidu. No. 10, Xibeiwang Road East, Beijing, PRC. +86-10-5679-5465
[2]Intel APAC R&D Co. Ltd. No. 880, Zixing Road, Shanghai, PRC. +86-21-6116-5000

Abstract. This paper is to address the resource utilization problem for high-performance data processing applications in a large IDC (Internet Data Center) environment. On one hand, each application calls for a best-fit infrastructure with a specific compute-storage ratio, to achieve the highest resource utilization while meeting its performance requirement. And such a ratio varies among applications. On the other hand, IDCs have always been trying to unify the infrastructures for lower TCO (Total Cost of Ownership). Therefore, it's getting harder and harder to adapt infrastructures to application needs. This issue results in significant waste of investment in large IDCs. Furthermore, the high-performance data processing applications always require the infrastructure to offer as high compute-storage performance as a DAS (Direct Attached Storage) server, which remains as a great challenge when addressing the resource utilization problem. This paper, as part of Baidu-Intel joint research program, first evaluates the state-of-the-art solutions, and then introduces a more practical infrastructure, the core of which is *rack-scale storage fabric*. This infrastructure disaggregates compute units and storage units by a SAS (Serial Attached SCSI) fabric, and allows to compose *logical servers* with arbitrary computer-storage ratios within a rack. And the experiments in Baidu's research environment show that the logical servers exhibit the similar throughput/IOPS as DAS servers, and also their compute-storage ratios can best-fit the needs of different Hadoop applications.

1 Introduction

Different applications often exhibit different resource demands. And even one application would have different resource demands at different phases of its lifecycle. The resource demand of an application is majorly represented by a ratio of its needs for compute resource (e.g. CPU and memory) to its needs for storage resource (e.g. disks), called *compute-storage ratio*. In another words, if the infrastructure that hosts a specific application matched the compute-storage ratio of this application, the application would be able to fully utilize the resources of this infrastructure. Otherwise, the infrastructure would be underutilized, which, in large-scale IDC environments, would result in significant waste of investment.

On the other hand, there is a solid trend that the IDC users keep simplifying their infrastructures, in order to reduce TCO (Total Cost of Ownership), because fewer types of infrastructures would lead to lower price and easier maintenance. Recently such standardizations, like OCP [5] and Scorpio [6], even intend to create unified and standardized infrastructures across the industry. As a result, the tension between the diversification of applications and the simplification of infrastructures keep increasing, which makes it impossible to find a best-fit infrastructure for each specific application, and so very often there are resources not fully utilized. In this context, the industry have been researching and developing many solutions to improve IDC resource utilizations, such as Mesos [4], OpenStack [8], flat datacenter storage [7], and Intel Rack Scale Architecture [10].

Moreover, a lot of IDC applications are distributed and high-performance data processing software, which require high throughput and low latency for the compute to access the data in the storage. For this sake, those applications have been often designed as being aware of the data locality, i.e. to process a piece of data right on the server where it is stored. In another words, the performance relies on a condition that the connection between each compute and each corresponding storage would be as fast as that of a normal DAS server, which has disks closely attached to CPUs via PCIe and/or SAS technologies. For instance, each SATA disk should offer about 150MB/s sequential read throughput to the corresponding CPU. This applies to many popular data processing frameworks, like Hadoop, Spark, MPP, and so on. Therefore, improving the resource utilization for those distributed high-performance data processing applications must always retain the above condition. Otherwise, it would significantly compromise the performance.

[a] Corresponding author: albert.hu@intel.com

 DOI: 10.1051/matecconf/20167604040

This paper is organized as follows. First, Section 2 evaluates the state-of-the-art solutions. Next, Section 3 introduces a rack-scale storage fabric solution and how it is implemented at Baidu, from both hardware and software perspectives. Following that, Section 4 provides a cost comparison to other network based solutions as well as to normal DAS server. Section 5 first records a unit test for throughput/IOPS, proving storage fabric retains as high compute-storage performance as a normal DAS server, and, second, shows solution benchmarks, demonstrating this solution can build the best-fit infrastructures for different Hadoop applications. At last, Section 6 concludes the paper.

2 Related Work

Virtualization [8] or container [4] technologies are widely used to collocate different applications on each of the normal servers, hoping that the composite compute-storage ratio of multiple applications would match the server's compute-storage ratio. However, these solutions encounter the following problems in practice.

First, the introduction of virtualization or container increased the software complexity and cost. Second, for virtual machine based solutions, the hypervisors will cause certain performance overheads and increase maintenance cost as well. Third, more importantly, the number of virtual machines or containers on each server has to be limited in a production environment due to application's complexity and scheduling overheads. Thus, usually, one server can only host two or three virtual machines or containers of the corresponding distributed applications. Unfortunately, it'll be very hard for so few applications to compose a desired compute-storage ratio that matches the underlying infrastructure.

Second, using traditional networked storage service, e.g. NAS, SAN, etc., to disaggregate the storage from the compute is the most common way to address resource utilization problems. This method offers the maximum flexibility, because, in theory, one can compose any compute unit and any storage unit from anywhere in an IDC. However, it is not suitable for high-performance data processing applications. The top problem is performance limitation: (1) Traditional network structure can never offer as good compute-storage performance as that in a normal DAS server in a scalable way. (2) The networked storage services have to introduce quite a few software stacks in between compute and storage, which would certainly cause overheads and downgrade the compute-storage performance.

Third, in order to relief the performance limitation of traditional network based disaggregation, [7] used CLOS network to seek high compute-storage performance. Though CLOS network can theoretically offer a full bisectional bandwidth, this method still has a few road blocks in implementation. First of all, changing the IDC network will be much more complicated than changing the servers. Since most of the IDC networks are never designed as CLOS, changing traditional network to CLOS will be too expensive and too time-consuming to be practicable. Second, CLOS network actually has performance penalties, and hence it cannot achieve its ideal performance. For example, no perfect load-balance that can ensure full utilization of all links, the TCP in cast issue getting worse [7], etc. Moreover, as [7] does, in order to achieve such an IDC-scale disaggregation, there must be a powerful and complicated management system to provide the necessary runtime services. Such a complicated system must take time and efforts to develop and maintain, which will definitely increase the TCO.

3 Rack-scale storage fabric

This section will first define a generic *zone-scale storage fabric* architecture, and then describe the implementations in Baidu's specific environment.

3.1. A Generic Architecture

The overall system architecture is illustrated in Figure 1. All compute and storage resources are divided into many zones. In each zone, there are a pool of compute units and a pool of storage units, plus a storage fabric in between these two pools. Each upstream port (USP) of the storage fabric is attached to one compute unit, and each downstream port (DSP) of the storage fabric is attached to one storage unit.

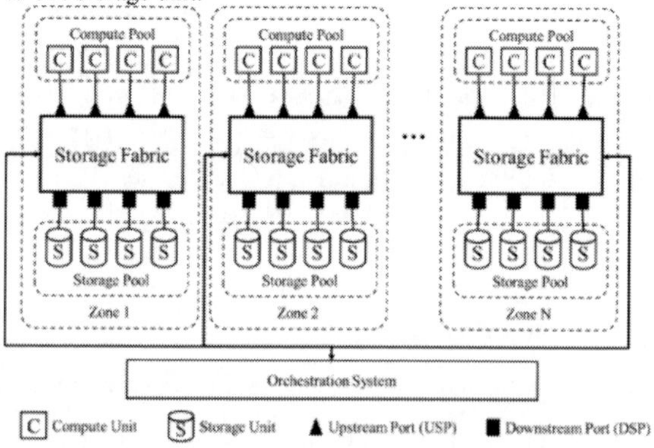

Figure 1. A Generic Zone-Scale Storage Fabric Architecture

First of all, the storage fabric allows users, via an orchestration system, to configure its internal links between USPs and DSPs. Once a USP and a DSP is configured to be linked up, the corresponding compute unit and storage unit are composed together, and then the software on the compute unit can access the data in the storage unit.

A compute unit can be composed with multiple storage units, and then makes up a new system, called *logical server*. In each zone, one can compose one or multiple logical servers to host a specific application, then all such logical servers across multiple zones make up the infrastructure for this application. Thus, if all the logical servers are composed with a compute-storage ratio that matches the application's compute-storage ratio, the whole infrastructure will best-fit this application.

Besides, each compute unit should be able to boot and execute a software environment independently from the storage units. Also, the storage protocols must support to hot-insert/remove a storage unit to/from a compute unit, without disrupting the software environment on that compute unit. In this way, adjusting the infrastructure will have minimum impact to the applications.

3.2 Implementation

This section will introduce our implementation for the above zone-scale storage fabric architecture, called *rack-scale storage fabric* solution, specifically fitting Baidu's business environment. This section will first explain the key requirements that drive our designs, and then describe the details of our prototype system that has been deployed and tested in Baidu research environment.

3.2.1 Requirements in Baidu's Environment

In Baidu's environment, a compute unit corresponds to a *server node*, which majorly consists of one or two CPUs, memory, network interfaces, as well as a local or remote disk installed with OS and applications. On the other hand, a storage unit corresponds to a *disk*, e.g. a SATA HDD (hard disk), or a SATA SSD (solid state disk).

The profiles of Baidu's high-performance data processing applications indicate the following requirements.

Requirement 1. A server node may need to access at max. 20 SATA HDDs, or, equivalently, 5 SATA SSDs. This translates to 30~40Gbps throughput and ~200,000 IOPS that a logical server would perform at maximum.

Requirement 2. Statistically, each server node may need to access in average 10 SATA HDDs, or, equivalently, 2 SATA SSDs. That's to say, the average compute-storage ratio of each zone should be equal to 1:10 (HDD) or 1:2 (SSD).

Requirement 3. Baidu's profiles tell that usually collocating 5 or more applications together would easily get any desired composite compute-storage ratio, e.g. 1:10 (HDD). This means there must be enough server nodes in each zone, so that at least 5 or more applications can be collocated there at the same time.

There're two more constraints when implementing the solution at Baidu.

Requirement 4. It's very much desirable to keep the IDC network infrastructure unchanged.

Requirement 5. The form of the rack has to be retained, because of Baidu's strategic investments in Scorpio [6] and the large amount of Scorpio-compliant racks been already deployed.

3.2.2 Hardware Configurations

Figure 2 is a photo of one rack of our prototype system that has been deployed and tested in Baidu's research environment. In this implementation, each rack contains 2 zones. And each zone contains 8 server nodes, so that the number of compute units in each zone is more than 5. In another words, **Requirement 3** has been met.

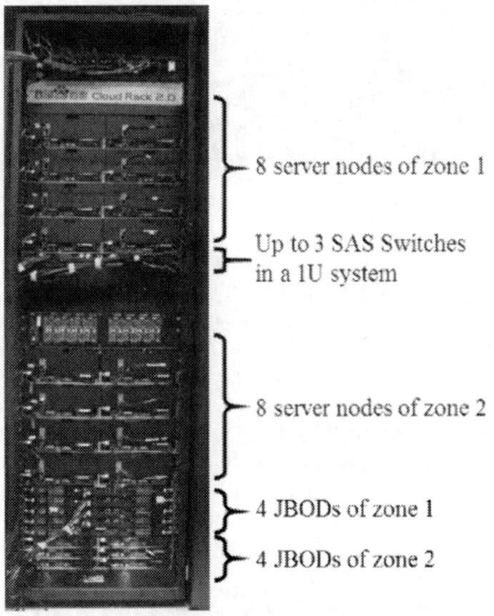

Figure 2. A Full-Rack Implementation at Baidu

Each zone also has 4 SAS JBODs. Each JBOD can be populated with max 20 SATA disks (both HDDs and SSDs can be used there). So, in HDD case, the compute-storage ratio of each zone is 8 server nodes vs. 80 HDDs, i.e. 1:10. In this way, **Requirement 2** has been met, too.

Each zone contains a SAS switch. Each server node has a SAS HBA (Host Bus Adapter), and each JBOD has a SAS expander. SAS cables are used to connect HBAs and expanders to SAS switch. In each zone, the SAS switch and the SAS expanders together make up a storage fabric. The USPs of this storage fabric are those SAS switch ports connected to server node's HBAs, and the DSPs are those SAS expander ports connected to disks.

In our prototype, server node is specially designed as 3U height, in order to leave enough space to test different vendors' HBAs. The current SAS HBA has two 48Gbps SFF8644 ports (x4 SAS 12G each), one of which is being used in our prototype to connect to SAS switch. So, the USP bandwidth (48Gbps) of each server node is designed to be enough to access 20 HDDs.

At the other end of the SAS switch, there are SAS JBODs. The embedded SAS expander in each JBOD gives each of the 20 disks a 12Gbps SAS port, which provides enough bandwidth for even a SSD. Connected to SAS switch are up to four 48Gbps SFF8644 ports (x4 SAS 12G each), two of which in this prototype is being used. So, the outstanding bandwidth (96Gbps) of each JBOD is more than enough to serve 20 enterprise SATA HDDs, and also enough to serve up to 10 SSDs. And, internally, the SAS expander provides a full-bandwidth fan-out from the four SFF8644 ports to the 20 disks.

Figure 3 is the prototype of our SAS switch system. It contains three separated SAS switches in a 1U height chassis, one for each zone, plus one network bridge board for remote management purpose. In this prototype, since each rack just contains two zones, only two SAS switches in that 1U system are being used.

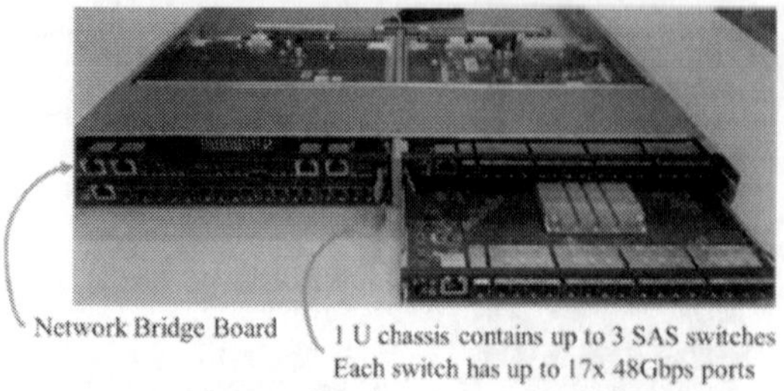

Figure 3. SAS Switch System

The current SAS switch prototype has totally 17 48Gbps SFF8644 ports (x4 SAS 12G each). In this prototype, 8 ports are connected to the 8 HBA ports on the 8 server nodes, and another 8 ports are connected to the 8 ports on the 4 SAS JBODs. The SAS switch can provide a full-bandwidth switching.

With all above designs, there is no bottleneck for a server node to access the max 20 HDDs, because the outstanding bandwidth of each HBA and each JBOD are enough, and the SAS switch and SAS expander are all full-bandwidth switching. Therefore, **Requirement 1** has been met. Last, this prototype doesn't need to change either IDC's network (**Requirement 4**) or rack infrastructures (**Requirement 5**). So, all the aforementioned requirements have been met, and this implementation can fit into Baidu's environment.

3.2.3 Orchestration Mechanism

Another key component of our implementation is an orchestration system that offers IDC operators with a semantics to identify any specific compute unit (i.e. server node) and any specific storage unit (i.e. HDD, SSD), determines whether they can be composed together through a storage fabric, and then does the composition by telling the storage fabric to link up the corresponding USP and DSP. There are two problems that an orchestration system needs to be implemented to solve.

(1) One problem is how to dynamically configure the storage fabric, so that the links between its USPs and DSPs can be changed, and these changes won't disrupt the software environments on the compute units.

For this, on one hand, SAS protocol has been working very well on disk hot-plug/unplug, i.e. doing the logical server composition/de-composition wouldn't disrupt the software environments on logical servers. On the other hand, in order for orchestration system to manipulate the compute-storage composition, the SAS switch has been developed to expose a set of remote management APIs, following Intel Rack Scale Architecture definitions [10]. By calling these APIs, our orchestration system can easily manipulate the links between USPs and DSPs.

(2) The other problem is how to obtain the correspondences between each server node and its attached USP, and the correspondences between each disk and its attached DSPs, regardless the states (e.g. powered on or off) of server node and disks.

First, the orchestration system identifies each server node according to the descriptive information, e.g. serial numbers, etc., that is provided by the BMC (Baseboard Management Controller) on the server node. When a server node is first-time added to a rack, it is required to power-on once, during which its BIOS (Basic Input/Output System) can fetch the SAS addresses of its HBA ports and persistently store them to its BMC, and then the BMC sends this information to the orchestration system. In this way, the orchestration system can get a mapping between each server node and the SAS addresses of its HBA ports.

On the other side, the SAS switch can also record the SAS addresses of the HBA ports that are physically connected to its USPs. Then, through management APIs, the orchestration system can get another mapping between each USP and the SAS addresses of the HBA ports that are connected to the USP.

With the above two mapping information, the orchestration system can corresponds each server node to its attached USPs.

Second, the SAS switch itself can retrieve both the descriptive information (e.g. serial number, etc.) and the SAS addresses of each attached disk, then come up with a correspondence between each disk and its attached DSP. Then, the orchestration system can get this correspondences via SAS switch management APIs.

With these, when IDC operator wants to compose a specific server node with a specific disk, the orchestration system will be able to tell that it should be which USP and which DSP of SAS fabric that should be linked up.

4 Cost Analysis

4.1 BOM Cost Comparison

This section will first compare BOM (Bill of Material) costs among a CLOS network based disaggregation (see Section 2) and two rack-scale disaggregation solutions. One is based on intra-rack network, which can be implemented to achieve similar performance to our solution. The other is our solution. See Figure 4.

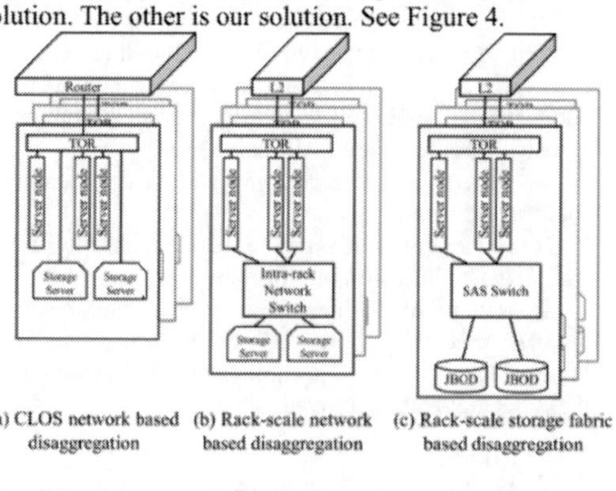

Figure 4. Three Configuration for BOM Cost comparison

Config. 1. A simple CLOS network based disaggregation. As illustrated in Figure (a), the network consists of 2 layers of switches. One is TOR (Top of the Rack) switches, and the other is Router switches [7]. Both compute-storage and compute-compute traffics go through this single network.

Config. 2. A simple intra-rack network based disaggregation. As illustrated in Figure (b), there are two sets of networks. The first set includes a single 2-layer network for the normal compute-compute traffics across the racks, which consists of a layer of TOR switches and a layer of L2 switches. The second set includes many separated intra-rack networks, one for each rack, to support the compute-storage traffics within each rack.

Config. 3. Our rack-scale storage fabric based disaggregation. As shown in Figure (c), it is similar to Config. 2, except two major differences. First, storage server changes to SAS JBOD. Second, each intra-rack network for compute-storage traffics is replaced by a SAS switch.

For clarity, let's define the following denotations.

B: the total bandwidth needed by compute-storage traffics. In fact, since the traffics at compute side and the traffics at storage side are symmetric, the total outstanding bandwidth of all compute units and the total outstanding bandwidth of all storage units equal to *(B/2)*.

k·B: the total bandwidth needed by the original compute-compute traffics, where ***k*** is a ratio of this bandwidth to the compute-storage one.

Px: *a* unit cost for ingredient *x* to offer a unit of bandwidth. E.g. P_{TOR} means unit cost of TOR switch.

h: the convergence rate of multi-layer switches, in terms of bandwidth. $0 < h \leq 1$. This only applies to the first set of networks, i.e. for compute-compute traffics, in Config. 2 and 3.

For simplicity, let's assume all types of network switches have the similar unit prices, i.e. $P_{router} = P_{L2} = P_{TOR} = P_{intra\_rack\_net\_switch}$. Also, without impacting the sufficiency, one can set $h = 1$ for Config. 2 and 3, i.e. there no convergence from TORs to L2 switches, which is the most expensive configuration for both Config. 2 and 3. Then, even in this case, we can first calculate the total cost difference between Config. 1 and 2 as below.

$$\mathrm{Diff}_{(1-2)} = B \cdot (P_{router} + P_{net\_cable} + 2 \cdot P_{TOR} - P_{intra\_rack\_net\_switch})$$

Mathematically, this is always a positive value, because we assume the unit prices of all kinds of network switches are similar. This formula actually means Config. 1 has to spend more money building an IDC-scale CLOS network for high-performance compute-storage traffics, than Config. 2 that only needs to build many small-scale networks within each rack.

Then, we can calculate the difference between Config. 2 and 3, as below.

$$\mathrm{Diff}_{(2\text{-}3)} = (B/2) \cdot \{[2 \cdot (P_{net\_cable} - P_{SAS\_cable}) + 2 \cdot (P_{intra\_rack\_net\_switch} - P_{SAS\_switch}) + (P_{NIC} - P_{SAS\_HBA})] + (P_{storage\_server} + P_{NIC} - P_{JBOD})\}$$

Mathematically, the first part of this formula includes 3 unit price differences, i.e. (1) between network cables (P_{net_cable}) and SAS cables (P_{SAS_cable}), (2) between the intra-rack network switch ($P_{intra\_rack\_net\_switch}$) and the SAS switch ($P_{SAS\_switch}$), and (3) between the NICs (P_{NIC}) and SAS HBAs (P_{SAS_HBA}) on the server nodes. By investigating the SAS 12G products and the 40Gbps network products in the marketplaces, it was concluded that all these three differences are actually trivial, and the SAS products even have cost advantages in some cases. On the other hand, this formula has a second part, which is the cost difference between storage servers and their NICs in Config. 2 and the SAS JBODs in Config. 3. This part is definitely a non-trivial positive value, because even the lowest-end storage server, which consists of CPU, memory, motherboards, etc., must be more costly than a JBOD, which is basically a SAS expander.

So, summing up the two parts, the difference is always a positive value, which means Config. 3 is cheaper than Config. 2. Actually, the root causes are, first, with the same performance (12G SAS vs. 40Gbps network), the network products have no cost advantage over SAS products, and, second, an intra-rack network based disaggregation always needs to use expensive storage servers, while rack-scale storage fabric only needs to use the cheaper SAS JBODs.

4.2 Cost Adder for Storage Fabric

For ROI (Return of Investment) analysis, it has been estimated how much extra investment would need be added, to enable our storage fabric based disaggregation, comparing to an original infrastructure that is just made up by normal DAS servers.

Without exposing Baidu's pricing data, Table transforms the absolute costs to percentages. You can see the total BOM increase would be less than 5%. Note that this only compares to normal servers. So, if counting in other ingredients in an original infrastructures, e.g. racks, which are basically the same between two options, this percentage will be even smaller.

Table 1. BOM Cost Adder (%) to Enable Storage Fabric

	SAS HBA	SAS cables	SAS switch	JBOD
Additional cost amortized to each server node (%)	2.57%	0.51%	1.03%	0.43%
Total (%)	4.543%			

On the other hand, based on Baidu's current resource utilization profile for high-performance data processing applications, it is very promising that the cost saving out of the higher resource utilization would be fairly enough to justify this small percentage of extra BOM investment.

5 Experimental Results

5.1 Unit Tests

The key advantage of storage fabric is to retain as high performance as a DAS server. Though the hardware configuration was designed to provide a sufficient bandwidth (see Section 3.2.2), quantitative performance testing are necessary to verify that our rack-scale storage fabric not cause any performance loss.

To verify the effect of SAS fabric on performance of a logical server, a server node (with a 48Gbps HBA port) is composed with 20 HDDs. Then we measured the throughput/IOPS of this logical server. As a fair comparison, we also tested a DAS server using the same type and number of server node and HDDs.

Table 2 shows the logical server performs very similarly to a 20-HDD DAS server. Also, note, per HDD's specification, which only discloses 160 MB/s sequential read peak bandwidth, our testing is valid.

Table 2. Performance comparison between logical server and DAS server

	Logical server Throughput /IOPS	DAS server Throughput /IOPS
Random read 4K	1,753 IOPS	1,700 IOPS
Random read 256K	2,535 IOPS	1,500 IOPS
Random write 4K	3,581 IOPS	3,760 IOPS
Random write 256K	3,730 IOPS	2,840 IOPS
Sequential read 4K	1,554 MB/s	1,297 MB/s
Sequential read 256K	3,210 MB/s	3,202 MB/s
Sequential write 4K	1,336 MB/s	1,170 MB/s
Sequential write 256K	2,563 MB/s	3,112 MB/s

5.2 Solution Benchmarks

In order to quantify the system-level effects, we deployed Hadoop benchmarks on our prototype system to simulate high-performance data processing applications.

We used BigBench [3] benchmark tool suite to simulate a real-life business scenario, where a retailer company wants to analyze a large amount of its sales data and figure out valuable information from them. This benchmark standardizes a series of queries, and implements them as a HIVE [9] application running on MapReduce [2] engine and HDFS [1] storage. It will measure how many queries an application can execute every hour, called queries per hour (QPH), to indicate if the application can meet a performance requirement.

On our prototype, one can compose different types of logical servers, in terms of compute-storage ratio, to best-fit different BigBench applications that have different performance requirements. We tested 7 BigBench applications. Their datasets are of the same size, but each application has a different performance requirement, ranging from 2 QPH to 5 QPH. Table 3 records the actual performances, as well as the different infrastructure configurations, of these 7 applications. From these test results, it can be concluded that each application can not only meet their performance requirement but also very well utilized the resources.

Table 3. BigBench Applications on Best-Fit Infrastructures

App No.	Expected QPH	#of server nodes	# of hard disks	Compute -storage ratio	Actual QPH
1	2	4	64	1 : 16	**1.92**
2	2.5	6	64	1 : 11	**2.67**
3	3	8	64	1 : 8	**3.36**
4	3.5	10	64	1 : 6.4	**3.72**
5	4	12	64	1 : 5.3	**4.23**
6	4.5	14	64	1 : 4.6	**4.96**
7	5	16	64	1 : 4	**5.55**

6 Summary

This paper introduced a *rack-scale storage fabric* solution to address resource utilization problem. The implementation uses SAS switch and SAS expanders to make up a storage fabric to disaggregate compute unit and storage unit, and an orchestration system was developed to configure underlying switch fabric. Our practical experience paves the way to build shareable data center infrastructure for high performance data processing applications with efficient resource utilization.

Our solution demonstrated many advantages. First, our *rack-scale storage fabric* accelerates new application deployment regardless of the limitation of underlying infrastructure, as logical server can be composed easily from compute resource pool and storage resource pool.

Second, compute resource and storage resource are separated from a normal server, each can independently upgrade depending on which resource in shortage. Plus, our orchestration system also provides a rack-wide view of resource discovery and management capability to help relieve labor of data center operators.

Third, all the components are final products, except that SAS switches are very close to production. Building such a system will not be limited by technique challenge or business ecosystem.

REFERENCES

[1] Borthakur D. The Hadoop Distributed File System. Hadoop Project Website. (2007).

[2] Dean J, Ghemawat S. MapReduce: Simplified Data Processing on Large Clusters. *Communications of the ACM.* **51**, pp: 107-113(2008).

[3] Ghazal A, Rabl T, Hu M, Raab F, Poess M, Crolotte A, Jacobsen HA. BigBench: Towards an Industry Standard Benchmark for Big Data Analytics. *In Proceedings of the 2013 ACM SIGMOD international conference on Management of Data.* pp: 1197-1208 (2013).

[4] Hindman B, Konwinski A, Zaharia M, Ghodsi A, Joseph AD, Katz RH, Shenker S, Stoica I. Mesos: A Platform for Fine-Grained Resource Sharing in the Data Center. In NSDI, **11** (2011).

[5] http://www.opencompute.org/

[6] http://www.opendatacenter.cn/

[7] Nightingale EB, Elson J, Fan J, Hofmann O, Howell J, Suzue Y. Flat Datacenter Storage. *10th USENIX Symposium on Operating Systems Design and Implementation,* pp: 1-15 (2012).

[8] Sefraoui O, Aissaoui M, Eleuldj M. OpenStack: Toward an Open-Source Solution for Cloud Computing. *International Journal of Computer Applications.* **55** (2012).

[9] Thusoo A, Sarma JS, Jain N, Shao Z, Chakka P, Anthony S, Liu H, Wyckoff P, Murthy R. Hive: A Warehousing Solution Over A Map-Reduce Framework. *In Proceedings of the VLDB Endowment.* pp: 1626-1629 (2009).

[10] Kyathsandra, Jay, and Eric Dahlen. "Intel rack scale architecture overview ", *INTEROP,* (2013).

MATEC Web of Conferences 76, 04041 (2016) DOI: 10.1051/matecconf/20167604041
CSCC 2016

A Web Based Framework for Pre-release Testing of Mobile Applications

Abeer Hamdy[1,2,a], Osman Ibrahim[1], Ahmed Hazem[1]

[1] Informatics and Computer science Faculty, The British University in Egypt, Cairo, Egypt
[2] Computers and Systems department, Electronics Research Institute, Cairo, Egypt

Abstract. Mobile applications are becoming an integral part of daily life and of business's marketing plan. They are helpful in promoting for the business, attracting and retaining customers. Software testing is vital to ensure the delivery of high quality mobile applications that could be accessed across different platforms and meet business and technical requirements. This paper proposes a web based tool, namely Pons, for the distribution of pre-release mobile applications for the purpose of manual testing. Pons facilities building, running, and manually testing Android applications directly in the browser. It gets the developers and end users engaged in testing the applications in one place, alleviates the tester's burden of installing and maintaining testing environments, and provides a platform for developers to rapidly iterate on the software and integrate changes over time. Thus, it speeds up the pre-release testing process, reduces its cost and increases customer satisfaction.

1 Introduction

Mobile platforms have been getting powerful and sophisticated which facilitates the development of a vast number of mobile applications that serve the business world. It became a business practice for small and large corporations to have a mobile application. Corporations use mobile applications for several purposes including promotion for and selling their products, better communication and engagement with customers. Examples of those applications include Uber [1], AEMC [2] and Empire loan [3]. Uber is a service that offers users safe and reliable transportation. Uber has a network of tens of thousands (maybe even hundreds of thousands) of drivers who respond to user requests for rides. While, Empire Loan has a chain of pawn shops that people can buy and sell merchandise in. AEMC is a worldwide energy monitoring company manufactures hardware that monitors energy consumption in large buildings and facilities.

In this extremely competitive business world, companies seek to release applications that are smart, simple and function well on different mobile devices with different hardware configurations, screen sizes and resolutions, different versions of operating systems, and across different mobile networks. Various testing methodologies were suggested for testing the different aspects of mobile applications before they are released which include usability testing [4],[5], GUI testing [6], [7], performance testing, compatibility testing, privacy testing [8]. Testing could be performed manually or automatically [6], [7]. Automatic testing is useful for big scenarios which are time consuming when run manually or for regression testing. While manual testing allows testers to perform ad-hoc tests, it is important in the pre-release stage. However, the existing platforms for pre-release distribution of mobile applications for the purpose of manual testing are badly-designed and often lead to various problems [8] such as:

1. Download and installation takes up a lot of time: To start testing an application, it must be downloaded and installed on a mobile device. Such process delays the development progress.
2. Feedback is cluttered among different mediums: In order to gather feedback, developers usually have to arrange for a way through which testers can leave their comments. Most of testing tools does not offer a medium for developer and testers to collaborate and communicate, leaving them to traditional communication practices (such as email communications). This leads to cluttered feedback, resulting in confusion for the developer and longer times in processing issues, feature requests, and bug reports.
3.Testing is done in isolation and out of context: Testing of mobile applications is often isolated and is done out of context. That is either due to testers having access to the software but not to the developer while carrying out their task, or by developers themselves trying to imitate the tester behavior without taking into consideration their perspectives are almost always quite different.
4. No over-the-air updates: Existing solutions does not offer developers a way to update the software over-the-air. Essentially, this means more time is spent building a new version of the application to be distributed, which can be a huge amount of time depending on the complexity of the components used and the size of the application itself.

[a] Corresponding author: abeer.hamdy@bue.edu.eg

This paper proposes a web based tool, namely Pons, which:

1. Provides a platform for distributing the pre-release of mobile applications for the purpose of manual testing.
2. Facilitates building, running and manually testing mobile applications in a browser.
3. Manages the process of manual testing for the purpose of speeding up the testing process and reducing its effort and cost.
4. Allows the testers to focus on testing mobile applications without having to worry about getting the platform up and running or the environment configured.
5. Provides a medium for both of developers and testers to collaborate and communicate without isolation from the application they are working on, Consequently, speeding up the testing process.

The paper is organized as follows: Section 2 provides the structure of Pons, while, section 3 discusses its development. Section 4 concludes the paper and discusses how Pons can be extended in the future.

2 Pons architecture

Pons is a web-based tool that facilitates pre-release distribution and engage the mobile application developers and clients /testers in a constructive closed feedback loop to achieve the business objectives of the applications. It comprises four main components, as demonstrated by figure 1, which are: 1) A web application, 2) Containers which work as a sandbox environment to build the mobile applications [9], 3) Version control management component to keep track of the different versions of the mobile application [10], and 4) Live streaming component to stream the mobile application to the client [11]. The roles of these components and their development are discussed in the following section.

3 Pons development and technologies

The following subsections discuss the technologies used in developing the different components of Pons and the role of each of them.

3.1 Web application component

Pons's web application is implemented as a single page application (SPA) which comprises two separate applications, front-end and back-end, that communicate using a JSON-based API [14], as depicted by figure 2. The front-end is built using a JavaScript web application framework Ember.JS [12]. While, the back-end is built using the Ruby on Rail framework [13].

For the past couple of years, there has been a growing trend in web development that promotes moving the application logic and user interface rendering (among other things) to the client. These applications have come to be known as single page applications (SPA). Figure 3 outlines the architecture of SPAs. In such an architecture the back-end application is responsible for the data layer (manipulating and storing data, along with exposing a REST API that is consumed by clients), while the front-end application is responsible for application-logic and the presentation layers (view rendering, and handling requests, among other tasks).

As Pons web application is developed as a SPA, its back-end is different from typical Ruby on Rail application in removing the entire View layer (since no template generation or view rendering is to be done on the server-side). This means Ruby on Rail application would serve as a back-end, providing persistence and data management through a REST API. Figure 4 outlines the architecture of Pons's Ruby on Rail application. As shown in the figure, there is no "Action View" module (as in typical Ruby on Rail) while there is a new module called ActiveModel::Serializers. This new module is responsible for serializing and deserializing JSON requests and responses. The rationale behind moving view rendering away from the server-side in Pons can be narrowed down to the following two reasons: i. Performance: Instead of having to send a full-blown HTTP request over the network each time a user interacts with the application, the entire payload is loaded upfront (hence the name, single page refers to that payload which is loaded on the first request only), allowing for communications with the server to be minimal, that is, to be only for fetching data. This has the advantage of keeping the user interface snappy and responsive. The overall performance of the application increases consequently. ii. Coherence: Rendering on the server side adds a layer of complexity, arising from the fact developers by nature already do some rendering on the client (most notably, in the form of UI interactivity, such as sliders, widgets, and rich text editors). This actually means having state and behaviour of UI duplicated, both on the client and the server, implemented using two different programming languages and running on two different machines. Rendering on the client eliminates this problem, and keeps the UI logic consistent and coherent.

This decision does not mean that client-side rendering is bullet-proof. As with any other kind of technical choice, opting for client-side rendering has its own disadvantages and technical debt. However, this project assumes that its benefits outweigh its problems.

Pons's front end is developed using Ember.js. Ember.js is based on the Model-View-Controller (MVC) paradigm. Ember facilitates creating complex front-end applications. Figure 5 outlines the interaction between different components in an Ember.js application, while Fig.6 describes how a request is routed and handled by Emper components.

3.2 Version management component

Generally speaking, version (Release) Management is the practice of keeping track of changes in a set of files, in order to retrieve them later on. Tools for controlling software versions are called Version Control Management Systems (VCMS). These systems provide a number of important functions that are vital to any software development activity [4] such as assigning a unique identifier to each version, storing and listing all changes to the code and providing a storage management to ensure code is not stored multiple times as new versions are recorded. VCMS also allow a single file to be edited concurrently by more than one developer.

Pons adopts a distributed version control management system called GIT [10]. GIT organizes the code into repositories, which are basically folders organized in a specific structure or format. Aside from that physical structure, a repository is also structured in a logical way, dividing the code inside to branches, tags and commits. A branch is a deviation from the original codeine, giving a developer the chance to write experimental code without worrying about the original version of his/her work. This has the advantage of allowing context switching without having a huge impact on the system: one can create a branch, do some work, go back to original branch, fix something, then return to the new branch and merge his/her work.

Mobile application developer should have a GITHub account to be able to use Pons in developing an application. Any client, to start accessing an existing mobile application, should request a permission through Pons.

3.3 Containers

Pons utilizes a container technology called Docker [14], [15], [16]. Docker is a portable container that wraps up a piece of software in a complete file system that contains everything it needs to run: code, runtime, system tools, and system libraries. Container is a lightweight alternative to a full-fledged virtual machine such as KVM [17]. Containers isolate applications from each other and the underlying infrastructure while providing an added layer of protection for the application. This guarantees that it will always run the same, regardless of the environment it is running in. Virtual machines run their own kernel and operating system instances and provide good isolation but that comes with the cost of having overhead. While containers are less isolated but have much lower overhead as both of the kernel and operating system instances are shared.

Docker is an extension to the capabilities of Linux containers (LXCs) [18], it wraps Linux containers and provide better abstraction and tooling. It was started as a side project and only open-sourced in 2013. It should be mentioned that Docker containers are based on open standards allowing containers to run on all major Linux distributions and Microsoft operating systems with support for every infrastructure. Pons utilizes Docker to create an LXC based container each time an Android application is built; to sandbox, the application and streamline the whole build/running process as depicted by figure 7.

Pons utilizes Docker by predefining Docker images that contain the necessary services and tools to build android applications, starting from the operating system up to the software development kit (SDK). A container is then built using one of these images to store the source code of a mobile application at specific moment of history in a sandbox environment.

Ready-made Docker images (snapshots of a container) are stored on a highly scalable server application called Docker registry [16]. There are two types of registries for Docker, public and private. Pons uses the private Docker registry to keep Docker images on the same server and consequently pulling them would be much faster, and obviously, to keep them private since Dockers public registry can be accessed by anyone. Docker pulls and pushes (stores and retrieves) images and repositories from/to the private Docker registry installed on the server. An alternative would be to pre-build these images and store (pull) them on the local Docker instance, which has the same effect as keeping them in a private registry in terms of speed and security.

The images stored are built in a down-top approach as shown in figure 8, meaning that each one would be depending on the other from the top down to the base image which will only include the operating system (in our case, Ubuntu). Such setup would allow for better configuration, as one can only include what is needed for a specific build.

Docker provides an application-programming interface (API) [9] to control a Docker instance remotely. This API is used by Pons to control the Docker daemon, to create, build and delete images and containers.

3.4 Open SSH

Due to a Docker limitation that prevents a Linux container from running more than one process, OpenSSH is employed by Pons. OpenSSH [19] is a collection of network-level utilities aimed at facilitating secure connections between different machines. The rationale behind installing an OpenSSH server in each container is to allow running different commands and executing multiple processes inside the container such as: Cloning a GIT repository, Creating an Android emulator.

Issuing commands to the container is done through Rye [20], which is a Ruby library that allow running SSH commands on multiple machines. This setup works as outlined in figure 9.

DOI: 10.1051/matecconf/20167604041

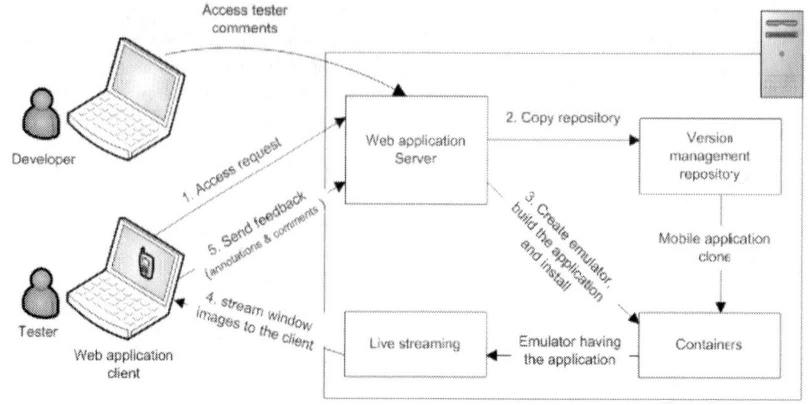

Figure1. Pons Architecture

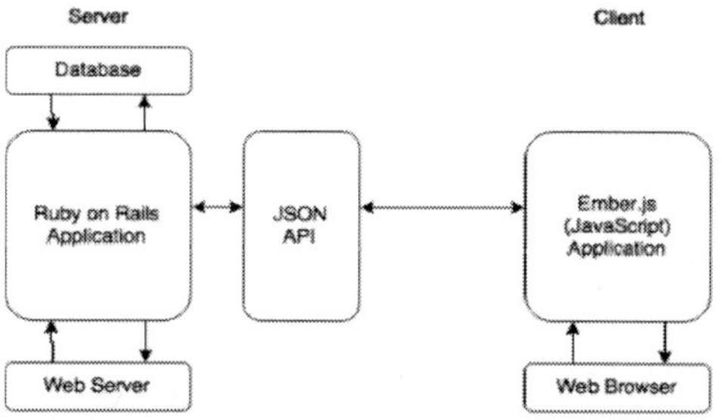

Figure 2. Pons web application architecture.

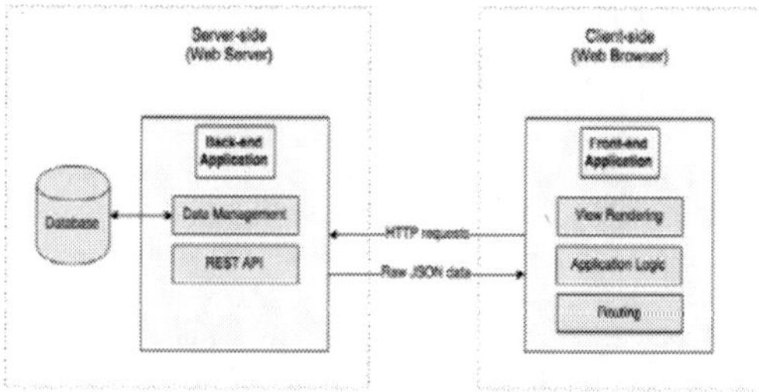

Figure 3. Single Page application (SPA) architecture.

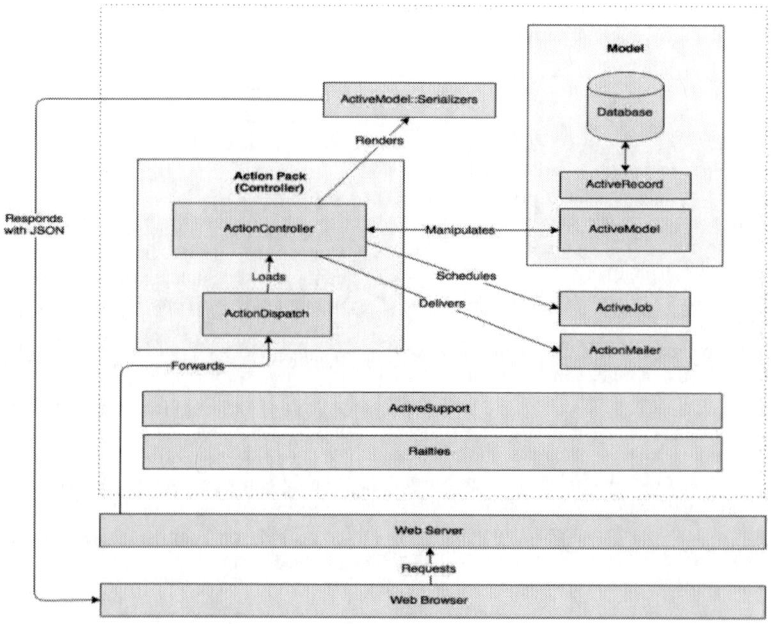

Figure 4. Pons's Ruby on Rails application

DOI: 10.1051/matecconf/20167604041

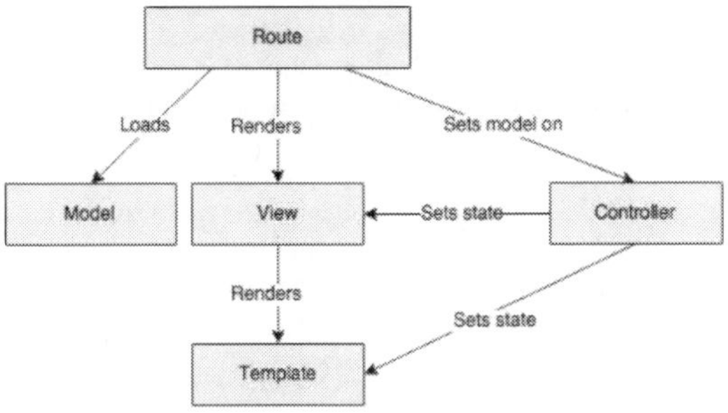

Figure 5. Ember.js application architecture

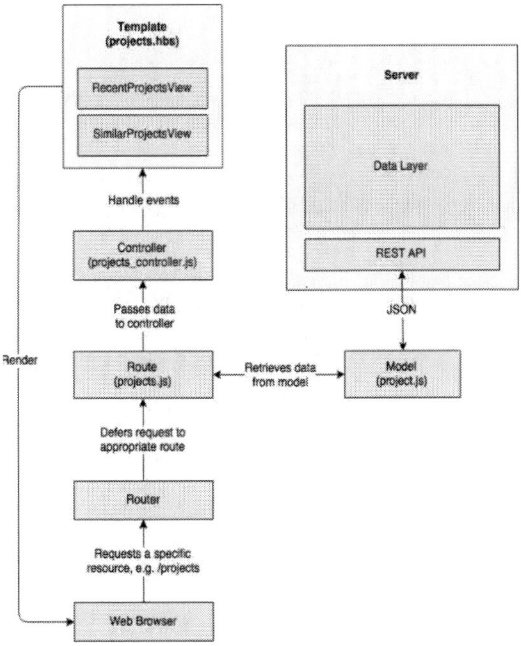

Figure 6. Request routing in Ember

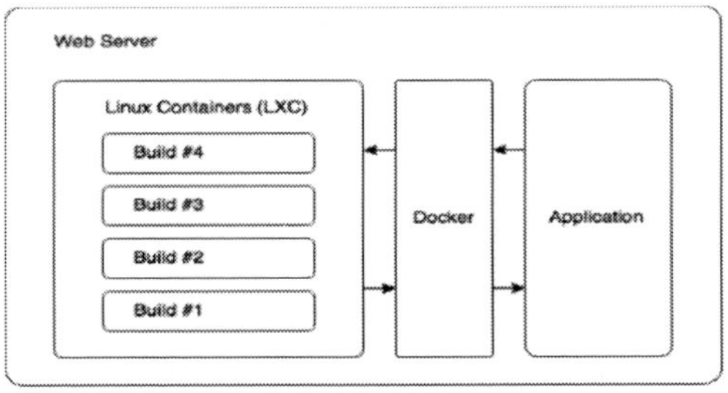

Figure 7. LXC containers (Application: Back end of Pons's web application).

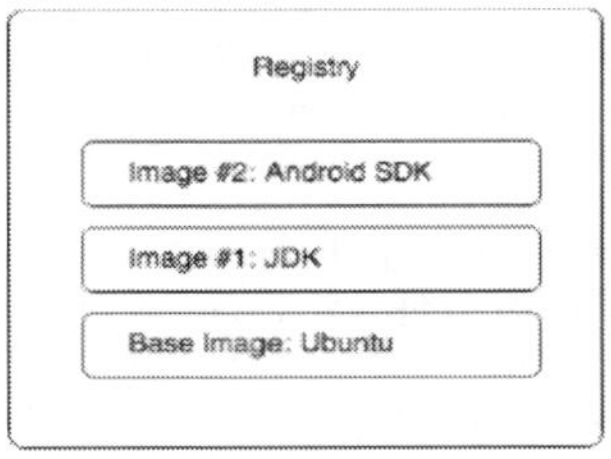

Figure 8. Docker Images.

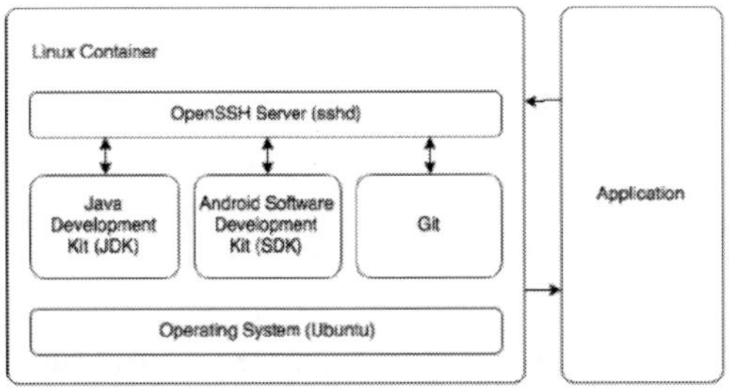

Figure 9. Communication between different components using OpenSSH.

3.5 Live Streaming and display

Delivering media as a stream is an alternative to downloading. Pons displays the Android emulator running inside a container by utilizing one of the live streaming tools called "X Persistent Remote Applications" (Xpra) [11]. Xpra is an Open Source Software tool that is used for directing a display from a remote host to a local machine. Xpra was installed on one of the Docker images, which the containers are built on. To display the streamed contents at the client side, Pons uses Xpra's HTML5 client This client establishes connection with the Xpra server installed in the container, receives buffer and images and decodes them as appropriate, before displaying them using HTML5 Canvas API.

3.6 Pre-release testing procedures

The basic procedures of building and streaming a mobile application to the browser of a client for the purpose of testing are as follows:

1. Client asks for a permission to get access to the repository containing the mobile application source code hosted on GitHub.

2. Pons grants the client an authentication token and saves it in its record, to keep track of this client.
3. Pons clone the repository that has the source code of the latest version of the Android application.
4. Upon obtaining the source code, Pons creates a Linux container (LXC) using Docker. The container will be based on a certain Docker image that can be
accessed from a private Docker registry. The registery is hosted on the server that hosts the backend of Pons's web application.
5. Pons copies the repository into the container, creates an Android emulator to be used while building the application, starts an OpenSSH server and assigning a specific port number for it then run Ant [21] to build the mobile application.
6. Pons starts the Android emulator, and then install the Android application it using SSH commands.
7. Xpra live streams the emulator to the client. An HTML5 canvas element displays the video streaming. On top of that element, there is another canvas element used as an overlay for drawing annotations and leaving comments by the tester.

4 Conclusion and future work

Testing is critical to ensure the development of a high quality mobile application that meets the business requirements and achieve the customer satisfaction. Pre-release distribution for the purpose of manual testing is crucial. However, testing pre-release is tedious and time-consuming process, with many problems hindering application development. Along with that, communication remains a stumbling block between developers and testers. It is often broken, and both are usually isolated from the software under testing.
Pons was proposed to alleviate problems existing with pre-release mobile testing. Pons facilitates building mobile applications and running them directly in the browser. When an application runs and its environment is ready for manual testing, a peer-reviewing session starts, allowing developers and testers to engage in a meaningful feedback loop, in which they can submit feature requests, report bugs and software faults, and handle them as appropriate.
Currently, we are extending Pons to work for automated testing of mobile software as well.

References

1. Uber: https://play.google.com/store/apps/details?id=com.ubercab&hl=en.
2. AEMC: http://www.aemc.com/HTML-email/PR_Update_Clamp_On_Models_407_607/AEMC_PRU_407-607_0914.html
3. Empire Loan: https://play.google.com/store/apps/details?id=com.empireloan.cashcam&hl=en.
4. A. Sonderegger, S. Schmutz, J. Sauer, The influence of age in usability testing, applied ergonomic, vol 52, PP. 291-300, (2016).
5. M. Masood, M. Thigambaram, The Usability of Mobile Applications for Preschoolers, 7th World Conference on Educational Sciences, (WCES-2015), NovotelAthens Convention Center, Athens, Greece, (2015).
6. D. Zhang and B. Adipat. Challenges, methodologies, and issues in the usability testing of mobile applications. International Journal of Human-Computer Interaction, PP. 293-308, (2005).
7. D. Amaltano, A. R. Fasolino, P. Tramontana, S. Decarmine, and A. Memon, Using GUI ripping for automated testing of android applications. In Proceedings of the 27th IEEE/ACM International Conference on Automated Software Engineering, pages 258-26, (2012).
8. C. Hu and I. Neamtiu. Automating GUI testing for android applications. In Proceedings of the 6th International Workshop on Automation of Software Test, PP. 77-83, (2011).
9. J. Turnbull. The Docker Book: Containerization is the new virtualization. James Turnbull, (2014).
10. J. Loeliger and M. McCullough. Version Control with Git: Powerful tools and techniques for collaborative software development. "O'Reilly Media, Inc.", (2012).
11. Xpra live streaming: https://www.xpra.org/, (2015).
12. D. Flanagan. JavaScript: the genitive guide. O'Reilly Media, Inc., (2006).
13. Ruby on Rails Guides: http://guides.rubyonrails.org/, (2015).
14. N. Nurseitov, M. Paulson, R. Reynolds, and C. Izurieta. Comparison of Json and Xml data interchange formats: A case study. Caine, PP. 157-162, (2009).
15. Docker: Https://www.docker.com/.
16. D. Merkel. Docker: lightweight linux containers for consistent development and deployment. Linux Journal, (2014).
17. Virtual machine KVM: www.linux-kvm.org.
18. Linux Containers LXC: https://linuxcontainers.org/, (2015).
19. Openssh: www.openssh.com
20. D. Berube. Practical Ruby Gems. Apress, (2007).
21. Ant: ant.apache.org/
22. J. Humble and D. Farley. Continuous Delivery: Reliable Software Releases Through Build, Test, and Deployment Automation. Addison-Wesley Professional, 1st edition, (2010).

The Impact on locomotor skills in children. The promotion of significant Knowledge supported by the use of videogames.

Yaneth P. Caviativa [1]

[1] Universidad Manuela Beltrán. Av. Circunvalar No. 60-00, Bogotá, Colombia

Abstract. Research on attentional processes and their relationship to the maturation of locomotor patterns involved in the use of some types of video games. For this reason, the aim of this study is to identify the influence of the practice of virtual reality games in attentional processes related to the jump motor pattern in children of 5 years. The research was conducted by a quantitative study design using SPSS crosstabulation longitudinal observational period with a pre-test, post-test and a control group. There are few studies on the effect of virtual reality games in the development of locomotor patterns, the study is consistent with research that finds positive effects of this type of games in learning motor activities. In this investigation it was found According to statistical chi-square can conclude that the development of motor skills SI influences meaningful learning of children, Most children engaged in meaningful learning, but they have a necessary guide or a process to follow, according to research must always be supervised by an adult sometimes do not need any supervision, in addition to the significant knowledge not articulated with educational processes guided by the teacher before the motor skills expected

1 Introduction

Videogames are a worldwide reality, which impact has increased in children and teenagers due to multiple occupations such as academicals and familiar, and so they fill familiar weaknesses like unavailable time to spend with relatives, by using these games in their free time very often, and it becomes much more appealing when the access to internet makes easier this activity.

Communication and Information Technologies (CIT), as well as virtual reality games, have become strategically allies in learning processes, since interaction increases motivation, a process that lies behind learning. In this sense (Gómez, 2013) affirms that:

> "The presence and interaction are two fundamental properties of virtual reality systems. It is called presence to the sensation of "being in" the virtual environment. Subjects that go through virtual reality environments do not have the sensation of observing these from the outside, but being part of them. This feature has made the investigators to think that simulation, for instance, of phobic situations through virtual reality could be used as an intermediate way of exposition between real life and imagination. Likewise, in investigation of cognitive rehabilitation, new options can be offered through games of virtual reality where by using the mouse of computer, the patient can interact with the virtual world." [1]

Due these findings, it can be inferred that there is a relation between the use of virtual reality games and maturity of basic locomotor patterns. it allowed to prove significant development of locomotor patterns like running and jumping. In the experience they were stimulated through the video game.
Even though the different uses of virtual reality games, some studies have seen negative effects derived from its practice, especially for visual system [2] and muscleskeletal system [3].

Researches recommend increasing the investigations about attentional processes and their relation with maturity of locomotor patterns involved in the usage of

Corresponding author: janeth.caviativa@umb.edu.co

these types of videogames. For this reason the objective of the present study is to identify the influence of the practice of virtual reality games on attentional processes related to the jump motor pattern in 5 years old children.

2 Videogames

A videogame is an informatic interactive program destined to entertainment that can work in different devices: computers, consoles, cellphones, etc.; it integrates audio and video, and allows enjoying experiences that, in many cases, would be very difficult to live in reality.

Among the features of videogames there can be found: graphics quality (in the beginning in two dimensions, nowadays in three), the control of the game should be easy and intuitive, and sound (from speaker to surroundings) [4]

There are different types of videogames, such as named adventure games (with intelligence tests or puzzles solving to advance), arcade (skill activities), sports, strategy (coordinate actions), role (where the player moves a character and evolves throughout the game according to his decisions), and simulation (some kind of action is simulated, for example, flying a plane) [4]

Virtual reality games are classified in an exclusive range of tools, in which the user can venture creatively, until the limit of their imagination allows it. There lays, possibly, the mayor attraction, since imagination and creativity have the opportunity of happening in an artificial and unlimited "world". The origin of these games is the defense department of the United States of America, where they were created as material for an aviation class in the 70's to complete flying simulations by practicing and not risking lives [5]

3 Learning and psychomotor development

Da Fonseca, (2010), affirms that:

> "Maturity without the opportunity of "motor experiences" leaves to half way the development and the capacity of learning in children. We are born with an inconclusive relation between body and brain that has no ways of communication or interaction. It is the development of motor skills what will proportionate that narrow communication between the center and the periphery of the body. The motor skills are related and develop simultaneously with emotional functioning. Which is, body and its manifestation, in whichever of its ambits, contain in their basis, an emotional component. [6]

Thus, the function of motor skills in the capacity of learning is very important when the child has initiated his preschool level and the teachers expect that the students are ready in their physic and mental functions so they continue to receive knowledge.

> "There is a reciprocal action between mental functions motor functions, psychological development and neurological development. The experiences that each child has with his body and his motor system will be a very important factor to fortify the development of their neural network system, and at the same time, the development of the neural system eases on the children the exploration and discovering of their capacities to practice different types of movements, promoting so, their autonomy, development of their identity and the organization of their thoughts." [7]

In children, the ideal is that the motor skills of their movement have progression throughout years, which is why:

> Psychomotor skill is an activity that gives a psychological significance to movement, in which each new ability develops from other less organized that allows to integrate and coordinate functions of psychic life with the movement, becoming a basic element in learning, since promotes the efficient cognitive process. Psychomotor skill is an activity that eases the integral development of the child. [8]

This association is shown in the early stages of the child when their cognitive process are produced by their motor activity, by manipulating and moving objects in their environment, to create significance as a result of the construction of learning by their context, generating that the child stimulates his/her own motor processes and motor abilities. This interrelation should be reinforced by the combination of teaching (mental learning) with motor activities such as using virtual reality games (motor learning).

Motor learning, and so significant learning, can be influenced by virtual reality games through the influence in premotor cortex. This cortex has direct connections with the primary motor area and contributes with the 30% of axons that conform corticospinal and corticobulbar tract. The premotor cortex is constituted by two components: lateral and medial.

The lateral component facilitates the development of conditional tasks with visual hints, while the medial component participates in the selection and beginning of movements through internal signs more than external motivations [9], virtual reality games can influence directly in processes of motor learning proportionating visual hints and having an impact directly on motivation.

4 Significant learning

As López (2015) affirms:

> Significant learning is an active restructuration of perceptions, ideas, concepts and schemes that the apprentice possesses in their cognitive structure. We could characterize their posture as constructivist; learning is not a simple passive assimilation of literal information, since subject transforms and structures it. Study materials and external information interact and interrelate with the previous schemes of knowledge and personal characteristics of the apprentice [10].

We could say that the significant learning constructs with the experience of each perception and so acquiring knowledge, experiences and generating new concepts.

Children can be considered as an active processor of information, and it is said that learning is systematic and organized, since in its more elaborated stage, consists in something very complex which cannot be reduced to simple memory tasks. Also it is worth pointing out the importance of learning by discovery according to the new facts that the subject perceives, infers, relates and generates ideas. With this one can say that it is not necessary that any significant learning in classroom should happen by discovery.

The previous knowledge of the student is considered in terms of knowledge schemes, which consist in representation that a person possesses in a specifically moment of their history about a piece of reality. These schemes include different types of knowledge about reality, such as: facts, experiences, personal anecdotes, attitudes, rules, etc. There are different types of significant learning since each one of them is related to requirements of human being to acquire beneficial knowledge for their own usage.

5 Motor patterns

Children develop skills in movement in a progressive way, from first involuntary moves to highly complex skills. Early childhood period (2 to 7 years) is critic for the development of elemental motor patterns. Children that do not develop mature motor patterns during this period, frequently present difficulties in carrying out complex motor abilities such as sport gestures.

Locomotor patterns are those movements that allow children the exploration of space. Like walking, running, high and extension jumping, leap, gallop and climb. [11]:

6 Methodology

This investigation work was developed through a quantitative study with a observational period of experimental and longitudinal type, with pre and post measures in a control and experimental group during six months. It was developed with the interaction of a videogame towards significant learning for locomotor development in these children.

The population of the study fulfilled the following inclusion criteria: children of preschool who belong to Manuela Beltrán school in Bogotá, who have not practiced real sport games, and the sign of informed assent and consent.

Later, the size and weight of children were compared obtaining their body mass index (BMI) with the help of the statistic program used in educative levels SPSS indicating chi-square, and with the help of contingency chart lower than 0,05, it could be identified if there is an influence of videogames over locomotor patterns of jumping in preschool children.

7 Results

The total population of the study was 30 children; from which 15 belong to control group and 15 to intervention group. The characteristics of size and weight of both populations are presented in chart 1. From this data (weight and size) the BMI was obtained.

Chart 1.

			BMI < 16	
			Selected	Total
Control	No	Recount	6	6
		% within control	100.0%	100.0%
		% within BMI < 16	37.5%	37.5%
		% of total	37.5%	37.5%
	Yes	Recount	10	10
		% within control	100.0%	100.0%
		% within BMI < 16	62.5%	62.5%
		% of total	62.5%	62.5%
Total		Recount	16	16
		% within control	100.0%	100.0%
		% within BMI < 16	100.0%	100.0%
		% of total	100.0%	100.0%

Chi-square tests

a. It will not be calculated any statistic because

	Value
Chi-square of Pearson	.[a]
Number of valid cases	16

BMI < 16 is a constant.

Chart 2.

Summary of cases processing

	Cases					
	Valid		Lost		Total	
	N	Percentage	N	Percentage	N	Percentage
Control * BMI < 16	16	100.0%	0	0.0%	16	100.0%

There is influence of videogames over locomotor pattern in preschool children since they learn by discovery generating a significant learning.

Besides we can conclude that significance in significant learning of videogames in preschool children helps in abilities like jumping helping therefore their motor skills.

Virtual reality games give a motor learning. Through the participation that children have in motor exercises in the scholar age, maturity in brain starts to increase in the experience of learning, at the same time with the perception and interaction with their scholar, family and social environment, which favors that the knowledge is received with pleasure and displayed for children as easy and fun.

8 Conclusion

In this investigation, it was found that according to chi-square statistic, it can be concluded that development in motor skills DOES influence in significant learning of boys and girls. Most of them do activities of significant learning, but do not have a necessary guidance or a procedure to follow. According to investigation they have to be always supervised by an adult but sometimes they do not need to have any kind of supervision, besides that significant knowledge does not articulate with didactic processes orientated by the teacher in the face of the expected motor skill.

In the beginning, they were only a group of exercises that were used to fix some weakness, disability or difficulty. But with the pass of the years, now is very important in childhood education, and even more so in early years of childhood due to the existence of interdependence between motor, affective and intellectual development.

> "The strategy itself can be determined being also a group of actions directed to the consecution of a goal, implying steps to be taken to obtain significant learning, and so securing the consecution of an objective: taking into account the capacity of thoughts which allows advancement in function of effectiveness criteria" [12].

Its final purpose is to regulate activity in people, its application allows to select, evaluate, persist or abandon different actions to achieve goals that we will propound, they are independent; imply auto direction; the existence of an objective and the conscious of that objective exists and auto control; the supervision and evaluation of the own behavior in function of objectives that guide them and the possibility of printing modifications on it whenever its necessary and according to the necessities and contexts where these didactic strategies are going to be applied.

Virtual reality videogames help as strategies in significant learning since they focus the attention and stimulate activity, jumping and motor skills in children of preschool age.

Acknowledgment

The author would like to thank Richard Jose De Sousa Da Silva for his translating collaboration and adjustment of the text to the corresponding and required format.

References

[1] GÓMEZ MORA, M. Aplicación de realidad virtual en la rehabilitación cognitiva. En: Revista Vínculos. Ciencia, Tecnología y Sociedad. Enero-junio, 2013. Vol 10, no 1. 130-135.

[2] MURCIA P. L., Incidencia del uso de los videojuegos en alteraciones visuales, ergonómicas en niños de 9 a 14 años [en línea]. En: Ciencia y Tecnología para la salud visual y ocular. 2004. Disponible en internet [citado en 18 Noviembre de 2013].

[3] BELTRÁN V. J., VALENCIA A., MOLINA J. P., Los videojuegos activos y la salud de los jóvenes: revisión de la investigación. En: Revista internacional de medicina y ciencias de la actividad física y el deporte, Marzo, 2011, Vol. 11, no 41, p. 203-219.

[4] GALEÓN. Historia de los Video juegos, [en línea] 2012. Disponible en internet: www.historia-videojuegos.galeon.com [citado en 25 Junio de 2012].

[5] PÁEZ A., Realidad Virtual, [en línea] Monografias.com, 2007. Disponible en internet: http://www.monografias.com/trabajos53/realidad-virtual/realidad-virtual.shtml [citado en 25 Junio de 2012].

[6] Da Fonseca, V. (2010, p. 304). Manual de observación Psicomotríz. Obtenido de https://books.google.com.ec/books?id=kNrRlgjAoYEC&printsec=frontco ver#v=onepage&q&f=false

[7] Vásquez, M. (14 de Julio de 2014, p. 12). Experiencias de aprendizaje sobre corporalidad y movimiento. Obtenido de http://es.slideshare.net/miriamcita/20130726181559 0libro2corporalidad

[8] Ortega, X. (5 de Febrero de 2013). Trabajos del libro e Psicomotricidad. Obtenido de http://xjog60.blogspot.com/2013/02/6-mepp.html

[9] PURVES, D. Neurociencia. Editorial Médica Panamericana. 2007.

[10] López, W. (2015, p. 26). La percepción visual y su incidencia en el desarrollo del aprendizaje significativo. Obtenido de http://repo.uta.edu.ec/bitstream/123456789/18605/1/TESIS%20con%20fir mas.pdf

[11] Mc CLENAGHAN Y GALLAHUE. Movimientos fundamentales su desarrollo y su rehabilitación. Editorial Panamericana. 1985.

[12] Sarmiento, A. (2012). Definicion de estrategia didactica. Obtenido de https://antonio6519.wordpress.com/2009/10/05/definicion-de-estrategiadidactica/

Concurrent and Distributed Applications with ActoDeS

Federico Bergenti[1], Eleonora Iotti[2], Agostino Poggi[2] and Michele Tomaiuolo[2]

[1]DMI, University of Parma, 43124 Parma Italy
[2]DII, University of Parma, 43124 Parma Italy

Abstract. ActoDeS is a software framework for the development of large concurrent and distributed systems. This software framework takes advantage of the actor model and of an its implementation that makes easy the development of the actor code by delegating the management of events (i.e., the reception of messages) to the execution environment. Moreover, it allows the development of scalable and efficient applications through the possibility of using different implementations of the components that drive the execution of actors. In particular, the paper introduces the software framework and presents the results of its experimentation.

1 Introduction

Concurrent and distributed programming tools and frameworks have lately received enormous interest because multi-core processors make concurrency an essential ingredient of efficient program execution and because distributed architectures are inherently concurrent. However, distributed and concurrent programming is hard and largely different from sequential programming. Programmers have more concerns when it comes to taming parallelism. In fact, distributed and concurrent programs are usually bigger than equivalent sequential ones and models of distributed and concurrent programming languages are different from familiar and popular sequential languages [1, 2].

Message passing is the most attractive solution because it is a concurrent model that is not based on the sharing of data and so its techniques can be used in distributed computation too.

One of the well-known theoretical and practical models of message passing is the actor model [3]. Using such a model, programs become collections of independent active objects (actors) that exchange messages and have no mutable shared state. Actors can help developers to avoid issues such as deadlock, live-lock and starvation, which are common problems for shared memory based approaches.

There are a multitude of actor oriented libraries and languages, and each of them implements some variants of actor semantics. However, such libraries and languages use either thread-based programming, which makes easy the development of programs, or event-based programming, which is far more practical to develop large and efficient concurrent systems, but also is more difficult to use.

This paper presents an actor based software framework, called ActoDeS (Actor Development System), that has the suitable features for both simplifying the development of large and distributed complex systems and guarantying scalable and efficient applications. The next section presents related work. Section 3 introduces the software framework and provides details about its implementation. Sections 4 shows how to write the code of an application and how to configure it through a simple application. Section 5 presents the experimentation of the software framework. Finally, section 6 concludes the paper by discussing its main features and the directions for future work.

2 Related Work

Several actor-oriented libraries and languages have been proposed in last decades and a large part of them uses Java as implementation language [4]. The rest of the section presents some of the most interesting works.

Salsa [5] is an actor-based language for mobile and Internet computing that provides three significant mechanisms based on the actor model: token-passing continuations, join continuations, and first-class continuations. In Salsa each actor has its own thread, and so it limits the scalability. Moreover, message-passing performance suffers from the overhead of reflective method calls.

Kilim [6] is a framework used to create robust and massively concurrent actor systems in Java. It takes advantage of code annotations and of a bytecode post-processor to simplify the writing of the code. However, it provides only a very simplified implementation of the actor model where each actor (called task in Kilim) has a mailbox and a method defining its behavior. Moreover, it does not provide remote messaging capabilities.

Scala [7] is an object-oriented and functional programming language that provides an implementation

[a] Corresponding author: Agostino.poggi@unipr.it

DOI: 10.1051/matecconf/20167604043

of the actor model unifying thread based and event based programming models. In fact, in Scala an actor can suspend with a full thread stack (receive) or can suspend with just a continuation closure (react). Therefore, scalability can be obtained by sacrificing program simplicity.

Akka [8] is an alternative toolkit and runtime system for developing event-based actors in Scala, but also providing APIs for developing actor-based systems in Java. One of its distinguishing features is the hierarchical organization of actors, so that a parent actor that creates some children actors is responsible for handling their failures.

Jetlang [9] provides a high performance Java threading library that should be used for message based concurrency. The library is designed specifically for high performance in-memory messaging and does not provide remote messaging capabilities.

AmbientTalk [10] is a distributed object-oriented programming language that is implemented on an actor-based and event driven concurrency model, which makes it highly suitable for composing service objects across a mobile network. It provides an actor implementation based on communicating event loops [8]. However, each actor is always associated with its own JVM thread and so it limits the scalability of applications on the number of actors for JVM.

3 ActoDES

ActoDeS is an actor based software framework that has the goal of both simplifying the development of concurrent and distributed complex systems and guarantying an efficient execution of applications.

ActoDeS is implemented by using the Java language and takes advantage of preexistent Java software libraries and solutions for supporting concurrency and distribution. ActoDeS has a layered architecture composed of an application and a runtime layer. The application layer provides the software components that an application developer needs to extend or directly use for implementing the specific actors of an application. The runtime layer provides the software components that implement the ActoDeS middleware infrastructures to support the development of standalone and distributed applications.

3.1. Actors

In ActoDeS an application is based on a set of interacting actors that perform tasks concurrently. An actor is an autonomous concurrent object, which interacts with other actors by exchanging asynchronous messages [3]. Moreover, it can create new actors, update its local state, change its behavior and kill itself.

Communication between actors is buffered: incoming messages are stored in a mailbox until the actor is ready to process them; moreover, an actor can set a timeout for waiting for a new message and then can execute some actions if the timeout fires. Each actor has a system-wide unique identifier called reference that allows it to be reached in a location transparent way. An actor can send messages only to the actors of which it knows the reference, that is, the actors it created and of which it received the references from other actors. After its creation, an actor can change several times its behavior until it kills itself. Each behavior has the main duty of processing a set of specific messages through a set of message handlers called cases. Therefore, if an unexpected message arrives, then the actor mailbox maintains it until a next behavior will be able to process it.

An actor can be viewed as a logical thread that implements an event loop [10, 11]. This event loop perpetually processes events that represent: the reception of messages, the behavior exchanges and the firing of timeouts. The life of an actor starts from the initialization of its behavior that then processes the received messages and the firing of message reception timeouts. During its life, an actor can move from a behavior to another one more times, and its life ends when it kills itself.

ActoDeS provides different actor implementations and the use of one or of another implementation represents one of the factors that mainly influence the performance of an application. In particular, actor implementations can be divided in two classes: active actors, i.e., actors that have their own thread of execution, and passive actors, i.e., actors that share a single thread of execution. In this last case, the scheduler has the duty of guaranteeing a fair execution of all the actors.

The implementation of an actor is based on four main components: a reference, a mailbox, a behavior and a state. Figure 1 shows a graphical representation of the architecture of an actor.

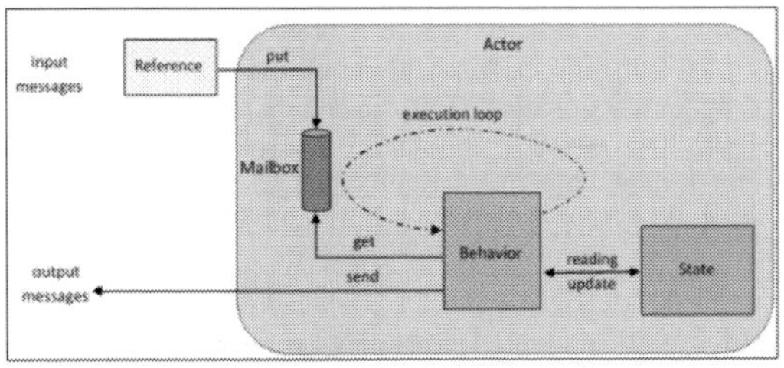

Figure 1. Actor architecture.

A reference supports the sending of messages to the actor it represents. Therefore, an actor needs to have the reference of another actor for sending it a message. In particular, an actor has the reference of another actor if either it created such an actor (in fact, the creation method returns the reference of the new actor) or it received a message that either has been sent by such an actor (in fact, each message contains the reference of the sender) or whose content enclosed its reference.

References act as identifiers of the actors of an application. To guarantee it and to simplify the implementation, an actor space acts as "container" for the actors running in the same Java Virtual Machine (JVM) and the string representation of a reference is composed of an actor identifier, an actor space identifier and the IP address of the computing node. In particular, the actor identifier is different for all the actors of the same actor space, and the actor space identifier is different for all the actor spaces of the same computing node.

A mailbox has the duty of maintaining the messages sent to its actor until it processes them. In particular, a behavior can process a set of specific messages leaving in the mailbox the messages that is not able to process. Such messages remain into the mailbox until the actor moves to a behavior that is able to process them. If all the behaviors of the actor cannot process such messages, then they remain into the queue for all the life of the actor. A mailbox has not an explicit limit on the number of messages that can maintain. However, it is clear that the (permanent) deposit of large numbers of messages in the mailboxes of the actors may reduce the performances of applications and may cause in some circumstances their failure.

As in the original actor model, in ActoDeS, a behavior had the main duty of processing the incoming messages and it perform it through a set of "case" methods that have the goal of processing the messages that match a specific message pattern.

Often the behaviors that drive the life of an actor need to share some information (e.g., a behavior may work on the results of the previous behaviors). It is possible thank to a state object. Of course, the kind of information that the behaviors of an actor need to share depends on the type of task they must perform in an application; therefore, the state of an actor must be specialized for the tasks it will perform (i.e., different behaviors can have different state representations).

A message is an object that contains a set of fields maintaining the typical header information, and the message content. Moreover, each message is different from any other one. In fact, messages of the same sender have a different identifier and messages of different senders have a different sender reference.

A message pattern is an object that can apply a combination of constraint objects on the value of all the fields of a message. ActoDeS provides a set of predefines constraints, but new ones can be easily added. In particular, one of such constraints allows the application of a pattern to the value of a message field. Therefore, the addition of field patterns (the current implementation offer only a regular expression pattern) will allow the definition of sophisticated filters on the values of all the message fields and in particular on the content of the message.

An actor has not direct access to the local state of the other actors and can share data with them only through the exchange of messages and through the creation of actors. Therefore, to avoid the problems due to the concurrent access to mutable data, both message passing and actor creation should have call-by-value semantics. This may require making a copy of the data even on shared memory platforms, but, as it is done by the large part of the actor libraries implemented in Java, ActoDeS does not make data copies because such operations would be the source of an important overhead. However, it encourages the programmers to use immutable objects (by implementing as immutable all the predefined message content objects) and delegates the appropriate use of mutable object to them

3.2 Actor Spaces

Depending on the complexity of the application and on the availability of computing and communication resources, one or more actor spaces can manage the actors of the application. An actor space acts as "container" for a set of actors and provides them the services necessary for their execution. In particular, an actor space takes advantage of two special actors: the scheduler and the service provider. The scheduler manages the concurrent execution of the actors of the actor space. The service provider enables the actors of an application to perform new kinds of action (e.g., to broadcast a message or to move from an actor space to another one). Figure 2 shows a graphical representation of the architecture of an ActoDeS distributed application.

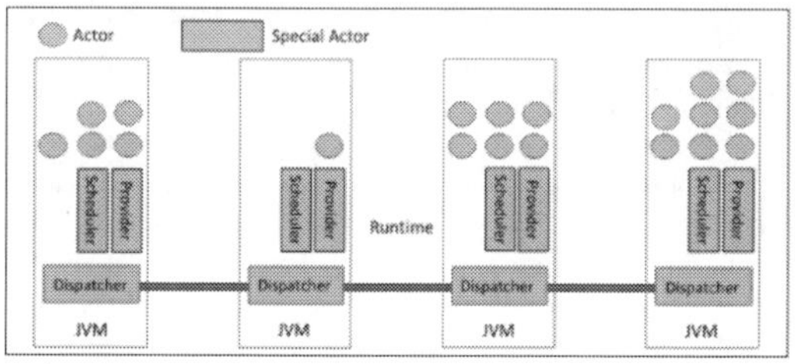

Figure 2. Distributed ActoDeS application architecture.

An actor space has the duty of supporting the execution of the actions of its actors and of enhancing them with new kinds of action. To do it, an actor space takes advantage of two main runtime components (i.e., the dispatcher and the registry) and of two special actors (the scheduler and the service provider).

The dispatcher has the duty of supporting the communication with the actors of the other actor spaces of the application. In particular, it creates connections to/from the other actor spaces, manages the reception of messages from the input connections, maps remote references to the appropriate output connections and uses them delivering messages to remote actors.

The registry supports the creation of actors and the reception of the messages coming from remote actors. In particular, it has the duties of creating new references and of providing the reference of a local actor to the dispatcher when it is managing a message coming from a remote actor. In fact, while the reference of a local actor allows the direct delivery of messages, the reference of a remote actor delegates the delivery of messages to the dispatcher of the actor space. Such a dispatcher delivers the message to the dispatcher of the actor space where the remote actor lives and the latter dispatcher takes advantage of the registry for mapping the remote reference to the local reference of the actor.

The scheduler is a special actor that manages the execution of the "normal" actors of an actor space. Of course, the duties of a scheduler depend on the implementation of the actors of the actor space and, in particular, on the type of threading solutions associated with them. In fact, while the Java runtime environment mainly manages the execution of active actors, ActoDeS schedulers completely manage the execution of passive actors.

The service provider is a special actor that offers a set of services for enabling the "normal" actors of an application to perform new kinds of actions. Of course, the actors of the application can require the execution of such services by sending a message to the service provider. In particular, the current implementation of the software framework provides services for supporting the broadcast of messages, the exchange of messages through the "publish and subscribe" pattern, the mobility of actors, the interaction with users through emails and the creation of actors (useful for creating actors in other actor spaces).

Moreover, an actor space can enable the execution of an additional runtime component called logger. The logger has the possibility to store (or to send to another application) the relevant information about the execution of the actors of the actor space (e.g., creation and deletion of actors, exchange and processing of messages, and behavior replacements). The logger can provide both textual and binary information that can be useful for understanding the activities of the application and for identifying the causes and of possible execution problems. In particular, the binary information contains real copies of the objects of the application (e.g., messages and copies of the actor state). Therefore, such an information can be used to feed other applications (e.g., monitoring and simulation tools).

Finally, the actor space provides a runtime component, called configurator, whose duty is to simplify the configuration of an application by supporting both a declarative and procedural configuration of the actor spaces of the application. In fact, such a configuration can be defined as a properties file or as a piece of code that calls the API provided by the configurator.

3.3 Application configuration

The quality of the execution of an ActoDeS application mainly depends on the implementation of the actors and of the schedulers of its actor spaces. Another important factor that influences its execution is the implementation of the runtime components that support the exchange of messages between both local and remote actors.

However, a combination of such implementations, that maximizes the quality of execution of an application, could be a bad configuration for another type of application. Moreover, different instances of the same application can work in different conditions (e.g., different number of users to serve, different amount of data to process) and so they may require different configurations.

As introduced in a previous section, actor implementations can be divided in two classes that allow to an actor either to have its own thread (active actor) or to share a single thread with the other actors of the actor space (passive actor).

The use of active actors has the advantage of delegating the scheduling to the JVM with the advantage of guaranteeing actors to have a fair access to the computational resources of the actor space.

However, this solution suffers from high memory consumption and context-switching overhead and so it can be used in actor spaces with a limited number of actors. Therefore, when the number of actors in an actor space is high, the best solution is the use of passive actors whose execution is managed by a scheduler provided by the ActoDeS framework. Such a scheduler uses a simple not preemptive round-robin scheduling algorithm and so the implementation of the passive actor has the duty of guaranteeing a fair access to the computational resources of the actor space, for example, by limiting the number of messages that an actor can process in a single execution cycle.

Moreover, in some particular applications is not possible to distribute in equal parts the tasks among the actors of an actor space and so there are some actors that should have a priority on the access to the computational resources of the actor space. Often in this situation, a good solution is the combination of active and passive actors.

In an actor-based system where the computation is mainly based on the exchange and processing of messages, the efficiency of the communication supports is a key parameter for the quality of applications. In ActoDeS both local and remote communication can be provided by replaceable components. In particular, the current implementation of the software framework supports the communication among the actor spaces through four kinds of connector that respectively use ActiveMQ [12], Java RMI [13], MINA [14] and ZeroMQ [15]. Moreover, when in an application the large part of communication is based on broadcast and multicast messages, the traditional individual mailbox can be replaced by a mailbox that transparent extracts the messages for its actor from a single queue shared with all the other actors of the actor space. In this case, such actors have a passive implementation and are called shared actors.

Finally, in some kinds of application there is a massive number of actors, but few of them are simultaneously executed. In this case both the active and passive implementations provide a bad scalability because of the cost of maintaining the threads or for the cost of cycling on a large number of inactive actors. An efficient implementation, derived from the passive one, tries to reduce the overhead of cycling on inactive actors. In particular, every actor has a counter that maintains the current number of consecutive inactivity cycles and the scheduler remove such an actor from the scheduling list when its counter reaches a specific value. When it happens, the actor is saved in maintained in the memory of the JVM (temporary-saved actor) or saved in a persistent storage (persistent-saved actor). A saved actor is reloaded in the scheduling list when another actor sends it a message.

3.4 Scalability and performance

The scalability and performance of the different implementations of actors and scheduling actors can be analyzed by comparing the execution times of three simple applications on a laptop with an Intel Core i7-4712HQ - 2.30GHz, 16 GB RAM, Windows 10 - 64bit, Java 8, 8 GB heap size. These examples involve four kinds of configuration: active (i.e., the actor space contains active actors), passive (i.e., the actor space contains passive actors), shared (i.e., the actor space contains passive actors whose mailboxes get messages from a unique message queue), and temporary-saved, (i.e., the actor space contains passive actors and the inactive ones may be save in the memory).

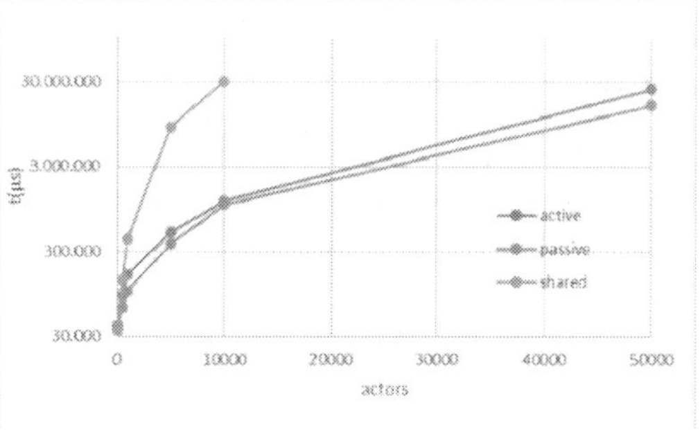

Figure 3. Messaging example performance.

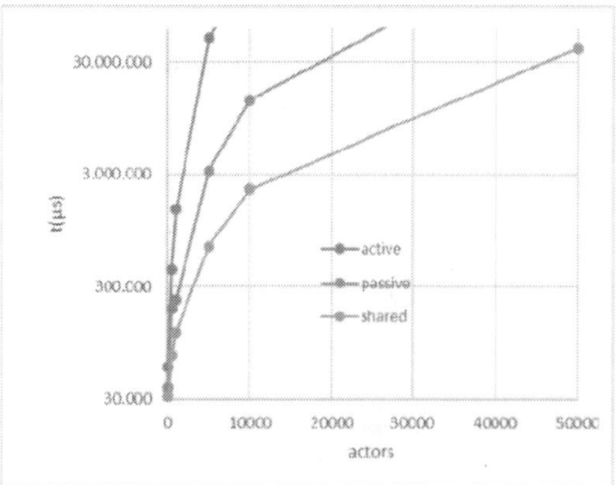

Figure 4. Broadcasting example performance.

The first application is based on the point-to-point exchange of messages between the actors of an actor space. The application starts an actor that creates a certain number of actors, sends 1000 messages to each of them and then waits for their answers. Figure 3 shows the execution time of the application from 100 to 50.000 actors using the active, passive and shared configurations. The best performances are obtained with the passive configuration when the number of actors increases. The second application is based on the broadcasting of messages to the actors of an actor space. The application starts an actor that creates a certain number of actors and then sends a broadcast message. Each actor receives the broadcast message, then, in its response, sends another broadcast message, and finally waits for all the broadcast messages. Figure 4 shows the execution time of the application from 100 to 50.000 actors using the active, passive and shared configurations. The best performances are obtained with the shared configuration.

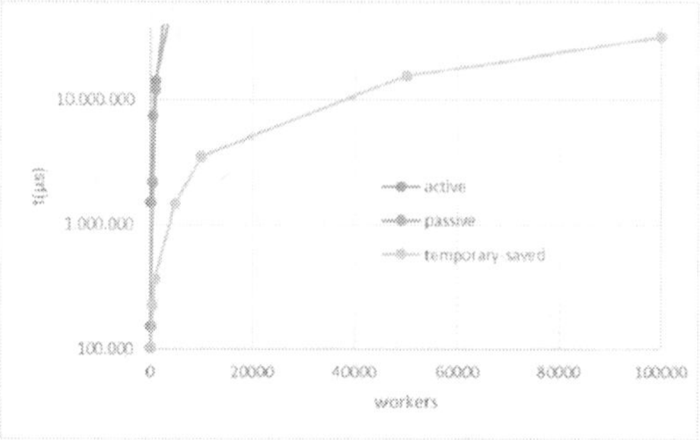

Figure 5. Master-workers example performance.

Finally, the third application can be viewed as a master - worker application. In particular, the master needs to perform a number of tasks equals to the number of workers and assigns them sequentially to one of the workers that it selects randomly. Every task consists of 1000 request - reply interactions between the master and the selected worker. Figure 5 shows the execution time of the application from 100 to 100.000 workers using the active, passive and temporary-saved actors. For high numbers of actors only the use of temporary actors provides reasonable performances

4 An Example of Application

One of the most used examples for highlight the problem due to the concurrent access to a shared resource is the bounded buffer. Its implementation with ActoDeS involves the definition of the behaviors that drive the actors representing the bounded buffer and the producers and consumers acting on it. In particular, the bounded buffer can be defined by the "EmptyBuffer", "PartialBuffer" and "FullBuffer" behaviors that defines the three relevant state of the actor. Every behavior of the buffer has a set of cases for processing the messages coming from the producers and consumers and for killing its actor when it receiver a message that concludes the application.

For example, Figure 6 shows the two "initialize" methods that define the code of the "EmptyBuffer" behavior. The first method initializes the buffer after the creation of the actor and calls the second method. The second method is directly call when the actor moves to such a behavior, defines the case for processing the request from a producer, inherits the case for killing its actor and binds the two cases to the corresponding message patterns.

The application is started by a "main" method that: defines the initialization values, the type of scheduler and the actor that the scheduler must create. This actor creates the actors that represent; the buffer, the consumers and the producers, then, at the end of a predefined "lifetime" asks the other actors to kill themselves, and, finally, terminates the application. Figure 7 shows the code of the "main" method that starts the application.

```
private static final MessagePattern PUTPATTERN =
    new MessagePattern(new MessagePatternField(
      MessageField.CONTENT, new IsInstance(Put.class)));

public void initialize(final Binder b, final Object[] v) {
  setState(new BufferState((Integer) v[0]));
  initialize(b);
}

public void initialize(final Binder b) {
  this.state = (BufferState) getState();

  Case c = (m) -> {
    this.state.add(((Put) m.getContent()).getElement());
    send(m, Done.DONE);

    if (this.state.size() == this.state.getCapacity()) {
      return new FullBuffer();
    }
    else {
      return new PartialBuffer();
    }
  }
  b.bind(PUTPATTERN, c);
  b.bind(KILLPATTERN, this.killCase);
}
```

Figure 6. The "EmptyBuffer" behavior.

```
public static void main(final String[] v) {
  final long lifetime     = 1000;
  final int size          = 10;
  final int producers     = 10;
  final int consumers     = 10;

  Configuration c = Controller.INSTANCE.getConfiguration();

  c.setScheduler(ThreadScheduler.class.getName());

  c.addActors(
    1, Initiator.class.getName(),
    lifetime, size, producers, consumers);

  Controller.INSTANCE.run();
}
```

Figure 7. The application "main" method.

5 Experimentation

We experimented and are experimenting ActoDeS in different application domains and, in particular, in the agent-based modelling and simulation (ABMS) [16], in the analysis of social networks [17, 18], in modelling e-business [19] and collaborative work services [20] and agent-based systems for the management of information in peer-to-peer [21], mobile [22] and pervasive environments [23, 24].

In particular, the analysis of large social networks is a suitable domain for testing the distribution of an application on different computing nodes. Our work on the modeling and simulation of social networks started some years ago when we used agent-based techniques for generating and analyzing different types of social network of limited size [17, 25]. Now we can take advantage of the ActoDeS software framework for coping with very large social networks. Therefore, in a ActoDeS system, actors represent the individuals of the social network and maintain their information. Moreover, such actors can exhibit different behaviors, allowing both to cooperate in the analysis of the social network and to simulate the behavior of the represented individuals by performing the actions that they can perform in the social network. Of course, some additional actors are necessary, in particular, for generating the social network and for driving its measurements.

The architecture we defined for such a kind of application is a distributed architecture based on a variable number of actor spaces. Each actor space maintains a set of actors that are managed by a temporary or persistent scheduler. Moreover, the service provider takes advantage of a naming service.

An important factor that simplifies the parallel construction of a social network is the availability of a universal unique identifier for each individual of the social network. Such an identifier permits to avoid the creation of actors representing the same individual in different actor spaces, thanks to the use of the naming service. In fact, the naming service allows to:

- maintain the binding between the references of the active actors with the identifiers of the corresponding individual;
- use the individual identifier to find an actor in the persistent storage;
- cooperate with the naming services of the actor spaces to decide if a new actor must be created.

Moreover, such a kind of application can take advantage of the fact that ActoDeS supports the migration of actors. It allows to define an initial distribution of the actors without any information about the structure of the network and then to move actors during the execution of the analysis and simulation tasks to reduce the overhead of the communication between the different computational nodes.

We started the experimentation of such a system by modelling some social networks with a number of individuals that vary from some thousands to some millions of individuals. We built such models by using the data maintained in the "Stanford Large Network Dataset Collection" [26] and up to now, we are using them for performing some simple measures (i.e., diameter, clustering coefficient and centrality). The first tests we did compare the performances of the system with a deployment on a different number of computing nodes (from one to four). The results of the tests showed that a single actor space can manage social networks with some millions of individuals, but the use of additional actor spaces on more computing nodes gives an important improvement in the performances. In fact, the advantages on performance of the partitioning of the model of large social networks on some computing nodes are relevant for both the creation and measurement phases, because it is necessary to move a smaller number of actors from the scheduler to the temporary or persistent storage and vice versa.

6 Conclusions

ActoDeS is a software framework that allows the development of efficient large actor based systems by combining the possibility to use different implementations of the components driving the execution of actors with the delegation of the management of the reception of messages to the execution environment.

ActoDeS is implemented by using the Java language and is an evolution of CoDE [27] that simplifies the definition of actor behaviors and provides more scalable and performant implementations. Moreover, it takes advantages of some implementation solutions used in JADE [28] for the definition of some internal components.

ActoDeS shares with Kilim [6], Scala [7] and Jetlang [9] the possibility to build applications that scale to a massive number of actors, but without the need of introducing new constructs that make complex the writing of actor based programs.

Moreover, ActoDeS has been designed for the development of distributed applications while the previous three actor based software were designed for applications running inside multi-core computers. In fact, the use of structured messages and message patterns makes possible the implementation of complex interactions in a distributed application because a message contains all the information for delivery it to the destination and then for building and sending a reply. Moreover, a message pattern filters the input messages on all the information contained in the message and not only on its content.

Current and future research activities are and will be dedicated to: i) extend the experimentation of the software framework, ii) provide a set of actor and scheduler implementations for ABMS and multi-agent applications, and iii) extend the functionalities provided by the software framework. In particular, future activities will be dedicated to the provision of a set of security and trust services and a set of coordination protocols to support the interaction between actor spaces of different organizations [29, 30] and the development of an ontology model and language for definition of the content exchanged by actors [31, 32].

References

1. C. Leopold, Parallel and Distributed Computing: A Survey of Models, Paradigms and Approaches, New York, NY, USA: John Wiley & Sons (2001)
2. M. Philippsen, A survey of concurrent object-oriented languages, Concurrency: Practice and Experience, vol. 12, no. 10, pp. 917-980 (2000)
3. G. A. Agha, Actors: A Model of Concurrent Computation in Distributed Systems, Cambridge, MA, USA: MIT Press (1986)
4. R. K. Karmani, A. Shali and G. A. Agha, Actor frameworks for the JVM platform: a comparative analysis, in Proc. of the 7th International Conference on Principles and Practice of Programming in Java, Calgary, Alberta, Canada, pp. 11-20 (2009)
5. C. Varela and G. A. Agha, Programming dynamically reconfigurable open systems with SALSA, SIGPLAN Notices, vol. 36, no. 12, pp. 20-34 (2001)
6. S. Srinivasan, and A. Mycroft, Kilim: Isolation-typed actors for Java, in Proc. of the ECOOP 2008 – Object-Oriented Programming Conference, Berlin, Germany, Springer, pp. 104-128 (2008)
7. P. Haller, and M. Odersky, Scala Actors: unifying thread-based and event-based programming, Theoretical Computer Science, vol. 410, no. 2-3, pp. 202–220 (2009)
8. Typesafe (2016), Akka software, Available from: http://akka.io.
9. M. Rettig (2016), Jetlang software. Available from: https://github.com/jetlang/.
10. J. Dedecker, T. Van Cutsem, S. Mostinckx, T. D'Hondt and W. De Meuter, Ambient-oriented programming in ambienttalk, in Proc. of the ECOOP 2006 – Object-Oriented Programming Conference, Berlin, Germany, Springer, pp. 230-254 (2006)
11. M. S. Miller, E. D. Tribble and J. Shapiro, Concurrency among strangers, in Trustworthy Global Computing, Berlin, Germany, Springer, pp. 195-229 (2005)
12. B. Snyder, D. Bosnanac and R. Davies, ActiveMQ in action, Westampton, NJ, USA, Manning (2001)
13. E. Pitt and K. McNiff, Java.rmi: the Remote Method Invocation Guide, Boston, MA, USA, Addison-Wesley (2001)
14. Apache Software Foundation (2016), Apache Mina Framework, Available from: http://mina.apache.org
15. P. Hintjens, ZeroMQ: Messaging for Many Applications, Sebastopol, CA, USA, O'Reilly, 2013.
16. A. Poggi, Agent based modeling and simulation with ActoMoS, Proc. of 16th Workshop on From Object to Agents (WOA 2015), Naples; Italy, pp. 91-96 (2015)
17. F. Bergenti, E. Franchi and A. Poggi, Agent-based interpretations of classic network models, Computational and Mathematical Organization Theory, vol. 19, no. 2, pp. 105-127 (2013)
18. E. Franchi, A. Poggi and M. Tomaiuolo, Open social networking for online collaboration, International Journal of e-Collaboration, vol. 9, no. 3, pp. 50-68 (2013)
19. A. Negri, A. Poggi, M. Tomaiuolo, and P. Turci, Agents for e-Business Applications, in 5th Int. Joint Conf. on Autonomous Agents and Multi-Agent Systems, Hakodate, Japan: ACM, pp. 907-914 (2006)
20. F. Bergenti, and A. Poggi. An agent-based approach to manage negotiation protocols in flexible CSCW systems, in Proc. of the fourth international conference on Autonomous agents, ACM, pp. 267-268. ACM (2000)
21. A. Poggi, and M. Tomaiuolo, A DHT-based multi-agent system for semantic information sharing, in New Challenges in Distributed Information Filtering and Retrieval, Berlin, Germany: Springer, pp. 197-213 (2013)

22. F. Bergenti, and A. Poggi, LEAP: A FIPA platform for handheld and mobile devices, Intelligent agents VIII. Berlin, Germany, Springer, pp. 436-446 (2001)
23. F. Bergenti, and A. Poggi, Ubiquitous Information Agents, International Journal on Cooperative Information Systems, Vol. 11, No. 3-4, pp. 231-244, (2002)
24. A. Poggi, HDS: a Software Framework for the Realization of Pervasive Applications, WSEAS Transactions on Computers, vol. 10, no. 9, pp. 1149-1159 (2010)
25. F. Bergenti, E. Franchi, E, and A. Poggi, Selected models for agent-based simulation of social networks, in Proc. 3rd Symposium on Social Networks and Multiagent Systems (SNAMAS'11), York, UK, pp. 27-32 (2011)
26. Stanford University (2016), SNAP: Stanford Large Network Dataset Collection, Available from: http://snap.stanford.edu/data/index.html.
27. F. Bergenti, A. Poggi, and M. Tomaiuolo, An Actor Based Software Framework for Scalable Applications, in Internet and Distributed Computing Systems, Berlin, Germany: Springer, pp. 26-35 (2014)
28. A. Poggi, M. Tomaiuolo, and P. Turci, Extending JADE for agent grid applications, in Enabling Technologies: Infrastructure for Collaborative Enterprises, Modena, Italy. IEEE Computer Society, pp. 352-357 (2004)
29. A. Poggi, M. Tomaiuolo and G. Vitaglione, A Security Infrastructure for Trust Management in Multi-agent Systems, in Trusting Agents for Trusting Electronic Societies, Theory and Applications in HCI and E-Commerce, LNCS, vol. 3577, Springer, Berlin, Germany, pp. 162-179 (2005)
30. F. Bergenti, and A. Poggi, An agent-based approach to manage negotiation protocols in flexible CSCW systems, in Proc. 4th International Conference on Autonomous Agents, Barcelona, Spain, ACM, pp. 267-268 (2000)
31. M. Tomaiuolo, P. Turci, F. Bergenti and A. Poggi, An ontology support for semantic aware agents, in Agent-Oriented Information Systems III, LNCS, vol. 3529, Springer, Berlin, Germany, pp. 140-153 (2006)
32. A. Poggi, Developing ontology based applications with O3L, WSEAS Trans. on Computers, vol, 8, no. 8, pp. 1286-1295 (2009)

MATEC Web of Conferences **76**, 04044 (2016) DOI: 10.1051/matecconf/20167604044
CSCC 2016

A model for the grasping analysis of an underactuated finger driven by unextensible tendon

Vincenzo Niola[1a], Cesare Rossi[1], Sergio Savino[1]

[1] *University of Naples "Federico II" Via Claudio 21, 80125, Naples ITALY*

Abstract. A grasping analysis is presented of an underactuated finger driven by unextensible tendon. The finger itself is one of those of a mechanical prosthesis that was principally conceived as human prosthesis. After a brief description of the whole system constituted by the mechanical hand, the model to predict the behavior of the finger during the grasping is presented; then some examples of grasping are presented. The model can be useful for both the under-actuated finger design and for the prediction of the capabilities of the whole hand.

1 Introduction

A number of Authors have investigated on mechanical grasping devices and hand prosthesis In particular [1-6]. These devices are based on mechanical systems using a number of motors [7-10] or on self-adapting devices using a single motor [11-13] .

Among the later, the authors of this contribution developed a new mechanical hand (Federica mechanical hand) based on a self-adaptive patented scheme (patent n. 0001415546 and n. 102015000059873, the latter pending) [14-18] that is briefly described in figure 1. In the figure a prototype is shown and a CAD design showing the working principle is also reported.

The hand is composed by five fingers, shown in figure 2, actuated by a single motor by means of a pulley system in cascade, which automatically distributes the tendon displacement to the phalanges. Each finger consists of three elements, representing respectively the distal, medial and proximal phalanges, joined by hinges, and activated by a single inelastic tendon. The grasp of an object of any shape is obtained by operating the main inelastic tendon, which, through the pulley system, distributes the force among the various fingers, and generates the closure of each finger according to the resistance offered by the object to be grasped in the contact points.

In this contribution, the authors focused themselves on the study of the grasping of the single finger in order to optimize the finger behavior during the grasping itself.

Some examples of contact between the finger phalanxes and a solid surface having a defined geometrical shape are considered.

The contact between the finger and a surface has been studied using the Simulink library called SimMechanics contact forces downloaded from the Mathworks. The library provides different blocks according to the type of surface to be treated. We focused mainly on two blocks, the "sphere to plane" and the "sphere to tube". The object of the study is the contact between the proximal phalanges, medial and distal and a sphere and, in addition, the contact between the tip of the finger shown schematically with a cylindrical surface and a sphere.

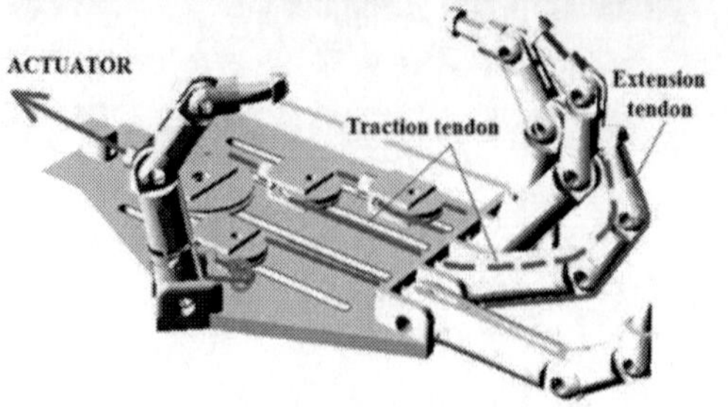

Figure 1. The underactuated, self-adapting mechanical hand.

[a] Vincenzo Niola: vincenzo.niola@unina.it

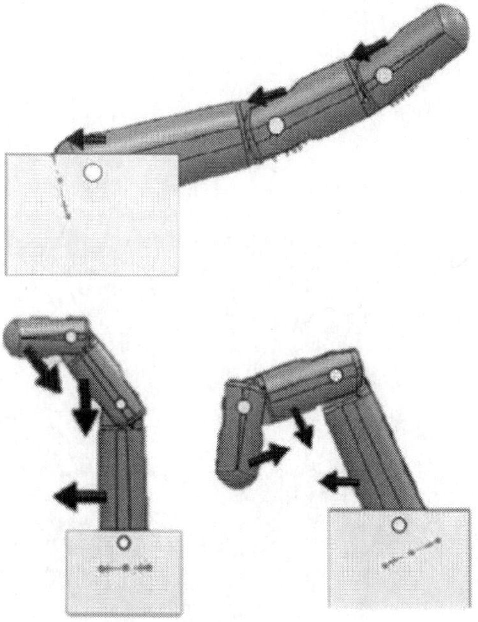

Figure 2. Scheme of the finger and closing simulation.

2 The contact between surfaces

The contact between the finger and a surface has been studied using the Simulink library called SimMechanics contact forces downloaded from the Mathworks. The library provides different blocks according to the type of surface to be treated. We focused mainly on two blocks, the "sphere to plane" and the "sphere to tube". The object of the study is the contact between the proximal phalanges, medial and distal and a surface and, in addition, the contact between the tip of the finger shown schematically with a cylindrical surface and a sphere.
The contact between two bodies was simulated with a force applied only along the direction of penetration of the two bodies. In figure 5 this force is shown as F_n, and it acts on the plane and on the sphere in the opposite direction. In the contact model, also the friction force is included; it acts as a tangential force in the contact point on both bodies. In figure 3 the friction force is shown as F_t.

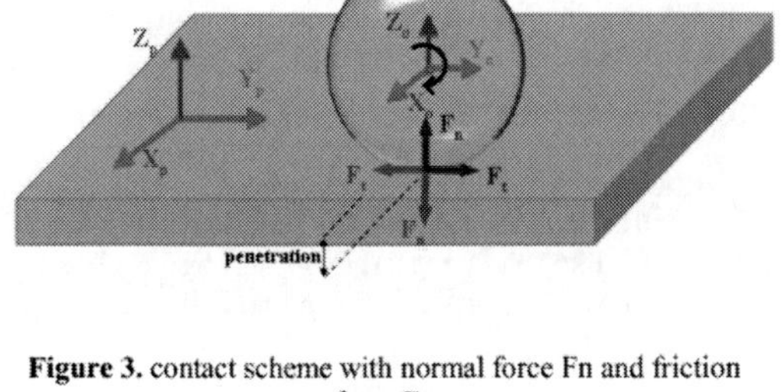

Figure 3. contact scheme with normal force Fn and friction force F_t.

The normal force F_n acts by opposing the penetration of the two bodies and the damping is zero when the penetration decreases.

$$F_n = \begin{cases} k \cdot Z_{penetration} + b \cdot v_{penetration} & \forall Z_{penetration} > 0, v_{penetration} > 0 \\ k \cdot Z_{penetration} & \forall Z_{penetration} > 0, v_{penetration} < 0 \\ 0 & \forall Z_{penetration} < 0 \end{cases} \quad (1)$$

Where $Z_{penetration}$ is the penetration between the two bodies , $v_{penetration}$ is the velocity of penetration, k is the contact stiffness and b is the contact damping.
The friction force Ft is the product of normal force and a coefficient of friction that is a function of the relative velocity at the contact point.
Examples of the tool to study the contact between a sphere and a plane or between a sphere and a tube are reported in fig. 4.
By using the original blocks of SimMechanics contact forces library we observed that it is not possible to model the edge effect between finger and ball. This circumstance is a drawback because many contact intermediate positions, i.e. those in which the ball is located between two fingers, are not correctly handled (a finger can penetrate the sphere).
In order to make the appropriate corrections we considered a simpler system constituted by a plane and a sphere; in fig. 5 mentioned drawback can be observed.

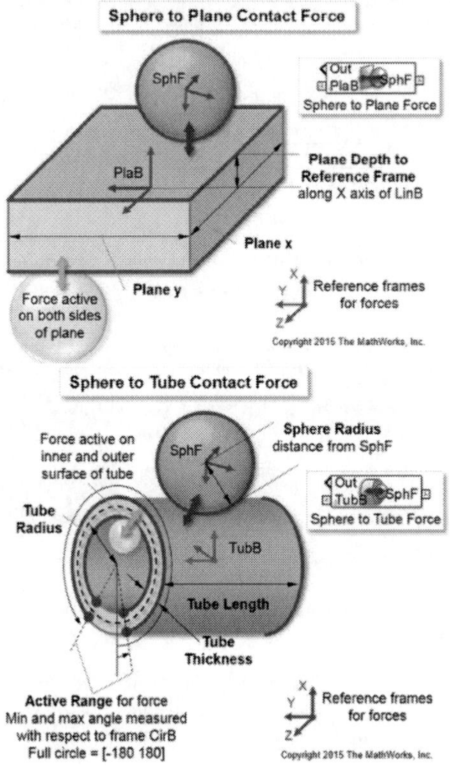

Figure 4. Contact between a sphere and a plane or between a sphere and a tube

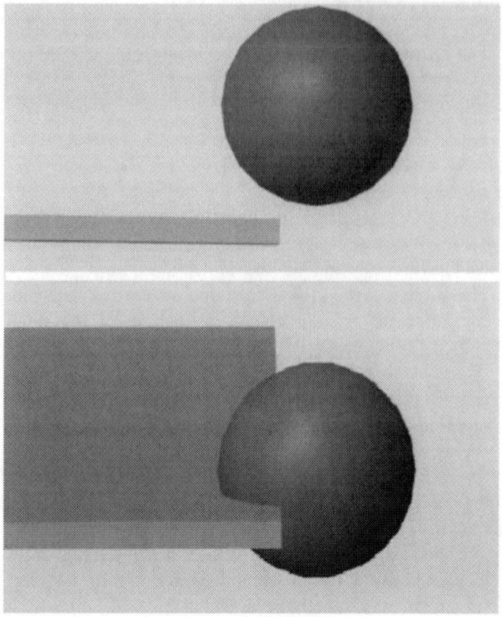

Figure5. Contact model without the "edge effect".

The main changes made to take account of the contact between the ball and the edge of the plan include the evaluation of the contact condition by introducing the following quantities:

$$dx_c = |x| - \frac{plane\_lengthx}{2} \quad (2)$$

$$dy_c = |y| - \frac{plane\_lengt}{2} \quad (3)$$

$$r_u = \sqrt{(sphere\_rad)^2 - (dx_c^2 + dy_c^2)} \quad (4)$$

Representing the distance of the sphere center from the edge of the plane, like it is possible to see in figure 6.

Figure 6. Point of contact of sphere when its center is out of plane.

Calculating the forces acting on the ball we reported the components of the normal force in the plane reference system according to the following equations:

$$F_z = \frac{F_n}{sphere-rad} \cdot \sqrt{sphere - rad^2 - dx_c^2 - dy_c^2} \quad (5)$$

$$F_x = \frac{\sqrt{F_n^2 - F_z^2}}{\sqrt{dx_c^2 + d\ _c^2}} \cdot dx_c \quad (6)$$

$$F_y = \frac{\sqrt{F_n^2 - F_z^2}}{\sqrt{dx_c^2 + dy_c^2}} \cdot dy_c \quad (7)$$

This in order to permit a correct impact between ball and plane and an eventual fall from the plane.
The sign of the moments of the forces acting on the sphere was changed in order to permit the correct rotation (clockwise or counter clockwise) depending on the contact of the sphere with the edge of the plane.
Similar expedients were adopted for the contact between ball and tube. In Figure 7 a wrong contact (up) and a wrong contact between ball and tube are shown.

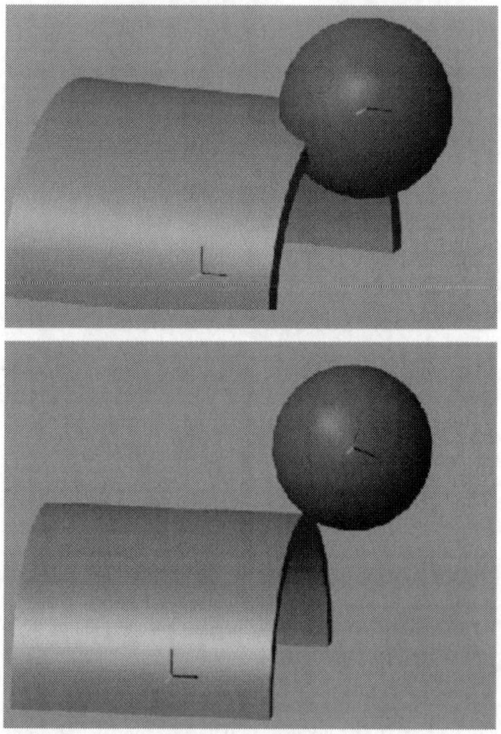

Figure 7. Contact model between sphere and tube without the "edge effect", and with "edge effect".

3 Simulation results

In this section some of the simulation results are reported.

3.1 The contact between finger and sphere

The blocks of the library SimMechanics Contact Forces, originally forecast in the model Federica hand, involve a situation like the one shown in figure 8, where penetration occurs between finger and ball.

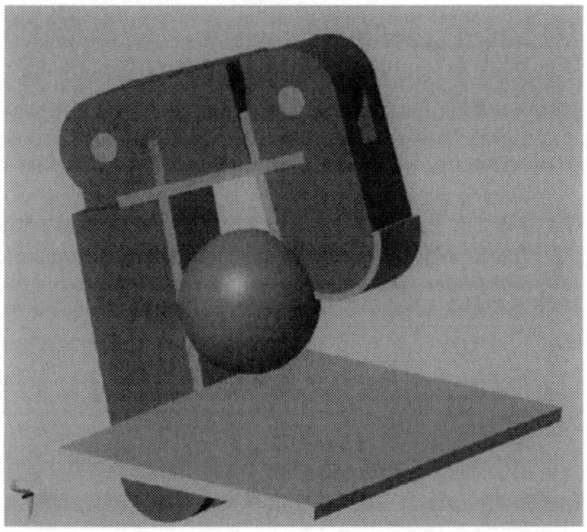

Figure 8. Finger in contact with sphere without "edge effect"

Thanks to the changes seen in the previous paragraphs, it is possible to evaluate all the intermediate positions; an example of this result is shown in figure 9.

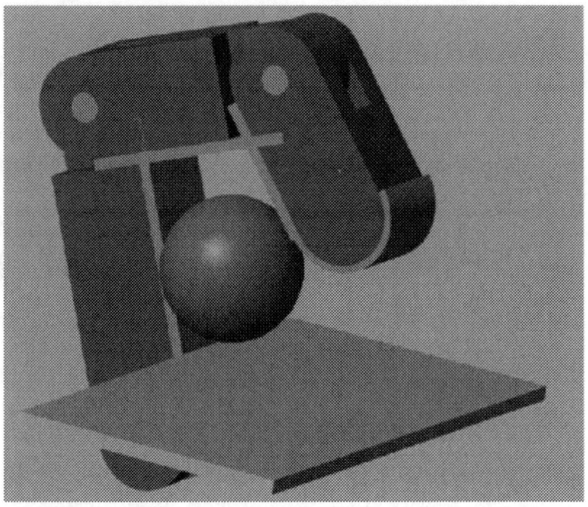

Figure 9. Finger in contact with sphere with "edge effect"

For each of the fingers, four blocks sphere to plane were used in order to simulate the contact between the inner surfaces of the phalanxes and the sphere and between the palm of the hand and the sphere and another block sphere to tube for the contact between the fingertip and the sphere.

In the simulations we assumed to grab spheres having different sizes that can be fixed on the palm in a specific position (using the weld joint block of SimMechanics) or can be free to move on the palm. The latter situation is supposed to be a result of an impact between the sphere and a finger phalanx before the sphere was grabbed; this was obtained by using the bushing joint block. The output variables of each contact block are analyzed in a subsystem called Grasp.

The grasping conditions require that a value based on the number of surfaces (i.e. the number of the phalanges) that touch the ball is assigned:

2 -> Object contact with at least 3 surfaces

1 -> Object contact with at least two surfaces

0.75 -> Object speed nothing compared to the palm

0.5 -> Object speed nothing compared to the phalanges

In figure 10 a graph showing the contact during the time is shown; the graph refers to the contact during the grasping of a sphere having unitary radius. The fluctuating trend in the graph is due to the fact that rebounds may occur due to elastic forces.

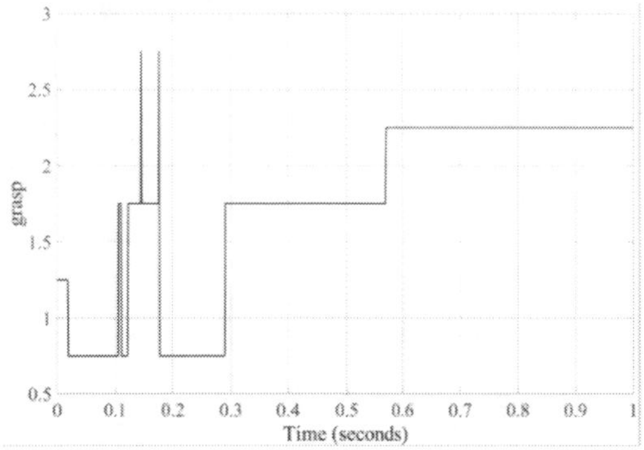

Figure 10. Grasp measure during a grasping task.

4 Conclusion

A model to analyze the grasping of an underactuated finger driven by unextensible tendon was presented. The finger itself is one of those of a mechanical prosthesis that was principally conceived as human prosthesis.

The reported examples seems to indicate that the model can predict the behavior of the finger during the grasping.

The model can be useful for both the under-actuated finger design and for the prediction of the capabilities of the whole hand. Also the actuator's optimum law of motion, computed by means of a previously proposed algorithm, [19], can represent a field of study that can be improved using the presented model.

Moreover, the model allows measuring the rotations of each phalanx, allowing to test the measurements carried out on real prototypes, by means of previously developed vision systems, [20-23].

The proposed method is also suitable to study several different topics (even very different from this one) the authors are investigating on. Among these, even the dynamics of the throwing machines (see e.g. [25-27]), as for the impact between their component is concerned can be studied.

ACKNOWLEDGEMENT

During this research a valuable help was provided by Mr. Francesco Iodice who was working for the bachelor's degree. The authors thank him for his diligence and his help.

References

1. Suárez, R., Roa, M. A., & Cornellà, J., Grasp quality measures. Technical University of Catalunya, Technical Report IOCDT-P-2006-10 (2006)
2. Roa, M. A., Suárez, R., Grasp quality measures: review and performance, Autonomous Robots, vol 38, Issue 1, pp 65-88 (2015)
3. Gabiccini, M., Farnioli, E., and Bicchi, A., Grasp and manipulation analysis for synergistic underactuated hands under general loading conditions, In International Conference of Ro-botics and Automation - ICRA 2012, pages 2836 – 2842, Saint Paul, MN, USA (2012).
4. Gabiccini, M., Farnioli, E., Bicchi, A., Grasp Analysis Tools for Synergistic Underactuated Robotic Hands. International Journal of Robotic Research, vol. 32, pp. 1553-1576 (2013)
5. Lotti, F., Vasura, G., Design aspects for advanced robot hands, In Proc. of IEEE/RSJ In-ternational Conference on Intelligent Robots and Systems, Lausanne, Switzerland, sep-tember 30 - October 4, 2002.
6. Roccella, S., Carrozza, M.C., Cappiello, G., Dario, P., Cabibihan, J.J., Zecca, M., Miwa, H., Itoh, K., Matsumoto, M., Takanishi, A., Design, fabrication and preliminary results of a Novel anthropomorphic hand for humanoid robotics: RCH- 1, Proceedings of 2004 IEEE/RSJ International Conference on Intelligent Robots and Systems, Sendai, Japan, September 28 - October 2, 2004
7. Hirose, S., Umetani, Y, The development of soft gripper for versatile robot hand, Mecha-nism and Machine Theory, vol. 13, pp. 351-359 (1978)
8. Catalano M. Grioli, G., Serio, A. , Farnioli, E., Piazza, C. and Bicchi, A., Adaptive Syner-gies for a Humanoid Robot Hand. In Proc. of IEEE-RAS International Conference on Hu-manoid Robots, Osaka (Japan), October 2012
9. Townsend, W., The BarretHand grasper - programmably flexible part handling and assem-bly, Industrial Robot: An International Journal, vol.27, no. 3, pp. 181-188 (2000)
10. Baril M., Laliberte T., Gosselin C., Routhier F., On the Design of a Mechanically Pro-grammable Underactuated Anthropo-morphic Prosthetic Gripper. Journal of Mechanical Design, issue 135, vol 12, doi:10.1115/1.4025493 (2013)
11. Dechev N., Cleghorn, W.L., Naumann, S., Multiple finger, passive adaptive grasp prosthetic hand, Mechanism and Machine Theory, vol. 36, pp 1157-1173 (2001)
12. Gosselin C., Pelletier, F., and Lalibertè, T. An Anthropomorphic Underactuated Robotic Hand with 15 Dofs and a Single Actuator. In Proc. of 2008 IEEE International Conference on Robotics and Automation, Pasadena (CA, USA), May 19-23 (2008)
13. Groenewegen, M. W., Aguirre, M. E., & Herder, J. L., Design of a Partially Compliant, Three-Phalanx Underactuated Prosthetic Finger. In ASME 2015 International Design Engineering Technical Conferences and Computers and Information in Engineering Conference American Society of Mechanical Engineers (2015)
14. Rossi, C., Savino, S., Mechanical Model of a Single Tendon Finger, Proc. of ICNAAM 2013: 11th International Conference of Numerical Analysis and Applied Mathematics, Rhodes, Greece, Sep 21-27 (2013)
15. Penta, F., Rossi, C., Savino, S., An Underactuated Finger for a Robotic Hand. International Journal of Mechanics and Control, Vol. 15, n.2, ISSN: 1590-8844 (2014)
16. Niola, V., Rossi, C., Savino, S. (2014). "A new mechanical hand: Theoretical studies and first prototyping", International Review of Mechanical Engineering, volume 8, issue 5, pp. 835-844, ISSN:19708734.
17. Niola, V., Penta, F., Rossi, C., Savino, S., An underactuated mechanical hand: Theoretical studies and prototyping, International Journal of Mechanics and Control, Volume 16, Issue 1, pp. 11-19 (2015)
18. Carbone G., Rossi C., Savino S., (2015). "Performance comparison between Federica Hand and LARM Hand", International Journal of Advanced Robotic Systems, 14 July 2015, Volume 12, DOI: 10.5772/60523, ISSN: 17298806
19. Niola, V., Rossi, C., Savino, S. and Strano, S., Robot trajectory planning by points and tangents. In Proceedings of the 10th WSEAS International Conference on Robotics, Control and Manufacturing Technology, ROCOM '10, Hangzhou, China, April 11-13, 2010, pp-91-96 (2010)
20. V. Niola, C. Rossi, S. Savino – "A New Real Time Shape Acquisition with a Laser Scanner: First Test Results" – ROBOTICS AND COMPUTER-INTEGRATED MANUFACTURING, issue 6, vol. 26, December 2010, pp 543-550, ISSN 0736-5845.
21. V. Niola, C. Rossi, Video acquisition of a robot arm trajectories in the work space, WSEAS Transactions on Computers, vol. 4, issue 7, pp. 830-836, (2005)
22. Niola, V., Quaremba, G., Amoresano, A., A study on infrared thermography processed trough the wavelet transform, Proceedings of the 8th WSEAS International Conference on System Science and Simulation in Engineering, ICOSSSE '09, pp 57-62 (2009)
23. M. Martorelli, C. Rossi, S. Savino, G. Staiano (2015) A Contactless Robot Kinematic Calibration Method by Digital Photogrammetry. International Journal of Mechanics and Control (JoMaC) vol. 16, No.2, ISSN: 1590-8844.
24. Rossi, C. Ancient throwing machines: A method to calculate their performance, Mechanism and Machine Theory, Volume 51, Pages 1-13 (2012).
25. Rossi, C., Russo, F., A reconstruction of the Greek-Roman repeating catapult, Mechanism and Machine Theory, Volume 45, Issue 1, pp 36-45 (2010)
26. Rossi, C., Pagano, S., A study on possible motors for siege towers, Journal of Mechanical Design, Transactions of the ASME, Volume 133, Issue 7, Article number 071009 (2011)

MATEC Web of Conferences 76, 04045 (2016) DOI: 10.1051/matecconf/20167604045
CSCC 2016

Simulation results of the grasping analysis of an underactuated finger

Vincenzo Niola[1a], Cesare Rossi[1], Sergio Savino[1]

[1] University of Naples "Federico II" Via Claudio 21, 80125, Naples ITALY

Abstract. The results of a number of simulations concerning the grasping analysis is presented. The grasping device consist in an under-actuated finger driven by un-extendible tendon that is one of the fingers of a mechanical prosthesis that was principally conceived as human prosthesis. The results, however, are useful for any similar finger to be used in grasping devices for industrial and agricultural applications, Aanalysis maps of the grasping were obtained which show the "robustness" of the socket. The method seems to be a suitable tool for the optimum design of such under-actuated fingers for grasping devices.

1 Introduction

In the last decades, grasping devices based on the human hand were widely studied an developed (see e.g. [1-13]); this both for human prostheses and for industrial or agricultural purposes. Among these studies the authors conceived developed and patented a new mechanical hand (Federica mechanical hand) based on a self-adaptive patented scheme (patent n. 0001415546 and n. 102015000059873, the latter pending) based on a self-adaptive scheme and under-actuated fingers operated by un-extendible tendons.

The main results of these investigations were reported in some papers and conference proceedings [14-18].

In figure 1 a scheme of the self-adapting system of the hand tendons and of one of the fingers are shown.

In figure 2 an hand prototype showing a correct grasping of a rather complex object by all the fingers is reported.

The study, the testing and the prototyping of the fingers and of the whole hand were presented in previous paper (see e.g. [14-18]).

Being the 3 phalanxes of the finger operated by an extension tendon and just one flexion tendon, the finger itself is underactuated, hence it becomes crucial a correct design of the phalanxes, of the tendon guide and of the hinges positions, in order to obtain a correct grasping of almost any possible object.

The grasping of an object can be very different depending on the position of the object respect to the grasping device. In the case of the single finger the figures 2 and 3 show that the quality of the grasp may be deeply different. In both the figures the grasping of a sphere is shown.

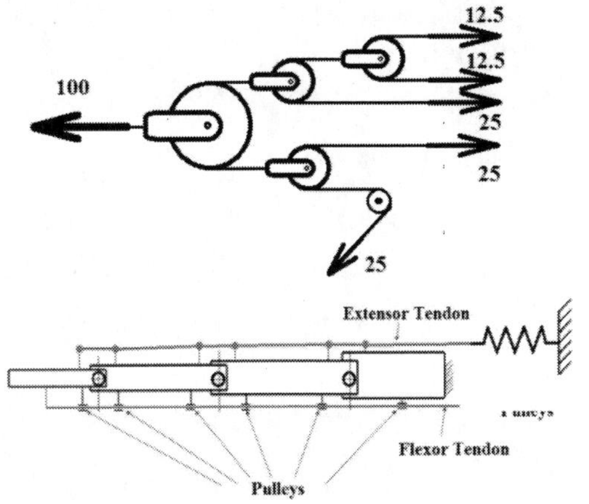

Figure 1. Schemes of the pulley system and of the finger.

In figure 3 an almost perfect grasping is shown: the inner surface of each of the phalanxes almost perfectly onto contact with the surface of the sphere. In figure 4, instead, the sphere is just roughly grasped since just the fingertip and the palm of the hand are onto contact with the surface of the sphere.

For the reasons above, it seemed to us interesting to propose and test a method to predict the grasping efficiency of each of the underactuated fingers that compose the mechanical hand we conceived.

[a] Vincenzo Niola: vincenzo.niola@unina.it

The method was presented in [19]; in the following some of the most significant results are presented.

Figure 2. An hand prototype correctly grasping an object.

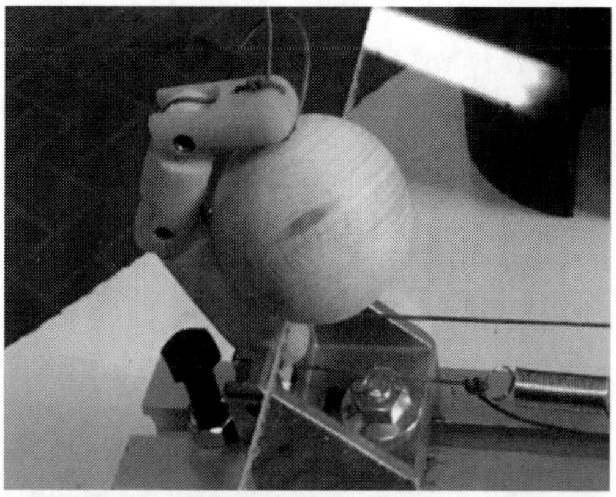

Figure 3. Good grasping of a sphere

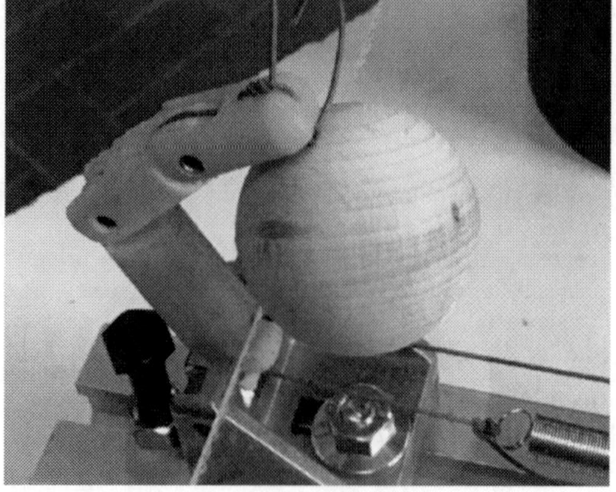

Figure 4. Instable grasping of a sphere

2 The contact between surfaces

The contact model was already described in [19] so we just briefly describe it.

The contact of the fingertip of each phalanx with the objects was simulated with an elastic damping reaction and a friction force between the bodies. In particular to analyze the contact of the finger with the object, each phalanx of the finger has been covered with a plain "skin", in this way the type of contact is always between a plane and a sphere. In figure 5 the model with the plain skin is shown.

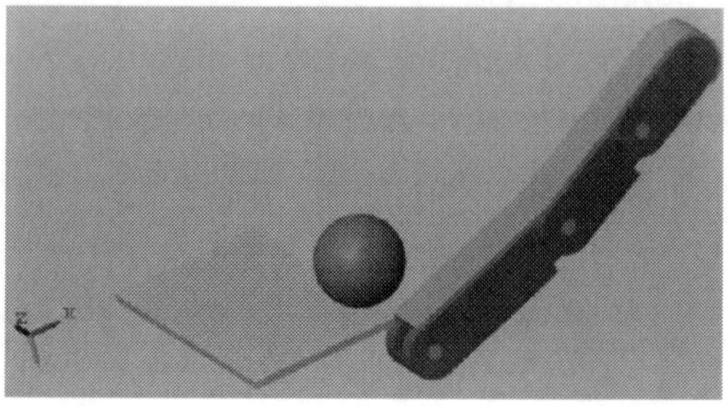

Figure 5. The multibody finger mode with plain "skin" to simulate the contact with the object.

The contact between two bodies was simulated with a force applied only along the direction of penetration of the two bodies. In figure 6 this force is shown as F_n, and it acts on the plane and on the sphere in the opposite direction.

In the contact model, also the friction force is included; it acts as a tangential force in the contact point on both bodies. In figure 6 the friction force is shown as F_t.

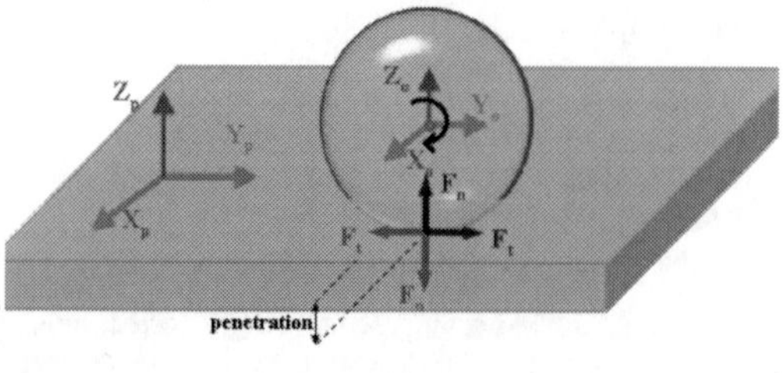

Figure 6. Contact scheme with normal force Fn and friction force Ft.

The normal force F_n acts by opposing the penetration of the two bodies and the damping is zero when the penetration decreases.

$$F_n = \begin{cases} k \cdot Z_{penetration} + b \cdot v_{penetration} & \forall Z_{penetration} > 0, v_{penetration} > 0 \\ k \cdot Z_{penetration} & \forall Z_{penetration} > 0, v_{penetration} < 0 \\ 0 & \forall Z_{penetration} < 0 \end{cases} \tag{1}$$

Where $Z_{penetration}$ is the penetration between the two bodies , $v_{penetration}$ is the velocity of penetration, k is the contact stiffness and b is the contact damping.

The friction force F_t is the product of normal force and a coefficient of friction that is a function of the relative velocity at the contact point.

$$F_t = F_n \cdot \mu, \qquad \mu = f(v_{CP}) \tag{2}$$

Where μ is the coefficient of friction and v_{CP} is the relative velocity at the contact point.

In particular the coefficient μ has the following expression (3).

$$\mu = f(v_{CP}) = \begin{cases} v_{CP} \cdot \mu_s / v_{thr} & v_{CP} < v_{trh} \\ \mu_s - v_{CP} \dfrac{\mu_s - \mu_k}{0.5 \cdot v_{thr}} & v_{trh} \le v_{CP} \le 1.5 \cdot v_{trh} \\ \mu_k & v_{CP} > 1.5 \cdot v_{trh} \end{cases} \tag{3}$$

Where μ_s is the static friction coefficient, μ_k is the kinetic friction coefficient and v_{thr} is a velocity threshold starting from which it is necessary to use the kinetic friction coefficient.

3 SIMULATION RESULTS

The multibody model finger that was developed was used to analyze the grasping efficiency while the position of the object was changed. The result consists in maps in which while the position of the object is changed, the grasping quality is evaluated. In the following examples the grasped object is represented by a sphere.

The robustness of the grasp is measured by analyzing different parameters. In particular, using the model, the following parameters are analyzed:

- the object's speed respect to the phalanges,
- the velocity of the object respect to the palm,
- the object contact with the phalanges and palm.

All these parameters were used to define a function of grasping G described by the expression (4):

$$G = \begin{cases} 0.50 \; if \; v_{obj}distal \cong 0 \cup v_{obj}medial \cong 0 \cup v_{obj}proximal \cong 0 \\ 0.75 \qquad if \; v_{obj}palm \cong 0 \\ 1.00 \qquad if \; the \; object \; is \; in \; contact \; with \; 2 \; surfaces \\ 2.00 \qquad if \; the \; object \; is \; in \; contact \; with \; at \; least \; 3 \; surfaces \end{cases} \tag{4}$$

Where:

v_{obj}distal, v_{obj}medial and v_{obj}proximal are the velocity of the object respect to the distal, medial and proximal phalanx, respectively;

v_{obj}palmi is the velocity of the object respect to the palm.

Naturally the function G also assumes composite values when more conditions simultaneously occur.

3.1 The grasping of the sphere by the finger

The grasping ability of a single finger of the Simulink model of Federica hand was tested; this was made both considering the object fixed and mobile. The simulations provide to move the ball in a plane orthogonal to the surface of the palm considering positions spaced of 2 mm. In the cases analyzed the ball center is situated in correspondence of the finger. Each simulation includes an analysis of approximately 300 positions and the result returns a graphic having different colored areas, depending on the contact. In figures 7 and 8 the cases of a fixed sphere of radius r = 1 cm and r = 1,15 cm are reported.

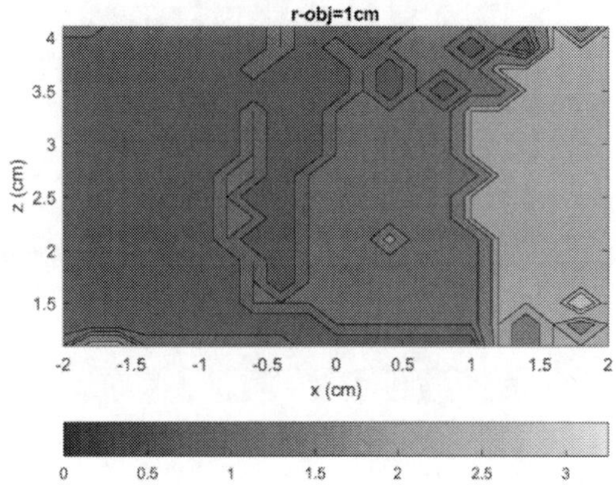

Figure 7. Results with fixed sphere of radius 1.0 cm.

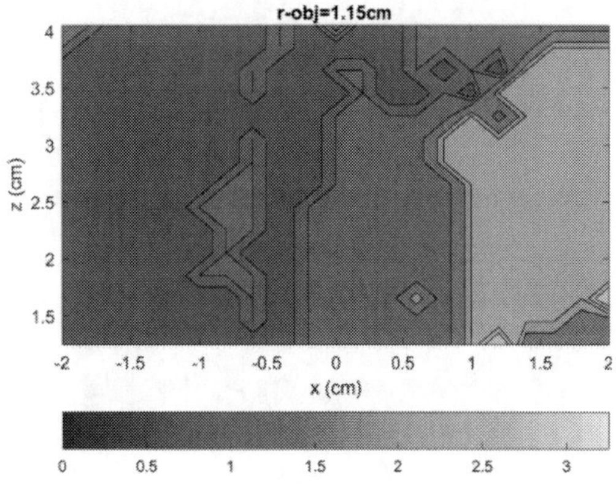

Figure 8. Results with fixed sphere of radius 1.15 cm.

The color to yellow indicates that contact is made with at least two surfaces. We note that the objects are of similar size, but the results in term of grasping are slightly better with the largest object because the contact area is larger.

When the object is movable, the grasping takes place in different areas; it often happens that the ball is grasped with the distal phalanx while the finger is fully extended.

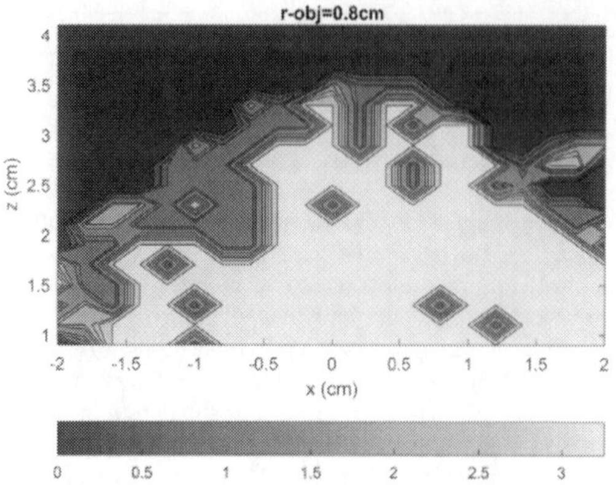

Figure 9. Results with moving sphere of radius 0.8 cm.

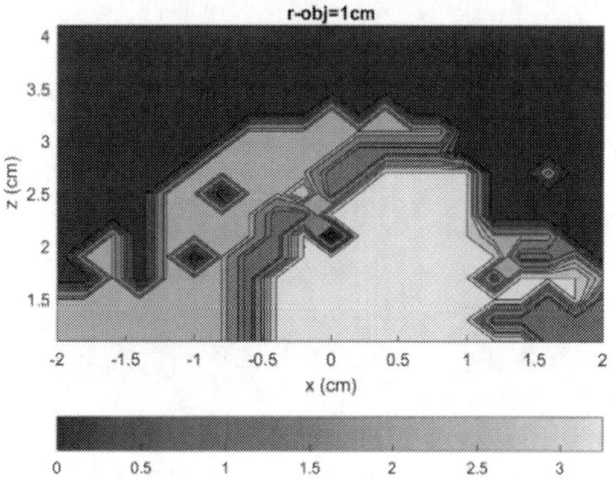

Figure 10. Results with moving sphere of radius 1.0 cm.

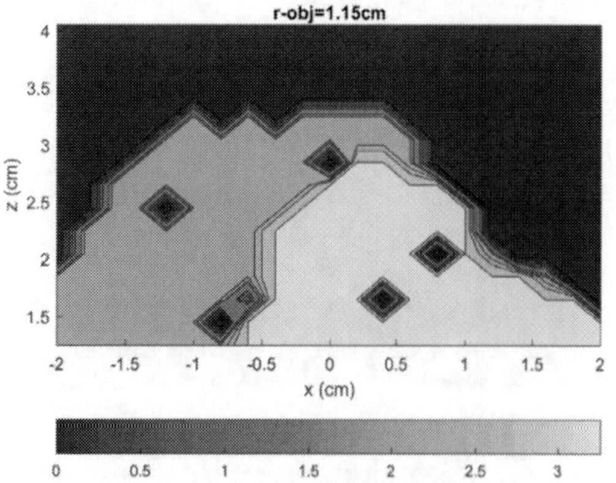

Figure 11. Results with moving sphere of radius 1.15 cm.

In figures 9, 10, 11 and 12 the cases with a ball of radius r = 0.8 cm, r = 1 cm, r=1.15 cm, and r=1.5 cm are analyzed.

The higher the object's radius, the most "elusive" the grasping is; the finger often fails to stop the ball that rolls and falls from the palm of the hand. This occurrence is more evident in figure 12, where the ball radius is r=1.5 cm and the area with a high value of G is very small.

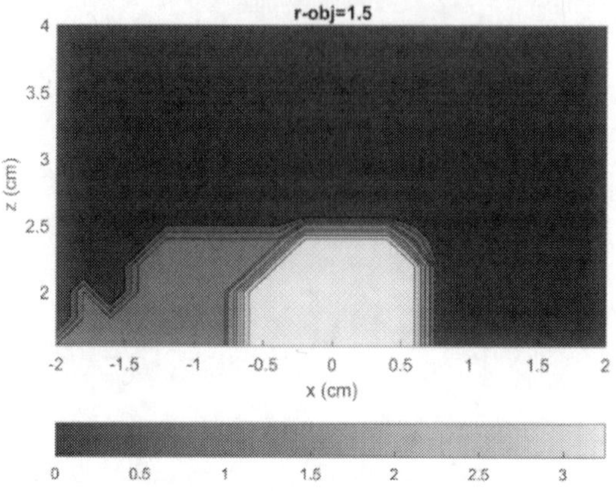

Figure 12. Results with moving sphere of radius 1.5 cm.

3.2 Finger with inclined surface

In the previous model the contact surfaces of the phalanxes are flat, and they have no inclination. A further investigation was carried on by tilting the contact surfaces of an angle of 5 °.

In particular, it must be observed that referring to the distal and medial phalanxes the tilted surface promotes the slip off of the object towards the inside part of the finger; the inclination of the proximal phalanx, instead, acts in the opposite way since it facilitates the positioning of the object towards the medial phalanx. In figure 13 the arrangement of the surfaces is shown.

Figure 13. Finger model with inclined contact surfaces.

With this new configuration the grasping is improved especially in the case of a mobile object.

Figure 14 shows the results of the analysis with the mobile sphere of radius r = 1.15 cm, and figure 15 shows the results with a mobile sphere of radius r = 1.5 cm.

The area where the better grasping occurs (high values of G) is increased respect the one referred to the case with inclined contact surfaces, figures 11 and 12.

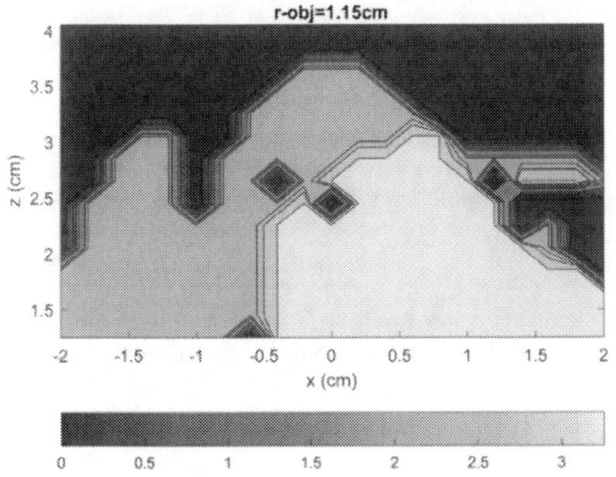

Figure 14. Results with moving ball of radius 1.15 cm and contact surfaces inclined.

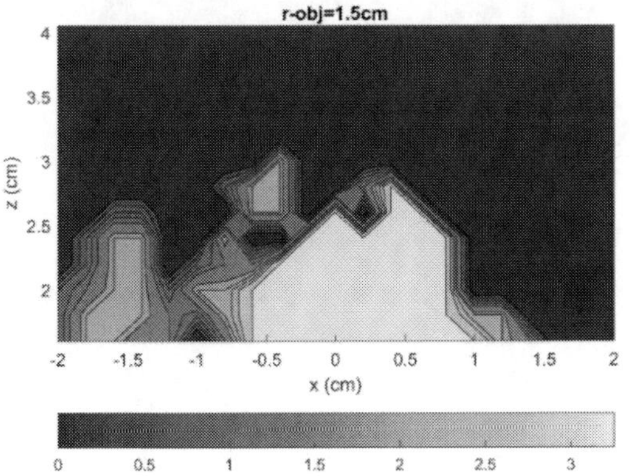

Figure 15. Results with moving ball of radius 1.5 cm and contact surfaces inclined.

4 Conclusion

The developed finger model was used to obtain analysis maps of the grasping that permit to evaluate the "robustness" of the grasping.

The reported results it appears that the proposed tool is a suitable instrument to analyze the grasping; in fact it permits to highlight the different results obtained by changing the parameters of the finger.

From the latter point of view, hence, the tool is also useful for the optimum finger design.

The next applications will concern the study of the results obtained with different contact surfaces (for example, truncated-spherical).

The dynamical behavior of the finger during the grasp can be also analyzed as function of different laws of motion, [20], of the only one actuator, by means of this model.

The finger model will then be extended to the entire hand studying the grasping quality of the whole gripping device, and comparing the virtual results relative to some points of the model with real measures acquired with vision systems, [21-24].

Finally, the proposed method is also suitable to study several different topics (even very different from this one) the authors are investigating on. Among these, even the dynamics of the throwing machines (see e.g. [25-27]), as for the impact between their component is concerned, can be studied.

ACKNOWLEDGEMENT

During this research a valuable help was provided by Mr. Francesco Iodice who was working for the bachelor's degree. The authors thank him for his diligence and his help.

References

1. Suárez, R., Roa, M. A., & Cornellà, J., Grasp quality measures. Technical University of Catalunya, Technical Report IOCDT-P-2006-10 (2006)
2. Roa, M. A., Suárez, R., Grasp quality measures: review and performance, Autonomous Robots, vol 38, Issue 1, pp 65-88 (2015)
3. Gabiccini, M., Farnioli, E., and Bicchi, A., Grasp and manipulation analysis for synergistic underactuated hands under general loading conditions, In International Conference of Ro-botics and Automation - ICRA 2012, pages 2836 – 2842, Saint Paul, MN, USA (2012).
4. Gabiccini, M., Farnioli, E., Bicchi, A., Grasp Analysis Tools for Synergistic Underactuated Robotic Hands. International Journal of Robotic Research, vol. 32, pp. 1553-1576 (2013)
5. Lotti, F., Vasura, G., Design aspects for advanced robot hands, In Proc. of IEEE/RSJ In-ternational Conference on Intelligent Robots and Systems, Lausanne, Switzerland, sep-tember 30 - October 4, 2002.
6. Roccella, S., Carrozza, M.C., Cappiello, G., Dario, P., Cabibihan, J.J., Zecca, M., Miwa, H., Itoh, K., Matsumoto, M., Takanishi, A., Design, fabrication and preliminary results of a Novel anthropomorphic hand for humanoid robotics: RCH- 1, Proceedings of 2004 IEEE/RSJ International Conference on Intelligent Robots and Systems, Sendai, Japan, September 28 - October 2, 2004
7. Hirose, S., Umetani, Y, The development of soft gripper for versatile robot hand, Mechanism and Machine Theory, vol. 13, pp. 351-359 (1978)
8. Catalano M. Grioli, G., Serio, A. , Farnioli, E., Piazza, C. and Bicchi, A., Adaptive Synergies for a Humanoid Robot Hand. In Proc. of IEEE-RAS International Conference on Humanoid Robots, Osaka (Japan), October 2012

9. Townsend, W., The BarretHand grasper - programmably flexible part handling and assem-bly, Industrial Robot: An International Journal, vol.27, no. 3, pp. 181-188 (2000)
10. Baril M., Laliberte T., Gosselin C., Routhier F., On the Design of a Mechanically Programmable Underactuated Anthropo-morphic Prosthetic Gripper. Journal of Mechanical Design, issue 135, vol 12, doi:10.1115/1.4025493 (2013)
11. Dechev N., Cleghorn, W.L., Naumann, S., Multiple finger, passive adaptive grasp prosthetic hand, Mechanism and Machine Theory, vol. 36, pp 1157-1173 (2001)
12. Gosselin C., Pelletier, F., and Laliberté, T. An Anthropomorphic Underactuated Robotic Hand with 15 Dofs and a Single Actuator. In Proc. of 2008 IEEE International Conference on Robotics and Automation, Pasadena (CA, USA), May 19-23 (2008)
13. Groenewegen, M. W., Aguirre, M. E., & Herder, J. L., Design of a Partially Compliant, Three-Phalanx Underactuated Prosthetic Finger. In ASME 2015 International Design Engineering Technical Conferences and Computers and Information in Engineering Conference American Society of Mechanical Engineers (2015)
14. Rossi, C., Savino, S., Mechanical Model of a Single Tendon Finger, Proc. of ICNAAM 2013: 11th International Conference of Numerical Analysis and Applied Mathematics, Rhodes, Greece, Sep 21-27 (2013)
15. Penta, F., Rossi, C., Savino, S., An Underactuated Finger for a Robotic Hand. International Journal of Mechanics and Control, Vol. 15, n.2, ISSN: 1590-8844 (2014)
16. Niola, V., Rossi, C., Savino, S. (2014). "A new mechanical hand: Theoretical studies and first prototyping", International Review of Mechanical Engineering, volume 8, issue 5, pp. 835-844, ISSN:19708734.
17. Niola, V., Penta, F., Rossi, C., Savino, S., An underactuated mechanical hand: Theoretical studies and prototyping, International Journal of Mechanics and Control, Volume 16, Issue 1, pp. 11-19 (2015)
18. Carbone G., Rossi C., Savino S., (2015). "Performance comparison between Federica Hand and LARM Hand", International Journal of Advanced Robotic Systems, 14 July 2015, Volume 12, DOI: 10.5772/60523, ISSN: 17298806
19. Rossi, C., Savino, S., Timpone, F., Multibody model for evaluate quality grasping of an underactuated mechanical finger, Proc. of RAAD 2016, 30 June-2 July, 2016, Belgrade.
20. Niola, V., Rossi, C., Savino, S. and Strano, S., Robot trajectory planning by points and tan-gents. In Proceedings of the 10th WSEAS International Conference on Robotics, Control and Manufacturing Technology, ROCOM '10, Hangzhou, China, April 11-13, 2010, pp-91-96 (2010)
21. V. Niola, C. Rossi, S. Savino – "A New Real Time Shape Acquisition with a Laser Scanner: First Test Results" – ROBOTICS AND COMPUTER-INTEGRATED MANUFACTURING, issue 6, vol. 26, December 2010, pp 543-550, ISSN 0736-5845.
22. V. Niola, C. Rossi, Video acquisition of a robot arm trajectories in the work space, WSEAS Transactions on Computers, vol. 4, issue 7, pp. 830-836, (2005)
23. Niola, V., Quaremba, G., Amoresano, A., A study on infrared thermography processed trough the wavelet transform, Proceedings of the 8th WSEAS International Conference on System Science and Simulation in Engineering, ICOSSSE '09, pp 57-62 (2009)
24. M. Martorelli, C. Rossi, S. Savino, G. Staiano (2015) A Contactless Robot Kinematic Calibration Method by Digital Photogrammetry. International Journal of Mechanics and Control (JoMaC) vol. 16, No.2, ISSN: 1590-8844.
25. Rossi, C. Ancient throwing machines: A method to calculate their performance 2012. Mechanism and Machine Theory.
26. Rossi, C., Russo, F., A reconstruction of the Greek-Roman repeating catapult, Mechanism and Machine Theory, Volume 45, Issue 1, pp 36-45 (2010)
27. Rossi, C., Pagano, S., A study on possible motors for siege towers, Journal of Mechanical Design, Transactions of the ASME, Volume 133, Issue 7, Article number 071009 (2011)

Mapping the Multi-instrumental Approaches to Teaching at Primary (Lower Secondary) Schools

Radek Nemec[1], Filip Sramek[1] and Andrea Berkova[1]

[1]University of Hradec Kralove, Faculty of Education, Czech Republic

Abstract. This article describes the results of the phone interviews across the Czech Republic at primary (lower secondary) schools focused on mapping the multi-instrumental approaches to teaching physics at primary schools. It was examined whether schools own some Computer-aided Assessment System or Online Homework System and if these systems are used. Equally, ownership of measurement systems using a computer and its use was checked. The use of a combination of these systems and their impact on the quality of education has been also examined. Results show that most schools do not use a combination of these systems and consequently this multi-instrumental approach but they think it might have benefits.

1 Introduction

Connecting of system CAA (Computer-aided assessment) [1] and SMPSL - measurement systems using computers [2] forms multi-instrumental tool as an element of change in the approach to the teaching of physics. The aim of this research is, with the help of interviews, to map the use of these systems and their combinations.

2 Used Instruments

Systems CAA (Computer-aided assessment) are suitable for testing and practicing mathematical knowledge. CAA platforms can help consolidate student´s understanding, support self-directed learning and make it easier for instructors to manage growing class sizes. These systems also contain special features such as working with graphs, series and mathematical symbols. In addition to practicing mathematical knowledge it is also available to use CAA platforms in physics. [3, 4]

SMPSL (measurement system using a computer) enables using sensors connected to the hardware of the system to a PC evaluation program. The evaluation is created using a graphical representation of values from the computer. It is a system that enables the collection, management and processing of data obtained with the measuring device that is connected to the computer. Such experiments are also called computer-aided experiments. [5, 6]

2.1 Research Methodology

Analysis was performed using a telephone interview at randomly selected primary schools in each region of the Czech Republic. For each region 3 schools were randomly selected. There are 13 regions plus capitol city. The list of schools was selected from the register of schools of the Ministry of Education, Youth and Sports. [7] A random analysis was conducted in scientist calculator from the list of schools.

The exact procedure for finding schools was as follows. There has to be contacts with teachers of physics. First, researcher finds a list of Czech primary schools on the website http://rejskol.msmt.cz/, where under "Type of school / facility" "B Primary-schools" is selected, then under "county / district:" the schools from particular regions can be found. After the list of schools was created, a scientific calculator was used to select 3 schools randomly from each region (plus Prague). These schools were subsequently searched on the Internet (to locate the physics teacher´s phone number or teachers' lounge).

Questions for the interview were determined as follows:

1. Do you own any CAA (Computer-aided assessment) systems? If so, which one?
2. Do you use these systems?
3. Do you have any Measurement systems using computers? If so, which one?
4. Do you use these systems?
5. Do you use the combination of these systems in teaching? (Multi-instrumental approach) Or a combination of other "educational" systems in teaching physics?
6. How often do you use this multi-instrumental approach?
7. Do you think that this approach affects the quality of pupils´ knowledge of physics?

[a] Corresponding author: radek.nemec@uhk.cz

6. ALT: If not, would you consider this approach, and why?

The following explanation was added for the first question. Explanation of what "CAA" is. Computer-aided assessment automatically creates and evaluates tasks (immediate feedback for students).
6. ALT means alternative question if this multi-instrumental approach was not used.

3 THE RESULTS

The results are processed using quantitative-qualitative research methods and are shown in the following tables and graphs.

Table 1 shows the results of question whether schools own any CAA (Computer-aided assessment) systems. If so, which one?

Table 1. Do you own any CAA (Computer-aided assessment) systems? If so, which one?

1. Do you own any CAA (Computer-aided assessment) systems? If so, which one?	
Yes	No
2	40

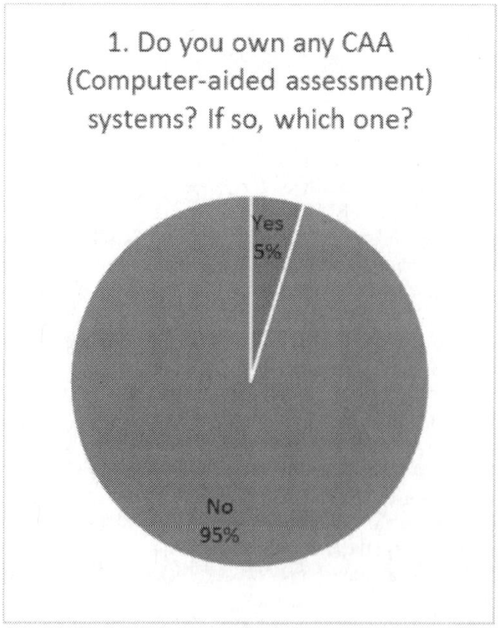

Fig. 1. Do you own any CAA (Computer-aided assessment) systems? If so, which one?

It is clear from Table 1 and Figure 1 that 95% of schools do not possess any CAA (Computer-aided Assessment) systems. In two cases, the answer was positive for system Moodle [8]. Learning Management System (LMS) Moodle is not a typical CAA system but under certain circumstances it can be considered as CAA system when Moodle quiz module is used.

Table 2 then shows the answer to the question 2 whether these systems are used at schools.

Table 2. Do you use CAA systems?

2. Do you use CAA systems?	
Yes	No
2	40

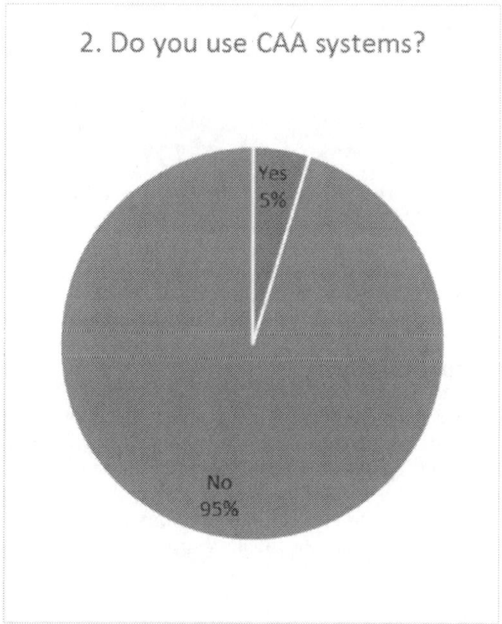

Fig. 2. Do you use CAA systems?

Table 2 and Figure 2 clearly indicate that if a school owns the CAA system, then it is used. The answer therefore directly follows the previous question. Although, it is just LMS Moodle which is used for CAA.

The third question dealt with the second component of the multi-instrumental approach in teaching physics. So, whether schools own any Measurement systems using computers. If so, which one?

Table 3. Do you own any Measurement systems using computers? If so, which one?

3. Do you have any Measurement systems using computers? If so, which one?	
Yes	No
7	35

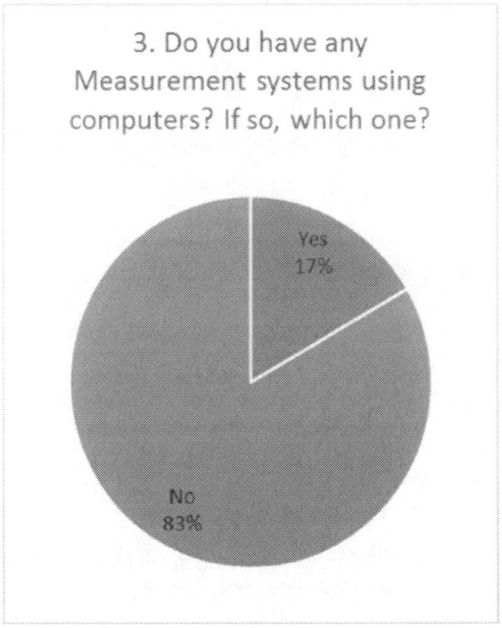

Fig. 3. Do you own any Measurement systems using systems? If so, which one?

From Table 3 and Figure 3, it is seen that in this area there is already an awareness of existence of this system. 17% of teachers from survey own Measurement systems using computers. It was system Vernier [9] or Pasco [10].

The fourth question, as well as question 2, follows the previous one. The question is: "Do you use Measurement systems using computers?"

Table 4. Do you use Measurement systems using computers?

4. Do you use Measurement systems using computers?	
Yes	No
6	36

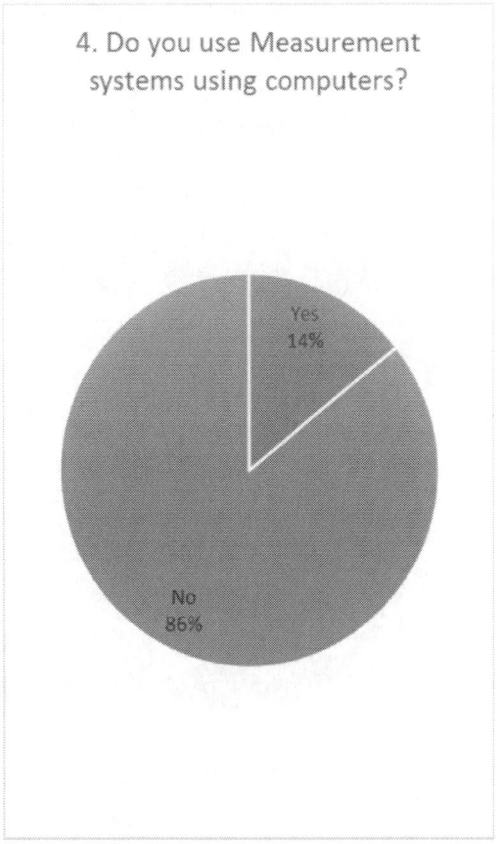

Fig. 4. Do you use Measurement systems using systems?

Table 4 and Figure 4 show that if a school owns the system, it is not used in all cases. See Table 3 or Figure 3.

The fifth question was: "Do you use the combination of these systems in teaching? (Multi-instrumental approach) Or a combination of other "educational" systems in teaching physics?"

Table 5. Do you use the combination of these systems in teaching? (Multi-instrumental approach) Or a combination of other "educational" systems in teaching physics?

5. Do you use the combination of these systems in teaching? (Multi-instrumental approach) Or a combination of other "educational" systems in teaching physics?	
Yes	No
2	40

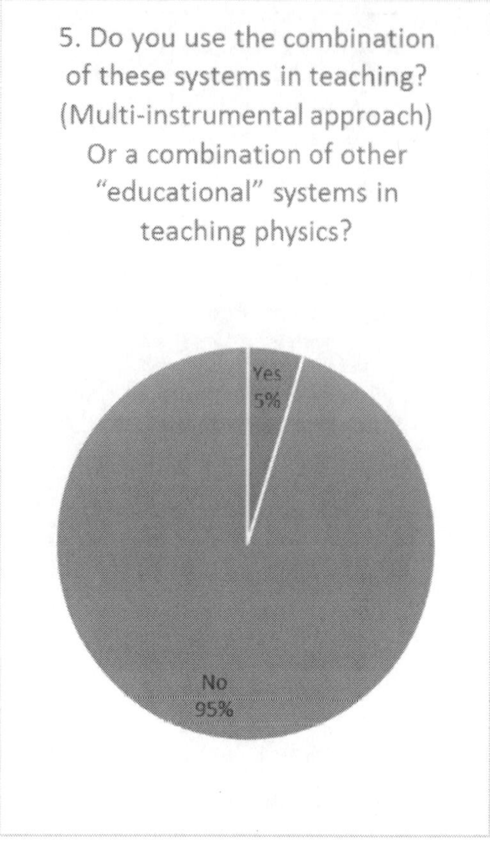

Fig. 5. Do you use the combination of these systems in teaching? (Multi-instrumental approach) Or a combination of other "educational" systems in teaching physics?

Table 5 and Figure 5 present a combination of these systems. From the results it is seen that in 95% it is not used. From straight answers of interview even in this 5% it is not a direct combination of SMPSL and CAA systems. The interviewees use internet applets. In these applets there is a partial use of the CAA and in terms of Measurement systems using computers it is a virtual laboratory.

Question 6 (How often do you use this multi-instrumental approach?) was not answered in any of the cases. It is therefore a thing that does not take place.

The seventh question (Do you think that this approach affects the quality of pupils´ knowledge of physics?) is purely subjective. There also appears the idea that teachers do not know: Alternatively, they developed answers as follows:

For clarity or understanding of pupils it should effect.

It has a positive effect.

I hope this can help with understanding of graphs.

Each new technology will help.

It is individual.

It's interesting to learn with that.

While drawing graphs and measurement addiction, it is more illustrative.

It's fun.

Good feedback.

Conversely:

The classical education is better.

It's too complicated.

See Table 6 and Figure 6.

Table 6. Do you think that this approach affects the quality of pupils´ knowledge of physics?

7. Do you think that this approach affects the quality of pupils´ knowledge of physics?		
Yes	No	I do not know
31	3	8

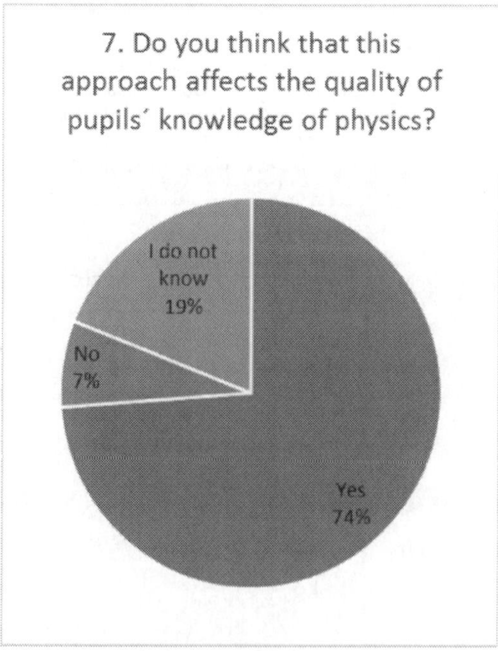

Fig. 6. Do you think that this approach affects the quality of pupils´ knowledge of physics?

As a last question, the alternative question to the question 6 followed: "If not, would you consider this approach, and why?"

Table 7. If not, would you consider this approach, and why?

6.ALT: If not, would you consider this approach, and why?		
Yes	No	I do not know
15	15	12

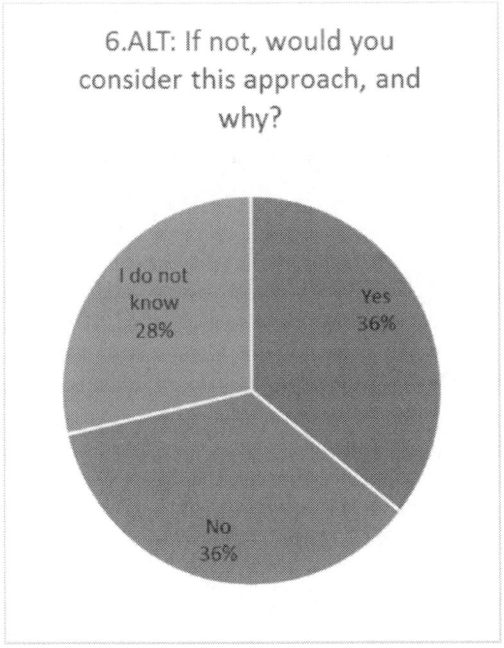

Fig. 7. If not, would you consider this approach, and why?

4 Conclusion

The results show that the system CAA (Computer-aided assessment) at primary schools in teaching physics is not used. Alternatively, the schools own and use LMS system Moodle. On the other hand, Measurement systems using computers are used or owned by 17% of respondents. In terms of combination of these systems in teaching or combination of other "educational" systems in teaching physics (Multi-instrumental approach) in 95% is disuse. The remaining 5%, however, does not use this combination directly, but the web applets. In terms of subjective opinion on this multi-instrumental approach, ¾ of opinion prevails that it could affect the quality of physics teaching at primary schools. Whether schools should consider this approach, it is based on 1/3 of "yes", 1/3 of "no" and 1/3 of "don´t know".

ACKNOWLEDGMENT

This research work has been supported by specific research project of University of Hradec Kralove, Faculty of Education in 2016 (No. 2142).

References

1. Berkova, A. (2015) Pocitacove hodnoceni matematickych znalosti studentu ve vyuce matematicke analyzy (Computer-aided assessment of students' mathematical knowledge in the subject of Mathematical analysis). *Media4u Magazine*. ISSN 1214-9187.
2. R. Nemec, J. Triska, J. Sedivy. System for Measurement Using a Computer in the School Laboratory. *International journal of education and information technologies*. 2014, 8(8), pp. 37-47. ISSN 2074-1316.
3. R. Nemec, A. Berkova, P. Hanzalova, (2016) The Connection of System SMPSL (System for measurement using a computer in the school laboratory) and CAA (Computer Aided Assessment) for Demonstration of Mathematical Modeling of Angle. *WSEAS Transactions on Information Science and Applications*. ISSN 1790-0832.
4. A. Berkova, J. Kulicka, (2015) Modelling and Simulation in Teaching of Future Teachers of Mathematics, *ICERI 2015 Proceedings (8th International Conference of Education, Research and Innovation)*, IATED, Seville, pp. 7525-7533.
5. R. Nemec, A Berkova, S. Hubalovsky, The Use of Method of Multidisciplinary Approach, Modeling and Simulation in Learning of Gear Ratios. *International Journal of Mathematics and Computers in Simulation*, volume 10, 2016 ISSN: 1998-0159
6. R. Nemec, S. Hubalovsky. Influence of Systems for Measurement using Computers to Popularity of Subject Physics at Elementary School – Some Results. In: *13th International Conference on Data Networks, Communications, Computers* (DNCOC 2015), Zakynthos Island, Greece, ISBN: 978-1-61804-355-9.
7. MŠMT. *Rejstřík škol a školských zařízení (Index of schools and school facilities)* [online]. 2016 [cit. 2016-03-01]. http://rejskol.msmt.cz/
8. *Moodle*. [online]. 2016 [cit. 2016-03-26]. https://moodle.com/
9. *Vernier*. [online]. 2016 [cit. 2016-04-01]. http://www.vernier.com/
10. *Pasco*. [online]. 2016 [cit. 2016-01-01]. https://www.pasco.com/

Cubic Spline Interpolation Reveals Different Evolutionary Trends of Various Species

Zhiqiang Li[1] and Peter Z. Revesz[1,a]

[1]Department of Computer Science, University of Nebraska-Lincoln, Lincoln, NE, 68588, USA

Abstract. Instead of being uniform in each branch of the biological evolutionary tree, the speed of evolution, measured in the number of mutations over a fixed number of years, seems to be much faster or much slower than average in some branches of the evolutionary tree. This paper describes an evolutionary trend discovery algorithm that uses cubic spline interpolation for various branches of the evolutionary tree. As shown in an example, within the vertebrate evolutionary tree, human evolution seems to be currently speeding up while the evolution of chickens is slowing down. The new algorithm can automatically identify those branches and times when something unusual has taken place, aiding data analytics of evolutionary data.

1 Introduction

Whereas evolutionary biologists in the past could be satisfied with piecing together an evolutionary tree of related species, now they can ask deeper questions, such as when was the evolutionary change most rapid or slow in any branch of the evolutionary tree [11]. In the past, evolutionary biologists could make only relatively subjective statements about the speed of evolution. However, the DNA data available today in many genome databases [5], [13] for an increasing number of living species and even from ancient DNA from fossils enables modern evolutionary biologists to make more precise and measurable statements about the speed of evolution. This is because the speed of biological evolution from an ancestor species to a descendant species can be measured in the number of genetic mutations.

Data analytics has the potential to make many fascinating discoveries about the evolutionary trends and their causes. Such a data analytics would bring together evolutionary biologists and data scientists. Towards this goal, we describe in this paper a novel evolutionary trend discovery (ETD) algorithm. The ETD algorithm estimates the different trends of evolution for various branches of the evolutionary tree. Our work already brings together cubic spline interpolation from numerical analysis, phylogenetic tree algorithms, and evolutionary biology.

This paper is organized as follows. Section 2 presents some related work. Section 3 describes a method to find evolutionary trends using the fossil record-based age estimates of ancestral species. Section 4 describes the experimental results. Finally Section 5 gives some conclusions and directions for future work

2 Related work

Given the genes of a set of related species, a hypothetical evolutionary tree, also called a phylogenetic tree, can be constructed using several different algorithms.

The UPGMA [12] and the Neighbor Joining (NJ) [10] algorithms are the most commonly used phylogenetic tree algorithms. The maximum likelihood method is also well known, although it less frequently used that UPGMA and Neighbor Joining because it requires more computational time. The Common Mutations Similarity Matrix (CMSM) algorithm of Revesz [6], the Incremental Phylogenetics by Repeated Insertions (IPRI) algorithm of Revesz and Li [4], and Wang's method [14] are some recently proposed phylogenetic tree algorithms. Many phylogenetic tree algorithms are reviewed in the textbooks [1]-[3].

The phylogenetic tree algorithms generate for a given set of genes of a set of related species a common ancestor/root node as well as internal nodes that correspond to the ancestral forms of various branches in the evolutionary tree. Moreover, the algorithms also associate with the root and each internal node an estimated gene (DNA sequence) based on all the descendant species.

There is a strong relationship between the biological classification of species and their evolutionary tree. In fact, the biological classification is often updated to match closer the constantly improving understanding of biological evolution.

For example, Table 1 lists the biological classification of fourteen vertebrate species. A phylogenetic tree generated for these fourteen species

[a] Corresponding author: revesz@cse.unl.edu

Table 1. The biological classification of forteen vertebrate species

Species	Phylum	Class	Order	Family
Human (*Homo sapiens*)	Chordata	Mammalia	Primates	Hominidae
Cattle (*Bos taurus*)	Chordata	Mammalia	Cetartiodactyla	Bovidae
Dog (*Canis familiaris*)	Chordata	Mammalia	Carnivora	Canidae
Brown rat (*Rattus norvegicus*)	Chordata	Mammalia	Rodentia	Muridae
Mouse (*Mus musculus*)	Chordata	Mammalia	Rodentia	Muridae
Hamster (*Mesocricetus auratus*)	Chordata	Mammalia	Rodentia	Cricetidae
Chicken (*Gallus gallus*)	Chordata	Aves	Galliformes	Phasianidae
Japanese quail (*Coturnix japonica*)	Chordata	Aves	Galliformes	Phasianidae
African clawed frog (*Xenopus laevis*)	Chordata	Amphibia	Anura	Pipidae
Japanese puffer fish (*Takifugu rubripes*)	Chordata	Actinopterygii	Tetraodontiformes	Tetraodontidae
Estuary cod fish (*Epinephelus coioides*)	Chordata	Actinopterygii	Perciformes	Serranidae
Ricefish (*Oryzias melastigma*)	Chordata	Actinopterygii	Beloniformes	Adrianichthyidae
Japanese ricefish (*Oryzias latipes*)	Chordata	Actinopterygii	Beloniformes	Adrianichthyidae
Zebrafish (*Danio rerio*)	Chordata	Actinopterygii	Cypriniformes	Cyprinidae

using the Common Mutations Similarity Matrix algorithm of Revesz [6] is shown in Figure 1.

The biological classification in Table 1 and the phylogenetic tree in Figure 1 correspond well with each other. In particular, the root, which is node 27, corresponds to the ancestors of vertebrates, the Chordata phylum. Node 24 represents the ancestor of fish, while node 26 represents the ancestor of every other vertebrate. Node 25 represents the ancestor of mammals, and node 21 represents the ancestor of rodents, etc. Biologists have used the extensive fossil record of vertebrates to estimate when each ancestor form existed. For example, the ancestor of all vertebrates is estimated to have lived about 525 million years ago. Some of the other known estimates of evolutionary biologists are listed in Table 2.

Our data analytics method also uses the cubic spline interpolation method from numerical analysis. A review and recent extension of the cubic spline method can be found in [7].

Table 2. Fossil-based age estimates of ancestral species.

Node Number	Classification	Million Years Ago
15	Beloniformes	N/A
16	Galliformes	85
18	Muridae	N/A
21	Rodentia	66
22	Amphibia	370
23	Primates	56
24	Actinopterygii	420
25	Mammalia	225
26	Non-Actinopterygii	420
27	Chordata	525

3 The evolutionary trend discovery algorithm

In this section we describe our *Evolutionary Trend Discovery* (ETD) algorithm. The pseudocode of our ETD algorithm is shown below. The ETD algorithm takes as input the following:

1. An evolutionary tree E.
2. A function T from internal nodes of E to millions of years ago, where for any internal node N, the value of $T(N)$ is the estimated evolutionary time from the root of E to N. The root R is always assumed to be at time 0.
3. A function A from nodes of E to amino acid sequences or DNA sequences.
4. A specific leaf node L.

The output of the ETD algorithm is the discovered evolutionary trend function D. In our description, the function D is a cubic spline interpolation function based on the combination of the genetic and temporal data that is associated with the path from the root to a leaf L. However, in theory, the trend function could be generated by several other numerical interpolation methods. Therefore the cubic spline interpolation is used here as an example of this general idea. Cubic spline interpolation gives an interpolating polynomial that is smoother than some other interpolating polynomials such as Lagrange polynomial and Newton polynomial.

 DOI: 10.1051/matecconf/20167604047

ALGORITHM ETD(E, T, A, L, D)

```
1 Find the tree E2 that is the same as E except that
pointers from the parents to the children are reversed.
2 Create arrays D1 and D2, and
  initialize i = path_length(L);
3 current_node = L;
4 while (current_node ≠ R)
5    D1[i] = T[current_node];
6    mutation_number = Hamming(A(current_node),
A(R));
7         D2[i] = mutation_number;
8    current_node = current_node.next(in E2);
9    i = i-1;
10 end
11 D1[i] = T(R);
12 D2[i] = 0;
13 D = Cubic_Spline(D1,D2);
14 Return D;
```

In the ETD algorithm we assume that we have available as a subroutine Hamming, which computes the Hamming Distance between two strings, and Cubic_Spline, which finds the cubic spine interpolation function with time D1 and corresponding values D2. The ETD algorithm allows us to investigate the evolutionary trend of a given species of interest using the changes in the number of mutations from the root to the leaf node corresponding to that species.

Example 1. Suppose that the ETD algorithm is called with the parameters where the tree is in Figure 1, the function *T* is in Table 2, the function *A* is the amino acids that are returned for each internal node by the CMSM algorithm and for each leaf node in Figure 1 the *TERT amino acid* (which is discussed in detail in Section 4), and the leaf node is 1. As can be seen in Figure 1, here L = node 1 and R = node 27. The path from L, which

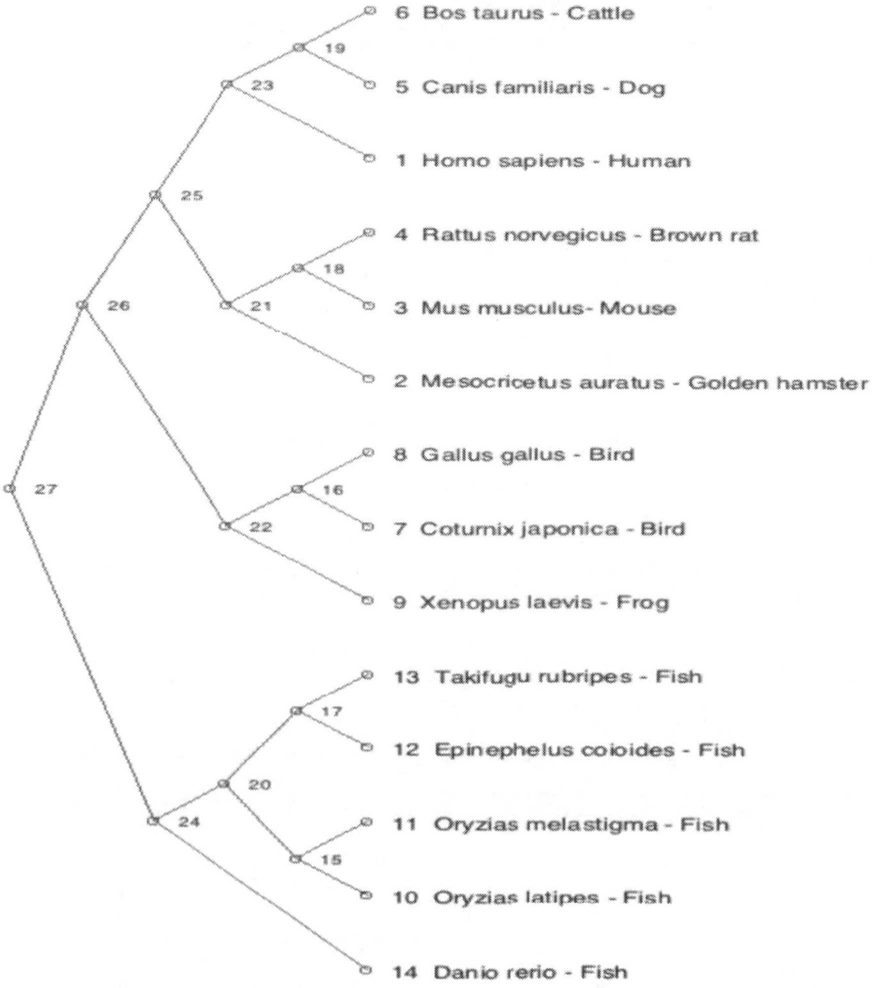

Figure 1. The CMSM phylogenetic tree based on vertebrate telomerase protein data.

corresponds to humans, to R, which is the ancestral vertebrate, is the following: 1 → 23 → 25 → 26 → 27. Hence the ETD algorithm will work as follows:

```
D1[4] = T(node 1)
D2[4] = Hamming(A(node 1), A(R)) = 83

D1[3] = T(node 23)
D2[3] = Hamming(A(node 23), A(R)) = 28

D1[2] = T(node 25)
D2[2] = Hamming(A(node 25), A(R)) = 11

D1[1] = T(node 26)
D2[1] = Hamming(A(node 26), A(R)) = 4

D1[0] = T(node 27)
D2[0] = 0
Build a cubic spline that satisfies D2 = D (D1).
```

4 Experimental results

As an example, we build an evolutionary tree based on the telomerase (TERT) protein family using the CMSM algorithm. Telomerase help protect eukaryote chromosomes during duplication and is generally present protein in eukaryotes. From the website http://telomerase.asu.edu we obtained 14 vertebrate telomerase proteins as our input data. After alignment, the length of each amino acid sequence was 1353. Figure 1 shows the evolution tree from CMSM.

We evaluate our evolutionary trend discovery algorithm using as test TERT data related to human and chicken evolution. Figure 2 shows the cubic spline interpolation results for both humans and chickens. Each unit on the x axis in Figure 2 is 1 million years. Both the human and the chicken evolutionary trend functions indicate that the overall number of mutations is increasing with time but at different rates. There are some small periods that can be considered errors in the

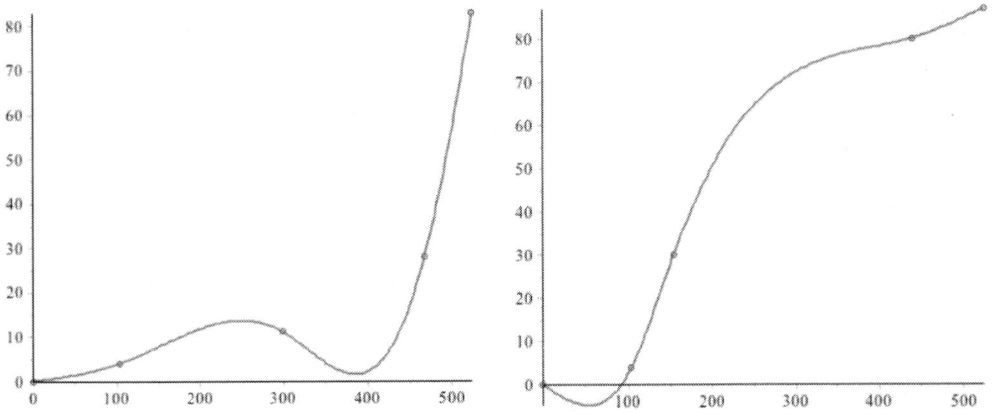

Figure 2. Cubic spline interpolation of the number of evolutionary mutations for human (left) and chicken (right). The x-axis is already known millions of years since the common ancestor of all vertebrates, and the y-axis is the number of mutations in the TERT proteins.

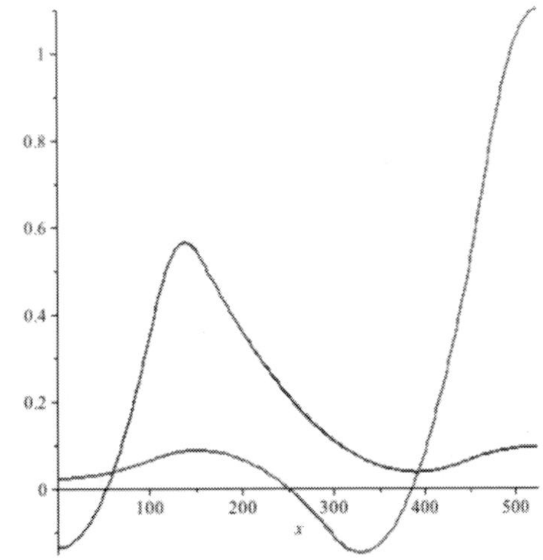

Figure 3. The above figure shows the first derivatives of the functions in Figure 2. The red curve shows the evolutionary trend function associated with humans and the purple curves shows the evolutionary trend function associated with chickens.

interpolation because the number of mutations should always increase. These blips of errors non-withstanding, the overall trends seem quite reasonable.

In order to check better the evolutionary trends, we also draw the curves of the first derivatives for the evolutionary trend functions as shown in Figure 3. The red curve stands for human evolution, and the purple curve represents chicken evolution from an ancestral vertebrate that lived around 500 million years ago. Figure 3 suggests that the evolution of humans involved a speeding up of the rate of evolutionary mutations. In contrast, the rate of evolutionary mutations slowed down for chickens around 200 million years ago. This result agrees with our intuition with biological evolution as birds have evolved from dinosaurs millions of years ago, and mammals have evolved more recently. There seems to be a more rapid evolution at the beginning of the appearance of radically new forms of species and adaptations to new modes of living, such as flying for birds, and then a decline in the rate of mutations and adaptations after a period of establishment of the new form. It would be interesting to check whether this pattern also appears when considering other genome or protein families and other examples of vertebrates from the mammalian and bird phyla.

5 Conclusions and future work

We plan to apply the ETD algorithm to other protein and genome families for both eukaryotes and bacteria. In the ETD algorithm, we also plan to use other estimated time function T. Some possibilities include the estimates obtained by the UPGMA algorithm that returns not only an evolutionary tree but also a time estimate for each internal node of the tree. Many other phylogenetic tree algorithms also a time function that may be useful. It remains to be seen which of these estimates is the best and what is the degree of consistency in the results when using all of these different estimates of T. The estimating of the time function T by some method is especially important in the case of species that do not have available as extensive fossil records as for the vertebrates.

In addition, in the future more complex data analytics would need to correlate the overall evolutionary trends with significant known events in the history of the earth, such as gradual changes in the atmospheric concentrations of carbon dioxide, oxygen and water vapor, temperature changes, water elevation changes etc. These may enable a deeper data analytics that identifies the significant factors that drive the speed of evolution.

References

1. D. Baum and S. Smith, *Tree Thinking: An Introduction to Phylogenetic Biology*, (Roberts and Company Publishers, 2012)
2. B.G. Hall, *Phylogenetic Trees Made Easy: A How to Manual*, 4th edition, (Sinauer Associates, 2011)
3. P. Lerney, M. Salemi, and A.-M Vandamme, editors. *The Phylogenetic Handbook: A Practical Approach to Phylogenetic Analysis and Hypothesis Testing*, 2nd edition, (Cambridge University Press, 2009)
4. P.Z. Revesz and Z. Li, "Incremental phylogenetics by repeated insertions: An evolutionary tree algorithm," *International Journal of Biology and Biomedical Engineering*, **10**, 1, 148-158, (2015)
5. P.Z. Revesz, *Introduction to Databases: From Biological to Spatio-Temporal*, (Springer, New York, 2010)
6. P.Z. Revesz, "An algorithm for constructing hypothetical evolutionary trees using common mutations similarity matrices," *Proc. 4th ACM International Conference on Bioinformatics and Computational Biology*, 731-734, (ACM Press, New York, 2013)
7. P.Z. Revesz, "A recurrence equation-based solution for the cubic spline interpolation problem," *International Journal of Mathematical Models and Methods in Applied Sciences*, **9**, 1, 446-452, (2015)
8. P.Z. Revesz and T. Triplet, "Classification integration and reclassification using constraint databases," *Artificial Intelligence in Medicine*, **49**, 2, 79-91, (2010)
9. P.Z. Revesz and T. Triplet, "Temporal data classification using linear classifiers," *Information Systems*, **36**, 1, 30-41, (2011)
10. N. Saitou and M. Nei, "The neighbor-joining method: A new method for reconstructing phylogenetic trees," *Molecular Biological Evolution*, **4**, 406-425, (1987)
11. M. Shortridge, T. Triplet, P.Z. Revesz, M. Griep, and R. Powers, "Bacterial protein structures reveal phylum dependent divergence," *Computational Biology and Chemistry*, **35**, 1, 24-33 (2011)
12. R.R. Sokal, and C. D. Michener, "A statistical method for evaluating systematic relationships," *University of Kansas Science Bulletin*, **38**, 1409-1438, (1958)
13. T. Triplet, M. Shortridge, M. Griep, J. Stark, R. Powers, and P.Z. Revesz, "PROFESS: A protein function, evolution, structure and sequence database," *Database -- The Journal of Biological Databases and Curation*, (2010)
14. S. Zhang and T. Wang, "A new distance-based approach for phylogenetic analysis of protein sequences," *International Journal of Biology and Biomedical Engineering*, **3**, 3, 35-42, (2009)

MATEC Web of Conferences 76, 04048 (2016) DOI: 10.1051/matecconf/20167604048
CSCC 2016

A Spatio-Temporal Analysis of Mitochondrial DNA Haplogroup I

Peter Z. Revesz[1,a]

[1] *Department of Computer Science, University of Nebraska-Lincoln, Lincoln, NE, 68588, USA*

Abstract. The recent recovery of ancient DNA from a growing number of human samples shows that mitochondrial DNA haplogroup I was introduced to Europe after the end of the Last Glacial Maximum. This paper provides a spatio-temporal analysis of the various subhaplogroups of mitochondrial DNA I. The study suggests that haplogroup I diversified into haplogroups I1, I2'3, I4 and I5 at specific regions in Eurasia and then spread southward to Crete and Egypt.

1 Introduction

Ancient mitochondrial DNA (mtDNA) provides important insights on the movement and spread of human populations out of Africa. In particular, European populations exhibit some remarkable changes after the end of the Last Glacial Maximum. The changes in the early postglacial period are thought to be the result of the arrival of new human population groups to Europe. These new populations brought to Europe the I and W mitochondrial DNAs [6]. The origin and exact spread of these two mitochondrial DNAs is little understood. This paper provides a spatio-temporal analysis of mtDNA I.

This paper is organized as follows. Section 2 presents some related work. Section 3 describes the source data and our data curating to refine and improve the haplogroup classifications and find the precise latitude and longitude coordinates of the location where each sample was discovered. Section 4 describes our spatio-temporal analysis of the curated data. Finally Section 5 gives some conclusions and directions for future work.

2 Related work

Several papers have attempted to trace the movement and spread of human populations based on ancient DNA data. Allentoft et al. [1] considers Eurasian populations and traces of Indo-European migrations in the Bronze Age. Other papers have made DNA-based connections between past and present day populations, such Brandt et al. [3] between ancient DNA and present Central Europeans and Vai et al. [14] between Medieval Lombards and present day Italians.

The difficulty of making connections between pairs of populations lies in the fact that most human populations are genetically fairly mixed, making the comparison of populations rely on complex statistical similarities according to several proposals including a recent one by the author [11]. For example, modern European human populations in every region contain a large number of mitochondrial DNA haplogroups. In contrast, Paleolithic human samples contain only a limited number of mtDNA haplogroups, mostly belonging to U. The genetics of European Neolithic human populations is relatively well-studied and traced back to Anatolia and the Near East [2], [4], [5]. However, mtDNA haplogroup I is associated neither with the Paleolithic nor with the Neolithic expansion. Hervella et al. [6] show that mtDNA haplogroup I occurs in Paternanbidea, Spain c. between 6000 BC. This early presence in Spain suggests that mtDNA I expanded to Eurasia from the Franco-Cantabrian glacial refugium after the Last Glacial Maximum. However, Olivieri et al. [8] argue that mtDNA haplogroup I originates from the Near East. That discrepancy and the uncertainty regarding the origin of the subhaplogroups of haplogroup I motivates the present study.

3 Source data and data curation

Several websites are specialized to record ancient mitochondrial DNA samples. Below we used the ancestral journals online database and website, which is available at the following Internet site: http://www.ancestraljourneys.org/ancientdna.shtml.

Table 1 lists from thirteen cultures fourteen samples that can be classified into one of the mtDNA haplogroups I1, I2, I3, I4 and I5. The Unetice culture had both I1 and I3 samples. For each of the sample locations, we found its latitude and longitude using Google map.

Some of the samples were classified as simply mtDNA I, but we could use the latest version of the mtDNA haplogroup classification table (Build 17, February 18, 2016) at www.PhyloTree.org to further refine the classification to I1, I2, I3, I4 or I5 haplogroup.

[a] Corresponding author: revesz@cse.unl.edu

Table 1. Cultures that contain mitochondrial DNA I1, I2, I3, I4 or I5 samples.

Type	Culture	Date	Place	Latitude	Longitude
Neolithic	Cami de Can Grau Granollers	3500-3000 BC	Cami de Can Grau Granollers, Barcelona, Spain	41.43	2.12
Bronze	Yamnaya	3000-2500 BC	Kirovohrad, Ukraine	48.30	32.16
Bronze	Bell Beaker	2600-2500 BC	Kromsdorf, Germany	50.98	11.37
Bronze	Minoan	2200-1700 BC	Charalambos cave, Crete, Greece	35.18	25.44
Bronze	Unetice	2200-1550 BC	Eulau, Germany	51.17	11.85
Bronze	Unetice	2200-1550 BC	Esperstedt, Germany	51.42	11.67
Bronze	Mezhovskaya	1598-1398 BC	Kapova cave, Russia	53.04	57.06
Bronze	Karasuk	1416-1268 BC	Sabinka, near Karasuk, Russia	53.43	78.03
Bronze	Vodokhranilische	1400-1000 BC	Vodokhranilische, Kazakhstan	49.52	49.86
Iron	Norabak	1209-1009 BC	Norabak, Armenia	40.13	45.86
Iron	Scythian	500-200 BC	Rostov-on-Don, Russia	47.14	39.42
Iron	Egyptian	402-385 BC	Faiyum Valley, Egypt	29.57	30.66
Medieval	Lombard	570-650 AD	Collegno, Italy	45.50	7.35
Medieval	Hungarian	975-1000 AD	Sárrétudvar, Hungary	47.25	21.17

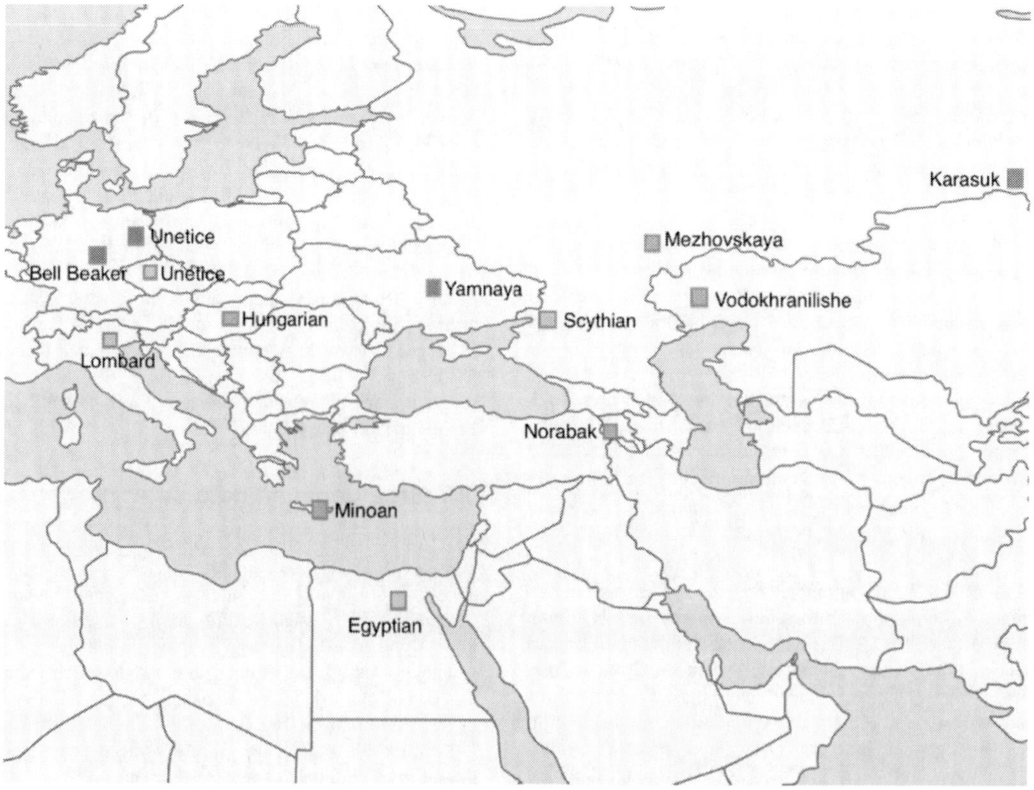

Figure 1. The distribution of mtDNA haplogroup samples I1 (blue), I2 and I3 (yellow), I4 (red) and I5 (green).

Table 2. Ancient DNA samples that belong to some branch of mtDNA haplogroup I. The samples and their classifications are from the website http://www.ancestraljourneys.org/ancientdna.shtml. Some of the classifications are updated. In case of updates, the original classification is on the left and the new classification is on the right of the > symbol.

CULTURE:		Cami de Can	Bell Beaker	Unetice	Yamnaya	Lombard	Egypt	Unetice	Scythian	Minoan	Hungarian	Mezhovskaya	Vodokhranilische	Norabak	Karasuk
YEAR:		3500-3000	2600-2500	2200-1550	3000-2500	570-650 AD	402-385	2200-1550	500-200	2200-1700	975-1000 AD	1598-1398	1400-1000	1209-1009	1416-1268
GROUP:		I1c1	I1a1	I1a1	I > I1a	I2a	I2	I3a	I3 > I3a	I5a	I > I5a	I5c > I5a2+	I > I5a4	I5c	I4a1
T10034C	I						x			x		x		x	x
G16129A!	I	x	x		x		x		x	x	x	x	x	x	x
455.1T	I1														
G6734A	I1														
G9966A	I1														
T16311C!	I1		x		x										
A3447G	I1a														
G8616t	I1a														
T16172C	I1a		x	x	x										
G203A	I1a1		x	x											
C16264T	I1c	x													
G16319A	I1c	x													
T16362C	I1c	x				x									
T9386C	I1c1														
C16270T	I1c1	x													
T152C!	I2'3						x					x			
G207A	I2'3						x								
A15758G	I2						x								
G16145A	I2a					x									
T239C	I3														
T16086C	I3a							x	x			x			
C16494T	I3b														
T2628C	I3c														
T8260C	I3d				x										
G8519A	I4														x
A10819G	I4a														x
T16304C	I4a1														x
C9851T	I4a2														
A2308G	I4b														
G4113A	I4b														
C13662T	I4b														
A14233G	I5													x	
T5074C	I5a														
C16148T	I5a									x	x				
T16086C	I5a2+							x	x			x			
C16294T	I5a4												x		
G709A	I5b														
C6506T	I5b														
C16169T	I5c											x		x	

In particular, we improved the classification of one Yamnaya sample from I to I1a, one Vodokhranilische sample from I to I5a4, and one Hungarian sample from I to I5a. In addition, we could refine the classification of a Scythian I3 sample to I3a. Table 2 gives a detailed explanation of the reason for these refinements. As Table 2 shows, there are still some ambiguities regarding the classification of a few samples. For example, the Mezhovskaya sample can be considered either I5c or I5a2 as shown in Table 2. The ancestral journeys online database contains some other mtDNA I samples that could not be further refined, including currently the earliest mtDNA haplogroup I sample from Paternanbidea, Spain from the Neolithic [6].

In Table 2 the first four data columns contain I1 samples, the next four contain I2 and I3 samples, the next five contain I5 samples, and the last contains a single I4 sample. The I2 and I3 haplogroups have a common ancestor called mtDNA I2'3. Therefore, in this paper we consider them as one group. We color-coded the haplogroups as blue for I1, golden for I2 and I3, green for I5, and red for I4. Using a similar color scheme, Figure 1 shows the location of each sample on a map.

4 Spatio-temporal analysis

At first we computed the centroid of each haplogroup. The result is shown in Table 3.

Table 3. The haplogroup centroid values.

Haplogroup	Latitude	Longitude
I1	47.97	14.375
I2'3	43.4075	22.275
I4	53.43	78.03
I5	45.024	39.878

The data in Table 3 needs to be considered together with the map in Figure 1. In combination, they allow us to draw some conclusions regarding the origin of the various haplogroups in this study. In particular the map suggest the following:

I1: This haplogroup is more western (with longitude 14.375) than other haplogroups and also more northern (47.97) than other haplogroups except for I4. Hence it is likely that this haplogroup originated in northwestern Europe.

I2'3: This haplogroup occurs in an old Unetice sample and three considerably more recent samples near the shores of the Mediterranean and Black Seas. Hence it is likely that this group also originated in northern Eurasia and the three later samples are the result of population movements facilitated by the seas.

I4: This haplogroup occurs only in one sample, which happens to be the easternmost of all the samples. Hence it is likely that this haplogroup originates somewhere in central Eurasia.

I5: This haplogroup seems to be concentrated between and above the Black and the Caspian Seas. Hence that area is the likely origin of haplogroup I5. The presence of haplogroup I5 in some Minoan samples may be explained as a population movement from the Black Sea to Crete. The Hungarian sample may be explained as another population movement from the region north of the Black Sea to present day Hungary.

Overall, the ancient mtDNA data suggests that the origin of the I1, I2'3, I4 and I5 haplogroups are all connected with various regions in Europe and western Asia.

5 Conclusions and future work

The spatio-temporal analysis of this paper can be extended in many ways using the methods described in [9]. In particular, we are interested in modeling the spread of human populations as spatio-temporal objects that are described using constraint databases [7]. This may be further combined with an extension of phylogenetic tree algorithms, such as the *Common Mutations Similarity Matrix* algorithm [10] and the *Incremental Phylogenetics by Repeated Insertions* algorithm [12]. Finally, the rate of evolution of the various subhaplogroups of mtDNA I is another interesting topic to be further explored perhaps by applying techniques similar to those in the study of bacterial evolution [13].

The extended study could also benefit from other ancient mtDNA I samples that may become available in the near future. The study of ancient human DNA is an exciting area of research, and in that study mtDNA haplogroup I plays an interesting role as a testimony to the earliest meeting of Paleolithic survivors in glacial refugia and newcomers to the European continent from either North Africa or the Near East.

References

1. M. Allentoft et al., Nature, **522**, 167-172 (11 June 2015)
2. R. Bollongino, O. Nehlich, M.P. Richards, J. Orschiedt, M.G. Thomas, C. Sell, Z. Fajkošová, A. Powell, J. Burger, Science, **342,** 6157, 479-481 (25 Oct. 2013)
3. G. Brandt et al., Science, **342**, 6155, 257-261 (2013).
4. P. Brotherton, Nature Comm., **4**, Art. No. 1764 (2013)
5. W. Haak, et al., PloS Bio., **8**, 11, (November 2010)
6. M. Hervella et al., Arch. and Anthrop. Sciences, **8**, 1, 97-106 (March 2016)
7. P.C. Kanellakis, G.M. Kuper, P.Z. Revesz, J. of Comp. and Sys. Sciences, **51**, 1, 26-52 (1995)
8. A. Olivieri, M. Pala, F. Gandini, B.H. Kashani, U.A. Perego, S.R. Woodward, V. Grugni, V. Battaglia, O. Semino, A. Achilli, M.B. Richards, A. Torroni, PLoS ONE, **8**, 7, (2013)

9. P.Z. Revesz, *Introduction to Databases: From Biological to Spatio-Temporal*, (Springer, New York, 2010)
10. P.Z. Revesz, Proc. 4th ACM Int. Conf. on Bioinfo. and Comp. Bio., 731-734, (ACM Press, New York, USA, 2013)
11. P.Z. Revesz, Int. J. of Bio. and Biomed. Eng., **10**, 1, 124-133 (2016)
12. P.Z. Revesz and Z. Li, Int. J. of Bio. and Biomed. Eng., **10**, 1, 148-158 (2016)
13. M. Shortridge, T. Triplet, P.Z. Revesz, M. Griep, R. Powers, Comp. Bio. and Chem., **35**, 1, 24-33, (2011)
14. S. Vai et al., PLoS ONE **10**, 1, (2015)

MATEC Web of Conferences **76**, 04049 (2016) DOI: 10.1051/matecconf/20167604049
CSCC 2016

Effect (Comparison between Elderly Person and Youth) of the Break in the Touch Typing Learning Comparison

Yumi Yamaguchi[1,a]

[1]*EDP Kansai University of International Studies, Japan*

Abstract. The technical education using the information appliance of the old worker is required. However, an elderly person is negative about the utilization of the information appliance. I experimented on, this study about an appropriate break to suppress fatigue of the elderly person, and to learn a touch typing technology effectively and made it clear. The experiment performed two kinds of touch typing learning by the Computer Based Training software. I performed an experiment of elderly person and "Consecutive learning short break models" "Massed practice long break models" which changed the interval of learning and the break by the touch typing software for youths. I performed a questionnaire to a subject to collect the subjective data of fatigue and the learning burden at the same time. As a result, I knew the thing that "the elderly person controlled fatigue by a learning method to put a break in diligently for a short time in this experiment, and could learn a touch typing skill" "having a long it than a youth as for the time to be concerned with the touch typing of the elderly person." that "the elderly person can learn a touch typing skill early by enjoying CBT learning."

1 Introduction

It is for the problem that is important effectively utilizing it in old workers to supplement lack of work force with the social progress with many Japanese elderly people [1].

In addition, the local government utilizes a web page as a place of the information disclosure necessary for a civic life. Therefore of the software that an elderly person utilizes an information appliance for life and collects necessary information was developed [2] In addition, the development of the special keyboard for elderly people is carried out [3]. However, the elderly person has cognitive hardness in psychology, and there is the characteristic that is hard to be able to support the new environment and situation flexibly [4].

Therefore the need of the PC utilization environment in consideration for the usability of the elderly person is pointed out [5].However, It doesn't generally spread for a stage of the development. It is a keyboard now to spread as an inputting tool of the information appliances widely. Therefore it is the technique that is indispensable to a thing and a worker of the current information-intensive society who the touch typing work using the keyboard utilizes an information appliance, and collect necessary information because it is. Therefore the technical education that can utilize the personal computer for elderly people is required now.

The conventional study of the touch typing using the keyboard of the elderly person clarified a psychology side and a relationship of the technical skill using spreadsheetware[5)], Development of the keyboard The precedent study about the appropriate break interval in the touch typing learning by the Computer Based Training software which I was going to perform in this study was poor. Computer Based Training (CBT) using the touch typing software spreads as the touch typing technology acquisition now.

However, as for the interval of learning for the acquisition of the touch typing technology and the appropriate break, it cannot be yet said that it is clear.
Therefore this study performed the experiment that changed the interval of learning and the break by the touch typing software for youths (freshman) with an elderly person, and I performed a statistical analysis, and a comparison considered the touch typing technology acquisition of the "short learning short break repetition model" "massed practice head break type" and the relations of the break.

2 Experiment

2.1 Design of the experiment

It is said that it is good that the abecedarian learning touch typing acquires a finger errand from home position (HP) by the touch typing learning software. The touch

[a] Corresponding author: y-yamaguchi@kuins.ac.jp

typing learning software is shown on the Web a lot.

It was done the screen display, and I chose "K/B trainer" [6] [7] with the reputation with plainness, and, by this experiment, a finger position from home position used it for an experiment from freeware in the Web. Key point of the typing acquirement law by the touch typing is"① I learn a key and the placement of the finger ② I memorize shooting with a finger. I changed a learning break interval by an experiment corresponding to each key point and experimented on three kinds. in an information processing room (for Windows) .

Experiment 1: I practiced learning a key position from the HP in correspondence with key point ①.

Experiment 2: I performed an experiment to input along a Japanese syllabary list in correspondence with key point ②.

I assumed it one set when I finished hitting one time of Japanese syllabary list. I prepared for learning time and two kinds of intervals of the break and tested it".

A experiment (Consecutive learning short break models),
B experiment (Massed practice long break models).

I classified subjects (elderly person, youth) in, "A experiment" and "B experiment" at random. In addition, I performed inventory survey of fatigue and the work awareness to all the members. I carried out a spare experiment, and the experiment method was decided.

1. Experiment1: (A to Z typing) five times of repetition
2. Break: Tea break (ten minutes)
3. Experiment2: (Typing of the Japanese syllabary list) ten times of repetition

2.2 Experiment method

2.2.1 Experiment 1

After explaining key to keyboard placement, and having ordered that "I return a finger to HP every typing by all means" learns HP than typing speed "memorizing the position of each key exactly" and should type it with an appropriate fingers. I started an experiment.

I tested five times consecutive typing without judging that it was in a state without fatigue, and sandwiching the break for short-term memory reinforcement of the placement of the keyboard.

2.2.2 Experiment 2

I directed it to type it being conscious of "accuracy" and "speedup of the typing". The software for the typing learning that I used this time displays a finger position to a screen graphically and is structure to warn by a beep in the case of a typing error. Therefore I cannot shift to the next key when I do not type a precise key. It is the structure which I notice a typing error and am easy to hit again.

The experiment assumed it one set until I finished hitting one time of Japanese syllabary list. I set two kinds of breaks in the inside that performed ten sets of experiments in total.

A Experiment (Consecutive learning short break models) :It is a short break of one minute every one set of learning

B Experiment (Massed practice long break models) : The learning that five sets continued including the break of nine minutes after five sets of consecutive learning.

2.3 Subject

48 elderly people (average age 67.4 years old, SD: 4.1) who participated in health club of University X,
56 University X first graders (average age 18.9 years old, SD: 0.2). There is experience using all the members word-processing software. There is no experience in the touch typing training. The elderly person who typed it by trade removed it. The university student with a word processor qualification from commercial high school removed it.

I classified it in A experiment group and B experimental group at random and performed experiment 2.The elderly person experiment posted an experiment assistant university student to each subject. I thereby had the environment that could ask you a question when I was in trouble

Experiment1 : 48 elderly people, youth 56

Experiment2 : 36 elderly people (20: A experiment (unfinishedanswer4)16, B experiment (unfinished answer 8)), youth 56

2.4 Questionnaire

For the middle (after five sets) and the end (after ten sets) of experiment 2, I performed the following questionnaires to check a fatigue degree and learning awareness of the learning

2.4.1 Question item

(A) This learning is difficult to do.
(B) This learning is tiring.
(C) This learning is interesting.
(D) This learning is effective.

2.4.2 Evaluation method

5th phases of evaluations
(1. not it at all, 2. a little, 3. to some extent, 4. considerably, 5. very much)

3 Result and Consideration

3.1 Experiment 1

I show a result of experiment 1 in figure 3.

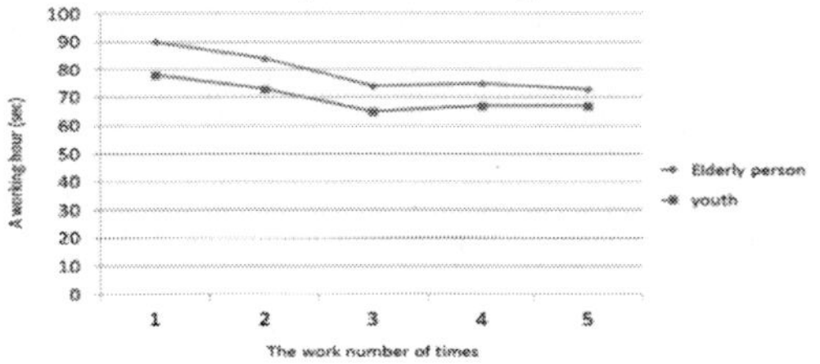

Figure 1 Experiment 1(A to Z) keying time

Significant difference was recognized than figure 1 in the working hour of a youth and the elderly person. But, I told "I return a finger to HP every typing by all means" learns HP than typing speed "memorizing the position of each key exactly" and should type it with an appropriate finger. Therefore I cannot evaluate a result provided this time for differences between youth and typing skill of the elderly person. Experiment 1 thought that it was in a learning process of the typing with both youth and elderly person memorizing HP and key position relations

I recognized shortening of the time to approximately 85% of youths, 81% of elderly people in comparison with the first by five times of consecutive keying experiments in the fifth mean working hour. Each person regarded the placement of the key as a process to learn.

3.2 Experiment 2

I show a result of experiment 2 in figure 2

I examined a result of figure 2 by analysis of variance two way layout. As a result, in the working hour of a youth and the elderly person, only the main effect of the age accepted significant difference ($P<0.01$). The significant difference was not seen in A experiment and B experiment.

Then, I analyzed contracted relations in progress and a working hour of the work number of times. In the first half (1~5) and the latter half (6~10), there was a difference in typing speed.

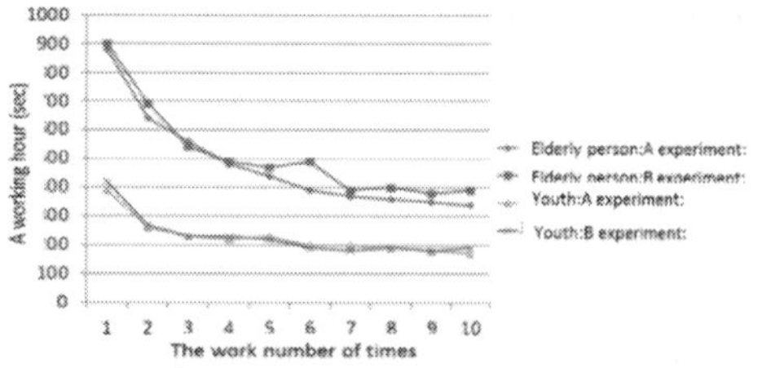

Figure 2. Experiment2 (Japanese syllabary list) typing time

The first half accepts shortening of the rapid working hour than figure 4. I thought with the process that this learned the position of the key which appeared quite frequently to vowel sounds from new typing, and learned a touch typing technology rapidly. It was reduced to half in acknowledgment of the acquisition of the steady technique in a working hour in comparison with the first time in the latter half.

Working hours of the elderly person are always longer than a youth. However, it decreased to the original working hour of the youth and an about the same standard in a working hour in the latter half of the elderly person. In the latter half, I did not do shortening of the sudden working hour like the first half. As a whole, a working hour shortened an elderly person and a youth by the acquisition of the touch typing skill together. The standard deviation of the elderly person in particular was big. However, it became fast, and the standard deviation reduced to progress of the learning, too.

From this, it was thought that individual difference greatly influenced the touch typing technology acquisition of the elderly person. I examined it in analysis of variance two way layout by age and an experiment method. However, significant difference was not recognized the main effect, interaction together probably because it was highly individual. In addition, the break that is long for the touch typing skill acquisition of the elderly person is inappropriate because experiment B accepted the temporary increase of the working hour just after a long break in elderly person group. "Interesting" answered the elderly person, "it is effective" than "I am tired" "difficult to do" about learning than a questionnaire result. "Difficult to do" "was tiring when I compared the tenth with the fifth of experiment A," but decreased. And "it is effective" increased "interesting".

Besides, the subject whom "interesting" answered, "it is effective" shortened a working hour. And "difficult to do" was long in one set of working hour of the subject whom I answered, "I am tired".

The youth felt, "it is hard to do it" in comparison with an elderly person, but the touch typing skill acquisition was early. In addition, "it was effective," but there was many it. "It was interesting," but there was few it.

A person feeling that an elderly person is interesting is in contrast to having learned a technique early. Age and the kind of the experiment influenced fatigue. Age in particular strongly influenced it.

Short learning short break repetition type of experiment A avoided the consciousness "that it was hard to do" for an elderly person than the above and was able to learn a touch typing skill. In addition, it became clear that the elderly person did not feel fatigue for a youth in a process of the skill even if I did the same touch typing learning.

I knew that it was possible for the technique acquisition effectively by enjoying that I put a short break diligently to maintain a touch typing skill when the elderly person reduced fatigue and learned it.

These were tendencies same as findings of the skill of the spreadsheet inflection technology of Umemuro [5] for elderly people. From this, I knew the fault if it was important to learn while enjoying it because an elderly person learned a computer utilization technology as well as the technical acquisition of the spreadsheet.

This experiment of the elderly person assumed it a repetition experiment of 10 set in consideration of the burden on subject, but the repetition number of times of the experiment is considered by the result in a skill process provided this time when I take similar skill process when I increase. A typing skill improved by utilizing CBT software, and learning it repeatedly, and shortening of the working hour knew that I was connected regardless of age in touch typing learning from experiment 1, a result of experiment 2.

4 Summary

1. The elderly person can learn a touch typing skill early by enjoying CBT learning.
2. The time to be concerned with the touch typing of the elderly person is longer than a youth。
3. The elderly person knew what controlled fatigue

by a learning method to classify a break into diligently for a short time, and could learn a touch typing skill in this experiment.

References

1. Ministry of Health, Labour and Welfare ,2015, public welfare labor whitepaper, http://www.mhlw.go.jp/wp/hakusyo/kousei/15/dl/2-02.pdf
2. Daiji Kobayashi: Experimental study about the Web accessibility of the elderly person, Nihonbashigakkann University bulletin **5**,15-27 (2006)
3. Masao Nogami: Development of a keyboard, the controller as the information support apparatus of the elderly person and the email software, Yamaguchi University Venture business laboratory, **6**.66 2002)
4. Kaoru Hoshi: *A psychological characteristic life and the welfare of the aging society,* (Open University Education Development Association,50-61,1994)
5. Hiroyuki Umemuro: Relations of the task recognition and the performance of the elderly person in the s kill acquisition process at the time of the data entry work introduction using the calculator, Japan Industrial Management Association, **47**,32-40(1996)
6. Iwata Design: A keyboard is easily usable, http://iwatadesign.com/
7. IT class support site (naruhodo.net), http://www.naruhodo.net/it

Patient-specific blood flow modelling for medical applications

Tatiana Dobroserdova[1,2,a], Sergey Simakov[2,1], Timur Gamilov[2,1], Roman Pryamonosov[1], and Ekaterina Sakharova[3]

[1] *Institute of Numerical Mathematics of the Russian Academy of Sciences, Gubkin str., 8, Moscow, 119333, Russia*
[2] *Moscow Institute of Physics and Technology, 9 Institutskiy per., Dolgoprudny, Russia*
[3] *Higher School of Economics National Research University, 20 Myasnitskaya Ulitsa, Moscow, Russia*

Abstract. Patient-specific blood flow modelling helps to predict surgical operation results, gives new noninvasive diagnostic methods, allows to investigate physiology of vascular pathologies. We develop numerical models for such medical applications. 1D blood flow model describes hemodynamics in the whole vascular network. 3D model of fluid flow can be embedded in the 1D model to zoom the domain of interest or to take into account pathologies or implants. We personalize the model, using patient-specific vascular structure and parameters. For some vascular regions extraction of patient-specific geometry can be automatic within developed technology. We verified the 1D model of blood flow. Two examples of real medical applications are presented. The method for FFR estimation is proposed. Also we used the 1D model for prediction of surgical occlusion treatment.

1 Introduction

Practical medicine has a lot of challenges where mathematical modelling can help significantly. Prediction of surgical operation impact based on numerical simulations (e.g. bypass surgery, stenting) for every certain patient [1] can become real in near future. New noninvasive diagnostic methods, for example estimation of fractional flow reserve [2, 3], are now suggested. New therapeutic methods like enhanced external counterpulsation are being successfully tested with numerical models. Parameters of the patient should be taken into account in the mentioned applications.

Segmentation of patient vascular tree is the basic problem of non-invasive prognostic methodologies. Many researches on blood vessel segmentation were presented and most of them are restricted to one region of interest (cerebral, coronary, abdominal aorta and leg vasculature). Coronary arteries segmentation and centerline extraction algorithms can be completely automated [4]. Techniques for cerebral arteries are often restricted to a braincase, excluding vertebral and carotid arteries, or require user administration. Abdominal aorta region is usually segmented with general methods.

In this paper we discuss out 1D blood flow model (Section 2). We also mention the possible way to adapt it for a real patient (Section 3). In section 4 we refer to the multiscale 1D-3D modelling as a method to take into account patient-specific pathologies or implants. In section 5 the model is verified. We present two real medical applications of numerical modelling in section 6.

[a] e-mail: DobroserdovaTK@gmail.com

2 1D model of global blood circulation

We consider blood as a viscous incompressible fluid. Every vessel is represented as a tube with elastic walls and the human vascular system is represented by the 1D graph. Blood flow in every vessel is described by the mass and momentum conservation laws [5, 6]:

$$\frac{\partial S}{\partial t} + \frac{\partial (S u)}{\partial x} = 0, \tag{1}$$

$$\frac{\partial u}{\partial t} + \frac{\partial (u^2/2 + p/\rho)}{\partial x} = \phi, \tag{2}$$

where S is the vessel cross-section area, u is the mean velocity, p is the mean pressure, ρ is the blood density. The term ϕ takes into account external forces, such as gravity or friction. The state equation designates elastic properties of the vessel wall and closes the system (1)–(2):

$$p = \rho c^2 f(S), \tag{3}$$

where c is the elasticity model parameter, $f(S)$ is known function [5].

The continuity of solution in vascular anastomoses is prescribed by the enforcing conservation of mass and total pressure continuity. This pair of boundary conditions does not include any additional model parameters and is appropriate for patient-specific modelling. At the same time it was verified for blood flow simulations [7].

For the numerical integration of the model equations (1)–(2), we use the grid-characteristic method [8].

3 Model initialization

The 1D model of global blood circulation describes hemodynamics in a 1D vascular network. Length, diameter, elastic parameter should be prescribed to every vessel.

Figure 1. Patient-specific 3D and 1D vascular networks.

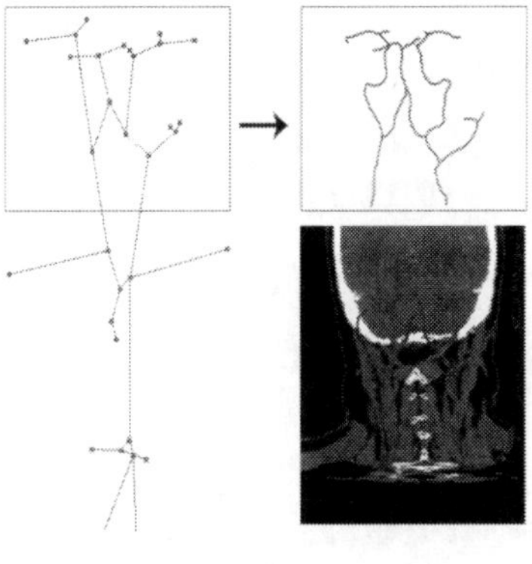

Figure 2. 1D-3D vascular network.

3.1 Reconstruction of the vascular tree

Patient-specific vascular system is recognized on MRI/CT scans. Segmentation of these scans allows us to reconstruct the 3D geometry of the system (fig. 1).

For some vascular regions extraction of patient specific geometry can be automatic. In case of coronary vessels it requires complex image processing and segmentation algorithms [2] utilizing Hough Circleness transformation and Isoperimetric Distance Trees for aorta initialization. Frangi Vesselness filter is used to find ostia points and segment vessels.

Other regions of circulatory system can be processed in semiautomatic manner. For instance, regions of abdominal aorta and main arteries in legs may be segmented with the tracking technique [1] in the absence of discontinuities, which can be eliminated manually.

Another region of interest is cerebral vasculature. One can take advantage of automatic coronary artery segmentation method [4] if bone intensities are darkened. If only ceCTA (or ceMRA) dataset is given, bone elimination should be done manually. In case when both contrast enhanced and not enhanced datasets are available, bones can be darkened with automatic techniques.

The 3D structure can be transformed into the 1D structure by extracting centerlines everywhere [1]. It is possible to calculate the length of every centerline and the diameter of the 3D vessel in every point during this algorithm.

3.2 Parameter initialization

Every vessel is considered as an elastic tube. Elastic parameters c of the vessel wall can not be measured *in vivo* with modern methods of diagnostics. It can be retrieved from the literature. The data depends on the individual parameters: age, weight, diseases, profession, smoking and etc. If any patient measurements are available (blood or pulse wave velocities, etc.) model parameters can be fitted to approximate it.

4 1D-3D modelling

1D model of global blood circulation describes hemodynamics in healthy vascular system. Medical applications often require blood flow simulations in the vascular network with pathologies or implants. Some pathologies like aneurysm, aorta dissection or placed implants have complex geometry and it is difficult to take them into account by the 1D model. Often the domain of interest should be considered as 3D. The example of multiscale geometry is presented on the fig.2: cerebral vessels are 3D and the rest vascular network is 1D.

The 3D model of fluid flow is based on the Navier-Stokes equations. Vessel walls can be treated as rigid in the 3D domain. It is the common assumption which helps to save computational time significantly. Also we do not need to tune elastic parameters of the wall which can not be measured for real patient.

Coupling boundary conditions should be specified on the interface between 1D and 3D models. The continuity of normal stress and either continuity of the fluid flux or continuity of linear combination of fluid and energy fluxes can be prescribed. In case of non-physiological reflected waves caused by inconsistency between elasticity effects in the 1D model and the non-compliance of the 3D model an auxiliary absorbing 0D device can be placed at the interface between 1D and 3D models [9]. A virtual device mimics the effect of the 3D model compliance and hence reduces pressure wave reflection and instabilities caused by the inconsistency.

5 Verification of the 1D blood flow model

The model of global blood circulation was verified with an experimental model [7]. The experimental model consists of 37 silicone tubes and represents the human arterial system including aorta and carotid arteries. All geometrical and material properties of the arterial network are known. The pulsative pump provides periodic output similar to the aortic flow. Pressure and flow were measured in several

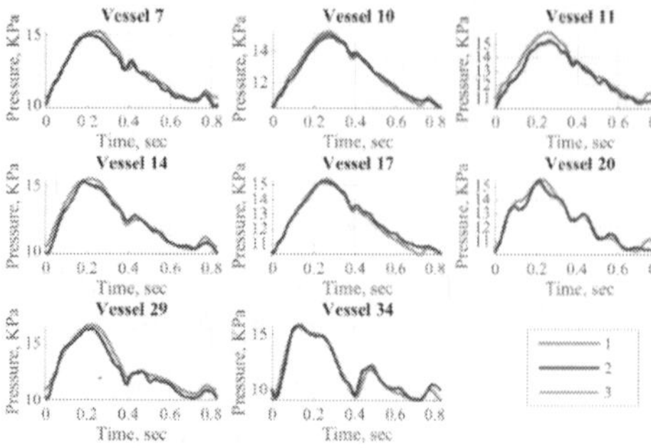

Figure 3. Comparison of pressure in several vessels. Red line (1): experimental measurements; Blue line (2): results of numerical simulation with described model; Black line (3): results of numerical simulation from [7].

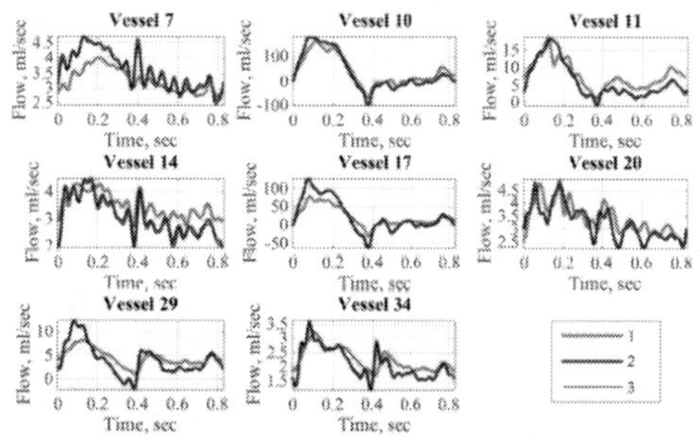

Figure 4. Comparison of fluid flow in several vessels. Red line (1): experimental measurements; Blue line (2): results of numerical simulation with described model; Black line (3): results of numerical simulation from [7].

places during the experiment. The results of the numerical simulation with model described in section 2 (blue line) are presented in fig. 3,4. They well correspond to the experimental data (red line) and to the numerical results of other groups (black line).

Model verification with real human data is rather challenging nowadays. Some parameters of the vascular system can not be measured. Qualitative tests based on patient-specific data were presented before [1, 10]. At the same time it is difficult to compare quantitative characteristics for such cases.

6 Medical applications

The described model can be used for a number of medical applications. Hemodynamic calculations help to assess blood pressure or velocity in various parts of cardiovascular system and predict results of a surgical treatment. Patient-specific data is crucial for such problems. Two examples of real medical applications are presented in the next section.

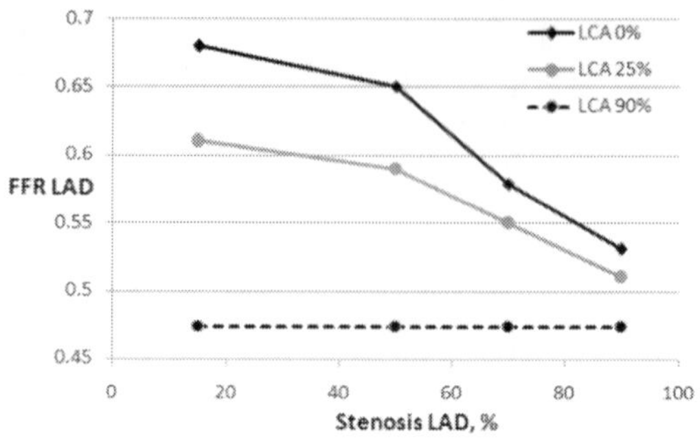

Figure 5. Comparison of FFR in LAD (distal stenosis) for different stenoses in LCA (proximal stenosis) and different stenosis degrees.

6.1 Fractional flow reserve estimation

Fractional flow reserve (FFR) measured during invasive coronary angiography is an independent prognosticator for patients with coronary artery diseases and the gold standard for decision making in coronary revascularization. Previously used parameter - percentage of closed lumen (degree of stenosis) - proved to be less accurate [11]. FFR is defined as a ratio between average pressure distal to the stenosis ($\bar{P}_{dist}$) and average aortic pressure ($\bar{P}_{aor}$) in the case of maximum possible hyperemia

$$FFR = \frac{\bar{P}_{dist}}{\bar{P}_{aor}}. \tag{4}$$

FFR measurement is an expensive and complicated procedure. Hemodynamic simulations can help to estimate FFR without surgical intervention.

Two anonymized patient cases with multiple stenosis of coronary arteries were investigated [2]. The 1D network was constructed on the basis of individual CT-scans. Functional model parameters were assigned to the network with the help of pulse wave velocity studies and other well-known medical and physiological literature. Personalised virtual FFR was computed. We demonstrated that our approach is capable to predict FFR with acceptable accuracy.

Blood flow model can also be used to study interaction between multiple stenoses and investigate changes in stenosis severety with patient's age. Figure 5 shows how proximal stenosis in left coronary artery (LCA) affects FFR in distal stenosis in left anterior descending artery (LAD).

6.2 Prediction of surgical atherosclerotic occlusion treatment

The 1D model of blood flow was used for presurgical patient-specific analysis of the hemodynamic changes due to atherosclerotic occlusion treatment in the femoral artery [1]. The vascular structure of lower extremities was reconstructed from MRI data of the patient. Unmeasured model parameter values (elasticities of vessel walls, resistances for boundary conditions) are fitted to match the available presurgical Doppler ultrasound measurements at some points before and after occlusion. These parameters were fitted to reach the best possible correspondance between calculated and measured peak velocities in a set of measurement points. These values also correspond to acceptable ranges for these parameters. Such ranges depend on general physiological and anatomical data, as well as on patient parameters such as height, weight, medical history.

The numerical simulations consider postsurgical blood flow through the left thigh arteries after occlusion treatment. Results of numerical modelling and measured values were compared. We observed quite good coincidence between these data sets: the maximum relative error is not greater than 20%. The error can be caused by the the physiological limitations during parameters fitting procedure and possible input data error.

7 Conclusions

In this paper we presented the model of global blood circulation. The described model was verified: the results of numerical experiments correspond to real data. We developed segmentation technology that allows us to get 3D patient-specific vessel geometry in automatic (for some regions) or semiautomatic manner. The 1D vascular tree can be reconstructed retrieving centerlines from 3D structure. Parameters were initialized depending on the patient peculiarity. It was used for practical medical applications. Noninvasive fractional flow reserve estimation and prediction of surgical operations are real thanks to numerical simulations.

Acknowledgement

The results of T.Dobroserdova and R.Pryamonosov presented in section 3.1 and 4 were supported by the Russian Federation President Grant for Young Scientists MK-6121.2015.1. Joint author results presented in other sections were supported by the Russian Science Foundation grant 14-31-00024.

References

[1] T. Gamilov, Yu. Ivanov, P. Kopylov, S. Simakov, Yu. Vassilevski. Patient-specific haemodynamic modeling after occlusion treatment in leg. Mathematical Modelling of Natural Phenomena.,**9(6)**: 85–97 (2014).

[2] T.Gamilov, Ph.Kopylov, R.Pryamonosov, S.Simakov. Virtual fractional flow reserve assesment in patient-specific coronary networks by 1D hemodynamic model. Rus. J. Num. Anal. Math. Mod., **5**: 269-276 (2015).

[3] E.Boileau, P.Nithiarasu. One-dimensional modelling of the coronary circulation. Application to noninvasive quantification of fractional flow reserve (FFR). Comp. Exper. Biomed. Sci. Meth. Appl., **21**: 137-155 (2015).

[4] Danilov A., Ivanov Y., Pryamonosov R., Vassilevski Y. Methods of graph network reconstruction in personalized medicine. Int J Numer Method Biomed Eng, doi: 10.1002/cnm.2754 (2015).

[5] A. Kholodov, S. Simakov. Computational study of oxygen concentration in human blood under low frequency disturbances. Mathematical models and computer simulations, **1(2)**:283-295 (2009).

[6] A. Quarteroni, L. Formaggia. Mathematical modelling and numerical simulation of the cardiovascular system. Handb. Numer. Anal., **12**: 3-127 (2004).

[7] K.Matthys, J.Alastruey, J.Peiro, A.Khir, P.Segers, P.Verdonck, K.Parker, S.Sherwin. Pulse wave propagation in a model human arterial network: assessment of 1D numerical simulations against in-vitro measurements. J. Biomech., **40(15)**:3476-3486 (2007).

[8] K.Magomedov, A.Kholodov. *Grid-characteristic Numerical Methods* (Nauka, Moscow, 1988).

[9] T.Dobroserdova, M.Olshanskii, S.Simakov. Multiscale coupling of compliant and rigid walls blood flow models. Int. J. Numer. Meth. Fluids, doi: 10.1002/fld.4241 (2016).

[10] S. Simakov, T. Gamilov, Y.N. Soe. Computational study of blood flow in lower extremities under intense physical load. Russian Journal of Numerical Analysis and Mathematical Modelling., **28(5)**: 485–504 (2013)

[11] B. De Bruyne, N.Pijls, G.Heyndrickx, D.Hodeige, R.Kirkeeide, K.Gould, Pressure-derived fractional flow reserve to assess serial epicardial stenoses: Theoretical basis and animal validation, Circulation, **15**: 1840-1847 (2000).

MATEC Web of Conferences 76, 05002 (2016) DOI: 10.1051/matecconf/20167605002
CSCC 2016

Is the Fractal Dimension of the Contour-lines a Reliable Tool for Classification of Medical Images?

Elena Hadzieva[1,a], Dijana C. Bogatinoska[1], Risto Petroski[1], Marija Shuminoska[1], Ljubinka Gjergjeska[1], Aleksandar Karadimce[1] and Vesna Trajkova[2]

[1]University of Information Science and Technology "St. Paul the Apostle" Partizanska bb, 6000 Ohrid, Macedonia
[2]General City Hospital "8-mi Septemvri", Dermatology Department, Pariska bb, 1000 Skopje, Macedonia

Abstract. When two-dimensional medical images are subject to fractal analysis, one of the methods used is to detect the contour of objects in the binary images and later to estimate the fractal dimension of the extracted contour. This scalar characteristic of the medical image should help in discrimination between normal and abnormal tissues. In this paper we expose the factors that affect the reliability of such examinations and put the fractal dimension in question as a valid criterion for description, classification and recognition in medical diagnosing.

1 Introduction

Fractal analysis is a mathematical field that deals with fractal characteristics of data. Its most important instrument is the fractal dimension, which can be defined on many ways and computed by different methods. The fractal dimension, roughly speaking, is a measure of complexity or irregularity of a fractal object. Medical images contain objects with typical fractal, non-Euclidean, structure - the fact that triggered the scientific community to apply the tools of fractal analysis in medical diagnosing. One of the most used approaches when using the fractal dimension as a diagnosing tool is the following. Normal and abnormal considered tissues (or cells) visually differ in smoothness; the first are smooth and even, the second are irregular, complex and odd. The first have lower complexity, i.e. lower fractal dimension, whilst the second have higher complexity, i.e. higher fractal dimension. Although this fractal approach for describing, classifying and recognition of medical images, as well as following and predicting the patient's condition, sounds reasonable and it is justified many times (see for example [1-6]), we have detected many ambiguities which put in question the reliability of the fractal dimension when applied in medical diagnosis or in some other field where natural objects are classified on the basis of the estimated values of the fractal dimension of their 2D contours.

Our experimentation began when we tried to reproduce closely the results met in several papers for successful application of fractal dimension in diagnosing cancer ([1-7]). We decided to work with skin cancer, taking into consideration the previously reported results and the dermatological ABCDE rule, according to which one of the most specific characteristic of melanoma moles is their irregular border. Thus, for melanoma moles higher fractal dimension is expected to be obtained, at least in statistical sense, compared to the fractal dimension of non-melanoma moles. We had an idea for establishing a new method for estimating the box-counting dimension of lines, for which we had a strong theoretical justification that it would be more robust than already used methods (a description of some methods is given in the review article [8]). And we planned to compare the published methods with our new method, in a proper application. Unfortunately, all our efforts to reproduce as much as possible the results from the papers, were unsuccessful, i.e. they were not giving neither expected results, nor any systematization or differentiation of melanoma and non-melanoma moles. Thus, we came to a challenge of answering the question: is the fractal dimension reliable or not to be used as a tool in medical diagnosing?

Deeper insight in our research is exposed in the following sections: Related Work, Theoretical Grounds, Data and Methods, Results and Discussion and Conclusion.

2 Related work

The authors in [6] compare the detection rate of malignant melanoma based on clinical visual investigation of about 65% with their approach based on fractal analysis, which gives significant 79.1% correctness. Moreover, the approach of Klein et al. in [2] gives high 97% of correctness in identifying malignant

[a] Elena Hadzieva: elena.hadzieva@uist.edu.mk

cells, which sounds remarkable compared to the current best tumor marker for pancreatic adenocarcinoma CA19-9 - it has its own sensitivity of 50 - 70% and applied jointly with two other tumor markers, the sensitivity is up to 85%. Dobrescu et al. in [7] claim that fractal and texture analyses can discriminate between the shapes of benign and malignant tumors. Fractal analysis and geometry have many applications other than diagnosing cancer. Indeed, they have application in image analysis in general, and especially in the medical fields (classifying ECG and EEG signals, brain, mammography, bone images, see for example the review given in [8]). All of these papers use the fractal dimension, computed with different methods, as one of the factors for classification and diagnosing.

On the other hand, there are papers that report about the non-reliability of the fractal dimension. Most of the fractal dimension estimators use the easy-to-implement box-counting method, for which the following drawbacks were recorded: binarization of the signal, construction of empty boxes, grid effect ([8]). Parameters tuning could improve the estimations by the box-counting method. However, it will be not clear whether the obtained differences in fractal dimensions are results of true differences in the images or results of certain "good" decisions made during the estimation process. In the same paper ([8]), the authors conclude that no comparative analysis was done (according to our knowledge, this is still the case), which could produce the most suitable method and improvements of existing results. The authors in [9] claim that the fractal dimension estimates depend on the estimator employed, the pixelization and resolution of the images and the structure identification technique used, and they kindly suggest that the previously reported results need revision. The authors of [10] come to a conclusion that fractal dimension depends on the edge detection algorithm used, in the sense that thicker line yields to higher dimensional values. Other authors (see [11]) treat the inconsistency of the fractal characteristics of medical images over large scale-ranges, proving that the fractal dimension depends on scale at which the object of interest is considered. Also, they propose a method for determining a scale or scale interval in which fractal dimension of observed tissue will have relevance in diagnosing (particularly, they work with breast cancer images, but their approach has wider application). It is known that medical images are "no reference model", i.e. they suffer from noise, that can not be objectively detected or measured. Reiss et al. in [12] found that the noise has significant effect on few commonly applied methods for computing the fractal dimension.

All of the authors cited in the last paragraph note different advantages and disadvantages in the process of calculating the fractal dimension, which they propose to be taken into consideration in order to avoid misreading of the results.

3 Theoretical grounds

When we think of fractals, we mainly think on "broken, irregular, complex, fragmented, grainy, ramified, strange, tangled and wrinkled shapes" ([13]), such as clouds, coastlines, edgy rocks, bushes, river basins, blood vessels, or lungs are. The theoretical definition of fractals can be met in many forms, but it seems like they are defined the best with the descriptive definition stated by Falconer in [14]: We refer to the subset of $\mathbb{R}^n$ as a fractal if:

- it has a fine structure, noticed even on arbitrarily small scales,
- it is too irregular to be described in traditional geometric language, both locally and globally,
- it often has some form of self-similarity, rigorous or approximate,
- its "fractal dimension" (defined in some way) is greater than its topological dimension,
- in most of the cases, it is defined in a very simple way, perhaps recursively.

Relating to the fourth item of the last definition, we will define dimensions mostly used to characterize fractals.

Definition 1 *([14], p. 29) Let $A \subset \mathbb{R}^m$. The number*

$$D_H(A) = \inf\{s|\mathcal{H}^s(A) = 0\} = \sup\{s|\mathcal{H}^s(A) = \infty\},$$

where

$$\mathcal{H}^s(A) = \lim_{\delta\to 0}\mathcal{H}^s_\delta(A),\ \mathcal{H}^s_\delta(A) = \inf\{\sum_{i=1}^{\infty}(\text{diam } U_i)^s :$$

U_i is a $\delta - cover\ of\ A\}$, *is called the Hausdorff dimension (or Hausdorff-Besicovitch dimension) of the set A.*

Although very satisfactory from theoretical point of view, in the sense that it satisfies all requirements from the pure mathematical definition of dimension, the Hausdorff dimension is almost useless for practical computational purposes.

Definition 2 *([15], p. 174) Let $A \in \mathcal{H}(\mathbb{R}^m)$ and let $N(A,\varepsilon)$ denote the smallest number of closed balls of radius $\varepsilon > 0$ needed to cover the set A. If*

$$D(A) = \lim_{\varepsilon\to 0}\frac{\ln(N(A,\varepsilon))}{\ln(1/\varepsilon)}$$

exists, then $D(A)$ is called the fractal dimension of A.

When the existence of the fractal dimension is ensured, it can be obtained if instead of balls, boxes of side length $\varepsilon_i = \frac{1}{2^i}$, $i \in \mathbb{N}$ are used. In such case, the fractal dimension is commonly called *box-counting fractal dimension* and it can be obtained by the formula

$$D(A) = \lim_{n\to\infty}\frac{\ln(N(A,n))}{\ln 2^n}, \quad (1)$$

where $(N(A,n))$ is the number of boxes with side-length $1/2^n$ that have nonempty intersection with *A*. Due to the limitation of the box-size with the size of the pixel, in practice, the fractal dimension is obtained when finite number of points $(\ln 2^i, \ln N(A,i))$ are fitted with a line, whose slope is then taken as approximation of the fractal dimension. This computational method is commonly known as basic box-counting method for the computation of the fractal dimension and it is mostly embedded in the software tools which estimate the fractal dimension.

4 Data and methods

We have recently analyzed more than 10 software tools used for computing the box-counting fractal dimension, applying them on artificially generated fractals and we have found that five best are (see [16]): Harfa (http://www.fch.vutbr.cz/lectures/imagesci/), FracLac (http://rsb.info.nih.gov/ij/plugins/fraclac), Fractalyse (http://www.fractalyse.org/), Fractal Count (http://www.pvv.org/~perchrh/imagej/fractal.html), and Fractal Analysis System (http://cse.naro.affrc.go.jp /sasaki/fractal/fractal-e.html). All of the tools are freely available (the last is available upon request), and all of them use the basic box-counting method or its variations. We tested them on artificial fractals (as the Sierpinsky triangle is), for which the fractal dimension is known (D = D (Sierp.tr.) = 1.5849), in order to configure and standardize the tools for further application.

HarFA (Harmonic and Fractal Image Analyser) is a software used to perform harmonic, wavelet and fractal analysis of digitized, especially biomedical images ([17]). It computes three fractal dimensions by using variations of traditional basic box counting method: DB, DBW, DW, which characterize properties of black plane DB, black-white border of black object DBW and properties of white background DW, respectively. The best result for the fractal dimension of the Sierpinski triangle, as our benchmark, was 1.5777, and it was obtained for values of the parameters of mesh varying from $4 = 2^2$ (minimum size of mesh square) to $512 = 2^9$ (maximum size of mesh square) and the number of steps between this values set to 10. The absolute percent error of this estimation is 0.73%.

FracLac is image analysis software developed as a plugin for ImageJ, which evolved to a suite of fractal analysis and morphology functions. The basic box counting algorithm, which is used for estimation of the fractal dimensions of images, was originally modified from ImageJ's box counting algorithm. FracLac is suitable to work with known fractals, as well as images of biological cells and other biological structures, including branching structures and textures. FracLac works on binary images (detects only black pixels on a white background, or white pixels on a black background), and on gray-scale images or grayscale images that have been converted to RGB. Using the Image Type option – Autoconvert to Binary, we can automatically threshold images to binary. We have used 4 grid positions and two different method for scaling: Power series and Block series. Benchmark testing with FracLac (Sierpinski triangle) gave D = 1.5640 for the method Power series and D = 1.5959 for Block series. The absolute percent errors of these estimations are 1-5%.

Fractalyse is an easy to use software, which is used to estimate the fractal dimension of black and white images, curves and networks. It works with black and white images in TIFF or BMP file formats. Two modules (counting and estimation) were used in the process of estimation of the fractal dimension using box counting method. The counting module offers an opportunity to choose box size (exponential or linear), and the type of the algorithm (grid or free box). The best estimated value for the fractal dimension of the Sierpinski triangle, as our benchmark testing, was D = 1.5290 obtained when using the exponential box size and grid algorithm. The absolute percent error of this estimation is 5%.

Fractal Count is another plugin for ImageJ, used for the estimation of the fractal dimension of the 2D and 3D binary images. The estimated values for the fractal dimension were obtained using the default values for the parameters. For the Sierpinski triangle, as our benchmark testing, the estimated value was D = 1.5504, which has absolute percent error of 3,5%.

Fractal analysis system for Windows is a free software developed to estimate the fractal dimensions of bitmap (bmp) images. The fractal dimension can be estimated on the entire image or on area of interest. The estimated value for the Sierpinski triangle was 1.5138, which is a result with 7% absolute error.

After establishing and configuring the software tools, we considered a set of 100 biomedical images of melanoma and non-melanoma moles, most of them obtained with the kind allowance of the first author of [18]-[21]. The images (out of which 30 are invasive malignant melanoma and 70 benign) are obtained from the EDRA Interactive Atlas of Dermoscopy and the dermatology practices of Dr. Ashfaq Marghoob (New York, NY), Dr. Harold Rabinovitz (Plantation, FL), and Dr. Scott Menzies (Sydney, Australia). These are 24-bit RGB color images with dimensions ranging from 577 × 391 pixels to 2556 × 1693 pixels.

The process of extracting the edge of the moles was mainly consisted of two parts:

1. Applying a thresholding algorithm which results in a black and white image, where the region of interest (the mole itself) is black, on a white background (the normal skin),
2. Cropping the pixels positioned on the edge between the black and white parts.

ImageJ as a suitable, widely used tool for manipulating images, has proven to be useful in our research as well. By default, ImageJ offers 17 threshold algorithms. To make sure they are all given a chance in a reasonable effort, an ImageJ Macro script was written and put in use (available on https://gist.github.com/9bdd6a6a2fb9fbef459d). These are the steps that were automatized:

- Open the mole image;
- Conversion to 8bit (gray-scale);
- Select and apply thresholding algorithm;
- Invert colors;
- Manual selection of the region of interest using Wand Tool;
- Run the Outline tool to get the area of interest outline;
- Finally, save the result for further calculation of the fractal dimension.

After this process was completed, we obtained 1700 = 17 × 100 one pixel wide edges ready for the calculation of the fractal dimension. By visual observation, we have discriminated 400 = 4 × 100 contour-lines appropriate for further investigation, obtained by the four ImageJ threshold algorithms: Default, Huang, Intermodes and Minimum.

5 Results and discussion

As said in the introduction, we were expecting to obtain the results which will discriminate between the melanoma and non-melanoma moles and later to choose the thresholding algorithm and the software tool for estimating fractal dimension which will give the best differentiation. Compared to many existing thresholding algorithms which result in smooth contours, our four chosen algorithms were producing pretty natural, fractal contours (see figures 2-5, 7-10). Figure 1 shows the original image of one randomly chosen melanoma mole and figures 2-5 show the four contours of this mole obtained by the chosen thresholding algorithms.

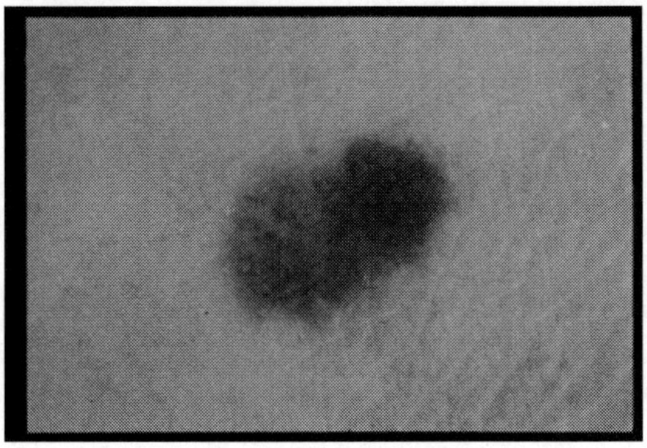

Figure 1. Original image of a melanoma mole.

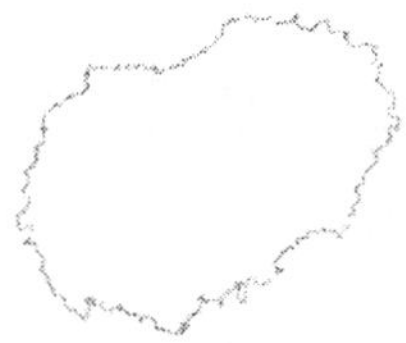

Figure 2. Contour of the mole from the Figure 1 obtained by the Default thresholding algorithm.

Figure 6 presents the original image of a randomly chosen non-melanoma mole, while figures 7-10 show the extracted outlines by Default, Huang, Intermodes and Minimum thresholding algorithm, respectively.

The distributions of the fractal dimensions of the contours extracted by the Default thresholding algorithm and computed by Harfa, Fraclac, Fractalyse, Fractal Count and Fractal Analysis System, are presented by the histograms given on Figures 11-15. The horizontal axis is for the values of fractal dimension, whilst the vertical is for the number of moles. The histograms, supported by the table 1 of means and standard deviation of the fractal dimensions of melanoma and non-melanoma moles, show that there is no good differentiation between melanoma and non-melanoma moles.

Figure 3. Contour of the mole from the Figure 1 obtained by the Huang thresholding algorithm.

Figure 4. Contour of the mole from the Figure 1 obtained by the Intermodes thresholding algorithm.

Figure 5. Contour of the mole from the Figure 1 obtained by the Minimum thresholding algorithm

It can be noted that, except in the FracLac case, the means of the fractal dimensions of melanoma moles are less than the appropriate means of the fractal dimensions of non-melanoma moles! Even in the FracLac case, if we consider the modes of the fractal dimensions, we wouldn't obtain satisfactory results. The values of the

DOI: 10.1051/matecconf/20167605002

standard deviations, give rice to the question of the accuracy and precision of the estimated fractal dimensions. At least two significant decimal figures are necessary in order to obtain clearer, more relevant classification.

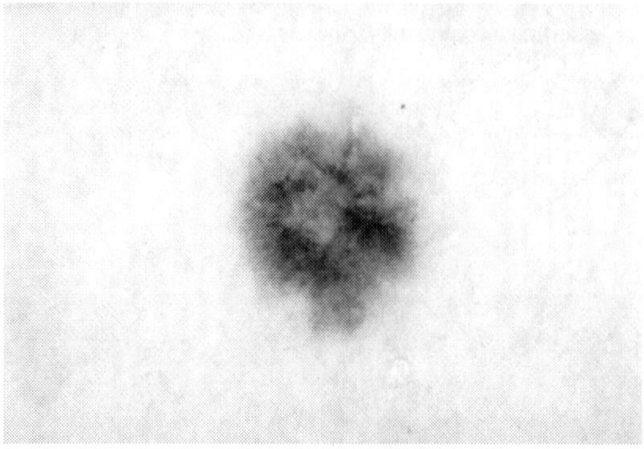

Figure 6. Original image of a non-melanoma mole.

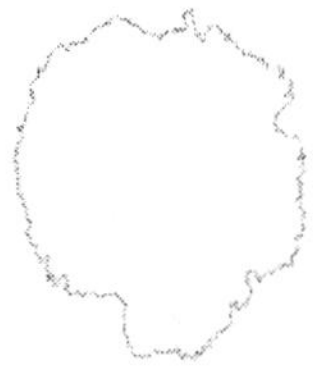

Figure 7. Contour of the mole from the Figure 6 obtained by the Default thresholding algorithm.

Figure 8. Contour of the mole from the Figure 6 obtained by the Huang thresholding algorithm.

Having in mind the obtained results and the accuracy of FracLac in estimating the fractal dimensions of artificial fractals previously considered ([16]), we decided to make another comparative analysis: to compute by FracLac the fractal dimensions of the contours obtained by the four different thresholding algorithms. The resulting fractal dimension of the contours obtained by the Default thresholding algorithm is already depicted in Figure 12.

Figure 9. Contour of the mole from the Figure 6 obtained by the Intermodes thresholding algorithm.

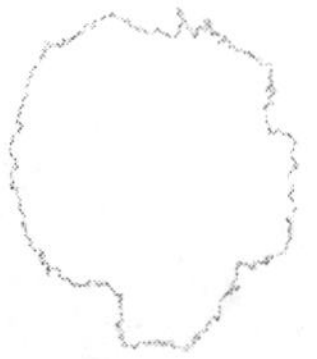

Figure 10. Contour of the mole from the Figure 6 obtained by the Minimum thresholding algorithm.

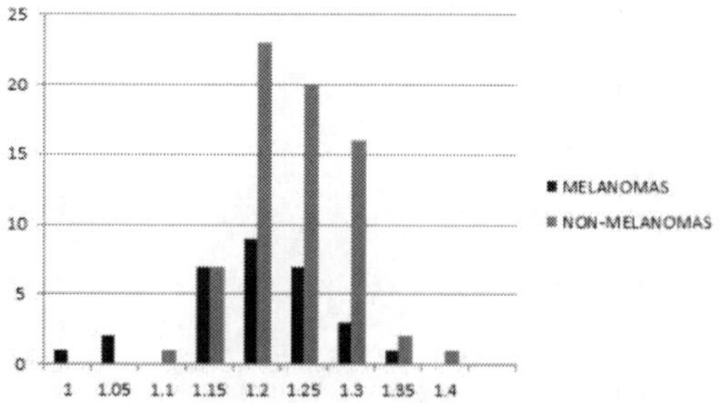

Figure 11. Histogram of the estimated fractal dimensions by Harfa, for outlines obtained by the Default thresholding algorithm.

Figures 16-18 show the histograms for the results obtained when the other three thresholding algorithms are employed, Huang, Intermodes and Minimum, respectively. The results for means and standard deviations of the fractal dimensions of melanoma and non-melanoma moles obtained with the last computations are resumed in Table 2. No new or different conclusion than previously stated.

Table 1. Table of means and standard deviations of the fractal dimensions of borderlines of melanoma and non-melanoma moles (thresholded by the Default thresholding algorithm), computed by different software tools

	Harfa	FracLac	Fractalyse	Fractal Count	Fractal Analysis System
Mean of fr. dim. – Mel.	1.1722	1.1792	1.1572	1.1473	1.1417
StDev of fr. dim. – Mel.	0.0761	0.0788	0.0685	0.0631	0.0633
Mean of fr. dim. – Non-mel.	1.2152	1.1650	1.1993	1.1712	1.1920
StDev of fr. dim. – Non-mel.	0.0526	0.0439	0.0556	0.0576	0.0558

Table 2. Table of means and standard deviations of the fractal dimensions of borderlines of melanoma and non-melanoma moles, thresholded by the Default, Intermodes, Huang and Minimum thresholding algorithm, computed by FracLac

	Default	Intermodes	Huang	Minimum
Mean of fr. dim. – Mel.	1.1792	1.1611	1.1614	1.1596
StDev of fr. dim. – Mel.	0.0788	0.0484	0.0631	0.0551
Mean of fr. dim. – Non-mel.	1.1650	1.1669	1.1684	1.1703
StDev of fr. dim. – Non-mel.	0.0439	0.0556	0.0507	0.0503

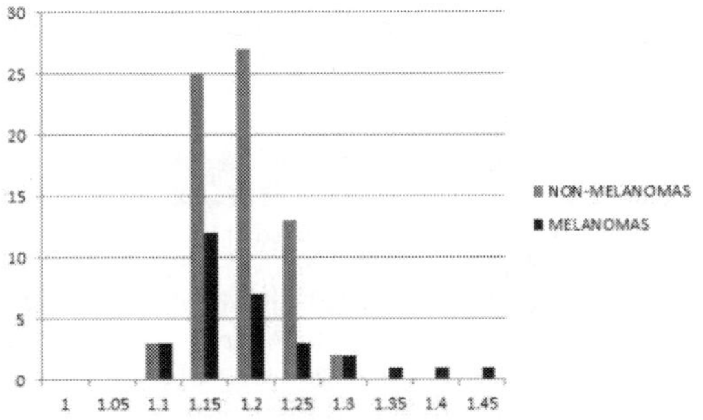

Figure 12. Histogram of the estimated fractal dimensions by FracLac, for contours obtained by the Default thresholding algorithm.

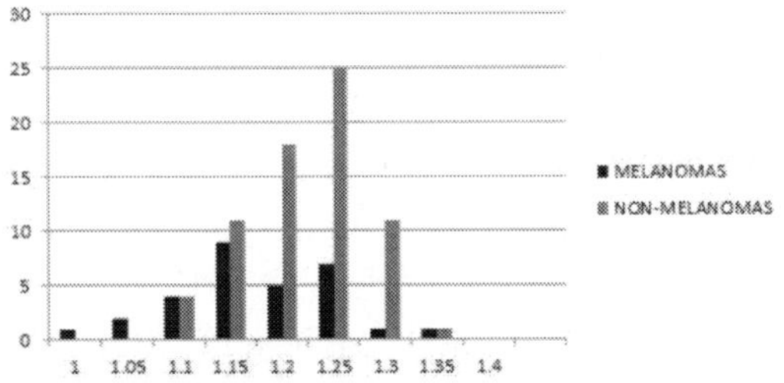

Figure 13. Histogram of the estimated fractal dimensions by Fractalyse, for contours obtained by the Default thresholding algorithm

Taking into consideration that there are many existing algorithms for extracting contour and many methods for estimating the fractal dimension (which contain many adjustable parameters), we might say that the results for the fractal dimension of the contours of images might be arbitrary and the classification non-accurate. We note that we are aware that what dermatologist understand as irregular border might be very different of what fractal analysts understand, i.e. melanoma moles might not be characterized by higher fractal dimension. Moreover, the dermatologists are not very sensitive on the exactness of the contour-line or contour thickness. Is it possible at all to choose the optimal contour-line?

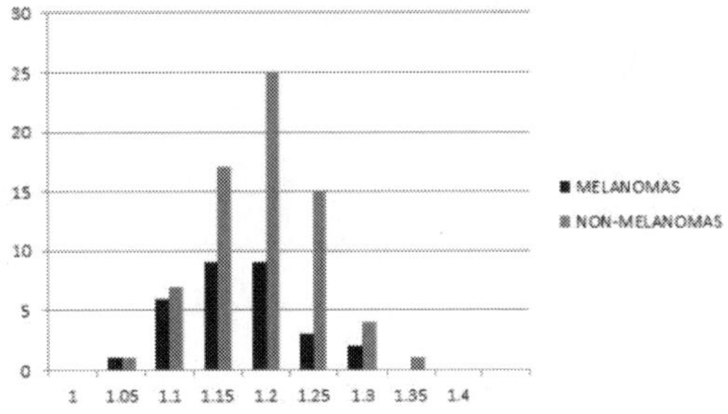

Figure 14. Histogram of the estimated fractal dimensions by Fractal Count, for contours obtained by the Default thresholding algorithm.

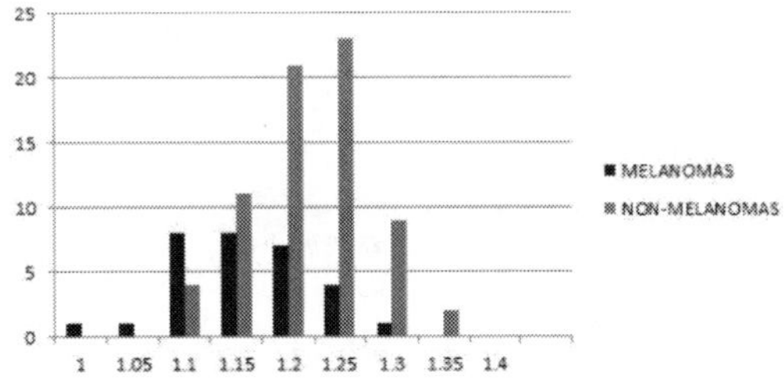

Figure 15. Histogram of the estimated fractal dimensions by Fractal Analysis System, for contours obtained by the Default thresholding algorithm.

What makes the fractal dimension a very relative scalar characteristic and too arbitrary to be reliable factor in classifying two-dimensional objects with fractal contour is described as follows:

DOI: 10.1051/matecconf/20167605002

1. The dependence of the images on the proficiency of the medical technician who makes and collects the images and on the type of the device that he uses;
2. The dependence of the fractal dimension on the quality of images, the structure identification technique used, edge detection algorithm, edge thickness, noise in the images and the estimator employed;
3. All the more or less random choices for the values of the parameters encountered.

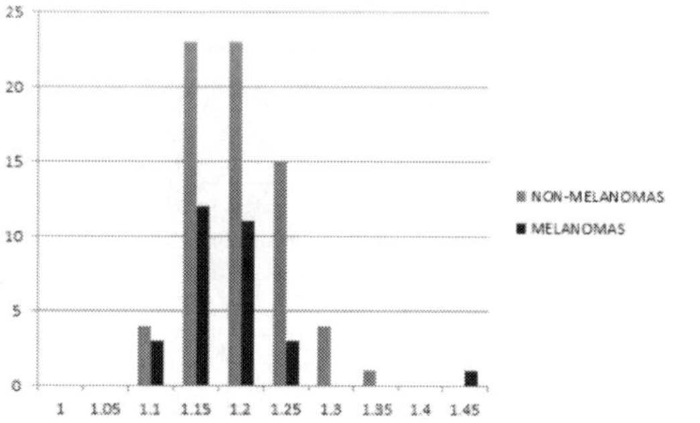

Figure 16. Histogram of computed fractal dimensions by FracLac, for contours obtained by the Huang thresholding algorithm.

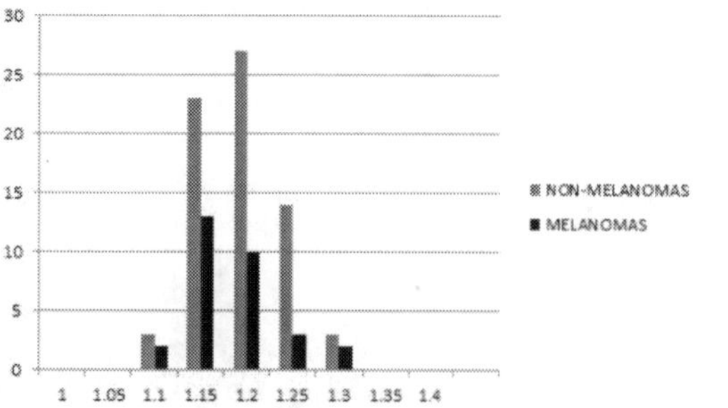

Figure 17. Histogram of computed fractal dimensions by FracLac, for contours obtained by the Intermodes thresholding algorithm.

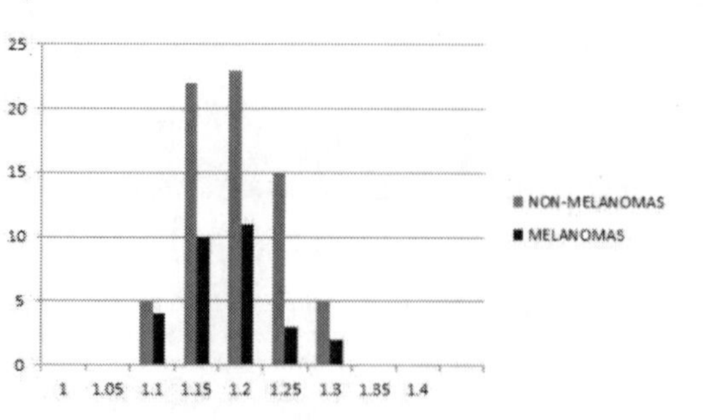

Figure 18. Histogram of computed fractal dimensions by FracLac, for contours obtained by the Minimum thresholding algorithm.

6 Conclusion

As it is noted ([22]), medical images typically suffer from at least one of the following deficiencies: low resolution, high level of noise, low contrast, geometric deformations, presence of imaging artifacts. Highly trained technicians and clinicians could bring these influences to a minimum. Additionally, in recent years there are lot of improvements in hardware, acquisition methods, signal processing techniques and mathematical methods. However, different papers show (see Section 2) that the fractal dimension depends on the following factors:

• the pixelization of the images,
• the resolution of the images,
• the edge-detection algorithm used,
• the scale at which the object is considered,
• the noise in the images,
• the thresholding algorithm, and
• the estimator used.

In our paper we give additional value to the last two factors, thresholding algorithm and the estimator used. We also try to highlight the struggle that occurs if well defined mathematical theory should be put in use. When the precisely, asymptotically defined scalar, as fractal dimension is, should characterize images dependent on many factors and limitations, many ambiguities happen. Deeper understanding of all positive and negative sides of the instruments of the fractal analysis, both from theoretical and practical aspects, is of crucial importance. Although in the papers considered in the Section 2, the authors give suggestions for the improvement of particular steps of the fractal analysis, there is a lot of randomness, arbitrariness, relativeness, beneficial and non-beneficial coincidences, that we suspect might yield to non-reliable results in practical applications.

Acknowledgment

The authors would like to thank to Zoran Ivanovski, Carlo Ciulla and Eustrat Zhupa, for their help in our work on this paper.

References

1. E. Claridge, P.N. Hall, M. Keefe, J.P. Allen, Shape Analysis for Classification of Malignant Melanoma, JBE **14** (3), 229-234 (1992)
2. K. Klein, T. Maier, V.C. Hirschfeld-Warneken, J.P. Spatz, Marker-Free Phenotyping of Tumor Cells by Fractal Analysis of Reflection Interference Contrast Microscopy Images, NL, ACS Publications, American Chemical Society, dx.doi.org/10.1021/nl4030402 | Nano Lett. 2013, **13**, 5474-5479 (2013)
3. P.Y. Kim, K.M. Iftekharuddin, P.G. Davey, M. Toth, A. Garas, G. Hollo, E.A. Essock, Novel Fractal Feature-Based Multiclass Glaucoma Detection and Progression Prediction, BHI, IEEE Journal of, **17**, no.2, pp.269-276 (March 2013), doi: 10.1109/TITB.2012.2218661

4. M. Mastrolonardo, E. Conte, J.P. Zbilut, 2006. A fractal analysis of skin pigmented lesions using the novel tool of the variogram technique, CSF, **28**, 1119-1135 (2006)
5. A. Piantanelli, P. Maponi, L. Scalise, S. Serresi, A. Cialabrini, A. Basso, Fractal characterisation of boundary irregularity in skin pigmented lesions, MBEC. Jul; **43** (4), 436-42 (2005)
6. E. Zagrouba, W. Barhoumi, A preliminary approach for the automated recognition of malignant melanoma, IAS, **23**, 121-135 (2004)
7. R. Dobrescu, M. Dobrescu, S. Mocanu and D. Popescu, Medical Images Classification for Skin Cancer Diagnosis Based on Combined Texture and Fractal Analysis, WSEAS Transactions on Biology and Biomedicine, **7**, no. 3, pp. 223-232 (2010)
8. R. Lopes, N. Betrouni, Fractal and multifractal analysis: A review, Medical Image Analysis, **13**, 634-649 (2009)
9. S. Criscuoli, M.P. Ras, I. Ermolli and M. Centrone, On the reliability of the fractal dimension measure of solar magnetic features and on its variation with solar activity, AA, **461**, 331-338 (2007), DOI: 10.1051/0004-6361:20065951
10. H. Ahammer, T.T.J. DeVaney, The influence of edge detection algorithms on the estimation of the fractal dimension of binary digital images, C, **14**(1):183-8 (2004)
11. B. Braverman, M. Tambasco, Scale-Specific Multifractal Medical Image Analysis, CMMM, **2013**, Hindawi Publishing Corporation, Article ID 262931, 11 pages, http://dx.doi.org/10.1155/2013/262931 (2013)
12. A.R. Martin, N. Sabathiel, H. Ahammer, Noise dependency of algorithms for calculating fractal dimensions in digital images, CSF, **78**, 39-46, (2015)
13. Mandelbrot, B., *The Fractal Geometry of Nature*, (W. H. Freeman, San Francisco, 1982)
14. K. J. Falconer, *Fractal Geometry. Mathematical foundations and Applications*, John Wiley and Sons, England (1990)
15. M. F. Barnsley, *Fractals everywhere*, Academic Press, USA (1988)
16. E. Hadzieva, D. C. Bogatinoska, Lj. Gjergjeska, M. Shuminoska, R. Petreski, Review of the Software Tools for Estimating the Fractal Dimension, S. Loshkovska, S. Koceski (Editors): ICT Innovations **2015**, Web Proceedings, ISSN 1857-7288, p. 201-211 (2015)
17. O. Zmeškal, M. Vesely, M. Nezadal, M. Buchniček, Fractal Analysis of Image Structures, HarFA - Harmonic and Fractal Image Analysis, 3-5, (2001)
18. M. E. Celebi, A. Aslandogan, W. V. Stoecker, Unsupervised Border Detection in Dermoscopy Images, SRT, **13**(4): 454–462 (2007)
19. M. E. Celebi, H. Kingravi, H. Iyatomi, A. Aslandogan, W. V. Stoecker, R. H. Moss, Border Detection in Dermoscopy Images Using Statistical Region Merging, SRT, **14**(3): 347–353 (2008)
20. M. E. Celebi, H. Iyatomi, G. Schaefer, W. V. Stoecker, Lesion Border Detection in Dermoscopy Images, CMIG, **33**(2): 148–153 (2009)
21. M. E. Celebi, Q. Wen, S. Hwang, H. Iyatomi, G. Schaefer, Lesion Border Detection in Dermoscopy Images Using Ensembles of Thresholding Methods, Skin Research and Technology, **19**(1): e252–258 (2013)
22. S. Angenent, E. Pichon, A. Tannenbaum, Mathematical Methods in Medical Image Processing, BAMS. **43**, 365-396 (2006).

MATEC Web of Conferences **76**, 05003 (2016) DOI: 10.1051/matecconf/20167605003
CSCC 2016

Data assimilation experiments with MPIESM climate model

Konstantin Belyaev[1], Andrey Kuleshov[2,a], Ingo Kirchner[3] and Natalia Tuchkova[4]

[1]*Shirshov Institute of Oceanology of RAS, Moscow, Russia*
[2]*Keldysh Institute of Applied Mathematics of RAS, Moscow, Russia*
[3]*Institute of Meteorology, Freie Universität Berlin, Berlin, Germany*
[4] Federal Research Center "Computer Science and Control" of RAS, Moscow, Russia

Abstract. Further development of data assimilation technique and its application in numerical experiments with state-of-the art Max Plank Institute Earth System model have been carried out. In particularly, the stability problem of assimilation is posed and discussed In the experiments the sea surface height data from archive Archiving, Validating and Interpolating Satellite Ocean have been used. All computations have been realized on cluster system of German Climate Computing Center. The results of numerical experiments with and without assimilation were recorded and analyzed. A special attention has been focused on the Arctic zone. It is shown that there is a good coincidence of model tendencies and independent data.

1 Introduction

Data assimilation methodology and the numerical climate modeling are among the most popular research directions over last 20 years. One of the frequently used versions of the numerical climate models is the Max Plank Institute Earth System model (MPIESM), created in Max Plank Institute for Meteorology in Hamburg, Germany. This model version is realized on cluster system in German Climate Computing Center (DKRZ) and consists of several modules including ocean block MPIOM, atmosphere block ECHAM6 and others which are executed in parallel. Details of the MPIESM and its realization can be found in particularly in [1].

Actual climate modeling research also often combines with data assimilation approaches. Data assimilation methods allow correcting the model output by data and obtaining the new initial conditions for future better forecast. The examples of data assimilation methods and their applications to the climate and weather predictions can be found, for instance, in [2]. An example of the MPIESM model in conjunction with data assimilation has been considered in [3].

Several issues are resolving in these types of research. First, the numerical model is turning on the real natural observations and eliminates the unrealistic and completely non-relevant scenarios which could be possible without assimilations. Secondly, the observed variables can correct not only the corresponding model components but also non observed model characteristics. Finally, the regions with badly data coverage can involve the observed information from more data richer domains through model connection and evaluate both local and global temporal and spatial variability.

These and others potential opportunities of correct combinations of models and assimilation methods require further developments all components which produce this progress. The model themselves, their numerical realization including modern parallel schemes and technologies, further information advance, data bases, data assimilation techniques and their mathematical realization lead to this progress. It is important to estimate the correction of data assimilation application for specific model and data base, and to prove that the resulted model fields are physically relevant.

2 Data assimilation method

In the current study the original data assimilation technique, developed earlier in [4, 5] is applied. The method has been applied earlier in conjunction with ocean circulation model HYCOM in [5]. In the current study the same technique is applied together with MPIESM. Along with the data assimilation block the entire model scheme is presented in Figure 1.

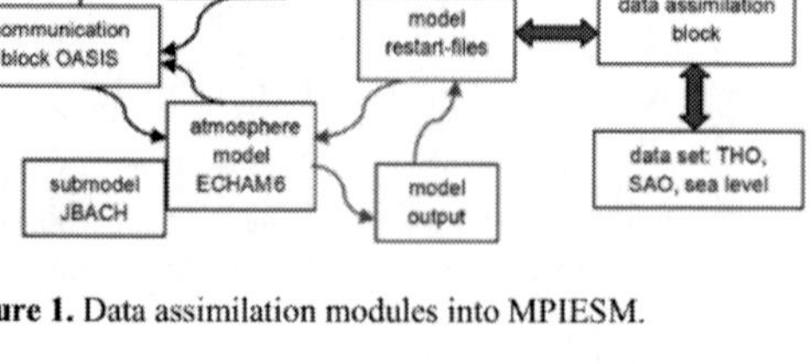

Figure 1. Data assimilation modules into MPIESM.

[a] Corresponding author: andrew_kuleshov@mail.ru

Let the dynamic numerical model be integrated on the time interval $[0,T]$ on the gridded spatial domain and $\mathbf{X}$ be the model state vector. Let the number of grid points be denoted as N_g and the number of unknown model variables be N_{mv}. Then the dimension of $\mathbf{X}$ will be $N_g \times N_{mv} = r$. Let $\mathbf{Y}$ be the observational vector, N_o is the number of observations and each with N_{ov} variables. Then the total dimension of the observational vector state is $N_o \times N_{ov} = N$. Normally, $N_{mv} \geq N_{ov}$ since not all model variables are observed. As it is usual in data assimilation theory two state vectors are introduced, namely the analysis and background states, $\mathbf{X}_a, \mathbf{X}_b$, respectively. They are linked by the equality

$$\mathbf{X}_a = \mathbf{X}_b + \mathbf{K}(\mathbf{Y} - \mathbf{H}\mathbf{X}_b), \tag{1}$$

where, matrix $\mathbf{K}$ is the so-called Kalman gain with dimension $r \times N$ while matrix $\mathbf{H}$ with dimension $N \times r$ is the observation operator that projects the model space into the observational space.

On time interval $[0,T]$ the discretization $0 = t_0 < t_1 < .... < t_{N_T} = T$, $t_{n+1} = t_n + \Delta t_n$ is introduced. On each time interval $[t_n, t_{n+1}]$, $n = 0,1,..., N_T - 1$ model equations are numerically solved and at instant time t_{n+1} data assimilation is performed by

$$\mathbf{X}_{a,n+1} = \mathbf{X}_{b,n+1} + \mathbf{K}_{n+1}(\mathbf{Y}_{n+1} - \mathbf{H}\mathbf{X}_{b,n+1}). \tag{2}$$

Model forecast can be written as a primitive for the function $\mathbf{\Lambda}$

$$\mathbf{X}(t_{n+1}) = \mathbf{X}(t_n) + \int_{t_n}^{t_{n+1}} \mathbf{\Lambda}(\mathbf{X}(\tau))d\tau, \tag{3}$$

where $\mathbf{\Lambda} = \dfrac{\partial \mathbf{X}}{\partial t}$. Then Equation (2) turns into a form

$$\mathbf{X}_{a,n+1} = \mathbf{X}_{an} + \int_{t_n}^{t_{n+1}} \mathbf{\Lambda}(\mathbf{X}(\tau))d\tau + $$
$$+\mathbf{K}_{n+1}\left(\mathbf{Y}_{n+1} - \mathbf{H}\mathbf{X}_{an} - \mathbf{H}\int_{t_n}^{t_{n+1}} \mathbf{\Lambda}(\mathbf{X}(\tau))d\tau\right). \tag{4}$$

The assimilation problem may be formulated as follows: find out the gain matrix $\mathbf{K}$ which will give minimum of the variance state vector $\mathbf{X}$ by minimizing (in the sense of the matrix norm) the diffusion matrix $\mathbf{KQK}'$ under the conditions that the main part of the correction is given by $(\mathbf{I} - \mathbf{KH})\mathbf{\Lambda} = \mathbf{C}$. According to this formulation vector $\mathbf{C}$ is an r-dimensional vector given at all grid points and having certain value for each model variable. In order to mathematically solve this optimization problem, the theory of conditional extremes will be applied.

The matrix $\mathbf{Q}$ is the symmetric and positively defined matrix with the dimension $N \times N$ as it follows from its definition. In the phase-space of rectangular matrices of the dimension $r \times N$ the scalar product is defined as

Now the minimization problem of the functional is considered

$$J(\mathbf{K}) = \|\mathbf{KQK}'\| = \text{tr}(\mathbf{KQK}') \to \min \tag{5}$$

under the condition

$$(\mathbf{I} - \mathbf{KH})\mathbf{\Lambda} = \mathbf{C}. \tag{6}$$

The matrix $\mathbf{KQK}'$ is symmetric and non-negatively defined, its trace is equalled to the sum of its diagonal elements, and also, it is equalled to the sum of eigenvalues of the matrix $\mathbf{KQK}'$. Function $J(\mathbf{K})$ is the convex, quadratic and smooth function of variable $\mathbf{K}$, its derivative is easily calculated. Hence, problem (5),(6) may be solved with the help of classical Lagrangian Multipliers Method.

The Lagrange function is introduced as follows

$$L(\mathbf{K}, \boldsymbol{\lambda}) = \|\mathbf{KQK}'\| + \langle \boldsymbol{\lambda}, \mathbf{KH\Lambda} + \mathbf{\Lambda} - \mathbf{C} \rangle,$$

where $\boldsymbol{\lambda} \in R^r$ are the Lagrangian multipliers.

According to the theory of Lagrangian Multipliers Method matrix $\mathbf{K}$ minimizes (5) and Lagrangian multipliers satisfy the equation

$$\frac{\partial L(\mathbf{K}, \boldsymbol{\lambda})}{\partial \mathbf{K}} = 0.$$

The derivative of the Lagrange function has a form

$$\frac{\partial L(\mathbf{K}, \boldsymbol{\lambda})}{\partial \mathbf{K}} = 2\mathbf{KQ} - \boldsymbol{\lambda}\,\mathbf{H\Lambda}'.$$

Set up it to zero we can find the matrix $\mathbf{K}$ giving the minimum of norm $\|\mathbf{KQK}'\|$ under conditions (6), as the solution of equations

$$\begin{aligned} &\mathbf{KQ} - \frac{1}{2}\boldsymbol{\lambda}\,\mathbf{H\Lambda}' = 0, \\ &(\mathbf{I} - \mathbf{KH})\mathbf{\Lambda} = \mathbf{C}. \end{aligned} \tag{7}$$

Equations (7) are matrix equations which are equivalent to $(r+1) \times N$ linear scalar equations containing the same number of unknown variables. Since the matrix $\mathbf{Q}$ is invertible this system of linear equations always has a unique solution.

The solution of system (7) can be obtained explicitly. It is the following

$$\mathbf{K} = \frac{(\mathbf{\Lambda} - \mathbf{C})(\mathbf{H\Lambda})'\mathbf{Q}^{-1}}{(\mathbf{H\Lambda})'\mathbf{Q}^{-1}\mathbf{H\Lambda}}.$$

Thus, the solution of the problem on the $(n+1)$th step is determined by formulas (2), where

$$\mathbf{K}_{n+1} = \frac{(\mathbf{\Lambda}_{n+1} - \mathbf{C}_{n+1})(\mathbf{H\Lambda}_{n+1})'\mathbf{Q}_{n+1}^{-1}}{(\mathbf{H\Lambda}_{n+1})'\mathbf{Q}_{n+1}^{-1}\mathbf{H\Lambda}_{n+1}},$$

$$\Lambda_{n+1} = \frac{X_{b,n+1} - X_{a,n}}{\Delta t_n}, \quad C_{n+1} = \frac{PY_{n+1} - X_{a,n}}{\Delta t_n},$$

P is the operator that interpolates the values of the vector of observed parameters for all spatial grid area. The projection operator **H** and the covariance matrix **Q** can be defined by its own way for each specific task. Description of the method has been completed. In the proposed method the calculation of the gain matrix takes into account the dynamics of the model alternatively to the classical Kalman filter [6].

3 Results of numerical simulation

The model experiments have been carried out as follows: first the spin up procedure during 250 years has been performed only for the ocean model MPIOM with climate NCEP forcing. Then entire ocean-land-atmosphere coupled model was running for 2 years started from initial conditions gotten after spin up. This data is set up as 2000 year. After that the numerical experiments with data assimilation (analysis) according to aforementioned method and without assimilation (control) have been executed as twin experiments started from 2001. Assimilations are executed from 2008 until 2010 each 3 months. Their results were compared in quantity and in quality between themselves and with the satellite observations data specifically for Arctic region.

In the current work data from archive AVISO (Archiving, Validating and Interpolating Satellite Ocean) dataset has been utilized. These data were downloaded from site www.ifremer.ocean.fr. Data were preprocessed and passed the quality control. Badly recognized or wrongly located data were rejected. Ice concentration data were downloaded from the site http://nsidc.org in Arctic zone (MASAM2: Daily 4-Km Arctic Sea Ice Concentration).

Some examples on 2016 year of model run are presented below. In assimilation experiments the analysis has been calculated each 3 months during full integration period. The difference of Surface Snow Thickness (SSTH) values between analysis and control run is shown on Figure 2. This Figure shows that after assimilation the SSTH valuable decreases which confirms the observed tendency as well as the tendencies given from other models. This decreasing is not uniform, its maximum is observed in Canadian shore and East Siberian. More weak signals are seen in Bare Sea. In general this result fits well to other calculations.

Figure 3 shows the difference between the assimilation and control run relatively the Sea Ice Thickness (SIT) The ice coverage thickness and ice concentration are considered as an important characteristics of Arctic zone. The Figure 3 confirms the tendencies that SIT mostly decreases everywhere in Arctic except relatively narrow zones near Canada shores. On a contrary, in Antarctic the SIT grows everywhere. This result also occurs in a good match with observed data and tendencies given by other models.

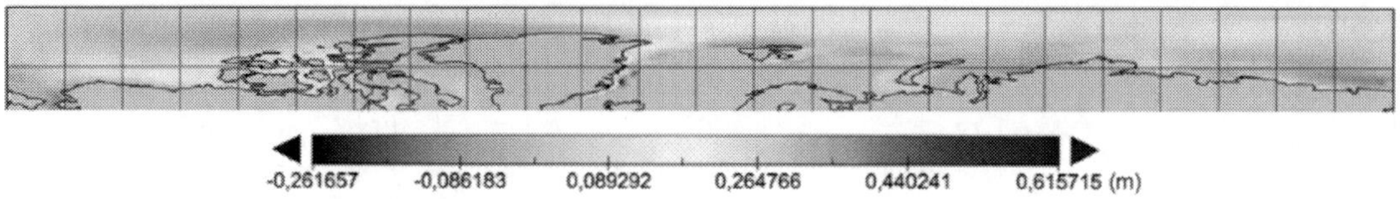

Figure 2. The difference of SSTH (analysis – control) (m) in Antarctic.

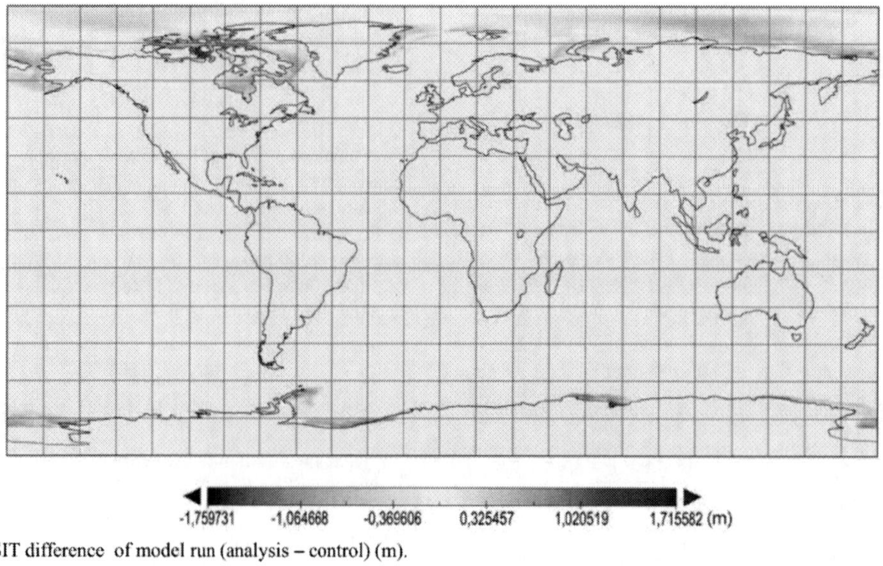

Figure 3. SIT difference of model run (analysis – control) (m).

Figure 4 demonstrates the zonal average of the difference of Sea Ice Thickness between the assimilation and control runs. In is clearly seen that in Antarctic zone this variable grows and grows substantially up to 20 sm (left part of the Figure 4) while in Arctic zone this average significantly falls up to 21 sm except very narrow zone. This also confirms the tendency that in Arctic the Ice thickness decreases over last years and observations of natural data in particular sea level match to this conclusion.

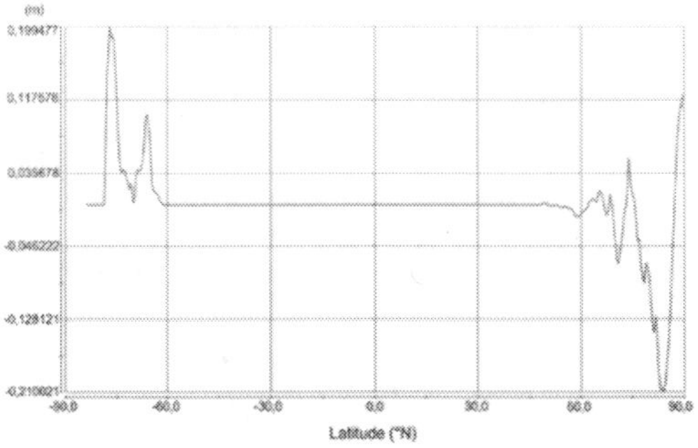

Figure 4. Zonal average of the difference of SIT (assimilation – control) (m).

4 Conclusions

The performed numerical experiments allow making a conclusion that the developed data assimilation method reduces the model error and leads to the results corresponding to the observed data.

Acknowledgements

This research has been supported by Russian Science Foundation, grant 14-11-00434.

References

1. H. Haak, Simulation of Low-Frequency Climate Variability in the North Atlantic Ocean and the Arctic, V.1, Max Planck Institute for Meteorology, 2004.
2. M. Ghil, P. Malnotte-Rizzoli, Adv. Geophys. **33**, 141-266 (1991).
3. K. Belyaev, N. Tuchkova, U. Cubasch, Oceanology **50**(3), 334-344 (2010).
4. C. A. S. Tanajura, and K. Belyaev, Appl. Math. Model. **33**, 2165-2174 (2009).
5. K.P.Belyaev, A.A. Kuleshov, C.A.S. Tanajura, N.P. Tuchkova, Proc. of the 19th Int. Conference CSCC-2015, 192-196 (2015).
6. G. Evensen, Ocean Dyn. **53**, 343-367 (2003).

Image Processing Based Signature Verification Technique to Reduce Fraud in Financial Institutions

Walid Hussein, Mostafa A. Salama and Osman Ibrahim

Faculty of Informatics and Computer Science, The British University in Egypt, Cairo, Egypt

Abstract. Handwritten signature is broadly utilized as personal verification in financial institutions ensures the necessity for a robust automatic signature verification tool. This tool aims to reduce fraud in all related financial transactions' sectors. This paper proposes an online, robust, and automatic signature verification technique using the recent advances in image processing and machine learning. Once the image of a handwritten signature for a customer is captured, several pre-processing steps are performed on it including filtration and detection of the signature edges. Afterwards, a feature extraction process is applied on the image to extract Speeded up Robust Features (SURF) and Scale-Invariant Feature Transform (SIFT) features. Finally, a verification process is developed and applied to compare the extracted image features with those stored in the database for the specified customer. Results indicate high accuracy, simplicity, and rapidity of the developed technique, which are the main criteria to judge a signature verification tool in banking and other financial institutions.

1 Introduction

A signature is a gained behavioural biometric of a user to declare his/her unique identity on printed documents. The demand of authorization based on signature is increased including credit card validation, security systems, banking system, checks, contracts, etc., as shown in figure 1. It is widely used as proof of identity and a socially accepted authentication method in daily life. The system stakeholders are person, organization or banks that need to verify signatures [1, 2]. The stakeholders are Bank's customers who must write their signature, and bank's employees have to verify if the sample signature is the original signature in database, to complete any transaction required on that account. Another customers are organizations' employees: any organization that still depend on paper works, employees must take supervisor's signature [3, 4].

Automatic signature verification system compete the current visual verification that depends mainly on the experience, mood and working environment of the verifier. Moreover, it is difficult for the eyes of any experts to precisely verify the ratios between lines and angles of a genuine signature to a fraud signature [5]. One reason is that signature is just a special way of handwriting that contains complex geometric patterns and often unreadable plots [6]. A signature forgery is replicating the genuine signature by the forger after careful practice. This type of forgeries is called the skilled forgery which harden the signature verification task. The other two types are random forgery where the forger does not know the shape of the original signature, and the simple forgery where the forger knows the shape of the original signature but does not practice enough to increase the similarity value between the fraud and the genuine signatures.

Fig. 1. An example of a handwritten signature to prove user identity on a banking check. Authentication of this signature is the key process to provide the user with an access to his/her bank account.

Automatic verification systems that authenticates the person's signature can be categorized as two types, an online (dynamic) and an offline (static) system [6, 7]. In online systems, dynamic data can be obtained from an online user display suchlike electronic tablet with an instructed pen and in this case, the input is a sequence of dynamic features about the user writing activity such as

Corresponding author: walid.hussein@bue.edu.eg

the applied pressure, speed of writing, etc. On the other hand, in the offline systems, signatures are written in a paper which is processed as two dimensional image and has been converted to the system with the aid of scanner or camera [8, 9]. The signature verification architecture usually starts by extracting the features of the genuine signatures followed by classification of a set of genuine and skilled test signatures. The offline features can be categorized as Global and local features, the Global features describe the image as whole the image size, while local features are commonly extracted by partitioning the image into a grid and extract the features in each of its parts [10, 11]. Lately, Interest points are picked using SIFT (Scale-Invariant Feature transform) [SIFT] and/or SURF (Speed-up Robust Features) [SIFT] to perform the signature verification task [12, 13]. These models extract the interest points in each image, then extract the features/descriptors for each interest point to verify the matching between signatures. The accuracy of the solution of these methods depends on the number of matches of the genuine signatures to other genuine and forged signatures [14, 15].

The work proposed in this paper uses a different approach in utilizing the SIFT/SURF extractors, where the matching depends on the summing up of the Euclidian distance between the interest points in the two images. The work applied here is based on the database of offline genuine and skilled forged signatures extracted in the work in [16] and in [17]. The results shows 95% classification accuracy which is higher than that of current research.

The rest of this paper is organized as follows: Section 2 presents the previous work of applying machine learning tools to perform the signature verification task. Section 3 describes the proposed approach, while the experimental work and discussion appear in section 4 and finally the conclusion is in section 5.

2 Materials and Methods

The signature image is initially pre-processed to facilitate the job of the feature extractor technique. The pre-processing includes the cropping of the signature area, removal of the noise, banalization of coloured image to grayscale one and finally edge detection or smoothing of the signature lines. Features are categorized into two types, global and grid features. Global features define the entire structure of the signature like the height, height-to-width ratio, and the image projection. Maximum horizontal and vertical projections represent the row and column that contain the maximum number of black pixels respectively. The second type of features is the grid features where a virtual grid is created of 12x8 segments for describing the detailed parts of the image. Pixels density, pixels distribution, and predominant axial slant are examples of the extracted grid features.
The training is applied on a set of genuine signatures using either a simple distance calculation method or a complex machine learning techniques. This approach is considered a unique method that multiple features are extracted which have global features such as statistical features, image gradient came from distribution of pixels in a signature image and descriptors, the classification contains variation between signature of the same user and done a distribution in distance space. For any tested signature the method gains a distribution which is compared with the saved distributions and a similarity between them is obtained. This method does not utilize set of forgery signature in the training. The approach utilizes the geometric center for feature extraction. This center gains both horizontal and vertical of the signature. The classification and description is done by Euclidean classifier which defines vectors between two signatures. This method tested by database of 20 writer, 10 signatures for genuine and 10 for forgeries. The method achieved 11.4% AER. The use of complex machine learning techniques like Hidden Markov model, support vector machine and neural network show better results in the domain of Hand-written signature verification. Lately, SIFT and SURF detectors and extractors show better results in the field of offline signature verification.

2.1 SIFT/SURF algorithms

Scale Invariant Feature Transform (SIFT) is powerful and successful approach to do feature detection. Speeded Up Robust Features (SURF) is based on the same steps and principle but it uses different schema and provides better and faster result. The SURF algorithm is divided into main two steps: firstly, interest points are detected. Secondly, interest point description is performed. Both of these steps depend on a scale space representation.

SIFT algorithm: SIFT Generates for the image, another images of 1/2, 1/4 and 1/8 of the original sizes. Then for each image apply the Gaussian blurring operator on the image of intensity function I(x, y) as shown in equation 1.

$$L(x, y, kn * \sigma) = G(x, y, kn * \sigma) * I(x, y) \qquad (1)$$

Equation 1 is applied for different scales for all image sizes (octave), such that $\sigma = kn*\sigma$ values where $k = 1.2$ and $n = 0, 1, 2, 3, 4$. Then apply the lablacian of Gaussian approximation, DOG, for each two successive layer in each octave as shown in equation 2.

$$DoG(x,y) = (L(x,y, kn*\sigma) - L(x,y, kn-1*\sigma) \qquad (2)$$

Then extract the potential interest points, by detecting the local extrema for each point in 3x3x3 neighbourhood window. Remove all points smaller than a specific threshold, and accept only points that match with the Harris corners. Finally, for each point of interest, 128 descriptor is extracted. It shows the orientation and magnitude of the 4x4 grids surrounding the interest point in the eight 45-angled regions.

SURF algorithm: Meanwhile, SURF excludes the step of creating different images in its processing. It uses Hessian matrix that expresses the local changes in area of each point in x and y direction as shown in equation 3.

$$H(p,\sigma) = \begin{bmatrix} L_{xx}(p,\sigma) & L_{xy}(p,\sigma) \\ L_{xy}(p,\sigma) & L_{yy}(p,\sigma) \end{bmatrix} \quad (3)$$

Where, $L_{xx}(p, \sigma)$ is the convolution of the image with the second derivative of the Gaussian as displayed in equation 4.

$$L_{xx}(p,\sigma) = I(p) * \frac{\partial^2 g(\sigma)}{\partial x^2} \quad (4)$$

A variable sized filter of a corresponding scale σ is used to form a scale space images. Afterwards, based on the sum of Haar wavelet responses, construct a square window centered around the interest point. This is to select dominant orientation of interest points (x,y) weighted Haar-wavelet responses (dx,dy). This allows the selection of only a single $\pi/3$ region along each of the selected orientation, out of the 8 regions in SIFT. The 4 values of orientation dx,dy and magnitude |dx|,|dy| of each point (x,y) is considered for the 4x4 grids in the 16x16 window around the interest point, which will form, 4x4x4, 64 descriptors vector for each feature.

3 The proposed signature verification model

The first step in the proposed verification system is the pre-processing of the image. In image pre-processing step, training and testing signature images are passed into this step. The main purpose of this phase is to make signature image ready for extracting features. The pre-processing phase includes grey scale conversion and binarization.

The image is converted into grey scale: Binary image is converted into grey scale to make process easier and feature extraction more accurate.

Binarizing image: In this step, grey scale image is converted to black and white image using a reasonable threshold. This will make signature clearer as it will be in black and the background will be in white. Threshold filtering is considered the simplest way to binarize an image. Threshold filtering does image binarization by using particular threshold value and intestines of image pixel. All pixels in the signature image with intestines equal all higher than specified threshold value will be converted to white otherwise, all pixels with intensities lower than threshold value will be converted to black which will make signature image black and white. The filter accepts grey scale images for processing, and the optimal threshold values differ from image to image and are obtained after deep investigation of the trained image. The next step is applying the SURF / SIFT feature extraction method as described above. The final step is the verification/matching method. This is done by calculating the Euclidean distance between the descriptors. For every key point in the descriptor in the original image, two closed neighbours are computed and the distance will be taken to match between them and find similarity. The matching of each two signatures is applied based on the number of key points in each one as shown in figure 2.

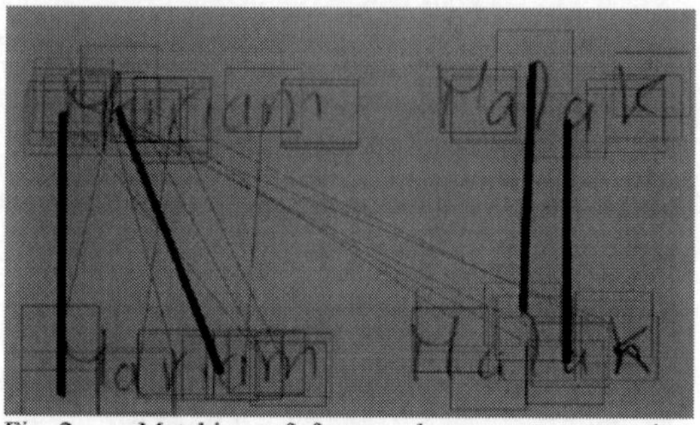

Fig. 2. Matching of features between two genuine signature images

4 Experimental Results

4.1 Accuracy of the proposed model

The proposed model is applied on two benchmark datasets available in [16] and [17]. For the first dataset [16], the results in figure 3 and 4 show that, the first 4 points are genuine-genuine matchings, while the rest of the points are genuine-forged matchings. In this test, 30 forged signatures are tested for verification of signatures of user one and user two. The defined threshold here is applied as the two points out of four which have the lowest Euclidian distance. Accordingly, the results shows nearly 85% classification accuracy of proving the forgery of user one and 92% classification accuracy for user two, as displayed in figure 3 and figure 4; respectively. Note that these results are based on the Euclidian distance values, not based on the number of matchings.

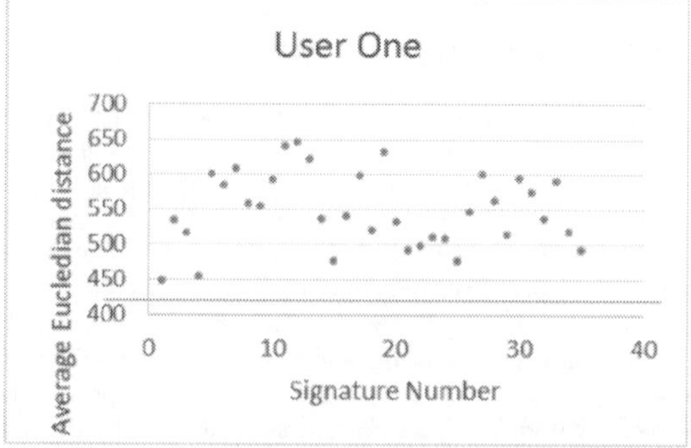

Fig. 3. Genuine-Genuine vs Genuine-Forged signatures for user one.

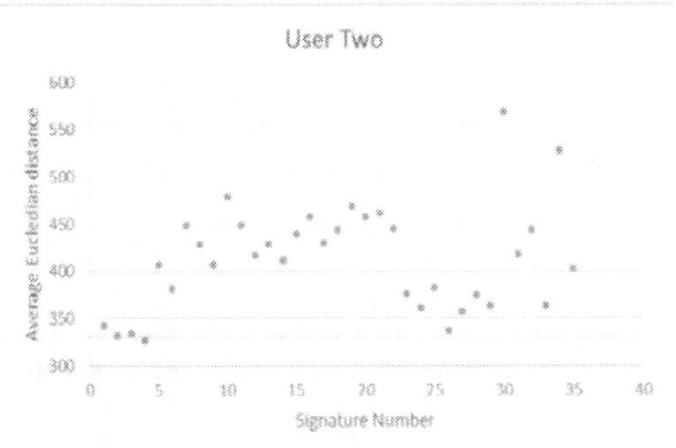

Fig. 4. Genuine-Genuine vs Genuine-Forged signatures for user two.

The same test is applied on the second dataset [17], but is applied by comparing between the first two genuine signatures and between the first genuine signature and another 3 forged signatures, the results are 100% verification accuracy of the forged signatures.

4.2 Parametric investigation of the model

A parametric study is applied in this work by changing threshold value in SURF detector. SURF detector depends on the Hessian matrix to find all interest points in a particular image. SURF divides the signature image into using second order Gaussian kernel and computes these kernels with box filter. The main function in EmguCV library is to detect interest points using SURF with Hessian threshold value. Experimental results show that best value for hessian Threshold could be from 300 to 500.

The SURF detector considers those features in the signature image whose hessian is larger than a specified hessian threshold. Therefore, as high specified threshold value, as less key points in the image will be taken by detector but with more accuracy. A low specified threshold, high key point will be taken.

When the Hessian threshold is 500, key points are 329 and when it is 100, key points are 1004. 1004 key points means many unnecessary key points is extracted from the feature , many calculation will be done which will increase the computational time of the algorithm and feature extracting will be not accurate. Therefore, after testing multiple signatures with different hessian threshold values best value for hessian threshold could be from 300 to 500.

The chart below in figure 5 shows the relation between hessian threshold value with the accuracy and the number of the detected points. Therefore, the relation of hessian threshold value and number of interest point is inversely proportional.as shown in fig.5, higher hessian threshold value will result in less key points and lower hessian threshold will result more key points.

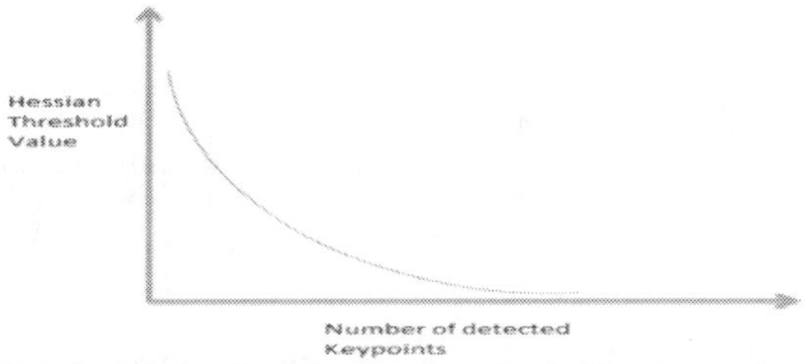

Fig. 5. Relation between hessian threshold value and Number of interest points.

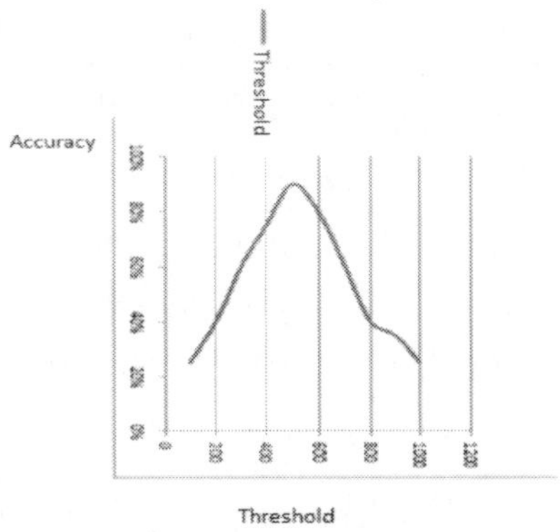

Fig. 6. Relation between hessian threshold value and Accuracy of SURF detector.

As shown in fig.6, after testing multiple signatures with different hessian threshold value shows that the best accuracy of the software is when hessian threshold value between 300 and 500. As shown in the figure 5 above, higher hessian threshold value high accuracy and lower threshold value low accuracy until 500 after hessian threshold; value bigger than 500 , gives less detected points in the signature image which will make accuracy of the software less so the best value of hessian threshold is 500.

5 Conclusion

Although the existence of an automatic signature verification tool is necessary, it is not yet applied in most of the financial institutions. The reason is that most of the currently available tools work with a highest accuracy of ca. 80%, which makes them not reliable in the verification task. For many years, researchers are trying to develop more robust signature verification tools using the advances in image processing algorithms.

The main objective of this work is to offer an economically and efficient offline handwritten signature verification system, in order to achieve the objective multiple methods have been reviewed and surf features algorithm is used in this paper as strong image descriptor. Databases of signatures were collected and saved containing known writer's signatures. The proposed model was successfully verified signatures of users with a lowest accuracy of 85%, indicating its promising implementation and making a room for more improvements to be researched and investigated.

The future work of the current study is to enhance the feature extraction step of the algorithm by adopting features related to cross correlation, and signature energy and skewness. Finally, an automatic feature extraction tool may be developed to predict the relevant features, which define each signature and reduce the verification effort.

References

1. J. Chambers, W. Yan, A. Garhwal, and M. Kankanhalli (2015) Currency security and forensics: a survey, Multimed Tools Appl vol. 74, pp. 4013-4043.
2. Bhanu Priya Taneja, Navdeep Kaur, (2015) Biometric System Based on Off-Line Signatures, International Journal of Advanced Research in Computer and Communication Engineering, vol. 4(5) , May 2015.
3. Maykin Warasart and Pramote Kuacharoen (2012) Paper-based Document Authentication using Digital Signature and QR Code, 2012 4TH International Conference on Computer Engineering and Technology (ICCET 2012).
4. Vijaypal Singh Dhaka, Mukta Rao, Manu Pratap Singh (2009) Signature Verification on Bank Checks Using Hopfield Neural Network, KARPAGAM Journal of Computer Science, vol 3(4).
5. Ilkhan Cüceloğlu,Hasan Ogul (2014) Detecting handwritten signatures in scanned documents, 19th Computer Vision Winter Workshop, Krtiny, Czech Republic, February 3–5, 2014.
6. Biswajit Halder, Rajkumar Darbar, Utpal Garain, Abhoy Ch. Mondal (2014) Analysis of Fluorescent Paper Pulps for Detecting Counterfeit Indian Paper Money, Information Systems Security, series Lecture Notes in Computer Science, vol. 8880, pp 411-424.
7. Jain, U.A.; Patil, N.N. (2014) A comparative study of various methods for offline signature verification, in Issues and Challenges in Intelligent Computing Techniques (ICICT), 2014 International Conference, pp.760-764, 7-8 Feb. 2014.
8. Anu Rathi, Divya Rathi, Parmanand Astya (2012) Offline Handwritten Signature Verification By Using Pixel Based Method, International Journal of Engineering Research & Technology, vol. 1(7), September - 2012.
9. Saroj Ramadas, Geethu P.C (2015) Comparative Study On Offline Handwritten Signature Verification Schemes, International Journal of Advanced Research Trends in Engineering and Technology (IJARTET), vol. 2(10), March 2015.
10. Karrar Neamah, Dzulkifli Mohamad, Tanzila Saba, Amjad Rehman (2014) Discriminative Features Mining for Offline Handwritten Signature Verification, 3D Res (2014) 5:2
11. Roy, Sayantan, Maheshkar Sushila (2014) Offline Signature Verification using Grid based and Centroid based Approach, International Journal of Computer Applications, vol. 86(8), pp. 0975–8887, January 2014.
12. Javier Ruiz-del-Solar, Christ Devia, Patricio Loncomilla, Felipe Concha (2012) Offline Signature Verification Using Local Interest Points and Descriptors, Progress in Pattern Recognition, Image Analysis and Applications, of the series Lecture Notes in Computer Science, vol. 5197, pp. 22-29.
13. Malik, M.I.; Liwicki, M.; Dengel, A.; Uchida, S.; Frinken, V. (2014) Automatic Signature Stability Analysis and Verification Using Local Features, in Frontiers in Handwriting Recognition (ICFHR), 2014 14th International Conference, pp. 621-626, 1-4 Sept. 2014.
14. Rajpal Kaur, Pooja Choudhary (2015) Offline Signature Verification in Punjabi based on SURF Features and Critical Point Matching using HMM, International Journal of Computer Applications , vol. 111(16), pp. 0975–8887, February 2015.
15. J. Ruiz-Shulcloper and W.G. Kropatsch (2008) Signature Verification Using Local Interest Points and Descriptors, CIARP 2008, LNCS 5197, pp. 22–29, 2008.
16. Javier Galbally, Moises Diaz-Cabrera, Miguel A. Ferrer, Marta Gomez-Barrero, Aythami Morales, Julian Fierrez (2015) On-line signature recognition through the combination of real dynamic data and synthetically generated static data, Pattern Recognition, vol. 48(9), September 2015, pp. 2921–2934.
17. Marcus Liwicki, Michael Blumenstein, Elisa van den Heuvel, Charles E.H. Berger, Reinoud D. Stoel, Bryan Found, Xiaohong Chen, Muhammad Imran Malik (2011) SigComp11: Signature Verification Competition for On- and Offline Skilled Forgeries, in proceedings of 11th Int. Conference on Document Analysis and Recognition.

Assessment of the infarct size with ST-elevation from high-resolution standard and orthogonal ECG leads

Mikhail Matveev

Institute of Biophysics and Biomedical Engineering, BAS, 1113 Sofia, Bulgaria

Abstract. The high-resolution electrocardiography is known to be a useful tool for extraction and analysis of low-amplitude signal components. We found the high-resolution standard and synthesized orthogonal electrocardiography leads may be useful for precise evaluation of the zone of acute myocardial infarct necrosis. We found high-resolution electrocardiography may be useful for precise location of the site of the myocardial necrosis and assessment of the severity of impaired left-ventricle systolic function of patients with ST-elevation myocardial infarct (STEMI) in the acute phase. High-resolution (1 MHz) ECG from 4 groups were collected: healthy controls (13), patients with anterior (10), inferior STEMI (19) and 12 patients with infero-lateral AMI). The three orthogonal leads X, Y, Z were synthesized from the 12-standard leads by known transformation. The possibility for facilitated and fast performance of this examination in clinical conditions, including emergency, the lack of necessity of specially trained staff for carrying out the examination and interpretation of the results, as well as the very low prime cost, make this electrophysiological method very suitable for application in the routine clinical practice for qualitative and quantitative assessment of patients with acute coronary syndromes.

1 Introduction

In principle the signal-averaged high-resolution electrocardiography (SAECG) is a technique involving computerized analysis of small segments of a standard electrocardiography (ECG) in order to detect late potentials [1,2]. It allows subtraction and analysis of low-amplitude components in the signal, containing important diagnostics information, but inadmissible for analysis using conventional 12-channel ECG. The high resolution SAECG and vectorcardiography (VCG) was employed recently as a method for qualitative and quantitative diagnosis of patients with acute myocardial infarct (AMI). The existing scarce data in world-wide literature about quantitative assessment of patients with AMI by SAECG suggest very high diagnostic value of this method [3-6]. In this research we studied the possibilities to create standards, characterizing ST-elevation myocardial infarct with different location and size using synthesized from SAECG orthogonal X, Y and Z leads and VCG loops.

2 ECG Data

High-resolution ECG recordings collected with the developed ECG data acquisition system [1]. The analysis involved 45 ECG recordings collected from 15 patients (average age 70±12.5 years) at the intensive coronary unit of the Department of Internal Medicine, Medical University - Sofia, all of them with clinical symptoms, ECG and laboratory signs for AMI with ST-elevation:

- typical angina pain with duration more than 30 min;
- ST-elevation above 1 mm in two or more neighbouring peripheral leads, or more than 2 mm in two or more neighbouring precordial leads;
- Serum creatine kinase (CK) activity levels above 180 U/L, MB-fraction of CK (MB-CK) above 15 U/L, MB-CK above 10% from the initial CK value;
- Onset of the clinical symptoms up to 24 hours before admission to hospital.

We involved into analysis recordings from *Public Accessible PTB Diagnostic ECG Database [2]* - high-resolution ECG database (12 standard leads + 3 orthogonal leads), because it is collected from healthy volunteers and patients with different heart diseases, which is supported with complete information about the diagnosis, haemodynamics and therapy for each patient. We randomly selected 13 healthy controls (age 43.4± 17.8 years) without history, ECG and laboratory indications for cardiovascular or non-cardiac disease, which could influence the ECG potentials. Moreover, we selected 41 patients (age 57.9±12.3 years) with acute AMI (19 patients with inferior AMI, 10 patients with anterior AMI, 12 patients with infero-lateral AMI), which have ECG recordings between 24 to 72 hours from the infarction date.

3 Methods

Corresponding author: mgm@biomed.bas.bg

We study an approach for analysis of high-resolution ECG recordings aiming to provide adequate information about the infarct size and localization. The method is based on assessment of the orthogonal leads X,Y,Z (OECG). Since the developed wireless ECG acquisition system operates only with 12 standard leads, we apply transformations (Eq.1) [3] to derive the synthesized orthogonal Xo,Yo, Zo leads:

$$\begin{aligned} Xo &= 0.4*II-0.8*(II+III)/3+0.2*V5+0.5*V6+0.1*V4 \\ Yo &= 0.3*III+0.8*II+0.5*(II+III)/3-0.2*V5-0.3*V6 \\ Zo &= -0.1*III-0.2*II+0.4*(II+III)/3-0.3*V1-0.1*V2-0.1*V3 \\ &-0.2*V4-0.1*V5+0.4*V6 \end{aligned} \quad (1)$$

Between lead I and lead II in the standard ECG, there is 60^0 zone with projection on the left ventricle, which is not directly reflected by any of the leads [4]. Therefore, to supply additional information, we apply synhresys of the orthogonal X, Y, Z leads, but lead *III*=2*(*II*+*avR*) is substituted in transformations (Eq.1) with inversion of the lead *avR* (-*avR*). In this way, we examined the possibility for improvement of the AMI diagnostics.

The most informative indexes extracted from the orthogonal leads, which show maximal deflection compared to the respective norms, are assessed for each infarct localization type. Taking for a basis an amplitude change of $\Delta A=1mm$ for these indexes, we calculate the equivalent increase in the serum enzyme activity [5]:

$$\Delta E = \Delta A * (E2 - E1)/(A2 - A1) \quad [U/L], \quad (2)$$

where $E1$ is the initial enzyme value [U/L], $E2$ is the peak enzyme activity [U/L], $A1$ is the initial index amplitude [mm], $A2$ corresponds to the index value when maximal amplitude change is reached [mm]. Since patients' admission to hospital after the beginning of the clinical symptoms varies in time and ECG recordings before AMI are usually missing, we substitute $A1$ with the mean value of the respective index for healthy controls. For the same reason (absence of initial 'normal' levels and physiologic variability of CK and CK-MB), we substitute $E1$ with the maximal norm level (180 U/L for CK, 15 U/L for CK-MB).

4 Results

The practical implementation of the high-resolution ECG acquisition system is demonstrated in Fig.1. Here is presented an example of ECG recordings (12 standard leads + synthesized orthogonal leads) from a patient with acute anterior AMI, which is admitted within 24 h from the beginning of the clinical symptoms. Taking into account that the high-resolution ECG recordings of the healthy controls do not contain any of the components, which are characteristic for the acute or undergone myocardionecrosis, we estimated the mean values of the indexes, which are known to show changes during lesion and myocardial necrosis [6, 7]. The indexes are measured from: (i) Frank orthogonal leads (X,Y,Z); (ii) the synthesized orthogonal leads (X1,Y1,Z1); (iii) the synthesized orthogonal leads with inversion of the lead *avR* (X2,Y2,Z2). The results are summarized in Table 1. to Table 4.

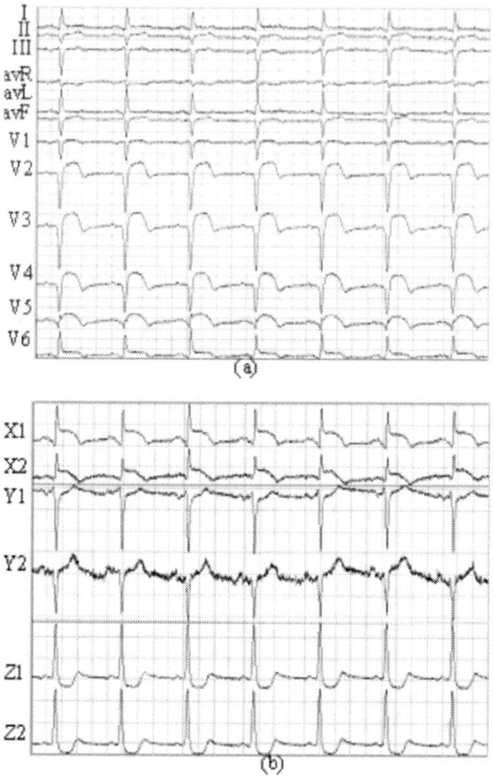

Figure 1. Example of high-resolution ECG recordings: (a) 12 standard leads; (b) synthesized orthogonal leads

Table 1. Indexes for healty controls (N=13).

OECG Leads	Q-wave amplitude [mm]	R-wave amplitude [mm]	ST-segment Elevation [mm]
X	1,6±1,4	15,7±6,8	-
X1	0,8±0,3	14,6±6,5	-
X2	0,7±06	4,95±4,0	-
Y	0,9±0,	10,3±5,7	-
Y1	1,4±0,6	10,0±6,6	-
Y2	1,6±1,1	24,9±11,98	0,85±0,2
Z	3,6±2,1	7,3±2,9	-
Z1	2,7±1,98	7,3±2,5	-
Z2	2,5±1,8	7,95±2,5	-

Table 2. Indexes for patients with inferior AMI (N=19).

OECG Leads	Q-wave amplitude [mm]	R-wave amplitude [mm]	ST-segment Elevation [mm]
X	2 (n=1)	12,6±4,33	2 (n=1)
X1	1.5 (n=1)	12,11±2.2	2 (n=1)
X2	1,25±0,35	[illegible]74±3,31	1,5 (n=1)
Y	2,43±1,66	6,[illegible]5±2,99	0,86±0,84
Y1	4,17±2,40	5,75±2,85	0,92±0,99
Y2	4,38±2,55	18,87±7,1	1,26±1,39
Z	5,32±3,39	6,83±3,69	0,13±0,28
Z1	5,11±3,87	8,36±4,47	0,21±0,38
Z2	4,48±3,64	8,5±4,57	0,21±0,38

Table 3. Indexes for patients with anterior AMI (N=10).

OECG Leads	Q-wave amplitude [mm]	R-wave amplitude [mm]	ST-segment Elevation [mm]
X	0,75±1,06	10,75±2,18	0,37±0,69
X1	0,75±1,06	10,0±2,07	0,37±0,69
X2	1,[illegible]±2,15	1,0±1,30	0,06±0,17
Y	1,37±1,66	9,56±4,51	0,68±1,27
Y1	1,44±2,49	7,68±5,47	1,0±1,38
Y2	2,37±2,66	25,62±10,5	1,25±1,77
Z	1,43±1,29	7,81±4,17	0
Z1	1,06±0,94	11,12±2,23	0
Z2	1,06±0,94	11,81±2,17	0

Table 4. Indexes for patients with inf.-lat. AMI (N=10).

OECG Leads	Q-wave amplitude [mm]	R-wave amplitude [mm]	ST-segment Elevation [mm]
X	1,3±1,25	15,5±3,83	0,35±0,57
X1	1,1±0,99	15,4±3,88	0,35±0,57
X2	0,55±0,95	[illegible]5±6,0	0,15±0,33
Y	3,6±2,13	5,6±2,35	0,4±0,45
Y1	6,35±2,59	0,95±1,70	0,5±0,57
Y2	6,25±4,03	15,05±8,8	1,15±0,91
Z	3,95±2,56	5,25±2,53	0,1±0,31
Z1	4,2±2,23	5,85±3,30	0,05±0,15
Z2	4,05±2,20	6,25±3,33	0

We determined the indexes, which show the most significant dynamics for the respective infarct localization compared to the norm of the healthy controls (Table 1):

- inferior AMI: Q-wave amplitude in Z1, Z2, Y1, Y2; R-wave amplitude in Y1 и Y2;
- anterior AMI: Q-wave amplitude in X2, Y2; R-wave amplitude in X, X1, X2, Y1;
- infero-lateral AMI: Q-wave amplitude in Y1,Y2, Z1, Z2; R-wave amplitude in Y1,Y2;

Table 5 contains the equivalent changes of the calculated serum activity (CK and CK-MB) for Q-wave and R-wave amplitude change of 1 mm. The correlation between the electrophysiological and enzyme variables gives the possibility for estimation of the volume of the necrotic tissue in gram/equivalents, after preliminary calculation on the basis of serum peak levels of the enzyme activity, taken from [4,6].

Table 5. Enzyme activity increase for 1 mm Q-wave and R-wave amplitude change.

Inferior AMI		
INDEX	CK [U/L]	CK-MB [U/L]
$Z1_Q$	348,6±168,5	26,8±3,7
$Z2_Q$	249,8±28,8	28,1±4,3
$Y1_Q$	433,2±48,9	14,8±2,7
$Y2_Q$	668,1±283,4	13,9±4,2
$Y1_R$	175,5±76,2	18,7±2,1
$Y2_R$	76,9±13,9	18,4±1,6
Infero-lateral AMI		
INDEX	CK [U/L]	CK-MB [U/L]
$Y1_Q$	166,55±88,9	14,1±3,9
$Y2_Q$	201,1±97,7	14,9±2,9
$Z1_Q$	263,0±288,4	28,1±4,9
$Z2_Q$	154,6±66,2	28,5±4,7
$Y1_R$	179,8±101,8	19,0±1,4
$Y2_R$	103,8±64,8	19,5±0,8
Anterior AMI		
INDEX	CK [U/L]	CK-MB [U/L]
$X2_Q$	266,0±193,7	15,6±6,7
$Y2_Q$	647,5±427,7	14,3±4,9
$X1_R$	159,6±63,7	5,48±2,3
$X2_R$	115,8±47,1	6,88±3,06
$Y1_R$	168,8±3,7	3,1±0,88

References

1. PTB Diagnostic ECG Database. URL: http://physionet.org/physiobank/database/ptbdb/.
2. Levkov Ch. Orthogonal electrocardiogram derived from the limb and chest electrodes of the conventional 12-lead system, Medical & Biol. Engineering & Computing, **25**:155-164 (1987).
3. Menown A., Adgey A. Improving the ECG classification of inferior and lateral myocardial infarction by inversion of lead aVR, Heart, **83**:657-660 (2000).
4. Hamidi E., Vl. Ivanov, M. Matveev. Size of the necrotic zone after acute myocardial infarct, estimated by electrocardiographic parameters and serial activity of serum enzymes for myocardial necrosis, Modern Medicine, **11**:39-44 (1987) (in bulgarian).
5. Birnbaum Y., G. Wagner. The initial electrocardiographic pattern in acute myocardial infarction: Correlation with infarct size, Journal of Electrocardiology, **32**:122-127 (1999).
6. Grøttum P., J. Kjekshus. A comparison of cumulated CK Release with three vectorcardiographic methods of estimating myocardial infarct size, Journal of Electrocardiology, **19**:337-346 (1986).
7. Matveev M., V. Krasteva, St. Naydenov, T. Donova. Possibilities of signal-averaged orthogonal and vector electrocardiography for locating and size evaluation of acute myocardial infarction with ST-elevation, Anatol J Cardiol. **Suppl.1**:193-197 (2007).

Segment-based Melody Matching for Query By Singing/Humming

Wen-Hsing Lai[a], Chi-Yong Lee

Department of Computer and Communication Engineering, National Kaohsiung First University of Science and Technology, No. 1, University Rd., Yanchao Dist., Kaohsiung City 824, Taiwan

Abstract. Segment-based melody matching approaches are proposed to solve the problems of pitch instability, tempo inconsistency, and puff noise of singing/humming in Query By Singing/Humming system. Instead of comparing frame by frame from the beginning and trying different scaling ratio, our segment-based approaches reduce the computation complexity by jumping to the possible segment boundary and using the segment ratio as scaling ratio. Our methods predict segment boundary candidates in query singing/humming and songs in database by detecting the abrupt change of pitch curve, match segment pair, scale each segment linearly and calculate the distance. The top 10 recognition rate of our method can reach 70.6%. Our method reduce computational load and performs better in situations of puff noise and inconsistent tempo than popular global Linear Scaling method.

1 Introduction

Due to the vigorous development of the Internet, a large amount of information flow on the web, which makes information more easily accessed. However, in this flood of information, how to find the information needed becomes a major issue and challenge. Keyword search engine is created, for quickly finding the information we want. Similar situation happens on the large amount of music on the Internet. When we think of a piece of music but do not know the song title or artist, how can we find it? Query By Singing/Humming, (QBSH) [1-7] is the technology developed for this demand.

QBSH is a melody recognition system by using a singing or humming query. The system will compare the singing or humming query with the songs stored in database, and report the most similar song to the user. The mostly used feature for recognition is frame-level pitch or note. Pitch information is generally gotten from pitch tracking algorithm [6]. The song with the smallest feature distance with the query is the most possible answer.

There are currently several techniques of QBSH. The most common ones are Linear Scaling (LS), Dynamic Time Warping (DTW) or their combinations [3][5]. Although the recognition rate of DTW, searching for the path of alignment with the minimum pitch distance, is higher, the computational complexity is also higher and the recognition time is longer. LS, which simply stretches or compresses the query pitch contour globally and matches it frame-by-frame (one pitch point per frame) with the target pitch contour, is simpler. It uses more intuitive linear stretch. Its computational complexity is lower and recognition speed is faster.

But when LS encounter the situation of short time puffs, which usually appears at the beginning of humming or singing, or unstable tempo, which is also very common especially for amateurs, the recognition rate will decline because of its simple global scaling. Besides, we do not know the singing or humming starting position in songs and we do not know the exact humming tempo variation, thus we generally need to compare from the beginning frame by frame with different scaling factor, which increases computational load. We try to solve the puff and unstable tempo problems and speed the recognition time by introducing segment-based approaches.

The segment-based methods we propose determine segment boundaries of query singing/humming and songs in database firstly, and then choose the possible segment matching pair, and stretch each segment by linear scaling. We hope the segment-based methods can eliminate the recognition inaccuracy caused by puff noise and tempo inconsistency. Since the query singing/humming may not start right from the very beginning frame, jumping to the possible segment boundary directly instead of comparing frame by frame from beginning can also reduce computational load.

This paper is organized as follows. The next section will introduce the background of LS, which our methods are based on. Then, the segment-based methods we propose are presented in the third section. Experimental results will be shown in the following section. Finally, conclusions and future works are discussed.

2 Linear Scaling

[a] Corresponding author: lwh@nkfust.edu.tw

In this paper, we propose segment-based Linear Scaling approaches. Segment boundaries are predicted and the query and songs in database are split into segments for matching. Inside each matching segment, LS matching is used. To understand it, the traditional LS is introduced in this section.

LS [6][7] is also called uniform scaling or global scaling. It is a frame-based method for melody recognition. Typical LS working on frame-level pitch uses interpolation to uniformly expand or compress the pitch curve of query singing/humming, and compare the scaled pitch curve with the songs in database. Different scaling ratio are tried and compared. Distances to all songs in database with different scaling ratio are calculated. The song in database with the minimum distance is the most likely song for the query singing/humming.

3 Segment-based approaches

In the segment-based methods we proposed, firstly, for query singing/humming and songs in database, we select the points with abrupt change of pitch as the segment boundary candidates. Secondly, from the segment boundary candidates in query singing/humming, four segment boundaries, the first, the last, the highest, and the second highest boundaries, are chosen. Between the segment boundaries, there are three segments. Because the query singing/humming does not necessarily correspond to the very beginning of midi in database, the corresponding matching segment boundary in midi is searched from the midi segment boundary candidates with the same rising or decreasing pitch trend. For all possible matching pairs, we calculate the distance of three segments. Inside segment, linear scaling is applied to stretch or compress the length. The scaling ratio is simply the ratio of segment length, so the query segment is scaled to the same length with the midi segment. Since the expansion or compression of segment and key shifting bring bias in calculating distance, distance normalization, which normalizes the distance by the length of the segment, and key transposition, which shifts the pitch to the same mean as that of midi song in database, are used. The segment pair with the shortest distance is the best match. After compare all the songs in database, the song with the shortest distance is the answer to the query singing/humming.

Our four approaches of the first step, selecting segment boundary candidates, are introduced in the following subsections. We call them "Cross *n* Semitones", "Moving Average", "Composite Moving Average", and "Combination of Cross *n* Semitones and Composite Moving Average".

3.1. Cross n Semitones

"Cross *n* Semitones" selects the points with pitch variation over *n* semitones within *m* frames as possible segment boundary candidates. If *n* is large, we get fewer candidate points. If *n* is small, we get more candidate points, but too small variation means they may be just caused by pitch drift phenomenon instead of song trend, and such selection of *n* may cause mistake. For convenience, when *n* equals 3, it is called "Cross 3 Semitones".

3.2 Moving Average

There are drifts in the pitch of query singing/humming. The technique of moving average on pitch curve can smooth out short-term fluctuations, reflecting the long-term trend, so we can reduce the interference in the process of selecting the segment boundary candidates. When the window length of moving average is *w*, we call it *w*MA. For example, 20MA means moving average with window length 20. The greater the *w* is, the smoother the pitch curve is. Over smooth curve reduces the influence of pitch drift, but loses the original pitch features, resulting a lot of songs look similar. On the other hand, if the *w* is small, it is less smooth, and keeps more original pitch features, but more vulnerable to the influence of pitch drift.

For convenience, we mark the segment boundary with continuously upward pitch frame as a positive boundary, and the segment boundary with consecutive decline pitch frame as a negative boundary. When we try to find the corresponding matching segment boundaries in song database, it is convenient that we only search from the segment boundary candidates in song database with the same rising (positive) or decreasing (negative) pitch trend.

If the pitch trend (upward or decline) value exceeds a threshold *t* we set, we mark it as a possible segment boundary candidates. The same procedure is done on songs in database to find the possible segment boundary candidates. Note that the moving average only applied in finding possible segment boundary candidates. When calculating the distance, the original pitch is used.

3.3 Composite Moving Average

Moving average curves with different *w* overlap at area with large dynamic pitch variation. Therefore, this overlapped point can be used as a possible segment boundary candidate. We call this method "Composite Moving Average". The number of moving average curves considered at one time is fixed as 3 in our experiment. The gap between the *w* is *g*. We express it as *w*MA(*g*). For example, 20MA(5) means composite moving average with window length 20, 15, and 10.

3.4 Combination of Cross n Semitones and Composite Moving Average

This method is a combination of "Cross *n* Semitones" and "Composite Moving Average". If a point is selected by both "Cross *n* Semitones" and "Composite Moving Average", then it is selected as a segment boundary candidate.

4 Experiments

DOI: 10.1051/matecconf/20167605006

4.1. Database

Two databases are used in our experiment. One is 2009 MIR-QbSH corpus including 35 singers, totally 829 songs. The recording is in wave format with 8kHz sampling rate, 8 bits per sample, and mono channel. Pitch files are also included. The frame size for pitch is 256 samples. The other database is called Mono-Midi including 342 midi songs, which is the corpus we collected from Internet.

4.2. Experimental results

We compare the top 1 and top 10 recognition rate of our four segment-based methods as shown in Table 1. A, B, C, D respectively indicate our segment-based methods using "Cross 3 Semitones with m=5", "20MA with t=10", "20MA(5) with t=35", and "Combination of Cross 3 Semitones with m=5 and 20MA(5) with t=35".

Two examples are also provided and observed. The first example is a query singing with puff noise at the beginning. As shown in Figure 1, the (lower) blue line is the singing pitch curve and the (upper) green line is the corresponding midi pitch curve. It is easy to see the puff noise at the beginning of the blue singing pitch curve. After applying our segment-based methods, the singing and midi pitch curves after segment-based scaling are shown in Figure 2. For comparison, the singing and midi pitch curves after applying traditional LS are also shown in Figure 3. Since our methods are segment-based, they are allowed to jump to the most matching segment boundary and exclude the noisy segment. Therefore, puff noise has less impact on the recognition results of our methods than others. For this example, the correct midi ranks 1, 1, 1, and 1 in experimental results by using our methods A, B, C, and D respectively. It ranks 154 and 139 by using traditional LS and DTW.

Another example is a query singing with inconsistent tempo. As shown in Figure 4, the blue line is the singing pitch curve and the green (stepwise) line is the corresponding midi pitch curve. The singing and midi pitch curves after applying traditional LS are shown in Figure 5. If we align the two curves at the position indicated by black (middle) arrow, we can see the inconsistent tempo costs shifting at the position indicated by (both side) red arrows. The singing and midi pitch curves after segment-based scaling by applying our segment-based methods are shown in Figure 6. The two pitch curves fits better than using traditional LS. For this example, the correct midi ranks 1, 1, 1, and 1 in experimental results by using our methods A, B, C, and D respectively. It ranks 86 and 1 by using LS and DTW.

Based on the above experimental results, the problems of puff noise and inconsistent tempo which usually encountered in singing/humming, can be solved by segment-based methods. DTW can solve tempo inconsistence problem, though, it carries more computational load.

Table 1. Comparion of the Recognition Rate of Our Four Segment-Based Approaches.

	A	B	C	D
Top 1	52.2%	55.4%	52.4%	56.2%
Top 10	60.3%	70.1%	70.6%	67.8%

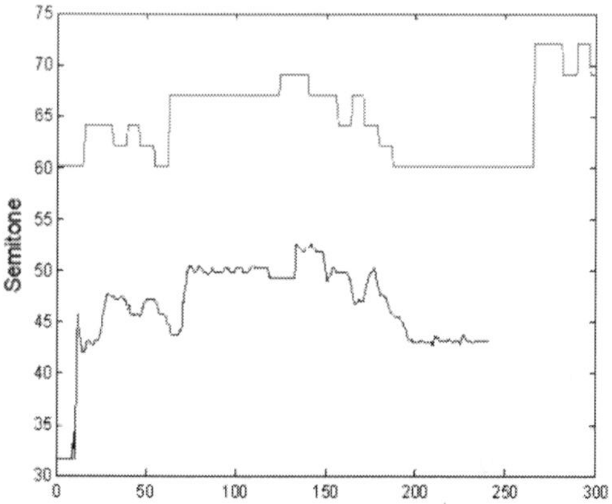

Figure 1. A singing example with puff noise at the beginning. The (lower) blue line is the singing pitch curve and the (upper) green line is the corresponding midi pitch curve.

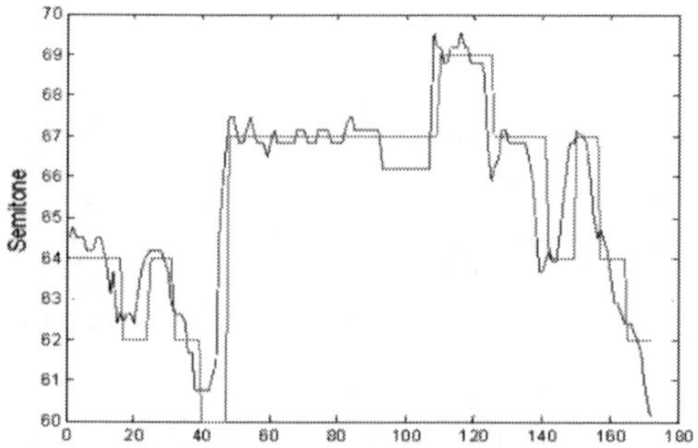

Figure 2. The singing and midi pitch curves after segment-based scaling. The blue line is the scaled singing pitch curve and the green (stepwise) line is the corresponding midi pitch curve.

DOI: 10.1051/matecconf/20167605006

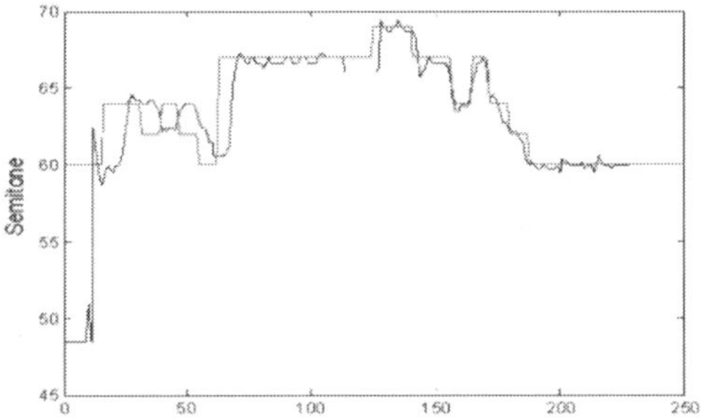

Figure 3. The singing and midi pitch curves after applying traditional LS. The blue line is the scaled singing pitch curve and the red (stepwise) line is the corresponding midi pitch curve.

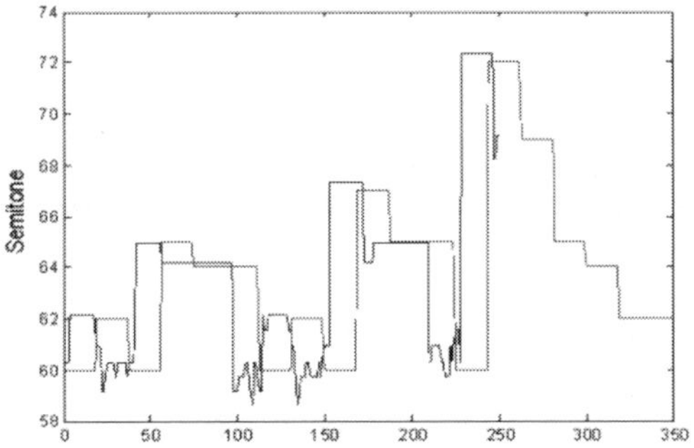

Figure 4. A singing example with inconsistent tempo. The blue line is the singing pitch curve and the green (stepwise) line is the corresponding midi pitch curve.

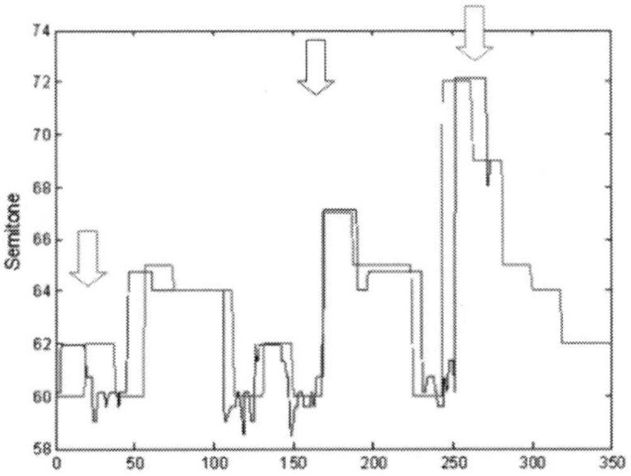

Figure 5. The singing and midi pitch curves after applying traditional LS. The blue line is the scaled singing pitch curve and the red (stepwise) line is the corresponding midi pitch curve.

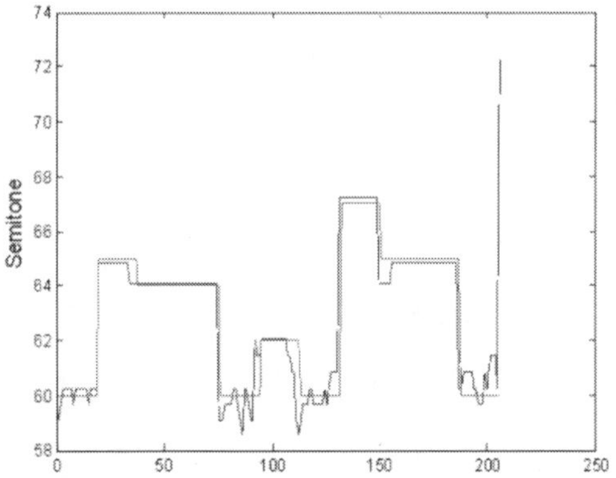

Figure 6. The singing and midi pitch curves after segment-based scaling. The blue line is the scaled singing pitch curve and the green (stepwise) line is the corresponding midi pitch curve.

5 Conclusions and future works

We propose four segment-based approaches to solve the problems of puff noise and inconsistent tempo in Query-By-Singing/Humming system. The segment-based methods also reduce the computation complexity by jumping to the possible segment boundary and using the segment ratio as scaling ratio, instead of comparing frame by frame from the very beginning and trying different scaling ratio in traditional LS method. Experimental results show that the best top 10 recognition rate is 70.6%. In addition, from our examples, it shows that segment-based method can solve the problems of puff noise and inconsistent tempo better than traditional global LS.

Improving the segment accuracy by observing and considering more features besides pitch variation will be the future work that we want to focus on.

References

1. Q. Wang, Z. Guo, G. Liu, C. Li, J. Guo, ICASSP, 3711 (2013)
2. C. C. Wang, C. H. Chen, C. Y. Kuo, L. T. Chiu, J. S. R. Jang, ICASSP, 477 (2012)
3. W. T. Kao, C. C. Wang, K. K. Chang, J. S. R. Jang, W. Liou, APSIPA, 1 (2013)
4. W. Cao, D. Jiang, J. Hou, Y. Qin, T. F. Zheng, Y. Liu, ICME, 942 (2009)
5. G. P. Nam, K. R. Park, INT J DISTRIB SENS N, 1 (2015)
6. S. Y. Cheng, *An Evaluation of Query By Singing/Humming Based on Various Pitch Tracking Methods* (Master Thesis, National Tsing Hua University, Taiwan, 2008)
7. H. Y. Zhuang, *Early Screening of Inappropriate Inputs for QBSH Systems*, (Master Thesis, National Tsing Hua University, Taiwan, 2009)

Intelligent Acquisition System Used in Mechanical Laboratory

Raluca Rob[1,a], Gelu Ovidiu Tirian[1] and Caius Panoiu[1]

[1]*Politehnica University of Timisoara, Department of Electrical Engineering and Industrial Informatics, Romania*

Abstract. The main purpose of this paper consists in determining of the parameters which characterize the functioning of the *Teves MK 60* as an ABS-ESP braking laboratory stand. This braking system model is used by the Volkswagen Golf and Bora the since 2002. The braking laboratory stand is able to simulate many operations which are able to give information concerning the ABS-ESP braking system comparing to the classical braking system. An application designed in LabVIEW comes to acquire and to process in real time the electrical signals generated by the *Teves MK 60* laboratory stand.

1 Introduction to *Brake Assist System*

Brake assist represents an active vehicle safety feature composed to help drivers come to a stop more quickly during an episode of emergency braking. Studies show that when making emergency stops, about half of all drivers do not press the brake fast enough or hard enough to make full use of their vehicle braking power.

Teves MK 60 system is designed as a laboratory stand where some operations can be simulated. The functioning of ABS system can be studied on each wheel separately. As well, the ABS pump supplying and control are monitored, and the functioning of the acceleration sensor and the rotation sensor.

A LabVIEW application is designed to process in real time or can record the variation of the electrical signals generated by the laboratory stand using a data acquisition board. A very important issue is that using this application, the user can track the emergency situation and detect faults in functioning of the ABS-ESP system. The LabVIEW application consists in two separate parts: the *acquisition application* and the *signal processing application*. Using the acquisition application, 12 sets of faults simulation were implemented. Each one consists in generating of one event that represents a single acquisition. In this scope, 12 set of measurement were generated. Each measurement was saved into a .txt file which can be loaded into the *signal processing application*.

2 Description of Teves MK60 stand

Teves MK60 laboratory stand is supplied to 230V and is presented in Figure 1. The connection to testers can be accomplished using a pin couple. The faults simulation can be made by acting appropriate switches.

On each wheel there is a sensor that measures wheel speed. The information is transmitted to the electronic control unit. Brake lines from the master cylinder fall into two distinct channels in ABS unit. Each of these channels can be closed by an electromagnetic valve actuation. Four of the eight valves are open continuously in normal state, while the others are closed. For reasons of safety, springs systems ensure that valves remain in their normal state, if power source is disconnected.

When moderate braking occurs, braking system operates as a normal two-circuit system. Braking pressure from the master cylinder acts directly the wheel cylinder through open channels.

If the wheel tends to lock, first the valves open and close and the brake pressure accumulated to this point remains constant. If the trend lock is still too high, other valves (which were closed by this point) are open. In the ABS unit, this channel is leading to the return electric pump drive unit, which starts when these valves open. The pump sends back the brake fluid through open valves to the channel between the central cylinder and closed brake valve. The brake pressure in the wheel cylinder decreases. At the same time, the pedal is prevented from no load operation, due to the pressure in relation to the central cylinder that is constant or a bit higher. If the wheel speed begins to increase, the first valve is opened again, the second valve closes and the adjustment process repeats.

Anti-lock braking system is disabled at speeds below 6 km / h. Braking pedal pulsating is due to the low pressure fluctuation during the regulation, because of sending back of the brake fluid to the return pump. Most vehicles have two separate brake circuits with two separate brake pumps, which are powered by the same electric motor shaft.

In Figure 2 it can be seen the connector couple where the acquisition system can be attached.

[a] Corresponding author: raluca.rob@fih.upt.ro

Figure 1. Teves MK60 laboratory stand.

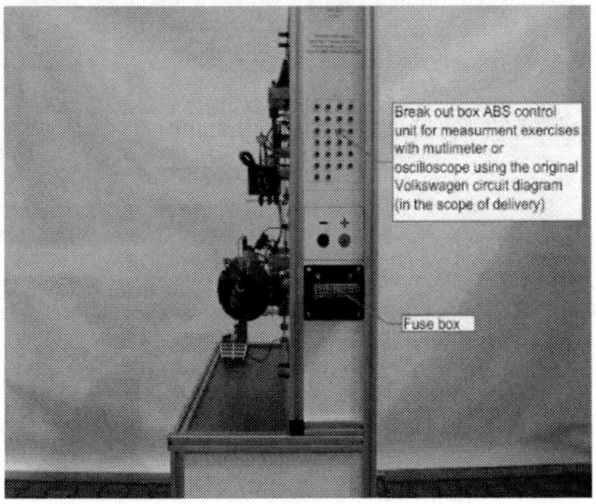

Figure 2. Connection couple for acquisition system connection.

3 Description of laboratory acquisition device

The data acquisition board used for acquiring the electric signals from Teves MK60 stand has the following characteristics:

- -16 analogic inputs, 250kS/s with 16 bit resolution;
- -2 analogic outputs, 740kS/s with 16 bit resolution;
- -24 TTL digital in/out;
- -1 digital trigger;
- -Windows, Linux compatibility.

3.1 Acquisition application

Using the acquisition application, the voltage samples are transformed into numeric data and stored into text documents. Using *DAQ Assistant.vi* subroutine, 12 analogical input channels were configured in order to acquire the possible faults. The maximum sampling rate for a single channel is 20kHz. Using a *while loop*, the application is able to generate and store the continuous information provided by the input signals into .txt files. The source code is presented in Figure 3.

3.2 Signal processing application

For each fault which is possible to occur, a measurement set was accomplished. Therefore, the signal processing application is able to load the samples from .txt files in order to process them. The faults which can be detected by the LabVIEW application consist in the followings:
-ABS faults on each wheel separately
-ABS pump supplying
-ABS pump controlling
-ABS system supplying
-acceleration sensor
-rotation sensor

3.2.1 Signal processing for ABS faults

In order to detect a fault to the ABS system on each wheel separately, each signal must be normed at input and output, as well. For filtering the signals, a nonlinear adapting filter OSLMS (Order Statistic Least Mean Square) was used. The scope of using this filter is to cancel the negaussian perturbations [1], [2].

Although the filtering, smoothing or prediction of the input signal is a linear operator depending on the input elements, the updating relations of the filter coefficients are nonlinear, so the filter that is used is considered as a nonlinear one.

It has been shown that the linear adaptive filters based on the gradient method and obtained by implementing the LMS algorithm uses an estimation of the gradient at the surface of the mean square error in order to update the filter coefficients. Such a strategy implies that the LMS algorithm is particularly vulnerable to the influence of the pulses, particularly in the case of the high amplitude pulse and short duration.

A problem that arises when using OSLMS filters is choosing the window length *L*, because the involved ordering transformations require extra calculus. [3], [4].

Generally, excepting the initialization process, one sample is changing on every step, the others remaining unchanged. For this reason, the sorting operation for updating each coefficient needs *L-1* comparisons. For *N* prediction coefficients, a number of $N \cdot log_2(L-1)$ comparisons are required. For implementing the OSLMS filter, a number of $N \cdot L$ multiplying operations and $N \cdot (L-1)$ adding operations appear on each iteration. This facts lead to an increasing of the calculus volume proportionally to the number of the prediction coefficients N and also to the window length *L*. [5], [6], [7], [8].

It puts a question about OSLMS filter to have improved performance regarding of the noise present at the input. Such a possibility is to adjust the OSLMS filter according to a parameter that is used in order to detect the presence of a pulse which represents the fault that occurs.

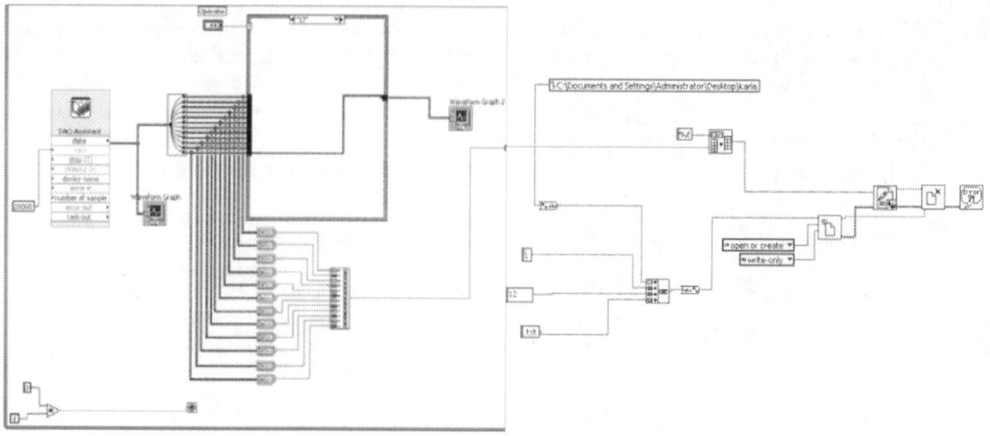

Figure 3. Source code for acquisition application.

This parameter noted with γ is measured at each iteration using the gradient estimated in the L points in the window. The parameter γ indicates the presence or the absence of the fault inside the window and in function of the decision, the algorithm switches between the applying of the MLMS filter-Median LMS filter (if the fault occurs) or LMS filter (if there is no fault).

Considering that $x_1, x_2, \cdots, x_L$ are the samples from the input signal in the L window length and $x_{(1)} \le x_{(2)} \le \cdots \le x_{(L)}$ represents the L sorted samples, the parameter γ has the following relation:

$$\gamma = \frac{\frac{1}{L} \cdot \sum_{i=1}^{L} (x_i - \bar{x})^4}{\left[\frac{1}{L} \cdot \sum_{i=1}^{L} (x_i - \bar{x})^2\right]^2} \qquad (1)$$

where $\bar{x} = \frac{1}{L} \cdot \sum_{i=1}^{L} x_i$ represents the average of the L samples.

The method that is implemented into LabVIEW application is based on calculating the samples average from the input window at n iteration, taking into consideration the samples average from the input window at n-1 iteration (Figure 4).

Considering that $x(n-L), x(n-L+1), \cdots, x(n-1)$ are the samples from the input window at n-1 iteration, having the average $\bar{x}_L(n-1)$, and $x(n-L+1), x(n-L+2), \cdots, x(n)$ are the samples from t

he input window at n iteration, having the average $\bar{x}_L(n)$, the recurrence relation is the following :

$$\bar{x}_L(n) = \bar{x}_L(n-1) - \frac{x(n-L) - x(n)}{L} \qquad (2)$$

In Figure 5 the signal variation for ABS faults with input norming, L = 250 samples is presented. Figure 6 uses the filtering algorithm for wheel 2 and Figure 7 the variation uses the output norming as well.

The LabVIEW application made possible to detect faults to ABS pump (ABS pump supplying, ABS pump command).

Pressure Release occurs when the control unit energizes the Outlet Valve while continuing to hold the Inlet Valve closed. The trapped brake fluid is released out of the calipers reducing braking pressure . At the same time the pump is switched on which draws in the released brake fluid and pumps it back into the pressure build-up circuit restoring the volume of brake fluid again in front of the Inlet valve. In Figure 8 the signal variation for ABS pump command with input norming (when the fault occurs), L = 250 samples is presented.

3.2.2 Signal processing for faults to acceleration and rotation sensors

For rotational speed, the rotation sensor produces a reference signal of 2.5 volts and a voltage input signal from 0.7 to 4.3 volts. This signal represents the rotational movement (yaw) of the vehicle from the neutral straight ahead position.

The sensor also integrates the transverse acceleration signal (side-ways acceleration). The signal range is 0.5V increasing to 4.5V as side forces (g-force) increase. This signal is combined with the rotation signal to determine when to start DSC regulation.

The signal processing is accomplished using the same OSLMS filtering algorithm. The front panel of the application which presents the variation of the signals generated by these sensors is presented in Figure 9.

3.2.3 Signal processing for faults to CAN protocol

CAN (Controller Area Network) is a real-time communication protocol which facilitates information exchange between car systems in order to optimize the controlling functions. If a fault occurs to CAN bus, the LabVIEW application is able to detect it and to display the signals variation. Figure 10 presents the signal variation for CAN bus and Figure 11 shows the source code for this subroutine.

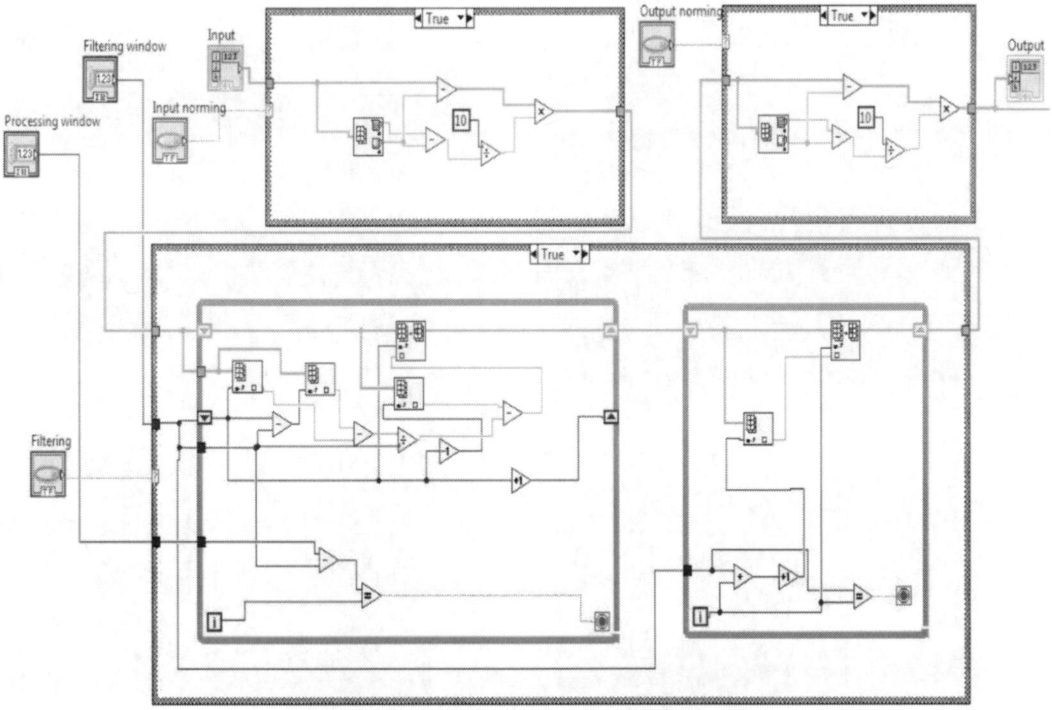

Figure 4. Source code for processing the ABS faults.

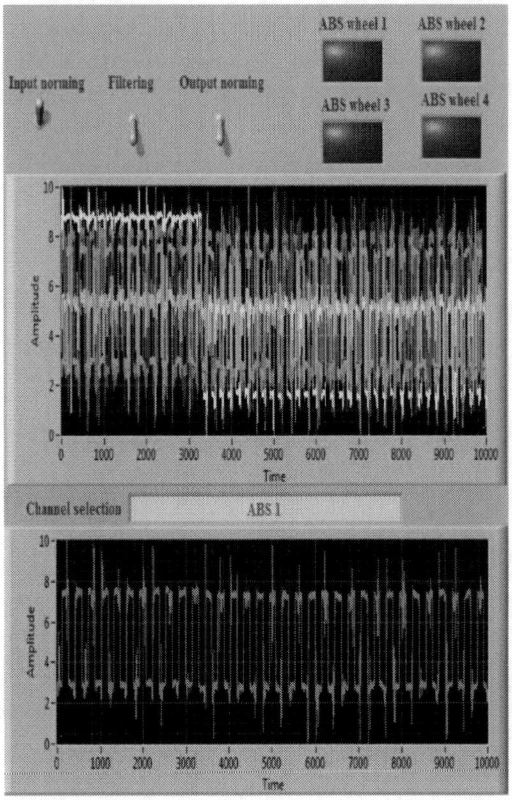

Figure 5. Signal variation for ABS faults with input norming, L=250samples.

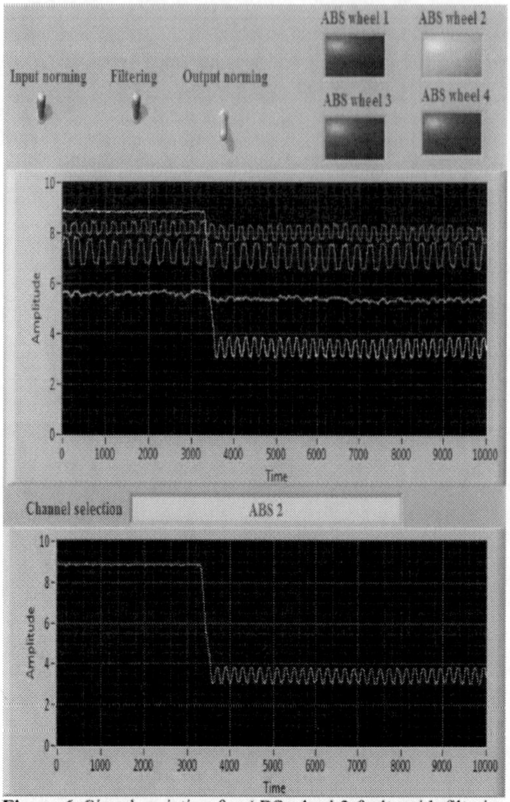

Figure 6. Signal variation for ABS wheel 2 faults with filtering (when the fault occurs), L=250samples.

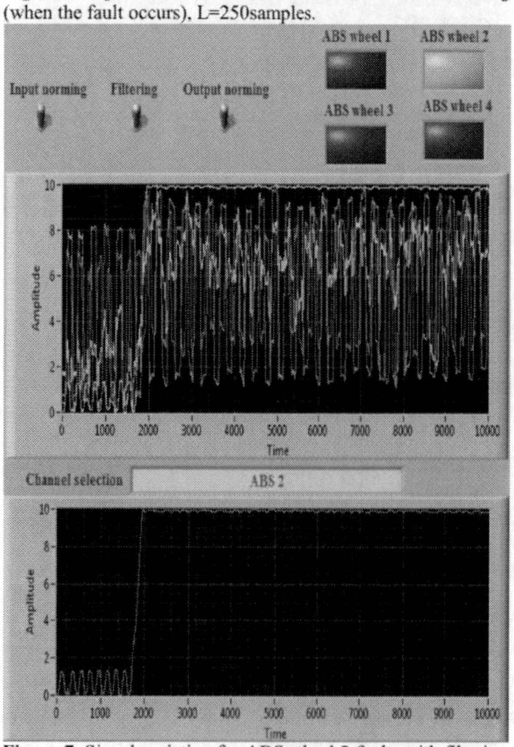

Figure 7. Signal variation for ABS wheel 2 faults with filtering and output norming (when the fault occurs), L=250samples.

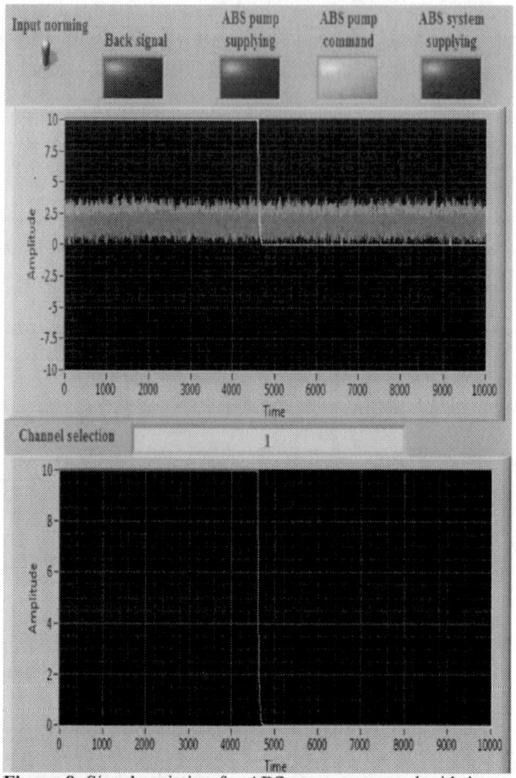

Figure 8. Signal variation for ABS pump command with input norming (when the fault occurs), L=250samples.

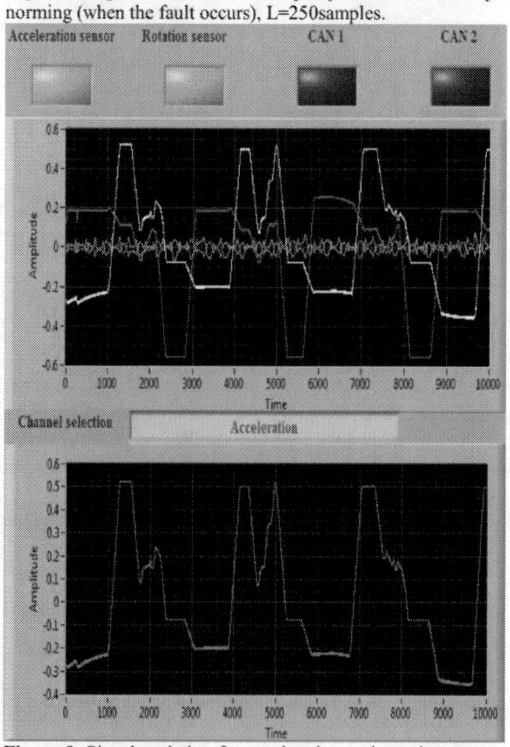

Figure 9. Signal variation for acceleration and rotation sensors (when the fault occurs), L=250samples.

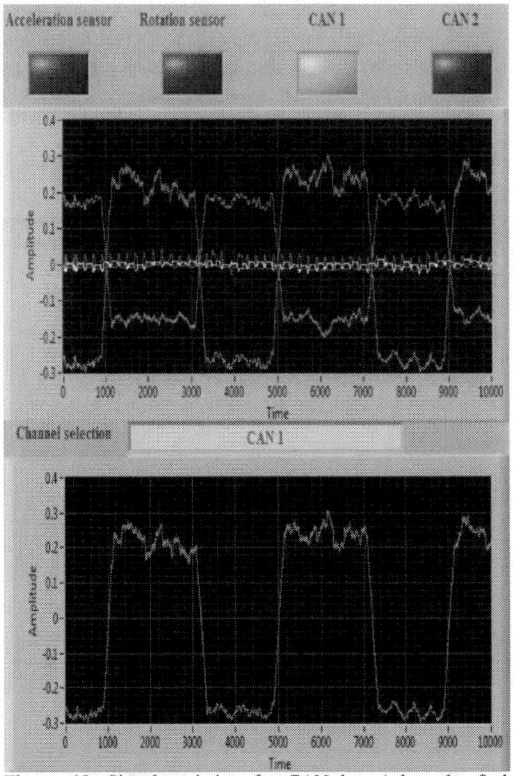

Figure 10. Signal variation for CAN bus (when the fault occurs), L=250samples.

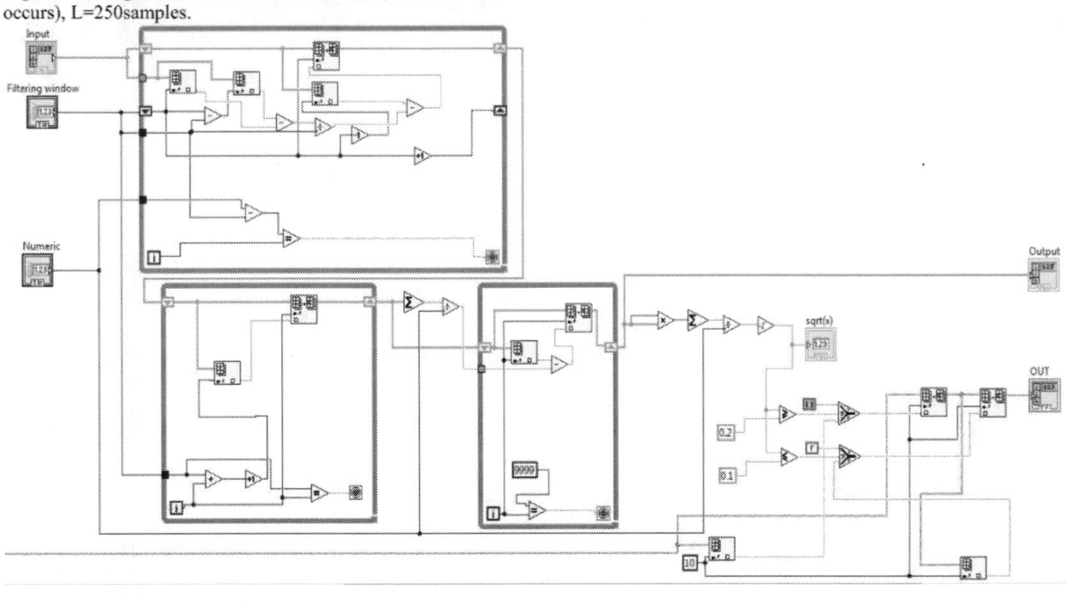

Figure 11. Source code for processing signal to CAN bus.

4 Conclusions

Signal processing applications are very useful in monitoring and processing data acquired from various devices. LabVIEW application described in this paper can work along with the ABS-ESP stand as an educational software.

The application provides facilities in studying the faults generated by TEVES MK60 stand. It works in real time with the stand functioning. The LabVIEW application is able to display the variation of the generated signal using an appropriate and facile interface with the user. The front panel of the application contains indicators which work in real time with the application.

Using the acquisition application, the information from the input signals (faults) is saved into .txt documents The algorithm of the signal processing application proposes an OSLMS filter which uses a parameter for detecting the input pulse. This method is based on computing the average of the samples from the input window at *n* iteration, considering as known the average of the samples from the input window at *n-1* iteration.

The signal processing application offers the possibility of comparing the results with any real testing systems in order to accomplish an educational method for mechanical students.

Acknowledgement

This work was supported by a grant of the Romanian National Authority for Scientific Research and Innovation, CNCS – UEFISCDI, project number PN-II-RU-TE-2014-4-1788.

References

1. C. Panoiu, L. Toma, M. Panoiu, R. Rob, *Properties of IIR-OSLMS adaptive filters* (Proceedings of the 27th IASTED International Conference on Modelling, Identification and Control MIC 2008, Innsbruck, Austria, pp. 460-465, 2008)
2. C. Panoiu, M. Panoiu, MALMS - *A new OSLMS filter* (Proceedings of the 4th IASTED International Conference Signal Processing, Pattern Recognition, and Applications, ~SPPRA 2007~, Innsbruck, Austria, pp.94-98, 2007)
3. http://www.bmwtech.ru/pdf/e46/ST034/14%20P2%20Traction%20and%20Stability%20Control%20Internet.pdf
4. Sabbioni, F. Cheli, V. D'Alessandro, *Analysis of ABS/ESP Control Logics Using a HIL Test Bench* (SAE Technical Paper 2011-01-0032, 2011)
5. H. Witter, M. Haiden, K. Talwar, ABS/ESP ECU *Testing with Sophisticated HIL Simulation Methods* (Symposium on International Automotive Technology 2009)
6. Fennel H., Ding E.L., *A model based failsafe system for the Continental TEVES Electronic Stability Program (ESP),* SAE Technical Paper 2000-01-1635, 2000, doi : 10.4271/2000-01-1635.
7. Tanneli M., *Friction curve peak detection by wheel deceleration measurement*, 2006 IEEE Intelligent Transportation Systems Conference, pp. 1592-1597, ISSN : 2153-0009.
8. Sathyanarayana A., Boyraz P., Purohit Z., Lubag R., *Driver adaptive and context aware active safety systems using CAN-bus signals*, Intelligent Vehicles Symposium (IV), 2010 IEEE, pp. 1236 – 1241, ISSN: 1931-0587.

MATEC Web of Conferences **76**, 05008 (2016) DOI: 10.1051/matecconf/20167605008
CSCC 2016

Calibration of low-cost triaxial magnetometer

Ales Kuncar[1,a], Martin Sysel[1], and Tomas Urbanek[1]

[1] *Tomas Bata University in Zlin, Faculty of Applied Informatics, Namesti T.G.Masaryka 5555, 760 01 Zlin, Czech Republic*

Abstract. Heading angle of magnetic compasses is estimated using the triaxial magnetometer readings. The accuracy of these readings is influenced by many factors such as sensor errors (scale factors, non-orthogonality, and offsets), and magnetic deviations (soft-iron and hard-iron interference). To calculate the true heading angle, the magnetic calibration of magnetometer is necessary. This research paper describes a calibration procedure for triaxial low-cost MEMS magnetometer. The proposed calibration method determines twelve calibration parameters in 3D arbitrary rotations of magnetometer.

1 Introduction

Advances in Micro-Electro-Mechanical System (MEMS) technologies have made a great role in wide range of engineering applications. Magnetometers have been used in geophysical research [1], military defence, mineral resources, drilling and mining practice [2]. These sensors measure the strength and direction of the local magnetic field. The measured magnetic field is a combination of the Earth's magnetic field and a magnetic field generated by nearby objects. Nevertheless, the main problem are errors such as zero deviation, scale factors, non-orthogonality, measurement noise, misalignment error, hard-iron and soft-iron interferences. The biggest effect comes from soft-iron and hard-iron interferences in the vicinity of the sensors. Before each application, calibration and compensation of such errors needs to be conducted.

There are two types of soft-iron and hard-iron interference compensation. The first methods use specific instruments like turntable, accelerometers or GPS (Global Positioning System). This method is able to reach high accuracy. The least-square method or ellipsoid fitting compensation method belongs in the second type. The traditional method for error compensation is mapping of the ellipsoid data to a sphere data.

Guo et al. [3] used Extended Kalman filter to compensate the soft-iron and hard-iron interference.

Kok et al. [4] presents a calibration algorithm using a maximum likelihood method and a additional inertial sensor.

Renaudin et al. [5] applied an adaptive least square estimator to ellipsoid fitting problem.

Liu et al. [6] describes calibration method using turntable and ellipsoid fitting method.

Cheuk et al. [7] used an evolutionary algorithm to minimize misalignment, scale and bias errors.

[a]Corresponding author: kuncar@fai.utb.cz

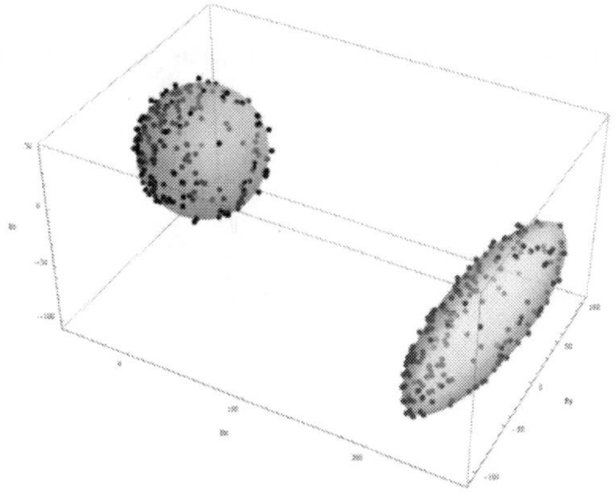

Figure 1. Calibrated (sphere) and raw magnetometer (ellipsoid) data.

The aim of this paper is to evaluate the calibration method which will account magnetometer sensor errors and magnetic interferences. In absence of magnetic interferences, the magnetometer will measure only the three components of the geomagnetic field. The vector magnitude is equal to the magnitude of geomagnetic field at a different orientation. The locus of the magnetometer readings lies on the surface of the sphere centred in zero field and the radius is equal to the magnitude of the geomagnetic field.

The hard-iron interference adds fixed offset in each axis to all measurements. That results in displacement of the sphere centred to the hard-iron offset; however, the geomagnetic field strength is still the same. The locus of the magnetometer measurements is distorted in each axis differently to a 3D ellipsoid in presence of soft-iron interference (Fig. 1).

The reminder of this paper is organized as follows. In section 2, the hardware and software for data collection is briefly introduced. The magnetometer error model and magnetometer calibration method is described in section 3 and section 4, respectively. The experimental results of magnetometer calibration is mentioned in section 5.

2 Equipment

This section provides an overview of the measurement chain. This chain includes control unit, inertial measurement unit (IMU) and software for data collection.

2.1 Control unit

The control unit STEVAL-MKI109V2, also known as "eMotion", is primarily designed to provide platform for the evaluation of STMicroelectronics' MEMS modules. This board consists of DIL24 socket to connect MEMS modules, other passive parts like LED diodes for signalization of its own inner states and "jumpers" to set the specific configuration, etc.

The board is controlled by the STM32F103RET6 high-performance 32-bit microcontroller based on ARM technology with 512 kB Flash memory functioning as bridge between the MEMS modules and a PC with graphical user interface (GUI) or dedicated software routines for customized applications. The board also includes:

- 16 MHz crystal oscillator
- Low noise voltage regulator lds3985xx30
- Low-capacity surge protector of USB interface
- Separating and impedance operational amplifiers for the signal adjustment of the MEMS modules

2.2 Inertial measurement unit

The STEVAL-MKI124V1 (Fig. 2) is a 10-axis module with IMU including triaxial gyroscope with intern thermometer (L3GD20), triaxial accelerometer and triaxial magnetometer (LSM303DLHC), and barometer (LPS331AP). All of these sensors are based on MEMS technology and factory tested, and trimmed, so no additional calibration is necessary. However, this factory calibration is appropriate only for basic applications. Advanced calibration had to be provided for application such as navigation systems.

Several different configurations allow for settings regarding specific usage. Sensor specifications are given in Table 1. and [8].

2.3 Software for data collection and visualization

The last part of the measurement chain is software Unico STSW-MKI109W. This software is used for interaction with sensors and provides:

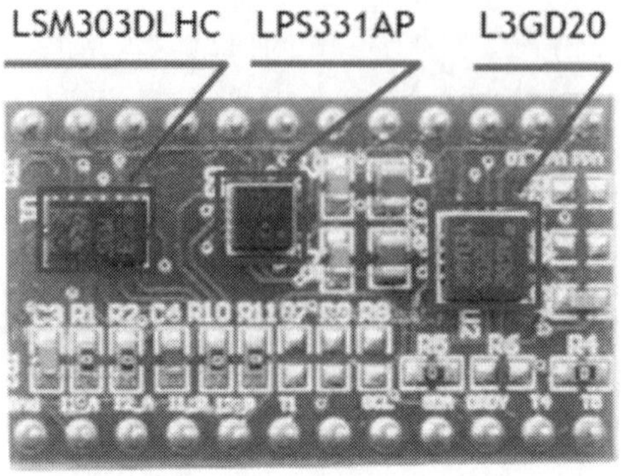

Figure 2. Inertial measurement unit STEVAL-MKI124V1.

- GUI for data collection and transfer
- subsystems for the storage and interpretation of the collected data in graphical or numerical format
- configuration of all the registers and the advanced features
- drivers for the data interpretation from the corresponding sensor
- drivers for the communication interface of the host computer

3 Magnetometer error model

The magnetometer readings are influenced by many sources of error like wideband measurement noise, stochastic biases, installation errors and magnetic interferences in the vicinity of the sensors. These magnetic interferences can be divided up into two groups: soft-iron and hard-iron interference. The hard-iron interference is caused by the presence of magnets or materials generating fixed or slightly time-varying magnetic field. The second type, soft-iron interference, occurs when a ferromagnetic materials is in the vicinity of the sensor or it can be even generated by the device itself. This will cause the distortion of magnetic field. The traditional method for compensation of such errors is equivalent to transforming the 3-D ellipsoid to the centre oriented sphere.

The magnetometer error model is,

$$R = M_m \cdot S \cdot SI \cdot (M + O + n) \tag{1}$$

In this model, the variables M_m, S and SI are matrices which interpret misalignment errors, scale factors and soft-iron biases, respectively. O and n are vectors representing hard-iron biases and wideband noise which distorts the true magnetic field measurements M.

1. **Misalignment error** is defined as angles between the magnetometer axis X_s, Y_s, Z_s and the device body axis X_d, Y_d, Z_d. This caused by imperfect mounting of sensor on the PCB (printed circuit board).

Table 1. Sensor characteristics.

	Accelerometer	Gyroscope	Magnetometer	Barometer
Full scale	±2g – ±16g	250 – 2000 dps	±1.3 – ±8.1 gauss	260 – 1260 mbar
Sensitivity	1 – 12 mg/LSB	8.75 – 70 mdps/LSB	230 – 1100 LSB/gauss	4096 LSB/mbar
Min. zero level	±60 mg	±10 – ±75 dps		
Zero level vs. temp	±0.5 mg/°C	±0.03 – ±0.04 dps/°C		
Noise density	220 $\mu g/\sqrt{Hz}$	0.03 dps/$\sqrt{Hz}$		
Cross-axis			±1 %FS/gauss	
Linearity		0.2 %FS		

$$M_m = \begin{bmatrix} m_{xx} & m_{xy} & m_{xz} \\ m_{yx} & m_{yy} & m_{yz} \\ m_{zx} & m_{zy} & m_{zz} \end{bmatrix} \quad (2)$$

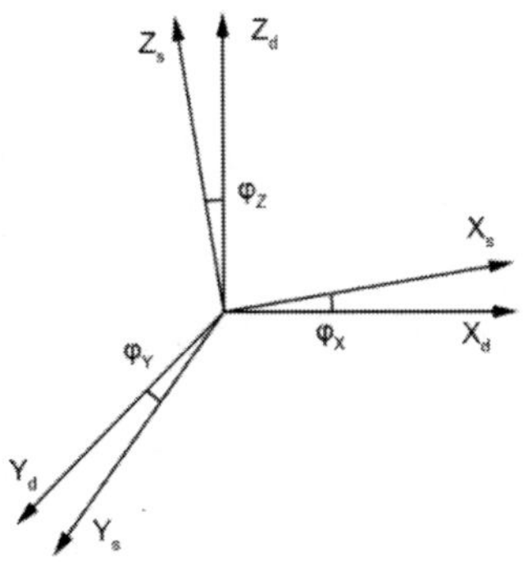

Figure 3. Misalignment error.

2. **Scale factor error** corresponds to constants of proportional relationship between the input and output of the magnetometer. The scale factor can be modelled as

$$S = diag\begin{pmatrix} s_x & s_y & s_z \end{pmatrix} \quad (3)$$

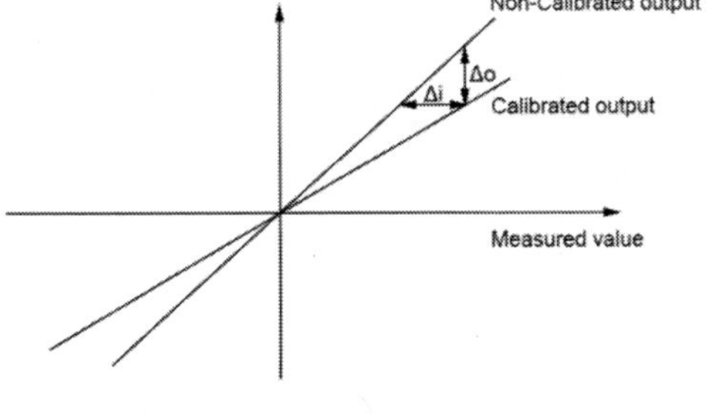

Figure 4. Scale factor error.

3. **Soft-Iron** error can be modelled as

$$SI = \begin{bmatrix} SI_{xx} & SI_{xy} & SI_{xz} \\ SI_{yx} & SI_{yy} & SI_{yz} \\ SI_{zx} & SI_{zy} & SI_{zz} \end{bmatrix} \quad (4)$$

4. **Hard-Iron** is equivalent to a bias and can be represented as

$$O = \begin{bmatrix} O_x & O_y & O_z \end{bmatrix}^T \quad (5)$$

4 Magnetometer calibration

The magnetometer calibration can be performed by 3 full rotations around each sensitive device body axes or 3D arbitrary rotations. The collected raw magnetometer data are used to determine the twelve unknown calibration parameters.

The relationship between the calibrated magnetometer data and the raw magnetometer measurements is expressed as [9]

$$\begin{bmatrix} M_x \\ M_y \\ M_z \end{bmatrix} = [M_m]_{3x3} \cdot \begin{bmatrix} \frac{1}{S_x} & 0 & 0 \\ 0 & \frac{1}{S_y} & 0 \\ 0 & 0 & \frac{1}{S_z} \end{bmatrix} \cdot [SI]_{3x3} \cdot \begin{bmatrix} R_x - O_x \\ R_y - O_y \\ R_z - O_z \end{bmatrix} \quad (6)$$

where

M_x, M_y, M_z are the correct magnetometer outputs,

M_m is a 3x3 misalignment matrix between the magnetometer axes and the device axes,

S_x, S_y, S_z are the scale factors,

R_x, R_y, R_z are the raw magnetometer readings,

SI is a 3x3 matrix of offsets caused by soft-iron interference,

O_x, O_y, O_z are the offsets caused by hard-iron interference.

Equation (6) can be simplified to [9]

$$\begin{bmatrix} M_x \\ M_y \\ M_z \end{bmatrix} = \begin{bmatrix} P_{11} & P_{12} & P_{13} \\ P_{21} & P_{22} & P_{23} \\ P_{31} & P_{32} & P_{33} \end{bmatrix} \cdot \begin{bmatrix} R_x - P_{10} \\ R_y - P_{20} \\ R_z - P_{30} \end{bmatrix} \quad (7)$$

where P_i are the twelve unknown calibration parameters.

DOI: 10.1051/matecconf/20167605008

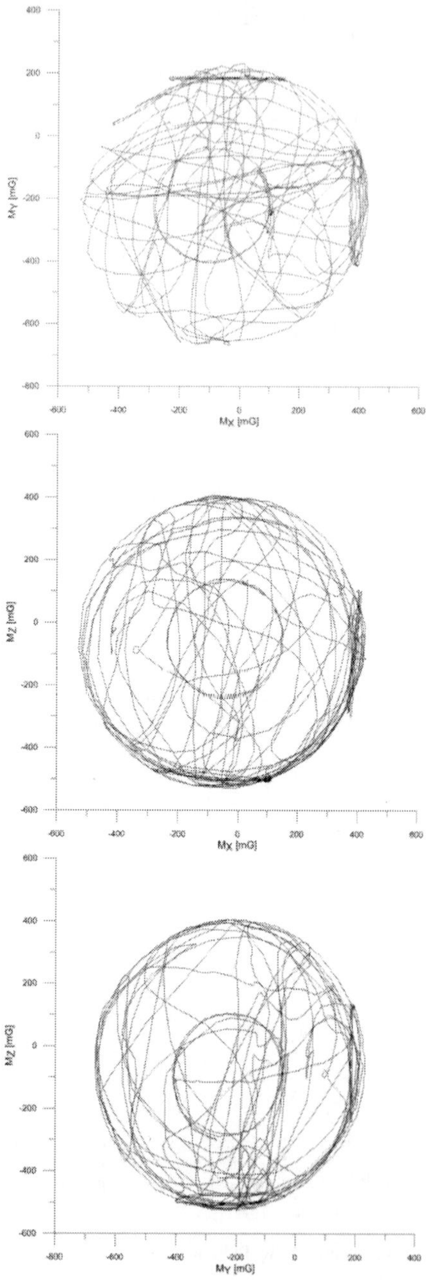

Figure 5. Slices of raw magnetometer measurements.

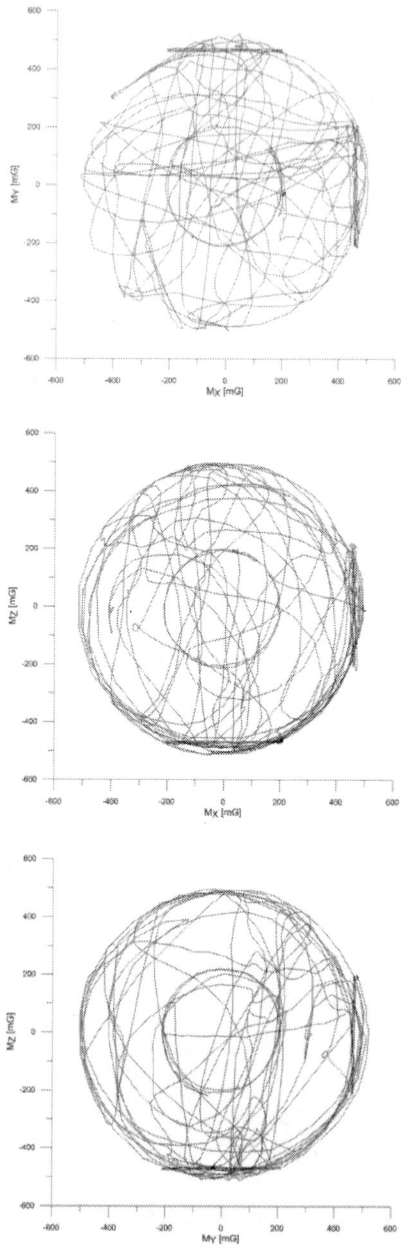

Figure 6. Slices of calibrated magnetometer measurements.

5 Experimental results

Data were measured while rotating the sensor in 3D arbitrary orientations. The true magnitude of the geomagnetic field in Zlin, Czech Republic (49.2306827° N, 17.6566617° E) is 48,996 nT which is 489.96 mGauss. The goal of this magnetometer calibration is to compensate the soft-iron and hard-iron interference.

As you can see in Fig. 5, the measured data before calibration shows signs of presence of the hard-iron interference. The effect of the soft-iron interference is very small so it can be ignored; however, it was also accounted for.

The ideal compensation of hard-iron and soft-iron interference changes the 3D ellipsoid to a sphere centred in zero field and radius of local magnetic field strength.

Fig. 6 shows the results after calibration. The data lies on the surface of the sphere centred in zero field with magnitude approximately 500 mGauss. The calculated transformation matrix is

$$\begin{bmatrix} 1.06 & -0.013 & -0.109 \\ -0.001 & 1.137 & 0.017 \\ 0.104 & -0.028 & 1.076 \end{bmatrix} \tag{8}$$

This matrix contains compensation of scale factor, misalignment errors, and soft-iron interference.

The offset caused by hard-iron interference is

$$\begin{bmatrix} -40.898 & -225.422 & -56.555 \end{bmatrix}^T \tag{9}$$

6 Conclusion

In applications, the effects of the hard-iron and soft-iron interference will distort the local magnetic field especially in low-cost magnetometers. These interferences needs to be accounted for and removed from the magnetometer measurements. Therefore, this paper describes a calibration method for low-cost triaxial magnetometer. This method does not require any additional equipment for data measurement. The data are collected while moving the sensor by the hand in arbitrary rotations.

In future work, we will use evolutionary algorithms for generating the calibration parameters.

Acknowledgement

This work was supported by Internal Grant Agency of Tomas Bata University in Zlin under the project No. IGA/FAI/2016/035.

References

[1] Jun Kawai, G. Uehara, T. Kohrin, H. Ogata, H. Kado, IEEE Transactions on Magnetics **35**, 3974 (1999)

[2] J. Haverinen, A. Kemppainen, *2011 IEEE International Symposium on Robotic and Sensors Environments (ROSE)* (IEEE, 2011), pp. 7–12, ISBN 978-1-4577-0819-0,

[3] Pengfei Guo, Haitao Qiu, Yunchun Yang, Zhang Ren, *2008 IEEE/ION Position, Location and Navigation Symposium* (IEEE, 2008), pp. 1167–1174, ISBN 978-1-4244-1536-6

[4] M. Kok, J. Hol, T. Schon, F. Gustafsson, H. Luinge, 2012 15th International Conference on Information Fusion (FUSION) pp. 787–793 (2012)

[5] V. Renaudin, M.H. Afzal, G. Lachapelle, Journal of Sensors **2010**, 1 (2010)

[6] Y. Liu, X. Li, X. Zhang, Y. Feng, Sensors **14**, 8485 (2014)

[7] C.M. Cheuk, T.K. Lau, K.W. Lin, Y. Liu, *2012 12th International Conference on Control Automation Robotics & Vision (ICARCV)* (IEEE, 2012), pp. 1341–1346, ISBN 978-1-4673-1872-3

[8] STMicroelectronics, Tech. rep., STMicroelectronics(2013)

[9] STMicroelectronics, Tech. rep., STMicroelectronics (2010)

Reverberation chamber and its verification for acoustic measurements

Pavel Drabek[1,a] and Martin Zalesak[1]

[1]*Tomas Bata University in Zlin, Faculty of Applied Informatics, Department of Automation and Control Engineering, Nad Stranemi 4511, Czech Republic*

Abstract. Reverberation rooms are useful for measurement of the acoustic quantities of machines that operate in long cycles, however, current reverberation chamber design practices often lead to known issues with reproducibility and repeatability of measured data. The problem is that construction process of these laboratories is performed according to the relevant standards requirements which are mainly focused on the volume of the room or on the absorption coefficient value of the boundary surfaces. Nevertheless, the inner-laboratory reproducibility of acoustic data is very difficult to achieve even when these diffusivity quantifiers are satisfied. This paper presents a verification process of an acoustic laboratory which proportions, shape and construction material of boundary surfaces are not in compliance with standards in every detail.

1 Introduction

One of the most fundamental factors affecting the inside enclosures is an excessive noise generated by equipment of environmental engineering [1]. From this perspective, it is necessary to approach the issues from the viewpoint of the entire chain of noise transmission into the buildings. It includes features of the sound source in terms of temporal, spectral and spatial aspects, of the sound propagation, and of individual sound transmission paths, and furthermore with noise receptiveness of individual humans. However, these features are not easy to measure; moreover, with respect to all requirements of gripping and placing, in case of the sound source. To determine acoustic parameters of these machines with higher accuracy, such as sound power, is requisite to perform the measurements in the acoustic laboratory. Certain types of acoustic measurements can be carried out in an environment which is free of reflections or environment which uses reflection in many directions as reverberation rooms. Reverberation rooms are useful for measurement of sound power, in particular, the sound power of machines that operate in long cycles, since the alternatives, the sound intensity method, and the free field method, are not very suitable for such sources [2]. However, the round robin evidence has shown that inter-laboratory reproducibility of acoustic data is difficult to achieve and high levels of measurement uncertainty remain even when design and construction process was carried out in accordance with recommended practices [3] [4].

The paper presents some aspects and results of the verification the newly build Laboratory of Environmental Engineering at Tomas Bata University in Zlin, Faculty of applied Informatics. This laboratory consists of Universal Compensate Calorimetric chamber which also serves as Reverberation chamber.

This chamber is used among other things to measure energy parameters and sound power level of equipment commonly used in buildings.

2 Reverberation chamber

The design of reverberation chamber is very complex concernment; moreover, when a multipurpose facility is concerned. The proposal of reverberation chamber depends on the prime purpose of usage. Acousticians use reverberation chamber to conduct various acoustical tests, including absorption and scattering coefficient measurements of acoustic materials, and determination of sound power levels of noise sources using sound pressure. European standards [5] and [6] are based on the already known facts in spatial acoustic and can be used as brief guidelines for the design of reverberation rooms. However, these standards assume diffuse field when the requirements, the volume, not rectangular shape and the sound absorption of the surfaces of the reverberant room, are satisfied. Following these assumptions could cause the sufficient diffuse sound field, but nevertheless, it is necessary to know the frequency range where the sound fields are adequately diffuse and where not. The measured data between the sound source and the diffuse sound field could be afflicted with great uncertainty in the predominantly non-diffuse section [7].

The reverberation chamber has a rectangular shape with dimensions 6,66 x 4,30 x 3,27 m and a volume of 93,66 m^3. According to the standards approach, the proportions, and shape of the chamber could appear to be a tricky problem. Its proportions should be selected so

[a] Corresponding author: pdrabek@fai.utb.cz

that the ratio of any two dimensions does not equal or closely approximate an integer [5]. In this case, however, the chamber dimension ratio it is almost the integer. This can result in the improper decomposition of eigenmodes from the chamber response at low frequencies. This is mostly because the acoustic energy is distributive very unevenly and direction of propagation is far from random.

The surrounding surfaces of the room consist of different materials, therefore, the sound absorbing qualities of the walls, floor, and ceiling can vary considerably within a frequency range of a few hertz. Particularly, ceiling and three walls are consists of PUR panels, remaining wall is formed by Cetris Farmacel panels and the floor is covered by an antiskid metal plate.

Figure 1. Reverberation chamber at FAI UTB in Zlin, CZ.

This multi-material concept is a rather awkward considering the fact very complicated evaluation of reverberant properties of the inner space at the design stadium. In the case of rectangular shape, the accuracy and reliability of results would be impaired by the interference of the direct sound with sound reflected from the boundaries [7]. In an attempt to avoid this regrettable phenomenon, it was applied a combination of two different geometric types of boundary diffusers (the tent and semicylinder type) and curved plexiglasses as hanging diffusers (see Figure 1). Generally, the diffusers can be used to break up the reflected wavefront and so disperse the focus while still maintaining the acoustic energy and avoiding absorption, however, it should be remembered that diffusers surface can cause significant diffraction from its edges [8]. The amount of diffraction depends on the wavelength and the size of the obstacle [9]. To minimalize the diffraction effect is recommended to accomplish an acoustic treatment. For boundary diffusers, this means using two different diffusers abreast and arranging them randomly or pseudorandomly on the wall. This will reduce periodicity and so improve dispersion [8].

3 Methods

The aim of the verification process was to specify the reverberant properties of acoustic test chambers with respect to the prime purpose of usage. This is a desirable goal of room acoustical efforts since differences in reverberant properties can cause significant errors in measured data [7]. For example, the absorption coefficients determined in reverberation chambers are commonly exaggerated by diffraction effects and care must be taken, where it is critical, to correctly take such effects into account. The appropriate proof can be that absorption coefficient tables published in the literature often contain values greater than 1 which is meaningless.

It is possible to conduct the evaluation of the acoustical behaviour of the chamber by different ways. First one established through theoretical modeling, second one using numerical simulations and third one based on the real measurements [10]. Description of a sound field in enclosures and evaluation of their reverberant characteristics are not simple, and several theoretical methods of different complexity have been developed for this. Numerical simulations are very useful, however, the accuracy of the prediction models is highly dependent on the quality of the input data, including the absorption coefficient of surfaces which often can not be determined correctly [8]. These two ways have the advantage to be able to obtain preliminary results when it is still on the drawing-board.

The verification described in this paper is based on several series of measurements which will be evaluated by impulse response of the chamber. This method was chosen because no absorption coefficient date was available for the individual surface materials for the chamber where the verification was carried out.

Reverberation time is the main parameter determining the indoor reverberation characteristics, thus, it is primarily used to assess the acoustic quality of enclosures [11]. For the purpose of analysing the structure of the impulse response characterizing the sound transmission through the chamber, this parameter was observed.

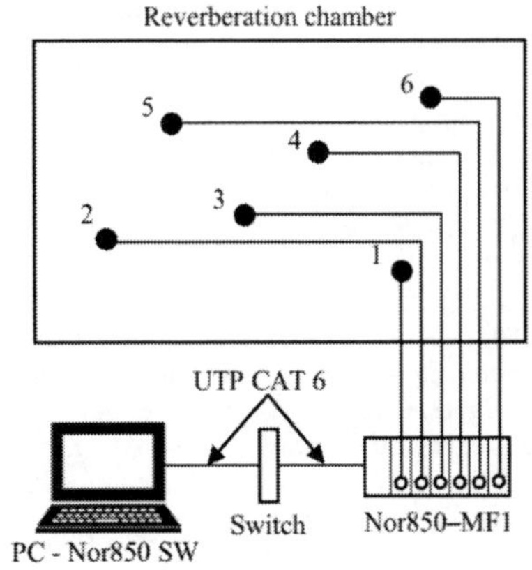

Figure 2. Scheme of measurement equipment (points 1-6 are consist of microphone GRAS GS-40AF and preamplifier Nor1209).

The standard equipment for this measurement is depicted schematically in Figure 2. The output voltage of the microphones and preamplifiers is fed to a multichannel Nor850 and then to a sound power module software which running the state-of-the-art Windows platform. This module enables connecting a number of individual measuring units through various communication channels including both standardized LAN and USB interfaces. Wireless communication through Bluetooth or WLAN is also available. It is very important to appropriately set the value of the sampling period. This setting controls the period length of each sample along the decay. In this case was chosen the lowest one, 5 ms.

The measurement was performed under conditions which are standardly used for determination of sound power levels of noise sources using sound pressure. The chamber was maintained at a temperature of 23°C and relative humidity of 50% and the range of mid frequencies, for which all measurements, was taken, extends from about 50 to 10 000 Hz. The following procedure is not required to comply with the same order.

First of all, was measured the background noise level in the room with the all devices turned off by measuring the time-averaged sound pressure level. In the case of acoustic laboratories, it is not so frequent, however, when the room impulse response is contaminated with high-level background noise the resulting accuracy is substantially reduced because of a distortion of decay curve slope during the late decay [11]. Secondly, the determination of the impulse sound generator suitability was done. In this case, the chamber was excitation by a balloon burst. Each third-octave bandwidth was examined, more specifically, the standard deviation and the amplitude of excitation peak of a sound pressure measured in six observation points. The minimum amplitude size depends on the chosen sound pressure drop which will be evaluated, usually 35 dB [12]. Finally, the last part of the process is to obtain several different decay curves.

If the sound field were completely diffuse, the decay should be the same throughout the chamber [7]. Since this ideal condition is hardly ever met in real enclosures, it is advisable to carry out several measurements for each frequency band at different microphone positions. This is even more important if the quantity to be evaluated is the early decay time, which may vary considerably from one place to the next within one inner space [7]. For this reason, the measurements were taken at least 3 locations of impulse source and with at least 6 microphone positions. The experimental arrangement consisted of a 1/2" omnidirectional microphones and inflated balloon inside the chamber. The subsequent analysis was achieved conveniently using a multichannel as a real-time analyser (Nor850 MF-1). Usually, the sound pressure level in the measure decay curves does not fall in a strictly linear way but contains random fluctuations which are due to complicated interferences between decaying normal modes [7].

The reverberation time was calculated using a linear least-squares regression [12] of the measured decay curve, from a level 5 dB below the initial level to 25 dB below, using a linear regression of ensemble averaged decay curves. It means that the decay curve is approximated by a straight line $\hat{L}_i$ [dB], at the time t_i [s] is defined as

$$\hat{L}_i = a + bt_i \tag{1}$$

Where is a value $\hat{L}_i$ at the time t=0 [dB],

b line tilt [dB/s].

According to linear least-squares regression method is estimation of value a and a line tilt b determine by following equations:

$$a = \overline{L} - b\overline{t} \tag{2}$$

$$b = \frac{\sum_{i=1}^{n}(t_i L_i) - m\overline{t}\overline{L}}{\sum_{i=1}^{n}(t_i^2) - m\overline{t}^{-2}} \tag{3}$$

Where

$$\overline{L} = \frac{1}{n}\sum_{i=1}^{n} L_i \tag{4}$$

$$\overline{t} = \frac{1}{n}\sum_{i=1}^{n} t_i \tag{5}$$

Estimation of reverberation time $\hat{T}$ is given by

$$\hat{T} = \frac{-60}{b}. \tag{6}$$

Another method of determining the decay curve consists in the reverse-time integration of squared impulse response which is described in [13].

4 Results

The main objective of measured results presented in the following was to examine a crucial acoustic properties of reverberation chamber at FAI UTB in Zlin for acoustic measurements. In other words, it was necessary to determine whether the inter-laboratory space is able to perform acoustic data with required reproducibility and specify the frequency range in which a given reverberation chamber can be used.

The background noise was measured in several days to be eliminated any temporal noises. Results and standards requirements are shown in Figure 3. As mentioned above the supporting constructions are consists of PUR panels. In fact, the entire chamber is surrounded by another compensation chamber formed by those same panels and thus considerably reduce the noise transmission between inner and external environment. As can be seen from the Figure 3 the background noise values are predominantly below the requirement values, nevertheless, this can not be achieved at the mid frequency 630 Hz. This phenomenon is most likely caused by the fact that the sandwich structure of PUR panel acts as oscillating plate and therefore at the resonant frequency sound will pass easier through the partitions, and so the sound insulation will be poorer [8]. Generally, it is important that the absorbing material is lightly packed, otherwise, it can form a vibration path bridging between the two partitions; this could greatly reduce the sound attenuation properties [8].

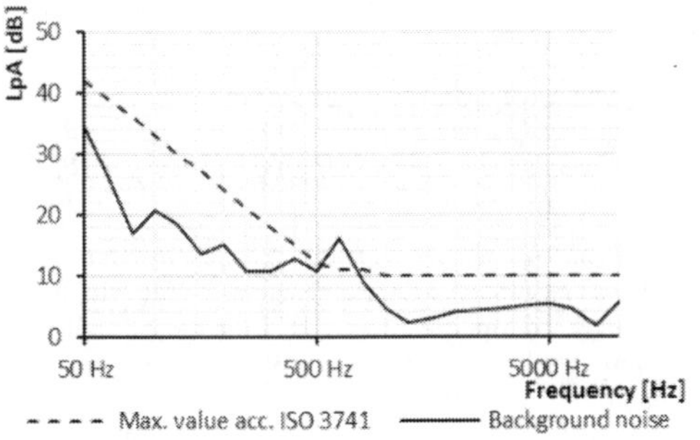

Figure 3. Graph of measured and permissible levels of background noise.

The determination of suitability of balloon burst as impulse sound source was done for three observation locations. According to the measured data can be said that the amount of energy emitted by a balloon burst depends greatly on air pressure inside a balloon, therefore, balloons do not provide repeatability results every time, especially at low frequency band. More about the comparison of different impulse sound sources is described in [14].

To properly characterize reverberant properties of the chamber, eighteen decay curves were obtained for each mid frequency band at different impulse sound source positions. Calculation results present in a clear way that in the analysed room reverberant response of the chamber and an initial amplitude of a sound decay strongly depend on the sound frequency, as indicated in Figure 4 and 5. They illustrate in each graphs only two curves because more of them would evocate confusing results.

It is obvious that a diffuse sound field will not be established in enclosures whose walls have the tendency to concentrate the reflected sound energy in certain regions [7]. For this reason, diffusers help to establish a diffuse sound field by continuously redistributing the energy in all possible directions. Upon each reflection is the fraction of energy diffusely scattered into non specular angles while the remaining energy is reflected into the specular reflection angle in the usual way. The diffuse energy is ambient energy spread throughout the room volume [8].

To assess the repeatability was very important to observe the initial slope of decay curves. In order to determine the decay times, the linear regression, according to the previous chapter, was used for finding fit lines to appropriate parts of the decay function. It is important to note that both decay times characterize a decrease in the sound energy level during the initial decay of sound. As can be seen from Figure 4, there are significant differences between each regression lines. For 50 Hz the excitation maximum peak sound pressure level was so low that the calculation could not be executed. At frequencies, 63 to 125 Hz can be observed quite wide variances of the slope of the regression lines. This indicates that it is extremely important to average over many source positions if the sound power of a source with a significant content of pure tones is to be determined in a reverberation chamber. However, this frequency range is not suitable for performing laboratory measurements with high accuracy. The frequencies 160 and 200 Hz also shows weaknesses as well though not so heavy. Nonetheless, there is no doubt that the inner space for these frequencies is not sufficiently diffuse.

Equally important was to compare the smoothness of the reverberation decay for the third-octaves from 50 Hz to 10 kHz. In general, the smoothness of the decay increases as frequency is increased, this can be seen in both Figures 4 and 5. The sound power emitted by an impulse source in a lightly damped chamber cannot be expected to be unaffected by the reverberant sound field even when it is placed far from the walls of the chamber, especially when the rectangular shape is assumed. This can be seen, for example, 50 Hz a large wave fluctuations are noted suggesting that in this case the beating effect is present. The beat information on the low-frequency reverberation decay makes possible a judgment on the degree of diffusion [11]. This effect increases the relative standard deviation of calculated reverberation times.

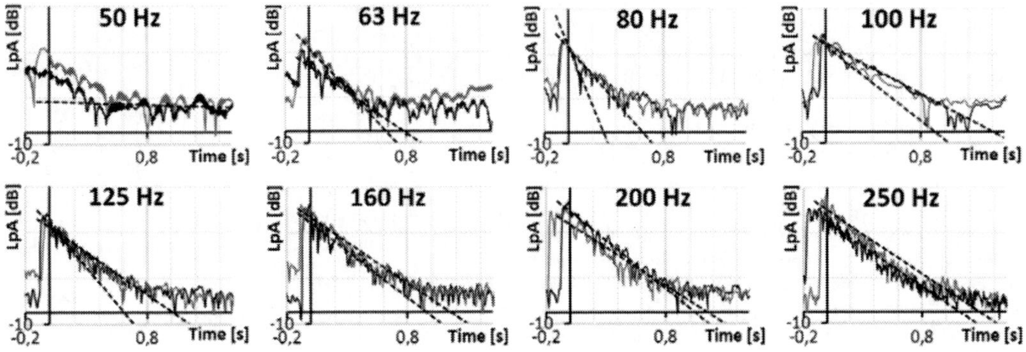

Figure 4. Temporal decay of level L_{pA} of pressure envelope for mid-frequencies of third-octave bandwidth about 50 to 250 Hz.

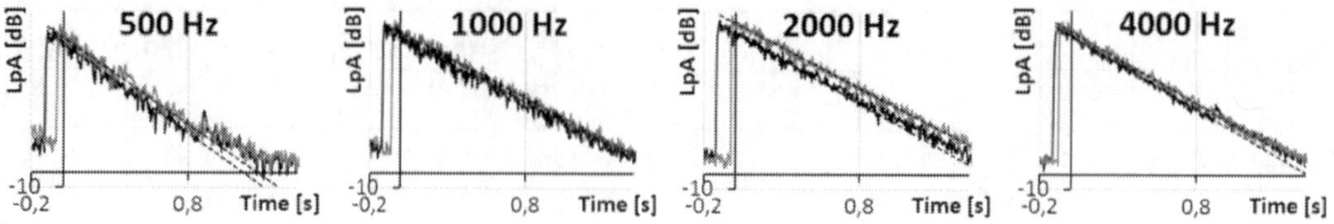

Figure 5. Temporal decay of level L_{pA} of pressure envelope for mid-frequencies of octave bandwidth about 500 to 4000 Hz.

For frequencies 63 and 80 Hz a characteristic property is a considerable different between decay times in the early and late stages of the decaying sound. A fundamental change of the response consists in a rapid decrease in a pressure in the initial stage of a sound decay. When the excitation impulse from the balloon burst energizes the inner space of the chamber, it excites one mode, and an instant later another mode. While the response shifts to the second mode, the first mode begins to decay. Before it decays very far, however, the random noise instantaneous frequency is once more back in the first mode, giving it another boost. All the modes of the room are in constant agitation, alternating between high and somewhat lower levels, as they begin to decay in between stimuli. It is strictly a random situation, but it can be said with confidence that each time the excitation noise is stopped, the modal excitation pattern will be somewhat different. These phenomena belong to the modal theory and it's well described in [8]. For the frequencies in Figure 5, the analysed time domain decreases almost linearly. These decays provide information that inner space is more stable than frequencies below 250 Hz. Within the mid-frequency 200 Hz of third-octave band will be located region where the transition boundary between the modal region where the room modes are well separated and the region of diffuse behaviour of a sound field, known also as the Schroeder region, where there is a high overlap of the room responses.

5 Conclusion

Reproducibility of acoustic data measured in acoustic laboratories is difficult to achieve for wide frequency bandwidth. For acoustic laboratories that perform measurements with high accuracy, it is necessary to know the frequency range where the sound fields are adequately diffuse and where not. In this paper were compared the decay curves obtained in several positions. These decays are not identical, and differences can be attributed to the non-uniform character of an acoustic field through the chamber. In particular, the fluctuations in the decays result from beats between closely spaced modes. Because the excitation level of the modes is constantly shifting, the form and degree of the beat pattern shift from one decay to another depending on where the random excitation happens. There is much information in each decay, and acoustical flaws can often be identified from aberrant decay shapes. The results are definitely signed by the fact that it has not been used impulse sound source which generates always the same pure-tone but balloon burst was used. In future will be the verification process made with a pistol shot.

The work could be extended to include the effects of edge diffraction, which previously in this paper have been shown to cause significant estimation errors in measured data. The work also needs to re-derive acoustic properties of all boundary walls using alternative reverberation time formulations to get absorption coefficients.

Acknowledgement

This work was supported by the Ministry of Education, Youth and Sports of the Czech Republic within the National Sustainability Programme project No. LO1303 (MSMT-7778/2014) and also by the Internal Grant Agency of Tomas Bata University in Zlin under the project No. IGA/CebiaTech/2016/001.

References

1. P. Drabek, Diploma thesis, (2014)
2. F. Jacobsen, *The Sound Field in a Reverberation Room*, (2011)
3. D. Bradley, M. Muller-Trapet, J. Adelgren, M. Vorlander, Building Acoustics, **21**, 145-152 (2014)
4. W. Weise, V. Wittstock, Building Acoustics, **12**, 3 (2005)
5. CSN EN ISO 3741, Standard, Urad pro technickou normalizaci, metrologii a statni zkusebnictvi, Prague, CZ (2011)
6. CSN EN ISO 354, Standard, Urad pro technickou normalizaci, metrologii a statni zkusebnictvi, Prague, CZ (2003)
7. H. Kuttruff, Room Acoustics, **5**, (2009)
8. T. Cox, P. D'Antonio, Acoustic Absorbers and Diffusers, **2**, (2009)
9. E. Deines, Dissertation, (2008)
10. M. Meissner, Archives of acoustics, **41**, 27-41 (2016)
11. M. Meissner, Archives of acoustics, **38**, 47-54 (2013)
12. CSN EN ISO 3382-2, Standard, Urad pro technickou normalizaci, metrologii a statni zkusebnictvi, Prague, CZ (2009)
13. M. Schroeder, Acoustical Society of America, **37**, 3, 400-412 (2016)
14. M. Horvat, K. Jambrosic, H. Domitrovic, Acoustics08 Paris, **17**, 3985-3990 (2008)

Monitoring and forecasting of intensive convective precipitation with the use of the mobile meteorological radar (MMR50)

David Šaur[1a] and Pavel Tomášek[1]

[1]Faculty of Applied Informatics, Tomas Bata University in Zlín, Namesti T.G.Masaryka 5555, 760 01 Zlin, Czech Republic

Abstract. This paper is focused on current possibilities of the measurement and predictions of intense convective precipitation through the mobile meteorological radar (MMR50). This meteorological radar equipment is part of the Information, Notification and Warning system of the Zlin Region in the Czech Republic, which consists of information and communication infrastructure for dealing with extraordinary events. The first chapter describes basic principles of radar precipitation measurement, e.g. radar estimate of rainfall intensity and radar products. The second chapter presents a methodology of measuring and predicting of intense convective precipitation using the mobile meteorological radar (MMR50), including other possibilities of precipitation forecast as NWP models, aerological, satellite, station measurements, statistics of historical situations, the risk of flash floods on the degree of soils saturation and the possibility of observation of dangerous accompanying phenomena. The last chapter deals with the verification of the principles of radar measurements and forecasts in a case study on 24th July 2015. Torrential rainfall in a combination with hail and strong wind gusts caused heavy flooding in the central part of Zlin region, which caused considerable material damage. Timely and quality information about the current and future formation and development of intense convective precipitation is essential for flood prevention measures. Acquired findings and conclusions can be used for crisis management in case of a possible occurrence of flash floods.

1 Introduction

The Zlín Region is one of the regions of the Czech Republic, which have been strongly affected by the impacts of local flash floods in the past decade. Three extensive flooding caused by persistent and intensive precipitation occurred in 1997-2006 (145 billion of material damages and the death toll of 88). This type of flooding is a specific with large expanse of the affected area. In contrast, flash floods have occurred regularly since 2007 until present (35 billion in material damages and the death toll of 41). This type of flooding affects the area of the very small size in the order of several km^2. Material damages are caused not only by torrential rainfall but also other hazardous atmospheric phenomena such as hail, strong wind gusts, tornadoes and atmospheric electrical discharges. Although, flash floods have not caused flood damage to the same extent as the second type of the flood, they occur at a substantially higher frequency.

In addition, current possibilities forecasting possibilities of flash floods probability are very limited. The forecasting of torrential rainfall is realized by NWP models and nowcasting systems. Both prediction methods achieve relatively low success rate, up to about 50%. Consequently, the Zlin Region has decided to actively solve this problem by creating the Information, Notification and Warning System of the Zlin Region. This system is formed by the backbone of information and communication infrastructure of the Zlin Region. The essence is its own internal network made of fiber optic cable, whose users are independent from the Internet and other external sources. The central unit is a server located on the regional managing workplace of the Crisis Staff of the Zlin Region. Information is distributed from this department to another 11 municipalities with extended powers. The main advantage is the efficient communication between the authorities of Crisis Management and the Integrated Rescue System of the Czech Republic before the occurrence and during extraordinary events [1].

Information, Notification and Warning System of the Zlin Region consist of many components, such as central dispatching, warning information systems, video conferencing systems, municipal camera surveillance systems, sensors and meteorological stations, chemical detection elements, substitute energy sources and the mobile meteorological radar (MMR50). This meteorological radar is a major tool intended for monitoring the current precipitation situation and very short-term forecasts for 30-60 minutes. The purpose of the device is to provide timely and relevant information on the weather situation, which may arise from a flash flood [2].

The main objective of this article is to describe the methodology of monitoring and forecasting of dangerous

[a] Corresponding author: saur@fai.utb.cz

weather phenomena by using the MMR50 meteorological radar.

2 Radar precipitation measurements

The mobile meteorological radar (MMR50) is a device intended for:

- Precipitation clouds detection,
- The intensity of precipitation estimation and
- The 3D information obtaining about the distribution of precipitation in the atmosphere.

2.1 Principle of radar precipitation measurement

The mobile meteorological radar (MMR50) consists of an antenna, which generates a narrow beam of high-energy pulses. When the beam encounters a particle of cloud, it is partially absorbed and then dispersed in all directions. Scattered rays are captured by the antenna where are subsequently amplified and detected by the radar receiver. The receiver calculates power of rays and the time from the pulse. The analog signal is digitized and processed by the special software. The resulting information is displayed to end users in the form of an image with radar reflections on a map [3], [4], [5].

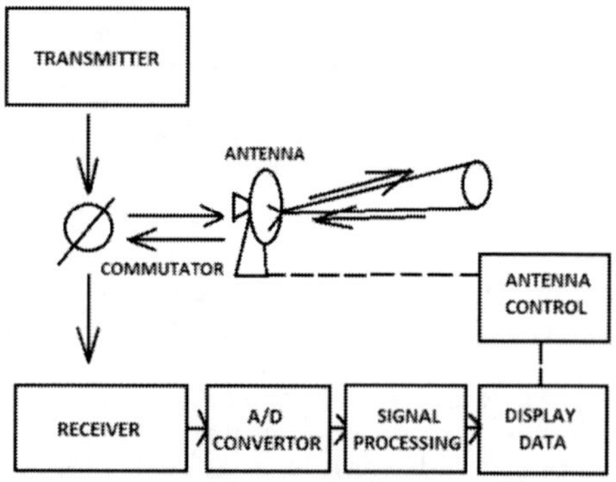

Figure 1. Scheme of the meteorological radar MMR50 [6].

The mobile meteorological radar (MMR50) also consists of other components such as radar units, elevation and azimuth drive including sensors, heating and cooling system, and power source part and the control computer [1].

Table 1. Parameters of the MMR50 meteorological radar [7].

Parameters	Values
Operating frequency	X-band (9410 MHz)
Transmitter Power Peak	50 kW
Antenna Elevation	-1°to +90°
Pulse Repetition Frequency	500 Hz
Maximum range	100 km

As can be seen in Table 1, The mobile meteorological radar (MMR50) operates at X-band with a wavelength of 3 cm. The advantage of this feature is higher detection sensitivity of intense precipitation but with a significantly higher attenuation, lower repetition frequency and maximum range than meteorological radars from the Czech Radar Network.

2.2 Radar estimation of the rainfall intensity

Fundamental radar parameter is the radar reflectivity. Radar reflectivity is the amount of energy reflected from precipitation of cloud particles, where N (D) denotes the spectrum of particle sizes and D_i represents the diameter of a droplet [3]:

$$Z = \Sigma D_i^6 = \int N(D) D^6 dD. \qquad (1)$$

Measured radar reflectivity is reported as 10 $\log Z_e$ [mm^6/m^3] in the unit of dBz.

Rainfall intensity I is dependent on the radar reflectivity Z determined using the Marshall-Palmer formula:

$$Z = aI^b \qquad (2)$$

where a and b are experimentally determined constants (a = 200, b = 1.6). Rainfall intensity I is calculated by the following formula [3], [4], [5]:

$$I = 10(Z\text{-}10\log(a))/10b. \qquad (3)$$

Table 2. The exponential dependence of radar reflectivity and intensity of precipitation [6].

Z [dBz]	I [mm/hr]	Meteorological targets
7	0,1	Weak rain
23	1	Moderate rain
39	10	Intensive rain
48	37	Intensive convective precipitation
52	65	Torrential rainfall
56	100	Intensive torrential rainfall
60	200	Hail, tornadoes

Table 2 shows that the radar reflectivity Z is changing exponentially dependent on the change of rainfall intensity.

2.3 3D information of the MMR50 meteorological radar

The mobile meteorological radar (MMR50) processes the input data into materials for analyzing and forecasting meteorological radar maps, and the subsequent distribution of documents to the Information, Notification and Warning System of the Zlin Region

3D radar information consists of the original volume of the radar data stored in Spherical coordinates which are converted into Cartesian coordinates. The result is product of radar reflectivity:

- -PPI (Plan Position Indicator) is the field of radar reflectivity measured at various elevation angles. The algorithm is based on bilinear interpolation for each pixel separately.
- -CAPPI (Constant Altitude Plan Position Indicator) the field of radar reflectivity calculated for a given altitude.
- -ColumnMax (Composite Reflexivity) is the maximum radar reflectivity in a vertical column of the atmosphere.
- -RHI (Range Height Indicator) is a vertical sectional view of the atmosphere where the main parameter is the azimuth. RHI algorithm is calculated as with the PPI.
- -Max Z the maximum field of radar reflectivity with side projections representing a vertical column of the atmosphere.
- -ECHOTOPS provides information on cloud altitude, with a maximum radar reflectivity.
- -VIL (Vertically Integrated Liquid) is a vertically integrated liquid water content determined by assuming the Marshall-Palmer distribution; VIL value is determined by the following formula:

$$VIL = 3{,}44.10^{-6} \int^{ht}_{hz} Z^{4/7} dh, \quad (4)$$

where Z [mm6.m-3] radar reflectivity, hz [m] height of the cloud base and ht [m] is the height of the cloud top. Summation over different levels of PPI is performed each surface element [3], [7].

These radar products (results) are used to specify the radar information in real time. The main objective is to obtain current information on the rainfall intensity and a probable occurrence of dangerous atmospheric phenomena.

3 Methodology of the measurement and forecasting of intensive convection precipitation

Radar results of the mobile meteorological radar (MMR50) provide us with information about the current state of the occurrence of precipitation in the atmosphere. One of the software components is an application Nowcast TITAN that provides predictive information about the intensity of precipitation equal or higher than 37 mm / hr. However, this predictive information is insufficient to assess the future occurrence of flash floods. Each meteorologist must have information on the conditions of air masses, satellite, aerological, station and other data.

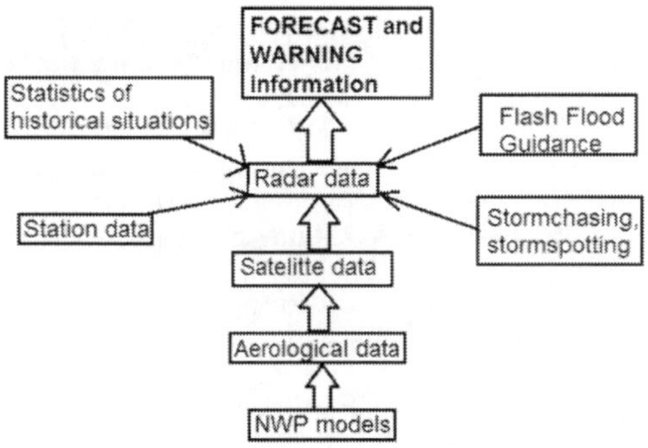

Figure 2. Scheme of the forecast and warning of the flash flood.

Complex intense convective precipitation forecast includes data from:

- -NWP models an aerological radiosonde (indices of convection, meteorological elements).
- -Satellite data (Infra-Red image and IR image in the thermal spectrum)
- -Radar data (outputs of the 6 radar products, statistics of historical situations, station data, the degree of the soil saturation and data from observations of thunderstorms).

3.1. Radar precipitation measurement

Analysis of the current rainfall situation contains the following information:

Table 3. Radar measurement intensive convective precipitation.

Radar products	Limits of measurement	Dangerous atmospheric phenomena
ColumnMax, Max Z	52 dBz	Moderate torrential rainfall
	56 dBz	Intensive torrential rainfall
	60 dBz	Hail, tornadoes
CAPPI	2 km	Torrential rainfall
RHI	2-4 km	Tornadoes
ECHOTOP	above 10 km	Torrential rainfall, hail, tornadoes
VIL	above 30 kg/m^2	Torrential rainfall, hail,

Probability prediction of the occurrence of dangerous accompanying phenomena must be combined with the outputs of NWP models, aerological, satellite and station measurements.

3.2 Very short-time forecast via MMR50 meteorological radar

The very short-term forecast is performed through the application of Nowcast TITAN. The principle of this system is simple. The algorithm marked on the map, such precipitation fields that have reached the radar reflectivity (Z=48 dBz), determines the direction of movement based on previous precipitation radar outputs and the red arrow indicates where the rainfall field will move during 30-60 minutes [1].

Comprehensive forecasting of flash floods is supplemented by information from:

- Statistics of historical weather situations.
- Degree of saturation of soils obtained from the Flash Flood Guidance.
- Observations of thunderstorms (Stormchasing and Stormspotting).

Statistics of historical weather events are intended to supplement the resulting predictions. The main selection criteria of historical weather situations is the direction of movement of precipitation (wind direction at 700 hPa), the synoptic situation and significant meteorological parameters (temperature, relative humidity at 2 meters above ground, wind direction and wind speed of 10 m above ground).

The degree of soil saturation is analyzed from the Flash Flood Guidance and demonstrates the probability of occurrence of flash floods by the permeability of the soil surface.

Observations from the terrain thunderstorms are supplementary information to nowcasting which can detect and confirm the presence of dangerous accompanying phenomena. Simultaneously, the purpose of the data is control and verification of radar precipitation measurements.

4 Case study on 24.7.2015

The methodology of measurements and predictions using the mobile meteorological radar (MMR50) was verified on a case study dated July 24, 2015. The central part of the Zlin Region was hit by local flash floods accompanied by hail and strong wind gusts.

The forecast of the weather situation was very complicated. Czech Hydrometeorological Institute did not deliver predictive warning information on the occurrence of the strong thunderstorms for this region.

The triggering mechanism of intensive convective precipitation was cold front on the western Slovakia, which had a tendency to go back to the east of the Czech Republic.

4.1. Outputs of radar precipitation measurement

Formation and development of intense convective precipitation were demonstrated at various radar products as ColumnMax, CAPPI 2km, Max Z, Range Height Indicator (RHI), ECHOTOP and Vertically Integrated Liquid (VIL) in real time between 17: 18-18: 13. These radar results show certain qualities and character of intensive convective precipitation clouds.

4.1.1 Radar products ColumnMax and CAPPI 2 km

Column Max is radar product which provides information about the maximum intensity of precipitation in the vertical column of the atmosphere. However, this output does not inform us about the current state of rainfall, but that a certain level of atmospheric precipitation occurs with the maximal intensity. Hence, the probable occurrence of rainfall is measured using CAPPI 2 km.

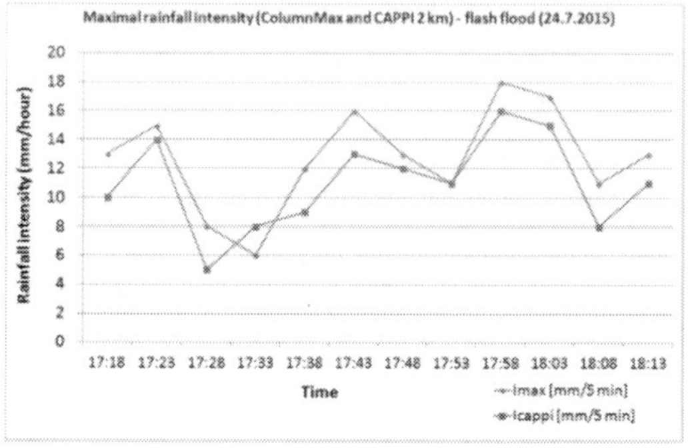

Figure 3. The current maximal intensity of precipitation measured by means of products Column Max and CAPPI 2 km.

Rainfall in mm/5 minutes is calculated from hourly precipitation intensity, divided by 12. Hour period had three peaks with the most intense rainfall. Rainfall intensity by product CAPPI 2 km achieved lower values than in ColumnMax, which determines the maximum intensity of precipitation in the whole atmosphere.

4.1.2 Radar product Max Z

Radar product Max Z contains information about the maximal intensity of precipitation in the column as ColumnMax and in addition horizontal and vertical distribution of rainfall intensity in different height levels.

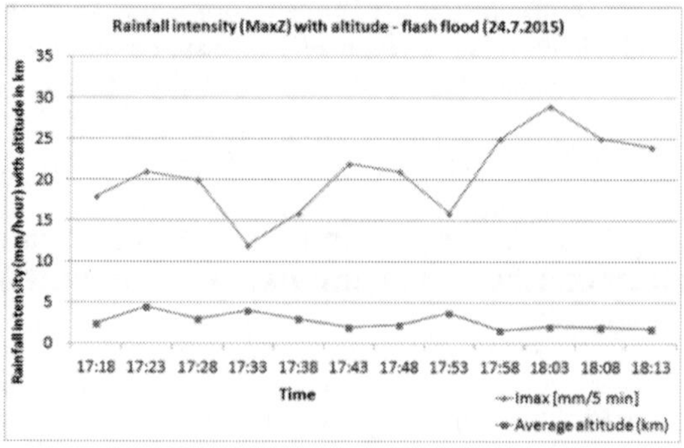

Figure 4. The current maximal rainfall intesity in different height levels (radar product Max Z).

Formation and development of convective precipitation clouds was clearly demonstrated by the outputs of the product Max Z. Intense convective precipitation occurred at the altitude of 3-5 km in the initial stages of development of convective storms; the mature stage in the levels of 2-4 km and the dissipating stage under 2 km. The most intense rainfall occurred mainly in the mature and dissipating stage of convective storms.

4.1.3 Radar product Range Height Indicator (RHI)

Range Height Indicator RHI gives information about the vertical and horizontal spatial distribution of rainfall intensity in the azimuth. The main purpose is to detect the area of Bounded Weak Echo Region (BWER) and HOOK Echo at an altitude of 2-4 km, which indicates the presence of supercell storms accompanied by tornadoes.

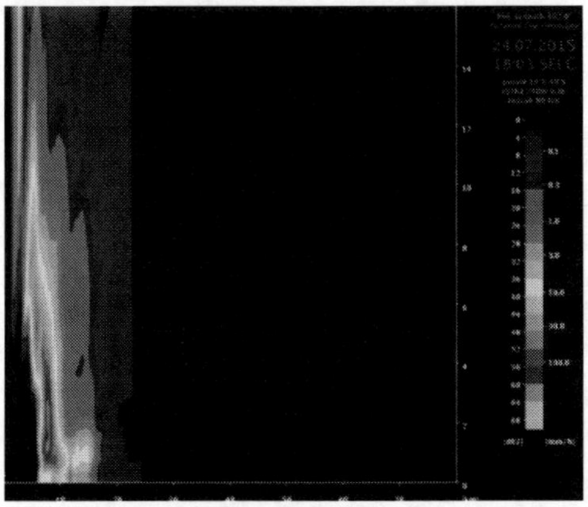

Figure 5. Vertical and horizontal distribution of rainfall intensity in the azimuth 102° (radar product RHI).

Figure 5 illustrates the distribution of rainfall intensity in the process of dissipating of convective storms. The most intensive reflections in the form of hail occurred at the level of 2 km and then below this level.

4.1.4 Radar product ECHOTOP

ECHOTOP radar product provides additional information about the occurrence of the maximum rainfall intensity at the highest altitude.

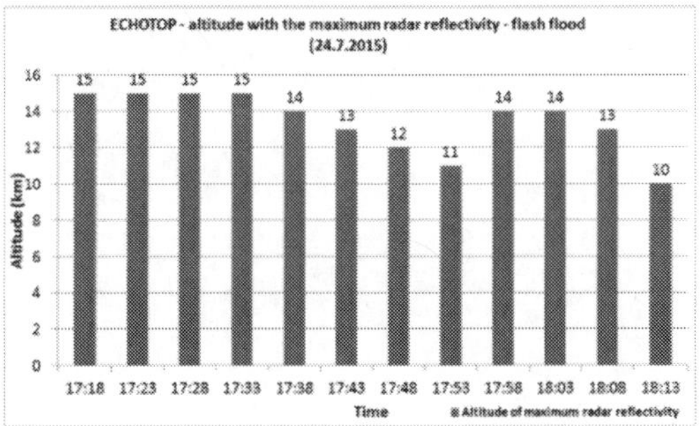

Figure 6. The height of the maximum rainfall intensity (radar product ECHOTOP).

Figure 6 shows that rainfall maximum intensity was present at an altitude of 15 km in the initial development of convective cells. Height occurrence of intense precipitation has gradually decreased (14-10 km) due to loss precipitation in the process of dissipating of convective storms.

4.1.4 Radar product Vertically Integrated Liquid VIL

Radar product VIL gives information about the amount of liquid water contained in the cloud in kg per m^2. This product is very important for the prediction of torrential rainfall which can cause the flash flood.

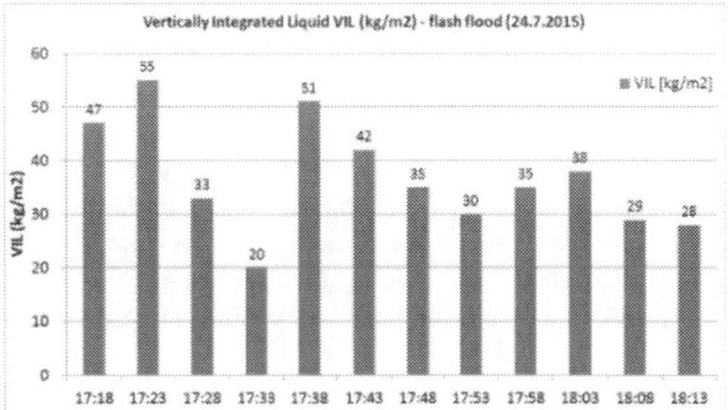

Figure 7. The quantity of liquid water contained in the convective precipitation clouds.

Figure 7 demonstrates the greatest amount of liquid water which was presented in convective precipitation clouds in the initial stage of development and the mature stage of convective storms. Torrential rainfall was measured in the district Vsetin and Zlin between 17 and 18 hours. Station precipitation measurements corresponded with radar outputs.

4.2. Outputs of forecasting precipitation using Nowcast TITAN

Very short-term forecast was implemented by software Nowcast TITAN. The output of was a graphical information about the current and future state of intense convective precipitation for 30-60 minutes in advance. Nowcast TITAN determines the area of municipalities with extended powers of the Zlin Region, for which it was calculated the forecast of precipitation locations and the direction of movement precipitation:

Table 4. Forecast precipitation of the Nowcast TITAN.

Time period	Measured precipitation in locations	Predicted precipitation in locations	Direction of precipitation motion
17:18-17:33	Vsetín, Rožnov, Vizovice	Vsetín, Walachian Meziříčí, Bystřice	Southeast (SE)
17:38-17:48	Vsetín, Vizovice, Zlín	Vsetín, Walachian Meziříčí, Zlín	Southeast (SE)
17:53-18:18	Vsetín, Bystřice, Zlín	Bystřice, Zlín, Holešov	East (E)

4.3. Other forecasting outputs

Outputs of the Nowcast TITAN were supplemented by other information, which is very important for predicting probability of occurrence of flash floods:

-NWP models predict rainfall intensity 30-50 mm / hr for the phenomenon of "Strong thunderstorms".

-Satellite measurements were measured maximum temperature cloud top -60 ° C which is typical for vertically developed convective clouds.

-The anticipated rate of precipitation was confirmed by statistics of historical situations in the areas of Vsetin, Vizovice, Zlín and Bystřice in the days 7.11 and 8.07. 2011.

-The highest degree of soil saturation (the highest risk of flash floods) was computed from the area Roznov, Vsetin, Zlín and Bystrice.

-Amateur meteorologists have confirmed the occurrence of thunderstorms accompanied by torrential rainfall and hailstorm in the municipalities Fryšták, Zlín-Štípa, Lukov, and Hrobice. Strong wind gusts were seen in Zlín-Malenovice which caused material damage to the roofs of houses.

5 Conclusion

The aim of the article was to provide information about current possibilities of monitoring and predictions of intense convective precipitation in the Zlin Region, Czech Republic. Principles of the methodology of measurements and predictions via the mobile meteorological radar (MMR50) were verified on a case study of the July 24, 2015 when the Zlin Region was hit by flash floods.

The most intense precipitation was predicted for area district the Vsetín, Zlin and Bystrice using the software Nowcast TITAN, which is part of the meteorological radar equipment. Convective precipitation over 30 mm / h was measured in the Vsetín district (ground meteorological station Huslenky 33.8 mm and Hošťálková 33.1 mm) and Zlin (ground meteorological station Zlín-Stipa 42.8 mm). Station measurements showed the 80% success rate in predictions of locations of intense convective precipitation. In addition, the occurrence of hailstorms and strong wind gusts was confirmed by observations of amateur meteorologists in the central part of the Zlin Region. These dangerous atmospheric phenomena caused material losses of tens of millions of crowns.

Future research will concentrate on the optimization of limits setting for individual radar products, the expansion of the database of historical weather events statistics and observation networks of amateur meteorologists. The main objective will be to ensure timely and quality information on the current and future state of intense convective precipitation, which may cause flash floods.

Acknowledgement

This work was supported by the Internal Grant Agency of Tomas Bata University under the project No. IGA/ FAI/ 2016/023 "Optimization of the System of Convective Precipitation Forecasts for Increase its Success Rate".

References

1. Information, Notification and Warning System of the Zlín Region, Integrated project, Zlín Region. 2012 Avalaible at: http://www.kr-zlinsky.cz/-informacni-vyrozumivaci-a-varovaci-system-zlinskeho-kraje-integrovany-projekt-cl-1392.html
2. IVVS Zlín Region - Information, Notification and Warning System" Avalaible at: http://www.colsys.cz/novinky/detail/ivvs-zlinskeho-kraje.htm
3. D. Rezacova, et al. Physics of clouds and precipitation. Prague: Academia, 2007. 574 pp. with. Fig.Gerstner; sv. 2. ISBN 978-80-200-1505-1.
4. Czech Hydrometeorological Institute Radar network CHMI. 2010-2011 Available at: http:// http://www.chmi.cz/files/portal/docs/meteo/rad/info_czrad/index.html
5. J. Kracmar, Meteorological radars. Czech Hydrometeorological Institute. 1997-2011. Available: http:// http://www.chmi.cz/files/portal/docs/meteo/rad/info_radar/index.html
6. D. Saur, R. Zak, J. Svejda. 19. International Conference on Systems (CSCC ´15), Special Session: Informatics in Control Theory and its Applications – Control Applications. Recent Advances in Systems. Zakynthos Island, Greece, July 16-20, 2015, s. 280-285. ISBN: 978-1-61804-321-4. ISSN: 1790-5117.
7. D. Saur, S. Plsek. International Journal of Circuits, Systems and Signal Processing. 2014, ISSN: 1998-4464. Avalaible at: http://www.naun.org/main/NAUN/circuitssystemssignal/2014/a192005-045.pdf

MATEC Web of Conferences 76, 05011 (2016) DOI: 10.1051/matecconf/20167605011
CSCC 2016

Measuring the lactose content in milk

Hana Vaskova[1,a] and Martina Buckova[2]

[1]*Tomas Bata University in Zlin, Faculty of Applied informatics, Department of Electronic and Measurements, 760 05 Zlin, Czech Republic*
[2]*Tomas Bata University in Zlin, Faculty of Technology, Department of Food Technology, 760 01 Zlin, Czech Republic*

Abstract. Raman spectroscopy has become a powerful and popular tool for food systems analyses lately. Based on characteristic vibrations of the studied material, the information on its content and structure can be answered. In the paper, Raman spectroscopy is studied for a purpose of lactose content in milk assessment. Lactose, the milk disaccharide, in a human organism decomposes during digestion by the act of enzyme lactase to more easily digestible monosaccharides – glucose and galactose. The lack of enzyme lactase causes symptoms of lactose intolerance what limits lactose-intolerant individuals in the intake of milk and dairy products. Lactose-free products in the diet can be a solution. Raman spectroscopy offers rapid measurement independent of the number of chemicals and other in the paper listed benefits. Raman spectra of lactose, glucose and galactose exhibit enough differences to distinguish the content of lactose in milk. C-O-H bending mode at 1087 cm^{-1} is used for lactose quantification. The method accuracy for measuring content of lactose was tested on dried milk droplets. Evaluation of the spectroscopic data was related to two different substances - phenylalanine contained generally in the milk and crystal violet used as an internal standard.

1 Introduction

Milk and dairy products are commonly considered as an important part of human diet as a good source of proteins, calcium, phosphorus, magnesium, and other crucial macro- and micronutrients.

The simple disaccharide lactose represents about 5% of the milk content. In a human organism is decomposed by an enzyme lactase to monosaccharides. Different extent of lactase deficiency is described in most of the world's population. Nowadays, approximately 70% of adult population worldwide suffer from lactose intolerance. In most cases the intolerance is gained during the lifetime as genetically programmed decrease of the amount of lactase; however, in a small content can be inborn. Many people should control lactose intake in their diet. A number of nutritional specialists warn of complete exclusion of dairy products from the diet because of the increased risk of inadequate intake of calcium and other minerals, resulting in risk of osteoporosis, etc.

To avoid elimination milk and dairy product from diet, producers have to manufacture lactose-free products. For meeting this requirement it is necessary to handle appropriate equipment for fast, simple and real-time determination of lactose content in milk or dairy products.

Raman spectroscopy is one of rapidly developing modern spectroscopic methods expanding into many industry sectors including dairy industry. Raman spectroscopy brings many advantages over conventional techniques.

[a] Corresponding author: vaskova@fai.utb.cz

2 Focus of the study

Lactose assessment is necessary in terms of food technology and analyses of food product in connection with nutritional value and also lactose intolerance. The development and use of modern methods offers fast experimental procedures independent of a number of chemical reagents. Using Raman spectroscopy for quantification requires finding signal of any constant part of sample, and a calibration set of samples. In this paper two procedures are presented - the constant share of protein phenylalanine as a natural part of milk; and addition of crystal violet to the samples as an internal standard.

3 Theory

3.1 Milk and lactose

Milk and dairy products are important part of human nutrition. Mammalian milk is first food for infants, and milk consumption lasts to adulthood in many parts of population on the world. In European and American population cow milk is the most frequently consumed, but sheep and goat milk is consumed also. The chemical composition of milk is influenced by animal species, environmental conditions, nutrition of animals, their lactation state and others. Main characteristics of milk are

Table 1. Average composition of goat, sheep, bovine and human milk [1].

	Milk			
	Bovine	Sheep	Goat	Human
Fat [%]	3,6	7,9	3,8	4,0
Lactose [%]	4,7	4,9	4,1	6,9
Protein [%]	3,2	6,2	3,4	1,2
Calcium [mg/100 g]	122	193	134	33
Phosphorus [mg/100 g]	119	158	121	43
Vitamin A [IU]	126	146	185	190
Vitamin D [IU]	2,0	0,18	2,3	1,4
Energy [kcal/100 g]	69	105	70	68

described in Table 1. Bovine milk is composed of 87% water, 4-5% lactose, 3-4% fat, 3% proteins, 0,8% minerals and 0,1% vitamins, on average.

As was mentioned above, lactose content can be individually important for many people. Lactose is the main carbohydrate present in milk. It is a disaccharide molecule composed by glucose and galactose. In human digestion there is enzyme called lactase (connected to small intestine membrane) that hydrolyses lactose to glucose and galactose. Chemical structure is shown in Figure 1. This lactase activity decreases significantly after weaning, but it is individual and it does not happen at the same grade [1].

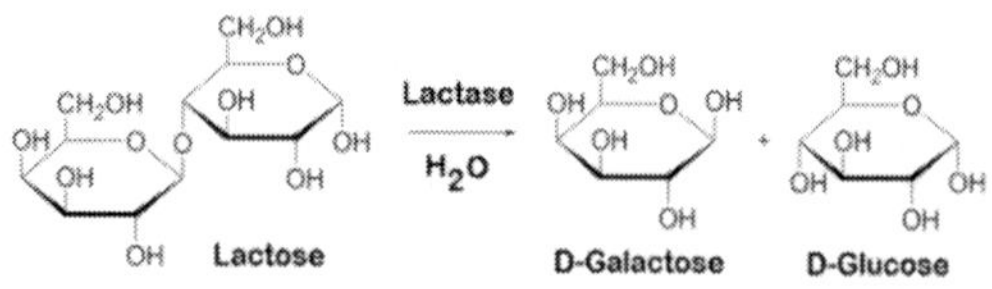

Figure 1. Chemical structure of lactose, glucose and galactose.

It is estimated approximately 70% adult population worldwide suffer from lactose intolerance. This is strongly influenced by human origin. In adult population in Europe and USA it is approximately 7-20%, in some Asian countries it is close to 100% [2]. Similar situation is in African countries. Lactose intolerance causes problems in gastrointestinal tract due to non-hydrolysed lactose, which is fermented by microorganisms in the colon. The main symptoms are flatulence, abdominal cramps and bloating, diarrhoea, nausea and others [1].

Some years ago, it was necessary to avoid all products with lactose content. Today, milk producers offer many kinds of milk and dairy products with low lactose content. Cheese, curd cheese and fermented dairy products content low amount of lactose due to their technological origin. On the other hand, products with high lactose content are milk, dried milk and cream. It is possible to found some lactose-free milk on the market.

3.2 Determination of lactose

Common methods for lactose determination in milk include gravimetric analysis, gas chromatography and most often high-performance liquid chromatography (HPLC). These methods are time consuming, need reagents and they are difficult for on-line analysis [3]. This is the reason for novel techniques development. For this purpose modern spectroscopy methods are often used. Near-infrared spectroscopy is one of those popular methods in dairy industry. However, it is necessary to adjust the determination due to water absorption interferences. Other new methods were developed using enzyme biosensors, which could be utilized for real-time lactose quantification in milk and dairy products [4].

3.3 Raman spectroscopy

Raman spectroscopy as a vibrational spectroscopic method reflects chemical composition and structure of materials. This feature makes the method proper for material identification. Moreover, considering the advantages of the method, Raman spectroscopy becomes popular and valuable part of laboratories around the world in recent years.

Raman spectroscopy provides very specific chemical „fingerprint“ of every single chemical substance in the form of the Raman spectrum. The method is based on so called Raman scattering. Raman scattering is an inelastic scattering resulting from an interaction of a photon and a molecule. In inelastic scattering photons have slightly changed wavelengths that are characteristic for specific bonds in surveyed material. Since most photons are on molecules scattered elastically (Rayleigh scattering without changing the wavelength), it is necessary to filter out of the spectrum of the strongly present wavelength of laser.

Although the fundamental phenomenon is known since thirties of the 20th century, its effective use in Raman spectroscopy occurs in about last decade. The rebirth of this method goes hand in hand with advances in a laser, detectors and computer technology. Raman spectroscopy brings many advantages as the method is relatively rapid, non-destructive, contactless, usable for measuring through transparent glass or polymeric covering layers or containers, applicable to all states of matter and different forms, without special requirements for sample preparation, usable as *in situ* analysis

The greatest drawback of the method is the fact that Raman scattering is a weak effect. Luminescence as much stronger quantum effect with bigger intensity can overlap Raman spectra and mask spectral information. Another disadvantage is eventual degradation of a sensitive sample when using intense laser beam.

Raman spectroscopy finds many applications in recent years in a number of scientific areas such as chemistry, biochemistry, material science, mineralogy, arts, medicine, also is used for pharmaceutical or forensic and security purposes.

4 Experimental part

4.1. Samples and chemicals

Samples were prepared from commonly sold milk (containing lactose) and lactose-free milk. Lactose, glucose and galactose from Sigma Aldrich were used as standards for HPLC calibration and to obtain Raman spectra of pure saccharides.

A set of samples were prepared from a common milk with additions of lactose to final amounts from 5,5 g/ 100 ml to 9,5 g/ 100 ml. Another set of samples contained also crystal violet (CV) as an internal standard [3].

After experiences with previous measurements of milk for milk fat content analyses [5] and the appearing luminescence at liquid milk samples, the form of dried milk droplets on aluminium plates was considered for the measurements and evaluation.

4.1.1 Sugar content in milk by HPLC

The accurate contents of individual monosaccharides and disaccharide were determined by HPLC. The data for common milk (LM) and lactose-free milk (LFM) are listed in Table 2.

Table 2. Content of lactose (LAC), glucose (GLU) and galactose (GAL) in milk. NS = not specified.

Sample	LAC [g/100 ml]	GLU [g/100 ml]	GAL [g/100 ml]
LM	5,46 ± 0,12	NS	NS
LFM	NS	2,34 ± 0,06	2,41 ± 0,05

4.1.2 Phenylalanine content in milk by IEC

Phenylalanine (Phe) is one of essential amino acids. It occurs in all organisms, especially as a apart of protein and must be supplied from a diet of animal of vegetable origin. Naturally it is found in a breast milk of mammlas.

Amount of phenylalanine and 14 other amino acids in milk samples obtained after acid hydrolysis was assessed using ion-exchange liquid chromatography (IEC) as described in [6]. Phenylalanine was determined in common milk, lactose-free milk and also in all tested samples. The content was considered as constant (0,93 ± 0,04) g/kg. Under this condition, it is possible to use peak corresponding to phenylalanine for spectra normalization as is shown below in the result section.

4.2 Instrumentation

4.2.1 Raman microscope

InVia Basis Raman microscope (Renishaw) was used to measure Raman spectra of all samples. The Raman microscope uses two lasers as light sources: argon ion laser with the maximum power 20 mW and 785 nm NIR diode laser with maximum output power 300mW. Both were tested, however, more accurate and by luminescence less affected results were those, obtained using NIR laser. A Leica DM 2500 confocal microscope with the resolution 2μm was coupled to the Raman spectrometer.

The acquisitions were collected with 5 s exposure time and 20 accumulations for milk and 1 s exposure time and 10 accumulations for carbohydrates. The samples were firstly scanned in common range 100 to 3200 cm^{-1} with 2 cm^{-1} spectral resolution. After determining the principle vibrational response the spectral range was then reduced to area from ca 300 to 1700 cm^{-1}.

4.2.2 HPLC-RI

Determination of lactose content in milk samples was carried on HPLC chromatograph Shimadzu LC-20AD Prominence with diferencial refractometric detector RID-20A, autosampler SIL 20AC (all Shimadzu Scientific Instruments) and Agilent Zorbax NH_2 column. Solution acetonitril: water in ratio 80:20 was used as mobile phase (acetonitil for HPLC, Sigma Aldrich).

4.2.3 IEC

Amount of phenylalanine in milk samples was determined by ion-exchange liquid chromatography (IEC). Amino Acid Analyzer AAA400 (Ingos, Prague, Czech Republic) was used for this analysis [6].

5 Results

All spectroscopic measurements were performed on dried milk droplets. Firstly Raman spectra of lactose, glucose and galactose were acquired. Spectrum of lactose, as can be seen in Figure 2, exhibits more peaks most likely due to the composition of two monosaccharides.

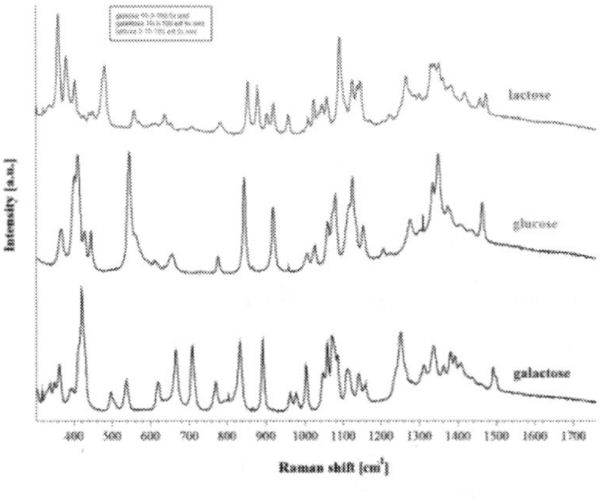

Figure 2. Raman spectra of lactose, galactose and glucose.

Secondly Raman spectra of milk and lactose-free milk were measured (see Figure 3). The Raman peaks of milk are listed in [5]. The main differences can be observed in region 400 cm^{-1} – 600 cm^{-1} area for endocyclic and exocyclic deformation bands [7], band 918 cm^{-1}

corresponding to glucose and mainly area around 1070 cm^{-1} – 1090 cm^{-1}. Here is clearly visible intense band 1087 cm^{-1} corresponding to lactose vibrations C-O-H bending mode. Band 1087 cm^{-1} is used for lactose content evaluation in sample sets.

Raman spectra of samples with addition of lactose were acquired. Baseline correction was applied on the spectral data in a uniform manner. Two methods were used for assessment of the lactose content. First method based on constant content of phenylalanine as was proved by HPLC. Second one uses CV as an internal standard.

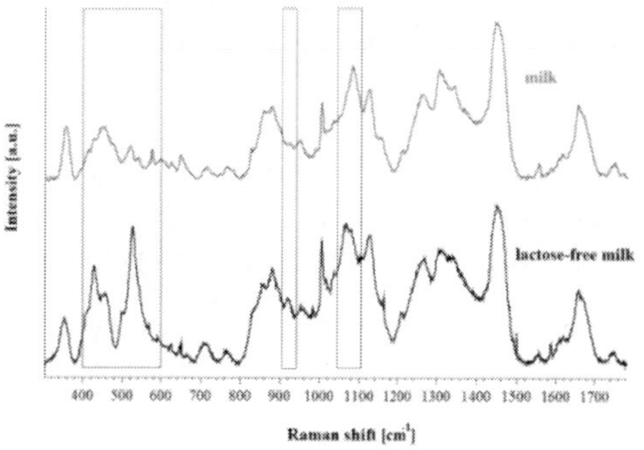

Figure 3. Raman spectra of milk and lactose-free milk.

5.1 Phenylalanine normalization

Raman spectra were normalized according to 1003 cm^{-1} band, which is characteristic for phenylalanine ring breathing band [8]. Phenylalanine is indicative of protein content in the sample. The dependence of the ratio of Raman intensities from bands 1087 cm^{-1} and 1003 cm^{-1} and the content of the lactose exhibits a steady increase, with quite well correlation as can be seen from Figure 4.

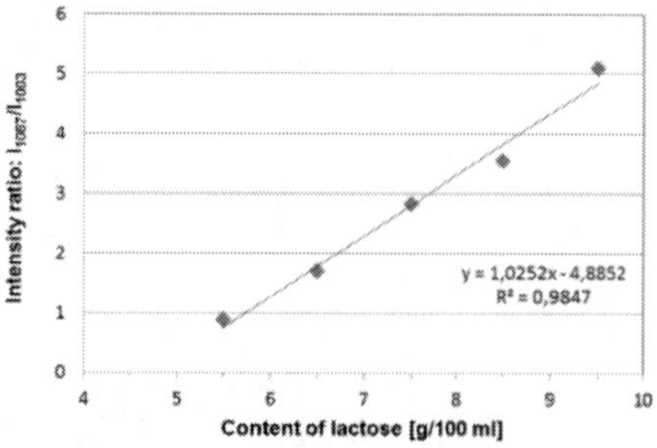

Figure 4. The increase of Raman intensity ratio I_{1087}/I_{1003} corresponding to content of lactose in milk using Phe as the standard.

5.2 Crystal violet normalization

As an internal standard CV was used and band 1173 cm^{-1} was taken for normalization as the most intense band in spectrum of CV, with a solitary position. Results acquired from Raman spectral data by linear regression shows (shown in Figure 5.) not so precise linear behavior (R^2 = 0,9122) in comparison with the phenylalanine normalization (R^2 = 0,9847). However, the linearly rising trend is observed also when using CV.

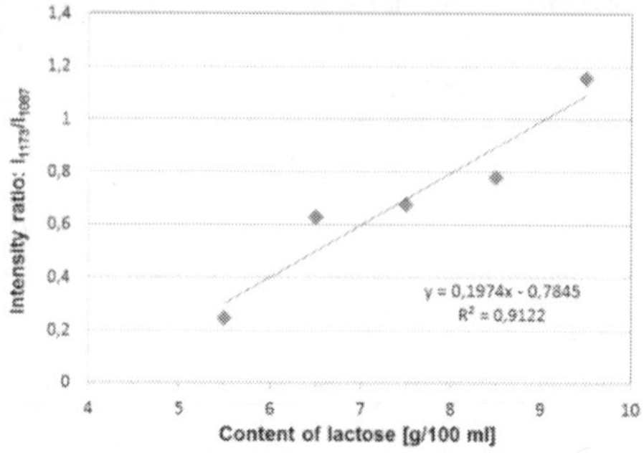

Figure 5. The increase of Raman intensity ratio I_{1173}/I_{1087} corresponding to content of lactose in milk using CV as an internal standard.

6 Conclusion

Raman spectroscopy was used as an innovative method for measuring the lactose content in milk. Measurements were performed on dried milk droplets in order to obtain more precise spectral response. Acquired spectral data show the possibility to distinguish different lactose concentrations on the basis of characteristic bands for lactose, phenylalanine or crystal violet. Normalization using phenylalanine exhibits better accuracy and also easier procedure without adding other substances. Raman spectroscopic evaluation brings advantages mainly in terms of simplicity, rapidity, no use of chemical reagents with the only demand to prepare the milk droplets.

Acknowledgement

This work was supported by the Ministry of Education, Youth and Sports of the Czech Republic within the National Sustainability Programme project No. LO1303 (MSMT-7778/2014) and also by the European Regional Development Fund under the project CEBIA-Tech No. CZ.1.05/2.1.00/03.0089

References

1. P.C. Pereira. Nutrition, **30**, 619-627, (2014).
2. S.B. Matthews, J.P. Waud, A.G. Roberts, A.K. Campbell Postgrad Med J, **81**, 167-73, (2005).
3. M Li, J. Chen, J. Xu, S. Fu, H. Gong. Analytical Letters, **48**, 1333-1340, (2015).
4. K. Kaniyamattam, A. De Vries. J. Dairy Sci., **97**, 2896-908, (2014).
5. H. Vaskova, M. Buckova, L. Zalesakova, Int. J. Biology Biomed Eng, **10**, 168-175,(2016).
6. F. Buňka, O. Kříž, A. Veličková, L. Buňková, S. Kráčmar. J. Food Compost Anal., **22**, 224-232, (2009)
7. J. De Gelder, K. De Gussem, P. Vandenabeele, L. Moens, J. Raman Spectrosc., ***38***, 1133-1147, (2007).
8. C.M. McGoverin, A. S. S. Clark, S. E. Holroyd, K. C. Gordon, Anal. Chim. Acta, **673**, 26-32, (2010)

MATEC Web of Conferences **76**, 05012 (2016) DOI: 10.1051/matecconf/20167605012
CSCC 2016

Raman microscopic detection of chromium compounds

Hana Vaskova[1,a]

[1] *Tomas Bata University in Zlin, Faculty of Applied informatics, Nad Stranemi 4511, 760 05 Zlin, Czech Republic*

Abstract. The paper is focused on performing Raman microscopy for the detection of trivalent and hexavalent chromium compounds. Raman spectroscopy has become a powerful method for material identification with the ability to differentiate the structure of the studied materials. It is important in the interests of human health and environmental protection to develop and use methods capable to measure not only the content of total chromium and but the content of toxic hexavalent chromium. Some of such methods are listed in the paper. Samples such as leather, leather processed to hydrolysate or leather waste material as well as the commonly used (yellow) paints, were used for the measurement. Evaluation was carried out on the basis of characteristic spectral features. Acquired Raman spectra show these features and can serve for qualitative analyses.

1 Introduction

Chromium finds wide industrial and commercial utilization already for decades. Suspected adverse health effects of prolonged exposure to chromium in particular on respiratory tract and skin has been known for a long time. The toxicity was clearly attributed to hexavalent form only in recent years. Problematic of hexavalent chromium belongs to widely discussed issues. It is realted to human health and the environmental impact. All things considered, both are inseparately connected.

Chromium exist predominantly in two forms as beneficial trivalent and mutagenic and toxic hexavalent chromium. Therefore measurements related to pottential hazard is complicated by duality of these two forms. This fact brings also stricter demands on the analytical methods to be able to differentiate compounds of trivalent and hexavalent in the samples as water, air, soil or stuff of an everyday life that are in direct contact with human organisms. One of the examples is leather goods. Aproximately 80% of the world production of leather is tanned using salts of trivalent chromium, which can oxidize under various conditions to toxic hexavalent form and cause health problems [1]. Another example is pained subjects. The colour scheme of some pigments is affected by both valences of chrome. Most of the matter subjects to ambient influences and thus changes. Neither for decades admired Sunflowers by Van Gogh, do not remain the same. Old Masters before the end of the 18th century used mineral pigments for shiny yellow colour, containing toxic elements such as chromium, lead or cadmium [2]. These pigments subject to reduction of hexavalent chromium in time and are changing the shiny yellow to green.

In this paper the attention is aimed on modern spectroscopic method Raman microscopy and its potential in a field of chemical component identification. On the set of samples with various share of trivalent and hexavalent chromium the advantages and contribution of the method is demonstrated.

2 Theory

2.1 Chromium

Chromium is one of the elements with a relatively high natural occurrence on Earth and in space. Chromium compounds appear in the environment also due to human activity as an adverse side product of industrial processes. This metallic element can exist in several oxidation states, however, the prevalent forms are two - trivalent chromium (CrIII) and hexavalent chromium (CrVI). Two forms with different properties and divergent impact on human health and environment.

2.1.1 Trivalent chromium

Trivalent chromium is a biogenic element and an essential part of human daily diet. Trace amounts help to control blood sugar (glucose) and stabilize blood fat levels. CrIII deficiency can cause fatigue, stress and decrease the body's ability to remove glucose from the blood. Compounds of trivalent chromium are benign due to low membrane permeability [3].

In the environment compounds of trivalent chromium are strongly bound to the soil particles and only small amounts penetrate from a soil to a groundwater.

[a] Corresponding author: vaskova@fai.utb.cz

Compounds of CrIII find applications for example in iron-chrome production, leather processing, manufacture of dyes and pigments, production of candles, cement.

2.1.2 Hexavalent chromium

In comparison to benign CrIII compounds, the CrVI compounds have mutagenic effects and are classified as carcinogens [4]. Compounds of hexavalent chromium cause allergic reactions, skin irritation and cancerous growth in nasal cavity, lung or in digestive tract. Significantly also affect the increase of heart disease.

The problematic of hexavalent chromium is connected also with the fact that compounds of CrIII can oxidize under various conditions to form CrVI compound. The conversion is known as well as some precursors, however the precise mechanism is complex and the details have not been clearly explained in literature yet.

Fortunately, human organisms abound by the defence mechanisms and have the ability to reduce CrVI to CrIII. To what extend is an issue for further research. Several sub-processes are discussed in [5]. Some studies show more dangerous impact of the instant high dose of CrVI compared to a similar dose obtained cumulatively in the longer term [6]. Other studies suggest, based on experimental and epidemiological data, on the incidence thresholds of CrVI in connection with carcinogenesis [7]. However, also the low-dose long-term contact with toxic elements should not be neglected.

Hexavalent chromium is a toxic element and is one of the heavy pollutants in the environment. CrVI compounds pollute air, watercourses usually as wastewaters from mainly metallurgical, leather and textile industries and penetrate into the soil from poorly secured landfills.

Compounds of CrVI find applications in metallurgical industry, chroming, welding of stainless steel, manufacture of dyes and pigments, production of chromium, printers, etc.

2.2 Methods for chromium detection

In the present time many methods allow measuring content of chromium. Often the content of chromium means total chromium (CrIII + CrVI). However, obtained results might be due to different classification of these two forms misleading in terms of safety, respectively hazard. More accurate evaluation arises from distinction of the benign and carcinogenic form, what is not always a rule when informing about chromium substances content. Separation techniques coupled with highly sensitive detection methods are needful for the analysis of the single chromium forms. For the detection of CrVI are recently used methods as [8]:

- Ultraviolet-visible spectrophotometry (UV-VIS) enables experimental identification of concentrations of hexavalent chromium in ppb in water and solutions. It is used as standard method. Detection limit of this method is about 50 μg/l.

- Inductively coupled plasma mass spectrometry (ICP-MS) is capable of detecting metals and several non-metals and to perform speciation of CrIII and CrVI in concentration in order 0,1g/μl.

- Inductively coupled plasma optical emission spectrometry (ICP-OAS) is analytical flame technique for detection of trace metals. For chromium the detection limit is similar as for ICP-MS.

- Atomic absorption spectroscopy (AAS), spectrometric analytical method used to determine the content of both, trace and major concentrations of individual elements in the analyzed solution.

- X-Ray fluorescence spectroscopy (XRF), atoms of energized sample give off specific X-rays characteristic of the element. The detection limit is several orders of magnitudes worse compared with ICP-MS.

Raman spectroscopy has the potential to recognize different chemical structures on the basis of molecular vibrations [9]. Raman spectroscopy/microscopy is the method discussed in this paper for the two chromium valences detection.

Problematic is often the detection limit of the methods together with allowed limits of the CrVI in different substances and environments, and also the availability of the measuring device for a specific application.

2.2.1 Raman microscopy

Raman microscopy incorporates the advantages of Raman spectroscopy and optical microscopy. Raman spectroscopy as a vibrational spectroscopic method reflects chemical composition and structure of materials. This feature makes the method proper for material identification. Together with the advantages of optical microscopy, Raman microscopy becomes popular and finds a valuable place in laboratories worldwide in recent years [9].

Raman spectroscopy provides very specific chemical „fingerprint“ of every single chemical substance in the form of the Raman spectrum. The method is based on Raman scattering - an inelastic scattering resulting from an interaction of a photon and a molecule. In inelastic scattering photons have slightly changed wavelengths that are characteristic for specific bonds in surveyed material. Since most photons are on molecules scattered elastically (Rayleigh scattering without changing the wavelength), it is necessary to filter out of the spectrum of the strongly present wavelength of laser.

Although the fundamental phenomenon is known since thirties of the 20th century, its effective use in Raman spectroscopy occurs in about last two decades. The rebirth of this method goes hand in hand with advances in a laser, detectors and computer technology. Raman spectroscopy brings many advantages as the method is relatively rapid, non-destructive, contactless, usable for measuring through transparent glass or polymeric covering layers or containers, applicable to all states of matter and different forms, without special requirements for sample preparation.

The greatest drawback of the method is the fact that Raman scattering is a weak effect. Luminescence as much stronger quantum effect with higher intensity can overlap Raman spectra and mask spectral information. Another disadvantage is eventual degradation of a sensitive sample when using intense laser beam.

Raman spectroscopy finds many applications in many scientific areas such as chemistry, biochemistry, material science, mineralogy, arts, medicine, also is used for pharmaceutical, forensic and security purposes.

In the last years an effort is made to produce various portable Raman spectrometers. Possibility of *in situ* and field analyses can be a significant advantage compared to laboratory techniques.

3 Experimental part

3.1. Samples and chemicals

Several types of samples containing chromium compounds were chosen for analyses by Raman microscopy. Samples are divided into two groups according to type or area of occurrence and also content of chromium.

3.1.1 Paints

Chromium exhibits many colours: yellow, orange, green, blue, violet, red, black and gray, depending on the compound. They are often present in pigments and dyes, which are used in different types of paints, colours and coatings. The attention was given to yellow paints in form of oil paint ($BaCrO_4$), enamel paint, painted board (by unknown colour) and powder pigment ($PbCrO_4$).

3.1.2 Leather

Salts of trivalent chromium are commonly used in leather industry for tanning hides. Due to oxidation and other effects traces of CrVI are also present in leather. The second group of samples with rather low concentrations of chromium is represented by the following forms: leather (pigskin); leather sample soaked in 0,1 % K_2CrO_7 solution; leather shavings (waste material of leather industry); dry matter of enzymatic hydrolyzate (resulting from the hydrolytic waste treatment) and ashes – incinerated leather sample.

3.2 Instrumentation

InVia Basis Raman microscope (Renishaw) was used to measure Raman spectra of all samples. The Raman microscope uses two lasers as light sources: argon ion laser with the maximum power 20 mW and 785 nm NIR diode laser with maximum output power 300mW. Both were tested, however, more accurate and by luminescence less affected results were those, obtained using diode NIR laser. A Leica DM 2500 confocal microscope with the resolution 2μm and 5x, 20x and 50x objecitves was coupled to the Raman spectrometer.

4 Results

All spectroscopic measurements were performed directly on the surface of the sample with no special treatment. Firstly, scanning was done in common range 100 cm^{-1} - 3200 cm^{-1} with 2 cm^{-1} spectral resolution. After determination of the principle vibrational response the spectral range was reduced to the area of interest i.e. 200 cm^{-1} - 1200 cm^{-1}.

4.1 Spectral data of paints

Raman spectra of paint samples were acquired and are shown in Figure 1. Spectra reveals two pairs of similarities. Powder pigment containing $PbCrO_4$ and paited board exhibit a clear conformity in comparison to oil paint and enamel paint. However, oil and enamel paints shows similar spectral pattern, too. Pigment in oil

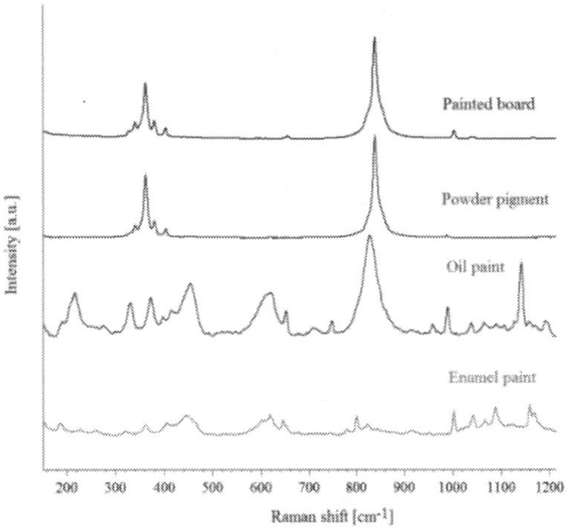

Figure 1. Raman spectra of three different yellow paints and powder pigment.

Table 1. Assignments of Ramam bands of $PbCrO_4$ [2]

Raman shift [cm^{-1}]	Characterisitc vibrace	
135	Cr-O lattice modes	
323	Cr-O bending area	
338		orthorhombic crystalline phase
358		monoclinic phase
377		
400		
839	CrO_4^{2-} symetric stretching	
855	CrO_4^{2-} antisymetric stretching	
987	SO_4^{2-} symetric stretching	

paint is known as lemon yellow, chemical composition is $BaCrO_4$. With respect to the distribution of peaks in the spectra, the same pigment base can be estimated for the enamel paint.

Peak positions of both pigments are confirmed by online spectral databases Raman Spectroscopic UCL Library and Database RRUFF. Assignments of Raman bands contained in $PbCrO_4$ are listed in Table 1.

4.2 Spectral data of leather samples

Raman spectroscopy has the potential to distinguish CrIII and CrVI valences [10]. The crucial peaks are about 550 cm^{-1} (symmetric stretching of Cr-O-Cr) for trivalent chromium and about 900 cm^{-1} (CrO_3 vibration) for hexavalent chromium. These peaks are demonstrated in Figure 2. In Figure 3, spectral response from leather shavings, dry matter of hydrolyzate, lather soaked in 0,1 % K_2CrO_7 solution and ash from the leather is depicted.

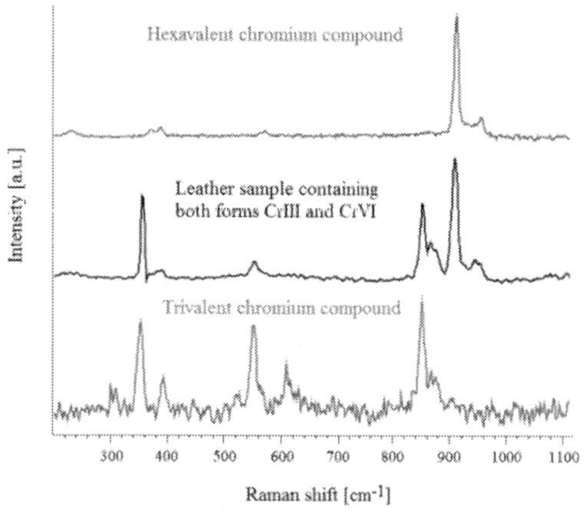

Figure 2. Raman spectra of leather containing trivalent and hexavalent chromium compounds.

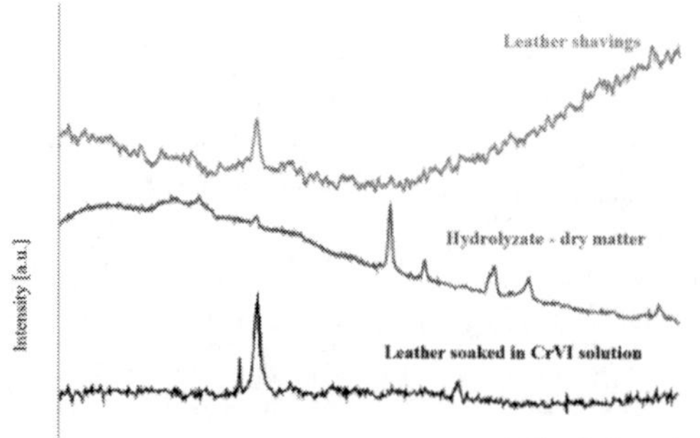

Figure 3. Raman spectra of leather shavings, collagenous protein hydrolyzate – dry matter, lather soaked in K_2CrO_7 solution, ash from leather.

Intensities of the spectra are not normalized. However, presence of CrIII in shavings is supposed after tanning as well as in soaked leather and ash. Low concentration of CrIII in enzymatic hydrolyzate agrees to the procedure of leather waste treatment [10]. On the other hand CrVI is in higher amounts present in soaked leather due to the K_2CrO_7 solution and in the ash due to oxidation during incineration.

5 Conclusion

Possibility to detect compounds of trivalent and hexavalent chromium was demonstrated on samples of paints and pigments and leather samples in different forms by Raman microscopy. Because of significantly different characteristics of these two oxidation states of chromium it is necessary to be able to distinguish benign and carcinogenic form and measure rather hexavalent chromium than total chromium. Raman spectroscopic evaluation brings advantages mainly in terms of simplicity, rapidity, no use of chemical reagents and no special requirements for the form of measured samples.

Acknowledgement

This work was supported by the Ministry of Education, Youth and Sports of the Czech Republic within the National Sustainability Programme project No. LO1303 (MSMT-7778/2014).

References

1. K. Kolomazník, M. Adámek, M. Anděl, M. Uhlířová, J Hazard Mater, **160**, 514-520, (2008).
2. L. Monico, *K.* Janssens, *E.* Hendriks, *B.G.* Brunetti, C. Miliani, J Raman Spectrosc, **45**, 1026–1033, (2014).
3. D. A. Eastmond, J. T. Macgregor, R. S. Slesinski, Crit. Rev. Toxicol., **39**,173-190, (2008).
4. Toxicological Review for Hexavalent Chromium [online], (2014).
5. EPA, Toxicolagical review of hexavalent chromium [online]. (1998).
6. S. de Flora, Carcinogenesis, **21**, 533-541, (2000).
7. J. Haney, N. Erraguntla, R. L. Sielken, C. Valdez-Flores, Regul. Toxicol. Pharmacol., **64**, 466-480, (2012).
8. N. Unceta, F. Séby, J. Malherbe, O. F. X. Donard, Anal Bioanal Chem, **397**, 1097–1111, (2010).
9. J. M. Chalmers, G. M. Howell, M. D. Hargreaves, *Infrared and Raman spectroscopy in forensic science*. [Wiley, Chichester, UK, 2012]
10. H. Vašková, *Modeling of Chemical Reactor for Leather Waste Dechromation*, (2015).

MATEC Web of Conferences 76, 05013 (2016) DOI: 10.1051/matecconf/20167605013
CSCC 2016

An Innovative Procedure for the Rolling Noise Evaluation

Massimo Viscardi[1a], Pasquale Napolitano[1], Stefano Ferraiuolo[2]

[1]University of Naples "Federico II", Dept. of Industrial Engineering, Via Claudio, 21 – 80125 Napoli - Italy
[2] HITACHI RAIL – Via Argine, 425 - 80147, Napoli - ITALY

Abstract: - Noise is often generated by pressure changes in the air induced by mechanical vibrations. The study of these phenomena is known as structural acoustics or, in a more fashionable way, virboacoustics. Vibroacoustics is the study of the mechanical waves in structures and how they interact with, and radiate into, adjacent media. In railway the most important noise source, based on fluid and structure interaction is the rolling noise. The aim of the paper is the development and implementation of a numerical method for the rail decay rate and combined roughness calculation according to the FprCEN/TR 16891:2015 and a subsequent evaluation of the excess noise level in accordance with the ISO/FDIS 3095: 2013. The tool, as a final results, will make possible the evaluation of the rail parameters without the involvement of long and expensive test campaign based on classical roughness measurement methods and will permit the compensation of the roughness induced excess noise level for a comparative comprehension of the acoustic experimental data.

1 Rolling Noise Generation

Between 1970 and 1980 there have been numerous studies on the wheel / rail noise generation, and in this area, the research is still open, especially regarding high speed trains. In this area there are several descriptive terms for various types of wheel/rail noise. The terms rolling noise and tangent track noise are both used here to refer to noise produced by rail and wheel roughness and material heterogeneity. Rolling noise also occurs at curved as well as tangent track. At systems with adequate ground rail and trued wheels, traction motor cooling fan and gearbox noise and undercar aerodynamic noise may contribute significantly to operational noise, and some care must be exercised in identifying the wheel/rail noise component. A representative example of 1/3-octave band wayside noise produced by a Bay Area Rapid Transit (BART) vehicle at various speeds are presented in figure 1. In this example, traction power equipment produces the peak in the spectrum at 250 Hz. At higher frequencies, wheel/rail noise dominates the spectrum, peaking at about 1,600 Hz. With trued wheels and smooth ground rail on ballast and ties, BART is one of the quietest vehicles in operation at U.S. transit systems. With normal rolling noise, the rail running surface will be free of spalls, checks, pitting, burns, corrugation, or other surface defects, which may not be entirely visible. The wheel and rail provide running surfaces which, under ideal conditions, should have similar characteristics for smoothness and low noise as any anti-friction bearing. From a practical perspective, ideal bearing surfaces are difficult to realize and maintain in track due to lack of lubricant, corrosion and contamination, and dynamic wheel/rail interaction forces.

2 Rolling Noise Sources

There are four mechanisms that are suggested in the literature, as the main causes of rolling noise.

These are:
- Rail and wheel roughness,
- Parameter variation, or moduli heterogeneity,
- Creep, and
- Aerodynamic noise.

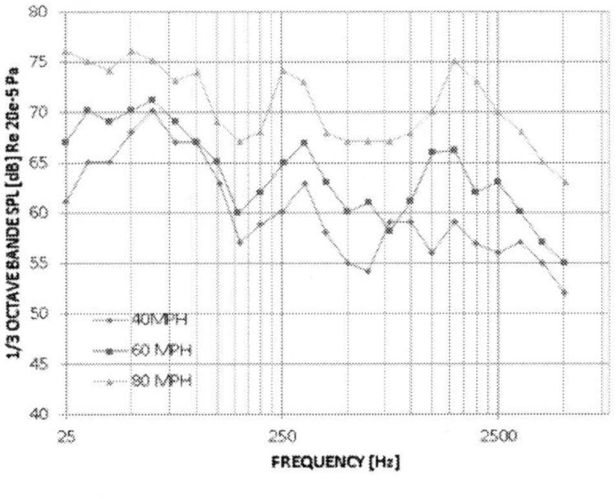

Figure 1: Pass-by noise for single car vehicle with aluminum centered wheels on ballast and tie track.

[a] Corresponding author: massimo.viscardi@unina.it

2.1 Wheel/Rail Roughness

Is probably the most significant cause of the wheel/rail noise. The surface roughness profile may be decomposed into a continuous spectrum of wavelengths. At wavelengths short relative to the contact patch dimension, the surface roughness is attenuated by averaging of the roughness across the contact patch, an effect which is described as contact patch filtering. Thus, fine regular grinding marks of dimensions less than, perhaps, 1.5mm should not produce significant noise compared to lower frequency components.

2.2 Parameter Variation

Parameter variation refers to the variation of rail and wheel steel moduli, rail support stiffness, and contact stiffness due to variation in rail head transverse radius-of-curvature. The influence of fractional changes in elastic moduli and of radius-of-curvature of the rail head as a function of wavelength necessary to generate wheel/rail noise equivalent to that generated by surface roughness is illustrated in the figure. Experimental data for the effect of modulus variation at this frequency have not yet been found. Rail head ball radius heterogeneity also induces a dynamic response in the wheel and rail. The variation of rail head curvature would have to be -on the order of 10% to 50% to produce a noise level similar to that produced by rail roughness alone. Data on rail head radii of curvature as a function of wavelength have not been obtained nor correlated with wayside noise. Also, railhead ball radius variation will normally accompany surface roughness, so that distinguishing between ball radius variation and roughness may be difficult in practice.

2.3 Dynamic Creep.

Dynamic creep may include both longitudinal and lateral dynamic creep, roll-slip in a direction parallel with the rail, and spin-creep of the wheel about a vertical axis normal to the wheel/rail contact area.

2.3.1 Longitudinal Creep

It is not considered significant by some researchers, as rolling noise levels are claimed to not increase significantly during braking or acceleration on smooth ground rail. However, qualitative changes of the sound of wheel/rail noise on newly ground rail with a grinding pattern in the rail running surface is observable to the ear as a train accelerates or decelerates, in contradiction to the notion that longitudinal creep is of no significance.

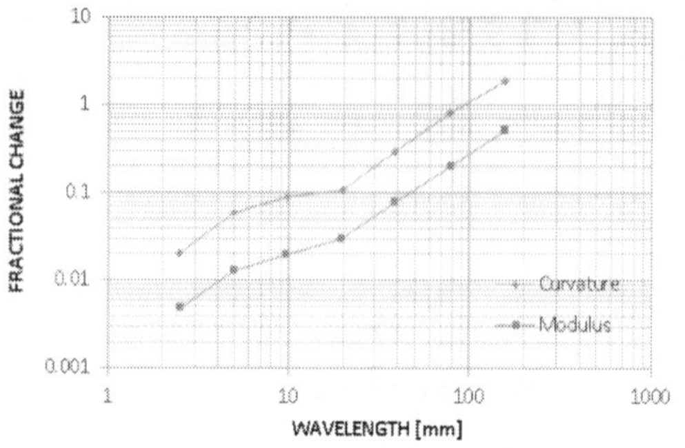

Figure 2: Change in elastic modules and railhead curvature required to generate wheel/rail excitation.

2.3.2 Lateral creep

It occurs during curve negotiation, and is responsible for the well-known wheel squeal phenomena resulting from stick-slip. Lateral creep may not be significant at tangent track, but lateral dynamic creep may occur during unloading cycles at high frequencies on abnormally rough or corrugated rail. Lateral dynamic creep is postulated by some to be responsible for short-pitch corrugation at tangent track. Therefore, lateral creep, at least in the broad sense, may be a significant source of noise.

2.3.3 Spin-creep

It is caused by wheel taper which produces a rolling radius differential between the field and gauge sides of the contact patch.

2.4 Aerodynamic Noise

Aerodynamic noise is caused by turbulent boundary layer noise about the wheel circumference as it moves forward and by undercar components which exhibit substantial aerodynamic roughness. Noise due to air turbulence about the wheel is usually not significant at train speeds representative of transit systems, while noise due to air turbulence in the truck area may be significant.

3 Tool Introduction

The tool has been developed according to the FprCEN/TR 16891:2015 in which the whole procedure is specified. In the procedure is described both the analytical procedure for decay rate and roughness calculation and the procedure for FRF estimation. Before show the tool implementation we will investigate the preliminary data needed to obtains results according to the regulation. At the end of the tool a second step, not mentioned in above standard, has been implemented for noise correction and prevision. The extra part developed want to answer at the following question: knowing the FRF of system how change the noise as function of roughness? The answer to this question acquire relevance for both train manufacturer and train regulation institution. In fact, the rolling noise maximum level, is given referred to rail with standard roughness curve reported in ISO/FDIS 3095.

3.1 Input Parameter

To detect the parameters, we need instruments that allow us, during the passage of the train, to detect not only the useful data to insert in the calculation formulas, but also the standard parameters of the train, as the number of axles and the speed of train during the pass-by. This instrumentation, is constituted by an accelerometer that can be mounted below the longitudinal axis, at the base of the rail, if you need only measure the vertical decay rate, otherwise, another accelerometer is positioned on the side of the railhead as shown in figure a, if you wanted to calculate the lateral decay rate. The number of accelerometers can also be increased if you need more measurements. The position b is more difficult. Indeed in that case we will have an angle which should be filled with the use of an angled pin so to ensure the verticality of the accelerometer. At the end of procedure, positioning the accelerometer as already illustrated, and using the methods described into ISO 5348 to mount the instrumentation, the result is shown in Figure 4. During the pass-by of the train, the instrumentation will detect:

- Vertical railhead vibration (acceleration signal) including the approach and departure of the train;
- Sound pressure time signal, if a transfer function is required;
- Train speed v;
- Train length ℓ, usually determined from known vehicle lengths;
- Number of axles N_{ax}, counted or estimated from the vibration or trigger signal;
- Optionally the axle pass-by trigger signal z(t).

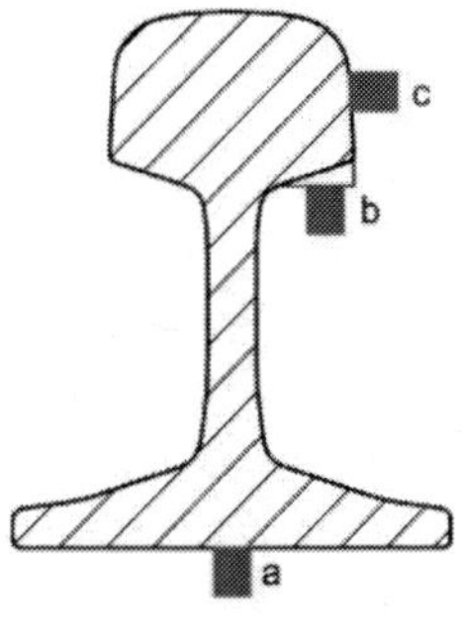

Figure 3: Suitable position of accelerometers

Figure 4: An accelerometer correctly positioned

4 Decay Rate Evaluation

To determine the track decay rate, an iterative method very close to that described in the standard EN 15461 is used. The rail vibration amplitude due to a single wheel is assumed to be described by an exponential function

$$A(x) \approx A(0)e^{\beta x} \quad (1)$$

Where x is the position away from the contact point along the rail; A(x) is the vibration amplitude along the rail; A(0) is the instantaneous amplitude at the position of the wheel contact point; β is a decay exponent. The decay rate in dB/m can be given as:

$$D_z = 20\log_{10}(e^{\beta}) \approx 8{,}686\beta \quad (2)$$

This decay rate is derived from the evaluation of the ratio of the integrated vibration energy over a length L2, potentially including the whole train pass-by versus the integrated vibration energy over a short length L1 directly around the wheels. L1 is taken as the shortest axle distance in the train (or part of the train).

A common minimum wheel distance is 1.8m, in which case the analysis length L1 extends from –0,9m to +0,9m around each wheel position. In summary, we have two quantities $A_{\Sigma L1}{}^2$ and $A_{\Sigma L2}{}^2$ that can be derived easily from the measurements of the acceleration signals.

We are interested to know how much is their ratio, which gives us the vibration energy ratio R for each third octave band frequency f_c.

$$R(f_c) = \frac{A^2_{\Sigma L1}}{A^2_{\Sigma L2}} \approx 1 - e^{-\beta L1} \quad (3)$$

We can see, in Figure 5, a typical pass-by spectrum measured by an accelerometer on the head of the rail along vertical direction. In Figure 6 a zoom of signal around a wheel for time T_x.

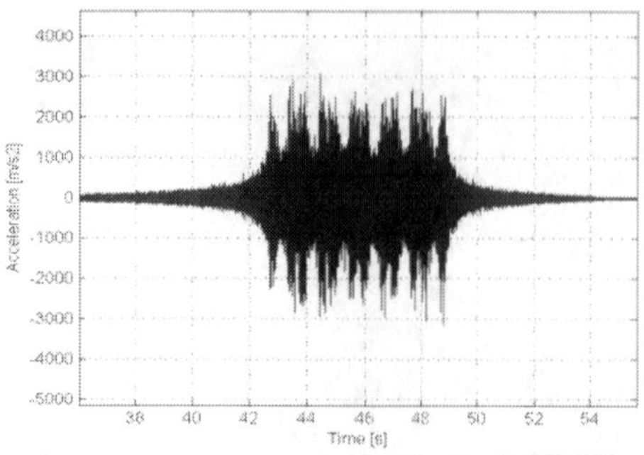

Figure 5: Time signal of vertical rail vibration; unfiltered time signal of whole pass-by with total integration time T indicated.

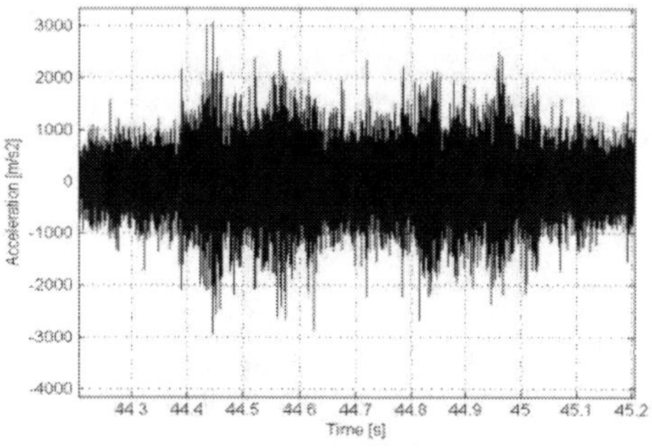

Figure 6: Time signal of vertical rail vibration; selected part of time signal indicated showing integration time T_x around each wheel.

4.1 Iteration Method

The T_x interval contains mainly energy from the single wheel, but also contributions from other wheels, particularly the nearby ones. T_x should be chosen slightly less than the smallest distance between wheels over the whole train to avoid overlap in energy summation. We can now derive very useful formulas for the purpose of the iterative process, whose steps are shown on the FprCEN/TR 16891:2015 standard. These formulas are:

$$\beta_k(f_c) = -\frac{\ln\left(1-\frac{R(f_c)N_{ax}}{w_k(f_c)}\right)}{L1} \quad (4)$$

$$w_k(f_c) = \sum_{j=1}^{N_{ax}} \sum_{i=1}^{N_{ax}} e^{-2\beta_{k-1}|x_j-x_i|} \quad (5)$$

The difference x_j-x_i is the distance between the current wheel j and another wheel i. The weighting coefficient w_k represents a sum of the squared contributions from all wheels, viewed from each wheel and then summated over all wheels. If the decay exponent is large, the effect of adjacent wheels is small and w_k quickly converges to

$$w_k = N_{ax} \quad (6)$$

If the decay is small then w_k becomes larger. Sufficient convergence is often achieved within around five steps.

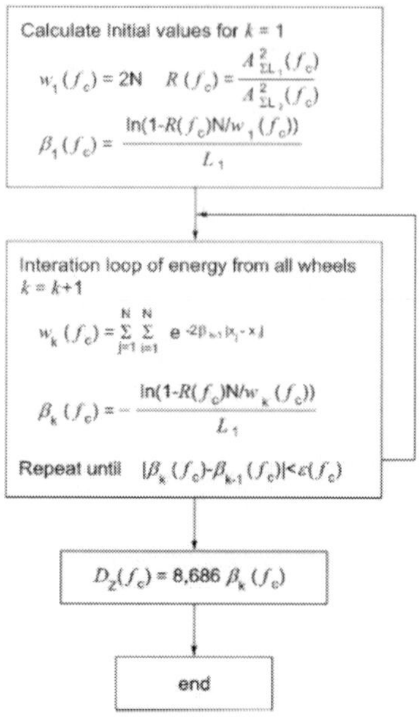

Figure 7: Logic of the energy iteration loop

The cycle showed in figure 7 is the core of standard and provide an accurate way for decay rate estimation. Usually the error $\varepsilon(f_c)$ is 0.1; a smaller value can be settled for an higher precision. At the end of the loop we have the decay rate as function of frequency. A typical curve of decay rate in dB/m is shown in figure 8.

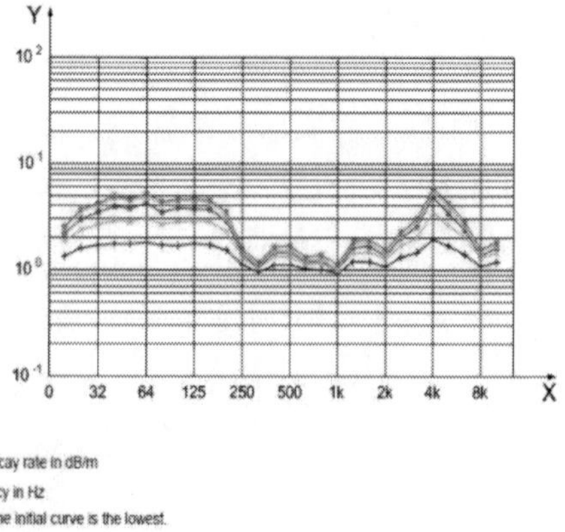

Figure 8: Convergence of a decay rate applying the iteration procedure

5 Combined Roughness Evaluation

The combined roughness for the whole train or part of a train with length ℓ is determined by the following formula:

$$L_{Rtot(f_c)} = L_{aeq,tp}(f_c, v) + 10\lg\left(\frac{D_z(f_c)\ell}{8{,}686N_{ax}}\right) - A_1(f_c) - A_2(f_c) - 40\lg(2\pi f_c) \quad (7)$$

The uncertainty in combined roughness can be reduced by using the average decay rate as input for the calculation of the above formula. If the combined roughness is averaged over several pass-by the averaging is done arithmetically.

5.1 Wavelength domain

Usually the roughness curve is reported as function of wavelength and not of frequency. The passage from one domain to another is done according the following equation

$$\lambda = \frac{v}{f} \quad (8)$$

Where v is the train speed in m/s and f is the frequency, usually a one-third octave band center. According to equation 8 with a single speed is impossible to investigate all the wavelength domain. To cover it completely a pass-by measure at different speeds must be performed. A general idea of wavelength range a single speed can cover a diagram is shown in figure 9.

The conversion performed applying equation 8 generates a non-centered spectrum. To normalize the wavelength domain to a standard spectrum a weight procedure must be applied to redefine the energy envelop over a standard one-third octave band spectrum.

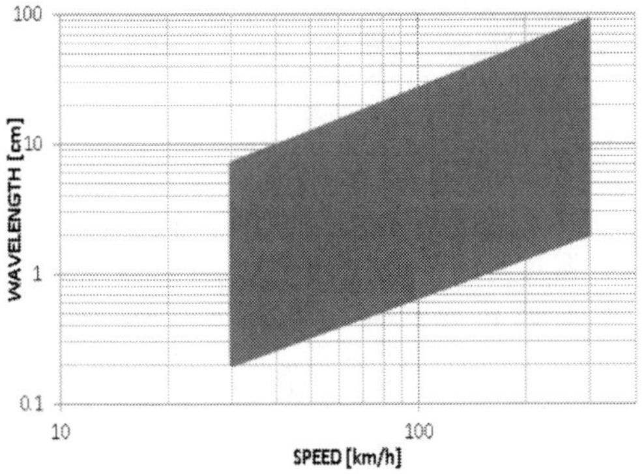

Figure 9: Approximate applicability range for determining combined roughness from rail vibration data during train pass-by

In table 1 is shown the standard spectrum for wavelength both for third and one-third octave bands.

Table 1: Standard octave and one third octave wavelengths

Octave band centre wavelength [mm] $\lambda_{c,oct}$	Third octave band centre wavelength [mm]		
	$\lambda_{c,third,1}$	$\lambda_{c,third,2}$	$\lambda_{c,third,3}$
500	630	500	400
250	315	250	200
125	160	125	100
63	80	63	50
31,50	40	31,50	25
16	20	16	12,50
8	10	8	6,30
4	5	4	3,15
2	2,50	2	1,60
1	1,25	1	0,80

To obtain roughness values at the preferred standard wavelengths λ_c the roughness levels derived at the neighboring wavelengths around a certain desired standard wavelength are used. First the neighboring wavelengths resulting from the frequency-to-wavelength transformation are located, which are named λ_- and λ_+ such that $\lambda_- < \lambda_c < \lambda_+$. Now the roughness level at wavelength λ_c can be calculated with:

$$L_{Rtot}(\lambda_c) = 10\lg\left\{\frac{\lambda_+ - \lambda_c}{\lambda_+ - \lambda_-}10^{\frac{L_{Rtot}(\lambda_-)}{10}} + \frac{\lambda_c - \lambda_-}{\lambda_+ - \lambda_-}10^{\frac{L_{Rtot}(\lambda_+)}{10}}\right\} \quad (9)$$

A correct conversion between one domain to another is only possible using the exact center wavelengths λ_c and center frequencies f_c, as defined in EN ISO 266.
Using the nominal center wavelengths in table above, for the conversion leads to an overlapping of wavelength bands and a small error regarding the conservation of energy in the order of 1 % or less. It may be required to have measurements at more than one speed so as to obtain a sufficient wavelength range for a particular application. Roughness spectra from multiple measurements may be averaged over common wavelengths, omitting or including points outside the common wavelength range.

6 Acoustic FRF Estimation

If rolling noise is the only significant source during a train pass-by, we can calculate the transfer function in two ways. The first is determined from the equivalent sound pressure level and combined roughness at speed v, and normalized to the axle density N_{ax}/l.
We use the following formula:

$$L_{HpRtot,nl}(f_c) = L_{peq,tp}(f_c) - L_{Rtot}(f_c, v) - 10\lg\left(\frac{N_{ax}}{\ell}\right) \quad (10)$$

The total transfer function L_(HpRtot,nl) (f_c) is independent from the roughness, train length and number of axles. It characterizes the vibro-acoustic properties of the vehicle, the track and the propagation area.

6.1 Power FRF Estimation

The second way is that the transfer function can also be defined in terms of sound power which is given for a defined length of track or vehicle and is normalized to the number of axles:

$$L_{HWRtot,n}(f_c) = L_W(f_c) - L_{Rtot}(f_c, v) - 10lg(N_{ax}) \quad (11)$$

7 Correction of the measured noise

ISO 3095 provides a reference roughness curve that represents the value should not be exceeded. Otherwise the standard admits a higher value and in fact the same ISO 3095 present a corrected roughness obtained with the following formula

$$L_c(f_c) = min[L_m(f_c), L_{ISO}(f_c)] \quad (12)$$

Where L_m indicate the measured roughness and L_{ISO} the standard one. In standard the equation 12 in expressed in wavelength domain but it cans be converted to frequency one.

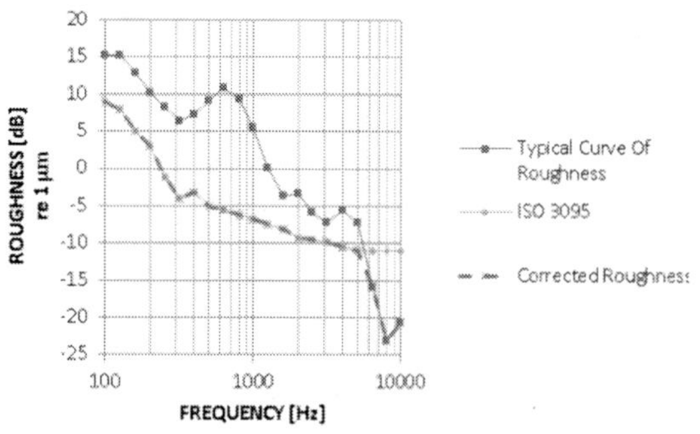

Figure 10: Typical roughness curve and standard one comparison; corrected roughness calculated according ISO 3095;

8 Conclusions

The tool described above and its implementation seems to offer a robust and affordable method for roughness evaluation. The tool provides a fast way to obtain a complex parameter starting from accelerometers measurements. The tool has two limits; first it results in a wheel/rail combined roughness and it doesn't provide any way to divide the rail roughness from wheel one. Second, the FRF calculated is independent from the train, wheel and rail types. It is a characteristic of the system and can't be used to provide data for other trains on the same rail or, that is the same, for that train on different rails. According to these limitations the tool remains a good way for roughness estimation for its simplicity and strength. Another approach of this standard is, surely, for rail real-time monitoring. A fixed accelerometer can analyzes trains pass-by for long period and advice when the roughness exceeds the threshold value for safety and noise comfort.

References

[1] Ente Italiano di Normazione, UNI/CT 050 , FprCEN/TR 16891 "Railway applications - Acoustics - Measurement method for combined roughness, track decay rates and transfer functions".
[2] ISO/FDIS 3095: 2013 "Acoustics — Railway applications — Measurement of noise emitted by railbound vehicles"
[3] Thompson, D.J., Wheel-Rail Noise Generation, Part I: Introduction and Interaction Model, Journal of Sound and Vibration,161, 1993a.
[4] Thompson, D.J., Wheel-Rail Noise Generation, Part II: Wheel Vibration, Journal of Sound and Vibration,161, 1993b.
[5] Thompson, D.J., Wheel-Rail Noise Generation, Part I: Inclusion of wheel rotation, Journal of Sound and Vibration,161, 1993c.
[6] Thompson, D.J., Experimental Analysis of Wave Propagation in Railway Propagation in Railway Track, Journal of Sound and Vibration, 203(5), 1997.
[7] James T. Nelson, Transit Cooperative Research Program - Wheel/Rail Noise Control Manual TCRP report 23.
[8] Rusciano, N., Viscardi, M., Ferraiuolo, S. Vibro acoustic characterization of a light metro rail traction system (2006) 13th International Congress on Sound and Vibration 2006, ICSV 2006, 7, pp. 5366-5374.
[9] Rusciano N., Scarselli G., Viscardi M., Ferraiolo S., Lecce L. "Vibro-acoustic characterization of a light metro vehicle (2003) Acta Acustica (Stuttgart), 89 (SUPP.), pp. S76.
[10] Iadevaia M., Viscardi M., Ferraiuolo S. "Structural vibration and sound power radiation modelling for a light train wheel" (2003) Proceedings of the Tenth International Congress on Sound and Vibration, pp. 1743-1748.

Computational modeling of heat and mass transfer processes in combustion chamber at power plant of Kazakhstan

Reinhard Leithner[1], Aliya Askarova[2], Saltanat Bolegenova[2], Symbat Bolegenova[2], Valeriy Maximov[2a], Shinar Ospanova[3], Aigul Ergalieva[3], Aizhan Nugymanova[3], Meruyert Beketayeva[3]

[1] *Technical University of Braunschweig, Institute of Energy and Process Systems Engineering, D-38023 Braunschweig, Germany*

[2] *SRI of Experimental and Theoretical Physic, Al-Farabi Kazakh National University, 050040, Almaty, Kazakhstan*

[3] *Al –Farabi Kazakh National University, Department of Physic and Technology, 050040 Almaty, Kazakhstan*

Abstract. In this paper the results obtained by the method of numerical modelling of Ekibastuz coal burning in furnace of Kazakhstan Power Plant. Numerical experiment was carried out on the basis of three-dimensional equations of convective heat and mass transfer, taking into account the heat propagation, heat radiation, chemical reactions and multiphase structure of the medium to predict the influence of different water content in coal on overall furnace operation and formation of combustion products.

1 Introduction

The power system of Kazakhstan is presented mostly by thermal power stations more than 70% of total amount of the electric power are generated. Thermal power stations work on solid fuel when pulverized coal combustion is predominant. Also natural gas and black oil can be used. Tendency of low grade coals usage to increase in domestic industry, it becomes especially important to develop and introduce new energy-saving technologies of solid fuel consumption and reduction in pollutant substance emissions. Applied technology of direct burning of low-grade coals in furnaces does not provide demanded reliability of working equipment and protection of environment from harmful combustion products due to approximately 50 % of pollutant emissions from stationary sources comes from thermal power enterprises and about 33 % are emitted by ferrous and non-ferrous metallurgy and mining.

Industrial implementation of any new technology is not possible without preliminary analysis of advantages and disadvantages suggested method. The rapid development in computer sciences gives the advance to computational techniques to be used for simulation of complex combustion processes in industrial furnaces.

Products of combustion contain different harmful substances and the emission of these components grows in to a great problem. Industrial development causes an increase in carbonaceous fuels' consumption. These fuels contain harmful and poisonous components such as carbonic oxide (CO), nitric oxide (NO), sulphur dioxide (SO_2), lead combinations and different hydrocarbons etc.

To decrease emissions of harmful substances various methods are applied, including special fire regimes (organization of combustion process), which suppresses the formation of harmful substances in flame and two-stage burning, when the burners work with low air surplus. In this way numerical experiments became one of the most effective and suitable means for detail analysis and in-depth study of physical and chemical phenomena.

In contrast to construction of an operating reduced model of the chamber, the three-dimensional modelling with the application of modern computer technology enables to carry out deep analysis of all chamber's parameters and save time and finances. At the same time, without additional inputs, it is possible to obtain the full set of characteristics of a convective heat and mass transfer process in reactive media, intervene flexibly in the process at any stage and reproduce separate technical solutions (the configuration of the fire chamber and assembly and construction burners), to model the formation of harmful dust and gaseous emissions and to investigate the influence of previous preparation of coal on its ignition and combustion stabilization.

2 Mathematical models

Combustion of coal-dust flame is a very complex physical-chemical process for mathematical analysis. In the boilers, where coal-dust fuel burns down in the air stream, many interrelated process occur. They are: complex aerodynamics, combustion under conditions of constantly changing temperature and component

[a] Corresponding author: Valeriy.Maximov@kaznu.kz

concentrations, heat exchange between the flame and the chamber surface. Simultaneously formation of carbon, nitrogen and sulphur oxide, corrosion hazardous and carcinogenic substances occurs.

A numerical experiment was carried out on the basis of three-dimensional equations of convective heat and mass transfer, taking into account the heat propagation, heat radiation, chemical reactions and the multiphase structure of the medium. To describe 3-D motion of reacting flows in chambers, the following set of differential equations was used [1]:

Continuity equation:

$$\frac{\partial \rho}{\partial \tau} = -\frac{\partial}{\partial x_i}(\rho u_i). \quad (1)$$

Momentum conservation law:

$$\frac{\partial}{\partial \tau}(\rho u_i) = -\frac{\partial}{\partial x_j}(\rho u_i u_j) + \frac{\partial}{\partial x_j}(\tau_{i,j}) - \frac{\partial p}{\partial x_j} + \rho f_i, \quad (2)$$

here: f_i – volume forces; $\tau_{i,j}$ – strain tensor.

Energy equation:

$$\frac{\partial}{\partial \tau}(\rho h) = -\frac{\partial}{\partial x_i}(\rho u_i h) - \frac{\partial q_i^{res}}{\partial x_j} + \frac{\partial p}{\partial \tau} + u_i \frac{\partial p}{\partial x_i} + \tau_{ij}\frac{\partial u_j}{\partial x_i} + s_q, \quad (3)$$

here: h – enthalpy; S_q – energy source.

Equation for substance components:

$$\frac{\partial}{\partial t}(\rho c_\beta) = -\frac{\partial}{\partial x_i}(\rho c_\beta u_i) - \frac{\partial j_i}{\partial x_i} + R_\beta, \quad (4)$$

where R_β – source of matter.

A standard k-ε model of turbulence has been used to close off the system and model turbulent viscosity [2,3]:

$$\frac{\partial}{\partial \tau}(\overline{\rho}k) = -\frac{\partial}{\partial x_i}(\overline{\rho u_i}k) + \frac{\partial}{\partial x_i}\left[\frac{\mu_{eff}}{\sigma_k}\frac{\partial k}{\partial x_i}\right] + P - \overline{\rho}\varepsilon, \quad (5)$$

$$\frac{\partial}{\partial \tau}(\overline{\rho}\varepsilon) = -\frac{\partial}{\partial x_i}(\overline{\rho u_i}\,\varepsilon) + \frac{\partial}{\partial x_i}\left[\frac{\mu_{eff}}{\sigma_\varepsilon}\frac{\partial \varepsilon}{\partial x_i}\right] + c_{\varepsilon 1}\frac{\varepsilon}{k}P - c_{\varepsilon 2}\overline{\rho}\frac{\varepsilon^2}{k}. \quad (6)$$

Point concentration of solid matter was determined by means of balance equations for monodispersion solid matter with the average particle diameter. To determine the mixture concentration the homogeneous model was used. Velocities of solid particles were considered to be equaled local gas velocity. Numerical model comprises sub-models for turbulent two-phase mixing, gas-phase chemical reactions, heterogeneous coal particle reactions (devolatilization, char oxidation), convective and six-flux radiant [4] heat transfer.

Calculation of turbulent flows with chemical reactions is based on the knowledge of chemical kinetics and modeling methods of turbulent transfer processes. To determine the source term in equation for components which is related to chemical reaction rate it's necessary to model correctly kinetics of chemical reactions. These reactions take place between fuel and oxidant in combustion space of the boiler. Local distribution of reacting components and temperature significantly influence on the reaction rates. The amount of energy, emitted in chemical reactions, the flame temperature and the nature of combustion products are very important characteristics in estimation of solid substances influence. Using the solid particles as fuel is most probable.

3 Coal combustion

The coal combustion model is divided into five sub-models for drying, pyrolysis (release of volatiles), and combustion of volatiles, carbon monoxide and residual char. Coal devolatilization is considered to run in a single step reaction forming a general hydrocarbon C_xH_y. The amount and composition of the hydrocarbon species have been taken from elementary and ultimate analysis of the coal. The model of coal dust combustion which is being used in this paper takes into account an integral oxidizing reaction of fuel components down to stable final products of reaction. Intermediate reactions and the formation of intermediate products haven't been taken into consideration. The model of integral reaction was used based on according to the fact that many chemical reactions proceed several stages. The slowest reaction determines the rate of the whole reaction.

The combustion of volatiles in the gas phase is assumed to be controlled by turbulent mixing, using the Eddy Dissipation Concept. The Eddy Dissipation Model according to Magnusson et al. is used to predict the combustion of the volatiles and the carbon monoxide formed during char combustion. Gaseous fuels are treated like volatiles. The char reaction rate is governed by the rate of oxygen diffusion to the surface and the kinetic rate of chemical reaction at the surface.

Simplified models are being used in this paper. These models take into account only chemical reactions of key components since the detail modelling of all passing reactions is possible only in the simple cases, because of large computational costs. Information about reactions and their kinetic data have been taken from [4].

Within the combustion of fossil fuel, nitric oxide is produced by different reaction paths. The main reactions are the oxidation of the molecular nitrogen in the air (thermal NO) and the oxidation of the fuel bounded nitrogen (fuel-NO). To describe the rates of forming and reducing nitric oxide during combustion global reaction schemes proposed by Mitchell and Tarbel [5] are used.

In this paper software package FLOREAN [1, 6-9] for 3-D modelling of coal-dust combustion in furnaces of real-sized boilers was used. This program enables to calculate velocity components u, v, w, temperature T, pressure P, concentration of combustion products and other characteristics of combustion process all over the combustion space and at its exit. Pressure is determined through the connection between the continuity equation

DOI: 10.1051/matecconf/20167606001

and the equation of motion by means of Patankar's Simple-method [10].

4 Results of CFD Studies

In present work CFD simulation tool was used to simulate and analyse low-grade coal combustion and flow properties of industrial furnaces of Kazakhstan Power Plants. The simulations of the furnaces of steam generators placed at Almaty Power Plant have been carried to predict the influence of different water content in coal on overall furnace operation and formation of combustion products.

Fig. 1 shows temperature distribution along the chamber height for burning of coal with different water content in initial air-fuel stream. The experimental data [11] are given here for coal burning with 7% moisture. Curve minimums caused by low temperature of fuel mixture supplied in the chamber space through the burners. Differences of calculated and experimental values of temperature are seen in the region of ignition and extinction. Figure 2 shows difference in temperature fields for different initial water content in burning coal. We can see that higher water content causes decrease in temperature in this section of combustion chamber.

Figures 3-8 show picture of fuel burning with the fields of oxygen, carbon oxide (CO) and carbon dioxide (CO_2), and nitrogen oxide (NO) concentration. The main formation regions of gases in the coal dust torch take place at the level of burners in the central part of the furnace volume.

The maximum difference of calculation and experiment (fig. 7) is seen in the region of ignition and extinction of flying matters. The main reason for this is that there is a determination of the gas burning rate by one stage model of pyrolysis where the set of kinetic constants for all the entire temperature range are used. The figures show that the regions with maximum difference coincide with regions having a high concentration of carbon oxide.

At the chamber furnace outlet we can see that decrease in coal moisture results in CO_2 decrease, (fig. 7) and simultaneous CO increase (fig. 5-6). Oxygen concentration (fig. 3, 4) in the total gas mixture at the outlet consequently increase with water content in coal (fig. 3-5). Same development is seen in the whole furnace volume (fig. 3, 5). Difference in NO formation for studied coal content is seen mostly in the region of burner location. At the furnace outlet the difference in NO concentrations is slight appearing (fig.8). The distribution character of all concentrations, listed in this paper is modelled sufficiently and it agrees with the experimental data [11].

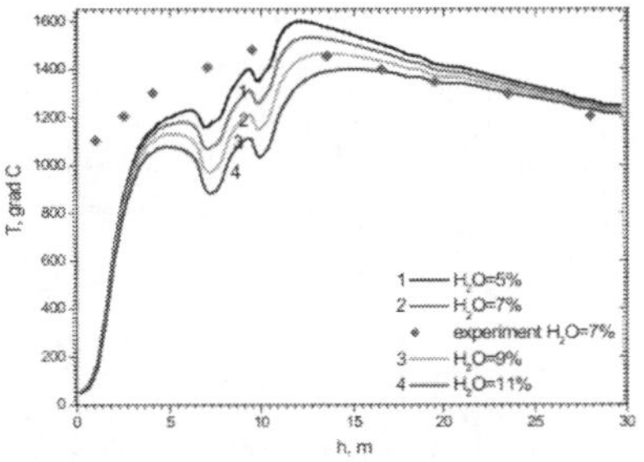

Figure 1. Temperature distribution along the chamber height for coal burning with different water content.

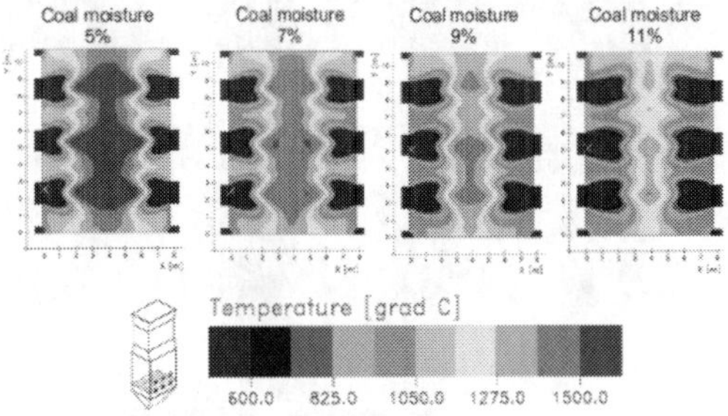

Figure 2. Temperature distribution in cross section of the furnace in the lower level of the burners for coal burning with different water content.

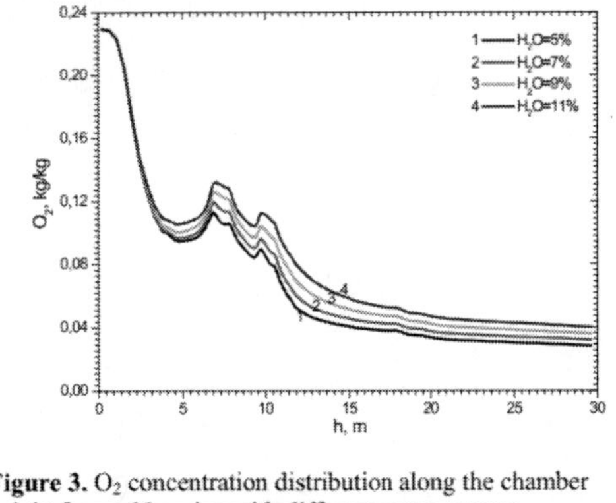

Figure 3. O_2 concentration distribution along the chamber height for coal burning with different water content.

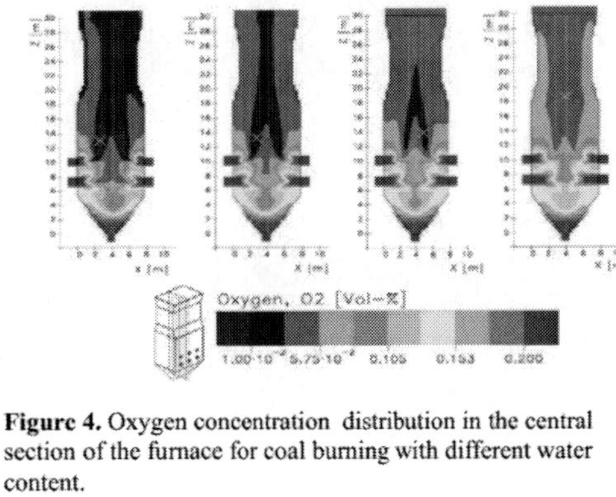

Figure 4. Oxygen concentration distribution in the central section of the furnace for coal burning with different water content.

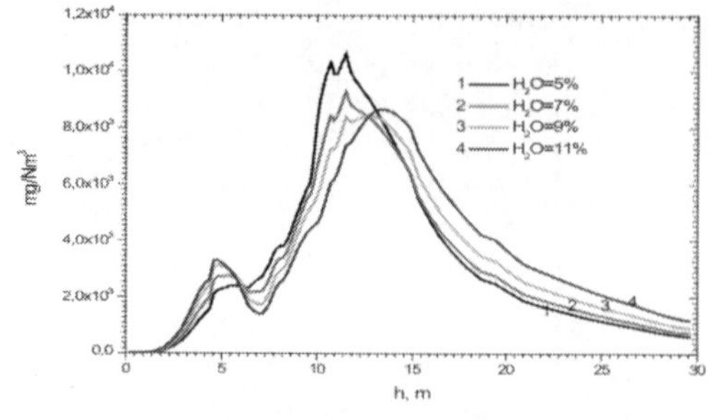

Figure 5. CO concentration distribution along the chamber height for coal burning with different water content.

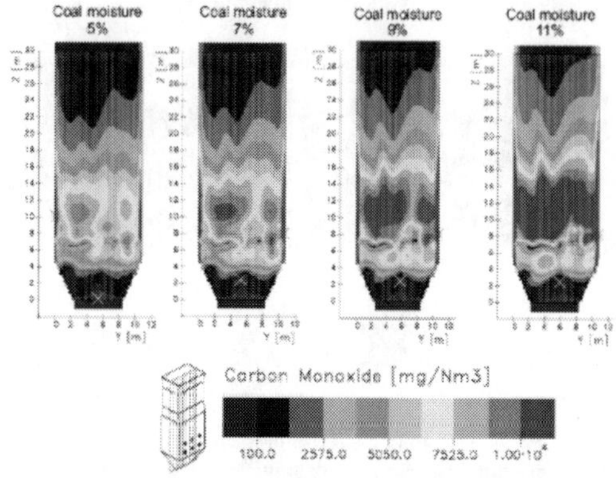

Figure 6. CO distribution in the central section of the furnace for coal burning with different water content.

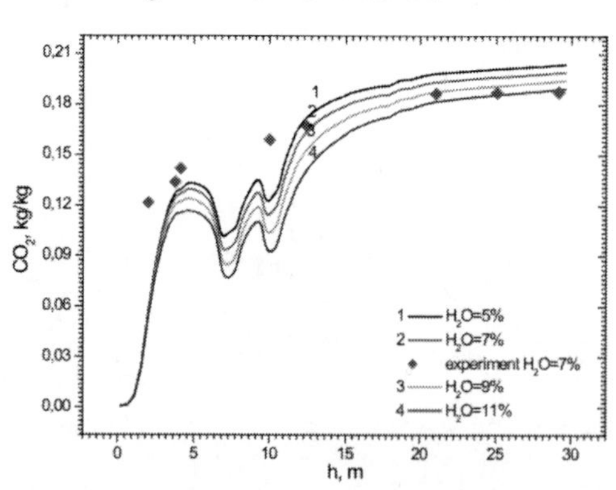

Figure 7. CO_2 concentration distribution along the chamber height for coal burning with different water content.

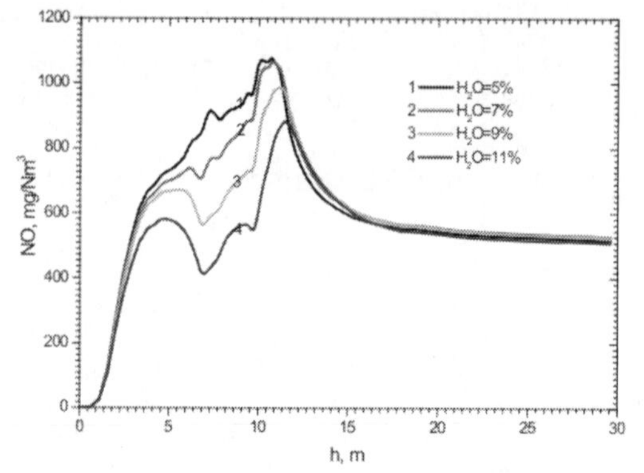

Figure 8. NO concentration distribution along the chamber height for coal burning with different water content.

5 Conclusions

In present work CFD simulation tool was used to numerically simulate and analyze low-grade coal combustion and flow properties of industrial furnaces of Kazakhstan Power Plants. The simulations of the furnaces of steam generator of Almaty Power Plant have been carried to predict the influence of different water content in coal on overall furnace operation and formation of combustion products. Results presented in the way of 3D-fields of temperatures, velocities and concentrations of the combustion products CO, CO2, NO_x etc.

CFD prediction of combustion process of combustion chamber can be very useful for engineers to choose an appropriate operating method to successful overall combustion optimization in furnaces to improve energy efficiency and control pollutant emissions.

This work was financially supported by the Ministry of Education and Science of the Republic of Kazakhstan – Grant №0115RK00599.

References

1. H. Müller, VDI-Verlag. **6**, 158 (1992)
2. B.E. Launder, Academic Press, 135 (1972)
3. B. Launder, D. Spalding, J. Comp. Met. Appl. Mech. Eng, (1974)
4. F.G. Lockwood, ASME Paper (1976)
5. J.W. Mitchell, J.M. Tarbell, AIChE J., **28** (1982)
6. R. Leithner, H. Müller, Second M.I.T. Conference on computational Fluid and Solid Mechanics (2003)
7. E.L. Karpenko, V.E. Messerle, et al., 7th International Fall Seminar on Propellants, Explosives and Pyrotechnics, **7** (2007)
8. A.S. Askarova, A.B. Ustimenko, S.A. Bolegenova, V.Yu. Maksimov, J. Thermophysics and aeromechanics, **21** (2014)
9. S.A. Bolegenova, V.Y. Maximov, A. Bekmukhamet, M.T. Beketayeva, Z.K. Gabitova, J. High temperature, **5** (2015)

10. A.S. Askarova, V.E. Messerle, S.A. Bolegenova, V.Yu. Maximov, Z.Kh. Gabitova, J. High temperature, **53** (2015)
11. V. Maximov, S. Bolegenova, M. Beketayeva, P. Safarik, J. Thermal science, **24** (2015)
12. E.I. Karpenko, V.E. Messerle, J. High Energy Chemistry, **40** (2006)
13. A. Askarowa, M.A. Buchmann, Gesell Energietech, Combustion and incineration - eighteenth dutch-german conference on flames, VDI Berichte, **1313** (1997)
14. S. Vockrodt, R. Leithner, A. Schiller, VDI Berichte, **1492** (1999)
15. M. Gorokhovski, A. Chtab-Desportes, I. Voloshina, AIP Conference Proceedings, **1207** (2010)
16. V.E. Messerle, A.B. Ustimenko, S.A. Bolegenova, V.Yu. Maximov, J. Thermophysics and Aeromechanics, **23** (2016)
17. S. Bolegenova, M. Beketayeva, Sh. Ospanova, V. Maximov, J. Applied Fluid Mechanics, **9** (2016)
18. M. Beketayeva, S.A. Bolegenova, S. Bolegenova, A. Bekmukhamet, V. Maximov, Int. J. Mech., **7** (2013)
19. Sh. Ospanova, S. Bolegenova, M. Beketayeva, V. Maximov, Int. J. Mech., **8** (2014)
20. S.V. Patankar, Hemisphere Publ. (1980)
21. B.K. Aliarov, B.P. Ustimenko, M.A. Buhman, Report № 01910010550. Kaz. SRIETP (1991)

AUTHOR INDEX

AUTHOR INDEX

AUTHOR INDEX